D0425267

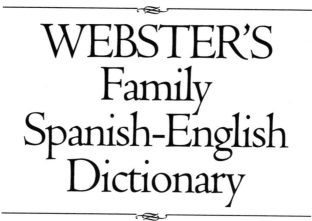

WEBSTER'S
Family
Spanish-English
Dictionary

WEBSTER'S
Family
Spanish-English
Dictionary

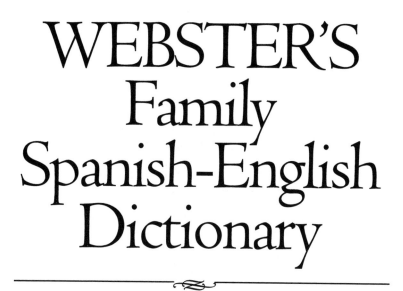

DELUXE EDITION

Created in Cooperation with the Editors of
Merriam-Webster

FEDERAL
STREET
PRESS

A Division of Merriam-Webster, Incorporated
Springfield, Massachusetts

Copyright © by Merriam-Webster, Incorporated

Federal Street Press is a trademark of
Federal Street Press, a division of Merriam-Webster, Incorporated.

All rights reserved. No part of this book covered by the
copyrights hereon may be reproduced or copied in any form or
by any means—graphic, electronic, or mechanical, including
photocopying, taping, or information storage and retrieval
systems—without written permission of the publisher.

This 2005 edition published by
Federal Street Press, a division of
Merriam-Webster, Incorporated
P.O. Box 281
Springfield, MA 01102

Federal Street Press books are available for bulk purchase
for sales promotion and premium use.
For details write the manager of special sales,
Federal Street Press, P.O. Box 281, Springfield, MA 01102

ISBN 10   1-892859-98-X

ISBN 13   978-1-892859-98-3

Printed in the United States of America

06 07 08 09   5 4 3

Contents

Preface

WEBSTER'S FAMILY SPANISH-ENGLISH DICTIONARY is a completely new dictionary designed to meet the needs of English and Spanish speakers in a time of ever-expanding communication among the countries of the Western Hemisphere. It is intended for language learners, teachers, office workers, tourists, business travelers—anyone who needs to communicate effectively in the Spanish and English languages as they are spoken and written in the Americas. This new dictionary provides accurate and up-to-date coverage of current vocabulary in both languages, as well as abundant examples of words used in context to illustrate idiomatic usage. The selection of Spanish words and idioms was based on evidence drawn from a wide variety of modern Latin-American sources and interpreted by trained Merriam-Webster bilingual lexicographers. The English entries were chosen by Merriam-Webster editors from the most recent Merriam-Webster dictionaries, and they represent the current basic vocabulary of American English.

All of this material is presented in a format which is based firmly upon and, in many important ways, is similar to the traditional styling found in the Merriam-Webster monolingual dictionaries. The reader who is familiar with Merriam-Webster dictionaries will immediately recognize this style, with its emphasis on convenience and ease of use, clarity and conciseness of the information presented, precise discrimination of senses, and frequent inclusion of example phrases showing words in actual use. Other features include pronunciations (in the International Phonetic Alphabet) for all English words, full coverage of irregular verbs in both languages, a section on basic Spanish grammar, tables of the most common Spanish and English abbreviations, and a detailed Explanatory Notes section which answers any questions the reader might have concerning the use of this book.

Webster's Family Spanish-English Dictionary represents the combined efforts of many members of the Merriam-Webster Editorial Department, along with advice and assistance from consultants outside the company. The primary defining work was done by Charlene M. Chateauneuf, Seán O'Mannion-Espejo, Karen L. Wilkinson, and Jocelyn Woods; early contributions to the text were also submitted by César Alegre, Hilton Alers, Marién Díaz, Anne Gatschet, and María D. Guijarro, with Victoria E. Neufeldt, Ph.D., and James L. Rader providing helpful suggestions regarding style. Proofreading was done by Susan L. Brady, Daniel B. Brandon, Charlene M. Chateauneuf, Deanna Stathis Chiasson, Seán O'Mannion-Espejo, James L. Rader, Donna L. Rickerby, Adrienne M. Scholz, Amy West, Karen L. Wilkinson, and Linda Picard Wood. Brian M. Sietsema, Ph.D., provided the pronunciations. Cross-reference services were provided by Donna L. Rickerby. Karen L. Levister assisted in inputting revisions. Carol Fugiel contributed many hours of clerical assistance and other valuable support. The editorial work relating to typesetting and production was begun by Jennifer S. Goss and continued by Susan L. Brady, who also offered helpful suggestions regarding format. Madeline L. Novak provided guidance on typographic matters. John M. Morse was responsible for the conception of this book as well as for numerous ideas and continued support along the way.

Eileen M. Haraty
Editor

Explanatory Notes

Entries

1. Main Entries

A boldface letter, word, or phrase appearing flush with the left-hand margin of each column of type is a main entry or entry word. The main entry may consist of letters set solid, of letters joined by a hyphen, or of letters separated by a space:

> **cafetalero¹, -ra** *adj* . . .
>
> **eye–opener** . . . *n* . . .
>
> **walk out** *vi* . . .

The main entry, together with the material that follows it on the same line and succeeding indented lines, constitutes a dictionary entry.

2. Order of Main Entries

Alphabetical order throughout the book follows the order of the English alphabet, with one exception: words beginning with the Spanish letter *ñ* follow all entries for the letter *n*. The main entries follow one another alphabetically letter by letter without regard to intervening spaces or hyphens; for example, *shake-up* follows *shaker*.

Homographs (words with the same spelling) having different parts of speech are usually given separate dictionary entries. These entries are distinguished by superscript numerals following the entry word:

> **hail¹** . . . *vt* . . .
>
> **hail²** *n* . . .
>
> **hail³** *interj* . . .
>
> **madrileño¹, -ña** *adj* . . .
>
> **madrileño², -ña** *n* . . .

Numbered homograph entries are listed in the following order: verb, adverb, adjective, noun, conjunction, preposition, pronoun, interjection, article.

Homographs having the same part of speech are normally included at the same dictionary entry, without regard to their different semantic origins. On the English-to-Spanish side, however, separate entries are made if the homographs have distinct inflected forms or if they have distinct pronunciations.

3. Guide Words

A pair of guide words is printed at the top of each page, indicating the first and last main entries that appear on that page:

factura · faringe

4. Variants

When a main entry is followed by the word *or* and another spelling, the two spellings are variants. Both are standard, and either one may be used according to personal inclination:

jailer *or* **jailor** ... *n* ...

quizá *or* **quizás** *adv* ...

Occasionally, a variant spelling is used only for a particular sense of a word. In these cases, the variant spelling is listed after the sense number of the sense to which it pertains:

electric ... *adj* **1** *or* **electrical** ...

Sometimes the entry word is used interchangeably with a longer phrase containing the entry word. For the purposes of this dictionary, such phrases are considered variants of the headword:

bunk² *n* **1** *or* **bunk bed** ...

angina *nf* **1** *or* **angina de pecho** : angina ...

Variant wordings of boldface phrases may also be shown:

> **madera** *nf*. . . **3 madera dura** *or* **madera noble** . . .
>
> **atención¹** *nf* . . . **2 poner atención** *or* **prestar atención** . . .

5. Run-On Entries

A main entry may be followed by one or more derivatives or by a homograph with a different functional label. These are run-on entries. Each is introduced by a boldface dash and each has a functional label. They are not defined, however, since their equivalents can be readily derived by adding the corresponding foreign-language suffix to the terms used to define the entry word or, in the case of homographs, simply substituting the appropriate part of speech:

> **illegal** . . . *adj* : ilegal — **illegally** *adv* (the Spanish adverb is *ilegalmente*)
>
> **transferir** . . . *vt* trasladar : to transfer — **transferible** *adj* (the English adjective is **transferable**)
>
> **Bosnian** *n* : bosnio *m*, -nia *f* — **Bosnian** *adj* (the Spanish adjective is *bosnio, -nia*)

On the Spanish side of the book, reflexive verbs are sometimes run on undefined:

> **enrollar** *vt* : to roll up, to coil — **enrollarse** *vr*

The absence of a definition means that *enrollarse* has the simple reflexive meaning "to become rolled up or coiled," "to roll itself up."

6. Bold Notes

A main entry may be followed by one or more phrases containing the entry word or an inflected form of the entry word. These are bold notes. Each bold note is defined at its own numbered sense:

álamo *nm* 1 : poplar 2 **álamo temblón**
: aspen

hold[1] . . . *vi* . . . 4 **to hold to :** . . . 5 **to**
hold with : . . .

If the bold note consists only of the entry word and a single preposition, the entry word is represented by a boldface swung dash ∼.

pegar . . . *vi* . . . 3 ∼ **con :** to match, to
go with . . .

The same bold note phrase may appear at two or more senses if it has more than one distinct meaning:

wear[1] . . . *vt* . . . 3 **to wear out :** gastar
⟨he wore out his shoes . . . ⟩ 4 **to wear**
out EXHAUST : agotar, fatigar ⟨to wear
oneself out . . . ⟩ . . .

estar . . . *vi* . . . 15 ∼ **por :** to be in favor
of 16 ∼ **por :** to be about to ⟨está por
cerrar . . . ⟩ . . .

If the use of the entry word is commonly restricted to one particular phrase, then a bold note may be given as the entry word's only sense:

ward[1] . . . *vt* **to ward off :** . . .

Pronunciation

1. Pronunciation of English Entry Words

The matter between a pair of brackets [ ] following the entry word of an English-to-Spanish entry indicates the pronunciation. The symbols used are explained in the International Phonetic Alphabet chart on page 58a.

The presence of variant pronunciations indicates that not all educated speakers pronounce words the same way. A second-place variant is not to be regarded as less acceptable than the pronunciation that is given first. It may, in fact, be used by as many educated speakers as the first variant, but the requirements of the printed page are such that one must precede the other:

tomato [tə'meɪt̬o, -'mɑ-] . . .

When a compound word has less than a full pronunciation, the missing part is to be supplied from the pronunciation at the entry for the unpronounced element of the compound:

gamma ray ['gæmə] . . .

ray ['reɪ] . . .

smoke[1] ['smoːk] . . .

smoke detector [dɪ'tɛktər] . . .

In general, no pronunciation is given for open compounds consisting of two or more English words that are main entries at their own alphabetical place:

water lily *n* : nenúfar *m*

Only the first entry in a series of numbered homographs is given a pronunciation if their pronunciations are the same:

dab[1] ['dæb] *vt* . . .

dab[2] *n* . . .

No pronunciation is shown for principal parts of verbs that are formed by regular suffixation, nor for other derivative words formed by common suffixes.

2. Pronunciation of Spanish Entry Words

Spanish pronunciation is highly regular, so no pronunciations are given for most Spanish-to-English entries. Exceptions have been made for certain words (such as foreign borrowings) whose Spanish pronunciations are not evident from their spellings:

pizza ['pitsa, 'pisa] . . .

footing ['fu̱,tɪŋ] . . .

Functional Labels

An italic label indicating a part of speech or some other functional classification follows the pronunciation or, if no pronunciation is given, the main entry. The eight traditional parts of speech, adjective, adverb, conjunction, interjection, noun, preposition, pronoun, and verb, are indicated as follows:

> **daily**[2] *adj* . . .
>
> **vagamente** *adv* . . .
>
> **and** . . . *conj* . . .
>
> **huy** *interj* . . .
>
> **jackal** . . . *n* . . .
>
> **para** *prep* . . .
>
> **neither**[3] *pron* . . .
>
> **leer** . . . *v* . . .

Verbs that are intransitive are labeled *vi,* and verbs that are transitive are labeled *vt.* Entries for verbs that are both transitive and intransitive are labeled *v;* if such an entry includes irregular verb inflections, it is labeled *v* immediately after the main entry, with the labels *vi* and *vt* serving to introduce transitive and intransitive subdivisions when both are present:

> **deliberar** *vi* : to deliberate
>
> **necessitate** . . . *vt* **-tated; -tating** : necesitar, requerir
>
> **satisfy** . . . *v* **-fied; -fying** *vt* . . . — *vi* . . .

Two other labels are used to indicate functional classifications of verbs: *v aux* (auxiliary verb) and *v impers* (impersonal verb).

> **may** . . . *v aux, past* **might** . . .
>
> **haber**[1] . . . *v aux* **1** : have . . . — *v impers*
> **1 hay** : there is, there are . . .

Gender Labels

In Spanish-to-English noun entries, the gender of the entry word is indicated by an italic *m* (masculine), *f* (feminine), or *mf* (masculine or feminine), immediately following the functional label:

magnesio *nm* . . .

galaxia *nf* . . .

turista *nmf* . . .

If both the masculine and feminine forms are shown for a noun referring to a person, the label is simply *n:*

director, -tora *n* . . .

Spanish noun equivalents of English entry words are also labeled for gender:

amnesia . . . *n* : amnesia *f*

earache . . . *n* : dolor *m* de oído

gamekeeper . . . *n* : guardabosque *mf*

Inflected Forms

1. Nouns

The plurals of nouns are shown in this dictionary when they are irregular, when plural suffixation brings about a change in accentuation or in the spelling of the root word, when an English noun ends in a consonant plus *-o* or in *-ey,* when an English noun ends in *-oo,* when an English noun is a compound that pluralizes any element but the last, when a noun has variant plurals, or whenever the dictionary user might have reasonable doubts regarding the spelling of a plural:

tooth . . . *n, pl* **teeth** . . .

garrafón *nm, pl* **-fones** . . .

potato . . . *n, pl* **-toes** . . .

> **abbey** ... *n, pl* **-beys** ...
>
> **cuckoo**[2] *n, pl* **-oos** ...
>
> **brother–in–law** ... *n, pl*
>   **brothers–in–law** ...
>
> **quail**[2] *n, pl* **quail** *or* **quails** ...
>
> **hábitat** *nm, pl* **-tats** ...
>
> **tahúr** *nm, pl* **tahúres** ...

Cutback inflected forms are used for most nouns on the English-to-Spanish side, regardless of the number of syllables. On the Spanish-to-English side, cutback inflections are given for nouns that have three or more syllables; plurals for shorter words are written out in full:

> **shampoo**[2] *n, pl* **-poos** ...
>
> **calamity** ... *n, pl* **-ties** ...
>
> **mouse** ... *n, pl* **mice** ...
>
> **sartén** *nmf, pl* **sartenes** ...
>
> **hámster** *nm, pl* **hámsters** ...
>
> **federación** *nf, pl* **-ciones** ...

If only one gender form has a plural which is irregular, that plural form will be given with the appropriate label:

> **campeón, -ona** *n, mpl* **-ones** : champi-
> on

The plurals of nouns are usually not shown when the base word is unchanged by the addition of the regular plural suffix or when the noun is unlikely to occur in the plural:

> **apple** ... *n* : manzana *f*
>
> **inglés**[3] *nm* : English (language)

Nouns that are plural in form and that regularly occur in plural constructions are labeled as *npl* (for English nouns), *nmpl* (for Spanish masculine nouns), or *nfpl* (for Spanish feminine nouns):

> **knickers** ... *npl* ...
>
> **enseres** *nmpl* ...
>
> **mancuernas** *nfpl* ...

Entry words that are unchanged in the plural are labeled *ns &
pl* (for English nouns), *nms & pl* (for Spanish masculine nouns),
nfs & pl (for Spanish feminine nouns), and *nmfs & pl* (for Spanish
gender-variable nouns):

> **deer** . . . *ns & pl* . . .
>
> **lavaplatos** *nms & pl* . . .
>
> **tesis** *nfs & pl* . . .
>
> **rompehuelgas** *nmfs & pl* . . .

2. Verbs

ENGLISH VERBS

The principal parts of verbs are shown in English-to-Spanish
entries when they are irregular, when suffixation brings about a
change in spelling of the root word, when the verb ends in *-ey,*
when there are variant inflected forms, or whenever it is believed
that the dictionary user might have reasonable doubts about the
spelling of an inflected form:

> **break¹** . . . *v* **broke** . . . ; **broken** . . . ;
> **breaking** . . .
>
> **drag¹** . . . *v* **dragged; dragging** . . .
>
> **monkey¹** . . . *vi* **-keyed; -keying** . . .
>
> **label¹** . . . *vt* **-beled** *or* **-belled; -beling**
> *or* **-belling** . . .
>
> **imagine** . . . *vt* **-ined; -ining** . . .

Cutback inflected forms are usually used when the verb has
two or more syllables:

> **multiply** . . . *v* **-plied; -plying** . . .
>
> **bevel¹** . . . *v* **-eled** *or* **-elled; -eling** *or*
> **-elling** . . .
>
> **forgo** *or* **forego** . . . *vt* **-went; -gone;**
> **-going** . . .
>
> **commit** . . . *vt* **-mitted; -mitting** . . .

The principal parts of an English verb are not shown when the
base word is unchanged by suffixation:

delay¹ ... *vt*

pitch¹ ... *vt*

SPANISH VERBS

Entries for irregular Spanish verbs are cross-referenced by number to the model conjugations appearing in the Conjugation of Spanish Verbs section:

abnegarse {49} *vr* ...

volver {89} *vi* ...

Entries for Spanish verbs with regular conjugations are not cross-referenced; however, model conjugations for regular Spanish verbs are included in the Conjugation of Spanish Verbs section beginning on page 38a.

Adverbs and Adjectives

The comparative and superlative forms of English adjective and adverb main entries are shown when suffixation brings about a change in spelling of the root word, when the inflection is irregular, and when there are variant inflected forms:

wet² *adj* **wetter; wettest** ...

good² *adj* **better** ... ; **best** ...

evil¹ ... *adj* **eviler** *or* **eviller; evilest** *or* **evillest** ...

The superlative forms of adjectives and adverbs of two or more syllables are usually cut back; the superlative is shown in full, however, when it is desirable to indicate the pronunciation of the inflected form:

early¹ ... *adv* **earlier; -est** ...

gaudy ... *adj* **gaudier; -est** ...

secure² *adj* **-curer; -est** ...

but

young¹ ... *adj* **younger** [ˈjʌŋgər]; **youngest** [-gəst] ...

At a few entries only the superlative form is shown:

mere *adj, superlative* **merest** . . .

The absence of the comparative form indicates that there is no evidence of its use.

The comparative and superlative forms of adjectives and adverbs are usually not shown when the base word is unchanged by suffixation:

quiet³ *adj* **1** . . .

Usage

1. Usage Labels

Two types of usage labels are used in this dictionary—regional and stylistic. Spanish words that are limited in use to a specific area or areas of Latin America, or to Spain, are given labels indicating the countries in which they are most commonly used:

guarachear *vi Cuba, PRi fam* . . .

bucket . . . *n* : . . . cubeta *f Mex*

The following regional labels are used in this book: *Arg* (Argentina), *Bol* (Bolivia), *CA* (Central America), *Car* (Caribbean), *Chile* (Chile), *Col* (Colombia), *CoRi* (Costa Rica), *Cuba* (Cuba), *DomRep* (Dominican Republic), *Ecua* (Ecuador), *Sal* (El Salvador), *Guat* (Guatemala), *Hond* (Honduras), *Mex* (Mexico), *Nic* (Nicaragua), *Pan* (Panama), *Par* (Paraguay), *Peru* (Peru), *PRi* (Puerto Rico), *Spain* (Spain), *Uru* (Uruguay), *Ven* (Venezuela).

Since this book focuses on the Spanish spoken in Latin America, only the most common regionalisms from Spain have been included in order to allow for more thorough coverage of Latin-American forms.

A number of Spanish words are given a *fam* (familiar) label as well, indicating that these words are suitable for informal contexts but would not normally be used in formal writing or speaking. The stylistic label *usu considered vulgar* is added for a word which is usually considered vulgar or offensive but whose widespread use justifies its inclusion in this book. The label is intended to warn the reader that the word in question may be inappropriate in polite conversation.

2. Usage Notes

Definitions are sometimes preceded by parenthetical usage notes that give supplementary semantic information:

> **not** ... *adv* **1** (*used to form a negative*)
> : no ...
>
> **within**[2] *prep* ... **2** (*in expressions of distance*) : ... **3** (*in expressions of time*)
> : ...
>
> **e**[2] *conj* (*used instead of* y *before words beginning with i or hi*) : ...
>
> **poder**[1] ... *v aux* ... **2** (*expressing possibility*) : ... **3** (*expressing permission*)
> : ...

Additional semantic orientation is also sometimes given in the form of parenthetical notes appearing within the definition:

> **calibrate** ... *vt* ... : calibrar (armas), graduar (termómetros)
>
> **palco** *nm* : box (in a theater or stadium)

Occasionally a usage note is used in place of a definition. This is usually done when the entry word has no single foreign-language equivalent. This type of usage note will be accompanied by examples of common use:

> **shall** ... *v aux* ... **1** (*used to express a command*) ⟨you shall do as I say : harás lo que te digo⟩ ...

3. Illustrations of Usage

Definitions are sometimes followed by verbal illustrations that show a typical use of the word in context or a common idiomatic usage. These verbal illustrations include a translation and are enclosed in angle brackets:

> **lejos** *adv* **1** : far away, distant ⟨a lo lejos
> : in the distance, far off⟩ ...
>
> **make**[1] ... **9** ... : ganar ⟨to make a liv-
> ing : ganarse la vida⟩ ...

Sense Division

A boldface colon is used to introduce a definition:

> **fable** ... *n* : fábula *f*

Boldface Arabic numerals separate the senses of a word that has more than one sense:

> **laguna** *nf* **1** : lagoon **2** : lacuna, gap

Whenever some information (such as a synonym, a boldface word or phrase, a usage note, a cross-reference, or a label) follows a sense number, it applies only to that specific numbered sense and not to any other boldface numbered senses:

> **abanico** *nm* ... **2** GAMA : ...
>
> **tonic**[2] *n* ... **2** *or* **tonic water** : ...
>
> **grillo** *nm* ... **2 grillos** *nmpl* : ...
>
> **fairy** ... *n, pl* **fairies** ... **2 fairy tale** : ...
>
> **myself** ... *pron* **1** (*used reflexively*) : ...
>
> **pike** ... *n* ... **3** → **turnpike**
>
> **atado**[2] *nm* ... **2** *Arg* : ...

Cross-References

Three different kinds of cross-references are used in this dictionary: synonymous, cognate, and inflectional. In each instance the cross-reference is readily recognized by the boldface arrow following the entry word.

Synonymous and cognate cross-references indicate that a definition at the entry cross-referred to can be substituted for the entry word:

scapula . . . → shoulder blade

amuck . . . → amok

An inflectional cross-reference is used to identify the entry word as an inflected form of another word (as a noun or verb):

fue, etc. → ir, ser

mice → mouse

Synonyms

At many entries or senses in this book, a synonym in small capital letters is provided before the boldface colon and the following defining text. These synonyms are all main entries or bold notes elsewhere in the book. They serve as a helpful guide to the meaning of the entry or sense and also give the reader an additional term that might be substituted in a similar context. On the English-to-Spanish side synonyms are particularly abundant, since special care has been taken to guide the English speaker—by means of synonyms, verbal illustrations, or usage notes—to the meaning of the Spanish terms at each sense of a multisense entry.

Spanish Grammar

Accentuation

Spanish word stress is generally determined according to the following rules:

- Words ending in a vowel, or in *-n* or *-s,* are stressed on the penultimate syllable (*za**pa**to,* **lla**man*).

- Words ending in a consonant other than *-n* or *-s* are stressed on the last syllable (*per**diz**, curiosi**dad***).

Exceptions to these rules have a written accent mark over the stressed vowel (***fá**cil, hablar**á**, **úl**timo*). There are also a few words which take accent marks in order to distinguish them from homonyms (*si, sí; que, qué; el, él; etc.*).

Adverbs ending in *-mente* have two stressed syllables since they retain both the stress of the root word and of the *-mente* suffix (***len**ta**men**te, di**fí**cil**men**te*). Many compounds also have two stressed syllables (*lim**pia**para**bri**sas*).

Punctuation and Capitalization

Questions and exclamations in Spanish are preceded by an inverted question mark ¿ and an inverted exclamation mark ¡, respectively:

¿Cuándo llamó Ana?
Y tú, ¿qué piensas?

¡No hagas eso!
Pero, ¡qué lástima!

In Spanish, unlike English, the following words are not capitalized:

- Names of days, months, and languages (*jueves, octubre, español*).

- Spanish adjectives or nouns derived from proper nouns (*los nicaragüenses, una teoría marxista*).

Articles

1. Definite Article

Spanish has five forms of the definite article: *el* (masculine singular), *la* (feminine singular), *los* (masculine plural), *las* (feminine plural), and *lo* (neuter). The first four agree in gender and number with the nouns they limit (*el carro*, the car; *las tijeras*, the scissors), although the form *el* is used with feminine singular nouns beginning with a stressed *a-* or *ha-* (*el águila, el hambre*).

The neuter article *lo* is used with the masculine singular form of an adjective to express an abstract concept (*lo mejor de este método*, the best thing about this method; *lo meticuloso de su trabajo*, the meticulousness of her work; *lo mismo para mí*, the same for me).

Whenever the masculine article *el* immediately follows the words *de* or *a*, it combines with them to form the contractions *del* and *al*, respectively (*viene **del** campo*, vi **al** hermano de Roberto).

The use of *el, la, los,* and *las* in Spanish corresponds largely to the use of *the* in English; some exceptions are noted below.

The definite article is used:

- When referring to something as a class (*los gatos son ágiles*, cats are agile; *me gusta el café*, I like coffee).

- In references to meals and in most expressions of time (*¿comiste el almuerzo?*, did you eat lunch?; *vino el año pasado*, he came last year; *son las dos*, it's two o'clock; *prefiero el verano*, I prefer summer; *la reunión es el lunes*, the meeting is on Monday; but: *hoy es lunes*, today is Monday).

- Before titles (except *don, doña, san, santo, santa, fray,* and *sor*) in third-person references to people (*la señora Rivera llamó*, Mrs. Rivera called; but: *hola, señora Rivera*, hello, Mrs. Rivera).

- In references to body parts and personal possessions (*me duele la cabeza*, my head hurts; *dejó el sombrero*, he left his hat).

- To mean "the one" or "the ones" when the subject is already understood (*la de madera*, the wooden one; *los que vi ayer*, the ones I saw yesterday).

The definite article is omitted:

- Before a noun in apposition, if the noun is not modified (*Caracas, capital de Venezuela;* but: *Pico Bolívar, la montaña más alta de Venezuela*).

- Before a number in a royal title (*Carlos Quinto*, Charles the Fifth).

2. Indefinite Article

The forms of the indefinite article in Spanish are *un* (masculine singular), *una* (feminine singular), *unos* (masculine plural), and *unas* (feminine plural). They agree in number and gender with the nouns they limit (*una mesa*, a table; *unos platos*, some plates), although the form *un* is used with feminine singular nouns beginning with a stressed *a-* or *ha-* (*un ala, un hacha*).

The use of *un, una, unos,* and *unas* in Spanish corresponds largely to the use of *a, an,* and *some* in English, with some exceptions:

- Indefinite articles are generally omitted before nouns identifying someone or something as a member of a class or category (*Paco es profesor/católico*, Paco is a professor/Catholic; *se llama páncreas*, it's called a pancreas).

- They are also often omitted in instances where quantity is understood from context (*vine sin chaqueta*, I came without a jacket; *no tengo carro*, I don't have a car).

Nouns

1. Gender

Nouns in Spanish are either masculine or feminine. A noun's gender can often be determined according to the following guidelines:

- Nouns ending in *-aje, -o,* or *-or* are usually masculine (*el traje, el libro, el sabor*), with some exceptions (*la mano, la foto, la labor,* etc.).

- Nouns ending in *-a, -dad, -ión, -tud,* or *-umbre* are usually feminine (*la alfombra, la capacidad, la excepción, la juventud, la certidumbre*). Exceptions include: *el día, el mapa,* and many learned borrowings ending in *-ma* (*el idioma, el tema*).

Most nouns referring to people or animals agree in gender with the subject (*el hombre, la mujer; el hermano, la hermana; el perro, la perra*). However, some nouns referring to people, including those ending in *-ista,* use the same form for both sexes (*el artista, la artista; el modelo, la modelo;* etc.).

A few names of animals exist in only one gender form (*la jirafa, el sapo,* etc.). In these instances, the adjectives *macho* and *hembra* are sometimes used to distinguish males and females (*una jirafa macho,* a male giraffe).

2. Pluralization

Plurals of Spanish nouns are formed as follows:

- Nouns ending in an unstressed vowel or an accented *-é* are pluralized by adding *-s* (*la vaca, las vacas; el café, los cafés*).

- Nouns ending in a consonant other than *-s,* or in a stressed vowel other than *-é,* are generally pluralized by adding *-es* (*el papel, los papeles; el rubí, los rubíes*). Exceptions include *papá* (*papás*) and *mamá* (*mamás*).

- Nouns with an unstressed final syllable ending in *-s* usually have a zero plural (*la crisis, las crisis; el jueves, los jueves*). Other nouns ending in *-s* add *-es* to form the plural (*el mes, los meses; el país, los países*).

- Nouns ending in *-z* are pluralized by changing the *-z* to *-c* and adding *-es* (*el lápiz, los lápices; la vez, las veces*).

- Many compound nouns have a zero plural (*el paraguas, los paraguas; el aguafiestas, los aguafiestas*).

- The plurals of *cualquiera* and *quienquiera* are *cualesquiera* and *quienesquiera,* respectively.

Adjectives

1. Gender and Number

Most adjectives agree in gender and number with the nouns they modify (un chico *alto*, una chica *alta*, unos chicos *altos*, unas chicas *altas*). Some adjectives, including those ending in *-e* and *-ista* (*fuerte, altruista*) and comparative adjectives ending in *-or* (*mayor, mejor*), vary only for number.

Adjectives whose masculine singular forms end in *-o* generally change the *-o* to *-a* to form the feminine (*pequeño* → *pequeña*). Masculine adjectives ending in *-án, -ón,* or *-dor,* and masculine adjectives of nationality which end in a consonant, usually add *-a* to form the feminine (*holgazán* → *holgazana*; *llorón* → *llorona*; *trabajador* → *trabajadora*; *irlandés* → *irlandesa*).

Adjectives are pluralized in much the same manner as nouns:

- The plurals of adjectives ending in an unstressed vowel or an accented *-é* are formed by adding an *-s* (un postre *rico*, unos postres *ricos;* una camisa *café*, unas camisas *cafés*).

- Adjectives ending in a consonant, or in a stressed vowel other than *-é*, are generally pluralized by adding *-es* (un niño *cortés*, unos niños *corteses;* una persona *iraní*, unas personas *iraníes*).

- Adjectives ending in *-z* are pluralized by changing the *-z* to *-c* and adding *-es* (una respuesta *sagaz*, unas respuestas *sagaces*).

2. Shortening

- The following masculine singular adjectives drop their final *-o* when they occur before a masculine singular noun: *bueno* (*buen*), *malo* (*mal*), *uno* (*un*), *alguno* (*algún*), *ninguno* (*ningún*), *primero* (*primer*), *tercero* (*tercer*).

- *Grande* shortens to *gran* before any singular noun.

- *Ciento* shortens to *cien* before any noun.

- The title *Santo* shortens to *San* before all masculine names except those beginning with *To-* or *Do-* (*San Juan, Santo Tomás*).

3. Position

Descriptive adjectives generally follow the nouns they modify (*una cosa útil, un actor famoso*). However, adjectives that express an inherent quality often precede the noun (*la blanca nieve*). Some adjectives change meaning depending on whether they occur before or after the noun: *un pobre niño*, a poor (pitiable) child; *un niño pobre*, a poor (not rich) child; *un gran hombre*, a great man; *un hombre grande*, a big man; *el único libro*, the only book; *el libro único*, the unique book, etc.

4. Comparative and Superlative Forms

The comparative of Spanish adjectives is generally rendered as *más . . . que* (more . . . than) or *menos . . . que* (less . . . than): *soy más alta que él*, I'm taller than he; *son menos inteligentes que tú*, they're less intelligent than you.

The superlative of Spanish adjectives usually follows the formula *definite article + (noun +) más/menos + adjective: ella es la estudiante más trabajadora*, she is the hardest-working student; *él es el menos conocido*, he's the least known.

A few Spanish adjectives have irregular comparative and superlative forms:

Adjective	Comparative/Superlative
bueno (good)	**mejor** (better, best)
malo (bad)	**peor** (worse, worst)
grande[1] (big, great), **viejo** (old)	**mayor** (greater, older; greatest, oldest)
pequeño[1] (little), **joven** (young)	**menor** (lesser, younger; least, youngest)
mucho (much), **muchos** (many)	**más** (more, most)
poco (little), **pocos** (few)	**menos** (less, least)

[1] These words have regular comparative and superlative forms when used in reference to physical size: *él es más grande que yo; nuestra casa es la más pequeña.*

ABSOLUTE SUPERLATIVE

The absolute superlative is formed by placing *muy* before the adjective, or by adding the suffix *-ísimo* (*ella es muy simpática* or *ella es simpatiquísima*, she is very nice). The absolute superlative using *-ísimo* is formed according to the following rules:

- Adjectives ending in a consonant other than *-z* simply add the *-ísimo* ending (*fácil → facilísimo*).

- Adjectives ending in *-z* change this consonant to *-c* and add *-ísimo* (*feliz → felicísimo*).

- Adjectives ending in a vowel or diphthong drop the vowel or diphthong and add *-ísimo* (*claro → clarísimo; amplio → amplísimo*).

- Adjectives ending in *-co* or *-go* change these endings to *qu* and *gu*, respectively, and add *-ísimo* (*rico → riquísimo; largo → larguísimo*).

- Adjectives ending in *-ble* change this ending to *-bil* and add *-ísimo* (*notable → notabilísimo*).

- Adjectives containing the stressed diphthong *ie* or *ue* will sometimes change these to *e* and *o*, respectively (*ferviente → fervientísimo* or *ferventísimo; bueno → buenísimo* or *bonísimo*).

Adverbs

Adverbs can be formed by adding the adverbial suffix *-mente* to virtually any adjective (*fácil → fácilmente*). If the adjective varies for gender, the feminine form is used as the basis for forming the adverb (*rápido → rápidamente*).

Pronouns

1. Personal Pronouns

The personal pronouns in Spanish are:

Person		Singular	Plural	
FIRST	**yo**	I	**nosotros, nosotras**	we
SECOND	**tú**	you (familiar)	**vosotros², vosotras²**	you, all of you
	vos¹	you		
	usted	you (formal)	**ustedes³**	you, all of you
THIRD	**él**	he	**ellos, ellas**	they
	ella	she		
	ello	it (neuter)		

[1] Familiar form used in addition to *tú* in South and Central America.

[2] Familiar form used in Spain.

[3] Formal form used in Spain; familiar and formal form used in Latin America.

FAMILIAR VS. FORMAL

The second person personal pronouns exist in both familiar and formal forms. The familiar forms are generally used when addressing relatives, friends, and children, although usage varies considerably from region to region; the formal forms are used in other contexts to show courtesy, respect, or emotional distance.

In Spain and in the Caribbean, *tú* is used exclusively as the familiar singular "you." In South and Central America, however, *vos* either competes with *tú* to varying degrees or replaces it entirely. (For a more detailed explanation of *vos* and its corresponding verb forms, refer to the Conjugation of Spanish Verbs section.)

The plural familiar form *vosotros, -as* is used only in Spain, where *ustedes* is reserved for formal contexts. In Latin America, *vosotros, -as* is not used, and *ustedes* serves as the all-purpose plural "you."

It should be noted that while *usted* and *ustedes* are regarded as second person pronouns, they take the third person form of the verb.

USAGE

In Spanish, personal pronouns are generally omitted (*voy al cine,* I'm going to the movies; *¿llamaron?,* did they call?), although they are sometimes used for purposes of emphasis or clarity (*se* *lo diré yo,* I will tell them; *vino ella, pero él se quedó,* she came, but he stayed behind). The forms *usted* and *ustedes* are usually included out of courtesy (*¿cómo está usted?,* how are you?).

Personal pronouns are not generally used in reference to inanimate objects or living creatures other than humans; in these instances, the pronoun is most often omitted (*¿es nuevo? no, es viejo,* is it new? no, it's old).

The neuter third person pronoun *ello* is reserved for indefinite subjects (as abstract concepts): *todo ello implica . . . ,* all of this implies . . . ; *por si ello fuera poco . . . ,* as if that weren't enough . . . . It most commonly appears in formal writing and speech. In less formal contexts, *ello* is often either omitted or replaced with *esto, eso,* or *aquello.*

2. Prepositional Pronouns

Prepositional pronouns are used as the objects of prepositions (*¿es para mí?,* is it for me?; *se lo dio a ellos,* he gave it to them).

The prepositional pronouns in Spanish are:

Singular		**Plural**	
mí	me	**nosotros, nosotras**	us
ti	you	**vosotros[1], vosotras[1]**	you
usted	you (formal)	**ustedes**	you
él	him	**ellos, ellas**	them
ella	her		
ello	it (neuter)		
sí	yourself, himself, herself, itself, oneself	**sí**	yourselves, themselves

[1] Used primarily in Spain.

When the preposition *con* is followed by *mí, ti,* or *sí,* both words are replaced by *conmigo, contigo,* and *consigo,* respectively (*¿vienes conmigo?,* are you coming with me?; *habló contigo,* he spoke with you; *no lo trajo consigo,* she didn't bring it with her).

3. Object Pronouns

DIRECT OBJECT PRONOUNS

Direct object pronouns represent the primary goal or result of the action of a verb. The direct object pronouns in Spanish are:

Singular		Plural	
me	me	**nos**	us
te	you	**os**[1]	you
le[2]	you, him	**les**[2]	you, them
lo	you, him, it	**los**	you, them
la	you, her, it	**las**	you, them

[1] Used only in Spain.
[2] Used mainly in Spain.

Agreement

The third person forms agree in both gender and number with the nouns they replace or the people they refer to (*pintó las paredes,* she painted the walls → *las pintó,* she painted them; *visitaron al señor Juárez,* they visited Mr. Juárez → *lo visitaron,* they visited him). The remaining forms vary only for number.

Position

Direct object pronouns are normally affixed to the end of an affirmative command, a simple infinitive, or a present participle (*¡hazlo!,* do it!; *es difícil hacerlo,* it's difficult to do it; *haciéndolo, aprenderás,* you'll learn by doing it). With constructions involving an auxiliary verb and an infinitive or present participle, the pronoun may occur either immediately before the construction or suffixed to it (*lo voy a hacer* or *voy a hacerlo,* I'm going to do it; *estoy haciéndolo* or *lo estoy haciendo,* I'm doing it). In all other cases, the pronoun immediately precedes the conjugated verb (*no lo haré,* I won't do it).

Regional Variation

In Spain and in a few areas of Latin America, *le* and *les* are used in place of *lo* and *los* when referring to or addressing people (*le vieron,* they saw him; *les vistió,* she dressed them). In most parts of Latin America, however, *los* and *las* are used for the second person plural in both formal and familiar contexts.

The second person plural familiar form *os* is restricted to Spain.

INDIRECT OBJECT PRONOUNS

Indirect object pronouns represent the secondary goal of the action of a verb (*me dio el regalo*, he gave me the gift; *les dije que no*, I told them no). The indirect object pronouns in Spanish are:

Singular		**Plural**	
me	(to, for, from) me	**nos**	(to, for, from) us
te	(to, for, from) you	**os**[1]	(to, for, from) you
le	(to, for, from) you, him, her, it	**les**	(to, for, from) you, them
se[2]		**se**[2]	

[1]Used only in Spain.
[2]See explanation below.

Position

Indirect object pronouns follow the same rules as direct object pronouns with regard to their position in relation to verbs. When they occur with direct object pronouns, the indirect object pronoun always precedes (*nos lo dio*, she gave it to us; *estoy trayéndotela*, I'm bringing it to you).

Use of *Se*

When the indirect object pronouns *le* or *les* occur before any direct object pronoun beginning with an *l-*, the indirect object pronouns *le* and *les* convert to *se* (*les mandé la carta*, I sent them the letter → *se la mandé*, I sent it to them; *vamos a comprarle los aretes*, let's buy her the earrings → *vamos a comprárselos*, let's buy them for her).

4. Reflexive Pronouns

Reflexive pronouns are used to refer back to the subject of the verb (*me hice daño*, I hurt myself; *se vistieron*, they got dressed, they dressed themselves; *nos lo compramos*, we bought it for ourselves).

The reflexive pronouns in Spanish are:

Singular		Plural	
me	myself	**nos**	ourselves
te	yourself	**os**[1]	yourselves
se	yourself, himself, herself, itself	**se**	yourselves, themselves

[1]Used only in Spain.

Reflexive pronouns are also used:

- When the verb describes an action performed to one's own body, clothing, etc. (*me quité los zapatos,* I took off my shoes; *se arregló el pelo,* he fixed his hair).

- In the plural, to indicate reciprocal action (*se hablan con frecuencia,* they speak with each other frequently).

- In the third person singular and plural, as an indefinite subject reference (*se dice que es verdad,* they say it's true; *nunca se sabe,* one never knows; *se escribieron miles de páginas,* thousands of pages were written).

It should be noted that many verbs which take reflexive pronouns in Spanish have intransitive equivalents in English (*ducharse,* to shower; *quejarse,* to complain; etc.).

5. Relative Pronouns

Relative pronouns introduce subordinate clauses acting as nouns or modifiers (*el libro que escribió* . . . , the book that he wrote . . . ; *las chicas a quienes conociste* . . . , the girls whom you met . . .). In Spanish, the relative pronouns are:

que (that, which, who, whom)

quien, quienes (who, whom, that, whoever, whomever)

el cual, la cual, los cuales, las cuales (which, who)

el que, la que, los que, las que (which, who, whoever)

lo cual (which)

lo que (what, which, whatever)

cuanto, cuanta, cuantos, cuantas (all those that, all that, whatever, whoever, as much as, as many as)

Relative pronouns are not omitted in Spanish as they often are in English: *el carro que vi ayer,* the car (that) I saw yesterday. When relative pronouns are used with prepositions, the preposition precedes the clause (*la película sobre la cual le hablé,* the film I spoke to you about).

The relative pronoun *que* can be used in reference to both people and things. Unlike other relative pronouns, *que* does not take the personal *a* when used as a direct object referring to a person (*el hombre que llamé,* the man that I called; but: *el hombre a quien llamé,* the man whom I called).

Quien is used only in reference to people. It varies in number with the explicit or implied antecedent (*las mujeres con quienes charlamos . . . ,* the women we chatted with; *quien lo hizo pagará,* whoever did it will pay).

El cual and *el que* vary for both number and gender, and are therefore often used in situations where *que* or *quien(es)* might create ambiguity: *nos contó algunas cosas sobre los libros, las cuales eran interesantes,* he told us some things about the books which (the things) were interesting.

Lo cual and *lo que* are used to refer back to a whole clause, or to something indefinite (*dijo que iría, lo cual me alegró,* he said he would go, which made me happy; *pide lo que quieras,* ask for whatever you want).

Cuanto varies for both number and gender with the implied antecedent: *conté a cuantas (personas) pude,* I counted as many (people) as I could. If an indefinite mass quantity is referred to, the masculine singular form is used (*anoté cuanto decía,* I jotted down whatever he said).

Possessives

1. Possessive Adjectives

UNSTRESSED FORMS

Singular		Plural	
mi(s)	my	**nuestro(s), nuestra(s)**	our
tu(s)	your	**vuestro(s)[1], vuestra(s)[1]**	your
su(s)	your, his, her, its	**su(s)**	your, their

[1] Used only in Spain.

STRESSED FORMS

Singular		Plural	
mío(s), **mía(s)**	my, mine, of mine	**nuestro(s),** **nuestra(s)**	our, ours, of ours
tuyo(s), **tuya(s)**	your, yours, of yours	**vuestro(s)[1],** **vuestra(s)[1]**	your, yours, of yours
suyo(s), **suya(s)**	your, yours, of yours; his, of his; her, hers, of hers; its, of its	**suyo(s),** **suya(s)**	your, yours, of yours; their, theirs, of theirs

[1]Used only in Spain.

The unstressed forms of possessive adjectives precede the nouns they modify (*mis zapatos,* my shoes; *nuestra escuela,* our school).

The stressed forms occur after the noun and are often used for purposes of emphasis (*el carro tuyo,* your car; *la pluma es mía,* the pen is mine; *unos amigos nuestros,* some friends of ours).

All possessive adjectives agree with the noun in number. The stressed forms, as well as the unstressed forms *nuestro* and *vuestro,* also vary for gender.

2. Possessive Pronouns

The possessive pronouns have the same forms as the stressed possessive adjectives (see table above). They are always preceded by the definite article, and they agree in number and gender with the nouns they replace (*las llaves mías,* my keys → *las mías,* mine; *los guantes nuestros,* our gloves → *los nuestros,* ours).

Demonstratives

1. Demonstrative Adjectives

The demonstrative adjectives in Spanish are:

Singular		Plural	
este, esta	this	**estos, estas**	these
ese, esa	that	**esos, esas**	those
aquel, aquella	that	**aquellos, aquellas**	those

Demonstrative adjectives agree with the nouns they modify in gender and number (*esta chica, aquellos árboles*). They normally precede the noun, but may occasionally occur after for purposes of emphasis or to express contempt: *en la época aquella de cambio,* in that era of change; *el perro ese ha ladrado toda la noche,* that (awful, annoying, etc.) dog barked all night long.

The forms *aquel, aquella, aquellos,* and *aquellas* are generally used in reference to people and things that are relatively distant from the speaker in space or time: *ese libro,* that book (a few feet away); *aquel libro,* that book (way over there).

2. Demonstrative Pronouns

The demonstrative pronouns in Spanish are orthographically identical to the demonstrative adjectives except that they take an accent mark over the stressed vowel (*éste, ése, aquél,* etc.). In addition, there are three neuter forms—*esto, eso,* and *aquello*—which are used when referring to abstract ideas or unidentified things (*¿te dijo eso?,* he said that to you?; *¿qué es esto?,* what is this?; *tráeme todo aquello,* bring me all that stuff).

Except for the neuter forms, demonstrative pronouns agree in gender and number with the nouns they replace (*esta silla,* this chair → *ésta,* this one; *aquellos vasos,* those glasses → *aquéllos,* those ones).

Abbreviations in This Work

adj	adjective	*nm*	masculine noun
adv	adverb	*nmf*	masculine or feminine noun
Arg	Argentina		
Bol	Bolivia	*nmfpl*	plural noun invariable for gender
Brit	British		
CA	Central America	*nmfs & pl*	noun invariable for both gender and number
Car	Caribbean region		
Col	Colombia		
conj	conjunction	*nmpl*	masculine plural noun
CoRi	Costa Rica		
DomRep	Dominican Republic	*nms & pl*	invariable singular or plural masculine noun
Ecua	Ecuador		
esp	especially	*npl*	plural noun
f	feminine	*ns & pl*	noun invariable for plural
fam	familiar or colloquial	*Pan*	Panama
fpl	feminine plural	*Par*	Paraguay
Guat	Guatemala	*pl*	plural
Hond	Honduras	*pp*	past participle
interj	interjection	*prep*	preposition
m	masculine	*PRi*	Puerto Rico
Mex	Mexico	*pron*	pronoun
mf	masculine or feminine	*s*	singular
		Sal	El Salvador
mfpl	masculine or feminine plural	*Uru*	Uruguay
		usu	usually
mpl	masculine plural	*v*	verb (transitive and intransitive)
n	noun		
nf	feminine noun	*v aux*	auxiliary verb
nfpl	feminine plural noun	*Ven*	Venezuela
		vi	intransitive verb
nfs & pl	invariable singular or plural feminine noun	*v impers*	impersonal verb
		vr	reflexive verb
Nic	Nicaragua	*vt*	transitive verb

Conjugation of Spanish Verbs

Simple Tenses

Tense	Regular Verbs Ending in -AR hablar	
PRESENT INDICATIVE	hablo	hablamos
	hablas	habláis
	habla	hablan
PRESENT SUBJUNCTIVE	hable	hablemos
	hables	habléis
	hable	hablen
PRETERIT INDICATIVE	hablé	hablamos
	hablaste	hablasteis
	habló	hablaron
IMPERFECT INDICATIVE	hablaba	hablábamos
	hablabas	hablabais
	hablaba	hablaban
IMPERFECT SUBJUNCTIVE	hablara	habláramos
	hablaras	hablarais
	hablara	hablaran
	or	
	hablase	hablásemos
	hablases	hablaseis
	hablase	hablasen
FUTURE INDICATIVE	hablaré	hablaremos
	hablarás	hablaréis
	hablará	hablarán
FUTURE SUBJUNCTIVE	hablare	habláremos
	hablares	hablareis
	hablare	hablaren
CONDITIONAL	hablaría	hablaríamos
	hablarías	hablaríais
	hablaría	hablarían
IMPERATIVE		hablemos
	habla	hablad
	hable	hablen
PRESENT PARTICIPLE (GERUND)	hablando	
PAST PARTICIPLE	hablado	

Regular Verbs Ending in -ER		Regular Verbs Ending in -IR	
comer		vivir	
como	comemos	vivo	vivimos
comes	coméis	vives	vivís
come	comen	vive	viven
coma	comamos	viva	vivamos
comas	comáis	vivas	viváis
coma	coman	viva	vivan
comí	comimos	viví	vivimos
comiste	comisteis	viviste	vivisteis
comió	comieron	vivió	vivieron
comía	comíamos	vivía	vivíamos
comías	comíais	vivías	vivíais
comía	comían	vivía	vivían
comiera	comiéramos	viviera	viviéramos
comieras	comierais	vivieras	vivierais
comiera	comieran	viviera	vivieran
or		*or*	
comiese	comiésemos	viviese	viviésemos
comieses	comieseis	vivieses	vivieseis
comiese	comiesen	viviese	viviesen
comeré	comeremos	viviré	viviremos
comerás	comeréis	vivirás	viviréis
comerá	comerán	vivirá	vivirán
comiere	comiéremos	viviere	viviéremos
comieres	comiereis	vivieres	viviereis
comiere	comieren	viviere	vivieren
comería	comeríamos	viviría	viviríamos
comerías	comeríais	vivirías	viviríais
comería	comerían	viviría	vivirían
	comamos		vivamos
come	comed	vive	vivid
coma	coman	viva	vivan
comiendo		viviendo	
comido		vivido	

Compound Tenses

1. Perfect Tenses

The perfect tenses are formed with *haber* and the past participle:

PRESENT PERFECT

      he hablado, etc. (*indicative*);
      haya hablado, etc. (*subjunctive*)

PAST PERFECT

      había hablado, etc. (*indicative*);
      hubiera hablado, etc. (*subjunctive*)
      or
      hubiese hablado, etc. (*subjunctive*)

PRETERIT PERFECT

      hube hablado, etc. (*indicative*)

FUTURE PERFECT

      habré hablado, etc. (*indicative*)

CONDITIONAL PERFECT

      habría hablado, etc. (*indicative*)

2. Progressive Tenses

The progressive tenses are formed with *estar* and the present participle:

PRESENT PROGRESSIVE

      estoy llamando, etc. (*indicative*);
      esté llamando, etc. (*subjunctive*)

IMPERFECT PROGRESSIVE

      estaba llamando, etc. (*indicative*);
      estuviera llamando, etc. (*subjunctive*)
      or
      estuviese llamando, etc. (*subjunctive*)

PRETERIT PROGRESSIVE

estuve llamando, etc. (*indicative*)

FUTURE PROGRESSIVE

estaré llamando, etc. (*indicative*)

CONDITIONAL PROGRESSIVE

estaría llamando, etc. (*indicative*)

PRESENT PERFECT PROGRESSIVE

he estado llamando, etc. (*indicative*);
haya estado llamando, etc. (*subjunctive*)

PAST PERFECT PROGRESSIVE

había estado llamando, etc. (*indicative*);
hubiera estado llamando, etc. (*subjunctive*)
or
hubiese estado llamando, etc. (*subjunctive*)

Use of *Vos*

In parts of South and Central America, *vos* often replaces or competes with *tú* as the second person familiar personal pronoun. It is particularly well established in the Río de la Plata region and much of Central America.

The pronoun *vos* often takes a distinct set of verb forms, usually in the present tense and the imperative. These vary widely from region to region; examples of the most common forms are shown below.

INFINITIVE FORM	hablar	comer	vivir
PRESENT INDICATIVE	vos hablás	vos comés	vos vivís
PRESENT SUBJUNCTIVE	vos hablés	vos comás	vos vivás
IMPERATIVE	hablá	comé	viví

In some areas, *vos* may take the *tú* or *vosotros* forms of the verb, while in others (as Uruguay), *tú* is combined with the *vos* verb forms.

Irregular Verbs

The *imperfect subjunctive,* the *future subjunctive,* the *conditional*, and most forms of the *imperative* are not included in the model conjugations list, but can be derived as follows:

The *imperfect subjunctive* and the *future subjunctive* are formed from the third person plural form of the preterit tense by removing the last syllable (*-ron*) and adding the appropriate suffix:

PRETERIT INDICATIVE, THIRD PERSON PLURAL (querer)	quisieron
IMPERFECT SUBJUNCTIVE (querer)	quisiera, quisieras, etc. *or* quisiese, quisieses, etc.
FUTURE SUBJUNCTIVE (querer)	quisiere, quisieres, etc.

The conditional uses the same stem as the future indicative:

FUTURE INDICATIVE (poner)	pondré, pondrás, etc.
CONDITIONAL (poner)	pondría, pondrías, etc.

The third person singular, first person plural, and third person plural forms of the *imperative* are the same as the corresponding forms of the present subjunctive.

The second person plural *(vosotros)* form of the *imperative* is formed by removing the final *-r* of the infinitive form and adding a *-d* (ex.: *oír → oíd*).

Model Conjugations of Irregular Verbs

The model conjugations below include the following simple tenses: the *present indicative* (IND), the *present subjunctive* (SUBJ), the *preterit indicative* (PRET), the *imperfect indicative* (IMPF), the *future indicative* (*FUT*), the second person singular form of the *imperative* (*IMPER*), the *present participle* or *gerund* (*PRP*), and the *past participle* (*PP*). Each set of conjugations is preceded by the corresponding infinitive form of the verb, shown in bold type. Only tenses containing irregularities are listed, and the irregular verb forms within each tense are displayed in bold type.

Each irregular verb entry in the Spanish-English section of this dictionary is cross-referred by number to one of the following model conjugations. These cross-reference numbers are shown in curly braces { } immediately following the entry's functional label.

1 **abolir** *(defective verb)* : *IND* abolimos, abolís *(other forms not used); SUBJ (not used); IMPER (only second person plural is used)*

2 **abrir** : *PP* abierto

3 **actuar** : *IND* **actúo, actúas, actúa,** actuamos, actuáis, **actúan;** *SUBJ* **actúe, actúes, actúe,** actuemos, actuéis, **actúen;** *IMPER* **actúa**

4 **adquirir** : *IND* **adquiero, adquieres, adquiere,** adquirimos, adquirís, **adquieren;** *SUBJ* **adquiera, adquieras, adquiera,** adquiramos, adquiráis, **adquieran;** *IMPER* **adquiere**

5 **airar** : *IND* **aíro, aíras, aíra,** airamos, airáis, **aíran;** *SUBJ* **aíre, aíres, aíre,** airemos, airéis, **aíren;** *IMPER* **aíra**

6 **andar** : *PRET* **anduve, anduviste, anduvo, anduvimos, anduvisteis, anduvieron**

7 **asir** : *IND* **asgo,** ases, ase, asimos, asís, asen; *SUBJ* **asga, asgas, asga, asgamos, asgáis, asgan**

8 **aunar** : *IND* **aúno, aúnas, aúna,** aunamos, aunáis, **aúnan;** *SUBJ* **aúne, aúnes, aúne,** aunemos, aunéis, **aúnen;** *IMPER* **aúna**

9 **avergonzar** : *IND* **avergüenzo, avergüenzas, avergüenza,** avergonzamos, avergonzáis, **avergüenzan;** *SUBJ* **avergüence, avergüences, avergüence,** avergoncemos, **avergoncéis, avergüencen;** *PRET* **avergoncé;** *IMPER* **avergüenza**

10 **averiguar** : *SUBJ* **averigüe, averigües, averigüe, averigüemos, averigüéis, averigüen;** *PRET* **averigüé,** averiguaste, averiguó, averiguamos, averiguasteis, averiguaron

11 **bendecir** : *IND* **bendigo, bendices, bendice,** bendecimos, bendecís, **bendicen;** *SUBJ* **bendiga, bendigas, bendiga, bendigamos, bendigáis, bendigan;** *PRET* **bendije, bendijiste, bendijo, bendijimos, bendijisteis, bendijeron;** *IMPER* **bendice**

12 **caber** : *IND* **quepo,** cabes, cabe, cabemos, cabéis, caben; *SUBJ* **quepa, quepas, quepa, quepamos, quepáis, quepan;** *PRET* **cupe, cupiste, cupo, cupimos, cupisteis, cupieron;** *FUT* **cabré, cabrás, cabrá, cabremos, cabréis, cabrán**

13 **caer** : *IND* **caigo,** caes, cae, caemos, caéis, caen; *SUBJ* **caiga, caigas, caiga, caigamos, caigáis, caigan;** *PRET* **caí, caíste, cayó, caímos, caísteis, cayeron;** *PRP* **cayendo;** *PP* **caído**

14 **cocer** : *IND* **cuezo, cueces, cuece,** cocemos, cocéis, **cuecen;** *SUBJ* **cueza, cuezas, cueza, cozamos, cozáis, cuezan;** *IMPER* **cuece**

15 **coger** : *IND* **cojo,** coges, coge, cogemos, cogéis, cogen; *SUBJ* **coja, cojas, coja, cojamos, cojáis, cojan**

16 **colgar** : *IND* **cuelgo, cuelgas, cuelga,** colgamos, colgáis, **cuelgan;** *SUBJ* **cuelgue, cuelgues, cuelgue, colguemos, colguéis, cuelguen;** *PRET* **colgué,** colgaste, colgó, colgamos, colgasteis, colgaron; *IMPER* **cuelga**

17 **concernir** *(defective verb; used only in the third person singular and plural of the present indicative, present subjunctive, and imperfect subjunctive) see* **25 discernir**

18 **conocer** : *IND* **conozco,** conoces, conoce, conocemos, conocéis, conocen; *SUBJ* **conozca, conozcas, conozca, conozcamos, conozcáis, conozcan**

19 **contar** : *IND* **cuento, cuentas, cuenta,** contamos, contáis, **cuentan;** *SUBJ* **cuente, cuentes, cuente,** contemos, contéis, **cuenten;** *IMPER* **cuenta**

20 **creer** : *PRET* **creí, creíste, creyó, creímos, creísteis, creyeron;** *PRP* **creyendo;** *PP* **creído**

21 **cruzar** : *SUBJ* **cruce, cruces, cruce, crucemos, crucéis, crucen;** *PRET* **crucé,** cruzaste, cruzó, cruzamos, cruzasteis, cruzaron

22 **dar** : *IND* **doy,** das, da, damos, **dais,** dan; *SUBJ* **dé,** des, **dé,** demos, **deis,** den; *PRET* **di, diste, dio, dimos, disteis, dieron**

23 **decir** : *IND* **digo, dices, dice,** decimos, decís, **dicen;** *SUBJ* **diga, digas, diga, digamos, digáis, digan;** *PRET* **dije, dijiste, dijo, dijimos,** dijisteis, **dijeron;** *FUT* **diré, dirás, dirá, diremos, diréis, dirán;** *IMPER* **di;** *PRP* **diciendo;** *PP* **dicho**

24 **delinquir** : *IND* **delinco,** delinques, delinque, delinquimos, delinquís, delinquen; *SUBJ* **delinca, delincas, delinca, delincamos, delincáis, delincan**

25 **discernir** : *IND* **discierno, disciernes, discierne,** discernimos, discernís, **disciernen;** *SUBJ* **discierna, disciernas, discierna,** discernamos, discernáis, **disciernan;** *IMPER* **discierne**

26 **distinguir** : *IND* **distingo,** distingues, distingue, distinguimos, distinguís, distinguen; *SUBJ* **distinga, distingas, distinga, distingamos, distingáis, distingan**

27 **dormir** : *IND* **duermo, duermes, duerme,** dormimos, dormís, **duermen;** *SUBJ* **duerma, duermas, duerma, durmamos, durmáis, duerman;** *PRET* dormí, dormiste, **durmió,** dormimos, dormisteis, **durmieron;** *IMPER* **duerme;** *PRP* **durmiendo**

28 **elegir** : *IND* **elijo, eliges, elige,** elegimos, elegís, **eligen;** *SUBJ* **elija, elijas, elija, elijamos, elijáis, elijan;** *PRET* elegí, elegiste, **eligió,** elegimos, elegisteis, **eligieron;** *IMPER* **elige;** *PRP* **eligiendo**

29 **empezar** : *IND* **empiezo, empiezas, empieza,** empezamos, empezáis, **empiezan;** *SUBJ* **empiece, empieces, empiece, empecemos, empecéis, empiecen;** *PRET* **empecé,** empezaste, empezó, empezamos, empezasteis, empezaron; *IMPER* **empieza**

30 **enraizar** : *IND* **enraízo, enraízas, enraíza,** enraizamos, enraizáis, **enraízan;** *SUBJ* **enraíce, enraíces, enraíce, enraicemos, enraicéis, enraícen;** *PRET* **enraicé,** enraizaste, enraizó, enraizamos, enraizasteis, enraizaron; *IMPER* **enraíza**

31 **erguir** : *IND* **irgo** *or* **yergo, irgues** *or* **yergues, irgue** *or* **yergue,** erguimos, erguís, **irguen** *or* **yerguen;** *SUBJ* **irga** *or* **yerga, irgas** *or* **yergas, irga** *or* **yerga, irgamos, irgáis, irgan** *or* **yergan;** *PRET* erguí, erguiste, **irguió,** erguimos, erguisteis, **irguieron;** *IMPER* **irgue** *or* **yergue;** *PRP* **irguiendo**

32 **errar** : *IND* **yerro, yerras, yerra,** erramos, erráis, **yerran;** *SUBJ*
yerre, yerres, yerre, erremos, erréis, **yerren;** *IMPER* **yerra**

33 **escribir** : *PP* **escrito**

34 **estar** : *IND* **estoy, estás, está,** estamos, estáis, **están;** *SUBJ* **esté,**
estés, esté, estemos, estéis, **estén;** *PRET* **estuve, estuviste,**
estuvo, estuvimos, estuvisteis, estuvieron; *IMPER* **está**

35 **exigir** : *IND* **exijo,** exiges, exige, exigimos, exigís, exigen; *SUBJ*
exija, exijas, exija, exijamos, exijáis, exijan

36 **forzar** : *IND* **fuerzo, fuerzas, fuerza,** forzamos, forzáis,
fuerzan; *SUBJ* **fuerce, fuerces, fuerce,** forcemos, **forcéis,**
fuercen; *PRET* **forcé,** forzaste, forzó, forzamos, forzasteis,
forzaron; *IMPER* **fuerza**

37 **freír** : *IND* **frío, fríes, fríe, freímos,** freís, **fríen;** *SUBJ* **fría, frías,**
fría, friamos, friáis, frían; *PRET* freí, **freíste, frió, freímos,**
freísteis, frieron; *IMPER* **fríe;** *PRP* **friendo;** *PP* **frito**

38 **gruñir** : *PRET* gruñí, gruñiste, **gruñó,** gruñimos, gruñisteis,
gruñeron; *PRP* **gruñendo**

39 **haber** : *IND* **he, has, ha, hemos,** habéis, **han;** *SUBJ* **haya, hayas,**
haya, hayamos, hayáis, hayan; *PRET* **hube, hubiste, hubo,**
hubimos, hubisteis, hubieron; *FUT* **habré, habrás, habrá,**
habremos, habréis, habrán; *IMPER* **he**

40 **hacer** : *IND* **hago,** haces, hace, hacemos, hacéis, hacen; *SUBJ*
haga, hagas, haga, hagamos, hagáis, hagan; *PRET* **hice,**
hiciste, hizo, hicimos, hicisteis, hicieron; *FUT* **haré, harás,**
hará, haremos, haréis, harán; *IMPER* **haz;** *PP* **hecho**

41 **huir** : *IND* **huyo, huyes, huye,** huimos, huís, **huyen;** *SUBJ* **huya,**
huyas, huya, huyamos, huyáis, huyan; *PRET* **huí,** huiste,
huyó, huimos, huisteis, **huyeron;** *IMPER* **huye;** *PRP* **huyendo**

42 **imprimir** : *PP* **impreso**

43 **ir** : *IND* **voy, vas, va, vamos, vais, van;** *SUBJ* **vaya, vayas, vaya,**
vayamos, vayáis, vayan; *PRET* **fui, fuiste, fue, fuimos, fuis-**
teis, fueron; *IMPF* **iba, ibas, iba, íbamos, ibais, iban;** *IMPER*
ve; *PRP* **yendo;** *PP* **ido**

44 **jugar** : *IND* **juego, juegas, juega,** jugamos, jugáis, **juegan;** *SUBJ*
juegue, juegues, juegue, juguemos, juguéis, jueguen; *PRET*

jugué, jugaste, jugó, jugamos, jugasteis, jugaron; *IMPER* **juega**

45 **lucir** : *IND* **luzco,** luces, luce, lucimos, lucís, lucen; *SUBJ* **luzca, luzcas, luzca, luzcamos, luzcáis, luzcan**

46 **morir** : *IND* **muero, mueres, muere,** morimos, morís, **mueren;** *SUBJ* **muera, mueras, muera, muramos, muráis, mueran;** *PRET* **morí,** moriste, **murió,** morimos, moristeis, **murieron;** *IMPER* **muere;** *PRP* **muriendo;** *PP* **muerto**

47 **mover** : *IND* **muevo, mueves, mueve,** movemos, movéis, **mueven;** *SUBJ* **mueva, muevas, mueva,** movamos, mováis, **muevan;** *IMPER* **mueve**

48 **nacer** : *IND* **nazco,** naces, nace, nacemos, nacéis, nacen; *SUBJ* **nazca, nazcas, nazca, nazcamos, nazcáis, nazcan**

49 **negar** : *IND* **niego, niegas, niega,** negamos, negáis, **niegan;** *SUBJ* **niegue, niegues, niegue, neguemos, neguéis, nieguen;** *PRET* **negué,** negaste, negó, negamos, negasteis, negaron; *IMPER* **niega**

50 **oír** : *IND* **oigo, oyes, oye, oímos,** oís, **oyen;** *SUBJ* **oiga, oigas, oiga, oigamos, oigáis, oigan;** *PRET* **oí, oíste, oyó, oímos, oísteis, oyeron;** *IMPER* **oye;** *PRP* **oyendo;** *PP* **oído**

51 **oler** : *IND* **huelo, hueles, huele,** olemos, oléis, **huelen;** *SUBJ* **huela, huelas, huela,** olamos, oláis, **huelan;** *IMPER* **huele**

52 **pagar** : *SUBJ* **pague, pagues, pague, paguemos, paguéis, paguen;** *PRET* **pagué,** pagaste, pagó, pagamos, pagasteis, pagaron

53 **parecer** : *IND* **parezco,** pareces, parece, parecemos, parecéis, parecen; *SUBJ* **parezca, parezcas, parezca, parezcamos, parezcáis, parezcan**

54 **pedir** : *IND* **pido, pides, pide,** pedimos, pedís, **piden;** *SUBJ* **pida, pidas, pida, pidamos, pidáis, pidan;** *PRET* **pedí,** pediste, **pidió,** pedimos, pedisteis, **pidieron;** *IMPER* **pide;** *PRP* **pidiendo**

55 **pensar** : *IND* **pienso, piensas, piensa,** pensamos, pensáis, **piensan;** *SUBJ* **piense, pienses, piense,** pensemos, penséis, **piensen;** *IMPER* **piensa**

56 **perder** : *IND* **pierdo, pierdes, pierde,** perdemos, perdéis, **pierden;** *SUBJ* **pierda, pierdas, pierda,** perdamos, perdáis, **pierdan;** *IMPER* **pierde**

57 **placer** : *IND* **plazco,** places, place, placemos, placéis, placen; *SUBJ* **plazca, plazcas, plazca, plazcamos, plazcáis, plazcan;** *PRET* plací, placiste, plació *or* **plugo,** placimos, placisteis, placieron *or* **pluguieron**

58 **poder** : *IND* **puedo, puedes, puede,** podemos, podéis, **pueden;** *SUBJ* **pueda, puedas, pueda,** podamos, podáis, **puedan;** *PRET* **pude, pudiste, pudo, pudimos, pudisteis, pudieron;** *FUT* **podré, podrás, podrá, podremos, podréis, podrán;** *IMPER* **puede;** *PRP* **pudiendo**

59 **podrir** *or* **pudrir** : *PP* **podrido** *(all other forms based on* pudrir*)*

60 **poner** : *IND* **pongo,** pones, pone, ponemos, ponéis, ponen; *SUBJ* **ponga, pongas, ponga, pongamos, pongáis, pongan;** *PRET* **puse, pusiste, puso, pusimos, pusisteis, pusieron;** *FUT* **pondré, pondrás, pondrá, pondremos, pondréis, pondrán;** *IMPER* **pon;** *PP* **puesto**

61 **producir** : *IND* **produzco,** produces, produce, producimos, producís, producen; *SUBJ* **produzca, produzcas, produzca, produzcamos, produzcáis, produzcan;** *PRET* **produje, produjiste, produjo, produjimos, produjisteis, produjeron**

62 **prohibir** : *IND* **prohíbo, prohíbes, prohíbe,** prohibimos, prohibís, **prohíben;** *SUBJ* **prohíba, prohíbas, prohíba,** prohibamos, prohibáis, **prohíban;** *IMPER* **prohíbe**

63 **proveer** : *PRET* proveí, **proveíste, proveyó, proveímos, proveísteis, proveyeron;** *PRP* **proveyendo;** *PP* **provisto**

64 **querer** : *IND* **quiero, quieres, quiere,** queremos, queréis, **quieren;** *SUBJ* **quiera, quieras, quiera,** queramos, queráis, **quieran;** *PRET* **quise, quisiste, quiso, quisimos, quisisteis, quisieron;** *FUT* **querré, querrás, querrá, querremos, querréis, querrán;** *IMPER* **quiere**

65 **raer** : *IND* rao *or* **raigo** *or* **rayo,** raes, rae, raemos, raéis, raen; *SUBJ* **raiga** *or* **raya, raigas** *or* **rayas, raiga** *or* **raya, raigamos** *or* **rayamos, raigáis** *or* **rayáis, raigan** *or* **rayan;** *PRET* **raí, raíste, rayó, raímos, raísteis, rayeron;** *PRP* **rayendo;** *PP* **raído**

66 **reír** : *IND* **río, ríes, ríe, reímos,** reís, **ríen;** *SUBJ* **ría, rías, ría, riamos, riáis, rían;** *PRET* reí, **reíste, rió,** reímos, **reísteis, rieron;** *IMPER* **ríe;** *PRP* **riendo;** *PP* **reído**

67 **reñir** : *IND* **riño, riñes, riñe,** reñimos, reñís, **riñen;** *SUBJ* **riña, riñas, riña, riñamos, riñáis, riñan;** *PRET* reñí, reñiste, **riñó,** reñimos, reñisteis, **riñeron;** *IMPER* riñe; *PRP* riñendo

68 **reunir** : *IND* **reúno, reúnes, reúne,** reunimos, reunís, **reúnen;** *SUBJ* **reúna, reúnas, reúna,** reunamos, reunáis, **reúnan;** *IMPER* **reúne**

69 **roer** : *IND* roo *or* **roigo** *or* **royo,** roes, roe, roemos, roéis, roen; *SUBJ* roa *or* **roiga** *or* **roya,** roas *or* **roigas** *or* **royas,** roa *or* **roiga** *or* **roya,** roamos *or* **roigamos** *or* **royamos,** roáis *or* **roigáis** *or* **royáis,** roan *or* **roigan** *or* **royan;** *PRET* roí, **roíste, royó, roímos, roísteis, royeron;** *PRP* **royendo;** *PP* **roído**

70 **romper** : *PP* **roto**

71 **saber** : *IND* **sé,** sabes, sabe, sabemos, sabéis, saben; *SUBJ* **sepa, sepas, sepa, sepamos, sepáis, sepan;** *PRET* **supe, supiste, supo, supimos, supisteis, supieron;** *FUT* **sabré, sabrás, sabrá, sabremos, sabréis, sabrán**

72 **sacar** : *SUBJ* **saque, saques, saque, saquemos, saquéis, saquen;** *PRET* **saqué,** sacaste, sacó, sacamos, sacasteis, sacaron

73 **salir** : *IND* **salgo,** sales, sale, salimos, salís, salen; *SUBJ* **salga, salgas, salga, salgamos, salgáis, salgan;** *FUT* **saldré, saldrás, saldrá, saldremos, saldréis, saldrán;** *IMPER* **sal**

74 **satisfacer** : *IND* **satisfago,** satisfaces, satisface, satisfacemos, satisfacéis, satisfacen; *SUBJ* **satisfaga, satisfagas, satisfaga, satisfagamos, satisfagáis, satisfagan;** *PRET* **satisfice, satisficiste, satisfizo, satisficimos, satisficisteis, satisficieron;** *FUT* **satisfaré, satisfarás, satisfará, satisfaremos, satisfaréis, satisfarán;** *IMPER* **satisfaz** *or* satisface; *PP* **satisfecho**

75 **seguir** : *IND* **sigo, sigues, sigue,** seguimos, seguís, **siguen;** *SUBJ* **siga, sigas, siga, sigamos, sigáis, sigan;** *PRET* seguí, seguiste, **siguió,** seguimos, seguisteis, **siguieron;** *IMPER* **sigue;** *PRP* **siguiendo**

76 **sentir** : *IND* **siento, sientes, siente,** sentimos, sentís, **sienten;** *SUBJ* **sienta, sientas, sienta, sintamos, sintáis, sientan;** *PRET*

sentí, sentiste, **sintió**, sentimos, sentisteis, **sintieron**; *IMPER*
siente; *PRP* **sintiendo**

77 **ser** : *IND* **soy, eres, es, somos, sois, son;** *SUBJ* **sea, seas, sea,**
seamos, seáis, sean; *PRET* **fui, fuiste, fue, fuimos, fuisteis,**
fueron; *IMPF* **era, eras, era, éramos, erais, eran;** *IMPER* **sé;**
PRP **siendo;** *PP* **sido**

78 **soler** *(defective verb; used only in the present, preterit, and imper-*
fect indicative, and the present and imperfect subjunctive) see
47 **mover**

79 **tañer** : *PRET* **tañí**, tañiste, **tañó**, tañimos, tañisteis, **tañeron;**
PRP **tañendo**

80 **tener** : *IND* **tengo, tienes, tiene,** tenemos, tenéis, **tienen;** *SUBJ*
tenga, tengas, tenga, tengamos, tengáis, tengan; *PRET* **tuve,**
tuviste, tuvo, tuvimos, tuvisteis, tuvieron; *FUT* **tendré, ten-**
drás, tendrá, tendremos, tendréis, tendrán; *IMPER* **ten**

81 **traer** : *IND* **traigo,** traes, trae, traemos, traéis, traen; *SUBJ*
traiga, traigas, traiga, traigamos, traigáis, traigan; *PRET*
traje, trajiste, trajo, trajimos, trajisteis, trajeron; *PRP*
trayendo; *PP* **traído**

82 **trocar** : *IND* **trueco, truecas, trueca,** trocamos, trocáis, **true-**
can; *SUBJ* **trueque, trueques, trueque, troquemos, troquéis,**
truequen; *PRET* **troqué,** trocaste, trocó, trocamos, trocasteis,
trocaron; *IMPER* **trueca**

83 **uncir** : *IND* **unzo,** unces, unce, uncimos, uncís, uncen; *SUBJ*
unza, unzas, unza, unzamos, unzáis, unzan

84 **valer** : *IND* **valgo,** vales, vale, valemos, valéis, valen; *SUBJ* **val-**
ga, valgas, valga, valgamos, valgáis, valgan; *FUT* **valdré,**
valdrás, valdrá, valdremos, valdréis, valdrán

85 **variar** : *IND* **varío, varías, varía,** variamos, variáis, **varían;**
SUBJ **varíe, varíes, varíe,** variemos, variéis, **varíen;** *IMPER*
varía

86 **vencer** : *IND* **venzo,** vences, vence, vencemos, vencéis, ven-
cen; *SUBJ* **venza, venzas, venza, venzamos, venzáis, venzan**

87 **venir** : *IND* **vengo, vienes, viene,** venimos, venís, **vienen;** *SUBJ*
venga, vengas, venga, vengamos, vengáis, vengan; *PRET*
vine, viniste, vino, vinimos, vinisteis, vinieron; *FUT* **vendré,**

vendrás, vendrá, vendremos, vendréis, vendrán; *IMPER* **ven;** *PRP* **viniendo**

88 **ver** : *IND* **veo, ves, ve, vemos, veis, ven;** *PRET* **vi, viste, vio, vimos, visteis, vieron;** *IMPER* **ve;** *PRP* **viendo;** *PP* **visto**

89 **volver** : *IND* **vuelvo, vuelves, vuelve,** volvemos, volvéis, **vuelven;** *SUBJ* **vuelva, vuelvas, vuelva,** volvamos, volváis, **vuelvan;** *IMPER* **vuelve;** *PP* **vuelto**

90 **yacer** : *IND* **yazco** *or* **yazgo** *or* **yago,** yaces, yace, yacemos, yacéis, yacen; *SUBJ* **yazca** *or* **yazga** *or* **yaga, yazcas** *or* **yazgas** *or* **yagas, yazca** *or* **yazga** *or* **yaga, yazcamos** *or* **yazgamos** *or* **yagamos, yazcáis** *or* **yazgáis** *or* **yagáis, yazcan** *or* **yazgan** *or* **yagan;** *IMPER* yace *or* yaz

Irregular English Verbs

INFINITIVE	PAST	PAST PARTICIPLE
arise	arose	arisen
awake	awoke	awoken *or* awaked
be	was, were	been
bear	bore	borne
beat	beat	beaten *or* beat
become	became	become
befall	befell	befallen
begin	began	begun
behold	beheld	beheld
bend	bent	bent
beseech	beseeched *or* besought	beseeched *or* besought
beset	beset	beset
bet	bet	bet
bid	bade *or* bid	bidden *or* bid
bind	bound	bound
bite	bit	bitten
bleed	bled	bled
blow	blew	blown
break	broke	broken
breed	bred	bred
bring	brought	brought
build	built	built
burn	burned *or* burnt	burned *or* burnt
burst	burst	burst
buy	bought	bought
can	could	—
cast	cast	cast
catch	caught	caught
choose	chose	chosen
cling	clung	clung
come	came	come
cost	cost	cost
creep	crept	crept
cut	cut	cut
deal	dealt	dealt
dig	dug	dug
do	did	done
draw	drew	drawn
dream	dreamed *or* dreamt	dreamed *or* dreamt
drink	drank	drunk *or* drank
drive	drove	driven
dwell	dwelled *or* dwelt	dwelled *or* dwelt

INFINITIVE	PAST	PAST PARTICIPLE
eat	ate	eaten
fall	fell	fallen
feed	fed	fed
feel	felt	felt
fight	fought	fought
find	found	found
flee	fled	fled
fling	flung	flung
fly	flew	flown
forbid	forbade	forbidden
forecast	forecast	forecast
forego	forewent	foregone
foresee	foresaw	foreseen
foretell	foretold	foretold
forget	forgot	forgotten *or* forgot
forgive	forgave	forgiven
forsake	forsook	forsaken
freeze	froze	frozen
get	got	got *or* gotten
give	gave	given
go	went	gone
grind	ground	ground
grow	grew	grown
hang	hung	hung
have	had	had
hear	heard	heard
hide	hid	hidden *or* hid
hit	hit	hit
hold	held	held
hurt	hurt	hurt
keep	kept	kept
kneel	knelt *or* kneeled	knelt *or* kneeled
know	knew	known
lay	laid	laid
lead	led	led
lean	leaned	leaned
leap	leaped *or* leapt	leaped *or* leapt
learn	learned	learned
leave	left	left
lend	lent	lent
let	let	let
lie	lay	lain
light	lit *or* lighted	lit *or* lighted
lose	lost	lost
make	made	made
may	might	—

INFINITIVE	PAST	PAST PARTICIPLE
mean	meant	meant
meet	met	met
mow	mowed	mowed *or* mown
pay	paid	paid
put	put	put
quit	quit	quit
read	read	read
rend	rent	rent
rid	rid	rid
ride	rode	ridden
ring	rang	rung
rise	rose	risen
run	ran	run
saw	sawed	sawed *or* sawn
say	said	said
see	saw	seen
seek	sought	sought
sell	sold	sold
send	sent	sent
set	set	set
shake	shook	shaken
shall	should	—
shear	sheared	sheared *or* shorn
shed	shed	shed
shine	shone *or* shined	shone *or* shined
shoot	shot	shot
show	showed	shown *or* showed
shrink	shrank *or* shrunk	shrunk *or* shrunken
shut	shut	shut
sing	sang *or* sung	sung
sink	sank *or* sunk	sunk
sit	sat	sat
slay	slew	slain
sleep	slept	slept
slide	slid	slid
sling	slung	slung
smell	smelled *or* smelt	smelled *or* smelt
sow	sowed	sown *or* sowed
speak	spoke	spoken
speed	sped *or* speeded	sped *or* speeded
spell	spelled	spelled
spend	spent	spent
spill	spilled	spilled
spin	spun	spun
spit	spit *or* spat	spit *or* spat
split	split	split

INFINITIVE	PAST	PAST PARTICIPLE
spoil	spoiled	spoiled
spread	spread	spread
spring	sprang *or* sprung	sprung
stand	stood	stood
steal	stole	stolen
stick	stuck	stuck
sting	stung	stung
stink	stank *or* stunk	stunk
stride	strode	stridden
strike	struck	struck
swear	swore	sworn
sweep	swept	swept
swell	swelled	swelled *or* swollen
swim	swam	swum
swing	swung	swung
take	took	taken
teach	taught	taught
tear	tore	torn
tell	told	told
think	thought	thought
throw	threw	thrown
thrust	thrust	thrust
tread	trod	trodden *or* trod
wake	woke	woken *or* waked
waylay	waylaid	waylaid
wear	wore	worn
weave	wove *or* weaved	woven *or* weaved
wed	wedded	wedded
weep	wept	wept
will	would	—
win	won	won
wind	wound	wound
withdraw	withdrew	withdrawn
withhold	withheld	withheld
withstand	withstood	withstood
wring	wrung	wrung
write	wrote	written

Spelling-to-Sound Correspondences in Spanish

For example words for the phonetic symbols below, see Pronunciation Symbols on page 58a.

VOWELS

a [a]

e [e] in open syllables (syllables ending with a vowel); [ɛ] in closed syllables (syllables ending with a consonant)

i [i]; before another vowel in the same syllable pronounced as [j] ([ʒ] or [ʃ] in Argentina and Uruguay; [ʤ] when at the beginning of a word in the Caribbean)

o [o] in open syllables (syllables ending with a vowel); [ɔ] in closed syllables (syllables ending with a consonant)

u [u]; before another vowel in the same syllable pronounced as [w]

y [i]; before another vowel in the same syllable pronounced as [j] ([ʒ] or [ʃ] in Argentina and Uruguay; [ʤ] when at the beginning of a word in the Caribbean)

CONSONANTS

b [b] at the beginning of a word or after m or n; [β] elsewhere

c [s] before i or e in Latin America and parts of southern Spain, [θ] in northern Spain; [k] elsewhere

ch [ʧ]; frequently [ʃ] in Chile and Panama; sometimes [ts] in Chile

d [d] at the beginning of a word or after n or l; [ð] elsewhere, frequently silent between vowels

f [f]; [Φ] in Honduras (no English equivalent for this sound; like [f] but made with both lips)

g [x] before i or e ([h] in the Caribbean and Central America); [g] at the beginning of a word or after n and not before i or e; [ɣ] elsewhere, frequently silent between vowels

gu [gw] at the beginning of a word before a, o; [ɣw] elsewhere before a, o; frequently just [w] between vowels; [g] at the beginning of a word before i, e; [ɣ] elsewhere before i, e; frequently silent between vowels

gü [gw] at the beginning of a word, [ɣw] elsewhere; frequently just [w] between vowels

h silent

j [x] ([h] in the Caribbean and Central America)

k [k]

l [l]

ll [j]; [ʒ] or [ʃ] in Argentina and Uruguay; [ʤ] when at the beginning of a word in the Caribbean;

[lʲ] in Bolivia, Paraguay, Peru, and parts of northern Spain (no English equivalent; like "lli" in *million*)

m [m]

n [n]; frequently [ŋ] at the end of a word when next word begins with a vowel

ñ [ɲ]

p [p]

qu [k]

r [r] (no English equivalent; a trilled sound) at the beginning of words; [t̮]/[ɾ] elsewhere

rr [r] (no English equivalent; a trilled sound)

s [s]; frequently [z] before

b, *d*, *g*, *m*, *n*, *l*, *r*; at the end of a word [h] or silent in many parts of Latin America and some parts of Spain

t [t]

v [b] at the beginning of a word or after *m* or *n*; [β] elsewhere

x [ks] or [gz] between vowels; [s] before consonants

z [s] in Latin America and parts of southern Spain, [θ] in northern Spain; at the end of a word [h] or silent in many parts of Latin America and some parts of Spain

Pronunciation Symbols

VOWELS

æ	ask, bat, glad
ɑ	cot, bomb
a	*New England* aunt, *British* ask, glass, *Spanish* casa
e	*Spanish* peso, jefe
ɛ	egg, bet, fed
ə	about, javelin, Alabama
ə	when italicized as in *ə*l, *ə*m, *ə*n, indicates a syllabic pronunciation of the consonant as in bottle, prism, button
i	very, any, thirty, *Spanish* piña
i:	eat, bead, bee
ɪ	id, bid, pit
o	Ohio, yellower, potato, *Spanish* óvalo
o:	oats, own, zone, blow
ɔ	awl, maul, caught, paw
ʊ	sure, should, could
u	*Spanish* uva, culpa
u:	boot, few, coo
ʌ	under, putt, bud
eɪ	eight, wade, bay
aɪ	ice, bite, tie
aʊ	out, gown, plow
ɔɪ	oyster, coil, boy
ər	further, stir
ɒ	*British* bond, god
:	indicates that the preceding vowel is long. Long vowels are almost always diphthongs in English, but not in Spanish.

CONSONANTS

b	baby, labor, cab
β	*Spanish* cabo, óvalo
d	day, ready, kid
dʒ	just, badger, fudge
ð	then, either, bathe
f	foe, tough, buff
g	go, bigger, bag
ɣ	*Spanish* tragar, daga
h	hot, aha
j	yes, vineyard
k	cat, keep, lacquer, flock
l	law, hollow, boil
m	mat, hemp, hammer, rim
n	new, tent, tenor, run
ŋ	rung, hang, swinger
ɲ	*Spanish* cabaña, piña
p	pay, lapse, top
r	rope, burn, tar
s	sad, mist, kiss
ʃ	shoe, mission, slush
t	toe, button, mat
ţ	indicates that some speakers of English pronounce this as a voiced alveolar flap [ɾ], as in later, catty, battle
ʧ	choose, batch
θ	thin, ether, bath
v	vat, never, cave
w	wet, software
x	*German* Bach, *Scots* loch, *Spanish* gente, jefe
z	zoo, easy, buzz
ʒ	jaborandi, azure, beige
h, k,	when italicized indicate
p, t	sounds which are present in the pronunciation of some speakers of English but absent in that of others, so that *whence* ['hwɛnţs] can be pronounced as ['wɛns], ['hwɛns], ['wɛnts], or ['hwɛnts]

STRESS MARKS

'	high stress	**pen**manship
ˌ	low stress	penman**ship**

Spanish–English
Dictionary

A

a¹ *nf* : first letter of the Spanish alphabet

a² *prep* **1** : to ⟨nos vamos a México : we're going to Mexico⟩ **2** (*used before direct or indirect objects referring to persons*) ⟨¿llamaste a tu papá? : did you call your dad?⟩ ⟨como a usted le guste : as you wish⟩ **3** : in the manner of ⟨papas a la francesa : french fries⟩ **4** : on, by means of ⟨a pie : on foot⟩ **5** : per, each ⟨tres pastillas al día : three pills per day⟩ **6** : at ⟨a las dos : at two o'clock⟩ ⟨al principio : at first⟩ **7** (*with infinitive*) ⟨enséñales a leer : teach them to read⟩ ⟨problemas a resolver : problems to be solved⟩

ábaco *nm* : abacus

abad *nm* : abbot

abadesa *nf* : abbess

abadía *nf* : abbey

abajo *adv* **1** : down ⟨póngalo más abajo : put it further down⟩ ⟨arriba y abajo : up and down⟩ **2** : downstairs **3** : under, beneath ⟨el abajo firmante : the undersigned⟩ **4** : down with ⟨¡abajo la inflación! : down with inflation!⟩ **5** ~ **de** : under, beneath **6 de** ~ : bottom ⟨el cajón de abajo : the bottom drawer⟩ **7 hacia** ~ *or* **para** ~ : downwards **8 cuesta abajo** : downhill **9 río abajo** : downstream

abalanzarse {21} *vr* : to hurl oneself, to rush

abanderado, -da *n* : standard-bearer

abandonado, -da *adj* **1** : abandoned, deserted **2** : neglected **3** : slovenly, unkempt

abandonar *vt* **1** DEJAR : to abandon, to leave **2** : to give up, to quit ⟨abandonaron la búsqueda : they gave up the search⟩ — **abandonarse** *vr* **1** : to neglect oneself **2** ~ **a** : to succumb to, to give oneself over to

abandono *nm* **1** : abandonment **2** : neglect **3** : withdrawal ⟨ganar por abandono : to win by default⟩

abanicar {72} *vt* : to fan — **abanicarse** *vr*

abanico *nm* **1** : fan **2** GAMA : range, gamut

abaratamiento *nm* : price reduction

abaratar *vt* : to lower the price of — **abaratarse** *vr* : to go down in price

abarcar {72} *vt* **1** : to cover, to include, to embrace **2** : to undertake **3** : to monopolize

abaritonado, -da *adj* : baritone

abarrotado, -da *adj* : packed, crammed

abarrotar *vt* : to fill up, to pack

abarrotería *nf CA, Mex* : grocery store

abarrotero, -ra *n Col, Mex* : grocer

abarrotes *nmpl* **1** : groceries, supplies **2 tienda de abarrotes** : general store, grocery store

abastecedor, -dora *n* : supplier

abastecer {53} *vt* : to supply, to stock — **abastecerse** *vr* : to stock up

abastecimiento → **abasto**

abasto *nm* : supply, supplying ⟨no da abasto : there isn't enough for all⟩

abatido, -da *adj* : dejected, depressed

abatimiento *nm* **1** : drop, reduction **2** : dejection, depression

abatir *vt* **1** DERRIBAR : to demolish, to knock down **2** : to shoot down **3** DEPRIMIR : to depress, to bring low — **abatirse** *vr* **1** DEPRIMIRSE : to get depressed **2** ~ **sobre** : to swoop down on

abdicación *nf, pl* **-ciones** : abdication

abdicar {72} *vt* : to relinquish, to abdicate

abdomen *nm, pl* **-dómenes** : abdomen

abdominal *adj* : abdominal

abecé *nm* : ABC's *pl*

abecedario *nm* ALFABETO : alphabet

abedul *nm* : birch (tree)

abeja *nf* : bee

abejorro *nm* : bumblebee

aberración *nf, pl* **-ciones** : aberration

aberrante *adj* : aberrant, perverse

abertura *nf* **1** : aperture, opening **2** AGUJERO : hole **3** : slit (in a skirt, etc.) **4** GRIETA : crack

abeto *nm* : fir (tree)

abierto¹ *pp* → **abrir**

abierto², -ta *adj* **1** : open **2** : candid, frank **3** : generous — **abiertamente** *adv*

abigarrado, -da *adj* : multicolored, variegated

abigeato *nm* : rustling (of livestock)

abismal *adj* : abysmal, vast

abismo *nm* : abyss, chasm ⟨al borde del abismo : on the brink of ruin⟩

abjurar *vi* ~ **de** : to abjure — **abjuración** *nf*

ablandamiento *nm* : softening, moderation

ablandar *vt* **1** SUAVIZAR : to soften **2** CALMAR : to soothe, to appease — *vi* : to moderate, to get milder — **ablandarse** *vr* **1** : to become soft, to soften **2** CEDER : to yield, to relent

ablución *nf, pl* **-ciones** : ablution

abnegación *nf, pl* **-ciones** : abnegation, self-denial

abnegado, -da *adj* : self-sacrificing, selfless

abnegarse {49} *vr* : to deny oneself

abobado, -da *adj* **1** : silly, stupid **2** : bewildered

abocarse {72} *vr* **1** DIRIGIRSE : to head, to direct oneself **2** DEDICARSE : to dedicate oneself

abochornar *vt* AVERGONZAR : to embarrass, to shame — **abochornarse** *vr*

abofetear *vt* : to slap

abogacía *nf* : law, legal profession

abogado, -da *n* : lawyer, attorney

abogar {52} *vi* ~ **por** : to plead for, to defend, to advocate

abolengo *nm* LINAJE : lineage, ancestry
abolición *nf, pl* -**ciones** : abolition
abolir {1} *vt* DEROGAR : to abolish, to repeal
abolladura *nf* : dent
abollar *vt* : to dent
abombar *vt* : to warp, to cause to bulge — **abombarse** *vr* : to decompose, to go bad
abominable *adj* ABORRECIBLE : abominable
abominación *nf, pl* -**ciones** : abomination
abominar *vt* ABORRECER : to abominate, to abhor
abonado, -da *n* : subscriber
abonar *vt* **1** : to pay **2** FERTILIZAR : to fertilize — **abonarse** *vr* : to subscribe
abono *nm* **1** : payment, installment **2** FERTILIZANTE : fertilizer **3** : season ticket
abordaje *nm* : boarding
abordar *vt* **1** : to address, to broach **2** : to accost, to waylay **3** : to come on board
aborigen[1] *adj, pl* -**rígenes** : aboriginal, native
aborigen[2] *nmf, pl* -**rígenes** : aborigine, indigenous inhabitant
aborrecer {53} *vt* ABOMINAR, ODIAR : to abhor, to detest, to hate
aborrecible *adj* ABOMINABLE, ODIOSO : abominable, detestable
aborrecimiento *nm* : abhorrence, loathing
abortar *vi* : to have an abortion — *vt* **1** : to abort **2** : to quash, to suppress
abortista *nmf* : abortionist
abortivo, -va *adj* : abortive
aborto *nm* **1** : abortion **2** : miscarriage
abotonar *vt* : to button — **abotonarse** *vr* : to button up
abovedado, -da *adj* : vaulted
abrasador, -dora *adj* : burning, scorching
abrasar *vt* QUEMAR : to burn, to sear, to scorch
abrasivo[1], **-va** *adj* : abrasive
abrasivo[2] *nm* : abrasive
abrazadera *nf* : clamp, brace
abrazar {21} *vt* : to hug, to embrace — **abrazarse** *vr*
abrazo *nm* : hug, embrace
abrebotellas *nms & pl* : bottle opener
abrelatas *nms & pl* : can opener
abrevadero *nm* BEBEDERO : watering trough
abreviación *nf, pl* -**ciones** : abbreviation
abreviar *vt* **1** : to abbreviate **2** : to shorten, to cut short
abreviatura → **abreviación**
abridor *nm* : bottle opener, can opener
abrigadero *nm* : shelter, windbreak
abrigado, -da *adj* **1** : sheltered **2** : warm, wrapped up (with clothing)
abrigar {52} *vt* **1** : to shelter, to protect **2** : to keep warm, to dress warmly **3** : to cherish, to harbor ⟨abrigar esper-

anzas : to cherish hopes⟩ — **abrigarse** *vr* : to dress warmly
abrigo *nm* **1** : coat, overcoat **2** : shelter, refuge
abril *nm* : April
abrillantador *nm* : polish
abrillantar *vt* : to polish, to shine
abrir {2} *vt* **1** : to open **2** : to unlock, to undo **3** : to turn on (a tap or faucet) — *vi* : to open, to open up — **abrirse** *vr* **1** : to open up **2** : to clear (of the skies)
abrochar *vt* : to button, to fasten — **abrocharse** *vr* : to fasten, to hook up
abrogación *nf, pl* -**ciones** : abrogation, annulment, repeal
abrogar {52} *vt* : to abrogate, to annul, to repeal
abrojo *nm* : bur (of a plant)
abrumador, -dora *adj* : crushing, overwhelming
abrumar *vt* **1** AGOBIAR : to overwhelm **2** OPRIMIR : to oppress, to burden
abrupto, -ta *adj* **1** : abrupt **2** ESCARPADO : steep — **abruptamente** *adv*
absceso *nm* : abscess
absolución *nf, pl* -**ciones** **1** : absolution **2** : acquittal
absolutismo *nm* : absolutism
absoluto, -ta *adj* **1** : absolute, unconditional **2 en ～** : not at all ⟨no me gustó en absoluto : I did not like it at all⟩ — **absolutamente** *adv*
absolver {89} *vt* **1** : to absolve **2** : to acquit
absorbente *adj* **1** : absorbent **2** : absorbing, engrossing
absorber *vt* **1** : to absorb, to soak up **2** : to occupy, to take up, to engross
absorción *nf, pl* -**ciones** : absorption
absorto, -ta *adj* : absorbed, engrossed
abstemio[1], **-mia** *adj* : abstemious, teetotal
abstemio[2], **-mia** *n* : teetotaler
abstención *nf, pl* -**ciones** : abstention
abstenerse {80} *vr* : to abstain, to refrain
abstinencia *nf* : abstinence
abstracción *nf, pl* -**ciones** : abstraction
abstracto, -ta *adj* : abstract
abstraer {81} *vt* : to abstract — **abstraerse** *vr* : to lose oneself in thought
abstraído, -da *adj* : preoccupied, withdrawn
abstruso, -sa *adj* : abstruse
abstuvo, etc. → **abstenerse**
absuelto *pp* → **absolver**
absurdo[1], **-da** *adj* DISPARATADO, RIDÍCULO : absurd, ridiculous — **absurdamente** *adv*
absurdo[2] *nm* : absurdity
abuchear *vt* : to boo, to jeer
abucheo *nm* : booing, jeering
abuela *nf* **1** : grandmother **2** : old woman **3 ¡tu abuela!** *fam* : no way!, forget about it!
abuelo *nm* **1** : grandfather **2** : old man **3 abuelos** *nmpl* : grandparents, ancestors

abulia *nf* : apathy, lethargy
abúlico, -ca *adj* : lethargic, apathetic
abultado, -da *adj* : bulging, bulky
abultar *vi* : to bulge — *vt* : to enlarge, to expand
abundancia *nf* : abundance
abundante *adj* : abundant, plentiful — **abundantemente** *adv*
abundar *vi* **1** : to abound, to be plentiful **2** ~ **en** : to be in agreement with
aburrido, -da *adj* **1** : bored, tired, fed up **2** TEDIOSO : boring, tedious
aburrimiento *nm* : boredom, weariness
aburrir *vt* : to bore, to tire — **aburrirse** *vr* : to get bored
abusado, -da *adj Mex fam* : sharp, on the ball
abusador, -dora *n* : abuser
abusar *vi* **1** : to go too far, to do something to excess **2** ~ **de** : to abuse (as drugs) **3** ~ **de** : to take unfair advantage of
abusivo, -va *adj* **1** : abusive **2** : outrageous, excessive
abuso *nm* **1** : abuse **2** : injustice, outrage
abyecto, -ta *adj* : despicable, contemptible
acá *adv* AQUÍ : here, over here ⟨¡ven acá! : come here!⟩
acabado¹, -da *adj* **1** : finished, done, completed **2** : old, worn-out
acabado² *nm* : finish ⟨un acabado brillante : a glossy finish⟩
acabar *vi* **1** TERMINAR : to finish, to end **2** ~ **de** : to have just (done something) ⟨acabo de ver a tu hermano : I just saw your brother⟩ **3** ~ **con** : to put an end to, to stamp out — *vt* TERMINAR : to finish — **acabarse** *vr* TERMINARSE : to come to an end, to run out ⟨se me acabó el dinero : I ran out of money⟩
acacia *nf* : acacia
academia *nf* : academy
académico¹, -ca *adj* : academic, scholastic — **académicamente** *adv*
académico², -ca *n* : academic, academician
acaecer {53} *vt* (*3rd person only*) : to happen, to take place
acalambrarse *vr* : to cramp up, to get a cramp
acallar *vt* : to quiet, to silence
acalorado, -da *adj* : emotional, heated
acaloramiento *nm* **1** : heat **2** : ardor, passion
acalorar *vt* : to heat up, to inflame — **acalorarse** *vr* : to get upset, to get worked up
acampada *nf* : camp, camping ⟨ir de acampada : to go camping⟩
acampar *vi* : to camp
acanalar *vt* **1** : to groove, to furrow **2** : to corrugate
acantilado *nm* : cliff
acanto *nm* : acanthus
acantonar *vt* : to station, to quarter
acaparador, -dora *adj* : greedy, selfish

acaparar *vt* **1** : to stockpile, to hoard **2** : to monopolize
acápite *nm* : paragraph
acariciar *vt* : to caress, to stroke, to pet
ácaro *nm* : mite
acarrear *vt* **1** : to haul, to carry **2** : to bring, to give rise to ⟨los problemas que acarrea : the problems that come along with it⟩
acarreo *nm* : transport, haulage
acartonarse *vr* **1** : to stiffen **2** : to become wizened
acaso *adv* **1** : perhaps, by any chance **2** **por si acaso** : just in case
acatamiento *nm* : compliance, observance
acatar *vt* : to comply with, to respect
acaudalado, -da *adj* RICO : wealthy, rich
acaudillar *vt* : to lead, to command
acceder *vi* ~ **a 1** : to accede to, to agree to **2** : to assume (a position) **3** : to gain access to
accesar *vt* : to access (on a computer)
accesibilidad *nf* : accessibility
accesible *adj* ASEQUIBLE : accessible, attainable
acceso *nm* **1** : access **2** : admittance, entrance
accesorio¹, -ria *adj* **1** : accessory **2** : incidental
accesorio² *nm* **1** : accessory **2** : prop (in the theater)
accidentado¹, -da *adj* **1** : eventful, turbulent **2** : rough, uneven **3** : injured
accidentado², -da *n* : accident victim
accidental *adj* : accidental, unintentional — **accidentalmente** *adv*
accidentarse *vr* : to have an accident
accidente *nm* **1** : accident **2** : unevenness **3** **accidente geográfico** : geographical feature
acción *nf, pl* **acciones 1** : action **2** ACTO : act, deed **3** : share, stock
accionamiento *nm* : activation
accionar *vt* : to put into motion, to activate — *vi* : to gesticulate
accionario, -ria *adj* : stock ⟨mercado accionario : stock market⟩
accionista *nmf* : stockholder, shareholder
acebo *nm* : holly
acechar *vt* **1** : to watch, to spy on **2** : to stalk, to lie in wait for
acecho *nm* **al acecho** : lying in wait
acedera *nf* : sorrel (herb)
acéfalo, -la *adj* : leaderless
aceitar *vt* : to oil
aceite *nm* **1** : oil **2** **aceite de ricino** : castor oil **3** **aceite de oliva** : olive oil
aceitera *nf* **1** : cruet (for oil) **2** : oilcan **3** *Mex* : oil refinery
aceitoso, -sa *adj* : oily
aceituna *nf* OLIVA : olive
aceituno *nm* OLIVO : olive tree
aceleración *nf, pl* **-ciones** : acceleration, speeding up
acelerado, -da *adj* : accelerated, speedy
acelerador *nm* : accelerator

aceleramiento *nm* → **aceleración**
acelerar *vt* **1** : to accelerate, to speed up **2** AGILIZAR : to expedite — *vi* : to accelerate (of an automobile) — **acelerarse** *vr* : to hasten, to hurry up
acelga *nf* : chard, Swiss chard
acendrado, -da *adj* : pure, unblemished
acendrar *vt* : to purify, to refine
acento *nm* **1** : accent **2** : stress, emphasis
acentuación *nf, pl* **-ciones** : accentuation
acentuado, -da *adj* : marked, pronounced
acentuar {3} *vt* **1** : to accent **2** : to emphasize, to stress — **acentuarse** *vr* : to become more pronounced
acepción *nf, pl* **-ciones** SIGNIFICADO : sense, meaning
aceptabilidad *nf* : acceptability
aceptable *adj* : acceptable
aceptación *nf, pl* **-ciones 1** : acceptance **2** APROBACIÓN : approval
aceptar *vt* **1** : to accept **2** : to approve
acequia *nf* **1** : irrigation ditch **2** *Mex* : sewer
acera *nf* : sidewalk
acerado, -da *adj* **1** : made of steel **2** : steely, tough
acerbo, -ba *adj* **1** : harsh, cutting ⟨comentarios acerbos : cutting remarks⟩ **2** : bitter — **acerbamente** *adv*
acerca *prep* ~ **de** : about, concerning
acercamiento *nm* : rapprochement, reconciliation
acercar {72} *vt* APROXIMAR, ARRIMAR : to bring near, to bring closer — **acercarse** *vr* APROXIMARSE, ARRIMARSE : to approach, to draw near
acería *nf* : steel mill
acerico *nm* : pincushion
acero *nm* : steel ⟨acero inoxidable : stainless steel⟩
acérrimo, -ma *adj* **1** : staunch, steadfast **2** : bitter ⟨un acérrimo enemigo : a bitter enemy⟩
acertado, -da *adj* CORRECTO : accurate, correct, on target — **acertadamente** *adv*
acertante[1] *adj* : winning
acertante[2] *nmf* : winner
acertar {55} *vt* : to guess correctly — *vi* **1** ATINAR : to be correct, to be on target **2** ~ **a** : to manage to
acertijo *nm* ADIVINANZA : riddle
acervo *nm* **1** : pile, heap **2** : wealth, heritage ⟨el acervo artístico del instituto : the artistic treasures of the institute⟩
acetato *nm* : acetate
acético, -ca *adj* : acetic ⟨ácido acético : acetic acid⟩
acetileno *nm* : acetylene
acetona *nf* **1** : acetone **2** : nail-polish remover
achacar {72} *vt* : to attribute, to impute ⟨te achaca todos sus problemas : he blames all his problems on you⟩
achacoso, -sa *adj* : frail, sickly

achaparrado, -da *adj* : stunted, scrubby ⟨árboles achaparrados : scrubby trees⟩
achaques *nmpl* : aches and pains
achatar *vt* : to flatten
achicar {72} *vt* **1** REDUCIR : to make smaller, to reduce **2** : to intimidate **3** : to bail out (water) — **achicarse** *vr* : to become intimidated
achicharrar *vt* : to scorch, to burn to a crisp
achicoria *nf* : chicory
achispado, -da *adj fam* : tipsy
achote *or* **achiote** *nm* : annatto seed
achuchón *nm, pl* **-chones 1** : push, shove **2** *fam* : squeeze, hug **3** *fam* : mild illness
aciago, -ga *adj* : fateful, unlucky
acicalar *vt* **1** PULIR : to polish **2** : to dress up, to adorn — **acicalarse** *vr* : to get dressed up
acicate *nm* **1** : spur **2** INCENTIVO : incentive, stimulus
acidez *nf, pl* **-deces 1** : acidity **2** : sourness **3 acidez estomacal** : heartburn
acidificar {72} *vt* : to acidify
ácido[1], **-da** *adj* AGRIO : acid, sour
ácido[2] *nm* : acid
acierto *nm* **1** : correct answer, right choice **2** : accuracy, skill, deftness
acimut *nm* : azimuth
acitronar *vt Mex* : to fry until crisp
aclamación *nf, pl* **-ciones** : acclaim, acclamation
aclamar *vt* : to acclaim, to cheer, to applaud
aclaración *nf, pl* **-ciones** CLARIFICACIÓN : clarification, explanation
aclarar *vt* **1** CLARIFICAR : to clarify, to explain, to resolve **2** : to lighten **3** **aclarar la voz** : to clear one's throat — *vi* **1** : to get light, to dawn **2** : to clear up — **aclararse** *vr* : to become clear
aclaratorio, -ria *adj* : explanatory
aclimatar *vt* : to acclimatize — **aclimatarse** *vr* ~ **a** : to get used to — **aclimatación** *nf*
acné *nm* : acne
acobardar *vt* INTIMIDAR : to frighten, to intimidate — **acobardarse** *vr* : to be frightened, to cower
acodarse *vr* ~ **en** : to lean (one's elbows) on
acogedor, -dora *adj* : cozy, warm, friendly
acoger {15} *vt* **1** REFUGIAR : to take in, to shelter **2** : to receive, to welcome — **acogerse** *vr* **1** REFUGIARSE : to take refuge **2** ~ **a** : to resort to, to avail oneself of
acogida *nf* **1** AMPARO, REFUGIO : refuge, protection **2** RECIBIMIENTO : reception, welcome
acolchar *vt* **1** : to pad (a wall, etc.) **2** : to quilt
acólito *nm* **1** MONAGUILLO : altar boy **2** : follower, helper, acolyte
acomedido, -da *adj* : helpful, obliging

acometer vt **1** ATACAR : to attack, to assail **2** EMPRENDER : to undertake, to begin — vi ~ **contra** : to rush against
acometida nf ATAQUE : attack, assault
acomodado, -da adj **1** : suitable, appropriate **2** : well-to-do, prosperous
acomodador, -dora n : usher, usherette f
acomodar vt **1** : to accommodate, to make room for **2** : to adjust, to adapt — **acomodarse** vr **1** : to settle in **2** ~ **a** : to adapt to
acomodaticio, -cia adj : accommodating, obliging
acomodo nm **1** : job, position **2** : arrangement, placement **3** : accommodation, lodging
acompañamiento nm : accompaniment
acompañante nmf **1** COMPAÑERO : companion **2** : accompanist
acompañar vt : to accompany, to go with
acompasado, -da adj : rhythmic, regular, measured
acomplejado, -da adj : full of complexes, neurotic
acondicionado, -da adj **1** : equipped, fitted-out **2 bien acondicionado** : in good shape, in a fit state
acondicionador nm **1** : conditioner **2 acondicionador de aire** : air conditioner
acondicionar vt **1** : to condition **2** : to fit out, to furnish
acongojado, -da adj : distressed, upset
acongojarse vr : to grieve, to become distressed
aconsejable adj : advisable
aconsejar vt : to advise, to counsel
acontecer {53} vt (3rd person only) : to occur, to happen
acontecimiento nm SUCESO : event
acopiar vt : to gather, to collect, to stockpile
acopio nm : collection, stock
acoplamiento nm : connection, coupling
acoplar vt : to couple, to connect — **acoplarse** vr : to fit together
acoquinar vt : to intimidate
acorazado¹, -da adj BLINDADO : armored
acorazado² nm : battleship
acordado, -da adj : agreed upon
acordar {19} vt **1** : to agree on **2** OTORGAR : to award, to bestow — **acordarse** vr RECORDAR : to remember, to recall
acorde¹ adj **1** : in agreement, in accordance **2** ~ **con** : in keeping with
acorde² nm : chord
acordeón nm, pl **-deones** : accordion — **acordeonista** nmf
acordonar vt **1** : to cordon off **2** : to lace up **3** : to mill (coins)
acorralar vt ARRINCONAR : to corner, to hem in, to corral
acortar vt : to shorten, to cut short — **acortarse** vr **1** : to become shorter **2** : to end early

acosar vt PERSEGUIR : to pursue, to hound, to harass
acoso nm ASEDIO : harassment ⟨acoso sexual : sexual harassment⟩
acostar {19} vt **1** : to lay (something) down **2** : to put to bed — **acostarse** vr **1** : to lie down **2** : to go to bed
acostumbrado, -da adj **1** HABITUADO : accustomed **2** HABITUAL : usual, customary
acostumbrar vt : to accustom — vi : to be accustomed, to be in the habit — **acostumbrarse** vr
acotación nf, pl **-ciones 1** : marginal note **2** : stage direction
acotado, -da adj : enclosed
acotamiento nm Mex : shoulder (of a road)
acotar vt **1** ANOTAR : to note, to annotate **2** DELIMITAR : to mark off (land), to demarcate
acre¹ adj **1** : acrid, pungent **2** MORDAZ : caustic, biting
acre² nm : acre
acrecentamiento nm : growth, increase
acrecentar {55} vt AUMENTAR : to increase, to augment
acreditación nf, pl **-ciones** : accreditation
acreditado, -da adj **1** : accredited, authorized **2** : reputable
acreditar vt **1** : to accredit, to authorize **2** : to credit **3** : to prove, to verify — **acreditarse** vr : to gain a reputation
acreedor¹, -dora adj : deserving, worthy
acreedor², -dora n : creditor
acribillar vt **1** : to riddle, to pepper (with bullets, etc.) **2** : to hound, to harass
acrílico nm : acrylic
acrimonia nf **1** : pungency **2** : acrimony
acrimonioso, -sa adj : acrimonious
acriollarse vr : to adopt local customs, to go native
acritud nf **1** : pungency, bitterness **2** : intensity, sharpness **3** : harshness, asperity
acrobacia nf : acrobatics
acróbata nmf : acrobat
acrobático, -ca adj : acrobatic
acrónimo nm : acronym
acta nf **1** : document, certificate ⟨acta de nacimiento : birth certificate⟩ **2 actas** nfpl : minutes (of a meeting)
actitud nf **1** : attitude **2** : posture, position
activación nf, pl **-ciones 1** : activation, stimulation **2** ACELERACIÓN : acceleration, speeding up
activar vt **1** : to activate **2** : to stimulate, to energize **3** : to speed up
actividad nf : activity
activista nmf : activist
activo¹, -va adj : active — **activamente** adv
activo² nm : assets pl ⟨activo y pasivo : assets and liabilities⟩

acto *nm* **1** ACCIÓN : act, deed **2** : act (in a play) **3 el acto sexual** : sexual intercourse **4 en el acto** : right away, on the spot **5 acto seguido** : immediately after

actor *nm* ARTISTA : actor

actriz *nf, pl* **actrices** ARTISTA : actress

actuación *nf, pl* **-ciones 1** : performance **2 actuaciones** *nfpl* DILIGENCIAS : proceedings

actual *adj* PRESENTE : present, current

actualidad *nf* **1** : present time ⟨en la actualidad : at present⟩ **2 actualidades** *nfpl* : current affairs

actualización *nf, pl* **-ciones** : updating, modernization

actualizar {21} *vt* : to modernize, to bring up to date

actualmente *adv* : at present, nowadays

actuar {3} *vi* : to act, to perform

actuarial *adj* : actuarial

actuario, -ria *n* : actuary

acuarela *nf* : watercolor

acuario *nm* : aquarium

Acuario *nmf* : Aquarius, Aquarian

acuartelar *vt* : to quarter (troops)

acuático, -ca *adj* : aquatic, water

acuchillar *vt* APUÑALAR : to knife, to stab

acuciante *adj* : pressing, urgent

acucioso, -sa → **acuciante**

acudir *vi* **1** : to go, to come (someplace for a specific purpose) ⟨acudió a la puerta : he went to the door⟩ ⟨acudimos en su ayuda : we came to her aid⟩ **2** : to be present, to show up ⟨acudí a la cita : I showed up for the appointment⟩ **3 ～ a** : to turn to, to have recourse to ⟨hay que acudir al médico : you must consult the doctor⟩

acueducto *nm* : aqueduct

acuerdo *nm* **1** : agreement **2 estar de acuerdo** : to agree **3 de acuerdo con** : in accordance with **4 de ～** : OK, all right

acuicultura *nf* : aquaculture

acullá *adv* : yonder, over there

acumulación *nf, pl* **-ciones** : accumulation

acumulador *nm* : storage battery

acumular *vt* : to accumulate, to amass — **acumularse** *vr* : to build up, to pile up

acumulativo, -va *adj* : cumulative — **acumulativamente** *adv*

acunar *vt* : to rock, to cradle

acuñar *vt* : to coin, to mint

acuoso, -sa *adj* : aqueous, watery

acupuntura *nf* : acupuncture

acurrucarse {72} *vr* : to cuddle, to nestle, to curl up

acusación *nf, pl* **-ciones 1** : accusation, charge **2 la acusación** : the prosecution

acusado¹, -da *adj* : prominent, marked

acusado², -da *n* : defendant

acusador, -dora *n* **1** : accuser **2** FISCAL : prosecutor

acusar *vt* **1** : to accuse, to charge **2** : to reveal, to betray ⟨sus ojos acusaban la desconfianza : his eyes revealed distrust⟩ — **acusarse** *vr* : to confess

acusativo *nm* : objective (in grammar)

acusatorio, -ria *adj* : accusatory

acuse *nm* **acuse de recibo** : acknowledgment of receipt

acústica *nf* : acoustics

acústico, -ca *adj* : acoustic

adagio *nm* **1** REFRÁN : adage, proverb **2** : adagio

adalid *nm* : leader, champion

adaptable *adj* : adaptable — **adaptabilidad** *nf*

adaptación *nf, pl* **-ciones** : adaptation, adjustment

adaptado, -da *adj* : suited, adapted

adaptador *nm* : adapter (in electricity)

adaptar *vt* **1** MODIFICAR : to adapt **2** : to adjust, to fit — **adaptarse** *vr* : to adapt oneself, to conform

adecentar *vt* : to tidy up

adecuación *nf, pl* **-ciones** ADAPTACIÓN : adaptation

adecuadamente *adv* : adequately

adecuado, -da *adj* **1** IDÓNEO : suitable, appropriate **2** : adequate

adecuar {8} *vt* : to adapt, to make suitable — **adecuarse** *vr* ～ **a** : to be appropriate for, to fit in with

adefesio *nm* : eyesore, monstrosity

adelantado, -da *adj* **1** : advanced, ahead **2** : fast (of a clock or watch) **3 por ～** : in advance

adelantamiento *nm* **1** : advancement **2** : speeding up

adelantar *vt* **1** : to advance, to move forward **2** : to overtake, to pass **3** : to reveal (information) in advance **4** : to advance, to lend (money) — **adelantarse** *vr* **1** : to advance, to get in front **2 ～ a** : to forestall, to preempt

adelante *adv* **1** : ahead, in front, forward **2 más adelante** : further on, later on **3 ¡adelante!** : come in!

adelanto *nm* **1** : advance, progress **2** : advance payment **3** : earliness ⟨llevamos una hora de adelanto : we're running an hour ahead of time⟩

adelfa *nf* : oleander

adelgazar {21} *vt* : to thin, to reduce — *vi* : to lose weight

ademán *nm, pl* **-manes 1** GESTO : gesture **2 ademanes** *nmpl* : manners

además *adv* **1** : besides, furthermore **2 ～ de** : in addition to, as well as

adenoides *nfpl* : adenoids

adentrarse *vr* ～ **en** : to go into, to penetrate

adentro *adv* : inside, within

adentros *nmpl* **decirse para sus adentros** : to say to oneself ⟨me dije para mis adentros que nunca regresaría : I told myself that I'd never go back⟩

adepto¹, -ta *adj* : supportive ⟨ser adepto a : to be a follower of⟩

adepto², -ta *n* PARTIDARIO : follower, supporter

aderezar {21} vt 1 SAZONAR : to season, to dress (salad) 2 : to embellish, to adorn
aderezo nm 1 : dressing, seasoning 2 : adornment, embellishment
adeudar vt 1 : to debit 2 DEBER : to owe
adeudo nm 1 DÉBITO : debit 2 Mex : debt, indebtedness
adherencia nf 1 : adherence, adhesiveness 2 : appendage, accretion
adherente adj : adhesive, sticky
adherirse {76} vr : to adhere, to stick
adhesión nf, pl -siones 1 : adhesion 2 : attachment, commitment (to a cause, etc.)
adhesivo[1], **-va** adj : adhesive
adhesivo[2] nm : adhesive
adicción nf, pl -ciones : addiction
adición nf, pl -ciones : addition
adicional adj : additional — **adicionalmente** adv
adicionar vt : to add
adictivo, -va adj : addictive
adicto[1], **-ta** adj 1 : addicted 2 : devoted, dedicated
adicto[2], **-ta** n 1 : addict 2 PARTIDARIO : supporter, advocate
adiestrador, -dora n : trainer
adiestramiento nm : training
adiestrar vt : to train
adinerado, -da adj : moneyed, wealthy
adiós nm, pl **adioses** 1 DESPEDIDA : farewell, good-bye 2 ¡adiós! : good-bye!
aditamento nm : attachment, accessory
aditivo nm : additive
adivinación nf, pl -ciones 1 : guess 2 : divination, prediction
adivinanza nf ACERTIJO : riddle
adivinar vt 1 : to guess 2 : to foretell, to predict
adivino, -na n : fortune-teller
adjetivo[1], **-va** adj : adjectival
adjetivo[2] nm : adjective
adjudicación nf, pl -ciones 1 : adjudication 2 : allocation, awarding, granting
adjudicar {72} vt 1 : to adjudge, to adjudicate 2 : to assign, to allocate ⟨adjudicar la culpa : to assign the blame⟩ 3 : to award, to grant
adjuntar vt : to enclose, to attach
adjunto[1], **-ta** adj : enclosed, attached
adjunto[2], **-ta** n : deputy, assistant
adjunto[3] nm : adjunct
administración nf, pl -ciones 1 : administration, management 2 **administración de empresas** : business administration
administrador, -dora n : administrator, manager
administrar vt : to administer, to manage, to run
administrativo, -va adj : administrative
admirable adj : admirable, impressive — **admirablemente** adv
admiración nf, pl -ciones : admiration

admirador, -dora n : admirer
admirar vt 1 : to admire 2 : to amaze, to astonish — **admirarse** vr : to be amazed
admirativo, -va adj : admiring
admisibilidad nf : admissibility
admisible adj : admissible, allowable
admisión nf, pl -siones : admission, admittance
admitir vt 1 : to admit, to let in 2 : to acknowledge, to concede 3 : to allow, to make room for ⟨la ley no admite cambios : the law doesn't allow for changes⟩
admonición nf, pl -ciones : admonition, warning
admonitorio, -ria adj : admonitory
ADN nm (ácido desoxirribonucleico) : DNA
adobar vt : to marinate
adobe nm : adobe
adobo nm 1 : marinade, seasoning 2 Mex : spicy marinade used for cooking pork
adoctrinamiento nm : indoctrination
adoctrinar vt : to indoctrinate
adolecer {53} vi PADECER : to suffer ⟨adolece de timidez : he suffers from shyness⟩
adolescencia nf : adolescence
adolescente[1] adj : adolescent, teenage
adolescente[2] nmf : adolescent, teenager
adonde conj : where ⟨el lugar adonde vamos es bello : the place where we're going is beautiful⟩
adónde adv : where ⟨¿adónde vamos? : where are we going?⟩
adondequiera adv : wherever, anywhere ⟨adondequiera que vayas : anywhere you go⟩
adopción nf, pl -ciones : adoption
adoptar vt 1 : to adopt (a measure), to take (a decision) 2 : to adopt (children)
adoptivo, -va adj 1 : adopted (children, country) 2 : adoptive (parents)
adoquín nm, pl **-quines** : paving stone, cobblestone
adorable adj : adorable, lovable
adoración nf, pl -ciones : adoration, worship
adorador[1], **-dora** adj : adoring, worshipping
adorador[2], **-dora** n : worshipper
adorar vt 1 : to adore, to worship
adormecer {53} vt 1 : to make sleepy, to lull to sleep 2 : to numb — **adormecerse** vr 1 : to doze off 2 : to go numb
adormecimiento nm 1 SUEÑO : drowsiness, sleepiness 2 INSENSIBILIDAD : numbness
adormilarse vr : to doze, to drowse
adornar vt DECORAR : to decorate, to adorn
adorno nm : ornament, decoration
adquirido, -da adj 1 : acquired 2 **mal adquirido** : ill-gotten
adquirir {4} vt 1 : to acquire, to gain 2 COMPRAR : to purchase

adquisición *nf, pl* **-ciones 1** : acquisition **2** COMPRA : purchase
adquisitivo, -va *adj* **poder adquisitivo** : purchasing power
adrede *adv* : intentionally, on purpose
adrenalina *nf* : adrenaline
adscribir {33} *vt* : to assign, to appoint — **adscribirse** *vr* ~ **a** : to become a member of
adscripción *nf, pl* **-ciones** : assignment, appointment
adscrito *pp* → **adscribir**
aduana *nf* : customs, customs office
aduanero[1], -ra *adj* : customs
aduanero[2], -ra *n* : customs officer
aducir {61} *vt* : to adduce, to offer as proof
adueñarse *vr* ~ **de** : to take possession of, to take over
adulación *nf, pl* **-ciones** : adulation, flattery
adulador[1], -dora *adj* : flattering
adulador[2], -dora *n* : flatterer, toady
adular *vt* LISONJEAR : to flatter
adulteración *nf, pl* **-ciones** : adulteration
adulterar *vt* : to adulterate
adulterio *nm* : adultery
adúltero[1], -ra *adj* : adulterous
adúltero[2], -ra *n* : adulterer
adultez *nf* : adulthood
adulto, -ta *adj & n* : adult
adusto, -ta *adj* : harsh, severe
advenedizo, -za *n* **1** : upstart, parvenu **2** : newcomer
advenimiento *nm* : advent
adverbio *nm* : adverb — **adverbial** *adj*
adversario[1], -ria *adj* : opposing, contrary
adversario[2], -ria *n* OPOSITOR : adversary, opponent
adversidad *nf* : adversity
adverso, -sa *adj* DESFAVORABLE : adverse, unfavorable — **adversamente** *adv*
advertencia *nf* AVISO : warning
advertir {76} *vt* **1** AVISAR : to warn **2** : to notice, to tell ⟨no advertí que estuviera enojada : I couldn't tell she was angry⟩
Adviento *nm* : Advent
adyacente *adj* : adjacent
aéreo, -rea *adj* **1** : aerial, air **2 correo aéreo** : airmail
aeróbic *nm* : aerobics
aeróbico, -ca *adj* : aerobic
aerobio, -bia *adj* : aerobic
aerodinámica *nf* : aerodynamics
aerodinámico, -ca *adj* : aerodynamic, streamlined
aeródromo *nm* : airfield
aeroespacial *adj* : aerospace
aerolínea *nf* : airline
aeromozo, -za *n* : flight attendant, steward *m*, stewardess *f*
aeronáutica *nf* : aeronautics
aeronáutico, -ca *adj* : aeronautical
aeronave *nf* : aircraft

aeropostal *adj* : airmail
aeropuerto *nm* : airport
aerosol *nm* : aerosol, aerosol spray
aeróstata *nmf* : balloonist
aerotransportado, -da *adj* : airborne
aerotransportar *vt* : to airlift
afabilidad *nf* : affability
afable *adj* : affable — **afablemente** *adv*
afamado, -da *adj* : well-known, famous
afán *nm, pl* **afanes 1** ANHELO : eagerness, desire **2** EMPEÑO : effort, determination
afanador, -dora *n Mex* : cleaning person, cleaner
afanarse *vr* : to toil, to strive
afanosamente *adv* : zealously, industriously, busily
afanoso, -sa *adj* **1** : eager, industrious **2** : arduous, hard
afear *vt* : to make ugly, to disfigure
afección *nf, pl* **-ciones 1** : fondness, affection **2** : illness, complaint
afectación *nf, pl* **-ciones** : affectation
afectado, -da *adj* **1** : affected, mannered **2** : influenced **3** : afflicted **4** : feigned
afectar *vt* **1** : to affect **2** : to upset **3** : to feign, to pretend
afectísimo, -ma *adj* **suyo afectísimo** : yours truly
afectivo, -va *adj* : emotional
afecto[1], -ta *adj* **1** : affected, afflicted **2** : fond, affectionate
afecto[2] *nm* CARIÑO : affection
afectuoso, -sa *adj* CARIÑOSO : affectionate, caring
afeitadora *nf* : shaver, electric razor
afeitar *vt* RASURAR : to shave — **afeitarse** *vr*
afelpado, -da *adj* : plush
afeminado, -da *adj* : effeminate
aferrado, -da *adj* : obstinate, stubborn
aferrarse {55} *vr* : to cling, to hold on
affidávit *nm, pl* **-dávits** : affidavit
afgano, -na *adj & n* : Afghan
AFI *nm* (Alfabeto Fonético Internacional) : IPA
afianzar {21} *vt* **1** : to secure, to strengthen **2** : to guarantee, to vouch for — **afianzarse** *vr* ESTABLECERSE : to establish oneself
afiche *nm* : poster
afición *nf, pl* **-ciones 1** : enthusiasm, penchant, fondness ⟨afición al deporte : love of sports⟩ **2** PASATIEMPO : hobby
aficionado[1], -da *adj* ENTUSIASTA : enthusiastic, keen
aficionado[2], -da *n* **1** ENTUSIASTA : enthusiast, fan **2** : amateur
áfido *nm* : aphid
afiebrado, -da *adj* : feverish
afilado, -da *adj* **1** : sharp **2** : long, pointed ⟨una nariz afilada : a sharp nose⟩
afilador *nm* : sharpener
afilalápices *nms & pl* : pencil sharpener
afilar *vt* : to sharpen
afiliación *nf, pl* **-ciones** : affiliation

afiliado[1], **-da** *adj* : affiliated
afiliado[2], **-da** *n* : member
afiliarse *vr* : to become a member, to join, to affiliate
afín *adj, pl* **afines** 1 PARECIDO : related, similar ⟨la biología y disciplinas afines : biology and related disciplines⟩ 2 PRÓXIMO : adjacent, nearby
afinación *nf, pl* **-ciones** 1 : tune-up 2 : tuning (of an instrument)
afinador, -dora *n* : tuner (of musical instruments)
afinar *vt* 1 : to perfect, to refine 2 : to tune (an instrument) — *vi* : to sing or play in tune
afincarse {72} *vr* : to establish oneself, to settle in
afinidad *nf* : affinity, similarity
afirmación *nf, pl* **-ciones** 1 : statement 2 : affirmation
afirmar *vt* 1 : to state, to affirm 2 REFORZAR : to make firm, to strengthen
afirmativo, -va *adj* : affirmative — **afirmativamente** *adv*
aflicción *nf, pl* **-ciones** DESCONSUELO, PESAR : grief, sorrow
afligido, -da *adj* : grief-stricken, sorrowful
afligir {35} *vt* 1 : to distress, to upset 2 : to afflict — **afligirse** *vr* : to grieve
aflojar *vt* 1 : to loosen, to slacken 2 *fam* : to pay up, to fork over — *vi* : to slacken, to ease up — **aflojarse** *vr* : to become loose, to slacken
afloramiento *nm* : outcropping, emergence
aflorar *vi* : to come to the surface, to emerge
afluencia *nf* 1 : flow, influx 2 : abundance, plenty
afluente *nm* : tributary
afluir {41} *vi* 1 : to flock ⟨la gente afluía a la frontera : people were flocking to the border⟩ 2 : to flow
aforismo *nm* : aphorism
aforo *nm* 1 : appraisal, assessment 2 : maximum capacity (of a theater, highway, etc.)
afortunado, -da *adj* : fortunate, lucky — **afortunadamente** *adv*
afrecho *nm* : bran, mash
afrenta *nf* : affront, insult
afrentar *vt* : to affront, to dishonor, to insult
africano, -na *adj & n* : African
afroamericano, -na *adj & n* : Afro-American
afrodisiaco *or* **afrodisíaco** *nm* : aphrodisiac
afrontamiento *nm* : confrontation
afrontar *vt* : to confront, to face up to
afrutado, -da *adj* : fruity
afuera *adv* 1 : out ⟨¡afuera! : get out!⟩ 2 : outside, outdoors
afueras *nfpl* ALEDAÑOS : outskirts
agachadiza *nf* : snipe (bird)
agachar *vt* : to lower (a part of the body) ⟨agachar la cabeza : to bow one's head⟩

— **agacharse** *vr* : to crouch, to stoop, to bend down
agalla *nf* 1 BRANQUIA : gill 2 **tener agallas** *fam* : to have guts, to have courage
agarradera *nf* ASA, ASIDERO : handle, grip
agarrado, -da *adj fam* : cheap, stingy
agarrar *vt* 1 : to grab, to grasp 2 : to catch, to take — *vi* **agarrar y** *fam* : to do (something) abruptly ⟨el día siguiente agarró y se fue : the next day he up and left⟩ — **agarrarse** *vr* 1 : to hold on, to cling 2 *fam* : to get into a fight ⟨se agarraron a golpes : they came to blows⟩
agarre *nm* : grip, grasp
agarrotarse *vr* 1 : to stiffen up 2 : to seize up
agasajar *vt* : to fête, to wine and dine
agasajo *nm* : lavish attention
ágata *nf* : agate
agave *nm* : agave
agazaparse *vr* 1 AGACHARSE : to crouch 2 : to hide
agencia *nf* : agency, office
agenciar *vt* : to obtain, to procure — **agenciarse** *vr* : to manage, to get by
agenda *nf* 1 : agenda 2 : appointment book
agente *nmf* 1 : agent 2 **agente de viajes** : travel agent 3 **agente de bolsa** : stockbroker 4 **agente de tráfico** : traffic officer
agigantado, -da *adj* GIGANTESCO : gigantic
agigantar *vt* 1 : to increase greatly, to enlarge 2 : to exaggerate
ágil *adj* 1 : agile, nimble 2 : sharp, lively (of a response, etc.) — **ágilmente** *adv*
agilidad *nf* : agility, nimbleness
agilizar {21} *vt* ACELERAR : to expedite, to speed up
agitación *nf, pl* **-ciones** 1 : agitation 2 NERVIOSISMO : nervousness
agitado, -da *adj* 1 : agitated, excited 2 : choppy, rough, turbulent
agitador, -dora *n* PROVOCADOR : agitator
agitar *vt* 1 : to agitate, to shake 2 : to wave, to flap 3 : to stir up — **agitarse** *vr* 1 : to toss about, to flap around 2 : to get upset
aglomeración *nf, pl* **-ciones** 1 : conglomeration, mass 2 GENTÍO : crowd
aglomerar *vt* : to cluster, to amass — **aglomerarse** *vr* : to crowd together
aglutinar *vt* : to bring together, to bind
agnóstico, -ca *adj & n* : agnostic
agobiado, -da *adj* : weary, worn-out, weighted-down
agobiante *adj* 1 : exhausting, overwhelming 2 : stifling, oppressive
agobiar *vt* 1 OPRIMIR : to oppress, to burden 2 ABRUMAR : to overwhelm 3 : to wear out, to exhaust
agonía *nf* : agony, death throes
agonizante *adj* : dying

agonizar {21} *vi* **1** : to be dying **2** : to be in agony **3** : to dim, to fade

agorero, -ra *adj* : ominous

agostar *vt* **1** : to parch **2** : to wither — **agostarse** *vr*

agosto *nm* **1** : August **2 hacer uno su agosto** : to make a fortune, to make a killing

agotado, -da *adj* **1** : exhausted, used up **2** : sold out **3** FATIGADO : worn-out, tired

agotador, -dora *adj* : exhausting

agotamiento *nm* FATIGA : exhaustion

agotar *vt* **1** : to exhaust, to use up **2** : to weary, to wear out — **agotarse** *vr*

agraciado¹, -da *adj* **1** : attractive **2** : fortunate

agraciado², -da *n* : winner

agradable *adj* GRATO, PLACENTERO : pleasant, agreeable — **agradablemente** *adv*

agradar *vi* : to be pleasing ⟨nos agradó mucho el resultado : we were very pleased with the result⟩

agradecer {53} *vt* **1** : to be grateful for **2** : to thank

agradecido, -da *adj* : grateful, thankful

agradecimiento *nm* : gratitude, thankfulness

agrado *nm* **1** GUSTO : taste, liking ⟨no es de su agrado : it's not to his liking⟩ **2** : graciousness, agreeableness **3 con ~** : with pleasure, willingly ⟨lo haré con agrado : I will be happy to do it⟩

agrandar *vt* **1** : to exaggerate **2** : to enlarge — **agrandarse** *vr*

agrario, -ria *adj* : agrarian, agricultural

agravación *nf, pl* **-ciones** : aggravation, worsening

agravante *adj* : aggravating

agravar *vt* **1** : to increase (weight), to make heavier **2** EMPEORAR : to aggravate, to worsen — **agravarse** *vr*

agraviar *vt* INJURIAR, OFENDER : to offend, to insult

agravio *nm* INJURIA : affront, offense, insult

agredir {1} *vt* : to assail, to attack

agregado¹, -da *n* **1** : attaché **2** : assistant professor

agregado² *nm* **1** : aggregate **2** AÑADIDURA : addition, something added

agregar {52} *vt* **1** AÑADIR : to add, to attach **2** : to appoint — **agregarse** *vr* : to join

agresión *nf, pl* **-siones** **1** : aggression **2** ATAQUE : attack

agresividad *nf* : aggressiveness, aggression

agresivo, -va *adj* : aggressive — **agresivamente** *adv*

agresor¹, -sora *adj* : hostile, attacking

agresor², -sora *n* **1** : aggressor **2** : assailant, attacker

agreste *adj* **1** CAMPESTRE : rural **2** : wild, untamed

agriar *vt* **1** : to sour, to make sour **2** : to embitter — **agriarse** *vr* : to turn sour

agrícola *adj* : agricultural

agricultor, -tora *n* : farmer, grower

agricultura *nf* : agriculture, farming

agridulce *adj* **1** : bittersweet **2** : sweet-and-sour

agrietar *vt* : to crack — **agrietarse** *vr* **1** : to crack **2** : to chap

agrimensor, -sora *n* : surveyor

agrimensura *nf* : surveying

agrio, agria *adj* **1** ÁCIDO : sour **2** : caustic, acrimonious

agriparse *vr* : to catch the flu

agroindustria *nf* : agribusiness

agronomía *nf* : agronomy

agropecuario, -ria *adj* : pertaining to livestock and agriculture

agrupación *nf, pl* **-ciones** GRUPO : group, association

agrupamiento *nm* : grouping, concentration

agrupar *vt* : to group together

agua *nf* **1** : water **2 agua oxigenada** : hydrogen peroxide **3 aguas negras** *or* **aguas residuales** : sewage **4 como agua para chocolate** *Mex fam* : furious **5 echar aguas** *Mex fam* : to keep an eye out, to be on the lookout

aguacate *nm* : avocado

aguacero *nm* : shower, downpour

aguado, -da *adj* **1** DILUIDO : watered-down, diluted **2** CA, Col, Mex fam : soft, flabby **3** Mex, Peru fam : dull, boring

aguafiestas *nmfs & pl* : killjoy, stick-in-the-mud, spoilsport

aguafuerte *nm* : etching

aguamanil *nm* : ewer, pitcher

aguanieve *nf* : sleet ⟨caer aguanieve : to be sleeting⟩

aguantar *vt* **1** SOPORTAR : to bear, to tolerate, to withstand **2** : to hold **3 aguantar las ganas** : to resist an urge ⟨no pude aguantar las ganas de reír : I couldn't keep myself from laughing⟩ — *vi* : to hold out, to last — **aguantarse** *vr* **1** : to resign oneself **2** : to restrain oneself

aguante *nm* **1** TOLERANCIA : tolerance, patience **2** RESISTENCIA : endurance, strength

aguar {10} *vt* **1** : to water down, to dilute **2 aguar la fiesta** *fam* : to spoil the party

aguardar *vt* ESPERAR : to wait for, to await — *vi* : to be in store

aguardiente *nm* : clear brandy

aguarrás *nm* : turpentine

agudeza *nf* **1** : keenness, sharpness **2** : shrillness **3** : witticism

agudizar {21} *vt* : to intensify, to heighten

agudo, -da *adj* **1** : acute, sharp **2** : shrill, high-pitched **3** PERSPICAZ : clever, shrewd

agüero *nm* AUGURIO, PRESAGIO : augury, omen

aguijón *nm, pl* **-jones** **1** : stinger (of a bee, etc.) **2** : goad

aguijonear *vt* : to goad
águila *nf* **1** : eagle **2 águila o sol** *Mex* : heads or tails
aguileño, -ña *adj* : aquiline
aguilera *nf* : aerie, eagle's nest
aguilón *nm, pl* **-lones** : gable
aguinaldo *nm* **1** : Christmas bonus, year-end bonus **2** *PRi, Ven* : Christmas carol
agüitarse *vr Mex fam* : to have the blues, to feel discouraged
aguja *nf* **1** : needle **2** : steeple, spire
agujerear *vt* : to make a hole in, to pierce
agujero *nm* **1** : hole **2 agujero negro** : black hole (in astronomy)
agujeta *nf* **1** *Mex* : shoelace **2 agujetas** *nfpl* : muscular soreness or stiffness
agusanado, -da *adj* : worm-eaten
aguzar {21} *vt* **1** : to sharpen ⟨aguzar el ingenio : to sharpen one's wits⟩ **2 aguzar el oído** : to prick up one's ears
ah *interj* : oh!
ahí *adv* **1** : there ⟨ahí está : there it is⟩ **2 por ~** : somewhere, thereabouts **3 de ahí que** : with the result that, so that
ahijado, -da *n* : godchild, godson *m*, goddaughter *f*
ahijar {5} *vt* : to adopt (a child)
ahínco *nm* : eagerness, zeal
ahogar {52} *vt* **1** : to drown **2** : to smother **3** : to choke back, to stifle — **ahogarse** *vr*
ahogo *nm* : breathlessness, suffocation
ahondar *vt* : to deepen — *vi* : to elaborate, to go into detail
ahora *adv* **1** : now **2 ahora mismo** : right now **3 hasta ~** : so far **4 por ~** : for the time being
ahorcar {72} *vt* : to hang, to kill by hanging — **ahorcarse** *vr*
ahorita *adv fam* : right now, right away
ahorquillado, -da *adj* : forked
ahorrador, -dora *adj* : thrifty
ahorrar *vt* **1** : to save (money) **2** : to spare, to conserve — *vi* : to save up — **ahorrarse** *vr* : to spare oneself
ahorrativo, -va *adj* : thrifty, frugal
ahorro *nm* : saving ⟨cuenta de ahorros : savings account⟩
ahuecar {72} *vt* **1** : to hollow out **2** : to cup (one's hands) **3** : to plump up, to fluff up
ahuizote *nm Mex fam* : annoying person, pain in the neck
ahumar {8} *vt* : to smoke, to cure
ahuyentar *vt* **1** : to scare away, to chase away **2** : to banish, to dispel ⟨ahuyentar las dudas : to dispel doubts⟩
airado, -da *adj* FURIOSO : angry, irate
airar {5} *vt* : to make angry, to anger
aire *nm* **1** : air **2 aire acondicionado** : air-conditioning **3 darse aires** : to give oneself airs
airear *vt* : to air, to air out — **airearse** *vr* : to get some fresh air
airoso, -sa *adj* **1** : elegant, graceful **2 salir airoso** : to come out winning
aislacionismo *nm* : isolationism

aislacionista *adj & nmf* : isolationist
aislado, -da *adj* : isolated, alone
aislador *nm* : insulator (part)
aislamiento *nm* **1** : isolation **2** : insulation
aislante *nm* : insulator, nonconductor
aislar {5} *vt* **1** : to isolate **2** : to insulate
ajado, -da *adj* **1** : worn, shabby **2** : wrinkled, crumpled
ajar *vt* : to wear out, to spoil
ajardinado, -da *adj* : landscaped
ajedrecista *nmf* : chess player
ajedrez *nm, pl* **-dreces** **1** : chess **2** : chess set
ajeno, -na *adj* **1** : alien **2** : of another, of others ⟨propiedad ajena : somebody else's property⟩ **3 ~ a** : foreign to **4 ~ de** : devoid of, free from
ajetreado, -da *adj* : hectic, busy
ajetrearse *vr* : to bustle about, to rush around
ajetreo *nm* : hustle and bustle, fuss
ají *nm, pl* **ajíes** : chili pepper
ajo *nm* : garlic
ajonjolí *nm, pl* **-líes** : sesame
ajuar *nm* : trousseau
ajustable *adj* : adjustable
ajustado, -da *adj* **1** CEÑIDO : tight, tight-fitting **2** : close, tight ⟨una ajustada victoria : a close victory⟩
ajustar *vt* **1** : to adjust, to adapt **2** : to take in (clothing) **3** : to settle, to resolve — **ajustarse** *vr* : to fit, to conform
ajuste *nm* **1** : adjustment **2** : tightening
ajusticiar *vt* EJECUTAR : to execute, to put to death
al *prep* (contraction of a and el) → **a²**
ala *nf* **1** : wing **2** : brim (of a hat)
Alá *nm* : Allah
alabanza *nf* ELOGIO : praise
alabar *vt* : to praise — **alabarse** *vr* : to boast
alabastro *nm* : alabaster
alabear *vt* : to warp — **alabearse** *vr*
alabeo *nm* : warp, warping
alacena *nf* : cupboard, larder
alacrán *nm, pl* **-cranes** ESCORPIÓN : scorpion
alado, -da *adj* : winged
alambique *nm* : still (to distill alcohol)
alambre *nm* **1** : wire **2 alambre de púas** : barbed wire
alameda *nf* **1** : poplar grove **2** : tree-lined avenue
álamo *nm* **1** : poplar **2 álamo temblón** : aspen
alar *nm* : eaves *pl*
alarde *nm* **1** : show, display **2 hacer alarde de** : to make show of, to boast about
alardear *vi* PRESUMIR : to boast, to brag
alargado, -da *adj* : elongated, slender
alargamiento *nm* : lengthening, extension, elongation
alargar {52} *vt* **1** : to extend, to lengthen **2** PROLONGAR : to prolong — **alargarse** *vr*

alarido *nm* : howl, shriek
alarma *nf* : alarm
alarmante *adj* : alarming — **alarmante-mente** *adv*
alarmar *vt* : to alarm
alazán *nm, pl* **-zanes** : sorrel (color or animal)
alba *nf* AMANECER : dawn, daybreak
albacea *nmf* TESTAMENTARIO : executor, executrix *f*
albahaca *nf* : basil
albanés, -nesa *adj & n, mpl* **-neses** : Albanian
albañil *nmf* : bricklayer, mason
albañilería *nf* : bricklaying, masonry
albaricoque *nm* : apricot
albatros *nm* : albatross
albedrío *nm* : will ⟨libre albedrío : free will⟩
alberca *nf* **1** : reservoir, tank **2** *Mex* : swimming pool
albergar {52} *vt* ALOJAR : to house, to lodge, to shelter
albergue *nm* **1** : shelter, refuge **2** : hostel
albino, -na *adj & n* : albino — **albinismo** *nm*
albóndiga *nf* : meatball
albor *nm* **1** : dawning, beginning **2** BLANCURA : whiteness
alborada *nf* : dawn
alborear *v impers* : to dawn
alborotado, -da *adj* **1** : excited, agitated **2** : rowdy, unruly
alborotador¹, -dora *adj* **1** : noisy, boisterous **2** : rowdy, unruly
alborotador², -dora *n* : agitator, troublemaker, rioter
alborotar *vt* **1** : to excite, to agitate **2** : to incite, to stir up — **alborotarse** *vr* **1** : to get excited **2** : to riot
alboroto *nm* **1** : disturbance, ruckus **2** MOTÍN : riot
alborozado, -da *adj* : jubilant
alborozar {21} *vt* : to gladden, to cheer
alborozo *nm* : joy, elation
álbum *nm* : album ⟨álbum de recortes : scrapbook⟩
albúmina *nf* : albumin
albur *nm* **1** : chance, risk **2** *Mex* : pun
alca *nf* : auk
alcachofa *nf* : artichoke
alcahuete, -ta *n* CHISMOSO : gossip
alcaide *nm* : warden (in a prison)
alcalde, -desa *n* : mayor
alcaldía *nf* **1** : mayoralty **2** AYUNTAMIENTO : city hall
álcali *nm* : alkali
alcalino, -na *adj* : alkaline — **alcalinidad** *nf*
alcance *nm* **1** : reach **2** : range, scope
alcancía *nf* **1** : piggy bank, money box **2** : collection box (for alms, etc.)
alcanfor *nm* : camphor
alcantarilla *nf* CLOACA : sewer, drain
alcanzar {21} *vt* **1** : to reach **2** : to catch up with **3** LOGRAR : to achieve, to at-

tain — *vi* **1** DAR : to suffice, to be enough **2** ~ **a** : to manage to
alcaparra *nf* : caper
alcapurria *nf PRi* : stuffed fritter made with taro and green banana
alcaravea *nf* : caraway
alcatraz *nm, pl* **-traces** : gannet
alcázar *nm* : fortress, castle
alce¹, etc. → **alzar**
alce² *nm* : moose, European elk
alcoba *nf* : bedroom
alcohol *nm* : alcohol
alcohólico, -ca *adj & n* : alcoholic
alcoholismo *nm* : alcoholism
alcoholizarse {21} *vr* : to become an alcoholic
alcornoque *nm* **1** : cork oak **2** *fam* : idiot, fool
alcurnia *nf* : ancestry, lineage
aldaba *nf* : door knocker
aldea *nf* : village
aldeano¹, -na *adj* : village, rustic
aldeano², -na *n* : villager
aleación *nf, pl* **-ciones** : alloy
alear *vt* : to alloy
aleatorio, -ria *adj* : random, fortuitous — **aleatoriamente** *adv*
alebrestar *vt* : to excite, to make nervous — **alebrestarse** *vr*
aledaño, -ña *adj* : bordering, neighboring
aledaños *nmpl* AFUERAS : outskirts, surrounding area
alegar {52} *vt* : to assert, to allege — *vi* DISCUTIR : to argue
alegato *nm* **1** : allegation, claim **2** *Mex* : argument, summation (in law) **3** : argument, dispute
alegoría *nf* : allegory
alegórico, -ca *adj* : allegorical
alegrar *vt* : to make happy, to cheer up — **alegrarse** *vr* : to be glad, to rejoice
alegre *adj* **1** : glad, cheerful **2** : colorful, bright **3** *fam* : tipsy
alegremente *adv* : happily, cheerfully
alegría *nf* : joy, cheer, happiness
alejado, -da *adj* : remote
alejamiento *nm* **1** : removal, separation **2** : estrangement
alejar *vt* **1** : to remove, to move away **2** : to estrange, to alienate — **alejarse** *vr* **1** : to move away, to stray **2** : to drift apart
alelado, -da *adj* **1** : bewildered, stupefied **2** : foolish, stupid
aleluya *interj* : hallelujah!, alleluia!
alemán¹, -mana *adj & n, mpl* **-manes** : German
alemán² *nm* : German (language)
alentador, -dora *adj* : encouraging
alentar {55} *vt* : to encourage, to inspire — *vi* : to breathe
alerce *nm* : larch
alérgeno *nm* : allergen
alergia *nf* : allergy
alérgico, -ca *adj* : allergic
alero *nm* **1** : eaves *pl* **2** : forward (in basketball)

alerón *nm, pl* **-rones** : aileron
alerta[1] *adv* : on the alert
alerta[2] *adj & nf* : alert
alertar *vt* : to alert
aleta *nf* **1** : fin **2** : flipper **3** : small wing
aletargado, -da *adj* : lethargic, sluggish, torpid
aletargarse {52} *vr* : to feel drowsy, to become lethargic
aletear *vi* : to flutter, to flap one's wings
aleteo *nm* : flapping, flutter
alevín *nm, pl* **-vines** **1** : fry, young fish **2** PRINCIPIANTE : beginner
alevosía *nf* **1** : treachery **2** : premeditation
alevoso, -sa *adj* : treacherous
alfabético, -ca *adj* : alphabetical — **alfabéticamente** *adv*
alfabetismo *nm* : literacy
alfabetizado, -da *adj* : literate
alfabetizar {21} *vt* : to alphabetize
alfabeto *nm* : alphabet
alfalfa *nf* : alfalfa
alfanje *nm* : cutlass, scimitar
alfarería *nf* : pottery
alfarero, -ra *n* : potter
alféizar *nm* : sill, windowsill
alfeñique *nm fam* : wimp, weakling
alférez *nmf, pl* **-reces** **1** : second lieutenant **2** : ensign
alfil *nm* : bishop (in chess)
alfiler *nm* **1** : pin **2** BROCHE : brooch
alfiletero *nm* : pincushion
alfombra *nf* : carpet, rug
alfombrado *nm* : carpeting
alfombrar *vt* : to carpet
alfombrilla *nf* : small rug, mat
alforfón *nm, pl* **-fones** : buckwheat
alforja *nf* : saddlebag
alforza *nf* : pleat, tuck
alga *nf* **1** : aquatic plant, alga **2** : seaweed
algarabía *nf* **1** : gibberish, babble **2** : hubbub, uproar
álgebra *nf* : algebra
algebraico, -ca *adj* : algebraic
álgido, -da *adj* **1** : critical, decisive **2** : icy cold
algo[1] *adv* : somewhat, rather ⟨es simpático, pero algo tacaño : he's nice but rather stingy⟩
algo[2] *pron* **1** : something **2** ~ **de** : some, a little ⟨tengo algo de dinero : I've got some money⟩
algodón *nm, pl* **-dones** : cotton
algoritmo *nm* : algorithm
alguacil *nm* : constable
alguien *pron* : somebody, someone
alguno[1] **, -na** *adj* (**algún** *before masculine singular nouns*) **1** : some, any ⟨algún día : someday, one day⟩ **2** (*in negative constructions*) : not any, not at all ⟨no tengo noticia alguna : I have no news at all⟩ **3 algunas veces** : sometimes
alguno[2] **, -na** *pron* **1** : one, someone, somebody ⟨alguno de ellos : one of them⟩ **2 algunos, -nas** *pron pl* : some,

a few ⟨algunos quieren trabajar : some want to work⟩
alhaja *nf* : jewel, gem
alhajar *vt* : to adorn with jewels
alharaca *nf* : fuss
alhelí *nm* : wallflower
aliado[1] **, -da** *adj* : allied
aliado[2] **, -da** *n* : ally
alianza *nf* : alliance
aliarse {85} *vr* : to form an alliance, to ally oneself
alias *adv & nm* : alias
alicaído, -da *adj* : depressed, discouraged
alicates *nmpl* PINZAS : pliers
aliciente *nm* **1** INCENTIVO : incentive **2** ATRACCIÓN : attraction
alienación *nf, pl* **-ciones** : alienation, derangement
alienar *vt* ENAJENAR : to alienate
aliento *nm* **1** : breath **2** : courage, strength **3 dar aliento a** : to encourage
aligerar *vt* **1** : to lighten **2** ACELERAR : to hasten, to quicken
alijo *nm* : cache, consignment (of contraband)
alimaña *nf* : pest, vermin
alimentación *nf, pl* **-ciones** NUTRICIÓN : nutrition, nourishment
alimentar *vt* **1** NUTRIR : to feed, to nourish **3** MANTENER : to support (a family) **3** FOMENTAR : to nurture, to foster — **alimentarse** *vr* ~ **con** : to live on
alimentario, -ria → **alimenticio**
alimenticio, -cia *adj* **1** : nutritional, food, dietary **2** : nutritious, nourishing
alimento *nm* : food, nourishment
aliñar *vt* **1** : to dress (salad) **2** CONDIMENTAR : to season
alineación *nf, pl* **-ciones** **1** : alignment **2** : lineup (in sports)
alineamiento *nm* : alignment
alinear *vt* **1** : to align **2** : to line up — **alinearse** *vr* **1** : to fall in, to line up **2** ~ **con** : to align oneself with
aliño *nm* : seasoning, dressing
alipús *nm, pl* **-puses** *Mex fam* : booze, drink
alisar *vt* : to smooth
aliso *nm* : alder
alistamiento *nm* : enlistment, recruitment
alistar *vt* **1** : to recruit **2** : to make ready — **alistarse** *vr* **1** : to join up, to enlist **2** : to get ready
aliteración *nf, pl* **-ciones** : alliteration
aliviar *vt* MITIGAR : to relieve, to alleviate, to soothe — **aliviarse** *vr* : to recover, to get better
alivio *nm* : relief
aljaba *nf* : quiver (for arrows)
aljibe *nm* : cistern, well
allá *adv* **1** : there, over there **2 más allá** : farther away **3 más allá de** : beyond **4 allá tú** : that's up to you

allanamiento nm 1 : (police) raid 2 allanamiento de morada : breaking and entering
allanar vt 1 : to raid, to search 2 : to resolve, to solve 3 : to smooth, to level out
allegado[1], -da adj : close, intimate
allegado[2], -da n : close friend, relation ⟨parientes y allegados : friends and relations⟩
allegar {52} vt : to gather, to collect
allende[1] adv : beyond, on the other side
allende[2] prep : beyond ⟨allende las montañas : beyond the mountains⟩
allí adv : there, over there ⟨allí mismo : right there⟩ ⟨hasta allí : up to that point⟩
alma nf 1 : soul 2 : person, human being 3 no tener alma : to be pitiless 4 tener el alma en un hilo : to have one's heart in one's mouth
almacén nm, pl -cenes 1 BODEGA : warehouse, storehouse 2 TIENDA : shop, store 3 gran almacén Spain : department store
almacenaje → almacenamiento
almacenamiento nm : storage ⟨almacenamiento de datos : data storage⟩
almacenar vt : to store, to put in storage
almacenero, -ra n : shopkeeper
almacenista nm MAYORISTA : wholesaler
almádena nf : sledgehammer
almanaque nm : almanac
almeja nf : clam
almendra nf 1 : almond 2 : kernel
almendro nm : almond tree
almiar nm : haystack
almíbar nm : syrup
almidón nm, pl -dones : starch
almidonar vt : to starch
alminar nm MINARETE : minaret
almirante nm : admiral
almizcle nm : musk
almohada nf : pillow
almohadilla nf 1 : small pillow, cushion 2 : bag, base (in baseball)
almohadón nm, pl -dones : bolster, cushion
almohazar {21} vt : to curry (a horse)
almoneda nf SUBASTA : auction
almorranas nfpl HEMORROIDES : hemorrhoids, piles
almorzar {36} vi : to have lunch — vt : to have for lunch
almuerzo nm : lunch
alocado, -da adj 1 : crazy 2 : wild, reckless 3 : silly, scatterbrained
alocución nf, pl -ciones : speech, address
áloe or aloe nm : aloe
alojamiento nm : lodging, accommodations pl
alojar vt ALBERGAR : to house, to lodge — alojarse vr : to lodge, to room
alondra nf : lark, skylark
alpaca nf : alpaca

alpinismo nm : mountain climbing, mountaineering
alpinista nmf : mountain climber
alpino, -na adj : Alpine, alpine
alpiste nm : birdseed
alquilar vt ARRENDAR : to rent, to lease
alquiler nm ARRENDAMIENTO : rent, rental
alquimia nf : alchemy
alquimista nmf : alchemist
alquitrán nm, pl -tranes BREA : tar
alquitranar vt : to tar, to cover with tar
alrededor[1] adv 1 : around, about ⟨todo temblaba alrededor : all around things were shaking⟩ 2 ∼ de : around, approximately ⟨alrededor de quince personas : around fifteen people⟩
alrededor[2] prep ∼ de : around, about ⟨corrió alrededor de la casa : she ran around the house⟩ ⟨llegaré alrededor de diciembre : I will get there around December⟩
alrededores nmpl ALEDAÑOS : surroundings, outskirts
alta nf 1 : admission, entry, enrollment 2 dar de alta : to release, to discharge (a patient)
altanería nf ALTIVEZ, ARROGANCIA : arrogance, haughtiness
altanero, -ra adj ALTIVO, ARROGANTE : arrogant, haughty — altaneramente adv
altar nm : altar
altavoz nm, pl -voces ALTOPARLANTE : loudspeaker
alteración nf, pl -ciones 1 MODIFICACIÓN : alteration, modification 2 PERTURBACIÓN : disturbance, disruption
alterado, -da adj : upset
alterar vt 1 MODIFICAR : to alter, to modify 2 PERTURBAR : to disturb, to disrupt — alterarse vr : to get upset, to get worked up
altercado nm DISCUSIÓN, DISPUTA : altercation, argument, dispute
alternador nm : alternator
alternancia nf : alternation, rotation
alternar vi 1 : to alternate 2 : to mix, to socialize — vt : to alternate — alternarse vr : to take turns
alternativa nf OPCIÓN : alternative, option
alternativo, -va adj 1 : alternating 2 : alternative — alternativamente adv
alterno, -na adj : alternate ⟨corriente alterna : alternating current⟩
alteza nf 1 : loftiness, lofty height 2 Alteza : Highness
altibajos nmpl 1 : unevenness (of terrain) 2 : ups and downs
altímetro nm : altimeter
altiplanicie nf → altiplano
altiplano nm : high plateau, upland
altisonante adj 1 : pompous, affected (of language) 2 Mex : rude, obscene (of language)
altitud nf : altitude

altivez *nf, pl* **-veces** ALTANERÍA, ARRO-
GANCIA : arrogance, haughtiness
altivo, -va *adj* ALTANERO, ARROGANTE
: arrogant, haughty
alto¹ *adv* **1** : high **2** : loud, loudly
alto², -ta *adj* **1** : tall, high **2** : loud ⟨en
voz alta : aloud, out loud⟩
alto³ *nm* **1** ALTURA : height, elevation
2 : stop, halt **3 altos** *nmpl* : upper floors
alto⁴ *interj* : halt!, stop!
altoparlante *nm* ALTAVOZ : loudspeaker
altozano *nm* : hillock
altruismo *nm* : altruism
altruista¹ *adj* : altruistic
altruista² *nmf* : altruist
altura *nf* **1** : height **2** : altitude **3** : loftiness, nobleness **4 a la altura de** : near,
up by ⟨en la avenida San Antonio a la
altura de la Calle Tres : on San Antonio Avenue up near Third Street⟩ **5 a
estas alturas** : at this point, at this
stage of the game
alubia *nf* : kidney bean
alucinación *nf, pl* **-ciones** : hallucination
alucinante *adj* : hallucinatory
alucinar *vi* : to hallucinate
alucinógeno¹, -na *adj* : hallucinogenic
alucinógeno² *nm* : hallucinogen
alud *nm* AVALANCHA : avalanche, landslide
aludido, -da *n* **1** : person in question ⟨el
aludido : the aforesaid⟩ **2 darse por
aludido** : to take it personally
aludir *vi* : to allude, to refer
alumbrado *nm* ILUMINACIÓN : lighting
alumbramiento *nm* **1** : lighting **2**
: childbirth
alumbrar *vt* **1** ILUMINAR : to light, to illuminate **2** : to give birth to
alumbre *nm* : alum
aluminio *nm* : aluminum
alumnado *nm* : student body
alumno, -na *n* **1** : pupil, student **2**
ex–alumno, -na : alumnus, alumna *f*
ex–alumnos, -nas *npl* : alumni, alum-
nae *f*
alusión *nf, pl* **-siones** : allusion, reference
alusivo, -va *adj* **1** : allusive **2** ～ **a** : in
reference to, regarding
aluvión *nm, pl* **-viones** : flood, barrage
alza *nf* SUBIDA : rise ⟨precios en alza
: rising prices⟩
alzamiento *nm* LEVANTAMIENTO : uprising, insurrection
alzar {21} *vt* **1** ELEVAR, LEVANTAR : to
lift, to raise **2** : to erect — **alzarse** *vr*
LEVANTARSE : to rise up
ama *nf* → **amo**
amabilidad *nf* : kindness
amable *adj* : kind, nice — **amablemente**
adv
amado¹, -da *adj* : beloved, darling
amado², -da *n* : sweetheart, loved one
amaestrar *vt* : to train (animals)
amafiarse *vr Mex fam* : to conspire, to
be in cahoots

amagar {52} *vt* **1** : to show signs of (an
illness, etc.) **2** : to threaten — *vi* **1** : to
be imminent, to threaten **2** : to feint,
to dissemble
amago *nm* **1** AMENAZA : threat **2** : sign,
hint
amainar *vi* : to abate, to ease up, to die
down
amalgama *nf* : amalgam
amalgamar *vt* : to amalgamate, to unite
amamantar *v* : to breast-feed, to nurse,
to suckle
amanecer¹ {53} *v impers* **1** : to dawn **2**
: to begin to show, to appear **3** : to
wake up (in the morning)
amanecer² *nm* ALBA : dawn, daybreak
amanerado, -da *adj* : affected, mannered
amansar *vt* **1** : to tame **2** : to soothe, to
calm down — **amansarse** *vr*
amante¹ *adj* : loving, fond
amante² *nmf* : lover
amañar *vt* : to rig, to fix, to tamper with
— **amañarse** *vr* **amañárselas** : to manage
amaño *nm* **1** : skill, dexterity **2** : trick,
ruse
amapola *nf* : poppy
amar *vt* : to love — **amarse** *vr*
amargado, -da *adj* : embittered, bitter
amargar {52} *vt* **1** : to make bitter, to embitter — *vi* : to taste bitter
amargo¹, -ga *adj* : bitter — **amargamente** *adv*
amargo² *nm* : bitterness, tartness
amargura *nf* **1** : bitterness **2** : grief, sorrow
amarilis *nf* : amaryllis
amarillear *vi* : to yellow, to turn yellow
amarillento, -ta *adj* : yellowish
amarillismo *nm* : yellow journalism,
sensationalism
amarillo¹, -lla *adj* : yellow
amarillo² *nm* : yellow
amarra *nf* **1** : mooring, mooring line **2**
soltar las amarras de : to loosen one's
grip on
amarrar *vt* : to moor (a boat) **2** ATAR
: to fasten, to tie up, to tie down
amartillar *vt* : to cock (a gun)
amasar *vt* **1** : to amass **2** : to knead **3**
: to mix, to prepare
amasijo *nm* : jumble, hodgepodge
amasio, -sia *n* : lover, paramour
amateur *adj & nmf* : amateur — **ama-
teurismo** *nm*
amatista *nf* : amethyst
amatorio, -ria *adj* : amatory, sexual
⟨poesía amatoria : love poems⟩
amazona *nf* **1** : Amazon (in mythology)
2 : horsewoman
amazónico, -ca *adj* : amazonian
ambages *nmpl sin* ～ : without hesitation, straight to the point
ámbar *nm* **1** : amber **2 ámbar gris** : ambergris
ambición *nf, pl* **-ciones** : ambition
ambicionar *vt* : to aspire to, to seek

ambicioso, -sa *adj* : ambitious — **am-biciosamente** *adv*
ambidextro, -tra *adj* : ambidextrous
ambientación *nf, pl* -ciones : setting, atmosphere
ambiental *adj* : environmental — **ambientalmente** *adv*
ambientalista *nmf* : environmentalist
ambientar *vt* : to give atmosphere to, to set (in literature and drama) — **ambientarse** *vr* : to adjust, to get one's bearings
ambiente *nm* 1 : atmosphere 2 : environment 3 : surroundings *pl*
ambigüedad *nf* : ambiguity
ambiguo, -gua *adj* : ambiguous
ámbito *nm* : domain, field, area
ambivalencia *nf* : ambivalence
ambivalente *adj* : ambivalent
ambos, -bas *adj & pron* : both
ambulancia *nf* : ambulance
ambulante *adj* 1 : traveling, itinerant 2 **vendedor ambulante** : street vendor
ameba *nf* : amoeba
amedrentar *vt* : to frighten, to intimidate — **amedrentarse** *vr*
amén *nm* 1 : amen 2 ~ **de** : in addition to, besides 3 **en un decir amén** : in an instant
amenaza *nf* : threat, menace
amenazador, -dora *adj* : threatening, menacing
amenazante → **amenazador**
amenazar {21} *v* : to threaten
amenguar {10} *vt* 1 : to diminish 2 : to belittle, to dishonor
amenidad *nf* : pleasantness, amenity
amenizar {21} *vt* 1 : to make pleasant 2 : to brighten up, to add life to
ameno, -na *adj* : agreeable, pleasant
amento *nm* : catkin
americano, -na *adj & n* : American
amerindio, -dia *adj & n* : Amerindian
ameritar *vt* MERECER : to deserve
ametralladora *nf* : machine gun
amianto *nm* : asbestos
amiba → **ameba**
amigable *adj* : friendly, amicable — **amigablemente** *adv*
amígdala *nf* : tonsil
amigdalitis *nf* : tonsilitis
amigo[1], -ga *adj* : friendly, close
amigo[2], -ga *n* : friend
amigote *nm* : crony, pal
amilanar *vt* 1 : to frighten 2 : to daunt, to discourage — **amilanarse** *vr* : to lose heart
aminoácido *nm* : amino acid
aminorar *vt* : to reduce, to lessen — *vi* : to diminish
amistad *nf* : friendship
amistoso, -sa *adj* : friendly — **amistosamente** *adv*
amnesia *nf* : amnesia
amnésico, -ca *adj & n* : amnesiac, amnesic
amnistía *nf* : amnesty
amnistiar {85} *vt* : to grant amnesty to

amo, ama *n* 1 : master *m*, mistress *f* 2 : owner, keeper (of an animal) 3 **ama de casa** : housewife 4 **ama de llaves** : housekeeper
amodorrado, -da *adj* : drowsy
amolar {19} *vt* 1 : to grind, to sharpen 2 : to pester, to annoy
amoldable *adj* : adaptable
amoldar *vt* 1 : to mold 2 : to adapt, to adjust — **amoldarse** *vr*
amonestación *nf, pl* -ciones 1 APERCIBIMIENTO : admonition, warning 2 **amonestaciones** *nfpl* : banns
amonestar *vt* APERCIBIR : to admonish, to warn
amoníaco *or* amoniaco *nm* : ammonia
amontonamiento *nm* : accumulation, piling up
amontonar *vt* 1 APILAR : to pile up, to heap up 2 : to collect, to gather 3 : to hoard — **amontonarse** *vr*
amor *nm* 1 : love 2 : loved one, beloved 3 **amor propio** : self-esteem 4 **hacer el amor** : to make love
amoral *adj* : amoral
amoratado, -da *adj* : black-and-blue, bruised, livid
amordazar {21} *vt* 1 : to gag, to muzzle 2 : to silence
amorfo, -fa *adj* : shapeless, amorphous
amorío *nm* : love affair, fling
amoroso, -sa *adj* 1 : loving, affectionate 2 : amorous ⟨una mirada amorosa : an amorous glance⟩ 3 : charming, cute — **amorosamente** *adv*
amortiguación *nf* : cushioning, absorption
amortiguador *nm* : shock absorber
amortiguar {10} *vt* : to soften (an impact)
amortizar {21} *vt* : to amortize, to pay off — **amortización** *nf*
amotinado[1], -da *adj* : rebellious, insurgent, mutinous
amotinado[2], -da *n* : rebel, insurgent, mutineer
amotinamiento *nm* : uprising, rebellion
amotinar *vt* : to incite (to riot), to agitate — **amotinarse** *vr* 1 : to riot, to rebel 2 : to mutiny
amparar *vt* : to safeguard, to protect — **ampararse** *vr* 1 ~ **de** : to take shelter from 2 ~ **en** : to have recourse to
amparo *nm* ACOGIDA, REFUGIO : protection, refuge
amperímetro *nm* : ammeter
amperio *nm* : ampere
ampliable *adj* : expandable, enlargeable, extendible
ampliación *nf, pl* -ciones : expansion, extension
ampliar {85} *vt* 1 : to expand, to extend 2 : to widen 3 : to enlarge (photographs) 4 : to elaborate on, to develop (ideas)
amplificador *nm* : amplifier
amplificar {72} *vt* : to amplify — **amplificación** *nf*

amplio, -plia *adj* : broad, wide, ample — **ampliamente** *adv*

amplitud *nf* **1** : breadth, extent **2** : spaciousness

ampolla *nf* **1** : blister **2** : vial, ampoule

ampollar *vt* : to blister — **ampollarse** *vr*

ampolleta *nf* **1** : small vial **2** : hourglass **3** *Chile* : light bulb

ampulosidad *nf* : pompousness, bombast

ampuloso, -sa *adj* GRANDILOCUENTE : pompous, bombastic — **ampulosamente** *adv*

amputar *vt* : to amputate — **amputación** *nf*

amueblar *vt* : to furnish

amuleto *nm* TALISMÁN : amulet, charm

amurallar *vt* : to wall in, to fortify

anacardo *nm* : cashew nut

anaconda *nf* : anaconda

anacrónico, -ca *adj* : anachronistic

anacronismo *nm* : anachronism

ánade *nmf* **1** : duck **2 ánade real** : mallard

anagrama *nm* : anagram

anal *adj* : anal

anales *nmpl* : annals

analfabetismo *nm* : illiteracy

analfabeto, -ta *adj* & *n* : illiterate

analgésico[1], -ca *adj* : analgesic, painkilling

analgésico[2] *nm* : painkiller, analgesic

análisis *nm* : analysis

analista *nmf* **1** : analyst **2** : annalist

analítico, -ca *adj* : analytical, analytic — **analíticamente** *adv*

analizar {21} *vt* : to analyze

analogía *nf* : analogy

analógico, -ca *adj* **1** : analogical **2** : analog ⟨computadora analógica : analog computer⟩

análogo, -ga *adj* : analogous, similar

ananá *or* **ananás** *nm, pl* **-nás** : pineapple

anaquel *nm* REPISA : shelf

anaranjado[1], -da *adj* NARANJA : orange-colored

anaranjado[2] *nm* NARANJA : orange (color)

anarquía *nf* : anarchy

anárquico, -ca *adj* : anarchic

anarquismo *nm* : anarchism

anarquista *adj* & *nmf* : anarchist

anatema *nm* : anathema

anatomía *nf* : anatomy — **anatomista** *nmf*

anatómico, -ca *adj* : anatomical — **anatómicamente** *adv*

anca *nf* **1** : haunch, hindquarter **2 ancas de rana** : frogs' legs

ancestral *adj* **1** : ancient, traditional **2** : ancestral

ancestro *nm* ASCENDIENTE : ancestor, forefather *m*

ancho[1], -cha *adj* **1** : wide, broad **2** : ample, loose-fitting

ancho[2] *nm* : width, breadth

anchoa *nf* : anchovy

anchura *nf* : width, breadth

ancianidad *nf* SENECTUD : old age

anciano[1], -na *adj* : aged, old, elderly

anciano[2], -na *n* : elderly person

ancla *nf* : anchor

ancladero → **anclaje**

anclaje *nm* : anchorage

anclar *v* FONDEAR : to anchor

andadas *nfpl* **1** : tracks **2 volver a las andadas** : to go back to one's old ways, to backslide

andador[1] *nm* **1** : walker, baby walker **2** *Mex* : walkway

andador[2], -dora *n* : walker, one who walks

andadura *nf* : course, journey ⟨su agotadora andadura al campeonato : his exhausting journey to the championship⟩

andaluz, -luza *adj* & *n, mpl* **-luces** : Andalusian

andamiaje *nm* **1** : scaffolding **2** ESTRUCTURA : structure, framework

andamio *nm* : scaffold

andanada *nf* **1** : volley, broadside **2 soltar una andanada a** : to reprimand

andanzas *nfpl* : adventures

andar[1] {6} *vi* **1** CAMINAR : to walk **2** IR : to go, to travel **3** FUNCIONAR : to run, to function ⟨el auto anda bien : the car runs well⟩ **4** : to ride ⟨andar a caballo : to ride on horseback⟩ **5** : to be ⟨anda sin dinero : he's broke⟩ — *vt* : to walk, to travel

andar[2] *nm* : walk, gait

andas *nfpl* : stand (for a coffin), bier

andén *nm, pl* **andenes** **1** : (train) platform **2** *CA, Col* : sidewalk

andino, -na *adj* : Andean

andorrano, -na *adj* & *n* : Andorran

andrajos *nmpl* : rags, tatters

andrajoso, -sa *adj* : ragged, tattered

andrógino, -na *adj* : androgynous

andurriales *nmpl* : remote place

anea *nf* : cattail

anduvo, etc. → **andar**

anécdota *nf* : anecdote

anecdótico, -ca *adj* : anecdotal

anegar {52} *vt* **1** INUNDAR : to flood **2** AHOGAR : to drown **3** : to overwhelm — **anegarse** *vr* : to be flooded

anejo *nm* → **anexo[2]**

anemia *nf* : anemia

anémico, -ca *adj* : anemic

anémona *nf* : anemone

anestesia *nf* : anesthesia

anestesiar *vt* : to anesthetize

anestésico[1], -ca *adj* : anesthetic

anestésico[2] *nm* : anesthetic

anestesista *nmf* : anesthetist

aneurisma *nmf* : aneurysm

anexar *vt* : to annex, to attach

anexión *nf, pl* **-xiones** : annexation

anexo[1], -xa *adj* : attached, joined, annexed

anexo[2] *nm* **1** : annex **2** : supplement (to a book), appendix

anfetamina *nf* : amphetamine

anfibio[1], **-bia** *adj* : amphibious
anfibio[2] *nm* : amphibian
anfiteatro *nm* **1** : amphitheater **2** : lecture hall
anfitrión, -triona *n, mpl* **-triones** : host, hostess *f*
ánfora *nf* **1** : amphora **2** *Mex, Peru* : ballot box
ángel *nm* : angel
angelical *adj* : angelic, angelical
angélico, -ca *adj* → **angelical**
angina *nf* **1** *or* **angina de pecho** : angina **2** *Mex* : tonsil
anglicano, -na *adj & n* : Anglican
angloparlante[1] *adj* : English-speaking
angloparlante[2] *nmf* : English speaker
anglosajón, -jona *adj & n, mpl* **-jones** : Anglo-Saxon
angoleño, -ña *adj & n* : Angolan
angora *nf* : angora
angostar *vt* : to narrow — **angostarse** *vr*
angosto, -ta *adj* : narrow
angostura *nf* : narrowness
anguila *nf* : eel
angular *adj* : angular — **angularidad** *nf*
ángulo *nm* **1** : angle **2** : corner **3** **ángulo muerto** : blind spot
anguloso, -sa *adj* : angular, sharp ⟨una cara angulosa : an angular face⟩ — **angulosidad** *nf*
angustia *nf* **1** CONGOJA : anguish, distress **2** : anxiety, worry
angustiar *vt* **1** : to anguish, to distress **2** : to worry — **angustiarse** *vr*
angustioso, -sa *adj* **1** : anguished, distressed **2** : distressing, worrisome
anhelante *adj* : yearning, longing
anhelar *vt* : to yearn for, to crave
anhelo *nm* : longing, yearning
anidar *vi* **1** : to nest **2** : to make one's home, to dwell — *vt* : to shelter
anillo *nm* SORTIJA : ring
ánima *n* ALMA : soul
animación *nf, pl* **-ciones** **1** : animation **2** VIVEZA : liveliness
animado, -da *adj* **1** : animated, lively **2** : cheerful — **animadamente** *adv*
animador, -dora *n* **1** : (television) host **2** : cheerleader
animadversión *nf, pl* **-siones** ANIMOSIDAD : animosity, antagonism
animal[1] *adj* **1** : animal **2** ESTÚPIDO : stupid, idiotic **3** : rough, brutish
animal[2] *nm* : animal
animal[3] *nmf* **1** IDIOTA : idiot, fool **2** : brute, beastly person
animar *vt* **1** ALENTAR : to encourage, to inspire **2** : to animate, to enliven **3** : to brighten up, to cheer up — **animarse** *vr*
anímico, -ca *adj* : mental ⟨estado anímico : state of mind⟩
ánimo *nm* **1** ALMA : spirit, soul **2** : mood, spirits *pl* **3** : encouragement **4** PROPÓSITO : intention, purpose ⟨sociedad sin ánimo de lucro : nonprofit organization⟩ **5** : energy, vitality

animosidad *nf* ANIMADVERSIÓN : animosity, ill will
animoso, -sa *adj* : brave, spirited
aniñado, -da *adj* : childlike
aniquilación *nf* → **aniquilamiento**
aniquilamiento *nm* : annihilation, extermination
aniquilar *vt* **1** : to annihilate, to wipe out **2** : to overwhelm, to bring to one's knees — **aniquilarse** *vr*
anís *nm* **1** : anise **2** **semilla de anís** : aniseed
aniversario *nm* : anniversary
ano *nm* : anus
anoche *adv* : last night
anochecer[1] {53} *v impers* : to get dark
anochecer[2] *nm* : dusk, nightfall
anodino, -na *adj* : insipid, dull
ánodo *nm* : anode
anomalía *nf* : anomaly
anómalo, -la *adj* : anomalous
anonadado, -da *adj* : dumbfounded, speechless
anonadar *vt* : to dumbfound, to stun
anonimato *nm* : anonymity
anónimo, -ma *adj* : anonymous — **anónimamente** *adv*
anorexia *nf* : anorexia
anoréxico, -ca *adj* : anorexic
anormal *adj* : abnormal — **anormalmente** *adv*
anormalidad *nf* : abnormality
anotación *nf, pl* **-ciones** **1** : annotation, note **2** : scoring (in sports) ⟨lograron una anotación : they managed to score a goal⟩
anotar *vt* **1** : to annotate **2** APUNTAR, ESCRIBIR : to write down, to jot down **3** : to score (in sports) — *vi* : to score
anquilosado, -da *adj* **1** : stiff-jointed **2** : stagnated, stale
anquilosamiento *nm* **1** : stiffness (of joints) **2** : stagnation, paralysis
anquilosarse *vr* **1** : to stagnate **2** : to become stiff or paralyzed
anquilostoma *nm* : hookworm
ánsar *nm* : goose
ansarino *nm* : gosling
ansia *nf* **1** INQUIETUD : apprehensiveness, uneasiness **2** ANGUSTIA : anguish, distress **3** ANHELO : longing, yearning
ansiar {85} *vt* : to long for, to yearn for
ansiedad *nf* : anxiety
ansioso, -sa *adj* **1** : anxious, worried **2** : eager — **ansiosamente** *adv*
antagónico, -ca *adj* : conflicting, opposing
antagonismo *nm* : antagonism
antagonista[1] *adj* : antagonistic
antagonista[2] *nmf* : antagonist, opponent
antagonizar {21} *vt* : to antagonize
antaño *adv* : yesteryear, long ago
antártico, -ca *adj* **1** : antarctic **2** **círculo antártico** : antarctic circle
ante[1] *nm* **1** : elk, moose **2** : suede
ante[2] *prep* **1** : before, in front of **2** : considering, in view of **3** **ante todo** : first and foremost, above all

anteanoche *adv* : the night before last
anteayer *adv* : the day before yesterday
antebrazo *nm* : forearm
antecedente[1] *adj* : previous, prior
antecedente[2] *nm* **1** : precedent **2 antecedentes** *nmpl* : record, background
anteceder *v* : to precede
antecesor, -sora *n* **1** ANTEPASADO : ancestor **2** PREDECESOR : predecessor
antedicho, -cha *adj* : aforesaid, above
antelación *nf, pl* **-ciones** **1** : advance notice **2 con ~** : in advance, beforehand
antemano *adv* **de ~** : in advance ⟨se lo agradezco de antemano : I thank you in advance⟩
antena *nf* : antenna
antenoche → anteanoche
anteojera *nf* **1** : eyeglass case **2 anteojeras** *nfpl* : blinders
anteojos *nmpl* GAFAS : glasses, eyeglasses
antepasado[1], **-da** *adj* : before last ⟨el domingo antepasado : the Sunday before last⟩
antepasado[2], **-da** *n* ANTECESOR : ancestor
antepecho *nm* **1** : guardrail **2** : ledge, sill
antepenúltimo, -ma *adj* : third from last
anteponer {60} *vt* **1** : to place before ⟨anteponer al interés de la nación el interés de la comunidad : to place the interests of the community before national interest⟩ **2** : to prefer
anteproyecto *nm* **1** : draft, proposal **2 anteproyecto de ley** : bill
antera *nf* : anther
anterior *adj* **1** : previous **2** : earlier ⟨tiempos anteriores : earlier times⟩ **3** : anterior, forward, front
anterioridad *nf* **1** : priority **2 con ~** : beforehand, in advance
anteriormente *adv* : previously, beforehand
antes *adv* **1** : before, earlier **2** : formerly, previously **3** : rather, sooner ⟨antes prefiero morir : I'd rather die⟩ **4 ~ de** : before, previous to ⟨antes de hoy : before today⟩ **5 antes que** : before ⟨antes que llegue Luis : before Luis arrives⟩ **6 cuanto antes** : as soon as possible **7 antes bien** : on the contrary
antesala *nf* **1** : anteroom, waiting room, lobby **2** : prelude, prologue
antiaborto, -ta *adj* : antiabortion
antiácido *nm* : antacid
antiadherente *adj* : nonstick
antiaéreo, -rea *adj* : antiaircraft
antiamericano, -na *adj* : anti-American
antibalas *adj* : bulletproof
antibiótico[1], **-ca** *adj* : antibiotic
antibiótico[2] *nm* : antibiotic
antichoque *adj* : shockproof
anticipación *nf, pl* **-ciones** **1** : expectation, anticipation **2 con ~** : in advance

anticipado, -da *adj* **1** : advance, early **2 por ~** : in advance
anticipar *vt* **1** : to anticipate, to forestall, to deal with in advance **2** : to pay in advance — **anticiparse** *vr* **1** : to be early **2** ADELANTARSE : to get ahead
anticipo *nm* **1** : advance (payment) **2** : foretaste, preview
anticlerical *adj* : anticlerical
anticlimático, -ca : anticlimactic
anticlímax *nm* : anticlimax
anticomunismo *nm* : anticommunism
anticomunista *adj & nmf* : anticommunist
anticoncepción *nf, pl* **-ciones** : birth control, contraception
anticonceptivo *nm* : contraceptive
anticongelante *nm* : antifreeze
anticuado, -da *adj* : antiquated, outdated
anticuario[1], **-ria** *adj* : antique, antiquarian
anticuario[2], **-ria** *n* : antiquarian, antiquary
anticuario[3] *nm* : antique shop
anticuerpo *nm* : antibody
antidemocrático, -ca *adj* : antidemocratic
antideportivo, -va *adj* : unsportsmanlike
antidepresivo *nm* : antidepressant
antídoto *nm* : antidote
antidrogas *adj* : antidrug
antier → anteayer
antiestético, -ca *adj* : unsightly, unattractive
antifascista *adj & nmf* : antifascist
antifaz *nm, pl* **-faces** : mask
antifeminista *adj & nmf* : antifeminist
antífona *nf* : anthem
antígeno *nm* : antigen
antigualla *nf* **1** : antique **2** : relic, old thing
antiguamente *adv* **1** : formerly, once **2** : long ago
antigüedad *nf* **1** : antiquity **2** : seniority **3** : age ⟨con siglos de antigüedad : centuries-old⟩ **4 antigüedades** *nfpl* : antiques
antiguo, -gua *adj* **1** : ancient, old **2** : former **3** : old-fashioned ⟨a la antigua : in the old-fashioned way⟩ **4 Antiguo Testamento** : Old Testament
antihigiénico, -ca *adj* INSALUBRE : unhygienic, unsanitary
antihistamínico *nm* : antihistamine
antiimperialismo *nm* : anti-imperialism
antiimperialista *adj & nmf* : anti-imperialist
antiinflacionario, -ria *adj* : anti-inflationary
antiinflamatorio, -ria *adj* : anti-inflammatory
antillano[1], **-na** *adj* CARIBEÑO : Caribbean, West Indian
antillano[2], **-na** *n* : West Indian
antílope *nm* : antelope
antimilitarismo *nm* : antimilitarism

antimilitarista *adj & nmf* : antimilitarist
antimonio *nm* : antimony
antimonopolista *adj* : antimonopoly, antitrust
antinatural *adj* : unnatural, perverse
antipatía *nf* : aversion, dislike
antipático, -ca *adj* : obnoxious, unpleasant
antipatriótico, -ca *adj* : unpatriotic
antirrábico, -ca *adj* : antirabies ⟨vacuna antirrábica : rabies vaccine⟩
antirreglamentario, -ria *adj* 1 : unlawful, illegal 2 : foul (in sports)
antirrevolucionario, -ria *adj & n* : antirevolutionary
antirrobo, -ba *adj* : antitheft
antisemita *adj* : anti-Semitic
antisemitismo *nm* : anti-Semitism
antiséptico¹, -ca *adj* : antiseptic
antiséptico² *nm* : antiseptic
antisocial *adj* : antisocial
antitabaco *adj* : antismoking
antiterrorista *adj* : antiterrorist
antítesis *nf* : antithesis
antitoxina *nf* : antitoxin
antitranspirante *nm* : antiperspirant
antojadizo, -za *adj* CAPRICHOSO : capricious
antojarse *vr* 1 APETECER : to be appealing, to be desirable ⟨se me antoja un helado : I feel like having ice cream⟩ 2 : to seem, to appear ⟨los árboles se antojaban fantasmas : the trees seemed like ghosts⟩
antojitos *nmpl Mex* : traditional Mexican snack foods
antojo *nm* 1 CAPRICHO : whim 2 : craving
antología *nf* 1 : anthology 2 de ～ *fam* : fantastic, incredible
antónimo *nm* : antonym
antonomasia *nf* por ～ : par excellence
antorcha *nf* : torch
antracita *nf* : anthracite
antro *nm* 1 : cave, den 2 : dive, seedy nightclub
antropofagia *nf* CANIBALISMO : cannibalism
antropófago¹, -ga *adj* : cannibalistic
antropófago², -ga *n* CANÍBAL : cannibal
antropoide *adj & nmf* : anthropoid
antropología *nf* : anthropology
antropológico, -ca *adj* : anthropological
antropólogo, -ga *n* : anthropologist
anual *adj* : annual, yearly — **anualmente** *adv*
anualidad *nf* : annuity
anuario *nm* : yearbook, annual
anudar *vt* : to knot, to tie in a knot — **anudarse** *vr*
anuencia *nf* : consent
anulación *nf, pl* **-ciones** : annulment, nullification
anular *vt* : to annul, to cancel
anunciador, -dora *n* → **anunciante**
anunciante *nmf* : advertiser
anunciar *vt* 1 : to announce 2 : to advertise

anuncio *nm* 1 : announcement 2 : advertisement, commercial
anzuelo *nm* 1 : fishhook 2 morder el anzuelo : to take the bait
añadido *nm* : addition
añadidura *nf* 1 : additive, addition 2 por ～ : in addition, furthermore
añadir *vt* 1 AGREGAR : to add 2 AUMENTAR : to increase
añejar *vt* : to age, to ripen
añejo, -ja *adj* 1 : aged, vintage 2 : aged, old, musty, stale
añicos *nmpl* : smithereens, bits ⟨hacer(se) añicos : to shatter⟩
añil *nm* 1 : indigo 2 : bluing
año *nm* 1 : year ⟨en el año 1990 : in (the year) 1990⟩ ⟨tiene diez años : she is ten years old⟩ 2 : grade ⟨cuarto año : fourth grade⟩ 3 año bisiesto : leap year 4 año luz : light-year 5 Año Nuevo : New Year
añoranza *nf* : longing, yearning
añorar *vt* 1 DESEAR : to long for 2 : to grieve for, to miss — *vi* : to mourn, to grieve
añoso, -sa *adj* : aged, old
aorta *nf* : aorta
apabullante *adj* : overwhelming, crushing
apabullar *vt* : to overwhelm
apacentar {55} *vt* : to pasture, to put to pasture
apache *adj & nmf* : Apache
apachurrado, -da *adj fam* : depressed, down
apachurrar *vt* : to crush, to squash
apacible *adj* : gentle, mild, calm — **apaciblemente** *adv*
apaciguador, -dora *adj* : calming
apaciguamiento *nm* : appeasement
apaciguar {10} *vt* APLACAR : to appease, to pacify — **apaciguarse** *vr* : to calm down
apadrinar *vt* 1 : to be a godparent to 2 : to sponsor, to support
apagado, -da *adj* 1 : off, out ⟨la luz está apagada : the light is off⟩ 2 : dull, subdued
apagador *nm Mex* : switch
apagar {52} *vt* 1 : to turn off, to shut off 2 : to extinguish, to put out — **apagarse** *vr* 1 : to go out, to fade 2 : to wane, to die down
apagón *nm, pl* **-gones** : blackout (of power)
apalancamiento *nm* : leverage
apalancar {72} *vt* 1 : to jack up 2 : to pry open
apalear *vt* : to beat up, to thrash
apantallar *vt Mex* : to dazzle, to impress
apañar *vt* 1 : to seize, to grasp 2 : to repair, to mend — **apañarse** *vr* : to manage, to get along
apaño *nm fam* 1 : patch 2 HABILIDAD : skill, knack
apapachar *vt Mex fam* : to cuddle, to caress — **apapacharse** *vr*

aparador *nm* **1** : sideboard, cupboard **2** ESCAPARATE, VITRINA : shop window
aparato *nm* **1** : machine, appliance, apparatus ⟨aparato auditivo : hearing aid⟩ ⟨aparato de televisión : television set⟩ **2** : system ⟨aparato digestivo : digestive system⟩ **3** : display, ostentation ⟨sin aparato : without ceremony⟩ **4** **aparatos** *nmpl* : braces (for the teeth)
aparatoso, -sa *adj* **1** : ostentatious **2** : spectacular
aparcamiento *nm Spain* **1** : parking **2** : parking lot
aparcar {72} *v Spain* : to park
aparcero, -ra *n* : sharecropper
aparear *vt* **1** : to mate (animals) **2** : to match up — **aparearse** *vr* : to mate
aparecer {53} *vi* **1** : to appear **2** PRESENTARSE : to show up **3** : to turn up, to be found — **aparecerse** *vr* : to appear
aparejado, -da *adj* **1** ir aparejado con : to go hand in hand with **2** llevar aparejado : to entail
aparejar *vt* **1** PREPARAR : to prepare, to make ready **2** : to harness (a horse) **3** : to fit out (a ship)
aparejo *nm* **1** : equipment, gear **2** : harness, saddle **3** : rig, rigging (of a ship)
aparentar *vt* **1** : to seem, to appear ⟨no aparentas tu edad : you don't look your age⟩ **2** FINGIR : to feign, to pretend
aparente *adj* **1** : apparent **2** : showy, striking — **aparentemente** *adv*
aparición *nf, pl* -ciones **1** : appearance **2** PUBLICACIÓN : publication, release **3** FANTASMA : apparition, vision
apariencia *nf* **1** ASPECTO : appearance, look **2** en ~ : seemingly, apparently
apartado *nm* **1** : section, paragraph **2** apartado postal : post office box
apartamento *nm* DEPARTAMENTO : apartment
apartar *vt* **1** ALEJAR : to move away, to put at a distance **2** : to put aside, to set aside, to separate — **apartarse** *vr* **1** : to step aside, to move away **2** DESVIARSE : to stray
aparte¹ *adv* **1** : apart, aside ⟨modestia aparte : if I say so myself⟩ **2** : separately **3** ~ de : apart from, besides
aparte² *adj* : separate, special
aparte³ *nm* : aside (in theater)
apartheid *nm* : apartheid
apasionado, -da *adj* : passionate, enthusiastic — **apasionadamente** *adv*
apasionante *adj* : fascinating, exciting
apasionar *vt* : to enthuse, to excite — **apasionarse** *vr*
apatía *nf* : apathy
apático, -ca *adj* : apathetic
apearse *vr* **1** DESMONTAR : to dismount **2** : to get out of or off (a vehicle)
apedrear *vt* : to stone, to throw stones at
apegado, -da *adj* : attached, close, devoted ⟨es muy apegado a su familia : he is very devoted to his family⟩

apegarse {52} *vr* ~ a : to become attached to, to grow fond of
apego *nm* AFICIÓN : attachment, fondness, inclination
apelación *nf, pl* -ciones : appeal (in court)
apelar *vi* **1** : to appeal **2** ~ a : to resort to
apelativo *nm* APELLIDO : last name, surname
apellidarse *vr* : to have for a last name ⟨¿cómo se apellida? : what is your last name?⟩
apellido *nm* : last name, surname
apelotonar *vt* : to roll into a ball, to bundle up
apenar *vt* : to aggrieve, to sadden — **apenarse** *vr* **1** : to be saddened **2** : to become embarrassed
apenas¹ *adv* : hardly, scarcely
apenas² *conj* : as soon as
apéndice *nm* **1** : appendix **2** : appendage
apendicectomía *nf* : appendectomy
apendicitis *nf* : appendicitis
apercibimiento *nm* **1** : preparation **2** AMONESTACIÓN : warning
apercibir *vt* **1** DISPONER : to prepare, to make ready **2** AMONESTAR : to warn **3** OBSERVAR : to observe, to perceive — **apercibirse** *vr* **1** : to get ready **2** ~ de : to notice
aperitivo *nm* **1** : appetizer **2** : aperitif
apero *nm* : tool, implement
apertura *nf* **1** : opening, aperture **2** : commencement, beginning **3** : openness
apesadumbrar *vt* : to distress, to sadden — **apesadumbrarse** *vr* : to be weighed down
apestar *vt* **1** : to infect with the plague **2** : to corrupt — *vi* : to stink
apestoso, -sa *adj* : stinking, foul
apetecer {53} *vt* **1** : to crave, to long for ⟨apeteció la fama : he longed for fame⟩ **2** : to appeal to ⟨me apetece un bistec : I feel like having a steak⟩ ⟨¿cuándo te apetece ir? : when do you want to go?⟩ — *vi* : to be appealing
apetecible *adj* : appetizing, appealing
apetito *nm* : appetite
apetitoso, -sa *adj* : appetizing
apiario *nm* : apiary
ápice *nm* **1** : apex, summit **2** PIZCA : bit, smidgen
apicultor, -tora *n* : beekeeper
apicultura *nf* : beekeeping
apilar *vt* AMONTONAR : to heap up, to pile up — **apilarse** *vr*
apiñado, -da *adj* : jammed, crowded
apiñar *vt* : to pack, to cram — **apiñarse** *vr* : to crowd together, to huddle
apio *nm* : celery
apisonadora *nf* : steamroller
apisonar *vt* : to pack down, to tamp
aplacamiento *nm* : appeasement
aplacar {72} *vt* APACIGUAR : to appease, to placate — **aplacarse** *vr* : to calm down

aplanadora *nf* : steamroller
aplanar *vt* : to flatten, to level
aplastante *adj* : crushing, overwhelming
aplastar *vt* : to crush, to squash
aplaudir *v* : to applaud
aplauso *nm* **1** : applause, clapping **2** : praise, acclaim
aplazamiento *nm* : postponement
aplazar {21} *vt* : to postpone, to defer
aplicable *adj* : applicable — **aplicabilidad** *nf*
aplicación *nf, pl* **-ciones 1** : application **2** : diligence, dedication
aplicado, -da *adj* : diligent, industrious
aplicador *nm* : applicator
aplicar {72} *vt* : to apply — **aplicarse** *vr* : to apply oneself
aplique *or* **apliqué** *nm* : appliqué
aplomar *vt* : to plumb, to make vertical
aplomo *nm* : aplomb, composure
apocado, -da *adj* : timid
apocalipsis *nms & pl* : apocalypse ⟨el Libro del Apocalipsis : the Book of Revelation⟩
apocalíptico, -ca *adj* : apocalyptic
apocamiento *nm* : timidity
apocarse {72} *vr* **1** : to shy away, to be intimidated **2** : to humble oneself, to sell oneself short
apócrifo, -fa *adj* : apocryphal
apodar *vt* : to nickname, to call — **apodarse** *vr*
apoderado, -da *n* : proxy, agent
apoderar *vt* : to authorize, to empower — **apoderarse** *vr* ~ **de** : to seize, to take over
apodo *nm* SOBRENOMBRE : nickname
apogeo *nm* : acme, peak, zenith
apología *nf* : defense, apology
apoplejía *nf* : apoplexy, stroke
apopléctico, -ca *adj* : apoplectic
aporrear *vt* : to bang on, to beat, to bludgeon
aportación *nf, pl* **-ciones** : contribution
aportar *vt* CONTRIBUIR : to contribute, to provide
aporte *nm* → **aportación**
apostador, -dora *n* : bettor, better
apostar {19} *v* : to bet, to wager ⟨apuesto que no viene : I bet he's not coming⟩
apostasía *nf* : apostasy
apóstata *nmf* : apostate
apostilla *nf* : note
apostillar *vt* : to annotate
apóstol *nm* : apostle
apostólico, -ca *adj* : apostolic
apóstrofe *nmf* : apostrophe
apostura *nf* : elegance, gracefulness
apoyacabezas *nms & pl* : headrest
apoyapiés *nms & pl* : footrest
apoyar *vt* **1** : to support, to back **2** : to lean, to rest — **apoyarse** *vr* **1** ~ **en** : to lean on **2** ~ **en** : to be based on, to rest on
apoyo *nm* : support, backing
apreciable *adj* : appreciable, substantial, considerable

apreciación *nf, pl* **-ciones 1** : appreciation **2** : appraisal, evaluation
apreciar *vt* **1** ESTIMAR : to appreciate, to value **2** EVALUAR : to appraise, to assess — **apreciarse** *vr* : to appreciate, to increase in value
aprecio *nm* **1** ESTIMO : esteem, appreciation **2** EVALUACIÓN : appraisal, assessment
aprehender *vt* **1** : to apprehend, to capture **2** : to conceive of, to grasp
aprehensión *nf, pl* **-siones** : apprehension, capture, arrest
apremiante *adj* : pressing, urgent
apremiar *vt* INSTAR : to pressure, to urge — *vi* URGIR : to be urgent ⟨el tiempo apremia : time is of the essence⟩
apremio *nm* : pressure, urgency
aprender *v* : to learn — **aprenderse** *vr*
aprendiz, -diza *n, mpl* **-dices** : apprentice, trainee
aprendizaje *nm* : apprenticeship
aprensión *nf, pl* **-siones** : apprehension, dread
aprensivo, -va *adj* : apprehensive, worried
apresamiento *nm* : seizure, capture
apresar *vt* : to capture, to seize
aprestar *vt* : to make ready, to prepare — **aprestarse** *vr* : to get ready
apresuradamente *adv* **1** : hurriedly **2** : hastily, too fast
apresurado, -da *adj* : hurried, in a rush
apresuramiento *nm* : hurry, haste
apresurar *vt* : to quicken, to speed up — **apresurarse** *vr* : to hurry up, to make haste
apretado, -da *adj* **1** : tight **2** *fam* : cheap, tightfisted — **apretadamente** *adv*
apretar {55} *vt* **1** : to press, to push (a button) **2** : to tighten **3** : to squeeze — *vi* **1** : to press, to push **2** : to fit tightly, to be too tight ⟨los zapatos me aprietan : my shoes are tight⟩
apretón *nm, pl* **-tones 1** : squeeze **2**
apretón de manos : handshake
apretujar *vt* : to squash, to squeeze — **apretujarse** *vr*
aprieto *nm* APURO : predicament, difficulty ⟨estar en un aprieto : to be in a fix⟩
aprisa *adv* : quickly, hurriedly
aprisionar *vt* **1** : to imprison **2** : to trap, to box in
aprobación *nf, pl* **-ciones** : approval, endorsement
aprobar {19} *vt* **1** : to approve of **2** : to pass (a law, an exam) — *vi* : to pass (in school)
aprobatorio, -ria *adj* : approving
apropiación *nf, pl* **-ciones** : appropriation
apropiado, -da *adj* : appropriate, proper, suitable — **apropiadamente** *adv*
apropiarse *vr* ~ **de** : to take possession of, to appropriate
aprovechable *adj* : usable

aprovechado[1], **-da** *adj* **1** : diligent, hardworking **2** : pushy, opportunistic
aprovechado[2], **-da** *n* : pushy person, opportunist
aprovechamiento *nm* : use, exploitation
aprovechar *vt* : to take advantage of, to make good use of — *vi* **1** : to be of use **2** : to progress, to improve — **aprovecharse** *vr* ~ **de** : to take advantage of, to exploit
aprovisionamiento *nm* : provisions *pl*, supplies *pl*
aprovisionar *vt* : to provide, to supply (with provisions)
aproximación *nf, pl* **-ciones 1** : approximation, estimate **2** : rapprochement
aproximado, -da *adj* : approximate, estimated — **aproximadamente** *adv*
aproximar *vt* ACERCAR, ARRIMAR : to approximate, to bring closer — **aproximarse** *vr* ACERCARSE, ARRIMARSE : to approach, to move closer
aptitud *nf* : aptitude, capability
apto, -ta *adj* **1** : suitable, suited, fit **2** HÁBIL : capable, competent
apuesta *nf* : bet, wager
apuesto, -ta *adj* : elegant, good-looking
apuntador, -dora *n* : prompter
apuntalar *vt* : to prop up, to shore up
apuntar *vt* **1** : to aim, to point **2** ANOTAR : to write down, to jot down **3** INDICAR, SEÑALAR : to point to, to point out **4** : to prompt (in the theater) — *vi* **1** : to take aim **2** : to become evident — **apuntarse** *vr* **1** : to sign up, to enroll **2** : to score
apunte *nm* : note
apuñalar *vt* : to stab
apuradamente *adv* **1** : with difficulty **2** : hurriedly, hastily
apurado, -da *adj* **1** APRESURADO : rushed, pressured **2** : poor, needy **3** : difficult, awkward **4** : embarrassed
apurar *vt* **1** APRESURAR : to hurry, to rush **2** : to use up, to exhaust **3** : to trouble — **apurarse** *vr* **1** APRESURARSE : to hurry up **2** PREOCUPARSE : to worry
apuro *nm* **1** APRIETO : predicament, jam **2** : rush, hurry **3** : embarrassment
aquejar *vt* : to afflict
aquel, aquella *adj, mpl* **aquellos** : that, those
aquél, aquélla *pron, mpl* **aquéllos 1** : that (one), those (ones) **2** : the former
aquello *pron* (*neuter*) : that, that matter, that business ⟨aquello fue algo serio : that was something serious⟩
aquí *adv* **1** : here **2** : now ⟨de aquí en adelante : from now on⟩ **3 por** ~ : around here, hereabouts
aquiescencia *nf* : acquiescence, approval
aquietar *vt* : to allay, to calm — **aquietarse** *vr* : to calm down
aquilatar *vt* **1** : to assay **2** : to assess, to size up

ara *nf* **1** : altar **2 en aras de** : in the interests of, for the sake of
árabe[1] *adj & nmf* : Arab, Arabian
árabe[2] *nm* : Arabic (language)
arabesco *nm* : arabesque — **arabesco, -ca** *adj*
arábigo, -ga *adj* **1** : Arabic, Arabian **2 número arábigo** : Arabic numeral
arable *adj* : arable
arado *nm* : plow
aragonés, -nesa *adj & n, mpl* **-neses** : Aragonese
arancel *nm* : tariff, duty
arándano *nm* : blueberry
arandela *nf* : washer (for a faucet, etc.)
araña *nf* **1** : spider **2** : chandelier
arañar *v* : to scratch, to claw
arañazo *nm* : scratch
arar *v* : to plow
arbitraje *nm* **1** : arbitration **2** : refereeing (in sports)
arbitrar *v* **1** : to arbitrate **2** : to referee, to umpire
arbitrariedad *nf* **1** : arbitrariness **2** INJUSTICIA : injustice, wrong
arbitrario, -ria *adj* **1** : arbitrary **2** : unfair, unjust — **arbitrariamente** *adv*
arbitrio *nm* **1** ALBEDRÍO : will **2** JUICIO : judgment
árbitro, -tra *n* **1** : arbitrator, arbiter **2** : referee, umpire
árbol *nm* **1** : tree **2 árbol genealógico** : family tree
arbolado[1], **-da** *adj* : wooded
arbolado[2] *nm* : woodland
arboleda *nf* : grove, wood
arbóreo, -rea *adj* : arboreal
arbusto *nm* : shrub, bush, hedge
arca *nf* **1** : ark **2** : coffer, chest
arcada *nf* **1** : arcade, series of arches **2 arcadas** *nfpl* : retching ⟨hacer arcadas : to retch⟩
arcaico, -ca *adj* : archaic
arcángel *nm* : archangel
arcano, -na *adj* : arcane
arce *nm* : maple tree
arcén *nm, pl* **arcenes** : hard shoulder, berm
archidiócesis *nfs & pl* : archdiocese
archipiélago *nm* : archipelago
archivador *nm* : filing cabinet
archivar *vt* **1** : to file **2** : to archive
archivero, -ra *n* : archivist
archivista *nmf* : archivist
archivo *nm* **1** : file **2** : archive, archives *pl*
arcilla *nf* : clay
arco *nm* **1** : arch, archway **2** : bow (in archery) **3** : arc **4** : wicket (in croquet) **5** PORTERÍA : goal, goalposts *pl* **6 arco iris** : rainbow
arder *vi* **1** : to burn ⟨el bosque está ardiendo : the forest is in flames⟩ ⟨arder de ira : to burn with anger, to be seething⟩ **2** : to smart, to sting, to burn ⟨le ardía el estómago : he had heartburn⟩
ardid *nm* : scheme, ruse

ardiente *adj* **1** : burning **2** : ardent, passionate — **ardientemente** *adv*
ardilla *nf* **1** : squirrel **2** *or* **ardilla listada** : chipmunk
ardor *nm* **1** : heat **2** : passion, ardor
ardoroso, -sa *adj* : heated, impassioned
arduo, -dua *adj* : arduous, grueling — **arduamente** *adv*
área *nf* : area
arena *nf* **1** : sand ⟨arena movediza : quicksand⟩ **2** : arena
arenga *nf* : harangue, lecture
arengar {52} *vt* : to harangue, to lecture
arenilla *nf* **1** : fine sand **2 arenillas** *nfpl* : kidney stones
arenisca *nf* : sandstone
arenoso, -sa *adj* : sandy, gritty
arenque *nm* : herring
arepa *nf* : cornmeal bread
arete *nm* : earring
argamasa *nf* : mortar (cement)
argelino, -na *adj & n* : Algerian
argentino, -na *adj & n* : Argentinian, Argentine
argolla *nf* : hoop, ring
argón *nm* : argon
argot *nm* : slang
argucia *nf* : sophistry, subtlety
argüir {41} *vi* : to argue — *vt* **1** ARGUMENTAR : to contend, to argue **2** INFERIR : to deduce **3** PROBAR : to prove
argumentación *nf, pl* **-ciones** : line of reasoning, argument
argumentar *vt* : to argue, to contend
argumento *nm* **1** : argument, reasoning **2** : plot, story line
aria *nf* : aria
aridez *nf, pl* **-deces** : aridity, dryness
árido, -da *adj* : arid, dry
Aries *nmf* : Aries
ariete *nm* : battering ram
arisco, -ca *adj* : surly, sullen, unsociable
arista *nf* **1** : ridge, edge **2** : beard (of a plant) **3 aristas** *nfpl* : rough edges, complications, problems
aristocracia *nf* : aristocracy
aristócrata *nmf* : aristocrat
aristocrático, -ca *adj* : aristocratic
aritmética *nf* : arithmetic
aritmético, -ca *adj* : arithmetic, arithmetical — **aritméticamente** *adv*
arlequín *nm, pl* **-quines** : harlequin
arma *nf* **1** : weapon **2 armas** *nfpl* : armed forces **3 arma de fuego** : firearm
armada *nf* : navy, fleet
armadillo *nm* : armadillo
armado, -da *adj* **1** : armed **2** : assembled, put together **3** *PRi* : obstinate, stubborn
armador, -dora *n* : shipowner
armadura *nf* **1** : armor **2** ARMAZÓN : skeleton, framework
armamento *nm* : armament, arms *pl*, weaponry
armar *vt* **1** : to assemble, to put together **2** : to create, to cause ⟨armar un es-

cándalo : to cause a scene⟩ **3** : to arm — **armarse** *vr* **armarse de valor** : to steel oneself
armario *nm* **1** CLÓSET, ROPERO : closet **2** ALACENA : cupboard
armatoste *nm fam* : monstrosity, contraption
armazón *nmf, pl* **-zones 1** ESQUELETO : framework, skeleton ⟨armazón de acero : steel framework⟩ **2** : frames *pl* (of eyeglasses)
armenio, -nia *adj & n* : Armenian
armería *nf* **1** : armory **2** : arms museum **3** : gunsmith's shop **4** : gunsmith's craft
armiño *nm* : ermine
armisticio *nm* : armistice
armonía *nf* : harmony
armónica *nf* : harmonica
armónico, -ca *adj* **1** : harmonic **2** : harmonious — **armónicamente** *adv*
armonioso, -sa *adj* : harmonious — **armoniosamente** *adv*
armonizar {21} *vt* **1** : to harmonize **2** : to reconcile — *vi* : to harmonize, to blend together
arnés *nm, pl* **arneses** : harness
aro *nm* **1** : hoop **2** : napkin ring **3** *Arg, Chile, Uru* : earring
aroma *nm* : aroma, scent
aromático, -ca *adj* : aromatic
arpa *nf* : harp
arpegio *nm* : arpeggio
arpía *nf* : shrew, harpy
arpillera *nf* : burlap
arpista *nmf* : harpist
arpón *nm, pl* **arpones** : harpoon — **arponear** *vt*
arquear *vt* : to arch, to bend — **arquearse** *vr* : to bend, to bow
arqueología *nf* : archaeology
arqueológico, -ca *adj* : archaeological
arqueólogo, -ga *n* : archaeologist
arquero, -ra *n* **1** : archer **2** PORTERO : goalkeeper, goalie
arquetípico, -ca *adj* : archetypal
arquetipo *nm* : archetype
arquitecto, -ta *n* : architect
arquitectónico, -ca *adj* : architectural — **aquitectónicamente** *adv*
arquitectura *nf* : architecture
arrabal *nm* **1** : slum **2 arrabales** *nmpl* : outskirts, outlying area
arracada *nf* : hoop earring
arracimarse *vr* : to cluster together
arraigado, -da *adj* : deep-seated, ingrained
arraigar {52} *vi* : to take root, to become established — **arraigarse** *vr*
arraigo *nm* : roots *pl* ⟨con mucho arraigo : deep-rooted⟩
arrancar {72} *vt* **1** : to pull out, to tear out **2** : to pick, to pluck (a flower) **3** : to start (an engine) **4** : to boot (a computer) — *vi* **1** : to start an engine **2** : to get going — **arrancarse** *vr* : to pull out, to pull off

arrancón *nm, pl* **-cones** *Mex* **1** : sudden loud start (of a car) **2 carrera de arrancones** : drag race
arranque *nm* **1** : starter (of a car) **2** ARREBATO : outburst, fit **3 punto de arranque** : beginning, starting point
arrasar *vt* **1** : to level, to smooth **2** : to devastate, to destroy **3** : to fill to the brim
arrastrar *vt* **1** : to drag, to tow **2** : to draw, to attract — *vi* : to hang down, to trail — **arrastrarse** *vr* **1** : to crawl **2** : to grovel
arrastre *nm* **1** : dragging **2** : pull, attraction **3 red de arrastre** : dragnet, trawling net
arrayán *nm, pl* **-yanes 1** MIRTO : myrtle **2 arrayán brabántico** : bayberry, wax myrtle
arrear *vt* : to urge on, to drive — *vi* : to hurry along
arrebatado, -da *adj* **1** PRECIPITADO : impetuous, hotheaded, rash **2** : flushed, blushing
arrebatar *vt* **1** : to snatch, to seize **2** CAUTIVAR : to captivate — **arrebatarse** *vr* : to get carried away (with anger, etc.)
arrebato *nm* ARRANQUE : fit, outburst
arreciar *vi* : to intensify, to worsen
arrecife *nm* : reef
arreglado, -da *adj* **1** : fixed, repaired **2** : settled, sorted out **3** : neat, tidy **4** : smart, dressed-up
arreglar *vt* **1** COMPONER : to repair, to fix **2** : to tidy up ⟨arregla tu cuarto : pick up your room⟩ **3** : to solve, to work out ⟨quiero arreglar este asunto : I want to settle this matter⟩ — **arreglarse** *vr* **1** : to get dressed (up) ⟨arreglarse el pelo : to get one's hair done⟩ **2 arreglárselas** *fam* : to get by, to manage
arreglo *nm* **1** : repair **2** : arrangement **3** : agreement, understanding
arrellanarse *vr* : to settle (in a chair)
arremangarse {52} *vr* : to roll up one's sleeves
arremeter *vi* EMBESTIR : to attack, to charge
arremetida *nf* EMBESTIDA : attack, onslaught
arremolinarse *vr* **1** : to crowd around, to mill about **2** : to swirl (about)
arrendador, -dora *n* **1** : landlord, landlady *f* **2** : tenant, lessee
arrendajo *nm* : jay
arrendamiento *nm* **1** ALQUILER : rental, leasing **2 contrato de arrendamiento** : lease
arrendar {55} *vt* ALQUILAR : to rent, to lease
arrendatario, -ria *n* : tenant, lessee, renter
arreos *nmpl* GUARNICIONES : tack, harness, trappings
arrepentido, -da *adj* : repentant, remorseful

arrepentimiento *nm* : regret, remorse, repentance
arrepentirse {76} *vr* **1** : to regret, to be sorry **2** : to repent
arrestar *vt* DETENER : to arrest, to detain
arresto *nm* **1** DETENCIÓN : arrest **2 arrestos** *nmpl* : boldness, daring
arriar {85} *vt* **1** : to lower (a flag, etc.) **2** : to slacken (a rope, etc.)
arriate *nm Mex, Spain* : bed (for plants), border
arriba *adv* **1** : up, upwards **2** : above, overhead **3** : upstairs **4** ~ **de** : more than **5 de arriba abajo** : from top to bottom, from head to foot
arribar *vi* **1** : to arrive **2** : to dock, to put into port
arribista *nmf* : parvenu, upstart
arribo *nm* : arrival
arriendo *nm* ARRENDAMIENTO : rent, rental
arriero, -ra *n* : mule driver, muleteer
arriesgado, -da *adj* **1** : risky **2** : bold, daring
arriesgar {52} *vt* : to risk, to venture — **arriesgarse** *vr* : to take a chance
arrimado, -da *n Mex fam* : sponger, freeloader
arrimar *vt* ACERCAR, APROXIMAR : to bring closer, to draw near — **arrimarse** *vr* ACERCARSE, APROXIMARSE : to approach, to get close
arrinconar *vt* **1** ACORRALAR : to corner, to box in **2** : to push aside, to abandon
arroba *nf* : arroba (Spanish unit of measurement)
arrobamiento *nm* : rapture, ecstasy
arrobar *vt* : to enrapture, to enchant — **arrobarse** *vr*
arrocero¹, -ra *adj* : rice
arrocero², -ra *n* : rice grower
arrodillarse *vr* : to kneel (down)
arrogancia *nf* ALTANERÍA, ALTIVEZ : arrogance, haughtiness
arrogante *adj* ALTANERO, ALTIVO : arrogant, haughty
arrogarse {52} *vr* : to usurp, to arrogate
arrojado, -da *adj* : daring, fearless
arrojar *vt* **1** : to hurl, to cast, to throw **2** : to give off, to spew out **3** : to yield, to produce **4** *fam* : to vomit — **arrojarse** *vr* PRECIPITARSE : to throw oneself, to leap
arrojo *nm* : boldness, fearlessness
arrollador, -dora *adj* : sweeping, overwhelming
arrollar *vt* **1** : to sweep away, to carry away **2** : to crush, to overwhelm **3** : to run over (with a vehicle)
aropar *vt* : to clothe, to cover (up) — **aroparse** *vr*
arrostrar *vt* : to confront, to face (up to)
arroyo *nm* **1** RIACHUELO : brook, creek, stream **2** : gutter
arroz *nm, pl* **arroces** : rice
arrozal *nm* : rice field, rice paddy
arruga *nf* : wrinkle, fold, crease

arrugado, -da *adj* : wrinkled, creased, lined

arrugar {52} *vt* : to wrinkle, to crease, to pucker — **arrugarse** *vr*

arruinar *vt* : to ruin, to wreck — **arruinarse** *vr* **1** : to be ruined **2** : to fall into ruin, to go bankrupt

arrullar *vt* : to lull to sleep — *vi* : to coo

arrullo *nm* **1** : lullaby **2** : coo (of a dove)

arrumaco *nm fam* : kissing, cuddling

arrumbar *vt* **1** : to lay aside, to put away **2** : to floor, to leave speechless

arsenal *nm* : arsenal

arsénico *nm* : arsenic

arte *nmf (usually m in singular, f in plural)* **1** : art ⟨artes y oficios : arts and crafts⟩ ⟨bellas artes : fine arts⟩ **2** HABILIDAD : skill **3** : cunning, cleverness

artefacto *nm* **1** : artifact **2** DISPOSITIVO : device

artemisa *nf* : sagebrush

arteria *nf* : artery — **arterial** *adj*

arteriosclerosis *nf* : arteriosclerosis, hardening of the arteries

artero, -ra *adj* : wily, crafty

artesanal *adj* : pertaining to crafts or craftsmanship, handmade

artesanía *nf* **1** : craftsmanship **2** : handicrafts *pl*

artesano, -na *n* : artisan, craftsman *m*, craftsperson

artesiano, -na *adj* : artesian ⟨pozo artesiano : artesian well⟩

ártico, -ca *adj* : arctic

articulación *nf, pl* **-ciones 1** : articulation, pronunciation **2** COYUNTURA : joint

articular *vt* **1** : to articulate, to utter **2** : to connect with a joint **3** : to coordinate, to orchestrate

articulista *nmf* : columnist

artículo *nm* **1** : article, thing **2** : item, feature, report **3 artículo de comercio** : commodity **4 artículos de primera necesidad** : essentials **5 artículos de tocador** : toiletries

artífice *nmf* **1** ARTESANO : artisan **2** : mastermind, architect

artificial *adj* **1** : artificial, man-made **2** : feigned, false — **artificialmente** *adv*

artificio *nm* **1** HABILIDAD : skill **2** APARATO : device, appliance **3** ARDID : artifice, ruse

artificioso, -sa *adj* **1** : skillful **2** : cunning, deceptive

artillería *nf* : artillery

artillero, -ra *n* : artilleryman *m*, gunner

artilugio *nm* : gadget, contraption

artimaña *nf* : ruse, trick

artista *nmf* **1** : artist **2** ACTOR, ACTRIZ : actor, actress *f*

artístico, -ca *adj* : artistic — **artísticamente** *adv*

artrítico, -ca *adj* : arthritic

artritis *nfs & pl* : arthritis

artrópodo *nm* : arthropod

arveja *nf* GUISANTE : pea

arzobispado *nm* : archbishopric

arzobispo *nm* : archbishop

as *nm* : ace

asa *nf* AGARRADERA, ASIDERO : handle, grip

asado¹, -da *adj* : roasted, grilled, broiled

asado² *nm* **1** : roast **2** : barbecued meat **3** : barbecue, cookout

asador *nm* : spit, rotisserie

asaduras *nfpl* : entrails, offal

asalariado¹, -da *adj* : wage-earning, salaried

asalariado², -da *n* : wage earner

asaltante *nmf* **1** : mugger, robber **2** : assailant

asaltar *vt* **1** : to assault **2** : to mug, to rob **3 asaltar al poder** : to seize power

asalto *nm* **1** : assault **2** : mugging, robbery **3** : round (in boxing) **4 asalto al poder** : coup d'etat

asamblea *nf* : assembly, meeting

asambleísta *nmf* : assemblyman *m*, assemblywoman *f*

asar *vt* : to roast, to grill — **asarse** *vr fam* : to roast, to be dying from heat

asbesto *nm* : asbestos

ascendencia *nf* **1** : ancestry, descent **2** ~ **sobre** : influence over

ascendente *adj* : ascending, upward ⟨un curso ascendente : an upward trend⟩

ascender {56} *vt* **1** : to ascend, to rise up **2** : to be promoted ⟨ascendió a gerente : she was promoted to manager⟩ **3** ~ **a** : to amount to, to reach ⟨las deudas ascienden a 20 millones de pesos : the debt amounts to 20 million pesos⟩ — *vt* : to promote

ascendiente¹ *nmf* ANCESTRO : ancestor

ascendiente² *nm* INFLUENCIA : influence, ascendancy

ascensión *nf, pl* **-siones 1** : ascent, rise **2 Fiesta de la Ascensión** : Ascension Day

ascenso *nm* **1** : ascent, rise **2** : promotion

ascensor *nm* ELEVADOR : elevator

asceta *nmf* : ascetic

ascético, -ca *adj* : ascetic

ascetismo *nm* : asceticism

asco *nm* **1** : disgust ⟨¡qué asco! : that's disgusting!, how revolting!⟩ **2 darle asco (a alguien)** : to sicken, to revolt **3 estar hecho un asco** : to be filthy **4 hacerle ascos a** : to turn up one's nose at

ascua *nf* **1** BRASA : ember **2 estar en ascuas** *fam* : to be on edge

asear *vt* **1** : to wash, to clean **2** : to tidy up — **asearse** *vr*

asechanza *nf* : snare, trap

asechar *vt* : to set a trap for

asediar *vt* **1** SITIAR : to besiege **2** ACOSAR : to harass

asedio *nm* **1** : siege **2** ACOSO : harassment

asegurador¹, -dora *adj* **1** : insuring, assuring **2** : pertaining to insurance

asegurador², -dora *n* : insurer, underwriter
aseguradora *nf* : insurance company
asegurar *vt* **1** : to assure **2** : to secure **3** : to insure — **asegurarse** *vr* **1** CERCIORARSE : to make sure **2** : to take out insurance, to insure oneself
asemejar *vt* **1** : to make similar ⟨ese bigote te asemeja a tu abuelo : that mustache makes you look like your grandfather⟩ **2** *Mex* : to be similar to, to resemble — **asemejarse** *vr* ~ **a** : to look like, to resemble
asentaderas *nfpl fam* : bottom, buttocks *pl*
asentado, -da *adj* : settled, established
asentamiento *nm* : settlement
asentar {55} *vt* **1** : to lay down, to set down, to place **2** : to settle, to establish **3** *Mex* : to state, to affirm — **asentarse** *vr* **1** : to settle **2** ESTABLECERSE : to settle down, to establish oneself
asentimiento *nm* : assent, consent
asentir {76} *vt* : to consent, to agree
aseo *nm* : cleanliness
aséptico, -ca *adj* : aseptic, germ-free
asequible *adj* ACCESIBLE : accessible, attainable
aserción *nf* → **aserto**
aserradero *nm* : sawmill
aserrar {55} *vt* : to saw
aserrín *nm, pl* **-rrines** : sawdust
aserto *nm* : assertion, affirmation
asesinar *vt* **1** : to murder **2** : to assassinate
asesinato *nm* **1** : murder **2** : assassination
asesino¹, -na *adj* : murderous, homicidal
asesino², -na *n* **1** : murderer, killer **2** : assassin
asesor, -sora *n* : advisor, consultant
asesoramiento *nm* : advice, counsel
asesorar *vt* : to advise, to counsel — **asesorarse** *vr* ~ **de** : to consult
asesoría *nf* **1** : consulting, advising **2** : consultant's office
asestar {55} *vt* **1** : to aim, to point (a weapon) **2** : to deliver, to deal (a blow)
aseveración *nf, pl* **-ciones** : assertion, statement
aseverar *vt* : to assert, to state
asexual *adj* : asexual — **asexualmente** *adv*
asfaltado¹, -da *adj* : asphalted, paved
asfaltado² *nm* PAVIMENTO : pavement, asphalt
asfaltar *vt* : to pave, to blacktop
asfalto *nm* : asphalt
asfixia *nf* : asphyxia, asphyxiation, suffocation
asfixiar *vt* : to asphyxiate, to suffocate, to smother — **asfixiarse** *vr*
asga, etc. → **asir**
así¹ *adv* **1** : like this, like that **2** : so, thus ⟨así sea : so be it⟩ **3** ~ **de** : so, about so ⟨una caja así de grande : a box about so big⟩ **4 así que** : so, therefore **5** ~ **como** : as well as **6 así así** : so-so, fair
así² *adj* : such, such a ⟨un talento así es inestimable : a talent like that is priceless⟩
así³ *conj* AUNQUE : even if, even though ⟨no irá, así le paguen : he won't go, even if they pay him⟩
asiático¹, -ca *adj* : Asian, Asiatic
asiático², -ca *n* : Asian
asidero *nm* **1** AGARRADERA, ASA : grip, handle **2** AGARRE : grip, hold
asiduamente *adv* : regularly, frequently
asiduidad *nf* **1** : assiduousness **2** : regularity, frequency
asiduo, -dua *adj* **1** : assiduous **2** : frequent, regular
asiento *nm* **1** : seat, chair ⟨asiento trasero : back seat⟩ **2** : location, site
asignación *nf, pl* **-ciones** **1** : allocation **2** : appointment, designation **3** : allowance, pay **4** *PRi* : homework, assignment
asignar *vt* **1** : to assign, to allocate **2** : to appoint
asignatura *nf* MATERIA : subject, course
asilado, -da *n* : exile, refugee
asilo *nm* : asylum, refuge, shelter
asimetría *nf* : asymmetry
asimétrico, -ca *adj* : asymmetrical, asymmetric
asimilación *nf, pl* **-ciones** : assimilation
asimilar *vt* : to assimilate — **asimilarse** *vr* ~ **a** : to be similar to, to resemble
asimismo *adv* **1** IGUALMENTE : similarly, likewise **2** TAMBIÉN : as well, also
asir {7} *vt* : to seize, to grasp — **asirse** *vr* ~ **a** : to cling to
asistencia *nf* **1** : attendance **2** : assistance **3** : assist (in sports)
asistente¹ *adj* : attending, in attendance
asistente² *nmf* **1** : assistant **2 los asistentes** : those present, those in attendance
asistir *vi* : to attend, to be present ⟨asistir a clase : to attend class⟩ — *vt* : to aid, to assist
asma *nf* : asthma
asmático, -ca *adj* : asthmatic
asno *nm* BURRO : ass, donkey
asociación *nf, pl* **-ciones** **1** : association, relationship **2** : society, group, association
asociado¹, -da *adj* : associate, associated
asociado², -da *n* : associate, partner
asociar *vt* **1** : to associate, to connect **2** : to pool (resources) **3** : to take into partnership — **asociarse** *vr* **1** : to become partners **2** ~ **a** : to join, to become a member of
asolar {19} *vt* : to devastate, to destroy
asoleado, -da *adj* : sunny
asolear *vt* : to put in the sun — **asolearse** *vr* : to sunbathe
asomar *vt* : to show, to stick out — *vi* : to appear, to become visible — **aso-**

marse *vr* **1** : to show, to appear **2** : to lean out, to look out ⟨se asomó por la ventana : he leaned out the window⟩

asombrar *vt* MARAVILLAR : to amaze, to astonish — **asombrarse** *vr* : to marvel, to be amazed

asombro *nm* : amazement, astonishment

asombroso, -sa *adj* : amazing, astonishing — **asombrosamente** *adv*

asomo *nm* **1** : hint, trace **2 ni por asomo** : by no means

aspa *nf* : blade (of a fan or propeller)

aspaviento *nm* : exaggerated movement, fuss, flounce

aspecto *nm* **1** : aspect **2** APARIENCIA : appearance, look

aspereza *nf* RUDEZA : roughness, coarseness

áspero, -ra *adj* : rough, coarse, abrasive — **ásperamente** *adv*

aspersión *nf, pl* **-siones** : sprinkling

aspersor *nm* : sprinkler

aspiración *nf, pl* **-ciones** **1** : inhalation, breathing in **2** ANHELO : aspiration, desire

aspiradora *nf* : vacuum cleaner

aspirante *nmf* : applicant, candidate

aspirar *vi* ~ **a** : to aspire to — *vt* : to inhale, to breathe in

aspirina *nf* : aspirin

asquear *vt* : to sicken, to disgust

asquerosidad *nf* : filth, foulness

asqueroso, -sa *adj* : disgusting, sickening, repulsive — **asquerosamente** *adv*

asta *nf* **1** : flagpole ⟨a media asta : at half-mast⟩ **2** : horn, antler **3** : shaft (of a weapon)

ástaco *nm* : crayfish

astado, -da *adj* : horned

aster *nm* : aster

asterisco *nm* : asterisk

asteroide *nm* : asteroid

astigmatismo *nm* : astigmatism

astil *nm* : shaft (of an arrow or feather)

astilla *nf* **1** : splinter, chip **2 de tal palo, tal astilla** : like father, like son

astillar *vt* : to splinter — **astillarse** *vr*

astillero *nm* : dry dock, shipyard

astral *adj* : astral

astringente *adj & nm* : astringent — **astringencia** *nf*

astro *nm* **1** : heavenly body **2** : star

astrología *nf* : astrology

astrológico, -ca *adj* : astrological

astrólogo, -ga *n* : astrologer

astronauta *nmf* : astronaut

astronáutica *nf* : astronautics

astronáutico, -ca *adj* : astronautic, astronautical

astronave *nf* : spaceship

astronomía *nf* : astronomy

astronómico, -ca *adj* : astronomical — **astronómicamente** *adv*

astrónomo, -ma *n* : astronomer

astroso, -sa *adj* DESALIÑADO : slovenly, untidy

astucia *nf* **1** : astuteness, shrewdness **2** : cunning, guile

astuto, -ta *adj* **1** : astute, shrewd **2** : crafty, tricky — **astutamente** *adv*

asueto *nm* : time off, break

asumir *vt* **1** : to assume, to take on ⟨asumir el cargo : to take office⟩ **2** SUPONER : to assume, to suppose

asunción *nf, pl* **-ciones** : assumption

asunto *nm* **1** CUESTIÓN, TEMA : affair, matter, subject **2 asuntos** *nmpl* : affairs, business

asustadizo, -za *adj* : nervous, jumpy, skittish

asustado, -da *adj* : frightened, afraid

asustar *vt* ESPANTAR : to scare, to frighten — **asustarse** *vr*

atacante *nmf* : assailant, attacker

atacar {72} *v* : to attack

atado¹, -da *adj* : shy, inhibited

atado² *nm* **1** : bundle, bunch **2** *Arg* : pack (of cigarettes)

atadura *nf* LIGADURA : tie, bond

atajar *vt* **1** IMPEDIR : to block, to stop **2** INTERRUMPIR : to interrupt, to cut off **3** CONTENER : to hold back, to restrain — *vi* ~ **por** : to take a shortcut through

atajo *nm* : shortcut

atalaya *nf* **1** : watchtower **2** : vantage point

atañer {79} *vt* ~ **a** (*3rd person only*) : to concern, to have to do with ⟨eso no me atañe : that does not concern me⟩

ataque *nm* **1** : attack, assault **2** : fit ⟨ataque de risa : fit of laughter⟩ **3 ataque de nervios** : nervous breakdown **4 ataque cardíaco** *or* **ataque al corazón** : heart attack

atar *vt* AMARRAR : to tie, to tie up, to tie down — **atarse** *vr*

atarantado, -da *adj fam* **1** : restless **2** : dazed, stunned

atarantar *vt fam* : to daze, to stun

atarazana *nf* : shipyard

atardecer¹ {53} *v impers* : to get dark

atardecer² *nm* : late afternoon, dusk

atareado, -da *adj* : busy, overworked

atascar {72} *vt* **1** ATORAR : to block, to clog, to stop up **2** : to hinder — **atascarse** *vr* **1** : to become obstructed **2** : to get bogged down **3** PARARSE : to stall

atasco *nm* **1** : blockage **2** EMBOTELLAMIENTO : traffic jam

ataúd *nm* : coffin, casket

ataviar {85} *vt* **1** : to dress, to clothe — **ataviarse** *vr* : to dress up

atavío *nm* ATUENDO : dress, attire

ateísmo *nm* : atheism

atemorizar {21} *vt* : to frighten, to intimidate — **atemorizarse** *vr*

atemperar *vt* : to temper, to moderate

atención¹ *nf, pl* **-ciones** **1** : attention **2 poner atención** *or* **prestar atención** : to pay attention **3 llamar la atención** : to attract attention **4 en atención a** : in view of

atención² *interj* **1** : attention! **2** : watch out!

atender {56} vt 1 : to help, to wait on 2 : to look after, to take care of 3 : to heed, to listen to — vi : to pay attention
atenerse {80} vr : to abide ⟨tendrás que atenerte a las reglas : you will have to abide by the rules⟩
atentado nm : attack, assault
atentamente adv 1 : attentively, carefully 2 (used in correspondence) : sincerely, sincerely yours
atentar {55} vi ~ **contra** : to make an attempt on, to threaten ⟨atentaron contra su vida : they made an attempt on his life⟩
atento, -ta adj 1 : attentive, mindful 2 CORTÉS : courteous
atenuación nf, pl **-ciones** 1 : lessening 2 : understatement
atenuante¹ adj : extenuating, mitigating
atenuante² nmf : extenuating circumstance, excuse
atenuar {3} vt 1 MITIGAR : to extenuate, to mitigate 2 : to dim (light), to tone down (colors) 3 : to minimize, to lessen
ateo¹, atea adj : atheistic
ateo², atea n : atheist
aterciopelado, -da adj : velvety, downy
aterido, -da adj : freezing, frozen
aterrador, -dora adj : terrifying
aterrar {55} vt : to terrify, to frighten
aterrizaje nm : landing (of a plane)
aterrizar {21} vt : to land, to touch down
aterrorizar {21} vt 1 : to terrify 2 : to terrorize — **aterrorizarse** vr : to be terrified
atesorar vt : to hoard, to amass
atestado, -da adj : crowded, packed
atestar {55} vt 1 ATIBORRAR : to crowd, to pack 2 : to witness, to testify to — vi : to testify
atestiguar {10} vt : to testify to, to bear witness to — vi DECLARAR : to testify
atiborrar vt : to pack, to crowd — **atiborrarse** vr : to stuff oneself
ático nm 1 : penthouse 2 BUHARDILLA, DESVÁN : attic
atigrado, -da adj : tabby (of cats), striped (of fur)
atildado, -da adj : smart, neat, dapper
atildar vt 1 : to put a tilde over 2 : to clean up, to smarten up — **atildarse** vr : to get spruced up
atinar vi ACERTAR : to be accurate, to be on target
atingencia nf : bearing, relevance
atípico, -ca adj : atypical
atiplado, -da adj : shrill, high-pitched
atirantar vt : to make taut, to tighten
atisbar vt 1 : to spy on, to watch 2 : to catch a glimpse of, to make out
atisbo nm : glimpse, sign, hint
atizador nm : poker (for a fire)
atizar {21} vt 1 : to poke, to stir, to stoke (a fire) 2 : to stir up, to rouse 3 fam : to give, to land (a blow)
atlántico, -ca adj : Atlantic
atlas nm : atlas

atleta nmf : athlete
atlético, -ca adj : athletic
atletismo nm : athletics
atmósfera nf : atmosphere
atmosférico, -ca adj : atmospheric
atole nm Mex 1 : thick hot beverage prepared with corn flour 2 **darle atole con el dedo (a alguien)** : to string (someone) along
atollarse vr : to get stuck, to get bogged down
atolón nm, pl **-lones** : atoll
atolondrado, -da adj 1 ATURDIDO : bewildered, dazed 2 DESPISTADO : scatterbrained, absentminded
atómico, -ca adj : atomic
atomizador nm : atomizer
atomizar {21} vt FRAGMENTAR : to fragment, to break into bits
átomo nm : atom
atónito, -ta adj : astonished, amazed
atontar vt 1 : to stupefy 2 : to bewilder, to confuse
atorar vt ATASCAR : to block, to clog — **atorarse** vr 1 ATASCARSE : to get stuck 2 ATRAGANTARSE : to choke
atormentador, -dora n : tormenter
atormentar vt : to torment, to torture — **atormentarse** vr : to torment oneself, to agonize
atornillar vt : to screw (in, on, down)
atorrante nmf Arg : bum, loafer
atosigar {52} vt : to harass, to annoy
atracadero nm : dock, pier
atracador, -dora n : robber, mugger
atracar {72} vt : to dock, to land — vt : to hold up, to rob, to mug — **atracarse** vr fam ~ **de** : to gorge oneself with
atracción nf, pl **-ciones** : attraction
atraco nm : holdup, robbery
atractivo¹, -va adj : attractive
atractivo² nm : attraction, appeal, charm
atraer {81} vt : to attract — **atraerse** vr 1 : to attract (each other) 2 GANARSE : to gain, to win
atragantarse vr : to choke (on food)
atrancar {72} vt : to block, to bar — **atrancarse** vr
atrapada nf : catch
atrapar vt : to trap, to capture
atrás adv 1 DETRÁS : back, behind ⟨se quedó atrás : he stayed behind⟩ 2 ANTES : ago ⟨mucho tiempo atrás : long ago⟩ 3 **para** ~ or **hacia** ~ : backwards, toward the rear 4 ~ **de** : in back of, behind
atrasado, -da adj 1 : late, overdue 2 : backward 3 : old-fashioned 4 : slow (of a clock or watch)
atrasar vt : to delay, to put off — vi : to lose time — **atrasarse** vr : to fall behind
atraso nm 1 RETRASO : lateness, delay ⟨llegó con 20 minutos de atraso : he was 20 minutes late⟩ 2 : backwardness 3 **atrasos** nmpl : arrears

atravesar {55} *vt* **1** CRUZAR : to cross, to go across **2** : to pierce **3** : to lay across **4** : to go through (a situation or crisis) — **atravesarse** *vr* **1** : to be in the way ⟨se me atravesó : it blocked my path⟩ **2** : to interfere, to meddle
atrayente *adj* : attractive
atreverse *vr* **1** : to dare **2** : to be insolent
atrevido, -da *adj* **1** : bold, daring **2** : insolent
atrevimiento *nm* **1** : daring, boldness **2** : insolence
atribución *nf, pl* **-ciones** : attribution
atribuible *adj* IMPUTABLE : attributable, ascribable
atribuir {41} *vt* **1** : to attribute, to ascribe **2** : to grant, to confer — **atribuirse** *vr* : to take credit for
atribular *vt* : to afflict, to trouble — **atribularse** *vr*
atributo *nm* : attribute
atril *nm* : lectern, stand
atrincherar *vt* : to entrench — **atrincherarse** *vr* **1** : to dig in, to entrench oneself **2** ~ **en** : to hide behind
atrio *nm* **1** : atrium **2** : portico
atrocidad *nf* : atrocity
atrofia *nf* : atrophy
atrofiar *v* : to atrophy
atronador, -dora *adj* : thunderous, deafening
atropellado, -da *adj* **1** : rash, hasty **2** : brusque, abrupt
atropellamiento → **atropello**
atropellar *vt* **1** : to knock down, to run over **2** : to violate, to abuse — **atropellarse** *vr* : to rush through (a task), to trip over one's words
atropello *nm* : abuse, violation, outrage
atroz *adj, pl* **atroces** : atrocious, appalling — **atrozmente** *adv*
atuendo *nm* ATAVÍO : attire, costume
atufar *vt* : to vex, to irritate — **atufarse** *vr* **1** : to get angry **2** : to smell bad, to stink
atún *nm, pl* **atunes** : tuna fish, tuna
aturdimiento *nm* : bewilderment, confusion
aturdir *vt* **1** : to stun, to shock **2** : to bewilder, to confuse, to stupefy
atuvo, etc. → **atenerse**
audacia *nf* OSADÍA : boldness, audacity
audaz *adj, pl* **audaces** : bold, audacious, daring — **audazmente** *adv*
audible *adj* : audible
audición *nf, pl* **-ciones** **1** : hearing **2** : audition
audiencia *nf* : audience
audífono *nm* **1** : hearing aid **2** **audífonos** *nmpl* : headphones, earphones
audio *nm* : audio
audiovisual *adj* : audiovisual
auditar *vt* : to audit
auditivo, -va *adj* : auditory, hearing, aural ⟨aparato auditivo : hearing aid⟩
auditor, -tora *n* : auditor
auditoría *nf* : audit

auditorio *nm* **1** : auditorium **2** : audience
auge *nm* **1** : peak, height **2** : boom, upturn
augur *nm* : augur
augurar *vt* : to predict, to foretell
augurio *nm* AGÜERO, PRESAGIO : augury, omen
augusto, -ta *adj* : august
aula *nf* : classroom
aullar {8} *vt* : to howl, to wail
aullido *nm* : howl, wail
aumentar *vt* ACRECENTAR : to increase, to raise — *vi* : to rise, to increase, to grow
aumento *nm* INCREMENTO : increase, rise
aun *adv* **1** : even ⟨ni aun en coche llegaría a tiempo : I wouldn't arrive on time even if I drove⟩ **2 aun así** : even so **3 aun más** : even more
aún *adv* **1** TODAVÍA : still, yet ⟨¿aún no ha llegado el correo? : the mail still hasn't come?⟩ **2 más aún** : furthermore
aunar {8} *vt* : to join, to combine — **aunarse** *vr* : to unite
aunque *conj* **1** : though, although, even if, even though **2 aunque sea** : at least
aura *nf* **1** : aura **2** : turkey buzzard
áureo, -rea *adj* : golden
aureola *nf* **1** : halo **2** : aura (of power, fame, etc.)
aurícula *nf* : auricle
auricular *nm* : telephone receiver
aurora *nf* **1** : dawn **2 aurora boreal** : aurora borealis
ausencia *nf* : absence
ausentarse *vr* **1** : to leave, to go away **2** ~ **de** : to stay away from
ausente[1] *adj* : absent, missing
ausente[2] *nmf* **1** : absentee **2** : missing person
auspiciar *vt* **1** PATROCINAR : to sponsor **2** FOMENTAR : to foster, to promote
auspicios *nmpl* : sponsorship, auspices
austeridad *nf* : austerity
austero, -ra *adj* : austere
austral[1] *adj* : southern
austral[2] *nm* : former monetary unit of Argentina
australiano, -na *adj & n* : Australian
austriaco *or* **austríaco, -ca** *adj & n* : Austrian
autenticar {72} *vt* : to authenticate — **autenticación** *nf*
autenticidad *nf* : authenticity
auténtico, -ca *adj* : authentic — **auténticamente** *adv*
autentificar {72} *vt* : to authenticate — **autentificación** *nf*
autismo *nm* : autism
autista *adj* : autistic
auto *nm* : auto, car
autoayuda *nf* : self-help
autobiografía *nf* : autobiography
autobiográfico, -ca *adj* : autobiographical
autobús *nm, pl* **-buses** : bus

autocompasión *nf* : self-pity
autocontrol *nm* : self-control
autocracia *nf* : autocracy
autócrata *nmf* : autocrat
autocrático, -ca *adj* : autocratic
autóctono, -na *adj* : indigenous, native ⟨arte autóctono : indigenous art⟩
autodefensa *nf* : self-defense
autodestrucción *nf* : self-destruction —
autodestructivo, -va *adj*
autodeterminación *nf* : self-determination
autodidacta[1] *adj* : self-taught
autodidacta[2] *nmf* : self-taught person, autodidact
autodidacto[1], -ta *adj* → **autodidacta[1]**
autodidacto[2], -ta *n* → **autodidacta[2]**
autodisciplina *nf* : self-discipline
autoestima *nf* : self-esteem
autogobierno *nm* : self-government
autografiar *vt* : to autograph
autógrafo *nm* : autograph
autoinfligido, -da *adj* : self-inflicted
automación → **automatización**
autómata *nm* : automaton
automático, -ca *adj* : automatic — **automáticamente** *adv*
automatización *nf* : automation
automatizar {21} *vt* : to automate
automotor, -tora *adj* **1** : self-propelled **2** : automotive, car
automotriz[1] *adj, pl* **-trices** : automotive, car
automotriz[2] *nf, pl* **-trices** : automaker
automóvil *nm* : automobile
automovilista *nmf* : motorist
automovilístico, -ca *adj* : automobile, car ⟨accidente automovilístico : automobile accident⟩
autonombrado, -da *adj* : self-appointed
autonomía *nf* : autonomy
autónomo, -ma *adj* : autonomous — **autónomamente** *adv*
autopista *nf* : expressway, highway
autoproclamado, -da *adj* : self-proclaimed, self-appointed
autopropulsado, -da *adj* : self-propelled
autopsia *nf* : autopsy
autor, -tora *n* **1** : author **2** : perpetrator
autoría *nf* : authorship
autoridad *nf* : authority
autoritario, -ria *adj* : authoritarian
autorización *nf, pl* **-ciones** : authorization
autorizado, -da *adj* **1** : authorized **2** : authoritative
autorizar {21} *vt* : to authorize, to approve
autorretrato *nm* : self-portrait
autoservicio *nm* **1** : self-service restaurant **2** SUPERMERCADO : supermarket
autostop *nm* **1** : hitchhiking **2 hacer autostop** : to hitchhike
autostopista *nmf* : hitchhiker
autosuficiencia *nf* : self-sufficiency — **autosuficiente** *adj*
auxiliar[1] *vt* : to aid, to assist

auxiliar[2] *adj* : assistant, auxiliary
auxiliar[3] *nmf* **1** : assistant, helper **2 auxiliar de vuelo** : flight attendant
auxilio *nm* **1** : aid, assistance **2 primeros auxilios** : first aid
aval *nm* : guarantee, endorsement
avalancha *nf* ALUD : avalanche
avalar *vt* : to guarantee, to endorse
avaluar {3} *vt* : to evaluate, to appraise
avalúo *nm* : appraisal, evaluation
avance *nm* ADELANTO : advance
avanzado, -da *adj* **1** : advanced **2** : progressive
avanzar {21} *v* : to advance, to move forward
avaricia *nf* CODICIA : greed, avarice
avaricioso, -sa *adj* : avaricious, greedy
avaro[1], -ra *adj* : miserly, greedy
avaro[2], -ra *n* : miser
avasallador, -dora *adj* : overwhelming
avasallamiento *nm* : subjugation, domination
avasallar *vt* : to overpower, to subjugate
ave *nf* **1** : bird **2 aves de corral** : poultry **3 ave rapaz** *or* **ave de presa** : bird of prey
avecinarse *vr* : to approach, to come near
avecindarse *vr* : to settle, to take up residence
avellana *nf* : hazelnut, filbert
avellano *nm* : hazel
avena *nf* **1** : oat, oats *pl* **2** : oatmeal
avenencia *nf* : agreement, pact
avenida *nf* : avenue
avenir {87} *vt* : to reconcile, to harmonize — **avenirse** *vr* **1** : to agree, to come to terms **2** : to get along
aventajado, -da *adj* : outstanding
aventajar *vt* **1** : to be ahead of, to lead **2** : to surpass, to outdo
aventar {55} *vt* **1** : to fan **2** : to winnow **3** *Col, Mex* : to throw, to toss — **aventarse** *vr* **1** *Col, Mex* : to hurl oneself **2** *Mex fam* : to dare, to take a chance
aventón *nm, pl* **-tones** *Col, Mex fam* : ride, lift
aventura *nf* **1** : adventure **2** RIESGO : venture, risk **3** : love affair
aventurado, -da *adj* : hazardous, risky
aventurar *vt* : to venture, to risk — **aventurarse** *vr* : to take a risk
aventurero[1], -ra *adj* : adventurous
aventurero[2], -ra *n* : adventurer
avergonzado, -da *adj* **1** : ashamed **2** : embarrassed
avergonzar {9} *vt* APENAR : to shame, to embarrass — **avergonzarse** *vr* APENARSE : to be ashamed, to be embarrassed
avería *nf* **1** : damage **2** : breakdown, malfunction
averiado, -da *adj* **1** : damaged, faulty **2** : broken down
averiar {85} *vt* : to damage — **averiarse** *vr* : to break down
averiguación *nf, pl* **-ciones** : investigation, inquiry

averiguar {10} *vt* **1** : to find out, to ascertain **2** : to investigate
aversión *nf, pl* **-siones** : aversion, dislike
avestruz *nm, pl* **-truces** : ostrich
avezado, -da *adj* : seasoned, experienced
aviación *nf, pl* **-ciones** : aviation
aviador, -dora *n* : aviator, flyer
aviar {85} *vt* **1** : to prepare, to make ready **2** : to tidy up **3** : to equip, to supply
avicultor, -tora *n* : poultry farmer
avicultura *nf* : poultry farming
avidez *nf, pl* **-deces** : eagerness
ávido, -da *adj* : eager, avid — **ávidamente** *adv*
avieso, -sa *adj* **1** : twisted, distorted **2** : wicked, depraved
avinagrado, -da *adj* : vinegary, sour
avío *nm* **1** : preparation, provision **2** : loan (for agriculture or mining) **3** **avíos** *nmpl* : gear, equipment
avión *nm, pl* **aviones** : airplane
avioneta *nf* : light airplane
avisar *vt* **1** : to notify, to inform **2** : to advise, to warn
aviso *nm* **1** : notice **2** : advertisement, ad **3** ADVERTENCIA : warning **4** **estar sobre aviso** : to be on the alert
avispa *nf* : wasp
avispado, -da *adj fam* : clever, sharp
avispero *nm* : wasps' nest
avispón *nm, pl* **-pones** : hornet
avistar *vt* : to sight, to catch sight of
avituallar *vt* : to suppy with food, to provision
avivar *vt* **1** : to enliven, to brighten **2** : to strengthen, to intensify
avizorar *vt* **1** ACECHAR : to spy on, to watch **2** : to observe, to perceive ⟨se avizoran dificultades : difficulties are expected⟩
axila *nf* : underarm, armpit
axioma *nm* : axiom
axiomático, -ca *adj* : axiomatic
ay *interj* **1** : oh! **2** : ouch!, ow!
ayer[1] *adv* : yesterday
ayer[2] *nm* ANTAÑO : yesteryear, days gone by
ayote *nm CA, Mex* : squash, pumpkin
ayuda *nf* **1** : help, assistance **2** **ayuda de cámara** : valet
ayudante *nmf* : helper, assistant

ayudar *vt* : to help, to assist — **ayudarse** *vr* ~ **de** : to make use of
ayunar *vi* : to fast
ayunas *nfpl* **en** ~ : fasting ⟨este medicamento ha de tomarse en ayunas : this medication should be taken on an empty stomach⟩
ayuno *nm* : fast
ayuntamiento *nm* **1** : town hall, city hall **2** : town or city council
azabache *nm* : jet ⟨negro azabache : jet black⟩
azada *nf* : hoe
azafata *nf* **1** : stewardess *f* **2** : hostess *f* (on a TV show)
azafrán *nm, pl* **-franes** **1** : saffron **2** : crocus
azahar *nm* : orange blossom
azalea *nf* : azalea
azar *nm* **1** : chance ⟨juegos de azar : games of chance⟩ **2** : accident, misfortune **3** **al azar** : at random, randomly
azaroso, -sa *adj* **1** : perilous, hazardous **2** : turbulent, eventful
azimut *nm* : azimuth
azogue *nm* : mercury, quicksilver
azorar *vt* **1** : to alarm, to startle **2** : to fluster, to embarrass — **azorarse** *vr* : to get embarrassed
azotar *vt* **1** : to whip, to flog **2** : to lash, to batter **3** : to devastate, to afflict
azote *nm* **1** LÁTIGO : whip, lash **2** *fam* : spanking, licking **3** : calamity, scourge
azotea *nf* : flat roof, terraced roof
azteca *adj & nmf* : Aztec
azúcar *nmf* : sugar — **azucarar** *vt*
azucarado, -da *adj* : sweetened, sugary
azucarera *nf* : sugar bowl
azucarero, -ra *adj* : sugar ⟨industria azucarera : sugar industry⟩
azucena *nf* : white lily
azuela *nf* : adze
azufre *nm* : sulphur — **azufroso, -sa** *adj*
azul *adj & nm* : blue
azulado, -da *adj* : bluish
azulejo *nm* : ceramic tile, floor tile
azuloso, -sa *adj* : bluish
azulete *nm* : bluing
azur[1] *adj* CELESTE : azure
azur[2] *n* CELESTE : azure, sky blue
azuzar {21} *vt* : to incite, to egg on

B

b *nf* : second letter of the Spanish alphabet
baba *nf* **1** : spittle, saliva **2** : dribble, drool (of a baby) **3** : slime, ooze
babear *vi* **1** : to drool, to slobber **2** : to ooze
babel *nmf* : babel, chaos, bedlam
babero *nm* : bib
babor *nm* : port, port side

babosa *nf* : slug (mollusk)
babosada *nf CA, Mex* : silly act or remark
baboso, -sa *adj* **1** : drooling, slobbering **2** : slimy **3** *CA, Mex fam* : silly, dumb
babucha *nf* : slipper
babuino *nm* : baboon
bacalao *nm* : cod (fish)

bache *nm* **1** : pothole **2** *PRi* : deep puddle **3** : bad period, rough time ⟨bache económico : economic slump⟩
bachiller *nmf* : high school graduate
bachillerato *nm* : high school diploma
bacilo *nm* : bacillus
bacon *nm Spain* : bacon
bacteria *nf* : bacterium
bacteriano, -na *adj* : bacterial
bacteriología *nf* : bacteriology
bacteriológico, -ca *adj* : bacteriologic, bacteriological
bacteriólogo, -ga *n* : bacteriologist
báculo *nm* **1** : staff, stick **2** : comfort, support
badajo *nm* : clapper (of a bell)
badén *nm, pl* **badenes 1** : (paved) ford, channel **2** : dip, ditch (in a road) **3** : speed bump
bádminton *nm* : badminton
bafle *or* **baffle** *nm* **1** : baffle **2** : speaker, loudspeaker
bagaje *nm* **1** EQUIPAJE : baggage, luggage **2** : background ⟨bagaje cultural : cultural baggage⟩
bagatela *nf* : trifle, trinket
bagre *nm* : catfish
bahía *nf* : bay
bailar *vt* : to dance — *vi* **1** : to dance **2** : to spin **3** : to be loose, to be too big
bailarín[1], -rina *adj, mpl* **-rines 1** : dancing **2** : fond of dancing
bailarín[2], -rina *n, mpl* **-rines 1** : dancer **2** : ballet dancer, ballerina *f*
baile *nm* **1** : dance **2** : dance party, ball **3 llevarse al baile a** *Mex fam* : to take for a ride, to take advantage of
baja *nf* **1** DESCENSO : fall, drop **2** : slump, recession **3** : loss, casualty **4 dar de baja** : to discharge, to dismiss **5 darse de baja** : to withdraw, to drop out
bajada *nf* **1** : descent **2** : dip, slope **3** : decrease, drop
bajar *vt* **1** DESCENDER : to lower, to let down, to take down **2** REDUCIR : to reduce (prices) **3** INCLINAR : to lower, to bow (the head) **4** : to go down, to descend **5 bajar de categoría** : to downgrade — *vi* **1** : to drop, to fall **2** : to come down, to go down **3** : to ebb (of tides) — **bajarse** *vr* ~ **de** : to get off, to get out of (a vehicle)
bajeza *nf* **1** : low or despicable act **2** : baseness
bajío *nm* **1** : lowland **2** : shoal, sandbank, shallows
bajista *nmf* : bass player, bassist
bajo[1] *adv* **1** : down, low **2** : softly, quietly ⟨habla más bajo : speak more softly⟩
bajo[2], -ja *adj* **1** : low **2** : short (of stature) **3** : soft, faint, deep (of sounds) **4** : lower ⟨el bajo Amazonas : the lower Amazon⟩ **5** : lowered ⟨con la mirada baja : with lowered eyes⟩ **6** : base, vile **7 los bajos fondos** : the underworld

bajo[3] *nm* **1** : bass (musical instrument) **2** : first floor, ground floor **3** : hemline
bajo[4] *prep* : under, beneath, below
bajón *nm, pl* **bajones** : sharp drop, slump
bajorrelieve *nm* : bas-relief
bala *nf* **1** : bullet **2** : bale
balacera *nf* TIROTEO : shoot-out, gunfight
balada *nf* : ballad
balance *nm* **1** : balance **2** : balance sheet
balancear *vt* **1** : to balance **2** : to swing (one's arms, etc.) **3** : to rock (a boat) — **balancearse** *vr* **1** OSCILAR : to swing, to sway, to rock **2** VACILAR : to hesitate, to vacillate
balanceo *nm* **1** : swaying, rocking **2** : vacillation
balancín *nm, pl* **-cines 1** : rocking chair **2** SUBIBAJA : seesaw
balandra *nf* : sloop
balanza *nf* BÁSCULA : scales *pl*, balance
balar *vi* : to bleat
balaustrada *nf* : balustrade
balaustre *nm* : baluster
balazo *nm* **1** TIRO : shot, gunshot **2** : bullet wound
balboa *nf* : balboa (monetary unit of Panama)
balbucear *vi* **1** : to mutter, to stammer **2** : to prattle, to babble ⟨los niños están balbuceando : the children are prattling away⟩
balbuceo *nm* : mumbling, stammering
balbucir → **balbucear**
balcánico, -ca *adj* : Balkan
balcón *nm, pl* **balcones** : balcony
balde *nm* **1** CUBO : bucket, pail **2 en** ~ : in vain, to no avail
baldío[1], -día *adj* **1** : fallow, uncultivated **2** : useless, vain
baldío[2] *nm* **1** : wasteland **2** *Mex* : vacant lot
baldosa *nf* LOSETA : floor tile
balear *vt* : to shoot, to shoot at
balero *nm* **1** *Mex* : ball bearing **2** *Mex, PRi* : cup-and-ball toy
balido *nm* : bleat
balín *nm, pl* **balines** : pellet
balística *nf* : ballistics
balístico, -ca *adj* : ballistic
baliza *nf* **1** : buoy **2** : beacon (for aircraft)
ballena *nf* : whale
ballenero[1], -ra *adj* : whaling
ballenero[2], -ra *n* : whaler
ballenero[3] *nm* : whaleboat, whaler
ballesta *nf* **1** : crossbow **2** : spring (of an automobile)
ballet *nm* : ballet
balneario *nm* : spa, bathing resort
balompié *nm* FÚTBOL : soccer
balón *nm, pl* **balones** : ball
baloncesto *nm* BASQUETBOL : basketball
balsa *nf* **1** : raft **2** : balsa **3** : pond, pool
balsámico, -ca *adj* : soothing

bálsamo *nm* : balsam, balm
báltico, -ca *adj* : Baltic
baluarte *nm* BASTIÓN : bulwark, bastion
bambolear *vi* 1 : to sway, to swing 2 : to wobble — **bambolearse** *vr*
bamboleo *nm* 1 : swaying, swinging 2 : wobbling
bambú *nm, pl* bambúes *or* bambús : bamboo
banal *adj* : banal, trivial
banalidad *nf* : banality
banana *nf* : banana
bananero¹, -ra *adj* : banana
bananero² *nm* : banana tree
banano *nm* 1 : banana tree 2 *CA, Col* : banana
banca *nf* 1 : banking 2 BANCO : bench
bancada *nf* 1 : group, faction 2 : workbench
bancal *nm* 1 : terrace (in agriculture) 2 : plot (of land)
bancario, -ria *adj* : bank, banking
bancarrota *nf* QUIEBRA : bankruptcy
banco *nm* 1 : bank ⟨banco central : central bank⟩ ⟨banco de datos : data bank⟩ ⟨banco de arena : sandbank⟩ ⟨banco de sangre : blood bank⟩ 2 BANCA : stool, bench 3 : pew 4 : school (of fish)
banda *nf* 1 : band, strip 2 *Mex* : belt ⟨banda transportadora : conveyor belt⟩ 3 : band (of musicians) 4 : gang (of persons), flock (of birds) 5 **banda de rodadura** : tread (of a tire, etc.) 6 **banda sonora** *or* **banda de sonido** : sound track
bandada *nf* : flock (of birds), school (of fish)
bandazo *nm* : swerving, lurch
bandearse *vr* : to look after oneself, to cope
bandeja *nf* : tray, platter
bandera *nf* : flag, banner
banderazo *nm* : starting signal (in sports)
banderilla *nf* : banderilla, dart (in bullfighting)
banderín *nm, pl* -rines : pennant, small flag
bandidaje *nm* : banditry
bandido, -da *n* BANDOLERO : bandit, outlaw
bando *nm* 1 FACCIÓN : faction, side 2 EDICTO : proclamation
bandolerismo *nm* : banditry
bandolero, -ra *n* BANDIDO : bandit, outlaw
bangladesí *adj & nmf* : Bangladeshi
banjo *nm* : banjo
banquero, -ra *n* : banker
banqueta *nf* 1 : footstool, stool, bench 2 *Mex* : sidewalk
banquete *nm* : banquet
banquetear *v* : to feast
banquillo *nm* 1 : bench (in sports) 2 : dock, defendant's seat
bañadera *nf* → bañera

bañar *vt* 1 : to bathe, to wash 2 : to immerse, to dip 3 : to coat, to cover ⟨bañado en lágrimas : bathed in tears⟩ — **bañarse** *vr* 1 : to take a bath, to bathe 2 : to go for a swim
bañera *nf* TINA : bathtub
bañista *nmf* : bather
baño *nm* 1 : bath 2 : swim, dip 3 : bathroom 4 **baño María** : double boiler
baqueta *nf* 1 : ramrod 2 **baquetas** *nfpl* : drumsticks
bar *nm* : bar, tavern
baraja *nf* : deck of cards
barajar *vt* 1 : to shuffle (cards) 2 : to consider, to toy with
baranda *nf* : rail, railing
barandal *nm* 1 : rail, railing 2 : bannister, handrail
barandilla *nf Spain* : bannister, handrail, railing
barata *nf* 1 *Mex* : sale, bargain 2 *Chile* : cockroach
baratija *nf* : bauble, trinket
baratillo *nm* : rummage sale, flea market
barato¹ *adv* : cheap, cheaply ⟨te lo vendo barato : I'll sell it to you cheap⟩
barato², -ta *adj* : cheap, inexpensive
baratura *nf* 1 : cheapness 2 : cheap thing
barba *nf* 1 : beard, stubble 2 : chin
barbacoa *nf* : barbecue
bárbaramente *adv* : barbarously
barbaridad *nf* 1 : barbarity, atrocity 2 **¡qué barbaridad!** : that's outrageous!
barbarie *nf* : barbarism, savagery
bárbaro¹ *adv fam* : wildly ⟨anoche lo pasamos bárbaro : we had a wild time last night⟩
bárbaro², -ra *adj* 1 : barbarous, wild, uncivilized 2 *fam* : great, fantastic
bárbaro³, -ra *n* : barbarian
barbecho *nm* : fallow land ⟨dejar en barbecho : to leave fallow⟩
barbero, -ra *n* : barber
barbilla *nf* MENTÓN : chin
barbitúrico *nm* : barbiturate
barbudo¹, -da *adj* : bearded
barbudo² *nm* : bearded man
barca *nf* 1 : boat 2 **barca de pasaje** : ferryboat
barcaza *nf* : barge
barcia *nf* : chaff
barco *nm* 1 BARCA : boat 2 BUQUE, NAVE : ship
bardo *nm* : bard
bario *nm* : barium
barítono *nm* : baritone
barlovento *nm* : windward
barman *nm* : bartender
barniz *nm, pl* barnices 1 LACA : varnish, lacquer 2 : glaze (on ceramics, etc.)
barnizar {21} *vt* 1 : to varnish 2 : to glaze
barométrico, -ca *adj* : barometric
barómetro *nm* : barometer
barón *nm, pl* barones : baron

baronesa *nf* : baroness
baronet *nm* : baronet
barquero, -ra : boatman *m,* boatwoman *f*
barquillo *nm* : wafer, thin cookie or cracker
barra *nf* : bar
barraca *nf* 1 CABAÑA, CHOZA : hut, cabin 2 : booth, stall
barracuda *nf* : barracuda
barranca *nf* 1 : hillside, slope 2 → **barranco**
barranco *nm* : ravine, gorge
barredora *nf* : street sweeper (machine)
barrena *nf* 1 TALADRO : drill, auger, gimlet 2 : tailspin
barrenar *vt* 1 : to drill 2 : to undermine
barrendero, -ra *n* : sweeper, street cleaner
barrer *v* : to sweep — **barrerse** *vr* : to slide (in sports)
barrera *nf* OBSTÁCULO : barrier, obstacle ⟨barrera de sonido : sound barrier⟩
barreta *nf* : crowbar
barriada *nf* 1 : district, quarter 2 : slums *pl*
barrica *nf* BARRIL, TONEL : barrel, cask, keg
barricada *nf* : barricade
barrida *nf* 1 : sweep 2 : slide (in sports)
barrido *nm* : sweeping
barriga *nf* PANZA : belly, paunch
barrigón, -gona *adj, mpl* **-gones** *fam* : potbellied, paunchy
barril *nm* 1 BARRICA : barrel, keg 2 **cerveza de barril** : draft beer
barrio *nm* 1 : neighborhood, district 2 **barrios bajos** : slums *pl*
barro *nm* 1 LODO : mud 2 ARCILLA : clay 3 ESPINILLA, GRANO : pimple, blackhead
barroco, -ca *adj* : baroque
barroso, -sa *adj* ENLODADO : muddy
barrote *nm* : bar (on a window)
barrunto *nm* 1 SOSPECHA : suspicion 2 INDICIO : sign, indication, hint
bártulos *nmpl* : things, belongings ⟨liar los bártulos : to pack one's things⟩
barullo *nm* BULLA : racket, ruckus
basa *nf* : base, pedestal
basalto *nm* : basalt
basar *vt* FUNDAR : to base — **basarse** *vr* FUNDARSE ~ **en** : to be based on
báscula *nf* BALANZA : balance, scales *pl*
base *nf* 1 : base, bottom 2 : base (in baseball) 3 FUNDAMENTO : basis, foundation 4 **base de datos** : database 5 **a base de** : based on, by means of 6 **en base a** : based on, on the basis of
básico, -ca *adj* FUNDAMENTAL : basic — **básicamente** *adv*
basílica *nf* : basilica
basquetbol *or* **básquetbol** *nm* BALONCESTO : basketball
basset *nm* : basset hound
bastante[1] *adv* 1 : enough, sufficiently ⟨he trabajado bastante : I have worked enough⟩ 2 : fairly, rather, quite ⟨lle-

garon bastante temprano : they arrived quite early⟩
bastante[2] *adj* : enough, sufficient
bastante[3] *pron* : enough ⟨hemos visto bastante : we have seen enough⟩
bastar *vi* : to be enough, to suffice
bastardilla *nf* CURSIVA : italic type, italics *pl*
bastardo, -da *adj* & *n* : bastard
bastidor *nm* 1 : framework, frame 2 : wing (in theater) ⟨entre bastidores : backstage, behind the scenes⟩
bastilla *nf* : hem
bastión *nf, pl* **bastiones** BALUARTE : bastion, bulwark
basto, -ta *adj* : coarse, rough
bastón *nm, pl* **bastones** 1 : cane, walking stick 2 : baton 3 **bastón de mando** : staff (of authority)
basura *nf* DESECHOS : garbage, waste, refuse
basurero[1], **-ra** *n* : garbage collector
basurero[2] *nm Mex* : garbage can
bata *nf* 1 : bathrobe, housecoat 2 : smock, coverall, lab coat
batalla *nf* 1 : battle 2 : fight, struggle 3 **de** ~ : ordinary, everyday ⟨mis zapatos de batalla : my everyday shoes⟩
batallar *vi* LIDIAR, LUCHAR : to battle, to fight
batallón *nm, pl* **-llones** : battalion
batata *nf* : yam, sweet potato
batazo *nm* HIT : hit (in baseball)
bate *nm* : baseball bat
batea *nf* 1 : tray, pan 2 : flat-bottomed boat, punt
bateador, -dora *n* : batter, hitter
batear *vi* : to bat — *vt* : to hit
bateo *nm* : batting (in baseball)
batería *nf* 1 PILA : battery 2 : drum kit, drums *pl* 3 **batería de cocina** : kitchen utensils *pl*
baterista *nmf* : drummer
batido *nm* LICUADO : milk shake
batidor *nm* : eggbeater, whisk, mixer
batidora *nf* : (electric) mixer
batir *vt* 1 GOLPEAR : to beat, to hit 2 VENCER : to defeat 3 REVOLVER : to mix, to beat 4 : to break (a record) — **batirse** *vr* : to fight
batista *nf* : batiste, cambric
batuta *nf* 1 : baton 2 **llevar la batuta** : to be the leader, to call the tune
baúl *nm* : trunk, chest
bautismal *adj* : baptismal
bautismo *nm* : baptism, christening
bautista *adj* & *nmf* : Baptist
bautizar {21} *vt* : to baptize, to christen
bautizo → **bautismo**
bávaro, -ra *adj* & *n* : Bavarian
baya *nf* 1 : berry 2 **baya de saúco** : elderberry
bayeta *nf* : cleaning cloth
bayoneta *nf* : bayonet
baza *nf* 1 : trick (in card games) 2 **meter baza en** : to butt in on
bazar *nm* : bazaar
bazo *nm* : spleen

bazofia *nf* **1** : table scraps *pl* **2** : slop, swill **3** : hogwash, rubbish

bazuca *nf* : bazooka

beagle *nm* : beagle

beatificar {72} *vt* : to beatify — **beatificación** *nf*

beatífico, -ca *adj* : beatific

beatitud *nf* : beatitude

beato, -ta *adj* **1** : blessed **2** : pious, devout **3** : sanctimonious, overly devout

bebé *nm* : baby

bebedero *nm* **1** ABREVADERO : watering trough **2** *Mex* : drinking fountain

bebedor, -dora *n* : drinker

beber *v* TOMAR : to drink

bebida *nf* : drink, beverage

beca *nf* : grant, scholarship

becado, -da *n* : scholar, scholarship holder

becerro, -rra *n* : calf

begonia *nf* : begonia

beige *adj & nm* : beige

beisbol *or* **béisbol** *nm* : baseball

beisbolista *nmf* : baseball player

beldad *nf* BELLEZA, HERMOSURA : beauty

belén *nf, pl* **belenes** NACIMIENTO : Nativity scene

belga *adj & nmf* : Belgian

beliceño, -ña *adj & n* : Belizean

belicista[1] *adj* : militaristic

belicista[2] *nmf* : warmonger

bélico, -ca *adj* GUERRERO : war, fighting ⟨esfuerzos bélicos : war efforts⟩

belicosidad *nf* : bellicosity

belicoso, -sa *adj* **1** : warlike, martial **2** : aggressive, belligerent

beligerancia *nf* : belligerence

beligerante *adj & nmf* : belligerent

bellaco[1], -ca *adj* : sly, cunning

bellaco[2], -ca *n* : rogue, scoundrel

belleza *nf* BELDAD, HERMOSURA : beauty

bello, -lla *adj* **1** HERMOSO : beautiful **2** **bellas artes** : fine arts

bellota *nf* : acorn

bemol *nm* : flat (in music) — **bemol** *adj*

benceno *nm* : benzene

bendecir {11} *vt* **1** CONSAGRAR : to bless, to consecrate **2** ALABAR : to praise, to extol **3 bendecir la mesa** : to say grace

bendición *nf, pl* **-ciones** : benediction, blessing

bendiga, bendijo etc. → **bendecir**

bendito, -ta *adj* **1** : blessed, holy **2** : fortunate **3** : silly, simple-minded

benedictino, -na *adj & n* : Benedictine

benefactor[1], -tora *adj* : beneficent

benefactor[2], -tora *n* : benefactor, benefactress *f*

beneficencia *nf* : beneficence, charity

beneficiar *vt* : to benefit, to be of assistance to — **beneficiarse** *vr* : to benefit, to profit

beneficiario, -ria *n* : beneficiary

beneficio *nm* **1** GANANCIA, PROVECHO : gain, profit **2** : benefit

beneficioso, -sa *adj* PROVECHOSO : beneficial

benéfico, -ca *adj* : charitable, beneficent

benemérito, -ta *adj* : meritorious, worthy

beneplácito *nm* : approval, consent

benevolencia *nf* BONDAD : benevolence, kindness

benévolo, -la *adj* BONDADOSO : benevolent, kind, good

bengala *nf* **luz de bengala 1** : flare (signal) **2** : sparkler

bengalí[1] *adj & nmf* : Bengali

bengalí[2] *nm* : Bengali (language)

benignidad *nf* : mildness, kindness

benigno, -na *adj* : benign, mild

beninés, -nesa *adj & n* : Beninese

benjamín, -mina *n, mpl* **-mines** : youngest child

beodo[1], -da *adj* : drunk, inebriated

beodo[2], -da *n* : drunkard

berberecho *nm* : cockle

berbiquí *nm* : brace (in carpentry)

berenjena *nf* : eggplant

bergantín *nm, pl* **-tines** : brig (ship)

berilo *nm* : beryl

bermudas *nfpl* : Bermuda shorts

berrear *vi* **1** : to bellow, to low **2** : to bawl, to howl

berrido *nm* **1** : bellowing **2** : howl, scream

berrinche *nm fam* : tantrum, conniption

berro *nm* : watercress

berza *nf* : cabbage

besar *vt* : to kiss

beso *nm* : kiss

bestia[1] *adj* **1** : ignorant, stupid **2** : boorish, rude

bestia[2] *nf* : beast, animal

bestia[3] *nmf* **1** IGNORANTE : ignoramus **2** : brute

bestial *adj* **1** : bestial, beastly **2** *fam* : huge, enormous ⟨hace un frío bestial : it's terribly cold⟩ **3** *fam* : great, fantastic

besuquear *vt fam* : to cover with kisses — **besuquearse** *vr fam* : to neck, to smooch

betabel *nm Mex* : beet

betún *nm, pl* **betunes 1** : shoe polish **2** *Mex* : icing

bianual *adj* : biannual

biatlón *nm, pl* **-lones** : biathlon

biberón *nm, pl* **-rones** : baby's bottle

biblia *nf* **1** : bible **2 la Biblia** : the Bible

bíblico, -ca *adj* : biblical

bibliografía *nf* : bibliography

bibliográfico, -ca *adj* : bibliographic, bibliographical

bibliógrafo, -fa *n* : bibliographer

biblioteca *nf* : library

bibliotecario, -ria *n* : librarian

bicameral *adj* : bicameral

bicarbonato *nm* **1** : bicarbonate **2 bicarbonato de soda** : sodium bicarbonate, baking soda

bicentenario *nm* : bicentennial

bíceps *nms & pl* : biceps
bicho *nm* : small animal, bug, insect
bici *nf fam* : bike
bicicleta *nf* : bicycle
bicolor *adj* : two-tone
bicúspide *adj* : bicuspid
bidón *nm*, *pl* **bidones** : large can, (oil) drum
bien¹ *adv* **1** : well ⟨¿dormiste bien? : did you sleep well?⟩ **2** CORRECTAMENTE : correctly, properly, right ⟨hay que hacerlo bien : it must be done correctly⟩ **3** : very, quite ⟨el libro era bien divertido : the book was very amusing⟩ **4** : easily ⟨bien puede acabarlo en un día : he can easily finish it in a day⟩ **5** : willingly, readily ⟨bien lo aceptaré : I'll gladly accept it⟩ **6 bien que** : although **7 más bien** : rather
bien² *adj* **1** : well, OK, all right ⟨¿te sientes bien? : are you feeling all right?⟩ **2** : pleasant, agreeable ⟨las flores huelen bien : the flowers smell very nice⟩ **3** : satisfactory **4** : correct, right
bien³ *nm* **1** : good ⟨el bien y el mal : good and evil⟩ **2 bienes** *nmpl* : property, goods, possessions
bienal *adj & nf* : biennial — **bienalmente** *adv*
bienaventurado, -da *adj* **1** : blessed **2** : fortunate, happy
bienaventuranzas *nfpl* : Beatitudes
bienestar *nm* **1** : welfare, well-being **2** CONFORT : comfort
bienhechor¹, **-chora** *adj* : beneficent, benevolent
bienhechor², **-chora** *n* : benefactor, benefactress *f*
bienintencionado, -da *adj* : well-meaning
bienvenida *nf* **1** : welcome **2 dar la bienvenida a** : to welcome
bienvenido, -da *adj* : welcome
bies *nm* : bias (in sewing)
bife *nm Arg, Chile, Uru* : steak
bífido, -da *adj* : forked
bifocal *adj* : bifocal
bifocales *nmpl* : bifocals
bifurcación *nf*, *pl* **-ciones** : fork (in a river or road)
bifurcarse {72} *vr* : to fork
bigamia *nf* : bigamy
bígamo, -ma *n* : bigamist
bigote *nm* **1** : mustache **2** : whisker (of an animal)
bigotudo, -da *adj* : mustached, having a big mustache
bikini *nm* : bikini
bilateral *adj* : bilateral — **bilateralmente** *adv*
bilingüe *adj* : bilingual
bilioso, -sa *adj* **1** : bilious **2** : irritable
bilis *nf* : bile
billar *nm* : pool, billiards
billete *nm* **1** : bill ⟨un billete de cinco dólares : a five-dollar bill⟩ **2** BOLETO : ticket ⟨billete de ida y vuelta : round-trip ticket⟩

billetera *nf* : billfold, wallet
billón *nm*, *pl* **billones** **1** : billion (Great Britain) **2** : trillion (U.S.A.)
bimestral *adj* : bimonthly — **bimestralmente** *adv*
bimotor *adj* : twin-engined
binacional *adj* : binational
binario, -ria *adj* : binary
bingo *nm* : bingo
binocular *adj* : binocular
binoculares *nmpl* : binoculars
binomio *nm* **1** : binomial **2** PAREJA : pair, duo
biodegradable *adj* : biodegradable
biodegradarse *vr* : to biodegrade
biodiversidad *nf* : biodiversity
biofísica *nf* : biophysics
biofísico¹, **-ca** *adj* : biophysical
biofísico², **-ca** *n* : biophysicist
biografía *nf* : biography
biográfico, -ca *adj* : biographical
biógrafo, -fa *n* : biographer
biología *nf* : biology
biológico, -ca *adj* : biological, biologic — **biológicamente** *adv*
biólogo, -ga *n* : biologist
biombo *nm* MAMPARA : folding screen, room divider
biomecánica *nf* : biomechanics
biopsia *nf* : biopsy
bioquímica *nf* : biochemistry
bioquímico¹, **-ca** *adj* : biochemical
bioquímico², **-ca** *n* : biochemist
biosfera *or* **biósfera** *nf* : biosphere
biotecnología *nf* : biotechnology
biótico, -ca *adj* : biotic
bipartidismo *nm* : two-party system
bipartidista *adj* : bipartisan
bípedo *nm* : biped
birlar *vt fam* : to swipe, to pinch
birmano, -na *adj & n* : Burmese
bis¹ *adv* **1** : twice, again (in music) **2** : a, A ⟨artículo 47 bis : Article 47A⟩ ⟨calle Bolívar, número 70 bis : Bolívar Street, number 70A⟩
bis² *nm* : encore
bisabuelo, -la *n* : great-grandfather *m*, great-grandmother *f*, great-grandparent
bisagra *nf* : hinge
bisecar {72} *vt* : bisect — **bisección** *nf*
bisel *nm* : bevel
biselar *vt* : to bevel
bisexual *adj* : bisexual
bisiesto *adj* **año bisiesto** : leap year
bismuto *nm* : bismuth
bisnieto, -ta *n* : great-grandson *m*, great-granddaughter *f*, great-grandchild
bisonte *nm* : bison, buffalo
bisoñé *nm* : hairpiece, toupee
bisoño¹, **-ña** *adj* : inexperienced, green
bisoño², **-ña** *n* : rookie, greenhorn
bistec *nm* : steak, beefsteak
bisturí *nm* ESCALPELO : scalpel
bisutería *nf* : costume jewelry
bit *nm* : bit (unit of information)
bivalvo *nm* : bivalve
bizarría *nf* **1** : courage, gallantry **2** : generosity

bizarro, -rra *adj* **1** VALIENTE : courageous, valiant **2** GENEROSO : generous
bizco, -ca *adj* : cross-eyed
bizcocho *nm* **1** : sponge cake **2** : biscuit **3** *Mex* : breadstick
bizquera *nf* : crossed eyes, squint
blanco[1], **-ca** *adj* : white
blanco[2], **-ca** *n* : white person
blanco[3] *nm* **1** : white **2** : target, bull's-eye ⟨dar en el blanco : to hit the target, to hit the nail on the head⟩ **3** : blank space, blank ⟨un cheque en blanco : a blank check⟩
blancura *nf* : whiteness
blancuzco, -ca *adj* **1** : whitish, off-white **2** PÁLIDO : pale
blandir {1} *vt* : to wave, to brandish
blando, -da *adj* **1** SUAVE : soft, tender **2** : weak (in character) **3** : lenient
blandura *nf* **1** : softness, tenderness **2** : leniency
blanqueador *nm* : bleach, whitener
blanquear *vt* **1** : to whiten, to bleach **2** : to shut out (in sports) **3** : to launder (money) — *vi* : to turn white
blanquillo *nm CA, Mex* : egg
blasfemar *vi* : to blaspheme
blasfemia *nf* : blasphemy
blasfemo, -ma *adj* : blasphemous
blazer *nm* : blazer
bledo *nm* **no me importa un bledo** *fam* : I couldn't care less, I don't give a damn
blindado, -da *adj* ACORAZADO : armored
blindaje *nm* **1** : armor, armor plating **2** : shield (for cables, machinery, etc.)
bloc *nm, pl* **blocs** : writing pad, pad of paper
blof *nm Col, Mex* : bluff
blofear *vi Col, Mex* : to bluff
blondo, -da *adj* : blond, flaxen
bloque *nm* **1** : block **2** GRUPO : bloc ⟨el bloque comunista : the Communist bloc⟩
bloquear *vt* **1** OBSTRUIR : to block, to obstruct **2** : to blockade
bloqueo *nm* **1** OBSTRUCCIÓN : blockage, obstruction **2** : blockade
blusa *nf* : blouse
blusón *nm, pl* **blusones** : loose shirt, smock
boa *nf* : boa
boato *nm* : ostentation, show
bobada *nf* **1** : stupid remark or action **2 decir bobadas** : to talk nonsense
bobalicón, -cona *adj, mpl* **-cones** *fam* : silly, stupid
bobina *nf* CARRETE : bobbin, reel
bobo[1], **-ba** *adj* : silly, stupid
bobo[2], **-ba** *n* : fool, simpleton
boca *nf* **1** : mouth **2 boca arriba** : face up, on one's back **3 boca abajo** : face down, prone **4 boca de riego** : hydrant **5 en boca de** : according to
bocacalle *nf* : entrance to a street ⟨gire a la última bocacalle : take the last turning⟩
bocadillo *nm Spain* : sandwich

bocado *nm* **1** : bite, mouthful **2** FRENO : bit (of a bridle)
bocajarro *nm* **a** ~ : point-blank, directly
bocallave *nf* : keyhole
bocanada *nf* **1** : swig, swallow **2** : puff, mouthful (of smoke) **3** : gust (of air) **4** : stream (of people)
boceto *nm* : sketch, outline
bochinche *nm fam* : ruckus, uproar
bochorno *nm* **1** VERGÜENZA : embarrassment **2** : hot and humid weather **3** : hot flash
bochornoso, -sa *adj* **1** EMBARAZOSO : embarrassing **2** : hot and muggy
bocina *nf* **1** : horn, trumpet **2** : automobile horn **3** : mouthpiece (of a telephone) **4** *Mex* : loudspeaker
bocinazo *nm* : honk (of a horn)
bocio *nm* : goiter
bocón, -cona *n, mpl* **bocones** *fam* : blabbermouth, loudmouth
boda *nf* : wedding
bodega *nf* **1** : wine cellar **2** *Chile, Col, Mex* : storeroom, warehouse **3** (*in various countries*) : grocery store
bofetada *nf* CACHETADA : slap on the face
bofetear *vt* CACHETEAR : to slap
bofetón *nm* → **bofetada**
bofo, -fa *adj* : flabby
boga *nf* : fashion, vogue ⟨estar en boga : to be in style⟩
bogotano[1], **-na** *adj* : of or from Bogotá
bogotano[2], **-na** *n* : person from Bogotá
bohemio, -mia *adj & n* : bohemian, Bohemian
boicot *nm, pl* **boicots** : boycott
boicotear *vt* : to boycott
boina *nf* : beret
boiserie *nf* : wood paneling, wainscoting
boj *nm, pl* **bojes** : box (plant), boxwood
bola *nf* **1** : ball ⟨bola de nieve : snowball⟩ **2** *fam* : lie, fib **3** *Mex fam* : bunch, group ⟨una bola de rateros : a bunch of thieves⟩ **4** *Mex* : uproar, tumult
bolear *vt Mex* : to polish (shoes)
bolera *nf* : bowling alley
bolero *nm* : bolero
boleta *nf* **1** : ballot **2** : ticket **3** : receipt
boletería *nf* TAQUILLA : box office, ticket office
boletín *nm, pl* **-tines** **1** : bulletin **2** : journal, review **3 boletín de prensa** : press release
boleto *nm* BILLETE : ticket
boliche *nm* **1** BOLOS : bowling **2** *Arg* : bar, tavern
bólido *nm* **1** : race car **2** METEORO : meteor
bolígrafo *nm* : ballpoint pen
bolillo *nm* **2** *Mex* : roll, bun
bolívar *nm* : bolivar (monetary unit of Venezuela)
boliviano[1], **-na** *adj & n* : Bolivian
boliviano[2] *nm* : boliviano (monetary unit of Bolivia)

bollo *nm* : bun, sweet roll
bolo *nm* : bowling pin, tenpin
bolos *nmpl* BOLICHE : bowling
bolsa *nf* 1 : bag, sack 2 *Mex* : pocketbook, purse 3 *Mex* : pocket 4 **la Bolsa** : the stock market, the stock exchange 5 **bolsa de trabajo** : employment agency
bolsear *vi Mex* : to pick pockets
bolsillo *nm* 1 : pocket 2 **dinero de bolsillo** : pocket change, loose change
bolso *nm* : pocketbook, handbag
bomba *nf* 1 : bomb 2 : bubble 3 : pump ⟨bomba de gasolina : gas pump⟩
bombachos *nmpl* : baggy pants, bloomers
bombardear *vt* 1 : to bomb 2 : to bombard
bombardeo *nm* 1 : bombing, shelling 2 : bombardment
bombardero *nm* : bomber (airplane)
bombástico, -ca *adj* : bombastic
bombear *vt* : to pump
bombero, -ra *n* : firefighter, fireman *m*
bombilla *nf* : lightbulb
bombillo *nm CA, Col, Ven* : lightbulb
bombo *nm* 1 : bass drum 2 *fam* : exaggerated praise, hype ⟨con bombos y platillos : with great fanfare⟩
bombón *nm, pl* **bombones** 1 : bonbon, chocolate 2 *Mex* : marshmallow
bonachón¹, -chona *adj, mpl* **-chones** *fam* : good-natured, kindhearted
bonachón², -chona *n, mpl* **-chones** *fam* BUENAZO : kindhearted person
bonaerense¹ *adj* : of or from Buenos Aires
bonaerense² *nmf* : person from Buenos Aires
bonanza *nf* 1 PROSPERIDAD : prosperity ⟨bonanza económica : economic boom⟩ 2 : calm weather 3 : rich ore deposit, bonanza
bondad *nf* BENEVOLENCIA : goodness, kindness ⟨tener la bondad de hacer algo : to be kind enough to do something⟩
bondadoso, -sa *adj* BENÉVOLO : kind, kindly, good — **bondadosamente** *adv*
bonete *nm* : cap, mortarboard
boniato *nm* : sweet potato
bonificación *nf, pl* **-ciones** 1 : discount 2 : bonus, extra
bonito¹ *adv* : nicely, well ⟨¡qué bonito canta tu hermana! : your sister sings wonderfully!⟩
bonito², -ta *adj* LINDO : pretty, lovely ⟨tiene un apartamento bonito : she has a nice apartment⟩
bonito³ *nm* : bonito (tuna)
bono *nm* 1 : bond ⟨bono bancario : bank bond⟩ 2 : voucher
boqueada *nf* : gasp ⟨dar la última boqueada : to give one's last gasp⟩
boquear *vi* 1 : to gasp 2 : to be dying
boquete *nm* : gap, opening, breach
boquiabierto, -ta *adj* : open-mouthed, speechless, agape

boquilla *nf* : mouthpiece (of a musical instrument)
borbollar *vi* : to bubble
borbotar *or* **borbotear** *vi* : to boil, to bubble, to gurgle
borboteo *nm* : bubbling, gurgling
borda *nf* : gunwale
bordado *nm* : embroidery, needlework
bordar *v* : to embroider
borde *nm* 1 : border, edge 2 **al borde de** : on the verge of ⟨estoy al borde de la locura : I'm about to go crazy⟩
bordear *vt* 1 : to border, to skirt ⟨el Río Este bordea Manhattan : the East River borders Manhattan⟩ 2 : to border on ⟨bordea la irrealidad : it borders on unreality⟩ 3 : to line ⟨una calle bordeada de árboles : a street lined with trees⟩
bordillo *nm* : curb
bordo *nm* **a** ∼ : aboard, on board
boreal *adj* : northern
borgoña *nf* : burgundy
bórico, -ca *adj* : boric ⟨ácido bórico : boric acid⟩
boricua *adj & nmf fam* : Puerto Rican
borinqueño, -ña → **boricua**
borla *nf* 1 : pom-pom, tassel 2 : powder puff
boro *nm* : boron
borrachera *nf* : drunkenness ⟨agarró una borrachera : he got drunk⟩
borrachín, -china *n, mpl* **-chines** *fam* : lush, drunk
borracho¹, -cha *adj* EBRIO : drunk, intoxicated
borracho², -cha *n* : drunk, drunkard
borrador *nm* 1 : rough copy, first draft ⟨en borrador : in the rough⟩ 2 : eraser
borrar *vt* : to erase, to blot out — **borrarse** *vr* 1 : to fade, to fade away 2 : to resign, to drop out 3 *Mex fam* : to split, to leave ⟨me borro : I'm out of here⟩
borrascoso, -sa *adj* : gusty, blustery
borrego, -ga *n* 1 : lamb, sheep 2 : simpleton, fool
borrico → **burro**
borrón *nm, pl* **borrones** : smudge, blot ⟨borrón y cuenta nueva : let's start on a clean slate, let's start over again⟩
borronear *vt* : to smudge, to blot
borroso, -sa *adj* 1 : blurry, smudgy 2 CONFUSO : unclear, confused
boscoso, -sa *adj* : wooded
bosnio, -nia *adj & n* : Bosnian
bosque *nm* : woods, forest
bosquecillo *nm* : grove, copse, thicket
bosquejar *vt* ESBOZAR : to outline, to sketch
bosquejo *nm* 1 TRAZADO : outline, sketch 2 : draft
bostezar {21} *vi* : to yawn
bostezo *nm* : yawn
bota *nf* 1 : boot 2 : wineskin
botana *nf Mex* : snack, appetizer
botanear *vi Mex* : to have a snack
botánica *nf* : botany

botánico[1], **-ca** *adj* : botanical
botánico[2], **-ca** *n* : botanist
botar *vt* **1** ARROJAR : to throw, to fling, to hurl **2** TIRAR : to throw out, to throw away **3** : to launch (a ship)
bote *nm* **1** : small boat ⟨bote de remos : rowboat⟩ **2** : can, jar **3** : jump, bounce **4** *Mex fam* : jail
botella *nf* : bottle
botica *nf* FARMACIA : drugstore, pharmacy
boticario, -ria *n* FARMACÉUTICO : pharmacist, druggist
botín *nm, pl* **botines 1** : baby's bootee **2** : ankle boot **3** : booty, plunder
botiquín *nm, pl* **-quines 1** : medicine cabinet **2** : first-aid kit
botón *nm, pl* **botones 1** : button **2** : bud **3** INSIGNIA : badge
botones *nmfs & pl* : bellhop
botulismo *nm* : botulism
boulevard [ˌbuleˈvar] → **bulevar**
bouquet *nm* **1** : fragrance, bouquet (of wine) **2** RAMILLETE : bouquet (of flowers)
boutique *nf* : boutique
bóveda *nf* **1** : vault, dome **2** CRIPTA : crypt
bovino, -na *adj* : bovine
box *nm, pl* **boxes 1** : pit (in auto racing) **2** *Mex* : boxing
boxeador, -dora *n* : boxer
boxear *vi* : to box
boxeo *nm* : boxing
boya *nf* : buoy
boyante *adj* **1** : buoyant **2** : prosperous, thriving
bozal *nm* **1** : muzzle **2** : halter (for a horse)
bracear *vi* **1** : to wave one's arms **2** : to make strokes (in swimming)
bracero, -ra *n* : migrant worker, day laborer
braguero *nm* : truss (in medicine)
bragueta *nf* : fly, pants zipper
braille *adj & nm* : braille
bramante *nm* : twine, string
bramar *vi* **1** RUGIR : to roar, to bellow **2** : to howl (of the wind)
bramido *nm* : bellowing, roar
brandy *nm* : brandy
branquia *nf* AGALLA : gill
brasa *nf* ASCUA : ember, live coal
brasero *nm* : brazier
brasier *nm* *Col, Mex* : brassiere, bra
brasileño, -ña *adj & n* : Brazilian
bravata *nf* **1** JACTANCIA : boast, bravado **2** AMENAZA : threat
bravo, -va *adj* **1** FEROZ : ferocious, fierce ⟨un perro bravo : a ferocious dog⟩ **2** EXCELENTE : excellent, great ⟨¡bravo! : bravo!, well done!⟩ **3** : rough, rugged, wild **4** : annoyed, angry
bravucón, -cona *n, mpl* **-cones** : bully
bravuconadas *nfpl* : bravado
bravura *nf* **1** FEROCIDAD : fierceness, ferocity **2** VALENTÍA : bravery

braza *nf* **1** : breaststroke **2** : fathom (unit of length)
brazada *nf* : stroke (in swimming)
brazalete *nm* PULSERA : bracelet, bangle
brazo *nm* **1** : arm **2 brazo derecho** : right-hand man **3 brazos** *nmpl* : hands, laborers
brea *nf* ALQUITRÁN : tar, pitch
brebaje *nm* : potion, brew
brecha *nf* **1** : gap, breach ⟨estar siempre en la brecha : to be always there when needed, to stay in the thick of things⟩ **2** : gash
brécol *nm* : broccoli
brega *nf* **1** LUCHA : struggle, fight **2** : hard work
bregar {52} *vi* **1** LUCHAR : to struggle **2** : to toil, to work hard **3** ~ **con** : to deal with
brete *nm* : jam, tight spot
breve *adj* **1** CORTO : brief, short **2 en** ~ : shortly, in short — **brevemente** *adv*
brevedad *nf* : brevity, shortness
breviario *nm* : breviary
brezal *nm* : heath, moor
brezo *nm* : heather
bribón, -bona *n, mpl* **bribones** : rascal, scamp
bricolaje *or* **bricolage** *nm* : do-it-yourself
brida *nf* : bridle
brigada *nf* **1** : brigade **2** : gang, team, squad
brigadier *nm* : brigadier
brillante[1] *adj* : brilliant, bright — **brillantemente** *adv*
brillante[2] *nm* DIAMANTE : diamond
brillantez *nf* : brilliance, brightness
brillar *vi* : to shine, to sparkle
brillo *nm* **1** LUSTRE : luster, shine **2** : brilliance
brilloso, -sa *adj* LUSTROSO : lustrous, shiny
brincar {72} *vi* **1** SALTAR : to jump around, to leap about **2** : to frolic, to gambol
brinco *nm* **1** SALTO : jump, leap, skip **2 pegar un brinco** : to give a start, to jump
brindar *vi* : to drink a toast ⟨brindó por los vencedores : he toasted the victors⟩ — *vt* OFRECER, PROPORCIONAR : to offer, to provide — **brindarse** *vr* : to offer one's assistance, to volunteer
brindis *nm* : toast, drink ⟨hacer un brindis : to drink a toast⟩
brinque, etc. → **brincar**
brío *nm* **1** : force, determination **2** : spirit, verve
brioso, -sa *adj* : spirited, lively
briqueta *nf* : briquette
brisa *nf* : breeze
británico[1], **-ca** *adj* : British
británico[2], **-ca** *n* **1** : British person **2 los británicos** : the British
brizna *nf* **1** : strand, thread **2** : blade (of grass)

broca *nf* : drill bit
brocado *nm* : brocade
brocha *nf* : paintbrush
broche *nm* 1 ALFILER : brooch 2 : fastener, clasp 3 **broche de oro** : finishing touch
brocheta *nf* : skewer
brócoli *nm* : broccoli
broma *nf* 1 CHISTE : joke, prank 2 : fun, merriment 3 **en** ~ : in jest, jokingly
bromear *vi* : to joke, to fool around ⟨sólo estaba bromeando : I was only kidding⟩
bromista[1] *adj* : fun-loving, joking
bromista[2] *nmf* : joker, prankster
bromo *nm* : bromine
bronca *nf fam* : fight, quarrel, fuss
bronce *nm* : bronze
bronceado[1], **-da** *adj* 1 : tanned, suntanned 2 : bronze
bronceado[2] *nm* 1 : suntan, tan 2 : bronzing
broncearse *vr* : to get a suntan
bronco, -ca *adj* 1 : harsh, rough 2 : untamed, wild
bronquial *adj* : bronchial
bronquio *nm* : bronchial tube, bronchus
bronquitis *nf* : bronchitis
broqueta *nf* : skewer
brotar *vi* 1 : to bud, to sprout 2 : to spring up, to stream, to gush forth 3 : to break out, to appear
brote *nm* 1 : outbreak 2 : sprout, bud, shoot
broza *nf* 1 : brushwood 2 MALEZA : scrub, undergrowth
brujería *nf* HECHICERÍA : witchcraft, sorcery
brujo[1], **-ja** *adj* : bewitching
brujo[2], **-ja** *n* : warlock *m*, witch *f*, sorcerer
brújula *nf* : compass
bruma *nf* : haze, mist
brumoso, -sa *adj* : hazy, misty
bruñir {38} *vt* : to burnish, to polish (metals)
brusco, -ca *adj* 1 SÚBITO : sudden, abrupt 2 : curt, brusque — **bruscamente** *adv*
brusquedad *nf* 1 : abruptness, suddenness 2 : brusqueness
brutal *adj* 1 : brutal 2 *fam* : incredible, terrific — **brutalmente** *adv*
brutalidad *nf* CRUELDAD : brutality
brutalizar {21} *vt* : to brutalize, to maltreat
bruto[1], **-ta** *adj* 1 : gross ⟨peso bruto : gross weight⟩ ⟨ingresos brutos : gross income⟩ 2 : unrefined ⟨petróleo bruto : crude oil⟩ 3 : brutish, stupid
bruto[2], **-ta** *n* 1 : brute 2 : dunce, blockhead
bubónico, -ca *adj* : bubonic
bucal *adj* : oral
bucanero *nm* : buccaneer, pirate
buccino *nm* : whelk
buceador, -dora *n* : diver, scuba diver

bucear *vi* 1 : to dive, to swim underwater 2 : to explore, to delve
buceo *nm* 1 : diving, scuba diving 2 : exploration, searching
buche *nm* 1 : crop (of a bird) 2 *fam* : belly, gut 3 : mouthful ⟨hacer buches : to rinse one's mouth⟩
bucle *nm* 1 : curl, ringlet 2 : loop
bucólico, -ca *adj* : bucolic
budín *nm, pl* **budines** : pudding
budismo *nm* : Buddhism
budista *adj & nmf* : Buddhist
buen *adj* → **bueno**[1]
buenamente *adv* 1 : easily 2 : willingly
buenaventura *nf* 1 : good luck 2 : fortune, future ⟨le dijo la buenaventura : she told his fortune⟩
buenazo, -za *n fam* BONACHÓN : kindhearted person
bueno[1], **-na** *adj* (**buen** *before masculine singular nouns*) 1 : good ⟨una buena idea : a good idea⟩ 2 BONDADOSO : nice, kind 3 APROPIADO : proper, appropriate 4 SANO : well, healthy 5 : considerable, goodly ⟨una buena cantidad : a lot⟩ 6 **buenos días** : hello, good day 7 **buenas tardes** : good afternoon 8 **buenas noches** : good evening, good night
bueno[2] *interj* 1 : OK!, all right! 2 *Mex* : hello! (on the telephone)
buey *nm* : ox, steer
búfalo *nm* 1 : buffalo 2 **búfalo de agua** : water buffalo
bufanda *nf* : scarf, muffler
bufar *vi* : to snort
bufet *or* **bufé** *nm* : buffet-style meal
bufete *nm* 1 : law firm, law office 2 : writing desk
bufido *nm* : snort
bufo, -fa *adj* : comic
bufón, -fona *n, mpl* **bufones** : clown, buffoon, jester
bufonada *nf* 1 : jest, buffoonery 2 : sarcasm
buhardilla *nf* 1 ÁTICO, DESVÁN : attic 2 : dormer window
búho *nm* 1 : owl 2 *fam* : hermit, recluse
buhonero, -ra *n* MERCACHIFLE : peddler
buitre *nm* : vulture
bujía *nf* : spark plug
bula *nf* : papal bull
bulbo *nm* : bulb
bulboso, -sa *adj* : bulbous
bulevar *nm* : boulevard
búlgaro, -ra *adj & n* : Bulgarian
bulla *nf* BARULLO : racket, rowdiness
bullicio *nm* 1 : ruckus, uproar 2 : hustle and bustle
bullicioso, -sa *adj* : noisy, busy, turbulent
bullir {38} *vi* 1 HERVIR : to boil 2 MOVERSE : to stir, to bustle about
bulto *nm* 1 : package, bundle 2 : piece of luggage, bag 3 : size, bulk, volume 4 : form, shape 5 : lump (on the body), swelling, bulge

bumerán *nm, pl* **-ranes** : boomerang
búnker *nm, pl* **búnkers** : bunker
búnquer → **búnker**
buñuelo *nm* : fried pastry
buque *nm* BARCO : ship, vessel
burbuja *nf* : bubble, blister (on a surface)
burbujear *vi* **1** : to bubble **2** : to fizz
burbujeo *nm* : bubbling
burdel *nm* : brothel, whorehouse
burdo, -da *adj* **1** : coarse, rough **2** : crude, clumsy ⟨una burda mentira : a clumsy lie⟩ — **burdamente** *adj*
burgués, -guesa *adj & n, mpl* **burgueses** : bourgeois
burguesía *nf* : bourgeoisie, middle class
burla *nf* **1** : mockery, ridicule **2** : joke, trick **3 hacer burla de** : to make fun of, to mock
burlar *vt* ENGAÑAR : to trick, to deceive — **burlarse** *vr* ~ **de** : to make fun of, to ridicule
burlesco, -ca *adj* : burlesque, comic
burlón[1], -lona *adj, mpl* **burlones** : joking, mocking
burlón[2], -lona *n, mpl* **burlones** : joker
burocracia *nf* : bureaucracy
burócrata *nmf* : bureaucrat
burocrático, -ca *adj* : bureaucratic
burrada *nf fam* : stupid act, nonsense
burrito *nm* : burrito
burro[1], -rra *adj fam* : dumb, stupid

burro[2], -rra *n* **1** ASNO : donkey, ass **2** *fam* : dunce, poor student
burro[3] *nm* **1** : sawhorse **2** *Mex* : ironing board **3** *Mex* : stepladder
bursátil *adj* : stock-market
bursitis *nf* : bursitis
burundés, -desa *adj & n* : Burundian
bus *nm* : bus
busca *nf* : search
buscador, -dora *n* : hunter (for treasure, etc.), prospector
buscapersonas *nms & pl* : beeper, pager
buscapleitos *nmfs & pl* : troublemaker
buscar {72} *vt* **1** : to look for, to seek **2** : to pick up, to collect **3** : to provoke — *vi* : to look, to search ⟨buscó en los bolsillos : he searched through his pockets⟩
buscavidas *nmf & pl* **1** : busybody **2** : go-getter
busque, etc. → **buscar**
búsqueda *nf* : search
busto *nm* : bust
butaca *nf* **1** SILLÓN : armchair **2** : seat (in a theatre) **3** *Mex* : pupil's desk
butano *nm* : butane
buzo[1], -za *adj Mex fam* : smart, astute ⟨¡ponte buzo! : get with it!, get on the ball!⟩
buzo[2] *nm* : diver, scuba diver
buzón *nm, pl* **buzones** : mailbox
byte *nm* : byte

C

c *nf* : third letter of the Spanish alphabet
cabal *adj* **1** : exact, correct **2** : complete **3** : upright, honest
cabales *nmpl* **no estar en sus cabales** : not to be in one's right mind
cabalgar {52} *vi* : to ride (on horseback)
cabalgata *nf* : cavalcade, procession
cabalidad *nf* **a** ~ : thoroughly, conscientiously
caballa *nf* : mackerel
caballada *nf* **1** : herd of horses **2** *fam* : nonsense, stupidity, outrageousness
caballar *adj* EQUINO : horse, equine
caballeresco, -ca *adj* : gallant, chivalrous
caballería *nf* **1** : cavalry **2** : horse, mount **3** : knighthood, chivalry
caballeriza *nf* : stable
caballero[1] → **caballeroso**
caballero[2] *nm* **1** : gentleman **2** : knight
caballerosidad *nf* : chivalry, gallantry
caballeroso, -sa *adj* : gentlemanly, chivalrous
caballete *nm* **1** : ridge **2** : easel **3** : trestle (for a table, etc.) **4** : bridge (of the nose) **5** : sawhorse
caballista *nmf* : horseman *m*, horsewoman *f*
caballito *nm* **1** : rocking horse **2 caballito de mar** : seahorse **3 caballitos** *nmpl* : merry-go-round

caballo *nm* **1** : horse **2** : knight (in chess) **3 caballo de fuerza** *or* **caballo de vapor** : horsepower
cabalmente *adv* : fully, exactly
cabaña *nf* CHOZA : cabin, hut
cabaret *nm, pl* **-rets** : nightclub, cabaret
cabecear *vt* : to head (in soccer) — *vi* **1** : to nod one's head **2** : to lurch, to pitch
cabecera *nf* **1** : headboard **2** : head ⟨cabecera de la mesa : head of the table⟩ **3** : heading, headline **4** : headwaters *pl* **5 médico de cabecera** : family doctor **6 cabecera municipal** *CA, Mex* : downtown area
cabecilla *nmf* : ringleader, kingpin
cabellera *nf* : head of hair, mane
cabello *nm* : hair
cabelludo, -da *adj* **1** : hairy **2 cuero cabelludo** : scalp
caber {12} *vi* **1** : to fit, to go ⟨no sé si cabremos todos en el coche : I don't know if we'll all fit in the car⟩ **2** : to be possible ⟨no cabe duda alguna : there's no doubt about it⟩ ⟨cabe que llegue mañana : he may come tomorrow⟩
cabestrillo *nm* : sling ⟨llevo el brazo en cabestrillo : my arm is in a sling⟩
cabestro *nm* : halter (for an animal)
cabeza *nf* **1** : head **2 cabeza hueca** : scatterbrain **3 de** ~ : head first **4 dolor de cabeza** : headache

cabezada *nf* **1** : butt, blow with the head **2** : nod ⟨echar una cabezada : to take a nap, to doze off⟩

cabezal *nm* : bolster

cabezazo *nm* : butt, blow with the head

cabezón, -zona *adj, mpl* **-zones** *fam* **1** : having a big head **2** : pigheaded, stubborn

cabida *nf* **1** : room, space, capacity **2** **dar cabida a** : to accommodate, to hold

cabildear *vi* : to lobby

cabildeo *nm* : lobbying

cabildero, -ra *n* : lobbyist

cabildo *nm* AYUNTAMIENTO **1** : town or city hall **2** : town or city council

cabina *nf* **1** : cabin **2** : booth **3** : cab (of a truck), cockpit (of an airplane)

cabizbajo, -ja *adj* : dejected, downcast

cable *nm* : cable

cableado *nm* : wiring

cabo *nm* **1** : end ⟨al cabo de dos semanas : at the end of two weeks⟩ **2** : stub, end piece **3** : corporal **4** : cape, headland ⟨el Cabo Cañaveral : Cape Canaveral⟩ **5 al fin y al cabo** : after all, in the end **6 llevar a cabo** : to carry out, to do

caboverdiano, -na *adj & n* : Cape Verdean

cabrá, etc. → **caber**

cabra *nf* : goat

cabrestante *nm* : windlass

cabrío, -ría *adj* : goat, caprine

cabriola *nf* **1** : skip, jump **2 hacer cabriolas** : to prance

cabriolar *vi* : to prance

cabrito *nm* : kid, baby goat

cabús *nm, pl* **cabuses** *Mex* : caboose

cacahuate *or* **cacahuete** *nm* : peanut

cacalote *nm Mex* : crow

cacao *nm* : cacao, cocoa bean

cacarear *vi* : to crow, to cackle, to cluck — *vt fam* : to boast about, to crow about ⟨cacarear un huevo : to brag about an accomplishment⟩

cacareo *nm* **1** : clucking (of a hen), crowing (of a rooster) **2** : boasting

cacatúa *nf* : cockatoo

cace, etc. → **cazar**

cacería *nf* **1** CAZA : hunt, hunting **2** : hunting party

cacerola *nf* : pan, saucepan

cacha *nf* : butt (of a gun)

cachar *vt fam* : to catch

cacharro *nm* **1** *fam* : thing, piece of junk **2** *fam* : jalopy **3 cacharros** *nmpl* : pots and pans

cache *nm* : cache, cache memory

caché *nm* : cachet

cachear *vt* : to search, to frisk

cachemir *nm* : cashmere

cachetada *nf* BOFETADA : slap on the face

cachete *nm* : cheek

cachetear *vt* BOFETEAR : to slap

cachiporra *nf* : bludgeon, club, blackjack

cachirul *nm Mex fam* : cheating ⟨hacer cachirul : to cheat⟩

cachivache *nm fam* : thing ⟨mete tus cachivaches en el maletero : put your stuff in the trunk⟩

cacho *nm fam* : piece, bit

cachorro, -rra *n* **1** : cub **2** PERRITO : puppy

cachucha *nf Mex* : cap, baseball cap

cacique *nm* **1** : chief (of a tribe) **2** : boss (in politics)

cacofonía *nf* : cacophony

cacofónico, -ca *adj* : cacophonous

cacto *nm* : cactus

cactus → **cacto**

cada *adj* **1** : each ⟨cuestan diez pesos cada una : they cost ten pesos each⟩ **2** : every ⟨cada vez : every time⟩ **3** : such, some ⟨sales con cada historia : you come up with such crazy stories⟩ **4 cada vez más** : more and more, increasingly **5 cada vez menos** : less and less

cadalso *nm* : scaffold, gallows

cadáver *nm* : corpse, cadaver

cadavérico, -ca *adj* **1** : cadaverous **2** PÁLIDO : deathly pale

caddie *or* **caddy** *nmf, pl* **caddies** : caddy

cadena *nf* **1** : chain **2** : network, channel **3 cadena de montaje** : assembly line **4 cadena perpetua** : life sentence

cadencia *nf* : cadence, rhythm

cadencioso, -sa *adj* : rhythmic, rhythmical

cadera *nf* : hip

cadete *nmf* : cadet

cadmio *nm* : cadmium

caducar {72} *vi* : to expire

caducidad *nf* : expiration

caduco, -ca *adj* **1** : outdated, obsolete **2** : deciduous

caer {13} *vi* **1** : to fall, to drop **2** : to collapse **3** : to hang (down) **4 caer bien** *fam* : to be pleasant, to be likeable ⟨me caes bien : I like you⟩ **5 caer mal** *or* **caer gordo** *fam* : to be unpleasant, to be unlikeable — **caerse** *vr* : to fall down

café[1] *adj* : brown ⟨ojos cafés : brown eyes⟩

café[2] *nm* **1** : coffee **2** : café

cafeína *nf* : caffeine

cafetal *nm* : coffee plantation

cafetalero[1], -ra *adj* : coffee ⟨cosecha cafetalera : coffee harvest⟩

cafetalero[2], -ra *n* : coffee grower

cafetera *nf* : coffeepot, coffeemaker

cafetería *nf* **1** : coffee shop, café **2** : lunchroom, cafeteria

cafetero[1], -ra *adj* : coffee-producing

cafetero[2], -ra *n* : coffee grower

cafeticultura *nf Mex* : coffee industry

caguama *nf* **1** : large Caribbean turtle **2** *Mex* : large bottle of beer

caída *nf* **1** BAJA, DESCENSO : fall, drop **2** : collapse, downfall

caiga, etc. → **caer**

caimán *nm, pl* **caimanes** : alligator, caiman

caimito *nm* : star apple
caja *nf* **1** : box, case **2** : cash register, checkout counter **3** : bed (of a truck) **4** *fam* : coffin **5 caja fuerte** *or* **caja de caudales** : safe **6 caja de seguridad** : safe-deposit box **7 caja torácica** : rib cage
cajero, -ra *n* **1** : cashier **2** : teller **3 cajero automático** : automated teller machine, ATM
cajeta *nf Mex* : a sweet caramel-flavored spread
cajetilla *nf* : pack (of cigarettes)
cajón *nm, pl* **cajones 1** : drawer, till **2** : crate, case **3 cajón de estacionamiento** *Mex* : parking space
cajuela *nf Mex* : trunk (of a car)
cal *nf* : lime, quicklime
cala *nf* : cove, inlet
calabacín *nm, pl* **-cines** : zucchini
calabacita *nf Mex* : zucchini
calabaza *nf* **1** : pumpkin, squash **2** : gourd **3 dar calabazas a** : to give the brush-off to, to jilt
calabozo *nm* **1** : prison **2** : jail cell
calado[1], -da *adj* **1** : drenched **2** : open-worked
calado[2] *nm* **1** : draft (of a ship) **2** : open-work
calafatear *vt* : to caulk
calamar *nm* **1** : squid **2 calamares** *nmpl* : calamari
calambre *nm* **1** ESPASMO : cramp **2** : electric shock, jolt
calamidad *nf* DESASTRE : calamity, disaster
calamina *nf* : calamine
calamitoso, -sa *adj* : calamitous, disastrous
calaña *nf* : ilk, kind, sort ⟨una persona de mala calaña : a bad sort⟩
calar *vt* **1** : to soak through **2** : to pierce, to penetrate — *vi* : to catch on —
calarse *vr* : to get drenched
calavera[1] *nf* **1** : skull **2** *Mex* : taillight
calavera[2] *nm* : rake, rogue
calcar {72} *vt* **1** : to trace **2** : to copy, to imitate
calce, etc. → **calzar**
calceta *nf* : knee-high stocking
calcetería *nf* : hosiery
calcetín *nm, pl* **-tines** : sock
calcificar {72} *v* : to calcify — **calcificarse** *vr*
calcinar *vt* : to char, to burn
calcio *nm* : calcium
calco *nm* **1** : transfer, tracing **2** : copy, image
calcomanía *nf* : decal, transfer
calculador, -dora *adj* : calculating
calculadora *nf* : calculator
calcular *vt* **1** : to calculate, to estimate **2** : to plan, to scheme
cálculo *nm* **1** : calculation, estimation **2** : calculus **3** : plan, scheme **4 cálculo biliar** : gallstone **5 hoja de cálculo** : spreadsheet
caldas *nfpl* : hot springs

caldear *vt* : to heat, to warm —
caldearse *vr* **1** : to heat up **2** : to become heated, to get tense
caldera *nf* **1** : cauldron **2** : boiler
caldo *nm* **1** CONSOMÉ : broth, stock **2 caldo de cultivo** : culture medium, breeding ground
caldoso, -sa *adj* : watery
calefacción *nf, pl* **-ciones** : heating, heat
calefactor *nm* : heater
caleidoscopio → **calidoscopio**
calendario *nm* **1** : calendar **2** : timetable, schedule
caléndula *nf* : marigold
calentador *nm* : heater
calentamiento *nm* **1** : heating, warming **2** : warm-up (in sports)
calentar {55} *vt* **1** : to heat, to warm **2** *fam* : to annoy, to anger **3** *fam* : to excite, to turn on — **calentarse** *vr* **1** : to get warm, to heat up **2** : to warm up (in sports) **3** *fam* : to become sexually aroused **4** *fam* : to get mad
calentura *nf* **1** FIEBRE : temperature, fever **2** : cold sore
calibrador *nm* : gauge, calipers *pl*
calibrar *vt* : to calibrate — **calibración** *nf*
calibre *nm* **1** : caliber, gauge **2** : importance, excellence **3** : kind, sort ⟨un problema de grueso calibre : a serious problem⟩
calidad *nf* **1** : quality, grade **2** : position, status **3 en calidad de** : as, in the capacity of
cálido, -da *adj* **1** : hot ⟨un clima cálido : a hot climate⟩ **2** : warm ⟨una cálida bienvenida : a warm welcome⟩
calidoscopio *nm* : kaleidoscope
caliente *adj* **1** : hot, warm ⟨mantenerse caliente : to stay warm⟩ **2** : heated, fiery ⟨una disputa caliente : a heated argument⟩ **3** *fam* : sexually excited, horny
califa *nm* : caliph
calificación *nf, pl* **-ciones 1** NOTA : grade (for a course) **2** : rating, score **3** CLASIFICACIÓN : qualification, qualifying ⟨ronda de calificación : qualifying round⟩
calificar {72} *vt* **1** : to grade **2** : to describe, to rate ⟨la calificaron de buena alumna : they described her as a good student⟩ **3** : to qualify, to modify (in grammar)
calificativo[1], -va *adj* : qualifying
calificativo[2] *nm* : qualifier, epithet
caligrafía *nf* **1** ESCRITURA : handwriting **2** : calligraphy
calipso *nm* : calypso
calistenia *nf* : calisthenics
cáliz *nm, pl* **cálices 1** : chalice, goblet **2** : calyx
caliza *nf* : limestone
callado, -da *adj* : quiet, silent — **calladamente** *adv*
callar *vi* : to keep quiet, to be silent — *vt* **1** : to silence, to hush ⟨¡calla a los

niños! : keep the children quiet!⟩ **2** : to keep secret — **callarse** *vr* : to remain silent ⟨¡cállate! : be quiet!, shut up!⟩

calle *nf* : street, road

callejear *vi* : to wander about the streets, to hang out

callejero, -ra *adj* : street ⟨perro callejero : stray dog⟩

callejón *nm, pl* **-jones 1** : alley **2 callejón sin salida** : dead-end street

callo *nm* **1** : callus, corn **2 callos** *nmpl* : tripe

calloso, -sa *adj* : callous

calma *nf* : calm, quiet

calmante[1] *adj* : calming, soothing

calmante[2] *nm* : tranquilizer, sedative

calmar *vt* TRANQUILIZAR : to calm, to soothe — **calmarse** *vr* : to calm down

calmo, -ma *adj* TRANQUILO : calm, tranquil

calmoso, -sa *adj* **1** TRANQUILO : calm, quiet **2** LENTO : slow, sluggish

calor *nm* **1** : heat ⟨hace calor : it's hot outside⟩ ⟨tener calor : to feel hot⟩ **2** : warmth, affection **3** : ardor, passion

caloría *nf* : calorie

calórico, -ca *adj* : caloric

calorífico, -ca *adj* : caloric

calque, etc. → **calcar**

calumnia *nf* : slander, libel — **calumnioso, -sa** *adj*

calumniar *vt* : to slander, to libel

caluroso, -sa *adj* **1** : hot **2** : warm, enthusiastic

calva *nf* : bald spot, bald head

calvario *nm* **1** : Calvary **2** : Stations of the Cross *pl* **3 vivir un calvario** : to suffer great adversity

calvicie *nf* : baldness

calvo[1], **-va** *adj* : bald

calvo[2], **-va** *n* : bald person

calza *nf* : block, wedge

calzada *nf* : roadway, avenue

calzado *nm* : footwear

calzador *nm* : shoehorn

calzar {21} *vt* **1** : to wear (shoes) ⟨¿de cuál calza? : what is your shoe size?⟩ ⟨siempre calzaban tenis : they always wore sneakers⟩ **2** : to provide with shoes

calzo *nm* : chock, wedge

calzoncillos *nmpl* : underpants, briefs

calzones *nmpl* : underpants, panties

cama *nf* **1** : bed **2 cama elástica** : trampoline

camada *nf* : litter, brood

camafeo *nm* : cameo

camaleón *nm, pl* **-leones** : chameleon

cámara *nf* **1** : camera **2** : chamber, room **3** : house (in government) **4** : inner tube

camarada *nmf* **1** : comrade, companion **2** : colleague

camaradería *nf* : camaraderie

camarero, -ra *n* **1** MESERO : waiter, waitress *f* **2** : bellhop *m*, chambermaid *f* (in a hotel) **3** : steward *m*, stewardess *f* (on a ship, etc.)

camarilla *nf* : political clique

camarógrafo, -fa *n* : cameraman *m*, camerawoman *f*

camarón *nm, pl* **-rones 1** : shrimp **2** : prawn

camarote *nm* : cabin, stateroom

camastro *nm* : small hard bed, pallet

cambalache *nm fam* : swap

cambiante *adj* **1** : changing **2** VARIABLE : changeable, variable

cambiar *vt* **1** ALTERAR, MODIFICAR : to change **2** : to exchange, to trade — *vi* **1** : to change **2 cambiar de velocidad** : to shift gears — **cambiarse** *vr* **1** : to change (clothing) **2** MUDARSE : to move (to a new address)

cambio *nm* **1** : change, alteration **2** : exchange **3** : change (money) **4 en cambio** : instead **5 en cambio** : however, on the other hand

cambista *nmf* : exchange broker

camboyano, -na *adj & n* : Cambodian

cambur *nm Ven* : banana

camelia *nf* : camellia

camello *nm* : camel

camellón *nm, pl* **-llones** *Mex* : traffic island

camerino *nm* : dressing room

camerunés, -nesa *adj, mpl* **-neses** : Cameroonian

camilla *nf* : stretcher

camillero, -ra *n* : orderly (in a hospital)

caminante *nmf* : wayfarer, walker

caminar *vi* ANDAR : to walk, to move — *vt* : to walk, to cover (a distance)

caminata *nf* : hike, long walk

camino *nm* **1** : path, road **2** : journey ⟨ponerse en camino : to set off⟩ **3** : way ⟨a medio camino : halfway there⟩

camión *nm, pl* **camiones 1** : truck **2** *Mex* : bus

camionero, -ra *n* **1** : truck driver **2** *Mex* : bus driver

camioneta *nf* : light truck, van

camisa *nf* **1** : shirt **2 camisa de fuerza** : straitjacket

camiseta *nf* **1** : T-shirt **2** : undershirt

camisón *nm, pl* **-sones** : nightshirt, nightgown

camorra *nf fam* : fight, trouble ⟨buscar camorra : to pick a fight⟩

camote *nm* **1** : root vegetable similar to the sweet potato **2 hacerse camote** *Mex fam* : to get mixed up

campal *adj* : pitched, fierce ⟨batalla campal : pitched battle⟩

campamento *nm* : camp

campana *nf* : bell

campanada *nf* TAÑIDO : stroke (of a bell), peal

campanario *nm* : bell tower, belfry

campanilla *nf* **1** : small bell, handbell **2** : uvula

campante *adj* : nonchalant, smug ⟨seguir tan campante : to go on as if nothing had happened⟩

campaña *nf* 1 CAMPO : countryside, country 2 : campaign 3 **tienda de campaña** : tent
campañol *nm* : vole
campechana *nf Mex* : puff pastry
campechanía *nf* : geniality
campechano, -na *adj* : open, cordial, friendly
campeón, -peona *n, mpl* -peones : champion
campeonato *nm* : championship
cámper *nm* : camper (vehicle)
campero, -ra *adj* : country, rural
campesino, -na *n* : peasant, farm laborer
campestre *adj* : rural, rustic
camping *nm* 1 : camping 2 : campsite
campiña *nf* CAMPO : countryside, country
campista *nmf* : camper
campo *nm* 1 CAMPAÑA : countryside, country 2 : field ⟨campo de aviación : airfield⟩ ⟨su campo de responsabilidad : her field of responsibility⟩
camposanto *nm* : graveyard, cemetery
campus *nms & pl* : campus
camuflaje *nm* : camouflage
camuflajear *vt* : to camouflage
camuflar → camuflajear
can *nm* : hound, dog
cana *nf* 1 : gray hair 2 **salirle canas** : to go gray, to get gray hair 3 **echar una cana al aire** : to let one's hair down
canadiense *adj & nmf* : Canadian
canal[1] *nm* 1 : canal 2 : channel
canal[2] *nmf* : gutter, groove
canalé *nm* : rib, ribbing (in fabric)
canaleta *nf* : gutter
canalete *nm* : paddle
canalizar {21} *vt* : to channel
canalla[1] *adj fam* : low, rotten
canalla[2] *nmf fam* : bastard, swine
canapé *nm* 1 : hors d'oeuvre, canapé 2 SOFÁ : couch, sofa
canario[1], -ria *adj* : of or from the Canary Islands
canario[2], -ria *n* : Canarian, Canary Islander
canario[3] *nm* : canary
canasta *nf* 1 : basket 2 : canasta (card game)
cancel *nm* 1 : sliding door 2 : partition
cancelación *nf, pl* -ciones 1 : cancellation 2 : payment in full
cancelar *vt* 1 : to cancel 2 : to pay off, to settle
cáncer *nm* : cancer
Cáncer *nmf* : Cancer
cancerígeno[1], -na *adj* : carcinogenic
cancerígeno[2] *nm* : carcinogen
canceroso, -sa *adj* : cancerous
cancha *nf* : court, field (for sports)
canciller *nm* : chancellor
cancillería *nf* : chancellery, ministry
canción *nf, pl* canciones 1 : song 2 **canción de cuna** : lullaby
cancionero[1] *nm* : songbook
cancionero[2], -ra *n Mex* : songster, songstress *f*

candado *nm* : padlock
candela *nf* 1 : flame, fire 2 : candle
candelabro *nm* : candelabra
candelero *nm* 1 : candlestick 2 **estar en el candelero** : to be the center of attention
candente *adj* : red-hot
candidato, -ta *n* : candidate, applicant
candidatura *nf* : candidacy
candidez *nf* 1 : simplicity 2 INGENUIDAD : naïveté, ingenuousness
cándido, -da *adj* 1 : simple, unassuming 2 INGENUO : naive, ingenuous
candil *nm* : oil lamp
candilejas *nfpl* : footlights
candor *nm* : naïveté, innocence
candoroso, -sa *adj* : naive, innocent
canela *nf* : cinnamon
canesú *nm* : yoke (of clothing)
cangrejo *nm* JAIBA : crab
canguro *nm* 1 : kangaroo 2 **hacer de canguro** *Spain* : to baby-sit
caníbal[1] *adj* : cannibalistic
caníbal[2] *nmf* ANTROPÓFAGO : cannibal
canibalismo *nm* ANTROPOFAGIA : cannibalism
canibalizar {21} *vt* : to cannibalize
canica *nf* : marble ⟨jugar a las canicas : to play marbles⟩
caniche *nm* : poodle
canijo, -ja *adj* 1 *fam* : puny, weak 2 *Mex fam* : tough, hard ⟨un examen muy canijo : a very tough exam⟩
canilla *nf* 1 : shin, shinbone 2 *Arg, Uru* : faucet
canino[1], -na *adj* : canine
canino[2] *nm* 1 COLMILLO : canine (tooth) 2 : dog, canine
canje *nm* INTERCAMBIO : exchange, trade
canjear *vt* INTERCAMBIAR : to exchange, to trade
cannabis *nm* : cannabis
cano, -na *adj* : gray ⟨un hombre de pelo cano : a gray-haired man⟩
canoa *nf* : canoe
canon *nm, pl* cánones : canon
canónico, -ca *adj* 1 : canonical 2 **derecho canónico** : canon law
canónigo *nm* : canon (of a church)
canonizar {21} *vt* : to canonize — canonización *nf*
canoso, -sa → cano
cansado, -da *adj* 1 : tired ⟨estar cansado : to be tired⟩ 2 : tiresome, wearying ⟨ser cansado : to be tiring⟩
cansancio *nm* FATIGA : fatigue, weariness
cansar *vt* FATIGAR : to wear out, to tire — *vi* : to be tiresome — cansarse *vr* 1 : to wear oneself out 2 : to get bored
cansino, -na *adj* : slow, weary, lethargic
cantaleta *nf fam* : nagging ⟨la misma cantaleta : the same old story⟩
cantalupo *nm* : cantaloupe
cantante *nmf* : singer
cantar[1] *v* : to sing

cantar² *nm* : song, ballad
cántaro *nm* **1** : pitcher, jug **2 llover a cántaros** *fam* : to rain cats and dogs
cantata *nf* : cantata
cantera *nf* : quarry ⟨cantera de piedra : stone quarry⟩
cántico *nm* : canticle, chant
cantidad¹ *adv fam* : really ⟨ese carro me costó cantidad : that car cost me plenty⟩
cantidad² *nf* **1** : quantity **2** : sum, amount (of money) **3** *fam* : a lot, a great many ⟨había cantidad de niños en el parque : there were tons of kids in the park⟩
cantimplora *nf* : canteen, water bottle
cantina *nf* **1** : tavern, bar **2** : canteen, mess, dining quarters *pl*
cantinero, -ra *n* : bartender
canto *nm* **1** : singing **2** : chant ⟨canto gregoriano : Gregorian chant⟩ **3** : song (of a bird) **4** : edge, end ⟨de canto : on end, sideways⟩ **5 canto rodado** : boulder
cantón *nm, pl* **cantones 1** : canton **2** *Mex fam* : place, home
cantonés¹, -nesa *adj & n, mpl* **-neses** : Cantonese
cantonés² *nm, pl* **-neses** : Cantonese (language)
cantor¹, -tora *adj* **1** : singing **2 pájaro cantor** : songbird
cantor², -tora *n* **1** : singer **2** : cantor
caña *nf* **1** : cane ⟨caña de azúcar : sugarcane⟩ **2** : reed **3 caña de pescar** : fishing rod **4 caña del timón** : tiller (of a boat)
cañada *nf* : ravine, gully
cáñamo *nm* : hemp
cañaveral *nm* : sugarcane field
cañería *nf* TUBERÍA : pipes *pl*, piping
caño *nm* **1** : pipe **2** : spout **3** : channel (for navigation)
cañón *nm, pl* **cañones 1** : cannon **2** : barrel (of a gun) **3** : canyon
cañonear *vt* : to shell, to bombard
cañoneo *nm* : shelling, bombardment
cañonero *nm* : gunboat
caoba *nf* : mahogany
caolín *nm* : kaolin
caos *nm* : chaos
caótico, -ca *adj* : chaotic
capa *nf* **1** : cape, cloak **2** : coating **3** : layer, stratum **4** : (social) class, stratum
capacidad *nf* **1** : capacity **2** : capability, ability
capacitación *nf, pl* **-ciones** : training
capacitar *vt* : to train, to qualify
caparazón *nm, pl* **-zones** : shell, carapace
capataz *nmf, pl* **-taces** : foreman *m*, forewoman *f*
capaz *adj, pl* **capaces 1** APTO : capable, able **2** COMPETENTE : competent **3** : spacious ⟨capaz para : with room for⟩
capcioso, -sa *adj* : cunning, deceptive ⟨pregunta capciosa : trick question⟩

capea *nf* : amateur bullfight
capear *vt* **1** : to make a pass with the cape (in bullfighting) **2** : to dodge, to weather ⟨capear el temporal : to ride out the storm⟩
capellán *nm, pl* **-llanes** : chaplain
capilar *nm* : capillary — **capilar** *adj*
capilla *nf* : chapel
capirotada *nf Mex* : traditional bread pudding
capirotazo *nm* : flip, flick
capital¹ *adj* **1** : capital **2** : chief, principal
capital² *nm* : capital ⟨capital de riesgo : venture capital⟩
capital³ *nf* : capital, capital city
capitalino¹, -na *adj* : of or from a capital city
capitalino², -na *n* : inhabitant of a capital city
capitalismo *nm* : capitalism
capitalista *adj & nmf* : capitalist
capitalizar {21} *vt* : to capitalize — **capitalización** *nf*
capitán, -tana *n, mpl* **-tanes** : captain
capitanear *vt* : to captain, to command
capitanía *nf* : captaincy
capitel *nm* : capital (of a column)
capitolio *nm* : capitol
capitulación *nf, pl* **-ciones** : capitulation
capitular *vi* : to capitulate, to surrender
capítulo *nm* **1** : chapter, section **2** : matter, subject
capó *nm* : hood (of a car)
capón *nm, pl* **capones** : capon
caporal *nm* **1** : chief, leader **2** : foreman (on a ranch)
capota *nf* : top (of a convertible)
capote *nm* **1** : cloak, overcoat **2** : bullfighter's cape **3** *Mex* COFRE : hood (of a car)
capricho *nm* ANTOJO : whim, caprice
caprichoso, -sa *adj* ANTOJADIZO : capricious, fickle
Capricornio *nmf* : Capricorn
cápsula *nf* : capsule
captar *vt* **1** : to catch, to grasp **2** : to gain, to attract **3** : to harness, to collect (waters)
captor, -tora *n* : captor
captura *nf* : capture, seizure
capturar *vt* : to capture, to seize
capucha *nf* : hood, cowl
capuchina *nf* : nasturtium
capuchino *nm* **1** : Capuchin (monk) **2** : capuchin (monkey) **3** : cappuccino
capullo *nm* **1** : cocoon **2** : bud (of a flower)
caqui *adj & nm* : khaki
cara *nf* **1** : face **2** ASPECTO : look, appearance ⟨¡qué buena cara tiene ese pastel! : that cake looks delicious!⟩ **3** *fam* : nerve, gall **4 ~ a** *or* **de cara a** : facing **5 de cara a** : in view of, in the light of
carabina *nf* : carbine
caracol *nm* **1** : snail **2** CONCHA : conch, seashell **3** : cochlea **4** : ringlet

caracola *nf* : conch
carácter *nm, pl* **caracteres** 1 ÍNDOLE : character, kind, nature 2 TEMPERAMENTO : disposition, temperament 3 : letter, symbol ⟨caracteres chinos : Chinese characters⟩
característica *nf* RASGO : trait, feature, characteristic
característico, -ca *adj* : characteristic — **característicamente** *adv*
caracterizar {21} *vt* : to characterize — **caracterización** *nf*
caramba *interj* 1 (*expressing annoyance*) : darn!, heck! 2 (*expressing disgust or surprise*) : jeez!
carámbano *nm* : icicle
carambola *nf* 1 : carom 2 : ruse, trick ⟨por carambola : by a lucky chance⟩
caramelo *nm* 1 : caramel 2 DULCE : candy
caramillo *nm* 1 : pipe, small flute 2 : heap, pile
caraqueño¹, -ña *adj* : of or from Caracas
caraqueño², -ña *n* : person from Caracas
carátula *nf* 1 : title page 2 : cover, dust jacket 3 CARETA : mask 4 *Mex* : face, dial (of a clock or watch)
caravana *nf* 1 : caravan 2 : convoy, motorcade 3 REMOLQUE : trailer
caray → **caramba**
carbohidrato *nm* : carbohydrate
carbón *nm, pl* **carbones** 1 : coal 2 : charcoal
carbonatado, -da *adj* : carbonated
carbonato *nm* : carbonate
carboncillo *nm* : charcoal
carbonera *nf* : coal cellar, coal bunker (on a ship)
carbonero, -ra *adj* : coal
carbonizar {21} *vt* : to carbonize, to char
carbono *nm* : carbon
carbunco *or* **carbunclo** *nm* : carbuncle
carburador *nm* : carburetor
carburante *nm* : fuel
carca *nmf fam* : old fogy
carcacha *nf fam* : jalopy, wreck
carcaj *nm* : quiver (for arrows)
carcajada *nf* : loud laugh, guffaw ⟨reírse a carcajadas : to roar with laughter⟩
carcajearse *vr* : to roar with laughter, to be in stitches
cárcel *nf* PRISIÓN : jail, prison
carcelero, -ra *n* : jailer
carcinogénico, -ca *adj* : carcinogenic
carcinógeno *nm* CANCERÍGENO : carcinogen
carcinoma *nm* : carcinoma
carcomer *vt* : to eat away at, to consume
carcomido, -da *adj* 1 : worm-eaten 2 : decayed, rotten
cardán *nm, pl* **cardanes** : universal joint
cardar *vt* : to card, to comb
cardenal *nm* 1 : cardinal (in religion) 2 : bruise
cardíaco *or* **cardiaco, -ca** *adj* : cardiac, heart

cárdigan *nm, pl* **-gans** : cardigan
cardinal *adj* : cardinal
cardiología *nf* : cardiology
cardiólogo, -ga *n* : cardiologist
cardiovascular *adj* : cardiovascular
cardo *nm* : thistle
cardumen *nm* : school of fish
carear *vt* : to bring face-to-face
carecer {53} *vi* ~ **de** : to lack ⟨el cheque carecía de fondos : the check lacked funds⟩
carencia *nf* 1 FALTA : lack 2 ESCASEZ : shortage 3 DEFICIENCIA : deficiency
carente *adj* ~ **de** : lacking (in)
carero, -ra *adj fam* : pricey
carestía *nf* 1 : rise in cost ⟨la carestía de la vida : the high cost of living⟩ 2 : dearth, scarcity
careta *nf* MÁSCARA : mask
carey *nm* 1 : hawksbill turtle, sea turtle 2 : tortoiseshell
carga *nf* 1 : loading 2 : freight, load, cargo 3 : burden, responsibility 4 : charge ⟨carga eléctrica : electrical charge⟩ 5 : attack, charge
cargado, -da *adj* 1 : loaded 2 : bogged down, weighted down 3 : close, stuffy 4 : charged ⟨cargado de tensión : charged with tension⟩ 5 FUERTE : strong ⟨café cargado : strong coffee⟩ 6 **cargado de hombros** : stoop-shouldered
cargador¹, -dora *n* : longshoreman *m*, longshorewoman *f*
cargador² *nm* 1 : magazine (for a firearm) 2 : charger (for batteries)
cargamento *nm* : cargo, load
cargar {52} *vt* 1 : to carry 2 : to load, to fill 3 : to charge — *vi* 1 : to load 2 : to rest (in architecture) 3 ~ **sobre** : to fall upon
cargo *nm* 1 : burden, load 2 : charge ⟨a cargo de : in charge of⟩ 3 : position, office
cargue, etc. → **cargar**
carguero¹, -ra *adj* : freight, cargo ⟨tren carguero : freight train⟩
carguero² *nm* : freighter, cargo ship
cariarse *vr* : to decay (of teeth)
caribe *adj* : Caribbean ⟨el mar Caribe : the Caribbean Sea⟩
caribeño, -ña *adj* : Caribbean
caribú *nm* : caribou
caricatura *nf* 1 : caricature 2 : cartoon
caricaturista *nmf* : caricaturist, cartoonist
caricaturizar {21} *vt* : to caricature
caricia *nf* 1 : caress 2 **hacer caricias** : to pet, to stroke
caridad *nf* 1 : charity 2 LIMOSNA : alms *pl*
caries *nfs & pl* : cavity (in a tooth)
carillón *nm, pl* **-llones** 1 : carillon 2 : glockenspiel
cariño *nm* AFECTO : affection, love
cariñoso, -sa *adj* AFECTUOSO : affectionate, loving — **cariñosamente** *adv*
carioca¹ *adj* : of or from Rio de Janeiro

carioca² *nmf* : person from Rio de Janeiro
carisma *nf* : charisma
carismático, -ca *adj* : charismatic
carita *adj Mex fam* : cute (said of a man) ⟨tu primo se cree muy carita : your cousin thinks he's gorgeous⟩
caritativo, -va *adj* : charitable
cariz *nm, pl* **carices** : appearance, aspect
carmesí *adj & nm* : crimson
carmín *nm, pl* **carmines** 1 : carmine 2 **carmín de labios** : lipstick
carnada *nf* CEBO : bait
carnal *adj* 1 : carnal 2 **primo carnal** : first cousin
carnaval *nm* : carnival
carnaza *nf* : bait
carne *nf* 1 : meat ⟨carne molida : ground beef⟩ 2 : flesh ⟨carne de gallina : goose bumps⟩
carné → **carnet**
carnero *nm* 1 : ram, sheep 2 : mutton
carnet *nm* 1 : identification card, ID 2 : membership card 3 **carnet de conducir** *Spain* : driver's license
carnicería *nf* 1 : butcher shop 2 MATANZA : slaughter, carnage
carnicero, -ra *n* : butcher
carnívoro¹, -ra *adj* : carnivorous
carnívoro² *nm* : carnivore
carnoso, -sa *adj* : fleshy, meaty
caro¹ *adv* : dearly, a lot ⟨pagué caro : I paid a high price⟩
caro², -ra *adj* 1 : expensive, dear 2 QUERIDO : dear, beloved
carpa *nf* 1 : carp 2 : big top (of a circus) 3 : tent
carpelo *nm* : carpel
carpeta *nf* : folder, binder, portfolio (of drawings, etc.)
carpetazo *nm* **dar carpetazo a** : to shelve, to defer
carpintería *nf* 1 : carpentry 2 : carpenter's workshop
carpintero, -ra *n* : carpenter
carraspear *vi* : to clear one's throat
carraspera *nf* : hoarseness ⟨tener carraspera : to have a frog in one's throat⟩
carrera *nf* 1 : run, running ⟨a la carrera : at full speed⟩ ⟨de carrera : hastily⟩ 2 : race 3 : course of study 4 : career, profession 5 : run (in baseball)
carreta *nf* : cart, wagon
carrete *nm* 1 BOBINA : reel, spool 2 : roll of film
carretel → **carrete**
carretera *nf* : highway, road ⟨carretera de peaje : turnpike⟩
carretero, -ra *adj* : highway ⟨el sistema carretero nacional : the national highway system⟩
carretilla *nf* 1 : wheelbarrow 2 **carretilla elevadora** : forklift
carril *nm* 1 : lane ⟨carretera de doble carril : two-lane highway⟩ 2 : rail (on a railroad track)
carrillo *nm* : cheek, jowl

carrito *nm* : cart ⟨carrito de compras : shopping cart⟩
carrizo *nm* JUNCO : reed
carro *nm* 1 COCHE : car 2 : cart 3 *Chile, Mex* : coach (of a train) 4 **carro alegórico** : float (in a parade)
carrocería *nf* : bodywork, body (of a vehicle)
carroña *nf* : carrion
carroñero, -ra *n* : scavenger (animal)
carroza *nf* 1 : carriage 2 : float (in a parade)
carruaje *nm* : carriage
carrusel *nm* 1 : merry-go-round 2 : carousel ⟨carrusel de equipaje : luggage carousel⟩
carta *nf* 1 : letter 2 NAIPE : playing card 3 : charter, constitution 4 MENÚ : menu 5 : map, chart 6 **tomar cartas en** : to intervene in
cártamo *nm* : safflower
cartearse *vr* ESCRIBIRSE : to write to one another, to correspond
cartel *nm* : sign, poster
cártel *or* **cartel** *nm* : cartel
cartelera *nf* 1 : billboard 2 : marquee
cartera *nf* 1 BILLETERA : wallet, billfold 2 BOLSO : pocketbook, purse 3 : portfolio ⟨cartera de acciones : stock portfolio⟩
carterista *nmf* : pickpocket
cartero, -ra *n* : letter carrier, mailman *m*
cartilaginoso, -sa *adj* : cartilaginous, gristly
cartílago *nm* : cartilage
cartilla *nf* 1 : primer, reader 2 : booklet ⟨cartilla de ahorros : bankbook⟩
cartografía *nf* : cartography
cartógrafo, -fa *n* : cartographer
cartón *nm, pl* **cartones** 1 : cardboard ⟨cartón madera : fiberboard⟩ 2 : carton
cartucho *nm* : cartridge
cartulina *nf* : poster board, cardboard
carúncula *nf* : wattle (of a bird)
casa *nf* 1 : house, building 2 HOGAR : home 3 : household, family 4 : company, firm 5 **echar la casa por la ventana** : to spare no expense
casaca *nf* : jacket
casado¹, -da *adj* : married
casado², -da *n* : married person
casamentero, -ra *n* : matchmaker
casamiento *nm* 1 : marriage 2 BODA : wedding
casar *vt* : to marry — *vi* : to go together, to match up — **casarse** *vr* 1 : to get married 2 ~ **con** : to marry
casateniente *nmf Mex* : landlord, landlady *f*
cascabel¹ *nm* : small bell
cascabel² *nf* : rattlesnake
cascada *nf* CATARATA, SALTO : waterfall, cascade
cascajo *nm* 1 : pebble, rock fragment 2 *fam* : piece of junk
cascanueces *nms & pl* : nutcracker

cascar {72} *vt* : to crack (a shell) — **cascarse** *vr* : to crack, to chip

cáscara *nf* **1** : skin, peel, rind, husk **2** : shell (of a nut or egg)

cascarón *nm, pl* **-rones 1** : eggshell **2** *Mex* : shell filled with confetti

cascarrabias *nmfs & pl fam* : grouch, crab

casco *nm* **1** : helmet **2** : hull **3** : hoof **4** : fragment, shard **5** : center (of a town) **6** *Mex* : empty bottle **7 cascos** *nmpl* : headphones

caserío *nm* **1** : country house **2** : hamlet

casero¹, -ra *adj* **1** : domestic, household **2** : homemade

casero², -ra *n* DUEÑO : landlord *m*, landlady *f*

caseta *nf* : booth, stand, stall ⟨caseta telefónica : telephone booth⟩

casete → **cassette**

casi *adv* **1** : almost, nearly, virtually **2** (*in negative phrases*) : hardly ⟨casi nunca : hardly ever⟩

casilla *nf* **1** : booth **2** : pigeonhole **3** : box (on a form)

casino *nm* **1** : casino **2** : (social) club

caso *nm* **1** : case **2 en caso de** : in case of, in the event of **3 hacer caso de** : to pay attention to, to notice **4 hacer caso omiso de** : to ignore, to take no notice of **5 no venir al caso** : to be beside the point

caspa *nf* : dandruff

casque, etc. → **cascar**

casquete *nm* **1** : skullcap **2 casquete glaciar** : ice cap **3 casquete corto** *Mex* : crew cut

casquillo *nm* : case, casing (of a bullet)

cassette *nmf* : cassette

casta *nf* **1** : caste **2** : lineage, stock ⟨de casta : thoroughbred, purebred⟩ **3 sacar la casta** *Mex* : to come out ahead

castaña *nf* : chestnut

castañetear *vi* : to chatter (of teeth)

castaño¹, -ña *adj* : chestnut, brown

castaño² *nm* **1** : chestnut tree **2** : chestnut, brown

castañuela *nf* : castanet

castellano¹, -na *adj & n* : Castilian

castellano² *nm* ESPAÑOL : Spanish, Castilian (language)

castidad *nf* : chastity

castigar {52} *vt* : to punish

castigo *nm* : punishment

castillo *nm* **1** : castle **2 castillo de proa** : forecastle

casto, -ta *adj* : chaste, pure — **castamente** *adv*

castor *nm* : beaver

castración *nf, pl* **-ciones** : castration

castrar *vt* **1** : to castrate, to spay, to neuter, to geld **2** DEBILITAR : to weaken, to debilitate

castrense *adj* : military

casual *adj* **1** FORTUITO : fortuitous, accidental **2** *Mex* : casual (of clothing)

casualidad *nf* **1** : chance **2 por** ∼ or **de** ∼ : by chance, by any chance

casualmente *adv* : accidentally, by chance

casucha *or* **casuca** *nf* : shanty, hovel

cataclismo *nm* : cataclysm

catacumbas *nfpl* : catacombs

catador, -dora *n* : wine taster

catalán¹, -lana *adj & n, mpl* **-lanes** : Catalan

catalán² *nm* : Catalan (language)

catálisis *nf* : catalysis

catalítico, -ca *adj* : catalytic

catalizador *nm* **1** : catalyst **2** : catalytic converter

catalogar {52} *vt* : to catalog, to classify

catálogo *nm* : catalog

catamarán *nm, pl* **-ranes** : catamaran

cataplasma *nf* : poultice

catapulta *nf* : catapult

catapultar *vt* : to catapult

catar *vt* **1** : to taste, to sample **2** : to look at, to examine

catarata *nf* **1** CASCADA, SALTO : waterfall **2** : cataract

catarro *nm* RESFRIADO : cold, catarrh

catarsis *nf* : catharsis

catártico, -ca *adj* : cathartic

catástrofe *nf* DESASTRE : catastrophe, disaster

catastrófico, -ca *adj* DESASTROSO : catastrophic, disastrous

catcher *nmf* : catcher (in baseball)

catecismo *nm* : catechism

cátedra *nf* **1** : chair, professorship **2** : subject, class **3 libertad de cátedra** : academic freedom

catedral *nf* : cathedral

catedrático, -ca *n* PROFESOR : professor

categoría *nf* **1** CLASE : category **2** RANGO : rank, standing **3 categoría gramatical** : part of speech **4 de** ∼ : first-rate, outstanding

categórico, -ca *adj* : categorical, unequivocal — **categóricamente** *adv*

catéter *nm* : catheter

cátodo *nm* : cathode

catolicismo *nm* : Catholicism

católico, -ca *adj & n* : Catholic

catorce *adj & nm* : fourteen

catorceavo *adj* : fourteenth

catre *nm* : cot

catsup *nm* : ketchup

caucásico, -ca *adj & n* : Caucasian

cauce *nm* **1** LECHO : riverbed **2** : means *pl*, channel

caucho *nm* **1** GOMA : rubber **2** : rubber tree **3** *Ven* : tire

caución *nf, pl* **cauciones** FIANZA : bail, security

caudal *nm* **1** : volume of water **2** RIQUEZA : capital, wealth **3** ABUNDANCIA : abundance

caudilllaje *nm* : leadership

caudillo *nm* : leader, commander

causa *nf* **1** MOTIVO : cause, reason, motive ⟨a causa de : because of⟩ **2** IDEAL : cause ⟨morir por una causa : to die for a cause⟩ **3** : lawsuit
causal[1] *adj* : causal
causal[2] *nm* : cause, grounds *pl*
causalidad *nf* : causality
causante[1] *adj* ~ **de** : causing, responsible for
causante[2] *nmf Mex* : taxpayer
causar *vt* **1** : to cause **2** : to provoke, to arouse ⟨eso me causa gracia : that strikes me as being funny⟩
cáustico, -ca *adj* : caustic
cautela *nf* : caution, prudence
cautelar *adj* : precautionary, preventive
cauteloso, -sa *adj* : cautious, prudent — **cautelosamente** *adv*
cauterizar {21} *vt* : to cauterize
cautivador, -dora *adj* : captivating
cautivar *vt* HECHIZAR : to captivate, to charm
cautiverio *nm* : captivity
cautivo, -va *adj & n* : captive
cauto, -ta *adj* : cautious, careful
cavar *vt* : to dig — *vi* ~ **en** : to delve into, to probe
caverna *nf* : cavern, cave
cavernoso, -sa *adj* **1** : cavernous **2** : deep, resounding
caviar *nm* : caviar
cavidad *nf* : cavity
cavilar *vi* : to ponder, to deliberate
cayado *nm* : crook, staff, crosier
cayena *nf* : cayenne pepper
cayó, etc. → **caer**
caza[1] *nf* **1** CACERÍA : hunt, hunting **2** : game
caza[2] *nm* : fighter plane
cazador, -dora *n* **1** : hunter **2 cazador furtivo** : poacher
cazar {21} *vt* **1** : to hunt **2** : to catch, to bag **3** *fam* : to land (a job, a spouse) — *vi* : to go hunting
cazatalentos *nmfs & pl* : talent scout
cazo *nm* **1** : saucepan, pot **2** CUCHARÓN : ladle
cazuela *nf* **1** : pan, saucepan **2** : casserole
cazurro, -ra *adj* : sullen, surly
CD *nm* : CD, compact disk
cebada *nf* : barley
cebar *vt* **1** : to bait **2** : to feed, to fatten **3** : to prime (a pump, etc.) — **cebarse** *vr* ~ **en** : to take it out on
cebo *nm* **1** CARNADA : bait **2** : feed **3** : primer (for firearms)
cebolla *nf* : onion
cebolleta *nf* : scallion, green onion
cebollino *nm* **1** : chive **2** : scallion
cebra *nf* : zebra
cebú *nm, pl* **cebús** *or* **cebúes** : zebu (cattle)
cecear *vi* : to lisp
ceceo *nm* : lisp
cecina *nf* : dried beef, beef jerky
cedazo *nm* : sieve

ceder *vi* **1** : to yield, to give way **2** : to diminish, to abate **3** : to give in, to relent — *vt* : to cede, to hand over
cedro *nm* : cedar
cédula *nf* : document, certificate
céfiro *nm* : zephyr
cegador, -dora *adj* : blinding
cegar {49} *vt* **1** : to blind **2** : to block, to stop up — *vi* : to be blinded, to go blind
cegatón, -tona *adj, mpl* **-tones** *fam* : blind as a bat
ceguera *nf* : blindness
ceiba *nf* : ceiba, silk-cotton tree
ceja *nf* **1** : eyebrow ⟨fruncir las cejas : to knit one's brows⟩ **2** : flange, rim
cejar *vi* : to give in, to back down
celada *nf* : trap, ambush
celador, -dora *n* GUARDIA : guard, warden
celda *nf* : cell (of a jail)
celebración *nf, pl* **-ciones** : celebration
celebrado, -da *adj* CÉLEBRE, FAMOSO : famous, celebrated
celebrante *nmf* OFICIANTE : celebrant
celebrar *vt* **1** FESTEJAR : to celebrate **2** : to hold (a meeting) **3** : to say (Mass) **4** : to welcome, to be happy about — *vi* : to be glad — **celebrarse** *vr* **1** : to be celebrated, to fall **2** : to be held, to take place
célebre *adj* CELEBRADO, FAMOSO : celebrated, famous
celebridad *nf* **1** : celebrity **2** FAMA : fame, renown
celeridad *nf* : celerity, swiftness
celeste[1] *adj* **1** : celestial **2** : sky blue, azure
celeste[2] *nm* : sky blue
celestial *adj* : heavenly, celestial
celibato *nm* : celibacy
célibe *adj & nmf* : celibate
cello *nm* : cello
celo *nm* **1** : zeal, fervor **2** : heat (of females), rut (of males) **3 celos** *nmpl* : jealousy ⟨tenerle celos a alguien : to be jealous of someone⟩
celofán *nm, pl* **-fanes** : cellophane
celosía *nf* **1** : lattice window **2** : latticework, trellis
celoso, -sa *adj* **1** : jealous **2** : zealous — **celosamente** *adv*
celta[1] *adj* : Celtic
celta[2] *nmf* : Celt
célula *nf* : cell
celular *adj* : cellular
celuloide *nm* **1** : celluloid **2** : film, cinema
celulosa *nf* : cellulose
cementar *vt* : to cement
cementerio *nm* : cemetery
cemento *nm* : cement
cena *nf* : supper, dinner
cenador *nm* : arbor
cenagal *nm* : bog, quagmire
cenagoso, -sa *adj* : swampy
cenar *vi* : to have dinner, to have supper — *vt* : to have for dinner or supper

⟨anoche cenamos tamales : we had tamales for supper last night⟩
cencerro *nm* : cowbell
cenicero *nm* : ashtray
ceniciento, -ta *adj* : ashen
cenit *nm* : zenith, peak
ceniza *nf* **1** : ash **2 cenizas** *nfpl* : ashes (of a deceased person)
cenizo, -za *n* : jinx
cenote *nm Mex* : natural deposit of spring water
censar *vt* : to take a census of
censo *nm* : census
censor, -sora *n* : censor, critic
censura *nf* **1** : censorship **2** : censure, criticism
censurable *adj* : reprehensible, blameworthy
censurar *vt* **1** : to censor **2** : to censure, to criticize
centauro *nm* : centaur
centavo *nm* **1** : cent (in English-speaking countries) **2** : unit of currency in various Latin-American countries
centella *nf* **1** : lightning flash **2** : spark
centellear *vi* **1** : to twinkle **2** : to gleam, to sparkle
centelleo *nm* : twinkling, sparkle
centenar *nm* **1** : hundred **2 a centenares** : by the hundreds
centenario¹, -ria *adj & n* : centenarian
centenario² *nm* : centennial
centeno *nm* : rye
centésimo¹, -ma *adj* : hundredth
centésimo² *nm* : hundredth
centígrado *adj* : centigrade, Celsius
centigramo *nm* : centigram
centímetro *nm* : centimeter
centinela *nmf* : sentinel, sentry
central¹ *adj* **1** : central **2** PRINCIPAL : main, principal
central² *nf* **1** : main office, headquarters **2 central camionera** *Mex* : bus terminal
centralita *nf* : switchboard
centralizar {21} *vt* : to centralize — **centralización** *nf*
centrar *vt* **1** : to center **2** : to focus — **centrarse** *vr* ~ **en** : to focus on, to concentrate on
céntrico, -ca *adj* : central
centrífugo, -ga *adj* : centrifugal
centrípeto, -ta *adj* : centripetal
centro¹ *nmf* : center (in sports)
centro² *nm* **1** MEDIO : center ⟨centro de atención : center of attention⟩ ⟨centro de gravedad : center of gravity⟩ **2** : downtown **3 centro de mesa** : centerpiece
centroamericano, -na *adj & n* : Central American
ceñido, -da *adj* AJUSTADO : tight, tight-fitting
ceñir {67} *vt* **1** : to encircle, to surround **2** : to hug, to cling to ⟨me ciñe demasiado : it's too tight on me⟩ — **ceñirse** *vr* ~ **a** : to restrict oneself to, to stick to

ceño *nm* **1** : frown, scowl **2 fruncir el ceño** : to frown, to knit one's brows
cepa *nf* **1** : stump (of a tree) **2** : stock (of a vine) **3** LINAJE : ancestry, stock
cepillar *vt* **1** : to brush **2** : to plane (wood) — **cepillarse** *vr*
cepillo *nm* **1** : brush ⟨cepillo de dientes : toothbrush⟩ **2** : plane (for woodworking)
cepo *nm* : trap (for animals)
cera *nf* **1** : wax ⟨cera de abejas : beeswax⟩ **2** : polish
cerámica *nf* **1** : ceramics *pl* **2** : pottery
cerámico, -ca *adj* : ceramic
ceramista *nmf* ALFARERO : potter
cerca¹ *adv* **1** : close, near, nearby **2** ~ **de** : nearly, almost
cerca² *nf* **1** : fence **2** : (stone) wall
cercado *nm* : enclosure
cercanía *nf* **1** PROXIMIDAD : proximity, closeness **2 cercanías** *nfpl* : outskirts, suburbs
cercano, -na *adj* : near, close
cercar {72} *vt* **1** : to fence in, to enclose **2** : to surround
cercenar *vt* **1** : to cut off, to amputate **2** : to diminish, to curtail
cerceta *nf* : teal (duck)
cerciorarse *vr* ASEGURARSE ~ **de** : to make sure of, to verify
cerco *nm* **1** : siege **2** : cordon, circle **3** : fence
cerda *nf* **1** : bristle **2** : sow
cerdo *nm* **1** : pig, hog **2 carne de cerdo** : pork
cereal *nm* : cereal — **cereal** *adj*
cerebelo *nm* : cerebellum
cerebral *adj* : cerebral
cerebro *nm* : brain
ceremonia *nf* : ceremony — **ceremonial** *adj*
ceremonioso, -sa *adj* : ceremonious
cereza *nf* : cherry
cerezo *nm* : cherry tree
cerilla *nf* **1** : match **2** : earwax
cerillo *nm* (in various countries) : match
cerner {56} *vt* : to sift — **cernerse** *vr* **1** : to hover **2** ~ **sobre** : to loom over, to threaten
cernidor *nm* : sieve
cernir → **cerner**
cero *nm* : zero
ceroso, -sa *adj* : waxy
cerque, etc. → **cercar**
cerquita *adv fam* : very close, very near
cerrado, -da *adj* **1** : closed, shut **2** : thick, broad ⟨tiene un acento cerrado : she has a thick accent⟩ **3** : cloudy, overcast **4** : quiet, reserved **5** : dense, stupid
cerradura *nf* : lock
cerrajería *nf* : locksmith's shop
cerrajero, -ra *n* : locksmith
cerrar {55} *vt* **1** : to close, to shut **2** : to turn off **3** : to bring to an end — *vi* **1** : to close up, to lock up **2** : to close down — **cerrarse** *vr* **1** : to close **2** : to fasten, to button up **3** : to conclude, to end

cerrazón *nf, pl* **-zones** : obstinacy, stubbornness

cerro *nm* COLINA, LOMA : hill

cerrojo *nm* PESTILLO : bolt, latch

certamen *nm, pl* **-támenes** : competition, contest

certero, -ra *adj* : accurate, precise — **certeramente** *adv*

certeza *nf* : certainty

certidumbre *nf* : certainty

certificable *adj* : certifiable

certificación *nf, pl* **-ciones** : certification

certificado[1], **-da** *adj* 1 : certified 2 : registered (of mail)

certificado[2] *nm* 1 : certificate 2 : registered letter

certificar {72} *vt* 1 : to certify 2 : to register (mail)

cervato *nm* : fawn

cervecera *nf* : brewery

cervecería *nf* 1 : brewery 2 : beer hall, bar

cerveza *nf* : beer ⟨cerveza de barril : draft beer⟩

cervical *adj* : cervical

cerviz *nf, pl* **cervices** : nape of the neck, cervix

cesación *nf, pl* **-ciones** : cessation, suspension

cesante *adj* : laid off, unemployed

cesantía *nf* : unemployment

cesar *vi* : to cease, to stop — *vt* : to dismiss, to lay off

cesárea *nf* : cesarean, C-section

cese *nm* 1 : cessation, stop ⟨cese del fuego : cease-fire⟩ 2 : dismissal

cesio *nm* : cesium

cesión *nf, pl* **cesiones** : transfer, assignment ⟨cesión de bienes : transfer of property⟩

césped *nm* : lawn, grass

cesta *nf* 1 : basket 2 : jai alai racket

cesto *nm* 1 : hamper 2 : basket (in basketball) 3 **cesto de (la) basura** : wastebasket

cetrería *nf* : falconry

cetrino, -na *adj* : sallow

cetro *nm* : scepter

chabacano[1], **-na** *adj* : tacky, tasteless

chabacano[2] *nm Mex* : apricot

chacal *nm* : jackal

cháchara *nf fam* 1 : small talk, chatter 2 **chácharas** *nfpl* : trinkets, junk

chacharear *vi fam* : to chatter, to gab

chacra *nf Arg, Chile, Peru* : small farm

chadiano, -na *adj & n* : Chadian

chal *nm* MANTÓN : shawl

chalado[1], **-da** *adj fam* : crazy, nuts

chalado[2], **-da** *n* : nut, crazy person

chalán *nm, pl* **chalanes** *Mex* : barge

chalé → **chalet**

chaleco *nm* : vest

chalet *nm Spain* : house

chalupa *nf* 1 : small boat 2 *Mex* : small stuffed tortilla

chamaco, -ca *n Mex fam* : kid, boy *m*, girl *f*

chamarra *nf* 1 : sheepskin jacket 2 : poncho, blanket

chamba *nf Mex, Peru fam* : job, work

chambear *vi Mex, Peru fam* : to work

chamo, -ma *n Ven fam* 1 : kid, boy *m*, girl *f* 2 : buddy, pal

champaña *or* **champán** *nm* : champagne

champiñón *nm, pl* **-ñones** : mushroom

champú *nm, pl* **-pus** *or* **-púes** : shampoo

champurrado *nm Mex* : hot chocolate thickened with cornstarch

chamuco *nm Mex fam* : devil

chamuscar {72} *vt* : to singe, to scorch — **chamuscarse** *vr*

chamusquina *nf* : scorch

chance *nm* OPORTUNIDAD : chance, opportunity

chancho[1], **-cha** *adj fam* : dirty, filthy, gross

chancho[2], **-cha** *n* 1 : pig, hog 2 *fam* : slob

chanchullero, -ra *adj fam* : shady, crooked

chanchullo *nm fam* : shady deal, scam

chancla *nf* 1 : thong sandal, slipper 2 : old shoe

chancleta → **chancla**

chanclo *nm* 1 : clog 2 **chanclos** *nmpl* : overshoes, galoshes, rubbers

chancro *nm* : chancre

changarro *nm Mex* : small shop, stall

chango, -ga *n Mex* : monkey

chantaje *nm* : blackmail

chantajear *vt* : to blackmail

chantajista *nmf* : blackmailer

chanza *nf* 1 : joke, jest 2 *Mex fam* : chance, opportunity

chapa *nf* 1 : sheet, panel, veneer 2 : lock 3 : badge

chapado, -da *adj* 1 : plated 2 **chapado a la antigua** : old-fashioned

chapar *vt* 1 : to veneer 2 : to plate (metals)

chaparrón *nm, pl* **-rrones** 1 : downpour 2 : great quantity, torrent

chapeado, -da *adj Col, Mex* : flushed

chapopote *nm Mex* : tar, blacktop

chapotear *vi* : to splash about

chapucero[1], **-ra** *adj* 1 : crude, shoddy 2 *Mex fam* : dishonest

chapucero[2], **-ra** *n* 1 : sloppy worker, bungler 2 *Mex fam* : cheat, swindler

chapulín *nm, pl* **-lines** *CA, Mex* : grasshopper, locust

chapuza *nf* 1 : botched job 2 *Mex fam* : fraud, trick ⟨hacer chapuzas : to cheat⟩

chapuzón *nm, pl* **-zones** : dip, swim ⟨darse un chapuzón : to go for a quick dip⟩

chaqueta *nf* : jacket

charada *nf* : charades (game)

charango *nm* : traditional Andean stringed instrument

charca *nf* : pond, pool

charco *nm* : puddle, pool

charcutería *nf* : delicatessen
charla *nf* : chat, talk
charlar *vi* : to chat, to talk
charlatán[1], **-tana** *adj* : talkative, chatty
charlatán[2], **-tana** *n, mpl* **-tanes** 1 : chatterbox 2 FARSANTE : charlatan, phony
charlatanear *vi* : to chatter away
charol *nm* 1 : lacquer, varnish 2 : patent leather 3 : tray
charola *nf Bol, Mex, Peru* : tray
charreada *nf Mex* : charro show, rodeo
charretera *nf* : epaulet
charro[1], **-rra** *adj* 1 : gaudy, tacky 2 *Mex* : pertaining to charros
charro[2], **-rra** *n Mex* : charro (Mexican cowboy or cowgirl)
chascarrillo *nm fam* : joke, funny story
chasco *nm* 1 BROMA : trick, joke 2 DECEPCIÓN, DESILUSIÓN : disillusionment, disappointment
chasis *or* **chasís** *nm* : chassis
chasquear *vt* 1 : to click (the tongue, fingers, etc.) 2 : to snap (a whip)
chasquido *nm* 1 : click (of the tongue or fingers) 2 : snap, crack
chatarra *nf* : scrap metal
chato, -ta *adj* 1 : pug-nosed 2 : flat
chauvinismo *nm* : chauvinism
chauvinista[1] *adj* : chauvinistic
chauvinista[2] *nmf* : chauvinist
chaval, -vala *n fam* : kid, boy *m*, girl *f*
chavo[1], **-va** *adj Mex fam* : young
chavo[2], **-va** *n Mex fam* : kid, boy *m*, girl *f*
chavo[3] *nm fam* : cent, buck ⟨no tengo un chavo : I'm broke⟩
chayote *nm* : chayote (plant, fruit)
checar {72} *vt Mex* : to check, to verify
checo[1], **-ca** *adj & n* : Czech
checo[2] *nm* : Czech (language)
checoslovaco, -ca *adj & n* : Czechoslovakian
chef *nm* : chef
chelín *nm, pl* **chelines** : shilling
cheque[1], **etc.** → **checar**
cheque[2] *nm* 1 : check 2 **cheque de viajero** : traveler's check
chequear *vt* 1 : to check, to verify 2 : to check in (baggage)
chequeo *nm* 1 INSPECCIÓN : check, inspection 2 : checkup, examination
chequera *nf* : checkbook
chévere *adj fam* : great, fantastic
chic *adj & nm* : chic
chica → **chico**
chicano, -na *adj & n* : Chicano *m*, Chicana *f*
chicha *nf* : fermented alcoholic beverage made from corn
chícharo *nm* : pea
chicharra *nf* 1 CIGARRA : cicada 2 : buzzer
chicharrón *nm, pl* **-rrones** 1 : pork rind 2 **darle chicharrón a** *Mex fam* : to get rid of
chichón *nm, pl* **chichones** : bump, swelling

chicle *nm* : chewing gum
chicloso *nm Mex* : taffy
chico[1], **-ca** *adj* 1 : little, small 2 : young
chico[2], **-ca** *n* 1 : child, boy *m*, girl *f* 2 : young man *m*, young woman *f*
chicote *nm* LÁTIGO : whip, lash
chiffon → **chifón**
chiflado[1], **-da** *adj fam* : nuts, crazy
chiflado[2], **-da** *n fam* : crazy person, lunatic
chiflar *vi* : to whistle — *vt* : to whistle at, to boo — **chiflarse** *vr fam* ∼ **por** : to be crazy about
chiflido *nm* : whistle, whistling
chiflón *nm, pl* **chiflones** : draft (of air)
chifón *nm, pl* **chifones** : chiffon
chilango[1], **-ga** *adj Mex fam* : of or from Mexico City
chilango[2], **-ga** *n Mex fam* : person from Mexico City
chilaquiles *nmpl Mex* : shredded tortillas in sauce
chile *nm* : chili pepper
chileno, -na *adj & n* : Chilean
chillar *vi* 1 : to squeal, to screech 2 : to scream, to yell 3 : to be gaudy, to clash
chillido *nm* 1 : scream, shout 2 : squeal, screech, cry (of an animal)
chillo *nm PRi* : red snapper
chillón, -llona *adj, mpl* **chillones** 1 : piercing, shrill 2 : loud, gaudy
chilpayate *nmf Mex fam* : child, little kid
chimenea *nf* 1 : chimney 2 : fireplace
chimichurri *nm Arg* : traditional hot sauce
chimpancé *nm* : chimpanzee
china *nf* 1 : pebble, small stone 2 *PRi* : orange
chinchar *vt fam* : to annoy, to pester — **chincharse** *vr fam* : to put up with something, to grin and bear it
chinchayote *nm Mex* : chayote root
chinche[1] *nf* 1 : bedbug 2 *Ven* : ladybug 3 : thumbtack
chinche[2] *nmf fam* : nuisance, pain in the neck
chinchilla *nf* : chinchilla
chino[1], **-na** *adj* 1 : Chinese 2 *Mex* : curly, kinky
chino[2], **-na** *n* : Chinese person
chino[3] *nm* : Chinese (language)
chip *nm, pl* **chips** : chip ⟨chip de memoria : memory chip⟩
chipote *nm Mex fam* : bump (on the head)
chipotle *nm Mex* : type of chili pepper
chipriota *adj & nmf* : Cypriot
chiquear *vt Mex* : to spoil, to indulge
chiquero *nm* POCILGA : pigpen, pigsty
chiquillada *nf* : childish prank
chiquillo[1], **-lla** *adj* : very young, little
chiquillo[2], **-lla** *n* : kid, youngster
chiquito[1], **-ta** *adj* : tiny
chiquito[2], **-ta** *n* : little one, baby
chiribita *nf* 1 : spark 2 **chiribitas** *nfpl* : spots before the eyes
chiribitil *nm* 1 DESVÁN : attic, garret 2 : cubbyhole

chirigota *nf fam* : joke
chirimía *nf* : traditional reed pipe
chirimoya *nf* : cherimoya, custard apple
chiripa *nf* **1** : fluke **2 de ~** : by sheer luck
chirivía *nf* : parsnip
chirona *nf fam* : slammer, jail
chirriar {85} *vi* **1** : to squeak, to creak **2** : to screech — chirriante *adj*
chirrido *nm* **1** : squeak, squeaking **2** : screech, screeching
chirrión *nm, pl* chirriones *Mex* : whip, lash
chisme *nm* **1** : gossip, tale **2** *Spain fam* : gadget, thingamajig
chismear *vi* : to gossip
chismoso[1], -sa *adj* : gossipy, gossiping
chismoso[2], -sa *n* **1** : gossiper, gossip **2** *Mex fam* : tattletale
chispa[1] *adj* **1** *Mex fam* : lively, vivacious ⟨un perrito chispa : a frisky puppy⟩ **2** *Spain fam* : tipsy
chispa[2] *nf* **1** : spark **2 echar chispas** : to be furious
chispeante *adj* : sparkling, scintillating
chispear *vi* **1** : to give off sparks **2** : to sparkle
chisporrotear *vi* : to crackle, to sizzle
chiste *nm* **1** : joke, funny story **2 tener chiste** : to be funny **3 tener su chiste** *Mex* : to be tricky
chistoso[1], -sa *adj* **1** : funny, humorous **2** : witty
chistoso[2], -sa *n* : wit, joker
chivas *nfpl Mex fam* : stuff, odds and ends
chivo[1], -va *n* **1** : kid, young goat **2 chivo expiatorio** : scapegoat
chivo[2] *nm* **1** : billy goat **2** : fit of anger
chocante *adj* **1** : shocking **2** : unpleasant, rude
chocar {72} *vi* **1** : to crash, to collide **2** : to clash, to conflict **3** : to be shocking ⟨le chocó : he was shocked⟩ **4** *Mex, Ven fam* : to be unpleasant or obnoxious ⟨me choca tu jefe : I can't stand your boss⟩ — *vt* **1** : to shake (hands) **2** : to clink glasses
chochear *vi* **1** : to be senile **2 ~ por** : to dote on, to be soft on
chochín *nm, pl* -chines : wren
chocho, -cha *adj* **1** : senile **2** : doting
choclo *nm* **1** : ear of corn, corncob **2** : corn **3 meter el choclo** *Mex fam* : to make a mistake
chocolate *nm* **1** : chocolate **2** : hot chocolate, cocoa
chofer *or* chófer *nm* **1** : chauffeur **2** : driver
choke *nm* : choke (of an automobile)
chole *interj Mex fam* ¡ya chole! : enough!, cut it out!
cholo, -la *adj & n* : mestizo
cholla *nf fam* : head
chollo *nm Spain fam* : bargain
chongo *nm* **1** *Mex* : bun (chignon) **2** chongos *nmpl Mex* : dessert made with fried bread

choque[1], etc. → chocar
choque[2] *nm* **1** : crash, collision **2** : clash, conflict **3** : shock
chorizo *nm* : chorizo, sausage
chorrear *vi* **1** : to drip **2** : to pour out, to gush out
chorrito *nm* : squirt, splash
chorro *nm* **1** : flow, stream, jet **2** *Mex fam* : heap, ton
choteado, -da *adj Mex fam* : worn-out, stale ⟨esa canción está bien choteada : that song's been played to death⟩
chotear *vt* : to make fun of
choteo *nm* : joking around, kidding
chovinismo, chovinista → chauvinismo, chauvinista
choza *nf* BARRACA, CABAÑA : hut, shack
chubasco *nm* : downpour, storm
chuchería *nf* : knickknack, trinket
chueco, -ca *adj* **1** : crooked, bent **2** *Chile, Mex fam* : dishonest, shady
chulada *nf Mex, Spain fam* : cute or pretty thing ⟨¡qué chulada de vestido! : what a lovely dress!⟩
chulear *vt Mex fam* : to compliment
chuleta *nf* : cutlet, chop
chulo[1], -la *adj* **1** *fam* : cute, pretty **2** *Spain fam* : cocky, arrogant
chulo[2] *nm Spain* : pimp
chupada *nf* **1** : suck, sucking **2** : puff, drag (on a cigarette)
chupado, -da *adj fam* **1** : gaunt, skinny **2** : plastered, drunk
chupaflor *nm* COLIBRÍ : hummingbird
chupamirto *nm Mex* : hummingbird
chupar *vt* **1** : to suck **2** : to absorb **3** : to puff on **4** *fam* : to drink, to guzzle — *vi* : to suckle — chuparse *vr* **1** : to waste away **2** *fam* : to put up with **3** ¡chúpate esa! *fam* : take that!
chupete *nm* **1** : pacifier **2** *Chile, Peru* : lollipop
chupetear *vt* : to suck (at)
chupón *nm, pl* chupones **1** : sucker (of a plant) **2** : baby bottle, pacifier
churrasco *nm* **1** : steak **2** : barbecued meat
churro *nm* **1** : fried dough **2** *fam* : botch, mess **3** *fam* : attractive person, looker
chusco, -ca *adj* : funny, amusing
chusma *nf* GENTUZA : riffraff, rabble
chutar *vi* : to shoot (in soccer)
chute *nm* : shot (in soccer)
cianuro *nm* : cyanide
cibernética *nf* : cybernetics
cicatriz *nf, pl* -trices : scar
cicatrizarse {21} *vr* : to form a scar, to heal
cíclico, -ca *adj* : cyclical
ciclismo *nm* : bicycling
ciclista *nmf* : bicyclist
ciclo *nm* : cycle
ciclomotor *nm* : moped
ciclón *nm, pl* ciclones : cyclone
cicuta *nf* : hemlock
cidra *nf* : citron (fruit)
ciega, ciegue etc. → cegar

ciego¹, -ga *adj* **1** INVIDENTE : blind **2 a ciegas** : blindly **3 quedarse ciego** : to go blind — **ciegamente** *adv*
ciego², -ga *n* INVIDENTE : blind person
cielo *nm* **1** : sky **2** : heaven **3** : ceiling
ciempiés *nms & pl* : centipede
cien¹ *adj* **1** : a hundred, hundred ⟨las primeras cien páginas : the first hundred pages⟩ **2 cien por cien** *or* **cien por ciento** : a hundred percent, through and through, wholeheartedly
cien² *nm* : one hundred
ciénaga *nf* : swamp, bog
ciencia *nf* **1** : science **2** : learning, knowledge **3 a ciencia cierta** : for a fact, for certain
cieno *nm* : mire, mud, silt
científico¹, -ca *adj* : scientific — **científicamente** *adv*
científico², -ca *n* : scientist
ciento¹ *adj* (*used in compound numbers*) : one hundred ⟨ciento uno : one hundred and one⟩
ciento² *nm* **1** : hundred, group of a hundred **2 por ~** : percent
cierne, etc. → **cerner**
cierra, etc. → **cerrar**
cierre *nm* **1** : closing, closure **2** : fastener, clasp, zipper
cierto, -ta *adj* **1** : true, certain, definite ⟨lo cierto es que . . . : the fact is that . . . ⟩ **2** : certain, one ⟨cierto día de verano : one summer day⟩ ⟨bajo ciertas circunstancias : under certain circumstances⟩ **3 por ~** : in fact, as a matter of fact — **ciertamente** *adv*
ciervo, -va *n* : deer, stag *m*, hind *f*
cifra *nf* **1** : figure, number **2** : quantity, amount **3** CLAVE : code, cipher
cifrar *vt* **1** : to write in code **2** : to place, to pin ⟨cifró su esperanza en la lotería : he pinned his hopes on the lottery⟩ — **cifrarse** *vr* : to amount ⟨la multa se cifra en millares : the fine amounts to thousands⟩
cigarra *nf* CHICHARRA : cicada
cigarrera *nf* : cigarette case
cigarrillo *nm* : cigarette
cigarro *nm* **1** : cigarette **2** PURO : cigar
cigoto *nm* : zygote
cigüeña *nf* : stork
cilantro *nm* : cilantro, coriander
cilíndrico, -ca *adj* : cylindrical
cilindro *nm* : cylinder
cima *nf* CUMBRE : peak, summit, top
cimarrón, -rrona *adj, mpl* **-rrones** : untamed, wild
címbalo *nm* : cymbal
cimbel *nm* : decoy
cimbrar *vt* : to shake, to rock — **cimbrarse** *vr* : to sway, to swing
cimentar {55} *vt* **1** : to lay the foundation of, to establish **2** : to strengthen, to cement
cimientos *nmpl* : base, foundation(s)
cinc *nm* : zinc
cincel *nm* : chisel

cincelar *vt* **1** : to chisel **2** : to engrave
cincha *nf* : cinch, girth
cinchar *vt* : to cinch (a horse)
cinco *adj & nm* : five
cincuenta *adj & nm* : fifty
cincuentavo¹, -va *adj* : fiftieth
cincuentavo² *nm* : fiftieth (fraction)
cine *nm* **1** : cinema, movies *pl* **2** : movie theater
cineasta *nmf* : filmmaker
cinematográfico, -ca *adj* : movie, film, cinematic ⟨la industria cinematográfica : the film industry⟩
cingalés¹, -lesa *adj & n* : Sinhalese
cingalés² *nm* : Sinhalese (language)
cínico¹, -ca *adj* **1** : cynical **2** : shameless, brazen — **cínicamente** *adv*
cínico², -ca *n* : cynic
cinismo *nm* : cynicism
cinta *nf* **1** : ribbon **2** : tape ⟨cinta métrica : tape measure⟩ **3** : strap, belt ⟨cinta transportadora : conveyor belt⟩
cinto *nm* : strap, belt
cintura *nf* **1** : waist, waistline **2 meter en cintura** *fam* : to bring into line, to discipline
cinturón *nm, pl* **-rones** **1** : belt **2 cinturón de seguridad** : seat belt
ciñe, etc. → **ceñir**
ciprés *nm, pl* **cipreses** : cypress
circo *nm* : circus
circón *nm, pl* **circones** : zircon
circonio *nm* : zirconium
circuitería *nf* : circuitry
circuito *nm* : circuit
circulación *nf, pl* **-ciones** **1** : circulation **2** : movement **3** : traffic
circular¹ *vi* **1** : to circulate **2** : to move along **3** : to drive
circular² *adj* : circular
circular³ *nf* : circular, flier
circulatorio, -ria *adj* : circulatory
círculo *nm* **1** : circle **2** : club, group
circuncidar *vt* : to circumcise
circuncisión *nf, pl* **-siones** : circumcision
circundar *vt* : to surround — **circundante** *adj*
circunferencia *nf* : circumference
circunflejo, -ja *adj* **acento circunflejo** : circumflex
circunlocución *nf, pl* **-ciones** : circumlocution
circunloquio *nm* → **circunlocución**
circunnavegar {52} *vt* : to circumnavigate — **circunnavegación** *nf*
circunscribir {33} *vt* : to circumscribe, to constrict, to limit — **circunscribirse** *vr*
circunscripción *nf, pl* **-ciones** **1** : limitation, restriction **2** : constituency
circunscrito *pp* → **circunscribir**
circunspección *nf, pl* **-ciones** : circumspection, prudence
circunspecto, -ta *adj* : circumspect, prudent
circunstancia *nf* : circumstance
circunstancial *adj* : circumstantial, incidental

circunstante *nmf* **1** : onlooker, bystander **2 los circunstantes** : those present

circunvalación *nf, pl* **-ciones** : surrounding, encircling ⟨carretera de circunvalación : bypass, beltway⟩

circunvecino, -na *adj* : surrounding, neighboring

cirio *nm* : large candle

cirro *nm* : cirrus (cloud)

cirrosis *nf* : cirrhosis

ciruela *nf* **1** : plum **2 ciruela pasa** : prune

cirugía *nf* : surgery

cirujano, -na *n* : surgeon

cisma *nm* : schism, rift

cisne *nm* : swan

cisterna *nf* : cistern, tank

cita *nf* **1** : quote, quotation **2** : appointment, date

citable *adj* : quotable

citación *nf, pl* **-ciones** EMPLAZAMIENTO : summons, subpoena

citadino[1], -na *adj* : of the city, urban

citadino[2], -na *n* : city dweller

citado, -da *adj* : said, aforementioned

citar *vt* **1** : to quote, to cite **2** : to make an appointment with **3** : to summon (to court), to subpoena — **citarse** *vr* ~ **con** : to arrange to meet (someone)

cítara *nf* : zither

citatorio *nm* : subpoena

citoplasma *nm* : cytoplasm

cítrico[1], -ca *adj* : citric

cítrico[2] *nm* : citrus fruit

ciudad *nf* **1** : city, town **2 ciudad universitaria** : college or university campus **3 ciudad perdida** *Mex* : shantytown

ciudadanía *nf* **1** : citizenship **2** : citizenry, citizens *pl*

ciudadano[1], -na *adj* : civic, city

ciudadano[2], -na *n* **1** NACIONAL : citizen **2** HABITANTE : resident, city dweller

ciudadela *nf* : citadel, fortress

cívico, -ca *adj* **1** : civic **2** : public-spirited

civil[1] *adj* **1** : civil **2** : civilian

civil[2] *nmf* : civilian

civilidad *nf* : civility, courtesy

civilización *nf, pl* **-ciones** : civilization

civilizar {21} *vt* : to civilize

civismo *nm* : community spirit, civic-mindedness, civics

cizaña *nf* : discord, rift

clamar *vi* : to clamor, to raise a protest — *vt* : to cry out for

clamor *nm* : clamor, outcry

clamoroso, -sa *adj* : clamorous, resounding, thunderous

clan *nm* : clan

clandestinidad *nf* : secrecy ⟨en la clandestinidad : underground⟩

clandestino, -na *adj* : clandestine, secret

clara *nf* : egg white

claraboya *nf* : skylight

claramente *adv* : clearly

clarear *v impers* **1** : to clear, to clear up **2** : to get light, to dawn — *vi* : to go gray, to turn white

claridad *nf* **1** NITIDEZ : clarity, clearness **2** : brightness, light

clarificación *nf, pl* **-ciones** ACLARACIÓN : clarification, explanation

clarificar {72} *vt* ACLARAR : to clarify, to explain

clarín *nm, pl* **clarines** : bugle

clarinete *nm* : clarinet

clarividencia *nf* **1** : clairvoyance **2** : perspicacity, discernment

clarividente[1] *adj* **1** : clairvoyant **2** : perspicacious, discerning

clarividente[2] *nmf* : clairvoyant

claro[1] *adv* **1** : clearly ⟨habla más claro : speak more clearly⟩ **2** : of course, surely ⟨¡claro!, ¡claro que sí! : absolutely!, of course!⟩ ⟨claro que entendió : of course she understood⟩

claro[2], -ra *adj* **1** : bright, clear **2** : pale, fair, light **3** : clear, evident

claro[3] *nm* **1** : clearing **2 claro de luna** : moonlight

clase *nf* **1** : class **2** ÍNDOLE, TIPO : sort, kind, type

clasicismo *nm* : classicism

clásico[1], -ca *adj* **1** : classic **2** : classical

clásico[2] *nm* : classic

clasificación *nf, pl* **-ciones** **1** : classification, sorting out **2** : rating **3** CALIFICACIÓN : qualification (in competitions)

clasificado, -da *adj* : classified ⟨aviso clasificado : classified ad⟩

clasificar {72} *vt* **1** : to classify, to sort out **2** : to rate, to rank — *vi* CALIFICAR : to qualify (in competitions) — **clasificarse** *vr*

claudicación *nf, pl* **-ciones** : surrender, abandonment of one's principles

claudicar {72} *vi* : to back down, to abandon one's principles

claustro *nm* : cloister

claustrofobia *nf* : claustrophobia

claustrofóbico, -ca *adj* : claustrophobic

cláusula *nf* : clause

clausura *nf* **1** : closure, closing **2** : closing ceremony **3** : cloister

clausurar *vt* **1** : to close, to bring to a close **2** : to close down

clavadista *nmf* : diver

clavado[1], -da *adj* **1** : nailed, fixed, stuck **2** *fam* : punctual, on the dot **3** *fam* : identical ⟨es clavado a su padre : he's the image of his father⟩

clavado[2] *nm* : dive

clavar *vt* **1** : to nail, to hammer **2** HINCAR : to plunge, to stick **3** : to fix (one's eyes) on — **clavarse** *vr* : to stick oneself (with a sharp object)

clave[1] *adj* : key, essential

clave[2] *nf* **1** CIFRA : code **2** : key ⟨la clave del misterio : the key to the mystery⟩ **3** : clef **4** : keystone

clavel *nm* : carnation

clavelito *nm* : pink (flower)

clavicémbalo *nm* : harpsichord
clavícula *nf* : collarbone
clavija *nf* **1** : plug **2** : peg, pin
clavo *nm* **1** : nail ⟨clavo grande : spike⟩ **2** : clove **3 dar en el clavo** : to hit the nail on the head
claxon *nm, pl* **cláxones** : horn (of an automobile)
clemencia *nf* : clemency, mercy
clemente *adj* : merciful
cleptomanía *nf* : kleptomania
cleptómano, -na *n* : kleptomaniac
clerecía *nf* : ministry, ministers *pl*
clerical *adj* : clerical
clérigo, -ga *n* : cleric, member of the clergy
clero *nm* : clergy
cliché *nm* **1** : cliché **2** : stencil **3** : negative (of a photograph)
cliente, -ta *n* : customer, client
clientela *nf* : clientele, customers *pl*
clima *nm* **1** : climate **2** AMBIENTE : atmosphere, ambience
climático, -ca *adj* : climatic
climatización *nf, pl* **-ciones** : air-conditioning
climatizar {21} *vt* : to air-condition — **climatizado, -da** *adj*
clímax *nm* : climax
clínica *nf* : clinic
clínico, -ca *adj* : clinical — **clínicamente** *adv*
clip *nm, pl* **clips** **1** : clip **2** : paper clip
clítoris *nms & pl* : clitoris
cloaca *nf* ALCANTARILLA : sewer
clocar {82} *vi* : to cluck
cloche *nm* CA, Car, Col, Ven : clutch (of an automobile)
clon *nm* : clone
cloqué, etc. → **clocar**
cloquear *vi* : to cluck
clorar *vt* : to chlorinate — **cloración** *nf*
cloro *nm* : chlorine
clorofila *nf* : chlorophyll
cloroformo *nm* : chloroform
cloruro *nm* : chloride
clóset *nm, pl* **clósets** **1** : closet **2** : cupboard
club *nm* : club
clueca, clueque etc. → **clocar**
coa *nf Mex* : hoe
coacción *nf, pl* **-ciones** : coercion, duress
coaccionar *vt* : to coerce
coactivo, -va *adj* : coercive
coagular *v* : to clot, to coagulate — **coagulación** *nf*
coágulo *nm* : clot
coalición *nf, pl* **-ciones** : coalition
coartada *nf* : alibi
coartar *vt* : to restrict, to limit
cobalto *nm* : cobalt
cobarde[1] *adj* : cowardly
cobarde[2] *nmf* : coward
cobardía *nf* : cowardice
cobaya *nf* : guinea pig
cobertizo *nm* : shed, shelter
cobertor *nm* COLCHA : bedspread, quilt

cobertura *nf* **1** : coverage **2** : cover, collateral
cobija *nf* FRAZADA, MANTA : blanket
cobijar *vt* : to shelter — **cobijarse** *vr* : to take shelter
cobra *nf* : cobra
cobrador, -dora *n* **1** : collector **2** : conductor (of a bus or train)
cobrar *vt* **1** : to charge **2** : to collect, to draw, to earn **3** : to acquire, to gain **4** : to recover, to retrieve **5** : to cash (a check) **6** : to claim, to take (a life) **7** : to shoot (game), to bag — *vi* **1** : to be paid **2 llamar por cobrar** *Mex* : to call collect
cobre *nm* : copper
cobrizo, -za *adj* : coppery
cobro *nm* : collection (of money), cashing (of a check)
coca *nf* **1** : coca **2** *fam* : coke, cocaine
cocaína *nf* : cocaine
cocal *nm* : coca plantation
cocción *nf, pl* **cocciones** : cooking
cocear *vi* : to kick (of an animal)
cocer {14} *vt* **1** COCINAR : to cook **2** HERVIR : to boil
cochambre *nmf fam* : filth, grime
cochambroso, -sa *adj* : filthy, grimy
coche *nm* **1** : car, automobile **2** : coach, carriage **3 coche cama** : sleeping car **4 coche fúnebre** : hearse
cochecito *nm* : baby carriage, stroller
cochera *nf* : garage, carport
cochinada *nf fam* **1** : filthy language **2** : disgusting behavior **3** : dirty trick
cochinillo *nm* : suckling pig, piglet
cochino[1], **-na** *adj* **1** : dirty, filthy, disgusting **2** *fam* : rotten, lousy
cochino[2], **-na** *n* : pig, hog
cocido[1], **-da** *adj* **1** : boiled, cooked **2 bien cocido** : well-done
cocido[2] *nm* ESTOFADO, GUISADO : stew
cociente *nm* : quotient
cocimiento *nm* : cooking, baking
cocina *nf* **1** : kitchen **2** : stove **3** : cuisine, cooking
cocinar *v* : to cook
cocinero, -ra *n* : cook, chef
cocineta *nf Mex* : kitchenette
coco *nm* **1** : coconut **2** *fam* : head **3** *fam* : bogeyman
cocoa *nf* : cocoa, hot chocolate
cocodrilo *nm* : crocodile
cocotero *nm* : coconut palm
coctel *or* **cóctel** *nm* **1** : cocktail **2** : cocktail party
coctelera *nf* : cocktail shaker
codazo *nm* **1 darle un codazo a** : to elbow, to nudge **2 abrirse paso a codazos** : to elbow one's way through
codearse *vr* : to rub elbows, to hobnob
códice *nm* : codex, manuscript
codicia *nf* AVARICIA : avarice, covetousness
codiciar *vt* : to covet
codicilo *nm* : codicil
codicioso, -sa *adj* : avaricious, covetous

codificación *nf, pl* **-ciones 1** : codification **2** : coding, encoding
codificar {72} *vt* **1** : to codify **2** : to code, to encode
código *nm* **1** : code **2 código postal** : zip code **3 código morse** : Morse code
codo[1], **-da** *adj Mex* : cheap, stingy
codo[2], **-da** *n Mex* : tightwad, cheapskate
codo[3] *nm* : elbow
codorniz *nf, pl* **-nices** : quail
coeficiente *nm* **1** : coefficient **2 coeficiente intelectual** : IQ, intelligence quotient
coexistir *vi* : to coexist — **coexistencia** *nf*
cofa *nf* : crow's nest
cofre *nm* **1** BAÚL : trunk, chest **2** *Mex* CAPOTE : hood (of a car)
coger {15} *vt* **1** : to seize, to take hold of **2** : to catch **3** : to pick up **4** : to gather, to pick **5** : to gore — **cogerse** *vr* AGARRARSE : to hold on
cogida *nf* **1** : gathering, harvest **2** : goring
cognición *nf, pl* **-ciones** : cognition
cognitivo, -va *adj* : cognitive
cogollo *nm* **1** : heart (of a vegetable) **2** : bud, bulb **3** : core, crux ⟨el cogollo de la cuestión : the heart of the matter⟩
cogote *nm* : scruff, nape
cohabitar *vi* : to cohabit — **cohabitación** *nf*
cohechar *vt* SOBORNAR : to bribe
cohecho *nm* SOBORNO : bribe, bribery
coherencia *nf* : coherence — **coherente** *adj*
cohesión *nf, pl* **-siones** : cohesion
cohesivo, -va *adj* : cohesive
cohete *nm* : rocket
cohibición *nf, pl* **-ciones 1** : (legal) restraint **2** INHIBICIÓN : inhibition
cohibido, -da *adj* : inhibited, shy
cohibir {62} *vt* : to inhibit, to make self-conscious — **cohibirse** *vr* : to feel shy or embarrassed
cohorte *nf* : cohort
coima *nf Arg, Chile, Peru* : bribe
coimear *vt Arg, Chile, Peru* : to bribe
coincidencia *nf* : coincidence
coincidente *adj* **1** : coincident **2** ACORDE : coinciding
coincidir *vi* **1** : to coincide **2** : to agree
coito *nm* : sexual intercourse, coitus
coja, etc. → **coger**
cojear *vi* **1** : to limp **2** : to wobble, to rock **3 cojear del mismo pie** : to be two of a kind
cojera *nf* : limp
cojín *nm, pl* **cojines** : cushion, throw pillow
cojinete *nm* **1** : bearing, bushing **2 cojinete de bola** : ball bearing
cojo[1], **-ja** *adj* **1** : limping, lame **2** : wobbly **3** : weak, ineffectual
cojo[2], **-ja** *n* : lame person

cojones *nmpl usu considered vulgar* **1** : testicles *pl* **2** : guts *pl*, courage
col *nf* **1** REPOLLO : cabbage **2 col de Bruselas** : Brussels sprout **3 col rizada** : kale
cola *nf* **1** RABO : tail ⟨cola de caballo : ponytail⟩ **2** FILA : line (of people) ⟨hacer cola : to wait in line⟩ **3** : cola, drink **4** : train (of a dress) **5** : tails *pl* (of a tuxedo) **6** PEGAMENTO : glue **7** *fam* : buttocks *pl*, rear end
colaboracionista *nmf* : collaborator, traitor
colaborador, -dora *n* **1** : contributor (to a periodical) **2** : collaborator
colaborar *vi* : to collaborate — **colaboración** *nf*
colación *nf, pl* **-ciones 1** : light meal **2** : comparison, collation ⟨sacar a colación : to bring up, to broach⟩ **3** : conferral (of a degree)
colador *nm* **1** : colander, strainer **2** *PRi* : small coffeepot
colapso *nm* **1** : collapse **2** : standstill
colar {19} *vt* : to strain, to filter — **colarse** *vr* **1** : to sneak in, to cut in line, to gate-crash **2** : to slip up, to make a mistake
colateral[1] *adj* : collateral — **colateralmente** *adv*
colateral[2] *nm* : collateral
colcha *nf* COBERTOR : bedspread, quilt
colchón *nm, pl* **colchones 1** : mattress **2** : cushion, padding, buffer
colchoneta *nf* : mat (for gymnastic sports)
colear *vi* **1** : to wag its tail **2 vivito y coleando** *fam* : alive and kicking
colección *nf, pl* **-ciones** : collection
coleccionar *vt* : to collect, to keep a collection of
coleccionista *nmf* : collector
colecta *nf* : collection (of donations)
colectar *vt* : to collect
colectividad *nf* : community, group
colectivo[1], **-va** *adj* : collective — **colectivamente** *adv*
colectivo[2] *nm* **1** : collective **2** *Arg, Bol, Peru* : city bus
colector[1], **-tora** *n* : collector ⟨colector de impuestos : tax collector⟩
colector[2] *nm* **1** : sewer **2** : manifold (of an engine)
colega *nmf* **1** : colleague **2** HOMÓLOGO : counterpart **3** *fam* : buddy
colegiado[1], **-da** *adj* : collegiate
colegiado[2], **-da** *n* **1** ÁRBITRO : referee **2** : member (of a professional association)
colegial[1], **-giala** *adj* **1** : school, collegiate **2** *Mex fam* : green, inexperienced
colegial[2], **-giala** *n* : schoolboy *m*, schoolgirl *f*
colegiatura *nf Mex* : tuition
colegio *nm* **1** : school **2** : college ⟨colegio electoral : electoral college⟩ **3** : professional association

colegir {28} vt 1 JUNTAR : to collect, to gather 2 INFERIR : to infer, to deduce
cólera¹ nm : cholera
cólera² nf FURIA, IRA : anger, rage
colérico, -ca adj 1 FURIOSO : angry 2 IRRITABLE : irritable
colesterol nm : cholesterol
coleta nf 1 : ponytail 2 : pigtail
coletazo nm : lash, flick (of a tail)
colgado, -da adj 1 : hanging, hanged 2 : pending 3 dejar colgado a : to disappoint, to let down
colgante¹ adj : hanging, dangling
colgante² nm : pendant, charm (on a bracelet)
colgar {16} vt 1 : to hang (up), to put up 2 AHORCAR : to hang (someone) 3 : to hang up (a telephone) 4 fam : to fail (an exam) — colgarse vr 1 : to hang, to be suspended 2 AHORCARSE : to hang oneself 3 : to hang up a telephone
colibrí nm CHUPAFLOR : hummingbird
cólico nm : colic
coliflor nf : cauliflower
colilla nf : butt (of a cigarette)
colina nf CERRO, LOMA : hill
colindante adj CONTIGUO : adjacent, neighboring
colindar vi : to adjoin, to be adjacent
coliseo nm : coliseum
colisión nf, pl -siones : collision
colisionar vi : to collide
collage nm : collage
collar nm 1 : collar (for an animal) 2 : necklace ⟨collar de perlas : string of pearls⟩
colmado, -da adj : heaping
colmar vt 1 : to fill to the brim 2 : to fulfill, to satisfy 3 : to heap, to shower ⟨me colmaron de regalos : they showered me with gifts⟩
colmena nf : beehive
colmenar nm APIARIO : apiary
colmillo nm 1 CANINO : canine (tooth), fang 2 : tusk
colmilludo, -da adj Mex, PRi : astute, shrewd, crafty
colmo nm : height, extreme, limit ⟨el colmo de la locura : the height of folly⟩ ⟨¡eso es el colmo! : that's the last straw!⟩
colocación nf, pl -ciones 1 : placement, placing 2 : position, job 3 : investment
colocar {72} vt 1 PONER : to place, to put 2 : to find a job for 3 : to invest — colocarse vr 1 SITUARSE : to position oneself 2 : to get a job
colofón nm, pl -fones 1 : ending, finale 2 : colophon
colofonia nf : rosin
colombiano, -na adj & n : Colombian
colon nm : (intestinal) colon
colón nm, pl colones : Costa Rican and Salvadoran unit of currency
colonia nf 1 : colony 2 : cologne 3 Mex : residential area, neighborhood
colonial adj : colonial

colonización nf, pl -ciones : colonization
colonizador¹, -dora adj : colonizing
colonizador², -dora n : colonizer, colonist
colonizar {21} vt : to colonize, to settle
colono, -na n 1 : settler, colonist 2 : tenant farmer
coloquial adj : colloquial
coloquio nm 1 : discussion, talk 2 : conference, symposium
color nm 1 : color 2 : paint, dye 3 colores nmpl : colored pencils
coloración nf, pl -ciones : coloring, coloration
colorado¹, -da adj 1 ROJO : red 2 ponerse colorado : to blush 3 chiste colorado Mex : off-color joke
colorado² nm ROJO : red
colorante nm : coloring ⟨colorante de alimentos : food coloring⟩
colorear vt : to color — vi 1 : to redden 2 : to ripen
colorete nm : rouge, blusher
colorido nm : color, coloring
colorín nm, pl -rines 1 : bright color 2 : goldfinch
colosal adj : colossal
coloso nm : colossus
coludir vi : to be in collusion, to conspire
columna nf 1 : column 2 columna vertebral : spine, backbone
columnata nf : colonnade
columnista nmf : columnist
columpiar vt : to push (on a swing) — columpiarse vr : to swing
columpio nm : swing
colusión nf, pl -siones : collusion
colza nf : rape (plant)
coma¹ nm : coma
coma² nf : comma
comadre nf 1 : godmother of one's child 2 : mother of one's godchild 3 fam : neighbor, female friend 4 fam : gossip
comadrear vi fam : to gossip
comadreja nf : weasel
comadrona nf : midwife
comanche nmf : Comanche
comandancia nf 1 : command headquarters 2 : command
comandante nmf 1 : commander, commanding officer 2 : major
comandar vt : to command, to lead
comando nm 1 : commando 2 : command (for computers)
comarca nf REGIÓN : region
comarcal adj REGIONAL : regional, local
comatoso, -sa adj : comatose
combar vt : to bend, to curve — combarse vr 1 : to bend, to buckle 2 : to warp, to bulge, to sag
combate nm 1 : combat 2 : fight, boxing match
combatiente nmf : combatant, fighter
combatir vt : to combat, to fight against — vi : to fight

combatividad *nf* : fighting spirit
combativo, -va *adj* : combative, spirited
combinación *nf, pl* **-ciones 1** : combination **2** : connection (in travel)
combinar *vt* **1** UNIR : to combine, to mix together **2** : to match, to put together — **combinarse** *vr* : to get together, to conspire
combo *nm* **1** : (musical) band **2** *Chile, Peru* : sledgehammer **3** *Chile, Peru* : punch
combustible[1] *adj* : combustible
combustible[2] *nm* : fuel
combustión *nf, pl* **-tiones** : combustion
comedero *nm* : trough, feeder
comedia *nf* : comedy
comediante *nmf* : actor, actress *f*
comedido, -da *adj* MESURADO : moderate, restrained
comediógrafo, -fa *n* : playwright
comedor *nm* : dining room
comején *nm, pl* **-jenes** : termite
comelón[1], **-lona** *adj, mpl* **-lones** *fam* : gluttonous
comelón[2], **-lona** *n, pl* **-lones** *fam* : big eater, glutton
comensal *nmf* : dinner guest
comentador, -dora *n* → **comentarista**
comentar *vt* **1** : to comment on, to discuss **2** : to mention, to remark
comentario *nm* **1** : comment, remark ⟨sin comentarios : no comment⟩ **2** : commentary
comentarista *nmf* : commentator
comenzar {29} *v* EMPEZAR : to begin, to start
comer[1] *vt* **1** : to eat **2** : to consume, to eat up, to eat into — *vi* **1** : to eat **2** CENAR : to have a meal **3 dar de comer** : to feed — **comerse** *vr* : to eat up
comer[2] *nm* : eating, dining
comercial *adj* & *nm* : commercial — **comercialmente** *adv*
comercializar {21} *vt* **1** : to commercialize **2** : to market
comerciante *nmf* : merchant, dealer
comerciar *vi* : to do business, to trade
comercio *nm* **1** : commerce, trade **2** NEGOCIO : business, place of business
comestible *adj* : edible
comestibles *nmpl* VÍVERES : groceries, food
cometa[1] *nm* : comet
cometa[2] *nf* : kite
cometer *vt* **1** : to commit **2 cometer un error** : to make a mistake
cometido *nm* : assignment, task
comezón *nf, pl* **-zones** PICAZÓN : itchiness, itching
comible *adj fam* : eatable, edible
comic *or* **cómic** *nm* : comic strip, comic book
comicastro, -tra *n* : second-rate actor, ham
comicidad *nf* HUMOR : humor, wit
comicios *nmpl* : elections, voting
cómico[1], **-ca** *adj* : comic, comical

cómico[2], **-ca** *n* HUMORISTA : comic, comedian, comedienne *f*
comida *nf* **1** : food **2** : meal **3** : dinner **4 comida basura** : junk food **5 comida rápida** : fast food
comidilla *nf* : talk, gossip
comienzo *nm* **1** : start, beginning **2 al comienzo** : at first **3 dar comienzo** : to begin
comillas *nfpl* : quotation marks ⟨entre comillas : in quotes⟩
comilón, -lona → **comelón, -lona**
comilona *nf fam* : feast
comino *nm* **1** : cumin **2 me vale un comino** *fam* : not to matter to someone ⟨no me importa un comino : I couldn't care less⟩
comisaría *nf* : police station
comisario, -ria *n* : commissioner
comisión *nf, pl* **-siones 1** : commission, committing **2** : committee **3** : percentage, commission ⟨comisión sobre las ventas : sales commission⟩
comisionado[1], **-da** *adj* : commissioned, entrusted
comisionado[2], **-da** *n* → **comisario**
comisionar *vt* : to commission
comité *nm* : committee
comitiva *nf* : retinue, entourage
como[1] *adv* **1** : around, about ⟨cuesta como 500 pesos : it costs around 500 pesos⟩ **2** : kind of, like ⟨tengo como mareos : I'm kind of dizzy⟩
como[2] *conj* **1** : how, as ⟨hazlo como dijiste que lo harías : do it the way you said you would⟩ **2** : since, given that ⟨como estaba lloviendo, no salí : since it was raining, I didn't go out⟩ **3** : if ⟨como lo vuelva a hacer lo arrestarán : if he does that again he'll be arrested⟩ **4 como quiera** : in any way
como[3] *prep* **1** : like, as ⟨ligero como una pluma : light as a feather⟩ **2 así como** : as well as
cómo *adv* **1** : how ⟨¿cómo estás? : how are you?⟩ ⟨¿a cómo están las manzanas? : how much are the apples?⟩ ⟨¿cómo? : excuse me?, what was that?⟩ ⟨¿se puede? ¡cómo no! : may I? please do!⟩
cómoda *nf* : bureau, chest of drawers
comodidad *nf* **1** : comfort **2** : convenience
comodín *nm, pl* **-dines 1** : joker, wild card **2** : all-purpose word or thing **3** : pretext, excuse
cómodo, -da *adj* **1** CONFORTABLE : comfortable **2** : convenient — **cómodamente** *adv*
comodoro *nm* : commodore
comoquiera *adv* **1** : in any way **2 comoquiera que** : in whatever way, however ⟨comoquiera que sea eso : however that may be⟩
compa *nm fam* : buddy, pal
compactar *vt* : to compact, to compress
compacto, -ta *adj* : compact

compadecer {53} vt : to sympathize with, to feel sorry for — compadecerse vr 1 ~ de : to take pity on, to commiserate with 2 ~ con : to fit, to accord (with)
compadre nm 1 : godfather of one's child 2 : father of one's godchild 3 fam : buddy, pal
compaginar vt 1 COORDINAR : to combine, to coordinate 2 : to collate
compañerismo nm : comradeship, camaraderie
compañero, -ra n : companion, mate, partner
compañía nf 1 : company ⟨llegó en compañía de su madre : he arrived with his mother⟩ 2 EMPRESA, FIRMA : firm, company
comparable adj : comparable
comparación nf, pl -ciones : comparison
comparado, -da adj : comparative ⟨literatura comparada : comparative literature⟩
comparar vt : to compare
comparativo[1], -va adj : comparative, relative — comparativamente adv
comparativo[2] nm : comparative degree or form
comparecencia nf 1 : appearance (in court) 2 orden de comparecencia : subpoena, summons
comparecer {53} vi : to appear (in court)
compartimiento or compartimento nm : compartment
compartir vt : to share
compás nm, pl -pases 1 : beat, rhythm, time 2 : compass
compasión nf, pl -siones : compassion, pity
compasivo, -va adj : compassionate, sympathetic
compatibilidad nf : compatibility
compatible adj : compatible
compatriota nmf PAISANO : compatriot, fellow countryman
compeler vt : to compel
compendiar vt : to summarize, to condense
compendio nm : summary
compenetración nf, pl -ciones : rapport, mutual understanding
compenetrarse vr 1 : to understand each other 2 ~ con : to identify oneself with
compensación nf, pl -ciones : compensation
compensar vt : to compensate for, to make up for — vi : to be worth one's while
compensatorio, -ria adj : compensatory
competencia nf 1 : competition, rivalry 2 : competence
competente adj : competent, able — competentemente adv
competición nf, pl -ciones : competition

competidor[1], -dora adj RIVAL : competing, rival
competidor[2], -dora n RIVAL : competitor, rival
competir {54} vi : to compete
competitividad nf : competitiveness
competitivo, -va adj : competitive — competitivamente adv
compilar vt : to compile — compilación nf
compinche nmf fam 1 : buddy, pal 2 : partner in crime, accomplice
complacencia nf : pleasure, satisfaction
complacer {57} vt : to please — complacerse vr ~ en : to take pleasure in
complaciente adj : obliging, eager to please
complejidad nf : complexity
complejo[1], -ja adj : complex
complejo[2] nm : complex
complementar vt : to complement, to supplement — complementarse vr
complementario, -ria adj : complementary
complemento nm 1 : complement, supplement 2 : supplementary pay, allowance
completamente adv : completely, totally
completar vt TERMINAR : to complete, to finish
completo, -ta adj 1 : complete 2 : perfect, absolute 3 : full, detailed
complexión nf, pl -xiones : (physical) constitution
complicación nf, pl -ciones : complication
complicado, -da adj : complicated
complicar {72} vt 1 : to complicate 2 : to involve — complicarse vr
cómplice nmf : accomplice
complicidad nf : complicity
complot nm, pl complots CONFABULACIÓN, CONSPIRACIÓN : conspiracy, plot
componenda nf : shady deal, scam
componente adj & nm : component, constituent
componer {60} vt 1 ARREGLAR : to fix, to repair 2 CONSTITUIR : to make up, to compose 3 : to compose, to write 4 : to set (a bone) — componerse vr 1 : to improve, to get better 2 ~ de : to consist of
comportamiento nm CONDUCTA : behavior, conduct
comportarse vr : to behave, to conduct oneself
composición nf, pl -ciones 1 OBRA : composition, work 2 : makeup, arrangement
compositor, -tora n : composer, songwriter
compostura nf 1 : composure 2 : mending, repair
compra nf 1 : purchase 2 ir de compras : to go shopping 3 orden de compra : purchase order

comprador, -dora *n* : buyer, shopper
comprar *vt* : to buy, to purchase
compraventa *nf* : buying and selling
comprender *vt* **1** ENTENDER : to comprehend, to understand **2** ABARCAR : to cover, to include — *vi* : to understand ⟨ya comprendo! : now I understand!⟩
comprensible *adj* : understandable — **comprensiblemente** *adv*
comprensión *nf, pl* **-siones 1** : comprehension, understanding, grasp **2** : understanding, sympathy
comprensivo, -va *adj* : understanding
compresa *nf* **1** : compress **2** *or* **compresa higiénica** : sanitary napkin
compresión *nf, pl* **-siones** : compression
compresor *nm* : compressor
comprimido *nm* PÍLDORA, TABLETA : pill, tablet
comprimir *vt* : to compress
comprobable *adj* : verifiable, provable
comprobación *nf, pl* **-ciones** : verification, confirmation
comprobante *nm* **1** : proof ⟨comprobante de identidad : proof of identity⟩ **2** : voucher, receipt ⟨comprobante de ventas : sales slip⟩
comprobar {19} *vt* **1** : to verify, to check **2** : to prove
comprometedor, -dora *adj* : compromising
comprometer *vt* **1** : to compromise **2** : to jeopardize **3** : to commit, to put under obligation — **comprometerse** *vr* **1** : to commit oneself **2** ~ **con** : to get engaged to
comprometido, -da *adj* **1** : compromising, awkward **2** : committed, obliged **3** : engaged (to be married)
compromiso *nm* **1** : obligation, commitment **2** : engagement ⟨anillo de compromiso : engagement ring⟩ **3** : agreement **4** : awkward situation, fix
compuerta *nf* : floodgate
compuesto[1] *pp* → **componer**
compuesto[2]**, -ta** *adj* **1** : fixed, repaired **2** : compound, composite **3** : decked out, spruced up **4** ~ **de** : made up of, consisting of
compuesto[3] *nm* : compound
compulsión *nf, pl* **-siones** : compulsion
compulsivo, -va *adj* **1** : compelling, urgent **2** : compulsive — **compulsivamente** *adv*
compungido, -da *adj* : contrite, remorseful
compungirse {35} *vr* : to feel remorse
compuso, etc. → **componer**
computable *adj* : countable ⟨años computables : years accrued⟩ ⟨ingresos computables : qualifying income⟩
computación *nf, pl* **-ciones** : computing, computers *pl*
computador *nm* → **computadora**
computadora *nf* **1** : computer **2 computadora portátil** : laptop computer

computar *vt* : to compute, to calculate
computarizar {21} *vt* : to computerize
cómputo *nm* : computation, calculation
comulgar {52} *vi* : to receive Communion
común *adj, pl* **comunes 1** : common **2 común y corriente** : ordinary, regular **3 por lo común** : generally, as a rule
comuna *nf* : commune
comunal *adj* : communal
comunicación *nf, pl* **-ciones 1** : communication **2** : access, link **3** : message, report
comunicado *nm* **1** : communiqué **2 comunicado de prensa** : press release
comunicar {72} *vt* **1** : to communicate, to convey **2** : to notify — **comunicarse** *vr* ~ **con 1** : to contact, to get in touch with **2** : to be connected to
comunicativo, -va *adj* : communicative, talkative
comunidad *nf* : community
comunión *nf, pl* **-niones 1** : communion, sharing **2** : Communion
comunismo *nm* : communism, Communism
comunista *adj & nmf* : communist
comúnmente *adv* : commonly
con *prep* **1** : with ⟨vengo con mi padre : I'm going with my father⟩ ⟨¡con quién hablas? : who are you speaking to?⟩ **2** : in spite of ⟨con todo : in spite of it all⟩ **3** : to, towards ⟨ella es amable con los niños : she is kind to the children⟩ **4** : by ⟨con llegar temprano : by arriving early⟩ **5 con (tal) que** : as long as, so long as
conato *nm* : attempt, effort ⟨conato de robo : attempted robbery⟩
cóncavo, -va *adj* : concave
concebible *adj* : conceivable
concebir {54} *vt* **1** : to conceive **2** : to conceive of, to imagine — *vi* : to conceive, to become pregnant
conceder *vt* **1** : to grant, to bestow **2** : to concede, to admit
concejal, -jala *n* : councilman *m*, councilwoman *f*, alderman *m*, alderwoman *f*
concejo *nm* : council ⟨concejo municipal : town council⟩
concentración *nf, pl* **-ciones** : concentration
concentrado *nm* : concentrate
concentrar *vt* : to concentrate — **concentrarse** *vr*
concéntrico, -ca *adj* : concentric
concepción *nf, pl* **-ciones** : conception
concepto *nm* NOCIÓN : concept, idea, opinion
conceptuar {3} *vt* : to regard, to judge
concernir {17} *vi* : to be of concern
concertar {55} *vt* **1** : to arrange, to set up **2** : to agree on, to settle **3** : to harmonize — *vi* : to be in harmony
concesión *nf, pl* **-siones 1** : concession **2** : awarding, granting
concha *nf* : conch, seashell

conciencia *nf* **1** : conscience **2** : consciousness, awareness
concientizar {21} *vt* : to make aware —
concientizarse *vr* ~ **de** : to realize, to become aware of
concienzudo, -da *adj* : conscientious
concierto *nm* **1** : concert **2** : agreement **3** : concerto
conciliador¹, -dora *adj* : conciliatory
conciliador², -dora *n* : arbitrator, peacemaker
conciliar *vt* : to conciliate, to reconcile — **conciliación** *nf*
conciliatorio, -ria *adj* → **conciliador¹**
concilio *nm* : (church) council
conciso, -sa *adj* : concise — **concisión** *nf*
conciudadano, -na *n* : fellow citizen
cónclave *nm* : conclave, private meeting
concluir {41} *vt* **1** TERMINAR : to conclude, to finish **2** DEDUCIR : to deduce, to infer — *vi* : to end, to conclude
conclusión *nf, pl* **-siones** : conclusion
concluyente *adj* : conclusive
concomitante *adj* : concomitant
concordancia *nf* : agreement, accordance
concordar {19} *vi* : to agree, to coincide — *vt* : to reconcile
concordia *nf* : concord, harmony
concretar *vt* **1** : to pinpoint, to specify **2** : to fulfill, to realize — **concretarse** *vr* : to become real, to take shape
concretizar → **concretar**
concreto¹, -ta *adj* **1** : concrete, actual **2** : definite, specific ⟨en concreto : specifically⟩ — **concretamente** *adv*
concreto² *nm* HORMIGÓN : concrete
concubina *nf* : concubine
concurrencia *nf* **1** : audience, turnout **2** : concurrence
concurrente *adj* : concurrent — **concurrentemente** *adv*
concurrido, -da *adj* : busy, crowded
concurrir *vi* **1** : to converge, to come together **2** : to concur, to agree **3** : to take part, to participate **4** : to attend, to be present ⟨concurrir a una reunión : to attend a meeting⟩ **5** ~ **a** : to contribute to
concursante *nmf* : contestant, competitor
concursar *vt* : to compete in — *vi* : to compete, to participate
concurso *nm* **1** : contest, competition **2** : concurrence, coincidence **3** : crowd, gathering **4** : cooperation, assistance
condado *nm* **1** : county **2** : earldom
conde, -desa *n* : count *m*, earl *m*, countess *f*
condecoración *nf, pl* **-ciones** : decoration, medal
condecorar *vt* : to decorate, to award (a medal)
condena *nf* **1** REPROBACIÓN : disapproval, condemnation **2** SENTENCIA : sentence, conviction

condenable *adj* : reprehensible
condenación *nf, pl* **-ciones** **1** : condemnation **2** : damnation
condenado¹, -da *adj* **1** : fated, doomed **2** : convicted, sentenced **3** *fam* : darn, damned
condenado², -da *n* : convict
condenar *vt* **1** : to condemn **2** : to sentence **3** : to board up, to wall up — **condenarse** *vr* : to be damned
condensación *nf, pl* **-ciones** : condensation
condensar *vt* : to condense
condesa *nf* → **conde**
condescendencia *nf* : condescension
condescender {56} *vi* **1** : to condescend **2** : to agree, to acquiesce
condición *nf, pl* **-ciones** **1** : condition, state **2** : capacity, position **3** **condiciones** *nfpl* : conditions, circumstances ⟨condiciones de vida : living conditions⟩
condicional *adj* : conditional — **condicionalmente** *adv*
condicionamiento *nm* : conditioning
condicionar *vt* **1** : to condition, to determine **2** ~ **a** : to be contingent on, to depend on
condimentar *vt* SAZONAR : to season, to spice
condimento *nm* : condiment, seasoning, spice
condiscípulo, -la *n* : classmate
condolencia *nf* : condolence, sympathy
condolerse {47} *vr* : to sympathize
condominio *nm* : condominium, condo
condón *nm, pl* **condones** : condom
cóndor *nm* : condor
conducción *nf, pl* **-ciones** **1** : conduction (of electricity, etc.) **2** DIRECCIÓN : management, direction
conducir {61} *vt* **1** DIRIGIR, GUIAR : to direct, to lead **2** MANEJAR : to drive (a vehicle) — *vi* **1** : to drive a vehicle **2** ~ **a** : to lead to — **conducirse** *vr* PORTARSE : to behave, to conduct oneself
conducta *nf* COMPORTAMIENTO : conduct, behavior
conducto *nm* : conduit, channel, duct
conductor¹, -tora *adj* : conducting, leading
conductor², -tora *n* : driver
conductor³ *nm* : conductor (of electricity, etc.)
conectar *vt* : to connect — *vi* ~ **con** : to link up with, to communicate with
conector *nm* : connector
conejera *nf* : rabbit hutch
conejillo *nm* **conejillo de Indias** : guinea pig
conejo, -ja *n* : rabbit
conexión *nf, pl* **-xiones** : connection
confabulación *nf, pl* **-ciones** COMPLOT, CONSPIRACIÓN : plot, conspiracy
confabularse *vr* : to plot, to conspire
confección *nf, pl* **-ciones** **1** : preparation **2** : tailoring, dressmaking
confeccionar *vt* : to make, to produce, to prepare

confederación *nf, pl* **-ciones** : confederation

confederarse *vr* : to confederate, to form a confederation

conferencia *nf* **1** REUNIÓN : conference, meeting **2** : lecture

conferenciante *nmf* : lecturer

conferencista → **conferenciante**

conferir {76} *vt* : to confer, to bestow

confesar {55} *v* : to confess — **confesarse** *vr* : to go to confession

confesión *nf, pl* **-siones 1** : confession **2** : creed, denomination

confesionario *nm* : confessional

confesor *nm* : confessor

confeti *nm* : confetti

confiable *adj* : trustworthy, reliable

confiado, -da *adj* **1** : confident, self-confident **2** : trusting — **confiadamente** *adv*

confianza *nf* **1** : trust ⟨de poca confianza : untrustworthy⟩ **2** : confidence, self-confidence

confianzudo, -da *adj* : forward, presumptuous

confiar {85} *vi* : to have trust, to be trusting — *vt* **1** : to confide **2** : to entrust — **confiarse** *vr* **1** : to be overconfident **2** ~ **a** : to confide in

confidencia *nf* : confidence, secret

confidencial *adj* : confidential — **confidencialmente** *adv*

confidencialidad *nf* : confidentiality

confidente *nmf* **1** : confidant, confidante *f* **2** : informer

configuración *nf, pl* **-ciones** : configuration, shape

configurar *vt* : to shape, to form

confín *nm, pl* **confines** : boundary, limit

confinamiento *nm* : confinement

confinar *vt* **1** : to confine, to limit **2** : to exile — *vi* ~ **con** : to border on

confirmación *nf, pl* **-ciones** : confirmation

confirmar *vt* : to confirm, to substantiate

confiscación *nf, pl* **-ciones** : confiscation

confiscar {72} *vt* DECOMISAR : to confiscate, to seize

confitado, -da *adj* : candied

confite *nm* : comfit, candy

confitería *nf* **1** DULCERÍA : candy store, confectionery **2** : tearoom, café

confitero, -ra *n* : confectioner

confitura *nf* : preserves, jam

conflagración *nf, pl* **-ciones 1** : conflagration, fire **2** : war

conflictivo, -va *adj* **1** : troubled **2** : controversial

conflicto *nm* : conflict

confluencia *nf* : junction, confluence

confluir {41} *vi* **1** : to converge, to join **2** : to gather, to assemble

conformar *vt* **1** : to form, to create **2** : to constitute, to make up — **conformarse** *vr* **1** RESIGNARSE : to resign oneself **2** : to comply, to conform **3** ~ **con** : to content oneself with, to be satisfied with

conforme¹ *adj* **1** : content, satisfied **2** ~ **a** : in accordance with

conforme² *conj* : as ⟨entreguen sus tareas conforme vayan saliendo : hand in your homework as you leave⟩

conformidad *nf* **1** : agreement, consent **2** : resignation

confort *nm* : comfort

confortable *adj* CÓMODO : comfortable

confortar *vt* CONSOLAR : to comfort, to console

confraternidad *nf* : brotherhood, fraternity

confraternización *nf, pl* **-ciones** : fraternization

confraternizar *vi* : to fraternize

confrontación *nf, pl* **-ciones** : confrontation

confrontar *vt* **1** ENCARAR : to confront **2** : to compare **3** : to bring face-to-face — *vi* : to border — **confrontarse** *vr* ~ **con** : to face up to

confundir *vt* : to confuse, to mix up — **confundirse** *vr* : to make a mistake, to be confused ⟨confundirse de número : to get the wrong number⟩

confusión *nf, pl* **-siones** : confusion

confuso, -sa *adj* **1** : confused, mixed-up **2** : obscure, indistinct

congelación *nf, pl* **-ciones 1** : freezing **2** : frostbite

congelado, -da *adj* HELADO : frozen

congelador *nm* HELADORA : freezer

congelamiento *nm* → **congelación**

congelar *vt* : to freeze — **congelarse** *vr*

congeniar *vi* : to get along (with someone)

congénito, -ta *adj* : congenital

congestión *nf, pl* **-tiones** : congestion

congestionado, -da *adj* : congested

congestionamiento *nm* → **congestión**

congestionarse *vr* **1** : to become flushed **2** : to become congested

conglomerado¹, -da *adj* : conglomerate, mixed

conglomerado² *nm* : conglomerate, conglomeration

congoja *nf* ANGUSTIA : anguish, grief

congoleño, -ña *adj & n* : Congolese

congraciarse *vr* : to ingratiate oneself

congratular *vt* FELICITAR : to congratulate

congregación *nf, pl* **-ciones** : congregation, gathering

congregar {52} *vt* : to bring together — **congregarse** *vr* : to congregate, to assemble

congresista *nmf* : congressman *m*, congresswoman *f*

congreso *nm* : congress, conference

congruencia *nf* **1** : congruence **2** COHERENCIA : coherence — **congruente** *adj*

cónico, -ca *adj* : conical, conic

conífera *nf* : conifer

conífero, -ra *adj* : coniferous
conjetura *nf* : conjecture, guess
conjeturar *vt* : to guess, to conjecture
conjugación *nf, pl* -**ciones** : conjugation
conjugar {52} *vt* 1 : to conjugate 2 : to combine
conjunción *nf, pl* -**ciones** : conjunction
conjuntivo, -va *adj* : connective ⟨tejido conjuntivo : connective tissue⟩
conjunto¹, -ta *adj* : joint
conjunto² *nm* 1 : collection, group 2 : ensemble, outfit ⟨conjunto musical : musical ensemble⟩ 3 : whole, entirety ⟨en conjunto : as a whole, altogether⟩
conjurar *vt* 1 : to exorcise 2 : to avert, to ward off — *vi* CONSPIRAR : to conspire, to plot
conjuro *nm* 1 : exorcism 2 : spell
conllevar *vt* 1 : to bear, to suffer 2 IMPLICAR : to entail, to involve
conmemorar *vt* : to commemorate — **conmemoración** *nf*
conmemorativo, -va *adj* : commemorative, memorial
conmigo *pron* : with me ⟨habló conmigo : he talked with me⟩
conminar *vt* AMENAZAR : to threaten, to warn
conmiseración *nf, pl* -**ciones** : pity, commiseration
conmoción *nf, pl* -**ciones** 1 : shock, upheaval 2 *or* **conmoción cerebral** : concussion
conmocionar *vt* : to shake, to shock
conmovedor, -dora *adj* EMOCIONANTE : moving, touching
conmover {47} *vt* 1 EMOCIONAR : to move, to touch 2 : to shake up — **conmoverse** *vr*
conmutador *nm* 1 : switch 2 : switchboard
conmutar *vt* 1 : to commute (a sentence) 2 : to switch, to exchange
connivencia *nf* : connivance
connotación *nf, pl* -**ciones** : connotation
connotar *vt* : to connote, to imply
cono *nm* : cone
conocedor¹, -dora *adj* : knowledgeable
conocedor², -dora *n* : connoisseur, expert
conocer {18} *vt* 1 : to know, to be acquainted with ⟨ya lo conocí : I've already met him⟩ 2 : to meet 3 RECONOCER : to recognize — **conocerse** *vr* 1 : to know each other 2 : to meet 3 : to know oneself
conocido¹, -da *adj* 1 : familiar 2 : well-known, famous
conocido², -da *n* : acquaintance
conocimiento *nm* 1 : knowledge 2 SENTIDO : consciousness
conque *conj* : so, so then, and so ⟨¡ah, conque esas tenemos! : oh, so that's what's going on!⟩
conquista *nf* : conquest
conquistador¹, -dora *adj* : conquering

conquistador², -dora *n* : conqueror
conquistar *vt* : to conquer
consabido, -da *adj* : usual, typical
consagración *nf, pl* -**ciones** : consecration
consagrar *vt* 1 : to consecrate 2 DEDICAR : to dedicate, to devote
consciencia → **conciencia**
consciente *adj* : conscious, aware — **conscientemente** *adv*
conscripción *nf, pl* -**ciones** : conscription, draft
conscripto, -ta *n* : conscript, inductee
consecución *nf, pl* -**ciones** : attainment
consecuencia *nf* 1 : consequence, result ⟨a consecuencia de : as a result of⟩ 2 **en** ~ : accordingly
consecuente *adj* : consistent — **consecuentemente** *adv*
consecutivo, -va *adj* : consecutive, successive — **consecutivamente** *adv*
conseguir {75} *vt* 1 : to get, to obtain 2 : to achieve, to attain 3 : to manage to ⟨consiguió acabar el trabajo : she managed to finish the job⟩
consejero, -ra *n* : adviser, counselor
consejo *nm* 1 : advice, counsel 2 : council ⟨consejo de guerra : court-martial⟩
consenso *nm* : consensus
consentido, -da *adj* : spoiled, pampered
consentimiento *nm* : consent, permission
consentir {76} *vt* 1 PERMITIR : to consent to, to allow 2 MIMAR : to pamper, to spoil — *vi* ~ **en** : to agree to, to approve of
conserje *nmf* : custodian, janitor, caretaker
conserva *nf* 1 : preserve(s), jam 2 **conservas** *nfpl* : canned goods
conservación *nf, pl* -**ciones** : conservation, preservation
conservacionista *nmf* : conservationist
conservador¹, -dora *adj & n* : conservative
conservador² *nm* : preservative
conservadurismo *nf* : conservatism
conservante *nm* : preservative
conservar *vt* 1 : to preserve 2 GUARDAR : to keep, to conserve
conservatorio *nm* : conservatory
considerable *adj* : considerable — **considerablemente** *adv*
consideración *nf, pl* -**ciones** 1 : consideration 2 : respect 3 **de** ~ : considerable, important
considerado, -da *adj* 1 : considerate, thoughtful 2 : respected
considerar *vt* 1 : to consider, to think over 2 : to judge, to deem 3 : to treat with respect
consigna *nf* 1 ESLOGAN : slogan 2 : assignment, orders *pl* 3 : checkroom
consignación *nf, pl* -**ciones** 1 : consignment 2 ASIGNACIÓN : allocation
consignar *vt* 1 : to consign 2 : to record, to write down 3 : to assign, to allocate

consigo *pron* : with her, with him, with you, with oneself ⟨se llevó las llaves consigo : she took the keys with her⟩
consiguiente *adj* **1** : resulting, consequent **2 por ~** : consequently, as a result
consistencia *nf* : consistency
consistente *adj* **1** : firm, strong, sound **2** : consistent — **consistentemente** *adv*
consistir *vi* **1 ~ en** : to consist of **2 ~ en** : to lie in, to consist in
consola *nf* : console
consolación *nf, pl* **-ciones** : consolation ⟨premio de consolación : consolation prize⟩
consolar {19} *vt* CONFORTAR : to console, to comfort
consolidar *vt* : to consolidate — **consolidación** *nf*
consomé *nm* CALDO : consommé, clear soup
consonancia *nf* **1** : consonance, harmony **2 en consonancia con** : in accordance with
consonante[1] *adj* : consonant, harmonious
consonante[2] *nf* : consonant
consorcio *nm* : consortium
consorte *nmf* : consort, spouse
conspicuo, -cua *adj* : eminent, famous
conspiración *nf, pl* **-ciones** COMPLOT, CONFABULACIÓN : conspiracy, plot
conspirador, -dora *n* : conspirator
conspirar *vi* CONJURAR : to conspire, to plot
constancia *nf* **1** PRUEBA : proof, certainty **2** : record, evidence ⟨que quede constancia : for the record⟩ **3** : perseverance, constancy
constante[1] *adj* : constant — **constantemente** *adv*
constante[2] *nf* : constant
constar *vi* **1** : to be evident, to be on record ⟨que conste : believe me, have no doubt⟩ **2 ~ de** : to consist of
constatación *nf, pl* **-ciones** : confirmation, proof
constatar *vt* **1** : to verify **2** : to state
constelación *nf, pl* **-ciones** : constellation
consternación *nf, pl* **-ciones** : consternation, dismay
consternar *vt* : to dismay, to appall
constipación *nf, pl* **-ciones** : constipation
constipado[1], **-da** *adj* **estar constipado** : to have a cold
constipado[2] *nm* RESFRIADO : cold
constiparse *vr* : to catch a cold
constitución *nf, pl* **-ciones** : constitution — **constitucional** *adj* — **constitucionalmente** *adv*
constitucionalidad *nf* : constitutionality
constituir {41} *vt* **1** FORMAR : to constitute, to make up, to form **2** FUNDAR : to establish, to set up — **constituirse**

vr ~ en : to set oneself up as, to become
constitutivo, -va *adj* : constituent, component
constituyente *adj & nmf* : constituent
constreñir {67} *vt* **1** FORZAR, OBLIGAR : to constrain, to oblige **2** LIMITAR : to restrict, to limit
construcción *nf, pl* **-ciones** : construction, building
constructivo, -va *adj* : constructive — **constructivamente** *adv*
constructor, -tora *n* : builder
constructora *nf* : construction company
construir {41} *vt* : to build, to construct
consuelo *nm* : consolation, comfort
consuetudinario, -ria *adj* **1** : customary, habitual **2 derecho consuetudinario** : common law
cónsul *nmf* : consul — **consular** *adj*
consulado *nm* : consulate
consulta *nf* **1** : consultation **2** : inquiry
consultar *vt* : to consult
consultor[1], **-tora** *adj* : consulting ⟨firma consultora : consulting firm⟩
consultor[2], **-tora** *n* : consultant
consultorio *nm* : office (of a doctor or dentist)
consumación *nf, pl* **-ciones** : consummation
consumado, -da *adj* : consummate, perfect
consumar *vt* **1** : to consummate, to complete **2** : to commit, to carry out
consumible *adj* : consumable
consumición *nf, pl* **-ciones** **1** : consumption **2** : drink (in a restaurant)
consumido, -da *adj* : thin, emaciated
consumidor, -dora *n* : consumer
consumir *vt* : to consume — **consumirse** *vr* : to waste away
consumo *nm* : consumption
contabilidad *nf* **1** : accounting, bookkeeping **2** : accountancy
contabilizar {21} *vt* : to enter, to record (in accounting)
contable[1] *adj* : countable
contable[2] *nmf Spain* : accountant, bookkeeper
contactar *vt* : to contact — *vi ~ con* : to get in touch with, to contact
contacto *nm* : contact
contado[1], **-da** *adj* **1** : counted ⟨tenía los días contados : his days were numbered⟩ **2** : rare, scarce ⟨en contadas ocasiones : on rare occasions⟩
contado[2] *nm* **al contado** : cash ⟨pagar al contado : to pay in cash⟩
contador[1], **-dora** *n* : accountant
contador[2] *nm* : meter ⟨contador de agua : water meter⟩
contaduría *nf* **1** : accounting office **2** CONTABILIDAD : accountancy
contagiar *vt* **1** : to infect **2** : to transmit (a disease) — **contagiarse** *vr* **1** : to be contagious **2** : to become infected
contagio *nm* : contagion, infection

contagioso, -sa *adj* : contagious, catching
contaminación *nf, pl* **-ciones** : contamination, pollution
contaminante *nm* : pollutant, contaminant
contaminar *vt* : to contaminate, to pollute
contar {19} *vt* **1** : to count **2** : to tell **3** : to include — *vi* **1** : to count (up) **2** : to matter, to be of concern ⟨eso no cuenta : that doesn't matter⟩ **3** ~ **con** : to rely on, to count on — **contarse** *vr* ~ **entre** : to be numbered among
contemplación *nf, pl* **-ciones** : contemplation — **contemplativo, -va** *adj*
contemplar *vt* **1** : to contemplate, to ponder **2** : to gaze at, to look at
contemporáneo, -nea *adj & n* : contemporary
contención *nf, pl* **-ciones** : containment, holding
contencioso, -sa *adj* : contentious
contender {56} *vi* **1** : to contend, to compete **2** : to fight
contendiente *nmf* : contender
contenedor *nm* **1** : container, receptacle **2** : Dumpster™
contener {80} *vt* **1** : to contain, to hold **2** ATAJAR : to restrain, to hold back — **contenerse** *vr* : to restrain oneself
contenido¹, -da *adj* : restrained, reserved
contenido² *nm* : contents *pl*, content
contentar *vt* : to please, to make happy — **contentarse** *vr* : to be satisfied, to be pleased
contento¹, -ta *adj* : contented, glad, happy
contento² *nm* : joy, happiness
contestación *nf, pl* **-ciones 1** : answer, reply **2** : protest
contestar *vt* RESPONDER : to answer — *vi* **1** RESPONDER : to answer, to reply **2** REPLICAR : to answer back
contexto *nm* : context
contienda *nf* **1** : dispute, conflict **2** : contest, competition
contigo *pron* : with you ⟨voy contigo : I'm going with you⟩
contiguo, -gua *adj* COLINDANTE : contiguous, adjacent
continencia *nf* : continence
continente *nm* : continent — **continental** *adj*
contingencia *nf* : contingency, eventuality
contingente *adj & nm* : contingent
continuación *nf, pl* **-ciones 1** : continuation **2 a** ~ : next ⟨lo demás sigue a continuación : the rest follows⟩ **3 a continuación de** : after, following
continuar {3} *v* : to continue
continuidad *nf* : continuity
continuo, -nua *adj* : continuous, steady, constant — **continuamente** *adv*
contonearse *vr* : to sway one's hips
contoneo *nm* : swaying, wiggling (of the hips)

contorno *nm* **1** : outline **2 contornos** *nmpl* : outskirts
contorsión *nf, pl* **-siones** : contortion
contra¹ *nf* **1** *fam* : difficulty, snag **2 llevar la contra a** : to oppose, to contradict
contra² *nm* : con ⟨los pros y los contras : the pros and cons⟩
contra³ *prep* : against
contraalmirante *nm* : rear admiral
contraatacar {72} *v* : to counterattack — **contraataque** *nm*
contrabajo *nm* : double bass
contrabalancear *vt* : to counterbalance — **contrabalanza** *nf*
contrabandear *v* : to smuggle
contrabandista *nmf* : smuggler, black marketeer
contrabando *nm* **1** : smuggling **2** : contraband
contracción *nf, pl* **-ciones** : contraction
contracepción *nf, pl* **-ciones** : contraception
contraceptivo *nm* ANTICONCEPTIVO : contraceptive
contrachapado *nm* : plywood
contracorriente *nf* **1** : crosscurrent **2 ir a contracorriente** : to go against the tide
contractual *adj* : contractual
contradecir {11} *vt* DESMENTIR : to contradict — **contradecirse** *vr* DESDECIRSE : to contradict oneself
contradicción *nf, pl* **-ciones** : contradiction
contradictorio, -ria *adj* : contradictory
contraer {81} *vt* **1** : to contract (a disease) **2** : to establish by contract ⟨contraer matrimonio : to get married⟩ **3** : to tighten, to contract — **contraerse** *vr* : to contract, to tighten up
contrafuerte *nm* : buttress
contragolpe *nm* **1** : counterblow **2** : backlash
contrahecho, -cha *adj* : deformed, hunchbacked
contraindicado, -da *adj* : contraindicated — **contraindicación** *nf*
contralor, -lora *n* : comptroller
contralto *nmf* : contralto
contramaestre *nm* **1** : boatswain **2** : foreman
contramandar *vt* : to countermand
contramano *nm* **a** ~ : the wrong way (on a street)
contramedida *nf* : countermeasure
contraorden *nf* : countermand
contraparte *nf* **1** : counterpart **2 en** ~ : on the other hand
contrapartida *nf* : compensation
contrapelo *nm* **a** ~ : in the wrong direction, against the grain
contrapeso *nm* : counterbalance
contraponer {60} *vt* **1** : to counter, to oppose **2** : to contrast, to compare
contraposición *nf, pl* **-ciones** : comparison
contraproducente *adj* : counterproductive

contrapunto *nm* : counterpoint
contrariar {85} *vt* **1** : to contradict, to oppose **2** : to vex, to annoy
contrariedad *nf* **1** : setback, obstacle **2** : vexation, annoyance
contrario, -ria *adj* **1** : contrary, opposite ⟨al contrario : on the contrary⟩ **2** : conflicting, opposed
contrarrestar *vt* : to counteract
contrarrevolución *nf, pl* -**ciones** : counterrevolution — **contrarrevolucionario, -ria** *adj & n*
contrasentido *nm* : contradiction
contraseña *nf* : password
contrastante *adj* : contrasting
contrastar *vt* **1** : to resist **2** : to check, to confirm — *vi* : to contrast
contraste *nm* : contrast
contratar *vt* **1** : to contract for **2** : to hire, to engage
contratiempo *nm* **1** PERCANCE : mishap, accident **2** DIFICULTAD : setback, difficulty
contratista *nmf* : contractor
contrato *nm* : contract
contravenir {87} *vt* : to contravene, to infringe
contraventana *nf* : shutter
contribución *nf, pl* -**ciones** : contribution
contribuidor, -dora *n* : contributor
contribuir {41} *vt* **1** APORTAR : to contribute **2** : to pay (in taxes) — *vi* **1** : contribute, to help out **2** : to pay taxes
contribuyente[1] *adj* : contributing
contribuyente[2] *nmf* : taxpayer
contrición *nf, pl* -**ciones** : contrition
contrincante *nmf* : rival, opponent
contrito, -ta *adj* : contrite, repentant
control *nm* **1** : control **2** : inspection, check **3** : checkpoint, roadblock
controlador, -dora *n* : controller ⟨controlador aéreo : air traffic controller⟩
controlar *vt* **1** : to control **2** : to monitor, to check
controversia *nf* : controversy
controversial → **controvertido**
controvertido, -da *adj* : controversial
controvertir {76} *vt* : to dispute, to argue about — *vi* : to argue, to debate
contubernio *nm* : conspiracy
contumacia *nf* : obstinacy, stubbornness
contumaz *adj, pl* -**maces** : obstinate, stubbornly disobedient
contundencia *nf* **1** : forcefulness, weight **2** : severity
contundente *adj* **1** : blunt ⟨un objeto contundente : a blunt instrument⟩ **2** : forceful, convincing — **contundentemente** *adv*
contusión *nf, pl* -**siones** : bruise, contusion
contuvo, etc. → **contener**
convalecencia *nf* : convalescence
convalecer {53} *vi* : to convalesce, to recover

convaleciente *adj & nmf* : convalescent
convección *nf, pl* -**ciones** : convection
convencer {86} *vt* : to convince, to persuade — **convencerse** *vr*
convencimiento *nm* : belief, conviction
convención *nf, pl* -**ciones** **1** : convention, conference **2** : pact, agreement **3** : convention, custom
convencional *adj* : conventional — **convencionalmente** *adv*
convencionalismo *nm* : conventionality
conveniencia *nf* **1** : convenience **2** : fitness, suitability, advisability
conveniente *adj* **1** : convenient **2** : suitable, advisable
convenio *nm* PACTO : agreement, pact
convenir {87} *vi* **1** : to be suitable, to be advisable **2** : to agree
convento *nm* **1** : convent **2** : monastery
convergencia *nf* : convergence
convergente *adj* : convergent, converging
converger {15} *vi* **1** : to converge **2** ∼ **en** : to concur on
conversación *nf, pl* -**ciones** : conversation
conversador, -dora *n* : conversationalist, talker
conversar *vi* : to converse, to talk
conversión *nf, pl* -**siones** : conversion
converso, -sa *n* : convert
convertible *adj & nm* : convertible
convertidor *nm* : converter
convertir {76} *vt* **1** : to convert **2** : to transform, to change **3** : to exchange (money) — **convertirse** *vr* ∼ **en** : to turn into
convexo, -xa *adj* : convex
convicción *nf, pl* -**ciones** : conviction
convicto[1], -**ta** *adj* : convicted
convicto[2], -**ta** *n* : convict, prisoner
convidado, -da *n* : guest
convidar *vt* **1** INVITAR : to invite **2** : to offer
convincente *adj* : convincing — **convincentemente** *adv*
convivencia *nf* **1** : coexistence **2** : cohabitation
convivir *vi* **1** : to coexist **2** : to live together
convocación *nf, pl* -**ciones** : convocation
convocar {72} *vt* : to convoke, to call together
convocatoria *nf* : summons, call
convoy *nm* : convoy
convulsión *nf, pl* -**siones** **1** : convulsion **2** : agitation, upheaval
convulsionar *vt* : to shake, to convulse — **convulsionarse** *vr*
convulsivo, -va *adj* : convulsive
conyugal *adj* : conjugal
cónyuge *nmf* : spouse, partner
coñac *nm* : cognac, brandy
cooperación *nf, pl* -**ciones** : cooperation
cooperador, -dora *adj* : cooperative

cooperar *vi* : to cooperate
cooperativa *nf* : cooperative, co-op
cooperativo, -va *adj* : cooperative
cooptar *vt* : to co-opt
coordenada *nf* : coordinate
coordinación *nf, pl* **-ciones** : coordination
coordinador, -dora *n* : coordinator
coordinar *vt* COMPAGINAR : to coordinate, to combine
copa *nf* **1** : wineglass, goblet **2** : drink ⟨irse de copas : to go out drinking⟩ **3** : cup, trophy
copar *vt* **1** : to take ⟨ya está copado el puesto : the job is already taken⟩ **2** : to fill, to crowd
copartícipe *nmf* : joint partner
copete *nm* **1** : tuft (of hair) **2 estar hasta el copete** : to be completely fed up
copia *nf* **1** : copy **2** : imitation, replica
copiadora *nf* : photocopier
copiar *vt* : to copy
copiloto *nmf* : copilot
copioso, -sa *adj* : copious, abundant
copla *nf* **1** : popular song or ballad **2** : couplet, stanza
copo *nm* **1** : snowflake **2 copos de avena** : rolled oats **3 copos de maíz** : cornflakes
copra *nf* : copra
cópula *nf* : copulation
copular *vi* : to copulate
coque *nm* : coke (fuel)
coqueta *nf* : dressing table
coquetear *vi* : to flirt
coqueteo *nm* : flirting, coquetry
coqueto[1], -ta *adj* : flirtatious, coquettish
coqueto[2], -ta *n* : flirt
coraje *nm* **1** VALOR : valor, courage **2** IRA : anger ⟨darle coraje a alguien : to make someone angry⟩
corajudo, -da *adj* : brave
coral[1] *nm* **1** : coral **2** : chorale
coral[2] *nf* : choir
Corán *nm* **el Corán** : the Koran
coraza *nf* **1** : armor, armor plating **2** : shell (of an animal)
corazón *nm, pl* **-zones 1** : heart ⟨de todo corazón : wholeheartedly⟩ ⟨de buen corazón : kindhearted⟩ **2** : core **3** : darling, sweetheart
corazonada *nf* : hunch, impulse
corbata *nf* : tie, necktie
corcel *nm* : steed, charger
corchete *nm* **1** : hook and eye, clasp **2** : square bracket
corcho *nm* : cork
corcholata *nf Mex* : cap, bottle top
corcovear *vi* : to buck
cordel *nm* : cord, string
cordero *nm* : lamb
cordial[1] *adj* : cordial, affable — **cordialmente** *adv*
cordial[2] *nm* : cordial (liqueur)
cordialidad *nf* : cordiality, warmth
cordillera *nf* : mountain range
córdoba *nf* : Nicaraguan unit of currency

cordón *nm, pl* **cordones 1** : cord ⟨cordón umbilical : umbilical cord⟩ **2** : cordon
cordura *nf* **1** : sanity **2** : prudence, good judgment
coreano[1], -na *adj & n* : Korean
coreano[2] *nm* : Korean (language)
corear *vt* : to chant, to chorus
coreografía *nf* : choreography
coreografiar {85} *vt* : to choreograph
coreográfico, -ca *adj* : choreographic
coreógrafo, -fa *n* : choreographer
corista *nmf* **1** : chorister **2** : chorus girl *f*
cormorán *nm, pl* **-ranes** : cormorant
cornada *nf* : goring, butt (with the horns)
córnea *nf* : cornea
cornear *vt* : to gore
cornejo *nm* : dogwood (tree)
corneta *nf* : bugle, horn, cornet
cornisa *nf* : cornice
cornudo, -da *adj* : horned
coro *nm* **1** : choir **2** : chorus
corola *nf* : corolla
corolario *nm* : corollary
corona *nf* **1** : crown **2** : wreath, garland **3** : corona (in astronomy)
coronación *nf, pl* **-ciones** : coronation
coronar *vt* **1** : to crown **2** : to reach the top of, to culminate
coronario, -ria *adj* : coronary
coronel, -nela *n* : colonel
coronilla *nf* **1** : crown (of the head) **2 estar hasta la coronilla** : to be completely fed up
corpiño *nm* **1** : bodice **2** *Arg* : brassiere, bra
corporación *nf, pl* **-ciones** : corporation
corporal *adj* : corporal, bodily
corporativo, -va *adj* : corporate
corpóreo, -rea *adj* : corporeal, physical
corpulencia *nf* : corpulence, stoutness, sturdiness
corpulento, -ta *adj* ROBUSTO : robust, stout, sturdy
corpúsculo *nm* : corpuscle
corral *nm* **1** : farmyard **2** : corral, pen, stockyard **3** *or* **corralito** : playpen
correa *nf* : strap, belt
correcaminos *nms & pl* : roadrunner
corrección *nf, pl* **-ciones 1** : correction **2** : correctness, propriety **3** : rebuke, reprimand **4 corrección de pruebas** : proofreading
correccional *nm* REFORMATORIO : reformatory
correctivo, -va *adj* : corrective ⟨lentes correctivos : corrective lenses⟩
correcto, -ta *adj* **1** : correct, right **2** : courteous, polite — **correctamente** *adv*
corrector, -tora *n* : proofreader
corredizo, -za *adj* : sliding ⟨puerta corrediza : sliding door⟩
corredor[1], -dora *n* **1** : runner, racer **2** : agent, broker ⟨corredor de bolsa : stockbroker⟩
corredor[2] *nm* PASILLO : corridor, hallway

correduría *nf* → **corretaje**

corregir {28} *vt* **1** ENMENDAR : to correct, to emend **2** : to reprimand **3 corregir pruebas** : to proofread — **corregirse** *vr* : to reform, to mend one's ways

correlación *nf, pl* **-ciones** : correlation

correo *nm* **1** : mail ⟨correo aéreo : airmail⟩ **2** : post office

correoso, -sa *adj* : leathery, rough

correr *vi* **1** : to run, to race **2** : to rush **3** : to flow — *vt* **1** : to travel over, to cover **2** : to move, to slide, to roll, to draw (curtains) **3 correr un riesgo** : to run a risk — **correrse** *vr* **1** : to move along **2** : to run, to spill over

correspondencia *nf* **1** : correspondence, mail **2** : equivalence **3** : connection, interchange

corresponder *vi* **1** : to correspond **2** : to pertain, to belong **3** : to be appropriate, to fit **4** : to reciprocate — **corresponderse** *vr* : to write to each other

correspondiente *adj* : corresponding, respective

corresponsal *nmf* : correspondent

corretaje *nm* : brokerage

corretear *vi* **1** VAGAR : to loiter, to wander about **2** : to run around, to scamper about — *vt* : to pursue, to chase

corrida *nf* **1** : run, dash **2** : bullfight

corrido[1], **-da** *adj* **1** : straight, continuous **2** : worldly, experienced

corrido[2] *nm* : Mexican narrative folk song

corriente[1] *adj* **1** : common, everyday **2** : current, present **3** *Mex* : cheap, trashy **4 perro corriente** *Mex* : mutt

corriente[2] *nf* **1** : current ⟨corriente alterna : alternating current⟩ ⟨direct current : corriente continua⟩ **2** : draft **3** TENDENCIA : tendency, trend

corrillo *nm* : small group, clique

corro *nm* : ring, circle (of people)

corroboración *nf, pl* **-ciones** : corroboration

corroborar *vt* : to corroborate

corroer {69} *vt* **1** : to corrode **2** : to erode, to wear away

corromper *vt* **1** : to corrupt **2** : to rot — **corromperse** *vr*

corrompido, -da *adj* CORRUPTO : corrupt, rotten

corrosión *nf, pl* **-siones** : corrosion

corrosivo, -va *adj* : corrosive

corrugar {52} *vt* : to corrugate — **corrugación** *nf*

corrupción *nf, pl* **-ciones** **1** : decay **2** : corruption

corruptela *nf* : corruption, abuse of power

corrupto, -ta *adj* CORROMPIDO : corrupt

corsario *nm* : privateer

corsé *nm* : corset

cortada *nf* : cut, gash

cortador, -dora *n* : cutter

cortadora *nf* : cutter, slicer

cortadura *nf* : cut, slash

cortafuegos *nms & pl* **1** : firebreak **2** : firewall (program)

cortante *adj* : cutting, sharp

cortar *vt* **1** : to cut, to slice, to trim **2** : to cut out, to omit **3** : to cut off, to interrupt **4** : to block, to close off **5** : to curdle (milk) — *vi* **1** : to cut **2** : to break up **3** : to hang up (the telephone) — **cortarse** *vr* **1** : to cut oneself ⟨cortarse el pelo : to cut one's hair⟩ **2** : to be cut off **3** : to sour (of milk)

cortauñas *nms & pl* : nail clippers

corte[1] *nm* **1** : cut, cutting ⟨corte de pelo : haircut⟩ **2** : style, fit

corte[2] *nf* **1** : court ⟨corte suprema : supreme court⟩ **2 hacer la corte a** : to court, to woo

cortejar *vt* GALANTEAR : to court, to woo

cortejo *nm* **1** GALANTEO : courtship **2** : retinue, entourage

cortés *adj* : courteous, polite — **cortésmente** *adv*

cortesano[1], **-na** *adj* : courtly

cortesano[2], **-na** *n* : courtier

cortesía *nf* **1** : courtesy, politeness **2 de** ~ : complimentary, free

corteza *nf* **1** : bark **2** : crust **3** : peel, rind **4** : cortex ⟨corteza cerebral : cerebral cortex⟩

cortijo *nm* : farmhouse

cortina *nf* : curtain

cortisona *nf* : cortisone

corto, -ta *adj* **1** : short (in length or duration) **2** : scarce **3** : timid, shy **4 corto de vista** : nearsighted

cortocircuito *nm* : short circuit

corvejón *nm, pl* **-jones** JARRETTE : hock

corvo, -va *adj* : curved, bent

cosa *nf* **1** : thing, object **2** : matter, affair **3 otra cosa** : anything else, something else

cosecha *nf* : harvest, crop

cosechador, -dora *n* : harvester, reaper

cosechadora *nf* : harvester (machine)

cosechar *vt* **1** : to harvest, to reap **2** : to win, to earn, to garner — *vi* : to harvest

coser *vt* **1** : to sew **2** : to stitch up — *vi* : to sew

cosmético[1], **-ca** *adj* : cosmetic

cosmético[2] *nm* : cosmetic

cósmico, -ca *adj* : cosmic

cosmonauta *nmf* : cosmonaut

cosmopolita *adj & nmf* : cosmopolitan

cosmos *nm* : cosmos

cosquillas *nfpl* **1** : tickling **2 hacer cosquillas** : to tickle

cosquilleo *nm* : tickling sensation, tingle

cosquilloso, -sa *adj* : ticklish

costa *nf* **1** : coast, shore **2** : cost ⟨a toda costa : at all costs⟩

costado *nm* **1** : side **2 al costado** : alongside

costar {19} *v* : to cost ⟨¿cuánto cuesta? : how much does it cost?⟩

costarricense *adj & nmf* : Costa Rican

costarriqueño, -ña → **costarricense**

coste → **costo**

costear *vt* : to pay for, to finance

costero, -ra *adj* : coastal, coast
costilla *nf* 1 : rib 2 : chop, cutlet 3 *fam* : better half, wife
costo *nm* 1 : cost, price 2 costo de vida : cost of living
costoso, -sa *adj* : costly, expensive
costra *nf* 1 : crust 2 POSTILLA : scab
costumbre *nf* 1 : custom 2 HÁBITO : habit
costura *nf* 1 : seam 2 : sewing, dressmaking 3 alta costura : haute couture
costurera *nf* : seamstress *f*
cotejar *vt* : to compare, to collate
cotejo *nm* : comparison, collation
cotidiano, -na *adj* : daily, everyday ⟨la vida cotidiana : daily life⟩
cotización *nf, pl* -ciones 1 : market price 2 : quote, estimate
cotizado, -da *adj* : in demand, sought after
cotizar {21} *vt* : to quote, to value — cotizarse *vr* : to be worth
coto *nm* 1 : enclosure, reserve 2 poner coto a : to put a stop to
cotorra *nf* 1 : small parrot 2 *fam* : chatterbox, windbag
cotorrear *vi fam* : to chatter, to gab, to blab
cotorreo *nm fam* : chatter, prattle
coyote *nm* 1 : coyote 2 *Mex fam* : smuggler (of illegal immigrants)
coyuntura *nf* 1 ARTICULACIÓN : joint 2 : occasion, moment
coz *nf, pl* coces : kick (of an animal)
crac *nm, pl* cracs : crash (of the stock market)
cozamos, etc. → cocer
craneal *adj* : cranial
cráneo *nf* : cranium, skull — craneano, -na *adj*
cráter *nm* : crater
crayón *nm, pl* -yones : crayon
creación *nf, pl* -ciones : creation
creador[1], -dora *adj* : creative, creating
creador[2], -dora *n* : creator
crear *vt* 1 : to create, to cause 2 : to originate
creatividad *nf* : creativity
creativo, -va *adj* : creative
crecer {53} *vi* 1 : to grow 2 : to increase
crecida *nf* : flooding, floodwater
crecido, -da *adj* 1 : grown, grown-up 2 : large (of numbers)
creciente *adj* 1 : growing, increasing 2 luna creciente : waxing moon
crecientemente *adv* : increasingly
crecimiento *nm* 1 : growth 2 : increase
credencial *adj* cartas credenciales : credentials
credenciales *nfpl* : documents, documentation, credentials
credibilidad *nf* : credibility
crédito *nm* : credit
credo *nm* : creed, credo
credulidad *nf* : credulity
crédulo, -la *adj* : credulous, gullible
creencia *nf* : belief
creer {20} *v* 1 : to believe 2 : to suppose, to think ⟨creo que sí : I think so⟩

— creerse *vr* 1 : to believe, to think 2 : to regard oneself as ⟨se cree guapísimo : he thinks he's so handsome⟩
creíble *adj* : believable, credible
creído, -da *adj* 1 *fam* : conceited 2 : confident, sure
crema *nf* 1 : cream 2 la crema y nata : the pick of the crop
cremación *nf, pl* -ciones : cremation
cremallera *nf* : zipper
cremar *vt* : to cremate
cremoso, -sa *adj* : creamy
crepa *nf Mex* : crepe (pancake)
crepe *or* crep *nmf* : crepe (pancake)
crepé *nm* 1 → crespón 2 papel crepé : crepe paper
crepitar *vi* : to crackle
crepúsculo *nm* : twilight
crescendo *nm* : crescendo
crespo, -pa *adj* : curly, frizzy
crespón *nm, pl* crespones : crepe (fabric)
cresta *nf* 1 : crest 2 : comb (of a rooster)
creta *nf* : chalk (mineral)
cretino, -na *n* : cretin
creyente *nmf* : believer
creyó, etc. → creer
crezca, etc. → crecer
cría *nf* 1 : breeding, rearing 2 : young 3 : litter
criadero *nm* : hatchery
criado[1], -da *adj* 1 : raised, brought up 2 bien criado : well-bred
criado[2], -da *n* : servant, maid *f*
criador, -dora *n* : breeder
crianza *nf* : upbringing, rearing
criar {85} *vt* 1 : to breed 2 : to bring up, to raise
criatura *nf* 1 : baby, child 2 : creature
criba *nf* : sieve, screen
cribar *vt* : to sift
cric *nm, pl* crics : jack
crimen *nm, pl* crímenes : crime
criminal *adj & nmf* : criminal
crin *nf* 1 : mane 2 : horsehair
criollo[1], -lla *adj* 1 : Creole 2 : native, national ⟨comida criolla : native cuisine⟩
criollo[2], -lla *n* : Creole
criollo[3] *nm* : Creole (language)
cripta *nf* : crypt
críptico, -ca *adj* 1 : cryptic, coded 2 : enigmatic, cryptic
criptón *nm* : krypton
críquet *nm* : cricket (game)
crisálida *nf* : chrysalis, pupa
crisantemo *nm* : chrysanthemum
crisis *nf* 1 : crisis 2 crisis nerviosa : nervous breakdown
crisma *nf fam* : head ⟨romperle la crisma a alguien : to knock someone's block off⟩
crisol *nm* 1 : crucible 2 : melting pot
crispar *vt* 1 : to cause to contract 2 : to irritate, to set on edge ⟨eso me crispa : that gets on my nerves⟩ — crisparse *vr* : to tense up

cristal *nm* **1** VIDRIO : glass, piece of glass **2** : crystal
cristalería *nf* **1** : glassware shop ⟨como chivo en cristalería : like a bull in a china shop⟩ **2** : glassware, crystal
cristalino[1], **-na** *adj* : crystalline, clear
cristalino[2] *nm* : lens (of the eye)
cristalizar {21} *vi* : to crystallize — **cristalización** *nf*
cristiandad *nf* : Christendom
cristianismo *nm* : Christianity
cristiano, -na *adj & n* : Christian
Cristo *nm* : Christ
criterio *nm* **1** : criterion **2** : judgment, sense
crítica *nf* **1** : criticism **2** : review, critique
criticar {72} *vt* : to criticize
crítico[1], **-ca** *adj* : critical — **críticamente** *adv*
crítico[2], **-ca** *n* : critic
criticón[1], **-cona** *adj, mpl* **-cones** *fam* : hypercritical, captious
criticón[2], **-cona** *n, mpl* **-cones** *fam* : faultfinder, critic
croar *vi* : to croak
croata *adj & nmf* : Croatian
crocante *adj* : crunchy
croché *or* **crochet** *nm* : crochet
cromático, -ca *adj* : chromatic
cromo *nm* **1** : chromium, chrome **2** : picture card, sports card
cromosoma *nm* : chromosome
crónica *nf* **1** : news report **2** : chronicle, history
crónico, -ca *adj* : chronic
cronista *nmf* **1** : reporter, newscaster **2** HISTORIADOR : chronicler, historian
cronología *nf* : chronology
cronológico, -ca *adj* : chronological — **cronológicamente** *adv*
cronometrador, -dora *n* : timekeeper
cronometrar *vt* : to time, to clock
cronómetro *nm* : chronometer
croquet *nm* : croquet
croqueta *nf* : croquette
croquis *nm* : rough sketch
cruce[1], etc. → **cruzar**
cruce[2] *nm* **1** : crossing, cross **2** : crossroads, intersection ⟨cruce peatonal : crosswalk⟩
crucero *nm* **1** : cruise **2** : cruiser, warship **3** *Mex* : intersection
crucial *adj* : crucial — **crucialmente** *adv*
crucificar {72} *vt* : to crucify
crucifijo *nm* : crucifix
crucifixión *nf, pl* **-fixiones** : crucifixion
crucigrama *nm* : crossword puzzle
crudo[1], **-da** *adj* **1** : raw **2** : crude, harsh
crudo[2] *nm* : crude oil
cruel *adj* : cruel — **cruelmente** *adv*
crueldad *nf* : cruelty
cruento, -ta *adj* : bloody
crujido *nm* **1** : rustling **2** : creaking **3** : crackling (of a fire) **4** : crunching
crujiente *adj* : crunchy, crisp
crujir *vi* **1** : to rustle **2** : to creak, to crack **3** : to crunch

crup *nm* : croup
crustáceo *nm* : crustacean
crutón *nm, pl* **crutones** : crouton
cruz *nf, pl* **cruces** : cross
cruza *nf* : cross (hybrid)
cruzada *nf* : crusade
cruzado[1], **-da** *adj* : crossed ⟨espadas cruzadas : crossed swords⟩
cruzado[2] *nm* **1** : crusader **2** : Brazilian unit of currency
cruzar {21} *vt* **1** : to cross **2** : to exchange (words, greetings) **3** : to cross, to interbreed — **cruzarse** *vr* **1** : to intersect **2** : to meet, to pass each other
cuaderno *nm* LIBRETA : notebook
cuadra *nf* **1** : city block **2** : stable
cuadrado[1], **-da** *adj* : square
cuadrado[2] *nm* : square ⟨elevar al cuadrado : to square (a number)⟩
cuadragésimo[1] *adj* : fortieth, forty-
cuadragésimo[2], **-ma** *n* : fortieth, forty- (in a series)
cuadrante *nm* **1** : quadrant **2** : dial
cuadrar *vi* : to conform, to agree — *vt* : to square — **cuadrarse** *vr* : to stand at attention
cuadriculado *nm* : grid (on a map, etc.)
cuadrilátero *nm* **1** : quadrilateral **2** : ring (in sports)
cuadrilla *nf* : gang, team, group
cuadro *nm* **1** : square ⟨una blusa a cuadros : a checkered blouse⟩ **2** : painting, picture **3** : baseball diamond, infield **4** : panel, board, cadre
cuadrúpedo *nm* : quadruped
cuadruple *adj* : quadruple
cuadruplicar {72} *vt* : to quadruple — **cuadruplicarse** *vr*
cuajada *nf* : curd
cuajar *vi* **1** : to curdle **2** COAGULAR : to clot, to coagulate **3** : to set, to jell **4** : to be accepted ⟨su idea no cuajó : his idea didn't catch on⟩ — *vt* **1** : to curdle **2** ~ **de** : to fill with
cual[1] *prep* : like, as
cual[2] *pron* **1** el cual, la cual, los cuales, las cuales : who, whom, which ⟨la razón por la cual te dije : the reason I said it⟩ **2** lo cual : which ⟨se rió, lo cual me dio rabia : he laughed, which made me mad⟩ **3** cada cual : everyone, everybody
cuál[1] *adj* : which, what ⟨¿cuáles libros? : which books?⟩
cuál[2] *pron* **1** (*in questions*) : which (one), what (one) ⟨¿cuál es el mejor? : which one is the best?⟩ ⟨¿cuál es tu apellido? : what is your last name?⟩ **2 cuál más, cuál menos** : some more, some less
cualidad *nf* : quality, trait
cualitativo, -va *adj* : qualitative — **cualitativamente** *adv*
cualquier *adj* → **cualquiera**[1]
cualquiera[1] (**cualquier** *before nouns*) *adj, pl* **cualesquiera 1** : any, whichever ⟨cualquier persona : any person⟩ **2** : everyday, ordinary ⟨un hombre cualquiera : an ordinary man⟩

cualquiera[2] *pron, pl* **cualesquiera 1** : anyone, anybody, whoever **2** : whatever, whichever

cuán *adv* : how ⟨¡cuán risible fue todo eso! : how funny it all was!⟩

cuando[1] *conj* **1** : when ⟨cuando llegó : when he arrived⟩ **2** : since, if ⟨cuando lo dices : if you say so⟩ **3 cuando más** : at the most **4 de vez en cuando** : from time to time

cuando[2] *prep* : during, at the time of ⟨cuando la guerra : during the war⟩

cuándo *adv & conj* **1** : when ⟨¿cuándo llegará? : when will she arrive?⟩ ⟨no sabemos cuándo será : we don't know when it will be⟩ **2 ¿de cuándo acá?** : since when?, how come?

cuantía *nf* **1** : quantity, extent **2** : significance, import

cuántico, -ca *adj* : quantum ⟨teoría cuántica : quantum theory⟩

cuantioso, -sa *adj* **1** : abundant, considerable **2** : heavy, grave ⟨cuantiosos daños : heavy damage⟩

cuantitativo, -va *adj* : quantitative — **cuantitativamente** *adv*

cuanto[1] *adv* **1** : as much as ⟨come cuanto puedas : eat as much as you can⟩ **2 cuanto antes** : as soon as possible **3 en ~** : as soon as **4 en cuanto a** : as for, as regards

cuanto[2], **-ta** *adj* : as many, whatever ⟨llévate cuantas flores quieras : take as many flowers as you wish⟩

cuanto[3], **-ta** *pron* **1** : as much as, all that, everything ⟨tengo cuanto deseo : I have all that I want⟩ **2 unos cuantos, unas cuantas** : a few

cuánto[1] *adv* : how much, how many ⟨¿a cuánto están las manzanas? : how much are the apples?⟩ ⟨no sé cuánto desean : I don't know how much they want⟩

cuánto[2], **-ta** *adj* : how much, how many ⟨¿cuántos niños tiene? : how many children do you have?⟩

cuánto[3] *pron* : how much, how many ⟨¿cuántos quieren participar? : how many want to take part?⟩ ⟨¿cuánto cuesta? : how much does it cost?⟩

cuarenta *adj & nm* : forty

cuarentavo[1], **-va** *adj* : fortieth

cuarentavo[2] *nm* : fortieth (fraction)

cuarentena *nf* **1** : group of forty **2** : quarantine

Cuaresma *nf* : Lent

cuartear *vt* **1** : to quarter **2** : to divide up — **cuartearse** *vr* AGRIETARSE : to crack, to split

cuartel *nm* **1** : barracks, headquarters **2** : mercy ⟨una guerra sin cuartel : a merciless war⟩

cuartelazo *nm* : coup d'état

cuarteto *nm* : quartet

cuartilla *nf* : sheet (of paper)

cuarto[1], **-ta** *adj* : fourth

cuarto[2], **-ta** *n* : fourth (in a series)

cuarto[3] *nm* **1** : quarter, fourth ⟨cuarto de galón : quart⟩ **2** HABITACIÓN : room

cuarzo *nm* : quartz

cuate, -ta *n Mex* **1** : twin **2** *fam* : buddy, pal

cuatrero, -ra *n* : rustler

cuatrillizo, -za *n* : quadruplet

cuatro *adj & nm* : four

cuatrocientos[1], **-tas** *adj* : four hundred

cuatrocientos[2] *nms & pl* : four hundred

cuba *nf* BARRIL : cask, barrel

cubano, -na *adj & n* : Cuban

cubertería *nf* : flatware, silverware

cubeta *nf* **1** : keg, cask **2** : bulb (of a thermometer) **3** *Mex* : bucket, pail

cúbico, -ca *adj* : cubic, cubed

cubículo *nm* : cubicle

cubierta *nf* **1** : covering **2** FORRO : cover, jacket (of a book) **3** : deck

cubierto[1] *pp* → **cubrir**

cubierto[2] *nm* **1** : cover, shelter ⟨bajo cubierto : under cover⟩ **2** : table setting **3** : utensil, piece of silverware

cubil *nm* : den, lair

cúbito *nm* : ulna

cubo *nm* **1** : cube **2** BALDE : pail, bucket, can ⟨cubo de basura : garbage can⟩ **3** : hub (of a wheel)

cubrecama *nm* COLCHA : bedspread

cubrir {2} *vt* : to cover — **cubrirse** *vr*

cucaracha *nf* : cockroach, roach

cuchara *nf* : spoon

cucharada *nf* : spoonful

cucharilla *or* **cucharita** *nf* : teaspoon

cucharón *nm, pl* **-rones** : ladle

cuchichear *vi* : to whisper

cuchicheo *nm* : whisper

cuchilla *nf* **1** : kitchen knife, cleaver **2** : blade ⟨cuchilla de afeitar : razor blade⟩ **3** : crest, ridge

cuchillada *nf* : stab, knife wound

cuchillo *nm* : knife

cuclillas *nfpl* **en ~** : squatting, crouching

cuco[1], **-ca** *adj fam* : pretty, cute

cuco[2] *nm* : cuckoo

cucurucho *nm* : ice-cream cone

cuece, cueza etc. → **cocer**

cuela, etc. → **colar**

cuelga, cuelgue etc. → **colgar**

cuello *nm* **1** : neck **2** : collar (of a shirt) **3 cuello del útero** : cervix

cuenca *nf* **1** : river basin **2** : eye socket

cuenco *nm* **1** : bowl, basin

cuenta[1], etc. → **contar**

cuenta[2] *nf* **1** : calculation, count **2** : account **3** : check, bill **4 darse cuenta** : to realize **5 tener en cuenta** : to bear in mind

cuentagotas *nfs & pl* **1** : dropper **2 con ~** : little by little

cuentista *nmf* **1** : short story writer **2** *fam* : liar, fibber

cuento *nm* **1** : story, tale **2 cuento de hadas** : fairy tale **3 sin ~** : countless

cuerda *nf* **1** : cord, rope, string **2 cuerdas vocales** : vocal cords **3 darle cuerda a** : to wind up (a clock, a toy, etc.)

cuerdo, -da *adj* : sane, sensible
cuerno *nm* **1** : horn, antler **2** : cusp (of the moon) **3** : horn (musical instrument)
cuero *nm* **1** : leather, hide **2 cuero cabelludo** : scalp
cuerpo *nm* **1** : body **2** : corps
cuervo *nm* : crow, raven
cuesta[1], etc. → **costar**
cuesta[2] *nf* **1** : slope ⟨cuesta arriba : uphill⟩ **2 a cuestas** : on one's back
cuestión *nf, pl* **-tiones** ASUNTO, TEMA : matter, affair
cuestionable *adj* : questionable, dubious
cuestionar *vt* : to question
cuestionario *nm* **1** : questionnaire **2** : quiz
cueva *nf* : cave
cuidado *nm* **1** : care **2** : worry, concern **3 tener cuidado** : to be careful **4 ¡cuidado!** : watch out!, be careful!
cuidador, -dora *n* : caretaker
cuidadoso, -sa *adj* : careful, attentive — **cuidadosamente** *adv*
cuidar *vt* **1** : to take care of, to look after **2** : to pay attention to — *vi* **1 ~ de** : to look after **2 cuidar de que** : to make sure that — **cuidarse** *vr* : to take care of oneself
culata *nf* : butt (of a gun)
culatazo *nf* : kick, recoil
culebra *nf* SERPIENTE : snake
culi *nmf* : coolie
culinario, -ria *adj* : culinary
culminante *adj* **punto culminante** : peak, high point, climax
culminar *vi* : to culminate — **culminación** *nf*
culo *nm* **1** *fam* : backside, behind **2** : bottom (of a glass)
culpa *nf* **1** : fault, blame ⟨echarle la culpa a alguien : to blame someone⟩ **2** : sin
culpabilidad *nf* : guilt
culpable[1] *adj* : guilty
culpable[2] *nmf* : culprit, guilty party
culpar *vt* : to blame
cultivado, -da *adj* **1** : cultivated, farmed **2** : cultured
cultivador, -dora *n* : cultivator
cultivar *vt* **1** : to cultivate **2** : to foster
cultivo *nm* **1** : cultivation, farming **2** : crop
culto[1], **-ta** *adj* : cultured, educated
culto[2] *nm* **1** : worship **2** : cult
cultura *nf* : culture
cultural *adj* : cultural — **culturalmente** *adv*
cumbre *nf* CIMA : top, peak, summit
cumpleaños *nms & pl* : birthday
cumplido[1], **-da** *adj* **1** : complete, full **2** : courteous, correct
cumplido[2] *nm* : compliment, courtesy ⟨por cumplido : out of courtesy⟩ ⟨andarse con cumplidos : to stand on ceremony, to be formal⟩
cumplimentar *vt* **1** : to congratulate **2** : to carry out, to perform

cumplimiento *nm* **1** : completion, fulfillment **2** : performance
cumplir *vt* **1** : to accomplish, to carry out **2** : to comply with, to fulfill **3** : to attain, to reach ⟨su hermana cumple los 21 el viernes : her sister will be 21 on Friday⟩ — *vi* **1** : to expire, to fall due **2** : to fulfill one's obligations ⟨cumplir con el deber : to do one's duty⟩ ⟨cumplir con la palabra : to keep one's word⟩ — **cumplirse** *vr* **1** : to come true, to be fulfilled ⟨se cumplieron sus sueños : her dreams came true⟩ **2** : to run out, to expire
cúmulo *nm* **1** MONTÓN : heap, pile **2** : cumulus
cuna *nf* **1** : cradle **2** : birthplace ⟨Puerto Rico es la cuna de la música salsa : Puerto Rico is the birthplace of salsa music⟩
cundir *vi* **1** : to propagate, to spread ⟨cundió el pánico en el vecindario : panic spread throughout the neighborhood⟩ **2** : to progress, to make headway
cuneta *nf* : ditch (in a road), gutter
cuña *nf* : wedge
cuñado, -da *n* : brother-in-law *m*, sister-in-law *f*
cuño *nm* : die (for stamping)
cuota *nf* **1** : fee, dues **2** : quota, share **3** : installment, payment
cupé *nm* : coupe
cupo[1], etc. → **caber**
cupo[2] *nm* **1** : quota, share **2** : capacity, room
cupón *nm, pl* **cupones 1** : coupon, voucher **2 cupón federal** : food stamp
cúpula *nf* : dome, cupola
cura[1] *nm* : priest
cura[2] *nf* **1** CURACIÓN, TRATAMIENTO : cure, treatment **2** : dressing, bandage
curación *nf, pl* **-ciones** CURA, TRATAMIENTO : cure, treatment
curandero, -ra *nm* **1** : witch doctor **2** : quack, charlatan
curar *vt* **1** : to cure, to heal **2** : to treat, to dress **3** CURTIR : to tan **4** : to cure (meat) — *vi* : to get well, to recover — **curarse** *vr*
curativo, -va *adj* : curative, healing
curiosear *vi* **1** : to snoop, to pry **2** : to browse — *vt* : to look over, to check
curiosidad *nf* **1** : curiosity **2** : curio
curioso, -sa *adj* **1** : curious, inquisitive **2** : strange, unusual, odd — **curiosamente** *adv*
currículo → **currículum**
currículum *nm, pl* **-lums 1** : résumé, curriculum vitae **2** : curriculum, course of study
curry [ˈkurri] *nm, pl* **-rries 1** : curry powder **2** : curry (dish)
cursar *vt* **1** : to attend (school), to take (a course) **2** : to dispatch, to pass on
cursi *adj fam* : affected, pretentious
cursilería *nf* **1** : vulgarity, poor taste **2** : pretentiousness

cursiva *nf* BASTARDILLA : italic type, italics *pl*
curso *nm* **1** : course, direction **2** : school year **3** : course, subject (in school)
cursor *nm* : cursor
curtido, -da *adj* : weather-beaten, leathery (of skin)
curtidor, -dora *n* : tanner
curtiduría *nf* : tannery
curtir *vt* **1** : to tan **2** : to harden, to weather — **curtirse** *vr*
curva *nf* : curve, bend
curvar *vt* : to bend

curvatura *nf* : curvature
curvilíneo, -nea *adj* : curvaceous, shapely
curvo, -va *adj* : curved, bent
cúspide *nf* : zenith, apex, peak
custodia *nf* : custody
custodiar *vt* : to guard, to look after
custodio, -dia *n* : keeper, guardian
cúter *nm* : cutter (boat)
cutícula *nf* : cuticle
cutis *nms & pl* : skin, complexion
cuyo, -ya *adj* **1** : whose, of whom, of which **2 en cuyo caso** : in which case

D

d *nf* : fourth letter of the Spanish alphabet
dable *adj* : feasible, possible
dactilar *adj* **huellas dactilares** : fingerprints
dádiva *nf* : gift, handout
dadivoso, -sa *adj* : generous
dado, -da *adj* **1** : given **2 dado que** : given that, since
dador, -dora *n* : giver, donor
dados *nmpl* : dice
daga *nf* : dagger
dalia *nf* : dahlia
dálmata *nm* : dalmatian
daltónico, -ca *adj* : color-blind
daltonismo *nm* : color blindness
dama *nf* **1** : lady **2 damas** *nfpl* : checkers
damasco *nm* : damask
damisela *nf* : damsel
damnificado, -da *n* : victim (of a disaster)
damnificar {72} *vt* : to damage, to injure
dance, etc. → **danzar**
dandi *nm* : dandy, fop
danés[1], -nesa *adj* : Danish
danés[2], -nesa *n, mpl* **daneses** : Dane, Danish person
danza *nf* : dance, dancing ⟨danza folklórica : folk dance⟩
danzante, -ta *n* BAILARÍN : dancer
danzar {21} *v* BAILAR : to dance
dañar *vt* **1** : to damage, to spoil **2** : to harm, to hurt — **dañarse** *vr*
dañino, -na *adj* : harmful
daño *nm* **1** : damage **2** : harm, injury **3 hacer daño a** : to harm, to damage **4 daños y perjuicios** : damages
dar {22} *vt* **1** : to give **2** ENTREGAR : to deliver, to hand over **3** : to hit, to strike **4** : to yield, to produce **5** : to perform **6** : to give off, to emit **7 ~ como** *or* **~ por** : to regard as, to consider — *vi* **1** ALCANZAR : to suffice, to be enough ⟨no me da para dos pasajes : I don't have enough for two fares⟩ **2 ~ a** *or* **~ sobre** : to overlook, to look out on **3 ~ con** : to run into **4 ~ con** : to hit upon (an idea) **5 dar de sí** : to give, to stretch — **darse** *vr* **1** : to give in, to

surrender **2** : to occur, to arise **3** : to grow, to come up **4 ~ con** *or* **~ contra** : to hit oneself against **5 dárselas de** : to boast about ⟨se las da de muy listo : he thinks he's very smart⟩
dardo *nm* : dart
datar *vt* : to date — *vi* **~ de** : to date from, to date back to
dátil *nm* : date (fruit)
dato *nm* **1** : fact, piece of information **2 datos** *nmpl* : data, information
dé → **dar**
de *prep* **1** : of ⟨la casa de Pepe : Pepe's house⟩ ⟨un niño de tres años : a three-year-old boy⟩ **2** : from ⟨es de Managua : she's from Managua⟩ ⟨salió del edificio : he left the building⟩ **3** : in, at ⟨a las tres de la mañana : at three in the morning⟩ ⟨salen de noche : they go out at night⟩ **4** : than ⟨más de tres : more than three⟩
deambular *vi* : to wander, to roam
debacle *nf* : debacle
debajo *adv* **1** : underneath, below, on the bottom **2 ~ de** : under, underneath **3 por ~** : below, beneath
debate *nm* : debate
debatir *vt* : to debate, to discuss — **debatirse** *vr* : to struggle
debe *nm* : debit column, debit
deber[1] *vt* : to owe — *v aux* **1** : must, have to ⟨debo ir a la oficina : I must go to the office⟩ **2** : should, ought to ⟨deberías buscar trabajo : you ought to look for work⟩ **3** (*expressing probability*) : must ⟨debe ser mexicano : he must be Mexican⟩ — **deberse** *vr* **~ a** : to be due to
deber[2] *nm* **1** OBLIGACIÓN : duty, obligation **2 deberes** *nmpl, Spain* : homework
debidamente *adv* : properly, duly
debido, -da *adj* **1** : right, proper, due **2 ~ a** : due to, owing to
débil *adj* : weak, feeble — **débilmente** *adv*
debilidad *nf* : weakness, debility, feebleness
debilitamiento *nm* : debilitation, weakening

debilitar *vt* : to debilitate, to weaken — **debilitarse** *vr*
debilucho[1], **-cha** *adj* : weak, frail
debilucho[2], **-cha** *n* : weakling
debitar *vt* : to debit
débito *nm* **1** DEUDA : debt **2** : debit
debut [de'but] *nm, pl* **debuts** : debut
debutante[1] *nmf* : beginner, newcomer
debutante[2] *nf* : debutante *f*
debutar *vi* : to debut, to make a debut
década *nf* DECENIO : decade
decadencia *nf* **1** : decadence **2** : decline
decadente *adj* **1** : decadent **2** : declining
decaer {13} *vi* **1** : to decline, to decay, to deteriorate **2** FLAQUEAR : to weaken, to flag
decaiga, etc. → **decaer**
decano, -na *n* **1** : dean **2** : senior member
decantar *vt* : to decant
decapitar *vt* : to decapitate, to behead
decayó, etc. → **decaer**
decena *nf* : group of ten
decencia *nf* : decency
decenio *nm* DÉCADA : decade
decente *adj* : decent — **decentemente** *adv*
decepción *nf, pl* **-ciones** : disappointment, letdown
decepcionante *adj* : disappointing
decepcionar *vt* : to disappoint, to let down — **decepcionarse** *vr*
deceso *nm* DEFUNCIÓN : death, passing
dechado *nm* **1** : sampler (of embroidery) **2** : model, paragon
decibelio *or* **decibel** *nm* : decibel
decidido, -da *adj* : decisive, determined, resolute — **decididamente** *adv*
decidir *vt* **1** : to decide, to determine ⟨no he decidido nada : I haven't made a decision⟩ **2** : to persuade, to decide ⟨su padre lo decidió a estudiar : his father persuaded him to study⟩ — *vi* : to decide — **decidirse** *vr* : to make up one's mind
decimal *adj* : decimal
décimo, -ma *adj* : tenth — **décimo, -ma** *n*
decimoctavo[1], **-va** *adj* : eighteenth
decimoctavo[2], **-va** *n* : eighteenth (in a series)
decimocuarto[1], **-ta** *adj* : fourteenth
decimocuarto[2], **-ta** *n* : fourteenth (in a series)
decimonoveno[1], **-na** *or* **decimonono, -na** *adj* : nineteenth
decimonoveno[2], **-na** *or* **decimonono, -na** *n* : nineteenth (in a series)
decimoquinto[1], **-ta** *adj* : fifteenth
decimoquinto[2], **-ta** *n* : fifteenth (in a series)
decimoséptimo[1], **-ma** *adj* : seventeenth
decimoséptimo[2], **-ma** *n* : seventeenth (in a series)
decimosexto[1], **-ta** *adj* : sixteenth
decimosexto[2], **-ta** *n* : sixteenth (in a series)

decimotercero[1], **-ra** *adj* : thirteenth
decimotercero[2], **-ra** *n* : thirteenth (in a series)
decir[1] {23} *vt* **1** : to say ⟨dice que no quiere ir : she says she doesn't want to go⟩ **2** : to tell ⟨dime lo que estás pensando : tell me what you're thinking⟩ **3** : to speak, to talk ⟨no digas tonterías : don't talk nonsense⟩ **4** : to call ⟨me dicen Rosy : they call me Rosy⟩ **5 es decir** : that is to say **6 querer decir** : to mean — **decirse** *vr* **1** : to say to oneself **2** : to be said ⟨¿cómo se dice "lápiz" en francés? : how do you say "pencil" in French?⟩
decir[2] *nm* DICHO : saying, expression
decisión *nf, pl* **-siones** : decision, choice
decisivo, -va *adj* : decisive, conclusive — **decisivamente** *adv*
declamar *vi* : to declaim — *vt* : to recite
declaración *nf, pl* **-ciones** **1** : declaration, statement **2** TESTIMONIO : deposition, testimony **3 declaración de derechos** : bill of rights **4 declaración jurada** : affidavit
declarado, -da *adj* : professed, open — **declaradamente** *adv*
declarar *vt* : to declare, to state — *vi* ATESTIGUAR : to testify — **declararse** *vr* **1** : to declare oneself, to make a statement **2** : to confess one's love **3** : to plead (in court) ⟨declararse inocente : to plead not guilty⟩
declinación *nf, pl* **-ciones** **1** : drop, downward trend **2** : declination **3** : declension (in grammar)
declinar *vt* : to decline, to turn down — *vi* **1** : to draw to a close **2** : to diminish, to decline
declive *nm* **1** DECADENCIA : decline **2** : slope, incline
decodificador *nm* : decoder
decolar *vi* *Chile, Col, Ecua* : to take off (of an airplane)
decolorar *vt* : to bleach — **decolorarse** *vr* : to fade
decomisar *vt* CONFISCAR : to seize, to confiscate
decomiso *nm* : seizure, confiscation
decoración *nf, pl* **-ciones** **1** : decoration **2** : decor **3** : stage set, scenery
decorado *nm* : stage set, scenery
decorador, -dora *n* : decorator
decorar *vt* ADORNAR : to decorate, to adorn
decorativo, -va *adj* : decorative, ornamental
decoro *nm* : decorum, propriety
decoroso, -sa *adj* : decent, proper, respectable
decrecer {53} *vi* : to decrease, to wane, to diminish — **decreciente** *adj*
decrecimiento *nm* : decrease, decline
decrépito, -ta *adj* : decrepit
decretar *vt* : to decree, to order
decreto *nm* : decree
decúbito *nm* : horizontal position ⟨en decúbito prono : prone⟩ ⟨en decúbito supino : supine⟩

dedal *nm* : thimble
dedalera *nf* DIGITAL : foxglove
dedicación *nf, pl* -ciones : dedication, devotion
dedicar {72} *vt* CONSAGRAR : to dedicate, to devote — **dedicarse** *vr* ~ **a** : to devote oneself to, to engage in
dedicatoria *nf* : dedication (of a book, song, etc.)
dedo *nm* **1** : finger ⟨dedo meñique : little finger⟩ **2 dedo del pie** : toe
deducción *nf, pl* -ciones : deduction
deducible *adj* **1** : deducible, inferable **2** : deductible
deducir {61} *vt* **1** INFERIR : to deduce **2** DESCONTAR : to deduct
defecar {72} *vi* : to defecate — **defecación** *nf*
defecto *nm* **1** : defect, flaw, shortcoming **2 en su defecto** : lacking that, in the absence of that
defectuoso, -sa *adj* : defective, faulty
defender {56} *vt* : to defend, to protect — **defenderse** *vr* **1** : to defend oneself **2** : to get by, to know the basics ⟨su inglés no es perfecto pero se defiende : his English isn't perfect but he gets by⟩
defendible *adj* : defensible, tenable
defensa¹ *nf* : defense
defensa² *nmf* : defender, back (in sports)
defensiva *nf* : defensive, defense
defensivo, -va *adj* : defensive — **defensivamente** *adv*
defensor¹, -sora *adj* : defending, defense
defensor², -sora *n* **1** : defender, advocate **2** : defense counsel
defeño, -ña *n* : person from the Federal District (Mexico City)
deferencia *nf* : deference
deficiencia *nf* : deficiency, flaw
deficiente *adj* : deficient
déficit *nm, pl* -cits **1** : deficit **2** : shortage, lack
definición *nf, pl* -ciones : definition
definido, -da *adj* : definite, well-defined
definir *vt* **1** : to define **2** : to determine
definitivamente *adv* **1** : finally **2** : permanently, for good **3** : definitely, absolutely
definitivo, -va *adj* **1** : definitive, conclusive **2 en definitiva** : all in all, on the whole **3 en definitiva** *Mex* : permanently, for good
deflación *nf, pl* -ciones : deflation
deforestación *nf, pl* -ciones : deforestation
deformación *nf, pl* -ciones **1** : deformation **2** : distortion
deformar *vt* **1** : to deform, to disfigure **2** : to distort — **deformarse** *vr*
deforme *adj* : deformed, misshapen
deformidad *nf* : deformity
defraudación *nf, pl* -ciones : fraud
defraudar *vt* **1** ESTAFAR : to defraud, to cheat **2** : to disappoint
defunción *nf, pl* -ciones DECESO : death, passing

degeneración *nf, pl* -ciones **1** : degeneration **2** : degeneracy, depravity
degenerado, -da *adj* DEPRAVADO : degenerate
degenerar *vi* : to degenerate
degenerativo, -va *adj* : degenerative
degollar {19} *vt* **1** : to slit the throat of, to slaughter **2** DECAPITAR : to behead **3** : to ruin, to destroy
degradación *nf, pl* -ciones **1** : degradation **2** : demotion
degradar *vt* **1** : to degrade, to debase **2** : to demote
degustación *nf, pl* -ciones : tasting, sampling
degustar *vt* : to taste
deidad *nf* : deity
deificar {72} *vt* : to idolize, to deify
dejado, -da *adj* **1** : slovenly **2** : careless, lazy
dejar *vt* **1** : to leave **2** ABANDONAR : to abandon, to forsake **3** : to let be, to let go **4** PERMITIR : to allow, to permit — *vi* ~ **de** : to stop, to quit ⟨dejar de fumar : to quit smoking⟩ — **dejarse** *vr* **1** : to let oneself be ⟨se deja insultar : he lets himself be insulted⟩ **2** : to forget, to leave ⟨me dejé las llaves en el carro : I left the keys in the car⟩ **3** : to neglect oneself, to let oneself go **4** : to grow ⟨nos estamos dejando el pelo largo : we're growing our hair long⟩
dejo *nm* **1** : aftertaste **2** : touch, hint **3** : (regional) accent
del (*contraction of* **de** *and* **el**) → **de**
delación *nf, pl* -ciones : denunciation, betrayal
delantal *nm* **1** : apron **2** : pinafore
delante *adv* **1** ENFRENTE : ahead, in front **2** ~ **de** : before, in front of
delantera *nf* **1** : front, front part, front row ⟨tomar la delantera : to take the lead⟩ **2** : forward line (in sports)
delantero¹, -ra *adj* **1** : front, forward **2 tracción delantera** : front-wheel drive
delantero², -ra *n* : forward (in sports)
delatar *vt* **1** : to betray, to reveal **2** : to denounce, to inform against
delegación *nf, pl* -ciones : delegation
delegado, -da *n* : delegate, representative
delegar {52} *vt* : to delegate
deleitar *vt* : to delight, to please — **deleitarse** *vr*
deleite *nm* : delight, pleasure
deletrear *vi* : to spell ⟨¿como se deletrea? : how do you spell it?⟩
deleznable *adj* **1** : brittle, crumbly **2** : slippery **3** : weak, fragile ⟨una excusa deleznable : a weak excuse⟩
delfín *nm, pl* **delfines 1** : dolphin **2** : dauphin, heir apparent
delgadez *nf* : thinness, skinniness
delgado, -da *adj* **1** FLACO : thin, skinny **2** ESBELTO : slender, slim **3** DELICADO : delicate, fine **4** AGUDO : sharp, clever
deliberación *nf, pl* -ciones : deliberation

deliberado, -da *adj* : deliberate, intentional — **deliberadamente** *adv*
deliberar *vi* : to deliberate
deliberativo, -va *adj* : deliberative
delicadeza *nf* **1** : delicacy, fineness **2** : gentleness, softness **3** : tact, discretion, consideration
delicado, -da *adj* **1** : delicate, fine **2** : sensitive, frail **3** : difficult, tricky **4** : fussy, hard to please **5** : tactful, considerate
delicia *nf* : delight
delicioso, -sa *adj* **1** RICO : delicious **2** : delightful
delictivo, -va *adj* : criminal
delictuoso, -sa → **delictivo**
delimitación *nf, pl* **-ciones** **1** : demarcation **2** : defining, specifying
delimitar *vt* **1** : to demarcate **2** : to define, to specify
delincuencia *nf* : delinquency, crime
delincuente¹ *adj* : delinquent
delincuente² *nmf* CRIMINAL : delinquent, criminal
delinear *vt* **1** : to delineate, to outline **2** : to draft, to draw up
delinquir {24} *vi* : to break the law
delirante *adj* : delirious
delirar *vi* **1** DESVARIAR : to be delirious **2** : to rave, to talk nonsense
delirio *nm* **1** DESVARÍO : delirium **2** DISPARATE : nonsense, ravings *pl* ⟨delirios de grandeza : delusions of grandeur⟩ **3** FRENESÍ : mania, frenzy ⟨¡fue el delirio! : it was wild!⟩
delito *nm* : crime, offense
delta *nm* : delta
demacrado, -da *adj* : emaciated, gaunt
demagogia *nf* : demagogy
demagógico, -ca *adj* : demagogic, demagogical
demagogo, -ga *n* : demagogue
demanda *nf* **1** : demand ⟨la oferta y la demanda : supply and demand⟩ **2** : petition, request **3** : lawsuit
demandado, -da *n* : defendant
demandante *nmf* : plaintiff
demandar *vt* **1** : to demand **2** REQUERIR : to call for, to require **3** : to sue, to file a lawsuit against
demarcar {72} *vt* : to demarcate — **demarcación** *nf*
demás¹ *adj* : remaining ⟨acabó las demás tareas : she finished the rest of the chores⟩
demás² *pron* **1** lo (la, los, las) demás : the rest, everyone else, everything else ⟨Pepe, Rosa, y los demás : Pepe, Rosa, and everybody else⟩ **2** estar por demás : to be of no use, to be pointless ⟨no estaría por demás : it couldn't hurt, it's worth a try⟩ **3** por demás : extremely **4** por lo demás : otherwise **5** y demás : and so on, et cetera
demasía *nf* en ~ : excessively, in excess
demasiado¹ *adv* **1** : too ⟨vas demasiado aprisa : you're going too fast⟩ **2** : too

much ⟨estoy comiendo demasiado : I'm eating too much⟩
demasiado², -da *adj* : too much, too many, excessive
demencia *nf* **1** : dementia **2** LOCURA : madness, insanity
demente¹ *adj* : insane, mad
demente² *nmf* : insane person
demeritar *vt* **1** : to detract from **2** : to discredit
demérito *nm* **1** : fault **2** : discredit, disrepute
democracia *nf* : democracy
demócrata¹ *adj* : democratic
demócrata² *nmf* : democrat
democrático, -ca *adj* : democratic — **democráticamente** *adv*
democratizar {21} *vt* : to democratize, to make democratic
demografía *nf* : demography
demográfico, -ca *adj* : demographic
demoledor, -dora *adj* : devastating
demoler {47} *vt* DERRIBAR, DERRUMBAR : to demolish, to destroy
demolición *nf, pl* **-ciones** : demolition
demonio *nm* DIABLO : devil, demon
demora *nf* : delay
demorar *vt* **1** RETRASAR : to delay **2** TARDAR : to take, to last ⟨la reparación demorará varios días : the repair will take several days⟩ — *vi* : to delay, to linger — **demorarse** *vr* **1** : to be slow, to take a long time **2** : to take too long
demostración *nf, pl* **-ciones** : demonstration
demostrar {19} *vt* : to demonstrate, to show
demostrativo, -va *adj* : demonstrative
demudar *vt* : to change, to alter — **demudarse** *vr* : to change one's expression
denegación *nf, pl* **-ciones** : denial, refusal
denegar {49} *vt* : to deny, to turn down
denigrante *adj* : degrading, humiliating
denigrar *vt* **1** DIFAMAR : to denigrate, to disparage **2** : to degrade, to humiliate
denodado, -da *adj* : bold, dauntless
denominación *nf, pl* **-ciones** **1** : name, designation **2** : denomination (of money)
denominador *nm* : denominator
denominar *vt* : to designate, to name
denostar {19} *vt* : to revile
denotar *vt* : to denote, to show
densidad *nf* : density, thickness
denso, -sa *adj* : dense, thick — **densamente** *adv*
dentado, -da *adj* SERRADO : serrated, jagged
dentadura *nf* **1** : teeth *pl* **2** dentadura postiza : dentures *pl*
dental *adj* : dental
dentellada *nf* **1** : bite **2** : tooth mark
dentera *nf* **1** : envy, jealousy **2** dar dentera : to set one's teeth on edge
dentición *nf, pl* **-ciones** **1** : teething **2** : dentition, set of teeth

dentífrico *nm* : toothpaste
dentista *nmf* : dentist
dentro *adv* **1** : in, inside **2** : indoors **3** ~ **de** : within, inside, in **4 dentro de poco** : soon, shortly **5 dentro de todo** : all in all, all things considered **6 por** ~ : inwardly, inside
denuedo *nm* : valor, courage
denuesto *nm* : insult
denuncia *nf* **1** : denunciation, condemnation **2** : police report
denunciante *nmf* : accuser (of a crime)
denunciar *vt* **1** : to denounce, to condemn **2** : to report (to the authorities)
deparar *vt* : to have in store for, to provide with ⟨no sabemos lo que nos depara el destino : we don't know what fate has in store for us⟩
departamental *adj* **1** : departmental **2 tienda departamental** *Mex* : department store
departamento *nm* **1** : department **2** APARTAMENTO : apartment
departir *vi* : to converse
dependencia *nf* **1** : dependence, dependency ⟨dependencia emocional : emotional dependence⟩ ⟨dependencia del alcohol : dependence on alcohol⟩ **2** : agency, branch office
depender *vi* **1** : to depend **2** ~ **de** : to depend on **3** ~ **de** : to be subordinate to
dependiente[1] *adj* : dependent
dependiente[2], **-ta** *n* : clerk, salesperson
deplorable *adj* : deplorable
deplorar *vt* **1** : to deplore **2** LAMENTAR : to regret
deponer {60} *vt* **1** : to depose, to overthrow **2** : to abandon (an attitude or stance) **3 deponer las armas** : to lay down one's arms — *vi* **1** TESTIFICAR : to testify, to make a statement **2** EVACUAR : to defecate
deportación *nf, pl* **-ciones** : deportation
deportar *vt* : to deport
deporte *nm* : sport, sports *pl* ⟨hacer deporte : to engage in sports⟩
deportista[1] *adj* **1** : fond of sports **2** : sporty
deportista[2] *nmf* **1** : sports fan **2** : athlete, sportsman *m*, sportswoman *f*
deportividad *nf Spain* : sportsmanship
deportivo, -va *adj* **1** : sports, sporting ⟨artículos deportivos : sporting goods⟩ **2** : sporty
deposición *nf, pl* **-ciones** **1** : statement, testimony **2** : removal from office
depositante *nmf* : depositor
depositar *vt* **1** : to deposit, to place **2** : to store — **depositarse** *vr* : to settle
depósito *nm* **1** : deposit **2** : warehouse, storehouse
depravación *nf, pl* **-ciones** : depravity
depravado, -da *adj* DEGENERADO : depraved, degenerate
depravar *vt* : to deprave, to corrupt
depreciación *nf, pl* **-ciones** : depreciation

depreciar *vt* : to depreciate, to reduce the value of — **depreciarse** *vr* : to lose value
depredación *nf* SAQUEO : depredation, plunder
depredador[1], **-dora** *adj* : predatory
depredador[2] *nm* **1** : predator **2** SAQUEADOR : plunderer
depresión *nf, pl* **-siones** **1** : depression **2** : hollow, recess **3** : drop, fall **4** : slump, recession
depresivo[1], **-va** *adj* **1** : depressive **2** : depressant
depresivo[2] *nm* : depressant
deprimente *adj* : depressing
deprimir *vt* **1** : to depress **2** : to lower — **deprimirse** *vr* ABATIRSE : to get depressed
depuesto *pp* → **deponer**
depuración *nf, pl* **-ciones** **1** PURIFICACIÓN : purification **2** PURGA : purge **3** : refinement, polish
depurar *vt* **1** PURIFICAR : to purify **2** PURGAR : to purge
depuso, etc. → **deponer**
derecha *nf* **1** : right **2** : right hand, right side **3** : right wing, right (in politics)
derechazo *nm* **1** : pass with the cape on the right hand (in bullfighting) **2** : right (in boxing) **3** : forehand (in tennis)
derechista[1] *adj* : rightist, right-wing
derechista[2] *nmf* : right-winger
derecho[1] *adv* **1** : straight **2** : upright **3** : directly
derecho[2], **-cha** *adj* **1** : right **2** : right-hand **3** RECTO : straight, upright, erect
derecho[3] *nm* **1** : right ⟨derechos humanos : human rights⟩ **2** : law ⟨derecho civil : civil law⟩ **3** : right side (of cloth or clothing)
deriva *nf* **1** : drift **2 a la deriva** : adrift
derivación *nf, pl* **-ciones** **1** : derivation **2** RAMIFICACIÓN : ramification, consequence
derivar *vi* **1** : to drift **2** ~ **de** : to come from, to derive from **3** ~ **en** : to result in — *vt* : to steer, to direct ⟨derivó la discusión hacia la política : he steered the discussion over to politics⟩ — **derivarse** *vr* : to be derived from, to arise from
dermatología *nf* : dermatology
dermatológico, -ca *adj* : dermatological
dermatólogo, -ga *n* : dermatologist
derogación *nf, pl* **-ciones** : abolition, repeal
derogar {52} *vt* ABOLIR : to abolish, to repeal
derramamiento *nm* **1** : spilling, overflowing **2 derramamiento de sangre** : bloodshed
derramar *vt* **1** : to spill **2** : to shed (tears, blood) — **derramarse** *vr* **1** : to spill over **2** : to scatter
derrame *nm* **1** : spilling, shedding **2** : leakage, overflow **3** : discharge, hemorrhage
derrapar *vi* : to skid

derrape *nm* : skid
derredor *nm* **al derredor** *or* **en derredor** : around, round about
derrengado, -da *adj* **1** : bent, twisted **2** : exhausted
derretir {54} *vt* : to melt, to thaw — **derretirse** *vr* **1** : to melt, to thaw **2** ~ **por** *fam* : to be crazy about
derribar *vt* **1** DEMOLER, DERRUMBAR : to demolish, to knock down **2** : to shoot down, to bring down (an airplane) **3** DERROCAR : to overthrow
derribo *nm* **1** : demolition, razing **2** : shooting down **3** : overthrow
derrocamiento *nm* : overthrow
derrocar {72} *vt* DERRIBAR : to overthrow, to topple
derrochador[1], **-dora** *adj* : extravagant, wasteful
derrochador[2], **-dora** *n* : spendthrift
derrochar *vt* : to waste, to squander
derroche *nm* : extravagance, waste
derrota *nf* **1** : defeat, rout **2** : course (at sea)
derrotar *vt* : to defeat
derrotero *nm* RUTA : course
derrotista *adj & nmf* : defeatist
derruir {41} *vt* : to demolish, to tear down
derrumbamiento *nm* : collapse
derrumbar *vt* **1** DEMOLER, DERRIBAR : to demolish, to knock down **2** DESPEÑAR : to cast down, to topple — **derrumbarse** *vr* DESPLOMARSE : to collapse, to break down
derrumbe *nm* **1** DESPLOME : collapse, fall ⟨el derrumbe del comunismo : the fall of Communism⟩ **2** : landslide
desabastecimiento *nm* : shortage, scarcity
desabasto *nm Mex* : shortage, scarcity
desabrido, -da *adj* : tasteless, bland
desabrigar {52} *vt* **1** : to undress **2** : to uncover **3** : to deprive of shelter
desabrochar *vt* : to unbutton, to undo — **desabrocharse** *vr* : to come undone
desacatar *vt* **1** DESAFIAR : to defy **2** DESOBEDECER : to disobey
desacato *nm* **1** : disrespect **2** : contempt (of court)
desacelerar *vi* : to decelerate, to slow down
desacertado, -da *adj* **1** : mistaken **2** : unwise
desacertar {55} *vi* ERRAR : to err, to be mistaken
desacierto *nm* ERROR : error, mistake
desaconsejable *adj* : inadvisable
desaconsejado, -da *adj* : ill-advised, unwise
desacorde *adj* **1** : conflicting **2** : discordant
desacostumbrado, -da *adj* : unaccustomed, unusual
desacreditar *vt* DESPRESTIGIAR : to discredit, to disgrace
desactivar *vt* : to deactivate, to defuse
desacuerdo *nm* : disagreement
desafiante *adj* : defiant

desafiar {85} *vt* RETAR : to defy, to challenge
desafilado, -da *adj* : blunt
desafinado, -da *adj* : out-of-tune, off-key
desafinarse *vr* : to go out of tune
desafío *nm* **1** RETO : challenge **2** RESISTENCIA : defiance
desafortunado, -da *adj* : unfortunate, unlucky — **desafortunadamente** *adv*
desafuero *nm* ABUSO : injustice, outrage
desagradable *adj* : unpleasant, disagreeable — **desagradablemente** *adv*
desagradar *vi* : to be unpleasant, to be disagreeable
desagradecido, -da *adj* : ungrateful
desagrado *nm* **1** : displeasure **2 con** ~ : reluctantly
desagravio *nm* **1** : apology **2** : amends, reparation
desagregarse {52} *vr* : to break up, to disintegrate
desaguar {10} *vi* : to drain, to empty
desagüe *nm* **1** : drain **2** : drainage
desahogado, -da *adj* **1** : well-off, comfortable **2** : spacious, roomy
desahogar {52} *vt* **1** : to relieve, to ease **2** : to give vent to — **desahogarse** *vr* **1** : to recover, to feel better **2** : to unburden oneself, to let off steam
desahogo *nm* **1** : relief, outlet **2 con** ~ : comfortably
desahuciar *vt* **1** : to deprive of hope **2** : to evict — **desahuciarse** *vr* : to lose all hope
desahucio *nm* : eviction
desairar {5} *vt* : to snub, to rebuff
desaire *nm* : rebuff, snub, slight
desajustar *vt* **1** : to disarrange, to put out of order **2** : to upset (plans)
desajuste *nm* **1** : maladjustment **2** : imbalance **3** : upset, disruption
desalentador, -dora *adj* : discouraging, disheartening
desalentar {55} *vt* DESANIMAR : to discourage, to dishearten — **desalentarse** *vr*
desaliento *nm* : discouragement
desaliñado, -da *adj* : slovenly, untidy
desalmado, -da *adj* : heartless, callous
desalojar *vt* **1** : to remove, to clear **2** EVACUAR : to evacuate, to vacate **3** : to evict
desalojo *nm* **1** : removal, expulsion **2** : evacuation **3** : eviction
desamor *nm* **1** FRIALDAD : indifference **2** ENEMISTAD : dislike, enmity
desamparado, -da *adj* DESVALIDO : helpless, destitute
desamparar *vt* : to abandon, to forsake
desamparo *nm* **1** : abandonment, neglect **2** : helplessness
desamueblado, -da *adj* : unfurnished
desandar {6} *vt* : to go back, to return to the starting point
desangelado, -da *adj* : dull, lifeless
desangrar *vt* : to bleed, to bleed dry — **desangrarse** *vr* **1** : to be bleeding **2** : to bleed to death

desanimar *vt* DESALENTAR : to discourage, to dishearten — **desanimarse** *vr*
desánimo *nm* DESALIENTO : discouragement, dejection
desanudar *vt* : to untie, to disentangle
desapacible *adj* : unpleasant, disagreeable
desaparecer {53} *vt* : to cause to disappear — *vi* : to disappear, to vanish
desaparecido[1], **-da** *adj* **1** : late, deceased **2** : missing
desaparecido[2], **-da** *n* : missing person
desaparición *nf, pl* **-ciones** : disappearance
desapasionado, -da *adj* : dispassionate, impartial — **desapasionadamente** *adv*
desapego *nm* : coolness, indifference
desapercibido, -da *adj* **1** : unnoticed **2** DESPREVENIDO : unprepared, off guard
desaprobación *nf, pl* **-ciones** : disapproval
desaprobar {19} *vt* REPROBAR : to disapprove of
desaprovechar *vt* MALGASTAR : to waste, to misuse — *vi* : to lose ground, to slip back
desarmador *nm Mex* : screwdriver
desarmar *vt* **1** : to disarm **2** DESMONTAR : to disassemble, to take apart
desarme *nm* : disarmament
desarraigado, -da *adj* : rootless
desarraigar {52} *vt* : to uproot, to root out
desarreglado, -da *adj* : untidy, disorganized
desarreglar *vt* **1** : to mess up **2** : to upset, to disrupt
desarreglo *nm* **1** : untidiness **2** : disorder, confusion
desarrollar *vt* : to develop — **desarrollarse** *vr* : to take place
desarrollo *nm* : development
desarticulación *nf, pl* **-ciones** **1** : dislocation **2** : breaking up, dismantling
desarticular *vt* **1** DISLOCAR : to dislocate **2** : to break up, to dismantle
desaseado, -da *adj* **1** : dirty **2** : messy, untidy
desastre *nm* CATÁSTROFE : disaster
desastroso, -sa *adj* : disastrous, catastrophic
desatar *vt* **1** : to undo, to untie **2** : to unleash **3** : to trigger, to precipitate — **desatarse** *vr* : to break out, to erupt
desatascar {72} *vt* : to unblock, to clear
desatención *nf, pl* **-ciones** **1** : absent-mindedness, distraction **2** : discourtesy
desatender {56} *vt* **1** : to disregard **2** : to neglect
desatento, -ta *adj* **1** DISTRAÍDO : absentminded **2** GROSERO : discourteous, rude
desatinado, -da *adj* : foolish, silly
desatino *nm* : folly, mistake

desautorizar {21} *vt* : to deprive of authority, to discredit
desavenencia *nf* DISCORDANCIA : disagreement, dispute
desayunar *vi* : to have breakfast — *vt* : to have for breakfast
desayuno *nm* : breakfast
desazón *nf, pl* **-zones** INQUIETUD : uneasiness, anxiety
desbalance *nm* : imbalance
desbancar {72} *vt* : to displace, to oust
desbandada *nf* : scattering, dispersal
desbarajuste *nm* DESORDEN : disarray, disorder, mess
desbaratar *vt* **1** ARRUINAR : to destroy, to ruin **2** DESCOMPONER : to break, to break down — **desbaratarse** *vr* : to fall apart
desbloquear *vt* **1** : to open up, to clear, to break through **2** : to free, to release
desbocado, -da *adj* : unbridled, rampant
desbocarse {72} *vr* : to run away, to bolt
desbordamiento *nm* : overflowing
desbordante *adj* : overflowing, bursting ⟨desbordante de energía : bursting with energy⟩
desbordar *vt* **1** : to overflow, to spill over **2** : to surpass, to exceed — **desbordarse** *vr*
descabellado, -da *adj* : outlandish, ridiculous
descafeinado, -da *adj* : decaffeinated
descalabrar *vt* : to hit on the head — **descalabrarse** *vr*
descalabro *nm* : setback, misfortune, loss
descalificación *nf, pl* **-ciones** **1** : disqualification **2** : disparaging remark
descalificar {72} *vt* **1** : to disqualify **2** DESACREDITAR : to discredit — **descalificarse** *vr*
descalzarse {21} *vr* : take off one's shoes
descalzo, -za *adj* : barefoot
descansado, -da *adj* **1** : rested, refreshed **2** : restful, peaceful
descansar *vi* : to rest, to relax — *vt* : to rest ⟨descansar la vista : to rest one's eyes⟩
descansillo *nm* : landing (of a staircase)
descanso *nm* **1** : rest, relaxation **2** : break **3** : landing (of a staircase) **4** : intermission
descapotable *adj & nm* : convertible
descarado, -da *adj* : brazen, impudent — **descaradamente** *adv*
descarga *nf* **1** : discharge **2** : unloading
descargar {52} *vt* **1** : to discharge **2** : to unload **3** : to release, to free **4** : to take out, to vent (anger, etc.) — **descargarse** *vr* **1** : to unburden oneself **2** : to quit **3** : to lose power
descargo *nm* **1** : unloading **2** : defense ⟨testigo de descargo : witness for the defense⟩
descarnado, -da *adj* : scrawny, gaunt
descaro *nm* : audacity, nerve

descarriado, -da *adj* : lost, gone astray
descarrilar *vi* : to derail — **descarrilarse** *vr*
descartar *vt* : to rule out, to reject — **descartarse** *vr* : to discard
descascarar *vt* : to peel, to shell, to husk — **descascararse** *vr* : to peel off, to chip
descendencia *nf* 1 : descendants *pl* 2 LINAJE : descent, lineage
descendente *adj* : downward, descending
descender {56} *vt* 1 : to descend, to go down 2 BAJAR : to lower, to take down, to let down — *vi* 1 : to descend, to come down 2 : to drop, to fall 3 ~ **de** : to be a descendant of
descendiente *adj & nm* : descendant
descenso *nm* 1 : descent 2 BAJA, CAÍDA : drop, fall
descentralizar {21} *vt* : to decentralize — **descentralizarse** *vr* — **descentralización** *nf*
descifrable *adj* : decipherable
descifrar *vt* : to decipher, to decode
descodificar {72} *vt* : to decode
descolgar {16} *vt* 1 : to take down, to let down 2 : to pick up, to answer (the telephone)
descollar {19} *vi* SOBRESALIR : to stand out, to be outstanding, to excel
descolorarse *vr* : to fade
descolorido, -da *adj* : discolored, faded
descomponer {60} *vt* 1 : to rot, to decompose 2 DESBARATAR : to break, to break down — **descomponerse** *vr* 1 : to break down 2 : to decompose
descomposición *nf, pl* **-ciones** 1 : breakdown, decomposition 2 : decay
descompresión *nf* : decompression
descompuesto[1] *pp* → **descomponer**
descompuesto[2]**, -ta** *adj* 1 : broken down, out of order 2 : rotten, decomposed
descomunal *adj* 1 ENORME : enormous, huge 2 EXTRAORDINARIO : extraordinary
desconcertante *adj* : disconcerting
desconcertar {55} *vt* : to disconcert — **desconcertarse** *vr*
desconchar *vt* : to chip — **desconcharse** *vr* : to chip off, to peel
desconcierto *nm* : uncertainty, confusion
desconectar *vt* 1 : to disconnect, to switch off 2 : to unplug
desconfiado, -da *adj* : distrustful, suspicious
desconfianza *nf* RECELO : distrust, suspicion
desconfiar {85} *vi* ~ **de** : to distrust, to be suspicious of
descongelar *vt* 1 : to thaw 2 : to defrost 3 : to unfreeze (assets — **descongelarse** *vr*
descongestionante *adj & nm* : decongestant

desconocer {18} *vt* 1 IGNORAR : to be unaware of 2 : to fail to recognize
desconocido[1]**, -da** *adj* : unknown, unfamiliar
desconocido[2]**, -da** *n* EXTRAÑO : stranger
desconocimiento *nm* : ignorance
desconsiderado, -da *adj* : inconsiderate, thoughtless — **desconsideradamente** *adj*
desconsolado, -da *adj* : disconsolate, heartbroken
desconsuelo *nm* AFLICCIÓN : grief, distress, despair
descontaminar *vt* : to decontaminate — **descontaminación** *nf*
descontar {19} *vt* 1 : to discount, to deduct 2 EXCEPTUAR : to except, to exclude
descontento[1]**, -ta** *adj* : discontented, dissatisfied
descontento[2] *nm* : discontent, dissatisfaction
descontrol *nm* : lack of control, disorder, chaos
descontrolarse *vr* : to get out of control, to be out of hand
descorazonado, -da *adj* : disheartened, discouraged
descorazonador, -dora *adj* : disheartening, discouraging
descorrer *vt* : to draw back
descortés *adj, pl* **-teses** : discourteous, rude
descortesía *nf* : discourtesy, rudeness
descrédito *nm* DESPRESTIGIO : discredit
descremado, -da *adj* : nonfat, skim
describir {33} *vt* : to describe
descripción *nf, pl* **-ciones** : description
descriptivo, -va *adj* : descriptive
descrito *pp* → **describir**
descuartizar {21} *vt* 1 : to cut up, to quarter 2 : to tear to pieces
descubierto[1] *pp* → **descubrir**
descubierto[2]**, -ta** *adj* 1 : exposed, revealed 2 **al descubierto** : out in the open
descubridor, -dora *n* : discoverer, explorer
descubrimiento *nm* : discovery
descubrir {2} *vt* 1 HALLAR : to discover, to find out 2 REVELAR : to uncover, to reveal — **descubrirse** *vr*
descuento *nm* REBAJA : discount
descuidado, -da *adj* 1 : neglectful, careless 2 : neglected, unkempt
descuidar *vt* : to neglect, to overlook — *vi* : to be careless — **descuidarse** *vr* 1 : to be careless, to drop one's guard 2 : to let oneself go
descuido *nm* 1 : carelessness, negligence 2 : slip, oversight
desde *prep* 1 : from 2 : since 3 **desde ahora** : from now on 4 **desde entonces** : since then 5 **desde hace** : for, since (a time) ⟨ha estado nevando desde hace dos días : it's been snowing for

two days⟩ **6 desde luego** : of course **7 desde que** : since, ever since **8 desde ya** : right now, immediately
desdecir {11} *vi* **1** ~ **de** : to be unworthy of **2** ~ **de** : to clash with — **desdecirse** *vr* **1** CONTRADECIRSE : to contradict oneself **2** RETRACTARSE : to go back on one's word
desdén *nm, pl* **desdenes** DESPRECIO : disdain, scorn
desdentado, -da *adj* : toothless
desdeñar *vt* DESPRECIAR : to disdain, to scorn, to despise
desdeñoso, -sa *adj* : disdainful, scornful — **desdeñosamente** *adv*
desdibujar *vt* : to blur — **desdibujarse** *vr*
desdicha *nf* **1** : misery **2** : misfortune
desdichado¹, -da *adj* **1** : unfortunate **2** : miserable, unhappy
desdichado², -da *n* : wretch
desdicho *pp* → **desdecir**
desdiga, desdijo etc. → **desdecir**
desdoblar *vt* DESPLEGAR : to unfold
deseable *adj* : desirable
desear *vt* **1** : to wish ⟨te deseo buena suerte : I wish you good luck⟩ **2** QUERER : to want, to desire
desecar {72} *vt* : to dry (flowers, etc.)
desechable *adj* : disposable
desechar *vt* **1** : to discard, to throw away **2** RECHAZAR : to reject
desecho *nm* **1** : reject **2 desechos** *nmpl* RESIDUOS : rubbish, waste
desembarazarse {21} *vr* ~ **de** : to get rid of
desembarcadero *nm* : jetty, landing pier
desembarcar {72} *vi* : to disembark — *vt* : to unload
desembarco *nm* **1** : landing, arrival **2** : unloading
desembarque → **desembarco**
desembocadura *nf* **1** : mouth (of a river) **2** : opening, end (of a street)
desembocar {72} *vi* ~ **en** *or* ~ **a 1** : to flow into, to join **2** : to lead to, to result in
desembolsar *vt* PAGAR : to disburse, to pay out
desembolso *nm* PAGO : disbursement, payment
desempacar {72} *v* : to unpack
desempate *nm* : tiebreaker, play-off
desempeñar *vt* **1** : to play (a role) **2** : to fulfill, to carry out **3** : to redeem (from a pawnshop) — **desempeñarse** *vr* : to function, to act
desempeño *nm* **1** : fulfillment, carrying out **2** : performance
desempleado¹, -da *adj* : unemployed
desempleado², -da *n* : unemployed person
desempleo *nm* : unemployment
desempolvar *vt* **1** : to dust off **2** : to resurrect, to revive
desencadenar *vt* **1** : to unchain **2** : to trigger, to unleash — **desencadenarse** *vr*

desencajar *vt* **1** : to dislocate **2** : to disconnect, to disengage
desencantar *vt* : to disenchant, to disillusion — **desencantarse** *vr*
desencanto *nm* : disenchantment, disillusionment
desenchufar *vt* : to disconnect, to unplug
desenfadado, -da *adj* **1** : uninhibited, carefree **2** : confident, self-assured
desenfado *nm* **1** DESENVOLTURA : self-assurance, confidence **2** : naturalness, ease
desenfrenadamente *adv* : wildly, with abandon
desenfrenado, -da *adj* : unbridled, unrestrained
desenfreno *nm* : abandon, unrestraint
desenganchar *vt* : to unhitch, to uncouple
desengañar *vt* : to disillusion, to disenchant — **desengañarse** *vr*
desengaño *nm* : disenchantment, disillusionment
desenlace *nm* : ending, outcome
desenlazar {21} *vt* **1** : to untie **2** : to clear up, to resolve
desenmarañar *vt* : to disentangle, to unravel
desenmascarar *vt* : to unmask, to expose
desenredar *vt* : to untangle, to disentangle
desenrollar *vt* : to unroll, to unwind
desentenderse {56} *vr* **1** ~ **de** : to want nothing to do with, to be uninterested in **2** ~ **de** : to pretend ignorance of
desenterrar {55} *vt* **1** EXHUMAR : to exhume **2** : to unearth, to dig up
desentonar *vi* **1** : to clash, to conflict **2** : to be out of tune, to sing off-key
desentrañar *vt* : to get to the bottom of, to unravel
desenvainar *vt* : to draw, to unsheathe (a sword)
desenvoltura *nf* **1** DESENFADO : confidence, self-assurance **2** ELOCUENCIA : eloquence, fluency
desenvolver {89} *vt* : to unwrap, to open — **desenvolverse** *vr* **1** : to unfold, to develop **2** : to manage, to cope
desenvuelto¹ *pp* → **desenvolver**
desenvuelto², -ta *adj* : confident, relaxed, self-assured
deseo *nm* : wish, desire
deseoso, -sa *adj* : eager, anxious
desequilibrar *vt* : to unbalance, to throw off balance — **desequilibrarse** *vr*
desequilibrio *nm* : imbalance
deserción *nf, pl* **-ciones** : desertion, defection
desertar *vi* **1** : to desert, to defect **2** ~ **de** : to abandon, to neglect
desertor, -tora *n* : deserter, defector
desesperación *nf, pl* **-ciones** : desperation, despair

desesperado, -da *adj* : desperate, despairing, hopeless — **desesperadamente** *adv*
desesperanza *nf* : despair, hopelessness
desesperar *vt* : to exasperate — *vi* : to despair, to lose hope — **desesperarse** *vr* : to become exasperated
desestimar *vt* **1** : to reject, to disallow **2** : to have a low opinion of
desfachatez *nf, pl* **-teces** : audacity, nerve, cheek
desfalcador, -dora *n* : embezzler
desfalcar {72} *vt* : to embezzle
desfalco *nm* : embezzlement
desfallecer {53} *vi* **1** : to weaken **2** : to faint
desfallecimiento *nm* **1** : weakness **2** : fainting
desfasado, -da *adj* **1** : out of sync **2** : out of step, behind the times
desfase *nm* : gap, lag ⟨desfase horario : jet lag⟩
desfavorable *adj* : unfavorable, adverse — **desfavorablemente** *adv*
desfavorecido, -da *adj* : underprivileged
desfigurar *vt* **1** : to disfigure, to mar **2** : to distort, to misrepresent
desfiladero *nm* : narrow gorge, defile
desfilar *vi* : to parade, to march
desfile *nm* : parade, procession
desfogar {52} *vt* **1** : to vent **2** *Mex* : to unclog, to unblock — **desfogarse** *vr* : to vent one's feelings, to let off steam
desforestación *nf, pl* **-ciones** : deforestation
desgajar *vt* **1** : to tear off **2** : to break apart — **desgajarse** *vr* : to come apart
desgana *nf* **1** INAPETENCIA : lack of appetite **2** APATÍA : apathy, unwillingness, reluctance
desgano *nm* → **desgana**
desgarbado, -da *adj* : ungainly
desgarrador, -dora *adj* : heartrending, heartbreaking
desgarradura *nf* : tear, rip
desgarrar *vt* **1** : to tear, to rip **2** : to break (one's heart) — **desgarrarse** *vr*
desgarre → **desgarro**
desgarro *nm* : tear
desgarrón *nm, pl* **-rrones** : rip, tear
desgastar *vt* **1** : to use up **2** : to wear away, to wear down
desgaste *nm* : deterioration, wear and tear
desglosar *vt* : to break down, to itemize
desglose *nm* : breakdown, itemization
desgobierno *nm* : anarchy, disorder
desgracia *nf* **1** : misfortune **2** : disgrace **3 por** ~ : unfortunately
desgraciadamente *adv* : unfortunately
desgraciado[1], -da *adj* **1** : unfortunate, unlucky **2** : vile, wretched
desgraciado[2], -da *n* : unfortunate person, wretch
desgranar *vt* : to shuck, to shell
deshabitado, -da *adj* : unoccupied, uninhabited

deshacer {40} *vt* **1** : to destroy, to ruin **2** DESATAR : to undo, to untie **3** : to break apart, to crumble **4** : to dissolve, to melt **5** : to break, to cancel — **deshacerse** *vr* **1** : to fall apart, to come undone **2** ~ **de** : to get rid of
deshecho[1] *pp* → **deshacer**
deshecho[2], -cha *adj* **1** : destroyed, ruined **2** : devastated, shattered **3** : undone, untied
desheredado, -da *adj* MARGINADO : dispossessed, destitute
desheredar *vt* : to disinherit
deshicieron, etc. → **deshacer**
deshidratar *vt* : to dehydrate — **deshidratación** *nf*
deshielo *nm* : thaw, thawing
deshilachar *vt* : to fray — **deshilacharse** *vr*
deshizo → **deshacer**
deshonestidad *nf* : dishonesty
deshonesto, -ta *adj* : dishonest
deshonra *nf* : dishonor, disgrace
deshonrar *vt* : to dishonor, to disgrace
deshonroso, -sa *adj* : dishonorable, disgraceful
deshuesar *vt* **1** : to pit (a fruit, etc.) **2** : to bone, to debone
deshumanizar {21} *vt* : to dehumanize — **deshumanización** *nf*
desidia *nf* **1** APATÍA : apathy, indolence **2** NEGLIGENCIA : negligence, sloppiness
desierto[1], -ta *adj* : deserted, uninhabited
desierto[2] *nm* : desert
designación *nf, pl* **-ciones** NOMBRAMIENTO : appointment, naming (to an office, etc.)
designar *vt* NOMBRAR : to designate, to appoint, to name
designio *nm* : plan
desigual *adj* **1** : unequal **2** DISPAREJO : uneven
desigualdad *nf* **1** : inequality **2** : unevenness
desilusión *nf, pl* **-siones** DESENCANTO, DESENGAÑO : disillusionment, disenchantment
desilusionar *vt* DESENCANTAR, DESENGAÑAR : to disillusion, to disenchant — **desilusionarse** *vr*
desinfectante *adj* & *nm* : disinfectant
desinfectar *vt* : to disinfect — **desinfección** *nf*
desinflar *vt* : to deflate — **desinflarse** *vr*
desinhibido, -da *adj* : uninhibited, unrestrained
desintegración *nf, pl* **-ciones** : disintegration
desintegrar *vt* : to disintegrate, to break up — **desintegrarse** *vr*
desinterés *nm* **1** : lack of interest, indifference **2** : unselfishness
desinteresado, -da *adj* GENEROSO : unselfish
desintoxicar {72} *vt* : to detoxify, to detox

desistir *vi* **1** : to desist, to stop **2** ~ **de** : to give up, to relinquish

deslave *nm Mex* : landslide

desleal *adj* INFIEL : disloyal — **deslealmente** *adv*

deslealtad *nf* : disloyalty

desleír {66} *vt* : to dilute, to dissolve

desligar {52} *vt* **1** : to separate, to undo **2** : to free (from an obligation) — **desligarse** *vr* ~ **de** : to extricate oneself from

deslindar *vt* **1** : to mark the limits of, to demarcate **2** : to define, to clarify

deslinde *nm* : demarcation

desliz *nm, pl* **deslices** : error, mistake, slip ⟨desliz de la lengua : slip of the tongue⟩

deslizar {21} *vt* **1** : to slide, to slip **2** : to slip in — **deslizarse** *vr* **1** : to slide, to glide **2** : to slip away

deslucido, -da *adj* **1** : unimpressive, dull **2** : faded, dingy, tarnished

deslucir {45} *vt* **1** : to spoil **2** : to fade, to dull, to tarnish **3** : to discredit

deslumbrar *vt* : to dazzle — **deslumbrante** *adj*

deslustrado, -da *adj* : dull, lusterless

deslustrar *vt* : to tarnish, to dull

deslustre *nm* : tarnish

desmán *nm, pl* **desmanes** **1** : outrage, abuse **2** : misfortune

desmandarse *vr* : to behave badly, to get out of hand

desmantelar *vt* DESMONTAR : to dismantle

desmañado, -da *adj* : clumsy, awkward

desmayado, -da *adj* **1** : fainting, weak **2** : dull, pale

desmayar *vi* : to lose heart, to falter — **desmayarse** *vr* DESVANECERSE : to faint, to swoon

desmayo *nm* **1** : faint, fainting **2 sufrir un desmayo** : to faint

desmedido, -da *adj* DESMESURADO : excessive, undue

desmejorar *vt* : to weaken, to make worse — *vi* : to decline (in health), to get worse

desmembramiento *nm* : dismemberment

desmembrar {55} *vt* **1** : to dismember **2** : to break up

desmemoriado, -da *adj* : absentminded, forgetful

desmentido *nm* : denial

desmentir {76} *vt* **1** NEGAR : to deny, to refute **2** CONTRADECIR : to contradict

desmenuzar {21} *vt* **1** : to break down, to scrutinize **2** : to crumble, to shred — **desmenuzarse** *vr*

desmerecer {53} *vt* : to be unworthy of — *vi* **1** : to decline in value **2** ~ **de** : to compare unfavorably with

desmesurado, -da *adj* DESMEDIDO : excessive, inordinate — **desmesuradamente** *adv*

desmigajar *vt* : to crumble — **desmigajarse** *vr*

desmilitarizado, -da *adj* : demilitarized

desmontar *vt* **1** : to clear, to level off **2** DESMANTELAR : to dismantle, to take apart — *vi* : to dismount

desmonte *nm* : clearing, leveling

desmoralizador, -dora *adj* : demoralizing

desmoralizar {21} *vt* DESALENTAR : to demoralize, to discourage

desmoronamiento *nm* : crumbling, falling apart

desmoronar *vt* : to wear away, to erode — **desmoronarse** *vr* : to crumble, to deteriorate, to fall apart

desmotadora *nf* : gin, cotton gin

desmovilizar {21} *vt* : to demobilize — **desmovilización** *nf*

desnaturalizar {21} *vt* **1** : to denature **2** : to distort, to alter

desnivel *nm* **1** : disparity, difference **2** : unevenness (of a surface)

desnivelado, -da *adj* **1** : uneven **2** : unbalanced

desnudar *vt* **1** : to undress **2** : to strip, to lay bare — **desnudarse** *vr* : to undress, to strip off one's clothing

desnudez *nf, pl* **-deces** : nudity, nakedness

desnudismo → **nudismo**

desnudista → **nudista**

desnudo¹, -da *adj* : nude, naked, bare

desnudo² *nm* : nude

desnutrición *nf, pl* **-ciones** MALNUTRICIÓN : malnutrition, undernourishment

desnutrido, -da *adj* MALNUTRIDO : malnourished, undernourished

desobedecer {53} *v* : to disobey

desobediencia *nf* : disobedience — **desobediente** *adj*

desocupación *nf, pl* **-ciones** : unemployment

desocupado, -da *adj* **1** : vacant, empty **2** : free, unoccupied **3** : unemployed

desocupar *vt* **1** : to empty **2** : to vacate, to move out of — **desocuparse** *vr* : to leave, to quit (a job)

desodorante *adj & nm* : deodorant

desolación *nf, pl* **-ciones** : desolation

desolado, -da *adj* **1** : desolate **2** : devastated, distressed

desolador, -dora *adj* **1** : devastating **2** : bleak, desolate

desollar *vt* : to skin, to flay

desorbitado, -da *adj* **1** : excessive, exorbitant **2 con los ojos desorbitados** : with eyes popping out of one's head

desorden *nm, pl* **desórdenes** **1** DESBARAJUSTE : disorder, mess **2** : disorder, disturbance, upset

desordenado, -da *adj* **1** : untidy, messy **2** : disorderly, unruly

desordenar *vt* : to mess up — **desordenarse** *vr* : to get messed up

desorganización *nf, pl* **-ciones** : disorganization

desorganizar {21} *vt* : to disrupt, to disorganize

desorientación *nf, pl* **-ciones** : disorientation, confusion

desorientar *vt* : to disorient, to mislead, to confuse — **desorientarse** *vr* : to become disoriented, to lose one's way

desovar *vi* : to spawn

despachar *vt* **1** : to complete, to conclude **2** : to deal with, to take care of, to handle **3** : to dispatch, to send off **4** *fam* : to finish off, to kill — **despacharse** *vr fam* : to gulp down, to polish off

despacho *nm* **1** : dispatch, shipment **2** OFICINA : office, study

despacio *adv* LENTAMENTE, LENTO : slowly, slow ⟨¡despacio! : take it easy!, easy does it!⟩

desparasitar *vt* : to worm (an animal), to delouse

desparpajo *nm fam* **1** : self-confidence, nerve **2** *CA* : confusion, muddle

desparramar *vt* **1** : to spill, to splatter **2** : to spread, to scatter

despatarrarse *vr* : to sprawl (out)

despavorido, -da *adj* : terrified, horrified

despecho *nm* **1** : spite **2 a despecho de** : despite, in spite of

despectivo, -va *adj* **1** : contemptuous, disparaging **2** : derogatory, pejorative

despedazar {21} *vt* : to cut to pieces, to tear apart

despedida *nf* **1** : farewell, good-bye **2 despedida de soltera** : bridal shower

despedir {54} *vt* **1** : to see off, to show out **2** : to dismiss, to fire **3** EMITIR : to give off, to emit ⟨despedir un olor : to give off an odor⟩ — **despedirse** *vr* : to take one's leave, to say good-bye

despegado, -da *adj* **1** : separated, detached **2** : cold, distant

despegar {52} *vt* : to remove, to detach — *vi* : to take off, to lift off, to blast off

despegue *nm* : takeoff, liftoff

despeinado, -da *adj* : disheveled, tousled ⟨estoy despeinada : my hair's a mess⟩

despeinarse *vr* **1** : to mess up one's hair **2** : to become disheveled ⟨me despeiné : my hair got messed up⟩

despejado, -da *adj* **1** : clear, fair **2** : alert, clear-headed **3** : uncluttered, unobstructed

despejar *vt* **1** : to clear, to free **2** : to clarify — *vi* **1** : to clear up **2** : to punt (in sports)

despeje *nm* **1** : clearing **2** : punt (in sports)

despellejar *vt* : to skin (an animal)

despenalizar {21} *vt* : to legalize — **despenalización** *nf*

despensa *nf* **1** : pantry, larder **2** PROVISIONES : provisions *pl*, supplies *pl*

despeñar *vt* : to hurl down

despepitar *vt* : to seed, to remove the seeds from

desperdiciar *vt* **1** DESAPROVECHAR, MALGASTAR : to waste **2** : to miss, to miss out on

desperdicio *nm* **1** : waste **2 desperdicios** *nmpl* RESIDUOS : refuse, scraps, rubbish

desperdigar {52} *vt* DISPERSAR : to disperse, to scatter

desperfecto *nm* **1** DEFECTO : flaw, defect **2** : damage

despertador *nm* : alarm clock

despertar {55} *vi* **1** : to awaken, to wake up — *vt* **1** : to arouse, to wake **2** EVOCAR : to elicit, to evoke — **despertarse** *vr* : to wake (oneself) up

despiadado, -da *adj* CRUEL : cruel, merciless, pitiless — **despiadadamente** *adv*

despido *nm* : dismissal, layoff

despierto, -ta *adj* **1** : awake, alert **2** LISTO : clever, sharp ⟨con la mente despierta : with a sharp mind⟩

despilfarrador[1], **-dora** *adj* : extravagant, wasteful

despilfarrador[2], **-dora** *n* : spendthrift, prodigal

despilfarrar *vt* MALGASTAR : to squander, to waste

despilfarro *nm* : extravagance, wastefulness

despintar *vt* : to strip the paint from — **despintarse** *vr* : to fade, to wash off, to peel off

despistado[1], **-da** *adj* **1** DISTRAÍDO : absentminded, forgetful **2** CONFUSO : confused, bewildered

despistado[2], **-da** *n* : scatterbrain, absentminded person

despistar *vt* : to throw off the track, to confuse — **despistarse** *vr*

despiste *nm* **1** : absentmindedness **2** : mistake, slip

desplantador *nm* : garden trowel

desplante *nm* : insolence, rudeness

desplazamiento *nm* **1** : movement, displacement **2** : journey

desplazar {21} *vt* **1** : to replace, to displace **2** TRASLADAR : to move, to shift

desplegar {49} *vt* **1** : to display, to show, to manifest **2** DESDOBLAR : to unfold, to unfurl **3** : to spread (out) **4** : to deploy

despliegue *nm* **1** : display **2** : deployment

desplomarse *vr* **1** : to plummet, to fall **2** DERRUMBARSE : to collapse, to break down

desplome *nm* **1** : fall, drop **2** : collapse

desplumar *vt* : to pluck (a chicken, etc.)

despoblado[1], **-da** *adj* : uninhabited, deserted

despoblado[2] *nm* : open country, deserted area

despoblar {19} *vt* : to depopulate

despojar *vt* **1** : to strip, to clear **2** : to divest, to deprive — **despojarse** *vr* **1 ∼ de** : to remove (clothing) **2 ∼ de** : to relinquish, to renounce

despojos · destrozado

90

despojos *nmpl* **1** : remains, scraps **2** : plunder, spoils

desportilladura *nf* : chip, nick

desportillar *vt* : to chip — **desportillarse** *vr*

desposeer {20} *vt* : to dispossess

déspota *nmf* : despot, tyrant

despotismo *nm* : despotism — **despótico, -ca** *adj*

despotricar {72} *vi* : to rant and rave, to complain excessively

despreciable *adj* **1** : despicable, contemptible **2** : negligible ⟨nada despreciable : not inconsiderable, significant⟩

despreciar *vt* DESDEÑAR, MENOSPRECIAR : to despise, to scorn, to disdain

despreciativo, -va *adj* : scornful, disdainful

desprecio *nm* DESDÉN, MENOSPRECIO : disdain, contempt, scorn

desprender *vt* **1** SOLTAR : to detach, to loosen, to unfasten **2** EMITIR : to emit, to give off — **desprenderse** *vr* **1** : to come off, to come undone **2** : to be inferred, to follow **3** ~ **de** : to part with, to get rid of

desprendido, -da *adj* : generous, unselfish, disinterested

desprendimiento *nm* **1** : detachment **2** GENEROSIDAD : generosity **3** **desprendimiento de tierras** : landslide

despreocupación *nf, pl* **-ciones** : indifference, lack of concern

despreocupado, -da *adj* : carefree, easygoing, unconcerned

desprestigiar *vt* DESACREDITAR : to discredit, to disgrace — **desprestigiarse** *vr* : to lose prestige

desprestigio *nm* DESCRÉDITO : discredit, disrepute

desprevenido, -da *adj* DESAPERCIBIDO : unprepared, off guard, unsuspecting

desproporción *nf, pl* **-ciones** : disproportion, disparity

desproporcionado, -da : out of proportion

despropósito *nm* : piece of nonsense, absurdity

desprotegido, -da *adj* : unprotected, vulnerable

desprovisto, -ta *adj* ~ **de** : devoid of, lacking in

después *adv* **1** : afterward, later **2** : then, next **3** ~ **de** : after, next after ⟨después de comer : after eating⟩ **4** **después (de) que** : after ⟨después que lo acabé : after I finished it⟩ **5** **después de todo** : after all **6 poco después** : shortly after, soon thereafter

despuntado, -da *adj* : blunt, dull

despuntar *vt* : to blunt — *vi* **1** : to dawn **2** : to sprout **3** : to excel, to stand out

desquiciar *vt* **1** : to unhinge (a door) **2** : to drive crazy — **desquiciarse** *vr* : to go crazy

desquitarse *vr* **1** : to get even, to retaliate **2** ~ **con** : to take it out on

desquite *nm* : revenge

desregulación *nf, pl* **-ciones** : deregulation

desregular *vt* : to deregulate

desregularización *nf* → **desregulación**

destacadamente *adv* : outstandingly, prominently

destacado, -da *adj* **1** : outstanding, prominent **2** : stationed, posted

destacamento *nm* : detachment (of troops)

destacar {72} *vt* **1** ENFATIZAR, SUBRAYAR : to emphasize, to highlight, to stress **2** : to station, to post — *vi* : to stand out

destajo *nm* **1** : piecework **2 a** ~ : by the item, by the job

destapador *nm* : bottle opener

destapar *vt* **1** : to open, to take the top off **2** DESCUBRIR : to reveal, to uncover **3** : to unblock, to unclog

destape *nm* : uncovering, revealing

destartalado, -da *adj* : dilapidated, tumbledown

destellar *vi* **1** : to sparkle, to flash, to glint **2** : to twinkle

destello *nm* **1** : flash, sparkle, twinkle **2** : glimmer, hint

destemplado, -da *adj* **1** : out of tune **2** : irritable, out of sorts **3** : unpleasant (of weather)

desteñir {67} *vi* : to run, to fade — **desteñirse** *vr* DESCOLORARSE : to fade

desterrado[1], -da *adj* : banished, exiled

desterrado[2], -da *n* : exile

desterrar {55} *vt* **1** EXILIAR : to banish, to exile **2** ERRADICAR : to eradicate, to do away with

destetar *vt* : to wean

destiempo *adv* **a** ~ : at the wrong time

destierro *nm* EXILIO : exile

destilación *nf, pl* **-ciones** : distillation

destilador, -dora *n* : distiller

destilar *vt* **1** : to exude **2** : to distill

destilería *nf* : distillery

destinación *nf, pl* **-ciones** DESTINO : destination

destinado, -da *adj* : destined, bound

destinar *vt* **1** : to appoint, to assign **2** ASIGNAR : to earmark, to allot

destinatario, -ria *n* **1** : addressee **2** : payee

destino *nm* **1** : destiny, fate **2** DESTINACIÓN : destination **3** : use **4** : assignment, post

destitución *nf, pl* **-ciones** : dismissal, removal from office

destituir {41} *vt* : to dismiss, to remove from office

destorcer {14} *vt* : to untwist

destornillador *nm* : screwdriver

destornillar *vt* : to unscrew

destrabar *vt* **1** : to untie, to undo, to ease up **2** : to separate

destreza *nf* HABILIDAD : dexterity, skill

destronar *vt* : to depose, to dethrone

destrozado, -da *adj* **1** : ruined, destroyed **2** : devastated, brokenhearted

destrozar {21} *vt* **1** : to smash, to shatter **2** : to destroy, to wreck — **destrozarse** *vr*
destrozo *nm* **1** DAÑO : damage **2** : havoc, destruction
destrucción *nf, pl* -ciones : destruction
destructivo, -va *adj* : destructive
destructor[1], -tora *adj* : destructive
destructor[2] *nm* : destroyer (ship)
destruir {41} *vt* : to destroy — destruirse *vr*
desubicado, -da *adj* **1** : out of place **2** : confused, disoriented
desunión *nf, pl* -niones : disunity
desunir *vt* : to split, to divide
desusado, -da *adj* **1** INSÓLITO : unusual **2** OBSOLETO : obsolete, disused, antiquated
desuso *nm* : disuse, obsolescence ⟨caer en desuso : to fall into disuse⟩
desvaído, -da *adj* **1** : pale, washed-out **2** : vague, blurred
desvainar *vt* : to shell
desvalido, -da *adj* DESAMPARADO : destitute, helpless
desvalijar *vt* **1** : to ransack **2** : to rob
desvalorización *nf, pl* -ciones **1** DEVALUACIÓN : devaluation **2** : depreciation
desvalorizar {21} *vt* : to devalue
desván *nm, pl* desvanes ÁTICO, BUHARDILLA : attic
desvanecer {53} *vt* **1** DISIPAR : to make disappear, to dispel **2** : to fade, to blur — desvanecerse *vr* **1** : to vanish, to disappear **2** : to fade **3** DESMAYARSE : to faint, to swoon
desvanecimiento *nm* **1** : disappearance **2** DESMAYO : faint **3** : fading
desvariar {85} *vi* **1** DELIRAR : to be delirious **2** : to rave, to talk nonsense
desvarío *nm* DELIRIO : delirium
desvelado, -da *adj* : sleepless
desvelar *vt* **1** : to keep awake **2** REVELAR : to reveal, to disclose — desvelarse *vr* **1** : to stay awake **2** : to do one's utmost
desvelo *nm* **1** : sleeplessness **2** desvelos *nmpl* : efforts, pains
desvencijado, -da *adj* : dilapidated, rickety
desventaja *nf* : disadvantage, drawback
desventajoso, -sa *adj* : disadvantageous, unfavorable
desventura *nf* INFORTUNIO : misfortune
desventurado, -da *adj* : unfortunate, ill-fated
desvergonzado, -da *adj* : shameless, impudent
desvergüenza *nf* : shamelessness, impudence
desvestir {54} *vt* : to undress — desvestirse *vr* : to get undressed
desviación *nf, pl* -ciones **1** : deviation, departure **2** : detour, diversion
desviar {85} *vt* **1** : to change the course of, to divert **2** : to turn away, to de-

flect — desviarse *vr* **1** : to branch off **2** APARTARSE : to stray
desvinculación *nf, pl* -ciones : dissociation
desvincular *vt* ~ de : to separate from, to dissociate from — desvincularse *vr*
desvío *nm* **1** : diversion, detour **2** : deviation
desvirtuar {3} *vt* **1** : to impair, to spoil **2** : to detract from **3** : to distort, to misrepresent
detalladamente *adv* : in detail, at great length
detallar *vt* : to detail
detalle *nm* **1** : detail **2** al detalle : retail
detallista[1] *adj* **1** : meticulous **2** : retail
detallista[2] *nmf* **1** : perfectionist **2** : retailer
detección *nf, pl* -ciones : detection
detectar *vt* : to detect — detectable *adj*
detective *nmf* : detective
detector *nm* : detector ⟨detector de mentiras : lie detector⟩
detención *nf, pl* -ciones **1** ARRESTO : detention, arrest **2** : stop, halt **3** : delay, holdup
detener {80} *vt* **1** ARRESTAR : to arrest, to detain **2** PARAR : to stop, to halt **3** : to keep, to hold back — detenerse *vr* **1** : to stop **2** : to delay, to linger
detenidamente *adv* : thoroughly, at length
detenimiento *nm* con ~ : carefully, in detail
detentar *vt* : to hold, to retain
detergente *nm* : detergent
deteriorado, -da *adj* : damaged, worn
deteriorar *vt* ESTROPEAR : to damage, to spoil — deteriorarse *vr* **1** : to get damaged, to wear out **2** : to deteriorate, to worsen
deterioro *nm* **1** : deterioration, wear **2** : worsening, decline
determinación *nf, pl* -ciones **1** : determination, resolve **2** tomar una determinación : to make a decision
determinado, -da *adj* **1** : certain, particular **2** : determined, resolute
determinante[1] *adj* : determining, deciding
determinante[2] *nm* : determinant
determinar *vt* **1** : to determine **2** : to cause, to bring about — determinarse *vr* : to make up one's mind, to decide
detestar *vt* : to detest — detestable *adj*
detonación *nf, pl* -ciones : detonation
detonador *nm* : detonator
detonante[1] *adj* : detonating, explosive
detonante[2] *nm* **1** → detonador **2** : catalyst, cause
detonar *vi* : to detonate, to explode
detractor, -tora *n* : detractor, critic
detrás *adv* **1** : behind **2** ~ de : in back of **3** por ~ : from behind
detrimento *nm* : detriment ⟨en detrimento de : to the detriment of⟩
detuvo, etc. → detener

deuda *nf* **1** DÉBITO : debt **2 en deuda con** : indebted to
deudo, -da *n* : relative
deudor¹, -dora *adj* : indebted
deudor², -dora *n* : debtor
devaluación *nf, pl* **-ciones** DESVALORIZACIÓN : devaluation
devaluar {3} *vt* : to devalue — **devaluarse** *vr* : to depreciate
devanarse *vr* **devanarse los sesos** : to rack one's brains
devaneo *nm* **1** : flirtation, fling **2** : idle pursuit
devastador, -dora *adj* : devastating
devastar *vt* : to devastate — **devastación** *nf*
devenir {87} *vi* **1** : to come about **2** ~ **en** : to become, to turn into
devoción *nf, pl* **-ciones** : devotion
devolución *nf, pl* **-ciones** REEMBOLSO : return, refund
devolver {89} *vt* **1** : to return, to give back **2** REEMBOLSAR : to refund, to pay back **3** : to vomit, to bring up — *vi* : to vomit, to throw up — **devolverse** *vr* : to return, to come back, to go back
devorar *vt* **1** : to devour **2** : to consume
devoto¹, -ta *adj* : devout — **devotamente** *adv*
devoto², -ta *n* : devotee, admirer
di → **dar, decir**
día *nm* **1** : day ⟨todos los días : every day⟩ **2** : daytime, daylight ⟨de día : by day, in the daytime⟩ ⟨en pleno día : in broad daylight⟩ **3 al día** : up-to-date **4 en su día** : in due time
diabetes *nf* : diabetes
diabético, -ca *adj & n* : diabetic
diablillo *nm* : little devil, imp
diablo *nm* DEMONIO : devil
diablura *nf* **1** : prank **2 diabluras** *nfpl* : mischief
diabólico, -ca *adj* : diabolical, diabolic, devilish
diaconisa *nf* : deaconess
diácono *nm* : deacon
diacrítico, -ca *adj* : diacritic, diacritical
diadema *nf* : diadem, crown
diáfano, -na *adj* : diaphanous
diafragma *nm* : diaphragm
diagnosticar {72} *vt* : to diagnose
diagnóstico¹, -ca *adj* : diagnostic
diagnóstico² *nm* : diagnosis
diagonal *adj & nf* : diagonal — **diagonalmente** *adv*
diagrama *nm* **1** : diagram **2 diagrama de flujo** ORGANIGRAMA : flowchart
dial *nm* : dial (on a radio, etc.)
dialecto *nm* : dialect
dialogar {52} *vi* : to have a talk, to converse
diálogo *nm* : dialogue
diamante *nm* : diamond
diametral *adj* : diametric, diametrical — **diametralmente** *adv*
diámetro *nm* : diameter
diana *nf* **1** : target, bull's-eye **2 or toque de diana** : reveille

diapositiva *nf* : slide, transparency
diario¹ *adv* *Mex* : every day, daily
diario², -ria *adj* : daily, everyday — **diariamente** *adv*
diario³ *nm* **1** : diary **2** PERIÓDICO : newspaper
diarrea *nf* : diarrhea
diatriba *nf* : diatribe, tirade
dibujante *nmf* **1** : draftsman *m*, draftswoman *f* **2** CARICATURISTA : cartoonist
dibujar *vt* **1** : to draw, to sketch **2** : to portray, to depict
dibujo *nm* **1** : drawing **2** : design, pattern **3 dibujos animados** : (animated) cartoons
dicción *nf, pl* **-ciones** : diction
diccionario *nm* : dictionary
dícese → **decir**
dicha *nf* **1** SUERTE : good luck **2** FELICIDAD : happiness, joy
dicho¹ *pp* → **decir**
dicho², -cha *adj* : said, aforementioned
dicho³ *nm* DECIR : saying, proverb
dichoso, -sa *adj* **1** : blessed **2** FELIZ : happy **3** AFORTUNADO : fortunate, lucky
diciembre *nm* : December
diciendo → **decir**
dictado *nm* : dictation
dictador, -dora *n* : dictator
dictadura *nf* : dictatorship
dictamen *nm, pl* **dictámenes 1** : report **2** : judgment, opinion
dictaminar *vt* : to report — *vi* : to give an opinion, to pass judgment
dictar *vt* **1** : to dictate **2** : to pronounce (a judgment) **3** : to give, to deliver ⟨dictar una conferencia : to give a lecture⟩
dictatorial *adj* : dictatorial
didáctico, -ca *adj* : didactic
diecinueve *adj & nm* : nineteen
diecinueveavo¹, -va *adj* : nineteenth
diecinueveavo² *nm* : nineteenth (fraction)
dieciocho *adj & nm* : eighteen
dieciochoavo¹, -va *or* **dieciochavo, -va** *adj* : eighteenth
dieciochoavo² *or* **dieciochavo** *nm* : eighteenth (fraction)
dieciséis *adj & nm* : sixteen
dieciseisavo¹, -va *adj* : sixteenth
dieciseisavo² *nm* : sixteenth (fraction)
diecisiete *adj & nm* : seventeen
diecisieteavo¹, -va *adj* : seventeenth
diecisieteavo² *nm* : seventeenth
diente *nm* **1** : tooth ⟨diente canino : eyetooth, canine tooth⟩ **2** : tusk, fang **3** : prong, tine **4 diente de león** : dandelion
dieron, etc. → **dar**
diesel ['disel] *nm* : diesel
diestra *nf* : right hand
diestramente *adv* : skillfully, adroitly
diestro¹, -tra *adj* **1** : right **2** : skillful, accomplished
diestro² *nm* : bullfighter, matador
dieta *nf* : diet

dietética *nf* : dietetics
dietético, -ca *adj* : dietetic
dietista *nmf* : dietitian
diez *adj & nm, pl* dieces : ten
difamación *nf, pl* -ciones : defamation, slander
difamar *vt* : to defame, to slander
difamatorio, -ria *adj* : slanderous, defamatory, libelous
diferencia *nf* 1 : difference 2 a diferencia de : unlike, in contrast to
diferenciación *nf, pl* -ciones : differentiation
diferenciar *vt* : to differentiate between, to distinguish — diferenciarse *vr* : to differ
diferendo *nm* : dispute, conflict
diferente *adj* DISTINTO : different — diferentemente *adv*
diferir {76} *vt* DILATAR, POSPONER : to postpone, to put off — *vi* : to differ
difícil *adj* : difficult, hard
difícilmente *adv* 1 : with difficulty 2 : hardly
dificultad *nf* : difficulty
dificultar *vt* : to make difficult, to obstruct
dificultoso, -sa *adj* : difficult, hard
difteria *nf* : diphtheria
difundir *vt* 1 : to diffuse, to spread out 2 : to broadcast, to spread
difunto, -ta *adj & n* FALLECIDO : deceased
difusión *nf, pl* -siones 1 : spreading 2 : diffusion (of heat, etc.) 3 : broadcast, broadcasting ⟨los medios de difusión : the media⟩
difuso, -sa *adj* : diffuse, widespread
diga, etc. → decir
digerir {76} *vt* : to digest — digerible *adj*
digestión *nf, pl* -tiones : digestion
digestivo, -va *adj* : digestive
digital[1] *adj* : digital — digitalmente *adv*
digital[2] *nf* 1 DEDALERA : foxglove 2 : digitalis
dígito *nm* : digit
dignarse *vr* : to deign, to condescend ⟨no se dignó contestar : he didn't deign to answer⟩
dignatario, -ria *n* : dignitary
dignidad *nf* 1 : dignity 2 : dignitary
dignificar {72} *vt* : to dignify
digno, -na *adj* 1 HONORABLE : honorable 2 : worthy — dignamente *adv*
digresión *nf, pl* -ciones : digression
dije *nm* : charm (on a bracelet)
dijo, etc. → decir
dilación *nf, pl* -ciones : delay
dilapidar *vt* : to waste, to squander
dilatar *vt* 1 : to dilate, to widen, to expand 2 DIFERIR, POSPONER : to put off, to postpone — dilatarse *vr* 1 : to expand (of gases, metals, etc.) 2 *Mex* : to take long, to be long
dilatorio, -ria *adj* : dilatory, delaying
dilema *nm* : dilemma
diletante *nmf* : dilettante

diligencia *nf* 1 : diligence, care 2 : promptness, speed 3 : action, step 4 : task, errand 5 : stagecoach 6 diligencias *nfpl* : judicial procedures, formalities
diligente *adj* : diligent — diligentemente *adv*
dilucidar *vt* : to elucidate, to clarify
dilución *nf, pl* -ciones : dilution
diluir {41} *vt* : to dilute
diluviar *v impers* : to pour (with rain), to pour down
diluvio *nm* 1 : flood 2 : downpour
dimensión *nf, pl* -siones : dimension — dimensional *adj*
dimensionar *vt* : to measure, to gauge
diminutivo[1], -va *adj* : diminutive
diminutivo[2] *nm* : diminutive
diminuto, -ta *adj* : minute, tiny
dimisión *nf, pl* -siones : resignation
dimitir *vi* : to resign, to step down
dimos → dar
dinámica *nf* : dynamics
dinámico, -ca *adj* : dynamic — dinámicamente *adv*
dinamismo *nm* : energy, vigor
dinamita *nf* : dynamite
dinamitar *vt* : to dynamite
dínamo *or* dinamo *nm* : dynamo
dinastía *nf* : dynasty
dineral *nm* : fortune, large sum of money
dinero *nm* : money
dinosaurio *nm* : dinosaur
dintel *nm* : lintel
dio, etc. → dar
diocesano, -na *adj* : diocesan
diócesis *nfs & pl* : diocese
dios, diosa *n* : god, goddess *f*
Dios *nm* : God
diploma *nm* : diploma
diplomacia *nf* : diplomacy
diplomado[1], -da *adj* : qualified, trained
diplomado[2] *nm Mex* : seminar
diplomático[1], -ca *adj* : diplomatic — diplomáticamente *adv*
diplomático[2], -ca *n* : diplomat
diptongo *nm* : diphthong
diputación *nf, pl* -ciones : deputation, delegation
diputado, -da *n* : delegate, representative
dique *nm* : dike
dirá, etc. → decir
dirección *nf, pl* -ciones 1 : address 2 : direction 3 : management, leadership 4 : steering (of an automobile)
direccional[1] *adj* : directional
direccional[2] *nf* : directional, turn signal
directa *nf* : high gear
directamente *adv* : straight, directly
directiva *nf* 1 ORDEN : directive 2 DIRECTORIO, JUNTA : board of directors
directivo[1], -va *adj* : executive, managerial
directivo[2], -va *n* : executive, director
directo, -ta *adj* 1 : direct, straight, immediate 2 en ~ : live (in broadcasting)

director, -tora *n* **1** : director, manager, head **2** : conductor (of an orchestra)
directorial *adj* : managing, executive
directorio *nm* **1** : directory **2** DIRECTI-VA, JUNTA : board of directors
directriz *nf, pl* **-trices** : guideline
dirigencia *nf* : leaders *pl*, leadership
dirigente¹ *adj* : directing, leading
dirigente² *nmf* : director, leader
dirigible *nm* : dirigible, blimp
dirigir {35} *vt* **1** : to direct, to lead **2** : to address **3** : to aim, to point **4** : to conduct (music) — **dirigirse** *vr* ~ **a 1** : to go towards **2** : to speak to, to address
dirimir *vt* **1** : to resolve, to settle **2** : to annul, to dissolve (a marriage)
discapacidad *nf* MINUSVALÍA : disability, handicap
discapacitado¹, -da *adj* : disabled, handicapped
discapacitado², -da *n* : disabled person, handicapped person
discar {72} *v* : to dial
discernimiento *nm* : discernment
discernir {25} *v* : to discern, to distinguish
disciplina *nf* : discipline
disciplinar *vt* : to discipline — **disciplinario, -ria** *adj*
discípulo, -la *n* : disciple, follower
disc jockey [ˌdiskˈjoke, -ˈd͡ʒo-] *nmf* : disc jockey
disco *nm* **1** : phonograph record **2** : disc, disk ⟨disco compacto : compact disc⟩ **3** : discus
díscolo, -la *adj* : unruly, disobedient
disconforme *adj* : in disagreement
discontinuidad *nf* : discontinuity
discontinuo, -nua *adj* : discontinuous
discordancia *nf* DESAVENENCIA : conflict, disagreement
discordante *adj* **1** : discordant **2** : conflicting
discordia *nf* : discord
discoteca *nf* **1** : disco, discotheque **2** *CA, Mex* : record store
discreción *nf, pl* **-ciones** : discretion
discrecional *adj* : discretionary
discrepancia *nf* : discrepancy
discrepar *vi* **1** : to disagree **2** : to differ
discreto, -ta *adj* : discreet — **discretamente** *adv*
discriminación *nf, pl* **-ciones** : discrimination
discriminar *vt* **1** : to discriminate against **2** : to distinguish, to differentiate
discriminatorio, -ria *adj* : discriminatory
disculpa *nf* **1** : apology **2** : excuse
disculpable *adj* : excusable
disculpar *vt* : to excuse, to pardon — **disculparse** *vr* : to apologize
discurrir *vi* **1** : to flow **2** : to pass, to go by **3** : to ponder, to reflect
discurso *nm* **1** ORACIÓN : speech, address **2** : discourse, treatise

discusión *nf, pl* **-siones** **1** : discussion **2** ALTERCADO, DISPUTA : argument
discutible *adj* : arguable, debatable
discutidor, -dora *adj* : argumentative
discutir *vt* **1** : to discuss **2** : to dispute — *vi* ALTERCAR : to argue, to quarrel
disecar {72} *vt* **1** : to dissect **2** : to stuff (for preservation)
disección *nf, pl* **-ciones** : dissection
diseminación *nf, pl* **-ciones** : dissemination, spreading
diseminar *vt* : to disseminate, to spread
disensión *nf, pl* **-siones** : dissension, disagreement
disentería *nf* : dysentery
disentir {76} *vi* : to dissent, to disagree
diseñador, -dora *n* : designer
diseñar *vt* **1** : to design, to plan **2** : to lay out, to outline
diseño *nm* : design
disentimiento *nm* : dissent
disertación *nf, pl* **-ciones** **1** : lecture, talk **2** : dissertation
disertar *vi* : to lecture, to give a talk
disfraz *nm, pl* **disfraces 1** : disguise **2** : costume **3** : front, pretense
disfrazar {21} *vt* **1** : to disguise **2** : to mask, to conceal — **disfrazarse** *vr* : to wear a costume, to be in disguise
disfrutar *vt* : to enjoy — *vi* : to enjoy oneself, to have a good time
disfrute *nm* : enjoyment
disfunción *nf, pl* **-ciones** : dysfunction — **disfuncional** *adj*
disgresión → **digresión**
disgustar *vt* : to upset, to displease, to make angry — **disgustarse** *vr*
disgusto *nm* **1** : annoyance, displeasure **2** : argument, quarrel **3** : trouble, misfortune
disidencia *nf* : dissidence, dissent
disidente *adj* & *nmf* : dissident
disímbolo, -la *adj Mex* : dissimilar
disímil *adj* : dissimilar
disimulado, -da *adj* **1** : concealed, disguised **2** : furtive, sly
disimular *vi* : to dissemble, to pretend — *vt* : to conceal, to hide
disimulo *nm* **1** : dissembling, pretense **2** : slyness, furtiveness **3** : tolerance
disipar *vt* **1** : to dissipate, to dispel **2** : to squander — **disiparse** *vr*
diskette [diˈskɛt] *nm* : floppy disk, diskette
dislocar {72} *vt* : to dislocate — **dislocación** *nf*
disminución *nf, pl* **-ciones** : decrease, drop, fall
disminuir {41} *vt* REDUCIR : to reduce, to decrease, to lower — *vi* **1** : to lower **2** : to drop, to fall
disociación *nf, pl* **-ciones** : dissociation
disociar *vt* : to dissociate, to separate
disolución *nf, pl* **-ciones** **1** : dissolution, dissolving **2** : breaking up **3** : dissipation
disoluto, -ta *adj* : dissolute, dissipated

disolver {89} *vt* **1** : to dissolve **2** : to break up — **disolverse** *vr*

disonancia *nf* : dissonance — **disonante** *adj*

dispar *adj* **1** : different, disparate **2** DIVERSO : diverse **3** DESIGUAL : inconsistent

disparado, -da *adj* **salir disparado** *fam* : to take off in a hurry, to rush away

disparar *vi* **1** : to shoot, to fire **2** *Mex fam* : to pay — *vt* **1** : to shoot **2** *Mex fam* : to treat to, to buy — **dispararse** *vr* : to shoot up, to skyrocket

disparatado, -da *adj* ABSURDO, RIDÍCULO : absurd, ridiculous, crazy

disparate *nm* : silliness, stupidity ⟨decir disparates : to talk nonsense⟩

disparejo, -ja *adj* DESIGUAL : uneven

disparidad *nf* : disparity

disparo *nm* TIRO : shot

dispendio *nm* : wastefulness, extravagance

dispendioso, -sa *adj* : wasteful, extravagant

dispensa *nf* : dispensation

dispensable *adj* **1** : dispensable **2** : excusable

dispensar *vt* **1** : to dispense, to give, to grant **2** EXCUSAR : to excuse, to forgive **3** EXIMIR : to exempt

dispensario *nm* **1** : dispensary, clinic **2** *Mex* : dispenser

dispersar *vt* DESPERDIGAR : to disperse, to scatter

dispersión *nf, pl* -siones : dispersion

disperso, -sa *adj* : dispersed, scattered

displicencia *nf* : indifference, coldness, disdain

displicente *adj* : indifferent, cold, disdainful

disponer {60} *vt* **1** : to arrange, to lay out **2** : to stipulate, to order **3** : to prepare — *vi* ~ **de** : to have at one's disposal — **disponerse** *vr* ~ **a** : to prepare to, to be about to

disponibilidad *nf* : availability

disponible *adj* : available

disposición *nf, pl* -ciones **1** : disposition **2** : aptitude, talent **3** : order, arrangement **4** : willingness, readiness **5 última disposición** : last will and testament

dispositivo *nm* **1** APARATO, MECANISMO : device, mechanism **2** : force, detachment

dispuesto[1] *pp* → **disponer**

dispuesto[2], **-ta** *adj* PREPARADO : ready, prepared, disposed

dispuso, etc. → **disponer**

disputa *nf* ALTERCADO, DISCUSIÓN : dispute, argument

disputar *vi* : to argue, to contend, to vie — *vt* : to dispute, to question — **disputarse** *vr* : to be in competition for ⟨se disputan la corona : they're fighting for the crown⟩

disquera *nf* : record label, recording company

disquete → **diskette**

disquisición *nf, pl* -ciones **1** : formal discourse **2 disquisiciones** *nfpl* : digressions

distancia *nf* : distance

distanciamiento *nm* **1** : distancing **2** : rift, estrangement

distanciar *vt* **1** : to space out **2** : to draw apart — **distanciarse** *vr* : to grow apart, to become estranged

distante *adj* **1** : distant, far-off **2** : aloof

distar *vi* ~ **de** : to be far from ⟨dista de ser perfecto : he is far from perfect⟩

diste → **dar**

distender {56} *vt* : to distend, to stretch

distensión *nf, pl* -siones : distension

distinción *nf, pl* -ciones : distinction

distinguible *adj* : distinguishable

distinguido, -da *adj* : distinguished, refined

distinguir {26} *vt* **1** : to distinguish **2** : to honor — **distinguirse** *vr*

distintivo, -va *adj* : distinctive, distinguishing

distinto, -ta *adj* **1** DIFERENTE : different **2** CLARO : distinct, clear, evident

distorsión *nf, pl* -siones : distortion

distorsionar *vt* : to distort

distracción *nf, pl* -ciones **1** : distraction, amusement **2** : forgetfulness **3** : oversight

distraer {81} *vt* **1** : to distract **2** ENTRETENER : to entertain, to amuse — **distraerse** *vr* **1** : to get distracted **2** : to amuse oneself

distraídamente *adv* : absentmindedly

distraído[1] *pp* → **distraer**

distraído[2], **-da** *adj* **1** : distracted, preoccupied **2** DESPISTADO : absentminded

distribución *nf, pl* -ciones : distribution

distribuidor, -dora *n* : distributor

distribuir {41} *vt* : to distribute

distributivo, -va *adj* : distributive

distrital *adj* : district, of the district

distrito *nm* : district

distrofia *nf* : dystrophy ⟨distrofia muscular : muscular dystrophy⟩

disturbio *nm* : disturbance

disuadir *vt* : to dissuade, to discourage

disuasión *nf, pl* -siones : dissuasion

disuasivo, -va *adj* : deterrent, discouraging

disuasorio, -ria *adj* : discouraging

disuelto *pp* → **disolver**

disyuntiva *nf* : dilemma

DIU [ˈdiu] *nm* (dispositivo intrauterino) : IUD, intrauterine device

diurético[1], **-ca** *adj* : diuretic

diurético[2] *nm* : diuretic

diurno, -na *adj* : day, daytime

diva *nf* → **divo**

divagar {52} *vi* : to digress

diván *nm, pl* **divanes** : divan

divergencia *nf* : divergence, difference

divergente *adj* : divergent, differing

divergir {35} *vi* **1** : to diverge **2** : to differ, to disagree

diversidad *nf* : diversity, variety
diversificación *nf, pl* **-ciones** : diversification
diversificar {72} *vt* : to diversify
diversión *nf, pl* **-siones** ENTRETENIMIENTO : fun, amusement, diversion
diverso, -sa *adj* : diverse, various
divertido, -da *adj* 1 : amusing, funny 2 : entertaining, enjoyable
divertir {76} *vt* ENTRETENER : to amuse, to entertain — **divertirse** *vr* : to have fun, to have a good time
dividendo *nm* : dividend
dividir *vt* 1 : to divide, to split 2 : to distribute, to share out — **dividirse** *vr*
divieso *nm* : boil
divinidad *nf* : divinity
divino, -na *adj* : divine
divisa *nf* 1 : currency 2 LEMA : motto 3 : emblem, insignia
divisar *vt* : to discern, to make out
divisible *adj* : divisible
división *nf, pl* **-siones** : division
divisionismo *nm* : factionalism
divisivo, -va *adj* : divisive
divisor *nm* : denominator
divisorio, -ria *adj* : dividing
divo, -va *n* 1 : prima donna 2 : celebrity, star
divorciado¹, -da *adj* 1 : divorced 2 : split, divided
divorciado², -da *n* : divorcé *m*, divorcée *f*
divorciar *vt* : to divorce — **divorciarse** *vr* : to get a divorce
divorcio *nm* : divorce
divulgación *nf, pl* **-ciones** 1 : spreading, dissemination 2 : popularization
divulgar {52} *vt* 1 : to spread, to circulate 2 REVELAR : to divulge, to reveal 3 : to popularize — **divulgarse** *vr*
dizque *adv* : supposedly, apparently
dobladillar *vt* : to hem
dobladillo *nm* : hem
doblar *vt* 1 : to double 2 PLEGAR : to fold, to bend 3 : to turn ⟨doblar la esquina : to turn the corner⟩ 4 : to dub — *vi* 1 : to turn 2 : to toll, to ring — **doblarse** *vr* 1 : to fold up, to double over 2 : to give in, to yield
doble¹ *adj* : double — **doblemente** *adv*
doble² *nm* 1 : double 2 : toll (of a bell), knell
doble³ *nmf* : stand-in, double
doblegar {52} *vt* 1 : to fold, to crease 2 : to force to yield — **doblegarse** *vr* : to yield, to bow
doblez¹ *nm, pl* **dobleces** : fold, crease
doblez² *nmf* : duplicity, deceitfulness
doce *adj & nm* : twelve
doceavo¹, -va *adj* : twelfth
doceavo² *nm* : twelfth (fraction)
docena *nf* 1 : dozen 2 **docena de fraile** : baker's dozen
docencia *nf* : teaching
docente¹ *adj* : educational, teaching
docente² *n* : teacher, lecturer
dócil *adj* : docile — **dócilmente** *adv*

docilidad *nf* : docility
docto, -ta *adj* : learned, erudite
doctor, -tora *n* : doctor
doctorado *nm* : doctorate
doctrina *nf* : doctrine — **doctrinal** *adj*
documentación *nf, pl* **-ciones** : documentation
documental *adj & nm* : documentary
documentar *vt* : to document
documento *nm* : document
dogma *nm* : dogma
dogmático, -ca *adj* : dogmatic
dogmatismo *nm* : dogmatism
dólar *nm* : dollar
dolencia *nf* : ailment, malaise
doler {47} *vi* 1 : to hurt, to ache 2 : to grieve — **dolerse** *vr* 1 : to be distressed 2 : to complain
doliente *nmf* : mourner, bereaved
dolor *nm* 1 : pain, ache ⟨dolor de cabeza : headache⟩ 2 PENA, TRISTEZA : grief, sorrow
dolorido, -da *adj* 1 : sore, aching 2 : hurt, upset
doloroso, -sa *adj* 1 : painful 2 : distressing — **dolorosamente** *adv*
doloso, -sa *adj* : fraudulent — **dolosamente** *adv*
domador, -dora *n* : tamer
domar *vt* : to tame, to break in
domesticado, -da *adj* : domesticated, tame
domesticar {72} *vt* : to domesticate, to tame
doméstico, -ca *adj* : domestic, household
domiciliado, -da *adj* : residing
domiciliario, -ria *adj* 1 : home 2 **arresto domiciliario** : house arrest
domiciliarse *vr* RESIDIR : to reside
domicilio *nm* : home, residence ⟨cambio de domicilio : change of address⟩
dominación *nf, pl* **-ciones** : domination
dominancia *nf* : dominance
dominante *adj* 1 : dominant 2 : domineering
dominar *vt* 1 : to dominate 2 : to master, to be proficient at — *vi* : to predominate, to prevail — **dominarse** *vr* : to control oneself
domingo *nm* : Sunday
dominical *adj* : Sunday ⟨periódico dominical : Sunday newspaper⟩
dominicano, -na *adj & n* : Dominican
dominio *nm* 1 : dominion, power 2 : mastery 3 : domain, field
dominó *nm, pl* **-nós** 1 : domino (tile) 2 : dominoes *pl* (game)
domo *nm* : dome
don¹ *nm* 1 : gift, present 2 : talent
don² *nm* 1 : title of courtesy preceding a man's first name 2 **don nadie** : nobody, insignificant person
dona *nf Mex* : doughnut, donut
donación *nf, pl* **-ciones** : donation
donador, -dora *n* : donor
donaire *nm* 1 GARBO : grace, poise 2 : witticism

donante *nf* → donador
donar *vt* : to donate
donativo *nm* : donation
doncella *nf* : maiden, damsel
doncellez *nf* : maidenhood
donde[1] *conj* : where, in which ⟨el pueblo donde vivo : the town where I live⟩
donde[2] *prep* : over by ⟨lo encontré donde la silla : I found it over by the chair⟩
dónde *adv* : where ⟨¿dónde está su casa? : where is your house?⟩
dondequiera *adv* 1 : anywhere, no matter where 2 dondequiera que : wherever, everywhere
doña *nf* : title of courtesy preceding a woman's first name
doquier *adv* por ~ : everywhere, all over
dorado[1], -da *adj* : gold, golden
dorado[2], -da *nm* : gilt
dorar *vt* 1 : to gild 2 : to brown (food)
dormido, -da *adj* 1 : asleep 2 : numb ⟨tiene el pie dormido : her foot's numb, her foot's gone to sleep⟩
dormilón, -lona *n* : sleepyhead, late riser
dormir {27} *vt* : to put to sleep — *vi* : to sleep — dormirse *vr* : to fall asleep
dormitar *vi* : to snooze, to doze
dormitorio *nm* 1 : bedroom 2 : dormitory
dorsal[1] *adj* : dorsal
dorsal[2] *nm* : number (worn in sports)
dorso *nm* 1 : back ⟨el dorso de la mano : the back of the hand⟩ 2 *Mex* : backstroke
dos *adj & nm* : two
doscientos[1], -tas *adj* : two hundred
doscientos[2] *nms & pl* : two hundred
dosel *nm* : canopy
dosificación *nf, pl* -ciones : dosage
dosis *nfs & pl* 1 : dose 2 : amount, quantity
dossier *nm* : dossier
dotación *nf, pl* -ciones 1 : endowment, funding 2 : staff, personnel
dotado, -da *adj* 1 : gifted 2 ~ de : endowed with, equipped with
dotar *vt* : to provide, to equip 2 : to endow
dote *nf* 1 : dowry 2 dotes *nfpl* : talent, gift
doy → dar
draga *nf* : dredge
dragado *nm* : dredging
dragar {52} *vt* : to dredge
dragón *nm, pl* dragones 1 : dragon 2 : snapdragon
drague, etc. → dragar
drama *nm* : drama
dramático, -ca *adj* : dramatic — dramáticamente *adv*
dramatizar {21} *vt* : to dramatize — dramatización *nf*
dramaturgo, -ga *n* : dramatist, playwright

drástico, -ca *adj* : drastic — drásticamente *adv*
drenaje *nm* : drainage
drenar *vt* : to drain
drene *nm Mex* : drain
driblar *vi* : to dribble (in basketball)
drible *nm* : dribble (in basketball)
droga *nf* : drug
drogadicción *nf, pl* -ciones : drug addiction
drogadicto, -ta *n* : drug addict
drogar {52} *vt* : to drug — drogarse *vr* : to take drugs
drogue, etc. → drogar
droguería *nf* FARMACIA : drugstore
dromedario *nm* : dromedary
dual *adj* : dual
dualidad *nf* : duality
dualismo *nm* : dualism
ducha *nf* : shower ⟨darse una ducha : to take a shower⟩
ducharse *vr* : to take a shower
ducho, -cha *adj* : experienced, skilled, expert
dúctil *adj* : ductile
ducto *nm* 1 : duct, shaft 2 : pipeline
duda *nf* : doubt ⟨no cabe duda : there's no doubt about it⟩
dudar *vt* : to doubt — *vi* ~ en : to hesitate to ⟨no dudes en pedirme ayuda : don't hesitate to ask me for help⟩
dudoso, -sa *adj* 1 : doubtful 2 : dubious, questionable — dudosamente *adv*
duele, etc. → doler
duelo *nm* 1 : duel 2 LUTO : mourning
duende *nm* 1 : elf, goblin 2 ENCANTO : magic, charm ⟨una bailarina que tiene duende : a dancer with a certain magic⟩
dueño, -ña *n* 1 : owner, proprietor, proprietress *f* 2 : landlord, landlady *f*
duerme, etc. → dormir
dueto *nm* : duet
dulce[1] *adv* : sweetly, softly
dulce[2] *adj* 1 : sweet 2 : mild, gentle, mellow — dulcemente *adv*
dulce[3] *nm* : candy, sweet
dulcería *nf* : candy store
dulcificante *nm* : sweetener
dulzura *nf* 1 : sweetness 2 : gentleness, mellowness
duna *nf* : dune
dúo *nm* : duo, duet
duodécimo[1], -ma *adj* : twelfth
duodécimo[2], -ma *nm* : twelfth (in a series)
dúplex *nms & pl* : duplex apartment
duplicación *nf, pl* -ciones : duplication, copying
duplicado *nm* : duplicate, copy
duplicar {72} *vt* 1 : to double 2 : to duplicate, to copy
duplicidad *nf* : duplicity
duque *nm* : duke
duquesa *nf* : duchess
durabilidad *nf* : durability
durable → duradero

duración *nf, pl* -ciones : duration, length
duradero, -ra *adj* : durable, lasting
duramente *adv* 1 : harshly, severely 2 : hard
durante *prep* : during ⟨durante todo el día : all day long⟩ ⟨trabajó durante tres horas : he worked for three hours⟩
durar *vi* : to last, to endure
durazno *nm* 1 : peach 2 : peach tree

dureza *nf* 1 : hardness, toughness 2 : severity, harshness
durmiente[1] *adj* : sleeping
durmiente[2] *nmf* : sleeper
durmió, etc. → dormir
duro[1] *adv* : hard ⟨trabajé tan duro : I worked so hard⟩
duro[2], -ra *adj* 1 : hard, tough 2 : harsh, severe

E

e[1] *nf* : fifth letter of the Spanish alphabet
e[2] *conj* (*used instead of* y *before words beginning with* i- *or* hi-) : and
ebanista *nmf* : cabinetmaker
ebanistería *nf* : cabinetmaking
ébano *nm* : ebony
ebriedad *nf* EMBRIAGUEZ : inebriation, drunkenness
ebrio, -bria *adj* EMBRIAGADO : inebriated, drunk
ebullición *nf, pl* -ciones : boiling
eccéntrico → excéntrico
echar *vt* 1 LANZAR : to throw, to cast, to hurl 2 EXPULSAR : to throw out, to expel 3 EMITIR : to emit, give off 4 BROTAR : to sprout, to put forth 5 DESPEDIR : to fire, to dismiss 6 : to put in, to add 7 echar a perder : to spoil, to ruin 8 echar de menos : to miss ⟨echan de menos a su madre : they miss their mother⟩ — *vi* 1 : to start off 2 ~ a : to begin to — echarse *vr* 1 : to throw oneself 2 : to lie down 3 : to put on 4 ~ a : to start to 5 echarse a perder : to go bad, to spoil 6 echárselas de : to pose as
ecléctico, -ca *adj* : eclectic
eclesiástico[1], -ca *adj* : ecclesiastical, ecclesiastic
eclesiástico[2] *nm* CLÉRIGO : cleric, clergyman
eclipsar *vt* 1 : to eclipse 2 : to outshine, to surpass
eclipse *nm* : eclipse
eco *nm* : echo
ecografía *nf* : ultrasound scanning
ecología *nf* : ecology
ecológico, -ca *adj* : ecological — ecológicamente *adv*
ecologista *nmf* : ecologist, environmentalist
ecólogo, -ga *n* : ecologist
economía *nf* 1 : economy 2 : economics
económicamente *adv* : financially
económico, -ca *adj* : economic, economical
economista *nmf* : economist
economizar {21} *vt* : to save, to economize on — *vi* : to save up, to be frugal
ecosistema *nm* : ecosystem
ecuación *nf, pl* -ciones : equation
ecuador *nm* : equator

ecuánime *adj* 1 : even-tempered 2 : impartial
ecuanimidad *nf* 1 : equanimity 2 : impartiality
ecuatorial *adj* : equatorial
ecuatoriano, -na *adj* & *n* : Ecuadorian
ecuestre *adj* : equestrian
ecuménico, -ca *adj* : ecumenical
eczema *nm* : eczema
edad *nf* 1 : age ⟨¿qué edad tiene? : how old is she?⟩ 2 ÉPOCA, ERA : epoch, era
edema *nm* : edema
Edén *nm, pl* Edenes : Eden, paradise
edición *nf, pl* -ciones 1 : edition 2 : publication, publishing
edicto *nm* : edict, proclamation
edificación *nf, pl* -ciones 1 : edification 2 : construction, building
edificante *adj* : edifying
edificar {72} *vt* 1 : to edify 2 CONSTRUIR : to build, to construct
edificio *nm* : building, edifice
editar *vt* 1 : to edit 2 PUBLICAR : to publish
editor[1], -tora *adj* : publishing ⟨casa editora : publishing house⟩
editor[2], -tora *n* 1 : editor 2 : publisher
editora *nf* : publisher, publishing company
editorial[1] *adj* 1 : publishing 2 : editorial
editorial[2] *nm* : editorial
editorial[3] *nf* : publishing house
editorializar {21} *vi* : to editorialize
edredón *nm, pl* -dones COBERTOR, COLCHA : comforter, eiderdown, quilt
educable *adj* : educable, teachable
educación *nf, pl* -ciones 1 ENSEÑANZA : education 2 : manners *pl* — educacional *adj*
educado, -da *adj* : polite, well-mannered
educador, -dora *n* : educator
educando, -da *n* ALUMNO, PUPILO : pupil, student
educar {72} *vt* 1 : to educate 2 CRIAR : to bring up, to raise 3 : to train — educarse *vr* : to be educated
educativo, -va *adj* : educational
efectista *adj* : dramatic, sensational
efectivamente *adv* : really, actually
efectividad *nf* : effectiveness

efectivo¹, -va *adj* **1** : effective **2** : real, actual **3** : permanent, regular (of employment)
efectivo² *nm* : cash
efecto *nm* **1** : effect **2 en** ～ : actually, in fact **3 efectos** *nmpl* : goods, property ⟨efectos personales : personal effects⟩
efectuar {3} *vt* : to carry out, to bring about
efervescencia *nf* **1** : effervescence **2** : vivacity, high spirits *pl*
efervescente *adj* **1** : effervescent **2** : vivacious
eficacia *nf* **1** : effectiveness, efficacy **2** : efficiency
eficaz *adj, pl* **-caces 1** : effective **2** EFICIENTE : efficient — **eficazmente** *adv*
eficiencia *nf* : efficiency
eficiente *adj* EFICAZ : efficient — **eficientemente** *adv*
eficientizar {21} *vt Mex* : to streamline, to make more efficient
efigie *nf* : effigy
efímera *nf* : mayfly
efímero, -ra *adj* : ephemeral
efusión *nf, pl* **-siones 1** : effusion **2** : warmth, effusiveness **3 con** ～ : effusively
efusivo, -va *adj* : effusive — **efusivamente** *adv*
egipcio, -cia *adj & n* : Egyptian
eglefino *nm* : haddock
ego *nm* : ego
egocéntrico, -ca *adj* : egocentric, self-centered
egoísmo *nm* : selfishness, egoism
egoísta¹ *adj* : selfish, egoistic
egoísta² *nmf* : egoist, selfish person
egotismo *nm* : egotism, conceit
egotista¹ *adj* : egotistic, egotistical, conceited
egotista² *nmf* : egotist, conceited person
egresado, -da *n* : graduate
egresar *vi* : to graduate
egreso *nm* **1** : graduation **2 ingresos y egresos** : income and expenditure
eh *interj* **1** : hey! **2** : eh?, huh?
eje *nm* **1** : axle **2** : axis
ejecución *nf, pl* **-ciones** : execution
ejecutante *nmf* : performer
ejecutar *vt* **1** : to execute, to put to death **2** : to carry out, to perform
ejecutivo, -va *adj & n* : executive
ejecutor, -tora *n* : executor
ejemplar¹ *adj* : exemplary, model
ejemplar² *nm* **1** : copy (of a book, magazine, etc.) **2** : specimen, example
ejemplificar {72} *vt* : to exemplify, to illustrate
ejemplo *nm* **1** : example **2 por** ～ : for example **3 dar ejemplo** : to set an example
ejercer {86} *vi* ～ **de** : to practice as, to work as — *vt* **1** : to practice **2** : exercise (a right) **3** : to exert
ejercicio *nm* **1** : exercise **2** : practice
ejercitar *vt* **1** : to exercise **2** ADIESTRAR : to drill, to train

ejército *nm* : army
ejidal *adj Mex* : cooperative
ejido *nm* **1** : common land **2** *Mex* : cooperative
ejote *nm Mex* : green bean
el¹ *pron* (*referring to masculine nouns*) **1** : the one ⟨tengo mi libro y el tuyo : I have my book and yours⟩ ⟨de los cantantes me gusta el de México : I prefer the singer from México⟩ **2 el que** : he who, whoever, the one that ⟨el que vino ayer : the one who came yesterday⟩ ⟨el que trabaja duro estará contento : he who works hard will be happy⟩
el², la *art, pl* **los, las** : the ⟨los niños están en la casa : the boys are in the house⟩ ⟨me duele el pie : my foot hurts⟩
él *pron* : he, him ⟨él es mi amigo : he's my friend⟩ ⟨hablaremos con él : we will speak with him⟩
elaboración *nf, pl* **-ciones 1** PRODUCCIÓN : production, making **2** : preparation, devising
elaborado, -da *adj* : elaborate
elaborar *vt* **1** : to make, to produce **2** : to devise, to draw up
elasticidad *nf* : elasticity
elástico¹, -ca *adj* **1** FLEXIBLE : flexible **2** : elastic
elástico² *nm* **1** : elastic (material) **2** : rubber band
elección *nf, pl* **-ciones 1** SELECCIÓN : choice, selection **2** : election
electivo, -va *adj* : elective
electo, -ta *adj* : elect ⟨el presidente electo : the president-elect⟩
elector, -tora *n* : elector, voter
electorado *nm* : electorate
electoral *adj* : electoral, election
electricidad *nf* : electricity
electricista *nmf* : electrician
eléctrico, -ca *adj* : electric, electrical
electrificar {72} *vt* : to electrify — **electrificación** *nf*
electrizar {21} *vt* : to electrify, to thrill — **electrizante** *adj*
electrocardiógrafo *nm* : electrocardiograph
electrocardiograma *nm* : electrocardiogram
electrocutar *vt* : to electrocute — **electrocución** *nf*
electrodo *nm* : electrode
electrodoméstico *nm* : electric appliance
electroimán *nm, pl* **-manes** : electromagnet
electrólisis *nfs & pl* : electrolysis
electrolito *nm* : electrolyte
electromagnético, -ca *adj* : electromagnetic
electromagnetismo *nm* : electromagnetism
electrón *nm, pl* **-trones** : electron
electrónica *nf* : electronics
electrónico, -ca *adj* : electronic — **electrónicamente** *adv*

elefante, -ta *n* : elephant
elegancia *nf* : elegance
elegante *adj* : elegant, smart — **elegantemente** *adv*
elegía *nf* : elegy
elegíaco, -ca *adj* : elegiac
elegibilidad *nf* : eligibility
elegible *adj* : eligible
elegido, -da *adj* **1** : chosen, selected **2** : elected
elegir {28} *vt* **1** ESCOGER, SELECCIONAR : to choose, to select **2** : to elect
elemental *adj* **1** : elementary, basic **2** : fundamental, essential
elemento *nm* : element
elenco *nm* : cast (of actors)
elepé *nm* : long-playing record
elevación *nf, pl* **-ciones** : elevation, height
elevado, -da *adj* **1** : elevated, lofty **2** : high
elevador *nm* ASCENSOR : elevator
elevar *vt* **1** ALZAR : to raise, to lift **2** AUMENTAR : to raise, to increase **3** : to elevate (in a hierarchy), to promote **4** : to present, to submit — **elevarse** *vr* : to rise
elfo *nm* : elf
eliminación *nf, pl* **-ciones** : elimination, removal
eliminar *vt* **1** : to eliminate, to remove **2** : to do in, to kill
elipse *nf* : ellipse
elipsis *nf* : ellipsis
elíptico, -ca *adj* : elliptical, elliptic
elite *or* **élite** *nf* : elite
elixir *or* **elíxir** *nm* : elixir
ella *pron* : she, her ⟨ella es mi amiga : she is my friend⟩ ⟨nos fuimos con ella : we left with her⟩
ello *pron* : it ⟨es por ello que me voy : that's why I'm going⟩
ellos, ellas *pron pl* **1** : they, them **2 de ellos, de ellas** : theirs
elocución *nf, pl* **-ciones** : elocution
elocuencia *nf* : eloquence
elocuente *adj* : eloquent — **elocuentemente** *adv*
elogiar *vt* ENCOMIAR : to praise
elogio *nm* : praise
elote *nm* **1** *Mex* : corn, maize **2** *CA, Mex* : corncob
elucidación *nf, pl* **-ciones** ESCLARECIMIENTO : elucidation
elucidar *vt* ESCLARECER : to elucidate
eludir *vt* EVADIR : to evade, to avoid, to elude
emanación *nf, pl* **-ciones** : emanation
emanar *vi* ~ **de** : to emanate from — *vt* : to exude
emancipar *vt* : to emancipate — **emancipación** *nf*
embadurnar *vt* EMBARRAR : to smear, to daub
embajada *nf* : embassy
embajador, -dora *n* : ambassador
embalaje *nm* : packing, packaging
embalar *vt* EMPAQUETAR : to pack

embaldosar *vt* : to tile, to pave with tiles
embalsamar *vt* : to embalm
embalsar *vt* : to dam, to dam up
embalse *nm* : dam, reservoir
embarazada *adj* ENCINTA, PREÑADA : pregnant, expecting
embarazar {21} *vt* **1** : to obstruct, to hamper **2** PREÑAR : to make pregnant
embarazo *nm* : pregnancy
embarazoso, -sa *adj* : embarrassing, awkward
embarcación *nf, pl* **-ciones** : boat, craft
embarcadero *nm* : wharf, pier, jetty
embarcar {72} *vi* : to embark, to board — *vt* : to load
embarco *nm* : embarkation
embargar {52} *vt* **1** : to seize, to impound **2** : to overwhelm
embargo *nm* **1** : seizure **2** : embargo **3 sin** ~ : however, nevertheless
embarque *nm* **1** : embarkation **2** : shipment
embarrancar {72} *vi* **1** : to run aground **2** : to get bogged down
embarrar *vt* **1** : to cover with mud **2** EMBADURNAR : to smear
embarullar *vt fam* : to muddle, to confuse — **embarullarse** *vr fam* : to get mixed up
embate *nm* **1** : onslaught **2** : battering (of waves or wind)
embaucador, -dora *n* : swindler, deceiver
embaucar {72} *vt* : to trick, to swindle
embeber *vt* : to absorb, to soak up — *vi* : to shrink
embelesado, -da *adj* : spellbound
embelesar *vt* : to enchant, to captivate
embellecer {53} *vt* : to embellish, to beautify
embellecimiento *nm* : beautification, embellishment
embestida *nf* **1** : charge (of a bull) **2** ARREMETIDA : attack, onslaught
embestir {54} *vt* : to hit, to run into, to charge at — *vi* ARREMETER : to charge, to attack
emblanquecer {53} *vt* BLANQUEAR : to bleach, to whiten — **emblanquecerse** *vr* : to turn white
emblema *nm* : emblem
emblemático, -ca *adj* : emblematic
embolia *nf* : embolism
émbolo *nm* : piston
embolsarse *vr* **1** : to pocket (money) **2** : to collect (payment)
emborracharse *vr* EMBRIAGARSE : to get drunk
emborronar *vt* **1** : to blot, to smudge **2** GARABATEAR : to scribble
emboscada *nf* : ambush
emboscar {72} *vt* : to ambush — **emboscarse** *vr* : to lie in ambush
embotadura *nf* : bluntness, dullness
embotar *vt* **1** : to dull, to blunt **2** : to weaken, to enervate
embotellamiento *nm* ATASCO : traffic jam

embotellar *vt* ENVASAR : to bottle

embragar {52} *vi* : to engage the clutch

embrague *nm* : clutch

embravecerse {53} *vr* **1** : to get furious **2** : to get rough ⟨el mar se embraveció : the sea became tempestuous⟩

embriagado, -da *adj* : inebriated, drunk

embriagador, -dora *adj* : intoxicating

embriagarse {52} *vr* EMBORRACHARSE : to get drunk

embriaguez *nf* EBRIEDAD : drunkenness, inebriation

embrión *nm, pl* **embriones** : embryo

embrionario, -ria *adj* : embryonic

embrollo *nm* ENREDO : imbroglio, confusion

embrujar *vt* HECHIZAR : to bewitch

embrujo *nm* : spell, curse

embudo *nm* : funnel

embuste *nm* **1** MENTIRA : lie, fib **2** ENGAÑO : trick, hoax

embustero¹, -ra *adj* : lying, deceitful

embustero², -ra *n* : liar, cheat

embutido *nm* **1** : sausage **2** : inlaid work

embutir *vt* **1** : to cram, to stuff, to jam **2** : to inlay

emergencia *nf* **1** : emergency **2** : emergence

emergente *adj* **1** : emergent **2** : consequent, resultant

emerger {15} *vi* : to emerge, to surface

emético¹, -ca *adj* : emetic

emético² *nm* : emetic

emigración *nf, pl* **-ciones 1** : emigration **2** : migration

emigrante *adj & nmf* : emigrant

emigrar *vi* **1** : to emigrate **2** : to migrate

eminencia *nf* : eminence

eminente *adj* : eminent, distinguished

eminentemente *adv* : basically, essentially

emisario¹, -ria *n* : emissary

emisario² *nm* : outlet (of a body of water)

emisión *nf, pl* **-siones 1** : emission **2** : broadcast **3** : issue ⟨emisión de acciones : stock issue⟩

emisor *nm* TRANSMISOR : television or radio transmitter

emisora *nf* : radio station

emitir *vt* **1** : to emit, to give off **2** : to broadcast **3** : to issue **4** : to cast (a vote)

emoción *nf, pl* **-ciones** : emotion —

emocional *adj* — **emocionalmente** *adv*

emocionado, -da *adj* **1** : moved, affected by emotion **2** ENTUSIASMADO : excited

emocionante *adj* **1** CONMOVEDOR : moving, touching **2** EXCITANTE : exciting, thrilling

emocionar *vt* **1** CONMOVER : to move, to touch **2** : to excite, to thrill — **emocionarse** *vr*

emotivo, -va *adj* : emotional, moving

empacador, -dora *n* : packer

empacar {72} *vt* **1** EMPAQUETAR : to pack **2** : to bale — *vi* : to pack — **empacarse** *vr* **1** : to balk, to refuse to budge **2** *Col, Mex fam* : to eat ravenously, to devour

empachar *vt* **1** ESTORBAR : to obstruct **2** : to give indigestion to **3** DISFRAZAR : to disguise, to mask — **empacharse** *vr* **1** INDIGESTARSE : to get indigestion **2** AVERGONZARSE : to be embarrassed

empacho *nm* **1** INDIGESTIÓN : indigestion **2** VERGÜENZA : embarrassment **3** **no tener empacho en** : to have no qualms about

empadronarse *vr* : to register to vote

empalagar {52} *vt* **1** : to cloy, to surfeit **2** FASTIDIAR : to annoy, to bother

empalagoso, -sa *adj* MELOSO : cloying, excessively sweet

empalar *vt* : to impale

empalizada *nf* : palisade (fence)

empalmar *vt* **1** : to splice, to link **2** : to combine — *vi* : to meet, to converge

empalme *nm* **1** CONEXIÓN : connection, link **2** : junction

empanada *nf* : pie, turnover

empanadilla *nf* : meat or seafood pie

empanar *vt* : to bread

empantanado, -da *adj* : bogged down, delayed

empañar *vt* **1** : to steam up **2** : to tarnish, to sully

empapado, -da *adj* : soggy, sodden

empapar *vt* MOJAR : to soak, to drench — **empaparse** *vr* **1** : to get soaking wet **2 ~ de** : to absorb, to be imbued with

empapelar *vt* : to wallpaper

empaque *nm fam* **1** : presence, bearing **2** : pomposity **3** DESCARO : impudence, nerve

empaquetar *vt* EMBALAR : to pack, to package — **empaquetarse** *vr fam* : to dress up

emparedado *nm* : sandwich

emparedar *vt* : to wall in, to confine

emparejar *vt* **1** : to pair, to match up **2** : to make even — *vi* : to catch up — **emparejarse** *vr* : to pair up

emparentado, -da *adj* : related

emparentar {55} *vi* : to become related by marriage

emparrillado *nm Mex* : gridiron (in football)

empastar *vt* **1** : to fill (a tooth) **2** : to bind (a book)

empaste *nm* : filling (of a tooth)

empatar *vt* : to tie, to connect — *vi* : to result in a draw, to be tied — **empatarse** *vr Ven* : to hook up, to link together

empate *nm* : draw, tie

empatía *nf* : empathy

empecinado, -da *adj* TERCO : stubborn

empecinarse *vr* OBSTINARSE : to be stubborn, to persist

empedernido, -da *adj* INCORREGIBLE : hardened, inveterate

empedrado *nm* : paving, pavement

empedrar {55} vt : to pave (with stones)
empeine nm : instep
empellón nm, pl -llones : shove, push
empelotado, -da adj 1 Mex fam : madly in love 2 fam : stark naked
empeñado, -da adj : determined, committed
empeñar vt 1 : to pawn 2 : to pledge, to give (one's word) — empeñarse vr 1 : to insist stubbornly 2 : to make an effort
empeño nm 1 : pledge, commitment 2 : insistence 3 ESFUERZO : effort, determination 4 : pawning ⟨casa de empeños : pawnshop⟩
empeoramiento nm : worsening, deterioration
empeorar vi : to deteriorate, to get worse — vt : to make worse
empequeñecer {53} vi : to diminish, to become smaller — vt : to minimize, to make smaller
emperador nm : emperor
emperatriz nf, pl -trices : empress
empero conj : however, nevertheless
empezar {29} v COMENZAR : to start, to begin
empinado, -da adj : steep
empinar vt ELEVAR : to lift, to raise — empinarse vr : to stand on tiptoe
empírico, -ca adj : empirical — empíricamente adv
emplasto nm : poultice, dressing
emplazamiento nm 1 : location, site 2 CITACIÓN : summons, subpoena
emplazar {21} vt 1 CONVOCAR : to convene, to summon 2 : to subpoena 3 UBICAR : to place, to position
empleado, -da n : employee
empleador, -dora n PATRÓN : employer
emplear vt 1 : to employ 2 USAR : to use — emplearse vr 1 : to get a job 2 : to occupy oneself
empleo nm 1 OCUPACIÓN : employment, occupation, job 2 : use, usage
empobrecer {53} vt : to impoverish — vi : to become poor — empobrecerse vr
empobrecimiento nm : impoverishment
empollar vi : to brood eggs — vt : to incubate
empolvado, -da adj 1 : dusty 2 : powdered, powdery
empolvar vt 1 : to cover with dust 2 : to powder — empolvarse vr 1 : to gather dust 2 : to powder one's face
emporio nm 1 : center, capital, empire ⟨un emporio cultural : a cultural center⟩ ⟨un emporio financiero : a financial empire⟩ 2 : department store
empotrado, -da adj : built-in ⟨armarios empotrados : built-in cabinets⟩
empotrar vt : to build into, to embed
emprendedor, -dora adj : enterprising
emprender vt : to undertake, to begin

empresa nf 1 COMPAÑÍA, FIRMA : company, corporation, firm 2 : undertaking, venture
empresariado nm 1 : business world 2 : management, managers pl
empresarial adj : business, managerial, corporate
empresario, -ria n 1 : manager 2 : businessman m, businesswoman f 3 : impresario
empréstito nm : loan
empujar vi : to push, to shove — vt 1 : to push 2 PRESIONAR : to spur on, to press
empuje nm : impetus, drive
empujón nm, pl -jones : push, shove
empuñadura nf MANGO : hilt, handle
empuñar vt 1 ASIR : to grasp 2 empuñar las armas : to take up arms
emú nm : emu
emular vt IMITAR : to emulate — emulación nf
emulsión nf, pl -siones : emulsion
emulsionante nm : emulsifier
emulsionar vt : to emulsify
en prep 1 : in ⟨en el bolsillo : in one's pocket⟩ ⟨en una semana : in a week⟩ 2 : on ⟨en la mesa : on the table⟩ 3 : at ⟨en casa : at home⟩ ⟨en el trabajo : at work⟩ ⟨en ese momento : at that moment⟩
enagua nf : petticoat, slip
enajenación nf, pl -ciones 1 : transfer (of property) 2 : alienation 3 : absentmindedness
enajenado, -da adj : out of one's mind
enajenar vt 1 : to transfer (property) 2 : to alienate 3 : to enrapture — enajenarse vr 1 : to become estranged 2 : to go mad
enaltecer {53} vt : to praise, to extol
enamorado[1], -da adj : in love
enamorado[2], -da n : lover, sweetheart
enamoramiento nm : infatuation, crush
enamorar vt : to enamor, to win the love of — enamorarse vr : to fall in love
enamoriscarse {72} vr fam : to have a crush, to be infatuated
enamorizado, -da adj : amorous, passionate
enano[1], -na adj : tiny, minute
enano[2], -na n : dwarf, midget
enarbolar vt 1 : to hoist, to raise 2 : to brandish
enarcar {72} vt : to arch, to raise
enardecer {53} vt 1 : to arouse (anger, passions) 2 : to stir up, to excite — enardecerse vr
encabezado nm Mex : headline
encabezamiento nm 1 : heading 2 : salutation, opening
encabezar {21} vt 1 : to head, to lead 2 : to put a heading on
encabritarse vr 1 : to rear up 2 fam : to get angry
encadenar vt 1 : to chain 2 : to connect, to link 3 INMOVILIZAR : to immobilize

encajar *vi* : to fit, to fit together, to fit in — *vt* **1** : to insert, to stick **2** : to take, to cope with ⟨encajó el golpe : he withstood the blow⟩

encaje *nm* **1** : lace **2** : financial reserve

encajonar *vt* **1** : to box, to crate **2** : to cram in

encalar *vt* : to whitewash

encallar *vi* **1** : to run aground **2** : to get stuck

encallecido, -da *adj* : callused

encamar *vt* : to confine to a bed

encaminado, -da *adj* **1** : on the right track **2** ～ **a** : aimed at, designed to

encaminar *vt* **1** : to direct, to channel **2** : to head in the right direction — **encaminarse** *vr* ～ **a** : to head for, to aim at

encandilar *vt* : to dazzle

encanecer {53} *vi* : to gray, to go gray

encantado, -da *adj* **1** : charmed, bewitched **2** : delighted

encantador¹, -dora *adj* : charming, delightful

encantador², -dora *n* : magician

encantamiento *nm* : enchantment, spell

encantar *vt* **1** : to enchant, to bewitch **2** : to charm, to delight ⟨me encanta esta canción : I love this song⟩

encanto *nm* **1** : charm, fascination **2** HECHIZO : spell **3** : delightful person or thing

encañonar *vt* : to point (a gun) at, to hold up

encapotado, -da *adj* : cloudy, overcast

encapotarse *vr* : to cloud over, to become overcast

encaprichado, -da *adj* : infatuated

encaprichamiento *nm* : infatuation

encapuchado, -da *adj* : hooded

encarado, -da *adj* **estar mal encarado** *fam* : to be ugly-looking, to look mean

encaramar *vt* : to raise, to lift up — **encaramarse** *vr* : to perch

encarar *vt* CONFRONTAR : to face, to confront

encarcelación *nf* → encarcelamiento

encarcelamiento *nm* : incarceration, imprisonment

encarcelar *vt* : to incarcerate, to imprison

encarecer {53} *vt* **1** : to increase, to raise (price, value) **2** : to beseech, to entreat — **encarecerse** *vr* : to become more expensive

encarecidamente *adv* : insistently, urgently

encarecimiento *nm* : increase, rise (in price)

encargado¹, -da *adj* : in charge

encargado², -da *n* : manager, person in charge

encargar {52} *vt* **1** : to put in charge of **2** : to recommend, to advise **3** : to order, to request — **encargarse** *vr* ～ **de** : to take charge of

encargo *nm* **1** : errand **2** : job assignment **3** : order ⟨hecho de encargo : custom-made, made to order⟩

encariñarse *vr* ～ **con** : to become fond of, to grow attached to

encarnación *nf, pl* **-ciones** : incarnation, embodiment

encarnado¹, -da *adj* **1** : incarnate **2** : flesh-colored **3** : red **4** : ingrown

encarnado² *nm* : red

encarnar *vt* : to incarnate, to embody — **encarnarse** *vr* **encarnarse una uña** : to have an ingrown nail

encarnizado, -da *adj* **1** : bloodshot, inflamed **2** : fierce, bloody

encarnizar {21} *vt* : to enrage, to infuriate — **encarnizarse** *vr* : to be brutal, to attack viciously

encarrilar *vt* : to guide, to put on the right track

encasillar *vt* CLASIFICAR : to classify, to pigeonhole, to categorize

encausar *vt* : to prosecute, to charge

encauzar {21} *vt* : to channel, to guide — **encauzarse** *vr*

encebollado, -da *adj* : cooked with onions

encefalitis *nms & pl* : encephalitis

enceguecedor, -dora *n* : blinding

encendedor *nm* : lighter

encender {56} *vi* : to light — *vt* **1** : to light, to set fire to **2** PRENDER : to switch on **3** : to start (a motor) **4** : to arouse, to kindle — **encenderse** *vr* **1** : to get excited **2** : to blush

encendido¹, -da *adj* **1** : burning **2** : flushed **3** : fiery, passionate

encendido² *nm* : ignition

encerado *nm* **1** : waxing, polishing **2** : blackboard

encerar *vt* : to wax, to polish

encerrar {55} *vt* **1** : to lock up, to shut away **2** : to contain, to include **3** : to involve, to entail

encerrona *nf* **1** TRAMPA : trap, setup **2** **prepararle una encerrona a alguien** : to set a trap for someone, to set someone up

encestar *vi* : to make a basket (in basketball)

enchapado *nm* : plating, coating (of metal)

encharcamiento *nm* : flood, flooding

encharcar {72} *vt* : to flood, to swamp — **encharcarse** *vr*

enchilada *nf* : enchilada

enchilar *vt Mex* : to season with chili

enchuecar {72} *vt Chile, Mex fam* : to make crooked, to twist

enchufar *vt* **1** : to plug in **2** : to connect, to fit together

enchufe *nm* **1** : connection **2** : plug, socket

encía *nf* : gum (tissue)

encíclica *nf* : encyclical

enciclopedia *nf* : encyclopedia

enciclopédico, -ca *adj* : encyclopedic

encierro *nm* **1** : confinement **2** : enclosure

encima *adv* **1** : on top, above **2** ADEMÁS : as well, besides **3** ～ **de** : on, on top of, over **4 por encima de** : above, beyond ⟨por encima de la ley : above the law⟩ **5 echarse encima** : to take upon oneself **6 estar encima de** *fam* : to nag, to criticize **7 quitarse de encima** : to get rid of

encina *nf* : evergreen oak

encinta *adj* EMBARAZADA, PREÑADA : pregnant, expecting

enclaustrado, -da *adj* : cloistered, shut away

enclavado, -da *adj* : buried

enclenque *adj* : weak, sickly

encoger {15} *vt* **1** : to shrink, to make smaller **2** : to intimidate — *vi* : to shrink, to contract — **encogerse** *vr* **1** : to shrink **2** : to be intimidated, to cower, to cringe **3 encogerse de hombros** : to shrug (one's shoulders)

encogido, -da *adj* **1** : shriveled, shrunken **2** TÍMIDO : shy, inhibited

encogimiento *nm* **1** : shrinking, shrinkage **2** : shrug **3** TIMIDEZ : shyness

encolar *vt* : to paste, to glue

encolerizar {21} *vt* ENFURECER : to enrage, to infuriate — **encolerizarse** *vr*

encomendar {55} *vt* CONFIAR : to entrust, to commend — **encomendarse** *vr*

encomiable *adj* : commendable, praiseworthy

encomiar *vt* ELOGIAR : to praise, to pay tribute to

encomienda *nf* **1** : charge, mission **2** : royal land grant **3** : parcel

encomio *nm* : praise, eulogy

encomioso, -sa *adj* : eulogistic, laudatory

enconar *vt* **1** : to irritate, to anger **2** : to inflame — **enconarse** *vr* **1** : to become heated **2** : to fester

encono *nm* **1** RENCOR : animosity, rancor **2** : inflammation, infection

encontrado, -da *adj* : contrary, opposing

encontrar {19} *vt* **1** HALLAR : to find **2** : to encounter, to meet — **encontrarse** *vr* **1** REUNIRSE : to meet **2** : to clash, to conflict **3** : to be ⟨su abuelo se encuentra mejor : her grandfather is doing better⟩

encorvar *vt* : to bend, to curve — **encorvarse** *vr* : to hunch over, to stoop

encrespar *vt* **1** : to curl, to ruffle, to ripple **2** : to annoy, to irritate — **encresparse** *vr* **1** : to curl one's hair **2** : to become choppy **3** : to get annoyed

encrucijada *nf* : crossroads

encuadernación *nf, pl* **-ciones** : bookbinding

encuadernar *vt* EMPASTAR : to bind (a book)

encuadrar *vt* **1** ENMARCAR : to frame **2** ENCAJAR : to fit, to insert **3** COMPRENDER : to contain, to include

encubierto *pp* → **encubrir**

encubrimiento *nm* : cover-up

encubrir {2} *vt* : to cover up, to conceal

encuentro *nm* **1** : meeting, encounter **2** : conference, congress

encuerado, -da *adj fam* : naked

encuerar *vt fam* : to undress

encuesta *nf* **1** INVESTIGACIÓN, PESQUISA : inquiry, investigation **2** SONDEO : survey

encuestador, -dora *n* : pollster

encuestar *vt* : to poll, to take a survey of

encumbrado, -da *adj* **1** : lofty, high **2** : eminent, distinguished

encumbrar *vt* **1** : to exalt, to elevate **2** : to extol — **encumbrarse** *vr* : to reach the top

encurtir *vt* ESCABECHAR : to pickle

ende *adv* **por** ~ : therefore, consequently

endeble *adj* : feeble, weak

endeblez *nf* : weakness, frailty

endémico, -ca *adj* : endemic

endemoniado, -da *adj* : fiendish, diabolical

endentecer {53} *vi* : to teethe

enderezar {21} *vt* **1** : to straighten (out) **2** : to stand on end, to put upright

endeudado, -da *adj* : in debt, indebted

endeudamiento *nm* : indebtedness

endeudarse *vr* **1** : to go into debt **2** : to feel obliged

endiabladamente *adv* : extremely, diabolically

endiablado, -da *adj* **1** : devilish, diabolical **2** : complicated, difficult

endibia *or* **endivia** *nf* : endive

endilgar {52} *vt fam* : to spring, to foist ⟨me endilgó la responsabilidad : he saddled me with the responsibility⟩

endocrino, -na *adj* : endocrine

endogamia *nf* : inbreeding

endosar *vt* : to endorse

endoso *nm* : endorsement

endulzante *nm* : sweetener

endulzar {21} *vt* **1** : to sweeten **2** : to soften, to mellow — **endulzarse** *vr*

endurecer {53} *vt* : to harden, to toughen — **endurecerse** *vr*

enebro *nm* : juniper

eneldo *nm* : dill

enema *nm* : enema

enemigo, -ga *adj & n* : enemy

enemistad *nf* : enmity, hostility

enemistar *vt* : to make enemies of — **enemistarse** *vr* ~ **con** : to fall out with

energía *nf* : energy

enérgico, -ca *adj* **1** : energetic, vigorous **2** : forceful, emphatic — **enérgicamente** *adv*

energúmeno, -na *n fam* : lunatic, crazy person

enero *nm* : January

enervar *vt* **1** : to enervate **2** *fam* : to annoy, to get on one's nerves — **enervante** *adj*

enésimo, -ma *adj* : umpteenth, nth

enfadar *vt* **1** : to annoy, to make angry **2** *Mex fam* : to bore — **enfadarse** *vr* : to get angry, to get annoyed

enfado *nm* : anger, annoyance
enfadoso, -sa *adj* : irritating, annoying
enfardar *vt* : to bale
énfasis *nms & pl* : emphasis
enfático, -ca *adj* : emphatic — **enfáticamente** *adv*
enfatizar {21} *vt* DESTACAR, SUBRAYAR : to emphasize
enfermar *vt* : to make sick — *vi* : to fall ill, to get sick — **enfermarse** *vr*
enfermedad *nf* 1 INDISPOSICIÓN : sickness, illness 2 : disease
enfermería *nf* : infirmary
enfermero, -ra *n* : nurse
enfermizo, -za *adj* : sickly
enfermo¹, -ma *adj* : sick, ill
enfermo², -ma *n* 1 : sick person, invalid 2 PACIENTE : patient
enfilar *vt* 1 : to take, to go along ⟨enfiló la carretera de Montevideo : she went up the road to Montevideo⟩ 2 : to line up, to put in a row 3 : to string, to thread 4 : to aim, to direct — *vi* : to make one's way
enflaquecer {53} *vi* : to lose weight, to become thin — *vt* : to emaciate
enfocar {72} *vt* 1 : to focus (on) 2 : to consider, to look at
enfoque *nm* : focus
enfrascamiento *nm* : immersion, absorption
enfrascarse {72} *vr* ~ **en** : to immerse oneself in, to get caught up in
enfrentamiento *nm* : clash, confrontation
enfrentar *vt* : to confront, to face — **enfrentarse** *vr* 1 ~ **con** : to clash with 2 ~ **a** : to face up to
enfrente *adv* 1 DELANTE : in front 2 : opposite
enfriamiento *nm* 1 CATARRO : chill, cold 2 : cooling off, damper
enfriar {85} *vt* 1 : to chill, to cool 2 : to cool down, to dampen — *vi* : to get cold — **enfriarse** *vr* : to get chilled, to catch a cold
enfundar *vt* : to sheathe, to encase
enfurecer {53} *vt* ENCOLERIZAR : to infuriate — **enfurecerse** *vr* : to fly into a rage
enfurecido, -da *adj* : furious, raging
enfurruñarse *vr fam* : to sulk
engalanar *vt* : to decorate, to deck out — **engalanarse** *vr* : to dress up
enganchar *vt* 1 : to hook, to snag 2 : to attach, to hitch up — **engancharse** *vr* 1 : to get snagged, to get hooked 2 : to enlist
enganche *nm* 1 : hook 2 : coupling, hitch 3 *Mex* : down payment
engañar *vt* 1 EMBAUCAR : to trick, to deceive, to mislead 2 : to cheat on, to be unfaithful to — **engañarse** *vr* 1 : to be mistaken 2 : to deceive oneself
engaño *nm* 1 : deception, trick 2 : fake, feint (in sports)
engañoso, -sa *adj* 1 : deceitful 2 : misleading, deceptive

engarrotarse *vr* : to stiffen up, to go numb
engatusamiento *nm* : cajolery
engatusar *vt* : to coax, to cajole
engendrar *vt* 1 : to beget, to father 2 : to give rise to, to engender
engentarse *vr Mex* : to be in a daze
englobar *vt* : to include, to embrace
engomar *vt* : to glue
engordar *vt* : to fatten, to fatten up — *vi* : to gain weight
engorro *nm* : nuisance, bother
engorroso, -sa *adj* : bothersome
engranaje *nm* : gears *pl*, cogs *pl*
engranar *vt* : to mesh, to engage — *vi* : to mesh gears
engrandecer {53} *vt* 1 : to enlarge 2 : to exaggerate 3 : to exalt
engrandecimiento *nm* 1 : enlargement 2 : exaggeration 3 : exaltation
engrane *nm Mex* : cogwheel
engrapadora *nf* : stapler
engrapar *vt* : to staple
engrasar *vt* : to grease, to lubricate
engrase *nm* : greasing, lubrication
engreído, -da *adj* PRESUMIDO, VANIDOSO : vain, conceited, stuck-up
engreimiento *nm* ARROGANCIA : arrogance, conceit
engreír {66} *vt* ENVANECER : to make vain — **engreírse** *vr* : to become conceited
engrosar {19} *vt* : to enlarge, to increase, to swell — *vi* ENGORDAR : to gain weight
engrudo *nm* : paste
engullir {38} *vt* : to gulp down, to gobble up — **engullirse** *vr*
enharinar *vt* : to flour
enhebrar *vt* ENSARTAR : to string, to thread
enhiesto, -ta *adj* 1 : erect, upright 2 : lofty, towering
enhilar *vt* : to thread (a needle, etc.)
enhorabuena *nf* FELICIDADES : congratulations *pl*
enigma *nm* : enigma, mystery
enigmático, -ca *adj* : enigmatic — **enigmáticamente** *adv*
enjabonar *vt* : to soap up, to lather — **enjabonarse** *vr*
enjaezar {21} *vt* : to harness
enjalbegar {52} *vt* : to whitewash
enjambrar *vi* : to swarm
enjambre *nm* 1 : swarm 2 MUCHEDUMBRE : crowd, mob
enjaular *vt* 1 : to cage 2 *fam* : to jail, to lock up
enjuagar {52} *vt* : to rinse — **enjuagarse** *vr* : to rinse out
enjuague *nm* 1 : rinse 2 **enjuague bucal** : mouthwash
enjugar {52} *vt* : to wipe away (tears)
enjuiciar *vt* 1 : to indict, to prosecute 2 JUZGAR : to try
enjundioso, -sa *adj* : substantial, weighty
enjuto, -ta *adj* : lean, gaunt

enlace *nm* 1 : bond, link, connection 2 : liaison
enladrillado *nm* : brick paving
enladrillar *vt* : to pave with bricks
enlatar *vt* ENVASAR : to can
enlazar {21} *v* : to join, to link, to fit together
enlistar *vt* : to list — enlistarse *vr* : to enlist
enlodado, -da *adj* BARROSO : muddy
enlodar *vt* 1 : to cover with mud 2 : to stain, to sully — enlodarse *vr*
enlodazar → enlodar
enloquecedor, -dora *adj* : maddening
enloquecer {53} *vt* ALOCAR : to drive crazy — enloquecerse *vr* : to go crazy
enlosado *nm* : flagstone pavement
enlosar *vt* : to pave with flagstone
enlutarse *vr* : to go into mourning
enmaderado *nm* 1 : wood paneling 2 : hardwood floor
enmarañar *vt* 1 : to tangle 2 : to complicate 3 : to confuse, to mix up — enmarañarse *vr*
enmarcar {72} *vt* 1 ENCUADRAR : to frame 2 : to provide the setting for
enmascarar *vt* : to mask, to disguise
enmasillar *vt* : to putty, to caulk
enmendar {55} *vt* 1 : to amend 2 CORREGIR : to emend, to correct 3 COMPENSAR : to compensate for — enmendarse *vr* : to mend one's ways
enmienda *nf* 1 : amendment 2 : correction, emendation
enmohecerse {53} *vr* 1 : to become moldy 2 OXIDARSE : to rust, to become rusty
enmudecer {53} *vt* : to mute, to silence — *vi* : to fall silent
enmugrar *vt* : to soil, to make dirty — enmugrarse *vr* : to get dirty
ennegrecer {53} *vt* : to blacken, to darken — ennegrecerse *vr*
ennoblecer {53} *vt* 1 : to ennoble 2 : to embellish
enojadizo, -za *adj* IRRITABLE : irritable, cranky
enojado, -da *adj* 1 : annoyed 2 : angry, mad
enojar *vt* 1 : to anger 2 : to annoy, to upset — enojarse *vr*
enojo *nm* 1 CÓLERA : anger 2 : annoyance
enojón, -jona *adj, pl* -jones *Chile, Mex fam* : irritable, cranky
enojoso, -sa *adj* FASTIDIOSO, MOLESTOSO : annoying, irritating
enorgullecer {53} *vt* : to make proud — enorgullecerse *vr* : to pride oneself
enorme *adj* INMENSO : enormous, huge — enormemente *adv*
enormidad *nf* 1 : enormity, seriousness 2 : immensity, hugeness
enraizado, -da *adj* : deep-seated, deeply rooted
enraizar {30} *vi* : to take root
enramada *nf* : arbor, bower
enramar *vt* : to cover with branches

enrarecer {53} *vt* : to rarefy — enrarecerse *vr*
enredadera *nf* : climbing plant, vine
enredar *vt* 1 : to tangle up, to entangle 2 : to confuse, to complicate 3 : to involve, to implicate — enredarse *vr*
enredo *nm* 1 EMBROLLO : muddle, confusion 2 MARAÑA : tangle
enredoso, -sa *adj* : complicated, tricky
enrejado *nm* 1 : railing 2 : grating, grille 3 : trellis, lattice
enrevesado, -da *adj* : complicated, involved
enriquecer {53} *vt* : to enrich — enriquecerse *vr* : to get rich
enriquecido, -da *adj* : enriched
enriquecimiento *nm* : enrichment
enrojecer {53} *vt* : to make red, to redden — enrojecerse *vr* : to blush
enrolar *vt* RECLUTAR : to recruit — enrolarse *vr* INSCRIBIRSE : to enlist, to sign up
enrollar *vt* : to roll up, to coil — enrollarse *vr*
enronquecerse {53} *vr* : to become hoarse
enroscar {72} *vt* TORCER : to twist — enroscarse *vr* : to coil, to twine
ensacar {72} *vt* : to bag (up)
ensalada *nf* : salad
ensaladera *nf* : salad bowl
ensalmo *nm* : incantation, spell
ensalzar {21} *vt* 1 : to praise, to extol 2 EXALTAR : to exalt
ensamblaje *nm* : assembly
ensamblar *vt* 1 : to assemble 2 : to join, to fit together
ensanchar *vt* 1 : to widen 2 : to expand, to extend — ensancharse *vr*
ensanche *nm* 1 : widening 2 : expansion, development
ensangrentado, -da *adj* : bloody, bloodstained
ensañarse *vr* : to act cruelly, to be merciless
ensartar *vt* 1 ENHEBRAR : to string, to thread 2 : to skewer, to pierce
ensayar *vi* : to rehearse — *vt* 1 : to try out, to test 2 : to assay
ensayista *nmf* : essayist
ensayo *nm* 1 : essay 2 : trial, test 3 : rehearsal 4 : assay (of metals)
enseguida *adv* INMEDIATAMENTE : right away, immediately, at once
ensenada *nf* : cove, inlet
enseña *nf* 1 INSIGNIA : emblem, insignia 2 : standard, banner
enseñanza *nf* 1 EDUCACIÓN : education 2 : teaching
enseñar *vt* 1 : to teach 2 MOSTRAR : to show, to display — enseñarse *vr* ~ a : to learn to, to get used to
enseres *nmpl* : equipment, furnishings *pl* ⟨enseres domésticos : household goods⟩
ensillar *vt* : to saddle (up)
ensimismado, -da *adj* : absorbed, engrossed

ensimismarse *vr* : to lose oneself in thought

ensoberbecerse {53} *vr* : to become haughty

ensombrecer {53} *vt* : to cast a shadow over, to darken — **ensombrecerse** *vr*

ensoñación *nf, pl* **-ciones** : fantasy

ensopar *vt* **1** : to drench **2** : to dunk, to dip

ensordecedor, -dora *adj* : deafening, thunderous

ensordecer {53} *vt* : to deafen — *vi* : to go deaf

ensuciar *vt* : to soil, to dirty — **ensuciarse** *vr*

ensueño *nm* **1** : daydream, revery **2** FANTASÍA : illusion, fantasy

entablar *vt* **1** : to cover with boards **2** : to initiate, to enter into, to start

entallar *vt* AJUSTAR : to tailor, to fit, to take in — *vi* QUEDAR : to fit

ente *nm* **1** : being, entity **2** : body, organization ⟨ente rector : ruling body⟩ **3** *fam* : eccentric, crackpot

enteco, -ca *adj* : gaunt, frail

entenado, -da *n Mex* : stepchild, stepson *m*, stepdaughter *f*

entender[1] {56} *vt* **1** COMPRENDER : to understand **2** OPINAR : to think, to believe **3** : to mean, to intend **4** DEDUCIR : to infer, to deduce — *vi* **1** : to understand ⟨¡ya entiendo! : now I understand!⟩ **2** ~ **de** : to know about, to be good at **3** ~ **en** : to be in charge of — **entenderse** *vr* **1** : to be understood **2** : to get along well, to understand each other **3** ~ **con** : to deal with

entender[2] *nm* **a mi entender** : in my opinion

entendible *adj* : understandable

entendido[1], **-da** *adj* **1** : skilled, expert **2 tener entendido** : to understand, to be under the impression ⟨teníamos entendido que vendrías : we were under the impression you would come⟩ **3 darse por entendido** : to go without saying

entendido[2] *nm* : expert, authority, connoisseur

entendimiento *nm* **1** : intellect, mind **2** : understanding, agreement

enterado, -da *adj* : aware, well-informed ⟨estar enterado de : to be privy to⟩

enteramente *adv* : entirely, completely

enterar *vt* INFORMAR : to inform — **enterarse** *vr* INFORMARSE : to find out, to learn

entereza *nf* **1** INTEGRIDAD : integrity **2** FORTALEZA : fortitude **3** FIRMEZA : resolve

enternecedor, -dora *adj* CONMOVEDOR : touching, moving

enternecer {53} *vt* CONMOVER : to move, to touch

entero[1], **-ra** *adj* **1** : entire, whole **2** : complete, absolute **3** : intact — **enteramente** *adv*

entero[2] *nm* **1** : integer, whole number **2** : point (in finance)

enterramiento *nm* : burial

enterrar {55} *vt* : to bury

entibiar *vt* : to cool (down) — **entibiarse** *vr* : to become lukewarm

entidad *nf* **1** ENTE : entity **2** : body, organization **3** : firm, company **4** : importance, significance

entierro *nm* **1** : burial **2** : funeral

entintar *vt* : to ink

entoldado *nm* : awning

entomología *nf* : entomology

entomólogo, -ga *n* : entomologist

entonación *nf, pl* **-ciones** : intonation

entonar *vi* : to be in tune — *vt* **1** : to intone **2** : to tone up

entonces *adv* **1** : then **2 desde** ~ : since then **3 en aquel entonces** : in those days

entornado, -da *adj* ENTREABIERTO : half-closed, ajar

entornar *vt* ENTREABRIR : to leave ajar

entorno *nm* : surroundings *pl*, environment

entorpecer {53} *vt* **1** : to hinder, to obstruct **2** : to dull — **entorpecerse** *vr* : to dull the senses

entrada *nf* **1** : entrance, entry **2** : ticket, admission **3** : beginning, onset **4** : entrée **5** : cue (in music) **6 entradas** *nfpl* : income ⟨entradas y salidas : income and expenditures⟩ **7 tener entradas** : to have a receding hairline

entrado, -da *adj* **entrado en años** : elderly

entramado *nm* : framework

entrampar *vt* **1** ATRAPAR : to entrap, to ensnare **2** ENGAÑAR : to deceive, to trick

entrante *adj* **1** : next, upcoming ⟨el año entrante : next year⟩ **2** : incoming, new ⟨el presidente entrante : the president elect⟩

entraña *nf* **1** MEOLLO : core, heart, crux **2 entrañas** *nfpl* VÍSCERAS : entrails

entrañable *adj* : close, intimate

entrañar *vt* : to entail, to involve

entrar *vi* **1** : to enter, to go in, to come in **2** : to begin — *vt* **1** : to bring in, to introduce **2** : to access

entre *prep* **1** : between **2** : among

entreabierto[1] *pp* → **entreabrir**

entreabierto[2], **-ta** *adj* ENTORNADO : half-open, ajar

entreabrir {2} *vt* ENTORNAR : to leave ajar

entreacto *nm* : intermission, interval

entrecano, -na *adj* : grayish, graying

entrecejo *nm* **fruncir el entrecejo** : to knit one's brows

entrecomillar *vt* : to place in quotation marks

entrecortado, -da *adj* **1** : labored, difficult ⟨respiración entrecortada : shortness of breath⟩ **2** : faltering, hesitant ⟨con la voz entrecortada : with a catch in his voice⟩

entrecruzar {21} vt ENTRELAZAR : to interweave, to intertwine — **entrecruzarse** vr
entredicho nm 1 DUDA : doubt, question 2 : prohibition
entrega nf 1 : delivery 2 : handing over, surrender 3 : installment ⟨entrega inicial : down payment⟩
entregar {52} vt 1 : to deliver 2 DAR : to give, to present 3 : to hand in, to hand over — **entregarse** vr 1 : to surrender, to give in 2 : to devote oneself
entrelazar {21} vt ENTRECRUZAR : to interweave, to intertwine
entremedias adv 1 : in between, halfway 2 : in the meantime
entremés nm, pl -meses 1 APERITIVO : appetizer, hors d'oeuvre 2 : interlude, short play
entremeterse → entrometerse
entremetido nm → entrometido
entremezclar vt : to intermingle
entrenador, -dora n : trainer, coach
entrenamiento nm : training, drill, practice
entrenar vt : to train, to drill, to practice — **entrenarse** vr : to train, to spar (in boxing)
entreoír {50} vt : to hear indistinctly
entrepierna nf 1 : inner thigh 2 : crotch 3 : inseam
entrepiso nm ENTRESUELO : mezzanine
entresacar {72} vt 1 SELECCIONAR : to pick out, to select 2 : to thin out
entresuelo nm ENTREPISO : mezzanine
entretanto¹ adv : meanwhile
entretanto² nm en el entretanto : in the meantime
entretejer vt : to interweave
entretela nf : facing (of a garment)
entretener {80} vt 1 DIVERTIR : to entertain, to amuse 2 DISTRAER : to distract 3 DEMORAR : to delay, to hold up — **entretenerse** vr 1 : to amuse oneself 2 : to dally
entretenido, -da adj DIVERTIDO : entertaining, amusing
entretenimiento nm 1 : entertainment, pastime 2 DIVERSIÓN : fun, amusement
entrever {88} vt 1 : to catch a glimpse of 2 : to make out, to see indistinctly
entreverar vt : to mix, to intermingle
entrevero nm : confusion, disorder
entrevista nf : interview
entrevistador, -dora n : interviewer
entrevistar vt : to interview — **entrevistarse** vr REUNIRSE ∼ con : to meet with
entristecer {53} vt : to sadden
entrometerse vr : to interfere, to meddle
entrometido, -da n : meddler, busybody
entroncar {72} vt RELACIONAR : to establish a relationship between, to connect — vi 1 : to be related 2 : to link up, to be connected
entronque nm 1 : kinship 2 VÍNCULO : link, connection

entuerto nm : wrong, injustice
entumecer {53} vt : to make numb, to be numb — **entumecerse** vr : to go numb, to fall asleep
entumecido, -da adj 1 : numb 2 : stiff (of muscles, joints, etc.)
entumecimiento nm : numbness
enturbiar vt 1 : to cloud 2 : to confuse — **enturbiarse** vr
entusiasmar vt : to excite, to fill with enthusiasm — **entusiasmarse** vr : to get excited
entusiasmo nm : enthusiasm
entusiasta¹ adj : enthusiastic
entusiasta² nmf AFICIONADO : enthusiast
enumerar vt : to enumerate — **enumeración** nf
enunciación nf, pl -ciones : enunciation, statement
enunciar vt : to enunciate, to state
envainar vt : to sheathe
envalentonar vt : to make bold, to encourage — **envalentonarse** vr
envanecer {53} vt ENGREÍR : to make vain — **envanecerse** vr
envasar vt 1 EMBOTELLAR : to bottle 2 ENLATAR : to can 3 : to pack in a container
envase nm 1 : packaging, packing 2 : container 3 LATA : can 4 : empty bottle
envejecer {53} vt : to age, to make look old — vi : to age, to grow old
envejecido, -da adj : aged, old-looking
envejecimiento nm : aging
envenenamiento nm : poisoning
envenenar vt 1 : to poison 2 : to embitter
envergadura nf 1 : span, breadth, spread 2 : importance, scope
envés nm, pl enveses : reverse, opposite side
enviado, -da n : envoy, correspondent
enviar {85} vt 1 : to send 2 : to ship
envidia nf : envy, jealousy
envidiar vt : to envy — **envidiable** adj
envidioso, -sa adj : envious, jealous
envilecer {53} vt : to degrade, to debase
envilecimiento nm : degradation, debasement
envío nm 1 : shipment 2 : remittance
enviudar vi : to be widowed, to become a widower
envoltorio nm 1 : bundle, package 2 : wrapping, wrapper
envoltura nf : wrapper, wrapping
envolver {89} vt 1 : to wrap 2 : to envelop, to surround 3 : to entangle, to involve — **envolverse** vr 1 : to become involved 2 : to wrap oneself (up)
envuelto pp → envolver
enyerbar vt Mex : to bewitch
enyesar vt 1 : to plaster 2 ESCAYOLAR : to put in a plaster cast
enzima nf : enzyme
éon nm, pl eones : aeon
eperlano nm : smelt (fish)

épico, -ca *adj* : epic
epicúreo[1], **-rea** *adj* : epicurean
epicúreo[2], **-rea** *n* : epicure
epidemia *nf* : epidemic
epidémico, -ca *adj* : epidemic
epidermis *nf* : epidermis
epifanía *nf* : feast of the Epiphany (January 6th)
epigrama *nm* : epigram
epilepsia *nf* : epilepsy
epiléptico, -ca *adj & n* : epileptic
epílogo *nm* : epilogue
episcopal *adj* : episcopal
episcopaliano, -na *adj & n* : Episcopalian
episódico, -ca *adj* : episodic
episodio *nm* : episode
epístola *nf* : epistle
epitafio *nm* : epitaph
epíteto *nm* : epithet, name
epítome *nm* : summary, abstract
época *nf* **1** EDAD, ERA, PERÍODO : epoch, age, period **2** : time of year, season **3 de ~** : vintage, antique
epopeya *nf* : epic poem
equidad *nf* JUSTICIA : equity, justice, fairness
equilátero, -ra *adj* : equilateral
equilibrado, -da *adj* : well-balanced
equilibrar *vt* : to balance — **equilibrarse** *vr*
equilibrio *nm* **1** : balance, equilibrium ⟨perder el equilibrio : to lose one's balance⟩ ⟨equilibrio político : balance of power⟩ **2** : poise, aplomb
equilibrista *nmf* ACRÓBATA, FUNÁMBULO : acrobat, tightrope walker
equino, -na *adj* : equine
equinoccio *nm* : equinox
equipaje *nm* BAGAJE : baggage, luggage
equipamiento *nm* : equipping, equipment
equipar *vt* : to equip — **equiparse** *vr*
equiparable *adj* : comparable
equiparar *vt* **1** IGUALAR : to put on a same level, to make equal **2** COMPARAR : to compare
equipo *nm* **1** : team, crew **2** : gear, equipment
equitación *nf, pl* **-ciones** : horseback riding, horsemanship
equitativo, -va *adj* JUSTO : equitable, fair, just — **equitativamente** *adv*
equivalencia *nf* : equivalence
equivalente *adj & nm* : equivalent
equivaler {84} *vi* : to be equivalent
equivocación *nf, pl* **-ciones** ERROR : error, mistake
equivocado, -da *adj* : mistaken, wrong — **equivocadamente** *adv*
equivocar {72} *vt* : to mistake, to confuse — **equivocarse** *vr* : to make a mistake, to be wrong
equívoco[1], **-ca** *adj* AMBIGUO : ambiguous, equivocal
equívoco[2] *nm* : misunderstanding
era[1], **etc.** → **ser**
era[2] *nf* EDAD, ÉPOCA : era, age

erario *nm* : public treasury
erección *nf, pl* **-ciones** : erection, raising
eremita *nmf* ERMITAÑO : hermit
ergonomía *nf* : ergonomics
erguido, -da *adj* : erect, upright
erguir {31} *vt* : to raise, to lift up — **erguirse** *vr* : to straighten up
erial *nm* : uncultivated land
erigir {35} *vt* : to build, to erect — **erigirse** *vr* **~ en** : to set oneself up as
erizado, -da *adj* : bristly
erizarse {21} *vr* : to bristle, to stand on end
erizo *nm* **1** : hedgehog **2 erizo de mar** : sea urchin
ermitaño[1], **-ña** *n* EREMITA : hermit, recluse
ermitaño[2] *nm* : hermit crab
erogación *nf, pl* **-ciones** : expenditure
erogar {52} *vt* **1** : to pay out **2** : to distribute
erosión *nf, pl* **-siones** : erosion
erosionar *vt* : to erode
erótico, -ca *adj* : erotic
erotismo *nm* : eroticism
errabundo, -da *adj* ERRANTE, VAGABUNDO : wandering
erradicar {72} *vt* : to eradicate — **erradicación** *nf*
errado, -da *adj* : wrong, mistaken
errante *adj* ERRABUNDO, VAGABUNDO : errant, wandering
errar {32} *vt* FALLAR : to miss — *vi* **1** DESACERTAR : to be wrong, to be mistaken **2** VAGAR : to wander
errata *nf* : misprint, error
errático, -ca *adj* : erratic — **erráticamente** *adv*
erróneo, -nea *adj* EQUIVOCADO : erroneous, wrong — **erróneamente** *adv*
error *nm* EQUIVOCACIÓN : error, mistake
eructar *vi* : to belch, to burp
eructo *nm* : belch, burp
erudición *nf, pl* **-ciones** : erudition, learning
erudito[1], **-ta** *adj* LETRADO : erudite, learned
erudito[2], **-ta** *n* : scholar
erupción *nf, pl* **-ciones** **1** : eruption **2** SARPULLIDO : rash
eruptivo, -va *adj* : eruptive
es → **ser**
esbelto, -ta *adj* DELGADO : slender, slim
esbirro *nm* : henchman
esbozar {21} *vt* BOSQUEJAR : to sketch, to outline
esbozo *nm* **1** : sketch **2** : rough draft
escabechar *vt* **1** ENCURTIR : to pickle **2** *fam* : to kill, to rub out
escabeche *nm* : brine (for pickling)
escabechina *nf* MASACRE : massacre, bloodbath
escabel *nm* : footstool
escabroso, -sa *adj* **1** : rugged, rough **2** : difficult, tough **3** : risqué
escabullirse {38} *vr* : to slip away, to escape

escala *nf* **1** : scale **2** ESCALERA : ladder **3** : stopover

escalada *nf* : ascent, climb

escalador, -dora *n* ALPINISTA : mountain climber

escalafón *nm, pl* **-fones 1** : list of personnel **2** : salary scale, rank

escalar *vt* : to climb, to scale — *vi* **1** : to go climbing **2** : to escalate

escaldar *vt* : to scald

escalera *nf* **1** : ladder ⟨escalera de tijera : stepladder⟩ **2** : stairs *pl*, staircase **3 escalera mecánica** : escalator

escalfador *nm* : chafing dish

escalfar *vt* : to poach (eggs)

escalinata *nf* : flight of stairs

escalofriante *adj* : horrifying, blood-curdling

escalofrío *nm* : shiver, chill, shudder

escalón *nm, pl* **-lones 1** : echelon **2** : step, rung

escalonado, -da *adj* GRADUAL : gradual, staggered

escalonar *vt* **1** : to terrace **2** : to stagger, to alternate

escalpelo *nm* BISTURÍ : scalpel

escama *nf* **1** : scale (of fish or reptiles) **2** : flake (of skin)

escamar *vt* **1** : to scale (fish) **2** : to make suspicious

escamocha *nf Mex* : fruit salad

escamoso, -sa *adj* : scaly

escamotear *vt* **1** : to palm, to conceal **2** *fam* : to lift, to swipe **3** : to hide, to cover up

escandalizar {21} *vt* : to shock, to scandalize — *vi* : to make a fuss — **escandalizarse** *vr* : to be shocked

escándalo *nm* **1** : scandal **2** : scene, commotion

escandaloso, -sa *adj* **1** : shocking, scandalous **2** RUIDOSO : noisy, rowdy **3** : flagrant, outrageous — **escandalosamente** *adv*

escandinavo, -va *adj & n* : Scandinavian

escandir *vt* : to scan (poetry)

escanear *vt* : to scan

escáner *nm* : scanner, scan

escaño *nm* **1** : seat (in a legislative body) **2** BANCO : bench

escapada *nf* HUIDA : flight, escape

escapar *vi* HUIR : to escape, to flee, to run away — **escaparse** *vr* : to escape notice, to leak out

escaparate *nm* **1** : shop window **2** : showcase

escapatoria *nf* **1** : loophole, excuse, pretext ⟨no tener escapatoria : to have no way out⟩ **2** ESCAPADA : escape, flight

escape *nm* **1** FUGA : escape **2** : exhaust (from a vehicle)

escapismo *nm* : escapism

escápula *nf* OMÓPLATO : scapula, shoulder blade

escapulario *nm* : scapular

escarabajo *nm* : beetle

escaramuza *nf* **1** : skirmish **2** : scrimmage

escaramuzar {21} *vi* : to skirmish

escarapela *nf* : rosette (ornament)

escarbar *vt* **1** : to dig, to scratch up **2** : to poke, to pick **3** ~ **en** : to investigate, to pry into

escarcha *nf* **1** : frost **2** *Mex, PRi* : glitter

escarchar *vt* **1** : to frost (a cake) **2** : to candy (fruit)

escardar *vt* **1** : to weed, to hoe **2** : to weed out

escariar *vt* : to ream

escarlata *adj & nf* : scarlet

escarlatina *nf* : scarlet fever

escarmentar {55} *vt* : to punish, to teach a lesson to — *vi* : to learn one's lesson

escarmiento *nm* **1** : lesson, warning **2** CASTIGO : punishment

escarnecer {53} *vt* RIDICULIZAR : to ridicule, to mock

escarnio *nm* : ridicule, mockery

escarola *nf* : escarole

escarpa *nf* : escarpment, steep slope

escarpado, -da *adj* : steep, sheer

escarpia *nf* : hook, spike

escasamente *adv* : scarcely, barely

escasear *vi* : to be scarce, to run short

escasez *nf, pl* **-seces** : shortage, scarcity

escaso, -sa *adj* **1** : scarce, scant **2** ~ **de** : short of

escatimar *vt* : to skimp on, to be sparing with ⟨no escatimar esfuerzos : to spare no effort⟩

escayola *nf* **1** : plaster (for casts) **2** : plaster cast

escayolar *vt* : to put in a plaster cast

escena *nf* **1** : scene **2** : stage

escenario *nm* **1** ESCENA : stage **2** : setting, scene ⟨el escenario del crimen : the scene of the crime⟩

escénico, -ca *adj* **1** : scenic **2** : stage

escenificar {72} *vt* : to stage, to dramatize

escepticismo *nm* : skepticism

escéptico[1], -ca *adj* : skeptical

escéptico[2], -ca *n* : skeptic

escindirse *vr* **1** : to split **2** : to break away

escisión *nf, pl* **-siones 1** : split, division **2** : excision

esclarecer {53} *vt* **1** ELUCIDAR : to elucidate, to clarify **2** ILUMINAR : to illuminate, to light up

esclarecimiento *nm* ELUCIDACIÓN : elucidation, clarification

esclavitud *nf* : slavery

esclavización *nf, pl* **-ciones** : enslavement

esclavizar {21} *vt* : to enslave

esclavo, -va *n* : slave

esclerosis *nf* **esclerosis múltiple** : multiple sclerosis

esclusa *nf* : floodgate, lock (of a canal)

escoba *nf* : broom

escobilla *nf* : small broom, brush, whisk broom

escobillón *nm, pl* **-llones** : swab

escocer {14} *vi* ARDER : to smart, to sting — **escocerse** *vr* : to be sore
escocés¹, -cesa *adj, mpl* **-ceses** 1 : Scottish 2 : tartan, plaid
escocés², -cesa *n, mpl* **-ceses** : Scottish person, Scot
escocés³ *nm* 1 : Scots (language) 2 *pl* **-ceses** : Scotch (whiskey)
escofina *nf* : file, rasp
escoger {15} *vt* ELEGIR, SELECCIONAR : to choose, to select
escogido, -da *adj* : choice, select
escolar¹ *adj* : school
escolar² *nmf* : student, pupil
escolaridad *nf* : schooling ⟨escolaridad obligatoria : compulsory education⟩
escolarización *nf, pl* **-ciones** : education, schooling
escollo *nm* 1 : reef 2 OBSTÁCULO : obstacle
escolta *nmf* : escort
escoltar *vt* : to escort, to accompany
escombro *nm* 1 : debris, rubbish 2 **escombros** *nmpl* : ruins, rubble
esconder *vt* OCULTAR : to hide, to conceal
escondidas *nfpl* 1 : hide-and-seek 2 a ∼ : secretly, in secret
escondimiento *nm* : concealment
escondite *nm* 1 ENCONDRIJO : hiding place 2 ESCONDIDAS : hide-and-seek
escondrijo *nm* ESCONDITE : hiding place
escopeta *nf* : shotgun
escoplear *vt* : to chisel (out)
escoplo *nm* : chisel
escora *nf* : list, heeling
escorar *vi* : to list, to heel (of a boat)
escorbuto *nm* : scurvy
escoria *nf* 1 : slag, dross 2 HEZ : dregs *pl*, scum ⟨la escoria de la sociedad : the dregs of society⟩
Escorpio *or* **Escorpión** *nmf* : Scorpio
escorpión *nm, pl* **-piones** ALACRÁN : scorpion
escote *nm* 1 : low neckline 2 **pagar a escote** : to go dutch
escotilla *nf* : hatch, hatchway
escotillón *nf, pl* **-llones** : trapdoor
escozor *nm* : smarting, stinging
escriba *nm* : scribe
escribano, -na *n* 1 : court clerk 2 NOTARIO : notary public
escribir {33} *v* 1 : to write 2 : to spell — **escribirse** *vr* CARTEARSE : to write to one another, to correspond
escrito¹ *pp* → **escribir**
escrito², -ta *adj* : written
escrito³ *nm* 1 : written document 2 **escritos** *nmpl* : writings, works
escritor, -tora *n* : writer
escritorio *nm* : desk
escritorzuelo, -la *n* : hack (writer)
escritura *nf* 1 : writing, handwriting 2 : deed 3 **las Escrituras** : the Scriptures
escroto *nm* : scrotum
escrúpulo *nm* : scruple

escrupuloso, -sa *adj* 1 : scrupulous 2 METICULOSO : exact, meticulous — **escrupulosamente** *adv*
escrutador, -dora *adj* : penetrating, searching
escrutar *vt* ESCUDRIÑAR : to scrutinize, to examine closely
escrutinio *nm* : scrutiny
escuadra *nf* 1 : square (instrument) 2 : fleet, squadron
escuadrilla *nf* : squadron, formation, flight
escuadrón *nm, pl* **-drones** : squadron
escuálido, -da *adj* 1 : skinny, scrawny 2 INMUNDO : filthy, squalid
escuchar *vt* 1 : to listen to 2 : to hear — *vi* : to listen — **escucharse** *vr*
escudar *vt* : to shield — **escudarse** *vr* ∼ **en** : to hide behind
escudero *nm* : squire
escudo *nm* 1 : shield 2 **escudo de armas** : coat of arms
escudriñar *vt* 1 ESCRUTAR : to scrutinize 2 : to inquire into, to investigate
escuela *nf* : school
escueto, -ta *adj* 1 : plain, simple 2 : succinct, concise — **escuetamente** *adv*
escuincle, -cla *n Mex fam* : child, kid
esculcar {72} *vt* : to search
esculpir *vt* 1 : to sculpt 2 : to carve, to engrave — *vi* : to sculpt
escultor, -tora *n* : sculptor
escultórico, -ca *adj* : sculptural
escultura *nf* : sculpture
escultural *adj* : statuesque
escupidera *nf* : spittoon, cuspidor
escupir *v* : to spit
escupitajo *nm* : spit
escurridizo, -za *adj* : slippery, elusive
escurridor *nm* 1 : dish rack 2 : colander
escurrir *vt* 1 : to wring out 2 : to drain — *vi* 1 : to drain 2 : to drip, to drip-dry — **escurrirse** *vr* : to slip away
ese, esa *adj, mpl* **esos** : that, those
ése, ésa *pron, mpl* **ésos** : that one, those ones *pl*
esencia *nf* : essence
esencial *adj* : essential — **esencialmente** *adv*
esfera *nf* 1 : sphere 2 : face, dial (of a watch)
esférico¹, -ca *adj* : spherical
esférico² *nm* : ball (in sports)
esfinge *nf* : sphinx
esforzado, -da *adj* 1 : energetic, vigorous 2 VALIENTE : courageous, brave
esforzar {36} *vt* : to strain — **esforzarse** *vr* : to make an effort
esfuerzo *nm* 1 : effort 2 ÁNIMO, VIGOR : spirit, vigor 3 **sin** ∼ : effortlessly
esfumar *vt* : to tone down, to soften — **esfumarse** *vr* 1 : to fade away, to vanish 2 *fam* : to take off, to leave
esgrima *nf* : fencing (sport)
esgrimidor, -dora *n* : fencer
esgrimir *vt* 1 : to brandish, to wield 2 : to use, to resort to — *vi* : to fence

esguince *nm* : sprain, strain (of a muscle)

eslabón *nm, pl* -**bones** : link

eslabonar *vt* : to link, to connect, to join

eslavo[1], **-va** *adj* : Slavic

eslavo[2], **-va** *n* : Slav

eslogan *nm, pl* -**lóganes** : slogan

eslovaco, -ca *adj & n* : Slovakian, Slovak

esloveno, -na *adj & nm* : Slovene, Slovenian

esmaltar *vt* : to enamel

esmalte *nm* 1 : enamel 2 **esmalte de uñas** : nail polish

esmerado, -da *adj* : careful, painstaking

esmeralda *nf* : emerald

esmerarse *vr* : to take great pains, to do one's utmost

esmeril *nm* : emery

esmero *nm* : meticulousness, great care

esmoquin *nm, pl* -**quins** : tuxedo

esnob[1] *adj, pl* **esnobs** : snobbish

esnob[2] *nmf, pl* **esnobs** : snob

esnobismo *nm* : snobbery, snobbishness

eso *pron* (*neuter*) 1 : that ⟨eso no me gusta : I don't like that⟩ 2 ¡eso es! : that's it!, that's right! 3 **a eso de** : around ⟨a eso de las tres : around three o'clock⟩ 4 **en ～** : at that point, just then

esófago *nm* : esophagus

esos → **ese**

ésos → **ése**

esotérico, -ca *adj* : esoteric — **esotéricamente** *adv*

espabilado, -da *adj* : bright, smart

espabilarse *vr* 1 : to awaken 2 : to get a move on 3 : to get smart, to wise up

espacial *adj* 1 : space 2 : spatial

espaciar *vt* DISTANCIAR : to space out, to spread out

espacio *nm* 1 : space, room 2 : period, length (of time) 3 **espacio exterior** : outer space

espacioso, -sa *adj* : spacious, roomy

espada[1] *nf* 1 : sword 2 **espadas** *nfpl* : spades (in playing cards)

espada[2] *nm* MATADOR, TORERO : bullfighter, matador

espadaña *nf* 1 : belfry 2 : cattail

espadilla *nf* : scull, oar

espagueti *nm or* **espaguetis** *nmpl* : spaghetti

espalda *nf* 1 : back 2 **espaldas** *nfpl* : shoulders, back 3 **por la espalda** : from behind

espaldarazo *nm* 1 : recognition, support 2 : slap on the back

espaldera *nf* : trellis

espantajo *nm* : scarecrow

espantapájaros *nms & pl* : scarecrow

espantar *vt* ASUSTAR : to scare, to frighten — **espantarse** *vr*

espanto *nm* : fright, fear, horror

espantoso, -sa *adj* 1 : frightening, terrifying 2 : frightful, dreadful

español[1], **-ñola** *adj* : Spanish

español[2], **-ñola** *n* : Spaniard

español[3] *nm* CASTELLANO : Spanish (language)

esparadrapo *nm* : adhesive bandage, Band-Aid™

esparcimiento *nm* 1 DIVERSIÓN, RECREO : entertainment, recreation 2 DESCANSO : relaxation 3 DISEMINACIÓN : dissemination, spreading

esparcir {83} *vt* DISPERSAR : to scatter, to spread — **esparcirse** *vr* 1 : to spread out 2 DESCANSARSE : to take it easy 3 DIVERTIRSE : to amuse oneself

espárrago *nm* : asparagus

espartano, -na *adj* : severe, austere

espasmo *nm* : spasm

espasmódico, -ca *adj* : spasmodic

espástico, -ca *adj* : spastic

espátula *nf* : spatula

especia *nf* : spice

especial *adj & nm* : special

especialidad *nf* : specialty

especialista *nmf* : specialist, expert

especialización *nf, pl* -**ciones** : specialization

especializarse {21} *vr* : to specialize

especialmente *adv* : especially, particularly

especie *nf* 1 : species 2 CLASE, TIPO : type, kind, sort

especificación *nf, pl* -**ciones** : specification

especificar {72} *vt* : to specify

específico, -ca *adj* : specific — **específicamente** *adv*

espécimen *nm, pl* **especímenes** : specimen

especioso, -sa *adj* : specious

espectacular *adj* : spectacular — **espectacularmente** *adv*

espectáculo *nm* 1 : spectacle, sight 2 : show, performance

espectador, -dora *n* : spectator, onlooker

espectro *nm* 1 : ghost, specter 2 : spectrum

especulación *nf, pl* -**ciones** : speculation

especulador, -dora *n* : speculator

especular *vi* : to speculate

especulativo, -va *adj* : speculative

espejismo *nm* 1 : mirage 2 : illusion

espejo *nm* : mirror

espejuelos *nmpl* ANTEOJOS : spectacles, glasses

espeluznante *adj* : hair-raising, terrifying

espera *nf* : wait

esperado, -da *adj* : anticipated

esperanza *nf* : hope, expectation

esperanzado, -da *adj* : hopeful

esperanzador, -dora *adj* : encouraging, promising

esperanzar {21} *vt* : to give hope to

esperar *vt* 1 AGUARDAR : to wait for, to await 2 : to expect 3 : to hope ⟨espero poder trabajar : I hope to be able to work⟩ ⟨espero que sí : I hope so⟩ — *vi*

: to wait — **esperarse** *vr* **1** : to expect, to be hoped ⟨como podría esperarse : as would be expected⟩ **2** : to hold on, to hang on ⟨espérate un momento : hold on a minute⟩

esperma *nmf* : sperm

esperpéntico, -ca *adj* GROTESCO : grotesque

esperpento *nm fam* MAMARRACHO : sight, fright ⟨voy hecha un esperpento : I really look a sight⟩

espesante *nm* : thickener

espesar *vt* : to thicken — **espesarse** *vr*

espeso, -sa *adj* : thick, heavy, dense

espesor *nm* : thickness, density

espesura *nf* **1** : thickness **2** : thicket

espetar *vt* **1** : to blurt out **2** : to skewer

espía *nmf* : spy

espiar {85} *vt* : to spy on, to observe — *vi* : to spy

espiga *nf* **1** : ear (of wheat) **2** : spike (of flowers)

espigado, -da *adj* : willowy, slender

espigar {52} *vt* : to glean, to gather — **espigarse** *vr* : to grow quickly, to shoot up

espigón *nm, pl* **-gones** : breakwater

espina *nf* **1** : thorn **2** : spine ⟨espina dorsal : spinal column⟩ **3** : fish bone

espinaca *nf* **1** : spinach (plant) **2 espinacas** *nfpl* : spinach (food)

espinal *adj* : spinal

espinazo *nm* : backbone

espineta *nf* : spinet

espinilla *nf* **1** BARRO, GRANO : pimple **2** : shin

espino *nm* : hawthorn

espinoso, -sa *adj* **1** : thorny, prickly **2** : bony (of fish) **3** : knotty, difficult

espionaje *nm* : espionage

espiración *nf, pl* **-ciones** : exhalation

espiral *adj & nf* : spiral

espirar *vt* EXHALAR : to breathe out, to give off — *vi* : to exhale

espiritismo *nm* : spiritualism

espiritista *nmf* : spiritualist

espíritu *nm* **1** : spirit **2** ÁNIMO : state of mind, spirits *pl* **3 el Espíritu Santo** : the Holy Ghost

espiritual *adj* : spiritual — **espiritualmente** *adv*

espiritualidad *nf* : spirituality

espita *nf* : spigot, tap

esplendidez *nf, pl* **-deces** ESPLENDOR : magnificence, splendor

espléndido, -da *adj* **1** : splendid, magnificent **2** : generous, lavish — **espléndidamente** *adv*

esplendor *nm* ESPLENDIDEZ : splendor

esplendoroso, -sa *adj* MAGNÍFICO : magnificent, grand

espliego *nm* LAVANDA : lavender

espolear *vt* : to spur on

espoleta *nf* **1** DETONADOR : detonator, fuse **2** : wishbone

espolón *nm, pl* **-lones** : spur (of poultry), fetlock (of a horse)

espolvorear *vt* : to sprinkle, to dust

esponja *nf* **1** : sponge **2 tirar la esponja** : to throw in the towel

esponjado, -da *adj* : spongy

esponjoso, -sa *adj* **1** : spongy **2** : soft, fluffy

esponsales *nmpl* : betrothal, engagement

espontaneidad *nf* : spontaneity

espontáneo, -nea *adj* : spontaneous — **espontáneamente** *adv*

espora *nf* : spore

esporádico, -ca *adj* : sporadic — **esporádicamente** *adv*

esposar *vt* : to handcuff

esposas *nfpl* : handcuffs

esposo, -sa *n* : spouse, wife *f*, husband *m*

esprint *nm* : sprint

esprintar *vi* : to sprint

esprínter *nmf* : sprinter

espuela *nf* : spur

espuerta *nf* : two-handled basket

espulgar {52} *vt* **1** : to delouse **2** : to scrutinize

espuma *nf* **1** : foam **2** : lather **3** : froth, head (on beer)

espumar *vi* : to foam, to froth — *vt* : to skim off

espumoso, -sa *adj* : foamy, frothy

espurio, -ria *adj* : spurious

esputar *v* : to expectorate, to spit

esputo *nm* : spit, sputum

esqueje *nm* : cutting (from a plant)

esquela *nf* **1** : note **2** : notice, announcement

esquelético, -ca *adj* : emaciated, skeletal

esqueleto *nm* **1** : skeleton **2** ARMAZÓN : framework

esquema *nf* BOSQUEJO : outline, sketch, plan

esquemático, -ca *adj* : schematic

esquí *nm* **1** : ski **2 esquí acuático** : water ski, waterskiing

esquiador, -dora *n* : skier

esquiar {85} *vi* : to ski

esquife *nm* : skiff

esquila *nf* **1** CENCERRO : cowbell **2** : shearing

esquilar *vt* TRASQUILAR : to shear

esquimal *adj & nmf* : Eskimo

esquina *nf* : corner

esquinazo *nm* **1** : corner **2 dar esquinazo a** *fam* : to stand up, to give the slip to

esquirla *nf* : splinter (of bone, glass, etc.)

esquirol *nm* ROMPEHUELGAS : strikebreaker, scab

esquisto *nm* : shale

esquivar *vt* **1** EVADIR : to dodge, to evade **2** EVITAR : to avoid

esquivez *nf, pl* **-veces** **1** : aloofness **2** TIMIDEZ : shyness

esquivo, -va *adj* **1** HURAÑO : aloof, unsociable **2** : shy **3** : elusive, evasive

esquizofrenia *nf* : schizophrenia

esquizofrénico, -ca *adj & n* : schizophrenic

esta *adj* → este[1]

ésta → éste

estabilidad *nf* : stability

estabilización *nf, pl* -ciones : stabilization

estabilizador *nm* : stabilizer

estabilizar {21} *vt* : to stabilize — estabilizarse *vr*

estable *adj* : stable, steady

establecer {53} *vt* FUNDAR, INSTITUIR : to establish, to found, to set up — establecerse *vr* INSTALARSE : to settle, to establish oneself

establecimiento *nm* 1 : establishing 2 : establishment, institution, office

establo *nm* : stable

estaca *nf* : stake, picket, post

estacada *nf* 1 : picket fence 2 : stockade

estacar {72} *vt* 1 : to stake out 2 : to fasten down with stakes — estacarse *vr* : to remain rigid

estación *nf, pl* -ciones 1 : station ⟨estación de servicio : service station, gas station⟩ 2 : season

estacional *adj* : seasonal

estacionamiento *nm* 1 : parking 2 : parking lot

estacionar *vt* 1 : to place, to station 2 : to park — estacionarse *vr* 1 : to park 2 : to remain stationary

estacionario, -ria *adj* 1 : stationary 2 : stable

estada *nf* : stay

estadía *nf* ESTANCIA : stay, sojourn

estadio *nm* 1 : stadium 2 : phase, stage

estadista *nmf* : statesman

estadística *nf* 1 : statistic, figure 2 : statistics

estadístico[1], -ca *adj* : statistical — estadísticamente *adv*

estadístico[2], -ca *n* : statistician

estado *nm* 1 : state 2 : status ⟨estado civil : marital status⟩ 3 CONDICIÓN : condition

estadounidense *adj & nmf* AMERICANO, NORTEAMERICANO : American

estafa *nf* : swindle, fraud

estafador, -dora *n* : cheat, swindler

estafar *vt* DEFRAUDAR : to swindle, to defraud

estalactita *nf* : stalactite

estalagmita *nf* : stalagmite

estallar *vi* 1 REVENTAR : to burst, to explode, to erupt 2 : to break out

estallido *nm* 1 EXPLOSIÓN : explosion 2 : report (of a gun) 3 : outbreak, outburst

estambre *nm* 1 : worsted (fabric) 2 : stamen

estampa *nf* 1 ILUSTRACIÓN, IMAGEN : printed image, illustration 2 ASPECTO : appearance, demeanor

estampado[1], -da *adj* : patterned, printed

estampado[2] *nm* : print, pattern

estampar *vt* : to stamp, to print, to engrave

estampida *nf* : stampede

estampilla *nf* 1 : rubber stamp 2 SELLO, TIMBRE : postage stamp

estancado, -da *adj* : stagnant

estancamiento *nm* : stagnation

estancar {72} *vt* 1 : to dam up, to hold back 2 : to bring to a halt, to deadlock — estancarse *vr* 1 : to stagnate 2 : to be brought to a standstill, to be deadlocked

estancia *nf* 1 ESTADÍA : stay, sojourn 2 : ranch, farm

estanciero, -ra *n* : rancher, farmer

estanco, -ca *adj* : watertight

estándar *adj & nm* : standard

estandarización *nf, pl* -ciones : standardization

estandarizar {21} *vt* : to standardize

estandarte *nm* : standard, banner

estanque *nm* 1 : pool, pond 2 : tank, reservoir

estante *nm* REPISA : shelf

estantería *nf* : shelves *pl*, bookcase

estaño *nm* : tin

estaquilla *nf* 1 : peg 2 ESPIGA : spike

estar {34} *v aux* : to be ⟨estoy aprendiendo inglés : I'm learning English⟩ ⟨está terminado : it's finished⟩ — *vi* 1 (*indicating a state or condition*) : to be ⟨está muy alto : he's so tall, he's gotten very tall⟩ ⟨¿ya estás mejor? : are you feeling better now?⟩ ⟨estoy casado : I'm married⟩ 2 (*indicating location*) : to be ⟨están en la mesa : they're on the table⟩ ⟨estamos en la página 2 : we're on page 2⟩ 3 : to be at home ⟨¿está María? : is Maria in?⟩ 4 : to remain ⟨estaré aquí 5 días : I'll be here for 5 days⟩ 5 : to be ready, to be done ⟨estará para las diez : it will be ready by ten o'clock⟩ 6 : to agree ⟨¿estamos? : are we in agreement?⟩ ⟨estoy contigo : I'm with you⟩ 7 ¿cómo estás? : how are you? 8 ¡está bien! : all right!, that's fine! 9 ~ a : to cost 10 ~ a : to be ⟨¿a qué día estamos? : what's today's date?⟩ 11 ~ con : to have ⟨está con fiebre : she has a fever⟩ 12 ~ de : to be ⟨estoy de vacaciones : I'm on vacation⟩ ⟨está de director hoy : he's acting as director today⟩ 13 estar bien (mal) : to be well (sick) 14 ~ para : to be in the mood for 15 ~ por : to be in favor of 16 ~ por : to be about to ⟨está por cerrar : it's on the verge of closing⟩ 17 estar de más : to be unnecessary 18 estar que : to be (in a state or condition) ⟨está que echa chispas : he's hopping mad⟩ — estarse *vr* QUEDARSE : to stay, to remain ⟨¡estáte quieto! : be still!⟩

estarcir {83} *vt* : to stencil

estatal *adj* : state, national

estática *nf* : static

estático, -ca *adj* : static

estatizar {21} *vt* : to nationalize — estatización *nf*

estatua *nf* : statue

estatuilla *nf* : statuette, figurine
estatura *nf* : height, stature ⟨de mediana estatura : of medium height⟩
estatus *nm* : status, prestige
estatutario, -ria *adj* : statutory
estatuto *nm* : statute
este[1], esta *adj, mpl* **estos** : this, these
este[2] *adj* : eastern, east
este[3] *nm* **1** ORIENTE : east **2** : east wind **3 el Este** : the East, the Orient
éste, ésta *pron, mpl* **éstos 1** : this one, these ones *pl* **2** : the latter
estela *nf* **1** : wake (of a ship) **2** RASTRO : trail (of dust, smoke, etc.)
estelar *adj* : stellar
estelarizar {21} *vt Mex* : to star in, to be the star of
esténcil *nm* : stencil
estentóreo, -rea *adj* : loud, thundering
estepa *nf* : steppe
éster *nf* : ester
estera *nf* : mat
estercolero *nm* : dunghill
estéreo *adj & nm* : stereo
estereofónico, -ca *adj* : stereophonic
estereotipado, -da *adj* : stereotyped
estereotipar *vt* : to stereotype
estereotipo *nm* : stereotype
estéril *adj* **1** : sterile, germ-free **2** : infertile, barren **3** : futile, vain
esterilidad *nf* **1** : sterility **2** : infertility
esterilizar {21} *vt* **1** : to sterilize, to disinfect **2** : to sterilize (a person), to spay (an animal) — **esterilización** *nf*
esterlina *adj* : sterling
esternón *nm, pl* **-nones** : sternum
estero *nm* : estuary
estertor *nm* : death rattle
estética *nf* : aesthetics
estético, -ca *adj* : aesthetic — **estéticamente** *adv*
estetoscopio *nm* : stethoscope
estibador, -dora *n* : longshoreman, stevedore
estibar *vt* : to load (freight)
estiércol *nm* : dung, manure
estigma *nm* : stigma
estigmatizar {21} *vt* : to stigmatize, to brand
estilarse *vr* : to be in fashion
estilete *nm* : stiletto
estilista *nmf* : stylist
estilizar {21} *vt* : to stylize
estilo *nm* **1** : style **2** : fashion, manner **3** : stylus
estima *nf* ESTIMACIÓN : esteem, regard
estimable *adj* **1** : considerable **2** : estimable, esteemed
estimación *nf, pl* **-ciones 1** ESTIMA : esteem, regard **2** : estimate
estimado, -da *adj* : esteemed, dear ⟨Estimado señor Ortiz : Dear Mr. Ortiz⟩
estimar *vt* **1** APRECIAR : to esteem, to respect **2** EVALUAR : to estimate, to appraise **3** OPINAR : to consider, to deem
estimulación *nf, pl* **-ciones** : stimulation
estimulante[1] *adj* : stimulating
estimulante[2] *nm* : stimulant

estimular *vt* **1** : to stimulate **2** : to encourage
estímulo *nm* **1** : stimulus **2** INCENTIVO : incentive, encouragement
estío *nm* : summertime
estipendio *nm* **1** : salary **2** : stipend, remuneration
estipular *vt* : to stipulate — **estipulación** *nf*
estirado, -da *adj* **1** : stretched, extended **2** PRESUMIDO : stuck-up, conceited
estiramiento *nm* **1** : stretching **2 estiramiento facial** : face-lift
estirar *vt* : to stretch (out), to extend — **estirarse** *vr*
estirón *nm, pl* **-rones 1** : pull, tug **2 dar un estirón** : to grow quickly, to shoot up
estirpe *nf* LINAJE : lineage, stock
estival *adj* VERANIEGO : summer
esto *pron (neuter)* **1** : this ⟨¿qué es esto? : what is this?⟩ **2 en ~** : at this point **3 por ~** : for this reason
estocada *nf* **1** : final thrust (in bullfighting) **2** : thrust, lunge (in fencing)
estofa *nf* CLASE : class, quality ⟨de baja estofa : low-class, poor-quality⟩
estofado *nm* COCIDO, GUISADO : stew
estofar *vt* GUISAR : to stew
estoicismo *nm* : stoicism
estoico[1], -ca *adj* : stoic, stoical
estoico[2], -ca *n* : stoic
estola *nf* : stole
estomacal *adj* GÁSTRICO : stomach, gastric
estómago *nm* : stomach
estoniano, -na *adj & n* : Estonian
estonio, -nia *adj & n* : Estonian
estopa *nf* **1** : tow (yarn or cloth) **2** : burlap
estopilla *nf* : cheesecloth
estoque *nm* : rapier, sword
estorbar *vt* OBSTRUIR : to obstruct, to hinder — *vi* : to get in the way
estorbo *nm* **1** : obstacle, hindrance **2** : nuisance
estornino *nm* : starling
estornudar *vi* : to sneeze
estornudo *nm* : sneeze
estos *adj* → **este[1]**
éstos → **éste**
estoy → **estar**
estrabismo *nm* : squint
estrado *nm* **1** : dais, platform, bench (of a judge) **2 estrados** *nmpl* : courts of law
estrafalario, -ria *adj* ESTRAMBÓTICO, EXCÉNTRICO : eccentric, bizarre
estragar {52} *vt* DEVASTAR : to ruin, to devastate
estragón *nm* : tarragon
estragos *nmpl* **1** : ravages, destruction, devastation ⟨los estragos de la guerra : the ravages of war⟩ **2 hacer estragos en** or **causar estragos entre** : to play havoc with
estrambótico, -ca *adj* ESTRAFALARIO, EXCÉNTRICO : eccentric, bizarre

estrangulamiento *nm* : strangling, strangulation
estrangular *vt* AHOGAR : to strangle — **estrangulación** *nf*
estratagema *nf* ARTIMAÑA : stratagem, ruse
estratega *nmf* : strategist
estrategia *nf* : strategy
estratégico, -ca *adj* : strategic, tactical — **estratégicamente** *adv*
estratificación *nf, pl* **-ciones** : stratification
estratificado, -da *adj* : stratified
estrato *nm* : stratum, layer
estratosfera *nf* : stratosphere
estratosférico, -ca *adj* **1** : stratospheric **2** : astronomical, exorbitant
estrechamiento *nm* **1** : narrowing **2** : narrow point **3** : tightening, strengthening (of relations)
estrechar *vt* **1** : to narrow **2** : to tighten, to strengthen (a bond) **3** : to hug, to embrace **4 estrechar la mano de** : to shake hands with — **estrecharse** *vr*
estrechez *nf, pl* **-checes 1** : tightness, narrowness **2 estrecheces** *nfpl* : financial problems
estrecho¹, -cha *adj* **1** : tight, narrow **2** ÍNTIMO : close — **estrechamente** *adv*
estrecho² *nm* : strait, narrows
estrella *nf* **1** ASTRO : star ⟨estrella fugaz : shooting star⟩ **2** : destiny ⟨tener buena estrella : to be born lucky⟩ **3** : movie star **4 estrella de mar** : starfish
estrellado, -da *adj* **1** : starry **2** : star-shaped **3 huevos estrellados** : fried eggs
estrellamiento *nm* : crash, collision
estrellar *vt* : to smash, to crash — **estrellarse** *vr* : to crash, to collide
estrellato *nm* : stardom
estremecedor, -dora *adj* : horrifying
estremecer {53} *vt* : to cause to shake — *vi* : to tremble, to shake — **estremecerse** *vr* : to shudder, to shiver (with emotion)
estremecimiento *nm* : trembling, shaking, shivering
estrenar *vt* **1** : to use for the first time **2** : to premiere, to open — **estrenarse** *vr* : to make one's debut
estreno *nm* DEBUT : debut, premiere
estreñimiento *nm* : constipation
estreñirse {67} *vr* : to be constipated
estrépito *nm* ESTRUENDO : clamor, din
estrepitoso, -sa *adj* : clamorous, noisy — **estrepitosamente** *adv*
estrés *nm, pl* **estreses** : stress
estresante *adj* : stressful
estresar *vt* : to stress, to stress out
estría *nf* : fluting, groove
estribación *nf, pl* **-ciones 1** : spur, ridge **2 estribaciones** *nfpl* : foothills
estribar *vi* FUNDARSE ~ **en** : to be due to, to stem from
estribillo *nm* : refrain, chorus

estribo *nm* **1** : stirrup **2** : abutment, buttress **3 perder los estribos** : to lose one's temper
estribor *nm* : starboard
estricnina *nf* : strychnine
estricto, -ta *adj* SEVERO : strict, severe — **estrictamente** *adv*
estridente *adj* : strident, shrill, loud — **estridentemente** *adv*
estrofa *nf* : stanza, verse
estrógeno *nm* : estrogen
estropajo *nm* : scouring pad
estropear *vt* **1** ARRUINAR : to ruin, to spoil **2** : to break, to damage — **estropearse** *vr* **1** : to spoil, to go bad **2** : to break down
estropicio *nm* DAÑO : damage, breakage
estructura *nf* : structure, framework
estructuración *nf, pl* **-ciones** : structuring, structure
estructural *adj* : structural — **estructuralmente** *adv*
estructurar *vt* : to structure, to organize
estruendo *nm* ESTRÉPITO : racket, din, roar
estruendoso, -sa *adj* : resounding, thunderous
estrujar *vt* APRETAR : to press, to squeeze
estuario *nm* : estuary
estuche *nm* : kit, case
estuco *nm* : stucco
estudiado, -da *adj* : affected, mannered
estudiantado *nm* : student body, students *pl*
estudiante *nmf* : student
estudiantil *adj* : student ⟨la vida estudiantil : student life⟩
estudiar *v* : to study
estudio *nm* **1** : study **2** : studio **3 estudios** *nmpl* : studies, education
estudioso, -sa *adj* : studious
estufa *nf* **1** : stove, heater **2** *Col, Mex* : cooking stove, range
estupefacción *nf, pl* **-ciones** : stupefaction, astonishment
estupefaciente¹ *adj* : narcotic
estupefaciente² *nm* DROGA, NARCÓTICO : drug, narcotic
estupefacto, -ta *adj* : astonished, stunned
estupendo, -da *adj* MARAVILLOSO : stupendous, marvelous — **estupendamente** *adv*
estupidez *nf, pl* **-deces 1** : stupidity **2** : nonsense
estúpido¹, -da *adj* : stupid — **estúpidamente** *adv*
estúpido², -da *n* IDIOTA : idiot, fool
estupor *nm* **1** : stupor **2** : amazement
esturión *nm, pl* **-riones** : sturgeon
estuvo, etc. → **estar**
etano *nm* : ethane
etanol *nm* : ethanol
etapa *nf* FASE : stage, phase
etcétera¹ : et cetera, and so on
etcétera² *nmf* : et cetera
éter *nm* : ether

etéreo, -rea *adj* : ethereal, heavenly
eternidad *nf* : eternity
eternizar {21} *vt* PERPETUAR : to make eternal, to perpetuate — eternizarse *vr* *fam* : to take forever
eterno, -na *adj* : eternal, endless — eternamente *adv*
ética *nf* : ethics
ético, -ca *adj* : ethical — éticamente *adv*
etimología *nf* : etymology
etimológico, -ca *adj* : etymological
etimólogo, -ga *n* : etymologist
etíope *adj & nmf* : Ethiopian
etiqueta *nf* 1 : etiquette 2 : tag, label 3 de ~ : formal, dressy
etiquetar *vt* : to label
étnico, -ca *adj* : ethnic
etnología *nf* : ethnology
etnólogo, -ga *n* : ethnologist
eucalipto *nm* : eucalyptus
Eucaristía *nf* : Eucharist, communion
eucarístico, -ca *adj* : eucharistic
eufemismo *nm* : euphemism
eufemístico, -ca *adj* : euphemistic
eufonía *nf* : euphony
eufónico, -ca *adj* : euphonious
euforia *nf* : euphoria, joyousness
eufórico, -ca *adj* : euphoric, exuberant, joyous — eufóricamente *adv*
eunuco *nm* : eunuch
europeo, -pea *adj & n* : European
euskera *nm* : Basque (language)
eutanasia *nf* : euthanasia
evacuación *nf, pl* -ciones : evacuation
evacuar *vt* 1 : to evacuate, to vacate 2 : to carry out — *vi* : to have a bowel movement
evadir *vt* ELUDIR : to evade, to avoid — evadirse *vr* : to escape, to slip away
evaluación *nf, pl* -ciones : assessment, evaluation
evaluador, -dora *n* : assessor
evaluar {3} *vt* : to evaluate, to assess, to appraise
evangélico, -ca *adj* : evangelical — evangélicamente *adv*
evangelio *nm* : gospel
evangelismo *nm* : evangelism
evangelista *nm* : evangelist
evangelizador, -dora *n* : evangelist, missionary
evaporación *nf, pl* -ciones : evaporation
evaporar *vt* : to evaporate — evaporarse *vr* ESFUMARSE : to disappear, to vanish
evasión *nf, pl* -siones 1 : escape, flight 2 : evasion, dodge
evasiva *nf* : excuse, pretext
evasivo, -va *adj* : evasive
evento *nm* : event
eventual *adj* 1 : possible 2 : temporary ⟨trabajadores eventuales : temporary workers⟩ — eventualmente *adv*
eventualidad *nf* : possibility, eventuality
evidencia *nf* 1 : evidence, proof 2 poner en evidencia : to demonstrate, to make clear

evidenciar *vt* : to demonstrate, to show — evidenciarse *vr* : to be evident
evidente *adj* : evident, obvious, clear — evidentemente *adv*
eviscerar *vt* : to eviscerate
evitable *adj* : avoidable, preventable
evitar *vt* 1 : to avoid 2 PREVENIR : to prevent 3 ELUDIR : to escape, to elude
evocación *nf, pl* -ciones : evocation
evocador, -dora *adj* : evocative
evocar {72} *vt* 1 : to evoke 2 RECORDAR : to recall
evolución *nf, pl* -ciones 1 : evolution 2 : development, progress
evolucionar *vi* 1 : to evolve 2 : to change, to develop
evolutivo, -va *adj* : evolutionary
exabrupto *nm* : pointed remark
exacción *nf, pl* -ciones : levying, exaction
exacerbar *vt* 1 : to exacerbate, to aggravate 2 : to irritate, to exasperate
exactamente *adv* : exactly
exactitud *nf* PRECISIÓN : accuracy, precision, exactitude
exacto, -ta *adj* PRECISO : accurate, precise, exact
exageración *nf, pl* -ciones : exaggeration
exagerado, -da *adj* 1 : exaggerated 2 : excessive — exageradamente *adv*
exagerar *v* : to exaggerate
exaltación *nf, pl* -ciones 1 : exaltation 2 : excitement, agitation
exaltado[1], -da *adj* : excitable, hotheaded
exaltado[2], -da *n* : hothead
exaltar *vt* 1 ENSALZAR : to exalt, to extol 2 : to excite, to agitate — exaltarse *vr* ACALORARSE : to get overexcited
ex–alumno → alumno
examen *nm, pl* exámenes 1 : examination, test 2 : consideration, investigation
examinar *vt* 1 : to examine 2 INSPECCIONAR : to inspect — examinarse *vr* : to take an exam
exánime *adj* 1 : lifeless 2 : exhausted
exasperante *adj* : exasperating
exasperar *vt* IRRITAR : to exasperate, to irritate — exasperación *nf*
excavación *nf, pl* -ciones : excavation
excavadora *nf* : excavator
excavar *v* : to excavate, to dig
excedente[1] *adj* 1 : excessive 2 : excess, surplus
excedente[2] *nm* : surplus, excess
exceder *vt* : to exceed, to surpass — excederse *vr* : to go too far
excelencia *nf* 1 : excellence 2 : excellency ⟨Su Excelencia : His Excellency⟩
excelente *adj* : excellent — excelentemente *adv*
excelso, -sa *adj* : lofty, sublime
excentricidad *nf* : eccentricity
excéntrico, -ca *adj & n* : eccentric
excepción *nf, pl* -ciones : exception
excepcional *adj* EXTRAORDINARIO : exceptional, extraordinary, rare

excepto *prep* SALVO : except
exceptuar {3} *vt* EXCLUIR : to except, to exclude
excesivo, -va *adj* : excessive — **excesivamente** *adv*
exceso *nm* 1 : excess 2 **excesos** *nmpl* : excesses, abuses 3 **exceso de velocidad** : speeding
excitabilidad *nf* : excitability
excitación *nf, pl* -ciones : excitement
excitante *adj* : exciting
excitar *vt* : to excite, to arouse — **excitarse** *vr*
exclamación *nf, pl* -ciones : exclamation
exclamar *v* : to exclaim
excluir {41} *vt* EXCEPTUAR : to exclude, to leave out
exclusión *nf, pl* -siones : exclusion
exclusividad *nf* 1 : exclusiveness 2 : exclusive rights *pl*
exclusivista *adj & nmf* : exclusivist
exclusivo, -va *adj* : exclusive — **exclusivamente** *adv*
excomulgar {52} *vt* : to excommunicate
excomunión *nf, pl* -niones : excommunication
excreción *nf, pl* -ciones : excretion
excremento *nm* : excrement
excretar *vt* : to excrete
exculpar *vt* : to exonerate, to exculpate — **exculpación** *nf*
excursión *nf, pl* -siones : excursion, outing
excursionista *nmf* 1 : sightseer, tourist 2 : hiker
excusa *nf* 1 PRETEXTO : excuse 2 DISCULPA : apology
excusado *nm Mex* : toilet
excusar *vt* 1 : to excuse 2 : to exempt — **excusarse** *vr* : to apologize, to send one's regrets
execrable *adj* : detestable, abominable
exención *nf, pl* -ciones : exemption
exento, -ta *adj* 1 : exempt, free 2 **exento de impuestos** : tax-exempt
exequias *nfpl* FUNERALES : funeral rites
exhalación *nf, pl* -ciones 1 : exhalation 2 : shooting star ⟨salió como una exhalación : he took off like a shot⟩
exhalar *vt* ESPIRAR : to exhale, to give off
exhaustivo, -va *adj* : exhaustive — **exhaustivamente** *adv*
exhausto, -ta *adj* AGOTADO : exhausted, worn-out
exhibición *nf, pl* -ciones 1 : exhibition, show 2 : showing
exhibir *vt* : to exhibit, to show, to display — **exhibirse** *vr*
exhortación *nf, pl* -ciones : exhortation
exhortar *vt* : to exhort
exhumar *vt* DESENTERRAR : to exhume — **exhumación** *nf*
exigencia *nf* : demand, requirement
exigente *adj* : demanding, exacting
exigir {35} *vt* 1 : to demand, to require 2 : to exact, to levy

exiguo, -gua *adj* : meager
exiliado[1], -da *adj* : exiled, in exile
exiliado[2], -da *n* : exile
exiliar *vt* DESTERRAR : to exile, to banish — **exiliarse** *vr* : to go into exile
exilio *nm* DESTIERRO : exile
eximio, -mia *adj* : distinguished, eminent
eximir *vt* EXONERAR : to exempt
existencia *nf* 1 : existence 2 **existencias** *nfpl* MERCANCÍA : goods, stock
existente *adj* 1 : existing, in existence 2 : in stock
existir *vi* : to exist
éxito *nm* 1 TRIUNFO : success, hit 2 **tener éxito** : to be successful
exitoso, -sa *adj* : successful — **exitosamente** *adv*
éxodo *nm* : exodus
exoneración *nf, pl* -ciones EXENCIÓN : exoneration, exemption
exonerar *vt* 1 EXIMIR : to exempt, to exonerate 2 DESPEDIR : to dismiss
exorbitante *adj* : exorbitant
exorcismo *nm* : exorcism — **exorcista** *nmf*
exorcizar {21} *vt* : to exorcise
exótico, -ca *adj* : exotic
expandir *vt* EXPANSIONAR : to expand — **expandirse** *vr* : to spread
expansión *nf, pl* -siones 1 : expansion, spread 2 DIVERSIÓN : recreation, relaxation
expansionar *vt* EXPANDIR : to expand — **expansionarse** *vr* 1 : to expand 2 DIVERTIRSE : to amuse oneself, to relax
expansivo, -va *adj* : expansive
expatriado, -da *adj & n* : expatriate
expatriarse {85} *vr* 1 EMIGRAR : to emigrate 2 : to go into exile
expectación *nf, pl* -ciones : expectation, anticipation
expectante *adj* : expectant
expectativa *nf* 1 : expectation, hope 2 **expectativas** *nfpl* : prospects
expedición *nf, pl* -ciones : expedition
expediente *nm* 1 : expedient, means 2 ARCHIVO : file, dossier, record
expedir {54} *vt* 1 EMITIR : to issue 2 DESPACHAR : to dispatch, to send
expedito, -ta *adj* 1 : free, clear 2 : quick, easy
expeler *vt* : to expel, to eject
expendedor, -dora *n* : dealer, seller
expendio *nm* TIENDA : store, shop
expensas *nfpl* 1 : expenses, costs 2 **a expensas de** : at the expense of
experiencia *nf* 1 : experience 2 EXPERIMENTO : experiment
experimentación *nf, pl* -ciones : experimentation
experimental *adj* : experimental
experimentar *vi* : to experiment — *vt* 1 : to experiment with, to test out 2 : to experience
experimento *nm* EXPERIENCIA : experiment

experto, -ta *adj & n* : expert
expiación *nf, pl* **-ciones** : expiation, atonement
expiar {85} *vt* : to expiate, to atone for
expiración *nf, pl* **-ciones** VENCIMIENTO : expiration
expirar *vi* **1** FALLECER, MORIR : to pass away, to die **2** : to expire
explanada *nf* : esplanade, promenade
explayar *vt* : to extend — **explayarse** *vr* : to expound, to speak at length
explicable *adj* : explicable, explainable
explicación *nf, pl* **-ciones** : explanation
explicar {72} *vt* : to explain — **explicarse** *vr* : to understand
explicativo, -va *adj* : explanatory
explicitar *vt* : to state explicitly, to specify
explícito, -ta *adj* : explicit — **explícitamente** *adv*
exploración *nf, pl* **-ciones** : exploration
explorador, -dora *n* : explorer, scout
explorar *vt* : to explore — **exploratorio, -ria** *adj*
explosión *nf, pl* **-siones 1** ESTALLIDO : explosion **2** : outburst ⟨una explosión de ira : an outburst of anger⟩
explosionar *vi* : to explode
explosivo, -va *adj* : explosive
explotación *nf, pl* **-ciones 1** : exploitation **2** : operation, running
explotar *vt* **1** : to exploit **2** : to operate, to run — *vi* ESTALLAR, REVENTAR : to explode — **explotable** *adj*
exponencial *adj* : exponential — **exponencialmente** *adv*
exponente *nm* : exponent
exponer {60} *vt* **1** : to exhibit, to show, to display **2** : to explain, to present, to set forth **3** : to expose, to risk — *vi* : to exhibit
exportación *nf, pl* **-ciones 1** : exportation **2 exportaciones** *nfpl* : exports
exportador, -dora *n* : exporter
exportar *vt* : to export — **exportable** *adj*
exposición *nf, pl* **-ciones 1** EXHIBICIÓN : exposition, exhibition **2** : exposure **3** : presentation, statement
expositor, -tora *n* **1** : exhibitor **2** : exponent
exprés *nms & pl* **1** : express, express train **2** : espresso
expresamente *adv* : expressly, on purpose
expresar *vt* : to express — **expresarse** *vr*
expresión *nf, pl* **-siones** : expression
expresivo, -va *adj* **1** : expressive **2** CARIÑOSO : affectionate — **expresivamente** *adv*
expreso[1], -sa *adj* : express, specific
expreso[2] *nm* : express train, express
exprimidor *nm* : squeezer, juicer
exprimir *vt* **1** : to squeeze **2** : to exploit
expropiar *vt* : to expropriate, to commandeer — **expropiación** *nf*
expuesto[1] *pp* → **exponer**
expuesto[2], -ta *adj* **1** : exposed **2** : hazardous, risky

expulsar *vt* : to expel, to eject
expulsión *nf, pl* **-siones** : expulsion
expurgar {52} *vt* : to expurgate
expuso, etc. → **exponer**
exquisitez *nf, pl* **-teces 1** : exquisiteness, refinement **2** : delicacy, special dish
exquisito, -ta *adj* **1** : exquisite **2** : delicious
extasiarse {85} *vr* : to be in ecstasy, to be enraptured
éxtasis *nms & pl* : ecstasy, rapture
extático, -ca *adj* : ecstatic
extemporáneo, -nea *adj* **1** : unseasonable **2** : untimely
extender {56} *vt* **1** : to spread out, to stretch out **2** : to broaden, to expand ⟨extender la influencia : to broaden one's influence⟩ **3** : to draw up (a document), to write out (a check) — **extenderse** *vr* **1** : to spread **2** : to last
extendido, -da *adj* **1** : outstretched **2** : widespread
extensamente *adv* : extensively, at length
extensible *adj* : extensible, extendable
extensión *nf, pl* **-siones 1** : extension, stretching **2** : expanse, spread **3** : extent, range **4** : length, duration
extensivo, -va *adj* **1** : extensive **2 hacer extensivo** : to extend
extenso, -sa *adj* **1** : extensive, detailed **2** : spacious, vast
extenuar {3} *vt* : to exhaust, to tire out — **extenuarse** *vr* — **extenuante** *adj*
exterior[1] *adj* **1** : exterior, external **2** : foreign ⟨asuntos exteriores : foreign affairs⟩
exterior[2] *nm* **1** : outside **2** : abroad
exteriorizar {21} *vt* : to express, to reveal
exteriormente *adv* : outwardly
exterminar *vt* : to exterminate — **exterminación** *nf*
exterminio *nm* : extermination
externar *vt Mex* : to express, to display
externo, -na *adj* : external, outward
extinción *nf, pl* **-ciones** : extinction
extinguidor *nm* : fire extinguisher
extinguir {26} *vt* **1** APAGAR : to extinguish, to put out **2** : to wipe out — **extinguirse** *vr* **1** APAGARSE : to go out, to fade out **2** : to die out, to become extinct
extinto, -ta *adj* : extinct
extintor *nm* : extinguisher
extirpación *n, pl* **-ciones** : removal, excision
extirpar *vt* : to eradicate, to remove, to excise — **extirparse** *vr*
extorsión *nf, pl* **-siones 1** : extortion **2** : harm, trouble
extorsionar *vt* : to extort
extra[1] *adv* : extra
extra[2] *adj* **1** : additional, extra **2** : superior, top-quality
extra[3] *nmf* : extra (in movies)

extra[4] *nm* : extra expense ⟨paga extra : bonus⟩
extracción *nf, pl* **-ciones** : extraction
extracto *nm* **1** : extract ⟨extracto de vainilla : vanilla extract⟩ **2** : abstract, summary
extractor *nm* : extractor
extracurricular *adj* : extracurricular
extradición *nf, pl* **-ciones** : extradition
extraditar *vt* : to extradite
extraer {81} *vt* : to extract
extraído *pp* → **extraer**
extrajudicial *adj* : out-of-court
extramatrimonial *adj* : extramarital
extranjerizante *adj* : foreign-sounding, foreign-looking
extranjero[1], **-ra** *adj* : foreign
extranjero[2], **-ra** *n* : foreigner
extranjero[3] *nm* : foreign countries *pl* ⟨viajó al extranjero : he traveled abroad⟩ ⟨trabajan en el extranjero : they work overseas⟩
extrañamente *adv* : strangely, oddly
extrañamiento *nm* ASOMBRO : amazement, surprise, wonder
extrañar *vt* : to miss (someone) — **extrañarse** *vr* : to be surprised
extrañeza *nf* **1** : strangeness, oddness **2** : surprise
extraño[1], **-ña** *adj* **1** RARO : strange, odd **2** EXTRANJERO : foreign
extraño[2], **-ña** *n* DESCONOCIDO : stranger
extraoficial *adj* OFICIOSO : unofficial — **extraoficialmente** *adv*
extraordinario, -ria *adj* EXCEPCIONAL : extraordinary — **extraordinariamente** *adv*
extrasensorial *adj* : extrasensory ⟨percepción extrasensorial : extrasensory perception⟩
extraterrestre *adj & nmf* : extraterrestrial, alien

extravagancia *nf* : extravagance, outlandishness, flamboyance
extravagante *adj* : extravagant, outrageous, flamboyant
extraviar {85} *vt* **1** : to mislead, to lead astray **2** : to misplace, to lose — **extraviarse** *vr* : to get lost, to go astray
extravío *nm* **1** PÉRDIDA : loss, misplacement **2** : misconduct
extremado, -da *adj* : extreme — **extremadamente** *adv*
extremar *vt* : to carry to extremes — **extremarse** *vr* : to do one's utmost
extremidad *nf* **1** : extremity, tip, edge **2 extremidades** *nfpl* : extremities
extremista *adj & nmf* : extremist
extremo[1], **-ma** *adj* **1** : extreme, utmost **2** EXCESIVO : excessive **3 en caso extremo** : as a last resort
extremo[2] *nm* **1** : extreme, end **2 al extremo de** : to the point of **3 en ~** : in the extreme
extrovertido[1], **-da** *adj* : extroverted, outgoing
extrovertido[2], **-da** *n* : extrovert
extrudir *vt* : to extrude
exuberancia *nf* **1** : exuberance **2** : luxuriance, lushness
exuberante *adj* : exuberant, luxuriant — **exuberantemente** *adv*
exudar *vt* : to exude
exultación *nf, pl* **-ciones** : exultation, elation
exultante *adj* : exultant, elated — **exultantemente** *adv*
exultar *vi* : to exult, to rejoice
eyacular *vi* : to ejaculate — **eyaculación** *nf*
eyección *nf, pl* **-ciones** : ejection, expulsion
eyectar *vt* : to eject, to expel — **eyectarse** *vr*

F

f *nf* : sixth letter of the Spanish alphabet
fábrica *nf* FACTORÍA : factory
fabricación *nf, pl* **-ciones** : manufacture
fabricante *nmf* : manufacturer
fabricar {72} *vt* MANUFACTURAR : to manufacture, to make
fabril *adj* INDUSTRIAL : industrial, manufacturing
fábula *nf* **1** : fable **2** : fabrication, fib
fabuloso, -sa *adj* **1** : fabulous, fantastic **2** : mythical, fabled
facción *nf, pl* **facciones** **1** : faction **2 facciones** *nfpl* RASGOS : features
faccioso, -sa *adj* : factious
faceta *nf* : facet
facha *nf* : appearance, look ⟨estar hecho una facha : to look a sight⟩
fachada *nf* : facade
facial *adj* : facial

fácil *adj* **1** : easy **2** : likely, probable ⟨es fácil que no pase : it probably won't happen⟩
facilidad *nf* **1** : facility, ease **2 facilidades** *nfpl* : facilities, services **3 facilidades** *nfpl* : opportunities
facilitar *vt* **1** : to facilitate **2** : to provide, to supply
fácilmente *adv* : easily, readily
facsímil *or* **facsímile** *nm* **1** : facsimile, copy **2** : fax
facsimilar *adj* : facsimile
factibilidad *nf* : feasibility
factible *adj* : feasible, practicable
facticio, -cia *adj* : artificial, factitious
factor[1], **-tora** *n* **1** : agent, factor **2** : baggage clerk
factor[2] *nm* ELEMENTO : factor, element
factoría *nf* FÁBRICA : factory
factótum *nm* : factotum

factura *nf* **1** : making, manufacturing **2** : bill, invoice
facturación *nf, pl* **-ciones 1** : invoicing, billing **2** : check-in
facturar *vt* **1** : to bill, to invoice **2** : to check in
facultad *nf* **1** : faculty, ability ⟨facultades mentales : mental faculties⟩ **2** : authority, power **3** : school (of a university) ⟨facultad de derecho : law school⟩
facultar *vt* : to authorize, to empower
facultativo, -va *adj* **1** OPTATIVO : voluntary, optional **2** : medical ⟨informe facultativo : medical report⟩
faena *nf* : task, job, work ⟨faenas domésticas : housework⟩
faenar *vi* **1** : to work, to labor **2** PESCAR : to fish
fagot *nm* : bassoon
faisán *nm, pl* **faisanes** : pheasant
faja *nf* **1** : sash, belt **2** : girdle **3** : strip (of land)
fajar *vt* **1** : to wrap (a sash or girdle) around **2** : to hit, to thrash — **fajarse** *vr* **1** : to put on a sash or girdle **2** : to come to blows
fajín *nm, pl* **-jines** : sash, belt
fajo *nm* : bundle, sheaf ⟨un fajo de billetes : a wad of cash⟩
falacia *nf* : fallacy
falaz, -laza *adj, mpl* **falaces** FALSO : fallacious, false
falda *nf* **1** : skirt ⟨falda escocesa : kilt⟩ **2** REGAZO : lap (of the body) **3** VERTIENTE : side, slope
faldón *nm, pl* **-dones 1** : tail (of a shirt, etc.) **2** : full skirt **3** **faldón bautismal** : christening gown
falible *adj* : fallible
fálico, -ca *adj* : phallic
falla *nf* **1** : flaw, defect **2** : (geological) fault **3** : fault, failing
fallar *vi* **1** FRACASAR : to fail, to go wrong **2** : to rule (in a court of law) — *vt* **1** ERRAR : to miss (a target) **2** : to pronounce judgment on
fallecer {53} *vi* MORIR : to pass away, to die
fallecido, -da *adj & n* DIFUNTO : deceased
fallecimiento *nm* : demise, death
fallido, -da *adj* : failed, unsuccessful
fallo *nm* **1** SENTENCIA : sentence, judgment, verdict **2** : error, fault
falo *nm* : phallus, penis
falsamente *adv* : falsely
falsear *vt* **1** : to falsify, to fake **2** : to distort — *vi* **1** CEDER : to give way **2** : to be out of tune
falsedad *nf* **1** : falseness, hypocrisy **2** MENTIRA : falsehood, lie
falsete *nm* : falsetto
falsificación *nf, pl* **-ciones 1** : counterfeit, forgery **2** : falsification
falsificador, -dora *n* : counterfeiter, forger

falsificar {72} *vt* **1** : to counterfeit, to forge **2** : to falsify
falso, -sa *adj* **1** FALAZ : false, untrue **2** : counterfeit, forged
falta *nf* **1** CARENCIA : lack ⟨hacer falta : to be lacking, to be needed⟩ **2** DEFECTO : defect, fault, error **3** : offense, misdemeanor **4** : foul (in basketball), fault (in tennis)
faltar *vi* **1** : to be lacking, to be needed ⟨me falta tiempo : I don't have enough time⟩ **2** : to be absent, to be missing **3** QUEDAR : to remain, to be left ⟨faltan pocos días para la fiesta : the party is just a few days away⟩ **4** ¡no faltaba más! : don't mention it!, you're welcome!
falto, -ta *adj* ~ **de** : lacking (in), short of
fama *nf* **1** : fame **2** REPUTACIÓN : reputation **3 de mala fama** : disreputable
famélico, -ca *adj* HAMBRIENTO : starving, famished
familia *nf* **1** : family **2 familia política** : in-laws
familiar¹ *adj* **1** CONOCIDO : familiar **2** : familial, family **3** INFORMAL : informal
familiar² *nmf* PARIENTE : relation, relative
familiaridad *nf* **1** : familiarity **2** : informality
familiarizarse {21} *vr* ~ **con** : to familiarize oneself with
famoso¹, -sa *adj* CÉLEBRE : famous
famoso², -sa *n* : celebrity
fanal *nm* **1** : beacon, signal light **2** *Mex* : headlight
fanático, -ca *adj & n* : fanatic
fanatismo *nm* : fanaticism
fandango *nm* : fandango
fanfarria *nf* **1** : (musical) fanfare **2** : pomp, ceremony
fanfarrón¹, -rrona *adj, mpl* **-rrones** *fam* : bragging, boastful
fanfarrón², -rrona *n, mpl* **-rrones** *fam* : braggart
fanfarronada *nf* : boast, bluster
fanfarronear *vi* : to brag, to boast
fango *nm* LODO : mud, mire
fangosidad *nf* : muddiness
fangoso, -sa *adj* LODOSO : muddy
fantasear *vi* : to fantasize, to daydream
fantasía *nf* **1** : fantasy **2** : imagination
fantasioso, -sa *adj* : fanciful
fantasma *nm* : ghost, phantom
fantasmagórico, -ca *adj* : phantasmagoric
fantasmal *adj* : ghostly
fantástico, -ca *adj* **1** : fantastic, imaginary, unreal **2** *fam* : great, fantastic
faquir *nm* : fakir
farándula *nf* : show business, theater
faraón *nm, pl* **faraones** : pharaoh
fardo *nm* **1** : bale **2** : bundle
farfulla *nf* : jabbering
farfullar *v* : to jabber, to gabble
faringe *nf* : pharynx

faríngeo, -gea *adj* : pharyngeal
fariña *nf* : coarse manioc flour
farmacéutico[1], **-ca** *adj* : pharmaceutical
farmacéutico[2], **-ca** *n* : pharmacist
farmacia *nf* : drugstore, pharmacy
fármaco *nm* : medicine, drug
farmacodependencia *nf* : drug addiction
farmacología *nf* : pharmacology
faro *nm* **1** : lighthouse **2** : headlight
farol *nm* **1** : streetlight **2** : lantern, lamp **3** *fam* : bluff **4** *Mex* : headlight
farola *nf* **1** : lamppost **2** : streetlight
farolero, -ra *n fam* : bluffer
farra *nf* : spree, revelry
fárrago *nm* REVOLTIJO : hodgepodge, jumble
farsa *nf* **1** : farce **2** : fake, sham
farsante *nmf* CHARLATÁN : charlatan, fraud, phony
fascículo *nm* : fascicle, part (of a publication)
fascinación *nf, pl* **-ciones** : fascination
fascinante *adj* : fascinating
fascinar *vt* **1** : to fascinate **2** : to charm, to captivate
fascismo *nm* : fascism
fascista *adj & nmf* : fascist
fase *nf* : phase, stage
fastidiar *vt* **1** MOLESTAR : to annoy, to bother, to hassle **2** ABURRIR : to bore — *vi* : to be annoying or bothersome
fastidio *nm* **1** MOLESTIA : annoyance, nuisance, hassle **2** ABURRIMIENTO : boredom
fastidioso, -sa *adj* **1** MOLESTO : annoying, bothersome **2** ABURRIDO : boring
fatal *adj* **1** MORTAL : fatal **2** *fam* : awful, terrible **3** : fateful, unavoidable
fatalidad *nf* **1** : fatality **2** DESGRACIA : misfortune, bad luck
fatalismo *nm* : fatalism
fatalista[1] *adj* : fatalistic
fatalista[2] *nmf* : fatalist
fatalmente *adv* **1** : unavoidably **2** : unfortunately
fatídico, -ca *adj* : fateful, momentous
fatiga *nf* CANSANCIO : fatigue
fatigado, -da *adj* AGOTADO : weary, tired
fatigar {52} *vt* CANSAR : to fatigue, to tire — **fatigarse** *vr* : to wear oneself out
fatigoso, -sa *adj* : fatiguing, tiring
fatuidad *nf* **1** : fatuousness **2** VANIDAD : vanity, conceit
fatuo, -tua *adj* **1** : fatuous **2** PRESUMIDO : vain
fauces *nfpl* : jaws *pl*, maw
faul *nm, pl* **fauls** : foul, foul ball
fauna *nf* : fauna
fausto *nm* : splendor, magnificence
favor *nm* **1** : favor **2 a favor de** : in favor of **3 por** ~ : please
favorable *adj* : favorable — **favorablemente** *adv*
favorecedor, -dora *adj* : becoming, flattering
favorecer {53} *vt* **1** : to favor **2** : to look well on, to suit

favorecido, -da *adj* **1** : flattering **2** : fortunate
favoritismo *nm* : favoritism
favorito, -ta *adj & n* : favorite
fax *nm* : fax, facsimile
fayuca *nf Mex* **1** : contraband **2** : black market
fayuquero *nm Mex* : smuggler, black marketeer
faz *nf* **1** : face, countenance ⟨la faz de la tierra : the face of the earth⟩ **2** : side (of coins, fabric, etc.)
fe *nf* **1** : faith **2** : assurance, testimony ⟨dar fe de : to bear witness to⟩ **3** : intention, will ⟨de buena fe : bona fide, in good faith⟩
fealdad *nf* : ugliness
febrero *nm* : February
febril *adj* : feverish — **febrilmente** *adv*
fecal *adj* : fecal
fecha *nf* **1** : date **2 fecha de caducidad** *or* **fecha de vencimiento** : expiration date **3 fecha límite** : deadline
fechar *vt* : to date, to put a date on
fechoría *nf* : misdeed
fécula *nf* : starch
fecundar *vt* : to fertilize (an egg) — **fecundación** *nf*
fecundidad *nf* **1** : fecundity, fertility **2** : productiveness
fecundo, -da *adj* FÉRTIL : fertile, fecund
federación *nf, pl* **-ciones** : federation
federal *adj* : federal
federalismo *nm* : federalism
federalista *adj & nmf* : federalist
federar *vt* : to federate
fehaciente *adj* : reliable, irrefutable — **fehacientemente** *adv*
feldespato *nm* : feldspar
felicidad *nf* **1** : happiness **2** ¡**felicidades!** : best wishes!, congratulations!, happy birthday!
felicitación *nf, pl* **-ciones** **1** : congratulation ⟨¡felicitaciones! : congratulations!⟩ **2** : greeting card
felicitar *vt* CONGRATULAR : to congratulate — **felicitarse** *vr* ~ **de** : to be glad about
feligrés, -gresa *n, mpl* **-greses** : parishioner
feligresía *nf* : parish
felino, -na *adj & n* : feline
feliz *adj, pl* **felices** **1** : happy **2 Feliz Navidad** : Merry Christmas
felizmente *adv* **1** : happily **2** : fortunately, luckily
felonía *nf* : felony
felpa *nf* **1** : terry cloth **2** : plush
felpudo *nm* : doormat
femenil *adj* : women's, girls' ⟨futbol femenil : women's soccer⟩
femenino, -na *adj* **1** : feminine **2** : women's ⟨derechos femeninos : women's rights⟩ **3** : female
femineidad *nf* : femininity
feminidad *nf* : femininity
feminismo *nm* : feminism
feminista *adj & nmf* : feminist

femoral *adj* : femoral
fémur *nm* : femur, thighbone
fenecer {53} *vi* **1** : to die, to pass away **2** : to come to an end, to cease
fénix *nm* : phoenix
fenomenal *adj* **1** : phenomenal **2** *fam* : fantastic, terrific — **fenomenalmente** *adv*
fenómeno *nm* **1** : phenomenon **2** : prodigy, genius
feo[1] *adv* : badly, bad
feo[2], **fea** *adj* **1** : ugly **2** : unpleasant, nasty
féretro *nm* ATAÚD : coffin, casket
feria *nf* **1** : fair, market **2** : festival, holiday **3** *Mex* : change (money)
feriado, -da *adj* **día feriado** : public holiday
ferial *nm* : fairground
fermentar *v* : to ferment — **fermentación** *nf*
fermento *nm* : ferment
ferocidad *nf* : ferocity, fierceness
feroz *adj, pl* **feroces** FIERO : ferocious, fierce — **ferozmente** *adv*
férreo, -rrea *adj* **1** : iron **2** : strong, steely ⟨una voluntad férrea : an iron will⟩ **3** : strict, severe **4 vía férrea** : railroad track
ferretería *nf* **1** : hardware store **2** : hardware **3** : foundry, ironworks
férrico, -ca *adj* : ferric
ferrocarril *nm* : railroad, railway
ferrocarrilero → **ferroviario**
ferroso, -sa *adj* : ferrous
ferroviario, -ria *adj* : rail, railroad
ferry *nm, pl* **ferrys** : ferry
fértil *adj* FECUNDO : fertile, fruitful
fertilidad *nf* : fertility
fertilizante[1] *adj* : fertilizing ⟨droga fertilizante : fertility drug⟩
fertilizante[2] *nm* ABONO : fertilizer
fertilizar *vt* ABONAR : to fertilize — **fertilización** *nf*
ferviente *adj* FERVOROSO : fervent
fervor *nm* : fervor, zeal
fervoroso, -sa *adj* FERVIENTE : fervent, zealous
festejar *vt* **1** CELEBRAR : to celebrate **2** AGASAJAR : to entertain, to wine and dine **3** *Mex fam* : to thrash, to beat
festejo *nm* : celebration, festivity
festín *nm, pl* **festines** : banquet, feast
festinar *vt* : to hasten, to hurry up
festival *nm* : festival
festividad *nf* **1** : festivity **2** : (religious) feast, holiday
festivo, -va *adj* **1** : festive **2 día festivo** : holiday — **festivamente** *adv*
fetal *adj* : fetal
fetiche *nm* : fetish
fétido, -da *adj* : fetid, foul
feto *nm* : fetus
feudal *adj* : feudal — **feudalismo** *nm*
feudo *nm* **1** : fief **2** : domain, territory
fiabilidad *nf* : reliability, trustworthiness
fiable *adj* : trustworthy, reliable
fiado, -da *adj* : on credit

fiador, -dora *n* : bondsman, guarantor
fiambrería *nf* : delicatessen
fiambres *nfpl* : cold cuts
fianza *nf* **1** CAUCIÓN : bail, bond **2** : surety, deposit
fiar {85} *vt* **1** : to sell on credit **2** : to guarantee — **fiarse** *vr* ~ **de** : to place trust in
fiasco *nm* FRACASO : fiasco, failure
fibra *nf* **1** : fiber **2 fibra de vidrio** : fiberglass
fibrilar *vi* : to fibrillate — **fibrilación** *nf*
fibroso, -sa *adj* : fibrous
ficción *nf, pl* **ficciones** **1** : fiction **2** : fabrication, lie
ficha *nf* **1** : index card **2** : file, record **3** : token **4** : domino, checker, counter, poker chip
fichar *vt* **1** : to open a file on **2** : to sign up — *vi* : to punch in, to punch out
fichero *nm* **1** : card file **2** : filing cabinet
ficticio, -cia *adj* : fictitious
fidedigno, -na *adj* FIABLE : reliable, trustworthy
fideicomisario, -ria *n* : trustee
fideicomiso *nm* : trusteeship, trust ⟨guardar en fideicomiso : to hold in trust⟩
fidelidad *nf* : fidelity, faithfulness
fideo *nm* : noodle
fiduciario[1], **-ria** *adj* : fiduciary
fiduciario[2], **-ria** *n* : trustee
fiebre *nf* **1** CALENTURA : fever, temperature ⟨fiebre amarilla : yellow fever⟩ ⟨fiebre palúdica : malaria⟩ **2** : fever, excitement
fiel[1] *adj* **1** : faithful, loyal **2** : accurate — **fielmente** *adv*
fiel[2] *nm* **1** : pointer (of a scale) **2 los fieles** : the faithful
fieltro *nm* : felt
fiera *nf* **1** : wild animal, beast **2** : fiend, demon ⟨una fiera para el trabajo : a demon for work⟩
fiereza *nf* : fierceness, ferocity
fiero, -ra *adj* FEROZ : fierce, ferocious
fierro *nm* HIERRO : iron
fiesta *nf* **1** : party, fiesta **2** : holiday, feast day
figura *nf* **1** : figure **2** : shape, form **3 figura retórica** : figure of speech
figurado, -da *adj* : figurative — **figuradamente** *adv*
figurar *vi* **1** : to figure, to be included ⟨Rivera figura entre los más grandes pintores de México : Rivera is among Mexico's greatest painters⟩ **2** : to be prominent, to stand out — *vt* : to represent ⟨esta línea figura el horizonte : this line represents the horizon⟩ — **figurarse** *vr* : to imagine, to think ⟨¡figúrate el lío en que se metió! : imagine the mess she got into!⟩
fijación *nf, pl* **-ciones** **1** : fixation, obsession **2** : fixing, establishing **3** : fastening, securing
fijador *nm* **1** : fixative **2** : hair spray

fijamente *adv* : fixedly
fijar *vt* **1** : to fasten, to affix **2** ES-TABLECER : to establish, to set up **3** CONCRETAR : to set, to fix ⟨fijar la fecha : to set the date⟩ — **fijarse** *vr* **1** : to settle, to become fixed **2** ~ **en** : to notice, to pay attention to
fijeza *nf* **1** : firmness (of convictions) **2** : persistence, constancy ⟨mirar con fijeza a : to stare at⟩
fijiano, -na *adj & n* : Fijian
fijo, -ja *adj* **1** : fixed, firm, steady **2** PER-MANENTE : permanent
fila *nf* **1** HILERA : line, file ⟨ponerse en fila : to get in line⟩ **2** : rank, row **3** **filas** *nfpl* : ranks ⟨cerrar filas : to close ranks⟩
filamento *nm* : filament
filantropía *nf* : philanthropy
filantrópico, -ca *adj* : philanthropic
filántropo, -pa *n* : philanthropist
filatelia *nf* : philately, stamp collecting
filatelista *nmf* : stamp collector, philatelist
fildeador, -dora *n* : fielder
filete *nm* **1** : fillet **2** SOLOMILLO : sirloin **3** : thread (of a screw)
filiación *nf, pl* **-ciones 1** : affiliation, connection **2** : particulars *pl,* (police) description
filial¹ *adj* : filial
filial² *nf* : affiliate, subsidiary
filibustero *nm* : freebooter, pirate
filigrana *nf* **1** : filigree **2** : watermark (on paper)
filipino, -na *adj & n* : Filipino
filmación *nf, pl* **-ciones** : filming, shooting
filmar *vt* : to film, to shoot
filme *or* **film** *nm* PELÍCULA : film, movie
filmina *nf* : slide, transparency
filo *nm* **1** : cutting edge, blade **2** : edge ⟨al filo del escritorio : at the edge of the desk⟩ ⟨al filo de la medianoche : at the stroke of midnight⟩
filología *nf* : philology
filólogo, -ga *n* : philologist
filón *nm, pl* **filones 1** : seam, vein (of minerals) **2** *fam* : successful business, gold mine
filoso, -sa *adj* : sharp
filosofar *vi* : to philosophize
filosofía *nf* : philosophy
filosófico, -ca *adj* : philosophic, philosophical — **filosóficamente** *adv*
filósofo, -fa *n* : philosopher
filtración *nf* : seepage, leaking
filtrar *v* : to filter — **filtrarse** *vr* : to seep through, to leak
filtro *nm* : filter
filudo, -da *adj* : sharp
fin *nm* **1** : end **2** : purpose, aim, objective **3** **en** ~ : in short **4** **fin de semana** : weekend **5** **por** ~ : finally, at last
finado, -da *adj & n* DIFUNTO : deceased
final¹ *adj* : final, ultimate — **finalmente** *adv*

final² *nm* : end, conclusion, finale
final³ *nf* : final, play-off
finalidad *nf* **1** : purpose, aim **2** : finality
finalista *nmf* : finalist
finalización *nf* : completion, end
finalizar {21} *v* : to finish, to end
financiación *nf, pl* **-ciones** : financing, funding
financiamiento *nm* → **financiación**
financiar *vt* : to finance, to fund
financiero¹, -ra *adj* : financial
financiero², -ra *n* : financier
financista *nmf* : financier
finanzas *nfpl* : finances, finance ⟨altas finanzas : high finance⟩
finca *nf* **1** : farm, ranch **2** : country house
fineza *nf* FINURA, REFINAMIENTO : refinement
fingido, -da *adj* : false, feigned
fingimiento *nm* : pretense
fingir {35} *v* : to feign, to pretend
finiquitar *vt* **1** : to settle (an account) **2** : to conclude, to bring to an end
finiquito *nm* : settlement (of an account)
finito, -ta *adj* : finite
finja, etc. → **fingir**
finlandés, -desa *adj & n* : Finnish
fino, -na *adj* **1** : fine, excellent **2** : delicate, slender **3** REFINADO : refined **4** : sharp, acute ⟨olfato fino : keen sense of smell⟩ **5** : subtle
finta *nf* : feint
fintar *or* **fintear** *vi* : to feint
finura *nf* **1** : fineness, high quality **2** FINEZA, REFINAMIENTO : refinement
fiordo *nm* : fjord
fique *nm* : sisal
firma *nf* **1** : signature **2** : signing **3** EM-PRESA : firm, company
firmamento *nm* : firmament, sky
firmante *nmf* : signer, signatory
firmar *v* : to sign
firme *adj* **1** : firm, resolute **2** : steady, stable
firmemente *adv* : firmly
firmeza *nf* **1** : firmness, stability **2** : strength, resolve
firuletes *nmpl* : frills, adornments
fiscal¹ *adj* : fiscal — **fiscalmente** *adv*
fiscal² *nmf* : district attorney, prosecutor
fiscalizar {21} *vt* **1** : to audit, to inspect **2** : to oversee **3** : to criticize
fisco *nm* : national treasury, exchequer
fisgar {52} *vt* HUSMEAR : to pry into, to snoop on
fisgón, -gona *n, mpl* **fisgones** : snoop, busybody
fisgonear *vi* : to snoop, to pry
fisgue, etc. → **fisgar**
física *nf* : physics
físico¹, -ca *adj* : physical — **físicamente** *adv*
físico², -ca *n* : physicist
físico³ *nm* : physique, figure
fisiología *nf* : physiology

fisiológico, -ca *adj* : physiological, physiologic

fisiólogo, -ga *n* : physiologist

fisión *nf, pl* **fisiones** : fission — **fisionable** *adj*

fisonomía → **fisonomía**

fisioterapeuta *nmf* : physical therapist

fisioterapia *nf* : physical therapy

fisonomía *nf* : physiognomy, features *pl*

fistol *nm* *Mex* : tie clip

fisura *nf* : fissure, crevasse

fláccido, -da *or* **flácido, -da** *adj* : flaccid, flabby

flaco, -ca *adj* **1** DELGADO : thin, skinny **2** : feeble, weak ⟨una flaca excusa : a feeble excuse⟩

flagelar *vt* : to flagellate — **flagelación** *nf*

flagelo *nm* **1** : scourge, whip **2** : calamity

flagrante *adj* : flagrant, glaring, blatant — **flagrantemente** *adv*

flama *nf* LLAMA : flame

flamante *adj* **1** : bright, brilliant **2** : brand-new

flamear *vi* **1** LLAMEAR : to flame, to blaze **2** ONDEAR : to flap, to flutter

flamenco¹, -ca *adj* **1** : flamenco **2** : Flemish

flamenco², -ca *n* : Fleming, Flemish person

flamenco³ *nm* **1** : Flemish (language) **2** : flamingo **3** : flamenco (music or dance)

flanco *nm* : flank, side

flanquear *vt* : to flank

flaquear *vi* DECAER : to flag, to weaken

flaqueza *nf* **1** DEBILIDAD : frailty, feebleness **2** : thinness **3** : weakness, failing

flato *nm* : gloom, melancholy

flatulento, -ta *adj* : flatulent — **flatulencia** *nf*

flauta *nf* **1** : flute **2 flauta dulce** : recorder

flautín *nm, pl* **flautines** : piccolo

flautista *nmf* : flute player, flutist

flebitis *nf* : phlebitis

flecha *nf* : arrow

fleco *nm* **1** : bangs *pl* **2** : fringe

flema *nf* : phlegm

flemático, -ca *adj* : phlegmatic, stolid, impassive

flequillo *nm* : bangs *pl*

fletar *vt* **1** : to charter, to hire **2** : to load (freight)

flete *nm* **1** : charter fee **2** : shipping cost **3** : freight, cargo

fletero *nm* : shipper, carrier

flexibilidad *nf* : flexibility

flexibilizar {21} *vt* : to make more flexible

flexible¹ *adj* : flexible

flexible² *nm* **1** : flexible electrical cord **2** : soft hat

flirtear *vi* : to flirt

flojear *vi* **1** DEBILITARSE : to weaken, to flag **2** : to idle, to loaf around

flojedad *nf* : weakness

flojera *nf fam* **1** : lethargy, feeling of weakness **2** : laziness

flojo, -ja *adj* **1** SUELTO : loose, slack **2** : weak, poor ⟨está flojo en las ciencias : he's weak in science⟩ **3** PEREZOSO : lazy

flor *nf* **1** : flower **2 flor de Pascua** : poinsettia

flora *nf* : flora

floración *nf* : flowering ⟨en plena floración : in full bloom⟩

floral *adj* : floral

floreado, -da *adj* : flowered, flowery

florear *vi* FLORECER : to flower, to bloom — *vt* **1** : to adorn with flowers **2** *Mex* : to flatter, to compliment

florecer {53} *vi* **1** : to bloom, to blossom **2** : to flourish, to thrive

floreciente *adj* **1** : flowering **2** PRÓSPERO : flourishing, thriving

florecimiento *nm* : flowering

floreo *nm* : flourish

florería *nf* : flower shop, florist's

florero¹, -ra *n* : florist

florero² *nm* JARRÓN : vase

floresta *nf* **1** : glade, grove **2** BOSQUE : woods

florido, -da *adj* **1** : full of flowers **2** : florid, flowery ⟨escritos floridos : flowery prose⟩

florista *nmf* : florist

florituri *nf* : frill, embellishment

flota *nf* : fleet

flotabilidad *nf* : buoyancy

flotación *nf, pl* **-ciones** : flotation

flotador *nm* **1** : float **2** : life preserver

flotante *adj* : floating, buoyant

flotar *vi* : to float

flote *nm* **a ~** : afloat

flotilla *nf* : flotilla, fleet

fluctuar {3} *vi* **1** : to fluctuate **2** VACILAR : to vacillate — **fluctuación** *nf* — **fluctuante** *adj*

fluidez *nf* **1** : fluency **2** : fluidity

fluido¹, -da *adj* **1** : flowing **2** : fluent **3** : fluid

fluido² *nm* : fluid

fluir {41} *vi* : to flow

flujo *nm* **1** : flow **2** : discharge

flúor *nm* : fluorine

fluoración *nf, pl* **-ciones** : fluoridation

fluorescencia *nf* : fluorescence — **fluorescente** *adj*

fluorizar {21} *vt* : to fluoridate

fluoruro *nm* : fluoride

fluvial *adj* : fluvial, river

fluye, etc. → **fluir**

fobia *nf* : phobia

foca *nf* : seal (animal)

focal *adj* : focal

focha *nf* : coot

foco *nm* **1** : focus **2** : center, pocket **3** : lightbulb **4** : spotlight **5** : headlight

fofo, -fa *adj* **1** ESPONJOSO : soft, spongy **2** : flabby

fogaje *nm* **1** FUEGO : skin eruption, cold sore **2** BOCHORNO : hot and humid weather

fogata *nf* : bonfire
fogón *nm, pl* **fogones** : bonfire
fogonazo *nm* : flash, explosion
fogonero, -ra *n* : stoker (of a furnace), fireman
fogoso, -sa *adj* ARDIENTE : ardent
foguear *vt* : to inure, to accustom
foja *nf* : sheet (of paper)
folículo *nm* : follicle
folio *nm* : folio, leaf
folklore *nm* : folklore
folklórico, -ca *adj* : folk, traditional
follaje *nm* : foliage
folleto *nm* : pamphlet, leaflet, circular
fomentar *vt* **1** : to foment, to stir up **2** PROMOVER : to promote, to foster
fomento *nm* : promotion, encouragement
fonda *nf* **1** POSADA : inn **2** : small restaurant
fondeado, -da *adj fam* : rich, in the money
fondear *vt* **1** : to sound **2** : to sound out, to examine **3** *Mex* : to fund, to finance — *vi* ANCLAR : to anchor — **fondearse** *vr fam* : to get rich
fondeo *nm* **1** : anchoring **2** *Mex* : funding, financing
fondillos *mpl* : seat, bottom (of clothing)
fondo *nm* **1** : bottom **2** : rear, back, end **3** : depth **4** : background **5** : sea bed **6** : fund ⟨fondo de inversiones : investment fund⟩ **7** *Mex* : slip, petticoat **8 fondos** *nmpl* : funds, resources ⟨cheque sin fondos : bounced check⟩ **9 a ～** : thoroughly, in depth **10 en ～** : abreast
fonema *nm* : phoneme
fonética *nf* : phonetics
fonético, -ca *adj* : phonetic
fontanería *nf* PLOMERÍA : plumbing
fontanero, -ra *n* PLOMERO : plumber
footing [ˈfuˌtɪŋ] *nm* : jogging ⟨hacer footing : to jog⟩
foque *nm* : jib
forajido, -da *n* : bandit, fugitive, outlaw
foráneo, -nea *adj* : foreign, strange
forastero, -ra *n* : stranger, outsider
forcejear *vi* : to struggle
forcejeo *nm* : struggle
fórceps *nms & pl* : forceps *pl*
forense *adj* : forensic, legal
forestal *adj* : forest
forja *nf* FRAGUA : forge
forjar *vt* **1** : to forge **2** : to shape, to create ⟨forjar un compromiso : to hammer out a compromise⟩ **3** : to invent, to concoct
forma *nf* **1** : form, shape **2** MANERA, MODO : manner, way **3** : fitness ⟨estar en forma : to be fit, to be in shape⟩ **4 formas** *nfpl* : appearances, conventions
formación *nf, pl* **-ciones** **1** : formation **2** : training ⟨formación profesional : vocational training⟩

formal *adj* **1** : formal **2** : serious, dignified **3** : dependable, reliable
formaldehído *nm* : formaldehyde
formalidad *nf* **1** : formality **2** : seriousness, dignity **3** : dependability, reliability
formalizar {21} *vt* : to formalize, to make official
formalmente *adv* : formally
formar *vt* **1** : to form, to make **2** CONSTITUIR : to constitute, to make up **3** : to train, to educate — **formarse** *vr* **1** DESARROLLARSE : to develop, to take shape **2** EDUCARSE : to be educated
formatear *vt* : to format
formativo, -va *adj* : formative
formato *nm* : format
formidable *adj* **1** : formidable, tremendous **2** *fam* : fantastic, terrific
formón *nm, pl* **formones** : chisel
fórmula *nf* : formula
formulación *nf, pl* **-ciones** : formulation
formular *vt* **1** : to formulate, to draw up **2** : to make, to lodge (a protest or complaint)
formulario *nm* : form ⟨rellenar un formulario : to fill out a form⟩
fornicar {72} *vi* : to fornicate — **fornicación** *nf*
fornido, -da *adj* : well-built, burly, hefty
foro *nm* **1** : forum **2** : public assembly, open discussion
forraje *nm* **1** : forage, fodder **2** : foraging **3** *fam* : hodgepodge
forrajear *vt* : to forage
forrar *vt* **1** : to line (a garment) **2** : to cover (a book)
forro *nm* **1** : lining **2** CUBIERTA : book cover
forsitia *nf* : forsythia
fortachón, -chona *adj, pl* **-chones** *fam* : brawny, strong, tough
fortalecer {53} *vt* : to strengthen, to fortify — **fortalecerse** *vr*
fortalecimiento *nm* **1** : strengthening, fortifying **2** : fortifications
fortaleza *nf* **1** : fortress **2** FUERZA : strength **3** : resolution, fortitude
fortificación *nf, pl* **-ciones** : fortification
fortificar {72} *vt* **1** : to fortify **2** : to strengthen
fortín *nm, pl* **fortines** : small fort
fortuito, -ta *adj* : fortuitous
fortuna *nf* **1** SUERTE : fortune, luck **2** RIQUEZA : wealth, fortune
forzar {36} *vt* **1** OBLIGAR : to force, to compel **2** : to force open **3** : to strain ⟨forzar los ojos : to strain one's eyes⟩
forzosamente *adv* **1** : forcibly, by force **2** : necessarily, inevitably ⟨forzosamente tendrán que pagar : they'll have no choice but to pay⟩
forzoso, -sa *adj* **1** : forced, compulsory **2** : necessary, inevitable
fosa *nf* **1** : ditch, pit ⟨fosa séptica : septic tank⟩ **2** TUMBA : grave **3** : cavity ⟨fosas nasales : nasal cavities, nostrils⟩
fosfato *nm* : phosphate

fosforescencia *nf* : phosphorescence — **fosforescente** *adj*

fósforo *nm* **1** CERILLA : match **2** : phosphorus

fósil[1] *adj* : fossilized, fossil

fósil[2] *nm* : fossil

fosilizarse {21} *vr* : to fossilize, to become fossilized

foso *nm* **1** FOSA, ZANJA : ditch **2** : pit (of a theater) **3** : moat

foto *nf* : photo, picture

fotocopia *nf* : photocopy — **fotocopiar** *vt*

fotocopiadora *nf* COPIADORA : photocopier

fotoeléctrico, -ca *adj* : photoelectric

fotogénico, -ca *adj* : photogenic

fotografía *nf* **1** : photograph **2** : photography

fotografiar {85} *vt* : to photograph

fotográfico, -ca *adj* : photographic — **fotográficamente** *adv*

fotógrafo, -fa *n* : photographer

fotosíntesis *nf* : photosynthesis

fotosintético, -ca *adj* : photosynthetic

fracasado[1], **-da** *adj* : unsuccessful, failed

fracasado[2], **-da** *n* : failure

fracasar *vi* **1** FALLAR : to fail **2** : to fall through

fracaso *nm* FIASCO : failure

fracción *nf, pl* **fracciones 1** : fraction **2** : part, fragment **3** : faction, splinter group

fraccionamiento *nm* **1** : division, breaking up **2** *Mex* : residential area, housing development

fraccionar *vt* : to divide, to break up

fraccionario, -ria *adj* : fractional

fractura *nf* **1** : fracture **2 fractura complicada** : compound fracture

fracturarse *vr* QUEBRARSE, ROMPERSE : to fracture, to break ⟨fracturarse el brazo : to break one's arm⟩

fragancia *nf* : fragrance, scent

fragante *adj* : fragrant

fragata *nf* : frigate

frágil *adj* **1** : fragile **2** : frail, delicate

fragilidad *nf* **1** : fragility **2** : frailty, delicacy

fragmentar *vt* : to fragment — **fragmentación** *nf*

fragmentario, -ria *adj* : fragmentary, sketchy

fragmento *nm* **1** : fragment, shard **2** : bit, snippet **3** : excerpt, passage

fragor *nm* : clamor, din, roar

fragoroso, -sa *adj* : thunderous, deafening

fragoso, -sa *adj* **1** : rough, uneven **2** : thick, dense

fragua *nf* FORJA : forge

fraguar {10} *vt* **1** : to forge **2** : to conceive, to concoct, to hatch — *vi* : to set, to solidify

fraile *nm* : friar, monk

frambuesa *nf* : raspberry

francamente *adv* **1** : frankly, candidly **2** REALMENTE : really ⟨es francamente admirable : it's really impressive⟩

francés[1], **-cesa** *adj, mpl* **franceses** : French

francés[2], **-cesa** *n, mpl* **franceses** : French person, Frenchman *m*, Frenchwoman *f*

francés[3] *nm* : French (language)

franciscano, -na *adj & n* : Franciscan

francmasón, -sona *n, mpl* **-sones** : Freemason — **francmasonería** *nf*

franco[1], **-ca** *adj* **1** CÁNDIDO : frank, candid **2** PATENTE : clear, obvious **3** : free ⟨franco a bordo : free on board⟩

franco[2] *nm* : franc

francotirador, -dora *n* : sniper

franela *nf* : flannel

franja *nf* **1** : stripe, band **2** : border, fringe

franquear *vt* **1** : to clear **2** ATRAVESAR : to cross, to go through **3** : to pay the postage on

franqueo *nm* : postage

franqueza *nf* : frankness

franquicia *nf* **1** EXENCIÓN : exemption **2** : franchise

frasco *nm* : small bottle, flask, vial

frase *nf* **1** : phrase **2** ORACIÓN : sentence

frasear *vt* : to phrase

fraternal *adj* : fraternal, brotherly

fraternidad *nf* **1** : brotherhood **2** : fraternity

fraternizar {21} *vi* : to fraternize — **fraternización** *nf*

fraterno, -na *adj* : fraternal, brotherly

fratricida *adj* : fratricidal

fratricidio *nm* : fratricide

fraude *nm* : fraud

fraudulento, -ta *adj* : fraudulent — **fraudulentamente** *adv*

fray *nm* : brother (title of a friar) ⟨Fray Bartolomé : Brother Bartholomew⟩

frazada *nf* COBIJA, MANTA : blanket

frecuencia *nf* : frequency

frecuentar *vt* : to frequent, to haunt

frecuente *adj* : frequent — **frecuentemente** *adv*

fregadera *nf fam* : hassle, pain in the neck

fregadero *nm* : kitchen sink

fregado[1], **-da** *adj fam* : annoying, bothersome

fregado[2] *nm* **1** : scrubbing, scouring **2** *fam* : mess, muddle

fregar {49} *vt* **1** : to scrub, to scour, to wash ⟨fregar los trastes : to do the dishes⟩ ⟨fregar el suelo : to scrub the floor⟩ **2** *fam* : to annoy — *vi* **1** : to wash the dishes **2** : to clean, to scrub **3** *fam* : to be annoying

freidera *nf Mex* : frying pan

freír {37} *vt* : to fry — **freírse** *vr*

frenar *vt* **1** : to brake **2** DETENER : to curb, to check — *vi* : to apply the brakes — **frenarse** *vr* : to restrain oneself

frenesí *nm* : frenzy
frenético, -ca *adj* : frantic, frenzied — **frenéticamente** *adv*
freno *nm* **1** : brake **2** : bit (of a bridle) **3** : check, restraint **4 frenos** *nmpl Mex* : braces (for teeth)
frente¹ *nm* **1** : front ⟨al frente de : at the head of⟩ ⟨en frente : in front, opposite⟩ **2** : facade **3** : front line, sphere of activity **4** : front (in meteorology) ⟨frente frío : cold front⟩ **5 hacer frente a** : to face up to, to brave
frente² *nf* **1** : forehead, brow **2 frente a frente** : face to face
fresa *nf* **1** : strawberry **2** : drill (in dentistry)
fresco¹, -ca *adj* **1** : fresh **2** : cool **3** *fam* : insolent, nervy
fresco² *nm* **1** : coolness **2** : fresh air ⟨al fresco : in the open air, outdoors⟩ **3** : fresco
frescor *nm* : cool air ⟨el frescor de la noche : the cool of the evening⟩
frescura *nf* **1** : freshness **2** : coolness **3** : calmness **4** DESCARO : nerve, audacity
fresno *nm* : ash (tree)
freza *nf* : spawn, roe
frezar {21} *vi* DESOVAR : to spawn
friable *adj* : friable
frialdad *nf* **1** : coldness **2** INDIFEREN-CIA : indifference, unconcern
fríamente *adv* : coldly, indifferently
fricasé *nm* : fricassee
fricción *nf, pl* **fricciones 1** : friction **2** : rubbing, massage **3** : discord, disagreement ⟨fricción entre los hermanos : friction between the brothers⟩
friccionar *vt* **1** FROTAR : to rub **2** : to massage
friega¹, friegue, etc. → **fregar**
friega² *nf* **1** FRICCIÓN : rubdown, massage **2** : annoyance, bother
frigidez *nf* : (sexual) frigidity
frigorífico *nm Spain* : refrigerator
frijol *nm* : bean ⟨frijoles refritos : refried beans⟩
frío¹, fría *adj* **1** : cold **2** INDIFERENTE : cool, indifferent
frío² *nm* **1** : cold ⟨hace mucho frío esta noche : it's very cold tonight⟩ **2** IN-DIFERENCIA : coldness, indifference **3 tener frío** : to feel cold ⟨tengo frío : I'm cold⟩ **4 tomar frío** RESFRIARSE : to catch a cold
friolento, -ta *adj* : sensitive to cold
friolera *nf (used ironically or humorously)* : trifling amount ⟨una friolera de mil dólares : a mere thousand dollars⟩
friso *nm* : frieze
fritar *vt* : to fry
frito¹ *pp* → **freír**
frito², -ta *adj* **1** : fried **2** *fam* : worn-out, fed up ⟨tener frito a alguien : to get on someone's nerves⟩ **3** *fam* : fast asleep ⟨se quedó frito en el sofá : she fell asleep on the couch⟩
fritura *nf* **1** : frying **2** : fried food

frivolidad *nf* : frivolity
frívolo, -la *adj* : frivolous — **frívolamente** *adv*
fronda *nf* **1** : frond **2 frondas** *nfpl* : foliage
frondoso, -sa *adj* : leafy, luxuriant
frontal *adj* : frontal, head-on ⟨un choque frontal : a head-on collision⟩
frontalmente *adv* : head-on
frontera *nf* : border, frontier
fronterizo, -za *adj* : border, on the border ⟨estados fronterizos : neighboring states⟩
frontispicio *nm* : frontispiece
frotar *vt* **1** : to rub **2** : to strike (a match) — **frotarse** *vr* : to rub (together)
frote *nm* : rubbing, rub
fructífero, -ra *adj* : fruitful, productive
fructificar {72} *vi* **1** : to bear or produce fruit **2** : to be productive
fructuoso, -sa *adj* : fruitful
frugal *adj* : frugal, thrifty — **frugalmente** *adv*
frugalidad *adj* : frugality
frunce *nm* : gather (in cloth), pucker
fruncido *nm* : gathering, shirring
fruncir {83} *vt* **1** : to gather, to shirr **2 fruncir el ceño** : to knit one's brow, to frown **3 fruncir la boca** : to pucker up, to purse one's lips
frunza, etc. → **fruncir**
frustración *nf, pl* **-ciones** : frustration
frustrado, -da *adj* **1** : frustrated **2** : failed, unsuccessful
frustrante *adj* : frustrating
frustrar *vt* : to frustrate, to thwart — **frustrarse** *vr* FRACASAR : to fail, to come to nothing ⟨se frustraron sus esperanzas : his hopes were dashed⟩
fruta *nf* : fruit
frutal¹ *adj* : fruit, fruit-bearing
frutal² *nm* : fruit tree
frutilla *nf* : South American strawberry
fruto *nm* **1** : fruit, agricultural product ⟨los frutos de la tierra : the fruits of the earth⟩ **2** : result, consequence ⟨los frutos de su trabajo : the fruits of his labor⟩
fucsia *adj & nm* : fuchsia
fue, etc. → **ir, ser**
fuego *nm* **1** : fire **2** : light ⟨¿tienes fuego? : have you got a light?⟩ **3** : flame, burner (on a stove) **4** : ardor, passion **5** FOGAJE : skin eruption, cold sore **6 fuegos artificiales** *nmpl* : fireworks
fuelle *nm* : bellows
fuente *nf* **1** MANANTIAL : spring **2** : fountain **3** ORIGEN : source ⟨fuentes informativas : sources of information⟩ **4** : platter, serving dish
fuera *adv* **1** : outside, out **2** : abroad, away **3** ～ **de** : outside of, out of, beyond **4** ～ **de** : besides, in addition to ⟨fuera de eso : aside from that⟩ **5 fuera de lugar** : out of place, amiss
fuerce, fuerza etc. → **forzar**

fuero *nm* **1** JURISDICCIÓN : jurisdiction **2** : privilege, exemption **3 fuero interno** : conscience, heart of hearts
fuerte[1] *adv* **1** : strongly, tightly, hard **2** : loudly **3** : abundantly
fuerte[2] *adj* **1** : strong **2** : intense ⟨un fuerte dolor : an intense pain⟩ **3** : loud **4** : extreme, excessive
fuerte[3] *nm* **1** : fort, stronghold **2** : forte, strong point
fuerza *nf* **1** : strength, vigor ⟨fuerza de voluntad : willpower⟩ **2** : force ⟨fuerza bruta : brute force⟩ **3** : power, might ⟨fuerza de brazos : manpower⟩ **4 fuerzas** *nfpl* : forces ⟨fuerzas armadas : armed forces⟩ **5 a fuerza de** : by, by dint of
fuetazo *nm* : lash
fuga *nf* **1** HUIDA : flight, escape **2** : fugue **3** : leak ⟨fuga de gas : gas leak⟩
fugarse {52} *vr* **1** : to escape **2** HUIR : to flee, to run away **3** : to elope
fugaz *adj, pl* **fugaces** : brief, fleeting
fugitivo, -va *adj & n* : fugitive
fulana *nf* : hooker, slut
fulano, -na *n* : so-and-so, what's-his-name, what's-her-name ⟨fulano, mengano, y zutano : Tom, Dick, and Harry⟩ ⟨señora fulana de tal : Mrs. so-and-so⟩
fulcro *nm* : fulcrum
fulgor *nm* : brilliance, splendor
fulgurar *vi* : to shine brightly, to gleam, to glow
fulminante *adj* **1** : fulminating, explosive **2** : devastating, terrible ⟨una mirada fulminante : a withering look⟩
fulminar *vt* **1** : to strike with lightning **2** : to strike down ⟨fulminar a alguien con la mirada : to look daggers at someone⟩
fumador, -dora *n* : smoker
fumar *v* : to smoke
fumble *nm* : fumble (in football)
fumblear *vt* : to fumble (in football)
fumigante *nm* : fumigant
fumigar {52} *vt* : to fumigate — **fumigación** *nf*
funámbulo, -la *n* EQUILIBRISTA : tightrope walker
función *nf, pl* **funciones 1** : function **2** : duty **3** : performance, show
funcional *adj* : functional — **funcionalmente** *adv*
funcionamiento *nm* **1** : functioning **2 en** ~ : in operation
funcionar *vi* **1** : to function **2** : to run, to work
funcionario, -ria *n* : civil servant, official
funda *nf* **1** : case, cover, sheath **2** : pillowcase
fundación *nf, pl* **-ciones** : foundation, establishment
fundado, -da *adj* : well-founded, justified
fundador, -dora *n* : founder

fundamental *adj* BÁSICO : fundamental, basic — **fundamentalmente** *adv*
fundamentalismo *nm* : fundamentalism
fundamentalista *nmf* : fundamentalist
fundamentar *vt* **1** : to lay the foundations for **2** : to support, to back up **3** : to base, to found
fundamento *nm* : basis, foundation, groundwork
fundar *vt* **1** ESTABLECER, INSTITUIR : to found, to establish **2** BASAR : to base — **fundarse** *vr* ~ **en** : to be based on, to stem from
fundición *nf, pl* **-ciones 1** : founding, smelting **2** : foundry
fundir *vt* **1** : to melt down, to smelt **2** : to fuse, to merge **3** : to burn out (a lightbulb) — **fundirse** *vr* **1** : to fuse together, to blend, to merge **2** : to melt, to thaw **3** : to fade (in television or movies)
fúnebre *adj* **1** : funeral, funereal **2** LÚGUBRE : gloomy, mournful
funeral[1] *adj* : funeral, funerary
funeral[2] *nm* **1** : funeral **2 funerales** *nmpl* EXEQUIAS : funeral rites
funeraria *nf* **1** : funeral home, funeral parlor **2 director de funeraria** : funeral director, undertaker
funerario, -ria *adj* : funeral
funesto, -ta *adj* : terrible, disastrous ⟨consecuencias funestas : disastrous consequences⟩
fungicida[1] *adj* : fungicidal
fungicida[2] *nm* : fungicide
fungir {35} *vi* : to act, to function ⟨fungir de asesor : to act as a consultant⟩
fungoso, -sa *adj* : fungous
funja, etc. → **fungir**
furgón *nm, pl* **furgones 1** : van, truck **2** : freight car, boxcar **3 furgón de cola** : caboose
furgoneta *nf* : van
furia *nf* **1** CÓLERA, IRA : fury, rage **2** : violence, fury ⟨la furia de la tormenta : the fury of the storm⟩
furibundo, -da *adj* : furious
furiosamente *adv* : furiously, frantically
furioso, -sa *adj* **1** AIRADO : furious, irate **2** : intense, violent
furor *nm* **1** : fury, rage **2** : violence (of the elements) **3** : passion, frenzy **4** : enthusiasm ⟨hacer furor : to be all the rage⟩
furtivo, -va *adj* : furtive — **furtivamente** *adv*
furúnculo *nm* DIVIESO : boil
fuselaje *nm* : fuselage
fusible *nm* : (electrical) fuse
fusil *nm* : rifle
fusilar *vt* **1** : to shoot, to execute (by firing squad) **2** *fam* : to plagiarize, to pirate
fusilería *nf* **1** : rifles *pl*, rifle fire **2 descarga de fusilería** : fusillade
fusión *nf, pl* **fusiones 1** : fusion **2** : union, merger

fusionar *vt* **1** : to fuse **2** : to merge, to amalgamate — **fusionarse** *vr*

fusta *nf* : riding crop

fustigar {52} *vt* **1** AZOTAR : to whip, to lash **2** : to upbraid, to berate

futbol *or* **fútbol** *nm* **1** : soccer **2 futbol americano** : football

futbolista *nmf* : soccer player

futesa *nf* **1** : small thing, trifle **2 futesas** *nfpl* : small talk

fútil *adj* : trifling, trivial

futurista *adj* : futuristic

futuro[1], **-ra** *adj* : future

futuro[2] *nm* PORVENIR : future

G

g *nf* : seventh letter of the Spanish alphabet

gabán *nm, pl* **gabanes** : topcoat, overcoat

gabardina *nf* **1** : gabardine **2** : trench coat, raincoat

gabarra *nf* : barge

gabinete *nm* **1** : cabinet (in government) **2** : study, office (in the home) **3** : (professional) office

gablete *nm* : gable

gabonés, -nesa *adj & n, mpl* **-neses** : Gabonese

gacela *nf* : gazelle

gaceta *nf* : gazette, newspaper

gachas *nfpl* : porridge

gacho, -cha *adj* **1** : drooping, turned downward **2** *Mex fam* : nasty, awful **3 ir a gachas** *fam* : to go on all fours

gaélico[1], **-ca** *adj* : Gaelic

gaélico[2] *nm* : Gaelic (language)

gafas *nfpl* ANTEOJOS : eyeglasses, glasses

gaita *nf* : bagpipes *pl*

gajes *nmpl* **gajes del oficio** : occupational hazards

gajo *nm* **1** : broken branch (of a tree) **2** : cluster, bunch (of fruit) **3** : segment (of citrus fruit)

gala *nf* **1** : gala ⟨vestido de gala : formal dress⟩ ⟨tener algo a gala : to be proud of something⟩ **2 galas** *nfpl* : finery, attire

galáctico, -ca *adj* : galactic

galán *nm, pl* **galanes** **1** : ladies' man, gallant **2** : leading man, hero **3** : boyfriend, suitor

galano, -na *adj* **1** : elegant **2** *Mex* : mottled

galante *adj* : gallant, attentive — **galantemente** *adv*

galantear *vt* **1** CORTEJAR : to court, to woo **2** : to flirt with

galanteo *nm* **1** CORTEJO : courtship **2** : flirtation, flirting

galantería *nf* **1** : gallantry, attentiveness **2** : compliment

galápago *nm* : aquatic turtle

galardón *nm, pl* **-dones** : award, prize

galardonado, -da *adj* : prize-winning

galardonar *vt* : to give an award to

galaxia *nf* : galaxy

galeno *nm fam* : physician, doctor

galeón *nm, pl* **galeones** : galleon

galera *nf* : galley

galería *nf* **1** : gallery, balcony (in a theater) ⟨galería comercial : shopping mall⟩ **2** : corridor, passage

galerón *n, mpl* **-rones** *Mex* : large hall

galés[1], **-lesa** *adj* : Welsh

galés[2], **-lesa** *n, mpl* **galeses** **1** : Welshman *m*, Welshwoman *f* **2 los galeses** : the Welsh

galés[3] *nm* : Welsh (language)

galgo *nm* : greyhound

galimatías *nms & pl* : gibberish, nonsense

galio *nm* : gallium

gallardete *nm* : pennant, streamer

gallardía *nf* **1** VALENTÍA : bravery **2** APOSTURA : elegance, gracefulness

gallardo, -da *adj* **1** VALIENTE : brave **2** APUESTO : elegant, graceful

gallear *vi* : to show off, to strut around

gallego[1], **-ga** *adj* **1** : Galician **2** *fam* : Spanish

gallego[2], **-ga** *n* **1** : Galician **2** *fam* : Spaniard

galleta *nf* **1** : cookie **2** : cracker

gallina *nf* **1** : hen **2 gallina de Guinea** : guinea fowl

gallinazo *nm* : vulture, buzzard

gallinero *nm* : chicken coop, henhouse

gallito, -ta *adj fam* : cocky, belligerent

gallo *nm* **1** : rooster, cock **2** *fam* : squeak or crack in the voice **3** *Mex* : serenade **4 gallo de pelea** : gamecock

galo[1], **-la** *adj* **1** : Gaulish **2** : French

galo[2], **-la** *n* : Frenchman *m*, Frenchwoman *f*

galocha *nf* : galosh

galón *nm, pl* **galones** **1** : gallon **2** : stripe (military insignia)

galopada *nf* : gallop

galopante *adj* : galloping ⟨inflación galopante : galloping inflation⟩

galopar *vi* : to gallop

galope *nm* : gallop

galpón *nm, pl* **galpones** : shed, storehouse

galvanizar {21} *vt* : to galvanize — **galvanización** *nf*

gama *nf* **1** : range, spectrum, gamut **2** → **gamo**

gamba *nf* : large shrimp, prawn

gamberro, -rra *n Spain* : hooligan, troublemaker

gambiano, -na *adj & n* : Gambian

gambito *nm* : gambit (in chess)

gameto *nm* : gamete

gamo, -ma *n* : fallow deer
gamuza *nf* **1** : suede **2** : chamois
gana *nf* **1** : desire, inclination **2 de buena gana** : willingly, readily, gladly **3 de mala gana** : reluctantly, halfheartedly **4 tener ganas de** : to feel like, to be in the mood for ⟨tengo ganas de bailar : I feel like dancing⟩ **5 ponerle ganas a algo** : to put effort into something
ganadería *nf* **1** : cattle raising, stockbreeding **2** : cattle ranch **3** GANADO : cattle *pl*, livestock
ganadero¹, -ra *adj* : cattle, ranching
ganadero², -ra *n* : rancher, stockbreeder
ganado *nm* **1** : cattle *pl*, livestock **2 ganado ovino** : sheep *pl* **3 ganado porcino** : swine *pl*
ganador¹, -dora *adj* : winning
ganador², -dora *n* : winner
ganancia *nf* **1** : profit **2 ganancias** *nfpl* : winnings, gains
ganancioso, -sa *adj* : profitable
ganar *vt* **1** : to win **2** : to gain ⟨ganar tiempo : to buy time⟩ **3** : to earn ⟨ganar dinero : to make money⟩ **4** : to acquire, to obtain — *vi* **1** : to win **2** : to profit ⟨salir ganando : to come out ahead⟩ — **ganarse** *vr* **1** : to gain, to win ⟨ganarse a alguien : to win someone over⟩ **2** : to earn ⟨ganarse la vida : to make a living⟩ **3** : to deserve
gancho *nm* **1** : hook **2** : clothes hanger **3** : hairpin, bobby pin **4** Col : safety pin
gandul¹ *nm* CA, Car, Col : pigeon pea
gandul², -dula *n fam* : idler, lazybones
gandulear *vi* : to idle, to loaf, to lounge about
ganga *nf* : bargain
ganglio *nm* **1** : ganglion **2** : gland
gangrena *nf* : gangrene — **gangrenoso, -sa** *adj*
gángster *nmf, pl* **gángsters** : gangster
gansada *nf* : silly thing, nonsense
ganso, -sa *n* **1** : goose, gander *m* **2** : idiot, fool
gañido *nm* : yelp (of a dog)
gañir {38} *vi* : to yelp
garabatear *v* : to scribble, to scrawl, to doodle
garabato *nm* **1** : doodle **2 garabatos** *nmpl* : scribble, scrawl
garaje *nm* : garage
garante *nmf* : guarantor
garantía *nf* **1** : guarantee, warranty **2** : security ⟨garantía de trabajo : job security⟩
garantizar {21} *vt* : to guarantee
garapiña *nf* : pineapple drink
garapiñar *vt* : to candy
garbanzo *nm* : chickpea, garbanzo
garbo *nm* **1** DONAIRE : grace, poise **2** : jauntiness
garboso, -sa *adj* **1** : graceful **2** : elegant, stylish
garceta *nf* : egret

gardenia *nf* : gardenia
garfio *nm* : hook, gaff, grapnel
gargajo *nm fam* : phlegm
garganta *nf* **1** : throat **2** : neck (of a person or a bottle) **3** : ravine, narrow pass
gargantilla *nf* : choker, necklace
gárgara *nf* **1** : gargle, gargling **2 hacer gárgaras** : to gargle
gargarizar *vi* : to gargle
gárgola *nf* : gargoyle
garita *nf* **1** : cabin, hut **2** : sentry box, lookout post
garoso, -sa *adj* Col, Ven : gluttonous, greedy
garra *nf* **1** : claw **2** : hand, paw **3 garras** *nfpl* : claws, clutches ⟨caer en las garras de alguien : to fall into someone's clutches⟩
garrafa *nf* : decanter, carafe
garrafal *adj* : terrible, monstrous
garrafón *nm, pl* **-fones** : large decanter, large bottle
garrapata *nf* : tick
garrobo *nm* CA : large lizard, iguana
garrocha *nf* **1** PICA : lance, pike **2** : pole ⟨salto con garrocha : pole vault⟩
garrotazo *nm* : blow (with a club)
garrote *nm* **1** : club, stick **2** Mex : brake
garúa *nf* : drizzle
garuar {3} *v impers* LLOVIZNAR : to drizzle
garza *nf* : heron
gas *nm* : gas, vapor, fumes *pl* ⟨gas lagrimógeno : tear gas⟩
gasa *nf* : gauze
gasear *vt* **1** : to gas **2** : to aerate (a liquid)
gaseosa *nf* REFRESCO : soda, soft drink
gaseoso, -sa *adj* **1** : gaseous **2** : carbonated, fizzy
gasoducto *nm* : gas pipeline
gasolina *nf* : gasoline, gas
gasolinera *nf* : gas station, service station
gastado, -da *adj* **1** : spent **2** : worn, worn-out
gastador¹, -dora *adj* : extravagant, spendthrift
gastador², -dora *n* : spendthrift
gastar *vt* **1** : to spend **2** CONSUMIR : to consume, to use up **3** : to squander, to waste **4** : to wear ⟨gasta un bigote : he sports a mustache⟩ — **gastarse** *vr* **1** : to spend, to expend **2** : to run down, to wear out
gasto *nm* **1** : expense, expenditure **2** DETERIORO : wear **3 gastos generales** *or* **gastos indirectos** : overhead
gástrico, -ca *adj* : gastric
gastritis *nf* : gastritis
gastronomía *nf* : gastronomy
gastronómico, -ca *adj* : gastronomic
gastrónomo, -ma *n* : gourmet
gatas *adv* **andar a gatas** : to crawl, to go on all fours
gatear *vi* **1** : to crawl **2** : to climb, to clamber (up)

gatillero *nm Mex* : gunman
gatillo *nm* : trigger
gatito, -ta *n* : kitten
gato[1], -ta *n* : cat
gato[2] *nm* : jack (for an automobile)
gauchada *nf Arg, Uru* : favor, kindness
gaucho *nm* : gaucho
gaveta *nf* 1 CAJÓN : drawer 2 : till
gavilla *nf* 1 : gang, band 2 : sheaf
gaviota *nf* : gull, seagull
gay ['ge, 'gai] *adj* : gay (homosexual)
gaza *nf* : loop
gazapo *nm* 1 : young rabbit 2 : misprint, error
gazmoñería *nf* MOJIGATERÍA : prudery, primness
gazmoño[1], -ña *adj* : prudish, prim
gazmoño[2], -ña *n* MOJIGATO : prude, prig
gaznate *nm* : throat, gullet
gazpacho *nm* : gazpacho
géiser *or* **géyser** *nm* : geyser
gel *nm* : gel
gelatina *nf* : gelatin
gélido, -da *adj* : icy, freezing cold
gelificarse *vr* : to jell
gema *nf* : gem
gemelo[1], -la *adj & n* MELLIZO : twin
gemelo[2] *nm* 1 : cuff link 2 **gemelos** *nmpl* BINOCULARES : binoculars
gemido *nm* : moan, groan, wail
Géminis *nmf* : Gemini
gemir {54} *vi* : to moan, to groan, to wail
gen *or* **gene** *nm* : gene
gendarme *nmf* POLICÍA : police officer, policeman *m*, policewoman *f*
gendarmería *nf* : police
genealogía *nf* : genealogy
genealógico, -ca *adj* : genealogical
generación *nf, pl* **-ciones** 1 : generation ⟨tercera generación : third generation⟩ 2 : generating, creating 3 : class ⟨la generación del '97 : the class of '97⟩
generacional *adj* : generation, generational
generador *nm* : generator
general[1] *adj* 1 : general 2 **en** ~ *or* **por lo general** : in general, generally
general[2] *nmf* 1 : general 2 **general de división** : major general
generalidad *nf* 1 : generality, generalization 2 : majority
generalización *nf, pl* **-ciones** 1 : generalization 2 : escalation, spread
generalizado, -da *adj* : generalized, widespread
generalizar {21} *vi* : to generalize — *vt* : to spread, to spread out — **generalizarse** *vr* : to become widespread
generalmente *adv* : usually, generally
generar *vt* : to generate — **generarse** *vr*
genérico, -ca *adj* : generic
género *nm* 1 : genre, class, kind ⟨el género humano : the human race, mankind⟩ 2 : gender (in grammar) 3 **géneros** *nmpl* : goods, commodities
generosidad *nf* : generosity
generoso, -sa *adj* 1 : generous, unselfish 2 : ample — **generosamente** *adv*

genética *nf* : genetics
genético, -ca *adj* : genetic — **genéticamente** *adv*
genetista *nmf* : geneticist
genial *adj* 1 AGRADABLE : genial, pleasant 2 : brilliant ⟨una obra genial : a work of genius⟩ 3 *fam* FORMIDABLE : fantastic, terrific
genialidad *nf* 1 : genius 2 : stroke of genius 3 : eccentricity
genio *nm* 1 : genius 2 : temper, disposition ⟨de mal genio : bad-tempered⟩ 3 : genie
genital *adj* : genital
genitales *nmpl* : genitals, genitalia
genocidio *nm* : genocide
genotipo *nm* : genotype
gente *nf* 1 : people 2 : relatives *pl*, folks *pl* 3 **gente menuda** *fam* : children, kids *pl* 4 **ser buena gente** : to be nice, to be kind
gentil[1] *adj* 1 AMABLE : kind 2 : gentile
gentil[2] *nmf* : gentile
gentileza *nf* 1 AMABILIDAD : kindness 2 CORTESÍA : courtesy
gentilicio, -cia *adj* 1 : national, tribal 2 : family
gentío *nm* MUCHEDUMBRE, MULTITUD : crowd, mob
gentuza *nf* CHUSMA : riffraff, rabble
genuflexión *nf, pl* **-xiones** 1 : genuflection 2 **hacer una genuflexión** : to genuflect
genuino, -na *adj* : genuine — **genuinamente** *adv*
geofísica *nf* : geophysics
geofísico, -ca *adj* : geophysical
geografía *nf* : geography
geográfico, -ca *adj* : geographic, geographical — **geográficamente** *adv*
geógrafo, -fa *n* : geographer
geología *nf* : geology
geológico, -ca *adj* : geologic, geological — **geológicamente** *adv*
geólogo, -ga *n* : geologist
geometría *nf* : geometry
geométrico, -ca *adj* : geometric, geometrical — **geométricamente** *adv*
geopolítica *nf* : geopolitics
geopolítico, -ca *adj* : geopolitical
georgiano, -na *adj & n* : Georgian
geranio *nm* : geranium
gerbo *nm* : gerbil
gerencia *nf* : management, administration
gerencial *adj* : managerial
gerente *nmf* : manager, director
geriatría *nf* : geriatrics
geriátrico, -ca *adj* : geriatric
germanio *nm* : germanium
germano, -na *adj* : Germanic, German
germen *nm, pl* **gérmenes** : germ
germicida *nf* : germicide
germinación *nf, pl* **-ciones** : germination
germinar *vi* : to germinate, to sprout
gerontología *nf* : gerontology
gerundio *nm* : gerund

gesta *nf* : deed, exploit
gestación *nf, pl* **-ciones** : gestation
gesticulación *nf, pl* **-ciones** : gesturing, gesticulation
gesticular *vi* : to gesticulate, to gesture
gestión *nf, pl* **gestiones 1** TRÁMITE : procedure, step **2** ADMINISTRACIÓN : management **3 gestiones** *nfpl* : negotiations
gestionar *vt* **1** : to negotiate, to work towards **2** ADMINISTRAR : to manage, to handle
gesto *nm* **1** ADEMÁN : gesture **2** : facial expression **3** MUECA : grimace
gestor¹, -tora *adj* : facilitating, negotiating, managing
gestor², -tora *n* : facilitator, manager
géyser → **géiser**
ghanés, -nesa *adj & n, mpl* **ghaneses** : Ghanaian
ghetto → **gueto**
giba *nf* **1** : hump (of an animal) **2** : hunchback (of a person)
gibón *nm, pl* **gibones** : gibbon
giboso¹, -sa *adj* : hunchbacked, humpbacked
giboso², -sa *n* : hunchback, humpback
gigabyte *nm* : gigabyte
gigante¹ *adj* : giant, gigantic
gigante², -ta *n* : giant
gigantesco, -ca *adj* : gigantic, huge
gime, etc. → **gemir**
gimnasia *nf* : gymnastics
gimnasio *nm* : gymnasium, gym
gimnasta *nmf* : gymnast
gimnástico, -ca *adj* : gymnastic
gimotear *vi* LLORIQUEAR : to whine, to whimper
gimoteo *nm* : whimpering
ginebra *nf* : gin
ginecología *nf* : gynecology
ginecológico, -ca *adj* : gynecologic, gynecological
ginecólogo, -ga *n* : gynecologist
ginseng *nm* : ginseng
gira *nf* : tour
giralda *nf* : weather vane
girar *vi* **1** : to turn around, to revolve **2** : to swing around, to swivel — *vt* **1** : to turn, to twist, to rotate **2** : to draft (checks) **3** : to transfer (funds)
girasol *nm* MIRASOL : sunflower
giratorio, -ria *adj* : revolving
giro *nm* **1** VUELTA : turn, rotation **2** : change of direction ⟨giro de 180 grados : U-turn, about-face⟩ **3 giro bancario** : bank draft **4 giro postal** : money order
giroscopio *or* **giróscopo** *nm* : gyroscope
gis *nm Mex* : chalk
gitano, -na *adj & n* : Gypsy
glacial *adj* : glacial, icy — **glacialmente** *adv*
glaciar *nm* : glacier
gladiador *nm* : gladiator
gladiolo *or* **gladíolo** *nm* : gladiolus
glándula *nf* : gland — **glandular** *adj*

glaseado *nm* : glaze, icing
glasear *vt* : to glaze
glaucoma *nm* : glaucoma
glicerina *nf* : glycerin, glycerol
glicinia *nf* : wisteria
global *adj* **1** : global, worldwide **2** : full, comprehensive **3** : total, overall
globalizar {21} *vt* **1** ABARCAR : to include, to encompass **2** : to extend worldwide
globalmente *adv* : globally, as a whole
globo *nm* **1** : globe, sphere **2** : balloon **3 globo ocular** : eyeball
glóbulo *nm* **1** : globule **2** : blood cell, corpuscle
gloria *nf* **1** : glory **2** : fame, renown **3** : delight, enjoyment **4** : star, legend ⟨las glorias del cine : the great names in motion pictures⟩
glorieta *nf* **1** : rotary, traffic circle **2** : bower, arbor
glorificar {72} *vt* ALABAR : to glorify — **glorificación** *nf*
glorioso, -sa *adj* : glorious — **gloriosamente** *adv*
glosa *nf* **1** : gloss **2** : annotation, commentary
glosar *vt* **1** : to gloss **2** : to annotate, to comment on (a text)
glosario *nm* : glossary
glotis *nf* : glottis
glotón¹, -tona *adj, mpl* **glotones** : gluttonous
glotón², -tona *n, mpl* **glotones** : glutton
glotón³ *nm, pl* **glotones** : wolverine
glotonería *nf* GULA : gluttony
glucosa *nf* : glucose
glutinoso, -sa *adj* : glutinous
gnomo [ˈnomo] *nm* : gnome
gobernación *nf, pl* **-ciones** : governing, government
gobernador, -dora *n* : governor
gobernante¹ *adj* : ruling, governing
gobernante² *nmf* : ruler, leader, governor
gobernar {55} *vt* **1** : to govern, to rule **2** : to steer, to sail (a ship) — *vi* **1** : to govern **2** : to steer
gobierno *nm* : government
goce¹, etc. → **gozar**
goce² *nm* **1** PLACER : enjoyment, pleasure **2** : use, possession
gol *nm* : goal (in soccer)
golear *vt* : to rout, to score many goals against (in soccer)
goleta *nf* : schooner
golf *nm* : golf
golfista *nmf* : golfer
golfo *nm* : gulf, bay
golondrina *nf* **1** : swallow (bird) **2 golondrina de mar** : tern
golosina *nf* : sweet, snack
goloso, -sa *adj* : fond of sweets ⟨ser goloso : to have a sweet tooth⟩
golpazo *nm* : heavy blow, bang, thump
golpe *nm* **1** : blow ⟨caerle a golpes a alguien : to give someone a beating⟩ **2** : knock **3 de** ~ : suddenly **4 de un**

golpe : all at once, in one fell swoop **5**
golpe de estado : coup, coup d'etat **6**
golpe de suerte : stroke of luck
golpeado, -da *adj* **1** : beaten, hit **2**
: bruised (of fruit) **3** : dented
golpear *vt* **1** : to beat (up), to hit **2** : to
slam, to bang, to strike — *vi* **1** : to
knock (at a door) **2** : to beat ⟨la lluvia
golpeaba contra el tejado : the rain beat
against the roof⟩ — **golpearse** *vr*
golpetear *v* : to knock, to rattle, to tap
golpeteo *nm* : banging, knocking, tapping
goma *nf* **1** : gum ⟨goma de mascar
: chewing gum⟩ **2** CAUCHO : rubber
⟨goma espuma : foam rubber⟩ **3** PEGA-
MENTO : glue **4** : rubber band **5** *Arg*
: tire **6** *or* **goma de borrar** : eraser
gomita *nf* : rubber band
gomoso, -sa *adj* : gummy, sticky
góndola *nf* : gondola
gong *nm* : gong
gonorrea *nf* : gonorrhea
gorda *nf Mex* : thick corn tortilla
gordinflón¹, -flona *adj, mpl* **-flones** *fam*
: chubby, pudgy
gordinflón², -flona *n, mpl* **-flones** *fam*
: chubby person
gordo¹, -da *adj* **1** : fat **2** : thick **3** : fatty, greasy, oily **4** : unpleasant ⟨me cae
gorda tu tía : I can't stand your aunt⟩
gordo², -da *n* : fat person
gordo³ *nm* **1** GRASA : fat **2** : jackpot
gordura *nf* : fatness, flab
gorgojo *nm* : weevil
gorgotear *vi* : to gurgle, to bubble
gorgoteo *nm* : gurgle
gorila *nm* : gorilla
gorjear *vi* : to chirp, to tweet, to warble **2** : to gurgle
gorjeo *nm* **1** : chirping, warbling **2**
: gurgling
gorra *nf* **1** : bonnet **2** : cap **3 de** ~ *fam*
: for free, at someone else's expense
⟨vivir de gorra : to sponge, to freeload⟩
gorrear *vt fam* : to bum, to scrounge —
vi fam : to freeload
gorrero, -ra *n fam* : freeloader, sponger
gorrión *nm, pl* **gorriones** : sparrow
gorro *nm* **1** : cap **2 estar hasta el gorro** : to be fed up
gorrón, -rrona *n, mpl* **gorrones** *fam*
: freeloader, scrounger
gorronear *vt fam* : to bum, to scrounge
— *vi fam* : to freeload
gota *nf* **1** : drop ⟨una gota de sudor : a
bead of sweat⟩ ⟨como dos gotas de
agua : like two peas in a pod⟩ ⟨sudar
la gota gorda : to sweat buckets, to
work very hard⟩ **2** : gout
gotear *v* **1** : to drip **2** : to leak — *v
impers* LLOVIZNAR : to drizzle
goteo *nm* : drip, dripping
gotera *nf* **1** : leak **2** : stain (from dripping water)
gotero *nm* : (medicine) dropper
gótico, -ca *adj* : Gothic
gourmet *nmf* : gourmet

gozar {21} *vi* **1** : to enjoy oneself, to have
a good time **2** ~ **de** : to enjoy, to have,
to possess ⟨gozar de buena salud : to
enjoy good health⟩ **3** ~ **con** : to take
delight in
gozne *nm* BISAGRA : hinge
gozo *nm* **1** : joy **2** PLACER : enjoyment,
pleasure
gozoso, -sa *adj* : joyful
grabación *nf, pl* **-ciones** : recording
grabado *nm* **1** : engraving **2 grabado
al aguafuerte** : etching
grabador, -dora *n* : engraver
grabadora *nf* : tape recorder
grabar *vt* **1** : to engrave **2** : to record,
to tape — *vi* **grabar al aguafuerte** : to
etch — **grabarse** *vr* **grabársele a alguien en la memoria** : to become en-
graved on someone's mind
gracia *nf* **1** : grace **2** : favor, kindness
3 : humor, wit ⟨su comentario no me
hizo gracia : I wasn't amused by his re-
mark⟩ **4 gracias** *nfpl* : thanks ⟨¡gracias! : thank you!⟩ ⟨dar gracias : to give
thanks⟩
grácil *adj* **1** : graceful **2** : delicate, slender, fine
gracilidad *nf* : gracefulness
gracioso, -sa *adj* **1** CHISTOSO : funny,
amusing **2** : cute, attractive
grada *nf* **1** : harrow **2** PELDAÑO : step,
stair **3 gradas** *nfpl* : bleachers, grandstand
gradación *nf, pl* **-ciones** : gradation,
scale
gradar *vt* : to harrow, to hoe
gradería *nf* : tiers *pl*, stands *pl*, rows *pl*
(in a theater)
gradiente *nf* : gradient, slope
grado *nm* **1** : degree (in meteorology
and mathematics) ⟨grado centígrado
: degree centigrade⟩ **2** : extent, level,
degree ⟨en grado sumo : greatly, to the
highest degree⟩ **3** RANGO : rank **4**
: year, class (in education) **5 de buen
grado** : willingly, readily
graduable *adj* : adjustable
graduación *nf, pl* **-ciones** **1** : graduation (from a school) **2** GRADO : rank
3 : alcohol content, proof
graduado¹, -da *adj* **1** : graduated **2
lentes graduados** : prescription lens-
es
graduado², -da *n* : graduate
gradual *adj* : gradual — **gradualmente**
adv
graduar {3} *v* **1** : to regulate, to adjust
2 CALIBRAR : to calibrate, to gauge —
graduarse *vr* ~ : to graduate (from a
school)
graffiti *or* **grafiti** *nmpl* : graffiti *pl*
gráfica *nf* → **gráfico²**
gráfico¹, -ca *adj* : graphic — **gráficamente** *adv*
gráfico² *nm* **1** : graph, chart **2** : graphic (for a computer, etc.) **3 gráfico de
barras** : bar graph
grafismo *nm* : graphics *pl*

grafito *nm* : graphite
gragea *nf* **1** : coated pill or tablet **2**
grageas *nfpl* : sprinkles, jimmies
grajo *nm* : rook (bird)
grama *nf* : grass
gramática *nf* : grammar
gramatical *adj* : grammatical — **gramaticalmente** *adv*
gramo *nm* : gram
gran → **grande**
grana *nf* : scarlet, deep red
granada *nf* **1** : pomegranate **2** : grenade ⟨granada de mano : hand grenade⟩
granadero *nm* **1** : grenadier **2** **granaderos** *nmpl Mex* : riot squad
granadino, -na *adj & n* : Grenadian
granado, -da *adj* **1** DISTINGUIDO : distinguished **2** : choice, select
granate *nm* **1** : garnet **2** : deep red, maroon
grande *adj* (**gran** *before singular nouns*) **1** : large, big ⟨un libro grande : a big book⟩ **2** ALTO : tall **3** NOTABLE : great ⟨un gran autor : a great writer⟩ **4** (*indicating intensity*) : great ⟨con gran placer : with great pleasure⟩ **5** : old, grown-up ⟨hijos grandes : grown children⟩
grandeza *nf* **1** MAGNITUD : greatness, size **2** : nobility **3** : generosity, graciousness **4** : grandeur, magnificence
grandilocuencia *nf* : grandiloquence — **grandilocuente** *adj*
grandiosidad *nf* : grandeur
grandioso, -sa *adj* **1** MAGNÍFICO : grand, magnificent **2** : grandiose
granel *adv* **1 a ~** : galore, in great quantities **2 a ~** : in bulk ⟨vender a granel : to sell in bulk⟩
granero *nm* : barn, granary
granito *nm* : granite
granizada *nf* : hailstorm
granizar {21} *v impers* : to hail
granizo *nm* : hail
granja *nf* : farm
granjear *vt* : to earn, to win — **granjearse** *vr* : to gain, to earn
granjero, -ra *n* : farmer
grano *nm* **1** PARTÍCULA : grain, particle ⟨un grano de arena : a grain of sand⟩ **2** : grain (of rice, etc.), bean (of coffee), seed **3** : grain (of wood or rock) **4** BARRO, ESPINILLA : pimple **5 ir al grano** : to get to the point
granuja *nmf* PILLUELO : rascal, urchin
granular[1] *vt* : to granulate — **granularse** *vr* : to break out in spots
granular[2] *adj* : granular, grainy
granza *nf* : chaff
grapa *nf* **1** : staple **2** : clamp
grapadora *nf* ENGRAPADORA : stapler
grapar *vt* ENGRAPAR : to staple
grasa *nf* **1** : grease **2** : fat **3** *Mex* : shoe polish
grasiento, -ta *adj* : greasy, oily
graso, -sa *adj* **1** : fatty **2** : greasy, oily
grasoso, -sa *adj* GRASIENTO : greasy, oily

gratificación *nf, pl* **-ciones 1** SATISFACCIÓN : gratification **2** : bonus **3** RECOMPENSA : recompense, reward
gratificar {72} *vt* **1** SATISFACER : to satisfy, to gratify **2** RECOMPENSAR : to reward **3** : to give a bonus to
gratinado, -da *adj* : au gratin
gratis[1] *adv* GRATUITAMENTE : free, for free, gratis
gratis[2] *adj* GRATUITO : free, gratis
gratitud *nf* : gratitude
grato, -ta *adj* AGRADABLE, PLACENTERO : pleasant, agreeable — **gratamente** *adv*
gratuitamente *adv* **1** : gratuitously **2** GRATIS : free, for free, gratis
gratuito, -ta *adj* **1** : gratuitous, unwarranted **2** GRATIS : free, gratis
grava *nf* : gravel
gravamen *nm, pl* **-vámenes 1** : burden, obligation **2** : (property) tax
gravar *vt* **1** : to burden, to encumber **2** : to levy (a tax)
grave *adj* **1** : grave, important **2** : serious, somber **3** : serious (of an illness)
gravedad *nf* **1** : gravity ⟨centro de gravedad : center of gravity⟩ **2** : seriousness, severity
gravemente *adv* : gravely, seriously
gravilla *nf* : (fine) gravel
gravitación *nf, pl* **-ciones** : gravitation
gravitacional *adj* : gravitational
gravitar *vi* **1** : to gravitate **2 ~ sobre** : to rest on **3 ~ sobre** : to loom over
gravoso, -sa *adj* ONEROSO : burdensome, onerous **2** : costly
graznar *vi* : to caw, to honk, to quack, to squawk
graznido *nm* : cawing, honking, quacking, squawking
gregario, -ria *adj* : gregarious
gregoriano, -na *adj* : Gregorian
gremial *adj* SINDICAL : union, labor
gremio *nm* SINDICATO : union, guild
greña *nf* **1** : mat, tangle **2 greñas** *nfpl* MELENAS : shaggy hair, mop
greñudo, -da *n* HIPPIE, MELENUDO : longhair, hippie
grey *nf* : congregation, flock
griego[1]**, -ga** *adj & n* : Greek
griego[2] *nm* : Greek (language)
grieta *nf* : crack, crevice
grifo *nm* **1** : faucet ⟨agua del grifo : tap water⟩ **2** : griffin
grillete *nm* : shackle
grillo *nm* **1** : cricket **2 grillos** *nmpl* : fetters, shackles
grima *nf* **1** : disgust, uneasiness **2 darle grima a alguien** : to get on someone's nerves
gringo, -ga *adj & n* YANQUI : Yankee, gringo
gripa *nf Col, Mex* : flu
gripe *nf* : flu
gris *adj* **1** : gray **2** : overcast, cloudy
grisáceo, -cea *adj* : grayish
gritar *v* : to shout, to scream, to cry
gritería *nf* : shouting, clamor

grito *nm* : shout, scream, cry ⟨a grito pelado : at the top of one's voice⟩
groenlandés, -desa *adj & n* : Greenlander
grogui *adj fam* : dazed, groggy
grosella *nf* 1 : currant 2 **grosella espinosa** : gooseberry
grosería *nf* 1 : insult, coarse language 2 : rudeness, discourtesy
grosero¹, -ra *adj* 1 : rude, fresh 2 : coarse, vulgar
grosero², -ra *n* : rude person
grosor *nm* : thickness
grosso *adj* **a grosso modo** : roughly, broadly, approximately
grotesco, -ca *adj* : grotesque, hideous
grúa *nf* 1 : crane (machine) 2 : tow truck
gruesa *nf* : gross
grueso¹, -sa *adj* 1 : thick, bulky 2 : heavy, big 3 : heavyset, stout
grueso² *nm* 1 : thickness 2 : main body, mass 3 **en ~** : in bulk
grulla *nf* : crane (bird)
grumo *nm* : lump, glob
gruñido *nm* : growl, grunt
gruñir {38} *vi* 1 : to growl, to grunt 2 : to grumble
gruñón¹, -ñona *adj, mpl* **gruñones** *fam* : grumpy, crabby
gruñón², -ñona *n, mpl* **gruñones** *fam* : grumpy person, nag
grupa *nf* : rump, hindquarters *pl*
grupo *nm* : group
gruta *nf* : grotto, cave
guacal *nm Col, Mex, Ven* : crate
guacamayo *nm* : macaw
guacamole *or* **guacamol** *nm* : guacamole
guacamote *nm Mex* : yuca, cassava
guachinango → **huachinango**
guacho, -cha *adj* 1 *Arg, Col, Chile, Peru* : orphaned 2 *Chile, Peru* : odd, unmatched
guadaña *nf* : scythe
guagua *nf* 1 *Arg, Col, Chile, Peru* : baby 2 *Cuba, PRi* : bus
guaira *nf* 1 *CA* : traditional flute 2 *Peru* : smelting furnace
guajiro, -ra *n Cuba* : peasant
guajolote *nm Mex* : turkey
guanábana *nf* : guanabana, soursop (fruit)
guanaco *nm* : guanaco
guandú *nm CA, Car, Col* : pigeon pea
guango, -ga *adj Mex* 1 : loose-fitting, baggy 2 : slack, loose
guano *nm* : guano
guante *nm* 1 : glove ⟨guante de boxeo : boxing glove⟩ 2 **arrojarle el guante (a alguien)** : to throw down the gauntlet (to someone)
guantelete *nm* : gauntlet
guapo, -pa *adj* 1 : handsome, good-looking, attractive 2 : elegant, smart 3 *fam* : bold, dashing
guapura *nf fam* : handsomeness, attractiveness, good looks *pl* ⟨¡qué guapura! : what a vision!⟩

guarache → **huarache**
guarachear *vi Cuba, PRi fam* : to go on a spree, to go out on the town
guaraní¹ *adj & nmf* : Guarani
guaraní² *nm* : Guarani (language of Paraguay)
guarda *nmf* 1 GUARDIÁN : security guard 2 : keeper, custodian
guardabarros *nms & pl* : fender, mudguard
guardabosque *nmf* : forest ranger, gamekeeper
guardacostas¹ *nmfs & pl* : coastguardsman
guardacostas² *nms & pl* : coast guard vessel
guardaespaldas *nmfs & pl* : bodyguard
guardafangos *nms & pl* : fender, mudguard
guardameta *nmf* ARQUERO, PORTERO : goalkeeper, goalie
guardapelo *nm* : locket
guardapolvo *nm* 1 : dustcover 2 : duster, housecoat
guardar *vt* 1 : to guard 2 : to maintain, to preserve 3 CONSERVAR : to put away 4 RESERVAR : to save 5 : to keep (a secret or promise) — **guardarse** *vr* 1 **~ de** : to refrain from 2 **~ de** : to guard against, to be careful not to
guardarropa *nm* 1 : cloakroom, checkroom 2 ARMARIO : closet, wardrobe
guardería *nf* : nursery, day-care center
guardia¹ *nf* 1 : guard, defense 2 : guard duty, watch 3 **en ~** : on guard
guardia² *nmf* 1 : sentry, guardsman, guard 2 : police officer, policeman *m*, policewoman *f*
guardiamarina *nmf* : midshipman
guardián, -diana *n, mpl* **guardianes** 1 GUARDA : security guard, watchman 2 : guardian, keeper 3 **perro guardián** : watchdog
guarecer {53} *vt* : to shelter, to protect — **guarecerse** *vr* : to take shelter
guarida *nf* 1 : den, lair 2 : hideout
guarismo *nm* : figure, numeral
guarnecer {53} *vt* 1 : to adorn 2 : to garnish 3 : to garrison
guarnición *nf, pl* **-ciones** 1 : garnish 2 : garrison 3 : decoration, trimming, setting (of a jewel)
guaro *nm CA* : liquor distilled from sugarcane
guasa *nf fam* 1 : joking, fooling around 2 **de ~** : in jest, as a joke
guasón¹, -sona *adj, mpl* **guasones** *fam* : funny, witty
guasón², -sona *n, mpl* **guasones** *fam* : joker, clown
guatemalteco, -ca *adj & n* : Guatemalan
guau *interj* : wow!
guayaba *nf* : guava (fruit)
gubernamental *adj* : governmental
gubernativo, -va → **gubernamental**
gubernatura *nf Mex* : governing body
guepardo *nm* : cheetah
güero, -ra *adj Mex* : blond, fair

guerra *nf* **1** : war ⟨declarar la guerra : to declare war⟩ ⟨guerra sin cuartel : all-out war⟩ **2** : warfare **3** LUCHA : conflict, struggle
guerrear *vi* : to wage war
guerrero[1], **-ra** *adj* **1** : war, fighting **2** : warlike
guerrero[2], **-ra** *n* : warrior
guerrilla *nf* : guerrilla warfare
guerrillero, -ra *adj & n* : guerrilla
gueto *nm* : ghetto
guía[1] *nf* **1** : directory, guidebook **2** ORIENTACIÓN : guidance, direction ⟨la conciencia me sirve como guía : conscience is my guide⟩
guía[2] *nmf* : guide, leader ⟨guía de turismo : tour guide⟩
guiar {85} *vt* **1** : to guide, to lead **2** CONDUCIR : to manage — **guiarse** *vr* : to be guided by, to go by
guija *nf* : pebble
guijarro *nm* : pebble
guillotina *nf* : guillotine — **guillotinar** *vt*
guinda[1] *adj & nm Mex* : burgundy (color)
guinda[2] *nf* : morello (cherry)
guineo *nm Car* : banana
guinga *nf* : gingham
guiñada → **guiño**
guiñar *vi* : to wink
guiño *nm* : wink
guión *nm, pl* **guiones 1** : script, screenplay **2** : hyphen, dash **3** ESTANDARTE : standard, banner
guirnalda *nf* : garland
guisa *nf* **1** : manner, fashion **2 a guisa de** : like, by way of **3 de tal guisa** : in such a way

guisado ESTOFADO *nm* : stew
guisante *nm* : pea
guisar *vt* **1** ESTOFAR : to stew **2** *Spain* : to cook
guiso *nm* **1** : stew **2** : casserole
güisqui → **whisky**
guita *nf* : string, twine
guitarra *nf* : guitar
guitarrista *nmf* : guitarist
gula *nf* GLOTONERÍA : gluttony, greed
gusano *nm* **1** LOMBRIZ : worm, earthworm ⟨gusano de seda : silkworm⟩ **2** : caterpillar, maggot, grub
gustar *vt* **1** : to taste **2** : to like ⟨¿gustan pasar? : would you like to come in?⟩ — *vi* **1** : to be pleasing ⟨me gustan los dulces : I like sweets⟩ ⟨a María le gusta Carlos : Maria is attracted to Carlos⟩ ⟨no me gusta que me griten : I don't like to be yelled at⟩ **2 ~ de** : to like, to enjoy ⟨no gusta de chismes : she doesn't like gossip⟩ **3 como guste** : as you wish, as you like
gustativo, -va *adj* : taste ⟨papilas gustativas : taste buds⟩
gusto *nm* **1** : flavor, taste **2** : taste, style **3** : pleasure, liking **4** : whim, fancy ⟨a gusto : at will⟩ **5 a ~** : comfortable, at ease **6 al gusto** : to taste, as one likes **7 mucho gusto** : pleased to meet you
gustosamente *adv* : gladly
gustoso, -sa *adj* **1** : willing, glad ⟨nuestra empresa participará gustosa : our company will be pleased to participate⟩ **2** : zesty, tasty
gutural *adj* : guttural

H

h *nf* : eighth letter of the Spanish alphabet
ha → **haber**
haba *nf* : broad bean
habanero[1], **-ra** *adj* : of or from Havana
habanero[2], **-ra** *n* : native or resident of Havana
haber[1] {39} *v aux* **1** : have, has ⟨no ha llegado el envío : the shipment hasn't arrived⟩ **2 ~ de** : must ⟨ha de ser tarde : it must be late⟩ — *v impers* **1 hay** : there is, there are ⟨hay dos mensajes : there are two messages⟩ ⟨¿qué hay de nuevo? : what's new?⟩ **2 hay que** : it is necessary ⟨hay que trabajar más rápido : you have to work faster⟩
haber[2] *nm* **1** : assets *pl* **2** : credit, credit side **3 haberes** *nmpl* : salary, income, remuneration
habichuela *nf* **1** : bean, kidney bean **2** : green bean
hábil *adj* **1** : able, skillful **2** : working ⟨días hábiles : working days⟩
habilidad *nf* CAPACIDAD : ability, skill
habilidoso, -sa *adj* : skillful, clever

habilitación *nf, pl* **-ciones 1** : authorization **2** : furnishing, equipping
habilitar *vt* **1** : to enable, to authorize, to empower **2** : to equip, to furnish
hábilmente *adv* : skillfully, expertly
habitable *adj* : habitable, inhabitable
habitación *nf, pl* **-ciones 1** CUARTO : room **2** DORMITORIO : bedroom **3** : habitation, occupancy
habitante *nmf* : inhabitant, resident
habitar *vt* : to inhabit — *vi* : to reside, to dwell
hábitat *nm, pl* **-tats** : habitat
hábito *nm* **1** : habit, custom **2** : habit (of a monk or nun)
habitual *adj* : habitual, customary — **habitualmente** *adv*
habituar {3} *vt* : to accustom, to habituate — **habituarse** *vr* **~ a** : to get used to, to grow accustomed to
habla *nf* **1** : speech **2** : language, dialect **3 de ~** : speaking ⟨de habla inglesa : English-speaking⟩
hablado, -da *adj* **1** : spoken **2 mal hablado** : foulmouthed

hablador[1], **-dora** *adj* : talkative
hablador[2], **-dora** *n* : chatterbox
habladuría *nf* 1 : rumor 2 **habladurías** *nfpl* : gossip, scandal
hablante *nmf* : speaker
hablar *vi* 1 : to speak, to talk ⟨hablar en broma : to be joking⟩ 2 ~ **de** : to mention, to talk about 3 **dar que hablar** : to make people talk — *vt* 1 : to speak (a language) 2 : to talk about, to discuss ⟨háblalo con tu jefe : discuss it with your boss⟩ — **hablarse** *vr* 1 : to speak to each other, to be on speaking terms 2 **se habla inglés (etc.)** : English (etc.) spoken
habrá, etc. → **haber**
hacedor, -dora *n* : creator, maker, doer
hacendado, -da *n* : landowner
hacer {40} *vt* 1 : to make 2 : to do, to perform 3 : to force, to oblige ⟨los hice esperar : I made them wait⟩ — *vi* : to act ⟨haces bien : you're doing the right thing⟩ — *v impers* 1 (*referring to weather*) ⟨hacer frío : to be cold⟩ ⟨hace viento : it's windy⟩ 2 **hace** : ago ⟨hace mucho tiempo : a long time ago, for a long time⟩ 3 **no le hace** : it doesn't matter, it makes no difference 4 **hacer falta** : to be necessary, to be needed — **hacerse** *vr* 1 : to become 2 : to pretend, to act, to play ⟨hacerse el tonto : to play dumb⟩ 3 : to seem ⟨el examen se me hizo difícil : the exam seemed difficult to me⟩ 4 : to get, to grow ⟨se hace tarde : it's growing late⟩
hacha *nf* : hatchet, ax
hachazo *nm* : blow, chop (with an ax)
hachís *nm* : hashish
hacia *prep* 1 : toward, towards ⟨hacia abajo : downward⟩ ⟨hacia adelante : forward⟩ 2 : near, around, about ⟨hacia las seis : about six o'clock⟩
hacienda *nf* 1 : estate, ranch, farm 2 : property 3 : livestock 4 **la Hacienda** : department of revenue, tax office
hacinar *vt* 1 : to pile up, to stack 2 : to overcrowd — **hacinarse** *vr* : to crowd together
hada *nf* : fairy
hado *nm* : destiny, fate
haga, etc. → **hacer**
haitiano, -na *adj & n* : Haitian
hala *interj Spain* 1 (*expressing encouragement or disbelief*) : come on! 2 (*expressing surprise*) : wow! 3 (*expressing protest*) : hey!
halagador[1], **-dora** *adj* : flattering
halagador[2], **-dora** *adj* : flatterer
halagar {52} *vt* : to flatter, to compliment
halago *nm* : flattery, praise
halagüeño, -ña *adj* 1 : flattering 2 : encouraging, promising
halar *vt CA, Car* → **jalar**
halcón *nm, pl* **halcones** : hawk, falcon
halibut *nm, pl* **-buts** : halibut
hálito *nm* 1 : breath 2 : gentle breeze

hallar *vt* 1 ENCONTRAR : to find 2 DESCUBRIR : to discover, to find out — **hallarse** *vr* 1 : to be situated, to find oneself 2 : to feel ⟨no se halla bien : he doesn't feel comfortable, he feels out of place⟩
hallazgo *nm* 1 : discovery 2 : find ⟨¡es un verdadero hallazgo! : it's a real find!⟩
halo *nm* 1 : halo 2 : aura
halógeno *nm* : halogen
hamaca *nf* : hammock
hambre *nf* 1 : hunger 2 : starvation 3 **tener hambre** : to be hungry 4 **dar hambre** : to make hungry
hambriento, -ta *adj* : hungry, starving
hambruna *nf* : famine
hamburguesa *nf* : hamburger
hampa *nf* : criminal underworld
hampón, -pona *n, mpl* **hampones** : criminal, thug
hámster ['xamster] *nm, pl* **hámsters** : hamster
han → **haber**
handicap *or* **hándicap** ['handi̦kap] *nm, pl* **-caps** : handicap (in sports)
hangar *nm* : hangar
hará, etc. → **hacer**
haragán[1], **-gana** *adj, mpl* **-ganes** : lazy, idle
haragán[2], **-gana** *n, mpl* **-ganes** HOLGAZÁN : slacker, good-for-nothing
haraganear *vi* : to be lazy, to waste one's time
haraganería *nf* : laziness
harapiento, -ta *adj* : ragged, tattered
harapos *nmpl* ANDRAJOS : rags, tatters
hardware ['hard̦wer] *nm* : computer hardware
harén *nm, pl* **harenes** : harem
harina *nf* 1 : flour 2 **harina de maíz** : cornmeal
hartar *vt* 1 : to glut, to satiate 2 FASTIDIAR : to tire, to irritate, to annoy — **hartarse** *vr* : to be weary, to get fed up
harto[1] *adv* : most, extremely, very
harto[2], **-ta** *adj* 1 : full, satiated 2 : fed up
hartura *nf* 1 : surfeit 2 : abundance, plenty
has → **haber**
hasta[1] *adv* : even
hasta[2] *prep* 1 : until, up until ⟨hasta entonces : until then⟩ ⟨¡hasta luego! : see you later!⟩ 2 : as far as ⟨nos fuimos hasta Managua : we went all the way to Managua⟩ 3 : up to ⟨hasta cierto punto : up to a certain point⟩ 4 **hasta que** : until
hastiar {85} *vt* 1 : to make weary, to bore 2 : to disgust, to sicken — **hastiarse** *vr* ~ **de** : to get tired of
hastío *nm* 1 TEDIO : tedium 2 REPUGNANCIA : disgust
hato *nm* 1 : flock, herd 2 : bundle (of possessions)
hawaiano, -na *adj & n* : Hawaiian
hay → **haber**[1]

haya[1], etc. → **haber**
haya[2] *nf* : beech (tree and wood)
hayuco *nm* : beechnut
haz[1] → **hacer**
haz[2] *nm, pl* **haces** **1** FARDO : bundle **2** : beam (of light)
haz[3] *nf, pl* **haces** **1** : face **2** **haz de la tierra** : surface of the earth
hazaña *nf* PROEZA : feat, exploit
hazmerreír *nm fam* : laughingstock
he[1] {39} → **haber**
he[2] *v impers* **he aquí** : here is, here are, behold
hebilla *nf* : buckle, clasp
hebra *nf* : strand, thread
hebreo[1], -brea *adj & n* : Hebrew
hebreo[2] *nm* : Hebrew (language)
hecatombe *nf* **1** MATANZA : massacre **2** : disaster
heces → **hez**
hechicería *nf* **1** BRUJERÍA : sorcery, witchcraft **2** : curse, spell
hechicero[1], -ra *adj* : bewitching, enchanting
hechicero[2], -ra *n* : sorcerer, sorceress *f*
hechizar {21} *vt* **1** EMBRUJAR : to bewitch **2** CAUTIVAR : to charm
hechizo *nm* **1** SORTILEGIO : spell, enchantment **2** ENCANTO : charm, fascination
hecho[1] *pp* → **hacer**
hecho[2], -cha *adj* **1** : made, done **2** : ready-to-wear **3** : complete, finished ⟨hecho y derecho : full-fledged⟩
hecho[3] *nm* **1** : fact **2** : event ⟨hechos históricos : historic events⟩ **3** : act, action **4** **de ~** : in fact, in reality
hechura *nf* **1** : style **2** : craftsmanship, workmanship **3** : product, creation
hectárea *nf* : hectare
heder {56} *vi* : to stink, to reek
hediondez *nf, pl* **-deces** : stink, stench
hediondo, -da *adj* MALOLIENTE : foul-smelling, stinking
hedor *nm* : stench, stink
hegemonía *nf* **1** : dominance **2** : hegemony (in politics)
helada *nf* : frost (in meteorology)
heladería *nf* : ice-cream parlor, ice-cream stand
helado[1], -da *adj* **1** GÉLIDO : icy, freezing cold **2** CONGELADO : frozen
helado[2] *nm* : ice cream
heladora *nf* CONGELADOR : freezer
helar {55} *v* CONGELAR : to freeze — *v impers* : to produce frost ⟨anoche heló : there was frost last night⟩ — **helarse** *vr*
helecho *nm* : fern, bracken
hélice *nf* **1** : spiral, helix **2** : propeller
helicóptero *nm* : helicopter
helio *nm* : helium
helipuerto *nm* : heliport
hembra *adj & nf* : female
hemisférico, -ca *adj* : hemispheric, hemispherical
hemisferio *nm* : hemisphere
hemofilia *nf* : hemophilia

hemofílico, -ca *adj & n* : hemophiliac
hemoglobina *nf* : hemoglobin
hemorragia *nf* **1** : hemorrhage **2** **hemorragia nasal** : nosebleed
hemorroides *nfpl* ALMORRANAS : hemorrhoids, piles
hemos → **haber**
henchido, -da *adj* : swollen, bloated
henchir {54} *vt* **1** : to stuff, to fill **2** : to swell, to swell up — **henchirse** *vr* **1** : to stuff oneself **2** LLENARSE : to fill up, to be full
hender {56} *vt* : to cleave, to split
hendidura *nf* : crack, crevice, fissure
henequén *nm, pl* **-quenes** : sisal hemp
heno *nm* : hay
hepatitis *nf* : hepatitis
heráldica *nf* : heraldry
heráldico, -ca *adj* : heraldic
heraldo *nm* : herald
herbario, -ria *adj* : herbal
herbicida *nm* : herbicide, weed killer
herbívoro[1], -ra *adj* : herbivorous
herbívoro[2] *nm* : herbivore
herbolario, -ria *n* : herbalist
hercio *nm* : hertz
hercúleo, -lea *adj* : herculean
heredar *vt* : to inherit
heredero, -ra *n* : heir, heiress *f*
hereditario, -ria *adj* : hereditary
hereje *nmf* : heretic
herejía *nf* : heresy
herencia *nf* **1** : inheritance **2** : heritage **3** : heredity
herético, -ca *adj* : heretical
herida *nf* : injury, wound
herido[1], -da *adj* **1** : injured, wounded **2** : hurt, offended
herido[2], -da *n* : injured person, casualty
herir {76} *vt* **1** : to injure, to wound **2** : to hurt, to offend
hermafrodita *nmf* : hermaphrodite
hermanar *vt* **1** : to unite, to bring together **2** : to match up, to twin (cities)
hermanastro, -tra *n* : half brother *m*, half sister *f*
hermandad *nf* **1** FRATERNIDAD : brotherhood ⟨hermandad de mujeres : sisterhood, sorority⟩ **2** : association
hermano, -na *n* : sibling, brother *m*, sister *f*
hermético, -ca *adj* : hermetic, watertight — **herméticamente** *adv*
hermoso, -sa *adj* BELLO : beautiful, lovely — **hermosamente** *adv*
hermosura *nf* BELLEZA : beauty, loveliness
hernia *nf* : hernia
héroe *nm* : hero
heroicidad *nf* : heroism, heroic deed
heroico, -ca *adj* : heroic — **heroicamente** *adv*
heroína *nf* **1** : heroine **2** : heroin
heroísmo *nm* : heroism
herpes *nms & pl* **1** : herpes **2** : shingles
herradura *nf* : horseshoe
herraje *nm* : ironwork

herramienta *nf* : tool
herrar {55} *vt* : to shoe (a horse)
herrería *nf* : blacksmith's shop
herrero, -ra *n* : blacksmith
herrumbre *nf* ORÍN : rust
herrumbroso, -sa *adj* OXIDADO : rusty
hertzio *nm* : hertz
hervidero *nm* 1 : mass, swarm 2 : hotbed (of crime, etc.)
hervidor *nm* : kettle
hervir {76} *vi* 1 BULLIR : to boil, to bubble 2 ∼ de : to teem with, to be swarming with — *vt* : to boil
hervor *nm* 1 : boiling 2 : fervor, ardor
heterogeneidad *nf* : heterogeneity
heterogéneo, -nea *adj* : heterogeneous
heterosexual *adj & nmf* : heterosexual
heterosexualidad *nf* : heterosexuality
hexágono *nm* : hexagon — **hexagonal** *adj*
hez *nf, pl* **heces** 1 ESCORIA : scum, dregs *pl* 2 : sediment, lees *pl* 3 **heces** *nfpl* : feces, excrement
hiato *nm* : hiatus
hibernar *vi* : to hibernate — **hibernación** *nf*
híbrido[1], **-da** *adj* : hybrid
híbrido[2] *nm* : hybrid
hicieron, etc. → **hacer**
hidalgo, -ga *n* : nobleman *m,* noblewoman *f*
hidrante *nm* CA, Col : hydrant
hidratar *vt* : to moisturize — **hidratante** *adj*
hidrato *nm* 1 : hydrate 2 **hidrato de carbono** : carbohydrate
hidráulico, -ca *adj* : hydraulic
hidroavión *nm, pl* **-viones** : seaplane
hidrocarburo *nm* : hydrocarbon
hidroeléctrico, -ca *adj* : hydroelectric
hidrofobia *nf* RABIA : hydrophobia, rabies
hidrófugo, -ga *adj* : water-repellent
hidrógeno *nm* : hydrogen
hidroplano *nm* : hydroplane
hiede, etc. → **heder**
hiedra *nf* 1 : ivy 2 **hiedra venenosa** : poison ivy
hiel *nf* 1 BILIS : bile 2 : bitterness
hiela, etc. → **helar**
hielo *nm* 1 : ice 2 : coldness, reserve ⟨romper el hielo : to break the ice⟩
hiena *nf* : hyena
hiende, etc. → **hender**
hierba *nf* 1 : herb 2 : grass 3 **mala hierba** : weed
hierbabuena *nf* : mint, spearmint
hiere, etc. → **herir**
hierra, etc. → **herrar**
hierro *nm* 1 : iron ⟨hierro fundido : cast iron⟩ 2 : branding iron
hierve, etc. → **hervir**
hígado *nm* : liver
higiene *nf* : hygiene
higiénico, -ca *adj* : hygienic — **higiénicamente** *adv*
higienista *nmf* : hygienist
higo *nm* 1 : fig 2 **higo chumbo** : prickly pear (fruit)

higrómetro *nm* : hygrometer
higuera *nf* : fig tree
hijastro, -tra *n* : stepson *m,* stepdaughter *f*
hijo, -ja *n* 1 : son *m,* daughter *f* 2 **hijos** *nmpl* : children, offspring
híjole *interj* Mex : wow!, good grief!
hilacha *nf* 1 : ravel, loose thread 2 **mostrar la hilacha** : to show one's true colors
hilado *nm* 1 : spinning 2 HILO : yarn, thread
hilar *vt* 1 : to spin (thread) 2 : to consider, to string together (ideas) — *vi* 1 : to spin 2 **hilar delgado** : to split hairs
hilarante *adj* 1 : humorous, hilarious 2 **gas hilarante** : laughing gas
hilaridad *nf* : hilarity
hilera *nf* FILA : file, row, line
hilo *nm* 1 : thread ⟨colgar de un hilo : to hang by a thread⟩ ⟨hilo dental : dental floss⟩ 2 LINO : linen 3 : (electric) wire 4 : theme, thread (of a discourse) 5 : trickle (of water, etc.)
hilvanar *vt* 1 : to baste, to tack 2 : to piece together
himnario *nm* : hymnal
himno *nm* 1 : hymn 2 **himno nacional** : national anthem
hincapié *nm* **hacer hincapié en** : to emphasize, to stress
hincar {72} *vt* CLAVAR : to stick, to plunge — **hincarse** *vr* **hincarse de rodillas** : to kneel down, to fall to one's knees
hinchado, -da *adj* 1 : swollen, inflated 2 : pompous, overblown
hinchar *vt* 1 INFLAR : to inflate 2 : to exaggerate — **hincharse** *vr* 1 : to swell up 2 : to become conceited, to swell with pride
hinchazón *nf, pl* **-zones** : swelling
hinche, etc. → **henchir**
hindi *nm* : Hindi
hindú *adj & nmf* : Hindu
hinduismo *nm* : Hinduism
hiniesta *nf* : broom (plant)
hinojo *nm* 1 : fennel 2 **de hinojos** : on bended knee
hinque, etc. → **hincar**
hipar *vi* : to hiccup
hiperactividad *nf* : hyperactivity
hiperactivo, -va *adj* : hyperactive, overactive
hipérbole *nf* : hyperbole
hiperbólico, -ca *adj* : hyperbolic, exaggerated
hipercrítico, -ca *adj* : hypercritical
hipermetropía *nf* : farsightedness
hipersensibilidad *nf* : hypersensitivity
hipersensible *adj* : hypersensitive
hipertensión *nf, pl* **-siones** : hypertension, high blood pressure
hip-hop [ˌxipˈxop] *nm* : hip-hop (music)
hípico, -ca *adj* : equestrian ⟨concurso hípico : horse show⟩
hipil → **huipil**
hipnosis *nfs & pl* : hypnosis

hipnótico, -ca *adj* : hypnotic
hipnotismo *nm* : hypnotism
hipnotizador¹, -dora *adj* **1** : hypnotic **2** : spellbinding, mesmerizing
hipnotizador², -dora *n* : hypnotist
hipnotizar {21} *vt* : to hypnotize
hipo *nm* : hiccup, hiccups *pl*
hipocampo *nm* : sea horse
hipocondría *nf* : hypochondria
hipocondríaco, -ca *adj & n* : hypochondriac
hipocresía *nf* : hypocrisy
hipócrita¹ *adj* : hypocritical — **hipócritamente** *adv*
hipócrita² *nmf* : hypocrite
hipodérmico, -ca *adj* **aguja hipodérmica** : hypodermic needle
hipódromo *nm* : racetrack
hipopótamo *nm* : hippopotamus
hipoteca *nf* : mortgage
hipotecar {72} *vt* **1** : to mortgage **2** : to compromise, to jeopardize
hipotecario, -ria *adj* : mortgage
hipotensión *nf* : low blood pressure
hipotenusa *nf* : hypotenuse
hipótesis *nfs & pl* : hypothesis
hipotético, -ca *adj* : hypothetical — **hipotéticamente** *adv*
hippie *or* **hippy** ['hipi] *nmf, pl* **hippies** [-pis] : hippie
hiriente *adj* : hurtful, offensive
hirió, etc. → **herir**
hirsuto, -ta *adj* **1** : hirsute, hairy **2** : bristly, wiry
hirviente *adj* : boiling
hirvió, etc. → **hervir**
hisopo *nm* **1** : hyssop **2** : cotton swab
hispánico, -ca *adj & n* : Hispanic
hispano¹, -na *adj* : Hispanic ⟨de habla hispana : Spanish-speaking⟩
hispano², -na *n* : Hispanic (person)
hispanoamericano¹, -na *adj* LATINOAMERICANO : Latin-American
hispanoamericano², -na *n* LATINOAMERICANO : Latin American
hispanohablante¹ *adj* : Spanish-speaking
hispanohablante² *nmf* : Spanish speaker
histerectomía *nf* : hysterectomy
histeria *nf* **1** : hysteria **2** : hysterics
histérico, -ca *adj* : hysterical — **histéricamente** *adv*
histerismo *nm* **1** : hysteria **2** : hysterics
historia *nf* **1** : history **2** NARRACIÓN, RELATO : story
historiador, -dora *n* : historian
historial *nm* **1** : record, document **2** CURRÍCULUM : résumé, curriculum vitae
histórico, -ca *adj* **1** : historical **2** : historic, important — **históricamente** *adv*
historieta *nf* : comic strip
histrionismo *nm* : histrionics, acting
hit ['hit] *nm, pl* **hits** **1** ÉXITO : hit, popular song **2** : hit (in baseball)
hito *nm* : milestone, landmark

hizo → **hacer**
hobby ['hɔbi] *nm, pl* **hobbies** [-bis] : hobby
hocico *nm* : snout, muzzle
hockey ['hɔke, -ki] *nm* : hockey
hogar *nm* **1** : home **2** : hearth, fireplace
hogareño, -ña *adj* **1** : home-loving **2** : domestic, homelike
hogaza *nf* : large loaf (of bread)
hoguera *nf* **1** FOGATA : bonfire **2 morir en la hoguera** : to burn at the stake
hoja *nf* **1** : leaf, petal, blade (of grass) **2** : sheet (of paper), page (of a book) ⟨hoja de cálculo : spreadsheet⟩ **3** FORMULARIO : form ⟨hoja de pedido : order form⟩ **4** : blade (of a knife) ⟨hoja de afeitar : razor blade⟩
hojalata *nf* : tinplate
hojaldre *nm* : puff pastry
hojarasca *nf* : fallen leaves *pl*
hojear *vt* : to leaf through (a book or magazine)
hojuela *nf* **1** : leaflet, young leaf **2** : flake
hola *interj* : hello!, hi!
holandés¹, -desa *adj, mpl* **-deses** : Dutch
holandés², -desa *n, mpl* **-deses** : Dutch person, Dutchman *m*, Dutchwoman *f* ⟨los holandeses : the Dutch⟩
holandés³ *nm* : Dutch (language)
holgadamente *adv* : comfortably, easily ⟨vivir holgadamente : to be well-off⟩
holgado, -da *adj* **1** : loose, baggy **2** : at ease, comfortable
holganza *nf* : leisure, idleness
holgazán¹, -zana *adj, mpl* **-zanes** : lazy
holgazán², -zana *n, mpl* **-zanes** HARAGÁN : slacker, idler
holgazanear *vi* HARAGANEAR : to laze around, to loaf
holgazanería *nf* PEREZA : idleness, laziness
holgura *nf* **1** : looseness **2** COMODIDAD : comfort, ease
holístico, -ca *adj* : holistic
hollar {19} *vt* : to tread on, to trample
hollín *nm, pl* **hollines** TIZNE : soot
holocausto *nm* : holocaust
holograma *nm* : hologram
hombre *nm* **1** : man ⟨el hombre : man, mankind⟩ **2 hombre de estado** : statesman **3 hombre de negocios** : businessman **4 hombre lobo** : werewolf
hombrera *nf* **1** : shoulder pad **2** : epaulet
hombría *nf* : manliness
hombro *nm* : shoulder ⟨encogerse de hombros : to shrug one's shoulders⟩
hombruno, -na *adj* : mannish
homenaje *nm* : homage, tribute ⟨rendir homenaje a : to pay tribute to⟩
homenajear *vt* : to pay homage to, to honor
homeopatía *nf* : homeopathy
homicida¹ *adj* : homicidal, murderous
homicida² *nmf* ASESINO : murderer
homicidio *nm* ASESINATO : homicide, murder

homilía *nf* : homily, sermon
homófono *nm* : homophone
homogeneidad *nf* : homogeneity
homogeneización *nf* : homogenization
homogeneizar {21} *vt* : to homogenize
homogéneo, -nea *adj* : homogeneous
homógrafo *nm* : homograph
homologación *nf, pl* **-ciones** 1 : sanctioning, approval 2 : parity
homologar {52} *vt* 1 : to sanction 2 : to bring into line
homólogo¹, -ga *adj* : homologous, equivalent
homólogo², -ga *n* : counterpart
homónimo¹, -ma *n* TOCAYO : namesake
homónimo² *nm* : homonym
homosexual *adj & nmf* : homosexual
homosexualidad *nf* : homosexuality
honda *nf* : sling
hondo¹ *adv* : deeply
hondo², -da *adj* PROFUNDO : deep ⟨en lo más hondo de : in the depths of⟩ — **hondamente** *adv*
hondonada *nf* 1 : hollow, depression 2 : ravine, gorge
hondura *nf* : depth
hondureño, -ña *adj & n* : Honduran
honestidad *nf* 1 : decency, modesty 2 : honesty, uprightness
honesto, -ta *adj* 1 : decent, virtuous 2 : honest, honorable — **honestamente** *adv*
hongo *nm* 1 : fungus 2 : mushroom
honor *nm* 1 : honor ⟨en honor a la verdad : to be quite honest⟩ 2 **honores** *nmpl* : honors ⟨hacer los honores : to do the honors⟩
honorable *adj* HONROSO : honorable — **honorablemente** *adv*
honorario, -ria *adj* : honorary
honorarios *nmpl* : payment, fees (for professional services)
honorífico, -ca *adj* : honorary ⟨mención honorífica : honorable mention⟩
honra *nf* 1 : dignity, self-respect ⟨tener a mucha honra : to take great pride in⟩ 2 : good name, reputation
honradamente *adv* : honestly, decently
honradez *nf, pl* **-deces** : honesty, integrity, probity
honrado, -da *adj* 1 HONESTO : honest, upright 2 : honored
honrar *vt* 1 : to honor 2 : to be a credit to ⟨su generosidad lo honra : his generosity does him credit⟩
honroso, -sa *adj* HONORABLE : honorable — **honrosamente** *adv*
hora *nf* 1 : hour ⟨media hora : half an hour⟩ ⟨a la última hora : at the last minute⟩ ⟨a la hora en punto : on the dot⟩ ⟨horas de oficina : office hours⟩ 2 : time ⟨¿qué hora es? : what time is it?⟩ 3 CITA : appointment
horario *nm* : schedule, timetable, hours *pl* ⟨horario de visita : visiting hours⟩
horca *nf* 1 : gallows *pl* 2 : pitchfork
horcajadas *nfpl* a ~ : astride, astraddle
horcón *nm, pl* **horcones** : wooden post, prop

horda *nf* : horde
horizontal *adj* : horizontal — **horizontalmente** *adv*
horizonte *nm* : horizon, skyline
horma *nf* 1 : shoe tree 2 : shoemaker's last
hormiga *nf* : ant
hormigón *nm, pl* **-gones** CONCRETO : concrete
hormigonera *nf* : cement mixer
hormigueo *nm* 1 : tingling, pins and needles *pl* 2 : uneasiness
hormiguero *nm* 1 : anthill 2 : swarm (of people)
hormona *nf* : hormone — **hormonal** *adj*
hornacina *nf* : niche, recess
hornada *nf* : batch
hornear *vt* : to bake
hornilla *nf* : burner (of a stove)
horno *nm* 1 : oven ⟨horno crematorio : crematorium⟩ ⟨horno de microondas : microwave oven⟩ 2 : kiln
horóscopo *nm* : horoscope
horqueta *nf* 1 : fork (in a river or road) 2 : crotch (in a tree) 3 : small pitchfork
horquilla *nf* 1 : hairpin, bobby pin 2 : pitchfork
horrendo, -da *adj* : horrendous, horrible
horrible *adj* : horrible, dreadful — **horriblemente** *adv*
horripilante *adj* : horrifying, hair-raising
horripilar *vt* : to horrify, to terrify
horror *nm* : horror, dread
horrorizado, -da *adj* : terrified
horrorizar {21} *vt* : to horrify, to terrify — **horrorizarse** *vr*
horroroso, -sa *adj* 1 : horrifying, terrifying 2 : dreadful, bad
hortaliza *nf* 1 : vegetable 2 **hortalizas** *nfpl* : garden produce
hortera *adj* *Spain fam* : tacky, gaudy
hortícola *adj* : horticultural
horticultor, -ra *n* : horticulturist
horticultura *nf* : horticulture
hosco, -ca *adj* : sullen, gloomy
hospedaje *nm* : lodging, accommodations *pl*
hospedar *vt* : to provide with lodging, to put up — **hospedarse** *vr* : to stay, to lodge
hospicio *nm* : orphanage
hospital *nm* : hospital
hospitalario, -ria *adj* : hospitable
hospitalidad *nf* : hospitality
hospitalización *nf, pl* **-ciones** : hospitalization
hospitalizar {21} *vt* : to hospitalize — **hospitalizarse** *vr*
hostería *nf* POSADA : inn
hostia *nf* : host, Eucharist
hostigamiento *nm* : harassment
hostigar {52} *vt* ACOSAR, ASEDIAR : to harass, to pester
hostil *adj* : hostile

hostilidad *nf* **1** : hostility, antagonism **2 hostilidades** *nfpl* : (military) hostilities

hostilizar {21} *vt* : to harass

hotel *nm* : hotel

hotelero[1], **-ra** *adj* : hotel ⟨la industria hotelera : the hotel business⟩

hotelero[2], **-ra** *n* : hotel manager, hotelier

hoy *adv* **1** : today ⟨hoy mismo : right now, this very day⟩ **2** : now, nowadays ⟨de hoy en adelante : from now on⟩

hoyo *nm* AGUJERO : hole

hoyuelo *nm* : dimple

hoz *nf, pl* **hoces** : sickle

hozar {21} *vi* : to root (of a pig)

huachinango *nm Mex* : red snapper

huarache *nm* : huarache sandal

hubo, etc. → **haber**

hueco[1], **-ca** *adj* **1** : hollow, empty **2** : soft, spongy **3** : hollow-sounding, resonant **4** : proud, conceited **5** : superficial

hueco[2] *nm* **1** : hole, hollow, cavity **2** : gap, space **3** : recess, alcove

huele, etc. → **oler**

huelga *nf* **1** PARO : strike **2 hacer huelga** : to strike, to go on strike

huelguista *nmf* : striker

huella[1], **etc.** → **hollar**

huella[2] *nf* **1** : footprint ⟨seguir las huellas de alguien : to follow in someone's footsteps⟩ **2** : mark, impact ⟨dejar huella : to leave one's mark⟩ ⟨sin dejar huella : without a trace⟩ **3 huella digital** *or* **huella dactilar** : fingerprint

huérfano[1], **-na** *adj* **1** : orphan, orphaned **2** : defenseless **3** ～ **de** : lacking, devoid of

huérfano[2], **-na** *n* : orphan

huerta *nf* **1** : large vegetable garden, truck farm **2** : orchard **3** : irrigated land

huerto *nm* **1** : vegetable garden **2** : orchard

hueso *nm* **1** : bone **2** : pit, stone (of a fruit)

huésped[1], **-peda** *n* INVITADO : guest

huésped[2] *nm* : host ⟨organismo huésped : host organism⟩

huestes *nfpl* **1** : followers **2** : troops, army

huesudo, -da *adj* : bony

hueva *nf* : roe, spawn

huevo *nm* : egg ⟨huevos revueltos : scrambled eggs⟩

huida *nf* : flight, escape

huidizo, -za *adj* **1** ESCURRIDIZO : elusive, slippery **2** : shy, evasive

huipil *nm CA, Mex* : traditional sleeveless blouse or dress

huir {41} *vi* **1** ESCAPAR : to escape, to flee **2** ～ **de** : to avoid

huiro *nm Chile, Peru* : seaweed

huizache *nm* : huisache, acacia

hule *nm* **1** : oilcloth, oilskin **2** *Mex* : rubber **3 hule espuma** *Mex* : foam rubber

humanidad *nf* **1** : humanity, mankind **2** : humaneness **3 humanidades** *nfpl* : humanities *pl*

humanismo *nm* : humanism

humanista *nmf* : humanist

humanístico, -ca *adj* : humanistic

humanitario, -ria *adj & n* : humanitarian

humano[1], **-na** *adj* **1** : human **2** BENÉVOLO : humane, benevolent — **humanamente** *adv*

humano[2] *nm* : human being, human

humareda *nf* : cloud of smoke

humeante *adj* **1** : smoky **2** : smoking, steaming

humear *vi* **1** : to smoke **2** : to steam

humectante[1] *adj* : moisturizing

humectante[2] *nm* : moisturizer

humedad *nf* **1** : humidity **2** : dampness, moistness

humedecer {53} *vt* **1** : to humidify **2** : to moisten, to dampen

húmedo, -da *adj* **1** : humid **2** : moist, damp

humidificador *nm* : humidifier

humidificar {72} *vt* : to humidify

humildad *nf* **1** : humility **2** : lowliness

humilde *adj* **1** : humble **2** : lowly ⟨gente humilde : poor people⟩

humildemente *adv* : meekly, humbly

humillación *nf, pl* **-ciones** : humiliation

humillante *adj* : humiliating

humillar *vt* : to humiliate — **humillarse** *vr* : to humble oneself ⟨humillarse a hacer algo : to stoop to doing something⟩

humo *nm* **1** : smoke, steam, fumes **2 humos** *nmpl* : airs *pl*, conceit

humor *nm* **1** : humor **2** : mood, temper ⟨está de buen humor : she's in a good mood⟩

humorada *nf* **1** BROMA : joke, witticism **2** : whim, caprice

humorismo *nm* : humor, wit

humorista *nmf* : humorist, comedian, comedienne *f*

humorístico, -ca *adj* : humorous — **humorísticamente** *adv*

humoso, -sa *adj* : smoky, steamy

humus *nm* : humus

hundido, -da *adj* **1** : sunken **2** : depressed

hundimiento *nm* **1** : sinking **2** : collapse, ruin

hundir *vt* **1** : to sink **2** : to destroy, to ruin — **hundirse** *vr* **1** : to sink down **2** : to cave in **3** : to break down, to go to pieces

húngaro[1], **-ra** *adj & n* : Hungarian

húngaro[2] *nm* : Hungarian (language)

huracán *nm, pl* **-canes** : hurricane

huraño, -ña *adj* **1** : unsociable, aloof **2** : timid, skittish (of an animal)

hurgar {52} *vt* : to poke, to jab, to rake (a fire) — *vi* ～ **en** : to rummage in, to poke through

hurgue, etc. → **hurgar**

hurón *nm, pl* **hurones** : ferret

huronear *vi* : to pry, to snoop

hurra *interj* : hurrah!, hooray!
hurtadillas *nfpl* **a ~** : stealthily, on the sly
hurtar *vt* ROBAR : to steal
hurto *nm* **1** : theft, robbery **2** : stolen property, loot
husmear *vt* **1** : to follow the scent of, to track **2** : to sniff out, to pry into — *vi* **1** : to pry, to snoop **2** : to sniff around (of an animal)
huso *nm* **1** : spindle **2 huso horario** : time zone
huy *interj* : ow!, ouch!
huye, etc. → **huir**

I

i *nf* : ninth letter of the Spanish alphabet
iba, etc. → **ir**
ibérico, -ca *adj* : Iberian
ibero, -ra *or* **íbero, -ra** *adj & n* : Iberian
iberoamericano, -na *adj* HISPANOAMERICANO, LATINOAMERICANO : Latin-American
ibis *nfs & pl* : ibis
ice, etc. → **izar**
iceberg *nm, pl* **icebergs** : iceberg
icono *nm* : icon
iconoclasia *nf* : iconoclasm
iconoclasta *nmf* : iconoclast
ictericia *nf* : jaundice
ida *nf* **1** : going, departure **2 ida y vuelta** : round-trip **3 idas y venidas** : comings and goings
idea *nf* **1** : idea, notion **2** : opinion, belief **3** PROPÓSITO : intention
ideal *adj & nm* : ideal — **idealmente** *adv*
idealismo *nm* : idealism
idealista[1] *adj* : idealistic
idealista[2] *nmf* : idealist
idealizar {21} *vt* : to idealize — **idealización** *nf*
idear *vt* : to devise, to think up
ideario *nm* : ideology
ídem *nm* : idem, the same, ditto
idéntico, -ca *adj* : identical, alike — **idénticamente** *adv*
identidad *nf* : identity
identificable *adj* : identifiable
identificación *nf, pl* **-ciones 1** : identification, identifying **2** : identification document, ID
identificar {72} *vt* : to identify — **identificarse** *vr* **1** : to identify oneself **2 ~ con** : to identify with
ideología *nf* : ideology — **ideológicamente** *adv*
ideológico, -ca *adj* : ideological
idílico, -ca *adj* : idyllic
idilio *nm* : idyll
idioma *nm* : language ⟨el idioma inglés : the English language⟩
idiomático, -ca *adj* : idiomatic — **idiomáticamente** *adv*
idiosincrasia *nf* : idiosyncrasy
idiosincrásico, -ca *adj* : idiosyncratic
idiota[1] *adj* : idiotic, stupid, foolish
idiota[2] *nmf* : idiot, foolish person
idiotez *nf, pl* **-teces 1** : idiocy **2** : idiotic act or remark ⟨¡no digas idioteces! : don't talk nonsense!⟩
ido *pp* → **ir**

idólatra[1] *adj* : idolatrous
idólatra[2] *nmf* : idolater
idolatrar *vt* : to idolize
idolatría *nf* : idolatry
ídolo *nm* : idol
idoneidad *nf* : suitability
idóneo, -nea *adj* ADECUADO : suitable, fitting
iglesia *nf* : church
iglú *nm* : igloo
ignición *nf, pl* **-ciones** : ignition
ignífugo, -ga *adj* : fire-resistant, fireproof
ignominia *nf* : ignominy, disgrace
ignominioso, -sa *adj* : ignominious, shameful
ignorancia *nf* : ignorance
ignorante[1] *adj* : ignorant
ignorante[2] *nmf* : ignorant person, ignoramus
ignorar *vt* **1** : to ignore **2** DESCONOCER : to be unaware of ⟨lo ignoramos por absoluto : we have no idea⟩
ignoto, -ta *adj* : unknown
igual[1] *adv* **1** : in the same way **2 por ~** : equally
igual[2] *adj* **1** : equal **2** IDÉNTICO : the same, alike **3** : even, smooth **4** SEMEJANTE : similar **5** CONSTANTE : constant
igual[3] *nmf* : equal, peer
igualación *nf* **1** : equalization **2** : leveling, smoothing **3** : equating (in mathematics)
igualado, -da *adj* **1** : even (of a score) **2** : level **3** *Mex* : disrespectful
igualar *vt* **1** : to equalize **2** : to tie ⟨igualar el marcador : to even the score⟩
igualdad *nf* **1** : equality **2** UNIFORMIDAD : evenness, uniformity
igualmente *adv* **1** : equally **2** ASIMISMO : likewise
iguana *nf* : iguana
ijada *nf* : flank, loin, side
ijar *nm* → **ijada**
ilegal[1] *adj* : illegal, unlawful — **ilegalmente** *adv*
ilegal[2] *nmf CA, Mex* : illegal alien
ilegalidad *nf* : illegality, unlawfulness
ilegibilidad *nf* : illegibility
ilegible *adj* : illegible — **ilegiblemente** *adv*
ilegitimidad *nf* : illegitimacy
ilegítimo, -ma *adj* : illegitimate, unlawful

ileso, -sa *adj* : uninjured, unharmed
ilícito, -ta *adj* : illicit — **ilícitamente** *adv*
ilimitado, -da *adj* : unlimited
ilógico, -ca *adj* : illogical — **ilógicamente** *adv*
iluminación *nf, pl* **-ciones** 1 : illumination 2 ALUMBRADO : lighting
iluminado, -da *adj* : illuminated, lighted
iluminar *vt* 1 : to illuminate, to light (up) 2 : to enlighten
ilusión *nf, pl* **-siones** 1 : illusion, delusion 2 ESPERANZA : hope ⟨hacerse ilusiones : to get one's hopes up⟩
ilusionado, -da *adj* ESPERANZADO : hopeful, eager
ilusionar *vt* : to build up hope, to excite — **ilusionarse** *vr* : to get one's hopes up
iluso¹, -sa *adj* : naive, gullible
iluso², -sa *n* SOÑADOR : dreamer, visionary
ilusorio, -ria *adj* ENGAÑOSO : illusory, misleading
ilustración *nf, pl* **-ciones** 1 : illustration 2 : erudition, learning ⟨la Ilustración : the Enlightenment⟩
ilustrado, -da *adj* 1 : illustrated 2 DOCTO : learned, erudite
ilustrador, -dora *n* : illustrator
ilustrar *vt* 1 : to illustrate 2 ACLARAR, CLARIFICAR : to explain
ilustrativo, -va *adj* : illustrative
ilustre *adj* : illustrious, eminent
imagen *nf, pl* **imágenes** : image, picture
imaginable *adj* : imaginable, conceivable
imaginación *nf, pl* **-ciones** : imagination
imaginar *vt* : to imagine — **imaginarse** *vr* 1 : to suppose, to imagine 2 : to picture
imaginario, -ria *adj* : imaginary
imaginativo, -va *adj* : imaginative — **imaginativamente** *adv*
imaginería *nf* 1 : imagery 2 : image making (in religion)
imán *nm, pl* **imanes** : magnet
imantar *vt* : to magnetize
imbatible *adj* : unbeatable
imbécil¹ *adj* : stupid, idiotic
imbécil² *nmf* 1 : imbecile 2 *fam* : idiot, dope
imborrable *adj* : indelible
imbuir {41} *vt* : to imbue — **imbuirse** *vr*
imitación *nf, pl* **-ciones** 1 : imitation 2 : mimicry, impersonation
imitador¹, -dora *adj* : imitative
imitador², -dora *n* 1 : imitator 2 : mimic
imitar *vt* 1 : to imitate, to copy 2 : to mimic, to impersonate
imitativo, -va *adj* → **imitador¹**
impaciencia *nf* : impatience
impacientar *vt* : to make impatient, to exasperate — **impacientarse** *vr*
impaciente *adj* : impatient — **impacientemente** *adv*
impactado, -da *adj* : shocked, stunned
impactante *adj* 1 : shocking 2 : impressive, powerful

impactar *vt* 1 GOLPEAR : to hit 2 IMPRESIONAR : to impact, to affect — **impactarse** *vr*
impacto *nm* 1 : impact, effect 2 : shock, collision
impagable *adj* 1 : unpayable 2 : priceless
impago *nm* : nonpayment
impalpable *adj* INTANGIBLE : impalpable, intangible
impar¹ *adj* : odd ⟨números impares : odd numbers⟩
impar² *nm* : odd number
imparable *adj* : unstoppable
imparcial *adj* : impartial — **imparcialmente** *adv*
imparcialidad *nf* : impartiality
impartir *vt* : to impart, to give
impasible *adj* : impassive, unmoved — **impasiblemente** *adv*
impasse *nm* : impasse
impávido, -da *adj* : undaunted, unperturbed
impecable *adj* INTACHABLE : impeccable, faultless — **impecablemente** *adv*
impedido, -da *adj* : disabled, crippled
impedimento *nm* 1 : impediment, obstacle 2 : disability
impedir {54} *vt* 1 : to prevent, to block 2 : to impede, to hinder
impeler *vt* 1 : to drive, to propel 2 : to impel
impenetrable *adj* : impenetrable — **impenetrabilidad** *nf*
impenitente *adj* : unrepentant, impenitent
impensable *adj* : unthinkable
impensado, -da *adj* : unforeseen, unexpected
imperante *adj* : prevailing
imperar *vi* 1 : to reign, to rule 2 PREDOMINAR : to prevail
imperativo¹, -va *adj* : imperative
imperativo² *nm* : imperative
imperceptible *adj* : imperceptible — **imperceptiblemente** *adv*
imperdible *nm* *Spain* : safety pin
imperdonable *adj* : unpardonable, unforgivable
imperecedero, -ra *adj* 1 : imperishable 2 INMORTAL : immortal, everlasting
imperfección *nf, pl* **-ciones** 1 : imperfection 2 DEFECTO : defect, flaw
imperfecto¹, -ta *adj* : imperfect, flawed
imperfecto² *nm* : imperfect tense
imperial *adj* : imperial
imperialismo *nm* : imperialism
imperialista *adj & nmf* : imperialist
impericia *nf* : lack of skill, incompetence
imperio *nm* : empire
imperioso, -sa *adj* 1 : imperious 2 : pressing, urgent — **imperiosamente** *adv*
impermeabilizante *adj* : water-repellent
impermeabilizar {21} *vt* : to waterproof
impermeable¹ *adj* 1 : impervious 2 : impermeable, waterproof
impermeable² *nm* : raincoat

impersonal *adj* : impersonal — **impersonalmente** *adv*
impertinencia *nf* INSOLENCIA : impertinence, insolence
impertinente *adj* **1** INSOLENTE : impertinent, insolent **2** INOPORTUNO : inappropriate, uncalled-for **3** IRRELEVANTE : irrelevant
imperturbable *adj* : imperturbable, impassive, stolid
ímpetu *nm* **1** : impetus, momentum **2** : vigor, energy **3** : force, violence
impetuoso, -sa *adj* : impetuous, impulsive — **impetuosamente** *adv*
impiedad *nf* : impiety
impío, -pía *adj* : impious, ungodly
implacable *adj* : implacable, relentless — **implacablemente** *adv*
implantación *nf, pl* **-ciones 1** : implantation **2** ESTABLECIMIENTO : establishment, introduction
implantado, -da *adj* : well-established
implantar *vt* **1** : to implant **2** ESTABLECER : to establish, to introduce — **implantarse** *vr*
implante *nm* : implant
implementar *vt* : to implement — **implementarse** *vr* — **implementación** *nf*
implemento *nm* : implement, tool
implicación *nf, pl* **-ciones** : implication
implicar {72} *vt* **1** ENREDAR, ENVOLVER : to involve, to implicate **2** : to imply
implícito, -ta *adj* : implied, implicit — **implícitamente** *adv*
implorar *vt* : to implore
implosión *nf, pl* **-siones** : implosion — **implosivo, -va** *adj*
implosionar *vi* : to implode
imponderable *adj & nm* : imponderable
imponente *adj* : imposing, impressive
imponer {60} *vt* **1** : to impose **2** : to confer — *vi* : to be impressive, to command respect — **imponerse** *vr* **1** : to take on (a duty) **2** : to assert oneself **3** : to prevail
imponible *adj* : taxable
impopular *adj* : unpopular — **impopularidad** *nf*
importación *nf, pl* **-ciones 1** : importation **2 importaciones** *nfpl* : imports
importado, -da *adj* : imported
importador¹, -dora *adj* : importing
importador², -dora *n* : importer
importancia *nf* : importance
importante *adj* : important — **importantemente** *adv*
importar *vi* : to matter, to be important ⟨no le importa lo que piensen : she doesn't care what they think⟩ — *vt* : to import
importe *nm* **1** : price, cost **2** : sum, amount
importunar *vt* : to bother, to inconvenience — *vi* : to be inconvenient
importuno, -na *adj* **1** : inopportune, inconvenient **2** : bothersome, annoying
imposibilidad *nf* : impossibility

imposibilitado, -da *adj* **1** : disabled, crippled **2 verse imposibilitado** : to be unable (to do something)
imposibilitar *vt* **1** : to make impossible **2** : to disable, to incapacitate — **imposibilitarse** *vr* : to become disabled
imposible *adj* : impossible
imposición *nf, pl* **-ciones 1** : imposition **2** EXIGENCIA : demand, requirement **3** : tax **4** : deposit
impositivo, -va *adj* : tax ⟨tasa impositiva : tax rate⟩
impostor, -tora *n* : impostor
impostura *nf* **1** : fraud, imposture **2** CALUMNIA : slander
impotencia *nf* **1** : impotence, powerlessness **2** : impotence (in medicine)
impotente *adj* **1** : powerless **2** : impotent
impracticable *adj* : impracticable
imprecisión *nf, pl* **-siones 1** : imprecision, vagueness **2** : inaccuracy
impreciso, -sa *adj* **1** : imprecise, vague **2** : inaccurate
impredecible *adj* : unpredictable
impregnar *vt* : to impregnate
imprenta *nf* **1** : printing **2** : printing shop, press
imprescindible *adj* : essential, indispensable
impresentable *adj* : unpresentable, unfit
impresión *nf, pl* **-siones 1** : print, printing **2** : impression, feeling
impresionable *adj* : impressionable
impresionante *adj* : impressive, incredible, amazing — **impresionantemente** *adv*
impresionar *vt* **1** : to impress, to strike **2** : to affect, to move — *vi* : to make an impression — **impresionarse** *vr* : to be affected, to be removed
impresionismo *nm* : impressionism
impresionista¹ *adj* : impressionist, impressionistic
impresionista² *nmf* : impressionist
impreso¹ *pp* → **imprimir**
impreso², -sa *adj* : printed
impreso³ *nm* PUBLICACIÓN : printed matter, publication
impresor, -sora *n* : printer
impresora *nf* : (computer) printer
imprevisible *adj* : unforeseeable
imprevisión *nf, pl* **-siones** : lack of foresight, thoughtlessness
imprevisto¹, -ta *adj* : unexpected, unforeseen
imprevisto² *nm* : unexpected occurrence, contingency
imprimir {42} *vt* **1** : to print **2** : to imprint, to stamp, to impress
improbabilidad *nf* : improbability
improbable *adj* : improbable, unlikely
improcedente *adj* **1** : inadmissible **2** : inappropriate, improper
improductivo, -va *adj* : unproductive
improperio *nm* : affront, insult
impropiedad *nf* : impropriety

impropio, -pia *adj* **1** : improper, incorrect **2** INADECUADO : unsuitable, inappropriate
improvisación *nf, pl* **-ciones** : improvisation, ad-lib
improvisado, -da *adj* : improvised, ad-lib
improvisar *v* : to improvise, to ad-lib
improviso *adj* **de ~** : all of a sudden, unexpectedly
imprudencia *nf* INDISCRECIÓN : imprudence, indiscretion
imprudente *adj* INDISCRETO : imprudent, indiscreet — **imprudentemente** *adv*
impúdico, -ca *adj* : shameless, indecent
impuesto[1] *pp* → **imponer**
impuesto[2] *nm* : tax
impugnar *vt* : to challenge, to contest
impulsar *vt* : to propel, to drive
impulsividad *nf* : impulsiveness
impulsivo, -va *adj* : impulsive — **impulsivamente** *adv*
impulso *nm* **1** : drive, thrust **2** : impulse, urge
impune *adj* : unpunished
impunemente *adv* : with impunity
impunidad *nf* : impunity
impureza *nf* : impurity
impuro, -ra *adj* : impure
impuso, etc. → **imponer**
imputable *adj* ATRIBUIBLE : attributable
imputación *nf, pl* **-ciones** **1** : attribution, imputation **2** : accusation
imputar *vt* ATRIBUIR : to impute, to attribute
inacabable *adj* : endless
inacabado, -da *adj* INCONCLUSO : unfinished
inaccesibilidad *nf* : inaccessibility
inaccesible *adj* **1** : inaccessible **2** : unattainable
inacción *nf, pl* **-ciones** : inactivity, inaction
inaceptable *adj* : unacceptable
inactividad *nf* : inactivity, idleness
inactivo, -va *adj* : inactive, idle
inadaptado[1]**, -da** *adj* : maladjusted
inadaptado[2]**, -da** *n* : misfit
inadecuación *nf, pl* **-ciones** : inadequacy
inadecuado, -da *adj* **1** : inadequate **2** IMPROPIO : inappropriate — **inadecuadamente** *adv*
inadmisible *adj* **1** : inadmissible **2** : unacceptable
inadvertencia *nf* : oversight
inadvertidamente *adv* : inadvertently
inadvertido, -da *adj* **1** : unnoticed ⟨pasar inadvertido : to go unnoticed⟩ **2** DESPISTADO, DISTRAÍDO : inattentive, distracted
inagotable *adj* : inexhaustible
inaguantable *adj* INSOPORTABLE : insufferable, unbearable
inalámbrico, -ca *adj* : wireless, cordless
inalcanzable *adj* : unreachable, unattainable

inalienable *adj* : inalienable
inalterable *adj* **1** : unalterable, unchangeable **2** : impassive **3** : colorfast
inamovible *adj* : immovable, fixed
inanición *nf, pl* **-ciones** : starvation
inanimado, -da *adj* : inanimate
inapelable *adj* : indisputable
inapetencia *nf* : lack of appetite
inaplicable *adj* : inapplicable
inapreciable *adj* **1** : imperceptible, negligible **2** : invaluable
inapropiado, -da *adj* : inappropriate, unsuitable
inarticulado, -da *adj* : inarticulate, unintelligible — **inarticuladamente** *adv*
inasequible *adj* : unattainable, inaccessible
inasistencia *nf* AUSENCIA : absence
inatacable *adj* : unassailable, indisputable
inaudible *adj* : inaudible
inaudito, -ta *adj* : unheard-of, unprecedented
inauguración *nf, pl* **-ciones** : inauguration
inaugural *adj* : inaugural, opening
inaugurar *vt* **1** : to inaugurate **2** : to open
inca *adj & nmf* : Inca
incalculable *adj* : incalculable
incalificable *adj* : indescribable
incandescencia *nf* : incandescence — **incandescente** *adj*
incansable *adj* INFATIGABLE : tireless — **incansablemente** *adv*
incapacidad *nf* **1** : inability, incapacity **2** : disability, handicap
incapacitado, -da *adj* **1** : disqualified **2** : disabled, handicapped
incapacitar *vt* **1** : to incapacitate, to disable **2** : to disqualify
incapaz *adj, pl* **-paces** **1** : incapable, unable **2** : incompetent, inept
incautación *nf, pl* **-ciones** : seizure, confiscation
incautar *vt* CONFISCAR : to confiscate, to seize — **incautarse** *vr*
incauto, -ta *adj* : unwary, unsuspecting
incendiar *vt* : to set fire to, to burn (down) — **incendiarse** *vr* : to catch fire
incendiario[1]**, -ria** *adj* : incendiary, inflammatory
incendiario[2]**, -ria** *n* : arsonist
incendio *nm* **1** : fire **2 incendio premeditado** : arson
incensario *nm* : censer
incentivar *vt* : to encourage, to stimulate
incentivo *nm* : incentive
incertidumbre *nf* : uncertainty, suspense
incesante *adj* : incessant — **incesantemente** *adv*
incesto *nm* : incest
incestuoso, -sa *adj* : incestuous
incidencia *nf* **1** : incident **2** : effect, impact **3 por ~** : by chance, accidentally

incidental *adj* : incidental
incidentalmente *adv* : by chance
incidente *nm* : incident, occurrence
incidir *vi* **1** ~ **en** : to fall into, to enter into ⟨incidimos en el mismo error : we fell into the same mistake⟩ **2** ~ **en** : to affect, to influence, to have a bearing on
incienso *nm* : incense
incierto, -ta *adj* **1** : uncertain **2** : untrue **3** : unsteady, insecure
incineración *nf, pl* **-ciones 1** : incineration **2** : cremation
incinerador *nm* : incinerator
incinerar *vt* **1** : to incinerate **2** : to cremate
incipiente *adj* : incipient
incisión *nf, pl* **-siones** : incision
incisivo¹, -va *adj* : incisive
incisivo² *nm* : incisor
inciso *nm* : digression, aside
incitación *nf, pl* **-ciones** : incitement
incitador¹, -dora *n* : instigator, agitator
incitador², -dora *adj* : provocative
incitante *adj* : provocative
incitar *vt* : to incite, to rouse
incivilizado, -da *adj* : uncivilized
inclemencia *nf* : inclemency, severity
inclemente *adj* : inclement
inclinación *nf, pl* **-ciones 1** PROPENSIÓN : inclination, tendency **2** : incline, slope
inclinado, -da *adj* **1** : sloping **2** : inclined, apt
inclinar *vt* : to tilt, to lean, to incline ⟨inclinar la cabeza : to bow one's head⟩ — **inclinarse** *vr* **1** : to lean, to lean over **2** ~ **a** : to be inclined to
incluir {41} *vt* : to include
inclusión *nf, pl* **-siones** : inclusion
inclusive *adv* : inclusively, up to and including
inclusivo, -va *adj* : inclusive
incluso *adv* **1** AUN : even, in fact ⟨es importante e incluso crucial : it is important and even crucial⟩ **2** : inclusively
incógnita *nf* **1** : unknown quantity (in mathematics) **2** : mystery
incógnito, -ta *adj* **1** : unknown **2 de incógnito** : incognito
incoherencia *nf* : incoherence
incoherente *adj* : incoherent — **incoherentemente** *adv*
incoloro, -ra *adj* : colorless
incombustible *adj* : fireproof
incomible *adj* : inedible
incomodar *vt* **1** : to make uncomfortable **2** : to inconvenience — **incomodarse** *vr* : to put oneself out, to take the trouble
incomodidad *nf* **1** : discomfort, awkwardness **2** MOLESTIA : inconvenience, bother
incómodo, -da *adj* **1** : uncomfortable, awkward **2** INCONVENIENTE : inconvenient
incomparable *adj* : incomparable

incompatibilidad *nf* : incompatibility
incompatible *adj* : incompatible, uncongenial
incompetencia *nf* : incompetence
incompetente *adj & nmf* : incompetent
incompleto, -ta *adj* : incomplete
incomprendido, -da *adj* : misunderstood
incomprensible *adj* : incomprehensible
incomprensión *nf, pl* **-siones** : lack of understanding, incomprehension
incomunicación *nf, pl* **-ciones** : lack of communication
incomunicado, -da *adj* **1** : cut off, isolated **2** : in solitary confinement
inconcebible *adj* : inconceivable, unthinkable — **inconcebiblemente** *adv*
inconcluso, -sa *adj* INACABADO : unfinished
incondicional *adj* : unconditional — **incondicionalmente** *adv*
inconexo, -xa *adj* : unconnected, disconnected
inconfesable *adj* : unspeakable, shameful
inconforme *adj & nmf* : nonconformist
inconformidad *nf* : nonconformity
inconformista *adj & nmf* : nonconformist
inconfundible *adj* : unmistakable, obvious — **inconfundiblemente** *adv*
incongruencia *nf* : incongruity
incongruente *adj* : incongruous
inconmensurable *adj* : vast, immeasurable
inconquistable *adj* : unyielding
inconsciencia *nf* **1** : unconsciousness, unawareness **2** : irresponsibility
inconsciente¹ *adj* **1** : unconscious, unaware **2** : reckless, needless — **inconscientemente** *adv*
inconsciente² *nm* **el inconsciente** : the unconscious
inconsecuente *adj* : inconsistent — **inconsecuencia** *nf*
inconsiderado, -da *adj* : inconsiderate, thoughtless
inconsistencia *nf* : inconsistency
inconsistente *adj* **1** : weak, flimsy **2** : inconsistent, weak (of an argument)
inconsolable *adj* : inconsolable — **inconsolablemente** *adv*
inconstancia *nf* : inconstancy
inconstante *adj* : inconstant, fickle, changeable
inconstitucional *adj* : unconstitutional
inconstitucionalidad *nf* : unconstitutionality
incontable *adj* INNUMERABLE : countless, innumerable
incontenible *adj* : uncontrollable, unstoppable
incontestable *adj* INCUESTIONABLE, INDISCUTIBLE : irrefutable, indisputable
incontinencia *nf* : incontinence — **incontinente** *adj*
incontrolable *adj* : uncontrollable
incontrolado, -da *adj* : uncontrolled, out of control

incontrovertible *adj* : indisputable
inconveniencia *nf* **1** : inconvenience, trouble **2** : unsuitability, inappropriateness **3** : tactless remark
inconveniente[1] *adj* **1** INCÓMODO : inconvenient **2** INAPROPIADO : improper, unsuitable
inconveniente[2] *nm* : obstacle, problem, snag ⟨no tengo inconveniente en hacerlo : I don't mind doing it⟩
incorporación *nf, pl* **-ciones** : incorporation
incorporar *vt* **1** : to incorporate **2** : to add, to include — **incorporarse** *vr* **1** : to sit up **2** ～ **a** : to join
incorpóreo, -rea *adj* : incorporeal, bodiless
incorrección *n, pl* **-ciones** : impropriety, improper word or action
incorrecto, -ta *adj* : incorrect — **incorrectamente** *adv*
incorregible *adj* : incorrigible — **incorregibilidad** *nf*
incorruptible *adj* : incorruptible
incredulidad *nf* : incredulity, skepticism
incrédulo[1], **-la** *adj* : incredulous, skeptical
incrédulo[2], **-la** *n* : skeptic
increíble *adj* : incredible, unbelievable — **increíblemente** *adv*
incrementar *vt* : to increase — **incrementarse** *vr*
incremento *nm* AUMENTO : increase
incriminar *vt* : to incriminate — **incriminación** *nf*
incriminatorio, -ria *adj* : incriminating, incriminatory
incruento, -ta *adj* : bloodless
incrustación *nf, pl* **-ciones** : inlay
incrustar *vt* **1** : to embed **2** : to inlay — **incrustarse** *vr* : to become embedded
incubación *nf, pl* **-ciones** : incubation
incubadora *nf* : incubator
incubar *v* : to incubate
incuestionable *adj* INCONTESTABLE, INDISCUTIBLE : unquestionable, indisputable — **incuestionablemente** *adv*
inculcar {72} *vt* : to inculcate, to instill
inculpar *vt* ACUSAR : to accuse, to charge
inculto, -ta *adj* **1** : uncultured, ignorant **2** : uncultivated, fallow
incumbencia *nf* : obligation, responsibility
incumbir *vi* (*3rd person only*) ～ **a** : to be incumbent upon, to be of concern to ⟨a mí no me incumbe : it's not my concern⟩
incumplido, -da *adj* : irresponsible, unreliable
incumplimiento *nm* **1** : nonfulfillment, neglect **2 incumplimiento de contrato** : breach of contract
incumplir *vt* : to fail to carry out, to break (a promise, a contract)
incurable *adj* : incurable
incurrir *vi* **1** ～ **en** : to incur ⟨incurrir en gastos : to incur expenses⟩ **2** ～ **en** : to fall into, to commit ⟨incurrió en un error : he made a mistake⟩

incursión *nf, pl* **-siones** : incursion, raid
incursionar *vi* **1** : to raid **2** ～ **en** : to go into, to enter ⟨el actor incursionó en el baile : the actor worked in dance for awhile⟩
indagación *nf, pl* **-ciones** : investigation, inquiry
indagar {52} *vt* : to inquire into, to investigate
indebido, -da *adj* : improper, undue — **indebidamente** *adv*
indecencia *nf* : indecency, obscenity
indecente *adj* : indecent, obscene
indecible *adj* : indescribable, inexpressible
indecisión *nf, pl* **-siones** : indecision
indeciso, -sa *adj* **1** IRRESOLUTO : indecisive **2** : undecided
indeclinable *adj* : unavoidable
indecoro *nm* : impropriety, indecorousness
indecoroso, -sa *adj* : indecorous, unseemly
indefectible *adj* : unfailing, sure
indefendible *adj* : indefensible
indefenso, -sa *adj* : defenseless, helpless
indefinible *adj* : indefinable
indefinido, -da *adj* **1** : undefined, vague **2** INDETERMINADO : indefinite — **indefinidamente** *adv*
indeleble *adj* : indelible — **indeleblemente** *adv*
indelicado, -da *adj* : indelicate, tactless
indemnización *nf, pl* **-ciones 1** : indemnity **2 indemnización por despido** : severance pay
indemnizar {21} *vt* : to indemnify, to compensate
independencia *nf* : independence
independiente *adj* : independent — **independientemente** *adv*
independizarse {21} *vr* : to become independent, to gain independence
indescifrable *adj* : indecipherable
indescriptible *adj* : indescribable — **indescriptiblemente** *adv*
indeseable *adj* & *nmf* : undesirable
indestructible *adj* : indestructible
indeterminación *nf, pl* **-ciones** : indeterminacy
indeterminado, -da *adj* **1** INDEFINIDO : indefinite **2** : indeterminate
indexar *vt* INDICIAR : to index (wages, prices, etc.)
indicación *nf, pl* **-ciones 1** : sign, signal **2** : direction, instruction **3** : suggestion, hint
indicado, -da *adj* **1** APROPIADO : appropriate, suitable **2** : specified, indicated ⟨al día indicado : on the specified day⟩
indicador *nm* **1** : gauge, dial, meter **2** : indicator ⟨indicadores económicos : economic indicators⟩
indicar {72} *vt* **1** SEÑALAR : to indicate **2** ENSEÑAR, MOSTRAR : to show
indicativo[1], **-va** *adj* : indicative
indicativo[2] *nm* : indicative (mood)

índice *nm* **1** : index **2** : index finger, forefinger **3** INDICIO : indication

indiciar *vt* : to index (prices, wages, etc.)

indicio *nm* : indication, sign

indiferencia *nf* : indifference

indiferente *adj* **1** : indifferent, unconcerned **2 ser indiferente** : to be of no concern ⟨me es indiferente : it doesn't matter to me⟩

indígena[1] *adj* : indigenous, native

indígena[2] *nmf* : native

indigencia *nf* MISERIA : poverty, destitution

indigente *adj & nmf* : indigent

indigestarse *vr* **1** EMPACHARSE : to have indigestion **2** *fam* : to nauseate, to disgust ⟨ese tipo se me indigesta : that guy makes me sick⟩

indigestión *nf, pl* **-tiones** EMPACHO : indigestion

indigesto, -ta *adj* : indigestible, difficult to digest

indignación *nf, pl* **-ciones** : indignation

indignado, -da *adj* : indignant

indignante *adj* : outrageous, infuriating

indignar *vt* : to outrage, to infuriate — **indignarse** *vr*

indignidad *nf* : indignity

indigno, -na *adj* : unworthy

índigo *nm* : indigo

indio[1], **-dia** *adj* **1** : American Indian, Indian, Amerindian **2** : Indian (from India)

indio[2], **-dia** *n* **1** : American Indian **2** : Indian (from India)

indirecta *nf* **1** : hint, innuendo **2 echar indirectas** *or* **lanzar indirectas** : to drop a hint, to insinuate

indirecto, -ta *adj* : indirect — **indirectamente** *adv*

indisciplina *nf* : indiscipline, unruliness

indisciplinado, -da *adj* : undisciplined, unruly

indiscreción *nf, pl* **-ciones 1** IMPRUDENCIA : indiscretion **2** : tactless remark

indiscreto, -ta *adj* IMPRUDENTE : indiscreet, imprudent — **indiscretamente** *adv*

indiscriminado, -da *adj* : indiscriminate — **indiscriminadamente** *adv*

indiscutible *adj* INCONTESTABLE, INCUESTIONABLE : indisputable, unquestionable — **indiscutiblemente** *adv*

indispensable *adj* : indispensable — **indispensablemente** *adv*

indisponer {60} *vt* **1** : to spoil, to upset **2** : to make ill — **indisponerse** *vr* **1** : to become ill **2** ~ **con** : to fall out with

indisposición *nf, pl* **-ciones** : indisposition, illness

indispuesto, -ta *adj* : unwell, indisposed

indistinguible *adj* : indistinguishable

indistintamente *adv* **1** : indistinctly **2** : indiscriminately

indistinto, -ta *adj* : indistinct, vague, faint

individual *adj* : individual — **individualmente** *adv*

individualidad *nf* : individuality

individualismo *nm* : individualism

individualista[1] *adj* : individualistic

individualista[2] *nmf* : individualist

individualizar {21} *vt* : to individualize

individuo *nm* : individual, person

indivisible *adj* : indivisible — **indivisibilidad** *nf*

indocumentado, -da *n* : illegal immigrant

índole *nf* **1** : nature, character **2** CLASE, TIPO : sort, kind

indolencia *nf* : indolence, laziness

indolente *adj* : indolent, lazy

indoloro, -ra *adj* : painless

indomable *adj* **1** : indomitable **2** : unruly, unmanageable

indómito, -ta *adj* : indomitable

indonesio, -sia *adj & n* : Indonesian

inducción *nf, pl* **-ciones** : induction

inducir {61} *vt* **1** : to induce, to cause **2** : to infer, to deduce

inductivo, -va *adj* : inductive

indudable *adj* : unquestionable, beyond doubt

indudablemente *adv* : undoubtedly, unquestionably

indulgencia *nf* **1** : indulgence, leniency **2** : indulgence (in religion)

indulgente *adj* : indulgent, lenient

indultar *vt* : to pardon, to reprieve

indulto *nm* : pardon, reprieve

indumentaria *nf* : clothing, attire

industria *nf* : industry

industrial[1] *adj* : industrial

industrial[2] *nmf* : industrialist, manufacturer

industrialización *nf, pl* **-ciones** : industrialization

industrializar {21} *vt* : to industrialize

industrioso, -sa *adj* : industrious

inédito, -ta *adj* **1** : unpublished **2** : unprecedented

inefable *adj* : ineffable

ineficacia *nf* **1** : inefficiency **2** : ineffectiveness

ineficaz *adj, pl* **-caces 1** : inefficient **2** : ineffective — **ineficazmente** *adv*

ineficiencia *nf* : inefficiency

ineficiente *adj* : inefficient — **ineficientemente** *adv*

inelegancia *nf* : inelegance — **inelegante** *adj*

inelegible *adj* : ineligible — **inelegibilidad** *nf*

ineludible *adj* : inescapable, unavoidable — **ineludiblemente** *adv*

ineptitud *nf* : ineptitude, incompetence

inepto, -ta *adj* : inept, incompetent

inequidad *nf* : inequity

inequitativo, -va *adj* : inequitable

inequívoco, -ca *adj* : unequivocal, unmistakable — **inequívocamente** *adv*

inercia *nf* **1** : inertia **2** : apathy, passivity **3 por** ~ : out of habit

inerme *adj* : unarmed, defenseless

inerte *adj* : inert
inescrupuloso, -sa *adj* : unscrupulous
inescrutable *adj* : inscrutable
inesperado, -da *adj* : unexpected — **inesperadamente** *adv*
inestabilidad *nf* : instability, unsteadiness
inestable *adj* : unstable, unsteady
inestimable *adj* : inestimable, invaluable
inevitabilidad *nf* : inevitability
inevitable *adj* : inevitable, unavoidable — **inevitablemente** *adv*
inexactitud *nf* : inaccuracy
inexacto, -ta *adj* : inexact, inaccurate
inexcusable *adj* : inexcusable, unforgivable
inexistencia *nf* : lack, nonexistence
inexistente *adj* : nonexistent
inexorable *adj* : inexorable — **inexorablemente** *adv*
inexperiencia *nf* : inexperience
inexperto, -ta *adj* : inexperienced, unskilled
inexplicable *adj* : inexplicable — **inexplicablemente** *adv*
inexplorado, -da *adj* : unexplored
inexpresable *adj* : inexpressible
inexpresivo, -va *adj* : inexpressive, expressionless
inexpugnable *adj* : impregnable
inextinguible *adj* **1** : inextinguishable **2** : unquenchable
inextricable *adj* : inextricable — **inextricablemente** *adv*
infalibilidad *nf* : infallibility
infalible *adj* : infallible — **infaliblemente** *adv*
infame *adj* **1** : infamous **2** : loathsome, vile ⟨tiempo infame : terrible weather⟩
infamia *nf* : infamy, disgrace
infancia *nf* **1** NIÑEZ : infancy, childhood **2** : children *pl* **3** : beginnings *pl*
infante *nm* **1** : infante, prince **2** : infantryman
infantería *nf* : infantry
infantil *adj* **1** : childish, infantile **2** : child's, children's
infantilismo *nm* **1** : infantilism **2** INMADUREZ : childishness
infarto *nm* : heart attack
infatigable *adj* : indefatigable, tireless — **infatigablemente** *adv*
infección *nf, pl* **-ciones** : infection
infeccioso, -sa *adj* : infectious
infectar *vt* : to infect — **infectarse** *vr*
infecto, -ta *adj* **1** : infected **2** : repulsive, sickening
infecundidad *nf* : infertility
infecundo, -da *adj* : infertile, barren
infelicidad *nf* : unhappiness
infeliz[1] *adj, pl* **-lices** **1** : unhappy **2** : hapless, unfortunate, wretched
infeliz[2] *nmf, pl* **-lices** : wretch
inferencia *nf* : inference
inferior[1] *adj* : inferior, lower
inferior[2] *nmf* : inferior, underling
inferioridad *nf* : inferiority

inferir {76} *vt* **1** DEDUCIR : to infer, to deduce **2** : to cause (harm or injury), to inflict
infernal *adj* : infernal, hellish
infestación *n, pl* **-ciones** : infestation
infestar *vt* **1** : to infest **2** : to overrun, to invade
inficción *nf, pl* **-ciones** *Mex* : pollution
infidelidad *nf* : unfaithfulness, infidelity
infiel[1] *adj* : unfaithful, disloyal
infiel[2] *nmf* : infidel, heathen
infierno *nm* **1** : hell **2 el quinto infierno** : the middle of nowhere
infiltrar *vt* : to infiltrate — **infiltrarse** *vr* — **infiltración** *nf*
infinidad *nf* **1** : infinity **2** SINFÍN : great number, huge quantity ⟨una infinidad de veces : countless times⟩
infinitesimal *adj* : infinitesimal
infinitivo *nm* : infinitive
infinito[1] *adv* : infinitely, vastly
infinito[2], **-ta** *adj* **1** : infinite **2** : limitless, endless **3 hasta lo infinito** : ad infinitum — **infinitamente** *adv*
infinito[3] *nm* : infinity
inflable *adj* : inflatable
inflación *nf, pl* **-ciones** : inflation
inflacionario, -ria *adj* : inflationary
inflacionista → **inflacionario**
inflamable *adj* : flammable
inflamación *nf, pl* **-ciones** : inflammation
inflamar *vt* : to inflame
inflamatorio, -ria *adj* : inflammatory
inflar *vt* HINCHAR : to inflate — **inflarse** *vr* **1** : to swell **2** : to become conceited
inflexibilidad *nf* : inflexibility
inflexible *adj* : inflexible, unyielding
inflexión *nf, pl* **-xiones** : inflection
infligir {35} *vt* : to inflict
influencia *nf* INFLUJO : influence
influenciable *adj* : easily influenced, suggestible
influenciar *vt* : to influence
influenza *nf* : influenza
influir {41} *vt* : to influence — *vi* ~ **en** *or* ~ **sobre** : to have an influence on, to affect
influjo *nm* INFLUENCIA : influence
influyente *adj* : influential
información *nf, pl* **-ciones** **1** : information **2** INFORME : report, inquiry **3** NOTICIAS : news
informado, -da *adj* : informed ⟨bien informado : well-informed⟩
informador, -dora *n* : informer, informant
informal *adj* **1** : unreliable (of persons) **2** : informal, casual — **informalmente** *adv*
informalidad *nf* : informality
informante *nmf* : informant
informar *vt* ENTERAR : to inform — *vi* : to report — **informarse** *vr* ENTERARSE : to get information, to find out
informática *nf* : computer science, computing

informativo¹, -va *adj* : informative
informativo² *nm* : news program, news
informatización *nf, pl* **-ciones** : computerization
informatizar {21} *vt* : to computerize
informe¹ *adj* AMORFO : shapeless, formless
informe² *nm* **1** : report **2** : reference (for employment) **3 informes** *nmpl* : information, data
infortunado, -da *adj* : unfortunate, unlucky
infortunio *nm* **1** DESGRACIA : misfortune **2** CONTRATIEMPO : mishap
infracción *nf, pl* **-ciones** : violation, offense, infraction
infractor, -tora *n* : offender
infraestructura *nf* : infrastructure
infrahumano, -na *adj* : subhuman
infranqueable *adj* **1** : impassable **2** : insurmountable
infrarrojo, -ja *adj* : infrared
infrecuente *adj* : infrequent
infringir {35} *vt* : to infringe, to breach
infructuoso, -sa *adj* : fruitless — **infructuosamente** *adv*
ínfulas *nfpl* **1** : conceit **2 darse ínfulas** : to put on airs
infundado, -da *adj* : unfounded, baseless
infundio *nm* : false story, lie, tall tale ⟨todo eso son infundios : that's a pack of lies⟩
infundir *vt* **1** : to instill **2 infundir ánimo a** : to encourage **3 infundir miedo a** : to intimidate
infusión *nf, pl* **-siones** : infusion
ingeniar *vt* : to devise, to think up — **ingeniarse** *vr* : to manage, to find a way
ingeniería *nf* : engineering
ingeniero, -ra *n* : engineer
ingenio *nm* **1** : ingenuity **2** CHISPA : wit, wits **3** : device, apparatus **4 ingenio azucarero** : sugar refinery
ingenioso, -sa *adj* **1** : ingenious **2** : clever, witty — **ingeniosamente** *adv*
ingente *adj* : huge, enormous
ingenuidad *nf* : naïveté, ingenuousness
ingenuo¹, -nua *adj* CÁNDIDO : naive — **ingenuamente** *adv*
ingenuo², -nua *n* : naive person
ingerencia → injerencia
ingerir {76} *vt* : to ingest, to consume
ingestión *nf, pl* **-tiones** : ingestion
ingle *nf* : groin
inglés¹, -glesa *adj, mpl* **ingleses** : English
inglés², -glesa *n, mpl* **ingleses** : Englishman *m*, Englishwoman *f*
inglés³ *nm* : English (language)
inglete *nm* : miter joint
ingobernable *adj* : ungovernable, lawless
ingratitud *nf* : ingratitude
ingrato¹, -ta *adj* **1** : ungrateful **2** : thankless
ingrato², -ta *n* : ingrate
ingrediente *nm* : ingredient

ingresar *vt* **1** : to admit ⟨ingresaron a Luis al hospital : Luis was admitted into the hospital⟩ **2** : to deposit — *vi* **1** : to enter, to go in **2** ~ **en** : to join, to enroll in
ingreso *nm* **1** : entrance, entry **2** : admission **3 ingresos** *nmpl* : income, earnings *pl*
íngrimo, -ma *adj* : all alone, all by oneself
inhábil *adj* : unskillful, clumsy
inhabilidad *nf* **1** : unskillfulness **2** : unfitness
inhabilitar *vt* **1** : to disqualify, to bar **2** : to disable
inhabitable *adj* : uninhabitable
inhabituado, -da *adj* ~ **a** : unaccustomed to
inhalador *nm* : inhaler
inhalante *nm* : inhalant
inhalar *vt* : to inhale — **inhalación** *nf*
inherente *adj* : inherent
inhibición *nf, pl* **-ciones** COHIBICIÓN : inhibition
inhibir *vt* : to inhibit — **inhibirse** *vr*
inhóspito, -ta *adj* : inhospitable
inhumación *nf, pl* **-ciones** : interment, burial
inhumanidad *nf* : inhumanity
inhumano, -na *adj* : inhuman, cruel, inhumane
inhumar *vt* : to inter, to bury
iniciación *nf, pl* **-ciones** **1** : initiation **2** : introduction
iniciado, -da *n* : initiate
iniciador¹, -dora *adj* : initiatory
iniciador², -dora *n* : initiator, originator
inicial¹ *adj* : initial, original — **inicialmente** *adv*
inicial² *nf* : initial (letter)
iniciar *vt* COMENZAR : to initiate, to begin — **iniciarse** *vr*
iniciativa *nf* : initiative
inicio *nm* COMIENZO : beginning
inicuo, -cua *adj* : iniquitous, wicked
igualado, -da *adj* : unequaled
inimaginable *adj* : unimaginable
inimitable *adj* : inimitable
ininteligible *adj* : unintelligible
ininterrumpido, -da *adj* : uninterrupted, continuous — **ininterrumpidamente** *adv*
iniquidad *nf* : iniquity, wickedness
injerencia *nf* : interference
injerirse {76} *vr* ENTROMETERSE, INMISCUIRSE : to meddle, to interfere
injertar *vt* : to graft
injerto *nm* : graft ⟨injerto de piel : skin graft⟩
injuria *nf* AGRAVIO : affront, insult
injuriar *vt* INSULTAR : to insult, to revile
injurioso, -sa *adj* : insulting, abusive
injusticia *nf* : injustice, unfairness
injustificable *adj* : unjustifiable
injustificadamente *adv* : unjustifiably, unfairly
injustificado, -da *adj* : unjustified, unwarranted

injusto, -ta *adj* : unfair, unjust — **injustamente** *adv*

inmaculado, -da *adj* : immaculate, spotless

inmadurez *nf, pl* **-reces** : immaturity

inmaduro, -ra *adj* 1 : immature 2 : unripe

inmediaciones *nfpl* : environs, surrounding area

inmediatamente *adv* ENSEGUIDA : immediately

inmediatez *nf, pl* **-teces** : immediacy

inmediato, -ta *adj* 1 : immediate 2 CONTIGUO : adjoining 3 **de ~** : immediately, right away 4 **~ a** : next to, close to

inmejorable *adj* : excellent, unbeatable

inmemorial *adj* : immemorial ⟨tiempos inmemoriales : time immemorial⟩

inmensidad *nf* : immensity, vastness

inmenso, -sa *adj* ENORME : immense, huge, vast — **inmensamente** *adv*

inmensurable *adj* : boundless, immeasurable

inmerecido, -da *adj* : undeserved — **inmerecidamente** *adv*

inmersión *nf, pl* **-siones** : immersion

inmerso, -sa *adj* 1 : immersed 2 : involved, absorbed

inmigración *nf, pl* **-ciones** : immigration

inmigrado, -da *adj & n* : immigrant

inmigrante *adj & nmf* : immigrant

inmigrar *vi* : to immigrate

inminencia *nf* : imminence

inminente *adj* : imminent — **inminentemente** *adv*

inmiscuirse {41} *vr* ENTROMETERSE, INJERIRSE : to meddle, to interfere

inmobiliario, -ria *adj* : real estate, property

inmoderación *n, pl* **-ciones** : immoderation, intemperance

inmoderado, -da *adj* : immoderate, excessive — **inmoderamente** *adv*

inmodestia *nf* : immodesty — **inmodesto, -ta** *adj*

inmolar *vt* : to immolate — **inmolación** *nf*

inmoral *adj* : immoral

inmoralidad *nf* : immorality

inmortal *adj & nmf* : immortal

inmortalidad *nf* : immortality

inmortalizar {21} *vt* : to immortalize

inmotivado, -da *adj* 1 : unmotivated 2 : groundless

inmovible *adj* : immovable, fixed

inmóvil *adj* 1 : still, motionless 2 : steadfast

inmovilidad *nf* : immobility

inmovilizar {21} *vt* : to immobilize

inmueble *nm* : building, property

inmundicia *nf* : dirt, filth, trash

inmundo, -da *adj* : dirty, filthy, nasty

inmune *adj* : immune

inmunidad *nf* : immunity

inmunizar {21} *vt* : to immunize — **inmunización** *nf*

inmunología *nf* : immunology

inmunológico, -ca *adj* : immune ⟨sistema inmunológico : immune system⟩

inmutabilidad *nf* : immutability

inmutable *adj* : immutable, unchangeable

innato, -ta *adj* : innate, inborn

innecesario, -ria *adj* : unnecessary — **innecesariamente** *adv*

innegable *adj* : undeniable

innoble *adj* : ignoble — **innoblemente** *adv*

innovación *nf, pl* **-ciones** : innovation

innovador, -dora *adj* : innovative

innovar *vt* : to introduce — *vi* : to innovate

innumerable *adj* INCONTABLE : innumerable, countless

inobjetable *adj* : indisputable, unobjectionable

inocencia *nf* : innocence

inocente¹ *adj* 1 : innocent 2 INGENUO : naive — **inocentemente** *adv*

inocente² *nmf* : innocent person

inocentón¹, -tona *adj, mpl* **-tones** : naive, gullible

inocentón², -tona *n, mpl* **-tones** : simpleton, dupe

inocuidad *nf* : harmlessness

inocular *vt* : to inoculate, to vaccinate — **inoculación** *nf*

inocuo, -cua *adj* : innocuous, harmless

inodoro¹, -ra *adj* : odorless

inodoro² *nm* : toilet

inofensivo, -va *adj* : inoffensive, harmless

inolvidable *adj* : unforgettable

inoperable *adj* : inoperable

inoperante *adj* : ineffective, inoperative

inopinado, -da *adj* : unexpected — **inopinadamente** *adv*

inoportuno, -na *adj* : untimely, inopportune, inappropriate

inorgánico, -ca *adj* : inorganic

inoxidable *adj* 1 : rustproof 2 **acero inoxidable** : stainless steel

inquebrantable *adj* : unshakable, unwavering

inquietante *adj* : disturbing, worrisome

inquietar *vt* PREOCUPAR : to disturb, to upset, to worry — **inquietarse** *vr*

inquieto, -ta *adj* 1 : anxious, uneasy, worried 2 : restless

inquietud *nf* 1 : anxiety, uneasiness, worry 2 AGITACIÓN : restlessness

inquilinato *nm* : tenancy

inquilino, -na *n* : tenant, occupant

inquina *nf* 1 : aversion, dislike 2 : ill will ⟨tener inquina a alguien : to have a grudge against someone⟩

inquirir {4} *vi* : to make inquiries — *vt* : to investigate

inquisición *nf, pl* **-ciones** : investigation, inquiry

inquisidor, -dora *adj* : inquisitive

inquisitivo, -va *adj* : inquisitive, curious — **inquisitivamente** *adv*

insaciable *adj* : insatiable

insalubre *adj* 1 : unhealthy 2 ANTIHIGIÉNICO : unsanitary

insalubridad *nf* : unhealthiness
insalvable *adj* : insuperable, insurmountable
insano, -na *adj* 1 LOCO : insane, mad 2 INSALUBRE : unhealthy
insatisfacción *nf, pl* -ciones : dissatisfaction
insatisfactorio *nm* : unsatisfactory
insatisfecho, -cha *adj* 1 : dissatisfied 2 : unsatisfied
inscribir {33} *vt* 1 MATRICULAR : to enroll, to register 2 GRABAR : to engrave — **inscribirse** *vr* : to register, to sign up
inscripción *nf, pl* -ciones 1 MATRÍCULA : enrollment, registration 2 : inscription
inscrito *pp* → **inscribir**
insecticida[1] *adj* : insecticidal
insecticida[2] *nm* : insecticide
insecto *nm* : insect
inseguridad *nf* 1 : insecurity 2 : lack of safety 3 : uncertainty
inseguro, -ra *adj* 1 : insecure 2 : unsafe 3 : uncertain
inseminar *vt* : to inseminate — **inseminación** *nf*
insensatez *nf, pl* -teces : foolishness, stupidity
insensato[1], **-ta** *adj* : foolish, senseless
insensato[2], **-ta** *n* : fool
insensibilidad *nf* : insensitivity
insensible *adj* : insensitive, unfeeling
inseparable *adj* : inseparable — **inseparablemente** *adv*
inserción *nf, pl* -ciones : insertion
insertar *vt* : to insert
inservible *adj* INÚTIL : useless, unusable
insidia *nf* 1 : snare, trap 2 : malice
insidioso, -sa *adj* : insidious
insigne *adj* : noted, famous
insignia *nf* ENSEÑA : insignia, emblem, badge
insignificancia *nf* 1 : insignificance 2 NIMIEDAD : trifle, triviality
insignificante *adj* : insignificant
insincero, -ra *adj* : insincere — **insinceridad** *nf*
insinuación *nf, pl* -ciones : insinuation, hint
insinuante *adj* : suggestive
insinuar {3} *vt* : to insinuate, to hint at — **insinuarse** *vr* 1 ~ **a** : to make advances to 2 ~ **en** : to worm one's way into
insipidez *nf, pl* -deces : insipidness, blandness
insípido, -da *adj* : insipid, bland
insistencia *nf* : insistence
insistente *adj* : insistent — **insistentemente** *adv*
insistir *v* : to insist
insociable *adj* : unsociable
insolación *nf, pl* -ciones : sunstroke
insolencia *nf* IMPERTINENCIA : insolence
insolente *adj* IMPERTINENTE : insolent
insólito, -ta *adj* : rare, unusual

insoluble *adj* : insoluble — **insolubilidad** *nf*
insolvencia *nf* : insolvency, bankruptcy
insolvente *adj* : insolvent, bankrupt
insomne *adj* & *nmf* : insomniac
insomnio *nm* : insomnia
insondable *adj* : fathomless, deep
insonorizado, -da *adj* : soundproof
insoportable *adj* INAGUANTABLE : unbearable, intolerable
insoslayable *adj* : unavoidable, inescapable
insospechado, -da *adj* : unexpected, unforeseen
insostenible *adj* : untenable
inspección *nf, pl* -ciones : inspection
inspeccionar *vt* : to inspect
inspector, -tora *n* : inspector
inspiración *nf, pl* -ciones 1 : inspiration 2 INHALACIÓN : inhalation
inspirador, -dora *adj* : inspiring
inspirar *vt* : to inspire — *vi* INHALAR : to inhale
instalación *nf, pl* -ciones : installation
instalar *vt* 1 : to install 2 : to instate — **instalarse** *vr* ESTABLECERSE : to settle, to establish oneself
instancia *nf* 1 : petition, request 2 **en última instancia** : as a last resort
instantánea *nf* : snapshot
instantáneo, -nea *adj* : instantaneous — **instantáneamente** *adv*
instante *nm* 1 : instant, moment 2 **al instante** : immediately 3 **a cada instante** : frequently, all the time 4 **por instantes** : constantly, incessantly
instar *vt* APREMIAR : to urge, to press — *vi* URGIR : to be urgent or pressing ⟨insta que vayamos pronto : it is imperative that we leave soon⟩
instauración *nf, pl* -ciones : establishment
instaurar *vt* : to establish
instigador, -dora *n* : instigator
instigar {52} *vt* : to instigate, to incite
instintivo, -va *adj* : instinctive — **instintivamente** *adv*
instinto *nm* : instinct
institución *nf, pl* -ciones : institution
institucional *adj* : institutional — **institucionalmente** *adv*
institucionalización *nf, pl* -ciones : institutionalization
institucionalizar {21} *vt* : to institutionalize
instituir {41} *vt* ESTABLECER, FUNDAR : to institute, to establish, to found
instituto *nm* : institute
institutriz *nf, pl* -trices : governess *f*
instrucción *nf, pl* -ciones 1 EDUCACIÓN : education 2 **instrucciones** *nfpl* : instructions, directions
instructivo, -va *adj* : instructive, educational
instructor, -tora *n* : instructor
instruir {41} *vt* 1 ADIESTRAR : to instruct, to train 2 ENSEÑAR : to educate, to teach

instrumentación *nf, pl* **-ciones** : orchestration
instrumental *adj* : instrumental
instrumentar *vt* : to orchestrate
instrumentista *nmf* : instrumentalist
instrumento *nm* : instrument
insubordinado, -da *adj* : insubordinate — **insubordinación** *nf*
insubordinarse *vr* : to rebel
insuficiencia *nf* **1** : insufficiency, inadequacy **2 insuficiencia cardíaca** : heart failure
insuficiente *adj* : insufficient, inadequate — **insuficientemente** *adv*
insufrible *adj* : insufferable
insular *adj* : insular
insularidad *nf* : insularity
insulina *nf* : insulin
insulso, -sa *adj* **1** INSÍPIDO : insipid, bland **2** : dull
insultante *adj* : insulting
insultar *vt* : to insult
insulto *nm* : insult
insumos *nmpl* : supplies ⟨insumos agrícolas : agricultural supplies⟩
insuperable *adj* : insuperable, insurmountable
insurgente *adj & nmf* : insurgent — **insurgencia** *nf*
insurrección *nf, pl* **-ciones** : insurrection, uprising
insustancial *adj* : insubstantial, flimsy
insustituible *adj* : irreplaceable
intachable *adj* : irreproachable, faultless
intacto, -ta *adj* : intact
intangible *adj* IMPALPABLE : intangible, impalpable
integración *nf, pl* **-ciones** : integration
integral *adj* **1** : integral, essential **2 pan integral** : whole grain bread
integrante[1] *adj* : integrating, integral
integrante[2] *nmf* : member
integrar *vt* : to make up, to compose — **integrarse** *vr* : to integrate, to fit in
integridad *nf* **1** RECTITUD : integrity, honesty **2** : wholeness, completeness
integrismo *nm* : fundamentalism
integrista *adj & nmf* : fundamentalist
íntegro, -gra *adj* **1** : honest, upright **2** ENTERO : whole, complete **3** : unabridged
intelecto *nm* : intellect
intelectual *adj & nmf* : intellectual — **intelectualmente** *adv*
intelectualidad *nf* : intelligentsia
inteligencia *nf* : intelligence
inteligente *adj* : intelligent — **inteligentemente** *adv*
inteligible *adj* : intelligible — **inteligibilidad** *nf*
intemperancia *adj* : intemperance, excess
intemperie *nf* **1** : bad weather, elements *pl* **2 a la intemperie** : in the open air, outside
intempestivo, -va *adj* : inopportune, untimely — **intempestivamente** *adv*

intención *nf, pl* **-ciones** : intention, plan
intencionado, -da → **intencional**
intencional *adj* : intentional — **intencionalmente** *adv*
intendencia *nf* : management, administration
intendente *nmf* : quartermaster
intensidad *nf* : intensity
intensificación *nf, pl* **-ciones** : intensification
intensificar {72} *vt* : to intensify — **intensificarse** *vr*
intensivo, -va *adj* : intensive — **intensivamente** *adv*
intenso, -sa *adj* : intense — **intensamente** *adv*
intentar *vt* : to attempt, to try
intento *nm* **1** PROPÓSITO : intent, intention **2** TENTATIVA : attempt, try
interacción *nf, pl* **-ciones** : interaction
interactivo, -va *adj* : interactive
interactuar {3} *vi* : to interact
intercalar *vt* : to intersperse, to insert
intercambiable *adj* : interchangeable
intercambiar *vt* CANJEAR : to exchange, to trade
intercambio *nm* CANJE : exchange, trade
interceder *vi* : to intercede
intercepción *nf, pl* **-ciones** : interception
interceptar *vt* **1** : to intercept, to block **2 interceptar las líneas** : to wiretap
intercesión *nf, pl* **-siones** : intercession
intercomunicación *nf, pl* **-ciones** : intercommunication
interconexión *nf, pl* **-xiones** : interconnection
interconfesional *adj* : interdenominational
interdepartamental *adj* : interdepartmental
interdependencia *nf* : interdependence — **interdependiente** *adj*
interdicción *nf, pl* **-ciones** : interdiction, prohibition
interés *nm, pl* **-reses** : interest
interesado, -da *adj* **1** : interested **2** : selfish, self-seeking
interesante *adj* : interesting
interesar *vt* : to interest — *vi* : to be of interest, to be interesting — **interesarse** *vr*
interestatal *adj* : interstate ⟨autopista interestatal : interstate highway⟩
interestelar *adj* : interstellar
interfase → **interfaz**
interfaz *nf, pl* **-faces** : interface
interferencia *nf* : interference, static
interferir {76} *vi* : to interfere, to meddle — *vt* : to interfere with, to obstruct
intergaláctico, -ca *adj* : intergalactic
intergubernamental *adj* : intergovernmental
interín[1] *or* **ínterin** *adv* : meanwhile
interín[2] *or* **ínterin** *nm, pl* **-rines** : meantime, interim ⟨en el interín : in the meantime⟩

interinamente *adv* : temporarily
interino, -na *adj* : acting, temporary, interim
interior[1] *adj* : interior, inner
interior[2] *nm* **1** : interior, inside **2** : inland region
interiormente *adv* : inwardly
interjección *nf, pl* -ciones : interjection
interlocutor, -tora *n* : interlocutor, speaker
interludio *nm* : interlude
intermediario, -ria *adj & n* : intermediary, go-between
intermedio[1], **-dia** *adj* : intermediate
intermedio[2] *nm* **1** : intermission **2 por intermedio de** : by means of
interminable *adj* : interminable, endless — **interminablemente** *adv*
intermisión *nf, pl* -siones : intermission, pause
intermitente[1] *adj* **1** : intermittent **2** : flashing, blinking (of a light) — **intermitentemente** *adv*
intermitente[2] *nm* : blinker, turn signal
internacional *adj* : international — **internacionalmente** *adv*
internacionalismo *nm* : internationalism
internacionalizar {21} *vt* : to internationalize
internado *nm* : boarding school
internar *vt* : to commit, to confine — **internarse** *vr* **1** : to penetrate, to advance into **2 ~ en** : to go into, to enter
internista *nmf* : internist
interno[1], **-na** *adj* : internal — **internamente** *adv*
interno[2], **-na** *n* **1** : intern **2** : inmate, internee
interpelación *nf, pl* -ciones : appeal, plea
interpelar *vt* : to question (formally)
interpersonal *adj* : interpersonal
interpolar *vt* : to insert, to interpolate
interponer {60} *vt* : to interpose — **interponerse** *vr* : to intervene
interpretación *nf, pl* -ciones : interpretation
interpretar *vt* **1** : to interpret **2** : to play, to perform
interpretativo, -va *adj* : interpretive
intérprete *nmf* **1** TRADUCTOR : interpreter **2** : performer
interpuesto *pp* → interponer
interracial *adj* : interracial
interrelación *nf, pl* -ciones : interrelationship
interrelacionar *vi* : to interrelate
interrogación *nf, pl* -ciones **1** : interrogation, questioning **2 signo de interrogación** : question mark
interrogador, -dora *n* : interrogator, questioner
interrogante[1] *adj* : questioning
interrogante[2] *nm* **1** : question mark **2** : query
interrogar {52} *vt* : to interrogate, to question

interrogativo, -va *adj* : interrogative
interrogatorio *nm* : interrogation, questioning
interrumpir *v* : to interrupt
interrupción *nf, pl* -ciones : interruption
interruptor *nm* **1** : (electrical) switch **2** : circuit breaker
intersección *nf, pl* -ciones : intersection
intersticio *nm* : interstice — **intersticial** *adj*
interuniversitario, -ria *adj* : intercollegiate
interurbano, -na *adj* **1** : intercity **2** : long-distance ⟨llamadas interurbanas : long-distance calls⟩
intervalo *nm* : interval
intervención *nf, pl* -ciones **1** : intervention **2** : audit **3 intervención quirúrgica** : operation
intervencionista *adj & nmf* : interventionist
intervenir {87} *vi* **1** : to take part **2** INTERCEDER : to intervene, to intercede — *vt* **1** : to control, to supervise **2** : to audit **3** : to operate on **4** : to tap (a telephone)
interventor, -tora *n* **1** : inspector **2** : auditor, comptroller
intestado, -da *adj* : intestate
intestinal *adj* : intestinal
intestino *nm* : intestine
intimar *vi* ~ **con** : to become friendly with — *vt* : to require, to call on
intimidación *nf, pl* -ciones : intimidation
intimidad *nf* **1** : intimacy **2** : privacy, private life
intimidar *vt* ACOBARDAR : to intimidate
íntimo, -ma *adj* **1** : intimate, close **2** PRIVADO : private — **íntimamente** *adv*
intitular *vt* : to entitle, to title
intocable *adj* : untouchable
intolerable *adj* : intolerable, unbearable
intolerancia *nf* : intolerance
intolerante[1] *adj* : intolerant
intolerante[2] *nmf* : intolerant person, bigot
intoxicación *nf, pl* -ciones : poisoning
intoxicante *nm* : poison
intoxicar {72} *vt* : to poison
intranquilidad *nf* PREOCUPACIÓN : worry, anxiety
intranquilizar {21} *vt* : to upset, to make uneasy — **intranquilizarse** *vr* : to get worried, to be anxious
intranquilo, -la *adj* PREOCUPADO : uneasy, worried
intransigencia *nf* : intransigence
intransigente *adj* : intransigent, unyielding
intransitable *adj* : impassable
intransitivo, -va *adj* : intransitive
intrascendente *adj* : unimportant, insignificant
intratable *adj* **1** : intractable **2** : awkward **3** : unsociable
intravenoso, -sa *adj* : intravenous

intrepidez *nf* : fearlessness
intrépido, -da *adj* : intrepid, fearless
intriga *nf* : intrigue
intrigante *nmf* : schemer
intrigar {52} *v* : to intrigue — **intrigante** *adj*
intrincado, -da *adj* : intricate, involved
intrínseco, -ca *adj* : intrinsic — **intrínsecamente** *adv*
introducción *nf, pl* **-ciones** : introduction
introducir {61} *vt* **1** : to introduce **2** : to bring in **3** : to insert **4** : to input, to enter — **introducirse** *vr* : to penetrate, to get into
introductorio, -ria *adj* : introductory
intromisión *nf, pl* **-siones** : interference, meddling
introspección *nf, pl* **-ciones** : introspection
introspectivo, -va *adj* : introspective
introvertido[1], -da *adj* : introverted
introvertido[2], -da *n* : introvert
intrusión *nf, pl* **-siones** : intrusion
intruso[1], -sa *adj* : intrusive
intruso[2], -sa *n* : intruder
intuición *nf, pl* **-ciones** : intuition
intuir {41} *vt* : to intuit, to sense
intuitivo, -va *adj* : intuitive — **intuitivamente** *adv*
inundación *nf, pl* **-ciones** : flood, inundation
inundar *vt* : to flood, to inundate
inusitado, -da *adj* : unusual, uncommon — **inusitadamente** *adv*
inusual *adj* : unusual, uncommon — **inusualmente** *adv*
inútil[1] *adj* INSERVIBLE : useless — **inútilmente** *adv*
inútil[2] *nmf* : good-for-nothing
inutilidad *nf* : uselessness
inutilizar {21} *vt* **1** : to make useless **2** INCAPACITAR : to disable, to put out of commission
invadir *vt* : to invade
invalidar *vt* : to nullify, to invalidate
invalidez *nf, pl* **-deces** **1** : invalidity **2** : disablement
inválido, -da *adj & n* : invalid
invalorable *adj* : invaluable
invariable *adj* : invariable — **invariablemente** *adv*
invasión *nf, pl* **-siones** : invasion
invasivo, -va *adj* : invasive
invasor[1], -sora *adj* : invading
invasor[2], -sora *n* : invader
invectiva *nf* : invective, abuse
invencibilidad *nf* : invincibility
invencible *adj* **1** : invincible **2** : insurmountable
invención *nf, pl* **-ciones** **1** INVENTO : invention **2** MENTIRA : fabrication, lie
inventar *vt* **1** : to invent **2** : to fabricate, to make up
inventariar {85} *vt* : to inventory
inventario *nm* : inventory
inventiva *nf* : ingenuity, inventiveness
inventivo, -va *adj* : inventive

invento *nm* INVENCIÓN : invention
inventor, -tora *n* : inventor
invernadero *nm* : greenhouse, hothouse
invernal *adj* : winter, wintry
invernar {55} *vi* **1** : to spend the winter **2** HIBERNAR : to hibernate
inverosímil *adj* : unlikely, far-fetched
inversión *nf, pl* **-siones** **1** : inversion **2** : investment
inversionista *nmf* : investor
inverso[1], -sa *adj* **1** : inverse, inverted **2** CONTRARIO : opposite **3 a la inversa** : on the contrary, vice versa **4 en orden inverso** : in reverse order — **inversamente** *adv*
inverso[2] *n* : inverse
inversor, -sora *n* : investor
invertebrado[1], -da *adj* : invertebrate
invertebrado[2] *nm* : invertebrate
invertir {76} *vt* **1** : to invert, to reverse **2** : to invest — *vi* : to make an investment — **invertirse** *vr* : to be reversed
investidura *nf* : investiture, inauguration
investigación *nf, pl* **-ciones** **1** ENCUESTA, INDAGACIÓN : investigation, inquiry **2** : research
investigador[1], -dora *adj* : investigative
investigador[2], -dora *n* **1** : investigator **2** : researcher
investigar {52} *vt* **1** INDAGAR : to investigate **2** : to research — *vi* ~ **sobre** : to do research into
investir {54} *vt* **1** : to empower **2** : to swear in, to inaugurate
inveterado, -da *adj* : inveterate, deep-seated
invicto, -ta *adj* : undefeated
invidente[1] *adj* CIEGO : blind, sightless
invidente[2] *nmf* CIEGO : blind person
invierno *nm* : winter, wintertime
inviolable *adj* : inviolable — **inviolabilidad** *nf*
inviolado, -da *adj* : inviolate, pure
invisibilidad *nf* : invisibility
invisible *adj* : invisible — **invisiblemente** *adv*
invitación *nf, pl* **-ciones** : invitation
invitado, -da *n* : guest
invitar *vt* : to invite
invocación *nf, pl* **-ciones** : invocation
invocar {72} *vt* : to invoke, to call on
involucramiento *nm* : involvement
involucrar *vt* : to implicate, to involve — **involucrarse** *vr* : to get involved
involuntario, -ria *adj* : involuntary — **involuntariamente** *adv*
invulnerable *adj* : invulnerable
inyección *nf, pl* **-ciones** : injection, shot
inyectado, -da *adj* **ojos inyectados** : bloodshot eyes
inyectar *vt* : to inject
ion *nm* : ion
iónico, -ca *adj* : ionic
ionizar {21} *vt* : to ionize — **ionización** *nf*
ionosfera *nf* : ionosphere
ir {43} *vi* **1** : to go ⟨ir a pie : to go on foot, to walk⟩ ⟨ir a caballo : to ride

horseback⟩ ⟨ir a casa : to go home⟩ **2** : to lead, to extend, to stretch ⟨el camino va de Cali a Bogotá : the road goes from Cali to Bogotá⟩ **3** FUN-CIONAR : to work, to function ⟨esta computadora ya no va : this computer doesn't work anymore⟩ **4** : to get on, to get along ⟨¿cómo te va? : how are you?, how's it going?⟩ ⟨el negocio no va bien : the business isn't doing well⟩ **5** : to suit ⟨ese vestido te va bien : that dress really suits you⟩ **6** ～ **con** : to be ⟨ir con prisa : to be in a hurry⟩ **7** ～ **por** : to follow, to go along ⟨fueron por la costa : they followed the shoreline⟩ **8 dejarse ir** : to let oneself go **9 ir a parar** : to end up **10 vamos a ver** : let's see — *v aux* **1** (*with present participle*) ⟨ir caminando : to walk⟩ ⟨¡voy corriendo! : I'll be right there!⟩ **2** ～ **a** : to be going to ⟨voy a hacerlo : I'm going to do it⟩ ⟨el avión va a despegar : the plane is about to take off⟩ — **irse** *vr* **1** : to leave, to go ⟨¡vámonos! : let's go!⟩ ⟨todo el mundo se fue : everyone left⟩ **2** ESCAPARSE : to leak **3** GASTARSE : to be used up, to be gone

ira *nf* CÓLERA, FURIA : wrath, anger
iracundo, -da *adj* : irate, angry
iraní *adj & nmf* : Iranian
iraquí *adj & nmf* : Iraqi
irascible *adj* : irascible, irritable — **irascibilidad** *nf*
irga, irgue etc. → **erguir**
iridio *nm* : iridium
iridiscencia *nf* : iridescence — **iridiscente** *adj*
iris *nms & pl* **1** : iris **2 arco iris** : rainbow
irlandés[1], **-desa** *adj, mpl* **-deses** : Irish
irlandés[2], **-desa** *n, pl* **-deses** : Irish person, Irishman *m*, Irishwoman *f*
irlandés[3] *nm* : Irish (language)
ironía *nf* : irony
irónico, -ca *adj* : ironic, ironical — **irónicamente** *adv*
irracional *adj* : irrational — **irracionalmente** *adv*
irracionalidad *nf* : irrationality
irradiación *nf, pl* **-ciones** : irradiation
irradiar *vt* : to radiate, to irradiate
irrazonable *adj* : unreasonable
irreal *adj* : unreal
irrebatible *adj* : unanswerable, irrefutable
irreconciliable *adj* : irreconcilable
irreconocible *adj* : unrecognizable
irrecuperable *adj* : irrecoverable, irretrievable
irredimible *adj* : irredeemable
irreductible *adj* : unyielding
irreemplazable *adj* : irreplaceable
irreflexión *nf, pl* **-xiones** : thoughtlessness, impetuosity
irreflexivo, -va *adj* : rash, unthinking — **irreflexivamente** *adv*
irrefrenable *adj* : uncontrollable, unstoppable ⟨un impulso irrefrenable : an irresistible urge⟩

irrefutable *adj* : irrefutable
irregular *adj* : irregular — **irregularmente** *adv*
irregularidad *nf* : irregularity
irrelevante *adj* : irrelevant — **irrelevancia** *nf*
irreligioso, -sa *adj* : irreligious
irremediable *adj* : incurable — **irremediablemente** *adv*
irreparable *adj* : irreparable
irreprimible *adj* : irrepressible
irreprochable *adj* : irreproachable
irresistible *adj* : irresistible — **irresistiblemente** *adv*
irresolución *nf, pl* **-ciones** : indecision, hesitation
irresoluto, -ta *adj* INDECISO : undecided
irrespeto *nm* : disrespect
irrespetuoso, -sa *adj* : disrespectful — **irrespetuosamente** *adv*
irresponsabilidad *nf* : irresponsibility
irresponsable *adj* : irresponsible — **irresponsablemente** *adv*
irrestricto, -ta *adj* : unrestricted, unconditional
irreverencia *nf* : disrespect
irreverente *adj* : disrespectful
irreversible *adj* : irreversible
irrevocable *adj* : irrevocable — **irrevocablemente** *adv*
irrigar {52} *vt* : to irrigate — **irrigación** *nf*
irrisible *adj* : laughable
irrisión *nf, pl* **-siones** : derision, ridicule
irrisorio, -ria *adj* RISIBLE : ridiculous, ludicrous
irritabilidad *nf* : irritability
irritable *adj* : irritable
irritación *nf, pl* **-ciones** : irritation
irritante *adj* : irritating
irritar *vt* : to irritate — **irritación** *nf*
irrompible *adj* : unbreakable
irrumpir *vi* ～ **en** : to burst into
irrupción *nf, pl* **-ciones** **1** : irruption **2** : invasion
isla *nf* : island
islámico, -ca *adj* : Islamic, Muslim
islandés[1], **-desa** *adj, mpl* **-deses** : Icelandic
islandés[2], **-desa** *n, mpl* **-deses** : Icelander
islandés[3] *nm* : Icelandic (language)
isleño, -ña *n* : islander
islote *nm* : islet
isometría *nfs & pl* : isometrics
isométrico, -ca *adj* : isometric
isósceles *adj* : isosceles ⟨triángulo isósceles : isosceles triangle⟩
isótopo *nm* : isotope
israelí *adj & nmf* : Israeli
istmo *nm* : isthmus
itacate *nm Mex* : pack, provisions *pl*
italiano[1], **-na** *adj & n* : Italian
italiano[2] *nm* : Italian (language)
iterbio *nm* : ytterbium
itinerante *adj* AMBULANTE : traveling, itinerant
itinerario *nm* : itinerary, route

itrio *nm* : yttrium
izar {21} *vt* : to hoist, to raise ⟨izar la bandera : to raise the flag⟩

izquierda *nf* : left
izquierdista *adj & nmf* : leftist
izquierdo, -da *adj* : left

J

j *nf* : tenth letter of the Spanish alphabet
ja *interj* 1 : ha! 2 ja, ja : ha-ha!
jabalí *nm* : wild boar
jabalina *nf* : javelin
jabón *nm, pl* jabones : soap
jabonar *vt* ENJABONAR : to soap up, to lather — jabonarse *vr*
jabonera *nf* : soap dish
jabonoso, -sa *adj* : soapy
jaca *nf* 1 : pony 2 YEGUA : mare
jacal *nm Mex* : shack, hut
jacinto *nm* : hyacinth
jactancia *nf* 1 : boastfulness 2 : boasting, bragging
jactancioso[1], -sa *adj* : boastful
jactancioso[2], -sa *n* : boaster, braggart
jactarse *vr* : to boast, to brag
jade *nm* : jade
jadear *vi* : to pant, to gasp, to puff — jadeante *adj*
jadeo *nm* : panting, gasping, puffing
jaez *nm, pl* jaeces 1 : harness 2 : kind, sort, ilk 3 jaeces *nmpl* : trappings
jaguar *nm* : jaguar
jai alai *nm* : jai alai
jaiba *nf* CANGREJO : crab
jalapeño *nm Mex* : jalapeño pepper
jalar *vt* 1 : to pull, to tug 2 *fam* : to attract, to draw in ⟨las ideas nuevas lo jalan : new ideas appeal to him⟩ — *vi* 1 : to pull, to pull together 2 *fam* : to hurry up, to get going 3 *Mex fam* : to be in working order ⟨esta máquina no jala : this machine doesn't work⟩
jalbegue *nm* : whitewash
jalea *nf* : jelly
jalear *vt* : to encourage, to urge on
jaleo *nm* 1 *fam* : uproar, ruckus, racket 2 *fam* : confusion, hassle 3 : cheering and clapping (for a dance)
jalón *nm, pl* jalones 1 : milestone, landmark 2 TIRÓN : pull, tug
jalonar *vt* : to mark, to stake out
jalonear *vt Mex, Peru fam* : to tug at — *vi* 1 *fam* : to pull, to tug 2 *CA fam* : to haggle
jamaica *nf* : hibiscus
jamaicano, -na → jamaiquino
jamaiquino, -na *adj & n* : Jamaican
jamás *adv* 1 NUNCA : never 2 nunca jamás *or* jamás de los jamases : never ever 3 para siempre jamás : for ever and ever
jamba *nf* : jamb
jamelgo *nm* : nag (horse)
jamón *nm, pl* jamones : ham
Januká *nmf* : Hanukkah
japonés[1], -nesa *adj & n, mpl* -neses : Japanese

japonés[2] *nm, pl* -neses : Japanese (language)
jaque *nm* 1 : check (in chess) ⟨jaque mate : checkmate⟩ 2 tener en jaque : to intimidate, to bully
jaqueca *nf* : headache, migraine
jarabe *nm* 1 : syrup 2 : Mexican folk dance
jarana *nf* 1 *fam* : revelry, partying, spree 2 *fam* : joking, fooling around 3 : small guitar
jaranear *vi fam* : to go on a spree, to party
jarcia *nf* 1 : rigging 2 : fishing tackle
jardín *nm, pl* jardines 1 : garden 2 jardín de niños : kindergarten 3 los jardines *nmpl* : the outfield
jardinería *nf* : gardening
jardinero, -ra *n* 1 : gardener 2 : outfielder (in baseball)
jarra *nf* 1 : pitcher, jug 2 : stein, mug 3 de jarras *or* en jarras : akimbo
jarrete *nm* 1 : back of the knee 2 CORVEJÓN : hock
jarro *nm* 1 : pitcher, jug 2 : mug
jarrón *nm, pl* jarrones FLORERO : vase
jaspe *nm* : jasper
jaspeado, -da *adj* 1 VETEADO : streaked, veined 2 : speckled, mottled
jaula *nf* : cage
jauría *nf* : pack of hounds
javanés, -nesa *adj & n* : Javanese
jazmín *nm, pl* jazmines : jasmine
jazz ['jas, 'dʒas] *nm* : jazz
jeans ['jins, 'dʒins] *nmpl* : jeans
jeep ['jip, 'dʒip] *nm, pl* jeeps : jeep
jefatura *nf* 1 : leadership 2 : headquarters ⟨jefatura de policía : police headquarters⟩
jefe, -fa *n* 1 : chief, head, leader ⟨jefe de bomberos : fire chief⟩ 2 : boss
Jehová *nm* : Jehovah
jején *nm, pl* jejenes : gnat, small mosquito
jengibre *nm* : ginger
jeque *nm* : sheikh, sheik
jerarca *nmf* : leader, chief
jerarquía *nf* 1 : hierarchy 2 RANGO : rank
jerárquico, -ca *adj* : hierarchical
jerbo *nm* : gerbil
jerez *nm, pl* jereces : sherry
jerga *nf* 1 : jargon, slang 2 : coarse cloth
jerigonza *nf* GALIMATÍAS : mumbo jumbo, gibberish
jeringa *nf* : syringe
jeringar {52} *vt* 1 : to inject 2 *fam* JOROBAR : to annoy, to pester — *vi fam*

JOROBAR : to be annoying, to be a nuisance
jeringuear → jeringar
jeringuilla → jeringa
jeroglífico *nm* : hieroglyphic
jersey *nm, pl* jerseys 1 : jersey (fabric) 2 *Spain* : sweater
Jesucristo *nm* : Jesus Christ
jesuita *adj & nm* : Jesuit
Jesús *nm* 1 : Jesus 2 ¡Jesús! : goodness!, good heavens!
jeta *nf* 1 : snout 2 *fam* : face, mug
jíbaro, -ra *adj* 1 : Jivaro 2 : rustic, rural
jibia *nf* : cuttlefish
jícama *nf* : jicama
jícara *nf Mex* : calabash
jilguero *nm* : European goldfinch
jinete *nmf* : horseman, horsewoman *f*, rider
jinetear *vt* 1 : to ride, to perform (on horseback) 2 DOMAR : to break in (a horse) — *vi* CABALGAR : to ride horseback
jingoísmo [ˌjɪŋɡoˈizmo, ˌdʒɪŋ-] *nm* : jingoism
jingoísta *adj* : jingoist, jingoistic
jiote *nm Mex* : rash
jira *nf* : outing, picnic
jirafa *nf* 1 : giraffe 2 : boom microphone
jirón *nm, pl* jirones : shred, rag ⟨hecho jirones : in tatters⟩
jitomate *nm Mex* : tomato
jockey [ˈjɔki, ˈdʒɔ-] *nmf, pl* jockeys [-kis] : jockey
jocosidad *nf* : humor, jocularity
jocoso, -sa *adj* : playful, jocular — jocosamente *adv*
jofaina *nf* : washbowl
jogging [ˈjɔɡɪŋ, ˈdʒɔ-] *nm* : jogging
jolgorio *nm* : merrymaking, fun
jonrón *nm, pl* jonrones : home run
jordano, -na *adj & n* : Jordanian
jornada *nf* 1 : expedition, day's journey 2 jornada de trabajo : working day 3 jornadas *nfpl* : conference, congress
jornal *nm* 1 : day's pay 2 a ～ : by the day
jornalero, -ra *n* : day laborer
joroba *nf* 1 GIBA : hump 2 *fam* : nuisance, pain in the neck
jorobado¹, -da *adj* GIBOSO : hunchbacked, humpbacked
jorobado², -da *n* GIBOSO : hunchback, humpback
jorobar *vt fam* JERINGAR : to bother, to annoy — *vi fam* JERINGAR : to be annoying, to be a nuisance
jorongo *nm Mex* : full-length poncho
jota *nf* 1 : jot, bit ⟨no entiendo ni jota : I don't understand a word of it⟩ ⟨no se ve ni jota : you can't see a thing⟩ 2 : jack (in playing cards)
joven¹ *adj, pl* jóvenes 1 : young 2 : youthful
joven² *nmf, pl* jóvenes : young man *m*, young woman *f*, young person

jovial *adj* : jovial, cheerful — jovialmente *adv*
jovialidad *nf* : joviality, cheerfulness
joya *nf* 1 : jewel, piece of jewelry 2 : treasure, gem ⟨la nueva empleada es una joya : the new employee is a real gem⟩
joyería *nf* 1 : jewelry store 2 : jewelry 3 joyería de fantasía : costume jewelry
joyero, -ra *n* : jeweler
juanete *nm* : bunion
jubilación *nf, pl* -ciones 1 : retirement 2 PENSIÓN : pension
jubilado¹, -da *adj* : retired, in retirement
jubilado², -da *nmf* : retired person, retiree
jubilar *vt* 1 : to retire, to pension off 2 *fam* : to get rid of, to discard — jubilarse *vr* : to retire
jubileo *nm* : jubilee
júbilo *nm* : jubilation, joy
jubiloso, -sa *adj* : jubilant, joyous
judaico, -ca *adj* : Judaic, Jewish
judaísmo *nm* : Judaism
judía *nf* 1 : bean 2 *or* judía verde : green bean, string bean
judicatura *nf* 1 : judiciary, judges *pl* 2 : office of judge
judicial *adj* : judicial — judicialmente *adv*
judío¹, -día *adj* : Jewish
judío², -día *n* : Jewish person, Jew
judo [ˈjuðo, ˈdʒu-] *nm* : judo
juega, juegue, etc. → jugar
juego *nm* 1 : play, playing ⟨poner en juego : to bring into play⟩ 2 : game, sport ⟨juego de cartas : card game⟩ ⟨Juegos Olímpicos : Olympic Games⟩ 3 : gaming, gambling ⟨estar en juego : to be at stake⟩ 4 : set ⟨un juego de llaves : a set of keys⟩ 5 hacer juego : to go together, to match 6 juego de manos : conjuring trick, sleight of hand
juerga *nf* : partying, binge ⟨irse de juerga : to go on a spree⟩
juerguista *nmf* : reveler, carouser
jueves *nms & pl* : Thursday
juez¹ *nmf, pl* jueces 1 : judge 2 ÁRBITRO : umpire, referee
juez², jueza *n* → juez¹
jugada *nf* 1 : play, move 2 : trick ⟨hacer una mala jugada : to play a dirty trick⟩
jugador, -dora *n* 1 : player 2 : gambler
jugar {44} *vi* 1 : to play ⟨jugar a la pelota : to play ball⟩ 2 APOSTAR : to gamble, to bet 3 : to joke, to kid — *vt* 1 : to play ⟨jugar un papel : to play a role⟩ ⟨jugar una carta : to play a card⟩ 2 : to bet — jugarse *vr* 1 : to risk, to gamble away ⟨jugarse la vida : to risk one's life⟩ 2 jugarse el todo por el todo : to risk everything
jugarreta *nf fam* : prank, dirty trick
juglar *nm* : minstrel

jugo *nm* **1** : juice **2** : substance, essence ⟨sacarle el jugo a algo : to get the most out of something⟩
jugosidad *nf* : juiciness, succulence
jugoso, -sa *adj* : juicy
juguete *nm* : toy
juguetear *vi* **1** : to play, to cavort, to frolic **2** : to toy, to fiddle
juguetería *nf* : toy store
juguetón, -tona *adj, mpl* **-tones** : playful — **juguetonamente** *adv*
juicio *nm* **1** : good judgment, reason, sense **2** : opinion ⟨a mi juicio : in my opinion⟩ **3** : trial ⟨llevar a juicio : to take to court⟩
juicioso, -sa *adj* : judicious, wise — **juiciosamente** *adv*
julio *nm* : July
juncia *nf* : sedge
junco *nm* **1** : reed, rush **2** : junk (boat)
jungla *nf* : jungle
junio *nm* : June
junquillo *nm* : jonquil
junta *nf* **1** : board, committee ⟨junta directiva : board of directors⟩ **2** REUNIÓN : meeting, session **3** : junta **4** : joint, gasket
juntamente *adv* **1** : jointly, together ⟨juntamente con : together with⟩ **2** : at the same time
juntar *vt* **1** UNIR : to unite, to combine, to put together **2** REUNIR : to collect, to gather together, to assemble **3** : to close partway ⟨juntar la puerta : to leave the door ajar⟩ — **juntarse** *vr* **1** : to join together **2** : to socialize, to get together
junto, -ta *adj* **1** UNIDO : joined, united **2** : close, adjacent ⟨colgaron los dos retratos juntos : they hung the two paintings side by side⟩ **3** (*used adverbially*) : together ⟨llegamos juntos : we arrived together⟩ **4** ~ **a** : next to, alongside of **5** ~ **con** : together with, along with
juntura *nf* : joint, coupling
Júpiter *nm* : Jupiter
jura *nf* : oath, pledge ⟨jura de bandera : pledge of allegiance⟩

jurado¹ *nm* : jury
jurado², -da *n* : juror
juramento *nm* **1** : oath ⟨juramento hipocrático : Hippocratic oath⟩ **2** : swearword, oath
jurar *vt* **1** : to swear ⟨jurar lealtad : to swear loyalty⟩ **2** : to take an oath ⟨el alcalde juró su cargo : the mayor took the oath of office⟩ — *vi* : to curse, to swear
jurídico, -ca *adj* : legal
jurisdicción *nf, pl* **-ciones** : jurisdiction
jurisdiccional *adj* : jurisdictional, territorial
jurisprudencia *nf* : jurisprudence, law
jurista *nmf* : jurist
justa *nf* **1** : joust **2** TORNEO : tournament, competition
justamente *adv* **1** PRECISAMENTE : precisely, exactly **2** : justly, fairly
justar *vi* : to joust
justicia *nf* **1** : justice, fairness ⟨hacerle justicia a : to do justice to⟩ ⟨ser de justicia : to be only fair⟩ **2 la justicia** : the law ⟨tomarse la justicia por su mano : to take the law into one's own hands⟩
justiciero, -ra *adj* : righteous, avenging
justificable *adj* : justifiable
justificación *nf, pl* **-ciones** : justification
justificante *nm* **1** : justification **2** : proof, voucher
justificar {72} *vt* **1** : to justify **2** : to excuse, to vindicate
justo¹ *adv* **1** : justly **2** : right, exactly ⟨justo a tiempo : just in time⟩ **3** : tightly
justo², -ta *adj* **1** : just, fair **2** : right, exact **3** : tight ⟨estos zapatos me quedan muy justos : these shoes are too tight⟩
justo³, -ta *n* : just person ⟨los justos : the just⟩
juvenil *adj* **1** : juvenile, young, youthful **2** ADOLESCENTE : teenage
juventud *nf* **1** : youth **2** : young people
juzgado *nm* TRIBUNAL : court, tribunal
juzgar {52} *vt* **1** : to try, to judge (a case in court) **2** : to pass judgment on **3** CONSIDERAR : to consider, to deem
juzgue, etc. → **juzgar**

K

k *nf* : eleventh letter of the Spanish alphabet
káiser *nm* : kaiser
kaki → **caqui**
kaleidoscopio → **caleidoscopio**
kamikaze *adj & nm* : kamikaze
kampucheano, -na *adj & n* : Kampuchean
kan *nm* : khan
karaoke *nm* : karaoke
karate *or* **kárate** *nm* : karate
kayac *or* **kayak** *nm, pl* **kayacs** *or* **kayaks** : kayak

keniano, -na *adj & n* : Kenyan
kepí *nm* : kepi
kermesse *or* **kermés** [kɛrˈmɛs] *nf, pl* **kermesses** *or* **kermeses** [-ˈmɛsɛs] : charity fair, bazaar
kerosene *or* **kerosén** *or* **keroseno** *nm* : kerosene, paraffin
kibutz *or* **kibbutz** *nms & pl* : kibbutz
kilo *nm* **1** : kilo, kilogram **2** *fam* : large amount
kilobyte [ˌkiloˈbait] *nm* : kilobyte
kilociclo *nm* : kilocycle
kilogramo *nm* : kilogram

kilohertzio *nm* : kilohertz
kilometraje *nm* : distance in kilometers, mileage
kilométrico, -ca *adj fam* : endless, very long
kilómetro *nm* : kilometer
kilovatio *nm* : kilowatt
kimono *nm* : kimono
kinder ['kɪndər] → **kindergarten**
kindergarten [ˌkɪndər'gartɛn] *nm, pl* **kindergartens** [-tɛns] : kindergarten, nursery school
kinesiología *nf* : physical therapy

kinesiólogo, -ga *n* : physical therapist
kiosco → **quiosco**
kit *nm, pl* **kits** : kit
kiwi ['kiwi] *nm* **1** : kiwi (bird) **2** : kiwifruit
klaxon → **claxon**
knockout [nɔ'kaut] → **nocaut**
koala *nm* : koala bear
kriptón *nm* : krypton
kurdo[1]**, -da** *adj* : Kurdish
kurdo[2]**, -da** *n* : Kurd
kuwaití [kuˌwai'ti] *adj & nmf* : Kuwaiti

L

l *nf* : twelfth letter of the Spanish alphabet
la[1] *pron* **1** : her, it ⟨llámala hoy : call her today⟩ ⟨sacó la botella y la abrió : he took out the bottle and opened it⟩ **2** *(formal)* : you ⟨no la vi a usted, Señora Díaz : I didn't see you, Mrs. Díaz⟩ **3** : the one ⟨mi casa y la de la puerta roja : my house and the one with the red door⟩ **4 la que** : the one who
la[2] *art* → **el**[2]
laberíntico, -ca *adj* : labyrinthine
laberinto *nm* : labyrinth, maze
labia *nf fam* : gift of gab ⟨tu amigo tiene labia : your friend has a way with words⟩
labial *adj* : labial, lip ⟨lápiz labial : lipstick⟩
labio *nm* **1** : lip **2 labio leporino** : harelip
labor *nf* : work, labor
laborable *adj* **1** : arable **2 día laborable** : workday, business day
laboral *adj* : work, labor ⟨costos laborales : labor costs⟩
laborar *vi* : to work
laboratorio *nm* : laboratory, lab
laboriosidad *nf* : industriousness, diligence
laborioso, -sa *adj* **1** : laborious, hard **2** : industrious, hardworking
labrado[1]**, -da** *adj* **1** : cultivated, tilled **2** : carved, wrought
labrado[2] *nm* : cultivated field
labrador, -dora *n* : farmer
labranza *nf* : farming
labrar *vt* **1** : to carve, to work (metal) **2** : to cultivate, to till **3** : to cause, to bring about
laca *nf* **1** : lacquer, shellac **2** : hair spray **3 laca de uñas** : nail polish
lacayo *nm* : lackey
lace, etc. → **lazar**
lacear *vt* : to lasso
laceración *nf, pl* **-ciones** : laceration
lacerante *adj* : hurtful, wounding
lacerar *vt* **1** : to lacerate, to cut **2** : to hurt, to wound (one's feelings)
lacio, -cia *adj* **1** : limp, lank **2 pelo lacio** : straight hair

lacónico, -ca *adj* : laconic — **lacónicamente** *adv*
lacra *nf* **1** : scar, mark (on the skin) **2** : stigma, blemish
lacrar *vt* : to seal (with wax)
lacrimógeno, -na *adj* **gas lacrimógeno** : tear gas
lacrimoso, -sa *adj* : tearful, moving
lactancia *nf* **1** : lactation **2** : breastfeeding
lactante *nmf* : nursing infant, suckling
lactar *v* : to breast-feed
lácteo, -tea *adj* **1** : dairy **2 Vía Láctea** : Milky Way
láctico, -ca *adj* : lactic
lactosa *nf* : lactose
ladeado, -da *adj* : crooked, tilted, lopsided
ladear *vt* : to tilt, to tip — **ladearse** *vr* : to bend (over)
ladera *nf* : slope, hillside
ladino[1]**, -na** *adj* **1** : cunning, shrewd **2** *CA, Mex* : mestizo
ladino[2]**, -na** *n* **1** : trickster **2** *CA, Mex* : Spanish-speaking Indian **3** *CA, Mex* : mestizo
lado *nm* **1** : side **2** PARTE : place ⟨miró por todos lados : he looked everywhere⟩ **3 al lado de** : next to, beside **4 de ~** : tilted, sideways ⟨está de lado : it's lying on its side⟩ **5 hacerse a un lado** : to step aside **6 lado a lado** : side by side **7 por otro lado** : on the other hand
ladrar *vi* : to bark
ladrido *nm* : bark (of a dog), barking
ladrillo *nm* **1** : brick **2** AZULEJO : tile
ladrón, -drona *n, mpl* **ladrones** : robber, thief, burglar
lagartija *nf* : small lizard
lagarto *nm* **1** : lizard **2 lagarto de Indias** : alligator
lago *nm* : lake
lágrima *nf* : tear, teardrop
lagrimear *vi* **1** : to water (of eyes) **2** : to weep easily
laguna *nf* **1** : lagoon **2** : lacuna, gap
laicado *nm* : laity
laico[1]**, -ca** *adj* : lay, secular
laico[2]**, -ca** *n* : layman *m*, laywoman *f*

laja *nf* : slab
lama[1] *nf* : slime, ooze
lama[2] *nm* : lama
lamber *vt* : to lick
lamé *nm* : lamé
lamentable *adj* **1** : unfortunate, lamentable **2** : pitiful, sad
lamentablemente *adv* : unfortunately, regrettably
lamentación *nf, pl* **-ciones** : lamentation, groaning, moaning
lamentar *vt* **1** : to lament **2** : to regret ⟨lo lamento : I'm sorry⟩ — **lamentarse** *vr* : to grumble, to complain
lamento *nm* : lament, groan, cry
lamer *vt* **1** : to lick **2** : to lap against
lamida *nf* : lick
lámina *nf* **1** PLANCHA : sheet, plate **2** : plate, illustration
laminado[1], **-da** *adj* : laminated
laminado[2] *nm* : laminate
laminar *vt* : to laminate — **laminación** *nf*
lámpara *nf* : lamp
lampiño, -ña *adj* : hairless
lamprea *nf* : lamprey
lana *nf* **1** : wool ⟨lana de acero : steel wool⟩ **2** *Mex fam* : money, dough
lance[1], etc. → **lanzar**
lance[2] *nm* **1** INCIDENTE : event, incident **2** RIÑA : quarrel **3** : throw, cast (of a net, etc.) **4** : move, play (in a game), throw (of dice)
lancear *vt* : to spear
lanceta *nf* : lancet
lancha *nf* **1** : small boat, launch **2** **lancha motora** : motorboat, speedboat
langosta *nf* **1** : lobster **2** : locust
langostino *nm* : prawn, crayfish
languidecer {53} *vi* : to languish
languidez *nf, pl* **-deces** : languor, listlessness
lánguido, -da *adj* : languid, listless — **languidamente** *adv*
lanolina *nf* : lanolin
lanudo, -da *adj* : woolly
lanza *nf* : spear, lance
lanzadera *nf* **1** : shuttle (for weaving) **2 lanzadera espacial** : space shuttle
lanzado, -da *adj* **1** : impulsive, brazen **2** : forward, determined ⟨ir lanzado : to hurtle along⟩
lanzador, -dora *n* : thrower, pitcher
lanzallamas *nms & pl* : flamethrower
lanzamiento *nm* **1** : throw **2** : pitch (in baseball) **3** : launching, launch
lanzar {21} *vt* **1** : to throw, to hurl **2** : to pitch **3** : to launch — **lanzarse** *vr* **1** : to throw oneself (at, into) **2** ～ **a** : to embark upon, to undertake
laosiano, -na *adj & n* : Laotian
lapicero *nm* **1** : mechanical pencil **2** *CA, Peru* : ballpoint pen
lápida *nf* : marker, tombstone
lapidar *vt* APEDREAR : to stone
lapidario, -ria *adj & n* : lapidary
lápiz *nm, pl* **lápices** **1** : pencil **2 lápiz de labios** *or* **lápiz labial** : lipstick

lapón, -pona *adj & n, mpl* **lapones** : Lapp
lapso *nm* : lapse, space (of time)
lapsus *nms & pl* : error, slip
laptop *nm, pl* **laptops** : laptop
laquear *vt* : to lacquer, to varnish, to shellac
largamente *adv* **1** : at length, extensively **2** : easily, comfortably **3** : generously
largar {52} *vt* **1** SOLTAR : to let loose, to release **2** AFLOJAR : to loosen, to slacken **3** *fam* : to give, to hand over **4** *fam* : to hurl, to let fly (insults, etc.) — **largarse** *vr fam* : to scram, to beat it
largo[1], **-ga** *adj* **1** : long **2 a lo largo** : lengthwise **3 a lo largo de** : along **4 a la larga** : in the long run
largo[2] *nm* : length ⟨tres metros de largo : three meters long⟩
largometraje *nm* : feature film
largue, etc. → **largar**
larguero *nm* : crossbeam
largueza *nf* : generosity, largesse
larguirucho, -cha *adj fam* : lanky
largura *nf* : length
laringe *nf* : larynx
laringitis *nfs & pl* : laryngitis
larva *nf* : larva — **larval** *adj*
las → **el**[2], **los**[1]
lasaña *nf* : lasagna
lasca *nf* : chip, chipping
lascivia *nf* : lasciviousness, lewdness
lascivo, -va *adj* : lascivious, lewd — **lascivamente** *adv*
láser *nm* : laser
lasitud *nf* : lassitude, weariness
laso, -sa *adj* : languid, weary
lástima *nf* **1** : compassion, pity **2** PENA : shame, pity ⟨¡qué lástima! : what a shame!⟩
lastimadura *nf* : injury, wound
lastimar *vt* **1** DAÑAR, HERIR : to hurt, to injure **2** AGRAVIAR : to offend — **lastimarse** *vr* : to hurt oneself
lastimero, -ra *adj* : pitiful, wretched
lastimoso, -sa *adj* **1** : shameful **2** : pitiful, terrible
lastrar *vt* **1** : to ballast **2** : to burden, to encumber
lastre *nm* **1** : burden **2** : ballast
lata *nf* **1** : tinplate **2** : tin can **3** *fam* : pest, bother, nuisance **4 dar lata** *fam* : to bother, to annoy
latencia *nf* : latency
latente *adj* : latent
lateral[1] *adj* **1** : lateral, side **2** : indirect — **lateralmente** *adv*
lateral[2] *nm* : end piece, side
látex *nms & pl* : latex
latido *nm* : beat, throb ⟨latido del corazón : heartbeat⟩
latifundio *nm* : large estate
latigazo *nm* : lash (with a whip)
látigo *nm* AZOTE : whip
latín *nm* : Latin (language)
latino[1], **-na** *adj* **1** : Latin **2** *fam* : Latin-American

latino², -na *n fam* : Latin American
latinoamericano¹, -na *adj* HISPANO-AMERICANO : Latin American
latinoamericano, -na *n* : Latin American
latir *vi* **1** : to beat, to throb **2 latirle a uno** *Mex fam* : to have a hunch ⟨me late que no va a venir : I have a feeling he's not going to come⟩
latitud *nf* **1** : latitude **2** : breadth
lato, -ta *adj* **1** : extended, lengthy **2** : broad (in meaning)
latón *nm, pl* latones : brass
latoso¹, -sa *adj fam* : annoying, bothersome
latoso², -sa *n fam* : pest, nuisance
latrocinio *nm* : larceny
laúd *nm* : lute
laudable *adj* : laudable, praiseworthy
laudo *nm* : findings, decision
laureado, -da *adj & n* : laureate
laurear *vt* : to award, to honor
laurel *nm* **1** : laurel **2** : bay leaf **3 dormirse en sus laureles** : to rest on one's laurels
lava *nf* : lava
lavable *adj* : washable
lavabo *nm* **1** LAVAMANOS : sink, washbowl **2** : lavatory, toilet
lavadero *nm* : laundry room
lavado *nm* **1** : laundry, wash **2** : laundering ⟨lavado de dinero : money laundering⟩
lavadora *nf* : washing machine
lavamanos *nms & pl* LAVABO : sink, washbowl
lavanda *nf* ESPLIEGO : lavender
lavandería *nf* : laundry (service)
lavandero, -ra *n* : launderer, laundress *f*
lavaplatos *nms & pl* **1** : dishwasher **2** *Chile, Col, Mex* : kitchen sink
lavar *vt* **1** : to wash, to clean **2** : to launder (money) **3 lavar en seco** : to dry-clean — **lavarse** *vr* **1** : to wash oneself **2 lavarse las manos de** : to wash one's hands of
lavativa *nf* : enema
lavatorio *nm* : lavatory, washroom
lavavajillas *nms & pl* : dishwasher
laxante *adj & nm* : laxative
laxitud *nf* : laxity, slackness
laxo, -xa *adj* : lax, slack
lazada *nf* : bow, loop
lazar {21} *vt* : to rope, to lasso
lazo *nm* **1** VÍNCULO : link, bond **2** : bow, ribbon **3** : lasso, lariat
le *pron* **1** : to her, to him, to it ⟨¿qué le dijiste? : what did you tell him?⟩ **2** : from her, from him, from it ⟨el ladrón le robó la cartera : the thief stole his wallet⟩ **3** : for her, for him, for it ⟨cómprale flores a tu mamá : buy your mom some flowers⟩ **4** *(formal)* : to you, for you ⟨le traje un regalo : I brought you a gift⟩
leal *adj* : loyal, faithful — **lealmente** *adv*
lealtad *nf* : loyalty, allegiance

lebrel *nm* : hound
lección *nf, pl* lecciones : lesson
lechada *nf* **1** : whitewash **2** : grout
lechal *adj* : suckling, unweaned ⟨cordero lechal : suckling lamb⟩
leche *nf* **1** : milk ⟨leche en polvo : powdered milk⟩ ⟨leche de magnesia : milk of magnesia⟩ **2** : milky sap
lechera *nf* **1** : milk jug **2** : dairymaid *f*
lechería *nf* : dairy store
lechero¹, -ra *adj* : dairy
lechero², -ra *n* : milkman *m*, milk dealer
lecho *nm* **1** : bed ⟨un lecho de rosas : a bed of roses⟩ ⟨lecho de muerte : deathbed⟩ **2** : riverbed **3** : layer, stratum (in geology)
lechón, -chona *n, mpl* lechones : suckling pig
lechoso, -sa *adj* : milky
lechuga *nf* : lettuce
lechuza *nf* BÚHO : owl, barn owl
lectivo, -va *adj* : school ⟨año lectivo : school year⟩
lector¹, -tora *adj* : reading ⟨nivel lector : reading level⟩
lector², -tora *n* : reader
lector³ *nm* : scanner, reader ⟨lector óptico : optical scanner⟩
lectura *nf* **1** : reading **2** : reading matter
leer {20} *v* : to read
legación *nf, pl* -ciones : legation
legado *nm* **1** : legacy, bequest **2** : legate, emissary
legajo *nm* : dossier, file
legal *adj* : legal, lawful — **legalmente** *adv*
legalidad *nf* : legality, lawfulness
legalista *adj* : legalistic
legalizar {21} *vt* : to legalize — **legalización** *nf*
legar {52} *vt* **1** : to bequeath, to hand down **2** DELEGAR : to delegate
legendario, -ria *adj* : legendary
legible *adj* : legible
legión *nf, pl* legiones : legion
legionario, -ria *n* : legionnaire
legislación *nf* **1** : legislation, lawmaking **2** : laws *pl*, legislation
legislador¹, -dora *adj* : legislative
legislador², -dora *n* : legislator
legislar *vi* : to legislate
legislativo, -va *adj* : legislative
legislatura *nf* **1** : legislature **2** : term of office
legitimar *vt* **1** : to legitimize **2** : to authenticate — **legitimación** *nf*
legitimidad *nf* : legitimacy
legítimo, -ma *adj* **1** : legitimate **2** : genuine, authentic — **legítimamente** *adv*
lego¹, -ga *adj* **1** : secular, lay **2** : uninformed, ignorant
lego², -ga *n* : layperson, layman *m*, laywoman *f*
legua *nf* **1** : league **2 notarse a leguas** : to be very obvious ⟨se notaba a leguas : you could tell from a mile away⟩

legue, etc. → **legar**
legumbre *nf* **1** HORTALIZA : vegetable **2** : legume
leíble *adj* : readable
leída *nf* : reading, read ⟨de una leída : in one reading, at one go⟩
leído¹ *pp* → **leer**
leído², **-da** *adj* : well-read
lejanía *nf* : remoteness, distance
lejano, **-na** *adj* : remote, distant, far away
lejía *nf* **1** : lye **2** : bleach
lejos *adv* **1** : far away, distant ⟨a lo lejos : in the distance, far off⟩ ⟨desde lejos : from a distance⟩ **2** : long ago, a long way off ⟨está lejos de los 50 años : he's a long way from 50 years old⟩ **3 de** ~ : by far ⟨esta decisión fue de lejos la más fácil : this decision was by far the easiest⟩ **4** ~ **de** : far from ⟨lejos de ser reprobado, recibió una nota de B : far from failing, he got a B⟩
lelo, **-la** *adj* : silly, stupid
lema *nm* : motto, slogan
lencería *nf* : lingerie
lengua *nf* **1** : tongue ⟨morderse la lengua : to bite one's tongue⟩ **2** IDIOMA : language ⟨lengua materna : mother tongue, native language⟩ ⟨lengua muerta : dead language⟩
lenguado *nm* : sole, flounder
lenguaje *nm* **1** : language, speech **2 lenguaje gestual** *or* **lenguaje de gestos** : sign language **3 lenguaje de programación** : programming language
lengüeta *nf* **1** : tongue (of a shoe), tab, flap **2** : reed (of a musical instrument) **3** : barb, point
lengüetada *nf* **beber a lengüetadas** : to lap (up)
lenidad *nf* : leniency
lenitivo, **-va** *adj* : soothing
lente *nmf* **1** : lens ⟨lentes de contacto : contact lenses⟩ **2 lentes** *nmpl* ANTEOJOS : eyeglasses ⟨lentes de sol : sunglasses⟩
lenteja *nf* : lentil
lentejuela *nf* : sequin, spangle
lentitud *nf* : slowness
lento¹ *adv* DESPACIO : slowly
lento², **-ta** *adj* **1** : slow **2** : slow-witted, dull — **lentamente** *adv*
leña *nf* : wood, firewood
leñador, **-dora** *n* : lumberjack, woodcutter
leñera *nf* : woodshed
leño *nm* : log
leñoso, **-sa** *adj* : woody
Leo *nmf* : Leo
león, **-ona** *n,* *mpl* **leones 1** : lion, lioness *f* **2** (*in various countries*) : puma, cougar
leonado, **-da** *adj* : tawny
leonino, **-na** *adj* **1** : leonine **2** : one-sided, unfair
leopardo *nm* : leopard
leotardo *nm* MALLA : leotard, tights *pl*
leperada *nf* *Mex* : obscenity

lépero, **-ra** *adj* *Mex* : vulgar, coarse
lepra *nf* : leprosy
leproso¹, **-sa** *adj* : leprous
leproso², **-sa** *n* : leper
lerdo, **-da** *adj* **1** : clumsy **2** : dull, oafish, slow-witted
les *pron* **1** : to them ⟨dales una propina : give them a tip⟩ **2** : from them ⟨se les privó de su herencia : they were deprived of their inheritance⟩ **3** : for them ⟨les hice sus tareas : I did their homework for them⟩ **4** : to you *pl,* for you *pl* ⟨les compré un regalo : I bought you all a present⟩
lesbiana *nf* : lesbian — **lesbiano,** **-na** *adj*
lesbianismo *nm* : lesbianism
lesión *nf,* *pl* **lesiones** HERIDA : lesion, wound, injury ⟨una lesión grave : a serious injury⟩
lesionado, **-da** *adj* HERIDO : injured, wounded
lesionar *vt* : to injure, to wound — **lesionarse** *vr* : to hurt oneself
lesivo, **-va** *adj* : harmful, damaging
letal *adj* MORTÍFERO : deadly, lethal — **letalmente** *adv*
letanía *nf* **1** : litany **2** *fam* : spiel, song and dance
letárgico, **-ca** *adj* : lethargic
letargo *nm* : lethargy, torpor
letón¹, **-tona** *adj* & *n,* *mpl* **letones** : Latvian
letón² *nm* : Latvian (language)
letra *nf* **1** : letter **2** CALIGRAFÍA : handwriting, lettering **3** : lyrics *pl* **4 al pie de la letra** : word for word, by the book **5 letras** *nfpl* : arts (in education)
letrado¹, **-da** *adj* ERUDITO : learned, erudite
letrado², **-da** *n* : attorney-at-law, lawyer
letrero *nm* RÓTULO : sign, notice
letrina *nf* : latrine
letrista *nmf* : lyricist, songwriter
leucemia *nf* : leukemia
leva *nf* : cam
levadizo, **-za** *adj* **1** : liftable **2 puente levadizo** : drawbridge
levadura *nf* **1** : yeast, leavening **2 levadura en polvo** : baking powder
levantamiento *nm* **1** ALZAMIENTO : uprising **2** : raising, lifting ⟨levantamiento de pesas : weight lifting⟩
levantar *vt* **1** ALZAR : to lift, to raise **2** : to put up, to erect **3** : to call off, to adjourn **4** : to give rise to, to arouse ⟨levantar sospechas : to arouse suspicion⟩ — **levantarse** *vr* **1** : to rise, to stand up **2** : to get out of bed
levar *vt* **levar anclas** : to weigh anchor
leve *adj* **1** : light, slight **2** : trivial, unimportant — **levemente** *adv*
levedad *nf* : lightness
levemente *adv* LIGERAMENTE : lightly, softly
leviatán *nm,* *pl* **-tanes** : leviathan
léxico¹, **-ca** *adj* : lexical
léxico² *nm* : lexicon, glossary
lexicografía *nf* : lexicography

lexicográfico, -ca *adj* : lexicographical, lexicographic
lexicógrafo, -fa *n* : lexicographer
ley *nf* **1** : law ⟨fuera de la ley : outside the law⟩ ⟨la ley de gravedad : the law of gravity⟩ **2** : purity (of metals) ⟨oro de ley : pure gold⟩
leyenda *nf* **1** : legend **2** : caption, inscription
leyó, etc. → **leer**
liar {85} *vt* **1** ATAR : to bind, to tie (up) **2** : to roll (a cigarette) **3** : to confuse — **liarse** *vr* : to get mixed up
libanés, -nesa *adj & n, mpl* **-neses** : Lebanese
libar *vt* **1** : to suck (nectar) **2** : to sip, to swig (liquor, etc.)
libelo *nm* **1** : libel, lampoon **2** : petition (in court)
libélula *nf* : dragonfly
liberación *nf, pl* **-ciones** : liberation, deliverance ⟨liberación de la mujer : women's liberation⟩
liberado, -da *adj* **1** : liberated ⟨una mujer liberada : a liberated woman⟩ **2** : freed, delivered
liberal *adj & nmf* : liberal
liberalidad *nf* : generosity, liberality
liberalismo *nm* : liberalism
liberalizar {21} *vt* : to liberalize — **liberalización** *nf*
liberar *vt* : to liberate, to free — **liberarse** *vr* : to get free of
liberiano, -na *adj & n* : Liberian
libertad *nf* **1** : freedom, liberty ⟨tomarse la libertad de : to take the liberty of⟩ **2 libertad bajo fianza** : bail **3 libertad condicional** : parole
libertador¹, -dora *adj* : liberating
libertador², -dora *n* : liberator
libertar *vt* LIBRAR : to set free
libertario, -ria *adj & n* : libertarian
libertinaje *nm* : licentiousness, dissipation
libertino¹, -na *adj* : licentious, dissolute
libertino², -na *n* : libertine
libidinoso, -sa *adj* : lustful, lewd
libido *nf* : libido
libio, -bia *adj & n* : Libyan
libra *nf* **1** : pound **2 libra esterlina** : pound sterling
Libra *nmf* : Libra
libramiento *nm* **1** : liberating, freeing **2** LIBRANZA : order of payment **3** *Mex* : beltway
libranza *nf* : order of payment
librar *vt* **1** LIBERTAR : to deliver, to set free **2** : to wage ⟨librar batalla : to do battle⟩ **3** : to issue ⟨librar una orden : to issue an order⟩ — **librarse** *vr* ~ **de** : to free oneself from, to get out of
libre¹ *adj* **1** : free ⟨un país libre : a free country⟩ ⟨libre de : free from, exempt from⟩ ⟨libre albedrío : free will⟩ **2** DESOCUPADO : vacant **3 día libre** : day off
libre² *nm Mex* : taxi
librea *nf* : livery

librecambio *nm* : free trade
libremente *adv* : freely
librería *nf* : bookstore
librero¹, -ra *n* : bookseller
librero² *nm Mex* : bookcase
libresco, -ca *adj* : bookish
libreta *nf* CUADERNO : notebook
libretista *nmf* **1** : librettist **2** : scriptwriter
libreto *nm* : libretto, script
libro *nm* **1** : book ⟨libro de texto : textbook⟩ **2 libros** *nmpl* : books (in bookkeeping), accounts ⟨llevar los libros : to keep the books⟩
licencia *nf* **1** : permission **2** : leave, leave of absence **3** : permit, license ⟨licencia de conducir : driver's license⟩
licenciado, -da *n* **1** : university graduate **2** ABOGADO : lawyer
licenciar *vt* **1** : to license, to permit, to allow **2** : to discharge **3** : to grant a university degree to — **licenciarse** *vr* : to graduate
licenciatura *nf* **1** : college degree **2** : course of study (at a college or university)
licencioso, -sa *adj* : licentious, lewd
liceo *nm* : secondary school, high school
licitación *nf, pl* **-ciones** : bid, bidding
licitar *vt* : to bid on
lícito, -ta *adj* **1** : lawful, licit **2** JUSTO : just, fair
licor *nm* **1** : liquor **2** : liqueur
licorera *nf* : decanter
licuado *nm* BATIDO : milk shake
licuadora *nf* : blender
licuar {3} *vt* : to liquefy — **licuarse** *vr*
lid *nf* **1** : fight, combat **2** : argument, dispute **3 lides** *nfpl* : matters, affairs **4 en buena lid** : fair and square
líder¹ *adj* : leading, foremost
líder² *nmf* : leader
liderar *vt* DIRIGIR : to lead, to head
liderato *nm* : leadership, leading
liderazgo → **liderato**
lidiar *vt* : to fight — *vi* BATALLAR, LUCHAR : to struggle, to battle, to wrestle
liebre *nf* : hare
liendre *nf* : nit
lienzo *nm* **1** : linen **2** : canvas, painting **3** : stretch of wall or fencing
liga *nf* **1** ASOCIACIÓN : league **2** GOMITA : rubber band **3** : garter
ligado, -da *adj* : linked, connected
ligadura *nf* **1** ATADURA : tie, bond **2** : ligature
ligamento *nm* : ligament
ligar {52} *vt* : to bind, to tie (up)
ligeramente *adv* **1** : slightly **2** LEVEMENTE : lightly, gently **3** : casually, flippantly
ligereza *nf* **1** : lightness **2** : flippancy **3** : agility
ligero, -ra *adj* **1** : light, lightweight **2** : slight, minor **3** : agile, quick **4** : light-hearted, superficial
lignito *nm* : lignite

ligue, etc. → **ligar**
lija *nf or* **papel de lija** : sandpaper
lijar *vt* : to sand
lila¹ *adj* : lilac, light purple
lila² *nf* : lilac
lima *nf* **1** : lime (fruit) **2** : file ⟨lima de uñas : nail file⟩
limadora *nf* : polisher
limar *vt* **1** : to file **2** : to polish, to put the final touch on **3** : to smooth over ⟨limar las diferencias : to iron out differences⟩
limbo *nm* **1** : limbo **2** : limb (in botany and astronomy)
limeño¹, -ña *adj* : of or from Lima, Peru
limeño², -ña *n* : person from Lima, Peru
limero *nm* : lime tree
limitación *nf, pl* **-ciones 1** : limitation **2** : limit, restriction ⟨sin limitación : unlimited⟩
limitado, -da *adj* **1** RESTRINGIDO : limited **2** : dull, slow-witted
limitar *vt* RESTRINGIR : to limit, to restrict — *vi* ~ **con** : to border on — **limitarse** *vr* ~ **a** : to limit oneself to
límite *nm* **1** : boundary, border **2** : limit ⟨el límite de mi paciencia : the limit of my patience⟩ ⟨límite de velocidad : speed limit⟩ **3 fecha límite** : deadline
limítrofe *adj* LINDANTE, LINDERO : bordering, adjoining
limo *nm* : slime, mud
limón *nm, pl* **limones 1** : lemon **2** : lemon tree **3 limón verde** *Mex* : lime
limonada *nf* : lemonade
limosna *nf* : alms, charity
limosnear *vi* : to beg (for alms)
limosnero, -ra *n* MENDIGO : beggar
limoso, -sa *adj* : slimy
limpiabotas *nmfs & pl* : bootblack
limpiador¹, -dora *adj* : cleaning
limpiador², -dora *n* : cleaning person, cleaner
limpiamente *adv* : cleanly, honestly, fairly
limpiaparabrisas *nms & pl* : windshield wiper
limpiar *vt* **1** : to clean, to cleanse **2** : to clean up, to remove defects **3** *fam* : to clean out (in a game) **4** *fam* : to swipe, to pinch — *vi* : to clean — **limpiarse** *vr*
limpiavidrios *nmfs & pl Mex* : windshield wiper
límpido, -da *adj* : limpid
limpieza *nf* **1** : cleanliness, tidiness **2** : cleaning **3** HONRADEZ : integrity, honesty **4** DESTREZA : skill, dexterity
limpio¹ *adv* : fairly
limpio², -pia *adj* **1** : clean, neat **2** : honest ⟨un juego limpio : a fair game⟩ **3** : free ⟨limpio de impurezas : pure, free from impurities⟩ **4** : clear, net ⟨ganancia limpia : clear profit⟩
limusina *nf* : limousine
linaje *nm* ABOLENGO : lineage, ancestry
linaza *nf* : linseed
lince *nm* : lynx

linchamiento *nm* : lynching
linchar *vt* : to lynch
lindante *adj* LIMÍTROFE, LINDERO : bordering, adjoining
lindar *vi* **1** ~ **con** : to border, to skirt **2** ~ **con** BORDEAR : to border on, to verge on
linde *nmf* : boundary, limit
lindero¹, -ra *adj* LIMÍTROFE, LINDANTE : bordering, adjoining
lindero² *nm* : boundary, limit
lindeza *nf* **1** : prettiness **2** : clever remark **3 lindezas** *nfpl, (used ironically)* : insults
lindo¹ *adv* **1** : beautifully, wonderfully ⟨canta lindo tu mujer : your wife sings beautifully⟩ **2 de lo lindo** : a lot, a great deal ⟨los zancudos nos picaban de lo lindo : the mosquitoes were biting away at us⟩
lindo², -da *adj* **1** BONITO : pretty, lovely **2** MONO : cute
línea *nf* **1** : line ⟨línea divisoria : dividing line⟩ ⟨línea de banda : sideline⟩ **2** : line, course, position ⟨línea de conducta : course of action⟩ ⟨en líneas generales : in general terms, along general lines⟩ **3** : line, service ⟨línea aérea : airline⟩ ⟨línea telefónica : telephone line⟩
lineal *adj* : linear
linfa *nf* : lymph
linfático, -ca *adj* : lymphatic
lingote *nm* : ingot
lingüista *nmf* : linguist
lingüística *nf* : linguistics
lingüístico, -ca *adj* : linguistic
linimento *nm* : liniment
lino *nm* **1** : linen **2** : flax
linóleo *nm* : linoleum
linterna *nf* **1** : lantern **2** : flashlight
lío *nm fam* **1** : confusion, mess **2** : hassle, trouble, jam ⟨meterse en un lío : to get into a jam⟩ **3** : affair, liaison
liofilizar {21} *vt* : to freeze-dry
lioso, -sa *adj fam* **1** : confusing, muddled **2** : troublemaking
liquen *nm* : lichen
liquidación *nf, pl* **-ciones 1** : liquidation **2** : clearance sale **3** : settlement, payment
liquidar *vt* **1** : to liquefy **2** : to liquidate **3** : to settle, to pay off **4** *fam* : to rub out, to kill
liquidez *nf, pl* **-deces** : liquidity
líquido¹, -da *adj* **1** : liquid, fluid **2** : net ⟨ingresos líquidos : net income⟩
líquido² *nm* **1** : liquid, fluid ⟨líquido de frenos : brake fluid⟩ **2** : ready cash, liquid assets
lira *nf* : lyre
lírica *nf* : lyric poetry
lírico, -ca *adj* : lyric, lyrical
lirio *nm* **1** : iris **2 lirio de los valles** MUGUETE : lily of the valley
lirismo *nm* : lyricism
lirón *nm, pl* **lirones** : dormouse
lisiado¹, -da *adj* : disabled, crippled

lisiado², -da *n* : disabled person, cripple
lisiar *vt* : to cripple, to disable — **lisiarse**
vr
liso, -sa *adj* 1 : smooth 2 : flat 3
: straight ⟨pelo liso : straight hair⟩ 4
: plain, unadorned ⟨liso y llano : plain
and simple⟩
lisonja *nf* : flattery
lisonjear *vt* ADULAR : to flatter
lista *nf* 1 : list 2 : roster, roll ⟨pasar lista
: to take attendance⟩ 3 : stripe, strip
4 : menu
listado¹, -da *adj* : striped
listado² *nm* : listing
listar *vt* : to list
listeza *nf* : smartness, alertness
listo, -ta *adj* 1 DISPUESTO, PREPARADO
: ready ⟨¿estás listo? : are you ready?⟩
2 : clever, smart
listón *nm, pl* listones 1 : ribbon 2 : strip
(of wood), lath 3 : high bar (in sports)
lisura *nf* : smoothness
litera *nf* : bunk bed, berth
literal *adj* : literal — **literalmente** *adv*
literario, -ria *adj* : literary
literato, -ta *n* : writer, author
literatura *nf* : literature
litigante *adj & nmf* : litigant
litigar {52} *vi* : to litigate, to be in litigation
litigio *nm* 1 : litigation, lawsuit 2 en ~
: in dispute
litigioso, -sa *adj* : litigious
litio *nm* : lithium
litografía *nf* 1 : lithography 2 : lithograph
litógrafo, -fa *n* : lithographer
litoral¹ *adj* : coastal
litoral² *nm* : shore, seaboard
litosfera *nf* : lithosphere
litro *nm* : liter
lituano¹, -na *adj & n* : Lithuanian
lituano² *nm* : Lithuanian (language)
liturgia *nf* : liturgy
litúrgico, -ca *adj* : liturgical — **litúrgi-
camente** *adv*
liviandad *nf* LIGEREZA : lightness
liviano, -na *adj* 1 : light, slight 2 IN-
CONSTANTE : fickle
lividez *nf* PALIDEZ : pallor
lívido, -da *adj* 1 AMORATADO : livid 2
PÁLIDO : pallid, extremely pale
living *nm* : living room
llaga *nf* : sore, wound
llama *nf* 1 : flame 2 : llama
llamada *nf* : call ⟨llamada a larga distancia : long-distance call⟩ ⟨llamada al
orden : call to order⟩
llamado¹, -da *adj* : named, called ⟨una
mujer llamada Rosa : a woman called
Rosa⟩
llamado² → **llamamiento**
llamador *nm* : door knocker
llamamiento *nm* : call, appeal
llamar *vt* 1 : to name, to call 2 : to call,
to summon 3 : to phone, to call up —
llamarse *vr* : to be called, to be named
⟨¿cómo te llamas? : what's your
name?⟩

llamarada *nf* 1 : flare-up, sudden blaze
2 : flushing (of the face)
llamativo, -va *adj* : flashy, showy, striking
llameante *adj* : flaming, blazing
llamear *vi* : to flame, to blaze
llana *nf* 1 : trowel 2 → **llano²**
llanamente *adv* : simply, plainly,
straightforwardly
llaneza *nf* : simplicity, naturalness
llano¹, -na *adj* 1 : even, flat 2 : frank,
open 3 LISO : plain, simple
llano² *nm* : plain
llanta *nf* 1 NEUMÁTICO : tire 2 : rim
llantén *nm, pl* llantenes : plantain
(weed)
llanto *nm* : crying, weeping
llanura *nf* : plain, prairie
llave *nf* 1 : key 2 : faucet 3 INTER-
RUPTOR : switch 4 : brace (punctuation mark) 5 **llave inglesa** : monkey
wrench
llavero *nm* : key chain, key ring
llegada *nf* : arrival
llegar {52} *vi* 1 : to arrive, to come 2 ~
a : to arrive at, to reach, to amount to
3 ~ a : to manage to ⟨llegó a terminar
la novela : she managed to finish the
novel⟩ 4 **llegar a ser** : to become ⟨llegó
a ser un miembro permanente : he became a permanent member⟩
llegue, etc. → **llegar**
llenar *vt* 1 : to fill, to fill up, to fill in 2
: to meet, to fulfill ⟨los regalos no
llenaron sus expectativas : the gifts did
not meet her expectations⟩ — **llenarse**
vr : to fill up, to become full
llenito, -ta *adj fam* REGORDETE : chubby, plump
lleno¹, -na *adj* 1 : full, filled 2 de ~
: completely, fully 3 **estar lleno de sí
mismo** : to be full of oneself
lleno² *nm* 1 *fam* : plenty, abundance 2
: full house, sellout
llevadero, -ra *adj* : bearable
llevar *vt* 1 : to take away, to carry ⟨me
gusta, me lo llevo : I like it, I'll take it⟩
2 : to wear 3 : to take, to lead ⟨lleva-
mos a Pedro al cine : we took Pedro to
the movies⟩ 4 **llevar a cabo** : to carry
out 5 **llevar adelante** : to carry on, to
keep going — *vi* : to lead ⟨un problema lleva al otro : one problem leads to
another⟩ — *v aux* : to have ⟨llevo mucho tiempo buscándolo : I've been
looking for it for a long time⟩ ⟨lleva
leído medio libro : he's halfway
through the book⟩ — **llevarse** *vr* 1 : to
take away, to carry off 2 : to get along
⟨siempre nos llevábamos bien : we always got along well⟩
llorar *vi* : to cry, to weep — *vt* : to mourn,
to bewail
lloriquear *vi* : to whimper, to whine
lloriqueo *nm* : whimpering, whining
llorón, -rona *n, mpl* llorones : crybaby,
whiner
lloroso, -sa *adj* : tearful, sad

llovedizo, -za *adj* : rain ⟨agua llovediza : rainwater⟩

llover {47} *v impers* : to rain ⟨está lloviendo : it's raining⟩ ⟨llover a cántaros : to rain cats and dogs⟩ — *vi* : to rain down, to shower ⟨le llovieron regalos : he was showered with gifts⟩

llovizna *nf* : drizzle, sprinkle

lloviznar *v impers* : to drizzle, to sprinkle

llueve, etc. → llover

lluvia *nf* 1 : rain, rainfall 2 : barrage, shower

lluvioso, -sa *adj* : rainy

lo¹ *pron* 1 : him, it ⟨lo vi ayer : I saw him yesterday⟩ ⟨lo entiendo : I understand it⟩ ⟨no lo creo : I don't believe so⟩ 2 (*formal, masculine*) : you ⟨disculpe, señor, no lo oí : excuse me sir, I didn't hear you⟩ 3 lo que : what, that which ⟨eso es lo que más le gusta : that's what he likes the most⟩

lo² *art* 1 : the ⟨lo mejor : the best, the best thing⟩ 2 : how ⟨sé lo bueno que eres : I know how good you are⟩

loa *nf* : praise

loable *adj* : laudable, praiseworthy — loablemente *adv*

loar *vt* : to praise, to laud

lobato, -ta *n* : wolf cub

lobby *nm* : lobby, pressure group

lobo, -ba *n* : wolf

lóbrego, -ga *adj* SOMBRÍO : gloomy, dark

lobulado, -da *adj* : lobed

lóbulo *nm* : lobe ⟨lóbulo de la oreja : earlobe⟩

locación *nf, pl* -ciones 1 : location (in moviemaking) 2 *Mex* : place

local¹ *adj* : local — localmente *adv*

local² *nm* : premises *pl*

localidad *nf* : town, locality

localización *nf, pl* -ciones 1 : locating, localization 2 : location

localizar {21} *vt* 1 UBICAR : to locate, to find 2 : to localize — localizarse *vr* UBICARSE : to be located ⟨se localiza en el séptimo piso : it is located on the seventh floor⟩

locatario, -ria *n* : tenant

loción *nf, pl* lociones : lotion

lócker *nm, pl* lóckers : locker

loco¹, -ca *adj* 1 DEMENTE : crazy, insane, mad 2 a lo loco : wildly, recklessly 3 volverse loco : to go mad

loco², -ca *n* 1 : crazy person, lunatic 2 hacerse el loco : to act the fool

locomoción *nf, pl* -ciones : locomotion

locomotor, -tora *adj* : locomotive

locomotora *nf* 1 : locomotive 2 : driving force

locuacidad *nf* : loquacity, talkativeness

locuaz *adj, pl* locuaces : loquacious, talkative

locución *nf, pl* -ciones : locution, phrase ⟨locución adverbial : adverbial phrase⟩

locura *nf* 1 : insanity, madness 2 : crazy thing, folly

locutor, -tora *n* : announcer

lodazal *nm* : bog, quagmire

lodo *nm* BARRO : mud, mire

lodoso, -sa *adj* : muddy

logaritmo *nm* : logarithm

logia *nf* : lodge ⟨logia masónica : Masonic lodge⟩

lógica *nf* : logic

lógico, -ca *adj* : logical — lógicamente *adv*

logística *nf* : logistics *pl*

logístico, -ca *adj* : logistic, logistical

logo → logotipo

logotipo *nm* : logo

logrado, -da *adj* : successful, well done

lograr *vt* 1 : to get, to obtain 2 : to achieve, to attain — lograrse *vr* : to be successful

logro *nm* : achievement, attainment

loma *nf* : hill, hillock

lombriz *nf, pl* lombrices : worm ⟨lombriz de tierra : earthworm, night crawler⟩ ⟨lombriz solitaria : tapeworm⟩ ⟨tener lombrices : to have worms⟩

lomo *nm* 1 : back (of an animal) 2 : loin ⟨lomo de cerdo : pork loin⟩ 3 : spine (of a book) 4 : blunt edge (of a knife)

lona *nf* : canvas

loncha *nf* LONJA, REBANADA : slice

lonche *nm* 1 ALMUERZO : lunch 2 *Mex* : submarine sandwich

lonchería *nf Mex* : luncheonette

londinense¹ *adj* : of or from London

londinense² *nmf* : Londoner

longaniza *nf* : spicy pork sausage

longevidad *nf* : longevity

longevo, -va *adj* : long-lived

longitud *nf* 1 LARGO : length ⟨longitud de onda : wavelength⟩ 2 : longitude

longitudinal *adj* : longitudinal

lonja *nf* LONCHA, REBANADA : slice

lontananza *nf* : background ⟨en lontananza : in the distance, far away⟩

lord *nm, pl* lores (*title in England*) : lord

loro *nm* : parrot

los¹, las *pron* 1 : them ⟨hice galletas y se las di a los nuevos vecinos : I made cookies and gave them to the new neighbors⟩ 2 : you ⟨voy a llevarlos a los dos : I am going to take both of you⟩ 3 los que, las que : those, who, the ones ⟨los que van a cantar deben venir temprano : those who are singing must come early⟩ 4 (*used with* haber) ⟨los hay en varios colores : they come in various colors⟩

los² *art* → el²

losa *nf* : flagstone, paving stone

loseta *nf* BALDOSA : floor tile

lote *nm* 1 : part, share 2 : batch, lot 3 : plot of land, lot

lotería *nf* : lottery

loto *nm* : lotus

loza *nf* 1 : crockery, earthenware 2 : china

lozanía *nf* 1 : healthiness, robustness 2 : luxuriance, lushness

lozano, -na *adj* **1** : robust, healthy-looking ⟨un rostro lozano : a smooth, fresh face⟩ **2** : lush, luxuriant
LSD *nm* : LSD
lubricante¹ *adj* : lubricating
lubricante² *nm* : lubricant
lubricar {72} *vt* : to lubricate, to oil — **lubricación** *nf*
lucero *nm* : bright star ⟨lucero del alba : morning star⟩
lucha *nf* **1** : struggle, fight **2** : wrestling
luchador, -dora *n* **1** : fighter **2** : wrestler
luchar *vi* **1** : to fight, to struggle **2** : to wrestle
luchón, -chona *adj, mpl* **luchones** *Mex* : industrious, hardworking
lucidez *nf, pl* **-deces** : lucidity, clarity
lucido, -da *adj* MAGNÍFICO : magnificent, splendid
lúcido, -da *adj* : lucid
luciérnaga *nf* : firefly, glowworm
lucimiento *nm* **1** : brilliance, splendor, sparkle **2** : triumph, success ⟨salir con lucimiento : to succeed with flying colors⟩
lucio *nm* : pike (fish)
lucir {45} *vi* **1** : to shine **2** : to look good, to stand out **3** : to seem, to appear ⟨ahora luce contento : he looks happy now⟩ — *vt* **1** : to wear, to sport **2** : to flaunt, to show off — **lucirse** *vr* **1** : to distinguish oneself, to excel **2** : to show off
lucrarse *vr* : to make a profit
lucrativo, -va *adj* : lucrative, profitable — **lucrativamente** *adv*
lucro *nm* GANANCIA : profit, gain
luctuoso, -sa *adj* : mournful, tragic
luego¹ *adv* **1** DESPUÉS : then, afterwards **2** : later (on) **3 desde ~** : of course **4 ¡hasta luego!** : see you later! **5 luego que** : as soon as **6 luego luego** *Mex fam* : right away, immediately
luego² *conj* : therefore ⟨pienso, luego existo : I think, therefore I am⟩
lugar *nm* **1** : place, position ⟨se llevó el primer lugar en su división : she took first place in her division⟩ **2** ESPACIO : space, room **3 dar lugar a** : to give rise to, to lead to **4 en lugar de** : instead of **5 lugar común** : cliché, platitude **6 tener lugar** : to take place
lugareño¹, -ña *adj* : village, rural
lugareño², -ña *n* : villager
lugarteniente *nmf* : lieutenant, deputy
lúgubre *adj* : gloomy, lugubrious
lujo *nm* **1** : luxury **2 de ~** : deluxe
lujoso, -sa *adj* : luxurious
lujuria *nf* : lust, lechery
lujurioso, -sa *adj* : lustful, lecherous
lumbago *nm* : lumbago
lumbar *adj* : lumbar
lumbre *nf* **1** FUEGO : fire **2** : brilliance, splendor **3 poner en la lumbre** : to put on the stove, to warm up
lumbrera *nf* **1** : skylight **2** : vent, port **3** : brilliant person, luminary
luminaria *nf* **1** : altar lamp **2** LUMBRERA : luminary, celebrity
luminiscencia *nf* : luminescence — **luminiscente** *adj*
luminosidad *nf* : luminosity, brightness
luminoso, -sa *adj* : shining, luminous
luna *nf* **1** : moon **2 luna de miel** : honeymoon
lunar¹ *adj* : lunar
lunar² *nm* **1** : mole, beauty spot **2** : defect, blemish **3** : polka dot
lunático, -ca *adj & n* : lunatic
lunes *nms & pl* : Monday
luneta *nf* **1** : lens (of eyeglasses) **2** : windshield (of an automobile) **3** : crescent
lupa *nf* : magnifying glass
lúpulo *nm* : hops (plant)
lustrar *vt* : to shine, to polish
lustre *nm* **1** BRILLO : luster, shine **2** : glory, distinction
lustroso, -sa *adj* BRILLOSO : lustrous, shiny
luto *nm* : mourning ⟨estar de luto : to be in mourning⟩
luz *nf, pl* **luces** **1** : light **2** : lighting **3** *fam* : electricity **4** : window, opening **5** : light, lamp **6** : span, spread (between supports) **7 a la luz de** : in light of **8 dar a luz** : to give birth **9 traje de luces** : matador's costume
luzca, etc. → lucir

M

m *nf* : thirteenth letter of the Spanish alphabet
macabro, -bra *adj* : macabre
macaco¹, -ca *adj* : ugly, misshapen
macaco², -ca *n* : macaque
macadán *nm, pl* **-danes** : macadam
macana *nf* **1** : club, cudgel **2** *fam* : nonsense, silliness **3** *fam* : lie, fib
macanudo, -da *adj fam* : great, fantastic
macarrón *nm, pl* **-rrones** **1** : macaroon **2 macarrones** *nmpl* : macaroni
maceta *nf* **1** : flowerpot **2** : mallet **3** *Mex fam* : head
macetero *nm* **1** : plant stand **2** TIESTO : flowerpot, planter
machacar {72} *vt* **1** : to crush, to grind **2** : to beat, to pound — *vi* : to insist, to go on (about)
machacón, -cona *adj, mpl* **-cones** : insistent, tiresome
machete *nm* : machete
machetear *vt* : to hack with a machete — *vi Mex fam* : to plod, to work tirelessly
machismo *nm* **1** : machismo **2** : male chauvinism
machista *nm* : male chauvinist

macho¹ *adj* **1** : male **2** : macho, virile, tough

macho² *nm* **1** : male **2** : he-man

machote *nm* **1** *fam* : tough guy, he-man **2** *CA, Mex* : rough draft, model **3** *Mex* : blank form

machucar {72} *vt* **1** : to pound, to beat, to crush **2** : to bruise

machucón *nm, pl* **-cones 1** MORETÓN : bruise **2** : smashing, pounding

macilento, -ta *adj* : gaunt, wan

macis *nm* : mace (spice)

macizo, -za *adj* **1** : solid ⟨oro macizo : solid gold⟩ **2** : strong, strapping **3** : massive

macrocosmo *nm* : macrocosm

mácula *nf* : blemish, stain

madeja *nf* **1** : skein, hank **2** : tangle (of hair)

madera *nf* **1** : wood **2** : lumber, timber **3 madera dura** *or* **madera noble** : hardwood

maderero, -ra *adj* : timber, lumber

madero *nm* : piece of lumber, plank

madrastra *nf* : stepmother

madrazo *nm Mex fam* : punch, blow ⟨se agarraron a madrazos : they beat each other up⟩

madre *nf* **1** : mother **2 madre política** : mother-in-law **3 la Madre Patria** : the mother country (said of Spain)

madrear *vt Mex fam* : to beat up

madreperla *nf* NÁCAR : mother-of-pearl

madreselva *nf* : honeysuckle

madriguera *nf* : burrow, den, lair

madrileño¹, -ña *adj* : of or from Madrid

madrileño², -ña *n* : person from Madrid

madrina *nf* **1** : godmother **2** : bridesmaid **3** : sponsor

madrugada *nf* **1** : early morning, wee hours **2** ALBA : dawn, daybreak

madrugador, -dora *n* : early riser

madrugar {52} *vi* **1** : to get up early **2** : to get a head start

madurar *v* **1** : to ripen **2** : to mature

madurez *nf, pl* **-reces 1** : maturity **2** : ripeness

maduro, -ra *adj* **1** : mature **2** : ripe

maestría *nf* **1** : mastery, skill **2** : master's degree

maestro¹, -tra *adj* **1** : masterly, skilled **2** : chief, main **3** : trained ⟨un elefante maestro : a trained elephant⟩

maestro², -tra *n* **1** : teacher (in grammar school) **2** : expert, master **3** : maestro

Mafia *nf* : Mafia

mafioso, -sa *n* : mafioso, gangster

magdalena *nf* : bun, muffin

magenta *adj & n* : magenta

magia *nf* : magic

mágico, -ca *adj* : magic, magical — **mágicamente** *adv*

magisterio *nm* **1** : teaching **2** : teachers *pl*, teaching profession

magistrado, -da *n* : magistrate, judge

magistral *adj* **1** : masterful, skillful **2** : magisterial

magistralmente *adv* : masterfully, brilliantly

magistratura *nf* : judgeship, magistracy

magma *nm* : magma

magnanimidad *nf* : magnanimity

magnánimo, -ma *adj* GENEROSO : magnanimous — **magnánimamente** *adv*

magnate *nmf* : magnate, tycoon

magnesia *nf* : magnesia

magnesio *nm* : magnesium

magnético, -ca *adj* : magnetic

magnetismo *nm* : magnetism

magnetizar {21} *vt* : to magnetize

magnetófono *nm* : tape recorder

magnetofónico, -ca *adj* **cinta magnetofónica** : magnetic tape

magnificar {72} *vt* **1** : to magnify **2** EXAGERAR : to exaggerate **3** ENSALZAR : to exalt, to extol, to praise highly

magnificencia *nf* : magnificence, splendor

magnífico, -ca *adj* ESPLENDOROSO : magnificent, splendid — **magníficamente** *adv*

magnitud *nf* : magnitude

magnolia *nf* : magnolia (flower)

magnolio *nm* : magnolia (tree)

mago, -ga *n* **1** : magician **2** : wizard (in folk tales, etc.) **3 los Reyes Magos** : the Magi

magro, -gra *adj* **1** : lean (of meat) **2** : meager

maguey *nm* : maguey

magulladura *nf* MORETÓN : bruise

magullar *vt* : to bruise — **magullarse** *vr*

mahometano¹, -na *adj* ISLÁMICO : Islamic, Muslim

mahometano², -na *n* : Muslim

mahonesa → **mayonesa**

maicena *nf* : cornstarch

mainframe ['meinˌfreim] *nm* : mainframe

maíz *nm* : corn, maize

maizal *nm* : cornfield

maja *nf* : pestle

majadería *nf* **1** TONTERÍA : stupidity, foolishness **2** *Mex* LEPERADA : insult, obscenity

majadero¹, -ra *adj* **1** : foolish, silly **2** *Mex* LÉPERO : crude, vulgar

majadero², -ra *n* **1** TONTO : fool **2** *Mex* : rude person, boor

majar *vt* : to crush, to mash

majestad *nf* : majesty ⟨Su Majestad : Your Majesty⟩

majestuosamente *adv* : majestically

majestuosidad *nf* : majesty, grandeur

majestuoso, -sa *adj* : majestic, stately

majo, -ja *adj Spain* **1** : nice, likeable **2** GUAPO : attractive, good-looking

mal¹ *adv* **1** : badly, poorly ⟨baila muy mal : he dances very badly⟩ **2** : wrong, incorrectly ⟨me entendió mal : she misunderstood me⟩ **3** : with difficulty, hardly ⟨mal puedo oírte : I can hardly hear you⟩ **4 de mal en peor** : from bad to worse **5 menos mal** : it could have been worse

mal² *adj* → **malo**
mal³ *nm* **1** : evil, wrong **2** DAÑO : harm, damage **3** DESGRACIA : misfortune **4** ENFERMEDAD : illness, sickness
malabar *adj* **juegos malabares** : juggling
malabarista *nmf* : juggler
malaconsejado, -da *adj* : ill-advised
malacostumbrado, -da *adj* CONSENTIDO : spoiled, pampered
malacostumbrar *vt* : to spoil
malagradecido, -da *adj* INGRATO : ungrateful
malaisio → **malasio**
malaquita *nf* : malachite
malaria *nf* PALUDISMO : malaria
malasio, -sia *adj & n* : Malaysian
malauiano, -na *adj & n* : Malawian
malaventura *nf* : misadventure, misfortune
malaventurado, -da *adj* MALHADADO : ill-fated, unfortunate
malayo, -ya *adj & n* : Malay, Malayan
malbaratar *vt* **1** MALGASTAR : to squander **2** : to undersell
malcriado¹, -da *adj* **1** : ill-bred, ill-mannered **2** : spoiled, pampered
malcriado², -da *n* : spoiled brat
maldad *nf* **1** : evil, wickedness **2** : evil deed
maldecir {11} *vt* : to curse, to damn — *vi* **1** : to curse, to swear **2** ~ **de** : to speak ill of, to slander, to defame
maldición *nf, pl* **-ciones** : curse
maldiga, maldijo etc. → **maldecir**
maldito, -ta *adj* **1** : cursed, damned ⟨¡maldita sea! : damn it all!⟩ **2** : wicked
maldoso, -sa *adj Mex* : mischievous
maleable *adj* : malleable
maleante *nmf* : crook, thug
malecón *nm, pl* **-cones** : jetty, breakwater
maleducado, -da *adj* : ill-mannered, rude
maleficio *nm* : curse, hex
maléfico, -ca *adj* : evil, harmful
malentender {56} *vt* : to misunderstand
malentendido *nm* : misunderstanding
malestar *nm* **1** : discomfort **2** IRRITACIÓN : annoyance **3** INQUIETUD : uneasiness, unrest
maleta *nf* : suitcase, bag ⟨haz tus maletas : pack your bags⟩
maletero¹, -ra *n* : porter
maletero² *nm* : trunk (of an automobile)
maletín *nm, pl* **-tines** **1** PORTAFOLIO : briefcase **2** : overnight bag, satchel
malevolencia *nf* : malevolence, wickedness
malévolo, -la *adj* : malevolent, wicked
maleza *nf* **1** : thicket, underbrush **2** : weeds *pl*
malformación *nf, pl* **-ciones** : malformation
malgache *adj & nmf* : Madagascan
malgastar *vt* : to squander (resources), to waste (time, effort)
malhablado, -da *adj* : foul-mouthed

malhadado, -da *adj* MALAVENTURADO : ill-fated
malhechor, -chora *n* : criminal, delinquent, wrongdoer
malherir {76} *vt* : to injure seriously
malhumor *nm* : bad mood, sullenness
malhumorado, -da *adj* : bad-tempered, cross
malicia *nf* **1** : wickedness, malice **2** : mischief, naughtiness **3** : cunning, craftiness
malicioso, -sa *adj* **1** : malicious **2** PÍCARO : mischievous
malignidad *nf* **1** : malignancy **2** MALDAD : evil
maligno, -na *adj* **1** : malignant ⟨un tumor maligno : a malignant tumor⟩ **2** : evil, harmful, malign
malinchismo *nm Mex* : preference for foreign goods or people — **malinchista** *adj*
malintencionado, -da *adj* : malicious, spiteful
malinterpretar *vt* : to misinterpret
malla *nf* **1** : mesh **2** LEOTARDO : leotard, tights *pl* **3** **malla de baño** : bathing suit
mallorquín, -quina *adj & n* : Majorcan
malnutrición *nf, pl* **-ciones** DESNUTRICIÓN : malnutrition
malnutrido, -da *adj* DESNUTRIDO : malnourished, undernourished
malo¹, -la *adj* (**mal** *before masculine singular nouns*) **1** : bad ⟨mala suerte : bad luck⟩ **2** : wicked, naughty **3** : cheap, poor (quality) **4** : harmful ⟨malo para la salud : bad for one's health⟩ **5** (*using the form* **mal**) : unwell ⟨estar mal del corazón : to have heart trouble⟩ **6** **estar de malas** : to be in a bad mood
malo², -la *n* : villain, bad guy (in novels, movies, etc.)
malogrado, -da *adj* : failed, unsuccessful
malograr *vt* **1** : to spoil, to ruin **2** : to waste (an opportunity, time) — **malograrse** *vr* **1** FRACASAR : to fail **2** : to die young
malogro *nm* **1** : untimely death **2** FRACASO : failure
maloliente *adj* HEDIONDO : foul-smelling, smelly
malparado, -da *adj* **salir malparado** *or* **quedar malparado** : to come out of (something) badly, to end up in a bad state
malpensado, -da *adj* : distrustful, suspicious, nasty-minded
malquerencia *nf* AVERSIÓN : ill will, dislike
malquerer {64} *vt* : to dislike
malquiso, etc. → **malquerer**
malsano, -na *adj* : unhealthy
malsonante *adj* : rude, offensive ⟨palabras malsonantes : foul language⟩
malta *nf* : malt
malteada *nf* : malted milk ⟨malteada de chocolate : chocolate malt⟩

maltés, -tesa *adj & n, mpl* **malteses** : Maltese
maltratar *vt* **1** : to mistreat, to abuse **2** : to damage, to spoil
maltrato *nm* : mistreatment, abuse
maltrecho, -cha *adj* : battered, damaged
malucho, -cha *adj fam* : sick, under the weather
malva *adj & nm* : mauve
malvado¹, -da *adj* : evil, wicked
malvado², -da *n* : evildoer, wicked person
malvavisco *nm* : marshmallow
malvender *vt* : to sell at a loss
malversación *nf, pl* **-ciones** : misappropriation (of funds), embezzlement
malversador, -dora *n* : embezzler
malversar *vt* : to embezzle
malvivir *vi* : to live badly, to just scrape by
mamá *nf fam* : mom, mama
mamar *vi* **1** : to suckle **2 darle de mamar a** : to breast-feed — *vt* **1** : to suckle, to nurse **2** : to learn from childhood, to grow up with — **mamarse** *vr fam* : to get drunk
mamario, -ria *adj* : mammary
mamarracho *nm fam* **1** ESPERPENTO : mess, sight **2** : laughingstock, fool **3** : rubbish, junk
mambo *nm* : mambo
mami *nf fam* : mommy
mamífero¹, -ra *adj* : mammalian
mamífero² *nm* : mammal
mamila *nf* **1** : nipple **2** *Mex* : baby bottle, pacifier
mamografía *nf* : mammogram
mamola *nf* : pat, chuck under the chin
mamotreto *nm fam* **1** : huge book, tome **2** ARMATOSTE : hulk, monstrosity
mampara *nf* BIOMBO : screen, room divider
mamparo *nm* : bulkhead
mampostería *nf* : masonry, stonemasonry
mampostero *nm* : mason, stonemason
mamut *nm, pl* **mamuts** : mammoth
maná *nm* : manna
manada *nf* **1** : flock, herd, pack **2** *fam* : horde, mob ⟨llegaron en manada : they came in droves⟩
manantial *nm* **1** FUENTE : spring **2** : source
manar *vi* **1** : to flow **2** : to abound
manatí *nm* : manatee
mancha *nf* **1** : stain, spot, mark ⟨mancha de sangre : bloodstain⟩ **2** : blemish, blot ⟨una mancha en su reputación : a blemish on his reputation⟩ **3** : patch
manchado, -da *adj* : stained
manchar *vt* **1** ENSUCIAR : to stain, to soil **2** DESHONRAR : to sully, to tarnish — **mancharse** *vr* : to get dirty
mancillar *vt* : to sully, to besmirch
manco, -ca *adj* : one-armed, one-handed
mancomunar *vt* : to combine, to pool — **mancomunarse** *vr* : to unite, to join together

mancomunidad *nf* **1** : commonwealth **2** : association, confederation
mancuernas *nfpl* : cuff links
mancuernillas *nf Mex* : cuff links
mandadero, -ra *n* : errand boy *m*, errand girl *f*, messenger
mandado *nm* **1** : order, command **2** : errand ⟨hacer los mandados : to run errands, to go shopping⟩
mandamás *nmf, pl* **-mases** *fam* : boss, bigwig, honcho
mandamiento *nm* **1** : commandment **2** : command, order, warrant ⟨mandamiento judicial : warrant, court order⟩
mandar *vt* **1** ORDENAR : to command, to order **2** ENVIAR : to send ⟨te manda saludos : he sends you his regards⟩ **3** ECHAR : to hurl, to throw **4** ¿mande? *Mex* : yes?, pardon? — *vi* : to be the boss, to be in charge — **mandarse** *vr Mex* : to take liberties, to take advantage
mandarín *nm* : Mandarin
mandarina *nf* : mandarin orange, tangerine
mandatario, -ria *n* **1** : leader (in politics) ⟨primer mandatario : head of state⟩ **2** : agent (in law)
mandato *nm* **1** : term of office **2** : mandate
mandíbula *nf* **1** : jaw **2** : mandible
mandil *nm* **1** DELANTAL : apron **2** : horse blanket
mandilón *nm, pl* **-lones** *fam* : wimp, coward
mandioca *nf* **1** : manioc, cassava **2** : tapioca
mando *nm* **1** : command, leadership **2** : control (for a device) ⟨mando a distancia : remote control⟩ **3 al mando de** : in charge of **4 al mando de** : under the command of
mandolina *nf* : mandolin
mandón, -dona *adj, mpl* **mandones** : bossy, domineering
mandonear *vt fam* MANGONEAR : to boss around
mandrágora *nf* : mandrake
manecilla *nf* : hand (of a clock), pointer
manejable *adj* **1** : manageable **2** : docile, easily led
manejar *vt* **1** CONDUCIR : to drive (a car) **2** OPERAR : to handle, to operate **3** : to manage **4** : to manipulate (a person) — *vi* : to drive — **manejarse** *vr* **1** COMPORTARSE : to behave **2** : to get along, to manage
manejo *nm* **1** : handling, operation **2** : management
manera *nf* **1** MODO : way, manner, fashion **2 de cualquier manera** *or* **de todas maneras** : anyway, anyhow **3 de manera que** : so, in order that **4 de ninguna manera** : by no means, absolutely not **5 manera de ser** : personality, demeanor

manga *nf* **1** : sleeve **2** MANGUERA : hose
manganeso *nm* : manganese
mangle *nm* : mangrove
mango *nm* **1** : hilt, handle **2** : mango
mangonear *vt fam* : to boss around, to bully — *vi* **1** : to be bossy **2** : to loaf, to fool around
mangosta *nf* : mongoose
manguera *nf* : hose
manguito *nm* **1** : muff **2** : sleeve (of a pipe, etc.), hose (of a car)
maní *nm, pl* **maníes** : peanut
manía *nf* **1** OBSESIÓN : mania, obsession **2** : craze, fad **3** : odd habit, peculiarity **4** : dislike, aversion
maníaco¹, -ca *adj* : maniacal
maníaco², -ca *n* : maniac
maniatar *vt* : to tie the hands of, to manacle
maniático¹, -ca *adj* **1** MANÍACO : maniacal **2** : obsessive **3** : fussy, finicky
maniático², -ca *n* **1** MANÍACO : maniac, lunatic **2** : obsessive person, fanatic **3** : eccentric, crank
manicomio *nm* : insane asylum, madhouse
manicura *nf* : manicure
manicuro, -ra *n* : manicurist
manido, -da *adj* : hackneyed, stale, trite
manifestación *nf, pl* **-ciones 1** : manifestation, sign **2** : demonstration, rally
manifestante *nmf* : demonstrator
manifestar {55} *vt* **1** : to demonstrate, to show **2** : to declare — **manifestarse** *vr* **1** : to be or become evident **2** : to state one's position ⟨se han manifestado a favor del acuerdo : they have declared their support for the agreement⟩ **3** : to demonstrate, to rally
manifiesto¹, -ta *adj* : manifest, evident, clear — **manifiestamente** *adv*
manifiesto² *nm* : manifesto
manija *nf* MANGO : handle
manilla → **manecilla**
manillar *nm* : handlebars *pl*
maniobra *nf* : maneuver, stratagem
maniobrar *v* : to maneuver
manipulación *nf, pl* **-ciones** : manipulation
manipulador¹, -dora *adj* : manipulating, manipulative
manipulador², -dora *n* : manipulator
manipular *vt* **1** : to manipulate **2** MANEJAR : to handle
maniquí¹ *nmf, pl* **-quíes** : mannequin, model
maniquí² *nm, pl* **-quíes** : mannequin, dummy
manirroto¹, -ta *adj* : extravagant
manirroto², -ta *n* : spendthrift
manivela *nf* : crank
manjar *nm* : delicacy, special dish
mano¹ *nf* **1** : hand **2** : coat (of paint or varnish) **3 a** ∼ : by hand **4 a** ∼ *or* **a la mano** : handy, at hand, nearby **5 darse la mano** : to shake hands **6 de la mano** : hand in hand ⟨la política y la economía van de la mano : politics and economics go hand in hand⟩ **7 de primera mano** : firsthand, at firsthand **8 de segunda mano** : secondhand ⟨ropa de segunda mano : secondhand clothing⟩ **9 mano a mano** : one-on-one **10 mano de obra** : labor, manpower **11 mano de mortero** : pestle **12 echar una mano** : to lend a hand **13 mano negra** *Mex fam* : shady dealings *pl*
mano², -na *n Mex fam* : buddy, pal ⟨¡oye, mano! : hey man!⟩
manojo *nm* PUÑADO : handful, bunch
manopla *nf* **1** : mitten, mitt **2** : brass knuckles *pl*
manosear *vt* **1** : to handle or touch excessively **2** ACARICIAR : to fondle, to caress
manotazo *nm* : slap, smack, swipe
manotear *vi* : to wave one's hands, to gesticulate
mansalva *adv* **a** ∼ : at close range
mansarda *nf* BUHARDILLA : attic
mansedumbre *nf* **1** : gentleness, meekness **2** : tameness
mansión *nf, pl* **-siones** : mansion
manso, -sa *adj* **1** : gentle, meek **2** : tame — **mansamente** *adv*
manta *nf* **1** COBIJA, FRAZADA : blanket **2** : poncho **3** *Mex* : coarse cotton fabric
manteca *nf* **1** GRASA : lard, fat **2** : butter
mantecoso, -sa *adj* : buttery
mantel *nm* **1** : tablecloth **2** : altar cloth
mantelería *nf* : table linen
mantener {80} *vt* **1** SUSTENTAR : to support, to feed ⟨mantener uno su familia : to support one's family⟩ **2** CONSERVAR : to keep, to preserve **3** CONTINUAR : to keep up, to sustain ⟨mantener una correspondencia : to keep up a correspondence⟩ **4** AFIRMAR : to maintain, to affirm — **mantenerse** *vr* **1** : to support oneself, to subsist **2 mantenerse firme** : to hold one's ground
mantenimiento *nm* **1** : maintenance, upkeep **2** : sustenance, food **3** : preservation
mantequera *nf* **1** : churn **2** : butter dish
mantequería *nf* **1** : creamery, dairy **2** : grocery store
mantequilla *nf* : butter
mantilla *nf* : mantilla
mantis *nf* **mantis religiosa** : praying mantis
manto *nm* **1** : cloak **2** : mantle (in geology)
mantón *nm, pl* **-tones** CHAL : shawl
mantuvo, etc. → **mantener**
manual¹ *adj* **1** : manual ⟨trabajo manual : manual labor⟩ **2** : handy, manageable — **manualmente** *adv*
manual² *nm* : manual, handbook
manualidades *nfpl* : handicrafts (in schools)
manubrio *nm* **1** : handle, crank **2** : handlebars *pl*

manufactura *nf* **1** FABRICACIÓN : manufacture **2** : manufactured item, product **3** FÁBRICA : factory
manufacturar *vt* FABRICAR : to manufacture
manufacturero¹, -ra *adj* : manufacturing
manufacturero², -ra *n* FABRICANTE : manufacturer
manuscrito¹, -ta *adj* : handwritten
manuscrito² *nm* : manuscript
manutención *nf, pl* **-ciones** : maintenance, support
manzana *nf* **1** : apple **2** CUADRA : block (enclosed by streets or buildings) **3** *or* **manzana de Adán** : Adam's apple
manzanal *nm* **1** : apple orchard **2** MANZANO : apple tree
manzanar *nm* : apple orchard
manzanilla *nf* **1** : chamomile **2** : chamomile tea
manzano *nm* : apple tree
maña *nf* **1** : dexterity, skill **2** : cunning, guile **3 mañas** *or* **malas mañas** *nfpl* : bad habits, vices
mañana *nf* **1** : morning **2** : tomorrow
mañanero, -ra *adj* MATUTINO : morning ⟨rocío mañanero : morning dew⟩
mañanitas *nfpl Mex* : birthday serenade
mañoso, -sa *adj* **1** HÁBIL : skillful **2** ASTUTO : cunning, crafty **3** : fussy, finicky
mapa *nm* CARTA : map
mapache *nm* : raccoon
mapamundi *nm* : map of the world
maqueta *nf* : model, mock-up
maquillador, -dora *n* : makeup artist
maquillaje *nm* : makeup
maquillarse *vr* : to put on makeup, to make oneself up
máquina *nf* **1** : machine ⟨máquina de coser : sewing machine⟩ ⟨máquina de escribir : typewriter⟩ **2** LOCOMOTORA : engine, locomotive **3** : machine (in politics) **4 a toda máquina** : at full speed
maquinación *nf, pl* **-ciones** : machination, scheme, plot
maquinal *adj* : mechanical, automatic — **maquinalmente** *adv*
maquinar *vt* : to plot, to scheme
maquinaria *nf* **1** : machinery **2** : mechanism, works *pl*
maquinilla *nf* **1** : small machine or device **2** *CA, Car* : typewriter
maquinista *nmf* **1** : machinist **2** : railroad engineer
mar *nmf* **1** : sea ⟨un mar agitado : a rough sea⟩ ⟨hacerse a la mar : to set sail⟩ **2 alta mar** : high seas
maraca *nf* : maraca
maraña *nf* **1** : thicket **2** ENREDO : tangle, mess
marasmo *nm* : paralysis, stagnation
maratón *nm, pl* **-tones** : marathon
maravilla *nf* **1** : wonder, marvel ⟨a las mil maravillas : wonderfully, marvelously⟩ ⟨hacer maravillas : to work wonders⟩ **2** : marigold
maravillar *vt* ASOMBRAR : to astonish, to amaze — **maravillarse** *vr* : to be amazed, to marvel
maravilloso, -sa *adj* ESTUPENDO : wonderful, marvelous — **maravillosamente** *adv*
marbete *nm* **1** ETIQUETA : label, tag **2** *PRi* : registration sticker (of a car)
marca *nf* **1** : mark **2** : brand, make **3** : trademark ⟨marca registrada : registered trademark⟩ **4** : record (in sports) ⟨batir la marca : to beat the record⟩
marcado, -da *adj* : marked ⟨un marcado contraste : a marked contrast⟩
marcador *nm* **1** TANTEADOR : scoreboard **2** : marker, felt-tipped pen **3 marcador de libros** : bookmark
marcaje *nm* **1** : scoring (in sports) **2** : guarding (in sports)
marcapasos *nms & pl* : pacemaker
marcar {72} *vt* **1** : to mark **2** : to brand (livestock) **3** : to indicate, to show **4** RESALTAR : to emphasize **5** : to dial (a telephone) **6** : to guard (an opponent) **7** ANOTAR : to score (a goal, a point) — *vi* **1** ANOTAR : to score **2** : to dial
marcha *nf* **1** : march **2** : hike, walk ⟨ir de marcha : to go hiking⟩ **3** : pace, speed ⟨a toda marcha : at top speed⟩ **4** : gear (of an automobile) ⟨marcha atrás : reverse, reverse gear⟩ **5 en ~** : in motion, in gear, under way
marchar *vi* **1** IR : to go, to travel **2** ANDAR : to walk **3** FUNCIONAR : to work, to go **4** : to march — **marcharse** *vr* : to leave
marchitar *vi* : to make wither, to wilt — **marchitarse** *vr* **1** : to wither, to shrivel up, to wilt **2** : to languish, to fade away
marchito, -ta *adj* : withered, faded
marcial *adj* : martial, military
marco *nm* **1** : frame, framework **2** : goalposts *pl* **3** AMBIENTE : setting, atmosphere **4** : mark (unit of currency)
marea *nf* : tide
mareado, -da *adj* **1** : dizzy, lightheaded **2** : queasy, nauseous **3** : seasick
marear *vt* **1** : to make sick ⟨los gases me marearon : the fumes made me sick⟩ **2** : to bother, to annoy — **marearse** *vr* **1** : to get sick, to become nauseated **2** : to feel dizzy **3** : to get tipsy
marejada *nf* **1** : surge, swell (of the sea) **2** : undercurrent, ferment, unrest
maremoto *nm* : tidal wave
mareo *nm* **1** : dizzy spell **2** : nausea **3** : seasickness, motion sickness **4** : annoyance, vexation
marfil *nm* : ivory
margarina *nf* : margarine
margarita *nf* **1** : daisy **2** : margarita (cocktail)
margen¹ *nf, pl* **márgenes** : bank (of a river), side (of a street)

margen² *nm, pl* **márgenes** 1 : edge, border 2 : margin ⟨margen de ganancia : profit margin⟩
marginación *nf, pl* **-ciones** : marginalization, exclusion
marginado¹, -da *adj* 1 DESHEREDADO : outcast, alienated, dispossessed 2 **clases marginadas** : underclass
marginado², -da *n* : outcast, misfit
marginal *adj* : marginal, fringe
marginalidad *nf* : marginality
marginar *vt* : to ostracize, to exclude
mariachi *nm* : mariachi musician or band
maridaje *nm* : marriage, union
maridar *vt* UNIR : to marry, to unite
marido *nm* ESPOSO : husband
marihuana *or* **mariguana** *or* **marijuana** *nf* : marihuana
marimacho *nmf fam* 1 : mannish woman 2 : tomboy
marimba *nf* : marimba
marina *nf* 1 : coast, coastal area 2 : navy, fleet ⟨marina mercante : merchant marine⟩
marinada *nf* : marinade
marinar *vt* : to marinate
marinero¹, -ra *adj* 1 : seaworthy 2 : sea, marine
marinero² *nm* : sailor
marino¹, -na *adj* : marine, sea
marino² *nm* : sailor, seaman
marioneta *nf* TÍTERE : puppet, marionette
mariposa *nf* 1 : butterfly 2 **mariposa nocturna** : moth
mariquita¹ *nf* : ladybug
mariquita² *nm fam* : sissy, wimp
mariscal *nm* 1 : marshal 2 **mariscal de campo** : field marshal (in the military), quarterback (in football)
marisco *nm* 1 : shellfish 2 **mariscos** *nmpl* : seafood
marisma *nf* : marsh, salt marsh
marital *adj* : marital, married ⟨la vida marital : married life⟩
marítimo, -ma *adj* : maritime, shipping ⟨la industria marítima : the shipping industry⟩
marmita *nf* : (cooking) pot
mármol *nm* : marble
marmóreo, -rea *adj* : marble, marmoreal
marmota *nf* 1 : marmot 2 **marmota de América** : woodchuck, groundhog
maroma *nf* 1 : rope 2 : acrobatic stunt 3 *Mex* : somersault
marque, etc. → **marcar**
marqués, -quesa *n, mpl* **marqueses** : marquis *m*, marquess *m*, marquise *f*, marchioness *f*
marquesina *nf* : marquee, canopy
marqueta *nf Mex* : block (of chocolate), lump (of sugar or salt)
marranada *nf* 1 : disgusting thing 2 : dirty trick
marrano¹, -na *adj* : filthy, disgusting
marrano², -na *n* 1 CERDO : pig, hog 2 : dirty pig, slob

marrar *vt* : to miss (a target) — *vi* : to fail, to go wrong
marras *adv* 1 : long ago 2 **de ~** : said, aforementioned ⟨el individuo de marras : the individual in question⟩
marrasquino *nm* : maraschino
marrón *adj & nm, pl* **marrones** CASTAÑO : brown
marroquí *adj & nmf, pl* **-quíes** : Moroccan
marsopa *nf* : porpoise
marsupial *nm* : marsupial
marta *nf* 1 : marten 2 **marta cebellina** : sable (animal)
Marte *nm* : Mars
martes *nms & pl* : Tuesday
martillar *v* : to hammer
martillazo *nm* : blow with a hammer
martillo *nm* 1 : hammer 2 **martillo neumático** : jackhammer
martinete *nm* 1 : heron 2 : pile driver
mártir *nmf* : martyr
martirio *nm* 1 : martyrdom 2 : ordeal, torment
martirizar {21} *vt* 1 : to martyr 2 ATORMENTAR : to torment
marxismo *nm* : Marxism
marxista *adj & nmf* : Marxist
marzo *nm* : March
mas *conj* PERO : but
más¹ *adv* 1 : more ⟨¿hay algo más grande? : is there anything bigger?⟩ 2 : most ⟨Luis es el más alto : Luis is the tallest⟩ 3 : longer ⟨el sabor dura más : the flavor lasts longer⟩ 4 : rather ⟨más querría andar : I would rather walk⟩ 5 a **~** : besides, in addition 6 **más allá** : further 7 **qué... más...** : what ..., what a ... ⟨qué día más bonito! : what a beautiful day!⟩
más² *adj* 1 : more ⟨dáme dos kilos más : give me two more kilos⟩ 2 : most ⟨la que ganó más dinero : the one who earned the most money⟩ 3 : else ⟨¿quién más quiere vino? : who else wants wine?⟩
más³ *n* : plus sign
más⁴ *prep* : plus ⟨tres más dos es igual a cinco : three plus two equals five⟩
más⁵ *pron* 1 : more ⟨¿tienes más? : do you have more?⟩ 2 **a lo más** : at most 3 **de ~** : extra, excess 4 **más o menos** : more or less, approximately 5 **por más que** : no matter how much ⟨por más que corras no llegarás a tiempo : no matter how fast you run you won't arrive on time⟩
masa *nf* 1 : mass, volume ⟨masa atómica : atomic mass⟩ ⟨producción en masa : mass production⟩ 2 : dough, batter 3 **masas** *nfpl* : people, masses ⟨las masas populares : the common people⟩ 4 **masa harina** *Mex* : corn flour (for tortillas, etc.)
masacrar *vt* : to massacre
masacre *nf* : massacre
masaje *nm* : massage
masajear *vt* : to massage

masajista *nmf* : masseur *m*, masseuse *f*
mascar {72} *v* MASTICAR : to chew
máscara *nf* 1 CARETA : mask 2 : appearance, pretense 3 **máscara antigás** : gas mask
mascarada *nf* : masquerade
mascarilla *nf* 1 : mask (in medicine) ⟨mascarilla de oxígeno : oxygen mask⟩ 2 : facial mask (in cosmetology)
mascota *nf* : mascot
masculinidad *nf* : masculinity
masculino, -na *adj* 1 : masculine, male 2 : manly 3 : masculine (in grammar)
mascullar *v* : to mumble, to mutter
masificado, -da *adj* : overcrowded
masilla *nf* : putty
masivamente *adv* : en masse
masivo, -va *adj* : mass ⟨comunicación masiva : mass communication⟩
masón *nm, pl* **masones** FRANCMASÓN : Mason, Freemason
masonería *nf* FRANCMASONERÍA : Masonry, Freemasonry
masónico, -ca *adj* : Masonic
masoquismo *nm* : masochism
masoquista[1] *adj* : masochistic
masoquista[2] *nmf* : masochist
masque, etc. → **mascar**
masticar {72} *v* MASCAR : to chew, to masticate
mástil *nm* 1 : mast 2 ASTA : flagpole 3 : neck (of a stringed instrument)
mastín *nm, pl* **mastines** : mastiff
mástique *nm* : putty, filler
mastodonte *nm* : mastodon
masturbación *nf, pl* **-ciones** : masturbation
masturbarse *vr* : to masturbate
mata *nf* 1 ARBUSTO : bush, shrub 2 : plant ⟨mata de tomate : tomato plant⟩ 3 : sprig, tuft 4 **mata de pelo** : mop of hair
matadero *nm* : slaughterhouse, abattoir
matado, -da *adj Mex* : strenuous, exhausting
matador *nm* TORERO : matador, bullfighter
matamoscas *nms & pl* : flyswatter
matanza *nf* MASACRE : slaughter, butchering
matar *vt* 1 : to kill 2 : to slaughter, to butcher 3 APAGAR : to extinguish, to put out (fire, light) 4 : to tone down (colors) 5 : to pass, to waste (time) 6 : to trump (in card games) — *vi* : to kill — **matarse** *vr* 1 : to be killed 2 SUICIDARSE : to commit suicide 3 *fam* : to exhaust oneself ⟨se mató tratando de terminarlo : he knocked himself out trying to finish it⟩
matasanos *nms & pl fam* : quack
matasellar *vt* : to cancel (a stamp), to postmark
matasellos *nms & pl* : postmark
matatena *nf Mex* : jacks
mate[1] *adj* : matte, dull
mate[2] *nm* 1 : maté 2 **jaque mate** : checkmate ⟨darle mate a *or* darle jaque mate a : to checkmate⟩

matemática → **matemáticas**
matemáticas *nfpl* : mathematics, math
matemático[1], **-ca** *adj* : mathematical —
matemáticamente *adv*
matemático[2], **-ca** *n* : mathematician
materia *nf* 1 : matter ⟨materia gris : gray matter⟩ 2 : material ⟨materia prima : raw material⟩ 3 : (academic) subject 4 **en materia de** : on the subject of, concerning
material[1] *adj* 1 : material, physical, real 2 **daños materiales** : property damage
material[2] *nm* 1 : material ⟨material de construcción : building material⟩ 2 EQUIPO : equipment, gear
materialismo *nm* : materialism
materialista[1] *adj* : materialistic
materialista[2] *nmf* 1 : materialist 2 *Mex* : truck driver
materializar {21} *vt* : to bring to fruition, to realize — **materializarse** *vr* : to materialize, to come into being
materialmente *adv* 1 : materially, physically ⟨materialmente imposible : physically impossible⟩ 2 : really, absolutely
maternal *adj* : maternal, motherly
maternidad *nf* 1 : maternity, motherhood 2 : maternity hospital, maternity ward
materno, -na *adj* : maternal
matinal *adj* MATUTINO : morning ⟨la pálida luz matinal : the pale morning light⟩
matinée *or* **matiné** *nf* : matinee
matiz *nm, pl* **matices** 1 : hue, shade 2 : nuance
matización *nf, pl* **-ciones** 1 : tinting, toning, shading 2 : clarification (of a statement)
matizar {21} *vt* 1 : to tinge, to tint (colors) 2 : to vary, to modulate (sounds) 3 : to qualify (statements)
matón *nm, pl* **matones** : thug, bully
matorral *nm* 1 : thicket 2 : scrub, scrubland
matraca *nf* 1 : rattle, noisemaker 2 **dar la matraca a** : to pester, to nag
matriarca *nf* : matriarch
matriarcado *nm* : matriarchy
matrícula *nf* 1 : list, roll, register 2 INSCRIPCIÓN : registration, enrollment 3 : license plate, registration number
matriculación *nf, pl* **-ciones** : matriculation, registration
matricular *vt* 1 INSCRIBIR : to enroll, to register (a person) 2 : to register (a vehicle) — **matricularse** *vr* : to matriculate
matrimonial *adj* : marital, matrimonial ⟨la vida matrimonial : married life⟩
matrimonio *nm* 1 : marriage, matrimony 2 : married couple
matriz *nf, pl* **matrices** 1 : uterus, womb 2 : original, master copy 3 : main office, headquarters 4 : stub (of a check) 5 : matrix ⟨matriz de puntos : dot matrix⟩

matrona *nf* : matron
matronal *adj* : matronly
matutino¹, -na *adj* : morning ⟨la edición matutina : the morning edition⟩
matutino² *nm* : morning paper
maullar {8} *vi* : to meow
maullido *nm* : meow
mauritano, -na *adj & n* : Mauritanian
mausoleo *nm* : mausoleum
maxilar *nm* : jaw, jawbone
máxima *nf* : maxim
máxime *adv* ESPECIALMENTE : especially, principally
maximizar {21} *vt* : to maximize
máximo¹, -ma *adj* : maximum, greatest, highest
máximo² *nm* **1** : maximum **2 al máximo** : to the utmost **3 como** ～ : at the most, at the latest
maya¹ *adj & nmf* : Mayan
maya² *nmf* : Maya, Mayan
mayo *nm* : May
mayonesa *nf* : mayonnaise
mayor¹ *adj* **1** (*comparative of* **grande**) : bigger, larger, greater, elder, older **2** (*superlative of* **grande**) : biggest, largest, greatest, eldest, oldest **3** : grown-up, mature **4** : main, major **5 mayor de edad** : of (legal) age **6 al por mayor** *or* **por** ～ : wholesale
mayor² *nmf* **1** : major (in the military) **2** : adult
mayoral *nm* CAPATAZ : foreman, overseer
mayordomo *nm* : butler, majordomo
mayoreo *nm* : wholesale
mayores *nmpl* : grown-ups, elders
mayoría *nf* **1** : majority **2 en su mayoría** : on the whole
mayorista¹ *adj* ALMACENISTA : wholesale
mayorista² *nmf* : wholesaler
mayoritariamente *adv* : primarily, chiefly
mayoritario, -ria *adj & n* : majority ⟨un consenso mayoritario : a majority consensus⟩
mayormente *adv* : primarily, chiefly
mayúscula *nf* : capital letter
mayúsculo, -la *adj* **1** : capital, uppercase **2** : huge, terrible ⟨un problema mayúsculo : a huge problem⟩
maza *nf* **1** : mace (weapon) **2** : drumstick **3** *fam* : bore, pest
mazacote *nm* **1** : concrete **2** : lumpy mess (of food) **3** : eyesore, crude work of art
mazapán *nm, pl* **-panes** : marzipan
mazmorra *nf* CALABOZO : dungeon
mazo *nm* **1** : mallet **2** : pestle **3** MANOJO : handful, bunch
mazorca *nf* **1** CHOCLO : cob, ear of corn **2 pelar la mazorca** *Mex fam* : to smile from ear to ear
me *pron* **1** : me ⟨me vieron : they saw me⟩ **2** : to me, for me, from me ⟨dame el libro : give me the book⟩ ⟨me lo compró : he bought it for me⟩ ⟨me robaron la cartera : they stole my pocketbook⟩

3 : myself, to myself, for myself, from myself ⟨me preparé una buena comida : I cooked myself a good dinner⟩ ⟨me equivoqué : I made a mistake⟩
mecánica *nf* : mechanics
mecánico¹, -ca *adj* : mechanical — **mecánicamente** *adv*
mecánico², -ca *n* **1** : mechanic **2** : technician ⟨mecánico dental : dental technician⟩
mecanismo *nm* : mechanism
mecanización *nf, pl* **-ciones** : mechanization
mecanizar {21} *vt* : to mechanize
mecanografía *nf* : typing
mecanografiar {85} *vt* : to type
mecanógrafo, -fa *n* : typist
mecate *nm* CA, Mex, Ven : rope, twine, cord
mecedor *nm* : glider (seat)
mecedora *nf* : rocking chair
mecenas *nmfs & pl* : patron (of the arts), sponsor
mecenazgo *nm* PATROCINIO : sponsorship, patronage
mecer {86} *vt* **1** : to rock **2** COLUMPIAR : to push (on a swing) — **mecerse** *vr* : to rock, to swing, to sway
mecha *nf* **1** : fuse **2** : wick **3 mechas** *nfpl* : highlights (in hair)
mechero *nm* **1** : burner **2** *Spain* : lighter
mechón *nm, pl* **mechones** : lock (of hair)
medalla *nf* : medal, medallion
medallista *nmf* : medalist
medallón *nm, pl* **-llones** **1** : medallion **2** : locket
media *nf* **1** CALCETÍN : sock **2** : average, mean **3 medias** *nfpl* : stockings, hose, tights **4 a medias** : by halves, half and half, halfway ⟨ir a medias : to go halves⟩ ⟨verdad a medias : half-truth⟩
mediación *nf, pl* **-ciones** : mediation
mediado, -da *adj* **1** : half full, half empty, half over **2** : halfway through ⟨mediada la tarea : halfway through the job⟩
mediador, -dora *n* : mediator
mediados *nmpl* **a mediados de** : halfway through, in the middle of ⟨a mediados del mes : towards the middle of the month, mid-month⟩
medialuna *nf* **1** : crescent **2** : croissant, crescent roll
medianamente *adv* : fairly, moderately
medianero, -ra *adj* **1** : dividing **2** : mediating
medianía *nf* **1** : middle position **2** : mediocre person, mediocrity
mediano, -na *adj* **1** : medium, average ⟨la mediana edad : middle age⟩ **2** : mediocre
medianoche *nf* : midnight
mediante *prep* : through, by means of ⟨Dios mediante : God willing⟩
mediar *vi* **1** : to mediate **2** : to be in the middle, to be halfway through **3** : to elapse, to pass ⟨mediaron cinco años entre el inicio de la guerra y el armisti-

cio : five years passed between the start of the war and the armistice⟩ **4** : to be a consideration ⟨media el hecho de que cuesta mucho : one must take into account that it is costly⟩ **5** : to come up, to happen ⟨medió algo urgente : something pressing came up⟩

mediatizar {21} *vt* : to influence, to interfere with

medicación *nf, pl* **-ciones** : medication, treatment

medicamento *nm* : medication, medicine, drug

medicar {72} *vt* : to medicate — **medicarse** *vr* : to take medicine

medicina *nf* : medicine

medicinal *adj* **1** : medicinal **2** : medicated

medicinar *vt* : to give medication to, to dose

medición *nf, pl* **-ciones** : measuring, measurement

médico[1], -ca *adj* : medical ⟨una receta médica : a doctor's prescription⟩

médico[2], -ca *n* DOCTOR : doctor, physician

medida *nf* **1** : measurement, measure ⟨hecho a medida : custom-made⟩ **2** : measure, step ⟨tomar medidas : to take steps⟩ **3** : moderation, prudence ⟨sin medida : immoderately⟩ **4** : extent, degree ⟨en gran medida : to a great extent⟩

medidor *nm* : meter, gauge

medieval *adj* : medieval — **medievalista** *nmf*

medievo → **medioevo**

medio[1] *adv* **1** : half ⟨está medio dormida : she's half asleep⟩ **2** : rather, kind of ⟨está medio aburrida esta fiesta : this party is rather boring⟩

medio[2], -dia *adj* **1** : half ⟨una media hora : half an hour⟩ ⟨medio hermano : half brother⟩ ⟨a media luz : in the half-light⟩ ⟨son las tres y media : it's half past three, it's three-thirty⟩ **2** : midway, halfway ⟨a medio camino : halfway there⟩ **3** : middle ⟨la clase media : the middle class⟩ **4** : average ⟨la temperatura media : the average temperature⟩

medio[3] *nm* **1** CENTRO : middle, center ⟨en medio de : in the middle of, amid⟩ **2** AMBIENTE : milieu, environment **3** : medium, spiritualist **4** : means *pl*, way ⟨por medio de : by means of⟩ ⟨los medios de comunicación : the media⟩ **5 medios** *nmpl* : means, resources

mediocampista *nmf* : midfielder

mediocre *adj* : mediocre, average

mediocridad *nf* : mediocrity

mediodía *nm* : noon, midday

medioevo *nm* : Middle Ages

medir {54} *vt* **1** : to measure **2** : to weigh, to consider ⟨medir los riesgos : to weigh the risks⟩ — *vi* : to measure — **medirse** *vr* : to be moderate, to exercise restraint

meditabundo, -da *adj* PENSATIVO : pensive, thoughtful

meditación *nf, pl* **-ciones** : meditation, thought

meditar *vi* : to meditate, to think ⟨meditar sobre la vida : to contemplate life⟩ — *vt* **1** : to think over, to consider **2** : to plan, to work out

meditativo, -va *adj* : pensive

mediterráneo, -nea *adj* : Mediterranean

medrar *vi* **1** PROSPERAR : to prosper, to thrive **2** AUMENTAR : to increase, to grow

medro *nm* PROSPERIDAD : prosperity, growth

medroso, -sa *adj* : fainthearted, fearful

médula *nf* **1** : marrow, pith **2 médula espinal** : spinal cord

medular *adj* : fundamental, core ⟨el punto medular : the crux of the matter⟩

medusa *nf* : jellyfish, medusa

megabyte *nm* : megabyte

megáfono *nm* : megaphone

megahercio *nm* : megahertz

megahertzio *nm* : megahertz

megatón *nm, pl* **-tones** : megaton

megavatio *nm* : megawatt

mejicano → **mexicano**

mejilla *nf* : cheek

mejillón *nm, pl* **-llones** : mussel

mejor[1] *adv* **1** : better ⟨Carla cocina mejor que Ana : Carla cooks better than Ann⟩ **2** : best ⟨ella es la que lo hace mejor : she's the one who does it best⟩ **3** : rather ⟨mejor morir que rendirme : I'd rather die than give up⟩ **4** : it's better that ... ⟨mejor te vas : you'd better go⟩ **5 a lo mejor** : maybe, perhaps

mejor[2] *adj* **1** (*comparative of* **bueno**) : better ⟨a falta de algo mejor : for lack of something better⟩ **2** (*comparative of* **bien**) : better ⟨está mucho mejor : he's much better⟩ **3** (*superlative of* **bueno**) : best, the better ⟨mi mejor amigo : my best friend⟩ **4** (*superlative of* **bien**) : best, the better ⟨duermo mejor en un clima seco : I sleep best in a dry climate⟩ **5** PREFERIBLE : preferable, better **6 lo mejor** : the best thing, the best part

mejor[3] *nmf* (*with definite article*) : the better (one), the best (one)

mejora *nf* : improvement

mejoramiento *nm* : improvement

mejorana *nf* : marjoram

mejorar *vt* : to improve, to make better — *vi* : to improve, to get better — **mejorarse** *vr*

mejoría *nf* : improvement, betterment

mejunje *nm* : concoction, brew

melancolía *nf* : melancholy, sadness

melancólico, -ca *adj* : melancholy, sad

melanoma *nm* : melanoma

melaza *nf* : molasses

melena *nf* **1** : mane **2** : long hair **3 melenas** *nfpl* GREÑAS : shaggy hair, mop

melenudo¹, -da *adj fam* : longhaired
melenudo², -da *n* GREÑUDO : longhair, hippie
melindres *nmpl* 1 : affectation, airs *pl* 2 : finickiness
melindroso¹, -sa *adj* 1 : affected 2 : fussy, finicky
melindroso², -sa *n* : finicky person, fussbudget
melisa *nf* : lemon balm
mella *nf* 1 : dent, nick 2 **hacer mella en** : to have an effect on, to make an impression on
mellado, -da *adj* 1 : chipped, dented 2 : gap-toothed
mellar *vt* : to dent, to nick
mellizo, -za *adj & n* GEMELO : twin
melocotón *nm, pl* **-tones** : peach
melodía *nf* : melody, tune
melódico, -ca *adj* : melodic
melodioso, -sa *adj* : melodious
melodrama *nm* : melodrama
melodramático, -ca *adj* : melodramatic
melón *nm, pl* **melones** : melon, cantaloupe
meloso, -sa *adj* 1 : honeyed, sweet 2 EMPALAGOSO : cloying, saccharine
membrana *nf* 1 : membrane 2 **membrana interdigital** : web, webbing (of a bird's foot) — **membranoso, -sa** *adj*
membresía *nf* : membership, members *pl*
membrete *nm* : letterhead, heading
membrillo *nm* : quince
membrudo, -da *adj* FORNIDO : muscular, well-built
memez *nf, pl* **memeces** : stupid thing
memo, -ma *adj* : silly, stupid
memorabilia *nf* : memorabilia
memorable *adj* : memorable
memorándum *or* **memorando** *nm, pl* **-dums** *or* **-dos** 1 : memorandum, memo 2 : memo book, appointment book
memoria *nf* 1 : memory ⟨de memoria : by heart⟩ ⟨hacer memoria : to try to remember⟩ ⟨traer a la memoria : to call to mind⟩ 2 RECUERDO : remembrance, memory ⟨su memoria perdurará para siempre : his memory will live forever⟩ 3 : report ⟨memoria annual : annual report⟩ 4 **memorias** *nfpl* : memoirs
memorizar {21} *vt* : to memorize — **memorización** *nf*
mena *nf* : ore
menaje *nm* : household goods *pl*, furnishings *pl*
mención *nf, pl* **-ciones** : mention
mencionar *vt* : to mention, to refer to
mendaz *adj, pl* **mendaces** : mendacious, lying
mendicidad *nf* : begging
mendigar {52} *vi* : to beg — *vt* : to beg for
mendigo, -ga *n* LIMOSNERO : beggar
mendrugo *nm* : crust (of bread)

menear *vt* 1 : to shake (one's head) 2 : to sway, to wiggle (one's hips) 3 : to wag (a tail) 4 : to stir (a liquid) — **menearse** *vr* 1 : to wiggle one's hips 2 : to fidget
meneo *nm* 1 : movement 2 : shake, toss 3 : swaying, wagging, wiggling 4 : stir, stirring
menester *nm* 1 : activity, occupation, duties *pl* 2 **ser menester** : to be necessary ⟨es menester que vengas : you must come⟩
mengano, -na → **fulano**
mengua *nf* 1 : decrease, decline 2 : lack, want 3 : discredit, dishonor
menguar *vt* : to diminish, to lessen — *vi* 1 : to decline, to decrease 2 : to wane — **menguante** *adj*
meningitis *nf* : meningitis
menisco *nm* : meniscus, cartilage
menjurje → **mejunje**
menopausia *nf* : menopause
menor¹ *adj* 1 (*comparative of* **pequeño**) : smaller, lesser, younger 2 (*superlative of* **pequeño**) : smallest, least, youngest 3 : minor 4 **al por menor** : retail 5 **ser menor de edad** : to be a minor, to be underage
menor² *nmf* : minor, juvenile
menos¹ *adv* 1 : less ⟨llueve menos en agosto : it rains less in August⟩ 2 : least ⟨el coche menos caro : the least expensive car⟩ 3 ∼ **de** : less than, fewer than
menos² *adj* 1 : less, fewer ⟨tengo más trabajo y menos tiempo : I have more work and less time⟩ 2 : least, fewest ⟨la clase que tiene menos estudiantes : the class that has the fewest students⟩
menos³ *prep* 1 SALVO, EXCEPTO : except 2 : minus ⟨quince menos cuatro son once : fifteen minus four is eleven⟩
menos⁴ *pron* 1 : less, fewer ⟨no deberías aceptar menos : you shouldn't accept less⟩ 2 **al menos** *or* **por lo menos** : at least 3 **a menos que** : unless
menoscabar *vt* 1 : to lessen, to diminish 2 : to disgrace, to discredit 3 PERJUDICAR : to harm, to damage
menoscabo *nm* 1 : lessening, diminishing 2 : disgrace, discredit 3 : harm, damage
menospreciar *vt* 1 DESPRECIAR : to scorn, to look down on 2 : to underestimate, to undervalue
menosprecio *nm* DESPRECIO : contempt, scorn
mensaje *nm* : message
mensajero, -ra *n* : messenger
menso, -sa *adj Mex fam* : foolish, stupid
menstrual *adj* : menstrual
menstruar {3} *vi* : to menstruate — **menstruación** *nf*
mensual *adj* : monthly
mensualidad *nf* 1 : monthly payment, installment 2 : monthly salary
mensualmente *adv* : every month, monthly

mensurable *adj* : measurable
menta *nf* 1 : mint, peppermint 2 **menta verde** : spearmint
mentado, -da *adj* 1 : aforementioned 2 FAMOSO : renowned, famous
mental *adj* : mental, intellectual — **mentalmente** *adv*
mentalidad *nf* : mentality
mentar {55} *vt* 1 : to mention, to name 2 **mentar la madre a** *fam* : to insult, to swear at
mente *nf* : mind ⟨tener en mente : to have in mind⟩
mentecato[1], -ta *adj* : foolish, simple
mentecato[2], -ta *n* : fool, idiot
mentir {76} *vi* : to lie
mentira *nf* : lie
mentiroso[1], -sa *adj* EMBUSTERO : lying, untruthful
mentiroso[2], -sa *n* EMBUSTERO : liar
mentís *nm, pl* **mentises** : denial, repudiation ⟨dar el mentís a : to deny, to refute⟩
mentol *nm* : menthol
mentón *nm, pl* **mentones** BARBILLA : chin
mentor *nm* : mentor, counselor
menú *nm, pl* **menús** : menu
menudear *vi* : to occur frequently — *vt* : to do repeatedly
menudencia *nf* 1 : trifle 2 **menudencias** *nfpl* : giblets
menudeo *nm* : retail, retailing
menudillos *nmpl* : giblets
menudo[1], -da *adj* 1 : minute, small 2 a ~ FRECUENTEMENTE : often, frequently
menudo[2] *nm* 1 *Mex* : tripe stew 2 **menudos** *nmpl* : giblets
meñique *nm or* **dedo meñique** : little finger, pinkie
meollo *nm* 1 MÉDULA : marrow 2 SESO : brains *pl* 3 ENTRAÑA : essence, core ⟨el meollo del asunto : the heart of the matter⟩
mequetrefe *nm fam* : good-for-nothing
mercachifle *nm* : peddler, hawker
mercadeo *nm* : marketing
mercadería *nf* : merchandise, goods *pl*
mercado *nm* : market ⟨mercado de trabajo *or* mercado laboral : labor market⟩ ⟨mercado de valores *or* mercado bursátil : stock market⟩
mercadotecnia *nf* : marketing
mercancía *nf* : merchandise, goods *pl*
mercante *nmf* : merchant, dealer
mercantil *adj* COMERCIAL : commercial, mercantile
merced *nf* 1 : favor 2 ~ **a** : thanks to, due to 3 **a merced de** : at the mercy of
mercenario, -ria *adj & n* : mercenary
mercería *nf* : notions store
Mercosur *nm* : economic community consisting of Argentina, Brazil, Paraguay, and Uruguay
mercurio *nm* : mercury
Mercurio *nm* : Mercury (planet)

merecedor, -dora *adj* : deserving, worthy
merecer {53} *vt* : to deserve, to merit — *vi* : to be worthy
merecidamente *adv* : rightfully, deservedly
merecido *nm* : something merited, due ⟨recibieron su merecido : they got their just deserts⟩
merecimiento *nm* : merit, worth
merendar {55} *vi* : to have an afternoon snack — *vt* : to have as an afternoon snack
merendero *nm* 1 : lunchroom, snack bar 2 : picnic area
merengue *nm* 1 : meringue 2 : merengue (dance)
meridiano[1], -na *adj* 1 : midday 2 : crystal clear
meridiano[2] *nm* : meridian
meridional *adj* SUREÑO : southern
merienda *nf* : afternoon snack, tea
mérito *nm* : merit
meritorio[1], -ria *adj* : deserving, meritorious
meritorio[2], -ria *n* : intern, trainee
merluza *nf* : hake
merma *nf* 1 : decrease, cut 2 : waste, loss
mermar *vi* : to decrease, to diminish — *vt* : to reduce, to cut down
mermelada *nf* : marmalade, jam
mero[1], -ra *adv Mex fam* 1 : nearly, almost ⟨ya mero me caí : I almost fell⟩ 2 : just, exactly ⟨aquí mero : right here⟩
mero[2], -ra *adj* 1 : mere, simple 2 *Mex fam* (*used as an intensifier*) : very ⟨en el mero centro : in the very center of town⟩
mero[3] *nm* : grouper
merodeador, -dora *n* 1 : marauder 2 : prowler
merodear *vi* 1 : to maraud, to pillage 2 : to prowl around, to skulk
mes *nm* : month
mesa *nf* 1 : table 2 : committee, board
mesada *nf* : allowance, pocket money
mesarse *vr* : to pull at ⟨mesarse los cabellos : to tear one's hair⟩
mesero, -ra *n* CAMARERO : waiter, waitress *f*
meseta *nf* : plateau, tableland
Mesías *nm* : Messiah
mesón *nm, pl* **mesones** : inn
mesonero, -ra *nm* : innkeeper
mestizo[1], -za *adj* 1 : of mixed ancestry 2 HÍBRIDO : hybrid
mestizo[2], -za *n* : person of mixed ancestry
mesura *nf* 1 MODERACIÓN : moderation, discretion 2 CORTESÍA : courtesy 3 GRAVEDAD : seriousness, dignity
mesurado, -da *adj* COMEDIDO : moderate, restrained
mesurar *vt* : to moderate, to restrain, to temper — **mesurarse** *vr* : to restrain oneself
meta *nf* : goal, objective

metabólico, -ca *adj* : metabolic
metabolismo *nm* : metabolism
metabolizar {21} *vt* : to metabolize
metafísica *nf* : metaphysics
metafísico, -ca *adj* : metaphysical
metáfora *nf* : metaphor
metafórico, -ca *adj* : metaphoric, metaphorical
metal *nm* **1** : metal **2** : brass section (in an orchestra)
metálico, -ca *adj* : metallic, metal
metalistería *nf* : metalworking
metalurgia *nf* : metallurgy
metalúrgico[1]**, -ca** *adj* : metallurgical
metalúrgico[2]**, -ca** *n* : metallurgist
metamorfosis *nfs & pl* : metamorphosis
metano *nm* : methane
metedura *nf* **metedura de pata** : blunder, faux pas
meteórico, -ca *adj* : meteoric
meteorito *nm* : meteorite
meteoro *nm* : meteor
meteorología *nf* : meteorology
meteorológico, -ca *adj* : meteorologic, meteorological
meteorólogo, -ga *n* : meteorologist
meter *vt* **1** : to put (in) ⟨metieron su dinero en el banco : they put their money in the bank⟩ **2** : to fit, to squeeze ⟨puedes meter dos líneas más en esa página : you can fit two more lines on that page⟩ **3** : to place (in a job) ⟨lo metieron de barrendero : they got him a job as a street sweeper⟩ **4** : to involve ⟨lo metió en un buen lío : she got him in an awful mess⟩ **5** : to make, to cause ⟨meten demasiado ruido : they make too much noise⟩ **6** : to spread (a rumor) **7** : to strike (a blow) **8** : to take up, to take in (clothing) **9 a todo meter** : at top speed — **meterse** *vr* **1** : to get into, to enter **2** *fam* : to meddle ⟨no te metas en lo que no te importa : mind your own business⟩ **3 ~ con** *fam* : to pick a fight with, to provoke ⟨no te metas conmigo : don't mess with me⟩
metiche[1] *adj Mex fam* : nosy
metiche[2] *nmf Mex fam* : busybody
meticulosidad *nf* : thoroughness, meticulousness
meticuloso, -sa *adj* : meticulous, thorough — **meticulosamente** *adv*
metida *nf* **metida de pata** *fam* : blunder, gaffe, blooper
metódico, -ca *adj* : methodical — **metódicamente** *adv*
metodista *adj & nmf* : Methodist
método *nm* : method
metodología *nf* : methodology
metomentodo *nmf fam* : busybody
metraje *nm* : length (of a film) ⟨de largo metraje : feature-length⟩
metralla *nf* : shrapnel
metralleta *nf* : submachine gun
métrico, -ca *adj* **1** : metric **2 cinta métrica** : tape measure
metro *nm* **1** : meter **2** : subway
metrónomo *nm* : metronome

metrópoli *nf or* **metrópolis** *nfs & pl* : metropolis
metropolitano, -na *adj* : metropolitan
mexicanismo *nm* : Mexican word or expression
mexicano, -na *adj & n* : Mexican
mexicoamericano, -na *adj & n* : Mexican-American
meza, etc. → **mecer**
mezcla *nf* **1** : mixing **2** : mixture, blend **3** : mortar (masonry material)
mezclar *vt* **1** : to mix, to blend **2** : to mix up, to muddle **3** INVOLUCRAR : to involve — **mezclarse** *vr* **1** : to get mixed up (in) **2** : to mix, to mingle (socially)
mezclilla *nf Chile, Mex* : denim ⟨pantalones de mezclilla : jeans⟩
mezcolanza *nf* : jumble, hodgepodge
mezquindad *nf* **1** : meanness, stinginess **2** : petty deed, mean action
mezquino[1]**, -na** *adj* **1** : mean, petty **2** : stingy **3** : paltry
mezquino[2] *nm Mex* : wart
mezquita *nf* : mosque
mezquite *nm* : mesquite
mi *adj* : my
mí *pron* **1** : me ⟨es para mí : it's for me⟩ ⟨a mí no me importa : it doesn't matter to me⟩ **2 mí mismo, mí misma** : myself
miasma *nm* : miasma
miau *nm* : meow
mica *nf* : mica
mico *nm* : monkey, long-tailed monkey
micra *nf* : micron
microbio *nm* : microbe, germ
microbiología *nf* : microbiology
microbiológico, -ca *adj* : microbiological
microbús *nm, pl* **-buses** : minibus
microcomputadora *nf* : microcomputer
microcosmos *nms & pl* : microcosm
microficha *nf* : microfiche
microfilm *nm, pl* **-films** : microfilm
micrófono *nm* : microphone
micrómetro *nm* : micrometer
microonda *nf* : microwave
microondas *nms & pl* : microwave, microwave oven
microordenador *nm Spain* : microcomputer
microorganismo *nm* : microorganism
microprocesador *nm* : microprocessor
microscópico, -ca *adj* : microscopic
microscopio *nm* : microscope
mide, etc. → **medir**
miedo *nm* **1** TEMOR : fear ⟨le tiene miedo al perro : he's scared of the dog⟩ ⟨tenían miedo de hablar : they were afraid to speak⟩ **2 dar miedo** : to frighten
miedoso, -sa *adj* TEMEROSO : fearful
miel *nf* : honey
miembro *nm* **1** : member **2** EXTREMIDAD : limb, extremity
mienta, etc. → **mentar**
miente, etc. → **mentir**

mientras[1] *adv* **1** *or* **mientras tanto** : meanwhile, in the meantime **2 mientras más** : the more ⟨mientras más como, más quiero : the more I eat, the more I want⟩

mientras[2] *conj* **1** : while, as ⟨roncaba mientras dormía : he snored while he was sleeping⟩ **2** : as long as ⟨luchará mientras pueda : he will fight as long as he is able⟩ **3 mientras que** : while, whereas ⟨él es alto mientras que ella es muy baja : he is tall, whereas she is very short⟩

miércoles *nms & pl* : Wednesday

miga *nf* **1** : crumb **2 hacer buenas (malas) migas con** : to get along well (poorly) with

migaja *nf* **1** : crumb **2 migajas** *nfpl* SOBRAS : leftovers, scraps

migración *nf, pl* **-ciones** : migration

migrante *nmf* : migrant

migraña *nf* : migraine

migratorio, -ria *adj* : migratory

mijo *nm* : millet

mil[1] *adj* : thousand

mil[2] *nm* : one thousand, a thousand

milagro *nm* : miracle ⟨de milagro : miraculously⟩

milagroso, -sa *adj* : miraculous, marvelous — **milagrosamente** *adv*

milenio *nm* : millennium

milésimo, -ma *adj* : thousandth — **milésimo** *nm*

milicia *nf* **1** : militia **2** : military service

miligramo *nm* : milligram

mililitro *nm* : milliliter

milímetro *nm* : millimeter

militancia *nf* : militancy

militante[1] *adj* : militant

militante[2] *nmf* : militant, activist

militar[1] *vi* **1** : to serve (in the military) **2** : to be active (in politics)

militar[2] *adj* : military

militar[3] *nmf* SOLDADO : soldier

militarismo *nm* : militarism

militarista *adj & nmf* : militarist

militarizar {21} *vt* : to militarize

milla *nf* : mile

millar *nm* : thousand

millón *nm, pl* **millones** : million

millonario, -ria *n* : millionaire

millonésimo[1], **-ma** *adj* : millionth

millonésimo[2] *nm* : millionth

mil millones *nms & pl* : billion

milpa *nf CA, Mex* : cornfield

milpiés *nms & pl* : millipede

mimar *vt* CONSENTIR : to pamper, to spoil

mimbre *nm* : wicker

mimeógrafo *nm* : mimeograph

mímica *nf* **1** : mime, sign language **2** IMITACIÓN : mimicry

mimo *nm* **1** : pampering, indulgence ⟨hacerle mimos a alguien : to pamper someone⟩ **2** : mime

mimoso, -sa *adj* **1** : fussy, finicky **2** : affectionate, clinging

mina *nf* **1** : mine **2** : lead (for pencils)

minar *vt* **1** : to mine **2** DEBILITAR : to undermine

minarete *nm* ALMINAR : minaret

mineral *adj & nm* : mineral

minería *nf* : mining

minero[1], **-ra** *adj* : mining

minero[2], **-ra** *n* : miner, mine worker

miniatura *nf* : miniature

minicomputadora *nf* : minicomputer

minifalda *nf* : miniskirt

minifundio *nm* : small farm

minimizar {21} *vt* : to minimize

mínimo[1], **-ma** *adj* **1** : minimum ⟨salario mínimo : minimum wage⟩ **2** : least, smallest **3** : very small, minute

mínimo[2] *nm* **1** : minimum, least amount **2** : modicum, small amount **3 como** ~ : at least

minino, -na *n fam* : pussy, pussycat

miniserie *nf* : miniseries

ministerial *adj* : ministerial

ministerio *nm* : ministry, department

ministro, -tra *n* : minister, secretary ⟨primer ministro : prime minister⟩ ⟨Ministro de Defensa : Secretary of Defense⟩

minivan [ˌmini'ban, -'van] *nf, pl* **-vanes** : minivan

minoría *nf* : minority

minorista[1] *adj* : retail

minorista[2] *nmf* : retailer

minoritario, -ria *adj* : minority

mintió, etc. → **mentir**

minuciosamente *adv* **1** : minutely **2** : in great detail **3** : thoroughly, meticulously

minucioso, -sa *adj* **1** : minute **2** DETALLADO : detailed **3** : thorough, meticulous

minué *nm* : minuet

minúsculo, -la *adj* DIMINUTO : tiny, miniscule

minusvalía *nf* : disability, handicap

minusválido[1], **-da** *adj* : handicapped, disabled

minusválido[2], **-da** *n* : handicapped person

minuta *nf* **1** BORRADOR : rough draft **2** : bill, fee

minutero *nm* : minute hand

minuto *nm* : minute

mío[1], **mía** *adj* **1** : my, of mine ⟨¡Dios mío! : my God!, good heavens!⟩ ⟨una amiga mía : a friend of mine⟩ **2** : mine ⟨es mío : it's mine⟩

mío[2], **mía** *pron* (*with definite article*) : mine, my own ⟨tus zapatos son iguales a los míos : your shoes are just like mine⟩

miope *adj* : nearsighted, myopic

miopía *nf* : myopia, nearsightedness

mira *nf* **1** : sight (of a firearm or instrument) **2** : aim, objective ⟨con miras a : with the intention of, with a view to⟩ ⟨de amplias miras : broad-minded⟩ ⟨poner la mira en : to aim at, to aspire to⟩

mirada *nf* **1** : look, glance, gaze **2** EX-PRESIÓN : look, expression ⟨una mira-da de sorpresa : a look of surprise⟩
mirado, -da *adj* **1** : cautious, careful **2** : considerate **3 bien mirado** : well thought of **4 mal mirado** : disliked, dis-approved of
mirador *nm* : balcony, lookout, vantage point
miramiento *nm* **1** CONSIDERACIÓN : consideration, respect **2 sin mi-ramientos** : without due considera-tion, carelessly
mirar *vt* **1** : to look at **2** OBSERVAR : to watch **3** REFLEXIONAR : to consider, to think over — *vi* **1** : to look **2** : to face, to overlook **3** ~ **por** : to look af-ter, to look out for — **mirarse** *vr* **1** : to look at oneself **2** : to look at each other
mirasol *nm* GIRASOL : sunflower
miríada *nf* : myriad
mirlo *nm* : blackbird
mirra *nf* : myrrh
mirto *nm* ARRAYÁN : myrtle
misa *nf* : Mass
misantropía *nf* : misanthropy
misantrópico, -ca *adj* : misanthropic
misántropo, -pa *n* : misanthrope
miscelánea *nf* : miscellany
misceláneo, -nea *adj* : miscellaneous
miserable *adj* **1** LASTIMOSO : miserable, wretched **2** : paltry, meager **3** MEZQUINO : stingy, miserly **4** : despi-cable, vile
miseria *nf* **1** POBREZA : poverty **2** : mis-ery, suffering **3** : pittance, meager amount
misericordia *nf* COMPASIÓN : mercy, compassion
misericordioso, -sa *adj* : merciful
mísero, -ra *adj* **1** : wretched, miserable **2** : stingy **3** : paltry, meager
misil *nm* : missile
misión *nf, pl* **misiones** : mission
misionero, -ra *adj & n* : missionary
misiva *nf* : missive, letter
mismísimo, -ma *adj* (*used as an intensi-fier*) : very, selfsame ⟨el mismísimo día : that very same day⟩
mismo¹ *adv* (*used as an intensifier*) : right, exactly ⟨hazlo ahora mismo : do it right now⟩ ⟨te llamará hoy mismo : he'll definitely call you today⟩
mismo², -ma *adj* **1** : same **2** (*used as an intensifier*) : very ⟨en ese mismo mo-mento : at that very moment⟩ **3** : one-self ⟨lo hizo ella misma : she made it herself⟩ **4 por lo mismo** : for that rea-son
misoginia *nf* : misogyny
misógino *nm* : misogynist
misterio *nm* : mystery
misterioso, -sa *adj* : mysterious — **mis-teriosamente** *adv*
misticismo *nm* : mysticism
místico¹, -ca *adj* : mystic, mystical
místico², -ca *n* : mystic

mitad *nf* **1** : half ⟨mitad y mitad : half and half⟩ **2** MEDIO : middle ⟨a mitad de : halfway through⟩ ⟨por la mitad : in half⟩
mítico, -ca *adj* : mythical, mythic
mitigar {52} *vt* ALIVIAR : to mitigate, to alleviate — **mitigación** *nf*
mitin *nm, pl* **mítines** : (political) meet-ing, rally
mito *nm* LEYENDA : myth, legend
mitología *nf* : mythology
mitológico, -ca *adj* : mythological
mitosis *nfs & pl* : mitosis
mitra *nf* : miter (bishop's hat)
mixto, -ta *adj* **1** : mixed, joint **2** : co-educational
mixtura *nf* : mixture, blend
mnemónico, -ca *adj* : mnemonic
mobiliario *nm* : furniture
mocasín *nm, pl* **-sines** : moccasin
mocedad *nf* **1** JUVENTUD : youth **2** : youthful prank
mochila *nf* MORRAL : backpack, knap-sack
moción *nf, pl* **-ciones** **1** MOVIMIENTO : motion, movement **2** : motion (to a court or assembly)
moco *nm* **1** : mucus **2** *fam* : snot ⟨limpiarse los mocos : to wipe one's (runny) nose⟩
mocoso, -sa *n* : kid, brat
moda *nf* **1** : fashion, style **2 a la moda** *or* **de** ~ : in style, fashionable **3 moda pasajera** : fad
modales *nmpl* : manners
modalidad *nf* **1** CLASE : kind, type **2** MANERA : way, manner
modelar *vt* : to model, to mold — **mo-delarse** *vr* : to model oneself after, to emulate
modelo¹ *adj* : model ⟨una casa modelo : a model home⟩
modelo² *nm* : model, example, pattern
modelo³ *nmf* : model, mannequin
módem *or* **modem** ['moðɛm] *nm* : mo-dem
moderación *nf, pl* **-ciones** MESURA : moderation
moderado, -da *adj & n* : moderate — **moderadamente** *adv*
moderador, -dora *n* : moderator, chair
moderar *vt* **1** TEMPERAR : to temper, to moderate **2** : to curb, to reduce ⟨mod-erar gastos : to curb spending⟩ **3** PRE-SIDIR : to chair (a meeting) — **moder-arse** *vr* **1** : to restrain oneself **2** : to diminish, to calm down
modernidad *nf* **1** : modernity, modern-ness **2** : modern age
modernismo *nm* : modernism
modernista¹ *adj* : modernist, mod-ernistic
modernista² *nmf* : modernist
modernizar {21} *vt* : to modernize — **modernización** *nf*
moderno, -na *adj* : modern, up-to-date
modestia *nf* : modesty

modesto, -ta *adj* : modest — **modestamente** *adv*
modificación *nf, pl* **-ciones** : alteration
modificador¹, -dora *adj* : modifying, moderating
modificador² → **modificante**
modificante *nm* : modifier
modificar {72} *vt* ALTERAR : to modify, to alter, to adapt
modismo *nm* : idiom
modista *nmf* 1 : dressmaker 2 : fashion designer
modo *nm* 1 MANERA : way, manner, mode ⟨de un modo u otro : one way or another⟩ ⟨a mi modo de ver : to my way of thinking⟩ 2 : mood (in grammar) 3 : mode (in music) 4 **a modo de** : by way of, in the manner of, like ⟨a modo de ejemplo : by way of example⟩ 5 **de cualquier modo** : in any case, anyway 6 **de modo que** : so, in such a way that 7 **de todos modos** : in any case, anyway 8 **en cierto modo** : in a way, to a certain extent
modorra *nf* : drowsiness, lethargy
modular¹ *v* : to modulate — **modulación** *nf*
modular² *adj* : modular
módulo *nm* : module, unit
mofa *nf* 1 : mockery, ridicule 2 **hacer mofa de** : to make fun of, to ridicule
mofarse *vr* ~ **de** : to scoff at, to make fun of
mofeta *nf* ZORRILLO : skunk
mofle *nm* CA, Mex : muffler (of a car)
moflete *nm* *fam* : fat cheek
mofletudo, -da *adj* *fam* : fat-cheeked, chubby
mohín *nm, pl* **mohines** : grimace, face
mohino, -na *adj* : gloomy, melancholy
moho *nm* 1 : mold, mildew 2 : rust
mohoso, -sa *adj* 1 : moldy 2 : rusty
moisés *nm, pl* **moiseses** : bassinet, cradle
mojado¹, -da *adj* : wet
mojado², -da *n* Mex *fam* : illegal immigrant
mojar *vt* 1 : to wet, to moisten 2 : to dunk — **mojarse** *vr* : to get wet
mojigatería *nf* 1 : hypocrisy 2 GAZMOÑERÍA : primness, prudery
mojigato¹, -ta *adj* : prudish, prim — **mojigatamente** *adv*
mojigato², -ta *n* : prude, prig
mojón *nm, pl* **mojones** : boundary stone, marker
molar *nm* MUELA : molar
molcajete *nm* Mex : mortar
molde *nm* 1 : mold, form 2 **letras de molde** : printing, block lettering
moldear *vt* 1 FORMAR : to mold, to shape 2 : to cast
moldura *nf* : molding
mole¹ *nm* Mex 1 : spicy sauce made with chilies and usually chocolate 2 : meat served with mole sauce
mole² *nf* : mass, bulk
molécula *nf* : molecule — **molecular** *adj*

moler {47} *vt* 1 : to grind, to crush 2 CANSAR : to exhaust, to wear out
molestar *vt* 1 FASTIDIAR : to annoy, to bother 2 : to disturb, to disrupt — *vi* : to be a nuisance — **molestarse** *vr* ~ **en** : to take the trouble to
molestia *nf* 1 FASTIDIO : annoyance, bother, nuisance 2 : trouble ⟨se tomó la molestia de investigar : she took the trouble to investigate⟩ 3 MALESTAR : discomfort
molesto, -ta *adj* 1 ENOJADO : bothered, annoyed 2 FASTIDIOSO : bothersome, annoying
molestoso, -sa *adj* : bothersome, annoying
molido, -da *adj* 1 MACHACADO : ground, crushed 2 **estar molido** : to be exhausted
molienda *nf* : milling, grinding
molinero, -ra *n* : miller
molinillo *nm* : grinder, mill ⟨molinillo de café : coffee grinder⟩
molino *nm* 1 : mill 2 **molino de viento** : windmill
molla *nf* : soft fleshy part, flesh (of fruit), lean part (of meat)
molleja *nf* : gizzard
molusco *nm* : mollusk
momentáneamente *adv* : momentarily
momentáneo, -nea *adj* 1 : momentary 2 TEMPORARIO : temporary
momento *nm* 1 : moment, instant ⟨espera un momentito : wait just a moment⟩ 2 : time, period of time ⟨momentos difíciles : hard times⟩ 3 : present, moment ⟨los atletas del momento : the athletes of the moment, today's popular athletes⟩ 4 : momentum 5 **al momento** : right away, at once 6 **de** ~ : at the moment, for the moment 7 **de un momento a otro** : any time now 8 **por momentos** : at times
momia *nf* : mummy
monaguillo *nm* ACÓLITO : altar boy
monarca *nmf* : monarch
monarquía *nf* : monarchy
monárquico, -ca *n* : monarchist
monasterio *nm* : monastery
monástico, -ca *adj* : monastic
mondadientes *nms & pl* PALILLO : toothpick
mondar *vt* : to peel
mondongo *nm* ENTRAÑAS : innards *pl*, insides *pl*, guts *pl*
moneda *nf* 1 : coin 2 : money, currency
monedero *nm* : change purse
monetario, -ria *adj* : monetary, financial
mongol, -gola *adj & n* : Mongol, Mongolian
monitor¹, -tora *n* : instructor (in sports)
monitor² *nm* : monitor ⟨monitor de televisión : television monitor⟩
monitorear *vt* : to monitor
monja *nf* : nun
monje *nm* : monk
mono¹, -na *adj* *fam* : lovely, pretty, cute, darling

mono[2], **-na** *n* : monkey
monóculo *nm* : monocle
monogamia *nf* : monogamy
monógamo, -ma *adj* : monogamous
monografía *nf* : monograph
monograma *nm* : monogram
monolingüe *adj* : monolingual
monolítico, -ca *adj* : monolithic
monolito *nm* : monolith
monólogo *nm* : monologue
monomanía *nf* : obsession
monopatín *nm, pl* **-tines 1** : scooter **2** : skateboard
monopolio *nm* : monopoly
monopolizar {21} *vt* : to monopolize — **monopolización** *nf*
monosilábico, -ca *adj* : monosyllabic
monosílabo *nm* : monosyllable
monoteísmo *nm* : monotheism
monoteísta[1] *adj* : monotheistic
monoteísta[2] *nmf* : monotheist
monotonía *nf* **1** : monotony **2** : monotone
monótono, -na *adj* : monotonous — **monótonamente** *adv*
monóxido *nm* : monoxide ⟨monóxido de carbono : carbon monoxide⟩
monserga *nf* : gibberish, drivel
monstruo *nm* : monster
monstruosidad *nf* : monstrosity
monstruoso, -sa *adj* : monstrous — **monstruosamente** *adv*
monta *nf* **1** : sum, total **2** : importance, value ⟨de poca monta : unimportant, insignificant⟩
montaje *nm* **1** : assembling, assembly **2** : montage
montante *nm* : transom, fanlight
montaña *nf* **1** MONTE : mountain **2** **montaña rusa** : roller coaster
montañero, -ra *n* : mountaineer, mountain climber
montañoso, -sa *adj* : mountainous
montar *vt* **1** : to mount **2** ESTABLECER : to set up, to establish **3** ARMAR : to assemble, to put together **4** : to edit (a film) **5** : to stage, to put on (a show) **6** : to cock (a gun) **7 montar en bicicleta** : to get on a bicycle **8 montar a caballo** CABALGAR : to ride horseback
monte *nm* **1** MONTAÑA : mountain, mount **2** : woodland, scrubland ⟨monte bajo : underbrush⟩ **3** : outskirts (of a town), surrounding country **4 monte de piedad** : pawnshop
montés *adj, pl* **monteses** : wild (of animals or plants)
montículo *nm* **1** : mound, heap **2** : hillock, knoll
monto *nm* : amount, total
montón *nm, pl* **-tones 1** : heap, pile **2** *fam* : ton, load ⟨un montón de preguntas : a ton of questions⟩ ⟨montones de gente : loads of people⟩
montura *nf* **1** : mount (horse) **2** : saddle, tack **3** : setting, mounting (of jewelry) **4** : frame (of glasses)

monumental *adj fam* **1** : tremendous, terrific **2** : massive, huge
monumento *nm* : monument
monzón *nm, pl* **monzones** : monsoon
moño *nm* **1** : bun (chignon) **2** LAZO : bow, knot ⟨corbata de moño : bow tie⟩
moquear *vi* : to snivel
moquillo *nm* : distemper
mora *nf* **1** : blackberry **2** : mulberry
morada *nf* RESIDENCIA : dwelling, abode
morado[1], **-da** *adj* : purple
morado[2] *nm* : purple
morador, -dora *n* : dweller, inhabitant
moral[1] *adj* : moral — **moralmente** *adv*
moral[2] *nf* **1** MORALIDAD : ethics, morality, morals *pl* **2** ÁNIMO : morale, spirits *pl*
moraleja *nf* : moral (of a story)
moralidad *nf* : morality
moralista[1] *adj* : moralistic
moralista[2] *nmf* : moralist
morar *vi* : to dwell, to reside
moratoria *nf* : moratorium
mórbido, -da *adj* : morbid
morboso, -sa *adj* : morbid — **morbosidad** *nf*
morcilla *nf* : blood sausage, blood pudding
mordacidad *nf* : bite, sharpness
mordaz *adj* : caustic, scathing
mordaza *nf* **1** : gag **2** : clamp
mordedura *nf* : bite (of an animal)
morder {47} *v* : to bite
mordida *nf* **1** : bite **2** *CA, Mex* : bribe, payoff
mordisco *nm* : bite, nibble
mordisquear *vt* : to nibble (on), to bite
morena *nf* **1** : moraine **2** : moray (eel)
moreno[1], **-na** *adj* **1** : brunette **2** : dark, dark-skinned
moreno[2], **-na** *n* **1** : brunette **2** : dark-skinned person
moretón *nm, pl* **-tones** : bruise
morfina *nf* : morphine
morfología *nf* : morphology
morgue *nf* : morgue
moribundo[1], **-da** *adj* : dying, moribund
moribundo[2], **-da** *n* : dying person
morillo *nm* : andiron
morir {46} *vi* **1** FALLECER : to die **2** APAGARSE : to die out, to go out
mormón, -mona *adj & n, pl* **mormones** : Mormon
moro[1], **-ra** *adj* : Moorish
moro[2], **-ra** *n* **1** : Moor **2** : Muslim
morosidad *nf* **1** : delinquency (in payment) **2** : slowness
moroso, -sa *adj* **1** : delinquent, in arrears ⟨cuentas morosas : delinquent accounts⟩ **2** : slow, sluggish
morral *nm* MOCHILA : backpack, knapsack
morralla *nf* **1** : small fish **2** : trash, riffraff **3** *Mex* : small change
morriña *nf* : homesickness
morro *nm* HOCICO : snout

morsa *nf* : walrus
morse *nm* : Morse code
mortaja *nf* SUDARIO : shroud
mortal[1] *adj* 1 : mortal 2 FATAL : fatal, deadly — mortalmente *adv*
mortal[2] *nmf* : mortal
mortalidad *nf* : mortality
mortandad *nf* 1 : loss of life, death toll 2 : carnage, slaughter
mortero *nm* : mortar (bowl, cannon, or building material)
mortífero, -ra *adj* LETAL : deadly, fatal
mortificación *nf, pl* -ciones 1 : mortification 2 TORMENTO : anguish, torment
mortificar {72} *vt* 1 : to mortify 2 TORTURAR : to trouble, to torment — mortificarse *vr* : to be mortified, to feel embarrassed
mosaico *nm* : mosaic
mosca *nf* 1 : fly 2 mosca común : housefly
moscada *adj* nuez moscada : nutmeg
moscovita *adj & nmf* : Muscovite
mosquearse *vr* 1 : to become suspicious 2 : to take offense
mosquete *nm* : musket
mosquetero *nm* : musketeer
mosquitero *nm* : mosquito net
mosquito *nm* ZANCUDO : mosquito
mostachón *nm, pl* -chones : macaroon
mostaza *nf* : mustard
mostrador *nm* : counter (in a store)
mostrar {19} *vt* 1 : to show 2 EXHIBIR : to exhibit, to display — mostrarse *vr* : to show oneself, to appear
mota *nf* 1 : fleck, speck 2 : defect, blemish
mote *nm* SOBRENOMBRE : nickname
moteado, -da *adj* : dotted, spotted, dappled
motel *nm* : motel
motín *nm, pl* motines 1 : riot 2 : rebellion, mutiny
motivación *nf, pl* -ciones : motivation — motivacional *adj*
motivar *vt* 1 CAUSAR : to cause 2 IMPULSAR : to motivate
motivo *nm* 1 MÓVIL : motive 2 CAUSA : cause, reason 3 TEMA : theme, motif
moto *nf* : motorcycle, motorbike
motocicleta *nf* : motorcycle
motociclismo *nm* : motorcycling
motociclista *nmf* : motorcyclist
motor[1], -ra *adj* MOTRIZ : motor
motor[2] *nm* 1 : motor, engine 2 : driving force, cause
motorista *nmf* : motorist
motriz *adj, pl* motrices : driving
motu proprio *adv* de motu proprio [de 'motu'proprio] : voluntarily, of one's own accord
mousse ['mus] *nmf* : mousse
mover {47} *vt* 1 TRASLADAR : to move, to shift 2 AGITAR : to shake, to nod (the head) 3 ACCIONAR : to power, to drive 4 INDUCIR : to provoke, to cause 5 : to excite, to stir — moverse *vr* 1

: to move, to move over 2 : to hurry, to get a move on 3 : to get moving, to make an effort
movible *adj* : movable
movida *nf* : move (in a game)
móvil[1] *adj* : mobile
móvil[2] *nm* 1 MOTIVO : motive 2 : mobile
movilidad *nf* : mobility
movilizar {21} *vt* : to mobilize — movilización *nf*
movimiento *nm* : movement, motion ⟨movimiento del cuerpo : bodily movement⟩ ⟨movimiento sindicalista : labor movement⟩
mozo[1], -za *adj* : young, youthful
mozo[2], -za *n* 1 JOVEN : young man *m*, young woman *f*, youth 2 : helper, servant 3 *Arg, Chile, Col, Peru* : waiter *m*, waitress *f*
mucamo, -ma *n* : servant, maid *f*
muchacha *nf* : maid
muchacho, -cha *n* 1 : kid, boy *m*, girl *f* 2 JOVEN : young man *m*, young woman *f*
muchedumbre *nf* MULTITUD : crowd, multitude
mucho[1] *adv* 1 : much, a lot ⟨mucho más : much more⟩ ⟨le gusta mucho : he likes it a lot⟩ 2 : long, a long time ⟨tardó mucho en venir : he was a long time getting here⟩ 3 por mucho que : no matter how much
mucho[2], -cha *adj* 1 : a lot of, many, much ⟨mucha gente : a lot of people⟩ ⟨hace mucho tiempo que no lo veo : I haven't seen him in ages⟩ 2 muchas veces : often
mucho[3], -cha *pron* 1 : a lot, many, much ⟨hay mucho que hacer : there is a lot to do⟩ ⟨muchas no vinieron : many didn't come⟩ 2 cuando ∼ *or* como ∼ : at most 3 con ∼ : by far 4 ni mucho menos : not at all, far from it
mucílago *nm* : mucilage
mucosidad *nf* : mucus
mucoso, -sa *adj* : mucous, slimy
muda *nf* 1 : change ⟨muda de ropa : change of clothes⟩ 2 : molt, molting
mudanza *nf* 1 CAMBIO : change 2 TRASLADO : move, moving
mudar *v* 1 CAMBIAR : to change 2 : to molt, to shed — mudarse *vr* 1 TRASLADARSE : to move (one's residence) 2 : to change (clothes)
mudo[1], -da *adj* 1 SILENCIOSO : silent ⟨el cine mudo : silent films⟩ 2 : mute, dumb
mudo[2], -da *n* : mute
mueble *nm* 1 : piece of furniture 2 muebles *nmpl* : furniture, furnishings
mueblería *nf* : furniture store
mueca *nf* : grimace, face
muela *nf* 1 : tooth, molar ⟨dolor de muelas : toothache⟩ ⟨muela de juicio : wisdom tooth⟩ 2 : millstone 3 : whetstone
muele, etc. → moler

muelle[1] *adj* : soft, comfortable, easy
muelle[2] *nm* **1** : wharf, dock **2** RESORTE
: spring
muérdago *nm* : mistletoe
muerde, etc. → **morder**
muere, etc. → **morir**
muerte *nf* : death
muerto[1] *pp* → **morir**
muerto[2], **-ta** *adj* **1** : dead **2** : lifeless, flat,
dull **3** ~ **de** : dying of ⟨estoy muerto
de hambre : I'm dying of hunger⟩
muerto[3], **-ta** *nm* DIFUNTO : dead person,
deceased
muesca *nf* : nick, notch
muestra[1], **etc.** → **mostrar**
muestra[2] *nf* **1** : sample **2** SEÑAL : sign,
show ⟨una muestra de respeto : a show
of respect⟩ **3** EXPOSICIÓN : exhibition,
exposition **4** : pattern, model
mueve, etc. → **mover**
mugido *nm* : moo, lowing, bellow
mugir {35} *vi* : to moo, to low, to bellow
mugre *nf* SUCIEDAD : grime, filth
mugriento, -ta *adj* : filthy
muguete *nm* : lily of the valley
muja, etc. → **mugir**
mujer *nf* **1** : woman **2** ESPOSA : wife
mulato, -ta *adj* & *n* : mulatto
muleta *nf* : crutch
mullido, -da *adj* **1** : soft, fluffy **2**
: spongy, springy
mulo, -la *n* : mule
multa *nf* : fine
multar *vt* : to fine
multicolor *adj* : multicolored
multicultural *adj* : multicultural
multidisciplinario, -ria *adj* : multidisci-
plinary
multifacético, -ca *adj* : multifaceted
multifamiliar *adj* : multifamily
multilateral *adj* : multilateral
multimedia *nf* : multimedia
multimillonario, -ria *n* : multimillionaire
multinacional *adj* : multinational
múltiple *adj* : multiple
multiplicación *nf, pl* **-ciones** : multiplication
multiplicar {72} *v* **1** : to multiply **2** : to
increase — **multiplicarse** *vr* : to multiply, to reproduce
multiplicidad *nf* : multiplicity
múltiplo *nm* : multiple
multitud *nf* MUCHEDUMBRE : crowd,
multitude
multiuso, -sa *adj* : multipurpose
multivitamínico, -ca *adj* : multivitamin
mundano, -na *adj* : worldly, earthly
mundial *adj* : world, worldwide
mundialmente *adv* : worldwide, all over
the world

mundo *nm* **1** : world **2 todo el mundo**
: everyone, everybody
municiones *nfpl* : ammunition, munitions
municipal *adj* : municipal
municipio *nm* **1** : municipality **2** AYUN-
TAMIENTO : town council
muñeca *nf* **1** : doll **2** MANIQUÍ : mannequin **3** : wrist
muñeco *nm* **1** : doll, boy doll **2** MARI-
ONETA : puppet
muñón *nm, pl* **muñones** : stump (of an
arm or leg)
mural *adj* & *nm* : mural
muralista *nmf* : muralist
muralla *nf* : rampart, wall
murciélago *nm* : bat (animal)
murga *nf* : band of street musicians
murió, etc. → **morir**
murmullo *nm* **1** : murmur, murmuring
2 : rustling, rustle ⟨el murmullo de las
hojas : the rustling of the leaves⟩
murmurar *vt* **1** : to murmur, to mutter
2 : to whisper (gossip) — *vi* **1** : to murmur **2** CHISMEAR : to gossip
muro *nm* : wall
musa *nf* : muse
musaraña *nf* : shrew
muscular *adj* : muscular
musculatura *nf* : muscles *pl*, musculature
músculo *nm* : muscle
musculoso, -sa *adj* : muscular, brawny
muselina *nf* : muslin
museo *nm* : museum
musgo *nm* : moss
musgoso, -sa *adj* : mossy
música *nf* : music
musical *adj* : musical — **musicalmente**
adv
músico[1], **-ca** *adj* : musical
músico[2], **-ca** *n* : musician
musitar *vt* : to mumble, to murmur
muslo *nm* : thigh
musulmán, -mana *adj* & *n, mpl* **-manes**
: Muslim
mutación *nf, pl* **-ciones** : mutation
mutante *adj* & *nm* : mutant
mutar *v* : to mutate
mutilar *vt* : to mutilate — **mutilación** *nf*
mutis *nm* **1** : exit (in theater) **2** : silence
mutual *adj* : mutual
mutuo, -tua *adj* : mutual, reciprocal —
mutuamente *adv*
muy *adv* **1** : very, quite ⟨es muy inteligente : she's very intelligent⟩ ⟨muy
bien : very well, fine⟩ ⟨eso es muy
americano : that's typically American⟩
2 : too ⟨es muy grande para él : it's too
big for him⟩

N

n *nf* : fourteenth letter of the Spanish alphabet
nabo *nm* : turnip
nácar *nm* MADREPERLA : nacre, mother-of-pearl
nacarado, -da *adj* : pearly
nacer {48} *vi* 1 : to be born ⟨nací en Guatemala : I was born in Guatemala⟩ ⟨no nació ayer : he wasn't born yesterday⟩ 2 : to hatch 3 : to bud, to sprout 4 : to rise, to originate 5 **nacer para algo** : to be born to be something 6 **volver a nacer** : to have a lucky escape
nacido¹, -da *adj* 1 : born 2 **recién nacido** : newborn
nacido², -da *n* 1 **los nacidos** : those born (at a particular time) 2 **recién nacido** : newborn baby
naciente *adj* 1 : newfound, growing 2 : rising ⟨el sol naciente : the rising sun⟩
nacimiento *nm* 1 : birth 2 : source (of a river) 3 : beginning, origin 4 BELÉN : Nativity scene, crèche
nación *nf, pl* **naciones** : nation, country, people (of a country)
nacional¹ *adj* : national
nacional² *nmf* CIUDADANO : national, citizen
nacionalidad *nf* : nationality
nacionalismo *nm* : nationalism
nacionalista¹ *adj* : nationalist, nationalistic
nacionalista² *nmf* : nationalist
nacionalización *nf, pl* **-ciones** 1 : nationalization 2 : naturalization
nacionalizar {21} *vt* 1 : to nationalize 2 : to naturalize (as a citizen) — **nacionalizarse** *vr*
naco, -ca *adj Mex* : trashy, vulgar, common
nada¹ *adv* : not at all, not in the least ⟨no estamos nada cansados : we are not at all tired⟩
nada² *nf* 1 : nothingness 2 : smidgen, bit ⟨una nada le disgusta : the slightest thing upsets him⟩
nada³ *pron* 1 : nothing ⟨no estoy haciendo nada : I'm not doing anything⟩ 2 **casi nada** : next to nothing 3 **de ～** : you're welcome 4 **dentro de nada** : very soon, in no time 5 **nada más** : nothing else, nothing more
nadador, -dora *n* : swimmer
nadar *vi* 1 : to swim 2 **～ en** : to be swimming in, to be rolling in — *vt* : to swim
nadería *nf* : small thing, trifle
nadie *pron* : nobody, no one ⟨no vi a nadie : I didn't see anyone⟩
nadir *nm* : nadir
nado *nm* 1 *Mex* : swimming 2 **a ～** : swimming ⟨cruzó el río a nado : he swam across the river⟩
nafta *nf* 1 : naphtha 2 (*in various countries*) : gasoline

naftalina *nf* : naphthalene, mothballs *pl*
náhuatl¹ *adj & nmf, pl* **nahuas** : Nahuatl
náhuatl² *nm* : Nahuatl (language)
nailon → **nilón**
naipe *nm* : playing card
nalga *nf* 1 : buttock 2 **nalgas** *nfpl* : buttocks, bottom
nalgada *nf* : smack on the bottom, spanking
namibio, -bia *adj & n* : Namibian
nana *nf* 1 : lullaby 2 *fam* : grandma 3 *CA, Col, Mex, Ven* : nanny
nanay *interj fam* : no way!, not likely!
naranja¹ *adj & nm* : orange (color)
naranja² *nf* : orange (fruit)
naranjal *nm* : orange grove
naranjo *nm* : orange tree
narcisismo *nm* : narcissism
narcisista¹ *adj* : narcissistic
narcisista² *nmf* : narcissist
narciso *nm* : narcissus, daffodil
narcótico¹, -ca *adj* : narcotic
narcótico² *nm* : narcotic
narcotizar {21} *vt* : to drug, to dope
narcotraficante *nmf* : drug trafficker
narcotráfico *nm* : drug trafficking
narigón, -gona *adj, mpl* **-gones** : big-nosed
narigudo → **narigón**
nariz *nf, pl* **narices** 1 : nose ⟨sonar(se) la nariz : to blow one's nose⟩ 2 : sense of smell
narración *nf, pl* **-ciones** : narration, account
narrador, -dora *n* : narrator
narrar *vt* : to narrate, to tell
narrativa *nf* : narrative, story
narrativo, -va *adj* : narrative
narval *nm* : narwhal
nasa *nf* : creel
nasal *adj* : nasal
nata *nf* 1 : cream ⟨nata batida : whipped cream⟩ 2 : skin (on boiled milk)
natación *nf, pl* **-ciones** : swimming
natal *adj* : native, natal
natalicio *nm* : birthday ⟨el natalicio de George Washington : George Washington's birthday⟩
natalidad *nf* : birthrate
natillas *nfpl* : custard
natividad *nf* : birth, nativity
nativo, -va *adj & n* : native
nato, -ta *adj* : born, natural
natural¹ *adj* 1 : natural 2 : normal ⟨como es natural : naturally, as expected⟩ 3 **～ de** : native of, from 4 **de tamaño natural** : life-size
natural² *nm* 1 CARÁCTER : disposition, temperament 2 : native ⟨un natural de Venezuela : a native of Venezuela⟩
naturaleza *nf* 1 : nature ⟨la madre naturaleza : mother nature⟩ 2 ÍNDOLE : nature, disposition, constitution ⟨la naturaleza humana : human nature⟩ 3 **naturaleza muerta** : still life

naturalidad *nf* : simplicity, naturalness
naturalismo *nm* : naturalism
naturalista[1] *adj* : naturalistic
naturalista[2] *nmf* : naturalist
naturalización *nf, pl* **-ciones** : naturalization
naturalizar {21} *vt* : to naturalize — **naturalizarse** *vr* NACIONALIZARSE : to become naturalized
naturalmente *adv* **1** : naturally, inherently **2** : of course
naufragar {52} *vi* **1** : to be shipwrecked **2** FRACASAR : to fail, to collapse
naufragio *nm* **1** : shipwreck **2** FRACASO : failure, collapse
náufrago[1], **-ga** *adj* : shipwrecked, castaway
náufrago[2], **-ga** *n* : shipwrecked person, castaway
náusea *nf* **1** : nausea **2 dar náuseas** : to nauseate, to disgust **3 náuseas matutinas** : morning sickness
nauseabundo, -da *adj* : nauseating, sickening
náutica *nf* : navigation
náutico, -ca *adj* : nautical
nautilo *nm* : nautilus
navaja *nf* **1** : pocketknife, penknife ⟨navaja de muelle : switchblade⟩ **2 navaja de afeitar** : straight razor, razor blade
navajo, -ja *adj & n* : Navajo
naval *adj* : naval
nave *nf* **1** : ship ⟨nave capitana : flagship⟩ ⟨nave espacial : spaceship⟩ **2** : nave ⟨nave lateral : aisle⟩ **3 quemar uno sus naves** : to burn one's bridges
navegabilidad *nf* : navigability
navegable *adj* : navigable
navegación *nf, pl* **-ciones** : navigation
navegante[1] *adj* : sailing, seafaring
navegante[2] *nmf* : navigator
navegar {52} *v* : to navigate, to sail
Navidad *nf* : Christmas, Christmastime ⟨Feliz Navidad : Merry Christmas⟩
navideño, -ña *adj* : Christmas
naviero, -ra *adj* : shipping
náyade *nf* : naiad
nazca, etc. → **nacer**
nazi *adj & nmf* : Nazi
nazismo *nm* : Nazism
nébeda *nf* : catnip
neblina *nf* : light fog, mist
neblinoso, -sa *adj* : misty, foggy
nebulosa *nf* : nebula
nebulosidad *nf* : mistiness, haziness
nebuloso, -sa *adj* **1** : hazy, misty **2** : nebulous, vague
necedad *nf* : stupidity, foolishness ⟨decir necedades : to talk nonsense⟩
necesariamente *adv* : necessarily
necesario, -ria *adj* **1** : necessary **2 si es necesario** : if need be **3 hacerse necesario** : to be required
neceser *nm* : toilet kit, vanity case
necesidad *nf* **1** : need, necessity **2** : poverty, want **3 necesidades** *nfpl* : hardships **4 hacer sus necesidades** : to relieve oneself

necesitado, -da *adj* : needy
necesitar *vt* **1** : to need **2** : to necessitate, to require — *vi* ~ **de** : to have need of
necio[1], **-cia** *adj* **1** : foolish, silly, dumb **2** *fam* : naughty
necio[2], **-cia** *n* ESTÚPIDO : fool, idiot
necrología *nf* : obituary
necrópolis *nfs & pl* : cemetery
néctar *nm* : nectar
nectarina *nf* : nectarine
neerlandés[1], **-desa** *adj, mpl* **-deses** HOLANDÉS : Dutch
neerlandés[2], **-desa** *n, mpl* **-deses** HOLANDÉS : Dutch person, Dutchman *m*
nefando, -da *adj* : unspeakable, heinous
nefario, -ria *adj* : nefarious
nefasto, -ta *adj* **1** : ill-fated, unlucky **2** : disastrous, terrible
negación *nf, pl* **-ciones** **1** : negation, denial **2** : negative (in grammar)
negar {49} *vt* **1** : to deny **2** REHUSAR : to refuse **3** : to disown — **negarse** *vr* **1** : to refuse **2** : to deny oneself
negativa *nf* **1** : denial **2** : refusal
negativo[1], **-va** *adj* : negative
negativo[2] *nm* : negative (of a photograph)
negligé *nm* : negligee
negligencia *nf* : negligence
negligente *adj* : neglectful, negligent — **negligentemente** *adv*
negociable *adj* : negotiable
negociación *nf, pl* **-ciones** **1** : negotiation **2 negociación colectiva** : collective bargaining
negociador, -dora *n* : negotiator
negociante *nmf* : businessman *m*, businesswoman *f*
negociar *vt* : to negotiate — *vi* : to deal, to do business
negocio *nm* **1** : business, place of business **2** : deal, transaction **3 negocios** *nmpl* : commerce, trade, business
negrero, -ra *n* **1** : slave trader **2** *fam* : slave driver, brutal boss
negrita *nf* : boldface (type)
negro[1], **-gra** *adj* **1** : black, dark **2** BRONCEADO : suntanned **3** : gloomy, awful, desperate ⟨la cosa se está poniendo negra : things are looking bad⟩ **4 mercado negro** : black market
negro[2], **-gra** *n* **1** : dark-skinned person, black person **2** *fam* : darling, dear
negro[3] *nm* : black (color)
negrura *nf* : blackness
negruzco, -ca *adj* : blackish
nene, -na *n* : baby, small child
nenúfar *nm* : water lily
neocelandés → **neozelandés**
neoclasicismo *nm* : neoclassicism
neoclásico, -ca *adj* : neoclassical
neófito, -ta *n* : neophyte, novice
neologismo *nm* : neologism
neón *nm, pl* **neones** : neon
neoyorquino[1], **-na** *adj* : of or from New York

neoyorquino², **-na** *n* : New Yorker
neozelandés¹, **-desa** *adj, mpl* **-deses**
: of or from New Zealand
neozelandés², **-desa** *n, mpl* **-deses**
: New Zealander
nepalés, **-lesa** *adj & n, mpl* **-leses**
: Nepali
nepotismo *nm* : nepotism
neptunio *nm* : neptunium
Neptuno *nm* : Neptune
nervio *nm* **1** : nerve **2** : tendon, sinew,
gristle (in meat) **3** : energy, drive **4**
: rib (of a vault) **5 nervios** *nmpl*
: nerves ⟨estar mal de los nervios : to
be a bundle of nerves⟩ ⟨ataque de
nervios : nervous breakdown⟩
nerviosamente *adv* : nervously
nerviosidad → **nerviosismo**
nerviosismo *nf* : nervousness, anxiety
nervioso, **-sa** *adj* **1** : nervous, nerve ⟨sistema nervioso : nervous system⟩ **2**
: high-strung, restless, anxious ⟨ponerse nervioso : to get nervous⟩ **3** : vigorous, energetic
nervudo, **-da** *adj* : sinewy, wiry
neta *nf Mex fam* : truth ⟨la neta es que
me cae mal : the truth is, I don't like
her⟩
netamente *adv* : clearly, obviously
neto, **-ta** *adj* **1** : net ⟨peso neto : net
weight⟩ **2** : clear, distinct
neumático¹, **-ca** *adj* : pneumatic
neumático² *nm* LLANTA : tire
neumonía *nf* PULMONÍA : pneumonia
neural *adj* : neural
neuralgia *nf* : neuralgia
neuritis *nf* : neuritis
neurología *nf* : neurology
neurológico, **-ca** *adj* : neurological,
neurologic
neurólogo, **-ga** *n* : neurologist
neurosis *nfs & pl* : neurosis
neurótico, **-ca** *adj & n* : neurotic
neutral *adj* : neutral
neutralidad *nf* : neutrality
neutralizar {21} *vt* : to neutralize — **neutralización** *nf*
neutro, **-tra** *adj* **1** : neutral **2** : neuter
neutrón *nm, pl* **neutrones** : neutron
nevada *nf* : snowfall
nevado, **-da** *adj* **1** : snowcapped **2**
: snow-white
nevar {55} *v impers* : to snow
nevasca *nf* : snowstorm, blizzard
nevera *nf* REFRIGERADOR : refrigerator
nevería *nf Mex* : ice cream parlor
nevisca *nf* : light snowfall, flurry
nevoso, **-sa** *adj* : snowy
nexo *nm* VÍNCULO : link, connection,
nexus
ni *conj* **1** : neither, nor ⟨afuera no hace
ni frío ni calor : it's neither cold nor
hot outside⟩ **2 ni que** : not even if, not
as if ⟨ni que me pagaran : not even if
they paid me⟩ ⟨ni que fuera (yo) su
madre : it's not as if I were his mother⟩ **3 ni siquiera** : not even ⟨ni siquiera
nos llamaron : they didn't even call us⟩

nicaragüense *adj & nmf* : Nicaraguan
nicho *nm* : niche
nicotina *nf* : nicotine
nido *nm* **1** : nest **2** : hiding place, den
niebla *nf* : fog, mist
niega, **niegue** etc. → **negar**
nieto, **-ta** *n* **1** : grandson *m*, granddaughter *f* **2 nietos** *nmpl* : grandchildren
nieva, etc. → **nevar**
nieve *nf* **1** : snow **2** *Cuba, Mex, PRi*
: sherbet
nigeriano, **-na** *adj & n* : Nigerian
nigua *nf* : sand flea, chigger
nihilismo *nm* : nihilism
nilón *or* **nilon** *nm, pl* **nilones** : nylon
nimbo *nm* **1** : halo **2** : nimbus
nimiedad *nf* INSIGNIFICANCIA : trifle,
triviality
nimio, **-mia** *adj* INSIGNIFICANTE : insignificant, trivial
ninfa *nf* : nymph
ningunear *vt Mex fam* : to disrespect
ninguno¹, **-na** (**ningún** *before masculine
singular nouns*) *adj, mpl* **ningunos** : no,
none ⟨no es ninguna tonta : she's no
fool⟩ ⟨no debe hacerse en ningún momento : that should never be done⟩
ninguno², **-na** *pron* **1** : neither, none
⟨ninguno de los dos ha vuelto aún : neither one has returned yet⟩ **2** : no one,
no other ⟨te quiero más que a ninguna : I love you more than any other⟩
niña *nf* **1** PUPILA : pupil (of the eye) **2
la niña de los ojos** : the apple of one's
eye
niñada *nf* **1** : childishness **2** : trifle, silly thing
niñería → **niñada**
niñero, **-ra** *n* : baby-sitter, nanny
niñez *nf, pl* **niñeces** INFANCIA : childhood
niño, **-ña** *n* : child, boy *m*, girl *f*
niobio *nm* : niobium
nipón, **-pona** *adj & n, mpl* **nipones**
JAPONÉS : Japanese
níquel *nm* : nickel
nitidez *nf, pl* **-deces** CLARIDAD : clarity, vividness, sharpness
nítido, **-da** *adj* CLARO : clear, vivid, sharp
nitrato *nm* : nitrate
nítrico, **-ca** *adj* **ácido nítrico** : nitric acid
nitrito *nm* : nitrite
nitrógeno *nm* : nitrogen
nitroglicerina *nf* : nitroglycerin
nivel *nm* **1** : level, height ⟨nivel del mar
: sea level⟩ **2** : level, standard ⟨nivel
de vida : standard of living⟩
nivelar *vt* : to level (out)
nixtamal *nm Mex* : limed corn used for
tortillas
no *adv* **1** : no ⟨¿quieres ir al mercado?
no, voy más tarde : do you want to go
shopping? no, I'm going later⟩ **2** : not
⟨no hagas eso! : don't do that!⟩ ⟨creo
que no : I don't think so⟩ **3** : non- ⟨no
fumador : non-smoker⟩ **4 ¡como no!**
: of course! **5 no bien** : as soon as, no
sooner

nobelio *nm* : nobelium
noble[1] *adj* : noble — noblemente *adv*
noble[2] *nmf* : nobleman *m*, noblewoman *f*
nobleza *nf* 1 : nobility 2 HONRADEZ : honesty, integrity
nocaut *nm* : knockout, KO
noche *nf* 1 : night, nighttime, evening 2 buenas noches : good evening, good night 3 de noche *or* por la noche : at night 4 hacerse de noche : to get dark
Nochebuena *nf* : Christmas Eve
nochecita *nf* : dusk
Nochevieja *nf* : New Year's Eve
noción *nf, pl* nociones 1 CONCEPTO : notion, concept 2 nociones *nfpl* : smattering, rudiments *pl*
nocivo, -va *adj* DAÑINO : harmful, noxious
noctámbulo, -la *n* 1 : sleepwalker 2 : night owl
nocturno[1], -na *adj* : night, nocturnal
nocturno[2] *nm* : nocturne
nodriza *nf* : wet nurse
nódulo *nm* : nodule
nogal *nm* 1 : walnut tree 2 *Mex* : pecan tree 3 nogal americano : hickory
nómada[1] *adj* : nomadic
nómada[2] *nmf* : nomad
nomás *adv* : only, just ⟨lo hice nomás porque sí : I did it just because⟩ ⟨nomás de recordarlo me enojo : I get angry just remembering it⟩ ⟨nomás faltan dos semanas para Navidad : there are only two weeks left till Christmas⟩
nombradía *nf* RENOMBRE : fame, renown
nombrado, -da *adj* : famous, well-known
nombramiento *nm* : appointment, nomination
nombrar *vt* 1 : to appoint 2 : to mention, to name
nombre *nm* 1 : name ⟨nombre de pluma : pseudonym, pen name⟩ ⟨en nombre : on behalf of⟩ ⟨sin nombre : nameless⟩ 2 : noun ⟨nombre propio : proper noun⟩ 3 : fame, renown
nomenclatura *nf* : nomenclature
nomeolvides *nmfs & pl* : forget-me-not
nómina *nf* : payroll
nominación *nf, pl* -ciones : nomination
nominal *adj* : nominal — nominalmente *adv*
nominar *vt* : to nominate
nominativo[1], -va *adj* : nominative
nominativo[2] *nm* : nominative (case)
nomo *nm* : gnome
non[1] *adj* IMPAR : odd, not even
non[2] *nm* : odd number
nonagésimo[1], -ma *adj* : ninetieth, ninety-
nonagésimo[2], -ma *n* : ninetieth, ninety- (in a series)
nono, -na *adj* : ninth — nono *nm*
nopal *nm* : nopal, cactus
nopalitos *nmpl Mex* : pickled cactus leaves
noquear *vt* : to knock out, to KO

norcoreano, -na *adj & n* : North Korean
nordeste[1] *or* noreste *adj* 1 : northeastern 2 : northeasterly
nordeste[2] *or* noreste *nm* : northeast
nórdico, -ca *adj & n* 1 ESCANDINAVO : Scandinavian 2 : Norse
noreste → nordeste
noria *nf* 1 : waterwheel 2 : Ferris wheel
norirlandés[1], -desa *adj, mpl* -deses : Northern Irish
norirlandés[2], -desa *n, mpl* -deses : person from Northern Ireland
norma *nf* 1 : rule, regulation 2 : norm, standard
normal *adj* 1 : normal, usual 2 : standard 3 escuela normal : teacher-training college
normalidad *nf* : normality, normalcy
normalización *nf, pl* -ciones *nf* 1 REGULARIZACIÓN : normalization 2 ESTANDARIZACIÓN : standardization
normalizar {21} *vt* 1 REGULARIZAR : to normalize 2 ESTANDARIZAR : to standardize — normalizarse *vr* : to return to normal
normalmente *adv* GENERALMENTE : ordinarily, generally
noroeste[1] *adj* 1 : northwestern 2 : northwesterly
noroeste[2] *nm* : northwest
norte[1] *adj* : north, northern
norte[2] *nm* 1 : north 2 : north wind 3 META : aim, objective
norteamericano, -na *adj & n* 1 : North American 2 AMERICANO, ESTADOUNIDENSE : American, native or inhabitant of the United States
norteño[1], -ña *adj* : northern
norteño[2], -ña *n* : Northerner
noruego[1], -ga *adj & n* : Norwegian
noruego[2] *nm* : Norwegian (language)
nos *pron* 1 : us ⟨nos enviaron a la frontera : they sent us to the border⟩ 2 : ourselves ⟨nos divertimos muchísimo : we enjoyed ourselves a great deal⟩ 3 : each other, one another ⟨nos vimos desde lejos : we saw each other from far away⟩ 4 : to us, for us, from us ⟨nos lo dio : he gave it to us⟩ ⟨nos lo compraron : they bought it from us⟩
nosotros, -tras *pron* 1 : we ⟨nosotros llegamos ayer : we arrived yesterday⟩ 2 : us ⟨ven con nosotros : come with us⟩ 3 nosotros mismos : ourselves ⟨lo arreglamos nosotros mismos : we fixed it ourselves⟩
nostalgia *nf* 1 : nostalgia, longing 2 : homesickness
nostálgico, -ca *adj* 1 : nostalgic 2 : homesick
nota *nf* 1 : note, message 2 : announcement ⟨nota de prensa : press release⟩ 3 : grade, mark (in school) 4 : characteristic, feature, touch 5 : note (in music) 6 : bill, check (in a restaurant)

notable *adj* **1** : notable, noteworthy **2** : outstanding
notación *nf, pl* **-ciones** : notation
notar *vt* **1** : to notice ⟨hacer notar algo : to point out something⟩ **2** : to tell ⟨la diferencia se nota inmediatamente : you can tell the difference right away⟩ — **notarse** *vr* **1** : to be evident, to show **2** : to feel, to seem
notario, -ria *n* : notary, notary public
noticia *nf* **1** : news item, piece of news **2 noticias** *nfpl* : news
noticiero *nm* : news program, newscast
noticioso, -sa *adj* : news ⟨agencia noticiosa : news agency⟩
notificación *nf, pl* **-ciones** : notification
notificar {72} *vt* : to notify, to inform
notoriedad *nf* **1** : knowledge, obviousness **2** : fame, notoriety
notorio, -ria *adj* **1** OBVIO : obvious, evident **2** CONOCIDO : well-known
novato¹, -ta *adj* : inexperienced, new
novato², -ta *n* : beginner, novice
novecientos¹, -tas *adj* : nine hundred
novecientos² *nms & pl* : nine hundred
novedad *nf* **1** : newness, novelty **2** : innovation
novedoso, -sa *adj* : original, novel
novel *adj* NOVATO : inexperienced, new
novela *nf* **1** : novel **2** : soap opera
novelar *vt* : to fictionalize, to make a novel out of
novelesco, -ca *adj* **1** : fictional **2** : fantastic, fabulous
novelista *nmf* : novelist
novena *nf* : novena
noveno, -na *adj* : ninth — **noveno, -na** *n*
noventa *adj & nm* : ninety
noventavo¹, -va *adj* : ninetieth
noventavo² *nm* : ninetieth (fraction)
noviazgo *nm* **1** : courtship, relationship **2** : engagement, betrothal
novicio, -cia *n* **1** : novice (in religion) **2** PRINCIPIANTE : novice, beginner
noviembre *nm* : November
novilla *nf* : heifer
novillada *nf* : bullfight featuring young bulls
novillero, -ra *n* : apprentice bullfighter
novillo *nm* : young bull
novio, -via *n* **1** : boyfriend *m*, girlfriend *f* **2** PROMETIDO : fiancé *m*, fiancée *f* **3** : bridegroom *m*, bride *f*
novocaína *nf* : novocaine
nubarrón *nm, pl* **-rrones** : storm cloud
nube *nf* **1** : cloud ⟨andar en las nubes : to have one's head in the clouds⟩ ⟨por las nubes : sky-high⟩ **2** : cloud (of dust), swarm (of insects, etc.)
nublado¹, -da *adj* **1** NUBOSO : cloudy, overcast **2** : clouded, dim
nublado² *nm* **1** : storm cloud **2** AMENAZA : menace, threat
nublar *vt* **1** : to cloud **2** OSCURECER : to obscure — **nublarse** *vr* : to get cloudy
nubosidad *nf* : cloudiness
nuboso, -sa *adj* NUBLADO : cloudy

nuca *nf* : nape, back of the neck
nuclear *adj* : nuclear
núcleo *nm* **1** : nucleus **2** : center, heart, core
nudillo *nm* : knuckle
nudismo *nm* : nudism
nudista *adj & nmf* : nudist
nudo *nm* **1** : knot ⟨nudo de rizo : square knot⟩ ⟨un nudo en la garganta : a lump in one's throat⟩ **2** : node **3** : junction, hub ⟨nudo de comunicaciones : communication center⟩ **4** : crux, heart (of a problem, etc.)
nudoso, -sa *adj* : knotty, gnarled
nuera *nf* : daughter-in-law
nuestro¹, -tra *adj* : our
nuestro², -tra *pron* (*with definite article*) : ours, our own ⟨el nuestro es más grande : ours is bigger⟩ ⟨es de los nuestros : it's one of ours⟩
nuevamente *adv* : again, anew
nuevas *nfpl* : tidings *pl*
nueve *adj & nm* : nine
nuevecito, -ta *adj* : brand-new
nuevo, -va *adj* **1** : new ⟨una casa nueva : a new house⟩ ⟨¿qué hay de nuevo? : what's new?⟩ **2 de ~** : again, once more **3 Nuevo Testamento** : New Testament
nuez *nf, pl* **nueces 1** : nut **2** : walnut **3** *Mex* : pecan **4 nuez de Adán** : Adam's apple **5 nuez moscada** : nutmeg
nulidad *nf* **1** : nullity **2** : incompetent person ⟨¡es una nulidad! : he's hopeless!⟩
nulo, -la *adj* **1** : null, null and void **2** INEPTO : useless, inept ⟨es nula para la cocina : she's hopeless at cooking⟩
numen *nm* : poetic muse, inspiration
numerable *adj* : countable
numeración *nf, pl* **-ciones 1** : numbering **2** : numbers *pl*, numerals *pl* ⟨numeración romana : Roman numerals⟩
numerador *nm* : numerator
numeral *adj* : numeral
numerar *vt* : to number
numerario, -ria *adj* : long-standing, permanent ⟨profesor numerario : tenured professor⟩
numérico, -ca *adj* : numerical — **numéricamente** *adv*
número *nm* **1** : number ⟨número impar : odd number⟩ ⟨número ordinal : ordinal number⟩ ⟨número arábico : Arabic numeral⟩ ⟨número quebrado : fraction⟩ **2** : issue (of a publication) **3 sin ~** : countless
numeroso, -sa *adj* : numerous
numismática *nf* : numismatics
nunca *adv* **1** : never, ever ⟨nunca es tarde : it's never too late⟩ ⟨no trabaja casi nunca : he hardly ever works⟩ **2 nunca más** : never again **3 nunca jamás** : never ever
nuncio *nm* : harbinger, herald
nupcial *adj* : nuptial, wedding
nupcias *nfpl* : nuptials *pl*, wedding

nutria *nf* **1** : otter **2** : nutria
nutrición *nf, pl* **-ciones** : nutrition, nourishment
nutrido, -da *adj* **1** : nourished ⟨mal nutrido : undernourished, malnourished⟩ **2** : considerable, abundant ⟨de nutrido : full of, abounding in⟩
nutriente *nm* : nutrient
nutrimento *nm* : nutriment
nutrir *vt* **1** ALIMENTAR : to feed, to nourish **2** : to foster, to provide
nutritivo, -va *adj* : nourishing, nutritious

nylon → **nilón**
ñ *nf* : fifteenth letter of the Spanish alphabet
ñame *nm* : yam
ñandú *nm* : rhea
ñapa *nf* : extra amount ⟨de ñapa : for good measure⟩
ñoñear *vi fam* : to whine
ñoño, -ña *adj fam* : whiny, fussy ⟨no seas tan ñoño : don't be such a wimp⟩
ñoquis *nmpl* : gnocchi *pl*
ñu *nm* : gnu, wildebeest

O

o¹ *nf* : sixteenth letter of the Spanish alphabet
o² *conj* (**u** *before words beginning with o- or ho-*) **1** : or ⟨¿vienes con nosotros o te quedas? : are you coming with us or staying?⟩ **2** : either ⟨o vienes con nosotros o te quedas : either you come with us or you stay⟩ **3 o sea** : that is to say, in other words
oasis *nms & pl* : oasis
obcecado, -da *adj* **1** : blinded ⟨obcecado por la ira : blinded by rage⟩ **2** : stubborn, obstinate
obcecar {72} *vt* : to blind (by emotions) — **obcecarse** *vr* : to become stubborn
obedecer {53} *vt* : to obey ⟨obedecer órdenes : to obey orders⟩ ⟨obedece a tus padres : obey your parents⟩ — *vi* **1** : to obey **2** ~ **a** : to respond to **3** ~ **a** : to be due to, to result from
obediencia *nf* : obedience
obediente *adj* : obedient — **obedientemente** *adv*
obelisco *nm* : obelisk
obertura *nf* : overture
obesidad *nf* : obesity
obeso, -sa *adj* : obese
óbice *nm* : obstacle, impediment
obispado *nm* DIÓCESIS : bishopric, diocese
obispo *nm* : bishop
obituario *nm* : obituary
objeción *nf, pl* **-ciones** : objection ⟨ponerle objeciones a algo : to object to something⟩
objetar *v* : to object ⟨no tengo nada que objetar : I have no objections⟩
objetividad *nf* : objectivity
objetivo¹, -va *adj* : objective — **objetivamente** *adv*
objetivo² *nm* **1** META : objective, goal, target **2** : lens
objeto *nm* **1** COSA : object, thing **2** OBJETIVO : objective, purpose ⟨con objeto de : in order to, with the aim of⟩ **3 objeto volador no identificado** : unidentified flying object
objetor, -tora *n* : objector ⟨objetor de conciencia : conscientious objector⟩
oblea *nf* **1** : wafer **2 hecho una oblea** *fam* : skinny as a rail

oblicuo, -cua *adj* : oblique — **oblicuamente** *adv*
obligación *nf, pl* **-ciones 1** DEBER : obligation, duty **2** : bond, debenture
obligado, -da *adj* **1** : obliged **2** : obligatory, compulsory **3** : customary
obligar {52} *vt* : to force, to require, to oblige — **obligarse** *vr* : to commit oneself, to undertake (to do something)
obligatorio, -ria *adj* : mandatory, required, compulsory
obliterar *vt* : to obliterate, to destroy — **obliteración** *nf*
oblongo, -ga *adj* : oblong
obnubilación *nf, pl* **-ciones** : bewilderment, confusion
obnubilar *vt* : to daze, to bewilder
oboe¹ *nm* : oboe
oboe² *nmf* : oboist
obra *nf* **1** : work ⟨obra de arte : work of art⟩ ⟨obra de teatro : play⟩ ⟨obra de consulta : reference work⟩ **2** : deed ⟨una buena obra : a good deed⟩ **3** : construction work **4 obra maestra** : masterpiece **5 obras públicas** : public works **6 por obra de** : thanks to, because of
obrar *vt* : to work, to produce ⟨obrar milagros : to work miracles⟩ — *vi* **1** : to act, to behave ⟨obrar con cautela : to act with caution⟩ **2 obrar en poder de** : to be in possession of
obrero¹, -ra *adj* : working ⟨la clase obrera : the working class⟩
obrero², -ra *n* : worker, laborer
obscenidad *nf* : obscenity
obsceno, -na *adj* : obscene
obscurecer, obscuridad, obscuro → **oscurecer, oscuridad, oscuro**
obsequiar *vt* REGALAR : to give, to present ⟨lo obsequiaron con una placa : they presented him with a plaque⟩
obsequio *nm* REGALO : gift, present
obsequiosidad *nf* : attentiveness, deference
obsequioso, -sa *adj* : obliging, attentive
observable *adj* : observable
observación *nf, pl* **-ciones 1** : observation, watching **2** : remark, comment
observador¹, -dora *adj* : observant

observador², -dora *n* : observer, watcher
observancia *nf* : observance
observante *adj* : observant ⟨los judíos observantes : observant Jews⟩
observar *vt* **1** : to observe, to watch ⟨estábamos observando a los niños : we were watching the children⟩ **2** NOTAR : to notice **3** ACATAR : to obey, to abide by **4** COMENTAR : to remark, to comment
observatorio *nm* : observatory
obsesión *nf, pl* **-siones** : obsession
obsesionar *vt* : to obsess, to preoccupy excessively — **obsesionarse** *vr*
obsesivo, -va *adj* : obsessive
obseso, -sa *adj* : obsessed
obsolescencia *nf* DESUSO : obsolescence — **obsolescente** *adj*
obsoleto, -ta *adj* DESUSADO : obsolete
obstaculizar {21} *vt* IMPEDIR : to obstruct, to hinder
obstáculo *nm* IMPEDIMENTO : obstacle
obstante¹ *conj* **no obstante** : nevertheless, however
obstante² *prep* **no obstante** : in spite of, despite ⟨mantuvo su inocencia no obstante la evidencia : he maintained his innocence in spite of the evidence⟩
obstar *v impers* ～ **a** *or* ～ **para** : to hinder, to prevent ⟨eso no obsta para que me vaya : that doesn't prevent me from leaving⟩
obstetra *nmf* TOCÓLOGO : obstetrician
obstetricia *nf* : obstetrics
obstétrico, -ca *adj* : obstetric, obstetrical
obstinación *nf, pl* **-ciones** **1** TERQUEDAD : obstinacy, stubbornness **2** : perseverance, tenacity
obstinado, -da *adj* **1** TERCO : obstinate, stubborn **2** : persistent — **obstinadamente** *adv*
obstinarse *vr* EMPECINARSE : to be obstinate, to be stubborn
obstrucción *nf, pl* **-ciones** : obstruction, blockage
obstruccionismo *nm* : obstructionism, filibustering
obstruccionista *adj* : obstructionist, filibustering
obstructor, -tora *adj* : obstructive
obstruir {41} *vt* BLOQUEAR : to obstruct, to block, to clog — **obstruirse** *vr*
obtención *nf* : obtaining, procurement
obtener {80} *vt* : to obtain, to secure, to get — **obtenible** *adj*
obturador *nm* : shutter (of a camera)
obtuso, -sa *adj* : obtuse
obtuvo, etc. → **obtener**
obús *nm, pl* **obuses** **1** : mortar (weapon) **2** : mortar shell
obviar *vt* : to get around (a difficulty), to avoid
obvio, -via *adj* : obvious — **obviamente** *adv*
oca *nf* : goose

ocasión *nf, pl* **-siones** **1** : occasion, time **2** : opportunity, chance **3** : bargain **4 de** ～ : secondhand **5 aviso de ocasión** *Mex* : classified ad
ocasional *adj* **1** : occasional **2** : chance, fortuitous
ocasionalmente *adv* **1** : occasionally **2** : by chance
ocasionar *vt* CAUSAR : to cause, to occasion
ocaso *nm* **1** ANOCHECER : sunset, sundown **2** DECADENCIA : decline, fall
occidental *adj* : western, occidental
occidente *nm* **1** OESTE, PONIENTE : west **2 el Occidente** : the West
oceánico, -ca *adj* : oceanic
océano *nm* : ocean
oceanografía *nf* : oceanography
oceanográfico, -ca *adj* : oceanographic
ocelote *nm* : ocelot
ochenta *adj* & *nm* : eighty
ochentavo¹, -va *adj* : eightieth
ochentavo² *nm* : eightieth (fraction)
ocho *adj* & *nm* : eight
ochocientos¹, -tas *adj* : eight hundred
ochocientos² *ms* & *pl* : eight hundred
ocio *nm* **1** : free time, leisure **2** : idleness
ociosidad *nf* : idleness, inactivity
ocioso, -sa *adj* **1** INACTIVO : idle, inactive **2** INÚTIL : pointless, useless
ocre *nm* : ocher
octágono *nm* : octagon — **octagonal** *adj*
octava *nf* : octave
octavo, -va *adj* : eighth — **octavo, -va** *n*
octeto *nm* **1** : octet **2** : byte
octogésimo¹, -ma *adj* : eightieth, eighty-
octogésimo², -ma *n* : eightieth, eighty- (in a series)
octubre *nm* : October
ocular *adj* **1** : ocular, eye ⟨músculos oculares : eye muscles⟩ **2 testigo ocular** : eyewitness
oculista *nmf* : oculist, ophthalmologist
ocultación *nf, pl* **-ciones** : concealment
ocultar *vt* ESCONDER : to conceal, to hide — **ocultarse** *vr*
oculto, -ta *adj* **1** ESCONDIDO : hidden, concealed **2** : occult
ocupación *nf, pl* **-ciones** **1** : occupation, activity **2** : occupancy **3** EMPLEO : employment, job
ocupacional *adj* : occupational, job-related
ocupado, -da *adj* **1** : busy **2** : taken ⟨este asiento está ocupado : this seat is taken⟩ **3** : occupied ⟨territorios ocupados : occupied territories⟩ **4 señal de ocupado** : busy signal
ocupante *nmf* : occupant
ocupar *vt* **1** : to occupy, to take possession of **2** : to hold (a position) **3** : to employ, to keep busy **4** : to fill (space, time) **5** : to inhabit (a dwelling) **6** : to bother, to concern — **ocuparse** *vr* ～ **de 1** : to be concerned with **2** : to take care of

ocurrencia *nf* **1** : occurrence, event **2** : witticism **3** : bright idea

ocurrente *adj* **1** : witty **2** : clever, sharp

ocurrir *vi* : to occur, to happen — **ocurrirse** *vr* ~ **a** : to occur to, to strike ⟨se me ocurrió una mejor idea : a better idea occurred to me⟩

oda *nf* : ode

odiar *vt* ABOMINAR, ABORRECER : to hate

odio *nm* : hate, hatred

odioso, -sa *adj* ABOMINABLE, ABORRECIBLE : hateful, detestable

odisea *nf* : odyssey

odontología *nf* : dentistry, dental surgery

odontólogo, -ga *n* : dentist, dental surgeon

oeste¹ *adj* **1** : west, western ⟨la región oeste : the western region⟩ **2** : westerly

oeste² *nm* **1** : west, West **2** : west wind

ofender *vt* AGRAVIAR : to offend, to insult — *vi* : to offend, to be insulting — **ofenderse** *vr* : to take offense

ofensa *nf* : offense, insult

ofensiva *nf* : offensive ⟨pasar a la ofensiva : to go on the offensive⟩

ofensivo, -va *adj* : offensive, insulting

ofensor, -sora *n* : offender

oferente *nmf* **1** : supplier **2** FUENTE : source ⟨un oferente no identificado : an unidentified source⟩

oferta *nf* **1** : offer **2** : sale, bargain ⟨las camisas están en oferta : the shirts are on sale⟩ **3 oferta y demanda** : supply and demand

ofertar *vt* OFRECER : to offer

oficial¹ *adj* : official — **oficialmente** *adv*

oficial² *nmf* **1** : officer, police officer, commissioned officer (in the military) **2** : skilled worker

oficializar {21} *vt* : to make official

oficiante *nmf* : celebrant

oficiar *vt* **1** : to inform officially **2** : to officiate at, to celebrate (Mass) — *vi* ~ **de** : to act as

oficina *nf* : office

oficinista *nmf* : office worker

oficio *nm* **1** : trade, profession ⟨es electricista de oficio : he's an electrician by trade⟩ **2** : function, role **3** : official communication **4** : experience ⟨tener oficio : to be experienced⟩ **5** : religious ceremony

oficioso, -sa *adj* **1** EXTRAOFICIAL : unofficial **2** : officious — **oficiosamente** *adv*

ofrecer {53} *vt* **1** : to offer **2** : to provide, to give **3** : to present (an appearance, etc.) — **ofrecerse** *vr* **1** : to offer oneself, to volunteer **2** : to open up, to present itself

ofrecimiento *nm* : offer, offering

ofrenda *nf* : offering

oftalmología *nf* : ophthalmology

oftalmólogo, -ga *n* : ophthalmologist

ofuscación *nf, pl* **-ciones** : blindness, confusion

ofuscar {72} *vt* **1** : to blind, to dazzle **2** CONFUNDIR : to bewilder, to confuse — **ofuscarse** *vr* ~ **con** : to be blinded by

ogro *nm* : ogre

ohm *nm, pl* **ohms** : ohm

ohmio → **ohm**

oídas *nfpl* **de** ~ : by hearsay

oído *nm* **1** : ear ⟨oído interno : inner ear⟩ **2** : hearing ⟨duro de oído : hard of hearing⟩ **3 tocar de oído** : to play by ear

oiga, etc. → **oír**

oír {50} *vi* : to hear — *vt* **1** : to hear **2** ESCUCHAR : to listen to **3** : to pay attention to, to heed **4** ¡**oye**! *or* ¡**oiga**! : listen!, excuse me!, look here!

ojal *nm* : buttonhole

ojalá *interj* **1** : I hope so!, if only!, God willing! **2** : I hope, I wish, hopefully ⟨¡ojalá que le vaya bien! : I hope things go well for her!⟩ ⟨¡ojalá no llueva! : hopefully it won't rain!⟩

ojeada *nf* : glimpse, glance ⟨echar una ojeada : to have a quick look⟩

ojear *vt* : to eye, to have a look at

ojete *nm* : eyelet

ojiva *nf* : warhead

ojo *nm* **1** : eye **2** : judgment, sharpness ⟨tener buen ojo para : to be a good judge of, to have a good eye for⟩ **3** : hole (in cheese), eye (in a needle), center (of a storm) **4** : span (of a bridge) **5 a ojos vistas** : openly, publicly **6 andar con ojo** : to be careful **7 ojo de agua** *Mex* : spring, source **8** ¡**ojo**! : look out!, pay attention!

ola *nf* **1** : wave **2 ola de calor** : heat wave

oleada *nf* : swell, wave ⟨una oleada de protestas : a wave of protests⟩

oleaje *nm* : waves *pl*, surf

óleo *nm* **1** : oil **2** : oil painting

oleoducto *nm* : oil pipeline

oleoso, -sa *adj* : oily

oler {51} *vt* **1** : to smell **2** INQUIRIR : to pry into, to investigate **3** AVERIGUAR : to smell out, to uncover — *vi* **1** : to smell ⟨huele mal : it smells bad⟩ **2** ~ **a** : to smell like, to smell of ⟨huele a pino : it smells like pine⟩ — **olerse** *vr* : to have a hunch, to suspect

olfatear *vt* **1** : to sniff **2** : to sense, to sniff out

olfativo, -va *adj* : olfactory

olfato *nm* **1** : sense of smell **2** : nose, instinct

oligarquía *nf* : oligarchy

olimpiada *or* **olimpíada** *nf* **1** : Olympiad **2** *or* **olimpiadas** *nfpl* : Olympics *pl*

olímpico, -ca *adj* : Olympic

olisquear *vt* : to sniff at

oliva *nf* ACEITUNA : olive ⟨aceite de oliva : olive oil⟩

olivo *nm* : olive tree

olla *nf* **1** : pot ⟨olla de presión : pressure cooker⟩ **2 olla podrida** : Spanish stew

olmeca *adj & nmf* : Olmec
olmo *nm* : elm
olor *nm* : smell, odor
oloroso, -sa *adj* : scented, fragrant
olote *nm Mex* : cob, corncob
olvidadizo, -za *adj* : forgetful, absent-minded
olvidar *vt* **1** : to forget, to forget about ⟨olvida lo que pasó : forget about what happened⟩ **2** : to leave behind ⟨olvidé mi chequera en la casa : I left my checkbook at home⟩ — **olvidarse** *vr* : to forget ⟨se me olvidó mi cuaderno : I forgot my notebook⟩ ⟨se le olvidó llamarme : he forgot to call me⟩
olvido *nm* **1** : forgetfulness **2** : oblivion **3** DESCUIDO : oversight
omaní *adj & nmf* : Omani
ombligo *nm* : navel, belly button
ombudsman *nmfs & pl* : ombudsman
omelette *nmf* : omelet
ominoso, -sa *adj* : ominous — **ominosamente** *adv*
omisión *nf, pl* **-siones** : omission, neglect
omiso, -sa *adj* **1** NEGLIGENTE : neglectful **2 hacer caso omiso de** : to ignore
omitir *vt* **1** : to omit, to leave out **2** : to fail to ⟨omitió dar su nombre : he failed to give his name⟩
ómnibus *n, pl* **-bus** *or* **-buses** : bus, coach
omnipotencia *nf* : omnipotence
omnipotente *adj* TODOPODEROSO : omnipotent, almighty
omnipresencia *nf* : ubiquity, omnipresence
omnipresente *adj* : ubiquitous, omnipresent
omnisciente *adj* : omniscient — **omnisciencia** *nf*
omnívoro, -ra *adj* : omnivorous
omóplato *or* **omoplato** *nm* : shoulder blade
once *adj & nm* : eleven
onceavo¹, -va *adj* : eleventh
onceavo² *nm* : eleventh (fraction)
onda *nf* **1** : wave, ripple, undulation ⟨onda sonora : sound wave⟩ **2** : wave (in hair) **3** : scallop (on clothing) **4** *fam* : wavelength, understanding ⟨agarrar la onda : to get the point⟩ ⟨en la onda : on the ball, with it⟩ **5 ¿qué onda?** *fam* : what's happening?, what's up?
ondear *vi* : to ripple, to undulate, to flutter
ondulación *nf, pl* **-ciones** : undulation
ondulado, -da *adj* **1** : wavy ⟨pelo ondulado : wavy hair⟩ **2** : undulating
ondulante *adj* : undulating
ondular *vt* : to wave (hair) — *vi* : to undulate, to ripple
oneroso, -sa *adj* GRAVOSO : onerous, burdensome
ónix *nm* : onyx
onza *nf* : ounce

opacar {72} *vt* **1** : to make opaque or dull **2** : to outshine, to overshadow
opacidad *nf* **1** : opacity **2** : dullness
opaco, -ca *adj* **1** : opaque **2** : dull
ópalo *nm* : opal
opción *nf, pl* **opciones 1** ALTERNATIVA : option, choice **2** : right, chance ⟨tener opción a : to be eligible for⟩
opcional *adj* : optional — **opcionalmente** *adv*
ópera *nf* : opera
operación *nf, pl* **-ciones 1** : operation **2** : transaction, deal
operacional *adj* : operational
operador, -dora *n* **1** : operator **2** : cameraman, projectionist
operante *adj* : operating, working
operar *vt* **1** : to produce, to bring about **2** INTERVENIR : to operate on **3** *Mex* : to operate, to run (a machine) — *vi* **1** : to operate, to function **2** : to deal, to do business — **operarse** *vr* **1** : to come about, to take place **2** : to have an operation
operario, -ria *n* : laborer, worker
operático, -ca → **operístico**
operativo¹, -va *adj* **1** : operating ⟨capacidad operativa : operating capacity⟩ **2** : operative
operativo² *nm* : operation ⟨operativo militar : military operation⟩
opereta *nf* : operetta
operístico, -ca *adj* : operatic
opiato *nm* : opiate
opinable *adj* : arguable
opinar *vi* **1** : to think, to have an opinion **2** : to express an opinion **3 opinar bien de** : to think highly of — *vt* : to think ⟨opinamos lo mismo : we're of the same opinion, we're in agreement⟩
opinión *nf, pl* **-niones** : opinion, belief
opio *nm* : opium
oponente *nmf* : opponent
oponer {60} *vt* **1** CONTRAPONER : to oppose, to place against **2 oponer resistencia** : to resist, to put up a fight — **oponerse** *vr* ~ **a** : to object to, to be against
oporto *nm* : port (wine)
oportunamente *adv* **1** : at the right time, opportunely **2** : appropriately
oportunidad *nf* : opportunity, chance
oportunismo *nm* : opportunism
oportunista¹ *adj* : opportunistic
oportunista² *nmf* : opportunist
oportuno, -na *adj* **1** : opportune, timely **2** : suitable, appropriate
oposición *nf, pl* **-ciones** : opposition
opositor, -tora *n* ADVERSARIO : opponent
oposum *nm* ZARIGÜEYA : opossum
opresión *nf, pl* **-siones 1** : oppression **2 opresión de pecho** : tightness in the chest
opresivo, -va *adj* : oppressive
opresor¹, -sora *adj* : oppressive
opresor², -sora *n* : oppressor

oprimir *vt* **1** : to oppress **2** : to press, to squeeze ⟨oprima el botón : push the button⟩

oprobio *nm* : opprobrium, shame

optar *vi* **1** ~ **por** : to opt for, to choose **2** ~ **a** : to aspire to, to apply for ⟨dos candidatos optan a la presidencia : two candidates are running for president⟩

optativo, -va *adj* FACULTATIVO : optional

óptica *nf* **1** : optics **2** : optician's shop **3** : viewpoint

óptico¹, -ca *adj* : optical, optic

óptico², -ca *n* : optician

optimismo *nm* : optimism

optimista¹ *adj* : optimistic

optimista² *nmf* : optimist

óptimo, -ma *adj* : optimum, optimal

optometría *nf* : optometry — **optometrista** *nmf*

opuesto¹ *pp* → **oponer**

opuesto² *adj* **1** : opposite, contrary **2** : opposed

opulencia *nf* : opulence — **opulento, -ta** *adj*

opus *nm* : opus

opuso, etc. → **oponer**

ora *conj* : now ⟨los matices eran variados, ora verdes, ora ocres : the hues were varied, now green, now ocher⟩

oración *nf, pl* **-ciones 1** DISCURSO : oration, speech **2** PLEGARIA : prayer **3** FRASE : sentence, clause

oráculo *nm* : oracle

orador, -dora *n* : speaker, orator

oral *adj* : oral — **oralmente** *adv*

órale *interj Mex fam* **1** : sure!, OK! ⟨¿los dos por cinco pesos? ¡órale! : both for five pesos? you've got a deal!⟩ **2** : come on! ⟨¡órale, vámonos! : come on, let's go!⟩

orangután *nm, pl* **-tanes** : orangutan

orar *vi* REZAR : to pray

oratoria *nf* : oratory

oratorio *nm* **1** CAPILLA : oratory, chapel **2** : oratorio

orbe *nm* **1** : orb, sphere **2** GLOBO : globe, world

órbita *nf* **1** : orbit **2** : eye socket **3** ÁMBITO : sphere, field

orbitador *nm* : space shuttle, orbiter

orbital *adj* : orbital

orbitar *v* : to orbit

orden¹ *nm, pl* **órdenes 1** : order ⟨todo está en orden : everything's in order⟩ ⟨por orden cronológico : in chronological order⟩ **2 orden del día** : agenda (at a meeting) **3 orden público** : law and order

orden² *nf, pl* **órdenes 1** : order ⟨una orden religiosa : a religious order⟩ ⟨una orden de tacos : an order of tacos⟩ **orden de compra** : purchase order **3 estar a la orden del día** : to be the order of the day, to be prevalent

ordenación *nf, pl* **-ciones 1** : ordination **2** : ordering, organizing

ordenadamente *adv* : in an orderly fashion, neatly

ordenado, -da *adj* : orderly, neat

ordenador *nm Spain* : computer

ordenamiento *nm* **1** : ordering, organizing **2** : code (of laws)

ordenanza¹ *nf* REGLAMENTO : ordinance, regulation

ordenanza² *nm* : orderly (in the armed forces)

ordenar *vt* **1** MANDAR : to order, to command **2** ARREGLAR : to put in order, to arrange **3** : to ordain (a priest)

ordeñar *vt* : to milk

ordeño *nm* : milking

ordinal *nm* : ordinal (number)

ordinariamente *adv* **1** : usually **2** : coarsely

ordinariez *nf* : coarseness, vulgarity

ordinario, -ria *adj* **1** : ordinary **2** : coarse, common, vulgar **3 de** ~ : usually

orear *vt* : to air

orégano *nm* : oregano

oreja *nf* : ear

orfanato *nm* : orphanage

orfanatorio *nm Mex* : orphanage

orfebre *nmf* : goldsmith, silversmith

orfebrería *nf* : articles of gold or silver

orfelinato *nm* : orphanage

orgánico, -ca *adj* : organic — **orgánicamente** *adv*

organigrama *nm* : organization chart, flowchart

organismo *nm* **1** : organism **2** : agency, organization

organista *nmf* : organist

organización *nf, pl* **-ciones** : organization

organizador¹, -dora *adj* : organizing

organizador², -dora *n* : organizer

organizar {21} *vt* : to organize, to arrange — **organizarse** *vr* : to get organized

organizativo, -va *adj* : organizational

órgano *nm* : organ

orgasmo *nm* : orgasm

orgía *nf* : orgy

orgullo *nm* : pride

orgulloso, -sa *adj* : proud — **orgullosamente** *adv*

orientación *nf, pl* **-ciones 1** : orientation **2** DIRECCIÓN : direction, course **3** GUÍA : guidance, direction

oriental¹ *adj* **1** : eastern **2** : oriental **3** *Arg, Uru* : Uruguayan

oriental² *nmf* **1** : Easterner **2** : Oriental **3** *Arg, Uru* : Uruguayan

orientar *vt* **1** : to orient, to position **2** : to guide, to direct — **orientarse** *vr* **1** : to orient oneself, to get one's bearings **2** ~ **hacia** : to turn towards, to lean towards

oriente *nm* **1** : east, East **2 el Oriente** : the Orient

orifice *nmf* : goldsmith

orificio *nm* : orifice, opening

origen *nm, pl* **orígenes 1** : origin **2** : lineage, birth **3 dar origen a** : to give rise to **4 en su origen** : originally

original *adj & nm* : original — **originalmente** *adv*

originalidad *nf* : originality

originar *vt* : to originate, to give rise to — **originarse** *vr* : to originate, to begin

originario, -ria *adj* ~ **de** : native of

originariamente *adv* : originally

orilla *nf* **1** BORDE : border, edge **2** : bank (of a river) **3** : shore

orillar *vt* **1** : to skirt, to go around **2** : to trim, to edge (cloth) **3** : to settle, to wind up **4** *Mex* : to pull over (a vehicle)

orín *nm* **1** HERRUMBRE : rust **2 orines** *nmpl* : urine

orina *nf* : urine

orinación *nf* : urination

orinal *nm* : urinal (vessel)

orinar *vi* : to urinate — **orinarse** *vr* : to wet oneself

oriol *nm* OROPÉNDOLA : oriole

oriundo, -da *adj* ~ **de** : native of

orla *nf* : border, edging

orlar *vt* : to edge, to trim

ornamentación *nf, pl* **-ciones** : ornamentation

ornamental *adj* : ornamental

ornamentar *vt* ADORNAR : to ornament, to adorn

ornamento *nm* : ornament, adornment

ornar *vt* : to adorn, to decorate

ornitología *nf* : ornithology

ornitólogo, -ga *n* : ornithologist

ornitorrinco *nm* : platypus

oro *nm* : gold

orondo, -da *adj* **1** : rounded, potbellied (of a container) **2** *fam* : smug, self-satisfied

oropel *nm* : glitz, glitter, tinsel

oropéndola *nf* : oriole

orquesta *nf* : orchestra — **orquestal** *adj*

orquestar *vt* : to orchestrate — **orquestación** *nf*

orquídea *nf* : orchid

ortiga *nf* : nettle

ortodoncia *nf* : orthodontics

ortodoncista *nmf* : orthodontist

ortodoxia *nf* : orthodoxy

ortodoxo, -xa *adj* : orthodox

ortografía *nf* : orthography, spelling

ortográfico, -ca *adj* : orthographic, spelling

ortopedia *nf* : orthopedics

ortopédico, -ca *adj* : orthopedic

ortopedista *nmf* : orthopedist

oruga *nf* **1** : caterpillar **2** : track (of a tank, etc.)

orzuelo *nm* : sty, stye (in the eye)

os *pron pl* (*objective form of* **vosotros**) *Spain* **1** : you, to you **2** : yourselves, to yourselves **3** : each other, to each other

osa *nf* → **oso**

osadía *nf* **1** VALOR : boldness, daring **2** AUDACIA : audacity, nerve

osado, -da *adj* **1** : bold, daring **2** : audacious, impudent — **osadamente** *adv*

osamenta *nf* : skeletal remains *pl*, bones *pl*

osar *vi* : to dare

oscilación *nf, pl* **-ciones** **1** : oscillation **2** : fluctuation **3** : vacillation, wavering

oscilar *vi* **1** BALANCEARSE : to swing, to sway, to oscillate **2** FLUCTUAR : to fluctuate **3** : to vacillate, to waver

oscuramente *adv* : obscurely

oscurecer {53} *vt* **1** : to darken **2** : to obscure, to confuse, to cloud **3 al oscurecer** : at dusk, at nightfall — *v impers* : to grow dark, to get dark — **oscurecerse** *vr* : to darken, to dim

oscuridad *nf* **1** : darkness **2** : obscurity

oscuro, -ra *adj* **1** : dark **2** : obscure **3 a oscuras** : in the dark, in darkness

óseo, ósea *adj* : skeletal, bony

ósmosis *or* **osmosis** *nf* : osmosis

oso, osa *n* **1** : bear **2 Osa Mayor** : Big Dipper **3 Osa Menor** : Little Dipper **4 oso blanco** : polar bear **5 oso hormiguero** : anteater **6 oso de peluche** : teddy bear

ostensible *adj* : ostensible, apparent — **ostensiblemente** *adv*

ostentación *nf, pl* **-ciones** : ostentation, display

ostentar *vt* **1** : to display, to flaunt **2** POSEER : to have, to hold ⟨ostenta el récord mundial : he holds the world record⟩

ostentoso, -sa *adj* : ostentatious, showy — **ostentosamente** *adv*

osteópata *nmf* : osteopath

osteopatía *n* : osteopathy

osteoporosis *nf* : osteoporosis

ostión *nm, pl* **ostiones** **1** *Mex* : oyster **2** *Chile* : scallop

ostra *nf* : oyster

ostracismo *nm* : ostracism

otear *vt* : to scan, to survey, to look over

otero *nm* : knoll, hillock

otomana *nf* : ottoman (mueble)

otomano, -na *adj & n* : Ottoman

otoñal *adj* : autumn, autumnal

otoño *nm* : autumn, fall

otorgamiento *nm* : granting, awarding

otorgar {52} *vt* **1** : to grant, to award **2** : to draw up, to frame (a legal document)

otro¹, otra *adj* **1** : other **2** : another ⟨en otro juego, ellos ganaron : in another game, they won⟩ **3 otra vez** : again **4 de otra manera** : otherwise **5 otra parte** : elsewhere **6 en otro tiempo** : once, formerly

otro², otra *pron* **1** : another one ⟨dame otro : give me another⟩ **2** : other one ⟨el uno o el otro : one or the other⟩ **3 los otros, las otras** : the others, the rest ⟨me dio una y se quedó con las otras : he gave me one and kept the rest⟩

ovación *nf, pl* **-ciones** : ovation

ovacionar *vt* : to cheer, to applaud

oval → ovalado
ovalado, -da *adj* : oval
óvalo *nm* : oval
ovárico, -ca *adj* : ovarian
ovario *nm* : ovary
oveja *nf* 1 : sheep, ewe 2 oveja negra : black sheep
overol *nm* : overalls *pl*
ovillar *vt* : to roll into a ball
ovillo *nm* 1 : ball (of yarn) 2 : tangle
ovni *or* OVNI *nm* (objeto volador no identificado) : UFO
ovoide *adj* : ovoid, ovoidal
ovulación *nf, pl* -ciones : ovulation
ovular *vi* : to ovulate
óvulo *nm* : ovum

oxidación *nf, pl* -ciones 1 : oxidation 2 : rusting
oxidado, -da *adj* : rusty
oxidar *vt* 1 : to cause to rust 2 : to oxidize — oxidarse *vr* : to rust, to become rusty
óxido *nm* 1 HERRUMBRE, ORÍN : rust 2 : oxide
oxigenar *vt* 1 : to oxygenate 2 : to bleach (hair)
oxígeno *nm* : oxygen
oxiuro *nm* : pinworm
oye, etc. → oír
oyente *nmf* 1 : listener 2 : auditor, auditing student
ozono *nm* : ozone

P

p *nf* : seventeenth letter of the Spanish alphabet
pabellón *nm, pl* -llones 1 : pavilion 2 : summerhouse, lodge 3 : flag (of a vessel)
pabilo *nm* MECHA : wick
paca *nf* FARDO : bale
pacana *nf* : pecan
pacer {48} *v* : to graze, to pasture
paces → paz
pachanga *nf fam* : party, bash
paciencia *nf* : patience
paciente *adj & nmf* : patient — pacientemente *adv*
pacificación *nf, pl* -ciones : pacification
pacíficamente *adv* : peacefully, peaceably
pacificar {72} *vt* : to pacify, to calm — pacificarse *vr* : to calm down, to abate
pacífico, -ca *adj* : peaceful, pacific
pacifismo *nm* : pacifism
pacifista *adj & nmf* : pacifist
pacotilla *nf* de ~ : shoddy, trashy
pactar *vt* : to agree on — *vi* : to come to an agreement
pacto *nm* CONVENIO : pact, agreement
padecer {53} *vt* : to suffer, to endure — *vi* ADOLECER ~ de : to suffer from
padecimiento *nm* 1 : suffering 2 : ailment, condition
padrastro *nm* 1 : stepfather 2 : hangnail
padre[1] *adj Mex fam* : fantastic, great
padre[2] *nm* 1 : father 2 padres *nmpl* : parents
padrenuestro *nm* : Lord's Prayer, paternoster
padrino *nm* 1 : godfather 2 : best man 3 : sponsor, patron
padrón *nm, pl* padrones : register, roll ⟨padrón municipal : city register⟩
paella *nf* : paella
paga *nf* 1 : payment 2 : pay, wages *pl*
pagadero, -ra *adj* : payable
pagado, -da *adj* 1 : paid 2 pagado de sí mismo : self-satisfied, smug
pagador, -dora *n* : payer

paganismo *nm* : paganism
pagano, -na *adj & n* : pagan
pagar {52} *vt* : to pay, to pay for, to repay — *vi* : to pay
pagaré *nm* VALE : promissory note, IOU
página *nf* : page
pago *nm* 1 : payment 2 en pago de : in return for
pagoda *nf* : pagoda
pague, etc. → pagar
país *nm* 1 NACIÓN : country, nation 2 REGIÓN : region, territory
paisaje *nm* : scenery, landscape
paisano, -na *n* COMPATRIOTA : compatriot, fellow countryman
paja *nf* 1 : straw 2 *fam* : trash, tripe
pajar *nm* : hayloft, haystack
pajarera *nf* : aviary
pájaro *nm* : bird ⟨pájaro cantor : songbird⟩ ⟨pájaro bobo : penguin⟩ ⟨pájaro carpintero : woodpecker⟩
pajita *nf* : (drinking) straw
pajote *nm* : straw, mulch
pala *nf* 1 : shovel, spade 2 : blade (of an oar or a rotor) 3 : paddle, racket
palabra *nf* 1 VOCABLO : word 2 PROMESA : word, promise ⟨un hombre de palabra : a man of his word⟩ 3 HABLA : speech 4 : right to speak ⟨tener la palabra : to have the floor⟩
palabrería *nf* : empty talk
palabrota *nf* : swearword
palacio *nm* 1 : palace, mansion 2 palacio de justicia : courthouse
paladar *nm* 1 : palate 2 GUSTO : taste
paladear *vt* SABOREAR : to savor
paladín *nm, pl* -dines : champion, defender
palanca *nf* 1 : lever, crowbar 2 *fam* : leverage, influence 3 palanca de cambio *or* palanca de velocidad : gearshift
palangana *nf* : washbowl
palanqueta *nf* : jimmy, small crowbar
palco *nm* : box (in a theater or stadium)
palear *vt* 1 : to shovel 2 : to paddle
palenque *nm* 1 ESTACADA : stockade, palisade 2 : arena, ring

paleontología *nf* : paleontology
paleontólogo, -ga *n* : paleontologist
palestino, -na *adj & n* : Palestinian
palestra *nf* : arena ⟨salir a la palestra : to join the fray⟩
paleta *nf* **1** : palette **2** : trowel **3** : spatula **4** : blade, vane **5** : paddle **6** *CA, Mex* : lollipop, Popsicle
paletilla *nf* : shoulder blade
paliar *vt* MITIGAR : to alleviate, to palliate
paliativo¹, -va *adj* : palliative
paliativo² *nm* : palliative
palidecer {53} *vi* : to turn pale
palidez *nf, pl* **-deces** : paleness, pallor
pálido, -da *adj* : pale
palillo *nm* **1** MONDADIENTES : toothpick **2 palillos** *nmpl* : chopsticks **3 palillo de tambor** : drumstick
paliza *nf* : beating, pummeling ⟨darle una paliza a : to beat, to thrash⟩
palma *nf* **1** : palm (of the hand) **2** : palm (tree or leaf) **3 batir palmas** : to clap, to applaud **4 llevarse la palma** *fam* : to take the cake
palmada *nf* **1** : pat **2** : slap **3** : clap
palmarés *nm* : record (of achievements)
palmario, -ria *adj* MANIFIESTO : clear, manifest
palmeado, -da *adj* : webbed
palmear *vt* : to slap on the back — *vi* : to clap, to applaud
palmera *nf* : palm tree
palmo *nm* **1** : span, small amount **2 palmo a palmo** : bit by bit, inch by inch **3 dejar con un palmo de narices** : to disappoint
palmotear *vi* : to applaud
palmoteo *nm* : clapping, applause
palo *nm* **1** : stick, pole, post **2** : shaft, handle ⟨palo de escoba : broomstick⟩ **3** : mast, spar **4** : wood **5** : blow (with a stick) **6** : suit (of cards)
paloma *nf* **1** : pigeon, dove **2 paloma mensajera** : carrier pigeon
palomilla *nf* : moth
palomitas *nfpl* : popcorn
palpable *adj* : palpable, tangible
palpar *vt* : to feel, to touch
palpitación *nf, pl* **-ciones** : palpitation
palpitar *vi* : to palpitate, to throb — **palpitante** *adj*
palta *nf* : avocado
paludismo *nm* MALARIA : malaria
palurdo, -da *n* : boor, yokel, bumpkin
pampa *nf* : pampa
pampeano, -na *adj* : pampean, pampas
pampero → **pampeano**
pan *nm* **1** : bread **2** : loaf of bread **3** : cake, bar ⟨pan de jabón : bar of soap⟩ **4 pan dulce** *CA, Mex* : traditional pastry **5 pan tostado** : toast **6 ser pan comido** *fam* : to be a piece of cake, to be a cinch
pana *nf* : corduroy
panacea *nf* : panacea
panadería *nf* : bakery, bread shop
panadero, -ra *n* : baker

panal *nm* : honeycomb
panameño, -ña *adj & n* : Panamanian
pancarta *nf* : placard, sign
pancita *nf Mex* : tripe
páncreas *nms & pl* : pancreas
panda *nmf* : panda
pandeado, -da *adj* : warped
pandearse *vr* **1** : to warp **2** : to bulge, to sag
pandemonio *or* **pandemónium** *nm* : pandemonium
pandereta *nf* : tambourine
pandero *nm* : tambourine
pandilla *nf* **1** : group, clique **2** : gang
panecito *nm* : roll, bread roll
panegírico¹, -ca *adj* : eulogistic, panegyrical
panegírico² *nm* : eulogy, panegyric
panel *nm* : panel — **panelista** *nmf*
panera *nf* : bread box
panfleto *nm* : pamphlet
pánico *nm* : panic
panorama *nm* **1** VISTA : panorama, view **2** : scene, situation ⟨el panorama nacional : the national scene⟩ **3** PERSPECTIVA : outlook
panorámico, -ca *adj* : panoramic
panqueque *nm* : pancake
pantaletas *nfpl* : panties
pantalla *nf* **1** : screen, monitor **2** : lampshade **3** : fan
pantalón *nm, pl* **-lones 1** : pants *pl*, trousers *pl* **2 pantalones vaqueros** : jeans **3 pantalones de mezclilla** *Chile, Mex* : jeans **4 pantalones de montar** : jodhpurs
pantano *nm* **1** : swamp, marsh, bayou **2** : reservoir **3** : obstacle, difficulty
pantanoso, -sa *adj* **1** : marshy, swampy **2** : difficult, thorny
panteón *nm, pl* **-teones 1** CEMENTERIO : cemetery **2** : pantheon, mausoleum
pantera *nf* : panther
pantimedias *nfpl Mex* : panty hose
pantomima *nf* : pantomime
pantorrilla *nf* : calf (of the leg)
pantufla *nf* ZAPATILLA : slipper
panza *nf* BARRIGA : belly, paunch
panzón, -zona *adj, mpl* **panzones** : potbellied, paunchy
pañal *nm* : diaper
pañería *nf* **1** : cloth, material **2** : fabric store
pañito *nm* : doily
paño *nm* **1** : cloth **2** : rag, dust cloth **3 paño de cocina** : dishcloth **4 paño higiénico** : sanitary napkin
pañuelo *nm* **1** : handkerchief **2** : scarf
papa¹ *nm* : pope
papa² *nf* **1** : potato **2 papa dulce** : sweet potato **3 papas fritas** : potato chips, french fries **4 papas a la francesa** *Mex* : french fries
papá *nm fam* **1** : dad, pop **2 papás** *nmpl* : parents, folks
papada *nf* **1** : double chin, jowl **2** : dewlap
papagayo *nm* LORO : parrot

papal *adj* : papal
papalote *nm Mex* : kite
papaya *nf* : papaya
papel *nm* **1** : paper, piece of paper **2** : role, part **3 papel de estaño** : tinfoil **4 papel de empapelar** *or* **papel pintado** : wallpaper **5 papel higiénico** : toilet paper **6 papel de lija** : sandpaper
papeleo *nm* : paperwork, red tape
papelera *nf* : wastebasket
papelería *nf* : stationery store
papelero, -ra *adj* : paper
papeleta *nf* **1** : ballot **2** : ticket, slip
paperas *nfpl* : mumps
papi *nm fam* : daddy, papa
papilla *nf* **1** : pap, mash **2 hacer papilla** : to beat to a pulp
papiro *nm* : papyrus
paquete *nm* BULTO : package, parcel
paquistaní *adj & nmf* : Pakistani
par¹ *adj* : even (in number)
par² *nm* **1** : pair, couple **2** : equal, peer ⟨sin par : matchless, peerless⟩ **3** : par (in golf) **4** : rafter **5 de par en par** : wide open
par³ *nf* **1** : par ⟨por encima de la par : above par⟩ **2 a la par que** : at the same time as, as well as ⟨interesante a la par que instructivo : both interesting and informative⟩
para *prep* **1** : for ⟨para ti : for you⟩ ⟨alta para su edad : tall for her age⟩ ⟨una cita para el lunes : an appointment for Monday⟩ **2** : to, towards ⟨para la derecha : to the right⟩ ⟨van para el río : they're heading towards the river⟩ **3** : to, in order to ⟨lo hace para molestarte : he does it to annoy you⟩ **4** : around, by (a time) ⟨para mañana estarán listos : they'll be ready by tomorrow⟩ **5 para adelante** : forwards **6 para atrás** : backwards **7 para que** : so, so that, in order that ⟨te lo digo para que sepas : I'm telling you so you'll know⟩
parabién *nm, pl* **-bienes** : congratulations *pl*
parábola *nf* **1** : parable **2** : parabola
parabrisas *nms & pl* : windshield
paracaídas *nms & pl* : parachute
paracaidista *nmf* **1** : parachutist **2** : paratrooper
parachoques *nms & pl* : bumper
parada *nf* **1** : stop ⟨parada de autobús : bus stop⟩ **2** : catch, save, parry (in sports) **3** DESFILE : parade
paradero *nm* : whereabouts
paradigma *nm* : paradigm
paradisíaco, -ca *or* **paradisiaco, -ca** *adj* : heavenly
parado, -da *adj* **1** : motionless, idle, stopped **2** : standing (up) **3** : confused, bewildered **4 bien (mal) parado** : in good (bad) shape ⟨salió bien parado : it turned out well for him⟩
paradoja *nf* : paradox
paradójico, -ca *adj* : paradoxical
parafernalia *nf* : paraphernalia

parafina *nf* : paraffin
parafrasear *vt* : to paraphrase
paráfrasis *nfs & pl* : paraphrase
paraguas *nms & pl* : umbrella
paraguayo, -ya *adj & n* : Paraguayan
paraíso *nm* **1** : paradise, heaven **2 paraíso fiscal** : tax shelter
paraje *nm* : spot, place
paralelismo *nm* : parallelism, similarity
paralelo¹, -la *adj* : parallel
paralelo² *nm* : parallel
paralelogramo *nm* : parallelogram
parálisis *nfs & pl* **1** : paralysis **2** : standstill **3 parálisis cerebral** : cerebral palsy
paralítico, -ca *adj & n* : paralytic
paralizar {21} *vt* **1** : to paralyze **2** : to bring to a standstill — **paralizarse** *vr*
parámetro *nm* : parameter
páramo *nm* : barren plateau, moor
parangón *nm, pl* **-gones** **1** : comparison **2 sin ~** : incomparable
paraninfo *nm* : auditorium, assembly hall
paranoia *nf* : paranoia
paranoico, -ca *adj & n* : paranoid
parapeto *nm* : parapet, rampart
parapléjico, -ca *adj & n* : paraplegic
parar *vt* **1** DETENER : to stop **2** : to stand, to prop — *vi* **1** CESAR : to stop **2** : to stay, to put up **3 ir a parar** : to end up, to wind up — **pararse** *vr* **1** : to stop **2** ATASCARSE : to stall (out) **3** : to stand up, to get up
pararrayos *nms & pl* : lightning rod
parasitario, -ria *adj* : parasitic
parasitismo *nm* : parasitism
parásito *nm* : parasite
parasol *nm* SOMBRILLA : parasol
parcela *nf* : parcel, tract of land
parcelar *vt* : to parcel (land)
parchar *vt* : to patch, to patch up
parche *nm* : patch
parcial *adj* : partial — **parcialmente** *adv*
parcialidad *nf* : partiality, bias
parco, -ca *adj* **1** : sparing, frugal **2** : moderate, temperate
pardo, -da *adj* : brownish grey
pardusco → **pardo**
parecer¹ {53} *vi* **1** : to seem, to look, to appear to be ⟨parece bien fácil : it looks very easy⟩ ⟨así parece : so it seems⟩ ⟨pareces una princesa : you look like a princess⟩ **2** : to think, to have an opinion ⟨me parece que sí : I think so⟩ **3** : to like, to be in agreement ⟨si te parece : if you like, if it's all right with you⟩ — **parecerse** *vr* **~ a** : to resemble
parecer² *nm* **1** OPINIÓN : opinion **2** ASPECTO : appearance ⟨al parecer : apparently⟩
parecido¹, -da *adj* **1** : similar, alike **2 bien parecido** : good-looking
parecido² *nm* : resemblance, similarity
pared *nf* : wall
pareja *nf* **1** : couple, pair **2** : partner, mate

parejo, -ja *adj* **1** : even, smooth, level **2** : equal, similar

parentela *nf* : relations *pl*, kinfolk

parentesco *nm* : relationship, kinship

paréntesis *nms & pl* **1** : parenthesis **2** : digression

parentético, -ca *adj* : parenthetic, parenthetical

paria *nmf* : pariah, outcast

paridad *nf* : parity, equality

pariente *nmf* : relative, relation

parir *vi* : to give birth — *vt* : to give birth to, to bear

parking *nm* : parking lot

parlamentar *vi* : to talk, to parley

parlamentario¹, -ria *adj* : parliamentary

parlamentario², -ria *n* : member of parliament

parlamento *nm* **1** : parliament **2** : negotiations *pl*, talks *pl*

parlanchín¹, -china *adj, mpl* **-chines** : chatty, talkative

parlanchín², -china *n, mpl* **-chines** : chatterbox

parlante *nm* ALTOPARLANTE : loudspeaker

parlotear *vi fam* : to gab, to chat, to prattle

parloteo *nm fam* : prattle, chatter

paro *nm* **1** HUELGA : strike **2** : stoppage, stopping **3 paro forzoso** : layoff

parodia *nf* : parody

parodiar *vt* : to parody

paroxismo *nm* **1** : fit, paroxysm **2** : peak, height ⟨llevaral paroxismo : to carry to the extreme⟩

parpadear *vi* **1** : to blink **2** : to flicker

parpadeo *nm* **1** : blink, blinking **2** : flickering

párpado *nm* : eyelid

parque *nm* **1** : park **2 parque de atracciones** : amusement park

parquear *vt* : to park — **parquearse** *vr*

parqueo *nm* : parking

parquet *or* **parqué** *nm* : parquet

parquímetro *nm* : parking meter

parra *nf* : vine, grapevine

párrafo *nm* : paragraph

parranda *nf fam* : party, spree

parrilla *nf* **1** : broiler, grill **2** : grate

parrillada *nf* BARBACOA : barbecue

párroco *nm* : parish priest

parroquia *nf* **1** : parish **2** : parish church **3** : customers *pl*, clientele

parroquial *adj* : parochial

parroquiano, -na *nm* **1** : parishioner **2** : customer, patron

parsimonia *nf* **1** : calm **2** : parsimony, thrift

parsimonioso, -sa *adj* **1** : calm, unhurried **2** : parsimonious, thrifty

parte¹ *nm* : report, dispatch

parte² *nf* **1** : part, share **2** : part, place ⟨en alguna parte : somewhere⟩ ⟨por todas partes : everywhere⟩ **3** : party (in negotiations, etc.) **4 de parte de** : on behalf of **5 ¿de parte de quién?** : may I ask who's calling? **6 tomar parte** : to take part

partero, -ra *n* : midwife

partición *nf, pl* **-ciones** : division, sharing

participación *nf, pl* **-ciones** **1** : participation **2** : share, interest **3** : announcement, notice

participante *nmf* **1** : participant **2** : competitor, entrant

participar *vi* **1** : to participate, to take part **2 ~ en** : to have a share in — *vt* : to announce, to notify

partícipe *nmf* : participant

participio *nm* : participle

partícula *nf* : particle

particular¹ *adj* **1** : particular, specific **2** : private, personal **3** : special, unique

particular² *nm* **1** : matter, detail **2** : individual

particularidad *nf* : characteristic, peculiarity

particularizar {21} *vt* **1** : to distinguish, to characterize **2** : to specify

partida *nf* **1** : departure **2** : item, entry **3** : certificate ⟨partida de nacimiento : birth certificate⟩ **4** : game, match, hand **5** : party, group

partidario, -ria *n* : follower, supporter

partido *nm* **1** : (political) party **2** : game, match ⟨partido de futbol : soccer game⟩ **3** APOYO : support, following **4** PROVECHO : profit, advantage ⟨sacar partido de : to profit from⟩

partir *vt* **1** : to cut, to split **2** : to break, to crack **3** : to share (out), to divide — *vi* **1** : to leave, to depart **2 ~ de** : to start from **3 a partir de** : as of, from ⟨a partir de hoy : as of today⟩ — **partirse** *vr* **1** : to smash, to split open **2** : to chap

partisano, -na *adj & n* : partisan

partitura *nf* : (musical) score

parto *nm* **1** : childbirth, delivery, labor ⟨estar de parto : to be in labor⟩ **2** : product, creation, brainchild

parvulario *nm* : nursery school

párvulo, -la *n* : toddler, preschooler

pasa *nf* **1** : raisin **2 pasa de Corinto** : currant

pasable *adj* : passable, tolerable — **pasablemente** *adv*

pasada *nf* **1** : passage, passing **2** : pass, wipe, coat (of paint) **3 de ~** : in passing **4 mala pasada** : dirty trick

pasadizo *nm* : passageway, corridor

pasado¹, -da *adj* **1** : past ⟨el año pasado : last year⟩ ⟨pasado mañana : the day after tomorrow⟩ ⟨pasadas las siete : after seven o'clock⟩ **2** : stale, bad, overripe **3** : old-fashioned, out-of-date **4** : overripe, slightly spoiled

pasado² *nm* : past

pasador *nm* **1** : bolt, latch **2** : barrette **3** *Mex* : bobby pin

pasaje *nm* **1** : ticket (for travel) **2** TARIFA : fare **3** : passageway **4** : passengers *pl*

pasajero¹, -ra *adj* : passing, fleeting

pasajero², -ra *n* : passenger

pasamanos *nms & pl* **1** : handrail **2**
: bannister
pasante *nmf* : assistant
pasaporte *nm* : passport
pasar *vi* **1** : to pass, to go by, to come
by **2** : to come in, to enter ⟨¿se puede
pasar? : may we come in?⟩ **3** : to happen ⟨¿qué pasa? : what's happening?,
what's going on?⟩ **4** : to manage, to get
by **5** : to be over, to end **6** ~ **de** : to
exceed, to go beyond **7** ~ **por** : to pretend to be — *vt* **1** : to pass, to give ⟨¿me
pasas la sal? : would you pass me the
salt?⟩ **2** : to pass (a test) **3** : to go over,
to cross **4** : to spend (time) **5** : to tolerate **6** : to go through, to suffer **7** : to
show (a movie, etc.) **8** : to overtake, to
pass, to surpass **9** : to pass over, to wipe
up **10 pasarlo bien** *or* **pasarla bien** : to
have a good time **11 pasarlo mal** *or*
pasarla mal : to have a bad time, to
have a hard time **12 pasar por alto** : to
overlook, to omit — **pasarse** *vr* **1** : to
move, to pass, to go away **2** : to slip
one's mind, to forget **3** : to go too far
pasarela *nf* **1** : gangplank **2** : footbridge
3 : runway, catwalk
pasatiempo *nm* : pastime, hobby
Pascua *nf* **1** : Easter **2** : Passover **3**
: Christmas **4 Pascuas** *nfpl* : Christmas season
pase *nm* **1** PERMISO : pass, permit **2**
pase de abordar *Mex* : boarding pass
pasear *vi* : to take a walk, to go for a
ride — *vt* **1** : to take for a walk **2** : to
parade around, to show off —
pasearse *vr* : to walk around
paseo *nm* **1** : walk, stroll **2** : ride **3** EX-
CURSIÓN : outing, trip **4** : avenue, walk
5 *or* **paseo marítimo** : boardwalk
pasiflora *nf* : passionflower
pasillo *nm* CORREDOR : hallway, corridor, aisle
pasión *nf, pl* **pasiones** : passion
pasional *adj* : passionate ⟨crimen pasional : crime of passion⟩
pasionaria → **pasiflora**
pasivo¹, -va *adj* : passive — **pasiva-
mente** *adv*
pasivo² *nm* **1** : liability ⟨activos y pa-
sivos : assets and liabilities⟩ **2** : debit
side (of an account)
pasmado, -da *adj* : stunned, flabber-
gasted
pasmar *vt* : to amaze, to stun — **pas-
marse** *vr*
pasmo *nm* **1** : shock, astonishment **2**
: wonder, marvel
pasmoso, -sa *adj* : incredible, amazing
— **pasmosamente** *adv*
paso¹, -sa *adj* : dried ⟨ciruela pasa
: prune⟩
paso² *nm* **1** : passage, passing ⟨de paso
: in passing, on the way⟩ **2** : way, path
⟨abrirse paso : to make one's way⟩ **3**
: crossing ⟨paso de peatones : cross-
walk⟩ ⟨paso a desnivel : underpass⟩
⟨paso elevado : overpass⟩ **4** : step

⟨paso a paso : step by step⟩ **5** : pace,
gait ⟨a buen paso : quickly, at a good
rate⟩
pasta *nf* **1** : paste ⟨pasta de dientes *or*
pasta dental : toothpaste⟩ **2** : pasta **3**
: pastry dough **4 libro en pasta dura**
: hardcover book **5 tener pasta de** : to
have the makings of
pastar *vi* : to graze — *vt* : to put to pasture
pastel¹ *adj* : pastel
pastel² *nm* **1** : cake ⟨pastel de cumpleaños : birthday cake⟩ **2** : pie, turnover
3 : pastel
pastelería *nf* : pastry shop
pasteurización *nf, pl* **-ciones** : pasteurization
pasteurizar {21} *vt* : to pasteurize
pastilla *nf* **1** COMPRIMIDO, PÍLDORA
: pill, tablet **2** : lozenge ⟨pastilla para
la tos : cough drop⟩ **3** : cake (of soap),
bar (of chocolate)
pastizal *nm* : pasture, grazing land
pasto *nm* **1** : pasture **2** HIERBA : grass,
lawn
pastor, -tora *n* **1** : shepherd, shepherdess *f* **2** : minister, pastor
pastoral *adj & nf* : pastoral
pastorear *vt* : to shepherd, to tend
pastorela *nf* **1** : pastoral, pastourelle **2**
Mex : a traditional Christmas play
pastoso, -sa *adj* **1** : pasty, doughy **2**
: smooth, mellow (of sounds)
pata *nf* **1** : paw, leg (of an animal) **2**
: foot, leg (of furniture) **3 patas de gallo** : crow's-feet **4 meter la pata** *fam* : to
put one's foot in it, to make a blunder
patada *nf* **1** PUNTAPIÉ : kick **2** : stamp
(of the foot)
patalear *vi* **1** : to kick **2** : to stamp one's
feet
pataleta *nf fam* : tantrum
patán¹ *adj, pl* **patanes** : boorish, crude
patán² *nm, pl* **patanes** : boor, lout
patata *nf Spain* : potato
pateador, -dora *n* : kicker (in sports)
patear *vt* : to kick — *vi* : to stamp one's
foot
patentar *vt* : to patent
patente¹ *adj* EVIDENTE : obvious, patent
— **patentemente** *adv*
patente² *nf* : patent
paternal *adj* : fatherly, paternal
paternidad *nf* **1** : fatherhood, paternity
2 : parenthood **3** : authorship
paterno, -na *adj* : paternal ⟨abuela pa-
terna : paternal grandmother⟩
patético, -ca *adj* : pathetic, moving
patetismo *nm* : pathos
patíbulo *nm* : gallows, scaffold
patillas *nfpl* : sideburns
patín *nm, pl* **patines** : skate ⟨patín de
ruedas : roller skate⟩
patinador, -dora *n* : skater
patinaje *nm* : skating
patinar *vi* **1** : to skate **2** : to skid, to slip
3 *fam* : to slip up, to blunder
patinazo *nm* **1** : skid **2** *fam* : blunder,
slipup

patineta *nf* **1** : scooter **2** : skateboard
patinete *nm* : scooter
patio *nm* **1** : courtyard, patio **2 patio de recreo** : playground
patito, -ta *n* : duckling
pato, -ta *n* **1** : duck **2 pato real** : mallard **3 pagar el pato** *fam* : to take the blame
patología *nf* : pathology
patológico, -ca *adj* : pathological
patólogo, -ga *n* : pathologist
patraña *nf* : tall tale, humbug, nonsense
patria *nf* : native land
patriarca *nm* : patriarch — **patriarcal** *adj*
patriarcado *nm* : patriarchy
patrimonio *nm* : patrimony, legacy
patrio, -tria *adj* **1** : native, home ⟨suelo patrio : native soil⟩ **2** : paternal
patriota[1] *adj* : patriotic
patriota[2] *nmf* : patriot
patriotería *nf* : jingoism, chauvinism
patriotero[1], **-ra** *adj* : jingoistic, chauvinistic
patriotero[2], **-ra** *n* : jingoist, chauvinist
patriótico, -ca *adj* : patriotic
patriotismo *nm* : patriotism
patrocinador, -dora *n* : sponsor, patron
patrocinar *vt* : to sponsor
patrocinio *nm* : sponsorship, patronage
patrón[1], **-trona** *n, mpl* **patrones 1** JEFE : boss **2** : patron saint
patrón[2] *nm, pl* **patrones 1** : standard **2** : pattern (in sewing)
patronal *adj* **1** : management, employers' ⟨sindicato patronal : employers' association⟩ **2** : pertaining to a patron saint ⟨fiesta patronal : patron saint's day⟩
patronato *nm* **1** : board, council **2** : foundation, trust
patrono, -na *n* **1** : employer **2** : patron saint
patrulla *nf* **1** : patrol **2** : police car, cruiser
patrullar *v* : to patrol
patrullero *nm* **1** : police car **2** : patrol boat
paulatino, -na *adj* : gradual
paupérrimo, -ma *adj* : destitute, poverty-stricken
pausa *nf* : pause, break
pausado[1] *adv* : slowly, deliberately ⟨habla más pausado : speak more slowly⟩
pausado[2], **-da** *adj* : slow, deliberate — **pausadamente** *adv*
pauta *nf* **1** : rule, guideline **2** : lines *pl* (on paper)
pava *nf Arg, Bol, Chile* : kettle
pavimentar *vt* : to pave
pavimento *nm* : pavement
pavo, -va *n* **1** : turkey **2 pavo real** : peacock **3 comer pavo** : to be a wallflower
pavón *nm, pl* **pavones** : peacock
pavonearse *vr* : to strut, to swagger
pavoneo *nm* : strut, swagger
pavor *nm* TERROR : dread, terror

pavoroso, -sa *adj* ATERRADOR : dreadful, terrifying
payasada *nf* BUFONADA : antic, buffoonery
payasear *vi* : to clown around
payaso, -sa *n* : clown
paz *nf, pl* **paces 1** : peace **2 dejar en paz** : to leave alone **3 hacer las paces** : to make up, to reconcile
pazca, etc. → **pacer**
PC *nmf* : PC, personal computer
peaje *nm* : toll
peatón *nm, pl* **-tones** : pedestrian
peatonal *adj* : pedestrian
peca *nf* : freckle
pecado *nm* : sin
pecador[1], **-dora** *adj* : sinful, sinning
pecador[2], **-dora** *n* : sinner
pecaminoso, -sa *adj* : sinful
pecar {72} *vi* **1** : to sin **2 ～ de** : to be too much (something) ⟨no pecan de amabilidad : they're not overly friendly⟩
pécari *or* **pecarí** *nm* : peccary
pececillo *nm* : small fish
pecera *nf* : fishbowl, fish tank
pecho *nm* **1** : chest **2** SENO : breast, bosom **3** : heart, courage **4 dar el pecho** : to breast-feed **5 tomar a pecho** : to take to heart
pechuga *nf* : breast (of fowl)
pecoso, -sa *adj* : freckled
pectoral *adj* : pectoral
peculado *nm* : embezzlement
peculiar *adj* **1** CARACTERÍSTICO : particular, characteristic **2** RARO : peculiar, uncommon
peculiaridad *nf* : peculiarity
pecuniario, -ria *adj* : pecuniary
pedagogía *nf* : pedagogy
pedagógico, -ca *adj* : pedagogic, pedagogical
pedagogo, -ga *n* : educator, pedagogue
pedal *nm* : pedal
pedalear *vi* : to pedal
pedante[1] *adj* : pedantic
pedante[2] *nmf* : pedant
pedantería *nf* : pedantry
pedazo *nm* TROZO : piece, bit, chunk ⟨caerse a pedazos : to fall to pieces⟩ ⟨hacer pedazos : to tear into shreds, to smash to pieces⟩
pedernal *nm* : flint
pedestal *nm* : pedestal
pedestre *adj* : commonplace, pedestrian
pediatra *nmf* : pediatrician
pediatría *nf* : pediatrics
pediátrico, -ca *adj* : pediatric
pedido *nm* **1** : order (of merchandise) **2** : request
pedigrí *nm* : pedigree
pedir {54} *vt* **1** : to ask for, to request ⟨le pedí un préstamo a Claudia : I asked Claudia for a loan⟩ **2** : to order (food, merchandise) **3 pedir disculpas** *or* **pedir perdón** : to apologize — *vi* **1** : to order **2** : to beg

pedrada *nf* **1** : blow (with a rock or stone) ⟨la ventana se quebró de una pedrada : the window was broken by a rock⟩ **2** *fam* : cutting remark, dig

pedregal *nm* : rocky ground

pedregoso, -sa *adj* : rocky, stony

pedrera *nf* CANTERA : quarry

pedrería *nf* : precious stones *pl*, gems *pl*

pegado, -da *adj* **1** : glued, stuck, stuck together **2** ∼ **a** : right next to

pegajoso, -sa *adj* **1** : sticky, gluey **2** : catchy ⟨una tonada pegajosa : a catchy tune⟩

pegamento *nm* : adhesive, glue

pegar {52} *vt* **1** : to glue, to stick, to paste **2** : to attach, to sew on **3** : to infect with, to give ⟨me pegó el resfriado : he gave me his cold⟩ **4** GOLPEAR : to hit, to deal, to strike ⟨me pegaron un puntapié : they gave me a kick⟩ **5** : to give (out with) ⟨pegó un grito : she let out a yell⟩ — *vi* **1** : to adhere, to stick **2** ∼ **en** : to hit, to strike (against) **3** ∼ **con** : to match, to go with — **pegarse** *vr* **1** GOLPEARSE : to hit oneself, to hit each other **2** : to stick, to take hold **3** : to be contagious **4** *fam* : to tag along, to stick around

pegote *nm* **1** : sticky mess **2** *Mex* : sticker, adhesive label

pegue, etc. → **pegar**

peinado *nm* : hairstyle, hairdo

peinador, -dora *n* : hairdresser

peinar *vt* : to comb — **peinarse** *vr*

peine *nm* : comb

peineta *nf* : ornamental comb

peladez *nf*, *pl* **-deces** *Mex fam* : obscenity, bad language

pelado, -da *adj* **1** : bald, hairless **2** : peeled **3** : bare, barren **4** : broke, penniless **5** *Mex fam* : coarse, crude

pelador *nm* : peeler

pelagra *nf* : pellagra

pelaje *nm* : coat (of an animal), fur

pelar *vt* **1** : to peel, to shell **2** : to skin **3** : to pluck **4** : to remove hair from **5** *fam* : to clean out (of money) — **pelarse** *vr* **1** : to peel **2** *fam* : to get a haircut **3** *Mex fam* : to split, to leave

peldaño *nm* **1** : step, stair **2** : rung

pelea *nf* **1** LUCHA : fight **2** : quarrel

pelear *vi* **1** LUCHAR : to fight **2** DISPUTAR : to quarrel — **pelearse** *vr*

peleón, -ona *adj*, *mpl* **-ones** *Spain* : quarrelsome, argumentative

peleonero, -ra *adj Mex* : quarrelsome

peletería *nf* **1** : fur shop **2** : fur trade

peletero, -ra *n* : furrier

peliagudo, -da *adj* : tricky, difficult, ticklish

pelícano *nm* : pelican

película *nf* **1** : movie, film **2** : (photographic) film **3** : thin covering, layer

peligrar *vi* : to be in danger

peligro *nm* **1** : danger, peril **2** : risk ⟨correr peligro de : to run the risk of⟩

peligroso, -sa *adj* : dangerous, hazardous

pelirrojo[1], -ja *adj* : red-haired, redheaded

pelirrojo[2], -ja *n* : redhead

pellejo *nm* **1** : hide, skin **2 salvar el pellejo** : to save one's neck

pellizcar {72} *vt* **1** : to pinch **2** : to nibble on

pellizco *nm* : pinch

pelo *nm* **1** : hair **2** : fur **3** : pile, nap **4 a pelo** : bareback **5 con pelos y señales** : in great detail **6 no tener pelos en la lengua** : to not mince words, to be blunt **7 tomarle el pelo a alguien** : to tease someone, to pull someone's leg

pelón, -lona *adj*, *mpl* **pelones 1** : bald **2** *fam* : broke **3** *Mex fam* : tough, difficult

pelota *nf* **1** : ball **2** *fam* : head **3 en pelotas** *fam* : naked **4 pelota vasca** : jai alai **5 pasar la pelota** *fam* : to pass the buck

pelotón *nm*, *pl* **-tones** : squad, detachment

peltre *nm* : pewter

peluca *nf* : wig

peluche *nm* : plush (fabric)

peludo, -da *adj* : hairy, shaggy, bushy

peluquería *nf* **1** : hairdresser's, barber shop **2** : hairdressing

peluquero, -ra *n* : barber, hairdresser

peluquín *nm*, *pl* **-quines** TUPÉ : hairpiece, toupee

pelusa *nf* : lint, fuzz

pélvico, -ca *adj* : pelvic

pelvis *nfs & pl* : pelvis

pena *nf* **1** CASTIGO : punishment, penalty ⟨pena de muerte : death penalty⟩ **2** AFLICCIÓN : sorrow, grief ⟨morir de pena : to die of a broken heart⟩ ⟨¡qué pena! : what a shame!, how sad!⟩ **3** DOLOR : pain, suffering **4** DIFICULTAD : difficulty, trouble ⟨a duras penas : with great difficulty⟩ **5** VERGÜENZA : shame, embarrassment **6 valer la pena** : to be worthwhile

penacho *nm* **1** : crest, tuft **2** : plume (of feathers)

penal[1] *adj* : penal

penal[2] *nm* CÁRCEL : prison, penitentiary

penalidad *nf* **1** : hardship **2** : penalty, punishment

penalizar {21} *vt* : to penalize

penalty *nm* : penalty (in sports)

penar *vt* : to punish, to penalize — *vi* : to suffer, to grieve

pendenciero, -ra *adj* : argumentative, quarrelsome

pender *vi* **1** : to hang **2** : to be pending

pendiente[1] *adj* **1** : pending **2 estar pendiente de** : to be watchful of, to be on the lookout for

pendiente[2] *nm Spain* : earring

pendiente[3] *nf* : slope, incline

pendón *nm*, *pl* **pendones** : banner

péndulo *nm* : pendulum

pene *nm* : penis

penetración *nf, pl* **-ciones 1** : penetration **2** : insight
penetrante *adj* **1** : penetrating, piercing **2** : sharp, acute **3** : deep (of a wound)
penetrar *vi* **1** : to penetrate, to sink in **2** ~ **por** *or* ~ **en** : to pierce, to go in, to enter into ⟨el frío penetra por la ventana : the cold comes right in through the window⟩ — *vt* **1** : to penetrate, to permeate **2** : to pierce ⟨el dolor penetró su corazón : sorrow pierced her heart⟩ **3** : to fathom, to understand
penicilina *nf* : penicillin
península *nf* : peninsula — **peninsular** *adj*
penitencia *nf* : penance, penitence
penitenciaría *nf* : penitentiary
penitente *adj & nmf* : penitent
penol *nm* : yardarm
penoso, -sa *adj* **1** : painful, distressing **2** : difficult, arduous **3** : shy, bashful
pensado, -da *adj* **1 bien pensado** : well thought-out **2 en el momento menos pensado** : when least expected **3 poco pensado** : badly thought-out **4 mal pensado** : evil-minded
pensador, -dora *n* : thinker
pensamiento *nm* **1** : thought **2** : thinking **3** : pansy
pensar {55} *vi* **1** : to think **2** ~ **en** : to think about — *vt* **1** : to think **2** : to think about **3** : to intend, to plan on — **pensarse** *vr* : to think over
pensativo, -va *adj* : pensive, thoughtful
pensión *nf, pl* **pensiones 1** JUBILACIÓN : pension **2** : boarding house **3 pensión alimenticia** : alimony
pensionado, -da *n* → **pensionista**
pensionista *nmf* **1** JUBILADO : pensioner, retiree **2** : boarder, lodger
pentágono *nm* : pentagon — **pentagonal** *adj*
pentagrama *nm* : staff (in music)
penúltimo, -ma *adj* : next to last, penultimate
penumbra *nf* : semidarkness
penuria *nf* **1** ESCASEZ : shortage, scarcity **2** : poverty
peña *nf* : rock, crag
peñasco *nm* : crag, large rock
peñón → **peñasco**
peón *nm, pl* **peones 1** : laborer, peon **2** : pawn (in chess)
peonía *nf* : peony
peor¹ *adv* (*comparative of* **mal**) : worse ⟨se llevan peor que antes : they get along worse than before⟩ **2** (*superlative of* **mal**) : worst ⟨me fue peor que a nadie : I did the worst of all⟩
peor² *adj* **1** (*comparative of* **malo**) : worse ⟨es peor que el original : it's worse than the original⟩ **2** (*superlative of* **malo**) : worst ⟨el peor de todos : the worst of all⟩
pepa *nf* : seed, pit (of a fruit)
pepenador, -dora *n CA, Mex* : scavenger
pepenar *vt CA, Mex* : to scavenge, to scrounge

pepinillo *nm* : pickle, gherkin
pepino *nm* : cucumber
pepita *nf* **1** : seed, pip **2** : nugget **3** *Mex* : dried pumpkin seed
peque, etc. → **pecar**
pequeñez *nf, pl* **-ñeces 1** : smallness **2** : trifle, triviality **3 pequeñez de espíritu** : pettiness
pequeño¹, -ña *adj* **1** : small, little ⟨un libro pequeño : a small book⟩ **2** : young **3** BAJO : short
pequeño², -ña *n* : child, little one
pera *nf* : pear
peraltar *vt* : to bank (a road)
perca *nf* : perch (fish)
percal *nm* : percale
percance *nm* : mishap, misfortune
percatarse *vr* ~ **de** : to notice, to become aware of
percebe *nm* : barnacle
percepción *nf, pl* **-ciones 1** : perception **2** : idea, notion **3** COBRO : receipt (of payment), collection
perceptible *adj* : perceptible, noticeable — **perceptiblemente** *adv*
percha *nf* **1** : perch **2** : coat hanger **3** : coatrack, coat hook
perchero *nm* : coatrack
percibir *vt* **1** : to perceive, to notice, to sense **2** : to earn, to draw (a salary)
percudido, -da *adj* : grimy
percudir *vt* : to make grimy — **percudirse** *vr*
percusión *nf, pl* **-siones** : percussion
percusor *or* **percutor** *nm* : hammer (of a firearm)
perdedor¹, -dora *adj* : losing
perdedor², -dora *n* : loser
perder {56} *vt* **1** : to lose **2** : to miss ⟨perdimos la oportunidad : we missed the opportunity⟩ **3** : to waste (time) — *vi* : to lose — **perderse** *vr* EXTRAVIARSE : to get lost, to stray
perdición *nf, pl* **-ciones** : perdition, damnation
pérdida *nf* **1** : loss **2 pérdida de tiempo** : waste of time
perdidamente *adv* : hopelessly
perdido, -da *adj* **1** : lost **2** : inveterate, incorrigible ⟨es un caso perdido : he's a hopeless case⟩ **3** : in trouble, done for **4 de** ~ *Mex fam* : at least
perdigón *nm, pl* **-gones** : shot, pellet
perdiz *nf, pl* **perdices** : partridge
perdón¹ *nm, pl* **perdones** : forgiveness, pardon
perdón² *interj* : excuse me!, sorry!
perdonable *adj* : forgivable
perdonar *vt* **1** DISCULPAR : to forgive, to pardon **2** : to exempt, to excuse
perdurable *adj* : lasting
perdurar *vi* : to last, to endure, to survive
perecedero, -ra *adj* : perishable
perecer {53} *vi* : to perish, to die
peregrinación *nf, pl* **-ciones** : pilgrimage
peregrinaje *nm* → **peregrinación**

peregrino¹, -na *adj* **1** : unusual, odd **2** MIGRATORIO : migratory
peregrino², -na *n* : pilgrim
perejil *nm* : parsley
perenne *adj* : perennial
perentorio, -ria *adj* **1** : peremptory **2** URGENTE : urgent **3** FIJO : fixed, set
pereza *nf* FLOJERA, HOLGAZANERÍA : laziness, idleness
perezoso¹, -sa *adj* FLOJO, HOLGAZÁN : lazy
perezoso² *nm* : sloth (animal)
perfección *nf, pl* **-ciones** : perfection
perfeccionamiento *nm* : perfecting, refinement
perfeccionar *vt* : to perfect, to refine
perfeccionismo *nm* : perfectionism
perfeccionista *nmf* : perfectionist
perfecto, -ta *adj* : perfect — **perfectamente** *adv*
perfidia *nf* : perfidy, treachery
pérfido, -da *adj* : perfidious
perfil *nm* **1** : profile **2 de ~** : sideways, from the side **3 perfiles** *nmpl* RASGOS : features, characteristics
perfilar *vt* : to outline, to define — **perfilarse** *vr* **1** : to be outlined, to be silhouetted **2** : to take shape
perforación *nf, pl* **-ciones 1** : perforation **2** : drilling
perforadora *nf* **1** : hole punch (for paper) **2** : drill (in mining, etc.)
perforar *vt* **1** : to perforate, to pierce **2** : to drill, to bore
perfumar *vt* : to perfume, to scent — **perfumarse** *vr*
perfume *nm* : perfume, scent
pergamino *nm* : parchment
pérgola *nf* : pergola, arbor
pericia *nf* : skill, expertise
pericial *adj* : expert ⟨testigo pericial : expert witness⟩
perico *nm* COTORRA : small parrot
periferia *nf* : periphery
periférico¹, -ca *adj* : peripheral
periférico² *nm* **1** *CA, Mex* : beltway **2** : peripheral
perilla *nf* **1** : goatee **2** : pommel (on a saddle) **3** *Col, Mex* : knob, handle **4 perilla de la oreja** : earlobe **5 de perillas** *fam* : handy, just right
perímetro *nm* : perimeter
periódico¹, -ca *adj* : periodic — **periódicamente** *adv*
periódico² *nm* DIARIO : newspaper
periodismo *nm* : journalism
periodista *nmf* : journalist
periodístico, -ca *adj* : journalistic, news
período *or* **periodo** *nm* : period
peripecia *nf* VICISITUD : vicissitude, reversal ⟨las peripecias de su carrera : the ups and downs of her career⟩
periquito *nm* **1** : parakeet **2 periquito australiano** : budgerigar
periscopio *nm* : periscope
perito, -ta *adj & n* : expert
perjudicar {72} *vt* : to harm, to be detrimental to

perjudicial *adj* : harmful, detrimental
perjuicio *nm* **1** : harm, damage **2 en perjuicio de** : to the detriment of
perjurar *vi* : to perjure oneself
perjurio *nm* : perjury
perjuro, -ra *n* : perjurer
perla *nf* **1** : pearl **2 de perlas** *fam* : wonderfully ⟨me viene de perlas : it suits me just fine⟩
permanecer {53} *vi* **1** QUEDARSE : to remain, to stay **2** SEGUIR : to remain, to continue to be
permanencia *nf* **1** : permanence, continuance **2** ESTANCIA : stay
permanente¹ *adj* **1** : permanent **2** : constant — **permanentemente** *adv*
permanente² *nf* : permanent (wave)
permeabilidad *nf* : permeability
permeable *adj* : permeable
permisible *adj* : permissible, allowable
permisividad *nf* : permissiveness
permisivo, -va *adv* : permissive
permiso *nm* **1** : permission **2** : permit, license **3** : leave, furlough **4 con ~** : excuse me, pardon me
permitir *vt* : to permit, to allow — **permitirse** *vr*
permuta *nf* : exchange
permutar *vt* INTERCAMBIAR : to exchange
pernicioso, -sa *adj* : pernicious, destructive
pernil *nm* **1** : haunch (of an animal) **2** : leg (of meat), ham **3** : trouser leg
perno *nm* : bolt, pin
pernoctar *vi* : to stay overnight, to spend the night
pero¹ *nm* **1** : fault, defect ⟨ponerle peros a : to find fault with⟩ **2** : objection
pero² *conj* : but
perogrullada *nf* : truism, platitude, cliché
peroné *nm* : fibula
perorar *vi* : to deliver a speech
perorata *nf* : oration, long-winded speech
peróxido *nm* : peroxide
perpendicular *adj & nf* : perpendicular
perpetrar *vt* : to perpetrate
perpetuar {3} *vt* ETERNIZAR : to perpetuate
perpetuidad *nf* : perpetuity
perpetuo, -tua *adj* : perpetual — **perpetuamente** *adv*
perplejidad *nf* : perplexity
perplejo, -ja *adj* : perplexed, puzzled
perrada *nf fam* : dirty trick
perrera *nf* : kennel, dog pound
perrero, -ra *n* : dogcatcher
perrito, -ta *n* CACHORRO : puppy, small dog
perro, -rra *n* **1** : dog, bitch *f* **2 perro caliente** : hot dog **3 perro salchicha** : dachshund **4 perro faldero** : lapdog **5 perro cobrador** : retriever
persa¹ *adj & nmf* : Persian
persa² *nm* : Persian (language)

persecución *nf, pl* **-ciones 1** : pursuit, chase **2** : persecution
perseguidor, -dora *n* **1** : pursuer **2** : persecutor
perseguir {75} *vt* **1** : to pursue, to chase **2** : to persecute **3** : to pester, to annoy
perseverancia *nf* : perseverance
perseverar *vi* : to persevere
persiana *nf* : blind, venetian blind
persignarse *vr* SANTIGUARSE : to cross oneself, to make the sign of the cross
persistir *vi* : to persist — **persistencia** *nf* — **persistente** *adj*
persona *nf* : person
personaje *nm* **1** : character (in drama or literature) **2** : personage, celebrity
personal[1] *adj* : personal — **personalmente** *adv*
personal[2] *nm* : personnel, staff
personalidad *nf* : personality
personalizar {21} *vt* : to personalize
personificar {72} *vi* : to personify — **personificación** *nf*
perspectiva *nf* **1** : perspective, view **2** : prospect, outlook
perspicacia *nf* : shrewdness, perspicacity, insight
perspicaz *adj, pl* **-caces** : shrewd, perspicacious
persuadir *vt* : to persuade — **persuadirse** *vr* : to become convinced
persuasión *nf, pl* **-siones** : persuasion
persuasivo, -va *adj* : persuasive
pertenecer {53} *vi* : to belong
perteneciente *adj* ~ **a** : belonging to
pertenencia *nf* **1** : membership **2** : ownership **3 pertenencias** *nfpl* : belongings, possessions
pértiga *nf* GARROCHA : pole ⟨salto de pértiga : pole vault⟩
pertinaz *adj, pl* **-naces 1** OBSTINADO : obstinate **2** PERSISTENTE : persistent
pertinencia *nf* : pertinence, relevance — **pertinente** *adj*
pertrechos *nmpl* : equipment, gear
perturbación *nf, pl* **-ciones** : disturbance, disruption
perturbador, -dora *adj* **1** INQUIETANTE : disturbing, troubling **2** : disruptive
perturbar *vt* **1** : to disturb, to trouble **2** : to disrupt
peruano, -na *adj & n* : Peruvian
perversidad *nf* : perversity, depravity
perversión *nf, pl* **-siones** : perversion
perverso, -sa *adj* : wicked, depraved
pervertido[1], **-da** *adj* DEPRAVADO : perverted, depraved
pervertido[2], **-da** *n* : pervert
pervertir {76} *vt* : to pervert, to corrupt
pesa *nf* **1** : weight **2 levantamiento de pesas** : weightlifting
pesadamente *adv* **1** : heavily **2** : slowly, clumsily
pesadez *nf, pl* **-deces 1** : heaviness **2** : slowness **3** : tediousness
pesadilla *nf* : nightmare

pesado[1], **-da** *adj* **1** : heavy **2** : slow **3** : irritating, annoying **4** : tedious, boring **5** : tough, difficult
pesado[2], **-da** *n fam* : bore, pest
pesadumbre *nf* AFLICCIÓN : grief, sorrow, sadness
pésame *nm* : condolences *pl* ⟨mi más sentido pésame : my heartfelt condolences⟩
pesar[1] *vt* **1** : to weigh **2** EXAMINAR : to consider, to think over — *vi* **1** : to weigh ⟨¿cuánto pesa? : how much does it weigh?⟩ **2** : to be heavy **3** : to weigh heavily, to be a burden ⟨no le pesa : it's not a burden on him⟩ ⟨pesa sobre mi corazón : it weighs upon my heart⟩ **4** INFLUIR : to carry weight, to have bearing **5** (*with personal pronouns*) : to grieve, to sadden ⟨me pesa mucho : I'm very sorry⟩ **6 pese a** : in spite of, despite
pesar[2] *nm* **1** AFLICCIÓN, PENA : sorrow, grief **2** REMORDIMIENTO : remorse **3 a pesar de** : in spite of, despite
pesaroso, -sa *adj* **1** : sad, mournful **2** ARREPENTIDO : sorry, regretful
pesca *nf* : fishing
pescadería *nf* : fish market
pescado *nm* : fish (as food)
pescador, -dora *n* : fisherman *m*, fisherwoman *f*
pescar {72} *vt* **1** : to fish for **2** : to catch **3** *fam* : to get a hold of, to land — *vi* : to fish, to go fishing
pescuezo *nm* : neck
pesebre *nm* : manger
pesero *nm Mex* : minibus
peseta *nf* : peseta (Spanish unit of currency)
pesimismo *nm* : pessimism
pesimista[1] *adj* : pessimistic
pesimista[2] *nmf* : pessimist
pésimo, -ma *adj* : dreadful, abominable
peso *nm* **1** : weight, heaviness **2** : burden, responsibility **3** : weight (in sports) **4** BÁSCULA : scales *pl* **5** : peso
pesque, etc. → **pescar**
pesquería *nf* : fishery
pesquero[1], **-ra** *adj* : fishing ⟨pueblo pesquero : fishing village⟩
pesquero[2] *nm* : fishing boat
pesquisa *nf* INVESTIGACIÓN : inquiry, investigation
pestaña *nf* **1** : eyelash **2** : flange, rim
pestañear *vi* : to blink
pestañeo *nm* : blink
peste *nf* **1** : plague, pestilence **2** : stench, stink **3** : nuisance, pest
pesticida *nm* : pesticide
pestilencia *nf* **1** : stench, foul odor **2** : pestilence
pestilente *adj* **1** : foul, smelly **2** : pestilent
pestillo *nm* CERROJO : bolt, latch
petaca *nf* **1** *Mex* : suitcase **2 petacas** *nfpl Mex fam* : bottom, behind
pétalo *nm* : petal
petardear *vi* : to backfire

petardeo *nm* : backfiring
petardo *nm* : firecracker
petate *nm Mex* : mat
petición *nf, pl* -ciones : petition, request
peticionar *vt* : to petition
peticionario, -ria *n* : petitioner
petirrojo *nm* : robin
peto *nm* : bib (of clothing)
pétreo, -trea *adj* : stone, stony
petrificar {72} *vt* : to petrify
petróleo *nm* : oil, petroleum
petrolero¹, -ra *adj* : oil ⟨industria petrolera : oil industry⟩
petrolero² *nm* : oil tanker
petrolífero, -ra *adj* → **petrolero¹**
petulancia *nf* INSOLENCIA : insolence, petulance
petulante *adj* INSOLENTE : insolent, petulant — **petulantemente** *adv*
petunia *nf* : petunia
peyorativo, -va *adj* : pejorative
pez¹ *nm, pl* **peces** 1 : fish 2 **pez de colores** : goldfish 3 **pez espada** : swordfish 4 **pez gordo** : big shot
pez² *nf, pl* **peces** : pitch, tar
pezón *nm, pl* **pezones** : nipple
pezuña *nf* : hoof ⟨pezuña hendida : cloven hoof⟩
pi *nf* : pi
piadoso, -sa *adj* 1 : compassionate, merciful 2 DEVOTO : pious, devout
pianista *nmf* : pianist, piano player
piano *nm* : piano
piar {85} *vi* : to chirp, to cheep, to tweet
pibe, -ba *n Arg, Uru fam* : kid, child
pica *nf* 1 : pike, lance 2 : goad (in bullfighting) 3 : spade (in playing cards)
picada *nf* 1 : bite, sting (of an insect) 2 : sharp descent
picadillo *nm* 1 : minced meat, hash 2 **hacer picadillo a** : to beat to a pulp
picado, -da *adj* 1 : perforated 2 : minced, chopped 3 : decayed (of teeth) 4 : choppy, rough 5 *fam* : annoyed, miffed
picador *nm* : picador
picadura *nf* 1 : sting, bite 2 : prick, puncture 3 : decay, cavity
picaflor *nm* COLIBRÍ : hummingbird
picana *nf* : goad, prod
picante¹ *adj* 1 : hot, spicy 2 : sharp, cutting 3 : racy, risqué
picante² *nm* 1 : spiciness 2 : hot spices *pl*, hot sauce
picaporte *nm* 1 : latch 2 : door handle 3 ALDABA : door knocker
picar {72} *vt* 1 : to sting, to bite 2 : to peck at 3 : to nibble on 4 : to prick, to puncture, to punch (a ticket) 5 : to grind, to chop 6 : to goad, to incite 7 : to pique, to provoke — *vi* 1 : to itch 2 : to sting 3 : to be spicy 4 : to nibble 5 : to take the bait 6 ~ **en** : to dabble in 7 **picar muy alto** : to aim too high — **picarse** *vr* 1 : to get a cavity, to decay 2 : to get annoyed, to take offense
picardía *nf* 1 : cunning, craftiness 2 : prank, dirty trick

picaresco, -ca *adj* 1 : picaresque 2 : rascally, roguish
pícaro¹, -ra *adj* 1 : mischievous 2 : cunning, sly 3 : off-color, risqué
pícaro², -ra *n* 1 : rogue, scoundrel 2 : rascal
picazón *nf, pl* -zones COMEZÓN : itch
picea *nf* : spruce (tree)
pichel *nm* : pitcher, jug
pichón, -chona *n, mpl* **pichones** 1 : young pigeon, squab 2 *Mex fam* : novice, greenhorn
picnic *nm* : picnic
pico *nm* 1 : peak 2 : point, spike 3 : beak, bill 4 : pick, pickax 5 **y pico** : and a little, and a bit ⟨las siete y pico : a little after seven⟩ ⟨dos metros y pico : a bit over two meters⟩
picor *nm* : itch, irritation
picoso, -sa *adj Mex* : very hot, spicy
picota *nf* 1 : pillory, stock 2 **poner a alguien en la picota** : to put someone on the spot
picotada *nf* → **picotazo**
picotazo *nm* : peck (of a bird)
picotear *vt* : to peck — *vi* : to nibble, to pick
pictórico, -ca *adj* : pictorial
picudo, -da *adj* 1 : pointy, sharp 2 ~ **para** *Mex fam* : clever at, good at
pide, etc. → **pedir**
pie *nm* 1 : foot ⟨a pie : on foot⟩ ⟨de pie : on one's feet, standing⟩ 2 : base, bottom, stem, foot ⟨pie de la cama : foot of the bed⟩ ⟨pie de una lámpara : base of a lamp⟩ ⟨pie de la escalera : bottom of the stairs⟩ ⟨pie de una copa : stem of a glass⟩ 3 : foot (in measurement) ⟨pie cuadrado : square foot⟩ 4 : cue (in theater) 5 **dar pie a** : to give cause for, to give rise to 6 **en pie de igualdad** : on equal footing
piedad *nf* 1 COMPASIÓN : mercy, pity 2 DEVOCIÓN : piety, devotion
piedra *nf* 1 : stone 2 : flint (of a lighter) 3 : hailstone 4 **piedra de afilar** : whetstone, grindstone 5 **piedra angular** : cornerstone 6 **piedra arenisca** : sandstone 7 **piedra caliza** : limestone 8 **piedra imán** : lodestone 9 **piedra de molino** : millstone 10 **piedra de toque** : touchstone
piel *nf* 1 : skin 2 CUERO : leather, hide ⟨piel de venado : deerskin⟩ 3 : fur, pelt 4 CÁSCARA : peel, skin 5 **piel de gallina** : goose bumps *pl* ⟨me pone la piel de gallina : it gives me goose bumps⟩
piélago *nm* **el piélago** : the deep, the ocean
piensa, etc. → **pensar**
pienso *nm* : feed, fodder
pierde, etc. → **perder**
pierna *nf* : leg
pieza *nf* 1 ELEMENTO : piece, part, component ⟨vestido de dos piezas : two-piece dress⟩ ⟨pieza de recambio : spare part⟩ ⟨pieza clave : key element⟩ 2 : piece (in chess) 3 OBRA : piece, work

⟨pieza de teatro : play⟩ 4 : room, bedroom
pifia *nf fam* : goof, blunder
pigargo *nm* : osprey
pigmentación *nf, pl* -**ciones** : pigmentation
pigmento *nm* : pigment
pigmeo, -mea *adj & n* : pygmy, Pygmy
pijama *nm* : pajamas *pl*
pila *nf* 1 BATERÍA : battery ⟨pila de linterna : flashlight battery⟩ 2 MONTÓN : pile, heap 3 : sink, basin, font ⟨pila bautismal : baptismal font⟩ ⟨pila para pájaros : birdbath⟩
pilar *nm* 1 : pillar, column 2 : support, mainstay
píldora *nf* PASTILLA : pill
pillaje *nm* : pillage, plunder
pillar *vt* 1 *fam* : to catch ⟨¡cuidado! ¡nos pillarán! : watch out! they'll catch us!⟩ 2 *fam* : to grasp, to catch on ⟨¿no lo pillas? : don't you get it?⟩
pillo¹, -lla *adj* : cunning, crafty
pillo², -lla *n* 1 : rascal, brat 2 : rogue, scoundrel
pilluelo, -la *n* : urchin
pilón *nm, pl* **pilones** 1 PILA : basin 2 : pillar, tower (for cables), pylon (of a bridge) 3 *Mex* : extra, lagniappe
pilotar *vt* : to pilot, to drive
pilote *nm* : pile (stake)
pilotear → **pilotar**
piloto *nm* 1 : pilot, driver 2 : pilot light
piltrafa *nf* 1 : poor quality meat 2 : wretch 3 **piltrafas** *nfpl* : food scraps
pimentero *nm* : pepper shaker
pimentón *nm, pl* -**tones** 1 : paprika 2 : cayenne pepper
pimienta *nf* 1 : pepper (condiment) 2 **pimienta de Jamaica** : allspice
pimiento *nm* : pepper (fruit) ⟨pimiento verde : green pepper⟩
pináculo *nm* 1 : pinnacle (of a building) 2 : peak, acme
pincel *nm* : paintbrush
pincelada *nf* 1 : brushstroke 2 **últimas pinceladas** : final touches
pinchar *vt* 1 PICAR : to puncture (a tire) 2 : to prick, to stick 3 : to goad, to tease, to needle — *vi* 1 : to be prickly 2 : to get a flat tire 3 *fam* : to get beaten, to lose out — **pincharse** *vr* : to give oneself an injection
pinchazo *nm* 1 : prick, jab 2 : puncture, flat tire
pingüe *adj* 1 : rich, huge (of profits) 2 : lucrative
pingüino *nm* : penguin
pininos *or* **pinitos** *nmpl* : first steps ⟨hacer pininos : to take one's first steps, to toddle⟩
pino *nm* : pine, pine tree
pinta *nf* 1 : dot, spot 2 : pint 3 *fam* : aspect, appearance ⟨las peras tienen buena pinta : the pears look good⟩ 4 **pintas** *nfpl Mex* : graffiti
pintadas *nfpl* : graffiti

pintar *vt* 1 : to paint 2 : to draw, to mark 3 : to describe, to depict — *vi* 1 : to paint, to draw 2 : to look ⟨no pinta bien : it doesn't look good⟩ 3 *fam* : to count ⟨aquí no pinta nada : he has no say here⟩ — **pintarse** *vr* 1 MAQUILLARSE : to put on makeup 2 **pintárselas solo** *fam* : to manage by oneself, to know it all
pintarrajear *vt* : to daub (with paint)
pinto, -ta *adj* : speckled, spotted
pintor, -tora *n* 1 : painter 2 **pintor de brocha gorda** : housepainter, dauber
pintoresco, -ca *adj* : picturesque, quaint
pintura *nf* 1 : paint 2 : painting (art, work of art)
pinza *nf* 1 : clothespin 2 : claw, pincer 3 : pleat, dart 4 **pinzas** *nfpl* : tweezers 5 **pinzas** *nfpl* ALICATES : pliers, pincers
pinzón *nm, pl* **pinzones** : finch
piña *nf* 1 : pineapple 2 : pine cone
piñata *nf* : piñata
piñón *nm, pl* **piñones** 1 : pine nut 2 : pinion
pío¹, pía *adj* 1 DEVOTO : pious, devout 2 : piebald, pied, dappled
pío² *nm* : peep, tweet, cheep
piocha *nf* 1 : pickax 2 *Mex* : goatee
piojo *nm* : louse
piojoso, -sa *adj* 1 : lousy 2 : filthy
pionero¹, -ra *adj* : pioneering
pionero², -ra *n* : pioneer
pipa *nf* : pipe (for smoking)
pipián *nm, pl* **pipianes** *Mex* : a spicy sauce or stew
pipiolo, -la *n* *fam* 1 : greenhorn, novice 2 : kid, youngster
pique¹, etc. → **picar**
pique² *nm* 1 : pique, resentment 2 : rivalry, competition 3 **a pique de** : about to, on the verge of 4 **irse a pique** : to sink, to founder
piqueta *nf* : pickax
piquete *nm* 1 : picketers *pl*, picket line 2 : squad, detachment 3 *Mex* : prick, jab
piquetear *vt* 1 : to picket 2 *Mex* : to prick, to jab
pira *nf* : pyre
piragua *nf* : canoe — **piragüista** *nmf*
pirámide *nf* : pyramid
piraña *nf* : piranha
pirata¹ *adj* : bootleg, pirated
pirata² *nmf* 1 : pirate 2 : bootlegger 3 **pirata aéreo** : hijacker
piratear *vt* 1 : to hijack, to commandeer 2 : to bootleg, to pirate
piratería *nf* : piracy, bootlegging
piromanía *nf* : pyromania
pirómano, -na *n* : pyromaniac
piropo *nm* : flirtatious compliment
pirotecnia *nf* : fireworks *pl*, pyrotechnics *pl*
pirotécnico, -ca *adj* : fireworks, pyrotechnic
pírrico, -ca *adj* : Pyrrhic
pirueta *nf* : pirouette
pirulí *nm* : cone-shaped lollipop

pisada · planta

pisada *nf* **1** : footstep **2** HUELLA : footprint

pisapapeles *nms & pl* : paperweight

pisar *vt* **1** : to step on, to set foot in **2** : to walk all over, to mistreat — *vi* : to step, to walk, to tread

piscina *nf* **1** : swimming pool **2** : fish pond

Piscis *nmf* : Pisces

piso *nm* **1** PLANTA : floor, story **2** SUELO : floor **3** *Spain* : apartment

pisotear *vt* **1** : to stamp on, to trample **2** PISAR : to walk all over **3** : to flout, to disregard

pisotón *nm, pl* **-tones** : stamp, step ⟨sufrieron empujones y pisotones : they were pushed and stepped on⟩

pista *nf* **1** RASTRO : trail, track ⟨siguen la pista de los sospechosos : they're on the trail of the suspects⟩ **2** : clue **3** CAMINO : road, trail **4** : track, racetrack **5** : ring, arena, rink **6 pista de aterrizaje** : runway, airstrip **7 pista de baile** : dance floor

pistacho *nm* : pistachio

pistilo *nm* : pistil

pistola *nf* **1** : pistol, handgun **2** : spray gun

pistolera *nf* : holster

pistolero *nm* : gunman

pistón *nm, pl* **pistones** : piston

pita *nf* **1** : agave **2** : pita fiber **3** : twine

pitar *vi* **1** : to blow a whistle **2** : to whistle, to boo **3** : to beep, to honk, to toot — *vt* : to whistle at, to boo

pitido *nm* **1** : whistle, whistling **2** : beep, honk, toot

pito *nm* **1** SILBATO : whistle **2 no me importa un pito** *fam* : I don't give a damn

pitón *nm, pl* **pitones** **1** : python **2** : point of a bull's horn

pituitario, -ria *adj* : pituitary

pívot *nmf, pl* **pívots** : center (in basketball)

pivote *nm* : pivot

piyama *nmf* : pajamas *pl*

pizarra *nf* **1** : slate **2** : blackboard **3** : scoreboard

pizarrón *nm, pl* **-rrones** : blackboard, chalkboard

pizca *nf* **1** : pinch ⟨una pizca de canela : a pinch of cinnamon⟩ **2** : speck, trace ⟨ni pizca : not a bit⟩ **3** *Mex* : harvest

pizcar {72} *vt Mex* : to harvest

pizque, etc. → pizcar

pizza ['pitsa, 'pisa] *nf* : pizza

pizzería *nf* : pizzeria, pizza parlor

placa *nf* **1** : sheet, plate **2** : plaque, nameplate **3** : plate (in photography) **4** : badge, insignia **5 placa de matrícula** : license plate, tag **6 placa dental** : plaque, tartar

placebo *nm* : placebo

placenta *nf* : placenta, afterbirth

placentero, -ra *adj* AGRADABLE, GRATO : pleasant, agreeable

placer[1] {57} *vi* GUSTAR : to be pleasing ⟨hazlo como te plazca : do it however you please⟩

placer[2] *nm* **1** : pleasure, enjoyment **2 a ~** : as much as one wants

plácido, -da *adj* TRANQUILO : placid, calm

plaga *nf* **1** : plague, infestation, blight **2** CALAMIDAD : disaster, scourge

plagado, -da *adj* **~ de** : filled with, covered with

plagar {52} *vt* : to plague

plagiar *vt* **1** : to plagiarize **2** SECUESTRAR : to kidnap, to abduct

plagiario, -ria *n* **1** : plagiarist **2** SECUESTRADOR : kidnapper, abductor

plagio *nm* **1** : plagiarism **2** SECUESTRO : kidnapping, abduction

plague, etc. → plagar

plan *nm* **1** : plan, strategy, program ⟨plan de inversiones : investment plan⟩ ⟨plan de estudios : curriculum⟩ **2** PLANO : plan, diagram **3** : attitude, intent, purpose ⟨ponte en plan serio : be serious⟩ ⟨estamos en plan de divertirnos : we're looking to have some fun⟩

plana *nf* **1** : page ⟨noticias en primera plana : front-page news⟩ **2 plana mayor** : staff (in the military)

plancha *nf* **1** : iron, ironing **2** : grill, griddle ⟨a la plancha : grilled⟩ **3** : sheet, plate ⟨plancha para hornear : baking sheet⟩ **4** *fam* : blunder, blooper

planchada *nf* : ironing, pressing

planchado *nm* → planchada

planchar *v* : to iron

planchazo *nm fam* : goof, blunder

plancton *nm* : plankton

planeación *nf* → planeamiento

planeador *nm* : glider (aircraft)

planeamiento *nm* : plan, planning

planear *vt* : to plan — *vi* : to glide (in the air)

planeo *nm* : gliding, soaring

planeta *nm* : planet

planetario[1], **-ria** *adj* **1** : planetary **2** : global, worldwide

planetario[2] *nm* : planetarium

planicie *nf* : plain

planificación *nf* : planning ⟨planificación familiar : family planning⟩

planificar {72} *vt* : to plan

planilla *nf* **1** LISTA : list **2** NÓMINA : payroll **3** TABLA : chart, table **4** *Mex* : slate, ticket (of candidates) **5 planilla de cálculo** *Arg, Chile* : spreadsheet

plano[1], **-na** *adj* : flat, level, plane

plano[2] *nm* **1** PLAN : map, plan **2** : plane (surface) **3** NIVEL : level ⟨en un plano personal : on a personal level⟩ **4** : shot (in photography) **5 de ~** : flatly, outright, directly ⟨se negó de plano : he flatly refused⟩

planta *nf* **1** : plant ⟨planta de interior : houseplant⟩ **2** FÁBRICA : plant, factory **3** PISO : floor, story **4** : staff, employees *pl* **5** : sole (of the foot)

plantación *nf, pl* **-ciones 1** : plantation **2** : planting
plantado, -da *adj* **1** : planted **2 dejar plantado** : to stand up (a date), to dump (a lover)
plantar *vt* **1** : to plant, to sow ⟨plantar de flores : to plant with flowers⟩ **2** : to put in, to place **3** *fam* : to plant, to land ⟨plantar un beso : to plant a kiss⟩ **4** *fam* : to leave, to jilt — **plantarse** *vr* **1** : to stand firm **2** *fam* : to arrive, to show up **3** *fam* : to balk
planteamiento *nm* **1** : approach, position ⟨el planteamiento feminista : the feminist viewpoint⟩ **2** : explanation, exposition **3** : proposal, suggestion, plan
plantear *vt* **1** : to set forth, to bring up, to suggest **2** : to establish, to set up **3** : to create, to pose (a problem) — **plantearse** *vr* **1** : to think about **2** : to arise
plantel *nm* **1** : educational institution **2** : staff, team
planteo → **planteamiento**
plantilla *nf* **1** : insole **2** : pattern, template, stencil **3** *Mex, Spain* : staff, roster of employees
plantío *nm* : field (planted with a crop)
plantón *nm, pl* **plantones 1** : seedling **2** : long wait ⟨darle a alguien un plantón : to stand someone up⟩
plañidero[1], -ra *adj* : mournful
plañidero[2], -ra *nf* : hired mourner
plañir {38} *v* : to mourn, to lament
plasma *nm* : plasma
plasmar *vt* : to express, to give form to — **plasmarse** *vr*
plasta *nf* : soft mass, lump
plástica *nf* : modeling, sculpture
plasticidad *nf* : plasticity
plástico[1], -ca *adj* : plastic
plástico[2] *nm* : plastic
plastificar {72} *vt* : to laminate
plata *nf* **1** : silver **2** : money
plataforma *nf* **1** ESTRADO, TARIMA : platform, dais **2** : platform (in politics) **3** : springboard, stepping stone **4 plataforma continental** : continental shelf **5 plataforma de lanzamiento** : launchpad **6 plataforma petrolífera** : oil rig (at sea)
platal *nm* : large sum of money, fortune
platanal *nm* : banana plantation
platanero[1], -ra *adj* : banana, banana-producing
platanero[2], -ra *n* : banana grower
plátano *nm* **1** : banana **2** : plantain **3 plátano macho** *Mex* : plantain
platea *nf* : orchestra, pit (in a theater)
plateado, -da *adj* **1** : silver, silvery **2** : silver-plated
plática *nf* **1** : talk, lecture **2** : chat, conversation
platicar {72} *vi* : to talk, to chat — *vt Mex* : to tell, to say
platija *nf* : flatfish, flounder

platillo *nm* **1** : saucer ⟨platillo volador : flying saucer⟩ **2** : cymbal **3** *Mex* : dish ⟨platillos típicos : local dishes⟩
platino *nm* : platinum
plato *nm* **1** : plate, dish ⟨lavar los platos : to do the dishes⟩ **2** : serving, helping **3** : course (of a meal) **4** : dish ⟨plato típico : typical dish⟩ **5** : home plate (in baseball) **6 plato hondo** : soup bowl
plató *nm* : set (in the movies)
platónico, -ca *adj* : platonic
playa *nf* : beach, seashore
playera *nf* **1** : canvas sneaker **2** *CA, Mex* : T-shirt
plaza *nf* **1** : square, plaza **2** : marketplace **3** : room, space, seat (in a vehicle) **4** : post, position **5 plaza fuerte** : stronghold, fortified city **6 plaza de toros** : bullring
plazca, etc. → **placer**
plazo *nm* **1** : period, term ⟨un plazo de cinco días : a period of five days⟩ ⟨a largo plazo : long-term⟩ **2** ABONO : installment ⟨pagar a plazos : to pay in installments⟩
pleamar *nf* : high tide
plebe *nf* : common people, masses *pl*
plebeyo[1], -ya *adj* : plebeian
plebeyo[2], -ya *n* : plebeian, commoner
plegable *adj* : folding, collapsible
plegadizo → **plegable**
plegar {49} *vt* DOBLAR : to fold, to bend — **plegarse** *vr* : to give in, to yield
plegaria *nf* ORACIÓN : prayer
pleito *nm* **1** : lawsuit **2** : fight, argument, dispute
plenamente *adv* COMPLETAMENTE : fully, completely
plenario, -ria *adj* : plenary, full
plenilunio *nm* : full moon
plenipotenciario, -ria *n* : plenipotentiary
plenitud *nf* : fullness, abundance
pleno, -na *adj* COMPLETO ((*often used as an intensifier*)) : full, complete ⟨en pleno uso de sus facultades : in full command of his faculties⟩ ⟨en plena noche : in the middle of the night⟩ ⟨en pleno corazón de la ciudad : right in the heart of the city⟩
plétora *nf* : plethora
pleuresía *nf* : pleurisy
pliega, pliegue etc. → **plegar**
pliego *nm* **1** HOJA : sheet of paper **2** : sealed document
pliegue *nm* **1** DOBLEZ : crease, fold **2** : pleat
plisar *vt* : to pleat
plomada *nf* **1** : plumb line **2** : sinker
plomería *nf* FONTANERÍA : plumbing
plomero, -ra *n* FONTANERO : plumber
plomizo, -za *adj* : leaden
plomo *nm* **1** : lead **2** : plumb line **3** : fuse **4** *fam* : bore, drag **5 a～** : plumb, straight
plugo, etc. → **placer**
pluma *nf* **1** : feather **2** : pen **3 pluma fuente** : fountain pen

plumaje *nm* : plumage
plumero *nm* : feather duster
plumilla *nf* : nib
plumón *nm, pl* **plumones** : down
plumoso, -sa *adj* : feathery, downy
plural *adj & nm* : plural
pluralidad *nf* : plurality
pluralizar {21} *vt* : to pluralize
pluriempleado, -da *adj* : holding more than one job
pluriempleo *nm* : moonlighting
plus *nm* : bonus
plusvalía *nf* : appreciation, capital gain
Plutón *nm* : Pluto
plutocracia *nf* : plutocracy
plutonio *nm* : plutonium
población *nf, pl* **-ciones 1** : population **2** : city, town, village
poblado¹, -da *adj* **1** : inhabited, populated **2** : full, thick ⟨cejas pobladas : bushy eyebrows⟩
poblado² *nm* : village, settlement
poblador, -dora *n* : settler
poblar {19} *vt* **1** : to populate, to inhabit **2** : to settle, to colonize **3 ~ de** : to stock with, to plant with — **poblarse** *vr* : to fill up, to become crowded
pobre¹ *adj* **1** : poor, impoverished **2** : unfortunate ⟨¡pobre de mí! : poor me!⟩ **3** : weak, deficient ⟨una dieta pobre : a poor diet⟩
pobre² *nmf* : poor person ⟨los pobres : the poor⟩ ⟨¡pobre! : poor thing!⟩
pobremente *adv* : poorly
pobreza *nf* : poverty
pocilga *nf* CHIQUERO : pigsty, pigpen
pocillo *nm* : small coffee cup, demitasse
poción *nf, pl* **pociones** : potion
poco¹ *adv* **1** : little, not much ⟨poco probable : not very likely⟩ ⟨come poco : he doesn't eat much⟩ **2** : a short time, a while ⟨tardaremos poco : we won't be very long⟩ **3 poco antes** : shortly before **4 poco después** : shortly after
poco², -ca *adj* **1** : little, not much, (a) few ⟨tengo poco dinero : I don't have much money⟩ ⟨en no pocas ocasiones : on more than a few occasions⟩ ⟨poca gente : few people⟩ **2 pocas veces** : rarely
poco³, -ca *pron* **1** : little, few ⟨le falta poco para terminar : he's almost finished⟩ ⟨uno de los pocos que quedan : one of the remaining few⟩ **2 un poco** : a little, a bit ⟨un poco de vino : a little wine⟩ ⟨un poco extraño : a bit strange⟩ **3 a ~ Mex** (*used to express disbelief*) ⟨¿a poco no se te hizo difícil? : you mean you didn't find it difficult?⟩ **4 de a poco** : little by little **5 hace poco** : not long ago **6 poco a poco** : little by little **7 dentro de poco** : shortly, in a little while **8 por ~** : nearly, almost
podar *vt* : to prune, to trim
poder¹ {58} *v aux* **1** : to be able to, can ⟨no puede hablar : he can't speak⟩ **2** (*expressing possibility*) : might, may ⟨puede llover : it may rain at any moment⟩ ⟨¿cómo puede ser? : how can that be?⟩ **3** (*expressing permission*) : can, may ⟨¿puedo ir a la fiesta? : can I go to the party?⟩ ⟨¿se puede? : may I come in?⟩ — *vi* **1** : to beat, to defeat ⟨cree que le puede a cualquiera : he thinks he can beat anyone⟩ **2** : to be possible ⟨¿crees que vendrán? — puede (que sí) : do you think they'll come? — maybe⟩ **3 ~ con** : to cope with, to manage ⟨¡no puedo con estos niños! : I can't handle these children!⟩ **4 no poder más** : to have had enough ⟨no puede más : she can't take anymore⟩ **5 no poder menos que** : to not be able to help ⟨no pudo menos que asombrarse : she couldn't help but be amazed⟩
poder² *nm* **1** : control, power ⟨poder adquisitivo : purchasing power⟩ **2** : authority ⟨el poder legislativo : the legislature⟩ **3** : possession ⟨está en mi poder : it's in my hands⟩ **4** : strength, force ⟨poder militar : military might⟩
poderío *nm* **1** : power **2** : wealth, influence
poderoso, -sa *adj* **1** : powerful **2** : wealthy, influential **3** : effective
podiatría *nf* : podiatry
podio *nm* : podium
pódium → **podio**
podología *nf* : podiatry, chiropody
podólogo, -ga *n* : podiatrist, chiropodist
podrá, etc. → **poder**
podredumbre *nf* **1** : decay, rottenness **2** : corruption
podrido, -da *adj* **1** : rotten, decayed **2** : corrupt
podrir → **pudrir**
poema *nm* : poem
poesía *nf* **1** : poetry **2** POEMA : poem
poeta *nmf* : poet
poético, -ca *adj* : poetic, poetical
pogrom *nm* : pogrom
póker *or* **poker** *nm* : poker (card game)
polaco¹, -ca *adj* : Polish
polaco², -ca *n* : Pole, Polish person
polaco³ *nm* : Polish (language)
polar *adj* : polar
polarizar {21} *vt* : to polarize — **polarizarse** *vr* — **polarización** *nf*
polea *nf* : pulley
polémica *nf* CONTROVERSIA : controversy, polemics
polémico, -ca *adj* CONTROVERTIDO : controversial, polemical
polen *nm, pl* **pólenes** : pollen
policía¹ *nf* : police
policía² *nmf* : police officer, policeman *m*, policewoman *f*
policíaco, -ca *or* **policiaco, -ca** *adj* : police ⟨novela policíaca : detective story⟩
policial *adj* : police
poliéster *nm* : polyester
poligamia *nf* : polygamy
polígamo¹, -ma *adj* : polygamous
polígamo², -ma *n* : polygamist
polígono *nm* : polygon — **poligonal** *adj*

poliinsaturado, -da *adj* : polyunsaturated
polilla *nf* : moth
polimerizar {21} *vt* : to polymerize
polímero *nm* : polymer
polinesio, -sia *adj & n* : Polynesian
polinizar {21} *vt* : to pollinate — **polinización** *nf*
polio *nf* : polio
poliomielitis *nf* : poliomyelitis, polio
polisón *nm, pl* **-sones** : bustle (on clothing)
politécnico, -ca *adj* : polytechnic
politeísmo *nm* : polytheism — **politeísta** *adj & nmf*
política *nf* **1** : politics **2** : policy
políticamente *adv* : politically
político[1], **-ca** *adj* **1** : political **2** : tactful, politic **3** : by marriage ⟨padre político : father-in-law⟩
político[2], **-ca** *n* : politician
póliza *nf* : policy ⟨póliza de seguros : insurance policy⟩
polizón *nm, pl* **-zones** : stowaway ⟨viajar de polizón : to stow away⟩
polka *nf* : polka
polla *nf* APUESTA : bet
pollera *nf* **1** : chicken coop **2** : skirt
pollero, -ra *n* **1** : poulterer **2** : poultry farm **3** *Mex fam* COYOTE : smuggler of illegal immigrants
pollito, -ta *n* : chick, young bird, fledgling
pollo, -lla *n* **1** : chicken **2** POLLITO : chick **3** JOVEN : young man *m*, young lady *f*
polluelo *nm* → **pollito**
polo *nm* **1** : pole ⟨el Polo Norte : the North Pole⟩ ⟨polo negativo : negative pole⟩ **2** : polo (sport) **3** : polo shirt **4** : focal point, center **5 polo opuesto** : exact opposite
polución *nf, pl* **-ciones** CONTAMINACIÓN : pollution
polvareda *nf* **1** : cloud of dust **2** : uproar, fuss
polvera *nf* : compact (for face powder)
polvo *nm* **1** : dust **2** : powder **3 polvos** *nmpl* : face powder **4 polvos de hornear** : baking powder **5 hacer polvo** *fam* : to crush, to shatter ⟨vas a hacer polvo el reloj : you're going to destroy your watch⟩
pólvora *nf* **1** : gunpowder **2** : fireworks *pl*
polvoriento, -ta *adj* : dusty, powdery
polvorín *nm, pl* **-rines** : magazine, storehouse (for explosives)
pomada *nf* : ointment, cream
pomelo *nm* : grapefruit
pómez *nf or* **piedra pómez** : pumice
pomo *nm* **1** : pommel (on a sword) **2** : knob, handle **3** : perfume bottle
pompa *nf* **1** : bubble **2** : pomp, splendor **3 pompas fúnebres** : funeral
pompón *nm, pl* **pompones** BORLA : pom-pom
pomposidad *nf* **1** : pomp, splendor **2** : pomposity, ostentation

pomposo, -sa *adj* : pompous — **pomposamente** *adv*
pómulo *nm* : cheekbone
pon → **poner**
ponchadura *nf Mex* : puncture, flat (tire)
ponchar *vt* **1** : to strike out (in baseball) **2** *Mex* : to puncture — **poncharse** *vr* **1** *Col, Ven* : to strike out (in baseball) **2** *Mex* : to blow out (of a tire)
ponche *nm* **1** : punch (drink) **2 ponche de huevo** : eggnog
poncho *nm* : poncho
ponderación *nf, pl* **-ciones** **1** : consideration, deliberation **2** : high praise
ponderar *vt* **1** : to weigh, to consider **2** : to speak highly of
pondrá, etc. → **poner**
ponencia *nf* **1** DISCURSO : paper, presentation, address **2** INFORME : report
ponente *nmf* : speaker, presenter
poner {60} *vt* **1** COLOCAR : to put, to place ⟨pon el libro en la mesa : put the book on the table⟩ **2** AGREGAR, AÑADIR : to put in, to add **3** : to put on (clothes) **4** CONTRIBUIR : to contribute **5** ESCRIBIR : to put in writing ⟨no le puso su nombre : he didn't put his name on it⟩ **6** IMPONER : to set, to impose **7** EXPONER : to put, to expose ⟨lo puso en peligro : she put him in danger⟩ **8** : to prepare, to arrange ⟨poner la mesa : to set the table⟩ **9** : to name ⟨le pusimos Ana : we called her Ana⟩ **10** ESTABLECER : to set up, to establish ⟨puso un restaurante : he opened up a restaurant⟩ **11** INSTALAR : to install, to put in **12** (*with an adjective or adverb*) : to make ⟨siempre lo pones de mal humor : you always put him in a bad mood⟩ **13** : to turn on, to switch on **14** SUPONER : to suppose ⟨pongamos que no viene : supposing he doesn't come⟩ **15** : to lay (eggs) **16** ~ **a** : to start (someone doing something) ⟨lo puse a trabajar : I put him to work⟩ **17** ~ **de** : to place as ⟨la pusieron de directora : they made her director⟩ **18** ~ **en** : to put in (a state or condition) ⟨poner en duda : to call into question⟩ — *vi* **1** : to contribute **2** : to lay eggs — **ponerse** *vr* **1** : to move (into a position) ⟨ponerse de pie : to stand up⟩ **2** : to put on, to wear **3** : to become, to turn ⟨se puso colorado : he turned red⟩ **4** : to set (of the sun or moon)
poni *or* **poney** *nm* : pony
ponga, etc. → **poner**
poniente *nm* **1** OCCIDENTE : west **2** : west wind
ponqué *nm Col, Ven* : cake
pontifical *adj* : pontifical
pontificar {72} *vi* : to pontificate
pontífice *nm* : pontiff, pope
pontón *nm, pl* **pontones** : pontoon
ponzoña *nf* VENENO : poison — **ponzoñoso, -sa** *adj*

popa *nf* **1** : stern **2 a ~** : astern, abaft, aft

popelín *nm, pl* **-lines** : poplin

popelina *nf* : poplin

popote *nm Mex* : (drinking) straw

populachero, -ra *adj* : common, popular, vulgar

populacho *nm* : rabble, masses *pl*

popular *adj* **1** : popular **2** : traditional **3** : colloquial

popularidad *nf* : popularity

popularizar {21} *vt* : to popularize — **popularizarse** *vr*

populista *adj & nmf* : populist — **populismo** *nm*

populoso, -sa *adj* : populous

popurrí *nm* : potpourri

por *prep* **1** : for, during ⟨se quedaron allí por la semana : they stayed there during the week⟩ ⟨por el momento : for now, at the moment⟩ **2** : around, during ⟨por noviembre empieza a nevar : around November it starts to snow⟩ ⟨por la mañana : in the morning⟩ **3** : around (a place) ⟨debe estar por allí : it must be over there⟩ ⟨por todas partes : everywhere⟩ **4** : by, through, along ⟨por la puerta : through the door⟩ ⟨pasé por tu casa : I stopped by your house⟩ ⟨por la costa : along the coast⟩ **5** : for, for the sake of ⟨lo hizo por su madre : he did it for his mother⟩ ⟨¡por Dios! : for heaven's sake!⟩ **6** : because of, on account of ⟨llegué tarde por el tráfico : I arrived late because of the traffic⟩ ⟨dejar por imposible : to give up as impossible⟩ **7** : per ⟨60 millas por hora : 60 miles per hour⟩ ⟨por docena : by the dozen⟩ **8** : for, in exchange for, instead of ⟨su hermana habló por él : his sister spoke on his behalf⟩ **9** : by means of ⟨hablar por teléfono : to talk on the phone⟩ ⟨por escrito : in writing⟩ **10** : as for ⟨por mí : as far as I'm concerned⟩ **11** : times ⟨tres por dos son seis : three times two is six⟩ **12** SEGÚN : from, according to ⟨por lo que dices : judging from what you're telling me⟩ **13** : as, for ⟨por ejemplo : for example⟩ **14** : by ⟨hecho por mi abuela : made by my grandmother⟩ ⟨por correo : by mail⟩ **15** : for, in order to ⟨lucha por ganar su respeto : he struggles to win her respect⟩ **16 estar por** : to be about to **17 por ciento** : percent **18 por favor** : please **19 por lo tanto** : therefore, consequently **20 ¿por qué?** : why? **21 por que → porque 22 por . . . que** : no matter how ⟨por mucho que intente : no matter how hard I try⟩ **23 por si** *or* **por si acaso** : just in case

porcelana *nf* : china, porcelain

porcentaje *nm* : percentage

porche *nm* : porch

porción *nf, pl* **porciones** **1** : portion **2** PARTE : part, share **3** RACIÓN : serving, helping

pordiosear *vi* MENDIGAR : beg

pordiosero, -ra *n* MENDIGO : beggar

porfiado, -da *adj* OBSTINADO, TERCO : obstinate, stubborn — **porfiadamente** *adv*

porfiar {85} *vi* : to insist, to persist

pormenor *nm* DETALLE : detail

pormenorizar {21} *vi* : to go into detail — *vt* : to tell in detail

pornografía *nf* : pornography

pornográfico, -ca *adj* : pornographic

poro *nm* : pore

poroso, -sa *adj* : porous — **porosidad** *nf*

poroto *nm Arg, Chile, Uru* : bean

porque *conj* **1** : because **2** *or* **por que** : in order that

porqué *nm* : reason, cause

porquería *nf* **1** SUCIEDAD : dirt, filth **2** : nastiness, vulgarity **3** : worthless thing, trifle **4** : junk food

porra *nf* **1** : nightstick, club **2** *Mex* : cheer, yell ⟨los aficionados le echaban porras : the fans cheered him on⟩

porrazo *nm* **1** : blow, whack **2 de golpe y porrazo** : suddenly

porrista *nmf* **1** : cheerleader **2** : fan, supporter

portaaviones *nms & pl* : aircraft carrier

portada *nf* **1** : title page **2** : cover **3** : facade, front

portador, -dora *n* : carrier, bearer

portafolio *or* **portafolios** *nm, pl* **-lios** **1** MALETÍN : briefcase **2** : portfolio (of investments)

portal *nm* **1** : portal, doorway **2** VESTÍBULO : vestibule, hall

portar *vt* **1** : to carry, to bear **2** : to wear — **portarse** *vr* CONDUCIRSE : to behave ⟨pórtate bien : behave yourself⟩

portátil *adj* : portable

portaviandas *nms & pl* : lunch box

portaviones *nm* → **portaaviones**

portavoz *nmf, pl* **-voces** : spokesperson, spokesman *m*, spokeswoman *f*

portazo *nm* : slam (of a door)

porte *nm* **1** ASPECTO : bearing, demeanor **2** TRANSPORTE : transport, carrying ⟨porte pagado : postage paid⟩

portento *nm* MARAVILLA : marvel, wonder

portentoso, -sa *adj* MARAVILLOSO : marvelous, wonderful

porteño, -ña *adj* : of or from Buenos Aires

portería *nf* **1** ARCO : goal, goalposts *pl* **2** : superintendent's office

portero, -ra *n* **1** ARQUERO : goalkeeper, goalie **2** : doorman *m* **3** : janitor, superintendent

pórtico *nm* : portico

portilla *nf* : porthole

portón *nm, pl* **portones** **1** : main door **2** : gate

portugués¹, -guesa *adj & n, mpl* **-gueses** : Portuguese

portugués² *nm* : Portuguese (language)

porvenir *nm* FUTURO : future
pos *adv* **en pos de** : in pursuit of
posada *nf* **1** : inn **2** *Mex* : Advent celebration
posadero, -ra *n* : innkeeper
posar *vi* : to pose — *vt* : to place, to lay — **posarse** *vr* **1** : to land, to light, to perch **2** : to settle, to rest
posavasos *nms & pl* : coaster (for drinks)
posdata → postdata
pose *nf* : pose
poseedor, -dora *n* : possessor, holder
poseer {20} *vt* : to possess, to hold, to have
poseído, -da *adj* : possessed
posesión *nf, pl* **-siones** : possession
posesionarse *vr* ~ **de** : to take possession of, to take over
posesivo[1], **-va** *adj* : possessive
posesivo[2] *nm* : possessive case
posguerra *nf* : postwar period
posibilidad *nf* **1** : possibility **2 posibilidades** *nfpl* : means, income
posibilitar *vt* : to make possible, to permit
posible *adj* : possible — **posiblemente** *adv*
posición *nf, pl* **-ciones 1** : position, place **2** : status, standing **3** : attitude, stance
posicionar *vt* **1** : to position, to place **2** : to establish — **posicionarse** *vr*
positivo[1], **-va** *adj* : positive
positivo[2] *nm* : print (in photography)
poso *nm* **1** : sediment, dregs *pl* **2** : grounds *pl* (of coffee)
posoperatorio, -ria *adj* : postoperative
posponer {60} *vt* **1** : to postpone **2** : to put behind, to subordinate
pospuso, etc. → posponer
posta *nf* : relay race
postal[1] *adj* : postal
postal[2] *nf* : postcard
postdata *nf* : postscript
poste *nm* : post, pole ⟨poste de teléfonos : telephone pole⟩
póster *or* **poster** *nm, pl* **pósters** *or* **posters** : poster, placard
postergación *nf, pl* **-ciones** : postponement, deferring
postergar {52} *vt* **1** : to delay, to postpone **2** : to pass over (an employee)
posteridad *nf* : posterity
posterior *adj* **1** ULTERIOR : later, subsequent **2** TRASERO : back, rear
postgrado *nm* : graduate course
postgraduado, -da *n* : graduate student, postgraduate
postigo *nm* **1** CONTRAVENTANA : shutter **2** : small door, wicket gate
postilla *nf* : scab
postizo, -za *adj* : artificial, false ⟨dentadura postiza : dentures⟩
postnatal *adj* : postnatal
postor, -tora *n* : bidder ⟨mejor postor : highest bidder⟩

postración *nf, pl* **-ciones 1** : prostration **2** ABATIMIENTO : depression
postrado, -da *adj* **1** : prostrate **2 postrado en cama** : bedridden
potranco, -ca *n* → potro[1]
postrar *vt* DEBILITAR : to debilitate, to weaken — **postrarse** *vr* : to prostrate oneself
postre *nm* : dessert
postrero, -ra *adj* (**postrer** *before masculine singular nouns*) ÚLTIMO : last
postulación *nf, pl* **-ciones 1** : collection **2** : nomination (of a candidate)
postulado *nm* : postulate, assumption
postulante, -ta *n* **1** : postulant **2** : candidate, applicant
postular *vt* **1** : to postulate **2** : to nominate **3** : to propose — **postularse** *vr* : to run, to be a candidate
póstumo, -ma *adj* : posthumous — **póstumamente** *adv*
postura *nf* **1** : posture, position (of the body) **2** ACTITUD, POSICIÓN : position, stance
potable *adj* : drinkable, potable
potaje *nm* : thick vegetable soup, pottage
potasa *nf* : potash
potasio *nm* : potassium
pote *nm* **1** OLLA : pot **2** : jar, container
potencia *nf* **1** : power ⟨potencias extranjeras : foreign powers⟩ ⟨elevado a la tercera potencia : raised to the third power⟩ **2** : capacity, potency
potencial *adj & nm* : potential
potenciar *vt* : to promote, to foster
potenciómetro *nm* : dimmer, dimmer switch
potentado, -da *n* **1** SOBERANO : potentate, sovereign **2** MAGNATE : tycoon, magnate
potente *adj* **1** : powerful, strong **2** : potent, virile
potestad *nf* **1** AUTORIDAD : authority, jurisdiction **2 patria potestad** : custody, guardianship
potrero *nm* **1** : field, pasture **2** : cattle ranch
potro[1], **-tra** *n* : colt *m*, filly *f*
potro[2] *nm* **1** : rack (for torture) **2** : horse (in gymnastics)
pozo *nm* **1** : well ⟨pozo de petróleo : oil well⟩ **2** : deep pool (in a river) **3** : mine shaft **4** *Arg, Par, Uru* : pothole **5 pozo séptico** : cesspool
pozole *nm* *Mex* : spicy stew made with pork and hominy
práctica *nf* **1** : practice, experience **2** EJERCICIO : exercising ⟨la práctica de la medicina : the practice of medicine⟩ **3** APLICACIÓN : application, practice ⟨poner en práctica : to put into practice⟩ **4 prácticas** *nfpl* : training
practicable *adj* : practicable, feasible
prácticamente *adv* : practically
practicante[1] *adj* : practicing ⟨católicos practicantes : practicing Catholics⟩

practicante[2] *nmf* : practicer, practitioner

practicar {72} *vt* **1** : to practice **2** : to perform, to carry out **3** : to exercise (a profession) — *vi* : to practice

práctico, -ca *adj* : practical, useful

pradera *nf* : grassland, prairie

prado *nm* **1** CAMPO : field, meadow **2** : park

pragmático, -ca *adj* : pragmatic — **pragmáticamente** *adv*

pragmatismo *nm* : pragmatism

preámbulo *nm* **1** INTRODUCCIÓN : preamble, introduction **2** RODEO : evasion ⟨gastar preámbulos : to beat around the bush⟩

prebélico, -ca *adj* : antebellum

prebenda *nf* : privilege, perquisite

precalentar {55} *vt* : to preheat

precariedad *nf* : precariousness

precario, -ria *adj* : precarious — **precariamente** *adv*

precaución *nf, pl* **-ciones** **1** : precaution ⟨medidas de precaución : precautionary measures⟩ **2** PRUDENCIA : caution, care ⟨con precaución : cautiously⟩

precautorio, -ria *adj* : precautionary

precaver *vt* PREVENIR : to prevent, to guard against — **precaverse** *vr* PREVENIRSE : to take precautions, to be on guard

precavido, -da *adj* CAUTELOSO : cautious, prudent

precedencia *nf* : precedence, priority

precedente[1] *adj* : preceding, previous

precedente[2] *nm* : precedent

preceder *v* : to precede

precepto *nm* : rule, precept

preciado, -da *adj* : esteemed, prized, valuable

preciarse *vr* **1** JACTARSE : to boast, to brag **2** ~ **de** : to pride oneself on

precinto *nm* : seal

precio *nm* **1** : price **2** : cost, sacrifice ⟨a cualquier precio : whatever the cost⟩

preciosidad *nf* : beautiful thing ⟨este vestido es una preciosidad : this dress is lovely⟩

precioso, -sa *adj* **1** HERMOSO : beautiful, exquisite **2** VALIOSO : precious, valuable

precipicio *nm* **1** : precipice **2** RUINA : ruin

precipitación *nf, pl* **-ciones** **1** PRISA : haste, hurry, rush **2** : precipitation, rain, snow

precipitado, -da *adj* **1** : hasty, sudden **2** : rash — **precipitadamente** *adv*

precipitar *vt* **1** APRESURAR : to hasten, to speed up **2** ARROJAR : to hurl, to throw — **precipitarse** *vr* **1** APRESURARSE : to rush **2** : to act rashly **3** ARROJARSE : to throw oneself

precisamente *adv* JUSTAMENTE : precisely, exactly

precisar *vt* **1** : to specify, to determine exactly **2** NECESITAR : to need, to require — *vi* : to be necessary

precisión *nf, pl* **-siones** **1** EXACTITUD : precision, accuracy **2** CLARIDAD : clarity (of style, etc.) **3** NECESIDAD : necessity ⟨tener precisión de : to have need of⟩

preciso, -sa *adj* **1** EXACTO : precise **2** : very, exact ⟨en ese preciso instante : at that very instant⟩ **3** NECESARIO : necessary

precocidad *nf* : precocity

precocinar *vt* : to precook

preconcebir {54} *vt* : to preconceive

precondición *nf, pl* **-ciones** : precondition

preconizar {21} *vt* **1** : to recommend, to advocate **2** : to extol

precoz *adj, pl* **precoces** **1** : precocious **2** : early, premature — **precozmente** *adv*

precursor, -sora *n* : forerunner, precursor

predecesor, -sora *n* ANTECESOR : predecessor

predecir {11} *vt* : to foretell, to predict

predestinado, -da *adj* : predestined, fated

predestinar *vt* : to predestine — **predestinación** *nf*

predeterminar *vt* : to predetermine

prédica *nf* SERMÓN : sermon

predicado *nm* : predicate

predicador, -dora *n* : preacher

predicar {72} *v* : to preach

predicción *nf, pl* **-ciones** **1** : prediction **2** PRONÓSTICO : forecast ⟨predicción del tiempo : weather forecast⟩

prediga, predijo etc. → **predecir**

predilección *nf, pl* **-ciones** : predilection, preference

predilecto, -ta *adj* : favorite

predio *nm* : property, piece of land

predisponer {60} *vt* **1** : to predispose, to incline **2** : to prejudice, to bias

predisposición *nf, pl* **-ciones** **1** : predisposition, tendency **2** : prejudice, bias

predominante *adj* : predominant — **predominantemente** *adv*

predominar *vi* PREVALECER : to predominate, to prevail

predominio *nm* : predominance, prevalence

preeminente *adj* : preeminent — **preeminencia** *nf*

preescolar *adj* & *nm* : preschool

preestreno *nm* : preview

prefabricado, -da *adj* : prefabricated

prefacio *nm* : preface

prefecto *nm* : prefect

preferencia *nf* **1** : preference **2** PRIORIDAD : priority **3** ~ : preferably

preferencial *adj* : preferential

preferente *adj* : preferential, special ⟨trato preferente : special treatment⟩

preferentemente *adv* : preferably

preferible *adj* : preferable
preferido, -da *adj & n* : favorite
preferir {76} *vt* : to prefer
prefigurar *vt* : foreshadow, prefigure
prefijo *nm* : prefix
pregonar *vt* **1** : to proclaim, to announce **2** : to hawk (merchandise) **3** : to reveal, to disclose **4** : to extol
pregunta *nf* **1** : question **2 hacer una pregunta** : to ask a question
preguntar *vt* : to ask, to question — *vi* : to ask, to inquire — **preguntarse** *vr* : to wonder
preguntón, -tona *adj, mpl* **-tones** : inquisitive
prehistórico, -ca *adj* : prehistoric
prejuiciado, -da *adj* : prejudiced
prejuicio *nm* : prejudice
prejuzgar {52} *vt* : to prejudge
prelado *nm* : prelate
preliminar *adj & nm* : preliminary
preludio *nm* : prelude
prematrimonial *adj* : premarital
prematuro, -ra *adj* : premature
premeditación *nf, pl* **-ciones** : premeditation
premeditar *vt* : to premeditate, to plan
premenstrual *adj* : premenstrual
premiado, -da *adj* : winning, prizewinning
premiar *vt* **1** : to award a prize to **2** : to reward
premier *nmf* : premier, prime minister
premio *nm* **1** : prize ⟨premio gordo : grand prize, jackpot⟩ **2** : reward **3** : premium
premisa *nf* : premise, basis
premolar *nm* : bicuspid (tooth)
premonición *nf, pl* **-ciones** : premonition
premura *nf* : haste, urgency
prenatal *adj* : prenatal
prenda *nf* **1** : piece of clothing **2** : security, pledge
prendar *vt* **1** : to charm, to captivate **2** : to pawn, to pledge — **prendarse** *vr* ~ **de** : to fall in love with
prendedor *nm* : brooch, pin
prender *vt* **1** SUJETAR : to pin, to fasten **2** APRESAR : to catch, to apprehend **3** : to light (a cigarette, a match) **4** : to turn on ⟨prende la luz : turn on the light⟩ **5 prender fuego a** : to set fire to — *vi* **1** : to take root **2** : to catch fire **3** : to catch on
prensa *nf* **1** : printing press **2** : press ⟨conferencia de prensa : press conference⟩
prensar *vt* : to press
prensil *adj* : prehensile
preñado, -da *adj* **1** : pregnant **2** ~ **de** : filled with
preñar *vt* EMBARAZAR : to make pregnant
preñez *nf, pl* **preñeces** : pregnancy
preocupación *nf, pl* **-ciones** INQUIETUD : worry, concern
preocupante *adj* : worrisome

preocupar *vt* INQUIETAR : to worry, to concern — **preocuparse** *vr* APURARSE : to worry, to be concerned
preparación *nf, pl* **-ciones** **1** : preparation, readiness **2** : education, training **3** : (medicinal) preparation
preparado[1], -da *adj* **1** : ready, prepared **2** : trained
preparado[2] *nm* : preparation, mixture
preparar *vt* **1** : to prepare, to make ready **2** : to teach, to train, to coach — **prepararse** *vr*
preparativos *nmpl* : preparations
preparatoria *nf Mex* : high school
preparatorio, -ria *adj* : preparatory
preponderante *adj* : preponderant, predominant — **preponderancia** *nf* —
preponderantemente *adv*
preposición *nf, pl* **-ciones** : preposition — **preposicional** *adj*
prepotente *adj* : arrogant, domineering, overbearing — **prepotencia** *nf*
prerrogativa *nf* : prerogative, privilege
presa *nf* **1** : capture, seizure ⟨hacer presa de : to seize⟩ **2** : catch, prey ⟨presa de : prey to, seized with⟩ **3** : claw, fang **4** DIQUE : dam **5** : morsel, piece (of food)
presagiar *vt* : to presage, to portend
presagio *nm* : omen, portent
presbiterio *nm* : presbytery, sanctuary (of a church)
presbítero *nm* : presbyter
presciencia *nf* : prescience
prescindible *adj* : expendable, dispensable
prescindir *vi* **1** ~ **de** : to do without, to dispense with **2** DESATENDER : to ignore, to disregard **3** OMITIR : to omit, to skip
prescribir {33} *vt* : to prescribe
prescripción *nf, pl* **-ciones** : prescription
prescrito *pp* → **prescribir**
presencia *nf* **1** : presence **2** ASPECTO : appearance
presenciar *vt* : to be present at, to witness
presentable *adj* : presentable
presentación *nf, pl* **-ciones** **1** : presentation **2** : introduction **3** : appearance
presentador, -dora *n* : newscaster, anchorman *m*, anchorwoman *f*
presentar *vt* **1** : to present, to show **2** : to offer, to give **3** : to submit (a document), to launch (a product) **4** : to introduce (a person) — **presentarse** *vr* **1** : to show up, to appear **2** : to arise, to come up **3** : to introduce oneself
presente[1] *adj* **1** : present, in attendance **2** : present, current **3 tener presente** : to keep in mind
presente[2] *nm* **1** : present (time, tense) **2** : one present ⟨entre los presentes se encontraban ... : those present included ...⟩
presentimiento *nm* : premonition, hunch, feeling

presentir {76} *vt* : to sense, to intuit ⟨presentía lo que iba a pasar : he sensed what was going to happen⟩
preservación *nf, pl* **-ciones** : preservation
preservar *vt* **1** : to preserve **2** : to protect
preservativo *nm* CONDÓN : condom
presidencia *nf* **1** : presidency **2** : chairmanship
presidencial *adj* : presidential
presidente, -ta *n* **1** : president **2** : chair, chairperson **3** : presiding judge
presidiario, -ria *n* : convict, prisoner
presidio *nm* : prison, penitentiary
presidir *vt* **1** MODERAR : to preside over, to chair **2** : to dominate, to rule over
presilla *nf* : eye, loop, fastener
presión *nf, pl* **presiones 1** : pressure **2** **presión arterial** : blood pressure
presionar *vt* **1** : to pressure **2** : to press, to push — *vi* : to put on the pressure
preso¹, -sa *adj* : imprisoned
preso², -sa *n* : prisoner
prestado, -da *adj* **1** : borrowed, on loan **2 pedir prestado** : to borrow
prestamista *nmf* : moneylender, pawnbroker
préstamo *nm* : loan
prestar *vt* **1** : to lend, to loan **2** : to render (a service), to give (aid) **3 prestar atención** : to pay attention **4 prestar juramento** : to take an oath — **prestarse** *vr* : to lend oneself ⟨se presta a confusiones : it lends itself to confusion⟩
prestatario, -ria *n* : borrower
presteza *nf* : promptness, speed
prestidigitación *nf, pl* **-ciones** : sleight of hand, prestidigitation
prestidigitador, -dora *n* : conjurer, magician
prestigio *nm* : prestige — **prestigioso, -sa** *adj*
presto¹ *adv* : promptly, at once
presto², -ta *adj* **1** : quick, prompt **2** DISPUESTO, PREPARADO : ready
presumido, -da *adj* VANIDOSO : conceited, vain
presumir *vt* SUPONER : to presume, to suppose — *vi* **1** ALARDEAR : to boast, to show off **2** ~ **de** : to consider oneself ⟨presume de inteligente : he thinks he's intelligent⟩
presunción *nf, pl* **-ciones 1** SUPOSICIÓN : presumption, supposition **2** VANIDAD : conceit, vanity
presunto, -ta *adj* : presumed, supposed, alleged — **presuntamente** *adv*
presuntuoso, -sa *adj* : conceited
presuponer {60} *vt* : to presuppose
presupuestal *adj* : budget, budgetary
presupuestar *vi* : to budget — *vt* : to budget for
presupuestario, -ria *adj* : budget, budgetary
presupuesto *nm* **1** : budget, estimate **2** : assumption, supposition

presurizar {21} *vt* : to pressurize
presuroso, -sa *adj* : hasty, quick
pretencioso, -sa *adj* : pretentious
pretender *vt* **1** INTENTAR : to attempt, to try ⟨pretendo estudiar : I'm trying to study⟩ **2** AFIRMAR : to claim ⟨pretende ser pobre : he claims he's poor⟩ **3** : to seek, to aspire to ⟨¿qué pretendes tú? : what are you after?⟩ **4** CORTEJAR : to court **5 pretender que** : to expect ⟨¿pretendes que lo crea? : do you expect me to believe you?⟩
pretendiente¹ *nmf* **1** : candidate, applicant **2** : pretender, claimant (to a throne, etc.)
pretendiente² *nm* : suitor
pretensión *nf, pl* **-siones 1** : intention, hope, plan **2** : pretension ⟨sin pretensiones : unpretentious⟩
pretexto *nm* EXCUSA : pretext, excuse
pretil *nm* : parapet, railing
prevalecer {53} *vi* : to prevail, to triumph
prevaleciente *adj* : prevailing, prevalent
prevalerse {84} *vr* ~ **de** : to avail oneself of, to take advantage of
prevención *nf, pl* **-ciones 1** : prevention **2** : preparation, readiness **3** : precautionary measure **4** : prejudice, bias
prevenido, -da *adj* **1** PREPARADO : prepared, ready **2** ADVERTIDO : forewarned **3** CAUTELOSO : cautious
prevenir {87} *vt* **1** : to prevent **2** : to warn — **prevenirse** *vr* ~ **contra** *or* ~ **de** : to take precautions against
preventivo, -va *adj* : preventive, precautionary
prever {88} *vt* ANTICIPAR : to foresee, to anticipate
previo, -via *adj* **1** : previous, prior **2** : after, upon ⟨previo pago : after paying, upon payment⟩
previsible *adj* : foreseeable
previsión *nf, pl* **-siones 1** : foresight **2** : prediction, forecast **3** : precaution
previsor, -sora *adj* : farsighted, prudent
prieto, -ta *adj* **1** : blackish, dark **2** : dark-skinned, swarthy **3** : tight, compressed
prima *nf* **1** : premium **2** : bonus **3** → **primo**
primacía *nf* **1** : precedence, priority **2** : superiority, supremacy
primado *nm* : primate (bishop)
primario, -ria *adj* : primary
primate *nm* : primate
primavera *nf* **1** : spring (season) **2** PRÍMULA : primrose
primaveral *adj* : spring, springlike
primero¹ *adv* **1** : first **2** : rather, sooner
primero², -ra *adj* (**primer** *before masculine singular nouns*) **1** : first **2** : top, leading **3** : fundamental, basic **4 de primera** : first-rate
primero³, -ra *n* : first
primicia *nf* **1** : first fruits **2** : scoop, exclusive

primigenio, -nia *adj* : original, primary
primitivo, -va *adj* 1 : primitive 2 ORIG-INAL : original
primo, -ma *n* : cousin
primogénito, -ta *adj & n* : firstborn
primor *nm* 1 : skill, care 2 : beauty, elegance
primordial *adj* 1 : primordial 2 : basic, fundamental
primoroso, -sa *adj* 1 : exquisite, fine, delicate 2 : skillful
prímula *nf* : primrose
princesa *nf* : princess
principado *nm* : principality
principal[1] *adj* 1 : main, principal 2 : foremost, leading
principal[2] *nm* : capital, principal
príncipe *nm* : prince
principesco, -ca *adj* : princely
principiante[1] *adj* : beginning
principiante[2] *nmf* : beginner, novice
principiar *vt* EMPEZAR : to begin
principio *nm* 1 COMIENZO : beginning 2 : principle 3 al principio : at first 4 a principios de : at the beginning of ⟨a principios de agosto : at the beginning of August⟩ 5 en ~ : in principle
pringar {52} *vt* 1 : to dip (in grease) 2 : to soil, to spatter (with grease) — pringarse *vr*
pringoso, -sa *adj* : greasy
pringue[1], etc. → pringar
pringue[2] *nm* : grease, drippings *pl*
prior, priora *n* : prior *m*, prioress *f*
priorato *nm* : priory
prioridad *nf* : priority, precedence
prisa *nf* 1 : hurry, rush 2 a ~ or de ~ : quickly, fast 3 a toda prisa : as fast as possible 4 darse prisa : to hurry 5 tener prisa : to be in a hurry
prisión *nf*, *pl* prisiones 1 CÁRCEL : prison, jail 2 ENCARCELAMIENTO : imprisonment
prisionero, -ra *n* : prisoner
prisma *nm* : prism
prismáticos *nmpl* : binoculars
prístino, -na *adj* : pristine
privacidad *nf* : privacy
privación *nf*, *pl* -ciones 1 : deprivation 2 : privation, want
privado, -da *adj* : private — privadamente *adv*
privar *vt* 1 DESPOJAR : to deprive 2 : to stun, to knock out — privarse *vr* : to deprive oneself
privativo, -va *adj* : exclusive, particular
privilegiado, -da *adj* : privileged
privilegiar *vt* : to grant a privilege to, to favor
privilegio *nm* : privilege
pro[1] *nm* 1 : pro, advantage ⟨los pros y contras : the pros and cons⟩ 2 en pro de : for, in favor of
pro[2] *prep* : for, in favor of ⟨grupos pro derechos humanos : groups supporting human rights⟩
proa *nf* : bow, prow
probabilidad *nf* : probability

probable *adj* : probable, likely
probablemente *adv* : probably
probar {19} *vt* 1 : to demonstrate, to prove 2 : to test, to try out 3 : to try on (clothing) 4 : to taste, to sample — *vi* : to try — probarse *vr* : to try on (clothing)
probeta *nf* : test tube
probidad *nf* : probity
problema *nm* : problem
problemática *nf* : set of problems ⟨la problemática que debemos enfrentar : the problems we must face⟩
probóscide *nf* : proboscis
problemático, -ca *adj* : problematic
procaz *adj*, *pl* procaces 1 : insolent, impudent 2 : indecent
procedencia *nf* : origin, source
procedente *adj* 1 : proper, fitting 2 ~ de : coming from
proceder *vi* 1 AVANZAR : to proceed 2 : to act, to behave 3 : to be appropriate, to be fitting 4 ~ de : to originate from, to come from
procedimiento *nm* : procedure, process
prócer *nmf* : eminent person, leader
procesado, -da *n* : accused, defendant
procesador *nm* : processor ⟨procesador de textos : word processor⟩
procesamiento *nm* : processing ⟨procesamiento de datos : data processing⟩
procesar *vt* 1 : to prosecute, to try 2 : to process
procesión *nf*, *pl* -siones : procession
proceso *nm* 1 : process 2 : trial, proceedings *pl*
proclama *nf* : proclamation
proclamación *nf*, *pl* -ciones : proclamation
proclamar *vt* : to proclaim — proclamarse *vr*
proclive *adj* ~ a : inclined to, prone to
proclividad *nf* : proclivity, inclination
procrear *vi* : to procreate — procreación *nf*
procurador, -dora *n* ABOGADO : attorney
procurar *vt* 1 INTENTAR : to try, to endeavor 2 CONSEGUIR : to obtain, to procure 3 procurar hacer : to manage to do
prodigar {52} *vt* : to lavish, to be generous with
prodigio *nm* : wonder, marvel
prodigioso, -sa *adj* : prodigious, marvelous
pródigo[1], -ga *adj* 1 : generous, lavish 2 : wasteful, prodigal
pródigo[2], -ga *n* : spendthrift, prodigal
producción *nf*, *pl* -ciones 1 : production 2 producción en serie : mass production
producir {61} *vt* 1 : to produce, to make, to manufacture 2 : to cause, to bring about 3 : to bear (interest) — producirse *vr* : to take place, to occur
productividad *nf* : productivity
productivo, -va *adj* 1 : productive 2 LUCRATIVO : profitable

producto *nm* **1** : product **2** : proceeds *pl*, yield
productor, -tora *n* : producer
proeza *nf* HAZAÑA : feat, exploit
profanar *vt* : to profane, to desecrate — **profanación** *nf*
profano¹, -na *adj* **1** : profane **2** : worldly, secular
profano², -na *n* : nonspecialist
profecía *nf* : prophecy
proferir {76} *vt* **1** : to utter **2** : to hurl (insults)
profesar *vt* **1** : to profess, to declare **2** : to practice, to exercise
profesión *nf, pl* **-siones** : profession
profesional *adj & nmf* : professional — **profesionalmente** *adv*
profesionalismo *nm* : professionalism
profesionalizar {21} *vt* : to professionalize
profesionista *nmf Mex* : professional
profesor, -sora *n* **1** MAESTRO : teacher **2** : professor
profesorado *nm* **1** : faculty **2** : teaching profession
profeta *nm* : prophet
profético, -ca *adj* : prophetic
profetisa *nf* : prophetess, prophet
profetizar {21} *vt* : to prophesy
prófugo, -ga *adj & n* : fugitive
profundidad *nf* : depth, profundity
profundizar {21} *vt* **1** : to deepen **2** : to study in depth — *vi* ~ **en** : to go deeply into, to study in depth
profundo, -da *adj* **1** HONDO : deep **2** : profound — **profundamente** *adv*
profusión *nf, pl* **-siones** : abundance, profusion
profuso, -sa *adj* : profuse, abundant, extensive
progenie *nf* : progeny, offspring
progenitor, -tora *n* ANTEPASADO : ancestor, progenitor
progesterona *nf* : progesterone
prognóstico *nm* : prognosis
programa *nm* **1** : program **2** : plan **3 programa de estudios** : curriculum
programable *adj* : programmable
programación *nf, pl* **-ciones** **1** : programming **2** : planning
programador, -dora *n* : programmer
programar *vt* **1** : to schedule, to plan **2** : to program (a computer, etc.)
progresar *vi* : to progress, to make progress
progresista *adj & nmf* : progressive
progresivo, -va *adj* : progressive, gradual
progreso *nm* : progress
prohibición *nf, pl* **-ciones** : ban, prohibition
prohibir {62} *vt* : to prohibit, to ban, to forbid
prohibitivo, -va *adj* : prohibitive
prohijar {5} *vt* ADOPTAR : to adopt
prójimo *nm* : neighbor, fellow man
prole *nf* : offspring, progeny
proletariado *nm* : proletariat, working class

proletario, -ria *adj & n* : proletarian
proliferar *vi* : to proliferate — **proliferación** *nf*
prolífico, -ca *adj* : prolific
prolijo, -ja *adj* : wordy, long-winded
prólogo *nm* : prologue, preface, foreword
prolongación *nf, pl* **-ciones** : extension, lengthening
prolongar {52} *vt* **1** : to prolong **2** : to extend, to lengthen — **prolongarse** *vr* CONTINUAR : to last, to continue
promediar *vt* **1** : to average **2** : to divide in half — *vi* : to be half over
promedio *nm* **1** : average **2** : middle, midpoint
promesa *nf* : promise
prometedor, -dora *adj* : promising, hopeful
prometer *vt* : to promise — *vi* : to show promise — **prometerse** *vr* COMPROMETERSE : to get engaged
prometido¹, -da *adj* : engaged
prometido², -da *n* NOVIO : fiancé *m*, fiancée *f*
prominente *adj* : prominent — **prominencia** *nf*
promiscuo, -cua *adj* : promiscuous — **promiscuidad** *nf*
promisorio, -ria *adj* **1** : promising **2** : promissory
promoción *nf, pl* **-ciones** **1** : promotion **2** : class, year **3** : play-off (in soccer)
promocionar *vt* : to promote — **promocional** *adj*
promontorio *nm* : promontory, headland
promotor, -tora *n* : promoter
promover {47} *vt* **1** : to promote, to advance **2** FOMENTAR : to foster, to encourage **3** PROVOCAR : to provoke, to cause
promulgación *nf, pl* **-ciones** **1** : enactment **2** : proclamation, enactment
promulgar {52} *vt* **1** : to promulgate, to proclaim **2** : to enact (a law or decree)
prono, -na *adj* : prone
pronombre *nm* : pronoun
pronosticar {72} *vt* : to predict, to forecast
pronóstico *nm* **1** PREDICCIÓN : forecast, prediction **2** : prognosis
prontitud *nf* **1** PRESTEZA : promptness, speed **2 con** ~ : promptly, quickly
pronto¹ *adv* **1** : quickly, promptly **2** : soon **3 de** ~ : suddenly **4 lo más pronto posible** : as soon as possible **5 tan pronto como** : as soon as
pronto², -ta *adj* **1** RÁPIDO : quick, speedy, prompt **2** PREPARADO : ready
pronunciación *nf, pl* **-ciones** : pronunciation
pronunciado, -da *adj* **1** : pronounced, sharp, steep **2** : marked, noticeable
pronunciamiento *nm* **1** : pronouncement **2** : military uprising
pronunciar *vt* **1** : to pronounce, to say **2** : to give, to deliver (a speech) **3 pro-**

nunciar un fallo : to pronounce sentence — **pronunciarse** *vr* : to declare oneself
propagación *nf, pl* **-ciones** : propagation, spreading
propaganda *nf* 1 : propaganda 2 PUBLICIDAD : advertising
propagar {52} *vt* 1 : to propagate 2 : to spread, to disseminate — **propagarse** *vr*
propalar *vt* 1 : to divulge 2 : to spread
propano *nm* : propane
propasarse *vr* : to go too far, to overstep one's bounds
propensión *nf, pl* **-siones** INCLINACIÓN : inclination, propensity
propenso, -sa *adj* : prone, susceptible
propiamente *adv* 1 : properly, correctly 2 : exactly, precisely ⟨propiamente dicho : strictly speaking⟩
propiciar *vt* 1 : to propitiate 2 : to favor, to foster
propicio, -cia *adj* : favorable, propitious
propiedad *nf* 1 : property ⟨propiedad privada : private property⟩ 2 : ownership 3 CUALIDAD : property, quality 4 : suitability, appropriateness
propietario¹, -ria *adj* : proprietary
propietario², -ria *n* DUEÑO : owner, proprietor
propina *nf* : tip, gratuity
propinar *vt* : to give, to strike ⟨propinar una paliza : to give a beating⟩
propio, -pia *adj* 1 : own ⟨su propia casa : his own house⟩ ⟨sus recursos propios : their own resources⟩ 2 APROPIADO : appropriate, suitable 3 CARACTERÍSTICO : characteristic, typical 4 MISMO : oneself ⟨el propio director : the director himself⟩
proponer {60} *vt* 1 : to propose, to suggest 2 : to nominate — **proponerse** *vr* : to intend, to plan, to set out ⟨lo que se propone lo cumple : he does what he sets out to do⟩
proporción *nf, pl* **-ciones** 1 : proportion 2 : ratio (in mathematics) 3 **proporciones** *nfpl* : proportions, size ⟨de grandes proporciones : very large⟩
proporcionado, -da *adj* 1 : proportionate 2 : proportioned ⟨bien proporcionado : well-proportioned⟩ — **proporcionadamente** *adv*
proporcional *adj* : proportional — **proporcionalmente** *adv*
proporcionar *vt* 1 : to provide, to give 2 : to proportion, to adapt
proposición *nf, pl* **-ciones** : proposal, proposition
propósito *nm* 1 INTENCIÓN : purpose, intention 2 a ~ : by the way 3 a ~ : on purpose, intentionally
propuesta *nf* PROPOSICIÓN : proposal
propulsar *vt* 1 IMPULSAR : to propel, to drive 2 PROMOVER : to promote, to encourage
propulsión *nf, pl* **-siones** : propulsion
propulsor *nm* : propellant

propuso, etc. → **proponer**
prorrata *nf* 1 : share, quota 2 a ~ : pro rata, proportionately
prórroga *nf* 1 : extension, deferment 2 : overtime (in sports)
prorrogar {52} *vt* 1 : to extend (a deadline) 2 : to postpone
prorrumpir *vi* : to burst forth, to break out ⟨prorrumpí en lágrimas : I burst into tears⟩
prosa *nf* : prose
prosaico, -ca *adj* : prosaic, mundane
proscribir {33} *v* 1 PROHIBIR : to prohibit, to ban, to proscribe 2 DESTERRAR : to banish, to exile
proscripción *nf, pl* **-ciones** 1 PROHIBICIÓN : ban, proscription 2 DESTIERRO : banishment
proscrito¹ *pp* → **proscribir**
proscrito², -ta *n* 1 DESTERRADO : exile 2 : outlaw
prosecución *nf, pl* **-ciones** 1 : continuation 2 : pursuit
proseguir {75} *vt* 1 CONTINUAR : to continue 2 : to pursue (studies, goals) — *vi* : to continue, to go on
prosélito, -ta *n* : proselyte
prospección *nf, pl* **-ciones** : prospecting, exploration
prospectar *vi* : to prospect
prospecto *nm* : prospectus, leaflet, brochure
prosperar *vi* : to prosper, to thrive
prosperidad *nf* : prosperity
próspero, -ra *adj* : prosperous, flourishing
próstata *nf* : prostate
prostitución *nf, pl* **-ciones** : prostitution
prostituir {41} *vt* : to prostitute — **prostituirse** *vr* : to prostitute oneself
prostituto, -ta *n* : prostitute
protagonista *nmf* 1 : protagonist, main character 2 : leader
protagonizar {21} *vt* : to star in
protección *nf, pl* **-ciones** : protection
protector¹, -tora *adj* : protective
protector², -tora *n* 1 : protector, guardian 2 : patron
protector³ *nm* : protector, guard ⟨chaleco protector : chest protector⟩
protectorado *nm* : protectorate
proteger {15} *vt* : to protect, to defend — **protegerse** *vr*
protegido, -da *n* : protégé
proteína *nf* : protein
prótesis *nfs & pl* : prosthesis
protesta *nf* 1 : protest 2 *Mex* : promise, oath
protestante *adj & nmf* : Protestant
protestantismo *nm* : Protestantism
protestar *vi* : to protest, to object — *vt* 1 : to protest, to object to 2 : to declare, to profess
protocolo *nm* : protocol
protón *nm, pl* **protones** : proton
protoplasma *nm* : protoplasm
prototipo *nm* : prototype
protozoario *or* **protozoo** *nm* : protozoan

protuberancia *nf* : protuberance — **protuberante** *adj*
provecho *nm* : benefit, advantage
provechoso, -sa *adj* BENEFICIOSO : beneficial, profitable, useful — **provechosamente** *adv*
proveedor, -dora *n* : provider, supplier
proveer {63} *vt* : to provide, to supply — **proveerse** *vr* ~ **de** : to obtain, to supply oneself with
provenir {87} *vi* ~ **de** : to come from
provenzal¹ *adj* : Provençal
provenzal² *nmf* : Provençal
provenzal³ *nm* : Provençal (language)
proverbio *nm* REFRÁN : proverb — **proverbial** *adj*
providencia *nf* **1** : providence, foresight **2** : Providence, God **3 providencias** *nfpl* : steps, measures
providencial *adj* : providential
provincia *nf* : province — **provincial** *adj*
provinciano, -na *adj* : provincial, unsophisticated
provisión *nf, pl* **-siones** : provision
provisional *adj* : provisional, temporary
provisionalmente *adv* : provisionally, tentatively
provisorio, -ria *adj* : provisional, temporary
provisto *pp* → **proveer**
provocación *nf, pl* **-ciones** : provocation
provocador¹, -dora *adj* : provocative, provoking
provocador², -dora *n* AGITADOR : agitator
provocar {72} *vt* **1** CAUSAR : to provoke, to cause **2** IRRITAR : to provoke, to pique
provocativo, -va *adj* : provocative
proxeneta *nmf* : pimp *m*
próximamente *adv* : shortly, soon
proximidad *nf* **1** : nearness, proximity **2 proximidades** *nfpl* : vicinity
próximo, -ma *adj* **1** : near, close ⟨la Navidad está próxima : Christmas is almost here⟩ **2** SIGUIENTE : next, following ⟨la próxima semana : the following week⟩
proyección *nf, pl* **-ciones 1** : projection **2** : showing, screening (of a film) **3** : range, influence, diffusion
proyectar *vt* **1** : to plan **2** LANZAR : to throw, to hurl **3** : to project, to cast (light or shadow) **4** : to show, to screen (a film)
proyectil *nm* : projectile, missile
proyecto *nm* **1** : plan, project **2 proyecto de ley** : bill
proyector *nm* **1** : projector **2** : spotlight
prudencia *nf* : prudence, care, discretion
prudente *adj* : prudent, sensible, reasonable
prueba¹, etc. → **probar**
prueba² *nf* **1** : proof, evidence **2** : trial, test **3** : proof (in printing or photography) **4** : event, qualifying round (in sports) **5 a prueba de agua** : waterproof **6 prueba de fuego** : acid test **7 poner a prueba** : to put to the test
prurito *nm* **1** : itching **2** : desire, urge
psicoanálisis *nm* : psychoanalysis — **psicoanalista** *nmf*
psicoanalítico, -ca *adj* : psychoanalytic
psicoanalizar {21} *vt* : to psychoanalyze
psicología *nf* : psychology
psicológico, -ca *adj* : psychological — **psicológicamente** *adv*
psicólogo, -ga *n* : psychologist
psicópata *nmf* : psychopath
psicopático, -ca *adj* : psycopathic
psicosis *nfs & pl* : psychosis
psicosomático, -ca *adj* : psychosomatic
psicoterapeuta *nmf* : psychotherapist
psicoterapia *nf* : psychotherapy
psicótico, -ca *adj & n* : psychotic
psique *nf* : psyche
psiquiatra *nmf* : psychiatrist
psiquiatría *nf* : psychiatry
psiquiátrico¹, -ca *adj* : psychiatric
psiquiátrico² *nm* : mental hospital
psíquico, -ca *adj* : psychic
psiquis *nfs & pl* : psyche
psoriasis *nf* : psoriasis
ptomaína *nf* : ptomaine
púa *nf* **1** : barb ⟨alambre de púas : barbed wire⟩ **2** : tooth (of a comb) **3** : quill, spine
pubertad *nf* : puberty
pubiano → **púbico**
púbico, -ca *adj* : pubic
publicación *nf, pl* **-ciones** : publication
publicar {72} *vt* **1** : to publish **2** DIVULGAR : to divulge, to disclose
publicidad *nf* **1** : publicity **2** : advertising
publicista *nmf* : publicist
publicitar *vt* **1** : to publicize **2** : to advertise
publicitario, -ria *adj* : advertising, publicity ⟨agencia publicitaria : advertising agency⟩
público¹, -ca *adj* : public — **públicamente** *adv*
público² *nm* **1** : public **2** : audience, spectators *pl*
puchero *nm* **1** : pot **2** : stew **3** : pout ⟨hacer pucheros : to pout⟩
pucho *nm* **1** : waste, residue **2** : cigarette butt **3 a puchos** : little by little, bit by bit
púdico, -ca *adj* : chaste, modest
pudiente *adj* **1** : powerful **2** : rich, wealthy
pudín *nm, pl* **pudines** BUDÍN : pudding
pudo, etc. → **poder**
pudor *nm* : modesty, reserve
pudoroso, -sa *adj* : modest, reserved, shy
pudrir {59} *vt* **1** : to rot **2** *fam* : to annoy, to upset — **pudrirse** *vr* **1** : to rot **2** : to languish
pueblerino, -na *adj* : provincial, countrified

puebla, etc. → **poblar**
pueblo *nm* **1** NACIÓN : people **2** : common people **3** ALDEA, POBLADO : town, village
puede, etc. → **poder**
puente *nm* **1** : bridge ⟨puente levadizo : drawbridge⟩ **2** : denture, bridge **3** **puente aéreo** : airlift
puerco¹, -ca *adj* : dirty, filthy
puerco², -ca *n* **1** CERDO, MARRANO : pig, hog **2** : pig, dirty or greedy person **3 puerco espín** : porcupine
pueril *adj* : childish, puerile
puerro *nm* : leek
puerta *nf* **1** : door, entrance, gate **2 a puerta cerrada** : behind closed doors
puerto *nm* **1** : port, harbor **2** : mountain pass **3 puerto marítimo** : seaport
puertorriqueño, -ña *adj & n* : Puerto Rican
pues *conj* **1** : since, because, for ⟨no puedo ir, pues no tengo plata : I can't go, since I don't have any money⟩ ⟨lo hace, pues a él le gusta : he does it because he likes to⟩ **2** (*used interjectionally*) : well, then ⟨¡pues claro que sí! : well, of course!⟩ ⟨¡pues no voy! : well then, I'm not going!⟩
puesta *nf* **1** : setting ⟨puesta del sol : sunset⟩ **2** : laying (of eggs) **3 puesta a punto** : tune-up **4 puesta en marcha** : start, starting up
puestero, -ra *n* : seller, vendor
puesto¹ *pp* → **poner**
puesto², -ta *adj* : dressed ⟨bien puesto : well-dressed⟩
puesto³ *nm* **1** LUGAR, SITIO : place, position **2** : position, job **3** : kiosk, stand, stall **4 puesto que** : since, given that
pugilato *nm* BOXEO : boxing, pugilism
pugilista *nm* BOXEADOR : boxer, pugilist
pugna *nf* **1** CONFLICTO, LUCHA : conflict, struggle **2 en ∼** : at odds, in conflict
pugnar *vi* LUCHAR : to fight, to strive, to struggle
pugnaz *adj* : pugnacious
pujante *adj* : mighty, powerful
pujanza *nf* : strength, vigor ⟨pujanza económica : economic strength⟩
pulcritud *nf* **1** : neatness, tidiness **2** ESMERO : meticulousness
pulcro, -cra *adj* **1** : clean, neat **2** : exquisite, delicate, refined
pulga *nf* **1** : flea **2 tener malas pulgas** : to be bad-tempered
pulgada *nf* : inch
pulgar *nm* **1** : thumb **2** : big toe
pulir *vt* **1** : to polish, to shine **2** REFINAR : to refine, to perfect
pulla *nf* **1** : cutting remark, dig, gibe **2** : obscenity
pulmón *nm, pl* **pulmones** : lung
pulmonar *adj* : pulmonary
pulmonía *nf* NEUMONÍA : pneumonia
pulpa *nf* : pulp, flesh
pulpería *nf* : small grocery store

púlpito *nm* : pulpit
pulpo *nm* : octopus
pulsación *nf, pl* **-ciones** **1** : beat, pulsation, throb **2** : keystroke
pulsar *vt* **1** APRETAR : to press, to push **2** : to strike (a key) **3** : to assess — *vi* : to beat, to throb
pulsera *nf* : bracelet
pulso *nm* **1** : pulse ⟨tomarle el pulso a alguien : to take someone's pulse⟩ ⟨tomarle el pulso a la opinión : to sound out opinion⟩ **2** : steadiness (of hand) ⟨dibujo a pulso : freehand sketch⟩
pulular *vi* ABUNDAR : to abound, to swarm ⟨en el río pululan los peces : the river is teeming with fish⟩
pulverizador *nm* **1** : atomizer, spray **2** : spray gun
pulverizar {21} *vt* **1** : to pulverize, to crush **2** : to spray
puma *nf* : cougar, puma
puna *nf* : bleak Andean tableland
punción *nf, pl* **punciones** : puncture
punible *adj* : punishable
punitivo, -va *adj* : punitive
punce, etc. → **punzar**
punta *nf* **1** : tip, end ⟨punta del dedo : fingertip⟩ ⟨en la punta de la lengua : at the tip of one's tongue⟩ **2** : point (of a weapon or pencil) ⟨punta de lanza : spearhead⟩ **3** : point, headland **4** : bunch, lot ⟨una punta de ladrones : a bunch of thieves⟩ **5 a punta de** : by, by dint of
puntada *nf* **1** : stitch (in sewing) **2** PUNZADA : sharp pain, stitch, twinge **3** *Mex* : witticism, quip
puntal *nm* **1** : prop, support **2** : stanchion
puntapié *nm* PATADA : kick
puntazo *nm* CORNADA : wound (from a goring)
puntear *vt* **1** : to pluck (a guitar) **2** : to lead (in sports)
puntería *nf* : aim, marksmanship
puntero *nm* **1** : pointer **2** : leader
puntiagudo, -da *adj* : sharp, pointed
puntilla *nf* **1** : lace edging **2** : dagger (in bullfighting) **3 de puntillas** : on tiptoe
puntilloso, -sa *adj* : punctilious
punto *nm* **1** : dot, point **2** : period (in punctuation) **3** : item, question **4** : spot, place **5** : moment, stage, degree **6** : point (in a score) **7** : stitch **8 en ∼** : on the dot, sharp ⟨a las dos en punto : at two o'clock sharp⟩ **9 al punto** : at once **10 a punto fijo** : exactly, certainly **11 dos puntos** : colon **12 hasta cierto punto** : up to a point **13 punto decimal** : decimal point **14 punto de vista** : point of view **15 punto y coma** : semicolon **16 y punto** : period ⟨es el mejor que hay y punto : it's the best there is, period⟩ **17 puntos cardinales** : points of the compass

puntuación *nf, pl* **-ciones 1** : punctuation **2** : scoring, score, grade
puntual *adj* **1** : prompt, punctual **2** : exact, accurate — **puntualmente** *adv*
puntualidad *nf* **1** : promptness, punctuality **2** : exactness, accuracy
puntualizar {21} *vt* **1** : to specify, to state **2** : to point out
puntuar {3} *vt* : to punctuate — *vi* : to score points
punzada *nf* : sharp pain, twinge, stitch
punzante *adj* **1** : sharp **2** CÁUSTICO : biting, caustic
punzar {21} *vt* : to pierce, to puncture
punzón *nm, pl* **punzones 1** : awl **2** : hole punch
puñado *nm* **1** : handful **2 a puñados** : lots of, by the handful
puñal *nm* DAGA : dagger
puñalada *nf* : stab, stab wound
puñetazo *nm* : punch (with the fist)
puño *nm* **1** : fist **2** : handful, fistful **3** : cuff (of a shirt) **4** : handle, hilt
pupila *nf* : pupil (of the eye)
pupilo, -la *n* **1** : pupil, student **2** : ward, charge
pupitre *nm* : writing desk
puré *nm* : purée ⟨puré de papas : mashed potatoes⟩
pureza *nf* : purity
purga *nf* **1** : laxative **2** : purge
purgante *adj & nm* : laxative, purgative
purgar {52} *vt* **1** : to purge, to cleanse **2** : to liquidate (in politics) **3** : to give a

laxative to — **purgarse** *vr* **1** : to take a laxative **2** ~ **de** : to purge oneself of
purgatorio *nm* : purgatory
purgue, etc. → **purgar**
purificador *nm* : purifier
purificar {72} *vt* : to purify — **purificación** *nf*
puritano¹, -na *adj* : puritanical, puritan
puritano², -na *n* **1** : Puritan **2** : puritan
puro¹ *adv* : sheer, much ⟨de puro terco : out of sheer stubbornness⟩
puro², -ra *adj* **1** : pure ⟨aire puro : fresh air⟩ **2** : plain, simple, sheer ⟨por pura curiosidad : from sheer curiosity⟩ **3** : only, just ⟨emplean puras mujeres : they only employ women⟩ **4 pura sangre** : Thoroughbred horse
puro³ *nm* : cigar
púrpura *nf* : purple
purpúreo, -rea *adj* : purple
purpurina *nf* : glitter (for decoration)
pus *nm* : pus
pusilánime *adj* COBARDE : pusillanimous, cowardly
puso, etc. → **poner**
pústula *nf* : pustule, pimple
puta *nf* : whore, slut
putrefacción *nf, pl* **-ciones** : putrefaction
putrefacto, -ta *adj* **1** PODRIDO : putrid, rotten **2** : decayed
pútrido, -da *adj* : putrid, rotten
puya *nf* **1** : point (of a lance) **2 lanzar una puya** : to gibe, to taunt

Q

q *nf* : eighteenth letter of the Spanish alphabet
que¹ *conj* **1** : that ⟨dice que está listo : he says that he's ready⟩ ⟨espero que lo haga : I hope that he does it⟩ **2** : than ⟨más que nada : more than anything⟩ **3** *(implying permission or desire)* ⟨¡que entre! : send him in!⟩ ⟨¡que te vaya bien! : I wish you well!⟩ **4** *(indicating a reason or cause)* ⟨¡cuidado, que te caes! : be careful, you're about to fall!⟩ ⟨no provoques al perro, que te va a morder : don't provoke the dog or (else) he'll bite⟩ **5 es que** : the thing is that, I'm afraid that **6 yo que tú** : if I were you
que² *pron* **1** : who, that ⟨la niña que viene : the girl who is coming⟩ **2** : whom, that ⟨los alumnos que enseñé : the students that I taught⟩ **3** : that, which ⟨el carro que me gusta : the car that I like⟩ **4 el (la, lo, las, los) que** → **el¹, la¹, lo¹, los¹**
qué¹ *adv* : how, what ⟨¡qué bonito! : how pretty!⟩
qué² *adj* : what, which ⟨¿qué hora es? : what time is it?⟩
qué³ *pron* : what ⟨¿qué quieres? : what do you want?⟩

quebracho *nm* : quebracho (tree)
quebrada *nf* DESFILADERO : ravine, gorge
quebradizo, -za *adj* FRÁGIL : breakable, delicate, fragile
quebrado¹, -da *adj* **1** : bankrupt **2** : rough, uneven **3** ROTO : broken
quebrado² *nm* : fraction
quebrantamiento *nm* **1** : breaking **2** : deterioration, weakening
quebrantar *vt* **1** : to break, to split, to crack **2** : to weaken **3** : to violate (a law or contract)
quebranto *nm* **1** : break, breaking **2** AFLICCIÓN : affliction, grief **3** PÉRDIDA : loss
quebrar {55} *vt* **1** ROMPER : to break **2** DOBLAR : to bend, to twist — *vi* **1** : to go bankrupt **2** : to fall out, to break up — **quebrarse** *vr*
queda *nf* : curfew
quedar *vi* **1** PERMANECER : to remain, to stay **2** : to be ⟨quedamos contentos con las mejoras : we were pleased with the improvements⟩ **3** : to be situated ⟨queda muy lejos : it's very far, it's too far away⟩ **4** : to be left ⟨quedan sólo dos alternativas : there are only two options left⟩ **5** : to fit, to suit ⟨estos zap-

atos no me quedan : these shoes don't fit⟩ **6 quedar bien (mal)** : to turn out well (badly) **7** ~ **en** : to agree, to arrange ⟨¿en qué quedamos? : what's the arrangement, then?⟩ — **quedarse** *vr* **1** : to stay ⟨se quedó en casa : she stayed at home⟩ **2** : to keep on ⟨se quedó esperando : he kept on waiting⟩ **3 quedarse atrás** : to stay behind ⟨no quedarse atrás : to be no slouch⟩ **4** ~ **con** : to remain ⟨me quedé con hambre después de comer : I was still hungry after I ate⟩

quedo[1] *adv* : softly, quietly

quedo[2], **-da** *adj* : quiet, still

quehacer *nm* **1** : work **2 quehaceres** *nmpl* : chores

queja *nf* : complaint

quejarse *vr* **1** : to complain **2** : to groan, to moan

quejido *nm* **1** : groan, moan **2** : whine, whimper

quejoso, -sa *adj* : complaining, whining

quejumbroso, -sa *adj* : querulous, whining

quema *nf* **1** FUEGO : fire **2** : burning

quemado, -da *adj* **1** : burned, burnt **2** : annoyed **3** : burned-out

quemador *nm* : burner

quemadura *nf* : burn

quemar *vt* : to burn, to set fire to — *vi* : to be burning hot — **quemarse** *vr*

quemarropa *nf* a ~ : point-blank

quemazón *nf, pl* **-zones 1** : burning **2** : intense heat **3** : itch **4** : cutting remark

quena *nf* : Peruvian reed flute

quepa, etc. → **caber**

querella *nf* **1** : complaint **2** : lawsuit

querellante *nmf* : plaintiff

querellarse *vr* ~ **contra** : to bring suit against, to sue

querer[1] {64} *vt* **1** DESEAR : to want, to desire ⟨quiere ser profesor : he wants to be a teacher⟩ ⟨¿cuánto quieres por esta computadora? : how much do you want for this computer?⟩ **2** : to love, to like, to be fond of ⟨te quiero : I love you⟩ **3** (*indicating a request*) ⟨¿quieres pasarme la leche? : please pass the milk⟩ **4 querer decir** : to mean **5 sin** ~ : unintentionally — *vi* : like, want ⟨si quieras : if you like⟩

querer[2] *nm* : love, affection

querido[1], **-da** *adj* : dear, beloved

querido[2], **-da** *n* : dear, sweetheart

queroseno *nm* : kerosene

querrá, etc. → **querer**

querúbico, -ca *adj* : cherubic

querubín *nm, pl* **-bines** : cherub

quesadilla *nf* : quesadilla

quesería *nf* : cheese shop

queso *nm* : cheese

quetzal *nm* **1** : quetzal (bird) **2** : monetary unit of Guatemala

quicio *nm* **1 estar fuera de quicio** : to be beside oneself **2 sacar de quicio** : to exasperate, to drive crazy

quid *nm* : crux, gist ⟨el quid de la cuestión : the crux of the matter⟩

quiebra[1], **etc.** → **quebrar**

quiebra[2] *nf* **1** : break, crack **2** BANCARROTA : failure, bankruptcy

quien *pron, pl* **quienes 1** : who, whom ⟨no sé quien ganará : I don't know who will win⟩ ⟨las personas con quienes trabajo : the people with whom I work⟩ **2** : whoever, whomever ⟨quien quiere salir que salga : whoever wants to can leave⟩ **3** : anyone, some people ⟨hay quienes no están de acuerdo : some people don't agree⟩

quién *pron, pl* **quiénes 1** : who, whom ⟨¿quién sabe? : who knows?⟩ ⟨¿con quién hablo? : with whom am I speaking?⟩ **2 de** ~ : whose ⟨¿de quién es este libro? : whose book is this?⟩

quienquiera *pron, pl* **quienesquiera** : whoever, whomever

quiere, etc. → **querer**

quieto, -ta *adj* **1** : calm, quiet **2** INMÓVIL : still

quietud *nf* **1** : calm, tranquility **2** INMOVILIDAD : stillness

quijada *nf* : jaw, jawbone

quijotesco, -ca *adj* : quixotic

quilate *nm* : karat

quilla *nf* : keel

quimera *nf* : chimera, illusion

quimérico, -ca *adj* : chimeric, fanciful

química *nf* : chemistry

químico[1], **-ca** *adj* : chemical

químico[2], **-ca** *n* : chemist

quimioterapia *nf* : chemotherapy

quimono *nm* : kimono

quince *adj & nm* : fifteen

quinceañero, -ra *n* : fifteen-year-old, teenager

quinceavo[1], **-va** *adj* : fifteenth

quinceavo[2] *nm* : fifteenth (fraction)

quincena *nf* : two week period, fortnight

quincenal *adj* : bimonthly, twice a month

quincuagésimo[1], **-ma** *adj* : fiftieth, fifty-

quincuagésimo[2], **-ma** *n* : fiftieth, fifty- (in a series)

quingombó *nm* : okra

quiniela *nf* : sports lottery

quinientos[1], **-tas** *adj* : five hundred

quinientos[2] *nms & pl* : five hundred

quinina *nf* : quinine

quino *nm* : cinchona

quinqué *nm* : oil lamp

quinquenal *adj* : five-year ⟨un plan quinquenal : a five-year plan⟩

quinta *nf* : country house, villa

quintaesencia *nf* : quintessence — **quintaesencial** *adj*

quintal *nm* : hundredweight

quinteto *nm* : quintet

quintillizo, -za *n* : quintuplet

quinto, -ta *adj* : fifth — **quinto, -ta** *n*

quíntuplo, -la *adj* : quintuple, five-fold

quiosco *nm* **1** : kiosk **2** : newsstand **3 quiosco de música** : bandstand

quirófano *nm* : operating room

quiromancia *nf* : palmistry
quiropráctica *nf* : chiropractic
quiropráctico, -ca *n* : chiropractor
quirúrgico, -ca *adj* : surgical — **quirúrgicamente** *adv*
quiso, etc. → **querer**
quisquilloso[1], **-sa** *adj* : fastidious, fussy
quisquilloso[2], **-sa** *n* : fussy person, fussbudget
quiste *nm* : cyst
quitaesmalte *nm* : nail polish remover
quitamanchas *nms & pl* : stain remover

quitanieves *nms & pl* : snowplow
quitar *vt* **1** : to remove, to take away **2** : to take off (clothes) **3** : to get rid of, to relieve — **quitarse** *vr* **1** : to withdraw, to leave **2** : to take off (one's clothes) **3** ~ **de** : to give up (a habit) **4 quitar de encima** : to get rid of
quitasol *nm* : parasol
quiteño[1], **-ña** *adj* : of or from Quito
quiteño[2], **-ña** *n* : person from Quito
quizá *or* **quizás** *adv* : maybe, perhaps
quórum *nm, pl* **quórums** : quorum

R

r *nf* : nineteenth letter of the Spanish alphabet
rábano *nm* **1** : radish **2 rábano picante** : horseradish
rabí *nmf, pl* **rabíes** : rabbi
rabia *nf* **1** HIDROFOBIA : rabies, hydrophobia **2** : rage, anger
rabiar *vi* **1** : to rage, to be furious **2** : to be in great pain **3 a** ~ *fam* : like crazy, like mad
rabieta *nf* BERRINCHE : tantrum
rabino, -na *n* : rabbi
rabioso, -sa *adj* **1** : enraged, furious **2** : rabid
rabo *nm* **1** COLA : tail **2 el rabo del ojo** : the corner of one's eye
racha *nf* **1** : gust of wind **2** : run, series, string ⟨racha perdedora : losing streak⟩
racheado, -da *adj* : gusty, windy
racial *adj* : racial
racimo *nm* : bunch, cluster ⟨un racimo de uvas : a bunch of grapes⟩
raciocinio *nm* : reason, reasoning
ración *nf, pl* **raciones 1** : share, ration **2** PORCIÓN : portion, helping
racional *adj* : rátional, reasonable — **racionalmente** *adv*
racionalidad *nf* : rationality
racionalización *nf, pl* **-ciones** : rationalization
racionalizar {21} *vt* **1** : to rationalize **2** : to streamline
racionamiento *nm* : rationing
racionar *vt* : to ration
racismo *nm* : racism
racista *adj & nmf* : racist
radar *nm* : radar
radiación *nf, pl* **-ciones** : radiation, irradiation
radiactividad *nf* : radioactivity
radiactivo, -va *adj* : radioactive
radiador *nm* : radiator
radial *adj* **1** : radial **2** : radio, broadcasting ⟨emisora radial : radio transmitter⟩
radiante *adj* : radiant
radiar *vt* **1** : to radiate **2** : to irradiate **3** : to broadcast (on the radio)
radical[1] *adj* : radical, extreme — **radicalmente** *adv*

radical[2] *nmf* : radical
radicalismo *nm* : radicalism
radicar {72} *vi* **1** : to be found, to lie **2** ARRAIGAR : to take root — **radicarse** *vr* : to settle, to establish oneself
radio[1] *nm* **1** : radius **2** : radium
radio[2] *nmf* : radio
radioactividad *nf* : radioactivity
radioactivo, -va *adj* : radioactive
radioaficionado, -da *n* : ham radio operator
radiodifusión *nf, pl* **-siones** : radio broadcasting
radiodifusora *nf* : radio station
radioemisora *nf* : radio station
radiofaro *nm* : radio beacon
radiofónico, -ca *adj* : radio ⟨estación radiofónica pública : public radio station⟩
radiofrecuencia *nf* : radio frequency
radiografía *nf* : X ray (photograph)
radiografiar {85} *vt* : to x-ray
radiología *nf* : radiology
radiólogo, -ga *n* : radiologist
radón *nm* : radon
raer {65} *vt* RASPAR : to scrape, to scrape off
ráfaga *nf* **1** : gust (of wind) **2** : flash, burst ⟨una ráfaga de luz : a flash of light⟩
raid *nm* CA, Mex fam : lift, ride
raído, -da *adj* : worn, shabby
raiga, etc. → **raer**
raíz *nf, pl* **raíces 1** : root **2** : origin, source **3 a raíz de** : following, as a result of **4 echar raíces** : to take root
raja *nf* **1** : crack, slit **2** : slice, wedge
rajá *nm* : raja
rajadura *nf* : crack, split
rajar *vt* HENDER : to crack, to split — *vi* **1** *fam* : to chatter **2** *fam* : to boast, to brag — **rajarse** *vr* **1** : to crack, to split open **2** *fam* : to back out
rajatabla *adv* **a** ~ : strictly, to the letter
ralea *nf* : kind, sort, ilk ⟨son de la misma valea : they're two of a kind⟩
ralentí *nm* **dejar al ralentí** : to leave (a motor) idling
rallado, -da *adj* **1** : grated **2 pan rallado** : bread crumbs *pl*
rallador *nm* : grater

rallar *vt* : to grate
ralo, -la *adj* : sparse, thin
RAM *nf* : RAM, random-access memory
rama *nf* : branch
ramaje *nm* : branches *pl*
ramal *nm* **1** : branchline **2** : halter, strap
ramera *nf* : harlot, prostitute
ramificación *nf, pl* **-ciones** : ramification
ramificarse {72} *vr* : to branch out, to divide into branches
ramillete *nm* **1** RAMO : bouquet **2** : select group, cluster
ramo *nm* **1** : branch **2** RAMILLETE : bouquet **3** : division (of science or industry) **4 Domingo de Ramos** : Palm Sunday
rampa *nf* : ramp, incline
rana *nf* **1** : frog **2 rana toro** : bullfrog
ranchera *nf Mex* : traditional folk song
ranchería *nf* : settlement
ranchero, -ra *n* : rancher, farmer
rancho *nm* **1** : ranch, farm **2** : hut **3** : settlement, camp **4** : food, mess (for soldiers, etc.)
rancio, -cia *adj* **1** : aged, mellow (of wine) **2** : ancient, old **3** : rancid
rango *nm* **1** : rank, status **2** : high social standing **3** : pomp, splendor
ranúnculo *nm* : buttercup
ranura *nf* : groove, slot
rap *nm* : rap (music)
rapacidad *nf* : rapacity
rapar *vt* **1** : to crop **2** : to shave
rapaz[1] *adj, pl* **rapaces** : rapacious, predatory
rapaz[2], **-paza** *n, mpl* **rapaces** : youngster, child
rape *nm* : close haircut
rapé *nm* : snuff
rapero, -ra *n* : rapper, rap artist
rapidez *nf* : rapidity, speed
rápido[1] *adv* : quickly, fast ⟨¡manejas tan rápido! : you drive so fast!⟩
rápido[2], **-da** *adj* : rapid, quick — **rápidamente** *adv*
rápido[3] *nm* **1** : express train **2 rápidos** *nmpl* : rapids
rapiña *nf* **1** : plunder, pillage **2 ave de rapiña** : bird of prey
raposa *nf* : vixen (fox)
rapsodia *nf* : rhapsody
raptar *vt* SECUESTRAR : to abduct, to kidnap
rapto *nm* **1** SECUESTRO : kidnapping, abduction **2** ARREBATO : fit, outburst
raptor, -tora *n* SECUESTRADOR : kidnapper
raque *nm* : beachcombing
raquero, -ra *n* : beachcomber
raqueta *nf* **1** : racket (in sports) **2** : snowshoe
raquítico, -ca *adj* **1** : scrawny, weak **2** : measly, skimpy
raquitismo *nm* : rickets
raramente *adv* : seldom, rarely
rareza *nf* **1** : rarity **2** : peculiarity, oddity

raro, -ra *adj* **1** EXTRAÑO : odd, strange, peculiar **2** : unusual, rare **3** : exceptional **4 rara vez** : seldom, rarely
ras *nm* **a ras de** : level with
rasar *vt* **1** : to skim, to graze **2** : to level
rascacielos *nms & pl* : skyscraper
rascar {72} *vt* **1** : to scratch **2** : to scrape — **rascarse** *vr* : to scratch an itch
rasgadura *nf* : tear, rip
rasgar {52} *vt* : to rip, to tear — **rasgarse** *vr*
rasgo *nm* **1** : stroke (of a pen) ⟨a grandes rasgos : in broad outlines⟩ **2** CARACTERÍSTICA : trait, characteristic **3** : gesture, deed **4 rasgos** *nmpl* FACCIONES : features
rasgón *nm, pl* **rasgones** : rip, tear
rasgue, etc. → **rasgar**
rasguear *vt* : to strum
rasguñar *vt* **1** : to scratch **2** : to sketch, to outline
rasguño *nm* **1** : scratch **2** : sketch
raso[1], **-sa** *adj* **1** : level, flat **2 soldado raso** : private (in the army) ⟨los soldados rasos : the ranks⟩
raso[2] *nm* : satin
raspadura *nf* **1** : scratching, scraping **2 raspaduras** *nfpl* : scrapings
raspar *vt* **1** : to scrape **2** : to file down, to smooth — *vi* : to be rough
rasque, etc. → **rascar**
rastra *nf* **1** : harrow **2 a rastras** : by dragging, unwillingly
rastrear *vt* **1** : to track, to trace **2** : to comb, to search **3** : to trawl
rastrero, -ra *adj* **1** : creeping, crawling **2** : vile, despicable
rastrillar *vt* : to rake, to harrow
rastrillo *nm* **1** : rake **2 Mex** : razor
rastro *nm* **1** PISTA : trail, track **2** VESTIGIO : trace, sign
rastrojo *nm* : stubble (of plants)
rasuradora *nf Mex, CA* : electric razor, shaver
rasurar *vt* AFEITAR : to shave — **rasurarse** *vr*
rata[1] *nm fam* : pickpocket, thief
rata[2] *nf* **1** : rat **2** *Col, Pan, Peru* : rate, percentage
ratear *vt* : to pilfer, to steal
ratero, -ra *n* : petty thief
ratificación *nf, pl* **-ciones** : ratification
ratificar {72} *vt* **1** : to ratify **2** : to confirm
rato *nm* **1** : while **2 pasar el rato** : to pass the time **3 a cada rato** : all the time, constantly ⟨les sacaba dinero a cada rato : he was always taking money from them⟩ **4 al poco rato** : later, shortly after
ratón[1], **-tona** *n, mpl* **ratones** **1** : mouse **2 ratón de biblioteca** *fam* : bookworm
ratón[2] *nm, pl* **ratones** **1** : (computer) mouse **2** *CoRi* : biceps
ratonera *nf* : mousetrap
raudal *nm* **1** : torrent **2 a raudales** : in abundance

raya¹, etc. → **raer**
raya² *nf* **1** : line **2** : stripe **3** : skate, ray **4** : part (in the hair) **5** : crease (in clothing)
rayar *vt* **1** ARAÑAR : to scratch **2** : to scrawl on, to mark up ⟨rayaron las paredes : they covered the walls with graffiti⟩ — *vi* **1** : to scratch **2** AMANECER : to dawn, to break ⟨al rayar el alba : at break of day⟩ **3** ~ **con** : to be adjacent to, to be next to **4** ~ **en** : to border on, to verge on ⟨su respuesta raya en lo ridículo : his answer borders on the ridiculous⟩ — **rayarse** *vr*
rayo *nm* **1** : ray, beam ⟨rayo láser : laser beam⟩ ⟨rayo de gamma : gamma ray⟩ ⟨rayo de sol : sunbeam⟩ **2** RELÁMPAGO : lightning bolt **3 rayo X** : X-ray
rayón *nm, pl* **rayones** : rayon
raza *nf* **1** : race ⟨raza humana : human race⟩ **2** : breed, strain **3 de** ~ : thoroughbred, pedigreed
razón *nf, pl* **razones 1** MOTIVO : reason, motive ⟨en razón de : by reason of, because of⟩ **2** JUSTICIA : rightness, justice ⟨tener razón : to be right⟩ **3** : reasoning, sense ⟨perder la razón : to lose one's mind⟩ **4** : ratio, proportion
razonable *adj* : reasonable — **razonablemente** *adv*
razonado, -da *adj* : itemized, detailed
razonamiento *nm* : reasoning
razonar *v* : to reason, to think
reabastecimiento *nm* : replenishment
reabierto *pp* → **reabrir**
reabrir {2} *vt* : to reopen — **reabrirse** *vr*
reacción *nf, pl* **-ciones 1** : reaction **2 motor a reacción** : jet engine
reaccionar *vi* : to react, to respond
reaccionario, -ria *adj & n* : reactionary
reacio, -cia *adj* : resistant, opposed
reacondicionar *vt* : to recondition
reactivación *nf, pl* **-ciones** : reactivation, revival
reactivar *vt* : reactivate, revive
reactor *nm* **1** : reactor ⟨reactor nuclear : nuclear reactor⟩ **2** : jet engine **3** : jet airplane, jet
reafirmar *vt* : to reaffirm, to assert, to strengthen
reajustar *vt* : to readjust, to adjust
reajuste *nm* : readjustment ⟨reajuste de precios : price increase⟩
real *adj* **1** : real, true **2** : royal
realce *nm* **1** : embossing, relief **2 dar realce** : to highlight, to bring out
realeza *nf* : royalty
realidad *nf* **1** : reality **2 en** ~ : in truth, actually
realinear *vt* : to realign
realismo *nm* **1** : realism **2** : royalism
realista¹ *adj* **1** : realistic **2** : realist **3** : royalist
realista² *nmf* **1** : realist **2** : royalist
realización *nf, pl* **-ciones** : execution, realization

realizar {21} *vt* **1** : to carry out, to execute **2** : to produce, to direct (a film or play) **3** : to fulfill, to achieve **4** : to realize (a profit) — **realizarse** *vr* **1** : to come true **2** : to fulfill oneself
realmente *adv* : really, in reality
realzar {21} *vt* **1** : to heighten, to raise **2** : to highlight, to enhance
reanimación *nf, pl* **-ciones** : revival, resuscitation
reanimar *vt* **1** : to revive, to restore **2** : to resuscitate — **reanimarse** *vr* : to come around, to recover
reanudación *nf, pl* **-ciones** : resumption, renewal
reanudar *vt* : to resume, to renew — **reanudarse** *vr* : to resume, to continue
reaparecer {53} *vi* **1** : to reappear **2** : to make a comeback
reaparición *nf, pl* **-ciones** : reappearance
reapertura *nf* : reopening
reata *nf* **1** : rope **2** *Mex* : lasso, lariat **3 de** ~ : single file
reavivar *vt* : to revive, to reawaken
rebaja *nf* **1** : reduction **2** DESCUENTO : discount **3 rebajas** *nfpl* : sale
rebajar *vt* **1** : to reduce, to lower ⟨a precios rebajados : at reduced prices, on sale⟩ **2** : to lessen, to diminish **3** : to humiliate — **rebajarse** *vr* **1** : to humble oneself **2 rebajarse a** : to stoop to
rebanada *nf* : slice
rebañar *vt* : to mop up, to sop up
rebaño *nm* **1** : flock **2** : herd
rebasar *vt* **1** : to surpass, to exceed **2** *Mex* : to pass, to overtake
rebatiña *nf* : scramble, fight (over something)
rebatir *vt* REFUTAR : to refute
rebato *nm* **1** : surprise attack **2 tocar a rebato** : to sound the alarm
rebelarse *vr* : to rebel
rebelde¹ *adj* : rebellious, unruly
rebelde² *nmf* **1** : rebel **2** : defaulter
rebeldía *nf* **1** : rebelliousness **2 en** ~ : in default
rebelión *nf, pl* **-liones** : rebellion
rebobinar *vt* : to rewind
reborde *nm* : border, flange, rim
rebosante *adj* : brimming, overflowing ⟨rebosante de salud : brimming with health⟩
rebosar *vi* **1** : to overflow **2** ~ **de** : to abound in, to be bursting with — *vt* : to radiate
rebotar *vi* **1** : to bounce **2** : to ricochet, to rebound
rebote *nm* **1** : bounce **2** : rebound, ricochet
rebozar {21} *vt* : to coat in batter
rebozo *nm* **1** : shawl, wrap **2 sin** ~ : frankly, openly
rebullir {38} *v* : to move, to stir — **rebullirse** *vr*
rebuscado, -da *adj* : affected, pretentious
rebuscar {72} *vi* : to search thoroughly

rebuznar *vi* : to bray
rebuzno *nm* : bray, braying
recabar *vt* **1** : to gather, to obtain, to collect **2 recabar fondos** : to raise money
recado *nm* **1** : message ⟨mandar recado : to send word⟩ **2** *Spain* : errand
recaer {13} *vi* **1** : to relapse **2** ∼ **en** *or* ∼ **sobre** : to fall on, to fall to
recaída *nf* : relapse
recaiga, etc. → **recaer**
recalar *vi* : to arrive
recalcar {72} *vt* : to emphasize, to stress
recalcitrante *adj* : recalcitrant
recalentar {55} *vt* **1** : to reheat, to warm up **2** : to overheat
recámara *nf* **1** *Col, Mex, Pan* : bedroom **2** : chamber (of a firearm)
recamarera *nf Mex* : chambermaid
recambio *nm* **1** : spare part **2** : refill (for a pen, etc.)
recapacitar *vi* **1** : to reconsider **2** ∼ **en** : to reflect on, to weigh
recapitular *v* : to recapitulate — **recapitulación** *nf*
recargable *adj* : rechargeable
recargado, -da *adj* : overly elaborate or ornate
recargar {52} *vt* **1** : to recharge **2** : to overload
recargo *nm* : surcharge
recatado, -da *adj* MODESTO : modest, demure
recato *nm* PUDOR : modesty
recaudación *nf, pl* **-ciones** **1** : collection **2** : earnings *pl*, takings *pl*
recaudador, -dora *n* **recaudador de impuestos** : tax collector
recaudar *vt* : to collect
recaudo *nm* : safe place ⟨a (buen) recaudo : in safe keeping⟩
recayó, etc. → **recaer**
rece, etc. → **rezar**
recelo *nm* : distrust, suspicion
receloso, -sa *adj* : distrustful, suspicious
recepción *nf, pl* **-ciones** : reception
recepcionista *nmf* : receptionist
receptáculo *nm* : receptacle
receptividad *nf* : receptivity, receptiveness
receptivo, -va *adj* : receptive
receptor[1], -tora *adj* : receiving
receptor[2], -tora *n* **1** : recipient **2** : catcher (in baseball), receiver (in football)
receptor[3] *nm* : receiver ⟨receptor de televisión : television set⟩
recesión *nf, pl* **-siones** : recession
recesivo, -va *adj* : recessive
receso *nm* : recess, adjournment
receta *nf* **1** : recipe **2** : prescription
recetar *vt* : to prescribe (medications)
rechazar {21} *vt* **1** : to reject **2** : to turn down, to refuse
rechazo *nm* : rejection, refusal
rechifla *nf* : booing, jeering
rechinar *vi* **1** : to squeak **2** : to grind, to gnash ⟨hacer rechinar los dientes : to grind one's teeth⟩

rechoncho, -cha *adj fam* : chubby, squat
recibidor *nm* : vestibule, entrance hall
recibimiento *nm* : reception, welcome
recibir *vt* **1** : to receive, to get **2** : to welcome — *vi* : to receive visitors —
recibirse *vr* ∼ **de** : to qualify as
recibo *nm* : receipt
reciclable *adj* : recyclable
reciclado → **reciclaje**
reciclaje *nm* **1** : recycling **2** : retraining
reciclar *vt* **1** : to recycle **2** : to retrain
recién *adv* **1** : newly, recently ⟨recién nacido : newborn⟩ ⟨recién casados : newlyweds⟩ ⟨recién llegado : newcomer⟩ **2** : just, only just ⟨recién ahora me acordé : I just now remembered⟩
reciente *adj* : recent — **recientemente** *adv*
recinto *nm* **1** : enclosure **2** : site, premises *pl*
recio[1] *adv* **1** : strongly, hard **2** : loudly, loud
recio[2], -cia *adj* **1** : severe, harsh **2** : tough, strong
recipiente[1] *nm* : container, receptacle
recipiente[2] *nmf* : recipient
reciprocar {72} *vi* : to reciprocate
reciprocidad *nf* : reciprocity
recíproco, -ca *adj* : reciprocal, mutual
recitación *nf, pl* **-ciones** : recitation, recital
recital *nm* : recital
recitar *vt* : to recite
reclamación *nf, pl* **-ciones** **1** : claim, demand **2** QUEJA : complaint
reclamar *vt* **1** EXIGIR : to demand, to require **2** : to claim — *vi* : to complain
reclamo *nm* **1** : bird call, lure **2** : lure, decoy **3** : inducement, attraction **4** : advertisement **5** : complaint
reclinar *vt* : to rest, to lean — **reclinarse** *vr* : to recline, to lean back
recluir {41} *vt* : to confine, to lock up — **recluirse** *vr* : to shut oneself up, to withdraw
reclusión *nf, pl* **-siones** : imprisonment
recluso, -sa *n* **1** : inmate, prisoner **2** SOLITARIO : recluse
recluta *nmf* : recruit, draftee
reclutamiento *nm* : recruitment, recruiting
reclutar *vt* ENROLAR : to recruit, to enlist
recobrar *vt* : to recover, to regain — **recobrarse** *vr* : to recover, to recuperate
recocer {14} *vt* : to overcook, to cook again
recodo *nm* : bend
recogedor *nm* : dustpan
recoger {15} *vt* **1** : to collect, to gather **2** : to get, to retrieve, to pick up **3** : to clean up, to tidy (up)
recogido, -da *adj* : quiet, secluded
recogimiento *nm* **1** : collecting, gathering **2** : withdrawal **3** : absorption, concentration

recolección *nf, pl* **-ciones** 1 : collection ⟨recolección de basura : trash pickup⟩ 2 : harvest
recolectar *vt* 1 : to gather, to collect 2 : to harvest, to pick
recomendable *adj* : advisable, recommended
recomendación *nf, pl* **-ciones** : recommendation
recomendar {55} *vt* 1 : to recommend 2 ACONSEJAR : to advise
recompensa *nf* : reward, recompense
recompensar *vt* 1 PREMIAR : to reward 2 : to compensate
reconciliación *nf, pl* **-ciones** : reconciliation
reconciliar *vt* : to reconcile — **reconciliarse** *vr*
recóndito, -ta *adj* 1 : remote, isolated 2 : hidden, recondite 3 **en lo más recóndito de** : in the depths of
reconfortar *vt* : to comfort — **reconfortante** *adj*
reconocer {18} *vt* 1 : to recognize 2 : to admit 3 : to examine
reconocible *adj* : recognizable
reconocido, -da *adj* 1 : recognized, accepted 2 : grateful
reconocimiento *nm* 1 : acknowledgment, recognition, avowal 2 : (medical) examination 3 : reconnaissance
reconquista *nf* : reconquest
reconquistar *vt* 1 : to reconquer, to recapture 2 RECUPERAR : to regain, to recover
reconsiderar *vt* : to reconsider — **reconsideración** *nf*
reconstrucción *nf, pl* **-ciones** : reconstruction
reconstruir {41} *vt* : to rebuild, to reconstruct
reconversión *nf, pl* **-siones** : restructuring
reconvertir {76} *vt* 1 : to restructure 2 : to retrain
recopilación *nf, pl* **-ciones** 1 : summary 2 : collection, compilation
recopilar *vt* : to compile, to collect
récord *or* **record** [ˈrɛkɔr] *nm, pl* **récords** *or* **records** [-kɔrs] : record ⟨record mundial : world record⟩ — **récord** *or* **record** *adj*
recordar {19} *vt* 1 : to recall, to remember 2 : to remind — *vi* 1 ACORDARSE : to remember 2 DESPERTAR : to wake up
recordatorio¹, -ria *adj* : commemorative
recordatorio² *nm* : reminder
recorrer *vt* 1 : to travel through, to tour 2 : to cover (a distance) 3 : to go over, to look over
recorrido *nm* 1 : journey, trip 2 : path, route, course 3 : round (in golf)
recortar *vt* 1 : to cut, to reduce 2 : to cut out 3 : to trim, to cut off 4 : to outline — **recortarse** *vr* : to stand out ⟨los árboles se recortaban en el horizonte : the trees were silhouetted against the horizon⟩

recorte *nm* 1 : cut, reduction 2 : clipping ⟨recortes de periódicos : newspaper clippings⟩
recostar {19} *vt* : to lean, to rest — **recostarse** *vr* : to lie down, recline
recoveco *nm* 1 VUELTA : bend, turn 2 : nook, corner 3 **recovecos** *nmpl* : intricacies, ins and outs
recreación *nf, pl* **-ciones** 1 : re-creation 2 DIVERSIÓN : recreation, entertainment
recrear *vt* 1 : to re-create 2 : to entertain, to amuse — **recrearse** *vr* : to enjoy oneself
recreativo, -va *adj* : recreational
recreo *nm* 1 DIVERSIÓN : entertainment, amusement 2 : recess, break
recriminación *nf, pl* **-ciones** : reproach, recrimination
recriminar *vt* : to reproach — *vi* : to recriminate — **recriminarse** *vr*
recrudecer {53} *v* : to intensify, to worsen — **recrudecerse** *vr*
rectal *adj* : rectal
rectangular *adj* : rectangular
rectángulo *nm* : rectangle
rectificación *nf, pl* **-ciones** : rectification, correction
rectificar {72} *vt* 1 : to rectify, to correct 2 : to straighten (out)
rectitud *nf* 1 : straightness 2 : honesty, rectitude
recto¹ *adv* : straight
recto², -ta *adj* 1 : straight 2 : upright, honorable 3 : sound
recto³ *nm* : rectum
rector¹, -tora *adj* : governing, managing
rector², -tora *n* : rector
rectoría *nf* : rectory
recubierto *pp* → **recubrir**
recubrir {2} *vt* : to cover, to coat
recuento *nm* : recount, count ⟨un recuento de los votos : a recount of the votes⟩
recuerdo *nm* 1 : memory 2 : souvenir, memento 3 **recuerdos** *nmpl* : regards
recular *vi* 1 : to back up 2 REPLEGARSE : to retreat, to fall back 3 RETRACTARSE : to back down
recuperación *nf, pl* **-ciones** 1 : recovery, recuperation 2 **recuperación de datos** : data retrieval
recuperar *vt* 1 : to recover, to get back, to retrieve 2 : to recuperate 3 : to make up for ⟨recuperar el tiempo perdido : to make up for lost time⟩ — **recuperarse** *vr* ~ **de** : to recover from, to get over
recurrente *adj* : recurrent, recurring
recurrir *vi* 1 ~ **a** : to turn to, to appeal to 2 ~ **a** : to resort to 3 : to appeal (in law)
recurso *nm* 1 : recourse ⟨el último recurso : the last resort⟩ 2 : appeal (in law) 3 **recursos** *nmpl* : resources, means ⟨recursos naturales : natural resources⟩

red *nf* **1** : net, mesh **2** : network, system, chain **3** : trap, snare

redacción *nf, pl* **-ciones 1** : writing, composition **2** : editing

redactar *vt* **1** : to write, to draft **2** : to edit

redactor, -tora *n* : editor

redada *nf* **1** : raid **2** : catch, haul

redefinir *vt* : to redefine — **redefinición** *nf*

redención *nf, pl* **-ciones** : redemption

redentor[1]**, -tora** *adj* : redeeming

redentor[2]**, -tora** *n* : redeemer

redescubierto *pp* → **redescubrir**

redescubrir {2} *vt* : to rediscover

redicho, -cha *adj fam* : affected, pretentious

redil *nm* **1** : sheepfold **2 volver al redil** : to return to the fold

redimir *vt* : to redeem, to deliver (from sin)

rediseñar *vt* : to redesign

redistribuir {41} *vt* : to redistribute — **redistribución** *nf*

rédito *nm* : return, yield

redituar {3} *vt* : to produce, to yield

redoblar *vt* : to redouble, to strengthen — **redoblado, -da** *adj*

redoble *nm* : drum roll

redomado, -da *adj* **1** : sly, crafty **2** : utter, out-and-out

redonda *nf* **1** : region, surrounding area **2 a la redonda** ALREDEDOR : around ⟨de diez millas a la redonda : for ten miles around⟩

redondear *vt* : to round off, to round out

redondel *nm* **1** : ring, circle **2** : bullring, arena

redondez *nf* : roundness

redondo, -da *adj* **1** : round ⟨mesa redonda : round table⟩ **2** : great, perfect ⟨un negocio redondo : an excellent deal⟩ **3** : straightforward, flat ⟨un rechazo redondo : a flat refusal⟩ **4** *Mex* : round-trip **5 en ~** : around

reducción *nf, pl* **-ciones** : reduction, decrease

reducido, -da *adj* **1** : reduced, limited **2** : small

reducir {61} *vt* **1** DISMINUIR : to reduce, to decrease, to cut **2** : to subdue **3** : to boil down — **reducirse** *vr* ~ **a** : to come down to, to be nothing more than

redundancia *nf* : redundancy

redundante *adj* : redundant

reedición *nf, pl* **-ciones** : reprint

reelegir {28} *vt* : to reelect — **reelección** *nf*

reembolsable *adj* : refundable

reembolsar *vt* **1** : to refund, to reimburse **2** : to repay

reembolso *nm* : refund, reimbursement

reemplazable *adj* : replaceable

reemplazar {21} *vt* : to replace, to substitute

reemplazo *nm* : replacement, substitution

reencarnación *nf, pl* **-ciones** : reincarnation

reencuentro *nm* : reunion

reestablecer {53} *vt* : to reestablish

reestructurar *vt* : to restructure

reexaminar *vt* : to reexamine

refaccionar *vt* : to repair, to renovate

refacciones *nfpl* : repairs, renovations

referencia *nf* **1** : reference **2 hacer referencia a** : to refer to

referendo → **referéndum**

referéndum *nm, pl* **-dums** : referendum

referente *adj* ~ **a** : concerning

réferi *or* **referi** ['rɛfɛri] *nmf* : referee

referir {76} *vt* **1** : to relate, to tell **2** : to refer ⟨nos refirió al diccionario : she referred us to the dictionary⟩ — **referirse** *vr* ~ **a 1** : to refer to **2** ~ **a** : to be concerned, to be in reference to ⟨en lo que se refiere a la educación : as far as education is concerned⟩

refinado[1]**, -da** *adj* : refined

refinado[2] *nm* : refining

refinamiento *nm* **1** : refining **2** FINURA : refinement

refinanciar *vt* : to refinance

refinar *vt* : to refine

refinería *nf* : refinery

reflectante *adj* : reflective, reflecting

reflector[1]**, -tora** *adj* : reflecting

reflector[2] *nm* **1** : spotlight, searchlight **2** : reflector

reflejar *vt* : to reflect — **reflejarse** *vr* : to be reflected ⟨la decepción se refleja en su rostro : the disappointment shows on her face⟩

reflejo *nm* **1** : reflection **2** : reflex **3 reflejos** *nmpl* : highlights, streaks (in hair)

reflexión *nf, pl* **-xiones** : reflection, thought

reflexionar *vi* : to reflect, to think

reflexivo, -va *adj* **1** : reflective, thoughtful **2** : reflexive

reflujo *nm* : ebb, ebb tide

reforma *nf* **1** : reform **2** : alteration, renovation

reformador, -dora *n* : reformer

reformar *vt* **1** : to reform **2** : to change, to alter **3** : to renovate, to repair — **reformarse** *vr* : to mend one's ways

reformatorio *nm* : reformatory

reformular *vt* : to reformulate — **reformulación** *nf*

reforzar {36} *vt* **1** : to reinforce, to strengthen **2** : to encourage, to support

refracción *nf, pl* **-ciones** : refraction

refractar *vt* : to refract — **refractarse** *vr*

refractario, -ria *adj* : refractory, obstinate

refrán *nm, pl* **refranes** ADAGIO : proverb, saying

refregar {49} *vt* : to scrub

refrenar *vt* **1** : to rein in (a horse) **2** : to restrain, to check — **refrenarse** *vr* : to restrain oneself

refrendar *vt* **1** : to countersign, to endorse **2** : to stamp (a passport)

refrescante *adj* : refreshing

refrescar {72} *vt* **1** : to refresh, to cool **2** : to brush up (on) **3 refrescar la memoria** : to refresh one's memory — *vi* : to turn cooler
refresco *nm* : refreshment, soft drink
refriega *nf* : skirmish, scuffle
refrigeración *nf, pl* **-ciones 1** : refrigeration **2** : air-conditioning
refrigerador *nmf* NEVERA : refrigerator
refrigeradora *nf Col, Peru* : refrigerator
refrigerante *nm* : coolant
refrigerar *vt* **1** : to refrigerate **2** : to air-condition
refrigerio *nm* : snack, refreshments *pl*
refrito[1], **-ta** *adj* : refried
refrito[2] *nm* : rehash
refuerzo *nm* : reinforcement, support
refugiado, -da *n* : refugee
refugiar *vt* : to shelter — **refugiarse** *vr* ACOGERSE : to take refuge
refugio *nm* : refuge, shelter
refulgencia *nf* : brilliance, splendor
refulgir {35} *vi* : to shine brightly
refundir *vt* **1** : to recast (metals) **2** : to revise, to rewrite
refunfuñar *vi* : to grumble, to groan
refutar *vt* : to refute — **refutación** *nf*
regadera *nf* **1** : watering can **2** : shower head, shower **3** : sprinkler
regaderazo *nm Mex* : shower
regalar *vt* **1** OBSEQUIAR : to present (as a gift), to give away **2** : to regale, to entertain **3** : to flatter, to make a fuss over — **regalarse** *vr* : to pamper oneself
regalía *nf* : royalty, payment
regaliz *nm, pl* **-lices** : licorice
regalo *nm* **1** OBSEQUIO : gift, present **2** : pleasure, comfort **3** : treat
regañadientes *mpl* **a ~** : reluctantly, unwillingly
regañar *vt* : to scold, to give a talking to — *vi* **1** QUEJARSE : to grumble, to complain **2** REÑIR : to quarrel, to argue
regaño *nm fam* : scolding
regañón, -ñona *adj, mpl* **-ñones** *fam* : grumpy, irritable
regar {49} *vt* **1** : to irrigate **2** : to water **3** : to wash, to hose down **4** : to spill, to scatter
regata *nf* : regatta, yacht race
regate *nm* : dodge, feint
regatear *vt* **1** : to haggle over **2** ESCATIMAR : to skimp on, to be sparing with — *vi* : to bargain, to haggle
regateo *nm* : bargaining, haggling
regatón *nm, pl* **-tones** : ferrule, tip
regazo *nm* : lap (of a person)
regencia *nf* : regency
regenerar *vt* : to regenerate — **regenerarse** *vr* — **regeneración** *nf*
regentar *vt* : to run, to manage
regente *nmf* : regent
regidor, -dora *n* : town councillor
régimen *nm, pl* **regímenes 1** : regime **2** : diet **3** : rules, rules *pl* ⟨régimen de vida : lifestyle⟩
regimiento *nm* : regiment

regio, -gia *adj* **1** : great, magnificent **2** : regal, royal
región *nf, pl* **regiones** : region, area
regional *adj* : regional — **regionalmente** *adv*
regir {28} *vt* **1** : to rule **2** : to manage, to run **3** : to control, to govern ⟨las costumbres que rigen la conducta : the customs which govern behavior⟩ — *vi* : to apply, to be in force ⟨las leyes rigen en los tres países : the laws apply in all three countries⟩ — **regirse** *vr* ~ **por** : to go by, to be guided by
registrador[1], **-dora** *adj* **caja registradora** : cash register
registrador[2], **-dora** *n* : registrar, recorder
registrar *vt* **1** : to register, to record **2** GRABAR : to record, to tape **3** : to search, to examine — **registrarse** *vr* **1** INSCRIBIRSE : to register **2** OCURRIR : to happen, to occur
registro *nm* **1** : register **2** : registration **3** : registry, record office **4** : range (of a voice or musical instrument) **5** : search
regla *nf* **1** NORMA : rule, regulation **2** : ruler ⟨regla de cálculo : slide rule⟩ **3** MENSTRUACIÓN : period, menstruation
reglamentación *nf, pl* **-ciones 1** : regulation **2** : rules *pl*
reglamentar *vt* : to regulate, to set rules for
reglamentario, -ria *adj* : regulation, official ⟨equipo reglamentario : standard equipment⟩
reglamento *nm* : regulations *pl*, rules *pl* ⟨reglamento de tráfico : traffic regulations⟩
regocijar *vt* : to gladden, to delight — **regocijarse** *vr* : to rejoice
regocijo *nm* : delight, rejoicing
regordete, -ta *adj fam* LLENITO : chubby
regresar *vt* DEVOLVER : to give back — *vi* : to return, to come back, to go back
regresión *nf, pl* **-siones** : regression, return
regresivo, -va *adj* : regressive
regreso *nm* **1** : return **2 estar de regreso** : to be back, to be home
reguero *nm* **1** : irrigation ditch **2** : trail, trace **3 propagarse como reguero de pólvora** : to spread like wildfire
regulable *adj* : adjustable
regulación *nf, pl* **-ciones** : regulation, control
regulador[1], **-dora** *adj* : regulating, regulatory
regulador[2] *nm* **1** : regulator, governor **2 regulador de tiro** : damper (in a chimney)
regular[1] *vt* : to regulate, to control
regular[2] *adj* **1** : regular **2** : fair, OK, so-so **3** : medium, average **4 por lo regular** : in general, generally
regularidad *nf* : regularity

regularización *nf, pl* **-ciones** NORMALIZACIÓN : normalization
regularizar {21} *vt* NORMALIZAR : to normalize, to make regular
regularmente *adv* : regularly
regusto *nm* : aftertaste
rehabilitar *vt* **1** : to rehabilitate **2** : to reinstate **3** : renovate, to restore — **rehabilitación** *nf*
rehacer {40} *vt* **1** : to redo **2** : to remake, to repair, to renew — **rehacerse** *vr* **1** : to recover **2** ~ **de** : to get over
rehecho *pp* → **rehacer**
rehén *nm, pl* **rehenes** : hostage
rehicieron, etc. → **rehacer**
rehizo → **rehacer**
rehuir {41} *vt* : to avoid, to shun
rehusar {8} *v* : to refuse
reimprimir *vt* : to reprint
reina *nf* : queen
reinado *nm* : reign
reinante *adj* **1** : reigning **2** : prevailing, current
reinar *vi* **1** : to reign **2** : to prevail
reincidencia *nf* : recidivism, relapse
reincidente *nmf* : backslider, recidivist
reincidir *vi* : to backslide, to retrogress
reincorporar *vt* : to reinstate — **reincorporarse** *vr* ~ **a** : to return to, to rejoin
reiniciar *vt* **1** : to resume, to restart **2** : to reboot (a computer)
reino *nm* : kingdom, realm ⟨reino animal : animal kingdom⟩
reinstalar *vt* **1** : to reinstall **2** : to reinstate
reintegración *nf, pl* **-ciones** **1** : reinstatement, reintegration **2** : refund, reimbursement
reintegrar *vt* **1** : to reintegrate, reinstate **2** : to refund, to reimburse — **reintegrarse** *vr* ~ **a** : to return to, to rejoin
reír {66} *vi* : to laugh — *vt* : to laugh at — **reírse** *vr*
reiteración *nf, pl* **-ciones** : reiteration, repetition
reiterado, -da *adj* : repeated ⟨lo explicó en reiteradas ocasiones : he explained it repeatedly⟩ — **reiteradamente** *adv*
reiterar *vt* : to reiterate, to repeat
reiterativo, -va *adj* : repetitive, repetitious
reivindicación *nf, pl* **-ciones** **1** : demand, claim **2** : vindication
reivindicar {72} *vt* **1** : to vindicate **2** : to demand, to claim **3** : to restore
reja *nf* **1** : grille, grating ⟨entre rejas : behind bars⟩ **2** : plowshare
rejilla *nf* : grille, grate, screen
rejuvenecer {53} *vt* : to rejuvenate — *vi* : to be rejuvenated — **rejuvenecerse** *vr*
rejuvenecimiento *nm* : rejuvenation
relación *nf, pl* **-ciones** **1** : relation, connection, relevance **2** : relationship **3** RELATO : account **4** LISTA : list **5 con relación a** *or* **en relación con** : in re-

lation to, concerning **6 relaciones-públicas** : public relations
relacionar *vt* : to relate, to connect — **relacionarse** *vr* ~ **con** : to be connected to, to be linked with
relajación *nf, pl* **-ciones** : relaxation
relajado, -da *adj* **1** : relaxed, loose **2** : dissolute, depraved
relajante *adj* : relaxing
relajar *vt* : to relax, to slacken — *vi* : to be relaxing — **relajarse** *vr*
relajo *nm* **1** : commotion, ruckus **2** : joke, laugh ⟨lo hizo de relajo : he did it for a laugh⟩
relamerse *vr* : to smack one's lips, to lick one's chops
relámpago *nm* : flash of lightning
relampaguear *vi* : to flash
relanzar {21} *vt* : to relaunch
relatar *vt* : to relate, to tell
relatividad *nf* : relativity
relativo, -va *adj* **1** : relative **2 en lo relativo a** : with regard to, concerning — **relativamente** *adv*
relato *nm* **1** : story, tale **2** : account
releer {20} *vt* : to reread
relegar {52} *vt* **1** : to relegate **2 relegar al olvido** : to consign to oblivion
relevante *adj* : outstanding, important
relevar *vt* **1** : to relieve, to take over from **2** ~ **de** : to exempt from — **relevarse** *vr* : to take turns
relevo *nm* **1** : relief, replacement **2** : relay ⟨carrera de relevos : relay race⟩
relicario *nm* **1** : reliquary **2** : locket
relieve *nm* **1** : relief, projection ⟨mapa en relieve : relief map⟩ ⟨letras en relieve : embossed letters⟩ **2** : prominence, importance **3 poner en relieve** : to highlight, to emphasize
religión *nf, pl* **-giones** : religion
religiosamente *adv* : religiously, faithfully
religioso[1], -sa *adj* : religious
religioso[2], -sa *n* : monk *m*, nun *f*
relinchar *vi* : to neigh, to whinny
relincho *nm* : neigh, whinny
reliquia *nf* **1** : relic **2 reliquia de familia** : family heirloom
rellenar *vt* **1** : to refill **2** : to stuff, to fill **3** : to fill out
relleno[1], -na *adj* : stuffed, filled
relleno[2] *nm* : stuffing, filling
reloj *nm* **1** : clock **2** : watch **3 reloj de arena** : hourglass **4 reloj de pulsera** : wristwatch **5 como un reloj** : like clockwork
relojería *nf* **1** : watchmaker's shop **2** : watchmaking, clockmaking
reluciente *adj* : brilliant, shining
relucir {45} *vi* **1** : to glitter, to shine **2 salir a relucir** : to come to the surface **3 sacar a relucir** : to bring up, to mention
relumbrante *adj* : dazzling
relumbrar *vi* : to shine brightly
relumbrón *nm, pl* **-brones** **1** : flash, glare **2 de** ~ : flashy, showy

remachar *vt* **1** : to rivet **2** : to clinch (a nail) **3** : to stress, to drive home — *vi* : to smash, to spike (a ball)

remache *nm* **1** : rivet **2** : smash, spike (in sports)

remanente *nm* **1** : remainder, balance **2** : surplus

remanso *nm* : pool

remar *vi* **1** : to row, to paddle **2** : to struggle, to toil

remarcar {72} *vt* : to emphasize, to stress

rematado, -da *adj* : utter, complete

rematador, -dora *n* : auctioneer

rematar *vt* **1** : to finish off **2** : to auction — *vi* **1** : to shoot **2** : to end

remate *nm* **1** : shot (in sports) **2** : auction **3** : end, conclusion **4 como ~** : to top it off **5 de ~** : completely, utterly

remecer {86} *vt* : to sway, to swing

remedar *vt* **1** IMITAR : to imitate, to copy **2** : to mimic, to ape

remediar *vt* **1** : to remedy, to repair **2** : to help out, to assist **3** EVITAR : to prevent, to avoid

remedio *nm* **1** : remedy, cure **2** : solution **3** : option ⟨no me quedó más remedio : I had no other choice⟩ ⟨no hay remedio : it can't be helped⟩ **4 poner remedio a** : to put a stop to **5 sin ~** : unavoidable, inevitable

remedo *nm* : imitation

rememorar *vi* : to recall ⟨rememorar los viejos tiempos : to reminisce⟩

remendar {55} *vt* **1** : to mend, to patch, to darn **2** : to correct

remero, -ra *n* : rower

remesa *nf* **1** : remittance **2** : shipment

remezón *nm, pl* **-zones** : mild earthquake, tremor

remiendo *nm* **1** : patch **2** : correction

remilgado, -da *adj* **1** : prim, prudish **2** : affected

remilgo *nm* : primness, affectation

reminiscencia *nf* : reminiscence

remisión *nf, pl* **-siones 1** ENVÍO : sending, delivery **2** : remission **3** : reference, cross-reference

remiso, -sa *adj* **1** : lax, remiss **2** : reluctant

remitente¹ *nm* : return address

remitente² *nmf* : sender (of a letter, etc.)

remitir *vt* **1** : to send, to remit **2 ~ a** : to refer to, to direct to ⟨nos remitió al diccionario : he referred us to the dictionary⟩ — *vi* : to subside, to let up

remo *nm* **1** : paddle, oar **2** : rowing (sport)

remoción *nf, pl* **-ciones 1** : removal **2** : dismissal

remodelación *nf, pl* **-ciones 1** : remodeling **2** : reorganization, restructuring

remodelar *vt* **1** : to remodel **2** : to restructure

remojar *vt* **1** : to soak, to steep **2** : to dip, to dunk **3** : to celebrate with a drink

remojo *nm* **1** : soaking, steeping **2 poner en remojo** : to soak, to leave soaking

remolacha *nf* : beet

remolcador *nm* : tugboat

remolcar {72} *vt* : to tow, to haul

remolino *nm* **1** : whirlwind **2** : eddy, whirlpool **3** : crowd, throng **4** : cowlick

remolque *nm* **1** : towing, tow **2** : trailer **3 a ~** : in tow

remontar *vt* **1** : to overcome **2** SUBIR : to go up — **remontarse** *vr* **1** : to soar **2 ~ a** : to date from, to go back to

rémora *nf* : obstacle, hindrance

remorder {47} *vt* INQUIETAR : to trouble, to distress

remordimiento *nm* : remorse

remotamente *adv* : remotely, vaguely

remoto, -ta *adj* **1** : remote, unlikely ⟨hay una posibilidad remota : there is a slim possibility⟩ **2** : distant, far-off

remover {47} *vt* **1** : to stir **2** : to move around, to turn over **3** : to stir up **4** : to remove **5** : to dismiss

remozamiento *nm* : renovation

remozar {21} *vt* **1** : to renew, to brighten up **2** : to redo, to renovate

remuneración *nf, pl* **-ciones** : remuneration, pay

remunerar *vt* : to pay, to remunerate

remunerativo, -va *adj* : remunerative

renacer {48} *vi* : to be reborn, to revive

renacimiento *nm* **1** : rebirth, revival **2 el Renacimiento** : the Renaissance

renacuajo *nm* : tadpole, pollywog

renal *adj* : renal, kidney

rencilla *nf* : quarrel

renco, -ca *adj* : lame

rencor *nm* **1** : rancor, enmity, hostility **2 guardar rencor** : to hold a grudge

rencoroso, -sa *adj* : resentful, rancorous

rendición *nf, pl* **-ciones 1** : surrender, submission **2** : yield, return

rendido, -da *adj* **1** : submissive **2** : worn-out, exhausted **3** : devoted

rendija *nf* GRIETA : crack, split

rendimiento *nm* **1** : performance **2** : yield

rendir {54} *vt* **1** : to render, to give ⟨rendir las gracias : to give thanks⟩ ⟨rendir homenaje a : to pay homage to⟩ **2** : to yield **3** CANSAR : to exhaust — *vi* **1** CUNDIR : to progress, to make headway **2** : to last, to go a long way — **rendirse** *vr* : to surrender, to give up

renegado, -da *n* : renegade

renegar {49} *vi* **1 ~ de** : to renounce, to disown, to give up **2 ~ de** : to complain about — *vt* **1** : to deny vigorously **2** : to abhor, to hate

renegociar *vt* : to renegotiate — **renegociación** *nf*

renglón *nm, pl* **renglones 1** : line (of writing) **2** : merchandise, line (of products)

rengo, -ga *adj* : lame
renguear *vi* : to limp
reno *nm* : reindeer
renombrado, -da *adj* : renowned, famous
renombre *nm* NOMBRADÍA : renown, fame
renovable *adj* : renewable
renovación *nf, pl* **-ciones 1** : renewal ⟨renovación de un contrato : renewal of a contract⟩ **2** : change, renovation
renovar {19} *vt* **1** : to renew, to restore **2** : to renovate
renquear *vi* : to limp, to hobble
renquera *nf* COJERA : limp, lameness
renta *nf* **1** : income **2** : rent **3 impuesto sobre la renta** : income tax
rentable *adj* : profitable
rentar *vt* **1** : to produce, to yield **2** ALQUILAR : to rent
renuencia *nf* : reluctance, unwillingness
renuente *adj* : reluctant, unwilling
renuncia *nf* **1** : resignation **2** : renunciation **3** : waiver
renunciar *vi* **1** : to resign **2** ～ **a** : to renounce, to relinquish ⟨renunció al título : herelinquished the title⟩
reñido, -da *adj* **1** : tough, hard-fought **2** : at odds, on bad terms
reñir {67} *vi* **1** : to argue **2** ～ **con** : to fall out with, to go up against — *vt* : to scold, to reprimand
reo, rea *n* **1** : accused, defendant **2** : offender, culprit
reojo *nm* **de** ～ : out of the corner of one's eye ⟨una mirada de reojo : a sidelong glance⟩
reorganizar {21} *vt* : to reorganize — **reorganización** *nf*
repantigarse {52} *vr* : to slouch, to loll about
reparación *nf, pl* **-ciones 1** : reparation, amends **2** : repair
reparar *vt* **1** : to repair, to fix, to mend **2** : to make amends for **3** : to correct **4** : to restore, to refresh — *vi* **1** ～ **en** : to observe, to take notice of **2** ～ **en** : to consider, to think about
reparo *nm* **1** : repair, restoration **2** : reservation, qualm ⟨no tuvieron reparos en decírmelo : they didn't hesitate to tell me⟩ **3 poner reparos a** : to find fault with, to object to
repartición *nf, pl* **-ciones 1** : distribution **2** : department, division
repartidor¹, -dora *adj* : delivery ⟨camión repartidor : delivery truck⟩
repartidor², -dora *n* : delivery person, distributor
repartimiento *nm* → **repartición**
repartir *vt* **1** : to allocate **2** DISTRIBUIR : to distribute, to hand out **3** : to spread
reparto *nm* **1** : allocation **2** : distribution **3** : cast (of characters)
repasar *vt* **1** : to pass by again **2** : to review, to go over **3** : to mend
repaso *nm* **1** : review **2** : mending **3** : checkup, overhaul

repatriar {85} *vt* : to repatriate — **repatriación** *nf*
repavimentar *vt* : to resurface
repelente¹ *adj* : repellent, repulsive
repelente² *nm* : repellent ⟨repelente de insectos : insect repellent⟩
repeler *vt* **1** : to repel, to resist, to repulse **2** : to reject **3** : to disgust ⟨el sabor me repele : I find the taste repulsive⟩
repensar {55} *v* : to rethink, to reconsider
repente *nm* **1** : sudden movement, start ⟨de repente : suddenly⟩ **2** : fit, outburst ⟨un repente de ira : a fit of anger⟩
repentino, -na *adj* : sudden — **repentinamente** *adv*
repercusión *nf, pl* **-siones** : repercussion
repercutir *vi* **1** : to reverberate, to echo **2** ～ **en** : to have effects on, to have repercussions on
repertorio *nm* : repertoire
repetición *nf, pl* **-ciones 1** : repetition **2** : rerun, repeat
repetidamente *adv* : repeatedly
repetido, -da *adj* **1** : repeated, numerous **2 repetidas veces** : repeatedly, time and again
repetir {54} *vt* **1** : to repeat **2** : to have a second helping of — **repetirse** *vr* **1** : to repeat oneself **2** : to recur
repetitivo, -va *adj* : repetitive, repetitious
repicar {72} *vt* : to ring — *vi* : to ring out, to peal
repique *nm* : ringing, pealing
repisa *nf* : shelf, ledge ⟨repisa de chimenea : mantelpiece⟩ ⟨repisa de ventana : windowsill⟩
replantear *vt* : to redefine, to restate — **replantearse** *vr* : to reconsider
replegar {49} *vt* : to fold — **replegarse** *vr* RETIRARSE : to retreat, to withdraw
repleto, -ta *adj* **1** : replete, full **2** ～ **de** : packed with, crammed with
réplica *nf* **1** : reply **2** : replica, reproduction **3** *Chile, Mex* : aftershock
replicación *nf, pl* : replication
replicar {72} *vi* **1** : to reply, to retort **2** : to argue, to answer back
repliegue *nm* **1** : fold **2** : retreat, withdrawal
repollo *nm* COL : cabbage
reponer {60} *vt* **1** : to replace, to put back **2** : to reinstate **3** : to reply — **reponerse** *vr* : to recover
reportaje *nm* : article, story, report
reportar *vt* **1** : to check, to restrain **2** : to bring, to carry, to yield ⟨me reportó numerosos beneficios : it brought me many benefits⟩ **3** : to report — **reportarse** *vr* **1** CONTENERSE : to control oneself **2** PRESENTARSE : to report, to show up
reporte *nm* : report
reportear *vt* : to report on, to cover

reportero, -ra *n* **1** : reporter **2 reportero gráfico** : photojournalist
reposado, -da *adj* : calm
reposar *vi* **1** : to rest, to repose **2** : to stand, to settle ⟨deje reposar la masa media hora : let the dough stand for half an hour⟩ **3** : to lie, to be buried — **reposarse** *vr* : to settle
reposición *nf, pl* **-ciones 1** : replacement **2** : reinstatement **3** : revival
repositorio *nm* : repository
reposo *nm* : repose, rest
repostar *vi* **1** : to stock up **2** : to refuel
repostería *nf* **1** : confectioner's shop **2** : pastry-making
repostero, -ra *n* : confectioner
repreguntar *vt* : to cross-examine
repreguntas *nfpl* : cross-examination
reprender *vt* : to reprimand, to scold
reprensible *adj* : reprehensible
represa *nf* : dam
represalia *nf* **1** : reprisal, retaliation **2 tomar represalias** : to retaliate
represar *vt* : to dam
representación *nf, pl* **-ciones 1** : representation **2** : performance **3 en representación de** : on behalf of
representante *nmf* **1** : representative **2** : performer
representar *vt* **1** : to represent, to act for **2** : to perform **3** : to look, to appear as **4** : to symbolize, to stand for **5** : to signify, to mean — **representarse** *vr* : to imagine, to picture
representativo, -va *adj* : representative
represión *nf, pl* **-siones** : repression
represivo, -va *adj* : repressive
reprimenda *nf* : reprimand
reprimir *vt* **1** : to repress **2** : to suppress, to stifle
reprobable *adj* : reprehensible, culpable
reprobación *nf* : disapproval
reprobar {19} *vt* **1** DESAPROBAR : to condemn, to disapprove of **2** : to fail (a course)
reprobatorio, -ria *adj* : disapproving, admonitory
reprochable *adj* : reprehensible, reproachable
reprochar *vt* : to reproach — **reprocharse** *vr*
reproche *nm* : reproach
reproducción *nf, pl* **-ciones** : reproduction
reproducir {61} *vt* : to reproduce — **reproducirse** *vr* **1** : to breed, to reproduce **2** : to recur
reproductor, -tora *adj* : reproductive
reptar *vi* : to crawl, to slither
reptil[1] *adj* : reptilian
reptil[2] *nm* : reptile
república *nf* : republic
republicanismo *nm* : republicanism
republicano, -na *adj & n* : republican
repudiar *vt* : to repudiate — **repudiación** *nf*
repudio *nm* : repudiation
repuesto[1] *pp* → **reponer**

repuesto[2] *nm* **1** : spare part **2 de ~** : spare ⟨rueda de repuesto : spare wheel⟩
repugnancia *nf* : repugnance
repugnante *adj* : repulsive, repugnant, revolting
repugnar *vt* : to cause repugnance, to disgust — **repugnarse** *vr*
repujar *vt* : to emboss
repulsivo, -va *adj* : repulsive
repuntar *vt Arg, Chile* : to round up (cattle) — *vi* : to begin to appear — **repuntarse** *vr* : to fall out, to quarrel
repuso, etc. → **reponer**
reputación *nf, pl* **-ciones** : reputation
reputar *vt* : to consider, to deem
requerir {76} *vt* **1** : to require, to call for **2** : to summon, to send for
requesón *nm, pl* **-sones** : curd cheese, cottage cheese
réquiem *nm* : requiem
requisa *nf* **1** : requisition **2** : seizure **3** : inspection
requisar *vt* **1** : to requisition **2** : to seize **3** INSPECCIONAR : to inspect
requisito *nm* **1** : requirement **2 requisito previo** : prerequisite
res *nf* **1** : beast, animal **2** *CA, Mex* : beef **3 reses** *nfpl* : cattle ⟨60 reses : 60 head of cattle⟩
resabio *nm* **1** VICIO : bad habit, vice **2** DEJO : aftertaste
resaca *nf* **1** : undertow **2** : hangover
resaltar *vi* SOBRESALIR : to stand out **2 hacer resaltar** : to bring out, to highlight — *vt* : to stress, to emphasize
resarcimiento *nm* **1** : compensation **2** : reimbursement
resarcir {83} *vt* : to compensate, to indemnify — **resarcirse** *vr* **~ de** : to make up for
resbaladizo, -za *adj* **1** RESBALOSO : slippery **2** : tricky, ticklish, delicate
resbalar *vi* **1** : to slip, to slide **2** : to slip up, to make a mistake **3** : to skid — **resbalarse** *vr*
resbalón *nm, pl* **-lones** : slip
resbaloso, -sa *adj* : slippery
rescatar *vt* **1** : to rescue, to save **2** : to recover, to get back
rescate *nm* **1** : rescue **2** : recovery **3** : ransom
rescindir *vt* : to rescind, to annul, to cancel
rescisión *nf, pl* **-siones** : annulment, cancellation
rescoldo *nm* : embers *pl*
resecar {72} *vt* : to make dry, to dry up — **resecarse** *vr* : to dry up
reseco, -ca *adj* : dry, dried-up
resentido, -da *adj* : resentful
resentimiento *nm* : resentment
resentirse {76} *vr* **1** : to suffer, to be weakened **2** OFENDERSE : to be upset ⟨se resintió porque la insultaron : she got upset when they insulted her, she resented being insulted⟩ **3 ~ de** : to feel the effects of

reseña *nf* **1** : report, summary, review **2** : description

reseñar *vt* **1** : to review **2** DESCRIBIR : to describe

reserva *nf* **1** : reservation **2** : reserve **3** : confidence, privacy ⟨con la mayor reserva : in strictest confidence⟩ **4 de** ~ : spare, in reserve **5 reservas** *nfpl* : reservations, doubts

reservación *nf, pl* **-ciones** : reservation

reservado, -da *adj* **1** : reserved, reticent **2** : confidential

reservar *vt* : to reserve — **reservarse** *vr* **1** : to save oneself **2** : to conceal, to keep to oneself

reservorio *nm* : reservoir, reserve

resfriado *nm* CATARRO : cold

resfriar {85} *vt* : to cool — **resfriarse** *vr* **1** : to cool off **2** : to catch a cold

resfrío *nm* : cold

resguardar *vt* : to safeguard, to protect — **resguardarse** *vr*

resguardo *nm* **1** : safeguard, protection **2** : receipt, voucher **3** : border guard, coast guard

residencia *nf* **1** : residence **2** : boarding house

residencial *adj* : residential

residente *adj & nmf* : resident

residir *vi* **1** VIVIR : to reside, to dwell **2** ~ **en** : to lie in, to consist of

residual *adj* : residual

residuo *nm* **1** : residue **2** : remainder **3 residuos** *nmpl* : waste ⟨residuos nucleares : nuclear waste⟩

resignación *nf, pl* **-ciones** : resignation

resignar *vt* : to resign — **resignarse** *vr* ~ **a** : to resign oneself to

resina *nf* **1** : resin **2 resina epoxídica** : epoxy

resistencia *nf* **1** : resistance **2** AGUANTE : endurance, strength, stamina

resistente *adj* **1** : resistant **2** : strong, tough

resistir *vt* **1** : to stand, to bear, to tolerate **2** : to withstand — *vi* : to resist ⟨resistió hasta el último minuto : he held out until the last minute⟩ — **resistirse** *vr* ~ **a** : to be resistant to, to be reluctant

resollar {19} *vi* : to breathe heavily, to wheeze

resolución *nf, pl* **-ciones** **1** : resolution, settlement **2** : decision **3** : determination, resolve

resolver {89} *vt* **1** : to resolve, to settle **2** : to decide — **resolverse** *vr* : to make up one's mind

resonancia *nf* **1** : resonance **2** : impact, repercussions *pl*

resonante *adj* **1** : resonant **2** : tremendous, resounding ⟨un éxito resonante : a resounding success⟩

resonar {19} *vi* : to resound, to ring

resoplar *vi* **1** : to puff, to pant **2** : to snort

resoplo *nm* **1** : puffing, panting **2** : snort

resorte *nm* **1** MUELLE : spring **2** : elasticity **3** : influence, means *pl* ⟨tocar resortes : to pull strings⟩

resortera *nf Mex* : slingshot

respaldar *vt* : to back, to support, to endorse — **respaldarse** *vr* : to lean back

respaldo *nm* **1** : back (of an object) **2** : support, backing

respectar *vt* : to concern, to relate to ⟨por lo que a mí respecta : as far as I'm concerned⟩

respectivo, -va *adj* : respective — **respectivamente** *adv*

respecto *nm* **1** ~ **a** : in regard to, concerning **2 al respecto** : on this matter, in this respect

respetable *adj* : respectable — **respetabilidad** *nf*

respetar *vt* : to respect

respeto *nm* **1** : respect, consideration **2 respetos** *nmpl* : respects ⟨presentar sus respetos : to pay one's respects⟩

respetuosidad *nf* : respectfulness

respetuoso, -sa *adj* : respectful — **respetuosamente** *adv*

respingo *nm* : start, jump

respiración *nf, pl* **-ciones** : respiration, breathing

respiradero *nm* : vent, ventilation shaft

respirador *nm* : respirator

respirar *v* : to breathe

respiratorio, -ria *adj* : respiratory

respiro *nm* **1** : breath **2** : respite, break

resplandecer {53} *vi* **1** : to shine **2** : to stand out

resplandeciente *adj* **1** : resplendent, shining **2** : radiant

resplandor *nm* **1** : brightness, brilliance, radiance **2** : flash

responder *vt* : to answer — *vi* **1** : to answer, to reply, to respond **2** ~ **a** : to respond to ⟨responder al tratamiento : to respond to treatment⟩ **3** ~ **de** : to answer for, to vouch for (something) **4** ~ **por** : to vouch for (someone)

responsabilidad *nf* : responsibility

responsable *adj* : responsible — **responsablemente** *adv*

respuesta *nf* : answer, response

resquebrajar *vt* : to split, to crack — **resquebrajarse** *vr*

resquemor *nm* : resentment, bitterness

resquicio *nm* **1** : crack **2** : opportunity, chance **3** : trace ⟨sin un resquicio de remordimiento : without a trace of remorse⟩ **4 resquicio legal** : loophole

resta *nf* SUSTRACCIÓN : subtraction

restablecer {53} *vt* : to reestablish, to restore — **restablecerse** *vr* : to recover

restablecimiento *nm* **1** : reestablishment, restoration **2** : recovery

restallar *vi* : to crack, to crackle, to click

restallido *nm* : crack, crackle

restante *adj* **1** : remaining **2 lo restante, los restantes** : the rest

restañar *vt* : to stanch

restar *vt* **1** : to deduct, to subtract ⟨restar un punto : to deduct a point⟩

2 : to minimize, to play down — *vi* : to remain, to be left

restauración *nf, pl* **-ciones 1** : restoration **2** : catering, food service

restaurante *nm* : restaurant

restaurar *vt* : to restore

restitución *nf, pl* **-ciones** : restitution, return

restituir {41} *vt* : to return, to restore, to reinstate

resto *nm* **1** : rest, remainder **2 restos** *nmpl* : remains ⟨restos de comida : leftovers⟩ ⟨restos arqueológicos : archeological ruins⟩ **3 restos mortales** : mortal remains

restorán *nm, pl* **-ranes** : restaurant

restregadura *nf* : scrub, scrubbing

restregar {49} *vt* **1** : to rub **2** : to scrub — **restregarse** *vr*

restricción *nf, pl* **-ciones** : restriction, limitation

restrictivo, -va *adj* : restrictive

restringido, -da *adj* LIMITADO : limited, restricted

restringir {35} *vt* LIMITAR : to restrict, to limit

restructuración *nf* : restructuring

restructurar *vt* : to restructure

resucitación *nf* : resuscitation ⟨resucitación cardiopulmonar : CPR, cardiopulmonary resuscitation⟩

resucitar *vt* **1** : to resuscitate, to revive, to resurrect **2** : to revitalize

resuello *nm* **1** : puffing, heavy breathing, wheezing **2** : break, breather

resuelto[1] *pp* → **resolver**

resuelto[2]**, -ta** *adj* : determined, resolved, resolute

resulta *nf* **1** : consequence, result **2 a resultas de** *or* **de resultas de** : as a result of

resultado *nm* : result, outcome

resultante *adj & nf* : resultant

resultar *vi* **1** : to work, to work out ⟨mi idea no resultó : my idea didn't work out⟩ **2** : to prove, to turn out to be ⟨resultó bien simpático : he turned out to be very nice⟩ **3** ~ **en** : to lead to, to result in **4** ~ **de** : to be the result of

resumen *nm, pl* **-súmenes 1** : summary, summation **2 en** ~ : in summary, in short

resumidero *nm* : drain

resumir *v* : to summarize, to sum up

resurgimiento *nm* : resurgence

resurgir {35} *vi* : to reappear, to revive

resurrección *nf, pl* **-ciones** : resurrection

retablo *nm* **1** : tableau **2** : altarpiece

retador, -dora *n* : challenger (in sports)

retaguardia *nf* : rear guard

retahíla *nf* : string, series ⟨una retahíla de insultos : a volley of insults⟩

retaliación *nf, pl* **-ciones** : retaliation

retama *nf* : broom (plant)

retar *vt* DESAFIAR : to challenge, to defy

retardante *adj* : retardant

retardar *vt* **1** RETRASAR : to delay, to retard **2** : to postpone

retazo *nm* **1** : remnant, scrap **2** : fragment, piece ⟨retazos de su obra : bits and pieces from his writings⟩

retención *nf, pl* **-ciones 1** : retention **2** : deduction, withholding

retener {80} *vt* **1** : to retain, to keep **2** : to withhold **3** : to detain

retentivo, -va *adj* : retentive

reticencia *nf* **1** : reluctance, reticence **2** : insinuation

reticente *adj* **1** : reluctant, reticent **2** : insinuating, misleading

retina *nf* : retina

retintín *nm, pl* **-tines 1** : jingle, jangle **2 con** ~ : sarcastically

retirada *nf* **1** : retreat ⟨batirse en retirada : to withdraw, to beat a retreat⟩ **2** : withdrawal (of funds) **3** : retirement **4** : refuge, haven

retirado, -da *adj* **1** : remote, distant, far off **2** : secluded, quiet

retirar *vt* **1** : to remove, to take away, to recall **2** : to withdraw, to take out — **retirarse** *vr* **1** REPLEGARSE : to retreat, to withdraw **2** JUBILARSE : to retire

retiro *nm* **1** JUBILACIÓN : retirement **2** : withdrawal, retreat **3** : seclusion

reto *nm* DESAFÍO : challenge, dare

retocar {72} *vt* : to touch up

retoñar *vi* : to sprout

retoño *nm* : sprout, shoot

retoque *nm* : retouching

retorcer {14} *vt* **1** : to twist **2** : to wring — **retorcerse** *vr* **1** : to get twisted, to get tangled up **2** : to squirm, to writhe, to wiggle about

retorcijón *nm, pl* **-jones** : cramp, sharp pain

retorcimiento *nm* **1** : twisting, wringing **2** : deviousness

retórica *nf* : rhetoric

retórico, -ca *adj* : rhetorical — **retóricamente** *adv*

retornar *v* : to return

retorno *nm* : return

retozar {21} *vi* : to frolic, to romp

retozo *nm* : frolicking

retozón, -zona *adj, mpl* **-zones** : playful

retracción *nf, pl* **-ciones** : retraction, withdrawal

retractable *adj* : retractable

retractación *nf, pl* **-ciones** : retraction (of a statement, etc.)

retractarse *vr* **1** : to withdraw, to back down **2** ~ **de** : to take back, to retract

retraer {81} *vt* **1** : to bring back **2** : to dissuade — **retraerse** *vr* **1** RETIRARSE : to withdraw, to retire **2** REFUGIARSE : to take refuge

retraído, -da *adj* : withdrawn, retiring, shy

retraimiento *nm* **1** : shyness, timidity **2** : withdrawal

retrasado, -da *adj* **1** : retarded, mentally slow **2** : behind, in arrears **3**

: backward (of a country) **4** : slow (of a watch)
retrasar *vt* **1** DEMORAR, RETARDAR : to delay, to hold up **2** : to put off, to postpone — **retrasarse** *vr* **1** : to be late **2** : to fall behind
retraso *nm* **1** ATRASO : delay, lateness **2 retraso mental** : mental retardation
retratar *vt* **1** : to portray, to depict **2** : to photograph **3** : to paint a portrait of
retrato *nm* **1** : depiction, portrayal **2** : portrait, photograph
retrete *nm* : restroom, toilet
retribución *nf, pl* **-ciones 1** : pay, payment **2** : reward
retribuir {41} *vt* **1** : to pay **2** : to reward
retroactivo, -va *adj* : retroactive — **retroactivamente** *adv*
retroalimentación *nf, pl* **-ciones** : feedback
retroceder *vi* **1** : to move back, to turn back **2** : to back off, to back down **3** : to recoil (of a firearm)
retroceso *nm* **1** : backward movement **2** : backing down **3** : setback, relapse **4** : recoil
retrógrado, -da *adj* **1** : reactionary **2** : retrograde
retropropulsión *nf* : jet propulsion
retrospectiva *nf* : retrospective, hindsight
retrospectivo, -va *adj* **1** : retrospective **2 mirada retrospectiva** : backward glance
retrovisor *nm* : rearview mirror
retruécano *nm* : pun, play on words
retumbar *vi* **1** : to boom, to thunder **2** : to resound, to reverberate
retumbo *nm* : booming, thundering, roll
retuvo, etc. → **retener**
reubicar {72} *vt* : to relocate — **reubicación** *nf*
reuma *or* **reúma** *nmf* → **reumatismo**
reumático, -ca *adj* : rheumatic
reumatismo *nm* : rheumatism
reunión *nf, pl* **-niones 1** : meeting **2** : gathering, reunion
reunir {68} *vt* **1** : to unite, to join, to bring together **2** : to have, to possess ⟨reunieron los requisitos necesarios : they fulfilled the necessary requirements⟩ **3** : to gather, to collect, to raise (funds) — **reunirse** *vr* : to meet
reutilizable *adj* : reusable
reutilizar {21} *vt* : to recycle, to reuse
revalidar *vt* **1** : to confirm, to ratify **2** : to defend (a title)
revaluar {3} *vt* : to reevaluate — **revaluación** *n*
revancha *nf* **1** DESQUITE : revenge, requital **2** : rematch
revelación *nf, pl* **-ciones** : revelation
revelado *nm* : developing (of film)
revelador¹, -dora *adj* : revealing
revelador² *nm* : developer
revelar *vt* **1** : to reveal, to disclose **2** : to develop (film)
revendedor, -dora *n* **1** : scalper **2** DETALLISTA : retailer

revender *vt* **1** : to resell **2** : to scalp
reventa *nf* **1** : resale **2** : scalping
reventar {55} *vi* **1** ESTALLAR, EXPLOTAR : to burst, to blow up **2 ~ de** : to be bursting with — *vt* **1** : to burst **2** *fam* : to annoy, to rile
reventón *nm, pl* **-tones 1** : burst, bursting **2** : blowout, flat tire **3** *Mex fam* : bash, party
reverberar *vi* : to reverberate — **reverberación** *nf*
reverdecer {53} *vi* **1** : to grow green again **2** : to revive
reverencia *nf* **1** : reverence **2** : bow, curtsy
reverenciar *vt* : to revere, to venerate
reverendo¹, -da *adj* **1** : reverend **2** *fam* : total, absolute ⟨es un reverendo imbécil : he is a complete idiot⟩
reverendo², -da *n* : reverend
reverente *adj* : reverent
reversa *nf Col, Mex* : reverse (gear)
reversible *adj* : reversible
reversión *nf, pl* **-siones** : reversion
reverso *nm* **1** : back, other side **2 el reverso de la medalla** : the complete opposite
revertir {76} *vi* **1** : to revert, to go back **2 ~ en** : to result in, to end up as
revés *nm, pl* **reveses 1** : back, wrong side **2** : setback, reversal **3** : backhand (in sports) **4 al revés** : the other way around, upside down, inside out **5 al revés de** : contrary to
revestimiento *nm* : covering, facing (of a building)
revestir {54} *vt* **1** : to coat, to cover, to surface **2** : to conceal, to disguise **3** : to take on, to assume ⟨la reunión revistió gravedad : the meeting took on a serious note⟩
revisar *vt* **1** : to examine, to inspect, to check **2** : to check over, to overhaul (machinery) **3** : to revise
revisión *nf, pl* **-siones 1** : revision **2** : inspection, check
revisor, -sora *n* **1** : inspector **2** : conductor (on a train)
revista *nf* **1** : magazine, journal **2** : revue **3 pasar revista** : to review, to inspect
revistar *vt* : to review, to inspect
revitalizar {21} *vt* : to revitalize — **revitalización** *nf*
revivir *vi* : to revive, to come alive again — *vt* : to relive
revocación *nf, pl* **-ciones** : revocation, repeal
revocar {72} *vt* **1** : to revoke, to repeal **2** : to plaster (a wall)
revolcar {82} *vt* : to knock over, to knock down — **revolcarse** *vr* : to roll around, to wallow
revolcón *nm, pl* **-cones** *fam* : tumble, fall
revolotear *vi* : to flutter around, to flit
revoloteo *nm* : fluttering, flitting

revoltijo *nm* **1** FÁRRAGO : mess, jumble **2** *Mex* : traditional seafood dish
revoltoso, -sa *adj* : unruly, rebellious
revolución *nf, pl* **-ciones** : revolution
revolucionar *vt* : to revolutionize
revolucionario, -ria *adj & n* : revolutionary
revolver {89} *vt* **1** : to move about, to mix, to shake, to stir **2** : to upset (one's stomach) **3** : to mess up, to rummage through ⟨revolver la casa : to turn the house upside down⟩ — **revolverse** *vr* **1** : to toss and turn **2** VOLVERSE : to turn around
revólver *nm* : revolver
revoque *nm* : plaster
revuelo *nm* **1** : fluttering **2** : commotion, stir
revuelta *nf* : uprising, revolt
revuelto[1] *pp* → **revolver**
revuelto[2], **-ta** *adj* **1** : choppy, rough ⟨mar revuelto : rough sea⟩ **2** : untidy **3 huevos revueltos** : scrambled eggs
rey *nm* : king
reyerta *nf* : brawl, fight
rezagado, -da *n* : straggler, latecomer
rezagar {52} *vt* **1** : to leave behind **2** : to postpone — **rezagarse** *vr* : to fall behind, to lag
rezar {21} *vi* **1** : to pray **2** : to say ⟨como reza el refrán : as the saying goes⟩ **3 ~ con** : to concern, to have to do with — *vt* : to say, to recite ⟨rezar un Ave María : to say a Hail Mary⟩
rezo *nm* : prayer, praying
rezongar {52} *vi* : to gripe, to grumble
rezumar *v* : to ooze, to leak
ría[1], **etc.** → **reír**
ría[2] *nf* : estuary
riachuelo *nm* ARROYO : brook, stream
riada *nf* : flood
ribera *nf* : bank, shore
ribete *nm* **1** : border, trim **2** : frill, adornment **3 ribetes** *nmpl* : hint, touch ⟨tiene sus ribetes de genio : there's a touch of genius in him⟩
ribetear *vt* : to border, to edge, to trim
ricamente *adv* : richly, splendidly
rice, etc. → **rizar**
rico[1], **-ca** *adj* **1** : rich, wealthy **2** : fertile **3** : luxurious, valuable **4** : delicious **5** : adorable, lovely **6** : great, wonderful
rico[2], **-ca** *n* : rich person
ridiculez *nf, pl* **-leces** : ridiculousness, absurdity
ridiculizar {21} *vt* : to ridicule
ridículo[1], **-la** *adj* ABSURDO, DISPARATADO : ridiculous, ludicrous — **ridículamente** *adv*
ridículo[2], **-la** *n* **1 hacer el ridículo** : to make a fool of oneself **2 poner en ridículo** : to ridicule
ríe, etc. → **reír**
riega, riegue etc. → **regar**
riego *nm* : irrigation
riel *nm* : rail, track

rienda *nf* **1** : rein **2 dar rienda suelta a** : to give free rein to **3 llevar las riendas** : to be in charge **4 tomar las riendas** : to take control
riesgo *nm* : risk
riesgoso, -sa *adj* : risky
rifa *nf* : raffle
rifar *vt* : to raffle — *vi* : to quarrel, to fight
rifle *nm* : rifle
rige, rija etc. → **regir**
rigidez *nf, pl* **-deces** **1** : rigidity, stiffness ⟨rigidez cadavérica : rigor mortis⟩ **2** : inflexibility
rígido, -da *adj* **1** : rigid, stiff **2** : strict — **rígidamente** *adv*
rigor *nm* **1** : rigor, harshness **2** : precision, meticulousness **3 de ~** : usual ⟨la respuesta de rigor : the standard reply⟩ **4 de ~** : essential, obligatory **5 en ~** : strictly speaking, in reality
riguroso, -sa *adj* : rigorous — **rigurosamente** *adv*
rima *nf* **1** : rhyme **2 rimas** *nfpl* : verse, poetry
rimar *vi* : to rhyme
rimbombante *adj* **1** : grandiose, showy **2** : bombastic, pompous
rímel *or* **rimel** *nm* : mascara
rin *nm Col, Mex* : wheel, rim (of a tire)
rincón *nm, pl* **rincones** : corner, nook
rinde, etc. → **rendir**
rinoceronte *nm* : rhinoceros
riña *nf* **1** : fight, brawl **2** : dispute, quarrel
riñe, etc. → **reñir**
riñón *nm, pl* **riñones** : kidney
río[1] → **reír**
río[2] *nm* **1** : river **2** : torrent, stream ⟨un río de lágrimas : a flood of tears⟩
ripio *nm* **1** : debris, rubble **2** : gravel
riqueza *nf* **1** : wealth, riches *pl* **2** : richness **3 riquezas naturales** : natural resources
risa *nf* **1** : laughter, laugh **2 dar risa** : to make laugh ⟨me dio mucha risa : I found it very funny⟩ **3** *fam* **morirse de la risa** : to die laughing, to crack up
risco *nm* : crag, cliff
risible *adj* IRRISORIO : ludicrous, laughable
risita *nf* : giggle, titter, snicker
risotada *nf* : guffaw
ristra *nf* : string, series *pl*
risueño, -ña *adj* **1** : cheerful, pleasant **2** : promising
rítmico, -ca *adj* : rhythmical, rhythmic — **rítmicamente** *adv*
ritmo *nm* **1** : rhythm **2** : pace, tempo ⟨trabajó a ritmo lento : she worked at a slow pace⟩
rito *nm* : rite, ritual
ritual *adj & nm* : ritual — **ritualmente** *adv*
rival *adj & nmf* COMPETIDOR : rival
rivalidad *nf* : rivalry, competition
rivalizar {21} *vi* **~ con** : to rival, to compete with

rizado, -da *adj* **1** : curly **2** : ridged **3** : ripply, undulating
rizar {21} *vt* **1** : to curl **2** : to ripple, to ruffle (a surface) **3** : to crumple, to fold — **rizarse** *vr* **1** : to frizz **2** : to ripple
rizo *nm* **1** : curl **2** : loop (in aviation)
robalo *or* **róbalo** *nm* : sea bass
robar *vt* **1** : to steal **2** : to rob, to burglarize **3** SECUESTRAR : to abduct, to kidnap **4** : to captivate — *vi* ～ **en** : to break into
roble *nm* : oak
robo *nm* : robbery, theft
robot *nm, pl* **robots** : robot
robótica *nf* : robotics
robustecer {53} *vt* : to grow stronger, to strengthen
robustez *nf* : sturdiness, robustness
robusto, -ta *adj* : robust, sturdy
roca *nf* : rock, boulder
roce¹, etc. → **rozar**
roce² *nm* **1** : rubbing, chafing **2** : brush, graze, touch **3** : close contact, familiarity **4** : friction, disagreement
rociador *nm* : sprinkler
rociar {85} *vt* : to spray, to sprinkle
rocío *nm* **1** : dew **2** : shower, light rain
rock *or* **rock and roll** *nm* : rock, rock and roll
rocola *nf* : jukebox
rocoso, -sa *adj* : rocky
rodada *nf* : track (of a tire), rut
rodado, -da *adj* **1** : wheeled **2** : dappled (of a horse)
rodadura *nf* : rolling, taxiing
rodaja *nf* : round, slice
rodaje *nm* **1** : filming, shooting **2** : breaking in (of a vehicle)
rodamiento *nm* **1** : bearing ⟨rodamiento de bolas : ball bearings⟩ **2** : rolling
rodante *adj* : rolling
rodar {19} *vi* **1** : to roll, to roll down, to roll along ⟨rodé por la escalera : I tumbled down the stairs⟩ ⟨todo rodaba bien : everthing was going along well⟩ **2** GIRAR : to turn, to go around **3** : to move about, to travel ⟨andábamos rodando por todas partes : we drifted along from place to place⟩ — *vt* **1** : to film, to shoot **2** : to break in (a new vehicle)
rodear *vt* **1** : to surround **2** : to round up (cattle) — *vi* **1** : to go around **2** : to beat around the bush — **rodearse** *vr* ～ **de** : to surround oneself with
rodeo *nm* **1** : rodeo, roundup **2** DESVÍO : detour **3** : evasion ⟨andar con rodeos : to beat around the bush⟩ ⟨sin rodeos : without reservations⟩
rodilla *nf* : knee
rodillo *nm* **1** : roller **2** : rolling pin
rododendro *nm* : rhododendron
roedor¹, -dora *adj* : gnawing
roedor² *nm* : rodent
roer {69} *vt* **1** : to gnaw **2** : to eat away at, to torment
rogar {16} *vt* : to beg, to request — *vi* **1** : to beg, to plead **2** : to pray

roiga, etc. → **roer**
rojez *nf* : redness
rojizo, -za *adj* : reddish
rojo¹, -ja *adj* **1** : red **2 ponerse rojo** : to blush
rojo² *nm* : red
rol *nm* **1** : role **2** : list, roll
rollo *nm* **1** : roll, coil ⟨un rollo de cinta : a roll of tape⟩ ⟨en rollo : rolled up⟩ **2** *fam* : roll of fat **3** *fam* : boring speech, lecture
romance *nm* **1** : Romance language **2** : ballad **3** : romance **4 en buen romance** : simply stated, simply put
romano, -na *adj & n* : Roman
romanticismo *nm* : romanticism
romántico, -ca *adj* : romantic — **románticamente** *adv*
rombo *nm* : rhombus
romería *nf* **1** : pilgrimage, procession **2** : crowd, gathering
romero¹, -ra *n* PEREGRINO : pilgrim
romero² *nm* : rosemary
romo, -ma *adj* : blunt, dull
rompecabezas *nms & pl* : puzzle, riddle
rompehielos *nms & pl* : icebreaker (ship)
rompehuelgas *nmfs & pl* ESQUIROL : strikebreaker, scab
rompenueces *nms & pl* : nutcracker
rompeolas *ns & pl* : breakwater, jetty
romper {70} *vt* **1** : to break, to smash **2** : to rip, to tear **3** : to break off (relations), to break (a contract) **4** : to break through, to break down **5** GASTAR : to wear out — *vi* **1** : to break ⟨al romper del día : at the break of day⟩ **2** ～ **a** : to begin to, to burst out with ⟨romper a llorar : to burst into tears⟩ **3** ～ **con** : to break off with
rompope *nm CA, Mex* : drink similar to eggnog
ron *nm* : rum
roncar {72} *vi* **1** : to snore **2** : to roar
ronco, -ca *adj* **1** : hoarse **2** : husky (of the voice) — **roncamente** *adv*
ronda *nf* **1** : beat, patrol **2** : round (of drinks, of negotiations, of a game)
rondar *vt* **1** : to patrol **2** : to hang around ⟨siempre está rondando la calle : he's always hanging around the street⟩ **3** : to be approximately ⟨debe rondar los cincuenta : he must be about 50⟩ — *vi* **1** : to be on patrol **2** : to prowl around, to roam about
ronque, etc. → **roncar**
ronquera *nf* : hoarseness
ronquido *nm* **1** : snore **2** : roar
ronronear *vi* : to purr
ronroneo *nm* : purr, purring
ronzal *nm* : halter (for an animal)
ronzar {21} *v* **1** : to munch, to crunch
roña *nf* **1** : mange **2** : dirt, filth **3** *fam* : stinginess
roñoso, -sa *adj* **1** : mangy **2** : dirty **3** *fam* : stingy
ropa *nf* **1** : clothes *pl*, clothing **2 ropa interior** : underwear

ropaje *nm* : apparel, garments *pl*, regalia
ropero *nm* ARMARIO, CLÓSET : wardrobe, closet
rosa[1] *adj* : rose-colored, pink
rosa[2] *nm* : rose, pink (color)
rosa[3] *nf* : rose (flower)
rosáceo, -cea *adj* : pinkish
rosado[1], **-da** *adj* **1** : pink **2 vino rosado** : rosé
rosado[2] *nm* : pink (color)
rosal *nm* : rosebush
rosario *nm* **1** : rosary **2** : series ⟨un rosario de islas : a string of islands⟩
rosbif *nm* : roast beef
rosca *nf* **1** : thread (of a screw) ⟨una tapa a rosca : a screw top⟩ **2** : ring, coil
roseta *nf* : rosette
rosquilla *nf* : ring-shaped pastry, doughnut
rostro *nm* : face, countenance
rotación *nf, pl* **-ciones** : rotation
rotar *vt* : to rotate, to turn — *vi* : to turn, to spin
rotativo[1], **-va** *adj* : rotary
rotativo[2] *nm* : newspaper
rotatorio, -ria *adj* → **rotativo**[1]
roto[1] *pp* → **romper**
roto[2], **-ta** *adj* **1** : broken **2** : ripped, torn
rotonda *nf* **1** : traffic circle, rotary **2** : rotunda
rotor *nm* : rotor
rótula *nf* : kneecap
rotular *vt* **1** : to head, to entitle **2** : to label
rótulo *nm* **1** : heading, title **2** : label, sign
rotundo, -da *adj* **1** REDONDO : round **2** : categorical, absolute ⟨un éxito rotundo : a resounding success⟩ — **rotundamente** *adv*
rotura *nf* : break, tear, fracture
roya *nf* : plant rust
roya, etc. → **roer**
rozado, -da *adj* GASTADO : worn
rozadura *nf* **1** : scratch, abrasion **2** : rubbed spot, sore
rozar {21} *vt* **1** : to chafe, to rub against **2** : to border on, to touch on **3** : to graze, to touch lightly — **rozarse** *vr* ∼ **con** *fam* : to rub shoulders with
ruandés, -desa *adj & n* : Rwandan
ruano, -na *adj* : roan
rubí *nm, pl* **rubíes** : ruby
rubio, -bia *adj & n* : blond
rublo *nm* : ruble
rubor *nm* **1** : flush, blush **2** : rouge, blusher
ruborizarse {21} *vr* : to blush
rubrica *nf* : title, heading
rubricar {72} *vt* **1** : to sign with a flourish ⟨firmado y rubricado : signed and sealed⟩ **2** : to endorse, to sanction
rubro *nm* **1** : heading, title **2** : line, area (in business)
rudeza *nf* ASPEREZA : roughness, coarseness

rudimentario, -ria *adj* : rudimentary — **rudimentariamente** *adv*
rudimento *nm* : rudiment, basics *pl*
rudo, -da *adj* **1** : rough, harsh **2** : coarse, unpolished — **rudamente** *adv*
rueda[1], **etc.** → **rodar**
rueda[2] *nf* **1** : wheel **2** RODAJA : round slice **3** : circle, ring **4 rueda de andar** : treadmill **5 rueda de prensa** : press conference **6 ir sobre ruedas** : to go smoothly
ruedita *nf* : caster (on furniture)
ruedo *nm* **1** : bullring, arena **2** : rotation, turn **3** : hem
ruega, ruegue etc. → **rogar**
ruego *nm* : request, appeal, plea
rugido *nm* : roar
rugir {35} *vi* : to roar
ruibarbo *nm* : rhubarb
ruido *nm* : noise, sound
ruidoso, -sa *adj* : loud, noisy — **ruidosamente** *adv*
ruin *adj* **1** : base, despicable **2** : mean, stingy
ruina *nf* **1** : ruin, destruction **2** : downfall, collapse **3 ruinas** *nfpl* : ruins, remains
ruinoso, -sa *adj* : run-down, dilapidated **2** : ruinous, disastrous
ruiseñor *nm* : nightingale
ruja, etc. → **rugir**
ruleta *nf* : roulette
rulo *nm* : curler, roller
rumano, -na *n* : Romanian, Rumanian
rumbo *nm* **1** : direction, course ⟨con rumbo a : bound for, heading for⟩ ⟨perder el rumbo : to go off course, to lose one's bearings⟩ ⟨sin rumbo : aimless, aimlessly⟩ **2** : ostentation, pomp **3** : lavishness, generosity
rumiante *adj & nm* : ruminant
rumiar *vt* : to ponder, to mull over — *vi* **1** : to chew the cud **2** : to ruminate, to ponder
rumor *nm* **1** : rumor **2** : murmur
rumorearse *or* **rumorarse** *vr* : to be rumored ⟨se rumorea que se va : rumor has it that she's leaving⟩
rumoroso, -sa *adj* : murmuring, babbling ⟨un arroyo rumoroso : a babbling brook⟩
rupia *nf* : rupee
ruptura *nf* **1** : break **2** : breaking, breach (of a contract) **3** : breaking off, breakup
rural *adj* : rural
ruso[1], **-sa** *adj & n* : Russian
ruso[2] *nm* : Russian (language)
rústico[1], **-ca** *adj* : rural, rustic
rústico[2], **-ca** *n* : rustic, country dweller
ruta *nf* : route
rutina *nf* : routine, habit
rutinario, -ria *adj* : routine, ordinary ⟨visita rutinaria : routine visit⟩ — **rutinariamente** *adv*

S

s *nf* : twentieth letter of the Spanish alphabet
sábado *nm* **1** : Saturday **2** : Sabbath
sábalo *nm* : shad
sabana *nf* : savanna
sábana *nf* : sheet, bedsheet
sabandija *nf* BICHO : bug, small reptile, pesky creature
sabático, -ca *adj* : sabbatical
sabedor, -dora *adj* : aware, informed
sabelotodo *nmf fam* : know-it-all
saber[1] {71} *vt* **1** : to know **2** : to know how to, to be able to ⟨sabe tocar el violín : she can play the violin⟩ **3** : to learn, to find out **4 a** ~ : to wit, namely — *vi* **1** : to know, to suppose **2** : to be informed ⟨supimos del desastre : we heard about the disaster⟩ **3** : to taste ⟨esto no sabe bien : this doesn't taste right⟩ **4** ~ **a** : to taste like ⟨sabe a naranja : it tastes like orange⟩ — **saberse** *vr* : to know ⟨ese chiste no me lo sé : I don't know that joke⟩
saber[2] *nm* : knowledge, learning
sabiamente *adv* : wisely
sabido, -da *adj* : well-known
sabiduría *nf* **1** : wisdom **2** : learning, knowledge
sabiendas *adv* **1 a** ~ : knowingly **2 a sabiendas de que** : knowing full well that
sabio[1], **-bia** *adj* **1** PRUDENTE : wise, sensible **2** DOCTO : learned
sabio[2], **-bia** *n* **1** : wise person **2** : savant, learned person
sable *nm* : saber, cutlass
sabor *nm* **1** : flavor, taste **2 sin** ~ : flavorless
saborear *vt* **1** : to taste, to savor **2** : to enjoy, to relish
sabotaje *nm* : sabotage
saboteador, -dora *n* : saboteur
sabotear *vt* : to sabotage
sabrá, etc. → **saber**
sabroso, -sa *adj* **1** RICO : delicious, tasty **2** AGRADABLE : pleasant, nice, lovely
sabueso *nm* **1** : bloodhound **2** *fam* : detective, sleuth
sacacorchos *nms & pl* : corkscrew
sacapuntas *nms & pl* : pencil sharpener
sacar {72} *vt* **1** : to pull out, to take out ⟨saca el pollo del congelador : take the chicken out of the freezer⟩ **2** : to get, to obtain ⟨saqué un 100 en el examen : I got 100 on the exam⟩ **3** : to get out, to extract ⟨le saqué la información : I got the information from him⟩ **4** : to stick out ⟨sacar la lengua : to stick out one's tongue⟩ **5** : to bring out, to introduce ⟨sacar un libro : to publish a book⟩ ⟨sacaron una moda nueva : they introduced a new style⟩ **6** : to take (photos) **7** : to make (copies) — *vi* **1**

: to kick off (in soccer or football) **2** : to serve (in sports)
sacarina *nf* : saccharin
sacarosa *nf* : sucrose
sacerdocio *nm* : priesthood
sacerdotal *adj* : priestly
sacerdote, -tisa *n* : priest *m*, priestess *f*
saciar *vt* **1** HARTAR : to sate, to satiate **2** SATISFACER : to satisfy
saciedad *nf* : satiety
saco *nm* **1** : bag, sack **2** : sac **3** : jacket, sport coat
sacramento *nm* : sacrament — **sacramental** *adj*
sacrificar {72} *vt* : to sacrifice — **sacrificarse** *vr* : to sacrifice oneself, to make sacrifices
sacrificio *nm* : sacrifice
sacrilegio *nm* : sacrilege
sacrílego, -ga *adj* : sacrilegious
sacristán *nm, pl* **-tanes** : sexton, sacristan
sacristía *nf* : sacristy, vestry
sacro, -cra *adj* SAGRADO : sacred ⟨arte sacro : sacred art⟩
sacrosanto, -ta *adj* : sacrosanct
sacudida *nf* **1** : shaking **2** : jerk, jolt, shock **3** : shake-up, upheaval
sacudir *vt* **1** : to shake, to beat **2** : to jerk, to jolt **3** : to dust off **4** CONMOVER : to shake up, to shock — **sacudirse** *vr* : to shake off
sacudón *nm, pl* **-dones** : intense jolt or shake-up
sádico[1], **-ca** *adj* : sadistic
sádico[2], **-ca** *n* : sadist
sadismo *nm* : sadism
safari *nm* : safari
saga *nf* : saga
sagacidad *nf* : sagacity, shrewdness
sagaz *adj, pl* **sagaces** PERSPICAZ : shrewd, discerning, sagacious
Sagitario *nmf* : Sagittarius, Sagittarian
sagrado, -da *adj* : sacred, holy
sainete *nm* : comedy sketch, one-act farce ⟨este proceso es un sainete : these proceedings are a farce⟩
sajar *vt* : to lance, to cut open
sal[1] → **salir**
sal[2] *nf* **1** : salt **2** *CA, Mex* : misfortune, bad luck
sala *nf* **1** : living room **2** : room, hall ⟨sala de conferencias : lecture hall⟩ ⟨sala de urgencias : emergency room⟩ ⟨sala de baile : ballroom⟩
salado, -da *adj* **1** : salty **2 agua salada** : salt water
salamandra *nf* : salamander
salami *nm* : salami
salar *vt* **1** : to salt **2** : to spoil, to ruin **3** *CoRi, Mex* : to jinx, to bring bad luck
salarial *adj* : salary, salary-related
salario *nm* **1** : salary **2 salario mínimo** : minimum wage
salaz *adj, pl* **salaces** : salacious, lecherous

salchicha *nf* 1 : sausage 2 : frankfurter, wiener

salchichón *nf, pl* **-chones** : a type of deli meat

salchichonería *nf Mex* 1 : delicatessen 2 : cold cuts *pl*

saldar *vt* : to settle, to pay off ⟨saldar una cuenta : to settle an account⟩

saldo *nm* 1 : settlement, payment 2 : balance ⟨saldo de cuenta : account balance⟩ 3 : remainder, leftover merchandise

saldrá, etc. → salir

salero *nm* 1 : saltshaker 2 : wit, charm

salga, etc. → salir

salida *nf* 1 : exit ⟨salida de emergencia : emergency exit⟩ 2 : leaving, departure 3 SOLUCIÓN : way out, solution 4 : start (of a race) 5 OCURRENCIA : wisecrack, joke 6 **salida del sol** : sunrise

saliente[1] *adj* 1 : departing, outgoing 2 : projecting 3 DESTACADO : salient, prominent

saliente[2] *nm* 1 : projection, protrusion 2 **ventana en saliente** : bay window

salinidad *nf* : salinity, saltiness

salino, -na *adj* : saline ⟨solución salina : saline solution⟩

salir {73} *vi* 1 : to go out, to come out, to get out ⟨salimos todas las noches : we go out every night⟩ ⟨su libro acaba de salir : her book just came out⟩ 2 PARTIR : to leave, to depart 3 APARECER : to appear ⟨salió en todos los diarios : it came out in all the papers⟩ 4 : to project, to stick out 5 : to cost, to come to 6 RESULTAR : to turn out, to prove 7 : to come up, to occur ⟨salga lo que salga : whatever happens⟩ ⟨salió una oportunidad : an opportunity came up⟩ 8 ~ **a** : to take after, to look like, to resemble 9 ~ **con** : to go out with, to date — **salirse** *vr* 1 : to escape, to get out, to leak out 2 : to come loose, to come off 3 **salirse con la suya** : to get one's own way

saliva *nf* : saliva

salivar *vi* : to salivate

salmo *nm* : psalm

salmón[1] *adj* : salmon-colored

salmón[2] *nm, pl* **salmones** : salmon

salmuera *nf* : brine

salobre *adj* : brackish, briny

salón *nm, pl* **salones** 1 : hall, large room ⟨salón de clase : classroom⟩ ⟨salón de baile : ballroom⟩ 2 : salon ⟨salón de belleza : beauty salon⟩ 3 : parlor, sitting room

salpicadera *nf Mex* : fender

salpicadura *nf* : spatter, splash

salpicar {72} *vt* 1 : to spatter, to splash 2 : to sprinkle, to scatter about

salpimentar {55} *vt* 1 : to season (with salt and pepper) 2 : to spice up

salsa *nf* 1 : sauce ⟨salsa picante : hot sauce⟩ ⟨salsa inglesa : Worcestershire sauce⟩ ⟨salsa tártara : tartar sauce⟩ 2

: gravy 3 : salsa (music) 4 **salsa mexicana** : salsa (sauce)

salsero, -ra *n* : salsa musician

saltador, -dora *n* : jumper

saltamontes *nms & pl* : grasshopper

saltar *vi* 1 BRINCAR : to jump, to leap 2 : to bounce 3 : to come off, to pop out 4 : to shatter, to break 5 : to explode, to blow up — *vt* 1 : to jump, to jump over 2 : to skip, to miss — **saltarse** *vr* OMITIR : to skip, to omit ⟨me salté ese capítulo : I skipped that chapter⟩

saltarín, -rina *adj, mpl* **-rines** : leaping, hopping ⟨frijol saltarín : jumping bean⟩

salteado, -da *adj* 1 : sautéed 2 : jumbled up ⟨los episodios se transmitieron salteados : the episodes were broadcast in random order⟩

salteador *nm* : highwayman

saltear *vt* 1 SOFREÍR : to sauté 2 : to skip around, to skip over

saltimbanqui *nmf* : acrobat

salto *nm* 1 BRINCO : jump, leap, skip 2 : jump, dive (in sports) 3 : gap, omission 4 **dar saltos** : to jump up and down 5 *or* **salto de agua** CATARATA : waterfall

saltón, -tona *adj, mpl* **saltones** : bulging, protruding

salubre *adj* : healthful, salubrious

salubridad *nf* : healthfulness, health

salud *nf* 1 : health ⟨buena salud : good health⟩ 2 **¡salud!** : bless you! (when someone sneezes) 3 **¡salud!** : cheers!, to your health!

saludable *adj* 1 SALUBRE : healthful 2 SANO : healthy, well

saludar *vt* 1 : to greet, to say hello to 2 : to salute — **saludarse** *vr*

saludo *nm* 1 : greeting, regards *pl* 2 : salute

salutación *nf, pl* **-ciones** : salutation

salva *nf* 1 : salvo, volley 2 **salva de aplausos** : round of applause

salvación *nf, pl* **-ciones** 1 : salvation 2 RESCATE : rescue

salvado *nm* : bran

salvador, -dora *n* 1 : savior, rescuer 2 **el Salvador** : the Savior

salvadoreño, -ña *adj & n* : Salvadoran, El Salvadoran

salvaguardar *vt* : to safeguard

salvaguardia *or* **salvaguarda** *nf* : safeguard, defense

salvajada *nf* ATROCIDAD : atrocity, act of savagery

salvaje[1] *adj* 1 : wild ⟨animales salvajes : wild animals⟩ 2 : savage, cruel 3 : primitive, uncivilized

salvaje[2] *nmf* : savage

salvajismo *nm* : savagery

salvamento *nm* 1 : rescuing, lifesaving 2 : salvation 3 : refuge

salvar *vt* 1 : to save, to rescue 2 : to cover (a distance) 3 : to get around (an obstacle), to overcome (a difficulty) 4

: to cross, to jump across **5 salvando** : except for, excluding — **salvarse** *vr* **1** : to survive, to escape **2** : to save one's soul

salvavidas[1] *nms & pl* **1** : life preserver **2 bote salvavidas** : lifeboat

salvavidas[2] *nmf* : lifeguard

salvedad *nf* **1** EXCEPCIÓN : exception **2** : proviso, stipulation

salvia *nf* : sage (plant)

salvo[1], **-va** *adj* **1** : unharmed, sound ⟨sano y salvo : safe and sound⟩ **2 a ~** : safe from danger

salvo[2] *prep* **1** EXCEPTO : except (for), save ⟨todos asistirán salvo Jaime : all will attend except for Jaime⟩ **2 salvo que** : unless ⟨salvo que llueva : unless it rains⟩

salvoconducto *nm* : safe-conduct

samba *nf* : samba

San *adj* → **santo**[1]

sanar *vt* : to heal, to cure — *vi* : to get well, to recover

sanatorio *nm* **1** : sanatorium **2** : clinic, private hospital

sanción *nf, pl* **sanciones** : sanction

sancionar *vt* **1** : to penalize, to impose a sanction on **2** : to sanction, to approve

sancochar *vt* : to parboil

sandalia *nf* : sandal

sándalo *nm* : sandalwood

sandez *nf, pl* **sandeces** ESTUPIDEZ : nonsense, silly thing to say

sandía *nf* : watermelon

sandwich ['sandwiʧ, 'saŋgwiʧ] *nm, pl* **sandwiches** [-dwiʧɛs, -gwi-] EMPAREDADO : sandwich

saneamiento *nm* **1** : cleaning up, sanitation **2** : reorganizing, streamlining

sanear *vt* **1** : to clean up, to sanitize **2** : to reorganize, to streamline

sangrante *adj* **1** : bleeding **2** : flagrant, blatant

sangrar *vi* : to bleed — *vt* : to indent (a paragraph, etc.)

sangre *nf* **1** : blood **2 a sangre fría** : in cold blood **3 a sangre y fuego** : by violent force **4 pura sangre** : thoroughbred

sangría *nf* **1** : bloodletting **2** : sangria (wine punch) **3** : drain, draining ⟨una sangría fiscal : a financial drain⟩ **4** : indentation, indenting

sangriento, -ta *adj* **1** : bloody **2** : cruel

sanguijuela *nf* **1** : leech, bloodsucker **2** : sponger, leech

sanguinario, -ria *adj* : bloodthirsty

sanguíneo, -nea *adj* **1** : blood ⟨vaso sanguíneo : blood vessel⟩ **2** : sanguine, ruddy

sanidad *nf* **1** : health **2** : public health, sanitation

sanitario[1], **-ria** *adj* **1** : sanitary **2** : health ⟨centro sanitario : health center⟩

sanitario[2], **-ria** *n* : sanitation worker

sanitario[3] *nm Col, Mex, Ven* : toilet ⟨los sanitarios : the toilets, the restroom⟩

sano, -na *adj* **1** SALUDABLE : healthy **2** : wholesome **3** : whole, intact

santiaguino, -na *adj* : of or from Santiago, Chile

santiamén *nm* **en un santiamén** : in no time at all

santidad *nf* : holiness, sanctity

santificar {72} *vt* : to sanctify, to consecrate, to hallow

santiguarse {10} *vr* PERSIGNARSE : to cross oneself

santo[1], **-ta** *adj* **1** : holy, saintly ⟨el Santo Padre : the Holy Father⟩ ⟨una vida santa : a saintly life⟩ **2 Santo, Santa** (San *before names of masculine saints except those beginning with D or T*) : Saint ⟨Santa Clara : Saint Claire⟩ ⟨Santo Tomás : Saint Thomas⟩ ⟨San Francisco : Saint Francis⟩

santo[2], **-ta** *n* : saint

santo[3] *nm* **1** : saint's day **2** CUMPLEAÑOS : birthday

santuario *nm* : sanctuary

santurrón, -rrona *adj, mpl* **-rrones** : overly pious, sanctimonious — **santurronamente** *adv*

saña *nf* **1** : fury, rage **2** : viciousness ⟨con saña : viciously⟩

sapo *nm* : toad

saque[1], etc. → **sacar**

saque[2] *nm* **1** : kickoff (in soccer or football) **2** : serve, service (in sports)

saqueador, -dora *n* DEPREDADOR : plunderer, looter

saquear *vt* : to sack, to plunder, to loot

saqueo *nm* DEPREDACIÓN : sacking, plunder, looting

sarampión *nm* : measles *pl*

sarape *nm CA, Mex* : serape, blanket

sarcasmo *nm* : sarcasm

sarcástico, -ca *adj* : sarcastic

sarcófago *nm* : sarcophagus

sardina *nf* : sardine

sardónico, -ca *adj* : sardonic

sarga *nf* : serge

sargento *nmf* : sergeant

sarna *nf* : mange

sarnoso, -sa *adj* : mangy

sarpullido *nm* ERUPCIÓN : rash

sarro *nm* **1** : deposit, coating **2** : tartar, plaque

sarta *nf* **1** : string, series (of insults, etc.) **2** : string (of pearls, etc.)

sartén *nmf, pl* **sartenes** **1** : frying pan **2 tener la sartén por el mango** : to call the shots, to be in control

sasafrás *nm* : sassafras

sastre, -tra *n* : tailor

sastrería *nf* **1** : tailoring **2** : tailor's shop

Satanás *or* **Satán** *nm* : Satan, the devil

satánico, -ca *adj* : satanic

satélite *nm* : satellite

satín *or* **satén** *nm, pl* **satines** *or* **satenes** : satin

satinado, -da *adj* : satiny, glossy

sátira *nf* : satire

satírico, -ca *adj* : satirical, satiric

satirizar {21} *vt* : to satirize

sátiro *nm* : satyr
satisfacción *nf, pl* **-ciones** : satisfaction
satisfacer {74} *vt* **1** : to satisfy **2** : to fulfill, to meet **3** : to pay, to settle —
satisfacerse *vr* **1** : to be satisfied **2** : to take revenge
satisfactorio, -ria *adj* : satisfactory —
satisfactoriamente *adv*
satisfecho, -cha *adj* : satisfied, content, pleased
saturación *nf, pl* **-ciones** : saturation
saturar *vt* **1** : to saturate, to fill up **2** : to satiate, to surfeit
saturnismo *nm* : lead poisoning
Saturno *nm* : Saturn
sauce *nm* : willow
saúco *nm* : elder (tree)
saudí *or* **saudita** *adj & nmf* : Saudi, Saudi Arabian
sauna *nmf* : sauna
savia *nf* : sap
saxofón *nm, pl* **-fones** : saxophone
sazón[1] *nf, pl* **sazones** **1** : flavor, seasoning **2** : ripeness, maturity ⟨en sazón : in season, ripe⟩ **3 a la sazón** : at that time, then
sazón[2] *nmf, pl* **sazones** *Mex* : flavor, seasoning
sazonar *vt* CONDIMENTAR : to season, to spice
scanner *nm* → **escáner**
sé → **saber, ser**
se *pron* **1** : to him, to her, to you, to them ⟨se los daré a ella : I'll give them to her⟩ **2** : each other, one another ⟨se abrazaron : they hugged each other⟩ **3** : himself, herself, itself, yourself, yourselves, themselves ⟨se afeitó antes de salir : he shaved before leaving⟩ **4** (*used in passive constructions*) ⟨se dice que es hermosa : they say she's beautiful⟩ ⟨se habla inglés : English spoken⟩
sea, etc. → **ser**
sebo *nm* **1** : grease, fat **2** : tallow **3** : suet
secado *nm* : drying
secador *nm* : hair dryer
secadora *nf* **1** : dryer, clothes dryer **2** *Mex* : hair dryer
secante *nm* : blotting paper, blotter
secar {72} *v* : to dry — **secarse** *vr* **1** : to get dry **2** : to dry up
sección *nf, pl* **secciones** **1** : section ⟨sección transversal : cross section⟩ **2** : department, division
seco, -ca *adj* **1** : dry **2** DISECADO : dried ⟨fruta seca : dried fruit⟩ **3** : thin, lean **4** : curt, brusque **5** : sharp ⟨un golpe seco : a sharp blow⟩ **6 a secas** : simply, just ⟨se llama Chico, a secas : he's just called Chico⟩ **7 en ~** : abruptly, suddenly ⟨frenar en seco : to make a sudden stop⟩
secoya *nf* : sequoia, redwood
secreción *nf, pl* **-ciones** : secretion
secretar *vt* : to secrete
secretaría *nf* **1** : secretariat, administrative department **2** *Mex* : ministry, cabinet office

secretariado *nm* **1** : secretariat **2** : secretarial profession
secretario, -ria *n* : secretary — **secretarial** *adj*
secreto[1], **-ta** *adj* **1** : secret **2** : secretive — **secretamente** *adv*
secreto[2] *nm* **1** : secret **2** : secrecy
secta *nf* : sect
sectario, -ria *adj & n* : sectarian
sector *nm* : sector
secuaz *nmf, pl* **secuaces** : follower, henchman, underling
secuela *nf* : consequence, sequel ⟨las secuelas de la guerra : the aftermath of the war⟩
secuencia *nf* : sequence
secuestrador, -dora *n* **1** : kidnapper, abductor **2** : hijacker
secuestrar *vt* **1** RAPTAR : to kidnap, to abduct **2** : to hijack, to commandeer **3** CONFISCAR : to confiscate, to seize
secuestro *nm* **1** RAPTO : kidnapping, abduction **2** : hijacking **3** : seizure, confiscation
secular *adj* : secular — **secularismo** *nm* — **secularización** *nf*
secundar *vt* : to support, to second
secundaria *nf* **1** : secondary education, high school **2** *Mex* : junior high school, middle school
secundario, -ria *adj* : secondary
secuoya *nf* : sequoia
sed *nf* **1** : thirst ⟨tener sed : to be thirsty⟩ **2 tener sed de** : to hunger for, to thirst for
seda *nf* : silk
sedación *nf, pl* **-ciones** : sedation
sedal *nm* : fishing line
sedán *nm, pl* **sedanes** : sedan
sedante *adj & nm* CALMANTE : sedative
sedar *vt* : to sedate
sede *nf* **1** : seat, headquarters **2** : venue, site **3 la Santa Sede** : the Holy See
sedentario, -ria *adj* : sedentary
sedición *nf, pl* **-ciones** : sedition — **sedicioso, -sa** *adj*
sediento, -ta *adj* : thirsty, thirsting
sedimentación *nf, pl* **-ciones** : sedimentation
sedimentario, -ria *adj* : sedimentary
sedimento *nm* : sediment
sedoso, -sa *adj* : silky, silken
seducción *nf, pl* **-ciones** : seduction
seducir {61} *vt* **1** : to seduce **2** : to captivate, to charm
seductivo, -va *adj* : seductive
seductor[1], **-tora** *adj* **1** SEDUCTIVO : seductive **2** ENCANTADOR : charming, alluring
seductor[2], **-tora** *n* : seducer
segador, -dora *n* : harvester
segar {49} *vt* **1** : to reap, to harvest, to cut **2** : to sever abruptly ⟨una vida segada por la enfermedad : a life cut short by illness⟩
seglar[1] *adj* LAICO : lay, secular
seglar[2] *nm* LAICO : layperson, layman *m*, laywoman *f*

segmentación *nf, pl* **-ciones** : segmentation

segmentado, -da *adj* : segmented

segmento *nm* : segment

segregar {52} *vt* **1** : to segregate **2** SECRETAR : to secrete

seguida *nf* **en** ~ : right away, immediately ⟨vuelvo en seguida : I'll be right back⟩

seguidamente *adv* **1** : next, immediately after **2** : without a break, continuously

seguido[1] *adv* **1** RECTO : straight, straight ahead **2** : often, frequently

seguido[2]**, -da** *adj* **1** CONSECUTIVO : consecutive, successive ⟨tres días seguidos : three days in a row⟩ **2** : straight, unbroken **3** ~ **por** *or* ~ **de** : followed by

seguidor, -dora *n* : follower, supporter

seguimiento *nm* **1** : following, pursuit **2** : continuation **3** : tracking, monitoring

seguir {75} *vt* **1** : to follow ⟨el sol sigue la lluvia : sunshine follows the rain⟩ ⟨seguiré tu consejo : I'll follow your advice⟩ ⟨me siguieron con la mirada : they followed me with their eyes⟩ **2** : to go along, to keep on ⟨seguimos toda la carretera panamericana : we continued along the PanAmerican Highway⟩ ⟨siguió hablando : he kept on talking⟩ ⟨seguir el curso : to stay on course⟩ **3** : to take (a course, a treatment) — *vi* **1** : to go on, to keep going ⟨sigue adelante : keep going, carry on⟩ **2** : to remain, to continue to be ⟨¿todavía sigues aquí? : you're still here?⟩ ⟨sigue con vida : she's still alive⟩ **3** : to follow, to come after ⟨la frase que sigue : the following sentence⟩

según[1] *adv* : it depends ⟨según y como : it all depends on⟩

según[2] *conj* **1** COMO, CONFORME : as, just as ⟨según lo dejé : just as I left it⟩ **2** : depending on how ⟨según se vea : depending on how one sees it⟩

según[3] *prep* **1** : according to ⟨según los rumores : according to the rumors⟩ **2** : depending on ⟨según los resultados : depending on the results⟩

segundo[1]**, -da** *adj* : second ⟨el segundo lugar : second place⟩

segundo[2]**, -da** *n* **1** : second (in a series) **2** : second (person), second-in-command

segundo[3] *nm* : second ⟨sesenta segundos : sixty seconds⟩

seguramente *adv* **1** : for sure, surely **2** : probably

seguridad *nf* **1** : safety, security **2** : (financial) security ⟨seguridad social : Social Security⟩ **3** CERTEZA : certainty, assurance ⟨con toda seguridad : with complete certainty⟩ **4** : confidence, self-confidence

seguro[1] *adv* : certainly, definitely ⟨va a llover, seguro : it's going to rain for sure⟩ ⟨¡seguro que sí! : of course!⟩

seguro[2]**, -ra** *adj* **1** : safe, secure **2** : sure, certain ⟨estoy segura que es él : I'm sure that's him⟩ **3** : reliable, trustworthy **4** : self-assured

seguro[3] *nm* **1** : insurance ⟨seguro de vida : life insurance⟩ **2** : fastener, clasp **3** *Mex* : safety pin

seis *adj & nm* : six

seiscientos[1]**, -tas** *adj* : six hundred

seiscientos[2] *nms & pl* : six hundred

selección *nf, pl* **-ciones 1** ELECCIÓN : selection, choice **2 selección natural** : natural selection

seleccionar *vt* ELEGIR : to select, to choose

selectivo, -va *adj* : selective — **selectivamente** *adv*

selecto, -ta *adj* **1** : choice, select **2** EXCLUSIVO : exclusive

selenio *nm* : selenium

sellar *vt* **1** : to seal **2** : to stamp

sello *nm* **1** : seal **2** ESTAMPILLA, TIMBRE : postage stamp **3** : hallmark, characteristic

selva *nf* **1** BOSQUE : woods *pl*, forest ⟨selva húmeda : rain forest⟩ **2** JUNGLA : jungle

selvático, -ca *adj* **1** : forest, jungle ⟨sendero selvático : jungle path⟩ **2** : wild

semáforo *nm* **1** : traffic light **2** : stop signal

semana *nf* : week

semanal *adj* : weekly — **semanalmente** *adv*

semanario *nm* : weekly (publication)

semántica *nf* : semantics

semántico, -ca *adj* : semantic

semblante *nm* **1** : countenance, face **2** : appearance, look

semblanza *nf* : biographical sketch, profile

sembrado *nm* : cultivated field

sembrador, -dora *n* : planter, sower

sembradora *nf* : seeder (machine)

sembrar {55} *vt* **1** : to plant, to sow **2** : to scatter, to strew ⟨sembrar el pánico : to spread panic⟩

semejante[1] *adj* **1** PARECIDO : similar, alike **2** TAL : such ⟨nunca he visto cosa semejante : I have never seen such a thing⟩

semejante[2] *nm* PRÓJIMO : fellowman

semejanza *nf* PARECIDO : similarity, resemblance

semejar *vi* : to resemble, to look like — **semejarse** *vr* : to be similar, to look alike

semen *nm* : semen

semental *nm* : stud (animal) ⟨caballo semental : stallion⟩

semestre *nm* : semester

semicírculo *nm* : semicircle, half circle

semiconductor *nm* : semiconductor

semidiós *nm, pl* **-dioses** : demigod *m*

semifinal *nf* : semifinal

semifinalista[1] *adj* : semifinal

semifinalista[2] *nmf* : semifinalist

semiformal *adj* : semiformal
semilla *nf* : seed
semillero *nm* **1** : seedbed **2** : hotbed, breeding ground
seminario *nm* **1** : seminary **2** : seminar, graduate course
seminarista *nm* : seminarian
semiprecioso, -sa *adj* : semiprecious
semita[1] *adj* : Semitic
semita[2] *nmf* : Semite
sémola *nf* : semolina
sempiterno, -na *adj* ETERNO : eternal, everlasting
senado *nm* : senate
senador, -dora *n* : senator
sencillamente *adv* : simply, plainly
sencillez *nf* : simplicity
sencillo[1]**, -lla** *adj* **1** : simple, easy **2** : plain, unaffected **3** : single
sencillo[2] *nm* **1** : single (recording) **2** : small change (coins) **3** : one-way ticket
senda *nf* CAMINO, SENDERO : path, way
sendero *nm* CAMINO, SENDA : path, way
sendos, -das *adj pl* : each, both ⟨llevaban sendos vestidos nuevos : they were each wearing a new dress⟩
senectud *nf* ANCIANIDAD : old age
senegalés, -lesa *adj & n, mpl* **-leses** : Senegalese
senil *adj* : senile — **senilidad** *nf*
seno *nm* **1** : breast, bosom ⟨los senos : the breasts⟩ ⟨el seno de la familia : the bosom of the family⟩ **2** : sinus **3 seno materno** : womb
sensación *nf, pl* **-ciones 1** IMPRESIÓN : feeling ⟨tener la sensación : to have a feeling⟩ **2** : sensation ⟨causar sensación : to cause a sensation⟩
sensacional *adj* : sensational
sensacionalista *adj* : sensationalistic, lurid
sensatez *nf* **1** : good sense **2 con ∼** : sensibly
sensato, -ta *adj* : sensible, sound — **sensatamente** *adv*
sensibilidad *nf* **1** : sensitivity, sensibility **2** SENSACIÓN : feeling
sensibilizar {21} *vt* : to sensitize
sensible *adj* **1** : sensitive **2** APRECIABLE : considerable, significant
sensiblemente *adv* : considerably, significantly
sensiblería *nf* : sentimentality, mush
sensiblero, -ra *adj* : mawkish, sentimental, mushy
sensitivo, -va *adj* **1** : sense ⟨órganos sensitivos : sense organs⟩ **2** : sentient, capable of feeling
sensor *nm* : sensor
sensorial *adj* : sensory
sensual *adj* : sensual, sensuous — **sensualmente** *adv*
sensualidad *nf* : sensuality
sentado, -da *adj* **1** : sitting, seated **2** : established, settled ⟨dar por sentado : to take for granted⟩ ⟨dejar sentado : to make clear⟩ **3** : sensible, steady, judicious

sentar {55} *vt* **1** : to seat, to sit **2** : to establish, to set — *vi* **1** : to suit ⟨ese color te sienta : that color suits you⟩ **2** : to agree with (of food or drink) ⟨las cebollas no me sientan : onions don't agree with me⟩ **3** : to please ⟨le sentó mal el paseo : she didn't enjoy the trip⟩ — **sentarse** *vr* : to sit, to sit down ⟨siéntese, por favor : please have a seat⟩
sentencia *nf* **1** : sentence, judgment **2** : maxim, saying
sentenciar *vt* : to sentence
sentido[1]**, -da** *adj* **1** : heartfelt, sincere ⟨mi más sentido pésame : my sincerest condolences⟩ **2** : touchy, sensitive **3** : offended, hurt
sentido[2] *nm* **1** : sense ⟨sentido común : common sense⟩ ⟨los cinco sentidos : the five senses⟩ ⟨sin sentido : senseless⟩ **2** CONOCIMIENTO : consciousness **3** SIGNIFICADO : meaning, sense ⟨doble sentido : double entendre⟩ **4** : direction ⟨calle de sentido único : one-way street⟩
sentimental[1] *adj* **1** : sentimental **2** : love, romantic ⟨vida sentimental : love life⟩
sentimental[2] *nmf* : sentimentalist
sentimentalismo *nm* : sentimentality, sentimentalism
sentimiento *nm* **1** : feeling, emotion **2** PESAR : regret, sorrow
sentir {76} *vt* **1** : to feel, to experience ⟨no siento nada de dolor : I don't feel any pain⟩ ⟨sentía sed : he was feeling thirsty⟩ ⟨sentir amor : to feel love⟩ **2** PERCIBIR : to perceive, to sense ⟨sentir un ruido : to hear a noise⟩ **3** LAMENTAR : to regret, to feel sorry for ⟨lo siento mucho : I'm very sorry⟩ — *vi* **1** : to have feeling, to feel **2 sin ∼** : without noticing, inadvertently — **sentirse** *vr* **1** : to feel ⟨¿te sientes mejor? : are you feeling better?⟩ **2** *Chile, Mex* : to take offense
seña *nf* **1** : sign, signal **2 dar señas de** : to show signs of
señal *nf* **1** : signal **2** : sign ⟨señal de tráfico : traffic sign⟩ **3** INDICIO : indication ⟨en señal de : as a token of⟩ **4** VESTIGIO : trace, vestige **5** : scar, mark **6** : deposit, down payment
señalado, -da *adj* : distinguished, notable
señalador *nm* : marker ⟨señalador de libros : bookmark⟩
señalar *vt* **1** INDICAR : to indicate, to show **2** : to mark **3** : to point out, to stress **4** : to fix, to set — **señalarse** *vr* : to distinguish oneself
señor, -ñora *n* **1** : gentleman *m*, man *m*, lady *f*, woman *f*, wife *f* **2** : Sir *m*, Madam *f* ⟨estimados señores : Dear Sirs⟩ **3** : Mr. *m*, Mrs. *f* **4** : lord *m*, lady *f* ⟨el Señor : the Lord⟩
señoría *nf* **1** : lordship **2 Su Señoría** : Your Honor
señorial *adj* : stately, regal

señorío *nm* **1** : manor, estate **2** : dominion, power **3** : elegance, class
señorita *nf* **1** : young lady, young woman **2** : Miss
señuelo *nm* **1** : decoy **2** : bait
sépalo *nm* : sepal
sepa, etc. → **saber**
separación *nf, pl* **-ciones 1** : separation, division **2** : gap, space
separadamente *adv* : separately, apart
separado, -da *adj* **1** : separated **2** : separate ⟨vidas separadas : separate lives⟩ **3 por** ~ : separately
separar *vt* **1** : to separate, to divide **2** : to split up, to pull apart — **separarse** *vr*
sepelio *nm* : interment, burial
sepia[1] *adj & nm* : sepia
sepia[2] *nf* : cuttlefish
septentrional *adj* : northern
séptico, -ca *adj* : septic
septiembre *nm* : September
séptimo[1], -ma *adj* : seventh
séptimo[2] *nm* : seventh
septuagésimo[1], -ma *adj* : seventieth
septuagésimo[2] *nm* : seventieth
sepulcral *adj* **1** : sepulchral **2** : dismal, gloomy
sepulcro *nm* TUMBA : tomb, sepulchre
sepultar *vt* ENTERRAR : to bury
sepultura *nf* **1** : burial **2** TUMBA : grave, tomb
seque, etc. → **secar**
sequedad *nf* **1** : dryness **2** : brusqueness, curtness
sequía *nf* : drought
séquito *nm* : retinue, entourage
ser[1] {77} *vi* **1** : to be ⟨él es mi hermano : he is my brother⟩ ⟨Camila es linda : Camila is pretty⟩ **2** : to exist, to live ⟨ser, o no ser : to be or not to be⟩ **3** : to take place, to occur ⟨el concierto es el domingo : the concert is on Sunday⟩ **4** (*used with expressions of time, date, season*) ⟨son las diez : it's ten o'clock⟩ ⟨hoy es el 9 : today's the 9th⟩ **5** : to cost, to come to ⟨¿cuánto es? : how much is it?⟩ **6** (*with the future tense*) : to be able to be ⟨¿será posible? : can it be possible?⟩ **7** ~ **de** : to come from ⟨somos de Managua : we're from Managua⟩ **8** ~ **de** : to belong to ⟨ese lápiz es de Juan : that's Juan's pencil⟩ **9 es que** : the thing is that ⟨es que no lo conozco : it's just that I don't know him⟩ **10** ¡**sea**! : agreed!, all right! **11 sea. . . sea** : either. . . or — *v aux* (*used in passive constructions*) : to be ⟨la cuenta ha sido pagada : the bill has been paid⟩ ⟨él fue asesinado : he was murdered⟩
ser[2] *nm* : being ⟨ser humano : human being⟩
seráfico, -ca *adj* : angelic, seraphic
serbio[1], -bia *adj & n* : Serb, Serbian
serbio[2] *nm* : Serbian (language)
serbocroata[1] *adj* : Serbo-Croatian
serbocroata[2] *nm* : Serbo-Croatian (language)

serenar *vt* : to calm, to soothe — **serenarse** *vr* CALMARSE : to calm down
serenata *nf* : serenade
serendipia *nf* : serendipity
serenidad *nf* : serenity, calmness
sereno[1], -na *adj* **1** SOSEGADO : serene, calm, composed **2** : fair, clear (of weather) **3** : calm, still (of the sea) — **serenamente** *adv*
sereno[2] *nm* : night watchman
seriado, -da *adj* : serial
serial *nm* : serial (on radio or television)
seriamente *adv* : seriously
serie *nf* **1** : series **2** SERIAL : serial **3 fabricación en serie** : mass production **4 fuera de serie** : extraordinary, amazing
seriedad *nf* **1** : seriousness, earnestness **2** : gravity, importance
serio, -ria *adj* **1** : serious, earnest **2** : reliable, responsible **3** : important **4 en** ~ : seriously, in earnest — **seriamente** *adv*
sermón *nm, pl* **sermones 1** : sermon **2** *fam* : harangue, lecture
sermonear *vt fam* : to harangue, to lecture
serpentear *vi* : to twist, to wind — **serpenteante** *adj*
serpentina *nf* : paper streamer
serpiente *nf* : serpent, snake
serrado, -da *adj* DENTADO : serrated
serranía *nf* : mountainous area
serrano, -na *adj* : from the mountains
serrar {55} *vt* : to saw
serrín *nm, pl* **serrines** : sawdust
serruchar *vt* : to saw up
serrucho *nm* : saw, handsaw
servicentro *nm Peru* : gas station
servicial *adj* : obliging, helpful
servicio *nm* **1** : service **2** SAQUE : serve (in sports) **3 servicios** *nmpl* : restroom
servidor, -dora *n* **1** : servant **2 su seguro servidor** : yours truly (in correspondence)
servidumbre *nf* **1** : servitude **2** : help, servants *pl*
servil *adj* **1** : servile, subservient **2** : menial
servilismo *nm* : servility, subservience
servilleta *nf* : napkin
servir {54} *vt* **1** : to serve, to be of use to **2** : to serve, to wait **3** SURTIR : to fill (an order) — *vi* **1** : to work ⟨mi radio no sirve : my radio isn't working⟩ **2** : to be of use, to be helpful ⟨esa computadora no sirve para nada : that computer's perfectly useless⟩ — **servirse** *vr* **1** : to help oneself to **2** : to be kind enough ⟨sírvase enviarnos un catálogo : please send us a catalog⟩
sésamo *nm* AJONJOLÍ : sesame, sesame seeds *pl*
sesenta *adj & nm* : sixty
sesentavo[1], -va *adj* : sixtieth
sesentavo[2] *n* : sixtieth (fraction)
sesgado, -da *adj* **1** : inclined, tilted **2** : slanted, biased

sesgar {52} *vt* **1** : to cut on the bias **2** : to tilt **3** : to bias, to slant
sesgo *nm* : bias
sesgue, etc. → **sesgar**
sesión *nf, pl* **sesiones 1** : session **2** : showing, performance
sesionar *vi* REUNIRSE : to meet, to be in session
seso *nm* **1** : brains, intelligence **2 sesos** *nmpl* : brains (as food)
sesudo, -da *adj* **1** : prudent, sensible **2** : brainy
set *nm, pl* **sets** : set (in tennis)
seta *nf* : mushroom
setecientos[1], **-tas** *adj* : seven hundred
setecientos[2] *nms & pl* : seven hundred
setenta *adj & nm* : seventy
setentavo[1], **-va** *adj* : seventieth
setentavo[2] *nm* : seventieth
setiembre → **septiembre**
seto *nm* **1** : fence, enclosure **2 seto vivo** : hedge
seudónimo *nm* : pseudonym
severidad *nf* **1** : harshness, severity **2** : strictness
severo, -ra *adj* **1** : harsh, severe **2** ESTRICTO : strict — **severamente** *adv*
sexagésimo[1], **-ma** *adj* : sixtieth, sixty-
sexagésimo[2], **-ma** *n* : sixtieth, sixty- (in a series)
sexismo *nm* : sexism — **sexista** *adj & nmf*
sexo *nm* : sex
sextante *nm* : sextant
sexteto *nm* : sextet
sexto, -ta *adj* : sixth — **sexto, -ta** *n*
sexual *adj* : sexual, sex ⟨educación sexual : sex education⟩ — **sexualmente** *adv*
sexualidad *nf* : sexuality
sexy *adj, pl* **sexy** *or* **sexys** : sexy
shock ['ʃok, 'tʃok] *nm* : shock ⟨estado de shock : state of shock⟩
short *nm, pl* **shorts** : shorts *pl*
show *nm, pl* **shows** : show
si *conj* **1** : if ⟨lo haré si me pagan : I'll do it if they pay me⟩ ⟨si lo supiera te lo diría : if I knew it I would tell you⟩ **2** : whether, if ⟨no importa si funciona o no : it doesn't matter whether it works (or not)⟩ **3** (*expressing desire, protest, or surprise*) ⟨si supiera la verdad : if only I knew the truth⟩ ⟨¡si no quiero! : but I don't want to!⟩ **4 si bien** : although ⟨si bien se ha progresado : although progress has been made⟩ **5 si no** : otherwise, or else ⟨si no, no voy : otherwise I won't go⟩
sí[1] *adv* **1** : yes ⟨sí, gracias : yes, please⟩ ⟨creo que sí : I think so⟩ **2 sí que** : indeed, absolutely ⟨esta vez sí que ganaré : this time I'm sure to win⟩ **3 porque sí** *fam* : because, just because ⟨lo hizo porque sí : she did it just because⟩
sí[2] *nm* : yes ⟨dar el sí : to say yes, to express consent⟩
sí[3] *pron* **1 de por sí** *or* **en sí** : by itself, in itself, per se **2 fuera de sí** : beside

oneself **3 para sí (mismo)** : to himself, to herself, for himself, for herself **4 entre** ~ : among themselves
siamés, -mesa *adj & n, mpl* **siameses** : Siamese
sibilante *adj & nf* : sibilant
siciliano, -na *adj & n* : Sicilian
sico- → **psico-**
sicomoro *or* **sicómoro** *nm* : sycamore
SIDA *or* **sida** *nm* (síndrome de inmunodeficiencia adquirida) : AIDS
siderurgia *nf* : iron and steel industry
siderúrgico, -ca *adj* : steel, iron ⟨la industria siderúrgica : the steel industry⟩
sidra *nf* : hard cider
siega[1], **siegue, etc.** → **segar**
siega[2] *nf* **1** : harvesting **2** : harvest time **3** : harvested crop
siembra[1], **etc.** → **sembrar**
siembra[2] *nf* **1** : sowing **2** : sowing season **3** SEMBRADO : cultivated field
siempre *adv* **1** : always ⟨siempre tienes hambre : you're always hungry⟩ **2** : still ⟨¿siempre te vas? : are you still going?⟩ **3** *Mex* : after all ⟨siempre no fui : I didn't go after all⟩ **4 siempre que** : whenever, every time ⟨siempre que pasa : every time he walks by⟩ **5 para** ~ : forever, for good **6 siempre y cuando** : provided that
sien *nf* : temple (on the forehead)
sienta, etc. → **sentar**
siente, etc. → **sentir**
sierpe *nf* : serpent, snake
sierra[1], **etc.** → **serrar**
sierra[2] *nf* **1** : saw ⟨sierra de vaivén : jigsaw⟩ **2** CORDILLERA : mountain range **3** : mountains *pl* ⟨viven en la sierra : they live in the mountains⟩
siervo, -va *n* **1** : slave **2** : serf
siesta *nf* : nap, siesta
siete *adj & nm* : seven
sífilis *nf* : syphilis
sifón *nm, pl* **sifones** : siphon
siga, sigue etc. → **seguir**
sigilo *nm* : secrecy, stealth
sigiloso, -sa *adj* FURTIVO : furtive, stealthy — **sigilosamente** *adv*
sigla *nf* : acronym, abbreviation
siglo *nm* **1** : century **2** : age ⟨el Siglo de Oro : the Golden Age⟩ ⟨hace siglos que no te veo : I haven't seen you in ages⟩ **3** : world, secular life
signar *vt* : to sign (a treaty or agreement)
signatario, -ria *n* : signatory
significación *nf, pl* **-ciones 1** : significance, importance **2** : signification, meaning
significado *nm* **1** : sense, meaning **2** : significance
significante *adj* : significant
significar {72} *vt* **1** : to mean, to signify **2** : to express, to make known — **significarse** *vr* **1** : to draw attention, to become known **2** : to take a stance
significativo, -va *adj* **1** : significant, important **2** : meaningful — **significativamente** *adv*

signo *nm* **1** : sign ⟨signo de igual : equal sign⟩ ⟨un signo de alegría : a sign of happiness⟩ **2** : (punctuation) mark ⟨signo de interrogación : question mark⟩ ⟨signo de admiración : exclamation point⟩ ⟨signo de intercalación : caret⟩
siguiente *adj* : next, following
sílaba *nf* : syllable
silábico, -ca *adj* : syllabic
silbar *v* : to whistle
silbato *nm* PITO : whistle
silbido *nm* : whistle, whistling
silenciador *nm* **1** : muffler (of an automobile) **2** : silencer
silenciar *vt* **1** : to silence **2** : to muffle
silencio *nm* **1** : silence, quiet ⟨¡silencio! : be quiet!⟩ **2** : rest (in music)
silencioso, -sa *adj* : silent, quiet — **silenciosamente** *adv*
sílice *nf* : silica
silicio *nm* : silicon
silla *nf* **1** : chair **2 silla de ruedas** : wheelchair
sillón *nm, pl* **sillones** : armchair, easy chair
silo *nm* : silo
silueta *nf* **1** : silhouette **2** : figure, shape
silvestre *adj* : wild ⟨flor silvestre : wildflower⟩
silvicultor, -tora *n* : forester
silvicultura *nf* : forestry
sima *nf* ABISMO : chasm, abyss
simbólico, -ca *adj* : symbolic — **simbólicamente** *adj*
simbolismo *nm* : symbolism
simbolizar {21} *vt* : to symbolize
símbolo *nm* : symbol
simetría *nf* : symmetry
simétrico, -ca *adj* : symmetrical, symmetric
simiente *nf* : seed
símil *nm* **1** : simile **2** : analogy, comparison
similar *adj* SEMEJANTE : similar, alike
similitud *nf* : similarity, resemblance
simio *nm* : ape
simpatía *nf* **1** : liking, affection ⟨tomarle simpatía a : to take a liking to⟩ **2** : warmth, friendliness **3** : support, solidarity
simpático, -ca *adj* : nice, friendly, likeable
simpatizante *nf* : sympathizer, supporter
simpatizar {21} *vi* **1** : to get along, to hit it off ⟨simpaticé mucho con él : I really liked him⟩ **2** ~ **con** : to sympathize with, to support
simple[1] *adj* **1** SENCILLO : plain, simple, easy **2** : pure, mere ⟨por simple vanidad : out of pure vanity⟩ **3** : simpleminded, foolish
simple[2] *n* : fool, simpleton
simplemente *adv* : simply, merely, just
simpleza *nf* **1** : foolishness, simpleness **2** NECEDAD : nonsense
simplicidad *nf* : simplicity

simplificar {72} *vt* : to simplify — **simplificación** *nf*
simplista *adj* : simplistic
simposio *or* **simposium** *nm* : symposium
simulación *nf, pl* **-ciones** : simulation
simulacro *nm* : imitation, sham ⟨simulacro de juicio : mock trial⟩
simular *vt* **1** : to simulate **2** : to feign, to pretend
simultáneo, -nea *adj* : simultaneous — **simultáneamente** *adv*
sin *prep* **1** : without ⟨sin querer : unintentionally⟩ ⟨sin refinar : unrefined⟩ **2** **sin que** : without ⟨lo hicimos sin que él se diera cuenta : we did it without him noticing⟩
sinagoga *nf* : synagogue
sinceridad *nf* : sincerity
sincero, -ra *adj* : sincere, honest, true — **sinceramente** *adv*
síncopa *nf* : syncopation
sincopar *vt* : to syncopate
sincronizar {21} *vt* : to synchronize — **sincronización** *nf*
sindical *adj* GREMIAL : union, labor ⟨representante sindical : union representative⟩
sindicalización *nf, pl* **-ciones** : unionizing, unionization
sindicalizar {21} *vt* : to unionize — **sindicalizarse** *vr* **1** : to form a union **2** : to join a union
sindicar → **sindicalizar**
sindicato *nm* GREMIO : union, guild
síndrome *nm* : syndrome
sinecura *nf* : sinecure
sinfín *nm* : endless number ⟨un sinfín de problemas : no end of problems⟩
sinfonía *nf* : symphony
sinfónica *nf* : symphony orchestra
sinfónico, -ca *adj* : symphonic, symphony
singular[1] *adj* **1** : singular, unique **2** PARTICULAR : peculiar, odd **3** : singular (in grammar) — **singularmente** *adv*
singular[2] *nm* : singular
singularidad *nf* : uniqueness, singularity
singularizar {21} *vt* : to make unique or distinct — **singularizarse** *vr* : to stand out, to distinguish oneself
siniestrado, -da *adj* : damaged, wrecked ⟨zona siniestrada : disaster zone⟩
siniestro[1]**, -tra** *adj* **1** IZQUIERDO : left, left-hand **2** MALVADO : sinister, evil
siniestro[2] *nm* : accident, disaster
sinnúmero → **sinfín**
sino *conj* **1** : but, rather ⟨no será hoy, sino mañana : it won't be today, but tomorrow⟩ **2** EXCEPTO : but, except ⟨no hace sino despertar suspicacias : it does nothing but arouse suspicion⟩
sinónimo[1]**, -ma** *adj* : synonymous
sinónimo[2] *nm* : synonym
sinopsis *nfs & pl* RESUMEN : synopsis, summary
sinrazón *nf, pl* **-zones** : wrong, injustice

sinsabores *nmpl* : woes, troubles
sinsonte *nm* : mockingbird
sintáctico, -ca *adj* : syntactic, syntactical
sintaxis *nfs & pl* : syntax
síntesis *nfs & pl* 1 : synthesis, fusion 2 SINOPSIS : synopsis, summary
sintético, -ca *adj* : synthetic — sintéticamente *adv*
sintetizar {21} *vt* 1 : to synthesize 2 RESUMIR : to summarize
sintió, etc. → sentir
síntoma *nm* : symptom
sintomático, -ca *adj* : symptomatic
sintonía *nf* 1 : tuning in (of a radio) 2 en sintonía con : in tune with, attuned to
sintonizador *nm* : tuner, knob for tuning (of a radio, etc.)
sintonizar {21} *vt* : to tune (in) to — *vi* 1 : to tune in 2 ~ con : to be in tune with, to empathize with
sinuosidad *nf* : sinuosity
sinuoso, -sa *adj* 1 : winding, sinuous 2 : devious
sinvergüenza¹ *adj* 1 DESCARADO : shameless, brazen, impudent 2 TRAVIESO : naughty
sinvergüenza² *nmf* 1 : rogue, scoundrel 2 : brat, rascal
sionista *adj & nmf* : Zionist — sionismo *nm*
siqui- → psiqui-
siquiera *adv* 1 : at least ⟨dame siquiera un poquito : at least give me a little bit⟩ 2 (*in negative constructions*) : not even ⟨ni siquiera nos saludaron : they didn't even say hello to us⟩
sirena *nf* 1 : mermaid 2 : siren ⟨sirena de niebla : foghorn⟩
sirio, -ria *adj & n* : Syrian
sirope *nm* : syrup
sirve, etc. → servir
sirviente, -ta *n* : servant, maid *f*
sisal *nm* : sisal
sisear *vi* : to hiss
siseo *nm* : hiss
sísmico, -ca *adj* : seismic
sismo *nm* 1 TERREMOTO : earthquake 2 TEMBLOR : tremor
sismógrafo *nm* : seismograph
sistema *nm* : system
sistemático, -ca *adj* : systematic — sistemáticamente *adv*
sistematizar {21} *vt* : to systematize
sistémico, -ca *adj* : systemic
sitiar *vt* ASEDIAR : to besiege
sitio *nm* 1 LUGAR : place, site ⟨vámonos a otro sitio : let's go somewhere else⟩ 2 ESPACIO : room, space ⟨hacer sitio a : to make room for⟩ 3 : siege ⟨estado de sitio : state of siege⟩ 4 *Mex* : taxi stand
situación *nf, pl* -ciones : situation
situado, -da *adj* : situated, placed
situar {3} *vt* UBICAR : to situate, to place, to locate — situarse *vr* 1 : to be placed, to be located 2 : to make a place for oneself, to do well

sketch *nm* : sketch, skit
slip *nm* : briefs *pl*, underpants *pl*
smog *nm* : smog
smoking *nm* ESMOQUIN : tuxedo
snob → esnob
so *prep* : under ⟨so pena de : under penalty of⟩
sobaco *nm* : armpit
sobado, -da *adj* 1 : worn, shabby 2 : well-worn, hackneyed
sobar *vt* 1 : to finger, to handle 2 : to knead 3 : to rub, to massage 4 *fam* : to beat, to pummel
soberanía *nf* : sovereignty
soberano, -na *adj & n* : sovereign
soberbia *nf* 1 ORGULLO : pride, arrogance 2 MAGNIFICENCIA : magnificence
soberbio, -bia *adj* 1 : proud, arrogant 2 : grand, magnificent
sobornable *adv* : venal, bribable
sobornar *vt* : to bribe
soborno *nm* 1 : bribery 2 : bribe
sobra *nf* 1 : excess, surplus 2 de ~ : extra, to spare 3 sobras *nfpl* : leftovers, scraps
sobrado, -da *adj* : abundant, excessive, more than enough
sobrante¹ *adj* : remaining, superfluous
sobrante² *nm* : remainder, surplus
sobrar *vi* : to be in excess, to be superfluous ⟨más vale que sobre a que falte : it's better to have too much than not enough⟩
sobre¹ *nm* 1 : envelope 2 : packet ⟨un sobre de sazón : a packet of seasoning⟩
sobre² *prep* 1 : on, on top of ⟨sobre la mesa : on the table⟩ 2 : over, above 3 : about ⟨¿tiene libros sobre Bolivia? : do you have books on Bolivia?⟩ 4 sobre todo : especially, above all
sobrealimentar *vt* : to overfeed
sobrecalentar {55} *vt* : to overheat — sobrecalentarse *vr*
sobrecama *nmf* : bedspread
sobrecargar {52} *vt* : to overload, to overburden, to weigh down
sobrecoger {15} *vt* 1 : to surprise, to startle 2 : to scare — sobrecogerse *vr*
sobrecubierta *nf* : dust jacket
sobredosis *nfs & pl* : overdose
sobreentender {56} *vt* : to infer, to understand
sobreestimar *vt* : to overestimate, to overrate
sobreexcitado, -da *adj* : overexcited
sobreexponer {60} *vt* : to overexpose
sobregirar *vt* : to overdraw
sobregiro *nm* : overdraft
sobrehumano, -na *adj* : superhuman
sobrellevar *vt* : to endure, to bear
sobremanera *adv* : exceedingly
sobremesa *nf* : after-dinner conversation
sobrenatural *adj* : supernatural
sobrenombre *nm* APODO : nickname
sobrentender → sobreentender

sobrepasar *vt* : to exceed, to surpass —
  sobrepasarse *vr* PASARSE : to go too
  far
sobrepelliz *nf, pl* **-pellices** : surplice
sobrepeso *nm* **1** : excess weight **2**
  : overweight, obesity
sobrepoblación, sobrepoblado → **su-**
  perpoblación, superpoblado
sobreponer {60} *vt* **1** SUPERPONER : to
  superimpose **2** ANTEPONER : to put
  first, to give priority to — **sobrepon-**
  erse *vr* **1** : to pull oneself together **2**
  ~ **a** : to overcome
sobreprecio *nm* : surcharge
sobreproducción *nf, pl* **-ciones** : over-
  production
sobreproducir {61} *vt* : to overproduce
sobreprotector, -tora *adj* : overprotec-
  tive
sobreproteger {15} *vt* : to overprotect
sobresaliente[1] *adj* **1** : protruding, projecting **2** : outstanding, noteworthy **3**
  : significant, salient
sobresaliente[2] *nmf* : understudy
sobresalir {73} *vi* **1** : to protrude, to jut
  out, to project **2** : to stand out, to excel
sobresaltar *vt* : to startle, to frighten —
  sobresaltarse *vr*
sobresalto *nm* : start, fright
sobresueldo *nm* : bonus, additional pay
sobretasa *nf* : surcharge ⟨sobretasa a la
  gasolina : gas tax⟩
sobretodo *nm* : overcoat
sobrevalorar *or* **sobrevaluar** {3} *vt* : to
  overvalue, to overrate
sobrevender *vt* : to oversell
sobrevenir {87} *vi* ACAECER : to take
  place, to come about ⟨podrían sobrevenir complicaciones : complications could occur⟩
sobrevivencia → **supervivencia**
sobreviviente → **superviviente**
sobrevivir *vi* : to survive — *vt* : to outlive, to outlast
sobrevolar {19} *vt* : to fly over, to overfly
sobriedad *nf* : sobriety, moderation
sobrino, -na *n* : nephew *m*, niece *f*
sobrio, -bria *adj* : sober — **sobriamente**
  adv
socarrón, -rrona *adj, mpl* **-rrones** **1**
  : sly, cunning **2** : sarcastic
socavar *vt* : to undermine
sociabilidad *nf* : sociability
sociable *adj* : sociable
social *adj* : social — **socialmente** *adv*
socialista *adj & nmf* : socialist — **so-**
  cialismo *nm*
sociedad *nf* **1** : society **2** : company,
  enterprise **3 sociedad anónima** : incorporated company
socio, -cia *n* **1** : member **2** : partner
socioeconómico, -ca *adj* : socioeconomic
sociología *nf* : sociology
sociológico, -ca *adj* : sociological —
  sociológicamente *adv*

sociólogo, -ga *n* : sociologist
socorrer *vt* : to assist, to come to the aid
  of
socorrido, -da *adj* ÚTIL : handy, practical
socorrista *nmf* **1** : rescue worker **2**
  : lifeguard
socorro *nm* AUXILIO **1** : aid, help
  ⟨equipo de socorro : rescue team⟩ **2**
  ¡**socorro**! : help!
soda *nf* : soda, soda water
sodio *nf* : sodium
soez *adj, pl* **soeces** GROSERO : rude,
  vulgar — **soezmente** *adv*
sofá *nm* : couch, sofa
sofistería *nf* : sophistry — **sofista** *nmf*
sofisticación *nf, pl* **-ciones** : sophistication
sofisticado, -da *adj* : sophisticated
sofocante *adj* : suffocating, stifling
sofocar {72} *vt* **1** AHOGAR : to suffocate,
  to smother **2** EXTINGUIR : to extinguish, to put out (a fire) **3** APLASTAR
  : to crush, to put down ⟨sofocar una
  rebelión : to crush a rebellion⟩ — **so-**
  focarse *vr* **1** : to suffocate **2** *fam* : to
  get upset, to get mad
sofreír {66} *vt* : to sauté
sofrito[1], **-ta** *adj* : sautéed
sofrito[2] *nm* : seasoning sauce
softbol *nm* : softball
software *nm* : software
soga *nf* : rope
soja → **soya**
sojuzgar *vt* : to subdue, to conquer, to
  subjugate
sol *nm* **1** : sun **2** : Peruvian unit of currency
solamente *adv* SÓLO : only, just
solapa *nf* **1** : lapel (of a jacket) **2** : flap
  (of an envelope)
solapado, -da *adj* : secret, underhanded
solapar *vt* : to cover up, to keep secret
  — **solaparse** *vr* : to overlap
solar[1] {19} *vt* : to floor, to tile
solar[2] *adj* : solar, sun
solar[3] *nm* **1** TERRENO : lot, piece of
  land, site **2** *Cuba, Peru* : tenement
  building
solariego, -ga *adj* : ancestral
solaz *nm, pl* **solaces** **1** CONSUELO : solace, comfort **2** DESCANSO : relaxation, recreation
solazarse {21} *vr* : to relax, to enjoy oneself
soldado *nm* **1** : soldier **2 soldado raso**
  : private, enlisted man
soldador[1], **-dora** *n* : welder
soldador[2] *nm* : soldering iron
soldadura *nf* **1** : welding **2** : soldering,
  solder
soldar {19} *vt* **1** : to weld **2** : to solder
soleado, -da *adj* : sunny
soledad *nf* : loneliness, solitude
solemne *adj* : solemn — **solemne-**
  mente *adv*
solemnidad *nf* : solemnity

soler {78} *vi* : to be in the habit of, to tend to ⟨solía tomar café por la tarde : she usually drank coffee in the afternoon⟩ ⟨eso suele ocurrir : that frequently happens⟩
solera *nf* 1 : prop, support 2 : tradition
solicitante *nmf* : applicant
solicitar *vt* 1 : to request, to solicit 2 : to apply for ⟨solicitar empleo : to apply for employment⟩
solícito, -ta *adj* : solicitous, attentive, obliging
solicitud *nf* 1 : solicitude, concern 2 : request 3 : application
solidaridad *nf* : solidarity
solidario, -ria *adj* : supportive, united in support ⟨se declararon solidarios con la nueva ley : they declared their support for the new law⟩ ⟨espíritu solidario : spirit of solidarity⟩
solidarizar {21} *vi* : to be in solidarity ⟨solidarizamos con la huelga : we support the strike⟩
solidez *nf* 1 : solidity, firmness 2 : soundness (of an argument, etc.)
solidificar {72} *vt* : to solidify, to make solid — **solidificarse** *vr* — **solidificación** *nf*
sólido[1], -da *adj* 1 : solid, firm 2 : sturdy, well-made 3 : sound, well-founded — **sólidamente** *adv*
sólido[2] *nm* : solid
soliloquio *nm* : soliloquy
solista *nmf* : soloist
solitaria *nf* TENIA : tapeworm
solitario[1], -ria *adj* 1 : lonely 2 : lone, solitary 3 DESIERTO : deserted, lonely ⟨una calle solitaria : a deserted street⟩
solitario[2], -ria *n* : recluse, loner
solitario[3] *nm* : solitaire
sollozar {21} *vi* : to sob
sollozo *nm* : sob
solo[1], -la *adj* 1 : alone, by oneself 2 : lonely 3 ÚNICO : only, sole, unique ⟨hay un solo problema : there's only one problem⟩ 4 **a solas** : alone
solo[2] *nm* : solo
sólo *adv* SOLAMENTE : just, only ⟨sólo quieren comer : they just want to eat⟩
solomillo *nm* : sirloin, loin
solsticio *nm* : solstice
soltar {19} *vt* 1 : to let go of, to drop 2 : to release, to set free 3 AFLOJAR : to loosen, to slacken
soltería *nf* : bachelorhood, spinsterhood
soltero[1], -ra *adj* : single, unmarried
soltero[2], -ra *n* 1 : bachelor *m*, single man *m*, single woman *f* 2 **apellido de soltera** : maiden name
soltura *nf* 1 : looseness, slackness 2 : fluency (of language) 3 : agility, ease of movement
soluble *adj* : soluble — **solubilidad** *nf*
solución *nf, pl* **-ciones** 1 : solution (in a liquid) 2 : answer, solution
solucionar *vt* RESOLVER : to solve, to resolve — **solucionarse** *vr*

solvencia *nf* 1 : solvency 2 : settling, payment (of debts) 3 : reliability ⟨solvencia moral : trustworthiness⟩
solvente[1] *adj* 1 : solvent 2 : reliable, trustworthy
solvente[2] *nm* : solvent
somalí *adj & nmf* : Somalian
sombra *nf* 1 : shadow 2 : shade 3 **sombras** *nfpl* : darkness, shadows *pl* 4 **sin sombra de duda** : without a shadow of a doubt
sombreado, -da *adj* 1 : shady 2 : shaded, darkened
sombrear *vt* : to shade
sombrerero, -ra *n* : milliner, hatter
sombrero *nm* 1 : hat 2 **sin ~** : bareheaded 3 **sombrero hongo** : derby
sombrilla *nf* : parasol, umbrella
sombrío, -bría *adj* LÓBREGO : dark, somber, gloomy — **sombríamente** *adv*
someramente *adv* : cursorily, summarily
somero, -ra *adj* : superficial, cursory, shallow
someter *vt* 1 : to subjugate, to conquer 2 : to subordinate 3 : to subject (to treatment or testing) 4 : to submit, to present — **someterse** *vr* 1 : to submit, to yield 2 : to undergo
sometimiento *nm* 1 : submission, subjection 2 : presentation
somnífero[1], -ra *adj* : soporific
somnífero[2] *nm* : sleeping pill
somnolencia *nf* : drowsiness, sleepiness
somnoliento, -ta *adj* : drowsy, sleepy
somorgujo *or* **somormujo** *nm* : loon, grebe
somos → **ser**
son[1] → **ser**
son[2] *nm* 1 : sound ⟨al son de la trompeta : at the sound of the trumpet⟩ 2 : news, rumor 3 **en son de** : as, in the manner of, by way of ⟨en son de broma : as a joke⟩ ⟨en son de paz : in peace⟩
sonado, -da *adj* : celebrated, famous, much-discussed
sonaja *nf* : rattle
sonajero *nm* : rattle (toy)
sonámbulo, -la *n* : sleepwalker
sonar[1] {19} *vi* 1 : to sound ⟨suena bien : it sounds good⟩ 2 : to ring (bells) 3 : to look or sound familiar ⟨me suena ese nombre : that name rings a bell⟩ 4 **~ a** : to sound like — *vt* 1 : to ring 2 : to blow (a trumpet, a nose) — **sonarse** *vr* : to blow one's nose
sonar[2] *nm* : sonar
sonata *nf* : sonata
sonda *nf* 1 : sounding line 2 : probe 3 CATÉTER : catheter
sondar *vt* 1 : to sound, to probe (in medicine, drilling, etc.) 2 : to probe, to explore (outer space)
sondear *vt* 1 : to sound 2 : to probe 3 : to sound out, to test (opinions, markets)

sondeo *nm* **1** : sounding, probing **2** : drilling **3** ENCUESTA : survey, poll
soneto *nm* : sonnet
sónico, -ca *adj* : sonic
sonido *nm* : sound
sonoridad *nf* : sonority, resonance
sonoro, -ra *adj* **1** : resonant, sonorous, voiced (in linguistics) **2** : resounding, loud **3 banda sonora** : soundtrack
sonreír {66} *vi* : to smile
sonriente *adj* : smiling
sonrisa *nf* : smile
sonrojar *vt* : to cause to blush — **sonrojarse** *vr* : to blush
sonrojo *nm* RUBOR : blush
sonrosado, -da *adj* : rosy, pink
sonsacar {72} *vt* : to wheedle, to extract
sonsonete *nm* **1** : tapping **2** : drone **3** : mocking tone
soñador[1], -dora *adj* : dreamy
soñador[2], -dora *n* : dreamer
soñar {19} *v* **1** : to dream **2** ~ **con** : to dream about **3 soñar despierto** : to daydream
soñoliento, -ta *adj* : sleepy, drowsy
sopa *nf* **1** : soup **2 estar hecho una sopa** : to be soaked to the bone
sopera *nf* : soup tureen
sopesar *vt* : to weigh, to evaluate
soplar *vi* : to blow — *vt* : to blow on, to blow out, to blow off
soplete *nm* : blowtorch
soplido *nm* : puff
soplo *nm* : puff, gust
soplón, -plona *n, mpl* **soplones** *fam* : tattletale, sneak
sopor *nm* SOMNOLENCIA : drowsiness, sleepiness
soporífero, -ra *adj* : soporific
soportable *adj* : bearable, tolerable
soportar *vt* **1** SOSTENER : to support, to hold up **2** RESISTIR : to withstand, to resist **3** AGUANTAR : to bear, to tolerate
soporte *nm* : base, stand, support
soprano *nmf* : soprano
sor *nf* : Sister (religious title)
sorber *vt* **1** : to sip, to suck in **2** : to absorb, to soak up
sorbete *nm* : sherbet
sorbo *nm* **1** : sip, gulp, swallow **2 beber a sorbos** : to sip
sordera *nf* : deafness
sordidez *nf, pl* **-deces** : sordidness, squalor
sórdido, -da *adj* : sordid, dirty, squalid
sordina *nf* : mute (for a musical instrument)
sordo, -da *adj* **1** : deaf **2** : muted, muffled
sordomudo, -da *n* : deaf-mute
sorgo *nm* : sorghum
soriasis *nfs & pl* : psoriasis
sorna *nf* : sarcasm, mocking tone
sorprendente *adj* : surprising — **sorprendentemente** *adv*
sorprender *vt* : to surprise — **sorprenderse** *vr*

sorpresa *nf* : surprise
sorpresivo, -va *adj* **1** : surprising, surprise **2** IMPREVISTO : sudden, unexpected
sortear *vt* **1** RIFAR : to raffle, to draw lots for **2** : to dodge, to avoid
sorteo *nm* : drawing, raffle
sortija *nf* **1** ANILLO : ring **2** : curl, ringlet
sortilegio *nm* **1** HECHIZO : spell, charm **2** HECHICERÍA : sorcery
SOS *nm* : SOS
sosegado, -da *adj* SERENO : calm, tranquil, serene
sosegar {49} *vt* : to calm, to pacify — **sosegarse** *vr*
sosiego *nm* : tranquillity, serenity, calm
soslayar *vt* ESQUIVAR : to dodge, to evade
soslayo *nm* **de** ~ : obliquely, sideways ⟨mirar de soslayo : to look askance⟩
soso, -sa *adj* **1** INSÍPIDO : bland, flavorless **2** ABURRIDO : dull, boring
sospecha *nf* : suspicion
sospechar *vt* : to suspect — *vi* : to be suspicious
sospechosamente *adv* : suspiciously
sospechoso[1], -sa *adj* : suspicious, suspect
sospechoso[2], -sa *n* : suspect
sostén *nm, pl* **sostenes 1** APOYO : support **2** : sustenance **3** : brassiere, bra
sostener {80} *vt* **1** : to support, to hold up **2** : to hold ⟨sostenme la puerta : hold the door for me⟩ ⟨sostener una conversación : to hold a conversation⟩ **3** : to sustain, to maintain — **sostenerse** *vr* **1** : to stand, to hold oneself up **2** : to continue, to remain
sostenible *adj* : sustainable, tenable
sostenido[1], -da *adj* **1** : sustained, prolonged **2** : sharp (in music)
sostenido[2] *nm* : sharp (in music)
sostuvo, etc. → **sostener**
sotana *nf* : cassock
sótano *nm* : basement
sotavento *nm* : lee ⟨a sotavento : leeward⟩
soterrar {55} *vt* **1** : to bury **2** : to conceal, to hide away
soto *nm* : grove, copse
souvenir *nm, pl* **-nirs** RECUERDO : souvenir, memento
soviético, -ca *adj* : Soviet
soy → **ser**
soya *nf* : soy, soybean
spaghetti → **espagueti**
sport [ɛˈspor] *adj* : sport, casual
sprint [ɛˈsprin, -ˈsprint] *nm* : sprint — **sprinter** *nmf*
squash [ɛˈskwaʃ, -ˈskwatʃ] *nm* : squash (sport)
Sr. *nm* : Mr.
Sra. *nf* : Mrs., Ms.
Srta. *or* **Srita.** *nf* : Miss, Ms.
standard → **estándar**
stress → **estrés**
su *adj* **1** : his, her, its, their, one's ⟨su libro : her book⟩ ⟨sus consecuencias

: its consequences⟩ **2** (*formal*) : your ⟨tómese su medicina, señor : take your medicine, sir⟩
suave *adj* **1** BLANDO : soft **2** LISO : smooth **3** : gentle, mild **4** *Mex fam* : great, fantastic
suavemente *adj* : smoothly, gently, softly
suavidad *nf* : softness, smoothness, mellowness
suavizante *nm* : softener, fabric softener
suavizar {21} *vt* **1** : to soften, to smooth out **2** : to tone down — **suavizarse** *vr*
subacuático, -ca *adj* : underwater
subalterno¹, -na *adj* **1** SUBORDINADO : subordinate **2** SECUNDARIO : secondary
subalterno², -na *n* SUBORDINADO : subordinate
subarrendar {55} *vt* : to sublet
subasta *nf* : auction
subastador, -dora *n* : auctioneer
subastar *vt* : to auction, to auction off
subcampeón, -peona *n, mpl* **-peones** : runner-up
subcomité *nm* : subcommittee
subconsciente *adj & nm* : subconscious — **subconscientemente** *adv*
subcontratar *vt* : to subcontract
subcontratista *nmf* : subcontractor
subcultura *nf* : subculture
subdesarrollado, -da *adj* : underdeveloped
subdirector, -tora *n* : assistant manager
súbdito, -ta *n* : subject (of a monarch)
subdividir *vt* : to subdivide
subdivisión *nf, pl* **-siones** : subdivision
subestimar *vt* : to underestimate, to undervalue
subexponer {60} *vt* : to underexpose
subexposición *nf, pl* **-ciones** : underexposure
subgrupo *nm* : subgroup
subibaja *nm* : seesaw
subida *nf* **1** : ascent, climb **2** : rise, increase **3** : slope, hill ⟨ir de subida : to go uphill⟩
subido, -da *adj* **1** : intense, strong ⟨amarillo subido : bright yellow⟩ **2 subido de tono** : risqué
subir *vt* **1** : to bring up, to take up **2** : to climb, to go up **3** : to raise — *vi* **1** : to go up, to come up **2** : to rise, to increase **3** : to be promoted **4** ~ **a** : to get on, to mount ⟨subir a un tren : to get on a train⟩ — **subirse** *vr* **1** : to climb (up) **2** : to pull up (clothing) **3 subirse a la cabeza** : to go to one's head
súbito, -ta *adj* **1** REPENTINO : sudden **2 de** ~ : all of a sudden, suddenly — **súbitamente** *adv*
subjetivo, -va *adj* : subjective — **subjetivamente** *adv* — **subjetividad** *nf*
subjuntivo¹, -va *adj* : subjunctive
subjuntivo² *nm* : subjunctive
sublevación *nf, pl* **-ciones** ALZAMIENTO : uprising, rebellion

sublevar *vt* : to incite to rebellion — **sublevarse** *vr* : to rebel, to rise up
sublimar *vt* : to sublimate — **sublimación** *nf*
sublime *adj* : sublime
submarinismo *nm* : scuba diving
submarinista *nmf* : scuba diver
submarino¹, -na *adj* : submarine, undersea
submarino² *nm* : submarine
suboficial *nmf* : noncommissioned officer, petty officer
subordinado, -da *adj & n* : subordinate
subordinar *vt* : to subordinate — **subordinarse** *vr* — **subordinación** *nf*
subproducto *nm* : by-product
subrayar *vt* **1** : to underline, to underscore **2** ENFATIZAR : to highlight, to emphasize
subrepticio, -cia *adj* : surreptitious — **subrepticiamente** *adv*
subsahariano, -na *adj* : sub-Saharan
subsanar *vt* **1** RECTIFICAR : to rectify, to correct **2** : to overlook, to excuse **3** : to make up for
subscribir → **suscribir**
subsecretario, -ria *n* : undersecretary
subsecuente *adj* : subsequent — **subsecuentemente** *adv*
subsidiar *vt* : to subsidize
subsidiaria *nf* : subsidiary
subsidio *nm* : subsidy
subsiguiente *adj* : subsequent
subsistencia *nf* **1** : subsistence **2** : sustenance
subsistir *vi* **1** : to subsist, to live **2** : to endure, to survive
substancia → **sustancia**
subteniente *nmf* : second lieutenant
subterfugio *nm* : subterfuge
subterráneo¹, -nea *adj* : underground, subterranean
subterráneo² *nm* **1** : underground passage, tunnel **2** *Arg, Uru* : subway
subtítulo *nm* : subtitle, subheading
subtotal *nm* : subtotal
suburbano, -na *adj* : suburban
suburbio *nm* **1** : suburb **2** : slum (outside a city)
subvención *nf, pl* **-ciones** : subsidy, grant
subvencionar *vt* : to subsidize
subversivo, -va *adj & n* : subversive — **subversión** *nf*
subvertir {76} *vt* : to subvert
subyacente *adj* : underlying
subyugar {52} *vt* : to subjugate — **subyugación** *nf*
succión *nf, pl* **succiones** : suction
succionar *vt* : to suck up, to draw in
sucedáneo *nm* : substitute ⟨sucedáneo de azucar : sugar substitute⟩
suceder *vi* **1** OCURRIR : to happen, to occur ⟨¿qué sucede? : what's going on?⟩ ⟨suceda lo que sueda : come what may⟩ **2** ~ **a** : to follow, to succeed ⟨suceder al trono : to succeed to the throne⟩ ⟨a la primavera sucede el verano : summer follows spring⟩

sucesión *nf, pl* **-siones** **1** : succession **2** : sequence, series **3** : issue, heirs *pl*
sucesivamente *adv* : successively, consecutively ⟨y así sucesivamente : and so on⟩
sucesivo, -va *adj* : successive ⟨en los días sucesivos : in the days that followed⟩
suceso *nm* **1** : event, happening, occurrence **2** : incident, crime
sucesor, -sora *n* : successor
suciedad *nf* **1** : dirtiness, filthiness **2** MUGRE : dirt, filth
sucinto, -ta *adj* CONCISO : succinct, concise — **sucintamente** *adv*
sucio, -cia *adj* : dirty, filthy
sucre *nm* : Ecuadoran unit of currency
suculento, -ta *adj* : succulent
sucumbir *vi* : to succumb
sucursal *nf* : branch (of a business)
sudadera *nf* : sweatshirt
sudado, -da → **sudoroso**
sudafricano, -na *adj & n* : South African
sudamericano, -na *adj & n* : South American
sudanés, -nesa *adj & n, mpl* **-neses** : Sudanese
sudar *vi* TRANSPIRAR : to sweat, to perspire
sudario *nm* : shroud
sudeste → **sureste**
sudoeste → **suroeste**
sudor *nm* TRANSPIRACIÓN : sweat, perspiration
sudoroso, -sa *adj* : sweaty
sueco[1], -ca *adj* : Swedish
sueco[2], -ca *n* : Swede
sueco[3] *nm* : Swedish (language)
suegro, -gra *n* **1** : father-in-law *m*, mother-in-law *f* **2 suegros** *nmpl* : in-laws
suela *nf* : sole (of a shoe)
suelda, etc. → **soldar**
sueldo *nm* : salary, wage
suele, etc. → **soler**
suelo *nm* **1** : ground ⟨caerse al suelo : to fall down, to hit the ground⟩ **2** : floor, flooring **3** TIERRA : soil, land
suelta, etc. → **soltar**
suelto[1], -ta *adj* : loose, free, unattached
suelto[2] *nm* : loose change
suena, etc. → **sonar**
sueña, etc. → **soñar**
sueño *nm* **1** : dream **2** : sleep ⟨perder el sueño : to lose sleep⟩ **3** : sleepiness ⟨tener sueño : to be sleepy⟩
suero *nm* **1** : serum **2** : whey
suerte *nf* **1** FORTUNA : luck, fortune ⟨tener suerte : to be lucky⟩ ⟨por suerte : luckily⟩ **2** DESTINO : fate, destiny, lot **3** CLASE, GÉNERO : sort, kind ⟨toda suerte de cosas : all kinds of things⟩
suertudo, -da *adj fam* : lucky
suéter *nm* : sweater
suficiencia *nf* **1** : adequacy, sufficiency **2** : competence, fitness **3** : smugness, self-satisfaction
suficiente *adj* **1** BASTANTE : enough, sufficient ⟨tener suficiente : to have enough⟩ **2** : suitable, fit **3** : smug, complacent
suficientemente *adv* : sufficiently, enough
sufijo *nm* : suffix
suflé *nm* : soufflé
sufragar {52} *vt* **1** AYUDAR : to help out, to support **2** : to defray (costs) — *vi* : to vote
sufragio *nm* : suffrage, vote
sufrido, -da *adj* **1** : long-suffering, patient **2** : sturdy, serviceable (of clothing)
sufrimiento *nm* : suffering
sufrir *vt* **1** : to suffer ⟨sufrir una pérdida : to suffer a loss⟩ **2** : to tolerate, to put up with ⟨ella no lo puede sufrir : she can't stand him⟩ — *vi* : to suffer
sugerencia *nf* : suggestion
sugerir {76} *vt* **1** PROPONER, RECOMENDAR : to suggest, to recommend, to propose **2** : to suggest, to bring to mind
sugestión *nf, pl* **-tiones** : suggestion, prompting ⟨poder de sugestión : power of suggestion⟩
sugestionable *adj* : suggestible, impressionable
sugestionar *vt* : to influence, to sway — **sugestionarse** *vr* ∼ **con** : to talk oneself into, to become convinced of
sugestivo, -va *adj* **1** : suggestive **2** : interesting, stimulating
suicida[1] *adj* : suicidal
suicida[2] *nmf* : suicide victim, suicide
suicidarse *vr* : to commit suicide
suicidio *nm* : suicide
suite *nf* : suite
suizo, -za *adj & n* : Swiss
sujeción *nf, pl* **-ciones** **1** : holding, fastening **2** : subjection
sujetador *nm* **1** : fastener **2** : holder ⟨sujetador de tazas : cup holder⟩
sujetalibros *nms & pl* : bookend
sujetapapeles *nms & pl* CLIP : paper clip
sujetar *vt* **1** : to hold on to, to steady, to hold down **2** FIJAR : to fasten, to attach **3** DOMINAR : to subdue, to conquer — **sujetarse** *vr* **1** : to hold on, to hang on **2** ∼ **a** : to abide by
sujeto[1], -ta *adj* **1** : secure, fastened **2** ∼ **a** : subject to
sujeto[2] *nm* **1** INDIVIDUO : individual, character **2** : subject (in grammar)
sulfúrico, -ca *adj* : sulfuric
sulfuro *nm* : sulfur
sultán *nm, pl* **sultanes** : sultan
suma *nf* **1** CANTIDAD : sum, quantity **2** : addition
sumamente *adv* : extremely, exceedingly
sumar *vt* **1** : to add, to add up **2** : to add up to, to total — *vi* : to add up — **sumarse** *vr* ∼ **a** : to join
sumario[1], -ria *adj* SUCINTO : succinct, summary — **sumariamente** *adv*
sumario[2] *nm* : summary

sumergir {35} *vt* : to submerge, to immerse, to plunge — **sumergirse** *vr*
sumersión *nf, pl* **-siones** : submersion, immersion
sumidero *nm* : drain, sewer
suministrar *vt* : to supply, to provide
suministro *nm* : supply, provision
sumir *vt* SUMERGIR : to plunge, to immerse, to sink — **sumirse** *vr*
sumisión *nf, pl* **-siones 1** : submission **2** : submissiveness
sumiso, -sa *adj* : submissive, acquiescent, docile
sumo, -ma *adj* **1** : extreme, great, high ⟨la suma autoridad : the highest authority⟩ **2 a lo sumo** : at the most — **sumamente** *adv*
suntuoso, -sa *adj* : sumptuous, lavish — **suntuosamente** *adv*
supeditar *vt* SUBORDINAR : to subordinate — **supeditación** *nf*
super[1] *or* **súper** *adj fam* : super, great
super[2] *nm* SUPERMERCADO : market, supermarket
superable *adj* : surmountable
superabundancia *nf* : overabundance, superabundance — **superabundante** *adj*
superar *vt* **1** : to surpass, to exceed **2** : to overcome, to surmount — **superarse** *vr* : to improve oneself
superávit *nm, pl* **-vit** *or* **-vits** : surplus
superchería *nf* : trickery, fraud
supercomputadora *nf* : supercomputer
superestructura *nf* : superstructure
superficial *adj* : superficial — **superficialmente** *adv*
superficialidad *nf* : superficiality
superficie *nf* **1** : surface **2** : area ⟨la superficie de un triángulo : the area of a triangle⟩
superfluidad *nf* : superfluity
superfluo, -flua *adj* : superfluous
superintendente *nmf* : supervisor, superintendent
superior[1] *adj* **1** : superior **2** : upper ⟨nivel superior : upper level⟩ **3** : higher ⟨educación superior : higher education⟩ **4 ~ a** : above, higher than, in excess of
superior[2] *nm* : superior
superioridad *nf* : superiority
superlativo[1], **-va** *adj* : superlative
superlativo[2] *nm* : superlative
supermercado *nm* : supermarket
superpoblación *nf, pl* **-ciones** : overpopulation
superpoblado, -da *adj* : overpopulated
superponer {60} *vt* : to superimpose
superpotencia *nf* : superpower
superproducción → **sobreproducción**
supersónico, -ca *adj* : supersonic
superstición *nf, pl* **-ciones** : superstition
supersticioso, -sa *adj* : superstitious
supervisar *vt* : to supervise, to oversee
supervisión *nf, pl* **-siones** : supervision
supervisor, -sora *n* : supervisor, overseer

supervivencia *nf* : survival
superviviente *nmf* : survivor
supino, -na *adj* : supine
suplantar *vt* : to supplant, to replace
suplemental → **suplementario**
suplementario, -ria *adj* : supplementary, additional, extra
suplemento *nm* : supplement
suplencia *nf* : substitution, replacement
suplente *adj & nmf* : substitute ⟨equipo suplente : replacement team⟩
supletorio, -ria *adj* : extra, additional ⟨teléfono supletorio : extension phone⟩ ⟨cama supletoria : spare bed⟩
súplica *nf* : plea, entreaty
suplicar {72} *vt* IMPLORAR, ROGAR : to entreat, to implore, to supplicate
suplicio *nm* TORMENTO : ordeal, torture
suplir *vt* **1** COMPENSAR : to make up for, to compensate for **2** REEMPLAZAR : to replace, to substitute
supo, etc. → **saber**
suponer {60} *vt* **1** PRESUMIR : to suppose, to assume ⟨supongo que sí : I guess so, I suppose so⟩ ⟨se supone que van a llegar mañana : they're supposed to arrive tomorrow⟩ **2** : to imply, to suggest **3** : to involve, to entail ⟨el éxito supone mucho trabajo : success involves a lot of work⟩
suposición *nf, pl* **-ciones** PRESUNCIÓN : supposition, assumption
supositorio *nm* : suppository
supremacía *nf* : supremacy
supremo, -ma *adj* : supreme
supresión *nf, pl* **-siones 1** : suppression, elimination **2** : deletion
suprimir *vt* **1** : to suppress, to eliminate **2** : to delete
supuestamente *adv* : supposedly, allegedly
supuesto, -ta *adj* **1** : supposed, alleged **2 por ~** : of course, absolutely
supurar *vi* : to ooze, to discharge
supuso, etc. → **suponer**
sur[1] *adj* : southern, southerly, south
sur[2] *nm* **1** : south, South **2** : south wind
surafricano, -na → **sudafricano**
suramericano, -na → **sudamericano**
surcar {72} *vt* **1** : to plow (through) **2** : to groove, to score, to furrow
surco *nm* : groove, furrow, rut
sureño[1], **-ña** *adj* : southern, Southern
sureño[2], **-ña** *n* : Southerner
sureste[1] *adj* **1** : southeast, southeastern **2** : southeasterly
sureste[2] *nm* : southeast, Southeast
surf *nm* : surfing
surfear *vi* : to surf
surfing → **surf**
surfista *nmf* : surfer
surgimiento *nm* : rise, emergence
surgir {35} *vi* : to rise, to arise, to emerge
suroeste[1] *adj* **1** : southwest, southwestern **2** : southwesterly
suroeste[2] *nm* : southwest, Southwest
surtido[1], **-da** *adj* **1** : assorted, varied **2** : stocked, provisioned

surtido² *nm* : assortment, selection
surtidor *nm* **1** : jet, spout **2** *Arg, Chile, Spain* : gas pump
surtir *vt* **1** : to supply, to provide ⟨surtir un pedido : to fill an order⟩ **2 surtir efecto** : to have an effect — *vi* : to spout, to spurt up — **surtirse** *vr* : to stock up
susceptible *adj* : susceptible, sensitive — **susceptibilidad** *nf*
suscitar *vt* : to provoke, to give rise to
suscribir {33} *vt* **1** : to sign (a formal document) **2** : to endorse, to sanction — **suscribirse** *vr* ~ **a** : to subscribe to
suscripción *nf, pl* **-ciones 1** : subscription **2** : endorsement, sanction **3** : signing
suscriptor, -tora *n* : subscriber
susodicho, -cha *adj* : aforementioned, aforesaid
suspender *vt* **1** COLGAR : to suspend, to hang **2** : to suspend, to discontinue **3** : to suspend, to dismiss
suspensión *nf, pl* **-siones** : suspension
suspenso *nm* : suspense
suspicacia *nf* : suspicion, mistrust
suspicaz *adj, pl* **-caces** DESCONFIADO : suspicious, wary
suspirar *vi* : to sigh
suspiro *nm* : sigh
surque, etc. → **surcar**
suscrito *pp* → **suscribir**
sustancia *nf* **1** : substance **2 sin** ~ : shallow, lacking substance
sustancial *adj* **1** : substantial **2** ESENCIAL, FUNDAMENTAL : essential, fundamental — **sustancialmente** *adv*
sustancioso, -sa *adj* **1** NUTRITIVO : hearty, nutritious **2** : substantial, solid
sustantivo *nm* : noun

sustentación *nf, pl* **-ciones** SOSTÉN : support
sustentar *vt* **1** : to support, to hold up **2** : to sustain, to nourish **3** : to maintain, to hold (an opinion) — **sustentarse** *vr* : to support oneself
sustento *nm* **1** : means of support, livelihood **2** : sustenance, food
sustitución *nf, pl* **-ciones** : replacement, substitution
sustituir {41} *vt* **1** : to replace, to substitute for **2** : to stand in for
sustituto, -ta *n* : substitute, stand-in
susto *nm* : fright, scare
sustracción *nf, pl* **-ciones 1** RESTA : subtraction **2** : theft
sustraer {81} *vt* **1** : to remove, to take away **2** RESTAR : to subtract **3** : to steal — **sustraerse** *vr* ~ **a** : to avoid, to evade
susurrar *vi* **1** : to whisper **2** : to murmur **3** : to rustle (leaves, etc.) — *vt* : to whisper
susurro *nm* **1** : whisper **2** : murmur **3** : rustle, rustling
sutil *adj* **1** : delicate, thin, fine **2** : subtle
sutileza *nf* **1** : delicacy **2** : subtlety
sutura *nf* : suture
suturar *vt* : to suture
suyo¹, -ya *adj* **1** : his, her, its, theirs ⟨los libros suyos : his books⟩ ⟨un amigo suyo : a friend of hers⟩ ⟨esta casa es suya : this house is theirs⟩ **2** (*formal*) : yours ⟨¿este abrigo es suyo, señor? : is this your coat, sir?⟩
suyo², -ya *pron* **1** : his, hers, theirs ⟨mi guitarra y la suya : my guitar and hers⟩ ⟨ellos trajeron las suyas : they brought theirs, they brought their own⟩ **2** (*formal*) : yours ⟨usted olvidó la suya : you forgot yours⟩
switch *nm* : switch

T

t *nf* : twenty-first letter of the Spanish alphabet
taba *nf* : anklebone
tabacalero¹, -ra *adj* : tobacco ⟨industria tabacalera : tobacco industry⟩
tabacalero², -ra *n* : tobacco grower
tabaco *nm* : tobacco
tábano *nm* : horsefly
taberna *nf* : tavern, bar
tabernáculo *nm* : tabernacle
tabicar {72} *vt* : to wall up
tabique *nm* : thin wall, partition
tabla *nf* **1** : table, list ⟨tabla de multiplicar : multiplication table⟩ **2** : board, plank, slab ⟨tabla de planchar : ironing board⟩ **3** : plot, strip (of land) **4 tablas** *nfpl* : stage, boards *pl*
tablado *nm* **1** : floor **2** : platform, scaffold **3** : stage
tablero *nm* **1** : bulletin board **2** : board (in games) ⟨tablero de ajedrez : chess-

board⟩ ⟨tablero de damas : checkerboard⟩ **3** PIZARRA : blackboard **4** : switchboard **5 tablero de instrumentos** : dashboard, instrument panel
tableta *nf* **1** COMPRIMIDO, PÍLDORA : tablet, pill **2** : bar (of chocolate)
tabletear *vi* : to rattle, to clack
tableteo *nm* : clack, rattling
tablilla *nf* **1** : small board or tablet **2** : bulletin board **3** : splint
tabloide *nm* : tabloid
tablón *nm, pl* **tablones 1** : plank, beam **2 tablón de anuncios** : bulletin board
tabú¹ *adj* : taboo
tabú² *nm, pl* **tabúes** *or* **tabús** : taboo
tabulador *nm* : tabulator
tabular¹ *vt* : to tabulate
tabular² *adj* : tabular
taburete *nm* : footstool, stool
tacañería *nf* : miserliness, stinginess

tacaño¹, -ña *adj* MEZQUINO : stingy, miserly
tacaño², -ña *n* : miser, tightwad
tacha *nf* **1** : flaw, blemish, defect **2 poner tacha a** : to find fault with **3 sin ~** : flawless
tachadura *nf* : erasure, correction
tachar *vt* **1** : to cross out, to delete **2 ~ de** : to accuse of, to label as ⟨lo tacharon de mentiroso : they accused him of being a liar⟩
tachón *nm, pl* **tachones** : stud, hobnail
tachonar *vt* : to stud
tachuela *nf* : tack, hobnail, stud
tácito, -ta *adj* : tacit, implicit — **tácitamente** *adv*
taciturno, -na *adj* **1** : taciturn **2** : sullen, gloomy
tacle *nm* : tackle
taclear *vt* : to tackle (in football)
taco *nm* **1** : wad, stopper, plug **2** : pad (of paper) **3** : cleat **4** : heel (of a shoe) **5** : cue (in billiards) **6** : light snack, bite **7** : taco
tacón *nm, pl* **tacones** : heel (of a shoe) ⟨de tacón alto : high-heeled⟩
táctica *nf* : tactic, tactics *pl*
táctico¹, -ca *adj* : tactical
táctico², -ca *n* : tactician
táctil *adj* : tactile
tacto *nm* **1** : touch, touching, feel **2** DELICADEZA : tact
tafetán *nm, pl* **-tanes** : taffeta
tahúr *nm, pl* **tahúres** : gambler
tailandés¹, -desa *adj & n, pl* **-deses** : Thai
tailandés² *nm* : Thai (language)
taimado, -da *adj* **1** : crafty, sly **2** *Chile* : sullen, sulky
tajada *nf* **1** : slice **2 sacar tajada** *fam* : to get one's share
tajante *adj* **1** : cutting, sharp **2** : decisive, categorical
tajantemente *adj* : emphatically, categorically
tajar *vt* : to cut, to slice
tajo *nm* **1** : cut, slash, gash **2** ESCARPA : steep cliff
tal¹ *adv* **1** : so, in such a way **2 tal como** : just as ⟨tal como lo hice : just the way I did it⟩ **3 con tal que** : provided that, as long as **4 ¿qué tal?** : how are you?, how's it going?
tal² *adj* **1** : such, such a **2 tal vez** : maybe, perhaps
tal³ *pron* **1** : such a one, someone **2** : such a thing, something **3 tal para cual** : two of a kind
tala *nf* : felling (of trees)
taladrar *vt* : to drill
taladro *nm* : drill, auger ⟨taladro eléctrico : power drill⟩
talante *nm* **1** HUMOR : mood, disposition **2** VOLUNTAD : will, willingness
talar *vt* **1** : to cut down, to fell **2** DEVASTAR : to devastate, to destroy
talco *nm* **1** : talc **2** : talcum powder
talego *nm* : sack

talento *nm* : talent, ability
talentoso, -sa *adj* : talented, gifted
talismán *nm, pl* **-manes** AMULETO : talisman, charm
talla *nf* **1** ESTATURA : height **2** : size (in clothing) **3** : stature, status **4** : sculpture, carving
tallar *vt* **1** : to sculpt, to carve **2** : to measure (someone's height) **3** : to deal (cards)
tallarín *nf, pl* **-rines** : noodle
talle *nm* **1** : size **2** : waist, waistline **3** : figure, shape
taller *nm* **1** : shop, workshop **2** : studio (of an artist)
tallo *nm* : stalk, stem ⟨tallo de maíz : cornstalk⟩
talón *nm, pl* **talones** **1** : heel (of the foot) **2** : stub (of a check) **3 talón de Aquiles** : Achilles' heel
talud *nm* : slope, incline
tamal *nm* : tamale
tamaño¹, -ña *adj* : such a big ⟨¿crees tamaña mentira? : do you believe such a lie?⟩
tamaño² *nm* **1** : size **2 de tamaño natural** : life-size
tamarindo *nm* : tamarind
tambalearse *vr* **1** : to teeter **2** : to totter, to stagger, to sway — **tambaleante** *adj*
tambaleo *nm* : staggering, lurching, swaying
también *adv* : too, as well, also
tambor *nm* : drum
tamborilear *vi* : to drum, to tap
tamborileo *nm* : tapping, drumming
tamiz *nm* : sieve
tamizar {21} *vt* : to sift
tampoco *adv* : neither, not either ⟨ni yo tampoco : me neither⟩
tampón *nm, pl* **tampones** **1** : ink pad **2** : tampon
tam–tam *nm* : tom-tom
tan *adv* **1** : so, so very ⟨no es tan difícil : it is not that difficult⟩ **2** : as ⟨tan pronto como : as soon as⟩ **3 tan siquiera** : at least, at the least **4 tan sólo** : only, merely
tanda *nf* **1** : turn, shift **2** : batch, lot, series
tándem *nm* **1** : tandem (bicycle) **2** : duo, pair
tangente *adj & nf* : tangent — **tangencial** *adj*
tangible *adj* : tangible
tango *nm* : tango
tanino *nm* : tannin
tanque *nm* **1** : tank, reservoir **2** : tanker, tank (vehicle)
tanteador *nm* MARCADOR : scoreboard
tantear *vt* **1** : to feel, to grope **2** : to size up, to weigh — *vi* **1** : to keep score **2** : to feel one's way
tanteo *nm* **1** : estimate, rough calculation **2** : testing, sizing up **3** : scoring
tanto¹ *adv* **1** : so much ⟨tanto mejor : so much the better⟩ **2** : so long ⟨¿por qué

te tardaste tanto? : why did you take so long?⟩

tanto², -ta *adj* **1** : so much, so many, such ⟨no hagas tantas preguntas : don't ask so many questions⟩ ⟨tiene tanto encanto : he has such charm, he's so charming⟩ **2** : as much, as many ⟨come tantos dulces como yo : she eats as many sweets as I do⟩ **3** : odd, however many ⟨cuarenta y tantos años : forty-odd years⟩

tanto³ *nm* **1** : certain amount **2** : goal, point (in sports) **3 al tanto** : abreast, in the picture **4 un tanto** : somewhat, rather ⟨un tanto cansado : rather tired⟩

tanto⁴, -ta *pron* **1** : so much, so many ⟨tiene tanto que hacer : she has so much to do⟩ ⟨¡no me des tantos! : don't give me so many!⟩ **2 entre ~** : meanwhile **3 por lo tanto** : therefore

tañer {79} *vt* **1** : to ring (a bell) **2** : to play (a musical instrument)

tañido *nm* **1** CAMPANADA : ring, peal, toll **2** : sound (of an instrument)

tapa *nf* **1** : cover, top, lid **2** *Spain* : bar snack

tapacubos *nms & pl* : hubcap

tapadera *nf* **1** : cover, lid **2** : front, cover (for an organization or person)

tapar *vt* **1** CUBRIR : to cover, to cover up **2** OBSTRUIR : to block, to obstruct — **taparse** *vr*

tapete *nm* **1** : small rug, mat **2** : table cover **3 poner sobre el tapete** : to bring up for discussion

tapia *nf* : (adobe) wall, garden wall

tapiar *vt* **1** : to wall in **2** : to enclose, to block off

tapicería *nf* **1** : upholstery **2** TAPIZ : tapestry

tapicero, -ra *n* : upholsterer

tapioca *nf* : tapioca

tapir *nm* : tapir

tapiz *nm, pl* **tapices** : tapestry

tapizar {21} *vt* **1** : to upholster **2** : to cover, to carpet

tapón *nm, pl* **tapones** **1** : cork **2** : bottle cap **3** : plug, stopper

tapujo *nm* **1** : deceit, pretension **2 sin tapujos** : openly, frankly

taquigrafía *nf* : stenography, shorthand

taquigráfico, -ca *adj* : stenographic

taquígrafo, -fa *n* : stenographer

taquilla *nf* **1** : box office, ticket office **2** : earnings *pl*, take

taquillero, -ra *adj* : box-office, popular ⟨un éxito taquillero : a box-office success⟩

tarántula *nf* : tarantula

tararear *vt* : to hum

tardanza *nf* : lateness, delay

tardar *vi* **1** : to delay, to take a long time **2** : to be late **3 a más tardar** : at the latest — *vt* DEMORAR : to take (time) ⟨tarda una hora : it takes an hour⟩

tarde¹ *adv* **1** : late **2 tarde o temprano** : sooner or later

tarde² *nf* **1** : afternoon, evening **2 ¡buenas tardes!** : good afternoon!, good evening! **3 en la tarde** *or* **por la tarde** : in the afternoon, in the evening

tardío, -día *adj* : late, tardy

tardo, -da *adj* : slow

tarea *nf* **1** : task, job **2** : homework

tarifa *nf* **1** : rate ⟨tarifas postales : postal rates⟩ **2** : fare (for transportation) **3** : price list **4** ARANCEL : duty

tarima *nf* PLATAFORMA : dais, platform, stage

tarjeta *nf* : card ⟨tarjeta de crédito : credit card⟩ ⟨tarjeta postal : postcard⟩

tarro *nm* **1** : jar, pot **2** *Arg, Chile* : can, tin

tarta *nf* **1** : tart **2** : cake

tartaleta *nf* : tart

tartamudear *vi* : to stammer, to stutter

tartamudeo *nm* : stutter, stammer

tartán *nm, pl* **tartanes** : tartan, plaid

tártaro *nm* : tartar

tasa *nf* **1** : rate ⟨tasa de desempleo : unemployment rate⟩ **2** : tax, fee **3** : appraisal, valuation

tasación *nf, pl* **-ciones** : appraisal, assessment

tasador, -dora *n* : assessor, appraiser

tasar *vt* **1** VALORAR : to appraise, to value **2** : to set the price of **3** : to ration, to limit

tasca *nf* : cheap bar, dive

tatuaje *nm* : tattoo, tattooing

tatuar {3} *vt* : to tattoo

taurino, -na *adj* : bull, bullfighting

Tauro *nmf* : Taurus

tauromaquia *nf* : (art of) bullfighting

taxi *nm, pl* **taxis** : taxi, taxicab

taxidermia *nf* : taxidermy

taxidermista *nmf* : taxidermist

taxímetro *nm* : taximeter

taxista *nmf* : taxi driver

taza *nf* **1** : cup **2** : cupful **3** : (toilet) bowl **4** : basin (of a fountain)

tazón *nm, pl* **tazones** **1** : bowl **2** : large cup, mug

te *pron* **1** : you ⟨te quiero : I love you⟩ **2** : for you, to you, from you ⟨me gustaría dártelo : I would like to give it to you⟩ **3** : yourself, for yourself, to yourself, from yourself ⟨¡cálmate! : calm yourself!⟩ ⟨¿te guardaste uno? : did you keep one for yourself?⟩ **4** : thee

té *nm* **1** : tea **2** : tea party

tea *nf* : torch

teatral *adj* : theatrical — **teatralmente** *adv*

teatro *nm* **1** : theater **2 hacer teatro** : to put on an act, to exaggerate

teca *nf* : teak

techado *nm* **1** : roof **2 bajo techado** : under cover, indoors

techar *vt* : to roof, to shingle

techo *nm* **1** TEJADO : roof **2** : ceiling **3** : upper limit, ceiling

techumbre *nf* : roofing

tecla *nf* **1** : key (of a musical instrument or a machine) **2 dar en la tecla** : to hit the nail on the head

teclado *nm* : keyboard
teclear *vt* : to type in, to enter
técnica *nf* 1 : technique, skill 2 : technology
técnico[1], **-ca** *adj* : technical — **técnicamente** *adv*
técnico[2], **-ca** *n* : technician, expert, engineer
tecnología *nf* : technology
tecnológico, -ca *adj* : technological — **tecnológicamente** *adv*
tecolote *nm Mex* : owl
tedio *nm* : tedium, boredom
tedioso, -sa *adj* : tedious, boring — **tediosamente** *adv*
teja *nf* : tile
tejado *nm* TECHO : roof
tejedor, -dora *n* : weaver
tejer *vt* 1 : to knit, to crochet 2 : to weave 3 FABRICAR : to concoct, to make up, to fabricate
tejido *nm* 1 TELA : fabric, cloth 2 : weave, texture 3 : tissue ⟨tejido muscular : muscle tissue⟩
tejo *nm* 1 : yew 2 : hopscotch (children's game)
tejón *nm, pl* **tejones** : badger
tela *nf* 1 : fabric, cloth, material 2 **tela de araña** : spiderweb 3 **poner en tela de juicio** : to call into question, to doubt
telar *nm* : loom
telaraña *nf* : spiderweb, cobweb
tele *nf fam* : TV, television
telecomunicación *nf, pl* **-ciones** : telecommunication
teleconferencia *nf* : teleconference
teledifusión *nf, pl* **-siones** : television broadcasting
teledirigido, -da *adj* : remote-controlled
telefonear *v* : to telephone, to call
telefónico, -ca *adj* : phone, telephone ⟨llamada telefónica : phone call⟩
telefonista *nmf* : telephone operator
teléfono *nm* 1 : telephone 2 **llamar por teléfono** : to telephone, to make a phone call
telegrafiar {85} *v* : to telegraph
telegráfico, -ca *adj* : telegraphic
telégrafo *nm* : telegraph
telegrama *nm* : telegram
telenovela *nf* : soap opera
telepatía *nf* : telepathy
telepático, -ca *adj* : telepathic — **telepáticamente** *adv*
telescópico, -ca *adj* : telescopic
telescopio *nm* : telescope
telespectador, -dora *n* : television viewer
telesquí *nm, pl* **-squís** : ski lift
televidente *nmf* : television viewer
televisar *vt* : to televise
televisión *nf, pl* **-siones** : television, TV
televisivo, -va *adj* : television ⟨serie televisiva : television series⟩
televisor *nm* : television set
telón *nm, pl* **telones** 1 : curtain (in theater) 2 **telón de fondo** : backdrop, background

tema *nm* 1 ASUNTO : theme, topic, subject 2 MOTIVO : motif, central theme
temario *nm* 1 : set of topics (for study) 2 : agenda
temática *nf* : subject matter
temático, -ca *adj* : thematic
temblar {55} *vi* 1 : to tremble, to shake, to shiver ⟨le temblaban las rodillas : his knees were shaking⟩ 2 : to shudder, to be afraid ⟨tiemblo con sólo pensarlo : I shudder to think of it⟩
temblor *nm* 1 : shaking, trembling 2 : tremor, earthquake
tembloroso, -sa *adj* : tremulous, trembling, shaking ⟨con la voz temblorosa : with a shaky voice⟩
temer *vt* : to fear, to dread — *vi* : to be afraid
temerario, -ria *adj* : reckless, rash — **temerariamente** *adv*
temeridad *nf* 1 : temerity, recklessness, rashness 2 : rash act
temeroso, -sa *adj* MIEDOSO : fearful, frightened
temible *adj* : fearsome, dreadful
temor *nm* MIEDO : fear, dread
témpano *nm* : ice floe
temperamento *nm* : temperament — **temperamental** *adj*
temperancia *nf* : temperance
temperar *vt* MODERAR : to temper, to moderate — *vi* : to have a change of air
temperatura *nf* : temperature
tempestad *nf* 1 : storm, tempest 2 **tempestad de arena** : sandstorm
tempestuoso, -sa *adj* : tempestuous, stormy
templado, -da *adj* 1 : temperate, mild 2 : moderate, restrained 3 : warm, lukewarm 4 VALIENTE : courageous, bold
templanza *nf* 1 : temperance, moderation 2 : mildness (of weather)
templar *vt* 1 : to temper (steel) 2 : to restrain, to moderate 3 : to tune (a musical instrument) 4 : to warm up, to cool down — **templarse** *vr* 1 : to be moderate 2 : to warm up, to cool down
temple *nm* 1 : temper (of steel, etc.) 2 HUMOR : mood ⟨de buen temple : in a good mood⟩ 3 : tuning 4 VALOR : courage
templo *nm* 1 : temple 2 : church, chapel
tempo *nm* : tempo (in music)
temporada *nf* 1 : season, time ⟨temporada de béisbol : baseball season⟩ 2 : period, spell ⟨por temporadas : on and off⟩
temporal[1] *adj* 1 : temporal 2 : temporary
temporal[2] *nm* 1 : storm 2 **capear el temporal** : to weather the storm
temporalmente *adv* : temporarily
temporario, -ria *adj* : temporary — **temporariamente** *adv*
temporero[1], **-ra** *adj* : temporary, seasonal

temporero², -ra *n* : temporary or seasonal worker
temporizador *nm* : timer
tempranero, -ra *adj* **1** : early **2** : early-rising
temprano¹ *adv* : early ⟨lo más temprano posible : as soon as possible⟩
temprano², -na *adj* : early ⟨la parte temprana del siglo : the early part of the century⟩
ten → **tener**
tenacidad *nf* : tenacity, perseverance
tenaz *adj, pl* **tenaces** **1** : tenacious, persistent **2** : strong, tough
tenaza *nf, or* **tenazas** *nfpl* **1** : pliers, pincers **2** : tongs **3** : claw (of a crustacean)
tenazmente *adv* : tenaciously
tendedero *nm* : clothesline
tendencia *nf* **1** PROPENSIÓN : tendency, inclination **2** : trend
tendencioso, -sa *adj* : tendentious, biased
tendente → **tendiente**
tender {56} *vt* **1** EXTENDER : to spread out, to lay out **2** : to hang out (clothes) **3** : to lay (cables, etc.) **4** : to set (a trap) — *vi* ~ **a** : to tend to, to have a tendency towards — **tenderse** *vr* : to stretch out, to lie down
tendero, -ra *n* : shopkeeper, storekeeper
tendido *nm* **1** : laying (of cables, etc.) **2** : seats *pl*, section (at a bullfight)
tendiente *adj* ~ **a** : aimed at, designed to
tendón *nm, pl* **tendones** : tendon
tenebrosidad *nf* : darkness, gloom
tendrá, etc. → **tener**
tenebroso, -sa *adj* **1** OSCURO : gloomy, dark **2** SINIESTRO : sinister
tenedor¹, -dora *n* **1** : holder **2 tenedor de libros, tenedora de libros** : bookkeeper
tenedor² *nm* : table fork
tenencia *nf* **1** : possession, holding **2** : tenancy **3** : tenure
tener {80} *vt* **1** : to have ⟨tiene ojos verdes : she has green eyes⟩ ⟨tengo mucho que hacer : I have a lot to do⟩ ⟨tiene veinte años : he's twenty years old⟩ ⟨tiene un metro de largo : it's one meter long⟩ **2** : to hold ⟨ten esto un momento : hold this for a moment⟩ **3** : to feel, to make ⟨tengo frío : I'm cold⟩ ⟨eso nos tiene contentos : that makes us happy⟩ **4** ~ **por** : to think, to consider ⟨me tienes por loco : you think I'm crazy⟩ — *v aux* **1 tener que** : to have to ⟨tengo que salir : I have to leave⟩ ⟨tiene que estar aquí : it has to be here, it must be here⟩ **2** (*with past participle*) ⟨tenía pensado escribirte : I've been thinking of writing to you⟩ — **tenerse** *vr* **1** : to stand up **2** ~ **por** : to consider oneself ⟨me tengo por afortunado : I consider myself lucky⟩
tenería *nf* CURTIDURÍA : tannery
tenga, etc. → **tener**
tenia *nf* SOLITARIA : tapeworm

teniente *nmf* **1** : lieutenant **2 teniente coronel** : lieutenant colonel
tenis *nms & pl* **1** : tennis **2 tenis** *nmpl* : sneakers *pl*
tenista *nmf* : tennis player
tenor *nm* **1** : tenor **2** : tone, sense
tensar *vt* **1** : to tense, to make taut **2** : to draw (a bow) — **tensarse** *vr* : to become tense
tensión *nf, pl* **tensiones** **1** : tension, tautness **2** : stress, strain **3 tensión arterial** : blood pressure
tenso, -sa *adj* : tense
tentación *nf, pl* **-ciones** : temptation
tentáculo *nm* : tentacle, feeler
tentador¹, -dora *adj* : tempting
tentador², -dora *n* : tempter, temptress *f*
tentar {55} *vt* **1** TOCAR : to feel, to touch **2** PROBAR : to test, to try **3** ATRAER : to tempt, to entice
tentativa *nf* : attempt, try
tentempié *nm fam* : snack, bite
tenue *adj* **1** : tenuous **2** : faint, weak, dim **3** : light, fine **4** : thin, slender
teñir {67} *vt* **1** : to dye **2** : to stain
teodolito *nm* : theodolite, transit (for surveying)
teología *nf* : theology
teológico, -ca *adj* : theological
teólogo, -ga *n* : theologian
teorema *nm* : theorem
teoría *nf* : theory
teórico¹, -ca *adj* : theoretical — **teóricamente** *adv*
teórico², -ca *n* : theorist
teorizar {21} *vi* : to theorize
tepe *nm* : sod, turf
teponaztle *nm Mex* : traditional drum
tequila *nm* : tequila
terapeuta *nmf* : therapist
terapéutica *nf* : therapeutics
terapéutico, -ca *adj* : therapeutic
terapia *nf* **1** : therapy **2 terapia intensiva** : intensive care
tercer → **tercero**
tercermundista *adj* : third-world
tercero¹, -ra *adj* (**tercer** *before masculine singular nouns*) **1** : third **2 el Tercer Mundo** : the Third World
tercero², -ra *n* : third (in a series)
terceto *nm* **1** : tercet, triplet (in literature) **2** : trio (in music)
terciar *vt* **1** : to place diagonally **2** : to divide into three parts — *vi* **1** : to mediate **2** ~ **en** : to take part in
terciario, -ria *adj* : tertiary
tercio¹, -cia → **tercero**
tercio² *nm* : third ⟨dos tercios : two thirds⟩
terciopelo *nm* : velvet
terco, -ca *adj* OBSTINADO : obstinate, stubborn
tergiversación *nf, pl* **-ciones** : distortion
tergiversar *vt* : to distort, to twist
termal *adj* : thermal, hot
termas *nfpl* : hot springs
térmico, -ca *adj* : thermal, heat ⟨energía térmica : thermal energy⟩

terminación *nf, pl* **-ciones** : termination, conclusion

terminal[1] *adj* : terminal — **terminalmente** *adv*

terminal[2] *nm* (*in some regions f*) : (electric or electronic) terminal

terminal[3] *nf* (*in some regions m*) : terminal, station

terminante *adj* : final, definitive, categorical — **terminantemente** *adv*

terminar *vt* **1** CONCLUIR : to end, to conclude **2** ACABAR : to complete, to finish off — *vi* **1** : to finish **2** : to stop, to end — **terminarse** *vr* **1** : to run out **2** : to come to an end

término *nm* **1** CONCLUSIÓN : end, conclusion **2** : term, expression **3** : period, term of office **4 término medio** : happy medium **5 términos** *nmpl* : terms, specifications ⟨los términos del acuerdo : the terms of the agreement⟩

terminología *nf* : terminology

termita *nf* : termite

termo *nm* : thermos

termodinámica *nf* : thermodynamics

termómetro *nm* : thermometer

termostato *nm* : thermostat

ternera *nf* : veal

ternero, -ra *n* : calf

terno *nm* **1** : set of three **2** : three-piece suit

ternura *nf* : tenderness

terquedad *nf* OBSTINACIÓN : obstinacy, stubbornness

terracota *nf* : terra-cotta

terraplén *nm, pl* **-plenes** : terrace, embankment

terráqueo, -quea *adj* **1** : earth **2 globo terráqueo** : the earth, globe (of the earth)

terrateniente *nmf* : landowner

terraza *nf* **1** : terrace, veranda **2** : balcony (in a theater) **3** : terrace (in agriculture)

terremoto *nm* : earthquake

terrenal *adj* : worldly, earthly

terreno *nm* **1** : terrain **2** SUELO : earth, ground **3** : plot, tract of land **4 perder terreno** : to lose ground **5 preparar el terreno** : to pave the way

terrestre *adj* : terrestrial

terrible *adj* : terrible, horrible — **terriblemente** *adv*

terrier *nmf* : terrier

territorial *adj* : territorial

territorio *nm* : territory

terrón *nm, pl* **terrones 1** : clod (of earth) **2 terrón de azúcar** : lump of sugar

terror *nm* : terror

terrorífico, -ca *adj* : horrific, terrifying

terrorismo *nm* : terrorism

terrorista *adj & nmf* : terrorist

terroso, -sa *adj* : earthy ⟨colores terrosos : earthy colors⟩

terruño *nm* : native land, homeland

terso, -sa *adj* **1** : smooth **2** : glossy, shiny **3** : polished, flowing (of a style)

tersura *nf* **1** : smoothness **2** : shine

tertulia *nf* : gathering, group ⟨tertulia literaria : literary circle⟩

tesauro *nm* : thesaurus

tesis *nfs & pl* : thesis

tesón *nm* : persistence, tenacity

tesonero, -ra *adj* : persistent, tenacious

tesorería *nf* : treasurer's office

tesorero, -ra *n* : treasurer

tesoro *nm* **1** : treasure **2** : thesaurus

test *nm* : test

testaferro *nm* : figurehead

testamentario[1]**, -ria** *adj* : testamentary

testamentario[2]**, -ria** *n* ALBACEA : executor, executrix *f*

testamento *nm* : testament, will

testar *vi* : to draw up a will

testarudo, -da *adj* : stubborn, pigheaded

testículo *nm* : testicle

testificar {72} *v* : to testify

testigo *nmf* : witness

testimonial *adj* **1** : testimonial **2** : token

testimoniar *vi* : to testify

testimonio *nm* : testimony, statement

teta *nf* : teat

tétano *or* **tétanos** *nm* : tetanus, lockjaw

tetera *nf* **1** : teapot **2** : teakettle

tetilla *nf* **1** : teat **2** : nipple

tetina *nf* : nipple (on a bottle)

tétrico, -ca *adj* : somber, gloomy

textil *adj & nm* : textile

texto *nm* : text

textual *adj* : literal, exact — **textualmente** *adv*

textura *nf* : texture

tez *nf, pl* **teces** : complexion, coloring

ti *pron* **1** : you ⟨es para ti : it's for you⟩ **2 ti mismo, ti misma** : yourself **3** : thee

tía → **tío**

tiamina *nf* : thiamine

tianguis *nm Mex* : open-air market

tibetano[1]**, -na** *adj & n* : Tibetan

tibetano[2] *nm* : Tibetan (language)

tibia *nf* : tibia

tibieza *nf* **1** : tepidness **2** : halfheartedness

tibio, -bia *adj* **1** : lukewarm, tepid **2** : cool, unenthusiastic

tiburón *nm, pl* **-rones 1** : shark **2** : raider (in finance)

tic *nm* **1** : click, tick **2 tic nervioso** : tic

tico, -ca *adj & n fam* : Costa Rican

tictac *nm* **1** : ticking, tick-tock **2 hacer tictac** : to tick

tiembla, etc. → **temblar**

tiempo *nm* **1** : time ⟨justo a tiempo : just in time⟩ ⟨perder tiempo : to waste time⟩ ⟨tiempo libre : spare time⟩ **2** : period, age ⟨en los tiempos que corren : nowadays⟩ **3** : season, moment ⟨antes de tiempo : prematurely⟩ **4** : weather ⟨hace buen tiempo : the weather is fine, it's nice outside⟩ **5** : tempo (in music) **6** : half (in sports) **7** : tense (in grammar)

tienda *nf* **1** : store, shop **2** *or* **tienda de campaña** : tent

tiende, etc. → **tender**

tiene, etc. → **tener**
tienta[1], etc. → **tentar**
tienta[2] *nf* **andar a tientas** : to feel one's way, to grope around
tiernamente *adv* : tenderly
tierno, -na *adj* **1** : affectionate, tender **2** : tender, young
tierra *nf* **1** : land **2** SUELO : ground, earth **3** : country, homeland, soil **4 tierra natal** : native land **5 tierras altas** : highlands **6 la Tierra** : the Earth
tieso, -sa *adj* **1** : stiff, rigid **2** : upright, erect
tiesto *nm* **1** : potsherd **2** MACETA : flowerpot
tiesura *nf* : stiffness, rigidity
tifoidea *nf* : typhoid
tifoideo, -dea *adj* : typhoid ⟨fiebre tifoidea : typhoid fever⟩
tifón *nm, pl* **tifones** : typhoon
tifus *nm* : typhus
tigre, -gresa *n* **1** : tiger, tigress *f* **2** : jaguar
tijera *nf* **1** *or* **tijeras** *nfpl* : scissors **2 de** ∼ : folding ⟨escalera de tijera : stepladder⟩
tijereta *nf* : earwig
tijeretada *nf or* **tijeretazo** *nm* : cut, snip
tildar *vt* ∼ **de** : to brand as, to call ⟨lo tildaron de traidor : they branded him as a traitor⟩
tilde *nf* **1** : accent mark **2** : tilde (accent over ñ)
tilo *nm* : linden (tree)
timador, -dora *n* : swindler
timar *vt* : to swindle, to cheat
timbal *nm* **1** : kettledrum **2 timbales** *nmpl* : timpani
timbre *nm* **1** : bell ⟨tocar el timbre : to ring the doorbell⟩ **2** : tone, timbre **3** SELLO : seal, stamp **4** *CA, Mex* : postage stamp
timidez *nf* : timidity, shyness
tímido, -da *adj* : timid, shy — **tímidamente** *adv*
timo *nm fam* : swindle, trick, hoax
timón *nm, pl* **timones** : rudder ⟨estar al timón : to beat the helm⟩
timonel *nm* : helmsman, coxswain
timorato, -ta *adj* **1** : timorous **2** : sanctimonious
tímpano *nm* **1** : eardrum **2 tímpanos** *nmpl* : timpani, kettledrums
tina *nf* **1** BAÑERA : tub, bathtub **2** : vat
tinaco *nm Mex* : water tank
tinieblas *nfpl* **1** OSCURIDAD : darkness **2** : ignorance
tino *nm* **1** : good judgment, sense **2** : tact, sensitivity, insight
tinta *nf* : ink
tinte *nm* **1** : dye, coloring **2** : overtone ⟨tintes raciales : racial overtones⟩
tintero *nm* **1** : inkwell **2 quedarse en el tintero** : to remain unsaid
tintinear *vt* : to jingle, to clink, to tinkle
tintineo *nm* : clink, jingle, tinkle
tinto, -ta *adj* **1** : dyed, stained ⟨tinto en sangre : bloodstained⟩ **2** : red (of wine)

tintorería *nf* : dry cleaner (service)
tintura *nf* **1** : dye, tint **2** : tincture ⟨tintura de yodo : tincture of iodine⟩
tiña *nf* : ringworm
tiñe, etc. → **teñir**
tío, tía *n* **1** : uncle *m*, aunt *f*
tiovivo *nm* : merry-go-round
tipi *nm* : tepee
típico, -ca *adj* : typical — **típicamente** *adv*
tipificar {72} *vt* **1** : to classify, to categorize **2** : to typify
tiple *nm* : soprano
tipo[1] *nm* **1** CLASE : type, kind, sort **2** : figure, build, appearance **3** : rate ⟨tipo de interés : interest rate⟩ **4** : (printing) type, typeface **5** : style, model ⟨un vestido tipo 60's : a 60's-style dress⟩
tipo[2], **-pa** *n fam* : guy *m*, gal *f*, character
tipografía *nf* : typography, printing
tipográfico, -ca *adj* : typographic, typographical
tipógrafo, -fa *n* : printer, typographer
tique *or* **tiquet** *nm* **1** : ticket **2** : receipt
tira *nf* **1** : strip, strap **2 tira cómica** : comic, comic strip
tirabuzón *nm, pl* **-zones** : corkscrew
tirada *nf* **1** : throw **2** : distance, stretch **3** IMPRESIÓN : printing, issue
tiradero *nm Mex* **1** : dump **2** : mess, clutter
tirador[1] *nm* : handle, knob
tirador[2], **-dora** *n* : marksman *m*, markswoman *f*
tiragomas *nms & pl* : slingshot
tiranía *nf* : tyranny
tiránico, -ca *adj* : tyrannical
tiranizar {21} *vt* : to tyrannize
tirano[1], **-na** *adj* : tyrannical, despotic
tirano[2], **-na** *n* : tyrant
tirante[1] *adj* **1** : tense, strained **2** : taut
tirante[2] *nm* **1** : shoulder strap **2 tirantes** *nmpl* : suspenders
tirantez *nf* **1** : tautness **2** : tension, friction, strain
tirar *vt* **1** : to throw, to hurl, to toss **2** BOTAR : to throw away, to throw out, to waste **3** DERRIBAR : to knock down **4** : to shoot, to fire, to launch **5** : to take (a photo) **6** : to print, to run off — *vi* **1** : to pull, to draw **2** : to shoot **3** : to attract **4** : to get by, to manage ⟨va tirando : he's getting along, he's managing⟩ **5** ∼ **a** : to tend towards, to be rather ⟨tira a picante : it's a bit spicy⟩ — **tirarse** *vr* **1** : to throw oneself **2** *fam* : to spend (time)
tiritar *vi* : to shiver, to tremble
tiro *nm* **1** BALAZO, DISPARO : shot, gunshot **2** : shot, kick (in sports) **3** : flue **4** : team (of horses, etc.) **5 a** ∼ : within range **6 al tiro** : right away **7 tiro de gracia** : coup de grace, death blow
tiroideo, -dea *adj* : thyroid
tiroides *nmf* : thyroid, thyroid gland — **tiroides** *adj*

tirolés, -lesa *adj* : Tyrolean
tirón *nm, pl* **tirones 1** : pull, tug, yank **2 de un tirón** : all at once, in one go
tiroteo *nm* **1** : shooting **2** : gunfight, shoot-out
tirria *nf* **tener tirria a** *fam* : to have a grudge against
titánico, -ca *adj* : titanic, huge
titanio *nm* : titanium
títere *nm* : puppet
tití *nm* : marmoset
titilar *vi* : to twinkle, to flicker
titileo *nm* : twinkle, flickering
titiritero, -ra *n* **1** : puppeteer **2** : acrobat
titubear *vi* **1** : to hesitate **2** : to stutter, to stammer — **titubeante** *adj*
titubeo *nm* **1** : hesitation **2** : stammering
titulado, -da *adj* **1** : titled, entitled **2** : qualified
titular¹ *vt* : to title, to entitle — **titularse** *vr* **1** : to be called, to be entitled **2** : to receive a degree
titular² *adj* : titular, official
titular³ *nm* : headline
titular⁴ *nmf* **1** : owner, holder **2** : officeholder, incumbent
titularidad *nf* **1** : ownership, title **2** : position, office (with a title) **3** : starting position (in sports)
título *nm* **1** : title **2** : degree, qualification **3** : security, bond **4 a título de** : by way of, in the capacity of
tiza *nf* : chalk
tiznar *vt* : to blacken (with soot, etc.)
tizne *nm* HOLLÍN : soot
tiznón *nm, pl* **tiznones** : stain, smudge
tlapalería *nf Mex* : hardware store
TNT *nm* (trinitrotolueno) : TNT
toalla *nf* : towel
toallita *nf* : washcloth
tobillo *nm* : ankle
tobogán *nm, pl* **-ganes 1** : toboggan, sled **2** : slide, chute
tocadiscos *nms & pl* : record player, phonograph
tocado¹, -da *adj* **1** : bad, bruised (of fruit) **2** *fam* : touched, not all there
tocado² *nm* : headdress
tocador¹ *nm* **1** : dressing table, vanity table **2 artículos de tocador** : toiletries
tocador², -dora *n* : player (of music)
tocante *adj* ~ **a** : with regard to, regarding
tocar {72} *vt* **1** : to touch, to feel, to handle **2** : to touch on, to refer to **3** : to concern, to affect **4** : to play (a musical instrument) — *vi* **1** : to knock, to ring ⟨tocar a la puerta : to rap on the door⟩ **2** ~ **en** : to touch on, to border on ⟨eso toca en lo ridículo : that's almost ludicrous⟩ **3 tocarle a** : to fall to, to be up to, to be one's turn ⟨¿a quién le toca manejar? : whose turn is it to drive?⟩
tocayo, -ya *n* : namesake
tocineta *nf Col, Ven* : bacon
tocino *nm* **1** : bacon **2** : salt pork

tocología *nf* OBSTETRICIA : obstetrics
tocólogo, -ga *n* OBSTETRA : obstetrician
tocón *nm, pl* **toconés** CEPA : stump (of a tree)
todavía *adv* **1** AÚN : still, yet ⟨todavía puedes verlo : you can still see it⟩ **2** : even ⟨todavía más rápido : even faster⟩ **3 todavía no** : not yet
todo¹, -da *adj* **1** : all, whole, entire ⟨con toda sinceridad : with all sincerity⟩ ⟨toda la comunidad : the whole community⟩ **2** : every, each ⟨a todo nivel : at every level⟩ **3** : maximum ⟨a toda velocidad : at top speed⟩ **4 todo el mundo** : everyone, everybody
todo² *nm* : whole
todo³, -da *pron* **1** : everything, all, every bit ⟨lo sabe todo : he knows it all⟩ ⟨es todo un soldado : he's every inch a soldier⟩ **2 todos, -das** *pl* : everybody, everyone, all
todopoderoso, -sa *adj* OMNIPOTENTE : almighty, all-powerful
toga *nf* **1** : toga **2** : gown, robe (for magistrates, etc.)
toldo *nm* : awning, canopy
tolerable *adj* : tolerable — **tolerablemente** *adv*
tolerancia *nf* : tolerance, toleration
tolerante *adj* : tolerant — **tolerantemente** *adv*
tolerar *vt* : to tolerate
tolete *nm* : oarlock
tolva *nf* : hopper (container)
toma *nf* **1** : taking, seizure, capture **2** DOSIS : dose **3** : take, shot **4 toma de corriente** : wall socket, outlet **5 toma y daca** : give-and-take
tomar *vt* **1** : to take ⟨tomé el libro : I took the book⟩ ⟨tomar un taxi : to take a taxi⟩ ⟨tomar una foto : to take a photo⟩ ⟨toma dos años : it takes two years⟩ ⟨tomaron medidas drásticas : they took drastic measures⟩ **2** BEBER : to drink **3** CAPTURAR : to capture, to seize **4 tomar el sol** : to sunbathe **5 tomar tierra** : to land — *vi* : to drink (alcohol) — **tomarse** *vr* **1** : to take ⟨tomarse la molestia de : to take the trouble to⟩ **2** : to drink, to eat, to have
tomate *nm* : tomato
tomillo *nm* : thyme
tomo *nm* : volume, tome
ton *nm* **sin ton ni son** : without rhyme or reason
tonada *nf* **1** : tune, song **2** : accent
tonalidad *nf* : tonality
tonel *nm* BARRICA : barrel, cask
tonelada *nf* : ton
tonelaje *nm* : tonnage
tónica *nf* **1** : tonic (water) **2** : tonic (in music) **3** : trend, tone ⟨dar la tónica : to set the tone⟩
tónico¹, -ca *adj* : tonic
tónico² *nm* : tonic ⟨tónico capilar : hair tonic⟩
tono *nm* **1** : tone ⟨tono muscular : muscle tone⟩ **2** : shade (of colors) **3** : key (in music)

tontamente *adv* : foolishly, stupidly
tontear *vi* **1** : to fool around, to play the fool **2** : to flirt
tontería *nf* **1** : foolishness **2** : stupid remark or action **3 decir tonterías** : to talk nonsense
tonto[1], **-ta** *adj* **1** : dumb, stupid **2** : silly **3 a tontas y a locas** : without thinking, haphazardly
tonto[2], **-ta** *n* : fool, idiot
topacio *nm* : topaz
toparse *vr* ~ **con** : to bump into, to run into, to come across ⟨me topé con algunas dificultades : I ran into some problems⟩
tope *nm* **1** : limit, end ⟨hasta el tope : to the limit, to the brim⟩ **2** : stop, check, buffer ⟨tope de puerta : doorstop⟩ **3** : bump, collision **4** *Mex* : speed bump
tópico[1], **-ca** *adj* **1** : topical, external **2** : trite, commonplace
tópico[2] *nm* **1** : topic, subject **2** : cliché, trite expression
topo *nm* **1** : mole (animal) **2** *fam* : clumsy person, blunderer
topografía *nf* : topography
topográfico, -ca *adj* : topographic, topographical
topógrafo, -fa *n* : topographer
toque[1], etc. → **tocar**
toque[2] *nm* **1** : touch ⟨el último toque : the finishing touch⟩ ⟨un toque de color : a touch of color⟩ **2** : ringing, peal, chime **3** *Mex* : shock, jolt **4 toque de queda** : curfew **5 toque de diana** : reveille
toquetear *vt* : to touch, to handle, to finger
tórax *nm* : thorax
torbellino *nm* : whirlwind
torcedura *nf* **1** : twisting, buckling **2** : sprain
torcer {14} *vt* **1** : to bend, to twist **2** : to sprain **3** : to turn (a corner) **4** : to wring, to wring out **5** : to distort — *vi* : to turn — **torcerse** *vr*
torcido, -da *adj* **1** : twisted, crooked **2** : devious
tordo *nm* ZORZAL : thrush
torear *vt* **1** : to fight (bulls) **2** : to dodge, to sidestep
toreo *nm* : bullfighting
torero, -ra *n* MATADOR : bullfighter, matador
tormenta *nf* **1** : storm ⟨tormenta de nieve : snowstorm⟩ **2** : turmoil, frenzy
tormento *nm* **1** : torment, anguish **2** : torture
tormentoso, -sa *adj* : stormy, turbulent
tornado *nm* : tornado
tornamesa *nmf* : turntable
tornar *vt* **1** : to return, to give back **2** : to make, to render — *vi* : to go back — **tornarse** *vr* : to become, to turn into
tornasol *nm* **1** : reflected light **2** : sunflower **3** : litmus
tornear *vt* : to turn (in carpentry)
torneo *nm* : tournament

tornillo *nm* **1** : screw **2 tornillo de banco** : vise
torniquete *nm* **1** : tourniquet **2** : turnstile
torno *nm* **1** : lathe **2** : winch **3 torno de banco** : vise **4 en torno a** : around, about ⟨en torno a este asunto : about this issue⟩ ⟨en torno suyo : around him⟩
toro *nm* : bull
toronja *nf* : grapefruit
toronjil *nm* : balm, lemon balm
torpe *adj* **1** DESMAÑADO : clumsy, awkward **2** : stupid, dull — **torpemente** *adv*
torpedear *vt* : to torpedo
torpedo *nm* : torpedo
torpeza *nf* **1** : clumsiness, awkwardness **2** : stupidity **3** : blunder
torre *nf* **1** : tower ⟨torre de perforación : oil rig⟩ **2** : turret **3** : rook, castle (in chess)
torrencial *adj* : torrential — **torrencialmente** *adv*
torrente *nm* **1** : torrent **2 torrente sanguíneo** : bloodstream
torreón *nm*, *pl* **-rreones** : tower (of a castle)
torreta *nf* : turret (of a tank, ship, etc.)
tórrido, -da *adj* : torrid
torsión *nf*, *pl* **torsiones** : torsion — **torsional** *adj*
torso *nm* : torso, trunk
torta *nf* **1** : torte, cake **2** *Mex* : sandwich
tortazo *nm* *fam* : blow, wallop
tortilla *nf* **1** : tortilla **2** *or* **tortilla de huevo** : omelet
tórtola *nf* : turtledove
tortuga *nf* **1** : turtle, tortoise **2 tortuga de agua dulce** : terrapin **3 tortuga boba** : loggerhead
tortuoso, -sa *adj* : tortuous, winding
tortura *nf* : torture
torturador, -dora *n* : torturer
torturar *vt* : to torture, to torment
torvo, -va *adj* : grim, stern, baleful
torzamos, etc. → **torcer**
tos *nf* **1** : cough **2 tos ferina** : whooping cough
tosco, -ca *adj* : rough, coarse
toser *vi* : to cough
tosquedad *nf* : crudeness, coarseness, roughness
tostada *nf* **1** : piece of toast **2** : tostada
tostador *nm* **1** : toaster **2** : roaster (for coffee)
tostar {19} *vt* **1** : to toast **2** : to roast (coffee) **3** : to tan — **tostarse** *vr* : to get a tan
tostón *nm*, *pl* **tostones** *Car* : fried plantain chip
total[1] *adv* : in the end, so ⟨total, que no fui : in short, I didn't go⟩
total[2] *adj* & *nm* : total — **totalmente** *adv*
totalidad *nf* : totality, whole
totalitario, -ria *adj* & *n* : totalitarian
totalitarismo *nm* : totalitarianism

totalizar {21} vt : total, to add up to
tótem nm, pl **tótems** : totem
totopo nm CA, Mex : tortilla chip
totuma nf : calabash
tour ['tur] nm, pl **tours** : tour, excursion
toxicidad nf : toxicity
tóxico[1], **-ca** adj : toxic, poisonous
tóxico[2] nm : poison
toxicomanía nf : drug addiction
toxicómano, -na n : drug addict
toxina nf : toxin
tozudez nf : stubbornness, obstinacy
tozudo, -da adj : stubborn, obstinate —
  tozudamente adv
traba nf **1** : tie, bond **2** : obstacle, hindrance
trabajador[1], **-dora** adj : hardworking
trabajador[2], **-dora** n : worker
trabajar vi **1** : to work ⟨trabaja mucho
  : he works hard⟩ ⟨trabajo de secretaria
  : I work as a secretary⟩ **2** : to strive
  ⟨trabajan por mejores oportunidades
  : they're striving for better opportunities⟩ **3** : to act, to perform ⟨trabajar
  en una película : to be in a movie⟩ —
  vt **1** : to work (metal) **2** : to knead **3**
  : to till **4** : to work on ⟨tienes que trabajar el español : you need to work on
  your Spanish⟩
trabajo nm **1** : work, job **2** LABOR
  : labor, work ⟨tengo mucho trabajo : I
  have a lot of work to do⟩ **3** TAREA : task
  4 ESFUERZA : effort **5 costar trabajo**
  : to be difficult **6 tomarse el trabajo**
  : to take the trouble **7 trabajo en
  equipo** : teamwork **8 trabajos** nmpl
  : hardships, difficulties
trabajoso, -sa adj LABORIOSO : laborious — **trabajosamente** adv
trabalenguas nms & pl : tongue twister
trabar vt **1** : to join, to connect **2** : to
  impede, to hold back **3** : to strike up
  (a conversation), to form (a friendship)
  4 : to thicken (sauces) — **trabarse** vr
  1 : to jam **2** : to become entangled **3**
  : to be tongue-tied, to stammer
trabucar {72} vt : to confuse, to mix up
trabuco nm : blunderbuss
tracalero, -ra adj Mex : dishonest, tricky
tracción nf : traction
trace, etc. → trazar
tracto nm : tract
tractor nm : tractor
tradición nf, pl **-ciones** : tradition
tradicional adj : traditional — **tradicionalmente** adv
traducción nf, pl **-ciones** : translation
traducible adj : translatable
traducir {61} vt **1** : to translate **2** : to
  convey, to express — **traducirse** vr ~
  en : to result in
traductor, -tora n : translator
traer {81} vt **1** : to bring ⟨trae una ensalada : bring a salad⟩ **2** CAUSAR : to
  cause, to bring about ⟨el problema
  puede traer graves consecuencias : the
  problem could have serious consequences⟩ **3** : to carry, to have ⟨todos
  los periódicos traían las mismas noti-

cias : all of the newspapers carried the
  same news⟩ **4** LLEVAR : to wear —
traerse vr **1** : to bring along **2 traérselas** : to be difficult
traficante nmf : dealer, trafficker
traficar {72} vi **1** : to trade, to deal **2** ~
  con : to traffic in
tráfico nm **1** : trade **2** : traffic
tragaluz nf, pl **-luces** : skylight, fanlight
tragar {52} v : to swallow — **tragarse** vr
tragedia nf : tragedy
trágico, -ca adj : tragic — **trágicamente**
  adv
trago nm **1** : swallow, swig **2** : drink,
  liquor **3 trago amargo** : hard time
trague, etc. → tragar
traición nf, pl **traiciones 1** : treason **2**
  : betrayal, treachery
traicionar vt : to betray
traicionero, -ra → traidor
traidor[1], **-dora** adj : traitorous, treasonous
traidor[2], **-dora** n : traitor
traiga, etc. → traer
tráiler or **trailer** nm : trailer
traílla nf **1** : leash **2** : harrow
traje nm **1** : suit **2** : dress **3** : costume
  4 traje de baño : bathing suit
trajín nm, pl **trajines 1** : transport **2** fam
  : hustle and bustle
trajinar vt : to transport, to carry — vi
  : to rush around
trajo, etc. → traer
trama nf **1** : plot **2** : weave, weft (fabric)
tramar vt **1** : to plot, to plan **2** : to weave
tramitar vt : to transact, to negotiate, to
  handle
trámite nm : procedure, step
tramo nm **1** : stretch, section **2** : flight
  (of stairs)
trampa nf **1** : trap **2 hacer trampas** : to
  cheat
trampear vt : to cheat
trampero, -ra n : trapper
trampilla nf : trapdoor
trampolín nm, pl **-lines 1** : diving board
  2 : trampoline **3** : springboard ⟨un
  trampolín al éxito : a springboard to
  success⟩
tramposo[1], **-sa** adj : crooked, cheating
tramposo[2], **-sa** n : cheat, swindler
tranca nf **1** : stick, club **2** : bar, crossbar
trancar {72} vt : to bar (a door or window)
trancazo nm GOLPE : blow, hit
trance nm **1** : critical juncture, tough
  time **2** : trance **3 en trance de** : in the
  process of ⟨en trance de extinción : on
  the verge of extinction⟩
tranco nm **1** : stride **2** UMBRAL : threshold
tranque, etc. → trancar
tranquilidad nf : tranquility, peace
tranquilizador, -dora adj **1** : soothing **2**
  : reassuring
tranquilizante[1] adj **1** : reassuring **2**
  : tranquilizing

tranquilizante[2] *nm* : tranquilizer
tranquilizar {21} *vt* CALMAR : to calm down, to soothe ⟨tranquilizar la conciencia : to ease the conscience⟩ — **tranquilizarse** *vr*
tranquilo, -la *adj* CALMO : calm, tranquil ⟨una vida tranquila : a quiet life⟩ — **tranquilamente** *adv*
transacción *nf, pl* **-ciones** : transaction
transar *vi* TRANSIGIR : to give way, to compromise — *vt* : to buy and sell
transatlántico[1], **-ca** *adj* : transatlantic
transatlántico[2] *nm* : ocean liner
transbordador *nm* **1** : ferry **2 transbordador espacial** : space shuttle
transbordar *v* : to transfer
transbordo *nm* : transfer
transcendencia → **trascendencia**
transcender → **trascender**
transcribir {33} *vt* : to transcribe
transcrito *pp* → **transcribir**
transcripción *nf, pl* **-ciones** : transcription
transcurrir *vi* : to elapse, to pass
transcurso *nm* : course, progression ⟨en el transcurso de cien años : over the course of a hundred years⟩
transeúnte *nmf* **1** : passerby **2** : transient
transferencia *nf* : transfer, transference
transferir {76} *vt* TRASLADAR : to transfer — **transferible** *adj*
transfigurar *vt* : to transfigure, to transform — **transfiguración** *nf*
transformación *nf, pl* **-ciones** : transformation, conversion
transformador *nm* : transformer
transformar *vt* **1** CONVERTIR : to convert **2** : to transform, to change, to alter — **transformarse** *vr*
transfusión *nf, pl* **-siones** : transfusion
transgredir {1} *vt* : to transgress — **transgresión** *nf*
transgresor, -sora *n* : transgressor
transición *nf, pl* **-ciones** : transition ⟨período de transición : transition period⟩
transido, -da *adj* : overcome, beset ⟨transido de dolor : racked with pain⟩
transigir {35} *vi* **1** : to give in, to compromise **2** ~ **con** : to tolerate, to put up with
transistor *nm* : transistor
transitable *adj* : passable
transitar *vi* : to go, to pass, to travel ⟨transitar por la ciudad : to travel through the city⟩
transitivo, -va *adj* : transitive
tránsito *nm* **1** TRÁFICO : traffic ⟨hora de máximo tránsito : rush hour⟩ **2** : transit, passage, movement **3** : death, passing
transitorio, -ria *adj* **1** : transitory **2** : provisional, temporary — **transitoriamente** *adv*
translúcido, -da *adj* : translucent
translucir → **traslucir**
transmisible *adj* : transmissible

transmisión *nf, pl* **-siones** **1** : transmission, broadcast **2** : transfer **3** : transmission (of an automobile)
transmisor *nm* : transmitter
transmitir *vt* **1** : to transmit, to broadcast **2** : to pass on, to transfer — *vi* : to transmit, to broadcast
transparencia *nf* : transparency
transparentar *vt* : to reveal, to betray — **transparentarse** *vr* **1** : to be transparent **2** : to show through
transparente[1] *adj* : transparent — **transparentemente** *adv*
transparente[2] *nm* : shade, blind
transpiración *nf, pl* **-ciones** SUDOR : perspiration, sweat
transpirado, -da *adj* : sweaty
transpirar *vi* **1** SUDAR : to perspire, to sweat **2** : to transpire
transplantar, transplante → **trasplantar, trasplante**
transponer {60} *vt* **1** : to transpose, to move about **2** TRASPLANTAR : to transplant — **transponerse** *vr* **1** OCULTARSE : to hide **2** PONERSE : to set, to go down (of the sun or moon) **3** DORMITAR : to doze off
transportación *nf, pl* **-ciones** : transportation
transportador *nm* **1** : protractor **2** : conveyor
transportar *vt* **1** : to transport, to carry **2** : to transmit **3** : to transpose (music) — **transportarse** *vr* : to get carried away
transporte *nm* : transport, transportation
transportista *nmf* : hauler, carrier, trucker
transpuso, etc. → **transponer**
transversal *adj* : transverse, cross ⟨corte transversal : cross section⟩
transversalmente *adv* : obliquely
transverso, -sa *adj* : transverse
tranvía *nm* : streetcar, trolley
trapeador *nm* : mop
trapear *vt* : to mop
trapecio *nm* **1** : trapezoid **2** : trapeze
trapezoide *nm* : trapezoid
trapo *nm* **1** : cloth, rag ⟨trapo de polvo : dust cloth⟩ **2 soltar el trapo** : to burst into tears **3 trapos** *nmpl fam* : clothes
tráquea *nf* : trachea, windpipe
traquetear *vi* : to clatter, to jolt
traqueteo *nm* **1** : jolting **2** : clattering, clatter
tras *prep* **1** : after ⟨día tras día : day after day⟩ ⟨uno tras otro : one after another⟩ **2** : behind ⟨tras la puerta : behind the door⟩
trasbordar, trasbordo → **transbordar, transbordo**
trascendencia *nf* **1** : importance, significance **2** : transcendence
trascendental *adj* **1** : transcendental **2** : important, momentous
trascendente *adj* **1** : important, significant **2** : transcendent

trascender {56} *vi* **1** : to leak out, to become known **2** : to spread, to have a wide effect **3** ~ **a** : to smell of ⟨la casa trascendía a flores : the house smelled of flowers⟩ **4** ~ **de** : to transcend, to go beyond — *vt* : to transcend
trasero[1], **-ra** *adj* POSTERIOR : rear, back
trasero[2] *nm* : buttocks
trasfondo *nm* **1** : background, backdrop **2** : undertone, undercurrent
trasformación → **transformación**
trasgo *nm* : goblin, imp
trasgredir → **transgredir**
trasladar *vt* **1** TRANSFERIR : to transfer, to move **2** POSPONER : to postpone **3** TRADUCIR : to translate **4** COPIAR : to copy, to transcribe — **trasladarse** *vr* MUDARSE : to move, to relocate
traslado *nm* **1** : transfer, move **2** : copy
traslapar *vt* : to overlap — **traslaparse** *vr*
traslapo *nm* : overlap
traslúcido, -da → **translúcido**
traslucir {45} *vi* : to reveal, to show — **traslucirse** *vr* : to show through
trasmano *nm* **a** ~ : out of the way, out of reach
trasmisión, trasmitir → **transmisión, transmitir**
trasnochar *vi* : to stay up all night
trasparencia *nf* **trasparente** → **transparencia, transparente**
traspasar *vt* **1** PERFORAR : to pierce, to go through **2** : to go beyond ⟨traspasar los límites : to overstep the limits⟩ **3** ATRAVESAR : to cross, to go across **4** : to sell, to transfer
traspaso *nm* : transfer, sale
traspié *nm* **1** : stumble **2** : blunder
traspiración → **transpiración**
trasplantar *vt* : to transplant
trasplante *nm* : transplant
trasponer → **transponer**
trasportar → **transportar**
trasquilar *vt* ESQUILAR : to shear
traste *nm* **1** : fret (on a guitar) **2** *CA, Mex, PRi* : kitchen utensil ⟨lavar los trastes : to do the dishes⟩ **3 dar al traste con** : to ruin, to destroy **4 irse al traste** : to fall through
trastornar *vt* : to disturb, to upset, to disrupt — **trastornarse** *vr*
trastorno *nm* **1** : disorder ⟨trastorno mental : mental disorder⟩ **2** : disturbance, upset
trastos *nmpl* **1** : implements, utensils **2** *fam* : pieces of junk, stuff
trasunto *nm* : image, likeness
tratable *adj* **1** : friendly, sociable **2** : treatable
tratado *nm* **1** : treatise **2** : treaty
tratamiento *nm* : treatment
tratante *nmf* : dealer, trader
tratar *vi* **1** ~ **con** : to deal with, to have contact with ⟨no trato mucho con los clientes : I don't have much contact with customers⟩ **2** ~ **de** : to try to ⟨estoy tratando de comer : I am trying to

eat⟩ **3** ~ **de** *or* ~ **sobre** : to be about, to concern ⟨el libro trata de las plantas : the book is about plants⟩ **4** ~ **en** : to deal in ⟨trata en herramientas : he deals in tools⟩ — *vt* **1** : to treat ⟨tratan bien a sus empleados : they treat their employees well⟩ **2** : to handle ⟨trató el tema con delicadeza : he handled the subject tactfully⟩ — **tratarse** *vr* ~ **de** : to be about, to concern
trato *nm* **1** : deal, agreement **2** : relationship, dealings *pl* **3** : treatment ⟨malos tratos : ill-treatment⟩
trauma *nm* : trauma
traumático, -ca *adj* : traumatic — **traumáticamente** *adv*
traumatismo *nm* : injury ⟨traumatismo cervical : whiplash⟩
través *nm* **1 a través de** : across, through **2 al través** : crosswise, across **3 de través** : sideways
travesaño *nm* **1** : crossbar **2** : crossbeam, crosspiece, transom (of a window)
travesía *nf* : voyage, crossing (of the sea)
travesura *nf* **1** : prank, mischievous act **2 travesuras** *nfpl* : mischief
travieso, -sa *adj* : mischievous, naughty — **traviesamente** *adv*
trayecto *nm* **1** : journey **2** : route **3** : trajectory, path
trayectoria *nf* : course, path, trajectory
trayendo → **traer**
traza *nf* **1** DISEÑO : design, plan **2** : appearance
trazado *nm* **1** BOSQUEJO : outline, sketch **2** PLAN : plan, layout
trazar {21} *vt* **1** : to trace **2** : to draw up, to devise **3** : to outline, to sketch
trazo *nm* **1** : stroke, line **2** : sketch, outline
trébol *nm* **1** : clover, shamrock **2** : club (playing card)
trece *adj & nm* : thirteen
treceavo[1], **-va** *adj* : thirteenth
treceavo[2] *nm* : thirteenth (fraction)
trecho *nm* **1** : stretch, period ⟨de trecho en trecho : at intervals⟩ **2** : distance, space
tregua *nf* **1** : truce **2** : lull, respite **3 sin** ~ : relentless, unrelenting
treinta *adj & nm* : thirty
treintavo[1], **-va** *adj* : thirtieth
treintavo[2] *nm* : thirtieth (fraction)
tremendo, -da *adj* **1** : tremendous, enormous **2** : terrible, dreadful **3** *fam* : great, super
trementina *nf* AGUARRÁS : turpentine
trémulo, -la *adj* **1** : trembling, shaky **2** : flickering
tren *nm* **1** : train **2** : set, assembly ⟨tren de aterrizaje : landing gear⟩ **3** : speed, pace ⟨a todo tren : at top speed⟩
trence, etc. → **trenzar**
trenza *nf* : braid, pigtail
trenzar {21} *vt* : to braid — **trenzarse** *vr* : to get involved
trepador, -dora *adj* : climbing ⟨rosal trepador : rambling rose⟩

trepadora *nf* **1** : climbing plant, climber **2** : nuthatch
trepar *vi* **1** : to climb ⟨trepar a un árbol : to climb up a tree⟩ **2** : to creep, to spread (of a plant)
trepidación *nf, pl* **-ciones** : vibration
trepidante *adj* **1** : vibrating **2** : fast, frantic
trepidar *vi* **1** : to shake, to vibrate **2** : to hesitate, to waver
tres *adj & nm* : three
trescientos¹, -tas *adj* : three hundred
trescientos² *nms & pl* : three hundred
treta *nf* : trick, ruse
tríada *nf* : triad
triángulo *nm* : triangle — **triangular** *adj*
tribal *adj* : tribal
tribu *nf* : tribe
tribulación *nf, pl* **-ciones** : tribulation
tribuna *nf* **1** : dais, platform **2** : stands *pl*, bleachers *pl*, grandstand
tribunal *nm* : court, tribunal
tributar *vt* : to pay, to render — *vi* : to pay taxes
tributario¹, -ria *adj* : tax ⟨evasión tributaria : tax evasion⟩
tributario² *nm* : tributary
tributo *nm* **1** : tax **2** : tribute
triciclo *nm* : tricycle
tricolor *adj* : tricolor, tricolored
tridente *nm* : trident
tridimensional *adj* : three-dimensional, 3-D
trienal *adj* : triennial
trifulca *nf fam* : row, ruckus
trigésimo¹, -ma *adj* : thirtieth, thirty-
trigésimo², -ma *n* : thirtieth, thirty- (in a series)
trigo *nm* **1** : wheat **2 trigo rubión** : buckwheat
trigonometría *nf* : trigonometry
trigueño, -ña *adj* **1** : light brown (of hair) **2** MORENO : dark, olive-skinned
trillado, -da *adj* : trite, hackneyed
trilladora *nf* : thresher, threshing machine
trillar *vt* : to thresh
trillizo, -za *n* : triplet
trilogía *nf* : trilogy
trimestral *adj* : quarterly — **trimestralmente** *adv*
trinar *vi* **1** : to thrill **2** : to warble
trinchar *vt* : to carve, to cut up
trinchera *nf* **1** : trench, ditch **2** : trench coat
trineo *nm* : sled, sleigh
trinidad *nf* **la Trinidad** : the Trinity
trino *nm* : trill, warble
trinquete *nm* : ratchet
trío *nm* : trio
tripa *nf* **1** INTESTINO : gut, intestine **2 tripas** *nfpl fam* : belly, tummy, insides *pl* ⟨dolerle a uno las tripas : to have a stomach ache⟩
tripartito, -ta *adj* : tripartite
triple *adj & nm* : triple
triplicado *nm* : triplicate
triplicar {72} *vt* : to triple, to treble

trípode *nm* : tripod
tripulación *nf, pl* **-ciones** : crew
tripulante *nmf* : crew member
tripular *vt* : to man
tris *nm* **estar en un tris de** : to be within an inch of, to be very close to
triste *adj* **1** : sad, gloomy ⟨ponerse triste : to become sad⟩ **2** : desolate, dismal ⟨una perspectiva triste : a dismal outlook⟩ **3** : sorry, sorry-looking ⟨la triste verdad : the sorry truth⟩
tristeza *nf* DOLOR : sadness, grief
tristón, -tona *adj, mpl* **-tones** : melancholy, downhearted
tritón *nm, pl* **tritones** : newt
triturar *vt* : to crush, to grind
triunfal *adj* : triumphal, triumphant — **triunfalmente** *adv*
triunfante *adj* : triumphant, victorious
triunfar *vi* : to triumph, to win
triunfo *nm* **1** : triumph, victory **2** ÉXITO : success **3** : trump (in card games)
triunvirato *nm* : triumvirate
trivial *adj* **1** : trivial **2** : trite, commonplace
trivialidad *nf* : triviality
triza *nf* **1** : shred, bit **2 hacer trizas** : to tear into shreds, to smash to pieces
trocar {82} *vt* **1** CAMBIAR : to exchange, to trade **2** CAMBIAR : to change, to alter, to transform **3** CONFUNDIR : to confuse, to mix up
trocha *nf* : path, trail
troce, etc. → trozar
trofeo *nm* : trophy
tromba *nf* **1** : whirlwind **2 tromba de agua** : downpour, cloudburst
trombón *nm, pl* **trombones 1** : trombone **2** : trombonist — **trombonista** *nmf*
trombosis *nf* : thrombosis
trompa *nf* **1** : trunk (of an elephant), proboscis (of an insect) **2** : horn ⟨trompa de caza : hunting horn⟩ **3** : tube, duct (in the body)
trompada *nf fam* **1** : punch, blow **2** : bump, collision (of persons)
trompeta *nf* : trumpet
trompetista *nmf* : trumpet player, trumpeter
trompo *nm* : spinning top
tronada *nf* : thunderstorm
tronar {19} *vi* **1** : to thunder, to roar **2** : to be furious, to rage **3** CA, Mex fam : to shoot — *v impers* : to thunder ⟨está tronando : it's thundering⟩
tronchar *vt* **1** : to snap, to break off **2** : to cut off (relations)
tronco *nm* **1** : trunk (of a tree) **2** : log **3** : torso
trono *nm* **1** : throne **2** *fam* : toilet
tropa *nf* **1** : troop, soldiers *pl* **2** : crowd, mob **3** : herd (of livestock)
tropel *nm* : mob, swarm
tropezar {29} *vi* **1** : to trip, to stumble **2** : to slip up, to blunder **3** ~ **con** : to run into, to bump into **4** ~ **con** : to come up against (a problem)

tropezón *nm, pl* **-zones** 1 : stumble 2 : mistake, slip

tropical *adj* : tropical

trópico *nm* 1 : tropic ⟨trópico de Cáncer : tropic of Cancer⟩ 2 **el trópico** : the tropics

tropiezo *nm* 1 CONTRATIEMPO : snag, setback 2 EQUIVOCACIÓN : mistake, slip

troqué, etc. → **trocar**

troquel *nm* : die (for stamping)

trotamundos *nmf* : globe-trotter

trotar *vi* 1 : to trot 2 : to jog 3 *fam* : to rush about

trote *nm* 1 : trot 2 *fam* : rush, bustle 3 **de ~** : durable, for everyday use

trovador, -dora *n* : troubadour

trozar {21} *vt* : to cut up, to dice

trozo *nm* 1 PEDAZO : piece, bit, chunk 2 : passage, extract

trucha *nf* : trout

truco *nm* 1 : trick 2 : knack

truculento, -ta *adj* : horrifying, gruesome

trueca, trueque etc. → **trocar**

truena, etc. → **tronar**

trueno *nm* : thunder

trueque *nm* : barter, exchange

trufa *nf* : truffle

truncar {72} *vt* 1 : to truncate, to cut short 2 : to thwart, to frustrate ⟨truncó sus esperanzas : she shattered their hopes⟩

trunco, -ca *adj* 1 : truncated 2 : unfinished, incomplete

trunque, etc. → **truncar**

tu *adj* 1 : your ⟨tu vestido : your dress⟩ ⟨toma tus vitaminas : take your vitamins⟩ 2 : thy

tú *pron* 1 : you ⟨tú eres mi hijo : you are my son⟩ 2 : thou

tuba *nf* : tuba

tubérculo *nm* : tuber

tuberculosis *nf* : tuberculosis

tuberculoso, -sa *adj* : tuberculous, tubercular

tubería *nf* : pipes *pl*, tubing

tuberoso, -sa *adj* : tuberous

tubo *nm* 1 : tube ⟨tubo de ensayo : test tube⟩ 2 : pipe ⟨tubo de desagüe : drainpipe⟩ 3 **tubo digestivo** : alimentary canal

tubular *adj* : tubular

tuerca *nf* : nut ⟨tuercas y tornillos : nuts and bolts⟩

tuerce, etc. → **torcer**

tuerto, -ta *adj* : one-eyed, blind in one eye

tuerza, etc. → **torcer**

tuesta, etc. → **tostar**

tuétano *nm* : marrow

tufo *nm* 1 : fume, vapor 2 *fam* : stench, stink

tugurio *nm* : hovel

tulipán *nm, pl* **-panes** : tulip

tumba *nf* 1 SEPULCRO : tomb 2 FOSA : grave 3 : felling of trees

tumbar *vt* 1 : to knock down 2 : to fell, to cut down — *vi* : to fall down —

tumbarse *vr* ACOSTARSE : to lie down

tumbo *nm* 1 : tumble, fall 2 **dar tumbos** : to jolt, to bump around

tumor *nm* : tumor

túmulo *nm* : burial mound

tumulto *nm* 1 ALBOROTO : commotion, tumult 2 MOTÍN : riot 3 MULTITUD : crowd

tumultuoso, -sa *adj* : tumultuous

tuna *nf* : prickly pear (fruit)

tundra *nf* : tundra

tunecino, -na *adj* & *n* : Tunisian

túnel *nm* : tunnel

tungsteno *nm* : tungsten

túnica *nf* : tunic

tupé *nm* PELUQUÍN : toupee

tupido, -da *adj* 1 DENSO : dense, thick 2 OBSTRUIDO : obstructed, blocked up

turba *nf* 1 : peat 2 : mob, throng

turbación *nf, pl* **-ciones** 1 : disturbance 2 : alarm, concern 3 : confusion

turbante *nm* : turban

turbar *vt* 1 : to disturb, to disrupt 2 : to worry, to upset 3 : to confuse

turbina *nf* : turbine

turbio, -bia *adj* 1 : cloudy, murky, turbid 2 : dim, blurred 3 : shady, crooked

turbopropulsor *nm* : turboprop

turborreactor *nm* : turbojet

turbulencia *nf* : turbulence

turbulento, -ta *adj* : turbulent

turco[1], **-ca** *adj* : Turkish

turco[2], **-ca** *n* : Turk

turco[3] *nm* : Turkish (language)

turgente *adj* : turgid, swollen

turismo *nm* : tourism, tourist industry

turista *nmf* : tourist, vacationer

turístico, -ca *adj* : tourist, travel

turnar *vi* : to take turns, to alternate

turno *nm* 1 : turn ⟨ya te tocará tu turno : you'll get your turn⟩ 2 : shift, duty ⟨turno de noche : night shift⟩ 3 **por turno** : alternately

turón *nm, pl* **turones** : polecat

turquesa *nf* : turquoise

turrón *nm, pl* **turrones** : nougat

tusa *nf* : corn husk

tutear *vt* : to address as *tú*

tutela *nf* 1 : guardianship 2 : tutelage, protection

tuteo *nm* : addressing as *tú*

tutor, -tora *n* 1 : tutor 2 : guardian

tuvo, etc. → **tener**

tuyo[1], **-ya** *adj* : yours, of yours ⟨un amigo tuyo : a friend of yours⟩ ⟨¿es tuya esta casa? : is this house yours?⟩

tuyo[2], **-ya** *pron* 1 : yours ⟨ése es el tuyo : that one is yours⟩ ⟨trae la tuya : bring your own⟩ 2 **los tuyos** : your relations, your friends ⟨¿vendrán los tuyos? : are your folks coming?⟩

tweed ['twið] *nm* : tweed

U

u¹ *nf* : twenty-second letter of the Spanish alphabet

u² *conj* (*used instead of* **o** *before words beginning with* o- *or* ho-) : or

ualabí *nm* : wallaby

uapití *nm* : American elk, wapiti

ubicación *nf, pl* **-ciones** : location, position

ubicar {72} *vt* **1** SITUAR : to place, to put, to position **2** LOCALIZAR : to locate, to find — **ubicarse** *vr* **1** LOCALIZARSE : to be placed, to be located **2** SITUARSE : to position oneself

ubicuidad *nf* OMNIPRESENCIA : ubiquity

ubicuo, -cua *adj* OMNIPRESENTE : ubiquitous

ubre *nf* : udder

ucraniano¹, -na *adj & n* : Ukranian

ucraniano² *nm* : Ukranian (language)

Ud., Uds. → **usted**

ufanarse *vr* ~ **de** : to boast about, to pride oneself on

ufano, -na *adj* **1** ORGULLOSO : proud **2** : self-satisfied, smug

ugandés, -desa *adj & n, mpl* **-deses** : Ugandan

ukelele *nm* : ukulele

úlcera *nf* : ulcer — **ulceroso, -sa** *adj*

ulcerar *vt* : to ulcerate — **ulcerarse** *vr* — **ulceración** *nf*

ulceroso, -sa *adj* : ulcerous

ulterior *adj* : later, subsequent — **ulteriormente** *adv*

últimamente *adv* : lately, recently

ultimar *vt* **1** CONCLUIR : to complete, to finish, to finalize **2** MATAR : to kill

último, -ma *adj* **1** : last, final ⟨la última galleta : the last cookie⟩ ⟨en último caso : as a last resort⟩ **2** : last, latest, most recent ⟨su último viaje a España : her last trip to Spain⟩ ⟨en los últimos años : in recent years⟩ **3 por** ~ : finally

ultrajar *vt* INSULTAR : to offend, to outrage, to insult

ultraje *nm* INSULTO : outrage, insult

ultramar *nm* **de** ~ *or* **en** ~ : overseas, abroad

ultranza *nf* **1 a** ~ : to the extreme ⟨lo defendió a ultranza : she defended him fiercely⟩ **2 a** ~ : extreme, out-and-out ⟨perfeccionismo a ultranza : rabid perfectionism⟩

ultrarrojo, -ja *adj* : infrared

ultravioleta *adj* : ultraviolet

ulular *vi* **1** : to hoot **2** : to howl, to wail

ululato *nm* : hoot (of an owl), wail (of a person)

umbilical *adj* : umbilical ⟨cordón umbilical : umbilical cord⟩

umbral *nm* : threshold, doorstep

un¹ *adj* → **uno¹**

un², una *art, mpl* **unos 1** : a, an **2 unos** *or* **unas** *pl* : some, a few ⟨hace unas se-manas : a few weeks ago⟩ **3 unos** *or* **unas** *pl* : about, approximately ⟨unos veinte años antes : about twenty years before⟩

unánime *adj* : unanimous — **unánimemente** *adv*

unanimidad *nf* **1** : unanimity **2 por** ~ : unanimously

unción *nf, pl* **-ciones** : unction

uncir {83} *vt* : to yoke

undécimo¹, -ma *adj* : eleventh

undécimo², -ma *n* : eleventh (in a series)

ungir {35} *vt* : to anoint

ungüento *nm* : ointment, salve

únicamente *adv* : only, solely

unicelular *adj* : unicellular

único¹, -ca *adj* **1** : only, sole **2** : unique, extraordinary

único², -ca *n* : only one ⟨los únicos que vinieron : the only ones who showed up⟩

unicornio *nm* : unicorn

unidad *nf* **1** : unity **2** : unit

unidireccional *adj* : unidirectional

unido, -da *adj* **1** : joined, united **2** : close ⟨unos amigos muy unidos : very close friends⟩

unificar {72} *vt* : to unify — **unificación** *nf*

uniformado, -da *adj* : uniformed

uniformar *vt* ESTANDARIZAR : to standardize, to make uniform

uniforme¹ *adj* : uniform — **uniformemente** *adv*

uniforme² *nm* : uniform

uniformidad *nf* : uniformity

unilateral *adj* : unilateral — **unilateralmente** *adv*

unión *nf, pl* **uniones 1** : union **2** JUNTURA : joint, coupling

unir *vt* **1** JUNTAR : to unite, to join, to link **2** COMBINAR : to combine, to blend — **unirse** *vr* **1** : to join together **2** : to combine, to mix together **3** ~ **a** : to join ⟨se unieron al grupo : they joined the group⟩

unísono *nm* : unison ⟨al unísono : in unison⟩

unitario, -ria *adj* : unitary, unit ⟨precio unitario : unit price⟩

universal *adj* : universal — **universalmente** *adv*

universidad *nf* : university

universitario¹, -ria *adj* : university, college

universitario², -ria *n* : university student, college student

universo *nm* : universe

unja, etc. → **ungir**

uno¹, una *adj* (**un** *before masculine singular nouns*) : one ⟨una silla : one chair⟩ ⟨tiene treinta y un años : he's thirty-one years old⟩ ⟨el tomo uno : volume one⟩

uno² *nm* : one, number one

uno³, una *pron* **1** : one (number) ⟨uno por uno : one by one⟩ ⟨es la una : it's one o'clock⟩ **2** : one (person or thing) ⟨una es mejor que las otras : one (of them) is better than the others⟩ ⟨hacerlo uno mismo : to do it oneself⟩ **3 unos, unas** *pl* : some (ones), some people **4 uno y otro** : both **5 unos y otros** : all of them **6 el uno al otro** : one another, each other ⟨se enseñaron los unos a los otros : they taught each other⟩

untar *vt* **1** : to anoint **2** : to smear, to grease **3** : to bribe

unza, etc. → **uncir**

uña *nf* **1** : fingernail, toenail **2** : claw, hoof, stinger

uranio *nm* : uranium

Urano *nm* : Uranus

urbanidad *nf* : urbanity, courtesy

urbanización *nf, pl* **-ciones** : housing development, residential area

urbanizar {21} *vt* : to develop (an area)

urbano, -na *adj* **1** : urban **2** CORTÉS : urbane, polite

urbe *nf* : large city, metropolis

urdimbre *nf* : warp (in a loom)

urdu *nm* : Urdu

uretra *nf* : urethra

urgencia *nf* **1** : urgency **2** EMERGENCIA : emergency

urgente *adj* : urgent — **urgentemente** *adv*

urgir {35} *v impers* : to be urgent, to be pressing ⟨me urge localizarlo : I urgently need to find him⟩ ⟨el tiempo urge : time is running out⟩

urinario¹, -ria *adj* : urinary

urinario² *nm* : urinal (place)

urja, etc. → **urgir**

urna *nf* **1** : urn **2** : ballot box ⟨acudir a las urnas : to go to the polls⟩

urogallo *nm* : grouse (bird)

urraca *nf* **1** : magpie **2 urraca de América** : blue jay

urticaria *nf* : hives

uruguayo, -ya *adj & n* : Uruguayan

usado, -da *adj* **1** : used, secondhand **2** : worn, worn-out

usanza *nf* : custom, usage

usar *vt* **1** EMPLEAR, UTILIZAR : to use, to make use of **2** CONSUMIR : to consume, to use (up) **3** LLEVAR : to wear **4 de usar y tirar** : disposable — **usarse** *vr* **1** : to be used **2** : to be in fashion

uso *nm* **1** EMPLEO, UTILIZACIÓN : use ⟨de uso personal : for personal use⟩ ⟨hacer uso de : to make use of⟩ ⟨uso y desgaste : wear and tear⟩ **3** USANZA : custom, usage, habit ⟨al uso de : in the manner of, in the style of⟩

usted *pron* **1** (*formal form of address in most countries; often written as* **Ud.** *or* **Vd.**) : you **2 ustedes** *pl* (*often written as* **Uds.** *or* **Vds.**) : you, all of you

usual *adj* : usual, common, normal ⟨poco usual : not very common⟩ — **usualmente** *adv*

usuario, -ria *n* : user

usura *nf* : usury — **usurario, -ria** *adj*

usurero, -ra *n* : usurer

usurpador, -dora *n* : usurper

usurpar *vt* : to usurp — **usurpación** *nf*

utensilio *nm* : utensil, tool

uterino, -na *adj* : uterine

útero *nm* : uterus, womb

útil *adj* : useful, handy, helpful

útiles *nmpl* : implements, tools

utilidad *nf* **1** : utility, usefulness **2 utilidades** *nfpl* : profits

utilitario, -ria *adj* : utilitarian

utilizable *adj* : usable, fit for use

utilización *nf, pl* **-ciones** : utilization, use

utilizar {21} *vt* : to use, to utilize

útilmente *adv* : usefully

utopía *nf* : utopia

utópico, -ca *adj* : utopian

uva *nf* : grape

uvular *adj* : uvular

V

v *nf* : twenty-third letter of the Spanish alphabet

va → **ir**

vaca *nf* : cow

vacación *nf, pl* **-ciones 1** : vacation ⟨dos semanas de vacaciones : two weeks of vacation⟩ **2 estar de vacaciones** : to be on vacation **3 irse de vacaciones** : to go on vacation

vacacionar *vi Mex* : to vacation

vacacionista *nmf CA, Mex* : vacationer

vacante¹ *adj* : vacant, empty

vacante² *nf* : vacancy (for a job)

vaciado *nm* : cast, casting ⟨vaciado de yeso : plaster cast⟩

vaciar {85} *vt* **1** : to empty, to empty out, to drain **2** AHUECAR : to hollow out **3** : to cast (in a mold) — *vi* ~ **en** : to flow into, to empty into

vacilación *nf, pl* **-ciones** : hesitation, vacillation

vacilante *adj* **1** : hesitant, unsure **2** : shaky, unsteady **3** : flickering

vacilar *vi* **1** : to hesitate, to vacillate, to waver **2** : to be unsteady, to wobble **3** : to flicker **4** *fam* : to joke, to fool around

vacío¹, -cía *adj* **1** : vacant **2** : empty **3** : meaningless

vacío² *nm* **1** : emptiness, void **2** : space, gap **3** : vacuum **4 hacerle el vacío a alguien** : to ostracize someone, to give someone the cold shoulder

vacuidad *nf* : vacuity, vacuousness

vacuna *nf* : vaccine
vacunación *nf, pl* -ciones INOCU-LACIÓN : vaccination, inoculation
vacunar *vt* INOCULAR : to vaccinate, to inoculate
vacuno[1], -na *adj* : bovine ⟨ganado vacuno : beef cattle⟩
vacuno[2] *nm* : bovine
vacuo, -cua *adj* : empty, shallow, inane
vadear *vt* : to ford, to wade across
vado *nm* : ford
vagabundear *vi* : to wander, to roam about
vagabundo[1], -da *adj* 1 ERRANTE : wandering 2 : stray
vagabundo[2], -da *n* : vagrant, bum, vagabond
vagamente *adv* : vaguely
vagancia *nf* 1 : vagrancy 2 PEREZA : laziness, idleness
vagar {52} *vi* ERRAR : to roam, to wander
vagina *nf* : vagina — vaginal *adj*
vago[1], -ga *adj* 1 : vague 2 PEREZOSO : lazy, idle
vago[2], -ga *n* 1 : idler, loafer 2 VAGABUNDO : vagrant, bum
vagón *nm, pl* vagones : car (of a train)
vague, etc. → vagar
vaguear *vi* 1 : to loaf, to lounge around 2 VAGAR : to wander
vaguedad *nf* : vagueness
vahído *nm* : dizzy spell
vaho *nm* 1 : breath 2 : vapor, steam (on glass, etc.)
vaina *nf* 1 : sheath, scabbard 2 : pod (of a pea or bean) 3 *fam* : nuisance, bother
vainilla *nf* : vanilla
vaivén *nm, pl* vaivenes 1 : swinging, swaying, rocking 2 : change, fluctuation ⟨los vaivenes de la vida : life's ups and downs⟩
vajilla *nf* : dishes *pl*, set of dishes
valdrá, etc. → valer
vale *nm* 1 : voucher 2 PAGARÉ : promissory note, IOU
valedero, -ra *adj* : valid
valentía *nf* : courage, valor
valer {84} *vt* 1 : to be worth ⟨valen una fortuna : they're worth a fortune⟩ ⟨no vale protestar : there's no point in protesting⟩ ⟨valer la pena : to be worth the trouble⟩ 2 : to cost ⟨¿cuánto vale? : how much does it cost?⟩ 3 : to earn, to gain ⟨le valió una reprimenda : it earned him a reprimand⟩ 4 : to protect, to aid ⟨¡válgame Dios! : God help me!⟩ 5 : to be equal to — *vi* 1 : to have value ⟨sus consejos no valen para nada : his advice is worthless⟩ 2 : to be valid, to count ⟨¡eso no vale! : that doesn't count!⟩ 3 hacerse valer : to assert oneself 4 más vale : it's better ⟨más vale que te vayas : you'd better go⟩ — valerse *vr* 1 ∼ de : to take advantage of 2 valerse solo *or* valerse por sí mismo : to look after oneself 3 *Mex* : to be fair ⟨no se vale : it's not fair⟩

valeroso, -sa *adj* : brave, valiant
valet ['balet, -'le] *nm* : jack (in playing cards)
valga, etc. → valer
valía *nf* : value, worth
validar *vt* : to validate — validación *nf*
validez *nf* : validity
válido, -da *adj* : valid
valiente *adj* 1 : brave, valiant 2 (*used ironically*) : fine, great ⟨¡valiente amiga! : what a fine friend!⟩ — valientemente *adv*
valija *nf* : suitcase, valise
valioso, -sa *adj* PRECIOSO : valuable, precious
valla *nf* 1 : fence, barricade 2 : hurdle (in sports) 3 : obstacle, hindrance
vallar *vt* : to fence, to put a fence around
valle *nm* : valley, vale
valor *nm* 1 : value, worth, importance 2 CORAJE : courage, valor 3 valores *nmpl* : values, principles 4 valores *nmpl* : securities, bonds 5 sin ∼ : worthless
valoración *nf, pl* -ciones 1 EVALUACIÓN : valuation, appraisal, assessment 2 APRECIACIÓN : appreciation
valorar *vt* 1 EVALUAR : to evaluate, to appraise, to assess 2 APRECIAR : to value, to appreciate
valorizarse {21} *vr* : to appreciate, to increase in value — valorización *nf*
vals *nm* : waltz
valsar *vi* : to waltz
valuación *nf, pl* -ciones : valuation, appraisal
valuar {3} *vt* : to value, to appraise, to assess
válvula *nf* 1 : valve 2 válvula reguladora : throttle
vamos → ir
vampiro *nm* : vampire
van → ir
vanadio *nm* : vanadium
vanagloriarse *vr* : to boast, to brag
vanamente *adv* : vainly, in vain
vandalismo : vandalism
vándalo *nm* : vandal — vandalismo *nm*
vanguardia *nf* 1 : vanguard 2 : avante-garde 3 a la vanguardia : at the forefront
vanidad *nf* : vanity
vanidoso, -sa *adj* PRESUMIDO : vain, conceited
vano, -na *adj* 1 INÚTIL : vain, useless 2 : vain, worthless ⟨vanas promesas : empty promises⟩ 3 en ∼ : in vain, of no avail
vapor *nm* 1 : vapor, steam 2 : steamer, steamship 3 al vapor : steamed
vaporizador *nm* : vaporizer
vaporizar {21} *vt* : to vaporize — vaporizarse *vr* — vaporización *nf*
vaporoso, -sa *adj* 1 : vaporous 2 : sheer, airy
vapulear *vt* : to beat, to thrash
vaquero[1], -ra *adj* : cowboy ⟨pantalón vaquero : jeans⟩

vaquero[2], **-ra** *n* : cowboy *m*, cowgirl *f*
vaqueros *nmpl* JEANS : jeans
vaquilla *nf* : heifer
vara *nf* 1 : pole, stick, rod 2 : staff (of office) 3 : lance, pike (in bullfighting) 4 : yardstick 5 **vara de oro** : goldenrod
varado, -da *adj* 1 : beached, aground 2 : stranded
varar *vt* : to beach (a ship), to strand — *vi* : to run aground
variable *adj & nf* : variable — **variabilidad** *nf*
variación *nf, pl* **-ciones** : variation
variado, -da *adj* : varied, diverse
variante *adj & nf* : variant
varianza *nf* : variance
variar {85} *vt* 1 : to change, to alter 2 : to diversify — *vi* 1 : to vary, to change 2 **variar de opinión** : to change one's mind
varicela *nf* : chicken pox
varices *or* **várices** *nfpl* : varicose veins
varicoso, -sa *adj* : varicose
variedad *nf* DIVERSIDAD : variety, diversity
varilla *nf* 1 : rod, bar 2 : spoke (of a wheel) 3 : rib (of an umbrella)
vario, -ria *adj* 1 : varied, diverse 2 : variegated, motley 3 : changeable 4 **varios, varias** *pl* : various, several
variopinto, -ta *adj* : diverse, assorted, motley
varita *nf* : wand ⟨varita mágica : magic wand⟩
varón *nm, pl* **varones** 1 HOMBRE : man, male 2 NIÑO : boy
varonil *adj* 1 : masculine, manly 2 : mannish
vas → **ir**
vasallo *nm* : vassal — **vasallaje** *nm*
vasco[1], **-ca** *adj & n* : Basque
vasco[2] *nm* : Basque (language)
vascular *adj* : vascular
vasija *nf* : container, vessel
vaso *nm* 1 : glass, tumbler 2 : glassful 3 : vessel ⟨vaso sanguíneo : blood vessel⟩
vástago *nm* 1 : offspring, descendant 2 : shoot (of a plant)
vastedad *nf* : vastness, immensity
vasto, -ta *adj* : vast, immense
vataje *nm* : wattage
vaticinar *vt* : to predict, to foretell
vaticinio *nm* : prediction, prophecy
vatio *nm* : watt
vaya, etc. → **ir**
Vd., Vds. → **usted**
ve, etc. → **ir, ver**
vea, etc. → **ver**
vecinal *adj* : local
vecindad *nf* 1 : neighborhood, vicinity 2 **casa de vecindad** : tenement
vecindario *nm* 1 : neighborhood, area 2 : residents *pl*
vecino, -na *n* 1 : neighbor 2 : resident, inhabitant
veda *nf* 1 PROHIBICIÓN : prohibition 2 : closed season (for hunting or fishing)

vedar *vt* 1 : to prohibit, to ban 2 IMPEDIR : to impede, to prevent
vega *nf* : fertile lowland
vegetación *nf, pl* **-ciones** 1 : vegetation 2 **vegetaciones** *nfpl* : adenoids
vegetal *adj & nm* : vegetable, plant
vegetar *vi* : to vegetate
vegetarianismo *nm* : vegetarianism
vegetariano, -na *adj & n* : vegetarian
vegetativo, -va *adj* : vegetative
vehemente *adj* : vehement — **vehemencia** *nf*
vehículo *nm* : vehicle — **vehicular** *adj*
veía, etc. → **ver**
veinte *adj & nm* : twenty
veinteavo[1], **-va** *adj* : twentieth
veinteavo[2] *nm* : twentieth (fraction)
veintena *nf* : group of twenty, score ⟨una veintena de participantes : about twenty participants⟩
vejación *nf, pl* **-ciones** : ill-treatment, humiliation
vejar *vt* : to mistreat, to ridicule, to harass
vejete *nm* : old fellow, codger
vejez *nf* : old age
vejiga *nf* 1 : bladder 2 AMPOLLA : blister
vela *nf* 1 VIGILIA : wakefulness ⟨pasé la noche en vela : I stayed awake all night⟩ 2 : watch, vigil, wake 3 : candle 4 : sail
velada *nf* : evening party, soirée
velado, -da *adj* 1 : veiled, hidden 2 : blurred 3 : muffled
velador[1], **-dora** *n* : guard, night watchman
velador[2] *nm* 1 : candlestick 2 : night table
velar *vt* 1 : to hold a wake over 2 : to watch over, to sit up with 3 : to blur, to expose (a photo) 4 : to veil, to conceal — *vi* 1 : to stay awake 2 ~ **por** : to watch over, to look after
velatorio *nm* VELORIO : wake (for the dead)
veleidad *nf* 1 : fickleness 2 : whim, caprice
veleidoso, -sa : fickle, capricious
velero *nm* 1 : sailing ship 2 : sailboat
veleta *nf* : weather vane
vello *nm* 1 : body hair 2 : down, fuzz
vellocino *nm* : fleece
vellón *nm, pl* **vellones** 1 : fleece, sheepskin 2 *PRi* : nickel (coin)
vellosidad *nf* : downiness, hairiness
velloso, -sa *adj* : downy, fluffy, hairy
velo *nm* : veil
velocidad *nf* 1 : speed, velocity ⟨velocidad máxima : speed limit⟩ 2 MARCHA : gear (of an automobile)
velocímetro *nm* : speedometer
velocista *nmf* : sprinter
velorio *nm* VELATORIO : wake (for the dead)
velour *nm* : velour, velours
veloz *adj, pl* **veloces** : fast, quick, swift — **velozmente** *adv*
ven → **venir**

vena *nf* **1** : vein ⟨vena yugular : jugular vein⟩ **2** : vein, seam, lode **3** : grain (of wood) **4** : style ⟨en vena lírica : in a lyrical vein⟩ **5** : strain, touch ⟨una vena de humor : a touch of humor⟩ **6** : mood
venado *nm* **1** : deer **2** : venison
venal *adj* : venal — **venalidad** *nf*
vencedor, -dora *n* : winner, victor
vencejo *nm* : swift (bird)
vencer {86} *vt* **1** DERROTAR : to vanquish, to defeat **2** SUPERAR : to overcome, to surmount — *vi* **1** GANAR : to win, to triumph **2** CADUCAR : to expire ⟨el plazo vence el jueves : the deadline is Thursday⟩ **3** : to fall due, to mature — **vencerse** *vr* **1** DOMINARSE : to control oneself **2** : to break, to collapse
vencido, -da *adj* **1** : defeated **2** : expired **3** : due, payable **4 darse por vencido** : to give up
vencimiento *nm* **1** : defeat **2** : expiration **3** : maturity (of a loan)
venda *nf* : bandage
vendaje *nm* : bandage, dressing
vendar *vt* **1** : to bandage **2 vendar los ojos** : to blindfold
vendaval *nm* : gale, strong wind
vendedor, -dora *n* : salesperson, salesman *m*, saleswoman *f*
vender *vt* **1** : to sell **2** : to sell out, to betray — **venderse** *vr* **1** : to be sold ⟨se vende : for sale⟩ **2** : to sell out
vendetta *nf* : vendetta
vendible *adj* : salable, marketable
vendimia *nf* : grape harvest
vendrá, etc. → **venir**
veneno *nm* **1** : poison **2** : venom
venenoso, -sa *adj* : poisonous, venomous
venerable *adj* : venerable
veneración *nf, pl* **-ciones** : veneration, reverence
venerar *vt* : to venerate, to revere
venéreo, -rea *adj* : venereal
venero *nm* **1** VENA : seam, lode, vein **2** MANANTIAL : spring **3** FUENTE : origin, source
venezolano, -na *adj & n* : Venezuelan
venga, etc. → **venir**
vengador, -dora *n* : avenger
venganza *nf* : vengeance, revenge
vengar {52} *vt* : to avenge — **vengarse** *vr* : to get even, to revenge oneself
vengativo, -va *adj* : vindictive, vengeful
vengue, etc. → **vengar**
venia *nf* **1** PERMISO : permission, leave **2** PERDÓN : pardon **3** : bow (of the head)
venial *adj* : venial
venida *nf* **1** LLEGADA : arrival, coming **2** REGRESO : return **3 idas y venidas** : comings and goings
venidero, -ra *adj* : coming, future
venir {87} *vi* **1** : to come ⟨lo vi venir : I saw him coming⟩ ⟨¡venga! : come on!⟩ **2** : to arrive ⟨vinieron en coche : they came by car⟩ **3** : to come, to originate ⟨sus zapatos vienen de Italia : her shoes

are from Italy⟩ **4** : to come, to be available ⟨viene envuelto en plástico : it comes wrapped in plastic⟩ **5** : to come back, to return **6** : to affect, to overcome ⟨me vino un vahído : a dizzy spell came over me⟩ **7** : to fit ⟨te viene un poco grande : it's a little big for you⟩ **8** (*with the present participle*) : to have been ⟨viene entrenando diariamente : he's been training daily⟩ **9 ~ a** (*with the infinitive*) : to end up, to turn out ⟨viene a ser lo mismo : it comes out the same⟩ **10 que viene** : coming, next ⟨el año que viene : next year⟩ **11 venir bien** : to be suitable, to be just right — **venirse** *vr* **1** : to come, to arrive **2** : to come back **3 venirse abajo** : to fall apart, to collapse
venta *nf* **1** : sale **2 venta al por menor** *or* **venta al detalle** : retail sales
ventaja *nf* **1** : advantage **2** : lead, head start **3 ventajas** *nfpl* : perks, extras
ventajoso, -sa *adj* **1** : advantageous **2** : profitable — **ventajosamente** *adv*
ventana *nf* **1** : window (of a building) **2 ventana de la nariz** : nostril
ventanal *nm* : large window
ventanilla *nf* **1** : window (of a vehicle or airplane) **2** : ticket window, box office
ventero, -ra *n* : innkeeper
ventilación *nf, pl* **-ciones** : ventilation
ventilador *nm* **1** : ventilator **2** : fan
ventilar *vt* **1** : to ventilate, to air out **2** : to air, to discuss **3** : to make public, to reveal — **ventilarse** *vr* : to get some air
ventisca *nf* : snowstorm, blizzard
ventisquero *nm* : snowdrift
ventosear *vi* : to break wind
ventosidad *nf* : wind, flatulence
ventoso, -sa *adj* : windy
ventrículo *nm* : ventricle
ventrílocuo, -cua *n* : ventriloquist
ventriloquia *nf* : ventriloquism
ventura *nf* **1** : fortune, luck, chance **2** : happiness **3 a la ventura** : at random, as it comes
venturoso, -sa *adj* **1** AFORTUNADO : fortunate, lucky **2** : successful
Venus *nm* : Venus
venza, etc. → **vencer**
ver[1] {88} *vt* **1** : to see ⟨vimos la película : we saw the movie⟩ **2** ENTENDER : to understand ⟨ya lo veo : now I get it⟩ **3** EXAMINAR : to examine, to look into ⟨lo veré : I'll take a look at it⟩ **4** JUZGAR : to see, to judge ⟨a mi manera de ver : to my way of thinking⟩ **5** VISITAR : to meet with, to visit **6** AVERIGUAR : to find out **7 a ver** *or* **vamos a ver** : let's see — *vi* **1** : to see **2** ENTERARSE : to learn, to find out **3** ENTENDER : to understand — **verse** *vr* **1** HALLARSE : to find oneself **2** PARECER : to look, to appear **3** ENCONTRARSE : to see each other, to meet
ver[2] *nm* **1** : looks *pl*, appearance **2** : opinion ⟨a mi ver : in my view⟩

vera *nf* : side ⟨a la vera del camino : alongside the road⟩
veracidad *nf* : truthfulness, veracity
veranda *nf* : veranda
veraneante *nmf* : summer vacationer
veranear *vi* : to spend the summer
veraniego, -ga *adj* 1 ESTIVAL : summer ⟨el sol veraniego : the summer sun⟩ 2 : summery
verano *nm* : summer
veras *nfpl* **de** ~ : really, truly
veraz *adj, pl* **veraces** : truthful, veracious
verbal *adj* : verbal — **verbalmente** *adv*
verbalizar {21} *vt* : to verbalize, to express
verbena *nf* 1 FIESTA : festival, fair 2 : verbena, vervain
verbigracia *adv* : for example
verbo *nm* : verb
verborrea *nf* : verbiage
verbosidad *nf* : verbosity, wordiness
verboso, -sa *adj* : verbose, wordy
verdad *nf* 1 : truth 2 **de** ~ : really, truly 3 ¿**verdad?** : right?, isn't that so?
verdaderamente *adv* : really, truly
verdadero, -dera *adj* 1 REAL, VERÍDICO : true, real 2 AUTÉNTICO : genuine
verde[1] *adj* 1 : green (in color) 2 : green, unripe 3 : inexperienced, green 4 : dirty, risqué
verde[2] *nm* : green
verdear *vi* : to turn green, to become verdant
verdín *nm, pl* **verdines** : slime, scum
verdor *nm* 1 : greenness 2 : verdure
verdoso, -sa *adj* : greenish
verdugo *nm* 1 : executioner, hangman 2 : tyrant
verdugón *nm, pl* **-gones** : welt, wheal
verdura *nf* : vegetable(s), green(s)
vereda *nf* 1 SENDA : path, trail 2 : sidewalk, pavement
veredicto *nm* : verdict
verga *nf* : spar, yard (of a ship)
vergonzoso, -sa *adj* 1 : disgraceful, shameful 2 : bashful, shy — **vergonzosamente** *adv*
vergüenza *nf* 1 : disgrace, shame 2 : embarrassment 3 : bashfulness, shyness
vericueto *nm* : rough terrain
verídico, -ca *adj* 1 REAL, VERDADERO : true, real 2 VERAZ : truthful
verificación *nf, pl* **-ciones** 1 : verification 2 : testing, checking
verificador, -dora *n* : inspector, tester
verificar {72} *vt* 1 : to verify, to confirm 2 : to test, to check 3 : to carry out, to conduct — **verificarse** *vr* 1 : to take place, to occur 2 : to come true
verja *nf* 1 : rails *pl* (of a fence) 2 : grating, grille 3 : gate
vermut *nm, pl* **vermuts** : vermouth
vernáculo, -la *adj* : vernacular
vernal *adj* : vernal, spring
verosímil *adj* 1 : probable, likely 2 : credible, realistic

verosimilitud *nf* 1 : probability, likeliness 2 : verisimilitude
verraco *nm* : boar
verruga *nf* : wart
versado, -da *adj* ~ **en** : versed in, knowledgeable about
versar *vi* ~ **sobre** : to deal with, to be about
versátil *adj* 1 : versatile 2 : fickle
versatilidad *nf* 1 : versatility 2 : fickleness
versículo *nm* : verse (in the Bible)
versión *nf, pl* **versiones** 1 : version 2 : translation
verso *nm* : verse
versus *prep* : versus, against
vértebra *nf* : vertebra — **vertebral** *adj*
vertebrado[1]**, -da** *adj* : vertebrate
vertebrado[2] *nm* : vertebrate
vertedero *nm* 1 : garbage dump 2 DESAGÜE : drain, outlet
verter {56} *vt* 1 : to pour 2 : to spill, to shed 3 : to empty out 4 : to express, to voice 5 : to translate, to render — *vi* : to flow
vertical *adj & nf* : vertical — **verticalmente** *adv*
vértice *nm* : vertex, apex
vertido *nm* : spilling, spill
vertiente *nf* 1 : slope 2 : aspect, side, element
vertiginoso, -sa *adj* : vertiginous — **vertiginosamente** *adv*
vértigo *nm* : vertigo, dizziness
vesícula *nf* 1 : vesicle 2 **vesícula biliar** : gallbladder
vesicular *adj* : vesicular
vestíbulo *nm* : vestibule, hall, lobby, foyer
vestido *nm* 1 : dress, costume, clothes *pl* 2 : dress (garment)
vestidor *nm* : dressing room
vestiduras *nfpl* 1 : clothing, raiment, regalia 2 *or* **vestiduras sacerdotales** : vestments
vestigio *nm* : vestige, sign, trace
vestimenta *nf* ROPA : clothing, clothes *pl*
vestir {54} *vt* 1 : to dress, to clothe 2 LLEVAR : to wear 3 ADORNAR : to decorate, to dress up — *vi* 1 : to dress ⟨vestir bien : to dress well⟩ 2 : to look good, to suit the occasion — **vestirse** *vr* 1 : to get dressed 2 ~ **de** : to dress up as ⟨se vistieron de soldados : they dressed up as soldiers⟩ 3 ~ **de** : to wear, to dress in
vestuario *nm* 1 : wardrobe 2 : dressing room, locker room
veta *nf* 1 : grain (in wood) 2 : vein, seam, lode 3 : trace, streak ⟨una veta de terco : a stubborn streak⟩
vetar *vt* : to veto
veteado, -da *adj* : streaked, veined
veterano, -na *adj & n* : veteran
veterinaria *nf* : veterinary medicine
veterinario[1]**, -ria** *adj* : veterinary
veterinario[2]**, -ria** *n* : veterinarian

veto *nm* : veto

vetusto, -ta *adj* ANTIGUO : ancient, very old

vez *nf, pl* **veces 1** : time, occasion ⟨a la vez : at the same time⟩ ⟨a veces : at times, occasionally⟩ ⟨de vez en cuando : from time to time⟩ **2** (*with numbers*) : time ⟨una vez : once⟩ ⟨de una vez : all at once⟩ ⟨de una vez para siempre : once and for all⟩ ⟨dos veces : twice⟩ **3** : turn ⟨a su vez : in turn⟩ ⟨en vez de : instead of⟩ ⟨hacer las veces de : to act as, to stand in for⟩

vía[1] *nf* **1** RUTA, CAMINO : road, route, way ⟨Vía Láctea : Milky Way⟩ **2** MEDIO : means, way ⟨por vía oficial : through official channels⟩ **3** : track, line (of a railroad) **4** : tract, passage ⟨por vía oral : orally⟩ **5 en vías de** : in the process of ⟨en vías de solución : on the road to a solution⟩ **6 por** ~ : by (in transportation) ⟨por vía aérea : by air, airmail⟩

vía[2] *prep* : via

viable *adj* : viable, feasible — **viabilidad** *nf*

viaducto *nm* : viaduct

viajante *mf* : traveling salesman, traveling saleswoman

viajar *vi* : to travel, to journey

viaje *nm* : trip, journey ⟨viaje de negocios : business trip⟩

viajero[1]**, -ra** *adj* : traveling

viajero[2]**, -ra** *n* **1** : traveler **2** PASAJERO : passenger

vial *adj* : road, traffic

viático *nm* : travel allowance, travel expenses *pl*

víbora *nf* : viper

vibración *nf, pl* **-ciones** : vibration

vibrador *nm* : vibrator

vibrante *adj* **1** : vibrant **2** : vibrating

vibrar *vi* : to vibrate

vibratorio, -ria *adj* : vibratory

vicario, -ria *n* : vicar

vicealmirante *nmf* : vice admiral

vicepresidente, -ta *n* : vice president — **vicepresidencia** *nf*

viceversa *adv* : vice versa, conversely

viciado, -da *adj* : stuffy, close

viciar *vt* **1** : to corrupt **2** : to invalidate **3** FALSEAR : to distort **4** : to pollute, to adulterate

vicio *nm* **1** : vice, depravity **2** : bad habit **3** : defect, blemish

vicioso, -sa *adj* : depraved, corrupt

vicisitud *nf* : vicissitude

víctima *nf* : victim

victimario, -ria *n* ASESINO : killer, murderer

victimizar {21} *vt Arg, Mex* : to victimize

victoria *nf* : victory — **victorioso, -sa** *adj* — **victoriosamente** *adv*

victoriano, -na *adj* : Victorian

vid *nf* : vine, grapevine

vida *nf* **1** : life ⟨la vida cotidiana : everyday life⟩ **2** : life span, lifetime **3** BI-

OGRAFÍA : biography, life **4** : way of life, lifestyle **5** : livelihood ⟨ganarse la vida : to earn one's living⟩ **6** VIVEZA : liveliness **7 media vida** : half-life

vidente *nmf* **1** : psychic, clairvoyant **2** : sighted person

video *or* **vídeo** *nm* : video

videocasete *or* **videocassette** *nm* : videocassette

videocasetera *or* **videocassettera** *nf* : videocassette recorder, VCR

videocinta *nf* : videotape

videograbar *vt* : to videotape

vidriado *nm* : glaze

vidriar *vt* : to glaze (pottery, tile, etc.)

vidriera *nf* **1** : stained-glass window **2** : glass door or window **3** : store window

vidriero, -ra *n* : glazier

vidrio *nm* **1** : glass, piece of glass **2** : windowpane

vidrioso, -sa *adj* **1** : brittle, fragile **2** : slippery **3** : glassy, glazed (of eyes) **4** : touchy, delicate

vieira *nf* **1** : scallop **2** : scallop shell

viejo[1]**, -ja** *adj* **1** ANCIANO : old, elderly **2** ANTIGUO : former, longstanding ⟨viejas tradiciones : old traditions⟩ ⟨viejos amigos : old friends⟩ **3** GASTADO : old, worn, worn-out

viejo[2]**, -ja** *n* ANCIANO : old man *m*, old woman *f*

viene, etc. → venir

viento *nm* **1** : wind **2 hacer viento** : to be windy **3 contra viento y marea** : against all odds **4 viento alisio** : trade wind **5 viento en popa** : splendidly, successfully

vientre *nm* **1** : abdomen, belly **2** : womb **3** : bowels *pl*

viernes *nms & pl* : Friday

vierte, etc. → verter

vietnamita[1] *adj & nmf* : Vietnamese

vietnamita[2] *nm* : Vietnamese (language)

viga *nf* **1** : beam, rafter, girder **2 viga voladiza** : cantilever

vigencia *nf* **1** : validity **2** : force, effect ⟨entrar en vigencia : to go into effect⟩

vigente *adj* : valid, in force

vigésimo[1]**, -ma** *adj* : twentieth, twenty- ⟨la vigésima segunda edición : the twenty-second edition⟩

vigésimo[2]**, -ma** *n* : twentieth, twenty- (in a series)

vigía *nmf* : lookout

vigilancia *nf* : vigilance, watchfulness ⟨bajo vigilancia : under surveillance⟩

vigilante[1] *adj* : vigilant, watchful

vigilante[2] *nmf* : watchman, guard

vigilar *vt* **1** CUIDAR : to look after, to keep an eye on **2** GUARDAR : to watch over, to guard — *vi* **1** : to be watchful **2** : to keep watch

vigilia *nf* **1** VELA : wakefulness **2** : night work **3** : vigil (in religion)

vigor *nm* **1** : vigor, energy, strength **2** VIGENCIA : force, effect

vigorizante *adj* : invigorating

vigorizar {21} *vt* : to strengthen, to invigorate
vigoroso, -sa *adj* : vigorous — **vigorosamente** *adv*
VIH *nm* (virus de inmunodeficiencia humana) : HIV
vikingo, -ga *adj & n* : Viking
vil *adj* : vile, despicable
vileza *nf* **1** : vileness **2** : despicable action, villainy
vilipendiar *vt* : to vilify, to revile
villa *nf* **1** : town, village **2** : villa
villancico *nm* : carol, Christmas carol
villano, -na *n* **1** : villain **2** : peasant
vilo *nm* **1 en** ～ : in the air **2 en** ～ : uncertain, in suspense
vinagre *nm* : vinegar
vinagrera *nf* : cruet (for vinegar)
vinatería *nf* : wine shop
vinculación *nf, pl* **-ciones 1** : linking **2** RELACIÓN : bond, link, connection
vincular *vt* CONECTAR, RELACIONAR : to tie, to link, to connect
vínculo *nm* LAZO : tie, link, bond
vindicación *nf, pl* **-ciones** : vindication
vindicar *vt* **1** : to vindicate **2** : to avenge
vinilo *nm* : vinyl
vino¹, etc. → **venir**
vino² *nm* : wine
viña *nf* : vineyard
viñedo *nm* : vineyard
vio, etc. → **ver**
viola *nf* : viola
violación *nf, pl* **-ciones 1** : violation, offense **2** : rape
violador¹, -dora *n* : violator, offender
violador² *nm* : rapist
violar *vt* **1** : to rape **2** : to violate (a law or right) **3** PROFANAR : to desecrate
violencia *nf* : violence
violentamente *adv* : by force, violently
violentar *vt* **1** FORZAR : to break open, to force **2** : to distort (words or ideas) — **violentarse** *vr* : to force oneself
violento, -ta *adj* **1** : violent **2** EMBARAZOSO, INCÓMODO : awkward, embarassing
violeta¹ *adj & nm* : violet (color)
violeta² *nf* : violet (flower)
violín *nm, pl* **-lines** : violin
violinista *nmf* : violinist
violonchelista *nmf* : cellist
violonchelo *nm* : cello, violoncello
VIP *nmf, pl* **VIPs** : VIP
vira *nf* : welt (of a shoe)
virago *nf* : virago, shrew
viraje *nm* **1** : turn, swerve **2** : change
viral *adj* : viral
virar *vi* : to tack, to turn, to veer
virgen¹ *adj* : virgin ⟨lana virgen : virgin wool⟩
virgen² *nmf, pl* **vírgenes** : virgin ⟨la Santísima Virgen : the Blessed Virgin⟩
virginal *adj* : virginal, chaste
virginidad *nf* : virginity
Virgo *nmf* : Virgo
vírico, -ca *adj* : viral
viril *adj* : virile — **virilidad** *nf*

virrey, -rreina *n* : viceroy *m*, vicereine *f*
virtual *adj* : virtual — **virtualmente** *adv*
virtud *nf* **1** : virtue **2 en virtud de** : by virtue of
virtuosismo *nm* : virtuosity
virtuoso¹, -sa *adj* : virtuous — **virtuosamente** *adv*
virtuoso², -sa *n* : virtuoso
viruela *nf* **1** : smallpox **2** : pockmark
virulencia *nf* : virulence
virulento, -ta *adj* : virulent
virus *nm* : virus
viruta *nf* : shaving
visa *nf* : visa
visado *nm Spain* : visa
visaje *nm* : face, grimace ⟨hacer visajes : to make faces⟩
visceral *adj* : visceral
vísceras *nfpl* : viscera, entrails
visconde, -desa *n* : viscount *m*, viscountess *f*
viscosidad *nf* : viscosity
viscoso, -sa *adj* : viscous
visera *nf* : visor
visibilidad *nf* : visibility
visible *adj* : visible — **visiblemente** *adv*
visión *nf, pl* **visiones 1** : vision, eyesight **2** : view, perspective **3** : vision, illusion ⟨ver visiones : to be seeing things⟩
visionario, -ria *adj & n* : visionary
visita *nf* **1** : visit, call **2** : visitor **3 ir de visita** : to go visiting
visitador, -dora *n* : visitor, frequent caller
visitante¹ *adj* : visiting
visitante² *nmf* : visitor
visitar *vt* : to visit
vislumbrar *vt* **1** : to discern, to make out **2** : to begin to see, to have an inkling of
vislumbre *nf* : glimmer, gleam
viso *nm* **1** APARIENCIA : appearance ⟨tener visos de : to seem, to show signs of⟩ **2** DESTELLO : glint, gleam **3** : sheen, iridescence
visón *nm, pl* **visones** : mink
víspera *nf* **1** : eve, day before **2**
vísperas *nfpl* : vespers
vista *nf* **1** VISIÓN : vision, eyesight **2** MIRADA : look, gaze, glance **3** PANORAMA : view, vista, panorama **4** : hearing (in court) **5 a primera vista** : at first sight **6 en vista de** : in view of **7 hacer la vista gorda** : to turn a blind eye **8 ¡hasta la vista!** : so long!, see you! **9 perder de vista** : to lose sight of **10 punto de vista** : point of view
vistazo *nm* : glance, look
viste, etc. → **ver¹, vestir**
visto¹ *pp* → **ver**
visto², -ta *adj* **1** : obvious, clear **2** : in view of, considering **3 estar bien visto** : to be approved of **4 estar mal visto** : to be frowned upon **5 por lo visto** : apparently **6 nunca visto** : unheard-of **7 visto que** : since, given that
visto³ *nm* **visto bueno** : approval

vistoso, -sa *adj* : colorful, bright
visual *adj* : visual — **visualmente** *adv*
visualización *nf, pl* **-ciones** : visualization
visualizar {21} *vt* **1** : to visualize **2** : to display (on a screen)
vital *adj* **1** : vital **2** : lively, dynamic
vitalicio, -cia *adj* : life, lifetime
vitalidad *nf* : vitality
vitamina *nf* : vitamin
vitamínico, -ca *adj* : vitamin ⟨complejos vitamínicos : vitamin compounds⟩
vitorear *vt* : to cheer, to acclaim
vitral *nm* : stained-glass window
vítreo, -rea *adj* : vitreous, glassy
vitrina *nf* **1** : showcase, display case **2** : store window
vitriolo *nm* : vitriol
vituperar *vt* : to condemn, to vituperate against
vituperio *nm* : vituperation, censure
viudez *nf* : widowerhood, widowhood
viudo, -da *n* : widower *m*, widow *f*
vivacidad *nf* VIVEZA : vivacity, liveliness
vivamente *adv* **1** : in a lively manner **2** : vividly **3** : strongly, acutely ⟨lo recomendamos vivamente : we strongly recommend it⟩
vivaque *nm* : bivouac
vivaquear *vi* : to bivouac
vivar *vi* : to cheer
vivaz *adj, pl* **vivaces** **1** : lively, vivacious **2** : clever, sharp **3** : perennial
víveres *nmpl* : provisions, supplies, food
vivero *nm* **1** : nursery (for plants) **2** : hatchery, fish farm
viveza *nf* **1** VIVACIDAD : liveliness **2** BRILLO : vividness, brightness **3** ASTUCIA : cleverness, sharpness
vívido, -da *adj* : vivid, lively
vividor, -dora *n* : sponger, parasite
vivienda *nf* **1** : housing **2** MORADA : dwelling, home
viviente *adj* : living
vivificar {72} *vt* : to vivify, to give life to
vivir[1] *vi* **1** : to live, to be alive **2** SUBSISTIR : to subsist, to make a living **3** RESIDIR : to reside **4** : to spend one's life ⟨vive para trabajar : she lives to work⟩ **5** ~ **de** : to live on — *vt* **1** : to live ⟨vivir su vida : to live one's life⟩ **2** EXPERIMENTAR : to go through, to experience
vivir[2] *nm* **1** : life, lifestyle **2 de mal vivir** : disreputable
vivisección *nf, pl* **-ciones** : vivisection
vivo, -va *adj* **1** : alive **2** INTENSO : vivid, bright, intense **3** ANIMADO : lively, vivacious **4** ASTUTO : sharp, clever **5 en** ~ : live ⟨transmisión en vivo : live broadcast⟩ **6 al rojo vivo** : red-hot
vizconde, -desa *n* : viscount *m*, viscountess *f*
vocablo *nm* PALABRA : word
vocabulario *nm* : vocabulary
vocación *nf, pl* **-ciones** : vocation
vocacional *adj* : vocational
vocal[1] *adj* : vocal

vocal[2] *nmf* : member (of a committee, board, etc.)
vocal[3] *nf* : vowel
vocalista *nmf* CANTANTE : singer, vocalist
vocalizar {21} *vi* : to vocalize
vocear *v* : to shout
vocerío *nm* : clamor, shouting
vocero, -ra *n* PORTAVOZ : spokesperson, spokesman *m*, spokeswoman *f*
vociferante *adj* : vociferous
vociferar *vi* GRITAR : to shout, to yell
vodevil *nm* : vaudeville
vodka *nm* : vodka
voladizo[1], **-za** *adj* : projecting
voladizo[2] *nm* : projection
volador, -dora *adj* : flying
volando *adv* : quickly, in a hurry
volante[1] *adj* : flying
volante[2] *nm* **1** : steering wheel **2** FOLLETO : flier, circular **3** : shuttlecock **4** : flywheel **5** : balance wheel (of a watch) **6** : ruffle, flounce
volar {19} *vi* **1** : to fly **2** CORRER : to hurry, to rush ⟨el tiempo vuela : time flies⟩ ⟨pasar volando : to fly past⟩ **3** DIVULGARSE : to spread ⟨unos rumores volaban : rumors were spreading around⟩ **4** DESAPARECER : to disappear ⟨el dinero ya voló : the money's already gone⟩ — *vt* **1** : to blow up, to demolish **2** : to irritate
volátil *adj* : volatile — **volatilidad** *nf*
volatilizar {21} *vt* : to volatize — **volatilizarse** *vr*
volcán *nm, pl* **volcanes** : volcano
volcánico, -ca *adj* : volcanic
volcar {82} *vt* **1** : to upset, to knock over, to turn over **2** : to empty out **3** : to make dizzy **4** : to cause a change of mind in **5** : to irritate — *vi* **1** : to overturn, to tip over **2** : to capsize — **volcarse** *vr* **1** : to overturn **2** : to do one's utmost
volea *nf* : volley (in sports)
volear *vi* : to volley (in sports)
voleibol *nm* : volleyball
voleo *nm* **al voleo** : haphazardly, at random
volframio *nm* : wolfram, tungsten
volición *nf, pl* **-ciones** : volition
volqué, etc. → **volcar**
voltaje *nm* : voltage
voltear *vt* **1** : to turn over, to turn upside down **2** : to reverse, to turn inside out **3** : to turn ⟨voltear la cara : to turn one's head⟩ **4** : to knock down — *vi* **1** : to roll over, to do somersaults **2** : to turn ⟨volteó a la izquierda : he turned left⟩ — **voltearse** *vr* **1** : to turn around **2** : to change one's allegiance
voltereta *nf* : somersault, tumble
voltio *nm* : volt
volubilidad *nf* : fickleness, changeableness
voluble *adj* : fickle, changeable
volumen *nm, pl* **-lúmenes** **1** TOMO : volume, book **2** : capacity, size, bulk **3** CANTIDAD : amount ⟨el volumen de

ventas : the volume of sales⟩ **4** : volume, loudness

voluminoso, -sa *adj* : voluminous, massive, bulky

voluntad *nf* **1** : will, volition **2** DESEO : desire, wish **3** INTENCIÓN : intention **4 a voluntad** : at will **5 buena voluntad** : good will **6 mala voluntad** : ill will **7 fuerza de voluntad** : willpower

voluntario¹, -ria *adj* : voluntary — **voluntariamente** *adv*

voluntario², -ria *n* : volunteer

voluntarioso, -sa *adj* **1** : stubborn **2** : willing, eager

voluptuosidad *nf* : voluptuousness

voluptuoso, -sa *adj* : voluptuous — **voluptuosamente** *adv*

voluta *nf* : spiral, column (of smoke)

volver {89} *vi* **1** : to return, to come or go back ⟨volver a casa : to return home⟩ **2** : to revert ⟨volver al tema : to get back to the subject⟩ **3 ~ a** : to do again ⟨volvieron a llamar : they called again⟩ **4 volver en sí** : to come to, to regain consciousness — *vt* **1** : to turn, to turn over, to turn inside out **2** : to return, to repay, to restore **3** : to cause, to make ⟨la volvía loca : it was driving her crazy⟩ — **volverse** *vr* **1** : to become ⟨se volvió deprimido : he became depressed⟩ **2** : to turn around

vomitar *vi* : to vomit — *vt* **1** : to vomit **2** : to spew out (lava, etc.)

vómito *nm* **1** : vomiting **2** : vomit

voracidad *nf* : voracity

vorágine *nf* : whirlpool, maelstrom

voraz *adj, pl* **voraces** : voracious — **vorazmente** *adv*

vórtice *nm* **1** : whirlpool, vortex **2** TORBELLINO : whirlwind

vos *pron* (*in some regions of Latin America*) : you

vosear *vt* : to address as *vos*

vosotros, -tras *pron pl Spain* **1** : you, yourselves **2** : ye

votación *nf, pl* **-ciones** : vote, voting

votante *nmf* : voter

votar *vi* : to vote — *vt* : to vote for

votivo, -va *adj* : votive

voto *nm* **1** : vote **2** : vow (in religion) **3 votos** *nmpl* : good wishes

voy → **ir**

voz *nf, pl* **voces 1** : voice **2** : opinion, say **3** GRITO : shout, yell **4** : sound **5** VOCABLO : word, term **6** : rumor **7 a**

voz en cuello : at the top of one's lungs **8 dar voces** : to shout **9 en voz alta** : aloud, in a loud voice **10 en voz baja** : softly, in a low voice

vudú *nm* : voodoo

vuelco *nm* : upset, overturning ⟨me dio un vuelco el corazón : my heart skipped a beat⟩

vuela, etc. → **volar**

vuelca, vuelque etc. → **volcar**

vuelo *nm* **1** : flight, flying ⟨alzar el vuelo : to take flight⟩ **2** : flight (of an aircraft) ⟨vuelo espacial : space flight⟩ **3** : flare, fullness (of clothing) **4 al vuelo** : on the wing

vuelta *nf* **1** GIRO : turn ⟨se dio la vuelta : he turned around⟩ **2** REVOLUCIÓN : circle, revolution ⟨dio la vuelta al mundo : she went around the world⟩ ⟨las ruedas daban vueltas : the wheels were spinning⟩ **3** : flip, turn ⟨le dio la vuelta : she flipped it over⟩ **4** : bend, curve ⟨a la vuelta de la esquina : around the corner⟩ **5** REGRESO : return ⟨de ida y vuelta : round trip⟩ ⟨a vuelta de correo : return mail⟩ **6** : round, lap (in sports or games) **7** PASEO : walk, drive, ride ⟨dio una vuelta : he went for a walk⟩ **8** DORSO, REVÉS : back, other side ⟨a la vuelta : on the back⟩ **9** : cuff (of pants) **10 darle vueltas** : to think over **11 estar de vuelta** : to be back

vuelto *pp* → **volver**

vuelve, etc. → **volver**

vuestro¹, -stra *adj Spain* : your, of yours ⟨vuestros coches : your cars⟩ ⟨una amiga vuestra : a friend of yours⟩

vuestro², -stra *pron Spain,* (*with definite article*) : yours ⟨la vuestra es más grande : yours is bigger⟩ ⟨esos son los vuestros : those are yours⟩

vulcanizar {21} *vt* : to vulcanize

vulgar *adj* **1** : common **2** : vulgar

vulgaridad *nf* : vulgarity

vulgarismo *nm* : vulgarism

vulgarizar {21} *vt* : to vulgarize, to popularize

vulgarmente *adv* : vulgarly, popularly

vulgo *nm* **el vulgo** : the masses, common people

vulnerable *adj* : vulnerable — **vulnerabilidad** *nf*

vulnerar *vt* **1** : to injure, to damage (one's reputation or honor) **2** : to violate, to break (a law or contract)

W

w *nf* : twenty-fourth letter of the Spanish alphabet

wafle *nm* : waffle

waflera *nf* : waffle iron

wapití *nm* : wapiti, elk

whisky *nm, pl* **whiskys** *or* **whiskies** : whiskey

wigwam *nm* : wigwam

X

x *nf* : twenty-fifth letter of the Spanish alphabet
xenofobia *nf* : xenophobia
xenófobo[1], -ba *adj* : xenophobic

xenófobo[2], -ba *n* : xenophobe
xenón *nm* : xenon
xerocopiar *vt* : to photocopy, to xerox
xilófono *nm* : xylophone

Y

y[1] *nf* : twenty-sixth letter of the Spanish alphabet
y[2] *conj* (**e** *before words beginning with i- or hi-*) **1** : and ⟨mi hermano y yo : my brother and I⟩ ⟨¿y los demás? : and (what about) the others?⟩ **2** (*used in numbers*) ⟨cincuenta y cinco : fifty-five⟩ **3** *fam* : well ⟨y por supuesto : well, of course⟩
ya[1] *adv* **1** : already ⟨ya terminó : she's finished already⟩ **2** : now, right now ⟨¡hazlo ya! : do it now!⟩ ⟨ya mismo : right away⟩ **3** : later, soon ⟨ya iremos : we'll go later on⟩ **4** : no longer, anymore ⟨ya no fuma : he no longer smokes⟩ **5** (*used for emphasis*) ⟨¡ya lo sé! : I know!⟩ ⟨ya lo creo : of course⟩ **6 no ya** : not only ⟨no ya lloran sino gritan : they're not only crying but screaming⟩ **7 ya que** : now that, since ⟨ya que sabe la verdad : now that she knows the truth⟩
ya[2] *conj* **ya . . . ya** : whether . . . or, first . . . then ⟨ya le gusta, ya no : first he likes it, then he doesn't⟩
yac *nm* : yak
yacer {90} *vi* : to lie ⟨en esta tumba yacen sus abuelos : his grandparents lie in this grave⟩
yacimiento *nm* : bed, deposit ⟨yacimiento petrolífero : oil field⟩
yaga, etc. → yacer
yanqui *adj & nmf* : Yankee
yarda *nf* : yard
yate *nm* : yacht
yaz, yazca, yazga etc. → yacer
yedra *nf* : ivy
yegua *nf* : mare
yelmo *nm* : helmet
yema *nf* **1** : bud, shoot **2** : yolk (of an egg) **3 yema del dedo** : fingertip
yemenita *adj & nmf* : Yemenite
yen *nm* : yen (currency)
yendo → ir

yerba *nf* **1** *or* **yerba mate** : maté **2** → hierba
yerga, yergue etc. → erguir
yermo[1], -ma *adj* : barren, deserted
yermo[2] *nm* : wasteland
yerno *nm* : son-in-law
yerra, etc. → errar
yerro *nm* : blunder, mistake
yerto, -ta *adj* : rigid, stiff
yesca *nf* : tinder
yeso *nm* **1** : plaster **2** : gypsum
yo[1] *nm* : ego, self
yo[2] *pron* **1** : I **2** : me ⟨todos menos yo : everyone except me⟩ ⟨tan bajo como yo : as short as me⟩ **3 soy yo** : it is I, it's me
yodado, -da *adj* : iodized
yodo *nm* : iodine
yoduro *nm* : iodide
yoga *nm* : yoga
yogui *nm* : yogi
yogurt *or* **yogur** *nm* : yogurt
yola *nf* : yawl
yoyo *or* **yoyó** *nm* : yo-yo
yuca *nf* **1** : yucca (plant) **2** : cassava, manioc
yucateco[1], -ca *adj* : of or from the Yucatán
yucateco[2], -ca *n* : person from the Yucatán
yudo → judo
yugo *nm* : yoke
yugoslavo, -va *adj & n* : Yugoslavian
yugular *adj* : jugular ⟨vena yugular : jugular vein⟩
yungas *nfpl Bol, Chile, Peru* : warm tropical valleys
yunque *nm* : anvil
yunta *nf* : yoke, team (of oxen)
yuppy *nmf, pl* **yuppies** : yuppie
yute *nm* : jute
yuxtaponer {60} *vt* : to juxtapose — **yuxtaposición** *nf*

Z

z *nf* : twenty-seventh letter of the Spanish alphabet
zacate *nm CA, Mex* **1** : grass, forage **2** : hay
zafacón *nm, pl* **-cones** *Car* : wastebasket
zafar *vt* : to loosen, to untie — **zafarse**

vr **1** : to loosen up, to come undone **2** : to get free of
zafio, -fia *adj* : coarse, crude
zafiro *nm* : sapphire
zaga *nf* **1** : defense (in sports) **2 a la zaga** *or* **en ~** : behind, in the rear
zagual *nm* : paddle (of a canoe)

zaguán *nm, pl* **zaguanes** : front hall, vestibule
zaherir {76} *vt* **1** : to criticize sharply **2** : to wound, to mortify
zahones *nmpl* : chaps
zaino, -na *adj* : chestnut (color)
zalamería *nf* : flattery, sweet talk
zalamero[1], **-ra** *adj* : flattering, fawning
zalamero[2], **-ra** *n* : flatterer
zambiano, -na *adj & nmf* : Zambian
zambullida *nf* : dive, plunge
zambullirse {38} *vr* : to dive, to plunge
zanahoria *nf* : carrot
zancada *nf* : stride, step
zancadilla *nf* **1** : trip, stumble **2** *fam* : trick, ruse
zancos *nmpl* : stilts
zancuda *nf* : wading bird
zancudo *nm* MOSQUITO : mosquito
zángano *nm* : drone, male bee
zanja *nf* : ditch, trench
zanjar *vt* ACLARAR : to settle, to clear up, to resolve
zapallo *nm Arg, Chile, Peru, Uru* : pumpkin
zapapico *nm* : pickax
zapata *nf* : brake shoe
zapatería *nf* **1** : shoemaker's, shoe factory **2** : shoe store
zapatero[1], **-ra** *adj* : dry, tough, poorly cooked
zapatero[2], **-ra** *n* : shoemaker, cobbler
zapatilla *nf* **1** PANTUFLA : slipper **2** *or* **zapatilla de deporte** : sneaker
zapato *nm* : shoe
zar, zarina *n* : czar *m*, czarina *f*
zarandear *vt* **1** : to sift, to sieve **2** : to shake, to jostle, to jiggle
zarapito *nm* : curlew
zarcillo *nm* **1** : earring **2** : tendril (of a plant)
zarigüeya *nf* : opossum
zarista *adj & nmf* : czarist
zarpa *nf* : paw
zarpar *vi* : to set sail, to raise anchor
zarza *nf* : bramble, blackberry bush
zarzamora *nf* **1** : blackberry **2** : bramble, blackberry bush

zarzaparrilla *nf* : sarsaparilla
zepelin *nm, pl* **-lines** : zeppelin
zigoto *nm* : zygote
zigzag *nm, pl* **zigzags** *or* **zigzagues** : zigzag
zigzaguear *vi* : to zigzag
zimbabuense *adj & nmf* : Zimbabwean
zinc *nm* : zinc
zinnia *nf* : zinnia
zíper *nm CA, Mex* : zipper
zircón *nm, pl* **zircones** : zircon
zócalo *nm Mex* : main square
zodíaco *or* **zodiaco** *nm* : zodiac — **zodíacal** *adj*
zombi *or* **zombie** *nmf* : zombie
zona *nf* : zone, district, area
zonzo[1], **-za** *adj* : stupid, silly
zonzo[2], **-za** *n* : idiot, nitwit
zoo *nm* : zoo
zoología *nf* : zoology
zoológico[1], **-ca** *adj* : zoological
zoológico[2] *nm* : zoo
zoólogo, -ga *n* : zoologist
zoom *nm* : zoom lens
zopilote *nm CA, Mex* : buzzard
zoquete *nmf fam* : oaf, blockhead
zorrillo *nm* MOFETA : skunk
zorro[1], **-rra** *adj* : sly, crafty
zorro[2], **-rra** *n* **1** : fox, vixen **2** : sly crafty person
zorzal *nm* : thrush
zozobra *nf* : anxiety, worry
zozobrar *vi* : to capsize
zueco *nm* : clog (shoe)
zulú[1] *adj & nmf* : Zulu
zulú[2] *nm* : Zulu (language)
zumaque *nm* : sumac
zumbar *vi* : to buzz, to hum — *vt fam* **1** : to hit, to thrash **2** : to make fun of
zumbido *nm* : buzzing, humming
zumo *nf* JUGO : juice
zurcir {83} *vt* : to darn, to mend
zurdo[1], **-da** *adj* : left-handed
zurdo[2], **-da** *n* : left-handed person
zurza, etc. → **zurcir**
zutano, -na → **fulano**

English–Spanish
Dictionary

A

a¹ ['eɪ] *n, pl* **a's** *or* **as** ['eɪz] : primera letra del alfabeto inglés

a² [ə, 'eɪ] *art* (**an** /ən/, 'æn] before vowel or silent h) **1** : un *m*, una *f* ⟨a house : una casa⟩ ⟨half an hour : media hora⟩ ⟨what a surprise! : ¡qué sorpresa!⟩ **2** PER : por, a la, al ⟨30 kilometers an hour : 30 kilómetros por hora⟩ ⟨twice a month : dos veces al mes⟩

aardvark ['ɑrd,vɑrk] *n* : oso *m* hormiguero

aback [ə'bæk] *adv* **1** : por sorpresa **2 to be taken aback** : quedarse desconcertado

abacus ['æbəkəs] *n, pl* **abaci** ['æbə,saɪ, -,ki:] *or* **abacuses** : ábaco *m*

abaft [ə'bæft] *adv* : a popa

abalone [,æbə'lo:ni] *n* : abulón *m*, oreja *f* marina

abandon¹ [ə'bændən] *vt* **1** DESERT, FORSAKE : abandonar, desamparar (a alguien), desertar de (algo) **2** GIVE UP, SUSPEND : renunciar a, suspender ⟨he abandoned the search : suspendió la búsqueda⟩ **3** EVACUATE, LEAVE : abandonar, evacuar, dejar ⟨to abandon ship : abandonar el buque⟩ **4 to abandon oneself** : entregarse, abandonarse

abandon² *n* : desenfreno *m* ⟨with wild abandon : desenfrenadamente⟩

abandoned [ə'bændənd] *adj* **1** DESERTED : abandonado **2** UNRESTRAINED : desenfrenado, desinhibido

abandonment [ə'bændənmənt] *n* : abandono *m*, desamparo *m*

abase [ə'beɪs] *vt* **abased; abasing** : degradar, humillar, rebajar

abash [ə'bæʃ] *vt* : avergonzar, abochornar

abashed [ə'bæʃt] *adj* : avergonzado

abate [ə'beɪt] *vi* **abated; abating** : amainar, menguar, disminuir

abattoir ['æbə,twɑr] *n* : matadero *m*

abbess ['æbɪs, -,bɛs, -bəs] *n* : abadesa *f*

abbey ['æbi] *n, pl* **-beys** : abadía *f*

abbot ['æbət] *n* : abad *m*

abbreviate [ə'bri:vi,eɪt] *vt* **-ated; -ating** : abreviar

abbreviation [ə,bri:vi'eɪʃən] *n* : abreviación *f*, abreviatura *f*

ABC's [,eɪ,bi:'si:z] *npl* : abecé *m*

abdicate ['æbdɪ,keɪt] *v* **-cated; -cating** : abdicar

abdication [,æbdɪ'keɪʃən] *n* : abdicación *f*

abdomen ['æbdəmən, æb'do:mən] *n* : abdomen *m*, vientre *m*

abdominal [æb'dɑmənəl] *adj* : abdominal — **abdominally** *adv*

abduct [æb'dʌkt] *vt* : raptar, secuestrar

abduction [æb'dʌkʃən] *n* : rapto *m*, secuestro *m*

abductor [æb'dʌktər] *n* : raptor *m*, -tora *f*; secuestrador *m*, -dora *f*

abed [ə'bɛd] *adv & adj* : en cama

aberrant [æ'bɛrənt, 'æbərənt] *adj* **1** ABNORMAL : anormal, aberrante **2** ATYPICAL : anómalo, atípico

aberration [,æbə'reɪʃən] *n* **1** : aberración *f* **2** DERANGEMENT : perturbación *f* mental

abet [ə'bɛt] *vt* **abetted; abetting** ASSIST : ayudar ⟨to aid and abet : ser cómplice de⟩

abeyance [ə'beɪənts] *n* : desuso *m*, suspensión *f*

abhor [əb'hɔr, æb-] *vt* **-horred; -horring** : abominar, aborrecer

abhorrence [əb'hɔrənts, æb-] *n* : aborrecimiento *m*, odio *m*

abhorrent [əb'hɔrənt, æb-] *adj* : abominable, aborrecible, odioso

abide [ə'baɪd] *v* **abode** [ə'bo:d] *or* **abided; abiding** *vt* STAND : soportar, tolerar ⟨I can't abide them : no los puedo ver⟩ — *vi* **1** ENDURE : quedar, permanecer **2** DWELL : morar, residir **3 to abide by** : atenerse a

ability [ə'bɪləṭi] *n, pl* **-ties 1** CAPABILITY : aptitud *f*, capacidad *f*, facultad *f* **2** COMPETENCE : competencia *f* **3** TALENT : talento *m*, don *m*, habilidad *f*

abject ['æb,dʒɛkt, æb'-] *adj* **1** WRETCHED : miserable, desdichado **2** HOPELESS : abatido, desesperado **3** SERVILE : servil ⟨abject flattery : halagos serviles⟩ — **abjectly** *adv*

abjure [æb'dʒʊr] *vt* **-jured; -juring** : abjurar de

ablaze [ə'bleɪz] *adj* **1** BURNING : ardiendo, en llamas **2** RADIANT : resplandeciente, radiante

able ['eɪbəl] *adj* **abler; ablest 1** CAPABLE : capaz, hábil **2** COMPETENT : competente

ablution [ə'blu:ʃən] *n* : ablución *f* ⟨to perform one's ablutions : lavarse⟩

ably ['eɪbli] *adv* : hábilmente, eficientemente

abnormal [æb'nɔrməl] *adj* : anormal — **abnormally** *adv*

abnormality [,æbnər'mæləṭi, -nɔr-] *n, pl* **-ties** : anormalidad *f*

aboard¹ [ə'bord] *adv* : a bordo

aboard² *prep* : a bordo de

abode¹ → **abide**

abode² [ə'bo:d] *n* : morada *f*, residencia *f*, vivienda *f*

abolish [ə'bɑlɪʃ] *vt* : abolir, suprimir

abolition [,æbə'lɪʃən] *n* : abolición *f*, supresión *f*

abominable [ə'bɑmənəbəl] *adj* DETESTABLE : abominable, aborrecible, espantoso

abominate [ə'bɑmə,neɪt] *vt* **-nated; -nating** : abominar, aborrecer

abomination [ə,bɑmə'neɪʃən] *n* : abominación *f*

aboriginal [,æbə'rɪdʒənəl] *adj* : aborigen, indígena

aborigine [,æbə'rɪdʒəni] *n* NATIVE : aborigen *mf*, indígena *mf* abort [ə'bɔrt] vt 1 : abortar (en medicina) 2 CALL OFF : suspender, abandonar — vi : abortar, hacerse un aborto

abortion [ə'bɔrʃən] n : aborto m

abortive [ə'bɔrţɪv] adj UNSUCCESSFUL : fracasado, frustrado, malogrado

abound [ə'baʊnd] vi to abound in : abundar en, estar lleno de

about¹ [ə'baʊt] adv 1 APPROXIMATELY : aproximadamente, casi, más o menos 2 AROUND : por todas partes, alrededor ⟨the children are running about : los niños están corriendo por todas partes⟩ 3 to be about to : estar a punto de 4 to be up and about : estar levantado

about² prep 1 AROUND : alrededor de 2 CONCERNING : de, acerca de, sobre ⟨he always talks about politics : siempre habla de política⟩

above¹ [ə'bʌv] adv 1 OVERHEAD : por encima, arriba 2 : más arriba ⟨as stated above : como se indica más arriba⟩

above² adj : anterior, antedicho ⟨for the above reasons : por las razones antedichas⟩

above³ prep 1 OVER : encima de, arriba de, sobre 2 : superior a, por encima de ⟨he's above those things : él está por encima de esas cosas⟩ 3 : más de, superior a ⟨he earns above $50,000 : gana más de $50,000⟩ ⟨a number above 10 : un número superior a 10⟩ 4 above all : sobre todo

aboveboard¹ [ə'bʌv'bord, -,bord] adv open and aboveboard : sin tapujos

aboveboard² adj : legítimo, sincero

abrade [ə'breɪd] vt abraded; abrading 1 ERODE : erosionar, corroer 2 SCRAPE : escoriar, raspar

abrasion [ə'breɪʒən] n 1 SCRAPE, SCRATCH : raspadura f, rasguño m 2 EROSION : erosión f

abrasive¹ [ə'breɪsɪv] adj 1 ROUGH : abrasivo, áspero 2 BRUSQUE, IRRITATING : brusco, irritante

abrasive² n : abrasivo m

abreast [ə'brɛst] adv 1 : en fondo, al lado ⟨to march three abreast : marchar de tres en fondo⟩ 2 to keep abreast : mantenerse al día

abridge [ə'brɪʤ] vt abridged; abridging : compendiar, resumir

abridgment or abridgement [ə'brɪʤmənt] n : compendio m, resumen m

abroad [ə'brɔd] adv 1 ABOUT, WIDELY : por todas partes, en todas direcciones ⟨the news spread abroad : la noticia corrió por todas partes⟩ 2 OVERSEAS : en el extranjero, en el exterior

abrogate ['æbrə,geɪt] vt -gated; -gating : abrogar

abrupt [ə'brʌpt] adj 1 SUDDEN : abrupto, repentino, súbito 2 BRUSQUE, CURT : brusco, cortante — abruptly adv

abscess ['æb,sɛs] n : absceso m

abscond [æb'skɑnd] vi : huir, fugarse

absence ['æbsənts] n 1 : ausencia f (de una persona) 2 LACK : falta f, carencia f

absent¹ [æb'sɛnt] vt to absent oneself : ausentarse

absent² ['æbsənt] adj : ausente

absentee [,æbsən'ti:] n : ausente mf

absentminded [,æbsənt'maɪndəd] adj : distraído, despistado

absentmindedly [,æbsənt'maɪndədli] adv : distraídamente

absentmindedness [,æbsənt'maɪndədnəs] n : distracción f, despiste m

absolute ['æbsə,lu:t, ,æbsə'lu:t] adj 1 COMPLETE, PERFECT : completo, pleno, perfecto 2 UNCONDITIONAL : absoluto, incondicional 3 DEFINITE : categórico, definitivo

absolutely ['æbsə,lu:tli, ,æbsə'lu:tli] adv 1 COMPLETELY : completamente, absolutamente 2 CERTAINLY : desde luego ⟨do you agree? absolutely! : ¿estás de acuerdo? ¡desde luego!⟩

absolution [,æbsə'lu:ʃən] n : absolución f

absolutism ['æbsə,lu:,tɪzəm] n : absolutismo m

absolve [əb'zɑlv, æb-, -'sɑlv] vt -solved; -solving : absolver, perdonar

absorb [əb'zɔrb, æb-, -'sɔrb] vt 1 : absorber, embeber (un líquido), amortiguar (un golpe, la luz) 2 ENGROSS : absorber 3 ASSIMILATE : asimilar

absorbed [əb'zɔrbd, æb-, -'sɔrbd] adj ENGROSSED : absorto, ensimismado

absorbency [əb'zɔrbəntsi, æb-, -'sɔr-] n : absorbencia f

absorbent [əb'zɔrbənt, æb-, -'sɔr-] adj : absorbente

absorbing [əb'zɔrbɪŋ, æb-, -'sɔr-] adj : absorbente, fascinante

absorption [əb'zɔrpʃən, æb-, -'sɔrp-] n 1 : absorción f 2 CONCENTRATION : concentración f

abstain [əb'steɪn, æb-] vi : abstenerse

abstainer [əb'steɪnər, æb-] n : abstemio m, -mia f

abstemious [æb'sti:miəs] adj : abstemio, sobrio — abstemiously adv

abstention [əb'stɛntʃən, æb-] n : abstención f

abstinence ['æbstənənts] n : abstinencia f

abstract¹ [æb'strækt, 'æb,-] vt 1 EXTRACT : abstraer, extraer 2 SUMMARIZE : compendiar, resumir

abstract² adj : abstracto — abstractly [æb'stræktli, 'æb,-] adv

abstract³ ['æb,strækt] n : resumen m, compendio m, sumario m

abstraction [æb'strækʃən] n 1 : abstracción f, idea f abstracta 2 ABSENTMINDEDNESS : distracción f

abstruse [əb'stru:s, æb-] adj : abstruso, recóndito — abstrusely adv

absurd [əb'sərd, -'zərd] adj : absurdo, ridículo, disparatado — absurdly adv

absurdity [əb'sərdəti, -'zər-] *n, pl* **-ties 1** : absurdo *m* **2** NONSENSE : disparate *m*, despropósito *m*

abundance [ə'bʌndənts] *n* : abundancia *f*

abundant [ə'bʌndənt] *adj* : abundante, cuantioso, copioso

abundantly [ə'bʌndəntli] *adv* : abundantemente, en abundancia

abuse¹ [ə'bju:z] *vt* **abused; abusing 1** MISUSE : abusar de **2** MISTREAT : maltratar **3** REVILE : insultar, injuriar, denostar

abuse² [ə'bju:s] *n* **1** MISUSE : abuso *m* **2** MISTREATMENT : abuso *m*, maltrato *m* **3** INSULTS : insultos *mpl*, improperios *mpl* ⟨a string of abuse : una serie de improperios⟩

abuser [ə'bju:zər] *n* : abusador *m*, -dora *f*

abusive [ə'bju:sɪv] *adj* **1** ABUSING : abusivo **2** INSULTING : ofensivo, injurioso, insultante — **abusively** *adv*

abut [ə'bʌt] *v* **abutted; abutting** *vt* : bordear — *vi* **to abut on** : colindar con

abutment [ə'bʌtmənt] *n* **1** BUTTRESS : contrafuerte *m*, estribo *m* **2** CLOSENESS : contigüidad *f*

abysmal [ə'bɪzməl] *adj* **1** DEEP : abismal, insondable **2** TERRIBLE : atroz, desastroso

abysmally [ə'bɪzməli] *adv* : desastrosamente, terriblemente

abyss [ə'bɪs, 'æbɪs] *n* : abismo *m*, sima *f*

acacia [ə'keɪʃə] *n* : acacia *f*

academic¹ [ˌækə'dɛmɪk] *adj* **1** : académico **2** THEORETICAL : teórico — **academically** [-mɪkli] *adv*

academic² *n* : académico *m*, -ca *f*

academician [ˌækədə'mɪʃən] *n* → **academic**

academy [ə'kædəmi] *n, pl* **-mies** : academia *f*

acanthus [ə'kænʲθəs] *n* : acanto *m*

accede [æk'si:d] *vi* **-ceded; -ceding 1** AGREE : acceder, consentir **2** ASCEND : subir, acceder ⟨he acceded to the throne : subió al trono⟩

accelerate [ɪk'sɛləˌreɪt, æk-] *v* **-ated; -ating** *vt* : acelerar, apresurar — *vi* : acelerar (dícese de un carro)

acceleration [ɪkˌsɛlə'reɪʃən, æk-] *n* : aceleración *f*

accelerator [ɪk'sɛləˌreɪtər, æk-] *n* : acelerador *m*

accent¹ ['ækˌsɛnt, æk'sɛnt] *vt* : acentuar

accent² ['ækˌsɛnt, -sənt] *n* **1** : acento *m* **2** EMPHASIS, STRESS : énfasis *m*, acento *m*

accentuate [ɪk'sɛnʧuˌeɪt, æk-] *vt* **-ated; -ating** : acentuar, poner énfasis en

accept [ɪk'sɛpt, æk-] *vt* **1** : aceptar **2** ACKNOWLEDGE : admitir, reconocer

acceptability [ɪkˌsɛptə'bɪləti, æk-] *n* : aceptabilidad *f*

acceptable [ɪk'sɛptəbəl, æk-] *adj* : aceptable, admisible — **acceptably** [-bli] *adv*

acceptance [ɪk'sɛptənts, æk-] *n* : aceptación *f*, aprobación *f*

access¹ ['ækˌsɛs] *vt* : obtener acceso a, entrar a

access² *n* : acceso *m*

accessibility [ɪkˌsɛsə'bɪləti] *n, pl* **-ties** : accesibilidad *f*

accessible [ɪk'sɛsəbəl, æk-] *adj* : accesible, asequible

accession [ɪk'sɛʃən, æk-] *n* **1** : ascenso *f*, subida *f* (al trono, etc.) **2** ACQUISITION : adquisición *f*

accessory¹ [ɪk'sɛsəri, æk-] *adj* : auxiliar

accessory² *n, pl* **-ries 1** : accesorio *m*, complemento *m* **2** ACCOMPLICE : cómplice *mf*

accident ['æksədənt] *n* **1** MISHAP : accidente *m* **2** CHANCE : casualidad *f*

accidental [ˌæksə'dɛntəl] *adj* : accidental, casual, imprevisto, fortuito

accidentally [ˌæksə'dɛntəli, -'dɛntli] *adv* **1** BY CHANCE : por casualidad **2** UNINTENTIONALLY : sin querer, involuntariamente

acclaim¹ [ə'kleɪm] *vt* : aclamar, elogiar

acclaim² *n* : aclamación *f*, elogio *m*

acclamation [ˌæklə'meɪʃən] *n* : aclamación *f*

acclimate ['ækləˌmeɪt, ə'klaɪmət] → **acclimatize**

acclimatize [ə'klaɪməˌtaɪz] *v* **-tized; -tizing 1** : aclimatar **2 to acclimatize oneself** : aclimatarse

accolade ['ækəˌleɪd, -ˌlad] *n* **1** PRAISE : elogio *m* **2** AWARD : galardón *m*

accommodate [ə'kɑməˌdeɪt] *vt* **-dated; -dating 1** ADAPT : acomodar, adaptar **2** SATISFY : tener en cuenta, satisfacer **3** HOLD : dar cabida a, tener cabida para

accommodation [əˌkɑmə'deɪʃən] *n* **1** : adaptación *f*, adecuación *f* **2** accommodations *npl* LODGING : alojamiento *m*, hospedaje *m*

accompaniment [ə'kʌmpənəmənt, -'kʌm-] *n* : acompañamiento *m*

accompanist [ə'kʌmpənɪst, -'kɑm-] *n* : acompañante *mf*

accompany [ə'kʌmpəni, -'kɑm-] *vt* **-nied; -nying** : acompañar

accomplice [ə'kɑmpləs, -'kʌm-] *n* : cómplice *mf*

accomplish [ə'kɑmplɪʃ, -'kʌm-] *vt* : efectuar, realizar, lograr, llevar a cabo

accomplished [ə'kɑmplɪʃt, -'kʌm-] *adj* : consumado, logrado

accomplishment [ə'kɑmplɪʃmənt, -'kʌm-] *n* **1** ACHIEVEMENT : logro *m*, éxito *m* **2** SKILL : destreza *f*, habilidad *f*

accord¹ [ə'kɔrd] *vt* GRANT : conceder, otorgar — *vi* **to accord with** : concordar con, conformarse con

accord² *n* **1** AGREEMENT : acuerdo *m*, convenio *m* **2** VOLITION : voluntad *f*

⟨on one's own accord : voluntariamente, de motu proprio⟩
accordance [ə'kɔrdənts] n 1 ACCORD
: acuerdo m, conformidad f 2 **in accordance with** : conforme a, según, de
acuerdo con
accordingly [ə'kɔrdɪŋli] adv 1 CORRE-
SPONDINGLY : en consecuencia 2 CON-
SEQUENTLY : por consiguiente, por lo
tanto
according to [ə'kɔrdɪŋ] prep : según, de
acuerdo con, conforme a
accordion [ə'kɔrdiən] n : acordeón m
accordionist [ə'kɔrdiənɪst] n : acordeonista mf
accost [ə'kɔst] vt : abordar, dirigirse a
account[1] [ə'kaunt] vt : considerar, estimar ⟨he accounts himself lucky : se
considera afortunado⟩ — vi **to account for** : dar cuenta de, explicar
account[2] n 1 : cuenta f ⟨savings account
: cuenta de ahorros⟩ 2 EXPLANATION
: versión f, explicación f 3 REPORT : relato m, informe m 4 IMPORTANCE : importancia f ⟨to be of no account : no
tener importancia⟩ 5 **on account of**
BECAUSE OF : a causa de, debido a, por
6 **on no account** : de ninguna manera
accountability [ə,kauntə'bɪləṭi] n : responsabilidad f
accountable [ə'kauntəbəl] adj : responsable
accountant [ə'kauntənt] n : contador m,
-dora f; contable mf Spain
accounting [ə'kauntɪŋ] n : contabilidad
f
accoutrements or **accouterments** [ə-
'ku:trəmənts, -'ku:ṭər-] npl 1 EQUIP-
MENT : equipo m, avíos mpl 2 ACCES-
SORIES : accesorios mpl 3 TRAPPINGS
: símbolos mpl ⟨the accoutrements of
power : los símbolos del poder⟩
accredit [ə'krɛdət] vt : acreditar, autorizar
accreditation [ə,krɛdə'teɪʃən] n : acreditación f, homologación f
accretion [ə'kri:ʃən] n 1 : acrecentamiento m (proceso) 2 : acreción f,
acrecencia f (producto)
accrual [ə'kru:əl] n : incremento m, acumulación f
accrue [ə'kru:] vi **-crued; -cruing** : acumularse, aumentarse
accumulate [ə'kju:mjə,leɪt] v **-lated;
-lating** vt : acumular, amontonar — vi
: acumularse, amontonarse
accumulation [ə,kju:mjə'leɪʃən] n : acumulación f, amontonamiento m
accuracy ['ækjərəsi] n : exactitud f, precisión f
accurate ['ækjərət] adj : exacto, correcto, fiel, preciso — **accurately** adv
accusation [,ækjə'zeɪʃən] n : acusación
f
accusatory [ə'kju:zə,tori] adj : acusatorio
accuse [ə'kju:z] vt **-cused; -cusing**
: acusar, delatar, denunciar

accused [ə'kju:zd] ns & pl DEFENDANT
: acusado m, -da f
accuser [ə'kju:zər] n : acusador m, -dora
f
accustom [ə'kʌstəm] vt : acostumbrar,
habituar
ace ['eɪs] n : as m
acerbic [ə'sərbɪk, æ-] adj : acerbo, mordaz
acetate ['æsə,teɪt] n : acetato m
acetic [ə'si:ṭɪk] adj : acético
acetone ['æsə,to:n] n : acetona f
acetylene [ə'sɛṭələn, -ṭə,li:n] n : acetileno m
ache[1] ['eɪk] vi **ached; aching** 1 : doler
2 **to ache for** : anhelar, ansiar
ache[2] n : dolor m
achieve [ə'tʃi:v] vt **achieved; achieving**
: lograr, alcanzar, conseguir, realizar
achievement [ə'tʃi:vmənt] n : logro m,
éxito m, realización f
acid[1] ['æsəd] adj 1 SOUR : ácido, agrio
2 CAUSTIC, SHARP : acerbo, mordaz —
acidly adv
acid[2] n : ácido m
acidic [ə'sɪdɪk, æ-] adj : ácido
acidity [ə'sɪdəṭi, æ-] n, pl **-ties** : acidez f
acknowledge [ɪk'nɑlɪdʒ, æk-] vt **-edged;
-edging** 1 ADMIT : reconocer, admitir
2 RECOGNIZE : reconocer 3 **to acknowledge receipt of** : acusar recibo
de
acknowledgment [ɪk'nɑlɪdʒmənt, æk-] n
1 RECOGNITION : reconocimiento m 2
THANKS : agradecimiento m
acme ['ækmi] n : colmo m, apogeo m,
cúspide f
acne ['ækni] n : acné m
acolyte ['ækə,laɪt] n : acólito m
acorn ['eɪ,kɔrn, -kərn] n : bellota f
acoustic [ə'ku:stɪk] or **acoustical**
[-stɪkəl] adj : acústico — **acoustically**
adv
acoustics [ə'ku:stɪks] ns & pl : acústica
f
acquaint [ə'kweɪnt] vt 1 INFORM : enterar, informar 2 FAMILIARIZE : familiarizar 3 **to be acquainted with**
: conocer a (una persona), estar al tanto de (un hecho)
acquaintance [ə'kweɪntənts] n 1
KNOWLEDGE : conocimiento m 2
: conocido m, -da f ⟨friends and ac-
quaintances : amigos y conocidos⟩
acquiesce [,ækwi'ɛs] vi **-esced; -escing**
: consentir, conformarse
acquiescence [,ækwi'ɛsənts] n : consentimiento m, aquiescencia f
acquire [ə'kwaɪr] vt **-quired; -quiring**
: adquirir, obtener
acquisition [,ækwə'zɪʃən] n : adquisición f
acquisitive [ə'kwɪzəṭɪv] adj : adquisitivo, codicioso
acquit [ə'kwɪt] vt **-quitted; -quitting** 1
: absolver, exculpar 2 **to acquit oneself** : comportarse, defenderse
acquittal [ə'kwɪṭəl] n : absolución f, exculpación f

acre ['eɪkər] n : acre m
acreage ['eɪkərɪʤ] n : superficie f en acres
acrid ['ækrəd] adj 1 BITTER : acre 2 CAUSTIC : acre, mordaz — acridly adv
acrimonious [ˌækrə'mo:niəs] adj : áspero, cáustico, sarcástico
acrimony ['ækrəˌmo:ni] n, pl -nies : acrimonia f
acrobat ['ækrəˌbæt] n : acróbata mf, saltimbanqui mf
acrobatic [ˌækrə'bæṭɪk] adj : acrobático
acrobatics [ˌækrə'bæṭɪks] ns & pl : acrobacia f
acronym ['ækrəˌnɪm] n : acrónimo m
across¹ [ə'krɔs] adv 1 CROSSWISE : al través 2 : a través, del otro lado ⟨he's already across : ya está del otro lado⟩ 3 : de ancho ⟨40 feet across : 40 pies de ancho⟩
across² prep 1 : al otro lado de ⟨across the street : al otro lado de la calle⟩ 2 : a través de ⟨a log across the road : un tronco a través del camino⟩
acrylic [ə'krɪlɪk] n : acrílico m
act¹ ['ækt] vi 1 PERFORM : actuar, interpretar 2 FEIGN, PRETEND : fingir, simular 3 BEHAVE : comportarse 4 FUNCTION : actuar, servir, funcionar 5 : tomar medidas ⟨he acted to save the business : tomó medidas para salvar el negocio⟩ 6 to act as : servir de, hacer de
act² n 1 DEED : acto m, hecho m, acción f 2 DECREE : ley f, decreto m 3 : acto m (en una obra de teatro), número m (en un espectáculo) 4 PRETENSE : fingimiento m
action ['ækʃən] n 1 DEED : acción f, acto m, hecho m 2 BEHAVIOR : actuación f, comportamiento m 3 LAWSUIT : demanda f 4 MOVEMENT : movimiento m 5 COMBAT : combate m 6 PLOT : acción f, trama f 7 MECHANISM : mecanismo m
activate ['æktəˌveɪt] vt -vated; -vating : activar
activation [ˌæktə'veɪʃən] n : activación f
active ['æktɪv] adj 1 MOVING : activo, en movimiento 2 LIVELY : vigoroso, enérgico 3 : en actividad ⟨an active volcano : un volcán en actividad⟩ 4 OPERATIVE : vigente
actively ['æktɪvli] adv : activamente, enérgicamente
activist ['æktɪvɪst] n : activista mf — activist adj
activity [æk'tɪvəṭi] n, pl -ties 1 MOVEMENT : actividad f, movimiento m 2 VIGOR : vigor m, energía f 3 OCCUPATION : actividad f, ocupación f
actor ['æktər] n : actor m, artista mf
actress ['æktrəs] n : actriz f
actual ['æktʃuəl] adj : real, verdadero
actuality [ˌæktʃu'æləṭi] n, pl -ties : realidad f

actually ['æktʃuəli, -ʃəli] adv : realmente, en realidad
actuary ['æktʃuˌɛri] n, pl -aries : actuario m, -ria f de seguros
acumen [ə'kju:mən] n : perspicacia f
acupuncture ['ækjuˌpʌŋktʃər] n : acupuntura f
acute [ə'kju:t] adj acuter; acutest 1 SHARP : agudo 2 PERCEPTIVE : perspicaz, sagaz 3 KEEN : fino, muy desarrollado, agudo ⟨an acute sense of smell : un fino olfato⟩ 4 SEVERE : grave 5 acute angle : ángulo m agudo
acutely [ə'kju:tli] adv : intensamente ⟨to be acutely aware : estar perfectamente consciente⟩
acuteness [ə'kju:tnəs] n : agudeza f
ad ['æd] → advertisement
adage ['ædɪʤ] n : adagio m, refrán m, dicho m
adamant ['ædəmənt, -ˌmænt] adj : firme, categórico, inflexible — adamantly adv
Adam's apple ['ædəmz] n : nuez f de Adán
adapt [ə'dæpt] vt : adaptar, ajustar — vi : adaptarse
adaptability [əˌdæptə'bɪləṭi] n : adaptabilidad f, flexibilidad f
adaptable [ə'dæptəbəl] adj : adaptable, amoldable
adaptation [ˌæˌdæp'teɪʃən, -dəp-] n 1 : adaptación f, modificación f 2 VERSION : versión f
adapter [ə'dæptər] n : adaptador m
add ['æd] vt 1 : añadir, agregar ⟨to add a comment : añadir una observación⟩ 2 : sumar ⟨add these numbers : suma estos números⟩ — vi : sumar (en total)
adder ['ædər] n : víbora f
addict¹ [ə'dɪkt] vt : causar adicción en
addict² ['ædɪkt] n 1 : adicto m, -ta f 2 drug addict : drogadicto m, -ta f; toxicómano m, -na f
addiction [ə'dɪkʃən] n 1 : adicción f, dependencia f 2 drug addiction : drogadicción f
addictive [ə'dɪktɪv] adj : adictivo
addition [ə'dɪʃən] n 1 : adición f, añadidura f 2 in ~ : además, también
additional [ə'dɪʃənəl] adj : extra, adicional, de más
additionally [ə'dɪʃənəli] adv : además, adicionalmente
additive ['ædəṭɪv] n : aditivo m
addle ['ædəl] vt -dled; -dling : confundir, enturbiar
address¹ [ə'drɛs] vt 1 : dirigirse a, pronunciar un discurso ante ⟨to address a jury : dirigirse a un jurado⟩ 2 : dirigir, ponerle la dirección a ⟨to address a letter : dirigir una carta⟩
address² [ə'drɛs, 'æˌdrɛs] n 1 SPEECH : discurso m, alocución f 2 : dirección f (de una residencia, etc.)
addressee [ˌæˌdrɛ'si:, ə-] n : destinatario m, -ria f

adduce [ə-'duːs, 'djuːs] *vt* -duced; -ducing : aducir
adenoids ['æd,nɔɪd, -dən,ɔɪd] *npl* : adenoides *fpl*
adept [ə'dɛpt] *adj* : experto, hábil — adeptly *adv*
adequacy ['ædɪkwəsi] *n, pl* -cies : cantidad *f* suficiente
adequate ['ædɪkwət] *adj* 1 SUFFICIENT : adecuado, suficiente 2 ACCEPTABLE, PASSABLE : adecuado, aceptable
adequately ['ædɪkwətli] *adv* : suficientemente, apropiadamente
adhere [æd'hɪr, əd-] *vi* -hered; -hering 1 STICK : pegarse, adherirse 2 to adhere to : adherirse a (una política, etc.), cumplir con (una promesa)
adherence [æd'hɪrənts, əd-] *n* : adhesión *f*, adherencia *f*, observancia *f* (de una ley, etc.)
adherent[1] [æd'hɪrənt, əd-] *adj* : adherente, adhesivo, pegajoso
adherent[2] *n* : adepto *m*, -ta *f*; partidario *m*, -ria *f*
adhesion [æd'hiːʒən, əd-] *n* : adhesión *f*
adhesive[1] [æd'hiːsɪv, əd-, -zɪv] *adj* : adhesivo
adhesive[2] *n* : adhesivo *m*, pegamento *m*
adjacent [ə'dʒeɪsənt] *adj* : adyacente, colindante, contiguo
adjective ['ædʒɪktɪv] *n* : adjetivo *m* — adjectival [,ædʒɪk'taɪvəl] *adj*
adjoin [ə'dʒɔɪn] *vt* : lindar con, colindar con
adjoining [ə'dʒɔɪnɪŋ] *adj* : contiguo, colindante
adjourn [ə'dʒərn] *vt* : levantar, suspender ⟨the meeting is adjourned : se levanta la sesión⟩ — *vi* : aplazarse
adjournment [ə'dʒərnmənt] *n* : suspensión *f*, aplazamiento *m*
adjudicate [ə'dʒuːdɪ,keɪt] *vt* -cated; -cating : juzgar, arbitrar
adjudication [ə,dʒuːdɪ'keɪʃən] *n* 1 JUDGING : arbitrio *m* (judicial) 2 JUDGMENT : fallo *m*
adjunct ['æ,dʒʌŋkt] *n* : adjunto *m*, complemento *m*
adjust [ə'dʒʌst] *vt* : ajustar, arreglar, regular — *vi* to adjust to : adaptarse a
adjustable [ə'dʒʌstəbəl] *adj* : ajustable, regulable, graduable
adjustment [ə'dʒʌstmənt] *n* : ajuste *m*, modificación *f*
ad–lib[1] ['æd'lɪb] *v* -libbed; -libbing : improvisar
ad–lib[2] *adj* : improvisado
administer [æd'mɪnəstər, əd-] *vt* : administrar
administration [æd,mɪnə'streɪʃən, əd-] *n* 1 MANAGING : administración *f*, dirección *f* 2 GOVERNMENT, MANAGEMENT : administración *f*, gobierno *m*
administrative [æd'mɪnə,streɪt̬ɪv, əd-] *adj* : administrativo — administratively *adv*
administrator [æd'mɪnə,streɪt̬ər, əd-] *n* : administrador *m*, -dora *f*

admirable ['ædmərəbəl] *adj* : admirable, loable — admirably *adv*
admiral ['ædmərəl] *n* : almirante *mf*
admiration [,ædmə'reɪʃən] *n* : admiración *f*
admire [æd'maɪr] *vt* -mired; -miring : admirar
admirer [æd'maɪrər] *n* : admirador *m*, -dora *f*
admiring [æd'maɪrɪŋ] *adj* : admirativo, de admiración
admiringly [æd'maɪrɪŋli] *adv* : con admiración
admissible [æd'mɪsəbəl] *adj* : admisible, aceptable
admission [æd'mɪʃən] *n* 1 ADMITTANCE : entrada *f*, admisión *f* 2 ACKNOWLEDGMENT : reconocimiento *m*, admisión *f*
admit [æd'mɪt, əd-] *vt* -mitted; -mitting 1 : admitir, dejar entrar ⟨the museum admits children : el museo deja entrar a los niños⟩ 2 ACKNOWLEDGE : reconocer, admitir
admittance [æd'mɪtənts, əd-] *n* : admisión *f*, entrada *f*, acceso *m*
admittedly [æd'mɪt̬ədli, əd-] *adv* : la verdad es que, lo cierto es que ⟨admittedly we went too fast : la verdad es que fuimos demasiado de prisa⟩
admonish [æd'mɑnɪʃ, əd-] *vt* : amonestar, reprender
admonition [,ædmə'nɪʃən] *n* : admonición *f*
ado [ə'duː] *n* 1 FUSS : ruido *m*, alboroto *m* 2 TROUBLE : dificultad *f*, lío *m* 3 without further ado : sin más preámbulos
adobe [ə'doːbi] *n* : adobe *m*
adolescence [,ædəl'ɛsənts] *n* : adolescencia *f*
adolescent[1] [,ædəl'ɛsənt] *adj* : adolescente, de adolescencia
adolescent[2] *n* : adolescente *mf*
adopt [ə'dɑpt] *vt* : adoptar
adoption [ə'dɑpʃən] *n* : adopción *f*
adoptive [ə'dɑptɪv] *adj* : adoptivo
adorable [ə'dorəbəl] *adj* : adorable, encantador
adorably [ə'dorəbli] *adv* : de manera adorable
adoration [,ædə'reɪʃən] *n* : adoración *f*
adore [ə'dor] *vt* adored; adoring 1 WORSHIP : adorar 2 LOVE : querer, adorar 3 LIKE : encantarle (algo a uno), gustarle mucho (algo a uno) ⟨I adore your new dress : me encanta tu vestido nuevo⟩
adorn [ə'dorn] *vt* : adornar, ornar, engalanar
adornment [ə'dornmənt] *n* : adorno *m*, decoración *f*
adrenaline [ə'drenələn] *n* : adrenalina *f*
adrift [ə'drɪft] *adj & adv* : a la deriva
adroit [ə'drɔɪt] *adj* : diestro, hábil — adroitly *adv*
adroitness [ə'drɔɪtnəs] *n* : destreza *f*, habilidad *f*

adult¹ [ə'dʌlt, 'æˌdʌlt] *adj* : adulto
adult² *n* : adulto *m*, -ta *f*
adulterate [ə'dʌltəˌreɪt] *vt* **-ated; -ating** : adulterar
adulterous [ə'dʌltərəs] *adj* : adúltero
adultery [ə'dʌltəri] *n, pl* **-teries** : adulterio *m*
adulthood [ə'dʌltˌhʊd] *n* : adultez *f*, edad *f* adulta
advance¹ [æd'væn*t*s, əd-] *v* **-vanced; -vancing** *vt* **1** : avanzar, adelantar ⟨to advance troops : avanzar las tropas⟩ **2** PROMOTE : ascender, promover **3** PROPOSE : proponer, presentar **4** : adelantar, anticipar ⟨they advanced me next month's salary : me adelantaron el sueldo del próximo mes⟩ — *vi* **1** PROCEED : avanzar, adelantarse **2** PROGRESS : progresar
advance² *adj* : anticipado ⟨advance notice : previo aviso⟩
advance³ *n* **1** PROGRESSION : avance *m* **2** PROGRESS : adelanto *m*, mejora *f*, progreso *m* **3** RISE : aumento *m*, alza *f* **4** LOAN : anticipo *m*, préstamo *m* **5** in ∼ : por adelantado
advanced [æd'væn*t*st, əd-] *adj* **1** DEVELOPED : avanzado, desarrollado **2** PRECOCIOUS : adelantado, precoz **3** HIGHER : superior
advancement [æd'væn*t*smənt, əd-] *n* **1** FURTHERANCE : fomento *m*, adelantamiento *m*, progreso *m* **2** PROMOTION : ascenso *m*
advantage [əd'væntɪdʒ, æd-] *n* **1** SUPERIORITY : ventaja *f*, superioridad *f* **2** GAIN : provecho *m*, partido *m* **3 to take advantage of** : aprovecharse de
advantageous [ˌædˌvæn'teɪdʒəs, -vən-] *adj* : ventajoso, provechoso — **advantageously** *adv*
advent ['ædˌvɛnt] *n* **1 Advent** : Adviento *m* **2** ARRIVAL : advenimiento *m*, venida *f*
adventure [æd'vɛntʃər, əd-] *n* : aventura *f*
adventurer [æd'vɛntʃərər, əd-] *n* : aventurero *m*, -ra *f*
adventurous [æd'vɛntʃərəs, əd-] *adj* **1** : intrépido, aventurero ⟨an adventurous traveler : un viajero intrépido⟩ **2** RISKY : arriesgado, aventurado
adverb ['ædˌvərb] *n* : adverbio *m* — **adverbial** [æd'vərbiəl] *adj*
adversary ['ædvərˌseri] *n, pl* **-saries** : adversario *m*, -ria *f*
adverse [æd'vərs, 'ædˌ] *adj* **1** OPPOSING : opuesto, contrario **2** UNFAVORABLE : adverso, desfavorable — **adversely** *adv*
adversity [æd'vərsəti, əd-] *n, pl* **-ties** : adversidad *f*
advertise ['ædvərˌtaɪz] *v* **-tised; -tising** *vt* : anunciar, hacerle publicidad a — *vi* : hacer publicidad, hacer propaganda
advertisement ['ædvərˌtaɪzmənt; æd 'vərtəzmənt] *n* : anuncio *m*

advertiser ['ædvərˌtaɪzər] *n* : anunciante *mf*
advertising ['ædvərˌtaɪzɪŋ] *n* : publicidad *f*, propaganda *f*
advice [æd'vaɪs] *n* : consejo *m*, recomendación *f* ⟨take my advice : sigue mis consejos⟩
advisability [ædˌvaɪzə'bɪləti, əd-] *n* : conveniencia *f*
advisable [æd'vaɪzəbəl, əd-] *adj* : aconsejable, recomendable, conveniente
advise [æd'vaɪz, əd-] *v* **-vised; -vising** *vt* **1** COUNSEL : aconsejar, asesorar **2** RECOMMEND : recomendar **3** INFORM : informar, notificar — *vi* : dar consejo
adviser *or* **advisor** [æd'vaɪzər, əd-] *n* : consejero *m*, -ra *f*; asesor *m*, -sora *f*
advisory [æd'vaɪzəri, əd-] *adj* **1** : consultivo **2 in an advisory capacity** : como asesor
advocacy ['ædvəkəsi] *n* : promoción *f*, apoyo *m*
advocate¹ ['ædvəˌkeɪt] *vt* **-cated; -cating** : recomendar, abogar por, ser partidario de
advocate² ['ædvəkət] *n* : defensor *m*, -sora *f*; partidario *m*, -ria *f*
adze ['ædz] *n* : azuela *f*
aeon ['iːən, 'iːˌɑn] *n* : eón *m*, siglo *m*, eternidad *f*
aerate ['ærˌeɪt] *vt* **-ated; -ating** : gasear (un líquido), oxigenar (la sangre)
aerial¹ ['æriəl] *adj* : aéreo
aerial² *n* : antena *f*
aerie ['æri, 'ɪri, 'eɪəri] *n* : aguilera *f*
aerobic [ˌær'oːbɪk] *adj* : aerobio, aeróbico ⟨aerobic exercises : ejercicios aeróbicos⟩
aerobics [ˌær'oːbɪks] *ns & pl* : aeróbic *m*
aerodynamic [ˌæroːdaɪ'næmɪk] *adj* : aerodinámico — **aerodynamically** [-mɪkli] *adv*
aerodynamics [ˌæroːdaɪ'næmɪks] *n* : aerodinámica *f*
aeronautical [ˌærə'nɔtɪkəl] *adj* : aeronáutico
aeronautics [ˌærə'nɔtɪks] *n* : aeronáutica *f*
aerosol ['ærəˌsɔl] *n* : aerosol *m*
aerospace¹ ['æroˌspeɪs] *adj* : aeroespacial
aerospace² *n* : espacio *m*
aesthetic [ɛs'θɛtɪk] *adj* : estético — **aesthetically** [-tɪkli] *adv*
aesthetics [ɛs'θɛtɪks] *n* : estética *f*
afar [ə'fɑr] *adv* : lejos, a lo lejos
affability [ˌæfə'bɪləti] *n* : afabilidad *f*
affable ['æfəbəl] *adj* : afable — **affably** *adv*
affair [ə'fær] *n* **1** MATTER : asunto *m*, cuestión *f*, caso *m* **2** EVENT : ocasión *f*, acontecimiento *m* **3** LIAISON : amorío *m*, aventura *f* **4 business affairs** : negocios *mpl* **5 current affairs** : actualidades *fpl*
affect [ə'fɛkt, æ-] *vt* **1** INFLUENCE, TOUCH : afectar, tocar **2** FEIGN : fingir

affectation [ˌæˌfɛkˈteɪʃən] *n* : afectación *f*

affected [əˈfɛktəd, æ-] *adj* **1** FEIGNED : afectado, fingido **2** MOVED : conmovido

affecting [əˈfɛktɪŋ, æ-] *adj* : conmovedor

affection [əˈfɛkʃən] *n* : afecto *m*, cariño *m*

affectionate [əˈfɛkʃənət] *adj* : afectuoso, cariñoso — **affectionately** *adv*

affidavit [ˌæfəˈdeɪvət, ˈæfəˌ-] *n* : declaración *f* jurada, afidávit *m*

affiliate[1] [əˈfɪliˌeɪt] *v* **-ated; -ating** *vt* : afiliar, asociar ⟨to be affiliated with : estar afiliado a⟩

affiliate[2] [əˈfɪliət] *n* : afiliado *m*, -da *f* (persona), filial *f* (organización)

affiliation [əˌfɪliˈeɪʃən] *n* : afiliación *f*, filiación *f*

affinity [əˈfɪnəti] *n, pl* **-ties** : afinidad *f*

affirm [əˈfərm] *vt* : afirmar, aseverar, declarar

affirmation [ˌæfərˈmeɪʃən] *n* : afirmación *f*, aserto *m*, declaración *f*

affirmative[1] [əˈfərmətɪv] *adj* : afirmativo ⟨affirmative action : acción afirmativa⟩

affirmative[2] *n* **1** : afirmativa *f* **2 to answer in the affirmative** : responder afirmativamente, dar una respuesta afirmativa

affix [əˈfɪks] *vt* : fijar, poner, pegar

afflict [əˈflɪkt] *vt* **1** : afligir, aquejar **2 to be afflicted with** : padecer de, sufrir de

affliction [əˈflɪkʃən] *n* **1** TRIBULATION : aflicción *f*, tribulación *f* **2** AILMENT : enfermedad *f*, padecimiento *m*

affluence [ˈæˌfluːənts; æˈfluː-, ə-] *n* : afluencia *f*, abundancia *f*, prosperidad *f*

affluent [ˈæˌfluːənt; æˈfluː-, ə-] *adj* : próspero, adinerado

afford [əˈford] *vt* **1** : tener los recursos para, permitirse el lujo de ⟨I can afford it : puedo permitírmelo, tengo con que comprarlo⟩ **2** PROVIDE : ofrecer, proporcionar, dar

affront[1] [əˈfrʌnt] *vt* : afrentar, insultar, ofender

affront[2] *n* : afrenta *f*, insulto *m*, ofensa *f*

Afghan [ˈæfˌgæn, -gən] *n* : afgano *m*, -na *f* — **Afghan** *adj*

afire [əˈfaɪr] *adj* : ardiendo, en llamas

aflame [əˈfleɪm] *adj* : llameante, en llamas

afloat [əˈfloːt] *adv & adj* : a flote

afoot [əˈfʊt] *adj* **1** WALKING : a pie, andando **2** UNDER WAY : en marcha ⟨something suspicious is afoot : algo sospechoso se está tramando⟩

aforementioned [əˈforˈmɛntʃənd] *adj* : antedicho, susodicho

aforesaid [əˈforˌsɛd] *adj* : antes mencionado, antedicho

afraid [əˈfreɪd] *adj* **1 to be afraid** : tener miedo **2 to be afraid that** : temerse que ⟨I'm afraid not : me temo que no⟩

afresh [əˈfrɛʃ] *adv* **1** : de nuevo, otra vez **2 to start afresh** : volver a empezar

African [ˈæfrɪkən] *n* : africano *m*, -na *f* — **African** *adj*

Afro–American[1] [ˌæfroəˈmɛrɪkən] *adj* : afroamericano *m*, -na *f*

Afro–American[2] *n* : afroamericano

aft [ˈæft] *adv* : a popa

after[1] [ˈæftər] *adv* **1** AFTERWARD : después **2** BEHIND : detrás, atrás

after[2] *adj* : posterior, siguiente ⟨in after years : en los años posteriores⟩

after[3] *conj* : después de, después de que ⟨after we ate : después de que comimos, después de comer⟩

after[4] *prep* **1** FOLLOWING : después de, tras ⟨after Saturday : después del sábado⟩ ⟨day after day : día tras día⟩ **2** BEHIND : tras de, después de ⟨I ran after the dog : corrí tras del perro⟩ **3** CONCERNING : por ⟨they asked after you : preguntaron por ti⟩ **4 after all** : después de todo

aftereffect [ˈæftərɪˌfɛkt] *n* : efecto *m* secundario

afterlife [ˈæftərˌlaɪf] *n* : vida *f* venidera, vida *f* después de la muerte

aftermath [ˈæftərˌmæθ] *n* : consecuencias *fpl*, resultados *mpl*

afternoon [ˌæftərˈnuːn] *n* : tarde *f*

aftertaste [ˈæftərˌteɪst] *n* : resabio *m*, regusto *m*

afterthought [ˈæftərˌθɔt] *n* : ocurrencia *f* tardía, idea *f* tardía

afterward [ˈæftərwərd] *or* **afterwards** [-wərdz] *adv* : después, luego ⟨soon afterward : poco después⟩

again [əˈgɛn, -ˈgɪn] *adv* **1** ANEW, OVER : de nuevo, otra vez **2** BESIDES : además **3 then again** : por otra parte ⟨I may stay, then again I may not : puede ser que me quede, por otra parte, puede que no⟩

against [əˈgɛntst, -ˈgɪntst] *prep* **1** TOUCHING : contra ⟨against the wall : contra la pared⟩ **2** OPPOSING : contra, en contra de ⟨I will vote against the proposal : votaré en contra de la propuesta⟩ ⟨against the grain : a contrapelo⟩

agape [əˈgeɪp] *adj* : boquiabierto

agate [ˈægət] *n* : ágata *f*

age[1] [ˈeɪʤ] *vi* **aged; aging** : envejecer, madurar

age[2] *n* **1** : edad *f* ⟨ten years of age : diez años de edad⟩ ⟨to be of age : ser mayor de edad⟩ **2** PERIOD : era *f*, siglo *m*, época *f* **3 old age** : vejez *f* **4 ages** *npl* : siglos *mpl*, eternidad *f*

aged *adj* **1** [ˈeɪʤəd, ˈeɪʤd] OLD : anciano, viejo, vetusto **2** [ˈeɪʤd] (*indicating a specified age*) ⟨a girl aged 10 : una niña de 10 años de edad⟩

ageless [ˈeɪʤləs] *adj* **1** YOUTHFUL : eternamente joven **2** TIMELESS : eterno, perenne

agency [ˈeɪʤəntsi] *n, pl* **-cies** : agencia *f*, oficina *f* ⟨travel agency : agencia de viajes⟩ **2 through the agency of** : a través de, por medio de

agenda [ə'ʤndə] *n* : agenda *f*, orden *m* del día

agent ['eɪʤənt] *n* **1** MEANS : agente *m*, medio *m*, instrumento *m* **2** REPRESENTATIVE : agente *mf*, representante *mf*

aggravate ['ægrə,veɪt] *vt* **-vated; -vating 1** WORSEN : agravar, empeorar **2** ANNOY : irritar, exasperar

aggravation [,ægrə'veɪʃən] *n* **1** WORSENING : empeoramiento *m* **2** ANNOYANCE : molestia *f*, irritación *f*, exasperación *f*

aggregate¹ ['ægrɪ,geɪt] *vt* **-gated; -gating** : juntar, sumar

aggregate² ['ægrɪgət] *adj* : total, global, conjunto

aggregate³ ['ægrɪgət] *n* **1** CONGLOMERATE : agregado *m*, conglomerado *m* **2** WHOLE : total *m*, conjunto *m*

aggression [ə'grɛʃən] *n* **1** ATTACK : agresión *f* **2** AGGRESSIVENESS : agresividad *f*

aggressive [ə'grɛsɪv] *adj* : agresivo — **aggressively** *adv*

aggressiveness [ə'grɛsɪvnəs] *n* : agresividad *f*

aggressor [ə'grɛsər] *n* : agresor *m*, -sora *f*

aggrieved [ə'gri:vd] *adj* : ofendido, herido

aghast [ə'gæst] *adj* : espantado, aterrado, horrorizado

agile ['æʤəl] *adj* : ágil

agility [ə'ʤɪləti] *n, pl* **-ties** : agilidad *f*

agitate ['æʤə,teɪt] *v* **-tated; -tating** *vt* **1** SHAKE : agitar **2** UPSET : inquietar, perturbar — *vi* **to agitate against** : hacer campaña en contra de

agitation [,æʤə'teɪʃən] *n* : agitación *f*, inquietud *f*

agitator ['æʤə,teɪtər] *n* : agitador *m*, -dora *f*

agnostic [æg'nɑstɪk] *n* : agnóstico *m*, -ca *f*

ago [ə'go:] *adv* : hace ⟨two years ago : hace dos años⟩ ⟨long ago : hace tiempo, hace mucho tiempo⟩

agog [ə'gɑg] *adj* : ansioso, curioso

agonize ['ægə,naɪz] *vi* **-nized; -nizing** : tormentarse, angustiarse

agonizing ['ægə,naɪzɪŋ] *adj* : angustioso, terrible — **agonizingly** [-zɪŋli] *adv*

agony ['ægəni] *n, pl* **-nies 1** PAIN : dolor *m* **2** ANGUISH : angustia *f*

agrarian [ə'grɛriən] *adj* : agrario

agree [ə'gri:] *v* **agreed; agreeing** *vt* ACKNOWLEDGE : estar de acuerdo ⟨he agreed that I was right : estuvo de acuerdo en que tenía razón⟩ — *vi* **1** CONCUR : estar de acuerdo **2** CONSENT : ponerse de acuerdo **3** TALLY : concordar **4 to agree with** : sentarle bien (a alguien) ⟨this climate agrees with me : este clima me sienta bien⟩

agreeable [ə'gri:əbəl] *adj* **1** PLEASING : agradable, simpático **2** WILLING : dispuesto **3** AGREEING : de acuerdo, conforme

agreeably [ə'gri:əbli] *adv* : agradablemente

agreement [ə'gri:mənt] *n* **1** : acuerdo *m*, conformidad *f* ⟨in agreement with : de acuerdo con⟩ **2** CONTRACT, PACT : acuerdo *m*, pacto *m*, convenio *m* **3** CONCORD, HARMONY : concordia *f*

agriculture ['ægrɪ,kʌltʃər] *n* : agricultura *f* — **agricultural** [,ægrɪ'kʌltʃərəl] *adj*

aground [ə'graʊnd] *adj* : encallado, varado

ahead [ə'hɛd] *adv* **1** : al frente, delante, adelante ⟨he walked ahead : caminó delante⟩ **2** BEFOREHAND : por adelantado, con antelación **3** LEADING : a la delantera **4 to get ahead** : adelantar, progresar

ahead of *prep* **1** : al frente de, delante de, antes de **2 to get ahead of** : adelantarse a

ahoy [ə'hɔɪ] *interj* **ship ahoy!** : ¡barco a la vista!

aid¹ ['eɪd] *vt* : ayudar, auxiliar

aid² *n* **1** HELP : ayuda *f*, asistencia *f* **2** ASSISTANT : asistente *mf*

aide ['eɪd] *n* : ayudante *mf*

AIDS ['eɪdz] *n* : SIDA *m*, sida *m*

ail ['eɪl] *vt* : molestar, afligir — *vi* : sufrir, estar enfermo

aileron ['eɪlə,rɑn] *n* : alerón *m*

ailment ['eɪlmənt] *n* : enfermedad *f*, dolencia *f*, achaque *m*

aim¹ ['eɪm] *vt* **1** : apuntar (un arma), dirigir (una observación) **2** INTEND : proponerse, querer ⟨he aims to do it tonight : se propone hacerlo esta noche⟩ — *vi* **1** POINT : apuntar **2 to aim at** : aspirar a

aim² *n* **1** MARKSMANSHIP : puntería *f* **2** GOAL : propósito *m*, objetivo *m*, fin *m*

aimless ['eɪmləs] *adj* : sin rumbo, sin objeto

aimlessly ['eɪmləsli] *adv* : sin rumbo, sin objeto

air¹ ['ær] *vt* **1** : airear, ventilar ⟨to air out a mattress : airear un colchón⟩ **2** EXPRESS : airear, manifestar, comunicar **3** BROADCAST : transmitir, emitir

air² *n* **1** : aire *m* **2** MELODY : aire *m* **3** APPEARANCE : aire *m*, aspecto *m* **4 airs** *npl* : aires *mpl*, afectación *f* **5 by ~** : por avión (dícese de una carta), en avión (dícese de una persona) **6 to be on the air** : estar en el aire, estar emitiendo

airborne ['ær,born] *adj* **1** : aerotransportado ⟨airborne troops : tropas aerotransportadas⟩ **2** FLYING : volando, en el aire

air–condition [,ærkən'dɪʃən] *vt* : climatizar, condicionar con el aire

air conditioner [,ærkən'dɪʃənər] *n* : acondicionador *m* de aire

air–conditioning [ˌærkənˈdɪʃənɪŋ] *n* : aire *m* acondicionado

aircraft [ˈærˌkræft] *ns & pl* **1** : avión *m*, aeronave *f* **2 aircraft carrier** : portaaviones *m*

airfield [ˈærˌfiːld] *n* : aeródromo *m*, campo *m* de aviación

air force *n* : fuerza *f* aérea

airlift [ˈærˌlɪft] *n* : puente *m* aéreo, transporte *m* aéreo

airline [ˈærˌlaɪn] *n* : aerolínea *f*, línea *f* aérea

airliner [ˈærˌlaɪnər] *n* : avión *m* de pasajeros

airmail[1] [ˈærˌmeɪl] *vt* : enviar por vía aérea

airmail[2] *n* : correo *m* aéreo

airman [ˈærmən] *n, pl* **-men** [-mən, -ˌmɛn] **1** AVIATOR : aviador *m*, -dora *f* **2** : soldado *m* de la fuerza aérea

airplane [ˈærˌpleɪn] *n* : avión *m*

airport [ˈærˌport] *n* : aeropuerto *m*

airship [ˈærˌʃɪp] *n* : dirigible *m*, zepelín *m*

airstrip [ˈærˌstrɪp] *n* : pista *f* de aterrizaje

airtight [ˈærˈtaɪt] *adj* : hermético, herméticamente cerrado

airwaves [ˈærˌweɪvz] *npl* : radio *m*, televisión *f*

airy [ˈæri] *adj* **airier** [-iər]; **-est 1** DELICATE, LIGHT : delicado, ligero **2** BREEZY : aireado, bien ventilado

aisle [ˈaɪl] *n* : pasillo *m*, nave *f* lateral (de una iglesia)

ajar [əˈdʒɑr] *adj* : entreabierto, entornado

akimbo [əˈkɪmbo] *adj & adv* : en jarras

akin [əˈkɪn] *adj* **1** RELATED : emparentado **2** SIMILAR : semejante, parecido

alabaster [ˈæləˌbæstər] *n* : alabastro *m*

alacrity [əˈlækrəti] *n* : presteza *f*, prontitud *f*

alarm[1] [əˈlɑrm] *vt* **1** WARN : alarmar, alertar **2** FRIGHTEN : asustar

alarm[2] *n* **1** WARNING : alarma *f*, alerta *f* **2** APPREHENSION, FEAR : aprensión *f*, inquietud *f*, temor *m* **3 alarm clock** : despertador *m*

alarming [əˈlɑrmɪŋ] *adj* : alarmante

alas [əˈlæs] *interj* : ¡ay!

Albanian [ælˈbeɪniən] *n* : albanés *m*, -nesa *f* — **Albanian** *adj*

albatross [ˈælbəˌtrɔs] *n, pl* **-tross** or **-trosses** : albatros *m*

albeit [ɔlˈbiːət, æl-] *conj* : aunque

albino [ælˈbaɪno] *n, pl* **-nos** : albino *m*, -na *f*

album [ˈælbəm] *n* : álbum *m*

albumen [ælˈbjuːmən] *n* **1** : clara *f* de huevo **2** → **albumin**

albumin [ælˈbjuːmən] *n* : albúmina *f*

alchemist [ˈælkəmɪst] *n* : alquimista *mf*

alchemy [ˈælkəmi] *n, pl* **-mies** : alquimia *f*

alcohol [ˈælkəˌhɔl] *n* **1** ETHANOL : alcohol *m*, etanol *m* **2** LIQUOR : alcohol *m*, bebidas *fpl* alcohólicas

alcoholic[1] [ˌælkəˈhɔlɪk] *adj* : alcohólico

alcoholic[2] *n* : alcohólico *m*, -ca *f*

alcoholism [ˈælkəhɔˌlɪzəm] *n* : alcoholismo *m*

alcove [ˈælˌkoːv] *n* : nicho *m*, hueco *m*

alderman [ˈɔldərmən] *n, pl* **-men** [-mən, -ˌmɛn] : concejal *mf*

ale [ˈeɪl] *n* : cerveza *f*

alert[1] [əˈlərt] *vt* : alertar, poner sobre aviso

alert[2] *adj* **1** WATCHFUL : alerta, vigilante **2** QUICK : listo, vivo

alert[3] *n* : alerta *f*, alarma *f*

alertly [əˈlərtli] *adv* : con listeza

alertness [əˈlərtnəs] *n* **1** WATCHFULNESS : vigilancia *f* **2** ASTUTENESS : listeza *f*, viveza *f*

alfalfa [ælˈfælfə] *n* : alfalfa *f*

alga [ˈælɡə] *n, pl* **-gae** [ˈælˌdʒiː] : alga *f*

algebra [ˈældʒəbrə] *n* : álgebra *m*

algebraic [ˌældʒəˈbreɪk] *adj* : algebraico — **algebraically** [-ɪkli] *adv*

Algerian [ælˈdʒɪriən] *n* : argelino *m*, -na *f* — **Algerian** *adj*

algorithm [ˈælɡəˌrɪðəm] *n* : algoritmo *m*

alias[1] [ˈeɪliəs] *adv* : alias

alias[2] *n* : alias *m*

alibi[1] [ˈæləˌbaɪ] *vi* : ofrecer una coartada

alibi[2] *n* **1** : coartada *f* **2** EXCUSE : pretexto *m*, excusa *f*

alien[1] [ˈeɪliən] *adj* **1** STRANGE : ajeno, extraño **2** FOREIGN : extranjero, foráneo **3** EXTRATERRESTRIAL : extraterrestre

alien[2] *n* **1** FOREIGNER : extranjero *m*, -ra *f*; forastero *m*, -ra *f* **2** EXTRATERRESTRIAL : extraterrestre *mf*

alienate [ˈeɪliəˌneɪt] *vt* **-ated; -ating** ESTRANGE : alienar, enajenar **2 to alienate oneself** : alejarse, distanciarse

alienation [ˌeɪliəˈneɪʃən] *n* : alienación *f*, enajenación *f*

alight [əˈlaɪt] *vi* **1** DISMOUNT : bajarse, apearse **2** LAND : posarse, aterrizar

align [əˈlaɪn] *vt* : alinear

alignment [əˈlaɪnmənt] *n* : alineación *f*, alineamiento *m*

alike[1] [əˈlaɪk] *adv* : igual, del mismo modo

alike[2] *adj* : igual, semejante, parecido

alimentary [ˌæləˈmɛntəri] *adj* **1** : alimenticio **2 alimentary canal** : tubo *m* digestivo

alimony [ˈæləˌmoːni] *n, pl* **-nies** : pensión *f* alimenticia

alive [əˈlaɪv] *adj* **1** LIVING : vivo, viviente **2** LIVELY : animado, activo **3** ACTIVE : vigente, en uso **4** AWARE : consciente ⟨alive to the danger : consciente del peligro⟩

alkali [ˈælkəˌlaɪ] *n, pl* **-lies** [-ˌlaɪz] or **-lis** [-ˌlaɪz] : álcali *m*

alkaline [ˈælkələn, -ˌlaɪn] *adj* : alcalino

all[1] [ˈɔl] *adv* **1** COMPLETELY : todo, completamente **2** : igual ⟨the score is 14 all : es 14 iguales, están empatados a 14⟩

3 all the better : tanto mejor **4 all the more** : aún más, todavía más

all² *adj* : todo ⟨all the children : todos los niños⟩ ⟨in all likelihood : con toda probabilidad, con la mayor probabilidad⟩

all³ *pron* **1** : todo, -da ⟨they ate it all : lo comieron todo⟩ ⟨that's all : eso es todo⟩ ⟨enough for all : suficiente para todos⟩ **2 all in all** : en general **3 not at all** (*in negative constructions*) : en absoluto, para nada

Allah ['ɑlɑ, ɑ'lɑ] *n* : Alá *m*

all–around [ˌɔlə'raʊnd] *adj* : completo, amplio

allay [ə'leɪ] *vt* **1** ALLEVIATE : aliviar, mitigar **2** CALM : aquietar, calmar

allegation [ˌælɪ'geɪʃən] *n* : alegato *m*, acusación *f*

allege [ə'lɛdʒ] *vt* **-leged; -leging 1** : alegar, afirmar **2 to be alleged** : decirse, pretenderse ⟨she is alleged to be wealthy : se dice que es adinerada⟩

alleged [ə'lɛdʒd, ə'lɛdʒəd] *adj* : presunto, supuesto

allegedly [ə'lɛdʒədli] *adv* : supuestamente, según se alega

allegiance [ə'li:dʒənts] *n* : lealtad *f*, fidelidad *f*

allegorical [ˌælə'gɔrɪkəl] *adj* : alegórico

allegory ['ælə,gori] *n, pl* **-ries** : alegoría *f*

alleluia [ˌɑlə'lu:jə, ˌæ-] → **hallelujah**

allergen ['ælərdʒən] *n* : alérgeno *m*

allergic [ə'lərdʒɪk] *adj* : alérgico

allergy ['ælərdʒi] *n, pl* **-gies** : alergia *f*

alleviate [ə'li:vi,eɪt] *vt* **-ated; -ating** : aliviar, mitigar, paliar

alleviation [ə,li:vi'eɪʃən] *n* : alivio *m*

alley ['æli] *n, pl* **-leys 1** : callejón *m* **2 bowling alley** : bolera *f*

alliance [ə'laɪənts] *n* : alianza *f*, coalición *f*

alligator ['ælə,geɪtər] *n* : caimán *m*

alliteration [ə,lɪtə'reɪʃən] *n* : aliteración *f*

allocate ['ælə,keɪt] *vt* **-cated; -cating** : asignar, adjudicar

allocation [ˌælə'keɪʃən] *n* : asignación *f*, reparto *m*, distribución *f*

allot [ə'lɑt] *vt* **-lotted; -lotting** : repartir, distribuir, asignar

allotment [ə'lɑtmənt] *n* : reparto *m*, asignación *f*, distribución *f*

allow [ə'laʊ] *vt* **1** PERMIT : permitir, dejar **2** ALLOT : conceder, dar **3** ADMIT, CONCEDE : admitir, conceder — *vi* **to allow for** : tener en cuenta

allowable [ə'laʊəbəl] *adj* **1** PERMISSIBLE : permisible, lícito **2** : deducible ⟨allowable expenditure : gasto deducible⟩

allowance [ə'laʊənts] *n* **1** : complemento *m* (para gastos, etc.), mesada *f* (para niños) **2 to make allowance(s)** : tener en cuenta, disculpar

alloy ['æ,lɔɪ] *n* : aleación *f*

all–purpose ['ɔl'pərpəs] *adj* : multiuso ⟨all-purpose flour : harina común⟩

all right¹ *adv* **1** YES : sí, por supuesto **2** WELL : bien ⟨I did all right : me fue bien⟩ **3** DEFINITELY : bien, ciertamente, sin duda ⟨he's sick all right : está bien enfermo⟩

all right² *adj* **1** OK : bien ⟨are you all right? : ¿estás bien?⟩ **2** SATISFACTORY : bien, bueno ⟨your work is all right : tu trabajo es bueno⟩

all–round [ˌɔl'raʊnd] → **all–around**

allspice ['ɔlspaɪs] *n* : pimienta *f* de Jamaica

allude [ə'lu:d] *vi* **-luded; -luding** : aludir, referirse

allure¹ [ə'lʊr] *vt* **-lured; -luring** : cautivar, atraer

allure² *n* : atractivo *m*, encanto *m*

allusion [ə'lu:ʒən] *n* : alusión *f*

ally¹ [ə'laɪ, 'æ,laɪ] *vi* **-lied; -lying** : aliarse

ally² ['æ,laɪ, ə'laɪ] *n* : aliado *m*, -da *f*

almanac ['ɔlmə,næk, 'æl-] *n* : almanaque *m*

almighty [ɔl'maɪti] *adj* : omnipotente, todopoderoso

almond ['ɑmənd, 'ɑl-, 'æ-, 'æl-] *n* : almendra *f*

almost ['ɔl,mo:st, ɔl'mo:st] *adv* : casi, prácticamente

alms ['ɑmz, 'ɑlmz, 'ælmz] *ns & pl* : limosna *f*, caridad *f*

aloe ['ælo:] *n* : áloe *m*

aloft [ə'lɔft] *adv* : en alto, en el aire

alone¹ [ə'lo:n] *adv* : sólo, solamente, únicamente

alone² *adj* : solo ⟨they're alone in the house : están solos en la casa⟩

along¹ [ə'lɔŋ] *adv* **1** FORWARD : adelante ⟨farther along : más adelante⟩ ⟨move along! : ¡circulen, por favor!⟩ **2 to bring along** : traer **3 ~ with** : con, junto con **4 all along** : desde el principio

along² *prep* **1** : por, a lo largo de ⟨along the coast : a lo largo de la costa⟩ **2** : en, en el curso de, por ⟨along the way : en el curso del viaje⟩

alongside¹ [ə,lɔŋ'saɪd] *adv* : al costado, al lado

alongside² *or* **alongside of** *prep* : junto a, al lado de

aloof [ə'lu:f] *adj* : distante, reservado

aloofness [ə'lu:fnəs] *n* : reserva *f*, actitud *f* distante

aloud [ə'laʊd] *adv* : en voz alta

alpaca [æl'pækə] *n* : alpaca *f*

alphabet ['ælfə,bɛt] *n* : alfabeto *m*

alphabetical [ˌælfə'bɛtɪkəl] *or* **alphabetic** [-'bɛtɪk] *adj* : alfabético — **alphabetically** [-tɪkli] *adv*

alphabetize ['ælfəbə,taɪz] *vt* **-ized; -izing** : alfabetizar, poner en orden alfabético

alpine ['æl,paɪn] *adj* : alpino

already [ɔl'rɛdi] *adv* : ya

also ['ɔl,so:] *adv* : también, además

altar ['ɔltər] *n* : altar *m*

alter ['ɔltər] *vt* : alterar, cambiar, modificar

alteration [ˌɔltəˈreɪʃən] *n* : alteración *f*, cambio *m*, modificación *f*
altercation [ˌɔltərˈkeɪʃən] *n* : altercado *m*, disputa *f*
alternate¹ [ˈɔltərˌneɪt] *v* **-nated; -nating** : alternar
alternate² [ˈɔltərnət] *adj* **1** : alterno ⟨alternate cycles of inflation and depression : ciclos alternos de inflación y depresión⟩ **2** : uno sí y otro no ⟨he cooks on alternate days : cocina un día sí y otro no⟩
alternate³ [ˈɔltərnət] *n* : suplente *mf*; sustituto *m*, -ta *f*
alternately [ˈɔltərnətli] *adv* : alternativemente, por turno
alternating current [ˈɔltərˌneɪtɪŋ] *n* : corriente *f* alterna
alternation [ˌɔltərˈneɪʃən] *n* : alternancia *f*, rotación *f*
alternative¹ [ɔlˈtərnətɪv] *adj* : alternativo
alternative² *n* : alternativa *f*
alternator [ˈɔltərˌneɪtər] *n* : alternador *m*
although [ɔlˈðoː] *conj* : aunque, a pesar de que
altitude [ˈæltəˌtuːd, -ˌtjuːd] *n* : altitud *f*, altura *f*
alto [ˈælˌtoː] *n*, *pl* **-tos** : alto *mf*, contralto *mf*
altogether [ˌɔltəˈɡɛðər] *adv* **1** COMPLETELY : completamente, totalmente, del todo **2** ON THE WHOLE : en suma, en general
altruism [ˈæltruˌɪzəm] *n* : altruismo *m*
altruistic [ˌæltruˈɪstɪk] *adj* : altruista — **altruistically** [-tɪkli] *adv*
alum [ˈæləm] *n* : alumbre *m*
aluminum [əˈluːmənəm] *n* : aluminio *m*
alumna [əˈlʌmnə] *n*, *pl* **-nae** [-ˌniː] : exalumna *f*
alumnus [əˈlʌmnəs] *n*, *pl* **-ni** [-ˌnaɪ] : exalumno *m*
always [ˈɔlwiz, -ˌweɪz] *adv* **1** INVARIABLY : siempre, invariablemente **2** FOREVER : para siempre
am → **be**
amalgam [əˈmælɡəm] *n* : amalgama *f*
amalgamate [əˈmælɡəˌmeɪt] *vt* **-ated; -ating** : amalgamar, unir, fusionar
amalgamation [əˌmælɡəˈmeɪʃən] *n* : fusión *f*, unión *f*
amaryllis [ˌæməˈrɪləs] *n* : amarilis *f*
amass [əˈmæs] *vt* : amasar, acumular
amateur [ˈæmətʃər, -tər, -ˌtʊr, -ˌtjʊr] *n* **1** : amateur *mf* **2** BEGINNER : principiante *mf*; aficionado *m*, -da *f*
amateurish [ˈæməˌtʃərɪʃ, -ˌtər-, -ˌtʊr-, -ˌtjʊr-] *adj* : amateur, inexperto
amaze [əˈmeɪz] *vt* **amazed; amazing** : asombrar, maravillar, pasmar
amazement [əˈmeɪzmənt] *n* : asombro *m*, sorpresa *f*
amazing [əˈmeɪzɪŋ] *adj* : asombroso, sorprendente — **amazingly** [-zɪŋli] *adv*
Amazon [ˈæməˌzɑn] *n* : amazona *f* (en mitología)
Amazonian [ˌæməˈzoːniən] *adj* : amazónico

ambassador [æmˈbæsədər] *n* : embajador *m*, -dora *f*
amber [ˈæmbər] *n* : ámbar *m*
ambergris [ˈæmbərˌɡrɪs, -ˌɡriːs] *n* : ámbar *m* gris
ambidextrous [ˌæmbɪˈdɛkstrəs] *adj* : ambidextro — **ambidextrously** *adv*
ambience *or* **ambiance** [ˈæmbiənts, ˈɑmbiˌɑnts] *n* : ambiente *m*, atmósfera *f*
ambiguity [ˌæmbəˈɡjuːəti] *n*, *pl* **-ties** : ambigüedad *f*
ambiguous [æmˈbɪɡjuəs] *adj* : ambiguo
ambition [æmˈbɪʃən] *n* : ambición *f*
ambitious [æmˈbɪʃəs] *adj* : ambicioso — **ambitiously** *adv*
ambivalence [æmˈbɪvələnts] *n* : ambivalencia *f*
ambivalent [æmˈbɪvələnt] *adj* : ambivalente
amble¹ [ˈæmbəl] *vi* **-bled; -bling** : ir tranquilamente, pasearse despreocupadamente
amble² *n* : paseo *m* tranquilo
ambulance [ˈæmbjələnts] *n* : ambulancia *f*
ambush¹ [ˈæmˌbʊʃ] *vt* : emboscar
ambush² *n* : emboscada *f*, celada *f*
ameliorate [əˈmiːljəˌreɪt] *v* **-rated; -rating** IMPROVE : mejorar
amelioration [əˌmiːljəˈreɪʃən] *n* : mejora *f*
amen [ˈeɪˈmɛn, ˈɑ-] *interj* : amén
amenable [əˈmiːnəbəl, -ˈmɛ-] *adj* RESPONSIVE : susceptible, receptivo, sensible
amend [əˈmɛnd] *vt* **1** IMPROVE : mejorar, enmendar **2** CORRECT : enmendar, corregir
amendment [əˈmɛndmənt] *n* : enmienda *f*
amends [əˈmɛndz] *ns* & *pl* : compensación *f*, reparación *f*, desagravio *m*
amenity [əˈmɛnəti, -ˈmiː-] *n*, *pl* **-ties 1** PLEASANTNESS : lo agradable, amenidad *f* **2** amenities *npl* : servicios *mpl*, comodidades *fpl*
American [əˈmɛrɪkən] *n* : americano *m*, -na *f* — **American** *adj*
American Indian *n* : indio *m* (americano), india *f* (americana)
amethyst [ˈæməθəst] *n* : amatista *f*
amiability [ˌeɪmiːəˈbɪləti] *n* : amabilidad *f*, afabilidad *f*
amiable [ˈeɪmiːəbəl] *adj* : amable, afable — **amiably** [-bli] *adv*
amicable [ˈæmɪkəbəl] *adj* : amigable, amistoso, cordial — **amicably** [-bli] *adv*
amid [əˈmɪd] *or* **amidst** [əˈmɪdst] *prep* : en medio de, entre
amino acid [əˈmiːnoː] *n* : aminoácido *m*
amiss¹ [əˈmɪs] *adv* : mal, fuera de lugar ⟨to take amiss : tomar a mal, llevar a mal⟩
amiss² *adj* **1** WRONG : malo, inoportuno **2 there's something amiss** : pasa algo, algo anda mal
ammeter [ˈæˌmiːtər] *n* : amperímetro *m*

ammonia [ə'mo:njə] *n* : amoníaco *m*
ammunition [ˌæmjə'nɪʃən] *n* **1** : municiones *fpl* **2** ARGUMENTS : argumentos *mpl*
amnesia [æm'ni:ʒə] *n* : amnesia *f*
amnesty ['æmnəsti] *n, pl* -**ties** : amnistía *f*
amoeba [ə'mi:bə] *n, pl* -**bas** *or* -**bae** [-ˌbi:] : ameba *f*
amoebic [ə'mi:bɪk] *adj* : amébico
amok [ə'mʌk, -'mɑk] *adv* **to run amok** : correr a ciegas, enloquecerse, desbocarse (dícese de la economía, etc.)
among [ə'mʌŋ] *prep* : entre
amoral [eɪ'mɔrəl] *adj* : amoral
amorous ['æmərəs] *adj* **1** PASSIONATE : enamoradizo, apasionado **2** ENAMORED : enamorado **3** LOVING : amoroso, cariñoso
amorously ['æmərəsli] *adv* : con cariño
amorphous [ə'mɔrfəs] *adj* : amorfo, informe
amortize ['æmərˌtaɪz, ə'mɔr-] *vt* -**tized**; -**tizing** : amortizar
amount[1] [ə'maunt] *vi* **to amount to 1** : equivaler a, significar ⟨that amounts to treason : eso equivale a la traición⟩ **2** : ascender (a) ⟨my debts amount to $2000 : mis deudas ascienden a $2000⟩
amount[2] *n* : cantidad *f*, suma *f*
ampere ['æmˌpɪr] *n* : amperio *m*
ampersand ['æmpərˌsænd] *n* : el signo &
amphetamine [æm'fɛtˌəˌmi:n] *n* : anfetamina *f*
amphibian [æm'fɪbiən] *n* : anfibio *m*
amphibious [æm'fɪbiəs] *adj* : anfibio
amphitheater ['æmfəˌθi:ətər] *n* : anfiteatro *m*
ample ['æmpəl] *adj* -**pler**; -**plest 1** LARGE, SPACIOUS : amplio, extenso, grande **2** ABUNDANT : abundante, generoso
amplifier ['æmpləˌfaɪər] *n* : amplificador *m*
amplify ['æmpləˌfaɪ] *vt* -**fied**; -**fying** : amplificar
amply ['æmpli] *adv* : ampliamente, abundantemente, suficientemente
amputate ['æmpjəˌteɪt] *vt* -**tated**; -**tating** : amputar
amputation [ˌæmpjə'teɪʃən] *n* : amputación *f*
amuck [ə'mʌk] → **amok**
amulet ['æmjələt] *n* : amuleto *m*, talismán *m*
amuse [ə'mju:z] *vt* **amused**; **amusing 1** ENTERTAIN : entretener, distraer **2** : hacer reír, divertir ⟨the joke amused us : la broma nos hizo reír⟩
amusement [ə'mju:zmənt] *n* **1** ENTERTAINMENT : diversión *f*, entretenimiento *m*, pasatiempo *m* **2** LAUGHTER : risa *f*
an *art* → **a**[2]
anachronism [ə'nækrəˌnɪzəm] *n* : anacronismo *m*
anachronistic [əˌnækrə'nɪstɪk] *adj* : anacrónico

anaconda [ˌænə'kɑndə] *n* : anaconda *f*
anagram ['ænəˌɡræm] *n* : anagrama *m*
anal ['eɪnəl] *adj* : anal
analgesic [ˌænəl'dʒi:zɪk, -sɪk] *n* : analgésico *m*
analog ['ænəˌlɔɡ] *adj* : analógico
analogical [ˌænə'lɑdʒɪkəl] *adj* : analógico — **analogically** [-kli] *adv*
analogous [ə'næləɡəs] *adj* : análogo
analogy [ə'nælədʒi] *n, pl* -**gies** : analogía *f*
analysis [ə'næləsəs] *n, pl* -**yses** [-ˌsi:z] **1** : análisis *m* **2** PSYCHOANALYSIS : psicoanálisis *m*
analyst ['ænəlɪst] *n* **1** : analista *mf* **2** PSYCHOANALYST : psicoanalista *mf*
analytic [ˌænə'lɪtɪk] *or* **analytical** [-tɪkəl] *adj* : analítico — **analytically** [-tɪkli] *adv*
analyze ['ænəˌlaɪz] *vt* -**lyzed**; -**lyzing** : analizar
anarchic [æ'nɑrkɪk] *adj* : anárquico — **anarchically** [-kɪkli] *adv*
anarchism ['ænərˌkɪzəm, -nɑr-] *n* : anarquismo *m*
anarchist ['ænərkɪst, -nɑr-] *n* : anarquista *mf*
anarchy ['ænərki, -nɑr-] *n* : anarquía *f*
anathema [ə'næθəmə] *n* : anatema *m*
anatomic [ˌænə'tɑmɪk] *or* **anatomical** [-mɪkəl] *adj* : anatómico — **anatomically** [-mɪkli] *adv*
anatomy [ə'nætəmi] *n, pl* -**mies** : anatomía *f*
ancestor ['ænˌsɛstər] *n* : antepasado *m*, -da *f*; antecesor *m*, -sora *f*
ancestral [æn'sɛstrəl] *adj* : ancestral, de los antepasados
ancestry ['ænˌsɛstri] *n* **1** DESCENT : ascendencia *f*, linaje *m*, abolengo *m* **2** ANCESTORS : antepasados *mpl*, -das *fpl*
anchor[1] ['æŋkər] *vt* **1** MOOR : anclar, fondear **2** FASTEN : sujetar, asegurar, fijar
anchor[2] *n* **1** : ancla *f* **2** : presentador *m*, -dora *f* (en televisión)
anchorage ['æŋkərɪdʒ] *n* : anclaje *m*
anchovy ['ænˌtʃo:vi, æn'tʃo:-] *n, pl* -**vies** *or* -**vy** : anchoa *f*
ancient ['eɪntʃənt] *adj* **1** : antiguo ⟨ancient history : historia antigua⟩ **2** OLD : viejo
ancients ['eɪntʃənts] *npl* : los antiguos *mpl*
and ['ænd] *conj* **1** : y (**e** *before words beginning with* i- *or* hi-) **2** : con ⟨ham and eggs : huevos con jamón⟩ **3** : a ⟨go and see : ve a ver⟩ **4** : de ⟨try and finish it soon : trata de terminarlo pronto⟩
Andalusian [ˌændə'lu:ʒən] *n* : andaluz *m*, -luza *f* — **Andalusian** *adj*
Andean ['ændiən] *adj* : andino
andiron ['ænˌdaɪərn] *n* : morillo *m*
Andorran [æn'dɔrən] *n* : andorrano *m*, -na *f* — **Andorran** *adj*
androgynous [æn'drɑdʒənəs] *adj* : andrógino
anecdotal [ˌænɪk'do:t̬əl] *adj* : anecdótico

anecdote ['ænɪk,do:t] *n* : anécdota *f*
anemia [ə'ni:miə] *n* : anemia *f*
anemic [ə'ni:mɪk] *adj* : anémico
anemone [ə'nɛməni] *n* : anémona *f*
anesthesia [,ænəs'θi:ʒə] *n* : anestesia *f*
anesthetic[1] [,ænəs'θtɪk] *adj* : anestésico
anesthetic[2] *n* : anestésico *m*
anesthetist [ə'nɛsθətɪst] *n* : anestesista *mf*
anesthetize [ə'nɛsθə,taɪz] *vt* -**tize; -tized** : anestesiar
aneurysm ['ænjə,rɪzəm] *n* : aneurisma *mf*
anew [ə'nu:, -'nju:] *adv* : de nuevo, otra vez, nuevamente
angel ['eɪndʒəl] *n* : ángel *m*
angelic [æn'dʒɛlɪk] *or* **angelical** [-lɪkəl] *adj* : angélico, angelical — **angelically** [-lɪkli] *adv*
anger[1] ['æŋgər] *vt* : enojar, enfadar
anger[2] *n* : enojo *m*, enfado *m*, ira *f*, cólera *f*, rabia *f*
angina [æn'dʒaɪnə] *n* : angina *f*
angle[1] ['æŋgəl] *v* **angled; angling** *vt* DIRECT, SLANT : orientar, dirigir — *vi* FISH : pescar (con caña)
angle[2] *n* **1** : ángulo *m* **2** POINT OF VIEW : perspectiva *f*, punto *m* de vista
angler ['æŋglər] *n* : pescador *m*, -dora *f*
Anglican ['æŋglɪkən] *n* : anglicano *m*, -na *f* — **Anglican** *adj*
Anglo-Saxon[1] [,æŋglo'sæksən] *adj* : anglosajón
Anglo-Saxon[2] *n* : anglosajón *m*, -jona *f*
Angolan [æŋ'go:lən, æn-] *n* : angoleño *m*, -ña *f* — **Angolan** *adj*
angora [æŋ'gorə, æn-] *n* : angora *f*
angrily ['æŋgrəli] *adv* : furiosamente, con ira
angry ['æŋgri] *adj* -**grier; -est** : enojado, enfadado, furioso
anguish ['æŋgwɪʃ] *n* : angustia *f*, congoja *f*
anguished ['æŋgwɪʃt] *adj* : angustiado, acongojado
angular ['æŋgjələr] *adj* : angular (dícese de las formas), anguloso (dícese de las caras)
animal ['ænəməl] *n* **1** : animal *m* **2** BRUTE : bruto *m*, -ta *f*
animate[1] ['ænə,meɪt] *vt* -**mated; -mating** : animar
animate[2] ['ænəmət] *adj* : animado
animated ['ænə,meɪtəd] *adj* **1** LIVELY : animado, vivo, vivaz **2 animated cartoon** : dibujos *mpl* animados
animation [,ænə'meɪʃən] *n* : animación *f*
animosity [,ænə'masəti] *n*, *pl* -**ties** : animosidad *f*, animadversión *f*
anise ['ænəs] *n* : anís *m*
aniseed ['ænəs,si:d] *n* : anís *m*, semilla *f* de anís
ankle ['æŋkəl] *n* : tobillo *m*
anklebone ['æŋkəl,bo:n] *n* : taba *f*
annals ['ænəlz] *npl* : anales *mpl*, crónica *f*
anneal [ə'ni:l] *vt* **1** TEMPER : templar **2** STRENGTHEN : fortalecer

annex[1] [ə'nɛks, 'æ,nɛks] *vt* : anexar
annex[2] ['æ,nɛks, -nɪks] *n* : anexo *m*, anejo *m*
annexation [,æ,nɛk'seɪʃən] *n* : anexión *f*
annihilate [ə'naɪə,leɪt] *vt* -**lated; -lating** : aniquilar
annihilation [ə,naɪə'leɪʃən] *n* : aniquilación *f*, aniquilamiento *m*
anniversary [,ænə'vərsəri] *n*, *pl* -**ries** : aniversario *m*
annotate ['ænə,teɪt] *vt* -**tated; -tating** : anotar
annotation [,ænə'teɪʃən] *n* : anotación *f*
announce [ə'naʊnts] *vt* -**nounced; -nouncing** : anunciar
announcement [ə'naʊntsmənt] *n* : anuncio *m*
announcer [ə'naʊntsər] *n* : anunciador *m*, -dora *f*; comentarista *mf*; locutor *m*, -tora *f*
annoy [ə'nɔɪ] *vt* : molestar, fastidiar, irritar
annoyance [ə'nɔɪənts] *n* **1** IRRITATION : irritación *f*, fastidio *m* **2** NUISANCE : molestia *f*, fastidio *m*
annoying [ə'nɔɪɪŋ] *adj* : molesto, fastidioso, engorroso — **annoyingly** [-ɪŋli] *adv*
annual[1] ['ænjʊəl] *adj* : anual — **annually** *adv*
annual[2] *n* **1** : planta *f* anual **2** YEARBOOK : anuario *m*
annuity [ə'nu:əti] *n*, *pl* -**ties** : anualidad *f*
annul [ə'nʌl] *vt* **annulled; annulling** : anular, invalidar
annulment [ə'nʌlmənt] *n* : anulación *f*
anode ['æ,no:d] *n* : ánodo *m*
anoint [ə'nɔɪnt] *vt* : ungir
anomalous [ə'naməlⱥs] *adj* : anómalo
anomaly [ə'naməli] *n*, *pl* -**lies** : anomalía *f*
anonymity [,ænə'nɪməti] *n* : anonimato *m*
anonymous [ə'nanəməs] *adj* : anónimo — **anonymously** *adv*
anorexia [,ænə'rɛksiə] *n* : anorexia *f*
anorexic [,ænə'rɛksɪk] *adj* : anoréxico
another[1] [ə'nʌðər] *adj* : otro
another[2] *pron* : otro, otra
answer[1] ['æntsər] *vt* **1** : contestar (a), responder (a) ⟨to answer the telephone : contestar el teléfono⟩ **2** FULFILL : satisfacer **3 to answer for** : ser responsable de, pagar por ⟨she'll answer for that mistake : pagará por ese error⟩ — *vi* : contestar, responder
answer[2] *n* **1** REPLY : respuesta *f*, contestación *f* **2** SOLUTION : solución *f*
answerable ['æntsərəbəl] *adj* : responsable
ant ['ænt] *n* : hormiga *f*
antacid [ænt'æsəd, 'æn,tæ-] *n* : antiácido *m*
antagonism [æn'tægə,nɪzəm] *n* : antagonismo *m*, hostilidad *f*
antagonist [æn'tægənɪst] *n* : antagonista *mf*

antagonistic [æn,tægə'nıstık] *adj* : antagonista, hostil
antagonize [æn'tægə,naız] *vt* -nized; -nizing : antagonizar
antarctic [ænt'arktık, -'artık] *adj* : antártico
antarctic circle *n* : círculo *m* antártico
anteater ['ænt,i:tər] *n* : oso *m* hormiguero
antebellum [,æntı'bɛləm] *adj* : prebélico
antecedent[1] [,æntə'si:dənt] *adj* : antecedente, precedente
antecedent[2] *n* : antecedente *mf*; precursor *m*, -sora *f*
antelope ['æntəl,o:p] *n*, *pl* -lope or -lopes : antílope *m*
antenna [æn'tɛnə] *n*, *pl* -nae [-,ni:, -,naı] or -nas : antena *f*
anterior [æn'tıriər] *adj* : anterior
anthem ['ænθəm] *n* : himno *m* ⟨national anthem : himno nacional⟩
anther ['ænθər] *n* : antera *f*
anthill ['ænt,hıl] *n* : hormiguero *m*
anthology [æn'θalədʒi] *n*, *pl* -gies : antología *f*
anthracite ['ænθrə,saıt] *n* : antracita *f*
anthropoid[1] ['ænθrə,pɔıd] *adj* : antropoide
anthropoid[2] *n* : antropoide *mf*
anthropological [,ænθrəpə'ladʒıkəl] *adj* : antropológico
anthropologist [,ænθrə'palədʒıst] *n* : antropólogo *m*, -ga *f*
anthropology [,ænθrə'palədʒi] *n* : antropología *f*
antiabortion [,æntiə'bɔrʃən, ,æntaı-] *adj* : antiaborto
antiaircraft [,ænti'ær,kræft, ,æntaı-] *adj* : antiaéreo
anti–American [,æntiə'mɛrıkən, ,æntaı-] *adj* : antiamericano
antibiotic[1] [,æntibaı'atık, ,æntaı-, -bi-] *adj* : antibiótico
antibiotic[2] *n* : antibiótico *m*
antibody ['ænti,badi] *n*, *pl* -bodies : anticuerpo *m*
antic[1] ['æntık] *adj* : extravagante, juguetón
antic[2] *n* : payasada *f*, travesura *f*
anticipate [æn'tısə,peıt] *vt* -pated; -pating 1 FORESEE : anticipar, prever 2 EXPECT : esperar, contar con
anticipation [æn,tısə'peıʃən] *n* 1 FORESIGHT : previsión *f* 2 EXPECTATION : anticipación *f*, expectación *f*, esperanza *f*
anticipatory [æn'tısəpə,tori] *adj* : en anticipación, en previsión
anticlimactic [,æntiklaı'mæktık] *adj* : anticlimático, decepcionante
anticlimax [,ænti'klaı,mæks] *n* : anticlímax *m*
anticommunism [,ænti'kamjə,nızəm, ,æntaı-] *n* : anticomunismo *m*
anticommunist[1] [,ænti'kamjənıst, ,æntaı-] *adj* : anticomunista
anticommunist[2] *n* : anticomunista *mf*

antidemocratic [,ænti,dɛmə'kræṭık, ,æntaı-] *adj* : antidemocrático
antidepressant [,æntidi'prɛsənt] *n* : antidepresivo *m* — antidepressant *adj*
antidote ['ænti,do:t] *n* : antídoto *m*
antidrug [,ænti'drʌg, ,æntaı-; 'ænti,drʌg, 'æntaı-] *adj* : antidrogas
antifascist [,ænti'fæʃıst, ,æntaı-] *adj* : antifascista
antifeminist [,ænti'fɛmənıst, ,æntaı-] *adj* : antifeminista
antifreeze ['ænti,fri:z] *n* : anticongelante *m*
antigen ['æntıdʒən, -,dʒɛn] *n* : antígeno *m*
antihistamine [,ænti'hıstə,mi:n, -mən] *n* : antihistamínico *m*
anti–imperialism [,æntiım'pıriə,lızəm, ,æntaı-] *n* : antiimperialismo *m*
anti–imperialist [,æntiım'pıriəlıst, ,æntaı-] *adj* : antiimperialista
anti–inflammatory [,ætiın'flæmətori] *adj* : antiinflamatorio
anti–inflationary [,æntiın'fleıʃə,nɛri, ,æntaı-] *adj* : antiinflacionario
antimony ['æntə,mo:ni] *n* : antimonio *m*
antipathy [æn'tıpəθi] *n*, *pl* -thies : antipatía *f*, aversión *f*
antiperspirant [,ænti'pərspərənt, ,æntaı-] *n* : antitranspirante *m*
antiquarian[1] [,æntə'kweriən] *adj* : antiguo, anticuario ⟨an antiquarian book : un libro antiguo⟩
antiquarian[2] *n* : anticuario *m*, -ria *f*
antiquary ['æntə,kweri] *n* → antiquarian[2]
antiquated ['æntə,kweıṭəd] *adj* : anticuado, pasado de moda
antique[1] [æn'ti:k] *adj* 1 OLD : antiguo, de época ⟨an antique mirror : un espejo antiguo⟩ 2 OLD-FASHIONED : anticuado, pasado de moda
antique[2] *n* : antigüedad *f*
antiquity [æn'tıkwəṭi] *n*, *pl* -ties : antigüedad
antirevolutionary [,ænti,revə'lu:ʃə,nɛri, ,æntaı-] *adj* : antirrevolucionario
anti–Semitic [,æntisə'mıṭık, ,æntaı-] *adj* : antisemita
anti–Semitism [,ænti'sɛmə,tızəm, ,æntaı-] *n* : antisemitismo *m*
antiseptic[1] [,æntə'sɛptık] *adj* : antiséptico — antiseptically [-tıkli] *adv*
antiseptic[2] *n* : antiséptico *m*
antismoking [,ænti'smo:kıŋ, ,æntaı-] *adj* : antitabaco
antisocial [,ænti'so:ʃəl, ,æntaı-] *adj* 1 : antisocial 2 UNSOCIABLE : poco sociable
antitheft [,ænti'θɛft, ,æntaı-] *adj* : antirrobo
antithesis [æn'tıθəsıs] *n*, *pl* -eses [-,si:z] : antítesis *f*
antitoxin [,ænti'taksən, ,æntaı-] *n* : antitoxina *f*
antitrust [,ænti'trʌst, ,æntaı-] *adj* : antimonopolista
antler ['æntlər] *n* : asta *f*, cuerno *m*

antonym ['æntə,nɪm] *n* : antónimo *m*

anus ['eɪnəs] *n* : ano *m*

anvil ['ænvəl, -vɪl] *n* : yunque *m*

anxiety [æŋk'zaɪəti] *n, pl* -eties 1 UN-EASINESS : inquietud *f*, preocupación *f*, ansiedad *f* 2 APPREHENSION : ansiedad *f*, angustia *f*

anxious ['æŋkʃəs] *adj* 1 WORRIED : inquieto, preocupado, ansioso 2 WORRISOME : preocupante, inquietante 3 EAGER : ansioso, deseoso

anxiously ['æŋkʃəsli] *adv* : con inquietud, con ansiedad

any¹ ['ɛni] *adv* 1 : algo ⟨is it any better? : ¿está (algo) mejor?⟩ 2 : para nada ⟨it is not any good : no sirve para nada⟩

any² *adj* 1 : alguno ⟨is there any doubt? : ¿hay alguna duda?⟩ ⟨call me if you have any questions : llámeme si tiene alguna pregunta⟩ 2 : cualquier ⟨I can answer any question : puedo responder a cualquier pregunta⟩ 3 : todo ⟨in any case : en todo caso⟩ 4 : ningún ⟨he would not accept it under any circumstances : no lo aceptaría bajo ninguna circunstancia⟩

any³ *pron* 1 : alguno *m*, -na *f* ⟨are there any left? : ¿queda alguno?⟩ 2 : ninguno *m*, -na *f* ⟨I don't want any : no quiero ninguno⟩

anybody ['ɛni,bʌdi, -,bɑ-] → anyone

anyhow ['ɛni,haʊ] *adv* 1 HAPHAZARDLY : de cualquier manera 2 IN ANY CASE : de todos modos, en todo caso

anymore [,ɛni'mor] *adv* 1 : ya, ya más ⟨he doesn't dance anymore : ya no baila más⟩ 2 : todavía ⟨do they sing anymore? : ¿cantan todavía?⟩

anyone ['ɛni,wʌn] *pron* 1 : alguien ⟨is anyone here? : ¿hay alguien aquí?⟩ ⟨if anyone wants to come : si alguno quiere venir⟩ 2 : cualquiera ⟨anyone can play : cualquiera puede jugar⟩ 3 : nadie ⟨I don't want anyone here : no quiero a nadie aquí⟩

anyplace ['ɛni,pleɪs] → anywhere

anything ['ɛni,θɪŋ] *pron* 1 : algo, alguna cosa ⟨do you want anything? : ¿quieres algo?, ¿quieres alguna cosa?⟩ 2 : nada ⟨hardly anything : casi nada⟩ 3 : cualquier cosa ⟨I eat anything : como de todo⟩

anytime ['ɛni,taɪm] *adv* : en cualquier momento, a cualquier hora, cuando sea

anyway ['ɛni,weɪ] → anyhow

anywhere ['ɛni,hwɛr] *adv* 1 : en algún sitio, en alguna parte ⟨do you see it anywhere? : ¿lo ves en alguna parte?⟩ 2 : en ningún sitio, por ninguna parte ⟨I can't find it anywhere : no puedo encontrarlo por ninguna parte⟩ 3 : en cualquier parte, dondequiera, donde sea ⟨put it anywhere : ponlo dondequiera⟩

aorta [eɪ'ɔrtə] *n, pl* -tas *or* -tae [-ti, -taɪ] : aorta *f*

Apache [ə'pætʃi] *n, pl* Apache *or* Apaches : apache *mf*

apart [ə'pɑrt] *adv* 1 SEPARATELY : aparte, separadamente 2 ASIDE : aparte, a un lado 3 to fall apart : deshacerse, hacerse pedazos 4 to take apart : desmontar, desmantelar

apartheid [ə'pɑr,teɪt, -,taɪt] *n* : apartheid *m*

apartment [ə'pɑrtmənt] *n* : apartamento *m*, departamento *m*, piso *m Spain*

apathetic [,æpə'θɛtɪk] *adj* : apático, indiferente — apathetically [-tɪkli] *adv*

apathy ['æpəθi] *n* : apatía *f*, indiferencia *f*

ape¹ ['eɪp] *vt* aped; aping : imitar, remedar

ape² *n* : simio *m*; mono *m*, -na *f*

aperitif [ə,pɛrə'ti:f] *n* : aperitivo *m*

aperture ['æpərtʃər, -,tʃʊr] *n* : abertura *f*, rendija *f*, apertura *f* (en fotografía)

apex ['eɪ,pɛks] *n, pl* apexes *or* apices ['eɪpə,si:z, 'æ-] : ápice *m*, cúspide *f*, cima *f*

aphid ['eɪfɪd, 'æ-] *n* : áfido *m*

aphorism ['æfə,rɪzəm] *n* : aforismo *m*

aphrodisiac [,æfrə'di:zi,æk, -'dɪ-] *n* : afrodisíaco *m*

apiary ['eɪpi,ɛri] *n, pl* -aries : apiario *m*, colmenar *m*

apiece [ə'pi:s] *adv* : cada uno

aplenty [ə'plɛnti] *adj* : en abundancia

aplomb [ə'plɑm, -'plʌm] *n* : aplomo *m*

apocalypse [ə'pɑkə,lɪps] *n* : apocalipsis *m*

apocalyptic [ə,pɑkə'lɪptɪk] *adj* : apocalíptico

apocrypha [ə'pɑkrəfə] *n* : textos *mpl* apócrifos

apocryphal [ə'pɑkrəfəl] *adj* : apócrifo

apologetic [ə,pɑlə'dʒɛtɪk] *adj* : lleno de disculpas

apologetically [ə,pɑlə'dʒɛtɪkli] *adv* : disculpándose, con aire de disculpas

apologize [ə'pɑlə,dʒaɪz] *vi* -gized; -gizing : disculparse, pedir perdón

apology [ə'pɑlədʒi] *n, pl* -gies : disculpa *f*, excusa *f*

apoplectic [,æpə'plɛktɪk] *adj* : apoplético

apoplexy ['æpə,plɛksi] *n* : apoplejía *f*

apostasy [ə'pɑstəsi] *n, pl* -sies : apostasía *f*

apostate [ə'pɑs,teɪt] *n* : apóstata *mf*

apostle [ə'pɑsəl] *n* : apóstol *m*

apostolic [,æpə'stɑlɪk] *adj* : apostólico

apostrophe [ə'pɑstrə,fi:] *n* : apóstrofo *m* (ortográfico)

apothecary [ə'pɑθə,kɛri] *n, pl* -caries : boticario *m*, -ria *f*

appall [ə'pɔl] *vt* : consternar, horrorizar

apparatus [,æpə'rætəs, -'reɪ-] *n, pl* -tuses *or* -tus : aparato *m*, equipo *m*

apparel [ə'pærəl] *n* : atavío *m*, ropa *f*

apparent [ə'pærənt] *adj* 1 VISIBLE : visible 2 OBVIOUS : claro, evidente, manifiesto 3 SEEMING : aparente, ostensible

apparently [ə'pærəntli] *adv* : aparentemente, al parecer

apparition [ˌæpə'rɪʃən] *n* : aparición *f*, visión *f*

appeal¹ [ə'pi:l] *vt* : apelar ⟨to appeal a decision : apelar contra una decisión⟩ — *vi* **1 to appeal for** : pedir, solicitar **2 to appeal to** : atraer a ⟨that doesn't appeal to me : eso no me atrae⟩

appeal² *n* **1** : apelación *f* (en derecho) **2** PLEA : ruego *m*, súplica *f* **3** ATTRACTION : atracción *f*, atractivo *m*, interés *m*

appear [ə'pɪr] *vi* **1** : aparecer, aparecerse, presentarse ⟨he suddenly appeared : apareció de repente⟩ **2** COME OUT : aparecer, salir, publicarse **3** : comparecer (ante el tribunal), actuar (en el teatro) **4** SEEM : parecer

appearance [ə'pɪrənts] *n* **1** APPEARING : aparición *f*, presentación *f*, comparecencia *f* (ante un tribunal), publicación *f* (de un libro) **2** LOOK : apariencia *f*, aspecto *m*

appease [ə'pi:z] *vt* **-peased; -peasing 1** CALM, PACIFY : aplacar, apaciguar, sosegar **2** SATISFY : satisfacer, mitigar

appeasement [ə'pi:zmənt] *n* : aplacamiento *m*, apaciguamiento *m*

append [ə'pɛnd] *vt* : agregar, añadir, adjuntar

appendage [ə'pɛndɪdʒ] *n* **1** ADDITION : apéndice *m*, añadidura *f* **2** LIMB : miembro *m*, extremidad *f*

appendectomy [ˌæpən'dɛktəmi] *n, pl* **-mies** : apendicectomía *f*

appendicitis [ə,pɛndə'saɪtəs] *n* : apendicitis *f*

appendix [ə'pɛndɪks] *n, pl* **-dixes** *or* **-dices** [-də,si:z] : apéndice *m*

appetite ['æpə,taɪt] *n* **1** CRAVING : apetito *m*, deseo *m*, ganas *fpl* **2** PREFERENCE : gusto *m*, preferencia *f* ⟨the cultural appetites of today : los gustos culturales de hoy⟩

appetizer ['æpə,taɪzər] *n* : aperitivo *m*, entremés *m*, botana *f Mex*, tapa *f Spain*

appetizing ['æpə,taɪzɪŋ] *adj* : apetecible, apetitoso — **appetizingly** [-zɪŋli] *adv*

applaud [ə'plɔd] *v* : aplaudir

applause [ə'plɔz] *n* : aplauso *m*

apple ['æpəl] *n* : manzana *f*

appliance [ə'plaɪənts] *n* **1** : aparato *m* **2 household appliance** : electrodoméstico *m*, aparato *m* electrodoméstico

applicability [ˌæplɪkə'bɪləti, ə,plɪkə-] *n* : aplicabilidad *f*

applicable ['æplɪkəbəl, ə'plɪkə-] *adj* : aplicable, pertinente

applicant ['æplɪkənt] *n* : solicitante *mf*, aspirante *mf*; postulante *mf*; candidato *m*, -ta *f*

application [ˌæplə'keɪʃən] *n* **1** USE : aplicación *f*, empleo *m*, uso *m* **2** DILIGENCE : aplicación *f*, diligencia *f*, dedicación *f* **3** REQUEST : solicitud *f*, petición *f*, demanda *f*

applicator ['æplə,keɪtər] *n* : aplicador *m*

appliqué¹ [ˌæplə'keɪ] *vt* : decorar con apliques

appliqué² *n* : aplique *m*

apply [ə'plaɪ] *v* **-plied; -plying** *vt* **1** : aplicar (una sustancia, los frenos, el conocimiento) **2 to apply oneself** : dedicarse, aplicarse — *vi* **1** : aplicarse, referirse ⟨the rules apply to everyone : las reglas se aplican a todos⟩ **2 to apply for** : solicitar, pedir

appoint [ə'pɔɪnt] *vt* **1** NAME : nombrar, designar **2** FIX, SET : fijar, señalar, designar ⟨to appoint a date : fijar una fecha⟩ **3** EQUIP : equipar ⟨a well-appointed office : una oficina bien equipada⟩

appointee [ə,pɔɪn'ti:, ˌæ-] *n* : persona *f* designada

appointment [ə'pɔɪntmənt] *n* **1** APPOINTING : nombramiento *m*, designación *f* **2** ENGAGEMENT : cita *f*, hora *f* **3** POST : puesto *m*

apportion [ə'porʃən] *vt* : distribuir, repartir

apportionment [ə'porʃənmənt] *n* : distribución *f*, repartición *f*, reparto *m*

apposite ['æpəzət] *adj* : apropiado, oportuno, pertinente — **appositely** *adv*

appraisal [ə'preɪzəl] *n* : evaluación *f*, valoración *f*, tasación *f*, apreciación *f*

appraise [ə'preɪz] *vt* **-praised; -praising** : evaluar, valorar, tasar, apreciar

appraiser [ə'preɪzər] *n* : tasador *m*, -dora *f*

appreciable [ə'pri:ʃəbəl, -'prɪʃiə-] *adj* : apreciable, sensible, considerable — **appreciably** [-bli] *adv*

appreciate [ə'pri:ʃi,eɪt, -'prɪ-] *v* **-ated; -ating** *vt* **1** VALUE : apreciar, valorar **2** : agradecer ⟨we appreciate his frankness : agradecemos su franqueza⟩ **3** UNDERSTAND : darse cuenta de, entender — *vi* : apreciarse, valorizarse

appreciation [ə,pri:ʃi'eɪʃən, -,prɪ-] *n* **1** GRATITUDE : agradecimiento *m*, reconocimiento *m* **2** VALUING : apreciación *f*, valoración *f*, estimación *f* ⟨art appreciation : apreciación artística⟩ **3** UNDERSTANDING : comprensión *f*, entendimiento *m*

appreciative [ə'pri:ʃətɪv, -'prɪ-; ə'pri:ʃi ,eɪ-] *adj* **1** : apreciativo ⟨an appreciative audience : un público apreciativo⟩ **2** GRATEFUL : agradecido **3** ADMIRING : de admiración

apprehend [ˌæprɪ'hɛnd] *vt* **1** ARREST : aprehender, detener, arrestar **2** DREAD : temer **3** COMPREHEND : comprender, entender

apprehension [ˌæprɪ'hɛnʃən] *n* **1** ARREST : arresto *m*, detención *f*, aprehensión *f* **2** ANXIETY : aprensión *f*, ansiedad *f*, temor *m* **3** UNDERSTANDING : comprensión *f*, percepción *f*

apprehensive [ˌæprɪ'hɛnsɪv] *adj* : aprensivo, inquieto — **apprehensively** *adv*

apprentice¹ [ə'prɛntɪs] *vt* **-ticed; -ticing** : colocar de aprendiz
apprentice² *n* : aprendiz *m*, -diza *f*
apprenticeship [ə'prɛntɪsˌʃɪp] *n* : aprendizaje *f*
apprise [ə'praɪz] *vt* **-prised; -prising** : informar, avisar
approach¹ [ə'proːtʃ] *vt* **1** NEAR : acercarse a **2** APPROXIMATE : aproximarse a **3** : abordar, dirigirse a ⟨I approached my boss with the proposal : me dirigí a mi jefe con la propuesta⟩ **4** TACKLE : abordar, enfocar, considerar — *vi* : acercarse, aproximarse
approach² *n* **1** NEARING : acercamiento *m*, aproximación *f* **2** POSITION : enfoque *m*, planteamiento *m* **3** OFFER : propuesta *f*, oferta *f* **4** ACCESS : acceso *m*, vía *f* de acceso
approachable [ə'proːtʃəbəl] *adj* : accesible, asequible
approbation [ˌæprə'beɪʃən] *n* : aprobación *f*
appropriate¹ [ə'proːpriˌeɪt] *vt* **-ated; -ating 1** SEIZE : apropiarse de **2** ALLOCATE : destinar, asignar
appropriate² [ə'proːpriət] *adj* : apropiado, adecuado, idóneo — **appropriately** *adv*
appropriateness [ə'proːpriətnəs] *n* : idoneidad *f*, propiedad *f*
appropriation [əˌproːpri'eɪʃən] *n* **1** SEIZURE : apropiación *f* **2** ALLOCATION : asignación *f*
approval [ə'pruːvəl] *n* **1** : aprobación *f*, visto *m* bueno **2 on approval** : a prueba
approve [ə'pruːv] *vt* **-proved; -proving 1** : aprobar, sancionar, darle el visto bueno a **2 to approve of** : consentir en, aprobar ⟨he doesn't approve of smoking : está en contra del tabaco⟩
approximate¹ [ə'praksəˌmeɪt] *vt* **-mated; -mating** : aproximarse a, acercarse a
approximate² [ə'praksəmət] *adj* : aproximado
approximately [ə'praksəmətli] *adv* : aproximadamente, más o menos
approximation [əˌpraksə'meɪʃən] *n* : aproximación *f*
appurtenance [ə'pərtənənts] *n* : accesorio *m*
apricot ['æprəˌkɑt, 'eɪ-] *n* : albaricoque *m*, chabacano *m Mex*
April ['eɪprəl] *n* : abril *m*
apron ['eɪprən] *n* : delantal *m*, mandil *m*
apropos¹ [ˌæprə'poː, 'æprəˌpoː] *adv* : a propósito
apropos² *adj* : pertinente, oportuno, acertado
apropos of *prep* : a propósito de
apt ['æpt] *adj* **1** FITTING : apto, apropiado, acertado, oportuno **2** LIABLE : propenso, inclinado **3** CLEVER, QUICK : listo, despierto
aptitude ['æptəˌtuːd, -ˌtjuːd] *n* **1** : aptitud *f*, capacidad *f* ⟨aptitude test : prueba de aptitud⟩ **2** TALENT : talento *m*, facilidad *f*

aptly ['æptli] *adv* : acertadamente
aqua ['ækwə, 'ɑ-] *n* : color *m* aguamarina
aquarium [ə'kwæriəm] *n*, *pl* **-iums** *or* **-ia** [-iə] : acuario *m*
Aquarius [ə'kwæriəs] *n* : Acuario *mf*
aquatic [ə'kwɑṭɪk, -'kwæ-] *adj* : acuático
aqueduct ['ækwəˌdʌkt] *n* : acueducto *m*
aqueous ['eɪkwiəs, 'æ-] *adj* : acuoso
aquiline ['ækwəˌlaɪn, -lən] *adj* : aguileño
Arab¹ ['ærəb] *adj* : árabe
Arab² *n* : árabe *mf*
arabesque [ˌærə'bɛsk] *n* : arabesco *m*
Arabian¹ [ə'reɪbiən] *adj* : árabe
Arabian² *n* → **Arab²**
Arabic¹ ['ærəbɪk] *adj* : árabe
Arabic² *n* : árabe *m* (idioma)
arable ['ærəbəl] *adj* : arable, cultivable
arbiter ['ɑrbəṭər] *n* : árbitro *m*, -tra *f*
arbitrary ['ɑrbəˌtrɛri] *adj* : arbitrario — **arbitrarily** [ˌɑrbə'trɛrəli] *adv*
arbitrate ['ɑrbəˌtreɪt] *v* **-trated; -trating** : arbitrar
arbitration [ˌɑrbə'treɪʃən] *n* : arbitraje *m*
arbitrator ['ɑrbəˌtreɪṭər] *n* : árbitro *m*, -tra *f*
arbor ['ɑrbər] *n* : cenador *m*, pérgola *f*
arboreal [ɑr'boriəl] *adj* : arbóreo
arc¹ ['ɑrk] *vi* **arced; arcing** : formar un arco
arc² *n* : arco *m*
arcade [ɑr'keɪd] *n* **1** ARCHES : arcada *f* **2** MALL : galería *f* comercial
arcane [ɑr'keɪn] *adj* : arcano, secreto, misterioso
arch¹ ['ɑrtʃ] *vt* : arquear, enarcar — *vi* : formar un arco, arquearse
arch² *adj* **1** CHIEF : principal **2** MISCHIEVOUS : malicioso, pícaro
arch³ *n* : arco *m*
archaeological [ˌɑrkiə'lɑʤɪkəl] *adj* : arqueológico
archaeologist [ˌɑrki'ɑləʤɪst] *n* : arqueólogo *m*, -ga *f*
archaeology *or* **archeology** [ˌɑrki'ɑləʤi] *n* : arqueología *f*
archaic [ɑr'keɪɪk] *adj* : arcaico — **archaically** [-ɪkli] *adv*
archangel ['ɑrkˌeɪnʤəl] *n* : arcángel *m*
archbishop [ɑrtʃ'bɪʃəp] *n* : arzobispo *m*
archdiocese [ɑrtʃ'daɪəsəs, -ˌsiːz, -ˌsiːs] *n* : archidiócesis *f*
archer ['ɑrtʃər] *n* : arquero *m*, -ra *f*
archery ['ɑrtʃəri] *n* : tiro *m* al arco
archetypal [ˌɑrkɪ'taɪpəl] *adj* : arquetípico
archetype ['ɑrkɪˌtaɪp] *n* : arquetipo *m*
archipelago [ˌɑrkə'pɛləˌgoː, ˌɑrtʃə-] *n*, *pl* **-goes** *or* **-gos** [-goːz] : archipiélago *m*
architect ['ɑrkəˌtɛkt] *n* : arquitecto *m*, -ta *f*
architectural [ˌɑrkə'tɛktʃərəl] *adj* : arquitectónico — **architecturally** *adv*
architecture ['ɑrkəˌtɛktʃər] *n* : arquitectura *f*
archive ['ɑrˌkaɪv] *n* *or* **archives** ['ɑrˌkaɪvz] *npl* : archivo *m*

archivist ['ɑrkəvɪst, -ˌkaɪ-] *n* : archivero *m*, -ra *f*; archivista *mf*
archway ['ɑrtʃˌweɪ] *n* : arco *m*, pasadizo *m* abovedado
arctic ['ɑrktɪk, 'ɑrt̬-] *adj* **1** : ártico ⟨arctic regions : zonas árticas⟩ **2** FRIGID : glacial
arctic circle *n* : círculo *m* ártico
ardent ['ɑrdənt] *adj* **1** PASSIONATE : ardiente, fogoso, apasionado **2** FERVENT : ferviente, fervoroso — **ardently** *adv*
ardor ['ɑrdər] *n* : ardor *m*, pasión *f*, fervor *m*
arduous ['ɑrdʒuəs] *adj* : arduo, duro, riguroso — **arduously** *adv*
arduousness ['ɑrdʒuəsnəs] *n* : dureza *f*, rigor *m*
are → **be**
area ['ærɪə] *n* **1** SURFACE : área *f*, superficie *f* **2** REGION : área *f*, región *f*, zona *f* **3** FIELD : área *f*, terreno *m*, campo *m* (de conocimiento)
area code *n* : código *m* de la zona, prefijo *m* Spain
arena [ə'riːnə] *n* **1** : arena *f*, estadio *m* ⟨sports arena : estadio deportivo⟩ **2** : arena *f*, ruedo *m* ⟨the political arena : el ruedo político⟩
Argentine ['ɑrdʒənˌtaɪn, -ˌtiːn] *or* **Argentinean** *or* **Argentinian** [ˌɑrdʒən'tɪniən] *n* : argentino *m*, -na *f* — **Argentine** *or* **Argentinean** *or* **Argentinian** *adj*
argon ['ɑrˌgɑn] *n* : argón *m*
argot ['ɑrgət, -ˌgoː] *n* : argot *m*
arguable ['ɑrgjuəbəl] *adj* : discutible
argue ['ɑrˌgjuː] *v* -**gued**; -**guing** *vi* **1** REASON : argüir, argumentar, razonar **2** DISPUTE : discutir, pelear(se), alegar — *vt* **1** SUGGEST : sugerir **2** MAINTAIN : alegar, argüir, sostener **3** DISCUSS : discutir, debatir
argument ['ɑrgjəmənt] *n* **1** REASONING : argumento *m*, razonamiento *m* **2** DISCUSSION : discusión *f*, debate *m* **3** QUARREL : pelea *f*, riña *f*, disputa *f*
argumentative [ˌɑrgjə'mɛntət̬ɪv] *adj* : discutidor
argyle ['ɑrˌgaɪl] *n* : diseño *m* de rombos
aria ['ɑrɪə] *n* : aria *f*
arid ['ærəd] *adj* : árido
aridity [ə'rɪdət̬i, æ-] *n* : aridez *f*
Aries ['ɛriːz, -iˌiːz] *n* : Aries *mf*
arise [ə'raɪz] *vi* **arose** [ə'roːz]; **arisen** [ə'rɪzən]; **arising 1** ASCEND : ascender, subir, elevarse **2** ORIGINATE : originarse, surgir, presentarse **3** GET UP : levantarse
aristocracy [ˌærə'stɑkrəsi] *n, pl* -**cies** : aristocracia *f*
aristocrat [ə'rɪstəˌkræt] *n* : aristócrata *mf*
aristocratic [əˌrɪstə'kræt̬ɪk] *adj* : aristocrático, noble
arithmetic[1] [ˌærɪθ'mɛt̬ɪk] *or* **arithmetical** [-t̬ɪkəl] *adj* : aritmético
arithmetic[2] [ə'rɪθməˌtɪk] *n* : aritmética
ark ['ɑrk] *n* : arca *f*

arm[1] ['ɑrm] *vt* : armar — *vi* : armarse
arm[2] *n* **1** : brazo *m* (del cuerpo o de un sillón), manga *f* (de una prenda) **2** BRANCH : rama *f*, sección *f* **3** WEAPON : arma *f* ⟨to take up arms : tomar las armas⟩ **4** → **coat of arms**
armada [ɑr'mɑdə, -'meɪ-] *n* : armada *f*, flota *f*
armadillo [ˌɑrmə'dɪlo] *n, pl* -**los** : armadillo *m*
armament ['ɑrməmənt] *n* : armamento *m*
armchair ['ɑrmˌtʃɛr] *n* : butaca *f*, sillón *m*
armed ['ɑrmd] *adj* **1** : armado ⟨armed robbery : robo a mano armada⟩ **2** : armado ⟨armed forces : fuerzas *fpl* armadas
Armenian [ɑr'miːniən] *n* : armenio *m*, -nia *f* — **Armenian** *adj*
armistice ['ɑrməstɪs] *n* : armisticio *m*
armor ['ɑrmər] *n* : armadura *f*, coraza *f*
armored ['ɑrmərd] *adj* : blindado, acorazado
armory ['ɑrməri] *n, pl* -**mories** : arsenal *m* (almacén), armería *f* (museo), fábrica *f* de armas
armpit ['ɑrmˌpɪt] *n* : axila *f*, sobaco *m*
army ['ɑrmi] *n, pl* -**mies 1** : ejército *m* (militar) **2** MULTITUDE : legión *f*, multitud *f*, ejército *m*
aroma [ə'roːmə] *n* : aroma *f*
aromatic [ˌærə'mæt̬ɪk] *adj* : aromático
around[1] [ə'raʊnd] *adv* **1** : de circunferencia ⟨a tree three feet around : un árbol de tres pies de circunferencia⟩ **2** : alrededor, a la redonda ⟨for miles around : por millas a la redonda⟩ ⟨all around : por todos lados, todo alrededor⟩ **3** : por ahí ⟨they're somewhere around : deben estar por ahí⟩ **4** APPROXIMATELY : más o menos, aproximadamente ⟨around 5 o'clock : a eso de las 5⟩ **5 to turn around** : darse la vuelta, voltearse
around[2] *prep* **1** SURROUNDING : alrededor de, en torno a **2** THROUGH : por, en ⟨he traveled around Mexico : viajó por México⟩ ⟨around the house : en casa⟩ **3** : a la vuelta de ⟨around the corner : a la vuelta de la esquina⟩ **4** NEAR : alrededor de, cerca de
arousal [ə'raʊzəl] *n* : excitación *f*
arouse [ə'raʊz] *vt* **aroused; arousing 1** AWAKE : despertar **2** EXCITE : despertar, suscitar, excitar
arraign [ə'reɪn] *vt* : hacer comparecer (ante un tribunal)
arraignment [ə'reɪnmənt] *n* : orden *m* de comparecencia, acusación *f*
arrange [ə'reɪndʒ] *vt* -**ranged**; -**ranging 1** ORDER : arreglar, poner en orden, disponer **2** SETTLE : arreglar, fijar, concertar **3** ADAPT : arreglar, adaptar
arrangement [ə'reɪndʒmənt] *n* **1** ORDER : arreglo *m*, orden *m* **2** ARRANGING : disposición *f* ⟨floral arrangement : arreglo floral⟩ **3** AGREEMENT : arreglo *m*, acuerdo *m*, convenio *m* **4 arrange-**

ments *npl* : preparativos *mpl*, planes *mpl*

array¹ [ə'reɪ] *vt* 1 ORDER : poner en orden, presentar, formar 2 GARB : vestir, ataviar, engalanar

array² *n* 1 ORDER : orden *m*, formación *f* 2 ATTIRE : atavío *m*, galas *mpl* 3 RANGE, SELECTION : selección *f*, serie *f*, gama *f* ⟨an array of problems : una serie de problemas⟩

arrears [ə'rɪrz] *npl* : atrasos *mpl* ⟨to be in arrears : estar atrasado en los pagos⟩

arrest¹ [ə'rɛst] *vt* 1 APPREHEND : arrestar, detener 2 CHECK, STOP : detener, parar

arrest² *n* 1 APPREHENSION : arresto *m*, detención *f* ⟨under arrest : detenido⟩ 2 STOPPING : paro *m*

arrival [ə'raɪvəl] *n* : llegada *f*, venida *f*, arribo *m*

arrive [ə'raɪv] *vi* -rived; -riving 1 COME : llegar, arribar 2 SUCCEED : triunfar, tener éxito

arrogance ['ærəgənts] *n* : arrogancia *f*, soberbia *f*, altanería *f*, altivez *f*

arrogant ['ærəgənt] *adj* : arrogante, soberbio, altanero, altivo — **arrogantly** *adv*

arrogate ['ærə,geɪt] *vt* -gated; -gating to arrogate to oneself : arrogarse

arrow ['æro] *n* : flecha *f*

arrowhead ['æro,hɛd] *n* : punta *f* de flecha

arroyo [ə'rɔɪo] *n* : arroyo *m*

arsenal ['ɑrsənəl] *n* : arsenal *m*

arsenic ['ɑrsənɪk] *n* : arsénico *m*

arson ['ɑrsən] *n* : incendio *m* premeditado

arsonist ['ɑrsənɪst] *n* : incendiario *m*, -ria *f*; pirómano *m*, -na *f*

art ['ɑrt] *n* 1 : arte *m* 2 SKILL : destreza *f*, habilidad *f*, maña *f* 3 **arts** *npl* : letras *fpl* (en la educación) 4 **fine arts** : bellas artes *fpl*

arterial [ɑr'tɪriəl] *adj* : arterial

arteriosclerosis [ɑr,tɪrioʊsklə'roʊsɪs] *n* : arteriosclerosis *f*

artery ['ɑrtəri] *n, pl* -teries 1 : arteria *f* 2 THOROUGHFARE : carretera *f* principal, arteria *f*

artesian well [ɑr'tiːʒən] *n* : pozo *m* artesiano

artful ['ɑrtfəl] *adj* 1 INGENIOUS : ingenioso, diestro 2 CRAFTY : astuto, taimado, ladino, artero — **artfully** *adv*

arthritic [ɑr'θrɪtɪk] *adj* : artrítico

arthritis [ɑr'θraɪtəs] *n, pl* -tides [ɑr-'θrɪtə,diːz] : artritis *f*

arthropod ['ɑrθrə,pɑd] *n* : artrópodo *m*

artichoke ['ɑrtə,tʃoʊk] *n* : alcachofa *f*

article ['ɑrtɪkəl] *n* 1 ITEM : artículo *m*, objeto *m* 2 ESSAY : artículo *m* 3 CLAUSE : artículo *m*, cláusula *f* 4 : artículo *m* ⟨definite article : artículo determinado⟩

articulate¹ [ɑr'tɪkjə,leɪt] *vt* -lated; -lating 1 UTTER : articular, enunciar, expresar 2 CONNECT : articular (en anatomía)

articulate² [ɑr'tɪkjələt] *adj* **to be articulate** : poder articular palabras, expresarse bien

articulately [ɑr'tɪkjələtli] *adv* : elocuentemente, con fluidez

articulateness [ɑr'tɪkjələtnəs] *n* : elocuencia *f*, fluidez *f*

articulation [ɑr,tɪkjə'leɪʃən] *n* 1 JOINT : articulación *f* 2 UTTERANCE : articulación *f*, declaración *f* 3 ENUNCIATION : articulación *f*, pronunciación *f*

artifact ['ɑrtə,fækt] *n* : artefacto *m*

artifice ['ɑrtəfəs] *n* : artificio *m*

artificial [,ɑrtə'fɪʃəl] *adj* 1 SYNTHETIC : artificial, sintético 2 FEIGNED : artificial, falso, afectado

artificially [,ɑrtə'fɪʃəli] *adv* : artificialmente, con afectación

artillery [ɑr'tɪləri] *n, pl* -leries : artillería *f*

artisan ['ɑrtəzən, -sən] *n* : artesano *m*, -na *f*

artist ['ɑrtɪst] *n* : artista *mf*

artistic [ɑr'tɪstɪk] *adj* : artístico — **artistically** [-tɪkli] *adv*

artistry ['ɑrtəstri] *n* : maestría *f*, arte *m*

artless ['ɑrtləs] *adj* : sencillo, natural, ingenuo, cándido — **artlessly** *adv*

artlessness ['ɑrtləsnəs] *n* : ingenuidad *f*, candidez *f*

arty ['ɑrti] *adj* **artier; -est** : pretenciosamente artístico

as¹ ['æz] *adv* 1 : tan, tanto ⟨this one's not as difficult : éste no es tan difícil⟩ 2 : como ⟨some trees, as oak and pine : algunos árboles, como el roble y el pino⟩

as² *conj* 1 LIKE : como, igual que 2 WHEN, WHILE : cuando, mientras, a la vez que 3 BECAUSE : porque 4 THOUGH : aunque, por más que ⟨strange as it may appear : por extraño que parezca⟩ 5 **as is** : tal como está

as³ *prep* 1 : de ⟨I met her as a child : la conocí de pequeña⟩ 2 LIKE : como ⟨behave as a man : compórtate como un hombre⟩

as⁴ *pron* : que ⟨in the same building as my brother : en el mismo edificio que mi hermano⟩

asbestos [æz'bɛstəs, æs-] *n* : asbesto *m*, amianto *m*

ascend [ə'sɛnd] *vi* : ascender, subir — *vt* : subir, subir a, escalar

ascendancy [ə'sɛndəntsi] *n* : ascendiente *m*, predominio *m*

ascendant¹ [ə'sɛndənt] *adj* 1 RISING : ascendente 2 DOMINANT : superior, dominante

ascendant² *n* **to be in the ascendant** : estar en alza, ir ganando predominio

ascension [ə'sɛntʃən] *n* : ascensión *f*

ascent [ə'sɛnt] *n* 1 RISE : ascensión *f*, subida *f*, ascenso *m* 2 SLOPE : cuesta *f*, pendiente *f*

ascertain [,æsər'teɪn] *vt* : determinar, establecer, averiguar

ascertainable [,æsər'teɪnəbəl] *adj* : determinable, averiguable

ascetic¹ [ə'sɛtɪk] *adj* : ascético
ascetic² *n* : asceta *mf*
asceticism [ə'sɛtə,sɪzəm] *n* : ascetismo *m*
ascribable [ə'skraɪbəbəl] *adj* : atribuible, imputable
ascribe [ə'skraɪb] *vt* -**cribed**; -**cribing** : atribuir, imputar
aseptic [eɪ'sɛptɪk] *adj* : aséptico
asexual [ˌeɪ'sɛkʃʊəl] *adj* : asexual
as for *prep* CONCERNING : en cuanto a, respecto a, para
ash ['æʃ] *n* **1** : ceniza *f* ⟨to reduce to ashes : reducir a cenizas⟩ **2** : fresno *m* (árbol)
ashamed [ə'ʃeɪmd] *adj* : avergonzado, abochornado, apenado — **ashamedly** [ə'ʃeɪmədli] *adv*
ashen ['æʃən] *adj* : lívido, ceniciento, pálido
ashore [ə'ʃor] *adv* **1** : en tierra **2 to go ashore** : desembarcar
ashtray ['æʃ,treɪ] *n* : cenicero *m*
Asian¹ ['eɪʒən, -ʃən] *adj* : asiático
Asian² *n* : asiático *m*, -ca *f*
aside [ə'saɪd] *adv* **1** : a un lado ⟨to step aside : hacerse a un lado⟩ **2** : de lado, aparte ⟨jesting aside : bromas aparte⟩ **3 to set aside** : guardar, apartar, reservar
aside from *prep* **1** BESIDES : además de **2** EXCEPT : aparte de, menos
as if *conj* : como si
asinine ['æsən,aɪn] *adj* : necio, estúpido
ask ['æsk] *vt* **1** : preguntar ⟨ask him if he's coming : pregúntale si viene⟩ **2** REQUEST : pedir, solicitar ⟨to ask a favor : pedir un favor⟩ **3** INVITE : invitar — *vi* **1** INQUIRE : preguntar ⟨I asked about her children : pregunté por sus niños⟩ **2** REQUEST : pedir ⟨we asked for help : pedimos ayuda⟩
askance [ə'skænts] *adv* **1** SIDELONG : de reojo, de soslayo **2** SUSPICIOUSLY : con recelo, con desconfianza
askew [ə'skju:] *adj* : torcido, ladeado
asleep [ə'sli:p] *adj* **1** : dormido, durmiendo **2 to fall asleep** : quedarse dormido
as of *prep* : desde, a partir de
asparagus [ə'spærəgəs] *n* : espárrago *m*
aspect ['æ,spɛkt] *n* : aspecto *m*
aspen ['æspən] *n* : álamo *m* temblón
asperity [æ'spɛrəti, ə-] *n*, *pl* -**ties** : aspereza *f*
aspersion [ə'spərʒən] *n* : difamación *f*, calumnia *f*
asphalt ['æs,fɔlt] *n* : asfalto *m*
asphyxia [æ'sfɪksiə, ə-] *n* : asfixia *f*
asphyxiate [æ'sfɪksi,eɪt] *v* -**ated**; -**ating** *vt* : asfixiar — *vi* : asfixiarse
asphyxiation [æ,sfɪksi'eɪʃən] *n* : asfixia *f*
aspirant ['æspərənt, ə'spaɪrənt] *n* : aspirante *mf*, pretendiente *mf*
aspiration [ˌæspə'reɪʃən] *n* **1** DESIRE : aspiración *f*, anhelo *m*, ambición *f* **2** BREATHING : aspiración *f*

aspire [ə'spaɪr] *vi* -**pired**; -**piring** : aspirar
aspirin ['æsprən, 'æspə-] *n*, *pl* **aspirin** *or* **aspirins** : aspirina *f*
ass ['æs] *n* **1** : asno *m* **2** IDIOT : imbécil *mf*, idiota *mf*
assail [ə'seɪl] *vt* : atacar, asaltar
assailant [ə'seɪlənt] *n* : asaltante *mf*, atacante *mf*
assassin [ə'sæsən] *n* : asesino *m*, -na *f*
assassinate [ə'sæsən,eɪt] *vt* -**nated**; -**nating** : asesinar
assassination [ə,sæsən'eɪʃən] *n* : asesinato *m*
assault¹ [ə'sɔlt] *vt* : atacar, asaltar, agredir
assault² *n* : ataque *m*, asalto *m*, agresión *f*
assay¹ [æ'seɪ, 'æ,seɪ] *vt* : ensayar
assay² ['æ,seɪ, æ'seɪ] *n* : ensayo *m*
assemble [ə'sɛmbəl] *v* -**bled**; -**bling** *vt* **1** GATHER : reunir, recoger, juntar **2** CONSTRUCT : ensamblar, montar, construir — *vi* : reunirse, congregarse
assembly [ə'sɛmbli] *n*, *pl* -**blies** **1** MEETING : reunión *f* **2** CONSTRUCTING : ensamblaje *m*, montaje *m*
assemblyman [ə'sɛmblimən] *n*, *pl* -**men** [-mən, -,mɛn] : asambleísta *m*
assemblywoman [ə'sɛmbli,wʊmən] *n*, *pl* -**women** [-,wɪmən] : asambleísta *f*
assent¹ [ə'sɛnt] *vi* : asentir, consentir
assent² *n* : asentimiento *m*, aprobación *f*
assert [ə'sərt] *vt* **1** AFFIRM : afirmar, aseverar, mantener **2 to assert oneself** : imponerse, hacerse valer
assertion [ə'sərʃən] *n* : afirmación *f*, aseveración *f*, aserto *m*
assertive [ə'sərt̬ɪv] *adj* : firme, enérgico
assertiveness [ə'sərt̬ɪvnəs] *n* : seguridad *f* en sí mismo
assess [ə'sɛs] *vt* **1** IMPOSE : gravar (un impuesto), imponer **2** EVALUATE : evaluar, valorar, aquilatar
assessment [ə'sɛsmənt] *n* : evaluación *f*, valoración *f*
assessor [ə'sɛsər] *n* : evaluador *m*, -dora *f*; tasador *m*, -dora *f*
asset ['æ,sɛt] *n* **1** : ventaja *f*, recurso *m* **2 assets** *npl* : bienes *mpl*, activo *m* ⟨assets and liabilities : activo y pasivo⟩
assiduous [ə'sɪdʒʊəs] *adj* : diligente, aplicado, asiduo — **assiduously** *adv*
assign [ə'saɪn] *vt* **1** APPOINT : designar, nombrar **2** ALLOT : asignar, señalar **3** ATTRIBUTE : atribuir, dar, conceder
assignment [ə'saɪnmənt] *n* **1** TASK : función *f*, tarea *f*, misión *f* **2** HOMEWORK : tarea *f*, asignación *f* *PRi*, deberes *mpl Spain* **3** APPOINTMENT : nombramiento *m* **4** ALLOCATION : asignación *f*
assimilate [ə'sɪmə,leɪt] *v* -**lated**; -**lating** *vt* : asimilar — *vi* : adaptarse, integrarse
assimilation [ə,sɪmə'leɪʃən] *n* : asimilación *f*
assist¹ [ə'sɪst] *vt* : asistir, ayudar
assist² *n* : asistencia *f*, contribución *f*

assistance [ə'sɪstənts] *n* : asistencia *f*, ayuda *f*, auxilio *m*

assistant [ə'sɪstənt] *n* : ayudante *mf*, asistente *mf*

associate¹ [ə'soːʃiˌeɪt, -si-] *v* **-ated; -ating** *vt* **1** CONNECT, RELATE : asociar, relacionar **2 to be associated with** : estar relacionado con, estar vinculado a — *vi* **to associate with** : relacionarse con, frecuentar

associate² [ə'soːʃiət, -siət] *n* : asociado *m*, -da *f*; colega *mf*; socio *m*, -cia *f*

association [əˌsoːʃi'eɪʃən, -si-] *n* **1** ORGANIZATION : asociación *f*, sociedad *f* **2** RELATIONSHIP : asociación *f*, relación *f*

as soon as *conj* : en cuanto, tan pronto como

assorted [ə'sɔrtəd] *adj* : surtido

assortment [ə'sɔrtmənt] *n* : surtido *m*, variedad *f*, colección *f*

assuage [ə'sweɪdʒ] *vt* **-suaged; -suaging 1** EASE : aliviar, mitigar **2** CALM : calmar, aplacar **3** SATISFY : saciar, satisfacer

assume [ə'suːm] *vt* **-sumed; -suming 1** SUPPOSE : suponer, asumir **2** UNDERTAKE : asumir, encargarse de **3** TAKE ON : adquirir, adoptar, tomar ⟨to assume importance : tomar importancia⟩ **4** FEIGN : adoptar, afectar, simular

assumption [ə'sʌmpʃən] *n* : asunción *f*, presunción *f*

assurance [ə'ʃurənts] *n* **1** CERTAINTY : certidumbre *f*, certeza *f* **2** CONFIDENCE : confianza *f*, aplomo *m*, seguridad *f*

assure [ə'ʃur] *vt* **-sured; -suring** : asegurar, garantizar ⟨I assure you that I'll do it : te aseguro que lo haré⟩

assured [ə'ʃurd] *adj* **1** CERTAIN : seguro, asegurado **2** CONFIDENT : confiado, seguro de sí mismo

aster ['æstər] *n* : aster *m*

asterisk ['æstəˌrɪsk] *n* : asterisco *m*

astern [ə'stərn] *adv* **1** BEHIND : detrás, a popa **2** BACKWARDS : hacia atrás

asteroid ['æstəˌrɔɪd] *n* : asteroide *m*

asthma ['æzmə] *n* : asma *m*

asthmatic [æz'mætɪk] *adj* : asmático

as though → **as if**

astigmatism [ə'stɪgməˌtɪzəm] *n* : astigmatismo *m*

as to *prep* **1** ABOUT : sobre, acerca de **2** → **according to**

astonish [ə'stɑnɪʃ] *vt* : asombrar, sorprender, pasmar

astonishing [ə'stɑnɪʃɪŋ] *adj* : asombroso, sorprendente, increíble — **astonishingly** *adv*

astonishment [ə'stɑnɪʃmənt] *n* : asombro *m*, estupefacción *f*, sorpresa *f*

astound [ə'staund] *vt* : asombrar, pasmar, dejar estupefacto

astounding [ə'staundɪŋ] *adj* : asombroso, pasmoso — **astoundingly** *adv*

astraddle [ə'strædəl] *adv* : a horcajadas

astral ['æstrəl] *adj* : astral

astray [ə'streɪ] *adv* & *adj* : perdido, extraviado, descarriado

astride [ə'straɪd] *adv* : a horcajadas

astringency [ə'strɪndʒəntsi] *n* : astringencia *f*

astringent¹ [ə'strɪndʒənt] *adj* : astringente

astringent² *n* : astringente *m*

astrologer [ə'strɑlədʒər] *n* : astrólogo *m*, -ga *f*

astrological [ˌæstrə'lɑdʒɪkəl] *adj* : astrológico

astrology [ə'strɑlədʒi] *n* : astrología *f*

astronaut ['æstrəˌnɔt] *n* : astronauta *mf*

astronautic [ˌæstrə'nɔtɪk] *or* **astronautical** [-tɪkəl] *adj* : astronáutico

astronautics [ˌæstrə'nɔtɪks] *ns & pl* : astronáutica *f*

astronomer [ə'strɑnəmər] *n* : astrónomo *m*, -ma *f*

astronomical [ˌæstrə'nɑmɪkəl] *adj* **1** : astronómico **2** ENORMOUS : astronómico, enorme, gigantesco

astronomy [ə'strɑnəmi] *n, pl* **-mies** : astronomía *f*

astute [ə'stuːt, -'stjuːt] *adj* : astuto, sagaz, perspicaz — **astutely** *adv*

astuteness [ə'stuːtnəs, -'stjuːt-] *n* : astucia *f*, sagacidad *f*, perspicacia *f*

asunder [ə'sʌndər] *adv* : en dos, en pedazos ⟨to tear asunder : hacer pedazos⟩

as well as¹ *conj* : tanto como

as well as² *prep* BESIDES : además de, aparte de

as yet *adv* : aún, todavía

asylum [ə'saɪləm] *n* **1** REFUGE : refugio *m*, santuario *m*, asilo *m* **2 insane asylum** : manicomio *m*

asymmetrical [ˌeɪsə'metrɪkəl] *or* **asymmetric** [-'metrɪk] *adj* : asimétrico

asymmetry [ˌeɪ'sɪmətri] *n* : asimetría *f*

at ['æt] *prep* **1** : en ⟨at the top : en lo alto⟩ ⟨at peace : en paz⟩ ⟨at Ann's house : en casa de Ana⟩ **2** : a ⟨at the rear : al fondo⟩ ⟨at 10 o'clock : a las diez⟩ **3** : por ⟨at last : por fin⟩ ⟨to be surprised at something : sorprenderse por algo⟩ **4** : de ⟨he's laughing at you : está riéndose de ti⟩ **5** : para ⟨you're good at this : eres bueno para esto⟩

at all *adv* : en absoluto, para nada

ate → **eat**

atheism ['eɪθiˌɪzəm] *n* : ateísmo *m*

atheist ['eɪθiːst] *n* : ateo *m*, atea *f*

atheistic [ˌeɪθi'ɪstɪk] *adj* : ateo

athlete ['æθˌliːt] *n* : atleta *mf*

athletic [æθ'letɪk] *adj* : atlético

athletics [æθ'letɪks] *ns & pl* : atletismo *m*

Atlantic [ət'læntɪk, æt-] *adj* : atlántico

atlas ['ætləs] *n* : atlas *m*

ATM [ˌeɪˌtiː'em] *n* : cajero *m* automático

atmosphere ['ætməˌsfɪr] *n* **1** AIR : atmósfera *f*, aire *m* **2** AMBIENCE : ambiente *m*, atmósfera *f*, clima *m*

atmospheric [ˌætmə'sfɪrɪk, -'sfer-] *adj* : atmosférico — **atmospherically** [-ɪkli] *adv*

atoll ['æˌtɔl, 'eɪ-, -ˌtɑl] *n* : atolón *m*
atom ['æt̬əm] *n* **1** : átomo *m* **2** SPECK
: ápice *m*, pizca *f*
atomic [ə'tɑmɪk] *adj* : atómico
atomic bomb *n* : bomba *f* atómica
atomizer ['æt̬əˌmaɪzər] *n* : atomizador
m, pulverizador *m*
atone [ə'toːn] *vt* **atoned; atoning to**
atone for : expiar
atonement [ə'toːnmənt] *n* : expiación *f*,
desagravio *m*
atop¹ [ə'tɑp] *adj* : encima
atop² *prep* : encima de, sobre
atrium ['eɪtriəm] *n, pl* **atria** [-triə] *or* **atriums** **1** : atrio *m* **2** : aurícula *f* (del
corazón)
atrocious [ə'troːʃəs] *adj* : atroz — **atrociously** *adv*
atrocity [ə'trɑsət̬i] *n, pl* **-ties** : atrocidad
f
atrophy¹ ['ætrəfi] *vt* **-phied; -phying**
: atrofiar
atrophy² *n, pl* **-phies** : atrofia *f*
attach [ə'tætʃ] *vt* **1** FASTEN : sujetar, atar,
amarrar, pegar **2** JOIN : juntar, adjuntar **3** ATTRIBUTE : dar, atribuir ⟨I attached little importance to it : le di poca
importancia⟩ **4** SEIZE : embargar **5 to**
become attached to someone : encariñarse con alguien
attaché [ˌæt̬ə'ʃeɪ, ˌæˌtæ-, ə̩tæ-] *n* : agregado *m*, -da *f*
attachment [ə'tætʃmənt] *n* **1** ACCESSORY : accesorio *m* **2** CONNECTION
: conexión *f*, acoplamiento *m* **3** FONDNESS : apego *m*, cariño *m*, afición *f*
attack¹ [ə'tæk] *vt* **1** ASSAULT : atacar,
asaltar, agredir **2** TACKLE : acometer,
combatir, enfrentarse con
attack² *n* **1** : ataque *m*, asalto *m*,
acometida *f* ⟨to launch an attack : lanzar un ataque⟩ **2** : ataque *m*, crisis *f*
⟨heart attack : ataque cardíaco, infarto⟩ ⟨attack of nerves : crisis nerviosa⟩
attacker [ə'tækər] *n* : asaltante *mf*
attain [ə'teɪn] *vt* **1** ACHIEVE : lograr, conseguir, alcanzar, realizar **2** REACH : alcanzar, llegar a
attainable [ə'teɪnəbəl] *adj* : alcanzable,
realizable, asequible
attainment [ə'teɪnmənt] *n* : logro *m*, consecución *f*, realización *f*
attempt¹ [ə'tɛmpt] *vt* : intentar, tratar de
attempt² *n* : intento *m*, tentativa *f*
attend [ə'tɛnd] *vt* **1** : asistir a ⟨to attend
a meeting : asistir a una reunión⟩ **2**
: atender, ocuparse de, cuidar ⟨to attend a patient : atender a un paciente⟩
3 HEED : atender a, hacer caso de **4**
ACCOMPANY : acompañar
attendance [ə'tɛndənt̬s] *n* **1** ATTENDING
: asistencia *f* **2** TURNOUT : concurrencia *f*
attendant¹ [ə'tɛndənt] *adj* : concomitante, inherente
attendant² *n* : asistente *mf*, acompañante *mf*, guarda *mf*

attention [ə'tɛntʃən] *n* **1** : atención *f* **2**
to pay attention : prestar atención,
hacer caso **3 to stand at attention** : estar firme
attentive [ə'tɛntɪv] *adj* : atento — **attentively** *adv*
attentiveness [ə'tɛntɪvnəs] *n* **1**
THOUGHTFULNESS : cortesía *f*, consideración *f* **2** CONCENTRATION : atención *f*, concentración *f*
attest [ə'tɛst] *vt* : atestiguar, dar fe de
attestation [ˌæˌts'teɪʃən] *n* : testimonio
m
attic ['æt̬ɪk] *n* : ático *m*, desván *m*,
buhardilla *f*
attire¹ [ə'taɪr] *vt* **-tired; -tiring** : ataviar
attire² *n* : atuendo *m*, atavío *m*
attitude ['æt̬əˌtuːd, -ˌtjuːd] *n* **1** FEELING
: actitud *f* **2** POSTURE : postura *f*
attorney [ə'tərni] *n, pl* **-neys** : abogado
m, -da *f*
attract [ə'trækt] *vt* **1** : atraer **2 to attract**
attention : llamar la atención
attraction [ə'trækʃən] *n* : atracción *f*,
atractivo *m*
attractive [ə'træktɪv] *adj* : atractivo,
atrayente
attractively [ə'træktɪvli] *adv* : de manera atractiva, de buen gusto, hermosamente
attractiveness [ə'træktɪvnəs] *n* : atractivo *m*
attributable [ə'trɪbjut̬əbəl] *adj* : atribuible, imputable
attribute¹ [ə'trɪˌbjuːt] *vt* **-tributed; -tributing** : atribuir
attribute² ['ætrəˌbjuːt] *n* : atributo *m*,
cualidad *f*
attribution [ˌætrə'bjuːʃən] *n* : atribución
f
attune [ə'tuːn, -'tjuːn] *vt* **-tuned; -tuning**
1 ADAPT : adaptar, adecuar **2 to be attuned to** : estar en armonía con
atypical [ˌeɪ'tɪpɪkəl] *adj* : atípico
auburn ['ɔbərn] *adj* : castaño rojizo
auction¹ ['ɔkʃən] *vt* : subastar, rematar
auction² *n* : subasta *f*, remate *m*
auctioneer [ˌɔkʃə'nɪr] *n* : subastador *m*,
-dora *f*; rematador *m*, -dora *f*
audacious [ɔ'deɪʃəs] *adj* : audaz, atrevido
audacity [ɔ'dæsət̬i] *n, pl* **-ties** : audacia
f, atrevimiento *m*, descaro *m*
audible ['ɔdəbəl] *adj* : audible — **audibly** [-bli] *adv*
audience ['ɔdiənts] *n* **1** INTERVIEW : audiencia *f* **2** PUBLIC : audiencia *f*, público *m*, auditorio *m*, espectadores *mpl*
audio¹ ['ɔdiˌoː] *adj* : de sonido, de audio
audio² *n* : audio *m*
audiovisual [ˌɔdioˈvɪʒuəl] *adj* : audiovisual
audit¹ ['ɔdət] *vt* **1** : auditar (finanzas) **2**
: asistir como oyente a (una clase o un
curso)
audit² *n* : auditoría *f*
audition¹ [ɔ'dɪʃən] *vi* : hacer una audición

audition[2] *n* : audición *f*
auditor ['ɔdəṭər] *n* **1** : auditor *m*, -tora *f* (de finanzas) **2** STUDENT : oyente *mf*
auditorium [ˌɔdə'tɔriəm] *n, pl* **-riums** *or* **-ria** [-riə] : auditorio *m*, sala *f*
auditory ['ɔdəˌtori] *adj* : auditivo
auger ['ɔgər] *n* : taladro *m*, barrena *f*
augment [ɔg'mɛnt] *vt* : aumentar, incrementar
augmentation [ˌɔgmən'teɪʃən] *n* : aumento *m*, incremento *m*
augur[1] ['ɔgər] *vt* : augurar, presagiar — *vi* **to augur well** : ser de buen agüero
augur[2] *n* : augur *m*
augury ['ɔgjʊri, -gər-] *n, pl* **-ries** : augurio *m*, presagio *m*, agüero *m*
august [ɔ'gʌst] *adj* : augusto
August ['ɔgəst] *n* : agosto *m*
auk ['ɔk] *n* : alca *f*
aunt ['ænt, 'ant] *n* : tía *f*
aura ['ɔrə] *n* : aura *f*
aural ['ɔrəl] *adj* : auditivo
auricle ['ɔrɪkəl] *n* : aurícula *f*
aurora borealis [ə'rorəˌbori'æləs] *n* : aurora *f* boreal
auspices ['ɔspəsəz, -ˌsiːz] *npl* : auspicios *mpl*
auspicious [ɔ'spɪʃəs] *adj* : prometedor, propicio, de buen augurio
austere [ɔ'stɪr] *adj* : austero, severo, adusto — **austerely** *adv*
austerity [ɔ'stɛrəṭi] *n, pl* **-ties** : austeridad *f*
Australian [ɔ'streɪljən] *n* : australiano *m*, -na *f* — **Australian** *adj*
Austrian ['ɔstriən] *n* : austriaco *m*, -ca *f* — **Austrian** *adj*
authentic [ə'θɛntɪk, ɔ-] *adj* : auténtico, genuino — **authentically** [-tɪkli] *adv*
authenticate [ə'θɛntɪˌkeɪt, ɔ-] *vt* **-cated; -cating** : autenticar, autentificar
authenticity [ɔˌθɛn'tɪsəṭi] *n* : autenticidad *f*
author ['ɔθər] *n* **1** WRITER : escritor *m*, -tora *f*; autor *m*, -tora *f* **2** CREATOR : autor *m*, -tora *f*; creador *m*, -dora *f*; artífice *mf*
authoritarian [ɔˌθɔrə'tɛriən, ə-] *adj* : autoritario
authoritative [ə'θɔrəˌteɪṭɪv, ɔ-] *adj* **1** RELIABLE : fidedigno, autorizado **2** DICTATORIAL : autoritario, dictatorial, imperioso
authoritatively [ə'θɔrəˌteɪṭɪvli, ɔ-] *adv* **1** RELIABLY : con autoridad **2** DICTATORIALLY : de manera autoritaria
authority [ə'θɔrəṭi, ɔ-] *n, pl* **-ties** **1** EXPERT : autoridad *f*; experto *m*, -ta *f* **2** POWER : autoridad *f*, poder *m* **3** AUTHORIZATION : autorización *f*, licencia *f* **4 the authorities** : las autoridades **5 on good authority** : de buena fuente
authorization [ˌɔθərə'zeɪʃən] *n* : autorización *f*
authorize ['ɔθəˌraɪz] *vt* **-rized; -rizing** : autorizar, facultar
authorship ['ɔθərˌʃɪp] *n* : autoría *f*
autism ['ɔˌtɪzəm] *n* : autismo *m*

autistic [ɔ'tɪstɪk] *adj* : autista
auto ['ɔṭo] → **automobile**
autobiographical [ˌɔṭoˌbaɪə'græfɪkəl] *adj* : autobiográfico
autobiography [ˌɔṭobaɪ'agrəfi] *n, pl* **-phies** : autobiografía *f*
autocracy [ɔ'takrəsi] *n, pl* **-cies** : autocracia *f*
autocrat ['ɔṭəˌkræt] *n* : autócrata *mf*
autocratic [ˌɔṭə'kræṭɪk] *adj* : autocrático — **autocratically** [-tɪkli] *adv*
autograph[1] ['ɔṭəˌgræf] *vt* : autografiar
autograph[2] *n* : autógrafo *m*
automaker ['ɔṭoːmeɪkər] *n* : fabricante *mf* de autos, automotriz *f*
automate ['ɔṭəˌmeɪt] *vt* **-mated; -mating** : automatizar
automatic [ˌɔṭə'mæṭɪk] *adj* : automático — **automatically** [-tɪkli] *adv*
automation [ˌɔṭə'meɪʃə n] *n* : automatización *f*
automaton [ɔ'taməˌtan] *n, pl* **-atons** *or* **-ata** [-ṭə, -ˌṭa] : autómata *m*
automobile [ˌɔṭəmo'biːl, -'moːˌbiːl] *n* : automóvil *m*, auto *m*, carro *m*, coche *m*
automotive [ˌɔṭə'moːṭɪv] *adj* : automotor
autonomous [ɔ'tanəməs] *adj* : autónomo — **autonomously** *adv*
autonomy [ɔ'tanəmi] *n, pl* **-mies** : autonomía *f*
autopsy ['ɔˌtapsi, -təp-] *n, pl* **-sies** : autopsia *f*
autumn ['ɔṭəm] *n* : otoño *m*
autumnal [ɔ'tʌmnəl] *adj* : otoñal
auxiliary[1] [ɔg'zɪljəri, -'zɪləri] *adj* : auxiliar
auxiliary[2] *n, pl* **-ries** : auxiliar *mf*, ayudante *mf*
avail[1] [ə'veɪl] *vt* **to avail oneself** : aprovecharse, valerse
avail[2] *n* **1** : provecho *m*, utilidad *f* **2 to no avail** : en vano **3 to be of no avail** : no servir de nada, ser inútil
availability [əˌveɪlə'bɪləṭi] *n, pl* **-ties** : disponibilidad *f*
available [ə'veɪləbəl] *adj* : disponible
avalanche ['ævəˌlæntʃ] *n* : avalancha *f*, alud *m*
avarice ['ævərəs] *n* : avaricia *f*, codicia *f*
avaricious [ˌævə'rɪʃəs] *adj* : avaricioso, codicioso
avenge [ə'vɛnʤ] *vt* **avenged; avenging** : vengar
avenger [ə'vɛnʤər] *n* : vengador *m*, -dora *f*
avenue ['ævəˌnuː, -ˌnjuː] *n* **1** : avenida *f* **2** MEANS : vía *f*, camino *m*
average[1] ['ævrɪʤ, 'ævə-] *vt* **-aged; -aging** **1** : hacer un promedio de ⟨he averages 8 hours a day : hace un promedio de 8 horas diarias⟩ **2** : calcular el promedio de, promediar (en matemáticas)
average[2] *adj* **1** MEAN : medio ⟨the average temperature : la temperatura media⟩ **2** ORDINARY : común, ordinario ⟨the average man : el hombre común⟩

average³ *n* : promedio *m*
averse [əˈvərs] *adj* : reacio, opuesto
aversion [əˈvərʒən] *n* : aversión *f*
avert [əˈvərt] *vt* **1** : apartar, desviar ⟨he averted his eyes from the scene : apartó los ojos de la escena⟩ **2** AVOID, PREVENT : evitar, prevenir
aviary [ˈeɪviˌɛri] *n, pl* **-aries** : pajarera *f*
aviation [ˌeɪviˈeɪʃən] *n* : aviación *f*
aviator [ˈeɪviˌeɪtər] *n* : aviador *m*, -dora *f*
avid [ˈævɪd] *adj* **1** GREEDY : ávido, codicioso **2** ENTHUSIASTIC : ávido, entusiasta, ferviente — **avidly** *adv*
avocado [ˌævəˈkɑdo, ˌɑvə-] *n, pl* **-dos** : aguacate *m*, palta *f*
avocation [ˌævəˈkeɪʃən] *n* : pasatiempo *m*, afición *f*
avoid [əˈvɔɪd] *vt* **1** SHUN : evitar, eludir **2** FORGO : evitar, abstenerse de ⟨I always avoided gossip : siempre evitaba los chismes⟩ **3** EVADE : evitar ⟨if I can avoid it : si puedo evitarlo⟩
avoidable [əˈvɔɪdəbəl] *adj* : evitable
avoidance [əˈvɔɪdənts] *n* : el evitar
avoirdupois [ˌævərdəˈpɔɪz] *n* : sistema *m* inglés de pesos y medidas
avow [əˈvaʊ] *vt* : reconocer, confesar
avowal [əˈvaʊəl] *n* : reconocimiento *m*, confesión *f*
await [əˈweɪt] *vt* : esperar
awake¹ [əˈweɪk] *v* **awoke** [əˈwoːk]; **awoken** [əˈwoːkən] *or* **awaked; awaking** : despertar
awake² *adj* : despierto
awaken [əˈweɪkən] → **awake¹**
award¹ [əˈwɔrd] *vt* : otorgar, conceder, conferir
award² *n* **1** PRIZE : premio *m*, galardón *m* **2** MEDAL : condecoración *f*
aware [əˈwær] *adj* : consciente ⟨to be aware of : darse cuenta de, estar consciente de⟩
awareness [əˈwærnəs] *n* : conciencia *f*, conocimiento *m*
awash [əˈwɔʃ] *adj* : inundado
away¹ [əˈweɪ] *adv* **1** : de aquí ⟨go away! : ¡fuera de aquí!, ¡vete!⟩ **2** : de distancia ⟨10 miles away : 10 millas de distancia, queda a 10 millas⟩ **3 far away** : lejos, a lo lejos **4 right away** : en segui-

da, ahora mismo **5 to be away** : estar ausente, estar de viaje **6 to give away** : regalar (una posesión), revelar (un secreto) **7 to go away** : irse, largarse **8 to put away** : guardar **9 to turn away** : volver la cara
away² *adj* **1** ABSENT : ausente ⟨away for the week : ausente por la semana⟩ **2 away game** : partido *m* que se juega fuera
awe¹ [ˈɔ] *vt* **awed; awing** : abrumar, asombrar, impresionar
awe² *n* : asombro *m*
awesome [ˈɔsəm] *adj* **1** IMPOSING : imponente, formidable **2** AMAZING : asombroso
awestruck [ˈɔˌstrʌk] *adj* : asombrado
awful [ˈɔfəl] *adj* **1** AWESOME : asombroso **2** DREADFUL : horrible, terrible, atroz **3** ENORMOUS : enorme, tremendo ⟨an awful lot of people : muchísima gente, la mar de gente⟩
awfully [ˈɔfəli] *adv* **1** EXTREMELY : terriblemente, extremadamente **2** BADLY : muy mal, espantosamente
awhile [əˈhwaɪl] *adv* : un rato, algún tiempo
awkward [ˈɔkwərd] *adj* **1** CLUMSY : torpe, desmañado **2** EMBARRASSING : embarazoso, delicado — **awkwardly** *adv*
awkwardness [ˈɔkwərdnəs] *n* **1** CLUMSINESS : torpeza *f* **2** INCONVENIENCE : incomodidad *f*
awl [ˈɔl] *n* : punzón *m*
awning [ˈɔnɪŋ] *n* : toldo *m*
awry [əˈraɪ] *adj* **1** ASKEW : torcido **2 to go awry** : salir mal, fracasar
ax *or* **axe** [ˈæks] *n* : hacha *m*
axiom [ˈæksiəm] *n* : axioma *m*
axiomatic [ˌæksiəˈmætɪk] *adj* : axiomático
axis [ˈæksɪs] *n, pl* **axes** [-ˌsiːz] : eje *m*
axle [ˈæksəl] *n* : eje *m*
aye¹ [ˈaɪ] *adv* : sí
aye² *n* : sí *m*
azalea [əˈzeɪljə] *n* : azalea *f*
azimuth [ˈæzəməθ] *n* : azimut *m*, acimut *m*
Aztec [ˈæzˌtɛk] *n* : azteca *mf*
azure¹ [ˈæʒər] *adj* : azur, celeste
azure² *n* : azur *m*

B

b [ˈbiː] *n, pl* **b's** *or* **bs** [ˈbiːz] : segunda letra del alfabeto inglés
babble¹ [ˈbæbəl] *vi* **-bled; -bling 1** PRATTLE : balbucear **2** CHATTER : charlatanear, parlotear *fam* **3** MURMUR : murmurar
babble² *n* : balbuceo *m* (de bebé), parloteo *m* (de adultos), murmullo *m* (de voces, de un arroyo)
babe [ˈbeɪb] *n* → **baby³**
babel [ˈbeɪbəl, ˈbæ-] *n* : babel *f*, caos *m*

baboon [bæˈbuːn] *n* : babuino *m*
baby¹ [ˈbeɪbi] *vt* **-bied; -bying** : mimar, consentir
baby² *adj* **1** : de niño ⟨a baby carriage : un cochecito⟩ ⟨baby talk : habla infantil⟩ **2** TINY : pequeño, minúsculo
baby³ *n, pl* **-bies** : bebé *m*; niño *m*, -ña *f*
babyhood [ˈbeɪbiˌhʊd] *n* : niñez *f*, primera infancia *f*
babyish [ˈbeɪbiɪʃ] *adj* : infantil, pueril

baby–sit [ˈbeɪbiˌsɪt] *vi* **-sat** [-ˌsæt]; **-sitting** : cuidar niños, hacer de canguro *Spain*

baby–sitter [ˈbeɪbiˌsɪt̬ər] *n* : niñero *m*, -ra *f*; canguro *mf Spain*

baccalaureate [ˌbækəˈlɔriət] *n* : licenciatura *f*

bachelor [ˈbætʃələr] *n* **1** : soltero *m* **2** : licenciado *m*, -da *f* ⟨bachelor of arts degree : licenciatura en filosofía y letras⟩

bacillus [bəˈsɪləs] *n, pl* **-li** [-ˌlaɪ] : bacilo *m*

back¹ [ˈbæk] *vt* **1** *or* **to back up** SUPPORT : apoyar, respaldar **2** *or* **to back up** REVERSE : darle marcha atrás a (un vehículo) **3** : estar detrás de, formar el fondo de ⟨trees back the garden : unos árboles están detrás del jardín⟩ — *vi* **1** *or* **to back up** : retroceder **2** **to back away** : echarse atrás **3** **to back down** *or* **to back out** : volverse atrás, echarse para atrás

back² *adv* **1** : atrás, hacia atrás, detrás ⟨to move back : moverse atrás⟩ ⟨back and forth : de acá para allá⟩ **2** AGO : atrás, antes, ya ⟨some years back : unos años atrás, ya unos años⟩ ⟨10 months back : hace diez meses⟩ **3** : de vuelta, de regreso ⟨we're back : estamos de vuelta⟩ ⟨she ran back : volvió corriendo⟩ ⟨to call back : llamar de nuevo⟩

back³ *adj* **1** REAR : de atrás, posterior, trasero **2** OVERDUE : atrasado **3** **back pay** : atrasos *mpl*

back⁴ *n* **1** : espalda *f* (de un ser humano), lomo *m* (de un animal) **2** : respaldo *m* (de una silla), espalda *f* (de ropa) **3** REVERSE : reverso *m*, dorso *m*, revés *m* **4** REAR : fondo *m*, parte *f* de atrás **5** : defensa *mf* (en deportes)

backache [ˈbækˌeɪk] *n* : dolor *m* de espalda

backbite [ˈbækˌbaɪt] *v* **-bit** [-ˌbɪt]; **-bitten** [-ˌbɪtən]; **-biting** *vt* : calumniar, hablar mal de — *vi* : murmurar

backbiter [ˈbækˌbaɪt̬ər] *n* : calumniador *m*, -dora *f*

backbone [ˈbækˌboːn] *n* **1** : columna *f* vertebral **2** FIRMNESS : firmeza *f*, carácter *m*

backdrop [ˈbækˌdrɑp] *n* : telón *m* de fondo

backer [ˈbækər] *n* **1** SUPPORTER : partidario *m*, -ria *f* **2** SPONSOR : patrocinador *m*, -dora *f*

backfire¹ [ˈbækˌfaɪr] *vi* **-fired; -firing 1** : petardear (dícese de un automóvil) **2** FAIL : fallar, salir el tiro por la culata

backfire² *n* : petardeo *m*, explosión *f*

background [ˈbækˌɡraʊnd] *n* **1** : fondo *m* (de un cuadro, etc.), antecedentes *mpl* (de una situación) **2** EXPERIENCE, TRAINING : experiencia *f* profesional, formación *f*

backhand¹ [ˈbækˌhænd] *adv* : de revés, con el revés

backhand² *n* : revés *m*

backhanded [ˈbækˌhændəd] *adj* **1** : dado con el revés, de revés **2** INDIRECT : indirecto, ambiguo

backing [ˈbækɪŋ] *n* **1** SUPPORT : apoyo *m*, respaldo *m* **2** REINFORCEMENT : refuerzo *m* **3** SUPPORTERS : partidarios *mpl*, -rias *fpl*

backlash [ˈbækˌlæʃ] *n* : reacción *f* violenta

backlog [ˈbækˌlɔɡ] *n* : atraso *m*, trabajo *m* acumulado

backpack¹ [ˈbækˌpæk] *vi* : viajar con mochila

backpack² *n* : mochila *f*

backrest [ˈbækˌrɛst] *n* : respaldo *m*

backside [ˈbækˌsaɪd] *n* : trasero *m*

backslide [ˈbækˌslaɪd] *vi* **-slid** [-ˌslɪd]; **-slid** *or* **-slidden** [-ˌslɪdən]; **-sliding** : recaer, reincidir

backstage [ˌbækˈsteɪdʒ, ˈbækˌ-] *adv & adj* : entre bastidores

backtrack [ˈbækˌtræk] *vi* : dar marcha atrás, volverse atrás

backup [ˈbækˌʌp] *n* **1** SUPPORT : respaldo *m*, apoyo *m* **2** : copia *f* de seguridad (para computadoras)

backward¹ [ˈbækwərd] *or* **backwards** [-wərdz] *adv* **1** : hacia atrás **2** : de espaldas ⟨he fell backwards : se cayó de espaldas⟩ **3** : al revés ⟨you're doing it backwards : lo estás haciendo al revés⟩ **4** **to bend over backwards** : hacer todo lo posible

backward² *adj* **1** : hacia atrás ⟨a backward glance : una mirada hacia atrás⟩ **2** RETARDED : retrasado **3** SHY : tímido **4** UNDERDEVELOPED : atrasado

backwardness [ˈbækwərdnəs] *n* : atraso *m* (dícese de una región), retraso *m* (dícese de una persona)

backwoods [ˌbækˈwʊdz] *npl* : monte *m*, región *f* alejada

bacon [ˈbeɪkən] *n* : tocino *m*, tocineta *f Col, Ven*, bacon *m Spain*

bacterial [bækˈtɪriəl] *adj* : bacteriano

bacteriologist [bækˌtɪriˈɑlədʒɪst] *n* : bacteriólogo *m*, -ga *f*

bacteriology [bækˌtɪriˈɑlədʒi] *n* : bacteriología *f*

bacterium [bækˈtɪriəm] *n, pl* **-ria** [-iə] : bacteria *f*

bad¹ [ˈbæd] *adv* → **badly**

bad² *adj* **1** : malo **2** ROTTEN : podrido **3** SERIOUS, SEVERE : grave **4** DEFECTIVE : defectuoso ⟨a bad check : un cheque sin fondos⟩ **5** HARMFUL : perjudicial **6** CORRUPT, EVIL : malo, corrompido **7** NAUGHTY : travieso **8** **from bad to worse** : de mal en peor **9** **too bad!** : ¡qué lástima!

bad³ *n* : lo malo ⟨the good and the bad : lo bueno y lo malo⟩

bade → **bid**

badge [ˈbædʒ] *n* : insignia *f*, botón *m*, chapa *f*

badger¹ [ˈbædʒər] *vt* : fastidiar, acosar, importunar

badger² *n* : tejón *m*
badly ['bædli] *adv* **1** : mal **2** URGENT-LY : mucho, con urgencia **3** SEVERE-LY : gravemente
badminton ['bæd₁mɪntən, -₁mɪt-] *n* : bádminton *m*
badness ['bædnəs] *n* : maldad *f*
baffle¹ ['bæfəl] *vi* **-fled; -fling 1** PERPLEX : desconcertar, confundir **2** FRUS-TRATE : frustrar
baffle² *n* : deflector *m*, bafle *m* (acústico)
bafflement ['bæfəlmənt] *n* : desconcierto *m*, confusión *f*
bag¹ ['bæg] *v* **bagged; bagging** *vi* SAG : formar bolsas — *vt* **1** : ensacar, poner en una bolsa **2** : cobrar (en la caza), cazar
bag² *n* **1** : bolsa *f*, saco *m* **2** HANDBAG : cartera *f*, bolso *m*, bolsa *f* Mex **3** SUIT-CASE : maleta *f*, valija *f*
bagatelle [₁bægə'tɛl] *n* : bagatela *f*
bagel ['beɪgəl] *n* : rosquilla *f* de pan
baggage ['bægɪʤ] *n* : equipaje *m*
baggy ['bægi] *adj* **-gier; -est** : holgado, ancho
bagpipe ['bæg₁paɪp] *n* *or* **bagpipes** ['bæg₁paɪps] *npl* : gaita *f*
bail¹ ['beɪl] *vt* **1** : achicar (agua de un bote) **2 to bail out** : poner en libertad (de una cárcel) bajo fianza **3 to bail out** EXTRICATE : sacar de apuros
bail² *n* : fianza *f*, caución *f*
bailiff ['beɪləf] *n* : alguacil *mf*
bailiwick ['beɪli₁wɪk] *n* : dominio *m*
bailout ['beɪl₁aʊt] *n* : rescate *m* (financiero)
bait¹ ['beɪt] *vt* **1** : cebar (un anzuelo o cepo) **2** HARASS : acosar
bait² *n* : cebo *m*, carnada *f*
bake¹ ['beɪk] *vt* **baked; baking** : hornear, hacer al horno
bake² *n* : fiesta con platos hechos al horno
baker ['beɪkər] *n* : panadero *m*, -ra *f*
baker's dozen *n* : docena *f* de fraile
bakery ['beɪkəri] *n*, *pl* **-ries** : panadería *f*
bakeshop ['beɪk₁ʃɑp] *n* : pastelería *f*, panadería *f*
baking powder *n* : levadura *f* en polvo
baking soda → **sodium bicarbonate**
balance¹ ['bælənts] *v* **-anced; -ancing** *vt* **1** : hacer el balance de (una cuenta) ⟨to balance the books : cuadrar las cuentas⟩ **2** EQUALIZE : balancear, equilibrar **3** HARMONIZE : armonizar — *vi* : balancearse
balance² *n* **1** SCALES : balanza *f*, báscula *f* **2** COUNTERBALANCE : contrapeso *m* **3** EQUILIBRIUM : equilibrio *m* **4** REMAINDER : balance *m*, resto *m*
balanced ['bælən*t*st] *adj* : equilibrado, balanceado
balcony ['bælkəni] *n*, *pl* **-nies 1** : balcón *m*, terraza *f* (de un edificio) **2** : galería *f* (de un teatro)

bald ['bɔld] *adj* **1** : calvo, pelado, pelón **2** PLAIN : simple, puro ⟨the bald truth : la pura verdad⟩
balding ['bɔldɪŋ] *adj* : quedándose calvo
baldly ['bɔldli] *adv* : sin reparos, sin rodeos, francamente
baldness ['bɔldnəs] *n* : calvicie *f*
bale¹ ['beɪl] *vt* **baled; baling** : empacar, hacer balas de
bale² *n* : bala *f*, fardo *m*, paca *f*
baleful ['beɪlfəl] *adj* **1** DEADLY : mortífero **2** SINISTER : siniestro, funesto, torvo ⟨a baleful glance : una mirada torva⟩
balk¹ ['bɔk] *vt* : obstaculizar, impedir — *vi* **1** : plantarse *fam* (dícese de un caballo, etc.) **2 to balk at** : resistirse a, mostrarse reacio a
balk² *n* : obstáculo *m*
Balkan ['bɔlkən] *adj* : balcánico
balky ['bɔki] *adj* **balkier; -est** : reacio, obstinado, terco
ball¹ ['bɔl] *vt* : apelotonar, ovillar
ball² *n* **1** : pelota *f*, bola *f*, balón *m*, ovillo *m* (de lana) **2** : juego *m* con pelota o bola **3** DANCE : baile *m*, baile *m* de etiqueta
ballad ['bæləd] *n* : romance *m*, balada *f*
balladeer [₁bælə'dɪr] *n* : cantante *mf* de baladas
ballast¹ ['bæləst] *vt* : lastrar
ballast² *n* : lastre *m*
ball bearing *n* : cojinete *m* de bola
ballerina [₁bælə'ri:nə] *n* : bailarina *f*
ballet [bæ'leɪ, 'bæ₁leɪ] *n* : ballet *m*
ballistic [bə'lɪstɪk] *adj* : balístico
ballistics [bə'lɪstɪks] *ns* & *pl* : balística *f*
balloon¹ [bə'lu:n] *vi* **1** : viajar en globo **2** SWELL : hincharse, inflarse
balloon² *n* : globo *m*
balloonist [bə'lu:nɪst] *n* : aeróstata *mf*
ballot¹ ['bælət] *vi* : votar
ballot² *n* **1** : papeleta *f* (de voto) **2** BAL-LOTING : votación *f* **3** VOTE : voto *m*
ballpoint pen ['bɔl₁pɔɪnt] *n* : bolígrafo *m*
ballroom ['bɔl₁ru:m, -₁rʊm] *n* : sala *f* de baile
ballyhoo ['bæli₁hu:] *n* : propaganda *f*, publicidad *f*, bombo *m* *fam*
balm ['bɑm, 'bɑlm] *n* : bálsamo *f*, ungüento *m*
balmy ['bɑmi, 'bɑl-] *adj* **balmier; -est 1** MILD : templado, agradable **2** SOOTH-ING : balsámico **3** CRAZY : chiflado *fam*, chalado *fam*
baloney [bə'lo:ni] *n* NONSENSE : tonterías *fpl*, estupideces *fpl*
balsa ['bɔlsə] *n* : balsa *f*
balsam ['bɔlsəm] *n* **1** : bálsamo *m* **2** *or* **balsam fir** : abeto *m* balsámico
Baltic ['bɔltɪk] *adj* : báltico
baluster ['bæləstər] *n* : balaustre *m*
balustrade ['bælə₁streɪd] *n* : balaustrada *f*
bamboo [bæm'bu:] *n* : bambú *m*
bamboozle [bæm'bu:zəl] *vt* **-zled; -zling** : engañar, embaucar

ban¹ ['bæn] *vt* **banned; banning** : prohibir, proscribir

ban² *n* : prohibición *f*, proscripción *f*

banal [bə'nɑl, bə'næl, 'beɪnəl] *adj* : banal, trivial

banality [bə'nælət̬i] *n, pl* **-ties** : banalidad *f*, trivialidad *f*

banana [bə'nænə] *n* : banano *m*, plátano *m*, banana *f*, cambur *m Ven*, guineo *m Car*

band¹ ['bænd] *vt* **1** BIND : fajar, atar **2 to band together** : unirse, juntarse

band² *n* **1** STRIP : banda *f*, cinta *f* (de un sombrero, etc.) **2** STRIPE : franja *f* **3** : banda *f* (de radiofrecuencia) **4** RING : anillo *m* **5** GROUP : banda *f*, grupo *m*, conjunto *m* ⟨jazz band : conjunto de jazz⟩

bandage¹ ['bændɪdʒ] *vt* **-daged; -daging** : vendar

bandage² *n* : vendaje *m*, venda *f*

bandanna *or* **bandana** [bæn'dænə] *n* : pañuelo *m* (de colores)

bandit ['bændət] *n* : bandido *m*, -da *f*; bandolero *m*, -ra *f*

banditry ['bændətri] *n* : bandolerismo *m*, bandidaje *m*

bandstand ['bænd,stænd] *n* : quiosco *m* de música

bandwagon ['bænd,wægən] *n* **1** : carroza *f* de músicos **2 to jump on the bandwagon** : subirse al carro, seguir la moda

bandy¹ ['bændi] *vt* **-died; -dying 1** EXCHANGE : intercambiar **2 to bandy about** : circular, propagar

bandy² *adj* : arqueado, torcido ⟨bandy-legged : de piernas arqueadas⟩

bane ['beɪn] *n* **1** POISON : veneno *m* **2** RUIN : ruina *f*, pesadilla *f*

baneful ['beɪnfəl] *adj* : nefasto, funesto

bang¹ ['bæŋ] *vt* **1** STRIKE : golpear, darse ⟨he banged his elbow against the door : se dio con el codo en la puerta⟩ **2** SLAM : cerrar (la puerta) con un portazo — *vi* **1** SLAM : cerrarse de un golpe **2 to bang on** : aporrear, golpear ⟨she was banging on the table : aporreaba la mesa⟩

bang² *adv* : directamente, exactamente

bang³ *n* **1** BLOW : golpe *m*, porrazo *m*, trancazo *m* **2** EXPLOSION : explosión *f*, estallido *m* **3** SLAM : portazo *m* **4 bangs** *npl* : flequillo *m*, fleco *m*

Bangladeshi [,bɑŋglə'dɛʃi, ,bæŋ-, ,bʌŋ-, -'deɪ-] *n* : bangladesí *mf* — **Bangladeshi** *adj*

bangle ['bæŋgəl] *n* : brazalete *m*, pulsera *f*

banish ['bænɪʃ] *vt* **1** EXILE : desterrar, exiliar **2** EXPEL : expulsar

banishment ['bænɪʃmənt] *n* **1** EXILE : destierro *m*, exilio *m* **2** EXPULSION : expulsión *f*

banister ['bænəstər] *n* **1** BALUSTER : balaustre *m* **2** HANDRAIL : pasamanos *m*, barandilla *f*, barandal *m*

banjo ['bæn,dʒo:] *n, pl* **-jos** : banjo *m*

bank¹ ['bæŋk] *vt* **1** TILT : peraltar (una carretera), ladear (un avión) **2** HEAP : amontonar **3** : cubrir (un fuego) **4** : depositar (dinero en un banco) — *vi* **1** : ladearse (dícese de un avión) **2** : tener una cuenta (en un banco) **3 to bank on** : contar con

bank² *n* **1** MASS : montón *m*, montículo *m*, masa *f* **2** : orilla *f*, ribera *f* (de un río) **3** : peralte *m* (de una carretera) **4** : banco *m* ⟨World Bank : Banco Mundial⟩ ⟨banco de sangre : blood bank⟩

bankbook ['bæŋk,bʊk] *n* : libreta *f* bancaria, libreta *f* de ahorros

banker ['bæŋkər] *n* : banquero *m*, -ra *f*

banking ['bæŋkɪŋ] *n* : banca *f*

bankrupt¹ ['bæŋ,krʌpt] *vt* : hacer quebrar, llevar a la quiebra, arruinar

bankrupt² *adj* **1** : en bancarrota, en quiebra **2** ~ **of** LACKING : carente de, falto de

bankrupt³ *n* : fallido *m*, -da *f*; quebrado *m*, -da *f*

bankruptcy ['bæŋ,krʌptsi] *n, pl* **-cies** : ruina *f*, quiebra *f*, bancarrota *f*

banner¹ ['bænər] *adj* : excelente

banner² *n* : estandarte *m*, bandera *f*

banns ['bænz] *npl* : amonestaciones *fpl*

banquet¹ ['bæŋkwət] *vi* : celebrar un banquete

banquet² *n* : banquete *m*

banter¹ ['bæntər] *vi* : bromear, hacer bromas

banter² *n* : bromas *fpl*

baptism ['bæp,tɪzəm] *n* : bautismo *m*

baptismal [bæp'tɪzməl] *adj* : bautismal

Baptist ['bæptɪst] *n* : bautista *mf* — **Baptist** *adj*

baptize [bæp'taɪz, 'bæp,taɪz] *vt* **-tized; -tizing** : bautizar

bar¹ ['bɑr] *vt* **barred; barring 1** OBSTRUCT : obstruir, bloquear **2** EXCLUDE : excluir **3** PROHIBIT : prohibir **4** SECURE : atrancar, asegurar ⟨bar the door! : ¡atranca la puerta!⟩

bar² *n* **1** : barra *f*, barrote *m* (de una ventana), tranca *f* (de una puerta) **2** BARRIER : barrera *f*, obstáculo *m* **3** LAW : abogacía *f* **4** STRIPE : franja *f* **5** COUNTER : mostrador *m*, barra *f* **6** TAVERN : bar *m*, taberna *f*

bar³ *prep* **1** : excepto, con excepción de **2 bar none** : sin excepción

barb ['bɑrb] *n* **1** POINT : púa *f*, lengüeta *f* **2** GIBE : pulla *f*

barbarian¹ [bɑr'bæriən] *adj* **1** : bárbaro **2** CRUDE : tosco, bruto

barbarian² *n* : bárbaro *m*, -ra *f*

barbaric [bɑr'bærɪk] *adj* **1** PRIMITIVE : primitivo **2** CRUEL : brutal, cruel

barbarity [bɑr'bærət̬i] *n, pl* **-ties** : barbaridad *f*

barbarous ['bɑrbərəs] *adj* **1** UNCIVILIZED : bárbaro **2** MERCILESS : despiadado, cruel

barbarously ['bɑrbərəsli] *adv* : bárbaramente

barbecue¹ [ˈbɑrbɪˌkju:] vt **-cued; -cuing** : asar a la parrilla
barbecue² n : barbacoa f, parrillada f
barbed [ˈbɑrbd] adj **1** : con púas ⟨barbed wire : alambre de púas⟩ **2** BITING : mordaz
barber [ˈbɑrbər] n : barbero m, -ra f
barbiturate [bɑrˈbɪtʃərət] n : barbitúrico m
bard [ˈbɑrd] n : bardo m
bare¹ [ˈbær] vt **bared; baring** : desnudar
bare² adj **1** NAKED : desnudo **2** EXPOSED : descubierto, sin protección **3** EMPTY : desprovisto, vacío **4** MINIMUM : mero, mínimo ⟨the bare necessities : las necesidades mínimas⟩ **5** PLAIN : puro, sencillo
bareback [ˈbærˌbæk] or **barebacked** [-ˌbækt] adv & adj : a pelo
barefaced [ˈbærˌfeɪst] adj : descarado
barefoot [ˈbærˌfʊt] or **barefooted** [-ˌfʊtəd] adv & adj : descalzo
bareheaded [ˈbærˈhɛdəd] adv & adj : sin sombrero, con la cabeza descubierta
barely [ˈbærli] adv : apenas, por poco
bareness [ˈbærnəs] n : desnudez f
bargain¹ [ˈbɑrgən] vi HAGGLE : regatear, negociar — vt BARTER : trocar, cambiar
bargain² n **1** AGREEMENT : acuerdo m, convenio m ⟨to strike a bargain : cerrar un trato⟩ **2** : ganga f ⟨bargain price : precio de ganga⟩
barge¹ [ˈbɑrdʒ] vi **barged; barging 1** : mover con torpeza **2 to barge in** : entrometerse, interrumpir
barge² n : barcaza f, gabarra f
bar graph n : gráfico m de barras
baritone [ˈbærəˌtoːn] n : barítono m
barium [ˈbæriəm] n : bario m
bark¹ [ˈbɑrk] vi : ladrar — vt or **to bark out** : gritar ⟨to bark out an order : dar una orden a gritos⟩
bark² n **1** : ladrido m (de un perro) **2** : corteza f (de un árbol) **3** or **barque** : tipo de embarcación con velas de proa y popa
barley [ˈbɑrli] n : cebada f
barn [ˈbɑrn] n : granero m (para cosechas), establo m (para ganado)
barnacle [ˈbɑrnɪkəl] n : percebe m
barnyard [ˈbɑrnˌjɑrd] n : corral m
barometer [bəˈrɑmətər] n : barómetro m
barometric [ˌbærəˈmɛtrɪk] adj : barométrico
baron [ˈbærən] n **1** : barón m **2** TYCOON : magnate mf
baroness [ˈbærənɪs, -nəs, -ˌnɛs] n : baronesa f
baronet [ˌbærəˈnɛt, ˈbærənət] n : baronet m
baronial [bəˈroːniəl] adj **1** : de barón **2** STATELY : señorial, majestuoso
baroque [bəˈroːk, -ˈrɑk] adj : barroco
barracks [ˈbærəks] ns & pl : cuartel m
barracuda [ˌbærəˈkuːdə] n, pl **-da** or **-das** : barracuda f

barrage [bəˈrɑʒ, -ˈrɑdʒ] n **1** : descarga f (de artillería) **2** DELUGE : aluvión m ⟨a barrage of questions : un aluvión de preguntas⟩
barred [ˈbɑrd] adj : excluido, prohibido
barrel¹ [ˈbærəl] v **-reled** or **-relled; -reling** or **-relling** vt : embarrilar — vi : ir disparado
barrel² n **1** : barril m, tonel m **2** : cañón m (de un arma de fuego), cilindro m (de una cerradura)
barren [ˈbærən] adj **1** STERILE : estéril (dícese de las plantas o la mujer), árido (dícese del suelo) **2** DESERTED : yermo, desierto
barrette [bɑˈrɛt, bə-] n : pasador m, broche m para el cabello
barricade¹ [ˈbærəˌkeɪd, ˌbærəˈ-] vt **-caded; -cading** : cerrar con barricadas
barricade² n : barricada f
barrier [ˈbæriər] n **1** : barrera f **2** OBSTACLE : obstáculo m, impedimento m
barring [ˈbɑrɪŋ] prep : excepto, salvo, a excepción de
barrio [ˈbɑrio, ˈbær-] n : barrio m
barroom [ˈbɑrˌruːm, -ˌrʊm] n : bar m
barrow [ˈbærˌoː] → wheelbarrow
bartender [ˈbɑrˌtɛndər] n : camarero m, -ra f; barman m
barter¹ [ˈbɑrtər] vt : cambiar, trocar
barter² n : trueque m, permuta f
basalt [bəˈsɔlt, ˈbeɪˌ-] n : basalto m
base¹ [ˈbeɪs] vt **based; basing** : basar, fundamentar, establecer
base² adj **baser; basest 1** : de baja ley (dícese de un metal) **2** CONTEMPTIBLE : vil, despreciable
base³ n, pl **bases** : base f
baseball [ˈbeɪsˌbɔl] n : beisbol m, béisbol m
baseless [ˈbeɪsləs] adj : infundado
basely [ˈbeɪsli] adv : vilmente
basement [ˈbeɪsmənt] n : sótano m
baseness [ˈbeɪsnəs] n : vileza f, bajeza f
bash¹ [ˈbæʃ] vt : golpear violentamente
bash² n **1** BLOW : golpe m, porrazo m, madrazo m Mex fam **2** PARTY : fiesta f, juerga f fam
bashful [ˈbæʃfəl] adj : tímido, vergonzoso, penoso
bashfulness [ˈbæʃfəlnəs] n : timidez f
basic¹ [ˈbeɪsɪk] adj **1** FUNDAMENTAL : básico, fundamental **2** RUDIMENTARY : básico, elemental **3** : básico (en química)
basic² n : fundamento m, rudimento m
basically [ˈbeɪsɪkli] adv : fundamentalmente
basil [ˈbeɪzəl, ˈbæzəl] n : albahaca f
basilica [bəˈsɪlɪkə] n : basílica f
basin [ˈbeɪsən] n **1** WASHBOWL : palangana f, lavamanos m, lavabo m **2** : cuenca f (de un río)
basis [ˈbeɪsəs] n, pl **bases** [-ˌsiːz] **1** BASE : base f, pilar m **2** FOUNDATION : fundamento m, base f **3 on a weekly basis** : semanalmente

bask ['bæsk] *vi* : disfrutar, deleitarse ⟨to bask in the sun : disfrutar del sol⟩
basket ['bæskət] *n* : cesta *f*, cesto *m*, canasta *f*
basketball ['bæskət,bɔl] *n* : baloncesto *m*, basquetbol *m*
bas-relief [,bɑrɪ'li:f] *n* : bajorrelieve *m*
bass¹ ['bæs] *n*, *pl* **bass** *or* **basses** : róbalo *m* (pesca)
bass² ['beɪs] *n* : bajo *m* (tono, voz, cantante)
bass drum *n* : bombo *m*
basset hound ['bæsət,haʊnd] *n* : basset *m*
bassinet [,bæsə'nɛt] *n* : moisés *m*, cuna *f*
bassist ['beɪsɪst] *n* : bajista *mf*
bassoon [bə'su:n, bæ-] *n* : fagot *m*
bass viol ['beɪs'vaɪəl, -,o:l] → **double bass**
bastard¹ ['bæstərd] *adj* : bastardo
bastard² *n* : bastardo *m*, -da *f*
bastardize ['bæstər,daɪz] *vt* **-ized; -izing** DEBASE : degradar, envilecer
baste ['beɪst] *vt* **basted; basting** 1 STITCH : hilvanar 2 : bañar (con su jugo durante la cocción)
bastion ['bæstʃən] *n* : bastión *m*, baluarte *m*
bat¹ ['bæt] *vt* **batted; batting** 1 HIT : batear 2 **without batting an eye** : sin pestañear
bat² *n* 1 : murciélago *m* (animal) 2 : bate *m* ⟨baseball bat : bate de beisbol⟩
batch ['bætʃ] *n* : hornada *f*, tanda *f*, grupo *m*, cantidad *f*
bate ['beɪt] *vt* **bated; bating** 1 : aminorar, reducir 2 **with bated breath** : con ansiedad, aguantando la respiración
bath ['bæθ, 'bɑθ] *n*, *pl* **baths** ['bæðz, 'bæθs, 'bɑðz, 'bɑθs] 1 BATHING : baño *m* ⟨to take a bath : bañarse⟩ 2 : baño *m* (en fotografía, etc.) 3 BATHROOM : baño *m*, cuarto *m* de baño 4 SPA : balneario *m* 5 LOSS : pérdida *f*
bathe ['beɪð] *v* **bathed; bathing** *vt* 1 WASH : bañar, lavar 2 SOAK : poner en remojo 3 FLOOD : inundar ⟨to bathe with light : inundar de luz⟩ — *vi* : bañarse, ducharse
bather ['beɪðər] *n* : bañista *mf*
bathrobe ['bæθ,ro:b] *n* : bata *f* (de baño)
bathroom ['bæθ,ru:m, -,rʊm] *n* : baño *m*, cuarto *m* de baño
bathtub ['bæθ,tʌb] *n* : bañera *f*, tina *f* (de baño)
batiste [bə'ti:st] *n* : batista *f*
baton [bə'tɑn] *n* : batuta *f*, bastón *m*
battalion [bə'tæljən] *n* : batallón *m*
batten ['bætən] *vt* **to batten down the hatches** : cerrar las escotillas
batter¹ ['bætər] *vt* 1 BEAT : aporrear, golpear 2 MISTREAT : maltratar
batter² *n* 1 : masa *f* para rebozar 2 HITTER : bateador *m*, -dora *f*
battering ram *n* : ariete *m*
battery ['bætəri] *n*, *pl* **-teries** 1 : lesiones *fpl* ⟨assault and battery : agresión con lesiones⟩ 2 ARTILLERY : batería *f* 3 : batería *f*, pila *f* (de electricidad) 4 SERIES : serie *f*
batting ['bætɪŋ] *n* 1 *or* **cotton batting** : algodón *m* en láminas 2 : bateo *m* (en beisbol)
battle¹ ['bætəl] *vi* **-tled; -tling** : luchar, pelear
battle² *n* : batalla *f*, lucha *f*, pelea *f*
battle-ax ['bætəl,æks] *n* : hacha *f* de guerra
battlefield ['bætəl,fi:ld] *n* : campo *m* de batalla
battlements ['bætəlmənts] *npl* : almenas *fpl*
battleship ['bætəl,ʃɪp] *n* : acorazado *m*
batty ['bæti] *adj* **-tier; -est** : chiflado *fam*, chalado *fam*
bauble ['bɔbəl] *n* : chuchería *f*, baratija *f*
Bavarian [bə'vɛriən] *n* : bávaro *m*, -ra *f* — **Bavarian** *adj*
bawdiness ['bɔdinəs] *n* : picardía *f*
bawdy ['bɔdi] *adj* **bawdier; -est** : subido de tono, verde, colorado *Mex*
bawl¹ ['bɔl] *vi* : llorar a gritos
bawl² *n* : grito *m*, alarido *m*
bawl out *vt* SCOLD : regañar
bay¹ ['beɪ] *vi* HOWL : aullar
bay² *adj* : castaño, zaino (dícese de los caballos)
bay³ *n* 1 : bahía *f* ⟨Bay of Campeche : Bahía de Campeche⟩ 2 *or* **bay horse** : caballo *m* castaño 3 LAUREL : laurel *m* 4 HOWL : aullido *m* 5 : saliente *m* ⟨bay window : ventana en saliente⟩ 6 COMPARTMENT : área *f*, compartimento *m* 7 **at ~** : acorralado
bayberry ['beɪ,bɛri] *n*, *pl* **-ries** : arrayán *m* brabántico
bayonet¹ [,beɪə'nɛt, 'beɪə,nɛt] *vt* **-neted; -neting** : herir *o* matar) con bayoneta
bayonet² *n* : bayoneta *f*
bayou ['baɪ,u:, -,o:] *n* : pantano *m*
bazaar [bə'zɑr] *n* 1 : bazar *m* 2 SALE : venta *f* benéfica
bazooka [bə'zu:kə] *n* : bazuca *f*
BB ['bi:bi] *n* : balín *m*
be ['bi:] *v* **was** ['wəz, 'wɑz]; **were** ['wər]; **been** ['bɪn]; **being; am** ['æm]; **is** ['ɪz]; **are** ['ɑr] *vi* 1 (*expressing equality*) : ser ⟨José is a doctor : José es doctor⟩ ⟨I'm Ann's sister : soy la hermana de Ana⟩ 2 (*expressing quality*) : ser ⟨the tree is tall : el árbol es alto⟩ ⟨you're silly! : ¡eres tonto!⟩ 3 (*expressing origin or possession*) : ser ⟨she's from Managua : es de Managua⟩ ⟨it's mine : es mío⟩ 4 (*expressing location*) : estar ⟨my mother is at home : mi madre está en casa⟩ ⟨the cups are on the table : las tazas están en la mesa⟩ 5 (*expressing existence*) : ser, existir ⟨to be or not to be : ser, o no ser⟩ ⟨I think, therefore I am : pienso, luego existo⟩ 6 (*expressing a state of being*) : estar, tener ⟨how are you? : ¿cómo estás?⟩ ⟨I'm cold : tengo frío⟩ ⟨she's 10 years old : tiene 10 años⟩ ⟨they're both sick : están en-

fermos los dos⟩ — *v impers* **1** (*indicating time*) : ser ⟨it's eight o'clock : son las ocho⟩ ⟨it's Friday : hoy es viernes⟩ **2** (*indicating a condition*) : hacer, estar ⟨it's sunny : hace sol⟩ ⟨it's very dark outside : está bien oscuro afuera⟩ — *v aux* **1** (*expressing progression*) : estar ⟨what are you doing?—I'm working : ¿qué haces?—estoy trabajando⟩ **2** (*expressing occurrence*) : ser ⟨it was finished yesterday : fue acabado ayer, se acabó ayer⟩ ⟨it was cooked in the oven : se cocinó en el horno⟩ **3** (*expressing possibility*) : poderse ⟨can she be trusted? : ¿se puede confiar en ella?⟩ **4** (*expressing obligation*) : deber ⟨you are to stay here : debes quedarte aquí⟩ ⟨he was to come yesterday : se esperaba que viniese ayer⟩

beach[1] ['bi:tʃ] *vt* : hacer embarrancar, hacer varar, hacer encallar

beach[2] *n* : playa *f*

beachcomber ['bi:tʃ,ko:mər] *n* : raquero *m*, -ra *f*

beachhead ['bi:tʃ,hɛd] *n* : cabeza *f* de playa

beacon ['bi:kən] *n* : faro *m*

bead[1] ['bi:d] *vi* : formarse en gotas

bead[2] *n* **1** : cuenta *f* **2** DROP : gota *f* **3 beads** *npl* NECKLACE : collar *m*

beady ['bi:di] *adj* **beadier; -est 1** : de forma de cuenta **2 beady eyes** : ojos *mpl* pequeños y brillantes

beagle ['bi:gəl] *n* : beagle *m*

beak ['bi:k] *n* : pico *m*

beaker ['bi:kər] *n* **1** CUP : taza *f* alta **2** : vaso *m* de precipitados (en un laboratorio)

beam[1] ['bi:m] *vi* **1** SHINE : brillar **2** SMILE : sonreír radiantemente — *vt* BROADCAST : transmitir, emitir

beam[2] *n* **1** : viga *f*, barra *f* **2** RAY : rayo *m*, haz *m* de luz **3** : haz *m* de radiofaro (para guiar pilotos, etc.)

bean ['bi:n] *n* **1** : habichuela *f*, frijol *m* **2 broad bean** : haba *f* **3 string bean** : judía *f*

bear[1] ['bær] *v* **bore** ['bor]; **borne** ['bɔrn]; **bearing** *vt* **1** CARRY : llevar, portar **2** : dar a luz (un niño) **3** PRODUCE : dar (frutas, cosechas) **4** ENDURE, SUPPORT : soportar, resistir, aguantar — *vi* **1** TURN : doblar, dar la vuelta ⟨bear right : doble a la derecha⟩ **2 to bear up** : resistir

bear[2] *n*, *pl* **bears** *or* **bear** : oso *m*, osa *f*

bearable ['bærəbəl] *adj* : soportable

beard ['bɪrd] *n* **1** : barba *f* **2** : arista *f* (de plantas)

bearded ['bɪrdəd] *adj* : barbudo, de barba

bearer ['bærər] *n* : portador *m*, -dora *f*

bearing ['bærɪŋ] *n* **1** CONDUCT, MANNERS : comportamiento *m*, modales *mpl* **2** SUPPORT : soporte *f* **3** SIGNIFICANCE : relación *f*, importancia *f* ⟨to have no bearing on : no tener nada que ver con⟩ **4** : cojinete *m*, rodamiento *m*

(de una máquina) **5** COURSE, DIRECTION : dirección *f*, rumbo *m* ⟨to get one's bearings : orientarse⟩

beast ['bi:st] *n* **1** : bestia *f*, fiera *f* ⟨beast of burden : animal de carga⟩ **2** BRUTE : bruto *m*, -ta *f*; bestia *mf*

beastly ['bi:stli] *adj* : detestable, repugnante

beat[1] ['bi:t] *v* **beat; beaten** ['bi:tən] *or* **beat; beating** *vt* **1** STRIKE : golpear, pegar, darle una paliza (a alguien) **2** DEFEAT : vencer, derrotar **3** AVOID : anticiparse a, evitar ⟨to beat the crowd : evitar el gentío⟩ **4** MASH, WHIP : batir — *vi* THROB : palpitar, latir

beat[2] *adj* EXHAUSTED : derrengado, muy cansado ⟨I'm beat! : ¡estoy molido!⟩

beat[3] *n* **1** : golpe *m*, redoble *m* (de un tambor), latido *m* (del corazón) **2** RHYTHM : ritmo *m*, tiempo *m*

beater ['bi:tər] *n* **1** : batidor *m*, -dora *f* **2** EGGBEATER : batidor *m*

beatific [,bi:ə'tɪfɪk] *adj* : beatífico

beatitude [bi'ætə,tu:d] *n* **1** : beatitud *f* **2 the Beatitudes** : las bienaventuranzas

beau ['bo:] *n*, *pl* **beaux** *or* **beaus** : pretendiente *m*, galán *m*

beautification [,bju:təfə'keɪʃən] *n* : embellecimiento *m*

beautiful ['bju:tɪfəl] *adj* : hermoso, bello, lindo, precioso

beautifully ['bju:tɪfəli] *adv* **1** ATTRACTIVELY : hermosamente **2** EXCELLENTLY : maravillosamente, excelentemente

beauty ['bju:ti] *n*, *pl* **-ties** : belleza *f*, hermosura *f*, beldad *f*

beauty shop *or* **beauty salon** *n* : salón *m* de belleza

beaver ['bi:vər] *n* : castor *m*

because [bɪ'kʌz, -'kɔz] *conj* : porque

because of *prep* : por, a causa de, debido a

beck ['bɛk] *n* **to be at the beck and call of** : estar a la entera disposición de, estar sometido a la voluntad de

beckon ['bɛkən] *vi* **to beckon to someone** : hacerle señas a alguien

become [bɪ'kʌm] *v* **-came** [-'keɪm]; **-come; -coming** *vi* : hacerse, volverse, ponerse ⟨he became famous : se hizo famoso⟩ ⟨to become sad : ponerse triste⟩ **2** : acostumbrarse a ⟩ — *vt* **1** BEFIT : ser apropiado para **2** SUIT : favorecer, quedarle bien (a alguien) ⟨that dress becomes you : ese vestido te favorece⟩

becoming [bɪ'kʌmɪŋ] *adj* **1** SUITABLE : apropiado **2** FLATTERING : favorecedor

bed[1] ['bɛd] *v* **bedded; bedding** *vt* : acostar — *vi* : acostarse

bed[2] *n* **1** : cama *f*, lecho *m* **2** : cauce *m* (de un río), fondo *m* (del mar) **3** : arriate *m* (para plantas) **4** LAYER, STRATUM : estrato *m*, capa *f*

bedbug [ˈbɛdˌbʌg] *n* : chinche *f*
bedclothes [ˈbɛdˌkloːðz, -ˌkloːz] *npl* : ropa *f* de cama, sábanas *fpl*
bedding [ˈbɛdɪŋ] *n* **1** → **bedclothes 2** : cama *f* (para animales)
bedeck [bɪˈdɛk] *vt* : adornar, engalanar
bedevil [bɪˈdɛvəl] *vt* **-iled** *or* **-illed; -iling** *or* **-illing** : acosar, plagar
bedlam [ˈbɛdləm] *n* : locura *f*, caos *m*, alboroto *m*
bedraggled [bɪˈdrægəld] *adj* : desaliñado, despeinado
bedridden [ˈbɛdˌrɪdən] *adj* : postrado en cama
bedrock [ˈbɛdˌrak] *n* : lecho *m* de roca
bedroom [ˈbɛdˌruːm, -ˌrʊm] *n* : dormitorio *m*, habitación *f*, pieza *f*, recámara *f Col, Mex, Pan*
bedspread [ˈbɛdˌsprd] *n* : cubrecama *m*, colcha *f*, cobertor *m*
bee [ˈbiː] *n* **1** : abeja *f* (insecto) **2** GATHERING : círculo *m*, reunión *f*
beech [ˈbiːtʃ] *n, pl* **beeches** *or* **beech** : haya *f*
beechnut [ˈbiːtʃˌnʌt] *n* : hayuco *m*
beef¹ [ˈbiːf] *vt* **to beef up** : fortalecer, reforzar — *vi* COMPLAIN : quejarse
beef² *n, pl* **beefs** [ˈbiːfs] *or* **beeves** [ˈbiːvz] : carne *f* de vaca, carne *f* de res *CA, Mex*
beefsteak [ˈbiːfˌsteɪk] *n* : filete *m*, bistec *m*
beehive [ˈbiːˌhaɪv] *n* : colmena *f*
beekeeper [ˈbiːˌkiːpər] *n* : apicultor *m*, -tora *f*
beeline [ˈbiːˌlaɪn] *n* **to make a beeline for** : ir derecho a, ir directo hacia
been → **be**
beep¹ [ˈbiːp] *v* : pitar
beep² *n* : pitido *m*
beeper [ˈbiːpər] *n* : busca *m*, buscapersonas *m*
beer [ˈbɪr] *n* : cerveza *f*
beeswax [ˈbiːzˌwæks] *n* : cera *f* de abejas
beet [ˈbiːt] *n* : remolacha *f*, betabel *m Mex*
beetle [ˈbiːt̬əl] *n* : escarabajo *m*
befall [bɪˈfɔl] *v* **-fell** [-ˈfl]; **-fallen** [-ˈfɔlən] *vt* : sucederle a, acontecerle a — *vi* : acontecer
befit [bɪˈfɪt] *vt* **-fitted; -fitting** : convenir a, ser apropiado para
before¹ [bɪˈfor] *adv* **1** : antes ⟨before and after : antes y después⟩ **2** : anterior ⟨the month before : el mes anterior⟩
before² *conj* : antes que ⟨he would die before surrendering : moriría antes que rendirse⟩
before³ *prep* **1** : antes de ⟨before eating : antes de comer⟩ **2** : delante de, ante ⟨I stood before the house : estaba parada delante de la casa⟩ ⟨before the judge : ante el juez⟩
beforehand [bɪˈforˌhænd] *adv* : antes, por adelantado, de antemano, con anticipación
befriend [bɪˈfrɛnd] *vt* : hacerse amigo de

befuddle [bɪˈfʌdəl] *vt* **-dled; -dling** : aturdir, ofuscar, confundir
beg [ˈbɛg] *v* **begged; begging** *vt* : pedir, mendigar, suplicar ⟨I begged him to go : le supliqué que fuera⟩ — *vi* : mendigar, pedir limosna
beget [bɪˈgɛt] *vt* **-got** [-ˈgɑt]; **-gotten** [-ˈgɑtən] *or* **-got; -getting** : engendrar
beggar [ˈbɛgər] *n* : mendigo *m*, -ga *f*; pordiosero *m*, -ra *f*
begin [bɪˈgɪn] *v* **-gan** [-ˈgæn]; **-gun** [-ˈgʌn]; **-ginning** *vt* : empezar, comenzar, iniciar — *vi* **1** START : empezar, comenzar, iniciarse **2** ORIGINATE : nacer, originarse **3 to begin with** : en primer lugar, para empezar
beginner [bɪˈgɪnər] *n* : principiante *mf*
beginning [bɪˈgɪnɪŋ] *n* : principio *m*, comienzo *m*
begone [bɪˈgɔn] *interj* : ¡fuera de aquí!
begonia [bɪˈgoːnjə] *n* : begonia *f*
begrudge [bɪˈgrʌdʒ] *vt* **-grudged; -grudging 1** : dar de mala gana **2** ENVY : envidiar, resentir
beguile [bɪˈgaɪl] *vt* **-guiled; -guiling 1** DECEIVE : engañar **2** AMUSE : divertir, entretener
behalf [bɪˈhæf, -ˈhaf] *n* **1** : favor *m*, beneficio *m*, parte *f* **2 on behalf of** *or* **in behalf of** : de parte de, en nombre de
behave [bɪˈheɪv] *vi* **-haved; -having** : comportarse, portarse
behavior [bɪˈheɪvjər] *n* : comportamiento *m*, conducta *f*
behead [bɪˈhd] *vt* : decapitar
behest [bɪˈhst] *n* **1** : mandato *m*, orden *f* **2 at the behest of** : a instancia de
behind¹ [bɪˈhaɪnd] *adv* : atrás, detrás ⟨to fall behind : quedarse atrás⟩
behind² *prep* **1** : atrás de, detrás de, tras ⟨behind the house : detrás de la casa⟩ ⟨one behind another : uno tras otro⟩ **2** : atrasado con, después de ⟨behind schedule : atrasado con el trabajo⟩ ⟨I arrived behind the others : llegué después de los otros⟩ **3** SUPPORTING : en apoyo de, detrás
behind³ [bɪˈhaɪnd, ˈbiːˌhaɪnd] *n* : trasero *m*
behold [bɪˈhoːld] *vt* **-held; -holding** : contemplar
beholder [bɪˈhoːldər] *n* : observador *m*, -dora *f*
behoove [bɪˈhuːv] *vt* **-hooved; -hooving** : convenirle a, corresponderle a ⟨it behooves us to help him : nos conviene ayudarlo⟩
beige¹ [ˈbeɪʒ] *adj* : beige
beige² *n* : beige *m*
being [ˈbiːɪŋ] *n* **1** EXISTENCE : ser *m*, existencia *f* **2** CREATURE : ser *m*, ente *m*
belabor [bɪˈleɪbər] *vt* **to belabor the point** : extenderse sobre el tema
belated [bɪˈleɪt̬əd] *adj* : tardío, retrasado
belch¹ [ˈbɛltʃ] *vi* **1** BURP : eructar **2** EXPEL : expulsar, arrojar
belch² *n* : eructo *m*

beleaguer [bɪ'li:gər] *vt* **1** BESIEGE : asediar, sitiar **2** HARASS : fastidiar, molestar
belfry ['bɛlfri] *n*, *pl* **-fries** : campanario *m*
Belgian ['bɛldʒən] *n* : belga *mf* — **Belgian** *adj*
belie [bɪ'laɪ] *vt* **-lied; -lying** **1** MISREPRESENT : falsear, ocultar **2** CONTRADICT : contradecir, desmentir
belief [bə'li:f] *n* **1** TRUST : confianza *f* **2** CONVICTION : creencia *f*, convicción *f* **3** FAITH : fe *f*
believable [bə'li:vəbəl] *adj* : verosímil, creíble
believe [bə'li:v] *v* **-lieved; -lieving** : creer
believer [bə'li:vər] *n* **1** : creyente *mf* **2** : partidario *m*, -ria *f*; entusiasta *mf* ⟨she's a great believer in vitamins : ella es una gran partidaria de las vitaminas⟩
belittle [bɪ'lɪtəl] *vt* **-littled; -littling** **1** DISPARAGE : menospreciar, denigrar, rebajar **2** MINIMIZE : minimizar, quitar importancia a
Belizean [bə'li:ziən] *n* : beliceño *m*, -ña *f* — **Belizean** *adj*
bell[1] ['bɛl] *vt* : ponerle un cascabel a
bell[2] *n* : campana *f*, cencerro *m* (para una vaca o cabra), cascabel *m* (para un gato), timbre *m* (de teléfono, de la puerta)
belle ['bɛl] *n* : belleza *f*, beldad *f*
bellhop ['bɛl,hɑp] *n* : botones *m*
bellicose ['bɛlɪ,ko:s] *adj* : belicoso *m* — **bellicosity** [,bɛlɪ'kɑsəti] *n*
belligerence [bə'lɪdʒərənts] *n* : agresividad *f*, beligerancia *f*
belligerent[1] [bə'lɪdʒərənt] *adj* : agresivo, beligerante
belligerent[2] *n* : beligerante *mf*
bellow[1] ['bɛ,lo:] *vi* : bramar, mugir — *vt* : gritar
bellow[2] *n* : bramido *m*, grito *m*
bellows ['bɛ,lo:z] *ns & pl* : fuelle *m*
bellwether ['bɛl,wɛðər] *n* : líder *mf*
belly[1] ['bɛli] *vi* **-lied; -lying** SWELL : hincharse, inflarse
belly[2] *n*, *pl* **-lies** : abdomen *m*, vientre *m*, barriga *f*, panza *f*
belong [bɪ'lɔŋ] *vi* **1** : pertenecer (a), ser propiedad (de) ⟨it belongs to her : pertenece a ella, es suyo, es de ella⟩ **2** : ser parte (de), ser miembro (de) ⟨he belongs to the club : es miembro del club⟩ **3** : deber estar, ir ⟨your coat belongs in the closet : tu abrigo va en el ropero⟩
belongings [bɪ'lɔŋɪŋz] *npl* : pertenencias *fpl*, efectos *mpl* personales
beloved[1] [bɪ'lʌvəd, -'lʌvd] *adj* : querido, amado
beloved[2] *n* : amado *m*, -da *f*; enamorado *m*, -da *f*; amor *m*
below[1] [bɪ'lo:] *adv* : abajo
below[2] *prep* **1** : abajo de, debajo de ⟨below the window : debajo de la ventana⟩ **2** : por debajo de, bajo ⟨below average : por debajo del promedio⟩ ⟨5 degrees below zero : 5 grados bajo cero⟩

belt[1] ['bɛlt] *vt* **1** : ceñir con un cinturón, ponerle un cinturón a **2** THRASH : darle una paliza a, darle un trancazo a
belt[2] *n* **1** : cinturón *m*, cinto *m* (para el talle) **2** BAND, STRAP : cinta *f*, correa *f*, banda *f* Mex **3** AREA : frente *m*, zona *f*
beltway ['bɛlt,weɪ] *n* : carretera *f* de circunvalación; periférico *m* CA, Mex; libramiento *m* Mex
bemoan [bɪ'mo:n] *vt* : lamentarse de
bemuse [bɪ'mju:z] *vt* **-mused; -musing** **1** BEWILDER : confundir, desconcertar **2** ENGROSS : absorber
bench ['bɛntʃ] *n* **1** SEAT : banco *m*, escaño *m*, banca *f* **2** : estrado *m* (de un juez) **3** COURT : tribunal *m*
bend[1] ['bɛnd] *v* **bent** ['bnt;]; **bending** *vt* : torcer, doblar, curvar, flexionar — *vi* **1** : torcerse, agacharse ⟨to bend over : inclinarse⟩ **2** TURN : torcer, hacer una curva
bend[2] *n* **1** TURN : vuelta *f*, recodo *m* **2** CURVE : curva *f*, ángulo *m*, codo *m*
beneath[1] [bɪ'ni:θ] *adv* : bajo, abajo, debajo
beneath[2] *prep* : bajo de, abajo de, por debajo de
benediction [,bɛnə'dɪkʃən] *n* : bendición *f*
benefactor ['bɛnə,fæktər] *n* : benefactor *m*, -tora *f*
beneficence [bə'nɛfəsənts] *n* : beneficencia *f*
beneficent [bə'nɛfəsənt] *adj* : benéfico, caritativo
beneficial [,bɛnə'fɪʃəl] *adj* : beneficioso, provechoso — **beneficially** *adv*
beneficiary [,bɛnə'fɪʃi,ɛri, -'fɪʃəri] *n*, *pl* **-ries** : beneficiario *m*, -ria *f*
benefit[1] ['bɛnəfɪt] *vt* : beneficiar — *vi* : beneficiarse
benefit[2] *n* **1** ADVANTAGE : beneficio *m*, ventaja *f*, provecho *m* **2** AID : asistencia *f*, beneficio *m* **3** : función *f* benéfica (para recaudar fondos)
benevolence [bə'nɛvələnts] *n* : bondad *f*, benevolencia *f*
benevolent [bə'nɛvələnt] *adj* : benévolo, bondadoso — **benevolently** *adv*
Bengali [bɛn'gɔli, bɛŋ-] *n* **1** : bengalí *mf* **2** : bengalí *m* (idioma) — **Bengali** *adj*
benign [bɪ'naɪn] *adj* **1** GENTLE, KIND : benévolo, amable **2** FAVORABLE : propicio, favorable **3** MILD : benigno ⟨a benign tumor : un tumor benigno⟩
Beninese [bə,nɪ'ni:z, -,ni:-, -'ni:s; ,bnɪ'-] *n* : beninés *m*, -nesa *f* — **Beninese** *adj*
bent ['bɛnt] *n* : aptitud *f*, inclinación *f*
benumb [bɪ'nʌm] *vt* : entumecer
benzene ['bɛn,zi:n] *n* : benceno *m*
bequeath [bɪ'kwi:θ, -'kwi:ð] *vt* : legar, dejar en testamento
bequest [bɪ'kwɛst] *n* : legado *m*
berate [bɪ'reɪt] *vt* **-rated; -rating** : reprender, regañar
bereaved[1] [bɪ'ri:vd] *adj* : que está de luto, afligido (por la muerte de alguien)

bereaved² *n* **the bereaved** : los deudos del difunto (o de la difunta)
bereavement [bɪ'ri:vmənt] *n* **1** SORROW : dolor *m*, pesar *m* **2** LOSS : pérdida *f*
bereft [bɪ'rɛft] *adj* : privado, desprovisto
beret [bə'reɪ] *n* : boina *f*
beriberi [ˌbɛri'bɛri] *n* : beriberi *m*
berm ['bərm] *n* : arcén *m*
berry ['bɛri] *n, pl* **-ries** : baya *f*
berserk [bər'sərk, -'zərk] *adj* **1** : enloquecido **2 to go beserk** : volverse loco
berth¹ ['bərθ] *vi* : atracar
berth² *n* **1** DOCK : atracadero *m* **2** ACCOMMODATION : litera *f*, camarote *m* **3** POSITION : trabajo *m*, puesto *m*
beryl ['bɛrəl] *n* : berilo *m*
beseech [bɪ'si:tʃ] *vt* **-seeched** *or* **-sought** [-'sɔt]; **-seeching** : suplicar, implorar, rogar
beset [bɪ'sɛt] *vt* **-set; -setting 1** HARASS : acosar **2** SURROUND : rodear
beside [bɪ'saɪd] *prep* : al lado de, junto a
besides¹ [bɪ'saɪdz] *adv* **1** ALSO : además, también, aparte **2** MOREOVER : además, por otra parte
besides² *prep* **1** : además de, aparte de ⟨six others besides you : seis otros además de ti⟩ **2** EXCEPT : excepto, fuera de, aparte de
besiege [bɪ'si:dʒ] *vt* **-sieged; -sieging** : asediar, sitiar, cercar
besmirch [bɪ'smərtʃ] *vt* : ensuciar, mancillar
best¹ ['bɛst] *vt* : superar, ganar a
best² *adv* (*superlative of* **well**) : mejor ⟨as best I can : lo mejor que puedo⟩
best³ *adj* (*superlative of* **good**) : mejor ⟨my best friend : mi mejor amigo⟩
best⁴ *n* **1 the best** : lo mejor, el mejor, la mejor, los mejores, las mejores **2 at ∼** : a lo más **3 to do one's best** : hacer todo lo posible
bestial ['bɛstʃəl, 'bi:s-] *adj* **1** : bestial **2** BRUTISH : brutal, salvaje
best man *n* : padrino *m*
bestow [bɪ'sto:] *vt* : conferir, otorgar, conceder
bestowal [bɪ'sto:əl] *n* : concesión *f*, otorgamiento *m*
bet¹ ['bɛt] *v* **bet; betting** *vt* : apostar — *vi* **to bet on** : apostarle a
bet² *n* : apuesta *f*
betoken [bɪ'to:kən] *vt* : denotar, ser indicio de
betray [bɪ'treɪ] *vt* **1** : traicionar ⟨to betray one's country : traicionar uno a su patria⟩ **2** DIVULGE, REVEAL : delatar, revelar ⟨to betray a secret : revelar un secreto⟩
betrayal [bɪ'treɪəl] *n* : traición *f*, delación *f*, revelación *f* ⟨betrayal of trust : abuso de confianza⟩
betrothal [bɪ'tro:ðəl, -'trɔ-] *n* : esponsales *mpl*, compromiso *m*
betrothed [bɪ'tro:ðd, -'trɔθt] *n* FIANCÉ : prometido *m*, -da *f*

better¹ ['bɛtər] *vt* **1** IMPROVE : mejorar **2** SURPASS : superar
better² *adv* (*comparative of* **well**) **1** : mejor **2** MORE : más ⟨better than 50 miles : más de 50 millas⟩
better³ *adj* (*comparative of* **good**) **1** : mejor ⟨the weather is better today : hace mejor tiempo hoy⟩ ⟨I was sick, but now I'm better : estuve enfermo, pero ahora estoy mejor⟩ **2** : mayor ⟨the better part of a month : la mayor parte de un mes⟩
better⁴ *n* **1** : el mejor, la mejor ⟨the better of the two : el mejor de los dos⟩ **2 to get the better of** : vencer a, quedar por encima de, superar
betterment ['bɛtərmənt] *n* : mejoramiento *m*, mejora *f*
bettor *or* **better** ['bɛtər] *n* : apostador *m*, -dora *f*
between¹ [bɪ'twi:n] *adv* **1** : en medio, por lo medio **2 in ∼** : intermedio
between² *prep* : entre
bevel¹ ['bɛvəl] *v* **-eled** *or* **-elled; -eling** *or* **-elling** *vt* : biselar — *vi* INCLINE : inclinarse
bevel² *n* : bisel *m*
beverage ['bɛvrɪdʒ, 'bɛvə-] *n* : bebida *f*
bevy ['bɛvi] *n, pl* **bevies** : grupo *m* (de personas), bandada *f* (de pájaros)
bewail [bɪ'weɪl] *vt* : lamentarse de, llorar
beware [bɪ'wær] *vi* **to beware of** : tener cuidado con ⟨beware of the dog! : ¡cuidado con el perro!⟩ — *vt* : guardarse de, cuidarse de
bewilder [bɪ'wɪldər] *vt* : desconcertar, dejar perplejo
bewilderment [bɪ'wɪldərmənt] *n* : desconcierto *m*, perplejidad *f*
bewitch [bɪ'wɪtʃ] *vt* **1** : hechizar, embrujar **2** CHARM : cautivar, encantar
bewitchment [bɪ'wɪtʃmənt] *n* : hechizo *m*
beyond¹ [bi'jɑnd] *adv* **1** FARTHER, LATER : más allá, más lejos (en el espacio), más adelante (en el tiempo) **2** MORE : más ⟨$50 and beyond : $50 o más⟩
beyond² *n* **the beyond** : el más allá, lo desconocido
beyond³ *prep* **1** : más allá de ⟨beyond the frontier : más allá de la frontera⟩ **2** : fuera de ⟨beyond one's reach : fuera de su alcance⟩ **3** BESIDES : además de
biannual [ˌbaɪ'ænjʊəl] *adj* : bianual — **biannually** *adv*
bias¹ ['baɪəs] *vt* **-ased** *or* **-assed; -asing** *or* **-assing 1** : predisponer, sesgar, influir en, afectar **2 to be biased against** : tener prejuicio contra
bias² *n* **1** : sesgo *m*, bies *m* (en la costura) **2** PREJUDICE : prejuicio *m* **3** TENDENCY : inclinación *f*, tendencia *f*
biased ['baɪəst] *adj* : tendencioso, parcial
bib ['bɪb] *n* **1** : peto *m* **2** : babero *m* (para niños)
Bible ['baɪbəl] *n* : Biblia *f*
biblical ['bɪblɪkəl] *adj* : bíblico

bibliographer [ˌbɪbliˈɑgrəfər] *n* : bibliógrafo *m*, -fa *f*
bibliographic [ˌbɪbliəˈgræfɪk] *adj* : bibliográfico
bibliography [ˌbɪbliˈɑgrəfi] *n*, *pl* **-phies** : bibliografía *f*
bicameral [ˌbaɪˈkæmərəl] *adj* : bicameral
bicarbonate [ˌbaɪˈkɑrbənət, -ˌneɪt] *n* : bicarbonato *m*
bicentennial [ˌbaɪsɛnˈtɛniəl] *n* : bicentenario *m*
biceps [ˈbaɪˌsɛps] *ns & pl* : bíceps *m*
bicker¹ [ˈbɪkər] *vi* : pelear, discutir, reñir
bicker² *n* : pelea *f*, riña *f*, discusión *f*
bicuspid [baɪˈkʌspɪd] *n* : premolar *m*, diente *m* bicúspide
bicycle¹ [ˈbaɪsɪkəl, -ˌsɪ-] *vi* **-cled; -cling** : ir en bicicleta
bicycle² *n* : bicicleta *f*
bicycling [ˈbaɪsɪkəlɪŋ] *n* : ciclismo *m*
bicyclist [ˈbaɪsɪkəlɪst] *n* : ciclista *mf*
bid¹ [ˈbɪd] *vt* **bade** [ˈbæd, ˈbeɪd] *or* **bid; bidden** [ˈbɪdən] *or* **bid; bidding** **1** ORDER : pedir, mandar **2** INVITE : invitar **3** SAY : dar, decir ⟨to bid good evening : dar las buenas noches⟩ ⟨to bid farewell to : decir adiós a⟩ **4** : ofrecer (en una subasta), declarar (en juegos de cartas)
bid² *n* **1** OFFER : oferta *f* (en una subasta), declaración *f* (en juegos de cartas) **2** INVITATION : invitación *f* **3** ATTEMPT : intento *m*, tentativa *f*
bidder [ˈbɪdər] *n* : postor *m*, -tora *f*
bide [ˈbaɪd] *v* **bode** [ˈboːd] *or* **bided; biding** *vt* : esperar, aguardar ⟨to bide one's time : esperar el momento oportuno⟩ — *vi* DWELL : morar, vivir
biennial [baɪˈɛniəl] *adj* : bienal — **biennially** *adv*
bier [ˈbɪr] *n* **1** STAND : andas *fpl* **2** COFFIN : ataúd *m*, féretro *m*
bifocals [ˈbaɪˌfoːkəlz] *npl* : lentes *mpl* bifocales, bifocales *mpl*
big [ˈbɪg] *adj* **bigger; biggest** **1** LARGE : grande **2** PREGNANT : embarazada **3** IMPORTANT, MAJOR : importante, grande ⟨a big decision : una gran decisión⟩ **4** POPULAR : popular, famoso, conocido
bigamist [ˈbɪgəmɪst] *n* : bígamo *m*, -ma *f*
bigamous [ˈbɪgəməs] *adj* : bígamo
bigamy [ˈbɪgəmi] *n* : bigamia *f*
Big Dipper → **dipper**
bighorn [ˈbɪgˌhɔrn] *n*, *pl* **-horn** *or* **-horns** *or* **bighorn sheep** : oveja *f* salvaje de las montañas
bight [ˈbaɪt] *n* : bahía *f*, ensenada *f*, golfo *m*
bigot [ˈbɪgət] *n* : intolerante *mf*
bigoted [ˈbɪgətəd] *adj* : intolerante, prejuiciado, fanático
bigotry [ˈbɪgətri] *n*, *pl* **-tries** : intolerancia *f*
big shot *n* : pez *m* gordo *fam*, mandamás *mf*

bigwig [ˈbɪgˌwɪg] → **big shot**
bike [ˈbaɪk] *n* **1** : bicicleta *f*, bici *f fam* **2** : motocicleta *f*, moto *f*
bikini [bəˈkiːni] *n* : bikini *m*
bilateral [baɪˈlætərəl] *adj* : bilateral — **bilaterally** *adv*
bile [ˈbaɪl] *n* **1** : bilis *f* **2** IRRITABILITY : mal genio *m*
bilingual [baɪˈlɪŋgwəl] *adj* : bilingüe
bilious [ˈbɪliəs] *adj* **1** : bilioso **2** IRRITABLE : bilioso, colérico
bilk [ˈbɪlk] *vt* : burlar, estafar, defraudar
bill¹ [ˈbɪl] *vt* : pasarle la cuenta a — *vi* : acariciar ⟨to bill and coo : acariciarse⟩
bill² *n* **1** LAW : proyecto *m* de ley, ley *f* **2** INVOICE : cuenta *f*, factura *f* **3** POSTER : cartel *m* **4** PROGRAM : programa *m* (del teatro) **5** : billete *m* ⟨a five-dollar bill : un billete de cinco dólares⟩ **6** BEAK : pico *m*
billboard [ˈbɪlˌbɔrd] *n* : cartelera *f*
billet¹ [ˈbɪlət] *vt* : acuartelar, alojar
billet² *n* : alojamiento *m*
billfold [ˈbɪlˌfoːld] *n* : billetera *f*, cartera *f*
billiards [ˈbɪljərdz] *n* : billar *m*
billion [ˈbɪljən] *n*, *pl* **billions** *or* **billion** : mil millones *mpl*
billow¹ [ˈbɪlo] *vi* : hincharse, inflarse
billow² *n* **1** WAVE : ola *f* **2** CLOUD : nube *f* ⟨a billow of smoke : un nube de humo⟩
billowy [ˈbɪlowi] *adj* : ondulante
billy goat [ˈbɪliˌgoːt] *n* : macho *m* cabrío
bin [ˈbɪn] *n* : cubo *m*, cajón *m*
binary [ˈbaɪnəri, -ˌnɛri] *adj* : binario *m*
bind [ˈbaɪnd] *vt* **bound** [ˈbaʊnd]; **binding** **1** TIE : atar, amarrar **2** OBLIGATE : obligar **3** UNITE : aglutinar, ligar, unir **4** BANDAGE : vendar **5** : encuadernar (un libro)
binder [ˈbaɪndər] *n* **1** FOLDER : carpeta *f* **2** : encuadernador *m*, -dora *f* (de libros)
binding [ˈbaɪndɪŋ] *n* **1** : encuadernación *f* (de libros) **2** COVER : cubierta *f*, forro *m*
binge [ˈbɪndʒ] *n* : juerga *f*, parranda *f fam*
bingo [ˈbɪnˌgoː] *n*, *pl* **-gos** : bingo *m*
binocular [baɪˈnɑkjələr, bə-] *adj* : binocular
binoculars [bəˈnɑkjələrz, baɪ-] *npl* : binoculares *mpl*
biochemical¹ [ˌbaɪoˈkɛmɪkəl] *adj* : bioquímico
biochemical² *n* : bioquímico *m*
biochemist [ˌbaɪoˈkɛmɪst] *n* : bioquímico *m*, -ca *f*
biochemistry [ˌbaɪoˈkɛməstri] *n* : bioquímica *f*
biodegradable [ˌbaɪodɪˈgreɪdəbəl] *adj* : biodegradable
biodegradation [ˌbaɪodɛgrəˈdeɪʃən] *n* : biodegradación *f*
biodegrade [ˌbaɪodɪˈgreɪd] *vi* **-graded; -grading** : biodegradarse

biodiversity [ˌbaɪodə'vərsəṭi, -daɪ-] *n, pl* **-ties** : bioversidad *f*
biographer [baɪ'ɑɡrəfər] *n* : biógrafo *m*, -fa *f*
biographical [ˌbaɪə'ɡræfɪkəl] *adj* : biográfico
biography [baɪ'ɑɡrəfi, bi:-] *n, pl* **-phies** : biografía *f*
biologic [ˌbaɪə'lɑʤɪk] *or* **biological** [-ʤɪkəl] *adj* : biológico
biologist [baɪ'ɑləʤɪst] *n* : biólogo *m*, -ga *f*
biology [baɪ'ɑləʤi] *n* : biología *f*
biophysical [ˌbaɪo'fɪzɪkəl] *adj* : biofísico
biophysicist [ˌbaɪo'fɪzəsɪst] *n* : biofísico *m*, -ca *f*
biophysics [ˌbaɪo'fɪzɪks] *ns & pl* : biofísica *f*
biopsy ['baɪˌɑpsi] *n, pl* **-sies** : biopsia *f*
biosphere ['baɪəˌsfɪr] *n* : biosfera *f*, biósfera *f*
biotechnology [ˌbaɪotɛk'nɑləʤi] *n* : biotecnología *f*
biotic [baɪ'ɑtɪk] *adj* : biótico
bipartisan [baɪ'pɑrṭəzən, -sən] *adj* : bipartidista, de dos partidas
biped ['baɪˌpɛd] *n* : bípedo *m*
birch ['bərtʃ] *n* : abedul *m*
bird ['bərd] *n* : pájaro *m* (pequeño), ave *f* (grande)
birdbath ['bərdˌbæθ, -ˌbɑθ] *n* : pila *f* para pájaros
bird dog *n* : perro *m*, -rra *f* de caza
bird of prey *n* : ave *f* rapaz, ave *f* de presa
birdseed ['bərdˌsiːd] *n* : alpiste *m*
bird's—eye ['bərdzˌaɪ] *adj* **1** : visto desde arriba ⟨bird's-eye view : vista aérea⟩ **2** CURSORY : rápido, somero
birth ['bərθ] *n* **1** : nacimiento *m*, parto *m* **2** ORIGIN : origen *m*, nacimiento *m*
birthday ['bərθˌdeɪ] *n* : cumpleaños *m*, aniversario *m*
birthmark ['bərθˌmɑrk] *n* : mancha *f* de nacimiento
birthplace ['bərθˌpleɪs] *n* : lugar *m* de nacimiento
birthrate ['bərθˌreɪt] *n* : índice *m* de natalidad
birthright ['bərθˌraɪt] *n* : derecho *m* de nacimiento
biscuit ['bɪskət] *n* : bizcocho *m*
bisect ['baɪˌsɛkt, ˌbaɪ'-] *vt* : bisecar
bisexual [ˌbaɪ'sɛkʃʊəl] *adj* : bisexual
bishop ['bɪʃəp] *n* **1** : obispo *m* **2** : alfil *m* (en ajedrez)
bismuth ['bɪzməθ] *n* : bismuto *m*
bison ['baɪzən, -sən] *ns & pl* : bisonte *m*
bistro ['biːstro, 'bɪs-] *n, pl* **-tros** : bar *m*, restaurante *m* pequeño
bit ['bɪt] *n* **1** FRAGMENT, PIECE : pedazo *m*, trozo *m* ⟨a bit of luck : un poco de suerte⟩ **2** : freno *m*, bocado *m* (de una brida) **3** : broca *f* (de un taladro) **4** : bit *m* (de información)
bitch¹ ['bɪtʃ] *vi* COMPLAIN : quejarse, reclamar

bitch² *n* : perra *f*
bite¹ ['baɪt] *v* **bit** ['bɪt]; **bitten** ['bɪtən]; **biting** *vt* **1** : morder **2** STING : picar **3** PUNCTURE : punzar, pinchar **4** GRIP : agarrar — *vi* **1** : morder ⟨that dog bites : ese perro muerde⟩ **2** STING : picar (dícese de un insecto), cortar (dícese del viento) **3** : picar ⟨the fish are biting now : ya están picando los peces⟩ **4** GRAB : agarrarse
bite² *n* **1** BITING : mordisco *m*, dentellada *f* **2** SNACK : bocado *m* ⟨a bite to eat : algo de comer⟩ **3** : picadura *f* (de un insecto), mordedura *f* (de un animal) **4** SHARPNESS : mordacidad *f*, penetración *f*
biting *adj* **1** PENETRATING : cortante, penetrante **2** CAUSTIC : mordaz, sarcástico
bitter ['bɪṭər] *adj* **1** ACRID : amargo, acre **2** PENETRATING : cortante, penetrante ⟨bitter cold : frío glacial⟩ **3** HARSH : duro, amargo ⟨to the bitter end : hasta el final⟩ **4** INTENSE, RELENTLESS : intenso, extremo, implacable ⟨bitter hatred : odio implacable⟩
bitterly ['bɪṭərli] *adv* : amargamente
bitterness ['bɪṭərnəs] *n* : amargura *f*
bittersweet ['bɪṭərˌswiːt] *adj* : agridulce
bivalve ['baɪˌvælv] *n* : bivalvo *m* — **bivalve** *adj*
bivouac¹ ['bɪvəˌwæk, 'bɪvˌwæk] *vi* **-ouacked; -ouacking** : acampar, vivaquear
bivouac² *n* : vivaque *m*
bizarre [bə'zɑr] *adj* : extraño, singular, estrafalario, estrambótico — **bizarrely** *adv*
blab ['blæb] *vi* **blabbed; blabbing** : parlotear *fam*, cotorrear *fam*
black¹ ['blæk] *vt* : ennegrecer
black² *adj* **1** : negro (color, raza) **2** SOILED : sucio **3** DARK : oscuro, negro **4** WICKED : malvado, perverso, malo **5** GLOOMY : negro, sombrío, deprimente
black³ *n* **1** : negro *m* (color) **2** : negro *m*, -gra *f* (persona)
black—and—blue [ˌblækən'bluː] *adj* : amoratado
blackball ['blækˌbɔl] *vt* **1** OSTRACIZE : hacerle el vacío a, aislar **2** BOYCOTT : boicotear
blackberry ['blækˌbɛri] *n, pl* **-ries** : mora *f*
blackbird ['blækˌbərd] *n* : mirlo *m*
blackboard ['blækˌbɔrd] *n* : pizarra *f*, pizarrón *m*
blacken ['blækən] *vt* **1** BLACK : ennegrecer **2** DEFAME : deshonrar, difamar, manchar
blackhead ['blækˌhɛd] *n* : espinilla *f*, punto *m* negro
black hole *n* : agujero *m* negro
blackjack ['blækˌʤæk] *n* **1** : cachiporra *f* (arma) **2** : veintiuna *f* (juego de cartas)
blacklist¹ ['blækˌlɪst] *vt* : poner en la lista negra

blacklist² *n* : lista *f* negra
blackmail¹ ['blæk,meɪl] *vt* : chantajear, hacer chantaje a
blackmail² *n* : chantaje *m*
blackmailer ['blæk,meɪlər] *n* : chantajista *mf*
blackout ['blæk,aʊt] *n* 1 : apagón *m* (de poder eléctrico) 2 FAINT : desmayo *m*, desvanecimiento *m*
black out *vt* : dejar sin luz — *vi* FAINT : perder el conocimiento, desmayarse
blacksmith ['blæk,smɪθ] *n* : herrero *m*
blacktop ['blæk,tɑp] *n* : asfalto *m*
bladder ['blædər] *n* : vejiga *f*
blade ['bleɪd] *n* : hoja *f* (de un cuchillo), cuchilla *f* (de un patín), pala *f* (de un remo o una hélice), brizna *f* (de hierba)
blamable ['bleɪməbəl] *adj* : culpable
blame¹ ['bleɪm] *vt* **blamed; blaming** : culpar, echar la culpa a
blame² *n* : culpa *f*
blameless ['bleɪmləs] *adj* : intachable, sin culpa, inocente — **blamelessly** *adv*
blameworthiness ['bleɪm,wərðinəs] *n* : culpa *f*, culpabilidad *f*
blameworthy ['bleɪm,wərði] *adj* : culpable, reprochable, censurable
blanch ['blæntʃ] *vt* WHITEN : blanquear — *vi* PALE : palidecer
bland ['blænd] *adj* : soso, insulso, desabrido ⟨a bland smile : una sonrisa insulsa⟩ ⟨a bland diet : una dieta fácil de digerir⟩
blandishments ['blændɪʃmənts] *npl* : lisonjas *fpl*, halagos *mpl*
blandly ['blændli] *adv* : de manera insulsa
blandness ['blændnəs] *n* : lo insulso, lo desabrido
blank¹ ['blæŋk] *vt* OBLITERATE : borrar
blank² *adj* 1 DAZED : perplejo, desconcertado 2 EXPRESSIONLESS : sin expresión, inexpresivo 3 : en blanco (dícese de un papel), liso (dícese de una pared) 4 EMPTY : vacío, en blanco ⟨a blank stare : una mirada vacía⟩ ⟨his mind went blank : se quedó en blanco⟩
blank³ *n* 1 SPACE : espacio *m* en blanco 2 FORM : formulario *m* 3 CARTRIDGE : cartucho *m* de fogueo 4 *or* **blank key** : llave *f* ciega
blanket¹ [blæŋkət] *vt* : cubrir
blanket² *adj* : global
blanket³ *n* : manta *f*, cobija *f*, frazada *f*
blankly ['blæŋkli] *adv* : sin comprender
blankness ['blæŋknəs] *n* 1 PERPLEXITY : desconcierto *m*, perplejidad *f* 2 EMPTINESS : vacío *m*, vacuidad *f*
blare¹ ['blær] *vi* **blared; blaring** : resonar
blare² *n* : estruendo *m*
blarney ['blɑrni] *n* : labia *f* *fam*
blasé [blɑ'zeɪ] *adj* : displicente, indiferente
blaspheme [blæs'fiːm, 'blæs,-] *vi* **-phemed; -pheming** : blasfemar
blasphemer [blæs'fiːmər, 'blæs,-] *n* : blasfemo *m*, -ma *f*

blasphemous ['blæsfəməs] *adj* : blasfemo
blasphemy ['blæsfəmi] *n, pl* **-mies** : blasfemia *f*
blast¹ ['blæst] *vt* 1 BLOW UP : volar, hacer volar 2 ATTACK : atacar, arremeter contra
blast² *n* 1 GUST : ráfaga *f* 2 EXPLOSION : explosión *f*
blast–off ['blæst,ɔf] *n* : despegue *m*
blast off *vi* : despegar
blatant ['bleɪtənt] *adj* : descarado — **blatantly** ['bleɪtəntli] *adv*
blaze¹ ['bleɪz] *v* **blazed; blazing** *vi* SHINE : arder, brillar, resplandecer — *vt* MARK : marcar, señalar ⟨to blaze a trail : abrir un camino⟩
blaze² *n* 1 FIRE : fuego *m* 2 BRIGHTNESS : resplandor *m*, brillantez *f* 3 OUTBURST : arranque *m* ⟨a blaze of anger : un arranque de cólera⟩ 4 DISPLAY : alarde *m*, llamarada *f* ⟨a blaze of color : un derroche de color⟩
blazer ['bleɪzər] *n* : chaqueta *f* deportiva, blazer *m*
bleach¹ ['bliːtʃ] *vt* : blanquear, decolorar
bleach² *n* : lejía *f*, blanqueador *m*
bleachers ['bliːtʃərz] *ns & pl* : gradas *fpl*, tribuna *f* descubierta
bleak ['bliːk] *adj* 1 DESOLATE : inhóspito, sombrío, desolado 2 DEPRESSING : deprimente, triste, sombrío
bleakly ['bliːkli] *adv* : sombríamente
bleakness ['bliːknəs] *n* : lo inhóspito, lo sombrío
blear ['blɪr] *adj* : empañado, nublado
bleary ['blɪri] *adj* 1 : adormilado, fatigado 2 **bleary–eyed** : con los ojos nublados
bleat¹ ['bliːt] *vi* : balar
bleat² *n* : balido *m*
bleed ['bliːd] *v* **bled** ['blɛd]; **bleeding** *vi* 1 : sangrar 2 GRIEVE : sufrir, afligirse 3 EXUDE : exudar (dícese de una planta), correrse (dícese de los colores) — *vt* 1 : sangrar (a una persona), purgar (frenos) 2 **to bleed someone dry** : sacarle todo el dinero a alguien
blemish¹ ['blɛmɪʃ] *vt* : manchar, marcar
blemish² *n* : imperfección *f*, mancha *f*, marca *f*
blend¹ ['blɛnd] *vt* 1 MIX : mezclar 2 COMBINE : combinar, aunar
blend² *n* : mezcla *f*, combinación *f*
blender ['blɛndər] *n* : licuadora *f*
bless ['blɛs] *vt* **blessed** ['blɛst]; **blessing** 1 CONSECRATE : bendecir, consagrar 2 : bendecir ⟨may God bless you! : ¡que Dios te bendiga!⟩ 3 **to bless with** : dotar de 4 **to bless oneself** : santiguarse
blessed ['blɛsəd] *or* **blest** ['blɛst] *adj* : bienaventurado, bendito, dichoso
blessedly ['blɛsədli] *adv* : felizmente, alegremente, afortunadamente
blessing ['blɛsɪŋ] *n* 1 : bendición *f* 2 APPROVAL : aprobación *f*, consentimiento *m*

blew → blow
blight[1] ['blaɪt] vt : arruinar, infestar
blight[2] n 1 : añublo m 2 PLAGUE : peste f, plaga f 3 DECAY : deterioro m, ruina f
blimp ['blɪmp] n : dirigible m
blind[1] ['blaɪnd] vt 1 : cegar, dejar ciego 2 DAZZLE : deslumbrar
blind[2] adj 1 SIGHTLESS : ciego 2 INSENSITIVE : ciego, insensible, sin razón 3 CLOSED : sin salida ⟨blind alley : callejón sin salida⟩
blind[3] n 1 : persiana f (para una ventana) 2 COVER : escondite m, escondrijo m
blinders ['blaɪndərz] npl : anteojeras fpl
blindfold[1] ['blaɪnd,fo:ld] vt : vendar los ojos
blindfold[2] n : venda f (para los ojos)
blinding ['blaɪndɪŋ] adj : enceguecedor, cegador ⟨with blinding speed : con una rapidez inusitada⟩
blindly ['blaɪndli] adv : a ciegas, ciegamente
blindness ['blaɪndnəs] n : ceguera f
blink[1] ['blɪŋk] vi 1 WINK : pestañear, parpadear 2 : brillar intermitentemente
blink[2] n : pestañeo m, parpadeo m
blinker ['blɪŋkər] n : intermitente m, direccional f
bliss ['blɪs] n 1 HAPPINESS : dicha f, felicidad f absoluta 2 PARADISE : paraíso m
blissful ['blɪsfəl] adj : dichoso, feliz — **blissfully** adv
blister[1] ['blɪstər] vi : ampollarse
blister[2] n : ampolla f (en la piel o una superficie), burbuja f (en una superficie)
blithe ['blaɪθ, 'blaɪð] adj **blither; blithest** 1 CAREFREE : despreocupado 2 CHEERFUL : alegre, risueño — **blithely** adv
blitz[1] ['blɪts] vt 1 BOMBARD : bombardear 2 : atacar con rapidez
blitz[2] n 1 : bombardeo m aéreo 2 CAMPAIGN : ataque m, acometida f
blizzard ['blɪzərd] n : tormenta f de nieve, ventisca f
bloat ['blo:t] vi : hincharse, inflarse
blob ['blɑb] n : gota f, mancha f, borrón m
bloc ['blɑk] n : bloque m
block[1] ['blɑk] vt 1 OBSTRUCT : obstruir, bloquear 2 CLOG : atascar, atorar
block[2] n 1 PIECE : bloque m ⟨building blocks : cubos de construcción⟩ ⟨auction block : plataforma de subastas⟩ ⟨starting block : taco de salida⟩ 2 OBSTRUCTION : obstrucción f, bloqueo m 3 : cuadra f, manzana f (de edificios) ⟨to go around the block : dar la vuelta a la cuadra⟩ 4 BUILDING : edificio m (de apartamentos, oficinas, etc.) 5 GROUP, SERIES : serie f, grupo m ⟨a block of tickets : una serie de entradas⟩ 6 **block and tackle** : aparejo m de poleas

blockade[1] [blɑ'keɪd] vt **-aded; -ading** : bloquear
blockade[2] n : bloqueo m
blockage ['blɑkɪdʒ] n : bloqueo m, obstrucción f
blockhead ['blɑk,hɛd] n : bruto m, -ta f; estúpido m, -da f
blond[1] or **blonde** ['blɑnd] adj : rubio, güero Mex, claro (dícese de la madera)
blond[2] or **blonde** n : rubio m, -bia f; güero m, -ra f Mex
blood ['blʌd] n 1 : sangre f 2 LIFEBLOOD : vida f, alma f 3 LINEAGE : linaje m, sangre f
blood bank n : banco m de sangre
bloodcurdling ['blʌd,kərdəlɪŋ] adj : espeluznante, aterrador
blooded ['blʌdəd] adj : de sangre ⟨cold-blooded animal : animal de sangre fría⟩
bloodhound ['blʌd,haʊnd] n : sabueso m
bloodless ['blʌdləs] adj 1 : incruento, sin derramamiento de sangre 2 LIFELESS : desanimado, insípido, sin vida
bloodmobile ['blʌdmo,bi:l] n : unidad f móvil para donantes de sangre
blood pressure n : tensión f, presión f (arterial)
bloodshed ['blʌd,ʃɛd] n : derramamiento m de sangre
bloodshot ['blʌd,ʃɑt] adj : inyectado de sangre
bloodstain ['blʌd,steɪn] n : mancha f de sangre
bloodstained ['blʌd,steɪnd] adj : manchado de sangre
bloodstream ['blʌd,stri:m] n : torrente m sanguíneo, corriente f sanguínea
bloodsucker ['blʌd,sʌkər] n : sanguijuela f
bloodthirsty ['blʌd,θərsti] adj : sanguinario
blood vessel n : vaso m sanguíneo
bloody ['blʌdi] adj **bloodier; -est** : ensangrentado, sangriento
bloom[1] ['blu:m] vi 1 FLOWER : florecer 2 MATURE : madurar
bloom[2] n 1 FLOWER : flor f ⟨to be in bloom : estar en flor⟩ 2 FLOWERING : floración f ⟨in full bloom : en plena floración⟩ 3 : rubor m (de la tez) ⟨in the bloom of youth : en plena juventud, en la flor de la vida⟩
bloomers ['blu:mərz] npl : bombachos mpl
blooper ['blu:pər] n : metedura f de pata fam
blossom[1] ['blɑsəm] vi : florecer, dar flor
blossom[2] n : flor f
blot[1] ['blɑt] vt **blotted; blotting** 1 SPOT : emborronar, borronear 2 DRY : secar
blot[2] n 1 STAIN : mancha f, borrón m 2 BLEMISH : mancha f, tacha f
blotch[1] ['blɑtʃ] vt : emborronar, borronear
blotch[2] n : mancha f, borrón m
blotchy ['blɑtʃi] adj **blotchier; -est** : lleno de manchas

blotter ['blɑṭər] *n* : hoja *f* de papel secante, secante *m*

blouse ['blaʊs, 'blaʊz] *n* : blusa *f*

blow¹ ['blo:] *v* **blew** ['blu:]; **blown** ['blo:n]; **blowing** *vi* **1** : soplar, volar ⟨the wind is blowing hard : el viento está soplando con fuerza⟩ ⟨it blew out the door : voló por la puerta⟩ ⟨the window blew shut : se cerró la ventana⟩ **2** SOUND : sonar ⟨the whistle blew : sonó el silbato⟩ **3 to blow out** : fundirse (dícese de un fusible eléctrico), reventarse (dícese de una llanta) **4 to blow off** : dejar plantado (a alguien), flatar a (una cita, etc.) — *vt* **1** : soplar, echar ⟨to blow smoke : echar humo⟩ **2** SOUND : tocar, sonar **3** SHAPE : soplar, dar forma a ⟨to blow glass : soplar vidrio⟩ **4** BUNGLE : echar a perder

blow² *n* **1** PUFF : soplo *m*, soplido *m* **2** GALE : vendaval *f* **3** HIT, STROKE : golpe *m* **4** CALAMITY : golpe *m*, desastre *m* **5 to come to blows** : llegar a las manos

blower ['blo:ər] *n* FAN : ventilador *m*

blowout ['blo:,aʊt] *n* : reventón *m*

blowtorch ['blo:,tɔrtʃ] *n* : soplete *m*

blow up *vi* EXPLODE : estallar, hacer explosión — *vt* BLAST : volar, hacer volar

blubber¹ ['blʌbər] *vi* : lloriquear

blubber² *n* : esperma *f* de ballena

bludgeon ['blʌdʒən] *vt* : aporrear

blue¹ ['blu:] *adj* **bluer; bluest 1** : azul **2** MELANCHOLY : melancólico, triste

blue² *n* : azul *m*

blueberry ['blu:,bɛri] *n*, *pl* **-ries** : arándano *m*

bluebird ['blu:,bərd] *n* : azulejo *m*

blue cheese *n* : queso *m* azul

blueprint ['blu:,prɪnt] *n* **1** : plano *m*, proyecto *m*, cianotipo *m* **2** PLAN : anteproyecto *m*, programa *m*

blues ['blu:z] *npl* **1** DEPRESSION : depresión *f*, melancolía *f* **2** : blues *m* ⟨to sing the blues : cantar blues⟩

bluff¹ ['blʌf] *vi* : hacer un farol, blofear *Col, Mex*

bluff² *adj* **1** STEEP : escarpado **2** FRANK : campechano, franco, directo

bluff³ *n* **1** : farol *m*, blof *m Col, Mex* **2** CLIFF : acantilado *m*, risco *m*

bluing *or* **blueing** ['blu:ɪŋ] *n* : añil *m*, azulete *m*

bluish ['blu:ɪʃ] *adj* : azulado

blunder¹ ['blʌndər] *vi* **1** STUMBLE : tropezar, dar traspiés **2** ERR : cometer un error, tropezar, meter la pata *fam*

blunder² *n* : error *m*, fallo *m* garrafal, metedura *f* de pata *fam*

blunderbuss ['blʌndər,bʌs] *n* : trabuco *m*

blunt¹ ['blʌnt] *vt* : despuntar (aguja o lápiz), desafilar (cuchillo o tijeras), suavizar (crítica)

blunt² *adj* **1** DULL : desafilado, despuntado **2** DIRECT : directo, franco, categórico

bluntly ['blʌntli] *adv* : sin rodeos, francamente, bruscamente

bluntness ['blʌntnəs] *n* **1** DULLNESS : falta *f* de filo, embotadura *f* **2** FRANKNESS : franqueza *f*

blur¹ ['blər] *vt* **blurred; blurring** : desdibujar, hacer borroso

blur² *n* **1** SMEAR : mancha *f*, borrón *m* **2** : aspecto *m* borroso ⟨everything was just a blur : todo se volvió borroso⟩

blurb ['blərb] *n* : propaganda *f*, nota *f* publicitaria

blurry ['bləri] *adj* : borroso

blurt ['blərt] *vt* : espetar, decir impulsivamente

blush¹ ['blʌʃ] *vi* : ruborizarse, sonrojarse, hacerse colorado

blush² *n* : rubor *m*, sonrojo *m*

bluster¹ ['blʌstər] *vi* **1** BLOW : soplar con fuerza **2** BOAST : fanfarronear, echar bravatas

bluster² *n* : fanfarronada *f*, bravatas *fpl*

blustery ['blʌstəri] *adj* : borrascoso, tempestuoso

boa ['bo:ə] *n* : boa *f*

boar ['bor] *n* : cerdo *m* macho, verraco *m*

board¹ ['bord] *vt* **1** : embarcarse en, subir a bordo de (una nave o un avión), subir a (un tren o carro) **2** LODGE : hospedar, dar hospedaje con comidas a **3 to board up** : cerrar con tablas

board² *n* **1** PLANK : tabla *f*, tablón *m* **2** : tablero *m* ⟨chessboard : tablero de ajedrez⟩ **3** MEALS : comida *f* ⟨board and lodging : comida y alojamiento⟩ **4** COMMITTEE, COUNCIL : junta *f*, consejo *m*

boarder ['bordər] *n* LODGER : huésped *m*, -peda *f*

boardinghouse ['bordɪŋ,haʊs] *n* : casa *f* de huéspedes

boarding school *n* : internado *m*

boardwalk ['bord,wɔk] *n* : paseo *m* marítimo

boast¹ ['bo:st] *vi* : alardear, presumir, jactarse

boast² *n* : jactancia *f*, alarde *m*

boaster ['bo:stər] *n* : presumido *m*, -da *f*; fanfarrón *m*, -rrona *f fam*

boastful ['bo:stfəl] *adj* : jactancioso, fanfarrón *fam*

boastfully ['bo:stfəli] *adv* : de manera jactanciosa

boat¹ ['bo:t] *vt* : transportar en barco, poner a bordo

boat² *n* : barco *m*, embarcación *f*, bote *m*, barca *f*

boatman ['bo:tmən] *n*, *pl* **-men** [-mən, -,mɛn] : barquero *m*

boatswain ['bo:sən] *n* : contramaestre *m*

bob¹ ['bɑb] *v* **bobbed; bobbing** *vi* **1** : balancearse, mecerse ⟨to bob up and down : subir y bajar⟩ **2** *or* **to bob up** APPEAR : presentarse, surgir — *vt* **1** : inclinar (la cabeza o el cuerpo) **2** CUT : cortar, recortar ⟨she bobbed her hair : se cortó el pelo⟩

bob² *n* **1** : inclinación *f* (de la cabeza, del cuerpo), sacudida *f* **2** FLOAT : flotador *m*, corcho *m* (de pesca) **3** : pelo *m* corto
bobbin [ˈbabən] *n* : bobina *f*, carrete *m*
bobby pin [ˈbabiˌpɪn] *n* : horquilla *f*
bobcat [ˈbabˌkæt] *n* : lince *m* rojo
bobolink [ˈbabəˌlɪŋk] *n* : tordo *m* arrocero
bobsled [ˈbabˌslɛd] *n* : bobsleigh *m*
bobwhite [ˈbabˈʰwaɪt] *n* : codorniz *m* (del Nuevo Mundo)
bode¹ [ˈboːd] *v* **boded; boding** *vt* : presagiar, augurar — *vi* **to bode well** : ser de buen agüero
bode² → **bide**
bodice [ˈbadəs] *n* : corpiño *m*
bodied [ˈbadid] *adj* : de cuerpo ⟨leanbodied : de cuerpo delgado⟩ ⟨ablebodied : no discapacitado⟩
bodiless [ˈbadiləs, ˈbadələs] *adj* : incorpóreo
bodily¹ [ˈbadəli] *adv* : en peso ⟨to lift someone bodily : levantar a alguien en peso⟩
bodily² *adj* : corporal, del cuerpo ⟨bodily harm : daños corporales⟩
body [ˈbadi] *n, pl* **bodies 1** : cuerpo *m*, organismo *m* **2** CORPSE : cadáver *m* **3** PERSON : persona *f*, ser *m* humano **4** : nave *f* (de una iglesia), carrocería (de un automóvil), fuselaje *m* (de un avión), casco *m* (de una nave) **5** COLLECTION, MASS : conjunto *m*, grupo *m*, masa *f* ⟨in a body : todos juntos, en masa⟩ **6** ORGANIZATION : organismo *m*, organización *f*
bodyguard [ˈbadiˌgard] *n* : guardaespaldas *mf*
bog¹ [ˈbag, ˈbɔg] *vt* **bogged; bogging** : empantanar, inundar ⟨to get bogged down : empantanarse⟩
bog² *n* : lodazal *m*, ciénaga *f*, cenagal *m*
bogey [ˈbʊgi, ˈboː-] *n, pl* **-geys** : terror *m*, coco *m fam*
boggle [ˈbagəl] *vi* **-gled; -gling** : quedarse atónito, quedarse pasmado ⟨the mind boggles! : ¡es increíble!⟩
boggy [ˈbagi, ˈbɔ-] *adj* **boggier; -est** : cenagoso
bogus [ˈboːgəs] *adj* : falso, fingido, falaz
bohemian [boːˈhiːmiən] *n* : bohemio *m*, -mia *f* — **bohemian** *adj*
boil¹ [ˈbɔɪl] *vi* **1** : hervir **2 to make one's blood boil** : hervirle la sangre a uno — *vt* **1** : hervir, hacer hervir ⟨to boil water : hervir agua⟩ **2** : cocer, hervir ⟨to boil potatoes : cocer papas⟩
boil² *n* **1** BOILING : hervor *m* **2** : furúnculo *m*, divieso *m* (en medicina)
boiler [ˈbɔɪlər] *n* : caldera *f*
boisterous [ˈbɔɪstərəs] *adj* : bullicioso, escandaloso — **boisterously** *adv*
bold [ˈboːld] *adj* **1** COURAGEOUS : valiente **2** INSOLENT : insolente, descarado **3** DARING : atrevido, audaz — **boldly** *adv*
boldface [ˈboːldˌfeɪs] *or* **boldface type** *n* : negrita *f*

boldness [ˈboːldnəs] *n* **1** COURAGE : valor *m*, coraje *m* **2** INSOLENCE : atrevimiento *m*, insolencia *f*, descaro *m* **3** DARING : audacia *f*
bolero [bəˈlɛro] *n, pl* **-ros** : bolero *m*
Bolivian [bəˈlɪviən] *n* : boliviano *m*, -na *f* — **Bolivian** *adj*
boll [ˈboːl] *n* : cápsula *f* (del algodón)
boll weevil *n* : gorgojo *m* del algodón
bologna [bəˈloːni] *n* : salchicha *f* ahumada
bolster¹ [ˈboːlstər] *vt* **-stered; -stering** : reforzar, reafirmar ⟨to bolster morale : levantar la moral⟩
bolster² *n* : cabezal *m*, almohadón *m*
bolt [ˈboːlt] *vt* **1** : atornillar, sujetar con pernos ⟨bolted to the floor : sujetado con pernos al suelo⟩ **2** : cerrar con pestillo, echar el cerrojo a ⟨to bolt the door : echar el cerrojo a la puerta⟩ **3 to bolt down** : engullir ⟨she bolted down her dinner : engulló su comida⟩ — *vi* : echar a correr, salir corriendo ⟨he bolted from the room : salió corriendo de la sala⟩
bolt² *n* **1** LATCH : pestillo *m*, cerrojo *m* **2** : tornillo *m*, perno *m* ⟨nuts and bolts : tuercas y tornillos⟩ **3** : rollo *m* ⟨a bolt of cloth : un rollo de tela⟩ **4 lightning bolt** : relámpago *m*, rayo *m*
bomb¹ [ˈbam] *vt* : bombardear
bomb² *n* : bomba *f*
bombard [bamˈbard, bəm-] *vt* : bombardear
bombardier [ˌbambəˈdɪr] *n* : bombardero *m*, -ra *f*
bombardment [bamˈbardmənt] *n* : bombardeo *m*
bombast [ˈbamˌbæst] *n* : grandilocuencia *f*, ampulosidad *f*
bombastic [bamˈbæstɪk] *adj* : grandilocuente, ampuloso, bombástico
bomber [ˈbamər] *n* : bombardero *m*
bombproof [ˈbamˌpruːf] *adj* : a prueba de bombas
bombshell [ˈbamˌʃɛl] *n* : bomba *f* ⟨a political bombshell : una bomba política⟩
bona fide [ˈboːnəˌfaɪd, ˈba-, ˌboːnəˈfaɪdi] *adj* **1** : de buena fe ⟨a bona fide offer : una oferta de buena fe⟩ **2** GENUINE : genuino, auténtico
bonanza [bəˈnænzə] *n* : bonanza *f*
bonbon [ˈbanˌban] *n* : bombón *m*
bond¹ [ˈband] *vt* **1** INSURE : dar fianza a, asegurar **2** STICK : adherir, pegar — *vi* : adherirse, pegarse
bond² *n* **1** LINK, TIE : vínculo *m*, lazo *m* **2** BAIL : fianza *f*, caución *f* **3** : bono *m* ⟨stocks and bonds : acciones y bonos⟩ **4 bonds** *npl* FETTERS : cadenas *fpl*
bondage [ˈbandɪdʒ] *n* : esclavitud *f*
bondholder [ˈbandˌhoːldər] *n* : tenedor *m*, -dora *f* de bonos
bondsman [ˈbandzmən] *n, pl* **-men** [-mən, -ˌmɛn] **1** SLAVE : esclavo *m* **2** SURETY : fiador *m*, -dora *f*
bone¹ [ˈboːn] *vt* **boned; boning** : deshuesar

bone² *n* : hueso *m*
boneless ['boːnləs] *adj* : sin huesos, sin espinas
boner ['boːnər] *n* : metedura *f* de pata, metida *f* de pata
bonfire ['bɑn,faɪr] *n* : hoguera *f*, fogata *f*, fogón *m*
bonito [bə'niːt̬o] *n*, *pl* -tos *or* -to : bonito *m*
bonnet ['bɑnət] *n* : sombrero *m* (de mujer), gorra *f* (de niño)
bonus ['boːnəs] *n* 1 : prima *f*, bonificación *f* (pagado al empleado) 2 ADVANTAGE, BENEFIT : beneficio *m*, provecho *m*
bony ['boːni] *adj* **bonier; -est** : huesudo
boo¹ ['buː] *vt* : abuchear
boo² *n*, *pl* **boos** : abucheo *m*
booby ['buːbi] *n*, *pl* **-bies** : bobo *m*, -ba *f*; tonto *m*, -ta *f*
book¹ ['bʊk] *vt* : reservar ⟨to book a flight : reservar un vuelo⟩
book² *n* 1 : libro *m* 2 **the Book** : la Biblia 3 **by the book** : según las reglas
bookcase ['bʊk,keɪs] *n* : estantería *f*, librero *m Mex*
bookend ['bʊk,ɛnd] *n* : sujetalibros *m*
bookie ['bʊki] → **bookmaker**
bookish ['bʊkɪʃ] *adj* : libresco
bookkeeper ['bʊk,kiːpər] *n* : tenedor *m*, -dora *f* de libros; contable *mf Spain*
bookkeeping ['bʊk,kiːpɪŋ] *n* : contabilidad *f*, teneduría *f* de libros
booklet ['bʊklət] *n* : folleto *m*
bookmaker ['bʊk,meɪkər] *n* : corredor *m*, -dora *f* de apuestas
bookmark ['bʊk,mɑrk] *n* : señalador *m* de libros, marcador *m* de libros
bookseller ['bʊk,slər] *n* : librero *m*, -ra *f*
bookshelf ['bʊk,ʃɛlf] *n*, *pl* **-shelves** 1 : estante *m* 2 **bookshelves** *npl* : estantería *f*
bookstore ['bʊk,stor] *n* : librería *f*
bookworm ['bʊk,wərm] *n* : ratón *m* de biblioteca *fam*
boom¹ ['buːm] *vi* 1 THUNDER : tronar, resonar 2 FLOURISH, PROSPER : estar en auge, prosperar
boom² *n* 1 BOOMING : bramido *m*, estruendo *m* 2 FLOURISHING : auge *m* ⟨population boom : auge de población⟩
boomerang ['buːmə,ræŋ] *n* : bumerán *m*
boon¹ ['buːn] *adj* **boon companion** : amigo *m*, -ga *f* del alma
boon² *n* : ayuda *f*, beneficio *m*, adelanto *m*
boondocks ['buːn,dɑks] *npl* : área *f* rural remota, región *f* alejada
boor ['bʊr] *n* : grosero *m*, -ra *f*
boorish ['bʊrɪʃ] *adj* : grosero
boost¹ ['buːst] *vt* 1 LIFT : levantar, alzar 2 INCREASE : aumentar, incrementar 3 PROMOTE : promover, fomentar, hacer publicidad por

boost² *n* 1 THRUST : impulso *m*, empujón *m* 2 ENCOURAGEMENT : estímulo *m*, aliento *m* 3 INCREASE : aumento *m*, incremento *m*
booster ['buːstər] *n* 1 SUPPORTER : partidario *m*, -ria *f* 2 **booster rocket** : cohete *m* propulsor 3 **booster shot** : vacuna *f* de refuerzo
boot¹ ['buːt] *vt* KICK : dar una patada a, patear
boot² *n* 1 : bota *f*, botín *m* 2 KICK : puntapié *m*, patada *f*
bootee *or* **bootie** ['buːt̬i] *n* : botita *f*, botín *m*
booth ['buːθ] *n*, *pl* **booths** ['buːðz, 'buːθs] : cabina *f* (de teléfono, de votar), caseta *f* (de información), barraca *f* (a una feria)
bootlegger ['buːt,lɛgər] *n* : contrabandista *mf* del alcohol
booty ['buːt̬i] *n*, *pl* **-ties** : botín *m*
booze ['buːz] *n fam* : alcohol *m*
borax ['bor,æks] *n* : bórax *m*
border¹ ['bordər] *vt* 1 EDGE : ribetear, bordear 2 BOUND : limitar con, lindar con — *vi* VERGE : rayar, lindar ⟨that borders on absurdity : eso raya en el absurdo⟩
border² *n* 1 EDGE : borde *m*, orilla *f* 2 TRIM : ribete *m* 3 FRONTIER : frontera *f*
bore¹ ['bor] *vt* **bored; boring** 1 PIERCE : taladrar, perforar ⟨to bore metals : taladrar metales⟩ 2 OPEN : hacer, abrir ⟨to bore a tunnel : abrir un túnel⟩ 3 WEARY : aburrir
bore² → **bear¹**
bore³ *n* 1 : pesado *m*, -da *f* (persona aburrida) 2 TEDIOUSNESS : pesadez *f*, lo aburrido 3 DIAMETER : calibre *m*
boredom ['bordəm] *n* : aburrimiento *m*
boring ['borɪŋ] *adj* : aburrido, pesado
born ['born] *adj* 1 : nacido 2 : nato ⟨she's a born singer : es una cantante nata⟩ ⟨he's a born leader : nació para mandar⟩
borne *pp* → **bear¹**
boron ['bor,ɑn] *n* : boro *m*
borough ['bəro] *n* : distrito *m* municipal
borrow ['bɑro] *vt* 1 : pedir prestado, tomar prestado 2 APPROPRIATE : apropiarse de, adoptar
borrower ['bɑrəwər] *n* : prestatario *m*, -ria *f*
Bosnian ['bɑzniən, 'bɔz-] *n* : bosnio *m*, -nia *f* — **Bosnian** *adj*
bosom¹ ['bʊzəm, 'buː-] *adj* : íntimo
bosom² *n* 1 CHEST : pecho *m* 2 BREAST : pecho *m*, seno *m* 3 CLOSENESS : seno *m* ⟨in the bosom of her family : en el seno de su familia⟩
bosomed ['bʊzəmd, 'buː-] *adj* : con busto ⟨big-bosomed : con mucho busto⟩
boss¹ ['bɔs] *vt* 1 SUPERVISE : dirigir, supervisar 2 **to boss around** : mandonear *fam*, mangonear *fam*
boss² *n* : jefe *m*, -fa *f*; patrón *m*, -trona *f*
bossy ['bɔsi] *adj* **bossier; -est** : mandón *fam*, autoritario, dominante

botanist [ˈbɑtənɪst] *n* : botánico *m*, -ca *f*
botany [ˈbɑtəni] *n* : botánica *f* — **botanical** [bəˈtænɪkəl] *adj*
botch[1] [ˈbɑtʃ] *vt* : hacer una chapuza de, estropear
botch[2] *n* : chapuza *f*
both[1] [ˈboːθ] *adj* : ambos, los dos, las dos ⟨both books : ambos libros, los dos libros⟩
both[2] *conj* : tanto como ⟨both Ann and her mother are tall : tanto Ana como su madre son altas⟩
both[3] *pron* : ambos *m*, -bas *f*; los dos, las dos
bother[1] [ˈbɑðər] *vt* **1** IRK : preocupar ⟨nothing's bothering me : nada me preocupa⟩ ⟨what's bothering him? : ¿qué le pasa?⟩ **2** PESTER : molestar, fastidiar — *vi* to bother to : molestarse en, tomar la molestia de
bother[2] *n* **1** TROUBLE : molestia *f*, problemas *mpl* **2** ANNOYANCE : molestia *f*, fastidio *m*
bothersome [ˈbɑðərsəm] *adj* : molesto, fastidioso
bottle[1] [ˈbɑtəl] *vt* **bottled; bottling** : embotellar, envasar
bottle[2] *n* : botella *f*, frasco *m*
bottleneck [ˈbɑtəlˌnɛk] *n* **1** : cuello *m* de botella (en un camino) **2** : embotellamiento *m*, atasco *m* (de tráfico) **3** OBSTACLE : obstáculo *m*
bottom[1] [ˈbɑtəm] *adj* : más bajo, inferior, de abajo
bottom[2] *n* **1** : fondo *m* (de una caja, de una taza, del mar), pie *m* (de una escalera, de una página, una montaña), asiento *m* (de una silla), parte *f* de abajo (de una pila) **2** CAUSE : origen *m*, causa *f* ⟨to get to the bottom of : llegar al fondo de⟩ **3** BUTTOCKS : trasero *m*, nalgas *fpl*
bottomless [ˈbɑtəmləs] *adj* : sin fondo, sin límites
botulism [ˈbɑtʃəˌlɪzəm] *n* : botulismo *m*
boudoir [bəˈdwɑr, buˈ-; ˈbuˌ-, ˈbu-] *n* : tocador *m*
bough [ˈbaʊ] *n* : rama *f*
bought → **buy**[1]
bouillon [ˈbuːˌjɑn; ˈbʊlˌjɑn, -jən] *n* : caldo *m*
boulder [ˈboːldər] *n* : canto *m* rodado, roca *f* grande
boulevard [ˈbʊləˌvɑrd, ˈbuː-] *n* : bulevar *m*, boulevard *m*
bounce[1] [ˈbaʊnts] *v* **bounced; bouncing** *vt* : hacer rebotar — *vi* : rebotar
bounce[2] *n* : rebote *m*
bouncy [ˈbaʊntsi] *adj* **bouncier; -est 1** LIVELY : vivo, exuberante, animado **2** RESILIENT : elástico, flexible **3** : que rebota (dícese de una pelota)
bound[1] [ˈbaʊnd] *vt* : delimitar, rodear — *vi* LEAP : saltar, dar brincos
bound[2] *adj* **1** OBLIGED : obligado **2** : encuadernado, empastado ⟨a book bound in leather : un libro encuadernado en cuero⟩ **3** DETERMINED : decidido, empeñado **4** to be bound to : ser seguro que, tener que, no caber duda que ⟨it was bound to happen : tenía que suceder⟩ **5** bound for : con rumbo a ⟨bound for Chicago : con rumbo a Chicago⟩ ⟨to be homeward bound : ir camino a casa⟩
bound[3] *n* **1** LIMIT : límite *m* **2** LEAP : salto *m*, brinco *m*
boundary [ˈbaʊndri, -dəri] *n, pl* **-aries** : límite *m*, línea *f* divisoria, linde *mf*
boundless [ˈbaʊndləs] *adj* : sin límites, infinito
bounteous [ˈbaʊntiəs] *adj* **1** GENEROUS : generoso **2** ABUNDANT : copioso, abundante — **bounteously** *adv*
bountiful [ˈbaʊntɪfəl] *adj* **1** GENEROUS, LIBERAL : munificente, pródigo, generoso **2** ABUNDANT : copioso, abundante
bounty [ˈbaʊnti] *n, pl* **-ties 1** GENEROSITY : generosidad *f*, munificencia *f* **2** REWARD : recompensa *f*
bouquet [boːˈkeɪ, buːˈ-] *n* **1** : ramo *m*, ramillete *m* **2** FRAGRANCE : bouquet *m*, aroma *m*
bourbon [ˈbərbən, ˈbʊr-] *n* : bourbon *m*, whisky *m* americano
bourgeois[1] [ˈbʊrʒˌwɑ, bʊrʒˈwɑ] *adj* : burgués
bourgeois[2] *n* : burgués *m*, -guesa *f*
bourgeoisie [ˌbʊrʒˌwɑˈzi] *n* : burguesía *f*
bout [ˈbaʊt] *n* **1** : encuentro *m*, combate *m* (en deportes) **2** ATTACK : ataque *m* (de una enfermedad) **3** PERIOD, SPELL : período *m* (de actividad)
boutique [buːˈtiːk] *n* : boutique *f*
bovine[1] [ˈboːˌvaɪn, -ˌviːn] *adj* : bovino, vacuno
bovine[2] *n* : bovino *m*
bow[1] [ˈbaʊ] *v* **1** : hacer una reverencia, inclinarse **2** SUBMIT : ceder, resignarse, someterse — *vt* **1** LOWER : inclinar, bajar **2** BEND : doblar
bow[2] [ˈbaʊ] *n* **1** BOWING : reverencia *f*, inclinación *f* **2** : proa *f* (de un barco)
bow[3] [ˈboː] *vi* CURVE : arquearse, doblarse
bow[4] [ˈboː] *n* **1** ARCH, CURVE : arco *m*, curva *f* **2** : arco *m* (arma o vara para tocar varios instrumentos de música) **3** : lazo *m*, moño *m* ⟨to tie a bow : hacer un moño⟩
bowels [ˈbaʊəls] *npl* **1** INTESTINES : intestinos *mpl* **2** : entrañas *fpl* ⟨in the bowels of the earth : en las entrañas de la tierra⟩
bower [ˈbaʊər] *n* : enramada *f*
bowl[1] [ˈboːl] *vi* : jugar a los bolos
bowl[2] *n* : tazón *m*, cuenco *m*
bowler [ˈboːlər] *n* : jugador *m*, -dora *f* de bolos
bowling [ˈboːlɪŋ] *n* : bolos *mpl*
box[1] [ˈbɑks] *vt* **1** PACK : empaquetar, embalar, encajonar **2** SLAP : bofetear, cachetear — *vi* : boxear

box² *n* **1** CONTAINER : caja *f*, cajón *m* **2** COMPARTMENT : compartimento *m*, palco *m* (en el teatro) **3** SLAP : bofetada *f*, cachetada *f* **4** : boj *m* (planta)

boxcar ['bɑks,kɑr] *n* : vagón *m* de carga, furgón *m*

boxer ['bɑksər] *n* : boxeador *m*, -dora *f*

boxing ['bɑksɪŋ] *n* : boxeo *m*

box office *n* : taquilla *f*, boletería *f*

boxwood ['bɑks,wʊd] *n* : boj *m*

boy ['bɔɪ] *n* **1** : chico *m*, muchacho *m* **2** *or* **little boy** : niño *m*, chico *m* **3** SON : hijo *m*

boycott¹ ['bɔɪ,kɑt] *vt* : boicotear

boycott² *n* : boicot *m*

boyfriend ['bɔɪ,frɛnd] *n* **1** FRIEND : amigo *m* **2** SWEETHEART : novio *m*

boyhood ['bɔɪ,hʊd] *n* : niñez *f*

boyish ['bɔɪɪʃ] *adj* : de niño, juvenil

bra ['brɑ] → **brassiere**

brace¹ ['breɪs] *v* **braced; bracing** *vt* **1** PROP UP, SUPPORT : apuntalar, apoyar, sostener **2** INVIGORATE : vigorizar **3** REINFORCE : reforzar — *vi* **to brace oneself** PREPARE : prepararse

brace² *n* **1** : berbiquí *m* ⟨brace and bit : berbiquí y barrena⟩ **2** CLAMP, REINFORCEMENT : abrazadera *f*, refuerzo *m* **3** : llave *f* (signo de puntuación) **4** **braces** *npl* : aparatos *mpl* (de ortodoncia), frenos *mpl Mex*

bracelet ['breɪslət] *n* : brazalete *m*, pulsera *f*

bracken ['brækən] *n* : helecho *m*

bracket¹ ['brækət] *vt* **1** SUPPORT : asegurar, apuntalar **2** : poner entre corchetes **3** CATEGORIZE, GROUP : catalogar, agrupar

bracket² *n* **1** SUPPORT : soporte *m* **2** : corchete *m* (marca de puntuación) **3** CATEGORY, CLASS : clase *f*, categoría *f*

brackish ['brækɪʃ] *adj* : salobre

brad ['bræd] *n* : clavo *m* con cabeza pequeña, clavito *m*

brag¹ ['bræg] *vi* **bragged; bragging** : alardear, fanfarronear, jactarse

brag² *n* : alarde *m*, jactancia *f*, fanfarronada *f*

braggart ['brægərt] *n* : fanfarrón *m*, -rrona *f fam*; jactancioso *m*, -sa *f*

braid¹ ['breɪd] *vt* : trenzar

braid² *n* : trenza *f*

braille ['breɪl] *n* : braille *m*

brain¹ ['breɪn] *vt* : romper la crisma a, aplastar el cráneo a

brain² *n* **1** : cerebro *m* **2** **brains** *npl* INTELLECT : inteligencia *f*, sesos *mpl*

brainless ['breɪnləs] *adj* : estúpido, tonto

brainstorm ['breɪn,stɔrm] *n* : idea *f* brillante, idea *f* genial

brainy ['breɪni] *adj* **brainier; -est** : inteligente, listo

braise ['breɪz] *vt* **braised; braising** : cocer a fuego lento, estofar

brake¹ ['breɪk] *v* **braked; braking** : frenar

brake² *n* : freno *m*

bramble ['bræmbəl] *n* : zarza *f*, zarzamora *f*

bran ['bræn] *n* : salvado *m*

branch¹ ['bræntʃ] *vi* **1** : echar ramas (dícese de una planta) **2** DIVERGE : ramificarse, separarse

branch² *n* **1** : rama *f* (de una planta) **2** EXTENSION : ramal *m* (de un camino, un ferrocarril, un río), rama *f* (de una familia o un campo de estudiar), sucursal *f* (de una empresa), agencia *f* (del gobierno)

brand¹ ['brænd] *vt* **1** : marcar (ganado) **2** LABEL : tachar, tildar ⟨they branded him as a liar : lo tacharon de mentiroso⟩

brand² *n* **1** : marca *f* (de ganado) **2** STIGMA : estigma *m* **3** MAKE : marca *f* ⟨brand name : marca de fábrica⟩

brandish ['brændɪʃ] *vt* : blandir

brand–new ['brænd'nu:, -'nju:] *adj* : nuevo, flamante

brandy ['brændi] *n, pl* **-dies** : brandy *m*

brash ['bræʃ] *adj* **1** IMPULSIVE : impulsivo, impetuoso **2** BRAZEN : excesivamente desenvuelto, descarado

brass ['bræs] *n* **1** : latón *m* **2** GALL, NERVE : descaro *m*, cara *f fam* **3** OFFICERS : mandamases *mpl fam*

brassiere [brə'zɪr, brɑ-] *n* : sostén *m*, brasier *m Col, Mex*

brassy ['bræsi] *adj* **brassier; -est** : dorado

brat ['bræt] *n* : mocoso *m*, -sa *f*; niño *m* mimado, niña *f* mimada

bravado [brə'vɑdo] *n, pl* **-does** *or* **-dos** : bravuconadas *fpl*, bravatas *fpl*

brave¹ ['breɪv] *vt* **braved; braving** : afrontar, hacer frente a

brave² *adj* **braver; bravest** : valiente, valeroso — **bravely** *adv*

brave³ *n* : guerrero *m* indio

bravery ['breɪvəri] *n* : valor *m*, valentía *f*

bravo ['brɑ,vo:] *n, pl* **-vos** : bravo *m*

brawl¹ ['brɔl] *vi* : pelearse, pegarse

brawl² *n* : pelea *f*, reyerta *f*

brawn ['brɔn] *n* : fuerza *f* muscular

brawny ['brɔni] *adj* **brawnier; -est** : musculoso

bray¹ ['breɪ] *vi* : rebuznar

bray² *n* : rebuzno *m*

brazen ['breɪzən] *adj* **1** : de latón **2** BOLD : descarado, directo

brazenly ['breɪzənli] *adv* : descaradamente, insolentemente

brazenness ['breɪzənnəs] *n* : descaro *m*, atrevimiento *m*

brazier ['breɪʒər] *n* : brasero *m*

Brazilian [brə'zɪljən] *n* : brasileño *m*, -ña *f* — **Brazilian** *adj*

Brazil nut [brə'zɪl,nʌt] *n* : nuez *f* de Brasil

breach¹ ['bri:tʃ] *vt* **1** PENETRATE : abrir una brecha en, penetrar **2** VIOLATE : infringir, violar

breach² *n* **1** VIOLATION : infracción *f*, violación *f* ⟨breach of trust : abuso de confianza⟩ **2** GAP, OPENING : brecha *f*

bread¹ ['brɛd] *vt* : empanar

bread² *n* : pan *m*

breadth ['brɛtθ] *n* : ancho *m*, anchura *f*

breadwinner ['brɛd₁wɪnər] *n* : sostén *m* de la familia

break¹ ['breɪk] *v* **broke** ['bro:k]; **broken** ['bro:kən]; **breaking** *vt* **1** SMASH : romper, quebrar **2** VIOLATE : infringir, violar, romper **3** SURPASS : batir, superar **4** CRUSH, RUIN : arruinar, deshacer, destrozar ⟨to break one's spirit : quebrantar su espíritu⟩ **5** : dar, comunicar ⟨to break the news : dar las noticias⟩ **6** INTERRUPT : cortar, interrumpir — *vi* **1** : romperse, quebrarse ⟨my calculator broke : se me rompió la calculadora⟩ **2** DISPERSE : dispersarse, despejarse **3** : estallar (dícese de una tormenta), romper (dícese del día) **4** CHANGE : cambiar (dícese del tiempo o de la voz) **5** DECREASE : bajar ⟨my fever broke : me bajó la fiebre⟩ **6** : divulgarse, revelarse ⟨the news broke : la noticia se divulgó⟩ **7 to break into** : forzar, abrir **8 to break out of** : escaparse de **9 to break through** : penetrar

break² *n* **1** : ruptura *f*, rotura *f*, fractura *f* (de un hueso), claro *m* (entre las nubes), cambio *m* (del tiempo) **2** CHANCE : oportunidad *f* ⟨a lucky break : un golpe de suerte⟩ **3** REST : descanso *m* ⟨to take a break : tomar(se) un descanso⟩

breakable ['breɪkəbəl] *adj* : quebradizo, frágil

breakage ['breɪkɪdʒ] *n* **1** BREAKING : rotura *f* **2** DAMAGE : destrozos *mpl*, daños *mpl*

breakdown ['breɪk₁daʊn] *n* **1** : avería *f* (de máquinas), interrupción *f* (de comunicaciones), fracaso *m* (de negociaciones) **2** ANALYSIS : análisis *m*, desglose *m* **3** *or* **nervous breakdown** : crisis *f* nerviosa

break down *vi* **1** : estropearse, descomponerse ⟨the machine broke down : la máquina se descompuso⟩ **2** FAIL : fracasar **3** CRY : echarse a llorar — *vt* **1** DESTROY : derribar, echar abajo **2** OVERCOME : vencer (la resistencia), disipar (sospechas) **3** ANALYZE : analizar, descomponer

breaker ['breɪkər] *n* **1** WAVE : ola *f* grande **2** : interruptor *m* automático (de electricidad)

breakfast¹ ['brɛkfəst] *vi* : desayunar

breakfast² *n* : desayuno *m*

breakneck ['breɪk₁nɛk] *adj* **at breakneck speed** : a una velocidad vertiginosa

break out *vi* **1** : salirse ⟨she broke out in spots : le salieron granos⟩ **2** ERUPT : estallar (dícese de una guerra, la violencia, etc.) **3** ESCAPE : fugarse, escaparse

breakup ['breɪk₁əp] *n* **1** DIVISION : desintegración *f* **2** : ruptura *f*

break up *vt* **1** DIVIDE : dividir **2** : disolver (una muchedumbre, una pelea, etc.) — *vi* **1** BREAK : romperse **2** SEPARATE : deshacerse, separarse ⟨I broke up with him : terminé con él⟩

breast ['brɛst] *n* **1** : pecho *m*, seno *m* (de una mujer) **2** CHEST : pecho *m*

breastbone ['brɛst₁bo:n] *n* : esternón *m*

breast–feed ['brɛst₁fi:d] *vt* **-fed** [-₁fɛd]; **-feeding** : amamantar, darle de mamar (a un niño)

breath ['brɛθ] *n* **1** BREATHING : aliento *m* ⟨to hold one's breath : aguantar la respiración⟩ **2** BREEZE : soplo *m* ⟨a breath of fresh air : un soplo de aire fresco⟩

breathe ['bri:ð] *v* **breathed; breathing** *vi* **1** : respirar **2** LIVE : vivir, respirar — *vt* **1** : respirar, aspirar ⟨to breathe fresh air : respirar el aire fresco⟩ **2** UTTER : decir ⟨I won't breathe a word of this : no diré nada de esto⟩

breathless ['brɛθləs] *adj* : sin aliento, jadeante

breathlessly ['brɛθləsli] *adv* : entrecortadamente, jadeando

breathlessness ['brɛθləsnəs] *n* : dificultad *f* al respirar

breathtaking ['brɛθ₁teɪkɪŋ] *adj* IMPRESSIVE : impresionante, imponente

breeches ['brɪtʃəz, 'bri:-] *npl* : pantalones *mpl*, calzones *mpl*, bombachos *mpl*

breed¹ ['bri:d] *v* **bred** ['brɛd]; **breeding** *vt* **1** : criar (animales) **2** ENGENDER : engendrar, producir ⟨familiarity breeds contempt : la confianza hace perder el respeto⟩ **3** RAISE, REAR : criar, educar — *vi* REPRODUCE : reproducirse

breed² *n* **1** : variedad *f* (de plantas), raza *f* (de animales) **2** CLASS : clase *f*, tipo *m*

breeder ['bri:dər] *n* : criador *m*, -dora *f* (de animales); cultivador *m*, -dora *f* (de plantas)

breeze¹ ['bri:z] *vi* **breezed; breezing** : pasar con ligereza ⟨to breeze in : entrar como si nada⟩

breeze² *n* : brisa *f*, soplo *m* (de aire)

breezy ['bri:zi] *adj* **breezier; -est 1** AIRY, WINDY : aireado, ventoso **2** LIVELY : animado, alegre **3** NONCHALANT : despreocupado

brethren → **brother**

brevity ['brɛvəti] *n, pl* **-ties** : brevedad *f*, concisión *f*

brew¹ ['bru:] *vt* **1** : fabricar, elaborar (cerveza) **2** FOMENT : tramar, maquinar, fomentar — *vi* **1** : fabricar cerveza **2** : amenazar ⟨a storm is brewing : una tormenta amenaza⟩

brew² *n* **1** BEER : cerveza *f* **2** POTION : brebaje *m*

brewer ['bru:ər] *n* : cervecero *m*, -ra *f*

brewery ['bru:əri, 'bruri] *n, pl* **-eries** : cervecería *f*

briar ['braɪər] → **brier**

bribe¹ ['braɪb] *vt* **bribed; bribing** : sobornar, cohechar, coimear *Arg, Chile, Peru*

bribe² *n* : soborno *m*, cohecho *m*, coima *f Arg, Chile, Peru*, mordida *f CA, Mex*

bribery ['braɪbəri] *n, pl* **-eries** : soborno *m*, cohecho *m*, coima *f*, mordida *f CA, Mex*

bric–a–brac ['brɪkə‚bræk] *npl* : baratijas *fpl*, chucherías *fpl*

brick¹ ['brɪk] *vt* **to brick up** : tabicar, tapiar

brick² *n* : ladrillo *m*

bricklayer ['brɪk‚leɪər] *n* : albañil *mf*

bricklaying ['brɪk‚leɪɪŋ] *n* : albañilería *f*

bridal ['braɪdəl] *adj* : nupcial, de novia

bride ['braɪd] *n* : novia *f*

bridegroom ['braɪd‚gru:m] *n* : novio *m*

bridesmaid ['braɪdz‚meɪd] *n* : dama *f* de honor

bridge¹ ['brɪdʒ] *vt* **bridged; bridging 1** : tender un puente sobre **2 to bridge the gap** : salvar las diferencias

bridge² *n* **1** : puente *m* **2** : caballete *m* (de la nariz) **3** : puente *m* de mando (de un barco) **4** DENTURE : puente *m* (dental) **5** : bridge *m* (juego de naipes)

bridle¹ ['braɪdəl] *v* **-dled; -dling** *vt* **1** : embridar (un caballo) **2** RESTRAIN : refrenar, dominar, contener — *vi* **to bridle at** : molestarse por, picarse por

bridle² *n* : brida *f*

brief¹ ['bri:f] *vt* : dar órdenes a, instruir

brief² *adj* : breve, sucinto, conciso

brief³ *n* **1** : resumen *m*, sumario *m* **2 briefs** *npl* : calzoncillos *mpl*

briefcase ['bri:f‚keɪs] *n* : portafolio *m*, maletín *m*

briefly ['bri:fli] *adv* : brevemente, por poco tiempo ⟨to speak briefly : discursar en pocas palabras⟩

brier ['braɪər] *n* **1** BRAMBLE : zarza *f*, rosal *m* silvestre **2** HEATH : brezo *m* veteado

brig ['brɪg] *n* **1** : bergantín *m* (barco) **2** : calabozo *m* (en un barco)

brigade [brɪ'geɪd] *n* : brigada *f*

brigadier general [‚brɪgə'dɪr] *n* : general *m* de brigada

brigand ['brɪgənd] *n* : bandolero *m*, -ra *f*; forajido *m*, -da *f*

bright ['braɪt] *adj* **1** : brillante (dícese del sol, de los ojos), vivo (dícese de un color), claro, fuerte **2** CHEERFUL : alegre, animado ⟨bright and early : muy temprano⟩ **3** INTELLIGENT : listo, inteligente ⟨a bright idea : una idea luminosa⟩

brighten ['braɪtən] *vt* **1** ILLUMINATE : iluminar **2** ENLIVEN : alegrar, animar — *vi* **1** : hacerse más brillante **2 to brighten up** : animarse, alegrarse, mejorar

brightly ['braɪtli] *adv* : vivamente, intensamente, alegremente

brightness ['braɪtnəs] *n* **1** LUMINOSITY : luminosidad *f*, brillantez *f*, resplandor *m*, brillo *m* **2** CHEERFULNESS : alegría *f*, ánimo *m*

brilliance ['brɪljənts] *n* **1** BRIGHTNESS : resplandor *m*, fulgor *m*, brillo *m*, brillantez *f* **2** INTELLIGENCE : inteligencia *f*, brillantez *f*

brilliancy ['brɪljəntsi] → **brilliance**

brilliant ['brɪljənt] *adj* : brillante

brilliantly ['brɪljəntli] *adv* : brillantemente, con brillantez

brim¹ ['brɪm] *vi* **brimmed; brimming 1** *or* **to brim over** : desbordarse, rebosar **2 to brim with tears** : llenarse de lágrimas

brim² *n* **1** : ala *f* (de un sombrero) **2** : borde *m* (de una taza o un vaso)

brimful ['brɪm'fʊl] *adj* : lleno hasta el borde, repleto, rebosante

brimless ['brɪmləs] *adj* : sin ala

brimstone ['brɪm‚sto:n] *n* : azufre *m*

brindled ['brɪndəld] *adj* : manchado, pinto

brine ['braɪn] *n* **1** : salmuera *f*, escabeche *m* (para encurtir) **2** OCEAN : océano *m*, mar *m*

bring ['brɪŋ] *vt* **brought** ['brɔt]; **bringing 1** CARRY : traer ⟨bring me some coffee : tráigame un café⟩ **2** PRODUCE : traer, producir, conseguir ⟨his efforts will bring him success : sus esfuerzos le conseguirán el éxito⟩ **3** PERSUADE : convencer, persuadir **4** YIELD : rendir, alcanzar, venderse por ⟨to bring a good price : alcanzar un precio alto⟩ **5 to bring to an end** : terminar (con) **6 to bring to light** : sacar a la luz

bring about *vt* : ocasionar, provocar, determinar

bring forth *vt* PRODUCE : producir

bring out *vt* : sacar, publicar (un libro, etc.)

bring to *vt* REVIVE : resucitar

bring up *vt* **1** REAR : criar **2** MENTION : sacar, mencionar

brininess ['braɪnɪnəs] *n* : salinidad *f*

brink ['brɪŋk] *n* : borde *m*

briny ['braɪni] *adj* **brinier; -est** : salobre

briquette *or* **briquet** [brɪ'kɛt] *n* : briqueta *f*

brisk ['brɪsk] *adj* **1** LIVELY : rápido, enérgico, brioso **2** INVIGORATING : fresco, estimulante

brisket ['brɪskət] *n* : falda *f*

briskly ['brɪskli] *adv* : rápidamente, enérgicamente, con brío

briskness ['brɪsknəs] *n* : brío *m*, rapidez *f*

bristle¹ ['brɪsəl] *vi* **-tled; -tling 1** : erizarse, ponerse de punta **2** : enfurecerse, enojarse ⟨she bristled at the suggestion : se enfureció ante tal sugerencia⟩ **3** : estar plagado, estar repleto ⟨a city bristling with tourists : una ciudad repleta de turistas⟩

bristle² *n* : cerda *f* (de un animal), pelo *m* (de una planta)

bristly ['brɪsəli] *adj* **bristlier; -est** : áspero y erizado

British¹ ['brɪtɪʃ] *adj* : británico

British² *n* **the British** *npl* : los británicos

brittle [ˈbrɪtəl] *adj* **-tler; -tlest** : frágil, quebradizo
brittleness [ˈbrɪtəlnəs] *n* : fragilidad *f*
broach [ˈbroːtʃ] *vt* BRING UP : mencionar, abordar, sacar
broad [ˈbrɔd] *adj* **1** WIDE : ancho **2** SPACIOUS : amplio, extenso **3** FULL : pleno ⟨in broad daylight : en pleno día⟩ **4** OBVIOUS : claro, evidente **5** TOLERANT : tolerante, liberal **6** GENERAL : general **7** ESSENTIAL : principal, esencial ⟨the broad outline : los rasgos esenciales⟩
broadcast¹ [ˈbrɔdˌkæst] *vt* **-cast; -casting 1** SCATTER : esparcir, diseminar **2** CIRCULATE, SPREAD : divulgar, difundir, propagar **3** TRANSMIT : transmitir, emitir
broadcast² *n* **1** TRANSMISSION : transmisión *f*, emisión *f* **2** PROGRAM : programa *m*, emisión *f*
broadcaster [ˈbrɔdˌkæstər] *n* : presentador *m*, -dora *f*; locutor *m*, -tora *f*
broadcloth [ˈbrɔdˌklɔθ] *n* : paño *m* fino
broaden [ˈbrɔdən] *vt* : ampliar, ensanchar — *vi* : ampliarse, ensancharse
broadloom [ˈbrɔdˌluːm] *adj* : tejido en telar ancho
broadly [ˈbrɔdli] *adv* **1** GENERALLY : en general, aproximadamente **2** WIDELY : extensivamente
broad–minded [ˈbrɔdˈmaɪndəd] *adj* : tolerante, de amplias miras
broad–mindedness [brɔdˈmaɪndədnəs] *n* : tolerancia *f*
broadside [ˈbrɔdˌsaɪd] *n* **1** VOLLEY : andanada *f* **2** ATTACK : ataque *m*, invectiva *f*, andanada *f*
brocade [broˈkeɪd] *n* : brocado *m*
broccoli [ˈbrɑkəli] *n* : brócoli *m*, brécol *m*
brochure [broˈʃʊr] *n* : folleto *m*
brogue [ˈbroːg] *n* : acento *m* irlandés
broil¹ [ˈbrɔɪl] *vt* : asar a la parrilla
broil² *n* : asado *m*
broiler [ˈbrɔɪlər] *n* **1** GRILL : parrilla *f* **2** : pollo *m* para asar
broke¹ [ˈbroːk] → break¹
broke² *adj* : pelado, arruinado ⟨to go broke : arruinarse, quebrar⟩
broken [ˈbroːkən] *adj* **1** DAMAGED, SHATTERED : roto, quebrado, fracturado **2** IRREGULAR, UNEVEN : accidentado, irregular, recortado **3** VIOLATED : roto, quebrantado **4** INTERRUPTED : interrumpido, discontinuo **5** CRUSHED : abatido, quebrantado ⟨a broken man : un hombre destrozado⟩ **6** IMPERFECT : mal ⟨to speak broken English : hablar el inglés con dificultad⟩
brokenhearted [ˌbroːkənˈhɑrtəd] *adj* : descorazonado, desconsolado
broker¹ [ˈbroːkər] *vt* : hacer corretaje de
broker² *n* **1** : agente *mf*; corredor *m*, -dora *f* **2** → stockbroker
brokerage [ˈbroːkərɪdʒ] *n* : corretaje *m*, agencia *f* de corredores

bromine [ˈbroːˌmiːn] *n* : bromo *m*
bronchitis [branˈkaɪtəs, braŋ-] *n* : bronquitis *f*
bronze¹ [ˈbrɑnz] *vt* **bronzed; bronzing** : broncear
bronze² *n* : bronce *m*
brooch [ˈbroːtʃ, ˈbruːtʃ] *n* : broche *m*, prendedor *m*
brood¹ [ˈbruːd] *vt* **1** INCUBATE : empollar, incubar **2** PONDER : sopesar, considerar — *vi* **1** INCUBATE : empollar **2** REFLECT : rumiar, reflexionar **3** WORRY : ponerse melancólico, inquietarse
brood² *adj* : de cría
brood³ *n* : nidada *f* (de pájaros), camada *f* (de mamíferos)
brooder [ˈbruːdər] *n* **1** THINKER : pensador *m*, -dora *f* **2** INCUBATOR : incubadora *f*
brook¹ [ˈbrʊk] *vt* TOLERATE : tolerar, admitir
brook² *n* : arroyo *m*
broom [ˈbruːm, ˈbrʊm] *n* **1** : retama *f*, hiniesta *f* **2** : escoba *f* (para barrer)
broomstick [ˈbruːmˌstɪk, ˈbrʊm-] *n* : palo *m* de escoba
broth [ˈbrɔθ] *n, pl* **broths** [ˈbrɔθs, ˈbrɔðz] : caldo *m*
brothel [ˈbrɑθəl, ˈbrɔ-] *n* : burdel *m*
brother [ˈbrʌðər] *n, pl* **brothers** *also* **brethren** [ˈbrɔðrən, -ðərn] **1** : hermano *m* **2** KINSMAN : pariente *m*, familiar *m*
brotherhood [ˈbrʌðərˌhʊd] *n* **1** FELLOWSHIP : fraternidad *f* **2** ASSOCIATION : hermandad *f*
brother–in–law [ˈbrʌðərɪnˌlɔ] *n, pl* **brothers–in–law** : cuñado *m*
brotherly [ˈbrʌðərli] *adj* : fraternal
brought → bring
brow [ˈbraʊ] *n* **1** EYEBROW : ceja *f* **2** FOREHEAD : frente *f* **3** : cima *f* ⟨the brow of a hill : la cima de una colina⟩
browbeat [ˈbraʊˌbiːt] *vt* **-beat; -beaten** [-ˌbiːtən] *or* **-beat; -beating** : intimidar
brown¹ [ˈbraʊn] *vt* **1** : dorar (en cocina) **2** TAN : broncear — *vi* **1** : dorarse (en cocina) **2** TAN : broncearse
brown² *adj* : marrón, café, castaño (dícese del pelo), moreno (dícese de la piel)
brown³ *n* : marrón *m*, café *m*
brownish [ˈbraʊnɪʃ] *adj* : pardo
browse [ˈbraʊz] *vi* **browsed; browsing 1** GRAZE : pacer **2** LOOK : mirar, echar un vistazo
bruin [ˈbruːɪn] *n* BEAR : oso *m*
bruise¹ [ˈbruːz] *vt* **bruised; bruising 1** : contusionar, machucar, magullar (a una persona) **2** DAMAGE : dañar (frutas) **3** CRUSH : majar **4** HURT : herir (los sentimientos)
bruise² *n* : moretón *m*, cardenal *m*, magulladura *f* (dícese de frutas)
brunch [ˈbrʌntʃ] *n* : combinación *f* de desayuno y almuerzo
brunet¹ *or* **brunette** [bruːˈnɛt] *adj* : moreno
brunet² *or* **brunette** *n* : moreno *m*, -na *f*

brunt ['brʌnt] *n* **to bear the brunt of** : llevar el peso de, aguantar el mayor impacto de
brush¹ ['brʌʃ] *vt* **1** : cepillar ⟨to brush one's teeth : cepillarse uno los dientes⟩ **2** SWEEP : barrer, quitar con un cepillo **3** GRAZE : rozar **4 to brush off** DISREGARD : hacer caso omiso de, ignorar — *vi* **to brush up on** : repasar, refrescar, dar un repaso a
brush² *n* **1** *or* **brushwood** ['brʌʃˌwʊd] : broza *f* **2** SCRUB, UNDERBRUSH : maleza *f* **3** : cepillo *m*, pincel *m* (de artista), brocha *f* (de pintor) **4** TOUCH : roce *m* **5** SKIRMISH : escaramuza *f*
brush–off ['brʌʃˌɔf] *n* **to give the brush–off to** : dar calabazas a
brusque ['brʌsk] *adj* : brusco — **brusquely** *adv*
brussels sprout ['brʌsəlzˌspraʊt] *n* : col *f* de Bruselas
brutal ['bru:təl] *adj* : brutal, cruel, salvaje — **brutally** *adv*
brutality [bru:'tælət̬i] *n*, *pl* **-ties** : brutalidad *f*
brutalize ['bru:t̬əlˌaɪz] *vt* **-ized; -izing** : brutalizar, maltratar
brute¹ ['bru:t] *adj* : bruto ⟨brute force : fuerza bruta⟩
brute² *n* **1** BEAST : bestia *f*, animal *m* **2** : bruto *m*, -ta *f*; bestia *mf* (persona)
brutish ['bru:t̬ɪʃ] *adj* **1** : de animal **2** CRUEL : brutal, salvaje **3** STUPID : bruto, estúpido
bubble¹ ['bʌbəl] *vi* **-bled; -bling** : burbujear ⟨to bubble over with joy : rebosar de alegría⟩
bubble² *n* : burbuja *f*
bubbly ['bʌbəli] *adj* **bubblier; -est 1** BUBBLING : burbujeante **2** LIVELY : vivaz, lleno de vida
bubonic plague [bu:'bɑnɪk, 'bju:-] *n* : peste *f* bubónica
buccaneer [ˌbʌkə'nɪr] *n* : bucanero *m*
buck¹ ['bʌk] *vi* **1** : corcovear (dícese de un caballo o un burro) **2** JOLT : dar sacudidas **3 to buck against** : resistirse a, rebelarse contra **4 to buck up** : animarse, levantar el ánimo — *vt* OPPOSE : oponerse a, ir en contra de
buck² *n*, *pl* **buck** *or* **bucks 1** : animal *m* macho, ciervo *m* (macho) **2** DOLLAR : dólar *m* **3 to pass the buck** *fam* : pasar la pelota *fam*
bucket ['bʌkət] *n* : balde *m*, cubo *m*, cubeta *f Mex*
bucketful ['bʌkətˌfʊl] *n* : balde *m* lleno
buckle¹ ['bʌkəl] *v* **-led; -ling** *vt* **1** FASTEN : abrochar **2** BEND, TWIST : combar, torcer — *vi* **1** BEND, TWIST : combarse, torcerse, doblarse (dícese de las rodillas) **2 to buckle down** : ponerse a trabajar con esmero **3 to buckle up** : abrocharse
buckle² *n* **1** : hebilla *f* **2** TWISTING : torcedura *f*
buckshot ['bʌkˌʃɑt] *n* : perdigón *m*
buckskin ['bʌkˌskɪn] *n* : gamuza *f*

bucktooth ['bʌkˌtu:θ] *n* : diente *m* saliente, diente *m* salido
buckwheat ['bʌkˌʍi:t] *n* : trigo *m* rubión, alforfón *m*
bucolic [bju:'kɑlɪk] *adj* : bucólico
bud¹ ['bʌd] *v* **budded; budding** *vt* GRAFT : injertar — *vi* : brotar, hacer brotes
bud² *n* : brote *m*, yema *f*, capullo *m* (de una flor)
Buddhism ['bu:ˌdɪzəm, 'bʊ-] *n* : budismo *m*
Buddhist ['bu:dɪst, 'bʊ-] *n* : budista *mf* — **Buddhist** *adj*
buddy ['bʌdi] *n*, *pl* **-dies** : amigo *m*, -ga *f*; compinche *mf fam*; cuate *m*, -ta *f Mex fam*
budge ['bʌdʒ] *vi* **budged; budging 1** MOVE : moverse, desplazarse **2** YIELD : ceder
budget¹ ['bʌdʒət] *vt* : presupuestar (gastos), asignar (dinero) — *vi* : presupuestar, planear el presupuesto
budget² *n* : presupuesto
budgetary ['bʌdʒəˌteri] *adj* : presupuestario
buff¹ ['bʌf] *vt* POLISH : pulir, sacar brillo a, lustrar
buff² *adj* : beige, amarillento
buff³ *n* **1** : beige *m*, amarillento *m* **2** ENTHUSIAST : aficionado *m*, -da *f*; entusiasta *mf*
buffalo ['bʌfəˌlo:] *n*, *pl* **-lo** *or* **-loes 1** : búfalo *m* **2** BISON : bisonte *m*
buffer ['bʌfər] *n* **1** BARRIER : barrera *f* ⟨buffer state : estado tapón⟩ **2** SHOCK ABSORBER : amortiguador *m*
buffet¹ ['bʌfət] *vt* : golpear, zarandear, sacudir
buffet² *n* BLOW : golpe *m*
buffet³ [ˌbʌ'feɪ, ˌbu:-] *n* **1** : bufete *m*, bufé *m* (comida) **2** SIDEBOARD : aparador *m*
buffoon [ˌbʌ'fu:n] *n* : bufón *m*, -fona *f*; payaso *m*, -sa *f*
buffoonery [ˌbʌ'fu:nəri] *n*, *pl* **-eries** : bufonada *f*, payasada *f*
bug¹ ['bʌg] *vt* **bugged; bugging 1** PESTER : fastidiar, molestar **2** : ocultar micrófonos en
bug² *n* **1** INSECT : bicho *m*, insecto *m* **2** DEFECT : defecto *m*, falla *f*, problema *m* **3** GERM : microbio *m*, virus *m* **4** MICROPHONE : micrófono *m*
bugaboo ['bʌgəˌbu:] → **bogey**
bugbear ['bʌgˌbær] *n* : pesadilla *f*, coco *m*
buggy ['bʌgi] *n*, *pl* **-gies** : calesa *f* (tirada por caballos), cochecito *m* (para niños)
bugle ['bju:gəl] *n* : clarín *m*, corneta *f*
bugler ['bju:gələr] *n* : corneta *mf*
build¹ ['bɪld] *v* **built** ['bɪlt]; **building** *vt* **1** CONSTRUCT : construir, edificar, ensamblar, levantar **2** DEVELOP : desarrollar, elaborar, forjar **3** INCREASE : incrementar, aumentar — *vi* **to build up** : aumentar, intensificar
build² *n* PHYSIQUE : físico *m*, complexión *f*

builder ['bɪldər] *n* : constructor *m*, -tora *f*; contratista *mf*
building ['bɪldɪŋ] *n* **1** EDIFICE : edificio *m* **2** CONSTRUCTION : construcción *f*
built-in ['bɪlt'ɪn] *adj* **1** : empotrado ⟨built-in cabinets : armarios empotrados⟩ **2** INHERENT : incorporado, intrínseco
bulb ['bʌlb] *n* **1** : bulbo *m* (de una planta), cabeza *f* (de ajo), cubeta *f* (de un termómetro) **2** LIGHTBULB : bombilla *f*, foco *m*, bombillo *m* CA, Col, Ven
bulbous ['bʌlbəs] *adj* : bulboso
Bulgarian [bʌl'gæriən, bʊl-] *n* **1** : búlgaro *m*, -ra *f* **2** : búlgaro *m* (idioma) — **Bulgarian** *adj*
bulge¹ ['bʌldʒ] *vi* **bulged; bulging** : abultar, sobresalir
bulge² *n* : bulto *m*, protuberancia *f*
bulk¹ ['bʌlk] *vt* : hinchar — *vi* EXPAND, SWELL : ampliarse, hincharse
bulk² *n* **1** SIZE, VOLUME : volumen *m*, tamaño *m* **2** FIBER : fibra *f* **3** MASS : mole *f* **4 the bulk of** : la mayor parte de **5 in ~** : en grandes cantidades
bulkhead ['bʌlk,hɛd] *n* : mamparo *m*
bulky ['bʌlki] *adj* **bulkier; -est** : voluminoso, grande
bull¹ ['bʊl] *adj* : macho
bull² *n* **1** : toro *m*, macho *m* (de ciertas especies) **2** : bula *f* (papal) **3** DECREE : decreto *m*, edicto *m*
bulldog ['bʊl,dɔg] *n* : bulldog *m*
bulldoze ['bʊl,do:z] *vt* **-dozed; -dozing 1** LEVEL : nivelar (el terreno), derribar (un edificio) **2** FORCE : forzar ⟨he bulldozed his way through : se abrió paso a codazos⟩
bulldozer ['bʊl,do:zər] *n* : bulldozer *m*
bullet ['bʊlət] *n* : bala *f*
bulletin ['bʊlətən, -ləʇən] *n* **1** NOTICE : comunicado *m*, anuncio *m*, boletín *m* **2** NEWSLETTER : boletín *m* (informativo)
bulletin board *n* : tablón *m* de anuncios
bulletproof ['bʊlət,pru:f] *adj* : antibalas, a prueba de balas
bullfight ['bʊl,faɪt] *n* : corrida *f* (de toros)
bullfighter ['bʊl,faɪʇər] *n* : torero *m*, -ra *f*; matador *m*
bullfrog ['bʊl,frɔg] *n* : rana *f* toro
bullheaded ['bʊl'hɛdəd] *adj* : testarudo
bullion ['bʊljən] *n* : oro *m* en lingotes, plata *f* en lingotes
bullock ['bʊlək] *n* **1** STEER : buey *m*, toro *m* castrado **2** : toro *m* joven, novillo *m*
bull's-eye ['bʊlz,aɪ] *n, pl* **bull's-eyes** : diana *f*, blanco *m*
bully¹ ['bʊli] *vt* **-lied; -lying** : intimidar, amedrentar, mangonear
bully² *n, pl* **-lies** : matón *m*; bravucón *m*, -cona *f*
bulrush ['bʊl,rʌʃ] *n* : especie *f* de junco
bulwark ['bʊl,wərk, -,wɔrk; 'bʌl,wərk] *n* : baluarte *m*, bastión *f*
bum¹ ['bʌm] *v* **bummed; bumming** *vi* **to bum around** : vagabundear, vagar — *vt* : gorronear *fam*, sablear *fam*

bum² *adj* : inútil, malo ⟨a bum rap : una acusación falsa⟩
bum³ *n* **1** LOAFER : vago *m*, -ga *f* **2** HOBO, TRAMP : vagabundo *m*, -da *f*
bumblebee ['bʌmbəl,bi:] *n* : abejorro *m*
bump¹ ['bʌmp] *vt* : chocar contra, golpear contra, dar ⟨to bump one's head : darse (un golpe) en la cabeza⟩ — *vi* **to bump into** MEET : encontrarse con, tropezarse con
bump² *n* **1** BULGE : bulto *m*, protuberancia *f* **2** IMPACT : golpe *m*, choque *m* **3** JOLT : sacudida *f*
bumper¹ ['bʌmpər] *adj* : extraordinario, récord ⟨a bumper crop : una cosecha abundante⟩
bumper² *n* : parachoques *mpl*
bumpkin ['bʌmpkən] *n* : palurdo *m*, -da *f*
bumpy ['bʌmpi] *adj* **bumpier; -est** : desigual, lleno de baches (dícese de un camino), agitado (dícese de un vuelo en avión)
bun ['bʌn] *n* : bollo *m*
bunch¹ ['bʌntʃ] *vt* : agrupar, amontonar — *vi* **to bunch up** : amontonarse, agruparse, fruncirse (dícese de una tela)
bunch² *n* : grupo *m*, montón *m*, ramo *m* (de flores)
bundle¹ ['bʌndəl] *vt* **-dled; -dling** : liar, atar
bundle² *n* **1** : fardo *m*, atado *m*, bulto *m*, haz *m* (de palos) **2** PARCEL : paquete *m* **3** LOAD : montón *m* ⟨a bundle of money : un montón de dinero⟩
bungalow ['bʌŋgə,lo:] *n* : tipo de casa de un solo piso
bungle¹ ['bʌŋgəl] *vt* **-gled; -gling** : echar a perder, malograr
bungle² *n* : chapuza *f*, desatino *m*
bungler ['bʌŋgələr] *n* : chapucero *m*, -ra *f*; inepto *m*, -ta *f*
bunion ['bʌnjən] *n* : juanete *m*
bunk¹ ['bʌŋk] *vi* : dormir (en una litera)
bunk² *n* **1** *or* **bunk bed** : litera *f* **2** NONSENSE : tonterías *fpl*, bobadas *fpl*
bunker ['bʌŋkər] *n* **1** : carbonera *f* (en un barco) **2** SHELTER : búnker *m*
bunny ['bʌni] *n, pl* **-nies** : conejo *m*, -ja *f*
buoy¹ ['bu:i, 'bɔɪ] *vt* **to buoy up 1** : mantener a flote **2** CHEER, HEARTEN : animar, levantar el ánimo a
buoy² *n* : boya *f*
buoyancy ['bɔɪəntsi, 'bu:jən-] *n* **1** : flotabilidad *f* **2** OPTIMISM : confianza *f*, optimismo *m*
buoyant ['bɔɪənt, 'bu:jənt] *adj* : boyante, flotante
bur *or* **burr** ['bər] *n* : abrojo *m* (de una planta)
burden¹ ['bərdən] *vt* : cargar, oprimir
burden² *n* : carga *f*, peso *m*
burdensome ['bərdənsəm] *adj* : oneroso
burdock ['bər,dɑk] *n* : bardana *f*
bureau ['bjʊro] *n* **1** CHEST OF DRAWERS : cómoda *f* **2** DEPARTMENT : departamento *m* (del gobierno) **3** AGENCY

: agencia *f* ⟨travel bureau : agencia de viajes⟩
bureaucracy [bjʊ'rɑkrəsi] *n, pl* **-cies** : burocracia *f*
bureaucrat ['bjʊrə,kræt] *n* : burócrata *mf*
bureaucratic [,bjʊrə'kræṭɪk] *adj* : burocrático
burgeon ['bərdʒən] *vi* : florecer, retoñar, crecer
burglar ['bərglər] *n* : ladrón *m*, -drona *f*
burglarize ['bərglə,raɪz] *vt* **-ized; -izing** : robar
burglary ['bərgləri] *n, pl* **-glaries** : robo *m*
burgle ['bərgəl] *vt* **-gled; -gling** : robar
burgundy ['bərgəndi] *n, pl* **-dies** : borgoña *m*, vino *m* de Borgoña
burial ['bɛriəl] *n* : entierro *m*, sepelio *m*
burlap ['bər,læp] *n* : arpillera *f*
burlesque[1] [bər'lɛsk] *vt* **-lesqued; -lesquing** : parodiar
burlesque[2] *n* **1** PARODY : parodia *f* **2** REVUE : revista *f* (musical)
burly ['bərli] *adj* **-lier; -liest** : fornido, corpulento, musculoso
Burmese [,bər'mi:z, -'mi:s] *n* : birmano *m*, -na *f* — **Burmese** *adj*
burn[1] ['bərn] *v* **burned** ['bərnd, 'bərnt] *or* **burnt** ['bərnt]; **burning** *vt* **1** : quemar, incendiar ⟨to burn a building : incendiar un edificio⟩ ⟨I burned my hand : me quemé la mano⟩ **2** CONSUME : usar, gastar, consumir — *vi* **1** : arder (dícese de un fuego o un edificio), quemarse (dícese de la comida, etc.) **2** : estar prendido, estar encendido ⟨we left the lights burning : dejamos las luces encendidas⟩ **3 to burn out** : consumirse, apagarse **4 to burn with** : arder de ⟨he was burning with jealousy : ardía de celos⟩
burn[2] *n* : quemadura *f*
burner ['bərnər] *n* : quemador *m*
burnish ['bərnɪʃ] *vt* : bruñir
burp[1] ['bərp] *vi* : eructar — *vt* : hacer eructar
burp[2] *n* : eructo *m*
burr → **bur**
burro ['bəro, 'bʊr-] *n, pl* **-os** : burro *m*
burrow[1] ['bəro] *vi* **1** : cavar, hacer una madriguera **2 to burrow into** : hurgar en — *vt* : cavar, excavar
burrow[2] *n* : madriguera *f*, conejera *f* (de un conejo)
bursar ['bərsər] *n* : administrador *m*, -dora *f*
bursitis [bər'saɪṭəs] *n* : bursitis *f*
burst[1] ['bərst] *v* **burst; bursting** *vi* **1** : reventarse (dícese de una llanta o un globo), estallar (dícese de obuses o fuegos artificiales), romperse (dícese de un dique) **2 to burst in** : irrumpir en **3 to burst into** : empezar a, echar a ⟨to burst into tears : echarse a llorar⟩ — *vt* : reventar
burst[2] *n* **1** EXPLOSION : estallido *m*, explosión *f*, reventón *m* (de una llanta) **2** OUTBURST : arranque *m* (de actividad,

de velocidad), arrebato *m* (de ira), salva *f* (de aplausos)
Burundian [bʊ'ru:ndiən, -'rʊn-] *n* : burundés *m*, -desa *f* — **Burundian** *adj*
bury ['bɛri] *vt* **buried; burying 1** INTER : enterrar, sepultar **2** HIDE : esconder, ocultar **3 to bury oneself in** : enfrascarse en
bus[1] ['bʌs] *v* **bused** *or* **bussed** ['bʌst]; **busing** *or* **bussing** ['bʌsɪŋ] *vt* : transportar en autobús — *vi* : viajar en autobús
bus[2] *n* : autobús *m*, bus *m*, camión *m* *Mex*, colectivo *m* *Arg, Bol, Peru*
busboy ['bʌs,bɔɪ] *n* : ayudante *mf* de camarero
bush ['bʊʃ] *n* **1** SHRUB : arbusto *m*, mata *f* **2** THICKET : maleza *f*, matorral *m*
bushel ['bʊʃəl] *n* : medida de áridos igual a 35.24 litros
bushing ['bʊʃɪŋ] *n* : cojinete *m*
bushy ['bʊʃi] *adj* **bushier; -est** : espeso, poblado ⟨bushy eyebrows : cejas pobladas⟩
busily ['bɪzəli] *adv* : afanosamente, diligentemente
business ['bɪznəs, -nəz] *n* **1** OCCUPATION : ocupación *f*, oficio *m* **2** DUTY, MISSION : misión *f*, deber *m*, responsabilidad *f* **3** ESTABLISHMENT, FIRM : empresa *f*, firma *f*, negocio *m*, comercio *m* **4** COMMERCE : negocios *mpl*, comercio *m* **5** AFFAIR, MATTER : asunto *m*, cuestión *f*, cosa *f* ⟨it's none of your business : no es asunto tuyo⟩
businessman ['bɪznəs,mæn, -nəz-] *n, pl* **-men** [-mən, -,mɛn] : empresario *m*, hombre *m* de negocios
businesswoman ['bɪznəs,wʊmən, -nəz-] *n, pl* **-women** [-,wɪmən] : empresaria *f*, mujer *f* de negocios
bust[1] ['bʌst] *vt* **1** BREAK, SMASH : romper, estropear, destrozar **2** TAME : domar, amansar (un caballo) — *vi* **1** : romperse, estropearse
bust[2] *n* **1** : busto *m* (en la escultura) **2** BREASTS : pecho *m*, senos *mpl*, busto *m*
bustle[1] ['bʌsəl] *vi* **-tled; -tling to bustle about** : ir y venir, trajinar, ajetrearse
bustle[2] *n* **1** *or* **hustle and bustle** : bullicio *m*, ajetreo *m* **2** : polisón *m* (en la ropa feminina)
busy[1] ['bɪzi] *vt* **busied; busying to busy oneself with** : ocuparse con, ponerse a, entretenerse con
busy[2] *adj* **busier; -est 1** OCCUPIED : ocupado, atareado ⟨he's busy working : está ocupado en su trabajo⟩ ⟨the telephone was busy : el teléfono estaba ocupado⟩ **2** BUSTLING : concurrido, animado ⟨a busy street : una calle concurrida, una calle con mucho tránsito⟩
busybody ['bɪzi,bɑdi] *n, pl* **-bodies** : entrometido *m*, -da *f*; metiche *mf* *fam*; metomentodo *mf*
but[1] ['bʌt] *conj* **1** THAT : que ⟨there is no doubt but he is lazy : no cabe duda

que sea perezoso⟩ **2** WITHOUT : sin que **3** NEVERTHELESS : pero, no obstante, sin embargo ⟨I called her but she didn't answer : la llamé pero no contestó⟩ **4** YET : pero ⟨he was poor but proud : era pobre pero orgulloso⟩

but² *prep* EXCEPT : excepto, menos ⟨everyone but Carlos : todos menos Carlos⟩ ⟨the last but one : el penúltimo⟩

butcher¹ [ˈbʊtʃər] *vt* **1** SLAUGHTER : matar (animales) **2** KILL : matar, asesinar, masacrar **3** BOTCH : estropear, hacer una chapuza

butcher² *n* **1** : carnicero *m*, -ra *f* **2** KILLER : asesino *m*, -na *f* **3** BUNGLER : chapucero *m*, -ra *f*

butler [ˈbʌtlər] *n* : mayordomo *m*

butt¹ [ˈbʌt] *vt* **1** : embestir (con los cuernos), darle un cabezazo a **2** ABUT : colindar con, bordear — *vi* **to butt in 1** INTERRUPT : interrumpir **2** MEDDLE : entrometerse, meterse

butt² *n* **1** BUTTING : embestida *f* (de cuernos), cabezazo *m* **2** TARGET : blanco *m* ⟨the butt of their jokes : el blanco de sus bromas⟩ **3** BOTTOM, END : extremo *m*, culata *f* (de un rifle), colilla *f* (de un cigarrillo)

butte [ˈbjuːt] *n* : colina *f* empinada y aislada

butter¹ [ˈbʌtər] *vt* **1** : untar con mantequilla **2 to butter up** : halagar

butter² *n* : mantequilla *f*

buttercup [ˈbʌtərˌkʌp] *n* : ranúnculo *m*

butterfat [ˈbʌtərˌfæt] *n* : grasa *f* de la leche

butterfly [ˈbʌtərˌflaɪ] *n*, *pl* **-flies** : mariposa *f*

buttermilk [ˈbʌtərˌmɪlk] *n* : suero *m* de la leche

butternut [ˈbʌtərˌnʌt] *n* : nogal *m* ceniciento (árbol)

butterscotch [ˈbʌtərˌskɑtʃ] *n* : caramelo *m* duro hecho con mantequilla

buttery [ˈbʌtəri] *adj* : mantecoso

buttocks [ˈbʌtəks, -ˌtɑks] *npl* : nalgas *fpl*, trasero *m*

button¹ [ˈbʌtən] *vt* : abrochar, abotonar — *vi* : abrocharse, abotonarse

button² *n* : botón *m*

buttonhole¹ [ˈbʌtənˌhoːl] *vt* **-holed; -holing** : acorralar

buttonhole² *n* : ojal *m*

buttress¹ [ˈbʌtrəs] *vt* : apoyar, reforzar

buttress² *n* **1** : contrafuerte *m* (en la arquitectura) **2** SUPPORT : apoyo *m*, sostén *m*

buxom [ˈbʌksəm] *adj* : con mucho busto, con mucho pecho

buy¹ [ˈbaɪ] *vt* **bought** [ˈbɔt]; **buying** : comprar

buy² *n* BARGAIN : compra *f*, ganga *f*

buyer [ˈbaɪər] *n* : comprador *m*, -dora *f*

buzz¹ [ˈbʌz] *vi* : zumbar (dícese de un insecto), sonar (dícese de un teléfono o un despertador)

buzz² *n* **1** : zumbido *m* (de insectos) **2** : murmullo *m*, rumor *m* (de voces)

buzzard [ˈbʌzərd] *n* VULTURE : buitre *m*, zopilote *m* CA, Mex

buzzer [ˈbʌzər] *n* : timbre *m*, chicharra *f*

buzzword [ˈbʌzˌwərd] *n* : palabra *f* de moda

by¹ [ˈbaɪ] *adv* **1** NEAR : cerca ⟨he lives close by : vive muy cerca⟩ **2 to stop by** : pasar por casa, hacer una visita **3 to go by** : pasar ⟨they rushed by : pasaron corriendo⟩ **4 to put by** : reservar, poner a un lado **5 by and by** : poco después, dentro de poco **6 by and large** : en general

by² *prep* **1** NEAR : cerca de, al lado de, junto a **2** VIA : por ⟨she left by the door : salió por la puerta⟩ **3** PAST : por, por delante de ⟨they walked by him : pasaron por delante de él⟩ **4** DURING : de, durante ⟨by night : de noche⟩ **5** (*in expressions of time*) : para ⟨we'll be there by ten : estaremos allí para las diez⟩ ⟨by then : para entonces⟩ **6** (*indicating cause or agent*) : por, de, a ⟨built by the Romans : construido por los romanos⟩ ⟨a book by Borges : un libro de Borges⟩ ⟨made by hand : hecho a mano⟩

by and by *adv* : dentro de poco

bygone¹ [ˈbaɪˌɡɔn] *adj* : pasado

bygone² *n* **let bygones be bygones** : lo pasado, pasado está

bylaw *or* **byelaw** [ˈbaɪˌlɔ] *n* : norma *f*, reglamento *m*

by-line [ˈbaɪˌlaɪn] *n* : data *f*

bypass¹ [ˈbaɪˌpæs] *vt* : evitar

bypass² *n* **1** BELTWAY : carretera *f* de circunvalación **2** DETOUR : desvío *m*

by-product [ˈbaɪˌprɑdəkt] *n* : subproducto *m*, producto *m* derivado

bystander [ˈbaɪˌstændər] *n* : espectador *m*, -dora *f*

byte [ˈbaɪt] *n* : byte *m*

byway [ˈbaɪˌweɪ] *n* : camino *m* (apartado), carretera *f* secundaria

byword [ˈbaɪˌwərd] *n* **1** PROVERB : proverbio *m*, refrán *m* **2 to be a byword for** : estar sinónimo de

C

c ['si:] *n, pl* **c's** *or* **cs** : tercera letra del alfabeto inglés

cab ['kæb] *n* **1** TAXI : taxi *m* **2** : cabina *f* (de un camión o una locomotora) **3** CARRIAGE : coche *m* de caballos

cabal [kə'bɑl, -'bæl] *n* **1** INTRIGUE, PLOT : conspiración *f*, complot *m*, intriga *f* **2** : grupo *m* de conspiradores

cabaret [ˌkæbə'reɪ] *n* : cabaret *m*

cabbage ['kæbɪʤ] *n* : col *f*, repollo *m*

cabbie *or* **cabby** ['kæbi] *n* : taxista *mf*

cabin ['kæbən] *n* **1** HUT : cabaña *f*, choza *f*, barraca *f* **2** STATEROOM : camarote *m* **3** : cabina *f* (de un automóvil o avión)

cabinet ['kæbnət] *n* **1** CUPBOARD : armario *m* **2** : gabinete *m*, consejo *m* de ministros **3** **medicine cabinet** : botiquín *m*

cabinetmaker ['kæbnətˌmeɪkər] *n* : ebanista *mf*

cabinetmaking ['kæbnətˌmeɪkɪŋ] *n* : ebanistería *f*

cable¹ ['keɪbəl] *vt* **-bled; -bling** : enviar un cable, telegrafiar

cable² *n* **1** : cable *m* (para colgar o sostener algo) **2** : cable *m* eléctrico **3** → **cablegram**

cablegram ['keɪbəlˌgræm] *n* : telegrama *m*, cable *m*

caboose [kə'buːs] *n* : furgón *m* de cola, cabús *m* *Mex*

cabstand ['kæbˌstænd] *n* : parada *f* de taxis

cacao [kə'kaʊ, -'keɪo] *n, pl* **cacaos** : cacao *m*

cache¹ ['kæʃ] *vt* **cached; caching** : esconder, guardar en un escondrijo

cache² *n* **1** : escondite *m*, escondrijo *m* ⟨cache of weapons : escondite de armas⟩ **2** : cache *m* ⟨cache memory : memoria cache⟩

cachet [kæ'ʃeɪ] *n* : caché *m*, prestigio *m*

cackle¹ ['kækəl] *vi* **-led; -ling 1** CLUCK : cacarear **2** : reírse o carcajearse estridentemente ⟨he was cackling with delight : estaba carcajeándose de gusto⟩

cackle² *n* **1** : cacareo *m* (de una polla) **2** LAUGH : risa *f* estridente

cacophony [kæ'kɑfəni, -'kɔ-] *n, pl* **-nies** : cacofonía *f*

cactus ['kæktəs] *n, pl* **cacti** [-ˌtaɪ] *or* **-tuses** : cacto *m*, cactus *m*

cadaver [kə'dævər] *n* : cadáver *m*

cadaverous [kə'dævərəs] *adj* : cadavérico

caddie¹ *or* **caddy** ['kædi] *vi* **caddied; caddying** : trabajar de caddie, hacer de caddie

caddie² *or* **caddy** *n, pl* **-dies** : caddie *mf*

caddy ['kædi] *n, pl* **-dies** : cajita *f* para té

cadence ['keɪdənts] *n* : cadencia *f*, ritmo *m*

cadenced ['keɪdəntst] *adj* : cadencioso, rítmico

cadet [kə'dɛt] *n* : cadete *mf*

cadmium ['kædmiəm] *n* : cadmio *m*

cadre ['kæˌdreɪ, 'kɑ-, -ˌdriː] *n* : cuadro *m* (de expertos)

café [kæ'feɪ, kə-] *n* : café *m*, cafetería *f*

cafeteria [ˌkæfə'tɪriə] *n* : cafetería *f*, restaurante *m* de autoservicio

caffeine [kæ'fiːn] *n* : cafeína *f*

cage¹ ['keɪʤ] *vt* **caged; caging** : enjaular

cage² *n* : jaula *f*

cagey ['keɪʤi] *adj* **-gier; -est 1** CAUTIOUS : cauteloso, astuto **2** SHREWD : astuto, vivo — **cagily** [-ʤəli] *adv*

caisson ['keɪˌsɑn, -sən] *n* **1** : cajón *m* de municiones **2** : cajón *m* hidráulico

cajole [kə'ʤoːl] *vt* **-joled; -joling** : engatusar

cajolery [kə'ʤoːləri] *n* : engatusamiento *m*

cake¹ ['keɪk] *v* **caked; caking** *vt* : cubrir ⟨caked with mud : cubierto de barro⟩ — *vi* : endurecerse

cake² *n* **1** : torta *f*, bizcocho *m*, pastel *m* **2** : pastilla *f* (de jabón) **3 to take the cake** : llevarse la palma, ser el colmo

calabash ['kæləˌbæʃ] *n* : calabaza *f*

calamari [ˌkɑlə'mari] *ns & pl* : calamares *mpl*

calamine ['kæləˌmaɪn] *n* : calamina *f* ⟨calamine lotion : loción de calamina⟩

calamitous [kə'læmətəs] *adj* : desastroso, catastrófico, calamitoso — **calamitously** *adv*

calamity [kə'læməti] *n, pl* **-ties** : desastre *m*, desgracia *f*, calamidad *f*

calcium ['kælsiəm] *n* : calcio *m*

calcium carbonate ['kɑrbəˌneɪt, -nət] *n* : carbonato *m* de calcio

calculable ['kælkjələbəl] *adj* : calculable, computable

calculate ['kælkjəˌleɪt] *v* **-lated; -lating** *vt* **1** COMPUTE : calcular, computar **2** ESTIMATE : calcular, creer **3** INTEND : planear, tener la intención de ⟨I calculated on spending $100 : planeaba gastar $100⟩ — *vi* : calcular, hacer cálculos

calculated ['kælkjəˌleɪtəd] *adj* **1** ESTIMATED : calculado **2** DELIBERATE : intencional, premeditado, deliberado

calculating ['kælkjəˌleɪtɪŋ] *adj* SHREWD : calculador, astuto

calculation [ˌkælkjə'leɪʃən] *n* : cálculo *m*

calculator ['kælkjəˌleɪtər] *n* : calculadora *f*

calculus ['kælkjələs] *n, pl* **-li** [-ˌlaɪ] **1** : cálculo *m* ⟨differential calculus : cálculo diferencial⟩ **2** TARTAR : sarro *m* (dental)

caldron ['kɔldrən] → **cauldron**

calendar ['kæləndər] *n* **1** : calendario *m* **2** SCHEDULE : calendario *m*, programa *m*, agenda *f*

calf ['kæf, 'kaf] *n, pl* **calves** ['kævz, 'kavz] **1** : becerro *m*, -rra *f*; ternero *m*, -ra *f* (de vacunos) **2** : cría *f* (de otros mamíferos) **3** : pantorrilla *f* (de la pierna)
calfskin ['kæf,skɪn] *n* : piel *f* de becerro
caliber *or* **calibre** ['kæləbər] *n* **1** : calibre *m* ⟨a .38 caliber gun : una pistola de calibre .38⟩ **2** ABILITY : calibre *m*, valor *m*, capacidad *f*
calibrate ['kælə,breɪt] *vt* **-brated; -brating** : calibrar (armas), graduar (termómetros)
calibration [,kælə'breɪʃən] *n* : calibrado *m*, calibración *f*
calico ['kælɪ,ko:] *n, pl* **-coes** *or* **-cos 1** : calicó *m*, percal *m* **2** *or* **calico cat** : gato *m* manchado
calipers ['kæləpərz] *npl* : calibrador *m*
caliph *or* **calif** ['keɪləf, 'kæ-] *n* : califa *m*
calisthenics [,kæləs'θɛnɪks] *ns & pl* : calistenia *f*
calk ['kɔk] → **caulk**
call¹ ['kɔl] *vi* **1** CRY, SHOUT : gritar, vociferar **2** VISIT : hacer (una) visita, visitar **3 to call for** : exigir, requerir, necesitar ⟨it calls for patience : requiere mucha paciencia⟩ — *vt* **1** SUMMON : llamar, convocar **2** TELEPHONE : llamar por teléfono, telefonear **3** NAME : llamar, apodar
call² *n* **1** SHOUT : grito *m*, llamada *f* **2** : grito *m* (de un animal), reclamo *m* (de un pájaro) **3** SUMMONS : llamada *f* **4** DEMAND : llamado *m*, petición *f* **5** VISIT : visita *f* **6** DECISION : decisión *f* (en deportes) **7** *or* **telephone call** : llamada *f* (telefónica)
call down *vt* REPRIMAND : reprender, reñir
caller ['kɔlər] *n* **1** VISITOR : visita *f* **2** : persona *f* que llama (por teléfono)
calligraphy [kə'lɪgrəfi] *n, pl* **-phies** : caligrafía *f*
calling ['kɔlɪŋ] *n* : vocación *f*, profesión *f*
calliope [kə'laɪə,pi:, 'kæli,o:p] *n* : órgano *m* de vapor
call off *vt* CANCEL : cancelar, suspender
callous¹ ['kæləs] *vt* : encallecer
callous² *adj* **1** CALLUSED : calloso, encallecido **2** UNFEELING : insensible, desalmado, cruel
callously ['kæləsli] *adv* : cruelmente, insensiblemente
callousness ['kæləsnəs] *n* : insensibilidad *f*, crueldad *f*
callow ['kælo] *adj* : inexperto, inmaduro
callus ['kæləs] *n* : callo *m*
callused ['kæləst] *adj* : encallecido, calloso
calm¹ ['kam, 'kalm] *vt* : tranquilizar, calmar, sosegar — *vi* : tranquilizarse, calmarse ⟨calm down! : ¡tranquilízate!⟩
calm² *adj* **1** TRANQUIL : calmo, tranquilo, sereno, ecuánime **2** STILL : en calma (dícese del mar), sin viento (dícese del aire)

calm³ *n* : tranquilidad *f*, calma *f*
calmly ['kamli, 'kalm-] *adv* : con calma, tranquilamente
calmness ['kamnəs, 'kalm-] *n* : calma *f*, tranquilidad *f*
caloric [kə'lɔrɪk] *adj* : calórico (dícese de los alimentos), calorífico (dícese de la energía)
calorie ['kæləri] *n* : caloría *f*
calumniate [kə'lʌmni,eɪt] *vt* **-ated; -ating** : calumniar, difamar
calumny ['kæləmni] *n, pl* **-nies** : calumnia *f*, difamación *f*
calve ['kæv, 'kav] *vi* **calved; calving** : parir (dícese de los mamíferos)
calves → **calf**
calypso [kə'lɪp,so:] *n, pl* **-sos** : calipso *m*
calyx ['keɪlɪks, 'kæ-] *n, pl* **-lyxes** *or* **-lyces** [-lə,si:z] : cáliz *m*
cam ['kæm] *n* : leva *f*
camaraderie [,kam'radəri, ,kæm-; ,kamə'ra-] *n* : compañerismo *m*, camaradería *f*
Cambodian [kæm'bo:diən] *n* : camboyano *m*, -na *f* — **Cambodian** *adj*
came → **come**
camel ['kæməl] *n* : camello *m*
camellia [kə'mi:ljə] *n* : camelia *f*
cameo ['kæmi,o:] *n, pl* **-eos 1** : camafeo *m* **2** *or* **cameo performance** : actuación *f* especial
camera ['kæmrə, 'kæmərə] *n* : cámara *f*, máquina *f* fotográfica
Cameroonian [,kæmə'ru:niən] *n* : camerunés *m*, -nesa *f*
camouflage¹ ['kæmə,flaʒ, -,flaʤ] *vt* **-flaged; -flaging** : camuflajear, camuflar
camouflage² *n* : camuflaje *m*
camp¹ ['kæmp] *vi* : acampar, ir de camping
camp² *n* **1** : campamento *m* **2** FACTION : campo *m*, bando *m* ⟨in the same camp : del mismo bando⟩ **3 to pitch camp** : acampar, poner el campamento **4 to break camp** : levantar el campamento
campaign¹ [kæm'peɪn] *vi* : hacer (una) campaña
campaign² *n* : campaña *f*
campanile [,kæmpə'ni:,li:, -'ni:l] *n, pl* **-niles** *or* **-nili** [-'ni:,li:] : campanario *m*
camper ['kæmpər] *n* **1** : campista *mf* (persona) **2** : cámper *m* (vehículo)
campground ['kæmp,graʊnd] *n* : campamento *m*, camping *m*
camphor ['kæmpfər] *n* : alcanfor *m*
campsite ['kæmp,saɪt] *n* : campamento *m*, camping *m*
campus ['kæmpəs] *n* : campus *m*, recinto *m* universitario
can¹ ['kæn] *v aux, past* **could** ['kʊd]; *present s & pl* **can 1** : poder ⟨could you help me? : ¿podría ayudarme?⟩ **2** : saber ⟨she can't drive yet : todavía no sabe manejar⟩ **3** MAY : poder, tener permiso para ⟨can I sit down? : ¿puedo sentarme?⟩ **4** : poder ⟨it can't be! : ¡no

puede ser!〉 〈where can they be?
: ¿dónde estarán?〉
can² [ˈkæn] *vt* **canned; canning** **1** : enlatar, envasar 〈to can tomatoes : en-
latar tomates〉 **2** DISMISS, FIRE : despedir, echar
can³ *n* : lata *f*, envase *m*, cubo *m* 〈a can
of beer : una lata de cerveza〉 〈garbage
can : cubo de basura〉
Canadian [kəˈneɪdiən] *n* : canadiense *mf*
— **Canadian** *adj*
canal [kəˈnæl] *n* **1** : canal *m*, tubo *m* 〈al-
imentary canal : tubo digestivo〉 **2**
: canal *m* 〈Panama Canal : Canal de
Panamá〉
canapé [ˈkænəpi, -ˌpeɪ] *n* : canapé *m*
canary [kəˈnɛri] *n, pl* **-naries** : canario
m
cancel [ˈkæntsəl] *vt* **-celed** *or* **-celled;**
-celing *or* **-celling** : cancelar
cancellation [ˌkæntsəˈleɪʃən] *n* : cancelación *f*
cancer [ˈkæntsər] *n* : cáncer *m*
Cancer *n* : Cáncer *mf*
cancerous [ˈkæntsərəs] *adj* : canceroso
candelabrum [ˌkændəˈlɑbrəm, -ˈlæ-] *or*
candelabra [-brə] *n, pl* **-bra** *or* **-bras**
: candelabro *m*
candid [ˈkændɪd] *adj* **1** FRANK : franco,
sincero, abierto **2** : natural, espontáneo (en la fotografía)
candidacy [ˈkændədəsi] *n, pl* **-cies**
: candidatura *f*
candidate [ˈkændəˌdeɪt, -dət] *n* : candidato *m*, -ta *f*
candidly [ˈkændɪdli] *adv* : con franqueza
candied [ˈkændid] *adj* : confitado
candle [ˈkændəl] *n* : vela *f*, candela *f*,
cirio *m* (ceremonial)
candlestick [ˈkændəlˌstɪk] *n* : candelero
m
candor [ˈkændər] *n* : franqueza *f*
candy [ˈkændi] *n, pl* **-dies** : dulce *m*,
caramelo *m*
cane¹ [ˈkeɪn] *vt* **caned; caning** **1**
: tapizar (muebles) con mimbre **2**
FLOG : azotar con una vara
cane² *n* **1** : bastón *m* (para andar), vara
f (para castigar) **2** REED : caña *f*, mimbre *m* (para muebles)
canine¹ [ˈkeɪˌnaɪn] *adj* : canino
canine² *n* **1** DOG : canino *m*; perro *m*,
-rra *f* **2** *or* **canine tooth** : colmillo *m*,
diente *m* canino
canister [ˈkænəstər] *n* : lata *f*, bote *m*
canker [ˈkæŋkər] *n* : úlcera *f* bucal
cannery [ˈkænəri] *n, pl* **-ries** : fábrica *f*
de conservas
cannibal [ˈkænəbəl] *n* : caníbal *mf*; antropófago *m*, -ga *f*
cannibalism [ˈkænəbəˌlɪzəm] *n* : canibalismo *m*, antropofagia *f*
cannibalize [ˈkænəbəˌlaɪz] *vt* **-ized;**
-izing : canibalizar
cannily [ˈkænəli] *adv* : astutamente,
sagazmente
cannon [ˈkænən] *n, pl* **-nons** *or* **-non**
: cañón *m*

cannot (**can not**) [ˈkænˌɑt, kəˈnɑt] →
can¹
canny [ˈkæni] *adj* **-nier; -est** SHREWD
: astuto, sagaz
canoe¹ [kəˈnuː] *vt* **-noed; -noeing** : ir en
canoa
canoe² *n* : canoa *f*, piragua *f*
canon [ˈkænən] *n* **1** : canon *m* 〈canon
law : derecho canónico〉 **2** WORKS
: canon *m* 〈the canon of American literature : el canon de la literatura amer-
icana〉 **3** : canónigo *m* (de una catedral) **4** STANDARD : canon *m*, norma *f*
canonical [kəˈnɑnɪkəl] *adj* : canónico
canonize [ˈkænəˌnaɪz] *vt* **-ized; -izing**
: canonizar
canopy [ˈkænəpi] *n, pl* **-pies** : dosel *m*,
toldo *m*
cant¹ [ˈkænt] *vt* TILT : ladear, inclinar —
vi **1** SLANT : ladearse, inclinarse, escorar (dícese de un barco) **2** : hablar in-
sinceramente
cant² *n* **1** SLANT : plano *m* inclinado **2**
JARGON : jerga *f* **3** : palabras *fpl* insin-
ceras
can't [ˈkænt, ˈkant] (*contraction of* **can**
not) → **can¹**
cantaloupe [ˈkæntəlˌoːp] *n* : melón *m*,
cantalupo *m*
cantankerous [kænˈtæŋkərəs] *adj* : irritable, irascible — **cantankerously** *adv*
cantankerousness [kænˈtæŋkərəsnəs]
n : irritabilidad *f*, irascibilidad *f*
cantata [kənˈtɑtə] *n* : cantata *f*
canteen [kænˈtiːn] *n* **1** FLASK : cantimplora *f* **2** CAFETERIA : cantina *f*, comedor *m* **3** : club *m* para actividades sociales y recreativas
canter¹ [ˈkæntər] *vi* : ir a medio galope
canter² *n* : medio galope *m*
cantilever [ˈkæntəˌliːvər, -ˌlɛvər] *n* **1**
: viga *f* voladiza **2 cantilever bridge**
: puente *m* voladizo
canto [ˈkænˌtoː] *n, pl* **-tos** : canto *m*
canton [ˈkæntən, -ˌtan] *n* : cantón *m*
Cantonese [ˌkæntəˈniːz, -ˈiːs] *n* **1** : cantonés *m*, -nesa *f* **2** : cantonés *m* (idioma) — **Cantonese** *adj*
cantor [ˈkæntər] *n* : solista *mf*
canvas [ˈkænvəs] *n* **1** : lona *f* **2** SAILS
: velas *fpl* (de un barco) **3** : lienzo *m*,
tela *f* (de pintar) **4** PAINTING : pintura
f, óleo *m*, cuadro *m*
canvass¹ [ˈkænvəs] *vt* **1** SOLICIT : solicitar votos o pedidos de, hacer campaña
entre **2** SOUND OUT : sondear (opiniones, etc.)
canvass² *n* SURVEY : sondeo *m*, encuesta *f*
canyon [ˈkænjən] *n* : cañón *m*
cap¹ [ˈkæp] *vt* **capped; capping** **1** COV-
ER : tapar (un recipiente), enfundar (un
diente), cubrir (una montaña) **2** CLI-
MAX : coronar, ser el punto culminante
de 〈to cap it all off : para colmo〉 **3**
LIMIT : limitar, poner un tope a
cap² *n* **1** : gorra *f*, gorro *m*, cachucha *f*
Mex 〈baseball cap : gorra de béisbol〉

2 COVER, TOP : tapa *f*, tapón *m* (de botellas), corcholata *f Mex* **3** LIMIT : tope *m*, límite *m*

capability [ˌkeɪpəˈbɪləti] *n, pl* **-ties** : capacidad *f*, habilidad *f*, competencia *f*

capable [ˈkeɪpəbəl] *adj* : competente, capaz, hábil — **capably** [-bli] *adv*

capacious [kəˈpeɪʃəs] *adj* : amplio, espacioso, de gran capacidad

capacity[1] [kəˈpæsəti] *adj* : completo, total ⟨a capacity crowd : un lleno completo⟩

capacity[2] *n, pl* **-ties** **1** ROOM, SPACE : capacidad *f*, cabida *f*, espacio *m* **2** CAPABILITY : habilidad *f*, competencia *f* **3** FUNCTION, ROLE : calidad *f*, función *f* ⟨in his capacity as ambassador : en su calidad de embajador⟩

cape [ˈkeɪp] *n* **1** : capa *f* **2** : cabo *m* ⟨Cape Horn : el Cabo de Hornos⟩

caper[1] [ˈkeɪpər] *vi* : dar saltos, correr y brincar

caper[2] *n* **1** : alcaparra *f* ⟨olives and capers : aceitunas y alcaparras⟩ **2** ANTIC, PRANK : broma *f*, travesura *f* **3** LEAP : brinco *m*, salto *m*

Cape Verdean [ˈkeɪpˈvərdiən] *n* : caboverdiano *m*, -na *f* — **Cape Verdean** *adj*

capful [ˈkæpˌfʊl] *n* : tapa *f*, tapita *f*

capillary[1] [ˈkæpəˌlɛri] *adj* : capilar

capillary[2] *n, pl* **-ries** : capilar *m*

capital[1] [ˈkæpətəl] *adj* **1** : capital ⟨capital punishment : pena capital⟩ **2** : mayúsculo (dícese de las letras) **3** : de capital ⟨capital assets : activo fijo⟩ ⟨capital gain : ganancia de capital, plusvalía⟩ **4** EXCELLENT : excelente, estupendo

capital[2] *n* **1** *or* **capital city** : capital *f*, sede *f* del gobierno **2** WEALTH : capital *m* **3** *or* **capital letter** : mayúscula *f* **4** : capitel *m* (de una columna)

capitalism [ˈkæpətəlˌɪzəm] *n* : capitalismo *m*

capitalist[1] [ˈkæpətəlɪst] *or* **capitalistic** [ˌkæpətəlˈɪstɪk] *adj* : capitalista

capitalist[2] *n* : capitalista *mf*

capitalization [ˌkæpətələˈzeɪʃən] *n* : capitalización *f*

capitalize [ˈkæpətəlˌaɪz] *v* **-ized; -izing** *vt* **1** FINANCE : capitalizar, financiar **2** : escribir con mayúscula — *vi* to **capitalize on** : sacar partido de, aprovechar

capitol [ˈkæpətəl] *n* : capitolio *m*

capitulate [kəˈpɪtʃəˌleɪt] *vi* **-lated; -lating** : capitular

capitulation [kəˌpɪtʃəˈleɪʃən] *n* : capitulación *f*

capon [ˈkeɪˌpan, -pən] *n* : capón *m*

cappuccino [ˌkapəˈtʃiːnoː] *n* : capuchino *m* (café)

caprice [kəˈpriːs] *n* : capricho *m*, antojo *m*

capricious [kəˈprɪʃəs, -ˈpriː-] *adj* : caprichoso — **capriciously** *adv*

Capricorn [ˈkæprɪˌkɔrn] *n* : Capricornio *mf*

capsize [ˈkæpˌsaɪz, kæpˈsaɪz] *v* **-sized; -sizing** *vi* : volcar, volcarse — *vt* : hacer volcar

capstan [ˈkæpstən, -ˌstæn] *n* : cabrestante *m*

capsule [ˈkæpsəl, -ˌsuːl] *n* **1** : cápsula *f* (en la farmacéutica y botánica) **2** **space capsule** : cápsula *f* espacial

captain[1] [ˈkæptən] *vt* : capitanear

captain[2] *n* **1** : capitán *m*, -tana *f* **2** HEADWAITER : jefe *m*, -fa *f* de comedor **3** **captain of industry** : magnate *mf*

caption[1] [ˈkæpʃən] *vt* : ponerle una leyenda a (una ilustración), titular (un artículo), subtitular (una película)

caption[2] *n* **1** HEADING : titular *m*, encabezamiento *m* **2** : leyenda *f* (al pie de una ilustración) **3** SUBTITLE : subtítulo *m*

captivate [ˈkæptəˌveɪt] *vt* **-vated; -vating** CHARM : cautivar, hechizar, encantar

captivating [ˈkæptəˌveɪtɪŋ] *adj* : cautivador, hechicero, encantador

captive[1] [ˈkæptɪv] *adj* : cautivo

captive[2] *n* : cautivo *m*, -va *f*

captivity [kæpˈtɪvəti] *n* : cautiverio *m*

captor [ˈkæptər] *n* : captor *m*, -tora *f*

capture[1] [ˈkæpʃər] *vt* **-tured; -turing** **1** SEIZE : capturar, apresar **2** CATCH : captar ⟨to capture one's interest : captar el interés de uno⟩

capture[2] *n* : captura *f*, apresamiento *m*

car [ˈkɑr] *n* **1** AUTOMOBILE : automóvil *m*, coche *m*, carro *m* **2** : vagón *m*, coche *m* (de un tren) **3** : cabina *f* (de un ascensor)

carafe [kəˈræf, -ˈrɑf] *n* : garrafa *f*

caramel [ˈkɑrməl; ˈkærəməl, -ˌmɛl] *n* **1** : caramelo *m*, azúcar *f* quemada **2** *or* **caramel candy** : caramelo *m*, dulce *m* de leche

carat [ˈkærət] *n* : quilate *m*

caravan [ˈkærəˌvæn] *n* : caravana *f*

caraway [ˈkærəˌweɪ] *n* : alcaravea *f*

carbine [ˈkɑrˌbaɪn, -ˌbiːn] *n* : carabina *f*

carbohydrate [ˌkɑrboˈhaɪˌdreɪt, -drət] *n* : carbohidrato *m*, hidrato *m* de carbono

carbon [ˈkɑrbən] *n* **1** : carbono *m* **2** → **carbon paper** **3** → **carbon copy**

carbonated [ˈkɑrbəˌneɪtəd] *adj* : carbonatado (dícese del agua), gaseoso (dícese de las bebidas)

carbon copy *n* **1** : copia *f* al carbón **2** DUPLICATE : duplicado *m*, copia *f* exacta

carbon paper *n* : papel *m* carbón

carbuncle [ˈkɑrˌbʌŋkəl] *n* : carbunco *m*

carburetor [ˈkɑrbəˌreɪtər, -bjə-] *n* : carburador *m*

carcass [ˈkɑrkəs] *n* : cuerpo *m* (de un animal muerto)

carcinogen [kɑrˈsɪnədʒən, ˈkɑrsənəˌdʒɛn] *n* : carcinógeno *m*, cancerígeno *m*

carcinogenic [ˌkɑrsənoˈdʒɛnɪk] *adj* : carcinogénico

carcinoma [ˌkɑrsəˈnoːmə] *n* : carcinoma *m*

card[1] [ˈkɑrd] *vt* : cardar (fibras)
card[2] *n* **1** : carta *f*, naipe *m* ⟨to play cards : jugar a las cartas⟩ ⟨a deck of cards : una baraja⟩ **2** : tarjeta *f* ⟨birthday card : tarjeta de cumpleaños⟩ ⟨business card : tarjeta (de visita)⟩
cardboard [ˈkɑrdˌbord] *n* : cartón *m*, cartulina *f*
cardiac [ˈkɑrdiˌæk] *adj* : cardíaco, cardiaco
cardigan [ˈkɑrdɪgən] *n* : cárdigan *m*, chaqueta *f* de punto
cardinal[1] [ˈkɑrdənəl] *adj* FUNDAMENTAL : cardinal, fundamental
cardinal[2] *n* : cardenal *m*
cardinal number *n* : número *m* cardinal
cardinal point *n* : punto *m* cardinal
cardiologist [ˌkɑrdiˈɑləʤɪst] *n* : cardiólogo *m*, -ga *f*
cardiology [ˌkɑrdiˈɑləʤi] *n* : cardiología *f*
cardiovascular [ˌkɑrdioˈvæskjələr] *adj* : cardiovascular
care[1] [ˈkær] *v* **cared; caring** *vi* **1** : importarle a uno ⟨they don't care : no les importa⟩ **2** : preocuparse, inquietarse ⟨she cares about the poor : se preocupa por los pobres⟩ **3 to care for** TEND : cuidar (de), atender, encargarse de **4 to care for** CHERISH : querer, sentir cariño por **5 to care for** LIKE : gustarle (algo a uno) ⟨I don't care for your attitude : tu actitud no me agrada⟩ — *vt* WISH : desear, querer ⟨if you care to go : si deseas ir⟩
care[2] *n* **1** ANXIETY : inquietud *f*, preocupación *f* **2** CAREFULNESS : cuidado *m*, atención *f* ⟨handle with care : manejar con cuidado⟩ **3** CHARGE : cargo *m*, cuidado *m* **4 to take care of** : cuidar (de), atender, encargarse de
careen [kəˈriːn] *vi* **1** SWAY : oscilar, balancearse **2** CAREER : ir a toda velocidad
career[1] [kəˈrɪr] *vi* : ir a toda velocidad
career[2] *n* VOCATION : vocación *f*, profesión *f*, carrera *f*
carefree [ˈkærˌfriː, ˌkærˈ-] *adj* : despreocupado
careful [ˈkærfəl] *adj* **1** CAUTIOUS : cuidadoso, cauteloso **2** PAINSTAKING : cuidadoso, esmerado, meticuloso
carefully [ˈkærfəli] *adv* : con cuidado, cuidadosamente
carefulness [ˈkærfəlnəs] *n* **1** CAUTION : cuidado *m*, cautela *f* **2** METICULOUSNESS : esmero *m*, meticulosidad *f*
caregiver [ˈkærˌgɪvər] *n* : persona *f* que cuida a niños o enfermos
careless [ˈkærləs] *adj* : descuidado, negligente — **carelessly** *adv*
carelessness [ˈkærləsnəs] *n* : descuido *m*, negligencia *f*
caress[1] [kəˈrɛs] *vt* : acariciar
caress[2] *n* : caricia *f*
caret [ˈkærət] *n* : signo *m* de intercalación
caretaker [ˈkɛrˌteɪkər] *n* : conserje *mf*; velador *m*, -dora *f*

cargo [ˈkɑrˌgoː] *n, pl* **-goes** *or* **-gos** : cargamento *m*, carga *f*
Caribbean [kærəˈbiːən, kəˈrɪbiən] *adj* : caribeño ⟨the Caribbean Sea : el mar Caribe⟩
caribou [ˈkærəˌbuː] *n, pl* **-bou** *or* **-bous** : caribú *m*
caricature[1] [ˈkærɪkəˌʧʊr] *vt* **-tured; -turing** : caricaturizar
caricature[2] *n* : caricatura *f*
caricaturist [ˈkærɪkəˌʧʊrɪst] *n* : caricaturista *mf*
caries [ˈkærˌiːz] *ns & pl* : caries *f*
carillon [ˈkærəˌlɑn] *n* : carillón *m*
carmine [ˈkɑrmən, -ˌmaɪn] *n* : carmín *m*
carnage [ˈkɑrnɪʤ] *n* : matanza *f*, carnicería *f*
carnal [ˈkɑrnəl] *adj* : carnal
carnation [kɑrˈneɪʃən] *n* : clavel *m*
carnival [ˈkɑrnəvəl] *n* : carnaval *m*, feria *f*
carnivore [ˈkɑrnəˌvor] *n* : carnívoro *m*
carnivorous [kɑrˈnɪvərəs] *adj* : carnívoro
carol[1] [ˈkærəl] *vi* **-oled** *or* **-olled; -oling** *or* **-olling** : cantar villancicos
carol[2] *n* : villancico *m*
caroler *or* **caroller** [ˈkærələr] *n* : persona *f* que canta villancicos
carom[1] [ˈkærəm] *vi* **1** REBOUND : rebotar ⟨the bullet caromed off the wall : la bala rebotó contra el muro⟩ **2** : hacer carambola (en billar)
carom[2] *n* : carambola *f*
carouse [kəˈrauz] *vt* **-roused; -rousing** : irse de parranda, irse de juerga
carousel *or* **carrousel** [ˌkærəˈsɛl, ˈkærəˌ-] *n* : carrusel *m*, tiovivo *m*
carouser [kəˈrauzər] *n* : juerguista *mf*
carp[1] [ˈkɑrp] *vi* **1** COMPLAIN : quejarse **2 to carp at** : criticar
carp[2] *n, pl* **carp** *or* **carps** : carpa *f*
carpel [ˈkɑrpəl] *n* : carpelo *m*
carpenter [ˈkɑrpəntər] *n* : carpintero *m*, -ra *f*
carpentry [ˈkɑrpəntri] *n* : carpintería *f*
carpet[1] [ˈkɑrpət] *vt* : alfombrar
carpet[2] *n* : alfombra *f*
carpeting [ˈkɑrpətɪŋ] *n* : alfombrado *m*
carport [ˈkɑrˌport] *n* : cochera *f*, garaje *m* abierto
carriage [ˈkærɪʤ] *n* **1** TRANSPORT : transporte *m* **2** POSTURE : porte *m*, postura *f* **3 horse-drawn carriage** : carruaje *m*, coche *m* **4 baby carriage** : cochecito *m*
carrier [ˈkæriər] *n* **1** : transportista *mf*, empresa *f* de transportes **2** : portador *m*, -dora *f* (de una enfermedad) **3 aircraft carrier** : portaaviones *m*
carrier pigeon *n* : paloma *f* mensajera
carrion [ˈkæriən] *n* : carroña *f*
carrot [ˈkærət] *n* : zanahoria *f*
carry [ˈkæri] *v* **-ried; -rying** *vt* **1** TRANSPORT : llevar, cargar, transportar (cargamento), conducir (electricidad), portar (un virus) ⟨to carry a bag : cargar una bolsa⟩ ⟨to carry money : llevar dinero encima, traer dinero consi-

go⟩ 2 BEAR : soportar, aguantar, resistir (peso) 3 STOCK : vender, tener en abasto 4 ENTAIL : llevar, implicar, acarrear 5 WIN : ganar (una elección o competición), aprobar (una moción) 6 **to carry oneself** : portarse, comportarse ⟨he carried himself honorably : se comportó dignamente⟩ — vi : oírse, proyectarse ⟨her voice carries well : su voz se puede oír desde lejos⟩
carryall ['kæri,ɔl] n : bolsa f de viaje
carry away vt **to get carried away** : exaltarse, entusiasmarse
carry on vt CONDUCT : realizar, ejercer, mantener ⟨to carry on research : realizar investigaciones⟩ ⟨to carry on a correspondence : mantener una correspondencia⟩ — vi 1 : portarse de manera escandalosa o inapropiada ⟨it's embarrassing how he carries on : su manera de comportarse da vergüenza⟩ 2 CONTINUE : seguir, continuar
carry out vt 1 PERFORM : llevar a cabo, realizar 2 FULFILL : cumplir
cart¹ ['kɑrt] vt : acarrear, llevar
cart² n : carreta f, carro m
cartel [kɑr'tɛl] n : cártel m
cartilage ['kɑrt̬əlɪdʒ] n : cartílago m
cartilaginous [,kɑrt̬əl'ædʒənəs] adj : cartilaginoso
cartographer [kɑr'tɑgrəfər] n : cartógrafo m, -fa f
cartography [kɑr'tɑgrəfi] n : cartografía f
carton ['kɑrt̬ən] n : caja f de cartón
cartoon [kɑr'tu:n] n 1 : chiste m (gráfico), caricatura f ⟨a political cartoon : un chiste político⟩ 2 COMIC STRIP : tira f cómica, historieta f 3 or animated cartoon : dibujo m animado
cartoonist [kɑr'tu:nɪst] n : caricaturista mf, dibujante mf (de chistes)
cartridge ['kɑrtrɪdʒ] n : cartucho m
carve ['kɑrv] vt **carved; carving** 1 : tallar (madera), esculpir (piedra), grabar ⟨he carved his name in the bark : grabó su nombre en la corteza⟩ 2 SLICE : cortar, trinchar (carne)
cascade¹ [kæs'keɪd] vi **-caded; -cading** : caer en cascada
cascade² n : cascada f, salto m de agua
case¹ ['keɪs] vt **cased; casing** 1 BOX, PACK : embalar, encajonar 2 INSPECT : observar, inspeccionar (antes de cometer un delito)
case² n 1 : caso m ⟨an unusual case : un caso insólito⟩ ⟨ablative case : caso ablativo⟩ ⟨a case of the flu : un caso de gripe⟩ 2 BOX : caja f 3 CONTAINER : funda f, estuche m 4 **in any case** : de todos modos, en cualquier caso 5 **in case** : como precaución ⟨just in case : por si acaso⟩ 6 **in case of** : en caso de
casement ['keɪsmənt] n : ventana f con bisagras
cash¹ ['kæʃ] vt : convertir en efectivo, cobrar, cambiar (un cheque)

cash² n : efectivo m, dinero m en efectivo
cashew ['kæ,ʃu:, kə'ʃu:] n : anacardo m
cashier¹ [kə'ʃɪr] vt : destituir, despedir
cashier² n : cajero m, -ra f
cashmere ['kæʒ,mɪr, 'kæʃ-] n : cachemir m
casino [kə'si:,no:] n, pl **-nos** : casino m
cask ['kæsk] n : tonel m, barrica f, barril m
casket ['kæskət] n COFFIN : ataúd m, féretro m
cassava [kə'sɑvə] n : mandioca f, yuca f
casserole ['kæsə,ro:l] n 1 : cazuela f 2 : guiso m, guisado m ⟨tuna casserole : guiso de atún⟩
cassette [kə'sɛt, kæ-] n : cassette mf
cassock ['kæsək] n : sotana f
cast¹ ['kæst] vt **cast; casting** 1 THROW : tirar, echar, arrojar ⟨the die is cast : la suerte está echada⟩ 2 : depositar (un voto) 3 : asignar (papeles en una obra de teatro) 4 MOLD : moldear, fundir, vaciar 5 **to cast off** ABANDON : desamparar, abandonar
cast² n 1 THROW : lance m, lanzamiento m 2 APPEARANCE : aspecto m, forma f 3 : elenco m, reparto m (de una obra de teatro) 4 **plaster cast** : molde m de yeso, escayola f
castanets [,kæstə'nɛts] npl : castañuelas fpl
castaway¹ ['kæstə,weɪ] adj : náufrago
castaway² n : náufrago m, -ga f
caste ['kæst] n : casta f
caster ['kæstər] n : ruedita f (de un mueble)
castigate ['kæstə,geɪt] vt **-gated; -gating** : castigar severamente, censurar, reprobar
Castilian [kæ'stɪljən] n 1 : castellano m, -na f 2 : castellano m (idioma) — **Castilian** adj
cast iron n : hierro m fundido
castle ['kæsəl] n 1 : castillo m 2 : torre f (en ajedrez)
cast-off ['kæst,ɔf] adj : desechado
castoff ['kæst,ɔf] n : desecho m
castrate ['kæs,treɪt] vt **-trated; -trating** : castrar
castration [kæ'streɪʃən] n : castración f
casual ['kæʒuəl] adj 1 FORTUITOUS : casual, fortuito 2 INDIFFERENT : indiferente, despreocupado 3 INFORMAL : informal — **casually** ['kæʒuəli, 'kæʒəli] adv
casualness ['kæʒuəlnəs] n 1 FORTUITOUSNESS : casualidad f 2 INDIFFERENCE : indiferencia f, despreocupación f 3 INFORMALITY : informalidad f
casualty ['kæʒuəlti, 'kæʒəl-] n, pl **-ties** 1 ACCIDENT : accidente m serio, desastre m 2 VICTIM : víctima f, baja f; herido m, -da f
cat ['kæt] n : gato m, -ta f
cataclysm ['kæt̬ə,klɪzəm] n : cataclismo m

cataclysmal [ˌkæt̬ə'klızməl] or cataclysmic [ˌkæt̬ə'klızmık] adj : catastrófico
catacombs ['kæt̬ə,ko:mz] npl : catacumbas fpl
Catalan ['kæt̬ələn, -ˌlæn] n 1 : catalán m, catalana f 2 : catalán m (idioma) — Catalan adj
catalog¹ or catalogue ['kæt̬ə,lɔg] vt -loged or -logued; -loging or -loguing : catalogar
catalog² n : catálogo m
catalyst ['kæt̬ələst] n : catalizador m
catalytic [ˌkæt̬əl'ıtık] adj : catalítico
catamaran [ˌkæt̬əmə'ræn, 'kæt̬əmə-ˌræn] n : catamarán m
catapult¹ ['kæt̬ə,pʌlt, -ˌpʊlt] vt : catapultar
catapult² n : catapulta f
cataract ['kæt̬ə,rækt] n : catarata f
catarrh [kə'tɑr] n : catarro m
catastrophe [kə'tæstrə,fi:] n : catástrofe f
catastrophic [ˌkæt̬ə'strɑfık] adj : catastrófico — catastrophically [-fıkli] adv
catcall ['kæt,kɔl] n : rechifla f, abucheo m
catch¹ ['kætʃ, 'kɛtʃ] v caught ['kɔt]; catching vt 1 CAPTURE, TRAP : capturar, agarrar, atrapar, coger 2 : agarrar, pillar fam, tomar de sorpresa ⟨they caught him red-handed : lo pillaron con las manos en la masa⟩ 3 GRASP : agarrar, captar 4 ENTANGLE : enganchar, enredar 5 : tomar (un tren, etc.) 6 : contagiarse de ⟨to catch a cold : contagiarse de un resfriado, resfriarse⟩ — vi 1 GRASP : agarrar 2 HOOK : engancharse 3 IGNITE : prender, agarrar
catch² n 1 CATCHING : captura f, atrapada f, parada f (de una pelota) 2 : redada f (de pescado), presa f (de caza) ⟨he's a good catch : es un buen partido⟩ 3 LATCH : pestillo m, pasador m 4 DIFFICULTY, TRICK : problema m, trampa f, truco m
catcher ['kætʃər, 'kɛ-] n : catcher mf; receptor m, -tora f (en béisbol)
catching ['kætʃıŋ, 'kɛ-] adj : contagioso
catchup ['kætʃəp, 'kɛ-] → ketchup
catchword ['kætʃ,wərd, 'kɛtʃ-] n : eslogan m, lema m
catchy ['kætʃi, 'kɛ-] adj catchier; -est : pegajoso ⟨a catchy song : una canción pegajosa⟩
catechism ['kæt̬ə,kızəm] n : catecismo m
categorical [ˌkæt̬ə'gɔrıkəl] adj : categórico, absoluto, rotundo — categorically [-kli] adv
categorize ['kæt̬ıgə,raız] vt -rized; -rizing : clasificar, catalogar
category ['kæt̬ə,gori] n, pl -ries : categoría f, género m, clase f
cater ['keıt̬ər] vi 1 : proveer alimentos (para fiestas, bodas, etc.) 2 to cater to : atender a ⟨to cater to all tastes : atender a todos los gustos⟩

catercorner¹ ['kæt̬i,kɔrnər, 'kæt̬ə-, 'kıt̬i-] or cater–cornered [-ˌkɔrnərd] adv : diagonalmente, en diagonal
catercorner² or cater–cornered adj : diagonal
caterer ['keıt̬ərər] n : proveedor m, -dora f de comida
caterpillar ['kæt̬ər,pılər] n : oruga f
catfish ['kæt,fıʃ] n : bagre m
catgut ['kæt,gʌt] n : cuerda f de tripa
catharsis [kə'θɑrsıs] n, pl catharses [-ˌsi:z] : catarsis f
cathartic¹ [kə'θɑrt̬ık] adj : catártico
cathartic² n : purgante m
cathedral [kə'θi:drəl] n : catedral f
catheter ['kæθət̬ər] n : catéter m, sonda f
cathode ['kæ,θo:d] n : cátodo m
catholic ['kæθəlık] adj 1 BROAD, UNIVERSAL : liberal, universal 2 Catholic : católico
Catholic n : católico m, -ca f
Catholicism [kə'θɑlə,sızəm] n : catolicismo m
catlike ['kæt,laık] adj : gatuno, felino
catnap¹ ['kæt,næp] vi -napped; -napping : tomarse una siestecita
catnap² n : siesta f breve, siestecita f
catnip ['kæt,nıp] n : nébeda f
catsup ['kɛtʃəp, 'kætsəp] → ketchup
cattail ['kæt,teıl] n : espadaña f, anea f
cattiness ['kæt̬inəs] n : malicia f
cattle ['kæt̬əl] npl : ganado m, reses fpl
cattleman ['kæt̬əlmən, -ˌmæn] n, pl -men [-mən, -ˌmɛn] : ganadero m
catty ['kæt̬i] adj -tier; -est : malicioso, malintencionado
catwalk ['kæt,wɔk] n : pasarela f
Caucasian¹ [kɔ'keıʒən] adj : caucásico
Caucasian² n : caucásico m, -ca f
caucus ['kɔkəs] n : junta f de políticos
caught → catch
cauldron ['kɔldrən] n : caldera f
cauliflower ['kɑlı,flauər, 'kɔ-] n : coliflor f
caulk¹ ['kɔk] vt : calafatear (un barco), enmasillar (una grieta)
caulk² n : masilla f
causal ['kɔzəl] adj : causal
causality [kɔ'zælət̬i] n : causalidad f
cause¹ ['kɔz] vt caused; causing : causar, provocar, ocasionar
cause² n 1 ORIGIN : causa f, origen m 2 REASON : causa f, razón f, motivo m 3 LAWSUIT : litigio m, pleito m 4 MOVEMENT : causa f, movimiento m
causeless ['kɔzləs] adj : sin causa
causeway ['kɔz,weı] n : camino m elevado
caustic ['kɔstık] adj 1 CORROSIVE : cáustico, corrosivo 2 BITING : mordaz, sarcástico
cauterize ['kɔt̬ə,raız] vt -ized; -izing : cauterizar
caution¹ ['kɔʃən] vt : advertir
caution² n 1 WARNING : advertencia f, aviso m 2 CARE, PRUDENCE : precaución f, cuidado m, cautela f

cautionary ['kɔʃə,nɛri] *adv* : admonitorio ⟨cautionary tale : cuento moral⟩

cautious ['kɔʃəs] *adj* : cauteloso, cuidadoso, precavido

cautiously ['kɔʃəsli] *adv* : cautelosamente, con precaución

cautiousness ['kɔʃəsnəs] *n* : cautela *f*, precaución *f*

cavalcade [,kævəl'keɪd, 'kævəl,-] *n* **1** : cabalgata *f* **2** SERIES : serie *f*

cavalier¹ [,kævə'lɪr] *adj* : altivo, desdeñoso — **cavalierly** *adv*

cavalier² *n* : caballero *m*

cavalry ['kævəlri] *n*, *pl* **-ries** : caballería *f*

cave¹ ['keɪv] *vi* **caved; caving** *or* **to cave in** : derrumbarse

cave² *n* : cueva *f*

cavern ['kævərn] *n* : caverna *f*

cavernous ['kævərnəs] *adj* : cavernoso — **cavernously** *adv*

caviar *or* **caviare** ['kævi,ɑr, 'kɑ-] *n* : caviar *m*

cavity ['kævəti] *n*, *pl* **-ties 1** HOLE : cavidad *f*, hueco *m* **2** CARIES : caries *f*

cavort [kə'vɔrt] *vi* : brincar, hacer cabriolas

caw¹ ['kɔ] *vi* : graznar

caw² *n* : graznido *m*

cayenne pepper [,kaɪ'ɛn, ,keɪ-] *n* : pimienta *f* cayena, pimentón *m*

CD [,si:'di:] *n* : CD *m*, disco *m* compacto

CD-ROM [,si:,di:'ram] *n* : CD-ROM *m*

cease ['si:s] *v* **ceased; ceasing** *vt* : dejar de ⟨they ceased bickering : dejaron de discutir⟩ — *vi* : cesar, pasarse

ceaseless ['si:sləs] *adj* : incesante, continuo

cedar ['si:dər] *n* : cedro *m*

cede ['si:d] *vt* **ceded; ceding** : ceder, conceder

ceiling ['si:lɪŋ] *n* **1** : techo *m*, cielo *m* raso **2** LIMIT : límite *m*, tope *m*

celebrant ['sɛləbrənt] *n* : celebrante *mf*, oficiante *mf*

celebrate ['sɛlə,breɪt] *v* **-brated; -brating** *vt* **1** : celebrar, oficiar ⟨to celebrate Mass : celebrar la misa⟩ **2** : celebrar, festejar ⟨we're celebrating our anniversary : estamos celebrando nuestro aniversario⟩ **3** EXTOL : alabar, ensalzar, exaltar — *vi* : estar de fiesta, divertirse

celebrated ['sɛlə,breɪtəd] *adj* : célebre, famoso, renombrado

celebration [,sɛlə'breɪʃən] *n* : celebración *f*, festejos *mpl*

celebrity [sə'lɛbrəti] *n*, *pl* **-ties 1** RENOWN : fama *f*, renombre *m*, celebridad *f* **2** PERSONALITY : celebridad *f*, personaje *m*

celery ['sɛləri] *n*, *pl* **-eries** : apio *m*

celestial [sə'lɛstʃəl, -'lstiəl] *adj* **1** : celeste **2** HEAVENLY : celestial, paradisiaco

celibacy ['sɛləbəsi] *n* : celibato *m*

celibate¹ ['sɛləbət] *adj* : célibe

celibate² *n* : célibe *mf*

cell ['sɛl] *n* **1** : célula *f* (de un organismo) **2** : celda *f* (en una cárcel, etc.) **3** : elemento *m* (de una pila)

cellar ['sɛlər] *n* **1** BASEMENT : sótano *m* **2** : bodega *f* (de vinos)

cellist ['tʃɛlɪst] *n* : violonchelista *mf*

cello ['tʃɛ,lo:] *n*, *pl* **-los** : violonchelo *m*

cellophane ['sɛlə,feɪn] *n* : celofán *m*

cell phone *n* : teléfono *m* celular

cellular ['sɛljələr] *adj* : celular

celluloid ['sɛljə,lɔɪd] *n* : celuloide

cellulose ['sɛljə,lo:s] *n* : celulosa *f*

Celsius ['sɛlsiəs] *adj* : centígrado ⟨100 degrees Celsius : 100 grados centígrados⟩

Celt ['kɛlt, 'sɛlt] *n* : celta *mf*

Celtic¹ ['kɛltɪk, 'sɛl-] *adj* : celta

Celtic² *n* : celta *m*

cement¹ [sɪ'mɛnt] *vi* : unir o cubrir algo con cemento, cementar

cement² *n* **1** : cemento *m* **2** GLUE : pegamento *m*

cemetery ['sɛmə,tɛri] *n*, *pl* **-teries** : cementerio *m*, panteón *m*

censer ['sɛntsər] *n* : incensario *m*

censor¹ ['sɛntsər] *vt* : censurar

censor² *n* : censor *m*, -sora *f*

censorious [sɛn'soriəs] *adj* : de censura, crítico

censorship ['sɛntsər,ʃɪp] *n* : censura *f*

censure¹ ['sɛntʃər] *vt* **-sured; -suring** : censurar, criticar, reprobar — **censurable** [-tʃərəbəl] *adj*

censure² *n* : censura *f*, reproche *m* oficial

census ['sɛntsəs] *n* : censo *m*

cent ['sɛnt] *n* : centavo *m*

centaur ['sɛn,tɔr] *n* : centauro *m*

centennial¹ [sɛn'tɛniəl] *adj* : del centenario

centennial² *n* : centenario *m*

center¹ ['sɛntər] *vt* **1** : centrar **2** CONCENTRATE : concentrar, fijar, enfocar — *vi* : centrarse, enfocarse

center² *n* **1** : centro *m* ⟨center of gravity : centro de gravedad⟩ **2** : centro *mf* (en futbol americano), pívot *mf* (en basquetbol)

centerpiece ['sɛntər,pi:s] *n* : centro *m* de mesa

centigrade ['sɛntə,greɪd, 'san-] *adj* : centígrado

centigram ['sɛntə,græm, 'san-] *n* : centigramo *m*

centimeter ['sɛntə,mi:tər, 'san-] *n* : centímetro *m*

centipede ['sɛntə,pi:d] *n* : ciempiés *m*

central ['sɛntrəl] *adj* **1** : céntrico, central ⟨in a central location : en un lugar céntrico⟩ **2** MAIN, PRINCIPAL : central, fundamental, principal

Central American¹ *adj* : centroamericano

Central American² *n* : centroamericano *m*, -na *f*

centralization [,sɛntrələ'zeɪʃən] *n* : centralización *f*

centralize ['sɛntrə,laɪz] *vt* **-ized; -izing** : centralizar

centrally ['sɛntrəli] *adv* 1 centrally heated : con calefacción central 2 centrally located : céntrico, en un lugar céntrico
centre ['sɛntər] → center
centrifugal [sɛn'trɪfjəgəl, -'trɪfɪ-] *adj* : centrífugo
centrifugal force *n* : fuerza *f* centrífuga
century ['sɛntʃəri] *n*, *pl* -ries : siglo *m*
ceramic[1] [sə'ræmɪk] *adj* : de cerámica
ceramic[2] *n* 1 : objeto *m* de cerámica, cerámica *f* 2 ceramics *npl* : cerámica *f*
cereal[1] ['sɪriəl] *adj* : cereal
cereal[2] *n* : cereal *m*
cerebellum [,sɛrə'bɛləm] *n*, *pl* -bellums *or* -bella [-'bɛlə] : cerebelo *m*
cerebral [sə'ri:brəl, 'sɛrə-] *adj* : cerebral
cerebral palsy *n* : parálisis *f* cerebral
cerebrum [sə'ri:brəm, 'sɛrə-] *n*, *pl* -brums *or* -bra [-brə] : cerebro *m*
ceremonial[1] [,sɛrə'mo:niəl] *adj* : ceremonial
ceremonial[2] *n* : ceremonial *m*
ceremonious [,sɛrə'mo:niəs] *adj* 1 FORMAL : ceremonioso, formal 2 CEREMONIAL : ceremonial
ceremony ['sɛrə,mo:ni] *n*, *pl* -nies : ceremonia *f*
cerise [sə'ri:s] *n* : rojo *m* cereza
certain[1] ['sərtən] *adj* 1 DEFINITE : cierto, determinado ⟨a certain percentage : un porcentaje determinado⟩ 2 TRUE : cierto, con certeza ⟨I don't know for certain : no sé exactamente⟩ 3 : cierto, alguno ⟨it has a certain charm : tiene cierta gracia⟩ 4 INEVITABLE : seguro, inevitable 5 ASSURED : seguro, asegurado ⟨she's certain to do well : seguro que le irá bien⟩
certain[2] *pron* : ciertos *pl*, algunos *pl* ⟨certain of my friends : algunos de mis amigos⟩
certainly ['sərtənli] *adv* 1 DEFINITELY : ciertamente, seguramente 2 OF COURSE : por supuesto
certainty ['sərtənti] *n*, *pl* -ties : certeza *f*, certidumbre *f*, seguridad *f*
certifiable [,sərtə'faɪəbəl] *adj* : certificable
certificate [sər'tɪfɪkət] *n* : certificado *m*, acta *f* ⟨birth certificate : acta de nacimiento⟩
certification [,sərtəfə'keɪʃən] *n* : certificación *f*
certify ['sərtə,faɪ] *vt* -fied; -fying 1 VERIFY : certificar, verificar, confirmar 2 ENDORSE : endosar, aprobar oficialmente
certitude ['sərtə,tu:d, -,tju:d] *n* : certeza *f*, certidumbre *f*
cervical ['sərvɪkəl] *adj* 1 : cervical (dícese del cuello) 2 : del cuello del útero
cervix ['sərvɪks] *n*, *pl* -vices [-və-,si:z] *or* -vixes 1 NECK : cerviz *f* 2 *or* uterine cervix : cuello *m* del útero
cesarean[1] [sɪ'zæriən] *adj* : cesáreo

cesarean[2] *n* : cesárea *f*
cesium ['si:ziəm] *n* : cesio *m*
cessation [s'seɪʃən] *n* : cesación *f*, cese *m*
cesspool ['sɛs,pu:l] *n* : pozo *m* séptico
Chadian ['tʃædiən] *n* : chadiano *m*, -na *f* — Chadian *adj*
chafe ['tʃeɪf] *v* chafed; chafing *vi* : enojarse, irritarse — *vt* : rozar
chaff ['tʃæf] *n* 1 : barcia *f*, granzas *fpl* 2 to separate the wheat from the chaff : separar el grano de la paja
chafing dish ['tʃeɪfɪŋ,dɪʃ] *n* : escalfador *m*
chagrin[1] [ʃə'grɪn] *vt* : desilusionar, avergonzar
chagrin[2] *n* : desilusión *f*, disgusto *m*
chain[1] ['tʃeɪn] *vt* : encadenar
chain[2] *n* 1 : cadena *f* ⟨steel chain : cadena de acero⟩ ⟨restaurant chain : cadena de restaurantes⟩ 2 SERIES : serie *f* ⟨chain of events : serie de eventos⟩ 3 chains *npl* FETTERS : grillos *mpl*
chair[1] ['tʃɛr] *vt* : presidir, moderar
chair[2] *n* 1 : silla *f* 2 CHAIRMANSHIP : presidencia *f* 3 → chairman, chairwoman
chairman ['tʃɛrmən] *n*, *pl* -men [-mən, -,mɛn] : presidente *m*
chairmanship ['tʃɛrmən,ʃɪp] *n* : presidencia *f*
chairwoman ['tʃɛr,wumən] *n*, *pl* -women [-,wɪmən] : presidenta *f*
chaise longue ['ʃeɪz'lɔŋ] *n*, *pl* chaise longues [-lɔŋ, -'lɔŋz] : chaise longue *f*
chalet [ʃæ'leɪ] *n* : chalet *m*, chalé *m*
chalice ['tʃælɪs] *n* : cáliz *m*
chalk[1] ['tʃɔk] *vt* : escribir con tiza
chalk[2] *n* 1 LIMESTONE : creta *f*, caliza *f* 2 : tiza *f*, gis *m* *Mex* (para escribir)
chalkboard ['tʃɔk,bord] → blackboard
chalk up *vt* 1 ASCRIBE : atribuir, adscribir 2 SCORE : apuntarse, anotarse (una victoria, etc.)
chalky ['tʃɔki] *adj* chalkier; -est 1 : calcáreo 2 PALE : pálido 3 POWDERY : polvoriento
challenge[1] ['tʃælɪndʒ] *vt* -lenged; -lenging 1 DISPUTE : disputar, cuestionar, poner en duda 2 DARE : desafiar, retar 3 STIMULATE : estimular, incentivar
challenge[2] *n* : reto *m*, desafío *m*
challenger ['tʃælɪndʒər] *n* : retador *m*, -dora *f*; contendiente *mf*
chamber ['tʃeɪmbər] *n* 1 ROOM : cámara *f*, sala *f* ⟨the senate chamber : la cámara del senado⟩ 2 : recámara *f* (de un arma de fuego), cámara *f* (de combustión) 3 : cámara *f* ⟨chamber of commerce : cámara de comercio⟩ 4 chambers *npl* *or* judge's chambers : despacho *m* del juez
chambermaid ['tʃeɪmbər,meɪd] *n* : camarera *f*
chamber music *n* : música *f* de cámara
chameleon [kə'mi:ljən, -liən] *n* : camaleón *m*

chamois ['ʃæmi] *n, pl* chamois [-mi, -miz] : gamuza *f*

champ¹ ['ʧæmp, 'ʧɑmp] *vi* 1 : masticar ruidosamente 2 to champ at the bit : impacientarse, comerle a uno la impaciencia

champ² ['ʧæmp] *n* : campeón *m*, -peona *f*

champagne [ʃæm'peɪn] *n* : champaña *m*, champán *m*

champion¹ ['ʧæmpiən] *vt* : defender, luchar por (una causa)

champion² *n* 1 ADVOCATE, DEFENDER : paladín *m*; campeón *m*, -peona *f*; defensor *m*, -sora *f* 2 WINNER : campeón *m*, -peona *f* ⟨world champion : campeón mundial⟩

championship ['ʧæmpiən,ʃɪp] *n* : campeonato *m*

chance¹ ['ʧænʦ] *v* chanced; chancing *vi* 1 HAPPEN : ocurrir por casualidad 2 to chance upon : encontrar por casualidad — *vt* RISK : arriesgar

chance² *adj* : fortuito, casual ⟨a chance encounter : un encuentro casual⟩

chance³ *n* 1 FATE, LUCK : azar *m*, suerte *f*, fortuna *f* 2 OPPORTUNITY : oportunidad *f*, ocasión *f* 3 PROBABILITY : probabilidad *f*, posibilidad *f* 4 RISK : riesgo *m* 5 : boleto *m* (de una rifa o lotería) 6 by chance : por casualidad

chancellor ['ʧænʦələr] *n* 1 : canciller *m* 2 : rector *m*, -tora *f* (de una universidad)

chancre ['ʃæŋkər] *n* : chancro *m*

chancy ['ʧænʦi] *adj* chancier; -est : riesgoso, arriesgado

chandelier [,ʃændə'lɪr] *n* : araña *f* de luces

change¹ ['ʧeɪnʤ] *v* changed; changing *vt* 1 ALTER : cambiar, alterar, modificar 2 EXCHANGE : cambiar de, intercambiar ⟨to change places : cambiar de sitio⟩ — *vi* 1 VARY : cambiar, variar, transformarse ⟨you haven't changed : no has cambiado⟩ 2 *or* to change clothes : cambiarse (de ropa)

change² *n* 1 ALTERATION : cambio *m* 2 : cambio *m*, vuelto *m* ⟨two dollars change : dos dólares de vuelto⟩ 3 COINS : cambio *m*, monedas *fpl*

changeable ['ʧeɪnʤəbəl] *adj* : cambiante, variable

changeless ['ʧeɪnʤləs] *adj* : invariable, constante

changer ['ʧeɪnʤər] *n* 1 : cambiador *m* ⟨record changer : cambiador de discos⟩ 2 *or* money changer : cambista *mf* (de dinero)

channel¹ ['ʧænəl] *vt* -neled *or* -nelled; -neling *or* -nelling : encauzar, canalizar

channel² *n* 1 RIVERBED : cauce *m* 2 STRAIT : canal *m*, estrecho *m* ⟨English Channel : Canal de la Mancha⟩ 3 COURSE, MEANS : vía *f*, conducto *m* ⟨the usual channels : las vías normales⟩ 4 : canal *m* (de televisión)

chant¹ ['ʧænt] *v* : salmodiar, cantar

chant² *n* 1 : salmodia *f* 2 Gregorian chant : canto *m* gregoriano

Chanukah ['xɑnəkə, 'hɑ-] → Hanukkah

chaos ['keɪˌɑs] *n* : caos *m*

chaotic [keɪ'ɑtɪk] *adj* : caótico — chaotically [-tɪkli] *adv*

chap¹ ['ʧæp] *vi* chapped; chapping : partirse, agrietarse

chap² *n* FELLOW : tipo *m*, hombre *m*

chapel ['ʧæpəl] *n* : capilla *f*

chaperon¹ *or* chaperone ['ʃæpəˌroːn] *vt* -oned; -oning : ir de chaperón, acompañar

chaperon² *or* chaperone *n* : chaperón *m*, -rona *f*; acompañante *mf*

chaplain ['ʧæplɪn] *n* : capellán *m*

chapter ['ʧæptər] *n* 1 : capítulo *m* (de un libro) 2 BRANCH : sección *f*, división *f* (de una organización)

char ['ʧɑr] *vt* charred; charring 1 BURN : carbonizar 2 SCORCH : chamuscar

character ['kærɪktər] *n* 1 LETTER, SYMBOL : carácter *m* ⟨Chinese characters : caracteres chinos⟩ 2 DISPOSITION : carácter *m*, personalidad *f* ⟨of good character : de buena reputación⟩ 3 : tipo *m*, personaje *m* peculiar ⟨he's quite a character! : ¡él es algo serio!⟩ 4 : personaje *m* (ficticio)

characteristic¹ [,kærɪktə'rɪstɪk] *adj* : característico, típico — characteristically [-tɪkli] *adv*

characteristic² *n* : característica *f*

characterization [,kærɪktərə'zeɪʃən] *n* : caracterización *f*

characterize ['kærɪktəˌraɪz] *vt* -ized; -izing : caracterizar

charades [ʃə'reɪdz] *ns & pl* : charada *f*

charcoal ['ʧɑrˌkoːl] *n* : carbón *m*

chard ['ʧɑrd] → Swiss chard

charge¹ ['ʧɑrʤ] *v* charged; charging *vt* 1 : cargar ⟨to charge the batteries : cargar las pilas⟩ 2 ENTRUST : encomendar, encargar 3 COMMAND : ordenar, mandar 4 ACCUSE : acusar ⟨charged with robbery : acusado de robo⟩ 5 : cargar a una cuenta, comprar a crédito — *vi* 1 : cargar (contra el enemigo) ⟨charge! : ¡a la carga!⟩ 2 : cobrar ⟨they charge too much : cobran demasiado⟩

charge² *n* 1 : carga *f* (eléctrica) 2 BURDEN : carga *f*, peso *m* 3 RESPONSIBILITY : cargo *m*, responsabilidad *f* ⟨to take charge of : hacerse cargo de⟩ 4 ACCUSATION : cargo *m*, acusación *f* 5 COST : costo *m*, cargo *m*, precio *m* 6 ATTACK : carga *f*, ataque *m*

charge card → credit card

chargeable ['ʧɑrʤəbəl] *adj* 1 : acusable, perseguible (dícese de un delito) 2 ~ to : a cargo de (una cuenta)

charger ['ʧɑrʤər] *n* : corcel *m*, caballo *m* (de guerra)

chariot ['ʧæriət] *n* : carro *m* (de guerra)

charisma [kə'rɪzmə] *n* : carisma *m*

charismatic [,kærəz'mætɪk] *adj* : carismático

charitable ['ʧærəṭəbəl] *adj* **1** GENER-
OUS : caritativo ⟨a charitable organization : una organización benéfica⟩ **2**
KIND, UNDERSTANDING : generoso,
benévolo, comprensivo — **charitably**
[-bli] *adv*
charitableness ['ʧærəṭəbəlnəs] *n* : caridad *f*
charity ['ʧærəṭi] *n, pl* **-ties 1** GENEROS-
ITY : caridad *f* **2** ALMS : caridad *f*,
limosna *f* **3** : organización *f* benéfica,
obra *f* de beneficencia
charlatan ['ʃɑrləṭən] *n* : charlatán *m*,
-tana *f*; farsante *mf*
charley horse ['ʧɑrli͵hɔrs] *n* : calambre
m
charm[1] ['ʧɑrm] *vt* : encantar, cautivar,
fascinar
charm[2] *n* **1** AMULET : amuleto *m*, talismán *m* **2** ATTRACTION : encanto *m*,
atractivo *m* ⟨it has a certain charm
: tiene cierto atractivo⟩ **3** : dije *m*, colgante *m* ⟨charm bracelet : pulsera de
dijes⟩
charmer ['ʧɑrmər] *n* : persona *f* encantadora
charming ['ʧɑrmɪŋ] *adj* : encantador,
fascinante
chart[1] ['ʧɑrt] *vt* **1** : trazar un mapa de,
hacer un gráfico de **2** PLAN : trazar,
planear ⟨to chart a course : trazar un
derrotero⟩
chart[2] *n* **1** MAP : carta *f*, mapa *m* **2** DI-
AGRAM : gráfico *m*, cuadro *m*, tabla *f*
charter[1] ['ʧɑrṭər] *vt* **1** : establecer los estatutos de (una organización) **2** RENT
: alquilar, fletar
charter[2] *n* **1** STATUTES : estatutos *mpl*
2 CONSTITUTION : carta *f*, constitución
f
chartreuse [ʃɑr'truːz, -'truːs] *n* : color *m*
verde-amarillo intenso
chary ['ʧæri] *adj* **charier; -est 1** WARY
: cauteloso, precavido **2** SPARING : parco
chase[1] ['ʧeɪs] *vt* **chased; chasing 1**
PURSUE : perseguir, ir a la caza de **2**
DRIVE : ahuyentar, echar ⟨he chased
the dog from the garden : ahuyentó al
perro del jardín⟩ **3** : grabar (metales)
chase[2] *n* **1** PURSUIT : persecución *f*,
caza *f* **2 the chase** HUNTING : caza *f*
chaser ['ʧeɪsər] *n* **1** PURSUER : perseguidor *m*, -dora *f* **2** : bebida *f* que se
toma después de un trago de licor
chasm ['kæzəm] *n* : abismo *m*, sima *f*
chassis ['ʧæsi, 'ʃæsi] *n, pl* **chassis** [-siz]
: chasis *m*, armazón *m*
chaste ['ʧeɪst] *adj* **chaster; -est 1** : casto **2** MODEST : modesto, puro **3** AUS-
TERE : austero, sobrio
chastely ['ʧeɪstli] *adv* : castamente
chasten ['ʧeɪsən] *vt* : castigar, sancionar
chasteness ['ʧeɪstnəs] *n* **1** MODESTY
: modestia *f*, castidad *f* **2** AUSTERITY
: sobriedad *f*, austeridad *f*

chastise ['ʧæs͵taɪz, ʧæs'-] *vt* **-tised;
-tising 1** REPRIMAND : reprender, corregir, reprobar **2** PUNISH : castigar
chastisement ['ʧæs͵taɪzmənt, ʧæs'taɪz-,
͵'ʧæstəz-] *n* : castigo *m*, corrección *f*
chastity ['ʧæstəti] *n* : castidad *f*, decencia *f*, modestia *f*
chat[1] ['ʧæt] *vi* **chatted; chatting** : charlar, platicar
chat[2] *n* : charla *f*, plática *f*
château [ʃæ'toː] *n, pl* **-teaus** [-'toːz] *or*
-teaux [-'toː, -'toːz] : mansión *f*
campestre
chattel ['ʧæṭəl] *n* : bienes *fpl* muebles,
enseres *mpl*
chatter[1] ['ʧæṭər] *vi* **1** : castañetear
(dícese de los dientes) **2** GAB : parlotear
fam, cotorrear *fam*
chatter[2] *n* **1** CHATTERING : castañeteo
m (de dientes) **2** GABBING : parloteo
m fam, cotorreo *m fam*, cháchara *f fam*
chatterbox ['ʧæṭər͵bɑks] *n* : parlanchín
m, -china *f*; charlatán *m*, -tana *f*;
hablador *m*, -dora *f*
chatty ['ʧæṭi] *adj* **chattier; chattiest 1**
TALKATIVE : parlanchín, charlatán **2**
CONVERSATIONAL : familiar, conversador ⟨a chatty letter : una carta llena
de noticias⟩
chauffeur[1] ['ʃoːfər, ʃoʹfər] *vi* : trabajar
de chofer privado — *vt* : hacer de
chofer para
chauffeur[2] *n* : chofer *m* privado
chauvinism ['ʃoːvə͵nɪzəm] *n* : chauvinismo *m*, patriotería *f*
chauvinist ['ʃoːvənɪst] *n* : chauvinista
mf; patriotero *m*, -ra *f*
chauvinistic [͵ʃoːvə'nɪstɪk] *adj* : chauvinista, patriotero
cheap[1] ['ʧiːp] *adv* : barato ⟨to sell cheap
: vender barato⟩
cheap[2] *adj* **1** INEXPENSIVE : barato,
económico **2** SHODDY : barato, mal hecho **3** STINGY : tacaño, agarrado *fam*,
codo *Mex*
cheapen ['ʧiːpən] *vt* : degradar, rebajar
cheaply ['ʧiːpli] *adv* : barato, a precio
bajo
cheapness ['ʧiːpnəs] *n* **1** : baratura *f*,
precio *m* bajo **2** STINGINESS : tacañería
f
cheapskate ['ʧiːp͵skeɪt] *n* : tacaño *m*,
-ña *f*; codo *m*, -da *f Mex*
cheat[1] ['ʧiːt] *vt* : defraudar, estafar, engañar — *vi* : hacer trampa
cheat[2] *n* **1** CHEATING : engaño *m*,
fraude *m*, trampa *f* **2** → **cheater**
cheater ['ʧiːṭər] *n* : estafador *m*, -dora *f*;
tramposo *m*, -sa *f*
check[1] ['ʧɛk] *vt* **1** HALT : frenar, parar,
detener **2** RESTRAIN : refrenar, contener, reprimir **3** VERIFY : verificar,
comprobar **4** INSPECT : revisar,
inspeccionar **5** MARK : marcar, señalar **6** : chequear, facturar
(maletas, equipaje) **7** CHECKER : marcar con cuadros **8 to check in** : registrarse en un hotel **9 to check out** : irse
de un hotel

check² *n* **1** HALT : detención *f* súbita, parada *f* **2** RESTRAINT : control *m*, freno *m* **3** INSPECTION : inspección *f*, verificación *f*, chequeo *m* **4** : cheque *m* ⟨to pay by check : pagar con cheque⟩ **5** VOUCHER : resguardo *m*, comprobante *m* **6** BILL : cuenta *f* (en un restaurante) **7** SQUARE : cuadro *m* **8** MARK : marca *f* **9** : jaque *m* (en ajedrez)

checkbook ['ʧɛk,bʊk] *n* : chequera *f*

checker¹ ['ʧɛkər] *vt* : marcar con cuadros

checker² *n* **1** : pieza *f* (en el juego de damas) **2** : verificador *m*, -dora *f* **3** CASHIER : cajero *m*, -ra *f*

checkerboard ['ʧɛkər,bord] *n* : tablero *m* de damas

checkers ['ʧɛkərz] *n* : damas *fpl*

checkmate¹ ['ʧɛk,meɪt] *vt* **-mated; -mating** **1** : dar jaque mate a (en ajedrez) **2** THWART : frustrar, arruinar

checkmate² *n* : jaque mate *m*

checkout ['ʧɛk,aʊt] *n or* **checkout counter** : caja *f*

checkpoint ['ʧɛk,pɔɪnt] *n* : puesto *m* de control

checkup ['ʧɛk,ʌp] *n* : examen *m* médico, chequeo *m*

cheddar ['ʧɛdər] *n* : queso *m* Cheddar

cheek ['ʧiːk] *n* **1** : mejilla *f*, cachete *m* **2** IMPUDENCE : insolencia *f*, descaro *m*

cheekbone ['ʧiːk,boːn] *n* : pómulo *m*

cheeky ['ʧiːki] *adj* **cheekier; -est** : descarado, insolente, atrevido

cheep¹ ['ʧiːp] *vi* : piar

cheep² *n* : pío *m*

cheer¹ ['ʧɪr] *vt* **1** ENCOURAGE : alentar, animar **2** GLADDEN : alegrar, levantar el ánimo a **3** ACCLAIM : aclamar, vitorear, echar porras a

cheer² *n* **1** CHEERFULNESS : alegría *f*, buen humor *m*, jovialidad *f* **2** APPLAUSE : aclamación *f*, ovación *f*, aplausos *mpl* ⟨three cheers for the chief! : ¡viva el jefe!⟩ **3 cheers!** : ¡salud!

cheerful ['ʧɪrfəl] *adj* : alegre, de buen humor

cheerfully ['ʧɪrfəli] *adv* : alegremente, jovialmente

cheerfulness ['ʧɪrfəlnəs] *n* : buen humor *m*, alegría *f*

cheerily ['ʧɪrəli] *adv* : alegremente

cheeriness ['ʧɪrinəs] *n* : buen humor *m*, alegría *f*

cheerleader ['ʧɪr,liːdər] *n* : porrista *mf*

cheerless ['ʧɪrləs] *adj* BLEAK : triste, sombrío

cheerlessly ['ʧɪrləsli] *adv* : desanimadamente

cheery ['ʧɪri] *adj* **cheerier; -est** : alegre, de buen humor

cheese ['ʧiːz] *n* : queso *m*

cheesecloth ['ʧiːz,klɔθ] *n* : estopilla *f*

cheesy ['ʧiːzi] *adj* **cheesier; -est** **1** : a queso **2** : que contiene queso **3** CHEAP : barato, de mala calidad

cheetah ['ʧiːtə] *n* : guepardo *m*

chef ['ʃɛf] *n* : chef *m*

chemical¹ ['kɛmɪkəl] *adj* : químico —
chemically [-mɪkli] *adv*

chemical² *n* : sustancia *f* química

chemise [ʃə'miːz] *n* **1** : camiseta *f*, prenda *f* interior de una pieza **2** : vestido *m* holgado

chemist ['kɛmɪst] *n* : químico *m*, -ca *f*

chemistry ['kɛmɪstri] *n, pl* **-tries** : química *f*

chemotherapy [,kiːmo'θɛrəpi, ,kɛmo-] *n, pl* **-pies** : quimioterapia *f*

chenille [ʃə'niːl] *n* : felpilla *f*

cherish ['ʧɛrɪʃ] *vt* **1** VALUE : apreciar, valorar **2** HARBOR : abrigar, albergar

cherry ['ʧɛri] *n, pl* **-ries** **1** : cereza *f* (fruta) **2** : cerezo *m* (árbol)

cherub ['ʧɛrəb] *n* **1** *pl* **-ubim** ['ʧɛrə,bɪm, 'ʧɛrjə-]** ANGEL : ángel *m*, querubín *m* **2** *pl* **-ubs** : niño *m* regordete, niña *f* regordeta

cherubic [ʧə'ruːbɪk] *adj* : querúbico, angelical

chess ['ʧɛs] *n* : ajedrez *m*

chessboard ['ʧɛs,bord] *n* : tablero *m* de ajedrez

chessman ['ʧɛsmən, -,mæn] *n, pl* **-men** [-mən, -,mɛn] : pieza *f* de ajedrez

chest ['ʧɛst] *n* **1** : cofre *m*, baúl *m* **2** : pecho *m* ⟨chest pains : dolores de pecho⟩

chestnut ['ʧɛst,nʌt] *n* **1** : castaña *f* (fruto) **2** : castaño *m* (árbol)

chest of drawers *n* : cómoda *f*

chevron ['ʃɛvrən] *n* : galón *m* (de un oficial militar)

chew¹ ['ʧuː] *vt* : masticar, mascar

chew² *n* : algo que se masca (como tabaco)

chewable ['ʧuːəbəl] *adj* : masticable

chewing gum *n* : goma *f* de mascar, chicle *m*

chewy ['ʧuːi] *adj* **chewier; -est** **1** : fibroso (dícese de las carnes o los vegetales) **2** : pegajoso, chicloso (dícese de los dulces)

chic¹ ['ʃiːk] *adj* : chic, elegante, de moda

chic² *n* : chic *m*, elegancia *f*

Chicano [ʧɪ'kɑno] *n* : chicano *m*, -na *f* — **Chicano** *adj*

chick ['ʧɪk] *n* : pollito *m*, -ta *f*; polluelo *m*, -la *f*

chicken ['ʧɪkən] *n* **1** FOWL : pollo *m* **2** COWARD : cobarde *mf*

chickenhearted ['ʧɪkən,hɑrtəd] *n* : miedoso, cobarde

chicken pox *n* : varicela *f*

chickpea ['ʧɪk,piː] *n* : garbanzo *m*

chicle ['ʧɪkəl] *n* : chicle *m* (resina)

chicory ['ʧɪkəri] *n, pl* **-ries** **1** : endibia *f* (para ensaladas) **2** : achicoria *f* (aditivo de café)

chide ['ʧaɪd] *vt* **chid** ['ʧɪd] *or* **chided; chid** *or* **chidden** ['ʧɪdən] *or* **chided; chiding** ['ʧaɪdɪŋ] : regañar, reprender

chief¹ ['ʧiːf] *adj* : principal, capital ⟨chief negotiator : negociador en jefe⟩ — **chiefly** *adv*

chief² *n* : jefe *m*, -fa *f*

chieftain [ˈʧiːftən] n : jefe m, -fa f (de una tribu)
chiffon [ʃɪˈfɑn, ˈʃɪ-] n : chifón m
chigger [ˈʧɪgər] n : nigua f
chignon [ˈʃiːnˌjɑn, -ˌjɔn] n : moño m, chongo m Mex
chilblain [ˈʧɪlˌbleɪn] n : sabañón m
child [ˈʧaɪld] n, pl **children** [ˈʧɪldrən] 1 BABY, YOUNGSTER : niño m, -ña f; criatura f 2 OFFSPRING : hijo m, -ja f; progenie f
childbearing[1] [ˈʧaɪlbɛrɪŋ] adj : relativo al parto ⟨of childbearing age : en edad fértil⟩
childbearing[2] → childbirth
childbirth [ˈʧaɪldˌbərθ] n : parto m
childhood [ˈʧaɪldˌhʊd] n : infancia f, niñez f
childish [ˈʧaɪldɪʃ] adj : infantil, inmaduro — **childishly** adv
childishness [ˈʧaɪldɪʃnəs] n : infantilismo m, inmadurez f
childless [ˈʧaɪldləs] adj : sin hijos
childlike [ˈʧaɪldˌlaɪk] adj : infantil, inocente ⟨a childlike imagination : una imaginación infantil⟩
childproof [ˈʧaɪldˌpruːf] adj : a prueba de niños
Chilean [ˈʧɪliən, ʧɪˈleɪən] n : chileno m, -na f — **Chilean** adj
chili or **chile** or **chilli** [ˈʧɪli] n, pl **chilies** or **chiles** or **chillies** 1 or **chili pepper** : chile m, ají m 2 : chile m con carne
chill[1] [ˈʧɪl] v : enfriar
chill[2] adj : frío, gélido ⟨a chill wind : un viento frío⟩
chill[3] n 1 CHILLINESS : fresco m, frío m 2 SHIVER : escalofrío m 3 DAMPER : enfriamiento m, frío m ⟨to cast a chill over : enfriar⟩
chilliness [ˈʧɪlinəs] n : frío m, fresco m
chilly [ˈʧɪli] adj **chillier; -est** : frío ⟨it's chilly tonight : hace frío esta noche⟩
chime[1] [ˈʧaɪm] v **chimed; chiming** vt : hacer sonar (una campana) — vi : sonar una campana, dar campanadas
chime[2] n 1 BELLS : juego m de campanitas sintonizadas, carillón m 2 PEAL : tañido m, campanada f
chime in vi : meterse en una conversación
chimera or **chimaera** [kaɪˈmɪrə, kə-] n : quimera f
chimney [ˈʧɪmni] n, pl **-neys** : chimenea f
chimney sweep n : deshollinador m, -dora f
chimp [ˈʧɪmp, ˈʃɪmp] → chimpanzee
chimpanzee [ˌʧɪmˌpænˈziː, ˌʃɪm-; ʧɪm ˈpænzi, ʃɪm-] n : chimpancé m
chin [ˈʧɪn] n : barbilla f, mentón m, barba f
china [ˈʧaɪnə] n 1 PORCELAIN : porcelana f, loza f 2 CROCKERY, TABLEWARE : loza f, vajilla f
chinchilla [ʧɪnˈʧɪlə] n : chinchilla f
Chinese [ˈʧaɪˈniːz, -ˈniːs] n 1 : chino m, -na f 2 : chino m (idioma) — **Chinese** adj

chink [ˈʧɪŋk] n : grieta f, abertura f
chintz [ˈʧɪnts] n : chintz m, chinz m
chip[1] [ˈʧɪp] v **chipped; chipping** vt : desportillar, desconchar, astillar (madera) — vi : desportillarse, desconcharse, descascararse (dícese de la pintura, etc.)
chip[2] n 1 : astilla f (de madera o vidrio), lasca f (de piedra) ⟨he's a chip off the old block : de tal palo, tal astilla⟩ 2 : bocado m pequeño (en rodajas o rebanadas) ⟨tortilla chips : totopos, tortillitas tostadas⟩ 3 : ficha f (de póker, etc.) 4 NICK : desportilladura f, mella f 5 : chip m ⟨memory chip : chip de memoria⟩
chip in v CONTRIBUTE : contribuir
chipmunk [ˈʧɪpˌmʌŋk] n : ardilla f listada
chipper [ˈʧɪpər] adj : alegre y vivaz
chiropodist [kəˈrɑpədɪst, ʃə-] n : podólogo m, -ga f
chiropody [kəˈrɑpədi, ʃə-] n : podología f
chiropractic [ˈkaɪrəˌpræktɪk] n : quiropráctica f
chiropractor [ˈkaɪrəˌpræktər] n : quiropráctico m, -ca f
chirp[1] [ˈʧərp] vi : gorjear (dícese de los pájaros), chirriar (dícese de los grillos)
chirp[2] n : gorjeo m (de un pájaro), chirrido m (de un grillo)
chisel[1] [ˈʧɪzəl] vt **-eled** or **-elled; -eling** or **-elling** 1 : cincelar, tallar, labrar 2 CHEAT : estafar, defraudar
chisel[2] n : cincel m (para piedras y metales), escoplo m (para madera), formón m
chiseler [ˈʧɪzələr] n SWINDLER : estafador m, -dora f; fraude mf
chit [ˈʧɪt] n : resguardo m, recibo m
chitchat [ˈʧɪt,ʧæt] n : cotorreo m, charla f
chivalric [ʃəˈvælrɪk] → chivalrous
chivalrous [ˈʃɪvəlrəs] adj 1 KNIGHTLY : caballeresco, relativo a la caballería 2 GENTLEMANLY : caballeroso, honesto, cortés
chivalrousness [ˈʃɪvəlrəsnəs] n : caballerosidad f, cortesía f
chivalry [ˈʃɪvəlri] n, pl **-ries** 1 KNIGHTHOOD : caballería f 2 CHIVALROUSNESS : caballerosidad f, nobleza f, cortesía f
chive [ˈʧaɪv] n : cebollino m
chloride [ˈklorˌaɪd] n : cloruro m
chlorinate [ˈklorəˌneɪt] vt **-nated; -nating** : clorar
chlorination [ˌklorəˈneɪʃən] n : cloración f
chlorine [ˈklorˌiːn] n : cloro m
chloroform [ˈklorəˌfɔrm] n : cloroformo m
chlorophyll [ˈklorəˌfɪl] n : clorofila f
chock–full [ˈʧɑkˈfʊl, ˈʧʌk-] adj : colmado, repleto
chocolate [ˈʧɑkələt, ˈʧɔk-] n 1 : chocolate m 2 BONBON : bombón m 3 : color m chocolate, marrón m

choice[1] [ˈʧɔɪs] *adj* **choicer; -est** : selecto, escogido, de primera calidad
choice[2] *n* **1** CHOOSING : elección *f*, selección *f* **2** OPTION : elección *f*, opción *f* ⟨I have no choice : no tengo alternativa⟩ **3** PREFERENCE : preferencia *f*, elección *f* **4** VARIETY : surtido *m*, selección *f* ⟨a wide choice : un gran surtido⟩
choir [ˈkwaɪr] *n* : coro *m*
choirboy [ˈkwaɪrˌbɔɪ] *n* : niño *m* de coro
choke[1] [ˈʧoːk] *v* **choked; choking** *vt* **1** ASPHYXIATE, STRANGLE : sofocar, asfixiar, ahogar, estrangular **2** BLOCK : tapar, obstruir — *vi* **1** SUFFOCATE : asfixiarse, sofocarse, ahogarse, atragantarse (con comida) **2** CLOG : taparse, obstruirse
choke[2] *n* **1** CHOKING : estrangulación *f* **2** : choke *m* (de un motor)
choker [ˈʧoːkər] *n* : gargantilla *f*
cholera [ˈkɑlərə] *n* : cólera *m*
cholesterol [kəˈlɛstəˌrɔl] *n* : colesterol *m*
choose [ˈʧuːz] *v* **chose** [ˈʧoːz]; **chosen** [ˈʧoːzən]; **choosing** *vt* **1** SELECT : escoger, elegir ⟨choose only one : escoja sólo uno⟩ **2** DECIDE : decidir ⟨he chose to leave : decidió irse⟩ **3** PREFER : preferir ⟨which one do you choose? : ¿cuál prefiere?⟩ — *vi* : escoger ⟨much to choose from : mucho de donde escoger⟩
choosy *or* **choosey** [ˈʧuːzi] *adj* **choosier; -est** : exigente, remilgado
chop[1] [ˈʧɑp] *vt* **chopped; chopping 1** MINCE : picar, cortar, moler (carne) **2 to chop down** : cortar, talar (un árbol)
chop[2] *n* **1** CUT : hachazo *m* (con una hacha), tajo *m* (con una cuchilla) **2** BLOW : golpe *m* (penetrante) ⟨karate chop : golpe de karate⟩ **3** : chuleta *f* ⟨pork chops : chuletas de cerdo⟩
chopper [ˈʧɑpər] → helicopter
choppy [ˈʧɑpi] *adj* **choppier; -est 1** : agitado, picado (dícese del mar) **2** DISCONNECTED : incoherente, inconexo
chops [ˈʧɑps] *npl* **1** : quijada *f*, mandíbula *f*, boca *f* (de una persona) **2 to lick one's chops** : relamerse
chopsticks [ˈʧɑpˌstɪks] *npl* : palillos *mpl*
choral [ˈkorəl] *adj* : coral
chorale [kəˈræl, -ˈrɑl] *n* **1** : coral *f* (composición musical vocal) **2** CHOIR, CHORUS : coral *f*, coro *m*
chord [ˈkɔrd] *n* **1** : acorde *m* (en música) **2** : cuerda *f* (en anatomía o geometría)
chore [ˈʧor] *n* **1** TASK : tarea *f* rutinaria **2** BOTHER, NUISANCE : lata *f fam*, fastidio *m* **3 chores** *npl* WORK : quehaceres *mpl*, faenas *fpl*
choreograph [ˈkoriəˌgræf] *vt* : coreografiar
choreographer [ˌkoriˈɑgrəfər] *n* : coreógrafo *m*, -fa *f*
choreographic [ˌkoriəˈgræfɪk] *adj* : coreográfico
choreography [ˌkoriˈɑgrəfi] *n, pl* **-phies** : coreografía *f*

chorister [ˈkorəstər] *n* : corista *mf*
chortle[1] [ˈʧortəl] *vi* **-tled; -tling** : reírse (con satisfacción o júbilo)
chortle[2] *n* : risa *f* (de satisfacción o júbilo)
chorus[1] [ˈkorəs] *vt* : corear
chorus[2] *n* **1** : coro *m* (grupo o composición musical) **2** REFRAIN : coro *m*, estribillo *m*
chose → choose
chosen [ˈʧoːzən] *adj* : elegido, selecto
chow [ˈʧau] *n* **1** FOOD : comida *f* **2** : chow-chow *m* (perro)
chowder [ˈʧaudər] *n* : sopa *f* de pescado
Christ [ˈkraɪst] *n* **1** : Cristo *m* **2 for Christ's sake** : ¡por Dios!
christen [ˈkrɪsən] *vt* **1** BAPTIZE : bautizar **2** NAME : bautizar con el nombre de
Christendom [ˈkrɪsəndəm] *n* : cristiandad *f*
christening [ˈkrɪsənɪŋ] *n* : bautismo *m*, bautizo *m*
Christian[1] [ˈkrɪsʧən] *adj* : cristiano
Christian[2] *n* : cristiano *m*, -na *f*
Christianity [ˌkrɪsʧiˈænəṭi, ˌkrɪsˈʧæ-] *n* : cristianismo *m*
Christian name *n* : nombre *m* de pila
Christmas [ˈkrɪsməs] *n* : Navidad *f* ⟨Christmas season : las Navidades⟩
chromatic [kroˈmæṭɪk] *adj* : cromático ⟨chromatic scale : escala cromática⟩
chrome [ˈkroːm] *n* : cromo *m* (metal)
chromium [ˈkroːmiəm] *n* : cromo *m* (elemento)
chromosome [ˈkroːməˌsoːm, -ˌzoːm] *n* : cromosoma *m*
chronic [ˈkrɑnɪk] *adj* : crónico — **chronically** [-nɪkli] *adv*
chronicle[1] [ˈkrɑnɪkəl] *vt* **-cled; -cling** : escribir (una crónica o historia)
chronicle[2] *n* : crónica *f*, historia *f*
chronicler [ˈkrɑnɪklər] *n* : historiador *m*, -dora *f*; cronista *mf*
chronological [ˌkrɑnəlˈɑʤɪkəl] *adj* : cronológico — **chronologically** [-kli] *adv*
chronology [krəˈnɑləʤi] *n, pl* **-gies** : cronología *f*
chronometer [krəˈnɑməṭər] *n* : cronómetro *m*
chrysalis [ˈkrɪsələs] *n, pl* **chrysalides** [krɪˈsæləˌdiːz] *or* **chrysalises** : crisálida *f*
chrysanthemum [krɪˈsænθəməm] *n* : crisantemo *m*
chubbiness [ˈʧʌbinəs] *n* : gordura *f*
chubby [ˈʧʌbi] *adj* **-bier; -est** : gordito, regordete, rechoncho
chuck [ˈʧʌk] *vt* **1** TOSS : tirar, lanzar, aventar *Col, Mex* **2 to chuck under the chin** : hacer la mamola
chuck[2] *n* **1** PAT : mamola *f*, palmada *f* **2** TOSS : lanzamiento *m* **3** *or* **chuck steak** : corte *m* de carne de res
chuckle[1] [ˈʧʌkəl] *vi* **-led; -ling** : reírse entre dientes
chuckle[2] *n* : risita *f*, risa *f* ahogada

chug¹ [ˈʧʌg] *vi* **chugged; chugging** : resoplar, traquetear

chug² *n* : resoplido *m*, traqueteo *m*

chum¹ [ˈʧʌm] *vi* **chummed; chumming** : ser camaradas, ser cuates *Mex fam*

chum² *n* : amigo *m*, -ga *f*; camarada *mf*; compinche *mf fam*

chummy [ˈʧʌmi] *adj* **-mier; -est** : amistoso ⟨they're very chummy : son muy amigos⟩

chump [ˈʧʌmp] *n* : tonto *m*, -ta *f*; idiota *mf*

chunk [ˈʧʌnk] *n* **1** PIECE : cacho *m*, pedazo *m*, trozo *m* **2** : cantidad *f* grande ⟨a chunk of money : mucho dinero⟩

chunky [ˈʧʌnki] *adj* **chunkier; -est 1** STOCKY : fornido, robusto **2** : que contiene pedazos

church [ˈʧərʧ] *n* **1** : iglesia *f* ⟨to go to church : ir a la iglesia⟩ **2** CHRISTIANS : iglesia *f*, conjunto *m* de fieles cristianos **3** DENOMINATION : confesión *f*, secta *f* **4** CONGREGATION : feligreses *mpl*, fieles *mpl*

churchgoer [ˈʧərʧˌgoːər] *n* : practicante *mf*

churchyard [ˈʧərʧˌjɑrd] *n* : cementerio *m* (junto a una iglesia)

churn¹ [ˈʧərn] *vt* **1** : batir (crema), hacer (mantequilla) **2** : agitar con fuerza, revolver — *vi* : agitarse, arremolinarse

churn² *n* : mantequera *f*

chute [ˈʃuːt] *n* : conducto *m* inclinado, vertedero *m* (para basuras)

chutney [ˈʧʌtni] *n, pl* **-neys** : chutney *m*

chutzpah [ˈhʊtspə, ˈxʊt-, -ˌspɑ] *n* : descaro *m*, frescura *f*, cara *f fam*

cicada [səˈkeɪdə, -ˈkɑ-] *n* : cigarra *f*, chicharra *f*

cider [ˈsaɪdər] *n* **1** : jugo *m* (de manzana, etc.) **2 hard cider** : sidra *f*

cigar [sɪˈgɑr] *n* : puro *m*, cigarro *m*

cigarette [ˌsɪgəˈrɛt, ˈsɪgəˌrɛt] *n* : cigarrillo *m*, cigarro *m*

cilantro [sɪˈlɑntroː, -ˈlæn-] *n* : cilantro *m*

cinch¹ [ˈsɪnʧ] *vt* **1** : cinchar (un caballo) **2** ASSURE : asegurar

cinch² *n* **1** : cincha *f* (para caballos) **2** : algo fácil o seguro ⟨it's a cinch : es bien fácil, es pan comido⟩

cinchona [sɪŋˈkoːnə] *n* : quino *m*

cinder [ˈsɪndər] *n* **1** EMBER : brasa *f*, ascua *f* **2 cinders** *npl* ASHES : cenizas *fpl*

cinema [ˈsɪnəmə] *n* : cine *m*

cinematic [ˌsɪnəˈmæṭɪk] *adj* : cinematográfico

cinnamon [ˈsɪnəmən] *n* : canela *f*

cipher [ˈsaɪfər] *n* **1** ZERO : cero *m* **2** CODE : cifra *f*, clave *f*

circa [ˈsərkə] *prep* : alrededor de, hacia ⟨circa 1800 : hacia el año 1800⟩

circle¹ [ˈsərkəl] *v* **-cled; -cling** *vt* **1** : encerrar en un círculo, poner un círculo alrededor de **2** : girar alrededor de, dar vueltas a ⟨we circled the building twice : le dimos vueltas al edificio dos veces⟩ — *vi* : dar vueltas

circle² *n* **1** : círculo *m* **2** CYCLE : ciclo *m* ⟨to come full circle : volver al punto de partida⟩ **3** GROUP : círculo *m*, grupo *m* (social)

circuit [ˈsərkət] *n* **1** BOUNDARY : circuito *m*, perímetro *m* (de una zona o un territorio) **2** TOUR : circuito *m*, recorrido *m*, tour *m* **3** : circuito *m* (eléctrico) ⟨a short circuit : un cortocircuito⟩

circuitous [ˌsərˈkjuːəţəs] *adj* : sinuoso, tortuoso

circuitry [ˈsərkətri] *n, pl* **-ries** : sistema *m* de circuitos

circular¹ [ˈsərkjələr] *adj* ROUND : circular, redondo

circular² *n* : circular *f*

circulate [ˈsərkjəˌleɪt] *v* **-lated; -lating** *vi* : circular — *vt* **1** : circular (noticias, etc.) **2** DISSEMINATE : hacer circular, divulgar

circulation [ˌsərkjəˈleɪʃən] *n* : circulación *f*

circulatory [ˈsərkjələˌtori] *adj* : circulatorio

circumcise [ˈsərkəmˌsaɪz] *vt* **-cised; -cising** : circuncidar

circumcision [ˌsərkəmˈsɪʒən, ˈsərkəmˌ-] *n* : circuncisión *f*

circumference [sərˈkʌmfrənts] *n* : circunferencia *f*

circumflex [ˈsərkəmˌflɛks] *n* : acento *m* circunflejo

circumlocution [ˌsərkəmloˈkjuːʃən] *n* : circunlocución *f*

circumnavigate [ˌsərkəmˈnævəˌgeɪt] *vt* **-gated; -gating** : circunnavegar

circumscribe [ˈsərkəmˌskraɪb] *vt* **-scribed; -scribing 1** : circunscribir, trazar una figura alrededor de **2** LIMIT : circunscribir, limitar

circumspect [ˈsərkəmˌspɛkt] *adj* : circunspecto, prudente, cauto

circumspection [ˌsərkəmˈspɛkʃən] *n* : circunspección *f*, cautela *f*

circumstance [ˈsərkəmˌstænts] *n* **1** EVENT : circunstancia *f*, acontecimiento *m* **2 circumstances** *npl* SITUATION : circunstancias *fpl*, situación *f* ⟨under the circumstances : dadas las circunstancias⟩ ⟨under no circumstances : de ninguna manera, bajo ningún concepto⟩ **3 circumstances** *npl* : situación *f* económica

circumstantial [ˌsərkəmˈstænʧəl] *adj* : circunstancial

circumvent [ˌsərkəmˈvɛnt] *vt* : evadir, burlar (una ley o regla), sortear (una responsabilidad o dificultad)

circumvention [ˌsərkəmˈvɛnʧən] *n* : evasión *f*

circus [ˈsərkəs] *n* : circo *m*

cirrhosis [səˈroːsɪs] *n, pl* **-rhoses** [-ˈroːˌsiːz] : cirrosis *f*

cirrus [ˈsɪrəs] *n, pl* **-ri** [ˈsɪrˌaɪ] : cirro *m*

cistern [ˈsɪstərn] *n* : cisterna *f*, aljibe *m*

citadel [ˈsɪţədəl, -ˌdɛl] *n* FORTRESS : ciudadela *f*, fortaleza *f*

citation [saɪ'teɪʃən] *n* 1 SUMMONS : emplazamiento *m*, citación *f*, convocatoria *f* (judicial) 2 QUOTATION : cita *f* 3 COMMENDATION : elogio *m*, mención *f* (de honor)
cite ['saɪt] *vt* **cited; citing** 1 ARRAIGN, SUBPOENA : emplazar, citar, hacer comparecer (ante un tribunal) 2 QUOTE : citar 3 COMMEND : elogiar, honrar (oficialmente)
citizen ['sɪtəzən] *n* : ciudadano *m*, -na *f*
citizenry ['sɪtəzənri] *n, pl* **-ries** : ciudadanía *f*, conjunto *m* de ciudadanos
citizenship ['sɪtəzən,ʃɪp] *n* : ciudadanía *f* ⟨Nicaraguan citizenship : ciudadanía nicaragüense⟩
citron ['sɪtrən] *n* : cidra *f*
citrus ['sɪtrəs] *n, pl* **-rus** *or* **-ruses** : cítrico *m*
city ['sɪt̬i] *n, pl* **cities** : ciudad *f*
civic ['sɪvɪk] *adj* : cívico
civics ['sɪvɪks] *ns & pl* : civismo *m*
civil ['sɪvəl] *adj* 1 : civil ⟨civil law : derecho civil⟩ 2 POLITE : cortés
civilian [sə'vɪljən] *n* : civil *mf* ⟨soldiers and civilians : soldados y civiles⟩
civility [sə'vɪlət̬i] *n, pl* **-ties** : cortesía *f*, educación *f*
civilization [,sɪvələ'zeɪʃən] *n* : civilización *f*
civilize ['sɪvə,laɪz] *vt* **-lized; -lizing** : civilizar — **civilized** *adj*
civil liberties *npl* : derechos *mpl* civiles
civilly ['sɪvəli] *adv* : cortésmente
civil rights *npl* : derechos *mpl* civiles
civil service *n* : administración *f* pública
civil war *n* : guerra *f* civil
clack¹ ['klæk] *vi* : tabletear
clack² *n* : tableteo *m*
clad ['klæd] *adj* 1 CLOTHED : vestido 2 COVERED : cubierto
claim¹ ['kleɪm] *vt* 1 DEMAND : reclamar, reivindicar ⟨she claimed her rights : reclamó sus derechos⟩ 2 MAINTAIN : afirmar, sostener ⟨they claim it's theirs : sostienen que es suyo⟩
claim² *n* 1 DEMAND : demanda *f*, reclamación *f* 2 DECLARATION : declaración *f*, afirmación *f* 3 **to stake a claim** : reclamar, reivindicar
claimant ['kleɪmənt] *n* : demandante *mf* (ante un juez), pretendiente *mf* (al trono, etc.)
clairvoyance [klær'vɔɪənts] *n* : clarividencia *f*
clairvoyant¹ [klær'vɔɪənt] *adj* : clarividente
clairvoyant² *n* : clarividente *mf*
clam ['klæm] *n* : almeja *f*
clamber ['klæmbər] *vi* : treparse o subirse torpemente
clammy ['klæmi] *adj* **-mier; -est** : húmedo y algo frío
clamor¹ ['klæmər] *vi* : gritar, clamar
clamor² *n* : clamor *m*
clamorous ['klæmərəs] *adj* : clamoroso, ruidoso, estrepitoso

clamp¹ ['klæmp] *vt* : sujetar con abrazaderas
clamp² *n* : abrazadera *f*
clan ['klæn] *n* : clan *m*
clandestine [klæn'dɛstɪn] *adj* : clandestino, secreto
clang¹ ['klæŋ] *vi* : hacer resonar (dícese de un objeto metálico)
clang² *n* : ruido *m* metálico fuerte
clangor ['klæŋər, -gər] *n* : estruendo *m* metálico
clank¹ ['klæŋk] *vi* : producir un ruido metálico seco
clank² *n* : ruido *m* metálico seco
clannish ['klænɪʃ] *adj* : exclusivista
clap¹ ['klæp] *v* **clapped; clapping** *vt* 1 SLAP, STRIKE : golpear ruidosamente, dar una palmada ⟨to clap one's hands : batir palmas, dar palmadas⟩ 2 APPLAUD : aplaudir — *vi* APPLAUD : aplaudir
clap² *n* 1 SLAP : palmada *f*, golpecito *m* 2 NOISE : ruido *m* seco ⟨a clap of thunder : un trueno⟩
clapboard ['klæbərd, 'klæp,bord] *n* : tabla *f* de madera (para revestir muros)
clapper ['klæpər] *n* : badajo *m* (de una campana)
clarification [,klærəfə'keɪʃən] *n* : clarificación *f*
clarify ['klærə,faɪ] *vt* **-fied; -fying** 1 EXPLAIN : aclarar 2 : clarificar (un líquido)
clarinet [,klærə'nɛt] *n* : clarinete *m*
clarion ['klæriən] *adj* : claro y sonoro
clarity ['klærət̬i] *n* : claridad *f*, nitidez *f*
clash¹ ['klæʃ] *vi* 1 : sonar, chocarse ⟨the cymbals clashed : los platillos sonaron⟩ 2 : chocar, enfrentarse ⟨the students clashed with the police : los estudiantes se enfrentaron con la policía⟩ 3 CONFLICT : estar en conflicto, oponerse 4 : desentonar (dícese de los colores), coincidir (dícese de los datos)
clash² *n* 1 : ruido *m* (producido por un choque) 2 CONFLICT, CONFRONTATION : enfrentamiento *m*, conflicto *m*, choque *m* 3 : desentono *m* (de colores), coincidencia *f* (de datos)
clasp¹ ['klæsp] *vt* 1 FASTEN : sujetar, abrochar 2 EMBRACE, GRASP : agarrar, sujetar, abrazar
clasp² *n* 1 FASTENING : broche *m*, cierre *m* 2 EMBRACE, SQUEEZE : apretón *m*, abrazo *m*
class¹ ['klæs] *vt* : clasificar, catalogar
class² *n* 1 KIND, TYPE : clase *f*, tipo *m*, especie *f* 2 : clase *f*, rango *m* social ⟨the working class : la clase obrera⟩ 3 LESSON : clase *f*, curso *m* ⟨English class : clase de inglés⟩ 4 : conjunto *m* de estudiantes, clase *f* ⟨the class of '97 : la promoción del 97⟩
classic¹ ['klæsɪk] *adj* : clásico
classic² *n* : clásico *m*, obra *f* clásica
classical ['klæsɪkəl] *adj* : clásico — **classically** [-kli] *adv*

classicism ['klæsəˌsɪzəm] *n* : clasicismo *m*

classification [ˌklæsəfə'keɪʃən] *n* : clasificación *f*

classified ['klæsəˌfaɪd] *adj* **1** : clasificado ⟨classified ads : avisos clasificados⟩ **2** RESTRICTED : confidencial, secreto ⟨classified documents : documentos secretos⟩

classify ['klæsəˌfaɪ] *vt* **-fied; -fying** : clasificar, catalogar

classless ['klæsləs] *adj* : sin clases

classmate ['klæsˌmeɪt] *n* : compañero *m*, -ra *f* de clase

classroom ['klæsˌruːm] *n* : aula *f*, salón *m* de clase

clatter¹ ['klæt̬ər] *vi* : traquetear, hacer ruido

clatter² *n* : traqueteo *m*, ruido *m*, estrépito *m*

clause ['klɔz] *n* : cláusula *f*

claustrophobia [ˌklɔstrə'foːbiə] *n* : claustrofobia *f*

claustrophobic [ˌklɔstrə'foːbɪk] *adj* : claustrofóbico

clavicle ['klævɪkəl] *n* : clavícula *f*

claw¹ ['klɔ] *v* : arañar

claw² *n* : garra *f*, uña *f* (de un gato), pinza *f* (de un crustáceo)

clay ['kleɪ] *n* : arcilla *f*, barro *m*

clayey ['kleɪi] *adj* : arcilloso

clean¹ ['kliːn] *vt* : limpiar, lavar, asear

clean² *adv* : limpio, limpiamente ⟨to play clean : jugar limpio⟩

clean³ *adj* **1** : limpio **2** UNADULTERATED : puro **3** IRREPROACHABLE : intachable, sin mancha ⟨to have a clean record : no tener antecedentes penales⟩ **4** DECENT : decente **5** COMPLETE : completo, absoluto ⟨a clean break with the past : un corte radical con el pasado⟩

cleaner ['kliːnər] *n* **1** : limpiador *m*, -dora *f* **2** : producto *m* de limpieza **3** DRY CLEANER : tintorería *f* (servicio)

cleanliness ['klɛnlinəs] *n* : limpieza *f*, aseo *m*

cleanly¹ ['kliːnli] *adv* : limpiamente, con limpieza

cleanly² ['klɛnli] *adj* **-lier; -est** : limpio, pulcro

cleanness ['kliːnnəs] *n* : limpieza *f*

cleanse ['klɛnz] *vt* **cleansed; cleansing** : limpiar, purificar

cleanser ['klɛnzər] *n* : limpiador *m*, purificador *m*

clear¹ ['klɪr] *vt* **1** CLARIFY : aclarar, clarificar (un líquido) **2** : despejar (una superficie), desatascar (un tubo), desmontar (una selva) ⟨to clear the table : levantar la mesa⟩ ⟨to clear one's throat : carraspear, aclararse la voz⟩ **3** EXONERATE : absolver, limpiar el nombre de **4** EARN : ganar, sacar (una ganancia de) **5** : pasar sin tocar ⟨he cleared the hurdle : saltó por encima de la valla⟩ **6 to clear up** RESOLVE : aclarar, resolver, esclarecer — *vi* **1** DISPERSE : irse, despejarse, disiparse **2** : ser compensado (dícese de un cheque) **3 to clear up** : despejar (dícese del tiempo), mejorarse (dícese de una enfermedad)

clear² *adv* : claro, claramente

clear³ *adj* **1** BRIGHT : claro, lúcido **2** FAIR : claro, despejado **3** TRANSPARENT : transparente, translúcido **4** EVIDENT, UNMISTAKABLE : evidente, claro, obvio **5** CERTAIN : seguro **6** UNOBSTRUCTED : despejado, libre

clear⁴ *n* **1 in the clear** : inocente, libre de toda sospecha **2 in the clear** SAFE : fuera de peligro

clearance ['klɪrənts] *n* **1** CLEARING : despeje *m* **2** SPACE : espacio *m* (libre), margen *m* **3** AUTHORIZATION : autorización *f*, despacho *m* (de la aduana)

clearing ['klɪrɪŋ] *n* : claro *m* (de un bosque)

clearly ['klɪrli] *adv* **1** DISTINCTLY : claramente, directamente **2** OBVIOUSLY : obviamente, evidentemente

cleat ['kliːt] *n* **1** : taco *m* **2 cleats** *npl* : zapatos *mpl* deportivos (con tacos)

cleavage ['kliːvɪʤ] *n* **1** CLEFT : hendidura *f*, raja *f* **2** : escote *m* (del busto)

cleave¹ ['kliːv] *vi* **cleaved** ['kliːvd] *or* **clove** ['kloːv]; **cleaving** ADHERE : adherirse, unirse

cleave² *vt* **cleaved; cleaving** SPLIT : hender, dividir, partir

cleaver ['kliːvər] *n* : cuchilla *f* de carnicero

clef ['klɛf] *n* : clave *f*

cleft ['klɛft] *n* : hendidura *f*, raja *f*, grieta *f*

clemency ['klɛmənʦi] *n* : clemencia *f*

clement ['klɛmənt] *adj* **1** MERCIFUL : clemente, piadoso **2** MILD : clemente, apacible

clench ['klɛnʧ] *vt* **1** CLUTCH : agarrar **2** TIGHTEN : apretar (el puño, los dientes)

clergy ['klərʤi] *n, pl* **-gies** : clero *m*

clergyman ['klərʤimən] *n, pl* **-men** [-mən, -ˌmɛn] : clérigo *m*

cleric ['klɛrɪk] *n* : clérigo *m*, -ga *f*

clerical ['klɛrɪkəl] *adj* **1** : clerical ⟨a clerical collar : un alzacuello⟩ **2** : de oficina ⟨clerical staff : personal de oficina⟩

clerk¹ ['klərk, *Brit* 'klɑrk] *vi* : trabajar de oficinista, trabajar de dependiente

clerk² *n* **1** : funcionario *m*, -ria *f* (de una oficina gubernamental) **2** : oficinista *mf*, empleado *m*, -da *f* de oficina **3** SALESPERSON : dependiente *m*, -ta *f*

clever ['klɛvər] *adj* **1** SKILLFUL : ingenioso, hábil **2** SMART : listo, inteligente, astuto

cleverly ['klɛvərli] *adv* **1** SKILLFULLY : ingeniosamente, hábilmente **2** INTELLIGENTLY : inteligentemente

cleverness ['klɛvərnəs] *n* **1** SKILL : ingenio *m*, habilidad *f* **2** INTELLIGENCE : inteligencia *f*

clew ['klu:] → **clue**
cliché [kli'ʃeɪ] n : cliché m, tópico m
click[1] ['klɪk] vt 1 : chasquear (los dedos, etc.) ⟨to click one's heels : dar un taconazo⟩ 2 : hacer clic en (un botón, etc.) — vi 1 : hacer clic 2 SNAP : chasquear 3 SUCCEED : tener éxito 4 GET ALONG : congeniar, llevarse bien
click[2] n : chasquido m (de los dedos, etc.), clic m (de un botón, etc.)
client ['klaɪənt] n : cliente m, -ta f
clientele [ˌklaɪən'tɛl, ˌkli:-] n : clientela f
cliff ['klɪf] n : acantilado m, precipicio m, risco m
climate ['klaɪmət] n : clima m
climatic [klaɪ'mætɪk, klə-] adj : climático
climax[1] ['klaɪˌmæks] vi : llegar al punto culminante, culminar — vt : ser el punto culminante de
climax[2] n : clímax m, punto m culminante
climb[1] ['klaɪm] vt : escalar, trepar a, subir a ⟨to climb a mountain : escalar una montaña⟩ — vi 1 RISE : subir, ascender ⟨prices are climbing : los precios están subiendo⟩ 2 : subirse, treparse ⟨to climb up a tree : treparse a un árbol⟩
climb[2] n : ascenso m, subida f
climber ['klaɪmər] n 1 : escalador m, -dora f ⟨a mountain climber : un alpinista⟩ 2 : trepadora f (planta)
clinch[1] ['klɪntʃ] vt 1 FASTEN, SECURE : remachar (un clavo), afianzar, abrochar 2 SETTLE : decidir, cerrar ⟨to clinch the title : ganar el título⟩
clinch[2] n : abrazo m, clinch m (en el boxeo)
clincher ['klɪntʃər] n : argumento m decisivo
cling ['klɪŋ] vi clung ['klʌŋ]; clinging 1 STICK : adherirse, pegarse 2 : aferrarse, agarrarse ⟨he clung to the railing : se aferró a la barandilla⟩
clinic ['klɪnɪk] n : clínica f
clinical ['klɪnɪkəl] adj : clínico — clinically [-kli] adv
clink[1] ['klɪŋk] vi : tintinear
clink[2] n : tintineo m
clip[1] ['klɪp] vt clipped; clipping 1 CUT : cortar, recortar 2 HIT : golpear, dar un puñetazo a 3 FASTEN : sujetar (con un clip)
clip[2] n 1 → clippers 2 BLOW : golpe m, puñetazo m 3 PACE : paso m rápido 4 FASTENER : clip m ⟨a paper clip : un sujetapapeles⟩
clipper ['klɪpər] n 1 : clíper m (buque de vela) 2 **clippers** npl : tijeras fpl ⟨nail clippers : cortauñas⟩
clique ['kli:k, 'klɪk] n : grupo m exclusivo, camarilla f (de políticos)
clitoris ['klɪtərəs, klɪ'tɔrəs] n, pl **clitorides** [-'tɔrəˌdi:z] : clítoris m
cloak[1] ['klo:k] vt : encubrir, envolver (en un manto de)

cloak[2] n : capa f, capote m, manto m ⟨under the cloak of darkness : al amparo de la oscuridad⟩
clobber ['klɑbər] vt : dar una paliza a
clock[1] ['klɑk] vt : cronometrar
clock[2] n 1 : reloj m (de pared), cronómetro m (en deportes o competencias) 2 **around the clock** : las veinticuatro horas
clockwise ['klɑkˌwaɪz] adv & adj : en la dirección de las manecillas del reloj
clockwork ['klɑkˌwərk] n : mecanismo m de relojería
clod ['klɑd] n 1 : terrón m 2 OAF : zoquete mf
clog[1] ['klɑg] v clogged; clogging vt 1 HINDER : estorbar, impedir 2 BLOCK : atascar, tapar — vi : atascarse, taparse
clog[2] n 1 OBSTACLE : traba f, impedimento m, estorbo m 2 : zueco m (zapato)
cloister[1] ['klɔɪstər] vt : enclaustrar
cloister[2] n : claustro m
clone ['klo:n] n 1 : clon m (de un organismo) 2 COPY : copia f, reproducción f
close[1] ['klo:z] v closed; closing vt : cerrar — vi 1 : cerrarse, cerrar 2 TERMINATE : concluirse, terminar 3 **to close in** APPROACH : acercarse, aproximarse
close[2] ['klo:s] adv : cerca, de cerca
close[3] adj closer; closest 1 CONFINING : restrictivo, estrecho 2 SECRETIVE : reservado 3 STRICT : estricto, detallado 4 STUFFY : cargado, bochornoso (dícese del tiempo) 5 TIGHT : apretado, entallado, ceñido ⟨it's a close fit : es muy apretado⟩ 6 NEAR : cercano, próximo 7 INTIMATE : íntimo ⟨close friends : amigos íntimos⟩ 8 ACCURATE : fiel, exacto 9 : reñido ⟨a close election : una elección muy reñida⟩
close[4] ['klo:z] n : fin m, final m, conclusión f
closely ['klo:sli] adv : cerca, de cerca
closeness ['klo:snəs] n 1 NEARNESS : cercanía f, proximidad f 2 INTIMACY : intimidad f
closet[1] ['klɑzət] vt **to be closeted with** : estar encerrado con
closet[2] n : armario m, guardarropa f, clóset m
closure ['klo:ʒər] n 1 CLOSING, END : cierre m, clausura f, fin m 2 FASTENER : cierre m
clot[1] ['klɑt] v clotted; clotting vt : coagular, cuajar — vi : cuajarse, coagularse
clot[2] n : coágulo m
cloth ['klɔθ] n, pl **cloths** ['klɔðz, 'klɔθs] 1 FABRIC : tela f 2 RAG : trapo m 3 TABLECLOTH : mantel m
clothe ['klo:ð] vt clothed or clad ['klæd]; clothing DRESS : vestir, arropar, ataviar
clothes ['klo:z, 'klo:ðz] npl 1 CLOTHING : ropa f 2 BEDCLOTHES : ropa f de cama
clothespin ['klo:zˌpɪn] n : pinza f (para la ropa)

clothing [ˈkloːðɪŋ] *n* : ropa *f*, indumentaria *f*
cloud¹ [ˈklaʊd] *vt* : nublar, oscurecer — *vi* **to cloud over** : nublarse
cloud² *n* : nube *f*
cloudburst [ˈklaʊdˌbərst] *n* : chaparrón *m*, aguacero *m*
cloudless [ˈklaʊdləs] *adj* : despejado, claro
cloudy [ˈklaʊdi] *adj* **cloudier; -est** : nublado, nuboso
clout¹ [ˈklaʊt] *vt* : bofetear, dar un tortazo a
clout² *n* **1** BLOW : golpe *m*, tortazo *m* **fam 2** INFLUENCE : influencia *f*, palanca *f fam*
clove¹ [ˈkloːv] *n* **1** : diente *m* (de ajo) **2** : clavo *m* (especia)
clove² → **cleave**
cloven hoof [ˈkloːvən] *n* : pezuña *f* hendida
clover [ˈkloːvər] *n* : trébol *m*
cloverleaf [ˈkloːvərˌliːf] *n, pl* **-leafs** *or* **-leaves** [-ˌliːvz] : intersección *f* en trébol
clown¹ [ˈklaʊn] *vi* : payasear, bromear ⟨stop clowning around : déjate de payasadas⟩
clown² *n* : payaso *m*, -sa *f*
clownish [ˈklaʊnɪʃ] *adj* **1** : de payaso **2** BOORISH : grosero — **clownishly** *adv*
cloying [ˈklɔɪɪŋ] *adj* : empalagoso, meloso
club¹ [ˈklʌb] *vt* **clubbed; clubbing** : aporrear, dar garrotazos a
club² *n* **1** CUDGEL : garrote *m*, porra *f* **2** : palo *m* ⟨golf club : palo de golf⟩ **3** : trébol *m* (naipe) **4** ASSOCIATION : club *m*
clubfoot [ˈklʌbˌfʊt] *n, pl* **-feet** : pie *m* deforme
clubhouse [ˈklʌbˌhaʊs] *n* : sede *f* de un club
cluck¹ [ˈklʌk] *vi* : cloquear, cacarear
cluck² *n* : cloqueo *m*, cacareo *m*
clue¹ [ˈkluː] *vt* **clued; clueing** *or* **cluing** *or* **to clue in** : dar una pista a, informar
clue² *n* : pista *f*, indicio *m*
clump¹ [ˈklʌmp] *vi* **1** : caminar con pisadas fuertes **2** LUMP : agruparse, aglutinarse — *vt* : amontonar
clump² *n* **1** : grupo *m* (de arbustos o árboles), terrón *m* (de tierra) **2** : pisada *f* fuerte
clumsily [ˈklʌmzəli] *adv* : torpemente, sin gracia
clumsiness [ˈklʌmzinəs] *n* : torpeza *f*
clumsy [ˈklʌmzi] *adj* **-sier; -est 1** AWKWARD : torpe, desmañado **2** TACTLESS : carente de tacto, poco delicado
clung → **cling**
clunky [ˈklʌŋki] *adj* : torpe, poco elegante
cluster¹ [ˈklʌstər] *vt* : agrupar, juntar — *vi* : agruparse, apiñarse, arracimarse
cluster² *n* : grupo *m*, conjunto *m*, racimo *m* (de uvas)

clutch¹ [ˈklʌtʃ] *vt* : agarrar, asir — *vi* **to clutch at** : tratar de agarrar
clutch² *n* **1** GRASP, GRIP : agarre *m*, apretón *m* **2** : embrague *m*, clutch *m* (de una máquina) **3 clutches** *npl* : garras *fpl* ⟨he fell into their clutches : cayó en sus garras⟩
clutter¹ [ˈklʌtər] *vt* : atiborrar o atestar de cosas, llenar desordenadamente
clutter² *n* : desorden *m*, revoltijo *m*
coach¹ [ˈkoːtʃ] *vt* : entrenar (atletas, artistas), preparar (alumnos)
coach² *n* **1** CARRIAGE : coche *m*, carruaje *m*, carroza *f* **2** : vagón *m* de pasajeros (de un tren) **3** BUS : autobús *m*, ómnibus *m* **4** : pasaje *m* aéreo de segunda clase **5** TRAINER : entrenador *m*, -dora *f*
coagulate [koˈægjəˌleɪt] *v* **-lated; -lating** *vt* : coagular, cuajar — *vi* : coagularse, cuajarse
coal [ˈkoːl] *n* **1** EMBER : ascua *f*, brasa *f* **2** : carbón *m* ⟨a coal mine : una mina de carbón⟩
coalesce [ˌkoːəˈlɛs] *vi* **-alesced; -alescing** : unirse
coalition [ˌkoːəˈlɪʃən] *n* : coalición *f*
coarse [ˈkors] *adj* **coarser; -est 1** : grueso (dícese de la arena o la sal), basto (dícese de las telas), áspero (dícese de la piel) **2** CRUDE, ROUGH : basto, tosco, ordinario **3** VULGAR : grosero — **coarsely** *adv*
coarsen [ˈkorsən] *vt* : hacer áspero o basto — *vi* : volverse áspero o basto
coarseness [ˈkorsnəs] *n* : aspereza *f*, tosquedad *f*
coast¹ [ˈkoːst] *vi* : deslizarse, rodar sin impulso
coast² *n* : costa *f*, litoral *m*
coastal [ˈkoːstəl] *adj* : costero
coaster [ˈkoːstər] *n* : posavasos *m*
coast guard *n* : guardia *f* costera, guardacostas *mpl*
coastline [ˈkoːstˌlaɪn] *n* : costa *f*
coat¹ [ˈkoːt] *vt* : cubrir, revestir, bañar (en un líquido)
coat² *n* **1** : abrigo *m* ⟨a sport coat : una chaqueta, un saco⟩ **2** : pelaje *m* (de animales) **3** LAYER : capa *f*, mano *f* (de pintura)
coating [ˈkoːtɪŋ] *n* : capa *f*
coat of arms *n* : escudo *m* de armas
coax [ˈkoːks] *vt* : engatusar, persuadir
cob [ˈkɑb] → **corncob**
cobalt [ˈkoːˌbɔlt] *n* : cobalto *m*
cobble [ˈkɑbəl] *vt* **cobbled; cobbling 1** : fabricar o remendar (zapatos) **2** **cobble together** : improvisar, hacer apresuradamente
cobbler [ˈkɑblər] *n* **1** SHOEMAKER : zapatero *m*, -ra *f* **2 fruit cobbler** : tarta *f* de fruta
cobblestone [ˈkɑbəlˌstoːn] *n* : adoquín *m*
cobra [ˈkoːbrə] *n* : cobra *f*
cobweb [ˈkɑbˌwɛb] *n* : telaraña *f*
coca [ˈkoːkə] *n* : coca *f*

cocaine [koˈkeɪn, ˈkoːˌkeɪn] *n* : cocaína *f*

cock¹ [ˈkɑk] *vt* 1 : ladear ⟨to cock one's head : ladear la cabeza⟩ 2 : montar, amartillar (un arma de fuego)

cock² *n* 1 ROOSTER : gallo *m* 2 FAUCET : grifo *m*, llave *f* 3 : martillo *m* (de un arma de fuego)

cockatoo [ˈkɑkəˌtuː] *n*, *pl* **-toos** : cacatúa *f*

cockeyed [ˈkɑkˌaɪd] *adj* 1 ASKEW : ladeado, torcido, chueco 2 ABSURD : disparatado, absurdo

cockfight [ˈkɑkˌfaɪt] *n* : pelea *f* de gallos

cockiness [ˈkɑkinəs] *n* : arrogancia *f*

cockle [ˈkɑkəl] *n* : berberecho *m*

cockpit [ˈkɑkˌpɪt] *n* : cabina *f*

cockroach [ˈkɑkˌroːtʃ] *n* : cucaracha *f*

cocktail [ˈkɑkˌteɪl] *n* 1 : coctel *m*, cóctel *m* 2 APPETIZER : aperitivo *m*

cocky [ˈkɑki] *adj* **cockier, -est** : creído, engreído

cocoa [ˈkoːˌkoː] *n* 1 CACAO : cacao *m* 2 : cocoa *f*, chocolate *m* (bebida)

coconut [ˈkoːkəˌnʌt] *n* : coco *m*

cocoon [kəˈkuːn] *n* : capullo *m*

cod [ˈkɑd] *n*, *pl* **cod** : bacalao *m*

coddle [ˈkɑdəl] *vt* **-dled; -dling** : mimar, consentir

code [ˈkoːd] *n* 1 : código *m* ⟨civil code : código civil⟩ 2 : código *m*, clave *f* ⟨secret code : clave secreta⟩

codeine [ˈkoːˌdiːn] *n* : codeína *f*

codex [ˈkoːˌdɛks] *n*, *pl* **-dexes** [-ˌdɛksəz] *or* **-dices** [-dəˌsiːz] : códice *m*

codger [ˈkɑdʒər] *n* : viejo *m*, vejete *m*

codify [ˈkɑdəˌfaɪ, ˈkoː-] *vt* **-fied; -fying** : codificar

coeducation [ˌkoːˌɛdʒəˈkeɪʃən] *n* : coeducación *f*, enseñanza *f* mixta

coeducational [ˌkoːˌɛdʒəˈkeɪʃənəl] *adj* : mixto

coefficient [ˌkoːəˈfɪʃənt] *n* : coeficiente *m*

coerce [koˈərs] *vt* **-erced; -ercing** : coaccionar, forzar, obligar

coercion [koˈərʒən, -ʃən] *n* : coacción *f*

coercive [koˈərsɪv] *adj* : coactivo

coexist [ˌkoːɪgˈzɪst] *vi* : coexistir

coexistence [ˌkoːɪgˈzɪstənts] *n* : coexistencia *f*

coffee [ˈkɔfi] *n* : café *m*

coffeepot [ˈkɔfiˌpɑt] *n* : cafetera *f*

coffee table *n* : mesa *f* de centro

coffer [ˈkɔfər] *n* : cofre *m*

coffin [ˈkɔfən] *n* : ataúd *m*, féretro *m*

cog [ˈkɑg] *n* : diente *m* (de una rueda dentada)

cogent [ˈkoːdʒənt] *adj* : convincente, persuasivo

cogitate [ˈkɑdʒəˌteɪt] *vi* **-tated; -tating** : reflexionar, meditar, discurrir

cogitation [ˌkɑdʒəˈteɪʃən] *n* : reflexión *f*, meditación *f*

cognac [ˈkoːnˌjæk] *n* : coñac *m*

cognate [ˈkɑgˌneɪt] *adj* : relacionado, afín

cognition [kɑgˈnɪʃən] *n* : cognición *f*

cognitive [ˈkɑgnəˌtɪv] *adj* : cognitivo

cogwheel [ˈkɑgˌhwiːl] *n* : rueda *f* dentada

cohabit [ˌkoːˈhæbət] *vi* : cohabitar

cohere [koˈhɪr] *vi* **-hered; -hering** 1 ADHERE : adherirse, pegarse 2 : ser coherente o congruente

coherence [koˈhɪrənts] *n* : coherencia *f*, congruencia *f*

coherent [koˈhɪrənt] *adj* : coherente, congruente — **coherently** *adv*

cohesion [koˈhiːʒən] *n* : cohesión *f*

cohesive [koːˈhiːsɪv, -zɪv] *adj* : cohesivo

cohort [ˈkoːˌhɔrt] *n* 1 : cohorte *f* (de soldados) 2 COMPANION : compañero *m*, -ra *f*; colega *mf*

coiffure [kwɑˈfjʊr] *n* : peinado *m*

coil¹ [ˈkɔɪl] *vt* : enrollar — *vi* : enrollarse, enroscarse

coil² *n* : rollo *m* (de cuerda, etc.), espiral *f* (de humo)

coin¹ [ˈkɔɪn] *vt* 1 MINT : acuñar (moneda) 2 INVENT : acuñar, crear, inventar ⟨to coin a phrase : como se suele decir⟩

coin² *n* : moneda *f*

coincide [ˌkoːɪnˈsaɪd, ˈkoːɪnˌsaɪd] *vi* **-cided; -ciding** : coincidir

coincidence [koˈɪntsədənts] *n* : coincidencia *f*, casualidad *f* ⟨what a coincidence! : ¡qué casualidad!⟩

coincident [koˈɪntsədənt] *adj* : coincidente, concurrente

coincidental [koˌɪntsəˈdɛntəl] *adj* : casual, accidental, fortuito

coitus [ˈkoːətəs] *n* : coito *m*

coke [ˈkoːk] *n* : coque *m*

colander [ˈkɑləndər, ˈkʌ-] *n* : colador *m*

cold¹ [ˈkoːld] *adj* : frío ⟨it's cold out : hace frío⟩ ⟨a cold reception : una fría recepción⟩ ⟨in cold blood : a sangre fría⟩

cold² *n* 1 : frío *m* ⟨to feel the cold : sentir frío⟩ 2 : resfriado *m*, catarro *m* ⟨to catch a cold : resfriarse⟩

cold–blooded [ˈkoːldˈblʌdəd] *adj* 1 CRUEL : cruel, despiadado 2 : de sangre fría (dícese de los reptiles, etc.)

coldly [ˈkoːldli] *adv* : fríamente, con frialdad

coldness [ˈkoːldnəs] *n* : frialdad *f* (de una persona o una actitud), frío *m* (de la temperatura)

coleslaw [ˈkoːlˌslɔ] *n* : ensalada *f* de col

colic [ˈkɑlɪk] *n* : cólico *m*

coliseum [ˌkɑləˈsiːəm] *n* : coliseo *m*, arena *f*

collaborate [kəˈlæbəˌreɪt] *vi* **-rated; -rating** : colaborar

collaboration [kəˌlæbəˈreɪʃə n] *n* : colaboración *f*

collaborator [kəˈlæbəˌreɪtər] *n* 1 COLLEAGUE : colaborador *m*, -dora *f* 2 TRAITOR : colaboracionista *mf*

collage [kəˈlɑʒ] *n* : collage *m*

collapse¹ [kəˈlæps] *vi* **-lapsed; -lapsing** 1 : derrumbarse, desplomarse, hundirse ⟨the building collapsed : el edificio se derrumbó⟩ **2** FALL : desplomarse, caerse ⟨he collapsed on the bed : se desplomó en la cama⟩ ⟨to collapse with laughter : morirse de risa⟩ **3** FAIL : fracasar, quebrar, arruinarse **4** FOLD : plegarse

collapse² *n* **1** FALL : derrumbe *m*, desplome *m* **2** BREAKDOWN, FAILURE : fracaso *m*, colapso *m* (físico), quiebra *f* (económica)

collapsible [kə'læpsəbəl] *adj* : plegable

collar¹ ['kɑlər] *vt* : agarrar, atrapar

collar² *n* : cuello *m*

collarbone ['kɑlər₁boːn] *n* : clavícula *f*

collate [kə'leɪt; 'kɑ₁leɪt, 'koː-] *vt* **-lated; -lating 1** COMPARE : cotejar, comparar **2** : ordenar, recopilar (páginas)

collateral¹ [kə'læʈərəl] *adj* : colateral

collateral² *n* : garantía *f*, fianza *f*, prenda *f*

colleague ['kɑ₁liːg] *n* : colega *mf*; compañero *m*, -ra *f*

collect¹ [kə'lɛkt] *vt* **1** GATHER : recopilar, reunir, recoger ⟨she collected her thoughts : puso en orden sus ideas⟩ **2** : coleccionar, juntar ⟨to collect stamps : coleccionar timbres⟩ **3** : cobrar (una deuda), recaudar (un impuesto) **4** DRAW : cobrar, percibir (un sueldo, etc.) — *vi* **1** ACCUMULATE : acumularse, juntarse **2** CONGREGATE : congregarse, reunirse

collect² *adv & adj* : por cobrar, a cobro revertido

collectible *or* **collectable** [kə'lɛktəbəl] *adj* : coleccionable

collection [kə'lɛkʃən] *n* **1** COLLECTING : colecta *f* (de contribuciones), cobro *m* (de deudas), recaudación *f* (de impuestos) **2** GROUP : colección *f* (de objetos), grupo *m* (de personas)

collective¹ [kə'lɛktɪv] *adj* : colectivo — **collectively** *adv*

collective² *n* : colectivo *m*

collector [kə'lɛktər] *n* **1** : coleccionista *mf* (de objetos) **2** : cobrador *m*, -dora *f* (de deudas)

college ['kɑlɪʤ] *n* **1** : universidad *f* **2** : colegio *m* (de electores o profesionales)

collegiate [kə'liːʤət] *adj* : universitario

collide [kə'laɪd] *vi* **-lided; -liding** : chocar, colisionar, estrellarse

collie ['kɑli] *n* : collie *mf*

collision [kə'lɪʒən] *n* : choque *m*, colisión *f*

colloquial [kə'loːkwiəl] *adj* : coloquial

colloquialism [kə'loːkwiə₁lɪzəm] *n* : expresión *f* coloquial

collusion [kə'luːʒən] *n* : colusión *f*

cologne [kə'loːn] *n* : colonia *f*

Colombian [kə'lʌmbiən] *n* : colombiano *m*, -na *f* — **Colombian** *adj*

colon¹ ['koːlən] *n*, *pl* **colons** *or* **cola** [-lə] : colon *m* (de los intestinos)

colon² *n*, *pl* **colons** : dos puntos *mpl* (signo ortográfico)

colonel ['kərnəl] *n* : coronel *m*

colonial¹ [kə'loːniəl] *adj* : colonial

colonial² *n* : colono *m*, -na *f*

colonist ['kɑlənɪst] *n* : colono *m*, -na *f*; colonizador *m*, -dora *f*

colonization [₁kɑlənə'zeɪʃən] *n* : colonización *f*

colonize ['kɑlə₁naɪz] *vt* **-nized; -nizing 1** : establecer una colonia en **2** SETTLE : colonizar

colonnade [₁kɑlə'neɪd] *n* : columnata *f*

colony ['kɑləni] *n*, *pl* **-nies** : colonia *f*

color¹ ['kʌlər] *vt* **1** : colorear, pintar **2** INFLUENCE : influir en, influenciar — *vi* BLUSH : sonrojarse, ruborizarse

color² *n* **1** : color *m* ⟨primary colors : colores primarios⟩ **2** INTEREST, VIVIDNESS : color *m*, colorido *m* ⟨local color : color local⟩

coloration [kʌlə'reɪʃən] *n* : coloración *f*

color-blind ['kʌlər₁blaɪnd] *adj* : daltónico

color blindness *n* : daltonismo *m*

colored ['kʌlərd] *adj* **1** : de color (dícese de los objetos) **2** : de color, negro (dícese de las personas)

colorfast ['kʌlər₁fæst] *adj* : que no se destiñe

colorful ['kʌlərfəl] *adj* **1** : lleno de colorido, de colores vivos **2** PICTURESQUE, STRIKING : pintoresco, llamativo

coloring ['kʌlərɪŋ] *n* **1** : color *m*, colorido *m* **2 food coloring** : colorante *m*

colorless ['kʌlərləs] *adj* **1** : incoloro, sin color **2** DULL : soso, aburrido

colossal [kə'lɑsəl] *adj* : colosal

colossus [kə'lɑsəs] *n*, *pl* **-si** [-₁saɪ] : coloso *m*

colt ['koːlt] *n* : potro *m*, potranco *m*

column ['kɑləm] *n* : columna *f*

columnist ['kɑləmnɪst, -ləmɪst] *n* : columnista *mf*

coma ['koːmə] *n* : coma *m*, estado *m* de coma

Comanche [kə'mænʧi] *n* : comanche *mf* — **Comanche** *adj*

comatose ['koːmə₁toːs, 'kɑ-] *adj* : comatoso, en estado de coma

comb¹ ['koːm] *vt* **1** : peinar (el pelo) **2** SEARCH : peinar, rastrear, registrar a fondo

comb² *n* **1** : peine *m* **2** : cresta *f* (de un gallo)

combat¹ [kəm'bæt, 'kɑm₁bæt] *vt* **-bated** *or* **-batted; -bating** *or* **-batting** : combatir, luchar contra

combat² ['kɑm₁bæt] *n* : combate *m*, lucha *f*

combatant [kəm'bætənt] *n* : combatiente *mf*

combative [kəm'bætɪv] *adj* : combativo

combination [₁kɑmbə'neɪʃən] *n* : combinación *f*

combine¹ [kəm'baɪn] *v* **-bined; -bining** *vt* : combinar, aunar — *vi* : combinarse, mezclarse

combine² ['kɑm₁baɪn] *n* **1** ALLIANCE : alianza *f* comercial o política **2** HARVESTER : cosechadora *f*

combustible [kəm'bʌstəbəl] *adj* : inflamable, combustible
combustion [kəm'bʌstʃən] *n* : combustión *f*
come ['kʌm] *vi* **came** ['keɪm]; **come**; **coming 1** APPROACH : venir, aproximarse ⟨here they come : acá vienen⟩ **2** ARRIVE : venir, llegar, alcanzar ⟨they came yesterday : vinieron ayer⟩ **3** ORIGINATE : venir, provenir ⟨this wine comes from France : este vino viene de Francia⟩ **4** AMOUNT : llegar, ascender ⟨the investment came to two million : la inversión llegó a dos millones⟩ **5 to come clean** : confesar, desahogar la conciencia **6 to come into** ACQUIRE : adquirir ⟨to come into a fortune : heredar una fortuna⟩ **7 to come off** SUCCEED : tener éxito, ser un éxito **8 to come out** : salir, aparecer, publicarse **9 to come to** REVIVE : recobrar el conocimiento, volver en sí **10 to come to pass** HAPPEN : acontecer **11 to come to terms** : llegar a un acuerdo
comeback ['kʌm,bæk] *n* **1** RETORT : réplica *f*, respuesta *f* **2** RETURN : retorno *m*, regreso *m* ⟨the champion announced his comeback : el campeón anunció su regreso⟩
come back *vi* **1** RETORT : replicar, contestar **2** RETURN : volver ⟨come back here! : ¡vuelve acá!⟩ ⟨that style's coming back : ese estilo está volviendo⟩
comedian [kə'mi:diən] *n* : cómico *m*, -ca *f*; humorista *mf*
comedienne [kə,mi:di'ɛn] *n* : cómica *f*, humorista *f*
comedy ['kɑmədi] *n*, *pl* **-dies** : comedia *f*
comely ['kʌmli] *adj* **-lier**; **-est** : bello, bonito
comet ['kɑmət] *n* : cometa *m*
comfort¹ ['kʌmpfərt] *vt* **1** CHEER : confortar, alentar **2** CONSOLE : consolar
comfort² *n* **1** CONSOLATION : consuelo *m* **2** WELL-BEING : confort *m*, bienestar *m* **3** CONVENIENCE : comodidad *f* ⟨the comforts of home : las comodidades del hogar⟩
comfortable ['kʌmpfərtəbəl, 'kʌmpftə-] *adj* : cómodo, confortable — **comfortably** ['kʌmpfərtəbli, 'kʌmpftə-] *adv*
comforter ['kʌmpfərtər] *n* QUILT : edredón *m*, cobertor *m*
comic¹ ['kɑmɪk] *adj* : cómico, humorístico
comic² *n* **1** COMEDIAN : cómico *m*, -ca *f*; humorista *mf* **2** *or* **comic book** : historieta *f*, cómic *m*
comical ['kɑmɪkəl] *adj* : cómico, gracioso, chistoso
comic strip *n* : tira *f* cómica, historieta *f*
coming ['kʌmɪŋ] *adj* : siguiente, próximo, que viene
comma ['kɑmə] *n* : coma *f*

command¹ [kə'mænd] *vt* **1** ORDER : ordenar, mandar **2** CONTROL, DIRECT : comandar, tener el mando de — *vi* **1** : dar órdenes **2** GOVERN : estar al mando *m*, gobernar
command² *n* **1** CONTROL, LEADERSHIP : mando *m*, control *m*, dirección *f* **2** ORDER : orden *f*, mandato *m* **3** MASTERY : maestría *f*, destreza *f*, dominio *m* **4** : tropa *f* asignada a un comandante
commandant ['kɑmən,dɑnt, -,dænt] *n* : comandante *mf*
commandeer [,kɑmən'dɪr] *vt* : piratear, secuestrar (un vehículo, etc.)
commander [kə'mændər] *n* : comandante *mf*
commandment [kə'mændmənt] *n* : mandamiento *m*, orden *f* ⟨the Ten Commandments : los diez mandamientos⟩
commando [kə'mændo:] *n* : comando *m*
commemorate [kə'mɛmə,reɪt] *vt* **-rated; -rating** : conmemorar
commemoration [kə,mɛmə'reɪʃən] *n* : conmemoración *f*
commemorative [kə'mɛmrətɪv, -'mɛmə,reɪtɪv] *adj* : conmemorativo
commence [kə'mɛnts] *v* **-menced; -mencing** *vt* : iniciar, comenzar — *vi* : iniciarse, comenzar
commencement [kə'mɛntsmənt] *n* **1** BEGINNING : inicio *m*, comienzo *m* **2** : ceremonia *f* de graduación
commend [kə'mɛnd] *vt* **1** ENTRUST : encomendar **2** RECOMMEND : recomendar **3** PRAISE : elogiar, alabar
commendable [kə'mɛndəbəl] *adj* : loable, meritorio, encomiable
commendation [,kɑmən'deɪʃən, -,mɛn-] *n* : elogio *m*, encomio *m*
commensurate [kə'mɛntsərət, -'mɛntʃərət] *adj* : proporcionado ⟨commensurate with : en proporción a⟩
comment¹ ['kɑ,mɛnt] *vi* **1** : hacer comentarios **2 to comment on** : comentar, hacer observaciones sobre
comment² *n* : comentario *m*, observación *f*
commentary ['kɑmən,tɛri] *n*, *pl* **-taries** : comentario *m*, crónica *f* (deportiva)
commentator ['kɑmən,teɪtər] *n* : comentarista *mf*, cronista *mf* (de deportes)
commerce ['kɑmərs] *n* : comercio *m*
commercial¹ [kə'mərʃəl] *adj* : comercial — **commercially** *adv*
commercial² *n* : comercial *m*
commercialize [kə'mərʃə,laɪz] *vt* **-ized; -izing** : comercializar
commiserate [kə'mɪzə,reɪt] *vi* **-ated; -ating** : compadecerse, consolarse
commiseration [kə,mɪzə'reɪʃən] *n* : conmiseración *f*
commission¹ [kə'mɪʃən] *vt* **1** : nombrar (un oficial) **2** : comisionar, encargar ⟨to commission a painting : encargar una pintura⟩

commission² *n* **1** : nombramiento *m* (al grado de oficial) **2** COMMITTEE : comisión *f*, comité *m* **3** COMMITTING : comisión *f*, realización *f* (de un acto) **4** PERCENTAGE : comisión *f* ⟨sales commissions : comisiones de venta⟩

commissioned officer *n* : oficial *mf*

commissioner [kə'mıʃənər] *n* **1** : comisionado *m*, -da *f*; miembro *m* de una comisión **2** : comisario *m*, -ria *f* (de policía, etc.)

commit [kə'mıt] *vt* **-mitted; -mitting 1** ENTRUST : encomendar, confiar **2** CONFINE : internar (en un hospital), encarcelar (en una prisión) **3** PERPETRATE : cometer ⟨to commit a crime : cometer un crimen⟩ **4 to commit oneself** : comprometerse

commitment [kə'mıtmənt] *n* **1** RESPONSIBILITY : compromiso *m*, responsabilidad *f* **2** DEDICATION : dedicación *f*, devoción *f* ⟨commitment to the cause : devoción a la causa⟩

committee [kə'mıti] *n* : comité *m*

commodious [kə'mo:diəs] *adj* SPACIOUS : amplio, espacioso

commodity [kə'madəti] *n, pl* **-ties** : artículo *m* de comercio, mercancía *f*, mercadería *f*

commodore ['kamə,dor] *n* : comodoro *m*

common¹ ['kamən] *adj* **1** PUBLIC : común, público ⟨the common good : el bien común⟩ **2** SHARED : común ⟨a common interest : un interés común⟩ **3** GENERAL : común, general ⟨it's common knowledge : todo el mundo lo sabe⟩ **4** ORDINARY : ordinario, común y corriente ⟨the common man : el hombre medio, el hombre de la calle⟩

common² *n* **1** : tierra *f* comunal **2 in ～** : en común

common cold *n* : resfriado *m* común

common denominator *n* : denominador *m* común

commoner ['kamənər] *n* : plebeyo *m*, -ya *f*

commonly ['kamənli] *adv* **1** FREQUENTLY : comúnmente, frecuentemente **2** USUALLY : normalmente

common noun *n* : nombre *m* común

commonplace¹ ['kamən,pleıs] *adj* : común, ordinario

commonplace² *n* : cliché *m*, tópico *m*

common sense *n* : sentido *m* común

commonwealth ['kamən,wɛlθ] *n* : entidad *f* política ⟨the British Commonwealth : la Mancomunidad Británica⟩

commotion [kə'mo:ʃən] *n* **1** RUCKUS : alboroto *m*, jaleo *m*, escándalo *m* **2** STIR, UPSET : revuelo *m*, conmoción *f*

communal [kə'mju:nəl] *adj* : comunal

commune¹ [kə'mju:n] *vi* **-muned; -muning** : estar en comunión

commune² ['ka,mju:n, kə'mju:n] *n* : comuna *f*

communicable [kə'mju:nıkəbəl] *adj* CONTAGIOUS : transmisible, contagioso

communicate [kə'mju:nə,keıt] *v* **-cated; -cating** *vt* **1** CONVEY : comunicar, expresar, hacer saber **2** TRANSMIT : transmitir (una enfermedad), contagiar — *vi* : comunicarse, expresarse

communication [kə,mju:nə'keıʃən] *n* : comunicación *f*

communicative [kə'mju:nı,keıṯıv, -kəṯıv] *adj* : comunicativo

communion [kə'mju:njən] *n* **1** SHARING : comunión *f* **2 Communion** : comunión *f*, eucaristía *f*

communiqué [kə'mju:nə,keı, -,mju:nə-'keı] *n* : comunicado *m*

communism *or* **Communism** ['kamjə-,nızəm] *n* : comunismo *m*

communist¹ *or* **Communist** ['kamjə-,nıst] *adj* : comunista ⟨the Communist Party : el Partido Comunista⟩

communist² *or* **Communist** *n* : comunista *mf*

communistic *or* **Communistic** [,kamjə-'nıstık] *adj* : comunista

community [kə'mju:nəti] *n, pl* **-ties** : comunidad *f*

commute [kə'mju:t] *v* **-muted; -muting** *vt* REDUCE : conmutar, reducir (una sentencia) — *vi* : viajar de la residencia al trabajo

commuter [kə'mju:ṯər] *n* : persona *f* que viaja diariamente al trabajo

compact¹ [kəm'pækt, 'kam,pækt] *vt* : compactar, consolidar, comprimir

compact² [kəm'pækt, 'kam,pækt] *adj* **1** DENSE, SOLID : compacto, macizo, denso **2** CONCISE : breve, conciso

compact³ ['kam,pækt] *n* **1** AGREEMENT : acuerdo *m*, pacto *m* **2** : polvera *f*, estuche *m* de maquillaje **3** *or* **compact car** : auto *m* compacto

compact disc ['kam,pækt'dısk] *n* : disco *m* compacto, compact disc *m*

compactly [kəm'pæktli, 'kam,pækt-] *adv* **1** DENSELY : densamente, macizamente **2** CONCISELY : concisamente, brevemente

companion [kəm'pænjən] *n* **1** COMRADE : compañero *m*, -ra *f*; acompañante *mf* **2** MATE : pareja *f* (de un zapato, etc.)

companionable [kəm'pænjənəbəl] *adj* : sociable, amigable

companionship [kəm'pænjən,ʃıp] *n* : compañerismo *m*, camaradería *f*

company ['kʌmpəni] *n, pl* **-nies 1** FIRM : compañía *f*, empresa *f* **2** GROUP : compañía *f* (de actores o soldados) **3** GUESTS : visita *f* ⟨we have company : tenemos visita⟩

comparable ['kampərəbəl] *adj* : comparable, parecido

comparative¹ [kəm'pærəṯıv] *adj* RELATIVE : comparativo, relativo — **comparatively** *adv*

comparative² *n* : comparativo *m*

compare¹ [kəm'pær] v **-pared; -paring** vt : comparar — vi **to compare with** : poder comparar con, tener comparación con

compare² n : comparación f ⟨beyond compare : sin igual, sin par⟩

comparison [kəm'pærəsən] n : comparación f

compartment [kəm'partmənt] n : compartimento m, compartimiento m

compass ['kʌmpəs, 'kam-] n **1** RANGE, SCOPE : alcance m, extensión f, límites mpl **2** : compás m (para trazar circunferencias) **3** : compás m, brújula f ⟨the points of the compass : los puntos cardinales⟩

compassion [kəm'pæʃən] n : compasión f, piedad f, misericordia f

compassionate [kəm'pæʃənət] adj : compasivo

compatibility [kəm,pætə'bıləti] n : compatibilidad f

compatible [kəm'pætəbəl] adj : compatible, afín

compatriot [kəm'peitriət, -'pæ-] n : compatriota mf; paisano m, -na f

compel [kəm'pɛl] vt **-pelled; -pelling** : obligar, compeler

compelling [kəm'pɛlıŋ] adj **1** FORCEFUL : fuerte **2** ENGAGING : absorbente **3** PERSUASIVE : persuasivo, convincente

compendium [kəm'pɛndiəm] n, pl **-diums** or **-dia** [-diə] : compendio m

compensate ['kampən,seit] v **-sated; -sating** vi **to compensate for** : compensar — vt : indemnizar, compensar

compensation [,kampən'seiʃən] n : compensación f, indemnización f

compensatory [kəm'pɛntsə,tori] adj : compensatorio

compete [kəm'pi:t] vi **-peted; -peting** : competir, contender, rivalizar

competence ['kampətənts] n : competencia f, aptitud f

competency ['kampətəntsi] → **competence**

competent ['kampətənt] adj : competente, capaz

competition [,kampə'tıʃən] n : competencia f, concurso m

competitive [kəm'pɛtətıv] adj : competitivo

competitor [kəm'pɛtətər] n : competidor m, -dora f

compilation [,kampə'leiʃən] n : recopilación f, compilación f

compile [kəm'pail] vt **-piled; -piling** : compilar, recopilar

complacency [kəm'pleisəntsi] n : satisfacción f consigo mismo, suficiencia f

complacent [kəm'pleisənt] adj : satisfecho de sí mismo, suficiente

complain [kəm'plein] vi **1** GRIPE : quejarse, regañar, rezongar **2** PROTEST : reclamar, protestar

complaint [kəm'pleint] n **1** GRIPE : queja f **2** AILMENT : afección f, dolencia f

3 ACCUSATION : reclamo m, acusación f

complement¹ ['kamplə,mɛnt] vt : complementar

complement² ['kampləmənt] n : complemento m

complementary [,kamplə'mɛntəri] adj : complementario

complete¹ [kəm'pli:t] vt **-pleted; -pleting 1** : completar, hacer entero ⟨this piece completes the collection : esta pieza completa la colección⟩ **2** FINISH : completar, acabar, terminar ⟨she completed her studies : completó sus estudios⟩

complete² adj **-pleter; -est 1** WHOLE : completo, entero, íntegro **2** FINISHED : terminado, acabado **3** TOTAL : completo, total, absoluto

completely [kəm'pli:tli] adv : completamente, totalmente

completion [kəm'pli:ʃən] n : finalización f, cumplimiento m

complex¹ [kam'plɛks, kəm-; 'kam-,plɛks] adj : complejo, complicado

complex² ['kam,plɛks] n : complejo m

complexion [kəm'plɛkʃən] n : cutis m, tez f ⟨of dark complexion : de tez morena⟩

complexity [kəm'plɛksəti, kam-] n, pl **-ties** : complejidad f

compliance [kəm'plaiənts] n : conformidad f ⟨in compliance with the law : conforme a la ley⟩

compliant [kəm'plaiənt] adj : dócil, sumiso

complicate ['kamplə,keit] vt **-cated; -cating** : complicar

complicated ['kamplə,keitəd] adj : complicado

complication [,kamplə'keiʃən] n : complicación f

complicity [kəm'plisəti] n, pl **-ties** : complicidad f

compliment¹ ['kamplə,mɛnt] vt : halagar, florear Mex

compliment² ['kampləmənt] n **1** : halago m, cumplido m **2 compliments** npl : saludos mpl ⟨give them my compliments : déles saludos de mi parte⟩

complimentary [,kamplə'mɛntəri] adj **1** FLATTERING : halagador, halagüeño **2** FREE : de cortesía, gratis

comply [kəm'plai] vi **-plied; -plying** : cumplir, acceder, obedecer

component¹ [kəm'po:nənt, 'kam-,po:-] adj : componente

component² n : componente m, elemento m, pieza f

compose [kəm'po:z] vt **-posed; -posing 1** : componer, crear ⟨to compose a melody : componer una melodía⟩ **2** CALM : calmar, serenar ⟨to compose oneself : serenarse⟩ **3** CONSTITUTE : constar, componer ⟨to be composed of : constar de⟩ **4** : componer (un texto a imprimirse)

composer [kəm'po:zər] n : compositor m, -tora f

composite¹ [kɑm'pɑzət, kəm-; 'kɑm-pəzət] adj : compuesto (de varias partes)

composite² n : compuesto m, mezcla f

composition [ˌkɑmpə'zɪʃən] n 1 MAKE-UP : composición f 2 ESSAY : ensayo m, trabajo m

compost ['kɑm̩po:st] n : abono m vegetal

composure [kəm'po:ʒər] n : compostura f, serenidad f

compound¹ [kɑm'paʊnd, kəm-; 'kɑm̩paʊnd] vt 1 COMBINE, COMPOSE : combinar, componer 2 AUGMENT : agravar, aumentar ⟨to compound a problem : agravar un problema⟩

compound² ['kɑm̩paʊnd; kɑm'paʊnd, kəm-] adj : compuesto ⟨compound interest : interés compuesto⟩

compound³ ['kɑm̩paʊnd] n 1 MIXTURE : compuesto m, mezcla f 2 ENCLOSURE : recinto m (de residencias, etc.)

compound fracture n : fractura f complicada

comprehend [ˌkɑmprɪ'hɛnd] vt 1 UNDERSTAND : comprender, entender 2 INCLUDE : comprender, incluir, abarcar

comprehensible [ˌkɑmprɪ'hɛntsəbəl] adj : comprensible

comprehension [ˌkɑmprɪ'hɛntʃən] n : comprensión f

comprehensive [ˌkɑmprɪ'hɛntsɪv] adj 1 INCLUSIVE : inclusivo, exhaustivo 2 BROAD : extenso, amplio

compress¹ [kəm'prɛs] vt : comprimir

compress² ['kɑm̩prɛs] n : compresa f

compression [kəm'prɛʃən] n : compresión f

compressor [kəm'prɛsər] n : compresor m

comprise [kəm'praɪz] vt -prised; -prising 1 INCLUDE : comprender, incluir 2 : componerse de, constar de ⟨the installation comprises several buildings : la instalación está compuesta de varios edificios⟩

compromise¹ ['kɑmprə̩maɪz] v -mised; -mising vi : transigir, avenirse — vt JEOPARDIZE : comprometer, poner en peligro

compromise² n : acuerdo m mutuo, compromiso m

comptroller [kən'tro:lər, 'kɑmp-̩tro:-] n : contralor m, -lora f; interventor m, -tora f

compulsion [kəm'pʌlʃən] n 1 COERCION : coacción f 2 URGE : compulsión f, impulso m

compulsive [kəm'pʌlsɪv] adj : compulsivo

compulsory [kəm'pʌlsəri] adj : obligatorio

compunction [kəm'pʌŋkʃən] n 1 QUALM : reparo m, escrúpulo m 2 REMORSE : remordimiento m

computation [ˌkɑmpjʊ'teɪʃən] n : cálculo m, cómputo m

compute [kəm'pju:t] vt -puted; -puting : computar, calcular

computer [kəm'pju:tər] n : computadora f, computador m, ordenador m Spain

computerize [kəm'pju:tə̩raɪz] vt -ized; -izing : computarizar, informatizar

comrade ['kɑm̩ræd] n : camarada mf; compañero m, -ra f

con¹ ['kɑn] vt conned; conning SWINDLE : estafar, timar

con² adv : contra

con³ n : contra m ⟨the pros and cons : los pros y los contras⟩

concave [kɑn'keɪv, 'kɑn̩keɪv] adj : cóncavo

conceal [kən'si:l] vt : esconder, ocultar, disimular

concealment [kən'si:lmənt] n : escondimiento m, ocultación f

concede [kən'si:d] vt -ceded; -ceding 1 ALLOW, GRANT : conceder 2 ADMIT : conceder, reconocer ⟨to concede defeat : reconocer la derrota⟩

conceit [kən'si:t] n : engreimiento m, presunción f

conceited [kən'si:t̬əd] adj : presumido, engreído, presuntuoso

conceivable [kən'si:vəbəl] adj : concebible, imaginable

conceivably [kən'si:vəbli] adv : posiblemente, de manera concebible

conceive [kən'si:v] v -ceived; -ceiving vi : concebir, embarazarse — vt IMAGINE : concebir, imaginar

concentrate¹ ['kɑntsən̩treɪt] v -trated; -trating vt : concentrar — vi : concentrarse

concentrate² n : concentrado m

concentration [ˌkɑntsən'treɪʃən] n : concentración f

concentric [kən'sɛntrɪk] adj : concéntrico

concept ['kɑn̩spt] n : concepto m, idea f

conception [kən'sɛpʃən] n 1 : concepción f (de un bebé) 2 IDEA : concepto m, idea f

concern¹ [kən'sərn] vt 1 : tratarse de, tener que ver con ⟨the novel concerns a sailor : la novela se trata de un marinero⟩ 2 INVOLVE : concernir, incumbir a, afectar ⟨that does not concern me : eso no me incumbe⟩

concern² n 1 AFFAIR : asunto m 2 WORRY : inquietud f, preocupación f 3 BUSINESS : negocio m

concerned [kən'sərnd] adj 1 ANXIOUS : preocupado, ansioso 2 INTERESTED, INVOLVED : interesado, afectado

concerning [kən'sərnɪŋ] prep REGARDING : con respecto a, acerca de, sobre

concert ['kɑn̩sərt] n 1 AGREEMENT : concierto m, acuerdo m 2 : concierto m (musical)

concerted [kən'sərt̬əd] adj : concertado, coordinado ⟨to make a concerted effort : coordinar los esfuerzos⟩

concertina [ˌkɑntsər'ti:nə] n : concertina f

concerto [kən'ʧɛrʈo:] n, pl -ti [-ʈi, -ˌtiː] or -tos : concierto m ⟨violin concerto : concierto para violín⟩
concession [kən'sɛʃən] n : concesión f
conch ['kaŋk, 'kanʧ] n, pl conchs ['kaŋks] or conches ['kanʧəz] : caracol m (animal), caracola f (concha)
conciliatory [kən'sɪliəˌtori] adj : conciliador, conciliatorio
concise [kən'saɪs] adj : conciso, breve — concisely adv
conclave ['kanˌkleɪv] n : cónclave m
conclude [kən'kluːd] v -cluded; -cluding vt 1 END : concluir, finalizar ⟨to conclude a meeting : concluir una reunión⟩ 2 DECIDE : concluir, llegar a la conclusión de — vi END : concluir, terminar
conclusion [kən'kluːʒən] n 1 INFERENCE : conclusión f 2 END : fin m, final m
conclusive [kən'kluːsɪv] adj : concluyente, decisivo — conclusively adv
concoct [kən'kakt, kan-] vt 1 PREPARE : preparar, confeccionar 2 DEVISE : inventar, tramar
concoction [kən'kakʃən] n : invención f, mejunje m, brebaje m
concomitant [kən'kamətənt] adj : concomitante
concord ['kanˌkord, 'kaŋ-] n 1 HARMONY : concordia f, armonía f 2 AGREEMENT : acuerdo m
concordance [kən'kordənts] n : concordancia f
concourse ['kanˌkors] n : explanada f, salón m (para pasajeros)
concrete1 ['kanˈkriːt, 'kanˌkriːt] adj 1 REAL : concreto ⟨concrete objects : objetos concretos⟩ 2 SPECIFIC : determinado, específico 3 : de concreto, de hormigón ⟨concrete walls : paredes de concreto⟩
concrete2 ['kanˌkriːt, kan'kriːt] n : concreto m, hormigón m
concur [kən'kər] vi concurred; concurring 1 COINCIDE : concurrir, coincidir 2 AGREE : concurrir, estar de acuerdo
concurrent [kən'kərənt] adj : concurrente, simultáneo
concussion [kən'kʌʃən] n : conmoción f cerebral
condemn [kən'dɛm] vt 1 CENSURE : condenar, reprobar, censurar 2 : declarar insalubre (alimentos), declarar ruinoso (un edificio) 3 SENTENCE : condenar ⟨condemned to death : condenado a muerte⟩
condemnation [ˌkanˌdɛm'neɪʃən] n : condena f, reprobación f
condensation [ˌkanˌdɛn'seɪʃən, -dən-] n : condensación f
condense [kən'dɛnts] v -densed; -densing vt 1 ABRIDGE : condensar, resumir 2 : condensar (vapor, etc.) — vi : condensarse

condescend [ˌkandɪ'sɛnd] vi 1 DEIGN : condescender, dignarse 2 to condescend to someone : tratar a alguien con condescendencia
condescension [ˌkandɪ'sɛntʃən] n : condescendencia f
condiment ['kandəmənt] n : condimento m
condition1 [kən'dɪʃən] vt 1 DETERMINE : condicionar, determinar 2 : acondicionar (el pelo o el aire), poner en forma (el cuerpo)
condition2 n 1 STIPULATION : condición f, estipulación f ⟨on the condition that : a condición de que⟩ 2 STATE : condición f, estado m ⟨in poor condition : en malas condiciones⟩ 3 conditions npl : condiciones fpl, situación f ⟨working conditions : condiciones del trabajo⟩
conditional [kən'dɪʃənəl] adj : condicional — conditionally adv
conditioner [kən'dɪʃənər] n : acondicionador m
condo ['kando:] → condominium
condolence [kən'do:lənts] n 1 SYMPATHY : condolencia f 2 condolences npl : pésame m
condom ['kandəm] n : condón m
condominium [ˌkandə'mɪniəm] n, pl -ums : condominio m
condone [kən'do:n] vt -doned; -doning : aprobar, perdonar, tolerar
condor ['kandər, -ˌdor] n : cóndor m
conducive [kən'duːsɪv, -'djuː-] adj : propicio, favorable
conduct1 [kən'dʌkt] vt 1 GUIDE : guiar, conducir ⟨to conduct a tour : guiar una visita⟩ 2 DIRECT : conducir, dirigir ⟨to conduct an orchestra : dirigir una orquesta⟩ 3 CARRY OUT : realizar, llevar a cabo ⟨to conduct an investigation : llevar a cabo una investigación⟩ 4 TRANSMIT : conducir, transmitir (calor, electricidad, etc.) 5 to conduct oneself BEHAVE : conducirse, comportarse
conduct2 ['kanˌdʌkt] n 1 MANAGEMENT : conducción f, dirección f, manejo m ⟨the conduct of foreign affairs : la conducción de asuntos exteriores⟩ 2 BEHAVIOR : conducta f, comportamiento m
conduction [kən'dʌkʃən] n : conducción f
conductivity [ˌkanˌdʌk'tɪvəti] n, pl -ties : conductividad f
conductor [kən'dʌktər] n 1 : conductor m, -tora f; revisor m, -sora f (en un tren); cobrador m, -dora f (en un bus); director m, -tora f (de una orquesta) 2 : conductor m (de electricidad, etc.)
conduit ['kanˌduːət, -ˌdjuː-] n : conducto m, canal m, vía f
cone ['ko:n] n 1 : piña f (fruto de las coníferas) 2 : cono m (en geometría) 3 ice–cream cone : cono m, barquillo m, cucurucho m
confection [kən'fɛkʃən] n : dulce m

confectioner [kən'fɛkʃənər] *n* : confitero *m*, -ra *f*
confederacy [kən'fɛdərəsi] *n, pl* -cies : confederación *f*
confederate[1] [kən'fɛdə‚reɪt] *v* -ated; -ating *vt* : unir, confederar — *vi* : confederarse, aliarse
confederate[2] [kən'fɛdərət] *adj* : confederado
confederate[3] *n* : cómplice *mf*; aliado *m*, -da *f*
confederation [kən‚fɛdə'reɪʃən] *n* : confederación *f*, alianza *f*
confer [kən'fər] *v* -ferred; -ferring *vt* : conferir, otorgar — *vi* to confer with : consultar
conference ['kɑnfrənts, -fərənts] *n* : conferencia *f* ⟨press conference : conferencia de prensa⟩
confess [kən'fɛs] *vt* : confesar — *vi* 1 : confesar ⟨the prisoner confessed : el detenido confesó⟩ 2 : confesarse (en religión)
confession [kən'fɛʃən] *n* : confesión *f*
confessional [kən'fɛʃənəl] *n* : confesionario *m*
confessor [kən'fɛsər] *n* : confesor *m*
confetti [kən'fɛti] *n* : confeti *m*
confidant ['kɑnfə‚dɑnt, -‚dænt] *n* : confidente *mf*
confide [kən'faɪd] *v* -fided; -fiding : confiar
confidence ['kɑnfədənts] *n* 1 TRUST : confianza *f* 2 SELF-ASSURANCE : confianza *f* en sí mismo, seguridad *f* en sí mismo 3 SECRET : confidencia *f*, secreto *m*
confident ['kɑnfədənt] *adj* 1 SURE : seguro 2 SELF-ASSURED : confiado, seguro de sí mismo
confidential [‚kɑnfə'dɛnʧəl] *adj* : confidencial — **confidentially** [‚kɑnfə'dɛnʧəli] *adv*
confidently ['kɑnfədəntli] *adv* : con seguridad, con confianza
configuration [kən‚fɪgjə'reɪʃən] *n* : configuración *f*
confine [kən'faɪn] *vt* -fined; -fining 1 LIMIT : confinar, restringir, limitar 2 IMPRISON : recluir, encarcelar, encerrar
confinement [kən'faɪnmənt] *n* : confinamiento *m*, reclusión *f*, encierro *m*
confines ['kɑn‚faɪnz] *npl* : límites *mpl*, confines *mpl*
confirm [kən'fərm] *vt* 1 RATIFY : ratificar 2 VERIFY : confirmar, verificar 3 : confirmar (en religión)
confirmation [‚kɑnfər'meɪʃən] *n* : confirmación *f*
confiscate ['kɑnfə‚skeɪt] *vt* -cated; -cating : confiscar, incautar, decomisar
confiscation [‚kɑnfə'skeɪʃən] *n* : confiscación *f*, incautación *f*, decomiso *m*
conflagration [‚kɑnflə'greɪʃən] *n* : conflagración *f*
conflict[1] [kən'flɪkt] *vi* : estar en conflicto, oponerse

conflict[2] ['kɑn‚flɪkt] *n* : conflicto *m* ⟨to be in conflict : estar en desacuerdo⟩
confluence ['kɑn‚flu:ənts, kən'flu:ənts] *n* : confluencia *f*
conform [kən'fɔrm] *vi* 1 ACCORD, COMPLY : ajustarse, adaptarse, conformarse ⟨it conforms with our standards : se ajusta a nuestras normas⟩ 2 CORRESPOND : corresponder, encajar ⟨to conform to the truth : corresponder a la verdad⟩
conformity [kən'fɔrməti] *n, pl* -ties : conformidad *f*
confound [kən'faʊnd, kɑn-] *vt* : confundir, desconcertar
confront [kən'frʌnt] *vt* : afrontar, enfrentarse a, encarar
confrontation [‚kɑnfrən'teɪʃən] *n* : enfrentamiento *m*, confrontación *f*
confuse [kən'fju:z] *vt* -fused; -fusing 1 PUZZLE : confundir, enturbiar 2 COMPLICATE : confundir, enredar, complicar ⟨to confuse the issue : complicar las cosas⟩
confusing [kən'fju:zɪŋ] *adj* : complicado, que confunde
confusion [kən'fju:ʒən] *n* 1 PERPLEXITY : confusión *f* 2 MESS, TURMOIL : confusión *f*, embrollo *m*, lío *m fam*
congeal [kən'dʒi:l] *vi* 1 FREEZE : congelarse 2 COAGULATE, CURDLE : coagularse, cuajarse
congenial [kən'dʒi:niəl] *adj* : agradable, simpático
congenital [kən'dʒɛnətəl] *adj* : congénito
congest [kən'dʒɛst] *vt* 1 : congestionar (en la medicina) 2 OVERCROWD : abarrotar, atestar, congestionar (el tráfico) — *vi* : congestionarse
congestion [kən'dʒɛstʃən] *n* : congestión *f*
conglomerate[1] [kən'glɑmərət] *adj* : conglomerado
conglomerate[2] [kən'glɑmərət] *n* : conglomerado *m*
conglomeration [kən‚glɑmə'reɪʃən] *n* : conglomerado *m*, acumulación *f*
Congolese [‚kɑŋgə'li:z, -'li:s] *n* : congoleño *m*, -ña *f* — **Congolese** *adj*
congratulate [kən'grædʒə‚leɪt, -'grætʃə-] *vt* -lated; -lating : felicitar
congratulation [kən‚grædʒə'leɪʃən, -‚grætʃə-] *n* : felicitación *f* ⟨congratulations! : ¡felicidades!, ¡enhorabuena!⟩
congregate ['kɑŋgrɪ‚geɪt] *v* -gated; -gating *vt* : congregar, reunir — *vi* : congregarse, reunirse
congregation [‚kɑŋgrɪ'geɪʃən] *n* 1 GATHERING : congregación *f*, fieles *mpl* (a un servicio religioso) 2 PARISHIONERS : feligreses *mpl*
congress ['kɑŋgrəs] *n* : congreso *m*
congressional [kən'grɛʃənəl, kɑn-] *adj* : del congreso
congressman ['kɑŋgrəsmən] *n, pl* -men [-mən, -‚mɛn] : congresista *m*, diputado *m*

congresswoman [ˈkɑŋɡrəsˌwʊmən] *n, pl* **-women** [-ˌwɪmən] : congresista *f*, diputada *f*

congruence [kənˈɡruːənts, ˈkɑŋɡruənts] *n* : congruencia *f*

congruent [kənˈɡruːənt, ˈkɑŋɡruənt] *adj* : congruente

conic [ˈkɑnɪk] → **conical**

conical [ˈkɑnɪkəl] *adj* : cónico

conifer [ˈkɑnəfər, ˈkoː-] *n* : conífera *f*

coniferous [koːˈnɪfərəs, kə-] *adj* : conífero

conjecture¹ [kənˈdʒɛktʃər] *v* **-tured; -turing** : conjeturar

conjecture² *n* : conjetura *f*, presunción *f*

conjugal [ˈkɑndʒɪɡəl, kənˈdʒuː-] *adj* : conyugal

conjugate [ˈkɑndʒəˌɡeɪt] *vt* **-gated; -gating** : conjugar

conjugation [ˌkɑndʒəˈɡeɪʃən] *n* : conjugación *f*

conjunction [kənˈdʒʌŋkʃən] *n* : conjunción *f* ⟨in conjunction with : en combinación con⟩

conjure [ˈkɑndʒər, ˈkʌn-] *v* **-jured; -juring** *vt* **1** ENTREAT : rogar, suplicar **2 to conjure up** : hacer aparecer (apariciones), evocar (memorias, etc.) — *vi* : practicar la magia

conjurer *or* **conjuror** [ˈkɑndʒərər, ˈkʌn-] *n* : mago *m*, -ga *f*; prestidigitador *m*, -dora *f*

connect [kəˈnɛkt] *vi* : conectar, enlazar, empalmar, comunicarse — *vt* **1** JOIN, LINK : conectar, unir, juntar, vincular **2** RELATE : relacionar, asociar (ideas)

connection [kəˈnɛkʃən] *n* : conexión *f*, enlace *m* ⟨professional connections : relaciones profesionales⟩

connective [kəˈnɛktɪv] *adj* : conectivo, conjuntivo ⟨connective tissue : tejido conjuntivo⟩

connector [kəˈnɛktər] *n* : conector *m*

connivance [kəˈnaɪvənts] *n* : connivencia *f*, complicidad *f*

connive [kəˈnaɪv] *vi* **-nived; -niving** CONSPIRE, PLOT : actuar en connivencia, confabularse, conspirar

connoisseur [ˌkɑnəˈsər, -ˈsʊr] *n* : conocedor *m*, -dora *f*; entendido *m*, -da *f*

connotation [ˌkɑnəˈteɪʃən] *n* : connotación *f*

connote [kəˈnoːt] *vt* **-noted; -noting** : connotar

conquer [ˈkɑŋkər] *vt* : conquistar, vencer

conqueror [ˈkɑŋkərər] *n* : conquistador *m*, -dora *f*

conquest [ˈkɑnˌkwɛst, ˈkɑŋ-] *n* : conquista *f*

conscience [ˈkɑntʃənts] *n* : conciencia *f*, consciencia *f* ⟨to have a clear conscience : tener la conciencia limpia⟩

conscientious [ˌkɑntʃiˈɛntʃəs] *adj* : concienzudo — **conscientiously** *adv*

conscious [ˈkɑntʃəs] *adj* **1** AWARE : consciente ⟨to become conscious of : darse cuenta de⟩ **2** ALERT, AWAKE : consciente **3** INTENTIONAL : intencional, deliberado

consciously [ˈkɑntʃəsli] *adv* INTENTIONALLY : intencionalmente, deliberadamente, a propósito

consciousness [ˈkɑntʃəsnəs] *n* **1** AWARENESS : conciencia *f*, consciencia *f* **2** : conocimiento *m* ⟨to lose consciousness : perder el conocimiento⟩

conscript¹ [kənˈskrɪpt] *vt* : reclutar, alistar, enrolar

conscript² [ˈkɑnˌskrɪpt] *n* : conscripto *m*, -ta *f*; recluta *mf*

consecrate [ˈkɑntsəˌkreɪt] *vt* **-crated; -crating** : consagrar

consecration [ˌkɑntsəˈkreɪʃən] *n* : consagración *f*, dedicación *f*

consecutive [kənˈsɛkjətɪv] *adj* : consecutivo, seguido ⟨on five consecutive days : cinco días seguidos⟩

consecutively [kənˈsɛkjətɪvli] *adv* : consecutivamente

consensus [kənˈsɛntsəs] *n* : consenso *m*

consent¹ [kənˈsɛnt] *vi* **1** AGREE : acceder, ponerse de acuerdo **2 to consent to do something** : consentir en hacer algo

consent² *n* : consentimiento *m*, permiso *m* ⟨by common consent : de común acuerdo⟩

consequence [ˈkɑntsəˌkwɛnts, -kwəntrs] *n* **1** RESULT : consecuencia *f*, secuela *f* **2** IMPORTANCE : importancia *f*, trascendencia *f*

consequent [ˈkɑntsəkwənt, -ˌkwɛnt] *adj* : consiguiente

consequential [ˌkɑntsəˈkwɛntʃəl] *adj* **1** CONSEQUENT : consiguiente **2** IMPORTANT : importante, trascendente, trascendental

consequently [ˈkɑntsəkwəntli, -ˌkwɛnt-] *adv* : por consiguiente, por ende, por lo tanto

conservation [ˌkɑntsərˈveɪʃən] *n* : conservación *f*, protección *f*

conservationist [ˌkɑntsərˈveɪʃənɪst] *n* : conservacionista *mf*

conservatism [kənˈsərvəˌtɪzəm] *n* : conservadurismo *m*

conservative¹ [kənˈsərvətɪv] *adj* **1** : conservador **2** CAUTIOUS : moderado, cauteloso ⟨a conservative estimate : un cálculo moderado⟩

conservative² *n* : conservador *m*, -dora *f*

conservatory [kənˈsərvəˌtori] *n, pl* **-ries** : conservatorio *m*

conserve¹ [kənˈsərv] *vt* **-served; -serving** : conservar, preservar

conserve² [ˈkɑnˌsərv] *n* PRESERVES : confitura *f*

consider [kənˈsɪdər] *vt* **1** CONTEMPLATE : considerar, pensar en ⟨we'd considered attending : habíamos pensado en asistir⟩ **2** : considerar, tener en cuenta ⟨consider the consequences : considera las consecuencias⟩ **3** JUDGE, REGARD : considerar, estimar

considerable [kən'sɪdərəbəl] *adj* : considerable — **considerably** [-bli] *adv*
considerate [kən'sɪdərət] *adj* : considerado, atento
consideration [kən,sɪdə'reɪʃən] *n* : consideración *f* ⟨to take into consideration : tener en cuenta⟩
considering [kən'sɪdərɪŋ] *prep* : teniendo en cuenta, visto
consign [kən'saɪn] *vt* **1** COMMIT, ENTRUST : confiar, encomendar **2** TRANSFER : consignar, transferir **3** SEND : consignar, enviar (mercancía)
consignment [kən'saɪnmənt] *n* **1** : envío *m*, remesa *f* **2 on** ~ : en consignación
consist [kən'sɪst] *vi* **1** LIE : consistir ⟨success consists in hard work : el éxito consiste en trabajar duro⟩ **2** : constar, componerse ⟨the set consists of 5 pieces : el juego se compone de 5 piezas⟩
consistency [kən'sɪstənʦi] *n, pl* **-cies 1** : consistencia *f* (de una mezcla o sustancia) **2** COHERENCE : coherencia *f* **3** UNIFORMITY : regularidad *f*, uniformidad *f*
consistent [kən'sɪstənt] *adj* **1** COMPATIBLE : compatible, coincidente ⟨consistent with policy : coincidente con la política⟩ **2** UNIFORM : uniforme, constante, regular — **consistently** [kən'sɪstəntli] *adv*
consolation [,kɑnʦə'leɪʃən] *n* **1** : consuelo *m* **2 consolation prize** : premio *m* de consolación
console¹ [kən'so:l] *vt* **-soled; -soling** : consolar
console² ['kɑn,so:l] *n* : consola *f*
consolidate [kən'sɑlə,deɪt] *vt* **-dated; -dating** : consolidar, unir
consolidation [kən,sɑlə'deɪʃən] *n* : consolidación *f*
consommé [,kɑnʦə'meɪ] *n* : consomé *m*
consonant ['kɑnʦənənt] *n* : consonante *m*
consort¹ [kən'sɔrt] *vi* : asociarse, relacionarse, tener trato ⟨to consort with criminals : tener trato con criminales⟩
consort² ['kɑn,sɔrt] *n* : consorte *mf*
consortium [kən'sɔrʃəm] *n, pl* **-tia** [-ʃə] *or* **-tiums** [-ʃəmz] : consorcio *m*
conspicuous [kən'spɪkjuəs] *adj* **1** OBVIOUS : visible, evidente **2** STRIKING : llamativo
conspicuously [kən'spɪkjuəsli] *adv* : de manera llamativa
conspiracy [kən'spɪrəsi] *n, pl* **-cies** : conspiración *f*, complot *m*, confabulación *f*
conspirator [kən'spɪrətər] *n* : conspirador *m*, -dora *f*
conspire [kən'spaɪr] *vi* **-spired; -spiring** : conspirar, confabularse
constable ['kɑnʦəbəl, 'kʌnʦə-] *n* : agente *mf* de policía (en un pueblo)
constancy ['kɑnʦənʦi] *n, pl* **-cies** : constancia *f*

constant¹ ['kɑnʦtənt] *adj* **1** FAITHFUL : leal, fiel **2** INVARIABLE : constante, invariable **3** CONTINUAL : constante, continuo
constant² *n* : constante *f*
constantly ['kɑnʦtəntli] *adv* : constantemente, continuamente
constellation [,kɑnʦtə'leɪʃən] *n* : constelación *f*
consternation [,kɑnʦtər'neɪʃən] *n* : consternación *f*
constipate ['kɑnʦtə,peɪt] *vt* **-pated; -pating** : estreñir
constipation ['kɑnʦtə'peɪʃən] *n* : estreñimiento *m*, constipación *f* (de vientre)
constituency [kən'stɪʧuənʦi] *n, pl* **-cies 1** : distrito *m* electoral **2** : residentes *mpl* de un distrito electoral
constituent¹ [kən'stɪʧuənt] *adj* **1** COMPONENT : constituyente, componente **2** : constituyente, constitutivo ⟨a constituent assembly : una asamblea constituyente⟩
constituent² *n* **1** COMPONENT : componente *m* **2** ELECTOR, VOTER : elector *m*, -tora *f*; votante *mf*
constitute ['kɑnʦtə,tu:t, -,tju:t] *vt* **-tuted; -tuting 1** ESTABLISH : constituir, establecer **2** COMPOSE, FORM : constituir, componer
constitution [,kɑnʦtə'tu:ʃən, -'tju:-] *n* : constitución *f*
constitutional [,kɑnʦtə'tu:ʃənəl, -'tju:-] *adj* : constitucional
constitutionality [,kɑnʦtə,tu:ʃə'næ-ləti, -,tju:-] *n* : constitucionalidad *f*
constrain [kən'streɪn] *vt* **1** COMPEL : constreñir, obligar **2** CONFINE : constreñir, limitar, restringir **3** RESTRAIN : contener, refrenar
constraint [kən'streɪnt] *n* : restricción *f*, limitación *f*
constrict [kən'strɪkt] *vt* : estrechar, apretar, comprimir
constriction [kən'strɪkʃən] *n* : estrechamiento *m*, compresión *f*
construct [kən'strʌkt] *vt* : construir
construction [kən'strʌkʃən] *n* : construcción *f*
constructive [kən'strʌktɪv] *adj* : constructivo
construe [kən'stru:] *vt* **-strued; -struing** : interpretar
consul ['kɑnʦəl] *n* : cónsul *mf*
consular ['kɑnʦələr] *adj* : consular
consulate ['kɑnʦələt] *n* : consulado *m*
consult [kən'sʌlt] *vt* : consultar — *vi* **to consult with** : consultar con, solicitar la opinión de
consultant [kən'sʌltənt] *n* : consultor *m*, -tora *f*; asesor *m*, -sora *f*
consultation [,kɑnʦəl'teɪʃən] *n* : consulta *f*
consumable [kən'su:məbəl] *adj* : consumible
consume [kən'su:m] *vt* **-sumed; -suming** : consumir, usar, gastar

consumer [kən'suːmər] *n* : consumidor *m*, -dora *f*

consummate¹ ['kɑntsə͵meɪt] *vt* -mated; -mating : consumar

consummate² [kən'sʌmət, 'kɑntsə-mət] *adj* : consumado, perfecto

consummation [͵kɑntsə'meɪʃən] *n* : consumación *f*

consumption [kən'sʌmpʃən] *n* **1** USE : consumo *m*, uso *m* ⟨consumption of electricity : consumo de electricidad⟩ **2** TUBERCULOSIS : tisis *f*, consunción *f*

contact¹ ['kɑn͵tækt, kən'-] *vt* : ponerse en contacto con, contactar (con)

contact² ['kɑn͵tækt] *n* **1** TOUCHING : contacto *m* ⟨to come into contact with : entrar en contacto con⟩ **2** TOUCH : contacto *m*, comunicación *f* ⟨to lose contact with : perder contacto con⟩ **3** CONNECTION : contacto *m* (en negocios) **4** → **contact lens**

contact lens ['kɑn͵tækt'lɛnz] *n* : lente *mf* de contacto, pupilente *m* Mex

contagion [kən'teɪdʒən] *n* : contagio *m*

contagious [kən'teɪdʒəs] *adj* : contagioso

contain [kən'teɪn] *vt* **1** : contener **2 to contain oneself** : contenerse

container [kən'teɪnər] *n* : recipiente *m*, envase *m*

containment [kən'teɪnmənt] *n* : contención *f*

contaminant [kən'tæmənənt] *n* : contaminante *m*

contaminate [kən'tæmə͵neɪt] *vt* -nated; -nating : contaminar

contamination [kən͵tæmə'neɪʃən] *n* : contaminación *f*

contemplate ['kɑntəm͵pleɪt] *v* -plated; -plating *vt* **1** VIEW : contemplar **2** PONDER : contemplar, considerar **3** CONSIDER, PROPOSE : proponerse, proyectar, pensar en ⟨to contemplate a trip : pensar en viajar⟩ — *vi* MEDITATE : meditar

contemplation [͵kɑntəm'pleɪʃən] *n* : contemplación *f*

contemplative [kən'tɛmplət̬ɪv, 'kɑntəm͵pleɪt̬ɪv] *adj* : contemplativo

contemporaneous [kən͵tɛmpə'reɪniəs] *adj* → **contemporary¹**

contemporary¹ [kən'tɛmpə͵rɛri] *adj* : contemporáneo

contemporary² *n, pl* -raries : contemporáneo *m*, -nea *f*

contempt [kən'tɛmpt] *n* **1** DISDAIN : desprecio *m*, desdén *m* ⟨to hold in contempt : despreciar⟩ **2** : desacato *m* (ante un tribunal)

contemptible [kən'tɛmptəbəl] *adj* : despreciable, vil

contemptuous [kən'tɛmptʃuəs] *adj* : despectivo, despreciativo, desdeñoso

contemptuously [kən'tɛmptʃuəsli] *adv* : despectivamente, con desprecio

contend [kən'tɛnd] *vi* **1** STRUGGLE : luchar, lidiar, contender ⟨to contend with a problem : lidiar con un proble-

ma⟩ **2** COMPETE : competir ⟨to contend for a position : competir por un puesto⟩ — *vt* **1** ARGUE, MAINTAIN : argüir, sostener, afirmar ⟨he contended that he was right : afirmó que tenía razón⟩ **2** CONTEST : protestar contra (una decisión, etc.), disputar

contender [kən'tɛndər] *n* : contendiente *mf*; aspirante *mf*; competidor *m*, -dora *f*

content¹ [kən'tɛnt] *vt* SATISFY : contentar, satisfacer

content² *adj* : conforme, contento, satisfecho

content³ *n* CONTENTMENT : contento *m*, satisfacción *f* ⟨to one's heart's content : hasta quedar satisfecho, a más no poder⟩

content⁴ ['kɑn͵tɛnt] *n* **1** MEANING : contenido *m*, significado *m* **2** PROPORTION : contenido *m*, proporción *f* ⟨fat content : contenido de grasa⟩ **3 contents** *npl* : contenido *m*, sumario *m* (de un libro) ⟨table of contents : índice de materias⟩

contented [kən'tɛntəd] *adj* : conforme, satisfecho ⟨a contented smile : una sonrisa de satisfacción⟩

contentedly [kən'tɛntədli] *adv* : con satisfacción

contention [kən'tɛntʃən] *n* **1** DISPUTE : disputa *f*, discusión *f* **2** COMPETITION : competencia *f*, contienda *f* **3** OPINION : argumento *m*, opinión *f*

contentious [kən'tɛntʃəs] *adj* : disputador, pugnaz, combativo

contentment [kən'tɛntmənt] *n* : satisfacción *f*, contento *m*

contest¹ [kən'tɛst] *vt* : disputar, cuestionar, impugnar ⟨to contest a will : impugnar un testamento⟩

contest² ['kɑn͵tɛst] *n* **1** STRUGGLE : lucha *f*, contienda *f* **2** GAME : concurso *m*, competencia *f*

contestable [kən'tɛstəbəl] *adj* : discutible, cuestionable

contestant [kən'tɛstənt] *n* : concursante *mf*; competidor *m*, -dora *f*

context ['kɑn͵tɛkst] *n* : contexto *m*

contiguous [kən'tɪgjuəs] *adj* : contiguo

continence ['kɑntənənts] *n* : continencia *f*

continent¹ ['kɑntənənt] *adj* : continente

continent² *n* : continente *m* — **continental** [͵kɑntən'ɛnt̬əl] *adj*

contingency [kən'tɪndʒəntsi] *n, pl* -cies : contingencia *f*, eventualidad *f*

contingent¹ [kən'tɪndʒənt] *adj* **1** POSSIBLE : contingente, eventual **2** ACCIDENTAL : fortuito, accidental **3 to be contingent on** : depender de, estar sujeto a

contingent² *n* : contingente *m*

continual [kən'tɪnjuəl] *adj* : continuo, constante — **continually** [kən-'tɪnjuəli, -'tɪnjəli] *adv*

continuance [kən'tɪnjuənts] *n* **1** CONTINUATION : continuación *f* **2** DURA-

TION : duración *f* 3 : aplazamiento *m* (de un proceso)
continuation [kən₁tɪnjʊˈeɪʃən] *n* : continuación *f*, prolongación *f*
continue [kənˈtɪnjuː] *v* -**tinued; -tinuing** *vi* 1 CARRY ON : continuar, seguir, proseguir ⟨please continue : continúe, por favor⟩ 2 ENDURE, LAST : continuar, prolongarse, durar 3 RESUME : continuar, reanudarse — *vt* 1 : continuar, seguir ⟨she continued writing : continuó escribiendo⟩ 2 RESUME : continuar, reanudar 3 EXTEND, PROLONG : continuar, prolongar
continuity [₁kɑntə-ˈnuːəti, -ˈnjuː-] *n, pl* -**ties** : continuidad *f*
continuous [kənˈtɪnjuəs] *adj* : continuo — **continuously** *adv*
contort [kənˈtɔrt] *vt* : torcer, retorcer, contraer (el rostro) — *vi* : contraerse, demudarse
contortion [kənˈtɔrʃən] *n* : contorsión *f*
contour [ˈkɑn₁tʊr] *n* 1 OUTLINE : contorno *m* 2 **contours** *npl* SHAPE : forma *f*, curvas *fpl* 3 **contour map** : mapa *m* topográfico
contraband [ˈkɑntrə₁bænd] *n* : contrabando *m*
contraception [₁kɑntrəˈsɛpʃən] *n* : anticoncepción *f*, contracepción *f*
contraceptive¹ [₁kɑntrəˈsɛptɪv] *adj* : anticonceptivo, contraceptivo
contraceptive² *n* : anticonceptivo *m*, contraceptivo *m*
contract¹ [kənˈtrækt, 1 *usu* ˈkɑn₁trækt] *vt* 1 : contratar (servicios profesionales) 2 : contraer (una enfermedad, una deuda) 3 TIGHTEN : contraer (un músculo) 4 SHORTEN : contraer (una palabra) — *vi* : contraerse, reducirse
contract² [ˈkɑn₁trækt] *n* : contrato *m*
contraction [kənˈtrækʃən] *n* : contracción *f*
contractor [ˈkɑn₁træktər, kənˈtræk-] *n* : contratista *mf*
contractual [kənˈtræktʃuəl] *adj* : contractual — **contractually** *adv*
contradict [₁kɑntrəˈdɪkt] *vt* : contradecir, desmentir
contradiction [₁kɑntrəˈdɪkʃən] *n* : contradicción *f*
contradictory [₁kɑntrəˈdɪktəri] *adj* : contradictorio
contralto [kənˈtræl₁to:] *n, pl* -**tos** : contralto *m* (voz), contralto *mf* (vocalista)
contraption [kənˈtræpʃən] *n* DEVICE : aparato *m*, artefacto *m*
contrary¹ [ˈkɑn₁trɛri, 2 *often* kənˈtrɛri] *adj* 1 OPPOSITE : contrario, opuesto 2 BALKY, STUBBORN : terco, testarudo 3 **contrary to** : al contrario de, en contra de ⟨contrary to the facts : en contra de los hechos⟩
contrary² [ˈkɑn₁trɛri] *n, pl* -**traries** 1 OPPOSITE : lo contrario, lo opuesto 2 **on the contrary** : al contrario, todo lo contrario

contrast¹ [kənˈtræst] *vi* DIFFER : contrastar, diferir — *vt* COMPARE : contrastar, comparar
contrast² [ˈkɑn₁træst] *n* : contraste *m*
contravene [₁kɑntrəˈviːn] *vt* -**vened; -vening** : contravenir, infringir
contribute [kənˈtrɪbjət] *v* -**uted; -uting** *vt* : contribuir, aportar (dinero, bienes, etc.) — *vi* : contribuir
contribution [₁kɑntrəˈbjuːʃən] *n* : contribución *f*
contributor [kənˈtrɪbjətər] *n* : contribuidor *m*, -dora *f*; colaborador *m*, -dora *f* (en periodismo)
contrite [ˈkɑn₁traɪt, kənˈtraɪt] *adj* REPENTANT : contrito, arrepentido
contrition [kənˈtrɪʃən] *n* : contrición *f*, arrepentimiento *m*
contrivance [kənˈtraɪvənts] *n* 1 DEVICE : aparato *m*, artefacto *m* 2 SCHEME : artimaña *f*, treta *f*, ardid *m*
contrive [kənˈtraɪv] *vt* -**trived; -triving** 1 DEVISE : idear, ingeniar, maquinar 2 MANAGE : lograr, ingeniárselas para ⟨she contrived a way out of the mess : se las ingenió para salir del enredo⟩
control¹ [kənˈtroːl] *vt* -**trolled; -trolling** : controlar, dominar
control² *n* 1 : control *m*, dominio *m*, mando *m* ⟨to be under control : estar bajo control⟩ 2 RESTRAINT : control *m*, limitación *f* ⟨birth control : control natal⟩ 3 : control *m*, dispositivo *m* de mando ⟨remote control : control remoto⟩
controllable [kənˈtroːləbəl] *adj* : controlable
controller [kənˈtroːlər, ˈkɑn₁-] *n* 1 → **comptroller** 2 : controlador *m*, -dora *f* ⟨air traffic controller : controlador aéreo⟩
controversial [₁kɑntrəˈvərʃəl, -siəl] *adj* : controvertido ⟨a controversial decision : una decisión controvertida⟩
controversy [ˈkɑntrə₁vərsi] *n, pl* -**sies** : controversia *f*
controvert [ˈkɑntrə₁vərt, ₁kɑntrəˈ-] *vt* : controvertir, contradecir
contusion [kənˈtuːʒən, -tjuː-] *n* BRUISE : contusión *f*, moretón *m*
conundrum [kəˈnʌndrəm] *n* RIDDLE : acertijo *m*, adivinanza *f*
convalesce [₁kɑnvəˈlɛs] *vi* -**lesced; -lescing** : convalecer
convalescence [₁kɑnvəˈlɛsənts] *n* : convalecencia *f*
convalescent¹ [₁kɑnvəˈlɛsənt] *adj* : convaleciente
convalescent² *n* : convaleciente *mf*
convection [kənˈvɛkʃən] *n* : convección *f*
convene [kənˈviːn] *v* -**vened; -vening** *vt* : convocar — *vi* : reunirse
convenience [kənˈviːnjənts] *n* 1 : conveniencia *f* ⟨at your convenience : cuando le resulte conveniente⟩ 2 AMENITY : comodidad *f* ⟨modern conveniences : comodidades modernas⟩

convenience store *n* : tienda *f* de conveniencia

convenient [kən'vi:njənt] *adj* : conveniente, cómodo — **conveniently** *adv*

convent ['kɑnvənt, -ˌvɛnt] *n* : convento *m*

convention [kən'vɛntʃən] *n* **1** PACT : convención *f*, convenio *m*, pacto *m* ⟨the Geneva Convention : la Convención de Ginebra⟩ **2** MEETING : convención *f*, congreso *m* **3** CUSTOM : convención *f*, convencionalismo *m*

conventional [kən'vɛntʃənəl] *adj* : convencional — **conventionally** *adv*

converge [kən'vərdʒ] *vi* **-verged; -verging** : converger, convergir

convergence [kən'vərdʒənts] *n* : convergencia *f*

convergent [kən'vərdʒənt] *adj* : convergente

conversant [kən'vərsənt] *adj* **conversant with** : versado con, experto en

conversation [ˌkɑnvər'seɪʃən] *n* : conversación *f*

conversational [ˌkɑnvər'seɪʃənəl] *adj* : familiar ⟨a conversational style : un estilo familiar⟩

converse¹ [kən'vərs] *vi* **-versed; -versing** : conversar

converse² [kən'vərs, 'kɑnˌvərs] *adj* : contrario, opuesto, inverso

conversely [kən'vərsli, 'kɑnˌvərs-] *adv* : a la inversa

conversion [kən'vərʒən] *n* **1** CHANGE : conversión *f*, transformación *f*, cambio *m* **2** : conversión *f* (a una religión)

convert¹ [kən'vərt] *vt* **1** : convertir (a una religión o un partido) **2** CHANGE : convertir, cambiar — *vi* : convertirse

convert² ['kɑnˌvərt] *n* : converso *m*, -sa *f*

converter *or* **convertor** [kən'vərtər] *n* : convertidor *m*

convertible¹ [kən'vərtəbəl] *adj* : convertible

convertible² *n* : convertible *m*, descapotable *m*

convex [kɑn'vɛks, 'kɑnˌ-, kən'-] *adj* : convexo

convey [kən'veɪ] *vt* **1** TRANSPORT : transportar, conducir **2** TRANSMIT : transmitir, comunicar, expresar (noticias, ideas, etc.)

conveyance [kən'veɪənts] *n* **1** TRANSPORT : transporte *m*, transportación *f* **2** COMMUNICATION : transmisión *f*, comunicación *f* **3** TRANSFER : transferencia *f*, traspaso *m* (de una propiedad)

conveyor [kən'veɪər] *n* : transportador *m*, -dora *f* ⟨conveyor belt : cinta transportadora⟩

convict¹ [kən'vɪkt] *vt* : declarar culpable

convict² ['kɑnˌvɪkt] *n* : preso *m*, -sa *f*; presidiario *m*, -ria *f*; recluso *m*, -sa *f*

conviction [kən'vɪkʃən] *n* **1** : condena *f* (de un acusado) **2** BELIEF : convicción *f*, creencia *f*

convince [kən'vɪnts] *vt* **-vinced; -vincing** : convencer

convincing [kən'vɪntsɪŋ] *adj* : convincente, persuasivo

convincingly [kən'vɪntsɪŋli] *adv* : de forma convincente

convivial [kən'vɪvjəl, -'vɪviəl] *adj* : jovial, festivo, alegre

conviviality [kənˌvɪvi'æləti] *n, pl* **-ties** : jovialidad *f*

convoke [kən'voːk] *vt* **-voked; -voking** : convocar

convoluted ['kɑnvəˌluːtəd] *adj* : intrincado, complicado

convoy ['kɑnˌvɔɪ] *n* : convoy *m*

convulse [kən'vʌls] *v* **-vulsed; -vulsing** *vt* : convulsionar ⟨convulsed with laughter : muerto de risa⟩ — *vi* : sufrir convulsiones

convulsion [kən'vʌlʃən] *n* : convulsión *f*

convulsive [kən'vʌlsɪv] *adj* : convulsivo — **convulsively** *adv*

coo¹ ['kuː] *vi* : arrullar

coo² *n* : arrullo *m* (de una paloma)

cook¹ ['kʊk] *vi* : cocinar — *vt* **1** : preparar (comida) **2 to cook up** CONCOCT : inventar, tramar

cook² *n* : cocinero *m*, -ra *f*

cookbook ['kʊkˌbʊk] *n* : libro *m* de cocina

cookery ['kʊkəri] *n, pl* **-eries** : cocina *f*

cookie *or* **cooky** ['kʊki] *n, pl* **-ies** : galleta *f* (dulce)

cooking ['kʊkɪŋ] *n* **1** COOKERY : cocina *f* **2** : cocción *f*, cocimiento *m* ⟨cooking time : tiempo de cocción⟩

cookout ['kʊkˌaʊt] *n* : comida *f* al aire libre

cool¹ ['kuːl] *vt* : refrescar, enfriar — *vi* **1** : refrescarse, enfriarse ⟨the pie is cooling : el pastel se está enfriando⟩ **2** : calmarse, tranquilizarse ⟨his anger cooled : su ira se calmó⟩

cool² *adj* **1** : fresco, frío ⟨cool weather : tiempo fresco⟩ **2** CALM : tranquilo, sereno **3** ALOOF : frío, distante

cool³ *n* **1** : fresco *m* ⟨the cool of the evening : el fresco de la tarde⟩ **2** COMPOSURE : calma *f*, serenidad *f*

coolant ['kuːlənt] *n* : refrigerante *m*

cooler ['kuːlər] *n* : nevera *f* portátil

coolie ['kuːli] *n* : culi *m*

coolly ['kuːlli] *adv* **1** CALMLY : con calma, tranquilamente **2** COLDLY : fríamente, con frialdad

coolness ['kuːlnəs] *n* **1** : frescura *f*, frescor *m* ⟨the coolness of the evening : el frescor de la noche⟩ **2** CALMNESS : tranquilidad *f*, serenidad *f* **3** COLDNESS, INDIFFERENCE : frialdad *f*, indiferencia *f*

coop¹ ['kuːp, 'kʊp] *vt or* **to coop up** : encerrar ⟨cooped up in the house : encerrado en la casa⟩

coop² *n* : gallinero *m*

co–op ['koːˌɑp] *n* → **cooperative²**

cooperate [ko'ɑpəˌreɪt] *vi* **-ated; -ating** : cooperar, colaborar

cooperation [ko͵apəˈreɪʃən] *n* : cooperación *f*, colaboración *f*
cooperative¹ [koˈapərətɪv, -ˈapə͵reɪtɪv] *adj* : cooperativo
cooperative² [koˈapərətɪv] *n* : cooperativa *f*
co–opt [koˈapt] *vt* **1** : nombrar como miembro, cooptar **2** APPROPRIATE : apropiarse de
coordinate¹ [koˈɔrdən͵eɪt] *v* **-nated; -nating** *vt* : coordinar — *vi* : coordinarse, combinar, acordar
coordinate² [koˈɔrdənət] *adj* **1** COORDINATED : coordinado **2** EQUAL : igual, semejante
coordinate³ [koˈɔrdənət] *n* : coordenada *f*
coordination [ko͵ɔrdənˈeɪʃən] *n* : coordinación *f*
coordinator [koˈɔrdən͵eɪtər] *n* : coordinador *m*, -dora *f*
cop [ˈkap] → **police officer**
cope [ˈkoːp] *vi* **coped; coping 1** : arreglárselas **2 to cope with** : hacer frente a, poder con ⟨I can't cope with all this! : ¡no puedo con todo esto!⟩
copier [ˈkapiər] *n* : copiadora *f*, fotocopiadora *f*
copilot [ˈkoː͵paɪlət] *n* : copiloto *m*
copious [ˈkoːpiəs] *adj* : copioso, abundante — **copiously** *adv*
copiousness [ˈkoːpiəsnəs] *n* : abundancia *f*
copper [ˈkapər] *n* : cobre *m*
coppery [ˈkapəri] *adj* : cobrizo
copra [ˈkoːprə, ˈka-] *n* : copra *f*
copse [ˈkaps] *n* THICKET : soto *m*, matorral *m*
copulate [ˈkapjə͵leɪt] *vi* **-lated; -lating** : copular
copulation [͵kapjəˈleɪʃən] *n* : cópula *f*, relaciones *fpl* sexuales
copy¹ [ˈkapi] *vt* **copied; copying 1** DUPLICATE : hacer una copia de, duplicar, reproducir **2** IMITATE : copiar, imitar
copy² *n*, *pl* **copies 1** : copia *f*, duplicado *m* (de un documento), reproducción *f* (de una obra de arte) **2** : ejemplar *m* (de un libro), número *m* (de una revista) **3** TEXT : manuscrito *m*, texto *m*
copyright¹ [ˈkapi͵raɪt] *vt* : registrar los derechos de
copyright² *n* : derechos *mpl* de autor
coral¹ [ˈkɔrəl] *adj* : de coral ⟨a coral reef : un arrecife de coral⟩
coral² *n* : coral *m*
coral snake *n* : serpiente *f* de coral
cord [ˈkɔrd] *n* **1** ROPE, STRING : cuerda *f*, cordón *m*, cordel *m* **2** : cuerda *f*, cordón *m*, médula *f* (en la anatomía) ⟨vocal cords : cuerdas vocales⟩ **3** : cuerda *f* ⟨a cord of firewood : una cuerda de leña⟩ **4** *or* **electric cord** : cable *m* eléctrico
cordial¹ [ˈkɔrdʒəl] *adj* : cordial — **cordially** *adv*
cordial² *n* : cordial *m*

cordiality [͵kɔrdʒiˈæləti] *n* : cordialidad *f*
cordless [ˈkɔrdləs] *adj* : inalámbrico
cordon¹ [ˈkɔrdən] *vt* **to cordon off** : acordonar
cordon² *n* : cordón *m*
corduroy [ˈkɔrdə͵rɔɪ] *n* **1** : pana *f* **2 corduroys** *npl* : pantalones *mpl* de pana
core¹ [ˈkor] *vt* **cored; coring** : quitar el corazón a (una fruta)
core² *n* **1** : corazón *m*, centro *m* (de algunas frutas) **2** CENTER : núcleo *m*, centro *m* **3** ESSENCE : núcleo *m*, meollo *m* ⟨to the core : hasta la médula⟩
coriander [ˈkori͵ændər] *n* : cilantro *m*
cork¹ [ˈkɔrk] *vt* : ponerle un corcho a
cork² *n* : corcho *m*
corkscrew [ˈkɔrk͵skruː] *n* : tirabuzón *m*, sacacorchos *m*
cormorant [ˈkɔrmərənt, -͵rænt] *n* : cormorán *m*
corn¹ [ˈkɔrn] *vt* : conservar en salmuera ⟨corned beef : carne en conserva⟩
corn² *n* **1** GRAIN : grano *m* **2** : maíz *m*, elote *m* *Mex* ⟨corn tortillas : tortillas de maíz⟩ **3** : callo *m* ⟨corn plaster : emplasto para callos⟩
corncob [ˈkɔrn͵kab] *n* : mazorca *f* (de maíz), choclo *m*, elote *m* *CA*, *Mex*
cornea [ˈkɔrniə] *n* : córnea *f*
corner¹ [ˈkɔrnər] *vt* **1** TRAP : acorralar, arrinconar **2** MONOPOLIZE : monopolizar, acaparar (un mercado) — *vi* : tomar una curva, doblar una esquina (en un automóvil)
corner² *n* **1** ANGLE : rincón *m*, esquina *f*, ángulo *m* ⟨the corner of a room : el rincón de una sala⟩ ⟨all corners of the world : todos los rincones del mundo⟩ ⟨to cut corners : atajar, economizar esfuerzos⟩ **2** INTERSECTION : esquina *f* **3** IMPASSE, PREDICAMENT : aprieto *m*, impasse *m* ⟨to be backed into a corner : estar acorralado⟩
cornerstone [ˈkɔrnər͵stoːn] *n* : piedra *f* angular
cornet [kɔrˈnɛt] *n* : corneta *f*
cornfield [ˈkɔrn͵fiːld] *n* : maizal *m*; milpa *f* *CA*, *Mex*
cornice [ˈkɔrnɪs] *n* : cornisa *f*
cornmeal [ˈkɔrn͵miːl] *n* : harina *f* de maíz
cornstalk [ˈkɔrn͵stɔk] *n* : tallo *m* del maíz
cornstarch [ˈkɔrn͵startʃ] *n* : maicena *f*, almidón *m* de maíz
cornucopia [͵kɔrnəˈkoːpiə, -njə-] *n* : cornucopia *f*
corolla [kəˈralə] *n* : corola *f*
corollary [ˈkɔrə͵lɛri] *n*, *pl* **-laries** : corolario *m*
corona [kəˈroːnə] *n* : corona *f* (del sol)
coronary¹ [ˈkɔrə͵nɛri] *adj* : coronario
coronary² *n*, *pl* **-naries 1** : trombosis *f* coronaria **2** HEART ATTACK : infarto *m*, ataque *m* al corazón
coronation [͵kɔrəˈneɪʃən] *n* : coronación *f*

coroner [ˈkɔrənər] *n* : médico *m* forense

corporal[1] [ˈkɔrpərəl] *adj* : corporal ⟨corporal punishment : castigos corporales⟩

corporal[2] *n* : cabo *m*

corporate [ˈkɔrpərət] *adj* : corporativo, empresarial

corporation [ˌkɔrpəˈreɪʃən] *n* : sociedad *f* anónima, corporación *f*, empresa *f*

corporeal [kɔrˈporiəl] *adj* **1** PHYSICAL : corpóreo **2** MATERIAL : material, tangible — **corporeally** *adv*

corps [ˈkor] *n*, *pl* **corps** [ˈkorz] : cuerpo *m* ⟨medical corps : cuerpo médico⟩ ⟨diplomatic corps : cuerpo diplomático⟩

corpse [ˈkɔrps] *n* : cadáver *m*

corpulence [ˈkɔrpjələnts] *n* : obesidad *f*, gordura *f*

corpulent [ˈkɔrpjələnt] *adj* : obeso, gordo

corpuscle [ˈkɔrˌpʌsəl] *n* : corpúsculo *m*, glóbulo *m* (sanguíneo)

corral[1] [kəˈræl] *vt* **-ralled; -ralling** : acorralar, encorralar (ganado)

corral[2] *n* : corral *m*

correct[1] [kəˈrɛkt] *vt* **1** RECTIFY : corregir, rectificar **2** REPRIMAND : corregir, reprender

correct[2] *adj* **1** ACCURATE, RIGHT : correcto, exacto ⟨to be correct : estar en lo cierto⟩ **2** PROPER : correcto, apropiado

correction [kəˈrɛkʃən] *n* : corrección *f*

corrective [kəˈrɛktɪv] *adj* : correctivo

correctly [kəˈrɛktli] *adv* : correctamente

correctness [kəˈrɛkt(t)nəs] *n* **1** ACCURACY : exactitud *f* **2** PROPRIETY : corrección *f*

correlate [ˈkɔrəˌleɪt] *vt* **-lated; -lating** : relacionar, poner en correlación

correlation [ˌkɔrəˈleɪʃən] *n* : correlación *f*

correspond [ˌkɔrəˈspand] *vi* **1** MATCH : corresponder, concordar, coincidir **2** WRITE : corresponderse, escribirse

correspondence [ˌkɔrəˈspandənts] *n* : correspondencia *f*

correspondent [ˌkɔrəˈspandənt] *n* : corresponsal *mf*

corresponding [kɔrəˈspandɪŋ, kɑr-] *adj* : correspondiente

correspondingly [ˌkɔrəˈspandɪŋli] *adv* : en consecuencia, de la misma manera

corridor [ˈkɔrədər, -ˌdɔr] *n* : corredor *m*, pasillo *m*

corroborate [kəˈrabəˌreɪt] *vt* **-rated; -rating** : corroborar

corroboration [kəˌrabəˈreɪʃən] *n* : corroboración *f*

corrode [kəˈroːd] *v* **-roded; -roding** *vt* : corroer — *vi* : corroerse

corrosion [kəˈroːʒən] *n* : corrosión *f*

corrosive [kəˈroːsɪv] *adj* : corrosivo

corrugate [ˈkɔrəˌgeɪt] *vt* **-gated; -gating** : ondular, acanalar, corrugar

corrugated [ˈkɔrəˌgeɪtəd] *adj* : ondulado, acanalado ⟨corrugated cardboard : cartón ondulado⟩

corrupt[1] [kəˈrʌpt] *vt* **1** PERVERT : corromper, pervertir, degradar (información) **2** BRIBE : sobornar

corrupt[2] *adj* : corrupto, corrompido

corruptible [kəˈrʌptəbəl] *adj* : corruptible

corruption [kəˈrʌpʃən] *n* : corrupción *f*

corsage [kɔrˈsaʒ, -ˈsaʤ] *n* : ramillete *m* que se lleva como adorno

corset [ˈkɔrsət] *n* : corsé *m*

cortex [ˈkɔrˌtɛks] *n*, *pl* **-tices** [ˈkɔrtəˌsiːz] *or* **-texes** : corteza *f* ⟨cerebral cortex : corteza cerebral⟩

cortisone [ˈkɔrtəˌsoːn, -zoːn] *n* : cortisona *f*

cosmetic[1] [kazˈmɛtɪk] *adj* : cosmético

cosmetic[2] *n* : cosmético *m*

cosmic [ˈkazmɪk] *adj* **1** : cósmico ⟨cosmic ray : rayo cósmico⟩ **2** VAST : grandioso, inmenso, vasto

cosmonaut [ˈkazməˌnɔt] *n* : cosmonauta *mf*

cosmopolitan[1] [ˌkazməˈpalətən] *adj* : cosmopolita

cosmopolitan[2] *n* : cosmopolita *mf*

cosmos [ˈkazməs, -ˌmoːs, -ˌmas] *n* : cosmos *m*, universo *m*

cost[1] [ˈkɔst] *v* **cost; costing** *vt* : costar ⟨how much does it cost? : ¿cuánto cuesta?, ¿cuánto vale?⟩ — *vi* : costar ⟨these cost more : éstos cuestan más⟩

cost[2] *n* : costo *m*, precio *m*, coste *m* ⟨cost of living : costo de vida⟩ ⟨victory at all costs : victoria a toda costa⟩

Costa Rican[1] [ˌkɔstəˈriːkən] *adj* : costarricense

Costa Rican[2] *n* : costarricense *mf*

costly [ˈkɔstli] *adj* : costoso, caro

costume [ˈkɑsˌtuːm, -ˌtjuːm] *n* **1** : traje *m* ⟨national costume : traje típico⟩ **2** : disfraz *m* ⟨costume party : fiesta de disfraces⟩ **3** OUTFIT : vestimenta *f*, traje *m*, conjunto *m*

cosy [ˈkoːzi] → **cozy**

cot [ˈkat] *n* : catre *m*

coterie [ˈkoːtəˌri, ˌkoːtəˈ-] *n* : tertulia *f*, círculo *m* (social)

cottage [ˈkɑtɪʤ] *n* : casita *f* (de campo)

cottage cheese *n* : requesón *m*

cotton [ˈkatən] *n* : algodón *m*

cottonmouth [ˈkatənˌmaʊθ] → **moccasin**

cottonseed [ˈkatənˌsiːd] *n* : semilla *f* de algodón

cotton swab → **swab**

cottontail [ˈkatənˌteɪl] *n* : conejo *m* de cola blanca

couch[1] [ˈkaʊʧ] *vt* : expresar, formular ⟨couched in strong language : expresado en lenguaje enérgico⟩

couch[2] *n* SOFA : sofá *m*

couch potato *n* : haragán *m*, -gana *f*; vago *m*, -ga *f*

cougar [ˈkuːgər] *n* : puma *m*

cough[1] [ˈkɔf] *vi* : toser

cough[2] *n* : tos *f*

could ['kʊd] → **can**

council ['kaʊn*t*səl] *n* **1** : concejo *m* ⟨city council : concejo municipal, ayuntamiento⟩ **2** MEETING : concejo *m*, junta *f* **3** BOARD : consejo *m* **4** : concilio *m* (eclesiástico)

councillor *or* **councilor** ['kaʊn*t*sələr] *n* : concejal *m*, -jala *f*

councilman ['kaʊn*t*səlmən] *n*, *pl* **-men** [-mən, -ˌmɛn] : concejal *m*

councilwoman ['kaʊn*t*səlˌwʊmən] *n*, *pl* **-women** [-ˌwɪmən] : concejala *f*

counsel[1] ['kaʊn*t*səl] *v* **-seled** *or* **-selled; -seling** *or* **-selling** *vt* ADVISE : aconsejar, asesorar, recomendar — *vi* CONSULT : consultar

counsel[2] *n* **1** ADVICE : consejo *m*, recomendación *f* **2** CONSULTATION : consulta *f* **3** **counsel** *ns & pl* LAWYER : abogado *m*, -da *f*

counselor *or* **counsellor** ['kaʊn*t*sələr] *n* : consejero *m*, -ra *f*; consultor *m*, -tora *f*; asesor *m*, -sora *f*

count[1] ['kaʊnt] *vt* : contar, enumerar — *vi* **1** : contar ⟨to count out loud : contar en voz alta⟩ **2** MATTER : contar, valer, importar ⟨that's what counts : eso es lo que cuenta⟩ **3** **to count on** : contar con

count[2] *n* **1** COMPUTATION : cómputo *m*, recuento *m*, cuenta *f* ⟨to lose count : perder la cuenta⟩ **2** CHARGE : cargo *m* ⟨two counts of robbery : dos cargos de robo⟩ **3** : conde *m* (noble)

countable ['kaʊntəbəl] *adj* : numerable

countdown ['kaʊntˌdaʊn] *n* : cuenta *f* atrás

countenance[1] ['kaʊntənən*t*s] *vt* **-nanced; -nancing** : permitir, tolerar

countenance[2] *n* FACE : semblante *m*, rostro *m*

counter[1] ['kaʊntər] *vt* **1** → **counteract** **2** OPPOSE : oponerse a, resistir — *vi* RETALIATE : responder, contraatacar

counter[2] *adv* **counter to** : contrario a, en contra de

counter[3] *adj* : contrario, opuesto

counter[4] *n* **1** PIECE : ficha *f* (de un juego) **2** : mostrador *m* (de un negocio), ventanilla *f* (en un banco) **3** : contador *m* (aparato) **4** COUNTERBALANCE : fuerza *f* opuesta, contrapeso *m*

counteract [ˌkaʊntərˈækt] *vt* : contrarrestar

counterattack ['kaʊntərəˌtæk] *n* : contraataque *m*

counterbalance[1] [ˌkaʊntərˈbælən*t*s] *vt* **-anced; -ancing** : contrapesar

counterbalance[2] ['kaʊntərˌbælən*t*s] *n* : contrapeso *m*

counterclockwise [ˌkaʊntərˈklɑkˌwaɪz] *adv & adj* : en el sentido opuesto al de las manecillas del reloj

counterfeit[1] ['kaʊntərˌfɪt] *vt* **1** : falsificar (dinero) **2** PRETEND : fingir, aparentar

counterfeit[2] *adj* : falso, inauténtico

counterfeit[3] *n* : falsificación *f*

counterfeiter ['kaʊntərˌfɪtər] *n* : falsificador *m*, -dora *f*

countermand ['kaʊntərˌmænd, ˌkaʊntər'-] *vt* : contramandar

countermeasure ['kaʊntərˌmɛʒər] *n* : contramedida *f*

counterpart ['kaʊntərˌpɑrt] *n* : homólogo *m*, contraparte *f Mex*

counterpoint ['kaʊntərˌpɔɪnt] *n* : contrapunto *m*

counterproductive [ˌkaʊntərprəˈdʌktɪv] *adj* : contraproducente

counterrevolution [ˌkaʊntərˌrɛvəˈluːʃən] *n* : contrarrevolución *f*

counterrevolutionary[1] [ˌkaʊntərˌrɛvəˈluːʃənˌɛri] *adj* : contrarrevolucionario

counterrevolutionary[2] *n*, *pl* **-ries** : contrarrevolucionario *m*, -ria *f*

countersign ['kaʊntərˌsaɪn] *n* : contraseña *f*

countess ['kaʊntɪs] *n* : condesa *f*

countless ['kaʊntləs] *adj* : incontable, innumerable

country[1] ['kʌntri] *adj* : campestre, rural

country[2] *n*, *pl* **-tries** **1** NATION : país *m*, nación *f*, patria *f* ⟨country of origin : país de origen⟩ ⟨love of one's country : amor a la patria⟩ **2** : campo *m* ⟨they left the city for the country : se fueron de la ciudad al campo⟩

countryman ['kʌntrimən] *n*, *pl* **-men** [-mən, -ˌmɛn] : compatriota *mf*; paisano *m*, -na *f*

countryside ['kʌntriˌsaɪd] *n* : campo *m*, campiña *f*

county ['kaʊnti] *n*, *pl* **-ties** : condado *m*

coup ['kuː] *n*, *pl* **coups** ['kuːz] **1** : golpe *m* maestro **2** *or* **coup d'etat** : golpe *m* (de estado), cuartelazo *m*

coupe ['kuːp] *n* : cupé *m*

couple[1] ['kʌpəl] *vt* **-pled; -pling** : acoplar, enganchar, conectar

couple[2] *n* **1** PAIR : par *m* ⟨a couple of hours : un par de horas, unas dos horas⟩ **2** : pareja *f* ⟨a young couple : una pareja joven⟩

coupling ['kʌplɪŋ] *n* : acoplamiento *m*

coupon ['kuːˌpɑn, 'kjuː-] *n* : cupón *m*

courage ['kərɪdʒ] *n* : valor *m*, valentía *f*, coraje *m*

courageous [kəˈreɪdʒəs] *adj* : valiente, valeroso

courier ['kʊriər, 'kəriər] *n* : mensajero *m*, -ra *f*

course[1] ['kors] *vi* **coursed; coursing** : correr (a toda velocidad)

course[2] *n* **1** PROGRESS : curso *m*, transcurso *m* ⟨to run its course : seguir su curso⟩ **2** DIRECTION : rumbo *m* (de un avión), derrota *f*, derrotero *m* (de un barco) **3** PATH, WAY : camino *m*, vía *f* ⟨course of action : línea de conducta⟩ **4** : plato *m* (de una cena) ⟨the main course : el plato principal⟩ **5** : curso *m* (académico) **6** **of course** : desde luego, por supuesto ⟨yes, of course! : ¡claro que sí!⟩

court¹ ['kort] *vt* woo : cortejar, galantear
court² *n* **1** PALACE : palacio *m* **2** RETINUE : corte *f*, séquito *m* **3** COURTYARD : patio *m* **4** : cancha *f* (de tenis, baloncesto, etc.) **5** TRIBUNAL : corte *f*, tribunal *m* ⟨the Supreme Court : la Corte Suprema⟩
courteous ['kərṭiəs] *adj* : cortés, atento, educado — **courteously** *adv*
courtesan ['korṭəzən, 'kər-] *n* : cortesana *f*
courtesy ['kərṭəsi] *n, pl* -sies : cortesía *f*
courthouse ['kort,haus] *n* : palacio *m* de justicia, juzgado *m*
courtier ['korṭiər, 'kortjər] *n* : cortesano *m*, -na *f*
courtly ['kortli] *adj* -lier; -est : distinguido, elegante, cortés
court–martial¹ ['kort,marʃəl] *vt* : someter a consejo de guerra
court–martial² *n, pl* **courts–martial** ['korts,marʃəl] : consejo *m* de guerra
court order *n* : mandamiento *m* judicial
courtroom ['kort,ru:m] *n* : tribunal *m*, corte *f*
courtship ['kort,ʃɪp] *n* : cortejo *m*, noviazgo *m*
courtyard ['kort,jard] *n* : patio *m*
cousin ['kʌzən] *n* : primo *m*, -ma *f*
couture [ku:'tur] *n* : industria *f* de la moda ⟨haute couture : alta costura⟩
cove ['ko:v] *n* : ensenada *f*, cala *f*
covenant ['kʌvənənt] *n* : pacto *m*, contrato *m*
cover¹ ['kʌvər] *vt* **1** : cubrir, tapar ⟨cover your head : tápate la cabeza⟩ ⟨covered with mud : cubierto de lodo⟩ **2** HIDE, PROTECT : encubrir, proteger **3** TREAT : tratar **4** INSURE : asegurar, cubrir
cover² *n* **1** SHELTER : cubierta *f*, abrigo *m*, refugio *m* ⟨to take cover : ponerse a cubierto⟩ ⟨under cover of darkness : al amparo de la oscuridad⟩ **2** LID, TOP : cubierta *f*, tapa *f* **3** : cubierta *f* (de un libro), portada *f* (de una revista) **4** covers *npl* BEDCLOTHES : ropa *f* de cama, cobijas *fpl*, mantas *fpl*
coverage ['kʌvərɪdʒ] *n* : cobertura *f*
coverlet ['kʌvərlət] *n* : cobertor *m*
covert¹ ['ko:,vərt, 'kʌvərt] *adj* : encubierto, secreto ⟨covert operations : operaciones encubiertas⟩
covert² ['kʌvərt, 'ko:-] *n* THICKET : espesura *f*, maleza *f*
cover–up ['kʌvər,ʌp] *n* : encubrimiento *m* (de algo ilícito)
covet ['kʌvət] *vt* : codiciar
covetous ['kʌvəṭəs] *adj* : codicioso
covey ['kʌvi] *n, pl* -eys **1** : bandada *f* pequeña (de codornices, etc.) **2** GROUP : grupo *m*
cow¹ ['kau] *vt* : intimidar, acobardar
cow² *n* : vaca *f*, hembra *f* (de ciertas especies)
coward ['kauərd] *n* : cobarde *mf*

cowardice ['kauərdɪs] *n* : cobardía *f*
cowardly ['kauərdli] *adj* : cobarde
cowboy ['kau,bɔɪ] *n* : vaquero *m*, cowboy *m*
cower ['kauər] *vi* : encogerse (de miedo), acobardarse
cowgirl ['kau,gərl] *n* : vaquera *f*
cowherd ['kau,hərd] *n* : vaquero *m*, -ra *f*
cowhide ['kau,haid] *n* : cuero *m*, piel *f* de vaca
cowl ['kaul] *n* : capucha *f* (de un monje)
cowlick ['kau,lɪk] *n* : remolino *m*
cowpuncher ['kau,pʌntʃər] → **cowboy**
cowslip ['kau,slɪp] *n* : prímula *f*, primavera *f*
coxswain ['kaksən, -,sweɪn] *n* : timonel *m*
coy ['kɔɪ] *adj* **1** SHY : tímido, cohibido **2** COQUETTISH : coqueto
coyote [kaɪ'o:ṭi, 'kaɪ,o:t] *n, pl* **coyotes** *or* **coyote** : coyote *m*
cozy ['ko:zi] *adj* -zier; -est : acogedor, cómodo
CPU [,si:,pi:'ju:] *n* (central processing unit) : CPU *f*
crab ['kræb] *n* : cangrejo *m*, jaiba *f*
crabby ['kræbi] *adj* -bier; -est : gruñón, malhumorado
crabgrass ['kræb,græs] *n* : garranchuelo *m*
crack¹ ['kræk] *vi* **1** : chasquear, restallar ⟨the whip cracked : el látigo restalló⟩ **2** SPLIT : rajarse, resquebrajarse, agrietarse **3** : quebrarse (dícese de la voz) — *vt* **1** : restallar, chasquear (un látigo, etc.) **2** SPLIT : rajar, agrietar, resquebrajar **3** BREAK : romper (un huevo), cascar (nueces), forzar (una caja fuerte) **4** SOLVE : resolver, descifrar (un código)
crack² *adj* FIRST-RATE : buenísimo, de primera
crack³ *n* **1** : chasquido *m*, restallido *m*, estallido *m* (de un arma de fuego), crujido *m* (de huesos) ⟨a crack of thunder : un trueno⟩ **2** WISECRACK : chiste *m*, ocurrencia *f*, salida *f* **3** CREVICE : raja *f*, grieta *f*, fisura *f* **4** BLOW : golpe *m* **5** ATTEMPT : intento *m*
crackdown ['kræk,daun] *n* : medidas *fpl* enérgicas
crack down *vt* : tomar medidas enérgicas
cracker ['krækər] *n* : galleta *f* (de soda, etc.)
crackle¹ ['krækəl] *vi* -led; -ling : crepitar, chisporrotear
crackle² *n* : crujido *m*, chisporroteo *m*
crackpot ['kræk,pat] *n* : excéntrico *m*, -ca *f*; chiflado *m*, -da *f*
crack–up ['kræk,ʌp] *n* **1** CRASH : choque *m*, estrellamiento *m* **2** BREAKDOWN : crisis *f* nerviosa
crack up *vt* **1** : estrellar (un vehículo) **2** : hacer reír **3** : elogiar ⟨it isn't all that it's cracked up to be : no es tan bueno como se dice⟩ — *vi* **1** : estrellarse **2** LAUGH : echarse a reír

cradle¹ [ˈkreɪdəl] *vt* **-dled; -dling** : acunar, mecer (a un niño)

cradle² *n* : cuna *f*

craft [ˈkræft] *n* **1** TRADE : oficio *m* ⟨the craft of carpentry : el oficio de carpintero⟩ **2** CRAFTSMANSHIP, SKILL : arte *m*, artesanía *f*, destreza *f* **3** CRAFTINESS : astucia *f*, maña *f* **4** *pl usually* **craft** BOAT : barco *m*, embarcación *f* **5** *pl usually* **craft** AIRCRAFT : avión *m*, aeronave *f*

craftiness [ˈkræftinəs] *n* : astucia *f*, maña *f*

craftsman [ˈkræftsmən] *n, pl* **-men** [-mən, -ˌmɛn] : artesano *m*, -na *f*

craftsmanship [ˈkræftsmənˌʃɪp] *n* : artesanía *f*, destreza *f*

crafty [ˈkræfti] *adj* **craftier; -est** : astuto, taimado

crag [ˈkræg] *n* : peñasco *m*

craggy [ˈkrægi] *adj* **-gier; -est** : peñascoso

cram [ˈkræm] *v* **crammed; cramming** *vt* **1** JAM : embutir, meter **2** STUFF : atiborrar, abarrotar ⟨crammed with people : atiborrado de gente⟩ — *vi* : estudiar a última hora, memorizar (para un examen)

cramp¹ [ˈkræmp] *vt* **1** : dar calambre en **2** RESTRICT : limitar, restringir, entorpecer ⟨to cramp someone's style : cortarle el vuelo a alguien⟩ — *vi or* **to cramp up** : acalambrarse

cramp² *n* **1** SPASM : calambre *m*, espasmo *m* (de los músculos) **2 cramps** *npl* : retorcijones *mpl* ⟨stomach cramps : retorcijones de estómago⟩

cranberry [ˈkrænˌbɛri] *n, pl* **-berries** : arándano *m* (rojo y agrio)

crane¹ [ˈkreɪn] *vt* **craned; craning** : estirar ⟨to crane one's neck : estirar el cuello⟩

crane² *n* **1** : grulla *f* (ave) **2** : grúa *f* (máquina)

cranial [ˈkreɪniəl] *adj* : craneal, craneano

cranium [ˈkreɪniəm] *n, pl* **-niums** *or* **-nia** [-niə] : cráneo *m*

crank¹ [ˈkræŋk] *vt or* **to crank up** : arrancar (con una manivela)

crank² *n* **1** : manivela *f*, manubrio *m* **2** ECCENTRIC : excéntrico *m*, -ca *f*

cranky [ˈkræŋki] *adj* **crankier; -est** : irritable, malhumorado, enojadizo

cranny [ˈkræni] *n, pl* **-nies** : grieta *f* ⟨every nook and cranny : todos los rincones⟩

crash¹ [ˈkræʃ] *vi* **1** SMASH : caerse con estrépito, estrellarse **2** COLLIDE : estrellarse, chocar **3** BOOM, RESOUND : retumbar, resonar — *vt* **1** SMASH : estrellar **2 to crash a party** : colarse en una fiesta **3 to crash one's car** : tener un accidente

crash² *n* **1** DIN : estrépito *m* **2** COLLISION : choque *m*, colisión *f* ⟨car crash : accidente automovilístico⟩ **3** FAILURE : quiebra *f* (de un negocio), crac *m* (de la bolsa)

crass [ˈkræs] *adj* : grosero, de mal gusto

crate¹ [ˈkreɪt] *vt* **crated; crating** : empacar en un cajón

crate² *n* : cajón *m* (de madera)

crater [ˈkreɪtər] *n* : cráter *m*

cravat [krəˈvæt] *n* : corbata *f*

crave [ˈkreɪv] *vt* **craved; craving** : ansiar, apetecer, tener muchas ganas de

craven [ˈkreɪvən] *adj* : cobarde, pusilánime

craving [ˈkreɪvɪŋ] *n* : ansia *f*, antojo *m*, deseo *m*

crawfish [ˈkrɔˌfɪʃ] → **crayfish**

crawl¹ [ˈkrɔl] *vi* **1** CREEP : arrastrarse, gatear (dícese de un bebé) **2** TEEM : estar plagado

crawl² *n* : paso *m* lento

crayfish [ˈkreɪˌfɪʃ] *n* **1** : ástaco *m* (de agua dulce) **2** : langostino *m* (de mar)

crayon [ˈkreɪˌɑn, -ən] *n* : crayón *m*

craze [ˈkreɪz] *n* : moda *f* pasajera, manía *f*

crazed [ˈkreɪzd] *adj* : enloquecido

crazily [ˈkreɪzəli] *adv* : locamente, erráticamente, insensatamente

craziness [ˈkreɪzinəs] *n* : locura *f*, demencia *f*

crazy [ˈkreɪzi] *adj* **-zier; -est 1** INSANE : loco, demente ⟨to go crazy : volverse loco⟩ **2** ABSURD, FOOLISH : loco, insensato, absurdo **3 like crazy** : como loco **4 to be crazy about** : estar loco por

creak¹ [ˈkriːk] *vi* : chirriar, rechinar, crujir

creak² *n* : chirrido *m*, crujido *m*

creaky [ˈkriːki] *adj* **creakier; -est** : chirriante, que cruje

cream¹ [ˈkriːm] *vt* **1** BEAT, MIX : batir, mezclar (azúcar y mantequilla, etc.) **2** : preparar (alimentos) con crema

cream² *n* **1** : crema *f* (de leche) **2** LOTION : crema *f*, loción *f* **3** ELITE : crema *f*, elite *f* ⟨the cream of the crop : la crema y nata, lo mejor⟩

creamery [ˈkriːməri] *n, pl* **-eries** : fábrica *f* de productos lácteos

creamy [ˈkriːmi] *adj* **creamier; -est** : cremoso

crease¹ [ˈkriːs] *vt* **creased; creasing 1** : plegar, poner una raya en (pantalones) **2** WRINKLE : arrugar

crease² *n* : pliegue *m*, doblez *m*, raya *f* (de pantalones)

create [kriˈeɪt] *vt* **-ated; -ating** : crear, hacer

creation [kriˈeɪʃən] *n* : creación *f*

creative [kriˈeɪtɪv] *adj* : creativo, original ⟨creative people : personas creativas⟩ ⟨a creative work : un obra original⟩

creatively [kriˈeɪtɪvli] *adv* : creativamente, con originalidad

creativity [ˌkriːeɪˈtɪvəti] *n* : creatividad *f*

creator [kriˈeɪtər] *n* : creador *m*, -dora *f*

creature [ˈkriːtʃər] *n* : ser *m* viviente, criatura *f*, animal *m*

credence ['kri:dənts] *n* : crédito *m*
credentials [krɪ'dɛnt∫əlz] *npl* : referencias *fpl* oficiales, cartas *fpl* credenciales
credibility [ˌkrɛdə'bɪləti] *n* : credibilidad *f*
credible ['krɛdəbəl] *adj* : creíble
credit[1] ['krɛdɪt] *vt* **1** BELIEVE : creer, dar crédito a **2** : ingresar, abonar ⟨to credit $100 to an account : ingresar $100 en (una) cuenta⟩ **3** ATTRIBUTE : atribuir ⟨they credit the invention to him : a él se le atribuye el invento⟩
credit[2] *n* **1** : saldo *m* positivo, saldo *m* a favor (de una cuenta) **2** : crédito *m* ⟨to buy on credit : comprar a crédito⟩ ⟨credit card : tarjeta de crédito⟩ **3** CREDENCE : crédito *m* ⟨I gave credit to everything he said : di crédito a todo lo que dijo⟩ **4** RECOGNITION : reconocimiento *m* **5** : orgullo *m*, honor *m* ⟨she's a credit to the school : ella es el orgullo de la escuela⟩
creditable ['krɛdɪtəbəl] *adj* : encomiable, loable — **creditably** [-bli] *adv*
credit card *n* : tarjeta de crédito
creditor ['krɛdɪtər] *n* : acreedor *m*, -dora *f*
credo ['kri:do:, 'kreɪ-] *n* : credo *m*
credulity [krɪ'du:ləti, -'dju:-] *n* : credulidad *f*
credulous ['krɛdʒələs] *adj* : crédulo
creed ['kri:d] *n* : credo *m*
creek ['kri:k, 'krɪk] *n* : arroyo *m*, riachuelo *m*
creel ['kri:l] *n* : nasa *f*, cesta *f* (de pescador)
creep[1] ['kri:p] *vi* **crept** ['krɛpt]; **creeping 1** CRAWL : arrastrarse, gatear **2** : moverse lentamente o sigilosamente ⟨he crept out of the house : salió sigilosamente de la casa⟩ **3** SPREAD : trepar (dícese de una planta)
creep[2] *n* **1** CRAWL : paso *m* lento **2** : asqueroso *m*, -sa *f* **3 creeps** *npl* : escalofríos *mpl* ⟨that gives me the creeps : eso me da escalofríos⟩
creeper ['kri:pər] *n* : planta *f* trepadora, trepadora *f*
creepy ['kri:pi] *adj* **1** SPOOKY : espeluznante **2** UNPLEASANT : asqueroso
cremate ['kri:ˌmeɪt] *vt* **-mated; -mating** : cremar
cremation [krɪ'meɪʃən] *n* : cremación *f*
Creole ['kri:ˌo:l] *n* **1** : criollo *m*, criolla *f* **2** : criollo *m* (idioma) — **Creole** *adj*
creosote ['kri:əˌso:t] *n* : creosota *f*
crepe *or* **crêpe** ['kreɪp] *n* **1** : crespón *m* (tela) **2** PANCAKE : crepe *mf*, crepa *f* Mex
crescendo [krɪ'ʃɛnˌdo:] *n, pl* **-dos** *or* **-does** : crescendo *m*
crescent ['krɛsənt] *n* : creciente *m*
crest ['krɛst] *n* **1** : cresta *f*, penacho *m* (de un ave) **2** PEAK, TOP : cresta *f* (de una ola), cima *f* (de una colina) **3** : emblema *m* (sobre un escudo de armas)
crestfallen ['krɛstˌfɔlən] *adj* : alicaído, abatido

cretin ['kri:tən] *n* : cretino *m*, -na *f*
crevasse [krɪ'væs] *n* : grieta *f*, fisura *f*
crevice ['krɛvɪs] *n* : grieta *f*, hendidura *f*
crew ['kru:] *n* **1** : tripulación *f* (de una nave) **2** TEAM : equipo *m* (de trabajadores o atletas)
crib ['krɪb] *n* **1** MANGER : pesebre *m* **2** GRANARY : granero *m* **3** : cuna *f* (de un bebé)
crick ['krɪk] *n* : calambre *m*, espasmo *m* muscular
cricket ['krɪkət] *n* **1** : grillo *m* (insecto) **2** : críquet *m* (juego)
crime ['kraɪm] *n* **1** : crimen *m*, delito *m* ⟨to commit a crime : cometer un delito⟩ **2** : crimen *m*, delincuencia *f* ⟨organized crime : crimen organizado⟩
criminal[1] ['krɪmənəl] *adj* : criminal
criminal[2] *n* : criminal *mf*, delincuente *mf*
crimp ['krɪmp] *vt* : ondular, rizar (el pelo), arrugar (una tela, etc.)
crimson ['krɪmzən] *n* : carmesí *m*
cringe ['krɪndʒ] *vi* **cringed; cringing** : encogerse
crinkle[1] ['krɪŋkəl] *v* **-kled; -kling** *vt* : arrugar — *vi* : arrugarse
crinkle[2] *n* : arruga *f*
crinkly ['krɪŋkəli] *adj* : arrugado
cripple[1] ['krɪpəl] *vt* **-pled; -pling 1** DISABLE : lisiar, dejar inválido **2** INCAPACITATE : inutilizar, incapacitar
cripple[2] *n* : lisiado *m*, -da *f*
crisis ['kraɪsɪs] *n, pl* **crises** [-ˌsi:z] : crisis *f*
crisp[1] ['krɪsp] *vt* : tostar, hacer crujiente
crisp[2] *adj* **1** CRUNCHY : crujiente, crocante **2** FIRM, FRESH : firme, fresco ⟨crisp lettuce : lechuga fresca⟩ **3** LIVELY : vivaz, alegre ⟨a crisp tempo : un ritmo alegre⟩ **4** INVIGORATING : fresco, vigorizante ⟨the crisp autumn air : el fresco aire otoñal⟩ — **crisply** *adv*
crisp[3] *n* : postre *m* de fruta (con pedacitos de masa dulce por encima)
crispy ['krɪspi] *adj* **crispier; -est** : crujiente ⟨crispy potato chips : papitas crujientes⟩
crisscross ['krɪsˌkrɔs] *vt* : entrecruzar
criterion [kraɪ'tɪriən] *n, pl* **-ria** [-ɪə] : criterio *m*
critic ['krɪtɪk] *n* **1** : crítico *m*, -ca *f* (de las artes) **2** FAULTFINDER : detractor *m*, -tora *f*; criticón *m*, -cona *f*
critical ['krɪtɪkəl] *adj* : crítico
critically ['krɪtɪkli] *adv* : críticamente ⟨critically ill : gravemente enfermo⟩
criticism ['krɪtəˌsɪzəm] *n* : crítica *f*
criticize ['krɪtəˌsaɪz] *vt* **-cized; -cizing 1** EVALUATE, JUDGE : criticar, analizar, evaluar **2** CENSURE : criticar, reprobar
critique [krɪ'ti:k] *n* : crítica *f*, evaluación *f*
croak[1] ['kro:k] *vi* : croar
croak[2] *n* : croar *m*, canto *m* (de la rana)
Croatian [kro'eɪʃən] *n* : croata *mf* — **Croatian** *adj*

crochet¹ [kro:ˈʃeɪ] *v* : tejer al croché
crochet² *n* : croché *m*, crochet *m*
crock [ˈkrɑk] *n* : vasija *f* de barro
crockery [ˈkrɑkəri] *n* : vajilla *f* (de barro)
crocodile [ˈkrɑkəˌdaɪl] *n* : cocodrilo *m*
crocus [ˈkroːkəs] *n*, *pl* **-cuses** : azafrán *m*
croissant [krəˈsɑnt] *n* : croissant *m*
crone [ˈkroːn] *n* : vieja *f* arpía, vieja *f* bruja
crony [ˈkroːni] *n*, *pl* **-nies** : amigote *m fam*; compinche *mf fam*
crook¹ [ˈkrʊk] *vt* : doblar (el brazo o el dedo)
crook² *n* **1** STAFF : cayado *m* (de pastor), báculo *m* (de obispo) **2** THIEF : ratero *m*, -ra *f*; ladrón *m*, -drona *f*
crooked [ˈkrʊkəd] *adj* **1** BENT : chueco, torcido **2** DISHONEST : deshonesto
crookedness [ˈkrʊkədnəs] *n* **1** : lo torcido, lo chueco **2** DISHONESTY : falta *f* de honradez
croon [ˈkruːn] *v* : cantar suavemente
crop¹ [ˈkrɑp] *v* **cropped; cropping** *vt* TRIM : recortar, cortar — *vi* **to crop up** : aparecer, surgir ⟨these problems keep cropping up : estos problemas no cesan de surgir⟩
crop² *n* **1** : buche *m* (de un ave o insecto) **2** WHIP : fusta *f* (de jinete) **3** HARVEST : cosecha *f*, cultivo *m*
croquet [ˌkroːˈkeɪ] *n* : croquet *m*
croquette [ˌkroːˈkɛt] *n* : croqueta *f*
cross¹ [ˈkrɔs] *vt* **1** : cruzar, atravesar ⟨to cross the street : cruzar la calle⟩ ⟨several canals cross the city : varios canales atraviesan la ciudad⟩ **2** CANCEL : tachar, cancelar ⟨he crossed his name off the list : tachó su nombre de la planilla⟩ **3** INTERBREED : cruzar (en genética)
cross² *adj* **1** : que atraviesa ⟨cross ventilation : ventilación que atraviesa un cuarto⟩ **2** CONTRARY : contrario, opuesto ⟨cross purposes : objetivos opuestos⟩ **3** ANGRY : enojado, de mal humor
cross³ *n* **1** : cruz *f* ⟨the sign of the cross : la señal de la cruz⟩ **2** : cruza *f* (en biología)
crossbones [ˈkrɔsˌboːnz] *npl* **1** : huesos *mpl* cruzados **2** → **skull**
crossbow [ˈkrɔsˌboː] *n* : ballesta *f*
crossbreed [ˈkrɔsˌbriːd] *vt* **-bred** [-ˌbrɛd]; **-breeding** : cruzar
crosscurrent [ˈkrɔsˌkərənt] *n* : contracorriente *f*
cross–examination [ˌkrɔsɪgˌzæməˈneɪʃən] *n* : repreguntas *fpl*, interrogatorio *m*
cross–examine [ˌkrɔsɪgˈzæmən] *vt* **-ined; -ining** : repreguntar
cross–eyed [ˈkrɔsˌaɪd] *adj* : bizco
crossing [ˈkrɔsɪŋ] *n* **1** INTERSECTION : cruce *m*, paso *m* ⟨pedestrian crossing : paso de peatones⟩ **2** VOYAGE : travesía *f* (del mar)

crossly [ˈkrɔsli] *adv* : con enojo, con enfado
cross–reference [ˌkrɔsˈrɛfrənts, -ˈrɛfərənts] *n* : referencia *f*, remisión *f*
crossroads [ˈkrɔsˌroːdz] *n* : cruce *m*, encrucijada *f*, crucero *m Mex*
cross section *n* **1** SECTION : corte *m* transversal **2** SAMPLE : muestra *f* representativa ⟨a cross section of the population : una muestra representativa de la población⟩
crosswalk [ˈkrɔsˌwɔk] *n* : cruce *m* peatonal, paso *m* de peatones
crossways [ˈkrɔsˌweɪz] → **crosswise**
crosswise¹ [ˈkrɔsˌwaɪz] *adv* : transversalmente, diagonalmente
crosswise² *adj* : transversal, diagonal
crossword puzzle [ˈkrɔsˌwərd] *n* : crucigrama *m*
crotch [ˈkrɑtʃ] *n* : entrepierna *f*
crotchety [ˈkrɑtʃəti] *adj* CRANKY : malhumorado, irritable, enojadizo
crouch [ˈkraʊtʃ] *vi* : agacharse, ponerse de cuclillas
croup [ˈkruːp] *n* : crup *m*
crouton [ˈkruːˌtɑn] *n* : crutón *m*
crow¹ [ˈkroː] *vi* **1** : cacarear, cantar (como un cuervo) **2** BRAG : alardear, presumir
crow² *n* **1** : cuervo *m* (ave) **2** : cantar *m* (del gallo)
crowbar [ˈkroːˌbɑr] *n* : palanca *f*
crowd¹ [ˈkraʊd] *vi* : aglomerarse, amontonarse — *vt* : atestar, atiborrar, llenar
crowd² *n* : multitud *f*, muchedumbre *f*, gentío *m*
crown¹ [ˈkraʊn] *vt* : coronar
crown² *n* : corona *f*
crow's nest *n* : cofa *f*
crucial [ˈkruːʃəl] *adj* : crucial, decisivo
crucible [ˈkruːsəbəl] *n* : crisol *m*
crucifix [ˈkruːsəˌfɪks] *n* : crucifijo *m*
crucifixion [ˌkruːsəˈfɪkʃən] *n* : crucifixión *f*
crucify [ˈkruːsəˌfaɪ] *vt* **-fied; -fying** : crucificar
crude [ˈkruːd] *adj* **cruder; -est 1** RAW, UNREFINED : crudo, sin refinar ⟨crude oil : petróleo crudo⟩ **2** VULGAR : grosero, de mal gusto **3** ROUGH : tosco, burdo, rudo
crudely [ˈkruːdli] *adv* **1** VULGARLY : groseramente **2** ROUGHLY : burdamente, de manera rudimentaria
crudity [ˈkruːdəti] *n*, *pl* **-ties 1** VULGARITY : grosería *f* **2** COARSENESS, ROUGHNESS : tosquedad *f*, rudeza *f*
cruel [ˈkruːəl] *adj* **-eler** *or* **-eller; -elest** *or* **-ellest** : cruel
cruelly [ˈkruːəli] *adv* : cruelmente
cruelty [ˈkruːəlti] *n*, *pl* **-ties** : crueldad *f*
cruet [ˈkruːɪt] *n* : vinagrera *f*, aceitera *f*
cruise¹ [ˈkruːz] *vi* **cruised; cruising 1** : hacer un crucero **2** : navegar o conducir a una velocidad constante ⟨cruising speed : velocidad de crucero⟩
cruise² *n* : crucero *m*

cruiser [ˈkruːzər] *n* **1** WARSHIP : crucero *m*, buque *m* de guerra **2** : patrulla *f* (de policía)
crumb [ˈkrʌm] *n* : miga *f*, migaja *f*
crumble [ˈkrʌmbəl] *v* -bled; -bling *vt* : desmigajar, desmenuzar — *vi* : desmigajarse, desmoronarse, desmenuzarse
crumbly [ˈkrʌmbli] *adj* : que se desmenuza fácilmente, friable
crumple [ˈkrʌmpəl] *v* -pled; -pling *vt* RUMPLE : arrugar — *vi* **1** WRINKLE : arrugarse **2** COLLAPSE : desplomarse
crunch¹ [ˈkrʌntʃ] *vt* **1** : ronzar (con los dientes) **2** : hacer crujir (con los pies, etc.) — *vi* : crujir
crunch² *n* : crujido *m*
crunchy [ˈkrʌntʃi] *adj* **crunchier; -est** : crujiente
crusade¹ [kruːˈseɪd] *vi* -saded; -sading : hacer una campaña (a favor de o contra algo)
crusade² *n* **1** : campaña *f* (de reforma, etc.) **2 Crusade** : cruzada *f*
crusader [kruːˈseɪdər] *n* **1** : cruzado *m* (en la Edad Media) **2** : campeón *m*, -peona *f* (de una causa)
crush¹ [ˈkrʌʃ] *vt* **1** SQUASH : aplastar, apachurrar **2** GRIND, PULVERIZE : triturar, machacar **3** SUPPRESS : aplastar, suprimir
crush² *n* **1** CROWD, MOB : gentío *m*, multitud *f*, aglomeración *f* **2** INFATUATION : enamoramiento *m*
crushing [ˈkrʌʃɪŋ] *adj* : aplastante, abrumador
crust [ˈkrʌst] *n* **1** : corteza *f*, costra *f* (de pan) **2** : tapa *f* de masa, pasta *f* (de un pastel) **3** LAYER : capa *f*, corteza *f* ⟨the earth's crust : la corteza terrestre⟩
crustacean [ˌkrʌsˈteɪʃən] *n* : crustáceo *m*
crusty [ˈkrʌsti] *adj* **crustier; -est 1** : de corteza dura **2** CROSS, GRUMPY : enojado, malhumorado
crutch [ˈkrʌtʃ] *n* : muleta *f*
crux [ˈkrʌks, ˈkrʊks] *n*, *pl* **cruxes** : quid *m*, esencia *f*, meollo *m* ⟨the crux of the problem : el quid del problema⟩
cry¹ [ˈkraɪ] *vi* **cried; crying 1** SHOUT : gritar ⟨they cried for more : a gritos pidieron más⟩ **2** WEEP : llorar
cry² *n*, *pl* **cries 1** SHOUT : grito *m* **2** WEEPING : llanto *m* **3** : chillido *m* (de un animal)
crybaby [ˈkraɪˌbeɪbi] *n*, *pl* **-bies** : llorón *m*, -rona *f*
crypt [ˈkrɪpt] *n* : cripta *f*
cryptic [ˈkrɪptɪk] *adj* : enigmático, críptico
crystal [ˈkrɪstəl] *n* : cristal *m*
crystalline [ˈkrɪstəlɪn] *adj* : cristalino
crystallize [ˈkrɪstəˌlaɪz] *v* -lized; -lizing *vt* : cristalizar, materializar ⟨to crystallize one's thoughts : cristalizar uno sus pensamientos⟩ — *vi* : cristalizarse
cub [ˈkʌb] *n* : cachorro *m*
Cuban [ˈkjuːbən] *n* : cubano *m*, -na *f* — **Cuban** *adj*

cubbyhole [ˈkʌbiˌhoːl] *n* : chiribitil *m*
cube¹ [ˈkjuːb] *vt* **cubed; cubing 1** : elevar (un número) al cubo **2** : cortar en cubos
cube² *n* **1** : cubo *m* **2 ice cube** : cubito *m* de hielo **3 sugar cube** : terrón *m* de azúcar
cubic [ˈkjuːbɪk] *adj* : cúbico
cubicle [ˈkjuːbɪkəl] *n* : cubículo *m*
cuckoo¹ [ˈkuːˌkuː, ˈkʊ-] *adj* : loco, chiflado
cuckoo² *n*, *pl* **-oos** : cuco *m*, cuclillo *m*
cucumber [ˈkjuːˌkʌmbər] *n* : pepino *m*
cud [ˈkʌd] *n* **to chew the cud** : rumiar
cuddle [ˈkʌdəl] *v* -dled; -dling *vi* : abrazarse tiernamente, acurrucarse — *vt* : abrazar
cudgel¹ [ˈkʌdʒəl] *vt* -geled *or* -gelled; -geling *or* -gelling : apalear, aporrear
cudgel² *n* : garrote *m*, porra *f*
cue¹ [ˈkjuː] *vt* **cued; cuing** *or* **cueing** : darle el pie a, darle la señal a
cue² *n* **1** SIGNAL : señal *f*, pie *m* (en teatro), entrada *f* (en música) **2** : taco *m* (de billar)
cuff¹ [ˈkʌf] *vt* : bofetear, cachetear
cuff² *n* **1** : puño *m* (de una camisa), vuelta *f* (de pantalones) **2** SLAP : bofetada *f*, cachetada *f* **3 cuffs** *npl* HANDCUFFS : esposas *fpl*
cuisine [kwɪˈziːn] *n* : cocina *f* ⟨Mexican cuisine : la cocina mexicana⟩
culinary [ˈkʌləˌneri, ˈkjuːlə-] *adj* : culinario
cull [ˈkʌl] *vt* : seleccionar, entresacar
culminate [ˈkʌlməˌneɪt] *vi* -nated; -nating : culminar
culmination [ˌkʌlməˈneɪʃən] *n* : culminación *f*, punto *m* culminante
culpable [ˈkʌlpəbəl] *adj* : culpable
culprit [ˈkʌlprɪt] *n* : culpable *mf*
cult [ˈkʌlt] *n* : culto *m*
cultivate [ˈkʌltəˌveɪt] *vt* -vated; -vating **1** TILL : cultivar, labrar **2** FOSTER : cultivar, fomentar **3** REFINE : cultivar, refinar ⟨to cultivate the mind : cultivar la mente⟩
cultivation [ˌkʌltəˈveɪʃən] *n* **1** : cultivo *m* ⟨under cultivation : en cultivo⟩ **2** CULTURE, REFINEMENT : cultura *f*, refinamiento *m*
cultural [ˈkʌltʃərəl] *adj* : cultural — **culturally** *adv*
culture [ˈkʌltʃər] *n* **1** CULTIVATION : cultivo *m* **2** REFINEMENT : cultura *f*, educación *f*, refinamiento *m* **3** CIVILIZATION : cultura *f*, civilización *f* ⟨the Incan culture : la cultura inca⟩
cultured [ˈkʌltʃərd] *adj* **1** EDUCATED, REFINED : culto, educado, refinado **2** : de cultivo, cultivado ⟨cultured pearls : perlas de cultivo⟩
culvert [ˈkʌlvərt] *n* : alcantarilla *f*
cumbersome [ˈkʌmbərsəm] *adj* : torpe y pesado, difícil de manejar
cumin [ˈkʌmən] *n* : comino *m*
cumulative [ˈkjuːmjələtɪv, -ˌleɪtɪv] *adj* : acumulativo

cumulus ['kju:mjələs] *n, pl* **-li** [-ˌlaɪ, -ˌli:] : cúmulo *m*

cunning¹ ['kʌnɪŋ] *adj* **1** CRAFTY : astuto, taimado **2** CLEVER : ingenioso, hábil **3** CUTE : mono, gracioso, lindo

cunning² *n* **1** SKILL : habilidad *f* **2** CRAFTINESS : astucia *f*, maña *f*

cup¹ ['kʌp] *vt* **cupped; cupping** : ahuecar (las manos)

cup² *n* **1** : taza *f* ⟨a cup of coffee : una taza de café⟩ **2** CUPFUL : taza *f* **3** : media pinta *f* (unidad de medida) **4** GOBLET : copa *f* **5** TROPHY : copa *f*, trofeo *m*

cupboard ['kʌbərd] *n* : alacena *f*, armario *m*

cupcake ['kʌpˌkeɪk] *n* : pastelito *m*

cupful ['kʌpˌfʊl] *n* : taza *f*

cupola ['kju:pələ, -ˌlo:] *n* : cúpula *f*

cur ['kər] *n* : perro *m* callejero, perro *m* corriente *Mex*

curate ['kjʊrət] *n* : cura *m*, párroco *m*

curator ['kjʊrˌeɪtər, kjʊˈreɪtər] *n* : conservador *m*, -dora *f* (de un museo); director *m*, -tora *f* (de un zoológico)

curb¹ ['kərb] *vt* : refrenar, restringir, controlar

curb² *n* **1** RESTRAINT : freno *m*, control *m* **2** : borde *m* de la acera

curd ['kərd] *n* : cuajada *f*

curdle ['kərdəl] *v* **-dled; -dling** *vi* : cuajarse — *vt* : cuajar ⟨to curdle one's blood : helarle la sangre a uno⟩

cure¹ ['kjʊr] *vt* **cured; curing 1** HEAL : curar, sanar **2** REMEDY : remediar **3** PROCESS : curar (alimentos, etc.)

cure² *n* **1** RECOVERY : curación *f*, recuperación *f* **2** REMEDY : cura *f*, remedio *m*

curfew ['kərˌfju:] *n* : toque *m* de queda

curio ['kjʊriˌo:] *n, pl* **-rios** : curiosidad *f*, objeto *m* curioso

curiosity [ˌkjʊriˈɑsəti] *n, pl* **-ties** : curiosidad *f*

curious ['kjʊriəs] *adj* **1** INQUISITIVE : curioso **2** STRANGE : curioso, raro

curl¹ ['kərl] *vt* **1** : rizar, ondular (el pelo) **2** COIL : enrollar **3** TWIST : torcer ⟨to curl one's lip : hacer una mueca⟩ — *vi* **1** : rizarse, ondularse **2 to curl up** : acurrucarse (con un libro, etc.)

curl² *n* **1** RINGLET : rizo *m* **2** COIL : espiral *f*, rosca *f*

curler ['kərlər] *n* : rulo *m*

curlew ['kərˌlu:, 'kərlˌju:] *n, pl* **-lews** *or* **-lew** : zarapito *m*

curly ['kərli] *adj* **curlier; -est** : rizado, crespo

currant ['kərənt] *n* **1** : grosella *f* (fruta) **2** RAISIN : pasa *f* de Corinto

currency ['kərəntsi] *n, pl* **-cies 1** PREVALENCE, USE : uso *m*, aceptación *f*, difusión *f* ⟨to be in currency : estar en uso⟩ **2** MONEY : moneda *f*, dinero *m*

current¹ ['kərənt] *adj* **1** PRESENT : actual ⟨current events : actualidades⟩ **2** PREVALENT : corriente, común — **currently** *adv*

current² *n* : corriente *f*

curriculum [kəˈrɪkjələm] *n, pl* **-la** [-lə] : currículum *m*, currículo *m*, programa *m* de estudio

curriculum vitae ['vi:ˌtaɪ, 'vaɪti] *n, pl* **curricula vitae** : currículum *m*, currículo *m*

curry¹ ['kəri] *vt* **-ried; -rying 1** GROOM : almohazar (un caballo) **2** : condimentar con curry **3 to curry favor** : congraciarse (con alguien)

curry² *n, pl* **-ries** : curry *m*

curse¹ ['kərs] *v* **cursed; cursing** *vt* **1** DAMN : maldecir **2** INSULT : injuriar, insultar, decir malas palabras a **3** AFFLICT : afligir — *vi* : maldecir, decir malas palabras

curse² *n* **1** : maldición *f* ⟨to put a curse on someone : echarle una maldición a alguien⟩ **2** AFFLICTION : maldición *f*, aflicción *f*, cruz *f*

cursor ['kərsər] *n* : cursor *m*

cursory ['kərsəri] *adj* : rápido, superficial, somero

curt ['kərt] *adj* : cortante, brusco, seco — **curtly** *adv*

curtail [kərˈteɪl] *vt* : acortar, limitar, restringir

curtailment [kərˈteɪlmənt] *n* : restricción *f*, limitación *f*

curtain ['kərtən] *n* : cortina *f* (de una ventana), telón *m* (en un teatro)

curtness ['kərtnəs] *n* : brusquedad *f*, sequedad *f*

curtsy¹ *or* **curtsey** ['kərtsi] *vt* **-sied** *or* **-seyed; -sying** *or* **-seying** : hacer una reverencia

curtsy² *or* **curtsey** *n, pl* **-sies** *or* **-seys** : reverencia *f*

curvature ['kərvəˌtʃʊr] *n* : curvatura *f*

curve¹ ['kərv] *v* **curved; curving** *vi* : torcerse, describir una curva — *vt* : encorvar

curve² *n* : curva *f*

cushion¹ ['kʊʃən] *vt* **1** : poner cojines o almohadones a **2** SOFTEN : amortiguar, mitigar, suavizar ⟨to cushion a blow : amortiguar un golpe⟩

cushion² *n* **1** : cojín *m*, almohadón *m* **2** PROTECTION : colchón *m*, protección *f*

cusp ['kʌsp] *n* : cúspide *f* (de un diente), cuerno *m* (de la luna)

cuspid ['kʌspɪd] *n* : diente *m* canino, colmillo *m*

custard ['kʌstərd] *n* : natillas *fpl*

custodian [ˌkʌˈsto:diən] *n* : custodio *m*, -dia *f*; guardián, chica *f*

custody ['kʌstədi] *n, pl* **-dies** : custodia *f*, cuidado *m* ⟨to be in custody : estar detenido⟩

custom¹ ['kʌstəm] *adj* : a la medida, a la orden

custom² *n* **1** : costumbre *f*, tradición *f* **2 customs** *npl* : aduana *f*

customarily [ˌkʌstəˈmɛrəli] *adv* : habitualmente, normalmente, de costumbre

customary ['kʌstə,mɛri] *adj* **1** TRADI-
TIONAL : tradicional **2** USUAL : habitual, de costumbre
customer ['kʌstəmər] *n* : cliente *m*, -ta *f*
custom–made ['kʌstəm'meɪd] *adj* : hecho a la medida
cut¹ ['kʌt] *v* **cut; cutting** *vt* **1** : cortar ⟨to
cut paper : cortar papel⟩ **2** : cortarse
⟨to cut one's finger : cortarse uno el
dedo⟩ **3** TRIM : cortar, recortar ⟨to
have one's hair cut : cortarse el pelo⟩
4 INTERSECT : cruzar, atravesar **5**
SHORTEN : acortar, abreviar **6** REDUCE
: reducir, rebajar ⟨to cut prices : rebajar los precios⟩ **7 to cut one's teeth**
: salirle los dientes a uno — *vi* **1** : cortar, cortarse **2 to cut in** : entrometerse
cut² *n* **1** : corte *m* ⟨a cut of meat : un
corte de carne⟩ **2** SLASH : tajo *m*, corte
m, cortadura *f* **3** REDUCTION : rebaja
f, reducción *f* ⟨a cut in the rates : una
rebaja en las tarifas⟩
cute ['kju:t] *adj* **cuter; -est** : mono *fam*,
lindo
cuticle ['kju:tɪkəl] *n* : cutícula *f*
cutlass ['kʌtləs] *n* : alfanje *m*
cutlery ['kʌtləri] *n* : cubiertos *mpl*
cutlet ['kʌtlət] *n* : chuleta *f*
cutter ['kʌtər] *n* **1** : cortadora *f* (implemento) **2** : cortador *m*, -dora *f* (persona) **3** : cúter *m* (embarcación)
cutthroat ['kʌt,θro:t] *adj* : despiadado,
desalmado ⟨cutthroat competition
: competencia feroz⟩
cutting¹ ['kʌtɪŋ] *adj* **1** : cortante ⟨a cutting wind : un viento cortante⟩ **2** CAUS-
TIC : mordaz

cutting² *n* : esqueje *m* (de una planta)
cuttlefish ['kʌtəl,fɪʃ] *n, pl* **-fish** *or*
-fishes : jibia *f*, sepia *f*
cyanide ['saɪə,naɪd, -nɪd] *n* : cianuro *m*
cycle¹ ['saɪkəl] *vi* **-cled; -cling** : andar en
bicicleta, ir en bicicleta
cycle² *n* **1** : ciclo *m* ⟨life cycle : ciclo de
vida, ciclo vital⟩ **2** BICYCLE : bicicleta
f **3** MOTORCYCLE : motocicleta *f*
cyclic ['saɪklɪk, 'sɪ-] *or* **cyclical** [-klɪkəl]
adj : cíclico
cyclist ['saɪklɪst] *n* : ciclista *mf*
cyclone ['saɪ,klo:n] *n* **1** : ciclón *m* **2**
TORNADO : tornado *m*
cyclopedia *or* **cyclopaedia** [,saɪklə-
'pi:diə] → **encyclopedia**
cylinder ['sɪləndər] *n* : cilindro *m*
cylindrical [sə'lɪndrɪkəl] *adj* : cilíndrico
cymbal ['sɪmbəl] *n* : platillo *m*, címbalo
m
cynic ['sɪnɪk] *n* : cínico *m*, -ca *f*
cynical ['sɪnɪkəl] *adj* : cínico
cynicism ['sɪnə,sɪzəm] *n* : cinismo *m*
cypress ['saɪprəs] *n* : ciprés *m*
Cypriot ['sɪpriət, -,at] *n* : chipriota *mf* —
Cypriot *adj*
cyst ['sɪst] *n* : quiste *m*
cytoplasm ['saɪtə,plæzəm] *n* : citoplasma *m*
czar ['zɑr, 'sɑr] *n* : zar *m*
czarina [zɑ'ri:nə, sə-] *n* : zarina *f*
Czech ['tʃɛk] *n* **1** : checo *m*, -ca *f* **2**
: checo *m* (idioma) — **Czech** *adj*
Czechoslovak [,tʃɛko'slo:,vɑk, -,væk] *or*
Czechoslovakian [-slo'vɑkiən, -'væ-] *n*
: checoslovaco *m*, -ca *f* — **Czechoslovak** *or* **Czechoslovakian** *adj*

D

d ['di:] *n, pl* **d's** *or* **ds** ['di:z] : cuarta
letra del alfabeto inglés
dab¹ ['dæb] *vt* **dabbed; dabbing** : darle
toques ligeros a, aplicar suavemente
dab² *n* **1** BIT : toque *m*, pizca *f*, poco *m*
⟨a dab of ointment : un toque de
ungüento⟩ **2** PAT : toque *m* ligero,
golpecito *m*
dabble ['dæbəl] *v* **-bled; -bling** *vt* SPAT-
TER : salpicar — *vi* **1** SPLASH
: chapotear **2** TRIFLE : jugar, interesarse superficialmente
dabbler ['dæbələr] *n* : diletante *mf*
dachshund ['dɑks,hʊnt, -,hʊnd; 'dɑk-
sənt, -sənd] *n* : perro *m* salchicha
dad ['dæd] *n* : papá *m fam*
daddy ['dædi] *n, pl* **-dies** : papi *m fam*
daffodil ['dæfə,dɪl] *n* : narciso *m*
daft ['dæft] *adj* : tonto, bobo
dagger ['dægər] *n* : daga *f*, puñal *m*
dahlia ['dæljə, 'dɑl-, 'deɪl-] *n* : dalia *f*
daily¹ ['deɪli] *adv* : a diario, diariamente
daily² *adj* : diario, cotidiano
daily³ *n, pl* **-lies** : diario *m*, periódico *m*
daintily ['deɪntəli] *adv* : delicadamente,
con delicadeza

daintiness ['deɪntinəs] *n* : delicadeza *f*,
finura *f*
dainty¹ ['deɪnti] *adj* **-tier; -est 1** DELI-
CATE : delicado **2** FASTIDIOUS : remilgado, melindroso **3** DELICIOUS : exquisito, sabroso
dainty² *n, pl* **-ties** DELICACY : exquisitez
f, manjar *m*
dairy ['dæri] *n, pl* **-ies 1** *or* **dairy store**
: lechería *f* **2** *or* **dairy farm** : granja *f*
lechera
dairymaid ['dæri,meɪd] *n* : lechera *f*
dairyman ['dærimən, -,mæn] *n, pl* **-men**
[-mən, -,mɛn] : lechero *m*
dais ['deɪəs] *n* : tarima *f*, estrado *m*
daisy ['deɪzi] *n, pl* **-sies** : margarita *f*
dale ['deɪl] *n* : valle *m*
dally ['dæli] *vi* **-lied; -lying 1** TRIFLE
: juguetear **2** DAWDLE : entretenerse,
perder tiempo
dalmatian [dæl'meɪʃən, dɔl-] *n* : dálmata *m*
dam¹ ['dæm] *vt* **dammed; damming**
: represar, embalsar
dam² *n* **1** : represa *f*, dique *m* **2** : madre
f (de animales domésticos)

damage¹ ['dæmɪʤ] vt **-aged; -aging** : dañar (un objeto o una máquina), perjudicar (la salud o una reputación)
damage² n **1** : daño m, perjuicio m **2 damages** npl : daños y perjuicios mpl
damaging ['dæməʤɪŋ] adj : perjudicial
damask ['dæməsk] n : damasco m
dame ['deɪm] n LADY : dama f, señora f
damn¹ ['dæm] vt **1** CONDEMN : condenar **2** CURSE : maldecir
damn² or **damned** ['dæmd] adj : condenado fam, maldito fam
damn³ n : pito m, bledo m, comino m ⟨it's not worth a damn : no vale un pito⟩ ⟨I don't give a damn : me importa un comino⟩
damnable ['dæmnəbəl] adj : condenable, detestable
damnation [dæm'neɪʃən] n : condenación f
damned¹ ['dæmd] adv VERY : muy
damned² adj **1** → **damnable 2** REMARKABLE : extraordinario
damp¹ ['dæmp] vt → **dampen**
damp² adj : húmedo
damp³ n MOISTURE : humedad f
dampen ['dæmpən] vt **1** MOISTEN : humedecer **2** DISCOURAGE : desalentar, desanimar
damper ['dæmpər] n **1** : regulador m de tiro (de una chimenea) **2** : sordina f (de un piano) **3 to put a damper on** : desanimar, apagar (el entusiasmo), enfriar
dampness ['dæmpnəs] n : humedad f
damsel ['dæmzəl] n : damisela f
dance¹ ['dænts] v **danced; dancing** : bailar
dance² n : baile m
dancer ['dæntsər] n : bailarín m, -rina f
dandelion ['dændəl,aɪən] n : diente m de león
dandruff ['dændrəf] n : caspa f
dandy¹ ['dændi] adj **-dier; -est** : excelente, magnífico, macanudo fam
dandy² n, pl **-dies 1** FOP : dandi m **2** : algo m excelente ⟨this new program is a dandy : este programa nuevo es algo excelente⟩
Dane ['deɪn] n : danés m, -nesa f
danger ['deɪnʤər] n : peligro m
dangerous ['deɪnʤərəs] adj : peligroso
dangle ['dæŋgəl] v **-gled; -gling** v HANG : colgar, pender — vt **1** SWING : hacer oscilar **2** PROFFER : ofrecer (como incentivo) **3 to keep someone dangling** : dejar a alguien en suspenso
Danish¹ ['deɪnɪʃ] adj : danés
Danish² n : danés m (idioma)
dank ['dæŋk] adj : frío y húmedo
dapper ['dæpər] adj : pulcro, atildado
dappled ['dæpəld] adj : moteado ⟨a dappled horse : un caballo rodado⟩
dare¹ ['dær] v **dared; daring** vi : osar, atreverse ⟨how dare you! : ¡cómo te atreves!⟩ — vt **1** CHALLENGE : desafiar, retar **2 to dare to do something** : atreverse a hacer algo, osar hacer algo

dare² n : desafío m, reto m
daredevil ['dær,dɛvəl] n : persona f temeraria
daring¹ ['dærɪŋ] adj : osado, atrevido, audaz
daring² n : arrojo m, coraje m, audacia f
dark ['dɑrk] adj **1** : oscuro (dícese del ambiente o de los colores), moreno (dícese del pelo o de la piel) **2** SOMBER : sombrío, triste
darken ['dɑrkən] vt **1** DIM : oscurecer **2** SADDEN : entristecer — vi : ensombrecerse, nublarse
darkly ['dɑrkli] adv **1** DIMLY : oscuramente **2** GLOOMILY : tristemente **3** MYSTERIOUSLY : misteriosamente, enigmáticamente
darkness ['dɑrknəs] n : oscuridad f, tinieblas f
darling¹ ['dɑrlɪŋ] adj **1** BELOVED : querido, amado **2** CHARMING : encantador, mono fam
darling² n **1** BELOVED : querido m, -da f; amado m, -da f; cariño m, -ña f **2** FAVORITE : preferido m, -da f; favorito m, -ta f
darn¹ ['dɑrn] vt : zurcir
darn² n **1** : zurcido m **2** → **damn³**
dart¹ ['dɑrt] vt THROW : lanzar, tirar — vi DASH : lanzarse, precipitarse
dart² n **1** : dardo m **2 darts** npl : juego m de dardos
dash¹ ['dæʃ] vt **1** SMASH : romper, estrellar **2** HURL : arrojar, lanzar **3** SPLASH : salpicar **4** FRUSTRATE : frustrar **5 to dash off** : hacer (algo) rápidamente — vi **1** SMASH : romperse, estrellarse **2** DART : lanzarse, irse apresuradamente
dash² n **1** BURST, SPLASH : arranque m, salpicadura f (de aguas) **2** : guión m largo (signo de puntuación) **3** DROP : gota f, pizca f **4** VERVE : brío m **5** RACE : carrera f ⟨a 100-meter dash : una carrera de 100 metros⟩ **6 to make a dash for it** : precipitarse (hacia), echarse a correr **7** → **dashboard**
dashboard ['dæʃ,bord] n : tablero m de instrumentos
dashing ['dæʃɪŋ] adj : gallardo, apuesto
data ['deɪt̬ə, 'dæ-, 'dɑ-] ns & pl : datos mpl, información f
database ['deɪt̬ə,beɪs, 'dæ-, 'dɑ-] n : base f de datos
date¹ ['deɪt] v **dated; dating** vt **1** : fechar (una carta, etc.), datar (un objeto) ⟨it was dated June 9 : estaba fechada el 9 de junio⟩ **2** : salir con ⟨she's dating my brother : sale con mi hermano⟩ — vi : datar
date² n **1** : fecha f ⟨to date : hasta la fecha⟩ **2** EPOCH, PERIOD : época f, período m **3** APPOINTMENT : cita f **4** COMPANION : acompañante mf **5** : dátil m (fruta)
dated ['deɪt̬əd] adj OUT-OF-DATE : anticuado, pasado de moda

datum · deal

datum ['deɪt̬əm, 'dæ-, 'dɑ-] *n*, *pl* **-ta** [-t̬ə] *or* **-tums** : dato *m*

daub¹ ['dɔb] *vt* : embadurnar

daub² *n* : mancha *f*

daughter ['dɔt̬ər] *n* : hija *f*

daughter–in–law ['dɔt̬ərɪn,lɔ] *n*, *pl* **daughters–in–law** : nuera *f*, hija *f* política

daunt ['dɔnt] *vt* : amilanar, acobardar, intimidar

dauntless ['dɔntləs] *adj* : intrépido, impávido

davenport ['dævən,port] *n* : sofá *m*

dawdle ['dɔdəl] *vi* **-dled; -dling 1** DALLY : demorarse, entretenerse, perder tiempo **2** LOITER : vagar, holgazanear, haraganear

dawn¹ ['dɔn] *vi* **1** : amanecer, alborear, despuntar ⟨Saturday dawned clear and bright : el sábado amaneció claro y luminoso⟩ **2 to dawn on** : hacerse obvio ⟨it dawned on me that she was right : me di cuenta de que tenía razón⟩

dawn² *n* **1** DAYBREAK : amanecer *m*, alba *f* **2** BEGINNING : albor *m*, comienzo *m* ⟨the dawn of history : los albores de la historia⟩ **3 from dawn to dusk** : de sol a sol

day ['deɪ] *n* **1** : día *m* **2** DATE : fecha *f* **3** TIME : día *m*, tiempo *m* ⟨in olden days : intaño⟩ **4** WORKDAY : jornada *f* laboral

daybreak ['deɪ,breɪk] *n* : alba *f*, amanecer *m*

day care *n* : servicio *m* de guardería infantil

daydream¹ ['deɪ,dri:m] *vi* : soñar despierto, fantasear

daydream² *n* : ensueño *m*, ensoñación *f*, fantasía *f*

daylight ['deɪ,laɪt] *n* **1** : luz *f* del día ⟨in broad daylight : a plena luz del día⟩ **2** → **daybreak 3** → **daytime**

daylight saving time *n* : hora *f* de verano

daytime ['deɪ,taɪm] *n* : horas *fpl* diurnas, día *m*

daze¹ ['deɪz] *vt* **dazed; dazing 1** STUN : aturdir **2** DAZZLE : deslumbrar, ofuscar

daze² *n* **1** : aturdimiento *m* **2 in a daze** : aturdido, atontado

dazzle¹ ['dæzəl] *vt* **-zled; -zling** : deslumbrar, ofuscar

dazzle² *n* : resplandor *m*, brillo *m*

DDT [,di:,di:'ti:] *n* : DDT *m*

deacon ['di:kən] *n* : diácono *m*

dead¹ ['dɛd] *adv* **1** ABRUPTLY : repentinamente, súbitamente ⟨to stop dead : parar en seco⟩ **2** ABSOLUTELY : absolutamente ⟨I'm dead certain : estoy absolutamente seguro⟩ **3** DIRECTLY : justo ⟨dead ahead : justo adelante⟩

dead² *adj* **1** LIFELESS : muerto **2** NUMB : entumecido **3** INDIFFERENT : indiferente, frío **4** INACTIVE : inactivo ⟨a dead volcano : un volcán inactivo⟩ **5** : desconectado (dícese del teléfono),

descargado (dícese de una batería) **6** EXHAUSTED : agotado, derrengado, muerto **7** OBSOLETE : obsoleto, muerto ⟨a dead language : una lengua muerta⟩ **8** EXACT : exacto ⟨in the dead center : justo en el blanco⟩

dead³ *n* **1 the dead** : los muertos **2 in the dead of night** : a las altas horas de la noche **3 in the dead of winter** : en pleno invierno

deadbeat ['dɛd,bi:t] *n* **1** LOAFER : vago *m*, -ga *f*; holgazán *m*, -zana *f* **2** FREELOADER : gorrón *m*, -rrona *f fam*; gorrero *m*, -ra *f fam*

deaden ['dɛdən] *vt* **1** : atenuar (un dolor), entorpecer (sensaciones) **2** DULL : deslustrar **3** DISPIRIT : desanimar **4** MUFFLE : amortiguar, reducir (sonidos)

dead–end ['dɛd'ɛnd] *adj* **1** : sin salida ⟨dead-end street : calle sin salida⟩ **2** : sin futuro ⟨a dead-end job : un trabajo sin porvenir⟩

dead end *n* : callejón *m* sin salida

dead heat *n* : empate *m*

deadline ['dɛd,laɪn] *n* : fecha *f* límite, fecha *f* tope, plazo *m* (determinado)

deadlock¹ ['dɛd,lɑk] *vt* : estancar — *vi* : estancarse, llegar a punto muerto

deadlock² *n* : punto *m* muerto, impasse *m*

deadly¹ ['dɛdli] *adv* : extremadamente, sumamente ⟨deadly serious : muy en serio⟩

deadly² *adj* **-lier; -est 1** LETHAL : mortal, letal, mortífero **2** ACCURATE : certero, preciso ⟨a deadly aim : una puntería infalible⟩ **3** CAPITAL : capital ⟨the seven deadly sins : los siete pecados capitales⟩ **4** DULL : funesto, aburrido **5** EXTREME : extremo, absoluto ⟨a deadly calm : una calma absoluta⟩

deadpan¹ ['dɛd,pæn] *adv* : de manera inexpresiva, sin expresión

deadpan² *adj* : inexpresivo, impasible

deaf ['dɛf] *adj* : sordo

deafen ['dɛfən] *vt* **-ened; -ening** : ensordecer

deafening ['dɛfənɪŋ] *adj* : ensordecedor

deaf–mute ['dɛf'mju:t] *n* : sordomudo *m*, -da *f*

deafness ['dɛfnəs] *n* : sordera *f*

deal¹ ['di:l] *v* **dealt; dealing** *vt* **1** APPORTION : repartir ⟨to deal justice : repartir la justicia⟩ **2** DISTRIBUTE : repartir, dar (naipes) **3** DELIVER : asestar, propinar ⟨to deal a blow : asestar un golpe⟩ — *vi* **1** : dar, repartir (en juegos de naipes) **2 to deal in** : comerciar en, traficar con (drogas) **3 to deal with** CONCERN : tratar de, tener que ver con ⟨the book deals with poverty : el libro trata de la pobreza⟩ **4 to deal with** HANDLE : tratar (con), encargarse de **5 to deal with** TREAT : tratar ⟨the judge dealt with him severely : el juez lo trató con severidad⟩ **6 to deal with** ACCEPT : aceptar (una situación o desgracia)

deal² *n* **1** : reparto *m* (de naipes) **2** AGREEMENT, TRANSACTION : trato *m*, acuerdo *m*, transacción *f* **3** TREATMENT : trato *m* ⟨he got a raw deal : le hicieron una injusticia⟩ **4** BARGAIN : ganga *f*, oferta *f* **5 a good deal** *or* **a great deal** : mucho, una gran cantidad
dealer ['di:lər] *n* : comerciante *mf*, traficante *mf*
dealership ['di:lər,ʃɪp] *n* : concesión *f*
dealings ['di:lɪŋz] *npl* **1** : relaciones *fpl* (personales) **2** TRANSACTIONS : negocios *mpl*, transacciones *fpl*
dean ['di:n] *n* **1** : deán *m* (del clero) **2** : decano *m*, -na *f* (de una facultad o profesión)
dear¹ ['dɪr] *adj* **1** ESTEEMED, LOVED : querido, estimado ⟨a dear friend : un amigo querido⟩ ⟨Dear Sir : Estimado Señor⟩ **2** COSTLY : caro, costoso
dear² *n* : querido *m*, -da *f*; amado *m*, -da *f*
dearly ['dɪrli] *adv* **1** : mucho ⟨I love them dearly : los quiero mucho⟩ **2** : caro ⟨to pay dearly : pagar caro⟩
dearth ['dərθ] *n* : escasez *f*, carestía *f*
death ['dɛθ] *n* **1** : muerte *f*, fallecimiento *m* ⟨to be the death of : matar⟩ **2** FATALITY : víctima *f* (mortal); muerto *m*, -ta *f* **3** END : fin *m* ⟨the death of civilization : el fin de la civilización⟩
deathbed ['dɛθ,bɛd] *n* : lecho *m* de muerte
deathblow ['dɛθ,blo:] *n* : golpe *m* mortal
deathless ['dɛθləs] *adj* : eterno, inmortal
deathly ['dɛθli] *adj* : de muerte, sepulcral (dícese del silencio), cadavérico (dícese de la palidez)
debacle [dɪ'bɑkəl, -'bæ-] *n* : desastre *m*, debacle *m*, fiasco *m*
debar [dɪ'bɑr] *vt* **-barred; -barring** : excluir, prohibir
debase [dɪ'beɪs] *vt* **-based; -basing** : degradar, envilecer
debasement [dɪ'beɪsmənt] *n* : degradación *f*, envilecimiento *m*
debatable [dɪ'beɪt̮əbəl] *adj* : discutible
debate¹ [dɪ'beɪt] *vt* **-bated; -bating** : debatir, discutir
debate² *n* : debate *m*, discusión *f*
debauch [dɪ'bɔtʃ] *vt* : pervertir, corromper
debauchery [dɪ'bɔtʃəri] *n, pl* **-eries** : libertinaje *m*, disipación *f*, intemperancia *f*
debilitate [dɪ'bɪlə,teɪt] *vt* **-tated; -tating** : debilitar
debility [dɪ'bɪləti] *n, pl* **-ties** : debilidad *f*
debit¹ ['dɛbɪt] *vt* : adeudar, cargar, debitar
debit² *n* : débito *m*, cargo *m*, debe *m*
debonair [ˌdɛbə'nær] *adj* : elegante y desenvuelto, apuesto
debris [də'bri:, deɪ-; 'deɪ,bri:] *n, pl* **-bris** [-'bri:z, -ˌbri:z] **1** RUBBLE, RUINS : es-

combros *mpl*, ruinas *fpl*, restos *mpl* **2** RUBBISH : basura *f*, deshechos *mpl*
debt ['dɛt] *n* **1** : deuda *f* ⟨to pay a debt : saldar una deuda⟩ **2** INDEBTEDNESS : endeudamiento *m*
debtor ['dɛt̮ər] *n* : deudor *m*, -dora *f*
debunk [di'bʌŋk] *vt* DISCREDIT : desacreditar, desprestigiar
debut¹ [deɪ'bju:, 'deɪ,bju:] *vi* : debutar
debut² *n* **1** : debut *m* (de un actor), estreno *m* (de una obra) **2** : debut *m*, presentación *f* (en sociedad)
debutante ['dɛbju,tɑnt] *n* : debutante *f*
decade ['dɛ,keɪd, dɛ'keɪd] *n* : década *f*
decadence ['dɛkədənts] *n* : decadencia *f*
decadent ['dɛkədənt] *adj* : decadente
decaf¹ ['di:ˌkæf] → **decaffeinated**
decaf² *n* : café *m* descafeinado
decaffeinated [di'kæfə,neɪt̮əd] *adj* : descafeinado
decal ['di:ˌkæl, di'kæl] *n* : calcomanía *f*
decamp [di'kæmp] *vi* : irse, largarse *fam*
decant [di'kænt] *vt* : decantar
decanter [di'kænt̮ər] *n* : licorera *f*, garrafa *f*
decapitate [di'kæpə,teɪt] *vt* **-tated; -tating** : decapitar
decay¹ [di'keɪ] *vi* **1** DECOMPOSE : descomponerse, pudrirse **2** DETERIORATE : deteriorarse **3** : cariarse (dícese de los dientes)
decay² *n* **1** DECOMPOSITION : descomposición *f* **2** DECLINE, DETERIORATION : decadencia *f*, deterioro *m* **3** : caries *f* (de los dientes)
decease¹ [di'si:s] *vi* **-ceased; -ceasing** : morir, fallecer
decease² *n* : fallecimiento *m*, defunción *f*, deceso *m*
deceit [di'si:t] *n* **1** DECEPTION : engaño *m* **2** DISHONESTY : deshonestidad *f*
deceitful [di'si:tfəl] *adj* : falso, embustero, engañoso, mentiroso
deceitfully [di'si:tfəli] *adv* : con engaño, con falsedad
deceitfulness [di'si:tfəlnəs] *n* : falsedad *f*, engaño *m*
deceive [di'si:v] *vt* **-ceived; -ceiving** : engañar, burlar
deceiver [di'si:vər] *n* : impostor *m*, -tora *f*
decelerate [di'sɛlə,reɪt] *vi* **-ated; -ating** : reducir la velocidad, desacelerar
December [di'sɛmbər] *n* : diciembre *m*
decency ['di:səntsi] *n, pl* **-cies** : decencia *f*, decoro *m*
decent ['di:sənt] *adj* **1** CORRECT, PROPER : decente, decoroso, correcto **2** CLOTHED : vestido, presentable **3** MODEST : púdico, modesto **4** ADEQUATE : decente, adecuado ⟨decent wages : paga adecuada⟩
decently ['di:səntli] *adv* : decentemente
decentralize [di'sɛntrə,laɪz] *v* **-lized; -lizing** [-ˌlaɪzɪŋ] *vt* : descentralizar — *vi* : descentralizarse
deception [di'sɛpʃən] *n* : engaño *m*

deceptive [dɪ'sɛptɪv] *adj* : engañoso, falaz — **deceptively** *adv*

decibel ['dɛsəbəl, -ˌbɛl] *n* : decibelio *m*

decide [dɪ'saɪd] *v* -cided; -ciding *vt* 1 CONCLUDE : decidir, llegar a la conclusión de ⟨he decided what to do : decidió qué iba a hacer⟩ 2 DETERMINE : decidir, determinar ⟨one blow decided the fight : un solo golpe determinó la pelea⟩ 3 CONVINCE : decidir ⟨her pleas decided me to help : sus súplicas me decidieron a ayudarla⟩ 4 RESOLVE : resolver — *vi* : decidirse

decided [dɪ'saɪdəd] *adj* 1 UNQUESTIONABLE : indudable 2 RESOLUTE : decidido, resuelto — **decidedly** *adv*

deciduous [dɪ'sɪdʒuəs] *adj* : caduco, de hoja caduca

decimal[1] ['dɛsəməl] *adj* : decimal

decimal[2] *n* : número *m* decimal

decipher [dɪ'saɪfər] *vt* : descifrar — **decipherable** [-əbəl] *adj*

decision [dɪ'sɪʒən] *n* : decisión *f*, determinación *f* ⟨to make a decision : tomar una decisión⟩

decisive [dɪ'saɪsɪv] *adj* 1 DECIDING : decisivo ⟨the decisive vote : el voto decisivo⟩ 2 CONCLUSIVE : decisivo, concluyente, contundente ⟨a decisive victory : una victoria contundente⟩ 3 RESOLUTE : decidido, resuelto, firme

decisively [dɪ'saɪsɪvli] *adv* : con decisión, de manera decisiva

decisiveness [dɪ'saɪsɪvnəs] *n* 1 FORCEFULNESS : contundencia *f* 2 RESOLUTION : firmeza *f*, decisión *f*, determinación *f*

deck[1] ['dɛk] *vt* 1 FLOOR : tumbar, derribar ⟨she decked him with one blow : lo tumbó de un solo golpe⟩ 2 to deck out : adornar, engalanar

deck[2] *n* 1 : cubierta *f* (de un barco) 2 *or* deck of cards : baraja *f* (de naipes)

declaim [dɪ'kleɪm] *v* : declamar

declaration [ˌdɛklə'reɪʃən] *n* : declaración *f*, pronunciamiento *m* (oficial)

declare [dɪ'klær] *vt* -clared; -claring : declarar, manifestar ⟨to declare war : declarar la guerra⟩ ⟨they declared their support : manifestaron su apoyo⟩

decline[1] [dɪ'klaɪn] *v* -clined; -clining *vi* 1 DESCEND : descender 2 DETERIORATE : deteriorarse, decaer ⟨her health is declining : su salud se está deteriorando⟩ 3 DECREASE : disminuir, decrecer, decaer 4 REFUSE : rehusar — *vt* 1 INFLECT : declinar 2 REFUSE, TURN DOWN : declinar, rehusar

decline[2] *n* 1 DETERIORATION : decadencia *f*, deterioro *m* 2 DECREASE : disminución *f*, descenso *m* 3 SLOPE : declive *m*, pendiente *f*

decode [dɪ'ko:d] *vt* -coded; -coding : descifrar (un mensaje), descodificar (una señal)

decoder [dɪ'ko:dər] *n* : descodificador *m*

decompose [ˌdi:kəm'po:z] *v* -posed; -posing *vt* 1 BREAK DOWN : descomponer 2 ROT : descomponer, pudrir — *vi* : descomponerse, pudrirse

decomposition [ˌdi:ˌkɑmpə'zɪʃən] *n* : descomposición *f*

decongestant [ˌdi:kən'dʒɛstənt] *n* : descongestionante *m*

decor *or* décor [deɪ'kɔr, 'deɪˌkɔr] *n* : decoración *f*

decorate ['dɛkəˌreɪt] *vt* -rated; -rating 1 ADORN : decorar, adornar 2 : condecorar ⟨he was decorated for bravery : lo condecoraron por valor⟩

decoration [ˌdɛkə'reɪʃən] *n* 1 ADORNMENT : decoración *f*, adorno *m* 2 : condecoración *f* (de honor)

decorative ['dɛkərəˌtɪv, -ˌreɪ-] *adj* : decorativo, ornamental, de adorno

decorator ['dɛkəˌreɪtər] *n* : decorador *m*, -dora *f*

decorum [dɪ'korəm] *n* : decoro *m*

decoy[1] ['di:ˌkɔɪ, dɪ'-] *vt* : atraer (con señuelo)

decoy[2] *n* : señuelo *m*, reclamo *m*, cimbel *m*

decrease[1] [dɪ'kri:s] *v* -creased; -creasing *vi* : decrecer, disminuir, bajar — *vt* : reducir, disminuir

decrease[2] ['di:ˌkri:s] *n* : disminución *f*, descenso *m*, bajada *f*

decree[1] [dɪ'kri:] *vt* -creed; -creeing : decretar

decree[2] *n* : decreto *m*

decrepit [dɪ'krɛpɪt] *adj* 1 FEEBLE : decrépito, débil 2 DILAPIDATED : deteriorado, ruinoso

decry [dɪ'kraɪ] *vt* -cried; -crying : censurar, criticar

dedicate ['dɛdɪˌkeɪt] *vt* -cated; -cating 1 : dedicar ⟨she dedicated the book to Carlos : le dedicó el libro a Carlos⟩ 2 : consagrar, dedicar ⟨to dedicate one's life : consagrar uno su vida⟩

dedication [ˌdɛdɪ'keɪʃən] *n* 1 DEVOTION : dedicación *f*, devoción *f* 2 : dedicatoria *f* (de un libro, una canción, etc.) 3 CONSECRATION : dedicación *f*

deduce [dɪ'du:s, -'dju:s] *vt* -duced; -ducing : deducir, inferir

deduct [dɪ'dʌkt] *vt* : deducir, descontar, restar

deductible [dɪ'dʌktəbəl] *adj* : deducible

deduction [dɪ'dʌkʃən] *n* : deducción *f*

deed[1] [dɪ:d] *vt* : ceder, transferir

deed[2] *n* 1 ACT : acto *m*, acción *f*, hecho *m* ⟨a good deed : una buena acción⟩ 2 FEAT : hazaña *f*, proeza *f* 3 TITLE : escritura *f*, título *m*

deem ['di:m] *vt* : considerar, juzgar

deep[1] ['di:p] *adv* : hondo, profundamente ⟨to dig deep : cavar hondo⟩

deep[2] *adj* 1 : hondo, profundo ⟨the deep end : la parte honda⟩ ⟨a deep wound : una herida profunda⟩ 2 WIDE : ancho 3 INTENSE : profundo, intenso 4 DARK : intenso, subido ⟨deep red : rojo subido⟩ 5 LOW : profundo ⟨a deep tone

: un tono profundo⟩ **6** ABSORBED : absorto ⟨deep in thought : absorto en la meditación⟩
deep³ *n* **1 the deep** : lo profundo, el piélago **2 the deep of night** : lo más profundo de la noche
deepen [ˈdiːpən] *vt* **1** : ahondar, profundizar **2** INTENSIFY : intensificar — *vi* **1** : hacerse más profundo **2** INTENSIFY : intensificarse
deeply [ˈdiːpli] *adv* : hondo, profundamente ⟨I'm deeply sorry : lo siento sinceramente⟩
deep–seated [ˈdiːpˈsiːt̬əd] *adj* : profundamente arraigado, enraizado
deer [ˈdɪr] *ns & pl* : ciervo *m*, venado *m*
deerskin [ˈdɪrˌskɪn] *n* : piel *f* de venado
deface [dɪˈfeɪs] *vt* **-faced; -facing** MAR : desfigurar
defacement [dɪˈfeɪsmənt] *n* : desfiguración *f*
defamation [ˌdɛfəˈmeɪʃən] *n* : difamación *f*
defamatory [dɪˈfæməˌtori] *adj* : difamatorio
defame [dɪˈfeɪm] *vt* **-famed; -faming** : difamar, calumniar
default¹ [dɪˈfɔlt, ˈdiːˌfɔlt] *vi* **1** : no cumplir (con una obligación), no pagar **2** : no presentarse (en un tribunal)
default² *n* **1** NEGLECT : omisión *f*, negligencia *f* **2** NONPAYMENT : impago *m*, falta *f* de pago **3 to win by default** : ganar por abandono
defaulter [dɪˈfɔltər] *n* : moroso *m*, -sa *f*; rebelde *mf* (en un tribunal)
defeat¹ [dɪˈfiːt] *vt* **1** FRUSTRATE : frustrar **2** BEAT : vencer, derrotar
defeat² *n* : derrota *f*, rechazo *m* (de legislación), fracaso *m* (de planes, etc.)
defecate [ˈdɛfɪˌkeɪt] *vi* **-cated; -cating** : defecar
defect¹ [dɪˈfɛkt] *vi* : desertar
defect² [ˈdiːˌfɛkt, dɪˈfɛkt] *n* : defecto *m*
defection [dɪˈfɛkʃən] *n* : deserción *f*, defección *f*
defective [dɪˈfɛktɪv] *adj* **1** FAULTY : defectuoso **2** DEFICIENT : deficiente
defector [dɪˈfɛktər] *n* : desertor *m*, -tora *f*
defend [dɪˈfɛnd] *vt* : defender
defendant [dɪˈfɛndənt] *n* : acusado *m*, -da *f*; demandado *m*, -da *f*
defender [dɪˈfɛndər] *n* **1** ADVOCATE : defensor *m*, -sora *f* **2** : defensa *mf* (en deportes)
defense [dɪˈfɛnts, ˈdiːˌfɛnts] *n* : defensa *f*
defenseless [dɪˈfɛntsləs] *adj* : indefenso
defensive¹ [dɪˈfɛntsɪv] *adj* : defensivo
defensive² *n* **on the defensive** : a la defensiva
defer³ [dɪˈfər] *v* **-ferred; -ferring** *vt* POSTPONE : diferir, aplazar, posponer — *vi* **to defer to** : deferir a
deference [ˈdɛfərənts] *n* : deferencia *f*
deferential [ˌdɛfəˈrɛntʃəl] *adj* : respetuoso
deferment [dɪˈfərmənt] *n* : aplazamiento *m*

defiance [dɪˈfaɪənts] *n* : desafío *m*
defiant [dɪˈfaɪənt] *adj* : desafiante, insolente
deficiency [dɪˈfɪʃəntsi] *n, pl* **-cies** : deficiencia *f*, carencia *f*
deficient [dɪˈfɪʃənt] *adj* : deficiente, carente
deficit [ˈdɛfəsɪt] *n* : déficit *m*
defile [dɪˈfaɪl] *vt* **-filed; -filing 1** DIRTY : ensuciar, manchar **2** CORRUPT : corromper **3** DESECRATE, PROFANE : profanar **4** DISHONOR : deshonrar
defilement [dɪˈfaɪlmənt] *n* **1** DESECRATION : profanación *f* **2** CORRUPTION : corrupción *f* **3** CONTAMINATION : contaminación *f*
define [dɪˈfaɪn] *vt* **-fined; -fining 1** BOUND : delimitar, demarcar **2** CLARIFY : aclarar, definir **3** : definir ⟨to define a word : definir una palabra⟩
definite [ˈdɛfənɪt] *adj* **1** CERTAIN : definido, determinado **2** CLEAR : claro, explícito **3** UNQUESTIONABLE : seguro, incuestionable
definite article *n* : artículo *m* definido
definitely [ˈdɛfənɪtli] *adv* **1** DOUBTLESSLY : indudablemente, sin duda **2** DEFINITIVELY : definitivamente, seguramente
definition [ˌdɛfəˈnɪʃən] *n* : definición *f*
definitive [dɪˈfɪnətɪv] *adj* **1** CONCLUSIVE : definitivo, decisivo **2** AUTHORITATIVE : de autoridad, autorizado
deflate [dɪˈfleɪt] *v* **-flated; -flating** *vt* **1** : desinflar (una llanta, etc.) **2** REDUCE : rebajar ⟨to deflate one's ego : bajarle los humos a uno⟩ — *vi* : desinflarse
deflation [dɪˈfleɪʃən] *n* **1** : desinflación *f* (de una llanta, etc.) **2** : deflación *f* (económica)
deflect [dɪˈflɛkt] *vt* : desviar — *vi* : desviarse
defoliant [dɪˈfoːliənt] *n* : defoliante *m*
deforestation [dɪˌfɔrəˈsteɪʃən] *n* : deforestación *f*, desforestación *f*
deform [dɪˈfɔrm] *vt* : deformar
deformation [ˌdiːˌfɔrˈmeɪʃən] *n* : deformación *f*
deformed [dɪˈfɔrmd] *adj* : deforme
deformity [dɪˈfɔrmət̬i] *n, pl* **-ties** : deformidad *f*
defraud [dɪˈfrɔd] *vt* : estafar, defraudar
defray [dɪˈfreɪ] *vt* : sufragar, costear
defrost [dɪˈfrɔst] *vt* : descongelar, deshelar — *vi* : descongelarse, deshelarse
deft [ˈdɛft] *adj* : hábil, diestro — **deftly** *adv*
defunct [dɪˈfʌŋkt] *adj* **1** DECEASED : difunto, fallecido **2** EXTINCT : extinto, fenecido
defuse [dɪˈfjuːz] *vt* : desactivar ⟨to defuse the situation : reducir las tensiones⟩
defy [dɪˈfaɪ] *vt* **-fied; -fying 1** CHALLENGE : desafiar, retar **2** DISOBEY : desobedecer **3** RESIST : resistir, hacer imposible, hacer inútil

degenerate[1] [di'dʒɛnəˌreɪt] *vi* **-ated; -ating** : degenerar

degenerate[2] [di'dʒɛnərət] *adj* : degenerado

degeneration [diˌdʒɛnə'reɪʃən] *n* : degeneración *f*

degenerative [di'dʒɛnərətɪv] *adj* : degenerative

degradation [ˌdɛgrə'deɪʃən] *n* : degradación *f*

degrade [di'greɪd] *vt* **-graded; -grading 1** : degradar, envilecer **2 to degrade oneself** : rebajarse

degrading [di'greɪdɪŋ] *adj* : degradante

degree [di'griː] *n* **1** EXTENT : grado *m* ⟨a third degree burn : una quemadura de tercer grado⟩ **2** : título *m* (de enseñanza superior) **3** : grado *m* (de un círculo, de la temperatura) **4 by degrees** : gradualmente, poco a poco

dehydrate [di'haɪˌdreɪt] *v* **-drated; -drating** *vt* : deshidratar — *vi* : deshidratarse

dehydration [ˌdiːhaɪ'dreɪʃən] *n* : deshidratación *f*

deice [ˌdiː'aɪs] *vt* **-iced; -icing** : deshelar, descongelar

deify ['diːəˌfaɪ, 'deɪ-] *vt* **-fied; -fying** : deificar

deign ['deɪn] *vi* : dignarse, condescender

deity ['diːəti, 'deɪ-] *n*, *pl* **-ties 1 the Deity** : Dios *m* **2** GOD, GODDESS : deidad *f*; dios *m*, diosa *f*

dejected [di'dʒɛktəd] *adj* : abatido, desalentado, desanimado

dejection [di'dʒɛkʃən] *n* : abatimiento *m*, desaliento *m*, desánimo *m*

delay[1] [di'leɪ] *vt* **1** POSTPONE : posponer, postergar **2** HOLD UP : retrasar, demorar — *vi* : tardar, demorar

delay[2] *n* **1** LATENESS : tardanza *f* **2** HOLDUP : demora *f*, retraso *m*

delectable [di'lɛktəbəl] *adj* **1** DELICIOUS : delicioso, exquisito **2** DELIGHTFUL : encantador

delegate[1] ['dɛlɪˌgeɪt] *v* **-gated; -gating** : delegar

delegate[2] ['dɛlɪgət, -ˌgeɪt] *n* : delegado *m*, -da *f*

delegation [ˌdɛlɪ'geɪʃən] *n* : delegación *f*

delete [di'liːt] *vt* **-leted; -leting** : suprimir, tachar, eliminar

deletion [di'liːʃən] *n* : supresión *f*, tachadura *f*, eliminación *f*

deli ['dɛli] → **delicatessen**

deliberate[1] [di'lɪbəˌreɪt] *v* **-ated; -ating** *vt* : deliberar sobre, reflexionar sobre, considerar — *vi* : deliberar

deliberate[2] [di'lɪbərət] *adj* **1** CONSIDERED : reflexionado, premeditado **2** INTENTIONAL : deliberado, intencional **3** SLOW : lento, pausado

deliberately [di'lɪbərətli] *adv* **1** INTENTIONALLY : adrede, a propósito **2** SLOWLY : pausadamente, lentamente

deliberation [diˌlɪbə'reɪʃən] *n* **1** CONSIDERATION : deliberación *f*, consideración *f* **2** SLOWNESS : lentitud *f*

delicacy ['dɛlɪkəsi] *n*, *pl* **-cies 1** : manjar *m*, exquisitez *f* ⟨caviar is a real delicacy : el caviar es un verdadero manjar⟩ **2** FINENESS : delicadeza *f* **3** FRAGILITY : fragilidad *f*

delicate ['dɛlɪkət] *adj* **1** SUBTLE : delicado ⟨a delicate fragrance : una fragancia delicada⟩ **2** DAINTY : delicado, primoroso, fino **3** FRAGILE : frágil **4** SENSITIVE : delicado ⟨a delicate matter : un asunto delicado⟩

delicately ['dɛlɪkətli] *adv* : delicadamente, con delicadeza

delicatessen [ˌdɛlɪkə'tɛsən] *n* : charcutería *f*, fiambrería *f*, salchichonería *f* *Mex*

delicious [di'lɪʃəs] *adj* : delicioso, exquisito, rico — **deliciously** *adv*

delight[1] [di'laɪt] *vt* : deleitar, encantar — *vi* **to delight in** : deleitarse con, complacerse en

delight[2] *n* **1** JOY : placer *m*, deleite *m*, gozo *m* **2** : encanto *m* ⟨your garden is a delight : su jardín es un encanto⟩

delightful [di'laɪtfəl] *adj* : delicioso, encantador

delightfully [di'laɪtfəli] *adv* : de manera encantadora, de maravilla

delineate [di'lɪniˌeɪt] *vt* **-eated; -eating** : delinear, trazar, bosquejar

delinquency [di'lɪŋkwəntsi] *n*, *pl* **-cies** : delincuencia *f*

delinquent[1] [di'lɪŋkwənt] *adj* **1** : delincuente **2** OVERDUE : vencido y sin pagar, moroso

delinquent[2] *n* : delincuente *mf* ⟨juvenile delinquent : delincuente juvenil⟩

delirious [di'lɪriəs] *adj* : delirante ⟨delirious with joy : loco de alegría⟩

delirium [di'lɪriəm] *n* : delirio *m*, desvarío *m*

deliver [di'lɪvər] *vt* **1** FREE : liberar, librar **2** DISTRIBUTE, HAND : entregar, repartir **3** : asistir en el parto de (un niño) **4** : pronunciar ⟨to deliver a speech : pronunciar un discurso⟩ **5** PROJECT : despachar, lanzar ⟨he delivered a fast ball : lanzó un pelota rápida⟩ **6** DEAL : propinar, asestar ⟨to deliver a blow : asestar un golpe⟩

deliverance [di'lɪvərənts] *n* : liberación *f*, rescate *m*, salvación *f*

deliverer [di'lɪvərər] *n* RESCUER : libertador *m*, -dora *f*; salvador *m*, -dora *f*

delivery [di'lɪvəri] *n*, *pl* **-eries 1** LIBERATION : liberación *f* **2** : entrega *f*, reparto *m* ⟨cash on delivery : entrega contra reembolso⟩ ⟨home delivery : servicio a domicilio⟩ **3** CHILDBIRTH : parto *m*, alumbramiento *m* **4** SPEECH : expresión *f* oral, modo *m* de hablar **5** THROW : lanzamiento *m*

dell ['dɛl] *n* : hondonada *f*, valle *m* pequeño

delta ['dɛltə] *n* : delta *m*

delude [di'luːd] *vt* **-luded; -luding 1** : engañar **2 to delude oneself** : engañarse

deluge[1] ['dɛl‚ju:ʤ, -‚ju:ʒ] *vt* **-uged; -uging 1** FLOOD : inundar **2** OVERWHELM : abrumar ⟨deluged with requests : abrumado de pedidos⟩
deluge[2] *n* **1** FLOOD : inundación *f* **2** DOWNPOUR : aguacero *m* **3** BARRAGE : aluvión *m*
delusion [di'lu:ʒən] *n* **1** : ilusión *f* (falsa) **2 delusions of grandeur** : delirios *mpl* de grandeza
deluxe [di'lʌks, -'lʊks] *adj* : de lujo
delve ['dɛlv] *vi* **delved; delving 1** DIG : escarbar **2 to delve into** PROBE : cavar en, ahondar en
demagogue ['dɛmə‚gɑg] *n* : demagogo *m*, demagoga *f*
demand[1] [di'mænd] *vt* : demandar, exigir, reclamar
demand[2] *n* **1** REQUEST : petición *f*, pedido *m*, demanda *f* ⟨by popular demand : a petición del público⟩ **2** CLAIM : reclamación *f*, exigencia *f* **3** MARKET : demanda *f* ⟨supply and demand : la oferta y la demanda⟩
demanding [di'mændɪŋ] *adj* : exigente
demarcation [‚di:‚mɑr'keɪʃən] *n* : demarcación *f*, deslinde *m*
demean [di'mi:n] *vt* : degradar, rebajar
demeanor [di'mi:nər] *n* : comportamiento *m*, conducta *f*
demented [di'mɛntəd] *adj* : demente, loco
dementia [di'mɛntʃə] *n* : demencia *f*
demerit [di'mɛrət] *n* : demérito *m*
demigod ['dɛmi‚gɑd, -‚gɔd] *n* : semidiós *m*
demise [di'maiz] *n* **1** DEATH : fallecimiento *m*, deceso *m* **2** END : hundimiento *m*, desaparición *f* (de una institución, etc.)
demitasse ['dɛmi‚tæs, -‚tɑs] *n* : taza *f* pequeña (de café)
demobilization [di‚mo:bələ'zeɪʃən] : desmovilización *f*
demobilize [di'mo:bə‚laiz] *vt* **-lized; -lizing** : desmovilizar
democracy [di'mɑkrəsi] *n, pl* **-cies** : democracia *f*
democrat ['dɛmə‚kræt] *n* : demócrata *mf*
democratic [‚dɛmə'krætɪk] *adj* : democrático — **democratically** [-tɪkli] *adv*
demographic [dɛmə'græfɪk] *adj* : demográfico
demolish [di'mɑlɪʃ] *vt* **1** RAZE : demoler, derribar, arrasar **2** DESTROY : destruir, destrozar
demolition [‚dɛmə'lɪʃən, ‚di:-] *n* : demolición *f*, derribo *m*
demon ['di:mən] *n* : demonio *m*, diablo *m*
demonstrably [di'mɑntstrəbli] *adv* : manifiestamente, claramente
demonstrate ['dɛmən‚streɪt] *vt* **-strated; -strating 1** SHOW : demostrar **2** PROVE : probar, demostrar **3** EXPLAIN : explicar, ilustrar

demonstration [‚dɛmən'streɪʃən] *n* **1** SHOW : muestra *f*, demostración *f* **2** RALLY : manifestación *f*
demonstrative [di'mɑntstrətɪv] *adj* **1** EFFUSIVE : efusivo, expresivo, demostrativo **2** : demostrativo (en lingüística) ⟨demonstrative pronoun : pronombre demostrativo⟩
demonstrator ['dɛmən‚streɪtər] *n* **1** : demostrador *m*, -dora *f* (de productos) **2** PROTESTER : manifestante *mf*
demoralize [di'mɔrə‚laiz] *vt* **-ized; -izing** : desmoralizar
demote [di'mo:t] *vt* **-moted; -moting** : degradar, bajar de categoría
demotion [di'mo:ʃən] *n* : degradación *f*, descenso *m* de categoría
demur [di'mər] *vi* **-murred; -murring 1** OBJECT : oponerse **2 to demur at** : ponerle objeciones a (algo)
demure [di'mjʊr] *adj* : recatado, modesto — **demurely** *adv*
den ['dɛn] *n* **1** LAIR : cubil *m*, madriguera *f* **2** HIDEOUT : guarida *f* **3** STUDY : estudio *m*, gabinete *m*
denature [di'neɪtʃər] *vt* **-tured; -turing** : desnaturalizar
denial [di'naiəl] *n* **1** REFUSAL : rechazo *m*, denegación *f*, negativa *f* **2** REPUDIATION : negación *f* (de una creencia, etc.), rechazo *m*
denigrate ['dɛni‚greɪt] *vt* **-grated; -grating** : denigrar
denim ['dɛnəm] *n* **1** : tela *f* vaquera, mezclilla *f* *Chile, Mex* **2 denims** *npl* → **jeans**
denizen ['dɛnəzən] *n* : habitante *mf*; morador *m*, -dora *f*
denomination [di‚nɑmə'neɪʃən] *n* **1** FAITH : confesión *f*, fe *f* **2** VALUE : denominación *f*, valor *m* (de una moneda)
denominator [di'nɑmə‚neɪtər] *n* : denominador *m*
denote [di'no:t] *vt* **-noted; -noting 1** INDICATE, MARK : indicar, denotar, señalar **2** MEAN : significar
denouement [‚deɪnu:'mɑ] *n* : desenlace *m*
denounce [di'naʊnts] *vt* **-nounced; -nouncing 1** CENSURE : denunciar, censurar **2** ACCUSE : denunciar, acusar, delatar
dense ['dɛnts] *adj* **denser; -est 1** THICK : espeso, denso ⟨dense vegetation : vegetación densa⟩ ⟨a dense fog : una niebla espesa⟩ **2** STUPID : estúpido, burro *fam*
densely ['dɛntsli] *adv* **1** THICKLY : densamente **2** STUPIDLY : torpemente
denseness ['dɛntsnəs] *n* **1** → **density 2** STUPIDITY : estupidez *f*
density ['dɛntsəti] *n, pl* **-ties** : densidad *f*
dent[1] ['dɛnt] *vt* : abollar, mellar
dent[2] *n* : abolladura *f*, mella *f*
dental ['dɛntəl] *adj* : dental
dental floss *n* : hilo *m* dental

dentifrice ['dɛntəfrɪs] *n* : dentífrico *m*, pasta *f* de dientes
dentist ['dɛntɪst] *n* : dentista *mf*
dentistry ['dɛntɪstri] *n* : odontología *f*
dentures ['dɛntʃərz] *npl* : dentadura *f* postiza
denude [di'nu:d, -'nju:d] *vt* **-nuded; -nuding** STRIP : desnudar, despojar
denunciation [di,nʌntsi'eɪʃən] *n* : denuncia *f*, acusación *f*
deny [di'naɪ] *vt* **-nied; -nying 1** REFUTE : desmentir, negar **2** DISOWN, REPUDIATE : negar, renegar de **3** REFUSE : denegar **4 to deny oneself** : privarse, sacrificarse
deodorant [di'o:dərənt] *n* : desodorante *m*
deodorize [di'o:də,raɪz] *vt* **-ized; -izing** : desodorizar
depart [di'pɑrt] *vt* : salirse de — *vi* **1** LEAVE : salir, partir, irse **2** DIE : morir
department [di'pɑrtmənt] *n* **1** DIVISION : sección *f* (de una tienda, una organización, etc.), departamento *m* (de una empresa, una universidad, etc.), ministerio *m* (del gobierno) **2** PROVINCE, SPHERE : esfera *f*, campo *m*, competencia *f*
departmental [di,pɑrt'mɛntəl, ,di:-] *adj* : departamental
department store *n* : grandes almacenes *mpl*
departure [di'pɑrtʃər] *n* **1** LEAVING : salida *f*, partida *f* **2** DEVIATION : desviación *f*
depend [di'pɛnd] *vi* **1** RELY : contar (con), confiar (en) ⟨depend on me! : ¡cuenta conmigo!⟩ **2 to depend on** : depender de ⟨success depends on hard work : el éxito depende de trabajar duro⟩ **3 that depends** : según, eso depende
dependable [di'pɛndəbəl] *adj* : responsable, digno de confianza, fiable
dependence [di'pɛndənts] *n* : dependencia *f*
dependency [di'pɛndəntsi] *n, pl* **-cies 1** → dependence **2** : posesión *f* (de una unidad política)
dependent[1] [di'pɛndənt] *adj* : dependiente
dependent[2] *n* : persona *f* a cargo de alguien
depict [di'pɪkt] *vt* **1** PORTRAY : representar **2** DESCRIBE : describir
depiction [di'pɪkʃən] *n* : representación *f*, descripción *f*
deplete [di'pli:t] *vt* **-pleted; -pleting 1** EXHAUST : agotar **2** REDUCE : reducir
depletion [di'pli:ʃən] *n* **1** EXHAUSTION : agotamiento *m* **2** REDUCTION : reducción *f*, disminución *f*
deplorable [di'plorəbəl] *adj* **1** CONTEMPTIBLE : deplorable, despreciable **2** LAMENTABLE : lamentable
deplore [di'plor] *vt* **-plored; -ploring 1** REGRET : deplorar, lamentar **2** CONDEMN : condenar, deplorar

deploy [di'plɔɪ] *vt* : desplegar
deployment [di'plɔɪmənt] *n* : despliegue *m*
deport [di'port] *vt* **1** EXPEL : deportar, expulsar (de un país) **2 to deport oneself** BEHAVE : comportarse
deportation [,di:,por'teɪʃən] *n* : deportación *f*
depose [di'po:z] *vt* **-posed; -posing** : deponer
deposit[1] [di'pɑzət] *vt* **-ited; -iting** : depositar
deposit[2] *n* **1** : depósito *m* (en el banco) **2** DOWN PAYMENT : entrega *f* inicial **3** : depósito *m*, yacimiento *m* (en geología)
deposition [,dɛpə'zɪʃən] *n* TESTIMONY : deposición *f*
depositor [di'pɑzətər] *n* : depositante *mf*
depository [di'pɑzə,tori] *n, pl* **-ries** : almacén *m*, depósito *m*
depot [*in sense 1 usu* 'dɛ,po:, *2 usu* 'di:-] *n* **1** STOREHOUSE : almacén *m*, depósito *m* **2** STATION, TERMINAL : terminal *mf*, estación *f* (de autobuses, ferrocarriles, etc.)
deprave [di'preɪv] *vt* **-praved; -praving** : depravar, pervertir
depraved [di'preɪvd] *adj* : depravado, degenerado
depravity [di'prævəti] *n, pl* **-ties** : depravación *f*
depreciate [di'pri:ʃi,eɪt] *v* **-ated; -ating** *vt* **1** DEVALUE : depreciar, devaluar **2** DISPARAGE : menospreciar, despreciar — *vi* : depreciarse, devaluarse
depreciation [di,pri:ʃi'eɪʃən] *n* : depreciación *f*, devaluación *f*
depress [di'prɛs] *vt* **1** PRESS, PUSH : apretar, presionar, pulsar **2** REDUCE : reducir, hacer bajar (precios, ventas, etc.) **3** SADDEN : deprimir, abatir, entristecer **4** DEVALUE : depreciar
depressant[1] [di'prɛsənt] *adj* : depresivo
depressant[2] *n* : depresivo *m*
depressed [di'prɛst] *adj* **1** DEJECTED : deprimido, abatido **2** : deprimido, en crisis (dícese de la economía)
depressing [di'prɛsɪŋ] *adj* : deprimente, triste
depression [di'prɛʃən] *n* **1** DESPONDENCY : depresión *f*, abatimiento *m* **2** : depresión *f* (en una superficie) **3** RECESSION : depresión *f* económica, crisis *f*
deprivation [,dɛprə'veɪʃən] *n* : privación *f*
deprive [di'praɪv] *vt* **-prived; -priving** : privar
depth ['dɛpθ] *n, pl* **depths** ['dɛpθs, 'dɛps] : profundidad *f*, fondo *m* ⟨to study in depth : estudiar a fondo⟩ ⟨in the depths of winter : en pleno invierno⟩
deputize ['dɛpju,taɪz] *vt* **-tized; -tizing** : nombrar como segundo
deputy ['dɛpjuti] *n, pl* **-ties** : suplente *mf*, sustituto *m*, -ta *f*
derail [di'reɪl] *v* : descarrilar

derailment [dɪ'reɪlmənt] *n* : descarrilamiento *m*
derange [dɪ'reɪndʒ] *vt* **-ranged; -ranging** **1** DISARRANGE : desarreglar, desordenar **2** DISTURB, UPSET : trastornar, perturbar **3** MADDEN : enloquecer, volver loco
derangement [dɪ'reɪndʒmənt] *n* **1** DISTURBANCE, UPSET : trastorno *m* **2** INSANITY : locura *f*, perturbación *f* mental
derby ['dərbi] *n, pl* **-bies 1** : derby *m* ⟨the Kentucky Derby : el Derby de Kentucky⟩ **2** : sombrero *m* hongo
deregulate [di'regju,leɪt] *vt* **-lated; -lating** : desregular
deregulation [di,regjʊ'leɪʃən] *n* : desregulación *f*
derelict¹ ['dɛrə,lɪkt] *adj* **1** ABANDONED : abandonado, en ruinas **2** REMISS : negligente, remiso
derelict² *n* **1** : propiedad *f* abandonada **2** VAGRANT : vagabundo *m*, -da *f*
deride [dɪ'raɪd] *vt* **-rided; -riding** : ridiculizar, burlarse de
derision [dɪ'rɪʒən] *n* : escarnio *m*, irrisión *f*, mofa *f*
derisive [dɪ'raɪsɪv] *adj* : burlón
derivation [,dɛrə'veɪʃən] *n* : derivación *f*
derivative¹ [dɪ'rɪvəṭɪv] *adj* **1** DERIVED : derivado **2** BANAL : carente de originalidad, banal
derivative² *n* : derivado *m*
derive [dɪ'raɪv] *v* **-rived; -riving** *vt* **1** OBTAIN : obtener, sacar **2** DEDUCE : deducir, inferir — *vi* : provenir, derivar, proceder
dermatologist [,dərmə'talədʒɪst] *n* : dermatólogo *m*, -ga *f*
dermatology [,dərmə'talədʒi] *n* : dermatología *f*
derogatory [dɪ'ragə,tori] *adj* : despectivo, despreciativo
derrick ['dɛrɪk] *n* **1** CRANE : grúa *f* **2** : torre *f* de perforación (sobre un pozo de petróleo)
descend [dɪ'sɛnd] *vt* : descender, bajar — *vi* **1** : descender, bajar ⟨he descended from the platform : descendió del estrado⟩ **2** DERIVE : descender, provenir **3** STOOP : rebajarse ⟨I descended to his level : me rebajé a su nivel⟩ **4** to descend upon : caer sobre, invadir
descendant¹ [dɪ'sɛndənt] *adj* : descendente
descendant² *n* : descendiente *mf*
descent [dɪ'sɛnt] *n* **1** : bajada *f*, descenso *m* ⟨the descent from the mountain : el descenso de la montaña⟩ **2** ANCESTRY : ascendencia *f*, linaje *f* **3** SLOPE : pendiente *f*, cuesta *f* **4** FALL : caída *f* **5** ATTACK : incursión *f*, ataque *m*
describe [dɪ'skraɪb] *vt* **-scribed; -scribing** : describir
description [dɪ'skrɪpʃən] *n* : descripción *f*

descriptive [dɪ'skrɪptɪv] *adj* : descriptivo ⟨descriptive adjective : adjetivo calificativo⟩
desecrate ['dɛsɪ,kreɪt] *vt* **-crated; -crating** : profanar
desecration [,dɛsɪ'kreɪʃən] *n* : profanación *f*
desegregate [di'sɛgrə,geɪt] *vt* **-gated; -gating** : eliminar la segregación racial de
desegregation [di,sɛgrə'geɪʃən] *n* : eliminación *f* de la segregación racial
desert¹ [dɪ'zərt] *vt* : abandonar (una persona o un lugar), desertar de (una causa, etc.) — *vi* : desertar
desert² ['dɛzərt] *adj* : desierto ⟨a desert island : una isla desierta⟩
desert³ *n* **1** ['dɛzərt] : desierto *m* (en geografía) **2** [dɪ'zərt] → **deserts**
deserter [dɪ'zərţər] *n* : desertor *m*, -tora *f*
desertion [dɪ'zərʃən] *n* : abandono *m*, deserción *f* (militar)
deserts [dɪ'zərts] *npl* : merecido *m* ⟨to get one's just deserts : llevarse uno su merecido⟩
deserve [dɪ'zərv] *vt* **-served; -serving** : merecer, ser digno de
deserving [dɪ'zərvɪŋ] *adj* : meritorio ⟨deserving of : digno de⟩
desiccate ['dɛsɪ,keɪt] *vt* **-cated; -cating** : desecar, deshidratar
design¹ [dɪ'zaɪn] *vt* **1** DEVISE : diseñar, concebir, idear **2** PLAN : proyectar **3** SKETCH : trazar, bosquejar
design² *n* **1** PLAN, SCHEME : plan *m*, proyecto *m* ⟨by design : a propósito, intencionalmente⟩ **2** SKETCH : diseño *m*, bosquejo *m* **3** PATTERN, STYLE : diseño *m*, estilo *m* **4 designs** *npl* INTENTIONS : propósitos *mpl*, designios *mpl*
designate ['dɛzɪg,neɪt] *vt* **-nated; -nating 1** INDICATE, SPECIFY : indicar, especificar **2** APPOINT : nombrar, designar
designation [,dɛzɪg'neɪʃən] *n* **1** NAMING : designación *f* **2** NAME : denominación *f*, nombre *m* **3** APPOINTMENT : designación *f*, nombramiento *m*
designer [dɪ'zaɪnər] *n* : diseñador *m*, -dora *f*
desirability [dɪ,zaɪrə'bɪləṭi] *n, pl* **-ties 1** ADVISABILITY : conveniencia *f* **2** ATTRACTIVENESS : atractivo *m*
desirable [dɪ'zaɪrəbəl] *adj* **1** ADVISABLE : conveniente, aconsejable **2** ATTRACTIVE : deseable, atractivo
desire¹ [dɪ'zaɪr] *vt* **-sired; -siring 1** WANT : desear **2** REQUEST : rogar, solicitar
desire² *n* : deseo *m*, anhelo *m*, ansia *m*
desist [dɪ'sɪst, -'zɪst] *vi* **to desist from** : desistir de, abstenerse de
desk ['dɛsk] *n* : escritorio *m*, pupitre *m* (en la escuela)
desktop ['dɛsk,tap] *adj* : de escritorio
desolate¹ ['dɛsə,leɪt, -zə-] *vt* **-lated; -lating** : devastar, desolar

desolate² [ˈdɛsələt, -zə-] *adj* **1** BARREN : desolado, desierto, yermo **2** DISCONSOLATE : desconsolado, desolado

desolation [ˌdɛsəˈleɪʃən, -zə-] *n* : desolación *f*

despair¹ [diˈspær] *vi* : desesperar, perder las esperanzas

despair² *n* : desesperación *f*, desesperanza *f*

desperate [ˈdɛspərət] *adj* **1** HOPELESS : desesperado, sin esperanzas **2** RASH : desesperado, precipitado **3** SERIOUS, URGENT : grave, urgente, apremiante ⟨a desperate need : una necesidad apremiante⟩

desperately [ˈdɛspərətli] *adv* : desesperadamente, urgentemente

desperation [ˌdɛspəˈreɪʃən] *n* : desesperación *f*

despicable [diˈspɪkəbəl, ˈdɛspɪ-] *adj* : vil, despreciable, infame

despise [diˈspaɪz] *vt* **-spised; -spising** : despreciar

despite [dəˈspaɪt] *prep* : a pesar de, aún con

despoil [diˈspɔɪl] *vt* : saquear

despondency [diˈspɑndənsi] *n* : desaliento *m*, desánimo *m*, depresión *f*

despondent [diˈspɑndənt] *adj* : desalentado, desanimado

despot [ˈdɛspət, -ˌpɑt] *n* : déspota *mf*; tirano *m*, -na *f*

despotic [dɛsˈpɑtɪk] *adj* : despótico

despotism [ˈdɛspəˌtɪzəm] *n* : despotismo *m*

dessert [diˈzərt] *n* : postre *m*

destination [ˌdɛstəˈneɪʃən] *n* : destino *m*, destinación *f*

destined [ˈdɛstənd] *adj* **1** FATED : predestinado **2** BOUND : destinado, con destino (a), con rumbo (a)

destiny [ˈdɛstəni] *n, pl* **-nies** : destino *m*

destitute [ˈdɛstəˌtuːt, -ˌtjuːt] *adj* **1** LACKING : carente, desprovisto **2** POOR : indigente, en miseria

destitution [ˌdɛstəˈtuːʃən, -ˈtjuː-] *n* : indigencia *f*, miseria *f*

destroy [diˈstrɔɪ] *vt* **1** KILL : matar **2** DEMOLISH : destruir, destrozar

destroyer [diˈstrɔɪər] *n* : destructor *m* (buque)

destructible [diˈstrʌktəbəl] *adj* : destructible

destruction [diˈstrʌkʃən] *n* : destrucción *f*, ruina *f*

destructive [diˈstrʌktɪv] *adj* : destructor, destructivo

desultory [ˈdɛsəlˌtori] *adj* **1** AIMLESS : sin rumbo, sin objeto **2** DISCONNECTED : inconexo

detach [diˈtætʃ] *vt* : separar, quitar, desprender

detached [diˈtætʃt] *adj* **1** SEPARATE : separado, suelto **2** ALOOF : distante, indiferente **3** IMPARTIAL : imparcial, objetivo

detachment [diˈtætʃmənt] *n* **1** SEPARATION : separación *f* **2** DETAIL : desta-

camento *m* (de tropas) **3** ALOOFNESS : reserva *f*, indiferencia *f* **4** IMPARTIALITY : imparcialidad *f*

detail¹ [diˈteɪl, ˈdiːˌteɪl] *vt* : detallar, exponer en detalle

detail² *n* **1** : detalle *m*, pormenor *m* **2** : destacamento *m* (de tropas)

detailed [diˈteɪld, ˈdiːˌteɪld] *adj* : detallado, minucioso

detain [diˈteɪn] *vt* **1** HOLD : detener **2** DELAY : entretener, demorar, retrasar

detect [diˈtɛkt] *vt* : detectar, descubrir

detection [diˈtɛkʃən] *n* : descubrimiento *m*

detective [diˈtɛktɪv] *n* : detective *mf* ⟨private detective : detective privado⟩

detector [diˈtɛktər] *n* : detector *m*

detention [diˈtɛnʃən] *n* : detención *m*

deter [diˈtər] *vt* **-terred; -terring** : disuadir, impedir

detergent [diˈtərdʒənt] *n* : detergente *m*

deteriorate [diˈtɪriəˌreɪt] *vi* **-rated; -rating** : deteriorarse, empeorar

deterioration [diˌtɪriəˈreɪʃən] *n* : deterioro *m*, empeoramiento *m*

determinant¹ [diˈtərmənənt] *adj* : determinante

determinant² *n* **1** : factor *m* determinante **2** : determinante *m* (en matemáticas)

determination [diˌtərməˈneɪʃən] *n* **1** DECISION : determinación *f*, decisión *f* **2** RESOLUTION : resolución *f*, determinación *f* ⟨with grim determination : con una firme resolución⟩

determine [diˈtərmən] *vt* **-mined; -mining 1** ESTABLISH : determinar, establecer **2** SETTLE : decidir **3** FIND OUT : averiguar **4** BRING ABOUT : determinar

determined [diˈtərmənd] *adj* RESOLUTE : decidido, resuelto

deterrent [diˈtərənt] *n* : medida *f* disuasiva

detest [diˈtɛst] *vt* : detestar, odiar, aborrecer

detestable [diˈtɛstəbəl] *adj* : detestable, odioso, aborrecible

dethrone [diˈθroːn] *vt* **-throned; -throning** : destronar

detonate [ˈdɛtənˌeɪt] *v* **-nated; -nating** *vt* : hacer detonar — *vi* : detonar, estallar

detonation [ˌdɛtəˈneɪʃən] *n* : detonación *f*

detour¹ [ˈdiːˌtʊr, diˈtʊr] *vi* : desviarse

detour² *n* : desvío *m*, rodeo *m*

detract [diˈtrækt] *vi* to **detract from** : restarle valor a, quitarle méritos a

detractor [diˈtræktər] *n* : detractor *m*, -tora *f*

detriment [ˈdɛtrəmənt] *n* : detrimento *m*, perjuicio *m*

detrimental [ˌdɛtrəˈmɛntəl] *adj* : perjudicial — **detrimentally** *adv*

devaluation [diˌvæljuˈeɪʃən] *n* : devaluación *f*

devalue [diˈvælˌjuː] *vt* **-ued; -uing** : devaluar, depreciar

devastate ['dɛvə₁steɪt] vt **-tated; -tating** : devastar, arrasar, asolar

devastation [₁dɛvə'steɪʃən] n : devastación f, estragos mpl

develop [di'vɛləp] vt **1** FORM, MAKE : desarrollar, elaborar, formar **2** : revelar (en fotografía) **3** FOSTER : desarrollar, fomentar **4** EXPLOIT : explotar (recursos), urbanizar (un área) **5** ACQUIRE : adquirir ⟨to develop an interest : adquirir un interés⟩ **6** CONTRACT : contraer (una enfermedad) — vi **1** GROW : desarrollarse **2** ARISE : aparecer, surgir

developed [di'vɛləpt] adj : avanzado, desarrollado

developer [di'vɛləpər] n **1** : inmobiliaria f, urbanizadora f **2** : revelador m (en fotografía)

development [di'vɛləpmənt] n **1** : desarrollo m ⟨physical development : desarrollo físico⟩ **2** : urbanización f (de un área), explotación f (de recursos), creación f (de inventos) **3** EVENT : acontecimiento m, suceso m ⟨to await developments : esperar acontecimientos⟩

deviant ['di:viənt] adj : desviado, anormal

deviate ['di:vi₁eɪt] v **-ated; -ating** vi : desviarse, apartarse — vt : desviar

deviation [₁di:vi'eɪʃən] n : desviación f

device [di'vaɪs] n **1** MECHANISM : dispositivo m, aparato m, mecanismo m **2** EMBLEM : emblema m

devil ['dɛvəl] vt **-iled** or **-illed; -iling** or **-illing 1** : sazonar con picante y especias **2** PESTER : molestar

devil² n **1** SATAN : el diablo, Satanás m **2** DEMON : diablo m, demonio m **3** FIEND : persona f diabólica; malvado m, -da f

devilish ['dɛvəlɪʃ] adj : diabólico

devilry ['dɛvəlri] n, pl **-ries** : diabluras fpl, travesuras fpl

devious ['di:viəs] adj **1** CRAFTY : taimado, artero **2** WINDING : tortuoso, sinuoso

devise [di'vaɪz] vt **-vised; -vising 1** INVENT : idear, concebir, inventar **2** PLOT : tramar

devoid [di'vɔɪd] adj ~ **of** : carente de, desprovisto de

devote [di'vo:t] vt **-voted; -voting 1** DEDICATE : consagrar, dedicar ⟨to devote one's life : dedicar uno su vida⟩ **2** **to devote oneself** : dedicarse

devoted [di'vo:t̬əd] adj **1** FAITHFUL : leal, fiel **2 to be devoted to someone** : tenerle mucho cariño a alguien

devotee [₁dɛvə'ti:, -'teɪ] n : devoto m, -ta f

devotion [di'vo:ʃən] n **1** DEDICATION : dedicación f, devoción f **2 devotions** PRAYERS : oraciones fpl, devociones fpl

devour [di'vaʊər] vt : devorar

devout [di'vaʊt] adj **1** PIOUS : devoto, piadoso **2** EARNEST, SINCERE : sincero, ferviente — **devoutly** adv

devoutness [di'vaʊtnəs] n : devoción f, piedad f

dew ['du:, 'dju:] n : rocío m

dewlap ['du₁læp, 'dju-] n : papada f

dew point n : punto m de condensación

dewy ['du:i, 'dju:i] adj **dewier; -est** : cubierto de rocío

dexterity [dɛk'stɛrəti] n, pl **-ties** : destreza f, habilidad f

dexterous ['dɛkstrəs] adj : diestro, hábil

dexterously ['dɛkstrəsli] adv : con destreza, con habilidad, hábilmente

dextrose ['dɛk₁stro:s] n : dextrosa f

diabetes [₁daɪə'bi:t̬iz] n : diabetes f

diabetic¹ [₁daɪə'bɛt̬ɪk] adj : diabético

diabetic² n : diabético m, -ca f

diabolic [₁daɪə'bɑlɪk] or **diabolical** [-lɪkəl] adj : diabólico, satánico

diacritical mark [₁daɪə'krɪt̬ɪkəl] n : signo m diacrítico

diadem ['daɪə₁dɛm, -dəm] n : diadema f

diagnose ['daɪɪg₁no:s, ₁daɪɪg'no:s] vt **-nosed; -nosing** : diagnosticar

diagnosis [₁daɪɪg'no:sɪs] n, pl **-noses** [-'no:₁si:z] : diagnóstico m

diagnostic [₁daɪɪg'nɑstɪk] adj : diagnóstico

diagonal¹ [daɪ'ægənəl] adj : diagonal, en diagonal

diagonal² n : diagonal f

diagonally [daɪ'ægənəli] adv : diagonalmente, en diagonal

diagram¹ ['daɪə₁græm] vt **-gramed** or **-grammed; -graming** or **-gramming** : hacer un diagrama de

diagram² n : diagrama m, gráfico m, esquema m

dial¹ ['daɪl] v **dialed** or **dialled; dialing** or **dialling** : marcar, discar

dial² n : esfera f (de un reloj), dial m (de un radio), disco m (de un teléfono)

dialect ['daɪə₁lɛkt] n : dialecto m

dialogue ['daɪə₁lɔg] n : diálogo m

diameter [daɪ'æmət̬ər] n : diámetro m

diamond ['daɪmənd, 'daɪə-] n **1** : diamante m, brillante m ⟨a diamond necklace : un collar de brillantes⟩ **2** : rombo m, forma f de rombo **3** : diamante m (en naipes) **4** INFIELD : cuadro m, diamante m (en béisbol)

diaper ['daɪpər, 'daɪə-] n : pañal m

diaphragm ['daɪə₁fræm] n : diafragma m

diarrhea [₁daɪə'ri:ə] n : diarrea f

diary ['daɪəri] n, pl **-ries** : diario m

diatribe ['daɪə₁traɪb] n : diatriba f

dice¹ ['daɪs] vt **diced; dicing** : cortar en cubos

dice² ns & pl **1** → **die²** **2** : dados mpl (juego)

dicker ['dɪkər] vt : regatear

dictate¹ ['dɪk₁teɪt, dɪk'teɪt] v **-tated; -tating** vt **1** : dictar ⟨to dictate a letter : dictar una carta⟩ **2** ORDER : mandar, ordenar — vi : dar órdenes

dictate² ['dɪk,teɪt] *n* **1** : mandato *m*, orden *f* **2 dictates** *npl* : dictados *mpl* ⟨the dictates of conscience : los dictados de la conciencia⟩

dictation [dɪk'teɪʃən] *n* : dictado *m*

dictator ['dɪk,teɪt̬ər] *n* : dictador *m*, -dora *f*

dictatorial [,dɪktə'toriəl] *adj* : dictatorial — **dictatorially** *adv*

dictatorship [dɪk'teɪt̬ər,ʃɪp, 'dɪk,-] *n* : dictadura *f*

diction ['dɪkʃən] *n* **1** : lenguaje *m*, estilo *m* **2** ENUNCIATION : dicción *f*, articulación *f*

dictionary ['dɪkʃə,neri] *n, pl* **-naries** : diccionario *m*

did → **do**

didactic [daɪ'dæktɪk] *adj* : didáctico

die¹ ['daɪ] *vi* **died** ['daɪd]; **dying** ['daɪɪŋ] **1** : morir **2** CEASE : morir, morirse ⟨a dying civilization : una civilización moribunda⟩ **3** STOP : apagarse, dejar de funcionar ⟨the motor died : el motor se apagó⟩ **4 to die down** SUBSIDE : amainar, disminuir **5 to die out** : extinguirse **6 to be dying for** *or* **to be dying to** : morirse por ⟨I'm dying to leave : me muero por irme⟩

die² ['daɪ] *n, pl* **dice** ['daɪs] : dado *m*

die³ *n, pl* **dies** ['daɪz] **1** STAMP : troquel *m*, cuño *m* **2** MOLD : matriz *f*, molde *m*

diesel ['di:zəl, -səl] *n* : diesel *m*

diet¹ ['daɪət] *vi* : ponerse a régimen, hacer dieta

diet² *n* : régimen *m*, dieta *f*

dietary ['daɪə,teri] *adj* : alimenticio, dietético

dietitian *or* **dietician** [,daɪə'tɪʃən] *n* : dietista *mf*

differ ['dɪfər] *vi* **-ferred; -ferring 1** : diferir, diferenciarse **2** VARY : variar **3** DISAGREE : discrepar, diferir, no estar de acuerdo

difference ['dɪfrənts, 'dɪfərənts] *n* : diferencia *f*

different ['dɪfrənt, 'dɪfərənt] *adj* : distinto, diferente

differentiate [,dɪfə'rentʃi,eɪt] *v* **-ated; -ating** *vt* **1** : hacer diferente **2** DISTINGUISH : distinguir, diferenciar — *vi* : distinguir

differentiation [,dɪfə,rentʃi'eɪʃən] *n* : diferenciación *f*

differently ['dɪfrəntli, 'dɪfərənt-] *adv* : de otra manera, de otro modo, distintamente

difficult ['dɪfɪ,kʌlt] *adj* : difícil

difficulty ['dɪfɪ,kʌlti] *n, pl* **-ties 1** : dificultad *f* **2** PROBLEM : problema *f*, dificultad *f*

diffidence ['dɪfədənts] *n* **1** SHYNESS : retraimiento *m*, timidez *f*, apocamiento *m* **2** RETICENCE : reticencia *f*

diffident ['dɪfədənt] *adj* **1** SHY : tímido, apocado, inseguro **2** RESERVED : reservado

diffuse¹ [dɪ'fju:z] *v* **-fused; -fusing** *vt* : difundir, esparcir — *vi* : difundirse, esparcirse

diffuse² [dɪ'fju:s] *adj* **1** WORDY : prolijo, verboso **2** WIDESPREAD : difuso

diffusion [dɪ'fju:ʒən] *n* : difusión *f*

dig¹ ['dɪg] *v* **dug** ['dʌg]; **digging** *vt* **1** : cavar, excavar ⟨to dig a hole : cavar un hoyo⟩ **2** EXTRACT : sacar ⟨to dig up potatoes : sacar papas del suelo⟩ **3** POKE, THRUST : clavar, hincar ⟨he dug me in the ribs : me dio un codazo en las costillas⟩ **4 to dig up** DISCOVER : descubrir, sacar a luz — *vi* : cavar, excavar

dig² *n* **1** POKE : codazo *m* **2** GIBE : pulla *f* **3** EXCAVATION : excavación *f*

digest¹ [daɪ'dʒest, dɪ-] *vt* **1** ASSIMILATE : digerir, asimilar **2** : digerir (comida) **3** SUMMARIZE : compendiar, resumir

digest² ['daɪ,dʒest] *n* : compendio *m*, resumen *m*

digestible [daɪ'dʒestəbəl, dɪ-] *adj* : digerible

digestion [daɪ'dʒestʃən, dɪ-] *n* : digestión *f*

digestive [daɪ'dʒestɪv, dɪ-] *adj* : digestivo ⟨the digestive system : el sistema digestivo⟩

digit ['dɪdʒət] *n* **1** NUMERAL : dígito *m*, número *m* **2** FINGER, TOE : dedo *m*

digital ['dɪdʒət̬əl] *adj* : digital — **digitally** *adv*

dignified ['dɪgnə,faɪd] *adj* : digno, decoroso

dignify ['dɪgnə,faɪ] *vt* **-fied; -fying** : dignificar, honrar

dignitary ['dɪgnə,teri] *n, pl* **-taries** : dignatario *m*, -ria *f*

dignity ['dɪgnəti] *n, pl* **-ties** : dignidad *f*

digress [daɪ'gres, də-] *vi* : desviarse del tema, divagar

digression [daɪ'greʃən, də-] *n* : digresión *f*

dike *or* **dyke** ['daɪk] *n* : dique *m*

dilapidated [də'læpə,deɪt̬əd] *adj* : ruinoso, desvencijado, destartalado

dilapidation [də,læpə'deɪʃən] *n* : deterioro *m*, estado *m* ruinoso

dilate [daɪ'leɪt, 'daɪ,leɪt] *v* **-lated; -lating** *vt* : dilatar — *vi* : dilatarse

dilemma [dɪ'lɛmə] *n* : dilema *m*

dilettante ['dɪlə,tɑnt, -,tænt] *n, pl* **-tantes** [-,tɑnts, -,tænts] *or* **-tanti** [,dɪlə'tɑnti, -'tæn-] : diletante *mf*

diligence ['dɪlədʒənts] *n* : diligencia *f*, aplicación *f*

diligent ['dɪlədʒənt] *adj* : diligente ⟨a diligent search : una búsqueda minuciosa⟩ — **diligently** *adv*

dill ['dɪl] *n* : eneldo *m*

dillydally ['dɪli,dæli] *vi* **-lied; lying** : demorarse, perder tiempo

dilute [daɪ'lu:t, də-] *vt* **-luted; -luting** : diluir, aguar

dilution [daɪ'lu:ʃən, də-] *n* : dilución *f*

dim¹ ['dɪm] *v* **dimmed; dimming** *vt* : atenuar (la luz), nublar (la vista), borrar (la memoria), opacar (una superficie) — *vi* : oscurecerse, apagarse

dim² *adj* **dimmer; dimmest 1** FAINT : oscuro, tenue (dícese de la luz), nublado (dícese de la vista), borrado (dícese de la memoria) **2** DULL : deslustrado **3** STUPID : tonto, torpe

dime ['daɪm] *n* : moneda *f* de diez centavos

dimension [də'mɛntʃən, daɪ-] *n* **1** : dimensión *f* **2 dimensions** *npl* EXTENT, SCOPE : dimensiones *fpl*, extensión *f*, medida *f*

diminish [də'mɪnɪʃ] *vt* LESSEN : disminuir, reducir, amainar — *vi* DWINDLE, WANE : menguar, reducirse

diminutive [də'mɪnjʊtɪv] *adj* : diminutivo, minúsculo

dimly ['dɪmli] *adv* : indistintamente, débilmente

dimmer ['dɪmər] *n* : potenciómetro *m*, conmutador *m* de luces (en automóviles)

dimness ['dɪmnəs] *n* : oscuridad *f*, debilidad *f* (de la vista), imprecisión *f* (de la memoria)

dimple ['dɪmpəl] *n* : hoyuelo *m*

din ['dɪn] *n* : estrépito *m*, estruendo *m*

dine ['daɪn] *vi* **dined; dining** : cenar

diner ['daɪnər] *n* **1** : comensal *mf* (persona) **2** : vagón *m* restaurante (en un tren) **3** : cafetería *f*, restaurante *m* barato

dinghy ['dɪŋi, 'dɪŋgi, 'dɪŋki] *n, pl* **-ghies** : bote *m*

dinginess ['dɪndʒinəs] *n* **1** DIRTINESS : suciedad *f* **2** SHABBINESS : lo gastado, lo deslucido

dingy ['dɪndʒi] *adj* **-gier; -est 1** DIRTY : sucio **2** SHABBY : gastado, deslucido

dinner ['dɪnər] *n* : cena *f*, comida *f*

dinosaur ['daɪnəˌsɔr] *n* : dinosaurio *m*

dint ['dɪnt] *n* **by dint of** : a fuerza de

diocese ['daɪəsəs, -ˌsiːz, -ˌsiːs] *n, pl* **-ceses** ['daɪəsəsəz] : diócesis *f*

dip¹ ['dɪp] *v* **dipped; dipping** *vt* **1** DUNK, PLUNGE : sumergir, mojar, meter **2** LADLE : servir con cucharón **3** LOWER : bajar, arriar (una bandera) — *vi* **1** DESCEND, DROP : bajar en picada, descender **2** SLOPE : bajar, inclinarse

dip² *n* **1** SWIM : chapuzón *m* **2** DROP : descenso *m*, caída *f* **3** SLOPE : cuesta *f*, declive *m* **4** SAUCE : salsa *f*

diphtheria [dɪf'θɪriə] *n* : difteria *f*

diphthong ['dɪfˌθɔŋ] *n* : diptongo *m*

diploma [də'ploːmə] *n, pl* **-mas** : diploma *m*

diplomacy [də'ploːməsi] *n* **1** : diplomacia *f* **2** TACT : tacto *m*, discreción *f*

diplomat ['dɪpləˌmæt] *n* **1** : diplomático *m*, -ca *f* (en relaciones internacionales) **2** : persona *f* diplomática

diplomatic [ˌdɪplə'mæt̪ɪk] *adj* : diplomático ⟨diplomatic immunity : inmunidad diplomática⟩

dipper ['dɪpər] *n* **1** LADLE : cucharón *m*, cazo *m* **2 Big Dipper** : Osa *f* Mayor **3 Little Dipper** : Osa *f* Menor

dire ['daɪr] *adj* **direr; direst 1** HORRIBLE : espantoso, terrible, horrendo **2** EXTREME : extremo ⟨dire poverty : pobreza extrema⟩

direct¹ [də'rɛkt, daɪ-] *vt* **1** ADDRESS : dirigir, mandar **2** AIM, POINT : dirigir **3** GUIDE : indicarle el camino (a alguien), orientar **4** MANAGE : dirigir ⟨to direct a film : dirigir una película⟩ **5** COMMAND : ordenar, mandar

direct² *adv* : directamente

direct³ *adj* **1** STRAIGHT : directo **2** FRANK : franco

direct current *n* : corriente *f* continua

direction [də'rɛkʃən, daɪ-] *n* **1** SUPERVISION : dirección *f* **2** INSTRUCTION, ORDER : instrucción *f*, orden *f* **3** COURSE : dirección *f*, rumbo *m* ⟨to change direction : cambiar de dirección⟩ **4 to ask directions** : pedir indicaciones

directional [də'rɛkʃənəl, daɪ-] *adj* : direccional

directive [də'rɛktɪv, daɪ-] *n* : directiva *f*

directly [də'rɛktli, daɪ-] *adv* **1** STRAIGHT : directamente ⟨directly north : directamente al norte⟩ **2** FRANKLY : francamente **3** EXACTLY : exactamente, justo ⟨directly opposite : justo enfrente⟩ **4** IMMEDIATELY : en seguida, inmediatamente

directness [də'rɛktnəs, daɪ-] *n* : franqueza *f*

director [də'rɛktər, daɪ-] *n* **1** : director *m*, -tora *f* **2 board of directors** : junta *f* directiva, directorio *m*

directory [də'rɛktəri, daɪ-] *n, pl* **-ries** : guía *f*, directorio *m* ⟨telephone directory : directorio telefónico⟩

dirge ['dərdʒ] *n* : canto *m* fúnebre

dirigible ['dɪrədʒəbəl, də'rɪdʒə-] *n* : dirigible *m*, zepelín *m*

dirt ['dərt] *n* **1** FILTH : suciedad *f*, mugre *f*, porquería *f* **2** SOIL : tierra *f*

dirtiness ['dərtinəs] *n* : suciedad *f*

dirty¹ ['dərti] *vt* **dirtied; dirtying** : ensuciar, manchar

dirty² *adj* **dirtier; -est 1** SOILED, STAINED : sucio, manchado **2** DISHONEST : sucio, deshonesto ⟨a dirty player : un jugador tramposo⟩ ⟨a dirty trick : una mala pasada⟩ **3** INDECENT : indecente, cochino ⟨a dirty joke : un chiste verde⟩

disability [ˌdɪsə'bɪləti] *n, pl* **-ties** : minusvalía *f*, discapacidad *f*, invalidez *f*

disable [dɪs'eɪbəl] *vt* **-abled; -abling** : dejar inválido, inutilizar, incapacitar

disabled [dɪs'eɪbəld] *adj* : minusválido, discapacitado

disabuse [ˌdɪsə'bjuːz] *vt* **-bused; -busing** : desengañar, sacar del error

disadvantage [ˌdɪsəd'væntɪdʒ] *n* : desventaja *f*

disadvantageous [ˌdɪsˌæd̪ˌvænˈteɪ-dʒəs] *adj* : desventajoso, desfavorable

disagree [ˌdɪsəˈgriː] *vi* **1** DIFFER : discrepar, no coincidir **2** DISSENT : disentir, discrepar, no estar de acuerdo
disagreeable [ˌdɪsəˈgriːəbəl] *adj* : desagradable
disagreement [ˌdɪsəˈgriːmənt] *n* **1** : desacuerdo *m* **2** DISCREPANCY : discrepancia *f* **3** ARGUMENT : discusión *f*, altercado *m*, disputa *f*
disappear [ˌdɪsəˈpɪr] *vi* : desaparecer, desvanecerse ⟨to disappear from view : perderse de vista⟩
disappearance [ˌdɪsəˈpɪrənts] *n* : desaparición *f*
disappoint [ˌdɪsəˈpɔɪnt] *vt* : decepcionar, defraudar, fallar
disappointing [ˌdɪsəˈpɔɪntɪŋ] *adj* : decepcionante
disappointment [ˌdɪsəˈpɔɪntmənt] *n* : decepción *f*, desilusión *f*, chasco *m*
disapproval [ˌdɪsəˈpruːvəl] *n* : desaprobación *f*
disapprove [ˌdɪsəˈpruːv] *vi* **-proved; -proving** : desaprobar, estar en contra
disapprovingly [ˌdɪsəˈpruːvɪŋli] *adv* : con desaprobación
disarm [dɪsˈɑrm] *vt* : desarmar
disarmament [dɪsˈɑrməmənt] *n* : desarme *m* ⟨nuclear disarmament : desarme nuclear⟩
disarrange [ˌdɪsəˈreɪndʒ] *vt* **-ranged; -ranging** : desarreglar, desordenar
disarray [ˌdɪsəˈreɪ] *n* : desorden *m*, confusión *f*, desorganización *f*
disaster [dɪˈzæstər] *n* : desastre *m*, catástrofe *f*
disastrous [dɪˈzæstrəs] *adj* : desastroso
disband [dɪsˈbænd] *vt* : disolver — *vi* : disolverse, dispersarse
disbar [dɪsˈbɑr] *vt* **-barred; -barring** : prohibir de ejercer la abogacía
disbelief [ˌdɪsbɪˈliːf] *n* : incredulidad *f*
disbelieve [ˌdɪsbɪˈliːv] *v* **-lieved; -lieving** : no creer, dudar
disburse [dɪsˈbərs] *vt* **-bursed; -bursing** : desembolsar
disbursement [dɪsˈbərsmənt] *n* : desembolso *m*
disc → **disk**
discard [dɪsˈkɑrd, ˈdɪsˌkɑrd] *vt* : desechar, deshacerse de, botar — *vi* : descartarse (en juegos de naipes)
discern [dɪˈsərn, -ˈzərn] *vt* : discernir, distinguir, percibir
discernible [dɪˈsərnəbəl, -ˈzər-] *adj* : perceptible, visible
discernment [dɪˈsərnmənt, -ˈzərn-] *n* : discernimiento *m*, criterio *m*
discharge¹ [dɪsˈtʃɑrdʒ, ˈdɪsˌ-] *v* **-charged; -charging** **1** UNLOAD : descargar (carga), desembarcar (pasajeros) **2** SHOOT : descargar, disparar **3** FREE : liberar, poner en libertad **4** DISMISS : despedir **5** EMIT : despedir (humo, etc.), descargar (electricidad) **6** : cumplir con (una obligación), saldar (una deuda) — *vi* **1** : descargarse (dícese de una batería) **2** OOZE : supurar

discharge² [ˈdɪsˌtʃɑrdʒ, dɪsˈ-] *n* **1** EMISSION : descarga *f* (de electricidad), emisión *f* (de gases) **2** DISMISSAL : despido *m* (del empleo), baja *f* (del ejército) **3** SECRETION : secreción *f*
disciple [dɪˈsaɪpəl] *n* : discípulo *m*, -la *f*
discipline¹ [ˈdɪsəplən] *vt* **-plined; -plining** **1** PUNISH : castigar, sancionar (a los empleados) **2** CONTROL : disciplinar **3** **to discipline oneself** : disciplinarse
discipline² *n* **1** FIELD : disciplina *f*, campo *m* **2** TRAINING : disciplina *f* **3** PUNISHMENT : castigo *m* **4** SELF-CONTROL : dominio *m* de sí mismo
disc jockey *n* : disc jockey *mf*
disclaim [dɪsˈkleɪm] *vt* DENY : negar
disclose [dɪsˈkloːz] *vt* **-closed; -closing** : revelar, poner en evidencia
disclosure [dɪsˈkloːʒər] *n* : revelación *f*
disco [ˈdɪskoː] *n* **1** → **discotheque 2** *or* **disco music** : disco *f*, música *f* disco
discolor [dɪsˈkʌlər] *vt* **1** BLEACH : decolorar **2** FADE : desteñir **3** STAIN : manchar — *vi* : decolorarse, desteñirse
discoloration [dɪsˌkʌləˈreɪʃən] *n* **1** FADING : decoloración *f* **2** STAIN : mancha *f*
discomfort [dɪsˈkʌmfərt] *n* **1** PAIN : molestia *f*, malestar *m* **2** UNEASINESS : inquietud *f*
disconcert [ˌdɪskənˈsərt] *vt* : desconcertar
disconcerting [ˌdɪskənˈsərt̬ɪŋ] *adj* : desconcertante
disconnect [ˌdɪskəˈnɛkt] *vt* : desconectar
disconnected [ˌdɪskəˈnɛktəd] *adj* : inconexo
disconsolate [dɪsˈkɑntsələt] *adj* : desconsolado
discontent [ˌdɪskənˈtɛnt] *n* : descontento *m*
discontented [ˌdɪskənˈtɛntəd] *adj* : descontento
discontinue [ˌdɪskənˈtɪnˌjuː] *vt* **-ued; -uing** : suspender, descontinuar
discontinuity [dɪsˌkɑntəˈnuːət̬i, -ˈnjuː-] *n, pl* **-ties** : discontinuidad *f*
discontinuous [ˌdɪskənˈtɪnjəwəs] *adj* : discontinuo
discord [ˈdɪsˌkɔrd] *n* **1** STRIFE : discordia *f*, discordancia *f* **2** : disonancia *f* (en música)
discordant [dɪsˈkɔrdənt] *adj* : discordante, discorde — **discordantly** *adv*
discotheque [ˈdɪskəˌtɛk, ˌdɪskəˈtɛk] *n* : discoteca *f*
discount¹ [ˈdɪsˌkaʊnt, dɪsˈ-] *vt* **1** REDUCE : descontar, rebajar (precios) **2** DISREGARD : descartar, ignorar
discount² [ˈdɪsˌkaʊnt] *n* : descuento *m*, rebaja *f*
discourage [dɪsˈkərɪdʒ] *vt* **-aged; -aging** **1** DISHEARTEN : desalentar, desanimar **2** DISSUADE : disuadir
discouragement [dɪsˈkərɪdʒmənt] *n* : desánimo *m*, desaliento *m*

discouraging [dɪsˈkərədʒɪŋ] *adj* : desalentador

discourse¹ [dɪsˈkors] *vi* -coursed; -coursing : disertar, conversar

discourse² [ˈdɪsˌkors] *n* 1 TALK : conversación *f* 2 SPEECH, TREATISE : discurso *m*, tratado *m*

discourteous [dɪsˈkərtiəs] *adj* : descortés — **discourteously** *adv*

discourtesy [dɪsˈkərtəsi] *n, pl* -sies : descortesía *f*

discover [dɪsˈkʌvər] *vt* : descubrir

discoverer [dɪsˈkʌvərər] *n* : descubridor *m*, -dora *f*

discovery [dɪsˈkʌvəri] *n, pl* -ries : descubrimiento *m*

discredit¹ [dɪsˈkrɛdət] *vt* 1 DISBELIEVE : no creer, dudar 2 : desacreditar, desprestigiar, poner en duda ⟨they discredited his research : desacreditaron sus investigaciones⟩

discredit² *n* 1 DISREPUTE : descrédito *m*, desprestigio *m* 2 DOUBT : duda *f*

discreet [dɪsˈkriːt] *adj* : discreto — **discreetly** *adv*

discrepancy [dɪsˈkrɛpəntsi] *n, pl* -cies : discrepancia *f*

discretion [dɪsˈkrɛʃən] *n* 1 CIRCUMSPECTION : discreción *f*, circunspección *f* 2 JUDGMENT : discernimiento *m*, criterio *m*

discretionary [dɪsˈkrɛʃəˌnɛri] *adj* : discrecional

discriminate [dɪsˈkrɪməˌneɪt] *v* -nated; -nating *vt* DISTINGUISH : distinguir, discriminar, diferenciar — *vi* : discriminar ⟨to discriminate against women : discriminar a las mujeres⟩

discrimination [dɪsˌkrɪməˈneɪʃən] *n* 1 PREJUDICE : discriminación *f* 2 DISCERNMENT : discernimiento *m*

discriminatory [dɪsˈkrɪmənəˌtori] *adj* : discriminatorio

discus [ˈdɪskəs] *n, pl* -cuses [-kəsəz] : disco *m*

discuss [dɪsˈkʌs] *vt* : hablar de, discutir, tratar (de)

discussion [dɪsˈkʌʃən] *n* : discusión *f*, debate *m*, conversación *f*

disdain¹ [dɪsˈdeɪn] *vt* : desdeñar, despreciar ⟨they disdained to reply : no se dignaron a responder⟩

disdain² *n* : desdén *m*

disdainful [dɪsˈdeɪnfəl] *adj* : desdeñoso — **disdainfully** *adv*

disease [dɪˈziːz] *n* : enfermedad *f*, mal *m*, dolencia *f*

diseased [dɪˈziːzd] *adj* : enfermo

disembark [ˌdɪsɪmˈbark] *v* : desembarcar

disembarkation [dɪsˌɛmˌbarˈkeɪʃən] *n* : desembarco *m*, desembarque *m*

disembodied [ˌdɪsɪmˈbadid] *adj* : incorpóreo

disenchant [ˌdɪsɪnˈtʃænt] *vt* : desilusionar, desencantar, desengañar

disenchantment [ˌdɪsɪnˈtʃæntmənt] *n* : desencanto *m*, desilusión *f*

disengage [ˌdɪsɪnˈgeɪdʒ] *vt* -gaged; -gaging 1 : soltar, desconectar (un mecanismo) 2 to disengage the clutch : desembragar

disentangle [ˌdɪsɪnˈtæŋgəl] *vt* -gled; -gling UNTANGLE : desenredar, desenmarañar

disfavor [dɪsˈfeɪvər] *n* : desaprobación *f*

disfigure [dɪsˈfɪgjər] *vt* -ured; -uring : desfigurar (a una persona), afear (un edificio, un área)

disfigurement [dɪsˈfɪgjərmənt] *n* : desfiguración *f*, afeamiento *m*

disfranchise [dɪsˈfrænˌtʃaɪz] *vt* -chised; -chising : privar del derecho a votar

disgrace¹ [dɪˈskreɪs] *vt* -graced; -gracing : deshonrar

disgrace² *n* 1 DISHONOR : desgracia *f*, deshonra *f* 2 SHAME : vergüenza *f* ⟨he's a disgrace to his family : es una vergüenza para su familia⟩

disgraceful [dɪˈskreɪsfəl] *adj* : vergonzoso, deshonroso, ignominioso

disgracefully [dɪˈskreɪsfəli] *adv* : vergonzosamente

disgruntle [dɪsˈgrʌntəl] *vt* -tled; -tling : enfadar, contrariar

disguise¹ [dɪˈskaɪz] *vt* -guised; -guising 1 : disfrazar, enmascarar (el aspecto) 2 CONCEAL : encubrir, disimular

disguise² *n* : disfraz *m*

disgust¹ [dɪˈskʌst] *vt* : darle asco (a alguien), asquear, repugnar ⟨that disgusts me : eso me da asco⟩

disgust² *n* : asco *m*, repugnancia *f*

disgusting [dɪˈskʌstɪŋ] *adj* : asqueroso, repugnante — **disgustingly** *adv*

dish¹ [ˈdɪʃ] *vt* SERVE : servir

dish² *n* 1 : plato *m* ⟨the national dish : el plato nacional⟩ 2 PLATE : plato *m* ⟨to wash the dishes : lavar los platos⟩ 3 serving dish : fuente *f*

dishcloth [ˈdɪʃˌklɔθ] *n* : paño *m* de cocina (para secar), trapo *m* de fregar (para lavar)

dishearten [dɪsˈhartən] *vt* : desanimar, desalentar

dishevel [dɪˈʃɛvəl] *vt* -eled *or* -elled; -eling *or* -elling : desarreglar, despeinar (el pelo)

disheveled *or* **dishevelled** [dɪˈʃɛvəld] *adj* : despeinado (dícese del pelo), desarreglado, desaliñado

dishonest [dɪˈsanəst] *adj* : deshonesto, fraudulento — **dishonestly** *adv*

dishonesty [dɪˈsanəsti] *n, pl* -ties : deshonestidad *f*, falta *f* de honradez

dishonor¹ [dɪˈsanər] *vt* : deshonrar

dishonor² *n* : deshonra *f*

dishonorable [dɪˈsanərəbəl] *adj* : deshonroso — **dishonorably** [-bli] *adv*

dishrag [ˈdɪʃˌræg] → **dishcloth**

dishwasher [ˈdɪʃˌwɔʃər] *n* : lavaplatos *m*, lavavajillas *m*

disillusion [ˌdɪsəˈluːʒən] *vt* : desilusionar, desencantar, desengañar

disillusionment [ˌdɪsəˈluːʒənmənt] *n* : desilusión *f*, desencanto *m*

disinclination [dɪsˌɪnkləˈneɪʃən, -ˌɪŋ-] *n* : aversión *f*

disinclined [ˌdɪsɪnˈklaɪnd] *adv* : poco dispuesto

disinfect [ˌdɪsɪnˈfɛkt] *vt* : desinfectar

disinfectant[1] [ˌdɪsɪnˈfɛktənt] *adj* : desinfectante

disinfectant[2] *n* : desinfectante *m*

disinherit [ˌdɪsɪnˈhɛrət] *vt* : desheredar

disintegrate [dɪsˈɪntəˌɡreɪt] *v* **-grated; -grating** *vt* : desintegrar, deshacer — *vi* : desintegrarse, deshacerse

disintegration [dɪsˌɪntəˈɡreɪʃən] *n* : desintegración *f*

disinterested [dɪsˈɪntərəstəd, -ˌrɛs-] *adj* **1** INDIFFERENT : indiferente **2** IMPARTIAL : imparcial, desinteresado

disinterestedness [dɪsˈɪntərəstədnəs, -ˌrɛs-] *n* : desinterés *m*

disjointed [dɪsˈʤɔɪntəd] *adj* : inconexo, incoherente

disk *or* **disc** [ˈdɪsk] *n* : disco *m*

disk drive *n* : unidad *f* de disco

diskette [ˌdɪsˈkɛt] *n* : diskette *m*, disquete *m*

dislike[1] [dɪsˈlaɪk] *vt* **-liked; -liking** : tenerle aversión a (algo), tenerle antipatía (a alguien), no gustarle (algo a uno)

dislike[2] *n* : aversión *f*, antipatía *f*

dislocate [ˈdɪsloˌkeɪt, dɪsˈloː-] *vt* **-cated; -cating** : dislocar

dislocation [ˌdɪsloˈkeɪʃən] *n* : dislocación *f*

dislodge [dɪsˈlɑʤ] *vt* **-lodged; -lodging** : sacar, desalojar, desplazar

disloyal [dɪsˈlɔɪəl] *adj* : desleal

disloyalty [dɪsˈlɔɪəlti] *n, pl* **-ties** : deslealtad *f*

dismal [ˈdɪzməl] *adj* **1** GLOOMY : sombrío, lúgubre, tétrico **2** DEPRESSING : deprimente, triste

dismantle [dɪsˈmæntəl] *vt* **-tled; -tling** : desmantelar, desmontar, desarmar

dismay[1] [dɪsˈmeɪ] *vt* : consternar

dismay[2] *n* : consternación *f*

dismember [dɪsˈmɛmbər] *vt* : desmembrar

dismiss [dɪsˈmɪs] *vt* **1** : dejar salir, darle permiso (a alguien) para retirarse **2** DISCHARGE : despedir, destituir **3** REJECT : descartar, desechar, rechazar

dismissal [dɪsˈmɪsəl] *n* **1** : permiso *m* para retirarse **2** DISCHARGE : despido *m* (de un empleado), destitución *f* (de un funcionario) **3** REJECTION : rechazo *m*

dismount [dɪsˈmaʊnt] *vi* : desmontar, bajarse, apearse

disobedience [ˌdɪsəˈbiːdiənts] *n* : desobediencia *f* — **disobedient** [-ənt] *adj*

disobey [ˌdɪsəˈbeɪ] *v* : desobedecer

disorder[1] [dɪsˈɔrdər] *vt* : desordenar, desarreglar

disorder[2] *n* **1** DISARRAY : desorden *m* **2** UNREST : disturbios *mpl*, desórdenes *mpl* **3** AILMENT : afección *f*, indisposición *f*, dolencia *f*

disorderly [dɪsˈɔrdərli] *adj* **1** UNTIDY : desordenado, desarreglado **2** UNRULY : indisciplinado, alborotado **3** **disorderly conduct** : conducta *f* escandalosa

disorganization [dɪsˌɔrɡənəˈzeɪʃən] *n* : desorganización *f*

disorganize [dɪsˈɔrɡəˌnaɪz] *vt* **-nized; -nizing** : desorganizar

disorient [dɪsˈɔriˌɛnt] *vt* : desorientar

disown [dɪsˈoːn] *vt* : renegar de, repudiar

disparage [dɪsˈpærɪʤ] *vt* **-aged; -aging** : menospreciar, denigrar

disparagement [dɪsˈpærɪʤmənt] *n* : menosprecio *m*

disparate [ˈdɪspərət, dɪsˈpærət] *adj* : dispar, diferente

disparity [dɪsˈpærəti] *n, pl* **-ties** : disparidad *f*

dispassionate [dɪsˈpæʃənət] *adj* : desapasionado, imparcial — **dispassionately** *adv*

dispatch[1] [dɪsˈpæʧ] *vt* **1** SEND : despachar, enviar **2** KILL : despachar, matar **3** HANDLE : despachar

dispatch[2] *n* **1** SENDING : envío *m*, despacho *m* **2** MESSAGE : despacho *m*, reportaje *m* (de un periodista), parte *m* (en el ejército) **3** PROMPTNESS : prontitud *f*, rapidez *f*

dispel [dɪsˈpɛl] *vt* **-pelled; -pelling** : disipar, desvanecer

dispensable [dɪˈspɛntsəbəl] *adj* : prescindible

dispensation [ˌdɪspɛnˈseɪʃən] *n* EXEMPTION : exención *m*, dispensa *f*

dispense [dɪsˈpɛnts] *v* **-pensed; -pensing** *vt* **1** DISTRIBUTE : repartir, distribuir, dar **2** ADMINISTER, BESTOW : administrar (justicia), conceder (favores, etc.) **3** : preparar y despachar (medicamentos) — *vi* **to dispense with** : prescindir de

dispenser [dɪsˈpɛntsər] *n* : dispensador *m*, distribuidor *m* automático

dispersal [dɪsˈpərsəl] *n* : dispersión *f*

disperse [dɪsˈpərs] *v* **-persed; -persing** *vt* : dispersar, diseminar — *vi* : dispersarse

dispersion [dɪˈspərʒən] *n* : dispersión *f*

dispirit [dɪˈspɪrət] *vt* : desalentar, desanimar

displace [dɪsˈpleɪs] *vt* **-placed; -placing** **1** : desplazar (un líquido, etc.) **2** REPLACE : reemplazar

displacement [dɪsˈpleɪsmənt] *n* **1** : desplazamiento *m* (de personas) **2** REPLACEMENT : sustitución *f*, reemplazo *m*

display[1] [dɪsˈpleɪ] *vt* : exponer, exhibir, mostrar

display[2] *n* **1** : muestra *f*, exposición *f*, alarde *m* **2** : visualizador *m* (de una computadora)

displease [dɪsˈpliːz] *vt* **-pleased; -pleasing** : desagradar a, disgustar, contrariar

displeasure [dɪsˈplɛʒər] *n* : desagrado *m*
disposable [dɪsˈpoːzəbəl] *adj* **1** : desechable ⟨disposable diapers : pañales desechables⟩ **2** AVAILABLE : disponible
disposal [dɪsˈpoːzəl] *n* **1** PLACEMENT : disposición *f*, colocación *f* **2** REMOVAL : eliminación *f* **3** to have at one's disposal : disponer de, tener a su disposición
dispose [dɪsˈpoːz] *v* -posed; -posing *vt* **1** ARRANGE : disponer, colocar **2** INCLINE : predisponer — *vi* **1** to dispose of DISCARD : desechar, deshacerse de **2** to dispose of HANDLE : despachar
disposition [ˌdɪspəˈzɪʃən] *n* **1** ARRANGEMENT : disposición *f* **2** TENDENCY : predisposición *f*, inclinación *f* **3** TEMPERAMENT : temperamento *m*, carácter *m*
dispossess [ˌdɪspəˈzɛs] *vt* : deposeer
disproportion [ˌdɪsprəˈporʃən] *n* : desproporción *f*
disproportionate [ˌdɪsprəˈporʃənət] *adj* : desproporcionado — **disproportionately** *adv*
disprove [dɪsˈpruːv] *vt* -proved; -proving : rebatir, refutar
disputable [dɪsˈpjuːṭəbəl, ˈdɪspjuṭəbəl] *adj* : disputable, discutible
dispute[1] [dɪsˈpjuːt] *v* -puted; -puting *vt* **1** QUESTION : discutir, cuestionar **2** OPPOSE : combatir, resistir — *vi* ARGUE, DEBATE : discutir
dispute[2] *n* **1** DEBATE : debate *m*, discusión *f* **2** QUARREL : disputa *f*, discusión *f*
disqualification [dɪsˌkwɑləfəˈkeɪʃən] *n* : descalificación *f*
disqualify [dɪsˈkwɑləˌfaɪ] *vt* -fied; -fying : descalificar, inhabilitar
disquiet[1] [dɪsˈkwaɪət] *vt* : inquietar
disquiet[2] *n* : ansiedad *f*, inquietud *f*
disregard[1] [ˌdɪsrɪˈgɑrd] *vt* : ignorar, no prestar atención a
disregard[2] *n* : indiferencia *f*
disrepair [ˌdɪsrɪˈpær] *n* : mal estado *m*
disreputable [dɪsˈrɛpjuṭəbəl] *adj* : de mala fama (dícese de una persona o un lugar), vergonzoso (dícese de la conducta)
disreputably [dɪsˈrɛpjuṭəbli] *adv* : vergonzosamente
disrepute [ˌdɪsrɪˈpjuːt] *n* : descrédito *m*, mala fama *f*, deshonra *f*
disrespect [ˌdɪsrɪˈspɛkt] *n* : falta *f* de respeto
disrespectful [ˌdɪsrɪˈspɛktfəl] *adj* : irrespetuoso — **disrespectfully** *adv*
disrobe [dɪsˈroːb] *v* -robed; -robing *vt* : desvestir, desnudar — *vi* : desvestirse, desnudarse
disrupt [dɪsˈrʌpt] *vt* : trastornar, perturbar
disruption [dɪsˈrʌpʃən] *n* : trastorno *m*
disruptive [dɪsˈrʌptɪv] *adj* : perjudicial, perturbador — **disruptively** *adv*
dissatisfaction [dɪsˌsæṭəsˈfækʃən] *n* : descontento *m*, insatisfacción *f*

dissatisfied [dɪsˈsæṭəsˌfaɪd] *adj* : descontento, insatisfecho
dissatisfy [dɪsˈsæṭəsˌfaɪ] *vt* -fied; -fying : no contentar, no satisfacer
dissect [dɪˈsɛkt] *vt* : disecar
dissection [dɪˈsɛkʃən] *n* : disección *f*
dissemble [dɪˈsɛmbəl] *v* -bled; -bling *vt* HIDE : ocultar, disimular — *vi* PRETEND : fingir, disimular
disseminate [dɪˈsɛməˌneɪt] *vt* -nated; -nating : diseminar, difundir, divulgar
dissemination [dɪˌsɛməˈneɪʃən] *n* : diseminación *f*, difusión *f*
dissension [dɪˈsɛntʃən] *n* : disensión *f*, desacuerdo *m*
dissent[1] [dɪˈsɛnt] *vi* : disentir
dissent[2] *n* : disentimiento *m*, disensión *f*
dissertation [ˌdɪsərˈteɪʃən] *n* **1** DISCOURSE : disertación *f*, discurso *m* **2** THESIS : tesis *f*
disservice [dɪsˈsərvɪs] *n* : perjuicio *m*
dissident[1] [ˈdɪsədənt] *adj* : disidente
dissident[2] *n* : disidente *mf*
dissimilar [dɪˈsɪmələr] *adj* : distinto, diferente, disímil
dissipate [ˈdɪsəˌpeɪt] *vt* -pated; -pating **1** DISPERSE : disipar, dispersar **2** SQUANDER : malgastar, desperdiciar, derrochar, disipar
dissipation [ˌdɪsəˈpeɪʃən] *n* : disipación *f*, libertinaje *m*
dissociate [dɪˈsoːʃiˌeɪt, -si-] *v* -ated [-ˌeɪṭəd], -ating [-ˌeɪṭɪŋ] *vt* : disociar ⟨to disassociate oneself : disociarse⟩ — *vi* : disociarse
dissociation [dɪˌsoːʃiˈeɪʃən, -si-] *n* : disociación *f*
dissolute [ˈdɪsəˌluːt] *adj* : disoluto
dissolution [ˌdɪsəˈluːʃən] *n* : disolución *f*
dissolve [dɪˈzɑlv] *v* -solved; -solving *vt* : disolver — *vi* : disolverse
dissonance [ˈdɪsənənts] *n* : disonancia *f*
dissuade [dɪˈsweɪd] *vt* -suaded; -suading : disuadir
distance[1] [ˈdɪstənts] *vt* -tanced [-tənts t]; -tancing [-təntsɪŋ] to distance oneself : distanciarse
distance[2] *n* **1** : distancia *f* ⟨the distance between two points : la distancia entre dos puntos⟩ ⟨in the distance : a lo lejos⟩ **2** RESERVE : actitud *f* distante, reserva *f* ⟨to keep one's distance : guardar las distancias⟩
distant [ˈdɪstənt] *adj* **1** FAR : distante, lejano **2** REMOTE : distante, lejano, remoto **3** ALOOF : distante, frío
distantly [ˈdɪstəntli] *adv* **1** LOOSELY : aproximadamente, vagamente **2** COLDLY : fríamente, con frialdad
distaste [dɪsˈteɪst] *n* : desagrado *m*, aversión *f*
distasteful [dɪsˈteɪstfəl] *adj* : desagradable, de mal gusto
distemper [dɪsˈtɛmpər] *n* : moquillo *m*
distend [dɪsˈtɛnd] *vt* : dilatar, hinchar — *vi* : dilatarse, hincharse

distill [dɪ'stɪl] vt : destilar
distillation [ˌdɪstə'leɪʃən] n : destilación f
distiller [dɪ'stɪlər] n : destilador m, -dora f
distillery [dɪ'stɪləri] n, pl -ries [-riz] : destilería f
distinct [dɪ'stɪŋkt] adj **1** DIFFERENT : distinto, diferente **2** CLEAR, UNMISTAKABLE : marcado, claro, evidente ⟨a distinct possibility : una clara posibilidad⟩
distinction [dɪ'stɪŋkʃən] n **1** DIFFERENTIATION : distinción f **2** DIFFERENCE : diferencia f **3** EXCELLENCE : distinción f, excelencia f ⟨a writer of distinction : un escritor destacado⟩
distinctive [dɪ'stɪŋktɪv] adj : distintivo, característico — **distinctively** adv
distinctiveness [dɪ'stɪŋktɪvnəs] n : peculiaridad f
distinctly [dɪ'stɪŋktli] adv : claramente, con claridad
distinguish [dɪs'tɪŋgwɪʃ] vt **1** DIFFERENTIATE : distinguir, diferenciar **2** DISCERN : distinguir ⟨he distinguished the sound of the piano : distinguió el sonido del piano⟩ **3 to distinguish oneself** : señalarse, distinguirse — vi DISCRIMINATE : distinguir
distinguishable [dɪs'tɪŋgwɪʃəbəl] adj : distinguible
distinguished [dɪs'tɪŋgwɪʃt] adj : distinguido
distort [dɪ'stɔrt] vt **1** MISREPRESENT : distorsionar, tergiversar **2** DEFORM : distorsionar, deformar
distortion [dɪ'stɔrʃən] n : distorsión f, deformación f, tergiversación f
distract [dɪ'strækt] vt : distraer, entretener
distracted [dɪ'stræktəd] adj : distraído
distraction [dɪ'strækʃən] n **1** INTERRUPTION : distracción f, interrupción f **2** CONFUSION : confusión f **3** AMUSEMENT : diversión f, entretenimiento m, distracción f
distraught [dɪ'strɔt] adj : afligido, turbado
distress¹ [dɪ'strɛs] vt : afligir, darle pena (a alguien), hacer sufrir
distress² n **1** SORROW : dolor m, angustia f, aflicción f **2** PAIN : dolor m **3 in ~** : en peligro
distressful [dɪ'strɛsfəl] adj : doloroso, penoso
distribute [dɪ'strɪˌbjuːt, -bjʊt] vt -uted; -uting : distribuir, repartir
distribution [ˌdɪstrə'bjuːʃən] n : distribución f, reparto m
distributive [dɪ'strɪbjʊṭɪv] adj : distributivo
distributor [dɪ'strɪbjʊṭər] n : distribuidor m, -dora f
district ['dɪsˌtrɪkt] n **1** REGION : región f, zona f, barrio m (de una ciudad) **2** : distrito m (zona política)
distrust¹ [dɪs'trʌst] vt : desconfiar de

distrust² n : desconfianza f, recelo m
distrustful [dɪs'trʌstfəl] adj : desconfiado, receloso, suspicaz
disturb [dɪ'stərb] vt **1** BOTHER : molestar, perturbar ⟨sorry to disturb you : perdone la molestia⟩ **2** DISARRANGE : desordenar **3** WORRY : inquietar, preocupar **4 to disturb the peace** : alterar el orden público
disturbance [dɪ'stərbənts] n **1** COMMOTION : alboroto m, disturbio m **2** INTERRUPTION : interrupción f
disuse [dɪs'juːs] n : desuso m
ditch¹ ['dɪtʃ] vt **1** : cavar zanjas en **2** DISCARD : deshacerse de, botar
ditch² n : zanja f, fosa f, cuneta f (en una carretera)
dither ['dɪðər] n **to be in a dither** : estar nervioso, ponerse como loco
ditto ['dɪṭoː] n, pl **-tos 1** : lo mismo, ídem m **2 ditto marks** : comillas fpl
ditty ['dɪṭi] n, pl **-ties** : canción f corta y simple
diurnal [daɪ'ərnəl] adj **1** DAILY : diario, cotidiano **2** : diurno ⟨a diurnal animal : un animal diurno⟩
divan ['daɪˌvæn, dɪ'-] n : diván m
dive¹ ['daɪv] vi **dived** or **dove** ['doːv]; **dived; diving 1** PLUNGE : tirarse al agua, zambullirse, dar un clavado **2** SUBMERGE : sumergirse **3** DROP : bajar en picada (dícese de un avión), caer en picada
dive² n **1** PLUNGE : zambullida f, clavado m (en el agua) **2** DESCENT : descenso m en picada **3** BAR, JOINT : antro m
diver ['daɪvər] n : saltador m, -dora f; clavadista mf
diverge [də'vərdʒ, daɪ-] vi **-verged; -verging 1** SEPARATE : divergir, separarse **2** DIFFER : divergir, discrepar
divergence [də'vərdʒənts, daɪ-] n : divergencia f — **divergent** [-ənt] adj
diverse [daɪ'vərs, də-, 'daɪˌvərs] adj : diverso, variado
diversification [daɪˌvərsəfə'keɪʃən, də-] n : diversificación f
diversify [daɪ'vərsəˌfaɪ, də-] vt **-fied; -fying** : diversificar, variar
diversion [daɪ'vərʒən, də-] n **1** DEVIATION : desviación f **2** AMUSEMENT, DISTRACTION : diversión f, distracción f, entretenimiento m
diversity [daɪ'vərsəṭi, də-] n, pl **-ties** : diversidad f
divert [də'vərt, daɪ-] vt **1** DEFLECT : desviar **2** DISTRACT : distraer **3** AMUSE : divertir, entretener
divest [daɪ'vɛst, də-] vt **1** UNDRESS : desnudar, desvestir **2 to divest of** : despojar de
divide [də'vaɪd] v **-vided; -viding** vt **1** HALVE : dividir, partir por la mitad **2** SHARE : repartir, dividir **3** : dividir (números) — vi : dividirse, dividir (en matemáticas)

dividend [ˈdɪvəˌdɛnd, -dənd] *n* **1** : dividendo *m* (en finanzas) **2** BONUS : beneficio *m*, provecho *m* **3** : dividendo *m* (en matemáticas)
divider [dɪˈvaɪdər] *n* **1** : separador *m* (para ficheros, etc.) **2** *or* **room divider** : mampara *f*, biombo *m*
divination [ˌdɪvəˈneɪʃən] *n* : adivinación *f*
divine¹ [dəˈvaɪn] *adj* **-viner; -est 1** : divino **2** SUPERB : divino, espléndido —
divinely *adv*
divine² *n* : clérigo *m*, eclesiástico *m*
divinity [dəˈvɪnəti] *n, pl* **-ties** : divinidad *f*
divisible [dɪˈvɪzəbəl] *adj* : divisible
division [dɪˈvɪʒən] *n* **1** DISTRIBUTION : división *f*, reparto *m* ⟨division of labor : distribución del trabajo⟩ **2** PART : división *f*, sección *f* **3** : división *f* (en matemáticas)
divisive [dəˈvaɪsɪv] *adj* : divisivo
divisor [dɪˈvaɪzər] *n* : divisor *m*
divorce¹ [dəˈvors] *v* **-vorced; -vorcing** *vt* : divorciar — *vi* : divorciarse
divorce² *n* : divorcio *m*
divorcé [dɪˌvorˈseɪ, -ˈsiː; -ˈvorˌ-] *n* : divorciado *m*
divorcée [dɪˌvorˈseɪ, -ˈsiː; -ˈvorˌ-] *n* : divorciada *f*
divulge [dəˈvʌldʒ, daɪ-] *vt* **-vulged; -vulging** : revelar, divulgar
dizzily [ˈdɪzəli] *adv* : vertiginosamente
dizziness [ˈdɪzinəs] *n* : mareo *m*, vahído *m*, vértigo *m*
dizzy [ˈdɪzi] *adj* **dizzier; -est 1** : mareado ⟨I feel dizzy : estoy mareado⟩ **2** : vertiginoso ⟨a dizzy speed : una velocidad vertiginosa⟩
DNA [ˌdiːˌɛnˈeɪ] *n* : ADN *m*
do [ˈduː] *v* **did** [ˈdɪd]; **done** [ˈdʌn]; **doing; does** [ˈdʌz] *vt* **1** CARRY OUT, PERFORM : hacer, realizar, llevar a cabo ⟨she did her best : hizo todo lo posible⟩ **2** PREPARE : preparar, hacer ⟨do your homework : haz tu tarea⟩ **3** ARRANGE : arreglar, peinar (el pelo) **4 to do in** RUIN : estropear, arruinar **5 to do in** KILL : matar, liquidar *fam* — *vi* **1** : hacer ⟨you did well : hiciste bien⟩ **2** FARE : estar, ir, andar ⟨how are you doing? : ¿cómo estás?, ¿cómo te va?⟩ **3** FINISH : terminar ⟨now I'm done : ya terminé⟩ **4** SERVE : servir, ser suficiente, alcanzar ⟨this will do for now : esto servirá por el momento⟩ **5 to do away with** ABOLISH : abolir, suprimir **6 to do away with** KILL : eliminar, matar **7 to do by** TREAT : tratar ⟨he does well by her : él la trata bien⟩ — *v aux* **1** (*used in interrogative sentences and negative statements*) ⟨do you know her? : ¿la conoces?⟩ ⟨I don't like that : a mí no me gusta eso⟩ **2** (*used for emphasis*) ⟨I do hope you'll come : espero que vengas⟩ **3** (*used as a substitute verb to avoid repetition*) ⟨do you speak English? yes, I do : ¿habla inglés? sí⟩

docile [ˈdɑsəl] *adj* : dócil, sumiso
dock¹ [ˈdɑk] *vt* **1** CUT : cortar **2** : descontar dinero de (un sueldo) — *vi* ANCHOR, LAND : fondear, atracar
dock² *n* **1** PIER : atracadero *m* **2** WHARF : muelle *m* **3** : banquillo *m* de los acusados (en un tribunal)
doctor¹ [ˈdɑktər] *vt* **1** TREAT : tratar, curar **2** ALTER : adulterar, alterar, falsificar (un documento)
doctor² *n* **1** : doctor *m*, -tora *f* ⟨Doctor of Philosophy : doctor en filosofía⟩ **2** PHYSICIAN : médico *m*, -ca *f*; doctor *m*, -tora *f*
doctorate [ˈdɑktərət] *n* : doctorado *m*
doctrine [ˈdɑktrɪn] *n* : doctrina *f*
document¹ [ˈdɑkjʊˌmɛnt] *vt* : documentar
document² [ˈdɑkjʊmənt] *n* : documento *m*
documentary¹ [ˌdɑkjʊˈmɛntəri] *adj* : documental
documentary² *n, pl* **-ries** : documental *m*
documentation [ˌdɑkjʊmənˈteɪʃən] *n* : documentación *f*
dodge¹ [ˈdɑdʒ] *v* **dodged; dodging** *vt* : esquivar, eludir, evadir (impuestos) — *vi* : echarse a un lado
dodge² *n* **1** RUSE : truco *m*, treta *f*, artimaña *f* **2** EVASION : regate *m*, evasión *f*
dodo [ˈdoːˌdoː] *n, pl* **-does** *or* **-dos** : dodo *m*
doe [ˈdoː] *n, pl* **does** *or* **doe** : gama *f*, cierva *f*
doer [ˈduːər] *n* : hacedor *m*, -dora *f*
does → **do**
doff [ˈdɑf, ˈdɔf] *vt* : quitarse ⟨to doff one's hat : quitarse el sombrero⟩
dog¹ [ˈdɔg, ˈdɑg] *vt* **dogged; dogging** : seguir de cerca, perseguir, acosar ⟨to dog someone's footsteps : seguir los pasos de alguien⟩ ⟨dogged by bad luck : perseguido por la mala suerte⟩
dog² *n* : perro *m*, -rra *f*
dogcatcher [ˈdɔgˌkætʃər] *n* : perrero *m*, -ra *f*
dog-eared [ˈdɔgˌɪrd] *adj* : con las esquinas dobladas
dogged [ˈdɔgəd] *adj* : tenaz, terco, obstinado
doggy [ˈdɔgi] *n, pl* **doggies** : perrito *m*, -ta *f*
doghouse [ˈdɔgˌhaʊs] *n* : casita *f* de perro
dogma [ˈdɔgmə] *n* : dogma *m*
dogmatic [dɔgˈmætɪk] *adj* : dogmático
dogmatism [ˈdɔgməˌtɪzəm] *n* : dogmatismo *m*
dogwood [ˈdɔgˌwʊd] *n* : cornejo *m*
doily [ˈdɔɪli] *n, pl* **-lies** : pañito *m*, -ta *f*
doings [ˈduːɪŋz] *npl* : eventos *mpl*, actividades *fpl*
doldrums [ˈdoːldrəmz, ˈdɑl-] *npl* **1** : zona *f* de las calmas ecuatoriales **2 to be in the doldrums** : estar abatido (dícese de una persona), estar estancado (dícese de una empresa)

dole ['do:l] *n* **1** ALMS : distribución *f* a los necesitados, limosna *f* **2** : subsidios *mpl* de desempleo

doleful ['do:lfəl] *adj* : triste, lúgubre

dolefully ['do:lfəli] *adv* : con pesar, de manera triste

dole out *vt* **doled out; doling out** : repartir

doll ['dɑl, 'dɔl] *n* : muñeco *m*, -ca *f*

dollar ['dɑlər] *n* : dólar *m*

dolly ['dɑli] *n, pl* **-lies 1** → **doll 2** : plataforma *f* rodante

dolphin ['dɑlfən, 'dɔl-] *n* : delfín *m*

dolt ['do:lt] *n* : imbécil *mf*; tonto *m*, -ta *f*

domain [do'meɪn, də-] *n* **1** TERRITORY : dominio *m*, territorio *m* **2** FIELD : campo *m*, esfera *f*, ámbito *m* ⟨the domain of art : el ámbito de las artes⟩

dome ['do:m] *n* : cúpula *f*, bóveda *f*

domestic¹ [də'mɛstɪk] *adj* **1** HOUSEHOLD : doméstico, casero **2** : nacional, interno ⟨domestic policy : política interna⟩ **3** TAME : domesticado

domestic² *n* : empleado *m* doméstico, empleada *f* doméstica

domestically [də'mɛstɪkli] *adv* : domésticamente

domesticate [də'mɛstɪˌkeɪt] *vt* **-cated; -cating** : domesticar

domicile ['dɑməˌsaɪl, 'do:-; 'dɑməsɪl] *n* : domicilio *m*

dominance ['dɑmənənts] *n* : dominio *m*, dominación *f*

dominant ['dɑmənənt] *adj* : dominante

dominate ['dɑməˌneɪt] *v* **-nated; -nating** : dominar

domination [ˌdɑmə'neɪʃən] *n* : dominación *f*

domineer [ˌdɑmə'nɪr] *vt* : dominar sobre, avasallar, tiranizar

Dominican [də'mɪnɪkən] *n* : dominicano *m*, -na *f* — **Dominican** *adj*

dominion [də'mɪnjən] *n* **1** POWER : dominio *m* **2** DOMAIN, TERRITORY : dominio *m*, territorio *m*

domino ['dɑməˌno:] *n, pl* **-noes** *or* **-nos 1** : dominó *m* **2 dominoes** *npl* : dominó *m* (juego)

don ['dɑn] *vt* **donned; donning** : ponerse

donate ['do:ˌneɪt, do:'-] *vt* **-nated; -nating** : donar, hacer un donativo de

donation [do:'neɪʃən] *n* : donación *f*, donativo *m*

done¹ ['dʌn] → **do**

done² *adj* **1** FINISHED : terminado, acabado, concluido **2** COOKED : cocinado

donkey ['dɑŋki, 'dʌŋ-] *n, pl* **-keys** : burro *m*, asno *m*

donor ['do:nər] *n* : donante *mf*; donador *m*, -dora *f*

don't ['do:nt] (*contraction of* **do not**) → **do**

doodle¹ ['du:dəl] *v* **-dled; -dling** : garabatear

doodle² *n* : garabato *m*

doom¹ ['du:m] *vt* : condenar

doom² *n* **1** JUDGMENT : sentencia *f*, condena *f* **2** DEATH : muerte *f* **3** FATE : destino *m* **4** RUIN : perdición *f*, ruina *f*

door ['dor] *n* : puerta *f*

doorbell ['dorˌbɛl] *n* : timbre *m*

doorknob ['dorˌnɑb] *n* : pomo *m*, perilla *f*

doorman ['dormən] *n, pl* **-men** [-mən, -ˌmɛn] : portero *m*

doormat ['dorˌmæt] *n* : felpudo *m*

doorstep ['dorˌstɛp] *n* : umbral *m*

doorway ['dorˌweɪ] *n* : entrada *f*, portal *m*

dope¹ ['do:p] *vt* **doped; doping** : drogar, narcotizar

dope² *n* **1** DRUG : droga *f*, estupefaciente *m*, narcótico *m* **2** IDIOT : idiota *mf*; tonto *m*, -ta *f* **3** INFORMATION : información *f*

dormant ['dɔrmənt] *adj* : inactivo, latente

dormer ['dɔrmər] *n* : buhardilla *f*

dormitory ['dɔrməˌtori] *n, pl* **-ries** : dormitorio *m*, residencia *f* de estudiantes

dormouse ['dɔrˌmaʊs] *n* : lirón *m*

dorsal ['dɔrsəl] *adj* : dorsal — **dorsally** *adv*

dory ['dori] *n, pl* **-ries** : bote *m* de fondo plano

dosage ['do:sɪʤ] *n* : dosis *f*

dose¹ ['do:s] *vt* **dosed; dosing** : medicinar

dose² *n* : dosis *f*

dossier ['dɔsˌjeɪ, 'dɑs-] *n* : dossier *m*

dot¹ ['dɑt] *vt* **dotted; dotting 1** : poner el punto sobre (una letra) **2** SCATTER : esparcir, salpicar

dot² *n* : punto *m* ⟨at six on the dot : a las seis en punto⟩ ⟨dots and dashes : puntos y rayas⟩

dote ['do:t] *vi* **doted; doting** : chochear

double¹ ['dʌbəl] *v* **-bled; -bling** *vt* **1** : doblar, duplicar (una cantidad), redoblar (esfuerzos) **2** FOLD : doblar, plegar **3 to double one's fist** : apretar el puño — *vi* **1** : doblarse, duplicarse **2 to double over** : retorcerse

double² *adj* : doble — **doubly** *adv*

double³ *n* : doble *mf*

double bass *n* : contrabajo *m*

double–cross [ˌdʌbəl'krɔs] *vt* : traicionar

double–crosser [ˌdʌbəl'krɔsər] *n* : traidor *m*, -dora *f*

double–jointed [ˌdʌbəl'ʤɔɪntəd] *adj* : con articulaciones dobles

double–talk ['dʌbəlˌtɔk] *n* : ambigüedades *fpl*, lenguaje *m* con doble sentido

doubt¹ ['daʊt] *vt* **1** QUESTION : dudar de, cuestionar **2** DISTRUST : desconfiar de **3** : dudar, creer poco probable ⟨I doubt it very much : lo dudo mucho⟩

doubt² *n* **1** UNCERTAINTY : duda *f*, incertidumbre *f* **2** DISTRUST : desconfianza *f* **3** SKEPTICISM : duda *f*, escepticismo *m*

doubtful ['dautfəl] *adj* **1** QUESTIONABLE : dudoso **2** UNCERTAIN : dudoso, incierto

doubtfully ['dautfəli] *adv* : dudosamente, sin estar convencido

doubtless ['dautləs] *or* **doubtlessly** *adv* : sin duda

douche¹ ['du:ʃ] *vt* **douched; douching** : irrigar

douche² *n* : ducha *f*, irrigación *f*

dough ['do:] *n* : masa *f*

doughnut *or* **donut** ['do:ˌnʌt] *n* : rosquilla *f*, dona *f Mex*

doughty ['dauṭi] *adj* **-tier; -est** : fuerte, valiente

dour ['dauər, 'dur] *adj* **1** STERN : severo, adusto **2** SULLEN : hosco, taciturno — **dourly** *adv*

douse ['daus, 'dauz] *vt* **doused; dousing 1** DRENCH : empapar, mojar **2** EXTINGUISH : extinguir, apagar

dove¹ ['do:v] → **dive**

dove² ['dʌv] *n* : paloma *f*

dovetail ['dʌvˌteɪl] *vi* : encajar, enlazar

dowdy ['daudi] *adj* **dowdier; -est** : sin gracia, poco elegante

dowel ['dauəl] *n* : clavija *f*

down¹ ['daun] *vt* **1** FELL : tumbar, derribar, abatir **2** DEFEAT : derrotar

down² *adv* **1** DOWNWARD : hacia abajo **2 to lie down** : acostarse, echarse **3 to put down (money)** : pagar un depósito (de dinero) **4 to sit down** : sentarse **5 to take down, to write down** : apuntar, anotar

down³ *adj* **1** DESCENDING : de bajada ⟨the down elevator : el ascensor de bajada⟩ **2** REDUCED : reducido, rebajado ⟨attendance is down : la concurrencia ha disminuido⟩ **3** DOWNCAST : abatido, deprimido

down⁴ *n* **1** : plumón *m* **2** : down *m* (en deportes) **3 ups and downs** : altibajos *mpl*

down⁵ *prep* **1** : (hacia) abajo ⟨down the mountain : montaña abajo⟩ ⟨I walked down the stairs : bajé por la escalera⟩ **2** ALONG : por, a lo largo de ⟨we ran down the beach : corrimos por la playa⟩ **3** : a través de ⟨down the years : a través de los años⟩

downcast ['daunˌkæst] *adj* **1** SAD : triste, abatido **2 with downcast eyes** : con los ojos bajos, con los ojos mirando al suelo

downfall ['daunˌfɔl] *n* : ruina *f*, perdición *f*

downgrade¹ ['daunˌgreɪd] *vt* **-graded; -grading** : bajar de categoría

downgrade² *n* : bajada *f*

downhearted ['daunˌhɑrṭəd] *adj* : desanimado, descorazonado

downhill ['daun'hɪl] *adv & adj* : cuesta abajo

download¹ ['daunˌlo:d] *vt* : descargar (un archivo)

download² *n* : descarga *f* (de archivos, etc.)

down payment *n* : entrega *f* inicial

downplay ['daunˌpleɪ] *vt* : minimizar

downpour ['daunˌpor] *n* : aguacero *m*, chaparrón *m*

downright¹ ['daunˌraɪt] *adv* THOROUGHLY : absolutamente, completamente

downright² *adj* : patente, manifiesto, absoluto ⟨a downright refusal : un rechazo categórico⟩

downside ['daunˌsaɪd] *n* : desventaja *f*

downstairs¹ ['daun'stærz] *adv* : abajo

downstairs² ['daunˌstærz] *adj* : del piso de abajo

downstairs³ ['daun'stærz, -ˌstærz] *n* : planta *f* baja

downstream ['daun'stri:m] *adv* : río abajo

down-to-earth [ˌdauntu'ərθ] *adj* : práctico, realista

downtown¹ [ˌdaun'taun] *adv* : hacia el centro, al centro, en el centro (de la ciudad)

downtown² *adj* : del centro (de la ciudad) ⟨downtown Chicago : el centro de Chicago⟩

downtown³ [ˌdaun'taun, 'daunˌtaun] *n* : centro *m* (de la ciudad)

downtrodden ['daunˌtrɑdən] *adj* : oprimido

downward ['daunwərd] *or* **downwards** [-wərdz] *adv & adj* : hacia abajo

downwind ['daun'wɪnd] *adv & adj* : en la dirección del viento

downy ['dauni] *adj* **downier; -est 1** : cubierto de plumón, plumoso **2** VELVETY : aterciopelado, velloso

dowry ['dauri] *n, pl* **-ries** : dote *f*

doze¹ ['do:z] *vi* **dozed; dozing** : dormitar

doze² *n* : sueño *m* ligero, cabezada *f*

dozen ['dʌzən] *n, pl* **dozens** *or* **dozen** : docena *f*

drab ['dræb] *adj* **drabber; drabbest 1** BROWNISH : pardo **2** DULL, LACKLUSTER : monótono, gris, deslustrado

draft¹ ['dræft, 'draft] *vt* **1** CONSCRIPT : reclutar **2** COMPOSE, SKETCH : hacer el borrador de, redactar

draft² *adj* **1** : de barril ⟨draft beer : cerveza de barril⟩ **2** : de tiro ⟨draft horses : caballos de tiro⟩

draft³ *n* **1** HAULAGE : tiro *m* **2** DRINK, GULP : trago *m* **3** OUTLINE, SKETCH : bosquejo *m*, borrador *m*, versión *f* **4** : corriente *f* de aire, chiflón *m*, tiro *m* (de una chimenea) **5** CONSCRIPTION : conscripción *f* **6 bank draft** : giro *m* bancario, letra *f* de cambio

draftee [dræf'ti:] *n* : recluta *mf*

draftsman ['dræftsmən] *n, pl* **-men** [-mən, -ˌmen] : dibujante *mf*

drafty ['dræfti] *adj* **draftier; -est** : con corrientes de aire

drag¹ ['dræg] *v* **dragged; dragging** *vt* **1** HAUL : arrastrar, jalar **2** DREDGE : dragar — *vi* **1** TRAIL : arrastrarse **2** LAG : rezagarse **3** : hacerse pesado, hacerse largo ⟨the day dragged on : el día se hizo largo⟩

drag² *n* **1** RESISTANCE : resistencia *f* (aerodinámica) **2** HINDRANCE : traba *f*, estorbo *m* **3** BORE : pesadez *f*, plomo *m fam*

dragnet ['dræg‚nɛt] *n* **1** : red *f* barredera (en pesca) **2** : operativo *m* policial de captura

dragon ['drægən] *n* : dragón *m*

dragonfly ['drægən‚flaɪ] *n*, *pl* **-flies** : libélula *f*

drain¹ ['dreɪn] *vt* **1** EMPTY : vaciar, drenar **2** EXHAUST : agotar, consumir — *vi* **1** : escurrir, escurrirse ⟨the dishes are draining : los platos están escurriéndose⟩ **2** EMPTY : desaguar **3 to drain away** : irse agotando

drain² *n* **1** : desagüe *m* **2** SEWER : alcantarilla *f* **3** GRATING : sumidero *m*, resumidero *m*, rejilla *f* **4** EXHAUSTION : agotamiento *m*, disminución *f* (de energía, etc.) ⟨to be a drain on : agotar, consumir⟩ **5 to throw down the drain** : tirar por la ventana

drainage ['dreɪnɪʤ] *n* : desagüe *m*, drenaje *m*

drainpipe ['dreɪn‚paɪp] *n* : tubo *m* de desagüe, caño *m*

drake ['dreɪk] *n* : pato *m* (macho)

drama ['drɑmə, 'dræ-] *n* **1** THEATER : drama *m*, teatro *m* **2** PLAY : obra *f* de teatro, drama *m*

dramatic [drə'mæṭɪk] *adj* : dramático — **dramatically** [-ṭɪkli] *adv*

dramatist ['dræmətɪst, 'drɑ-] *n* : dramaturgo *m*, -ga *f*

dramatization [‚dræmətə'zeɪʃən, ‚drɑ-] *n* : dramatización *f*

dramatize ['dræmə‚taɪz, 'drɑ-] *vt* **-tized; -tizing** : dramatizar

drank → **drink**

drape¹ ['dreɪp] *vt* **draped; draping 1** COVER : cubrir (con tela) **2** HANG : drapear, disponer los pliegues de

drape² *n* **1** HANG : caída *f* **2 drapes** *npl* : cortinas *fpl*

drapery ['dreɪpəri] *n*, *pl* **-eries 1** CLOTH : pañería *f*, tela *f* para cortinas **2 draperies** *npl* : cortinas *fpl*

drastic ['dræstɪk] *adj* **1** HARSH, SEVERE : drástico, severo **2** EXTREME : radical, excepcional — **drastically** [-tɪkli] *adv*

draught ['dræft, 'drɑft] *n* → **draft³**

draughty ['drɑfti] → **drafty**

draw¹ ['drɔ] *v* **drew** ['dru:]; **drawn** ['drɔn]; **drawing** *vt* **1** PULL : tirar de, jalar, correr (cortinas) **2** ATTRACT : atraer **3** PROVOKE : provocar, suscitar **4** INHALE : aspirar ⟨to draw breath : respirar⟩ **5** EXTRACT : sacar, extraer **6** TAKE : sacar ⟨to draw a number : sacar un número⟩ **7** COLLECT : cobrar, percibir (un sueldo, etc.) **8** BEND : tensar (un arco) **9** TIE : empatar (en deportes) **10** SKETCH : dibujar, trazar **11** FORMULATE : sacar, formular, llegar a ⟨to draw a conclusion : llegar a

una conclusión⟩ **12 to draw out** : hacer hablar (sobre algo), hacer salir de sí mismo **13 to draw up** DRAFT : redactar — *vi* **1** SKETCH : dibujar **2** TUG : tirar, jalar **3 to draw near** : acercarse **4 to draw to a close** : terminar, finalizar **5 to draw up** STOP : parar

draw² *n* **1** DRAWING, RAFFLE : sorteo *m* **2** TIE : empate *m* **3** ATTRACTION : atracción *f* **4** PUFF : chupada *f* (de un cigarrillo, etc.)

drawback ['drɔ‚bæk] *n* : desventaja *f*, inconveniente *m*

drawbridge ['drɔ‚brɪʤ] *n* : puente *m* levadizo

drawer ['drɔr, 'drɔər] *n* **1** ILLUSTRATOR : dibujante *mf* **2** : gaveta *f*, cajón *m* (en un mueble) **3 drawers** *npl* UNDERPANTS : calzones *mpl*

drawing ['drɔɪŋ] *n* **1** LOTTERY : sorteo *m*, lotería *f* **2** SKETCH : dibujo *m*, bosquejo *m*

drawl¹ ['drɔl] *vi* : hablar arrastrando las palabras

drawl² *n* : habla *f* lenta y con vocales prolongadas

dread¹ ['drɛd] *vt* : tenerle pavor a, temer

dread² *adj* : pavoroso, aterrado

dread³ *n* : pavor *m*, temor *m*

dreadful ['drɛdfəl] *adj* **1** DREAD : pavoroso **2** TERRIBLE : espantoso, atroz, terrible — **dreadfully** *adv*

dream¹ ['dri:m] *v* **dreamed** ['drɛmpt, 'dri:md] *or* **dreamt** ['drɛmpt]; **dreaming** *vi* **1** : soñar ⟨to dream about : soñar con⟩ **2** FANTASIZE : fantasear — *vt* **1** : soñar **2** IMAGINE : imaginarse **3 to dream up** : inventar, idear

dream² *n* **1** : sueño *m*, ensueño *m* **2 bad dream** NIGHTMARE : pesadilla *f*

dreamer ['dri:mər] *n* : soñador *m*, -dora *f*

dreamlike ['dri:m‚laɪk] *adj* : de ensueño

dreamy ['dri:mi] *adj* **dreamier; -est 1** DISTRACTED : soñador, distraído **2** DREAMLIKE : de ensueño **3** MARVELOUS : maravilloso

drearily ['drɪrəli] *adv* : sombríamente

dreary ['drɪri] *adj* **-rier; -est** : deprimente, lóbrego, sombrío

dredge¹ ['drɛʤ] *vt* **dredged; dredging 1** DIG : dragar **2** COAT : espolvorear, enharinar

dredge² *n* : draga *f*

dredger ['drɛʤər] *n* : draga *f*

dregs ['drɛgz] *npl* **1** LEES : posos *mpl*, heces *fpl* (de un líquido) **2** : heces *fpl*, escoria *f* ⟨the dregs of society : la escoria de la sociedad⟩

drench ['drɛntʃ] *vt* : empapar, mojar, calar

dress¹ ['drɛs] *vt* **1** CLOTHE : vestir **2** DECORATE : decorar, adornar **3** : preparar (pollo o pescado), aliñar (ensalada) **4** : curar, vendar (una herida) **5** FERTILIZE : abonar (la tierra) — *vi* **1** : vestirse **2 to dress up** : ataviarse, engalanarse, ponerse de etiqueta

dress² *n* **1** APPAREL : indumentaria *f*, ropa *f* **2** : vestido *m*, traje *m* (de mujer)

dresser ['drɛsər] *n* : cómoda *f* con espejo

dressing ['drɛsɪŋ] *n* **1** : vestirse *m* **2** : aderezo *m*, aliño *m* (de ensalada), relleno *m* (de pollo) **3** BANDAGE : vendaje *m*, gasa *f*

dressmaker ['drɛs,meɪkər] *n* : modista *mf*

dressmaking ['drɛs,meɪkɪŋ] *n* : costura *f*

dressy ['drɛsi] *adj* **dressier; -est** : de mucho vestir, elegante

drew → **draw**

dribble¹ ['drɪbəl] *vi* **-bled; -bling 1** DRIP : gotear **2** DROOL : babear **3** : driblar (en basquetbol)

dribble² *n* **1** TRICKLE : goteo *m*, hilo *m* **2** DROOL : baba *f* **3** : drible *m* (en basquetbol)

drier → **dry²**, **dryer**

driest *adj* → **dry²**

drift¹ ['drɪft] *vi* **1** : dejarse llevar por la corriente, ir a la deriva (dícese de un bote), ir sin rumbo (dícese de una persona) **2** ACCUMULATE : amontonarse, acumularse, apilarse

drift² *n* **1** DRIFTING : deriva *f* **2** HEAP, MASS : montón *m* (de arena, etc.), ventisquero *m* (de nieve) **3** MEANING : sentido *m*

drifter ['drɪftər] *n* : vagabundo *m*, -da *f*

driftwood ['drɪft,wʊd] *n* : madera *f* flotante

drill¹ ['drɪl] *vt* **1** BORE : perforar, taladrar **2** INSTRUCT : instruir por repetición — *vi* **1** TRAIN : entrenarse **2 to drill for oil** : perforar en busca de petróleo

drill² *n* **1** : taladro *m*, barrena *f* **2** EXERCISE, PRACTICE : ejercicio *m*, instrucción *f*

drily → **dryly**

drink¹ ['drɪŋk] *v* **drank** ['dræŋk]; **drunk** ['drʌŋk] *or* **drank; drinking** *vt* **1** : beber, tomar **2 to drink up** ABSORB : absorber — *vi* **1** : beber **2** : beber alcohol, tomar

drink² *n* **1** : bebida *f* **2** : bebida *f* alcohólica

drinkable ['drɪŋkəbəl] *adj* : potable

drinker ['drɪŋkər] *n* : bebedor *m*, -dora *f*

drip¹ ['drɪp] *vi* **dripped; dripping** : gotear, chorrear

drip² *n* **1** DROP : gota *f* **2** DRIPPING : goteo *m*

drive¹ ['draɪv] *v* **drove** ['droːv]; **driven** ['drɪvən]; **driving** *vt* **1** IMPEL : impeler, impulsar **2** OPERATE : guiar, conducir, manejar (un vehículo) **3** COMPEL : obligar, forzar **4** : clavar, hincar ⟨to drive a stake : clavar una estaca⟩ **5** *or* **to drive away** : ahuyentar, echar **6 to drive crazy** : volver loco — *vi* : manejar, conducir ⟨do you know how to drive? : ¿sabes manejar?⟩

drive² *n* **1** RIDE : paseo *m* en coche **2** CAMPAIGN : campaña *f* ⟨fund-raising drive : campaña para recaudar fondos⟩ **3** DRIVEWAY : camino *m* de entrada, entrada *f* **4** TRANSMISSION : transmisión *f* ⟨front-wheel drive : tracción delantera⟩ **5** ENERGY : dinamismo *m*, energía *f* **6** INSTINCT, NEED : instinto *m*, necesidad *f* básica **7** → **disk drive**

drivel ['drɪvəl] *n* : tontería *f*, estupidez *f*

driver ['draɪvər] *n* : conductor *m*, -tora *f*; chofer *m*

driveway ['draɪv,weɪ] *n* : camino *m* de entrada, entrada *f* (para coches)

drizzle¹ ['drɪzəl] *vi* **-zled; -zling** : lloviznar, garuar

drizzle² *n* : llovizna *f*, garúa *f*

droll ['droːl] *adj* : cómico, gracioso, chistoso — **drolly** *adv*

dromedary ['drɑmə,dɛri] *n, pl* **-daries** : dromedario *m*

drone¹ ['droːn] *vi* **droned; droning 1** BUZZ : zumbar **2** MURMUR : hablar con monotonía, murmurar

drone² *n* **1** : zángano *m* (abeja) **2** FREELOADER : gorrón *m*, -rrona *f fam*; parásito *m*, -ta *f* **3** BUZZ, HUM : zumbido *m*, murmullo *m*

drool¹ ['druːl] *vi* : babear

drool² *n* : baba *f*

droop¹ ['druːp] *vi* **1** HANG : inclinarse (dícese de la cabeza), encorvarse (dícese de los escombros), marchitarse (dícese de las flores) **2** FLAG : decaer, flaquear ⟨his spirits drooped : se desanimó⟩

droop² *n* : inclinación *f*, caída *f*

drop¹ ['drɑp] *v* **dropped; dropping** *vt* **1** : dejar caer, soltar ⟨she dropped the glass : se le cayó el vaso⟩ ⟨to drop a hint : dejar caer una indirecta⟩ **2** SEND : mandar ⟨drop me a line : mándame unas líneas⟩ **3** ABANDON : abandonar, dejar ⟨to drop the subject : cambiar de tema⟩ **4** LOWER : bajar ⟨he dropped his voice : bajó la voz⟩ **5** OMIT : omitir **6 to drop off** : dejar — *vi* **1** DRIP : gotear **2** FALL : caer(se) **3** DECREASE, DESCEND : bajar, descender ⟨the wind dropped : amainó el viento⟩ **4 to drop back** *or* **to drop behind** : rezagarse, quedarse atrás **5 to drop by** *or* **to drop in** : pasar

drop² *n* **1** : gota *f* (de líquido) **2** DECLINE : caída *f*, bajada *f*, descenso *m* **3** INCLINE : caída *f*, pendiente *f* ⟨a 20-foot drop : una caída de 20 pies⟩ **4** SWEET : pastilla *f*, dulce *m* **5 drops** *npl* : gotas *fpl* (de medicina)

droplet ['drɑplət] *n* : gotita *f*

dropper ['drɑpər] *n* : gotero *m*, cuentagotas *m*

dross ['drɑs, 'drɔs] *n* : escoria *f*

drought ['draʊt] *n* : sequía *f*

drove¹ → **drive**

drove² ['droːv] *n* : multitud *f*, gentío *m*, manada *f* (de ganado) ⟨in droves : en manada⟩

drown ['draʊn] *vt* **1** : ahogar **2** INUN-
DATE : anegar, inundar **3 to drown out**
: ahogar — *vi* : ahogarse
drowse¹ ['draʊz] *vi* **drowsed; drowsing**
DOZE : dormitar
drowse² *n* : sueño *m* ligero, cabezada *f*
drowsiness ['draʊzinəs] *n* : somnolencia *f*, adormecimiento *m*
drowsy ['draʊzi] *adj* **drowsier; -est**
: somnoliento, soñoliento
drub ['drʌb] *vt* **drubbed; drubbing 1**
BEAT, THRASH : golpear, apalear **2** DE-
FEAT : derrotar por completo
drudge¹ ['drʌdʒ] *vi* **drudged; drudging**
: trabajar como esclavo, trabajar duro
drudge² *n* : esclavo *m*, -va *f* del trabajo
drudgery ['drʌdʒəri] *n, pl* **-eries** : trabajo *m* pesado
drug¹ ['drʌg] *vt* **drugged; drugging**
: drogar, narcotizar
drug² *n* **1** MEDICATION : droga *f*, medicina *f*, medicamento *m* **2** NARCOTIC
: narcótico *m*, estupefaciente *m*, droga
f
druggist ['drʌgɪst] *n* : farmacéutico *m*,
-ca *f*
drugstore ['drʌg,stor] *n* : farmacia *f*,
botica *f*, droguería *f*
drum¹ ['drʌm] *v* **drummed; drumming**
vt : meter a fuerza ⟨he drummed it into
my head : me lo metió en la cabeza a
fuerza⟩ — *vi* : tocar el tambor
drum² *n* **1** : tambor *m* **2** : bidón *m* ⟨oil
drum : bidón de petróleo⟩
drummer ['drʌmər] *n* : baterista *mf*
drumstick ['drʌm,stɪk] *n* **1** : palillo *m*
(de tambor), baqueta *f* **2** : muslo *m* de
pollo
drunk¹ *pp* → **drink¹**
drunk² ['drʌŋk] *adj* : borracho, embriagado, ebrio
drunk³ *n* : borracho *m*, -cha *f*
drunkard ['drʌŋkərd] *n* : borracho *m*,
-cha *f*
drunken ['drʌŋkən] *adj* : borracho,
ebrio ⟨drunken driver : conductor
ebrio⟩ ⟨drunken brawl : pleito de bo-
rrachos⟩
drunkenly ['drʌŋkənli] *adv* : como un
borracho
drunkenness ['drʌŋkənnəs] *n* : borrachera *f*, embriaguez *f*, ebriedad *f*
dry¹ ['draɪ] *v* **dried; drying** *vt* : secar —
vi : secarse
dry² *adj* **drier; driest 1** : seco **2** THIRSTY
: sediento **3** : donde la venta de bebidas
alcohólicas está prohibida ⟨a dry county : un condado seco⟩ **4** DULL : aburrido, árido **5** : seco (dícese del vino),
brut (dícese de la champaña)
dry–clean ['draɪ,kli:n] *v* : limpiar en seco
dry cleaner *n* : tintorería *f* (servicio)
dry cleaning *n* : limpieza *f* en seco
dryer ['draɪər] *n* **1 hair dryer** : secador
m **2 clothes dryer** : secadora *f*
dry goods *npl* : artículos *mpl* de confección
dry ice *n* : hielo *m* seco

dryly ['draɪli] *adv* : secamente
dryness ['draɪnəs] *n* : sequedad *f*, aridez
f
dual ['du:əl, 'dju:-] *adj* : doble
dualism ['du:ə,lɪzəm] *n* : dualismo *m*
dub ['dʌb] *vt* **dubbed; dubbing 1** CALL
: apodar **2** : doblar (una película),
mezclar (una grabación)
dubious ['du:biəs, 'dju:-] *adj* **1** UNCER-
TAIN : dudoso, indeciso **2** QUESTION-
ABLE : sospechoso, dudoso, discutible
dubiously ['du:biəsli, 'dju:-] *adv* **1** UN-
CERTAINLY : dudosamente, con desconfianza **2** SUSPICIOUSLY : de modo
sospechoso, con recelo
duchess ['dʌtʃəs] *n* : duquesa *f*
duck¹ ['dʌk] *vt* **1** LOWER : agachar, bajar (la cabeza) **2** PLUNGE : zambullir
3 EVADE : eludir, evadir — *vi* **to duck
down** : agacharse
duck² *n, pl* **duck** *or* **ducks** : pato *m*,
-ta *f*
duckling ['dʌklɪŋ] *n* : patito *m*, -ta *f*
duct ['dʌkt] *n* : conducto *m*
ductile ['dʌktəl] *adj* : dúctil
dude ['du:d, 'dju:d] *n* **1** DANDY : dandi
m, dandy *m* **2** GUY : tipo *m*
due¹ ['du:, 'dju:] *adv* : justo a, derecho
hacia ⟨due north : derecho hacia el
norte⟩
due² *adj* **1** PAYABLE : pagadero, sin pagar **2** APPROPRIATE : debido, apropiado ⟨after due consideration : con las
debidas consideraciones⟩ **3** EXPECTED
: esperado ⟨the train is due soon : esperamos el tren muy pronto, el tren
debe llegar pronto⟩ **4 due to** : debido
a, por
due³ *n* **1 to give someone his (her) due**
: darle a alguien su merecido **2 dues**
npl : cuota *f*
duel¹ ['du:əl, 'dju:-] *vi* : batirse en duelo
duel² *n* : duelo *m*
duet [du'ɛt, dju-] *n* : dúo *m*
due to *prep* : debido a
dug → **dig**
dugout ['dʌg,aʊt] *n* **1** CANOE : piragua
f **2** SHELTER : refugio *m* subterráneo
duke ['du:k, 'dju:k] *n* : duque *m*
dull¹ ['dʌl] *vt* **1** DIM : opacar, quitar el
brillo a, deslustrar **2** BLUNT : embotar
(un filo), entorpecer (los sentidos),
aliviar (el dolor), amortiguar (sonidos)
dull² *adj* **1** STUPID : torpe, lerdo, lento
2 BLUNT : desafilado, despuntado **3**
LACKLUSTER : sin brillo, deslustrado **4**
BORING : aburrido, soso, pesado —
dully *adv*
dullness ['dʌlnəs] *n* **1** STUPIDITY : estupidez *f* **2** : embotamiento *m* (de los
sentidos) **3** MONOTONY : monotonía *f*,
insipidez *f* **4** : falta *f* de brillo **5** BLUNT-
NESS : falta *f* de filo, embotadura *f*
duly ['du:li, 'dju:-] *adv* PROPERLY : debidamente, a su debido tiempo
dumb ['dʌm] *adj* **1** MUTE : mudo **2** STU-
PID : estúpido, tonto, bobo — **dumbly**
adv

dumbbell [ˈdʌmˌbɛl] *n* **1** WEIGHT : pesa *f* **2** : estúpido *m*, -da *f*
dumbfound *or* **dumfound** [ˌdʌm-ˈfaʊnd] *vt* : dejar atónito, dejar sin habla
dummy [ˈdʌmi] *n, pl* **-mies 1** SHAM : imitación *f*, sustituto *m* **2** PUPPET : muñeco *m* **3** MANNEQUIN : maniquí *m* **4** IDIOT : tonto *m*, -ta *f*; idiota *mf*
dump¹ [ˈdʌmp] *vt* : descargar, verter
dump² *n* **1** : vertedero *m*, tiradero *m* *Mex* **2** **down in the dumps** : triste, deprimido
dumpling [ˈdʌmplɪŋ] *n* : bola *f* de masa hervida
dumpy [ˈdʌmpi] *adj* **dumpier; -est** : rechoncho, regordete
dun¹ [ˈdʌn] *vt* **dunned; dunning** : apremiar (a un deudor)
dun² *adj* : pardo (color)
dunce [ˈdʌnts] *n* : estúpido *m*, -da *f*; burro *m*, -rra *f fam*
dune [ˈduːn, ˈdjuːn] *n* : duna *f*
dung [ˈdʌŋ] *n* **1** FECES : excrementos *mpl* **2** MANURE : estiércol *m*
dungaree [ˌdʌŋɡəˈriː] *n* **1** DENIM : tela *f* vaquera, mezclilla *f Chile, Mex* **2** **dungarees** *npl* : pantalones *mpl* de trabajo hechos de tela vaquera
dungeon [ˈdʌndʒən] *n* : mazmorra *f*, calabozo *m*
dunk [ˈdʌŋk] *vt* : mojar, ensopar
duo [ˈduːoː, ˈdjuː-] *n, pl* **duos** : dúo *m*, par *m*
dupe¹ [ˈduːp, djuːp] *vt* **duped; duping** : engañar, embaucar
dupe² *n* : inocentón *m*, -tona *f*; simple *mf*
duplex¹ [ˈduːˌplɛks, ˈdjuː-] *adj* : doble
duplex² *n* : casa *f* de dos viviendas, dúplex *m*
duplicate¹ [ˈduːplɪˌkeɪt, ˈdjuː-] *vt* **-cated; -cating 1** COPY : duplicar, hacer copias de **2** REPEAT : repetir, reproducir
duplicate² [ˈduːplɪkət, ˈdjuː-] *adj* : duplicado ⟨a duplicate invoice : una factura por duplicado⟩
duplicate³ [ˈduːplɪkət, ˈdjuː-] *n* : duplicado *m*, copia *f*
duplication [ˌduːplɪˈkeɪʃən, ˌdjuː-] *n* **1** DUPLICATING : duplicación *f*, repetición *f* (de esfuerzos) **2** DUPLICATE : copia *f*, duplicado *m*
duplicity [dʊˈplɪsəti, ˌdjuː-] *n, pl* **-ties** : duplicidad *f*
durability [ˌdʊrəˈbɪləti, ˌdjʊr-] *n* : durabilidad *f* (de un producto) permanencia *f*
durable [ˈdʊrəbəl, ˈdjʊr-] *adj* : duradero
duration [dʊˈreɪʃən, djʊ-] *n* : duración *f*
duress [dʊˈrɛs, djʊ-] *n* : coacción *f*

during [ˈdʊrɪŋ, ˈdjʊr-] *prep* : durante
dusk [ˈdʌsk] *n* : anochecer *m*, crepúsculo *m*
dusky [ˈdʌski] *adj* **duskier; -est** : oscuro (dícese de los colores)
dust¹ [ˈdʌst] *vt* **1** : quitar el polvo de **2** SPRINKLE : espolvorear
dust² *n* : polvo *m*
duster [ˈdʌstər] *n* **1** *or* **dust cloth** : trapo *m* de polvo **2** HOUSECOAT : guardapolvo *m* **3** **feather duster** : plumero *m*
dustpan [ˈdʌstˌpæn] *n* : recogedor *m*
dusty [ˈdʌsti] *adj* **dustier; -est** : cubierto de polvo, polvoriento
Dutch¹ [ˈdʌtʃ] *adj* : holandés
Dutch² *n* **1** : holandés *m* (idioma) **2** **the Dutch** *npl* : los holandeses
Dutch treat *n* : invitación o pago a escote
dutiful [ˈduːtɪfəl, ˈdjuː-] *adj* : motivado por sus deberes, responsable
duty [ˈduːti, ˈdjuː-] *n, pl* **-ties 1** OBLIGATION : deber *m*, obligación *f*, responsabilidad *f* **2** TAX : impuesto *m*, arancel *m*
DVD [ˌdiːˌviːˈdiː] *n* : DVD *m*
dwarf¹ [ˈdwɔrf] *vt* STUNT : arrestar el crecimiento de **2** : hacer parecer pequeño
dwarf² *n, pl* **dwarfs** [ˈdwɔrfs] *or* **dwarves** [ˈdwɔrvz] : enano *m*, -na *f*
dwell [ˈdwɛl] *vi* **dwelled** *or* **dwelt** [ˈdwɛlt]; **dwelling 1** RESIDE : residir, morar, vivir **2** **to dwell on** : pensar demasiado en, insistir en
dweller [ˈdwɛlər] *n* : habitante *mf*
dwelling [ˈdwɛlɪŋ] *n* : morada *f*, vivienda *f*, residencia *f*
dwindle [ˈdwɪndəl] *vi* **-dled; -dling** : menguar, reducirse, disminuir
dye¹ [ˈdaɪ] *vt* **dyed; dyeing** : teñir
dye² *n* : tintura *f*, tinte *m*
dying → **die**
dyke → **dike**
dynamic [daɪˈnæmɪk] *adj* : dinámico
dynamics [daɪˈnæmɪks] *npl* : dinámica *f*
dynamite¹ [ˈdaɪnəˌmaɪt] *vt* **-mited; -miting** : dinamitar
dynamite² *n* : dinamita *f*
dynamo [ˈdaɪnəˌmoː] *n, pl* **-mos** : dínamo *m*, generador *m* de electricidad
dynasty [ˈdaɪnəsti, -ˌnæs-] *n, pl* **-ties** : dinastía *f*
dysentery [ˈdɪsənˌtɛri] *n, pl* **-teries** : disentería *f*
dysfunction [dɪsˈfʌŋkʃən] *n* : disfunción *f*
dystrophy [ˈdɪstrəfi] *n, pl* **-phies 1** : distrofia *f* **2** → **muscular dystrophy**

E

e [ˈiː] *n, pl* **e's** *or* **es** [ˈiːz] : quinta letra del alfabeto inglés

each¹ [ˈiːtʃ] *adv* : cada uno, por persona ⟨they cost $10 each : costaron $10 cada uno⟩

each² *adj* : cada ⟨each student : cada estudiante⟩ ⟨each and every one : todos sin excepción⟩

each³ *pron* **1** : cada uno *m*, cada una *f* ⟨each of us : cada uno de nosotros⟩ **2 each other** : el uno al otro, mutuamente ⟨we are helping each other : nos ayudamos el uno al otro⟩ ⟨they love each other : se aman⟩

eager [ˈiːgər] *adj* **1** ENTHUSIASTIC : entusiasta, ávido, deseoso **2** ANXIOUS : ansioso, impaciente

eagerly [ˈiːgərli] *adv* : con entusiasmo, ansiosamente

eagerness [ˈiːgərnəs] *n* : entusiasmo *m*, deseo *m*, impaciencia *f*

eagle [ˈiːgəl] *n* : águila *f*

ear [ˈɪr] *n* **1** : oído *m*, oreja *f* ⟨inner ear : oído interno⟩ ⟨big ears : orejas grandes⟩ **2 ear of corn** : mazorca *f*, choclo *m*

earache [ˈɪrˌeɪk] *n* : dolor *m* de oído

eardrum [ˈɪrˌdrʌm] *n* : tímpano *m*

earl [ˈərl] *n* : conde *m*

earlobe [ˈɪrˌloːb] *n* : lóbulo *m* de la oreja, perilla *f* de la oreja

early¹ [ˈərli] *adv* **earlier; -est** : temprano, pronto ⟨he arrived early : llegó temprano⟩ ⟨as early as possible : lo más pronto posible, cuanto antes⟩ ⟨ten minutes early : diez minutos de adelanto⟩

early² *adj* **earlier; -est** **1** (*referring to a beginning*) : primero ⟨the early stages : las primeras etapas⟩ ⟨in early May : a principios de mayo⟩ **2** (*referring to antiquity*) : primitivo, antiguo ⟨early man : el hombre primitivo⟩ ⟨early painting : la pintura antigua⟩ **3** (*referring to a designated time*) : temprano, antes de la hora, prematuro ⟨he was early : llegó temprano⟩ ⟨early fruit : frutas tempraneras⟩ ⟨an early death : una muerte prematura⟩

earmark [ˈɪrˌmɑrk] *vt* : destinar ⟨earmarked funds : fondos destinados⟩

earn [ˈərn] *vt* **1** : ganar ⟨to earn money : ganar dinero⟩ **2** DESERVE : ganarse, merecer

earnest¹ [ˈərnəst] *adj* : serio, sincero

earnest² *n* **in ⁓** : en serio, de verdad ⟨we began in earnest : empezamos de verdad⟩

earnestly [ˈərnəstli] *adv* **1** SERIOUSLY : con seriedad, en serio **2** FERVENTLY : de todo corazón

earnestness [ˈərnəstnəs] *n* : seriedad *f*, sinceridad *f*

earnings [ˈərnɪŋz] *npl* : ingresos *mpl*, ganancias *fpl*, utilidades *fpl*

earphone [ˈɪrˌfoːn] *n* : audífono *m*

earring [ˈɪrˌrɪŋ] *n* : zarcillo *m*, arete *m*, aro *m* *Arg, Chile, Uru*, pendiente *m* *Spain*

earshot [ˈɪrˌʃɑt] *n* : alcance *m* del oído

earth [ˈərθ] *n* **1** LAND, SOIL : tierra *f*, suelo *m* **2 the Earth** : la Tierra

earthen [ˈərθən, -ðən] *adj* : de tierra, de barro

earthenware [ˈərθənˌwær, -ðən-] *n* : loza *f*, vajillas *fpl* de barro

earthly [ˈərθli] *adj* : terrenal, mundano

earthquake [ˈərθˌkweɪk] *n* : terremoto *m*, temblor *m*

earthworm [ˈərθˌwərm] *n* : lombriz *f* (de tierra)

earthy [ˈərθi] *adj* **earthier; -est** **1** : terroso ⟨earthy colors : colores terrosos⟩ **2** DOWN-TO-EARTH : realista, práctico, llano **3** COARSE, CRUDE : basto, grosero, tosco ⟨earthy jokes : chistes groseros⟩

earwax [ˈɪrˌwæks] *n* → **wax²**

earwig [ˈɪrˌwɪg] *n* : tijereta *f*

ease¹ [ˈiːz] *v* **eased; easing** *vt* **1** ALLEVIATE : aliviar, calmar, hacer disminuir **2** LOOSEN, RELAX : aflojar (una cuerda), relajar (restricciones), descargar (tensiones) **3** FACILITATE : facilitar — *vi* : calmarse, relajarse

ease² *n* **1** CALM, RELIEF : tranquilidad *f*, comodidad *f*, desahogo *m* **2** FACILITY : facilidad *f* **3 at ⁓** : relajado, cómodo ⟨to put someone at ease : tranquilizar a alguien⟩

easel [ˈiːzəl] *n* : caballete *m*

easily [ˈiːzəli] *adv* **1** : fácilmente, con facilidad **2** UNQUESTIONABLY : con mucho, de lejos

easiness [ˈiːzinəs] *n* : facilidad *f*, soltura *f*

east¹ [ˈiːst] *adv* : al este

east² *adj* : este, del este, oriental ⟨east winds : vientos del este⟩

east³ *n* **1** : este *m* **2 the East** : el Oriente

Easter [ˈiːstər] *n* : Pascua *f* (de Resurrección)

easterly [ˈiːstərli] *adv & adj* : del este

eastern [ˈiːstərn] *adj* **1** : Oriental, del Este ⟨Eastern Europe : Europa del Este⟩ **2** : oriental, este

Easterner [ˈiːstərnər] *n* : habitante *mf* del este

eastward [ˈiːstwərd] *adv & adj* : hacia el este

easy [ˈiːzi] *adj* **easier; -est** **1** : fácil **2** LENIENT : indulgente

easygoing [ˌiːziˈgoːɪŋ] *adj* : acomodaticio, tolerante, poco exigente

eat [ˈiːt] *v* **ate** [ˈeɪt]; **eaten** [ˈiːtən]; **eating** *vt* **1** : comer **2** CONSUME : consumir, gastar, devorar ⟨expenses ate up profits : los gastos devoraron las ganancias⟩ **3** CORRODE : corroer — *vi* **1** : comer **2 to eat away at** *or* **to eat into** : comerse **3 to eat out** : comer fuera

eatable[1] ['iːṭəbəl] *adj* : comestible, comible *fam*

eatable[2] *n* **1** : algo para comer **2 eatables** *npl* : comestibles *mpl*, alimentos *mpl*

eater ['iːṭər] *n* : comedor *m*, -dora *f*

eaves ['iːvz] *npl* : alero *m*

eavesdrop ['iːvzˌdrɑp] *vi* **-dropped; -dropping** : escuchar a escondidas

eavesdropper ['iːvzˌdrɑpər] *n* : persona *f* que escucha a escondidas

ebb[1] ['ɛb] *vi* **1** : bajar, menguar (dícese de la marea) **2** DECLINE : decaer, disminuir

ebb[2] *n* **1** : reflujo *m* (de una marea) **2** DECLINE : decadencia *f*, declive *m*, disminución *f*

ebony[1] ['ɛbəni] *adj* **1** : de ébano **2** BLACK : de color ébano, negro

ebony[2] *n, pl* **-nies** : ébano *m*

ebullience [ɪ'bʊljənts, -'bʌl-] *n* : efervescencia *f*, vivacidad *f*

ebullient [ɪ'bʊljənt, -'bʌl-] *adj* : efervescente, vivaz

eccentric[1] [ɪk'sɛntrɪk] *adj* **1** : excéntrico ⟨an eccentric wheel : una rueda excéntrica⟩ **2** ODD, SINGULAR : excéntrico, extraño, raro — **eccentrically** [-trɪkli] *adv*

eccentric[2] *n* : excéntrico *m*, -ca *f*

eccentricity [ˌkˌsen'trɪsəṭi] *n, pl* **-ties** : excentricidad *f*

ecclesiastic [ɪˌkliːziˈæstɪk] *n* : eclesiástico *m*, clérigo *m*

ecclesiastical [ɪˌkliːziˈæstɪkəl] *or* **ecclesiastic** *adj* : eclesiástico — **ecclesiastically** *adv*

echelon ['ɛʃəˌlɑn] *n* **1** : escalón *m* (de tropas o aviones) **2** LEVEL : nivel *m*, esfera *f*, estrato *m*

echo[1] ['ɛˌkoː] *v* **echoed; echoing** *vi* : hacer eco, resonar — *vt* : repetir

echo[2] *n, pl* **echoes** : eco *m*

éclair [eɪ'klær, i-] *n* : pastel *m* relleno de crema

eclectic [ɛ'klɛktɪk, ɪ-] *adj* : ecléctico

eclipse[1] [ɪ'klɪps] *vt* **eclipsed; eclipsing** : eclipsar

eclipse[2] *n* : eclipse *m*

ecological [ˌiːkəˈlɑdʒɪkəl, ˌɛkə-] *adj* : ecológico — **ecologically** *adv*

ecologist [i'kɑlədʒɪst, ɛ-] *n* : ecólogo *m*, -ga *f*

ecology [i'kɑlədʒi, ɛ-] *n, pl* **-gies** : ecología *f*

economic [ˌiːkə'nɑmɪk, ˌɛkə-] *adj* : económico

economical [ˌiːkə'nɑmɪkəl, ˌɛkə-] *adj* : económico — **economically** *adv*

economics [ˌiːkə'nɑmɪks, ˌɛkə-] *n* : economía *f*

economist [i'kɑnəmɪst] *n* : economista *mf*

economize [i'kɑnəˌmaɪz] *v* **-mized; -mizing** : economizar, ahorrar

economy [i'kɑnəmi] *n, pl* **-mies** **1** : economía *f*, sistema *m* económico **2** THRIFT : economía *f*, ahorro *m*

ecosystem ['iːkoˌsɪstəm] *n* : ecosistema *m*

ecru ['ɛˌkruː, 'eɪ-] *n* : color *m* crudo

ecstasy ['ɛkstəsi] *n, pl* **-sies** : éxtasis *m*

ecstatic [ɛk'stæṭɪk, ɪk-] *adj* : extático

ecstatically [ɛk'stæṭɪkli, ɪk-] *adv* : con éxtasis, con gran entusiasmo

Ecuadoran [ˌɛkwəˈdorən] *or* **Ecuadorean** *or* **Ecuadorian** [-'doriən] *n* : ecuatoriano *m*, -na *f* — **Ecuadorean** *or* **Ecuadorian** *adj*

ecumenical [ˌɛkjʊ'mnɪkəl] *adj* : ecuménico

eczema [ɪg'ziːmə, 'ɛgzəmə, 'ɛksə-] *n* : eczema *m*

eddy[1] ['ɛdi] *vi* **eddied; eddying** : arremolinarse, hacer remolinos

eddy[2] *n, pl* **-dies** : remolino *m*

edema [ɪ'diːmə] *n* : edema *m*

Eden ['iːdən] *n* : Edén *m*

edge[1] ['ɛdʒ] *v* **edged; edging** *vt* **1** BORDER : bordear, ribetear, orlar **2** SHARPEN : afilar, aguzar **3** *or* **to edge one's way** : avanzar poco a poco **4 to edge out** : derrotar por muy poco — *vi* ADVANCE : ir avanzando (poco a poco)

edge[2] *n* **1** : filo *m* (de un cuchillo) **2** BORDER : borde *m*, orilla *f*, margen *m* **3** ADVANTAGE : ventaja *f*

edger ['ɛdʒər] *n* : cortabordes *m*

edgewise ['ɛdʒˌwaɪz] *adv* SIDEWAYS : de lado, de canto

edginess ['ɛdʒinəs] *n* : tensión *f*, nerviosismo *m*

edgy ['ɛdʒi] *adj* **edgier; -est** : tenso, nervioso

edible ['ɛdəbəl] *adj* : comestible

edict ['iːˌdɪkt] *n* : edicto *m*, mandato *m*, orden *f*

edification [ˌɛdəfəˈkeɪʃən] *n* : edificación *f*, instrucción *f*

edifice ['ɛdəfɪs] *n* : edificio *m*

edify ['ɛdəˌfaɪ] *vt* **-fied; -fying** : edificar

edit ['ɛdɪt] *vt* **1** : editar, redactar, corregir **2** *or* **to edit out** DELETE : recortar, cortar

edition [ɪ'dɪʃən] *n* : edición *f*

editor ['ɛdɪṭər] *n* : editor *m*, -tora *f*; redactor *m*, -tora *f*

editorial[1] [ˌɛdɪˈtoriəl] *adj* **1** : de redacción **2** : editorial ⟨an editorial comment : un comentario editorial⟩

editorial[2] *n* : editorial *m*

editorship ['ɛdəṭərˌʃɪp] *n* : dirección *f*

educable ['ɛdʒəkəbəl] *adj* : educable

educate ['ɛdʒəˌkeɪt] *vt* **-cated; -cating 1** TEACH : educar, enseñar **2** INSTRUCT : formar, educar, instruir **3** INFORM : informar, concientizar

education [ˌɛdʒəˈkeɪʃən] *n* : educación *f*

educational [ˌɛdʒəˈkeɪʃənəl] *adj* **1** : docente, de enseñanza ⟨an educational institution : una institución docente⟩ **2** PEDAGOGICAL : pedagógico **3** INSTRUCTIONAL : educativo, instructivo

educator ['ɛdʒəˌkeɪṭər] *n* : educador *m*, -dora *f*

eel ['iːl] *n* : anguila *f*

eerie ['ɪri] *adj* -rier; -est 1 SPOOKY : que da miedo, espeluznante 2 GHOSTLY : fantasmagórico

eerily ['ɪrəli] *adv* : de manera extraña y misteriosa

efface [ɪ'feɪs, -] *vt* -faced; -facing : borrar

effect¹ [ɪ'fɛkt] *vt* 1 CARRY OUT : efectuar, llevar a cabo 2 ACHIEVE : lograr, realizar

effect² *n* 1 RESULT : efecto *m*, resultado *m*, consecuencia *f* ⟨to no effect : sin resultado⟩ 2 MEANING : sentido *m* ⟨something to that effect : algo por el estilo⟩ 3 INFLUENCE : efecto *m*, influencia *f* 4 effects *npl* BELONGINGS : efectos *mpl*, pertenencias *fpl* 5 to go into effect : entrar en vigor 6 in ~ REALLY : en realidad, efectivamente

effective [ɪ'fɛktɪv] *adj* 1 EFFECTUAL : efectivo, eficaz 2 OPERATIVE : vigente — effectively *adv*

effectiveness [ɪ'fɛktɪvnəs] *n* : eficacia *f*, efectividad *f*

effectual [ɪ'fɛktʃuəl] *adj* : eficaz, efectivo — effectually *adv*

effeminate [ə'fɛmənət] *adj* : afeminado

effervesce [ˌɛfər'vɛs] *vi* -vesced; -vescing 1 : estar en efervescencia, burbujear (dícese de líquidos) 2 : estar eufórico, estar muy animado (dícese de las personas)

effervescence [ˌɛfər'vɛsənts] *n* 1 : efervescencia *f* 2 LIVELINESS : vivacidad *f*

effervescent [ˌɛfər'vɛsənt] *adj* 1 : efervescente 2 LIVELY, VIVACIOUS : vivaz, animado

effete ['ɛfiːt, ɪ-] *adj* 1 WORN-OUT : desgastado, agotado 2 DECADENT : decadente 3 EFFEMINATE : afeminado

efficacious [ˌɛfə'keɪʃəs] *adj* : eficaz, efectivo

efficacy ['ɛfɪkəsi] *n, pl* -cies : eficacia *f*

efficiency [ɪ'fɪʃəntsi] *n, pl* -cies : eficiencia *f*

efficient [ɪ'fɪʃənt] *adj* : eficiente — efficiently *adv*

effigy ['ɛfədʒi] *n, pl* -gies : efigie *f*

effluent ['ɛˌfluːənt, ɛ'fluː-] *n* : efluente *m* — effluent *adj*

effort ['ɛfərt] *n* 1 EXERTION : esfuerzo *m* 2 ATTEMPT : tentativa *f*, intento *m* ⟨it's not worth the effort : no vale la pena⟩

effortless ['ɛfərtləs] *adj* : fácil, sin esfuerzo

effortlessly ['ɛfərtləsli] *adv* : sin esfuerzo, fácilmente

effrontery [ɪ'frʌntəri] *n, pl* -teries : insolencia *f*, desfachatez *f*, descaro *m*

effusion [ɪ'fjuːʒən, ɛ-] *n* : efusión *f*

effusive [ɪ'fjuːsɪv, ɛ-] *adj* : efusivo — effusively *adv*

egg¹ ['ɛg] *vt* to egg on : incitar, azuzar, provocar

egg² *n* 1 : huevo *m* 2 OVUM : óvulo *m*

eggbeater ['ɛgˌbiːt̬ər] *n* : batidor *m* (de huevos)

eggnog ['ɛgˌnɑg] *n* : ponche *m* de huevo, rompope *m* CA, Mex

eggplant ['ɛgˌplænt] *n* : berenjena *f*

eggshell ['ɛgˌʃl] *n* : cascarón *m*

ego ['iːˌgoː] *n, pl* egos 1 SELF-ESTEEM : amor *m* propio 2 SELF : ego *m*, yo *m*

egocentric [ˌiːgoː'sɛntrɪk] *adj* : egocéntrico

egoism ['iːgoːˌwizəm] *n* : egoísmo *m*

egoist ['iːgoːwɪst] *n* : egoísta *mf*

egoistic [ˌiːˌgoː'wɪstɪk] *adj* : egoísta

egotism ['iːgoːˌtɪzəm] *n* : egotismo *m*

egotist ['iːgət̬ɪst] *n* : egotista *mf*

egotistic [ˌiːgə'tɪstɪk] *or* egotistical [-'tɪstɪkəl] *adj* : egotista — egotistically *adv*

egregious [ɪ'griːdʒəs] *adj* : atroz, flagrante, mayúsculo — egregiously *adv*

egress ['iːˌgrɛs] *n* : salida *f*

egret ['iːgrət, -ˌgrɛt] *n* : garceta *f*

Egyptian [ɪ'dʒɪpʃən] *n* 1 : egipcio *m*, -cia *f* 2 : egipcio *m* (idioma) — Egyptian *adj*

eiderdown ['aɪdərˌdaʊn] *n* 1 : plumón *m* 2 COMFORTER : edredón *m*

eight¹ ['eɪt] *adj* : ocho

eight² *n* : ocho *m*

eight hundred¹ *adj* : ochocientos

eight hundred² *n* : ochocientos *m*

eighteen¹ [eɪt'tiːn] *adj* : dieciocho

eighteen² *n* : dieciocho *m*

eighteenth¹ [eɪt'tiːnθ] *adj* : decimoctavo

eighteenth² *n* 1 : decimoctavo *m*, -va *f* (en una serie) 2 : dieciochoavo *m*, dieciochoava parte *f*

eighth¹ ['eɪtθ] *adj* : octavo

eighth² *n* 1 : octavo *m*, -va *f* (en una serie) 2 : octavo *m*, octava parte *f*

eightieth¹ ['eɪt̬iəθ] *adj* : octogésimo

eightieth² *n* 1 : octogésimo *m*, -ma *f* (en una serie) 2 : ochentavo *m*, ochentava parte *f*

eighty¹ ['eɪt̬i] *adj* : ochenta

eighty² *n, pl* eighties 1 : ochenta *m* 2 the eighties : los ochenta *mpl*

either¹ ['iːðər, 'aɪ-] *adj* 1 : cualquiera (de los dos) ⟨we can watch either movie : podemos ver cualquiera de las dos películas⟩ 2 : ninguno de los dos ⟨she wasn't in either room : no estaba en ninguna de las dos salas⟩ 3 EACH : cada ⟨on either side of the street : a cada lado de la calle⟩

either² *pron* 1 : cualquiera *mf* (de los dos) ⟨either is fine : cualquiera de los dos está bien⟩ 2 : ninguno *m*, -na *f* (de los dos) ⟨I don't like either : no me gusta ninguno⟩ 3 : algún *m*, alguna *f* ⟨is either of you interested? : ¿está alguno de ustedes (dos) interesado?⟩

either³ *conj* 1 : o, u ⟨either David or Daniel could go : puede ir (o) David o Daniel⟩ 2 : ni ⟨we won't watch either this movie or the other : no veremos ni esta película ni la otra⟩

ejaculate [i'dʒækjəˌleɪt] *v* -lated; -lating *vt* 1 : eyacular 2 EXCLAIM : exclamar — *vi* : eyacular

ejaculation [i͵ʤækjə'leɪʃən] *n* **1** : eyaculación *f* (en fisiología) **2** EXCLAMATION : exclamación *f*
eject [i'ʤɛkt] *vt* : expulsar, expeler
ejection [i'ʤɛkʃən] *n* : expulsión *f*
eke ['iːk] *vt* **eked; eking** *or* **to eke out** : ganar a duras penas
elaborate[1] [i'læbə͵reɪt] *v* **-rated; -rating** *vt* : elaborar, idear, desarrollar — *vi* **to elaborate on** : ampliar, entrar en detalles
elaborate[2] [i'læbərət] *adj* **1** DETAILED : detallado, minucioso, elaborado **2** COMPLICATED : complicado, intrincado, elaborado — **elaborately** *adv*
elaboration [i͵læbə'reɪʃən] *n* : elaboración *f*
elapse [i'læps] *vi* **elapsed; elapsing** : transcurrir, pasar
elastic[1] [i'læstɪk] *adj* : elástico
elastic[2] *n* **1** : elástico *m* **2** RUBBER BAND : goma *f*, gomita *f*, elástico *m*, liga *f*
elasticity [i͵læs'tɪsəti, ͵i:͵læs-] *n, pl* **-ties** : elasticidad *f*
elate [i'leɪt] *vt* **elated; elating** : alborozar, regocijar
elation [i'leɪʃən] *n* : euforia *f*, júbilo *m*, alborozo *m*
elbow[1] ['ɛl͵boː] *vt* : darle un codazo a
elbow[2] *n* : codo *m*
elder[1] ['ɛldər] *adj* : mayor
elder[2] *n* **1 to be someone's elder** : ser mayor que alguien **2** : anciano *m*, -na *f* (de un pueblo o una tribu) **3** : miembro *m* del consejo (en varias religiones)
elderberry ['ɛldər͵beri] *n, pl* **-berries** : baya *f* de saúco (fruta), saúco *m* (árbol)
elderly ['ɛldərli] *adj* : mayor, de edad, anciano
eldest ['ɛldəst] *adj* : mayor, de más edad
elect[1] [i'lɛkt] *vt* : elegir
elect[2] *adj* : electo ⟨the president-elect : el presidente electo⟩
elect[3] *npl* **the elect** : los elegidos *mpl*
election [i'lɛkʃən] *n* : elección *f*
elective[1] [i'lɛktɪv] *adj* **1** : electivo **2** OPTIONAL : facultativo, optativo
elective[2] *n* : asignatura *f* electiva
elector [i'lɛktər] *n* : elector *m*, -tora *f*
electoral [i'lɛktərəl] *adj* : electoral
electorate [i'lɛktərət] *n* : electorado *m*
electric [i'lɛktrɪk] *adj* **1** *or* **electrical** [-trɪkəl] : eléctrico **2** THRILLING : electrizante, emocionante
electrician [i͵lɛk'trɪʃən] *n* : electricista *mf*
electricity [i͵lɛk'trɪsəti] *n, pl* **-ties** : electricidad *f* **2** CURRENT : corriente *m* eléctrica
electrification [i͵lɛktrəfə'keɪʃən] *n* : electrificación *f*
electrify [i'lɛktrə͵faɪ] *vt* **-fied; -fying 1** : electrificar **2** THRILL : electrizar, emocionar
electrocardiogram [i͵lɛktro'kɑrdiə͵græm] *n* : electrocardiograma *m*
electrocardiograph [i͵lɛktro'kɑrdiə͵græf] *n* : electrocardiógrafo *m*

electrocute [i'lɛktrə͵kjuːt] *vt* **-cuted; -cuting** : electrocutar
electrocution [i͵lɛktrə'kjuːʃən] *n* : electrocución *f*
electrode [i'lɛk͵troːd] *n* : electrodo *m*
electrolysis [i͵lɛk'trɑləsɪs] *n* : electrólisis *f*
electrolyte [i'lɛktro͵laɪt] *n* : electrolito *m*
electromagnet [i͵lɛktro'mægnət] *n* : electroimán *m*
electromagnetic [i͵lɛktromæg'nɪtɪk] *adj* : electromagnético — **electromagnetically** [-tɪkli] *adv*
electromagnetism [i͵lɛktro'mægnə͵tɪzəm] *n* : electromagnetismo *m*
electron [i'lɛk͵trɑn] *n* : electrón *m*
electronic [i͵lɛk'trɑnɪk] *adj* : electrónico — **electronically** [-nɪkli] *adv*
electronic mail *n* : correo *m* electrónico
electronics [i͵lɛk'trɑnɪks] *n* : electrónica *f*
electroplate [i'lɛktrə͵pleɪt] *vt* **-plated; plating** : galvanizar mediante electrólisis
elegance ['ɛligənts] *n* : elegancia *f*
elegant ['ɛligənt] *adj* : elegante — **elegantly** *adv*
elegy ['ɛləʤi] *n, pl* **-gies** : elegía *f*
element ['ɛləmənt] *n* **1** COMPONENT : elemento *m*, factor *m* **2** : elemento *m* (en la química) **3** MILIEU : elemento *m*, medio *m* ⟨to be in one's element : estar en su elemento⟩ **4 elements** *npl* RUDIMENTS : elementos *mpl*, rudimentos *mpl*, bases *fpl* **5 the elements** WEATHER : los elementos *mpl*
elemental [͵ɛlə'mɛntəl] *adj* **1** BASIC : elemental, primario **2** : elemental (dícese de los elementos químicos)
elementary [͵ɛlə'mɛntri] *adj* **1** SIMPLE : elemental, simple, fundamental **2** : de enseñanza primaria
elementary school *n* : escuela *f* primaria
elephant ['ɛləfənt] *n* : elefante *m*, -ta *f*
elevate ['ɛlə͵veɪt] *vt* **-vated; -vating 1** RAISE : elevar, levantar, alzar **2** EXALT, PROMOTE : elevar, exaltar, ascender **3** ELATE : alborozar, regocijar
elevation [͵ɛlə'veɪʃən] *n* **1** : elevación *f* **2** ALTITUDE : altura *f*, altitud *f* **3** PROMOTION : ascenso *m*
elevator ['ɛlə͵veɪtər] *n* : ascensor *m*, elevador *m*
eleven[1] [ɪ'lɛvən] *adj* : once
eleven[2] *n* : once *m*
eleventh[1] [ɪlɛvənt θ] *adj* : undécimo
eleventh[2] *n* **1** : undécimo *m*, -ma *f* (en una serie) **2** : onceavo *m*, onceava parte *f*
elf ['ɛlf] *n, pl* **elves** ['ɛlvz] : elfo *m*, geniecillo *m*, duende *m*
elfin ['ɛlfən] *adj* **1** : de elfo, menudo **2** ENCHANTING, MAGIC : mágico, encantador
elfish ['ɛlfɪʃ] *adj* **1** : de elfo **2** MISCHIEVOUS : travieso
elicit [ɪ'lɪsət] *vt* : provocar

eligibility [ˌɛlədʒəˈbɪləti] *n, pl* **-ties** : elegibilidad *f*
eligible [ˈɛlədʒəbəl] *adj* 1 QUALIFIED : elegible 2 SUITABLE : idóneo
eliminate [ɪˈlɪmə₍neɪt] *vt* **-nated; -nating** : eliminar
elimination [ɪ₍lɪməˈneɪʃən] *n* : eliminación *f*
elite [eɪˈliːt, i-] *n* : elite *f*
elixir [iˈlɪksər] *n* : elixir *m*
elk [ˈɛlk] *n* : alce *m* (de Europa), uapití *m* (de América)
ellipse [ɪˈlɪps, -] *n* : elipse *f*
ellipsis [ɪˈlɪpsəs, -] *n, pl* **-lipses** [-₍siːz] 1 : elipsis *f* 2 : puntos *mpl* suspensivos (en la puntuación)
elliptical [ɪˈlɪptɪkəl, -] *or* elliptic [-tɪk] *adj* : elíptico
elm [ˈɛlm] *n* : olmo *m*
elocution [ˌɛləˈkjuːʃən] *n* : elocución *f*
elongate [iˈlɔŋ₍ɡeɪt] *vt* **-gated; -gating** : alargar
elongation [ˌiː₍lɔŋˈɡeɪʃən] *n* : alargamiento *m*
elope [iˈloːp] *vi* **eloped; eloping** : fugarse
elopement [iˈloːpmənt] *n* : fuga *f*
eloquence [ˈɛləkwənts] *n* : elocuencia *f*
eloquent [ˈɛləkwənt] *adj* : elocuente —
eloquently *adv*
El Salvadoran [ˌɛl₍sælvəˈdorən] *n* : salvadoreño *m*, -ña *f* — El Salvadoran *adj*
else¹ [ˈɛls] *adv* 1 DIFFERENTLY : de otro modo, de otra manera ⟨how else? : ¿de qué otro modo?⟩ 2 ELSEWHERE : de otro sitio, de otro lugar ⟨where else? : ¿en qué otro sitio?⟩ 3 or else OTHERWISE : si no, de lo contrario
else² *adj* 1 OTHER : otro ⟨anyone else : cualquier otro⟩ ⟨everyone else : todos los demás⟩ ⟨nobody else : ningún otro, nadie más⟩ ⟨somebody else : otra persona⟩ 2 MORE : más ⟨nothing else : nada más⟩ ⟨what else? : ¿qué más?⟩
elsewhere [ˈɛls₍hwɛr] *adv* : en otra parte, en otro sitio, en otro lugar
elucidate [iˈluːsə₍deɪt] *vt* **-dated; -dating** : dilucidar, elucidar, esclarecer
elucidation [i₍luːsəˈdeɪʃən] *n* : elucidación *f*, esclarecimiento *m*
elude [iˈluːd] *vt* **eluded; eluding** : eludir, evadir
elusive [iˈluːsɪv] *adj* 1 EVASIVE : evasivo, esquivo 2 SLIPPERY : huidizo, escurridizo 3 FLEETING, INTANGIBLE : impalpable, fugaz
elusively [iˈluːsɪvli] *adv* : de manera esquiva
elves → elf
emaciate [iˈmeɪʃi₍eɪt] *vt* **-ated; -ating** : enflaquecer
emaciation [i₍meɪsiˈeɪʃən, -ʃi-] *n* : enflaquecimiento *m*, escualidez *f*, delgadez *f* extrema
e-mail [ˈiː₍meɪl] *n* : e-mail *m*
emanate [ˈɛmə₍neɪt] *v* **-nated; -nating** *vi* : emanar, provenir, proceder — *vt* : emanar

emanation [ˌɛməˈneɪʃən] *n* : emanación *f*
emancipate [iˈmæntsə₍peɪt] *vt* **-pated; -pating** : emancipar
emancipation [i₍mæntsəˈpeɪʃən] *n* : emancipación *f*
emasculate [iˈmæskjə₍leɪt] *vt* **-lated; -lating** 1 CASTRATE : castrar, emascular 2 WEAKEN : debilitar
embalm [ɪmˈbɑm, ɛm-, -ˈbɑlm] *vt* : embalsamar
embankment [ɪmˈbæŋkmənt, ɛm-] *n* : terraplén *m*, muro *m* de contención
embargo¹ [ɪmˈbɑrɡo, ɛm-] *vt* **-goed; -going** : imponer un embargo sobre
embargo² *n, pl* **-goes** : embargo *m*
embark [ɪmˈbɑrk, ɛm-] *vi* : embarcar — *vi* 1 : embarcarse 2 to embark on START : emprender, embarcarse en
embarkation [ˌɛm₍bɑrˈkeɪʃən] *n* : embarque *m*, embarco *m*
embarrass [ɪmˈbærəs, ɛm-] *vt* : avergonzar, abochornar
embarrassing [ɪmˈbærəsɪŋ, ɛm-] *adj* : embarazoso, violento
embarrassment [ɪmˈbærəsmənt, ɛm-] *n* : vergüenza *f*, pena *f*
embassy [ˈɛmbəsi] *n, pl* **-sies** : embajada *f*
embed [ɪmˈbɛd, ɛm-] *vt* **-bedded; -bedding** : incrustar, empotrar, grabar (en la memoria)
embellish [ɪmˈbɛlɪʃ, ɛm-] *vt* : adornar, embellecer
embellishment [ɪmˈbɛlɪʃmənt, ɛm-] *n* : adorno *m*
ember [ˈɛmbər] *n* : ascua *f*, brasa *f*
embezzle [ɪmˈbɛzəl, ɛm-] *vt* **-zled; -zling** : desfalcar, malversar
embezzlement [ɪmˈbɛzəlmənt, ɛm-] *n* : desfalco *m*, malversación *f*
embezzler [ɪmˈbɛzələr, ɛm-] *n* : desfalcador *m*, -dora *f*; malversador *m*, -dora *f*
embitter [ɪmˈbɪtər, ɛm-] *vt* : amargar
emblem [ˈɛmbləm] *n* : emblema *m*, símbolo *m*
emblematic [ˌɛmbləˈmætɪk] *adj* : emblemático, simbólico
embodiment [ɪmˈbɑdɪmənt, ɛm-] *n* : encarnación *f*, personificación *f*
embody [ɪmˈbɑdi, ɛm-] *vt* **-bodied; -bodying** : encarnar, personificar
emboss [ɪmˈbɑs, ɛm-, -ˈbɔs] *vt* : repujar, grabar en relieve
embrace¹ [ɪmˈbreɪs, ɛm-] *vt* **-braced; -bracing** 1 HUG : abrazar 2 ADOPT, TAKE ON : adoptar, aceptar 3 INCLUDE : abarcar, incluir
embrace² *n* : abrazo *m*
embroider [ɪmˈbrɔɪdər, ɛm-] *vt* : bordar (una tela), adornar (una historia)
embroidery [ɪmˈbrɔɪdəri, ɛm-] *n, pl* **-deries** : bordado *m*
embroil [ɪmˈbrɔɪl, ɛm-] *vt* : embrollar, enredar
embryo [ˈɛmbri₍oː] *n, pl* **embryos** : embrión *m*

embryonic [ˌɛmbri'anɪk] *adj* : embrionario

emend [i'mɛnd] *vt* : enmendar, corregir

emendation [ˌiːˌmɛn'deɪʃən] *n* : enmienda *f*

emerald¹ ['ɛmrəld, 'ɛmə-] *adj* : verde esmeralda

emerald² *n* : esmeralda *f*

emerge [i'mərdʒ] *vi* emerged; emerging : emerger, salir, aparecer, surgir

emergence [i'mərdʒənts] *n* : aparición *f*, surgimiento *m*

emergency [i'mərdʒəntsi] *n, pl* -cies : emergencia *f*

emergent [i'mərdʒənt] *adj* : emergente

emery ['ɛməri] *n, pl* -eries : esmeril *m*

emetic¹ [i'mɛtɪk] *adj* : vomitivo, emético

emetic² *n* : vomitivo *m*, emético *m*

emigrant ['ɛmɪgrənt] *n* : emigrante *mf*

emigrate ['ɛməˌgreɪt] *vi* -grated; -grating : emigrar

emigration [ˌɛmə'greɪʃən] *n* : emigración *f*

eminence ['ɛmənənts] *n* 1 PROMINENCE : eminencia *f*, prestigio *m*, renombre *m* 2 DIGNITARY : eminencia *f*; dignatario *m*, -ria *f* ⟨Your Eminence : Su Eminencia⟩

eminent ['ɛmənənt] *adj* : eminente, ilustre

eminently ['ɛmənəntli] *adv* : sumamente

emissary ['ɛməˌsɛri] *n, pl* -saries : emisario *m*, -ria *f*

emission [i'mɪʃən] *n* : emisión *f*

emit [i'mɪt] *vt* emitted; emitting : emitir, despedir, producir

emote [i'moːt] *vi* emoted; emoting : exteriorizar las emociones

emotion [i'moːʃən] *n* : emoción *f*, sentimiento *m*

emotional [i'moːʃənəl] *adj* 1 : emocional, afectivo ⟨an emotional reaction : una reacción emocional⟩ 2 MOVING : emocionante, emotivo, conmovedor

emotionally [i'moːʃənəli] *adv* : emocionalmente

empathy ['ɛmpəθi] *n* : empatía *f*

emperor ['ɛmpərər] *n* : emperador *m*

emphasis ['ɛmfəsɪs] *n, pl* -phases [-ˌsiːz] : énfasis *m*, hincapié *m*

emphasize ['ɛmfəˌsaɪz] *vt* -sized; -sizing : enfatizar, destacar, subrayar, hacer hincapié en

emphatic [ɪm'fætɪk, ɛm-] *adj* : enfático, enérgico, categórico — emphatically [-ɪkli] *adv*

empire ['ɛmˌpaɪr] *n* : imperio *m*

empirical [ɪm'pɪrɪkəl, ɛm-] *adj* : empírico — empirically [-ɪkli] *adv*

employ¹ [ɪm'plɔɪ, ɛm-] *vt* 1 USE : usar, utilizar 2 HIRE : contratar, emplear 3 OCCUPY : ocupar, dedicar, emplear

employ² [ɪm'plɔɪ, ɛm-; 'ɪm-, 'ɛm-] *n* 1 : puesto *m*, cargo *m*, ocupación *f* 2 to be in the employ of : estar al servicio de, trabajar para

employee [ɪmˌplɔɪ'iː, ɛm-, -'plɔɪˌiː] *n* : empleado *m*, -da *f*

employer [ɪm'plɔɪər, ɛm-] *n* : patrón *m*, -trona *f*; empleador *m*, -dora *f*

employment [ɪm'plɔɪmənt, ɛm-] *n* : trabajo *m*, empleo *m*

empower [ɪm'pauər, ɛm-] *vt* : facultar, autorizar, conferirle poder a

empowerment [ɪm'pauərmənt, ɛm-] *n* : autorización *f*

empress ['ɛmprəs] *n* : emperatriz *f*

emptiness ['ɛmptinəs] *n* : vacío *m*, vacuidad *f*

empty¹ ['ɛmpti] *v* -tied; -tying *vt* : vaciar — *vi* : desaguar (dícese de un río)

empty² *adj* emptier; -est 1 : vacío 2 VACANT : desocupado, libre 3 MEANINGLESS : vacío, hueco, vano

empty–handed [ˌɛmpti'hændəd] *adj* : con las manos vacías

empty–headed [ˌɛmpti'hɛdəd] *adj* : cabeza hueca, tonto

emu ['iːˌmjuː] *n* : emú *m*

emulate ['ɛmjəˌleɪt] *vt* -lated; -lating : emular

emulation [ˌɛmjə'leɪʃən] *n* : emulación *f*

emulsifier [ɪ'mʌlsəˌfaɪər] *n* : emulsionante *m*

emulsify [ɪ'mʌlsəˌfaɪ] *vt* -fied; -fying : emulsionar

emulsion [ɪ'mʌlʃən] *n* : emulsión *f*

enable [ɪ'neɪbəl, ɛ-] *vt* -abled; -abling 1 EMPOWER : habilitar, autorizar, facultar 2 PERMIT : hacer posible, posibilitar, permitir

enact [ɪ'nækt, ɛ-] *vt* 1 : promulgar (un ley o decreto) 2 : representar (un papel en el teatro)

enactment [ɪ'næktmənt, ɛ-] *n* : promulgación *f*

enamel¹ [ɪ'næməl] *vt* -eled *or* -elled; -eling *or* -elling : esmaltar

enamel² *n* : esmalte *m*

enamor [ɪ'næmər] *vt* 1 : enamorar 2 to be enamored of : estar enamorado de (una persona), estar entusiasmado con (algo)

encamp [ɪn'kæmp, ɛn-] *vi* : acampar

encampment [ɪn'kæmpmənt, ɛn-] *n* : campamento *m*

encase [ɪn'keɪs, ɛn-] *vt* -cased; -casing : encerrar, revestir

encephalitis [ɪnˌsfə'laɪtəs, ɛn-] *n, pl* -litides ['lɪtəˌdiːz] : encefalitis *f*

enchant [ɪn'tʃænt, ɛn-] *vt* 1 BEWITCH : hechizar, encantar, embrujar 2 CHARM, FASCINATE : cautivar, fascinar, encantar

enchanting [ɪn'tʃæntɪŋ, ɛn-] *adj* : encantador

enchanter [ɪn'tʃæntər, ɛn-] *n* SORCERER : mago *m*, encantador *m*

enchantment [ɪn'tʃæntmənt, ɛn-] *n* 1 SPELL : encanto *m*, hechizo *m* 2 CHARM : encanto *m*

enchantress [ɪn'tʃæntrəs, ɛn-] *n* 1 SORCERESS : maga *f*, hechicera *f* 2 CHARMER : mujer *f* cautivadora

encircle [ɪn'sərkəl, ɛn-] *vt* -cled; -cling : rodear, ceñir, cercar

enclose [ɪn'kloːz, ɛn-] *vt* **-closed; -closing 1** SURROUND : encerrar, cercar, rodear **2** INCLUDE : incluir, adjuntar, acompañar ⟨please find enclosed : le enviamos adjunto⟩

enclosure [ɪn'kloːʒər, ɛn-] *n* **1** ENCLOSING : encierro *m* **2** : cercado *m* (de terreno), recinto *m* ⟨an enclosure for the press : un recinto para la prensa⟩ **3** ADJUNCT : anexo *m* (con una carta), documento *m* adjunto

encode [ɪn'koːd, ɛn-] *vt* : cifrar (mensajes, etc.), codificar (en informática)

encompass [ɪn'kʌmpəs, ɛn-, -'kɑm-] *vt* **1** SURROUND : circundar, rodear **2** INCLUDE : abarcar, comprender

encore ['ɑn,kor] *n* : bis *m*, repetición *f*

encounter¹ [ɪn'kaʊntər, ɛn-] *vt* **1** MEET : encontrar, encontrarse con, toparse con, tropezar con **2** FIGHT : combatir, luchar contra

encounter² *n* : encuentro *m*

encourage [ɪn'kərɪdʒ, ɛn-] *vt* **-aged; -aging 1** HEARTEN, INSPIRE : animar, alentar **2** FOSTER : fomentar, promover

encouragement [ɪn'kərɪdʒmənt, ɛn-] *n* : ánimo *m*, aliento *m*

encouraging [ɪn'kərədʒɪŋ, ɛn-] *adj* : alentador, esperanzador

encroach [ɪn'kroːtʃ, ɛn-] *vi* **to encroach on** : invadir, abusar (derechos), quitar (tiempo)

encroachment [ɪn'kroːtʃmənt, ɛn-] *n* : invasión *f*, usurpación *f*

encrust [ɪn'krʌst, ɛn-] *vt* **1** : recubrir con una costra **2** INLAY : incrustar ⟨encrusted with gems : incrustado de gemas⟩

encumber [ɪn'kʌmbər, ɛn-] *vt* **1** BLOCK : obstruir, estorbar **2** BURDEN : cargar, gravar

encumbrance [ɪn'kʌmbrənts, ɛn-] *n* : estorbo *m*, carga *f*, gravamen *m*

encyclopedia [ɪn,saɪklə'piːdiə, ɛn-] *n* : enciclopedia *f*

encyclopedic [ɪn,saɪklə'piːdɪk, ɛn-] *adj* : enciclopédico

end¹ ['ɛnd] *vt* **1** STOP : terminar, poner fin a **2** CONCLUDE : concluir, terminar — *vi* : terminar(se), acabar, concluir(se)

end² *n* **1** EXTREMITY : extremo *m*, final *m*, punta *f* **2** CONCLUSION : fin *m*, final *m* **3** AIM : fin *m*

endanger [ɪn'deɪndʒər, ɛn-] *vt* : poner en peligro

endear [ɪn'dɪr, ɛn-] *vt* **to endear oneself to** : ganarse la simpatía de, granjearse el cariño de

endearment [ɪn'dɪrmənt, ɛn-] *n* : expresión *f* de cariño

endeavor¹ [ɪn'dɛvər, ɛn-] *vt* : intentar, esforzarse por ⟨he endeavored to improve his work : intentó por mejorar su trabajo⟩

endeavor² *n* : intento *m*, esfuerzo *m*

endemic [ɛn'dɛmɪk, ɪn-] *adj* : endémico

ending ['ɛndɪŋ] *n* **1** CONCLUSION : final *m*, desenlace *m* **2** SUFFIX : sufijo *m*, terminación *f*

endive ['ɛn,daɪv, ,ɑn'diːv] *n* : endibia *f*, endivia *f*

endless ['ɛndləs] *adj* **1** INTERMINABLE : interminable, inacabable, sin fin **2** INNUMERABLE : innumerable, incontable

endlessly ['ɛndləsli] *adv* : interminablemente, eternamente, sin parar

endocrine ['ɛndəkrən, -,kraɪn, -,kriːn] *adj* : endocrino

endorse [ɪn'dɔrs, ɛn-] *vt* **-dorsed; -dorsing 1** SIGN : endosar, firmar **2** APPROVE : aprobar, sancionar

endorsement [ɪn'dɔrsmənt, ɛn-] *n* **1** SIGNATURE : endoso *m*, firma *f* **2** APPROVAL : aprobación *f*, aval *m*

endow [ɪn'daʊ, ɛn-] *vt* : dotar

endowment [ɪn'daʊmənt, ɛn-] *n* **1** FUNDING : dotación *f* **2** DONATION : donación *f*, legado *m* **3** ATTRIBUTE, GIFT : atributo *m*, dotes *fpl*

endurable [ɪn'dʊrəbəl, ɛn-, -'djʊr-] *adj* : tolerable, soportable

endurance [ɪn'dʊrənts, ɛn-, -'djʊr-] *n* : resistencia *f*, aguante *m*

endure [ɪn'dʊr, ɛn-, -'djʊr] *v* **-dured; -during** *vt* **1** BEAR : resistir, soportar, aguantar **2** TOLERATE : tolerar, soportar — *vi* LAST : durar, perdurar

enema ['ɛnəmə] *n* : enema *m*, lavativa *f*

enemy ['ɛnəmi] *n, pl* **-mies** : enemigo *m*, -ga *f*

energetic [,ɛnər'dʒɛtɪk] *adj* : enérgico, vigoroso — **energetically** [-tɪkli] *adv*

energize ['ɛnər,dʒaɪz] *vt* **-gized; -gizing 1** ACTIVATE : activar **2** INVIGORATE : vigorizar

energy ['ɛnərdʒi] *n, pl* **-gies 1** VITALITY : energía *f*, vitalidad *f* **2** EFFORT : esfuerzo *m*, energías *fpl* **3** POWER : energía *f* ⟨atomic energy : energía atómica⟩

enervate ['ɛnər,veɪt] *vt* **-vated; -vating** : enervar, debilitar

enfold [ɪn'foːld, ɛn-] *vt* : envolver

enforce [ɪn'fors, ɛn-] *vt* **-forced; -forcing 1** : hacer respetar, hacer cumplir (una ley, etc.) **2** IMPOSE : imponer ⟨to enforce obedience : imponer la obediencia⟩

enforcement [ɪn'forsmənt, ɛn-] *n* : imposición *f*

enfranchise [ɪn'fræn,tʃaɪz, ɛn-] *vt* **-chised; -chising** : conceder el voto a

enfranchisement [ɪn'fræn,tʃaɪzmənt, ɛn-] *n* : concesión *f* del voto

engage [ɪn'geɪdʒ, ɛn-] *v* **-gaged; -gaging** *vt* **1** ATTRACT : captar, atraer, llamar ⟨to engage one's attention : captar la atención⟩ **2** MESH : engranar ⟨to engage the clutch : embragar⟩ **3** COMMIT : comprometer ⟨to get engaged : comprometerse⟩ **4** HIRE : contratar **5** : entablar combate con (un enemigo)

— *vi* **1** PARTICIPATE : participar **2 to engage in combat** : entrar en combate

engagement [ɪn'geɪʤmənt, ɛn-] *n* **1** APPOINTMENT : cita *f*, hora *f* **2** BETROTHAL : compromiso *m*

engaging [ɪn'geɪʤɪŋ, ɛn-] *adj* : atractivo, encantador, interesante

engender [ɪn'ʤndər, ɛn-] *vt* **-dered; -dering** : engendrar

engine ['ɛnʤən] *n* **1** MOTOR : motor *m* **2** LOCOMOTIVE : locomotora *f*, máquina *f*

engineer[1] [ˌɛnʤə'nɪr] *vt* **1** : diseñar, construir (un sistema, un mecanismo, etc.) **2** CONTRIVE : maquinar, tramar, fraguar

engineer[2] *n* **1** : ingeniero *m*, -ra *f* **2** : maquinista *mf* (de locomotoras)

engineering [ˌɛnʤə'nɪrɪŋ] *n* : ingeniería *f*

English[1] ['ɪŋglɪʃ, 'ŋlɪʃ] *adj* : inglés

English[2] *n* **1** : inglés *m* (idioma) **2 the English** : los ingleses

Englishman ['ɪŋglɪʃmən, 'ŋlɪʃ-] *n, pl* **-men** [-mən, -ˌmɛn] : inglés *m*

Englishwoman ['ɪŋglɪʃˌwʊmən, 'ŋlɪʃ-] *n, pl* **-women** [-ˌwɪmən] : inglesa *f*

engrave [ɪn'greɪv, ɛn-] *vt* **-graved; -graving** : grabar

engraver [ɪn'greɪvər, ɛn-] *n* : grabador *m*, -dora *f*

engraving [ɪn'greɪvɪŋ, ɛn-] *n* : grabado *m*

engross [ɪn'groːs, ɛn-] *vt* : absorber

engrossed [ɪn'groːst, ɛn-] *adj* : absorto

engrossing [ɪn'groːsɪŋ, ɛn-] *adj* : fascinante, absorbente

engulf [ɪn'gʌlf, ɛn-] *vt* : envolver, sepultar

enhance [ɪn'hænts, ɛn-] *vt* **-hanced; -hancing** : realzar, aumentar, mejorar

enhancement [ɪn'hæntsmənt, ɛn-] *n* : mejora *f*, realce *m*, aumento *m*

enigma [ɪ'nɪgmə] *n* : enigma *m*

enigmatic [ˌɛnɪg'mætɪk, ˌiːnɪg-] *adj* : enigmático — **enigmatically** [-ʧɪkli] *adv*

enjoin [ɪn'ʤɔɪn, ɛn-] *vt* **1** COMMAND : ordenar, imponer **2** FORBID : prohibir, vedar

enjoy [ɪn'ʤɔɪ, ɛn-] *vt* **1** : disfrutar, gozar de ⟨did you enjoy the book? : ¿te gustó el libro?⟩ ⟨to enjoy good health : gozar de buena salud⟩ **2 to enjoy oneself** : divertirse, pasarlo bien

enjoyable [ɪn'ʤɔɪəbəl, ɛn-] *adj* : agradable, placentero, divertido

enjoyment [ɪn'ʤɔɪmənt, ɛn-] *n* : placer *m*, goce *m*, disfrute *m*, deleite *m*

enlarge [ɪn'larʤ, ɛn-] *v* **-larged; -larging** *vt* : extender, agrandar, ampliar — *vi* **1** : ampliarse **2 to enlarge upon** : extenderse sobre, entrar en detalles sobre

enlargement [ɪn'larʤmənt, ɛn-] *n* : expansión *f*, ampliación *f* (dícese de fotografías)

enlarger [ɪn'larʤər, ɛn-] *n* : ampliadora *f*

enlighten [ɪn'laɪtən, ɛn-] *vt* : iluminar, aclarar

enlightenment [ɪn'laɪtənmənt, ɛn-] *n* **1** : ilustración *f* ⟨the Enlightenment : la Ilustración⟩ **2** CLARIFICATION : aclaración *f*

enlist [ɪn'lɪst, ɛn-] *vt* **1** ENROLL : alistar, reclutar **2** SECURE : conseguir ⟨to enlist the support of : conseguir el apoyo de⟩ — *vi* : alistarse

enlisted man [ɪn'lɪstəd, ɛn-] *n* : soldado *m* raso

enlistment [ɪn'lɪstmənt, ɛn-] *n* : alistamiento *m*, reclutamiento *m*

enliven [ɪn'laɪvən, ɛn-] *vt* : animar, alegrar, darle vida a

enmity ['ɛnməti] *n, pl* **-ties** : enemistad *f*, animadversión *f*

ennoble [ɪ'noːbəl, ɛ-] *vt* **-bled; -bling** : ennoblecer

ennui [ˌɑn'wiː] *n* : hastío *m*, tedio *m*, fastidio *m*, aburrimiento *m*

enormity [ɪ'nɔrməti] *n, pl* **-ties** **1** ATROCITY : atrocidad *f*, barbaridad *f* **2** IMMENSITY : enormidad *f*, inmensidad *f*

enormous [ɪ'nɔrməs] *adj* : enorme, inmenso, tremendo — **enormously** *adv*

enough[1] [ɪ'nʌf] *adv* **1** : bastante, suficientemente **2 fair enough!** : ¡está bien!, ¡de acuerdo! **3 strangely enough** : por extraño que parezca **4 sure enough** : en efecto, sin duda alguna **5 well enough** : muy bien, bastante bien

enough[2] *adj* : bastante, suficiente ⟨do we have enough chairs? : ¿tenemos suficientes sillas?⟩

enough[3] *pron* : (lo) suficiente, (lo) bastante ⟨enough to eat : lo suficiente para comer⟩ ⟨it's not enough : no basta⟩ ⟨I've had enough! : ¡estoy harto!, ¡está bueno ya!⟩

enquire [ɪn'kwaɪr, ɛn-] **enquiry** ['ɪnˌkwaɪri, 'ɛn-, -kwəri; ɪn'kwaɪri, ɛn'-] → **inquire, inquiry**

enrage [ɪn'reɪʤ, ɛn-] *vt* **-raged; -raging** : enfurecer, encolerizar

enraged [ɪn'reɪʤd, ɛn-] *adj* : enfurecido, furioso

enrich [ɪn'rɪʧ, ɛn-] *vt* : enriquecer

enrichment [ɪn'rɪʧmənt, ɛn-] *n* : enriquecimiento *m*

enroll *or* **enrol** [ɪn'roːl, ɛn-] *v* **-rolled; -rolling** *vt* : matricular, inscribir — *vi* : matricularse, inscribirse

enrollment [ɪn'roːlmənt, ɛn-] *n* : matrícula *f*, inscripción *f*

en route [ɑ'ruːt, ɛn'raʊt] *adv* : de camino, por el camino

ensconce [ɪn'skants, ɛn-] *vt* **-sconced; -sconcing** : acomodar, instalar, establecer cómodamente

ensemble [ɑn'sambəl] *n* : conjunto *m*

enshrine [ɪn'ʃraɪn, ɛn-] *vt* **-shrined; -shrining** : conservar religiosamente, preservar

ensign ['ntsən, 'ɛnˌsaɪn] *n* **1** FLAG : enseña *f*, pabellón *m* **2** : alférez *mf* (de fragata)

enslave [ɪn'sleɪv, ɛn-] *vt* **-slaved; -slaving** : esclavizar

enslavement [ɪn'sleɪvmənt, ɛn-] *n* : esclavización *f*

ensnare [ɪn'snær, ɛn-] *vt* **-snared; -snaring** : atrapar

ensue [ɪn'suː, ɛn-] *vi* **-sued; -suing** : seguir, resultar

ensure [ɪn'ʃʊr, ɛn-] *vt* **-sured; -suring** : asegurar, garantizar

entail [ɪn'teɪl, ɛn-] *vt* : implicar, suponer, conllevar

entangle [ɪn'tæŋgəl, ɛn-] *vt* **-gled; -gling** : enredar

entanglement [ɪn'tæŋgəlmənt, ɛn-] *n* : enredo *m*

enter ['ɛntər] *vt* **1** : entrar en, entrar a **2** BEGIN : entrar en, comenzar, iniciar **3** RECORD : anotar, inscribir, dar entrada a ⟨to enter data : introducir datos⟩ **4** JOIN : entrar en, alistarse en, hacerse socio de — *vi* **1** : entrar **2 to enter into** : entrar en, firmar (un acuerdo), entablar (negociaciones, etc.)

enterprise ['ɛntər,praɪz] *n* **1** UNDERTAKING : empresa *f* **2** BUSINESS : empresa *f*, firma *f* **3** INITIATIVE : iniciativa *f*, empuje *m*

enterprising ['ɛntər,praɪzɪŋ] *adj* : emprendedor

entertain [,ɛntər'teɪn] *vt* **1** : recibir, agasajar ⟨to entertain guests : tener invitados⟩ **2** CONSIDER : considerar, contemplar **3** AMUSE : entretener, divertir

entertainer [,ɛntər'teɪnər] *n* : artista *mf*

entertaining [,ɛntər'teɪnɪŋ] *adj* : entretenido, divertido

entertainment [,ɛntər'teɪnmənt] *n* : entretenimiento *m*, diversión *f*

enthrall *or* **enthral** [ɪn'θrɔl, ɛn-] *vt* **-thralled; -thralling** : cautivar, embelesar

enthuse [ɪn'θuiz, ɛn-] *v* **-thused; -thusing** *vt* **1** EXCITE : entusiasmar **2** : decir con entusiasmo — *vi* **to enthuse over** : hablar con entusiasmo sobre

enthusiasm [ɪn'θuːzi,æzəm, ɛn-, -'θjuː-] *n* : entusiasmo *m*

enthusiast [ɪn'θuːzi,æst, ɛn-, -'θjuː-, -əst] *n* : entusiasta *mf*; aficionado *m*, -da *f*

enthusiastic [ɪn,θuːzi'æstɪk, ɛn-, -,θjuː-] *adj* : entusiasta, aficionado

enthusiastically [ɪn,θuːzi'æstɪkli, ɛn-, -,θjuː-] *adv* : con entusiasmo

entice [ɪn'taɪs, ɛn-] *vt* **-ticed; -ticing** : atraer, tentar

enticement [ɪn'taɪsmənt, ɛn-] *n* : tentación *f*, atracción *f*, señuelo *m*

entire [ɪn'taɪr, ɛn-] *adj* : entero, completo

entirely [ɪn'taɪrli, ɛn-] *adv* : completamente, totalmente

entirety [ɪn'taɪrti, ɛn-, -'taɪrəti] *n, pl* **-ties** : totalidad *f*

entitle [ɪn'taɪtəl, ɛn-] *vt* **-tled; -tling** **1** NAME : titular, intitular **2** : dar derecho a ⟨it entitles you to enter free : le

da derecho a entrar gratis⟩ **3 to be entitled to** : tener derecho a

entitlement [ɪn'taɪtəlmənt, ɛn-] *n* RIGHT : derecho *m*

entity ['ɛntəti] *n, pl* **-ties** : entidad *f*, ente *m*

entomologist [,ɛntə'mɑlədʒɪst] *n* : entomólogo *m*, -ga *f*

entomology [,ɛntə'mɑlədʒi] *n* : entomología *f*

entourage [,ɑntʊ'rɑʒ] *n* : séquito *m*

entrails ['ɛn,treɪlz, -trəlz] *npl* : entrañas *fpl*, vísceras *fpl*

entrance[1] [ɪn'trænts, ɛn-] *vt* **-tranced; -trancing** : encantar, embelesar, fascinar

entrance[2] ['ɛntrənts] *n* **1** ENTERING : entrada *f* ⟨to make an entrance : entrar en escena⟩ **2** ENTRY : entrada *f*, puerta *f* **3** ADMISSION : entrada *f*, ingreso *m* ⟨entrance examination : examen de ingreso⟩

entrant ['ɛntrənt] *n* : candidato *m*, -ta *f* (en un examen); participante *mf* (en un concurso)

entrap [ɪn'træp, ɛn-] *vt* **-trapped; -trapping** : atrapar, entrampar, hacer caer en una trampa

entrapment [ɪn'træpmənt, ɛn-] *n* : captura *f*

entreat [ɪn'triːt, ɛn-] *vt* : suplicar, rogar

entreaty [ɪn'triːti, ɛn-] *n, pl* **-treaties** : ruego *m*, súplica *f*

entrée *or* **entree** ['ɑn,treɪ, ,ɑn'-] *n* : plato *m* principal

entrench [ɪn'trɛntʃ, ɛn-] *vt* **1** FORTIFY : atrincherar (una posición militar) **2** : consolidar, afianzar ⟨firmly entrenched in his job : afianzado en su puesto⟩

entrepreneur [,ɑntrəprə'nər, -'njʊr] *n* : empresario *m*, -ria *f*

entrust [ɪn'trʌst, ɛn-] *vt* : confiar, encomendar

entry ['ɛntri] *n, pl* **-tries** **1** ENTRANCE : entrada *f* **2** NOTATION : entrada *f*, anotación *f*

entwine [ɪn'twaɪn, ɛn-] *vt* **-twined; -twining** : entrelazar, entretejer, entrecruzar

enumerate [ɪ'nuːmə,reɪt, ɛ-, -'njuː-] *vt* **-ated; -ating** **1** LIST : enumerar **2** COUNT : contar, enumerar

enumeration [ɪ,nuːmə'reɪʃən, ɛ-, -,njuː-] *n* : enumeración *f*, lista *f*

enunciate [ɪ'nʌntsi,eɪt, ɛ-] *vt* **-ated; -ating** **1** STATE : enunciar, decir **2** PRONOUNCE : articular, pronunciar

enunciation [ɪ,nʌntsi'eɪʃən, ɛ-] *n* **1** STATEMENT : enunciación *f*, declaración *f* **2** ARTICULATION : articulación *f*, pronunciación *f*, dicción *f*

envelop [ɪn'vləp, ɛn-] *vt* : envolver, cubrir

envelope ['ɛnvə,loːp, 'ɑn-] *n* : sobre *m*

enviable ['ɛnviəbəl] *adj* : envidiable

envious ['ɛnviəs] *adj* : envidioso — **enviously** *adv*

environment [ɪn'vaɪrənmənt, ɛn-, -'vaɪərn-] *n* : medio *m* (ambiente), ambiente *m*, entorno *m*
environmental [ɪn,vaɪrən'mɛntəl, ɛn-, -,vaɪərn-] *adj* : ambiental
environmentalist [ɪn,vaɪrən'mɛntəlɪst, ɛn-, -,vaɪərn-] *n* : ecologista *mf*
environs [ɪn'vaɪrənz, ɛn-, -'vaɪərnz] *npl* : alrededores *mpl*, entorno *m*, inmediaciones *fpl*
envisage [ɪn'vɪzɪʤ, ɛn-] *vt* **-aged; -aging 1** IMAGINE : imaginarse, concebir **2** FORESEE : prever
envision [ɪn'vɪʒən, ɛn-] *vt* : imaginar
envoy ['ɛn,vɔɪ, 'ɑn-] *n* : enviado *m*, -da *f*
envy[1] ['ɛnvi] *vt* **-vied; -vying** : envidiar
envy[2] *n, pl* **envies** : envidia *f*
enzyme ['ɛn,zaɪm] *n* : enzima *f*
eon ['iːən, iː,ɑn] → **aeon**
epaulet [,pə'lɛt] *n* : charretera *f*
ephemeral [ɪ'fɛmərəl, -'fiː-] *adj* : efímero, fugaz
epic[1] ['ɛpɪk] *adj* : épico
epic[2] *n* : poema *m* épico, epopeya *f*
epicure ['ɛpɪ,kjʊr] *n* : epicúreo *m*, -rea *f*; gastrónomo *m*, -ma *f*
epicurean [,ɛpɪkjʊ'riːən, -'kjʊriən] *adj* : epicúreo
epidemic[1] [,ɛpə'dɛmɪk] *adj* : epidémico
epidemic[2] *n* : epidemia *f*
epidermis [,ɛpə'dərməs] *n* : epidermis *f*
epigram ['ɛpə,græm] *n* : epigrama *m*
epilepsy ['ɛpə,lɛpsi] *n, pl* **-sies** : epilepsia *f*
epileptic[1] [,ɛpə'lɛptɪk] *adj* : epiléptico
epileptic[2] *n* : epiléptico *m*, -ca *f*
epilogue ['ɛpə,lɔg, -,lɑg] *n* : epílogo *m*
epiphany [ɪ'pɪfəni] *n, pl* **-nies 1 Epiphany** : Epifanía *f* **2 to have an epiphany** : tener una revelación
episcopal [ɪ'pɪskəpəl] *adj* : episcopal
Episcopalian [ɪ,pɪskə'peɪljən] *n* : episcopalista *mf*; episcopaliano *m*, -na *f*
episode ['ɛpə,soːd] *n* : episodio *m*
episodic [,ɛpə'sɑdɪk] *adj* : episódico
epistle [ɪ'pɪsəl] *n* : epístola *f*, carta *f*
epitaph ['ɛpə,tæf] *n* : epitafio *m*
epithet ['ɛpə,θɛt, -θət] *n* : epíteto *m*
epitome [ɪ'pɪtəmi] *n* **1** SUMMARY : epítome *m*, resumen *m* **2** EMBODIMENT : personificación *f*
epitomize [ɪ'pɪtə,maɪz] *vt* **-mized; -mizing 1** SUMMARIZE : resumir **2** EMBODY : ser la personificación de, personificar
epoch ['ɛpək, 'ɛ,pɑk, 'iː,pɑk] *n* : época *f*, era *f*
epoxy [ɪ'pɑksi] *n, pl* **epoxies** : resina *f* epoxídica
equable ['ɛkwəbəl, 'iː-] *adj* **1** CALM, STEADY : ecuánime **2** UNIFORM : estable (dícese de la temperatura), constante (dícese del clima), uniforme
equably ['ɛkwəbli, 'iː-] *adv* : con ecuanimidad
equal[1] ['iːkwəl] *vt* **equaled** *or* **equalled; equaling** *or* **equalling 1** : ser igual a

⟨two plus three equals five : dos más tres es igual a cinco⟩ **2** MATCH : igualar
equal[2] *adj* **1** SAME : igual **2** ADEQUATE : adecuado, capaz
equal[3] *n* : igual *mf*
equality [ɪ'kwɑləti] *n, pl* **-ties** : igualdad *f*
equalize ['iːkwə,laɪz] *vt* **-ized; -izing** : igualar, equiparar
equally ['iːkwəli] *adv* : igualmente, por igual
equanimity [,iːkwə'nɪməti, ,ɛ-] *n, pl* **-ties** : ecuanimidad *f*
equate [ɪ'kweɪt] *vt* **equated; equating** : equiparar, identificar
equation [ɪ'kweɪʒən] *n* : ecuación *f*
equator [ɪ'kweɪtər] *n* : ecuador *m*
equatorial [,iːkwə'toriəl, ,ɛ-] *adj* : ecuatorial
equestrian[1] [ɪ'kwɛstriən, ɛ-] *adj* : ecuestre
equestrian[2] *n* : jinete *mf*, caballista *mf*
equilateral [,iːkwə'lætərəl, ,ɛ-] *adj* : equilátero
equilibrium [,iːkwə'lɪbriəm, ,ɛ-] *n, pl* **-riums** *or* **-ria** [-briə] : equilibrio *m*
equine ['iː,kwaɪn, 'ɛ-] *adj* : equino, hípico
equinox ['iːkwə,nɑks, 'ɛ-] *n* : equinoccio *m*
equip [ɪ'kwɪp] *vt* **equipped; equipping 1** FURNISH : equipar **2** PREPARE : preparar
equipment [ɪ'kwɪpmənt] *n* : equipo *m*
equitable ['ɛkwətəbəl] *adj* : equitativo, justo, imparcial
equity ['ɛkwəti] *n, pl* **-ties 1** FAIRNESS : equidad *f*, imparcialidad *f* **2** VALUE : valor *m* líquido
equivalence [ɪ'kwɪvələnts] *n* : equivalencia *f*
equivalent[1] [ɪ'kwɪvələnt] *adj* : equivalente
equivalent[2] *n* : equivalente *m*
equivocal [ɪ'kwɪvəkəl] *adj* **1** AMBIGUOUS : equívoco, ambiguo **2** QUESTIONABLE : incierto, dudoso, sospechoso
equivocate [ɪ'kwɪvə,keɪt] *vi* **-cated; -cating** : usar lenguaje equívoco, andarse con evasivas
equivocation [ɪ,kwɪvə'keɪʃən] *n* : evasiva *f*, subterfugio *m*
era ['ɪrə, 'ɛrə, 'iːrə] *n* : era *f*, época *f*
eradicate [ɪ'rædə,keɪt] *vt* **-cated; -cating** : erradicar
erase [ɪ'reɪs] *vt* **erased; erasing** : borrar
eraser [ɪ'reɪsər] *n* : goma *f* de borrar, borrador *m*
erasure [ɪ'reɪʃər] *n* : tachadura *f*
ere[1] ['ɛr] *conj* : antes de que
ere[2] *prep* **1** : antes de **2 ere long** : dentro de poco
erect[1] [ɪ'rɛkt] *vt* **1** CONSTRUCT : erigir, construir **2** RAISE : levantar **3** ESTABLISH : establecer
erect[2] *adj* : erguido, derecho, erecto

erection · estimation

erection [ɪˈrɛkʃən] *n* **1** : erección *f* (en fisiología) **2** BUILDING : construcción *f*

ergonomics [ˌərɡəˈnɑmɪks] *npl* : ergonomía *f*

ermine [ˈərmən] *n* : armiño *m*

erode [ɪˈroːd] *vt* **eroded; eroding** : erosionar (el suelo), corroer (metales)

erosion [ɪˈroːʒən] *n* : erosión *f*, corrosión *f*

erotic [ɪˈrɑtɪk] *adj* : erótico — **erotically** [-tɪkli] *adv*

eroticism [ɪˈrɑtəˌsɪzəm] *n* : erotismo *m*

err [ˈɛr, ˈər] *vi* : cometer un error, equivocarse, errar

errand [ˈɛrənd] *n* : mandado *m*, encargo *m*, recado *m* *Spain* ⟨an errand of mercy : una misión de caridad⟩

errant [ˈɛrənt] *adj* **1** WANDERING : errante **2** ASTRAY : descarriado

erratic [ɪˈrætɪk] *adj* **1** INCONSISTENT : errático, irregular, inconsistente **2** ECCENTRIC : excéntrico, raro

erratically [ɪˈrætɪkli] *adv* : erráticamente, de manera irregular

erroneous [ɪˈroːniəs, ɛ-] *adj* : erróneo — **erroneously** *adv*

error [ˈɛrər] *n* : error *m*, equivocación *f* ⟨to be in error : estar equivocado⟩

ersatz [ˈɛrˌsɑts, ˈərˌsæts] *adj* : artificial, sustituto

erstwhile [ˈərstˌhwaɪl] *adj* : antiguo

erudite [ˈɛrəˌdaɪt, ˈɛrjʊ-] *adj* : erudito, letrado

erudition [ˌɛrəˈdɪʃən, ˌɛrjʊ-] *n* : erudición *f*

erupt [ɪˈrʌpt] *vi* **1** : hacer erupción (dícese de un volcán o un sarpullido) **2** : estallar (dícese de la cólera o la violencia)

eruption [ɪˈrʌpʃən] *n* : erupción *f*, estallido *m*

eruptive [ɪˈrʌptɪv] *adj* : eruptivo

escalate [ˈɛskəˌleɪt] *v* **-lated; -lating** *vt* : intensificar (un conflicto), aumentar (precios) — *vi* : intensificarse, aumentarse

escalation [ˌɛskəˈleɪʃən] *n* : intensificación *f*, escalada *f*, aumento *m*, subida *f*

escalator [ˈɛskəˌleɪtər] *n* : escalera *f* mecánica

escapade [ˈɛskəˌpeɪd] *n* : aventura *f*

escape[1] [ɪˈskeɪp, ɛ-] *v* **-caped; -caping** *vt* : escaparse de, librarse de, evitar — *vi* : escaparse, fugarse, huir

escape[2] *n* **1** FLIGHT : fuga *f*, huida *f*, escapada *f* **2** LEAKAGE : escape *m*, fuga *f* **3** : escapatoria *f*, evasión *f* ⟨to have no escape : no tener escapatoria⟩ ⟨escape from reality : evasión de la realidad⟩

escapee [ɪˌskeɪˈpiː, ˌɛ-] *n* : fugitivo *m*, -va *f*

escarole [ˈɛskəˌroːl] *n* : escarola *f*

escarpment [ɪsˈkɑrpmənt, ɛs-] *n* : escarpa *f*, escarpadura *f*

eschew [ɛˈʃuː, ɪsˈtʃuː] *vt* : evitar, rehuir, abstenerse de

escort[1] [ɪˈskɔrt, ɛ-] *vt* **1** : escoltar ⟨to escort a ship : escoltar un barco⟩ **2** ACCOMPANY : acompañar

escort[2] [ˈɛsˌkɔrt] *n* **1** : escolta *f* ⟨armed escort : escolta armada⟩ **2** COMPANION : acompañante *mf*; compañero *m*, -ra *f*

escrow [ˈɛsˌkroː] *n* **in escrow** : en depósito, en custodia de un tercero

Eskimo [ˈɛskəˌmoː] *n* **1** : esquimal *mf* **2** : esquimal *m* (idioma) — **Eskimo** *adj*

esophagus [ɪˈsɑfəɡəs, iː-] *n*, *pl* **-gi** [-ˌɡaɪ, -ˌdʒaɪ] : esófago *m*

esoteric [ˌɛsəˈtɛrɪk] *adj* : esotérico, hermético

especially [ɪˈspɛʃəli] *adv* : especialmente, particularmente

espionage [ˈɛspiəˌnɑʒ, -ˌnɑdʒ] *n* : espionaje *m*

espouse [ɪˈspaʊz, ɛ-] *vt* **espoused; espousing** **1** MARRY : casarse con **2** ADOPT, ADVOCATE : apoyar, adherirse a, adoptar

espresso [ɛˈsprɛˌsoː] *n*, *pl* **-sos** : café *m* exprés

essay[1] [ˈɛseɪ, ˈɛˌseɪ] *vt* : intentar, tratar

essay[2] [ˈɛˌseɪ] *n* **1** COMPOSITION : ensayo *m*, trabajo *m* **2** ATTEMPT : intento *m*

essayist [ˈɛˌseɪɪst] *n* : ensayista *mf*

essence [ˈɛsənts] *n* **1** CORE : esencia *f*, núcleo *m*, meollo *m* ⟨in essence : esencialmente⟩ **2** EXTRACT : esencia *f*, extracto *m* **3** PERFUME : esencia *f*, perfume *m*

essential[1] [ɪˈsɛntʃəl] *adj* : esencial, imprescindible, fundamental — **essentially** *adv*

essential[2] *n* : elemento *m* esencial, lo imprescindible

establish [ɪˈstæblɪʃ, ɛ-] *vt* **1** FOUND : establecer, fundar **2** SET UP : establecer, instaurar, instituir **3** PROVE : demostrar, probar

establishment [ɪˈstæblɪʃmənt, ɛ-] *n* **1** ESTABLISHING : establecimiento *m*, fundación *f*, instauración *f* **2** BUSINESS : negocio *m*, establecimiento *m* **3 the Establishment** : la clase dirigente

estate [ɪˈsteɪt, ɛ-] *n* **1** POSSESSIONS : bienes *mpl*, propiedad *f*, patrimonio *m* **2** PROPERTY : hacienda *f*, finca *f*, propiedad *f*

esteem[1] [ɪˈstiːm, ɛ-] *vt* : estimar, apreciar

esteem[2] *n* : estima *f*, aprecio *m*

ester [ˈɛstər] *n* : éster *m*

esthetic [ɛsˈθɛtɪk] → **aesthetic**

estimable [ˈɛstəməbəl] *adj* : estimable

estimate[1] [ˈɛstəˌmeɪt] *vt* **-mated; -mating** : calcular, estimar

estimate[2] [ˈɛstəmət] *n* **1** : cálculo *m* aproximado ⟨to make an estimate : hacer un cálculo⟩ **2** ASSESSMENT : valoración *f*, estimación *f*

estimation [ˌɛstəˈmeɪʃən] *n* **1** JUDGMENT : juicio *m*, opinión *f* ⟨in my estimation : en mi opinión, según mis cálculos⟩ **2** ESTEEM : estima *f*, aprecio *m*

estimator [ˈestəˌmeɪt̬ər] *n* : tasador *m*, -dora *f*
Estonian [ɛˈstoːniən] *n* : estonio *m*, -nia *f* — **Estonian** *adj*
estrange [ɪˈstreɪndʒ, ɛ-] *vt* **-tranged; -tranging** : enajenar, apartar, alejar
estrangement [ɪˈstreɪndʒmənt, ɛ-] *n* : alejamiento *m*, distanciamiento *m*
estrogen [ˈɛstrədʒən] *n* : estrógeno *m*
estrus [ˈɛstrəs] *n* : celo *m*
estuary [ˈɛstʃuˌwɛri] *n, pl* **-aries** : estuario *m*, -ría *f*
et cetera [ɛtˈsɛt̬ərə, -ˈsɛtrə] : etcétera
etch [ˈɛtʃ] *v* : grabar al aguafuerte
etching [ˈɛtʃɪŋ] *n* : aguafuerte *m*, grabado *m* al aguafuerte
eternal [ɪˈtərnəl, iː-] *adj* **1** EVERLASTING : eterno **2** INTERMINABLE : constante, incesante
eternally [ɪˈtərnəli, iː-] *adv* : eternamente, para siempre
eternity [ɪˈtərnət̬i, iː-] *n, pl* **-ties** : eternidad *f*
ethane [ˈɛˌθeɪn] *n* : etano *m*
ethanol [ˈɛθəˌnɔl, -ˌnoːl] *n* : etanol *m*
ether [ˈiːθər] *n* : éter *m*
ethereal [ɪˈθɪriəl, iː-] *adj* **1** CELESTIAL : etéreo, celeste **2** DELICATE : delicado
ethical [ˈɛθɪkəl] *adj* : ético — **ethically** *adv*
ethics [ˈɛθɪks] *ns & pl* **1** : ética *f* **2** MORALITY : ética *f*, moral *f*, moralidad *f*
Ethiopian [ˌiːθiˈoːpiən] *n* : etíope *mf* — **Ethiopian** *adj*
ethnic [ˈɛθnɪk] *adj* : étnico
ethnologist [ɛθˈnɑlədʒɪst] *n* : etnólogo *m*, -ga *f*
ethnology [ɛθˈnɑlədʒi] *n* : etnología *f*
etiquette [ˈɛt̬ɪkət, -ˌkɛt] *n* : etiqueta *f*, protocolo *m*
etymological [ˌɛt̬əməˈlɑdʒɪkəl] *adj* : etimológico
etymology [ˌɛt̬əˈmɑlədʒi] *n, pl* **-gies** : etimología *f*
eucalyptus [ˌjuːkəˈlɪptəs] *n, pl* **-ti** [-ˌtaɪ] *or* **-tuses** [-təsəz] : eucalipto *m*
Eucharist [ˈjuːkərɪst] *n* : Eucaristía *f*
eulogize [ˈjuːləˌdʒaɪz] *vt* **-gized; -gizing** : elogiar, encomiar
eulogy [ˈjuːlədʒi] *n, pl* **-gies** : elogio *m*, encomio *m*, panegírico *m*
eunuch [ˈjuːnək] *n* : eunuco *m*
euphemism [ˈjuːfəˌmɪzəm] *n* : eufemismo *m*
euphemistic [ˌjuːfəˈmɪstɪk] *adj* : eufemístico
euphony [ˈjuːfəni] *n, pl* **-nies** : eufonía *f*
euphoria [juˈforiə] *n* : euforia *f*
euphoric [juˈforɪk] *adj* : eufórico
European [ˌjʊrəˈpiːən] *n* : europeo *m*, europea *f* — **European** *adj*
euthanasia [ˌjuːθəˈneɪʒə, -ʒiə] *n* : eutanasia *f*
evacuate [ɪˈvækjuˌeɪt] *v* **-ated; -ating** *vt* VACATE : evacuar, desalojar — *vi* WITHDRAW : retirarse

evacuation [ɪˌvækjuˈeɪʃən] *n* : evacuación *f*, desalojo *m*
evade [ɪˈveɪd] *vt* **evaded; evading** : evadir, eludir, esquivar
evaluate [ɪˈvæljuˌeɪt] *vt* **-ated; -ating** : evaluar, valorar, tasar
evaluation [ɪˌvæljuˈeɪʃən] *n* : evaluación *f*, valoración *f*, tasación *f*
evangelical [ˌiːˌvænˈdʒɛlɪkəl, ˌɛvən-] *adj* : evangélico
evangelist [ɪˈvændʒəlɪst] *n* **1** : evangelista *m* **2** PREACHER : predicador *m*, -dora *f*
evaporate [ɪˈvæpəˌreɪt] *vi* **-rated; -rating** **1** VAPORIZE : evaporarse **2** VANISH : evaporarse, desvanecerse, esfumarse
evaporation [ɪˌvæpəˈreɪʃən] *n* : evaporación *f*
evasion [ɪˈveɪʒən] *n* : evasión *f*
evasive [ɪˈveɪsɪv] *adj* : evasivo
evasiveness [ɪˈveɪsɪvnəs] *n* : carácter *m* evasivo
eve [ˈiːv] *n* **1** : víspera *f* ⟨on the eve of the festivities : en vísperas de las festividades⟩ **2** → **evening**
even[1] [ˈiːvən] *vt* **1** LEVEL : allanar, nivelar, emparejar **2** EQUALIZE : igualar, equilibrar — *vi* **to even out** : nivelarse, emparejarse
even[2] *adv* **1** : hasta, incluso ⟨even a child can do it : hasta un niño puede hacerlo⟩ ⟨he looked content, even happy : se le veía satisfecho, incluso feliz⟩ **2** (*in negative constructions*) : ni siquiera ⟨he didn't even try : ni siquiera lo intentó⟩ **3** (*in comparisons*) : aún, todavía ⟨even better : aún mejor, todavía mejor⟩ **4 even if** : aunque **5 even so** : aun así **6 even though** : aun cuando, a pesar de que
even[3] *adj* **1** SMOOTH : uniforme, liso, parejo **2** FLAT : plano, llano **3** EQUAL : igual, igualado ⟨an even score : un marcador igualado⟩ **4** REGULAR : regular, constante ⟨an even pace : un ritmo constante⟩ **5** EXACT : exacto, justo **6** : par ⟨even number : número par⟩ **7 to be even** : estar en paz, estar a mano **8 to get even** : desquitarse, vengarse
evening [ˈiːvnɪŋ] *n* : tarde *f*, noche *f* ⟨in the evening : por la noche⟩
evenly [ˈiːvənli] *adv* **1** UNIFORMLY : de modo uniforme, de manera constante **2** FAIRLY : igualmente, equitativamente
evenness [ˈiːvənnəs] *n* : uniformidad *f*, igualdad *f*, regularidad *f*
event [ɪˈvɛnt] *n* **1** : acontecimiento *m*, suceso *m*, prueba *f* (en deportes) **2 in the event that** : en caso de que
eventful [ɪˈvɛntfəl] *adj* : lleno de incidentes, memorable
eventual [ɪˈvɛntʃuəl] *adj* : final, consiguiente
eventuality [ɪˌvɛntʃuˈæləti] *n, pl* **-ties** : eventualidad *f*
eventually [ɪˈvɛntʃuəli] *adv* : al fin, con el tiempo, algún día

ever ['ɛvər] *adv* **1** ALWAYS : siempre ⟨as ever : como siempre⟩ ⟨ever since : desde entonces⟩ **2** (*in questions*) : alguna vez, algún día ⟨have you ever been to Mexico? : ¿has estado en México alguna vez?⟩ **3** (*in negative constructions*) : nunca ⟨doesn't he ever work? : ¿es que nunca trabaja?⟩ ⟨nobody ever helps me : nadie nunca me ayuda⟩ **4** (*in comparisons*) : nunca ⟨better than ever : mejor que nunca⟩ **5** (*as intensifier*) ⟨I'm ever so happy! : ¡estoy tan y tan feliz!⟩ ⟨he looks ever so angry : parece estar muy enojado⟩

evergreen¹ ['ɛvər,griːn] *adj* : de hoja perenne

evergreen² *n* : planta *f* de hoja perenne

everlasting [,ɛvər'læstɪŋ] *adj* : eterno, perpetuo, imperecedero

evermore [,ɛvər'mor] *adv* : eternamente

every ['ɛvri] *adj* **1** EACH : cada ⟨every time : cada vez⟩ ⟨every other house : cada dos casas⟩ **2** ALL : todo ⟨every month : todos los meses⟩ ⟨every woman : toda mujer, todas las mujeres⟩ **3** COMPLETE : pleno, entero ⟨to have every confidence : tener plena confianza⟩

everybody ['ɛvri,bʌdi, -,bɑ-] *pron* : todos *mpl*, -das *fpl*; todo el mundo

everyday [,ɛvri'deɪ, 'ɛvri,-] *adj* : cotidiano, diario, corriente ⟨everyday clothes : ropa de todos los días⟩

everyone ['ɛvri,wʌn] → **everybody**

everything ['ɛvri,θɪŋ] *pron* : todo

everywhere ['ɛvri,ʍɛr] *adv* : en todas partes, por todas partes, dondequiera ⟨I looked everywhere : busqué en todas partes⟩ ⟨everywhere we go : dondequiera que vayamos⟩

evict [ɪ'vɪkt] *vt* : desalojar, desahuciar

eviction [ɪ'vɪkʃən] *n* : desalojo *m*, desahucio *m*

evidence ['ɛvədənts] *n* **1** INDICATION : indicio *m*, señal *m* ⟨to be in evidence : estar a la vista⟩ **2** PROOF : evidencia *f*, prueba *f* **3** TESTIMONY : testimonio *m*, declaración *f* ⟨to give evidence : declarar como testigo, prestar declaración⟩

evident ['ɛvidənt] *adj* : evidente, patente, manifiesto

evidently ['ɛvidəntli, ,ɛvi'dɛntli] *adv* **1** CLEARLY : claramente, obviamente **2** APPARENTLY : aparentemente, evidentemente, al parecer

evil¹ ['iːvəl, -vɪl] *adj* **eviler** *or* **eviller**; **evilest** *or* **evillest** **1** WICKED : malvado, malo, maligno **2** HARMFUL : nocivo, dañino, pernicioso **3** UNPLEASANT : desagradable ⟨an evil odor : un olor horrible⟩

evil² *n* **1** WICKEDNESS : mal *m*, maldad *f* **2** MISFORTUNE : desgracia *f*, mal *m*

evildoer [,iːvəl'duːər, ,iː'vɪl-] *n* : malvado *m*, -da *f*

evince [ɪ'vɪnts] *vt* **evinced; evincing** : mostrar, manifestar, revelar

eviscerate [ɪ'vɪsə,reɪt] *vt* **-ated; -ating** : eviscerar, destripar (un pollo, etc.)

evocation [,iːvo'keɪʃən, ,ɛ-] *n* : evocación *f*

evocative [i'vɑkətɪv] *adj* : evocador

evoke [i'voːk] *vt* **evoked; evoking** : evocar, provocar

evolution [,ɛvə'luːʃən, ,iː-] *n* : evolución *f*, desarrollo *m*

evolutionary [,ɛvə'luːʃə,nɛri, ,iː-] *adj* : evolutivo

evolve [i'vɑlv] *vi* **evolved; evolving** : evolucionar, desarrollarse

ewe ['juː] *n* : oveja *f*

exacerbate [ɪg'zæsər,beɪt] *vt* **-bated; -bating** : exacerbar

exact¹ [ɪg'zækt, ɛ-] *vt* : exigir, imponer, arrancar

exact² *adj* : exacto, preciso — **exactly** *adv*

exacting [ɪ'zæktɪŋ, ɛg-] *adj* : exigente, riguroso

exactitude [ɪg'zæktə,tuːd, ɛg-, -,tjuːd] *n* : exactitud *f*, precisión *f*

exaggerate [ɪg'zædʒə,reɪt, ɛg-] *v* **-ated; -ating** : exagerar

exaggerated [ɪg'zædʒə,reɪtəd, ɛg-] *adj* : exagerado — **exaggeratedly** *adv*

exaggeration [ɪg,zædʒə'reɪʃən, ɛg-] *n* : exageración *f*

exalt [ɪg'zɔlt, ɛg-] *vt* : exaltar, ensalzar, glorificar

exaltation [,ɛg,zɔl'teɪʃən, ,ɛk,sɔl-] *n* : exaltación *f*

exam [ɪg'zæm, ɛg-] → **examination**

examination [ɪg,zæmə'neɪʃən, ɛg-] *n* **1** TEST : examen *m* **2** INSPECTION : inspección *f*, revisión *f* **3** INVESTIGATION : examen *m*, estudio *m*

examine [ɪg'zæmən, ɛg-] *vt* **-ined; -ining** **1** TEST : examinar **2** INSPECT : inspeccionar, revisar **3** STUDY : examinar

example [ɪg'zæmpəl, ɛg-] *n* : ejemplo *m* ⟨for example : por ejemplo⟩ ⟨to set an example : dar ejemplo⟩

exasperate [ɪg'zæspə,reɪt, ɛg-] *vt* **-ated; -ating** : exasperar, sacar de quicio

exasperation [ɪg,zæspə'reɪʃən, ɛg-] *n* : exasperación *f*

excavate ['ɛkskə,veɪt] *vt* **-vated; -vating** : excavar

excavation [,ɛkskə'veɪʃən] *n* : excavación *f*

exceed [ɪk'siːd, ɛk-] *vt* **1** SURPASS : exceder, rebasar, sobrepasar **2** : exceder de, sobrepasar ⟨not exceeding two months : que no exceda de dos meses⟩

exceedingly [ɪk'siːdɪŋli, ɛk-] *adv* : extremadamente, sumamente

excel [ɪk'sɛl, ɛk-] *v* **-celled; -celling** *vi* : sobresalir, descollar, lucirse — *vt* : superar

excellence ['ɛksələnts] *n* : excelencia *f*

excellency ['ɛksələntsi] *n, pl* **-cies** : excelencia *f* ⟨His Excellency : Su Excelencia⟩

excellent ['ɛksələnt] *adj* : excelente, sobresaliente — **excellently** *adv*

except¹ [ɪk'sɛpt] *vt* : exceptuar, excluir
except² *conj* : pero, si no fuera por
except³ *prep* : excepto, menos, salvo ⟨everyone except Carlos : todos menos Carlos⟩
exception [ɪk'sɛpʃən] *n* **1** : excepción *f* **2 to take exception to** : ofenderse por, objetar a
exceptional [ɪk'sɛpʃənəl] *adj* : excepcional, extraordinario — **exceptionally** *adv*
excerpt¹ [ɛk'sərpt, ɛg'zərpt, 'ɛk͵-, 'g͵-] *vt* : escoger, seleccionar
excerpt² ['ɛk͵sərpt, 'ɛg͵zərpt] *n* : pasaje *m*, selección *f*
excess¹ ['ɛk͵sɛs, ɪk'sɛs] *adj* **1** : excesivo, de sobra **2 excess baggage** : exceso *m* de equipaje
excess² [ɪk'sɛs, 'ɛk͵sɛs] *n* **1** SUPERFLUITY : exceso *m*, superfluidad *f* ⟨an excess of energy : un exceso de energía⟩ **2** SURPLUS : excedente *m*, sobrante *m* ⟨in excess of : superior a⟩
excessive [ɪk'sɛsɪv, ɛk-] *adj* : excesivo, exagerado, desmesurado — **excessively** *adv*
exchange¹ [ɪks'tʃeɪndʒ, ɛks-; 'ɛks͵tʃeɪndʒ] *vt* **-changed; -changing** : cambiar, intercambiar, canjear
exchange² *n* **1** : cambio *m*, intercambio *m*, canje *m* **2 stock exchange** : bolsa *f* (de valores)
exchangeable [ɪks'tʃeɪndʒəbəl, ɛks-] *adj* : canjeable
excise¹ [ɪk'saɪz, ɛk-] *vt* **-cised; -cising** : extirpar
excise² ['ɛk͵saɪz] *n* **excise tax** : impuesto *m* interno, impuesto *m* sobre el consumo
excision [ɪk'sɪʒən, ɛk-] *n* : extirpación *f*, excisión *f*
excitability [ɪk͵saɪtə'bɪləti, ɛk-] *n* : excitabilidad *f*
excitable [ɪk'saɪt̬əbəl, ɛk-] *adj* : excitable
excitation [͵ɛk͵saɪ'teɪʃən] *n* : excitación *f*
excite [ɪk'saɪt, ɛk-] *vt* **-cited; -citing** **1** AROUSE, STIMULATE : excitar, mover, estimular **2** ANIMATE : entusiasmar, animar **3** EVOKE, PROVOKE : provocar, despertar, suscitar ⟨to excite curiosity : despertar la curiosidad⟩
excited [ɪk'saɪt̬əd, ɛk-] *adj* **1** STIMULATED : excitado, estimulado **2** ENTHUSIASTIC : entusiasmado, emocionado
excitedly [ɪk'saɪt̬ədli, ɛk-] *adv* : con excitación, con entusiasmo
excitement [ɪk'saɪtmənt, ɛk-] *n* **1** ENTHUSIASM : entusiasmo *m*, emoción *f* **2** AGITATION : agitación *f*, alboroto *m*, conmoción *f* **3** AROUSAL : excitación *f*
exciting [ɪk'saɪtɪŋ, ɛk-] *adj* **1** : emocionante **2** AROUSING : excitante
exclaim [ɪks'kleɪm, ɛk-] *v* : exclamar
exclamation [͵ɛksklə'meɪʃən] *n* : exclamación *f*
exclamation point *n* : signo *m* de admiración

exclamatory [ɪks'klæmə͵tori, ɛks-] *adj* : exclamativo
exclude [ɪks'klu:d, ɛks-] *vt* **-cluded; -cluding** **1** BAR : excluir, descartar, no admitir **2** EXPEL : expeler, expulsar
exclusion [ɪks'klu:ʒən, ɛks-] *n* : exclusión *f*
exclusive¹ [ɪks'klu:sɪv, ɛks-] *adj* **1** SOLE : exclusivo, único **2** SELECT : exclusivo, selecto
exclusive² *n* : exclusiva *f*
exclusively [ɪks'klu:sɪvli, ɛks-] *adv* : exclusivamente, únicamente
exclusiveness [ɪks'klu:sɪvnəs, ɛks-] *n* : exclusividad *f*
excommunicate [͵ɛkskə'mju:nə͵keɪt] *vt* **-cated; -cating** : excomulgar
excommunication [͵ɛkskə͵mju:nə'keɪʃən] *n* : excomunión *f*
excrement ['ɛkskrəmənt] *n* : excremento *m*
excrete [ɪk'skri:t, ɛk-] *vt* **-creted; -creting** : excretar
excretion [ɪk'skri:ʃən, ɛk-] *n* : excreción *f*
excruciating [ɪk'skru:ʃi͵eɪtɪŋ, ɛk-] *adj* : insoportable, atroz, terrible — **excruciatingly** *adv*
exculpate ['ɛkskəl͵peɪt] *vt* **-pated; -pating** : exculpar
excursion [ɪk'skərʒən, ɛk-] *n* **1** OUTING : excursión *f*, paseo *m* **2** DIGRESSION : digresión *f*
excuse¹ [ɪk'skju:z, ɛk-] *vt* **-cused; -cusing** **1** PARDON : disculpar, perdonar ⟨excuse me : con permiso, perdóneme, perdón⟩ **2** EXEMPT : eximir, disculpar **3** JUSTIFY : excusar, justificar
excuse² [ɪk'skju:s, ɛk-] *n* **1** JUSTIFICATION : excusa *f*, justificación *f* **2** PRETEXT : pretexto *m* **3 to make one's excuses to someone** : pedirle disculpas a alguien
execute ['ɛksɪ͵kju:t] *vt* **-cuted; -cuting** **1** CARRY OUT : ejecutar, llevar a cabo, desempeñar **2** ENFORCE : ejecutar, cumplir (un testamento, etc.) **3** KILL : ejecutar, ajusticiar
execution [͵ɛksɪ'kju:ʃən] *n* **1** PERFORMANCE : ejecución *f*, desempeño *m* **2** IMPLEMENTATION : cumplimiento *m* **3** : ejecución *f* (por un delito)
executioner [͵ɛksɪ'kju:ʃənər] *n* : verdugo *m*
executive¹ [ɪg'zɛkjət̬ɪv, ɛg-] *adj* : ejecutivo
executive² *n* : ejecutivo *m*, -va *f*
executor [ɪg'zɛkjət̬ər, ɛg-] *n* : albacea *m*, testamentario *m*
executrix [ɪg'zɛkjə͵trɪks, ɛg-] *n, pl* **executrices** [-͵zɛkjə'traɪ͵si:z] *or* **executrixes** [-'zɛkjə͵trɪksəz] : albacea *f*, testamentaria *f*
exemplary [ɪg'zɛmpləri, ɛg-] *adj* : ejemplar
exemplify [ɪg'zɛmplə͵faɪ, ɛg-] *vt* **-fied; -fying** : ejemplificar, ilustrar, demostrar

exempt¹ [ɪɡ'zɛmpt, ɛɡ-] vt : eximir, dispensar, exonerar
exempt² adj : exento, eximido
exemption [ɪɡ'zɛmpʃən, ɛɡ-] n : exención f
exercise¹ ['ɛksər,saɪz] v **-cised; -cising** vt **1** : ejercitar (el cuerpo) **2** USE : ejercer, hacer uso de — vi : hacer ejercicio
exercise² n **1** : ejercicio m **2 exercises** npl WORKOUT : ejercicios mpl físicos **3 exercises** npl CEREMONY : ceremonia f
exert [ɪɡ'zərt, ɛɡ-] vt **1** : ejercer, emplear **2 to exert oneself** : esforzarse
exertion [ɪɡ'zərʃən, ɛɡ-] n **1** USE : ejercicio m (de autoridad, etc.), uso m (de fuerza, etc.) **2** EFFORT : esfuerzo m, empeño m
exhalation [,ɛksə'leɪʃən, ,ɛkshə-] n : exhalación f, espiración f
exhale [ɛks'heɪl] v **-haled; -haling** vt **1** : exhalar, espirar **2** EMIT : exhalar, despedir, emitir — vi : espirar
exhaust¹ [ɪɡ'zɔst, ɛɡ-] vt **1** DEPLETE : agotar **2** TIRE : cansar, fatigar, agotar **3** EMPTY : vaciar
exhaust² n **1 exhaust fumes** : gases mpl de escape **2 exhaust pipe** : tubo m de escape **3 exhaust system** : sistema m de escape
exhausted [ɪɡ'zɔstəd, ɛɡ-] adj : agotado, derrengado
exhausting [ɪɡ'zɔstɪŋ, ɛɡ-] adj : extenuante, agotador
exhaustion [ɪɡ'zɔstʃən, ɛɡ-] n : agotamiento m
exhaustive [ɪɡ'zɔstɪv, ɛɡ-] adj : exhaustivo
exhibit¹ [ɪɡ'zɪbət, ɛɡ-] vt **1** DISPLAY : exhibir, exponer **2** PRODUCE, SHOW : mostrar, presentar
exhibit² n **1** OBJECT : objeto m expuesto **2** EXHIBITION : exposición f, exhibición f **3** EVIDENCE : prueba f instrumental
exhibition [,ɛksə'bɪʃən] n **1** : exposición f, exhibición f **2 to make an exhibition of oneself** : dar el espectáculo, hacer el ridículo
exhibitor [ɪɡ'zɪbətər] n : expositor m, -tora f
exhilarate [ɪɡ'zɪlə,reɪt, ɛɡ-] vt **-rated; -rating** : alegrar, levantar el ánimo de
exhilaration [ɪɡ,zɪlə'reɪʃən, ɛɡ-] n : alegría f, regocijo m, júbilo m
exhort [ɪɡ'zɔrt, ɛɡ-] vt : exhortar
exhortation [,ɛk,sɔr'teɪʃən, -sər-; ,ɛɡ-,zɔr-] n : exhortación f
exhumation [,ɛksju'meɪʃən, -hju-; ,ɛɡzu-, -zju-] n : exhumación f
exhume [ɪɡ'zu:m, -'zju:m; ɪks'ju:m, -'hju:m] vt **-humed; -huming** : exhumar, desenterrar
exigencies ['ɛksɪʤəntsiz, ɪɡ'zɪʤən,si:z] npl : exigencias fpl
exile¹ ['ɛɡ,zaɪl, 'ɛk,saɪl] vt **exiled; exiling** : exiliar, desterrar

exile² n **1** BANISHMENT : exilio m, destierro m **2** OUTCAST : exiliado m, -da f; desterrado m, -da f
exist [ɪɡ'zɪst, ɛɡ-] vi **1** BE : existir **2** LIVE : subsistir, vivir
existence [ɪɡ'zɪstənts, ɛɡ-] n : existencia f
existent [ɪɡ'zɪstənt, ɛɡ-] adj : existente
existing [ɪɡ'zɪstɪŋ] adj : existente
exit¹ ['ɛɡzət, 'ɛksət] vi : salir, hacer mutis (en el teatro) — vt : salir de
exit² n **1** DEPARTURE : salida f, partida f **2** EGRESS : salida f ⟨emergency exit : salida de emergencia⟩
exodus ['ɛksədəs] n : éxodo m
exonerate [ɪɡ'zɑnə,reɪt, ɛɡ-] vt **-ated; -ating** : exonerar, disculpar, absolver
exoneration [ɪɡ,zɑnə'reɪʃən, ɛɡ-] n : exoneración f
exorbitant [ɪɡ'zɔrbətənt, ɛɡ-] adj : exorbitante, excesivo
exorcise ['ɛk,sɔr,saɪz, -sər-] vt **-cised; -cising** : exorcizar
exorcism ['ɛksər,sɪzəm] n : exorcismo m
exotic¹ [ɪɡ'zɑtɪk, ɛɡ-] adj : exótico — **exotically** [-ɪkli] adv
exotic² n : planta f exótica
expand [ɪk'spænd, ɛk-] vt **1** ENLARGE : expandir, dilatar, aumentar, ampliar **2** EXTEND : extender — vi **1** ENLARGE : ampliarse, extenderse **2** : expandirse, dilatarse (dícese de los metales, gases, etc.)
expanse [ɪk'spænts, ɛk-] n : extensión f
expansion [ɪk'spænʃən, ɛk-] n **1** ENLARGEMENT : expansión f, ampliación f **2** EXPANSE : extensión f
expansive [ɪk'spæntsɪv, ɛk-] adj **1** : expansivo **2** OUTGOING : expansivo, comunicativo **3** AMPLE : ancho, amplio — **expansively** adv
expansiveness [ɪk'spæntsɪvnəs, ɛk-] n : expansibilidad f
expatriate¹ [ɛks'peɪtri,eɪt] vt **-ated; -ating** : expatriar
expatriate² [ɛks'peɪtriət, -,eɪt] adj : expatriado
expatriate³ [ɛks'peɪtriət, -,eɪt] n : expatriado m, -da f
expect [ɪk'spɛkt, ɛk-] vt **1** SUPPOSE : suponer, imaginarse **2** ANTICIPATE : esperar **3** COUNT ON, REQUIRE : contar con, esperar — vi **to be expecting** : estar embarazada
expectancy [ɪk'spɛktəntsi, ɛk-] n, pl **-cies** : expectativa f, esperanza f
expectant [ɪk'spɛktənt, ɛk-] adj **1** ANTICIPATING : expectante **2** EXPECTING : futuro ⟨expectant mother : futura madre⟩
expectantly [ɪk'spɛktəntli, ɛk-] adv : con expectación
expectation [,ɛk,spɛk'teɪʃən] n **1** ANTICIPATION : expectación f **2** EXPECTANCY : expectativa f
expedient¹ [ɪk'spi:diənt, ɛk-] adj : conveniente, oportuno
expedient² n : expediente m, recurso m

expedite ['ɛkspə,daɪt] vt -dited; -diting 1 FACILITATE : facilitar, dar curso a 2 HASTEN : acelerar

expedition [,ɛkspə'dɪʃən] n : expedición f

expeditious [,ɛkspə'dɪʃəs] adj : pronto, rápido

expel [ɪk'spɛl, ɛk-] vt -pelled; -pelling : expulsar, expeler

expend [ɪk'spɛnd, ɛk-] vt 1 DISBURSE : gastar, desembolsar 2 CONSUME : consumir, agotar

expendable [ɪk'spɛndəbəl, ɛk-] adj : prescindible

expenditure [ɪk'spɛndɪtʃər, ɛk-, -,tʃʊr] n : gasto m

expense [ɪk'spɛnts, ɛk-] n 1 COST : gasto m 2 **expenses** npl : gastos mpl, expensas fpl 3 **at the expense of** : a expensas de

expensive [ɪk'spɛntsɪv, ɛk-] adj : costoso, caro — **expensively** adv

experience¹ [ɪk'spɪriənts, ɛk-] vt -enced; -encing : experimentar (sentimientos), tener (dificultades), sufrir (una pérdida)

experience² n : experiencia f

experienced [ɪk'spɪriəntst, ɛk-] adj : con experiencia, experimentado

experiment¹ [ɪk'spɛrəmənt, ɛk-, -'spɪr-] vi : experimentar, hacer experimentos

experiment² n : experimento m

experimental [ɪk,spɛrə'mntəl, ɛk-, -,spɪr-] adj : experimental — **experimentally** adv

experimentation [ɪk,spɛrəmən'teɪʃən, ɛk-, -,spɪr-] n : experimentación f

expert¹ ['ɛk,spərt, ɪk'spərt] adj : experto, de experto, pericial (dícese de un testigo) — **expertly** adv

expert² ['ɛk,spərt] n : experto m, -ta f; perito m, -ta f; especialista mf

expertise [,ɛkspər'ti:z] n : pericia f, competencia f

expiate ['ɛkspi,eɪt] vt -ated; -ating : expiar

expiation [,ɛkspi'eɪʃən] n : expiación f

expiration [,ɛkspə'reɪʃən] n 1 EXHALATION : exhalación f, espiración f 2 DEATH : muerte f 3 TERMINATION : vencimiento m, caducidad f

expire [ɪk'spaɪr, ɛk-] vi -pired; -piring 1 EXHALE : espirar 2 DIE : expirar, morir 3 TERMINATE : caducar, vencer

explain [ɪk'spleɪn, ɛk-] vt : explicar

explanation [,ɛksplə'neɪʃən] n : explicación f

explanatory [ɪk'splænə,tori, ɛk-] adj : explicativo, aclaratorio

expletive ['ɛksplətɪv] n : improperio m, palabrota f fam, grosería f

explicable [ɛk'splɪkəbəl, 'ɛksplɪ-] adj : explicable

explicit [ɪk'splɪsət, ɛk-] adj : explícito, claro, categórico, rotundo — **explicitly** adv

explicitness [ɪk'splɪsətnəs, ɛk-] n : claridad f, carácter m explícito

explode [ɪk'splo:d, ɛk-] v -ploded; -ploding vt 1 BURST : hacer explosionar, hacer explotar 2 REFUTE : rebatir, refutar, desmentir — vi 1 BURST : explotar, estallar, reventar 2 SKYROCKET : dispararse

exploit¹ [ɪk'splɔɪt, ɛk-] vt : explotar, aprovecharse de

exploit² ['ɛk,splɔɪt] n : hazaña f, proeza f

exploitation [,ɛk,splɔɪ'teɪʃən] n : explotación f

exploration [,ɛksplə'reɪʃən] n : exploración f

exploratory [ɪk'splorə,tori, ɛk-] adj : exploratorio

explore [ɪk'splor, ɛk-] vt -plored; -ploring : explorar, investigar, examinar

explorer [ɪk'splorər, ɛk-] n : explorador m, -dora f

explosion [ɪk'splo:ʒən, ɛk-] n : explosión f, estallido m

explosive¹ [ɪk'splo:sɪv, ɛk-] adj : explosivo, fulminante — **explosively** adv

explosive² n : explosivo m

exponent [ɪk'spo:nənt, 'ɛk,spo:-] n 1 : exponente m 2 ADVOCATE : defensor m, -sora f; partidario m, -ria f

exponential [,ɛkspo'nɛntʃəl] adj : exponencial — **exponentially** adv

export¹ [ɛk'sport, 'ɛk,sport] vt : exportar

export² ['ɛk,sport] n 1 : artículo m de exportación 2 → exportation

exportation [,ɛk,spor'teɪʃən] n : exportación f

exporter [ɛk'sportər, 'ɛk,spor-] n : exportador m, -dora f

expose [ɪk'spo:z, ɛk-] vt -posed; -posing 1 : exponer (al peligro, a los elementos, a una enfermedad) 2 : exponer (una película a la luz) 3 DISCLOSE : descubrir, revelar, poner en evidencia 4 UNMASK : desenmascarar

exposé or **expose** [,ɛkspo'zeɪ] n : exposición f (de hechos), revelación f (de un escándalo)

exposed [ɪk'spo:zd, ɛk-] adj : descubierto, sin protección

exposition [,ɛkspə'zɪʃən] n : exposición f

exposure [ɪk'spo:ʒər, ɛk-] n 1 : exposición f 2 CONTACT : exposición f, experiencia f, contacto m 3 UNMASKING : desenmascaramiento m 4 ORIENTATION : orientación f ⟨a room with a northern exposure : una sala orientada al norte⟩

expound [ɪk'spaʊnd, ɛk-] vt : exponer, explicar — vi : hacer comentarios detallados

express¹ [ɪk'sprɛs, ɛk-] vt 1 SAY : expresar, comunicar 2 SHOW : expresar, manifestar, externar Mex 3 SQUEEZE : exprimir ⟨to express the juice from a lemon : exprimir el jugo de un limón⟩

express² adv : por correo exprés, por correo urgente

express³ *adj* **1** EXPLICIT : expreso, manifiesto **2** SPECIFIC : específico ⟨for that express purpose : con ese fin específico⟩ **3** RAPID : expreso, rápido
express⁴ *n* **1** : correo *m* exprés, correo *m* urgente **2** : expreso *m* (tren)
expression [ɪk'sprɛʃən, ɛk-] *n* **1** UTTERANCE : expresión *f* ⟨freedom of expression : libertad de expresión⟩ **2** : expresión *f* (en la matemática) **3** PHRASE : frase *f*, expresión *f* **4** LOOK : expresión *f*, cara *f*, gesto *m* ⟨with a sad expression : con un gesto de tristeza⟩
expressionless [ɪk'sprɛʃənləs, ɛk-] *adj* : inexpresivo
expressive [ɪk'sprɛsɪv, ɛk-] *adj* : expresivo
expressway [ɪk'sprɛs,weɪ, ɛk-] *n* : autopista *f*
expulsion [ɪk'spʌlʃən, ɛk-] *n* : expulsión *f*
expurgate ['ɛkspər,geɪt] *vt* -gated; -gating : expurgar
exquisite [ɛk'skwɪzət, 'ɛk,skwɪ-] *adj* **1** FINE : exquisito, delicado, primoroso **2** INTENSE : intenso, extremo
extant ['ɛkstənt, ɛk'stænt] *adj* : existente
extemporaneous [ɛk,stɛmpə'reɪniəs] *adj* : improvisado — **extemporaneously** *adv*
extend [ɪk'stɛnd, ɛk-] *vt* **1** STRETCH : extender, tender **2** PROLONG : prolongar, prorrogar **3** ENLARGE : agrandar, ampliar, aumentar **4** PROFFER : extender, dar, ofrecer — *vi* : extenderse
extended [ɪk'stɛndəd, ɛk-] *adj* LENGTHY : prolongado, largo
extension [ɪk'stɛnʧən, ɛk-] *n* **1** EXTENDING : extensión *f*, ampliación *f*, prórroga *f*, prolongación *f* **2** ANNEX : ampliación *f*, anexo *m* **3** : extensión *f* (de teléfono)
extensive [ɪk'stɛnsɪv, ɛk-] *adj* : extenso, vasto, amplio — **extensively** *adv*
extent [ɪk'stɛnt, ɛk-] *n* **1** SIZE : extensión *f*, magnitud *f* **2** DEGREE, SCOPE : alcance *m*, grado *m* ⟨to a certain extent : hasta cierto punto⟩
extenuate [ɪk'stɛnjə,weɪt, ɛk-] *vt* -ated; -ating : atenuar, aminorar, mitigar ⟨extenuating circumstances : circunstancias atenuantes⟩
extenuation [ɪk,stɛnjə'weɪʃən, ɛk-] *n* : atenuación *f*, aminoración *f*
exterior¹ [ɛk'stɪriər] *adj* : exterior
exterior² *n* : exterior *m*
exterminate [ɪk'stərmə,neɪt, ɛk-] *vt* -nated; -nating : exterminar
extermination [ɪk,stərmə'neɪʃən, ɛk-] *n* : exterminación *f*, exterminio *m*
exterminator [ɪk'stərmə,neɪtər, ɛk-] *n* : exterminador *m*, -dora *f*
external [ɪk'stərnəl, ɛk-] *adj* : externo, exterior — **externally** *adv*
extinct [ɪk'stɪŋkt, ɛk-] *adj* : extinto
extinction [ɪk'stɪŋkʃən, ɛk-] *n* : extinción *f*
extinguish [ɪk'stɪŋgwɪʃ, ɛk-] *vt* : extinguir, apagar

extinguisher [ɪk'stɪŋgwɪʃər, ɛk-] *n* : extinguidor *m*, extintor *m*
extirpate ['ɛkstər,peɪt] *vt* -pated; -pating : extirpar, exterminar
extol [ɪk'sto:l, ɛk-] *vt* -tolled; -tolling : exaltar, ensalzar, alabar
extort [ɪk'stɔrt, ɛk-] *vt* : extorsionar
extortion [ɪk'stɔrʃən, ɛk-] *n* : extorsión *f*
extra¹ ['ɛkstrə] *adv* : extra, más, extremadamente, super ⟨extra special : super especial⟩
extra² *adj* **1** ADDITIONAL : adicional, suplementario, de más **2** SUPERIOR : superior
extra³ *n* : extra *m*
extract¹ [ɪk'strækt, ɛk-] *vt* : extraer, sacar
extract² ['ɛk,strækt] *n* **1** EXCERPT : pasaje *m*, selección *f*, trozo *m* **2** : extracto *m* ⟨vanilla extract : extracto de vainilla⟩
extraction [ɪk'strækʃən, ɛk-] *n* : extracción *f*
extractor [ɪk'stræktər, ɛk-] *n* : extractor *m*
extracurricular [,ɛkstrəkə'rɪkjələr] *adj* : extracurricular
extradite ['ɛkstrə,daɪt] *vt* -dited; -diting : extraditar
extradition [,ɛkstrə'dɪʃən] *n* : extradición *f*
extramarital [,ɛkstrə'mærətəl] *adj* : extramatrimonial
extraneous [ɛk'streɪniəs] *adj* **1** OUTSIDE : extrínseco, externo **2** SUPERFLUOUS : superfluo, ajeno — **extraneously** *adv*
extraordinary [ɪk'strɔrdən,ɛri, ,ɛkstrə-'ɔrd-] *adj* : extraordinario, excepcional — **extraordinarily** [ɪk,strɔrdən'ɛrəli, ,kstrə,ord-] *adv*
extrasensory [,ɛkstrə'sɛntsəri] *adj* : extrasensorial
extraterrestrial¹ [,ɛkstrətə'rɛstriəl] *adj* : extraterrestre
extraterrestrial² *n* : extraterrestre *mf*
extravagance [ɪk'strævɪgənts, ɛk-] *n* **1** EXCESS : exceso *m*, extravagancia *f* **2** WASTEFULNESS : derroche *m*, despilfarro *m* **3** LUXURY : lujo *m*
extravagant [ɪk'strævɪgənt, ɛk-] *adj* **1** EXCESSIVE : excesivo, extravagante **2** WASTEFUL : despilfarrador, derrochador, gastador **3** EXORBITANT : costoso, exorbitante
extravagantly [ɪk'strævɪgəntli, ɛk-] *adv* **1** LAVISHLY : a lo grande **2** EXCESSIVELY : exageradamente, desmesuradamente
extravaganza [ɪk,strævə'gænzə, ɛk-] *n* : gran espectáculo *m*
extreme¹ [ɪk'stri:m, ɛk-] *adj* **1** UTMOST : extremo, sumo ⟨of extreme importance : de suma importancia⟩ **2** INTENSE : intenso, extremado ⟨extreme cold : frío extremado⟩ **3** EXCESSIVE : excesivo, extremo ⟨extreme views : opiniones extremas⟩ ⟨extreme measures : medidas excepcionales, medi-

das drásticas⟩ **4** OUTERMOST : extremo ⟨the extreme north : el norte extremo⟩
extreme² *n* **1** : extremo *m* **2 in the extreme** : en extremo, en sumo grado
extremely [ɪk'stri:mli, ɛk-] *adv* : sumamente, extremadamente, terriblemente
extremist [ɪk'stri:mɪst, ɛk-] *n* : extremista *mf* — **extremist** *adj*
extremity [ɪk'strɛməṭi, ɛk-] *n, pl* **-ties 1** EXTREME : extremo *m* **2 extremities** *npl* LIMBS : extremidades *fpl*
extricate ['ɛkstrə‚keɪt] *vt* **-cated; -cating** : librar, sacar
extrinsic [ɪk'strɪnzɪk, -'strɪntsɪk] *adj* : extrínseco
extrovert ['ɛkstrə‚vərt] *n* : extrovertido *m*, -da *f*
extroverted ['ɛkstrə‚vərṭəd] *adj* : extrovertido
extrude [ɪk'stru:d, ɛk-] *vt* **-truded; -truding** : extrudir, expulsar
exuberance [ɪg'zu:bərənts, ɛg-] *n* **1** JOYOUSNESS : euforia *f*, exaltación *f* **2** VIGOR : exuberancia *f*, vigor *m*
exuberant [ɪg'zu:bərənt, ɛg-] *adj* **1** JOYOUS : eufórico **2** LUSH : exuberante — **exuberantly** *adv*
exude [ɪg'zu:d, ɛg-] *vt* **-uded; -uding 1** OOZE : rezumar, exudar **2** EMANATE : emanar, irradiar
exult [ɪg'zʌlt, ɛg-] *vi* : exultar, regocijarse
exultant [ɪg'zʌltənt, ɛg-] *adj* : exultante, jubiloso — **exultantly** *adv*
exultation [‚ɛksəl'teɪʃən, ‚ɛgzəl-] *n* : exultación *f*, júbilo *m*, alborozo *m*

eye¹ ['aɪ] *vt* **eyed; eyeing** *or* **eying** : mirar, observar
eye² *n* **1** : ojo *m* **2** VISION : visión *f*, vista *f*, ojo *m* ⟨a good eye for bargains : un buen ojo para las gangas⟩ **3** GLANCE : mirada *f*, ojeada *f* **4** ATTENTION : atención *f* ⟨to catch one's eye : llamar la atención⟩ **5** POINT OF VIEW : punto *m* de vista ⟨in the eyes of the law : según la ley⟩ **6** : ojo *m* (de una aguja, una papa, una tormenta)
eyeball ['aɪ‚bɔl] *n* : globo *m* ocular
eyebrow ['aɪ‚braʊ] *n* : ceja *f*
eyedropper ['aɪ‚drɑpər] *n* : cuentagotas *f*
eyeglasses ['aɪ‚glæsəz] *npl* : anteojos *mpl*, lentes *mpl*, espejuelos *mpl*, gafas *fpl*
eyelash ['aɪ‚læʃ] *n* : pestaña *f*
eyelet ['aɪlət] *n* : ojete *m*
eyelid ['aɪ‚lɪd] *n* : párpado *m*
eye–opener ['aɪ‚o:pənər] *n* : revelación *f*, sorpresa *f*
eye–opening ['aɪ‚o:pənɪŋ] *adj* : revelador
eyepiece ['aɪ‚pi:s] *n* : ocular *m*
eyesight ['aɪ‚saɪt] *n* : vista *f*, visión *f*
eyesore ['aɪ‚sor] *n* : monstruosidad *f*, adefesio *m*
eyestrain ['aɪ‚streɪn] *n* : fatiga *f* visual, vista *f* cansada
eyetooth ['aɪ‚tu:θ] *n* : colmillo *m*
eyewitness ['aɪ‚wɪtnəs] *n* : testigo *mf* ocular, testigo *mf* presencial
eyrie ['aɪri] → aerie

F

f ['ɛf] *n, pl* **f's** *or* **fs** ['ɛfs] : sexta letra del alfabeto inglés
fable ['feɪbəl] *n* : fábula *f*
fabled ['feɪbəld] *adj* : legendario, fabuloso
fabric ['fæbrɪk] *n* **1** MATERIAL : tela *f*, tejido *m* **2** STRUCTURE : estructura *f* ⟨the fabric of society : la estructura de la sociedad⟩
fabricate ['fæbrɪ‚keɪt] *vt* **-cated; -cating 1** CONSTRUCT, MANUFACTURE : construir, fabricar **2** INVENT : inventar (excusas o mentiras)
fabrication [‚fæbrɪ'keɪʃən] *n* **1** LIE : mentira *f*, invención *f* **2** MANUFACTURE : fabricación *f*
fabulous ['fæbjələs] *adj* **1** LEGENDARY : fabuloso, legendario **2** INCREDIBLE : increíble, fabuloso ⟨fabulous wealth : riqueza fabulosa⟩ **3** WONDERFUL : magnífico, estupendo, fabuloso — **fabulously** *adv*
facade [fə'sɑd] *n* : fachada *f*
face¹ ['feɪs] *v* **faced; facing** *vt* **1** LINE : recubrir (una superficie), forrar (ropa) **2** CONFRONT : enfrentarse a, afrontar, hacer frente a ⟨to face the

music : afrontar las consecuencias⟩ ⟨to face the facts : aceptar la realidad⟩ **3** : estar de cara a, estar enfrente de ⟨she's facing her brother : está de cara a su hermano⟩ **4** OVERLOOK : dar a — *vi* : mirar (hacia), estar orientado (a)
face² *n* **1** : cara *f*, rostro *m* ⟨he told me to my face : me lo dijo a la cara⟩ **2** EXPRESSION : cara *f*, expresión *f* ⟨to pull a long face : poner mala cara⟩ **3** GRIMACE : mueca *f* ⟨to make faces : hacer muecas⟩ **4** APPEARANCE : fisonomía *f*, aspecto *m* ⟨the face of society : la fisonomía de la sociedad⟩ **5** EFFRONTERY : desfachatez *f* **6** PRESTIGE : prestigio *m* ⟨to lose face : desprestigiarse⟩ **7** FRONT, SIDE : cara *f* (de una moneda), esfera *f* (de un reloj), fachada *f* (de un edificio), pared *f* (de una montaña) **8** SURFACE : superficie *f*, faz *f* (de la tierra), cara *f* (de la luna) **9 in the face of** DESPITE : en medio de, en visto de, ante
facedown ['feɪs‚daʊn] *adv* : boca abajo
faceless ['feɪsləs] *adj* ANONYMOUS : anónimo
face–lift ['feɪs‚lɪft] *n* **1** : estiramiento *m*

facial **2** RENOVATION : renovación *f*, remozamiento *m*

facet ['fæsət] *n* **1** : faceta *f* (de una piedra) **2** ASPECT : faceta *f*, aspecto *m*

facetious [fə'si:ʃəs] *adj* : gracioso, burlón, bromista

facetiously [fə'si:ʃəsli] *adv* : en tono de burla

facetiousness [fə'si:ʃəsnəs] *n* : jocosidad *f*

face–to–face *adv & adj* : cara a cara

faceup ['feɪs'ʌp] *adv* : boca arriba

face value *n* : valor *m* nominal

facial[1] ['feɪʃəl] *adj* : de la cara, facial

facial[2] *n* : tratamiento *m* facial, limpieza *f* de cutis

facile ['fæsəl] *adj* SUPERFICIAL : superficial, simplista

facilitate [fə'sɪlə,teɪt] *vt* **-tated; -tating** : facilitar

facility [fə'sɪləti] *n*, *pl* **-ties 1** EASE : facilidad *f* **2** CENTER, COMPLEX : centro *m*, complejo *m* **3 facilities** *npl* AMENITIES : comodidades *fpl*, servicios *mpl*

facing ['feɪsɪŋ] *n* **1** LINING : entretela *f* (de una prenda) **2** : revestimiento *m* (de un edificio)

facsimile [fæk'sɪməli] *n* : facsímile *m*, facsímil *m*

fact ['fækt] *n* **1** : hecho *m* ⟨as a matter of fact : de hecho⟩ **2** INFORMATION : información *f*, datos *mpl* ⟨facts and figures : datos y cifras⟩ **3** REALITY : realidad *f* ⟨in fact : en realidad⟩

faction ['fækʃən] *n* : facción *m*, bando *m*

factional ['fækʃənəl] *adj* : entre facciones

factious ['fækʃəs] *adj* : faccioso, contencioso

factitious [fæk'tɪʃəs] *adj* : artificial, facticio

factor ['fæktər] *n* : factor *m*

factory ['fæktəri] *n*, *pl* **-ries** : fábrica *f*

factual ['fæktʃuəl] *adj* : basado en hechos, objetivo

factually ['fæktʃuəli] *adv* : en cuanto a los hechos

faculty ['fækəlti] *n*, *pl* **-ties 1** : facultad *f* ⟨the faculty of sight : las facultades visuales, el sentido de la vista⟩ **2** APTITUDE : aptitud *f*, facilidad *f* **3** TEACHERS : cuerpo *m* docente

fad ['fæd] *n* : moda *f* pasajera, manía *f*

fade ['feɪd] *v* **faded; fading** *vi* **1** WITHER : debilitarse (dícese de las personas), marchitarse (dícese de las flores y las plantas) **2** DISCOLOR : desteñirse, decolorarse **3** DIM : apagarse (dícese de la luz), perderse (dícese de los sonidos), fundirse (dícese de las imágenes) **4** VANISH : desvanecerse, decaer — *vt* DISCOLOR : desteñir

fag ['fæg] *vt* **fagged; fagging** EXHAUST : cansar, fatigar

fagot *or* **faggot** ['fægət] *n* : haz *m* de leña

Fahrenheit ['færən,haɪt] *adj* : Fahrenheit

fail[1] ['feɪl] *vi* **1** WEAKEN : fallar, deteriorarse **2** STOP : fallar, detenerse ⟨his heart failed : le falló el corazón⟩ **3** : fracasar, fallar ⟨her plan failed : su plan fracasó⟩ ⟨the crops failed : se perdió la cosecha⟩ **4** : quebrar ⟨a business about to fail : una empresa a punto de quebrar⟩ **5 to fail in** : faltar a, no cumplir con ⟨to fail in one's duties : faltar a sus deberes⟩ — *vt* **1** FLUNK : reprobar (un examen) **2** : fallar ⟨words fail me : las palabras me fallan, no encuentro palabras⟩ **3** DISAPPOINT : fallar, decepcionar ⟨don't fail me! : ¡no me falles!⟩

fail[2] *n* : fracaso *m*

failing ['feɪlɪŋ] *n* : defecto *m*

failure ['feɪljər] *n* **1** : fracaso *m*, malogro *m* ⟨crop failure : pérdida de la cosecha⟩ ⟨heart failure : insuficiencia cardíaca⟩ ⟨engine failure : falla mecánica⟩ **2** BANKRUPTCY : bancarrota *f*, quiebra *f* **3** : fracaso *m* (persona) ⟨he was a failure as a manager : como gerente, fue un fracaso⟩

faint[1] ['feɪnt] *vi* : desmayarse

faint[2] *adj* **1** COWARDLY, TIMID : cobarde, tímido **2** DIZZY : mareado ⟨faint with hunger : desfallecido de hambre⟩ **3** SLIGHT : leve, ligero, vago ⟨I haven't the faintest idea : no tengo la más mínima idea⟩ **4** INDISTINCT : tenue, indistinto, apenas perceptible

faint[3] *n* : desmayo *m*

fainthearted ['feɪnt'hɑrtəd] *adj* : cobarde, pusilánime

faintly ['feɪntli] *adv* : débilmente, ligeramente, levemente

faintness ['feɪntnəs] *n* **1** INDISTINCTNESS : lo débil, falta *f* de claridad **2** FAINTING : desmayo *m*, desfallecimiento *m*

fair[1] ['fær] *adj* **1** ATTRACTIVE, BEAUTIFUL : bello, hermoso, atractivo **2** (*relating to weather*) : bueno, despejado ⟨fair weather : tiempo despejado⟩ **3** JUST : justo, imparcial **4** ALLOWABLE : permisible **5** BLOND, LIGHT : rubio (dícese del pelo), blanco (dícese de la tez) **6** ADEQUATE : bastante, adecuado ⟨fair to middling : mediano, regular⟩ **7 fair game** : presa *f* fácil **8 to play fair** : jugar limpio

fair[2] *n* : feria *f*

fairground ['fær,graʊnd] *n* : parque *m* de diversiones

fairly ['færli] *adv* **1** IMPARTIALLY : imparcialmente, limpiamente, equitativamente **2** QUITE : bastante **3** MODERATELY : medianamente

fairness ['færnəs] *n* **1** IMPARTIALITY : imparcialidad *f*, justicia *f* **2** LIGHTNESS : blancura *f* (de la piel), lo rubio (del pelo)

fairy ['færi] *n*, *pl* **fairies 1** : hada *f* **2 fairy tale** : cuento *m* de hadas

fairyland ['færi,lænd] *n* **1** : país *m* de las hadas **2** : lugar *m* encantador

faith ['feɪθ] *n, pl* **faiths** ['feɪθs, 'feɪðz] **1** BELIEF : fe *f* **2** ALLEGIANCE : lealtad *f* **3** CONFIDENCE, TRUST : confianza *f*, fe *f* **4** RELIGION : religión *f*

faithful ['feɪθfəl] *adj* : fiel — **faithfully** *adv*

faithfulness ['feɪθfəlnəs] *n* : fidelidad *f*

faithless ['feɪθləs] *adj* **1** DISLOYAL : desleal **2** : infiel (en la religión) — **faithlessly** *adv*

faithlessness ['feɪθləsnəs] *n* : deslealtad *f*

fake¹ ['feɪk] *v* **faked; faking** *vt* **1** FALSIFY : falsificar, falsear **2** FEIGN : fingir — *vi* **1** PRETEND : fingir **2** : hacer un engaño, hacer una finta (en deportes)

fake² *adj* : falso, fingido, postizo

fake³ *n* **1** IMITATION : imitación *f*, falsificación *f* **2** IMPOSTOR : impostor *m*, -tora *f*; charlatán *m*, -tana *f*; farsante *mf* **3** FEINT : engaño *m*, finta *f* (en deportes)

faker ['feɪkər] *n* : impostor *m*, -tora *f*; charlatán *m*, -tana *f*; farsante *mf*

fakir [fə'kɪr, 'feɪkər] *n* : faquir *m*

falcon ['fælkən, 'fɔl-] *n* : halcón *m*

falconry ['fælkənri, 'fɔl-] *n* : cetrería *f*

fall¹ ['fɔl] *vi* **fell** ['fɛl]; **fallen** [fɔlən]; **falling** **1** : caer, caerse ⟨to fall out of bed : caer de la cama⟩ ⟨to fall down : caerse⟩ **2** HANG : caer **3** DESCEND : caer (dícese de la lluvia o de la noche), bajar (dícese de los precios), descender (dícese de la temperatura) **4** : caer (a un enemigo), rendirse ⟨the city fell : la ciudad se rindió⟩ **5** OCCUR : caer ⟨Christmas falls on a Friday : la Navidad cae en viernes⟩ **6** **to fall asleep** : dormirse, quedarse dormido **7** **to fall from grace** SIN : perder la gracia **8** **to fall sick** : caer enfermo, enfermarse **9** **to fall through** : fracasar, caer en la nada **10** **to fall to** : tocar a, corresponder a ⟨the task fell to him : le tocó hacerlo⟩

fall² *n* **1** TUMBLE : caída *f* ⟨to break one's fall : frenar uno su caída⟩ ⟨a fall of three feet : una caída de tres pies⟩ **2** FALLING : derrumbe *m* (de rocas), aguacero *m* (de lluvia), nevada *f* (de nieve), bajada *f* (de precios), disminución *f* (de cantidades) **3** AUTUMN : otoño *m* **4** DOWNFALL : caída *f*, ruina *f* **5** **falls** *npl* WATERFALL : cascada *f*, catarata *f*

fallacious [fə'leɪʃəs] *adj* : erróneo, engañoso, falaz

fallacy ['fæləsi] *n, pl* **-cies** : falacia *f*

fall back *vi* **1** RETREAT : retirarse, replegarse **2** **to fall back on** : recurrir a

fall guy *n* SCAPEGOAT : chivo *m* expiatorio

fallible ['fæləbəl] *adj* : falible

fallout ['fɔl,aʊt] *n* **1** : lluvia *f* radioactiva **2** CONSEQUENCES : secuelas *fpl*, consecuencias *fpl*

fallow¹ ['fælo] *vt* : barbechar

fallow² *adj* **to lie fallow** : estar en barbecho

fallow³ *n* : barbecho *m*

false ['fɔls] *adj* **falser; falsest** **1** UNTRUE : falso **2** ERRONEOUS : erróneo, equivocado **3** FAKE : falso, postizo **4** UNFAITHFUL : infiel **5** FRAUDULENT : fraudulento ⟨under false pretenses : por fraude⟩

falsehood ['fɔls,hʊd] *n* : mentira *f*, falsedad *f*

falsely ['fɔlsli] *adv* : falsamente, con falsedad

falseness ['fɔlsnəs] *n* : falsedad *f*

falsetto [fɔl'sɛto:] *n, pl* **-tos** : falsete *m*

falsification [,fɔlsəfə'keɪʃən] *n* : falsificación *f*, falseamiento *m*

falsify ['fɔlsə,faɪ] *vt* **-fied; fying** : falsificar, falsear

falsity ['fɔlsəti] *n, pl* **-ties** : falsedad *f*

falter ['fɔltər] *vi* **-tered; -tering** **1** TOTTER : tambalearse **2** STAMMER : titubear, tartamudear **3** WAVER : vacilar

faltering ['fɔltərɪŋ] *adj* : titubeante, vacilante

fame ['feɪm] *n* : fama *f*

famed ['feɪmd] *adj* : famoso, célebre, afamado

familial [fə'mɪljəl, -liəl] *adj* : familiar

familiar¹ [fə'mɪljər] *adj* **1** KNOWN : familiar, conocido ⟨to be familiar with : estar familiarizado con⟩ **2** INFORMAL : familiar, informal **3** INTIMATE : íntimo, de confianza **4** FORWARD : confianzudo, atrevido — **familiarly** *adv*

familiar² *n* : espíritu *m* guardián

familiarity [fə,mɪli'ærəţi, -,mɪl'jær-] *n, pl* **-ties** **1** KNOWLEDGE : conocimiento *m*, familiaridad *f* **2** INFORMALITY, INTIMACY : confianza *f*, familiaridad *f* **3** FORWARDNESS : exceso *m* de confianza, descaro *m*

familiarize [fə'mɪljə,raɪz] *vt* **-ized; -izing** **1** : familiarizar **2** **to familiarize oneself** : familiarizarse

family ['fæmli, 'fæmə-] *n, pl* **-lies** : familia *f*

family room *n* : living *m*, sala *f* (informal)

family tree *n* : árbol *m* genealógico

famine ['fæmən] *n* : hambre *f*, hambruna *f*

famish ['fæmɪʃ] *vi* **to be famished** : estar famélico, estar hambriento, morir de hambre *fam*

famous ['feɪməs] *adj* : famoso

famously ['feɪməsli] *adv* **to get on famously** : llevarse de maravilla

fan¹ ['fæn] *vt* **fanned; fanning** **1** : abanicar (a una persona), avivar (un fuego) **2** STIMULATE : avivar, estimular

fan² *n* **1** : ventilador *m*, abanico *m* **2** ADMIRER, ENTHUSIAST : aficionado *m*, -da *f*; entusiasta *mf*; admirador *m*, -dora *f*

fanatic¹ [fə'næţɪk] *or* **fanatical** [-ţɪ-kəl] *adj* : fanático

fanatic² *n* : fanático *m*, -ca *f*

fanaticism [fə'næṭə,sɪzəm] *n* : fanatismo *m*

fanciful ['fæntsɪfəl] *adj* **1** CAPRICIOUS : caprichoso, fantástico, extravagante **2** IMAGINATIVE : imaginativo — **fancifully** *adv*

fancy[1] ['fæntsi] *vt* **-cied; -cying 1** IMAGINE : imaginarse, figurarse ⟨fancy that! : ¡figúrate!, ¡imagínate!⟩ **2** CRAVE : apetecer, tener ganas de

fancy[2] *adj* **-cier; -est 1** ELABORATE : elaborado **2** LUXURIOUS : lujoso, elegante — **fancily** ['fæntsəli] *adv*

fancy[3] *n, pl* **-cies 1** LIKING : gusto *m*, afición *f* **2** WHIM : antojo *m*, capricho *m* **3** IMAGINATION : fantasía *f*, imaginación *f*

fandango [fæn'dæŋgo] *n, pl* **-gos** : fandango *m*

fanfare ['fæn,fær] *n* : fanfarria *f*

fang ['fæŋ] *n* : colmillo *m* (de un animal), diente *m* (de una serpiente)

fanlight ['fæn,laɪt] *n* : tragaluz *m*

fantasia [fæn'teɪʒə, -ziə; ,fæntə-'ziːə] *n* : fantasía *f*

fantasize ['fæntə,saɪz] *vi* **-sized; -sizing** : fantasear

fantastic [fæn'tæstɪk] *adj* **1** UNBELIEVABLE : fantástico, increíble, extraño **2** ENORMOUS : fabuloso, inmenso ⟨fantastic sums : sumas fabulosas⟩ **3** WONDERFUL : estupendo, fantástico, bárbaro *fam*, macanudo *fam* — **fantastically** [-tɪkli] *adv*

fantasy ['fæntəsi] *n, pl* **-sies** : fantasía *f*

far[1] ['fɑr] *adv* **farther** ['fɑrðər] *or* **further** ['fər-]; **farthest** *or* **furthest** [-ðəst] **1** : lejos ⟨far from here : lejos de aquí⟩ ⟨to go far : llegar lejos⟩ ⟨as far as Chicago : hasta Chicago⟩ ⟨far away : a lo lejos⟩ **2** MUCH : muy, mucho ⟨far bigger : mucho más grande⟩ ⟨far superior : muy superior⟩ ⟨it's by far the best : es con mucho el mejor⟩ **3** (*expressing degree or extent*) ⟨the results are far off : salieron muy inexactos los resultados⟩ ⟨to go so far as : decir tanto como⟩ ⟨to go far enough : tener el alcance necesario⟩ **4** (*expressing progress*) ⟨the work is far advanced : el trabajo está muy avanzado⟩ ⟨to take (something) too far : llevar (algo) demasiado lejos⟩ **5 far and wide** : por todas partes **6 far from it!** : ¡todo lo contrario! **7 so far** : hasta ahora, todavía

far[2] *adj* **farther** *or* **further; farthest** *or* **furthest 1** REMOTE : lejano, remoto ⟨the Far East : el Lejano Oriente, el Extremo Oriente⟩ ⟨a far country : un país lejano⟩ **2** LONG : largo ⟨a far journey : un viaje largo⟩ **3** EXTREME : extremo ⟨the far right : la extrema derecha⟩ ⟨at the far end of the room : en el otro extremo de la sala⟩

faraway ['fɑrə,weɪ] *adj* : remoto, lejano

farce ['fɑrs] *n* : farsa *f*

farcical ['fɑrsɪkəl] *adj* : absurdo, ridículo

fare[1] ['fær] *vi* **fared; faring** : ir, salir ⟨how did you fare? : ¿cómo te fue?⟩

fare[2] *n* **1** : pasaje *m*, billete *m*, boleto *m* ⟨half fare : medio pasaje⟩ **2** FOOD : comida *f*

farewell[1] [fær'wɛl] *adj* : de despedida

farewell[2] *n* : despedida *f*

far–fetched ['fɑr'fɛtʃt] *adj* : improbable, exagerado

farina [fə'riːnə] *n* : harina *f*

farm[1] ['fɑrm] *vt* **1** : cultivar, labrar **2** : criar (animales) — *vi* : ser agricultor

farm[2] *n* : granja *f*, hacienda *f*, finca *f*, estancia *f*

farmer ['fɑrmər] *n* : agricultor *m*, granjero *m*

farmhand ['fɑrm,hænd] *n* : peón *m*

farmhouse ['fɑrm,haʊs] *n* : granja *f*, vivienda *f* del granjero, casa *f* de hacienda

farming ['fɑrmɪŋ] *n* : labranza *f*, cultivo *m*, crianza *f* (de animales)

farmland ['fɑrm,lænd] *n* : tierras *fpl* de labranza

farmyard ['fɑrm,jɑrd] *n* : corral *m*

far–off ['fɑr,ɔf, -'ɔf] *adj* : remoto, distante, lejano

far–reaching ['fɑr'riːtʃɪŋ] *adj* : de gran alcance

farsighted ['fɑr,saɪṭəd] *adj* **1** : hipermétrope **2** JUDICIOUS : con visión de futuro, previsor, precavido

farsightedness ['fɑr,saɪṭədnəs] *n* **1** : hipermetropía *f* **2** PRUDENCE : previsión *f*

farther[1] ['fɑrðər] *adv* **1** AHEAD : más lejos (en el espacio), más adelante (en el tiempo) **2** MORE : más

farther[2] *adj* : más lejano, más remoto

farthermost ['fɑrðər,moːst] *adj* : (el) más lejano

farthest[1] ['fɑrðəst] *adv* **1** : lo más lejos ⟨I jumped farthest : salté lo más lejos⟩ **2** : lo más avanzado ⟨he progressed farthest : progresó al punto más avanzado⟩ **3** : más ⟨the farthest developed plan : el plan más desarrollado⟩

farthest[2] *adj* : más lejano

fascicle ['fæsɪkəl] *n* : fascículo *m*

fascinate ['fæsən,eɪt] *vt* **-nated; -nating** : fascinar, cautivar

fascinating ['fæsən,eɪṭɪŋ] *adj* : fascinante

fascination [,fæsən'eɪʃən] *n* : fascinación *f*

fascism ['fæʃ,ɪzəm] *n* : fascismo *m*

fascist[1] ['fæʃɪst] *adj* : fascista

fascist[2] *n* : fascista *mf*

fashion[1] ['fæʃən] *vt* : formar, moldear

fashion[2] *n* **1** MANNER : manera *f*, modo *m* **2** CUSTOM : costumbre *f* **3** STYLE : moda *f*

fashionable ['fæʃənəbəl] *adj* : de moda, chic

fashionably ['fæʃənəbli] *adv* : a la moda

fast[1] ['fæst] *vi* : ayunar

fast[2] *adv* **1** SECURELY : firmemente, seguramente ⟨to hold fast : agarrarse

bien⟩ **2** RAPIDLY : rápidamente, rápido, de prisa **3 to run fast** : ir adelantado (dícese de un reloj) **4** SOUNDLY
: profundamente ⟨fast asleep : profundamente dormido⟩
fast³ *adj* **1** SECURE : firme, seguro ⟨to
make fast : amarrar (un barco)⟩ **2**
FAITHFUL : leal ⟨fast friends : amigos
leales⟩ **3** RAPID : rápido, veloz **4** : adelantado ⟨my watch is fast : tengo el
reloj adelantado⟩ **5** DEEP : profundo
⟨a fast sleep : un sueño profundo⟩ **6**
COLORFAST : inalterable, que no destiñe **7** DISSOLUTE : extravagante, disi-
pado, disoluto
fast⁴ *n* : ayuno *m*
fasten ['fæsən] *vt* **1** ATTACH : sujetar,
atar **2** FIX : fijar ⟨to fasten one's eyes
on : fijar los ojos en⟩ **3** SECURE
: abrochar (ropa o cinturones), atar
(cordones), cerrar (una maleta) — *vi*
: abrocharse, cerrar
fastener ['fæsənər] *n* : cierre *m*, sujetador *m*
fastening ['fæsənɪŋ] *n* : cierre *m*, sujetador *m*
fast food *n* : comida *f* rápida
fastidious [fæs'tɪdiəs] *adj* : quisquilloso,
exigente — **fastidiously** *adv*
fat¹ ['fæt] *adj* **fatter; fattest 1** OBESE
: gordo, obeso **2** THICK : grueso
fat² *n* : grasa *f*
fatal ['feɪṭəl] *adj* **1** DEADLY : mortal **2**
ILL-FATED : malhadado, fatal **3** MO-
MENTOUS : fatídico
fatalism ['feɪṭəl‚ɪzəm] *n* : fatalismo *m*
fatalist ['feɪṭəlɪst] *n* : fatalista *mf*
fatalistic [‚feɪṭəl'ɪstɪk] *adj* : fatalista
fatality [feɪ'tæləti, fə-] *n*, *pl* **-ties** : víctima *f* mortal
fatally ['feɪṭəli] *adv* : mortalmente
fate ['feɪt] *n* **1** DESTINY : destino *m* **2**
END, LOT : final *m*, suerte *f*
fated ['feɪṭəd] *adj* : predestinado
fateful ['feɪtfəl] *adj* **1** MOMENTOUS
: fatídico, aciago **2** PROPHETIC
: profético — **fatefully** *adv*
father¹ ['fɑðər] *vt* : engendrar
father² *n* **1** : padre *m* ⟨my father and
my mother : mi padre y mi madre⟩ ⟨Fa-
ther Smith : el padre Smith⟩ **2 the Father** GOD : el Padre, Dios *m*
fatherhood ['fɑðər‚hʊd] *n* : paternidad *f*
father-in-law ['fɑðərɪn‚lɔ] *n*, *pl* **fa-
thers-in-law** : suegro *m*
fatherland ['fɑðər‚lænd] *n* : patria *f*
fatherless ['fɑðərləs] *adj* : huérfano de
padre, sin padre
fatherly ['fɑðərli] *adj* : paternal
fathom¹ ['fæðəm] *vt* UNDERSTAND : entender, comprender
fathom² *n* : braza *f*
fatigue¹ [fə'tiːg] *vt* **-tigued; -tiguing**
: fatigar, cansar
fatigue² *n* : fatiga *f*
fatness ['fætnəs] *n* : gordura *f* (de una
persona o un animal), grosor *m* (de un
objeto)

fatten ['fætən] *vt* : engordar, cebar
fatty ['fæti] *adj* **fattier; -est** : graso, grasoso, adiposo (dícese de los tejidos)
fatuous ['fætʃuəs] *adj* : necio, fatuo —
fatuously *adv*
faucet ['fɔsət] *n* : llave *f*, canilla *f* Arg,
Uru, grifo *m*
fault¹ ['fɔlt] *vt* : encontrar defectos a
fault² *n* **1** SHORTCOMING : defecto *m*,
falta *f* **2** DEFECT : falta *f*, defecto *m*,
falla *f* **3** BLAME : culpa *f* **4** FRACTURE
: falla *f* (geológica)
faultfinder ['fɔlt‚faɪndər] *n* : criticón *m*,
-cona *f*
faultfinding ['fɔlt‚faɪndɪŋ] *n* : crítica *f*
faultless ['fɔltləs] *adj* : sin culpa, sin im-
perfecciones, impecable
faultlessly ['fɔltləsli] *adv* : impecablemente, perfectamente
faulty ['fɔlti] *adj* **faultier; -est** : defectuoso, imperfecto — **faultily** ['fɔltəli] *adv*
fauna ['fɔnə] *n* : fauna *f*
faux ['foː] *adj* : de imitación
faux pas [‚foː'pɑ] *n*, *pl* **faux pas** [*same
or* -'pɑz] : metedura *f* de pata *fam*
favor¹ ['feɪvər] *vt* **1** SUPPORT : estar a favor de, ser partidario de, apoyar **2**
OBLIGE : hacerle un favor a **3** PREFER
: preferir **4** RESEMBLE : parecerse a,
salir a
favor² *n* : favor *m* ⟨in favor of : a favor
de⟩ ⟨an error in his favor : un error a
su favor⟩
favorable ['feɪvərəbəl] *adj* : favorable,
propicio
favorably ['feɪvərəbli] *adv* : favorablemente, bien
favorite¹ ['feɪvərət] *adj* : favorito,
preferido
favorite² *n* : favorito *m*, -ta *f*; preferido
m, -da *f*
favoritism ['feɪvərə‚tɪzəm] *n* : favoritismo *m*
fawn¹ ['fɔn] *vi* : adular, lisonjear
fawn² *n* : cervato *m*
fax ['fæks] *n* : facsímil *m*, facsímile *m*
faze ['feɪz] *vt* **fazed; fazing** : desconcertar, perturbar
fear¹ ['fɪr] *vt* : temer, tener miedo de —
vi : temer
fear² *n* : miedo *m*, temor *m* ⟨for fear of
: por temor a⟩
fearful ['fɪrfəl] *adj* **1** FRIGHTENING : espantoso, aterrador, horrible **2** FRIGHT-
ENED : temeroso, miedoso
fearfully ['fɪrfəli] *adv* **1** EXTREMELY : extremadamente, terriblemente **2** TIMID-
LY : con temor
fearless ['fɪrləs] *adj* : intrépido, impávido
fearlessly ['fɪrləsli] *adv* : sin temor
fearlessness ['fɪrləsnəs] *n* : intrepidez *f*,
impavidez *f*
fearsome ['fɪrsəm] *adj* : aterrador
feasibility [‚fiːzə'bɪləti] *n* : viabilidad *f*,
factibilidad *f*
feasible ['fiːzəbəl] *adj* : viable, factible,
realizable

feast[1] ['fi:st] *vi* : banquetear — *vt* **1** : agasajar, festejar **2 to feast one's eyes on** : regalarse la vista con

feast[2] *n* **1** BANQUET : banquete *m*, festín *m* **2** FESTIVAL : fiesta *f*

feat ['fi:t] *n* : proeza *f*, hazaña *f*

feather[1] ['fɛðər] *vt* **1** : emplumar **2 to feather one's nest** : hacer su agosto

feather[2] *n* **1** : pluma *f* **2 a feather in one's cap** : un triunfo personal

feathered ['fɛðərd] *adj* : con plumas

feathery ['fɛðəri] *adj* **1** DOWNY : plumoso **2** LIGHT : liviano

feature[1] ['fi:tʃər] *v* **-tured; -turing** *vt* **1** IMAGINE : imaginarse **2** PRESENT : presentar — *vi* : figurar

feature[2] *n* **1** CHARACTERISTIC : característica *f*, rasgo *m* **2** : largometraje *m* (en el cine), artículo *m* (en un periódico), documental *m* (en la televisión) **3 features** *npl* : rasgos *mpl*, facciones *fpl* ⟨delicate features : facciones delicadas⟩

February ['fɛbjuˌri, 'fɛbʊ-, 'fbrʊ-] *n* : febrero *m*

fecal ['fi:kəl] *adj* : fecal

feces ['fi:ˌsi:z] *npl* : heces *fpl*, excrementos *mpl*

feckless ['fɛkləs] *adj* : irresponsable

fecund ['fɛkənd, 'fi:-] *adj* : fecundo

fecundity [fɪ'kʌndəti, fɛ-] *n* : fecundidad *f*

federal ['fɛdrəl, -dərəl] *adj* : federal

federalism ['fɛdrəˌlɪzəm, -dərə-] *n* : federalismo *m*

federalist[1] ['fɛdrəlɪst, -dərə-] *adj* : federalista

federalist[2] *n* : federalista *mf*

federate ['fɛdəˌreɪt] *vt* **-ated; -ating** : federar

federation [ˌfɛdə'reɪʃən] *n* : federación *f*

fedora [fɪ'dorə] *n* : sombrero *m* flexible de fieltro

fed up *adj* : harto

fee ['fi:] *n* **1** : honorarios *mpl* (a un médico, un abogado, etc.) **2 entrance fee** : entrada *f*

feeble ['fi:bəl] *adj* **-bler; -blest 1** WEAK : débil, endeble **2** INEFFECTIVE : flojo, pobre, poco convincente

feebleminded [ˌfi:bəl'maɪndəd] *adj* **1** : débil mental **2** FOOLISH, STUPID : imbécil, tonto

feebleness ['fi:bəlnəs] *n* : debilidad *f*

feebly ['fi:bli] *adv* : débilmente

feed[1] ['fi:d] *v* **fed** ['fɛd]; **feeding** *vt* **1** : dar de comer a, nutrir, alimentar (a una persona) **2** : alimentar (un fuego o una máquina), proveer (información), introducir (datos) — *vi* : comer, alimentarse

feed[2] *n* **1** NOURISHMENT : alimento *m* **2** FODDER : pienso *m*

feedback ['fi:dˌbæk] *n* **1** : realimentación *f* (electrónica) **2** RESPONSE : reacción *f*

feeder ['fi:dər] *n* : comedero *m* (para animales)

feel[1] ['fi:l] *v* **felt** ['flt]; **feeling** *vi* **1** : sentirse, encontrarse ⟨I feel tired : me siento cansada⟩ ⟨he feels hungry : tiene hambre⟩ ⟨she feels like a fool : se siente como una idiota⟩ ⟨to feel like doing something : tener ganas de hacer algo⟩ **2** SEEM : parecer ⟨it feels like spring : parece primavera⟩ **3** THINK : parecerse, opinar, pensar ⟨how does he feel about that? : ¿qué opina él de eso?⟩ — *vt* **1** TOUCH : tocar, palpar **2** SENSE : sentir ⟨to feel the cold : sentir el frío⟩ **3** CONSIDER : sentir, creer, considerar ⟨to feel (it) necessary : creer necesario⟩

feel[2] *n* **1** SENSATION, TOUCH : sensación *f*, tacto *m* **2** ATMOSPHERE : ambiente *m*, atmósfera *f* **3 to have a feel for** : tener un talento especial para

feeler ['fi:lər] *n* : antena *f*, tentáculo *m*

feeling ['fi:lɪŋ] *n* **1** SENSATION : sensación *f*, sensibilidad *f* **2** EMOTION : sentimiento *m* **3** OPINION : opinión *f* **4 feelings** *npl* SENSIBILITIES : sentimientos *mpl* ⟨to hurt someone's feelings : herir los sentimientos de alguien⟩

feet → **foot**

feign ['feɪn] *vt* : simular, aparentar, fingir

feint[1] ['feɪnt] *vi* : fintar, fintear

feint[2] *n* : finta *f*

feldspar ['fɛldˌspar] *n* : feldespato *m*

felicitate [fɪ'lɪsəˌteɪt] *vt* **-tated; -tating** : felicitar, congratular

felicitation [fɪˌlɪsə'teɪʃən] *n* : felicitación *f*

felicitous [fɪ'lɪsətəs] *adj* : acertado, oportuno

feline[1] ['fi:ˌlaɪn] *adj* : felino

feline[2] *n* : felino *m*, -na *f*

fell[1] ['fɛl] *vt* : talar (un árbol), derribar (a una persona)

fell[2] → **fall**

fellow ['fɛˌlo:] *n* **1** COMPANION : compañero *m*, -ra *f*; camarada *mf* **2** ASSOCIATE : socio *m*, -cia *f* **3** MAN : tipo *m*, hombre *m*

fellowman [ˌfɛlo'mæn] *n*, *pl* **-men** : prójimo *m*, semejante *m*

fellowship ['fɛloˌʃɪp] *n* **1** COMPANIONSHIP : camaradería *f*, compañerismo *m* **2** ASSOCIATION : fraternidad *f* **3** GRANT : beca *f* (de investigación)

felon ['fɛlən] *n* : malhechor *m*, -chora *f*; criminal *mf*

felonious [fə'lo:niəs] *adj* : criminal

felony ['fɛləni] *n*, *pl* **-nies** : delito *m* grave

felt[1] ['fɛlt] *n* : fieltro *m*

felt[2] → **feel**

female[1] ['fi:ˌmeɪl] *adj* : femenino

female[2] *n* **1** : hembra *f* (de animal) **2** WOMAN : mujer *f*

feminine ['fɛmənən] *adj* : femenino

femininity [ˌfɛmə'nɪnəti] *n* : feminidad *f*, femineidad *f*

feminism ['fɛməˌnɪzəm] *n* : feminismo *m*

feminist[1] ['fɛmənɪst] *adj* : feminista

feminist[2] *n* : feminista *mf*

femoral ['fɛmərəl] *adj* : femoral
femur ['fi:mər] *n*, *pl* **femurs** *or* **femora** ['fɛmərə] : fémur *m*
fence[1] ['fɛnts] *v* **fenced; fencing** *vt* : vallar, cercar — *vi* : hacer esgrima
fence[2] *n* : cerca *f*, valla *f*, cerco *m*
fencer ['fɛntsər] *n* : esgrimista *mf*; esgrimidor *m*, -dora *f*
fencing ['fɛntsɪŋ] *n* **1** : esgrima *m* (deporte) **2** : materiales *mpl* para cercas **3** ENCLOSURE : cercado *m*
fend ['fɛnd] *vt* **to fend off** : rechazar (un enemigo), parar (un golpe), eludir (una pregunta) — *vi* **to fend for oneself** : arreglárselas sólo, valerse por sí mismo
fender ['fɛndər] *n* : guardabarros *mpl*, salpicadera *f Mex*
fennel ['fɛnəl] *n* : hinojo *m*
ferment[1] [fər'mɛnt] *v* : fermentar
ferment[2] ['fər,mɛnt] *n* **1** : fermento *m* (en la química) **2** TURMOIL : agitación *f*, conmoción *f*
fermentation [,fərmən'teɪʃən, -,mɛn-] *n* : fermentación *f*
fern ['fərn] *n* : helecho *m*
ferocious [fə'roːʃəs] *adj* : feroz — **ferociously** *adv*
ferociousness [fə'roːʃəsnəs] *n* : ferocidad *f*
ferocity [fə'rɑsəṭi] *n* : ferocidad *f*
ferret[1] ['fɛrət] *vi* SNOOP : hurgar, husmear — *vt* **to ferret out** : descubrir
ferret[2] *n* : hurón *m*
ferric ['fɛrɪk] *or* **ferrous** ['fɛrəs] *adj* : férrico
Ferris wheel ['fɛrɪs] *n* : noria *f*
ferry[1] ['fɛri] *vt* **-ried; -rying** : llevar, transportar
ferry[2] *n*, *pl* **-ries** : transbordador *m*, ferry *m*
ferryboat ['fɛri,boːt] *n* : transbordador *m*, ferry *m*
fertile ['fərṭəl] *adj* : fértil, fecundo
fertility [fər'tɪləṭi] *n* : fertilidad *f*
fertilization [,fərṭələ'zeɪʃən] *n* : fertilización *f* (del suelo), fecundación (de un huevo)
fertilize ['fərṭəl,aɪz] *vt* **-ized; -izing 1** : fecundar (un huevo) **2** : fertilizar, abonar (el suelo)
fertilizer ['fərṭəl,aɪzər] *n* : fertilizante *m*, abono *m*
fervent ['fərvənt] *adj* : ferviente, fervoroso, ardiente — **fervently** *adv*
fervid ['fərvɪd] *adj* : ardiente, apasionado — **fervidly** *adv*
fervor ['fərvər] *n* : fervor *m*, ardor *m*
fester ['fɛstər] *vi* : enconarse, supurar
festival ['fɛstəvəl] *n* : fiesta *f*, festividad *f*, festival *m*
festive ['fɛstɪv] *adj* : festivo — **festively** *adv*
festivity [fɛs'tɪvəṭi] *n*, *pl* **-ties** : festividad *f*, celebración *f*
festoon[1] [fɛs'tu:n] *vt* : adornar, engalanar
festoon[2] *n* GARLAND : guirnalda *f*
fetal ['fi:ṭəl] *adj* : fetal

fetch ['fɛtʃ] *vt* **1** BRING : traer, recoger, ir a buscar **2** REALIZE : realizar, venderse por ⟨the jewelry fetched $10,000 : las joyas se vendieron por $10,000⟩
fetching ['fɛtʃɪŋ] *adj* : atractivo, encantador
fête[1] ['feɪt, 'fɛt] *vt* **fêted; fêting** : festejar, agasajar
fête[2] *n* : fiesta *f*
fetid ['fɛṭəd] *adj* : fétido
fetish ['fɛṭɪʃ] *n* : fetiche *m*
fetlock ['fɛt,lɑk] *n* : espolón *m*
fetter ['fɛṭər] *vt* : encadenar, poner grillos a
fetters ['fɛṭərz] *npl* : grillos *mpl*, grilletes *mpl*, cadenas *fpl*
fettle ['fɛṭəl] *n* **in fine fettle** : en buena forma, en plena forma
fetus ['fi:ṭəs] *n* : feto *m*
feud[1] ['fju:d] *vi* : pelear, contender
feud[2] *n* : contienda *f*, enemistad *f* (heredada)
feudal ['fju:dəl] *adj* : feudal
feudalism ['fju:dəl,ɪzəm] *n* : feudalismo *m*
fever ['fi:vər] *n* : fiebre *f*, calentura *f*
feverish ['fi:vərɪʃ] *adj* **1** : afiebrado, con fiebre, febril **2** FRANTIC : febril, frenético
few[1] ['fju:] *adj* : pocos ⟨with few exceptions : con pocas excepciones⟩ ⟨a few times : varias veces⟩
few[2] *pron* **1** : pocos ⟨few (of them) were ready : pocos estaban listos⟩ **2 a few** : algunos, unos cuantos **3 few and far between** : contados
fewer ['fju:ər] *pron* : menos ⟨the fewer the better : cuantos menos mejor⟩
fez ['fɛz] *n*, *pl* **fezzes** : fez *m*
fiancé [,fi:,ɑn'seɪ, ,fi:'ɑn,seɪ] *n* : prometido *m*, novio *m*
fiancée [,fi:,ɑn'seɪ, ,fi:'ɑn,seɪ] *n* : prometida *f*, novia *f*
fiasco [fi'æs,ko:] *n*, *pl* **-coes** : fiasco *m*, fracaso *m*
fiat ['fi:,ɑt, -,æt, -ət; 'faɪət, -,æt] *n* : decreto *m*, orden *m*
fib[1] ['fɪb] *vi* **fibbed; fibbing** : decir mentirillas
fib[2] *n* : mentirilla *f*, bola *f fam*
fibber ['fɪbər] *n* : mentirosillo *m*, -lla *f*; cuentista *mf fam*
fiber *or* **fibre** ['faɪbər] *n* : fibra *f*
fiberboard ['faɪbər,bord] *n* : cartón *m* madera
fiberglass ['faɪbər,glæs] *n* : fibra *f* de vidrio
fibrillate ['fɪbrə,leɪt, 'faɪ-] *vi* **-lated; -lating** : fibrilar
fibrillation [,fɪbrə'leɪʃən, ,faɪ-] *n* : fibrilación *f*
fibrous ['faɪbrəs] *adj* : fibroso
fibula ['fɪbjələ] *n*, *pl* **-lae** [-,li:, -,laɪ] *or* **-las** : peroné *m*
fickle ['fɪkəl] *adj* : inconstante, voluble, veleidoso
fickleness ['fɪkəlnəs] *n* : volubilidad *f*, inconstancia *f*, veleidad *f*

fiction ['fɪkʃən] *n* : ficción *f*
fictional ['fɪkʃənəl] *adj* : ficticio
fictitious [fɪk'tɪʃəs] *adj* **1** IMAGINARY : ficticio, imaginario **2** FALSE : falso, ficticio
fiddle¹ ['fɪdəl] *vi* **-dled; -dling 1** : tocar el violín **2 to fiddle with** : juguetear con, toquetear
fiddle² *n* : violín *m*
fiddler ['fɪdlər, 'fɪdələr] *n* : violinista *mf*
fiddlesticks ['fɪdəl,stɪks] *interj* : ¡tonterías!
fidelity [fə'dɛləti, faɪ-] *n, pl* **-ties** : fidelidad *f*
fidget¹ ['fɪdʒət] *vi* **1** : moverse, estarse inquieto **2 to fidget with** : juguetear con
fidget² *n* **1** : persona *f* inquieta **2 fidgets** *npl* RESTLESSNESS : inquietud *f*
fidgety ['fɪdʒəti] *adj* : inquieto
fiduciary¹ [fə'duː:ʃiˌɛri, -'djuː:-, -ʃəri] *adj* : fiduciario
fiduciary² *n, pl* **-ries** : fiduciario *m*, -ria *f*
field¹ ['fiːld] *vt* : interceptar y devolver (una pelota), presentar (un candidato), sortear (una pregunta)
field² *adj* : de campaña, de campo ⟨field hospital : hospital de campaña⟩ ⟨field goal : gol de campo⟩ ⟨field trip : viaje de estudio⟩
field³ *n* **1** : campo *m* (de cosechas, de batalla, de magnetismo) **2** : campo *m*, cancha *f* (en deportes) **3** : campo *m* (de trabajo), esfera *f* (de actividades)
fielder ['fiːldər] *n* : jugador *m*, -dora *f* de campo; fildeador *m*, -dora *f*
field glasses *n* : binoculares *mpl*, gemelos *mpl*
fiend ['fiːnd] *n* **1** DEMON : demonio *m* **2** EVILDOER : persona *f* maligna; malvado *m*, -da *f* **3** FANATIC : fanático *m*, -ca *f*
fiendish ['fiːndɪʃ] *adj* : diabólico — **fiendishly** *adv*
fierce ['fɪrs] *adj* **fiercer; -est 1** FEROCIOUS : fiero, feroz **2** HEATED : acalorado **3** INTENSE : intenso, violento, fuerte — **fiercely** *adv*
fierceness ['fɪrsnəs] *n* **1** FEROCITY : ferocidad *f*, fiereza *f* **2** INTENSITY : intensidad *f*, violencia *f*
fieriness ['faɪərinəs] *n* : pasión *f*, ardor *m*
fiery ['faɪəri] *adj* **fierier; -est 1** BURNING : ardiente, llameante **2** GLOWING : encendido **3** PASSIONATE : acalorado, ardiente, fogoso
fiesta [fi'ɛstə] *n* : fiesta *f*
fife ['faɪf] *n* : pífano *m*
fifteen¹ [fɪf'tiːn] *adj* : quince
fifteen² *n* : quince *m*
fifteenth¹ [fɪf'tiːnθ] *adj* : decimoquinto
fifteenth² *n* **1** : decimoquinto *m*, -ta *f* (en una serie) **2** : quinceavo *m*, quinceava parte *f*
fifth¹ ['fɪfθ] *adj* : quinto

fifth² *n* **1** : quinto *m*, -ta *f* (en una serie) **2** : quinto *m*, quinta parte *f* **3** : quinta *f* (en la música)
fiftieth¹ ['fɪftiəθ] *adj* : quincuagésimo
fiftieth² *n* **1** : quincuagésimo *m*, -ma *f* (en una serie) **2** : cincuentavo *m*, cincuentava parte *f*
fifty¹ ['fɪfti] *adj* : cincuenta
fifty² *n, pl* **-ties** : cincuenta *m*
fifty–fifty¹ [ˌfɪfti'fɪfti] *adv* : a medias, mitad y mitad
fifty–fifty² *adj* **to have a fifty–fifty chance** : tener un cincuenta por ciento de posibilidades
fig ['fɪg] *n* : higo *m*
fight¹ ['faɪt] *v* **fought** ['fɔt]; **fighting** *vi* : luchar, combatir, pelear — *vt* : luchar contra, combatir contra
fight² *n* **1** COMBAT : lucha *f*, pelea *f*, combate *m* **2** MATCH : pelea *f*, combate *m* (en boxeo) **3** QUARREL : disputa *f*, pelea *f*, pleito *m*
fighter ['faɪtər] *n* **1** COMBATANT : luchador *m*, -dora *f*; combatiente *mf* **2** BOXER : boxeador *m*, -dora *f*
figment ['fɪgmənt] *n* **figment of the imagination** : producto *m* de la imaginación
figurative ['fɪgjərətɪv, -gə-] *adj* : figurado, metafórico
figuratively ['fɪgjərətɪvli, -gə-] *adv* : en sentido figurado, de manera metafórica
figure¹ ['fɪgjər, -gər] *v* **-ured; -uring** *vt* **1** CALCULATE : calcular **2** ESTIMATE : figurarse, calcular ⟨he figured it was possible : se figuró que era posible⟩ — *vi* **1** FEATURE, STAND OUT : figurar, destacar **2 that figures!** : ¡obvio!, ¡no me extraña nada!
figure² *n* **1** DIGIT : número *m*, cifra *f* **2** PRICE : precio *m*, cifra *f* **3** PERSONAGE : figura *f*, personaje *m* **4** : figura *f*, tipo *m*, físico *m* ⟨to have a good figure : tener buen tipo, tener un buen físico⟩ **5** DESIGN, OUTLINE : figura *f* **6 figures** *npl* : aritmética *f*
figurehead ['fɪgjərˌhɛd, -gər-] *n* : testaferro *m*, líder *mf* sin poder
figure of speech *n* : figura *f* retórica, figura *f* de hablar
figure out *vt* **1** UNDERSTAND : entender **2** RESOLVE : resolver (un problema, etc.)
figurine [ˌfɪgjə'riːn] *n* : estatuilla *f*
Fijian ['fiːdʒiən, fɪ'jiːən] *n* : fijiano *m*, -na *f* — **Fijian** *adj*
filament ['fɪləmənt] *n* : filamento *m*
filbert ['fɪlbərt] *n* : avellana *f*
filch ['fɪltʃ] *vt* : hurtar, birlar *fam*
file¹ ['faɪl] *v* **filed; filing** *vt* **1** CLASSIFY : clasificar **2** : archivar (documentos) **3** SUBMIT : presentar ⟨to file charges : presentar cargos⟩ **4** SMOOTH : limar — *vi* : desfilar, entrar (o salir) en fila
file² *n* **1** : lima *f* ⟨nail file : lima de uñas⟩ **2** DOCUMENTS : archivo *m* **3** LINE : fila *f*

filial ['fɪliəl, 'fɪljəl] *adj* : filial
filibuster¹ ['fɪlə,bʌstər] *vi* : practicar el obstruccionismo
filibuster² *n* : obstruccionismo *m*
filibusterer ['fɪlə,bʌstərər] *n* : obstruccionista *mf*
filigree ['fɪlə,gri:] *n* : filigrana *f*
Filipino [,fɪlə'pi:no:] *n* : filipino *m*, -na *f* — **Filipino** *adj*
fill¹ ['fɪl] *vt* **1** : llenar, ocupar ⟨to fill a cup : llenar una taza⟩ ⟨to fill a room : ocupar una sala⟩ **2** STUFF : rellenar **3** PLUG : tapar, rellenar, empastar (un diente) **4** SATISFY : cumplir con, satisfacer **5** *or* **to fill out** : llenar, re- llenar ⟨to fill out a form : rellenar un formulario⟩
fill² *n* **1** FILLING, STUFFING : relleno *m* **2 to eat one's fill** : comer lo suficiente **3 to have one's fill of** : estar harto de
filler ['fɪlər] *n* : relleno *m*
fillet¹ ['fɪlət, fɪ'leɪ, 'fɪ,leɪ] *vt* : cortar en filetes
fillet² *n* : filete *m*
fill in *vt* INFORM : informar, poner al corriente — *vi* **to fill in for** : reemplazar a
filling ['fɪlɪŋ] *n* **1** : relleno *m* **2** : empaste *m* (de un diente)
filling station → **gas station**
filly ['fɪli] *n*, *pl* **-lies** : potra *f*, potranca *f*
film¹ ['fɪlm] *vt* : filmar — *vi* : rodar
film² *n* **1** COATING : capa *f*, película *f* **2** : película *f* (fotográfica) **3** MOVIE : película *f*, filme *m*
filmmaker ['fɪlm,meɪkər] *n* : cineasta *mf*
filmy ['fɪlmi] *adj* **filmier; -est 1** GAUZY : diáfano, vaporoso **2** : cubierto de una película
filter¹ ['fɪltər] *vt* : filtrar
filter² *n* : filtro *m*
filth ['fɪlθ] *n* : mugre *f*, porquería *f*, roña *f*
filthiness ['fɪlθinəs] *n* : suciedad *f*
filthy ['fɪlθi] *adj* **filthier; -est 1** DIRTY : mugriento, sucio **2** OBSCENE : obsceno, indecente
filtration [fɪl'treɪʃən] *n* : filtración *f*
fin ['fɪn] *n* **1** : aleta *f* **2** : alerón *m* (de un automóvil o un avión)
finagle [fə'neɪgəl] *vt* **-gled; -gling** : arreglárselas para conseguir
final¹ ['faɪnəl] *adj* **1** DEFINITIVE : definitivo, final, inapelable **2** ULTIMATE : final **3** LAST : último, final
final² *n* **1** : final *f* (en deportes) **2 finals** *npl* : exámenes *mpl* finales
finale [fɪ'næli, -'nɑ-] *n* : final *m* ⟨grand finale : final triunfal⟩
finalist ['faɪnəlɪst] *n* : finalista *mf*
finality [faɪ'næləti, fə-] *n*, *pl* **-ties** : finalidad *f*
finalize ['faɪnəl,aɪz] *vt* **-ized; -izing** : finalizar
finally ['faɪnəli] *adv* **1** LASTLY : por último, finalmente **2** EVENTUALLY : por fin, al final **3** DEFINITIVELY : definitivamente

finance¹ [fə'nænts, 'faɪ,nænts] *vt* **-nanced; -nancing** : financiar
finance² *n* **1** : finanzas *fpl* **2 finances** *npl* RESOURCES : recursos *mpl* financieros
financial [fə'nænʧəl, faɪ-] *adj* : financiero, económico
financially [fə'nænʧəli, faɪ-] *adv* : económicamente
financier [,fɪnən'sɪr, ,faɪ,næn-] *n* : financiero *m*, -ra *f*; financista *mf*
financing [fə'næntsɪŋ, 'fæɪ,næntsɪŋ] *n* : financiación *f*, financiamiento *m*
finch ['fɪnʧ] *n* : pinzón *m*
find¹ ['faɪnd] *vt* **found** ['faʊnd]; **finding 1** LOCATE : encontrar, hallar ⟨I can't find it : no lo encuentro⟩ ⟨to find one's way : encontrar el camino, orientarse⟩ **2** DISCOVER, REALIZE : descubrir, darse cuenta de ⟨he found it difficult : descubrió que era difícil⟩ **3** DECLARE : declarar, hallar ⟨they found him guilty : lo declararon culpable⟩
find² *n* : hallazgo *m*
finder ['faɪndər] *n* : descubridor *m*, -dora *f*
finding ['faɪndɪŋ] *n* **1** FIND : hallazgo *m* **2 findings** *npl* : conclusiones *fpl*
find out *vt* DISCOVER : descubrir, averiguar — *vi* LEARN : enterarse
fine¹ ['faɪn] *vt* **fined; fining** : multar
fine² *adj* **finer; -est 1** PURE : puro (dícese del oro y de la plata) **2** THIN : fino, delgado **3** : fino ⟨fine sand : arena fina⟩ **4** SMALL : pequeño, minúsculo ⟨fine print : letras minúsculas⟩ **5** SUBTLE : sutil, delicado **6** EXCELLENT : excelente, magnífico, selecto **7** FAIR : bueno ⟨it's a fine day : hace buen tiempo⟩ **8** EXQUISITE : exquisito, delicado, fino **9 fine arts** : bellas artes *fpl*
fine³ *n* : multa *f*
finely ['faɪnli] *adv* **1** EXCELLENTLY : con arte **2** ELEGANTLY : elegantemente **3** PRECISELY : con precisión **4 to chop finely** : picar muy fino, picar en trozos pequeños
fineness ['faɪnnəs] *n* **1** EXCELLENCE : excelencia *f* **2** ELEGANCE : elegancia *f*, refinamiento *m* **3** DELICACY : delicadeza *f*, lo fino **4** PRECISION : precisión *f* **5** SUBTLETY : sutileza *f* **6** PURITY : ley *f* (de oro y plata)
finery ['faɪnəri] *n* : galas *fpl*, adornos *mpl*
finesse¹ [fə'nɛs] *vt* **-nessed; -nessing** : ingeniar
finesse² *n* **1** REFINEMENT : refinamiento *m*, finura *f* **2** TACT : delicadeza *f*, tacto *m*, diplomacia *f* **3** CRAFTINESS : astucia *f*
finger¹ ['fɪŋgər] *vt* **1** HANDLE : tocar, toquetear **2** ACCUSE : acusar, delatar
finger² *n* : dedo *m*
fingerling ['fɪŋgərlɪŋ] *n* : pez *m* pequeño y joven
fingernail ['fɪŋgər,neɪl] *n* : uña *f*
fingerprint¹ ['fɪŋgər,prɪnt] *vt* : tomar las huellas digitales a

fingerprint² *n* : huella *f* digital
fingertip ['fɪŋgər,tɪp] *n* : punta *f* del dedo, yema *f* del dedo
finicky ['fɪnɪki] *adj* : maniático, melindroso, mañoso
finish¹ ['fɪnɪʃ] *vt* **1** COMPLETE : acabar, terminar **2** : aplicar un acabado a (muebles, etc.)
finish² *n* **1** END : fin *m*, final *m* **2** REFINEMENT : refinamiento *m* **3** : acabado *m* ⟨a glossy finish : un acabado brillante⟩
finite ['faɪ,naɪt] *adj* : finito
fink ['fɪŋk] *n* : mequetrefe *mf fam*
Finn ['fɪn] *n* : finlandés *m*, -desa *f*
Finnish¹ ['fɪnɪʃ] *adj* : finlandés
Finnish² *n* : finlandés *m* (idioma)
fiord [fi'ɔrd] → **fjord**
fir ['fər] *n* : abeto *m*
fire¹ ['faɪr] *vt* **fired; firing 1** IGNITE, KINDLE : encender **2** ENLIVEN : animar, avivar **3** DISMISS : despedir **4** SHOOT : disparar **5** BAKE : cocer (cerámica)
fire² *n* **1** : fuego *m* **2** BURNING : incendio *m* ⟨fire alarm : alarma contra incendios⟩ ⟨to be on fire : estar en llamas⟩ **3** ENTHUSIASM : ardor *m*, entusiasmo *m* **4** SHOOTING : disparos *mpl*, fuego *m*
firearm ['faɪr,ɑrm] *n* : arma *f* de fuego
fireball ['faɪr,bɔl] *n* **1** : bola *f* de fuego **2** METEOR : bólido *m*
firebreak ['faɪr,breɪk] *n* : cortafuegos *m*
firebug ['faɪr,bʌg] *n* : pirómano *m*, -na *f*; incendiario *m*, -ria *f*
firecracker ['faɪr,krækər] *n* : petardo *m*
fire escape *n* : escalera *f* de incendios
firefighter ['faɪr,faɪtər] *n* : bombero *m*, -ra *f*
firefly ['faɪr,flaɪ] *n, pl* **-flies** : luciérnaga *f*
fireman ['faɪrmən] *n, pl* **-men** [-mən, -,mɛn] **1** FIREFIGHTER : bombero *m*, -ra *f* **2** STOKER : fogonero *m*, -ra *f*
fireplace ['faɪr,pleɪs] *n* : hogar *m*, chimenea *f*
fireproof¹ ['faɪr,pru:f] *vt* : hacer incombustible
fireproof² *adj* : incombustible, ignífugo
fireside¹ ['faɪr,saɪd] *adj* : informal ⟨fireside chat : charla informal⟩
fireside² *n* **1** HEARTH : chimenea *f*, hogar *m* **2** HOME : hogar *m*, casa *f*
firewall ['faɪr,wɔl] *n* : cortafuegos *m*
firewood ['faɪr,wʊd] *n* : leña *f*
fireworks ['faɪr,wərks] *npl* : fuegos *mpl* artificiales, pirotecnia *f*
firm¹ ['fərm] *vt or* **to firm up** : endurecer
firm² *adj* **1** VIGOROUS : fuerte, vigoroso **2** SOLID, UNYIELDING : firme, duro, sólido **3** UNCHANGING : firme, inalterable **4** RESOLUTE : firme, resuelto
firm³ *n* : empresa *f*, firma *f*, compañía *f*
firmament ['fərməmənt] *n* : firmamento *m*
firmly ['fərmli] *adv* : firmemente
firmness ['fərmnəs] *n* : firmeza *f*
first¹ ['fərst] *adv* **1** : primero ⟨finish your homework first : primero termina tu

tarea⟩ ⟨first and foremost : ante todo⟩ ⟨first of all : en primer lugar⟩ **2** : por primera vez ⟨I saw it first in Boston : lo vi por primera vez en Boston⟩
first² *adj* **1** : primero ⟨the first time : la primera vez⟩ ⟨at first sight : a primera vista⟩ ⟨in the first place : en primer lugar⟩ ⟨the first ten applicants : los diez primeros candidatos⟩ **2** FOREMOST : principal, primero ⟨first tenor : tenor principal⟩
first³ *n* **1** : primero *m*, -ra *f* **2** *or* **first gear** : primera *f* **3** at ~ : al principio
first aid *n* : primeros auxilios *mpl*
first–class¹ ['fərst'klæs] *adv* : en primera ⟨to travel first-class : viajar en primera⟩
first–class² *adj* : de primera
first class *n* : primera clase *f*
firsthand¹ ['fərst'hænd] *adv* : directamente
firsthand² *adj* : de primera mano
first lieutenant *n* : teniente *mf*; teniente primero *m*, teniente primera *f*
firstly ['fərstli] *adv* : primeramente, principalmente, en primer lugar
first–rate¹ ['fərst'reɪt] *adv* : muy bien
first–rate² *adj* : de primera, de primera clase
first sergeant *n* : sargento *mf*
firth ['fərθ] *n* : estuario *m*
fiscal ['fɪskəl] *adj* : fiscal — **fiscally** *adv*
fish¹ ['fɪʃ] *vi* **1** : pescar **2 to fish for** SEEK : buscar, rebuscar ⟨to fish for compliments : andar a la caza de cumplidos⟩ — *vt* : pescar
fish² *n, pl* **fish** *or* **fishes** : pez *m* (vivo), pescado *m* (para comer)
fisherman ['fɪʃərmən] *n, pl* **-men** [-mən, -,mɛn] : pescador *m*, -dora *f*
fishery ['fɪʃəri] *n, pl* **-eries 1** → **fishing 2** : zona *f* pesquera, pesquería *f*
fishhook ['fɪʃ,hʊk] *n* : anzuelo *m*
fishing ['fɪʃɪŋ] *n* : pesca *f*, industria *f* pesquera
fishing pole *n* : caña *f* de pescar
fish market *n* : pescadería *f*
fishy ['fɪʃi] *adj* **fishier; -est 1** : a pescado ⟨a fishy taste : un sabor a pescado⟩ **2** QUESTIONABLE : dudoso, sospechoso ⟨there's something fishy going on : aquí hay gato encerrado⟩
fission ['fɪʃən, -ʒən] *n* : fisión *f*
fissure ['fɪʃər] *n* : fisura *f*, hendidura *f*
fist ['fɪst] *n* : puño *m*
fistful ['fɪst,fʊl] *n* : puñado *m*
fisticuffs ['fɪstɪ,kʌfs] *npl* : lucha *f* a puñetazos
fit¹ ['fɪt] *v* **fitted; fitting** *vt* **1** MATCH : corresponder a, coincidir con ⟨the punishment fits the crime : el castigo corresponde al crimen⟩ **2** : quedar ⟨the dress doesn't fit me : el vestido no me queda⟩ **3** GO : caber, encajar en ⟨her key fits the lock : su llave encaja en la cerradura⟩ **4** INSERT, INSTALL : poner, colocar **5** ADAPT : adecuar, ajustar, adaptar **6** *or* **to fit out** EQUIP : equipar

— *vi* **1** : quedar, entallar ⟨these pants don't fit : estos pantalones no me quedan⟩ **2** CONFORM : encajar, cuadrar **3 to fit in** : encajar, estar integrado

fit² *adj* **fitter; fittest 1** SUITABLE : adecuado, apropiado, conveniente **2** QUALIFIED : calificado, competente **3** HEALTHY : sano, en forma

fit³ *n* **1** ATTACK : ataque *m*, acceso *m*, arranque *m* **2 to be a good fit** : quedar bien **3 to be a tight fit** : ser muy entallado (de ropa), estar apretado (de espacios)

fitful [ˈfɪtfəl] *adj* : irregular, intermitente — **fitfully** *adv*

fitness [ˈfɪtnəs] *n* **1** HEALTH : salud *f*, buena forma *f* (física) **2** SUITABILITY : idoneidad *f*

fitting¹ [ˈfɪtɪŋ] *adj* : adecuado, apropiado

fitting² *n* : accesorio *m*

five¹ [ˈfaɪv] *adj* : cinco

five² *n* : cinco *m*

five hundred¹ *adj* : quinientos

five hundred² *n* : quinientos *m*

fix¹ [ˈfɪks] *vt* **1** ATTACH, SECURE : sujetar, asegurar, fijar **2** ESTABLISH : fijar, concretar, establecer **3** REPAIR : arreglar, reparar **4** PREPARE : preparar ⟨to fix dinner : preparar la cena⟩ **5** : arreglar, amañar ⟨to fix a race : arreglar una carrera⟩ **6** RIVET : fijar (los ojos, la mirada, etc.)

fix² *n* **1** PREDICAMENT : aprieto *m*, apuro *m* **2** : posición *f* ⟨to get a fix on : establecer la posición de⟩

fixate [ˈfɪkˌseɪt] *vi* **-ated; -ating** : obsesionarse

fixation [fɪkˈseɪʃən] *n* : fijación *f*, obsesión *f*

fixed [ˈfɪkst] *adj* **1** STATIONARY : estacionario, inmóvil **2** UNCHANGING : fijo, inalterable **3** INTENT : fijo ⟨a fixed stare : una mirada fija⟩ **4 to be comfortably fixed** : estar en posición acomodada

fixedly [ˈfɪksədli] *adv* : fijamente

fixedness [ˈfɪksədnəs, ˈfɪkst-] *n* : rigidez *f*

fixture [ˈfɪkstʃər] *n* **1** : parte *f* integrante, elemento *m* fijo **2 fixtures** *npl* : instalaciones *fpl* (de una casa)

fizz¹ [ˈfɪz] *vi* : burbujear

fizz² *n* : efervescencia *f*, burbujeo *m*

fizzle¹ [ˈfɪzəl] *vi* **-zled; -zling 1** FIZZ : burbujear **2** FAIL : fracasar

fizzle² *n* : fracaso *m*, fiasco *m*

fjord [fiˈɔrd] *n* : fiordo *m*

flab [ˈflæb] *n* : gordura *f*

flabbergast [ˈflæbərˌgæst] *vt* : asombrar, pasmar, dejar atónito

flabby [ˈflæbi] *adj* **-bier; -est** : blando, fofo, aguado *CA, Col, Mex*

flaccid [ˈflæksəd, ˈflæsəd] *adj* : fláccido

flag¹ [ˈflæg] *vi* **flagged; flagging 1** : hacer señales con banderas **2** WEAKEN : flaquear, desfallecer

flag² *n* : bandera *f*, pabellón *m*, estandarte *m*

flagon [ˈflægən] *n* : jarra *f* grande

flagpole [ˈflægˌpoːl] *n* : asta *f*, mástil *m*

flagrant [ˈfleɪgrənt] *adj* : flagrante — **flagrantly** *adv*

flagship [ˈflægˌʃɪp] *n* : buque *m* insignia

flagstaff [ˈflægˌstæf] → **flagpole**

flagstone [ˈflægˌstoːn] *n* : losa *f*, piedra *f*

flail¹ [ˈfleɪl] *vt* **1** : trillar (grano) **2** : sacudir, agitar (los brazos)

flail² *n* : mayal *m*

flair [ˈflær] *n* : don *m*, facilidad *f*

flak [ˈflæk] *ns & pl* **1** : fuego *m* antiaéreo **2** CRITICISM : críticas *fpl*

flake¹ [ˈfleɪk] *vi* **flaked; flaking** : desmenuzarse, pelarse (dícese de la piel)

flake² *n* : copo *m* (de nieve), escama *f* (de la piel), astilla *f* (de madera)

flamboyance [flæmˈbɔɪənʦ] *n* : extravagancia *f*, rimbombancia *f*

flamboyant [flæmˈbɔɪənt] *adj* : exuberante, extravagante, rimbombante

flame¹ [ˈfleɪm] *vi* **flamed; flaming 1** BLAZE : arder, llamear **2** GLOW : brillar, encenderse

flame² *n* BLAZE : llama *f* ⟨to burst into flames : estallar en llamas⟩ ⟨to go up in flame : incendiarse⟩

flamethrower [ˈfleɪmˌθroːər] *n* : lanzallamas *m*

flamingo [fləˈmɪŋgo] *n*, *pl* **-gos** : flamenco *m*

flammable [ˈflæməbəl] *adj* : inflamable, flamable

flange [ˈflænʤ] *n* : reborde *m*, pestaña *f*

flank¹ [ˈflæŋk] *vt* **1** : flanquear (para defender o atacar) **2** BORDER, LINE : bordear

flank² *n* : ijada *f* (de un animal), costado *m* (de una persona), falda *f* (de una colina), flanco *m* (en un cuerpo de soldados)

flannel [ˈflænəl] *n* : franela *f*

flap¹ [ˈflæp] *v* **flapped; flapping** *vi* **1** : aletear ⟨the bird was flapping (its wings) : el pájaro aleteaba⟩ **2** FLUTTER : ondear, agitarse — *vt* : batir, agitar

flap² *n* **1** FLAPPING : aleteo *m*, aletazo *m* (de alas) **2** : soplada *f* (de un sobre), hoja *f* (de una mesa), faldón *m* (de una chaqueta)

flapjack [ˈflæpˌʤæk] → **pancake**

flare¹ [ˈflær] *vi* **flared; flaring 1** FLAME, SHINE : llamear, brillar **2 to flare up** : estallar, explotar (de cólera)

flare² *n* **1** FLASH : destello *m* **2** SIGNAL : (luz *f* de) bengala *f* **3 solar flare** : erupción *f* solar

flash¹ [ˈflæʃ] *vi* **1** SHINE, SPARKLE : destellar, brillar, relampaguear **2** : pasar como un relámpago ⟨an idea flashed through my mind : una idea me cruzó la mente como un relámpago⟩ — *vt* : despedir, lanzar (una luz), transmitir (un mensaje)

flash² *adj* SUDDEN : repentino

flash³ *n* **1** : destello *m* (de luz), fogonazo *m* (de una explosión) **2 flash of lightning** : relámpago *m* **3 in a flash** : de repente, de un abrir y cerrar los ojos

flashback ['flæʃˌbæk] *n* : flashback *m*

flashiness ['flæʃinəs] *n* : ostentación *f*

flashlight ['flæʃˌlaɪt] *n* : linterna *f*

flashy ['flæʃi] *adj* **flashier; -est** : llamativo, ostentoso

flask ['flæsk] *n* : frasco *m*

flat¹ ['flæt] *vt* **flatted; flatting 1** FLATTEN : aplanar, achatar **2** : bajar de tono (en música)

flat² *adv* **1** EXACTLY : exactamente ⟨in ten minutes flat : en diez minutos exactos⟩ **2** : desafinado, demasiado bajo (en la música)

flat³ *adj* **flatter; flattest 1** EVEN, LEVEL : plano, llano **2** SMOOTH : liso **3** DEFINITE : categórico, rotundo, explícito ⟨a flat refusal : una negativa categórica⟩ **4** DULL : aburrido, soso, monótono (dícese la voz) **5** DEFLATED : desinflado, pinchado, ponchado *Mex* **6** : bemol (en música) ⟨to sing flat : cantar desafinado⟩

flat⁴ *n* **1** PLAIN : llano *m*, terreno *m* llano **2** : bemol *m* (en la música) **3** APARTMENT : apartamento *m*, departamento *m* **4** *or* **flat tire** : pinchazo *m*, ponchadura *f Mex*

flatbed ['flætˌbɛd] *n* : camión *m* de plataforma

flatcar ['flætˌkɑr] *n* : vagón *m* abierto

flatfish ['flætˌfɪʃ] *n* : platija *f*

flat–footed ['flætˌfʊṭəd, ˌflæt'-] *adj* : de pies planos

flatly ['flætli] *adv* DEFINITELY : categóricamente, rotundamente

flatness ['flætnəs] *n* **1** EVENNESS : lo llano, lisura *f*, uniformidad *f* **2** DULLNESS : monotonía *f*

flat–out ['flæt'aʊt] *adj* **1** : frenético, a toda máquina ⟨a flat-out effort : un esfuerzo frenético⟩ **2** CATEGORICAL : descarado, rotundo, categórico

flatten ['flætən] *vt* : aplanar, achatar

flatter ['flætər] *vt* **1** OVERPRAISE : adular **2** COMPLIMENT : halagar **3** : favorecer ⟨the photo flatters you : la foto te favorece⟩

flatterer ['flætərər] *n* : adulador *m*, -dora *f*

flattering ['flætərɪŋ] *adj* **1** COMPLIMENTARY : halagador **2** BECOMING : favorecedor

flattery ['flætəri] *n, pl* **-ries** : halagos *mpl*

flatulence ['flætʃələn*ts*] *n* : flatulencia *f*, ventosidad *f*

flatulent ['flætʃələnt] *adj* : flatulento

flatware ['flætˌwær] *n* : cubertería *f*, cubiertos *mpl*

flaunt¹ ['flɔnt] *vt* : alardear, hacer alarde de

flaunt² *n* : alarde *m*, ostentación *f*

flavor¹ ['fleɪvər] *vt* : dar sabor a, sazonar

flavor² *n* **1** : gusto *m*, sabor *m* **2** FLAVORING : sazón *f*, condimento *m*

flavorful ['fleɪvərfəl] *adj* : sabroso

flavoring ['fleɪvərɪŋ] *n* : condimento *m*, sazón *f*

flavorless ['fleɪvərləs] *adj* : sin sabor

flaw ['flɔ] *n* : falla *f*, defecto *m*, imperfección *f*

flawed ['flɔd] *adj* : imperfecto, con defectos

flawless ['flɔləs] *adj* : impecable, perfecto — **flawlessly** *adv*

flax ['flæks] *n* : lino *m*

flaxen ['flæksən] *adj* : rubio, blondo (dícese del pelo)

flay ['fleɪ] *vt* **1** SKIN : desollar, despellejar **2** VILIFY : criticar con dureza, vilipendiar

flea ['fli:] *n* : pulga *f*

fleck¹ ['flɛk] *vt* : salpicar

fleck² *n* : mota *f*, pinta *f*

fledgling ['flɛʤlɪŋ] *n* : polluelo *m*, pollito *m*

flee ['fli:] *v* **fled** ['flɛd]; **fleeing** *vi* : huir, escapar(se) — *vt* : huir de

fleece¹ ['fli:s] *vt* **fleeced; fleecing 1** SHEAR : esquilar, trasquilar **2** SWINDLE : estafar, defraudar

fleece² *n* : lana *f*, vellón *m*

fleet¹ ['fli:t] *vi* : moverse con rapidez

fleet² *adj* SWIFT : rápido, veloz

fleet³ *n* : flota *f*

fleet admiral *n* : almirante *mf*

fleeting ['fli:tɪŋ] *adj* : fugaz, breve

flesh ['flɛʃ] *n* **1** : carne *f* (de seres humanos y animales) **2** : pulpa *f* (de frutas)

flesh out *vt* : desarrollar, darle cuerpo a

fleshy ['flɛʃi] *adj* **fleshier; -est** : gordo (dícese de las personas), carnoso (dícese de la fruta)

flew → **fly**

flex ['flɛks] *vt* : doblar, flexionar

flexibility [ˌflɛksə'bɪləṭi] *n, pl* **-ties** : flexibilidad *f*, elasticidad *f*

flexible ['flɛksəbəl] *adj* : flexible — **flexibly** [-bli] *adv*

flick¹ ['flɪk] *vt* : dar un capirotazo a (con el dedo) ⟨to flick a switch : darle al interruptor⟩ — *vi* **1** FLIT : revolotear **2 to flick through** : hojear (un libro)

flick² *n* : coletazo *m* (de una cola), capirotazo *m* (de un dedo)

flicker¹ ['flɪkər] *vi* **1** FLUTTER : revolotear, aletear **2** BLINK, TWINKLE : parpadear, titilar

flicker² *n* **1** : parpadeo *m*, titileo *m* **2** HINT, TRACE : indicio *m*, rastro *m* ⟨a flicker of hope : un rayo de esperanza⟩

flier ['flaɪər] *n* **1** AVIATOR : aviador *m*, -dora *f* **2** CIRCULAR : folleto *m* publicitario, circular *f*

flight ['flaɪt] *n* **1** : vuelo *m* (de aves o aviones), trayectoria *f* (de proyectiles) **2** TRIP : vuelo *m* **3** FLOCK, SQUADRON : bandada *f* (de pájaros), escuadrilla *f* (de aviones) **4** ESCAPE : huida *f*, fuga *f* **5 flight of fancy** : ilusiones *fpl*, fantasía *f* **6 flight of stairs** : tramo *m*

flight attendant *n* : auxiliar *mf* de vuelo

flightless ['flaɪtləs] *adj* : no volador

flighty ['flaɪt̬i] *adj* **flightier; -est** : caprichoso, frívolo

flimsy [flɪmzi] *adj* **flimsier; -est 1** LIGHT, THIN : ligero, fino **2** WEAK : endeble, poco sólido **3** IMPLAUSIBLE : pobre, flojo, poco convincente ⟨a flimsy excuse : una excusa floja⟩

flinch ['flɪntʃ] *vi* **1** WINCE : estremecerse **2** RECOIL : recular, retroceder

fling¹ ['flɪŋ] *vt* **flung** ['flʌŋ]; **flinging 1** THROW : lanzar, tirar, arrojar **2 to fling oneself** : lanzarse, tirarse, precipitarse

fling² *n* **1** THROW : lanzamiento *m* **2** ATTEMPT : intento *m* **3** AFFAIR : aventura *f* **4** BINGE : juerga *f*

flint ['flɪnt] *n* : pedernal *m*

flinty ['flɪnti] *adj* **flintier; -est 1** : de pedernal **2** STERN, UNYIELDING : severo, inflexible

flip¹ ['flɪp] *v* **flipped; flipping** *vt* **1** TOSS : tirar ⟨to flip a coin : echar a cara o cruz⟩ **2** OVERTURN : dar la vuelta a, voltear — *vi* **1** : moverse bruscamente **2 to flip through** : hojear (un libro)

flip² *adj* : insolente, descarado

flip³ *n* **1** FLICK : capirotazo *m*, golpe *m* ligero **2** SOMERSAULT : voltereta *f*

flip–flop ['flɪp‚flɑp] *n* **1** REVERSAL : giro *m* radical **2** THONG : chancla *f*, chancleta *f*

flippancy ['flɪpəntsi] *n*, *pl* **-cies** : ligereza *f*, falta *f* de seriedad

flippant ['flɪpənt] *adj* : ligero, frívolo, poco serio

flipper ['flɪpər] *n* : aleta *f*

flirt¹ ['flərt] *vi* **1** : coquetear, flirtear **2** TRIFLE : jugar ⟨to flirt with death : jugar con la muerte⟩

flirt² *n* : coqueto *m*, -ta *f*

flirtation [‚flər'teɪʃən] *n* : devaneo *m*, coqueteo *m*

flirtatious [‚flər'teɪʃəs] *adj* : insinuante, coqueto

flit ['flɪt] *vi* **flitted; flitting 1** : revolotear **2 to flit about** : ir y venir rápidamente

float¹ ['floːt] *vi* **1** : flotar **2** WANDER : vagar, errar — *vt* **1** : poner a flote, hacer flotar (un barco) **2** LAUNCH : hacer flotar (una empresa) **3** ISSUE : emitir (acciones en la bolsa)

float² *n* **1** : flotador *m*, corcho *m* (para pescar) **2** BUOY : boya *f* **3** : carroza *f* (en un desfile)

floating ['floːt̬ɪŋ] *adj* : flotante

flock¹ ['flɑk] *vi* **1** : moverse en rebaño **2** CONGREGATE : congregarse, reunirse

flock² *n* : rebaño *m* (de ovejas), bandada *f* (de pájaros)

floe ['floː] *n* : témpano *m* de hielo

flog ['flɑg] *vt* **flogged; flogging** : azotar, fustigar

flood¹ ['flʌd] *vt* : inundar, anegar

flood² *n* **1** INUNDATION : inundación *f* **2** TORRENT : avalancha *f*, diluvio *m*, torrente *m* ⟨a flood of tears : un mar de lágrimas⟩

floodlight ['flʌd‚laɪt] *n* : foco *m*

floodwater ['flʌd‚wɔt̬ər] *n* : crecida *f*, creciente *f*

floor¹ ['flor] *vt* **1** : solar, poner suelo a (una casa o una sala) **2** KNOCK DOWN : derribar, echar al suelo **3** NONPLUS : desconcertar, confundir, dejar perplejo

floor² *n* **1** : suelo *m*, piso *m* ⟨dance floor : pista de baile⟩ **2** STORY : piso *m*, planta *f* ⟨ground floor : planta baja⟩ ⟨second floor : primer piso⟩ **3** : mínimo *m* (de sueldos, precios, etc.)

floorboard ['flor‚bord] *n* : tabla *f* del suelo, suelo *m*, piso *m*

flooring ['florɪŋ] *n* : entarimado *m*

flop¹ ['flɑp] *vi* **flopped; flopping 1** FLAP : golpearse, agitarse **2** COLLAPSE : dejarse caer, desplomarse **3** FAIL : fracasar

flop² *n* **1** FAILURE : fracaso *m* **2 to take a flop** : caerse

floppy ['flɑpi] *adj* **-pier; -est 1** : blando, flexible **2 floppy disk** : diskette *m*, disquete *m*

flora ['florə] *n* : flora *f*

floral ['florəl] *adj* : floral, floreado

florid ['florɪd] *adj* **1** FLOWERY : florido **2** REDDISH : rojizo

florist ['florɪst] *n* : florista *mf*

floss¹ ['flɔs] *vi* : limpiarse los dientes con hilo dental

floss² *n* **1** : hilo *m* de seda (de bordar) **2** → **dental floss**

flotation [floˈteɪʃən] *n* : flotación *f*

flotilla [floˈtɪlə] *n* : flotilla *f*

flotsam ['flɑtsəm] *n* **1** : restos *mpl* flotantes (en el mar) **2 flotsam and jetsam** : desechos *mpl*, restos *mpl*

flounce¹ ['flaʊnts] *vi* **flounced; flouncing** : moverse haciendo aspavientos ⟨she flounced into the room : entró en la sala haciendo aspavientos⟩

flounce² *n* **1** RUFFLE : volante *m* **2** FLOURISH : aspaviento *m*

flounder¹ ['flaʊndər] *vi* **1** STRUGGLE : forcejear **2** STUMBLE : no saber qué hacer o decir, perder el hilo (en un discurso)

flounder² *n*, *pl* **flounder** *or* **flounders** : platija *f*

flour¹ ['flaʊər] *vt* : enharinar

flour² *n* : harina *f*

flourish¹ ['flərɪʃ] *vi* THRIVE : florecer, prosperar, crecer (dícese de las plantas) — *vt* BRANDISH : blandir

flourish² *n* : floritura *f*, floreo *m*

flourishing ['flərɪʃɪŋ] *adj* : floreciente, próspero

flout ['flaʊt] *vt* : desacatar, burlarse de

flow¹ ['floː] *vi* **1** COURSE : fluir, manar, correr **2** CIRCULATE : circular, correr ⟨traffic is flowing smoothly : el tránsito está circulando con fluidez⟩

flow² *n* **1** FLOWING : flujo *m*, circulación *f* **2** STREAM : corriente *f*, chorro *m*

flower¹ ['flaʊər] *vi* : florecer, florear

flower² *n* : flor *f*

flowered ['flaʊərd] *adj* : florido, floreado

floweriness ['flaʊərinəs] *n* : floritura *f*

flowering¹ ['flaʊərɪŋ] *adj* : floreciente

flowering² *n* : floración *f*, florecimiento *m*

flowerpot ['flaʊər,pɑt] *n* : maceta *f*, tiesto *m*, macetero *m*

flowery ['flaʊəri] *adj* **1** : florido **2** FLOWERED : floreado, de flores

flowing ['flo:ɪŋ] *adj* : fluido, corriente

flown → **fly**

flu ['flu:] *n* : gripe *f*, gripa *f Col, Mex*

fluctuate ['flʌktʃʊ,eɪt] *vi* **-ated; -ating** : fluctuar

fluctuation [,flʌktʃʊ'eɪʃən] *n* : fluctuación *f*

flue ['flu:] *n* : tiro *m*, salida *f* de humos

fluency ['flu:əntsi] *n* : fluidez *f*, soltura *f*

fluent ['flu:ənt] *adj* : fluido

fluently ['flu:əntli] *adv* : con soltura, con fluidez

fluff¹ ['flʌf] *vt* **1** : mullir ⟨to fluff up the pillows : mullir las almohadas⟩ **2** BUNGLE : echar a perder, equivocarse

fluff² *n* **1** FUZZ : pelusa *f* **2** DOWN : plumón *m*

fluffy ['flʌfi] *adj* **fluffier; -est 1** DOWNY : lleno de pelusa, velloso **2** SPONGY : esponjoso

fluid¹ ['flu:ɪd] *adj* : fluido

fluid² *n* : fluido *m*, líquido *m*

fluidity [flu'ɪdəṭi] *n* : fluidez *f*

fluid ounce *n* : onza *f* líquida (29.57 mililitros)

fluke ['flu:k] *n* : golpe *m* de suerte, chiripa *f*, casualidad *f*

flung → **fling**

flunk ['flʌŋk] *vt* FAIL : reprobar — *vi* : salir reprobando

fluorescence [,flʊr'ɛsənts, ,flɔr-] *n* : fluorescencia *f*

fluorescent [,flʊr'ɛsənt, ,flɔr-] *adj* : fluorescente

fluoridate ['flɔrə,deɪt, 'flʊr-] *vt* **-dated; -dating** : fluorizar

fluoridation [,flɔrə'deɪʃən, ,flʊr-] *n* : fluorización *f*, fluoración *f*

fluoride ['flɔr,aɪd, 'flʊr-] *n* : fluoruro *m*

fluorine ['flʊr,i:n] *n* : flúor *m*

fluorocarbon [,flʊro'karbən, ,flʊr-] *n* : fluorocarbono *m*

flurry ['fləri] *n, pl* **-ries 1** GUST : ráfaga *f* **2** SNOWFALL : nevisca *f* **3** BUSTLE : frenesí *m*, bullicio *m* **4** BARRAGE : aluvión *m*, oleada *f* ⟨a flurry of questions : un aluvión de preguntas⟩

flush¹ ['flʌʃ] *vt* **1** : limpiar con agua ⟨to flush the toilet : jalar la cadena⟩ **2** RAISE : hacer salir, levantar (en la caza) — *vi* BLUSH : ruborizarse, sonrojarse

flush² *adv* : al mismo nivel, a ras

flush³ *adj* **1** *or* **flushed** ['flʌʃt] : colorado, rojo, encendido (dícese de la cara) **2** FILLED : lleno a rebosar **3** ABUNDANT : copioso, abundante **4** AFFLUENT : adinerado **5** ALIGNED, SMOOTH : alineado, liso **6** flush against : pegado a, contra

flush⁴ *n* **1** FLOW, JET : chorro *m*, flujo *m* rápido **2** SURGE : arrebato *m*, arranque *m* ⟨a flush of anger : un arrebato de cólera⟩ **3** BLUSH : rubor *m*, sonrojo *m* **4** GLOW : resplandor *m*, flor *f* ⟨the flush of youth : la flor de la juventud⟩ ⟨in the flush of victory : en la euforia del triunfo⟩

fluster¹ ['flʌstər] *vt* : poner nervioso, aturdir

fluster² *n* : agitación *f*, confusión *f*

flute ['flu:t] *n* : flauta *f*

fluted ['flu:ṭəd] *adj* **1** GROOVED : estriado, acanalado **2** WAVY : ondulado

fluting ['flu:ṭɪŋ] *n* : estrías *fpl*

flutist ['flu:ṭɪst] *n* : flautista *mf*

flutter¹ ['flʌṭər] *vi* **1** : revolotear (dícese de un pájaro), ondear (dícese de una bandera), palpitar con fuerza (dícese del corazón) **2 to flutter about** : ir y venir, revolotear — *vt* : sacudir, batir

flutter² *n* **1** FLUTTERING : revoloteo *m*, aleteo *m* **2** COMMOTION, STIR : revuelo *m*, agitación *f*

flux ['flʌks] *n* **1** : flujo *m* (en física y medicina) **2** CHANGE : cambio *m* ⟨to be in a state of flux : estar cambiando continuamente⟩

fly¹ ['flaɪ] *v* **flew** ['flu:]; **flown** ['flo:n]; **flying** *vi* **1** : volar (dícese de los pájaros, etc.) **2** TRAVEL : volar (dícese de los aviones), ir en avión (dícese de los pasajeros) **3** FLOAT : flotar, ondear **4** FLEE : huir, escapar **5** RUSH : correr, irse volando **6** PASS : pasar (volando) ⟨how time flies! : ¡cómo pasa el tiempo!⟩ **7 to fly open** : abrir de golpe — *vt* : pilotar (un avión), hacer volar (una cometa)

fly² *n, pl* **flies 1** : mosca *f* ⟨to drop like flies : caer como moscas⟩ **2** : bragueta *f* (de pantalones, etc.)

flyer → **flier**

flying saucer *n* : platillo *m* volador

flypaper ['flaɪ,peɪpər] *n* : papel *m* matamoscas

flyspeck ['flaɪ,spɛk] *n* **1** : excremento *m* de mosca **2** SPECK : motita *f*, puntito *m*

flyswatter ['flaɪ,swɑṭər] *n* : matamoscas *m*

flywheel ['flaɪ,hwi:l] *n* : volante *m*

foal¹ ['fo:l] *vi* : parir

foal² *n* : potro *m*, -tra *f*

foam¹ ['fo:m] *vi* : hacer espuma

foam² *n* : espuma *f*

foamy ['fo:mi] *adj* **foamier; -est** : espumoso

focal ['fo:kəl] *adj* **1** : focal, central **2 focal point** : foco *m*, punto *m* de referencia

fo'c'sle ['fo:ksəl] → **forecastle**

focus[1] [ˈfoːkəs] v -cused or -cussed; -cusing or -cussing vt 1 : enfocar (un instrumento) 2 CONCENTRATE : concentrar, centrar — vi : enfocar, fijar la vista

focus[2] n, pl -ci [ˈfoːˌsaɪ, -ˌkaɪ] 1 : foco m ⟨to be in focus : estar enfocado⟩ 2 FOCUSING : enfoque m 3 CENTER : centro m, foco m

fodder [ˈfɑdər] n : pienso m, forraje m

foe [ˈfoː] n : enemigo m, -ga f

fog[1] [ˈfɔg, ˈfɑg] v fogged; fogging vt : empañar — vi to fog up : empañarse

fog[2] n : niebla f, neblina f

foggy [ˈfɔgi, ˈfɑ-] adj foggier; -est : nebuloso, brumoso

foghorn [ˈfɔgˌhɔrn, ˈfɑg-] n : sirena f de niebla

fogy [ˈfoːgi] n, pl -gies : carca mf fam, persona f chapada a la antigua

foible [ˈfɔɪbəl] n : flaqueza f, debilidad f

foil[1] [ˈfɔɪl] vt : frustrar, hacer fracasar

foil[2] n 1 : lámina f de metal, papel m de aluminio 2 CONTRAST : contraste m, complemento m 3 SWORD : florete m (en esgrima)

foist [ˈfɔɪst] vt : encajar, endilgar fam, colocar

fold[1] [ˈfoːld] vt 1 BEND : doblar, plegar 2 CLASP : cruzar (brazos), enlazar (manos), plegar (alas) 3 EMBRACE : estrechar, abrazar 4 to fold in : incorporar ⟨fold in the cream : incorpore la crema⟩ — vi 1 FAIL : fracasar 2 to fold up : doblarse, plegarse

fold[2] n 1 SHEEPFOLD : redil m (para ovejas) 2 FLOCK : rebaño m ⟨to return to the fold : volver al redil⟩ 3 CREASE : pliegue m, doblez m

folder [ˈfoːldər] n 1 CIRCULAR : circular f, folleto m 2 BINDER : carpeta f

foliage [ˈfoːliɪʤ, -liʤ] n : follaje m

folio [ˈfoːliˌoː] n, pl -lios : folio m

folk[1] [ˈfoːk] adj : popular, folklórico ⟨folk customs : costumbres populares⟩ ⟨folk dance : danza folklórica⟩

folk[2] n, pl folk or folks 1 PEOPLE : gente f 2 folks npl : familia f, padres mpl

folklore [ˈfoːkˌlor] n : folklore m

folklorist [ˈfoːkˌlorɪst] n : folklorista mf

folksy [ˈfoːksi] adj folksier; -est : campechano

follicle [ˈfɑlɪkəl] n : folículo m

follow [ˈfɑlo] vt 1 : seguir ⟨follow the guide : siga al guía⟩ ⟨she followed the road : siguió el camino, continuó por el camino⟩ 2 PURSUE : perseguir, seguir 3 OBEY : seguir, cumplir, observar 4 UNDERSTAND : entender — vi 1 : seguir 2 UNDERSTAND : entender 3 it follows that ... : se deduce que ...

follower [ˈfɑloər] n : seguidor m, -dora f

following[1] [ˈfɑloɪŋ] adj NEXT : siguiente

following[2] n FOLLOWERS : seguidores mpl

following[3] prep AFTER : después de

follow through vi to follow through with : continuar con, realizar

follow up vt : seguir (una sugerencia, etc.), investigar (una huella)

folly [ˈfɑli] n, pl -lies : locura f, desatino m

foment [foˈmɛnt] vt : fomentar

fond [ˈfɑnd] adj 1 LOVING : cariñoso, tierno 2 PARTIAL : aficionado 3 FERVENT : ferviente, fervoroso

fondle [ˈfɑndəl] vt -dled; -dling : acariciar

fondly [ˈfɑndli] adv : cariñosamente, afectuosamente

fondness [ˈfɑndnəs] n 1 LOVE : cariño m 2 LIKING : afición f

fondue [fɑnˈduː, -ˈdjuː] n : fondue f

font [ˈfɑnt] n 1 or baptismal font : pila f bautismal 2 FOUNTAIN : fuente f

food [ˈfuːd] n : comida f, alimento m

food chain n : cadena f alimenticia

foodstuffs [ˈfuːdˌstʌfs] npl : comestibles mpl

fool[1] [ˈfuːl] vi 1 JOKE : bromear, hacer el tonto 2 TOY : jugar, juguetear ⟨don't fool with the computer : no juegues con la computadora⟩ 3 to fool around : perder el tiempo ⟨he fools around instead of working : pierde el tiempo en vez de trabajar⟩ — vt DECEIVE : engañar, burlar

fool[2] n 1 IDIOT : idiota mf; tonto m, -ta f; bobo m, -ba f 2 JESTER : bufón m, -fona f

foolhardiness [ˈfuːlˌhardinəs] n : imprudencia f

foolhardy [ˈfuːlˌhardi] adj RASH : imprudente, temerario, precipitado

foolish [ˈfuːlɪʃ] adj 1 STUPID : insensato, estúpido 2 SILLY : idiota, tonto

foolishly [ˈfuːlɪʃli] adv : tontamente

foolishness [ˈfuːlɪʃnəs] n : insensatez f, estupidez f, tontería f

foolproof [ˈfuːlˌpruːf] adj : infalible

foot [ˈfʊt] n, pl feet [ˈfiːt] : pie m

footage [ˈfʊtɪʤ] n : medida f en pies, metraje m (en el cine)

football [ˈfʊtˌbɔl] n : futbol m americano, fútbol m americano

footbridge [ˈfʊtˌbrɪʤ] n : pasarela f, puente m peatonal

foothills [ˈfʊtˌhɪlz] npl : estribaciones fpl

foothold [ˈfʊtˌhoːld] n 1 : punto m de apoyo 2 to gain a foothold : afianzarse en una posición

footing [ˈfʊtɪŋ] n 1 BALANCE : equilibrio m 2 FOOTHOLD : punto m de apoyo 3 BASIS : base f ⟨on an equal footing : en igualdad⟩

footlights [ˈfʊtˌlaɪts] npl : candilejas fpl

footlocker [ˈfʊtˌlakər] n : baúl m pequeño, cofre m

footloose [ˈfʊtˌluːs] adj : libre y sin compromiso

footman [ˈfʊtmən] n, pl -men [-mən, -ˌmɛn] : lacayo m

footnote [ˈfʊtˌnoːt] n : nota f al pie de la página

footpath [ˈfʊtˌpæθ] n : sendero m, senda f, vereda f

footprint ['fʊt,prɪnt] *n* : huella *f*
footrace ['fʊt,reɪs] *n* : carrera *f* pedestre
footrest ['fʊt,rɛst] *n* : apoyapiés *m*, reposapiés *m*
footstep ['fʊt,stɛp] *n* 1 STEP : paso *m* 2 FOOTPRINT : huella *f*
footstool ['fʊt,stu:l] *n* : taburete *m*, escabel *m*
footwear ['fʊt,wær] *n* : calzado *m*
footwork ['fʊt,wərk] *n* : juego *m* de piernas, juego *m* de pies
fop ['fɑp] *n* : petimetre *m*, dandi *m*
for¹ ['fɔr] *conj* : puesto que, porque
for² *prep* 1 (*indicating purpose*) : para, de ⟨clothes for children : ropa para niños⟩ ⟨it's time for dinner : es la hora de comer⟩ 2 BECAUSE OF : por ⟨for fear of : por miedo de⟩ 3 (*indicating a recipient*) : para, por ⟨a gift for you : un regalo para ti⟩ 4 (*indicating support*) : por ⟨he fought for his country : luchó por su patria⟩ 5 (*indicating a goal*) : por, para ⟨a cure for cancer : una cura para el cáncer⟩ ⟨for your own good : por tu propio bien⟩ 6 (*indicating correspondence or exchange*) : por, para ⟨I bought it for $5 : lo compré por $5⟩ ⟨a lot of trouble for nothing : mucha molestia para nada⟩ 7 AS FOR : para, con respecto a 8 (*indicating duration*) : durante, por ⟨he's going for two years : se va por dos años⟩ ⟨I spoke for ten minutes : hablé (durante) diez minutos⟩ ⟨she has known it for three months : lo sabe desde hace tres meses⟩
forage¹ ['fɔrɪdʒ] *v* **-aged; -aging** *vi* : hurgar (en busca de alimento) — *vt* : buscar (provisiones)
forage² *n* : forraje *m*
foray ['fɔr,eɪ] *n* : incursión *f*
forbear¹ [fɔr'bær] *vi* **-bore** [-'bor]; **-borne** [-'born]; **-bearing** 1 ABSTAIN : abstenerse 2 : tener paciencia
forbear² → forbear
forbearance [fɔr'bærənts] *n* 1 ABSTAINING : abstención *f* 2 PATIENCE : paciencia *f*
forbid [fər'bɪd] *vt* **-bade** [-'bæd, -'beɪd]; **-bidden** [-'bɪdən]; **-bidding** 1 PROHIBIT : prohibir 2 PREVENT : impedir
forbidding [fər'bɪdɪŋ] *adj* 1 IMPOSING : imponente 2 DISAGREEABLE : desagradable, ingrato 3 GRIM : severo
force¹ ['fors] *vt* **forced; forcing** 1 COMPEL : obligar, forzar 2 : forzar ⟨to force open the window : forzar la ventana⟩ ⟨to force a lock : forzar una cerradura⟩ 3 IMPOSE : imponer, obligar
force² *n* 1 : fuerza *f* 2 **by force** : por la fuerza 3 **in force** : en vigor, en vigencia
forced ['forst] *adj* : forzado, forzoso
forceful ['forsfəl] *adj* : fuerte, energético, contundente
forcefully ['forsfəli] *adv* : con energía, con fuerza
forcefulness ['forsfəlnəs] *n* : contundencia *f*, fuerza *f*

forceps ['fɔrsəps, -,sɛps] *ns & pl* : fórceps *m*
forcible ['forsəbəl] *adj* 1 FORCED : forzoso 2 CONVINCING : contundente, convincente — **forcibly** [-bli] *adv*
ford¹ ['ford] *vt* : vadear
ford² *n* : vado *m*
fore¹ ['for] *adv* 1 FORWARD : hacia adelante 2 **fore and aft** : de popa a proa
fore² *adj* 1 FORWARD : delantero, de adelante 2 FORMER : anterior
fore³ *n* 1 : frente *m*, delantera *f* 2 **to come to the fore** : empezar a destacar, saltar a primera plana
fore-and-aft ['forən'æft, -ənd-] *adj* : longitudinal
forearm ['for,ɑrm] *n* : antebrazo *m*
forebear ['for,bær] *n* : antepasado *m*, -da *f*
foreboding [for'bo:dɪŋ] *n* : premonición *f*, presentimiento *m*
forecast¹ ['for,kæst] *vt* **-cast; -casting** : pronosticar, predecir
forecast² *n* : predicción *f*, pronóstico *m*
forecastle ['fo:ksəl] *n* : castillo *m* de proa
foreclose [for'klo:z] *vt* **-closed; -closing** : ejecutar (una hipoteca)
forefather ['for,fɑðər] *n* : antepasado *m*, ancestro *m*
forefinger ['for,fɪŋgər] *n* : índice *m*, dedo *m* índice
forefoot ['for,fʊt] *n* : pata *f* delantera
forefront ['for,frʌnt] *n* : frente *m*, vanguardia *f* ⟨in the forefront : a la vanguardia⟩
forego [for'go:] *vt* **-went; -gone; -going** 1 PRECEDE : preceder 2 → forgo
foregoing [for'go:ɪŋ] *adj* : precedente, anterior
foregone [for'gɔn] *adj* : previsto ⟨a foregone conclusion : un resultado inevitable⟩
foreground ['for,graʊnd] *n* : primer plano *m*
forehand¹ ['for,hænd] *adj* : directo, derecho
forehand² *n* : golpe *m* del derecho
forehead ['forəd, 'for,hɛd] *n* : frente *f*
foreign ['forən] *adj* 1 : extranjero, exterior ⟨foreign countries : países extranjeros⟩ ⟨foreign trade : comercio exterior⟩ 2 ALIEN : ajeno, extraño ⟨foreign to their nature : ajeno a su carácter⟩ ⟨a foreign body : un cuerpo extraño⟩
foreigner ['forənər] *n* : extranjero *m*, -ra *f*
foreknowledge [for'nɑlɪdʒ] *n* : conocimiento *m* previo
foreleg ['for,lɛg] *n* : pata *f* delantera
foreman ['formən] *n*, *pl* **-men** [-mən, -,mɛn] : capataz *mf* ⟨foreman of the jury : presidente del jurado⟩
foremost¹ ['for,mo:st] *adv* : en primer lugar
foremost² *adj* : más importante, principal, grande
forenoon ['for,nu:n] *n* : mañana *m*

forensic [fə'rɛntsɪk] adj **1** RHETORICAL : retórico, de argumentación **2** : forense ⟨forensic medicine : medicina forense⟩

foreordain [ˌforɔr'deɪn] vt : predestinar, predeterminar

forequarter ['for̩kwɔrtər] n : cuarto m delantero

forerunner ['for̩rʌnər] n : precursor m, -sora f

foresee [for'si:] vt **-saw; -seen; -seeing** : prever

foreseeable [for'si:əbəl] adj : previsible ⟨in the foreseeable future : en el futuro inmediato⟩

foreshadow [for'ʃædo:] vt : anunciar, prefigurar

foresight ['for̩saɪt] n : previsión f

foresighted ['for̩saɪtəd] adj : previsto

forest ['fɔrəst] n : bosque m (en zonas templadas), selva f (en zonas tropicales)

forestall [for'stɔl] vt **1** PREVENT : prevenir, impedir **2** PREEMPT : adelantarse a

forested ['fɔrəstəd] adj : arbolado

forester ['fɔrəstər] n : silvicultor m, -tora f

forestland ['fɔrəst̩lænd] n : zona f boscosa

forest ranger → ranger

forestry ['fɔrəstri] n : silvicultura f, ingeniería f forestal

foreswear → forswear

foretaste¹ ['for̩teɪst] vt **-tasted; -tasting** : anticipar

foretaste² n : anticipo m

foretell [for'tɛl] vt **-told; -telling** : predecir, pronosticar, profetizar

forethought ['for̩θɔt] n : previsión f, reflexión f previa

forever [fɔr'ɛvər] adv **1** PERPETUALLY : para siempre, eternamente **2** CONTINUALLY : siempre, constantemente

forevermore [fɔr̩ɛvər'mor] adv : por siempre jamás

forewarn [for'wɔrn] vt : prevenir, advertir

foreword ['forwərd] n : prólogo m

forfeit¹ ['fɔrfət] vt : perder el derecho a

forfeit² n **1** FINE, PENALTY : multa f **2** : prenda f (en un juego)

forge¹ ['fordʒ] v **forged; forging** vt **1** : forjar (metal o un plan) **2** COUNTERFEIT : falsificar — vi **to forge ahead** : avanzar, seguir adelante

forge² n : forja f

forger ['fordʒər] n : falsificador m, -dora f

forgery ['fordʒəri] n, pl **-eries** : falsificación f

forget [fər'gɛt] v **-got** [-'gɑt]; **-gotten** [-'gɑtən] or **-got; -getting** vt : olvidar — vi **to forget about** : olvidarse de, no acordarse de

forgetful [fər'gɛtfəl] adj : olvidadizo

forget-me-not [fər'gɛtmi̩nɑt] n : nomeolvides mf

forgettable [fər'gɛtəbəl] adj : poco memorable

forgivable [fər'gɪvəbəl] adj : perdonable

forgive [fər'gɪv] vt **-gave** [-'geɪv]; **-given** [-'gɪvən]; **-giving** : perdonar

forgiveness [fər'gɪvnəs] n : perdón m

forgiving [fər'gɪvɪŋ] adj : indulgente, comprensivo, clemente

forgo or **forego** [for'go:] vt **-went; -gone; -going** : privarse de, renunciar a

fork¹ ['fɔrk] vi : ramificarse, bifurcarse — vt **1** : levantar (con un tenedor, una horca, etc.) **2 to fork over** : desembolsar

fork² n **1** : tenedor m (utensilio de cocina) **2** PITCHFORK : horca f, horquilla f **3** : bifurcación f (de un río o camino), horqueta f (de un árbol)

forked ['fɔrkt, 'fɔrkəd] adj : bífido, ahorquillado

forklift ['fɔrk̩lɪft] n : carretilla f elevadora

forlorn [fɔr'lɔrn] adj **1** DESOLATE : abandonado, desolado, desamparado **2** SAD : triste **3** DESPERATE : desesperado

forlornly [fɔr'lɔrnli] adv **1** SADLY : con tristeza **2** HALFHEARTEDLY : sin ánimo

form¹ ['fɔrm] vt **1** FASHION, MAKE : formar **2** DEVELOP : moldear, desarrollar **3** CONSTITUTE : constituir, formar **4** ACQUIRE : adquirir (un hábito), formar (una idea) — vi : tomar forma, formarse

form² n **1** SHAPE : forma f, figura f **2** MANNER : manera f, forma f **3** DOCUMENT : formulario m **4** : forma f ⟨in good form : en buena forma⟩ ⟨true to form : en forma consecuente⟩ **5** MOLD : molde m **6** KIND, VARIETY : clase f, tipo m **7** : forma f (en gramática) ⟨plural forms : formas plurales⟩

formal¹ ['fɔrməl] adj **1** CEREMONIOUS : formal, de etiqueta, ceremonioso **2** OFFICIAL : formal, oficial, de forma

formal² n **1** BALL : baile m formal, baile m de etiqueta **2** or **formal dress** : traje m de etiqueta

formaldehyde [fɔr'mældə̩haɪd] n : formaldehído m

formality [fɔr'mæləti] n, pl **-ties** : formalidad f

formalize ['fɔrmə̩laɪz] vt **-ized; -izing** : formalizar

formally ['fɔrməli] adv : formalmente

format¹ ['fɔr̩mæt] vt **-matted; -matting** : formatear

format² n : formato m

formation [fɔr'meɪʃən] n **1** FORMING : formación f **2** SHAPE : forma f **3 in formation** : en formación

formative ['fɔrmətɪv] adj : formativo

former ['fɔrmər] adj **1** PREVIOUS : antiguo, anterior ⟨the former president : el antiguo presidente⟩ **2** : primero (de dos)

formerly ['fɔrmərli] adv : anteriormente, antes

formidable ['fɔrmədəbəl, fɔr'mɪdə-] *adj*
: formidable — **formidably** *adv*
formless ['fɔrmləs] *adj* : informe, amorfo
formula ['fɔrmjələ] *n, pl* **-las** *or* **-lae** [-ˌliː, -ˌlaɪ] **1** : fórmula *f* **2** **baby formula** : preparado *m* para biberón
formulate ['fɔrmjəˌleɪt] *vt* **-lated; -lating** : formular, hacer
formulation [ˌfɔrmjə'leɪʃən] *n* : formulación *f*
fornicate ['fɔrnəˌkeɪt] *vi* **-cated; -cating** : fornicar
fornication [ˌfɔrnə'keɪʃən] *n* : fornicación *f*
forsake [fər'seɪk] *vt* **-sook** [-'sʊk]; **-saken** [-'seɪkən]; **-saking 1** ABANDON : abandonar, desamparar **2** RELINQUISH : renunciar a
forswear [fɔr'swær] *v* **-swore; -sworn; -swearing** *vt* RENOUNCE : renunciar a — *vi* : perjurar
forsythia [fər'sɪθiə] *n* : forsitia *f*
fort ['fɔrt] *n* **1** STRONGHOLD : fuerte *m*, fortaleza *f*, fortín *m* **2** BASE : base *f* militar
forte ['fɔrt, 'fɔrˌteɪ] *n* : fuerte *m*
forth ['fɔrθ] *adv* **1** : adelante ⟨from this day forth : de hoy en adelante⟩ **2 and so forth** : etcétera
forthcoming [forθ'kʌmɪŋ, 'fɔrθˌ-] *adj* **1** COMING : próximo **2** DIRECT, OPEN : directo, franco, comunicativo
forthright ['fɔrθˌraɪt] *adj* : directo, franco — **forthrightly** *adv*
forthrightness ['fɔrθˌraɪtnəs] *n* : franqueza *f*
forthwith [forθ'wɪθ, -'wɪð] *adv* : inmediatamente, en el acto, enseguida
fortieth¹ ['fɔrṭiəθ] *adj* : cuadragésimo
fortieth² *n* **1** : cuadragésimo *m*, -ma *f* (en una serie) **2** : cuarentavo *m*, cuarentava parte *f*
fortification [ˌfɔrṭəfə'keɪʃən] *n* : fortificación *f*
fortify ['fɔrṭəˌfaɪ] *vt* **-fied; -fying** : fortificar
fortitude ['fɔrṭəˌtuːd, -ˌtjuːd] *n* : fortaleza *f*, valor *m*
fortnight ['fɔrtˌnaɪt] *n* : quince días *mpl*, dos semanas *fpl*
fortnightly¹ ['fɔrtˌnaɪtli] *adv* : cada quince días
fortnightly² *adj* : quincenal
fortress ['fɔrtrəs] *n* : fortaleza *f*
fortuitous [fɔr'tuːəṭəs, -'tjuː-] *adj* : fortuito, accidental
fortunate ['fɔrtʃənət] *adj* : afortunado
fortunately ['fɔrtʃənətli] *adv* : afortunadamente, con suerte
fortune ['fɔrtʃən] *n* **1** : fortuna *f* ⟨to seek one's fortune : buscar uno su fortuna⟩ **2** LUCK : suerte *f*, fortuna *f* **3** DESTINY, FUTURE : destino *m*, buenaventura *f* **4** : dineral *m*, platal *m* ⟨she spent a fortune : se gastó un dineral⟩
fortune–teller ['fɔrtʃənˌtɛlər] *n* : adivino *m*, -na *f*

fortune–telling ['fɔrtʃənˌtɛlɪŋ] *n* : adivinación *f*
forty¹ ['fɔrṭi] *adj* : cuarenta
forty² *n, pl* **forties** : cuarenta *m*
forum ['fɔrəm] *n, pl* **-rums** : foro *m*
forward¹ ['fɔrwərd] *vt* **1** PROMOTE : promover, adelantar, fomentar **2** SEND : remitir, enviar
forward² *adv* **1** : adelante, hacia adelante ⟨to go forward : irse adelante⟩ **2 from this day forward** : de aquí en adelante
forward³ *adj* **1** : hacia adelante, delantero **2** BRASH : atrevido, descarado
forward⁴ *n* : delantero *m*, -ra *f* (en deportes)
forwarder ['fɔrwərdər] *n* : agencia *f* de transportes, agente *mf* expedidor
forwardness ['fɔrwərdnəs] *n* : atrevimiento *m*, descaro *m*
forwards ['fɔrwərdz] *adv* → **forward²**
fossil¹ ['fɑsəl] *adj* : fósil
fossil² *n* : fósil *m*
fossilize ['fɑsəˌlaɪz] *vt* **-ized; -izing** : fosilizar — *vi* : fosilizarse
foster¹ ['fɔstər] *vt* : promover, fomentar
foster² *adj* : adoptivo ⟨foster child : niño adoptivo⟩
fought → **fight**
foul¹ ['faʊl] *vi* : cometer faltas (en deportes) — *vt* **1** DIRTY, POLLUTE : contaminar, ensuciar **2** TANGLE : enredar
foul² *adv* **1** → **foully 2** : contra las reglas
foul³ *adj* **1** REPULSIVE : asqueroso, repugnante **2** CLOGGED : atascado, obstruido **3** TANGLED : enredado **4** OBSCENE : obsceno **5** BAD : malo ⟨foul weather : mal tiempo⟩ **6** : antirreglamentario (en deportes)
foul⁴ *n* : falta *f*, faul *m*
foully ['faʊli] *adv* : asquerosamente
foulmouthed ['faʊlˌmæʊːðd, -ˌmaʊθt] *adj* : malhablado
foulness ['faʊlnəs] *n* **1** DIRTINESS : suciedad *f* **2** INCLEMENCY : inclemencia *f* **3** OBSCENITY : obscenidad *f*, grosería *f*
foul play *n* : actos *mpl* criminales
foul–up ['faʊlˌʌp] *n* : lío *m*, confusión *f*, desastre *m*
foul up *vt* SPOIL : estropear, arruinar — *vi* BUNGLE : echar todo a perder
found¹ → **find**
found² ['faʊnd] *vt* : fundar, establecer
foundation [faʊn'deɪʃən] *n* **1** FOUNDING : fundación *f* **2** BASIS : fundamento *m*, base *f* **3** INSTITUTION : fundación *f* **4** : cimientos *mpl* (de un edificio)
founder¹ ['faʊndər] *vi* SINK : hundirse, irse a pique
founder² *n* : fundador *m*, -dora *f*
founding ['faʊndɪŋ] *adj* : fundador ⟨the founding fathers : los fundadores⟩
foundling ['faʊndlɪŋ] *n* : expósito *m*, -ta *f*
foundry ['faʊndri] *n, pl* **-dries** : fundición *f*

fount ['faʊnt] *n* SOURCE : fuente *f*, origen *m*

fountain ['faʊntən] *n* **1** SPRING : fuente *f*, manantial *m* **2** SOURCE : fuente *f*, origen *m* **3** JET : chorro *m* (de agua), surtidor *m*

fountain pen *n* : pluma *f* fuente

four[1] ['for] *adj* : cuatro

four[2] *n* **1** : cuatro *m* **2** on all fours : a gatas

fourfold ['for,fo:ld, -'fo:ld] *adj* : cuadruple

four hundred[1] *adj* : cuatrocientos

four hundred[2] *n* : cuatrocientos *m*

fourscore ['for'skor] *adj* EIGHTY : ochenta *m*

fourteen[1] [for'ti:n] *adj* : catorce

fourteen[2] *n* : catorce *m*

fourteenth[1] [for'ti:nθ] *adj* : decimocuarto

fourteenth[2] *n* **1** : decimocuarto *m*, -ta *f* (en una serie) **2** : catorceavo *m*, catorceava parte *f*

fourth[1] ['forθ] *adj* : cuarto

fourth[2] *n* **1** : cuarto *m*, -ta *f* (en una serie) **2** : cuarto *m*, cuarta parte *f*

fowl ['faʊl] *n*, *pl* **fowl** *or* **fowls 1** BIRD : ave *f* **2** CHICKEN : pollo *m*

fox[1] ['faks] *vt* **1** TRICK : engañar **2** BAFFLE : confundir

fox[2] *n*, *pl* **foxes** : zorro *m*, -ra *f*

foxglove ['faks,glʌv] *n* : dedalera *f*, digital *f*

foxhole ['faks,ho:l] *n* : hoyo *m* para atrincherarse, trinchera *f* individual

foxy ['faksi] *adj* **foxier; -est** SHREWD : astuto

foyer ['fɔɪər, 'fɔɪ,jeɪ] *n* : vestíbulo *m*

fracas ['freɪkəs, 'fræ-] *n*, *pl* **-cases** [-kəsəz] : altercado *m*, pelea *f*, reyerta *f*

fraction ['frækʃən] *n* **1** : fracción *f*, quebrado *m* **2** PORTION : porción *f*, parte *f*

fractional ['frækʃənəl] *adj* **1** : fraccionario **2** TINY : minúsculo, mínimo, insignificante

fractious ['frækʃəs] *adj* **1** UNRULY : rebelde **2** IRRITABLE : malhumorado, irritable

fracture[1] ['fræktʃər] *vt* **-tured; -turing** : fracturar

fracture[2] *n* **1** : fractura *f* (de un hueso) **2** CRACK : fisura *f*, grieta *f*, falla *f* (geológica)

fragile ['frædʒəl, -,dʒaɪl] *adj* : frágil

fragility [frə'dʒɪləti] *n*, *pl* **-ties** : fragilidad *f*

fragment[1] ['fræg,mɛnt] *vt* : fragmentar — *vi* : fragmentarse, hacerse añicos

fragment[2] ['frægmənt] *n* : fragmento *m*, trozo *m*, pedazo *m*

fragmentary ['frægmən,teri] *adj* : fragmentario, incompleto

fragmentation [,frægmən'teɪʃən, -,mn-] *n* : fragmentación *f*

fragrance⟩ ['freɪgrənts] *n* : fragancia *f*, aroma *m*

fragrant ['freɪgrənt] *adj* : fragante, aromático — **fragrantly** *adv*

frail ['freɪl] *adj* : débil, delicado

frailty ['freɪlti] *n*, *pl* **-ties** : debilidad *f*, flaqueza *f*

frame[1] ['freɪm] *vt* **framed; framing 1** FORMULATE : formular, elaborar **2** BORDER : enmarcar, encuadrar **3** INCRIMINATE : incriminar

frame[2] *n* **1** BODY : cuerpo *m* **2** : armazón *f* (de un edificio, un barco, o un avión), bastidor *m* (de un automóvil), cuadro *m* (de una bicicleta), marco *m* (de un cuadro, una ventana, una puerta, etc.) **3 frames** *npl* : armazón *mf*, montura *f* (para anteojos) **4 frame of mind** : estado *m* de ánimo

framework ['freɪm,wərk] *n* **1** SKELETON, STRUCTURE : armazón *f*, estructura *f* **2** BASIS : marco *m*

franc ['fræŋk] *n* : franco *m*

franchise ['fræn,tʃaɪz] *n* **1** LICENSE : licencia *f* exclusiva, concesión *f* (en comercio) **2** SUFFRAGE : sufragio *m*

franchisee [,fræn,tʃaɪ'zi:, -tʃə-] *n* : concesionario *m*, -ria *f*

Franciscan [fræn'sɪskən] *n* : franciscano *m*, -na *f* — **Franciscan** *adj*

frank[1] ['fræŋk] *vt* : franquear

frank[2] *adj* : franco, sincero, cándido — **frankly** *adv*

frank[3] *n* : franqueo *m* (de correo)

frankfurter ['fræŋkfərtər, -,fər-] *or* **frankfurt** [-fərt] *n* : salchicha *f* (de Frankfurt, de Viena), perro *m* caliente

frankincense ['fræŋkən,sɛnts] *n* : incienso *m*

frankness ['fræŋknəs] *n* : franqueza *f*, sinceridad *f*, candidez *f*

frantic ['fræntɪk] *adj* : frenético, desesperado — **frantically** *adv*

fraternal [frə'tərnəl] *adj* : fraterno, fraternal

fraternity [frə'tərnəti] *n*, *pl* **-ties** : fraternidad *f*

fraternization [,frætərnə'zeɪʃən] *n* : fraternización *f*, confraternización *f*

fraternize ['frætər,naɪz] *vi* **-nized; -nizing** : fraternizar, confraternizar

fratricidal [,frætrə'saɪdəl] *adj* : fratricida

fratricide ['frætrə,saɪd] *n* : fratricidio *m*

fraud ['frɔd] *n* **1** DECEPTION, SWINDLE : fraude *m*, estafa *f*, engaño *m* **2** IMPOSTOR : impostor *m*, -tora *f*; farsante *mf*

fraudulent ['frɔdʒələnt] *adj* : fraudulento — **fraudulently** *adv*

fraught ['frɔt] *adj* **fraught with** : lleno de, cargado de

fray[1] ['freɪ] *vt* **1** WEAR : desgastar, deshilachar **2** IRRITATE : crispar, irritar (los nervios) — *vi* : desgastarse, deshilacharse

fray[2] *n* : pelea *f* ⟨to join the fray : salir a la palestra⟩ ⟨to return to the fray : volver a la carga⟩

frazzle¹ [ˈfræzəl] vt **-zled; -zling 1** FRAY : desgastar, deshilachar **2** EXHAUST : agotar, fatigar

frazzle² n EXHAUSTION : agotamiento m

freak [ˈfriːk] n **1** ODDITY : ejemplar m anormal, fenómeno m, rareza f **2** EN-THUSIAST : entusiasta mf

freakish [ˈfriːkɪʃ] adj : extraño, estrafalario, raro

freak out vi : ponerse como loco — vt : darle un ataque (a alguien)

freckle¹ [ˈfrɛkəl] vi **-led; -ling** : cubrirse de pecas

freckle² n : peca f

free¹ [ˈfriː] vt **freed; freeing 1** LIBERATE : libertar, liberar, poner en libertad **2** RELIEVE, RID : librar, eximir **3** RELEASE, UNTIE : desatar, soltar **4** UNCLOG : desatascar, destapar

free² adv **1** FREELY : libremente **2** GRATIS : gratuitamente, gratis

free³ adj **freer; freest 1** : libre ⟨free as a bird : libre como un pájaro⟩ **2** EXEMPT : libre ⟨tax-free : libre de impuestos⟩ **3** GRATIS : gratuito, gratis **4** VOLUNTARY : espontáneo, voluntario, libre **5** UNOCCUPIED : desocupado, libre **6** LOOSE : suelto

freebooter [ˈfriːˌbuːtər] n : pirata mf

freeborn [ˈfriːˈbɔrn] adj : nacido libre

freedom [ˈfriːdəm] n : libertad f

free-for-all [ˈfriːfərˌɔl] n : pelea f, batalla f campal

freelance¹ [ˈfriːˌlænts] vi **-lanced; -lancing** : trabajar por cuenta propia

freelance² adj : por cuenta propia, independiente

freeload [ˈfriːˌloːd] vi : gorronear fam, gorrear fam

freeloader [ˈfriːˌloːdər] n : gorrón m, -rrona f; gorrero m, -ra f; vividor m, -dora f

freely [ˈfriːli] adv **1** FREE : libremente **2** GRATIS : gratis, gratuitamente

freestanding [ˈfriːˈstændɪŋ] adj : de pie, no empotrado, independiente

freeway [ˈfriːˌweɪ] n : autopista f

freewill [ˈfriːˌwɪl] adj : de propia voluntad

free will n : libre albedrío m, propia voluntad f

freeze¹ [ˈfriːz] v **froze** [ˈfroːz]; **frozen** [ˈfroːzən]; **freezing** vi **1** : congelarse, helarse ⟨the water froze in the lake : el agua se congeló en el lago⟩ ⟨my blood froze : se me heló la sangre⟩ ⟨I'm freezing : me estoy helando⟩ **2** STOP : quedarse inmóvil — vt : helar, congelar (líquidos), congelar (alimentos, precios, activos)

freeze² n **1** FROST : helada f **2** FREEZING : congelación f, congelamiento m

freeze-dried [ˈfriːzˈdraɪd] adj : liofilizado

freeze-dry [ˈfriːzˈdraɪ] vt **-dried; -drying** : liofilizar

freezer [ˈfriːzər] n : congelador m

freezing [ˈfriːzɪŋ] adj : helando ⟨it's freezing! : ¡hace un frío espantoso!⟩

freezing point n : punto m de congelación

freight¹ [ˈfreɪt] vt : enviar como carga

freight² n **1** SHIPPING, TRANSPORT : transporte m, porte m, flete m **2** GOODS : mercancías fpl, carga f

freighter [ˈfreɪtər] n : carguero m, buque m de carga

French¹ [ˈfrɛntʃ] adj : francés

French² n **1** : francés m (idioma) **2 the French** npl : los franceses

french fries [ˈfrɛntʃˌfraɪz] npl : papas fpl fritas

Frenchman [ˈfrɛntʃmən] n, pl **-men** [-mən, -ˌmɛn] : francés m

Frenchwoman [ˈfrɛntʃˌwʊmən] n, pl **-women** [-ˌwɪmən] : francesa f

frenetic [frɪˈnɛtɪk] adj : frenético — **frenetically** [-tɪkli] adv

frenzied [ˈfrɛnzid] adj : frenético

frenzy [ˈfrɛnzi] n, pl **-zies** : frenesí m

frequency [ˈfriːkwəntsi] n, pl **-cies** : frecuencia f

frequent¹ [frɪˈkwɛnt, ˈfriːkwənt] vt : frecuentar

frequent² [ˈfriːkwənt] adj : frecuente — **frequently** adv

fresco [ˈfrɛsˌkoː] n, pl **-coes** : fresco m

fresh [ˈfrɛʃ] adj **1** : dulce ⟨freshwater : agua dulce⟩ **2** PURE : puro **3** : fresco ⟨fresh fruits : frutas frescas⟩ **4** CLEAN, NEW : limpio, nuevo ⟨fresh clothes : ropa limpia⟩ ⟨fresh evidence : evidencia nueva⟩ **5** REFRESHED : fresco, descansado **6** IMPERTINENT : descarado, impertinente

freshen [ˈfrɛʃən] vt : refrescar, arreglar — vi **to freshen up** : arreglarse, lavarse

freshet [ˈfrɛʃət] n : arroyo m desbordado

freshly [ˈfrɛʃli] adv : recientemente, recién

freshman [ˈfrɛʃmən] n, pl **-men** [-mən, -ˌmɛn] : estudiante mf de primer año universitario

freshness [ˈfrɛʃnəs] n : frescura f

freshwater [ˈfrɛʃˌwɔtər] n : agua f dulce

fret¹ [ˈfrɛt] vi **fretted; fretting** : preocuparse, inquietarse

fret² n **1** VEXATION : irritación f, molestia f **2** WORRY : preocupación f **3** : traste m (de un instrumento musical)

fretful [ˈfrɛtfəl] adj : fastidioso, quejoso, neurótico

fretfully [ˈfrɛtfəli] adv : ansiosamente, fastidiosamente, inquieto

fretfulness [ˈfrɛtfəlnəs] n : inquietud f, irritabilidad f

friable [ˈfraɪəbəl] adj : friable, pulverizable

friar [ˈfraɪər] n : fraile m

fricassee¹ [ˈfrɪkəˌsiː, ˌfrɪkəˈsiː] vt **-seed; -seeing** : cocinar al fricasé

fricassee² n : fricasé m

friction [ˈfrɪkʃən] n **1** RUBBING : fricción f **2** CONFLICT : fricción f, roce m

Friday [ˈfraɪˌdeɪ, -di] n : viernes m

fridge [ˈfrɪdʒ] → refrigerator

friend ['frɛnd] *n* : amigo *m*, -ga *f*

friendless ['frɛndləs] *adj* : sin amigos

friendliness ['frɛndlinəs] *n* : simpatía *f*, amabilidad *f*

friendly ['frɛndli] *adj* **-lier; -est 1** : simpático, amable, de amigo ⟨a friendly child : un niño simpático⟩ ⟨friendly advice : consejo de amigo⟩ **2** : agradable, acogedor ⟨a friendly atmosphere : un ambiente agradable⟩ **3** GOOD-NATURED : amigable, amistoso ⟨friendly competition : competencia amistosa⟩

friendship [frɛnd͵ʃɪp] *n* : amistad *f*

frieze ['fri:z] *n* : friso *m*

frigate ['frɪgət] *n* : fragata *f*

fright ['fraɪt] *n* : miedo *m*, susto *m*

frighten ['fraɪtən] *vt* : asustar, espantar

frightened ['fraɪtənd] *adj* : asustado, temeroso

frightening ['fraɪtənɪŋ] *adj* : espantoso, aterrador

frightful ['fraɪtfəl] *adj* **1** → **frightening 2** TREMENDOUS : espantoso, tremendo

frightfully ['fraɪtfəli] *adv* : terriblemente, tremendamente

frigid ['frɪdʒɪd] *adj* : glacial, extremadamente frío

frigidity [frɪ'dʒɪdəti] *n* **1** COLDNESS : frialdad *f* **2** : frigidez *f* (sexual)

frill ['frɪl] *n* **1** RUFFLE : volante *m* **2** EMBELLISHMENT : floritura *f*, adorno *m*

frilly ['frɪli] *adj* **frillier; -est 1** RUFFLY : con volantes **2** OVERDONE : recargado

fringe¹ ['frɪndʒ] *vt* **fringed; fringing** : orlar, bordear

fringe² *n* **1** BORDER : fleco *m*, orla *f* **2** EDGE : periferia *f*, margen *m* **3 fringe benefits** : incentivos *mpl*, extras *mpl*

frisk ['frɪsk] *vi* FROLIC : retozar, juguetear — *vt* SEARCH : cachear, registrar

friskiness ['frɪskinəs] *n* : vivacidad *f*

frisky ['frɪski] *adj* **friskier; -est** : retozón, juguetón

fritter¹ ['frɪtər] *vt* : desperdiciar, malgastar ⟨I frittered away the money : malgasté el dinero⟩

fritter² *n* : buñuelo *m*

frivolity [frɪ'vɑləti] *n, pl* **-ties** : frivolidad *f*

frivolous ['frɪvələs] *adj* : frívolo, de poca importancia

frivolously ['frɪvələsli] *adv* : frívolamente, a la ligera

frizz¹ ['frɪz] *vi* : rizarse, encresparse, ponerse chino *Mex*

frizz² *n* : rizos *mpl* muy apretados

frizzy ['frɪzi] *adj* **frizzier; -est** : rizado, crespo, chino *Mex*

fro ['fro:] *adv* **to and fro** : de aquí para allá, de un lado para otro

frock ['frɑk] *n* DRESS : vestido *m*

frog ['frɔg, 'frɑg] *n* **1** : rana *f* **2** FASTENER : alamar *m* **3 to have a frog in one's throat** : tener carraspera

frogman ['frɔg͵mæn, 'frɑg-, -mən] *n, pl* **-men** [-mən, -͵mɛn] : hombre *m* rana, submarinista *mf*

frolic¹ ['frɑlɪk] *vi* **-icked; -icking** : retozar, juguetear

frolic² *n* FUN : diversión *f*

frolicsome ['frɑlɪksəm] *adj* : juguetón

from ['frʌm, 'frɑm] *prep* **1** (*indicating a starting point*) : desde, de, a partir de ⟨from Cali to Bogota : de Cali a Bogotá⟩ ⟨where are you from? : ¿de dónde eres?⟩ ⟨from that time onward : desde entonces⟩ ⟨from tomorrow : a partir de mañana⟩ **2** (*indicating a source or sender*) : de ⟨a letter from my friend : una carta de mi amiga⟩ ⟨a quote from Shakespeare : una cita de Shakespeare⟩ **3** (*indicating distance*) : de ⟨10 feet from the entrance : a 10 pies de la entrada⟩ **4** (*indicating a cause*) : de ⟨red from crying : rojos de llorar⟩ ⟨he died from the cold : murió del frío⟩ **5** OFF, OUT OF : de ⟨she took it from the drawer : lo sacó del cajón⟩ **6** (*with adverbs or adverbial phrases*) : de, desde ⟨from above : desde arriba⟩ ⟨from among : de entre⟩

frond ['frɑnd] *n* : fronda *f*, hoja *f*

front¹ ['frʌnt] *vi* **1** FACE : dar, estar orientado ⟨the house fronts north : la casa da al norte⟩ **2** : servir de pantalla ⟨he fronts for his boss : sirve de pantalla para su jefe⟩

front² *adj* : delantero, de adelante, primero ⟨the front row : la primera fila⟩

front³ *n* **1** : frente *m*, parte *f* de adelante, delantera *f* ⟨the front of the class : el frente de la clase⟩ ⟨at the front of the train : en la parte delantera del tren⟩ **2** AREA, ZONE : frente *m*, zona *f* ⟨the Eastern front : el frente oriental⟩ ⟨on the educational front : en el frente de la enseñanza⟩ **3** FACADE : fachada *f* (de un edificio o una persona) **4** : frente *m* (en meteorología)

frontage ['frʌntɪdʒ] *n* : fachada *f*, frente *m*

frontal ['frʌntəl] *adj* : frontal, de frente

frontier [͵frʌn'tɪr] *n* : frontera *f*

frontiersman [͵frʌn'tɪrzmən] *n, pl* **-men** [-mən, -͵mɛn] : hombre *m* de la frontera

frontispiece ['frʌntəs͵pi:s] *n* : frontispicio *m*

frost¹ ['frɔst] *vt* **1** FREEZE : helar **2** ICE : escarchar (pasteles)

frost² *n* **1** : helada *f* (en meteorología) **2** : escarcha *f* ⟨frost on the window : escarcha en la ventana⟩

frostbite ['frɔst͵baɪt] *n* : congelación *f*

frostbitten ['frɔst͵bɪtən] *adj* : congelado (dícese de una persona), quemado (dícese de una planta)

frosting ['frɔstɪŋ] *n* ICING : glaseado *m*, betún *m Mex*

frosty ['frɔsti] *adj* **frostier; -est 1** CHILLY : helado, frío **2** COOL, UNFRIENDLY : frío, glacial

froth ['frɔθ] *n, pl* **froths** ['frɔθs, 'frɔðz] : espuma *f*

frothy ['frɔθi] *adj* **frothier; -est** : espumoso

frown[1] ['fraʊn] *vi* **1** : fruncir el ceño, fruncir el entrecejo **2 to frown at** : mirar (algo) con ceño, mirar (a alguien) con ceño

frown[2] *n* : ceño *m* (fruncido)

frowsy *or* **frowzy** ['fraʊzi] *adj* **frowsier** *or* **frowzier; -est** : desaliñado, desaseado

froze → **freeze**

frozen → **freeze**

frugal ['fru:gəl] *adj* : frugal, ahorrativo, parco — **frugally** *adv*

frugality [fru'gæləti] *n* : frugalidad *f*

fruit[1] ['fru:t] *vi* : dar fruto

fruit[2] *n* **1** : fruta *f* (término genérico), fruto *m* (término particular) **2 fruits** *npl* REWARDS : frutos *mpl* ⟨the fruits of his labor : los frutos de su trabajo⟩

fruitcake ['fru:t,keɪk] *n* : pastel *m* de frutas

fruitful ['fru:tfəl] *adj* : fructífero, provechoso

fruition [fru'ɪʃən] *n* **1** : cumplimiento *m*, realización *f* **2 to bring to fruition** : realizar

fruitless ['fru:tləs] *adj* : infructuoso, inútil — **fruitlessly** *adv*

fruity ['fru:ti] *adj* **fruitier; -est** : (con sabor) a fruta

frumpy ['frʌmpi] *adj* **frumpier; -est** : anticuado y sin atractivo

frustrate ['frʌs,treɪt] *vt* **-trated; -trating** : frustrar

frustrating ['frʌs,treɪt̬ɪŋ] *adj* : frustrante — **frustratingly** *adv*

frustration [,frʌs'treɪʃən] *n* : frustración *f*

fry[1] ['fraɪ] *vt* **fried; frying** : freír

fry[2] *n, pl* **fries 1** : fritura *f*, plato *m* frito **2** : fiesta *f* en que se sirven frituras **3** *pl* **fry** : alevín *m* (pez)

frying pan *n* : sartén *mf*

fuchsia ['fju:ʃə] *n* **1** : fucsia *f* (planta) **2** : fucsia *m* (color)

fuddle ['fʌdəl] *vt* **-dled; -dling** : confundir, atontar

fuddy-duddy ['fʌdi,dʌdi] *n, pl* **-dies** : persona *f* chapada a la antigua, carca *mf*

fudge[1] ['fʌʤ] *vt* **fudged; fudging 1** FALSIFY : amañar, falsificar **2** DODGE : esquivar

fudge[2] *n* : dulce *m* blando de chocolate y leche

fuel[1] ['fju:əl] *vt* **-eled** *or* **-elled; -eling** *or* **-elling 1** : abastecer de combustible **2** STIMULATE : estimular

fuel[2] *n* : combustible *m*, carburante *m* (para motores)

fugitive[1] ['fju:ʤət̬ɪv] *adj* **1** RUNAWAY : fugitivo **2** FLEETING : efímero, pasajero, fugaz

fugitive[2] *n* : fugitivo *m*, -va *f*

fugue ['fju:g] *n* : fuga *f*

fulcrum ['fʊlkrəm, 'fʌl-] *n, pl* **-crums** *or* **-cra** [-krə] : fulcro *m*

fulfill *or* **fulfil** [fʊl'fɪl] *vt* **-filled; -filling 1** PERFORM : cumplir con, realizar, llevar a cabo **2** SATISFY : satisfacer

fulfillment [fʊl'fɪlmənt] *n* **1** PERFORMANCE : cumplimiento *m*, ejecución *f* **2** SATISFACTION : satisfacción *f*, realización *f*

full[1] ['fʊl, 'fʌl] *adv* **1** VERY : muy ⟨full well : muy bien, perfectamente⟩ **2** ENTIRELY : completamente ⟨she swung full around : giró completamente⟩ **3** DIRECTLY : de lleno, directamente ⟨he looked me full in the face : me miró directamente a la cara⟩

full[2] *adj* **1** FILLED : lleno **2** COMPLETE : completo, detallado **3** MAXIMUM : todo, pleno ⟨at full speed : a toda velocidad⟩ ⟨in full bloom : en plena flor⟩ **4** PLUMP : redondo, llenito *fam*, regordete *fam* ⟨a full face : una cara redonda⟩ ⟨a full figure : un cuerpo llenito⟩ **5** AMPLE : amplio ⟨a full skirt : una falda amplia⟩

full[3] *n* **1 to pay in full** : pagar en su totalidad **2 to the full** : al máximo

full-fledged ['fʊl'flɛʤd] *adj* : hecho y derecho

fullness ['fʊlnəs] *n* **1** ABUNDANCE : plenitud *f*, abundancia *f* **2** : amplitud *f* (de una falda)

fully ['fʊli] *adv* **1** COMPLETELY : completamente, totalmente **2** : al menos, por lo menos ⟨fully half of them : al menos la mitad de ellos⟩

fulsome ['fʊlsəm] *adj* : excesivo, exagerado, efusivo

fumble[1] ['fʌmbəl] *v* **-bled; -bling** *vt* **1** : dejar caer, fumblear **2 to fumble one's way** : ir a tientas — *vi* **1** GROPE : hurgar, tantear **2 to fumble with** : manejar con torpeza

fumble[2] *n* : fumble *m* (en futbol americano)

fume[1] ['fju:m] *vi* **fumed; fuming 1** SMOKE : echar humo, humear **2** : estar furioso

fume[2] *n* : gas *m*, humo *m*, vapor *m*

fumigate ['fju:mə,geɪt] *vt* **-gated; -gating** : fumigar

fumigation [,fju:mə'geɪʃən] *n* : fumigación *f*

fun[1] ['fʌn] *adj* : divertido, entretenido

fun[2] *n* **1** AMUSEMENT : diversión *f*, entretenimiento *m* **2** ENJOYMENT : disfrute *m* **3 to have fun** : divertirse **4 to make fun of** : reírse de, burlarse de

function[1] ['fʌŋkʃən] *vi* : funcionar, desempeñarse, servir

function[2] *n* **1** PURPOSE : función *f* **2** GATHERING : reunión *f* social, recepción *f* **3** CEREMONY : ceremonia *f*, acto *m*

functional ['fʌŋkʃənəl] *adj* : funcional — **functionally** *adv*

functionary ['fʌŋkʃə,nɛri] *n, pl* **-aries** : funcionario *m*, -ria *f*

fund[1] ['fʌnd] *vt* : financiar

fund² *n* **1** SUPPLY : reserva *f*, cúmulo *m* **2** : fondo *m* ⟨investment fund : fondo de inversiones⟩ **3 funds** *npl* RESOURCES : fondos *mpl*

fundamental¹ [ˌfʌndəˈmɛntəl] *adj* **1** BASIC : fundamental, básico **2** PRINCIPAL : esencial, principal **3** INNATE : innato, intrínseco

fundamental² *n* : fundamento *m*

fundamentalism [ˌfʌndəˈmɛntəlˌɪzəm] *n* : integrismo *m*, fundamentalismo *m*

fundamentalist [ˌfʌndəˈmɛntəlɪst] *n* : integrista *mf*, fundamentalista *mf* — **fundamentalist** *adj*

fundamentally [ˌfʌndəˈmɛntəli] *adv* : fundamentalmente, básicamente

funding [ˈfʌndɪŋ] *n* : financiación *f*

fund–raiser [ˈfʌndˌreɪzər] *n* : función *f* para recaudar fondos

funeral¹ [ˈfjuːnərəl] *adj* **1** : funeral, funerario, fúnebre ⟨funeral procession : cortejo fúnebre⟩ **2 funeral home** : funeraria *f*

funeral² *n* : funeral *m*, funerales *mpl*

funereal [fjuˈnɪriəl] *adj* : fúnebre

fungal [ˈfʌŋgəl] *adj* : de hongos, micótico

fungicidal [ˌfʌndʒəˈsaɪdəl, ˌfʌngə-] *adj* : fungicida

fungicide [ˈfʌndʒəˌsaɪd, ˈfʌŋgə-] *n* : fungicida *m*

fungous [ˈfʌŋgəs] *adj* : fungoso

fungus [ˈfʌŋgəs] *n*, *pl* **fungi** [ˈfʌnˌdʒaɪ, ˈfʌnˌgaɪ] : hongo *m*

funk [ˈfʌŋk] *n* **1** FEAR : miedo *m* **2** DEPRESSION : depresión *f*

funky [ˈfʌŋki] *adj* **funkier; -est** ODD, QUAINT : raro, extraño, original

funnel¹ [ˈfʌnəl] *vt* **-neled; -neling** CHANNEL : canalizar, encauzar

funnel² *n* **1** : embudo *m* **2** SMOKESTACK : chimenea *f* (de un barco o vapor)

funnies [ˈfʌniz] *npl* : tiras *fpl* cómicas

funny [ˈfʌni] *adj* **funnier; -est 1** AMUSING : divertido, cómico **2** STRANGE : extraño, raro

fur¹ [ˈfər] *adj* : de piel

fur² *n* **1** : pelaje *m*, piel *f* **2** : prenda *f* de piel

furbish [ˈfərbɪʃ] *vt* : pulir, limpiar

furious [ˈfjʊriəs] *adj* **1** ANGRY : furioso **2** FRANTIC : violento, frenético, vertiginoso (dícese de la velocidad)

furiously [ˈfjʊriəsli] *adv* **1** ANGRILY : furiosamente **2** FRANTICALLY : frenéticamente

furlong [ˈfərˌlɔŋ] *n* : estadio *m* (201.2 m)

furlough¹ [ˈfərˌloː] *vt* : dar permiso a, dar licencia a

furlough² *n* LEAVE : permiso *m*, licencia *f*

furnace [ˈfərnəs] *n* : horno *m*

furnish [ˈfərnɪʃ] *vt* **1** SUPPLY : proveer, suministrar **2** : amueblar ⟨furnished apartment : departamento amueblado⟩

furnishings [ˈfərnɪʃɪŋz] *npl* **1** ACCESSORIES : accesorios *mpl* **2** FURNITURE : muebles *mpl*, mobiliario *m*

furniture [ˈfərnɪtʃər] *n* : muebles *mpl*, mobiliario *m*

furor [ˈfjʊrˌɔr, -ər] *n* **1** RAGE : furia *f*, rabia *f* **2** UPROAR : escándalo *m*, jaleo *m*, alboroto *m*

furrier [ˈfəriər] *n* : peletero *m*, -ra *f*

furrow¹ [ˈfəroː] *vt* **1** : surcar **2 to furrow one's brow** : fruncir el ceño

furrow² *n* **1** GROOVE : surco *m* **2** WRINKLE : arruga *f*, surco *m*

furry [ˈfəri] *adj* **furrier; -est** : peludo (dícese de un animal), peluche (dícese de un objeto)

further¹ [ˈfərðər] *vt* : promover, fomentar

further² *adv* **1** FARTHER : más lejos, más adelante **2** MOREOVER : además **3** MORE : más ⟨I'll consider it further in the morning : lo consideraré más en la mañana⟩

further³ *adj* **1** FARTHER : más lejano **2** ADDITIONAL : adicional, más

furtherance [ˈfərðərənts] *n* : promoción *f*, fomento *m*, adelantamiento *m*

furthermore [ˈfərðərˌmor] *adv* : además

furthermost [ˈfərðərˌmoːst] *adj* : más lejano, más distante

furthest [ˈfərðəst] → **farthest¹, farthest²**

furtive [ˈfərṭɪv] *adj* : furtivo, sigiloso — **furtively** *adv*

furtiveness [ˈfərṭɪvnəs] *n* STEALTH : sigilo *m*

fury [ˈfjʊri] *n*, *pl* **-ries 1** RAGE : furia *f*, ira *f* **2** VIOLENCE : furia *f*, furor *m*

fuse¹ [ˈfjuːz] *or* **fuze** *vt* **fused** *or* **fuzed; fusing** *or* **fuzing** : equipar con un fusible

fuse² *v* **fused; fusing** *vt* **1** SMELT : fundir **2** MERGE : fusionar, fundir — *vi* : fundirse, fusionarse

fuse³ *n* : fusible *m*

fuselage [ˈfjuːsəˌlɑʒ, -zə-] *n* : fuselaje *m*

fusillade [ˈfjuːsəˌlɑd, -ˌleɪd, ˌfjuːsəˈ-, -zə-] *n* : descarga *f* de fusilería

fusion [ˈfjuːʒən] *n* : fusión *f*

fuss¹ [ˈfʌs] *vi* **1** WORRY : preocuparse **2 to fuss with** : juguetear con, toquetear **3 to fuss over** : mimar

fuss² *n* **1** COMMOTION : alboroto *m*, escándalo *m* **2** ATTENTION : atenciones *fpl* **3** COMPLAINT : quejas *fpl*

fussbudget [ˈfʌsˌbʌdʒət] *n* : quisquilloso *m*, -sa *f*; melindroso *m*, -sa *f*

fussiness [ˈfʌsinəs] *n* **1** IRRITABILITY : irritabilidad *f* **2** ORNATENESS : lo recargado **3** METICULOUSNESS : meticulosidad *f*

fussy [ˈfʌsi] *adj* **fussier; -est 1** IRRITABLE : irritable, nervioso **2** OVERELABORATE : recargado **3** METICULOUS : meticuloso **4** FASTIDIOUS : quisquilloso, exigente

futile [ˈfjuːṭəl, ˈfjuːˌtaɪl] *adj* : inútil, vano

futility [fjuˈtɪləti] *n*, *pl* **-ties** : inutilidad *f*

future¹ [ˈfjuːtʃər] *adj* : futuro

future² *n* : futuro *m*

futuristic [ˌfjuːtʃəˈrɪstɪk] *adj* : futurista

fuze → **fuse¹**

fuzz ['fʌz] *n* : pelusa *f*
fuzziness ['fʌzinəs] *n* **1** DOWNINESS : vellosidad *f* **2** INDISTINCTNESS : falta *f* de claridad

fuzzy ['fʌzi] *adj* **fuzzier; -est 1** FLUFFY, FURRY : con pelusa, peludo **2** INDISTINCT : indistinto ⟨a fuzzy image : una imagen borrosa⟩

G

g ['dʒi:] *n, pl* **g's** *or* **gs** ['dʒi:z] : séptima letra del alfabeto inglés
gab¹ ['gæb] *vi* **gabbed; gabbing** : charlar, cotorrear *fam*, parlotear *fam*
gab² *n* CHATTER : cotorreo *m fam*, parloteo *m fam*
gabardine ['gæbər,di:n] *n* : gabardina *f*
gabby ['gæbi] *adj* **gabbier; -est** : hablador, parlanchín
gable ['geɪbəl] *n* : hastial *m*, aguilón *m*
Gabonese [,gæbə'ni:z, -'ni:s] *n* : gabonés *m*, -nesa *f* — **Gabonese** *adj*
gad ['gæd] *vi* **gadded; gadding** WANDER : deambular, vagar, callejear
gadfly ['gæd,flaɪ] *n, pl* **-flies 1** : tábano *m* (insecto) **2** FAULTFINDER : criticón *m*, -cona *f fam*
gadget ['gædʒət] *n* : artilugio *m*, aparato *m*
gadgetry ['gædʒətri] *n* : artilugios *mpl*, aparatos *mpl*
Gaelic ['geɪlɪk, 'gæ] *n* : gaélico *m* (idioma) — **Gaelic** *adj*
gaff ['gæf] *n* **1** : garfio *m* **2** → **gaffe**
gaffe ['gæf] *n* : metedura *f* de pata *fam*
gag¹ ['gæg] *v* **gagged; gagging** *vt* : amordazar ⟨to tie up and gag : atar y amordazar⟩ — *vi* **1** CHOKE : atragantarse **2** RETCH : hacer arcadas
gag² *n* **1** : mordaza *f* (para la boca) **2** JOKE : chiste *m*
gage → **gauge**
gaggle ['gægəl] *n* : bandada *f*, manada *f* (de gansos)
gaiety ['geɪəti] *n, pl* **-eties 1** MERRYMAKING : juerga *f* **2** MERRIMENT : alegría *f*, regocijo *m*
gaily ['geɪli] *adv* : alegremente
gain¹ ['geɪn] *vt* **1** ACQUIRE, OBTAIN : ganar, obtener, adquirir, conseguir ⟨to gain knowledge : adquirir conocimientos⟩ ⟨to gain a victory : obtener una victoria⟩ **2** REACH : alcanzar, llegar a **3** INCREASE : ganar, aumentar ⟨to gain weight : aumentar de peso⟩ **4** : adelantarse, ganar ⟨the watch gains two minutes a day : el reloj se adelanta dos minutos por día⟩ — *vi* **1** PROFIT : beneficiarse **2** INCREASE : aumentar
gain² *n* **1** PROFIT : beneficio *m*, ganancia *f*, lucro *m*, provecho *m* **2** INCREASE : aumento *m*
gainful ['geɪnfəl] *adj* : lucrativo, beneficioso, provechoso ⟨gainful employment : trabajo remunerado⟩
gait ['geɪt] *n* : paso *m*, andar *m*, manera *f* de caminar
gal ['gæl] *n* : muchacha *f*
gala¹ ['geɪlə, 'gæ-, 'gɑ-] *adj* : de gala

gala² *n* : gala *f*, fiesta *f*
galactic [gə'læktɪk] *adj* : galáctico
galaxy ['gæləksi] *n, pl* **-axies** : galaxia *f*
gale ['geɪl] *n* **1** WIND : vendaval *f*, viento *m* fuerte **2** **gales of laughter** : carcajadas *fpl*
gall¹ ['gɔl] *vt* **1** CHAFE : rozar **2** IRRITATE, VEX : irritar, molestar
gall² *n* **1** BILE : bilis *f*, hiel *f* **2** INSOLENCE : audacia *f*, insolencia *f*, descaro *m* **3** SORE : rozadura *f* (de un caballo) **4** : agalla *f* (de una planta)
gallant ['gælənt] *adj* **1** BRAVE : valiente, gallardo **2** CHIVALROUS, POLITE : galante, cortés
gallantry ['gæləntri] *n, pl* **-ries** : galantería *f*, caballerosidad *f*
gallbladder ['gɔl,blædər] *n* : vesícula *f* biliar
galleon ['gæljən] *n* : galeón *m*
gallery ['gæləri] *n, pl* **-leries 1** BALCONY : galería *f* (para espectadores) **2** CORRIDOR : pasillo *m*, galería *f*, corredor *m* **3** : galería *f* (para exposiciones)
galley ['gæli] *n, pl* **-leys** : galera *f*
gallium ['gæliəm] *n* : galio *m*
gallivant ['gælə,vænt] *vi* : callejear
gallon ['gælən] *n* : galón *m*
gallop¹ ['gæləp] *vi* : galopar
gallop² *n* : galope *m*
gallows ['gæ,loːz] *n, pl* **-lows** *or* **-lowses** [-,loːzəz] : horca *f*
gallstone ['gɔl,stoːn] *n* : cálculo *m* biliar
galore [gə'lor] *adj* : en abundancia ⟨bargains galore : muchísimas gangas⟩
galoshes [gə'lɑʃəz] *npl* : galochas *fpl*, chanclos *mpl*
galvanize ['gælvən,aɪz] *vt* **-nized; -nizing 1** STIMULATE : estimular, excitar, impulsar **2** : galvanizar (metales)
Gambian ['gæmbiən] *n* : gambiano *m*, -na *f* — **Gambian** *adj*
gambit ['gæmbɪt] *n* **1** : gambito *m* (en ajedrez) **2** STRATAGEM : estratagema *f*, táctica *f*
gamble¹ ['gæmbəl] *v* **-bled; -bling** *vi* : jugar, arriesgarse — *vt* **1** BET, WAGER : apostar, jugarse **2** RISK : arriesgar
gamble² *n* **1** BET : apuesta *f* **2** RISK : riesgo *m*
gambler ['gæmbələr] *n* : jugador *m*, -dora *f*
gambling ['gæmbəlɪŋ] *n* : juego *m*
gambol ['gæmbəl] *vi* **-boled** *or* **-bolled; -boling** *or* **-bolling** FROLIC : retozar, juguetear
game¹ ['geɪm] *adj* **1** READY : listo, dispuesto ⟨we're game for anything : es-

tamos listos para lo que sea⟩ **2** LAME : cojo

game² *n* **1** AMUSEMENT : juego *m*, diversión *f* **2** CONTEST : juego *m*, partido *m*, concurso *m* **3** : caza *f* ⟨big game : caza mayor⟩

gamecock ['geɪm,kɑk] *n* : gallo *m* de pelea

gamekeeper ['geɪm,ki:pər] *n* : guardabosque *mf*

gamely ['geɪmli] *adv* : animosamente

gamma ray ['gæmə] *n* : rayo *m* gamma

gamut ['gæmət] *n* : gama *f*, espectro *m* ⟨to run the gamut : pasar por toda la gama⟩

gamy *or* **gamey** ['geɪmi] *adj* **gamier; -est** : con sabor de animal de caza, fuerte

gander ['gændər] *n* **1** : ganso *m* (animal) **2** GLANCE : mirada *f*, vistazo *m*, ojeada *f*

gang¹ ['gæŋ] *vi* **to gang up** : agruparse, unirse

gang² *n* : banda *f*, pandilla *f*

gangling ['gæŋglɪŋ] *adj* LANKY : larguirucho *fam*

ganglion ['gæŋgliən] *n*, *pl* **-glia** [-gliə] : ganglio *m*

gangplank ['gæŋ,plæŋk] *n* : pasarela *f*

gangrene ['gæŋ,gri:n, 'gæn-; gæŋ'-, gæn'-] *n* : gangrena *f*

gangrenous ['gæŋgrənəs] *adj* : gangrenoso

gangster ['gæŋstər] *n* : gángster *mf*

gangway ['gæŋ,weɪ] *n* **1** : pasarela *f* **2 gangway!** : ¡abran paso!

gap ['gæp] *n* **1** BREACH, OPENING : espacio *m*, brecha *f*, abertura *f* **2** GORGE : desfiladero *m*, barranco *m* **3** : laguna *f* ⟨a gap in my education : una laguna en mi educación⟩ **4** INTERVAL : pausa *f*, intervalo *m* **5** DISPARITY : brecha *f*, disparidad *f*

gape¹ ['geɪp] *vi* **gaped; gaping 1** OPEN : abrirse, estar abierto **2** STARE : mirar fijamente con la boca abierta, mirar boquiabierto

gape² *n* **1** OPENING : abertura *f*, brecha *f* **2** STARE : mirada *f* boquiabierta

garage¹ [gə'rɑʒ, -'rɑʤ] *vt* **-raged; -raging** : dejar en un garaje

garage² *n* : garaje *m*, cochera *f*

garb¹ ['gɑrb] *vt* : vestir, ataviar

garb² *n* : vestimenta *f*, atuendo *f*

garbage ['gɑrbɪʤ] *n* : basura *f*, desechos *mpl*

garbageman ['gɑrbɪʤmən] *n*, *pl* **-men** [-mən, -ˌmɛn] : basurero *m*

garble ['gɑrbəl] *vt* **-bled; -bling** : tergiversar, distorsionar

garbled ['gɑrbəld] *adj* : incoherente, incomprensible

garden¹ ['gɑrdən] *vi* : trabajar en el jardín

garden² *n* : jardín *m*

gardener ['gɑrdənər] *n* : jardinero *m*, -ra *f*

gardenia [gɑr'di:njə] *n* : gardenia *f*

gardening ['gɑrdənɪŋ] *n* : jardinería *f*

gargantuan [gɑr'gænʧuən] *adj* : gigantesco, colosal

gargle¹ ['gɑrgəl] *vi* **-gled; -gling** : hacer gárgaras, gargarizar

gargle² *n* : gárgara *f*

gargoyle ['gɑr,gɔɪl] *n* : gárgola *f*

garish ['gærɪʃ] *adj* GAUDY : llamativo, chillón, charro — **garishly** *adv*

garland¹ ['gɑrlənd] *vt* : adornar con guirnaldas

garland² *n* : guirnalda *f*

garlic ['gɑrlɪk] *n* : ajo *m*

garment ['gɑrmənt] *n* : prenda *f*

garner ['gɑrnər] *vt* : recoger, cosechar

garnet ['gɑrnət] *n* : granate *m*

garnish¹ ['gɑrnɪʃ] *vt* : aderezar, guarnecer

garnish² *n* : aderezo *m*, guarnición *f*

garret ['gærət] *n* : buhardilla *f*, desván *m*

garrison¹ ['gærəsən] *vt* **1** QUARTER : acuartelar (tropas) **2** OCCUPY : guarnecer, ocupar (con tropas)

garrison² *n* **1** : guarnición *f* (ciudad) **2** FORT : fortaleza *f*, poste *m* militar

garrulous ['gærələs] *adj* : charlatán, parlanchín, garlero *Col fam*

garter ['gɑrtər] *n* : liga *f*

gas¹ ['gæs] *v* **gassed; gassing** *vt* : gasear — *vi* **to gas up** : llenar el tanque con gasolina

gas² *n*, *pl* **gases** ['gæsəz] **1** : gas *m* ⟨tear gas : gas lacrimógeno⟩ **2** GASOLINE : gasolina *f*

gaseous ['gæʃəs, 'gæsiəs] *adj* : gaseoso

gash¹ ['gæʃ] *vt* : hacer un tajo en, cortar

gash² *n* : cuchillada *f*, tajo *m*

gasket ['gæskət] *n* : junta *f*

gas mask *n* : máscara *f* antigás

gasoline ['gæsə,li:n, ˌgæsə'-] *n* : gasolina *f*, nafta *f*

gasp¹ ['gæsp] *vi* **1** : boquear ⟨to gasp with surprise : gritar de asombro⟩ **2** PANT : jadear, respirar con dificultad

gasp² *n* **1** : boqueada *f* ⟨a gasp of surprise : un grito sofocado⟩ **2** PANTING : jadeo *m*

gas station *n* : estación *f* de servicio, gasolinera *f*

gastric ['gæstrɪk] *adj* : gástrico ⟨gastric juice : jugo gástrico⟩

gastronomic [ˌgæstrə'nɑmɪk] *adj* : gastronómico

gastronomy [gæs'trɑnəmi] *n* : gastronomía *f*

gate ['geɪt] *n* : portón *m*, verja *f*, puerta *f*

gatekeeper ['geɪt,ki:pər] *n* : guarda *mf*; guardián *m*, -diana *f*

gateway ['geɪt,weɪ] *n* : puerta *f* (de acceso), entrada *f*

gather ['gæðər] *vt* **1** ASSEMBLE : juntar, recoger, reunir **2** HARVEST : recoger, cosechar **3** : fruncir (una tela) **4** INFER : deducir, suponer

gathering ['gæðərɪŋ] *n* : reunión *f*

gauche ['goːʃ] *adj* : torpe, falto de tacto

gaudy ['gɔdi] *adj* **gaudier; -est** : chillón, llamativo
gauge¹ ['geɪʤ] *vt* **gauged; gauging 1** MEASURE : medir **2** ESTIMATE, JUDGE : estimar, evaluar, juzgar
gauge² *n* **1** : indicador *m* ⟨pressure gauge : indicador de presión⟩ **2** CALIBER : calibre *m* **3** INDICATION : indicio *m*, muestra *f*
gaunt ['gɔnt] *adj* : demacrado, enjuto, descarnado
gauntlet ['gɔntlət] *n* : guante *m* ⟨to run the gauntlet of : exponerse a⟩
gauze ['gɔz] *n* : gasa *f*
gauzy ['gɔzi] *adj* **gauzier; -est** : diáfano, vaporoso
gave → **give**
gavel ['gævəl] *n* : martillo *m* (de un juez, un subastador, etc.)
gawk ['gɔk] *vi* GAPE : mirar boquiabierto
gawky ['gɔki] *adj* **gawkier; -est** : desmañado, torpe, desgarbado
gay ['geɪ] *adj* **1** MERRY : alegre **2** BRIGHT, COLORFUL : vistoso, vivo **3** HOMOSEXUAL : homosexual
gaze¹ ['geɪz] *vi* **gazed; gazing** : mirar (fijamente)
gaze² *n* : mirada *f* (fija)
gazelle [gə'zɛl] *n* : gacela *f*
gazette [gə'zɛt] *n* : gaceta *f*
gazetteer [ˌgæzə'tɪr] *n* : diccionario *m* geográfico
gear¹ ['gɪr] *vt* ADAPT, ORIENT : adaptar, ajustar, orientar ⟨a book geared to children : un libro adaptado a los niños⟩ — *vi* **to gear up** : prepararse
gear² *n* **1** CLOTHING : ropa *f* **2** BELONGINGS : efectos *mpl* personales **3** EQUIPMENT, TOOLS : equipo *m*, aparejo *m*, herramientas *fpl* ⟨fishing gear : aparejo de pescar⟩ ⟨landing gear : tren de aterrizaje⟩ **4** COGWHEEL : rueda *f* dentada **5** : marcha *f*, velocidad *f* (de un vehículo) ⟨to put in gear : poner en marcha⟩ ⟨to change gear(s) : cambiar de velocidad⟩
gearshift ['gɪrˌʃɪft] *n* : palanca *f* de cambio, palanca *f* de velocidad
geek ['giːk] *n fam* : intelectual *mf*
geese → **goose**
Geiger counter ['gaɪgərˌkaʊntər] *n* : contador *m* Geiger
gel ['ʤɛl] *n* : gel *m*
gelatin ['ʤɛlətən] *n* : gelatina *f*
gem ['ʤɛm] *n* : joya *f*, gema *f*, alhaja *f*
Gemini ['ʤɛməˌnaɪ] *n* : Géminis *mf*
gemstone ['ʤɛmˌstoːn] *n* : piedra *f* (semipreciosa o preciosa), gema *f*
gender ['ʤɛndər] *n* **1** SEX : sexo *m* **2** : género *m* (en la gramática)
gene ['ʤiːn] *n* : gen *m*, gene *m*
genealogical [ˌʤiːniə'lɑʤɪkəl] *adj* : genealógico
genealogy [ˌʤiːni'ɑləʤi, ˌʤɛ-, -'æ-] *n, pl* **-gies** : genealogía *f*
genera → **genus**

general¹ ['ʤɛnrəl, 'ʤɛnə-] *adj* : general ⟨in general : en general, por lo general⟩
general² *n* : general *mf*
generality [ˌʤɛnə'rælət̬i] *n, pl* **-ties** : generalidad *f*
generalization [ˌʤɛnrələ'zeɪʃən, ˌʤɛnərə-] *n* : generalización *f*
generalize ['ʤɛnrəˌlaɪz, 'ʤɛnərə-] *v* **-ized; -izing** : generalizar
generally ['ʤɛnrəli, 'ʤɛnərə-] *adv* : generalmente, por lo general, en general
generate ['ʤɛnəˌreɪt] *vt* **-ated; -ating** : generar, producir
generation [ˌʤɛnə'reɪʃən] *n* : generación *f*
generator ['ʤɛnəˌreɪt̬ər] *n* : generador *m*
generic [ʤə'nɛrɪk] *adj* : genérico
generosity [ˌʤɛnə'rɑsət̬i] *n, pl* **-ties** : generosidad *f*
generous ['ʤɛnərəs] *adj* **1** OPENHANDED : generoso, dadivoso, desprendido **2** ABUNDANT, AMPLE : abundante, amplio, generoso — **generously** *adv*
genetic [ʤə'nɛt̬ɪk] *adj* : genético — **genetically** [-t̬ɪkli] *adv*
geneticist [ʤə'nɛt̬əsɪst] *n* : genetista *mf*
genetics [ʤə'nɛt̬ɪks] *n* : genética *f*
genial ['ʤiːniəl] *adj* GRACIOUS : simpático, cordial, afable — **genially** *adv*
geniality [ˌʤiːni'ælət̬i] *n* : simpatía *f*, afabilidad *f*
genie ['ʤiːni] *n* : genio *m*
genital ['ʤɛnət̬əl] *adj* : genital
genitals ['ʤɛnət̬əlz] *npl* : genitales *mpl*
genius ['ʤiːnjəs] *n* : genio *m*
genocide ['ʤɛnəˌsaɪd] *n* : genocidio *m*
genre ['ʒɑnrə, 'ʒɑr] *n* : género *m*
genteel [ʤɛn'tiːl] *adj* : cortés, fino, refinado
gentile¹ ['ʤɛnˌtaɪl] *adj* : gentil
gentile² *n* : gentil *mf*
gentility [ʤɛn'tɪlət̬i] *n, pl* **-ties 1** : nobleza *f* (de nacimiento) **2** POLITENESS, REFINEMENT : cortesía *f*, refinamiento *m*
gentle ['ʤɛnt̬əl] *adj* **-tler; -tlest 1** NOBLE : bien nacido, noble **2** DOCILE : dócil, manso **3** KINDLY : bondadoso, amable **4** MILD : suave, apacible ⟨a gentle breeze : una brisa suave⟩ **5** SOFT : suave (dícese de un sonido), ligero (dícese del tacto) **6** MODERATE : moderado, gradual ⟨a gentle slope : una cuesta gradual⟩
gentleman ['ʤɛnt̬əlmən] *n, pl* **-men** [-mən, -ˌmɛn] : caballero *m*, señor *m*
gentlemanly ['ʤɛnt̬əlmənli] *adj* : caballeroso
gentleness ['ʤɛnt̬əlnəs] *n* : delicadeza *f*, suavidad *f*, ternura *f*
gentlewoman ['ʤɛnt̬əlˌwʊmən] *n, pl* **-women** [-ˌwɪmən] : dama *f*, señora *f*
gently ['ʤɛntli] *adv* **1** CAREFULLY, SOFTLY : con cuidado, suavemente, ligeramente **2** KINDLY : amablemente, con delicadeza

gentry [ˈdʒɛntri] *n, pl* **-tries** : aristocracia *f*

genuflect [ˈdʒɛnjʊˌflɛkt] *vi* : doblar la rodilla, hacer una genuflexión

genuflection [ˌdʒɛnjʊˈflɛkʃən] *n* : genuflexión *f*

genuine [ˈdʒɛnjuwən] *adj* **1** AUTHENTIC, REAL : genuino, verdadero, auténtico **2** SINCERE : sincero — **genuinely** *adv*

genus [ˈdʒiːnəs] *n, pl* **genera** [ˈdʒɛ-nərə] : género *m*

geographer [dʒiˈɑgrəfər] *n* : geógrafo *m*, -fa *f*

geographical [ˌdʒiːəˈgræfɪkəl] *or* **geographic** [-fɪk] *adj* : geográfico — **geographically** [-fɪkli] *adv*

geography [dʒiˈɑgrəfi] *n, pl* **-phies** : geografía *f*

geologic [ˌdʒiːəˈlɑdʒɪk] *or* **geological** [-dʒɪkəl] *adj* : geológico — **geologically** [-dʒɪkli] *adv*

geologist [dʒiˈɑlədʒɪst] *n* : geólogo *m*, -ga *f*

geology [dʒiˈɑlədʒi] *n* : geología *f*

geometric [ˌdʒiːəˈmɛtrɪk] *or* **geometrical** [-trɪkəl] *adj* : geométrico

geometry [dʒiˈɑmətri] *n, pl* **-tries** : geometría *f*

geopolitical [ˌdʒiːopəˈlɪtɪkəl] *adj* : geopolítico

Georgian [ˈdʒɔrdʒən] *n* **1** : georgiano *m* (idioma) **2** : georgiano *m*, -na *f* — **Georgian** *adj*

geranium [dʒəˈreɪniəm] *n* : geranio *m*

gerbil [ˈdʒɑrbəl] *n* : jerbo *m*, gerbo *m*

geriatric [ˌdʒɛriˈætrɪk] *adj* : geriátrico

geriatrics [ˌdʒɛriˈætrɪks] *n* : geriatría *f*

germ [ˈdʒərm] *n* **1** MICROORGANISM : microbio *m*, germen *m* **2** BEGINNING : germen *m*, principio *m* ⟨the germ of a plan : el germen de un plan⟩

German [ˈdʒərmən] *n* **1** : alemán *m*, -mana *f* **2** : alemán *m* (idioma) — **German** *adj*

germane [dʒərˈmeɪn] *adj* : relevante, pertinente

Germanic[1] [dʒərˈmænɪk] *adj* : germánico, germano

Germanic[2] *n* : germánico *m* (idioma)

germanium [dʒərˈmeɪniəm] *n* : germanio *m*

germ cell *n* : célula *f* germen

germicide [ˈdʒərməˌsaɪd] *n* : germicida *f*

germinate [ˈdʒərməˌneɪt] *v* **-nated; -nating** *vi* : germinar — *vt* : hacer germinar

germination [ˌdʒərməˈneɪʃən] *n* : germinación *f*

gerund [ˈdʒɛrənd] *n* : gerundio *m*

gestation [dʒɛˈsteɪʃən] *n* : gestación *f*

gesture[1] [ˈdʒɛstʃər] *vi* **-tured; -turing** : gesticular, hacer gestos

gesture[2] *n* **1** : gesto *m*, ademán *m* **2** SIGN, TOKEN : gesto *m*, señal *f* ⟨a gesture of friendship : una señal de amistad⟩

get [ˈgɛt] *v* **got** [ˈgɑt]; **got** *or* **gotten** [ˈgɑtən]; **getting** *vt* **1** OBTAIN : conseguir, obtener, adquirir **2** RECEIVE : recibir ⟨to get a letter : recibir una carta⟩ **3** EARN : ganar ⟨he gets $10 an hour : gana $10 por hora⟩ **4** FETCH : traer ⟨get me my book : tráigame el libro⟩ **5** CATCH : tomar (un tren, etc.), agarrar (una pelota, una persona, etc.) **6** CONTRACT : contagiarse de, contraer ⟨she got the measles : le dio el sarampión⟩ **7** PREPARE : preparar (una comida) **8** PERSUADE : persuadir, mandar a hacer ⟨I got him to agree : logré convencerlo⟩ **9** (*to cause to be*) ⟨to get one's hair cut : cortarse el pelo⟩ **10** UNDERSTAND : entender ⟨now I get it! : ¡ya entiendo!⟩ **11 to have got** : tener ⟨I've got a headache : tengo un dolor de cabeza⟩ **12 to have got to** : tener que ⟨you've got to come : tienes que venir⟩ — *vi* **1** BECOME : ponerse, volverse, hacerse ⟨to get angry : ponerse furioso, enojarse⟩ **2** GO, MOVE : ir, avanzar ⟨he didn't get far : no avanzó mucho⟩ **3** ARRIVE : llegar ⟨to get home : llegar a casa⟩ **4 to get to be** : llegar a ser ⟨she got to be the director : llegó a ser directora⟩ **5 to get ahead** : adelantarse, progresar **6 to get along** : llevarse bien (con alguien), congeniar **7 to get by** MANAGE : arreglárselas **8 to get over** OVERCOME : superar, consolarse de **9 to get together** MEET : reunirse **10 to get up** : levantarse

getaway [ˈgɛtəˌweɪ] *n* ESCAPE : fuga *f*, huida *f*, escapada *f*

geyser [ˈgaɪzər] *n* : géiser *m*

Ghanaian [ˈgɑniən, ˈgæ-] *n* : ghanés *m*, -nesa *f* — **Ghanaian** *adj*

ghastly [ˈgæstli] *adj* **-lier; -est 1** HORRIBLE : horrible, espantoso **2** PALE : pálido, cadavérico

gherkin [ˈgərkən] *n* : pepinillo *m*

ghetto [ˈgɛtoː] *n, pl* **-tos** *or* **-toes** : gueto *m*

ghost [ˈgoːst] *n* **1** : fantasma *f*, espectro *m* **2 the Holy Ghost** : el Espíritu Santo

ghostly [ˈgoːstli] *adv* : fantasmal

ghoul [ˈguːl] *n* **1** : demonio *m* necrófago **2** : persona *f* de gustos macabros

GI [ˌdʒiːˈaɪ] *n, pl* **GI's** *or* **GIs** : soldado *m* estadounidense

giant[1] [ˈdʒaɪənt] *adj* : gigante, gigantesco, enorme

giant[2] *n* : gigante *m*, -ta *f*

gibberish [ˈdʒɪbərɪʃ] *n* : galimatías *m*, jerigonza *f*

gibbon [ˈgɪbən] *n* : gibón *m*

gibe[1] [ˈdʒaɪb] *vi* **gibed; gibing** : mofarse, burlarse

gibe[2] *n* : pulla *f*, burla *f*, mofa *f*

giblets [ˈdʒɪbləts] *npl* : menudos *mpl*, menudencias *fpl*

giddiness [ˈgɪdinəs] *n* **1** DIZZINESS : vértigo *m*, mareo *m* **2** SILLINESS : frivolidad *f*, estupidez *f*

giddy ['gɪdi] *adj* **-dier; -est 1** DIZZY : mareado, vertiginoso **2** FRIVOLOUS, SILLY : frívolo, tonto

gift ['gɪft] *n* **1** TALENT : don *m*, talento *m*, dotes *fpl* **2** PRESENT : regalo *m*, obsequio *m*

gifted ['gɪftəd] *adj* TALENTED : talentoso

gig ['gɪg] *vi* : trabajo *m* (de duración limitada) ⟨to play a gig : tocar en un concierto⟩

gigabyte ['dʒɪgəˌbaɪt, 'gɪ-] *n* : gigabyte *m*

gigantic [dʒaɪ'gæntɪk] *adj* : gigantesco, enorme, colosal

giggle¹ ['gɪgəl] *vi* **-gled; -gling** : reírse tontamente

giggle² *n* : risita *f*, risa *f* tonta

gild ['gɪld] *vt* **gilded** *or* **gilt** ['gɪlt]; **gilding** : dorar

gill ['gɪl] *n* : agalla *f*, branquia *f*

gilt¹ ['gɪlt] *adj* : dorado

gilt² *n* : dorado *m*

gimlet ['gɪmlət] *n* **1** : barrena *f* (herramienta) **2** : bebida *f* de vodka o ginebra y limón

gimmick ['gɪmɪk] *n* **1** GADGET : artilugio *m* **2** CATCH : engaño *m*, trampa *f* **3** SCHEME, TRICK : ardid *m*, truco *m*

gin ['dʒɪn] *n* **1** : desmotadora *f* (de algodón) **2** : ginebra *f* (bebida alcohólica)

ginger ['dʒɪndʒər] *n* : jengibre *m*

ginger ale *n* : ginger ale *m*, gaseosa *f* de jengibre

gingerbread ['dʒɪndʒərˌbrɛd] *n* : pan *m* de jengibre

gingerly ['dʒɪndʒərli] *adv* : con cuidado, cautelosamente

gingham ['gɪŋəm] *n* : guinga *f*

ginseng ['dʒɪnˌsɪŋ, -ˌsɛŋ] *n* : ginseng *m*

giraffe [dʒə'ræf] *n* : jirafa *f*

gird ['gərd] *vt* **girded** *or* **girt** ['gərt]; **girding 1** BIND : ceñir, atar **2** ENCIRCLE : rodear **3 to gird oneself** : prepararse

girder ['gərdər] *n* : viga *f*

girdle¹ ['gərdəl] *vt* **-dled; -dling 1** GIRD : ceñir, atar **2** SURROUND : rodear, circundar

girdle² *n* : faja *f*

girl ['gərl] *n* **1** : chica *f*, muchacha *f* **2** *or* **little girl** : niña *f*, chica *f* **3** SWEETHEART : novia *f* **4** DAUGHTER : hija *f*

girlfriend ['gərlˌfrɛnd] *n* : novia *f*, amiga *f*

girlhood ['gərlˌhʊd] *n* : niñez *f*, juventud *f* (de una muchacha)

girlish ['gərlɪʃ] *adj* : de niña

girth ['gərθ] *n* **1** : circunferencia *f* (de un árbol, etc.), cintura *f* (de una persona) **2** CINCH : cincha *f* (para caballos, etc.)

gist ['dʒɪst] *n* : quid *m*, meollo *m*

give¹ ['gɪv] *v* **gave** ['geɪv]; **given** ['gɪvən]; **giving** *vt* **1** HAND, PRESENT : dar, regalar, obsequiar ⟨give it to me : dámelo⟩ ⟨they gave him a gold watch : le regalaron un reloj de oro⟩ **2** PAY : dar, pagar ⟨I'll give you $10 for this one : te daré $10 por éste⟩ **3** UTTER : dar, pronunciar ⟨to give a shout : dar un grito⟩ ⟨to give a speech : pronunciar un discurso⟩ ⟨to give a verdict : dictar sentencia⟩ **4** PROVIDE : dar ⟨to give one's word : dar uno su palabra⟩ ⟨to give a party : dar una fiesta⟩ **5** CAUSE : dar, causar, ocasionar ⟨to give trouble : causar problemas⟩ ⟨to give someone to understand : darle a entender a alguien⟩ **6** GRANT : dar, otorgar ⟨to give permission : dar permiso⟩ — *vi* **1** : hacer regalos **2** YIELD : ceder, romperse ⟨it gave under the weight of the crowd : cedió bajo el peso de la muchedumbre⟩ **3 to give in** *or* **to give up** SURRENDER : rendirse, entregarse **4 to give out** : agotarse, acabarse ⟨the supplies gave out : las provisiones se agotaron⟩

give² *n* FLEXIBILITY : flexibilidad *f*, elasticidad *f*

giveaway ['gɪvəˌweɪ] *n* **1** : revelación *f* involuntaria **2** GIFT : regalo *m*, obsequio *m*

given ['gɪvən] *adj* **1** INCLINED : dado, inclinado ⟨he's given to quarreling : es muy dado a discutir⟩ **2** SPECIFIC : dado, determinado ⟨at a given time : en un momento dado⟩

given name *n* : nombre *m* de pila

give up *vt* : dejar, renunciar a, abandonar ⟨to give up smoking : dejar de fumar⟩

gizzard ['gɪzərd] *n* : molleja *f*

glacial ['gleɪʃəl] *adj* : glacial — **glacially** *adv*

glacier ['gleɪʃər] *n* : glaciar *m*

glad ['glæd] *adj* **gladder; gladdest 1** PLEASED : alegre, contento ⟨she was glad I came : se alegró de que haya venido⟩ ⟨glad to meet you! : ¡mucho gusto!⟩ **2** HAPPY, PLEASING : feliz, agradable ⟨glad tidings : buenas nuevas⟩ **3** WILLING : dispuesto, gustoso ⟨I'll be glad to do it : lo haré con mucho gusto⟩

gladden ['glædən] *vt* : alegrar

glade ['gleɪd] *n* : claro *m*

gladiator ['glædiˌeɪtər] *n* : gladiador *m*

gladiolus [ˌglædi'oːləs] *n, pl* **-li** [-li, -ˌlaɪ] : gladiolo *m*, gladíolo *m*

gladly ['glædli] *adv* : con mucho gusto

gladness ['glædnəs] *n* : alegría *f*, gozo *m*

glamor *or* **glamour** ['glæmər] *n* : atractivo *m*, hechizo *m*, encanto *m*

glamorous ['glæmərəs] *adj* : atractivo, encantador

glance¹ ['glænts] *vi* **glanced; glancing 1** RICOCHET : rebotar ⟨it glanced off the wall : rebotó en la pared⟩ **2 to glance at** : mirar, echar un vistazo a **3 to glance away** : apartar los ojos

glance² *n* : mirada *f*, vistazo *m*, ojeada *f*

gland ['glænd] *n* : glándula *f*

glandular ['glændʒʊlər] *adj* : glandular

glare¹ ['glær] *vi* **glared; glaring 1** SHINE : brillar, relumbrar **2** STARE : mirar con ira, lanzar una mirada feroz

glare² *n* **1** BRIGHTNESS : resplandor *m*, luz *f* deslumbrante **2** : mirada *f* feroz
glaring ['glærɪŋ] *adj* **1** BRIGHT : deslumbrante, brillante **2** FLAGRANT, OBVIOUS : flagrante, manifiesto ⟨a glaring error : un error que salta a la vista⟩
glass ['glæs] *n* **1** : vidrio *m*, cristal *m* ⟨stained glass : vidrio de color⟩ **2** : vaso *m* ⟨a glass of milk : un vaso de leche⟩ **3 glasses** *npl* SPECTACLES : gafas *fpl*, anteojos *mpl*, lentes *mpl*, espejuelos *mpl*
glassblowing ['glæs,blo:ɪŋ] *n* : soplado *m* del vidrio
glassful ['glæs,fʊl] *n* : vaso *m*, copa *f*
glassware ['glæs,wær] *n* : cristalería *f*
glassy ['glæsi] *adj* **glassier; -est 1** VITREOUS : vítreo **2** : vidrioso ⟨glassy eyes : ojos vidriosos⟩
glaucoma [glaʊ'ko:mə, glɔ-] *n* : glaucoma *m*
glaze¹ ['gleɪz] *vt* **glazed; glazing 1** : ponerle vidrios a (una ventana, etc.) **2** : vidriar (cerámica) **3** : glasear (papel, verduras, etc.)
glaze² *n* : vidriado *m*, glaseado *m*, barniz *m*
glazier ['gleɪʒər] *n* : vidriero *m*, -ra *f*
gleam¹ ['gli:m] *vi* : brillar, destellar, relucir
gleam² *n* **1** LIGHT : luz *f* (oscura) **2** GLINT : destello *m* **3** GLIMMER : rayo *m*, vislumbre *f* ⟨a gleam of hope : un rayo de esperanza⟩
glean ['gli:n] *vt* : recoger, espigar
glee ['gli:] *n* : alegría *f*, júbilo *m*, regocijo *m*
gleeful ['gli:fəl] *adj* : lleno de alegría
glen ['glɛn] *n* : cañada *f*
glib ['glɪb] *adj* **glibber; glibbest 1** : simplista ⟨a glib reply : una respuesta simplista⟩ **2** : con mucha labia (dícese de una persona)
glibly ['glɪbli] *adv* : con mucha labia
glide¹ ['glaɪd] *vi* **glided; gliding** : deslizarse (en una superficie), planear (en el aire)
glide² *n* : planeo *m*
glider ['glaɪdər] *n* **1** : planeador *m* (aeronave) **2** : mecedor *m* (tipo de columpio)
glimmer¹ ['glɪmər] *vi* : brillar con luz trémula
glimmer² *n* **1** : luz *f* trémula, luz *f* tenue **2** GLEAM : rayo *m*, vislumbre *f* ⟨a glimmer of understanding : un rayo de entendimiento⟩
glimpse¹ ['glɪmps] *vt* **glimpsed; glimpsing** : vislumbrar, entrever
glimpse² *n* : mirada *f* breve ⟨to catch a glimpse of : alcanzar a ver, vislumbrar⟩
glint¹ ['glɪnt] *vi* GLEAM, SPARKLE : destellar, fulgurar
glint² *n* **1** SPARKLE : destello *m*, centelleo *m* **2 to have a glint in one's eye** : chispearle los ojos a uno
glisten¹ ['glɪsən] *vi* : brillar, centellear
glisten² *n* : brillo *m*, centelleo *m*

glitch ['glɪtʃ] *n* **1** MALFUNCTION : mal funcionamiento *m* **2** SNAG : problema *m*, complicación *f*
glitter¹ ['glɪtər] *vi* **1** SPARKLE : destellar, relucir, brillar **2** FLASH : relampaguear ⟨his eyes glittered in anger : le relampagueaban los ojos de ira⟩
glitter² *n* **1** BRIGHTNESS : brillo *m* **2** : purpurina *f* (para decoración)
glitz ['glɪts] *n* : oropel *m*
gloat ['glo:t] *vi* **to gloat over** : regodearse en
glob ['glɑb] *n* : plasta *f*, masa *f*, grumo *m*
global ['glo:bəl] *adj* **1** SPHERICAL : esférico **2** WORLDWIDE : global, mundial — **globally** *adv*
globe ['glo:b] *n* **1** SPHERE : esfera *f*, globo *m* **2** EARTH : globo *m*, Tierra *f* **3** : globo *m* terráqueo (modelo de la Tierra)
globe-trotter ['glo:b,trɑtər] *n* : trotamundos *mf*
globular ['glɑbjʊlər] *adj* : globular
globule ['glɑ,bju:l] *n* : glóbulo *m*
gloom ['glu:m] *n* **1** DARKNESS : penumbra *f*, oscuridad *f* **2** MELANCHOLY : melancolía *f*, tristeza *f*
gloomily ['glu:məli] *adv* : tristemente
gloomy ['glu:mi] *adj* **gloomier; -est 1** DARK : oscuro, tenebroso ⟨gloomy weather : tiempo gris⟩ **2** MELANCHOLY : melancólico **3** PESSIMISTIC : pesimista **4** DEPRESSING : deprimente, lúgubre
glorification [,glorəfə'keɪʃən] *n* : glorificación *f*
glorify ['glorə,faɪ] *vt* **-fied; -fying** : glorificar
glorious ['gloriəs] *adj* **1** ILLUSTRIOUS : glorioso, ilustre **2** MAGNIFICENT : magnífico, espléndido, maravilloso — **gloriously** *adv*
glory¹ ['glori] *vi* **-ried; -rying** EXULT : exultar, regocijarse
glory² *n, pl* **-ries 1** RENOWN : gloria *f*, fama *f*, honor *m* **2** PRAISE : gloria *f* ⟨glory to God : gloria a Dios⟩ **3** MAGNIFICENCE : magnificencia *f*, esplendor *m*, gloria *f* **4 to be in one's glory** : estar uno en su gloria
gloss¹ ['glɔs, 'glɑs] *vt* **1** EXPLAIN : glosar, explicar **2** POLISH : lustrar, pulir **3 to gloss over** : quitarle importancia a, minimizar
gloss² *n* **1** SHINE : lustre *m*, brillo *m* **2** EXPLANATION : glosa *f*, explicación *f* breve **3** → **glossary**
glossary ['glɔsəri, 'glɑ-] *n, pl* **-ries** : glosario *m*
glossy ['glɔsi, 'glɑ-] *adj* **glossier; -est** : brillante, lustroso, satinado (dícese del papel)
glove ['glʌv] *n* : guante *m*
glow¹ ['glo:] *vi* **1** SHINE : brillar, resplandecer **2** BRIM : rebosar ⟨to glow with health : rebosar de salud⟩

glow² *n* **1** BRIGHTNESS : resplandor *m*, brillo *m*, luminosidad *f* **2** FEELING : sensación *f* (de bienestar), oleada *f* (de sentimiento) **3** INCANDESCENCE : incandescencia *f*

glower ['glaʊər] *vi* : fruncir el ceño

glowworm ['gloː‚wərm] *n* : luciérnaga *f*

glucose ['gluː‚koːs] *n* : glucosa *f*

glue¹ ['gluː] *vt* **glued; gluing** *or* **glueing** : pegar, encolar

glue² *n* : pegamento *m*, cola *f*

gluey ['gluːi] *adj* **gluier; -est** : pegajoso

glum ['glʌm] *adj* **glummer; glummest 1** SULLEN : hosco, sombrío **2** DREARY, GLOOMY : sombrío, triste, melancólico

glut¹ ['glʌt] *vt* **glutted; glutting 1** SATIATE : saciar, hartar **2** : inundar (el mercado)

glut² *n* : exceso *m*, superabundancia *f*

glutinous ['gluːtənəs] *adj* STICKY : pegajoso, glutinoso

glutton ['glʌtən] *n* : glotón *m*, -tona *f*

gluttonous ['glʌtənəs] *adj* : glotón

gluttony ['glʌtəni] *n, pl* **-tonies** : glotonería *f*, gula *f*

gnarled ['nɑrld] *adj* **1** KNOTTY : nudoso **2** TWISTED : retorcido

gnash ['næʃ] *vt* : hacer rechinar (los dientes)

gnat ['næt] *n* : jején *m*

gnaw ['nɔ] *vt* : roer

gnome ['noːm] *n* : gnomo *m*

gnu ['nuː, 'njuː] *n, pl* **gnu** *or* **gnus** : ñu *m*

go¹ ['goː] *v* **went** ['wɛnt]; **gone** ['gɔn, 'gɑn]; **going; goes** ['goːz] *vi* **1** PROCEED : ir ⟨to go slow : ir despacio⟩ ⟨to go shopping : ir de compras⟩ **2** LEAVE : irse, marcharse, salir ⟨let's go! : ¡vámonos!⟩ ⟨the train went on time : el tren salió a tiempo⟩ **3** DISAPPEAR : desaparecer, pasarse, irse ⟨her fear is gone : se le ha pasado el miedo⟩ ⟨my pen is gone! : ¡mi pluma desapareció!⟩ **4** EXTEND : ir, extenderse, llegar ⟨this road goes to the river : este camino se extiende hasta el río⟩ ⟨to go from top to bottom : ir de arriba abajo⟩ **5** FUNCTION : funcionar, marchar ⟨the car won't go : el coche no funciona⟩ ⟨to get something going : poner algo en marcha⟩ **6** SELL : venderse ⟨it goes for $15 : se vende por $15⟩ **7** PROGRESS : ir, andar, seguir ⟨my exam went well : me fue bien en el examen⟩ ⟨how did the meeting go? : ¿qué tal la reunión?⟩ **8** BECOME : volverse, quedarse ⟨he's going crazy : está volviéndose loco⟩ ⟨the tire went flat : la llanta se desinfló⟩ **9** FIT : caber ⟨it will go through the door : cabe por la puerta⟩ **10** anything goes! : ¡todo vale! **11** to go : faltar ⟨only 10 days to go : faltan sólo 10 días⟩ **12** to go back on : faltar a (su promesa) **13** to go bad SPOIL : estropearse, echarse a perder **14** to go for : interesarse uno en, gustarle a uno (algo, alguien) ⟨I don't go for that : eso

no me interesa⟩ **15** to go off EXPLODE : estallar **16** to go with MATCH : armonizar con, hacer juego con — *v aux* to be going to : ir a ⟨I'm going to write a letter : voy a escribir una carta⟩ ⟨it's not going to last : no va a durar⟩

go² *n, pl* **goes 1** ATTEMPT : intento *m* ⟨to have a go at : intentar, probar⟩ **2** SUCCESS : éxito *m* **3** ENERGY : energía *f*, empuje *m* ⟨to be on the go : no parar, no descansar⟩

goad¹ ['goːd] *vt* : aguijonear (un animal), incitar (a una persona)

goad² *n* : aguijón *m*

goal ['goːl] *n* **1** : gol *m* (en deportes) ⟨to score a goal : anotar un gol⟩ **2** *or* **goalposts** : portería *f* **3** AIM, OBJECTIVE : meta *f*, objetivo *m*

goalie ['goːli] → **goalkeeper**

goalkeeper ['goːl‚kiːpər] *n* : portero *m*, -ra *f*; guardameta *mf*; arquero *m*, -ra *f*

goaltender ['goːl‚tɛndər] → **goalkeeper**

goat ['goːt] *n* **1** : cabra *f* (hembra) **2** billy goat : macho *m* cabrío, chivo *m*

goatee [goː'tiː] *n* : barbita *f* de chivo, piocha *f* Mex

goatskin ['goːt‚skɪn] *n* : piel *f* de cabra

gob ['gɑb] *n* : masa *f*, grumo *m*

gobble ['gɑbəl] *v* **-bled; -bling** *vt* to gobble up : tragar, engullir — *vi* : hacer ruidos de pavo

gobbledygook ['gɑbəldi‚gʊk, -‚guːk] *n* GIBBERISH : jerigonza *f*

goblet ['gɑblət] *n* : copa *f*

goblin ['gɑblən] *n* : duende *m*, trasgo *m*

god ['gɑd, 'gɔd] *n* **1** : dios *m* **2** God : Dios *m*

godchild ['gɑd‚tʃaɪld, 'gɔd-] *n, pl* **-children** : ahijado *m*, -da *f*

goddess ['gɑdəs, 'gɔ-] *n* : diosa *f*

godfather ['gɑd‚fɑðər, 'gɔd-] *n* : padrino *m*

godless ['gɑdləs, 'gɔd-] *adj* : ateo

godlike ['gɑd‚laɪk, 'gɔd-] *adj* : divino

godly ['gɑdli, 'gɔd-] *adj* **-lier; -est 1** DIVINE : divino **2** DEVOUT, PIOUS : piadoso, devoto, beato

godmother ['gɑd‚mʌðər, 'gɔd-] *n* : madrina *f*

godparents ['gɑd‚pærənts, 'gɔd-] *npl* : padrinos *mpl*

godsend ['gɑd‚sɛnd, 'gɔd-] *n* : bendición *f*, regalo *m* divino

goes → **go**

go-getter ['goː‚gɛtər] *n* : persona *f* ambiciosa, buscavidas *mf fam*

goggle ['gɑgəl] *vi* **-gled; -gling** : mirar con ojos desorbitados

goggles ['gɑgəlz] *npl* : gafas *fpl* (protectoras), anteojos *mpl*

goings-on [‚goːɪŋz'ɑn, -'ɔn] *npl* : sucesos *mpl*, ocurrencias *fpl*

goiter ['gɔɪtər] *n* : bocio *m*

gold ['goːld] *n* : oro *m*

golden ['goːldən] *adj* **1** : (hecho) de oro **2** : dorado, de color oro ⟨golden hair

: pelo rubio⟩ **3** FLOURISHING, PROS-PEROUS : dorado, próspero ⟨golden years : años dorados⟩ **4** FAVORABLE : favorable, excelente ⟨a golden opportunity : una excelente oportunidad⟩

goldenrod ['goːldən̩ɹɑd] *n* : vara *f* de oro

golden rule *n* : regla *f* de oro

goldfinch ['goːld̩fɪnt͡ʃ] *n* : jilguero *m*

goldfish ['goːld̩fɪʃ] *n* : pez *m* de colores

goldsmith ['goːld̩smɪθ] *n* : orífice *mf*, orfebre *mf*

golf[1] ['gɑlf, 'gɔlf] *vi* : jugar (al) golf

golf[2] *n* : golf *m*

golfer ['gɑlfər, 'gɔl-] *n* : golfista *mf*

gondola ['gɑndələ, gɑn'doːlə] *n* : góndola *f*

gone ['gɔn] *adj* **1** DEAD : muerto **2** PAST : pasado, ido **3** LOST : perdido, desaparecido **4 to be far gone** : estar muy avanzado **5 to be gone on** : estar loco por

goner ['gɔnər] *n* **to be a goner** : estar en las últimas

gong ['gɔŋ, 'gɑŋ] *n* : gong *m*

gonorrhea [ˌgɑnə'riːə] *n* : gonorrea *f*

good[1] ['gʊd] *adv* **1** (*used as an intensifier*) : bien ⟨a good strong rope : una cuerda bien fuerte⟩ **2** WELL : bien

good[2] *adj* **better** ['bɛt̬ər]; **best** ['bɛst] **1** PLEASANT : bueno, agradable ⟨good news : buenas noticias⟩ ⟨to have a good time : divertirse⟩ **2** BENEFICIAL : bueno, beneficioso ⟨good for a cold : beneficioso para los resfriados⟩ ⟨it's good for you : es bueno para uno⟩ **3** FULL : completo, entero ⟨a good hour : una hora entera⟩ **4** CONSIDERABLE : bueno, bastante ⟨a good many people : muchísima gente, un buen número de gente⟩ **5** ATTRACTIVE, DESIRABLE : bueno, bien ⟨a good salary : un buen sueldo⟩ ⟨to look good : quedar bien⟩ **6** KIND, VIRTUOUS : bueno, amable ⟨she's a good person : es buena gente⟩ ⟨that's good of you! : ¡qué amable!⟩ ⟨good deeds : buenas obras⟩ **7** SKILLED : bueno, hábil ⟨to be good at : tener facilidad para⟩ **8** SOUND : bueno, sensato ⟨good advice : buenos consejos⟩ **9** (*in greetings*) : bueno ⟨good morning : buenos días⟩ ⟨good afternoon (evening) : buenas tardes⟩ ⟨good night : buenas noches⟩

good[3] *n* **1** RIGHT : bien *m* ⟨to do good : hacer el bien⟩ **2** GOODNESS : bondad *f* **3** BENEFIT : bien *m*, provecho *m* ⟨it's for your own good : es por tu propio bien⟩ **4 goods** *npl* PROPERTY : efectos *mpl* personales, posesiones *fpl* **5 goods** *npl* WARES : mercancía *f*, mercadería *f*, artículos *mpl* **6 for ～** : para siempre

good–bye *or* **good–by** [gʊd'baɪ] *n* : adiós *m*

good–for–nothing [ˈgʊdfərˌnʌθɪŋ] *n* : inútil *mf*; haragán *m*, -gana *f*; holgazán *m*, -zana *f*

Good Friday *n* : Viernes *m* Santo

good–hearted ['gʊd'hɑrt̬əd] *adj* : bondadoso, benévolo, de buen corazón

good–looking ['gʊd'lʊkɪŋ] *adj* : bello, bonito, guapo

goodly ['gʊdli] *adj* **-lier; -est** : considerable, importante ⟨a goodly number : un número considerable⟩

good–natured ['gʊd'neɪt͡ʃərd] *adj* : amigable, amistoso, bonachón *fam*

goodness ['gʊdnəs] *n* **1** : bondad *f* **2 thank goodness!** : ¡gracias a Dios!, ¡menos mal!

good–tempered ['gʊd'tɛmpərd] *adj* : de buen genio

goodwill [ˌgʊd'wɪl] *n* **1** BENEVOLENCE : benevolencia *f*, buena voluntad *f* **2** : buen nombre *m* (de comercios), renombre *m* comercial

goody ['gʊdi] *n, pl* **goodies** : cosa *f* rica para comer, golosina *f*

gooey ['guːi] *adj* **gooier; gooiest** : pegajoso

goof[1] ['guːf] *vi* **1 to goof off** : holgazanear **2 to goof around** : hacer tonterías **3 to goof up** BLUNDER : cometer un error

goof[2] *n* **1** : bobo *m*, -ba *f*; tonto *m*, -ta *f* **2** BLUNDER : error *m*, planchazo *m fam*

goofy ['guːfi] *adj* **goofier; -est** SILLY : tonto, bobo

goose ['guːs] *n, pl* **geese** ['giːs] : ganso *m*, -sa *f*; ánsar *m*; oca *f*

gooseberry ['guːsˌbɛriː, 'guːz-] *n, pl* **-berries** : grosella *f* espinosa

goose bumps *npl* : carne *f* de gallina

gooseflesh ['guːsˌflɛʃ] → **goose bumps**

goose pimples → **goose bumps**

gopher ['goːfər] *n* : taltuza *f*

gore[1] ['gor] *vt* **gored; goring** : cornear

gore[2] *n* BLOOD : sangre *f*

gorge[1] ['gɔrd͡ʒ] *vt* **gorged; gorging** **1** SATIATE : saciar, hartar **2 to gorge oneself** : hartarse, atiborrarse, atracarse *fam*

gorge[2] *n* RAVINE : desfiladero *m*

gorgeous ['gɔrd͡ʒəs] *adj* : hermoso, espléndido, magnífico

gorilla [gə'rɪlə] *n* : gorila *m*

gory ['gori] *adj* **gorier; -est** BLOODY : sangriento

gosling ['gɑzlɪn, 'gɔz-] *n* : ansarino *m*

gospel ['gɑspəl] *n* **1** *or* **Gospel** : evangelio *m* ⟨the four Gospels : los cuatro evangelios⟩ **2 the gospel truth** : el evangelio, la pura verdad

gossamer ['gɑsəmər, 'gɑzə-] *adj* : tenue, sutil ⟨gossamer wings : alas tenues⟩

gossip[1] ['gɑsɪp] *vi* : chismear, contar chismes

gossip[2] *n* **1** : chismoso *m*, -sa *f* (persona) **2** RUMOR : chisme *m*, rumor *m*

gossipy ['gɑsɪpi] *adj* : chismoso

got → get

Gothic ['gɑθɪk] *adj* : gótico

gotten → get

gouge[1] ['gaʊd͡ʒ] *vt* **gouged; gouging** **1** : excavar, escoplear (con una gubia) **2** SWINDLE : estafar, extorsionar

gouge² n **1** CHISEL : gubia f, formón m **2** GROOVE : ranura f, hoyo m (hecho por un formón)

goulash ['guːˌlɑʃ, -ˌlæʃ] n : estofado m, guiso m al estilo húngaro

gourd ['gord, 'gʊrd] n : calabaza f

gourmand ['gʊrˌmɑnd] n **1** GLUTTON : glotón m, -tona f **2** → gourmet

gourmet ['gʊrˌmeɪ, gʊr'meɪ] n : gourmet mf; gastrónomo m, -ma f

gout ['gaʊt] n : gota f

govern ['gʌvərn] vt **1** RULE : gobernar **2** CONTROL, DETERMINE : determinar, controlar, guiar **3** RESTRAIN : dominar (las emociones, etc.) — vi : gobernar

governess ['gʌvərnəs] n : institutriz f

government ['gʌvərmənt] n : gobierno m

governmental [ˌgʌvər'mɛntəl] adj : gubernamental, gubernativo

governor ['gʌvənər, 'gʌvərnər] n **1** : gobernador m, - dora f (de un estado, etc.) **2** : regulador m (de una máquina)

governorship ['gʌvənərˌʃɪp, 'gʌvərnər-] n : cargo m de gobernador

gown ['gaʊn] n **1** : vestido m ⟨evening gown : traje de fiesta⟩ **2** : toga f (de magistrados, clérigos, etc.)

grab¹ ['græb] v **grabbed; grabbing** vt SNATCH : agarrar, arrebatar — vi : agarrarse

grab² n **1 to make a grab for** : tratar de agarrar **2 up for grabs** : disponible, libre

grace¹ ['greɪs] vt **graced; gracing 1** HONOR : honrar **2** ADORN : adornar, embellecer

grace² n **1** : gracia f ⟨by the grace of God : por la gracia de Dios⟩ **2** BLESSING : bendición f (de la mesa) **3** RESPITE : plazo m, gracia f ⟨a five days' grace (period) : un plazo de cinco días⟩ **4** GRACIOUSNESS : gentileza f, cortesía f **5** ELEGANCE : elegancia f, gracia f **6 to be in the good graces of** : estar en buenas relaciones con **7 with good grace** : de buena gana

graceful ['greɪsfəl] adj : lleno de gracia, garboso, grácil

gracefully ['greɪsfəli] adv : con gracia, con garbo

gracefulness ['greɪsfəlnəs] n : gracilidad f, apostura f, gallardía f

graceless ['greɪsləs] adj **1** DISCOURTEOUS : descortés **2** CLUMSY, INELEGANT : torpe, desgarbado, poco elegante

gracious ['greɪʃəs] adj : cortés, gentil, cordial

graciously ['greɪʃəsli] adv : gentilmente

graciousness ['greɪʃəsnəs] n : gentileza f

gradation [greɪ'deɪʃən, grə-] n : gradación f

grade¹ ['greɪd] vt **graded; grading 1** SORT : clasificar **2** LEVEL : nivelar **3** : calificar (exámenes, alumnos)

grade² n **1** QUALITY : categoría f, calidad f **2** RANK : grado m, rango m (mil-

itar) **3** YEAR : grado m, curso m, año m ⟨sixth grade : el sexto grado⟩ **4** MARK : nota f, calificación f (en educación) **5** SLOPE : cuesta f, pendiente f, gradiente f

grade school → elementary school

gradient ['greɪdiənt] n : gradiente f

gradual ['grædʒuəl] adj : gradual, paulatino

gradually ['grædʒuəli, 'grædʒəli] adv : gradualmente, poco a poco

graduate¹ ['grædʒuˌeɪt] v **-ated; -ating** vi : graduarse, licenciarse — vt : graduar ⟨a graduated thermometer : un termómetro graduado⟩

graduate² ['grædʒuət] adj : de postgrado ⟨graduate course : curso de postgrado⟩

graduate³ n **1** : licenciado m, -da f; graduado m, -da f (de la universidad) **2** : bachiller mf (de la escuela secundaria)

graduate student n : postgraduado m, -da f

graduation [ˌgrædʒu'eɪʃən] n : graduación f

graffiti [grə'fiːˌti, græ-] npl : pintadas fpl, graffiti mpl

graft¹ ['græft] vt : injertar

graft² n **1** : injerto m ⟨skin graft : injerto cutáneo⟩ **2** CORRUPTION : soborno m (político), ganancia f ilegal

grain ['greɪn] n **1** : grano m ⟨a grain of corn : un grano de maíz⟩ ⟨like a grain of sand : como grano de arena⟩ **2** CEREALS : cereales mpl **3** : veta f, vena f, grano m (de madera) **4** SPECK, TRACE : pizca f, ápice m ⟨a grain of truth : una pizca de verdad⟩ **5** grano m (unidad de peso)

gram ['græm] n : gramo m

grammar ['græmər] n : gramática f

grammar school → elementary school

grammatical [grə'mætɪkəl] adj : gramatical — **grammatically** [-kli] adv

granary ['greɪnəri, 'græ-] n, pl **-ries** : granero m

grand ['grænd] adj **1** FOREMOST : grande **2** IMPRESSIVE : impresionante, magnífico ⟨a grand view : una vista magnífica⟩ **3** LAVISH : grandioso, suntuoso, lujoso ⟨to live in a grand manner : vivir a lo grande⟩ **4** FABULOUS : fabuloso, magnífico ⟨to have a grand time : pasarlo estupendamente, pasarlo en grande⟩ **5 grand total** : total m, suma f total

grandchild ['grænˌtʃaɪld] n, pl **-children** : nieto m, -ta f

granddaughter ['grændˌdɔtər] n : nieta f

grandeur ['grændʒər] n : grandiosidad f, esplendor m

grandfather ['grændˌfɑðər] n : abuelo m

grandiose ['grændiˌoːs, ˌgrændi'-] adj **1** IMPOSING : imponente, grandioso **2** POMPOUS : pomposo, presuntuoso

grandma ['grænˌmɑ, -ˌmɔ] n : abuelita f, nana f

grandmother ['grænd,mʌðər] *n* : abuela *f*

grandpa ['græm,pɑ, -,pɔ] *n* : abuelito *m*

grandparents ['grænd,pærənts] *npl* : abuelos *mpl*

grandson ['grænd,sʌn] *n* : nieto *m*

grandstand ['grænd,stænd] *n* : tribuna *f*

granite ['grænɪt] *n* : granito *m*

grant¹ ['grænt] *vt* **1** ALLOW : conceder ⟨to grant a request : conceder una petición⟩ **2** BESTOW : conceder, dar, otorgar ⟨to grant a favor : otorgar un favor⟩ **3** ADMIT : reconocer, admitir ⟨I'll grant that he's clever : reconozco que es listo⟩ **4 to take for granted** : dar (algo) por sentado

grant² *n* **1** GRANTING : concesión *f*, otorgamiento *m* **2** SCHOLARSHIP : beca *f* **3** SUBSIDY : subvención *f*

granular ['grænjʊlər] *adj* : granular

granulated ['grænjʊ,leɪtəd] *adj* : granulado

grape ['greɪp] *n* : uva *f*

grapefruit ['greɪp,fru:t] *n* : toronja *f*, pomelo *m*

grapevine ['greɪp,vaɪn] *n* **1** : vid *f*, parra *f* **2 through the grapevine** : por vías secretas ⟨I heard it through the grapevine : me lo contaron⟩

graph ['græf] *n* : gráfica *f*, gráfico *m*

graphic ['græfɪk] *adj* **1** VIVID : vívido, gráfico **2 graphic arts** : artes gráficas

graphically ['græfɪkli] *adv* : gráficamente

graphite ['græ,faɪt] *n* : grafito *m*

grapnel ['græpnəl] *n* : rezón *m*

grapple ['græpəl] *v* **-pled; -pling** *vt* GRIP : agarrar (con un garfio) — *vi* STRUGGLE : forcejear, luchar (con un problema, etc.)

grasp¹ ['græsp] *vt* **1** GRIP, SEIZE : agarrar, asir **2** COMPREHEND : entender, comprender — *vi* **to grasp at** : aprovechar

grasp² *n* **1** GRIP : agarre *m* **2** CONTROL : control *m*, garras *fpl* **3** REACH : alcance *m* ⟨within your grasp : a su alcance⟩ **4** UNDERSTANDING : comprensión *f*, entendimiento *m*

grass ['græs] *n* **1** : hierba *f* (planta) **2** PASTURE : pasto *m*, zacate *m* CA, *Mex* **3** LAWN : césped *m*, pasto *m*

grasshopper ['græs,hɑpər] *n* : saltamontes *m*

grassland ['græs,lænd] *n* : pradera *f*

grassy ['græsi] *adj* **grassier; -est** : cubierto de hierba

grate¹ ['greɪt] *v* **grated; -ing** *vt* **1** : rallar (en cocina) **2** SCRAPE : rascar **3 to grate one's teeth** : hacer rechinar los dientes — *vi* **1** RASP, SQUEAK : chirriar **2** IRRITATE : irritar ⟨to grate on one's nerves : crisparle los nervios a uno⟩

grate² *n* **1** : parrilla *f* (para cocinar) **2** GRATING : reja *f*, rejilla *f*, verja *f* (en una ventana)

grateful ['greɪtfəl] *adj* : agradecido

gratefully ['greɪtfəli] *adv* : con agradecimiento

gratefulness ['greɪtfəlnəs] *n* : gratitud *f*, agradecimiento *m*

grater ['greɪtər] *n* : rallador *m*

gratification [,grætəfə'keɪʃən] *n* : gratificación *f*

gratify ['grætə,faɪ] *vt* **-fied; -fying 1** PLEASE : complacer **2** SATISFY : satisfacer, gratificar

grating ['greɪtɪŋ] *n* : reja *f*, rejilla *f*

gratis¹ ['grætəs, 'greɪ-] *adv* : gratis, gratuitamente

gratis² *adj* : gratis, gratuito

gratitude ['grætə,tu:d, -,tju:d] *n* : gratitud *f*, agradecimiento *m*

gratuitous [grə'tu:ətəs] *adj* : gratuito

gratuity [grə'tu:əti] *n, pl* **-ities** TIP : propina *f*

grave¹ ['greɪv] *adj* **graver; -est 1** IMPORTANT : grave, de mucha gravedad **2** SERIOUS, SOLEMN : grave, serio

grave² *n* : tumba *f*, sepultura *f*

gravel ['grævəl] *n* : grava *f*, gravilla *f*

gravelly ['grævəli] *adj* **1** : de grava **2** HARSH : áspero (dícese de la voz)

gravely ['greɪvli] *adv* : gravemente

gravestone ['greɪv,sto:n] *n* : lápida *f*

graveyard ['greɪv,jɑrd] *n* CEMETERY : cementerio *m*, panteón *m*, camposanto *m*

gravitate ['grævə,teɪt] *vi* **-tated; -tating** : gravitar

gravitation [,grævə'teɪʃən] *n* : gravitación *f*

gravitational [,grævə'teɪʃənəl] *adj* : gravitacional

gravity ['grævəti] *n, pl* **-ties 1** SERIOUSNESS : gravedad *f*, seriedad *f* **2** : gravedad *f* ⟨the law of gravity : la ley de la gravedad⟩

gravy ['greɪvi] *n, pl* **-vies** : salsa *f* (preparada con el jugo de la carne asada)

gray¹ ['greɪ] *vt* : hacer gris — *vi* : encanecer, ponerse gris

gray² *adj* **1** : gris (dícese del color) **2** : cano, canoso ⟨gray hair : pelo canoso⟩ ⟨to go gray : volverse cano⟩ **3** DISMAL, GLOOMY : gris, triste

gray³ *n* : gris *m*

grayish ['greɪɪʃ] *adj* : grisáceo

graze ['greɪz] *v* **grazed; grazing** *vi* : pastar, pacer — *vt* **1** : pastorear (ganado) **2** BRUSH : rozar **3** SCRATCH : raspar

grease¹ ['gri:s, 'gri:z] *vt* **greased; greasing** : engrasar, lubricar

grease² ['gri:s] *n* : grasa *f*

greasy ['gri:si, -zi] *adj* **greasier; -est 1** : grasiento **2** OILY : graso, grasoso

great ['greɪt] *adj* **1** LARGE : grande ⟨a great mountain : una montaña grande⟩ ⟨a great crowd : una gran muchedumbre⟩ **2** INTENSE : intenso, fuerte, grande ⟨great pain : gran dolor⟩ **3** EMINENT : grande, eminente, distinguido ⟨a great poet : un gran poeta⟩ **4** EXCELLENT, TERRIFIC : excelente, estupendo, fabuloso ⟨to have a great time : pasarlo en grande⟩ **5 a great while** : mucho tiempo

great–aunt [ˌgreɪt'ænt, -'ant] *n* : tía *f* abuela

greater ['greɪtər] (*comparative* of **great**) : mayor

greatest ['greɪtəst] (*superlative* of **great**) : el mayor, la mayor

great–grandchild [ˌgreɪt'grænd-ˌtʃaɪld] *n, pl* **-children** [-ˌtʃɪldrən] : bisnieto *m*, -ta *f*

great–grandfather [ˌgreɪt'grænd-ˌfɑðər] *n* : bisabuelo *m*

great–grandmother [ˌgreɪt'grænd-ˌmʌðər] *n* : bisabuela *f*

greatly ['greɪtli] *adv* **1** MUCH : mucho, sumamente ⟨to be greatly improved : haber mejorado mucho⟩ **2** VERY : muy ⟨greatly superior : muy superior⟩

greatness ['greɪtnəs] *n* : grandeza *f*

great–uncle [ˌgreɪt'ʌŋkəl] *n* : tío *m* abuelo

grebe ['griːb] *n* : somorgujo *m*

greed ['griːd] *n* **1** AVARICE : avaricia *f*, codicia *f* **2** GLUTTONY : glotonería *f*, gula *f*

greedily ['griːdəli] *adv* : con avaricia, con gula

greediness ['griːdinəs] → **greed**

greedy ['griːdi] *adj* **greedier; -est 1** AVARICIOUS : codicioso, avaricioso **2** GLUTTONOUS : glotón

Greek ['griːk] *n* **1** : griego *m*, -ga *f* **2** : griego *m* (idioma) — **Greek** *adj*

green[1] ['griːn] *adj* **1** : verde (dícese del color) **2** UNRIPE : verde, inmaduro **3** INEXPERIENCED : verde, novato

green[2] *n* **1** : verde *m* **2 greens** *npl* VEGETABLES : verduras *fpl*

greenery ['griːnəri] *n, pl* **-eries** : plantas *fpl* verdes, vegetación *f*

greenhorn ['griːnˌhɔrn] *n* : novato *m*, -ta *f*

greenhouse ['griːnˌhaʊs] *n* : invernadero *m*

greenhouse effect : efecto *m* invernadero

greenish ['griːnɪʃ] *adj* : verdoso

Greenlander ['griːnləndər, -ˌlæn-] *n* : groenlandés *m*, -desa *f*

greenness ['griːnnəs] *n* **1** : verdor *m* **2** INEXPERIENCE : inexperiencia *f*

green thumb *n* **to have a green thumb** : tener buena mano para las plantas

greet ['griːt] *vt* **1** : saludar ⟨to greet a friend : saludar a un amigo⟩ **2** : acoger, recibir ⟨they greeted him with boos : lo recibieron con abucheos⟩

greeting ['griːtɪŋ] *n* **1** : saludo *m* **2 greetings** *npl* REGARDS : saludos *mpl*, recuerdos *mpl*

gregarious [grɪ'gæriəs] *adj* : gregario (dícese de los animales), sociable (dícese de las personas) — **gregariously** *adv*

gregariousness [grɪ'gæriəsnəs] *n* : sociabilidad *f*

gremlin ['grɛmlən] *n* : duende *m*

grenade [grə'neɪd] *n* : granada *f*

Grenadian [grə'neɪdiən] *n* : granadino *m*, -na *f* — **Grenadian** *adj*

grew → **grow**

grey → **gray**

greyhound ['greɪˌhaʊnd] *n* : galgo *m*

grid ['grɪd] *n* **1** GRATING : rejilla *f* **2** NETWORK : red *f* (de electricidad, etc.) **3** : cuadriculado *m* (de un mapa)

griddle ['grɪdəl] *n* : plancha *f*

griddle cake → **pancake**

gridiron ['grɪdˌaɪərn] *n* **1** GRILL : parrilla *f* **2** : campo *m* de futbol americano

gridlock ['grɪdˌlɑk] *n* : atasco *m* completo (de una red de calles)

grief ['griːf] *n* **1** SORROW : dolor *m*, pena *f* **2** ANNOYANCE, TROUBLE : problemas *mpl*, molestia *f*

grievance ['griːvənts] *n* COMPLAINT : queja *f*

grieve ['griːv] *v* **grieved; grieving** *vt* DISTRESS : afligir, entristecer, apenar — *vi* **1** : sufrir, afligirse **2 to grieve for** *or* **to grieve over** : llorar, lamentar

grievous ['griːvəs] *adj* **1** OPPRESSIVE : gravoso, opresivo, severo **2** GRAVE, SERIOUS : grave, severo, doloroso

grievously ['griːvəsli] *adv* : gravemente, de gravedad

grill[1] ['grɪl] *vt* **1** : asar (a la parrilla) **2** INTERROGATE : interrogar

grill[2] *n* **1** : parrilla *f* (para cocinar) **2** : parrillada *f* (comida) **3** RESTAURANT : grill *m*

grille *or* **grill** ['grɪl] *n* : reja *f*, enrejado *m*

grim ['grɪm] *adj* **grimmer; grimmest 1** CRUEL : cruel, feroz **2** STERN : adusto, severo ⟨a grim expression : un gesto severo⟩ **3** GLOOMY : sombrío, deprimente **4** SINISTER : macabro, siniestro **5** UNYIELDING : inflexible, persistente ⟨with grim determination : con una voluntad de hierro⟩

grimace[1] ['grɪməs, grɪ'meɪs] *vi* **-maced; -macing** : hacer muecas

grimace[2] *n* : mueca *f*

grime ['graɪm] *n* : mugre *f*, suciedad *f*

grimly ['grɪmli] *adv* **1** STERNLY : severamente **2** RESOLUTELY : inexorablemente

grimy ['graɪmi] *adj* **grimier; -est** : mugriento, sucio

grin[1] ['grɪn] *vi* **grinned; grinning** : sonreír abiertamente

grin[2] *n* : sonrisa *f* abierta

grind[1] ['graɪnd] *v* **ground** ['graʊnd]; **grinding** *vt* **1** CRUSH : moler, machacar, triturar **2** SHARPEN : afilar **3** POLISH : pulir, esmerilar (lentes, espejos) **4 to grind one's teeth** : rechinarle los dientes a uno **5 to grind down** OPPRESS : oprimir, agobiar — *vi* **1** : funcionar con dificultad, rechinar ⟨to grind to a halt : pararse poco a poco, llegar a un punto muerto⟩ **2** STUDY : estudiar mucho

grind² *n* : trabajo *m* pesado ⟨the daily grind : la rutina diaria⟩

grinder ['graındər] *n* : molinillo *m* ⟨coffee grinder : molinillo de café⟩

grindstone ['graınd,sto:n] *n* : piedra *m* de afilar

grip¹ ['grıp] *vt* **gripped; gripping 1** GRASP : agarrar, asir **2** HOLD, INTEREST : captar el interés de

grip² *n* **1** GRASP : agarre *m*, asidero *m* ⟨to have a firm grip on something : agarrarse bien de algo⟩ **2** CONTROL, HOLD : control *m*, dominio *m* ⟨to lose one's grip on : perder el control de⟩ ⟨inflation tightened its grip on the economy : la inflación se afianzó en su dominio de la economía⟩ **3** UNDERSTANDING : comprensión *f*, entendimiento *m* ⟨to come to grips with : llegar a entender⟩ **4** HANDLE : asidero *m*, empuñadura *f* (de un arma)

gripe¹ ['graıp] *v* **griped; griping** *vt* IRRITATE, VEX : irritar, fastidiar, molestar — *vi* COMPLAIN : quejarse, rezongar

gripe² *n* : queja *f*

grippe ['grıp] *n* : influenza *f*, gripe *f*, gripa *f* Col, Mex

grisly ['grızli] *adj* **-lier; -est** : horripilante, horroroso, truculento

grist ['grıst] *n* : molienda *f* ⟨it's all grist for the mill : todo ayuda, todo es provechoso⟩

gristle ['grısəl] *n* : cartílago *m*

gristly ['grısli] *adj* **-tlier; -est** : cartilaginoso

grit¹ ['grıt] *vt* **gritted; gritting** : hacer rechinar (los dientes, etc.)

grit² *n* **1** SAND : arena *f* **2** GRAVEL : grava *f* **3** COURAGE : valor *m*, coraje *m* **4** **grits** *npl* : sémola *f* de maíz

gritty ['grıţi] *adj* **-tier; -est 1** : arenoso ⟨a gritty surface : una superficie arenosa⟩ **2** PLUCKY : valiente

grizzled ['grızəld] *adj* : entrecano

grizzly bear ['grızli] *n* : oso *m* pardo

groan¹ ['gro:n] *vi* **1** MOAN : gemir, quejarse **2** CREAK : crujir

groan² *n* **1** MOAN : gemido *m*, quejido *m* **2** CREAK : crujido *m*

grocer ['gro:sər] *n* : tendero *m*, -ra *f*

grocery ['gro:səri, -ʃəri] *n, pl* **-ceries 1** *or* **grocery store** : tienda *f* de comestibles, tienda *f* de abarrotes **2** **groceries** *npl* : comestibles *mpl*, abarrotes *mpl*

groggy ['grɑgi] *adj* **-gier; -est** : atontado, grogui, tambaleante

groin ['grɔın] *n* : ingle *f*

grommet ['grɑmət, 'grʌ-] *n* : arandela *f*

groom¹ ['gru:m, 'grʊm] *vt* **1** : cepillar, almohazar (un animal) **2** : arreglar, cuidar ⟨well-groomed : bien arreglado⟩ **3** PREPARE : preparar

groom² *n* **1** : mozo *m*, -za *f* de cuadra **2** BRIDEGROOM : novio *m*

groove¹ ['gru:v] *vt* **grooved; grooving** : acanalar, hacer ranuras en, surcar

groove² *n* **1** FURROW, SLOT : ranura *f*, surco *m* **2** RUT : rutina *f*

grope ['gro:p] *v* **groped; groping** *vi* : andar a tientas, tantear ⟨he groped for the switch : buscó el interruptor a tientas⟩ — *vt* **to grope one's way** : avanzar a tientas

gross¹ ['gro:s] *vt* : tener entrada bruta de, recaudar en bruto

gross² *adj* **1** FLAGRANT : flagrante, grave ⟨a gross error : un error flagrante⟩ ⟨a gross injustice : una injusticia grave⟩ **2** FAT : muy gordo, obeso **3** : bruto ⟨gross national product : producto nacional bruto⟩ **4** COARSE, VULGAR : grosero, basto

gross³ *n* **1** *pl* **gross** : gruesa *f* (12 docenas) **2** *or* **gross income** : ingresos *mpl* brutos

grossly ['gro:sli] *adv* **1** EXTREMELY : extremadamente ⟨grossly unfair : totalmente injusto⟩ **2** CRUDELY : groseramente

grotesque [gro:'tɛsk] *adj* : grotesco

grotesquely [gro:'tɛskli] *adv* : de forma grotesca

grotto ['grɑţo:] *n, pl* **-toes** : gruta *f*

grouch¹ ['graʊtʃ] *vi* : refunfuñar, rezongar

grouch² *n* **1** COMPLAINT : queja *f* **2** GRUMBLER : gruñón *m*, -ñona *f*; cascarrabias *mf fam*

grouchy ['graʊtʃi] *adj* **grouchier; -est** : malhumorado, gruñón

ground¹ ['graʊnd] *vt* **1** BASE : fundar, basar **2** INSTRUCT : enseñar los conocimientos básicos a ⟨to be well grounded in : ser muy entendido en⟩ **3** : conectar a tierra (un aparato eléctrico) **4** : varar, hacer encallar (un barco) **5** : restringir (un avión o un piloto) a la tierra

ground² *n* **1** EARTH, SOIL : suelo *m*, tierra *f* ⟨to dig (in) the ground : cavar la tierra⟩ ⟨to fall to the ground : caerse al suelo⟩ **2** LAND, TERRAIN : terreno *m* ⟨hilly ground : terreno alto⟩ ⟨to lose ground : perder terreno⟩ **3** BASIS, REASON : razón *f*, motivo *m* ⟨grounds for complaint : motivos de queja⟩ **4** BACKGROUND : fondo *m* **5** FIELD : campo *m*, plaza *f* ⟨parade ground : plaza de armas⟩ **6** : tierra *f* (para electricidad) **7** **grounds** *npl* PREMISES : recinto *m*, terreno *m* **8** **grounds** *npl* DREGS : posos *mpl* (de café)

ground³ → **grind**

groundhog ['graʊnd,hɔg] *n* : marmota *f* (de América)

groundless ['graʊndləs] *adj* : infundado

groundwork ['graʊnd,wərk] *n* **1** FOUNDATION : fundamento *m*, base *f* **2** PREPARATION : trabajo *m* preparatorio

group¹ ['gru:p] *vt* : agrupar

group² *n* : grupo *m*, agrupación *f*, conjunto *m*, compañía *f*

grouper ['gru:pər] *n* : mero *m*

grouse[1] ['graʊs] vi **groused; grousing** : quejarse, rezongar, refunfuñar

grouse[2] n, pl **grouse** or **grouses** : urogallo m (ave)

grout ['graʊt] n : lechada f

grove ['gro:v] n : bosquecillo m, arboleda f, soto m

grovel ['grɑvəl, 'grʌ-] vi **-eled** or **-elled; -eling** or **-elling 1** CRAWL : arrastrarse **2** : humillarse, postrarse ⟨to grovel before someone : postrarse ante alguien⟩

grow ['gro:] v **grew** ['gru:]; **grown** ['gro:n]; **growing** vi **1** : crecer ⟨palm trees grow on the islands : las palmas crecen en las islas⟩ ⟨my hair grows very fast : mi pelo crece muy rápido⟩ **2** DEVELOP, MATURE : desarrollarse, madurar **3** INCREASE : crecer, aumentar **4** BECOME : hacerse, volverse, ponerse ⟨she was growing angry : se estaba poniendo furiosa⟩ ⟨to grow dark : oscurecerse⟩ **5 to grow up** : hacerse mayor ⟨grow up! : ¡no seas niño!⟩ — vt **1** CULTIVATE, RAISE : cultivar **2** : dejar crecer ⟨to grow one's hair : dejarse crecer el pelo⟩

grower ['gro:ər] n : cultivador m, -dora f

growl[1] ['graʊl] vi : gruñir (dícese de un animal), refunfuñar (dícese de una persona)

growl[2] n : gruñido m

grown–up[1] ['gro:n,əp] adj : adulto, mayor

grown–up[2] n : adulto m, -ta f; persona f mayor

growth ['gro:θ] n **1** : crecimiento m ⟨to stunt one's growth : detener el crecimiento⟩ **2** INCREASE : aumento m, crecimiento m, expansión f **3** DEVELOPMENT : desarrollo m ⟨economic growth : desarrollo económico⟩ ⟨a five days' growth of beard : una barba de cinco días⟩ **4** LUMP, TUMOR : bulto m, tumor m

grub[1] ['grʌb] vi **grubbed; grubbing 1** DIG : escarbar **2** RUMMAGE : hurgar, buscar **3** DRUDGE : trabajar duro

grub[2] n **1** : larva f ⟨beetle grub : larva del escarabajo⟩ **2** DRUDGE : esclavo m, -va f del trabajo **3** FOOD : comida f

grubby ['grʌbi] adj **grubbier; -est** : mugriento, sucio

grudge[1] ['grʌdʒ] vt **grudged; grudging** : resentir, envidiar

grudge[2] n : rencor m, resentimiento m ⟨to hold a grudge : guardar rencor⟩

grueling or **gruelling** ['gru:lɪŋ, 'gru:ə-] adj : extenuante, agotador, duro

gruesome ['gru:səm] adj : horripilante, truculento, horroroso

gruff ['grʌf] adj **1** BRUSQUE : brusco ⟨a gruff reply : una respuesta brusca⟩ **2** HOARSE : ronco — **gruffly** adv

grumble[1] ['grʌmbəl] vi **-bled; -bling 1** COMPLAIN : refunfuñar, rezongar, quejarse **2** RUMBLE : hacer un ruido sordo, retumbar (dícese del trueno)

grumble[2] n **1** COMPLAINT : queja f **2** RUMBLE : ruido m sordo, estruendo m

grumbler ['grʌmbələr] n : gruñón m, -ñona f

grumpy ['grʌmpi] adj **grumpier; -est** : malhumorado, gruñón

grungy ['grʌndʒi] adj : sucio

grunt[1] ['grʌnt] vi : gruñir

grunt[2] n : gruñido m

guacamole [ˌgwɑkə'mo:li] n : guacamole m, guacamol m

guarantee[1] [ˌgærən'ti:] vt **-teed; -teeing 1** PROMISE : asegurar, prometer **2** : poner bajo garantía, garantizar (un producto o servicio)

guarantee[2] n **1** PROMISE : garantía f, promesa f ⟨lifetime guarantee : garantía de por vida⟩ **2** → **guarantor**

guarantor [ˌgærən'tɔr] n : garante mf; fiador m, -dora f

guaranty [ˌgærən'ti:] → **guarantee**

guard[1] ['gɑrd] vt **1** DEFEND, PROTECT : defender, proteger **2** : guardar, vigilar, custodiar ⟨to guard the frontier : vigilar la frontera⟩ ⟨she guarded my secret well : guardó bien mi secreto⟩ — vi **to guard against** : protegerse contra, evitar

guard[2] n **1** WATCHMAN : guarda mf ⟨security guard : guarda de seguridad⟩ **2** VIGILANCE : guardia f, vigilancia f ⟨to be on guard : estar en guardia⟩ ⟨to let one's guard down : bajar la guardia⟩ **3** SAFEGUARD : salvaguardia f, dispositivo m de seguridad (en una máquina) **4** PRECAUTION : precaución f, protección f

guardhouse ['gɑrd,haʊs] n : cuartel m de la guardia

guardian ['gɑrdiən] n **1** PROTECTOR : guardián m, -diana f; custodio m, -dia f **2** : tutor m, -tora f (de un niño)

guardianship ['gɑrdiən,ʃɪp] n : custodia f, tutela f

Guatemalan [ˌgwɑtə'mɑlən] n : guatemalteco m, -ca f — **Guatemalan** adj

guava ['gwɑvə] n : guayaba f

gubernatorial [ˌgu:bənə'tori:əl, ˌgju:-] adj : del gobernador

guerrilla or **guerilla** [gə'rɪlə] n : guerrillero m, -ra f

guess[1] ['gɛs] vt **1** CONJECTURE : adivinar, conjeturar ⟨guess what happened! : ¡adivina lo que pasó!⟩ **2** SUPPOSE : pensar, creer, suponer ⟨I guess so : supongo que sí⟩ **3** : adivinar correctamente, acertar ⟨to guess the answer : acertar la respuesta⟩ — vi : adivinar

guess[2] n : conjetura f, suposición f

guesswork ['gɛs,wərk] n : suposiciones fpl, conjeturas fpl

guest ['gɛst] n : huésped mf; invitado m, -da f

guffaw[1] [gə'fɔ] vi : reírse a carcajadas, carcajearse fam

guffaw[2] [gə'fɔ, 'gʌ,fɔ] n : carcajada f, risotada f

guidance ['gaɪdənts] *n* : orientación *f*, consejos *mpl*

guide¹ ['gaɪd] *vt* **guided; guiding 1** DIRECT, LEAD : guiar, dirigir, conducir **2** ADVISE, COUNSEL : aconsejar, orientar

guide² *n* : guía *f*

guidebook ['gaɪd,bʊk] *n* : guía *f* (para viajeros)

guideline ['gaɪd,laɪn] *n* : pauta *f*, directriz *f*

guild ['gɪld] *n* : gremio *m*, sindicato *m*, asociación *f*

guile ['gaɪl] *n* : astucia *f*, engaño *m*

guileless ['gaɪlləs] *adj* : inocente, cándido, sin malicia

guillotine¹ ['gɪlə,tiːn, 'giːjə,-] *vt* **-tined; -tining** : guillotinar

guillotine² *n* : guillotina *f*

guilt ['gɪlt] *n* : culpa *f*, culpabilidad *f*

guilty ['gɪlti] *adj* **guiltier; -est** : culpable

guinea fowl ['gɪni] *n* : gallina *f* de Guinea

guinea pig *n* : conejillo *m* de Indias, cobaya *f*

guise ['gaɪz] *n* : apariencia *f*, aspecto *m*, forma *f*

guitar [gə'tɑr, gɪ-] *n* : guitarra *f*

guitarist [gə'tɑrɪst, gɪ-] *n* : guitarrista *mf*

gulch ['gʌltʃ] *n* : barranco *m*, quebrada *f*

gulf ['gʌlf] *n* **1** : golfo *m* ⟨the Gulf of Mexico : el Golfo de México⟩ **2** GAP : brecha *f* ⟨the gulf between generations : la brecha entre las generaciones⟩ **3** CHASM : abismo *m*

gull ['gʌl] *n* : gaviota *f*

gullet ['gʌlət] *n* : garganta *f*

gullible ['gʌlɪbəl] *adj* : crédulo

gully ['gʌli] *n, pl* **-lies** : barranco *m*, hondonada *f*

gulp¹ ['gʌlp] *vt* **1** : engullir, tragar ⟨he gulped down the whiskey : engulló el whiskey⟩ **2** SUPPRESS : suprimir, reprimir, tragar ⟨to gulp down a sob : reprimir un sollozo⟩ — *vi* : tragar saliva, tener un nudo en la garganta

gulp² *n* : trago *m*

gum ['gʌm] *n* **1** CHEWING GUM : goma *f* de mascar, chicle *m* **2** **gums** *npl* : encías *fpl*

gumbo ['gʌm,boː] *n* : sopa *f* de quingombó

gumdrop ['gʌm,drɑp] *n* : pastilla *f* de goma

gummy ['gʌmi] *adj* **gummier; -est** : gomoso

gumption ['gʌmpʃən] *n* : iniciativa *f*, agallas *fpl fam*

gun¹ ['gʌn] *vt* **gunned; gunning 1** *or* **to gun down** : matar a tiros, asesinar **2** : acelerar (rápidamente) ⟨to gun the engine : acelerar el motor⟩

gun² *n* **1** CANNON : cañón *m* **2** FIREARM : arma *f* de fuego **3** SPRAY GUN : pistola *f* **4 to jump the gun** : adelantarse, salir antes de tiempo

gunboat ['gʌn,boːt] *n* : cañonero *m*

gunfight ['gʌn,faɪt] *n* : tiroteo *m*, balacera *f*

gunfire ['gʌn,faɪr] *n* : disparos *mpl*

gunman ['gʌnmən] *n, pl* **-men** [-mən, -,mɛn] : pistolero *m*, gatillero *m Mex*

gunner ['gʌnər] *n* : artillero *m*, -ra *f*

gunnysack ['gʌni,sæk] *n* : saco *m* de yute

gunpowder ['gʌn,paʊdər] *n* : pólvora *f*

gunshot ['gʌn,ʃɑt] *n* : disparo *m*, tiro *m*, balazo *m*

gunwale ['gʌnəl] *n* : borda *f*

guppy ['gʌpi] *n, pl* **-pies** : lebistes *m*

gurgle¹ ['gərgəl] *vi* **-gled; -gling 1** : borbotar, gorgotear (dícese de un líquido) **2** : gorjear (dícese de un niño)

gurgle² *n* **1** : borboteo *m*, gorgoteo *m* (de un líquido) **2** : gorjeo *m* (de un niño)

gush ['gʌʃ] *vi* **1** SPOUT : surgir, salir a chorros, chorrear **2** : hablar con entusiasmo efusivo ⟨she gushed with praise : se deshizo en elogios⟩

gust ['gʌst] *n* : ráfaga *f*, racha *f*

gusto ['gʌs,toː] *n, pl* **gustoes** : entusiasmo *m* ⟨with gusto : con deleite, con ganas⟩

gusty ['gʌsti] *adj* **gustier; -est** : racheado

gut¹ ['gʌt] *vt* **gutted; gutting 1** EVISCERATE : destripar (un pollo, etc.), limpiar (un pescado) **2** : destruir el interior de (un edificio)

gut² *n* **1** INTESTINE : intestino *m* **2 guts** *npl* INNARDS : tripas *fpl fam*, entrañas *fpl* **3 guts** *npl* COURAGE : valentía *f*, agallas *fpl*

gutter ['gʌtər] *n* **1** : canal *mf*, canaleta *f* (de un techo) **2** : cuneta *f*, arroyo *m* (de una calle)

guttural ['gʌtərəl] *adj* : gutural

guy ['gaɪ] *n* **1** *or* **guyline** : cuerda *f* tensora, cable *m* **2** FELLOW : tipo *m*, hombre *m*

guzzle ['gʌzəl] *vt* **-zled; -zling** : chupar, tragarse

gym ['dʒɪm] → **gymnasium**

gymnasium [dʒɪm'neɪziəm, -ʒəm] *n, pl* **-siums** *or* **-sia** [-ziːə, -ʒə] : gimnasio *m*

gymnast ['dʒɪmnəst, -,næst] *n* : gimnasta *mf*

gymnastic [dʒɪm'næstɪk] *adj* : gimnástico

gymnastics [dʒɪm'næstɪks] *ns & pl* : gimnasia *f*

gynecologist [,gaɪnə'kɑlədʒɪst, ,dʒɪnə-] *n* : ginecólogo *m*, -ga *f*

gynecology [,gaɪnə'kɑlədʒi, ,dʒɪnə-] *n* : ginecología *f*

gyp¹ ['dʒɪp] *vt* **gypped; gypping** : estafar, timar

gyp² *n* **1** SWINDLER : estafador *m*, -dora *f* **2** FRAUD, SWINDLE : estafa *f*, timo *m fam*

gypsum ['dʒɪpsəm] *n* : yeso *m*

Gypsy ['dʒɪpsi] *n, pl* **-sies** : gitano *m*, -na *f*

gyrate ['dʒaɪ,reɪt] *vi* **-rated; -rating** : girar, rotar

gyration [dʒaɪ'reɪʃən] *n* : giro *m*, rotación *f*

gyroscope ['dʒaɪrə,skoːp] *n* : giroscopio *m*, giróscopo *m*

H

h ['eɪʃ] *n, pl* **h's** *or* **hs** ['eɪʃəz] : octava letra del alfabeto inglés

ha ['hɑ] *interj* : ¡ja!

haberdashery ['hæbər,dæʃəri] *n, pl* **-eries** : tienda *f* de ropa para caballeros

habit ['hæbɪt] *n* **1** CUSTOM : hábito *m*, costumbre *f* **2** : hábito *m* (de un monje o una religiosa) **3** ADDICTION : dependencia *f*, adicción *f*

habitable ['hæbɪt̬əbəl] *adj* : habitable

habitat ['hæbɪ,tæt] *n* : hábitat *m*

habitation [,hæbɪ'teɪʃən] *n* **1** OCCUPANCY : habitación *f* **2** RESIDENCE : residencia *f*, morada *f*

habit–forming ['hæbɪt,fɔrmɪŋ] *adj* : que crea dependencia

habitual [hə'bɪtʃuəl] *adj* **1** CUSTOMARY : habitual, acostumbrado **2** INVETERATE : incorregible, empedernido — **habitually** *adv*

habituate [hə'bɪtʃu,eɪt] *vt* **-ated; -ating** : habituar, acostumbrar

hack¹ ['hæk] *vt* : cortar, tajear (a hachazos, etc.) ⟨to hack one's way : abrirse paso⟩ — *vi* **1** : hacer tajos **2** COUGH : toser

hack² *n* **1** CHOP : hachazo *m*, tajo *m* **2** HORSE : caballo *m* de alquiler **3** WRITER : escritor *m*, -tora *f* a sueldo; escritorzuelo *m*, -la *f* **4** COUGH : tos *f* seca

hackles ['hækəlz] *npl* **1** : pluma *f* erizada (de un ave), pelo *m* erizado (de un perro, etc.) **2 to get one's hackles up** : ponerse furioso

hackney ['hækni] *n, pl* **-neys** : caballo *m* de silla, caballo *m* de tiro

hackneyed ['hæknid] *adj* TRITE : trillado, gastado

hacksaw ['hæk,sɔ] *n* : sierra *f* para metales

had → **have**

haddock ['hædək] *ns & pl* : eglefino *m*

hadn't ['hædənt] (*contraction of* **had not**) → **have**

haft ['hæft] *n* : mango *m*, empuñadura *f*

hag ['hæg] *n* **1** WITCH : bruja *f*, hechicera *f* **2** CRONE : vieja *f* fea

haggard ['hægərd] *adj* : demacrado, macilento — **haggardly** *adv*

haggle ['hægəl] *vi* **-gled; -gling** : regatear

ha–ha [,hɑ'hɑ, 'hɑ'hɑ] *interj* : ¡ja, ja!

hail¹ ['heɪl] *vt* **1** GREET : saludar **2** SUMMON : llamar ⟨to hail a taxi : llamar un taxi⟩ — *vi* : granizar (en meteorología)

hail² *n* **1** : granizo *m* **2** BARRAGE : aluvión *m*, lluvia *f*

hail³ *interj* : ¡salve!

hailstone ['heɪl,sto:n] *n* : granizo *m*, piedra *f* de granizo

hailstorm ['heɪl,stɔrm] *n* : granizada *f*

hair ['hær] *n* **1** : pelo *m*, cabello *m* ⟨to get one's hair cut : cortarse el pelo⟩ **2** : vello *m* (en las piernas, etc.)

hairbreadth ['hær,brɛdθ] *or* **hairsbreadth** ['hærz-] *n* **by a hairbreadth** : por un pelo

hairbrush ['hær,brʌʃ] *n* : cepillo *m* (para el pelo)

haircut ['hær,kʌt] *n* : corte *m* de pelo

hairdo ['hær,du:] *n, pl* **-dos** : peinado *m*

hairdresser ['hær,drɛsər] *n* : peluquero *m*, -ra *f*

hairiness ['hærinəs] *n* : vellosidad *f*

hairless ['hærləs] *adj* : sin pelo, calvo, pelón

hairline ['hær,laɪn] *n* **1** : línea *f* delgada **2** : nacimiento *m* del pelo ⟨to have a receding hairline : tener entradas⟩

hairpin ['hær,pɪn] *n* : horquilla *f*

hair–raising ['hær,reɪzɪŋ] *adj* : espeluznante

hair spray *n* : laca *f*, fijador *m* (para el pelo)

hairstyle ['hær,staɪl] *n* : peinado *m*

hairy ['hæri] *adj* **hairier; -est** : peludo, velludo

Haitian ['heɪʃən, 'heɪtiən] *n* : haitiano *m*, -na *f* — **Haitian** *adj*

hake ['heɪk] *n* : merluza *f*

hale¹ ['heɪl] *vt* **haled; haling** : arrastrar, halar ⟨to hale to court : arrastrar al tribunal⟩

hale² *adj* : saludable, robusto

half¹ ['hæf, 'hɑf] *adv* : medio, a medias ⟨half cooked : medio cocido⟩

half² *adj* : medio, a medias ⟨a half hour : una media hora⟩ ⟨a half truth : una verdad a medias⟩

half³ *n, pl* **halves** ['hævz, 'hɑvz] **1** : mitad *f* ⟨half of my friends : la mitad de mis amigos⟩ ⟨in half : por la mitad⟩ **2** : tiempo *m* (en deportes)

half brother *n* : medio hermano *m*, hermanastro *m*

halfhearted ['hæf'hɑrt̬əd] *adj* : sin ánimo, poco entusiasta

halfheartedly ['hæf'hɑrt̬ədli] *adv* : con poco entusiasmo, sin ánimo

half–life ['hæf,laɪf] *n, pl* **half–lives** : media vida *f*

half sister *n* : media hermana *f*, hermanastra *f*

halfway¹ ['hæf'weɪ] *adv* : a medio camino, a mitad de camino

halfway² *adj* : medio, intermedio ⟨a halfway point : un punto intermedio⟩

half–wit ['hæf,wɪt] *n* : tonto *m*, -ta *f*; imbécil *mf*

half–witted ['hæf,wɪt̬əd] *adj* : estúpido

halibut ['hælɪbət] *ns & pl* : halibut *m*

hall ['hɔl] *n* **1** BUILDING : residencia *f* estudiantil, facultad *f* (de una universidad) **2** VESTIBULE : entrada *f*, vestíbulo *m*, zaguán *m* **3** CORRIDOR : corredor *m*, pasillo *m* **4** AUDITORIUM : sala *f*, salón *m* ⟨concert hall : sala de conciertos⟩ **5 city hall** : ayuntamiento *m*

hallelujah [,hælə'lu:jə, ,hɑ-] *interj* : ¡aleluya!

hallmark ['hɔl,mɑrk] n : sello m (distintivo)
hallow ['hæ,loː] vt : santificar, consagrar
hallowed ['hæ,loːd, 'hæ,loːəd, 'hɑ,loːd] adj : sagrado
Halloween [,hælə'wiːn, ,hɑ-] n : víspera f de Todos los Santos
hallucinate [hæ'luːsən,eɪt] vi -nated; -nating : alucinar
hallucination [hə,luːsən'eɪʃən] n : alucinación f
hallucinatory [hə'luːsənə,tori] adj : alucinante
hallucinogen [hə'luːsənədʒən] n : alucinógeno m
hallucinogenic [hə,luːsənə'dʒɛnɪk] adj : alucinógeno
hallway ['hɔl,weɪ] n 1 ENTRANCE : entrada f 2 CORRIDOR : corredor m, pasillo m
halo ['heɪ,loː] n, pl -los or -loes : aureola f, halo m
halt¹ ['hɔlt] vi : detenerse, pararse — vt 1 STOP : detener, parar (a una persona) 2 INTERRUPT : interrumpir (una actividad)
halt² n 1 : alto m, parada f 2 to come to a halt : pararse, detenerse
halter ['hɔltər] n 1 : cabestro m, ronzal m (para un animal) 2 : blusa f sin espalda
halting ['hɔltɪŋ] adj HESITANT : vacilante, titubeante — haltingly adv
halve ['hæv, 'hɑv] vt halved; halving 1 DIVIDE : partir por la mitad 2 REDUCE : reducir a la mitad
halves → half
ham ['hæm] n 1 : jamón m 2 or ham actor : comicastro m, -tra f 3 or ham radio operator : radioaficionado m, -da f 4 hams npl HAUNCHES : ancas fpl
hamburger ['hæm,bərgər] or hamburg [-,bərg] n 1 : carne f molida 2 : hamburguesa f (emparedado)
hamlet ['hæmlət] n VILLAGE : aldea f, poblado m
hammer¹ ['hæmər] vt 1 STRIKE : clavar, golpear 2 NAIL : clavar, martillar 3 to hammer out NEGOTIATE : elaborar, negociar, llegar a — vi : martillar, golpear
hammer² n 1 : martillo m 2 : percusor m, percutor m (de un arma de fuego)
hammock ['hæmək] n : hamaca f
hamper¹ ['hæmpər] vt : obstaculizar, dificultar
hamper² n : cesto m, canasta f
hamster ['hæmpstər] n : hámster m
hamstring ['hæm,strɪŋ] vt -strung [-,strʌŋ]; -stringing 1 : cortarle el tendón del corvejón a (un animal) 2 INCAPACITATE : incapacitar, inutilizar
hand¹ ['hænd] vt : pasar, dar, entregar
hand² n 1 : mano f ⟨made by hand : hecho a mano⟩ 2 POINTER : manecilla f, aguja f (de un reloj o instrumento) 3 SIDE : lado m ⟨on the other hand : por otro lado⟩ 4 HANDWRITING : letra f, escritura f 5 APPLAUSE : aplauso m 6 : mano f, cartas fpl (en juegos de naipes) 7 WORKER : obrero m, -ra f; trabajador m, -dora f 8 to ask for someone's hand (in marriage) : pedir la mano de alguien 9 to lend a hand : echar una mano
handbag ['hænd,bæg] n : cartera f, bolso m, bolsa f Mex
handball ['hænd,bɔl] n : frontón m, pelota f
handbill ['hænd,bɪl] n : folleto m, volante m
handbook ['hænd,bʊk] n : manual m
handcuff ['hænd,kʌf] vt : esposar, ponerle esposas (a alguien)
handcuffs ['hænd,kʌfs] npl : esposas fpl
handful ['hænd,fʊl] n : puñado m
handgun ['hænd,gʌn] n : pistola f, revólver m
handheld ['hænd,hɛld] adj : de mano
handicap¹ ['hændi,kæp] vt -capped; -capping 1 : asignar un handicap a (en deportes) 2 HAMPER : obstaculizar, poner en desventaja
handicap² n 1 DISABILITY : minusvalía f, discapacidad f 2 DISADVANTAGE : desventaja f, handicap m (en deportes)
handicapped ['hændi,kæpt] adj DISABLED : minusválido, discapacitado
handicraft ['hændi,kræft] n : artesanía f
handily ['hændəli] adv EASILY : fácilmente, con facilidad
handiwork ['hændi,wərk] n 1 WORK : trabajo m 2 CRAFTS : artesanías fpl
handkerchief ['hæŋkərtʃəf, -,tʃiːf] n, pl -chiefs : pañuelo m
handle¹ ['hændəl] v -dled; -dling 1 TOUCH : tocar 2 MANAGE : tratar, manejar, despachar 3 SELL : comerciar con, vender — vi : responder, conducirse (dícese de un vehículo)
handle² n : asa m, asidero m, mango m (de un cuchillo, etc.), pomo m (de una puerta), tirador m (de un cajón)
handlebars ['hændəl,bɑrz] npl : manubrio m, manillar m
handler ['hændələr] n : cuidador m, -dora f
handling ['hændəlɪŋ] n 1 MANAGEMENT : manejo m 2 TOUCHING : manoseo m 3 shipping and handling : porte m, transporte m
handmade ['hænd,meɪd] adj : hecho a mano
hand-me-downs ['hændmi,daʊnz] npl : ropa f usada
handout ['hænd,aʊt] n 1 AID : dádiva f, limosna f 2 LEAFLET : folleto m
handpick ['hænd'pɪk] vt : seleccionar con cuidado
handrail ['hænd,reɪl] n : pasamanos m, barandilla f, barandal m
handsaw ['hænd,sɔ] n : serrucho m
hands down adv 1 EASILY : con facilidad 2 UNQUESTIONABLY : con mucho, de lejos
handshake ['hænd,ʃeɪk] n : apretón m de manos

handsome ['hæn/səm] *adj* **-somer; -est 1** ATTRACTIVE : apuesto, guapo, atractivo **2** GENEROUS : generoso **3** SIZABLE : considerable
handsomely ['hæn/səmli] *adv* **1** ELEGANTLY : elegantemente **2** GENEROUSLY : con generosidad
handspring ['hænd,sprɪŋ] *n* : voltereta *f*
handstand ['hænd,stænd] *n* **to do a handstand** : pararse de manos
hand-to-hand ['hænd/tə'hænd] *adj* : cuerpo a cuerpo
handwriting ['hænd,raɪṭɪŋ] *n* : letra *f*, escritura *f*
handwritten ['hænd,rɪtən] *adj* : escrito a mano
handy ['hændi] *adj* **handier; -est 1** NEARBY : a mano, cercano **2** USEFUL : útil, práctico **3** DEXTEROUS : hábil
hang[1] ['hæŋ] *v* **hung** ['hʌŋ]; **hanging** *vt* **1** SUSPEND : colgar, tender, suspender **2** *past tense often* **hanged** EXECUTE : colgar, ahorcar **3 to hang one's head** : bajar la cabeza — *vi* **1** FALL : caer (dícese de las telas y la ropa) **2** DANGLE : colgar **3** HOVER : flotar, sostenerse en el aire **4** : ser ahorcado **5** DROOP : inclinarse **6 to hang up** : colgar ⟨he hung up on me : me colgó⟩
hang[2] *n* **1** DRAPE : caída *f* **2 to get the hang of something** : agarrarle la onda a algo
hangar ['hæŋər, 'hæŋgər] *n* : hangar *m*
hanger ['hæŋər] *n* : percha *f*, gancho *m* (para ropa)
hangman ['hæŋmən] *n, pl* **-men** [-mən, -,mɛn] : verdugo *m*
hangnail ['hæŋ,neɪl] *n* : padrastro *m*
hangout ['hæŋ,aut] *n* : lugar *m* popular, sitio *m* muy frecuentado
hangover ['hæŋ,o:vər] *n* : resaca *f*
hank ['hæŋk] *n* : madeja *f*
hanker ['hæŋkər] *vi* **to hanker for** : tener ansias de, tener ganas de
hankering ['hæŋkərɪŋ] *n* : ansia *f*, anhelo *m*
hansom ['hæn/səm] *n* : coche *m* de caballos
Hanukkah ['xɑnəkə, 'hɑ-] *n* : Januká, Hanukkah
haphazard [hæp'hæzərd] *adj* : casual, fortuito, al azar — **haphazardly** *adv*
hapless ['hæpləs] *adj* UNFORTUNATE : desafortunado, desventurado — **haplessly** *adv*
happen ['hæpən] *vi* **1** OCCUR : pasar, ocurrir, suceder, tener lugar **2** BEFALL : pasar, acontecer ⟨what happened to her? : ¿qué le ha pasado?⟩ **3** CHANCE : resultar, ocurrir por casualidad ⟨it happened that I wasn't home : resulta que estaba fuera de casa⟩ ⟨he happens to be right : da la casualidad de que tiene razón⟩
happening ['hæpənɪŋ] *n* : suceso *m*, acontecimiento *m*
happiness ['hæpinəs] *n* : felicidad *f*, dicha *f*

happy ['hæpi] *adj* **-pier; -est 1** JOYFUL : feliz, contento, alegre **2** FORTUNATE : afortunado, feliz — **happily** [-pəli] *adv*
happy-go-lucky ['hæpigo:'lʌki] *adj* : despreocupado
harangue[1] [hə'ræŋ] *vt* **-rangued; -ranguing** : arengar
harangue[2] *n* : arenga *f*
harass [hə'ræs, 'hærəs] *vt* **1** BESIEGE, HOUND : acosar, asediar, hostigar **2** ANNOY : molestar
harassment [hə'ræsmənt, 'hærəsmənt] *n* : acoso *m*, hostigamiento *m* ⟨sexual harrassment : acoso sexual⟩
harbinger ['hɑrbɪnʤər] *n* **1** HERALD : heraldo *m*, precursor *m* **2** OMEN : presagio *m*
harbor[1] ['hɑrbər] *vt* **1** SHELTER : dar refugio a, albergar **2** CHERISH, KEEP : abrigar, guardar, albergar ⟨to harbor doubts : guardar dudas⟩
harbor[2] *n* **1** REFUGE : refugio *m* **2** PORT : puerto *m*
hard[1] ['hɑrd] *adv* **1** FORCEFULLY : fuerte, con fuerza ⟨the wind blew hard : el viento sopló fuerte⟩ **2** STRENUOUSLY : duro, mucho ⟨to work hard : trabajar duro⟩ **3 to take something hard** : tomarse algo muy mal, estar muy afectado por algo
hard[2] *adj* **1** FIRM, SOLID : duro, firme, sólido **2** DIFFICULT : difícil, arduo **3** SEVERE : severo, duro ⟨a hard winter : un invierno severo⟩ **4** UNFEELING : insensible, duro **5** DILIGENT : diligente ⟨to be a hard worker : ser muy trabajador⟩ **6 hard liquor** : bebidas *fpl* fuertes **7 hard water** : agua *f* dura
hardcover ['hɑrd,kʌvər] *adj* : de pasta dura, de tapa dura
hard disk *n* : disco *m* duro
hard drive → **hard disk**
harden ['hɑrdən] *vt* : endurecer
hardheaded [,hɑrd'hɛdəd] *adj* **1** STUBBORN : testarudo, terco **2** REALISTIC : realista, práctico — **hardheadedly** *adv*
hard-hearted [,hɑrd'hɑrṭəd] *adj* : despiadado, insensible — **hard-heartedly** *adv*
hard-heartedness [,hɑrd'hɑrṭədnəs] *n* : dureza *f* de corazón
hardly ['hɑrdli] *adv* **1** SCARCELY : apenas, casi ⟨I hardly knew her : apenas la conocía⟩ ⟨hardly ever : casi nunca⟩ **2** NOT : difícilmente, poco, no ⟨they can hardly blame me! : ¡difícilmente pueden echarme la culpa!⟩ ⟨it's hardly likely : es poco probable⟩
hardness ['hɑrdnəs] *n* **1** FIRMNESS : dureza *f* **2** DIFFICULTY : dificultad *f* **3** SEVERITY : severidad *f*
hardship ['hɑrd,ʃɪp] *n* : dificultad *f*, privación *f*
hardware ['hɑrd,wær] *n* **1** TOOLS : ferretería *f* **2** : hardware *m* (de una computadora)
hardwood ['hɑrd,wʊd] *n* : madera *f* dura, madera *f* noble

hardworking ['hɑrd'wərkɪŋ] *adj* : trabajador

hardy ['hɑrdi] *adj* **-dier; -est** : fuerte, robusto, resistente (dícese de las plantas) — **hardily** [-dəli] *adv*

hare ['hær] *n, pl* **hare** *or* **hares** : liebre *f*

harebrained ['hær,breɪnd] *adj* : estúpido, absurdo, disparatado

harelip ['hær,lɪp] *n* : labio *m* leporino

harem ['hærəm] *n* : harén *m*

hark ['hɑrk] *vi* **1** (*used only in the imperative*) LISTEN : escuchar **2 hark back** RETURN : volver **3 hark back** RECALL : recordar

harlequin ['hɑrlɪkən, -kwən] *n* : arlequín *m*

harm[1] ['hɑrm] *vt* : hacerle daño a, perjudicar

harm[2] *n* : daño *m*, perjuicio *m*

harmful ['hɑrmfəl] *adj* : dañino, perjudicial — **harmfully** *adv*

harmless ['hɑrmləs] *adj* : inofensivo, inocuo — **harmlessly** *adv*

harmlessness ['hɑrmləsnəs] *n* : inocuidad *f*

harmonic [hɑr'mɑnɪk] *adj* : armónico — **harmonically** [-nɪkli] *adv*

harmonica [hɑr'mɑnɪkə] *n* : armónica *f*

harmonious [hɑr'mo:niəs] *adj* : armonioso — **harmoniously** *adv*

harmonize ['hɑrmə,naɪz] *v* **-nized; -nizing** : armonizar

harmony ['hɑrməni] *n, pl* **-nies** : armonía *f*

harness[1] ['hɑrnəs] *vt* **1** : enjaezar (un animal) **2** UTILIZE : utilizar, aprovechar

harness[2] *n* : arreos *mpl*, guarniciones *fpl*, arnés *m*

harp[1] ['hɑrp] *vi* **to harp on** : insistir sobre, machacar sobre

harp[2] *n* : arpa *m*

harpist ['hɑrpɪst] *n* : arpista *mf*

harpoon[1] [hɑr'pu:n] *vt* : arponear

harpoon[2] *n* : arpón *m*

harpsichord ['hɑrpsɪ,kɔrd] *n* : clavicémbalo *m*

harrow[1] ['hær,o:] *vt* **1** CULTIVATE : gradar, labrar (la tierra) **2** TORMENT : atormentar

harrow[2] *n* : grada *f*, rastra *f*

harry ['hæri] *vt* **-ried; -rying** HARASS : acosar, hostigar

harsh ['hɑrʃ] *adj* **1** ROUGH : áspero **2** SEVERE : duro, severo **3** : discordante (dícese de los sonidos) — **harshly** *adv*

harshness ['hɑrʃnəs] *n* **1** ROUGHNESS : aspereza *f* **2** SEVERITY : dureza *f*, severidad *f*

harvest[1] ['hɑrvəst] *v* : cosechar

harvest[2] *n* **1** HARVESTING : siega *f*, recolección *f* **2** CROP : cosecha *f*

harvester ['hɑrvəstər] *n* : segador *m*, -dora *f*; cosechadora *f* (máquina)

has → **have**

hash[1] ['hæʃ] *vt* **1** MINCE : picar **2 hash over** DISCUSS : discutir, repasar

hash[2] *n* **1** : picadillo *m* (comida) **2** JUMBLE : revoltijo *m*, fárrago *m*

hasn't ['hæzənt] (*contraction* of **has not**) → **has**

hasp ['hæsp] *n* : picaporte *m*, pestillo *m*

hassle[1] ['hæsəl] *vt* **-sled; -sling** : fastidiar, molestar

hassle[2] *n* **1** ARGUMENT : discusión *f*, disputa *f*, bronca *f* **2** FIGHT : pelea *f*, riña *f* **3** BOTHER, TROUBLE : problemas *mpl*, lío *m*

hassock ['hæsək] *n* **1** CUSHION : almohadón *m*, cojín *m* **2** FOOTSTOOL : escabel *m*

haste ['heɪst] *n* **1** : prisa *f*, apuro *m* **2 to make haste** : darse prisa, apurarse

hasten ['heɪsən] *vt* : acelerar, precipitar — *vi* : apresurarse, apurarse

hasty ['heɪsti] *adj* **hastier; -est** **1** HURRIED, QUICK : rápido, apresurado, apurado **2** RASH : precipitado — **hastily** [-təli] *adv*

hat ['hæt] *n* : sombrero *m*

hatch[1] ['hætʃ] *vt* **1** : incubar, empollar (huevos) **2** DEVISE : idear, tramar — *vi* : salir del cascarón

hatch[2] *n* : escotilla *f*

hatchery ['hætʃəri] *n, pl* **-ries** : criadero *m*

hatchet ['hætʃət] *n* : hacha *f*

hatchway ['hætʃ,weɪ] *n* : escotilla *f*

hate[1] ['heɪt] *vt* **hated; hating** : odiar, aborrecer, detestar

hate[2] *n* : odio *m*

hateful ['heɪtfəl] *adj* : odioso, aborrecible, detestable — **hatefully** *adv*

hatred ['heɪtrəd] *n* : odio *m*

hatter ['hætər] *n* : sombrerero *m*, -ra *f*

haughtiness ['hɔtinəs] *n* : altanería *f*, altivez *f*

haughty ['hɔti] *adj* **-tier; -est** : altanero, altivo — **haughtily** [-təli] *adv*

haul[1] ['hɔl] *vt* **1** DRAG, PULL : arrastrar, jalar **2** TRANSPORT : transportar

haul[2] *n* **1** PULL : tirón *m*, jalón *m* **2** CATCH : redada *f* **3** JOURNEY : viaje *m*, trayecto *m* ⟨it's a long haul : es un trayecto largo⟩

haulage ['hɔlɪdʒ] *n* : transporte *m*, tiro *m*

hauler ['hɔlər] *n* : transportista *mf*

haunch ['hɔntʃ] *n* **1** HIP : cadera *f* **2 haunches** *npl* HINDQUARTERS : ancas *fpl*, cuartos *mpl* traseros

haunt[1] ['hɔnt] *vt* **1** : aparecer en (dícese de un fantasma) **2** FREQUENT : frecuentar, rondar **3** PREOCCUPY : perseguir, obsesionar

haunt[2] *n* : guarida *f* (de animales o ladrones), lugar *m* predilecto

haunting ['hɔntɪŋ] *adj* : obsesionante, evocador — **hauntingly** *adv*

haute ['o:t] *adj* **1** : de moda, de categoría **2 haute couture** [,o:tku'tur] : alta costura *f* **3 haute cuisine** [,o:tkwɪ'zi:n] : alta cocina *f*

have ['hæv, *in sense 3 as an auxiliary verb usu* 'hæf] *v* **had** ['hæd]; **having; has** ['hæz, *in sense 3 as an auxiliary verb usu* 'hæs] *vt* **1** POSSESS : tener ⟨do you have change? : ¿tienes cambio?⟩ **2** EXPERI-ENCE, UNDERGO : tener, experimentar, sufrir ⟨I have a toothache : tengo un dolor de muelas⟩ **3** INCLUDE : tener, incluir ⟨April has 30 days : abril tiene 30 días⟩ **4** CONSUME : comer, tomar **5** RECEIVE : tener, recibir ⟨he had my permission : tenía mi permiso⟩ **6** ALLOW : permitir, dejar ⟨I won't have it! : ¡no lo permitiré!⟩ **7** HOLD : hacer ⟨to have a party : dar una fiesta⟩ ⟨to have a meeting : convocar una reunión⟩ **8** HOLD : tener ⟨he had me in his power : me tenía en su poder⟩ **9** BEAR : tener (niños) **10** (*indicating causation*) ⟨she had a dress made : mandó hacer un vestido⟩ ⟨to have one's hair cut : cortarse el pelo⟩ — *v aux* **1** : haber ⟨she has been very busy : ha estado muy ocupada⟩ ⟨I've lived here three years : hace tres años que vivo aquí⟩ **2** (*used in tags*) ⟨you've finished, haven't you? : ha terminado, ¿no?⟩ **3 to have to** : deber, tener que ⟨we have to leave : tenemos que salir⟩

haven ['heɪvən] *n* : refugio *m*

havoc ['hævək] *n* **1** DESTRUCTION : estragos *mpl*, destrucción *f* **2** CHAOS, DISORDER : desorden *m*, caos *m*

Hawaiian[1] [hə'waɪən] *adj* : hawaiano

Hawaiian[2] *n* : hawaiano *m*, -na *f*

hawk[1] ['hɔk] *vt* : pregonar, vender (mercancías) en la calle

hawk[2] *n* : halcón *m*

hawker ['hɔkər] *n* : vendedor *m*, -dora *f* ambulante

hawthorn ['hɔ,θɔrn] *n* : espino *m*

hay ['heɪ] *n* : heno *m*

hay fever *n* : fiebre *f* del heno

hayloft ['heɪ,lɔft] *n* : pajar *m*

hayseed ['heɪ,si:d] *n* : palurdo *m*, -da *f*

haystack ['heɪ,stæk] *n* : almiar *m*

haywire ['heɪ,waɪr] *adj* : descompuesto, desbaratado ⟨to go haywire : estropearse⟩

hazard[1] ['hæzərd] *vt* : arriesgar, aventurar

hazard[2] *n* **1** DANGER : peligro *m*, riesgo *m* **2** CHANCE : azar *m*

hazardous ['hæzərdəs] *adj* : arriesgado, peligroso

haze[1] ['heɪz] *vt* hazed; hazing : abrumar, acosar

haze[2] *n* : bruma *f*, neblina *f*

hazel ['heɪzəl] *n* **1** : avellano *m* (árbol) **2** : color *m* avellana

hazelnut ['heɪzəl,nʌt] *n* : avellana *f*

haziness ['heɪzinəs] *n* **1** MISTINESS : nebulosidad *f* **2** VAGUENESS : vaguedad *f*

hazy ['heɪzi] *adj* **hazier; -est 1** MISTY : brumoso, neblinoso, nebuloso **2** VAGUE : vago, confuso

he ['hi:] *pron* : él

head[1] ['hɛd] *vt* **1** LEAD : encabezar **2** DIRECT : dirigir — *vi* : dirigirse

head[2] *adj* MAIN : principal ⟨the head office : la oficina central, la sede⟩

head[3] *n* **1** : cabeza *f* ⟨from head to foot : de pies a cabeza⟩ **2** MIND : mente *f*, cabeza *f* **3** TIP, TOP : cabeza *f* (de un clavo, un martillo, etc.), cabecera *f* (de una mesa o un río), punta *f* (de una flecha), flor *m* (de un repollo, etc.), encabezamiento *m* (de una carta, etc.), espuma *f* (de cerveza) **4** DIRECTOR, LEADER : director *m*, -tora *f*; jefe *m*, -fa *f*; cabeza *f* (de una familia) **5** : cara *f* (de una moneda) ⟨heads or tails : cara o cruz⟩ **6** : cabeza *f* ⟨500 head of cattle : 500 cabezas de ganado⟩ ⟨$10 a head : $10 por cabeza⟩ **7 to come to a head** : llegar a un punto crítico

headache ['hɛd,eɪk] *n* : dolor *m* de cabeza, jaqueca *f*

headband ['hɛd,bænd] *n* : cinta *f* del pelo

headdress ['hɛd,drɛs] *n* : tocado *m*

headfirst ['hɛd'fərst] *adv* : de cabeza

headgear ['hɛd,gɪr] *n* : gorro *m*, casco *m*, sombrero *m*

heading ['hɛdɪŋ] *n* **1** DIRECTION : dirección *f* **2** TITLE : encabezamiento *m*, título *m* **3** : membrete *m* (de una carta)

headland ['hɛdlənd, -,lænd] *n* : cabo *m*

headlight ['hɛd,laɪt] *n* : faro *m*, foco *m*, farol *m* Mex

headline ['hɛd,laɪn] *n* : titular *m*

headlong[1] ['hɛd'lɔŋ] *adv* **1** HEADFIRST : de cabeza **2** HASTILY : precipitadamente

headlong[2] ['hɛd,lɔŋ] *adj* : precipitado

headmaster ['hɛd,mæstər] *n* : director *m*

headmistress ['hɛd,mɪstrəs, -'mɪs-] *n* : directora *f*

head–on ['hɛd'ɑn, -'ɔn] *adv & adj* : de frente

headphones ['hɛd,fo:nz] *npl* : audífonos *mpl*, cascos *mpl*

headquarters ['hɛd,kwɔrtərz] *ns & pl* **1** SEAT : oficina *f* central, sede *f* **2** : cuartel *m* general (de los militares)

headrest ['hɛd,rɛst] *n* : apoyacabezas *m*

headship ['hɛd,ʃɪp] *n* : dirección *f*

head start *n* : ventaja *f*

headstone ['hɛd,sto:n] *n* : lápida *f*

headstrong ['hɛd'strɔŋ] *adj* : testarudo, obstinado, empecinado

headwaiter ['hɛd'weɪtər] *n* : jefe *m*, -fa *f* de comedor

headwaters ['hɛd,wɔtərz, -,wɑ-] *npl* : cabecera *f*

headway ['hɛd,weɪ] *n* : progreso *m* ⟨to make headway against : avanzar contra⟩

heady ['hɛdi] *adj* **headier; -est 1** INTOXICATING : embriagador, excitante **2** SHREWD : astuto, sagaz

heal ['hi:l] *vt* : curar, sanar — *vi* **1** : sanar, curarse **2 to heal up** : cicatrizarse

healer ['hi:lər] *n* **1** : curandero *m*, -dera *f* **2** : curador *m*, -dora *f* (cosa)

health ['hɛlθ] *n* : salud *f*

healthful ['hɛlθfəl] *adj* : saludable, salubre — **healthfully** *adv*

healthy ['hɛlθi] *adj* **healthier; -est** : sano, bien — **healthily** [-θəli] *adv*

heap¹ ['hiːp] *vt* **1** PILE : amontonar, apilar **2** SHOWER : colmar

heap² *n* : montón *m*, pila *f*

hear ['hɪr] *v* **heard** ['hərd]; **hearing** *vt* **1** : oír ⟨do you hear me? : ¿me oyes?⟩ **2** HEED : oír, prestar atención a **3** LEARN : oír, enterarse de — *vi* **1** : oír ⟨to hear about : oír hablar de⟩ **2 to hear from** : tener noticias de

hearing ['hɪrɪŋ] *n* **1** : oído *m* ⟨hard of hearing : duro de oído⟩ **2** : vista *f* (en un tribunal) **3** ATTENTION : consideración *f*, oportunidad *f* de expresarse **4** EARSHOT : alcance *m* del oído

hearing aid *n* : audífono *m*

hearken ['harkən] *vt* : escuchar

hearsay ['hɪr,seɪ] *n* : rumores *mpl*

hearse ['hərs] *n* : coche *m* fúnebre

heart ['hart] *n* **1** : corazón *m* **2** CENTER, CORE : corazón *m*, centro *m* ⟨the heart of the matter : el meollo del asunto⟩ **3** FEELINGS : corazón *m*, sentimientos *mpl* ⟨a broken heart : un corazón destrozado⟩ ⟨to have a good heart : tener buen corazón⟩ ⟨to take something to heart : tomarse algo a pecho⟩ **4** COURAGE : valor *m*, corazón *m* ⟨to take heart : animarse, cobrar ánimos⟩ **5 hearts** *npl* : corazones *mpl* (en juegos de naipes) **6 by heart** : de memoria

heartache ['hart,eɪk] *n* : pena *f*, angustia *f*

heart attack *n* : infarto *m*, ataque *m* al corazón

heartbeat ['hart,biːt] *n* : latido *m* (del corazón)

heartbreak ['hart,breɪk] *n* : congoja *f*, angustia *f*

heartbreaking ['hart,breɪkɪŋ] *adj* : desgarrador, que parte el corazón

heartbroken ['hart,broːkən] *adj* : desconsolado, destrozado

heartburn ['hart,bərn] *n* : acidez *f* estomacal

hearten ['hartən] *vt* : alentar, animar

heartfelt ['hart,fɛlt] *adj* : sentido

hearth ['harθ] *n* : hogar *m*, chimenea *f*

heartily ['hartəli] *adv* **1** ENTHUSIASTICALLY : de buena gana, con entusiasmo **2** TOTALLY : totalmente, completamente

heartless ['hartləs] *adj* : desalmado, despiadado, cruel

heartsick ['hart,sɪk] *adj* : abatido, desconsolado

heartstrings ['hart,strɪŋz] *npl* : fibras *fpl* del corazón

heartwarming ['hart,wɔrmɪŋ] *adj* : conmovedor, emocionante

hearty ['harti] *adj* **heartier; -est 1** CORDIAL, WARM : cordial, caluroso **2** STRONG : fuerte ⟨to have a hearty appetite : ser de buen comer⟩ **3** SUBSTANTIAL : abundante, sustancioso ⟨a

hearty breakfast : un desayuno abundante⟩

heat¹ ['hiːt] *vt* : calentar

heat² *n* **1** WARMTH : calor *m* **2** HEATING : calefacción *f* **3** EXCITEMENT : calor *m*, entusiasmo *m* ⟨in the heat of the moment : en el calor del momento⟩ **4** ESTRUS : celo *m*

heated ['hiːtəd] *adj* **1** WARMED : calentado **2** IMPASSIONED : acalorado, apasionado

heater ['hiːtər] *n* : calentador *m*, estufa *f*, calefactor *m*

heath ['hiːθ] *n* **1** MOOR : brezal *m*, páramo *m* **2** HEATHER : brezo *m*

heathen¹ ['hiːðən] *adj* : pagano

heathen² *n, pl* **-thens** *or* **-then** : pagano *m*, -na *f*; infiel *mf*

heather ['hɛðər] *n* : brezo *m*

heave¹ ['hiːv] *v* **heaved** *or* **hove** ['hoːv]; **heaving** *vt* **1** LIFT, RAISE : levantar con esfuerzo **2** HURL : lanzar, tirar **3 to heave a sigh** : echar un suspiro, suspirar — *vi* **1** : subir y bajar, palpitar (dícese del pecho) **2 to heave up** RISE : levantarse

heave² *n* **1** EFFORT : gran esfuerzo *m* (para levantar algo) **2** THROW : lanzamiento *m*

heaven ['hɛvən] *n* **1** : cielo *m* ⟨for heaven's sake : por Dios⟩ **2 heavens** *npl* SKY : cielo *m* ⟨the heavens opened up : empezó a llover a cántaros⟩

heavenly ['hɛvənli] *adj* **1** : celestial, celeste **2** DELIGHTFUL : divino, encantador

heavily ['hɛvəli] *adv* **1** : pesadamente, con mucho peso **2** LABORIOUSLY : trabajosamente, penosamente **3** : mucho

heaviness ['hɛvinəs] *n* : peso *m*, pesadez *f*

heavy ['hɛvi] *adj* **heavier; -est 1** WEIGHTY : pesado **2** DENSE, THICK : denso, espeso, grueso **3** BURDENSOME : oneroso, gravoso **4** PROFOUND : profundo **5** SLUGGISH : lento, tardo **6** STOUT : corpulento **7** SEVERE : severo, duro, fuerte

heavy–duty ['hɛvi'duːt̬i, -'djuː-] *adj* : muy resistente, fuerte

heavyweight ['hɛvi,weɪt] *n* : peso *m* pesado (en deportes)

Hebrew¹ ['hiː,bruː] *adj* : hebreo

Hebrew² *n* **1** : hebreo *m*, -brea *f* **2** : hebreo *m* (idioma)

heck ['hɛk] *n* : ¡caramba!, ¡caray! ⟨a heck of a lot : un montón⟩ ⟨what the heck is ... ? : ¿que diablos es ... ?⟩

heckle ['hɛkəl] *vt* **-led; -ling** : interrumpir (a un orador)

hectare ['hɛk,tær] *n* : hectárea *f*

hectic ['hɛktɪk] *adj* : agitado, ajetreado — **hectically** [-tɪkli] *adv*

he'd ['hiːd] (*contraction of* **he had** *or* **he would**) → **have, would**

hedge¹ ['hɛdʒ] *v* **hedged; hedging** *vt* **1** : cercar con un seto **2 to hedge one's bet** : cubrirse — *vi* **1** : dar rodeos, con-

testar con evasivas **2 to hedge against** : cubrirse contra, protegerse contra
hedge² *n* **1** : seto *m* vivo **2** SAFEGUARD : salvaguardia *f*, protección *f*
hedgehog ['hɛʤ,hɔg, -hag] *n* : erizo *m*
heed¹ ['hi:d] *vt* : prestar atención a, hacer caso de
heed² *n* : atención *f*
heedless ['hi:dləs] *adj* : descuidado, despreocupado, inconsciente ⟨to be heedless of : hacer caso omiso de⟩ — **heedlessly** *adv*
heel¹ ['hi:l] *vi* : inclinarse
heel² *n* : talón *m* (del pie), tacón *m* (de calzado)
heft ['hɛft] *vt* : sopesar
hefty ['hɛfti] *adj* **heftier; -est** : robusto, fornido, pesado
hegemony [hɪ'ʤɛməni] *n, pl* **-nies** : hegemonía *f*
heifer ['hɛfər] *n* : novilla *f*
height ['haɪt] *n* **1** PEAK : cumbre *f*, cima *f*, punto *m* alto ⟨at the height of her career : en la cumbre de su carrera⟩ ⟨the height of stupidity : el colmo de la estupidez⟩ **2** TALLNESS : estatura *f* (de una persona), altura *f* (de un objeto) **3** ALTITUDE : altura *f*
heighten ['haɪtən] *vt* **1** : hacer más alto **2** INTENSIFY : aumentar, intensificar — *vi* : aumentarse, intensificarse
heinous ['heɪnəs] *adj* : atroz, abominable, nefando
heir ['ær] *n* : heredero *m*, -ra *f*
heiress ['ærəs] *n* : heredera *f*
heirloom ['ær,lu:m] *n* : reliquia *f* de familia
held → **hold**
helicopter ['hɛlə,kaptər] *n* : helicóptero *m*
helium ['hi:liəm] *n* : helio *m*
helix ['hi:lɪks] *n, pl* **helices** ['hɛlə,si:z, 'hi:-] *or* **helixes** ['hi:lɪksəz] : hélice *f*
hell ['hɛl] *n* : infierno *m*
he'll ['hi:l, 'hɪl] (*contraction of* **he shall** *or* **he will**) → **shall, will**
hellish ['hɛlɪʃ] *adj* : horroroso, infernal
hello [hə'lo:, hɛ-] *interj* : ¡hola!
helm ['hɛlm] *n* **1** : timón *m* **2 to take the helm** : tomar el mando
helmet ['hɛlmət] *n* : casco *m*
help¹ ['hɛlp] *vt* **1** AID, ASSIST : ayudar, auxiliar, socorrer, asistir **2** ALLEVIATE : aliviar **3** SERVE : servir ⟨help yourself! : ¡sírvete!⟩ **4** AVOID : evitar ⟨it can't be helped : no lo podemos evitar, no hay más remedio⟩ ⟨I couldn't help smiling : no pude menos que sonreír⟩
help² *n* **1** ASSISTANCE : ayuda *f* ⟨help! : ¡socorro!, ¡auxilio!⟩ **2** STAFF : personal *m* (en una oficina), servicio *m* doméstico
helper ['hɛlpər] *n* : ayudante *mf*
helpful ['hɛlpfəl] *adj* **1** OBLIGING : servicial, amable, atento **2** USEFUL : útil, práctico — **helpfully** *adv*
helpfulness ['hɛlpfəlnəs] *n* **1** KINDNESS : bondad *f*, amabilidad *f* **2** USEFULNESS : utilidad *f*

helping ['hɛlpɪŋ] *n* : porción *f*
helpless ['hɛlpləs] *adj* **1** POWERLESS : incapaz, impotente **2** DEFENSELESS : indefenso
helplessly ['hɛlpləsli] *adv* : en vano, inútilmente
helplessness ['hɛlpləsnəs] *n* POWERLESSNESS : incapacidad *f*, impotencia *f*
helter–skelter [,hɛltər'skɛltər] *adv* : atropelladamente, precipitadamente
hem¹ ['hɛm] *vt* **hemmed; hemming 1** : dobladillar **2 to hem in** : encerrar
hem² *n* : dobladillo *m*, bastilla *f*
hemisphere ['hɛmə,sfɪr] *n* : hemisferio *m*
hemispheric [,hɛmə'sfɪrɪk, -'sfr-] *or* **hemispherical** [-ɪkəl] *adj* : hemisférico
hemlock ['hɛm,lak] *n* : cicuta *f*
hemoglobin ['hi:mə,glo:bən] *n* : hemoglobina *f*
hemophilia [,hi:mə'fɪliə] *n* : hemofilia *f*
hemorrhage¹ ['hɛmərɪʤ] *vi* **-rhaged; -rhaging** : sufrir una hemorragia
hemorrhage² *n* : hemorragia *f*
hemorrhoids ['hɛmə,rɔɪdz, 'hɛm-,rɔɪdz] *npl* : hemorroides *fpl*, almorranas *fpl*
hemp ['hɛmp] *n* : cáñamo *m*
hen ['hɛn] *n* : gallina *f*
hence ['hɛnts] *adv* **1** : de aquí, de ahí ⟨10 years hence : de aquí a 10 años⟩ ⟨a dog bit me, hence my dislike of animals : un perro me mordió, de ahí mi aversión a los animales⟩ **2** THEREFORE : por lo tanto, por consiguiente
henceforth ['hɛnts,forθ, ,hɛnts'-] *adv* : de ahora en adelante
henchman ['hɛnʧmən] *n, pl* **-men** [-mən, -,mɛn] : secuaz *mf*, esbirro *m*
henpeck ['hɛn,pɛk] *vt* : dominar (al marido)
hepatitis [,hɛpə'taɪtəs] *n, pl* **-titides** [-'tɪtə,di:z] : hepatitis *f*
her¹ ['hər] *adj* : su, sus, de ella ⟨her house : su casa, la casa de ella⟩
her² ['hər, ər] *pron* **1** (*used as direct object*) : la ⟨I saw her yesterday : la vi ayer⟩ **2** (*used as indirect object*) : le, se ⟨he gave her the book : le dio el libro⟩ ⟨he sent it to her : se lo mandó⟩ **3** (*used as object of a preposition*) : ella ⟨we did it for her : lo hicimos por ella⟩ ⟨taller than her : más alto que ella⟩
herald¹ ['hɛrəld] *vt* ANNOUNCE : anunciar, proclamar
herald² *n* **1** MESSENGER : heraldo *m* **2** HARBINGER : precursor *m*
heraldic [he'rældɪk, hə-] *adj* : heráldico
heraldry ['hɛrəldri] *n, pl* **-ries** : heráldica *f*
herb ['ərb, 'hərb] *n* : hierba *f*
herbal ['ərbəl, 'hər-] *adj* : herbario
herbicide ['ərbə,saɪd, 'hər-] *n* : herbicida *m*
herbivore ['ərbə,vor, 'hər-] *n* : herbívoro *m*
herbivorous [,ər'bɪvərəs, ,hər-] *adj* : herbívoro
herculean [,hərkjə'li:ən, ,hər'kju:-liən] *adj* : hercúleo, sobrehumano

herd[1] [ˈhərd] *vt* : reunir en manada, conducir en manada — *vi* : ir en manada (dícese de los animales), apiñarse (dícese de la gente)

herd[2] *n* : manada *f*

herder [ˈhərdər] → **herdsman**

herdsman [ˈhərdzmən] *n, pl* **-men** [-mən, -ˌmɛn] : vaquero *m* (de ganado), pastor *m* (de ovejas)

here [ˈhɪr] *adv* 1 : aquí, acá ⟨come here! : ¡ven acá!⟩ ⟨right here : aquí mismo⟩ 2 NOW : en este momento, ahora, ya ⟨here he comes : ya viene⟩ ⟨here it's three o'clock (already) : ahora son las tres⟩ 3 : en este punto ⟨here we agree : estamos de acuerdo en este punto⟩ 4 **here you are!** : ¡toma!

hereabouts [ˈhɪrəˌbaʊts] *or* **hereabout** [-ˌbaʊt] *adv* : por aquí (cerca)

hereafter[1] [hɪrˈæftər] *adv* 1 : de aquí en adelante, a continuación 2 : en el futuro

hereafter[2] *n* **the hereafter** : el más allá

hereby [hɪrˈbaɪ] *adv* : por este medio

hereditary [həˈrɛdəˌtɛri] *adj* : hereditario

heredity [həˈrɛdəti] *n* : herencia *f*

herein [hɪrˈɪn] *adv* : aquí

hereof [hɪrˈʌv] *adv* : de aquí

hereon [hɪrˈɑn, -ˈɔn] *adv* : sobre esto

heresy [ˈhɛrəsi] *n, pl* **-sies** : herejía *f*

heretic [ˈhɛrəˌtɪk] *n* : hereje *mf*

heretical [həˈrɛtɪkəl] *adj* : herético

hereto [hɪrˈtuː] *adv* : a esto

heretofore [ˈhɪrtəˌfor] *adv* HITHERTO : hasta ahora

hereunder [hɪrˈʌndər] *adv* : a continuación, abajo

hereupon [hɪrəˈpɑn, -ˈpɔn] *adv* : con esto, en ese momento

herewith [hɪrˈwɪθ] *adv* : adjunto

heritage [ˈhɛrətɪdʒ] *n* : patrimonio *m* (nacional)

hermaphrodite [hərˈmæfrəˌdaɪt] *n* : hermafrodita *mf*

hermetic [hərˈmɛtɪk] *adj* : hermético — **hermetically** [-tɪkli] *adv*

hermit [ˈhərmət] *n* : ermitaño *m*, -ña *f*; eremita *mf*

hernia [ˈhərniə] *n, pl* **-nias** *or* **-niae** [-niˌiː, -niˌaɪ] : hernia *f*

hero [ˈhiːˌroː, ˈhɪrˌoː] *n, pl* **-roes** 1 : héroe *m* 2 PROTAGONIST : protagonista *mf*

heroic [hɪˈroːɪk] *adj* : heroico — **heroically** [-ɪkli] *adv*

heroics [hɪˈroːɪks] *npl* : actos *mpl* heroicos

heroin [ˈhɛroən] *n* : heroína *f*

heroine [ˈhɛroən] *n* 1 : heroína *f* 2 PROTAGONIST : protagonista *f*

heroism [ˈhɛroˌɪzəm] *n* : heroísmo *m*

heron [ˈhɛrən] *n* : garza *f*

herpes [ˈhərˌpiːz] *n* : herpes *m*

herring [ˈhɛrɪŋ] *n, pl* **-ring** *or* **-rings** : arenque *m*

hers [ˈhərz] *pron* : suyo, -ya; suyos, -yas; de ella ⟨these shoes are hers : estos zapatos son suyos⟩ ⟨hers are bigger : los de ella son más grandes⟩

herself [hərˈsɪlf] *pron* 1 (*used reflexively*) : se ⟨she dressed herself : se vistió⟩ 2 (*used emphatically*) : ella misma ⟨she fixed it herself : lo arregló ella misma, lo arregló por sí sola⟩

hertz [ˈhərts, ˈhrts] *ns* & *pl* : hercio *m*

he's [ˈhiːz] (*contraction of* he is *or* he has) → **be, have**

hesitancy [ˈhɛzətəntsi] *n, pl* **-cies** : vacilación *f*, titubeo *m*, indecisión *f*

hesitant [ˈhɛzətənt] *adj* : titubeante, vacilante — **hesitantly** *adv*

hesitate [ˈhɛzəˌteɪt] *vi* **-tated; -tating** : vacilar, titubear

hesitation [ˌhɛzəˈteɪʃən] *n* : vacilación *f*, indecisión *f*, titubeo *m*

heterogeneous [ˌhɛtərəˈdʒiːniəs, -njəs] *adj* : heterogéneo

heterosexual[1] [ˌhɛtəroˈsɛkʃuəl] *adj* : heterosexual

heterosexual[2] *n* : heterosexual *mf*

heterosexuality [ˌhɛtəroˌsɛkʃuˈæləti] *n* : heterosexualidad *f*

hew [ˈhjuː] *v* **hewed; hewed** *or* **hewn** [ˈhjuːn]; **hewing** *vt* 1 CUT : cortar, talar (árboles) 2 SHAPE : labrar, tallar — *vi* CONFORM : conformarse, ceñirse

hex[1] [ˈhɛks] *vt* : hacerle un maleficio (a alguien)

hex[2] *n* : maleficio *m*

hexagon [ˈhɛksəˌgɑn] *n* : hexágono *m*

hexagonal [hɛkˈsægənəl] *adj* : hexagonal

hey [ˈheɪ] *interj* : ¡eh!, ¡oye!

heyday [ˈheɪˌdeɪ] *n* : auge *m*, apogeo *m*

hi [ˈhaɪ] *interj* : ¡hola!

hiatus [haɪˈeɪtəs] *n* 1 : hiato *m* 2 PAUSE : pausa *f*

hibernate [ˈhaɪbərˌneɪt] *vi* **-nated; -nating** : hibernar, invernar

hibernation [ˌhaɪbərˈneɪʃən] *n* : hibernación *f*

hiccup[1] [ˈhɪkəp] *vi* **-cuped; -cuping** : hipar, tener hipo

hiccup[2] *n* : hipo *m* ⟨to have the hiccups : tener hipo⟩

hick [ˈhɪk] *n* BUMPKIN : palurdo *m*, -da *f*

hickory [ˈhɪkəri] *n, pl* **-ries** : nogal *m* americano

hidden [ˈhɪdən] *adj* : oculto

hide[1] [ˈhaɪd] *v* **hid** [ˈhɪd]; **hidden** [ˈhɪdən] *or* **hid; hiding** *vt* 1 CONCEAL : esconder 2 : ocultar ⟨to hide one's motives : ocultar uno sus motivos⟩ 3 SCREEN : tapar, no dejar ver — *vi* : esconderse

hide[2] *n* : piel *f*, cuero *m* ⟨to save one's hide : salvar el pellejo⟩

hide-and-seek [ˈhaɪdəndˈsiːk] *n* **to play hide-and-seek** : jugar a las escondidas

hidebound [ˈhaɪdˌbaʊnd] *adj* : rígido, conservador

hideous [ˈhɪdiəs] *adj* : horrible, horroroso, espantoso — **hideously** *adv*

hideout [ˈhaɪdˌaʊt] *n* : guarida *f*, escondrijo *m*

hierarchical [ˌhaɪəˈrɑrkɪkəl] *adj* : jerárquico

hierarchy ['haɪə,rɑrki] *n, pl* **-chies** : jerarquía *f*

hieroglyphic [,haɪərə'glɪfɪk] *n* : jeroglífico *m*

hi–fi ['haɪ'faɪ] *n* **1** → **high fidelity 2** : equipo *m* de alta fidelidad

high¹ ['haɪ] *adv* : alto

high² *adj* **1** TALL : alto ⟨a high wall : una pared alta⟩ **2** ELEVATED : alto, elevado ⟨high prices : precios elevados⟩ ⟨high blood pressure : presión alta⟩ **3** GREAT, IMPORTANT : grande, importante, alto ⟨a high number : un número grande⟩ ⟨high society : alta sociedad⟩ ⟨high hopes : grandes esperanzas⟩ **4** : alto (en música) **5** INTOXICATED : borracho, drogado

high³ *n* **1** : récord *m*, punto *m* máximo ⟨to reach an all-time high : batir el récord⟩ **2** : zona *f* de alta presión (en meteorología) **3** *or* **high gear** : directa *f* **4** **on high** : en las alturas

highbrow ['haɪ,braʊ] *n* : intelectual *mf*

higher ['haɪər] *adj* : superior

high fidelity *n* : alta fidelidad *f*

high–flown ['haɪ'floːn] *adj* : altisonante

high–handed ['haɪ'hændəd] *adj* : arbitrario

highlands ['haɪləndz] *npl* : tierras *fpl* altas, altiplano *m*

highlight¹ ['haɪ,laɪt] *vt* **1** EMPHASIZE : destacar, poner en relieve, subrayar **2** : ser el punto culminante de

highlight² *n* : punto *m* culminante

highly ['haɪli] *adv* **1** VERY : muy, sumamente **2** FAVORABLY : muy bien ⟨to speak highly of : hablar muy bien de⟩ ⟨to think highly of : tener en mucho a⟩

highness ['haɪnəs] *n* **1** HEIGHT : altura *f* **2** **Highness** : Alteza *f* ⟨Your Royal Highness : Su Alteza Real⟩

high–pitched ['haɪ'pɪtʃt] *adj* : agudo

high–rise ['haɪ,raɪz] *adj* : alto, de muchas plantas

high school *n* : escuela *f* superior, escuela *f* secundaria

high seas *npl* : alta mar *f*

high–spirited ['haɪ'spɪrətəd] *adj* : vivaz, muy animado, brioso

high–strung [,haɪ'strʌŋ] *adj* : nervioso, excitable

highway ['haɪ,weɪ] *n* : carretera *f*

highwayman ['haɪ,weɪmən] *n, pl* **-men** [-mən, -,mɛn] : salteador *m* (de caminos), bandido *m*

hijack¹ ['haɪ,dʒæk] *vt* : secuestrar

hijack² *n* : secuestro *m*

hijacker ['haɪ,dʒækər] *n* : secuestrador *m*, -dora *f*

hike¹ ['haɪk] *v* **hiked; hiking** *vi* : hacer una caminata — *vt* RAISE : subir

hike² *n* **1** : caminata *f*, excursión *f* **2** INCREASE : subida *f* (de precios)

hiker ['haɪkər] *n* : excursionista *mf*

hilarious [hɪ'læriəs, haɪ'-] *adj* : muy divertido, hilarante

hilarity [hɪ'lærəti, haɪ-] *n* : hilaridad *f*

hill ['hɪl] *n* **1** : colina *f*, cerro *m* **2** SLOPE : cuesta *f*, pendiente *f*

hillbilly ['hɪl,bɪli] *n, pl* **-lies** : palurdo *m*, -da *f* (de las montañas)

hillock ['hɪlək] *n* : loma *f*, altozano *m*, otero *m*

hillside ['hɪl,saɪd] *n* : ladera *f*, cuesta *f*

hilltop ['hɪl,tɑp] *n* : cima *f*, cumbre *f*

hilly ['hɪli] *adj* **hillier; -est** : montañoso, accidentado

hilt ['hɪlt] *n* : puño *m*, empuñadura *f*

him ['hɪm, əm] *pron* **1** (*used as direct object*) : lo ⟨I found him : lo encontré⟩ **2** (*used as indirect object*) : le, se ⟨we gave him a present : le dimos un regalo⟩ ⟨I sent it to him : se lo mandé⟩ **3** (*used as object of a preposition*) : él ⟨she was thinking of him : pensaba en él⟩ ⟨younger than him : más joven que él⟩

himself [hɪm'sɛlf] *pron* **1** (*used reflexively*) : se ⟨he washed himself : se lavó⟩ **2** (*used emphatically*) : él mismo ⟨he did it himself : lo hizo él mismo, lo hizo por sí solo⟩

hind¹ ['haɪnd] *adj* : trasero, posterior ⟨hind legs : patas traseras⟩

hind² *n* : cierva *f*

hinder ['hɪndər] *vt* : dificultar, impedir, estorbar

Hindi ['hɪndi:] *n* : hindi *m*

hindquarters [,haɪnd,kwɔrtərz] *npl* : cuartos *mpl* traseros

hindrance ['hɪndrənts] *n* : estorbo *m*, obstáculo *m*, impedimento *m*

hindsight ['haɪnd,saɪt] *n* : retrospectiva *f* ⟨with the benefit of hindsight : en retrospectiva, con la perspectiva que da la experiencia⟩

Hindu¹ ['hɪn,du:] *adj* : hindú

Hindu² *n* : hindú *mf*

Hinduism ['hɪndu:,ɪzəm] *n* : hinduismo *m*

hinge¹ ['hɪndʒ] *v* **hinged; hinging** *vt* : unir con bisagras — *vi* **to hinge on** : depender de

hinge² *n* : bisagra *f*, gozne *m*

hint¹ ['hɪnt] *vt* : insinuar, dar a entender — *vi* : soltar indirectas

hint² *n* **1** INSINUATION : insinuación *f*, indirecta *f* **2** TIP : consejo *m*, sugerencia *f* **3** TRACE : pizca *f*, indicio *m*

hinterland ['hɪntər,lænd, -lənd] *n* : interior *m* (de un país)

hip ['hɪp] *n* : cadera *f*

hip–hop ['hɪp,hɑp] *n* : hip-hop *m*

hippie ['hɪpi] *n* : hippie *mf*, hippy *mf*

hippopotamus [,hɪpə'pɑtəməs] *n, pl* **-muses** *or* **-mi** [-,maɪ] : hipopótamo *m*

hippo ['hɪpo:] *n, pl* **hippos** → **hippopotamus**

hire¹ ['haɪr] *vt* **hired; hiring 1** EMPLOY : contratar, emplear **2** RENT : alquilar, arrendar

hire² *n* **1** RENT : alquiler *m* ⟨for hire : se alquila⟩ **2** WAGES : paga *f*, sueldo *m* **3** EMPLOYEE : empleado *m*, -da *f*

his¹ ['hɪz, ɪz] *adj* : su, sus, de él ⟨his hat : su sombrero, el sombrero de él⟩

his² *pron* : suyo, -ya; suyos, suyas; de él ⟨the decision is his : la decisión es suya⟩ ⟨it's his, not hers : es de él, no de ella⟩

Hispanic¹ [hɪˈspænɪk] *adj* : hispano, hispánico
Hispanic² *n* : hispano *m*, -na *f*; hispánico *m*, -ca *f*
hiss¹ [ˈhɪs] *vi* : sisear, silbar — *vt* : decir entre dientes
hiss² *n* : siseo *m*, silbido *m*
historian [hɪˈstɔriən] *n* : historiador *m*, -dora *f*
historic [hɪˈstɔrɪk] *or* **historical** [-ɪkəl] *adj* : histórico — **historically** [-ɪkli] *adv*
history [ˈhɪstəri] *n*, *pl* **-ries** **1** : historia *f* **2** RECORD : historial *m*
histrionics [ˌhɪstriˈɑnɪks] *ns & pl* : histrionismo *m*
hit¹ [ˈhɪt] *v* **hit; hitting** *vt* **1** STRIKE : golpear, pegar, batear (una pelota) ⟨he hit the dog : le pegó al perro⟩ **2** : chocar contra, dar con, dar en (el blanco) ⟨the car hit a tree : el coche chocó contra un árbol⟩ **3** AFFECT : afectar ⟨the news hit us hard : la noticia nos afectó mucho⟩ **4** ENCOUNTER : tropezar con, toparse con ⟨to hit a snag : tropezar con un obstáculo⟩ **5** REACH : llegar a, alcanzar ⟨the price hit $10 a pound : el precio alcanzó los $10 dólares por libra⟩ ⟨to hit town : llegar a la ciudad⟩ ⟨to hit the headlines : ser noticia⟩ **6 to hit on** *or* **to hit upon** : dar con — *vi* : golpear
hit² *n* **1** BLOW : golpe *m* **2** : impacto *m* (de un arma) **3** SUCCESS : éxito *m*
hitch¹ [ˈhɪtʃ] *vt* **1** : mover con sacudidas **2** ATTACH : enganchar, atar, amarrar **3** → **hitchhike 4 to hitch up** : subirse (los pantalones, etc.)
hitch² *n* **1** JERK : tirón *m*, jalón *m* **2** OBSTACLE : obstáculo *m*, impedimento *m*, tropiezo *m*
hitchhike [ˈhɪtʃˌhaɪk] *vi* **-hiked; -hiking** : hacer autostop, ir de aventón *Col, Mex fam*
hitchhiker [ˈhɪtʃˌhaɪkər] *n* : autostopista *mf*
hither [ˈhɪðər] *adv* : acá, por aquí
hitherto [ˈhɪðərˌtu:, ˌhɪðərˈ-] *adv* : hasta ahora
hitter [ˈhɪtər] *n* BATTER : bateador *m*, -dora *f*
HIV [ˌeɪtʃˌaɪˈvi:] *n* (*human immunodeficiency virus*) : VIH *m*, virus *m* del sida
hive [ˈhaɪv] *n* **1** : colmena *f* **2** SWARM : enjambre *m* **3** : lugar *m* muy activo ⟨a hive of activity : un hervidero de actividad⟩
hives [ˈhaɪvz] *ns & pl* : urticaria *f*
hoard¹ [ˈhord] *vt* : acumular, atesorar
hoard² *n* : tesoro *m*, reserva *f*, provisión *f*
hoarfrost [ˈhorˌfrɔst] *n* : escarcha *f*
hoarse [ˈhors] *adj* **hoarser; -est** : ronco — **hoarsely** *adv*
hoarseness [ˈhorsnəs] *n* : ronquera *f*
hoary [ˈhori] *adj* **hoarier; -est 1** : cano, canoso **2** OLD : vetusto, antiguo
hoax¹ [ˈho:ks] *vt* : engañar, embaucar, bromear

hoax² *n* : engaño *m*, broma *f*
hobble¹ [ˈhɑbəl] *v* **-bled; -bling** *vi* LIMP : cojear, renguear — *vt* : manear (un animal)
hobble² *n* **1** LIMP : cojera *f*, rengo *m* **2** : maniota *f* (para un animal)
hobby [ˈhɑbi] *n*, *pl* **-bies** : pasatiempo *m*, afición *f*
hobgoblin [ˈhɑbˌgɑblən] *n* : duende *m*
hobnail [ˈhɑbˌneɪl] *n* : tachuela *f*
hobnob [ˈhɑbˌnɑb] *vi* **-nobbed; -nobbing** : codearse
hobo [ˈho:ˌbo:] *n*, *pl* **-boes** : vagabundo *m*, -da *f*
hock¹ [ˈhɑk] *vt* PAWN : empeñar
hock² *n* **in hock** : empeñado
hockey [ˈhɑki] *n* : hockey *m*
hodgepodge [ˈhɑdʒˌpɑdʒ] *n* : mezcolanza *f*
hoe¹ [ˈho:] *vt* **hoed; hoeing** : azadonar
hoe² *n* : azada *f*, azadón *m*
hog¹ [ˈhɔg, ˈhɑg] *vt* **hogged; hogging** : acaparar, monopolizar
hog² *n* **1** PIG : cerdo *m*, -da *f* **2** GLUTTON : glotón *m*, -tona *f*
hogshead [ˈhɔgzˌhɛd, ˈhɑgz-] *n* : tonel *m*
hoist¹ [ˈhɔɪst] *vt* : levantar, alzar, izar (una bandera, una vela)
hoist² *n* : grúa *f*
hold¹ [ˈho:ld] *v* **held** [ˈhɛld]; **holding** *vt* **1** POSSESS : tener ⟨to hold office : ocupar un puesto⟩ **2** RESTRAIN : detener, controlar ⟨to hold one's temper : controlar su mal genio⟩ **3** CLASP, GRASP : agarrar, coger ⟨to hold hands : agarrarse de la mano⟩ **4** : sujetar, mantener fijo ⟨hold this nail for me : sujétame este clavo⟩ **5** CONTAIN : contener, dar cabida a **6** SUPPORT : aguantar, sostener **7** REGARD : considerar, tener ⟨he held me responsible : me consideró responsable⟩ **8** CONDUCT : celebrar (una reunión), realizar (un evento), mantener (una conversación) — *vi* **1** : aguantar, resistir ⟨the rope will hold : la cuerda resistirá⟩ **2** : ser válido, valer ⟨my offer still holds : mi oferta todavía es válida⟩ **3 to hold forth** : perorar, arengar **4 to hold to** : mantenerse firme en **5 to hold with** : estar de acuerdo con
hold² *n* **1** GRIP : agarre *m*, llave *f* (en deportes) **2** CONTROL : control *m*, dominio *m* ⟨to get hold of oneself : controlarse⟩ **3** DELAY : demora *f* ⟨to put on hold : suspender temporalmente⟩ **4** : bodega *f* (en un barco o un avión) **5 to get hold of** : conseguir, localizar
holder [ˈho:ldər] *n* : poseedor *m*, -dora *f*; titular *mf*
holdings [ˈho:ldɪŋz] *npl* : propiedades *fpl*
hold out *vi* **1** LAST : aguantar, durar **2** RESIST : resistir
holdup [ˈho:ldˌʌp] *n* **1** ROBBERY : atraco *m* **2** DELAY : retraso *m*, demora *f*
hold up *vt* **1** ROB : robarle (a alguien), atracar, asaltar **2** DELAY : retrasar
hole [ˈho:l] *n* : agujero *m*, hoyo *m*

holiday ['hɑlə,deɪ] n 1 : día m feriado, fiesta f 2 VACATION : vacaciones fpl
holiness ['ho:linəs] n 1 : santidad f 2 His Holiness : Su Santidad
holistic [ho:'lɪstɪk] adj : holístico
holler¹ ['hɑlər] vi : gritar, chillar
holler² n : grito m, chillido m
hollow¹ ['hɑ,lo:] vt or to hollow out : ahuecar
hollow² adj -lower; -est 1 : hueco, hundido (dícese de las mejillas, etc.), cavernoso (dícese de un sonido) 2 EMPTY, FALSE : vacío, falso
hollow³ n 1 CAVITY : hueco m, depresión f, cavidad f 2 VALLEY : hondonada f, valle m
hollowness ['hɑ,lo:nəs] n 1 HOLLOW : hueco m, cavidad f 2 FALSENESS : falsedad f 3 EMPTINESS : vacuidad f
holly ['hɑli] n, pl -lies : acebo m
hollyhock ['hɑli,hɑk] n : malvarrosa f
holocaust ['hɑlə,kɔst, 'ho:-, 'hɔ-] n : holocausto m
hologram ['ho:lə,græm, 'hɑ-] n : holograma m
holster ['ho:lstər] n : pistolera f
holy ['ho:li] adj -lier; -est : santo, sagrado
Holy Ghost → Holy Spirit
Holy Spirit n the Holy Spirit : el Espíritu Santo
homage ['ɑmɪʤ, 'hɑ-] n : homenaje m
home ['ho:m] n 1 : casa f, hogar m, domicilio m ⟨to feel at home : sentirse en casa⟩ 2 INSTITUTION : residencia f, asilo m
homecoming ['ho:m,kʌmɪŋ] n : regreso m (a casa)
homegrown ['ho:m'gro:n] adj 1 : de cosecha propia 2 LOCAL : local
homeland ['ho:m,lænd] n : patria f, tierra f natal, terruño m
homeless ['ho:mləs] adj : sin hogar, sin techo
homely ['ho:mli] adj -lier; -est 1 DOMESTIC : casero, hogareño 2 UGLY : feo, poco atractivo
homemade ['ho:m'meɪd] adj : casero, hecho en casa
homemaker ['ho:m,meɪkər] n : ama f de casa, persona f que se ocupa de la casa
home plate n : base f del bateador
home run n : jonrón m
homesick ['ho:m,sɪk] adj : nostálgico ⟨to be homesick : echar de menos a la familia⟩
homesickness ['ho:m,sɪknəs] n : nostalgia f, morriña f
homespun ['ho:m,spʌn] adj : simple, sencillo
homestead ['ho:m,stɛd] n : estancia f, hacienda f
homeward¹ ['ho:mwərd] or homewards [-wərdz] adv : de vuelta a casa, hacia casa
homeward² adj : de vuelta, de regreso
homework ['ho:m,wərk] n : tarea f, deberes mpl Spain, asignación f PRi

homey ['ho:mi] adj homier; -est : hogareño
homicidal [,hɑmə'saɪdəl, ,ho:-] adj : homicida
homicide ['hɑmə,saɪd, 'ho:-] n : homicidio m
hominy ['hɑməni] n : maíz m descascarillado
homogeneity [,ho:məʤə'ni:əti, -'neɪ-] n, pl -ties : homogeneidad f
homogeneous [,ho:mə'ʤi:niəs, -njəs] adj : homogéneo — homogeneously adv
homogenize [ho:'mɑʤə,naɪz, hə-] vt -nized; -nizing : homogeneizar
homograph ['hɑmə,græf, 'ho:-] n : homógrafo m
homologous [ho:'mɑləgəs, hə-] adj : homólogo
homonym ['hɑmə,nɪm, 'ho:-] n : homónimo m
homophone ['hɑmə,fo:n, 'ho:-] n : homófono m
homosexual¹ [,ho:mə'sɛkʃuəl] adj : homosexual
homosexual² n : homosexual mf
homosexuality [,ho:mə,sɛkʃu'æləti] n : homosexualidad f
honcho ['hɑn,ʧo:] n : pez m gordo ⟨the head honcho : el jefe⟩
Honduran [hɑn'dʊrən, -'djʊr-] n : hondureño m, -ña f — Honduran adj
hone ['ho:n] vt honed; honing : afilar
honest ['ɑnəst] adj : honesto, honrado — honestly adv
honesty ['ɑnəsti] n, pl -ties : honestidad f, honradez f
honey ['hʌni] n, pl -eys : miel f
honeybee ['hʌni,bi:] n : abeja f
honeycomb ['hʌni,ko:m] n : panal m
honeymoon¹ ['hʌni,mu:n] vi : pasar la luna de miel
honeymoon² n : luna f de miel
honeysuckle ['hʌni,sʌkəl] n : madreselva f
honk¹ ['hɑŋk, 'hɔŋk] vi 1 : graznar (dícese del ganso) 2 : tocar la bocina (dícese de un vehículo), pitar
honk² n : graznido m (del ganso), bocinazo m (de un vehículo)
honor¹ ['ɑnər] vt 1 RESPECT : honrar 2 : cumplir con ⟨to honor one's word : cumplir con su palabra⟩ 3 : aceptar (un cheque, etc.)
honor² n 1 : honor m ⟨in honor of : en honor de⟩ 2 honors npl AWARDS : honores mpl, condecoraciones fpl 3 Your Honor : Su Señoría
honorable ['ɑnərəbəl] adj : honorable, honroso — honorably [-bli] adv
honorary ['ɑnə,rɛri] adj : honorario
hood ['hʊd] n 1 : capucha f 2 : capó m, bonete m Car (de un automóvil)
hooded ['hʊdəd] adj : encapuchado
hoodlum ['hʊdləm, 'hu:d-] n THUG : maleante mf, matón m
hoodwink ['hʊd,wɪŋk] vt : engañar

hoof ['hʊf, 'hu:f] *n, pl* **hooves** ['hʊvz, 'hu:vz] *or* **hoofs** : pezuña *f*, casco *m*
hoofed ['hʊft, 'hu:ft] *adj* : ungulado
hook[1] ['hʊk] *vt* : enganchar — *vi* : abrocharse, engancharse
hook[2] *n* : gancho *m*, percha *f*
hooked ['hʊkt] *adj* **1** : en forma de gancho **2 to be hooked on** : estar enganchado a
hooker ['hʊkər] *n* : prostituta *f*, fulana *f fam*
hookworm ['hʊk,wərm] *n* : anquilostoma *m*
hooligan ['hu:lɪgən] *n* : gamberro *m*, -rra *f*
hoop ['hu:p] *n* : aro *m*
hooray [hʊ'reɪ] → **hurrah**
hoot[1] ['hu:t] *vi* **1** SHOUT : gritar ⟨to hoot with laughter : morirse de risa, reírse a carcajadas⟩ **2** : ulular (dícese de un búho), tocar la bocina (dícese de un vehículo), silbar (dícese de un tren o un barco)
hoot[2] *n* **1** : ululato *m* (de un búho), silbido *m* (de un tren), bocinazo *m* (de un vehículo) **2** GUFFAW : carcajada *f*, risotada *f* **3 I don't give a hoot** : me vale un comino, me importa un pito
hop[1] ['hɑp] *vi* **hopped; hopping** : brincar, saltar
hop[2] *n* **1** LEAP : salto *m*, brinco *m* **2** FLIGHT : vuelo *m* corto **3** : lúpulo *m* (planta)
hope[1] ['ho:p] *v* **hoped; hoping** *vi* : esperar — *vt* : esperar que ⟨we hope she comes : esperamos que venga⟩ ⟨I hope not : espero que no⟩
hope[2] *n* : esperanza *f*
hopeful ['ho:pfəl] *adj* : esperanzado — **hopefully** *adv*
hopeless ['ho:pləs] *adj* **1** DESPAIRING : desesperado **2** IMPOSSIBLE : imposible ⟨a hopeless case : un caso perdido⟩
hopelessly ['ho:pləsli] *adv* **1** : sin esperanzas, desesperadamente **2** COMPLETELY : totalmente, completamente **3** IMPOSSIBLY : imposiblemente
hopelessness ['ho:pləsnəs] *n* : desesperanza *f*
hopper ['hɑpər] *n* : tolva *f*
hopscotch ['hɑp,skɑtʃ] *n* : tejo *m*
horde ['hord] *n* : horda *f*, multitud *f*
horizon [hə'raɪzən] *n* : horizonte *m*
horizontal [,hɔrə'zɑntəl] *adj* : horizontal — **horizontally** *adv*
hormone ['hɔr,mo:n] *n* : hormona *f* — **hormonal** [hɔr'mo:nəl] *adj*
horn ['hɔrn] *n* **1** : cuerno *m* (de un toro, una vaca, etc.) **2** : cuerno *m*, trompa *f* (instrumento musical) **3** : bocina *f*, claxon *m* (de un vehículo)
horned ['hɔrnd, 'hɔrnəd] *adj* : cornudo, astado, con cuernos
hornet ['hɔrnət] *n* : avispón *m*
horny ['hɔrni] *adj* **hornier; -est 1** CALLOUS : calloso **2** LUSTFUL *fam* : caliente *fam*
horoscope ['hɔrə,sko:p] *n* : horóscopo *m*

horrendous [hɔ'rɛndəs] *adj* : horrendo, horroroso, atroz
horrible ['hɔrəbəl] *adj* : horrible, espantoso, horroroso — **horribly** [-bli] *adv*
horrid ['hɔrɪd] *adj* : horroroso, horrible — **horridly** *adv*
horrific [hɔ'rɪfɪk] *adj* : terrorífico, horroroso
horrify ['hɔrə,faɪ] *vt* **-fied; -fying** : horrorizar
horrifying ['hɔrə,faɪɪŋ] *adj* : horripilante, horroroso
horror ['hɔrər] *n* : horror *m*
hors d'oeuvre [ɔr'dərv] *n, pl* **hors d'oeuvres** [-'dərvz] : entremés *m*
horse ['hɔrs] *n* : caballo *m*
horseback ['hɔrs,bæk] *n* **on ~** : a caballo
horse chestnut *n* : castaña *f* de Indias
horsefly ['hɔrs,flaɪ] *n, pl* **-flies** : tábano *m*
horsehair ['hɔrs,hær] *n* : crin *f*
horseman ['hɔrsmən] *n, pl* **-men** [-mən, -,mɛn] : jinete *m*, caballista *m*
horsemanship ['hɔrsmən,ʃɪp] *n* : equitación *f*
horseplay ['hɔrs,pleɪ] *n* : payasadas *fpl*
horsepower ['hɔrs,paʊər] *n* : caballo *m* de fuerza
horseradish ['hɔrs,rædɪʃ] *n* : rábano *m* picante
horseshoe ['hɔrs,ʃu:] *n* : herradura *f*
horsewhip ['hɔrs,hwɪp] *vt* **-whipped; -whipping** : azotar, darle fuetazos (a alguien)
horsewoman ['hɔrs,wʊmən] *n, pl* **-women** [-,wɪmən] : amazona *f*, jinete *f*, caballista *f*
horsey *or* **horsy** ['hɔrsi] *adj* **horsier; -est** : relacionado a los caballos, caballar
horticultural [,hɔrtə'kʌltʃərəl] *adj* : hortícola
horticulture ['hɔrtə,kʌltʃər] *n* : horticultura *f*
hose[1] ['ho:z] *vt* **hosed; hosing** : regar o lavar con manguera
hose[2] *n* **1** *pl* **hose** SOCKS : calcetines *mpl*, medias *fpl* **2** *pl* **hose** STOCKINGS : medias *fpl* **3** *pl* **hoses** : manguera *f*, manga *f*
hosiery ['ho:ʒəri, 'ho:ʒə-] *n* : calcetería *f*, medias *fpl*
hospice ['hɑspəs] *n* : hospicio *m*
hospitable [hɑ'spɪtəbəl, 'hɑs,pɪ-] *adj* : hospitalario — **hospitably** [-bli] *adv*
hospital ['hɑs,pɪtəl] *n* : hospital *m*
hospitality [,hɑspə'tæləti] *n, pl* **-ties** : hospitalidad *f*
hospitalization [,hɑs,pɪtələ'zeɪʃən] *n* : hospitalización *f*
hospitalize ['hɑs,pɪtəl,aɪz] *vt* **-ized; -izing** : hospitalizar
host[1] ['ho:st] *vt* : presentar (un programa de televisión, etc.)
host[2] *n* **1** : anfitrión *m*, -triona *f* (en la casa, a un evento); presentador *m*, -dora *f* (de un programa de televisión, etc.) **2** *or* **host organism** : huésped *m*

3 TROOPS : huestes *fpl* 4 MULTITUDE : multitud *f* ⟨for a host of reasons : por muchas razones⟩ 5 EUCHARIST : hostia *f*, Eucaristía *f*
hostage ['hɑstɪʤ] *n* : rehén *m*
hostel ['hɑstəl] *n* : albergue *m* juvenil
hostess ['ho:stɪs] *n* : anfitriona *f* (en la casa), presentadora *f* (de un programa)
hostile ['hɑstəl, -,taɪl] *adj* : hostil — **hostilely** *adv*
hostility [hɑs'tɪləti] *n*, *pl* **-ties** : hostilidad *f*
hot ['hɑt] *adj* **hotter; hottest** 1 : caliente, cálido, caluroso ⟨hot water : agua caliente⟩ ⟨a hot climate : un clima cálido⟩ ⟨a hot day : un día caluroso⟩ 2 ARDENT, FIERY : ardiente, acalorado ⟨to have a hot temper : tener mal genio⟩ 3 SPICY : picante 4 FRESH : reciente, nuevo ⟨hot news : noticias de última hora⟩ 5 EAGER : ávido 6 STOLEN : robado
hot air *n* : palabrería *f*
hotbed ['hɑt,bɛd] *n* 1 : semillero *m* (de plantas) 2 : hervidero *m*, semillero *m* (de crimen, etc.)
hot dog *n* : perro *m* caliente
hotel [ho:'tɛl] *n* : hotel *m*
hothead ['hɑt,hɛd] *n* : exaltado *m*, -da *f*
hotheaded ['hɑt'hɛdəd] *adj* : exaltado
hothouse ['hɑt,haʊs] *n* : invernadero *m*
hot plate *n* : placa *f* (de cocina)
hot rod *n* : coche *m* con motor modificado
hot water *n* **to get into hot water** : meterse en un lío
hound¹ ['haʊnd] *vt* : acosar, perseguir
hound² *n* : perro *m* (de caza)
hour ['aʊər] *n* : hora *f*
hourglass ['aʊər,glæs] *n* : reloj *m* de arena
hourly ['aʊərli] *adv & adj* : cada hora, por hora
house¹ ['haʊz] *vt* **housed; housing** : albergar, alojar, hospedar
house² ['haʊs] *n*, *pl* **houses** ['haʊzəz, -səz] 1 HOME : casa *f* 2 : cámara *f* (del gobierno) 3 BUSINESS : casa *f*, empresa *f*
houseboat ['haʊs,bo:t] *n* : casa *f* flotante
housebroken ['haʊs,bro:kən] *adj* : enseñado
housefly ['haʊs,flaɪ] *n*, *pl* **-flies** : mosca *f* común
household¹ ['haʊs,ho:ld] *adj* 1 DOMESTIC : doméstico, de la casa 2 FAMILIAR : conocido por todos
household² *n* : casa *f*, familia *f*
householder ['haʊs,ho:ldər] *n* : dueño *m*, -ña *f* de casa
housekeeper ['haʊs,ki:pər] *n* : ama *f* de llaves
housekeeping ['haʊs,ki:pɪŋ] *n* : gobierno *m* de la casa, quehaceres *mpl* domésticos
housemaid ['haʊs,meɪd] *n* : criada *f*, mucama *f*, muchacha *f*, sirvienta *f*
housewarming ['haʊs,wɔrmɪŋ] *n* : fiesta *f* de estreno de una casa

housewife ['haʊs,waɪf] *n*, *pl* **-wives** : ama *f* de casa
housework ['haʊs,wərk] *n* : faenas *fpl* domésticas, quehaceres *mpl* domésticos
housing ['haʊzɪŋ] *n* 1 HOUSES : vivienda *f* 2 COVERING : caja *f* protectora
hove → **heave**
hovel ['hʌvəl, 'hɑ-] *n* : casucha *f*, tugurio *m*
hover ['hʌvər, 'hɑ-] *vi* 1 : cernerse, sostenerse en el aire 2 **to hover about** : rondar
how ['haʊ] *adv* 1 : cómo ⟨how are you? : ¿cómo estás?⟩ ⟨I don't know how to fix it : no se cómo arreglarlo⟩ 2 : qué ⟨how beautiful! : ¡qué bonito!⟩ 3 : cuánto ⟨how old are you? : ¿cuántos años tienes?⟩ 4 **how about...?** : ¿qué te parece...?
however¹ [haʊ'ɛvər] *adv* 1 : por mucho que, por más que ⟨however hot it is : por mucho calor que haga⟩ 2 NEVERTHELESS : sin embargo, no obstante
however² *conj* : comoquiera que, de cualquier manera que
howl¹ ['haʊl] *vi* : aullar
howl² *n* : aullido *m*, alarido *m*
hub ['hʌb] *n* 1 CENTER : centro *m* 2 : cubo *m* (de una rueda)
hubbub ['hʌ,bʌb] *n* : algarabía *f*, alboroto *m*, jaleo *m*
hubcap ['hʌb,kæp] *n* : tapacubos *m*
huckster ['hʌkstər] *n* : buhonero *m*, -ra *f*; vendedor *m*, -dora *f* ambulante
huddle¹ ['hʌdəl] *vi* **-dled; -dling** 1 : apiñarse, amontonarse 2 **to huddle together** : acurrucarse
huddle² *n* : grupo *m* (cerrado) ⟨to go into a huddle : conferenciar en secreto⟩
hue ['hju:] *n* : color *m*, tono *m*
huff ['hʌf] *n* : enojo *m*, enfado *m* ⟨to be in a huff : estar enojado⟩
huffy ['hʌfi] *adj* **huffier; -est** : enojado, enfadado
hug¹ ['hʌg] *vt* **hugged; hugging** 1 EMBRACE : abrazar 2 : ir pegado a ⟨the road hugs the river : el camino está pegado al río⟩
hug² *n* : abrazo *m*
huge ['hju:ʤ] *adj* **huger; hugest** : inmenso, enorme — **hugely** *adv*
hulk ['hʌlk] *n* 1 : persona *f* fornida 2 : casco *m* (barco), armatoste *m* (edificio, etc.)
hulking ['hʌlkɪŋ] *adj* : grandote *fam*, pesado
hull¹ ['hʌl] *vt* : pelar
hull² *n* 1 HUSK : cáscara *f* 2 : casco *m* (de un barco, un avión, etc.)
hullabaloo ['hʌləbə,lu:] *n*, *pl* **-loos** : alboroto *m*, jaleo *m*
hum¹ ['hʌm] *v* **hummed; humming** *vi* 1 BUZZ : zumbar 2 : estar muy activo, moverse ⟨to hum with activity : bullir de actividad⟩ — *vt* : tararear (una melodía)

hum² *n* : zumbido *m*, murmullo *m*
human¹ ['hju:mən, 'ju:-] *adj* : humano
— **humanly** *adv*
human² *n* : ser *m* humano
humane [hju:'meɪn, ju:-] *adj* : humano, humanitario — **humanely** *adv*
humanism ['hju:mə,nɪzəm, 'ju:-] *n* : humanismo *m*
humanist¹ ['hju:mənɪst, 'ju:-] *n* : humanista *mf*
humanist² *or* **humanistic** [,hju:mə-'nɪstɪk, ,ju:-] *adj* : humanístico
humanitarian¹ [hju:,mænə'triən, ju:-] *adj* : humanitario
humanitarian² *n* : humanitario *m*, -ria *f*
humanity [hju:'mænəti, ju:-] *n, pl* -**ties** : humanidad *f*
humankind ['hju:mən'kaɪnd, 'ju:-] *n* : género *m* humano
humble¹ ['hʌmbəl] *vt* -**bled**; -**bling** 1 : humillar 2 **to humble oneself** : humillarse
humble² *adj* -**bler**; -**blest** : humilde, modesto — **humbly** ['hʌmbli] *adv*
humbug ['hʌm,bʌg] *n* 1 FRAUD : charlatán *m*, -tana *f*; farsante *mf* 2 NONSENSE : patrañas *fpl*, tonterías *fpl*
humdrum ['hʌm,drʌm] *adj* : monótono, rutinario
humid ['hju:məd, 'ju:-] *adj* : húmedo
humidifier [hju:'mɪdə,faɪər, ju:-] *n* : humidificador *m*
humidify [hju:'mɪdə,faɪ, ju:-] *vt* -**fied**; -**fying** : humidificar
humidity [hju:'mɪdəti, ju:-] *n, pl* -**ties** : humedad *f*
humiliate [hju:'mɪli,eɪt, ju:-] *vt* -**ated**; -**ating** : humillar
humiliating [hju:'mɪli,eɪtɪŋ, ju:-] *adj* : humillante
humiliation [hju:,mɪli'eɪʃən, ju:-] *n* : humillación *f*
humility [hju:'mɪləti, ju:-] *n* : humildad *f*
hummingbird ['hʌmɪŋ,bərd] *n* : colibrí *m*, picaflor *m*
hummock ['hʌmək] *n* : montículo *m*
humor¹ ['hju:mər, 'ju:-] *vt* : seguir el humor a, complacer
humor² *n* : humor *m*
humorist ['hju:mərɪst, 'ju:-] *n* : humorista *mf*
humorless ['hju:mərləs, 'ju:-] *adj* : sin sentido del humor ⟨a humorless smile : una sonrisa forzada⟩
humorous ['hju:mərəs, 'ju:-] *adj* : humorístico, cómico — **humorously** *adv*
hump ['hʌmp] *n* : joroba *f*, giba *f*
humpback ['hʌmp,bæk] *n* 1 HUMP : joroba *f*, giba *f* 2 HUNCHBACK : jorobado *m*, -da *f*; giboso *m*, -sa *f*
humpbacked ['hʌmp,bækt] *adj* : jorobado, giboso
humus ['hju:məs, 'ju:-] *n* : humus *m*
hunch¹ ['hʌntʃ] *vt* : encorvar — *vi or* **to hunch up** : encorvarse
hunch² *n* PREMONITION : presentimiento *m*

hunchback ['hʌntʃ,bæk] *n* 1 HUMP : joroba *f*, giba *f* 2 HUMPBACK : jorobado *m*, -da *f*; giboso *m*, -sa *f*
hunchbacked ['hʌntʃ,bækt] *adj* : jorobado, giboso
hundred¹ ['hʌndrəd] *adj* : cien, ciento
hundred² *n, pl* -**dreds** *or* -**dred** : ciento *m*
hundredth¹ ['hʌndrədθ] *adj* : centésimo
hundredth² *n* 1 : centésimo *m*, -ma *f* (en una serie) 2 : centésimo *m*, centésima parte *f*
hung → **hang**
Hungarian [hʌŋ'gæriən] *n* 1 : húngaro *m*, -ra *f* 2 : húngaro *m* (idioma) — **Hungarian** *adj*
hunger¹ ['hʌŋgər] *vi* 1 : tener hambre 2 **to hunger for** : ansiar, anhelar
hunger² *n* : hambre *m*
hungrily ['hʌŋgrəli] *adv* : ávidamente
hungry ['hʌŋgri] *adj* -**grier**; -**est** 1 : hambriento 2 **to be hungry** : tener hambre
hunk ['hʌŋk] *n* : trozo *m*, pedazo *m*
hunt¹ ['hʌnt] *vt* 1 PURSUE : cazar 2 **to hunt for** : buscar
hunt² *n* 1 PURSUIT : caza *f*, cacería *f* 2 SEARCH : búsqueda *f*, busca *f*
hunter ['hʌntər] *n* : cazador *m*, -dora *f*
hunting ['hʌntɪŋ] *n* : caza *f* ⟨to go hunting : ir de caza⟩
hurdle¹ ['hərdəl] *vt* -**dled**; -**dling** : saltar, salvar (un obstáculo)
hurdle² *n* : valla *f* (en deportes), obstáculo *m*
hurl ['hərl] *vt* : arrojar, tirar, lanzar
hurrah [hu'rɑ, -'rɔ] *interj* : ¡hurra!
hurricane ['hərə,keɪn] *n* : huracán *m*
hurried ['hərid] *adj* : apresurado, precipitado
hurriedly ['hərədli] *adv* : apresuradamente, de prisa
hurry¹ ['həri] *v* -**ried**; -**rying** *vi* : apurarse, darse prisa, apresurarse — *vt* : apurar, darle prisa (a alguien)
hurry² *n* : prisa *f*, apuro *f*
hurt¹ ['hərt] *v* **hurt**; **hurting** *vt* 1 INJURE : hacer daño a, herir, lastimar ⟨to hurt oneself : hacerse daño⟩ 2 DISTRESS, OFFEND : hacer sufrir, ofender, herir — *vi* : doler ⟨my foot hurts : me duele el pie⟩
hurt² *n* 1 INJURY : herida *f* 2 DISTRESS, PAIN : dolor *m*, pena *f*
hurtful ['hərtfəl] *adj* : hiriente, doloroso
hurtle ['hərtəl] *vi* -**tled**; -**tling** : lanzarse, precipitarse
husband¹ ['hʌzbənd] *vt* : economizar, bien administrar
husband² *n* : esposo *m*, marido *m*
husbandry ['hʌzbəndri] *n* 1 MANAGEMENT, THRIFT : economía *f*, buena administración *f* 2 AGRICULTURE : agricultura *f* ⟨animal husbandry : cría de animales⟩
hush¹ ['hʌʃ] *vt* 1 SILENCE : hacer callar, acallar 2 CALM : calmar, apaciguar
hush² *n* : silencio *m*

hush-hush [ˈhʌʃˌhʌʃ, ˌhʌʃˈhʌʃ] *adj* : muy secreto, confidencial
husk[1] [ˈhʌsk] *vt* : descascarar
husk[2] *n* : cáscara *f*
huskily [ˈhʌskəli] *adv* : con voz ronca
husky[1] [ˈhʌski] *adj* -kier; -est 1 HOARSE : ronco 2 BURLY : fornido
husky[2] *n, pl* -kies : perro *m*, -rra *f* esquimal
hustle[1] [ˈhəsəl] *v* -tled; -tling *vt* : darle prisa (a alguien), apurar ⟨they hustled me in : me hicieron entrar a empujones⟩ — *vi* : apurarse, ajetrearse
hustle[2] *n* BUSTLE : ajetreo *m*
hut [ˈhʌt] *n* : cabaña *f*, choza *f*, barraca *f*
hutch [ˈhʌtʃ] *n* 1 CUPBOARD : alacena *f* 2 rabbit hutch : conejera *f*
hyacinth [ˈhaɪəˌsɪnθ] *n* : jacinto *m*
hybrid[1] [ˈhaɪbrɪd] *adj* : híbrido
hybrid[2] *n* : híbrido *m*
hydrant [ˈhaɪdrənt] *n* : boca *f* de riego, hidrante *m CA, Col* ⟨fire hydrant : boca de incendios⟩
hydraulic [haɪˈdrɔlɪk] *adj* : hidráulico — hydraulically *adv*
hydrocarbon [ˌhaɪdroˈkɑrbən] *n* : hidrocarburo *m*
hydrochloric acid [ˌhaɪdroˈklorɪk] *n* : ácido *m* clorhídrico
hydroelectric [ˌhaɪdroɪˈlɛktrɪk] *adj* : hidroeléctrico
hydrogen [ˈhaɪdrədʒən] *n* : hidrógeno *m*
hydrogen bomb *n* : bomba *f* de hidrógeno
hydrogen peroxide *n* : agua *f* oxigenada, peróxido *m* de hidrógeno
hydrophobia [ˌhaɪdrəˈfoːbiə] *n* : hidrofobia *f*, rabia *f*
hydroplane [ˈhaɪdrəˌpleɪn] *n* : hidroplano *m*
hyena [haɪˈiːnə] *n* : hiena *f*
hygiene [ˈhaɪˌdʒiːn] *n* : higiene *f*
hygienic [haɪˈdʒɛnɪk, -ˈdʒiː-; ˌhaɪ-dʒiˈnɪk] *adj* : higiénico — hygienically [-nɪkli] *adv*
hygienist [haɪˈdʒiːnɪst, -ˈdʒɛ-; ˈhaɪ-ˌdʒiː-] *n* : higienista *mf*
hygrometer [haɪˈgrɑmətər] *n* : higrómetro *m*
hymn [ˈhɪm] *n* : himno *m*

hymnal [ˈhɪmnəl] *n* : himnario *m*
hype [ˈhaɪp] *n* : bombo *m* publicitario
hyperactive [ˌhaɪpərˈæktɪv] *adj* : hiperactivo
hyperactivity [ˌhaɪpərˌækˈtɪvəti] *n, pl* -ties : hiperactividad *f*
hyperbole [haɪˈpərbəli] *n* : hipérbole *f*
hyperbolic [ˌhaɪpərˈbalɪk] *adj* : hiperbólico
hypercritical [ˌhaɪpərˈkrɪtəkəl] *adj* : hipercrítico
hypersensitivity [ˌhaɪpərˌsɛntsəˈtɪ-vəti] *n* : hipersensibilidad *f*
hypertension [ˈhaɪpərˌtɛntʃən] *n* : hipertensión *f*
hyphen [ˈhaɪfən] *n* : guión *m*
hyphenate [ˈhaɪfənˌeɪt] *vt* -ated; -ating : escribir con guión
hypnosis [hɪpˈnoːsɪs] *n, pl* -noses [-ˌsiːz] : hipnosis *f*
hypnotic [hɪpˈnɑtɪk] *adj* : hipnótico, hipnotizador
hypnotism [ˈhɪpnəˌtɪzəm] *n* : hipnotismo *m*
hypnotize [ˈhɪpnəˌtaɪz] *vt* -tized; -tizing : hipnotizar
hypochondria [ˌhaɪpəˈkɑndriə] *n* : hipocondría *f*
hypochondriac [ˌhaɪpəˈkɑndriˌæk] *n* : hipocondríaco *m*, -ca *f*
hypocrisy [hɪpˈɑkrəsi] *n, pl* -sies : hipocresía *f*
hypocrite [ˈhɪpəˌkrɪt] *n* : hipócrita *mf*
hypocritical [ˌhɪpəˈkrɪtɪkəl] *adj* : hipócrita
hypodermic[1] [ˌhaɪpəˈdərmɪk] *adj* : hipodérmico
hypodermic[2] *n* : aguja *f* hipodérmica
hypotenuse [haɪˈpɑtənˌuːs, -ˌuːz, -ˌjuːs, -ˌjuːz] *n* : hipotenusa *f*
hypothesis [haɪˈpɑθəsɪs] *n, pl* -eses [-ˌsiːz] : hipótesis *f*
hypothetical [ˌhaɪpəˈθɛtɪkəl] *adj* : hipotético — hypothetically [-tɪkli] *adv*
hysteria [hɪsˈtɛriə, -tɪr-] *n* : histeria *f*, histerismo *m*
hysterical [hɪsˈtɛrɪkəl] *adj* : histérico — hysterically [-ɪkli] *adv*
hysterics [hɪsˈtɛrɪks] *n* : histeria *f*, histerismo *m*

I

i [ˈaɪ] *n, pl* i's *or* is [ˈaɪz] : novena letra del alfabeto inglés
I [ˈaɪ] *pron* : yo
Iberian [aɪˈbɪriən] *adj* : ibérico
ibis [ˈaɪbəs] *n, pl* ibis *or* ibises : ibis *f*
ice[1] [ˈaɪs] *v* iced; icing *vt* 1 FREEZE : congelar, helar 2 CHILL : enfriar 3 to ice a cake : escarchar un pastel — *vi* : helarse, congelarse
ice[2] *n* 1 : hielo *m* 2 SHERBET : sorbete *m*, nieve *f Cuba, Mex, PRi*

iceberg [ˈaɪsˌbərg] *n* : iceberg *m*
icebox [ˈaɪsˌbaks] → refrigerator
icebreaker [ˈaɪsˌbreɪkər] *n* : rompehielos *m*
ice cap *n* : casquete *m* glaciar
ice-cold [ˈaɪsˈkoːld] *adj* : helado
ice cream *n* : helado *m*, mantecado *m PRi*
Icelander [ˈaɪsˌlændər, -lən-] *n* : islandés *m*, -desa *f*
Icelandic[1] [aɪsˈlændɪk] *adj* : islandés

Icelandic² *n* : islandés *m* (idioma)
ice–skate [ˈaɪsˌskeɪt] *vi* **-skated; -skating** : patinar
ice skater *n* : patinador *m*, -dora *f*
ichthyology [ˌɪkthiˈɑləʤi] *n* : ictiología *f*
icicle [ˈaɪˌsɪkəl] *n* : carámbano *m*
icily [ˈaɪsəli] *adv* : fríamente, con frialdad ⟨he stared at me icily : me fijó la mirada con mucha frialdad⟩
icing [ˈaɪsɪŋ] *n* : glaseado *m*, betún *m* *Mex*
icon [ˈaɪˌkɑn, -kən] *n* : icono *m*
iconoclasm [aɪˈkɑnəˌklæzəm] *n* : iconoclasia *f*
iconoclast [aɪˈkɑnəˌklæst] *n* : iconoclasta *mf*
icy [ˈaɪsi] *adj* **icier; -est 1** : cubierto de hielo ⟨an icy road : una carretera cubierta de hielo⟩ **2** FREEZING : helado, gélido, glacial **3** ALOOF : frío, distante
id [ˈɪd] *n* : id *m*
I'd [ˈaɪd] (*contraction of* **I should** *or* **I would**) → **should, would**
idea [aɪˈdiːə] *n* : idea *f*
ideal¹ [aɪˈdiːəl] *adj* : ideal
ideal² *n* : ideal *m*
idealism [aɪˈdiːəˌlɪzəm] *n* : idealismo *m*
idealist [aɪˈdiːəlɪst] *n* : idealista *mf*
idealistic [aɪˌdiːəˈlɪstɪk] *adj* : idealista
idealistically [aɪˌdiːəˈlɪstɪkli] *adv* : con idealismo
idealization [aɪˌdiːələˈzeɪʃən] *n* : idealización *f*
idealize [aɪˈdiːəˌlaɪz] *vt* **-ized; -izing** : idealizar
ideally [aɪˈdiːəli] *adv* : perfectamente
identical [aɪˈdɛntɪkəl] *adj* : idéntico — **identically** [-tɪkli] *adv*
identifiable [aɪˌdɛntəˈfaɪəbəl] *adj* : identificable
identification [aɪˌdɛntəfəˈkeɪʃən] *n* **1** : identificación *f* **2 identification card** : carnet *m*, cédula *f* de identidad, identificación *f*
identify [aɪˈdɛntəˌfaɪ] *v* **-fied; -fying** *vt* : identificar — *vi* **to identify with** : identificarse con
identity [aɪˈdɛntəti] *n, pl* **-ties** : identidad *f*
ideological [ˌaɪdiəˈlɑʤɪkəl, ˌɪ-] *adj* : ideológico — **ideologically** [-ʤɪkli] *adv*
ideology [ˌaɪdiˈɑləʤi, ˌɪ-] *n, pl* **-gies** : ideología *f*
idiocy [ˈɪdiəsi] *n, pl* **-cies 1** : idiotez *f* **2** NONSENSE : estupidez *f*, tontería *f*
idiom [ˈɪdiəm] *n* **1** LANGUAGE : lenguaje *m* **2** EXPRESSION : modismo *m*, expresión *f* idiomática
idiomatic [ˌɪdiəˈmætɪk] *adj* : idiomático
idiosyncrasy [ˌɪdioˈsɪŋkrəsi] *n, pl* **-sies** : idiosincrasia *f*
idiosyncratic [ˌɪdiosɪnˈkrætɪk] *adj* : idiosincrásico — **idiosyncratically** [-tɪkli] *adv*
idiot [ˈɪdiət] *n* **1** : idiota *mf* (en medicina) **2** FOOL : idiota *mf*; tonto *m*, -ta *f*; imbécil *mf fam*

idiotic [ˌɪdiˈɑtɪk] *adj* : estúpido, idiota
idiotically [ˌɪdiˈɑtɪkli] *adv* : estúpidamente
idle¹ [ˈaɪdəl] *v* **idled; idling** *vi* **1** LOAF : holgazanear, flojear, haraganear **2** : andar al ralentí (dícese de un automóvil), marchar en vacío (dícese de una máquina) — *vt* : dejar sin trabajo
idle² *adj* **idler; idlest 1** VAIN : frívolo, vano, infundado ⟨idle curiosity : pura curiosidad⟩ **2** INACTIVE : inactivo, parado, desocupado **3** LAZY : holgazán, haragán, perezoso
idleness [ˈaɪdəlnəs] *n* **1** INACTIVITY : inactividad *f*, ociosidad *f* **2** LAZINESS : holgazanería *f*, flojera *f*, pereza *f*
idler [ˈaɪdələr] *n* : haragán *m*, -gana *f*; holgazán *m*, -zana *f*
idly [ˈaɪdəli] *adv* : ociosamente
idol [ˈaɪdəl] *n* : ídolo *m*
idolater *or* **idolator** [aɪˈdɑlətər] *n* : idólatra *mf*
idolatrous [aɪˈdɑlətrəs] *adj* : idólatra
idolatry [aɪˈdɑlətri] *n, pl* **-tries** : idolatría *f*
idolize [ˈaɪdəlaɪz] *vt* **-ized; -izing** : idolatrar
idyll [ˈaɪdəl] *n* : idilio *m*
idyllic [aɪˈdɪlɪk] *adj* : idílico
if [ˈɪf] *conj* **1** : si ⟨I would do it if I could : lo haría si pudiera⟩ ⟨if so : si es así⟩ ⟨as if : como sí⟩ ⟨if I were you : yo que tú⟩ **2** WHETHER : si ⟨I don't know if they're ready : no sé si están listos⟩ **3** THOUGH : aunque, si bien ⟨it's pretty, if somewhat old-fashioned : es lindo aunque algo anticuado⟩
igloo [ˈɪˌgluː] *n, pl* **-loos** : iglú *m*
ignite [ɪgˈnaɪt] *v* **-nited; -niting** *vt* : prenderle fuego a, encender — *vi* : prender, encenderse
ignition [ɪgˈnɪʃən] *n* **1** IGNITING : ignición *f*, encendido *m* **2** *or* **ignition switch** : encendido *m*, arranque *m* ⟨to turn on the ignition : arrancar el motor⟩
ignoble [ɪgˈnoːbəl] *adj* : innoble — **ignobly** *adv*
ignominious [ˌɪgnəˈmɪniəs] *adj* : ignominioso, deshonroso — **ignominiously** *adv*
ignominy [ˈɪgnəˌmɪni] *n, pl* **-nies** : ignominia *f*
ignoramus [ˌɪgnəˈreɪməs] *n* : ignorante *mf*; bestia *mf*; bruto *m*, -ta *f*
ignorance [ˈɪgnərənts] *n* : ignorancia *f*
ignorant [ˈɪgnərənt] *adj* **1** : ignorante **2 to be ignorant of** : no ser consciente de, desconocer, ignorar
ignorantly [ˈɪgnərəntli] *adv* : ignorantemente, con ignorancia
ignore [ɪgˈnor] *vt* **-nored; -noring** : ignorar, hacer caso omiso de, no hacer caso de
iguana [ɪˈgwɑnə] *n* : iguana *f*, garrobo *f* *CA*
ilk [ˈɪlk] *n* : tipo *m*, clase *f*, índole *f*
ill¹ [ˈɪl] *adv* **worse** [ˈwərs]; **worst** [ˈwərst] : mal ⟨to speak ill of : hablar mal de⟩

⟨he can ill afford to fail : mal puede permitirse el lujo de fracasar⟩
ill² *adj* **worse; worst 1** SICK : enfermo **2** BAD : malo ⟨ill luck : mala suerte⟩
ill³ *n* **1** EVIL : mal *m* **2** MISFORTUNE : mal *m*, desgracia *f* **3** AILMENT : enfermedad *f*
I'll ['aɪl] (*contraction of* **I shall** *or* **I will**) → **shall, will**
illegal [ɪl'li:gəl] *adj* : ilegal — **illegally** *adv*
illegality [ˌɪli'gæləti] *n* : ilegalidad *f*
illegibility [ɪlˌlɛdʒə'bɪləti] *n, pl* **-ties** : ilegibilidad *f*
illegible [ɪl'lɛdʒəbəl] *adj* : ilegible — **illegibly** [-bli] *adv*
illegitimacy [ˌɪlɪ'dʒɪtəməsi] *n* : ilegitimidad *f*
illegitimate [ˌɪlɪ'dʒɪtəmət] *adj* **1** BASTARD : ilegítimo, bastardo **2** UNLAWFUL : ilegítimo, ilegal — **illegitimately** *adv*
ill–fated ['ɪl'feɪtəd] *adj* : malhadado, infortunado, desventurado
illicit [ɪl'lɪsət] *adj* : ilícito — **illicitly** *adv*
illiteracy [ɪl'lɪtərəsi] *n, pl* **-cies** : analfabetismo *m*
illiterate¹ [ɪl'lɪtərət] *adj* : analfabeto
illiterate² *n* : analfabeto *m*, -ta *f*
ill–mannered [ˌɪl'manərd] *adj* : descortés, maleducado
ill–natured [ˌɪl'neɪtʃərd] *adj* : desagradable, de mal genio
ill–naturedly [ˌɪl'neɪtʃərdli] *adv* : desagradablemente
illness ['ɪlnəs] *n* : enfermedad *f*
illogical [ɪl'lɑdʒɪkəl] *adj* : ilógico — **illogically** [-kli] *adv*
ill–tempered [ˌɪl'tempərd] → **ill–natured**
ill–treat [ˌɪl'tri:t] *vt* : maltratar
ill–treatment [ˌɪl'tri:tmənt] *n* : maltrato *m*
illuminate [ɪ'lu:məˌneɪt] *vt* **-nated; -nating 1** : iluminar, alumbrar **2** ELUCIDATE : esclarecer, elucidar
illumination [ɪˌlu:mə'neɪʃən] *n* **1** LIGHTING : iluminación *f*, luz *f* **2** ELUCIDATION : esclarecimiento *m*, elucidación *f*
ill–use ['ɪl'ju:z] → **ill–treat**
illusion [ɪ'lu:ʒən] *n* : ilusión *f*
illusory [ɪ'lu:səri, -zəri] *adj* : engañoso, ilusorio
illustrate ['ɪləsˌtreɪʃən] *v* **-trated; -trating** : ilustrar
illustration [ˌɪlə'streɪʃən] *n* **1** PICTURE : ilustración *f* **2** EXAMPLE : ejemplo *m*, ilustración *f*
illustrative [ɪ'lʌstrətɪv, 'ɪləˌstreɪtɪv] *adj* : ilustrativo — **illustratively** *adv*
illustrator ['ɪləˌstreɪtər] *n* : ilustrador *m*, -dora *f*; dibujante *mf*
illustrious [ɪ'lʌstriəs] *adj* : ilustre, eminente, glorioso
illustriousness [ɪ'lʌstriəsnəs] *n* : eminencia *f*, prestigio *m*
ill will *n* : animosidad *f*, malquerencia *f*, mala voluntad *f*

I'm ['aɪm] (*contraction of* **I am**) → **be**
image¹ ['ɪmɪdʒ] *vt* **-aged; -aging** : imaginar, crear una imagen de
image² *n* : imagen *f*
imagery ['ɪmɪdʒri] *n, pl* **-eries 1** IMAGES : imágenes *fpl* **2** : imaginería *f* (en el arte)
imaginable [ɪ'mædʒənəbəl] *adj* : imaginable — **imaginably** [-bli] *adv*
imaginary [ɪ'mædʒəˌnɛri] *adj* : imaginario
imagination [ɪˌmædʒə'neɪʃən] *n* : imaginación *f*
imaginative [ɪ'mædʒənətɪv, -əˌneɪtɪv] *adj* : imaginativo — **imaginatively** *adv*
imagine [ɪ'mædʒən] *vt* **-ined; -ining** : imaginar(se)
imbalance [ɪm'bælənts] *n* : desajuste *m*, desbalance *m*, desequilibrio *m*
imbecile¹ ['ɪmbəsəl, -ˌsɪl] *or* **imbecilic** [ˌɪmbə'sɪlɪk] *adj* : imbécil, estúpido
imbecile² *n* **1** : imbécil *mf* (en medicina) **2** FOOL : idiota *mf*; imbécil *mf fam*; estúpido *m*, -da *f*
imbecility [ˌɪmbə'sɪləti] *n, pl* **-ties** : imbecilidad *f*
imbibe [ɪm'baɪb] *v* **-bibed; -bibing** *vt* **1** DRINK : beber **2** ABSORB : absorber, embeber — *vi* : beber
imbue [ɪm'bju:] *vt* **-bued; -buing** : imbuir
imitate ['ɪməˌteɪt] *vt* **-tated; -tating** : imitar, remedar
imitation¹ [ˌɪmə'teɪʃən] *adj* : de imitación, artificial
imitation² *n* : imitación *f*
imitative ['ɪməˌteɪtɪv] *adj* : imitativo, imitador, poco original
imitator ['ɪməˌteɪtər] *n* : imitador *m*, -dora *f*
immaculate [ɪ'mækjələt] *adj* **1** PURE : inmaculado, puro **2** FLAWLESS : impecable, intachable — **immaculately** *adv*
immaterial [ˌɪmə'tɪriəl] *adj* **1** INCORPOREAL : incorpóreo **2** UNIMPORTANT : irrelevante, sin importancia
immature [ˌɪmə'tʃʊr, -'tjʊr, -'tʊr] *adj* : inmaduro, verde (dícese de la fruta)
immaturity [ˌɪmə'tʃʊrəti, -'tjʊr-, -'tʊr-] *n, pl* **-ties** : inmadurez *f*, falta *f* de madurez
immeasurable [ɪ'mɛʒərəbəl] *adj* : inconmensurable, incalculable — **immeasurably** [-bli] *adv*
immediacy [ɪ'mi:diəsi] *n* : inmediatez *f*
immediate [ɪ'mi:diət] *adj* **1** INSTANT : inmediato, instantáneo ⟨immediate relief : alivio instantáneo⟩ **2** DIRECT : inmediato, directo ⟨the immediate cause of death : la causa directa de la muerte⟩ **3** URGENT : urgente, apremiante **4** CLOSE : cercano, próximo, inmediato ⟨her immediate family : sus familiares más cercanos⟩ ⟨in the immediate vicinity : en los alrededores, en las inmediaciones⟩
immediately [ɪ'mi:diətli] *adv* : inmediatamente, enseguida

immemorial [ˌɪməˈmoriəl] *adj* : inmemorial

immense [ɪˈmɛnts] *adj* : inmenso, enorme — **immensely** *adv*

immensity [ɪˈmɛntsəti] *n, pl* **-ties** : inmensidad *f*

immerse [ɪˈmərs] *vt* **-mersed; -mersing** 1 SUBMERGE : sumergir 2 **to immerse oneself in** : enfrascarse en

immersion [ɪˈmərʒən] *n* 1 : inmersión *f* (en un líquido) 2 : enfrascamiento *m* (en una actividad)

immigrant [ˈɪmɪgrənt] *n* : inmigrante *mf*

immigrate [ˈɪməˌgreɪt] *vi* **-grated; -grating** : inmigrar

immigration [ˌɪməˈgreɪʃən] *n* : inmigración *f*

imminence [ˈɪmənənts] *n* : inminencia *f*

imminent [ˈɪmənənt] *adj* : inminente — **imminently** *adv*

immobile [ɪmˈoːbəl] *adj* 1 FIXED, IMMOVABLE : inmovible, fijo 2 MOTIONLESS : inmóvil

immobility [ˌɪmoˈbɪləti] *n, pl* **-ties** : inmovilidad *f*

immobilize [ɪˈmoːbəˌlaɪz] *vt* **-lized; -lizing** : inmovilizar, paralizar

immoderate [ɪˈmɑdərət] *adj* : inmoderado, desmesurado, desmedido, excesivo — **immoderately** *adv*

immodest [ɪˈmɑdəst] *adj* 1 INDECENT : inmodesto, indecente, impúdico 2 CONCEITED : inmodesto, presuntuoso, engreído — **immodestly** *adv*

immodesty [ɪˈmɑdəsti] *n* : inmodestia *f*

immoral [ɪˈmɔrəl] *adj* : inmoral

immorality [ˌɪmɔˈræləti, ˌɪmə-] *n, pl* **-ties** : inmoralidad *f*

immorally [ɪˈmɔrəli] *adv* : de manera inmoral

immortal[1] [ɪˈmɔrtəl] *adj* : inmortal

immortal[2] *n* : inmortal *mf*

immortality [ˌɪmɔrˈtæləti] *n* : inmortalidad *f*

immortalize [ɪˈmɔrtəlˌaɪz] *vt* **-ized; -izing** : inmortalizar

immovable [ɪˈmuːvəbəl] *adj* 1 FIXED : fijo, inmovible 2 UNYIELDING : inflexible

immune [ɪˈmjuːn] *adj* 1 : inmune ⟨immune to smallpox : inmune a la viruela⟩ 2 EXEMPT : exento, inmune

immune system *n* : sistema *m* inmunológico

immunity [ɪˈmjuːnəti] *n, pl* **-ties** 1 : inmunidad *f* 2 EXEMPTION : exención *f*

immunization [ˌɪmjʊnəˈzeɪʃən] *n* : inmunización *f*

immunize [ˈɪmjʊˌnaɪz] *vt* **-nized; -nizing** : inmunizar

immunology [ˌɪmjʊˈnɑlədʒi] *n* : inmunología *f*

immutable [ɪˈmjuːtəbəl] *adj* : inmutable

imp [ˈɪmp] *n* RASCAL : diablillo *m*; pillo *m*, -lla *f*

impact[1] [ɪmˈpækt] *vt* 1 STRIKE : chocar con, impactar 2 AFFECT : afectar, impactar, impresionar — *vi* 1 STRIKE : hacer impacto, golpear 2 **to impact on** : tener un impacto sobre

impact[2] [ˈɪmˌpækt] *n* 1 COLLISION : impacto *m*, choque *m*, colisión *f* 2 EFFECT : efecto *m*, impacto *m*, consecuencias *fpl*

impacted [ɪmˈpæktəd] *adj* : impactado, incrustado (dícese de los dientes)

impair [ɪmˈpær] *vt* : perjudicar, dañar, afectar

impairment [ɪmˈpærmənt] *n* : perjuicio *m*, daño *m*

impala [ɪmˈpɑlə, -ˈpæ-] *n, pl* **impalas** *or* **impala** : impala *m*

impale [ɪmˈpeɪl] *vt* **-paled; -paling** : empalar

impanel [ɪmˈpænəl] *vt* **-eled** *or* **-elled; eling** *or* **-elling** : elegir (un jurado)

impart [ɪmˈpɑrt] *vt* 1 CONVEY : impartir, dar, conferir 2 DISCLOSE : revelar, divulgar

impartial [ɪmˈpɑrʃəl] *adj* : imparcial — **impartially** *adv*

impartiality [ɪmˌpɑrʃiˈæləti] *n, pl* **-ties** : imparcialidad *f*

impassable [ɪmˈpæsəbəl] *adj* : infranqueable, intransitable — **impassably** [-bli] *adv*

impasse [ˈɪmˌpæs] *n* 1 DEADLOCK : impasse *m*, punto *m* muerto 2 DEAD END : callejón *m* sin salida

impassioned [ɪmˈpæʃənd] *adj* : apasionado, vehemente

impassive [ɪmˈpæsɪv] *adj* : impasible, indiferente

impassively [ɪmˈpæsɪvli] *adv* : impasiblemente, sin emoción

impatience [ɪmˈpeɪʃənts] *n* : impaciencia *f*

impatient [ɪmˈpeɪʃənt] *adj* : impaciente — **impatiently** *adv*

impeach [ɪmˈpiːtʃ] *vt* : destituir (a un funcionario) de su cargo

impeachment [ɪmˈpiːtʃmənt] *n* 1 ACCUSATION : acusación *f* 2 DISMISSAL : destitución *f*

impeccable [ɪmˈpɛkəbəl] *adj* : impecable — **impeccably** [-bli] *adv*

impecunious [ˌɪmpɪˈkjuːniəs] *adj* : falto de dinero

impede [ɪmˈpiːd] *vt* **-peded; -peding** : impedir, dificultar, obstaculizar

impediment [ɪmˈpɛdəmənt] *n* 1 HINDRANCE : impedimento *m*, obstáculo *m* 2 **speech impediment** : defecto *m* del habla

impel [ɪmˈpɛl] *vt* **-pelled; -pelling** : impeler

impend [ɪmˈpɛnd] *vi* : ser inminente

impenetrable [ɪmˈpɛnətrəbəl] *adj* 1 : impenetrable ⟨an impenetrable forest : una selva impenetrable⟩ 2 INSCRUTABLE : incomprensible, inescrutable, impenetrable — **impenetrably** [-bli] *adv*

impenitent [ɪmˈpɛnətənt] *adj* : impenitente

imperative[1] [ɪm'pɛrətɪv] *adj* **1** AUTHOR-ITATIVE : imperativo, imperioso **2** NECESSARY : imprescindible — **imperatively** *adv*

imperative[2] *n* : imperativo *m*

imperceptible [ˌɪmpər'sɛptəbəl] *adj* : imperceptible — **imperceptibly** [-bli] *adv*

imperfect [ɪm'pərfɪkt] *adj* : imperfecto, defectuoso — **imperfectly** *adv*

imperfection [ɪmˌpər'fkʃən] *n* : imperfección *f*, defecto *m*

imperial [ɪm'pɪriəl] *adj* **1** : imperial **2** SOVEREIGN : soberano **3** IMPERIOUS : imperioso, señorial

imperialism [ɪm'pɪriəˌlɪzəm] *n* : imperialismo *m*

imperialist[1] [ɪm'pɪriəlɪst] *adj* : imperialista

imperialist[2] *n* : imperialista *mf*

imperialistic [ɪmˌpɪriːə'lɪstɪk] *adj* : imperialista

imperil [ɪm'pɛrəl] *vt* **-iled** *or* **-illed; -iling** *or* **-illing** : poner en peligro

imperious [ɪm'pɪriəs] *adj* : imperioso — **imperiously** *adv*

imperishable [ɪm'pɛrɪʃəbəl] *adj* : imperecedero

impermanent [ɪm'pərmənənt] *adj* : pasajero, inestable, efímero — **impermanently** *adv*

impermeable [ɪm'pərmiəbəl] *adj* : impermeable

impersonal [ɪm'pərsənəl] *adj* : impersonal — **impersonally** *adv*

impersonate [ɪm'pərsənˌeɪt] *vt* **-ated; -ating** : hacerse pasar por, imitar

impersonation [ɪmˌpərsən'eɪʃən] *n* : imitación *f*

impersonator [ɪm'pərsənˌeɪtər] *n* : imitador *m*, -dora *f*

impertinence [ɪm'pərtənənts] *n* : impertinencia *f*

impertinent [ɪm'pərtənənt] *adj* **1** IRRELEVANT : impertinente, irrelevante **2** INSOLENT : impertinente, insolente

impertinently [ɪm'pərtənəntli] *adv* : con impertinencia, impertinentemente

imperturbable [ˌɪmpər'tərbəbəl] *adj* : imperturbable

impervious [ɪm'pərviəs] *adj* **1** IMPENETRABLE : impermeable **2** INSENSITIVE : insensible ⟨impervious to criticism : insensible a la crítica⟩

impetuosity [ɪmˌpɛtʃʊ'ɑsəti] *n*, *pl* **-ties** : impetuosidad *f*

impetuous [ɪm'pɛtʃʊəs] *adj* : impetuoso, impulsivo

impetuously [ɪm'pɛtʃʊəsli] *adv* : de manera impulsiva, impetuosamente

impetus ['ɪmpətəs] *n* : ímpetu *m*, impulso *m*

impiety [ɪm'paɪəti] *n*, *pl* **-ties** : impiedad *f*

impinge [ɪm'pɪndʒ] *vi* **-pinged; -pinging 1 to impinge on** AFFECT : afectar a, incidir en **2 to impinge on** VIOLATE : violar, vulnerar

impious ['ɪmpiəs, ɪm'paɪəs] *adj* : impío, irreverente

impish ['ɪmpɪʃ] *adj* MISCHIEVOUS : pícaro, travieso

impishly ['ɪmpɪʃli] *adv* : con picardía

implacable [ɪm'plækəbəl] *adj* : implacable — **implacably** [-bli] *adv*

implant[1] [ɪm'plænt] *vt* **1** INCULCATE, INSTILL : inculcar, implantar **2** INSERT : implantar, insertar

implant[2] ['ɪmˌplænt] *n* : implante *m* (de pelo), injerto *m* (de piel)

implantation [ˌɪmˌplæn'teɪʃən] *n* : implantación *f*

implausibility [ɪmˌplɔzə'bɪləti] *n*, *pl* **-ties** : inverosimilitud *f*

implausible [ɪm'plɔzəbəl] *adj* : inverosímil, poco convincente

implement[1] ['ɪmpləˌmnt] *vt* : poner en práctica, implementar

implement[2] ['ɪmpləmənt] *n* : utensilio *m*, instrumento *m*, implemento *m*

implementation [ˌɪmpləmən'teɪʃən] *n* : implementación *f*, ejecución *f*, cumplimiento *m*

implicate ['ɪmpləˌkeɪt] *vt* **-cated; -cating** : implicar, involucrar

implication [ˌɪmplə'keɪʃən] *n* **1** CONSEQUENCE : implicación *f*, consecuencia *f* **2** INFERENCE : insinuación *f*, inferencia *f*

implicit [ɪm'plɪsət] *adj* **1** IMPLIED : implícito, tácito **2** ABSOLUTE : absoluto, completo ⟨implicit faith : fe ciega⟩ — **implicitly** *adv*

implied [ɪm'plaɪd] *adj* : implícito, tácito

implode [ɪm'plo:d] *vi* **-ploded; -ploding** : implosionar

implore [ɪm'plor] *vt* **-plored; -ploring** : implorar, suplicar

implosion [ɪm'plo:ʒən] *n* : implosión *f*

imply [ɪm'plaɪ] *vt* **-plied; -plying 1** SUGGEST : insinuar, dar a entender **2** INVOLVE : implicar, suponer ⟨rights imply obligations : los derechos implican unas obligaciones⟩

impolite [ˌɪmpə'laɪt] *adj* : descortés, maleducado

impoliteness [ˌɪmpə'laɪtnəs] *n* : descortesía *f*, falta *f* de educación

impolitic [ɪm'pɑləˌtɪk] *adj* : imprudente, poco político

imponderable[1] [ɪm'pɑndərəbəl] *adj* : imponderable

imponderable[2] *n* : imponderable *m*

import[1] [ɪm'port] *vt* **1** SIGNIFY : significar **2** : importar ⟨to import foreign cars : importar autos extranjeros⟩

import[2] ['ɪmˌport] *n* **1** SIGNIFICANCE : importancia *f*, significación *f* **2** → **importation**

importance [ɪm'portənts] *n* : importancia *f*

important [ɪm'portənt] *adj* : importante

importantly [ɪm'portəntli] *adv* **1** : con importancia **2 more importantly** : lo que es más importante

importation [ˌɪmˌpor'teɪʃən] *n* : importación *f*

importer [ɪm'portər] *n* : importador *m*, -dora *f*

importunate [ɪm'pɔrtʃənət] *adj* : importuno, insistente

importune [ˌɪmpər'tuːn, -'tjuːn; ɪm'pɔrtʃən] *vt* **-tuned; -tuning** : importunar, implorar

impose [ɪm'poːz] *v* **-posed; -posing** *vt* : imponer ⟨to impose a tax : imponer un impuesto⟩ — *vi* **to impose on** : abusar de, molestar ⟨to impose on her kindness : abusar de su bondad⟩

imposing [ɪm'poːzɪŋ] *adj* : imponente, impresionante

imposition [ˌɪmpə'zɪʃən] *n* : imposición *f*

impossibility [ɪmˌpɑsə'bɪləti] *n, pl* **-ties** : imposibilidad *f*

impossible [ɪm'pɑsəbəl] *adj* **1** : imposible ⟨an impossible task : una tarea imposible⟩ ⟨to make life impossible for : hacerle la vida imposible a⟩ **2** UNACCEPTABLE : inaceptable

impossibly [ɪm'pɑsəbli] *adv* : imposiblemente, increíblemente

impostor *or* **imposter** [ɪm'pɑstər] *n* : impostor *m*, -tora *f*

impotence ['ɪmpətənts] *n* : impotencia *f*

impotency ['ɪmpətəntsi] → **impotence**

impotent ['ɪmpətənt] *adj* : impotente

impound [ɪm'paʊnd] *vt* : incautar, embargar, confiscar

impoverish [ɪm'pɑvərɪʃ] *vt* : empobrecer

impoverishment [ɪm'pɑvərɪʃmənt] *n* : empobrecimiento *m*

impracticable [ɪm'præktɪkəbəl] *adj* : impracticable

impractical [ɪm'præktɪkəl] *adj* : poco práctico

imprecise [ˌɪmprɪ'saɪs] *adj* : impreciso

imprecisely [ˌɪmprɪ'saɪsli] *adv* : con imprecisión

impreciseness [ˌɪmprɪ'saɪsnəs] → **imprecision**

imprecision [ˌɪmprɪ'sɪʒən] *n* : imprecisión *f*, falta de precisión *f*

impregnable [ɪm'prɛgnəbəl] *adj* : inexpugnable, impenetrable, inconquistable

impregnate [ɪm'prɛgˌneɪt] *vt* **-nated; -nating 1** FERTILIZE : fecundar **2** PERMEATE, SATURATE : impregnar, empapar, saturar

impresario [ˌɪmprə'sɑriˌo, -'sær-] *n, pl* **-rios** : empresario *m*, -ria *f*

impress [ɪm'prɛs] *vt* **1** IMPRINT : imprimir, estampar **2** : impresionar, causar impresión a ⟨I was not impressed : no me hizo buena impresión⟩ **3 to impress (something) on someone** : recalcarle (algo) a alguien — *vi* : impresionar, hacer una impresión

impression [ɪm'prɛʃən] *n* **1** IMPRINT : marca *f*, huella *f*, molde *m* (de los dientes) **2** EFFECT : impresión *f*, efecto *m*, impacto *m* **3** PRINTING : impresión *f* **4** NOTION : impresión *f*, noción *f*

impressionable [ɪm'prɛʃənəbəl] *adj* : impresionable

impressionism [ɪm'prɛʃəˌnɪzəm] *n* : impresionismo *m*

impressionist [ɪm'prɛʃənɪst] *n* : impresionista *mf* — **impressionist** *adj*

impressive [ɪm'prɛsɪv] *adj* : impresionante — **impressively** *adv*

impressiveness [ɪm'prɛsɪvnəs] *n* : calidad de ser impresionante

imprint[1] [ɪm'prɪnt, 'ɪmˌ-] *vt* : imprimir, estampar

imprint[2] ['ɪmˌprɪnt] *n* : marca *f*, huella *f*

imprison [ɪm'prɪzən] *vt* **1** JAIL : encarcelar, aprisionar **2** CONFINE : recluir, encerrar

imprisonment [ɪm'prɪzənmənt] *n* : encarcelamiento *m*

improbability [ɪmˌprɑbə'bɪləti] *n, pl* **-ties** : improbabilidad *f*, inverosimilitud *f*

improbable [ɪm'prɑbəbəl] *adj* : improbable, inverosímil

impromptu[1] [ɪm'prɑmpˌtuː, -ˌtjuː] *adv* : sin preparación, espontáneamente

impromptu[2] *adj* : espontáneo, improvisado

impromptu[3] *n* : improvisación *f*

improper [ɪm'prɑpər] *adj* **1** INCORRECT : incorrecto, impropio **2** INDECOROUS : indecoroso

improperly [ɪm'prɑpərli] *adv* : incorrectamente, indebidamente

impropriety [ˌɪmprə'praɪəti] *n, pl* **-eties 1** INDECOROUSNESS : indecoro *m*, falta *f* de decoro **2** ERROR : impropiedad *f*, incorrección *f*

improve [ɪm'pruːv] *v* **-proved; -proving** : mejorar

improvement [ɪm'pruːvmənt] *n* : mejoramiento *m*, mejora *f*

improvidence [ɪm'prɑvədənts] *n* : imprevisión *f*

improvisation [ɪmˌprɑvə'zeɪʃən, ˌɪmprəvə-] *n* : improvisación *f*

improvise ['ɪmprəˌvaɪz] *v* **-vised; -vising** : improvisar

imprudence [ɪm'pruːdənts] *n* : imprudencia *f*, indiscreción *f*

imprudent [ɪm'pruːdənt] *adj* : imprudente, indiscreto

impudence ['ɪmpjədənts] *n* : insolencia *f*, descaro *m*

impudent ['ɪmpjədənt] *adj* : insolente, descarado — **impudently** *adv*

impugn [ɪm'pjuːn] *vt* : impugnar

impulse ['ɪmˌpʌls] *n* **1** : impulso *m* **2 on impulse** : sin reflexionar

impulsive [ɪm'pʌlsɪv] *adj* : impulsivo — **impulsively** *adv*

impulsiveness [ɪm'pʌlsɪvnəs] *n* : impulsividad *f*

impunity [ɪm'pjuːnəti] *n* **1** : impunidad *f* **2 with impunity** : impunemente

impure [ɪm'pjʊr] *adj* **1** : impuro ⟨impure thoughts : pensamientos impuros⟩ **2** CONTAMINATED : con impurezas, impuro

impurity [ɪm'pjʊrəti] *n, pl* **-ties** : impureza *f*

impute [ɪm'pju:t] *vt* **-puted; -puting** AT-TRIBUTE : imputar, atribuir

in¹ ['ɪn] *adv* **1** INSIDE : dentro, adentro ⟨let's go in : vamos adentro⟩ **2** HARVESTED : recogido ⟨the crops are in : las cosechas ya están recogidas⟩ **3 to be in** : estar ⟨is Linda in? : ¿está Linda?⟩ **4 to be in** : estar en poder ⟨the Democrats are in : los demócratas están en el poder⟩ **5 to be in for** : ser objeto de, estar a punto de ⟨they're in for a treat : los van a agasajar⟩ ⟨he's in for a surprise : se va a llevar una sorpresa⟩ **6 to be in on** : participar en, tomar parte en

in² *adj* **1** INSIDE : interior ⟨the in part : la parte interior⟩ **2** FASHIONABLE : de moda

in³ *prep* **1** (*indicating location or position*) ⟨in the lake : en el lago⟩ ⟨a pain in the leg : un dolor en la pierna⟩ ⟨in the sun : al sol⟩ ⟨in the rain : bajo la lluvia⟩ ⟨the best restaurant in Buenos Aires : el mejor restaurante de Buenos Aires⟩ **2** INTO : en, a ⟨he broke it in pieces : lo rompió en pedazos⟩ ⟨she went in the house : se metió a la casa⟩ **3** DURING : por, durante ⟨in the afternoon : por la tarde⟩ **4** WITHIN : dentro de ⟨I'll be back in a week : vuelvo dentro de una semana⟩ **5** (*indicating manner*) : en, con, de ⟨in Spanish : en español⟩ ⟨written in pencil : escrito con lápiz⟩ ⟨in this way : de esta manera⟩ **6** (*indicating states or circumstances*) ⟨to be in luck : tener suerte⟩ ⟨to be in love : estar enamorado⟩ ⟨to be in a hurry : tener prisa⟩ **7** (*indicating purpose*) : en ⟨in reply : en respuesta, como réplica⟩

in⁴ *n* **ins and outs** : pormenores *mpl*

inability [ˌɪnə'bɪləti] *n, pl* **-ties** : incapacidad *f*

inaccessibility [ˌɪnɪkˌsɛsə'bɪləti] *n, pl* **-ties** : inaccesibilidad *f*

inaccessible [ˌɪnɪk'sɛsəbəl] *adj* : inaccesible

inaccuracy [ɪn'ækjərəsi] *n, pl* **-cies 1** : inexactitud *f* **2** MISTAKE : error *m*

inaccurate [ɪn'ækjərət] *n* : inexacto, erróneo, incorrecto

inaccurately [ɪn'ækjərətli] *adv* : incorrectamente, con inexactitud

inaction [ɪn'ækʃən] *n* : inactividad *f*, inacción *f*

inactive [ɪn'æktɪv] *adj* : inactivo

inactivity [ˌɪnˌæk'tɪvəti] *n, pl* **-ties** : inactividad *f*, ociosidad *f*

inadequacy [ɪn'ædɪkwəsi] *n, pl* **-cies 1** INSUFFICIENCY : insuficiencia *f* **2** INCOMPETENCE : ineptitud *f*, incompetencia *f*

inadequate [ɪn'ædɪkwət] *adj* **1** INSUFFICIENT : insuficiente, inadecuado **2** INCOMPETENT : inepto, incompetente

inadmissible [ˌɪnæd'mɪsəbəl] *adj* : inadmisible

inadvertent [ˌɪnəd'vərtənt] *adj* : inadvertido, involuntario — **inadvertently** *adv*

inadvisable [ˌɪnæd'vaɪzəbəl] *adj* : desaconsejable

inalienable [ɪn'eɪljənəbəl, -'eɪliənə-] *adj* : inalienable

inane [ɪ'neɪn] *adj* **inaner; -est** : estúpido, idiota, necio

inanimate [ɪn'ænəmət] *adj* : inanimado, exánime

inanity [ɪ'nænəti] *n, pl* **-ties 1** STUPIDITY : estupidez *f* **2** NONSENSE : idiotez *f*, disparate *m*

inapplicable [ɪn'æplɪkəbəl, ˌɪnə-'plɪkə-bəl] *adj* IRRELEVANT : inaplicable, irrelevante

inappreciable [ˌɪnə'pri:ʃəbəl] *adj* : inapreciable, imperceptible

inappropriate [ˌɪnə'pro:priət] *adj* : inapropiado, inadecuado, impropio

inappropriateness [ˌɪnə'pro:priətnəs] *n* : lo inapropiado, impropiedad *f*

inapt [ɪn'æpt] *adj* **1** UNSUITABLE : inadecuado, inapropiado **2** INEPT : inepto

inarticulate [ˌɪnɑr'tɪkjələt] *adj* : inarticulado, incapaz de expresarse

inarticulately [ˌɪnɑr'tɪkjələtli] *adv* : inarticuladamente

inasmuch as [ˌɪnæz'mʌtʃæz] *conj* : ya que, dado que, puesto que

inattention [ˌɪnə'tɛntʃən] *n* : falta *f* de atención, distracción *f*

inattentive [ˌɪnə'tɛntɪv] *adj* : distraído, despistado

inattentively [ˌɪnə'tɛntɪvli] *adv* : distraídamente, sin prestar atención

inaudible [ɪn'ɔdəbəl] *adj* : inaudible

inaudibly [ɪn'ɔdəbli] *adv* : de forma inaudible

inaugural¹ [ɪ'nɔgjərəl, -gərəl] *adj* : inaugural, de investidura

inaugural² *n* **1** *or* **inaugural address** : discurso *m* de investidura **2** INAUGURATION : investidura *f* (de una persona)

inaugurate [ɪ'nɔgjə̩reɪt, -gə-] *vt* **-rated; -rating 1** BEGIN : inaugurar **2** INDUCT : investir ⟨to inaugurate the president : investir al presidente⟩

inauguration [ɪˌnɔgjə'reɪʃən, -gə-] *n* **1** : inauguración *f* (de un edificio, un sistema, etc.) **2** : investidura *f* (de una persona)

inauspicious [ˌɪnɔ'spɪʃəs] *adj* : desfavorable, poco propicio

inborn ['ɪn̩bɔrn] *adj* **1** CONGENITAL, INNATE : innato, congénito **2** HEREDITARY : hereditario

inbred ['ɪn̩brɛd] *adj* **1** : engendrado por endogamia **2** INNATE : innato

inbreed ['ɪn̩bri:d] *vt* **-bred; -breeding** : engendrar por endogamia

inbreeding ['ɪn̩bri:dɪŋ] *n* : endogamia *f*

Inca ['ɪŋkə] *n* : inca *mf*

incalculable [ɪn'kælkjələbəl] *adj* : incalculable — **incalculably** [-bli] *adv*

incandescence [ˌɪnkən'dɛsənts] *n* : incandescencia *f*

incandescent [ˌɪnkən'dɛsənt] *adj* **1** : incandescente **2** BRILLIANT : brillante

incantation [ˌɪnˌkæn'teɪʃən] *n* : conjuro *m*, ensalmo *m*

incapable [ɪn'keɪpəbəl] *adj* : incapaz

incapacitate [ˌɪnkə'pæsəˌteɪt] *vt* **-tated; -tating** : incapacitar

incapacity [ˌɪnkə'pæsəti] *n, pl* **-ties** : incapacidad *f*

incarcerate [ɪn'kɑrsəˌreɪt] *vt* **-ated; -ating** : encarcelar

incarceration [ɪnˌkɑrsə'reɪʃən] *n* : encarcelamiento *m*, encarcelación *f*

incarnate[1] [ɪn'kɑrˌneɪt] *vt* **-nated; -nating** : encarnar

incarnate[2] [ɪn'kɑrnət, -ˌneɪt] *adj* : encarnado

incarnation [ˌɪnˌkɑr'neɪʃən] *n* : encarnación *f*

incendiary[1] [ɪn'sɛndiˌri] *adj* : incendiario

incendiary[2] *n, pl* **-aries** : incendiario *m*, -ria *f*; pirómano *m*, -na *f*

incense[1] [ɪn'sɛnts] *vt* **-censed; -censing** : indignar, enfadar, enfurecer

incense[2] ['ɪnˌsɛnts] *n* : incienso *m*

incentive [ɪn'sɛntɪv] *n* : incentivo *m*, aliciente *m*, motivación *f*, acicate *m*

inception [ɪn'sɛpʃən] *n* : comienzo *m*, principio *m*

incessant [ɪn'sɛsənt] *adj* : incesante, continuo — **incessantly** *adv*

incest ['ɪnˌsɛst] *n* : incesto *m*

incestuous [ɪn'sɛstʃuəs] *adj* : incestuoso

inch[1] ['ɪntʃ] *v* : avanzar poco a poco

inch[2] *n* **1** : pulgada *f* **2 every inch** : absoluto, seguro ⟨every inch a winner : un seguro ganador⟩ **3 within an inch of** : a punto de

incidence ['ɪntsədənts] *n* **1** FREQUENCY : frecuencia *f*, índice *m* ⟨a high incidence of crime : un alto índice de crímenes⟩ **2 angle of incidence** : ángulo *m* de incidencia

incident[1] ['ɪntsədənt] *adj* : incidente

incident[2] *n* : incidente *m*, incidencia *f*, episodio *m* (en una obra de ficción)

incidental[1] [ˌɪntsə'dɛntəl] *adj* **1** SECONDARY : incidental, secundario **2** ACCIDENTAL : casual, fortuito

incidental[2] *n* **1** : algo incidental **2 incidentals** *npl* : imprevistos *mpl*

incidentally [ˌɪntsə'dɛntəli, -'dɛntli] *adv* **1** BY CHANCE : incidentalmente, casualmente **2** BY THE WAY : a propósito, por cierto

incinerate [ɪn'sɪnəˌreɪt] *vt* **-ated; -ating** : incinerar

incinerator [ɪn'sɪnəˌreɪtər] *n* : incinerador *m*

incipient [ɪn'sɪpiənt] *adj* : incipiente, naciente

incise [ɪn'saɪz] *vt* **-cised; -cising 1** ENGRAVE : grabar, cincelar, inscribir **2** : hacer una incisión en

incision [ɪn'sɪʒən] *n* : incisión *f*

incisive [ɪn'saɪsɪv] *adj* : incisivo, penetrante

incisively [ɪn'saɪsɪvli] *adv* : con agudeza

incisor [ɪn'saɪzər] *n* : incisivo *m*

incite [ɪn'saɪt] *vt* **-cited; -citing** : incitar, instigar

incitement [ɪn'saɪtmənt] *n* : incitación *f*

inclemency [ɪn'klɛmənˌtsi] *n, pl* **-cies** : inclemencia *f*

inclement [ɪn'klɛmənt] *adj* : inclemente, tormentoso

inclination [ˌɪnklə'neɪʃən] *n* **1** PROPENSITY : inclinación *f*, tendencia *f* **2** DESIRE : deseo *m*, ganas *fpl* **3** BOW : inclinación *f*

incline[1] [ɪn'klaɪn] *v* **-clined; -clining** *vi* **1** SLOPE : inclinarse **2** TEND : inclinarse, tender ⟨he is inclined to be late : tiende a llegar tarde⟩ — *vt* **1** LOWER : inclinar, bajar ⟨to incline one's head : bajar la cabeza⟩ **2** SLANT : inclinar **3** PREDISPOSE : predisponer

incline[2] ['ɪnˌklaɪn] *n* : inclinación *f*, pendiente *f*

inclined [ɪn'klaɪnd] *adj* **1** SLOPING : inclinado **2** PRONE : prono, dispuesto, dado

inclose, inclosure → **enclose, enclosure**

include [ɪn'klu:d] *vt* **-cluded; -cluding** : incluir, comprender

inclusion [ɪn'klu:ʒən] *n* : inclusión *f*

inclusive [ɪn'klu:sɪv] *adj* : inclusivo

incognito [ˌɪnˌkɑg'ni:ˌto, ɪn'kɑgnəˌto:] *adv & adj* : de incógnito

incoherence [ˌɪnko'hɪrənts, -'hɛr-] *n* : incoherencia *f*

incoherent [ˌɪnko'hɪrənt, -'hɛr-] *adj* : incoherente — **incoherently** *adv*

incombustible [ˌɪnkəm'bʌstəbəl] *adj* : incombustible

income ['ɪnˌkʌm] *n* : ingresos *mpl*, entradas *fpl*

income tax *n* : impuesto *m* sobre la renta

incoming ['ɪnˌkʌmɪŋ] *adj* **1** ARRIVING : que se recibe (dícese del correo), que llega (dícese de las personas), ascendente (dícese de la marea) **2** NEW : nuevo, entrante ⟨the incoming president : el nuevo presidente⟩ ⟨the incoming year : el año entrante⟩

incommunicado [ˌɪnkəˌmju:nə'kado] *adj* : incomunicado

incomparable [ɪn'kɑmpərəbəl] *adj* : incomparable, sin igual

incompatible [ˌɪnkəm'pæt̮əbəl] *adj* : incompatible

incompetence [ɪn'kɑmpət̮ənts] *n* : incompetencia *f*, impericia *f*, ineptitud *f*

incompetent [ɪn'kɑmpət̮ənt] *adj* : incompetente, inepto, incapaz

incomplete [ˌɪnkəm'pli:t] *adj* : incompleto — **incompletely** *adv*

incomprehensible [ˌɪnˌkɑmpri'hɛntsəbəl] *adj* : incomprensible

inconceivable [ˌɪnkən'si:vəbəl] *adj* **1** INCOMPREHENSIBLE : incomprensible **2** UNBELIEVABLE : inconcebible, increíble

inconceivably [ˌɪnkən'siːvəbli] *adv* : inconcebiblemente, increíblemente

inconclusive [ˌɪnkən'kluːsɪv] *adj* : inconcluyente, no decisivo

incongruity [ˌɪnkən'gruːəti, -ˌkɑn-] *n, pl* **-ties** : incongruencia *f*

incongruous [ɪn'kɑŋgruəs] *adj* : incongruente, inapropiado, fuera de lugar

incongruously [ɪn'kɑŋgruəsli] *adv* : de manera incongruente, inapropiadamente

inconsequential [ˌɪnˌkɑnsə'kwɛntʃəl] *adj* : intrascendente, de poco importancia

inconsiderable [ˌɪnkən'sɪdərəbəl] *adj* : insignificante

inconsiderate [ˌɪnkən'sɪdərət] *adj* : desconsiderado, sin consideración — **inconsiderately** *adv*

inconsistency [ˌɪnkən'sɪstəntsi] *n, pl* **-cies** : inconsecuencia *f*, inconsistencia *f*

inconsistent [ˌɪnkən'sɪstənt] *adj* : inconsecuente, inconsistente

inconsolable [ˌɪnkən'soːləbəl] *adj* : inconsolable — **inconsolably** [-bli] *adv*

inconspicuous [ˌɪnkən'spɪkjuəs] *adj* : discreto, no conspicuo, que no llama la atención

inconspicuously [ˌɪnkən'spɪkjuəsli] *adv* : discretamente, sin llamar la atención

incontestable [ˌɪnkən'tɛstəbəl] *adj* : incontestable, indiscutible — **incontestably** [-bli] *adv*

incontinence [ɪn'kɑntənənts] *n* : incontinencia *f*

incontinent [ɪn'kɑntənənt] *adj* : incontinente

inconvenience[1] [ˌɪnkən'viːnjənts] *vt* **-nienced; -niencing** : importunar, incomodar, molestar

inconvenience[2] *n* : incomodidad *f*, molestia *f*

inconvenient [ˌɪnkən'viːnjənt] *adj* : inconveniente, importuno, incómodo — **inconveniently** *adv*

incorporate [ɪn'kɔrpəˌreɪt] *vt* **-rated; -rating 1** INCLUDE : incorporar, incluir **2** : incorporar, constituir en sociedad (dícese de un negocio)

incorporation [ɪnˌkɔrpə'reɪʃən] *n* : incorporación *f*

incorporeal [ˌɪnˌkɔr'pɔriəl] *adj* : incorpóreo

incorrect [ˌɪnkə'rɛkt] *adj* **1** INACCURATE : incorrecto **2** WRONG : equivocado, erróneo **3** IMPROPER : impropio — **incorrectly** *adv*

incorrigible [ɪn'kɔrədʒəbəl] *adj* : incorregible

incorruptible [ˌɪnkə'rʌptəbəl] *adj* : incorruptible

increase[1] [ɪn'kriːs, 'ɪnˌkriːs] *v* **-creased; -creasing** *vi* GROW : aumentar, crecer, subir (dícese de los precios) — *vt* AUGMENT : aumentar, acrecentar

increase[2] ['ɪnˌkriːs, ɪn'kriːs] *n* : aumento *m*, incremento *m*, subida *f* (de precios)

increasing [ɪn'kriːsɪŋ, 'ɪnˌkriːsɪŋ] *adj* : creciente

increasingly [ɪn'kriːsɪŋli] *adv* : cada vez más

incredible [ɪn'krɛdəbəl] *adj* : increíble — **incredibly** [-bli] *adv*

incredulity [ˌɪnkrɪ'duːləti, -'djuː-] *n* : incredulidad *f*

incredulous [ɪn'krɛdʒələs] *adj* : incrédulo, escéptico

incredulously [ɪn'krɛdʒələsli] *adv* : con incredulidad

increment ['ɪŋkrəmənt, 'ɪn-] *n* : incremento *m*, aumento *m*

incremental [ˌɪŋkrə'mɛntəl, ˌɪn-] *adj* : de incremento

incriminate [ɪn'krɪməˌneɪt] *vt* **-nated; -nating** : incriminar

incrimination [ɪnˌkrɪmə'neɪʃən] *n* : incriminación *f*

incriminatory [ɪn'krɪmənəˌtori] *adj* : incriminatorio

incubate ['ɪŋkjʊˌbeɪt, 'ɪn-] *v* **-bated; -bating** *vt* : incubar, empollar — *vi* : incubar(se), empollar

incubation [ˌɪŋkjʊ'beɪʃən, ˌɪn-] *n* : incubación *f*

incubator ['ɪŋkjʊˌbeɪtər, 'ɪn-] *n* : incubadora *f*

inculcate [ɪn'kʌlˌkeɪt, 'ɪnˌkʌl-] *vt* **-cated; -cating** : inculcar

incumbency [ɪn'kʌmbəntsi] *n, pl* **-cies 1** OBLIGATION : incumbencia *f* **2** : mandato *m* (en la política)

incumbent[1] [ɪn'kʌmbənt] *adj* : obligatorio

incumbent[2] *n* : titular *mf*

incur [ɪn'kər] *vt* **incurred; incurring** : provocar (al enojo), incurrir en (gastos, obligaciones)

incurable [ɪn'kjʊrəbəl] *adj* : incurable, sin remedio

incursion [ɪn'kərʒən] *n* : incursión *f*

indebted [ɪn'dɛtəd] *adj* **1** : endeudado **2 to be indebted to** : estar en deuda con, estarle agradecido a

indebtedness [ɪn'dɛtədnəs] *n* : endeudamiento *m*

indecency [ɪn'diːsəntsi] *n, pl* **-cies** : indecencia *f*

indecent [ɪn'diːsənt] *adj* : indecente — **indecently** *adv*

indecipherable [ˌɪndɪ'saɪfərəbəl] *adj* : indescifrable

indecision [ˌɪndɪ'sɪʒən] *n* : indecisión *f*, irresolución *f*

indecisive [ˌɪndɪ'saɪsɪv] *adj* **1** INCONCLUSIVE : indeciso, que no es decisivo **2** IRRESOLUTE : indeciso, irresoluto, vacilante **3** INDEFINITE : indefinido — **indecisively** *adv*

indecorous [ɪn'dɛkərəs, ˌɪndɪ'korəs] *adj* : indecoroso — **indecorously** *adv*

indecorousness [ɪn'dkərəsnəs, ˌɪndɪ'korəs-] *n* : indecoro *m*

indeed [ɪn'diːd] *adv* **1** TRULY : verdaderamente, de veras **2** (*used as intensifier*) ⟨thank you very much indeed

: muchísimas gracias⟩ **3** OF COURSE : claro, por supuesto

indefatigable [ˌɪndɪˈfæṭɪgəbəl] *adj* : incansable, infatigable — **indefatigably** [-bli] *adv*

indefensible [ˌɪndɪˈfɛnsəbəl] *adj* **1** VULNERABLE : indefendible, vulnerable **2** INEXCUSABLE : inexcusable

indefinable [ˌɪndɪˈfaɪnəbəl] *adj* : indefinible

indefinite [ɪnˈdɛfənət] *adj* **1** : indefinido, indeterminado ⟨indefinite pronouns : pronombres indefinidos⟩ **2** VAGUE : vago, impreciso

indefinitely [ɪnˈdɛfənətli] *adv* : indefinidamente, por un tiempo indefinido

indelible [ɪnˈdɛləbəl] *adj* : indeleble, imborrable — **indelibly** [-bli] *adv*

indelicacy [ɪnˈdɛləkəsi] *n* : falta *f* de delicadeza

indelicate [ɪnˈdɛlɪkət] *adj* **1** IMPROPER : indelicado, indecoroso **2** TACTLESS : indiscreto, falto de tacto

indemnify [ɪnˈdɛmnəˌfaɪ] *vt* **-fied; -fying 1** INSURE : asegurar **2** COMPENSATE : indemnizar, compensar

indemnity [ɪnˈdɛmnəṭi] *n, pl* **-ties 1** INSURANCE : indemnidad *f* **2** COMPENSATION : indemnización *f*

indent [ɪnˈdɛnt] *vt* : sangrar (un párrafo)

indentation [ˌɪnˌdɛnˈteɪʃən] *n* **1** NOTCH : muesca *f*, mella *f* **2** INDENTING : sangría *f* (de un párrafo)

indenture[1] [ɪnˈdɛntʃər] *vt* **-tured; -turing** : ligar por contrato

indenture[2] *n* : contrato de aprendizaje

independence [ˌɪndəˈpɛndənts] *n* : independencia *f*

Independence Day *n* : día *m* de la Independencia (4 de julio en los EE.UU.)

independent[1] [ˌɪndəˈpɛndənt] *adj* : independiente — **independently** *adv*

independent[2] *n* : independiente *mf*

indescribable [ˌɪndɪˈskraɪbəbəl] *adj* : indescriptible, incalificable — **indescribably** [-bli] *adv*

indestructibility [ˌɪndɪˌstrʌktəˈbɪləṭi] *n* : indestructibilidad *f*

indestructible [ˌɪndɪˈstrʌktəbəl] *adj* : indestructible

indeterminate [ˌɪndɪˈtərmənət] *adj* **1** VAGUE : vago, impreciso, indeterminado **2** INDEFINITE : indeterminado, indefinido

index[1] [ˈɪnˌdɛks] *vt* **1** : ponerle un índice a (un libro o una revista) **2** : incluir en un índice ⟨all proper names are indexed : todos los nombres propios están incluidos en el índice⟩ **3** INDICATE : indicar, señalar **4** REGULATE : indexar, indiciar ⟨to index prices : indiciar los precios⟩

index[2] *n, pl* **-dexes** *or* **-dices** [ˈɪndəˌsiːz] **1** : índice *m* (de un libro, de precios) **2** INDICATION : indicio *m*, índice *m*, señal *f* ⟨an index of her character : una señal de su carácter⟩

index finger *n* FOREFINGER : dedo *m* índice

Indian [ˈɪndiən] *n* **1** : indio *m*, -dia *f* **2** → **American Indian** — **Indian** *adj*

indicate [ˈɪndəˌkeɪt] *vt* **-cated; -cating 1** POINT OUT : indicar, señalar **2** SHOW, SUGGEST : ser indicio de, ser señal de **3** EXPRESS : expresar, señalar **4** REGISTER : marcar, poner (una medida, etc.)

indication [ˌɪndəˈkeɪʃən] *n* : indicio *m*, señal *f*

indicative [ɪnˈdɪkəṭɪv] *adj* : indicativo

indicator [ˈɪndəˌkeɪṭər] *n* : indicador *m*

indict [ɪnˈdaɪt] *vt* : acusar, procesar (por un crímen)

indictment [ɪnˈdaɪtmənt] *n* : acusación *f*

indifference [ɪnˈdɪfrənts, -ˈdɪfə-] *n* : indiferencia *f*

indifferent [ɪnˈdɪfrənt, -ˈdɪfə-] *adj* **1** UNCONCERNED : indiferente **2** MEDIOCRE : mediocre

indifferently [ɪnˈdɪfrəntli, -ˈdɪfə-] *adv* **1** : con indiferencia, indiferentemente **2** SO-SO : de modo regular, más o menos

indigence [ˈɪndɪdʒənts] *n* : indigencia *f*

indigenous [ɪnˈdɪdʒənəs] *adj* : indígena, nativo

indigent [ˈɪndɪdʒənt] *adj* : indigente, pobre

indigestible [ˌɪndaɪˈdʒɛstəbəl, -dɪ-] *adj* : difícil de digerir

indigestion [ˌɪndaɪˈdʒɛstʃən, -dɪ-] *n* : indigestión *f*, empacho *m*

indignant [ɪnˈdɪgnənt] *adj* : indignado

indignantly [ɪnˈdɪgnəntli] *adv* : con indignación

indignation [ˌɪndɪgˈneɪʃən] *n* : indignación *f*

indignity [ɪnˈdɪgnəṭi] *n, pl* **-ties** : indignidad *f*

indigo [ˈɪndɪˌgoː] *n, pl* **-gos** *or* **-goes** : añil *m*, índigo *m*

indirect [ˌɪndəˈrɛkt, -daɪ-] *adj* : indirecto — **indirectly** *adv*

indiscernible [ˌɪndɪˈsərnəbəl, -ˈzər-] *adj* : imperceptible

indiscreet [ˌɪndɪˈskriːt] *adj* : indiscreto, imprudente — **indiscreetly** *adv*

indiscretion [ˌɪndɪˈskrɛʃən] *n* : indiscreción *f*, imprudencia *f*

indiscriminate [ˌɪndɪˈskrɪmənət] *adj* : indiscriminado

indiscriminately [ˌɪndɪˈskrɪmənətli] *adv* : sin discriminación, sin discernimiento

indispensable [ˌɪndɪˈspɛntsəbəl] *adj* : indispensable, necesario, imprescindible — **indispensably** [-bli] *adv*

indisposed [ˌɪndɪˈspoːzd] *adj* **1** ILL : indispuesto, enfermo **2** AVERSE, DISINCLINED : opuesto, reacio ⟨to be indisposed toward working : no tener ganas de trabajar⟩

indisputable [ˌɪndɪˈspjuːṭəbəl, ɪnˈdɪspjuṭə-] *adj* : indiscutible, incuestionable, incontestable — **indisputably** [-bli] *adv*

indistinct [ˌɪndɪ'stɪŋkt] *adj* : indistinto — **indistinctly** *adv*
indistinctness [ˌɪndɪ'stɪŋktnəs] *n* : falta *f* de claridad
indistinguishable [ˌɪndɪ'stɪŋgwɪʃəbəl] *adj* : indistinguible
individual[1] [ˌɪndə'vɪdʒuəl] *adj* **1** PERSONAL : individual, personal ⟨individual traits : características personales⟩ **2** SEPARATE : individual, separado **3** PARTICULAR : particular, propio
individual[2] *n* : individuo *m*
individualism [ˌɪndə'vɪdʒəwəˌlɪzəm] *n* : individualismo *m*
individualist [ˌɪndə'vɪdʒuəlɪst] *n* : individualista *mf*
individuality [ˌɪndəˌvɪdʒu'æləti] *n*, *pl* **-ties** : individualidad *f*
individually [ˌɪndə'vɪdʒuəli, -dʒəli] *adv* : individualmente
indivisible [ˌɪndɪ'vɪzəbəl] *adj* : indivisible
indoctrinate [ɪn'dɑktrəˌneɪt] *vt* **-nated; -nating 1** TEACH : enseñar, instruir **2** PROPAGANDIZE : adoctrinar
indoctrination [ɪnˌdɑktrə'neɪʃən] *n* : adoctrinamiento *m*
indolence ['ɪndələnts] *n* : indolencia *f*
indolent ['ɪndələnt] *adj* : indolente
indomitable [ɪn'dɑmətəbəl] *adj* : invencible, indomable, indómito — **indomitably** [-bli] *adv*
Indonesian [ˌɪndo'niːʒən, -ʃən] *n* : indonesio *m*, -sia *f* — **Indonesian** *adj*
indoor ['ɪn'dor] *adj* : interior (dícese de las plantas), para estar en casa (dícese de la ropa), cubierto (dícese de las piscinas, etc.), bajo techo (dícese de los deportes)
indoors ['ɪn'dorz] *adv* : adentro, dentro
indubitable [ɪn'duːbətəbəl, -'djuː-] *adj* : indudable, incuestionable, indiscutible
indubitably [ɪn'duːbətəbli, -'djuː-] *adv* : indudablemente
induce [ɪn'duːs, -'djuːs] *vt* **-duced; -ducing 1** PERSUADE : persuadir, inducir **2** CAUSE : inducir, provocar ⟨to induce labor : provocar un parto⟩
inducement [ɪn'duːsmənt, -'djuːs-] *n* **1** INCENTIVE : incentivo *m*, aliciente *m* **2** : inducción *f*, provocación *f* (de un parto)
induct [ɪn'dʌkt] *vt* **1** INSTALL : instalar, investir **2** ADMIT : admitir (como miembro) **3** CONSCRIPT : reclutar (al servicio militar)
inductee [ˌɪnˌdʌk'tiː] *n* : recluta *mf*, conscripto *m*, -ta *f*
induction [ɪn'dʌkʃən] *n* **1** INTRODUCTION : iniciación *f*, introducción *f* **2** : inducción *f* (en la lógica o la electricidad)
inductive [ɪn'dʌktɪv] *adj* : inductivo
indulge [ɪn'dʌldʒ] *v* **-dulged; -dulging** *vt* **1** GRATIFY : gratificar, satisfacer **2** SPOIL : consentir, mimar — *vi* **to indulge in** : permitirse

indulgence [ɪn'dʌldʒənts] *n* **1** SATISFYING : satisfacción *f*, gratificación *f* **2** HUMORING : complacencia *f*, indulgencia *f* **3** SPOILING : consentimiento *m* **4** : indulgencia *f* (en la religión)
indulgent [ɪn'dʌldʒənt] *adj* : indulgente, consentido — **indulgently** *adv*
industrial [ɪn'dʌstriəl] *adj* : industrial — **industrially** *adv*
industrialist [ɪn'dʌstriəlɪst] *n* : industrial *mf*
industrialization [ɪnˌdʌstriələ'zeɪ-ʃən] *n* : industrialización *f*
industrialize [ɪn'dʌstriəˌlaɪz] *vt* **-ized; -izing** : industrializar
industrious [ɪn'dʌstriəs] *adj* : diligente, industrioso, trabajador
industriously [ɪn'dʌstriəsli] *adv* : con diligencia, con aplicación
industriousness [ɪn'dʌstriəsnəs] *n* : diligencia *f*, aplicación *f*
industry ['ɪndəstri] *n*, *pl* **-tries 1** DILIGENCE : diligencia *f*, aplicación *f* **2** : industria *f* ⟨the steel industry : la industria siderúrgica⟩
inebriated [ɪ'niːbriˌeɪtəd] *adj* : ebrio, embriagado
inebriation [ɪˌniːbri'eɪʃən] *n* : ebriedad *f*, embriaguez *f*
ineffable [ɪn'ɛfəbəl] *adj* : inefable — **ineffably** [-bli] *adv*
ineffective [ˌɪnɪ'fɛktɪv] *adj* **1** INEFFECTUAL : ineficaz, inútil **2** INCAPABLE : incompetente, ineficiente, incapaz
ineffectively [ˌɪnɪ'fɛktɪvli] *adv* : ineficazmente, infructuosamente
ineffectual [ˌɪnɪ'fɛktʃuəl] *adj* : inútil, ineficaz — **ineffectually** *adv*
inefficiency [ˌɪnɪ'fɪʃəntsi] *n*, *pl* **-cies** : ineficiencia *f*, ineficacia *f*
inefficient [ˌɪnɪ'fɪʃənt] *adj* **1** : ineficiente, ineficaz **2** INCAPABLE, INCOMPETENT : incompetente, incapaz — **inefficiently** *adv*
inelegance [ɪn'ɛləgənts] *n* : inelegancia *f*
inelegant [ɪn'ɛləgənt] *adj* : inelegante, poco elegante
ineligibility [ɪnˌɛlədʒə'bɪləti] *n* : inelegibilidad *f*
ineligible [ɪn'ɛlədʒəbəl] *adj* : inelegible
inept [ɪ'nɛpt] *adj* : inepto ⟨inept at : incapaz para⟩
ineptitude [ɪ'nɛptəˌtuːd, -ˌtjuːd] *n* : ineptitud *f*, incompetencia *f*, incapacidad *f*
inequality [ˌɪnɪ'kwɑləti] *n*, *pl* **-ties** : desigualdad *f*
inert [ɪ'nərt] *adj* **1** INACTIVE : inerte, inactivo **2** SLUGGISH : lento
inertia [ɪ'nərʃə] *n* : inercia *f*
inescapable [ˌɪnɪ'skeɪpəbəl] *adj* : inevitable, ineludible — **inescapably** [-bli] *adv*
inessential [ˌɪnɪ'sɛntʃəl] *adj* : que no es esencial, innecesario
inestimable [ɪn'ɛstəməbəl] *adj* : inestimable, inapreciable

inevitability [ɪnˌɛvətəˈbɪləti] *n, pl* -ties : inevitabilidad *f*
inevitable [ɪnˈɛvətəbəl] *adj* : inevitable — **inevitably** [-bli] *adv*
inexact [ˌɪnɪɡˈzækt] *adj* : inexacto
inexactly [ˌɪnɪɡˈzæktli] *adv* : sin exactitud
inexcusable [ˌɪnɪkˈskjuːzəbəl] *adj* : inexcusable, imperdonable — **inexcusably** [-bli] *adv*
inexhaustible [ˌɪnɪɡˈzɔstəbəl] *adj* 1 INDEFATIGABLE : infatigable, incansable 2 ENDLESS : inagotable — **inexhaustibly** [-bli] *adv*
inexorable [ɪnˈɛksərəbəl] *adj* : inexorable — **inexorably** [-bli] *adv*
inexpensive [ˌɪnɪkˈspɛntsɪv] *adj* : barato, económico
inexperience [ˌɪnɪkˈspɪriənts] *n* : inexperiencia *f*
inexperienced [ˌɪnɪkˈspɪriəntst] *adj* : inexperto, novato
inexplicable [ˌɪnɪkˈsplɪkəbəl] *adj* : inexplicable — **inexplicably** [-bli] *adv*
inexpressible [ˌɪnɪkˈsprɛsəbəl] *adj* : inexpresable, inefable
inextricable [ˌɪnɪkˈstrɪkəbəl, ɪˈnɛk-ˌstrɪ-] *adj* : inextricable — **inextricably** [-bli] *adv*
infallibility [ɪnˌfæləˈbɪləti] *n* : infalibilidad *f*
infallible [ɪnˈfæləbəl] *adj* : infalible — **infallibly** [-bli] *adv*
infamous [ˈɪnfəməs] *adj* : infame — **infamously** *adv*
infamy [ˈɪnfəmi] *n, pl* -mies : infamia *f*
infancy [ˈɪnfəntsi] *n, pl* -cies : infancia *f*
infant [ˈɪnfənt] *n* : bebé *m*; niño *m*, -ña *f*
infantile [ˈɪnfənˌtaɪl, -təl, -ˌtiːl] *adj* : infantil, pueril
infantile paralysis → **poliomyelitis**
infantry [ˈɪnfəntri] *n, pl* -tries : infantería *f*
infatuated [ɪnˈfætʃʊˌeɪtəd] *adj* **to be infatuated with** : estar encaprichado con
infatuation [ɪnˌfætʃʊˈeɪʃən] *n* : encaprichamiento *m*, enamoramiento *m*
infect [ɪnˈfɛkt] *vt* : infectar, contagiar
infection [ɪnˈfɛkʃən] *n* : infección *f*, contagio *m*
infectious [ɪnˈfɛkʃəs] *adj* : infeccioso, contagioso
infer [ɪnˈfər] *vt* **inferred; inferring** 1 DEDUCE : deducir, inferir 2 SURMISE : concluir, suponer, tener entendido 3 IMPLY : sugerir, insinuar
inference [ˈɪnfərənts] *n* : deducción *f*, inferencia *f*, conclusión *f*
inferior¹ [ɪnˈfɪriər] *adj* : inferior, malo
inferior² *n* : inferior *mf*
inferiority [ɪnˌfɪriˈɔrəti] *n, pl* -ties : inferioridad *f* ⟨inferiority complex : complejo de inferioridad⟩
infernal [ɪnˈfərnəl] *adj* 1 : infernal ⟨infernal fires : fuegos infernales⟩ 2 DIABOLICAL : infernal, diabólico 3 DAMNABLE : maldito, condenado
inferno [ɪnˈfərˌnoː] *n, pl* -nos : infierno *m*

infertile [ɪnˈfərtəl, -ˌtaɪl] *adj* : estéril, infecundo
infertility [ˌɪnfərˈtɪləti] *n* : esterilidad *f*, infecundidad *f*
infest [ɪnˈfɛst] *vt* : infestar, plagar
infestation [ˌɪnˌfɛsˈteɪʃən] *n* : infestación *f*, plaga *f*
infidel [ˈɪnfədəl, -ˌdɛl] *n* : infiel *mf*
infidelity [ˌɪnfəˈdɛləti, -faɪ-] *n, pl* -ties 1 UNFAITHFULNESS : infidelidad *f* 2 DISLOYALTY : deslealtad *f*
infield [ˈɪnˌfiːld] *n* : cuadro *m*, diamante *m*
infiltrate [ɪnˈfɪlˌtreɪt, ˈɪnfɪl-] *v* -trated; -trating *vt* : infiltrar — *vi* : infiltrarse
infiltration [ˌɪnfɪlˈtreɪʃən] *n* : infiltración *f*
infinite [ˈɪnfənət] *adj* 1 LIMITLESS : infinito, sin límites 2 VAST : infinito, vasto, extenso
infinitely [ˈɪnfənətli] *adv* : infinitamente
infinitesimal [ˌɪnˌfɪnəˈtɛsəməl] *adj* : infinitésimo, infinitesimal — **infinitesimally** *adv*
infinitive [ɪnˈfɪnətɪv] *n* : infinitivo *m*
infinity [ɪnˈfɪnəti] *n, pl* -ties 1 : infinito *m* (en matemáticas, etc.) 2 : infinidad *f* ⟨an infinity of stars : una infinidad de estrellas⟩
infirm [ɪnˈfərm] *adj* 1 FEEBLE : enfermizo, endeble 2 INSECURE : inseguro
infirmary [ɪnˈfərməri] *n, pl* -ries : enfermería *f*, hospital *m*
infirmity [ɪnˈfərməti] *n, pl* -ties 1 FRAILTY : debilidad *f*, endeblez *f* 2 AILMENT : enfermedad *f*, dolencia *f* ⟨the infirmities of age : los achaques de la vejez⟩
inflame [ɪnˈfleɪm] *v* -flamed; -flaming *vt* 1 KINDLE : inflamar, encender 2 : inflamar (una herida) 3 STIR UP : encender, provocar, inflamar — *vi* : inflamarse
inflammable [ɪnˈflæməbəl] *adj* 1 FLAMMABLE : inflamable (la ropa) 2 IRASCIBLE : irascible, explosivo
inflammation [ˌɪnfləˈmeɪʃən] *n* : inflamación *f*
inflammatory [ɪnˈflæməˌtori] *adj* : inflamatorio, incendiario
inflatable [ɪnˈfleɪtəbəl] *adj* : inflable
inflate [ɪnˈfleɪt] *vt* -flated; -flating : inflar, hinchar
inflation [ɪnˈfleɪʃən] *n* : inflación *f*
inflationary [ɪnˈfleɪʃəˌneri] *adj* : inflacionario, inflacionista
inflect [ɪnˈflɛkt] *vt* 1 CONJUGATE, DECLINE : conjugar, declinar 2 MODULATE : modular (la voz)
inflection [ɪnˈflɛkʃən] *n* : inflexión *f*
inflexibility [ɪnˌflɛksəˈbɪləti] *n, pl* -ties : inflexibilidad *f*
inflexible [ɪnˈflɛksɪbəl] *adj* : inflexible
inflict [ɪnˈflɪkt] *vt* 1 : infligir, causar, imponer 2 **to inflict oneself on** : imponer uno su presencia (a alguien)
infliction [ɪnˈflɪkʃən] *n* : imposición *f*

influence¹ [ˈɪnˌfluːənts, ɪnˈfluːənts] *vt* **-enced; -encing** : influenciar, influir en
influence² *n* **1** : influencia *f*, influjo *m* ⟨to exert influence over : ejercer influencia sobre⟩ ⟨the influence of gravity : el influjo de la gravedad⟩ **2 under the influence** : bajo la influencia del alcohol, embriagado
influential [ˌɪnfluˈɛntʃəl] *adj* : influyente
influenza [ˌɪnfluˈɛnzə] *n* : gripe *f*, influenza *f*, gripa *f Col, Mex*
influx [ˈɪnˌflʌks] *n* : afluencia *f* (de gente), entrada *f* (de mercancías), llegada *f* (de ideas)
inform [ɪnˈfɔrm] *vt* : informar, notificar, avisar — *vi* **to inform on** : delatar, denunciar
informal [ɪnˈfɔrməl] *adj* **1** UNCEREMONIOUS : sin ceremonia, sin etiqueta **2** CASUAL : informal, familiar (dícese del lenguaje) **3** UNOFFICIAL : extraoficial
informality [ˌɪnfɔrˈmæləti, -fər-] *n, pl* **-ties** : informalidad *f*, familiaridad *f*, falta *f* de ceremonia
informally [ɪnˈfɔrməli] *adv* : sin ceremonias, de manera informal, informalmente
informant [ɪnˈfɔrmənt] *n* : informante *mf*; informador *m*, -dora *f*
information [ˌɪnfərˈmeɪʃən] *n* : información *f*
informative [ɪnˈfɔrmətɪv] *adj* : informativo, instructivo
informer [ɪnˈfɔrmər] *n* : informante *mf*; informador *m*, -dora *f*
infraction [ɪnˈfrækʃən] *n* : infracción *f*, violación *f*, transgresión *f*
infrared [ˌɪnfrəˈrɛd] *adj* : infrarrojo
infrastructure [ˈɪnfrəˌstrʌktʃər] *n* : infraestructura *f*
infrequent [ɪnˈfriːkwənt] *adj* : infrecuente, raro
infrequently [ɪnˈfriːkwəntli] *adv* : raramente, con poca frecuencia
infringe [ɪnˈfrɪndʒ] *v* **-fringed; -fringing** *vt* : infringir, violar — *vi* **to infringe on** : abusar de, violar
infringement [ɪnˈfrɪndʒmənt] *n* **1** VIOLATION : violación *f* (de la ley), incumplimiento *m* (de un contrato) **2** ENCROACHMENT : usurpación *f* (de derechos, etc.)
infuriate [ɪnˈfjʊriˌeɪt] *vt* **-ated; -ating** : enfurecer, poner furioso
infuriating [ɪnˈfjʊriˌeɪtɪŋ] *adj* : indignante, exasperante
infuse [ɪnˈfjuːz] *vt* **-fused; -fusing 1** INSTILL : infundir **2** STEEP : hacer una infusión de
infusion [ɪnˈfjuːʒən] *n* : infusión *f*
ingenious [ɪnˈdʒiːnjəs] *adj* : ingenioso — **ingeniously** *adv*
ingenue *or* **ingénue** [ˈɑndʒəˌnuː, ˈæn-; ˈæʒə-, ˈɑ-] *n* : ingenua *f*
ingenuity [ˌɪndʒəˈnuːəti, -ˈnjuː-] *n, pl* **-ities** : ingenio

ingenuous [ɪnˈdʒɛnjuəs] *adj* **1** FRANK : cándido, franco **2** NAIVE : ingenuo — **ingenuously** *adv*
ingenuousness [ɪnˈdʒɛnjuəsnəs] *n* **1** FRANKNESS : candidez *f*, candor *m* **2** NAÏVETÉ : ingenuidad *f*
ingest [ɪnˈdʒɛst] *vt* : ingerir
ingestion [ɪnˈdʒɛstʃən] *n* : ingestión *f*
inglorious [ɪnˈglɔriəs] *adj* : deshonroso, ignominioso
ingot [ˈɪŋgət] *n* : lingote *m*
ingrained [ɪnˈgreɪnd] *adj* : arraigado
ingrate [ˈɪnˌgreɪt] *n* : ingrato *m*, -ta *f*
ingratiate [ɪnˈgreɪʃiˌeɪt] *vt* **-ated; -ating** : conseguir la benevolencia de ⟨to ingratiate oneself with someone : congraciarse con alguien⟩
ingratiating [ɪnˈgreɪʃiˌeɪtɪŋ] *adj* : halagador, zalamero, obsequioso
ingratitude [ɪnˈgrætəˌtuːd, -ˌtjuːd] *n* : ingratitud *f*
ingredient [ɪnˈgriːdiənt] *n* : ingrediente *m*, componente *m*
ingrown [ˈɪnˌgroːn] *adj* **1** : crecido hacia adentro **2 ingrown toenail** : uña *f* encarnada
inhabit [ɪnˈhæbət] *vt* : vivir en, habitar, ocupar
inhabitable [ɪnˈhæbətəbəl] *adj* : habitable
inhabitant [ɪnˈhæbətənt] *n* : habitante *mf*
inhalant [ɪnˈheɪlənt] *n* : inhalante *m*
inhalation [ˌɪnhəˈleɪʃən, ˌɪnə-] *n* : inhalación *f*
inhale [ɪnˈheɪl] *v* **-haled; -haling** *vt* : inhalar, aspirar — *vi* : inspirar
inhaler [ɪnˈheɪlər] *n* : inhalador *m*
inhere [ɪnˈhɪr] *vi* **-hered; -hering** : ser inherente
inherent [ɪnˈhɪrənt, -ˈhɛr-] *adj* : inherente, intrínseco — **inherently** *adv*
inherit [ɪnˈhɛrət] *vt* : heredar
inheritance [ɪnˈhɛrətənts] *n* : herencia *f*
inheritor [ɪnˈhɛrətər] *n* : heredero *m*, -da *f*
inhibit [ɪnˈhɪbət] *vt* IMPEDE : inhibir, impedir
inhibition [ˌɪnhəˈbɪʃən, ˌɪnə-] *n* : inhibición *f*, cohibición *f*
inhuman [ɪnˈhjuːmən, -ˈjuː-] *adj* : inhumano, cruel — **inhumanly** *adv*
inhumane [ˌɪnhjuˈmeɪn, -ju-] *adj* INHUMAN : inhumano, cruel
inhumanity [ˌɪnhjuˈmænəti, -ju-] *n, pl* **-ties** : inhumanidad *f*, crueldad *f*
inimical [ɪˈnɪmɪkəl] *adj* **1** UNFAVORABLE : adverso, desfavorable **2** HOSTILE : hostil — **inimically** *adv*
inimitable [ɪˈnɪmətəbəl] *adj* : inimitable
iniquitous [ɪˈnɪkwətəs] *adj* : inicuo, malvado
iniquity [ɪˈnɪkwəti] *n, pl* **-ties** : iniquidad *f*
initial¹ [ɪˈnɪʃəl] *vt* **-tialed** *or* **-tialled; -tialing** *or* **-tialling** : poner las iniciales a, firmar con las iniciales
initial² *adj* : inicial, primero — **initially** *adv*

initial³ *n* : inicial *f*
initiate¹ [ɪˈnɪʃiˌeɪt] *vt* -ated; -ating 1 BE-
GIN : comenzar, iniciar 2 INDUCT : instruir 3 INTRODUCE : introducir, instruir
initiate² [ɪˈnɪʃiət] *n* : iniciado *m*, -da *f*
initiation [ɪˌnɪʃiˈeɪʃən] *n* : iniciación *f*
initiative [ɪˈnɪʃətɪv] *n* : iniciativa *f*
initiatory [ɪˈnɪʃiəˌtori] *adj* 1 INTRODUC-
TORY : introductorio 2 : de iniciación
⟨initiatory rites : ritos de iniciación⟩
inject [ɪnˈdʒɛkt] *vt* : inyectar
injection [ɪnˈdʒɛkʃən] *n* : inyección *f*
injudicious [ˌɪndʒuˈdɪʃəs] *adj* : imprudente, indiscreto, poco juicioso
injunction [ɪnˈdʒʌŋkʃən] *n* 1 ORDER : orden *f*, mandato *m* 2 COURT ORDER
: mandamiento *m* judicial
injure [ˈɪndʒər] *vt* -jured; -juring 1
WOUND : herir, lesionar 2 HURT : lastimar, dañar, herir 3 to injure oneself
: hacerse daño
injurious [ɪnˈdʒʊriəs] *adj* : perjudicial
⟨injurious to one's health : perjudicial
a la salud⟩
injury [ˈɪndʒəri] *n*, *pl* -ries 1 WRONG
: mal *m*, injusticia *f* 2 DAMAGE, HARM
: herida *f*, daño *m*, perjuicio *m*
injustice [ɪnˈdʒʌstəs] *n* : injusticia *f*
ink¹ [ˈɪŋk] *vt* : entintar
ink² *n* : tinta *f*
inkling [ˈɪŋklɪŋ] *n* : presentimiento *m*, indicio *m*, sospecha *f*
inkwell [ˈɪŋkˌwɛl] *n* : tintero *m*
inky [ˈɪŋki] *adj* 1 : manchado de tinta 2
BLACK : negro, impenetrable ⟨inky
darkness : negra oscuridad⟩
inland¹ [ˈɪnˌlænd, -lənd] *adv* : hacia el interior, tierra adentro
inland² *adj* : interior
inland³ *n* : interior *m*
in-law [ˈɪnˌlɔ] *n* 1 : pariente *m* político
2 **in-laws** *npl* : suegros *mpl*
inlay¹ [ɪnˈleɪ, ˈɪnˌleɪ] *vt* -laid [-ˈleɪd, -ˌleɪd];
-laying : incrustar, taracear
inlay² [ˈɪnˌleɪ] *n* 1 : incrustación *f* 2
: empaste *m* (de un diente)
inlet [ˈɪnˌlɛt, -lət] *n* : cala *f*, ensenada *f*
inmate [ˈɪnˌmeɪt] *n* : paciente *mf* (en un
hospital); preso *m*, -sa *f* (en una
prisión); interno *m*, -na *f* (en un asilo)
in memoriam [ˌɪnməˈmoriəm] *prep* : en
memoria de
inmost [ˈɪnˌmoːst] → **innermost**
inn [ˈɪn] *n* 1 : posada *f*, hostería *f*, fonda *f* 2 TAVERN : taberna *f*
innards [ˈɪnərdz] *npl* : entrañas *fpl*, tripas *fpl fam*
innate [ɪˈneɪt] *adj* 1 INBORN : innato 2
INHERENT : inherente
inner [ˈɪnər] *adj* : interior, interno
innermost [ˈɪnərˌmoːst] *adj* : más íntimo, más profundo
innersole [ˈɪnərˈsoːl] → **insole**
inning [ˈɪnɪŋ] *n* : entrada *f*
innkeeper [ˈɪnˌkiːpər] *n* : posadero *m*, -ra
f
innocence [ˈɪnəsənts] *n* : inocencia *f*

innocent¹ [ˈɪnəsənt] *adj* : inocente — **in-
nocently** *adv*
innocent² *n* : inocente *mf*
innocuous [ɪˈnɑkjəwəs] *adj* 1 HARM-
LESS : inocuo 2 INOFFENSIVE : inofensivo
innovate [ˈɪnəˌveɪt] *vi* -vated; -vating
: innovar
innovation [ˌɪnəˈveɪʃən] *n* : innovación
f, novedad *f*
innovative [ˈɪnəˌveɪtɪv] *adj* : innovador
innovator [ˈɪnəˌveɪtər] *n* : innovador *m*,
-dora *f*
innuendo [ˌɪnjuˈɛndo] *n*, *pl* -dos *or*
-does : insinuación *f*, indirecta *f*
innumerable [ɪˈnuːmərəbəl, -ˈnjuː-] *adj*
: innumerable
inoculate [ɪˈnɑkjəˌleɪt] *vt* -lated; -lating
: inocular
inoculation [ɪˌnɑkjəˈleɪʃən] *n* : inocu-
lación *f*
inoffensive [ˌɪnəˈfɛntsɪv] *adj* : inofensivo
inoperable [ɪnˈɑpərəbəl] *adj* : inoperable
inoperative [ɪnˈɑpərətɪv, -ˌreɪ-] *adj* : inoperante
inopportune [ɪnˌɑpərˈtuːn, -ˈtjuːn] *adj*
: inoportuno — **inopportunely** *adv*
inordinate [ɪnˈɔrdənət] *adj* : excesivo, inmoderado, desmesurado — **inordi-
nately** *adv*
inorganic [ˌɪnˌɔrˈgænɪk] *adj* : inorgánico
inpatient [ˈɪnˌpeɪʃənt] *n* : paciente *mf*
hospitalizado
input¹ [ˈɪnˌpʊt] *vt* **inputted** *or* **input**; **inputting** : entrar (datos, información)
input² *n* 1 CONTRIBUTION : aportación
f, contribución *f* 2 ENTRY : entrada *f*
(de datos) 3 ADVICE, OPINION : consejos *mpl*, opinión *f*
inquest [ˈɪnˌkwɛst] *n* INQUIRY, INVESTI-
GATION : investigación *f*, averiguación
f, pesquisa *f* (judicial)
inquire [ɪnˈkwaɪr] *v* -quired; -quiring *vt*
: preguntar, informarse de, inquirir ⟨he
inquired how to get in : preguntó como
entrar⟩ — *vi* 1 ASK : preguntar, informarse ⟨to inquire about : informarse
sobre⟩ ⟨to inquire after (someone)⟩
: preguntar por (alguien)⟩ 2 to inquire
into INVESTIGATE : investigar, inquirir
sobre
inquiringly [ɪnˈkwaɪrɪŋli] *adv* : inquisitivamente
inquiry [ˈɪnˌkwaɪri, ɪnˈkwaɪri; ˈɪnkwəri;
-ɪŋ-] *n*, *pl* -ries 1 QUESTION : pregunta
f ⟨to make inquiries about : pedir información sobre⟩ 2 INVESTIGATION
: investigación *f*, inquisición *f*, pesquisa
f
inquisition [ˌɪnkwəˈzɪʃən, ˌɪŋ-] *n* 1 : inquisición *f*, interrogatorio *m*, investigación *f* 2 the Inquisition : la Inquisición *f*
inquisitive [ɪnˈkwɪzətɪv] *adj* : inquisidor,
inquisitivo, curioso — **inquisitively**
adv

inquisitiveness [ɪn'kwɪzət̬ɪvnəs] *n* : curiosidad *f*
inquisitor [ɪn'kwɪzət̬ər] *n* : inquisidor *m*, -dora *f*; interrogador *m*, -dora *f*
inroad ['ɪn,roːd] *n* **1** ENCROACHMENT, INVASION : invasión *f*, incursión *f* **2 to make inroads into** : ocupar parte de (un tiempo), agotar parte de (ahorros, recursos), invadir (un territorio)
insane [ɪn'seɪn] *adj* **1** MAD : loco, demente ⟨to go insane : volverse loco⟩ **2** ABSURD : absurdo, insensato ⟨an insane scheme : un proyecto insensato⟩
insanely [ɪn'seɪnli] *adv* : como un loco ⟨insanely suspicious : loco de recelo⟩
insanity [ɪn'sænət̬i] *n, pl* **-ties 1** MADNESS : locura *f* **2** FOLLY : locura *f*, insensatez *f*
insatiable [ɪn'seɪʃəbəl] *adj* : insaciable — **insatiably** [-bli] *adv*
inscribe [ɪn'skraɪb] *vt* **-scribed; -scribing 1** ENGRAVE : inscribir, grabar **2** ENROLL : inscribir **3** DEDICATE : dedicar (un libro)
inscription [ɪn'skrɪpʃən] *n* : inscripción *f* (en un monumento), dedicación *f* (en un libro), leyenda *f* (de una ilustración, etc.)
inscrutable [ɪn'skruːt̬əbəl] *adj* : inescrutable, misterioso — **inscrutably** [-bli] *adv*
inseam ['ɪn,siːm] *n* : entrepierna *f*
insect ['ɪn,sɛkt] *n* : insecto *m*
insecticidal [ɪn,sɛktə'saɪdəl] *adj* : insecticida
insecticide [ɪn'sɛktə,saɪd] *n* : insecticida *m*
insecure [,ɪnsɪ'kjʊr] *adj* : inseguro, poco seguro — **insecurely** *adv*
insecurely [,ɪnsɪ'kjʊrli] *adv* : inseguramente
insecurity [,ɪnsɪ'kjʊrət̬i] *n, pl* **-ties** : inseguridad *f*
inseminate [ɪn'sɛmə,neɪt] *vt* **-nated; -nating** : inseminar
insemination [ɪn,sɛmə'neɪʃən] *n* : inseminación *f*
insensibility [ɪn,sɛntsə'bɪlət̬i] *n, pl* **-ties** : insensibilidad *f*
insensible [ɪn'sɛntsəbəl] *adj* **1** UNCONSCIOUS : inconsciente, sin conocimiento **2** NUMB : insensible, entumecido **3** UNAWARE : inconsciente
insensitive [ɪn'sɛntsət̬ɪv] *adj* : insensible
insensitivity [ɪn,sɛntsə'tɪvət̬i] *n, pl* **-ties** : insensibilidad *f*
inseparable [ɪn'sɛpərəbəl] *adj* : inseparable
insert¹ [ɪn'sərt] *vt* **1** : insertar, introducir, poner, meter ⟨insert your key in the lock : mete tu llave en la cerradura⟩ **2** INTERPOLATE : interpolar, intercalar
insert² ['ɪn,sərt] *n* : inserción *f*, hoja *f* insertada (en una revista, etc.)
insertion [ɪn'sərʃən] *n* : inserción *f*
inset ['ɪn,sɛt] *n* : página *f* intercalada (en un libro), entredós *m* (de encaje en la ropa)

inshore¹ ['ɪn'ʃor] *adv* : hacia la costa
inshore² *adj* : cercano a la costa, costero ⟨inshore fishing : pesca costera⟩
inside¹ [ɪn'saɪd, 'ɪn,saɪd] *adv* : adentro, dentro ⟨to run inside : correr para adentro⟩ ⟨inside and out : por dentro y por fuera⟩
inside² *adj* **1** : interior, de adentro, de dentro ⟨the inside lane : el carril interior⟩ **2** : confidencial ⟨inside information : información confidencial⟩
inside³ *n* **1** : interior *m*, parte *f* de adentro **2 insides** *npl* BELLY, GUTS : tripas *fpl fam* **3 inside out** : al revés
inside⁴ *prep* **1** INTO : al interior de **2** WITHIN : dentro de **3** (*referring to time*) : en menos de ⟨inside an hour : en menos de una hora⟩
inside of *prep* INSIDE : dentro de
insider [ɪn'saɪdər] *n* : persona *f* enterada
insidious [ɪn'sɪdiəs] *adj* : insidioso — **insidiously** *adv*
insidiousness [ɪn'sɪdiəsnəs] *n* : insidia *f*
insight ['ɪn,saɪt] *n* : perspicacia *f*, penetración *f*
insightful [ɪn'saɪtfəl] *adj* : perspicaz
insignia [ɪn'sɪgniə] *or* **insigne** [-,niː] *n, pl* **-nia** *or* **-nias** : insignia *f*, enseña *f*
insignificance [,ɪnsɪg'nɪfɪkənts] *n* : insignificancia *f*
insignificant [,ɪnsɪg'nɪfɪkənt] *adj* : insignificante
insincere [,ɪnsɪn'sɪr] *adj* : insincero, poco sincero
insincerely [,ɪnsɪn'sɪrli] *adv* : con poca sinceridad
insincerity [,ɪnsɪn'sɛrət̬i, -'sɪr-] *n, pl* **-ties** : insinceridad *f*
insinuate [ɪn'sɪnju,eɪt] *vt* **-ated; -ating** : insinuar
insinuation [ɪn,sɪnju'eɪʃən] *n* : insinuación *f*
insipid [ɪn'sɪpəd] *adj* : insípido
insist [ɪn'sɪst] *v* : insistir
insistence [ɪn'sɪstənts] *n* : insistencia *f*
insistent [ɪn'sɪstənt] *adj* : insistente — **insistently** *adv*
insofar as [,ɪnso'fɑræz] *conj* : en la medida en que, en tanto que, en cuanto a
insole ['ɪn,soːl] *n* : plantilla *f*
insolence ['ɪntsələnts] *n* : insolencia *f*
insolent ['ɪntsələnt] *adj* : insolente
insolubility [ɪn,saljʊ'bɪlət̬i] *n* : insolubilidad *f*
insoluble [ɪn'saljʊbəl] *adj* : insoluble
insolvency [ɪn'salvəntsi] *n, pl* **-cies** : insolvencia *f*
insolvent [ɪn'salvənt] *adj* : insolvente
insomnia [ɪn'samniə] *n* : insomnio *m*
insomuch as [,ɪnso'mʌtʃæz] → **inasmuch as**
insomuch that *conj* SO : así que, de manera que
inspect [ɪn'spɛkt] *vt* : inspeccionar, examinar, revisar
inspection [ɪn'spɛkʃən] *n* : inspección *f*, examen *m*, revisión *f*, revista *f* (de tropas)

inspector [ɪn'spɛktər] *n* : inspector *m*, -tora *f*
inspiration [ˌɪntspə'reɪʃən] *n* : inspiración *f*
inspirational [ˌɪntspə'reɪʃənəl] *adj* : inspirador
inspire [ɪn'spaɪr] *v* **-spired; -spiring** *vt* **1** INHALE : inhalar, aspirar **2** STIMULATE : estimular, animar, inspirar **3** INSTILL : inspirar, infundir — *vi* : inspirar
instability [ˌɪntstə'bɪləti] *n, pl* **-ties** : inestabilidad *f*
install [ɪn'stɔl] *vt* **-stalled; -stalling 1** : instalar ⟨to install the new president : instalar el presidente nuevo⟩ ⟨to install a fan : montar un abanico⟩ **2 to install oneself** : instalarse
installation [ˌɪntstə'leɪʃən] *n* : instalación *f*
installment [ɪn'stɔlmənt] *n* **1** : plazo *m*, cuota *f* ⟨to pay in four installments : pagar a cuatro plazos⟩ **2** : entrega *f* (de una publicación o telenovela) **3** INSTALLATION : instalación *f*
instance ['ɪntstənts] *n* **1** INSTIGATION : instancia *f* **2** EXAMPLE : ejemplo *m* ⟨for instance : por ejemplo⟩ **3** OCCASION : instancia *f*, caso *m*, ocasión *f* ⟨he prefers, in this instance, to remain anonymous : en este caso prefiere quedarse anónimo⟩
instant¹ ['ɪntstənt] *adj* **1** IMMEDIATE : inmediato, instantáneo ⟨an instant reply : una respuesta inmediata⟩ **2** : instantáneo ⟨instant coffee : café instantáneo⟩
instant² *n* : momento *m*, instante *m*
instantaneous [ˌɪntstən'teɪniəs] *adj* : instantáneo
instantaneously [ˌɪntstən'teɪniəsli] *adv* : instantáneamente, al instante
instantly ['ɪntstəntli] *adv* : al instante, instantáneamente
instead [ɪn'stɛd] *adv* **1** : en cambio, en lugar de eso, en su lugar ⟨Dad was going, but Mom went instead : papá iba a ir, pero mamá fue en su lugar⟩ **2** RATHER : al contrario
instead of *prep* : en vez de, en lugar de
instep ['ɪnˌstɛp] *n* : empeine *m*
instigate ['ɪntstəˌgeɪt] *vt* **-gated; -gating** INCITE, PROVOKE : instigar, incitar, provocar, fomentar
instigation [ˌɪntstə'geɪʃən] *n* : instancia *f*, incitación *f*
instigator ['ɪntstəˌgeɪtər] *n* : instigador *m*, -dora *f*; incitador *m*, -dora *f*
instill [ɪn'stɪl] *vt* **-stilled; -stilling** : inculcar, infundir
instinct ['ɪnˌstɪŋkt] *n* **1** TALENT : instinto *m*, don *m* ⟨an instinct for the right word : un don para escoger la palabra apropiada⟩ **2** : instinto *m* ⟨maternal instincts : instintos maternales⟩
instinctive [ɪn'stɪŋktɪv] *adj* : instintivo
instinctively [ɪn'stɪŋktɪvli] *adv* : instintivamente, por instinto
instinctual [ɪn'stɪŋktʃuəl] *adj* : instintivo

institute¹ ['ɪntstəˌtuːt, -ˌtjuːt] *vt* **-tuted; -tuting 1** ESTABLISH : establecer, instituir, fundar **2** INITIATE : iniciar, empezar, entablar
institute² *n* : instituto *m*
institution [ˌɪntstə'tuːʃən, -'tjuː-] *n* **1** ESTABLISHING : institución *f*, establecimiento *m* **2** CUSTOM : institución *f*, tradición *f* ⟨the institution of marriage : la institución del matrimonio⟩ **3** ORGANIZATION : institución *f*, organismo *m* **4** ASYLUM : asilo *m*
institutional [ˌɪntstə'tuːʃənəl, -'tjuː-] *adj* : institucional
institutionalize [ˌɪntstə'tuːʃənəˌlaɪz, -'tjuː-] *vt* **-ized; -izing 1** : institucionalizar ⟨institutionalized values : valores institucionalizados⟩ **2** : internar ⟨institutionalized orphans : huérfanos internados⟩
instruct [ɪn'strʌkt] *vt* **1** TEACH, TRAIN : instruir, adiestrar, enseñar **2** COMMAND : mandar, ordenar, dar instrucciones a
instruction [ɪn'strʌkʃən] *n* **1** TEACHING : instrucción *f*, enseñanza *f* **2** COMMAND : orden *f*, instrucción *f* **3 instructions** *npl* DIRECTIONS : instrucciones *fpl*, modo *m* de empleo
instructional [ɪn'strʌkʃənəl] *adj* : instructivo, educativo
instructive [ɪn'strʌktɪv] *adj* : instructivo
instructor [ɪn'strʌktər] *n* : instructor *m*, -tora *f*
instrument ['ɪntstrəmənt] *n* : instrumento *m*
instrumental [ˌɪntstrə'mɛntəl] *adj* : instrumental
instrumentalist [ˌɪntstrə'mɛntəlɪst] *n* : instrumentista *mf*
insubordinate [ˌɪnsə'bɔrdənət] *adj* : insubordinado
insubordination [ˌɪnsəˌbɔrdən'eɪʃən] *n* : insubordinación *f*
insubstantial [ˌɪnsəb'stæntʃəl] *adj* : insustancial, poco nutritivo (dícese de una comida), poco sólido (dícese de una estructura o un argumento)
insufferable [ɪn'sʌfərəbəl] *adj* UNBEARABLE : insufrible, intolerable, inaguantable, insoportable — **insufferably** [-bli] *adv*
insufficiency [ˌɪnsə'fɪʃəntsi] *n, pl* **-cies** : insuficiencia *f*
insufficient [ˌɪnsə'fɪʃənt] *adj* : insuficiente — **insufficiently** *adv*
insular ['ɪnsʊlər, -sjʊ-] *adj* **1** : isleño (dícese de la gente), insular (dícese del clima) ⟨insular residents : residentes de la isla⟩ **2** NARROW-MINDED : de miras estrechas
insularity [ˌɪntsʊ'lærəti, -sjʊ-] *n* : insularidad *f*
insulate ['ɪntsəˌleɪt] *vt* **-lated; -lating** : aislar
insulation [ˌɪntsə'leɪʃən] *n* : aislamiento *m*
insulator ['ɪntsəˌleɪtər] *n* : aislador *m* (pieza), aislante *m* (material)

insulin ['ɪntsələn] *n* : insulina *f*
insult¹ [ɪn'sʌlt] *vt* : insultar, ofender, injuriar
insult² ['ɪn,sʌlt] *n* : insulto *m*, injuria *f*, agravio *m*
insulting [ɪn'sʌltɪŋ] *adj* : ofensivo, injurioso, insultante
insultingly [ɪn'sʌltɪŋli] *adv* : ofensivamente, de manera insultante
insuperable [ɪn'su:pərəbəl] *adj* : insuperable — **insuperably** [-bli] *adv*
insurable [ɪn'ʃʊrəbəl] *adj* : asegurable
insurance [ɪn'ʃʊrənts, 'ɪn,ʃʊr-] *n* : seguro *m* ⟨life insurance : seguro de vida⟩ ⟨insurance company : compañía de seguros⟩
insure [ɪn'ʃʊr] *vt* **-sured; -suring 1** UNDERWRITE : asegurar **2** ENSURE : asegurar, garantizar
insured [ɪn'ʃʊrd] *n* : asegurado *m*, -da *f*
insurer [ɪn'ʃʊrər] *n* : asegurador *m*, -dora *f*
insurgent¹ [ɪn'sərdʒənt] *adj* : insurgente
insurgent² *n* : insurgente *mf*
insurmountable [,ɪnsər'maʊntəbəl] *adj* : insuperable, insalvable — **insurmountably** [-bli] *adv*
insurrection [,ɪnsə'rɛkʃən] *n* : insurrección *f*, levantamiento *m*, alzamiento *m*
intact [ɪn'tækt] *adj* : intacto
intake ['ɪn,teɪk] *n* **1** OPENING : entrada *f*, toma *f* ⟨fuel intake : toma de combustible⟩ **2** : entrada *f* (de agua o aire), consumo *m* (de sustancias nutritivas) **3** intake of breath : inhalación *f*
intangible [ɪn'tændʒəbəl] *adj* : intangible, impalpable — **intangibly** [-bli] *adv*
integer ['ɪntɪdʒər] *n* : entero *m*
integral ['ɪntɪgrəl] *adj* : integral, esencial
integrate ['ɪntə,greɪt] *v* **-grated; -grating** *vt* **1** UNITE : integrar, unir **2** DESEGREGATE : eliminar la segregación de — *vi* : integrarse
integration [,ɪntə'greɪʃən] *n* : integración *f*
integrity [ɪn'tɛgrəti] *n* : integridad *f*
intellect ['ɪntəl,ɛkt] *n* : intelecto *m*, inteligencia *f*, capacidad *f* intelectual
intellectual¹ [,ɪntə'lɛktʃʊəl] *adj* : intelectual — **intellectually** *adv*
intellectual² *n* : intelectual *mf*
intellectualism [,ɪntə'lɛktʃʊə,lɪzəm] *n* : intelectualismo *m*
intelligence [ɪn'tɛlədʒənts] *n* **1** : inteligencia *f* **2** INFORMATION, NEWS : inteligencia *f*, información *f*, noticias *fpl*
intelligent [ɪn'tɛlədʒənt] *adj* : inteligente — **intelligently** *adv*
intelligentsia [ɪn,tɛlə'dʒɛn/siə, -'gɛn-] *ns & pl* : intelectualidad *f*
intelligibility [ɪn,tɛlədʒə'bɪləti] *n* : inteligibilidad *f*
intelligible [ɪn'tɛlədʒəbəl] *adj* : inteligible, comprensible — **intelligibly** [-bli] *adv*
intemperance [ɪn'tɛmpərənts] *n* : inmoderación *f*, intemperancia *f*

intemperate [ɪn'tɛmpərət] *adj* : excesivo, inmoderado, desmedido
intend [ɪn'tɛnd] *vt* **1** MEAN : querer decir ⟨that's not what I intended : eso no es lo que quería decir⟩ **2** PLAN : tener planeado, proyectar, proponerse ⟨I intend to finish by Thursday : me propongo acabar para el jueves⟩
intended [ɪn'tɛndəd] *adj* **1** PLANNED : previsto, proyectado **2** INTENTIONAL : intencional, deliberado
intense [ɪn'tɛnts] *adj* **1** EXTREME : intenso, extremo ⟨intense pain : dolor intenso⟩ **2** : profundo, intenso ⟨to my intense relief : para mi alivio profundo⟩ ⟨intense enthusiasm : entusiasmo ardiente⟩
intensely [ɪn'tɛntsli] *adv* : sumamente, profundamente, intensamente
intensification [ɪn,tɛntsəfə'keɪʃən] *n* : intensificación *f*
intensify [ɪn'tɛntsə,faɪ] *v* **-fied; -fying** *vt* **1** STRENGTHEN : intensificar, redoblar ⟨to intensify one's efforts : redoblar uno sus esfuerzos⟩ **2** SHARPEN : intensificar, agudizar (dolor, ansiedad) — *vi* : intensificarse, hacerse más intenso
intensity [ɪn'tɛntsəti] *n, pl* **-ties** : intensidad *f*
intensive [ɪn'tɛntsɪv] *adj* : intensivo — **intensively** *adv*
intent¹ [ɪn'tɛnt] *adj* **1** FIXED : concentrado, fijo ⟨an intent stare : una mirada fija⟩ **2** intent on *or* intent upon : resuelto a, atento a
intent² *n* **1** PURPOSE : intención *f*, propósito *m* **2** for all intents and purposes : a todos los efectos, prácticamente
intention [ɪn'tɛnʃən] *n* : intención *f*, propósito *m*
intentional [ɪn'tɛnʃənəl] *adj* : intencional, deliberado
intentionally [ɪn'tɛnʃənəli] *adv* : a propósito, adrede
intently [ɪn'tɛntli] *adv* : atentamente, fijamente
inter [ɪn'tər] *vt* **-terred; -terring** : enterrar, inhumar
interact [,ɪntər'ækt] *vi* : interactuar, actuar recíprocamente, relacionarse
interaction [,ɪntər'ækʃən] *n* : interacción *f*, interrelación *f*
interactive [,ɪntər'æktɪv] *adj* : interactivo
interbreed [,ɪntər'bri:d] *v* **-bred** [-'brɛd]; **-breeding** *vt* : cruzar — *vi* : cruzarse
intercalate [ɪn'tərkə,leɪt] *vt* **-lated; -lating** : intercalar
intercede [,ɪntər'si:d] *vi* **-ceded; -ceding** : interceder
intercept [,ɪntər'sɛpt] *vt* : interceptar
interception [,ɪntər'sɛpʃən] *n* : intercepción *f*
intercession [,ɪntər'sɛʃən] *n* : intercesión *f*

interchange¹ [ˌɪntərˈtʃeɪndʒ] *vt* **-changed; -changing** : intercambiar
interchange² [ˈɪntərˌtʃeɪndʒ] *n* **1** EXCHANGE : intercambio *m*, cambio *m* **2** JUNCTION : empalme *m*, enlace *m* de carreteras
interchangeable [ˌɪntərˈtʃeɪndʒəbəl] *adj* : intercambiable
intercity [ˈɪntərˈsɪti] *adj* : interurbano
intercollegiate [ˌɪntərkəˈliːdʒət, -dʒiət] *adj* : interuniversitario
interconnect [ˌɪntərkəˈnɛkt] *vt* **1** : conectar, interconectar (en tecnología) **2** RELATE : interrelacionar — *vi* **1** : conectar **2** : interrelacionarse
intercontinental [ˌɪntərˌkɑntənˈnɛtəl] *adj* : intercontinental
intercourse [ˈɪntərˌkors] *n* **1** RELATIONS : relaciones *fpl*, trato *m* **2** COPULATION : acto *m* sexual, relaciones *fpl* sexuales, coito *m*
interdenominational [ˌɪntərdɪˌnɑməˈneɪʃənəl] *adj* : interconfesional
interdepartmental [ˌɪntərdɪˌpɑrtˈmɛntəl, -ˌdiː-] *adj* : interdepartamental
interdependence [ˌɪntərdɪˈpɛndənts] *n* : interdependencia *f*
interdependent [ˌɪntərdɪˈpɛndənt] *adj* : interdependiente
interdict [ˌɪntərˈdɪkt] *vt* **1** PROHIBIT : prohibir **2** : cortar (las líneas de comunicación o provisión del enemigo)
interest¹ [ˈɪntrəst, -təˌrɛst] *vt* : interesar
interest² *n* **1** SHARE, STAKE : interés *m*, participación *f* **2** BENEFIT : provecho *m*, beneficio *m*, interés *m* ⟨in the public interest : en el interés público⟩ **3** CHARGE : interés *m*, cargo *m* ⟨compound interest : interés compuesto⟩ **4** CURIOSITY : interés *m*, curiosidad *f* **5** COLOR : color *m*, interés *m* ⟨places of local interest : lugares de color local⟩ **6** HOBBY : afición *f*
interesting [ˈɪntrəstɪŋ, -təˌrɛstɪŋ] *adj* : interesante — **interestingly** *adv*
interface [ˈɪntərˌfeɪs] *n* **1** : punto *m* de contacto ⟨oil-water interface : punto de contacto entre el agua y el aceite⟩ **2** : interfaz *f* (de una computadora), interfase *f*
interfere [ˌɪntərˈfɪr] *vi* **-fered; -fering 1** INTERPOSE : interponerse, hacer interferencia ⟨to interfere with a play : obstruir una jugada⟩ **2** MEDDLE : entrometerse, interferir, intervenir **3** **to interfere with** DISRUPT : afectar (una actividad), interferir (la radiotransmisión) **4** **to interfere with** TOUCH : tocar ⟨someone interfered with my papers : alguien tocó mis papeles⟩
interference [ˌɪntərˈfɪrənts] *n* : interferencia *f*, intromisión *f*
intergalactic [ˌɪntərgəˈlæktɪk] *adj* : intergaláctico
intergovernmental [ˌɪntərˌgʌvərˈmɛntəl, -vərn-] *adj* : intergubernamental
interim¹ [ˈɪntərəm] *adj* : interino, provisional

interim² *n* **1** : interín *m*, intervalo *m* **2** **in the interim** : en el interín, mientras tanto
interior¹ [ɪnˈtɪriər] *adj* : interior
interior² *n* : interior *m*
interject [ˌɪntərˈdʒɛkt] *vt* : interponer, agregar
interjection [ˌɪntərˈdʒɛkʃən] *n* **1** : interjección *f* (en lingüística) **2** EXCLAMATION : exclamación *f* **3** INTERPOSITION, INTERRUPTION : interposición *f*, interrupción *f*
interlace [ˌɪntərˈleɪs] *vt* **-laced; -lacing 1** INTERWEAVE : entrelazar **2** INTERSPERSE : intercalar
interlock [ˌɪntərˈlɑk] *vt* **1** UNITE : trabar, unir **2** ENGAGE, MESH : engranar — *vi* : entrelazarse, trabarse
interloper [ˌɪntərˈloːpər] *n* **1** INTRUDER : intruso *m*, -sa *f* **2** MEDDLER : entrometido *m*, -da *f*
interlude [ˈɪntərˌluːd] *n* **1** INTERVAL : intervalo *m*, intermedio *m* (en el teatro) **2** : interludio *m* (en música)
intermarriage [ˌɪntərˈmærɪdʒ] *n* **1** : matrimonio *m* mixto (entre miembros de distintas razas o religiones) **2** : matrimonio *m* entre miembros del mismo grupo
intermarry [ˌɪntərˈmæri] *vi* **-married; -marrying 1** : casarse (con miembros de otros grupos) **2** : casarse entre sí (con miembros del mismo grupo)
intermediary¹ [ˌɪntərˈmiːdiˌɛri] *adj* : intermediario
intermediary² *n, pl* **-aries** : intermediario *m*, -ria *f*
intermediate¹ [ˌɪntərˈmiːdiət] *adj* : intermedio
intermediate² *n* GO-BETWEEN : intermediario *m*, -ria *f*; mediador *m*, -dora *f*
interment [ɪnˈtərmənt] *n* : entierro *m*
interminable [ɪnˈtərmənəbəl] *adj* : interminable, constante — **interminably** [-bli] *adv*
intermingle [ˌɪntərˈmɪŋgəl] *vt* **-mingled; -mingling** : entremezclar, mezclar — *vi* : entremezclarse
intermission [ˌɪntərˈmɪʃən] *n* : intermisión *f*, intervalo *m*, intermedio *m*
intermittent [ˌɪntərˈmɪtənt] *adj* : intermitente — **intermittently** *adv*
intermix [ˌɪntərˈmɪks] *vt* : entremezclar
intern¹ [ˈɪnˌtərn, ɪnˈtərn] *vt* : confinar (durante la guerra) — *vi* : servir de interno, hacer las prácticas
intern² [ˈɪnˌtərn] *n* : interno *m*, -na *f*
internal [ɪnˈtərnəl] *adj* : interno, interior ⟨internal bleeding : hemorragia interna⟩ ⟨internal affairs : asuntos interiores, asuntos domésticos⟩ — **internally** *adv*
international [ˌɪntərˈnæʃənəl] *adj* : internacional — **internationally** *adv*
internationalize [ˌɪntərˈnæʃənəˌlaɪz] *vt* **-ized; -izing** : internacionalizar
internee [ˌɪnˌtərˈniː] *n* : interno *m*, -na *f*
Internet [ˈɪntərˌnɛt] *n* : Internet *mf*

internist ['ɪn,tərnɪst] *n* : internista *mf*
interpersonal [,ɪntər'pərsənəl] *adj* : interpersonal
interplay ['ɪntər,pleɪ] *n* : interacción *f*, juego *m*
interpolate [ɪn'tərpə,leɪt] *vt* **-lated; -lating** : interpolar
interpose [,ɪntər'po:z] *v* **-posed; -posing** *vt* : interponer, interrumpir con — *vi* : interponerse
interposition [,ɪntərpə'zɪʃən] *n* : interposición *f*
interpret [ɪn'tərprət] *vt* : interpretar
interpretation [ɪn,tərprə'teɪʃən] *n* : interpretación *f*
interpretative [ɪn'tərprə,teɪt̬ɪv] *adj* : interpretativo
interpreter [ɪn'tərprət̬ər] *n* : intérprete *mf*
interpretive [ɪn'tərprət̬ɪv] *adj* : interpretativo
interracial [,ɪntər'reɪʃəl] *adj* : interracial
interrelate [,ɪntərɪ'leɪt] *v* **-related; -relating** : interrelacionar
interrelationship [,ɪntərɪ'leɪʃən,ʃɪp] *n* : interrelación *f*
interrogate [ɪn'tɛrə,geɪt] *vt* **-gated; -gating** : interrogar, someter a un interrogatorio
interrogation [ɪn,tɛrə'geɪʃən] *n* : interrogación *f*
interrogative[1] [,ɪntə'rɑgət̬ɪv] *adj* : interrogativo
interrogative[2] *n* : interrogativo *m*
interrogator [ɪn'tɛrə,geɪt̬ər] *n* : interrogador *m*, -dora *f*
interrogatory [,ɪntə'rɑgə,tɔri] *adj* → **interrogative**[1]
interrupt [,ɪntə'rʌpt] *v* : interrumpir
interruption [,ɪntə'rʌpʃən] *n* : interrupción *f*
intersect [,ɪntər'sɛkt] *vt* : cruzar, cortar — *vi* : cruzarse (dícese de los caminos), intersectarse (dícese de las líneas o figuras), cortarse
intersection [,ɪntər'sɛkʃən] *n* : intersección *f*, cruce *m*
intersperse [,ɪntər'spərs] *vt* **-spersed; -spersing** : intercalar, entremezclar
interstate [,ɪntər'steɪt] *adj* : interestatal
interstellar [,ɪntər'stɛlər] *adj* : interestelar
interstice [ɪn'tərstəs] *n*, *pl* **-stices** [-stə,si:z, -stəsəz] : intersticio *m*
intertwine [,ɪntər'twaɪn] *vi* **-twined; -twining** : entrelazarse
interval ['ɪntərvəl] *n* : intervalo *m*
intervene [,ɪntər'vi:n] *vi* **-vened; -vening** **1** ELAPSE : transcurrir, pasar ⟨the intervening years : los años intermediarios⟩ **2** INTERCEDE : intervenir, interceder, mediar
intervention [,ɪntər'vɛntʃən] *n* : intervención *f*
interview[1] ['ɪntər,vju:] *vt* : entrevistar — *vi* : hacer entrevistas
interview[2] *n* : entrevista *f*
interviewer ['ɪntər,vju:ər] *n* : entrevistador *m*, -dora *f*

interweave [,ɪntər'wi:v] *v* **-wove** [-'wo:v]; **-woven** [-'wo:vən]; **-weaving** *vt* : entretejer, entrelazar — *vi* INTERTWINE : entrelazarse, entretejerse
interwoven [,ɪntər'wo:vən] *adj* : entretejido
intestate [ɪn'tɛs,teɪt, -tət] *adj* : intestado
intestinal [ɪn'tɛstənəl] *adj* : intestinal
intestine [ɪn'tɛstən] *n* **1** : intestino *m* **2** **small intestine** : intestino *m* delgado **3** **large intestine** : intestino *m* grueso
intimacy ['ɪntəməsi] *n*, *pl* **-cies** **1** CLOSENESS : intimidad *f* **2** FAMILIARITY : familiaridad *f*
intimate[1] ['ɪntə,meɪt] *vt* **-mated; -mating** : insinuar, dar a entender
intimate[2] ['ɪntəmət] *adj* **1** CLOSE : íntimo, de confianza ⟨intimate friends : amigos íntimos⟩ **2** PRIVATE : íntimo, privado ⟨intimate clubs : clubes íntimos⟩ **3** INNERMOST, SECRET : íntimo, secreto ⟨intimate fantasies : fantasías secretas⟩
intimate[3] *n* : amigo *m* íntimo, amiga *f* íntima
intimidate [ɪn'tɪmə,deɪt] *vt* **-dated; -dating** : intimidar
intimidation [ɪn,tɪmə'deɪʃən] *n* : intimidación *f*
into ['ɪn,tu:] *prep* **1** (*indicating motion*) : en, a, contra, dentro de ⟨she got into bed : se metió en la cama⟩ ⟨to get into a plane : subir a un avión⟩ ⟨he crashed into the wall : chocó contra la pared⟩ ⟨looking into the sun : mirando al sol⟩ **2** (*indicating state or condition*) : a, en ⟨to burst into tears : echarse a llorar⟩ ⟨the water turned into ice : el agua se convirtió en hielo⟩ ⟨to translate into English : traducir al inglés⟩ **3** (*indicating time*) ⟨far into the night : hasta bien entrada la noche⟩ ⟨he's well into his eighties : tiene los ochenta bien cumplidos⟩ **4** (*in mathematics*) ⟨3 into 12 is 4 : 12 dividido por 3 es 4⟩
intolerable [ɪn'tɑlərəbəl] *adj* : intolerable — **intolerably** [-bli] *adv*
intolerance [ɪn'tɑlərənts] *n* : intolerancia *f*
intolerant [ɪn'tɑlərənt] *adj* : intolerante
intonation [,ɪnto'neɪʃən] *n* : entonación *f*
intone [ɪn'to:n] *vt* **-toned; -toning** : entonar
intoxicant [ɪn'tɑksɪkənt] *n* : bebida *f* alcohólica
intoxicate [ɪn'tɑksə,keɪt] *vt* **-cated; -cating** : emborrachar, embriagar
intoxicated [ɪn'tɑksə,keɪt̬əd] *adj* : borracho, embriagado
intoxicating [ɪn'tɑksə,keɪt̬ɪŋ] *adj* : embriagador
intoxication [ɪn,tɑksə'keɪʃən] *n* : embriaguez *f*
intractable [ɪn'træktəbəl] *adj* : obstinado, intratable
intramural [,ɪntrə'mjʊrəl] *adj* : interno, dentro de la universidad

intransigence [ɪn'trænʦədʒənʦs, -'trænzə-] *n* : intransigencia *f*
intransigent [ɪn'trænʦədʒənt, -'trænzə-] *adj* : intransigente
intransitive [ɪn'trænʦəṭɪv, -'trænzə-] *adj* : intransitivo
intravenous [ˌɪntrə'viːnəs] *adj* : intravenoso — **intravenously** *adv*
intrepid [ɪn'trɛpəd] *adj* : intrépido
intricacy ['ɪntrɪkəsi] *n, pl* **-cies** : complejidad *f*, lo intrincado
intricate ['ɪntrɪkət] *adj* : intrincado, complicado — **intricately** *adv*
intrigue¹ [ɪn'triːg] *v* **-trigued; -triguing** : intrigar
intrigue² ['ɪnˌtriːg, ɪn'triːg] *n* : intriga *f*
intriguing [ɪn'triːgɪŋ] *adj* : intrigante, fascinante
intrinsic [ɪn'trɪnzɪk, -'trɪnʦɪk] *adj* : intrínseco, esencial — **intrinsically** [-zɪkli, -sɪ-] *adv*
introduce [ˌɪntrə'duːs, -'djuːs] *vt* **-duced; -ducing 1** : presentar ⟨let me introduce my father : permítame presentar a mi padre⟩ **2** : introducir (algo nuevo), lanzar (un producto), presentar (una ley), proponer (una idea o un tema)
introduction [ˌɪntrə'dʌkʃən] *n* : introducción *f*, presentación *f*
introductory [ˌɪntrə'dʌktəri] *adj* : introductorio, preliminar, de introducción
introspection [ˌɪntrə'spɛkʃən] *n* : introspección *f*
introspective [ˌɪntrə'spɛktɪv] *adj* : introspectivo — **introspectively** *adv*
introvert ['ɪntrəˌvərt] *n* : introvertido *m*, -da *f*
introverted ['ɪntrəˌvərtəd] *adj* : introvertido
intrude [ɪn'truːd] *v* **-truded; -truding** *vi* **1** INTERFERE : inmiscuirse, entrometerse **2** DISTURB, INTERRUPT : molestar, estorbar, interrumpir — *vt* : introducir por fuerza
intruder [ɪn'truːdər] *n* : intruso *m*, -sa *f*
intrusion [ɪn'truːʒən] *n* : intrusión *f*
intrusive [ɪn'truːsɪv] *adj* : intruso
intuit [ɪn'tuːɪt, -'tjuː-] *vt* : intuir
intuition [ˌɪntu'ɪʃən, -tju-] *n* : intuición *f*
intuitive [ɪn'tuːəṭɪv, -'tjuː-] *adj* : intuitivo — **intuitively** *adv*
inundate ['ɪnənˌdeɪt] *vt* **-dated; -dating** : inundar
inundation [ˌɪnən'deɪʃən] *n* : inundación *f*
inure [ɪ'nʊr, -'njʊr] *vt* **-ured; -uring** : acostumbrar, habituar
invade [ɪn'veɪd] *vt* **-vaded; -vading** : invadir
invader [ɪn'veɪdər] *n* : invasor *m*, -sora *f*
invalid¹ [ɪn'væləd] *adj* : inválido, nulo
invalid² ['ɪnvələd] *adj* : inválido, discapacitado
invalid³ ['ɪnvələd] *n* : inválido *m*, -da *f*
invalidate [ɪn'væləˌdeɪt] *vt* **-dated; -dating** : invalidar
invalidity [ˌɪnvə'lɪdəṭi] *n, pl* **-ties** : invalidez *f*, falta de validez *f*

invaluable [ɪn'væljəbəl, -'væljʊə-] *adj* : invalorable, inestimable, inapreciable
invariable [ɪn'væriəbəl] *adj* : invariable, constante — **invariably** [-bli] *adv*
invasion [ɪn'veɪʒən] *n* : invasión *f*
invasive [ɪn'veɪsɪv] *adj* : invasivo
invective [ɪn'vɛktɪv] *n* : invectiva *f*, improperio *m*, vituperio *m*
inveigh [ɪn'veɪ] *vi* **to inveigh against** : arremeter contra, lanzar invectivas contra
inveigle [ɪn'veɪgəl, -'viː-] *vt* **-gled; -gling** : engatusar, embaucar, persuadir con engaños
invent [ɪn'vɛnt] *vt* : inventar
invention [ɪn'vɛnʧən] *n* : invención *f*, invento *m*
inventive [ɪn'vɛntɪv] *adj* : inventivo
inventiveness [ɪn'vɛntɪvnəs] *n* : ingenio *m*, inventiva *f*
inventor [ɪn'vɛntər] *n* : inventor *m*, -tora *f*
inventory¹ ['ɪnvənˌtɔri] *vt* **-ried; -rying** : inventariar
inventory² *n, pl* **-ries 1** LIST : inventario *m* **2** STOCK : existencias *fpl*
inverse¹ [ɪn'vərs, 'ɪnˌvərs] *adj* : inverso — **inversely** *adv*
inverse² *n* : inverso *m*
inversion [ɪn'vərʒən] *n* : inversión *f*
invert [ɪn'vərt] *vt* : invertir
invertebrate¹ [ɪn'vərṭəbrət, -ˌbreɪt] *adj* : invertebrado
invertebrate² *n* : invertebrado *m*
invest [ɪn'vɛst] *vt* **1** AUTHORIZE : investir, autorizar **2** CONFER : conferir **3** : invertir, dedicar ⟨he invested his savings in stocks : invirtió sus ahorros en acciones⟩ ⟨to invest one's time : dedicar uno su tiempo⟩
investigate [ɪn'vɛstəˌgeɪt] *v* **-gated; -gating** : investigar
investigation [ɪnˌvɛstə'geɪʃən] *n* : investigación *f*, estudio *m*
investigative [ɪn'vɛstəˌgeɪṭɪv] *adj* : investigador
investigator [ɪn'vɛstəˌgeɪṭər] *n* : investigador *m*, -dora *f*
investiture [ɪn'vɛstəˌʧʊr, -ʧər] *n* : investidura *f*
investment [ɪn'vɛstmənt] *n* : inversión *f*
investor [ɪn'vɛstər] *n* : inversor *m*, -sora *f*; inversionista *mf*
inveterate [ɪn'vɛṭərət] *adj* **1** DEEP-SEATED : inveterado, enraizado **2** HABITUAL : empedernido, incorregible
invidious [ɪn'vɪdiəs] *adj* **1** OBNOXIOUS : repugnante, odioso **2** UNJUST : injusto — **invidiously** *adv*
invigorate [ɪn'vɪgəˌreɪt] *vt* **-rated; -rating** : vigorizar, animar
invigorating [ɪn'vɪgəˌreɪṭɪŋ] *adj* : vigorizante, estimulante
invigoration [ɪnˌvɪgə'reɪʃən] *n* : animación *f*
invincibility [ɪnˌvɪnʦə'bɪləṭi] *n* : invencibilidad *f*

invincible [ɪn'vɪntsəbəl] *adj* : invencible — **invincibly** [-bli] *adv*
inviolable [ɪn'vaɪələbəl] *adj* : inviolable
inviolate [ɪn'vaɪələt] *adj* : inviolado, puro
invisibility [ɪn,vɪzə'bɪləti] *n* : invisibilidad *f*
invisible [ɪn'vɪzəbəl] *adj* : invisible — **invisibly** [-bli] *adv*
invitation [,ɪnvə'teɪʃən] *n* : invitación *f*
invite [ɪn'vaɪt] *vt* **-vited; -viting 1** ATTRACT : atraer, tentar ⟨a book that invites interest : un libro que atrae el interés⟩ **2** PROVOKE : provocar, buscar ⟨to invite trouble : buscarse problemas⟩ **3** ASK : invitar ⟨we invited them for dinner : los invitamos acenar⟩ **4** SOLICIT : solicitar, buscar (preguntas, comentarios, etc.)
inviting [ɪn'vaɪtɪŋ] *adj* : atractivo, atrayente
invocation [,ɪnvə'keɪʃən] *n* : invocación *f*
invoice¹ ['ɪn,vɔɪs] *vt* **-voiced; -voicing** : facturar
invoice² *n* : factura *f*
invoke [ɪn'vo:k] *vt* **-voked; -voking 1** : invocar, apelar a ⟨she invoked our aid : apeló a nuestra ayuda⟩ **2** CITE : invocar, citar ⟨to invoke a precedent : invocar un precedente⟩ **3** CONJURE UP : hacer aparecer, invocar
involuntary [ɪn'valən,teri] *adj* : involuntario — **involuntarily** [ɪn-,valən'trəli] *adv*
involve [ɪn'valv] *vt* **-volved; -volving 1** ENGAGE : ocupar (con una tarea, etc.) **2** IMPLICATE : involucrar, enredar, implicar ⟨to be involved in a crime : estar involucrado en un crimen⟩ **3** CONCERN : concernir, afectar **4** CONNECT : conectar, relacionar **5** ENTAIL, INCLUDE : suponer, incluir, consistir en ⟨what does the job involve? : ¿en qué consiste el trabajo?⟩ **6 to be involved with someone** : tener una relación (amorosa) con alguien
involved [ɪn'valvd] *adj* **1** COMPLEX, INTRICATE : complicado, complejo **2** CONCERNED : interesado, afectado
involvement [ɪn'valvmənt] *n* **1** PARTICIPATION : participación *f*, complicidad *f* **2** RELATIONSHIP : relación *f*
invulnerable [ɪn'vʌlnərəbəl] *adj* : invulnerable
inward¹ ['ɪnwərd] *or* **inwards** [-wərdz] *adv* : hacia adentro, hacia el interior
inward² *adj* INSIDE : interior, interno
inwardly ['ɪnwərdli] *adv* **1** MENTALLY, SPIRITUALLY : por dentro **2** INTERNALLY : internamente, interiormente **3** PRIVATELY : para sus adentros, para sí
iodide ['aɪə,daɪd] *n* : yoduro *m*
iodine ['aɪə,daɪn, -dən] *n* : yodo *m*, tintura *f* de yodo
iodize ['aɪə,daɪz] *vt* **-dized; -dizing** : yodar

ion ['aɪən, 'aɪ,an] *n* : ion *m*
ionic [aɪ'anɪk] *adj* : iónico
ionize ['aɪə,naɪz] *v* **ionized; ionizing** : ionizar
ionosphere [aɪ'anə,sfɪr] *n* : ionosfera *f*
iota [aɪ'o:tə] *n* : pizca *f*, ápice *m*
IOU [,aɪ,o'ju:] *n* : pagaré *m*, vale *m*
IPA [,aɪ,pi:'eɪ] *n* International Phonetic Alphabet : AFI *m*
IQ [,aɪ'kju:] *n* (*intelligence quotient*) : CI *m*, coeficiente *m* intelectual
Iranian [ɪ'reɪniən, -'ræ-, -'ra-; aɪ'-] *n* : iraní *mf* — **Iranian** *adj*
Iraqi [ɪ'raki:] *n* : iraquí *mf* — **Iraqi** *adj*
irascibility [ɪ,ræsə'bɪləti] *n* : irascibilidad *f*
irascible [ɪ'ræsəbəl] *adj* : irascible
irate [aɪ'reɪt] *adj* : furioso, airado, iracundo — **irately** *adv*
ire ['aɪr] *n* : ira *f*, cólera *f*
iridescence [,ɪrə'dɛsənts] *n* : iridiscencia *f*
iridescent [,ɪrə'dɛsənt] *adj* : iridiscente
iridium [ɪ'rɪdiəm] *n* : iridio *m*
iris ['aɪrəs] *n*, *pl* **irises** *or* **irides** ['aɪrə,di:z, 'ɪr-] **1** : iris *m* (del ojo) **2** : lirio *m* (planta)
Irish¹ ['aɪrɪʃ] *adj* : irlandés
Irish² **1** : irlandés *m* (idioma) **2 the Irish** *npl* : los irlandeses
Irishman ['aɪrɪʃmən] *n*, *pl* **-men** : irlandés *m*
Irishwoman ['aɪrɪʃ,wʊmən] *n*, *pl* **-women** : irlandesa *f*
irk ['ərk] *vt* : fastidiar, irritar, preocupar
irksome ['ərksəm] *adj* : irritante, fastidioso — **irksomely** *adv*
iron¹ ['aɪərn] *v* : planchar
iron² *n* **1** : hierro *m*, fierro *m* ⟨a will of iron : una voluntad de hierro, una voluntad férrea⟩ **2** : plancha *f* (para planchar la ropa)
ironclad ['aɪərn'klæd] *adj* **1** : acorazado, blindado **2** STRICT : riguroso, estricto
ironic [aɪ'ranɪk] *or* **ironical** [-nɪkəl] *adj* : irónico — **ironically** [-kli] *adv*
ironing ['aɪərnɪŋ] *n* **1** PRESSING : planchada *f* **2** : ropa *f* para planchar
ironing board *n* : tabla *f* (de planchar)
ironwork ['aɪərn,wərk] *n* **1** : obra *f* de hierro **2 ironworks** *npl* : fundición *f*
ironworker ['aɪərn,wərkər] *n* : fundidor *m*, -dora *f*
irony ['aɪrəni] *n*, *pl* **-nies** : ironía *f*
irradiate [ɪ'reɪdi,eɪt] *vt* **-ated; -ating** : irradiar, radiar
irradiation [ɪ,reɪdi'eɪʃən] *n* : irradiación *f*, radiación *f*
irrational [ɪ'ræʃənəl] *adj* : irracional — **irrationally** *adv*
irrationality [ɪ,ræʃə'næləti] *n*, *pl* **-ties** : irracionalidad *f*
irreconcilable [ɪ,rɛkən'saɪləbəl] *adj* : irreconciliable
irrecoverable [,ɪri'kʌvərəbəl] *adj* : irrecuperable — **irrecoverably** [-bli] *adv*

irredeemable [ˌɪrɪ'di:məbəl] *adj* 1 : irredimible (dícese de un bono) 2 HOPELESS : irremediable, irreparable
irreducible [ˌɪrɪ'du:səbəl, -'dju:-] *adj* : irreducible — **irreducibly** [-bli] *adv*
irrefutable [ˌɪrɪ'fju:təbəl, ɪr'rɛfjə-] *adj* : irrefutable
irregular[1] [ɪ'rɛgjələr] *adj* : irregular — **irregularly** *adv*
irregular[2] *n* 1 : soldado *m* irregular 2 **irregulars** *npl* : artículos *mpl* defectuosos
irregularity [ɪˌrɛgjə'lærəṭi] *n, pl* -**ties** : irregularidad *f*
irrelevance [ɪ'rɛləvənts] *n* : irrelevancia *f*
irrelevant [ɪ'rɛləvənt] *adj* : irrelevante
irreligious [ˌɪrɪ'lɪdʒəs] *adj* : irreligioso
irreparable [ɪ'rɛpərəbəl] *adj* : irreparable
irreplaceable [ˌɪrɪ'pleɪsəbəl] *adj* : irreemplazable, insustituible
irrepressible [ˌɪrɪ'prɛsəbəl] *adj* : incontenible, incontrolable
irreproachable [ɪrɪ'pro:tʃəbəl] *adj* : irreprochable, intachable
irresistible [ˌɪrɪ'zɪstəbəl] *adj* : irresistible — **irresistibly** [-bli] *adv*
irresolute [ɪ'rɛzəˌlu:t] *adj* : irresoluto, indeciso
irresolutely [ɪ'rɛzəˌlu:tli, -ˌrzə'lu:t-] *adv* : de manera indecisa
irresolution [ɪˌrɛzə'lu:ʃən] *n* : irresolución *f*
irrespective of [ˌɪrɪ'spɛktɪvəv] *prep* : sin tomar en consideración, sin tener en cuenta
irresponsibility [ˌɪrɪˌspɑntsə'bɪləṭi] *n, pl* -**ties** : irresponsabilidad *f*, falta *f* de responsabilidad
irresponsible [ˌɪrɪ'spɑntsəbəl] *adj* : irresponsable — **irresponsibly** [-bli] *adv*
irretrievable [ˌɪrɪ'tri:vəbəl] *adj* IRRECOVERABLE : irrecuperable
irreverence [ɪ'rɛvərənts] *n* : irreverencia *f*, falta *f* de respeto
irreverent [ɪ'rɛvərənt] *adj* : irreverente, irrespetuoso
irreversible [ˌɪrɪ'vərsəbəl] *adj* : irreversible
irrevocable [ɪ'rɛvəkəbəl] *adj* : irrevocable — **irrevocably** [-bli] *adv*
irrigate ['ɪrəˌgeɪt] *vt* -**gated**; -**gating** : irrigar, regar
irrigation [ˌɪrə'geɪʃən] *n* : irrigación *f*, riego *m*
irritability [ˌɪrəṭə'bɪləṭi] *n, pl* -**ties** : irritabilidad *f*
irritable ['ɪrəṭəbəl] *adj* : irritable, colérico
irritably ['ɪrəṭəbli] *adv* : con irritación
irritant[1] ['ɪrətənt] *adj* : irritante
irritant[2] *n* : agente *m* irritante
irritate ['ɪrəˌteɪt] *vt* -**tated**; -**tating** 1 ANNOY : irritar, molestar 2 : irritar (en medicina)
irritating ['ɪrəˌteɪṭɪŋ] *adj* : irritante
irritatingly ['ɪrəˌteɪṭɪŋli] *adv* : de modo irritante, fastidiosamente

irritation [ˌɪrə'teɪʃən] *n* : irritación *f*
is → **be**
Islam [ɪs'lɑm, ɪz-, -'læm; 'ɪsˌlɑm, 'ɪz-, -ˌlæm] *n* : el Islam
Islamic [ɪs'lɑmɪk, ɪz-, -'læ-] *adj* : islámico
island ['aɪlənd] *n* : isla *f*
islander ['aɪləndər] *n* : isleño *m*, -ña *f*
isle ['aɪl] *n* : isla *f*, islote *m*
islet ['aɪlət] *n* : islote *m*
isolate ['aɪsəˌleɪt] *vt* -**lated**; -**lating** : aislar
isolated ['aɪsəˌleɪṭəd] *adj* : aislado, solo
isolation [ˌaɪsə'leɪʃən] *n* : aislamiento *m*
isometric [ˌaɪsə'mɛtrɪk] *adj* : isométrico
isometrics [ˌaɪsə'mɛtrɪks] *ns & pl* : isometría *f*
isosceles [aɪ'sɑsəˌli:z] *adj* : isósceles
isotope ['aɪsəˌto:p] *n* : isótopo *m*
Israeli [ɪz'reɪli] *n* : israelí *mf* — **Israeli** *adj*
issue[1] ['ɪˌʃu:] *v* -**sued**; -**suing** *vi* 1 EMERGE : emerger, salir, fluir 2 DESCEND : descender (dícese de los padres o antepasados específicos) 3 EMANATE, RESULT : emanar, surgir, resultar — *vt* 1 EMIT : emitir 2 DISTRIBUTE : emitir, distribuir ⟨to issue a new stamp : emitir un sello nuevo⟩ 3 PUBLISH : publicar
issue[2] *n* 1 EMERGENCE, FLOW : emergencia *f*, flujo *m* 2 PROGENY : descendencia *f*, progenie *f* 3 OUTCOME, RESULT : desenlace *m*, resultado *m*, consecuencia *f* 4 MATTER, QUESTION : asunto *m*, cuestión *f* 5 PUBLICATION : publicación *f*, distribución *f*, emisión *f* 6 : número *m* (de un periódico o una revista)
isthmus ['ɪsməs] *n* : istmo *m*
it ['ɪt] *pron* 1 (*as subject; generally omitted*) : él, ella, ello ⟨it's a big building : es un edificio grande⟩ ⟨who was it? : ¿quién era?⟩ 2 (*as indirect object*) : le ⟨I'll give it some water : voy a darle agua⟩ 3 (*as direct object*) : lo, la ⟨give it to me : dámelo⟩ 4 (*as object of a preposition; generally omitted*) : él, ella, ello ⟨behind it : detrás, detrás de él⟩ 5 (*in impersonal constructions*) ⟨it's raining : está lloviendo⟩ ⟨it's 8 o'clock : son las ocho⟩ 6 (*as the implied subject or object of a verb*) ⟨it is necessary to study : es necesario estudiar⟩ ⟨to give it all one's got : dar lo mejor de sí⟩
Italian [ɪ'tæliən, aɪ-] *n* 1 : italiano *m*, -na *f* 2 : italiano *m* (idioma) — **Italian** *adj*
italic[1] [ɪ'tælɪk, aɪ-] *adj* : en cursiva, en bastardilla
italic[2] *n* : cursiva *f*, bastardilla *f*
italicize [ɪ'tæləˌsaɪz, aɪ-] *vt* -**cized**; -**cizing** : poner en cursiva
itch[1] ['ɪtʃ] *vi* 1 : picar ⟨her arm itched : le pica el brazo⟩ 2 : morirse ⟨they were itching to go outside : se morían por salir⟩ — *vt* : dar picazón, hacer picar

itch[2] *n* **1** ITCHING : picazón *f*, picor *m*, comezón *f* **2** RASH : sarpullido *m*, erupción *f* **3** DESIRE : ansia *f*, deseo *m*

itchy ['ɪtʃi] *adj* **itchier; -est** : que pica, que da comezón

it'd ['ɪtəd] (*contraction of* **it had** *or* **it would**) → **have, would**

item ['aɪtəm] *n* **1** OBJECT : artículo *m*, pieza *f* ⟨item of clothing : prenda de vestir⟩ **2** : punto *m* (en una agenda), número *m* (en el teatro), ítem *m* (en un documento) **3 news item** : noticia *f*

itemize ['aɪtə,maɪz] *vt* **-ized; -izing** : detallar, enumerar, listar

itinerant [aɪ'tɪnərənt] *adj* : itinerante, ambulante

itinerary [aɪ'tɪnə,rɛri] *n, pl* **-aries** : itinerario *m*

it'll ['ɪtəl] (*contraction of* **it shall** *or* **it will**) → **shall, will**

its ['ɪts] *adj* : su, sus ⟨its kennel : su perrera⟩ ⟨a city and its inhabitants : una ciudad y sus habitantes⟩

it's ['ɪts] (*contraction of* **it is** *or* **it has**) → **be, have**

itself [ɪt'sɛlf] *pron* **1** (*used reflexively*) : se ⟨the cat gave itself a bath : el gato se bañó⟩ **2** (*used for emphasis*) : (él) mismo, (ella) misma, sí (mismo), solo ⟨he is courtesy itself : es la misma cortesía⟩ ⟨in and of itself : por sí mismo⟩ ⟨it opened by itself : se abrió solo⟩

IUD [,aɪ,ju:'di:] *n* intrauterine device : DIU *m*, dispositivo *m* intrauterino

I've ['aɪv] (*contraction of* **I have**) → **have**

ivory ['aɪvəri] *n, pl* **-ries 1** : marfil *m* **2** : color *m* de marfil

ivy ['aɪvi] *n, pl* **ivies 1** : hiedra *f*, yedra *f* **2** → **poison ivy**

J

j ['dʒeɪ] *n, pl* **j's** *or* **js** ['dʒeɪz] : décima letra del alfabeto inglés

jab[1] ['dʒæb] *v* **jabbed; jabbing** *vt* **1** PUNCTURE : clavar, pinchar **2** POKE : dar, golpear (con la punta de algo) ⟨he jabbed me in the ribs : me dio un codazo en las costillas⟩ — *vi* **to jab at** : dar, golpear

jab[2] *n* **1** PRICK : pinchazo *m* **2** POKE : golpe *m* abrupto

jabber[1] ['dʒæbər] *v* : farfullar

jabber[2] *n* : galimatías *m*, farfulla *f*

jack[1] ['dʒæk] *vt* **to jack up 1** : levantar (con un gato) **2** INCREASE : subir, aumentar

jack[2] *n* **1** : gato *m*, cric *m* ⟨hydraulic jack : gato hidráulico⟩ **2** FLAG : pabellón *m* **3** SOCKET : enchufe *m* hembra **4** : jota *f*, valet *m* ⟨jack of hearts : jota de corazones⟩ **5 jacks** *npl* : cantillos *mpl*

jackal ['dʒækəl] *n* : chacal *m*

jackass ['dʒæk,æs] *n* : asno *m*, burro *m*

jacket ['dʒækət] *n* **1** : chaqueta *f* **2** COVER : sobrecubierta *f* (de un libro), carátula *f* (de un disco)

jackhammer ['dʒæk,hæmər] *n* : martillo *m* neumático

jack-in-the-box ['dʒækɪnðə,baks] *n* : caja *f* de sorpresa

jackknife[1] ['dʒæk,naɪf] *vi* **-knifed; -knifing** : doblarse como una navaja, plegarse

jackknife[2] *n* : navaja *f*

jack-of-all-trades *n* : persona *f* que sabe un poco de todo, persona *f* de muchos oficios

jack-o'-lantern ['dʒækə,læntərn] *n* : linterna *f* hecha de una calabaza

jackpot ['dʒæk,pat] *n* **1** : primer premio *m*, gordo *m* **2 to hit the jackpot** : sacarse la lotería, sacarse el gordo

jackrabbit ['dʒæk,ræbət] *n* : liebre *f* grande de Norteamérica

jade ['dʒeɪd] *n* : jade *m*

jaded ['dʒeɪdəd] *adj* **1** TIRED : agotado **2** BORED : hastiado

jagged ['dʒægəd] *adj* : dentado, mellado

jaguar ['dʒæg,war, 'dʒægju,war] *n* : jaguar *m*

jai alai ['haɪ,laɪ] *n* : jai alai *m*, pelota *f* vasca

jail[1] ['dʒeɪl] *vt* : encarcelar

jail[2] *n* : cárcel *f*

jailbreak ['dʒeɪl,breɪk] *n* : fuga *f*, huida *f* (de la cárcel)

jailer *or* **jailor** ['dʒeɪlər] *n* : carcelero *m*, -ra *f*

jalapeño [,halə'peɪnjo, ,hæ-, -'pi:no] *n* : jalapeño *m*

jalopy [dʒə'lapi] *n, pl* **-lopies** : cacharro *m fam*, carro *m* destartalado

jalousie ['dʒæləsi] *n* : celosía *f*

jam[1] ['dʒæm] *v* **jammed; jamming** *vt* **1** CRAM : apiñar, embutir **2** BLOCK : atascar, atorar **3 to jam on the brakes** : frenar en seco — *vi* STICK : atascarse, atrancarse

jam[2] *n* **1** *or* **traffic jam** : atasco *m*, embotellamiento *m* (de tráfico) **2** PREDICAMENT : lío *m*, aprieto *m*, apuro *m* **3** : mermelada *f* ⟨strawberry jam : mermelada de fresa⟩

Jamaican [dʒə'meɪkən] *n* : jamaiquino *m*, -na *f*; jamaicano *m*, -na *f* — **Jamaican** *adj*

jamb ['dʒæm] *n* : jamba *f*

jamboree [,dʒæmbə'ri:] *n* : fiesta *f* grande

jangle[1] ['dʒæŋgəl] *v* **-gled; -gling** *vi* : hacer un ruido metálico — *vt* **1** : hacer sonar **2 to jangle one's nerves** : irritar, crispar

jangle[2] *n* : ruido *m* metálico

janitor ['dʒænətər] *n* : portero *m*, -ra *f*; conserje *mf*

January ['dʒænju,ɛri] *n* : enero *m*

Japanese [,dʒæpə'ni:z, -'ni:s] *n* **1**

: japonés *m*, -nesa *f* **2** : japonés *m* (idioma) — **Japanese** *adj*
jar¹ ['ʤɑr] *v* **jarred; jarring** *vi* **1** GRATE : chirriar **2** CLASH : desentonar **3** SHAKE : sacudirse **4 to jar on** : crispar, enervar — *vt* JOLT : sacudir
jar² *n* **1** GRATING : chirrido *m* **2** JOLT : vibración *f*, sacudida *f* **3** : tarro *m*, bote *m*, pote *m* ⟨a jar of honey : un tarro de miel⟩
jargon ['ʤɑrgən] *n* : jerga *f*
jasmine ['ʤæzmən] *n* : jazmín *m*
jasper ['ʤæspər] *n* : jaspe *m*
jaundice ['ʤɔndɪs] *n* : ictericia *f*
jaundiced ['ʤɔndɪst] *adj* **1** : ictérico **2** EMBITTERED, RESENTFUL : amargado, resentido, negativo ⟨with a jaundiced eye : con una actitud de cinismo⟩
jaunt ['ʤɔnt] *n* : excursión *f*, paseo *m*
jauntily ['ʤɔntəli] *adv* : animadamente
jauntiness ['ʤɔntinəs] *n* : animación *f*, vivacidad *f*
jaunty ['ʤɔnti] *adj* **-tier; -est** **1** SPRIGHTLY : animado, alegre **2** RAKISH : desenvuelto, desenfadado
Javanese [ˌʤævə'ni:z, ˌʤɑ-, -'ni:s] *n* **1** : javanés *m* (idioma) **2** : javanés *m*, -nesa *f* — **Javanese** *adj*
javelin ['ʤævələn] *n* : jabalina *f*
jaw¹ ['ʤɔ] *vi* GAB : cotorrear *fam*, parlotear *fam*
jaw² *n* **1** : mandíbula *f*, quijada *f* **2** : mordaza *f* (de una herramienta) **3 the jaws of death** : las garras *f* de la muerte
jawbone ['ʤɔˌbo:n] *n* : mandíbula *f*
jay ['ʤeɪ] *n* : arrendajo *m*, chara *f* *Mex*, azulejo *m* *Mex*
jaybird ['ʤeɪˌbərd] → **jay**
jaywalk ['ʤeɪˌwɔk] *vi* : cruzar la calle sin prudencia
jaywalker ['ʤeɪˌwɔkər] *n* : peatón *m* imprudente
jazz¹ ['ʤæz] *vt* **to jazz up** : animar, alegrar
jazz² *n* : jazz *m*
jazzy ['ʤæzi] *adj* **jazzier; -est** **1** : con ritmo de jazz **2** FLASHY, SHOWY : llamativo, ostentoso
jealous ['ʤɛləs] *adj* : celoso, envidioso — **jealously** *adv*
jealousy ['ʤɛləsi] *n* : celos *mpl*, envidia *f*
jeans ['ʤi:nz] *npl* : jeans *mpl*, vaqueros *mpl*
jeep ['ʤi:p] *n* : jeep *m*
jeer¹ ['ʤɪr] *vi* **1** BOO : abuchear **2** SCOFF : mofarse, burlarse — *vt* RIDICULE : mofarse de, burlarse de
jeer² *n* **1** : abucheo *m* **2** TAUNT : mofa *f*, burla *f*
Jehovah [ʤɪ'ho:və] *n* : Jehová *m*
jell ['ʤɛl] *vi* **1** SET : gelificarse, cuajar **2** FORM : cuajar, formarse (una idea, etc.)
jelly¹ ['ʤɛli] *v* **jellied; jellying** *vi* **1** JELL : gelificarse, cuajar **2** : hacer jalea — *vt* : gelificar
jelly² *n*, *pl* **-lies** **1** : jalea *f* **2** GELATIN : gelatina *f*

jellyfish ['ʤɛliˌfɪʃ] *n* : medusa *f*
jeopardize ['ʤɛpərˌdaɪz] *vt* **-dized; -dizing** : arriesgar, poner en peligro
jeopardy ['ʤɛpərdi] *n* : peligro *m*, riesgo *m*
jerk¹ ['ʤərk] *vt* **1** JOLT : sacudir **2** TUG, YANK : darle un tirón a — *vi* JOLT : dar sacudidas ⟨the train jerked along : el tren iba moviéndose a sacudidas⟩
jerk² *n* **1** TUG : tirón *m*, jalón *m* **2** JOLT : sacudida *f* brusca **3** FOOL : estúpido *m*, -da *f*; idiota *mf*
jerkin ['ʤərkən] *n* : chaqueta *f* sin mangas, chaleco *m*
jerky ['ʤərki] *adj* **jerkier; -est** **1** : espasmódico (dícese de los movimientos) **2** CHOPPY : inconexo (dícese de la prosa) — **jerkily** [-kəli] *adv*
jerry–built ['ʤɛriˌbɪlt] *adj* : mal construido, chapucero
jersey ['ʤərzi] *n*, *pl* **-seys** : jersey *m*
jest¹ ['ʤɛst] *vi* : bromear
jest² *n* **1** : broma *f*, chiste *m*
jester ['ʤɛstər] *n* : bufón *m*, -fona *f*
Jesuit ['ʤɛzuət] *n* : jesuita *m* — **Jesuit** *adj*
Jesus ['ʤi:zəs, -zəz] *n* **1** : Jesús *m* **2 Jesus Christ** : Jesucristo *m* **3 Jesus (Christ)!** *fam* : ¡por Dios!
jet¹ ['ʤɛt] *v* **jetted; jetting** *vt* SPOUT : arrojar a chorros — *vi* **1** GUSH : salir a chorros, chorrear **2** FLY : viajar en avión, volar
jet² *n* **1** STREAM : chorro *m* **2** *or* **jet airplane** : avión *m* a reacción, reactor *m* **3** : azabache *m* (mineral) **4 jet engine** : reactor *m*, motor *m* a reacción **5 jet lag** : desajuste *m* de horario (debido a un vuelo largo)
jet–propelled *adj* : a reacción
jetsam ['ʤɛtsəm] *n* **flotsam and jetsam** : restos *mpl*, desechos *mpl*
jettison ['ʤɛtəsən] *vt* **1** : echar al mar **2** DISCARD : desechar, deshacerse de
jetty ['ʤɛti] *n*, *pl* **-ties** **1** PIER, WHARF : desembarcadero *m*, muelle *m* **2** BREAKWATER : malecón *m*, rompeolas *m*
Jew ['ʤu:] *n* : judío *m*, -día *f*
jewel ['ʤu:əl] *n* **1** : joya *f*, alhaja *f* **2** GEM : piedra *f* preciosa, gema *f* **3** : rubí *m* (de un reloj) **4** TREASURE : joya *f*, tesoro *m*
jeweler *or* **jeweller** ['ʤu:ələr] *n* : joyero *m*, -ra *f*
jewelry ['ʤu:əlri] *n* : joyas *fpl*, alhajas *fpl*
Jewish ['ʤu:ɪʃ] *adj* : judío
jib ['ʤɪb] *n* : foque *m* (de un barco)
jibe ['ʤaɪb] *vi* **jibed; jibing** AGREE : concordar
jiffy ['ʤɪfi] *n*, *pl* **-fies** : santiamén *m*, segundo *m*, momento *m*
jig¹ ['ʤɪg] *vi* **jigged; jigging** : bailar la giga
jig² *n* **1** : giga *f* **2 the jig is up** : se acabó la fiesta
jigger ['ʤɪgər] *n* : medida de 1 a 2 onzas (para licores)

jiggle¹ ['ʤɪgəl] *v* **-gled; -gling** *vt* : agitar o sacudir ligeramente — *vi* : agitarse, vibrar

jiggle² *n* : sacudida *f*, vibración *f*

jigsaw ['ʤɪg,sɔ] *n* **1** : sierra *f* de vaivén **2 jigsaw puzzle** : rompecabezas *m*

jilt ['ʤɪlt] *vt* : dejar plantado, dar calabazas a

jimmy¹ ['ʤɪmi] *vt* **-mied; -mying** : forzar con una palanqueta

jimmy² *n, pl* **-mies** : palanqueta *f*

jingle¹ ['ʤɪŋgəl] *v* **-gled; -gling** *vi* : tintinear — *vt* : hacer sonar

jingle² *n* **1** TINKLE : tintineo *m*, retintín *m* **2** : canción *f* rimada

jingoism ['ʤɪŋgo,ɪzəm] *n* : jingoísmo *m*, patriotería *f*

jingoistic [,ʤɪŋgo'ɪstɪk] *or* **jingoist** ['ʤɪŋgoɪst] *adj* : jingoísta, patriotero

jinx¹ ['ʤɪŋks] *vt* : traer mala suerte a, salar *CoRi, Mex*

jinx² *n* **1** : cenizo *m*, -za *f* **2 to put a jinx on** : echarle el mal de ojo a

jitters ['ʤɪt̬ərz] *npl* : nervios *mpl* ⟨he got the jitters : se puso nervioso⟩

jittery ['ʤɪt̬əri] *adj* : nervioso

job ['ʤab] *n* **1** : trabajo *m* ⟨he did odd jobs for her : le hizo algunos trabajos⟩ **2** CHORE, TASK : tarea *f*, quehacer *m* **3** EMPLOYMENT : trabajo *m*, empleo *m*, puesto *m*

jobber ['ʤabər] *n* MIDDLEMAN : intermediario *m*, -ria *f*

jock ['ʤak] *n* : deportista *mf*, atleta *mf*

jockey¹ ['ʤaki] *v* **-eyed; -eying** *vt* **1** MANIPULATE : manipular **2** MANEUVER : maniobrar — *vi* **to jockey for position** : maniobrar para conseguir algo

jockey² *n, pl* **-eys** : jockey *mf*

jocose [ʤo'koːs] *adj* : jocoso

jocular ['ʤakjulər] *adj* : jocoso — **jocularly** *adv*

jocularity [,ʤakju'lærət̬i] *n* : jocosidad *f*

jodhpurs ['ʤadpərz] *npl* : pantalones *mpl* de montar

jog¹ ['ʤag] *v* **jogged; jogging** *vt* **1** NUDGE : dar, empujar, codear **2 to jog one's memory** : refrescar la memoria — *vi* **1** RUN : correr despacio, trotar, hacer footing (como ejercicio) **2** TRUDGE : andar a trote corto

jog² *n* **1** PUSH, SHAKE : empujoncito *m*, sacudida *f* leve **2** TROT : trote *m* corto, footing *m* (en deportes) **3** TWIST : recodo *m*, vuelta *f*, curva *f*

jogger ['ʤagər] *n* : persona *f* que hace footing

join ['ʤɔɪn] *vt* **1** CONNECT, LINK : unir, juntar ⟨to join in marriage : unir en matrimonio⟩ **2** ADJOIN : lindar con, colindar con **3** MEET : reunirse con, encontrarse con ⟨we joined them for lunch : nos reunimos con ellos para almorzar⟩ **4** : hacerse socio de (una organización), afiliarse a (un partido), entrar en (una empresa) — *vi* **1** UNITE : unirse **2** MERGE : empalmar (dícese de las carreteras), confluir (dícese de

los ríos) **3 to join up** : hacerse socio, enrolarse

joiner ['ʤɔɪnər] *n* **1** CARPENTER : carpintero *m*, -ra *f* **2** : persona *f* que se une a varios grupos

joint¹ ['ʤɔɪnt] *adj* : conjunto, colectivo, mutuo ⟨a joint effort : un esfuerzo conjunto⟩ — **jointly** *adv*

joint² *n* **1** : articulación *f*, coyuntura *f* ⟨out of joint : dislocado⟩ **2** ROAST : asado *m* **3** JUNCTURE : juntura *f*, unión *f* **4** DIVE : antro *m*, tasca *f*

joist ['ʤɔɪst] *n* : viga *f*

joke¹ ['ʤoːk] *vi* **joked; joking** : bromear

joke² *n* **1** STORY : chiste *m* **2** PRANK : broma *f*

joker ['ʤoːkər] *n* **1** PRANKSTER : bromista *mf* **2** : comodín *m* (en los naipes)

jokingly ['ʤoːkɪŋli] *adv* : en broma

jollity ['ʤaləti] *n, pl* **-ties** MERRIMENT : alegría *f*, regocijo *m*

jolly ['ʤali] *adj* **-lier; -est** : alegre, jovial

jolt¹ ['ʤoːlt] *vi* JERK : dar tumbos, dar sacudidas — *vt* : sacudir

jolt² *n* **1** JERK : sacudida *f* brusca **2** SHOCK : golpe *m* (emocional)

jonquil ['ʤankwɪl] *n* : junquillo *m*

Jordanian [ʤɔr'deɪniən] *n* : jordano *m*, -na *f* — **Jordanian** *adj*

josh ['ʤaʃ] *vt* TEASE : tomarle el pelo (a alguien) — *vi* JOKE : bromear

jostle ['ʤasəl] *v* **-tled; -tling** *vi* **1** SHOVE : empujar, dar empellones **2** CONTEND : competir — *vt* **1** SHOVE : empujar **2 to jostle one's way** : abrirse paso a empellones

jot¹ ['ʤat] *vt* **jotted; jotting** : anotar, apuntar ⟨jot it down : apúntalo⟩

jot² *n* BIT : ápice *m*, jota *f*, pizca *f*

jounce¹ ['ʤæʊnts] *v* **jounced; jouncing** *vt* JOLT : sacudir — *vi* : dar tumbos, dar sacudidas

jounce² *n* JOLT : sacudida *f*, tumbo *m*

journal ['ʤərnəl] *n* **1** DIARY : diario *m* **2** PERIODICAL : revista *f*, publicación *f* periódica **3** NEWSPAPER : periódico *m*, diario *m*

journalism ['ʤərnəl,ɪzəm] *n* : periodismo *m*

journalist ['ʤərnəlɪst] *n* : periodista *mf*

journalistic [,ʤərnəl'ɪstɪk] *adj* : periodístico

journey¹ ['ʤərni] *vi* **-neyed; -neying** : viajar

journey² *n, pl* **-neys** : viaje *m*

journeyman ['ʤərnimən] *n, pl* **-men** [-mən, -,mn] : oficial *m*

joust¹ ['ʤaʊst] *vi* : justar

joust² *n* : justa *f*

jovial ['ʤoːviəl] *adj* : jovial — **jovially** *adv*

joviality [,ʤoːvi'æləti] *n* : jovialidad *f*

jowl ['ʤæʊl] *n* **1** JAW : mandíbula *f* **2** CHEEK : mejilla *f*, cachete *m*

joy ['ʤɔɪ] *n* **1** HAPPINESS : gozo *m*, alegría *f*, felicidad *f* **2** DELIGHT : placer *m*, deleite *m* ⟨the child is a real joy : el niño es un verdadero placer⟩

joyful ['dʒɔɪfəl] adj : gozoso, alegre, feliz — **joyfully** adv

joyless ['dʒɔɪləs] adj : sin alegría, triste

joyous ['dʒɔɪəs] adj : alegre, feliz, eufórico — **joyously** adv

joyousness ['dʒɔɪəsnəs] n : alegría f, felicidad f, euforia f

joyride ['dʒɔɪ,raɪd] n : paseo m temerario e irresponsable (en coche)

joystick ['dʒɔɪ,stɪk] n : joystick m

jubilant ['dʒu:bələnt] adj : jubiloso, alborozado — **jubilantly** adv

jubilation [,dʒu:bə'leɪʃən] n : júbilo m

jubilee ['dʒu:bə,li:] n 1 : quincuagésimo aniversario m 2 CELEBRATION : celebración f, festejos mpl

Judaic [dʒʊ'deɪk] adj : judaico

Judaism ['dʒu:də,ɪzəm, 'dʒu:di-, 'dʒu:-,deɪ-] n : judaísmo m

judge¹ ['dʒʌdʒ] vt **judged; judging** 1 ASSESS : evaluar, juzgar 2 DEEM : juzgar, considerar 3 TRY : juzgar (ante el tribunal) 4 **judging by** : a juzgar por

judge² n 1 : juez mf, jueza f 2 **to be a good judge of** : saber juzgar a, entender mucho de

judgment or **judgement** ['dʒʌdʒ-mənt] n 1 RULING : fallo m, sentencia f 2 OPINION : opinión f 3 DISCERNMENT : juicio m, discernimiento m

judgmental [,dʒʌdʒ'mntəl] adj : crítico — **judgmentally** adv

judicature ['dʒu:dɪkə,tʃʊr] n : judicatura f

judicial [dʒʊ'dɪʃəl] adj : judicial — **judicially** adv

judiciary¹ [dʒʊ'dɪʃi,ri, -'dɪʃəri] adj : judicial

judiciary² n 1 JUDICATURE : judicatura f 2 : poder m judicial

judicious [dʒʊ'dɪʃəs] adj SOUND, WISE : juicioso, sensato — **judiciously** adv

judo ['dʒu:,do:] n : judo m

jug ['dʒʌg] n 1 : jarra f, jarro m, cántaro m 2 JAIL : cárcel f, chirona f fam

juggernaut ['dʒʌgər,nɔt] n : gigante m, fuerza f irresistible ⟨a political juggernaut : un gigante político⟩

juggle ['dʒʌgəl] v **-gled; -gling** vt 1 : hacer juegos malabares con 2 MANIPULATE : manipular, jugar con — vi : hacer juegos malabares

juggler ['dʒʌgələr] n : malabarista mf

jugular ['dʒʌgjʊlər] adj : yugular ⟨jugular vein : vena yugular⟩

juice ['dʒu:s] n 1 : jugo m (de carne, de frutas) m, zumo m (de frutas) 2 ELECTRICITY : electricidad f, luz f

juicer ['dʒu:sər] n : exprimidor m

juiciness ['dʒu:sinəs] n : jugosidad f

juicy ['dʒu:si] adj **juicier; -est** 1 SUCCULENT : jugoso, suculento 2 PROFITABLE : jugoso, lucrativo 3 RACY : picante

jukebox ['dʒu:k,bɑks] n : rocola f, máquina f de discos

julep ['dʒu:ləp] n : bebida f hecha con whisky americano y menta

July [dʒʊ'laɪ] n : julio m

jumble¹ ['dʒʌmbəl] vt **-bled; -bling** : mezclar, revolver

jumble² n : revoltijo m, fárrago m, embrollo m

jumbo¹ ['dʒʌm,bo:] adj : gigante, enorme, de tamaño extra grande

jumbo² n, pl **-bos** : coloso m, cosa f de tamaño extra grande

jump¹ ['dʒʌmp] vi 1 LEAP : saltar, brincar 2 START : levantarse de un salto, sobresaltarse 3 MOVE, SHIFT : moverse, pasar ⟨to jump from job to job : pasar de un empleo a otro⟩ 4 INCREASE, RISE : dar un salto, aumentarse de golpe, subir bruscamente 5 BUSTLE : animarse, ajetrearse 6 **to jump to conclusions** : sacar conclusiones precipitadas — vt 1 : saltar ⟨to jump a fence : saltar una valla⟩ 2 SKIP : saltarse 3 ATTACK : atacar, asaltar 4 **to jump the gun** : precipitarse

jump² n 1 LEAP : salto m 2 START : sobresalto m, respingo m 3 INCREASE : subida f brusca, aumento m 4 ADVANTAGE : ventaja f ⟨we got the jump on them : les llevamos la ventaja⟩

jumper ['dʒʌmpər] n 1 : saltador m, -dora f (en deportes) 2 : jumper m, vestido m sin mangas

jumpy ['dʒʌmpi] adj **jumpier; -est** : asustadizo, nervioso

junction ['dʒʌŋkʃən] n 1 JOINING : unión f 2 : cruce m (de calles), empalme m (de un ferrocarril), confluencia f (de ríos)

juncture ['dʒʌŋktʃər] n 1 UNION : juntura f, unión f 2 MOMENT, POINT : coyuntura f ⟨at this juncture : en esta coyuntura, en este momento⟩

June ['dʒu:n] n : junio m

jungle ['dʒʌŋgəl] n : jungla f, selva f

junior¹ ['dʒu:njər] adj 1 YOUNGER : más joven ⟨John Smith, Junior : John Smith, hijo⟩ 2 SUBORDINATE : subordinado, subalterno

junior² n 1 : persona f de menor edad ⟨she's my junior : es menor que yo⟩ 2 SUBORDINATE : subalterno m, -na f; subordinado m, -da f 3 : estudiante mf de penúltimo año

juniper ['dʒu:nəpər] n : enebro m

junk¹ ['dʒʌŋk] vt : echar a la basura

junk² n 1 RUBBISH : desechos mpl, desperdicios mpl 2 STUFF : trastos mpl fam, cachivaches mpl fam 3 **piece of junk** : cacharro m, porquería f

junket ['dʒʌŋkət] n : viaje m (pagado con dinero público)

junta ['hʊntə, 'dʒʌn-, 'hʌn-] n : junta f militar

Jupiter ['dʒu:pətər] n : Júpiter m

jurisdiction [,dʒʊrəs'dɪkʃən] n : jurisdicción f

jurisprudence [,dʒʊrəs'pru:dənts] n : jurisprudencia f

jurist ['dʒʊrɪst] n : jurista mf; magistrado m, -da f

juror [ˈdʒurər] n : jurado m, -da f
jury[1] [ˈdʒuri] n, pl **-ries** : jurado m
just[1] [ˈdʒʌst] adv 1 EXACTLY : justo, precisamente, exactamente 2 POSSIBLY : posiblemente ⟨it just might work : tal vez resulte⟩ 3 BARELY : justo, apenas ⟨just in time : justo a tiempo⟩ 4 ONLY : sólo, solamente, nada más ⟨just us : sólo nosotros⟩ 5 QUITE : muy, simplemente ⟨it's just horrible! : ¡qué horrible!⟩ 6 **to have just (done something)** : acabar de (hacer algo) ⟨he just called : acaba de llamar⟩
just[2] adj : justo — **justly** adv
justice [ˈdʒʌstɪs] n 1 : justicia f 2 JUDGE : juez mf, jueza f

justification [ˌdʒʌstəfəˈkeɪʃən] n : justificación f
justify [ˈdʒʌstəˌfaɪ] vt **-fied; -fying** : justificar — **justifiable** [ˌdʒʌstəˈfaɪəbəl] adj
jut [ˈdʒʌt] vi **jutted; jutting** : sobresalir
jute [ˈdʒuːt] n : yute m
juvenile[1] [ˈdʒuːvəˌnaɪl, -vənəl] adj 1 : juvenil ⟨juvenile delincuent : delincuente juvenil⟩ ⟨juvenile court : tribunal de menores⟩ 2 CHILDISH : infantil
juvenile[2] n : menor mf
juxtapose [ˈdʒʌkstəˌpoːz] vt **-posed; -posing** : yuxtaponer
juxtaposition [ˌdʒʌkstəpəˈzɪʃən] n : yuxtaposición f

K

k [ˈkeɪ] n, pl **k's** or **ks** [ˈkeɪz] : undécima letra del alfabeto inglés
kaiser [ˈkaɪzər] n : káiser m
kale [ˈkeɪl] n : col f rizada
kaleidoscope [kəˈlaɪdəˌskoːp] n : calidoscopio m
kamikaze [ˌkɑmɪˈkɑzi] n : kamikaze m — **kamikaze** adj
kangaroo [ˌkæŋgəˈruː] n, pl **-roos** : canguro m
kaolin [ˈkeɪələn] n : caolín m
karaoke [ˌkæriˈoːki] n : karaoke m
karat [ˈkærət] n : quilate m
karate [kəˈrɑti] n : karate m
katydid [ˈkeɪtiˌdɪd] n : saltamontes m
kayak [ˈkaɪˌæk] n : kayac m, kayak m
keel[1] [ˈkiːl] vi **to keel over** : volcar (dícese de un barco), desplomarse (dícese de una persona)
keel[2] n : quilla f
keen [ˈkiːn] adj 1 SHARP : afilado, filoso ⟨a keen blade : una hoja afilada⟩ 2 PENETRATING : cortante, penetrante ⟨a keen wind : un viento cortante⟩ 3 ENTHUSIASTIC : entusiasta 4 ACUTE : agudo, fino ⟨keen hearing : oído fino⟩ ⟨keen intelligence : inteligencia aguda⟩
keenly [ˈkiːnli] adv 1 ENTHUSIASTICALLY : con entusiasmo 2 INTENSELY : vivamente, profundamente ⟨keenly aware of : muy consciente de⟩
keenness [ˈkiːnnəs] n 1 SHARPNESS : lo afilado, lo filoso 2 ENTHUSIASM : entusiasmo m 3 ACUTENESS : agudeza f
keep[1] [ˈkiːp] v **kept** [ˈkɛpt]; **keeping** vt 1 : cumplir (la palabra a uno), acudir a (una cita) 2 OBSERVE : observar (una fiesta) 3 GUARD : guardar, cuidar 4 CONTINUE : mantener ⟨to keep silence : mantener silencio⟩ 5 SUPPORT : mantener (una familia) 6 RAISE : criar (animales) 7 : llevar, escribir (un diario, etc.) 8 RETAIN : guardar, conservar, quedarse con 9 STORE : guardar 10 DETAIN : hacer quedar, detener 11 PRESERVE : guardar ⟨to keep a secret : guardar un secreto⟩ — vi 1 : conser-

varse (dícese de los alimentos) 2 CONTINUE : seguir, no dejar ⟨he keeps on pestering us : no deja de molestarnos⟩ 3 **to keep from** : abstenerse de ⟨I couldn't keep from laughing : no podía contener la risa⟩
keep[2] n 1 TOWER : torreón m (de un castillo), torre f del homenaje 2 SUSTENANCE : manutención f, sustento m 3 **for keeps** : para siempre
keeper [ˈkiːpər] n 1 : guarda mf (en un zoológico); conservador m, -dora f (en un museo) 2 GAMEKEEPER : guardabosque mf
keeping [ˈkiːpɪŋ] n 1 CONFORMITY : conformidad f, acuerdo m ⟨in keeping with : de acuerdo con⟩ 2 CARE : cuidado m ⟨in the keeping of : al cuidado de⟩
keepsake [ˈkiːpˌseɪk] n : recuerdo m
keep up vt CONTINUE, MAINTAIN : mantener, seguir con — vi 1 : mantenerse al corriente ⟨he kept up with the news : se mantenía al tanto de las noticias⟩ 2 CONTINUE : continuar 3 **to keep up with someone** : mantener contacto con alguien
keg [ˈkɛg] n : barril m
kelp [ˈkɛlp] n : alga f marina
ken [ˈkɛn] n 1 SIGHT : vista f, alcance m de la vista 2 UNDERSTANDING : comprensión f, alcance m del conocimiento ⟨it's beyond his ken : no lo puede entender⟩
kennel [ˈkɛnəl] n : caseta f para perros, perrera f
Kenyan [ˈkɛnjən, ˈkiːn-] n : keniano m, -na f — **Kenyan** adj
kept → **keep**
kerchief [ˈkərtʃəf, -ˌtʃiːf] n : pañuelo m
kernel [ˈkərnəl] n 1 : almendra f (de semillas y nueces) 2 : grano m (de cereales) 3 CORE : meollo m ⟨a kernel of truth : un fondo de verdad⟩
kerosene or **kerosine** [ˈkɛrəˌsiːn, ˌkɛrəˈ-] n : queroseno m, kerosén m, kerosene m

ketchup ['kɛtʃəp, 'kæ-] *n* : salsa *f* catsup
kettle ['kɛtəl] *n* **1** : hervidor *m*, pava *f* *Arg, Bol, Chile* **2** → teakettle
kettledrum ['kɛtəl₁drʌm] *n* : timbal *m*
key¹ ['ki:] *vt* **1** ATTUNE : adaptar, adecuar **2 to key up** : poner nervioso, inquietar
key² *adj* : clave, fundamental
key³ *n* **1** : llave *f* **2** SOLUTION : clave *f*, soluciones *fpl* **3** : tecla *f* (de un piano o una máquina) **4** : tono *m*, tonalidad *f* (en la música) **5** ISLET, REEF : cayo *m*, islote *m*
keyboard ['ki:₁bord] *n* : teclado *m*
keyhole ['ki:₁ho:l] *n* : bocallave *f*, ojo *m* (de una cerradura)
keynote¹ ['ki:₁no:t] *vt* -**noted; -noting 1** : establecer la tónica de (en música) **2** : pronunciar el discurso principal de
keynote² *n* **1** : tónica *f* (en música) **2** : idea *f* fundamental
keystone ['ki:₁sto:n] *n* : clave *f*, dovela *f*
keystroke ['ki:₁stro:k] *n* : pulsación *f* (de tecla)
khaki ['kæki, 'kɑ-] *n* : caqui *m*
khan ['kɑn, 'kæn] *n* : kan *m*
kibbutz [kə'bʊts, -'bu:ts] *n, pl* -**butzim** [-₁bʊt'si:m, -₁bu:t-] : kibutz *m*
kibitz ['kɪbɪts] *vi* : dar consejos molestos
kibitzer ['kɪbɪtsər, kɪ'bɪt-] *n* : persona *f* que da consejos molestos
kick¹ ['kɪk] *vi* **1** : dar patadas (dícese de una persona), cocear (dícese de un animal) **2** PROTEST : patalear, protestar **3** RECOIL : dar un culatazo (dícese de un arma de fuego) — *vt* : patear, darle una patada (a alguien)
kick² *n* **1** : patada *f*, puntapié *m*, coz *f* (de un animal) **2** RECOIL : culatazo *m* (de un arma de fuego) **3** : fuerza *f* ⟨a drink with a kick : una bebida fuerte⟩
kicker ['kɪkər] *n* : pateador *m*, -dora *f* (en deportes)
kickoff ['kɪk₁ɔf] *n* : saque *m* (inicial)
kick off *vi* **1** : hacer el saque inicial (en deportes) **2** BEGIN : empezar — *vt* : empezar
kid¹ ['kɪd] *v* **kidded; kidding** *vt* **1** FOOL : engañar **2** TEASE : tomarle el pelo (a alguien) — *vi* JOKE : bromear ⟨I'm only kidding : lo digo en broma⟩
kid² *n* **1** : chivo *m*, -va *f*; cabrito *m*, -ta *f* **2** CHILD : chico *m*, -ca *f*; niño *m*, -ña *f*
kidder ['kɪdər] *n* : bromista *mf*
kiddingly ['kɪdɪŋli] *adv* : en broma
kidnap ['kɪd₁næp] *vt* -**napped** *or* -**naped** [-₁næpt]; -**napping** *or* -**naping** [-₁næpɪŋ] : secuestrar, raptar
kidnapper *or* **kidnaper** ['kɪd₁næpər] *n* : secuestrador *m*, -dora *f*; raptor *m*, -tora *f*
kidnapping ['kɪd₁næpɪŋ] *n* : secuestro *m*
kidney ['kɪdni] *n, pl* -**neys** : riñón *m*
kidney bean *n* : frijol *m*
kill¹ ['kɪl] *vt* **1** : matar **2** END : acabar con, poner fin a **3 to kill time** : matar el tiempo

kill² *n* **1** KILLING : matanza *f* **2** PREY : presa *f*
killer ['kɪlər] *n* : asesino *m*, -na *f*
killjoy ['kɪl₁dʒɔɪ] *n* : aguafiestas *mf*
kiln ['kɪl, 'kɪln] *n* : horno *m*
kilo ['ki:₁lo:] *n, pl* -**los** : kilo *m*
kilobyte ['kɪlə₁baɪt] *n* : kilobyte *m*
kilocycle ['kɪlə₁saɪkəl] *n* : kilociclo *m*
kilogram ['kɪlə₁græm, 'ki:-] *n* : kilogramo *m*
kilohertz ['kɪlə₁hərts] *n* : kilohertzio *m*
kilometer [kɪ'lɑmətər, 'kɪlə₁mi:-] *n* : kilómetro *m*
kilowatt ['kɪlə₁wɑt] *n* : kilovatio *m*
kilt ['kɪlt] *n* : falda *f* escocesa
kilter ['kɪltər] *n* **1** ORDER : buen estado *m* **2 out of kilter** : descompuesto, estropeado
kimono [kə'mo:no, -nə] *n, pl* -**nos** : kimono *m*, quimono *m*
kin ['kɪn] *n* : familiares *mpl*, parientes *mpl*
kind¹ ['kaɪnd] *adj* : amable, bondadoso, benévolo
kind² *n* **1** ESSENCE : esencia *f* ⟨a difference in degree, not in kind : una diferencia cuantitativa y no cualitativa⟩ **2** CATEGORY : especie *f*, género *m* **3** TYPE : clase *f*, tipo *m*, índole *f*
kindergarten ['kɪndər₁gɑrtən, -dən] *n* : kinder *m*, kindergarten *m*, jardín *m* de infantes, jardín *m* de niños *Mex*
kindhearted [₁kaɪnd'hɑrtəd] *adj* : bondadoso, de buen corazón
kindle ['kɪndəl] *v* -**dled; -dling** *vt* **1** IGNITE : encender **2** AROUSE : despertar, suscitar — *vi* : encenderse
kindliness ['kaɪndlinəs] *n* : bondad *f*
kindling ['kɪndlɪŋ, 'kɪndlən] *n* : astillas *fpl*, leña *f*
kindly¹ ['kaɪndli] *adv* **1** AMIABLY : amablemente, bondadosamente **2** COURTEOUSLY : cortésmente, con cortesía ⟨we kindly ask you not smoke : les rogamos que no fumen⟩ **3** PLEASE : por favor **4 to take kindly to** : aceptar de buena gana
kindly² *adj* -**lier; -est** : bondadoso, amable
kindness ['kaɪndnəs] *n* : bondad *f*
kind of *adv* SOMEWHAT : un tanto, algo
kindred¹ ['kɪndrəd] *adj* SIMILAR : similar, afín ⟨kindred spirits : almas gemelas⟩
kindred² *n* **1** FAMILY : familia *f*, parentela *f* **2** → kin
kinfolk ['kɪn₁fo:k] *or* **kinfolks** [-₁fo:ks] *npl* → kin
king ['kɪŋ] *n* : rey *m*
kingdom ['kɪŋdəm] *n* : reino *m*
kingfisher ['kɪŋ₁fɪʃər] *n* : martín *m* pescador
kingly ['kɪŋli] *adj* -**lier; -est** : regio, real
king-size ['kɪŋ₁saɪz] *or* **king-sized** [-₁saɪzd] *adj* : de tamaño muy grande, extra largo (dícese de cigarrillos)
kink ['kɪŋk] *n* **1** : rizo *m* (en el pelo), vuelta *f* (en una cuerda) **2** CRAMP

: calambre *m* ⟨to have a kink in the neck : tener tortícolis⟩

kinky ['kɪŋki] *adj* **-kier; -est** : rizado (dícese del pelo), enroscado (dícese de una cuerda)

kinship ['kɪn,ʃɪp] *n* : parentesco *m*

kinsman ['kɪnzmən] *n, pl* **-men** [-mən, -,mɛn] : familiar *m*, pariente *m*

kinswoman ['kɪnz,wʊmən] *n, pl* **-women** [-,wɪmən] : familiar *f*, pariente *f*

kiosk ['ki:,ɑsk] *n* : quiosco *m*

kipper ['kɪpər] *n* : arenque *m* ahumado

kiss[1] ['kɪs] *vt* : besar — *vi* : besarse

kiss[2] *n* : beso *m*

kit ['kɪt] *n* **1** SET : juego *m*, kit *m* **2** CASE : estuche *m*, caja *f* **3 first–aid kit** : botiquín *m* **4 tool kit** : caja *f* de herramientas **5 travel kit** : neceser *m*

kitchen ['kɪtʃən] *n* : cocina *f*

kite ['kaɪt] *n* **1** : milano *m* (ave) **2** : cometa *f*, papalote *m Mex* ⟨to fly a kite : hacer volar una cometa⟩

kith ['kɪθ] *n* : amigos *mpl* ⟨kith and kin : amigos y parientes⟩

kitten ['kɪtən] *n* : gatito *m*, -ta *f*

kitty ['kɪti] *n, pl* **-ties 1** FUND, POOL : bote *m*, fondo *m* común **2** CAT : gato *m*, gatito *m*

kitty–corner ['kɪti,kɔrnər] *or* **kitty–cornered** [-nərd] → **catercorner**

kiwi ['ki:,wi:] *n* : kiwi *m*

kleptomania [,klɛptə'meɪniə] *n* : cleptomanía *f*

kleptomaniac [,klɛptə'meɪni,æk] *n* : cleptómano *m*, -na *f*

knack ['næk] *n* : maña *f*, facilidad *f*

knapsack ['næp,sæk] *n* : mochila *f*, morral *m*

knave ['neɪv] *n* : bellaco *m*, pícaro *m*

knead ['ni:d] *vt* **1** : amasar, sobar **2** MASSAGE : masajear

knee ['ni:] *n* : rodilla *f*

kneecap ['ni:,kæp] *n* : rótula *f*

kneel ['ni:l] *vi* **knelt** ['nɛlt] *or* **kneeled** ['ni:ld]; **kneeling** : arrodillarse, ponerse de rodillas

knell ['nɛl] *n* : doble *m*, toque *m* ⟨death knell : toque de difuntos⟩

knew → **know**

knickers ['nɪkərz] *npl* : pantalones *mpl* bombachos de media pierna

knickknack ['nɪk,næk] *n* : chuchería *f*, baratija *f*

knife[1] ['naɪf] *vt* **knifed** ['naɪft]; **knifing** : acuchillar, apuñalar

knife[2] *n, pl* **knives** ['naɪvz] : cuchillo *m*

knight[1] ['naɪt] *vt* : conceder el título de *Sir* a

knight[2] *n* **1** : caballero *m* ⟨knight errant : caballero andante⟩ **2** : caballo *m* (en ajedrez) **3** : uno que tiene el título de *Sir*

knighthood ['naɪt,hʊd] *n* **1** : caballería *f* **2** : título *m* de *Sir*

knightly ['naɪtli] *adj* : caballeresco

knit[1] ['nɪt] *v* **knit** *or* **knitted** ['nɪtəd]; **knitting** *vt* **1** UNITE : unir, enlazar **2** : tejer ⟨to knit a sweater : tejer un suéter⟩ **3**

to knit one's brows : fruncir el ceño — *vi* **1** : tejer **2** : soldarse (dícese de los huesos)

knit[2] *n* : prenda *f* tejida

knitter ['nɪtər] *n* : tejedor *m*, -dora *f*

knob ['nɑb] *n* **1** LUMP : bulto *m*, protuberancia *f* **2** HANDLE : perilla *f*, tirador *m*, botón *m*

knobbed ['nɑbd] *adj* **1** KNOTTY : nudoso **2** : que tiene perilla o botón

knobby ['nɑbi] *adj* **knobbier; -est 1** KNOTTY : nudoso **2 knobby knees** : rodillas *fpl* huesudas

knock[1] ['nɑk] *vt* **1** HIT, RAP : golpear, golpetear **2** : hacer chocar ⟨they knocked heads : se dieron en la cabeza⟩ **3** CRITICIZE : criticar — *vi* **1** RAP : dar un golpe, llamar (a la puerta) **2** COLLIDE : darse, chocar

knock[2] *n* : golpe *m*, llamada *f* (a la puerta), golpeteo *m* (de un motor)

knock down *vt* : derribar, echar al suelo

knocker ['nɑkər] *n* : aldaba *f*, llamador *m*

knock–kneed ['nɑk'ni:d] *adj* : patizambo

knockout ['nɑk,aʊt] *n* : nocaut *m*, knockout *m* (en deportes)

knock out *vt* : dejar sin sentido, poner fuera de combate (en el boxeo)

knoll ['no:l] *n* : loma *f*, otero *m*, montículo *m*

knot[1] ['nɑt] *v* **knotted; knotting** *vt* : anudar — *vi* : anudarse

knot[2] *n* **1** : nudo *m* (en cordel o madera), nódulo *m* (en los músculos) **2** CLUSTER : grupo *m* **3** : nudo *m* (unidad de velocidad)

knotty ['nɑti] *adj* **-tier; -est 1** GNARLED : nudoso **2** COMPLEX : espinoso, enredado, complejo

know ['no:] *v* **knew** ['nu:, 'nju:]; **known** ['no:n]; **knowing** *vt* **1** : saber ⟨he knows the answer : sabe la respuesta⟩ **2** : conocer (a una persona, un lugar) ⟨do you know Julia? : ¿conoces a Julia?⟩ **3** RECOGNIZE : reconocer **4** DISCERN, DISTINGUISH : distinguir, discernir **5 to know how to** : saber ⟨I don't know how to dance : no sé bailar⟩ — *vi* : saber

knowable ['no:əbəl] *adj* : conocible

knowing ['no:ɪŋ] *adj* **1** KNOWLEDGEABLE : informado ⟨a knowing look : una mirada de complicidad⟩ **2** ASTUTE : astuto **3** DELIBERATE : deliberado, intencional

knowingly ['no:ɪŋli] *adv* **1** : con complicidad ⟨she smiled knowingly : sonrió con una mirada de complicidad⟩ **2** DELIBERATELY : a sabiendas, adrede, a propósito

know–it–all ['no:ɪt,ɔl] *n* : sabelotodo *mf fam*

knowledge ['nɑlɪʤ] *n* **1** AWARENESS : conocimiento *m* **2** LEARNING : conocimientos *mpl*, saber *m*

knowledgeable ['nɑlɪʤəbəl] *adj* : informado, entendido, enterado

known ['noːn] *adj* : conocido, familiar
knuckle ['nʌkəl] *n* : nudillo *m*
koala [ko'wɑlə] *n* : koala *m*
kohlrabi [ˌkoːl'rɑbi, -'ræ-] *n, pl* -bies : colinabo *m*
Koran [kə'rɑn, -'ræn] *n* the Koran : el Corán
Korean [kə'riːən] *n* **1** : coreano *m*, -na *f* **2** : coreano *m* (idioma) — **Korean** *adj*
kosher ['koːʃər] *adj* : aprobado por la ley judía

kowtow [ˌkɑʊ'tɑʊ, 'kɑʊˌtɑʊ] *vi* **to kowtow to** : humillarse ante, doblegarse ante
krypton ['krɪpˌtɑn] *n* : criptón *m*
kudos ['kjuːˌdɑs, 'kuː-, -ˌdoːz] *n* : fama *f*, renombre *m*
kumquat ['kʌmˌkwɑt] *n* : naranjita *f* china
Kurd ['kʊrd, 'kərd] *n* : kurdo *m*, -da *f*
Kurdish ['kʊrdɪʃ, 'kər-] *adj* : kurdo
Kuwaiti [kʊ'weɪti] *n* : kuwaití *mf* — **Kuwaiti** *adj*

L

l ['ɛl] *n, pl* **l's** *or* **ls** ['lz] : duodécima letra del alfabeto inglés
lab ['læb] → **laboratory**
label[1] ['leɪbəl] *vt* -**beled** *or* -**belled**; -**beling** *or* -**belling** **1** : etiquetar, poner etiqueta a **2** BRAND, CATEGORIZE : calificar, tildar, tachar ⟨they labeled him as a fraud : lo calificaron de farsante⟩
label[2] *n* **1** : etiqueta *f*, rótulo *m* **2** DESCRIPTION : calificación *f*, descripción *f* **3** BRAND : marca *f*
labial ['leɪbiəl] *adj* : labial
labor[1] ['leɪbər] *vi* **1** WORK : trabajar **2** STRUGGLE : avanzar penosamente (dícese de una persona), funcionar con dificultad (dícese de un motor) **3 to labor under a delusion** : hacerse ilusiones, tener una falsa impresión — *vt* BELABOR : insistir en, extenderse sobre
labor[2] *n* **1** EFFORT, WORK : trabajo *m*, esfuerzos *mpl* **2** : parto *m* ⟨to be in labor : estar de parto⟩ **3** TASK : tarea *f*, labor *m* **4** WORKERS : mano *f* de obra
laboratory ['læbrəˌtori, lə'bɔrə-] *n, pl* -**ries** : laboratorio *m*
Labor Day *n* : Día *m* del Trabajo
laborer ['leɪbərər] *n* : peón *m*; trabajador *m*, -dora *f*
laborious [lə'boriəs] *adj* : laborioso, difícil
laboriously [lə'boriəsli] *adv* : laboriosamente, trabajosamente
labor union → **union**
labyrinth ['læbəˌrɪnθ] *n* : laberinto *m*
lace[1] ['leɪs] *vt* **laced; lacing** **1** TIE : acordonar, atar los cordones de **2** : adornar de encaje ⟨I laced the dress in white : adorné el vestido de encaje blanco⟩ **3** SPIKE : echar licor a
lace[2] *n* **1** : encaje *m* **2** SHOELACE : cordón *m* (de zapatos), agujeta *f Mex*
lacerate ['læsəˌreɪt] *vt* -**ated; -ating** : lacerar
laceration [ˌlæsə'reɪʃən] *n* : laceración *f*
lack[1] ['læk] *vt* : carecer de, no tener ⟨she lacks patience : carece de paciencia⟩ — *vi* : faltar ⟨they lack for nothing : no les falta nada⟩
lack[2] *n* : falta *f*, carencia *f*
lackadaisical [ˌlækə'deɪzɪkəl]   *adj*

: apático, indiferente, lánguido — **lackadaisically** [-kli] *adv*
lackey ['læki] *n, pl* -**eys** **1** FOOTMAN : lacayo *m* **2** TOADY : adulador *m*, -dora *f*
lackluster ['lækˌlʌstər] *adj* **1** DULL : sin brillo, apagado, deslustrado **2** MEDIOCRE : deslucido, mediocre
laconic [lə'kɑnɪk] *adj* : lacónico — **laconically** [-nɪkli] *adv*
lacquer[1] ['lækər] *vt* : laquear, pintar con laca
lacquer[2] *n* : laca *f*
lacrosse [lə'krɔs] *n* : lacrosse *f*
lactic acid ['læktɪk] *n* : ácido *m* láctico
lacuna [lə'kuːnə, -'kjuː-] *n, pl* -**nae** [-ˌniː, -ˌnɑɪ] *or* -**nas** : laguna *f*
lacy ['leɪsi] *adj* **lacier; -est** : de encaje, como de encaje
lad ['læd] *n* : muchacho *m*, niño *m*
ladder ['lædər] *n* : escalera *f*
laden ['leɪdən] *adj* : cargado
ladle[1] ['leɪdəl] *vt* -**dled; -dling** : servir con cucharón
ladle[2] *n* : cucharón *m*, cazo *m*
lady ['leɪdi] *n, pl* -**dies** **1** : señora *f*, dama *f* **2** WOMAN : mujer *f*
ladybird ['leɪdiˌbərd] → **ladybug**
ladybug ['leɪdiˌbʌg] *n* : mariquita *f*
lag[1] ['læg] *vi* **lagged; lagging** : quedarse atrás, retrasarse, rezagarse
lag[2] *n* **1** DELAY : retraso *m*, demora *f* **2** INTERVAL : lapso *m*, intervalo *m*
lager ['lɑgər] *n* : cerveza *f* rubia
laggard[1] ['lægərd] *adj* : retardado, retrasado
laggard[2] *n* : rezagado *m*, -da *f*
lagoon [lə'guːn] *n* : laguna *f*
laid → **lay**[1]
laid-back ['leɪd'bæk] *adj* : tranquilo, relajado
lain *pp* → **lie**[1]
lair ['lær] *n* : guarida *f*, madriguera *f*
laissez-faire [ˌlɛˌseɪ'fær, ˌleɪˌzeɪ-] *n* : liberalismo *m* económico
laity ['leɪəti] *n* the laity : los laicos, el laicado
lake ['leɪk] *n* : lago *m*
lama ['lɑmə] *n* : lama *m*
lamb ['læm] *n* **1** : cordero *m*, borrego *m* (animal) **2** : carne *f* de cordero

lambaste [læm'beɪst] *or* **lambast** [-'bæst] *vt* **-basted; -basting** **1** BEAT, THRASH : golpear, azotar, darle una paliza (a alguien) **2** CENSURE : arremeter contra, censurar

lame[1] ['leɪm] *vt* **lamed; laming** : lisiar, hacer cojo

lame[2] *adj* **lamer; lamest** **1** : cojo, renco, rengo **2** WEAK : pobre, débil, poco convincente ⟨a lame excuse : una excusa débil⟩

lamé [lɑ'meɪ, læ-] *n* : lamé *m*

lame duck *n* : persona *f* sin poder ⟨a lame-duck President : un presidente saliente⟩

lamely ['leɪmli] *adv* : sin convicción

lameness ['leɪmnəs] *n* **1** : cojera *f*, renquera *f* **2** : falta *f* de convicción, debilidad *f*, pobreza *f* ⟨the lameness of her response : la pobreza de su respuesta⟩

lament[1] [lə'mɛnt] *vt* **1** MOURN : llorar, llorar por **2** DEPLORE : lamentar, deplorar — *vi* : llorar

lament[2] *n* : lamento *m*

lamentable ['læməntəbəl, lə'mɛntə-] *adj* : lamentable, deplorable — **lamentably** [-bli] *adv*

lamentation [ˌlæmən'teɪʃən] *n* : lamentación *f*, lamento *m*

laminate[1] ['læməˌneɪt] *vt* **-nated; -nating** : laminar

laminate[2] ['læmənət] *n* : laminado *m*

laminated ['læməˌneɪtəd] *adj* : laminado

lamp ['læmp] *n* : lámpara *f*

lampoon[1] [læm'puːn] *vt* : satirizar

lampoon[2] *n* : sátira *f*

lamprey ['læmpri] *n, pl* **-preys** : lamprea *f*

lance[1] ['lænts] *vt* **lanced; lancing** : abrir con lanceta, sajar

lance[2] *n* : lanza *f*

lance corporal *n* : cabo *m* interino, soldado *m* de primera clase

lancet ['læntsət] *n* : lanceta *f*

land[1] ['lænd] *vt* **1** : desembarcar (pasajeros de un barco), hacer aterrizar (un avión) **2** CATCH : pescar, sacar (un pez) del agua **3** GAIN, SECURE : conseguir, ganar ⟨to land a job : conseguir empleo⟩ **4** DELIVER : dar, asestar ⟨he landed a punch : asestó un puñetazo⟩ — *vi* **1** : aterrizar, tomar tierra, atracar ⟨the plane just landed : el avión acaba de aterrizar⟩ ⟨the ship landed an hour ago : el barco atracó hace una hora⟩ **2** ALIGHT : posarse, aterrizar ⟨to land on one's feet : caer de pie⟩

land[2] *n* **1** GROUND : tierra *f* ⟨dry land : tierra firme⟩ **2** TERRAIN : terreno *m* **3** NATION : país *m*, nación *f* **4** DOMAIN : mundo *m*, dominio *m* ⟨the land of dreams : el mundo de los sueños⟩

landfill ['lændˌfɪl] *n* : vertedero *m* (de basuras)

landing ['lændɪŋ] *n* **1** : aterrizaje *m* (de aviones), desembarco *m* (de barcos) **2** : descansillo *m* (de una escalera)

landing field *n* : campo *m* de aterrizaje

landing strip → **airstrip**

landlady ['lændˌleɪdi] *n, pl* **-dies** : casera *f*, dueña *f*, arrendadora *f*

landless ['lændləs] *adj* : sin tierra

landlocked ['lændˌlɑkt] *adj* : sin salida al mar

landlord ['lændˌlɔrd] *n* : dueño *m*, casero *m*, arrendador *m*

landlubber ['lændˌlʌbər] *n* : marinero *m* de agua dulce

landmark ['lændˌmɑrk] *n* **1** : señal *f* (geográfica), punto *m* de referencia **2** MILESTONE : hito *m* ⟨a landmark in our history : un hito en nuestra historia⟩ **3** MONUMENT : monumento *m* histórico

landowner ['lændˌoːnər] *n* : hacendado *m*, -da *f*; terrateniente *mf*

landscape[1] ['lændˌskeɪp] *vt* **-scaped; -scaping** : ajardinar

landscape[2] *n* : paisaje *m*

landslide ['lændˌslaɪd] *n* **1** : desprendimiento *m* de tierras, derrumbe *m* **2** **landslide victory** : victoria *f* arrolladora

landward ['lændwərd] *adv* : en dirección de la tierra, hacia tierra

lane ['leɪn] *n* **1** PATH, WAY : camino *m*, sendero *m* **2** : carril *m* (de una carretera)

language ['læŋgwɪdʒ] *n* **1** : idioma *m*, lengua *f* ⟨the English language : el idioma inglés⟩ **2** : lenguaje *m* ⟨body language : lenguaje corporal⟩

languid ['læŋgwɪd] *adj* : lánguido — **languidly** *adv*

languish ['læŋgwɪʃ] *vi* **1** WEAKEN : languidecer, debilitarse **2** PINE : consumirse, suspirar (por) ⟨to languish for love : suspirar por el amor⟩ ⟨he languished in prison : estuvo pudriéndose en la cárcel⟩

languor ['læŋgər] *n* : languidez *f*

languorous ['læŋgərəs] *adj* : lánguido — **languorously** *adv*

lank ['læŋk] *adj* **1** THIN : delgado, larguirucho *fam* **2** LIMP : lacio

lanky ['læŋki] *adj* **lankier; -est** : delgado, larguirucho *fam*

lanolin ['lænəlɪn] *n* : lanolina *f*

lantern ['læntərn] *n* : linterna *f*, farol *m*

Laotian [leɪ'oːʃən, 'lauʃən] *n* : laosiano *m*, -na *f* — **Laotian** *adj*

lap[1] ['læp] *v* **lapped; lapping** *vt* **1** FOLD : plegar, doblar **2** WRAP : envolver **3** : lamer, besar ⟨waves were lapping the shore : las olas lamían la orilla⟩ **4** **to lap up** : beber a lengüetadas (como un gato) — *vi* OVERLAP : traslaparse

lap[2] *n* **1** : falda *f*, regazo *m* (del cuerpo) **2** OVERLAP : traslapo *m* **3** : vuelta *f* (en deportes) **4** STAGE : etapa *f* (de un viaje)

lapdog ['læpˌdɔg] *n* : perro *m* faldero

lapel [lə'pɛl] *n* : solapa *f*

lapp ['læp] *n* : lapón *m*, -pona *f* — **Lapp** *adj*

lapse[1] ['læps] *vi* **lapsed; lapsing** **1** FALL, SLIP : caer ⟨to lapse into bad habits : caer en malos hábitos⟩ ⟨to lapse into unconsciousness : perder el conocimiento⟩ ⟨to lapse into silence : quedarse callado⟩ **2** FADE : decaer, desvanecerse ⟨her dedication lapsed : su dedicación se desvaneció⟩ **3** CEASE : cancelarse, perderse **4** ELAPSE : transcurrir, pasar **5** EXPIRE : caducar

lapse² *n* **1** SLIP : lapsus *m*, desliz *m*, falla *f* ⟨a lapse of memory : una falla de memoria⟩ **2** INTERVAL : lapso *m*, intervalo *m*, período *m* **3** EXPIRATION : caducidad *f*

laptop¹ ['læp,tɑp] *adj* : portátil, laptop

laptop² *n* : laptop *m*

larboard ['lɑrbərd] *n* : babor *m*

larcenous ['lɑrsənəs] *adj* : de robo

larceny ['lɑrsəni] *n*, *pl* **-nies** : robo *m*, hurto *m*

larch ['lɑrtʃ] *n* : alerce *f*

lard ['lɑrd] *n* : manteca *f* de cerdo

larder ['lɑrdər] *n* : despensa *f*, alacena *f*

large ['lɑrdʒ] *adj* **larger; largest 1** BIG : grande **2** COMPREHENSIVE : amplio, extenso **3 by and large** : por lo general

largely ['lɑrdʒli] *adv* : en gran parte, en su mayoría

largeness ['lɑrdʒnəs] *n* : lo grande

largesse *or* **largess** [lɑr'ʒes, -'dʒes] *n* : generosidad *f*, largueza *f*

lariat ['læriət] *n* : lazo *m*

lark¹ ['lɑrk] *n* **1** FUN : diversión *f* ⟨what a lark! : ¡qué divertido!⟩ **2** : alondra *f* (pájaro)

larva ['lɑrvə] *n*, *pl* **-vae** [-,vi:, -,vaɪ] : larva *f* — **larval** [-vəl] *adj*

laryngitis [,lærən'dʒaɪtəs] *n* : laringitis *f*

larynx ['lærɪŋks] *n*, *pl* **-rynges** [lə'rɪn,dʒi:z] *or* **-ynxes** ['lærɪŋksəz] : laringe *f*

lasagna [lə'zɑnjə] *n* : lasaña *f*

lascivious [lə'sɪviəs] *adj* : lascivo

lasciviousness [lə'sɪviəsnəs] *n* : lascivia *f*, lujuria *f*

laser ['leɪzər] *n* : láser *m*

laser disc *n* : disco *m* láser

lash¹ ['læʃ] *vt* **1** WHIP : azotar **2** BIND : atar, amarrar

lash² *n* **1** WHIP : látigo *m* **2** STROKE : latigazo *m* **3** EYELASH : pestaña *f*

lass ['læs] *or* **lassie** ['læsi] *n* : muchacha *f*, chica *f*

lassitude ['læsə,tu:d, -,tju:d] *n* : lasitud *f*

lasso¹ ['læ,so:, læ'su:] *vt* : lazar

lasso² *n*, *pl* **-sos** *or* **-soes** : lazo *m*, reata *f Mex*

last¹ ['læst] *vi* **1** CONTINUE : durar ⟨how long will it last? : ¿cuánto durará?⟩ **2** ENDURE : aguantar, durar **3** SURVIVE : durar, sobrevivir **4** SUFFICE : durar, bastar — *vt* **1** : durar ⟨it will last a lifetime : durará toda la vida⟩ **2 to last out** : aguantar

last² *adv* **1** : en último lugar, al último ⟨we came in last : llegamos en último lugar⟩ **2** : por última vez, la última vez ⟨I saw him last in Bogota : lo vi por última vez en Bogotá⟩ **3** FINALLY : por último, en conclusión

last³ *adj* **1** FINAL : último, final **2** PREVIOUS : pasado ⟨last year : el año pasado⟩

last⁴ *n* **1** : el último, la última, lo último ⟨at last : por fin, al fin, finalmente⟩ **2** : horma *f* (de zapatero)

lasting ['læstɪŋ] *adj* : perdurable, duradero, estable

lastly ['læstli] *adv* : por último, finalmente

latch¹ ['lætʃ] *vt* : cerrar con picaporte

latch² *n* : picaporte *m*, pestillo *m*, pasador *m*

late¹ ['leɪt] *adv* **later; latest 1** : tarde ⟨to arrive late : llegar tarde⟩ ⟨to sleep late : dormir hasta tarde⟩ **2** : a última hora, a finales ⟨late in the month : a finales del mes⟩ **3** RECENTLY : recién, últimamente ⟨as late as last year : todavía en el año pasado⟩

late² *adj* **later; latest 1** TARDY : tardío, de retraso ⟨to be late : llegar tarde⟩ **2** : avanzado ⟨because of the late hour : a causa de la hora avanzada⟩ **3** DECEASED : difunto, fallecido **4** RECENT : reciente, último ⟨our late quarrel : nuestra última pelea⟩

latecomer ['leɪt,kʌmər] *n* : rezagado *m*, -da *f*

lately ['leɪtli] *adv* : recientemente, últimamente

lateness ['leɪtnəs] *n* **1** DELAY : retraso *m*, atraso *m*, tardanza *f* **2** : lo avanzado (de la hora)

latent ['leɪtənt] *adj* : latente — **latently** *adv*

lateral ['lætərəl] *adj* : lateral — **laterally** *adv*

latex ['leɪ,teks] *n*, *pl* **-tices** ['leɪtə,si:z, 'lætə-] *or* **-texes** : látex *m*

lath ['læθ, 'læð] *n*, *pl* **laths** *or* **lath** : listón *m*

lathe ['leɪð] *n* : torno *m*

lather¹ ['læðər] *vt* : enjabonar — *vi* : espumar, hacer espuma

lather² *n* **1** : espuma *f* (de jabón) **2** : sudor *m* (de caballo) **3 to get into a lather** : ponerse histérico

Latin¹ *adj* : latino

Latin² *n* **1** : latín *m* (idioma) **2** → **Latin American**

Latin–American ['lætənə'mrɪkən] *adj* : latinoamericano

Latin American *n* : latinoamericano *m*, -na *f*

latitude ['lætə,tu:d, -,tju:d] *n* : latitud *f*

latrine [lə'tri:n] *n* : letrina *f*

latte ['lɑ,teɪ] *n* : café *m* con leche

latter¹ ['lætər] *adj* **1** SECOND : segundo **2** LAST : último

latter² *pron* **the latter** : éste, ésta, éstos *pl*, éstas *pl*

lattice ['lætəs] *n* : enrejado *m*, celosía *f*

Latvian ['lætviən] *n* : letón *m*, -tona *f* — **Latvian** *adj*

laud¹ ['lɔd] *vt* : alabar, loar

laud² *n* : alabanza *f*, loa *f*

laudable ['lɔdəbəl] *adj* : loable — **laudably** [-bli] *adv*
laugh¹ ['læf] *vi* : reír, reírse
laugh² *n* **1** LAUGHTER : risa *f* **2** JOKE : chiste *m*, broma *f* ⟨he did it for a laugh : lo hizo en broma, lo hizo para divertirse⟩
laughable ['læfəbəl] *adj* : risible, de risa
laughingstock ['læfɪŋ,stɑk] *n* : hazmerreír *m*
laughter ['læftər] *n* : risa *f*, risas *fpl*
launch¹ ['lɔntʃ] *vt* **1** HURL : lanzar **2** : botar (un barco) **3** START : iniciar, empezar
launch² *n* **1** : lancha *f* (bote) **2** LAUNCHING : lanzamiento *m*
launder ['lɔndər] *vt* **1** : lavar y planchar (ropa) **2** : blanquear, lavar (dinero)
launderer ['lɔndərər] *n* : lavandero *m*, -ra *f*
laundress ['lɔndrəs] *n* : lavandera *f*
laundry ['lɔndri] *n, pl* **laundries** **1** : ropa *f* sucia, ropa *f* para lavar ⟨to do the laundry : lavar la ropa⟩ **2** : lavandería *f* (servicio de lavar)
laureate ['lɔriət] *n* : laureado *m*, -da *f* ⟨poet laureate : poeta laureado⟩
laurel ['lɔrəl] *n* **1** : laurel *m* (planta) **2** laurels *npl* : laureles *mpl* ⟨to rest on one's laurels : dormirse uno en sus laureles⟩
lava ['lɑvə, 'læ-] *n* : lava *f*
lavatory ['lævə,tori] *n, pl* **-ries** : baño *m*, cuarto *m* de baño
lavender ['lævəndər] *n* : lavanda *f*, espliego *m*
lavish¹ ['lævɪʃ] *vt* : prodigar (a), colmar (de)
lavish² *adj* **1** EXTRAVAGANT : pródigo, generoso, derrochador **2** ABUNDANT : abundante **3** LUXURIOUS : lujoso, espléndido
lavishly ['lævɪʃli] *adv* : con generosidad, espléndidamente ⟨to live lavishly : vivir a lo grande⟩
lavishness ['lævɪʃnəs] *n* : generosidad *f*, esplendidez *f*
law ['lɔ] *n* **1** : ley *f* ⟨to break the law : violar la ley⟩ **2** : derecho *m* ⟨criminal law : derecho criminal⟩ **3** : abogacía *f* ⟨to practice law : ejercer la abogacía⟩
law–abiding ['lɔə,baɪdɪŋ] *adj* : observante de la ley
lawbreaker ['lɔ,breɪkər] *n* : infractor *m*, -tora *f* de la ley
lawful ['lɔfəl] *adj* : legal, legítimo, lícito — **lawfully** *adv*
lawgiver ['lɔ,gɪvər] *n* : legislador *m*, -dora *f*
lawless ['lɔləs] *adj* : anárquico, ingobernable — **lawlessly** *adv*
lawlessness ['lɔləsnəs] *n* : anarquía *f*, desorden *m*
lawmaker ['lɔ,meɪkər] *n* : legislador *m*, -dora *f*
lawman ['lɔmən] *n, pl* **-men** [-,mɛn] : agente *m* del orden
lawn ['lɔn] *n* : césped *m*, pasto *m*

lawn mower *n* : cortadora *f* de césped
lawsuit ['lɔ,su:t] *n* : pleito *m*, litigio *m*, demanda *f*
lawyer ['lɔɪər, 'lɔjər] *n* : abogado *m*, -da *f*
lax ['læks] *adj* : laxo, relajado — **laxly** *adv*
laxative ['læksətɪv] *n* : laxante *m*
laxity ['læksəti] *n* : relajación *f*, descuido *m*, falta *f* de rigor
lay¹ ['leɪ] *vt* **laid** ['leɪd]; **laying** **1** PLACE, PUT : poner, colocar ⟨she laid it on the table : lo puso en la mesa⟩ ⟨to lay eggs : poner huevos⟩ **2** : hacer ⟨to lay a bet : hacer una apuesta⟩ **3** IMPOSE : imponer ⟨to lay a tax : imponer un impuesto⟩ ⟨to lay the blame on : echarle la culpa a⟩ **4 to lay out** PRESENT : presentar, exponer ⟨he laid out his plan : presentó su proyecto⟩ **5 to lay out** DESIGN : diseñar (el trazado de)
lay² → lie¹
lay³ *adj* SECULAR : laico, lego
lay⁴ *n* **1** : disposición *f*, configuración *f* ⟨the lay of the land : la configuración del terreno⟩ **2** BALLAD : romance *m*, balada *f*
layer ['leɪər] *n* **1** : capa *f* (de pintura, etc.), estrato *m* (de roca) **2** : gallina *f* ponedora
layman ['leɪmən] *n, pl* **-men** [-mən, -,mɛn] : laico *m*, lego *m*
layoff ['leɪ,ɔf] *n* : despido *m*
lay off *vt* : despedir
layout ['leɪ,aʊt] *n* : disposición *f*, distribución *f* (de una casa, etc.), trazado *m* (de una ciudad)
lay up *vt* **1** STORE : guardar, almacenar **2 to be laid up** : estar enfermo, tener que guardar cama
laywoman ['leɪ,wʊmən] *n, pl* **-women** [-,wɪmən] : laica *f*, lega *f*
laziness ['leɪzinəs] *n* : pereza *f*, flojera *f*
lazy ['leɪzi] *adj* **-zier; -est** : perezoso, holgazán — **lazily** ['leɪzəli] *adv*
leach ['li:tʃ] *vt* : filtrar
lead¹ ['li:d] *vt* **led** ['lɛd]; **leading** **1** GUIDE : conducir, llevar, guiar **2** DIRECT : dirigir **3** HEAD : encabezar, ir al frente de **4 to lead to** : resultar en, llevar a ⟨it only leads to trouble : sólo resulta en problemas⟩
lead² *n* : delantera *f*, primer lugar *m* ⟨to take the lead : tomar la delantera⟩
lead³ ['lɛd] *n* **1** : plomo *m* (metal) **2** : mina *f* (de lápiz) **3 lead poisoning** : saturnismo *m*
leaden ['lɛdən] *adj* **1** : plomizo ⟨a leaden sky : un ciel plomizo⟩ **2** HEAVY : pesado
leader ['li:dər] *n* : jefe *m*, -fa *f*; líder *mf*; dirigente *mf*; gobernante *mf*
leadership ['li:dər,ʃɪp] *n* : mando *m*, dirección *f*
leaf¹ ['li:f] *vi* **1** : echar hojas (dícese de un árbol) **2 to leaf through** : hojear (un libro)

leaf[2] *n, pl* **leaves** ['li:vz] **1** : hoja *f* (de plantas o libros) **2 to turn over a new leaf** : hacer borrón y cuenta nueva
leafless ['li:fləs] *adj* : sin hojas, pelado
leaflet ['li:flət] *n* : folleto *m*
leafy ['li:fi] *adj* **leafier; -est** : frondoso
league[1] ['li:g] *v* **leagued; leaguing** *vt* : aliar, unir — *vi* : aliarse, unirse
league[2] *n* **1** : legua *f* (medida de distancia) **2** ASSOCIATION : alianza *f*, sociedad *f*, liga *f*
leak[1] ['li:k] *vt* **1** : perder, dejar escapar (un líquido o un gas) **2** : filtrar (información) — *vi* **1** : gotear, escaparse, fugarse (dícese de un líquido o un gas) **2** : hacer agua (dícese de un bote) **3** : filtrarse, divulgarse (dícese de información)
leak[2] *n* **1** HOLE : agujero *m* (en recipientes), gotera *f* (en un tejado) **2** ESCAPE : fuga *f*, escape *m* **3** : filtración *f* (de información)
leakage ['li:kɪdʒ] *n* : escape *m*, fuga *f*
leaky ['li:ki] *adj* **leakier; -est** : agujereado (dícese de un recipiente), que hace agua (dícese de un bote), con goteras (dícese de un tejado)
lean[1] ['li:n] *vi* **1** BEND : inclinarse, ladearse **2** RECLINE : reclinarse **3** RELY : apoyarse (en), depender (de) **4** INCLINE, TEND : inclinarse, tender — *vt* : apoyar
lean[2] *adj* **1** THIN : delgado, flaco **2** : sin grasa, magro (dícese de la carne)
leanness ['li:nnəs] *n* : delgadez *f*
lean-to ['li:n,tu:] *n* : cobertizo *m*
leap[1] ['li:p] *vi* **leaped** ['li:pt, 'lɛpt] *or* **leapt; leaping** : saltar, brincar
leap[2] *n* : salto *m*, brinco *m*
leap year *n* : año *m* bisiesto
learn ['lərn] *vt* **1** : aprender ⟨to learn to sing : aprender a cantar⟩ **2** MEMORIZE : aprender de memoria **3** DISCOVER : saber, enterarse de — *vi* **1** : aprender ⟨to learn from experience : aprender por experiencia⟩ **2** FIND OUT : enterarse, saber
learned ['lərnəd] *adj* : erudito
learner ['lərnər] *n* : principiante *mf*, estudiante *mf*
learning ['lərnɪŋ] *n* : erudición *f*, saber *m*
lease[1] ['li:s] *vt* **leased; leasing** : arrendar
lease[2] *n* : contrato *m* de arrendamiento
leash[1] ['li:ʃ] *vt* : atraillar (un animal)
leash[2] *n* : traílla *f*
least[1] ['li:st] *adv* : menos ⟨when least expected : cuando menos se espera⟩
least[2] *adj* (*superlative of* **little**) : menor, más mínimo
least[3] *n* **1** : lo menos ⟨at least : por lo menos⟩ **2 to say the least** : por no decir más
leather ['lɛðər] *n* : cuero *m*
leathery ['lɛðəri] *adj* : curtido (dícese de la piel), correoso (dícese de la carne)

leave[1] ['li:v] *v* **left** ['lɛft]; **leaving** *vt* **1** BEQUEATH : dejar, legar **2** DEPART : dejar, salir(se) de **3** ABANDON : abandonar, dejar **4** FORGET : dejar, olvidarse de ⟨I left the books at the library : dejé los libros en la biblioteca⟩ **5 to be left** : quedar ⟨it's all I have left : es todo lo que me queda⟩ **6 to be left over** : sobrar **7 to leave out** : omitir, excluir — *vi* : irse, salir, partir, marcharse ⟨she left yesterday morning : se fue ayer por la mañana⟩
leave[2] *n* **1** PERMISSION : permiso *m* ⟨by your leave : con su permiso⟩ **2** *or* **leave of absence** : permiso *m*, licencia *f* ⟨maternity leave : licencia por maternidad⟩ **3 to take one's leave** : despedirse
leaven ['lɛvən] *n* : levadura *f*
leaves → **leaf**[2]
leaving ['li:vɪŋ] *n* **1** : salida *f*, partida *f* **2 leavings** *npl* : restos *mpl*, sobras *fpl*
Lebanese [,lɛbə'ni:z, -'ni:s] *n* : libanés *m*, -nesa *f* — **Lebanese** *adj*
lecherous ['lɛtʃərəs] *adj* : lascivo, libidinoso — **lecherously** *adv*
lechery ['lɛtʃəri] *n* : lascivia *f*, lujuria *f*
lecture[1] ['lɛktʃər] *v* **-tured; -turing** *vi* : dar clase, dictar clase, dar una conferencia — *vt* SCOLD : sermonear, echar una reprimenda a, regañar
lecture[2] *n* **1** : conferencia *f* **2** REPRIMAND : reprimenda *f*
lecturer ['lɛktʃərər] *n* **1** SPEAKER : conferenciante *mf* **2** TEACHER : profesor *m*, -sora *f*
led → **lead**[1]
ledge ['lɛdʒ] *n* : repisa *f* (de una pared), antepecho *m* (de una ventana), saliente *m* (de una montaña)
ledger ['lɛdʒər] *n* : libro *m* mayor, libro *m* de contabilidad
lee[1] ['li:] *adj* : de sotavento
lee[2] *n* : sotavento *m*
leech ['li:tʃ] *n* : sanguijuela *f*
leek ['li:k] *n* : puerro *m*
leer[1] ['lɪr] *vi* : mirar con lascivia
leer[2] *n* : mirada *f* lasciva
leery ['lɪri] *adj* : receloso
lees ['li:z] *npl* : posos *mpl*, heces *fpl*
leeward[1] ['li:wərd, 'lu:ərd] *adj* : de sotavento
leeward[2] *n* : sotavento *m*
leeway ['li:,weɪ] *n* : libertad *f*, margen *m*
left[1] ['lɛft] *adv* : hacia la izquierda
left[2] → **leave**[1]
left[3] *adj* : izquierdo
left[4] *n* : izquierda *f* ⟨on the left : a la izquierda⟩
left-hand ['lɛft'hand] *adj* **1** : de la izquierda **2** → **left-handed**
left-handed ['lɛft'handəd] *adj* **1** : zurdo (dícese de una persona) **2** : con doble sentido ⟨a left-handed compliment : un cumplido a medias⟩
leftist ['lɛftɪst] *n* : izquierdista *mf* — **leftist** *adj*
leftover ['lɛft,o:vər] *adj* : sobrante, que sobra

leftovers ['lɛft,oːvərz] *npl* : restos *mpl*, sobras *fpl*

left wing *n* **the left wing** : la izquierda

left–winger ['lɛft'wɪŋər] *n* : izquierdista *mf*

leg ['lɛg] *n* **1** : pierna *f* (de una persona, de carne, de ropa), pata *f* (de un animal, de muebles) **2** STAGE : etapa *f* (de un viaje), vuelta *f* (de una carrera)

legacy ['lɛgəsi] *n, pl* **-cies** : legado *m*, herencia *f*

legal ['liːgəl] *adj* **1** : legal, jurídico ⟨legal advisor : asesor jurídico⟩ ⟨the legal profession : la abogacía⟩ **2** LAWFUL : legítimo, legal

legalistic [,liːgə'lɪstɪk] *adj* : legalista

legality [li'gæləti] *n, pl* **-ties** : legalidad *f*

legalize ['liːgə,laɪz] *vt* **-ized; -izing** : legalizar

legally ['liːgəli] *adv* : legalmente

legate ['lɛgət] *n* : legado *m*

legation [lɪ'geɪʃən] *n* : legación *f*

legend ['lɛʤənd] *n* **1** STORY : leyenda *f* **2** INSCRIPTION : leyenda *f*, inscripción *f* **3** : signos *mpl* convencionales (en un mapa)

legendary ['lɛʤən,dɛri] *adj* : legendario

legerdemain [,lɛʤərdə'meɪn] → **sleight of hand**

leggings ['lɛgɪŋz, 'lɛgənz] *npl* : mallas *fpl*

legibility [,lɛʤə'bɪləti] *n* : legibilidad *f*

legible ['lɛʤəbəl] *adj* : legible

legibly ['lɛʤəbli] *adv* : de manera legible

legion ['liːʤən] *n* : legión *f*

legionnaire [,liːʤə'nær] *n* : legionario *m, -ria f*

legislate ['lɛʤəs,leɪt] *vi* **-lated; -lating** : legislar

legislation [,lɛʤəs'leɪʃən] *n* : legislación *f*

legislative ['lɛʤəs,leɪtɪv] *adj* : legislativo, legislador

legislator ['lɛʤəs,leɪtər] *n* : legislador *m*, -dora *f*

legislature ['lɛʤəs,leɪtʃər] *n* : asamblea *f* legislativa

legitimacy [lɪ'ʤɪtəməsi] *n* : legitimidad *f*

legitimate [lɪ'ʤɪtəmət] *adj* **1** VALID : legítimo, válido, justificado **2** LAWFUL : legítimo, legal

legitimately [lɪ'ʤɪtəmətli] *adv* : legítimamente

legitimize [lɪ'ʤɪtə,maɪz] *vt* **-mized; -mizing** : legitimar, hacer legítimo

legume ['lɛ,gjuːm, lɪ'gjuːm] *n* : legumbre *f*

leisure ['liːʒər, 'lɛ-] *n* **1** : ocio *m*, tiempo *m* libre ⟨a life of leisure : una vida de ocio⟩ **2 to take one's leisure** : reposar **3 at your leisure** : cuando te venga bien, cuando tengas tiempo

leisurely ['liːʒərli, 'lɛ-] *adj & adv* : lento, sin prisas

lemming ['lɛmɪŋ] *n* : lemming *m*

lemon ['lɛmən] *n* : limón *m*

lemonade [,lɛmə'neɪd] *n* : limonada *f*

lemony ['lɛməni] *adj* : a limón

lend ['lɛnd] *vt* **lent** ['lɛnt]; **lending 1** : prestar ⟨to lend money : prestar dinero⟩ **2** GIVE : dar ⟨it lends force to his criticism : da fuerza a su crítica⟩ **3 to lend oneself to** : prestarse a

length ['lɛŋθ] *n* **1** : longitud *f*, largo *m* ⟨10 feet in length : 10 pies de largo⟩ **2** DURATION : duración *f* **3** : trozo *m* (de madera), corte *m* (de tela) **4 to go to any lengths** : hacer todo lo posible **5 at ~** : extensamente ⟨to speak at length : hablar largo y tendido⟩

lengthen ['lɛŋθən] *vt* **1** : alargar ⟨can they lengthen the dress? : ¿se puede alargar el vestido?⟩ **2** EXTEND, PROLONG : prolongar, extender — *vi* : alargarse, crecer ⟨the days are lengthening : los días están creciendo⟩

lengthways ['lɛŋθ,weɪz] → **lengthwise**

lengthwise ['lɛŋθ,waɪz] *adv* : a lo largo, longitudinalmente

lengthy ['lɛŋθi] *adj* **lengthier; -est 1** OVERLONG : largo y pesado **2** EXTENDED : prolongado, largo

leniency ['liːniəntsi] *n, pl* **-cies** : lenidad *f*, indulgencia *f*

lenient ['liːniənt] *adj* : indulgente, poco severo

leniently ['liːniəntli] *adv* : con lenidad, con indulgencia

lens ['lɛnz] *n* **1** : cristalino *m* (del ojo) **2** : lente *mf* (de un instrumento o una cámara) **3** → **contact lens**

lent → **lend**

Lent ['lɛnt] *n* : Cuaresma *f*

lentil ['lɛntəl] *n* : lenteja *f*

Leo ['liːoː] *n* : Leo *mf*

leopard ['lɛpərd] *n* : leopardo *m*

leotard ['liːə,tɑrd] *n* : leotardo *m*, malla *f*

leper ['lɛpər] *n* : leproso *m*, -sa *f*

leprechaun ['lɛprə,kɑn] *n* : duende *m* (irlandés)

leprosy ['lɛprəsi] *n* : lepra *f* — **leprous** ['lɛprəs] *adj*

lesbian[1] ['lɛzbiən] *adj* : lesbiano

lesbian[2] *n* : lesbiana *f*

lesbianism ['lɛzbiə,nɪzəm] *n* : lesbianismo *m*

lesion ['liːʒən] *n* : lesión *f*

less[1] ['lɛs] *adv* (*comparative of* **little**[1]) : menos ⟨the less you know, the better : cuanto menos sepas, mejor⟩ ⟨less and less : cada vez menos⟩

less[2] *adj* (*comparative of* **little**[2]) : menos ⟨less than three : menos de tres⟩ ⟨less money : menos dinero⟩ ⟨nothing less than perfection : nada menos que la perfección⟩

less[3] *pron* : menos ⟨I'm earning less : estoy ganando menos⟩

less[4] *prep* : menos ⟨one month less two days : un mes menos dos días⟩

lessee [lɛ'siː] *n* : arrendatario *m*, -ria *f*

lessen ['lɛsən] *vt* : disminuir, reducir — *vi* : disminuir, reducirse

lesser ['lɛsər] *adj* : menor ⟨to a lesser degree : en menor grado⟩
lesson ['lɛsən] *n* **1** CLASS : clase *f*, curso *m* **2** : lección *f* ⟨the lessons of history : las lecciones de la historia⟩
lessor ['lɛ,sɔr, l'sɔr] *n* : arrendador *m*, -dora *f*
lest ['lɛst] *conj* : para (que) no ⟨lest we forget : para que no olvidemos⟩
let ['lɛt] *vt* **let; letting 1** ALLOW : dejar, permitir ⟨let me see it : déjame verlo⟩ **2** MAKE : hacer ⟨let me know : házmelo saber, avísame⟩ ⟨let them wait : que esperen, haz que esperen⟩ **3** RENT : alquilar **4** (*used in the first person plural imperative*) ⟨let's go! : ¡vamos!, ¡vámonos!⟩ ⟨let us pray : oremos⟩ **5 to let down** DISAPPOINT : fallar **6 to let off** FORGIVE : perdonar **7 to let out** REVEAL : revelar **8 to let up** ABATE : amainar, disminuir ⟨the pace never lets up : el ritmo nunca disminuye⟩
letdown *n* : chasco *m*, decepción *f*
lethal ['li:θəl] *adj* : letal — **lethally** *adv*
lethargic [lɪ'θɑrdʒɪk] *adj* : letárgico
lethargy ['lɛθərdʒi] *n* : letargo *m*
let on *vi* **1** ADMIT : reconocer ⟨don't let on! : ¡no digas nada!⟩ **2** PRETEND : fingir
let's ['lɛts] (*contraction of* **let us**) → **let**
letter[1] ['lɛţər] *vt* : marcar con letras, inscribir letras en
letter[2] *n* **1** : letra *f* (del alfabeto) **2** : carta *f* ⟨a letter to my mother : una carta a mi madre⟩ **3 letters** *npl* ARTS : letras *fpl* **4 to the letter** : al pie de la letra
lettering ['lɛţərɪŋ] *n* : letra *f*
lettuce ['lɛţəs] *n* : lechuga *f*
leukemia [lu:'ki:miə] *n* : leucemia *f*
levee ['lɛvi] *n* : dique *m*
level[1] ['lɛvəl] *vt* **-eled** *or* **-elled; -eling** *or* **-elling 1** FLATTEN : nivelar, aplanar **2** AIM : apuntar (una pistola), dirigir (una acusación) **3** RAZE : rasar, arrasar
level[2] *adj* **1** EVEN : llano, plano, parejo **2** CALM : tranquilo ⟨to keep a level head : no perder la cabeza⟩
level[3] *n* : nivel *m*
leveler ['lɛvələr] *n* : nivelador *m*, -dora *f*
levelheaded ['lɛvəl'hɛdəd] *adj* : sensato, equilibrado
levelly ['lɛvəli] *adv* CALMLY : con ecuanimidad *f*, con calma
levelness ['lɛvəlnəs] *n* : uniformidad *f*
lever ['lɛvər, 'li:-] *n* : palanca *f*
leverage ['lɛvərɪdʒ, 'li:-] *n* **1** : apalancamiento *m* (en física) **2** INFLUENCE : influencia *f*, palanca *f fam*
leviathan [lɪ'vaɪəθən] *n* : leviatán *m*, gigante *m*
levity ['lɛvəţi] *n* : ligereza *f*, frivolidad *f*
levy[1] ['lɛvi] *vt* **levied; levying 1** IMPOSE : imponer, exigir, gravar (un impuesto) **2** COLLECT : recaudar (un impuesto)
levy[2] *n, pl* **levies** : impuesto *m*, gravamen *m*
lewd ['lu:d] *adj* : lascivo — **lewdly** *adv*
lewdness ['lu:dnəs] *n* : lascivia *f*

lexical ['lɛksikəl] *adj* : léxico
lexicographer [,lɛksə'kɑgrəfər] *n* : lexicógrafo *m*, -fa *f*
lexicographical [,lɛksəko'græfɪkəl] *or* **lexicographic** [-'græfɪk] *adj* : lexicográfico
lexicography [,lɛksə'kɑgrəfi] *n* : lexicografía *f*
lexicon ['lɛksɪ,kɑn] *n, pl* **-ica** [-kə] *or* **-icons** : léxico *m*, lexicón *m*
liability [,laɪə'bɪləţi] *n, pl* **-ties 1** RESPONSIBILITY : responsabilidad *f* **2** SUSCEPTIBILITY : propensión *f* **3** DRAWBACK : desventaja *f* **4 liabilities** *npl* DEBTS : deudas *fpl*, pasivo *m*
liable ['laɪəbəl] *adj* **1** RESPONSIBLE : responsable **2** SUSCEPTIBLE : propenso **3** PROBABLE : probable ⟨it's liable to happen : es probable que suceda⟩
liaison ['li:ə,zɑn, li'eɪ-] *n* **1** CONNECTION : enlace *m*, relación *f* **2** AFFAIR : amorío *m*, aventura *f*
liar ['laɪər] *n* : mentiroso *m*, -sa *f*; embustero *m*, -ra *f*
libel[1] ['laɪbəl] *vt* **-beled** *or* **-belled; -beling** *or* **-belling** : difamar, calumniar
libel[2] *n* : difamación *f*, calumnia *f*
libeler ['laɪbələr] *n* : difamador *m*, -dora *f*; calumniador *m*, -dora *f*; libelista *mf*
libelous *or* **libellous** ['laɪbələs] *adj* : difamatorio, calumnioso, injurioso
liberal[1] ['lɪbrəl, 'lɪbərəl] *adj* **1** TOLERANT : liberal, tolerante **2** GENEROUS : generoso **3** ABUNDANT : abundante **4 liberal arts** : humanidades *fpl*, artes *fpl* liberales
liberal[2] *n* : liberal *mf*
liberalism ['lɪbrə,lɪzəm, 'lɪbərə-] *n* : liberalismo *m*
liberality [,lɪbə'ræləţi] *n, pl* **-ties** : liberalidad *f*, generosidad *f*
liberalize ['lɪbrə,laɪz, 'lɪbərə-] *vt* **-ized; -izing** : liberalizar
liberally ['lɪbrəli, 'lɪbərə-] *adv* **1** GENEROUSLY : generosamente **2** ABUNDANTLY : abundantemente **3** FREELY : libremente
liberate ['lɪbə,reɪt] *vt* **-ated; -ating** : liberar, libertar
liberation [,lɪbə'reɪʃən] *n* : liberación *f*
liberator ['lɪbə,reɪtər] *n* : libertador *m*, -dora *f*
Liberian [laɪ'bɪriən] *n* : liberiano *m*, -na *f* — **Liberian** *adj*
libertine ['lɪbər,ti:n] *n* : libertino *m*, -na *f*
liberty ['lɪbərţi] *n, pl* **-ties 1** : libertad *f* **2 to take the liberty of** : tomarse la libertad de **3 to take liberties with** : tomarse confianzas con, tomarse libertades con
libido [lə'bi:do:, -'baɪ-] *n, pl* **-dos** : libido *f* — **libidinous** [lə'bɪdənəs] *adj*
Libra ['li:brə] *n* : Libra *mf*
librarian [laɪ'brɛriən] *n* : bibliotecario *m*, -ria *f*
library ['laɪ,brɛri] *n, pl* **-braries** : biblioteca *f*

librettist [lɪ'brɛtɪst] *n* : libretista *mf*
libretto [lɪ'brɛ̜o] *n, pl* **-tos** *or* **-ti** [-ṭi:] : libreto *m*
Libyan ['lɪbiən] *n* : libio *m*, -bia *f* — **Libyan** *adj*
lice → **louse**
license[1] ['laɪsən*t*s] *vt* **licensed; licensing** : licenciar, autorizar, dar permiso a
license[2] *or* **licence** *n* **1** PERMISSION : licencia *f*, permiso *m* **2** PERMIT : licencia *f*, carnet *m Spain* ⟨driver's license : licencia de conducir⟩ **3** FREEDOM : libertad *f* **4** LICENTIOUSNESS : libertinaje *m*
licentious [laɪ'sɛn*t*ʃəs] *adj* : licencioso, disoluto — **licentiously** *adv*
licentiousness [laɪ'sɛn*t*ʃəsnəs] *n* : libertinaje *m*
lichen ['laɪkən] *n* : liquen *m*
licit ['lɪsət] *adj* : lícito
lick[1] ['lɪk] *vt* **1** : lamer **2** BEAT : darle una paliza (a alguien)
lick[2] *n* **1** : lamida *f*, lengüetada *f* ⟨a lick of paint : una mano de pintura⟩ **2** BIT : pizca *f*, ápice *m* **3 a lick and a promise** : una lavada a la carrera
licorice ['lɪkərɪʃ, -rəs] *n* : regaliz *m*, dulce *m* de regaliz
lid ['lɪd] *n* **1** COVER : tapa *f* **2** EYELID : párpado *m*
lie[2] ['laɪ] *vi* **lay** ['leɪ]; **lain** ['leɪn]; **lying** ['laɪɪŋ] **1** : acostarse, echarse ⟨I lay down : me acosté⟩ **2** : estar, estar situado, encontrarse ⟨the book lay on the table : el libro estaba en la mesa⟩ ⟨the city lies to the south : la ciudad se encuentra al sur⟩ **3** CONSIST : consistir **4 to lie in** : residir en ⟨the power lies in the people : el poder reside en el pueblo⟩
lie[2] *vi* **lied; lying** ['laɪɪŋ] : mentir
lie[3] *n* **1** UNTRUTH : mentira *f* ⟨to tell lies : decir mentiras⟩ **2** POSITION : posición *f*
liege ['li:dʒ] *n* : señor *m* feudal
lien ['li:n, 'li:ən] *n* : derecho *m* de retención
lieutenant [lu:'tɛnənt] *n* : teniente *mf*
lieutenant colonel *n* : teniente *mf* coronel
lieutenant commander *n* : capitán *m*, -tana *f* de corbeta
lieutenant general *n* : teniente *mf* general
life ['laɪf] *n, pl* **lives** ['laɪvz] **1** : vida *f* ⟨plant life : la vida vegetal⟩ **2** EXISTENCE : vida *f*, existencia *f* **3** BIOGRAPHY : biografía *f*, vida *f* **4** DURATION : duración *f*, vida *f* **5** LIVELINESS : vivacidad *f*, animación *f*
lifeblood ['laɪf,blʌd] *n* : parte *f* vital, sustento *m*
lifeboat ['laɪf,bo:t] *n* : bote *m* salvavidas
lifeguard ['laɪf,gɑrd] *n* : socorrista *mf*, salvavidas *mf*
lifeless ['laɪfləs] *adj* : sin vida, muerto
lifelike ['laɪf,laɪk] *adj* : que parece vivo, natural, verosímil

lifelong ['laɪf'lɔŋ] *adj* : de toda la vida ⟨a lifelong friend : un amigo de toda la vida⟩
life preserver *n* : salvavidas *m*
lifesaver ['laɪf,seɪvər] *n* **1** : salvación *f* **2** → **lifeguard**
lifesaving ['laɪf,seɪvɪŋ] *n* : socorrismo *m*
lifestyle ['laɪf,staɪl] *n* : estilo *m* de vida
lifetime ['laɪf,taɪm] *n* : vida *f*, curso *m* de la vida
lift[1] ['lɪft] *vt* **1** RAISE : levantar, alzar, subir **2** END : levantar ⟨to lift a ban : levantar una prohibición⟩ — *vi* **1** RISE : levantarse, alzarse **2** CLEAR UP : despejar ⟨the fog lifted : se disipó la niebla⟩
lift[2] *n* **1** LIFTING : levantamiento *m*, alzamiento *m* **2** BOOST : impulso *m*, estímulo *m* **3 to give someone a lift** : llevar en coche a alguien
liftoff ['lɪft,ɔf] *n* : despegue *m*
ligament ['lɪgəmənt] *n* : ligamento *m*
ligature ['lɪgə,tʃʊr, -tʃər] *n* : ligadura *f*
light[1] ['laɪt] *v* **lit** ['lɪt] *or* **lighted; lighting** *vt* **1** ILLUMINATE : iluminar, alumbrar **2** IGNITE : encender, prenderle fuego a — *vi* : encenderse, prender
light[2] *vi* **lighted** *or* **lit** ['lɪt]; **lighting** **1** LAND, SETTLE : posarse **2** DISMOUNT : bajarse, apearse
light[3] ['laɪt] *adv* **1** LIGHTLY : suavemente, ligeramente **2 to travel light** : viajar con poco equipaje
light[4] *adj* **1** LIGHTWEIGHT : ligero, liviano, poco pesado **2** EASY : fácil, ligero, liviano ⟨light reading : lectura fácil⟩ ⟨light work : trabajo liviano⟩ **3** GENTLE, MILD : fino, suave, leve ⟨a light breeze : una brisa suave⟩ ⟨a light rain : una lluvia fina⟩ **4** FRIVOLOUS : de poca importancia, superficial **5** BRIGHT : bien iluminado, claro **6** PALE : claro (dícese de los colores), rubio (dícese del pelo)
light[5] *n* **1** ILLUMINATION : luz *f* **2** DAYLIGHT : luz *f* del día **3** DAWN : amanecer *m*, madrugada *f* **4** LAMP : lámpara *f* ⟨to turn on off the light : apagar la luz⟩ **5** ASPECT : aspecto *m* ⟨in a new light : con otros ojos⟩ ⟨in the light of : en vista de, a la luz de⟩ **6** MATCH : fósforo *m*, cerillo *m* **7 to bring to light** : sacar a (la) luz
lightbulb ['laɪt,bʌlb] *n* : bombilla *f*, foco *m*, bombillo *m CA, Col, Ven*
lighten ['laɪtən] *vt* **1** ILLUMINATE : iluminar, dar más luz a **2** : aclararse (el pelo) **3** : aligerar (una carga, etc.) **4** RELIEVE : aliviar **5** GLADDEN : alegrar ⟨it lightened his heart : alegró su corazón⟩
lighter ['laɪtər] *n* : encendedor *m*
lighthearted ['laɪt'hɑrtəd] *adj* : alegre, despreocupado, desenfadado — **lightheartedly** *adv*
lightheartedness ['laɪt'hɑrtədnəs] *n* : desenfado *m*, alegría *f*
lighthouse ['laɪt,haʊs] *n* : faro *m*

lighting ['laɪt̮ɪŋ] *n* : iluminación *f*
lightly ['laɪtli] *adv* **1** GENTLY : suavemente **2** SLIGHTLY : ligeramente **3** FRIVOLOUSLY : a la ligera **4 to let off lightly** : tratar con indulgencia
lightness ['laɪtnəs] *n* **1** BRIGHTNESS : luminosidad *f*, claridad *f* **2** GENTLENESS : ligereza *f*, suavidad *f*, delicadeza *f* **3** : ligereza *f*, liviandad *f* (de peso)
lightning ['laɪtnɪŋ] *n* : relámpago *m*, rayo *m*
lightning bug → **firefly**
lightproof ['laɪt̮ˌpruːf] *adj* : impenetrable por la luz, opaco
lightweight ['laɪt̮ˌweɪt] *adj* : ligero, liviano, de poco peso
light–year ['laɪt̮ˌjɪr] *n* : año *m* luz
lignite ['lɪgˌnaɪt] *n* : lignito *m*
likable *or* **likeable** ['laɪkəbəl] *adj* : simpático, agradable
like¹ ['laɪk] *v* **liked; liking** *vt* **1** : agradar, gustarle (algo a uno) ⟨he likes rice : le gusta el arroz⟩ ⟨she doesn't like flowers : a ella no le gustan las flores⟩ ⟨I like you : me caes bien⟩ **2** WANT : querer, desear ⟨I'd like a hamburger : quiero una hamburguesa⟩ ⟨he would like more help : le gustaría tener más ayuda⟩ — *vi* : querer ⟨do as you like : haz lo que quieras⟩
like² *adj* : parecido, semejante, similar
like³ *n* **1** PREFERENCE : preferencia *f*, gusto *m* **2 the like** : cosa *f* parecida, cosas *fpl* por el estilo ⟨I've never seen the like : nunca he visto cosa parecida⟩
like⁴ *conj* **1** AS IF : como si ⟨they looked at me like I was crazy : se me quedaron mirando como si estuviera loca⟩ **2** AS : como, igual que ⟨she doesn't love you like I do : ella no te quiere como yo⟩
like⁵ *prep* **1** : como, parecido a ⟨she acts like my mother : se comporta como mi madre⟩ ⟨he looks like me : se parece a mí⟩ **2** : propio de, típico de ⟨that's just like her : eso es muy típico de ella⟩ **3** : como ⟨animals like cows : animales como vacas⟩ **4 like this, like that** : así ⟨do it like that : hazlo así⟩
likelihood ['laɪkliˌhʊd] *n* : probabilidad *f* ⟨in all likelihood : con toda probabilidad⟩
likely¹ ['laɪkli] *adv* : probablemente ⟨most likely he's sick : lo más probable es que esté enfermo⟩ ⟨they're likely to come : es probable que vengan⟩
likely² *adj* **-lier; -est 1** PROBABLE : probable ⟨to be likely to : ser muy probable que⟩ **2** SUITABLE : apropiado, adecuado **3** BELIEVABLE : verosímil, creíble **4** PROMISING : prometedor
liken ['laɪkən] *vt* : comparar
likeness ['laɪknəs] *n* **1** SIMILARITY : semejanza *f*, parecido *m* **2** PORTRAIT : retrato *m*
likewise ['laɪkˌwaɪz] *adv* **1** SIMILARLY : de la misma manera, asimismo **2** ALSO : también, además, asimismo

liking ['laɪkɪŋ] *n* **1** FONDNESS : afición *f* (por una cosa), simpatía *f* (por una persona) **2** TASTE : gusto *m* ⟨is it to your liking? : ¿te gusta?⟩
lilac ['laɪlək, -ˌlæk, -ˌlɑk] *n* : lila *f*
lilt ['lɪlt] *n* : cadencia *f*, ritmo *m* alegre
lily ['lɪli] *n*, *pl* **lilies 1** : lirio *m*, azucena *f* **2 lily of the valley** : lirio *m* de los valles, muguete *m*
lima bean ['laɪmə] *n* : frijol *m* de media luna
limb ['lɪm] *n* **1** APPENDAGE : miembro *m*, extremidad *f* **2** BRANCH : rama *f*
limber¹ ['lɪmbər] *vi or* **to limber up** : calentarse, prepararse
limber² *adj* : ágil (dícese de las personas), flexible (dícese de los objetos)
limbo ['lɪmˌboː] *n*, *pl* **-bos 1** : limbo *m* (en la religión) **2** OBLIVION : olvido *m* ⟨the project is in limbo : el proyecto ha caído en el olvido⟩
lime ['laɪm] *n* **1** : cal *f* (óxido) **2** : lima *f* (fruta), limón *m* verde *Mex*
limelight ['laɪmˌlaɪt] *n* **to be in the limelight** : ser el centro de atención, estar en el candelero
limerick ['lɪmərɪk] *n* : poema *m* jocoso de cinco versos
limestone ['laɪmˌstoːn] *n* : piedra *f* caliza, caliza *f*
limit¹ ['lɪmət] *vt* : limitar, restringir
limit² *n* **1** MAXIMUM : límite *m*, máximo *m* ⟨speed limit : límite de velocidad⟩ **2 limits** *npl* : límites *mpl*, confines *mpl* ⟨city limits : límites de la ciudad⟩ **3 that's the limit!** : ¡eso es el colmo!
limitation [ˌlɪmə'teɪʃən] *n* : limitación *f*, restricción *f*
limited ['lɪmət̮əd] *adj* : limitado, restringido
limitless ['lɪmət̮ləs] *adj* : ilimitado, sin límites
limousine ['lɪməˌziːn, ˌlɪmə'-] *n* : limusina *f*
limp¹ ['lɪmp] *vi* : cojear
limp² *adj* **1** FLACCID : fláccido **2** LANK : lacio (dícese del pelo) **3** WEAK : débil ⟨to feel limp : sentirse desfallecer, sentirse sin fuerzas⟩
limp³ *n* : cojera *f*
limpid ['lɪmpəd] *adj* : límpido, claro
limply ['lɪmpli] *adv* : sin fuerzas
limpness ['lɪmpnəs] *n* : flaccidez *f*, debilidad *f*
linden ['lɪndən] *n* : tilo *m*
line¹ ['laɪn] *v* **lined; lining** *vt* **1** : forrar, cubrir ⟨to line a dress : forrar un vestido⟩ ⟨to line the walls : cubrir las paredes⟩ **2** MARK : rayar, trazar líneas en **3** BORDER : bordear **4** ALIGN : alinear — *vi* **to line up** : ponerse en fila, hacer cola
line² *n* **1** CORD, ROPE : cuerda *f* **2** WIRE : cable *m* ⟨power line : cable eléctrico⟩ **3** : línea *f* (de teléfono) **4** ROW : fila *f*, hilera *f* **5** NOTE : nota *f*, líneas *fpl* ⟨drop me a line : mándame unas líneas⟩ **6** COURSE : línea *f* ⟨line of inquiry : línea

de investigación⟩ **7** AGREEMENT : conformidad *f* ⟨to be in line with : ser conforme a⟩ ⟨to fall into line : estar de acuerdo⟩ **8** OCCUPATION : ocupación *f*, rama *f*, especialidad *f* **9** LIMIT : línea *f*, límite *m* ⟨dividing line : línea divisoria⟩ ⟨to draw the line : fijar límites⟩ **10** SERVICE : línea *f* ⟨bus line : línea de autobuses⟩ **11** MARK : línea *f*, arruga *f* (de la cara)

lineage ['lɪnɪɪʤ] *n* : linaje *m*, abolengo *m*

lineal ['lɪniəl] *adj* : en línea directa

lineaments ['lɪniəmənts] *npl* : facciones *fpl* (de la cara), rasgos *mpl*

linear ['lɪniər] *adj* : lineal

linen ['lɪnən] *n* : lino *m*

liner ['laɪnər] *n* **1** LINING : forro *m* **2** SHIP : buque *m*, transatlántico *m*

lineup ['laɪn,ʌp] *n* **1** : fila *f* de sospechosos **2** : formación *f* (en deportes) **3** ALIGNMENT : alineación *f*

linger ['lɪŋgər] *vi* **1** TARRY : quedarse, entretenerse, rezagarse **2** PERSIST : persistir, sobrevivir

lingerie [,lɑndʒə'reɪ, ,lænʒə'ri:] *n* : ropa *f* íntima femenina, lencería *f*

lingo ['lɪŋgo] *n, pl* **-goes 1** LANGUAGE : idioma *m* **2** JARGON : jerga *f*

linguist ['lɪŋgwɪst] *n* : lingüista *mf*

linguistic [lɪŋ'gwɪstɪk] *adj* : lingüístico

linguistics [lɪŋ'gwɪstɪks] *n* : lingüística *f*

liniment ['lɪnəmənt] *n* : linimento *m*

lining ['laɪnɪŋ] *n* : forro *m*

link[1] ['lɪŋk] *vt* : unir, enlazar, conectar — *vi* **to link up** : unirse, conectar

link[2] *n* **1** : eslabón *m* (de una cadena) **2** BOND : conexión *f*, lazo *m*, vínculo *m*

linkage ['lɪŋkɪʤ] *n* : conexión *f*, unión *f*, enlace *m*

linoleum [lə'no:liəm] *n* : linóleo *m*

linseed oil ['lɪn,si:d] *n* : aceite *m* de linaza

lint ['lɪnt] *n* : pelusa *f*

lintel ['lɪntəl] *n* : dintel *m*

lion ['laɪən] *n* : león *m*

lioness ['laɪənɪs] *n* : leona *f*

lionize ['laɪə,naɪz] *vt* **-ized; -izing** : tratar a una persona como muy importante

lip ['lɪp] *n* **1** : labio *m* **2** EDGE, RIM : pico *m* (de una jarra), borde *m* (de una taza)

lipreading ['lɪp,ri:dɪŋ] *n* : lectura *f* de los labios

lipstick ['lɪp,stɪk] *n* : lápiz *m* de labios, barra *f* de labios

liquefy ['lɪkwə,faɪ] *v* **-fied; -fying** *vt* : licuar — *vi* : licuarse

liqueur [lɪ'kʊr, -'kər, -'kjʊr] *n* : licor *m*

liquid[1] ['lɪkwəd] *adj* : líquido

liquid[2] *n* : líquido *m*

liquidate ['lɪkwə,deɪt] *vt* **-dated; -dating** : liquidar

liquidation [,lɪkwə'deɪʃən] *n* : liquidación *f*

liquidity [lɪk'wɪdəti] *n* : liquidez *f*

liquor ['lɪkər] *n* : alcohol *m*, bebidas *fpl* alcohólicas, licor *m*

lisp[1] ['lɪsp] *vi* : cecear

lisp[2] *n* : ceceo *m*

lissome ['lɪsəm] *adj* **1** FLEXIBLE : flexible **2** LITHE : ágil y grácil

list[1] ['lɪst] *vt* **1** ENUMERATE : hacer una lista de, enumerar **2** INCLUDE : poner en una lista, incluir — *vi* : escorar (dícese de un barco)

list[2] *n* **1** ENUMERATION : lista *f* **2** SLANT : escora *f*, inclinación *f*

listen ['lɪsən] *vi* **1** : escuchar, oír **2 to listen to** HEED : prestar atención a, hacer caso de, escuchar **3 to listen to reason** : atender a razones

listener ['lɪsənər] *n* : oyente *mf*, persona *f* que sabe escuchar

listless ['lɪstləs] *adj* : lánguido, apático — **listlessly** *adv*

listlessness ['lɪstləsnəs] *n* : apatía *f*, languidez *f*, desgana *f*

lit ['lɪt] → **light**

litany ['lɪtəni] *n, pl* **-nies** : letanía *f*

liter ['li:tər] *n* : litro *m*

literacy ['lɪtərəsi] *n* : alfabetismo *m*

literal ['lɪtərəl] *adj* : literal — **literally** *adv*

literary ['lɪtə,rri] *adj* : literario

literate ['lɪtərət] *adj* : alfabetizado

literature ['lɪtərə,tʃʊr, -tʃər] *n* : literatura *f*

lithe ['laɪð, 'laɪθ] *adj* : ágil y grácil

lithesome ['laɪðsəm, 'laɪθ-] → **lissome**

lithium ['lɪθiəm] *n* : litio *m*

lithograph ['lɪθə,græf] *n* : litografía *f*

lithographer [lɪ'θɑgrəfər, 'lɪθə-,græfər] *n* : litógrafo *m*, -fa *f*

lithography [lɪ'θɑgrəfi] *n* : litografía *f*

lithosphere ['lɪθə,sfɪr] *n* : litosfera *f*

Lithuanian [,lɪθə'weɪniən] *n* **1** : lituano *m* (idioma) **2** : lituano *m*, -na *f* — **Lithuanian** *adj*

litigant ['lɪtɪgənt] *n* : litigante *mf*

litigate ['lɪtə,geɪt] *vi* **-gated; -gating** : litigar

litigation [,lɪtə'geɪʃən] *n* : litigio *m*

litmus paper ['lɪtməs] *n* : papel *m* de tornasol

litter[1] ['lɪtər] *vt* : tirar basura en, ensuciar — *vi* : tirar basura

litter[2] *n* **1** : camada *f*, cría *f* ⟨a litter of kittens : una cría de gatitos⟩ **2** STRETCHER : camilla *f* **3** RUBBISH : basura *f* **4** : arena *f* higiénica (para gatos)

little[1] ['lɪtəl] *adv* **less** ['lɛs]; **least** ['li:st] **1** : poco ⟨she sings very little : canta muy poco⟩ **2 little did I know that . . .** : no tenía la menor idea de que . . . **3 as little as possible** : lo menos posible

little[2] *adj* **littler** *or* **less** ['lɛs] *or* **lesser** ['lɛsər]; **littlest** *or* **least** ['li:st] **1** SMALL : pequeño **2** : poco ⟨they speak little Spanish : hablan poco español⟩ ⟨little by little : poco a poco⟩ **3** TRIVIAL : sin importancia, trivial

little[3] *n* **1** : poco *m* ⟨little has changed : poco ha cambiado⟩ **2 a little** : un poco, algo ⟨it's a little surprising : es algo sorprendente⟩

Little Dipper → **dipper**

liturgical [lə'tərʤɪkəl] *adj* : litúrgico — **liturgically** [-kli] *adv*

liturgy ['lɪʧərʤi] n, pl -gies : liturgia f
livable ['lɪvəbəl] adj : habitable
live¹ ['lɪv] vi lived; living 1 EXIST : vivir ⟨as long as I live : mientras viva⟩ ⟨to live from day to day : vivir al día⟩ 2 : llevar una vida, vivir ⟨he lived simply : llevó una vida sencilla⟩ 3 SUBSIST : mantenerse, vivir 4 RESIDE : vivir, residir
live² ['laɪv] adj 1 LIVING : vivo 2 BURNING : encendido ⟨a live coal : una brasa⟩ 3 : con corriente ⟨live wires : cables con corriente⟩ 4 : cargado, sin estallar ⟨a live bomb : una bomba sin estallar⟩ 5 CURRENT : de actualidad ⟨a live issue : un asunto de actualidad⟩ 6 : en vivo, en directo ⟨a live interview : una entrevista en vivo⟩
livelihood ['laɪvliˌhʊd] n : sustento m, vida f, medio m de vida
liveliness ['laɪvlinəs] n : animación f, vivacidad f
livelong ['lɪv'lɔŋ] adj : entero, completo
lively ['laɪvli] adj -lier; -est : animado, vivaz, vivo, enérgico
liven ['laɪvən] vt : animar — vi : animarse
liver ['lɪvər] n : hígado m
livery ['lɪvəri] n, pl -eries : librea f
lives → life
livestock ['laɪvˌstɑk] n : ganado m
live wire n : persona f vivaz y muy activa
livid ['lɪvəd] adj 1 BLACK-AND-BLUE : amoratado 2 PALE : lívido 3 ENRAGED : furioso
living¹ ['lɪvɪŋ] adj : vivo
living² n to make a living : ganarse la vida
living room n : living m, sala f de estar
lizard ['lɪzərd] n : lagarto m
llama ['lɑmə, 'jɑ-] n : llama f
load¹ ['lo:d] vt : cargar, embarcar
load² n 1 CARGO : carga f 2 WEIGHT : peso m 3 BURDEN : carga f, peso m 4 loads npl : montón m, pila f, cantidad f ⟨loads of work : un montón de trabajo⟩
loaf¹ ['lo:f] vi : holgazanear, flojear, haraganear
loaf² n, pl loaves ['lo:vz] 1 : pan m, pan m de molde, barra f de pan 2 meat loaf : pan m de carne
loafer ['lo:fər] n : holgazán m, -zana f; haragán m, -gana f; vago m, -ga f
loam ['lo:m] n : marga f, suelo m
loan¹ ['lo:n] vt : prestar
loan² n : préstamo m, empréstito m (del banco)
loath ['lo:θ, 'lo:ð] adj : poco dispuesto ⟨I am loath to say it : me resisto a decirlo⟩
loathe ['lo:ð] vt loathed; loathing : odiar, aborrecer
loathing ['lo:ðɪŋ] n : aversión f, odio m, aborrecimiento m
loathsome ['lo:θsəm, 'lo:ð-] adj : odioso, repugnante
lob¹ ['lɑb] vt lobbed; lobbing : hacerle un globo (a otro jugador)

lob² n : globo m (en deportes)
lobby¹ ['lɑbi] v -bied; -bying vt : presionar, ejercer presión sobre — vi to lobby for : presionar para (lograr algo)
lobby² n, pl -bies 1 FOYER : vestíbulo m 2 LOBBYISTS : grupo m de presión, lobby m
lobbyist ['lɑbiɪst] n : miembro m de un lobby
lobe ['lo:b] n : lóbulo m
lobed ['lo:bd] adj : lobulado
lobotomy [lə'bɑtəmi, lo-] n, pl -mies : lobotomía f
lobster ['lɑbstər] n : langosta f
local¹ ['lo:kəl] adj : local
local² n 1 : anestesia f local 2 the locals : los vecinos del lugar, los habitantes
locale [lo'kæl] n : lugar m, escenario m
locality [lo'kæləti] n, pl -ties : localidad f
localize ['lo:kəˌlaɪz] vt -ized; -izing : localizar
locally ['lo:kəli] adv : en la localidad, en la zona
locate ['lo:ˌkeɪt, lo'keɪt] v -cated; -cating vt 1 POSITION : situar, ubicar 2 FIND : localizar, ubicar — vi SETTLE : establecerse
location [lo'keɪʃən] n 1 POSITION : posición f, emplazamiento m, ubicación f 2 PLACE : lugar m, sitio m
lock¹ ['lɑk] vt 1 FASTEN : cerrar 2 CONFINE : encerrar ⟨they locked me in the room : me encerraron en la sala⟩ 3 IMMOBILIZE : bloquear (una rueda) — vi 1 : cerrarse (dícese de una puerta) 2 : trabarse, bloquearse (dícese de una rueda)
lock² n 1 : mechón m (de pelo) 2 FASTENER : cerradura f, cerrojo m, chapa f 3 : esclusa f (de un canal)
locker ['lɑkər] n : armario m, cajón m con llave, lócker m
locket ['lɑkət] n : medallón m, guardapelo m, relicario m
lockjaw ['lɑkˌʤɔ] n : tétano m
lockout ['lɑkˌaʊt] n : cierre m patronal, lockout m
locksmith ['lɑkˌsmɪθ] n : cerrajero m, -ra f
lockup ['lɑkˌʌp] n JAIL : cárcel f
locomotion [ˌlo:kə'mo:ʃən] n : locomoción f
locomotive¹ [ˌlo:kə'mo:tɪv] adj : locomotor
locomotive² n : locomotora f
locust ['lo:kəst] n 1 : langosta f, chapulín m CA, Mex 2 CICADA : cigarra f, chicharra f 3 : acacia f blanca (árbol)
locution [lo'kju:ʃən] n : locución f
lode ['lo:d] n : veta f, vena f, filón m
lodestar ['lo:dˌstɑr] n : estrella f polar
lodestone ['lo:dˌsto:n] n : piedra f imán
lodge¹ ['lɑʤ] v lodged; lodging vt 1 HOUSE : hospedar, alojar 2 FILE : presentar ⟨to lodge a complaint : presentar una demanda⟩ — vi 1 : posarse, meterse ⟨the bullet lodged in the door

: la bala se incrustó en la puerta⟩ 2
STAY : hospedarse, alojarse
lodge² *n* 1 : pabellón *m*, casa *f* de campo ⟨hunting lodge : refugio de caza⟩ 2
: madriguera *f* (de un castor) 3 : logia *f* ⟨Masonic lodge : logia masónica⟩
lodger ['lɑdʒər] *n* : inquilino *m*, -na *f*; huésped *m*, -peda *f*
lodging ['lɑdʒɪŋ] *n* 1 : alojamiento *m* 2
lodgings *npl* ROOMS : habitaciones *fpl*
loft ['lɔft] *n* 1 ATTIC : desván *m*, ático *m*, buhardilla *f* 2 : loft *m* (en un depósito comercial) 3 HAYLOFT : pajar *m* 4
: galería *f* ⟨choir loft : galería del coro⟩
loftily ['lɔftəli] *adv* : altaneramente, con altivez
loftiness ['lɔftinəs] *n* 1 NOBILITY : nobleza *f* 2 ARROGANCE : altanería *f*, arrogancia *f* 3 HEIGHT : altura *f*, elevación *f*
lofty ['lɔfti] *adj* **loftier; -est** 1 NOBLE
: noble, elevado 2 HAUGHTY : altivo, arrogante, altanero 3 HIGH : majestuoso, elevado
log¹ ['lɔg, 'lɑg] *vi* **logged; logging** 1 : talar (árboles) 2 RECORD : registrar, anotar 3 **to log on** : entrar (al sistema) 4 **to log off** : salir (del sistema)
log² *n* 1 : tronco *m*, leño *m* 2 RECORD
: diario *m*
logarithm ['lɔgə,rɪðəm, 'lɑ-] *n* : logaritmo *m*
logger ['lɔgər, 'lɑ-] *n* : leñador *m*, -dora *f*
loggerhead ['lɔgər,hd, 'lɑ-] *n* 1 : tortuga *f* boba 2 **to be at loggerheads** : estar en pugna, estar en desacuerdo
logic ['lɑdʒɪk] *n* : lógica *f* — **logical** ['lɑdʒɪkəl] *adj* — **logically** [-kli] *adv*
logistic [lə'dʒɪstɪk, lo-] *adj* : logístico
logistics [lə'dʒɪstɪks, lo-] *ns & pl* : logística *f*
logo ['lo:,go:] *n, pl* **logos** [-,go:z] : logotipo *m*
loin ['lɔɪn] *n* 1 : lomo *m* ⟨pork loin
: lomo de cerdo⟩ 2 **loins** *npl* : lomos *mpl* ⟨to gird one's loins : prepararse para la lucha⟩
loiter ['lɔɪtər] *vi* : vagar, perder el tiempo
loll ['lɑl] *vi* 1 SLOUCH : repantigarse 2
IDLE : holgazanear, hacer el vago
lollipop *or* **lollypop** ['lɑli,pɑp] *n* : dulce *m* en palito, chupete *m* *Chile, Peru*, paleta *f* *CA, Mex*
lone ['lo:n] *adj* 1 SOLITARY : solitario 2
ONLY : único
loneliness ['lo:nlinəs] *n* : soledad *f*
lonely ['lo:nli] *adj* **-lier; -est** 1 SOLITARY
: solitario, aislado 2 LONESOME : solo
⟨to feel lonely : sentirse muy solo⟩
loner ['lo:nər] *n* : solitario *m*, -ria *f*; recluso *m*, -sa *f*
lonesome ['lo:nsəm] *adj* : solo, solitario
long¹ ['lɔŋ] *vi* 1 **to long for** : añorar, desear, ansiar 2 **to long to** : anhelar, estar deseando ⟨they longed to see her
: estaban deseando verla, tenían muchas ganas de verla⟩

long² *adv* 1 : mucho, mucho tiempo ⟨it didn't take long : no llevó mucho tiempo⟩ ⟨will it last long? : ¿va a durar mucho?⟩ 2 **all day long** : todo el día 3 **as long as** *or* **so long as** : mientras, con tal que 4 **long before** : mucho antes 5 **so long!** : ¡hasta luego!, ¡adiós!
long³ *adj* **longer** ['lɔŋgər]; **longest** ['lɔŋgəst] 1 (*indicating length*)) : largo ⟨the dress is too long : el vestido es demasiado largo⟩ ⟨a long way from : bastante lejos de⟩ ⟨in the long run : a la larga⟩ 2 (*indicating time*)) : largo, prolongado ⟨a long illness : una enfermedad prolongada⟩ ⟨a long walk : un paseo largo⟩ ⟨at long last : por fin⟩ 3 **to be long on** : estar cargado de
long⁴ *n* 1 **before long** : dentro de poco 2 **the long and the short** : lo esencial, lo fundamental
longevity [lɑn'dʒvəti] *n* : longevidad *f*
longhand ['lɔŋ,hænd] *n* : escritura *f* a mano, escritura *f* cursiva
longhorn ['lɔŋ,hɔrn] *n* : longhorn *mf*
longing [lɔŋɪŋ] *n* : vivo deseo *m*, ansia *f*, anhelo *m*
longingly [lɔŋɪŋlli] *adv* : ansiosamente, con ansia
longitude ['lɑndʒə,tu:d, -,tju:d] *n* : longitud *f*
longitudinal [,lɑndʒə'tu:dənəl, -'tju:-] *adj* : longitudinal — **longitudinally** *adv*
long–lived ['lɔŋ'lɪvd, -'laɪvd] *adj* : longevo
longshoreman ['lɔŋ'ʃormən] *n, pl* **-men** [-mən, -,mɛn] : estibador *m*, -dora *f*
long–standing ['lɔŋ'stændɪŋ] *adj* : de larga data
long–suffering ['lɔŋ'sʌfərɪŋ] *adj* : paciente, sufrido
look¹ ['lʊk] *vi* 1 GLANCE : mirar ⟨to look out the window : mirar por la ventana⟩ 2 INVESTIGATE : buscar, mirar ⟨look in the closet : busca en el closet⟩ ⟨look before you leap : mira lo que haces⟩ 3 SEEM : parecer ⟨he looks happy
: parece estar contento⟩ ⟨I look like my mother : me parezco a mi madre⟩ 4 **to look after** : cuidar, cuidar de 5 **to look for** EXPECT : esperar 6 **to look for** SEEK
: buscar — *vt* : mirar
look² *n* 1 GLANCE : mirada *f* 2 EXPRESSION : cara *f* ⟨a look of disapproval : una cara de desaprobación⟩ 3 ASPECT : aspecto *m*, apariencia *f*, aire *m* 4 **looks** *npl* : belleza *f*
lookout ['lʊk,aʊt] *n* 1 : centinela *mf*, vigía *mf* 2 **to be on the lookout for** : estar al acecho de, andar a la caza de
loom¹ ['lu:m] *vi* 1 : aparecer, surgir ⟨the city loomed up in the distance : la ciudad surgió en la distancia⟩ 2 IMPEND
: amenazar, ser inminente 3 **to loom large** : cobrar mucha importancia
loom² *n* : telar *m*
loon ['lu:n] *n* : somorgujo *m*, somormujo *m*
loony *or* **looney** ['lu:ni] *adj* **-nier; -est**
: loco, chiflado *fam*

loop¹ [ˈluːp] *vt* **1** : hacer lazadas con **2 to loop around** : pasar alrededor de — *vi* **1** : rizar el rizo (dícese de un avión) **2** : serpentear (dícese de una carretera)

loop² *n* **1** : lazada *f* (en hilo o cuerda) **2** BEND : curva *f* **3** CIRCUIT : circuito *m* cerrado **4** : rizo *m* (en la aviación) ⟨to loop the loop : rizar el rizo⟩

loophole [ˈluːpˌhoːl] *n* : escapatoria *f*, pretexto *m*

loose¹ [ˈluːs] *vt* **loosed; loosing 1** RELEASE : poner en libertad, soltar **2** UNTIE : deshacer, desatar **3** DISCHARGE, UNLEASH : descargar, desatar

loose² → **loosely**

loose³ *adj* **looser; -est 1** INSECURE : flojo, suelto, poco seguro ⟨a loose tooth : un diente flojo⟩ **2** ROOMY : suelto, holgado ⟨loose clothing : ropa holgada⟩ **3** OPEN : suelto, abierto ⟨loose soil : suelo suelto⟩ ⟨a loose weave : una tejida abierta⟩ **4** FREE : suelto ⟨to break loose : soltarse⟩ **5** SLACK : flojo, flexible **6** APPROXIMATE : libre, aproximado ⟨a loose translation : una traducción aproximada⟩

loosely [ˈluːsli] *adv* **1** : sin apretar **2** ROUGHLY : aproximadamente, más o menos

loosen [ˈluːsən] *vt* : aflojar

loose-leaf [ˈluːsˈliːf] *adj* : de hojas sueltas

looseness [ˈluːsnəs] *n* **1** : aflojamiento *m*, holgura *f* (de ropa) **2** IMPRECISION : imprecisión *f*

loot¹ [ˈluːt] *vt* : saquear, robar

loot² *n* : botín *m*

looter [ˈluːt̬ər] *n* : saqueador *m*, -dora *f*

lop [ˈlɑp] *vt* **lopped; lopping** : cortar, podar

lope¹ [ˈloːp] *vi* **loped; loping** : correr a paso largo

lope² *n* : paso *m* largo

lopsided [ˈlɑpˌsaɪdəd] *adj* **1** CROOKED : torcido, chueco, ladeado **2** ASYMETRICAL : asimétrico

loquacious [loˈkweɪʃəs] *adj* : locuaz

lord [ˈlɔrd] *n* **1** : señor *m*, noble *m* **2** : lord *m* (en la Gran Bretaña) **3 the Lord** : el Señor **4 good Lord!** : ¡Dios mío!

lordly [ˈlɔrdli] *adj* **-lier; -est** HAUGHTY : arrogante, altanero

lordship [ˈlɔrdˌʃɪp] *n* : señoría *f*

Lord's Supper *n* : Eucaristía *f*

lore [ˈlor] *n* : saber *m* popular, tradición *f*

lose [ˈluːz] *v* **lost** [ˈlɔst]; **losing** [ˈluː-zɪŋ] *vt* **1** : perder ⟨I lost my umbrella : perdí mi paraguas⟩ ⟨to lose blood : perder sangre⟩ ⟨to lose one's voice : quedarse fónico⟩ ⟨to have nothing to lose : no tener nada que perder⟩ ⟨to lose no time : no perder tiempo⟩ ⟨to lose weight : perder peso, adelgazar⟩ ⟨to lose one's temper : perder los estribos, enojarse, enfadarse⟩ ⟨to lose sight of : perder de vista⟩ **2** : costar, hacer perder ⟨the errors lost him his job : los errores le

costaron su empleo⟩ **3** : atrasar ⟨my watch loses 5 minutes a day : mi reloj atrasa 5 minutos por día⟩ **4 to lose oneself** : perderse, ensimismarse — *vi* **1** : perder ⟨we lost to the other team : perdimos contra el otro equipo⟩ **2** : atrasarse ⟨the clock loses time : el reloj se atrasa⟩

loser [ˈluːzər] *n* : perdedor *m*, -dora *f*

loss [ˈlɔs] *n* **1** LOSING : pérdida *f* ⟨loss of memory : pérdida de memoria⟩ ⟨to sell at a loss : vender con pérdida⟩ ⟨to be at a loss to : no saber como⟩ **2** DEFEAT : derrota *f*, juego *m* perdido **3 losses** *npl* DEATHS : muertos *mpl*

lost [ˈlɔst] *adj* **1** : perdido ⟨a lost cause : una causa perdida⟩ ⟨lost in thought : absorto⟩ **2 to get lost** : perderse **3 to make up for lost time** : recuperar el tiempo perdido

lot [ˈlɑt] *n* **1** DRAWING : sorteo *m* ⟨by lot : por sorteo⟩ **2** SHARE : parte *f*, porción *f* **3** FATE : suerte *f* **4** LAND, PLOT : terreno *m*, solar *m*, lote *m*, parcela *f* ⟨parking lot : estacionamiento⟩ **5 a lot of** *or* **lots of** : mucho, un montón de, bastante ⟨lots of books : un montón de libros, muchos libros⟩ ⟨a lot of people : mucha gente⟩

loth [ˈloːθ, ˈloːð] → **loath**

lotion [ˈloːʃən] *n* : loción *f*

lottery [ˈlɑt̬əri] *n, pl* **-teries** : lotería *f*

lotus [ˈloːt̬əs] *n* : loto *m*

loud¹ [ˈlaʊd] *adv* : alto, fuerte ⟨out loud : en voz alta⟩

loud² *adj* **1** : alto, fuerte ⟨a loud voice : una voz alta⟩ **2** NOISY : ruidoso ⟨a loud party : una fiesta ruidosa⟩ **3** FLASHY : llamativo, chillón

loudly [ˈlaʊdli] *adv* : alto, fuerte, en voz alta

loudness [ˈlaʊdnəs] *n* : volumen *m*, fuerza *f* (del ruido)

loudspeaker [ˈlaʊdˌspiːkər] *n* : altavoz *m*, altoparlante *m*

lounge¹ [ˈlaʊndʒ] *vi* **lounged; lounging** : holgazanear, gandulear

lounge² *n* : salón *m*, sala *f* de estar

louse [ˈlaʊs] *n, pl* **lice** [ˈlaɪs] : piojo *m*

lousy [ˈlaʊzi] *adj* **lousier; -est 1** : piojoso, lleno de piojos **2** BAD : pésimo, muy malo

lout [ˈlaʊt] *n* : bruto *m*, patán *m*

louver *or* **louvre** [ˈluːvər] *n* : persiana *f*, listón *m* de persiana

lovable [ˈlʌvəbəl] *adj* : adorable, amoroso, encantador

love¹ [ˈlʌv] *v* **loved; loving** *vt* **1** : querer, amar ⟨I love you : te quiero⟩ **2** ENJOY : encantarle a alguien, ser (muy) aficionado a, gustarle mucho a uno (algo) ⟨she loves flowers : le encantan las flores⟩ ⟨he loves golf : es muy aficionado al golf⟩ ⟨I'd love to go with you : me gustaría mucho acompañarte⟩ — *vi* : querer, amar

love² *n* **1** : amor *m*, cariño *m* ⟨to be in love with : estar enamorado de⟩ ⟨to fall

in love with : enamorarse de〉 2 EN-
THUSIASM, INTEREST : amor *m*, afición
m, gusto *m* 〈love of music : afición a
la música〉 3 BELOVED : amor *m*; amado *m*, -da *f*; enamorado *m*, -da *f*
loveless ['lʌvləs] *adj* : sin amor
loveliness ['lʌvlinəs] *n* : belleza *f*, hermosura *f*
lovelorn ['lʌv,lɔrn] *adj* : herido de amor,
perdidamente enamorado
lovely ['lʌvli] *adj* -**lier**; -**est** : hermoso,
bello, lindo, precioso
lover ['lʌvər] *n* : amante *mf* (de personas); aficionado *m*, -da *f* (a alguna actividad)
loving ['lʌvɪŋ] *adj* : amoroso, cariñoso
lovingly ['lʌvɪŋli] *adv* : cariñosamente
low[1] ['lo:] *vi* : mugir
low[2] *adv* : bajo, profundo 〈to aim low
: apuntar bajo〉 〈to lie low : mantenerse escondido〉 〈to turn the lights
down low : bajar las luces〉
low[3] *adj* **lower** ['lo:ər]; -**est** 1 : bajo 〈a
low building : un edificio bajo〉 〈a low
bow : una profunda reverencia〉 2
SOFT : bajo, suave 〈in a low voice : en
voz baja〉 3 SHALLOW : bajo, poco profundo 4 HUMBLE : humilde, modesto
5 DEPRESSED : deprimido, bajo de
moral 6 INFERIOR : bajo, inferior 7
UNFAVORABLE : mal 〈to have a low
opinion of him : tener un mal concepto de él〉 8 **to be low on** : tener poco
de, estar escaso de
low[4] *n* 1 : punto *m* bajo 〈to reach an all-
time low : estar más bajo que nunca〉
2 *or* **low gear** : primera velocidad *f* 3
: mugido *m* (de una vaca)
lowbrow ['lo:,brau] *n* : persona *f* inculta
lower[1] ['lo:ər] *vt* 1 DROP : bajar 〈to lower one's voice : bajar la voz〉 2 : arriar, bajar 〈to lower the flag : arriar la
bandera〉 3 REDUCE : reducir, bajar 4
to lower oneself : rebajarse
lower[2] ['lo:ər] *adj* : inferior, más bajo, de
abajo
lowland ['lo:lənd, -,lænd] *n* : tierras *fpl*
bajas
lowly ['lo:li] *adj* -**lier**; -**est** : humilde,
modesto
loyal ['lɔɪəl] *adj* : leal, fiel — **loyally** *adv*
loyalist ['lɔɪəlɪst] *n* : partidario *m*, -ria *f*
del régimen
loyalty ['lɔɪəlti] *n*, *pl* -**ties** : lealtad *f*, fidelidad *f*
lozenge ['lɑzəndʒ] *n* : pastilla *f*
LSD [,ɛl,ɛs'di:] *n* : LSD *m*
lubricant ['lu:brɪkənt] *n* : lubricante *m*
lubricate ['lu:brɪ,keɪt] *vt* -**cated**; -**cating**
: lubricar — **lubrication** [,lu:brɪ-
'keɪʃən] *n*
lucid ['lu:səd] *adj* : lúcido, claro — **lu-
cidly** *adv*
lucidity [lu:'sɪdəti] *n* : lucidez *f*
luck ['lʌk] *n* 1 : suerte *f* 2 **to have bad
luck** : tener mala suerte 3 **good luck!**
: ¡(buena) suerte!
luckily ['lʌkəli] *adv* : afortunadamente,
por suerte

luckless ['lʌkləs] *adj* : desafortunado
lucky ['lʌki] *adj* **luckier**; -**est** 1 : afortunado, que tiene suerte 〈a lucky
woman : una mujer afortunada〉 2
FORTUITOUS : fortuito, de suerte 3 OP-
PORTUNE : oportuno 4 : de (la) suerte
〈lucky number : número de la suerte〉
lucrative ['lu:krətɪv] *adj* : lucrativo,
provechoso — **lucratively** *adv*
ludicrous ['lu:dəkrəs] *adj* : ridículo, absurdo — **ludicrously** *adv*
ludicrousness ['lu:dəkrəsnəs] *n* : ridiculez *f*, absurdo *m*
lug ['lʌg] *vt* **lugged**; **lugging** : arrastrar,
transportar con dificultad
luggage ['lʌgɪdʒ] *n* : equipaje *m*
lugubrious [lʊ'gu:briəs] *adj* : lúgubre —
lugubriously *adv*
lukewarm ['lu:k'wɔrm] *adj* 1 TEPID
: tibio 2 HALFHEARTED : poco entusiasta
lull[1] ['lʌl] *vt* 1 CALM, SOOTHE : calmar,
sosegar 2 **to lull to sleep** : arrullar,
adormecer
lull[2] *n* : calma *f*, pausa *f*
lullaby ['lʌlə,baɪ] *n*, *pl* -**bies** : canción *f*
de cuna, arrullo *m*, nana *f*
lumber[1] ['lʌmbər] *vt* : aserrar (madera)
— *vi* : moverse pesadamente
lumber[2] *n* : madera *f*
lumberjack ['lʌmbər,dʒæk] *n* : leñador
m, -dora *f*
lumberyard ['lʌmbər,jɑrd] *n* : almacén
m de maderas
luminary ['lu:mə,nɛri] *n*, *pl* -**naries**
: lumbrera *f*, luminaria *f*
luminescence [,lu:mə'nɛsənts] *n* : luminiscencia *f* — **luminescent** [-'nɛs-
ənt] *adj*
luminosity [,lu:mə'nɑsəti] *n*, *pl* -**ties**
: luminosidad *f*
luminous ['lu:mənəs] *adj* : luminoso —
luminously *adv*
lump[1] ['lʌmp] *vt* *or* **to lump together**
: juntar, agrupar, amontonar — *vi*
CLUMP : agruparse, aglutinarse
lump[2] *n* 1 GLOB : grumo *m* 2 PIECE
: pedazo *m*, trozo *m*, terrón *m* 〈a lump
of coal : un trozo de carbón〉 〈a lump
of sugar : un terrón de azúcar〉 3
SWELLING : bulto *m*, hinchazón *f*,
protuberancia *f* 4 **to have a lump in
one's throat** : tener un nudo en la garganta
lumpy ['lʌmpi] *adj* **lumpier**; -**est** 1
: lleno de grumos (dícese de una salsa)
2 UNEVEN : desigual, disparejo
lunacy ['lu:nəsi] *n*, *pl* -**cies** : locura *f*
lunar ['lu:nər] *adj* : lunar
lunatic[1] ['lu:nə,tɪk] *adj* : lunático, loco
lunatic[2] *n* : loco *m*, -ca *f*
lunch[1] ['lʌntʃ] *vi* : almorzar, comer
lunch[2] *n* : almuerzo *m*, comida *f*, lonche
m
luncheon ['lʌntʃən] *n* 1 : comida *f*, almuerzo *m* 2 **luncheon meat** : fiambres
fpl

lung ['lʌŋ] *n* : pulmón *m*
lunge[1] ['lʌndʒ] *vi* **lunged; lunging 1**
THRUST : atacar (en la esgrima) **2 to
lunge forward** : arremeter, lanzarse
lunge[2] *n* **1** : arremetida *f*, embestida *f* **2**
: estocada *f* (en la esgrima)
lurch[1] ['lərtʃ] *vi* **1** PITCH : cabecear, dar
bandazos, dar sacudidas **2** STAGGER
: tambalearse
lurch[2] *n* **1** : sacudida *f*, bandazo *m* (de
un vehículo) **2** : tambaleo *m* (de una
persona)
lure[1] ['lʊr] *vt* **lured; luring** : atraer
lure[2] *n* **1** ATTRACTION : atractivo *m* **2**
ENTICEMENT : señuelo *m*, aliciente
m **3** BAIT : cebo *m* artificial (en la
pesca)
lurid ['lʊrəd] *adj* **1** GRUESOME : espeluznante, horripilante **2** SENSA-
TIONAL : sensacionalista, chocante **3**
GAUDY : chillón
lurk ['lərk] *vi* : estar al acecho
luscious ['lʌʃəs] *adj* **1** DELICIOUS : delicioso, exquisito **2** SEDUCTIVE : seductor, cautivador
lush ['lʌʃ] *adj* **1** LUXURIANT : exuberante, lozano **2** LUXURIOUS : suntuoso,
lujoso
lust[1] ['lʌst] *vi* **to lust after** : desear (a una
persona), codiciar (riquezas, etc.)
lust[2] *n* **1** LASCIVIOUSNESS : lujuria *f*, lascivia *f* **2** CRAVING : deseo *m*, ansia *f*,
anhelo *m*
luster *or* **lustre** ['lʌstər] *n* **1** GLOSS,

SHEEN : lustre *m*, brillo *m* **2** SPLEN-
DOR : lustre *m*, esplendor *m*
lusterless ['lʌstərləs] *adj* : deslustrado,
sin brillo
lustful ['lʌstfəl] *adj* : lujurioso, lascivo,
lleno de deseo
lustrous ['lʌstrəs] *adj* : brillante, brilloso, lustroso
lusty ['lʌsti] *adj* **lustier; -est** : fuerte, robusto, vigoroso — **lustily** ['lʌstəli] *adv*
lute ['lu:t] *n* : laúd *m*
luxuriant [ˌlʌg'ʒʊriənt, ˌlʌk'ʃʊr-] *adj* **1**
: exuberante, lozano (dícese de las
plantas) **2** : abundante y hermoso
(dícese del pelo) — **luxuriantly** *adv*
luxuriate [ˌlʌg'ʒʊriˌeɪt, ˌlʌk'ʃʊr-] *vi*
-ated; -ating 1 : disfrutar **2 to luxuriate in** : deleitarse con
luxurious [ˌlʌg'ʒʊriəs, ˌlʌk'ʃʊr-] *adj* : lujoso, suntuoso — **luxuriously** *adv*
luxury ['lʌkʃəri, 'lʌgʒə-] *n, pl* **-ries** : lujo
m
lye ['laɪ] *n* : lejía *f*
lying → **lie**[1], **lie**[2]
lymph ['lɪmpf] *n* : linfa *f*
lymphatic [lɪm'fætɪk] *adj* : linfático
lynch ['lɪntʃ] *vt* : linchar
lynx ['lɪŋks] *n, pl* **lynx** *or* **lynxes** : lince
m
lyre ['laɪr] *n* : lira *f*
lyric[1] ['lɪrɪk] *adj* : lírico
lyric[2] *n* **1** : poema *m* lírico **2 lyrics** *npl*
: letra *f* (de una canción)
lyrical ['lɪrɪkəl] *adj* : lírico, elocuente

M

m ['ɛm] *n, pl* **m's** *or* **ms** ['ɛmz] : deci-
motercera letra del alfabeto inglés
ma'am ['mæm] → **madam**
macabre [mə'kɑb, -'kɑbər, -'kɑbrə] *adj*
: macabro
macadam [mə'kædəm] *n* : macadán *m*
macaroni [ˌmækə'ro:ni] *n* : macarrones
mpl
macaroon [ˌmækə'ru:n] *n* : macarrón *m*,
mostachón *m*
macaw [mə'kɔ] *n* : guacamayo *m*
mace ['meɪs] *n* **1** : maza *f* (arma o símbolo) **2** : macis *f* (especia)
machete [mə'ʃɛti] *n* : machete *m*
machination [ˌmækə'neɪʃən, ˌmæʃə-] *n*
: maquinación *f*, intriga *f*
machine[1] [mə'ʃi:n] *vt* **-chined; -chining**
: trabajar a máquina
machine[2] *n* **1** : máquina *f* ⟨machine
shop : taller de máquinas⟩ ⟨machine
language : lenguaje de la máquina⟩ **2**
: aparato *m*, maquinaria *f* (en política)
machine gun *n* : ametralladora *f*
machinery [mə'ʃi:nəri] *n, pl* **-eries 1**
: maquinaria *f* **2** WORKS : mecanismo
m
machinist [mə'ʃi:nɪst] *n* : maquinista *mf*
machismo [mɑ'tʃi:zmo:] *n* : machismo
m, masculinidad *f*

macho ['mɑtʃo:] *adj* : machote, macho
mackerel ['mækərəl] *n, pl* **-el** *or* **-els** : caballa *f*
mackinaw ['mækəˌnɔ] *n* : chaqueta *f* escocesa de lana
mad ['mæd] *adj* **madder; maddest 1** IN-
SANE : loco, demente **2** RABID : rabioso **3** FOOLISH : tonto, insensato **4**
ANGRY : enojado, furioso **5** CRAZY
: loco ⟨I'm mad about you : estoy loco
por ti⟩
Madagascan [ˌmædə'gæskən] *n* : malgache *mf* — **Madagascan** *adj*
madam ['mædəm] *n, pl* **mesdames**
[meɪ'dɑm, -'dæm] : señora *f*
madcap[1] ['mædˌkæp] *adj* ZANY : alocado, disparatado
madcap[2] *n* : alocado *m*, -da *f*
madden ['mædən] *vt* : enloquecer, enfurecer
maddening ['mædənɪŋ] *adj* : enloquecedor, exasperante ⟨I find it maddening : me saca de quicio⟩
made → **make**[1]
madhouse ['mædˌhaʊs] *n* : manicomio
m ⟨the office was a madhouse : la oficina parecía una casa de locos⟩
madly ['mædli] *adv* : como un loco, locamente

madman ['mæd,mæn, -mən] *n, pl* **-men** [-mən, -,mɛn] : loco *m*, demente *m*
madness ['mædnəs] *n* : locura *f*, demencia *f*
madwoman ['mæd,wumən] *n, pl* **-women** [-,wɪmən] : loca *f*, demente *f*
maelstrom ['meɪlstrəm] *n* : remolino *m*, vorágine *f*
maestro ['maɪ,stroː] *n, pl* **-stros** *or* **-stri** [-,striː] : maestro *m*
Mafia ['mɑfiə] *n* : Mafia *f*
magazine ['mægə,ziːn] *n* **1** STOREHOUSE : almacén *m*, polvorín *m* (de explosivos) **2** PERIODICAL : revista *f* **3** : cargador *m* (de un arma de fuego)
magenta [mə'dʒɛntə] *n* : magenta *f*, color *m* magenta
maggot ['mægət] *n* : gusano *m*
magic[1] ['mædʒɪk] *or* **magical** ['mædʒɪkəl] *adj* : mágico
magic[2] *n* : magia *f*
magically ['mædʒɪkli] *adv* : mágicamente ⟨they magically appeared : aparecieron como por arte de magia⟩
magician [mə'dʒɪʃən] *n* **1** SORCERER : mago *m*, -ga *f* **2** CONJURER : prestidigitador *m*, -dora *f*; mago *m*, -ga *f*
magistrate ['mædʒə,streɪt] *n* : magistrado *m*, -da *f*
magma ['mægmə] *n* : magma *m*
magnanimity [,mægnə'nɪməti] *n, pl* **-ties** : magnanimidad *f*
magnanimous [mæg'nænəməs] *adj* : magnánimo, generoso — **magnanimously** *adv*
magnate ['mæg,neɪt, -nət] *n* : magnate *mf*
magnesium [mæg'niːziəm, -ʒəm] *n* : magnesio *m*
magnet ['mægnət] *n* : imán *m*
magnetic [mæg'nɛtɪk] *adj* : magnético — **magnetically** [-tɪkli] *adv*
magnetic field *n* : campo *m* magnético
magnetism ['mægnə,tɪzəm] *n* : magnetismo *m*
magnetize ['mægnə,taɪz] *vt* **-tized; -tizing 1** : magnetizar, imantar **2** ATTRACT : magnetizar, atraer
magnification [,mægnəfə'keɪʃən] *n* : aumento *m*, ampliación *f*
magnificence [mæg'nɪfəsənts] *n* : magnificencia *f*
magnificent [mæg'nɪfəsənt] *adj* : magnífico — **magnificently** *adv*
magnify ['mægnə,faɪ] *vt* **-fied; -fying 1** ENLARGE : ampliar **2** EXAGGERATE : magnificar, exagerar
magnifying glass *n* : lupa *f*
magnitude ['mægnə,tuːd, -,tjuːd] *n* **1** GREATNESS : magnitud *f*, grandeza *f* **2** QUANTITY : cantidad *f* **3** IMPORTANCE : magnitud *f*, envergadura *f*
magnolia [mæg'noːljə] *n* : magnolia *f* (flor), magnolio *m* (árbol)
magpie ['mæg,paɪ] *n* : urraca *f*
mahogany [mə'hagəni] *n, pl* **-nies** : caoba *f*

maid ['meɪd] *n* **1** MAIDEN : doncella *f* **2** *or* **maidservant** ['meɪd,sərvənt] : sirvienta *f*, muchacha *f*, mucama *f*, criada *f*
maiden[1] ['meɪdən] *adj* **1** UNMARRIED : soltera **2** FIRST : primero ⟨maiden voyage : primera travesía⟩
maiden[2] *n* : doncella *f*
maidenhood ['meɪdən,hud] *n* : doncellez *f*
maiden name *n* : nombre *m* de soltera
mail[1] ['meɪl] *vt* : enviar por correo, echar al correo
mail[2] *n* **1** : correo *m* ⟨airmail : correo aéreo⟩ **2** : malla *f* ⟨coat of mail : cota de malla⟩
mailbox ['meɪl,baks] *n* : buzón *m*
mailman ['meɪl,mæn, -mən] *n, pl* **-men** [-mən, -,mn] : cartero *m*
maim ['meɪm] *vt* : mutilar, desfigurar, lisiar
main[1] ['meɪn] *adj* : principal, central ⟨the main office : la oficina central⟩
main[2] *n* **1** HIGH SEAS : alta mar *f* **2** : tubería *f* principal (de agua o gas), cable *m* principal (de un circuito) **3 with might and main** : con todas sus fuerzas
mainframe ['meɪn,freɪm] *n* : mainframe *m*, computadora *f* central
mainland ['meɪn,lænd, -lənd] *n* : continente *m*
mainly ['meɪnli] *adv* **1** PRINCIPALLY : principalmente, en primer lugar **2** MOSTLY : principalmente, en la mayor parte
mainstay ['meɪn,steɪ] *n* : pilar *m*, sostén *m* principal
mainstream[1] ['meɪn,striːm] *adj* : dominante, corriente, convencional
mainstream[2] *n* : corriente *f* principal
maintain [meɪn'teɪn] *vt* **1** SERVICE : dar mantenimiento a (una máquina) **2** PRESERVE : mantener, conservar ⟨to maintain silence : guardar silencio⟩ **3** SUPPORT : mantener, sostener **4** ASSERT : mantener, sostener, afirmar
maintenance ['meɪntənənts] *n* : mantenimiento *m*
maize ['meɪz] *n* : maíz *m*
majestic [mə'dʒɛstɪk] *adj* : majestuoso — **majestically** [-tɪkli] *adv*
majesty ['mædʒəsti] *n, pl* **-ties 1** : majestad *f* ⟨Your Majesty : su Majestad⟩ **2** SPLENDOR : majestuosidad *f*, esplendor *m*
major[1] ['meɪdʒər] *vi* **-jored; -joring** : especializarse
major[2] *adj* **1** GREATER : mayor **2** NOTEWORTHY : mayor, notable **3** SERIOUS : grave **4** : mayor (en la música)
major[3] *n* **1** : mayor *mf*, comandante *mf* (en las fuerzas armadas) **2** : especialidad *f* (universitaria)
Majorcan [ma'dʒɔrkən, mə-, -'jɔr-] : mallorquín *m*, -quina *f* — **Majorcan** *adj*
major general *n* : general *mf* de división

majority [mə'dʒɔrəṭi] *n, pl* **-ties 1**
ADULTHOOD : mayoría *f* de edad **2**
: mayoría*f*, mayor parte*f* ⟨the vast majority : la inmensa mayoría⟩
make¹ ['meɪk] *v* **made** ['meɪd;]; **making**
vt **1** CREATE : hacer ⟨to make noise
: hacer ruido⟩ **2** FASHION, MANUFAC-
TURE : hacer, fabricar ⟨she made a
dress : hizo un vestido⟩ **3** DEVISE,
FORM : desarrollar, elaborar, formar **4**
CONSTITUTE : hacer, constituir ⟨made
of stone : hecho de piedra⟩ **5** PREPARE
: hacer, preparar **6** RENDER : hacer,
poner ⟨it makes him nervous : lo pone
nervioso⟩ ⟨to make someone happy
: hacer feliz a alguien⟩ ⟨it made me sad
: me dio pena⟩ **7** PERFORM : hacer ⟨to
make a gesture : hacer un gesto⟩ **8**
COMPEL : hacer, forzar, obligar **9**
EARN : ganar ⟨to make a living : ganarse la vida⟩ — *vi* **1** HEAD : ir, dirigirse ⟨we made for home : nos fuimos
a casa⟩ **2 to make do** : arreglárselas **3
to make good** REPAY : pagar **4 to make
good** SUCCEED : tener éxito
make² *n* BRAND : marca *f*
make–believe¹ [,meɪkbə'li:v] *adj* : imaginario
make–believe² *n* : fantasía *f*, invención
f ⟨a world of make-believe : un mundo de ensueño⟩
make out *vt* **1** WRITE : hacer (un cheque)
2 DISCERN : distinguir, divisar **3** UN-
DERSTAND : comprender, entender —
vi : arreglárselas ⟨how did you make
out? : ¿qué tal te fue?⟩
maker ['meɪkər] *n* : fabricante *mf*
makeshift ['meɪk,ʃɪft] *adj* : provisional,
improvisado
makeup ['meɪk,ʌp] *n* **1** COMPOSITION
: composición *f* **2** CHARACTER : carácter *m*, temperamento *m* **3** COSMETICS
: maquillaje *m*
make up *vt* **1** INVENT : inventar **2** : recuperar ⟨she made up the time : recu-
peró las horas perdidas⟩ — *vi* RECON-
CILE : hacer las paces, reconciliarse
making ['meɪkɪŋ] *n* **1** : creación *f*, producción *f* ⟨in the making : en ciernes⟩
2 to have the makings of : tener
madera de (dícese de personas), tener
los ingredientes para
maladjusted [,mælə'dʒʌstəd] *adj* : inadaptado
malady ['mælədi] *n, pl* **-dies** : dolencia
f, enfermedad *f*, mal *m*
malaise [mə'leɪz, mæ-] *n* : malestar *m*
malapropism ['mælə,prɑ,pɪzəm] *n* : uso
m incorrecto y cómico de una palabra
malaria [mə'leriə] *n* : malaria *f*, paludismo *m*
malarkey [mə'lɑrki] *n* : tonterías *fpl*, estupideces *fpl*
Malawian [mə'lɑwiən] *n* : malauiano *m*,
-na *f* — **Malawian** *adj*
Malay [mə'leɪ, 'meɪ,leɪ] *n* **1** *or* **Malayan**
[mə'leɪən, meɪ-; 'meɪ,leɪən] : malayo *m*,

-ya *f* **2** : malayo *m* (idioma) — **Malay**
or **Malayan** *adj*
Malaysian [mə'leɪʒən, -ʃən] *n* : malasio
m, -sia*f*; malaisio *m*, -sia*f* — **Malaysian**
adj
male¹ ['meɪl] *adj* **1** : macho **2** MASCU-
LINE : masculino
male² *n* : macho *m* (de animales o plantas), varón *m* (de personas)
malefactor ['mælə,fæktər] *n* : malhechor *m*, -chora *f*
maleness ['meɪlnəs] *n* : masculinidad *f*
malevolence [mə'lɛvələnts] *n* : malevolencia *f*
malevolent [mə'lɛvələnt] *adj* : malévolo
malformation [,mælfɔr'meɪʃən] *n* : malformación *f*
malformed [mæl'fɔrmd] *adj* : mal formado, deforme
malfunction¹ [mæl'fʌŋkʃən] *vi* : funcionar mal
malfunction² *n* : mal funcionamiento *m*
malice ['mælɪs] *n* **1** : malicia *f*, malevolencia *f* **2 with malice aforethought**
: con premeditación
malicious [mə'lɪʃəs] *adj* : malicioso,
malévolo — **maliciously** *adv*
malign¹ [mə'laɪn] *vt* : calumniar, difamar
malign² *adj* : maligno
malignancy [mə'lɪgnəntsi] *n, pl* **-cies**
: malignidad *f*
malignant [mə'lɪgnənt] *adj* : maligno
malinger [mə'lɪŋgər] *vi* : fingirse enfermo
malingerer [mə'lɪŋgərər] *n* : uno que se
finge enfermo
mall ['mɔl] *n* **1** PROMENADE : alameda
f, paseo *m* (arbolado) **2** : centro *m* comercial ⟨shopping mall : galería comer-
cial⟩
mallard ['mælərd] *n, pl* **-lard** *or* **-lards**
: pato *m* real, ánade *mf* real
malleable ['mæliəbəl] *adj* : maleable
mallet ['mælət] *n* : mazo *m*
malnourished [mæl'nərɪʃt] *adj* : desnutrido, malnutrido
malnutrition [,mælnu'trɪʃən, -nju-] *n*
: desnutrición *f*, malnutrición *f*
malodorous [mæl'o:dərəs] *adj* : maloliente
malpractice [,mæl'præktəs] *n* : mala
práctica *f*, negligencia *f*
malt ['mɔlt] *n* : malta *f*
maltreat [mæl'tri:t] *vt* : maltratar
mama *or* **mamma** ['mɑmə] *n* : mamá *f*
mammal ['mæməl] *n* : mamífero *m*
mammalian [mə'meɪliən, mæ-] *adj*
: mamífero
mammary ['mæməri] *adj* **1** : mamario
2 mammary gland : glándula mamaria
mammogram ['mæmə,græm] *n* : mamografía *f*
mammoth¹ ['mæməθ] *adj* : colosal, gigantesco
mammoth² *n* : mamut *m*
man¹ ['mæn] *vt* **manned; manning** : tripular (un barco o avión), encargarse de
(un servicio)

man² *n, pl* **men** [ˈmɛn] **1** PERSON : hombre *m*, persona *f* **2** MALE : hombre *m* **3** MANKIND : humanidad *f*

manacles [ˈmænɪkəlz] *npl* HANDCUFFS : esposas *fpl*

manage [ˈmænɪʤ] *v* **-aged; -aging** *vt* **1** HANDLE : controlar, manejar **2** DIRECT : administrar, dirigir **3** CONTRIVE : lograr, ingeniárselas para — *vi* COPE : arreglárselas

manageable [ˈmænɪʤəbəl] *adj* : manejable

management [ˈmænɪʤmənt] *n* **1** DIRECTION : administración *f*, gestión *f*, dirección *f* **2** HANDLING : manejo *m* **3** MANAGERS : dirección *f*, gerencia *f*

manager [ˈmænɪʤər] *n* : director *m*, -tora *f*; gerente *mf*; administrador *m*, -dora *f*

managerial [ˌmænəˈʤɪriəl] *adj* : directivo, gerencial

mandarin [ˈmændərən] *n* **1** : mandarín *m* **2** *or* **mandarin orange** : mandarina *f*

mandate [ˈmænˌdeɪt] *n* : mandato *m*

mandatory [ˈmændəˌtori] *adj* : obligatorio

mandible [ˈmændəbəl] *n* : mandíbula *f*

mandolin [ˌmændəˈlɪn, ˈmændələn] *n* : mandolina *f*

mane [ˈmeɪn] *n* : crin *f* (de un caballo), melena *f* (de un león o una persona)

maneuver¹ [məˈnuːvər, -ˈnjuː-] *vt* **1** PLACE, POSITION : maniobrar, posicionar, colocar **2** MANIPULATE : manipular, maniobrar — *vi* : maniobrar

maneuver² *n* : maniobra *f*

manfully [ˈmænfəli] *adj* : valientemente

manganese [ˈmæŋgəˌniːz, -ˌniːs] *n* : manganeso *m*

mange [ˈmeɪnʤ] *n* : sarna *f*

manger [ˈmeɪnʤər] *n* : pesebre *m*

mangle [ˈmæŋgəl] *vt* **-gled; -gling** **1** CRUSH, DESTROY : aplastar, despedazar, destrozar **2** MUTILATE : mutilar ⟨to mangle a text : mutilar un texto⟩

mango [ˈmæŋˌgoː] *n, pl* **-goes** : mango *m*

mangrove [ˈmæŋˌgroːv, ˈmæŋ-] *n* : mangle *m*

mangy [ˈmeɪnʤi] *adj* **mangier; -est** **1** : sarnoso **2** SHABBY : gastado

manhandle [ˈmænˌhændəl] *vt* **-dled; -dling** : maltratar, tratar con poco cuidado

manhole [ˈmænˌhoːl] *n* : boca *f* de alcantarilla

manhood [ˈmænˌhʊd] *n* **1** : madurez *f* (de un hombre) **2** COURAGE, MANLINESS : hombría *f*, valor *m* **3** MEN : hombres *mpl*

manhunt [ˈmænˌhʌnt] *n* : búsqueda *f* (de un criminal)

mania [ˈmeɪniə, -njə] *n* : manía *f*

maniac [ˈmeɪniˌæk] *n* : maníaco *m*, -ca *f*; maniático *m*, -ca *f*

maniacal [məˈnaɪəkəl] *adj* : maníaco, maniaco

manicure¹ [ˈmænəˌkjʊr] *vt* **-cured; -curing** **1** : hacer la manicura a **2** TRIM : recortar

manicure² *n* : manicura *f*

manicurist [ˈmænəˌkjʊrɪst] *n* : manicuro *m*, -ra *f*

manifest¹ [ˈmænəˌfɛst] *vt* : manifestar

manifest² *adj* : manifiesto, patente — **manifestly** *adv*

manifestation [ˌmænəfəˈsteɪʃən] *n* : manifestación *f*

manifesto [ˌmænəˈfɛsˌtoː] *n, pl* **-tos** *or* **-toes** : manifiesto *m*

manifold¹ [ˈmænəˌfoːld] *adj* : diverso, variado

manifold² *n* : colector *m* (de escape)

manipulate [məˈnɪpjəˌleɪt] *vt* **-lated; -lating** : manipular

manipulation [məˌnɪpjəˈleɪʃən] *n* : manipulación *f*

manipulative [məˈnɪpjəˌleɪt̬ɪv, -lət̬ɪv] *adj* : manipulador

mankind [ˈmænˈkaɪnd, ˌkaɪnd] *n* : género *m* humano, humanidad *f*

manliness [ˈmænlinəs] *n* : hombría *f*, masculinidad *f*

manly [ˈmænli] *adj* **-lier; -est** : varonil, viril

man–made [ˈmænˈmeɪd] *adj* : artificial ⟨man-made fabrics : telas sintéticas⟩

manna [ˈmænə] *n* : maná *m*

mannequin [ˈmænɪkən] *n* **1** DUMMY : maniquí *m* **2** MODEL : modelo *mf*

manner [ˈmænər] *n* **1** KIND, SORT : tipo *m*, clase *f* **2** WAY : manera *f*, modo *m* **3** STYLE : estilo *m* (artístico) **4** **manners** *npl* CUSTOMS : costumbres *fpl* ⟨Victorian manners : costumbres victorianas⟩ **5** **manners** *npl* ETIQUETTE : modales *mpl*, educación *f*, etiqueta *f* ⟨good manners : buenos modales⟩

mannered [ˈmænərd] *adj* **1** AFFECTED, ARTIFICIAL : amanerado, afectado **2** **well–mannered** : educado, cortés **3** → **ill–mannered**

mannerism [ˈmænəˌrɪzəm] *n* : peculiaridad *f*, gesto *m* particular

mannerly [ˈmænərli] *adj* : cortés, bien educado

mannish [ˈmænɪʃ] *adj* : masculino, hombruno

man–of–war [ˌmænəˈwɔr, -əvˈwɔr] *n, pl* **men–of–war** [ˌmɛn-] WARSHIP : buque *m* de guerra

manor [ˈmænər] *n* **1** : casa *f* solariega, casa *f* señorial **2** ESTATE : señorío *m*

manpower [ˈmænˌpaʊər] *n* : personal *m*, mano *f* de obra

mansion [ˈmænʧən] *n* : mansión *f*

manslaughter [ˈmænˌslɔtər] *n* : homicidio *m* sin premeditación

mantel [ˈmæntəl] *n* : repisa *f* de chimenea

mantelpiece [ˈmæntəlˌpiːs] → **mantel**

mantis [ˈmæntəs] *n, pl* **-tises** *or* **-tes** [ˈmænˌtiːz] : mantis *f* religiosa

mantle [ˈmæntəl] *n* : manto *m*

manual¹ [ˈmænjʊəl] *adj* : manual — **manually** *adv*

manual² *n* : manual *m*

manufacture¹ [ˌmænjəˈfæktʃər] *vt* **-tured; -turing** 1 : fabricar, manufacturar, confeccionar (ropa), elaborar (comestibles)

manufacture² *n* : manufactura *f*, fabricación *f*, confección *f* (de ropa), elaboración *f* (de comestibles)

manufacturer [ˌmænjəˈfæktʃərər] *n* : fabricante *m*; manufacturero *m*, -ra *f*

manure [məˈnʊr, -ˈnjʊr] *n* : estiércol *m*

manuscript [ˈmænjəˌskrɪpt] *n* : manuscrito *m*

many¹ [ˈmɛni] *adj* **more** [ˈmor]; **most** [ˈmoːst] : muchos

many² *pron* : muchos *pl*, -chas *pl*

map¹ [ˈmæp] *vt* **mapped; mapping** 1 : trazar el mapa de 2 PLAN : planear, proyectar ⟨to map out a program : planear un programa⟩

map² *n* : mapa *m*

maple [ˈmeɪpəl] *n* : arce *m*

mar [ˈmɑr] *vt* **marred; marring** 1 SPOIL : estropear, echar a perder 2 DEFACE : desfigurar

maraschino [ˌmærəˈskiːnoː, -ˈʃiː-] *n, pl* **-nos** : cereza *f* al marrasquino

marathon [ˈmærəˌθɑn] *n* 1 RACE : maratón *m* 2 CONTEST : competencia *f* de resistencia

maraud [məˈrɔd] *vi* : merodear

marauder [məˈrɔdər] *n* : merodeador *m*, -dora *f*

marble [ˈmɑrbəl] *n* 1 : mármol *m* 2 : canica *f* ⟨to play marbles : jugar a las canicas⟩

march¹ [ˈmɑrtʃ] *vi* 1 : marchar, desfilar ⟨they marched past the grandstand : desfilaron ante la tribuna⟩ 2 : caminar con resolución ⟨she marched right up to him : se le acercó sin vacilación⟩

march² *n* 1 MARCHING : marcha *f* 2 PASSAGE : paso *m* (del tiempo) 3 PROGRESS : avance *m*, progreso *m* 4 : marcha *f* (en música)

March [ˈmɑrtʃ] *n* : marzo *m*

marchioness [ˈmɑrʃənɪs] *n* : marquesa *f*

Mardi Gras [ˈmɑrdiˌgrɑ] *n* : martes *m* de Carnaval

mare [ˈmær] *n* : yegua *f*

margarine [ˈmɑrdʒərən] *n* : margarina *f*

margin [ˈmɑrdʒən] *n* : margen *m*

marginal [ˈmɑrdʒənəl] *adj* 1 : marginal 2 MINIMAL : mínimo — **marginally** *adv*

marigold [ˈmærəˌgoːld] *n* : maravilla *f*, caléndula *f*

marijuana [ˌmærəˈhwɑnə] *n* : marihuana *f*

marina [məˈriːnə] *n* : puerto *m* deportivo

marinade [ˌmærəˈnɑd] *n* : adobo *m*, marinada *f*

marinate [ˈmærəˌneɪt] *vt* **-nated; -nating** : marinar

marine¹ [məˈriːn] *adj* 1 : marino ⟨marine life : vida marina⟩ 2 NAUTICAL : náutico, marítimo 3 : de la infantería de marina

marine² *n* : soldado *m* de marina

mariner [ˈmærɪnər] *n* : marinero *m*, marino *m*

marionette [ˌmæriəˈnɛt] *n* : marioneta *f*, títere *m*

marital [ˈmærətəl] *adj* 1 : matrimonial 2 **marital status** : estado *m* civil

maritime [ˈmærəˌtaɪm] *adj* : marítimo

marjoram [ˈmɑrdʒərəm] *n* : mejorana *f*

mark¹ [ˈmɑrk] *vt* 1 : marcar 2 CHARACTERIZE : caracterizar 3 SIGNAL : señalar 4 NOTICE : prestar atención a, hacer caso de 5 **to mark off** : demarcar, delimitar

mark² *n* 1 TARGET : blanco *m* 2 : marca *f*, señal *f* ⟨put a mark where you left off : pon una señal donde terminaste⟩ 3 INDICATION : señal *f*, indicio *m* 4 GRADE : nota *f* 5 IMPRINT : huella *f*, marca *f* 6 BLEMISH : marca *f*, imperfección *f*

marked [ˈmɑrkt] *adj* : marcado, notable — **markedly** [ˈmɑrkədli] *adv*

marker [ˈmɑrkər] *n* : marcador *m*

market¹ [ˈmɑrkət] *vt* : poner en venta, comercializar

market² *n* 1 MARKETPLACE : mercado *m* ⟨the open market : el mercado libre⟩ 2 DEMAND : demanda *f*, mercado *m* 3 STORE : tienda *f* 4 → **stock market**

marketable [ˈmɑrkətəbəl] *adj* : vendible

marketing [ˈmɑrkətɪŋ] *n* : mercadotecnia *f*, mercadeo *m*

marketplace [ˈmɑrkətˌpleɪs] *n* : mercado *m*

marksman [ˈmɑrksmən] *n, pl* **-men** [-mən, -ˌmn] : tirador *m*

marksmanship [ˈmɑrksmənˌʃɪp] *n* : puntería *f*

marlin [ˈmɑrlɪn] *n* : marlín *m*

marmalade [ˈmɑrməˌleɪd] *n* : mermelada *f*

marmoset [ˈmɑrməˌsɛt] *n* : tití *m*

marmot [ˈmɑrmət] *n* : marmota *f*

maroon¹ [məˈruːn] *vt* : abandonar, aislar

maroon² *n* : rojo *m* oscuro, granate *m*

marquee [mɑrˈkiː] *n* : marquesina *f*

marquess [ˈmɑrkwɪs] *or* **marquis** [ˈmɑrkwɪs, mɑrˈkiː] *n, pl* **-quesses** *or* **-quises** [-ˈkiːz, -ˈkizəz] *or* **-quis** [-ˈkiː, -ˈkiːz] : marqués *m*

marquise [mɑrˈkiːz] *n* → **marchioness**

marriage [ˈmærɪdʒ] *n* 1 : matrimonio *m* 2 WEDDING : casamiento *m*, boda *f*

marriageable [ˈmærɪdʒəbəl] *adj* **of marriageable age** : de edad de casarse

married [ˈmærid] *adj* 1 : casado 2 **to get married** : casarse

marrow [ˈmæroː] *n* : médula *f*, tuétano *m*

marry [ˈmæri] *vt* **-ried; -rying** 1 : casar ⟨the priest married them : el cura los casó⟩ 2 : casarse con ⟨she married John : se casó con John⟩

Mars [ˈmɑrz] *n* : Marte *m*
marsh [ˈmɑrʃ] *n* **1** : pantano *m* **2 salt marsh** : marisma *f*
marshal[1] [ˈmɑrʃəl] *vt* **-shaled** *or* **-shalled; -shaling** *or* **-shalling 1** : poner en orden, reunir **2** USHER : conducir
marshal[2] *n* **1** : maestro *m* de ceremonias **2** : mariscal *m* (en el ejército); jefe *m*, -fa *f* (de la policía, de los bomberos, etc.)
marshmallow [ˈmɑrʃˌmɛloː, -ˌmæloː] *n* : malvavisco *m*
marshy [ˈmɑrʃi] *adj* **marshier; -est** : pantanoso
marsupial [mɑrˈsuːpiəl] *n* : marsupial *m*
mart [ˈmɑrt] *n* MARKET : mercado *m*
marten [ˈmɑrtən] *n*, *pl* **-ten** *or* **-tens** : marta *f*
martial [ˈmɑrʃəl] *adj* : marcial
martin [ˈmɑrtən] *n* **1** SWALLOW : golondrina *f* **2** SWIFT : vencejo *m*
martyr[1] [ˈmɑrtər] *vt* : martirizar
martyr[2] *n* : mártir *mf*
martyrdom [ˈmɑrtərdəm] *n* : martirio *m*
marvel[1] [ˈmɑrvəl] *vi* **-veled** *or* **-velled; -veling** *or* **-velling** : maravillarse
marvel[2] *n* : maravilla *f*
marvelous [ˈmɑrvələs] *or* **marvellous** *adj* : maravilloso — **marvelously** *adv*
Marxism [ˈmɑrkˌsɪzəm] *n* : marxismo *m*
Marxist[1] [ˈmɑrksɪst] *adj* : marxista
Marxist[2] *n* : marxista *mf*
mascara [mæsˈkærə] *n* : rímel *m*, rimel *m*
mascot [ˈmæsˌkɑt, -kət] *n* : mascota *f*
masculine [ˈmæskjələn] *adj* : masculino
masculinity [ˌmæskjəˈlɪnəti] *n* : masculinidad *f*
mash[1] [ˈmæʃ] *vt* **1** : hacer puré de (papas, etc.) **2** CRUSH : aplastar, majar
mash[2] *n* **1** FEED : afrecho *m* **2** : malta *f* (para hacer bebidas alcohólicas) **3** PASTE, PULP : papilla *f*, pasta *f*
mask[1] [ˈmæsk] *vt* **1** CONCEAL, DISGUISE : enmascarar, ocultar **2** COVER : cubrir, tapar
mask[2] *n* : máscara *f*, careta *f*, mascarilla *f* (de un cirujano o dentista)
masochism [ˈmæsəˌkɪzəm, ˈmæzə-] *n* : masoquismo *m*
masochist [ˈmæsəˌkɪst, ˈmæzə-] *n* : masoquista *mf*
masochistic [ˌmæsəˈkɪstɪk, ˌmæzə-] *adj* : masoquista
mason [ˈmeɪsən] *n* **1** BRICKLAYER : albañil *mf* **2** *or* **stonemason** [ˈstoːnˌ-] : mampostero *m*, cantero *m*
masonry [ˈmeɪsənri] *n*, *pl* **-ries 1** BRICKLAYING : albañilería *f* **2** *or* **stonemasonry** [ˈstoːnˌ-] : mampostería *f*
masquerade[1] [ˌmæskəˈreɪd] *vi* **-aded; -ading 1** : disfrazarse (de), hacerse pasar (por) **2** : asistir a una mascarada
masquerade[2] *n* **1** : mascarada *f*, baile *m* de disfraces **2** FACADE : farsa *f*, fachada *f*
mass[1] [ˈmæs] *vi* : concentrarse, juntarse en masa — *vt* : concentrar

mass[2] *n* **1** : masa *f* ⟨atomic mass : masa atómica⟩ **2** BULK : mole *f*, volumen *m* **3** MULTITUDE : cantidad *f*, montón *m* (de cosas), multitud *f* (de gente) **4 the masses** : las masas, el pueblo, el populacho
Mass [ˈmæs] *n* : misa *f*
massacre[1] [ˈmæsɪkər] *vt* **-cred; -cring** : masacrar
massacre[2] *n* : masacre *f*
massage[1] [məˈsɑʒ, -ˈsɑdʒ] *vt* **-saged; -saging** : masajear
massage[2] *n* : masaje *m*
masseur [mæˈsər] *n* : masajista *m*
masseuse [mæˈsøz, -ˈsuːz] *n* : masajista *f*
massive [ˈmæsɪv] *adj* **1** BULKY : voluminoso, macizo **2** HUGE : masivo, enorme — **massively** *adv*
mast [ˈmæst] *n* : mástil *m*, palo *m*
master[1] [ˈmæstər] *vt* **1** SUBDUE : dominar **2** : llegar a dominar ⟨she mastered French : llegó a dominar el francés⟩
master[2] *n* **1** TEACHER : maestro *m*, profesor *m* **2** EXPERT : experto *m*, -ta *f*; maestro *m*, -tra *f* **3** : amo *m* (de animales o esclavos), señor *m* (de la casa) **4 master's degree** : maestría *f*
masterful [ˈmæstərfəl] *adj* **1** IMPERIOUS : autoritario, imperioso, dominante **2** SKILLFUL : magistral — **masterfully** *adv*
masterly [ˈmæstərli] *adj* : magistral
mastermind [ˈmæstərˌmaɪnd] *n* : cerebro *m*, artífice *mf*
masterpiece [ˈmæstərˌpiːs] *n* : obra *f* maestra
masterwork [ˈmæstərˌwərk] → **masterpiece**
mastery [ˈmæstəri] *n* **1** DOMINION : dominio *m*, autoridad *f* **2** SUPERIORITY : superioridad *f* **3** EXPERTISE : maestría *f*
masticate [ˈmæstəˌkeɪt] *v* **-cated; -cating** : masticar
mastiff [ˈmæstɪf] *n* : mastín *m*
mastodon [ˈmæstəˌdɑn] *n* : mastodonte *m*
masturbate [ˈmæstərˌbeɪt] *v* **-bated; -bating** *vi* : masturbarse — *vt* : masturbar
masturbation [ˌmæstərˈbeɪʃən] *n* : masturbación *f*
mat[1] [ˈmæt] *v* **matted; matting** *vt* TANGLE : enmarañar — *vi* : enmarañarse
mat[2] *n* **1** : estera *f* **2** TANGLE : maraña *f* **3** PAD : colchoneta *f* (de gimnasia) **4** *or* **matt** *or* **matte** [ˈmæt] FRAME : marco *m* (de cartón)
mat[3] → **matte**
matador [ˈmætəˌdor] *n* : matador *m*
match[1] [ˈmætʃ] *vt* **1** PIT : enfrentar, oponer **2** EQUAL, FIT : igualar, corresponder a, coincidir con **3** : combinar con, hacer juego con ⟨her shoes match her dress : sus zapatos hacen juego con su vestido⟩ — *vi* **1** CORRESPOND : concordar, coincidir **2** : hacer juego ⟨with a tie to match : con una corbata que hace juego⟩

match² n 1 EQUAL : igual mf ⟨he's no match for her : no puede competir con ella⟩ 2 FIGHT, GAME : partido m, combate m (en boxeo) 3 MARRIAGE : matrimonio m, casamiento m 4 : fósforo m, cerilla f, cerillo m in various countries) ⟨he lit a match : encendió un fósforo⟩ 5 to be a good match : hacer buena pareja (dícese de las personas), hacer juego (dícese de la ropa)

matchless ['mætʃləs] adj : sin igual, sin par

matchmaker ['mætʃˌmeɪkər] n : casamentero m, -ra f

mate¹ ['meɪt] v mated; mating vi 1 FIT : encajar 2 PAIR : emparejarse 3 (relating to animals) : aparearse, copular — vt : aparear, acoplar (animales)

mate² n 1 COMPANION : compañero m, -ra f; camarada mf 2 : macho m, hembra f (de animales) 3 : oficial mf (de un barco) ⟨first mate : primer oficial⟩ 4 : compañero m, -ra f; pareja f (de un zapato, etc.)

material¹ [mə'tɪriəl] adj 1 PHYSICAL : material, físico ⟨the material world : el mundo material⟩ ⟨material needs : necesidades materiales⟩ 2 IMPORTANT : importante, esencial 3 material evidence : prueba f sustancial

material² n 1 : material m 2 CLOTH : tejido m, tela f

materialism [mə'tɪriəˌlɪzəm] n : materialismo m

materialist [mə'tɪriəlɪst] n : materialista mf

materialistic [məˌtɪriə'lɪstɪk] adj : materialista

materialize [mə'tɪriəˌlaɪz] v -ized; -izing vt : materializar, hacer aparecer — vi : materializarse, aparecer

maternal [mə'tərnəl] adj MOTHERLY : maternal — maternally adv

maternity¹ [mə'tərnəti] adj : de maternidad ⟨maternity clothes : ropa de futura mamá⟩ ⟨maternity leave : licencia por maternidad⟩

maternity² n, pl -ties : maternidad f

math ['mæθ] → mathematics

mathematical [ˌmæθə'mætɪkəl] adj : matemático — mathematically adv

mathematician [ˌmæθəmə'tɪʃən] n : matemático m, -ca f

mathematics [ˌmæθə'mætɪks] ns & pl : matemáticas fpl, matemática f

matinee or matinée [ˌmætən'eɪ] n : matiné f

matriarch ['meɪtriˌɑrk] n : matriarca f

matriarchy ['meɪtriˌɑrki] n, pl -chies : matriarcado m

matriculate [mə'trɪkjəˌleɪt] v -lated; -lating vt : matricular — vi : matricularse

matriculation [məˌtrɪkjə'leɪʃən] n : matrícula f, matriculación f

matrimony ['mætrəˌmoːni] n : matrimonio m — matrimonial [ˌmætrə'moːniəl] adj

matrix ['meɪtrɪks] n, pl -trices ['meɪtrəˌsiːz, 'mæ-] or -trixes ['meɪtrɪksəz] : matriz f

matron ['meɪtrən] n : matrona f

matronly ['meɪtrənli] adj : de matrona, matronal

matte ['mæt] adj : mate, de acabado mate

matter¹ ['mætər] vi : importar ⟨it doesn't matter : no importa⟩

matter² n 1 QUESTION : asunto m, cuestión f ⟨a matter of taste : una cuestión de gusto⟩ 2 SUBSTANCE : materia f, sustancia f 3 matters npl CIRCUMSTANCES : situación f, cosas fpl ⟨to make matters worse : para colmo de males⟩ 4 to be the matter : pasar ⟨what's the matter? : ¿qué pasa?⟩ 5 as a matter of fact : en efecto, en realidad 6 for that matter : de hecho 7 no matter how much : por mucho que

matter–of–fact ['mætərəv'fækt] adj : práctico, realista

mattress ['mætrəs] n : colchón m

mature¹ [mə'tʊr, -'tjʊr, -'tʃʊr] vi -tured; -turing 1 : madurar 2 : vencer ⟨when does the loan mature? : ¿cuándo vence el préstamo?⟩

mature² adj -turer; -est 1 : maduro 2 DUE : vencido

maturity [mə'tʊrəti, -'tjʊr-, -'tʃʊr-] n : madurez f

maudlin ['mɔdlɪn] adj : sensiblero

maul¹ ['mɔl] vt 1 BEAT : golpear, pegar 2 MANGLE : mutilar 3 MANHANDLE : maltratar

maul² n MALLET : mazo m

Mauritanian [ˌmɔrə'teɪniən] n : mauritano m, -na f — Mauritanian adj

mausoleum [ˌmɔsə'liːəm, ˌmɔzə-] n, pl -leums or -lea [-'liːə] : mausoleo m

mauve ['moːv, 'mɔv] n : malva m

maven or mavin ['meɪvən] n EXPERT : experto m, -ta f

maverick ['mævrɪk, 'mævə-] n 1 : ternero m sin marcar 2 NONCONFORMIST : inconformista mf, disidente mf

mawkish ['mɔkɪʃ] adj : sensiblero

maxim ['mæksəm] n : máxima f

maximize ['mæksəˌmaɪz] vt -mized; -mizing : maximizar, llevar al máximo

maximum¹ ['mæksəməm] adj : máximo

maximum² n, pl -ma ['mæksəmə] or -mums : máximo m

may ['meɪ] v aux, past might ['maɪt] present s & pl may 1 (expressing permission) : poder ⟨you may go : puedes ir⟩ 2 (expressing possibility or probability) : poder ⟨you may be right : puede que tengas razón⟩ ⟨it may happen occasionally : puede pasar de vez en cuando⟩ 3 (expressing desires, intentions, or contingencies) ⟨may the best man win : que gane el mejor⟩ ⟨I laugh that I may not weep : me río para no llorar⟩ ⟨come what may : pase lo que pase⟩

May ['meɪ] n : mayo m

Maya ['maɪə] *or* **Mayan** ['maɪən] *n* : maya *mf* — **Maya** *or* **Mayan** *adj*

maybe ['meɪbi] *adv* PERHAPS : quizás, tal vez

mayfly ['meɪˌflaɪ] *n, pl* **-flies** : efímera *f*

mayhem ['meɪˌhɛm, 'meɪəm] *n* **1** MUTILATION : mutilación *f* **2** DEVASTATION : estragos *mpl*

mayonnaise ['meɪəˌneɪz] *n* : mayonesa *f*

mayor ['meɪər, 'mɛr] *n* : alcalde *m*, -desa *f*

mayoral ['meɪərəl, 'mɛrəl] *adj* : de alcalde

maze ['meɪz] *n* : laberinto *m*

me ['mi:] *pron* **1** : me ⟨she called me : me llamó⟩ ⟨give it to me : dámelo⟩ **2** (*after a preposition*) : mí ⟨for me : para mí⟩ ⟨with me : conmigo⟩ **3** (*after conjunctions and verbs*) : yo ⟨it's me : soy yo⟩ ⟨as big as me : tan grande como yo⟩ **4** (*emphatic use*) : yo ⟨me, too! : ¡yo también!⟩ ⟨who, me? : ¿quién, yo?⟩

meadow ['mɛdo:] *n* : prado *m*, pradera *f*

meadowland ['mɛdoˌlænd] *n* : pradera *f*

meadowlark ['mɛdoˌlɑrk] *n* : pájaro *m* cantor con el pecho amarillo

meager *or* **meagre** ['mi:gər] *adj* **1** THIN : magro, flaco **2** POOR, SCANTY : exiguo, escaso, pobre

meagerly ['mi:gərli] *adv* : pobremente

meagerness ['mi:gərnəs] *n* : escasez *f*, pobreza *f*

meal ['mi:l] *n* **1** : comida *f* ⟨a hearty meal : una comida sustanciosa⟩ **2** : harina *f* (de maíz, etc.)

mealtime ['mi:lˌtaɪm] *n* : hora *f* de comer

mean¹ ['mi:n] *vt* **meant** ['mɛnt]; **meaning 1** INTEND : querer, pensar, tener la intención de ⟨I didn't mean to do it : lo hice sin querer⟩ ⟨what do you mean to do? : ¿qué piensas hacer?⟩ **2** SIGNIFY : querer decir, significar ⟨what does that mean? : ¿qué quiere decir eso?⟩ **3** : importar ⟨health means everything : lo que más importa es la salud⟩

mean² *adj* **1** HUMBLE : humilde **2** NEGLIGIBLE : despreciable ⟨it's no mean feat : no es poca cosa⟩ **3** STINGY : mezquino, tacaño **4** CRUEL : malo, cruel ⟨to be mean to someone : tratar mal a alguien⟩ **5** AVERAGE, MEDIAN : medio

mean³ *n* **1** MIDPOINT : término *m* medio **2** AVERAGE : promedio *m*, media *f* aritmética **3** means *npl* WAY : medio *m*, manera *f*, vía *f* **4** means *npl* RESOURCES : medios *mpl*, recursos *mpl* **5** by all means : por supuesto, cómo no **6** by means of : por medio de **7** by no means : de ninguna manera, de ningún modo

meander [mi'ændər] *vi* **-dered; -dering 1** WIND : serpentear **2** WANDER : vagar, andar sin rumbo fijo

meaning ['mi:nɪŋ] *n* **1** : significado *m*, sentido *m* ⟨double meaning : doble sentido⟩ **2** INTENT : intención *f*, propósito *m*

meaningful ['mi:nɪŋfəl] *adj* : significativo — **meaningfully** *adv*

meaningless ['mi:nɪŋləs] *adj* : sin sentido

meanness ['mi:nnəs] *n* **1** CRUELTY : crueldad *f*, mezquindad *f* **2** STINGINESS : tacañería *f*

meantime¹ ['mi:nˌtaɪm] *adv* → **meanwhile¹**

meantime² *n* **1** : interín *m* **2 in the meantime** : entretanto, mientras tanto

meanwhile¹ ['mi:nˌʍaɪl] *adv* : entretanto, mientras tanto

meanwhile² *n* → **meantime²**

measles ['mi:zəlz] *ns & pl* : sarampión *m*

measly ['mi:zli] *adj* **-slier; -est** : miserable, mezquino

measurable ['mɛʒərəbəl, 'meɪ-] *adj* : mensurable — **measurably** [-bli] *adv*

measure¹ ['mɛʒər, 'meɪ-] *v* **-sured; -suring** : medir ⟨he measured the table : midió la mesa⟩ ⟨it measures 15 feet tall : mide 15 pies de altura⟩

measure² *n* **1** AMOUNT : medida *f*, cantidad *f* ⟨in large measure : en gran medida⟩ ⟨a full measure : una cantidad exacta⟩ ⟨a measure of proficiency : una cierta competencia⟩ ⟨for good measure : de ñapa, por añadidura⟩ **2** DIMENSIONS, SIZE : medida *f*, tamaño *m* **3** RULER : regla *f* ⟨tape measure : cinta métrica⟩ **4** MEASUREMENT : medida *f* ⟨cubic measure : medida de capacidad⟩ **5** MEASURING : medida *f* **6** measures *npl* : medidas *fpl* ⟨security measures : medidas de seguridad⟩

measureless ['mɛʒərləs, 'meɪ-] *adj* : inmensurable

measurement ['mɛʒərmənt, 'meɪ-] *n* **1** MEASURING : medición *f* **2** DIMENSION : medida *f*

measure up *vi* **to measure up to** : estar a la altura de

meat ['mi:t] *n* **1** FOOD : comida *f*. **2** : carne *f* ⟨meat and fish : carne y pescado⟩ **3** SUBSTANCE : sustancia *f*, esencia *f* ⟨the meat of the story : la sustancia del cuento⟩

meatball ['mi:tˌbɔl] *n* : albóndiga *f*

meaty ['mi:ti] *adj* **meatier; -est** : con mucha carne, carnoso

mechanic [mɪ'kænɪk] *n* : mecánico *m*, -ca *f*

mechanical [mɪ'kænɪkəl] *adj* : mecánico — **mechanically** *adv*

mechanics [mɪ'kænɪks] *ns & pl* **1** : mecánica *f* ⟨fluid mechanics : la mecánica de fluidos⟩ **2** MECHANISMS : mecanismos *mpl*, aspectos *mpl* prácticos

mechanism ['mɛkəˌnɪzəm] *n* : mecanismo *m*

mechanization [ˌmɛkənə'zeɪʃən] *n* : mecanización *f*

mechanize ['mɛkə,naɪz] *vt* -nized; -nizing : mecanizar
medal ['mɛdəl] *n* : medalla *f*, condecoración *f*
medalist ['mɛdəlɪst] *or* medallist *n* : medallista *mf*
medallion [mə'dæljən] *n* : medallón *m*
meddle ['mɛdəl] *vi* -dled; -dling : meterse, entrometerse
meddler ['mɛdələr] *n* : entrometido *m*, -da *f*
meddlesome ['mɛdəlsəm] *adj* : entrometido
media ['mi:diə] *npl* : medios *mpl* de comunicación
median¹ ['mi:diən] *adj* : medio
median² *n* : valor *m* medio
mediate ['mi:di,eɪt] *vi* -ated; -ating : mediar
mediation [,mi:di'eɪʃən] *n* : mediación *f*
mediator ['mi:di,eɪtər] *n* : mediador *m*, -dora *f*
medical ['mɛdɪkəl] *adj* : médico
medicate ['mɛdə,keɪt] *vt* -cated; -cating : medicar ⟨medicated powder : polvos medicinales⟩
medication [,mɛdə'keɪʃən] *n* **1** TREATMENT : tratamiento *m*, medicación *f* **2** MEDICINE : medicamento *m* ⟨to be on medication : estar medicado⟩
medicinal [mə'dɪsənəl] *adj* : medicinal
medicine ['mɛdəsən] *n* **1** MEDICATION : medicina *f*, medicamento *m* **2** : medicina *f* ⟨he's studying medicine : estudia medicina⟩
medicine man *n* : hechicero *m*
medieval *or* mediaeval [mɪ'di:vəl, ,mi:-, ,m-, -di'i:vəl] *adj* : medieval
mediocre [,mi:di'o:kər] *adj* : mediocre
mediocrity [,mi:di'ɑkrəti] *n, pl* -ties : mediocridad *f*
meditate ['mɛdə,teɪt] *vi* -tated; -tating : meditar
meditation [,mɛdə'teɪʃən] *n* : meditación *f*
meditative ['mɛdə,teɪtɪv] *adj* : meditabundo
medium¹ ['mi:diəm] *adj* : mediano ⟨of medium height : de estatura mediana, de estatura regular⟩
medium² *n, pl* -diums *or* -dia ['mi:-diə] **1** MEAN : punto *m* medio, término *m* medio ⟨happy medium : justo medio⟩ **2** MEANS : medio *m* **3** SUBSTANCE : medio *m*, sustancia *f* ⟨a viscous medium : un medio viscoso⟩ **4** : medio *m* de comunicación **5** : medio *m* (artístico)
medley ['mɛdli] *n, pl* -leys : popurrí *m* (de canciones)
meek ['mi:k] *adj* **1** LONG-SUFFERING : paciente, sufrido **2** SUBMISSIVE : sumiso, dócil, manso
meekly ['mi:kli] *adv* : dócilmente
meekness ['mi:knəs] *n* : mansedumbre *f*, docilidad *f*
meet¹ ['mi:t] *v* met ['mɛt]; meeting *vt* **1** ENCOUNTER : encontrarse con **2** JOIN

: unirse con **3** CONFRONT : enfrentarse a **4** SATISFY : satisfacer, cumplir con ⟨to meet costs : pagar los gastos⟩ **5** : conocer ⟨I met his sister : conocí a su hermana⟩ — *vi* ASSEMBLE : reunirse, congregarse
meet² *n* : encuentro *m*
meeting ['mi:tɪŋ] *n* **1** : reunión *f* ⟨to open the meeting : abrir la sesión⟩ **2** ENCOUNTER : encuentro *m* **3** : entrevista *f* (formal)
meetinghouse ['mi:tɪŋ,haʊs] *n* : iglesia *f* (de ciertas confesiones protestantes)
megabyte ['mɛgə,baɪt] *n* : megabyte *m*
megahertz ['mɛgə,hərts, -,hrts] *n* : megahercio *m*
megaphone ['mɛgə,fo:n] *n* : megáfono *m*
melancholy¹ ['mɛlən,kɑli] *adj* : melancólico, triste, sombrío
melancholy² *n, pl* -cholies : melancolía *f*
melanoma [,mɛlə'no:mə] *n, pl* -mas : melanoma *m*
meld ['mɛld] *vt* : fusionar, unir — *vi* : fusionarse, unirse
melee ['meɪ,leɪ, meɪ'leɪ] *n* BRAWL : reyerta *f*, riña *f*, pelea *f*
meliorate ['mi:ljə,reɪt, 'mi:liə-] → ameliorate
mellow¹ ['mɛlo:] *vt* : suavizar, endulzar — *vi* : suavizarse, endulzarse
mellow² *adj* **1** RIPE : maduro **2** MILD : apacible ⟨a mellow character : un carácter apacible⟩ ⟨mellow wines : vinos añejos⟩ **3** : suave, dulce ⟨mellow colors : colores suaves⟩ ⟨mellow tones : tonos dulces⟩
mellowness ['mɛlonəs] *n* : suavidad *f*, dulzura *f*
melodic [mə'lɑdɪk] *adj* : melódico —
melodically [-dɪkli] *adv*
melodious [mə'lo:diəs] *adj* : melodioso — melodiously *adv*
melodiousness [mə'lo:diəsnəs] *n* : calidad *f* de melódico
melodrama ['mɛlə,drɑmə, -,dræ-] *n* : melodrama *m*
melodramatic [,mɛlədrə'mætɪk] *adj* : melodramático — melodramatically [-tɪkli] *adv*
melody ['mɛlədi] *n, pl* -dies : melodía *f*, tonada *f*
melon ['mɛlən] *n* : melón *m*
melt ['mɛlt] *vt* **1** : derretir, disolver **2** SOFTEN : ablandar ⟨it melted his heart : ablandó su corazón⟩ — *vi* **1** : derretirse, disolverse **2** SOFTEN : ablandarse **3** DISAPPEAR : desvanecerse, esfumarse ⟨the clouds melted away : las nubes se desvanecieron⟩
melting point *n* : punto *m* de fusión
member ['mɛmbər] *n* **1** LIMB : miembro *m* **2** : miembro *m* (de un grupo); socio *m*, -cia *f* (de un club) **3** PART : miembro *m*, parte *f*
membership ['mɛmbər,ʃɪp] *n* **1** : membresía *f* ⟨application for membership

: solicitud de entrada⟩ **2** MEMBERS : membresía *f*, miembros *mpl*, socios *mpl*
membrane [ˈmɛmˌbreɪn] *n* : membrana *f* — **membranous** [ˈmɛmbrə-nəs] *adj*
memento [mɪˈmɛnˌtoː] *n, pl* **-tos** *or* **-toes** : recuerdo *m*
memo [ˈmɛmoː] *n, pl* **memos** : memorándum *m*
memoirs [ˈmɛmˌwɑrz] *npl* : memorias *fpl*, autobiografía *f*
memorabilia [ˌmɛmərəˈbiliə, -ˈbɪljə] *npl* **1** : objetos *mpl* de interés histórico **2** MEMENTOS : recuerdos *mpl*
memorable [ˈmɛmərəbəl] *adj* : memorable, notable — **memorably** [-bli] *adv*
memorandum [ˌmɛməˈrændəm] *n, pl* **-dums** *or* **-da** [-də] : memorándum *m*
memorial¹ [məˈmoriəl] *adj* : conmemorativo
memorial² *n* : monumento *m* conmemorativo
Memorial Day *n* : el último lunes de mayo (observado en Estados Unidos como día feriado para conmemorar a los caídos en guerra)
memorialize [məˈmoriəˌlaɪz] *vt* **-ized; -izing** COMMEMORATE : conmemorar
memorization [ˌmɛmərəˈzeɪʃən] *n* : memorización *f*
memorize [ˈmɛməˌraɪz] *vt* **-rized; -rizing** : memorizar, aprender de memoria
memory [ˈmɛmri, ˈmɛmə-] *n, pl* **-ries 1** : memoria *f* ⟨he has a good memory : tiene buena memoria⟩ **2** RECOLLECTION : recuerdo *m* **3** COMMEMORATION : memoria *f*, conmemoración *f*
men → **man²**
menace¹ [ˈmɛnəs] *vt* **-aced; -acing 1** THREATEN : amenazar **2** ENDANGER : poner en peligro
menace² *n* : amenaza *f*
menacing [ˈmɛnəsɪŋ] *adj* : amenazador, amenazante
menagerie [məˈnædʒəri, -ˈnæʒəri] *n* : colección *f* de animales salvajes
mend¹ [ˈmɛnd] *vt* **1** CORRECT : enmendar, corregir ⟨to mend one's ways : enmendarse⟩ **2** REPAIR : remendar, arreglar, reparar — *vi* HEAL : curarse
mend² *n* : remiendo *m*
mendicant [ˈmɛndɪkənt] *n* BEGGAR : mendigo *m*, -ga *f*
menhaden [mɛnˈheɪdən, mən-] *ns & pl* : pez *m* de la misma familia que los arenques
menial¹ [ˈmiːniəl] *adj* : servil, bajo
menial² *n* : sirviente *m*, -ta *f*
meningitis [ˌmɛnənˈdʒaɪtəs] *n, pl* **-gitides** [-ˈdʒɪtəˌdiːz] : meningitis *f*
menopause [ˈmɛnəˌpɔz] *n* : menopausia *f*
menorah [məˈnorə] *n* : candelabro *m* (usado en los oficios religiosos judíos)
menstrual [ˈmɛnstruəl] *adj* : menstrual
menstruate [ˈmɛnstruˌeɪt] *vi* **-ated; -ating** : menstruar
menstruation [ˌmɛnstruˈeɪʃən] *n* : menstruación *f*

mental [ˈmɛntəl] *adj* : mental ⟨mental hospital : hospital psiquiátrico⟩ — **mentally** *adv*
mentality [mɛnˈtæləti] *n, pl* **-ties** : mentalidad *f*
menthol [ˈmɛnˌθɔl, -ˌθoːl] *n* : mentol *m*
mentholated [ˌmɛnθəˌleɪtəd] *adj* : mentolado
mention¹ [ˈmɛntʃən] *vt* : mencionar, mentar, referirse a ⟨don't mention it! : ¡de nada!, ¡no hay de qué!⟩
mention² *n* : mención *f*
mentor [ˈmɛnˌtɔr, ˈmɛntər] *n* : mentor *m*
menu [ˈmɛnˌju:] *n* **1** : menú *m*, carta *f* (en un restaurante) **2** : menú *m* (de computadoras)
meow¹ [miːˈaʊ] *vi* : maullar
meow² *n* : maullido *m*, miau *m*
mercantile [ˈmərkənˌtiːl, -ˌtaɪl] *adj* : mercantil
mercenary¹ [ˈmərsənɛˌri] *adj* : mercenario
mercenary² *n, pl* **-naries** : mercenario *m*, -ria *f*
merchandise [ˈmərtʃənˌdaɪz, -ˌdaɪs] *n* : mercancía *f*, mercadería *f*
merchandiser [ˈmərtʃənˌdaɪzər] *n* : comerciante *mf*; vendedor *m*, -dora *f*
merchant [ˈmərtʃənt] *n* : comerciante *mf*
merchant marine *n* : marina *f* mercante
merciful [ˈmərsɪfəl] *adj* : misericordioso, clemente
mercifully [ˈmərsɪfli] *adv* **1** : con misericordia, con compasión **2** FORTUNATELY : afortunadamente
merciless [ˈmərsɪləs] *adj* : despiadado — **mercilessly** *adv*
mercurial [ˌmərˈkjuriəl] *adj* TEMPERAMENTAL : temperamental, volátil
mercury [ˈmərkjəri] *n, pl* **-ries** : mercurio *m*
Mercury *n* : Mercurio *m*
mercy [ˈmərsi] *n, pl* **-cies 1** CLEMENCY : misericordia *f*, clemencia *f* **2** BLESSING : bendición *f*
mere [ˈmɪr] *adj, superlative* **merest** : mero, simple
merely [ˈmɪrli] *adv* : solamente, simplemente
merge [ˈmərdʒ] *v* **merged; merging** *vi* : unirse, fusionarse (dícese de las compañías), confluir (dícese de los ríos, las calles, etc.) — *vt* : unir, fusionar, combinar
merger [ˈmərdʒər] *n* : unión *f*, fusión *f*
meridian [məˈrɪdiən] *n* : meridiano *m*
meringue [məˈræŋ] *n* : merengue *m*
merino [məˈriːno] *n, pl* **-nos 1** : merino *m*, -na *f* **2** *or* **merino wool** : lana *f* merino
merit¹ [ˈmɛrət] *vt* : merecer, ser digno de
merit² *n* : mérito *m*, valor *m*
meritorious [ˌmɛrəˈtoriəs] *adj* : meritorio
mermaid [ˈmərˌmeɪd] *n* : sirena *f*
merriment [ˈmɛrɪmənt] *n* : alegría *f*, júbilo *m*, regocijo *m*

merry ['mɛri] *adj* **-rier; -est** : alegre —
merrily ['mɛrəli] *adv*
merry-go-round ['mɛrigo,raʊnd] *n*
: carrusel *m*, tiovivo *m*
merrymaker ['mɛri,meɪkər] *n* : juerguista *mf*
merrymaking ['mɛri,meɪkɪŋ] *n* : juerga *f*
mesa ['meɪsə] *n* : mesa *f*
mesdames → **madam, Mrs.**
mesh¹ ['mɛʃ] *vi* **1** ENGAGE : engranar (dícese de las piezas mecánicas) **2** TANGLE : enredarse **3** COORDINATE : coordinarse, combinar
mesh² *n* **1** : malla *f* ⟨wire mesh : malla metálica⟩ **2** NETWORK : red *f* **3** MESHING : engranaje *m* ⟨in mesh : engranado⟩
mesmerize ['mɛzmə,raɪz] *vt* **-ized; -izing 1** HYPNOTIZE : hipnotizar **2** FASCINATE : cautivar, embelesar, fascinar
mess¹ ['mɛs] *vt* **1** SOIL : ensuciar **2 to mess up** DISARRANGE : desordenar, desarreglar **3 to mess up** BUNGLE : echar a perder — *vi* **1** PUTTER : entretenerse **2** INTERFERE : meterse, entrometerse ⟨don't mess with me : no te metas conmigo⟩
mess² *n* **1** : rancho *m* (para soldados, etc.) **2** DISORDER : desorden *m* ⟨your room is a mess : tienes el cuarto hecho un desastre⟩ **3** CONFUSION, TURMOIL : confusión *f*, embrollo *m*, lío *m fam*
message ['mɛsɪdʒ] *n* : mensaje *m*, recado *m*
messenger ['mɛsəndʒər] *n* : mensajero *m*, -ra *f*
Messiah [mə'saɪə] *n* : Mesías *m*
Messrs. → **Mr.**
messy ['mɛsi] *adj* **messier; -est** UNTIDY : desordenado, sucio
met → **meet**
metabolic [,mɛţə'balɪk] *adj* : metabólico
metabolism [mə'tæbə,lɪzəm] *n* : metabolismo *m*
metabolize [mə'tæbə,laɪz] *vt* **-lized; -lizing** : metabolizar
metal ['mɛţəl] *n* : metal *m*
metallic [mə'tælɪk] *adj* : metálico
metallurgical [,mɛţəl'ərdʒɪkəl] *adj* : metalúrgico
metallurgy ['mɛţəl,ərdʒi] *n* : metalurgia *f*
metalwork ['mɛţəl,wərk] *n* : objeto *m* de metal
metalworking ['mɛţəl,wərkɪŋ] *n* : metalistería *f*
metamorphosis [,mɛţə'mɔrfəsɪs] *n, pl* **-phoses** [-,siːz] : metamorfosis *f*
metaphor ['mɛţə,fɔr, -fər] *n* : metáfora *f*
metaphoric [,mɛţə'fɔrɪk] *or* **metaphorical** [-ɪkəl] *adj* : metafórico
metaphysical [,mɛţə'fɪzəkəl] *adj* : metafísico
metaphysics [,mɛţə'fɪzɪks] *n* : metafísica *f*

mete ['miːt] *vt* **meted; meting** ALLOT : repartir, distribuir ⟨to mete out punishment : imponer castigos⟩
meteor ['miːţiər, -ţi:,ɔr] *n* : meteoro *m*
meteoric [,miːţi'ɔrɪk] *adj* : meteórico
meteorite ['miːţiə,raɪt] *n* : meteorito *m*
meteorologic [,miːţi,ɔrə'ladʒɪk] *or* **meteorological** [-'ladʒɪkəl] *adj* : meteorológico
meteorologist [,miːţiə'ralədʒɪst] *n* : meteorólogo *m*, -ga *f*
meteorology [,miːţiə'ralədʒi] *n* : meteorología *f*
meter ['miːţər] *n* **1** : metro *m* ⟨it measures 2 meters : mide 2 metros⟩ **2** : contador *m*, medidor *m* (de electricidad, etc.) ⟨parking meter : parquímetro⟩ **3** : metro *m* (en literatura o música)
methane ['mɛ,θeɪn] *n* : metano *m*
method ['mɛθəd] *n* : método *m*
methodical [mə'θadɪkəl] *adj* : metódico — **methodically** *adv*
Methodist ['mɛθədɪst] *n* : metodista *mf* — **Methodist** *adj*
methodology [,mɛθə'dalədʒi] *n, pl* **-gies** : metodología *f*
meticulous [mə'tɪkjələs] *adj* : meticuloso — **meticulously** *adv*
meticulousness [mə'tɪkjələsnəs] *n* : meticulosidad *f*
metric ['mɛtrɪk] *or* **metrical** [-trɪkəl] *adj* : métrico
metric system *n* : sistema *m* métrico
metronome ['mɛtrə,noːm] *n* : metrónomo *m*
metropolis [mə'trapələs] *n* : metrópoli *f*, metrópolis *f*
metropolitan [,mɛtrə'palətən] *adj* : metropolitano
mettle ['mɛţəl] *n* : temple *m*, valor *m* ⟨on one's mettle : dispuesto a mostrar su valía⟩
Mexican ['mɛksɪkən] *n* : mexicano *m*, -na *f* — **Mexican** *adj*
mezzanine ['mɛzə,niːn, ,mɛzə'niːn] *n* **1** : entrepiso *m*, entresuelo *m* **2** : primer piso *m* (de un teatro)
miasma [maɪ'æzmə] *n* : miasma *m*
mica ['maɪkə] *n* : mica *f*
mice → **mouse**
micro ['maɪkro] *adj* : muy pequeño, microscópico
microbe ['maɪ,kro:b] *n* : microbio *m*
microbiology [,maɪkrobaɪ'alədʒi] *n* : microbiología *f*
microchip ['maɪkro,tʃɪp] *n* : microchip *m*
microcomputer ['maɪkrokəm,pju:ţər] *n* : microcomputadora *f*
microcosm ['maɪkro,kazəm] *n* : microcosmo *m*
microfilm ['maɪkro,fɪlm] *n* : microfilm *m*
micrometer [maɪ'kraməţər] *n* : micrómetro *m*
micron ['maɪ,kran] *n* : micrón *m*
microorganism [,maɪkro'ɔrgə,nɪzəm] *n* : microorganismo *m*, microbio *m*

microphone · milk 528

microphone ['maɪkrə,fo:n] *n* : micrófono *m*

microprocessor ['maɪkro,prɑ,ssər] *n* : microprocesador *m*

microscope ['maɪkrə,sko:p] *n* : microscopio *m*

microscopic [,maɪkrə'skɑpɪk] *adj* : microscópico

microscopy [maɪ'krɑskəpi] *n* : microscopía *f*

microwave ['maɪkrə,weɪv] *n* **1** : microonda *f* **2** *or* **microwave oven** : microondas *m*

mid ['mɪd] *adj* : medio ⟨mid morning : a media mañana⟩ ⟨in mid-August : a mediados de agosto⟩ ⟨in mid ocean : en alta mar⟩

midair ['mɪd'ær] *n* **in** ~ : en el aire ⟨to catch in midair : agarrar al vuelo⟩

midday ['mɪd'deɪ] *n* NOON : mediodía *m*

middle[1] ['mɪdəl] *adj* **1** CENTRAL : medio, del medio, de en medio **2** INTERMEDIATE : intermedio, mediano ⟨middle age : la mediana edad⟩

middle[2] *n* **1** CENTER : medio *m*, centro *m* ⟨fold it down the middle : dóblalo por la mitad⟩ **2** **in the middle of** : en medio de (un espacio), a mitad de (una actividad) ⟨in the middle of the month : a mediados del mes⟩

Middle Ages *npl* : Edad *f* Media

middle class *n* : clase *f* media

middleman ['mɪdəl,mæn] *n, pl* **-men** [-,mən, -,mɛn] : intermediario *m*, -ria *f*

middling ['mɪdlɪŋ, -lən] *adj* **1** MEDIUM, MIDDLE : mediano **2** MEDIOCRE : mediocre, regular

midfielder ['mɪd,fi:ldər] *n* : mediocampista *mf*

midge ['mɪdʒ] *n* : mosca *f* pequeña

midget ['mɪdʒət] *n* **1** : enano *m*, -na *f* (persona) **2** : cosa *f* diminuta

midland ['mɪdlənd, -,lænd] *n* : región *f* central (de un país)

midnight ['mɪd,naɪt] *n* : medianoche *f*

midpoint ['mɪd,pɔɪnt] *n* : punto *m* medio, término *m* medio

midriff ['mɪd,rɪf] *n* : diafragma *m*

midshipman ['mɪd,ʃɪpmən, ,mɪd'ʃɪp-] *n, pl* **-men** [-mən, -,mɛn] : guardiamarina *m*

midst[1] ['mɪdst] *n* : medio *m* ⟨in our midst : entre nosotros⟩ ⟨in the midst of : en medio de⟩

midst[2] *prep* : entre

midstream ['mɪd'stri:m, -,stri:m] *n* : medio *m* de la corriente ⟨in the midstream of his career : en medio de su carrera⟩

midsummer ['mɪd'sʌmər, -,sʌ-] *n* : pleno verano *m*

midtown ['mɪd,taʊn] *n* : centro *m* (de una ciudad)

midway ['mɪd,weɪ] *adv* HALFWAY : a mitad de camino

midweek ['mɪd,wi:k] *n* : medio *m* de la semana ⟨in midweek : a media semana⟩

midwife ['mɪd,waɪf] *n, pl* **-wives** [-,waɪvz] : partera *f*, comadrona *f*

midwinter ['mɪd'wɪntər, -,win-] *n* : pleno invierno *m*

midyear ['mɪd,jɪr] *n* : medio *m* del año ⟨at midyear : a mediados del año⟩

mien ['mi:n] *n* : aspecto *m*, porte *m*, semblante *m*

miff ['mɪf] *vt* : ofender

might[1] ['maɪt] (*used to express permission or possibility or as a polite alternative to* **may**) → **may** ⟨it might be true : podría ser verdad⟩ ⟨might I speak with Sarah? : ¿se puede hablar con Sarah?⟩

might[2] *n* : fuerza *f*, poder *m*

mightily ['maɪtəli] *adv* : con mucha fuerza, poderosamente

mighty[1] ['maɪti] *adv* VERY : muy ⟨mighty good : muy bueno, buenísimo⟩

mighty[2] *adj* **mightier; -est** **1** POWERFUL : poderoso, potente **2** GREAT : grande, imponente

migraine ['maɪ,greɪn] *n* : jaqueca *f*, migraña *f*

migrant ['maɪgrənt] *n* : trabajador *m*, -dora *f* ambulante

migrate ['maɪ,greɪt] *vi* **-grated; -grating** : emigrar

migration [maɪ'greɪʃən] *n* : migración *f*

migratory ['maɪgrə,tori] *adj* : migratorio

mild ['maɪld] *adj* **1** GENTLE : apacible, suave ⟨a mild disposition : un temperamento suave⟩ **2** LIGHT : leve, ligero ⟨a mild punishment : un castigo leve, un castigo poco severo⟩ **3** TEMPERATE : templado (dícese del clima) — **mildly** *adv*

mildew[1] ['mɪl,du:, -,dju:] *vi* : enmohecerse

mildew[2] *n* : moho *m*

mildness ['maɪldnəs] *n* : apacibilidad *f*, suavidad *f*

mile ['maɪl] *n* : milla *f*

mileage ['maɪlɪdʒ] *n* **1** ALLOWANCE : viáticos *mpl* (pagados por milla recorrida) **2** : distancia *f* recorrida (en millas), kilometraje *m*

milestone ['maɪl,sto:n] *n* LANDMARK : hito *m*, jalón *m* ⟨a milestone in his life : un hito en su vida⟩

milieu [mi:'lju:, -'jø] *n, pl* **-lieus** *or* **-lieux** [-'ju:z, -'jø] SURROUNDINGS : entorno *m*, medio *m*, ambiente *m*

militant[1] ['mɪlətənt] *adj* : militante, combativo

militant[2] *n* : militante *mf*

militarism ['mɪlətə,rɪzəm] *n* : militarismo *m*

militaristic [,mɪlətə'rɪstɪk] *adj* : militarista

military[1] ['mɪlə,teri] *adj* : militar

military[2] *n* **the military** : las fuerzas armadas

militia [mə'lɪʃə] *n* : milicia *f*

milk[1] ['mɪlk] *vt* **1** : ordeñar (una vaca, etc.) **2** EXPLOIT : explotar

milk² *n* : leche *f*
milkman ['mɪlk,mæn, -mən] *n, pl* **-men** [-mən, -,mɛn] : lechero *m*
milk shake *n* : batido *m*, licuado *m*
milkweed ['mɪlk,wi:d] *n* : algodoncillo *m*
milky ['mɪlki] *adj* **milkier; -est** : lechoso
Milky Way *n* : Vía *f* Láctea
mill¹ ['mɪl] *vt* : moler (granos), fresar (metales), acordonar (monedas) — *vi* **to mill about** : arremolinarse
mill² *n* **1** : molino *m* (para moler granos) **2** FACTORY : fábrica *f* ⟨textile mill : fábrica textil⟩ **3** GRINDER : molinillo *m*
millennium [mə'lɛniəm] *n, pl* **-nia** [-niə] *or* **-niums** : milenio *m*
miller ['mɪlər] *n* : molinero *m*, -ra *f*
millet ['mɪlət] *n* : mijo *m*
milligram ['mɪlə,græm] *n* : miligramo *m*
milliliter ['mɪlə,li:tər] *n* : mililitro *m*
millimeter ['mɪlə,mi:tər] *n* : milímetro *m*
milliner ['mɪlənər] *n* : sombrerero *m*, -ra *f* (de señoras)
millinery ['mɪlə,nɛri] *n* : sombreros *mpl* de señora
million¹ ['mɪljən] *adj* **a million** : un millón de
million² *n, pl* **millions** *or* **million** : millón *m*
millionaire [,mɪljə'nær, 'mɪljə,nær] *n* : millonario *m*, -ria *f*
millionth¹ ['mɪljənθ] *adj* : millonésimo
millionth² *n* : millonésimo *m*
millipede ['mɪlə,pi:d] *n* : milpiés *m*
millstone ['mɪl,sto:n] *n* : rueda *f* de molino, muela *f*
mime¹ ['maɪm] *v* **mimed; miming** *vt* MIMIC : imitar, remedar — *vi* PANTOMIME : hacer la mímica
mime² *n* **1** : mimo *mf* **2** PANTOMIME : pantomima *f*
mimeograph ['mɪmiə,græf] *n* : mimeógrafo *m*
mimic¹ ['mɪmɪk] *vt* **-icked; -icking** : imitar, remedar
mimic² *n* : imitador *m*, -dora *f*
mimicry ['mɪmɪkri] *n, pl* **-ries** : mímica *f*, imitación *f*
minaret [,mɪnə'rɛt] *n* : alminar *m*, minarete *m*
mince ['mɪnts] *v* **minced; mincing** *vt* **1** CHOP : picar, moler (carne) **2 not to mince one's words** : no tener uno pelos en la lengua — *vi* : caminar de manera afectada
mincemeat ['mɪnts,mi:t] *n* : mezcla *f* de fruta picada, sebo, y especias
mind¹ ['maɪnd] *vt* **1** TEND : cuidar, atender ⟨mind the children : cuida a los niños⟩ **2** OBEY : obedecer **3** : preocuparse por, sentirse molestado por ⟨I don't mind his jokes : sus bromas no me molestan⟩ **4** : tener cuidado con ⟨mind the ladder! : ¡cuidado con la escalera!⟩ — *vi* **1** OBEY : obedecer **2** CARE : importarle a uno ⟨I don't mind : no me importa, me es igual⟩
mind² *n* **1** MEMORY : memoria *f*, recuerdo *m* ⟨keep it in mind : téngalo en

cuenta⟩ **2** : mente *f* ⟨the mind and the body : la mente y el cuerpo⟩ **3** INTENTION : intención *f*, propósito *m* ⟨to have a mind to do something : tener intención de hacer algo⟩ **4** : razón *f* ⟨he's out of his mind : está loco⟩ **5** OPINION : opinión *f* ⟨to change one's mind : cambiar de opinión⟩ **6** INTELLECT : capacidad *f* intelectual
minded ['maɪndəd] *adj* **1** (*used in combination*) ⟨narrow-minded : de mentalidad cerrada⟩ ⟨health-minded : preocupado por la salud⟩ **2** INCLINED : inclinado
mindful ['maɪndfəl] *adj* AWARE : consciente — **mindfully** *adv*
mindless ['maɪndləs] *adj* **1** SENSELESS : estúpido, sin sentido ⟨mindless violence : violencia sin sentido⟩ **2** HEEDLESS : inconsciente
mindlessly ['maɪndləsli] *adv* **1** SENSELESSLY : sin sentido **2** HEEDLESSLY : inconscientemente
mine¹ ['maɪn] *vt* **mined; mining 1** : extraer (oro, etc.) **2** : minar (con artefactos explosivos)
mine² *n* : mina *f* ⟨gold mine : mina de oro⟩
mine³ *pron* : mío, mía ⟨that one's mine : ése es el mío⟩ ⟨some friends of mine : unos amigos míos⟩
minefield ['maɪn,fi:ld] *n* : campo *m* de minas
miner ['maɪnər] *n* : minero *m*, -ra *f*
mineral ['mɪnərəl] *n* : mineral *m* — **mineral** *adj*
mineralogy [,mɪnə'rɑlədʒi, -'ræ-] *n* : mineralogía *f*
mingle ['mɪŋgəl] *v* **-gled; -gling** *vt* MIX : mezclar — *vi* **1** MIX : mezclarse **2** CIRCULATE : circular
miniature¹ ['mɪniə,tʃʊr, 'mɪni,tʃʊr, -tʃər] *adj* : en miniatura, diminuto
miniature² *n* : miniatura *f*
minibus ['mɪni,bʌs] *n* : microbús *m*, pesera *f Mex*
minicomputer ['mɪnikəm,pju:tər] *n* : minicomputadora *f*
minimal ['mɪnəməl] *adj* : mínimo
minimally ['mɪnəməli] *adv* : en grado mínimo
minimize ['mɪnə,maɪz] *vt* **-mized; -mizing** : minimizar
minimum¹ ['mɪnəməm] *adj* : mínimo
minimum² *n, pl* **-ma** ['mɪnəmə] *or* **-mums** : mínimo *m*
miniseries ['mɪni,sɪri:z] *n* : miniserie *f*
miniskirt ['mɪni,skərt] *n* : minifalda *f*
minister¹ ['mɪnəstər] *vi* **to minister to** : cuidar (de), atender a
minister² *n* **1** : pastor *m*, -tora *f* (de una iglesia) **2** : ministro *m*, -tra *f* (en política)
ministerial [,mɪnə'stɪriəl] *adj* : ministerial
ministry ['mɪnəstri] *n, pl* **-tries 1** : ministerio *m* (en política) **2** : sacerdocio *m* (en el catolicismo), clerecía *f* (en el protestantismo)

minivan ['mɪni,væn] *n* : minivan *f*
mink ['mɪŋk] *n, pl* **mink** *or* **minks** : visón *m*
minnow ['mɪno:] *n, pl* **-nows** : pececillo *m* de agua dulce
minor[1] ['maɪnər] *adj* : menor
minor[2] *n* **1** : menor *mf* (de edad) **2** : asignatura *f* secundaria (de estudios)
minority [mə'nɔrəti, maɪ-] *n, pl* **-ties** : minoría *f*
minstrel ['mɪntstrəl] *n* : juglar *m*, trovador *m* (en el medioevo)
mint[1] ['mɪnt] *vt* : acuñar
mint[2] *adj* : sin usar ⟨in mint condition : como nuevo⟩
mint[3] *n* **1** : menta *f* ⟨mint tea : té de menta⟩ **2** : pastilla *f* de menta **3** : casa *f* de la moneda ⟨the U.S. Mint : la casa de la moneda de los EE.UU.⟩ **4** FORTUNE : dineral *m*, fortuna *f*
minuet [,mɪnju'ɛt] *n* : minué *m*
minus[1] ['maɪnəs] *n* **1** : cantidad *f* negativa **2 minus sign** : signo *m* de menos
minus[2] *prep* **1** : menos ⟨four minus two : cuatro menos dos⟩ **2** WITHOUT : sin ⟨minus his hat : sin su sombrero⟩
minuscule *or* **miniscule** ['mɪnəs,kju:l, mɪ'nʌs-] *adj* : minúsculo
minute[1] [maɪ'nu:t, mɪ-, -'nju:t] *adj* **-nuter; -est 1** TINY : diminuto, minúsculo **2** DETAILED : minucioso
minute[2] ['mɪnət] *n* **1** : minuto *m* ⟨ten minutes late : diez minutos de retraso⟩ **2** MOMENT : momento *m* **3 minutes** *npl* : actas *fpl* (de una reunión)
minutely [maɪ'nu:tli, mɪ-, -'nju:t-] *adv* : minuciosamente
miracle ['mɪrɪkəl] *n* : milagro *m*
miraculous [mə'rækjələs] *adj* : milagroso — **miraculously** *adv*
mirage [mɪ'rɑʒ, *chiefly Brit* 'mɪr,ɑʒ] *n* : espejismo *m*
mire[1] ['maɪr] *vi* **mired; miring** : atascarse
mire[2] *n* **1** MUD : barro *m*, lodo *m* **2** : atolladero *m* ⟨stuck in a mire of debt : agobiado por la deuda⟩
mirror[1] ['mɪrər] *vt* : reflejar
mirror[2] *n* : espejo *m*
mirth ['mərθ] *n* : alegría *f*, regocijo *m*
mirthful ['mərθfəl] *adj* : alegre, regocijado
misadventure [,mɪsəd'vɛntʃər] *n* : malaventura *f*, desventura *f*
misanthrope ['mɪsən,θro:p] *n* : misántropo *m*, -pa *f*
misanthropic [,mɪsən'θrɑpɪk] *adj* : misantrópico
misanthropy [mɪ'sænθrəpi] *n* : misantropía *f*
misapprehend [,mɪs,æprə'hɛnd] *vt* : entender mal
misapprehension [,mɪs,æprə'hɛntʃən] *n* : malentendido *m*
misappropriate [,mɪsə'pro:pri,eɪt] *vt* **-ated; -ating** : malversar
misbegotten [,mɪsbi'gɑtən] *adj* **1** ILLEGITIMATE : ilegítimo **2** : mal concebido ⟨misbegotten laws : leyes mal concebidas⟩

misbehave [,mɪsbi'heɪv] *vi* **-haved; -having** : portarse mal
misbehavior [,mɪsbi'heɪvjər] *n* : mala conducta *f*
miscalculate [mɪs'kælkjə,leɪt] *v* **-lated; -lating** : calcular mal
miscalculation [mɪs,kælkjə'leɪʃən] *n* : error *m* de cálculo, mal cálculo *m*
miscarriage [,mɪs'kærɪʤ, 'mɪs,kærɪʤ] *n* **1** : aborto *m* **2** FAILURE : fracaso *m*, malogro *m* ⟨a miscarriage of justice : una injusticia, un error judicial⟩
miscarry [,mɪs'kæri, 'mɪs,kæri] *vi* **-ried; -rying 1** ABORT : abortar **2** FAIL : malograrse, fracasar
miscellaneous [,mɪsə'leɪniəs] *adj* : misceláneo
miscellany ['mɪsə,leɪni] *n, pl* **-nies** : miscelánea *f*
mischance [mɪs'tʃænts] *n* : desgracia *f*, infortunio *m*, mala suerte *f*
mischief ['mɪstʃəf] *n* : diabluras *fpl*, travesuras *fpl*
mischievous ['mɪstʃəvəs] *adj* : travieso, pícaro
mischievously ['mɪstʃəvəsli] *adv* : de manera traviesa
misconception [,mɪskən'sɛpʃən] *n* : concepto *m* erróneo, idea *f* falsa
misconduct [mɪs'kɑndəkt] *n* : mala conducta *f*
misconstrue [,mɪskən'stru:] *vt* **-strued; -struing** : malinterpretar
misdeed [mɪs'di:d] *n* : fechoría *f*
misdemeanor [,mɪsdɪ'mi:nər] *n* : delito *m* menor
miser ['maɪzər] *n* : avaro *m*, -ra *f*; tacaño *m*, -ña *f*
miserable ['mɪzərəbəl] *adj* **1** UNHAPPY : triste, desdichado **2** WRETCHED : miserable, desgraciado ⟨a miserable hut : una choza miserable⟩ **3** UNPLEASANT : desagradable, malo ⟨miserable weather : tiempo malísimo⟩ **4** CONTEMPTIBLE : despreciable, mísero ⟨for a miserable $10 : por unos míseros diez dólares⟩
miserably ['mɪzərəbli] *adv* **1** SADLY : tristemente **2** WRETCHEDLY : miserablemente, lamentablemente **3** UNFORTUNATELY : desgraciadamente
miserly ['maɪzərli] *adj* : avaro, tacaño
misery ['mɪzəri] *n, pl* **-eries** : miseria *f*, sufrimiento *m*
misfire [mɪs'faɪr] *vi* **-fired; -firing** : fallar
misfit ['mɪs,fɪt] *n* : inadaptado *m*, -da *f*
misfortune [mɪs'fɔrtʃən] *n* : desgracia *f*, desventura *f*, infortunio *m*
misgiving [mɪs'gɪvɪŋ] *n* : duda *f*, recelo *m*
misguided [mɪs'gaɪdəd] *adj* : desacertado, equivocado, mal informado
mishap ['mɪs,hæp] *n* : contratiempo *m*, percance *m*, accidente *m*
misinform [,mɪsɪn'fɔrm] *vt* : informar mal
misinterpret [,mɪsɪn'tərprət] *vt* : malinterpretar

misinterpretation [ˌmɪsɪnˌtərprə'teɪ-ʃən] n : mala interpretación f, malentendido m

misjudge [mɪs'dʒʌdʒ] vt -judged; -judging : juzgar mal

mislay [mɪs'leɪ] vt -laid [-leɪd]; -laying : extraviar, perder

mislead [mɪs'liːd] vt -led [-'lɛd]; -leading : engañar

misleading [mɪs'liːdɪŋ] adj : engañoso

mismanage [mɪs'mænɪdʒ] vt -aged; -aging : administrar mal

mismanagement [mɪs'mænɪdʒmənt] n : mala administración f

misnomer [mɪs'noːmər] n : nombre m inapropiado

misogynist [mɪ'sɑdʒənɪst] n : misógino m

misogyny [mə'sɑdʒəni] n : misoginia f

misplace [mɪs'pleɪs] vt -placed; -placing : extraviar, perder

misprint ['mɪsˌprɪnt, mɪs'-] n : errata f, error m de imprenta

mispronounce [ˌmɪsprə'naʊnts] vt -nounced; -nouncing : pronunciar mal

mispronunciation [ˌmɪsprəˌnʌntsi'eɪʃən] n : pronunciación f incorrecta

misquote [mɪs'kwoːt] vt -quoted; -quoting : citar incorrectamente

misread [mɪs'riːd] vt -read; -reading 1 : leer mal ⟨she misread the sentence : leyó mal la frase⟩ 2 MISUNDERSTAND : malinterpretar ⟨they misread his intention : malinterpretaron su intención⟩

misrepresent [ˌmɪsˌrprɪ'zɛnt] vt : distorsionar, falsear, tergiversar

misrule¹ [mɪs'ruːl] vt -ruled; -ruling : gobernar mal

misrule² n : mal gobierno m

miss¹ ['mɪs] vt 1 : errar, faltar ⟨to miss the target : no dar en el blanco⟩ 2 : no encontrar, perder ⟨they missed each other : no se encontraron⟩ ⟨I missed the plane : perdí el avión⟩ 3 : echar de menos, extrañar ⟨we miss him a lot : lo echamos mucho de menos⟩ 4 OVERLOOK : pasar por alto, perder (una oportunidad, etc.) 5 AVOID : evitar ⟨they just missed hitting the tree : por muy poco chocan contra el árbol⟩ 6 OMIT : saltarse ⟨he missed breakfast : se saltó el desayuno⟩

miss² n 1 : fallo m (de un tiro, etc.) 2 FAILURE : fracaso m 3 : señorita f ⟨Miss Jones called us : nos llamó la señorita Jones⟩ ⟨excuse me, miss : perdone, señorita⟩

missal ['mɪsəl] n : misal m

misshapen [mɪs'ʃeɪpən] adj : deforme

missile ['mɪsəl] n 1 : misil m ⟨guided missile : misil guiado⟩ 2 PROJECTILE : proyectil m

missing ['mɪsɪŋ] adj 1 ABSENT : ausente ⟨who's missing? : ¿quién falta?⟩ 2 LOST : perdido, desaparecido ⟨missing persons : los desaparecidos⟩

mission ['mɪʃən] n 1 : misión f (mandada por una iglesia) 2 DELEGATION : misión f, delegación f, embajada f 3 TASK : misión f

missionary¹ ['mɪʃəˌnɛri] adj : misionero

missionary² n, pl -aries : misionero m, -ra f

missive ['mɪsɪv] n : misiva f

misspell [mɪs'spɛl] vt : escribir mal

misspelling [mɪs'spɛlɪŋ] n : falta f de ortografía

misstep ['mɪsˌstɛp] n : traspié m, tropezón m

mist ['mɪst] n 1 HAZE : neblina f, niebla f 2 SPRAY : rocío m

mistake¹ [mɪ'steɪk] vt -took [-'stʊk]; -taken [-'steɪkən]; -taking 1 MISINTERPRET : malinterpretar 2 CONFUSE : confundir ⟨he mistook her for Clara : la confundió con Clara⟩

mistake² n 1 MISUNDERSTANDING : malentendido m, confusión f 2 ERROR : error m ⟨I made a mistake : me equivoqué, cometí un error⟩

mistaken [mɪ'steɪkən] adj WRONG : equivocado — mistakenly adv

mister ['mɪstər] n : señor m ⟨watch out, mister : cuidado, señor⟩

mistiness ['mɪstinəs] n : nebulosidad f

mistletoe ['mɪsəlˌtoː] n : muérdago m

mistreat [mɪs'triːt] vt : maltratar

mistreatment [mɪs'triːtmənt] n : maltrato m, abuso m

mistress ['mɪstrəs] n 1 : dueña f, señora f (de una casa) 2 LOVER : amante f

mistrust¹ [mɪs'trʌst] vt : desconfiar de

mistrust² n : desconfianza f

mistrustful [mɪs'trʌstfəl] adj : desconfiado

misty ['mɪsti] adj mistier; -est 1 : neblinoso, nebuloso 2 TEARFUL : lloroso

misunderstand [ˌmɪsˌʌndər'stænd] vt -stood [-'stʊd]; -standing 1 : entender mal 2 MISINTERPRET : malinterpretar ⟨don't misunderstand me : no me malinterpretes⟩

misunderstanding [ˌmɪsˌʌndər'stændɪŋ] n 1 MISINTERPRETATION : malentendido m 2 DISAGREEMENT, QUARREL : disputa f, discusión f

misuse¹ [mɪs'juːz] vt -used; -using 1 : emplear mal 2 ABUSE, MISTREAT : abusar de, maltratar

misuse² [mɪs'juːs] n 1 : mal empleo m, mal uso m 2 WASTE : derroche m, despilfarro m 3 ABUSE : abuso m

mite ['maɪt] n 1 : ácaro m 2 BIT : poco m ⟨a mite tired : un poquito cansado⟩

miter or mitre ['maɪtər] n 1 : mitra f (de un obispo) 2 or miter joint : inglete m

mitigate ['mɪtəˌgeɪt] vt -gated; -gating : mitigar, aliviar

mitigation [ˌmɪtə'geɪʃən] n : mitigación f, alivio m

mitosis [maɪ'toːsɪs] n, pl -toses [-ˌsiːz] : mitosis f

mitt ['mɪt] n : manopla f, guante m (de béisbol)

mitten ['mɪtən] *n* : manopla *f*, mitón *m*
mix¹ ['mɪks] *vt* **1** COMBINE : mezclar **2** STIR : remover, revolver **3 to mix up** CONFUSE : confundir — *vi* : mezclarse
mix² *n* : mezcla *f*
mixer ['mɪksər] *n* **1** : batidora *f* (de la cocina) **2 cement mixer** : hormigonera *f*
mixture ['mɪkstʃər] *n* : mezcla *f*
mix–up ['mɪks,ʌp] *n* CONFUSION : confusión *f*, lío *m fam*
mnemonic [nɪ'mɑnɪk] *adj* : mnemónico
moan¹ ['mo:n] *vi* : gemir
moan² *n* : gemido *m*
moat ['mo:t] *n* : foso *m*
mob¹ ['mɑb] *vt* **mobbed; mobbing 1** ATTACK : atacar en masa **2** HOUND : acosar, rodear
mob² *n* **1** THRONG : multitud *f*, turba *f*, muchedumbre *f* **2** GANG : pandilla *f*
mobile¹ ['mo:bəl, -,bi:l, -,baɪl] *adj* : móvil ⟨mobile home : caravana, casa rodante⟩
mobile² ['mo,bi:l] *n* : móvil *m*
mobility [mo'bɪləti] *n* : movilidad *f*
mobilize ['mo:bə,laɪz] *vt* **-lized; -lizing** : movilizar
moccasin ['mɑkəsən] *n* **1** : mocasín *m* **2** *or* **water moccasin** : serpiente *f* venenosa de Norteamérica
mocha ['mo:kə] *n* **1** : mezcla *f* de café y chocolate **2** : color *m* chocolate
mock¹ ['mɑk, 'mɔk] *vt* **1** RIDICULE : burlarse de, mofarse de **2** MIMIC : imitar, remedar (de manera burlona)
mock² *adj* **1** SIMULATED : simulado **2** PHONY : falso
mockery ['mɑkəri, 'mɔ-] *n, pl* **-eries 1** JEER, TAUNT : burla *f*, mofa *f* ⟨to make a mockery of : burlarse de⟩ **2** FAKE : imitación *f* (burlona)
mockingbird ['mɑkɪŋ,bərd, 'mɔ-] *n* : sinsonte *m*
mode ['mo:d] *n* **1** FORM : modo *m*, forma *f* **2** MANNER : modo *m*, manera *f*, estilo *m* **3** FASHION : moda *f*
model¹ ['mɑdəl] *v* **-eled** *or* **-elled; -eling** *or* **-elling** *vt* SHAPE : modelar — *vi* : trabajar de modelo
model² *adj* **1** EXEMPLARY : modelo, ejemplar ⟨a model student : un estudiante modelo⟩ **2** MINIATURE : en miniatura
model³ *n* **1** PATTERN : modelo *m* **2** MINIATURE : modelo *m*, miniatura *f* **3** EXAMPLE : modelo *m*, ejemplo *m* **4** MANNEQUIN : modelo *mf* **5** DESIGN : modelo *m* ⟨the '97 model : el modelo '97⟩
modem ['mo:dəm, -,dɛm] *n* : módem *m*
moderate¹ ['mɑdə,reɪt] *v* **-ated; -ating** *vt* : moderar, temperar — *vi* **1** CALM : moderarse, calmarse **2** : fungir como moderador (en un debate, etc.)
moderate² ['mɑdərət] *adj* : moderado
moderate³ ['mɑdərət] *n* : moderado *m*, -da *f*

moderately ['mɑdərətli] *adv* **1** : con moderación **2** FAIRLY : medianamente
moderation [,mɑdə'reɪʃən] *n* : moderación *f*
moderator ['mɑdə,reɪtər] *n* : moderador *m*, -dora *f*
modern ['mɑdərn] *adj* : moderno
modernism ['mɑdər,nɪzəm] *n* : modernismo *m*
modernist ['mɑdərnɪst] *n* : modernista *mf* — **modernist** *adj*
modernity [mə'dərnəti] *n* : modernidad *f*
modernization [,mɑdərnə'zeɪʃən] *n* : modernización *f*
modernize ['mɑdər,naɪz] *v* **-ized; -izing** *vt* : modernizar — *vi* : modernizarse
modest ['mɑdəst] *adj* **1** HUMBLE : modesto **2** DEMURE : recatado, pudoroso **3** MODERATE : modesto, moderado — **modestly** *adv*
modesty ['mɑdəsti] *n* : modestia *f*
modicum ['mɑdɪkəm] *n* : mínimo *m*, pizca *f*
modification [,mɑdəfə'keɪʃən] *n* : modificación *f*
modifier ['mɑdə,faɪər] *n* : modificante *m*, modificador *m*
modify ['mɑdə,faɪ] *vt* **-fied; -fying** : modificar, calificar (en gramática)
modish ['mo:dɪʃ] *adj* STYLISH : a la moda, de moda
modular ['mɑdʒələr] *adj* : modular
modulate ['mɑdʒə,leɪt] *vt* **-lated; -lating** : modular
modulation [,mɑdʒə'leɪʃən] *n* : modulación *f*
module ['mɑ,dʒu:l] *n* : módulo *m*
mogul ['mo:gəl] *n* : magnate *mf*; potentado *m*, -da *f*
mohair ['mo:,hær] *n* : mohair *m*
moist ['mɔɪst] *adj* : húmedo
moisten ['mɔɪsən] *vt* : humedecer
moistness ['mɔɪstnəs] *n* : humedad *f*
moisture ['mɔɪstʃər] *n* : humedad *f*
moisturize ['mɔɪstʃə,raɪz] *vt* **-ized; -izing** : humedecer (el aire), humectar (la piel)
moisturizer ['mɔɪtʃə,raɪzər] *n* : crema *f* hidratante, crema *f* humectante
molar ['mo:lər] *n* : muela *f*, molar *m*
molasses [mə'læsəz] *n* : melaza *f*
mold¹ ['mo:ld] *vt* : moldear, formar (carácter, etc.) — *vi* : enmohecerse ⟨the bread will mold : el pan se enmohecerá⟩
mold² *n* **1** *or* **leaf mold** : mantillo *m* **2** FORM : molde *m* ⟨to break the mold : romper el molde⟩ **3** FUNGUS : moho *m*
molder ['mo:ldər] *vi* CRUMBLE : desmoronarse
molding ['mo:ldɪŋ] *n* : moldura *f* (en arquitectura)
moldy ['mo:ldi] *adj* **moldier; -est** : mohoso
mole ['mo:l] *n* **1** : lunar *m* (en la piel) **2** : topo *m* (animal)

molecule ['malɪˌkjuːl] *n* : molécula *f* —
molecular [mə'lɛkjələr] *adj*
molehill ['moːlˌhɪl] *n* : topera *f*
molest [mə'lɛst] *vt* **1** ANNOY, DISTURB
: molestar **2** : abusar (sexualmente)
mollify ['maləˌfaɪ] *vt* **-fied; -fying**
: apaciguar, aplacar
mollusk *or* **mollusc** ['maləsk] *n* : molusco *m*
mollycoddle ['malɪˌkadəl] *vt* **-dled;**
-dling PAMPER : consentir, mimar
molt ['moːlt] *vi* : mudar, hacer la muda
molten ['moːltən] *adj* : fundido
mom ['mam, 'mʌm] *n* : mamá *f*
moment ['moːmənt] *n* **1** INSTANT : momento *m* ⟨one moment, please : un momento, por favor⟩ **2** TIME : momento
m ⟨at the moment : de momento, ac-
tualmente⟩ ⟨from that moment : desde entonces⟩ **3** IMPORTANCE : importancia *f* ⟨of great moment : de gran
importancia⟩
momentarily [ˌmoːmən'tɛrəli] *adv* **1**
: momentáneamente **2** SOON : dentro
de poco, pronto
momentary ['moːmənˌtɛri] *adj* : momentáneo
momentous [moː'mɛntəs] *adj* : de suma
importancia, fatídico
momentum [moː'mɛntəm] *n, pl* **-ta** [-tə]
or **-tums 1** : momento *m* (en física) **2**
IMPETUS : ímpetu *m*, impulso *m*
mommy ['mami, 'mʌ-] *n* : mami *f*
monarch ['maˌnark, -nərk] *n* : monarca
mf
monarchism ['maˌnarˌkɪzəm, -nər-] *n*
: monarquismo *m*
monarchist ['maˌnarkɪst, -nər-] *n*
: monárquico *m*, -ca *f*
monarchy ['maˌnarki, -nər-] *n, pl* **-chies**
: monarquía *f*
monastery ['manəˌstɛri] *n, pl* **-teries**
: monasterio *m*
monastic [mə'næstɪk] *adj* : monástico
— **monastically** [-tɪkli] *adv*
Monday ['mʌnˌdeɪ, -di] *n* : lunes *m*
monetary ['manəˌtɛri, 'mʌnə-] *adj*
: monetario
money ['mʌni] *n, pl* **-eys** *or* **-ies** ['mʌniz]
: dinero *m*, plata *f*
moneyed ['mʌnid] *adj* : adinerado
moneylender ['mʌniˌlɛndər] *n* : prestamista *mf*
money order *n* : giro *m* postal
Mongol ['maŋgəl, -ˌgoːl] → **Mongolian**
Mongolian [man'goːliən, maŋ-] *n* : mongol *m*, -gola *f* — **Mongolian** *adj*
mongoose ['manˌguːs, 'maŋ-] *n, pl*
-gooses : mangosta *f*
mongrel ['maŋgrəl, 'mʌn-] *n* **1** : perro
m mestizo, perro *m* corriente *Mex* **2**
HYBRID : híbrido *m*
monitor[1] ['manətər] *vt* : controlar, monitorear
monitor[2] *n* **1** : ayudante *mf* (en una escuela) **2** : monitor *m* (de una computadora, etc.)
monk ['mʌŋk] *n* : monje *m*

monkey[1] ['mʌŋki] *vi* **-keyed; -keying 1**
to monkey around : hacer payasadas,
payasear **2 to monkey with** : juguetear
con
monkey[2] *n, pl* **-keys** : mono *m*, -na *f*
monkeyshines ['mʌŋkiˌʃaɪnz] *npl*
PRANKS : picardías *fpl*, travesuras *fpl*
monkey wrench *n* : llave *f* inglesa
monocle ['manɪkəl] *n* : monóculo *m*
monogamous [mə'nagəməs] *adj*
: monógamo
monogamy [mə'nagəmi] *n* : monogamia *f*
monogram[1] ['manəˌgræm] *vt*
-grammed; -gramming : marcar con
monograma ⟨monogrammed towels
: toallas con monograma⟩
monogram[2] *n* : monograma *m*
monograph ['manəˌgræf] *n* : monografía *f*
monolingual [ˌmanə'lɪŋgwəl] *adj* : monolingüe
monolith ['manəˌlɪθ] *n* : monolito *m*
monolithic [ˌmanə'lɪθɪk] *adj* : monolítico
monologue ['manəˌlɔg] *n* : monólogo *m*
monoplane ['manəˌpleɪn] *n* : mono-
plano *m*
monopolize [mə'napəˌlaɪz] *vt* **-lized;**
-lizing : monopolizar
monopoly [mə'napəli] *n, pl* **-lies** : monopolio *m*
monosyllabic [ˌmanəsə'læbɪk] *adj*
: monosilábico
monosyllable ['manoˌsɪləbəl] *n* : monosílabo *m*
monotheism ['manoθiːˌɪzəm] *n* : monoteísmo *m*
monotheistic [ˌmanoθiː'ɪstɪk] *adj* : monoteísta
monotone ['manəˌtoːn] *n* : voz *f* monó-
tona
monotonous [mə'natənəs] *adj* : monótono — **monotonously** *adv*
monotony [mə'natəni] *n* : monotonía *f*,
uniformidad *f*
monoxide [mə'nakˌsaɪd] *n* : monóxido
m
monsoon [man'suːn] *n* : monzón *m*
monster ['manstər] *n* : monstruo *m*
monstrosity [man'strasəti] *n, pl* **-ties**
: monstruosidad *f*
monstrous ['manstrəs] *adj* : monstruoso — **monstrously** *adv*
montage [man'taʒ] *n* : montaje *m*
month ['mʌnθ] *n* : mes *m*
monthly[1] ['mʌnθli] *adv* : mensualmente
monthly[2] *adj* : mensual
monthly[3] *n, pl* **-lies** : publicación *f* mensual
monument ['manjəmənt] *n* : monumento *m*
monumental [ˌmanjə'mɛntəl] *adj* : monumental — **monumentally** *adv*
moo[1] ['muː] *vi* : mugir
moo[2] *n* : mugido *m*
mood ['muːd] *n* : humor *m* ⟨to be in a
good mood : estar de buen humor⟩ ⟨to

be in the mood for : tener ganas de⟩ ⟨to be in no mood for : no estar para⟩
moodiness ['mu:dinəs] *n* **1** SADNESS : melancolía *f*, tristeza *f* **2** : cambios *mpl* de humor, carácter *m* temperamental
moody ['mu:di] *adj* **moodier; -est 1** GLOOMY : melancólico, deprimido **2** TEMPERAMENTAL : temperamental, de humor variable
moon ['mu:n] *n* : luna *f*
moonbeam ['mu:n‚bi:m] *n* : rayo *m* de luna
moonlight[1] ['mu:n‚laɪt] *vi* : estar pluriempleado
moonlight[2] *n* : claro *m* de luna, luz *f* de la luna
moonlit ['mu:n‚lɪt] *adj* : iluminado por la luna ⟨a moonlit night : una noche de luna⟩
moonshine ['mu:n‚ʃaɪn] *n* **1** MOONLIGHT : luz *f* de la luna **2** NONSENSE : disparates *mpl*, tonterías *fpl* **3** : whisky *m* destilado ilegalmente
moor[1] ['mʊr, 'mɔr] *vt* : amarrar
moor[2] *n* : brezal *m*, páramo *m*
Moor ['mʊr] *n* : moro *m*, -ra *f*
mooring ['mʊrɪŋ, 'mɔr-] *n* DOCK : atracadero *m*
Moorish ['mʊrɪʃ] *adj* : moro
moose ['mu:s] *ns & pl* : alce *m* (norteamericano)
moot ['mu:t] *adj* DEBATABLE : discutible
mop[1] ['mɑp] *vt* **mopped; mopping** : trapear
mop[2] *n* : trapeador *m*
mope ['mo:p] *vi* **moped; moping** : andar deprimido, quedar abatido
moped ['mo:‚pɛd] *n* : ciclomotor *m*
moraine [mə'reɪn] *n* : morena *f*
moral[1] ['mɔrəl] *adj* : moral ⟨moral judgment : juicio moral⟩ ⟨moral support : apoyo moral⟩ — **morally** *adv*
moral[2] *n* **1** : moraleja *f* (de un cuento, etc.) **2 morals** *npl* : moral *f*, moralidad *f*
morale [mə'ræl] *n* : moral *f*
moralist ['mɔrəlɪst] *n* : moralista *mf*
moralistic [‚mɔrə'lɪstɪk] *adj* : moralista
morality [mə'ræləti] *n, pl* **-ties** : moralidad *f*
morass [mə'ræs] *n* **1** SWAMP : ciénaga *f*, pantano *m* **2** CONFUSION, MESS : lío *m fam*, embrollo *m*
moratorium [‚mɔrə'toriəm] *n, pl* **-riums** *or* **-ria** [-iə] : moratoria *f*
moray ['mɔr‚eɪ, mə'reɪ] *n* : morena *f*
morbid ['mɔrbɪd] *adj* **1** : mórbido, morboso (en medicina) **2** GRUESOME : morboso, horripilante
morbidity [mɔr'bɪdəti] *n, pl* **-ties** : morbosidad *f*
more[1] ['mor] *adv* : más ⟨what more can I say? : ¿qué más puedo decir?⟩ ⟨more important : más importante⟩ ⟨once more : una vez más⟩
more[2] *adj* : más ⟨nothing more than that : nada más que eso⟩ ⟨more work : más trabajo⟩

more[3] *n* : más *m* ⟨the more you eat, the more you want : cuanto más comes, tanto más quieres⟩
more[4] *pron* : más ⟨more were found : se encontraron más⟩
moreover [mor'o:vər] *adv* : además
mores ['mɔr‚eɪz, -i:z] *npl* CUSTOMS : costumbres *fpl*, tradiciones *fpl*
morgue ['mɔrg] *n* : morgue *f*
moribund ['mɔrə‚bʌnd] *adj* : moribundo
Mormon ['mɔrmən] *n* : mormón *m*, -mona *f* — **Mormon** *adj*
morn ['mɔrn] → **morning**
morning ['mɔrnɪŋ] *n* : mañana *f* ⟨good morning! : ¡buenos días!⟩
Moroccan [mə'rɑkən] *n* : marroquí *mf* — **Moroccan** *adj*
moron ['mor‚ɑn] *n* **1** : retrasado *m*, -da *f* mental **2** DUNCE : estúpido *m*, -da *f*; tonto *m*, -ta *f*
morose [mə'ro:s] *adj* : hosco, sombrío — **morosely** *adv*
moroseness [mə'ro:snəs] *n* : malhumor *m*
morphine ['mɔr‚fi:n] *n* : morfina *f*
morphology [mɔr'fɑlədʒi] *n, pl* **-gies** : morfología *f*
morrow ['mɑro:] *n* : día *m* siguiente
Morse code ['mɔrs] *n* : código *m* morse
morsel ['mɔrsəl] *n* **1** BITE : bocado *m* **2** FRAGMENT : pedazo *m*
mortal[1] ['mɔrtəl] *adj* : mortal ⟨mortal blow : golpe mortal⟩ ⟨mortal fear : miedo mortal⟩ — **mortally** *adv*
mortal[2] *n* : mortal *mf*
mortality [mɔr'tæləti] *n* : mortalidad *f*
mortar ['mɔrtər] *n* **1** : mortero *m*, molcajete *m Mex* ⟨mortar and pestle : mortero y maja⟩ **2** : mortero *m* ⟨mortar shell : granada de mortero⟩ **3** CEMENT : mortero *m*, argamasa *f*
mortgage[1] ['mɔrgɪdʒ] *vt* **-gaged; -gaging** : hipotecar
mortgage[2] *n* : hipoteca *f*
mortification [‚mɔrtəfə'keɪʃən] *n* **1** : mortificación *f* **2** HUMILIATION : humillación *f*, vergüenza *f*
mortify ['mɔrtə‚faɪ] *vt* **-fied; -fying 1** : mortificar (en religión) **2** HUMILIATE : humillar, avergonzar
mortuary ['mɔrtʃə‚weri] *n, pl* **-aries** FUNERAL HOME : funeraria *f*
mosaic [mo'zeɪk] *n* : mosaico *m*
Moslem ['mɑzləm] → **Muslim**
mosque ['mɑsk] *n* : mezquita *f*
mosquito [mə'ski:ţo] *n, pl* **-toes** : mosquito *m*, zancudo *m*
moss ['mɔs] *n* : musgo *m*
mossy ['mɑsi] *adj* **-ier; -est** : musgoso
most[1] ['mo:st] *adv* : más ⟨the most interesting book : el libro más interesante⟩
most[2] *adj* **1** : la mayoría de, la mayor parte de ⟨most people : la mayoría de la gente⟩ **2** GREATEST : más (dícese de los números), mayor (dícese de las cantidades) ⟨the most ability : la mayor capacidad⟩

most[3] *n* : más *m*, máximo *m* ⟨the most I can do : lo más que puedo hacer⟩ ⟨three weeks at the most : tres semanas como máximo⟩

most[4] *pron* : la mayoría, la mayor parte ⟨most will go : la mayoría irá⟩

mostly ['mo:stli] *adv* MAINLY : en su mayor parte, principalmente

mote ['mo:t] *n* SPECK : mota *f*

motel [mo'tɛl] *n* : motel *m*

moth ['mɔθ] *n* : palomilla *f*, polilla *f*

mother[1] ['mʌðər] *vt* **1** BEAR : dar a luz a **2** PROTECT : cuidar de, proteger

mother[2] *n* : madre *f*

motherhood ['mʌðər,hʊd] *n* : maternidad *f*

mother-in-law ['mʌðərɪn,lɔ] *n, pl* **mothers-in-law** : suegra *f*

motherland ['mʌðər,lænd] *n* : patria *f*

motherly ['mʌðərli] *adj* : maternal

mother-of-pearl [,mʌðərəv'pərl] *n* : nácar *m*, madreperla *f*

motif [mo'ti:f] *n* : motivo *m*

motion[1] ['mo:ʃən] *vt* : hacerle señas (a alguien) ⟨she motioned us to come in : nos hizo señas para que entráramos⟩

motion[2] *n* **1** MOVEMENT : movimiento *m* ⟨to set in motion : poner en marcha⟩ **2** PROPOSAL : moción *f* ⟨to second a motion : apoyar una moción⟩

motionless ['mo:ʃənləs] *adj* : inmóvil, quieto

motion picture *n* MOVIE : película *f*

motivate ['mo:tə,veɪt] *vt* **-vated; -vating** : motivar, mover, inducir

motivation [,mo:tə'veɪʃən] *n* : motivación *f*

motive[1] ['mo:tɪv] *adj* : motor ⟨motive power : fuerza motriz⟩

motive[2] *n* : motivo *m*, móvil *m*

motley ['mɑtli] *adj* : abigarrado, variopinto

motor[1] ['mo:tər] *vi* : viajar en coche

motor[2] *n* : motor *m*

motorbike ['mo:tər,baɪk] *n* : motocicleta *f* (pequeña), moto *f*

motorboat ['mo:tər,bo:t] *n* : bote *m* a motor, lancha *f* motora

motorcar ['mo:tər,kɑr] *n* : automóvil *m*

motorcycle ['mo:tər,saɪkəl] *n* : motocicleta *f*

motorcyclist ['mo:tər,saɪkəlɪst] *n* : motociclista *mf*

motorist ['mo:tərɪst] *n* : automovilista *mf*, motorista *mf*

mottle ['mɑtəl] *vt* **-tled; -tling** : manchar, motear ⟨mottled skin : piel manchada⟩ ⟨a mottled surface : una superficie moteada⟩

motto ['mɑt̬o:] *n, pl* **-toes** : lema *m*

mould ['mo:ld] → **mold**

mound ['maʊnd] *n* **1** PILE : montón *m* **2** KNOLL : montículo *m* **3** burial mound : túmulo *m*

mount[1] ['maʊnt] *vt* **1** : montar a (un caballo), montar en (una bicicleta), subir a **2** : montar (artillería, etc.) — *vi* INCREASE : aumentar

mount[2] *n* **1** SUPPORT : soporte *m* **2** HORSE : caballería *f*, montura *f* **3** MOUNTAIN : monte *m*, montaña *f*

mountain ['maʊntən] *n* : montaña *f*

mountaineer [,maʊntən'ɪr] *n* : alpinista *mf*; montañero *m*, -ra *f*

mountaineering [,maʊntən'ɪrɪŋ] *n* : alpinismo *m*

mountainous ['maʊntənəs] *adj* : montañoso

mountaintop ['maʊntən,tɑp] *n* : cima *f*, cumbre *f*

mourn ['morn] *vt* : llorar (por), lamentar ⟨to mourn the death of : llorar la muerte de⟩ — *vi* : llorar, estar de luto

mourner ['mornər] *n* : doliente *mf*

mournful ['mornfəl] *adj* **1** SORROWFUL : lloroso, plañidero, triste **2** GLOOMY : deprimente, entristecedor — **mournfully** *adv*

mourning ['mornɪŋ] *n* : duelo *m*, luto *m*

mouse ['maʊs] *n, pl* **mice** ['maɪs] **1** : ratón *m*, -tona *f* **2** : ratón *m* (de una computadora)

mousetrap ['maʊs,træp] *n* : ratonera *f*

mousse ['mu:s] *n* : mousse *mf*

moustache ['mʌ,stæʃ, mə'stæʃ] → **mustache**

mouth[1] ['maʊð] *vt* **1** : decir con poca sinceridad, repetir sin comprensión **2** : articular en silencio ⟨she mouthed the words : formó las palabras con los labios⟩

mouth[2] ['maʊθ] *n* : boca *f* (de una persona o un animal), entrada *f* (de un túnel), desembocadura *f* (de un río)

mouthful ['maʊθ,fʊl] *n* : bocado *m* (de comida), bocanada *f* (de líquido o humo)

mouthpiece ['maʊθ,pi:s] *n* : boquilla *f* (de un instrumento musical)

mouthwash ['maʊθ,wɔʃ, -,wɑʃ] *n* : enjuague *m* bucal

movable ['mu:vəbəl] *or* **moveable** *adj* : movible, móvil

move[1] ['mu:v] *v* **moved; moving** *vi* **1** GO : ir **2** RELOCATE : mudarse, trasladarse **3** STIR : moverse ⟨don't move! : ¡no te muevas!⟩ **4** ACT : actuar — *vt* **1** : mover ⟨move it over there : ponlo allí⟩ ⟨he kept moving his feet : no dejaba de mover los pies⟩ **2** INDUCE, PERSUADE : inducir, persuadir, mover **3** TOUCH : conmover ⟨it moved him to tears : lo hizo llorar⟩ **4** PROPOSE : proponer

move[2] *n* **1** MOVEMENT : movimiento *m* **2** RELOCATION : mudanza *f* (de casa), traslado *m* **3** STEP : paso *m* ⟨a good move : un paso acertado⟩

movement ['mu:vmənt] *n* : movimiento *m*

mover ['mu:vər] *n* : persona *f* que hace mudanzas

movie ['mu:vi] *n* **1** : película *f* **2 movies** *npl* : cine *m*

moving ['mu:vɪŋ] *adj* **1** : en movimiento ⟨a moving target : un blanco móvil⟩

2 TOUCHING : conmovedor, emocionante

mow[1] ['moː] vt **mowed; mowed** or **mown** ['moːn]; **mowing** : cortar (la hierba)

mow[2] ['maʊ] n : pajar m

mower ['moːər] → **lawn mower**

Mr. ['mɪstər] n, pl **Messrs.** ['mɛsərz] : señor m

Mrs. ['mɪsəz, -səs, esp South 'mɪzəz, -zəs] n, pl **Mesdames** [meɪ'dɑm, -'dæm] : señora f

Ms. ['mɪz] n : señora f, señorita f

much[1] ['mʌtʃ] adv **more** ['mor]; **most** ['moːst] : mucho ⟨I'm much happier : estoy mucho más contenta⟩ ⟨she talks as much as I do : habla tanto como yo⟩

much[2] adj **more; most** : mucho ⟨it has much validity : tiene mucha validez⟩ ⟨too much time : demasiado tiempo⟩

much[3] pron : mucho, -cha ⟨I don't need much : no necesito mucho⟩

mucilage ['mjuːsəlɪdʒ] n : mucílago m

muck ['mʌk] n 1 MANURE : estiércol m 2 DIRT, FILTH : mugre f, suciedad f 3 MIRE, MUD : barro m, fango m, lodo m

mucous ['mjuːkəs] adj : mucoso ⟨mucous membrane : membrana mucosa⟩

mucus ['mjuːkəs] n : mucosidad f

mud ['mʌd] n : barro m, fango m, lodo m

muddle[1] ['mʌdəl] v **-dled; -dling** vt 1 CONFUSE : confundir 2 BUNGLE : echar a perder, malograr — vi : andar confundido ⟨to muddle through : arreglárselas⟩

muddle[2] n : confusión f, embrollo m, lío m

muddleheaded [,mʌdəl'hɛdəd, 'mʌdəl,-] adj CONFUSED : confuso, despistado

muddy[1] ['mʌdi] vt **-died; -dying** : llenar de barro

muddy[2] adj **-dier; -est** : barroso, fangoso, lodoso, enlodado ⟨you're all muddy : estás cubierto de barro⟩

muff[1] ['mʌf] vt BUNGLE : echar a perder, fallar (un tiro, etc.)

muff[2] n : manguito m

muffin ['mʌfən] n : magdalena f, mantecada f Mex

muffle ['mʌfəl] vt **-fled; -fling** 1 ENVELOP : cubrir, tapar 2 DEADEN : amortiguar (un sonido)

muffler ['mʌflər] n 1 SCARF : bufanda f 2 : silenciador m, mofle m CA, Mex (de un automóvil)

mug[1] ['mʌg] v **mugged; mugging** vi : posar (con afectación), hacer muecas ⟨mugging for the camera : haciendo muecas para la cámara⟩ — vt ASSAULT : asaltar, atracar

mug[2] n CUP : tazón m

mugger ['mʌgər] n : atracador m, -dora f

mugginess ['mʌginəs] n : bochorno m

muggy ['mʌgi] adj **-gier; -est** : bochornoso

mulatto [mʊ'lɑto, -'læ-] n, pl **-toes** or **-tos** : mulato m, -ta f

mulberry ['mʌl,bɛri] n, pl **-ries** : morera f (árbol), mora f (fruta)

mulch[1] ['mʌltʃ] vt : cubrir con pajote

mulch[2] n : pajote m

mule ['mjuːl] n 1 : mula f 2 : obstinado m, -da f; terco m, -ca f

mulish ['mjuːlɪʃ] adj : obstinado, terco

mull ['mʌl] vt **to mull over** : reflexionar sobre

mullet ['mʌlət] n, pl **-let** or **-lets** : mújol m, múgil m

multicolored [,mʌlti'kʌlərd, ,mʌltaɪ-] adj : multicolor, abigarrado

multicultural [,mʌlti'kʌltʃərəl] adj : multicultural

multifaceted [,mʌlti'fæsətəd, ,mʌltaɪ-] adj : multifacético

multifamily [,mʌlti'fæmli, ,mʌltaɪ-] adj : multifamiliar

multifarious [,mʌltə'færiəs] adj DIVERSE : diverso, variado

multilateral [,mʌlti'lætərəl, ,mʌltaɪ-] adj : multilateral

multimedia [,mʌlti'miːdiə, ,mʌltaɪ-] adj : multimedia

multimillionaire [,mʌlti,mɪljə'nær, ,mʌltaɪ-, -'mɪljə,nær] adj : multimillonario

multinational [,mʌlti'næʃənəl, ,mʌltaɪ-] adj : multinacional

multiple[1] ['mʌltəpəl] adj : múltiple

multiple[2] n : múltiplo m

multiple sclerosis [sklə'roːsɪs] n : esclerosis f múltiple

multiplication [,mʌltəplə'keɪʃən] n : multiplicación f

multiplicity [,mʌltə'plɪsəti] n, pl **-ties** : multiplicidad f

multiplier ['mʌltə,plaɪər] n : multiplicador m (en matemáticas)

multiply ['mʌltə,plaɪ] v **-plied; -plying** vt : multiplicar — vi : multiplicarse

multipurpose [,mʌlti'pərpəs, ,mʌltaɪ-] adj : multiuso

multitude ['mʌltə,tuːd, -,tjuːd] n 1 CROWD : multitud f, muchedumbre f 2 HOST : multitud f, gran cantidad f ⟨a multitude of ideas : numerosas ideas⟩

multivitamin [,mʌlti'vaɪtəmən, ,mʌltaɪ-] adj : multivitamínico

mum[1] ['mʌm] adj SILENT : callado

mum[2] n → **chrysanthemum**

mumble[1] ['mʌmbəl] v **-bled; -bling** vt : mascullar, musitar — vi : mascullar, hablar entre dientes, murmurar

mumble[2] n **to speak in a mumble** : hablar entre dientes

mummy ['mʌmi] n, pl **-mies** : momia f

mumps ['mʌmps] ns & pl : paperas fpl

munch ['mʌntʃ] v : mascar, masticar

mundane [,mʌn'deɪn, 'mʌn,-] adj 1 EARTHLY, WORLDLY : mundano, terrenal 2 COMMONPLACE : rutinario, ordinario

municipal [mjʊ'nɪsəpəl] adj : municipal

municipality [mjʊ,nɪsə'pæləti] n, pl **-ties** : municipio m

munitions [mjʊ'nɪʃənz] npl : municiones fpl

mural¹ ['mjʊrəl] *adj* : mural
mural² ['mjʊrəlɪst] *n* : mural *m*
murder¹ ['mərdər] *vt* : asesinar, matar —
vi : matar
murder² *n* : asesinato *m*, homicidio *m*
murderer ['mərdərər] *n* : asesino *m*, -na
f; homicida *mf*
murderess ['mərdərɪs, -də‚rɛs, -dərəs] *n*
: asesina *f*, homicida *f*
murderous ['mərdərəs] *adj* : asesino,
homicida
murk ['mərk] *n* DARKNESS : oscuridad *f*,
tinieblas *fpl*
murkiness ['mərkinəs] *n* : oscuridad *f*,
tenebrosidad *f*
murky ['mərki] *adj* **-kier; -est** : oscuro,
tenebroso
murmur¹ ['mərmər] *vi* 1 DRONE : murmurar 2 GRUMBLE : refunfuñar, regañar, rezongar — *vt* MUMBLE : murmurar
murmur² *n* 1 COMPLAINT : queja *f* 2
DRONE : murmullo *m*, rumor *m*
muscle¹ ['mʌsəl] *vi* **-cled; -cling** : meterse ⟨to muscle in on : meterse por la
fuerza en, entrometerse en⟩
muscle² *n* 1 : músculo *m* 2 STRENGTH
: fuerza *f*
muscular ['mʌskjələr] *adj* 1 : muscular
⟨muscular tissue : tejido muscular⟩ 2
BRAWNY : musculoso
muscular dystrophy *n* : distrofia *f* muscular
musculature ['mʌskjələ‚tʃʊr, -tʃər] *n*
: musculatura *f*
muse¹ ['mju:z] *vi* **mused; musing** PON-
DER, REFLECT : cavilar, meditar, reflexionar
muse² *n* : musa *f*
museum [mjʊ'zi:əm] *n* 1 : museo *m*
mush ['mʌʃ] *n* 1 : gachas *fpl* (de maíz)
2 SENTIMENTALITY : sensiblería *f*
mushroom¹ ['mʌʃ‚ru:m, -‚rʊm] *vi* GROW,
MULTIPLY : crecer rápidamente, multiplicarse
mushroom² *n* : hongo *m*, champiñón *m*,
seta *f*
mushy ['mʌʃi] *adj* **mushier; -est** 1 SOFT
: blando 2 MAWKISH : sensiblero
music ['mju:zɪk] *n* : música *f*
musical¹ [mju:zɪkəl] *adj* : musical, de
música — **musically** *adv*
musical² *n* : comedia *f* musical
music box *n* : cajita *f* de música
musician [mjʊ'zɪʃən] *n* : músico *m*, -ca
f
musk ['mʌsk] *n* : almizcle *m*
musket ['mʌskət] *n* : mosquete *m*
musketeer [‚mʌskə'tɪr] *n* : mosquetero
m
muskrat ['mʌsk‚ræt] *n*, *pl* **-rat** *or* **-rats**
: rata *f* almizclera
Muslim¹ ['mʌzləm, 'mʊs-, 'mʊz-] *adj*
: musulmán
Muslim² *n* : musulmán *m*, -mana *f*
muslin ['mʌzlən] *n* : muselina *f*
muss¹ ['mʌs] *vt* : desordenar, despeinar
(el pelo)

muss² *n* : desorden *m*
mussel ['mʌsəl] *n* : mejillón *m*
must¹ ['mʌst] *v aux* 1 (*expressing obligation or necessity*) : deber, tener que
⟨you must stop : debes parar⟩ ⟨we
must obey : tenemos que obedecer⟩ 2
(*expressing probability*) : deber (de),
haber de ⟨you must be tired : debes de
estar cansado⟩ ⟨it must be late : ha de
ser tarde⟩
must² *n* : necesidad *f* ⟨exercise is a must
: el ejercicio es imprescindible⟩
mustache ['mʌ‚stæʃ, mʌ'stæʃ] *n* : bigote
m, bigotes *mpl*
mustang ['mʌ‚stæŋ] *n* : mustang *m*
mustard ['mʌstərd] *n* : mostaza *f*
muster¹ ['mʌstər] *vt* 1 ASSEMBLE : reunir 2 **to muster up** : armarse de, cobrar (valor, fuerzas, etc.)
muster² *n* 1 INSPECTION : revista *f* (de
tropas) ⟨it didn't pass muster : no re-
sistió un examen minucioso⟩ 2 COL-
LECTION : colección *f*
mustiness ['mʌstinəs] *n* : lo mohoso
musty ['mʌsti] *adj* **mustier; -est** : mohoso, que huele a moho, que huele a
encerrado
mutant¹ ['mju:tənt] *adj* : mutante
mutant² *n* : mutante *m*
mutate ['mju:‚teɪt] *vi* **-tated; -tating** 1
: mutar (genéticamente) 2 CHANGE
: transformarse
mutation [mju:'teɪʃən] *n* : mutación *f*
(genética)
mute¹ ['mju:t] *vt* **muted; muting** MUF-
FLE : amortiguar, ponerle sordina a (un
instrumento musical)
mute² *adj* **muter; mutest** : mudo —
mutely *adv*
mute³ *n* 1 : mudo *m*, -da *f* (persona) 2
: sordina *f* (para un instrumento musical)
mutilate ['mju:tə‚leɪt] *vt* **-lated; -lating**
: mutilar
mutilation [‚mju:tə'leɪʃən] *n* : mutilación
f
mutineer [‚mju:tən'ɪr] *n* : amotinado *m*,
-da *f*
mutinous ['mju:tənəs] *adj* : amotinado
mutiny¹ ['mju:təni] *vi* **-nied; -nying**
: amotinarse
mutiny² *n*, *pl* **-nies** : amotinamiento *m*,
motín *m*
mutt ['mʌt] *n* MONGREL : perro *m* mestizo, perro *m* corriente *Mex*
mutter ['mʌtər] *vi* 1 MUMBLE : mascullar, hablar entre dientes, murmurar
2 GRUMBLE : refunfuñar, regañar, rezongar
mutton ['mʌtən] *n* : carne *f* de carnero
mutual ['mju:tʃuəl] *adj* 1 : mutuo ⟨mu-
tual respect : respeto mutuo⟩ 2 COM-
MON : común ⟨a mutual friend : un
amigo común⟩
mutually ['mju:tʃuəli, -tʃəli] *adv* 1 : mutuamente ⟨mutually beneficial : mutuamente beneficioso⟩ 2 JOINTLY
: conjuntamente

muzzle[1] ['mʌzəl] *vt* **-zled; -zling** : ponerle un bozal a (un animal), amordazar
muzzle[2] *n* **1** SNOUT : hocico *m* **2** : bozal *m* (para un perro, etc.) **3** : boca *f* (de un arma de fuego)
my[1] ['maɪ] *adj* : mi ⟨my parents : mis padres⟩
my[2] *interj* : ¡caramba!, ¡Dios mío!
myopia [maɪ'o:piə] *n* : miopía *f*
myopic [maɪ'o:pɪk, -'ɑ-] *adj* : miope
myriad[1] ['mɪriəd] *adj* INNUMERABLE : innumerable
myriad[2] *n* : miríada *f*
myrrh ['mər] *n* : mirra *f*
myrtle ['mərt̬əl] *n* : mirto *m*, arrayán *m*
myself [maɪ'sɛlf] *pron* **1** (*used reflexively*) : me ⟨I washed myself : me lavé⟩ **2** (*used for emphasis*) : yo mismo, yo misma ⟨I did it myself : lo hice yo mismo⟩
mysterious [mɪ'stɪriəs] *adj* : misterioso — **mysteriously** *adv*

mysteriousness [mɪ'stɪriəsnəs] *n* : lo misterioso
mystery ['mɪstəri] *n, pl* **-teries** : misterio *m*
mystic[1] ['mɪstɪk] *adj* : místico
mystic[2] *n* : místico *m*, -ca *f*
mystical ['mɪstɪkəl] *adj* : místico — **mystically** *adv*
mysticism ['mɪstə,sɪzəm] *n* : misticismo *m*
mystify ['mɪstə,faɪ] *vt* **-fied; -fying** : dejar perplejo, confundir
mystique [mɪ'sti:k] *n* : aura *f* de misterio
myth ['mɪθ] *n* : mito *m*
mythic ['mɪθɪk] *adj* : mítico
mythical ['mɪθɪkəl] *adj* : mítico
mythological [ˌmɪθə'lɑdʒɪkəl] *adj* : mitológico
mythology [mɪ'θɑlədʒi] *n, pl* **-gies** : mitología *f*

N

n ['ɛn] *n, pl* **n's** *or* **ns** ['ɛnz] : decimocuarta letra del alfabeto inglés
nab ['næb] *vt* **nabbed; nabbing** : prender, pillar *fam*, pescar *fam*
nadir ['neɪdər, 'neɪˌdɪr] *n* : nadir *m*, punto *m* más bajo
nag[1] ['næg] *v* **nagged; nagging** *vi* **1** COMPLAIN : quejarse, rezongar **2 to nag at** HASSLE : molestar, darle (la) lata (a alguien) — *vt* **1** PESTER : molestar, fastidiar **2** SCOLD : regañar, estarle encima a *fam*
nag[2] *n* **1** GRUMBLER : gruñón *m*, -ñona *f* **2** HORSE : jamelgo *m*
naiad ['neɪəd, 'naɪ-, -ˌæd] *n, pl* **-iads** *or* **-iades** [-əˌdi:z] : náyade *f*
nail[1] ['neɪl] *vt* : clavar, sujetar con clavos
nail[2] *n* **1** FINGERNAIL : uña *f* ⟨nail file : lima (de uñas)⟩ ⟨nail polish : laca de uñas⟩ **2** : clavo *m* ⟨to hit the nail on the head : dar en el clavo⟩
naive *or* **naïve** [nɑ'i:v] *adj* **-iver; -est 1** INGENUOUS : ingenuo, cándido **2** GULLIBLE : crédulo
naively [nɑ'i:vli] *adv* : ingenuamente
naïveté [ˌnɑˌi:və'teɪ, nɑ'i:vəˌ-] *n* : ingenuidad *f*
naked ['neɪkəd] *adj* **1** UNCLOTHED : desnudo **2** UNCOVERED : desenvainado (dícese de una espada), pelado (dícese de los árboles), expuesto al aire (dícese de una llama) **3** OBVIOUS, PLAIN : manifiesto, puro, desnudo ⟨the naked truth : la pura verdad⟩ **4 to the naked eye** : a simple vista
nakedly ['neɪkədli] *adv* : manifiestamente
nakedness ['neɪkədnəs] *n* : desnudez *f*
name[1] ['neɪm] *vt* **named; naming 1** CALL : llamar, bautizar, ponerle nombre a **2** MENTION : mentar, mencionar, dar el nombre de ⟨they have named a

suspect : han dado el nombre de un sospechoso⟩ **3** APPOINT : nombrar **4 to name a price** : fijar un precio
name[2] *adj* **1** KNOWN : de nombre ⟨name brand : marca conocida⟩ **2** PROMINENT : de renombre, de prestigio
name[3] *n* **1** : nombre *m* ⟨what is your name? : ¿cómo se llama?⟩ **2** SURNAME : apellido *m* **3** EPITHET : epíteto *m* ⟨to call somebody names : llamar a alguien de todo⟩ **4** REPUTATION : fama *f*, reputación *f* ⟨to make a name for oneself : darse a conocer, hacerse famoso⟩
nameless ['neɪmləs] *adj* **1** ANONYMOUS : anónimo **2** INDESCRIBABLE : indecible, indescriptible
namelessly ['neɪmləsli] *adv* : anónimamente
namely ['neɪmli] *adv* : a saber
namesake ['neɪmˌseɪk] *n* : tocayo *m*, -ya *f*; homónimo *m*, -ma *f*
Namibian [nə'mɪbiən] *n* : namibio *m*, -bia *f* — **Namibian** *adj*
nanny ['næni] *n, pl* **-nies** : niñera *f*; nana *f* CA, Col, Mex, Ven
nap[1] ['næp] *vi* **napped; napping 1** : dormir, dormir la siesta **2 to be caught napping** : estar desprevenido
nap[2] *n* **1** SLEEP : siesta *f* ⟨to take a nap : echarse una siesta⟩ **2** FUZZ, PILE : pelo *m*, pelusa *f* (de telas)
nape ['neɪp, 'næp] *n* : nuca *f*, cerviz *f*, cogote *m*
naphtha ['næfθə] *n* : nafta *f*
napkin ['næpkən] *n* : servilleta *f*
narcissism ['nɑrsəˌsɪzəm] *n* : narcisismo *m*
narcissist ['nɑrsəsɪst] *n* : narcisista *mf*
narcissistic [ˌnɑrsə'sɪstɪk] *adj* : narcisista
narcissus [nɑr'sɪsəs] *n, pl* **-cissus** *or*

-cissuses *or* **-cissi** [-ˈsɪˌsaɪ, -ˌsiː] : narciso *m*

narcotic¹ [nɑrˈkɑtɪk] *adj* : narcótico

narcotic² *n* : narcótico *m*, estupefaciente *m*

narrate [ˈnærˌeɪt] *vt* **-rated; -rating** : narrar, relatar

narration [næˈreɪʃən] *n* : narración *f*

narrative¹ [ˈnærətɪv] *adj* : narrativo

narrative² *n* : narración *f*, narrativa *f*, relato *m*

narrator [ˈnærˌeɪtər] *n* : narrador *m*, -dora *f*

narrow¹ [ˈnærˌoː] *vi* : estrecharse, angostarse ⟨the river narrowed : el río se estrechó⟩ — *vt* **1** : estrechar, angostar **2** LIMIT : restringir, limitar ⟨to narrow the search : limitar la búsqueda⟩

narrow² *adj* **1** : estrecho, angosto **2** LIMITED : estricto, limitado ⟨in the narrowest sense of the word : en el sentido más estricto de la palabra⟩ **3 to have a narrow escape** : escapar por un pelo

narrowly [ˈnæroli] *adv* **1** BARELY : por poco **2** CLOSELY : de cerca

narrow–minded [ˌnæroˈmaɪndəd] *adj* : de miras estrechas

narrowness [ˈnæronəs] *n* : estrechez *f*

narrows [ˈnæroːz] *npl* STRAIT : estrecho *m*

narwhal [ˈnɑrˌʍɑl, ˈnɑrwəl] *n* : narval *m*

nasal [ˈneɪzəl] *adj* : nasal, gangoso ⟨a nasal voice : una voz gangosa⟩

nasally [ˈneɪzəli] *adv* **1** : por la nariz **2** : con voz gangosa

nastily [ˈnæstəli] *adv* : con maldad, cruelmente

nastiness [ˈnæstinəs] *n* : porquería *f*

nasturtium [nəˈstərʃəm, næ-] *n* : capuchina *f*

nasty [ˈnæsti] *adj* **-tier; -est 1** FILTHY : sucio, mugriento **2** OBSCENE : obsceno **3** MEAN, SPITEFUL : malo, malicioso **4** UNPLEASANT : desagradable, feo **5** REPUGNANT : asqueroso, repugnante ⟨a nasty smell : un olor asqueroso⟩

natal [ˈneɪtəl] *adj* : natal

nation [ˈneɪʃən] *n* : nación *f*

national¹ [ˈnæʃənəl] *adj* : nacional

national² *n* : ciudadano *m*, -na *f*; nacional *mf*

nationalism [ˈnæʃənəˌlɪzəm] *n* : nacionalismo *m*

nationalist¹ [ˈnæʃənəlɪst] *adj* : nacionalista

nationalist² *n* : nacionalista *mf*

nationalistic [ˌnæʃənəˈlɪstɪk] *adj* : nacionalista

nationality [ˌnæʃəˈnæləti] *n, pl* **-ties** : nacionalidad *f*

nationalization [ˌnæʃənələˈzeɪʃən] *n* : nacionalización *f*

nationalize [ˈnæʃənəˌlaɪz] *vt* **-ized; -izing** : nacionalizar

nationally [ˈnæʃənəli] *adv* : a escala nacional, a nivel nacional

nationwide [ˈneɪʃənˈwaɪd] *adj* : en toda la nación, por todo el país

native¹ [ˈneɪtɪv] *adj* **1** INNATE : innato **2** : natal ⟨her native city : su ciudad natal⟩ **3** INDIGENOUS : indígena, autóctono

native² *n* **1** ABORIGINE : nativo *m*, -va *f*; indígena *mf* **2** : natural *m* ⟨he's a native of Mexico : es natural de México⟩

Native American → American Indian

nativity [nəˈtɪvəti, neɪ-] *n, pl* **-ties 1** BIRTH : navidad *f* **2 the Nativity** : la Natividad, la Navidad

natty [ˈnæti] *adj* **-tier; -est** : elegante, garboso

natural¹ [ˈnætʃərəl] *adj* **1** : natural, de la naturaleza ⟨natural woodlands : bosques naturales⟩ ⟨natural childbirth : parto natural⟩ **2** INNATE : innato, natural **3** UNAFFECTED : natural, sin afectación **4** LIFELIKE : natural, vivo

natural² *n* **to be a natural** : tener un talento innato (para algo)

natural gas *n* : gas *m* natural

natural history *n* : historia *f* natural

naturalism [ˈnætʃərəˌlɪzəm] *n* : naturalismo *m*

naturalist [ˈnætʃərəlɪst] *n* : naturalista *mf* — **naturalist** *adj*

naturalistic [ˌnætʃərəˈlɪstɪk] *adj* : naturalista

naturalization [ˌnætʃərələˈzeɪʃən] *n* : naturalización *f*

naturalize [ˈnætʃərəˌlaɪz] *vt* **-ized; -izing** : naturalizar

naturally [ˈnætʃərəli] *adv* **1** INHERENTLY : naturalmente, intrínsecamente **2** UNAFFECTEDLY : de manera natural **3** OF COURSE : por supuesto, naturalmente

naturalness [ˈnætʃərəlnəs] *n* : naturalidad *f*

natural science *n* : ciencias *fpl* naturales

nature [ˈneɪtʃər] *n* **1** : naturaleza *f* ⟨the laws of nature : las leyes de la naturaleza⟩ **2** KIND, SORT : índole *f*, clase *f* ⟨things of this nature : cosas de esta índole⟩ **3** DISPOSITION : carácter *m*, natural *m*, naturaleza *f* ⟨it is his nature to be friendly : es de natural simpático⟩ ⟨human nature : la naturaleza humana⟩

naught [ˈnɔt] *n* **1** : nada *f* ⟨to come to naught : reducirse a nada, fracasar⟩ **2** ZERO : cero *m*

naughtily [ˈnɔtəli] *adv* : traviesamente, con malicia

naughtiness [ˈnɔtinəs] *n* : mala conducta *f*, travesuras *fpl*, malicia *f*

naughty [ˈnɔti] *adj* **-tier; -est 1** MISCHIEVOUS : travieso, pícaro **2** RISQUÉ : picante, subido de tono

nausea [ˈnɔziə, ˈnɔʃə] *n* **1** SICKNESS : náuseas *fpl* **2** DISGUST : asco *m*

nauseate [ˈnɔziˌeɪt, -ʒi-, -si-, -ʃi-] *vt* **-ated; -ating 1** SICKEN : darle náuseas (a alguien) **2** DISGUST : asquear, darle asco (a alguien)

nauseating *adj* : nauseabundo, repugnante

nauseatingly [ˈnɔziˌeɪtɪŋli, -ʒi-, -si-, -ʃi-] *adv* : hasta el punto de dar asco ⟨nauseatingly sweet : tan dulce que da asco⟩

nauseous [ˈnɔʃəs, -ziəs] *adj* **1** SICK : mareado, con náuseas **2** SICKENING : nauseabundo

nautical [ˈnɔt̬ɪkəl] *adj* : náutico

nautilus [ˈnɔt̬ələs] *n, pl* **-luses** *or* **-li** [-ˌlaɪ, -ˌli:] : nautilo *m*

Navajo [ˈnævəˌhoː, ˈnɑ-] *n* : navajo *m*, -ja *f* — **Navajo** *adj*

naval [ˈneɪvəl] *adj* : naval

nave [ˈneɪv] *n* : nave *f*

navel [ˈneɪvəl] *n* : ombligo *m*

navigability [ˌnævɪgəˈbɪlət̬i] *n* : navegabilidad *f*

navigable [ˈnævɪgəbəl] *adj* : navegable

navigate [ˈnævəˌgeɪt] *v* **-gated; -gating** *vi* : navegar — *vt* **1** STEER : gobernar (un barco), pilotar (un avión) **2** : navegar por (un río, etc.)

navigation [ˌnævəˈgeɪʃən] *n* : navegación *f*

navigator [ˈnævəˌgeɪt̬ər] *n* : navegante *mf*

navy [ˈneɪvi] *n, pl* **-vies 1** FLEET : flota *f* **2** : marina *f* de guerra, armada *f* ⟨the United States Navy : la armada de los Estados Unidos⟩ **3** *or* **navy blue** : azul *m* marino

nay¹ [ˈneɪ] *adv* : no

nay² *n* : no *m*, voto *m* en contra

Nazi [ˈnɑtsi, ˈnæt-] *n* : nazi *mf*

Nazism [ˈnɑtˌsɪzəm, ˈnæt-] *or* **Naziism** [ˈnɑtsiˌɪzəm, ˈnæt-] *n* : nazismo *m*

Neanderthal man [niˈændərˌθɔl, -ˌtɔl] *n* : hombre *m* de Neanderthal

near¹ [ˈnɪr] *vt* **1** : acercarse a ⟨the ship is nearing port : el barco se está acercando al puerto⟩ **2** : estar a punto de ⟨she is nearing graduation : está a punto de graduarse⟩

near² *adv* **1** CLOSE : cerca ⟨my family lives quite near : mi familia vive muy cerca⟩ **2** NEARLY : casi ⟨I came near to finishing : casi terminé⟩

near³ *adj* **1** CLOSE : cercano, próximo **2** SIMILAR : parecido, semejante

near⁴ *prep* : cerca de

nearby¹ [nɪrˈbaɪ, ˈnɪrˌbaɪ] *adv* : cerca

nearby² *adj* : cercano

nearly [ˈnɪrli] *adv* **1** ALMOST : casi ⟨nearly asleep : casi dormido⟩ **2** **not nearly** : ni con mucho, ni mucho menos ⟨it was not nearly so bad as I had expected : no fue ni con mucho tan malo como esperaba⟩

nearness [ˈnɪrnəs] *n* : proximidad *f*

nearsighted [ˈnɪrˌsaɪt̬əd] *adj* : miope, corto de vista

nearsightedly [ˈnɪrˌsaɪt̬ədli] *adv* : con miopía

nearsightedness [ˈnɪrˌsaɪt̬ədnəs] *n* : miopía *f*

neat [ˈniːt] *adj* **1** CLEAN, ORDERLY : ordenado, pulcro, limpio **2** UNDILUTED : solo, sin diluir **3** SIMPLE, TASTEFUL : sencillo y de buen gusto **4** CLEVER : hábil, ingenioso ⟨a neat trick : un truco ingenioso⟩

neatly [ˈniːtli] *adv* **1** TIDILY : ordenadamente **2** CLEVERLY : ingeniosamente

neatness [ˈniːtnəs] *n* : pulcritud *f*, limpieza *f*, orden *m*

nebula [ˈnɛbjʊlə] *n, pl* **-lae** [-ˌli:, -ˌlaɪ] : nebulosa *f*

nebulous [ˈnɛbjʊləs] *adj* : nebuloso, vago

necessarily [ˌnɛsəˈsɛrəli] *adv* : necesariamente, forzosamente

necessary¹ [ˈnɛsəˌsɛri] *adj* **1** INEVITABLE : inevitable **2** COMPULSORY : necesario, obligatorio **3** ESSENTIAL : imprescindible, preciso, necesario

necessary² *n, pl* **-saries** : lo esencial, lo necesario

necessitate [nɪˈsɛsəˌteɪt] *vt* **-tated; -tating** : necesitar, requerir

necessity [nɪˈsɛsət̬i] *n, pl* **-ties 1** NEED : necesidad *f* **2** REQUIREMENT : requisito *m* indispensable **3** POVERTY : indigencia *f*, necesidad *f* **4** INEVITABILITY : inevitabilidad *f*

neck¹ [ˈnɛk] *vi* : besuquearse

neck² *n* **1** : cuello *m* (de una persona), pescuezo *m* (de un animal) **2** COLLAR : cuello *m* **3** : cuello *m* (de una botella), mástil *m* (de una guitarra)

neckerchief [ˈnɛkərˌtʃəf, -ˌtʃiːf] *n, pl* **-chiefs** [-tʃəfs, -ˌtʃiːfs] : pañuelo *m* (para el cuello), mascada *f Mex*

necklace [ˈnɛkləs] *n* : collar *m*

neckline [ˈnɛkˌlaɪn] *n* : escote *m*

necktie [ˈnɛkˌtaɪ] *n* : corbata *f*

nectar [ˈnɛktər] *n* : néctar *m*

nectarine [ˌnɛktəˈriːn] *n* : nectarina *f*

née *or* **nee** [ˈneɪ] *adj* : de soltera ⟨Mrs. Smith, née Whitman : la señora Smith, de soltera Whitman⟩

need¹ [ˈniːd] *vt* **1** : necesitar ⟨I need your help : necesito su ayuda⟩ ⟨I need money : me falta dinero⟩ **2** REQUIRE : requerir, exigir ⟨that job needs patience : ese trabajo exige paciencia⟩ **3 to need to** : tener que ⟨he needs to study : tiene que estudiar⟩ ⟨they need to be scolded : hay que reprenderlos⟩ — *v aux* **1** MUST : tener que, deber ⟨need you shout? : ¿tienes que gritar?⟩ **2 to be needed** : hacer falta ⟨you needn't worry : no hace falta que te preocupes, no hay por qué preocuparse⟩

need² *n* **1** NECESSITY : necesidad *f* ⟨in case of need : en caso de necesidad⟩ **2** LACK : falta *f* ⟨the need for better training : la falta de mejor capacitación⟩ ⟨to be in need : necesitar⟩ **3** POVERTY : necesidad *f*, indigencia *f* **4 needs** *npl* : requisitos *mpl*, carencias *fpl*

needful [ˈniːdfəl] *adj* : necesario

needle¹ [ˈniːdəl] *vt* **-dled; -dling** : pinchar

needle² *n* **1** : aguja *f* ⟨to thread a needle : enhebrar una aguja⟩ ⟨knitting needle : aguja de tejer⟩ 2 POINTER : aguja *f*, indicador *m*

needlepoint ['ni:dəl,pɔint] *n* 1 LACE : encaje *m* de mano 2 EMBROIDERY : bordado *m* en cañamazo

needless ['ni:dləs] *adj* : innecesario

needlessly ['ni:dləsli] *adv* : sin ninguna necesidad, innecesariamente

needlework ['ni:dəl,wərk] *n* : bordado *m*

needn't ['ni:dənt] (*contraction of* need not) → need

needy[1] ['ni:di] *adj* needier; -est : necesitado

needy[2] *n* the needy : los necesitados *mpl*

nefarious [nɪ'færiəs] *adj* : nefario, nefando, infame

negate [nɪ'geɪt] *vt* -gated; -gating 1 DENY : negar 2 NULLIFY : invalidar, anular

negation [nɪ'geɪʃən] *n* : negación *f*

negative[1] ['nɛgəṭɪv] *adj* : negativo

negative[2] *n* 1 : negación *f* (en lingüística) 2 : negativa *f* ⟨to answer in the negative : contestar con una negativa⟩ 3 : término *m* negativo (en matemáticas) 4 : negativo *m*, imagen *f* en negativo (en fotografía)

negatively ['nɛgəṭɪvli] *adv* : negativamente

neglect[1] [nɪ'glɛkt] *vt* 1 : desatender, descuidar ⟨to neglect one's health : descuidar la salud⟩ 2 : no cumplir con, faltar a ⟨to neglect one's obligations : faltar uno a sus obligaciones⟩ ⟨he neglected to tell me : omitió decírmelo⟩

neglect[2] *n* 1 : negligencia *f*, descuido *m*, incumplimiento *m* ⟨through neglect : por negligencia⟩ ⟨neglect of duty : incumplimiento del deber⟩ 2 in a state of neglect : abandonado, descuidado

neglectful [nɪ'glɛktfəl] *adj* : descuidado

negligee [,nɛglə'ʒeɪ] *n* : negligé *m*

negligence ['nɛglɪʤənts] *n* : descuido *m*, negligencia *f*

negligent ['nɛglɪʤənt] *adj* : negligente, descuidado — negligently *adv*

negligible ['nɛglɪʤəbəl] *adj* : insignificante, despreciable

negotiable [nɪ'go:ʃəbəl, -ʃiə-] *adj* : negociable

negotiate [nɪ'go:ʃi,eɪt] *v* -ated; -ating *vi* : negociar — *vt* 1 : negociar, gestionar ⟨to negotiate a treaty : negociar un trato⟩ 2 : salvar, franquear ⟨they negotiated the obstacles : salvaron los obstáculos⟩ ⟨to negotiate a turn : tomar una curva⟩

negotiation [nɪ,go:ʃi'eɪʃən, -si'eɪ-] *n* : negociación *f*

negotiator [nɪ'go:ʃi,eɪʈər, -si,eɪ-] *n* : negociador *m*, -dora *f*

Negro ['ni:,gro:] *n*, *pl* -groes : negro *m*, -gra *f*

neigh[1] ['neɪ] *vi* : relinchar

neigh[2] *n* : relincho *m*

neighbor[1] ['neɪbər] *vt* : ser vecino de, estar junto a ⟨her house neighbors mine : su casa está junto a la mía⟩ — *vi* : estar cercano, lindar, colindar ⟨her land neighbors on mine : sus tierras lindan con las mías⟩

neighbor[2] *n* 1 : vecino *m*, -na *f* 2 love thy neighbor : ama a tu prójimo

neighborhood ['neɪbər,hʊd] *n* 1 : barrio *m*, vecindad *f*, vecindario *m* 2 in the neighborhood of : alrededor de, cerca de

neighborly ['neɪbərli] *adv* : amable, de buena vecindad

neither[1] ['ni:ðər, 'naɪ-] *adj* : ninguno (de los dos)

neither[2] *conj* 1 : ni ⟨neither asleep nor awake : ni dormido ni despierto⟩ 2 NOR : ni (tampoco) ⟨I'm not asleep— neither am I : no estoy dormido—ni yo tampoco⟩

neither[3] *pron* : ninguno

nemesis ['nɛməsɪs] *n*, *pl* -eses [-,si:z] 1 RIVAL : rival *mf* 2 RETRIBUTION : justo castigo *m*

Neoclassical [,ni:o'klæsɪkəl] *adj* : neoclásico

neologism [ni'alə,ʤɪzəm] *n* : neologismo *m*

neon[1] ['ni:,an] *adj* : de neón ⟨neon sign : letrero de neón⟩

neon[2] *n* : neón *m*

neophyte ['ni:ə,faɪt] *n* : neófito *m*, -ta *f*

Nepali [nə'pɔli, -'pɑ-, -'pæ-] *n* : nepalés *m*, -lesa *f* — Nepali *adj*

nephew ['nɛ,fju:, *chiefly British* 'nɛ,vju:] *n* : sobrino *m*

nepotism ['nɛpə,tɪzəm] *n* : nepotismo *m*

Neptune ['nɛp,tu:n, -,tju:n] *n* : Neptuno *m*

nerd ['nərd] *n* : ganso *m*, -sa *f*

nerve ['nərv] *n* 1 : nervio *m* 2 COURAGE : coraje *m*, valor *m*, fuerza *f* de la voluntad ⟨to lose one's nerve : perder el valor⟩ 3 AUDACITY, GALL : atrevimiento *m*, descaro *m* ⟨of all the nerve! : ¡qué descaro!⟩ 4 nerves *npl* : nervios *mpl* ⟨a fit of nerves : un ataque de nervios⟩

nervous ['nərvəs] *adj* 1 : nervioso ⟨the nervous system : el sistema nervioso⟩ 2 EXCITABLE : nervioso, excitable ⟨to get nervous : excitarse, ponerse nervioso⟩ 3 FEARFUL : miedoso, temeroso

nervously ['nərvəsli] *adv* : nerviosamente

nervousness ['nərvəsnəs] *n* : nerviosismo *m*, nerviosidad *f*, ansiedad *f*

nervy ['nərvi] *adj* nervier; -est 1 COURAGEOUS : valiente 2 IMPUDENT : atrevido, descarado, fresco *fam* 3 NERVOUS : nervioso

nest[1] ['nɛst] *vi* : anidar

nest[2] *n* 1 : nido *m* (de un ave), avispero *m* (de una avispa), madriguera *f* (de un animal) 2 REFUGE : nido *m*, refugio *m* 3 SET : juego *m* ⟨a nest of tables : un juego de mesitas⟩

nestle ['nɛsəl] *vi* -tled; -tling : acurrucarse, arrimarse cómodamente

net¹ ['nɛt] *vt* **netted; netting 1** CATCH : pescar, atrapar con una red **2** CLEAR : ganar neto ⟨they netted $5000 : ganaron $5000 netos⟩ **3** YIELD : producir neto

net² *adj* : neto ⟨net weight : peso neto⟩ ⟨net gain : ganancia neta⟩

net³ *n* : red *f*, malla *f*

nether ['nɛðər] *adj* **1** : inferior, más bajo **2 the nether regions** : el infierno

nettle¹ ['nɛtəl] *vt* **-tled; -tling** : irritar, provocar, molestar

nettle² *n* : ortiga *f*

network ['nɛt͵wərk] *n* **1** SYSTEM : red *f* **2** CHAIN : cadena *f* ⟨a network of supermarkets : una cadena de supermercados⟩

neural ['nʊrəl, 'njʊr-] *adj* : neural

neuralgia [nʊ'rældʒə, njʊ-] *n* : neuralgia *f*

neuritis [nʊ'raɪtəs, njʊ-] *n, pl* **-ritides** [-'rɪtə͵diːz] *or* **-ritises** : neuritis *f*

neurological [͵nʊrə'lɑdʒɪkəl, ͵njʊr-] *or* **neurologic** [͵nʊrə'lɑdʒɪk, ͵njʊr-] *adj* : neurológico

neurologist [nʊ'rɑlədʒɪst, njʊ-] *n* : neurólogo *m*, -ga *f*

neurology [nʊ'rɑlədʒi, njʊ-] *n* : neurología *f*

neurosis [nʊ'roːsɪs, njʊ-] *n, pl* **-roses** [-͵siːz] : neurosis *f*

neurotic¹ [nʊ'rɑtɪk, njʊ-] *adj* : neurótico

neurotic² *n* : neurótico *m*, -ca *f*

neuter¹ ['nuːtər, 'njuː-] *vt* : castrar

neuter² *adj* : neutro

neutral¹ ['nuːtrəl, 'njuː-] *adj* **1** IMPARTIAL : neutral, imparcial ⟨to remain neutral : permanecer neutral⟩ **2** : neutro ⟨a neutral color : un color neutro⟩ **3** : neutro (en la química o la electricidad)

neutral² *n* : punto *m* muerto (de un automóvil)

neutrality [nuː'træləti:, njuː-] *n* : neutralidad *f*

neutralization [͵nuːtrələ'zeɪʃən, ͵njuː-] *n* : neutralización *f*

neutralize ['nuːtrə͵laɪz, 'njuː-] *vt* **-ized; -izing** : neutralizar

neutron ['nuː͵trɑn, 'njuː-] *n* : neutrón *m*

never ['nɛvər] *adv* **1** : nunca, jamás ⟨he never studies : nunca estudia⟩ **2 never again** : nunca más, nunca jamás **3 never mind** : no importa

nevermore [͵nɛvər'mor] *adv* : nunca más

nevertheless [͵nɛvərðə'lɛs] *adv* : sin embargo, no obstante

new ['nuː, 'njuː] *adj* **1** : nuevo ⟨a new dress : un vestido nuevo⟩ **2** RECENT : nuevo, reciente ⟨what's new? : ¿qué hay de nuevo?⟩ ⟨a new arrival : un recién llegado⟩ **3** DIFFERENT : nuevo, distinto ⟨this problem is new : este problema es distinto⟩ ⟨new ideas : ideas nuevas⟩ **4 like new** : como nuevo

newborn ['nuː͵bɔrn, 'njuː-] *adj* : recién nacido

newcomer ['nuː͵kʌmər, 'njuː-] *n* : recién llegado *m*, recién llegada *f*

newfangled ['nuː'fæŋɡəld, 'njuː-] *adj* : novedoso

newfound ['nuː'faʊnd, 'njuː-] *adj* : recién descubierto

newly ['nuːli, 'njuː-] *adv* : recién, recientemente

newlywed ['nuːli͵wɛd, 'njuː-] *n* : recién casado *m*, -da *f*

new moon *n* : luna *f* nueva

newness ['nuːnəs, 'njuː-] *n* : novedad *f*

news ['nuːz, 'njuːz] *n* : noticias *fpl*

newscast ['nuːz͵kæst, 'njuːz-] *n* : noticiero *m*, informativo *m*

newscaster ['nuːz͵kæstər, 'njuːz-] *n* : presentador *m*, -dora *f*; locutor *m*, -tora *f*

newsletter ['nuːz͵lɛtər, 'njuːz-] *n* : boletín *m* informativo

newsman ['nuːzmən, 'njuːz-, -͵mæn] *n, pl* **-men** [-mən, -͵mɛn] : periodista *m*, reportero *m*

newspaper ['nuːz͵peɪpər, 'njuːz-] *n* : periódico *m*, diario *m*

newspaperman ['nuːz͵peɪpər͵mæn, 'njuːz-] *n, pl* **-men** [-mən, -͵mɛn] **1** REPORTER : periodista *m*, reportero *m* **2** : dueño *m* de un periódico

newsprint ['nuːz͵prɪnt, 'njuːz-] *n* : papel *m* de prensa

newsstand ['nuːz͵stænd, 'njuːz-] *n* : quiosco *m*, puesto *m* de periódicos

newswoman ['nuːz͵wʊmən, 'njuːz-] *n, pl* **-women** [-͵wɪmən] : periodista *f*, reportera *f*

newsworthy ['nuːz͵wərði, 'njuːz-] *adj* : de interés periodístico

newsy ['nuːzi:, 'njuː-] *adj* **newsier; -est** : lleno de noticias

newt ['nuːt, 'njuːt] *n* : tritón *m*

New Testament *n* : Nuevo Testamento *m*

New Year *n* : Año *m* Nuevo

New Year's Day *n* : día *m* del Año Nuevo

New Yorker [nuː'jɔrkər, njuː-] *n* : neoyorquino *m*, -na *f*

New Zealander [nuː'ziːləndər, njuː-] *n* : neozelandés *m*, -desa *f*

next¹ ['nɛkst] *adv* **1** AFTERWARD : después, luego ⟨what will you do next? : ¿qué harás después?⟩ **2** NOW : después, ahora, entonces ⟨next I will sing a song : ahora voy a cantar una canción⟩ **3** : la próxima vez ⟨when next we meet : la próxima vez que nos encontremos⟩

next² *adj* **1** ADJACENT : contiguo, de al lado **2** COMING : que viene, próximo ⟨next Friday : el viernes que viene⟩ **3** FOLLOWING : siguiente ⟨the next year : el año siguiente⟩

next–door ['nɛkst'dor] *adj* : de al lado

next to¹ *adv* ALMOST : casi, prácticamente ⟨next to impossible : casi imposible⟩

next to[2] *prep* : junto a, al lado de
nexus ['nɛksəs] *n* : nexo *m*
nib ['nɪb] *n* : plumilla *f*
nibble[1] ['nɪbəl] *v* **-bled; -bling** *vt* : pellizcar, mordisquear, picar — *vi* : picar
nibble[2] *n* : mordisco *m*
Nicaraguan [ˌnɪkəˈrɑgwən] *n* : nicaragüense *mf* — **Nicaraguan** *adj*
nice ['naɪs] *adj* **nicer; nicest 1** REFINED : pulido, refinado **2** SUBTLE : fino, sutil **3** PLEASING : agradable, bueno, lindo ⟨nice weather : buen tiempo⟩ **4** RESPECTABLE : bueno, decente **5 nice and** : bien, muy ⟨nice and hot : bien caliente⟩ ⟨nice and slow : despacito⟩
nicely ['naɪsli] *adv* **1** KINDLY : amablemente **2** POLITELY : con buenos modales **3** ATTRACTIVELY : de buen gusto
niceness ['naɪsnəs] *n* : simpatía *f*, amabilidad *f*
nicety ['naɪsəti] *n, pl* **-ties 1** DETAIL, SUBTLETY : sutileza *f*, detalle *m* **2 niceties** *npl* : lujos *mpl*, detalles *mpl*
niche ['nɪtʃ] *n* **1** RECESS : nicho *m*, hornacina *f* **2** : nicho *m*, hueco *m* ⟨to make a niche for oneself : hacerse un hueco, encontrarse una buena posición⟩
nick[1] ['nɪk] *vt* : cortar, hacer una muesca en
nick[2] *n* **1** CUT : corte *m*, muesca *f* **2 in the nick of time** : en el momento crítico, justo a tiempo
nickel ['nɪkəl] *n* **1** : níquel *m* **2** : moneda *f* de cinco centavos
nickname[1] ['nɪkˌneɪm] *vt* **-named; -naming** : apodar
nickname[2] *n* : apodo *m*, mote *m*, sobrenombre *m*
nicotine ['nɪkəˌtiːn] *n* : nicotina *f*
niece ['niːs] *n* : sobrina *f*
Nigerian [naɪˈdʒɪriən] *n* : nigeriano *m*, -na *f* — **Nigerian** *adj*
niggardly ['nɪgərdli] *adj* : mezquino, tacaño
niggling ['nɪgəlɪŋ] *adj* **1** PETTY : insignificante **2** PERSISTENT : constante, persistente ⟨a niggling doubt : una duda constante⟩
nigh[1] ['naɪ] *adv* **1** NEARLY : casi **2 to draw nigh** : acercarse, avecinarse
nigh[2] *adj* : cercano, próximo
night[1] ['naɪt] *adj* : nocturno, de la noche ⟨the night sky : el cielo nocturno⟩ ⟨night shift : turno de la noche⟩
night[2] *n* **1** EVENING : noche *f* ⟨at night : de noche⟩ ⟨last night : anoche⟩ ⟨tomorrow night : mañana por la noche⟩ **2** DARKNESS : noche *f*, oscuridad *f* ⟨night fell : cayó la noche⟩
nightclothes ['naɪtˌkloːðz, -ˌkloːz] *npl* : ropa *f* de dormir
nightclub ['naɪtˌklʌb] *n* : cabaret *m*, club *m* nocturno
night crawler ['naɪtˌkrɔlər] *n* EARTHWORM : lombriz *f* (de tierra)
nightfall ['naɪtˌfɔl] *n* : anochecer *m*
nightgown ['naɪtˌgaʊn] *n* : camisón *m* (de noche)

nightingale ['naɪtənˌgeɪl, 'naɪtɪŋ-] *n* : ruiseñor *m*
nightly[1] ['naɪtli] *adv* : cada noche, todas las noches
nightly[2] *adj* : de todas las noches
nightmare ['naɪtˌmær] *n* : pesadilla *f*
nightmarish ['naɪtˌmærɪʃ] *adj* : de pesadilla
night owl *n* : noctámbulo *m*, -la *f*
nightshade ['naɪtˌʃeɪd] *n* : hierba *f* mora
nightshirt ['naɪtˌʃərt] *n* : camisa *f* de dormir
nightstick ['naɪtˌstɪk] *n* : porra *f*
nighttime ['naɪtˌtaɪm] *n* : noche *f*
nihilism ['naɪəˌlɪzəm] *n* : nihilismo *m*
nil ['nɪl] *n* : nada *f*, cero *m*
nimble ['nɪmbəl] *adj* **-bler; -blest 1** AGILE : ágil **2** CLEVER : hábil, ingenioso
nimbleness ['nɪmbəlnəs] *n* : agilidad *f*
nimbly ['nɪmbli] *adv* : con agilidad, ágilmente
nincompoop ['nɪnkəmˌpuːp, 'nɪŋ-] *n* FOOL : tonto *m*, -ta *f*; bobo *m*, -ba *f*
nine[1] ['naɪn] *adj* **1** : nueve **2 nine times out of ten** : casi siempre
nine[2] *n* : nueve *m*
nine hundred[1] *adj* : novecientos
nine hundred[2] *n* : novecientos *m*
ninepins ['naɪnˌpɪnz] *n* : bolos *mpl*
nineteen[1] [naɪnˈtiːn] *adj* : diecinueve
nineteen[2] *n* : diecinueve *m*
nineteenth[1] [naɪnˈtiːnθ] *adj* : decimonoveno, decimonono ⟨the nineteenth century : el siglo diecinueve⟩
nineteenth[2] *n* **1** : decimonoveno *m*, -na *f*; decimonono *m*, -na *f* (en una serie) **2** : diecinueveavo *m*, diecinueveava parte *f*
ninetieth[1] ['naɪntiəθ] *adj* : nonagésimo
ninetieth[2] *n* **1** : nonagésimo *m*, -ma *f* (en una serie) **2** : noventavo *m*, noventava parte *f*
ninety[1] ['naɪnti] *adj* : noventa
ninety[2] *n, pl* **-ties** : noventa *m*
ninth[1] ['naɪnθ] *adj* : noveno
ninth[2] *n* **1** : noveno *m*, -na *f* (en una serie) **2** : noveno *m*, novena parte *f*
ninny ['nɪni] *n, pl* **ninnies** FOOL : tonto *m*, -ta *f*; bobo *m*, -ba *f*
nip[1] ['nɪp] *vt* **nipped; nipping 1** PINCH : pellizcar **2** BITE : morder, mordisquear **3 to nip in the bud** : cortar de raíz
nip[2] *n* **1** TANG : sabor *m* fuerte **2** PINCH : pellizco *m* **3** NIBBLE : mordisco *m* **4** SWALLOW : trago *m*, traguito *m* **5 there's a nip in the air** : hace fresco
nipple ['nɪpəl] *n* : pezón *m* (de una mujer), tetilla *f* (de un hombre)
nippy ['nɪpi] *adj* **-pier; -est 1** SHARP : fuerte, picante **2** CHILLY : frío ⟨it's nippy today : hoy hace frío⟩
nit ['nɪt] *n* : liendre *f*
nitrate ['naɪˌtreɪt] *n* : nitrato *m*
nitric acid ['naɪtrɪk] *n* : ácido *m* nítrico
nitrite ['naɪˌtraɪt] *n* : nitrito *m*
nitrogen ['naɪtrədʒən] *n* : nitrógeno *m*
nitroglycerin *or* **nitroglycerine** [ˌnaɪtro-ˈglɪsərən] *n* : nitroglicerina *f*

nitwit ['nɪt,wɪt] *n* : zonzo *m*, -za *f*; bobo *m*, -ba *f*
no¹ ['no:] *adv* : no ⟨are you leaving?—no : ¿te vas?⟩—no⟩ ⟨no less than : no menos de⟩ ⟨to say no : decir que no⟩ ⟨like it or no : quieras o no quieras⟩
no² *adj* **1** : ninguno ⟨it's no trouble : no es ningún problema⟩ ⟨she has no money : no tiene dinero⟩ **2** (*indicating a small amount*) ⟨we'll be there in no time : llegamos dentro de poco, no tardamos nada⟩ **3** (*expressing a negation*) ⟨he's no liar : no es mentiroso⟩
no³ *n, pl* **noes** *or* **nos** ['no:z] **1** DENIAL : no *m* ⟨I won't take no for an answer : no aceptaré un no por respuesta⟩ **2** : vota *f* en contra ⟨the noes have it : se ha rechazado la moción⟩
nobility [no'bɪləti] *n* : nobleza *f*
noble¹ ['no:bəl] *adj* **-bler; -blest 1** ILLUSTRIOUS : noble, glorioso **2** ARISTOCRATIC : noble **3** STATELY : majestuoso, magnífico **4** LOFTY : noble, elevado ⟨noble sentiments : sentimientos elevados⟩
noble² *n* : noble *mf*, aristócrata *mf*
nobleman ['no:bəlmən] *n, pl* **-men** [-mən, -,mɛn] : noble *m*, aristócrata *m*
nobleness ['no:bəlnəs] *n* : nobleza *f*
noblewoman ['no:bəl,wumən] *n, pl* **-women** [-,wimən] : noble *f*, aristócrata *f*
nobly ['no:bli] *adv* : noblemente
nobody¹ ['no:bədi, -,badi] *n, pl* **-bodies** : don nadie *m* ⟨he's a mere nobody : es un don nadie⟩
nobody² *pron* : nadie
nocturnal [nak'tərnəl] *adj* : nocturno
nocturne ['nak,tərn] *n* : nocturno *m*
nod¹ ['nad] *v* **nodded; nodding** *vi* **1** : saludar con la cabeza, asentir con la cabeza **2 to nod off** : dormirse, quedarse dormido — *vt* : inclinar (la cabeza) ⟨to nod one's head in agreement : asentir con la cabeza⟩
nod² *n* : saludo *m* con la cabeza, señal *m* con la cabeza, señal *m* de asentimiento
node ['no:d] *n* : nudo *m* (de una planta)
nodule ['na,dʒu:l] *n* : nódulo *m*
noel [no'ɛl] *n* **1** CAROL : villancico *m* de Navidad **2 Noel** CHRISTMAS : Navidad *f*
noes → **no³**
noise¹ ['nɔɪz] *vt* **noised; noising** : rumorear, publicar
noise² *n* : ruido *m*
noiseless ['nɔɪzləs] *adj* : silencioso, sin ruido
noiselessly ['nɔɪzləsli] *adv* : silenciosamente
noisemaker ['nɔɪz,meɪkər] *n* : matraca *f*
noisiness ['nɔɪzinəs] *n* : ruido *m*
noisome ['nɔɪsəm] *adj* : maloliente, fétido
noisy ['nɔɪzi] *adj* **noisier; -est** : ruidoso — **noisily** ['nɔɪzəli] *adv*
nomad¹ ['no:,mæd] → **nomadic**

nomad² *n* : nómada *mf*
nomadic [no'mædɪk] *adj* : nómada
nomenclature ['no:mən,kleɪtʃər] *n* : nomenclatura *f*
nominal ['namənəl] *adj* **1** : nominal ⟨the nominal head of his party : el jefe nominal de su partido⟩ **2** TRIFLING : insignificante
nominally ['namənəli] *adv* : sólo de nombre, nominalmente
nominate ['namə,neɪt] *vt* **-nated; -nating 1** PROPOSE : proponer (como candidato), nominar **2** APPOINT : nombrar
nomination [,namə'neɪʃən] *n* **1** PROPOSAL : propuesta *f*, postulación *f* **2** APPOINTMENT : nombramiento *m*
nominative¹ ['namənətɪv] *adj* : nominativo
nominative² *n or* **nominative case** : nominativo *m*
nominee [,namə'ni:] *n* : candidato *m*, -ta *f*
nonaddictive [,nanə'dɪktɪv] *adj* : que no crea dependencia
nonalcoholic [,nan,ælkə'hɔlɪk] *adj* : sin alcohol, no alcohólico
nonaligned [,nanə'laɪnd] *adj* : no alineado
nonbeliever [,nanbə'li:vər] *n* : no creyente *mf*
nonbreakable [,nan'breɪkəbəl] *adj* : irrompible
nonce ['nants] *n* **for the nonce** : por el momento
nonchalance [,nanʃə'lants] *n* : indiferencia *f*, despreocupación *f*
nonchalant [,nanʃə'lant] *adj* : indiferente, despreocupado, impasible
nonchalantly [,nanʃə'lantli] *adv* : con aire despreocupado, con indiferencia
noncombatant [,nankəm'bætənt, -'kambə-] *n* : no combatiente *mf*
noncommissioned officer [,nankə'mɪʃənd] *n* : suboficial *mf*
noncommittal [,nankə'mɪtəl] *adj* : evasivo, que no se compromete
nonconductor [,nankən'dʌktər] *n* : aislante *m*
nonconformist [,nankən'fɔrmɪst] *n* : inconformista *mf*, inconforme *mf*
nonconformity [,nankən'fɔrməti] *n* : inconformidad *f*, no conformidad *f*
noncontagious [,nankən'teɪdʒəs] *adj* : no contagioso
nondenominational [,nandɪ,namə'neɪʃənəl] *adj* : no sectario
nondescript [,nandɪ'skrɪpt] *adj* : anodino, soso
nondiscriminatory [,nandɪ'skrɪmənə,tori] *adj* : no discriminatorio
nondrinker [,nan'drɪŋkər] *n* : abstemio *m*, -mia *f*
none¹ ['nʌn] *adv* : de ninguna manera, de ningún modo, nada ⟨he was none too happy : no se sintió nada contento⟩ ⟨I'm none the worse for it : no estoy peor por ello⟩ ⟨none too soon : a buena hora⟩

none[2] *pron* : ninguno, ninguna
nonentity [ˌnɑn'ɛntəti] *n, pl* **-ties** : persona *f* insignificante, nulidad *f*
nonessential [ˌnɑnɪ'sɛntʃəl] *adj* : secundario, no esencial
nonessentials [ˌnɑnɪ'sɛntʃəlz] *npl* : cosas *fpl* secundarias, cosas *fpl* accesorias
nonetheless [ˌnʌnðə'lɛs] *adv* : sin embargo, no obstante
nonexistence [ˌnɑnɪg'zɪstənts] *n* : inexistencia *f*
nonexistent [ˌnɑnɪg'zɪstənt] *adj* : inexistente
nonfat [ˌnɑn'fæt] *adj* : sin grasa
nonfattening [ˌnɑn'fætənɪŋ] *adj* : que no engorda
nonfiction [ˌnɑn'fɪkʃən] *n* : no ficción *f*
nonflammable [ˌnɑn'flæməbəl] *adj* : no inflamable
nonintervention [ˌnɑnˌɪntər'vɛntʃən] *n* : no intervención *f*
nonmalignant [ˌnɑnmə'lɪgnənt] *adj* : no maligno, benigno
nonnegotiable [ˌnɑnnɪ'goːʃəbəl, -ʃiə-] *adj* : no negociable
nonpareil[1] [ˌnɑnpə'rɛl] *adj* : sin parangón, sin par
nonpareil[2] *n* : persona *f* sin igual, cosa *f* sin par
nonpartisan [ˌnɑn'pɑrtəzən, -sən] *adj* : imparcial
nonpaying [ˌnɑn'peɪɪŋ] *adj* : que no paga
nonpayment [ˌnɑn'peɪmənt] *n* : impago *m*, falta *f* de pago
nonperson [ˌnɑn'pərsən] *n* : persona *f* sin derechos
nonplus [ˌnɑn'plʌs] *vt* **-plussed; -plussing** : confundir, desconcertar, dejar perplejo
nonprescription [ˌnɑnprɪ'skrɪpʃən] *adj* : disponible sin receta del médico
nonproductive [ˌnɑnprə'dʌktɪv] *adj* : improductivo
nonprofit [ˌnɑn'prɑfət] *adj* : sin fines lucrativos
nonproliferation [ˌnɑnprəˌlɪfə'reɪʃən] *adj* : no proliferación
nonresident [ˌnɑn'rɛzədənt, -ˌdɛnt] *n* : no residente *mf*
nonscheduled [ˌnɑn'skɛˌdʒuːld] *adj* : no programado, no regular
nonsectarian [ˌnɑnˌsɛk'tæriən] *adj* : no sectario
nonsense ['nɑnˌsɛnts, 'nɑntsənts] *n* : tonterías *fpl*, disparates *mpl*
nonsensical [nɑn'sɛntsɪkəl] *adj* ABSURD : absurdo, disparatado — **nonsensically** [-kli] *adv*
nonsmoker [ˌnɑn'smoːkər] *n* : no fumador *m*, -dora *f*; persona *f* que no fuma
nonstandard [ˌnɑn'stændərd] *adj* : no regular, no estándar
nonstick [ˌnɑn'stɪk] *adj* : antiadherente
nonstop[1] [ˌnɑn'stɑp] *adv* : sin parar ⟨he talked nonstop : habló sin parar⟩
nonstop[2] *adj* : directo, sin escalas ⟨nonstop flight : vuelo directo⟩

nonsupport [ˌnɑnsə'pɔrt] *n* : falta *f* de manutención
nontaxable [ˌnɑn'tæksəbəl] *adj* : exento de impuestos
nontoxic [ˌnɑn'tɑksɪk] *adj* : no tóxico
nonviolence [ˌnɑn'vaɪlənts, -'vaɪə-] *n* : no violencia *f*
nonviolent [ˌnɑn'vaɪlənt, -'vaɪə-] *adj* : pacífico, no violento
noodle ['nuːdəl] *n* : fideo *m*, tallarín *m*
nook ['nʊk] *n* : rincón *m*, recoveco *m*, escondrijo *m* ⟨in every nook and cranny : en todos los rincones⟩
noon ['nuːn] *n* : mediodía *m*
noonday ['nuːnˌdeɪ] *n* : mediodía *m* ⟨the noonday sun : el sol de mediodía⟩
no one *pron* NOBODY : nadie
noontime ['nuːnˌtaɪm] *n* : mediodía *m*
noose ['nuːs] *n* **1** LASSO : lazo *m* **2 hangman's noose** : dogal *m*, soga *f*
nor ['nɔr] *conj* : ni ⟨neither good nor bad : ni bueno ni malo⟩ ⟨nor I! : ¡ni yo tampoco!⟩
Nordic ['nɔrdɪk] *adj* : nórdico
norm ['nɔrm] *n* **1** STANDARD : norma *f*, modelo *m* **2** CUSTOM, RULE : regla *f* general, lo normal
normal ['nɔrməl] *adj* : normal — **normally** *adv*
normalcy ['nɔrməlsi] *n* : normalidad *f*
normality [nɔr'mæləti] *n* : normalidad *f*
normalize ['nɔrməˌlaɪz] *vt* : normalizar
Norse ['nɔrs] *adj* : nórdico
north[1] ['nɔrθ] *adv* : al norte
north[2] *adj* : norte, del norte ⟨the north coast : la costa del norte⟩
north[3] *n* **1** : norte *m* **2 the North** : el Norte *m*
North American *n* : norteamericano *m*, -na *f* — **North American** *adj*
northbound ['nɔrθˌbaʊnd] *adv* : con rumbo al norte
northeast[1] [nɔrθ'iːst] *adv* : hacia el nordeste
northeast[2] *adj* : nordeste, del nordeste
northeast[3] *n* : nordeste *m*, noreste *m*
northeasterly[1] [nɔrθ'iːstərli] *adv* : hacia el nordeste
northeasterly[2] *adj* : nordeste, del nordeste
northeastern [nɔrθ'iːstərn] *adj* : nordeste, del nordeste
northerly[1] ['nɔrðərli] *adv* : hacia el norte
northerly[2] *adj* : del norte ⟨a northerly wind : un viento del norte⟩
northern ['nɔrðərn] *adj* : norte, norteño, septentrional
Northerner ['nɔrðərnər] *n* : norteño *m*, -ña *f*
northern lights → aurora borealis
North Pole : Polo *m* Norte
North Star *n* : estrella *f* polar
northward ['nɔrθwərd] *adv & adj* : hacia el norte
northwest[1] [nɔrθ'wɛst] *adv* : hacia el noroeste
northwest[2] *adj* : del noroeste
northwest[3] *n* : noroeste *m*

northwesterly[1] [nɔrθ'wɛstərli] *adv* : hacia el noroeste

northwesterly[2] *adj* : del noroeste

northwestern [nɔrθ'wɛstərn] *adj* : noroeste, del noroeste

Norwegian [nɔr'wiːʤən] *n* **1** : noruego *m*, -ga *f* **2** : noruego *m* (idioma) — **Norwegian** *adj*

nose[1] ['noːz] *v* **nosed; nosing** *vt* **1** SMELL : olfatear **2** : empujar con el hocico ⟨the dog nosed open the bag : el perro abrió el saco con el hocico⟩ **3** EDGE, MOVE : mover poco a poco — *vi* **1** PRY : entrometerse, meter las narices **2** EDGE : avanzar poco a poco

nose[2] *n* **1** : nariz *f* (de una persona), hocico *m* (de un animal) ⟨to blow one's nose : sonarse las narices⟩ **2** SMELL : olfato *m*, sentido *m* del olfato **3** FRONT : parte *f* delantera, nariz *f* (de un avión), proa *f* (de un barco) **4** **to follow one's nose** : dejarse guiar por el instinto

nosebleed ['noːzˌbliːd] *n* : hemorragia *f* nasal

nosedive ['noːzˌdaɪv] *n* **1** : descenso *m* en picada (de un avión) **2** : caída *f* súbita (de precios, etc.)

nose–dive ['noːzˌdaɪv] *vi* : descender en picada, caer en picada

nostalgia [nɑ'stælʤə, nə-] *n* : nostalgia *f*

nostalgic [nɑ'stælʤɪk, nə-] *adj* : nostálgico

nostril ['nɑstrəl] *n* : ventana *f* de la nariz

nostrum ['nɑstrəm] *n* : panacea *f*

nosy *or* **nosey** ['noːzi] *adj* **nosier; -est** : entrometido

not ['nɑt] *adv* **1** (*used to form a negative*) : no ⟨she is not tired : no está cansada⟩ ⟨not to say something would be wrong : no decir nada sería injusto⟩ **2** (*used to replace a negative clause*) : no ⟨are we going or not? : ¿vamos a ir o no?⟩ ⟨of course not! : ¡claro que no!⟩

notable[1] ['noːtəbəl] *adj* **1** NOTEWORTHY : notable, de notar **2** DISTINGUISHED, PROMINENT : distinguido, destacado

notable[2] *n* : persona *f* importante, personaje *m*

notably ['noːtəbli] *adv* : notablemente, particularmente

notarize ['noːtəˌraɪz] *vt* **-rized; -rizing** : autenticar, autorizar

notary public ['noːtəri] *n, pl* **-ries public** *or* **-ry publics** : notario *m*, -ria *f*; escribano *m*, -na *f*

notation [noʊ'teɪʃən] *n* **1** NOTE : anotación *f*, nota *f* **2** : notación *f* ⟨musical notation : notación musical⟩

notch[1] ['nɑtʃ] *vt* : hacer una muesca en, cortar

notch[2] *n* : muesca *f*, corte *m*

note[1] ['noːt] *vt* **noted; noting** **1** NOTICE : notar, observar, tomar nota de **2** RECORD : anotar, apuntar

note[2] *n* **1** : nota *f* (musical) **2** COMMENT : nota *f*, comentario *m* **3** LETTER : nota *f*, cartita *f* **4** PROMINENCE : prestigio *m* ⟨a musician of note : un músico destacado⟩ **5** ATTENTION : atención *f* ⟨to take note of : prestar atención a⟩

notebook ['noːtˌbʊk] *n* **1** : libreta *f*, cuaderno *m* **2** : notebook *m* (computadora)

noted ['noːtəd] *adj* EMINENT : renombrado, eminente, celebrado

noteworthy ['noːtˌwərði] *adj* : notable, de notar, de interés

nothing[1] ['nʌθɪŋ] *adv* **1** : de ninguna manera ⟨nothing daunted, we carried on : sin amilanarnos, seguimos adelante⟩ **2** **nothing like** : no . . . en nada ⟨he's nothing like his brother : no se parece en nada a su hermano⟩

nothing[2] *n* **1** NOTHINGNESS : nada *f* **2** ZERO : cero *m* **3** : persona *f* de poca importancia, cero *m* **4** TRIFLE : nimiedad *f*

nothing[3] *pron* : nada ⟨there's nothing better : no hay nada mejor⟩ ⟨nothing else : nada más⟩ ⟨nothing but : solamente⟩ ⟨they mean nothing to me : ellos me son indiferentes⟩

nothingness ['nʌθɪŋnəs] *n* **1** VOID : vacío *m*, nada *f* **2** NONEXISTENCE : inexistencia *f* **3** TRIFLE : nimiedad *f*

notice[1] ['noːtɪs] *vt* **-ticed; -ticing** : notar, observar, advertir, darse cuenta de

notice[2] *n* **1** NOTIFICATION : aviso *m*, notificación *f* **2** ATTENTION : atención *f* ⟨to take notice of : prestar atención a⟩

noticeable ['noːtɪsəbəl] *adj* : evidente, perceptible — **noticeably** [-bli] *adv*

notification [ˌnoːtəfə'keɪʃən] *n* : notificación *f*, aviso *m*

notify ['noːtəˌfaɪ] *vt* **-fied; -fying** : notificar, avisar

notion ['noːʃən] *n* **1** IDEA : idea *f*, noción *f* **2** WHIM : capricho *m*, antojo *m* **3** **notions** *npl* : artículos *mpl* de mercería

notoriety [ˌnoːtə'raɪəti] *n* : mala fama *f*, notoriedad *f*

notorious [noʊ'toːriəs] *adj* : de mala fama, célebre, bien conocido

notwithstanding[1] [ˌnɑtwɪθ'stændɪŋ, -wɪð-] *adv* NEVERTHELESS : no obstante, sin embargo

notwithstanding[2] *conj* : a pesar de que

notwithstanding[3] *prep* : a pesar de, no obstante

nougat ['nuːgət] *n* : turrón *m*

nought ['nɔt, 'nɑt] → **naught**

noun ['naʊn] *n* : nombre *m*, sustantivo *m*

nourish ['nərɪʃ] *vt* **1** FEED : alimentar, nutrir, sustentar **2** FOSTER : fomentar, alentar

nourishing ['nərɪʃɪŋ] *adj* : alimenticio, nutritivo

nourishment ['nərɪʃmənt] *n* : nutrición *f*, alimento *m*, sustento *m*

novel[1] ['nɑvəl] *adj* : original, novedoso

novel² *n* : novela *f*
novelist ['nɑvəlɪst] *n* : novelista *mf*
novelty ['nɑvəlti] *n, pl* **-ties** **1** : novedad *f* **2 novelties** *npl* TRINKETS : baratijas *fpl*, chucherías *fpl*
November [noˈvɛmbər] *n* : noviembre *m*
novice ['nɑvɪs] *n* : novato *m*, -ta *f*; principiante *mf*; novicio *m*, -cia *f*
now¹ ['naʊ] *adv* **1** PRESENTLY : ahora, ya, actualmente ⟨from now on : de ahora en adelante⟩ ⟨long before now : ya hace tiempo⟩ ⟨now and then : de vez en cuando⟩ **2** IMMEDIATELY : ahora (mismo), inmediatamente ⟨do it right now! : ¡hazlo ahora mismo!⟩ **3** THEN : ya, entonces ⟨now they were ready : ya estaban listos⟩ **4** (*used to introduce a statement, a question, a command, or a transition*) ⟨now hear this! : ¡presten atención!⟩ ⟨now what do you think of that? : ¿qué piensas de eso?⟩
now² *n* (*indicating the present time*) ⟨until now : hasta ahora⟩ ⟨by now : ya⟩ ⟨ten years from now : dentro de 10 años⟩
now³ *conj* **now that** : ahora que, ya que
nowadays ['naʊəˌdeɪz] *adv* : hoy en día, actualmente, en la actualidad
nowhere¹ ['noːˌʍɛr] *adv* **1** : en ninguna parte, a ningún lado ⟨nowhere to be found : en ninguna parte, por ningún lado⟩ ⟨you're going nowhere : no estás yendo a ningún lado, no estás yendo a ninguna parte⟩ **2 nowhere near** : ni con mucho, nada cerca ⟨it's nowhere near here : no está nada cerca de aquí⟩
nowhere² *n* **1** : ninguna parte *f* **2 out of nowhere** : de la nada
noxious ['nɑkʃəs] *adj* : nocivo, dañino, tóxico
nozzle ['nɑzəl] *n* : boca *f*
nuance ['nuːˌɑnts, 'njuː-] *n* : matiz *m*
nub ['nʌb] *n* **1** KNOB, LUMP : protuberancia *f*, nudo *m* **2** GIST : quid *m*, meollo *m*
nuclear ['nuːkliər, 'njuː-] *adj* : nuclear
nucleus ['nuːkliəs, 'njuː-] *n, pl* **-clei** [-kliˌaɪ] : núcleo *m*
nude¹ ['nuːd, 'njuːd] *adj* **nuder; nudest** : desnudo
nude² *n* : desnudo *m*
nudge¹ ['nʌʤ] *vt* **nudged; nudging** : darle con el codo (a alguien)
nudge² *n* : toque *m* que se da con el codo
nudism ['nuːˌdɪzəm, 'njuː-] *n* : nudismo *m*
nudist ['nuːdɪst, 'njuː-] *n* : nudista *mf*
nudity ['nuːdəti, 'njuː-] *n* : desnudez *f*
nugget ['nʌgət] *n* : pepita *f*
nuisance ['nuːsənts, 'njuː-] *n* **1** BOTHER : fastidio *m*, molestia *f*, lata *f* **2** PEST : pesado *m*, -da *f fam*
null ['nʌl] *adj* : nulo ⟨null and void : nulo y sin efecto⟩
nullify ['nʌləˌfaɪ] *vt* **-fied; -fying** : invalidar, anular
nullity ['nələti] *n, pl* **-ties** : nulidad *f*
numb¹ ['nʌm] *vt* : entumecer, adormecer

numb² *adj* : entumecido, dormido ⟨numb with fear : paralizado de miedo⟩
number¹ ['nʌmbər] *vt* **1** COUNT, INCLUDE : contar, incluir **2** : numerar ⟨number the pages : numera las páginas⟩ **3** TOTAL : ascender a, sumar
number² *n* **1** : número *m* ⟨in round numbers : en números redondos⟩ ⟨telephone number : número de teléfono⟩ **2 a number of** : varios, unos pocos, unos cuantos
numberless ['nʌmbərləs] *adj* : innumerable, sin número
numbness ['nʌmnəs] *n* : entumecimiento *m*
numeral ['nuːmərəl, 'njuː-] *n* : número *m* ⟨Roman numeral : número romano⟩
numerator ['nuːməˌreɪtər, 'njuː-] *n* : numerador *m*
numeric [nʊˈmɛrɪk, njʊ-] *adj* : numérico
numerical [nʊˈmɛrɪkəl, njʊ-] *adj* : numérico — **numerically** [-kli] *adv*
numerous ['nuːmərəs, 'njuː-] *adj* : numeroso
numismatics [ˌnuːməzˈmætɪks, ˌnjuː-] *n* : numismática *f*
numskull ['nʌmˌskʌl] *n* : tonto *m*, -ta *f*; mentecato *m*, -ta *f*; zoquete *m fam*
nun ['nʌn] *n* : monja *f*
nuptial ['nʌpʃəl] *adj* : nupcial
nuptials ['nʌpʃəlz] *npl* WEDDING : nupcias *fpl*, boda *f*
nurse¹ ['nərs] *vt* **nursed; nursing** **1** SUCKLE : amamantar **2** : cuidar (de), atender ⟨to nurse the sick : cuidar a los enfermos⟩ ⟨to nurse a cold : curarse de un resfriado⟩
nurse² *n* **1** : enfermero *m*, -ra *f* **2** → **nursemaid**
nursemaid ['nərsˌmeɪd] *n* : niñera *f*
nursery ['nərsəri] *n, pl* **-eries** **1** *or* **day nursery** : guardería *f* **2** : vivero *m* (de plantas)
nursing home *n* : hogar *m* de ancianos, clínica *f* de reposo
nurture¹ ['nərtʃər] *vt* **-tured; -turing** **1** FEED, NOURISH : nutrir, alimentar **2** EDUCATE : criar, educar **3** FOSTER : alimentar, fomentar
nurture² *n* **1** UPBRINGING : crianza *f*, educación *f* **2** FOOD : alimento *m*
nut ['nʌt] *n* **1** : nuez *f* **2** : tuerca *f* ⟨nuts and bolts : tuercas y tornillos⟩ **3** LUNATIC : loco *m*, -ca *f*; chiflado *m*, -da *f fam* **4** ENTHUSIAST : fanático *m*, -ca *f*; entusiasta *mf*
nutcracker ['nʌtˌkrækər] *n* : cascanueces *m*
nuthatch ['nʌtˌhætʃ] *n* : trepador *m*
nutmeg ['nʌtˌmɛg] *n* : nuez *f* moscada
nutrient ['nuːtriənt, 'njuː-] *n* : nutriente *m*, alimento *m* nutritivo
nutriment ['nuːtrəmənt, 'njuː-] *n* : nutrimento *m*
nutrition [nʊˈtrɪʃən, njʊ-] *n* : nutrición *f*
nutritional [nʊˈtrɪʃənəl, njʊ-] *adj* : alimenticio
nutritious [nʊˈtrɪʃəs, njʊ-] *adj* : nutritivo, alimenticio

nuts ['nʌts] *adj* **1** FANATICAL : fanático
2 CRAZY : loco, chiflado *fam*
nutshell ['nʌt̩ʃɛl] *n* **1** : cáscara *f* de nuez
2 in a nutshell : en pocas palabras
nutty ['nʌt̬i] *adj* **-tier; -tiest** : loco, chiflado *fam*

nuzzle ['nʌzəl] *v* **-zled; -zling** *vi* NESTLE
: acurrucarse, arrimarse — *vt* : acariciar con el hocico
nylon ['naɪˌlɑn] *n* **1** : nilón *m* **2 nylons**
npl : medias *fpl* de nilón
nymph ['nɪmpf] *n* : ninfa *f*

O

o ['oː] *n, pl* **o's** *or* **os** ['oːz] **1** : decimo-
quinta letra del alfabeto inglés **2** ZERO
: cero *m*
O ['oː] → **oh**
oaf ['oːf] *n* : zoquete *m*; bruto *m*, -ta *f*
oafish ['oːfɪʃ] *adj* : torpe, lerdo
oak ['oːk] *n, pl* **oaks** *or* **oak** : roble *m*
oaken ['oːkən] *adj* : de roble
oar ['oːr] *n* : remo *m*
oarlock ['oːrˌlɑk] *n* : tolete *m*, escálamo
m
oasis [oʊˈeɪsɪs] *n, pl* **oases** [-ˌsiːz] : oasis
m
oat ['oːt] *n* : avena *f*
oath ['oːθ] *n, pl* **oaths** ['oːðz, 'oːθs] **1** : juramento *m* ⟨to take an oath : prestar
juramento⟩ **2** SWEARWORD : mala palabra *f*, palabrota *f*
oatmeal ['oːtˌmiːl] *n* : avena *f* ⟨instant
oatmeal : avena instantánea⟩
obdurate ['ɑbdʊrət, -djʊ-] *adj* : inflexible, firme, obstinado
obedience [oʊˈbiːdiənts] *n* : obediencia *f*
obedient [oʊˈbiːdiənt] *adj* : obediente —
obediently *adv*
obelisk ['ɑbəˌlɪsk] *n* : obelisco *m*
obese [oʊˈbiːs] *adj* : obeso
obesity [oʊˈbiːsət̬i] *n* : obesidad *f*
obey [oʊˈbeɪ] *v* **obeyed; obeying** : obedecer ⟨to obey the law : cumplir la ley⟩
obfuscate ['ɑbfəˌskeɪt] *vt* **-cated; -cat-
ing** : ofuscar, confundir
obituary [əˈbɪtʃuˌɛri] *n, pl* **-aries** : obituario *m*, necrología *f*
object[1] [əbˈdʒɛkt] *vt* : objetar — *vi*
: oponerse, poner reparos, hacer objeciones
object[2] ['ɑbdʒɪkt] *n* **1** : objeto *m* **2** OB-
JECTIVE, PURPOSE : objetivo *m*,
propósito *m* **3** : complemento *m* (en
gramática)
objection [əbˈdʒɛkʃən] *n* : objeción *f*
objectionable [əbˈdʒɛkʃənəbəl] *adj*
: ofensivo, indeseable — **objectionably**
[-bli] *adv*
objective[1] [əbˈdʒɛktɪv] *adj* **1** IMPARTIAL
: objetivo, imparcial **2** : de complemento, directo (en gramática)
objective[2] *n* **1** : objetivo *m* **2** *or* **objective case** : acusativo *m*
objectively [əbˈdʒɛktɪvli] *adv* : objetivamente
objectivity [ˌɑbˌdʒɛkˈtɪvət̬i] *n, pl* **-ties**
: objetividad *f*
obligate ['ɑbləˌgeɪt] *vt* **-gated; -gating**
: obligar
obligation [ˌɑbləˈgeɪʃən] *n* : obligación *f*

obligatory [əˈblɪgəˌtori] *adj* : obligatorio
oblige [əˈblaɪdʒ] *vt* **obliged; obliging 1**
COMPEL : obligar **2** : hacerle un favor
(a alguien), complacer ⟨to oblige a
friend : hacerle un favor a un amigo⟩
3 to be much obliged : estar muy
agradecido
obliging [əˈblaɪdʒɪŋ] *adj* : servicial, complaciente — **obligingly** *adv*
oblique [oʊˈbliːk] *adj* **1** SLANTING : oblicuo **2** INDIRECT : indirecto — **obliquely** *adv*
obliterate [əˈblɪt̬əˌreɪt] *vt* **-ated; -ating 1**
ERASE : obliterar, borrar **2** DESTROY
: destruir, eliminar
obliteration [əˌblɪt̬əˈreɪʃən] *n* : obliteración *f*
oblivion [əˈblɪviən] *n* : olvido *m*
oblivious [əˈblɪviəs] *adj* : inconsciente
— **obliviously** *adv*
oblong[1] ['ɑˌblɔŋ] *adj* : oblongo
oblong[2] *n* : figura *f* oblonga, rectángulo *m*
obnoxious [ɑbˈnɑkʃəs, əb-] *adj* : repugnante, odioso — **obnoxiously** *adv*
oboe ['oːˌboː] *n* : oboe *m*
oboist ['oːˌboɪst] *n* : oboe *mf*
obscene [ɑbˈsiːn, əb-] *adj* : obsceno, indecente — **obscenely** *adv*
obscenity [ɑbˈsɛnət̬i, əb-] *n, pl* **-ties** : obscenidad *f*
obscure[1] [ɑbˈskjʊr, əb-] *vt* **-scured;
-scuring 1** CLOUD, DIM : oscurecer,
nublar **2** HIDE : ocultar
obscure[2] *adj* **1** DIM : oscuro **2** REMOTE,
SECLUDED : recóndito **3** VAGUE : os-
curo, confuso, vago **4** UNKNOWN : desconocido ⟨an obscure poet : un poeta
desconocido⟩ — **obscurely** *adv*
obscurity [ɑbˈskjʊrət̬i, əb-] *n, pl* **-ties**
: oscuridad *f*
obsequious [ɑbˈsiːkwiəs] *adj* : servil, excesivamente atento
observable [əbˈzɑrvəbəl] *adj* : observable, perceptible
observance [əbˈzɑrvənts] *n* **1** FULFILL-
MENT : observancia *f*, cumplimiento *m*
2 PRACTICE : práctica *f*
observant [əbˈzɑrvənt] *adj* : observador
observation [ˌɑbsərˈveɪʃən, -zər-] *n* : observación *f*
observatory [əbˈzɑrvəˌtori] *n, pl* **-ries**
: observatorio *m*
observe [əbˈzɑrv] *v* **-served; -serving** *vt*
1 OBEY : observar, obedecer **2** CELE-
BRATE : celebrar, guardar (una práctica religiosa) **3** WATCH : observar, mi-

rar **4** REMARK : observar, comentar —
vi LOOK : mirar
observer [ab'zərvər] *n* : observador *m*,
-dora *f*
obsess [əb'sɛs] *vt* : obsesionar
obsession [ab'sɛʃən, əb-] *n* : obsesión *f*
obsessive [ab'sɛsɪv, əb-] *adj* : obsesivo
— **obsessively** *adv*
obsolescence [ˌɑbsə'lɛsənts] *n* : obsolescencia *f*
obsolescent [ˌɑbsə'lɛsənt] *adj* : obsolescente ⟨to become obsolescent : caer
en desuso⟩
obsolete [ˌɑbsə'li:t, 'ɑbsəˌ-] *adj* : obsoleto, anticuado
obstacle ['ɑbstɪkəl] *n* : obstáculo *m*, impedimento *m*
obstetric [əb'stɛtrɪk] *or* **obstetrical**
[-trɪkəl] *adj* : obstétrico
obstetrician [ˌɑbstə'trɪʃən] *n* : obstetra
mf; tocólogo *m*, -ga *f*
obstetrics [əb'stɛtrɪks] *ns & pl* : obstetricia *f*, tocología *f*
obstinacy ['ɑbstənəsi] *n, pl* -**cies** : obstinación *f*, terquedad *f*
obstinate ['ɑbstənət] *adj* : obstinado,
terco — **obstinately** *adv*
obstreperous [əb'strɛpərəs] *adj* **1**
CLAMOROUS : ruidoso, clamoroso **2**
UNRULY : rebelde, indisciplinado
obstruct [əb'strʌkt] *vt* : obstruir, bloquear
obstruction [əb'strʌkʃən] *n* : obstrucción *f*, bloqueo *m*
obstructive [əb'strʌktɪv] *adj* : obstructor
obtain [əb'teɪn] *vt* : obtener, conseguir
— *vi* PREVAIL : imperar, prevalecer
obtainable [əb'teɪnəbəl] *adj* : obtenible,
asequible
obtrude [əb'tru:d] *v* -**truded; -truding** *vt*
1 EXTRUDE : expulsar **2** IMPOSE : imponer — *vi* INTRUDE : inmiscuirse, entrometerse
obtrusive [əb'tru:sɪv] *adj* **1** IMPERTI-
NENT, MEDDLESOME : impertinente,
entrometido **2** PROTRUDING : prominente
obtuse [ɑb'tu:s, əb-, -'tju:s] *adj* : obtuso, torpe
obtuse angle *n* : ángulo obtuso
obviate ['ɑbviˌeɪt] *vt* -**ated; -ating** : obviar, evitar
obvious ['ɑbviəs] *adj* : obvio, evidente,
manifiesto
obviously ['ɑbviəsli] *adv* **1** CLEARLY
: obviamente, evidentemente **2** OF
COURSE : claro, por supuesto
occasion¹ [ə'keɪʒən] *vt* : ocasionar,
causar
occasion² *n* **1** OPPORTUNITY : oportunidad *f*, ocasión *f* **2** CAUSE : motivo *m*,
razón *f* **3** INSTANCE : ocasión *f* **4**
EVENT : ocasión *f*, acontecimiento *m*
5 on ~ : de vez en cuando, ocasionalmente
occasional [ə'keɪʒənəl] *adj* : ocasional
occasionally [ə'keɪʒənəli] *adv* : de vez
en cuando, ocasionalmente

occidental [ˌɑksə'dɛntəl] *adj* : oeste, del
oeste, occidental
occult¹ [ə'kʌlt, 'ɑˌkʌlt] *adj* **1** HIDDEN,
SECRET : oculto, secreto **2** ARCANE
: arcano, esotérico
occult² *n* **the occult** : las ciencias ocul-
tas
occupancy ['ɑkjəpəntsi] *n, pl* -**cies**
: ocupación *f*, habitación *f*
occupant ['ɑkjəpənt] *n* : ocupante *mf*
occupation [ˌɑkjə'peɪʃən] *n* : ocupación
f, profesión *f*, oficio *m*
occupational [ˌɑkjə'peɪʃənəl] *adj* : ocupacional
occupy ['ɑkjəˌpaɪ] *vt* -**pied; -pying** : ocupar
occur [ə'kər] *vi* **occurred; occurring 1**
EXIST : encontrarse, existir **2** HAPPEN
: ocurrir, acontecer, suceder, tener lugar **3** : ocurrirse ⟨it occurred to him
that . . . : se le ocurrió que . . . ⟩
occurrence [ə'kərənts] *n* : acontecimiento *m*, suceso *m*, ocurrencia *f*
ocean ['o:ʃən] *n* : océano *m*
oceanic [ˌo:ʃi'ænɪk] *adj* : oceánico
oceanography [ˌo:ʃə'nɑgrəfi] *n*
: oceanografía *f*
ocelot ['ɑsəˌlɑt, 'o:-] *n* : ocelote *m*
ocher *or* **ochre** ['o:kər] *n* : ocre *m*
o'clock [ə'klɑk] *adv* (*used in telling time*)
⟨it's ten o'clock : son las diez⟩ ⟨at six
o'clock : a las seis⟩
octagon ['ɑktəˌgɑn] *n* : octágono *m*
octagonal [ɑk'tægənəl] *adj* : octagonal
octave ['ɑktɪv] *n* : octava *f*
October [ɑk'to:bər] *n* : octubre *m*
octopus ['ɑktəˌpʊs, -pəs] *n, pl* -**puses** *or*
-**pi** [-ˌpaɪ] : pulpo *m*
ocular ['ɑkjələr] *adj* : ocular
oculist ['ɑkjəlɪst] *n* **1** OPHTHALMOLO-
GIST : oftalmólogo *m*, -ga *f*; oculista *mf*
2 OPTOMETRIST : optometrista *mf*
odd ['ɑd] *adj* **1** : sin pareja, suelto ⟨an
odd sock : un calcetín sin pareja⟩ **2**
UNEVEN : impar ⟨odd numbers
: números impares⟩ **3** : y pico, y tantos ⟨forty odd years ago : hace cuarenta
y pico años⟩ **4** : alguno, uno que otro
⟨odd jobs : algunos trabajos⟩ **5**
STRANGE : extraño, raro
oddball ['ɑdˌbɔl] *n* : excéntrico *m*, -ca *f*;
persona *f* rara
oddity ['ɑdəṭi] *n, pl* -**ties** : rareza *f*, cosa
f rara
oddly ['ɑdli] *adv* : de manera extraña
oddness ['ɑdnəs] *n* : rareza *f*, excentricidad *f*
odds ['ɑdz] *npl* **1** CHANCES : probabili-
dades *fpl* **2** : puntos *mpl* de ventaja (de
una apuesta) **3 to be at odds** : estar en
desacuerdo
odds and ends *npl* : costillas *fpl*, cosas
fpl sueltas, cachivaches *mpl*
ode ['o:d] *n* : oda *f*
odious ['o:diəs] *adj* : odioso — **odious-
ly** *adv*
odor ['o:dər] *n* : olor *m*
odorless ['o:dərləs] *adj* : inodoro, sin
olor

odorous ['o:dərəs] *adj* : oloroso
odyssey ['ɑdəsi] *n, pl* **-seys** : odisea *f*
o'er ['or] → **over**
of ['ʌv, 'əv] *prep* **1** FROM : de ⟨a man of the city : un hombre de la ciudad⟩ **2** (*indicating character or background*) : de ⟨a woman of great ability : una mujer de gran capacidad⟩ **3** (*indicating cause*) : de ⟨he died of the flu : murió de la gripe⟩ **4** BY : de ⟨the works of Shakespeare : las obras de Shakespeare⟩ **5** (*indicating contents, material, or quantity*) : de ⟨a house of wood : una casa de madera⟩ ⟨a glass of water : un vaso de agua⟩ **6** (*indicating belonging or connection*) : de ⟨the front of the house : el frente de la casa⟩ **7** ABOUT : sobre, de ⟨tales of the West : los cuentos del Oeste⟩ **8** (*indicating a particular example*) : de ⟨the city of Caracas : la ciudad de Caracas⟩ **9** FOR : por, a ⟨love of country : amor por la patria⟩ **10** (*indicating time or date*) ⟨five minutes of ten : las diez menos cinco⟩ ⟨the eighth of April : el ocho de abril⟩
off¹ ['ɔf] *adv* **1** (*indicating change of position or state*) ⟨to march off : marcharse⟩ ⟨he dozed off : se puso a dormir⟩ **2** (*indicating distance in space or time*) ⟨some miles off : a varias millas⟩ ⟨the holiday is three weeks off : faltan tres semanas para la fiesta⟩ **3** (*indicating removal*) ⟨the knob came off : se le cayó el pomo⟩ **4** (*indicating termination*) ⟨shut the television off : apaga la televisión⟩ **5** (*indicating suspension of work*) ⟨to take a day off : tomarse un día de descanso⟩ **6 off and on** : de vez en cuando
off² *adj* **1** FARTHER : más remoto, distante ⟨the off side of the building : el lado distante del edificio⟩ **2** STARTED : empezado ⟨to be off on a spree : irse de juerga⟩ **3** OUT : apagado ⟨the light is off : la luz está apagada⟩ **4** CANCELED : cancelado, suspendido **5** INCORRECT : erróneo, incorrecto **6** REMOTE : remoto, lejano ⟨an off chance : una posibilidad remota⟩ **7** FREE : libre ⟨I'm off today : hoy estoy libre⟩ **8 to be well off** : vivir con desahogo, tener bastante dinero
off³ *prep* **1** (*indicating physical separation*) : de ⟨she took it off the table : lo tomó de la mesa⟩ ⟨a shop off the main street : una tienda al lado de la calle principal⟩ **2** : a la costa de, a expensas de ⟨he lives off his sister : vive a expensas de su hermana⟩ **3** (*indicating the suspension of an activity*) ⟨to be off duty : estar libre⟩ ⟨he's off liquor : ha dejado el alcohol⟩ **4** BELOW : por debajo de ⟨he's off his game : está por debajo de su juego normal⟩
offal ['ɔfəl] *n* **1** RUBBISH, WASTE : desechos *mpl*, desperdicios *mpl* **2** VISCERA : vísceras *fpl*, asaduras *fpl*

offend [ə'fɛnd] *vt* **1** VIOLATE : violar, atentar contra **2** HURT : ofender ⟨to be easily offended : ser muy susceptible⟩
offender [ə'fɛndər] *n* : delincuente *mf*; infractor *m*, -tora *f*
offense *or* **offence** [ə'fɛnts, 'ɔ,fɛnts] *n* **1** INSULT : ofensa *f*, injuria *f*, agravio *m* ⟨to take offense : ofenderse⟩ **2** ASSAULT : ataque *m* **3** : ofensiva *f* (en deportes) **4** CRIME, INFRACTION : infracción *f*, delito *m*
offensive¹ [ə'fɛntsɪv, 'ɔ,fɛnt-] *adj* : ofensivo — **offensively** *adv*
offensive² *n* : ofensiva *f*
offer¹ ['ɔfər] *vt* **1** : ofrecer ⟨they offered him the job : le ofrecieron el puesto⟩ **2** PROPOSE : proponer, sugerir **3** SHOW : ofrecer, mostrar ⟨to offer resistance : ofrecer resistencia⟩
offer² *n* : oferta *f*, ofrecimiento *m*, propuesta *f*
offering ['ɔfərɪŋ] *n* : ofrenda *f*
offhand¹ ['ɔf'hænd] *adv* : sin preparación, sin pensarlo
offhand² *adj* **1** IMPROMPTU : improvisado **2** ABRUPT : brusco
office ['ɔfəs] *n* **1** : cargo *m* ⟨to run for office : presentarse como candidato⟩ **2** : oficina *f*, despacho *m*, gabinete *m* (en la casa) ⟨office hours : horas de oficina⟩
officeholder ['ɔfəs,ho:ldər] *n* : titular *mf*
officer ['ɔfəsər] *n* **1** *or* **police officer** : policía *mf*, agente *mf* de policía **2** OFFICIAL : oficial *mf*; funcionario *m*, -ria *f*; director *m*, -tora *f* (en una empresa) **3** COMMISSIONED OFFICER : oficial *mf*
official¹ [ə'fɪʃəl] *adj* : oficial — **officially** *adv*
official² *n* : funcionario *m*, -ria *f*; oficial *mf*
officiate [ə'fɪʃi,eɪt] *v* **-ated; -ating** *vi* **1** : arbitrar (en deportes) **2 to officiate at** : oficiar, celebrar — *vt* : arbitrar
officious [ə'fɪʃəs] *adj* : oficioso
offing ['ɔfɪŋ] *n* **in the offing** : en perspectiva
offset ['ɔf,sɛt] *vt* **-set; -setting** : compensar
offshoot ['ɔf,ʃu:t] *n* **1** OUTGROWTH : producto *m*, resultado *m* **2** BRANCH, SHOOT : retoño *m*, rama *f*, vástago *m* (de una planta)
offshore¹ ['ɔf'ʃor] *adv* : a una distancia de la costa
offshore² *adj* **1** : de (la) tierra ⟨an offshore wind : un viento que sopla de tierra⟩ **2** : (de) costa afuera, cercano a la costa ⟨an offshore island : una isla costera⟩
offspring ['ɔf,sprɪŋ] *ns & pl* **1** YOUNG : crías *fpl* (de los animales) **2** PROGENY : prole *f*, progenie *f*
off–white ['ɔf'hwaɪt] *adj* : blancuzco
often ['ɔfən, 'ɔftən] *adv* : muchas veces, a menudo, seguido

oftentimes ['ɔfən₁taɪmz, 'ɔftən-] *or* **ofttimes** ['ɔft₁taɪms] → **often**

ogle ['o:gəl] *vt* **ogled; ogling** : comerse con los ojos, quedarse mirando a

ogre ['o:gər] *n* : ogro *m*

oh ['o:] *interj* : ¡oh!, ¡ah!, ¡ay! ⟨oh, of course : ah, por supuesto⟩ ⟨oh no! : ¡ay no!⟩ ⟨oh really? : ¿de veras?⟩

ohm ['o:m] *n* : ohm *m*, ohmio *m*

oil¹ ['ɔɪl] *vt* : lubricar, engrasar, aceitar

oil² *n* **1** : aceite *m* **2** PETROLEUM : petróleo *m* **3** *or* **oil painting** : óleo *m*, pintura *f* al óleo **4** *or* **oil paint(s)** : óleo *m*

oilcloth ['ɔɪl₁klɔθ] *n* : hule *m*

oiliness ['ɔɪlinəs] *n* : lo aceitoso

oilskin ['ɔɪl₁skɪn] *n* **1** : hule *m* **2 oilskins** *npl* : impermeable *m*

oily ['ɔɪli] *adj* **oilier; -est** : aceitoso, grasiento, grasoso ⟨oily fingers : dedos grasientos⟩

ointment ['ɔɪntmənt] *n* : ungüento *m*, pomada *f*

OK¹ [₁o:'keɪ] *vt* **OK'd** *or* **okayed** [₁o:'keɪd]; **OK'ing** *or* **okaying** APPROVE, AUTHORIZE : dar el visto bueno a, autorizar, aprobar

OK² *or* **okay** [₁o:'keɪ] *adv* **1** WELL : bien **2** YES : sí, por supuesto

OK³ *adj* : bien ⟨he's OK : está bien⟩ ⟨it's OK with me : estoy de acuerdo⟩

OK⁴ *n* : autorización *f*, visto *m* bueno

okra ['o:krə, *South also* -kri] *n* : quingombó *m*

old¹ ['o:ld] *adj* **1** ANCIENT : antiguo ⟨old civilizations : civilizaciones antiguas⟩ **2** FAMILIAR : viejo ⟨old friends : viejos amigos⟩ ⟨the same old story : el mismo cuento⟩ **3** (*indicating a certain age*) ⟨he's ten years old : tiene diez años (de edad)⟩ **4** AGED : viejo, anciano ⟨an old woman : una anciana⟩ **5** FORMER : antiguo ⟨her old neighborhood : su antiguo barrio⟩ **6** WORN-OUT : viejo, gastado

old² *n* **1 the old** : los viejos, los ancianos **2 in the days of old** : antaño, en los tiempos antiguos

olden ['o:ldən] *adj* : de antaño, de antigüedad

old–fashioned ['o:ld'fæʃənd] *adj* : anticuado, pasado de moda

old maid *n* **1** SPINSTER : soltera *f* **2** FUSSBUDGET : maniático *m*, -ca *f*; melindroso *m*, -sa *f*

Old Testament *n* : Antiguo Testamento *m*

old–time ['o:ld'taɪm] *adj* : antiguo

old–timer ['o:ld'taɪmər] *n* **1** VETERAN : veterano *m*, -na *f* **2** *or* **oldster** : anciano *m*, -na *f*

old–world ['o:ld'wərld] *adj* : pintoresco (de antaño)

oleander ['o:li₁ændər] *n* : adelfa *f*

oleomargarine [₁o:lio'mɑrdʒərən] → **margarine**

olfactory [ɑl'fæktəri, ol-] *adj* : olfativo

oligarchy ['ɑlə₁gɑrki, 'o:lə-] *n, pl* **-chies** : oligarquía *f*

olive ['ɑlɪv, -ləv] *n* **1** : aceituna *f*, oliva *f* (fruta) **2** : olivo *m* (árbol) **3** *or* **olive green** : color *m* aceituna, verde *m* oliva

Olmec ['ɑl₁mɛk, 'o:l-] *n* : olmeca *mf* — **Olmec** *adj*

Olympic [ə'lɪmpɪk, o-] *adj* : olímpico

Olympic Games *npl* : Juegos *mpl* Olímpicos

Olympics [ə'lɪmpɪks, o-] *npl* : olimpiadas *fpl*

Omani [o'mɑni, -'mæ-] *n* : omaní *mf* — **Omani** *adj*

ombudsman ['ɑm₁bʊdzmən, ɑm-'bʊdz-] *n, pl* **-men** [-mən, -₁mɛn] : ombudsman *m*

omelet *or* **omelette** ['ɑmlət, 'ɑmə-] *n* : omelette *mf*, tortilla *f* (de huevo)

omen ['o:mən] *n* : presagio *m*, augurio *m*, agüero *m*

ominous ['ɑmənəs] *adj* : ominoso, agorero, de mal agüero

ominously ['ɑmənəsli] *adv* : de manera amenazadora

omission [o'mɪʃən] *n* : omisión *f*

omit [o'mɪt] *vt* **omitted; omitting 1** LEAVE OUT : omitir, excluir **2** NEGLECT : omitir ⟨they omitted to tell us : omitieron decírnoslo⟩

omnipotence [ɑm'nɪpətəns] *n* : omnipotencia *f* — **omnipotent** [ɑm-'nɪpətənt] *adj*

omnipresent [₁ɑmnɪ'prɛzənt] *adj* : omnipresente

omniscient [ɑm'nɪʃənt] *adj* : omnisciente

omnivorous [ɑm'nɪvərəs] *adj* **1** : omnívoro **2** AVID : ávido, voraz

on¹ ['ɑn, 'ɔn] *adv* **1** (*indicating contact with a surface*) ⟨put the top on : pon la tapa⟩ ⟨he has a hat on : lleva un sombrero puesto⟩ **2** (*indicating forward movement*) ⟨from that moment on : a partir de ese momento⟩ ⟨farther on : más adelante⟩ **3** (*indicating operation or an operating position*) ⟨turn the light on : prende la luz⟩

on² *adj* **1** (*being in operation*) ⟨the radio is on : el radio está prendido⟩ **2** (*taking place*) ⟨the game is on : el juego ha comenzado⟩ **3 to be on to** : estar enterado de

on³ *prep* **1** (*indicating position*) : en, sobre, encima de ⟨on the table : en (sobre, encima de) la mesa⟩ ⟨shadows on the wall : sombras en la pared⟩ ⟨on horseback : a caballo⟩ **2** AT, TO : a ⟨on the right : a la derecha⟩ **3** ABOARD, IN : en, a ⟨on the plane : en el avión⟩ ⟨he got on the train : subió al tren⟩ **4** (*indicating time*) ⟨she worked on Saturdays : trabajaba los sábados⟩ ⟨every hour on the hour : a la hora en punto⟩ **5** (*indicating means or agency*) : por ⟨he cut himself on a tin can : se cortó con una lata⟩ ⟨to talk on the telephone : hablar por teléfono⟩ **6** (*indicating a state or process*) : en ⟨on fire : en llamas⟩ ⟨on the increase : en aumento⟩ **7** (*indicating connection or membership*) : en ⟨on a committee : en una comisión⟩ **8** (*indicating an activity*) ⟨on vacation : de vacaciones⟩ ⟨on a diet : a dieta⟩ **9** ABOUT, CONCERNING : sobre ⟨a book on insects : un libro sobre insectos⟩ ⟨reflect on that : reflexiona sobre eso⟩

once¹ [ˈwʌnts] *adv* **1** : una vez ⟨once a month : una vez al mes⟩ ⟨once and for all : de una vez por todas⟩ **2** EVER : alguna vez **3** FORMERLY : antes, anteriormente

once² *adj* FORMER : antiguo

once³ *n* **1** : una vez **2 at ～** SIMULTANEOUSLY : al mismo tiempo, simultáneamente **3 at ～** IMMEDIATELY : inmediatamente, en seguida

once⁴ *conj* : una vez que, tan pronto como

once–over [ˌwʌntsˈoːvər, ˈwʌnts-] *n* **to give someone the once–over** : echarle un vistazo a alguien

oncoming [ˈɑnˌkʌmɪŋ, ˈɔn-] *adj* : que viene

one¹ [ˈwʌn] *adj* **1** (*being a single unit*) : un, una ⟨he only wants one apple : sólo quiere una manzana⟩ **2** (*being a particular one*) : un, una ⟨he arrived early one morning : llegó temprano una mañana⟩ **3** (*being the same*) : mismo, misma ⟨they're all members of one team : todos son miembros del mismo equipo⟩ ⟨one and the same thing : la misma cosa⟩ **4** SOME : alguno, alguna; un, una ⟨I'll see you again one day : algún día te veré otra vez⟩ ⟨at one time or another : en una u otra ocasión⟩

one² *n* **1** : uno *m* (número) **2** (*indicating the first of a set or series*) ⟨from day one : desde el primer momento⟩ **3** (*indicating a single person or thing*) ⟨the one (girl) on the right : la de la derecha⟩ ⟨he has the one but needs the other : tiene uno pero necesita el otro⟩

one³ *pron* **1** : uno, una ⟨one of his friends : una de sus amigas⟩ ⟨one never knows : uno nunca sabe, nunca se sabe⟩ ⟨to cut one's finger : cortarse el dedo⟩ **2 one and all** : todos, todo el mundo **3 one another** : el uno al otro, se ⟨they loved one another : se amaban⟩ **4 that one** : aquél, aquella **5 which one?** : ¿cuál?

one–on–one [wʌnɔnˈwʌn, -ɑn-] *adj* : uno a uno — **one–on–one** *adv*

onerous [ˈɑnərəs, ˈoːnə-] *adj* : oneroso, gravoso

oneself [ˌwʌnˈsɛlf] *pron* **1** (*used reflexively or for emphasis*) : se, sí mismo, uno mismo ⟨to control oneself : controlarse⟩ ⟨to talk to oneself : hablarse a sí mismo⟩ ⟨to do it oneself : hacérselo uno mismo⟩ **2 by ～** : solo

one–sided [ˈwʌnˈsaɪdəd] *adj* **1** : de un solo lado **2** LOPSIDED : asimétrico **3** BIASED : parcial, tendencioso **4** UNILATERAL : unilateral

onetime [ˈwʌnˈtaɪm] *adj* FORMER : antiguo

one–way [ˈwʌnˈweɪ] *adj* **1** : de sentido único, de una sola dirección ⟨a one-way street : una calle de sentido único⟩ **2** : de ida, sencillo ⟨a one-way ticket : un boleto de ida⟩

ongoing [ˈɑnˌgoːɪŋ] *adj* **1** CONTINUING : en curso, corriente **2** DEVELOPING : en desarrollo

onion [ˈʌnjən] *n* : cebolla *f*

online [ˈɔnˈlaɪn, ˈɑn-] *adj* : en línea

onlooker [ˈɔnˌlʊkər, ˈɑn-] *n* : espectador *m*, -dora *f*; circunstante *mf*

only¹ [ˈoːnli] *adv* **1** MERELY : sólo, solamente, nomás ⟨for only two dollars : por tan sólo dos dólares⟩ ⟨only once : sólo una vez, no más de una vez⟩ ⟨I only did it to help : lo hice por ayudar nomás⟩ **2** SOLELY : únicamente, sólo, solamente ⟨only he knows it : solamente él lo sabe⟩ **3** (*indicating a result*) ⟨it will only cause him problems : no hará más que crearle problemas⟩ **4 if only** : ojalá, por lo menos ⟨if only it were true! : ¡ojalá sea cierto!⟩ ⟨if he could only dance : si por lo menos pudiera bailar⟩

only² *adj* : único ⟨an only child : un hijo único⟩ ⟨the only chance : la única oportunidad⟩

only³ *conj* BUT : pero ⟨I would go, only I'm sick : iría, pero estoy enfermo⟩

onset [ˈɑnˌsɛt] *n* : comienzo *m*, llegada *f*

onslaught [ˈɑnˌslɔt, ˈɔn-] *n* : arremetida *f*, embestida *f*, embate *m*

onto [ˈɑnˌtuː, ˈɔn-] *prep* : sobre

onus [ˈoːnəs] *n* : responsabilidad *f*, carga *f*

onward¹ [ˈɑnwərd, ˈɔn-] *or* **onwards** *adv* FORWARD : adelante, hacia adelante

onward² *adj* : hacia adelante

onyx [ˈɑnɪks] *n* : ónix *m*

ooze¹ [ˈuːz] *v* **oozed; oozing** *vi* : rezumar — *vt* **1** : rezumar **2** EXUDE : irradiar, rebosar ⟨to ooze confidence : irradiar confianza⟩

ooze² *n* SLIME : cieno *m*, limo *m*

opacity [oˈpæsəti] *n, pl* **-ties** : opacidad *f*

opal [ˈoːpəl] *n* : ópalo *m*

opaque [oˈpeɪk] *adj* **1** : opaco **2** UNCLEAR : poco claro

open¹ [ˈoːpən] *vt* **1** : abrir ⟨open the door : abre la puerta⟩ **2** UNCOVER : destapar **3** UNFOLD : desplegar, abrir **4** CLEAR : abrir (un camino, etc.) **5** INAUGURATE : abrir (una tienda), inaugurar (una exposición, etc.) **6** INITIATE : iniciar, entablar, abrir ⟨to open the meeting : abrir la sesión⟩ ⟨to open a discussion : entablar un debate⟩ — *vi* **1** : abrirse **2** BEGIN : empezar, comenzar

open² *adj* **1** : abierto ⟨an open window : una ventana abierta⟩ **2** FRANK : abierto, franco, directo **3** UNCOV-

ERED : descubierto, abierto **4** EX-
TENDED : extendido, abierto ⟨with
open arms : con los brazos abiertos⟩ **5**
UNRESTRICTED : libre, abierto **6** UN-
DECIDED : pendiente, por decidir, sin
resolver ⟨an open question : una
cuestión pendiente⟩ **7** AVAILABLE : vacante, libre ⟨the job is open : el puesto
está vacante⟩
open³ *n* **in the open 1** OUTDOORS : al
aire libre **2** KNOWN : conocido, saca-
do a la luz
open-air ['o:pən'ær] *adj* OUTDOOR : al
aire libre
open-and-shut ['o:pənənd'ʃʌt] *adj*
: claro, evidente ⟨an open-and-shut
case : un caso muy claro⟩
opener ['o:pənər] *n* : destapador *m*,
abrelatas *m*, abridor *m*
openhanded [ˌo:pən'hændəd] *adj* : generoso, liberal
openhearted [ˌo:pən'hartəd] *adj* **1**
FRANK : franco, sincero **2** : generoso,
de gran corazón
opening ['o:pənɪŋ] *n* **1** BEGINNING
: comienzo *m*, principio *m*, apertura *f*
2 APERTURE : abertura *f*, brecha *f*, claro
m (en el bosque) **3** OPPORTUNITY
: oportunidad *f*
openly ['o:pənli] *adv* **1** FRANKLY : abiertamente, francamente **2** PUBLICLY
: públicamente, declaradamente
openness ['o:pənnəs] *n* : franqueza *f*
opera ['aprə, 'apərə] *n* **1** : ópera *f* **2** →
opus
opera glasses *npl* : gemelos *mpl* de
teatro
operate ['apəˌreɪt] *v* -ated; -ating *vi* **1**
ACT, FUNCTION : operar, funcionar, ac-
tuar **2 to operate on (someone)** : operar a (alguien) — *vt* **1** WORK : operar, manejar, hacer funcionar (una
máquina) **2** MANAGE : manejar, administrar (un negocio)
operatic [ˌapə'rætɪk] *adj* : operístico
operation [ˌapə'reɪʃən] *n* **1** FUNCTION-
ING : funcionamiento *m* **2** USE : uso
m, manejo *m* (de máquinas) **3**
SURGERY : operación *f*, intervención *f*
quirúrgica
operational [ˌapə'reɪʃənəl] *adj* : operacional, de operación
operative ['apərətɪv, -ˌreɪ-] *adj* **1** OPER-
ATING : vigente, en vigor **2** WORKING
: operativo **3** SURGICAL : quirúrgico
operator ['apəˌreɪtər] *n* : operador *m*,
-dora *f*
operetta [ˌapə'rɛtə] *n* : opereta *f*
ophthalmologist [ˌaf̩θæl'malədʒɪst,
-θə'ma-] *n* : oftalmólogo *m*, -ga *f*
ophthalmology [ˌaf̩θæl'malədʒi,
-θə'ma-] *n* : oftalmología *f*
opiate ['o:piət, -piˌeɪt] *n* : opiato *m*
opinion [ə'pɪnjən] *n* : opinión *f*
opinionated [ə'pɪnjəˌneɪtəd] *adj* : testarudo, dogmático
opium ['o:piəm] *n* : opio *m*
opossum [ə'pasəm] *n* : zarigüeya *f*, oposum *m*

opponent [ə'po:nənt] *n* : oponente *mf*;
opositor *m*, -tora *f*; contrincante *mf* (en
deportes)
opportune [ˌapər'tu:n, -'tju:n] *adj*
: oportuno — **opportunely** *adv*
opportunist [ˌapər'tu:nɪst, -'tju:-] *n*
: oportunista *mf*
opportunistic [ˌapərtu'nɪstɪk, -tju-] *adj*
: oportunista *mf*
opportunity [ˌapər'tu:nəti, -'tju:-] *n*, *pl*
-ties : oportunidad *f*, ocasión *f*, chance
m, posibilidades *fpl*
oppose [ə'po:z] *vt* **-posed; -posing 1** : ir
en contra de, oponerse a ⟨good oppos-
es evil : el bien se opone al mal⟩ **2** COM-
BAT : luchar contra, combatir, resistir
opposite¹ ['apəzət] *adv* : enfrente
opposite² *adj* **1** FACING : de enfrente
⟨the opposite side : el lado de enfrente⟩
2 CONTRARY : opuesto, contrario ⟨in
opposite directions : en direcciones
contrarias⟩ ⟨the opposite sex : el sexo
opuesto, el otro sexo⟩
opposite³ *n* : lo contrario, lo opuesto
opposite⁴ *prep* : enfrente de, frente a
opposition [ˌapə'zɪʃən] *n* **1** : oposición
f, resistencia *f* **2 in opposition to**
AGAINST : en contra de
oppress [ə'prɛs] *vt* **1** PERSECUTE
: oprimir, perseguir **2** BURDEN
: oprimir, agobiar
oppression [ə'prɛʃən] *n* : opresión *f*
oppressive [ə'prɛsɪv] *adj* **1** HARSH
: opresivo, severo **2** STIFLING : agobiante, sofocante ⟨oppressive heat
: calor sofocante⟩
oppressor [ə'prɛsər] *n* : opresor *m*, -sora
f
opprobrium [ə'pro:briəm] *n* : oprobio *m*
opt ['apt] *vi* : optar
optic ['aptɪk] *or* **optical** [-tɪkəl] *adj* : óptico
optical disk *n* : disco *m* óptico
optician [ap'tɪʃən] *n* : óptico *m*, -ca *f*
optics ['aptɪks] *npl* : óptica *f*
optimal ['aptəməl] *adj* : óptimo
optimism ['aptəˌmɪzəm] *n* : optimismo
m
optimist ['aptəmɪst] *n* : optimista *mf*
optimistic [ˌaptə'mɪstɪk] *adj* : optimista
optimistically [ˌaptə'mɪstɪkli] *adv* : con
optimismo, positivamente
optimum¹ ['aptəməm] *adj* → **optimal**
optimum² *n*, *pl* **-ma** ['aptəmə] : lo óptimo, lo ideal
option ['apʃən] *n* : opción *f* ⟨she has no
option : no tiene más remedio⟩
optional ['apʃənəl] *adj* : facultativo, optativo
optometrist [ap'tamətrɪst] *n* : optometrista *mf*
optometry [ap'tamətri] *n* : optometría *f*
opulence ['apjələnts] *n* : opulencia *f*
opulent ['apjələnt] *adj* : opulento
opus ['o:pəs] *n*, *pl* **opera** ['o:pərə, 'apə-]
: opus *m*, obra *f* (de música)
or ['ɔr] *conj* **1** (*indicating an alternative*)
: o (**u** *before words beginning with o or
ho*) ⟨coffee or tea : café o té⟩ ⟨one day

or another : un día u otro⟩ **2** (*following a negative*) : ni ⟨he didn't have his keys or his wallet : no llevaba ni sus llaves ni su billetera⟩
oracle ['ɔrəkəl] *n* : oráculo *m*
oral ['ɔrəl] *adj* : oral — **orally** *adv*
orange ['ɔrɪnʤ] *n* **1** : naranja *f*, china *f* PRi (fruto) **2** : naranja *m* (color), color *m* de china PRi
orangeade [,ɔrɪnʤ'eɪd] *n* : naranjada *f*
orangutan [ə'ræŋə,tæŋ, -'ræŋgə-, -,tæn] *n* : orangután *m*
oration [ə'reɪʃən] *n* : oración *f*, discurso *m*
orator ['ɔrətər] *n* : orador *m*, -dora *f*
oratorio [,ɔrə'tori,oː] *n, pl* **-rios** : oratorio *m*
oratory ['ɔrə,tori] *n, pl* **-ries** : oratoria *f*
orb ['ɔrb] *n* : orbe *m*
orbit¹ ['ɔrbət] *vt* **1** CIRCLE : girar alrededor de, orbitar **2** : poner en órbita (un satélite, etc.) — *vi* : orbitar
orbit² *n* : órbita *f*
orbital ['ɔrbətəl] *adj* : orbital
orchard ['ɔrtʃərd] *n* : huerto *m*
orchestra ['ɔrkəstrə] *n* : orquesta *f*
orchestral [or'kɛstrəl] *adj* : orquestal
orchestrate ['ɔrkə,streɪt] *vt* **-trated; -trating 1** : orquestar, instrumentar (en música) **2** ORGANIZE : arreglar, organizar
orchestration [,ɔrkə'streɪʃən] *n* : orquestación *f*
orchid ['ɔrkɪd] *n* : orquídea *f*
ordain [or'deɪn] *vt* **1** : ordenar (en religión) **2** DECREE : decretar, ordenar
ordeal [or'diːl, 'ɔr,diːl] *n* : prueba *f* dura, experiencia *f* terrible
order¹ ['ɔrdər] *vt* **1** ORGANIZE : arreglar, ordenar, poner en orden **2** COMMAND : ordenar, mandar **3** REQUEST : pedir, encargar ⟨to order a meal : pedir algo de comer⟩ — *vi* : hacer un pedido
order² *n* **1** : orden *f* ⟨a religious order : una orden religiosa⟩ **2** COMMAND : orden *f*, mandato *m* ⟨to give an order : dar una orden⟩ **3** REQUEST : orden *f*, pedido *m* ⟨purchase order : orden de compra⟩ **4** ARRANGEMENT : orden *m* ⟨in chronological order : por orden cronológico⟩ **5** DISCIPLINE : orden *m* ⟨law and order : el orden público⟩ **6 in order to** : para **7 out of order** : descompuesto, averiado **8 orders** *npl or* **holy orders** : órdenes *fpl* sagradas
orderliness ['ɔrdərlinəs] *n* : orden *m*
orderly¹ ['ɔrdərli] *adj* **1** METHODICAL : ordenado, metódico **2** PEACEFUL : pacífico, disciplinado
orderly² *n, pl* **-lies 1** : ordenanza *m* (en el ejército) **2** : camillero *m* (en un hospital)
ordinal ['ɔrdənəl] *n or* **ordinal number** : ordinal *m*, número *m* ordinal
ordinance ['ɔrdənənts] *n* : ordenanza *f*, reglamento *m*
ordinarily [,ɔrdən'ɛrəli] *adv* : ordinariamente, por lo general

ordinary ['ɔrdən,ɛri] *adj* **1** NORMAL, USUAL : normal, usual **2** AVERAGE : común y corriente, normal **3** MEDIOCRE : mediocre, ordinario
ordination [,ɔrdən'eɪʃən] *n* : ordenación *f*
ordnance ['ɔrdnənts] *n* : artillería *f*
ore ['or] *n* : mineral *m* (metalífero), mena *f*
oregano [ə'rɛgə,noː] *n* : orégano *m*
organ ['ɔrgən] *n* **1** : órgano *m* (instrumento) **2** : órgano *m* (del cuerpo) **3** PERIODICAL : publicación *f* periódica, órgano *m*
organic [or'gænɪk] *adj* : orgánico — **organically** *adv*
organism ['ɔrgə,nɪzəm] *n* : organismo *m*
organist ['ɔrgənɪst] *n* : organista *mf*
organization [,ɔrgənə'zeɪʃən] *n* **1** ORGANIZING : organización *f* **2** BODY : organización *f*, organismo *m*
organizational [,ɔrgənə'zeɪʃənəl] *adj* : organizativo
organize ['ɔrgə,naɪz] *vt* **-nized; -nizing** : organizar, arreglar, poner en orden
organizer ['ɔrgə,naɪzər] *n* : organizador *m*, -dora *f*
orgasm ['ɔr,gæzəm] *n* : orgasmo *m*
orgy ['ɔrʤi] *n, pl* **-gies** : orgía *f*
orient ['ori,ɛnt] *vt* : orientar
Orient *n* **the Orient** : el Oriente
oriental [,ori'ɛntəl] *adj* : del Oriente, oriental
Oriental *n* : oriental *mf*
orientation [,orien'teɪʃən] *n* : orientación *f*
orifice ['ɔrəfəs] *n* : orificio *m*
origin ['ɔrəʤən] *n* **1** ANCESTRY : origen *m*, ascendencia *f* **2** SOURCE : origen *m*, raíz *f*, fuente *f*
original¹ [ə'rɪʤənəl] *adj* : original
original² *n* : original *m*
originality [ə,rɪʤə'næləti] *n* : originalidad *f*
originally [ə'rɪʤənəli] *adv* **1** AT FIRST : al principio, originariamente **2** CREATIVELY : originalmente, con originalidad
originate [ə'rɪʤə,neɪt] *v* **-nated; -nating** *vt* : originar, iniciar, crear — *vi* **1** BEGIN : originarse, empezar **2** COME : provenir, proceder, derivarse
originator [ə'rɪʤə,neɪtər] *n* : creador *m*, -dora *f*; inventor *m*, -tora *f*
oriole ['ori,oːl, -iəl] *n* : oropéndola *f*
ornament¹ ['ɔrnəmənt] *vt* : adornar, decorar, ornamentar
ornament² *n* : ornamento *m*, adorno *m*, decoración *f*
ornamental [,ɔrnə'mɛntəl] *adj* : ornamental, de adorno, decorativo
ornamentation [,ɔrnəmən'teɪʃən, -mɛn-] *n* : ornamentación *f*
ornate [or'neɪt] *adj* : elaborado, recargado
ornery ['ɔrnəri, 'arnəri] *adj* **ornerier; -est** : de mal genio, malhumorado
ornithologist [,ɔrnə'θɑləʤɪst] *n* : ornitólogo *m*, -ga *f*

ornithology [ˌɔrnəˈθɑlədʒi] *n, pl* **-gies** : ornitología *f*

orphan¹ [ˈɔrfən] *vt* : dejar huérfano

orphan² *n* : huérfano *m*, -na *f*

orphanage [ˈɔrfənɪdʒ] *n* : orfelinato *m*, orfanato *m*

orthodontics [ˌɔrθəˈdɑntɪks] *n* : ortodoncia *f*

orthodontist [ˌɔrθəˈdɑntɪst] *n* : ortodoncista *mf*

orthodox [ˈɔrθəˌdɑks] *adj* : ortodoxo

orthodoxy [ˈɔrθəˌdɑksi] *n, pl* **-doxies** : ortodoxia *f*

orthographic [ˌɔrθəˈgræfɪk] *adj* : ortográfico

orthography [ɔrˈθɑgrəfi] *n, pl* **-phies** SPELLING : ortografía *f*

orthopedic [ˌɔrθəˈpiːdɪk] *adj* : ortopédico

orthopedics [ˌɔrθəˈpiːdɪks] *ns & pl* : ortopedia *f*

orthopedist [ˌɔrθəˈpiːdɪst] *n* : ortopedista *mf*

oscillate [ˈɑsəˌleɪt] *vi* **-lated; -lating** : oscilar

oscillation [ˌɑsəˈleɪʃən] *n* : oscilación *f*

osmosis [ɑzˈmoːsɪs, ɑs-] *n* : ósmosis *f*, osmosis *f*

osprey [ˈɑspri, -ˌpreɪ] *n* : pigargo *m*

ostensible [ɑˈstɛntsəbəl] *adj* APPARENT : aparente, ostensible — **ostensibly** [-bli] *adv*

ostentation [ˌɑstənˈteɪʃən] *n* : ostentación *f*, boato *m*

ostentatious [ˌɑstənˈteɪʃəs] *adj* : ostentoso — **ostentatiously** *adv*

osteopath [ˈɑstiəˌpæθ] *n* : osteópata *f*

osteopathy [ˌɑstiˈɑpəθi] *n* : osteopatía *f*

osteoporosis [ˌɑstiopəˈroːsɪs] *n, pl* **-roses** [-ˌsiːz] : osteoporosis *f*

ostracism [ˈɑstrəˌsɪzəm] *n* : ostracismo *m*

ostracize [ˈɑstrəˌsaɪz] *vt* **-cized; -cizing** : condenar al ostracismo, marginar, aislar

ostrich [ˈɑstrɪtʃ, ˈɔs-] *n* : avestruz *m*

other¹ [ˈʌðər] *adv* **other than** : aparte de, fuera de

other² *adj* : otro ⟨the other boys : los otros muchachos⟩ ⟨smarter than other people : más inteligente que los demás⟩ ⟨on the other hand : por otra parte, por otro lado⟩ ⟨every other day : cada dos días⟩

other³ *pron* : otro, otra ⟨one in front of the other : uno tras otro⟩ ⟨myself and three others : yo y tres otros, yo y tres más⟩ ⟨somewhere or other : en alguna parte⟩

otherwise¹ [ˈʌðərˌwaɪz] *adv* **1** DIFFERENTLY : de otro modo, de manera distinta ⟨he could not act otherwise : no pudo actuar de manera distinta⟩ **2** : eso aparte, por lo demás ⟨I'm dizzy, but otherwise I'm fine : estoy mareado pero, por lo demás, estoy bien⟩ **3** OR ELSE : de lo contrario, si no ⟨do what I tell you, otherwise you'll be sorry : haz

lo que te digo, de lo contrario, te arrepentirás⟩

otherwise² *adj* : diferente, distinto ⟨the facts are otherwise : la realidad es diferente⟩

otter [ˈɑtər] *n* : nutria *f*

Ottoman [ˈɑtəmən] *n* **1** : otomano *m*, -na *f* **2** : otomana *f* (mueble) — **Ottoman** *adj*

ouch [ˈaʊtʃ] *interj* : ¡ay!, ¡huy!

ought [ˈɔt] *v aux* : deber ⟨you ought to take care of yourself : deberías cuidarte⟩

oughtn't [ˈɔtənt] (*contraction of* **ought not**) → **ought**

ounce [ˈaʊnts] *n* : onza *f*

our [ˈɑr, ˈaʊr] *adj* : nuestro

ours [ˈaʊrz, ˈɑrz] *pron* : nuestro, nuestra ⟨a cousin of ours : un primo nuestro⟩

ourselves [ɑrˈsɛlvz, aʊr-] *pron* **1** (*used reflexively*) : nos, nosotros ⟨we amused ourselves : nos divertimos⟩ ⟨we were always thinking of ourselves : siempre pensábamos en nosotros⟩ **2** (*used for emphasis*) : nosotros mismos, nosotras mismas ⟨we did it ourselves : lo hicimos nosotros mismos⟩

oust [ˈaʊst] *vt* : desbancar, expulsar

ouster [ˈaʊstər] *n* : expulsión *f* (de un país, etc.), destitución *f* (de un puesto)

out¹ [ˈaʊt] *vi* : revelarse, hacerse conocido

out² *adv* **1** (*indicating direction or movement*) : para afuera ⟨she opened the door and looked out : abrió la puerta y miró para afuera⟩ **2** (*indicating a location away from home or work*) : fuera, afuera ⟨to eat out : comer afuera⟩ **3** (*indicating loss of control or possession*) ⟨they let the secret out : sacaron el secreto a la luz⟩ **4** (*indicating completion or discontinuance*) ⟨his money ran out : se le acabó el dinero⟩ ⟨to turn out the light : apagar la luz⟩ **5** OUTSIDE : fuera, afuera ⟨out in the garden : afuera en el jardín⟩ **6** ALOUD : en voz alta, en alto ⟨to cry out : gritar⟩

out³ *adj* **1** EXTERNAL : externo, exterior **2** OUTLYING : alejado, distante ⟨the out islands : las islas distantes⟩ **3** ABSENT : ausente **4** UNFASHIONABLE : fuera de moda **5** EXTINGUISHED : apagado

out⁴ *prep* **1** (*used to indicate an outward movement*) : por ⟨I looked out the window : miré por la ventana⟩ ⟨she ran out the door : corrió por la puerta⟩ **2** → **out of**

out-and-out [ˈaʊtənˈaʊt] *adj* UTTER : redomado, absoluto

outboard motor [ˈaʊtˌbord] *n* : motor *m* fuera de borde

outbound [ˈaʊtˌbaʊnd] *adj* : que sale, de salida

outbreak [ˈaʊtˌbreɪk] *n* : brote *m* (de una enfermedad), comienzo *m* (de guerra), ola *f* (de violencia), erupción *f* (de granos)

outbuilding ['aʊt,bɪldɪŋ] *n* : edificio *m* anexo

outburst ['aʊt,bərst] *n* : arranque *m*, arrebato *m*

outcast ['aʊt,kæst] *n* : marginado *m*, -da *f*; paria *mf*

outcome ['aʊt,kʌm] *n* : resultado *m*, desenlace *m*, consecuencia *f*

outcrop ['aʊt,krɑp] *n* : afloramiento *m*

outcry ['aʊt,kraɪ] *n, pl* **-cries** : clamor *m*, protesta *f*

outdated [,aʊt'deɪtəd] *adj* : anticuado, fuera de moda

outdistance [,aʊt'dɪstənts] *vt* **-tanced; -tancing** : aventajar, dejar atrás

outdo [,aʊt'du:] *vt* **-did** [-'dɪd]; **-done** [-'dʌn]; **-doing; -does** [-'dʌz] : superar

outdoor ['aʊt'dor] *adj* : al aire libre ⟨outdoor sports : deportes al aire libre⟩ ⟨outdoor clothing : ropa de calle⟩

outdoors[1] ['aʊt'dorz] *adv* : afuera, al aire libre

outdoors[2] *n* : aire *m* libre

outer ['aʊtər] *adj* **1** : exterior, externo **2 outer space** : espacio *m* exterior

outermost ['aʊtər,most] *adj* : más remoto, más exterior, extremo

outfield ['aʊt,fi:ld] *n* **the outfield** : los jardines

outfielder ['aʊt,fi:ldər] *n* : jardinero *m*, -ra *f*

outfit[1] ['aʊt,fɪt] *vt* **-fitted; -fitting** EQUIP : equipar

outfit[2] *n* **1** EQUIPMENT : equipo *m* **2** COSTUME, ENSEMBLE : traje *m*, conjunto *m* **3** GROUP : conjunto *m*

outgo ['aʊt,go:] *n, pl* **outgoes** : gasto *m*

outgoing ['aʊt,go:ɪŋ] *adj* **1** OUTBOUND : que sale **2** DEPARTING : saliente ⟨an outgoing president : un presidente saliente⟩ **3** EXTROVERTED : extrovertido, expansivo

outgrow [,aʊt'gro:] *vt* **-grew** [-'gru:]; **-grown** [-'gro:n]; **-growing 1** : crecer más que ⟨that tree outgrew all the others : ese árbol creció más que todos los otros⟩ **2 to outgrow one's clothes** : quedarle pequeña la ropa a uno

outgrowth ['aʊt,gro:θ] *n* **1** OFFSHOOT : brote *m*, vástago *m* (de una planta) **2** CONSEQUENCE : consecuencia *f*, producto *m*, resultado *m*

outing ['aʊtɪŋ] *n* : excursión *f*

outlandish [aʊt'lændɪʃ] *adj* : descabellado, muy extraño

outlast [,aʊt'læst] *vt* : durar más que

outlaw[1] ['aʊt,lɔ] *vt* : hacerse ilegal, declarar fuera de la ley, prohibir

outlaw[2] *n* : bandido *m*, -da *f*; bandolero *m*, -ra *f*; forajido *m*, -da *f*

outlay ['aʊt,leɪ] *n* : gasto *m*, desembolso *m*

outlet ['aʊt,lɛt, -lət] *n* **1** EXIT : salida *f*, escape *m* ⟨electrical outlet : toma de corriente⟩ **2** RELIEF : desahogo *m* **3** MARKET : mercado *m*, salida *f*

outline[1] ['aʊt,laɪn] *vt* **-lined; -lining 1** SKETCH : diseñar, esbozar, bosquejar **2** DEFINE, EXPLAIN : perfilar, delinear, explicar ⟨she outlined our responsibilities : delineó nuestras responsabilidades⟩

outline[2] *n* **1** PROFILE : perfil *m*, silueta *f*, contorno *m* **2** SKETCH : bosquejo *m*, boceto *m* **3** SUMMARY : esquema *m*, resumen *m*, sinopsis *m* ⟨an outline of world history : un esquema de la historia mundial⟩

outlive [,aʊt'lɪv] *vt* **-lived; -living** : sobrevivir a

outlook ['aʊt,lʊk] *n* **1** VIEW : vista *f*, panorama *f* **2** POINT OF VIEW : punto *m* de vista **3** PROSPECTS : perspectivas *fpl*

outlying ['aʊt,laɪɪŋ] *adj* : alejado, distante, remoto ⟨the outlying areas : las afueras⟩

outmoded [,aʊt'mo:dəd] *adj* : pasado de moda, anticuado

outnumber [,aʊt'nʌmbər] *vt* : superar en número a, ser más numeroso de

out of *prep* **1** (*indicating direction or movement from within*) : de, por ⟨we ran out of the house : salimos corriendo de la casa⟩ ⟨to look out of the window : mirar por la ventana⟩ **2** (*being beyond the limits of*) ⟨out of control : fuera de control⟩ ⟨to be out of sight : desaparecer de vista⟩ **3** OF : de ⟨one out of four : uno de cada cuatro⟩ **4** (*indicating absence or loss*) : sin ⟨out of money : sin dinero⟩ ⟨we're out of matches : nos hemos quedado sin fósforos⟩ **5** BECAUSE OF : por ⟨out of curiosity : por curiosidad⟩ **6** FROM : de ⟨made out of plastic : hecho de plástico⟩

out-of-date [,aʊtəv'deɪt] *adj* : anticuado, obsoleto, pasado de moda

out-of-door [,aʊtəv'dor] *or* **out-of-doors** [-'dorz] *→* **outdoor**

out-of-doors *n* *→* **outdoors**[2]

outpatient ['aʊt,peɪʃənt] *n* : paciente *m* externo, paciente *f* externa

outpost ['aʊt,po:st] *n* : puesto *m* avanzado

output[1] ['aʊt,pʊt] *vt* **-putted** *or* **-put; -putting** : producir

output[2] *n* : producción *f* (de una fábrica), rendimiento *m* (de una máquina), productividad *f* (de una persona)

outrage[1] ['aʊt,reɪʤ] *vt* **-raged; -raging 1** INSULT : ultrajar, injuriar **2** INFURIATE : indignar, enfurecer

outrage[2] *n* **1** ATROCITY : atropello *m*, atrocidad *f*, atentado *m* **2** SCANDAL : escándalo *m* **3** ANGER : ira *f*, furia *f*

outrageous [,aʊt'reɪʤəs] *adj* **1** SCANDALOUS : escandaloso, ofensivo, atroz **2** UNCONVENTIONAL : poco convencional, extravagante **3** EXORBITANT : exorbitante, excesivo (dícese de los precios, etc.)

outright[1] [,aʊt'raɪt] *adv* **1** COMPLETELY : por completo, totalmente ⟨to sell outright : vender por completo⟩ ⟨he refused it outright : lo rechazó rotundamente⟩ 2 DIRECTLY : directamente, sin reserva 3 INSTANTLY : al instante, en el acto

outright² [ˈaʊtˌraɪt] *adj* 1 COMPLETE : completo, absoluto, categórico ⟨an outright lie : una mentira absoluta⟩ 2 : sin reservas ⟨an outright gift : un regalo sin reservas⟩

outset [ˈaʊtˌsɛt] *n* : comienzo *m*, principio *m*

outshine [ˌaʊtˈʃaɪn] *vt* **-shone** [-ˈʃoːn, -ˈʃɑn] *or* **-shined**; **-shining** : eclipsar

outside¹ [ˌaʊtˈsaɪd, ˈaʊtˌ-] *adv* : fuera, afuera

outside² *adj* 1 : exterior, externo ⟨the outside edge : el borde exterior⟩ ⟨outside influences : influencias externas⟩ 2 REMOTE : remoto ⟨an outside chance : una posibilidad remota⟩

outside³ *n* 1 EXTERIOR : parte *f* de afuera, exterior *m* 2 MOST : máximo *m* ⟨three weeks at the outside : tres semanas como máximo⟩ 3 **from the outside** : desde afuera, desde fuera

outside⁴ *prep* : fuera de, afuera de ⟨outside my window : fuera de mi ventana⟩ ⟨outside regular hours : fuera del horario normal⟩ ⟨outside the law : afuera de la ley⟩

outside of *prep* 1 → **outside⁴** 2 → **besides²**

outsider [ˌaʊtˈsaɪdər] *n* : forastero *m*, -ra *f*

outskirts [ˈaʊtˌskərts] *npl* : afueras *fpl*, alrededores *mpl*

outsmart [ˌaʊtˈsmɑrt] → **outwit**

outspoken [ˌaʊtˈspoːkən] *adj* : franco, directo

outstanding [ˌaʊtˈstændɪŋ] *adj* 1 UNPAID : pendiente 2 NOTABLE : destacado, notable, excepcional, sobresaliente

outstandingly [ˌaʊtˈstændɪŋli] *adv* : excepcionalmente

outstretched [ˌaʊtˈstrɛtʃt] *adj* : extendido

outstrip [ˌaʊtˈstrɪp] *vt* **-stripped** *or* **-strip** [-ˈstrɪpt]; **-stripping** 1 : aventajar, dejar atrás ⟨he outstripped the other runners : aventajó a los otros corredores⟩ 2 SURPASS : aventajar, sobrepasar

outward¹ [ˈaʊtwərd] *or* **outwards** [-wərdz] *adv* : hacia afuera, hacia el exterior

outward² *adj* 1 : hacia afuera ⟨an outward flow : un flujo hacia afuera⟩ 2 : externo ⟨outward beauty : belleza externa⟩

outwardly [ˈaʊtwərdli] *adv* 1 EXTERNALLY : exteriormente 2 APPARENTLY : aparentemente ⟨outwardly friendly : aparentemente simpático⟩

outwit [ˌaʊtˈwɪt] *vt* **-witted**; **-witting** : ser más listo que

ova → **ovum**

oval¹ [ˈoːvəl] *adj* : ovalado, oval

oval² *n* : óvalo *m*

ovarian [oˈværiən] *adj* : ovárico

ovary [ˈoːvəri] *n*, *pl* **-ries** : ovario *m*

ovation [oˈveɪʃən] *n* : ovación *f*

oven [ˈʌvən] *n* : horno *m*

over¹ [ˈoːvər] *adv* 1 (*indicating movement across*) ⟨he flew over to London : voló a Londres⟩ ⟨come on over! : ¡ven acá!⟩ 2 (*indicating an additional amount*) ⟨the show ran 10 minutes over : el espectáculo terminó 10 minutos de tarde⟩ 3 ABOVE, OVERHEAD : por encima 4 AGAIN : otra vez, de nuevo ⟨over and over : una y otra vez⟩ ⟨to start over : volver a empezar⟩ 5 **all over** EVERYWHERE : por todas partes 6 **to fall over** : caerse 7 **to turn over** : poner boca abajo, voltear

over² *adj* 1 HIGHER, UPPER : superior 2 REMAINING : sobrante, que sobra 3 ENDED : terminado, acabado ⟨the work is over : el trabajo está terminado⟩

over³ *prep* 1 ABOVE : encima de, arriba de, sobre ⟨over the fireplace : encima de la chimenea⟩ ⟨the hawk flew over the hills : el halcón voló sobre los cerros⟩ 2 : más de ⟨over $50 : más de $50⟩ 3 ALONG : por, sobre ⟨to glide over the ice : deslizarse sobre el hielo⟩ 4 (*indicating motion through a place or thing*) ⟨they showed me over the house : me mostraron la casa⟩ 5 ACROSS : por encima de, sobre ⟨he jumped over the ditch : saltó por encima de la zanja⟩ 6 UPON : sobre ⟨a cape over my shoulders : una capa sobre los hombros⟩ 7 ON : por ⟨to speak over the telephone : hablar por teléfono⟩ 8 DURING : en, durante ⟨over the past 25 years : durante los últimos 25 años⟩ 9 BECAUSE OF : por ⟨they fought over the money : se pelearon por el dinero⟩

overabundance [ˌoːvərəˈbʌndənts] *n* : superabundancia *f*

overabundant [ˌoːvərəˈbʌndənt] *adj* : superabundante

overactive [ˌoːvərˈæktɪv] *adj* : hiperactivo

overall [ˌoːvərˈɔl] *adj* : total, global, de conjunto

overalls [ˈoːvərˌɔlz] *npl* : overol *m*

overawe [ˌoːvərˈɔ] *vt* **-awed**; **-awing** : intimidar, impresionar

overbearing [ˌoːvərˈbærɪŋ] *adj* : dominante, imperioso, prepotente

overblown [ˌoːvərˈbloːn] *adj* 1 INFLATED : inflado, exagerado 2 BOMBASTIC : grandilocuente, rimbombante

overboard [ˈoːvərˌbord] *adv* : por la borda, al agua

overburden [ˌoːvərˈbərdən] *vt* : sobrecargar, agobiar

overcast [ˈoːvərˌkæst] *adj* CLOUDY : nublado

overcharge [ˌoːvərˈtʃɑrdʒ] *vt* **-charged**; **-charging** : cobrarle de más (a alguien)

overcoat [ˈoːvərˌkoːt] *n* : abrigo *m*

overcome [ˌoːvərˈkʌm] *v* **-came** [-ˈkeɪm]; **-come**; **-coming** *vt* 1 CON-

QUER : vencer, derrotar, superar **2** OVERWHELM : abrumar, agobiar — *vi* : vencer

overconfidence [ˌoːvərˈkɑnfədən/s] *n* : exceso *m* de confianza

overconfident [ˌoːvərˈkɑnfədənt] *adj* : demasiado confiado

overcook [ˌoːvərˈkʊk] *vt* : recocer, cocer demasiado

overcrowded [ˌoːvərˈkraʊdəd] *adj* **1** PACKED : abarrotado, atestado de gente **2** OVERPOPULATED : super-poblado

overdo [ˌoːvərˈduː] *vt* -did [-ˈdɪd]; -done [-ˈdʌn]; -doing; -does [-ˈdʌz] **1** : hac-er demasiado **2** EXAGGERATE : ex-agerar **3** OVERCOOK : recocer

overdose [ˈoːvərˌdoːs] *n* : sobredosis *f*

overdraft [ˈoːvərˌdræft] *n* : sobregiro *m*, descubierto *m*

overdraw [ˌoːvərˈdrɔ] *vt* -drew [-ˈdruː]; -drawn [-ˈdrɔn]; -drawing **1** : sobregi-rar ⟨my account is overdrawn : tengo la cuenta en descubierto⟩ **2** EXAG-GERATE : exagerar

overdue [ˌoːvərˈduː] *adj* **1** UNPAID : ven-cido y sin pagar **2** TARDY : de retraso, tardío

overeat [ˌoːvərˈiːt] *vi* -ate [-ˈeɪt]; -eaten [-ˈiːtən]; -eating : comer demasiado

overelaborate [ˌoːvərɪˈlæbərət] *adj* : re-cargado

overestimate [ˌoːvərˈɛstəˌmeɪt] *vt* -mated; -mating : sobreestimar

overexcited [ˌoːvərɪkˈsaɪtəd] *adj* : so-breexcitado

overexpose [ˌoːvərɪkˈspoːz] *vt* -posed; -posing : sobreexponer

overfeed [ˌoːvərˈfiːd] *vt* -fed [-ˈfɛd]; -feeding : sobrealimentar

overflow¹ [ˌoːvərˈfloː] *vt* **1** : desbordar **2** INUNDATE : inundar — *vi* : desbor-darse, rebosar

overflow² [ˈoːvərˌfloː] *n* **1** : derrame *m*, desbordamiento *m* (de un río) **2** SUR-PLUS : exceso *m*, excedente *m*

overfly [ˌoːvərˈflaɪ] *vt* -flew [-ˈfluː]; -flown [-ˈfloːn]; -flying : sobrevolar

overgrown [ˌoːvərˈgroːn] *adj* **1** : cu-bierto ⟨overgrown with weeds : cu-bierto de malas hierbas⟩ **2** : demasia-do grande

overhand¹ [ˈoːvərˌhænd] *adv* : por enci-ma de la cabeza

overhand² *adj* : por lo alto (tirada)

overhang¹ [ˌoːvərˈhæŋ] *v* -hung [-ˈhʌŋ]; -hanging *vt* **1** : sobresalir por encima de **2** THREATEN : amenazar — *vi* : so-bresalir

overhang² [ˈoːvərˌhæŋ] *n* : saliente *mf*

overhaul [ˌoːvərˈhɔl] *vt* **1** : revisar ⟨to overhaul an engine : revisar un motor⟩ **2** OVERTAKE : adelantar

overhead¹ [ˌoːvərˈhɛd] *adv* : por encima, arriba, por lo alto

overhead² [ˈoːvərˌhɛd] *adj* : de arriba

overhead³ [ˈoːvərˌhɛd] *n* : gastos *mpl* generales

overhear [ˌoːvərˈhɪr] *vt* -heard; -hearing : oír por casualidad

overheat [ˌoːvərˈhiːt] *vt* : recalentar, so-brecalentar, calentar demasiado

overjoyed [ˌoːvərˈdʒɔɪd] *adj* : rebosante de alegría

overkill [ˈoːvərˌkɪl] *n* : exceso *m*, exce-dente *m*

overland¹ [ˈoːvərˌlænd, -lənd] *adv* : por tierra

overland² *adj* : terrestre, por tierra

overlap¹ [ˌoːvərˈlæp] *v* -lapped; -lapping *vt* : traslapar — *vi* : traslaparse, sola-parse

overlap² [ˈoːvərˌlæp] *n* : traslapo *m*

overlay¹ [ˌoːvərˈleɪ] *vt* -laid [-ˈleɪd]; -laying : recubrir, revestir

overlay² [ˈoːvərˌleɪ] *n* : revestimiento *m*

overload [ˌoːvərˈloːd] *vt* : sobrecargar

overlong [ˌoːvərˈlɔŋ] *adj* : excesiva-mente largo, largo y pesado

overlook [ˌoːvərˈlʊk] *vt* **1** INSPECT : in-speccionar, revisar **2** : tener vista a, dar a ⟨a house overlooking the valley : una casa que tiene vista al valle⟩ **3** MISS : pasar por alto **4** EXCUSE : dejar pasar, disculpar

overly [ˈoːvərli] *adv* : demasiado

overnight¹ [ˌoːvərˈnaɪt] *adv* **1** : por la noche, durante la noche **2** : de la noche a la mañana ⟨we can't do it overnight : no podemos hacerlo de la noche a la mañana⟩

overnight² [ˈoːvərˈnaɪt] *adj* **1** : de noche ⟨an overnight stay : una estancia de una noche⟩ ⟨an overnight bag : una bolsa de viaje⟩ **2** SUDDEN : repentino

overpass [ˈoːvərˌpæs] *n* : paso *m* eleva-do, paso *m* a desnivel *Mex*

overpopulated [ˌoːvərˈpɑpjəˌleɪtəd] *adj* : sobrepoblado

overpower [ˌoːvərˈpaʊər] *vt* **1** CON-QUER, SUBDUE : vencer, superar **2** OVERWHELM : abrumar, agobiar ⟨overpowered by the heat : sofocado por el calor⟩

overpraise [ˌoːvərˈpreɪz] *vt* -praised; -praising : alabar demasiado

overrate [ˌoːvərˈreɪt] *vt* -rated; -rating : sobrevalorar, sobrevaluar

override [ˌoːvərˈraɪd] *vt* -rode [-ˈroːd]; -ridden [-ˈrɪdən]; -riding **1** : predomi-nar sobre, contar más que ⟨hunger overrode our manners : el hambre pre-dominó sobre los modales⟩ **2** ANNUL : anular, invalidar ⟨to override a veto : anular un veto⟩

overrule [ˌoːvərˈruːl] *vt* -ruled; -ruling : anular (una decisión), desautorizar (una persona), denegar (un pedido)

overrun [ˌoːvərˈrʌn] *v* -ran [-ˈræn]; -running *vt* **1** INVADE : invadir **2** IN-FEST : infestar, plagar **3** EXCEED : ex-ceder, rebasar — *vi* : rebasar el tiem-po previsto

overseas¹ [ˌoːvərˈsiːz] *adv* : en el ex-tranjero ⟨to travel overseas : viajar al extranjero⟩

overseas[2] ['o:vər,si:z] *adj* : extranjero, exterior

oversee [,o:vər'si:] *vt* **-saw** [-'sɔ]; **-seen** [-'si:n]; **-seeing** SUPERVISE : supervisar

overseer ['o:vər,si:ər] *n* : supervisor *m*, -sora *f*; capataz *mf*

overshadow [,o:vər'ʃæ,do:] *vt* 1 DARKEN : oscurecer, ensombrecer 2 ECLIPSE, OUTSHINE : eclipsar

overshoe ['o:vər,ʃu:] *n* : chanclo *m*

overshoot [,o:vər'ʃu:t] *vt* **-shot** [-'ʃɑt]; **-shooting** : pasarse de ⟨to overshoot the mark : pasarse de la raya⟩

oversight ['o:vər,saɪt] *n* : descuido *m*, inadvertencia *f*

oversleep [,o:vər'sli:p] *vi* **-slept** [-'slɛpt]; **-sleeping** : no despertarse a tiempo, quedarse dormido

overspread [,o:vər'sprɛd] *vt* **-spread**; **-spreading** : extenderse sobre

overstaffed [,o:vər'stæft] *adj* : con exceso de personal

overstate [,o:vər'steɪt] *vt* **-stated**; **-stating** EXAGGERATE : exagerar

overstatement [,o:vər'steɪtmənt] *n* : exageración *f*

overstep [,o:vər'stɛp] *vt* **-stepped**; **-stepping** EXCEED : sobrepasar, traspasar, exceder

overt [o'vərt, 'o:,vərt] *adj* : evidente, manifiesto, patente

overtake [,o:vər'teɪk] *vt* **-took** [-'tʊk]; **-taken** [-'teɪkən]; **-taking** : pasar, adelantar, rebasar *Mex*

overthrow[1] [,o:vər'θro:] *vt* **-threw** [-'θru:]; **-thrown** [-'θro:n]; **-throwing** 1 OVERTURN : dar la vuelta a, volcar 2 DEFEAT, TOPPLE : derrocar, derribar, deponer

overthrow[2] ['o:vər,θro:] *n* : derrocamiento *m*, caída *f*

overtime ['o:vər,taɪm] *n* 1 : horas *fpl* extras (de trabajo) 2 : prórroga *f* (en deportes)

overtly [o'vərtli, 'o:,vərt-] *adv* OPENLY : abiertamente

overtone ['o:vər,to:n] *n* 1 : armónico *m* (en música) 2 HINT, SUGGESTION : tinte *m*, insinuación *f*

overture ['o:vər,tʃʊr, -tʃər] *n* 1 PROPOSAL : propuesta *f* 2 : obertura *f* (en música)

overturn [,o:vər'tərn] *vt* 1 UPSET : dar la vuelta a, volcar 2 NULLIFY : anular, invalidar — *vi* TURN OVER : volcar, dar un vuelco

overuse [,o:vər'ju:z] *vt* **-used**; **-using** : abusar de

overview ['o:vər,vju:] *n* : resumen *m*, visión *f* general

overweening [,o:vər'wi:nɪŋ] *adj* 1 ARROGANT : arrogante, soberbio 2 IMMODERATE : desmesurado

overweight [,o:vər'weɪt] *adj* : demasiado gordo, demasiado pesado

overwhelm [,o:vər'hwɛlm] *vt* 1 CRUSH, DEFEAT : aplastar, arrollar 2 SUBMERGE : inundar, sumergir 3 OVERPOWER : abrumar, agobiar ⟨overwhelmed by remorse : abrumado de remordimiento⟩

overwhelming [,o:vər'hwɛlmɪŋ] *adj* 1 CRUSHING : abrumador, apabullante 2 SWEEPING : arrollador, aplastante ⟨an overwhelming majority : una mayoría aplastante⟩

overwork [,o:vər'wərk] *vt* 1 : hacer trabajar demasiado 2 OVERUSE : abusar de — *vi* : trabajar demasiado

overwrought [,o:vər'rɔt] *adj* : alterado, sobreexcitado

ovoid ['o:,vɔɪd] *or* **ovoidal** [o'vɔɪdəl] *adj* : ovoide

ovulate ['avjə,leɪt, 'o:-] *vi* **-lated**; **-lating** : ovular

ovulation [,avjə'leɪʃən, ,o:-] *n* : ovulación *f*

ovum ['o:vəm] *n*, *pl* **ova** [-və] : óvulo *m*

owe ['o:] *vt* **owed**; **owing** : deber ⟨you owe me $10 : me debes $10⟩ ⟨he owes his wealth to his father : le debe su riqueza a su padre⟩

owing to *prep* : debido a

owl ['aʊl] *n* : búho *m*, lechuza *f*, tecolote *m Mex*

own[1] ['o:n] *vt* 1 POSSESS : poseer, tener, ser dueño de 2 ADMIT : reconocer, admitir — *vi* **to own up** : reconocer (algo), admitir (algo)

own[2] *adj* : propio, personal, particular ⟨his own car : su propio coche⟩

own[3] *pron* my; (your, his/her, our, their); **own** : el mío, la mía; el tuyo, la tuya; el suyo, la suya; el nuestro, la nuestra ⟨to each his own : cada uno a lo suyo⟩ ⟨money of my own : mi propio dinero⟩ ⟨to be on one's own : estar solo⟩

owner ['o:nər] *n* : dueño *m*, -ña *f*; propietario *m*, -ria *f*

ownership ['o:nər,ʃɪp] *n* : propiedad *f*

ox ['aks] *n*, *pl* **oxen** ['aksən] : buey *m*

oxidation [,aksə'deɪʃən] *n* : oxidación *f*

oxide ['ak,saɪd] *n* : óxido *m*

oxidize ['aksə,daɪz] *vt* **-dized**; **-dizing** : oxidar

oxygen ['aksɪdʒən] *n* : oxígeno *m*

oyster ['ɔɪstər] *n* : ostra *f*, ostión *m Mex*

ozone ['o:,zo:n] *n* : ozono *m*

P

p ['pi:] *n, pl* **p's** *or* **ps** ['pi:z] : decimosexta letra del alfabeto inglés

pace[1] ['peɪs] *v* **paced; pacing** *vi* : caminar, ir y venir — *vt* **1** : caminar por ⟨she paced the floor : caminaba de un lado a otro del cuarto⟩ **2 to pace a runner** : marcarle el ritmo a un corredor

pace[2] *n* **1** STEP : paso *m* **2** RATE : paso *m*, ritmo *m* ⟨to set the pace : marcar el paso, marcar la pauta⟩

pacemaker ['peɪs,meɪkər] *n* : marcapasos *m*

pacific [pə'sɪfɪk] *adj* : pacífico

pacifier ['pæsə,faɪər] *n* : chupete *m*, chupón *m*, mamila *f Mex*

pacifism ['pæsə,fɪzəm] *n* : pacifismo *m*

pacifist ['pæsəfɪst] *n* : pacifista *mf*

pacify ['pæsə,faɪ] *vt* **-fied; -fying 1** SOOTHE : apaciguar, pacificar **2** : pacificar (un país, una región, etc.)

pack[1] ['pæk] *vt* **1** PACKAGE : empaquetar, embalar, envasar **2** : empacar, meter (en una maleta) ⟨to pack one's bag : hacer la maleta⟩ **3** FILL : llenar, abarrotar ⟨a packed theater : un teatro abarrotado⟩ **4 to pack off** SEND : mandar — *vi* : empacar, hacer las maletas

pack[2] *n* **1** BUNDLE : bulto *m*, fardo *m* **2** BACKPACK : mochila *f* **3** PACKAGE : paquete *m*, cajetilla *f* (de cigarrillos, etc.) **4** : manada *f* (de lobos, etc.), jauría *f* (de perros) ⟨a pack of thieves : una pandilla de ladrones⟩

package[1] ['pækɪdʒ] *vt* **-aged; -aging** : empaquetar, embalar

package[2] *n* : paquete *m*, bulto *m*

packaging ['pækɪdʒɪŋ] *n* **1** : embalaje *m* **2** WRAPPING : envoltorio *m*

packer ['pækər] *n* : empacador *m*, -dora *f*

packet ['pækət] *n* : paquete *m*

packing ['pækɪŋ] *n* : embalaje *m*

pact ['pækt] *n* : pacto *m*, acuerdo *m*

pad[1] ['pæd] *vt* **padded; padding 1** FILL, STUFF : rellenar, acolchar (una silla, una pared) **2** : meter paja en, rellenar ⟨to pad a speech : rellenar un discurso⟩

pad[2] *n* **1** CUSHION : almohadilla *f* ⟨a shoulder pad : una hombrera⟩ **2** TABLET : bloc *m* (de papel) **3** *or* **lily pad** : hoja *f* grande (de un nenúfar) **4 ink pad** : tampón *m* **5 launching pad** : plataforma *f* (de lanzamiento)

padding ['pædɪŋ] *n* **1** FILLING : relleno *m* **2** : paja *f* (en un discurso, etc.)

paddle[1] ['pædəl] *v* **-dled; -dling** *vt* **1** : hacer avanzar (una canoa) con canalete **2** HIT : azotar, darle nalgadas a (con una pala o paleta) — *vi* **1** : remar (en una canoa) **2** SPLASH : chapotear, mojarse los pies

paddle[2] *n* **1** : canalete *m*, zagual *m* (de una canoa, etc.) **2** : pala *f*, paleta *f* (en deportes)

paddock ['pædək] *n* **1** PASTURE : potrero *m* **2** : paddock *m*, cercado *m* (en un hipódromo)

paddy ['pædi] *n, pl* **-dies** : arrozal *m*

padlock[1] ['pæd,lɑk] *vt* : cerrar con candado

padlock[2] *n* : candado *m*

pagan[1] ['peɪgən] *adj* : pagano

pagan[2] *n* : pagano *m*, -na *f*

paganism ['peɪgən,ɪzəm] *n* : paganismo *m*

page[1] ['peɪdʒ] *vt* **paged; paging** : llamar por altavoz

page[2] *n* **1** BELLHOP : botones *m* **2** : página *f* (de un libro, etc.)

pageant ['pædʒənt] *n* **1** SPECTACLE : espectáculo *m* **2** PROCESSION : desfile *m*

pageantry ['pædʒəntri] *n* : pompa *f*, fausto *m*

pager ['peɪdʒər] *n* BEEPER : buscapersonas *m*

pagoda [pə'goːdə] *n* : pagoda *f*

paid → **pay**

pail ['peɪl] *n* : balde *m*, cubo *m*, cubeta *f Mex*

pailful ['peɪl,fʊl] *n* : balde *m*, cubo *m*, cubeta *f Mex*

pain[1] ['peɪn] *vt* : doler

pain[2] *n* **1** PENALTY : pena *f* ⟨under pain of death : so pena de muerte⟩ **2** SUFFERING : dolor *m*, malestar *m*, pena *f* (mental) **3 pains** *npl* EFFORT : esmero *m*, esfuerzo *m* ⟨to take pains : esmerarse⟩

painful ['peɪnfəl] *adj* : doloroso — **painfully** *adv*

painkiller ['peɪn,kɪlər] *n* : analgésico *m*

painless ['peɪnləs] *adj* : indoloro, sin dolor

painlessly ['peɪnləsli] *adv* : sin dolor

painstaking ['peɪn,steɪkɪŋ] *adj* : esmerado, cuidadoso, meticuloso — **painstakingly** *adv*

paint[1] ['peɪnt] *v* : pintar

paint[2] *n* : pintura *f*

paintbrush ['peɪnt,brʌʃ] *n* : pincel *m* (de un artista), brocha *f* (para pintar casas, etc.)

painter ['peɪntər] *n* : pintor *m*, -tora *f*

painting ['peɪntɪŋ] *n* : pintura *f*

pair[1] ['pær] *vt* : emparejar, poner en parejas — *vi* : emparejarse

pair[2] *n* : par *m* (de objetos), pareja *f* (de personas o animales) ⟨a pair of scissors : unas tijeras⟩

pajamas [pə'dʒɑməz, -'dʒæ-] *npl* : pijama *m*, piyama *mf*

Pakistani [,pækɪ'stæni, ,pɑkɪ'stɑni] *n* : paquistaní *mf* — **Pakistani** *adj*

pal ['pæl] *n* : amigo *m*, -ga *f*; compinche *mf fam*; chamo *m*, -ma *f Ven fam*; cuate *m*, -ta *f Mex*

palace ['pæləs] *n* : palacio *m*

palatable ['pælətəbəl] *adj* : sabroso

palate ['pælət] *n* **1** : paladar *m* (de la boca) **2** TASTE : paladar *m*, gusto *m*

palatial [pə'leɪʃəl] *adj* : suntuoso, espléndido

palaver [pə'lævər, -'lɑ-] *n* : palabrería *f*

pale¹ ['peɪl] *v* **paled; paling** *vi* : palidecer — *vt* : hacer pálido

pale² *adj* **paler; palest 1** : pálido ⟨to turn pale : palidecer, ponerse pálido⟩ **2** : claro (dícese de los colores)

paleness ['peɪlnəs] *n* : palidez *f*

paleontologist [ˌpeɪliˌɑn'tɑlədʒɪst] *n* : paleontólogo *m*, -ga *f*

paleontology [ˌpeɪliˌɑn'tɑlədʒi] *n* : paleontología *f*

Palestinian [ˌpælə'stɪniən] *n* : palestino *m*, -na *f* — **Palestinian** *adj*

palette ['pælət] *n* : paleta *f* (para mezclar pigmentos)

palisade [ˌpælə'seɪd] *n* **1** FENCE : empalizada *f*, estacada *f* **2** CLIFFS : acantilado *m*

pall¹ ['pɔl] *vi* : perder su sabor, dejar de gustar

pall² *n* **1** : paño *m* mortuorio (sobre un ataúd) **2** COVER : cortina *f* (de humo, etc.) **3 to cast a pall over** : ensombrecer

pallbearer ['pɔlˌberər] *n* : portador *m*, -dora *f* del féretro

pallet ['pælət] *n* **1** BED : camastro *m* **2** PLATFORM : plataforma *f* de carga

palliative ['pæliˌeɪtɪv, 'pæljətɪv] *adj* : paliativo

pallid ['pæləd] *adj* : pálido

pallor ['pælər] *n* : palidez *f*

palm¹ ['pɑm, 'pɑlm] *vt* **1** CONCEAL : escamotear (un naipe, etc.) **2 to palm off** : encajar, endilgar *fam* ⟨he palmed it off on me : me lo endilgó⟩

palm² *n* **1** *or* **palm tree** : palmera *f* **2** : palma *f* (de la mano)

Palm Sunday *n* : Domingo *m* de Ramos

palomino [ˌpælə'miːˌnoː] *n*, *pl* **-nos** : caballo *m* de color dorado

palpable ['pælpəbəl] *adj* : palpable — **palpably** [-bli] *adv*

palpitate ['pælpəˌteɪt] *vi* **-tated; -tating** : palpitar

palpitation [ˌpælpə'teɪʃən] *n* : palpitación *f*

palsy ['pɔlzi] *n*, *pl* **-sies 1** : parálisis *f* **2** → **cerebral palsy**

paltry ['pɔltri] *adj* **-trier; -est** : mísero, mezquino, insignificante ⟨a paltry excuse : una mala excusa⟩

pampas ['pæmpəz, 'pɑmpəs] *npl* : pampa *f*

pamper ['pæmpər] *vt* : mimar, consentir, chiquear *Mex*

pamphlet ['pæmpflət] *n* : panfleto *m*, folleto *m*

pan¹ ['pæn] *vt* **panned; panning** CRITICIZE : poner por los suelos — *vi* **to pan for gold** : cribar el oro con batea, lavar oro

pan² *n* **1** : cacerola *f*, cazuela *f* **2 frying pan** : sartén *mf*, freidera *f Mex*

panacea [ˌpænə'siːə] *n* : panacea *f*

Panamanian [ˌpænə'meɪniən] *n* : panameño *m*, -ña *f* — **Panamanian** *adj*

pancake ['pænˌkeɪk] *n* : panqueque *m*

pancreas ['pæŋkriəs, 'pæn-] *n* : páncreas *m*

panda ['pændə] *n* : panda *mf*

pandemonium [ˌpændə'moːniəm] *n* : pandemonio *m*, pandemónium *m*

pander ['pændər] *vi* **to pander to** : satisfacer, complacer (a alguien) ⟨to pander to popular taste : satisfacer el gusto popular⟩

pane ['peɪn] *n* : cristal *m*, vidrio *m*

panel¹ ['pænəl] *vt* **-eled** *or* **-elled; -eling** *or* **-elling** : adornar con paneles

panel² *n* **1** : lista *f* de nombres (de un jurado, etc.) **2** GROUP : panel *m*, grupo *m* ⟨discussion panel : panel de discusión⟩ **3** : panel *m* (de una pared, etc.) **4 instrument panel** : tablero *m* de instrumentos

paneling ['pænəlɪŋ] *n* : paneles *mpl*

pang ['pæŋ] *n* : puntada *f*, punzada *f*

panic¹ ['pænɪk] *v* **-icked; -icking** *vt* : llenar de pánico — *vi* : ser presa de pánico

panic² *n* : pánico *m*

panicky ['pænɪki] *adj* : presa de pánico

panorama [ˌpænə'ræmə, -'rɑ-] *n* : panorama *m*

panoramic [ˌpænə'ræmɪk, -'rɑ-] *adj* : panorámico

pansy ['pænzi] *n*, *pl* **-sies** : pensamiento *m*

pant¹ ['pænt] *vi* : jadear, resoplar

pant² *n* : jadeo *m*, resoplo *m*

pantaloons [ˌpæntə'luːnz] → **pants**

pantheon ['pænˌθiˌɑn, -ən] *n* : panteón *m*

panther ['pænθər] *n* : pantera *f*

panties ['pæntiz] *npl* : calzones *mpl*; pantaletas *fpl Mex*, *Ven*; bragas *fpl Spain*

pantomime¹ ['pæntəˌmaɪm] *v* **-mimed; -miming** *vt* : representar mediante la pantomima — *vi* : hacer la mímica

pantomime² *n* : pantomima *f*

pantry ['pæntri] *n*, *pl* **-tries** : despensa *f*

pants ['pænts] *npl* **1** TROUSERS : pantalón *m*, pantalones *mpl* **2** → **panties**

panty hose ['pænti] *ns* & *pl* : medias *fpl*, panties *mfpl*, pantimedias *fpl Mex*

pap ['pæp] *n* : papilla *f* (para bebés, etc.)

papa ['pɑpə] *n* : papá *m*

papal ['peɪpəl] *adj* : papal

papaya [pə'paɪə] *n* : papaya *f* (fruta)

paper¹ ['peɪpər] *vt* WALLPAPER : empapelar

paper² *adj* : de papel

paper³ *n* **1** : papel *m* ⟨a piece of paper : un papel⟩ **2** DOCUMENT : papel *m*, documento *m* **3** NEWSPAPER : periódico *m*, diario *m*

paperback ['peɪpərˌbæk] *n* : libro *m* en rústica

paper clip *n* : clip *m*, sujetapapeles *m*

paperweight ['peɪpərˌweɪt] *n* : pisapapeles *m*

paperwork ['peɪpərˌwərk] n : papeleo m
papery ['peɪpəri] adj : parecido al papel
papier-mâché [ˌpeɪpərməˈʃeɪ, ˌpæ-ˌpjeɪmæˈʃeɪ] n : papel m maché
papoose [pæˈpuːs, pə-] n : niño m, -ña f de los indios norteamericanos
paprika [pəˈpriːkə, pæ-] n : pimentón m, paprika f
papyrus [pəˈpaɪrəs] n, pl -ruses or -ri [-ri, -ˌraɪ] : papiro m
par ['pɑr] n 1 VALUE : valor m (nominal), par f ⟨below par : debajo de la par⟩ 2 EQUALITY : igualdad f ⟨to be on a par with : estar al mismo nivel que⟩ 3 : par m (en golf)
parable ['pærəbəl] n : parábola f
parabola [pəˈræbələ] n : parábola f (en matemáticas)
parachute¹ ['pærəˌʃuːt] vi -chuted; -chuting : lanzarse en paracaídas
parachute² n : paracaídas m
parachutist ['pærəˌʃuːtɪst] n : paracaidista mf
parade¹ [pəˈreɪd] vi -raded; -rading 1 MARCH : desfilar 2 SHOW OFF : pavonearse, lucirse
parade² n 1 PROCESSION : desfile m 2 DISPLAY : alarde m
paradigm ['pærəˌdaɪm] n : paradigma m
paradise ['pærəˌdaɪs, -ˌdaɪz] n : paraíso m
paradox ['pærəˌdɑks] n : paradoja f
paradoxical [ˌpærəˈdɑksɪkəl] adj : paradójico — paradoxically adv
paraffin ['pærəfən] n : parafina f
paragon ['pærəˌɡɑn, -ɡən] n : dechado m
paragraph¹ ['pærəˌɡræf] vt : dividir en párrafos
paragraph² n : párrafo m, acápite m
Paraguayan [ˌpærəˈɡwaɪən, -ˈɡweɪ-] n : paraguayo m, -ya f — Paraguayan adj
parakeet ['pærəˌkiːt] n : periquito m
paralegal [ˌpærəˈliːɡəl] n : asistente mf de abogado
parallel¹ ['pærəˌlɛl, -ləl] vt 1 MATCH, RESEMBLE : ser paralelo a, ser análogo a, corresponder con 2 : extenderse en línea paralela con ⟨the road parallels the river : el camino se extiende a lo largo del río⟩
parallel² adj : paralelo
parallel³ n 1 : línea f paralela, superficie f paralela 2 : paralelo m (en geografía) 3 SIMILARITY : paralelismo m, semejanza f
parallelogram [ˌpærəˈlɛləˌɡræm] n : paralelogramo m
paralysis [pəˈræləsɪs] n, pl -yses [-ˌsiːz] : parálisis f
paralyze ['pærəˌlaɪz] vt -lyzed; -lyzing : paralizar
parameter [pəˈræmətər] n : parámetro m
paramount ['pærəˌmaʊnt] adj : supremo ⟨of paramount importance : de suma importancia⟩
paranoia [ˌpærəˈnɔɪə] n : paranoia f

paranoid ['pærəˌnɔɪd] adj : paranoico
parapet ['pærəpət, -ˌpɛt] n : parapeto m
paraphernalia [ˌpærəfəˈneɪljə, -fər-] ns & pl : parafernalia f
paraphrase¹ ['pærəˌfreɪz] vt -phrased; -phrasing : parafrasear
paraphrase² n : paráfrasis f
paraplegic¹ [ˌpærəˈpliːdʒɪk] adj : parapléjico
paraplegic² n : parapléjico m, -ca f
parasite ['pærəˌsaɪt] n : parásito m
parasitic [ˌpærəˈsɪtɪk] adj : parasitario
parasol ['pærəˌsɔl] n : sombrilla f, quitasol m, parasol m
paratrooper ['pærəˌtruːpər] n : paracaidista mf (militar)
parboil ['pɑrˌbɔɪl] vt : sancochar, cocer a medias
parcel¹ ['pɑrsəl] vt -celed or -celled; -celing or -celling or to parcel out : repartir, parcelar (tierras)
parcel² n 1 LOT : parcela f, lote m 2 PACKAGE : paquete m, bulto m
parch ['pɑrtʃ] vt : resecar
parchment ['pɑrtʃmənt] n : pergamino m
pardon¹ ['pɑrdən] vt 1 FORGIVE : perdonar, disculpar ⟨pardon me! : ¡perdone!, ¡disculpe la molestia!⟩ 2 REPRIEVE : indultar (a un delincuente)
pardon² n 1 FORGIVENESS : perdón m 2 REPRIEVE : indulto m
pardonable ['pɑrdənəbəl] adj : perdonable, disculpable
pare ['pær] vt pared; paring 1 PEEL : pelar 2 TRIM : recortar 3 REDUCE : reducir ⟨he pared it (down) to 50 pages : lo redujo a 50 páginas⟩
parent ['pærənt] n 1 : madre f, padre m 2 parents npl : padres mpl
parentage ['pærəntɪdʒ] n : linaje m, abolengo m, origen m
parental [pəˈrɛntəl] adj : de los padres
parenthesis [pəˈrɛnθəsɪs] n, pl -theses [-ˌsiːz] : paréntesis m
parenthetic [ˌpærənˈθɛtɪk] or parenthetical [-tɪkəl] adj : parentético — parenthetically [-tɪkli] adv
parenthood ['pærəntˌhʊd] n : paternidad f
parfait [pɑrˈfeɪ] n : postre m elaborado con frutas y helado
pariah [pəˈraɪə] n : paria mf
parish ['pærɪʃ] n : parroquia f
parishioner [pəˈrɪʃənər] n : feligrés m, -gresa f
parity ['pærəti] n, pl -ties : paridad f
park¹ ['pɑrk] vt : estacionar, parquear, aparcar Spain — vi : estacionarse, parquearse, aparcar Spain
park² n : parque m
parka ['pɑrkə] n : parka f
parking ['pɑrkɪŋ] n : estacionamiento m, aparcamiento m Spain
parkway ['pɑrkˌweɪ] n : carretera f ajardinada, bulevar m
parley¹ ['pɑrli] vi : parlamentar, negociar

parley² *n, pl* **-leys** : negociación *f*, parlamento *m*

parliament ['pɑrləmənt, 'pɑrljə-] *n* : parlamento *m*

parliamentary [ˌpɑrlə'mɛntəri, ˌpɑrljə-] *adj* : parlamentario

parlor ['pɑrlər] *n* **1** : sala *f*, salón *m* (en una casa) **2** : salón *m* ⟨beauty parlor : salón de belleza⟩ **3 funeral parlor** : funeraria *f*

parochial [pə'ro:kiəl] *adj* **1** : parroquial **2** PROVINCIAL : pueblerino, de miras estrechas

parody¹ ['pærədi] *vt* **-died; -dying** : parodiar

parody² *n, pl* **-dies** : parodia *f*

parole [pə'ro:l] *n* : libertad *f* condicional

paroxysm ['pærək,sizəm, pə'rɑk-] *n* : paroxismo *m*

parquet ['pɑr,keɪ, pɑr'keɪ] *n* : parquet *m*, parqué *m*

parrakeet → **parakeet**

parrot ['pærət] *n* : loro *m*, papagayo *m*

parry¹ ['pæri] *v* **-ried; -rying** *vi* : parar un golpe — *vt* EVADE : esquivar (una pregunta, etc.)

parry² *n, pl* **-ries** : parada *f*

parsimonious [ˌpɑrsə'mo:niəs] *adj* : tacaño, mezquino

parsley ['pɑrsli] *n* : perejil *m*

parsnip ['pɑrsnip] *n* : chirivía *f*

parson ['pɑrsən] *n* : pastor *m*, -tora *f*; clérigo *m*

parsonage ['pɑrsənɪʤ] *n* : rectoría *f*, casa *f* del párroco

part¹ ['pɑrt] *vi* **1** SEPARATE : separarse, despedirse ⟨we should part as friends : debemos separarnos amistosamente⟩ **2** OPEN : abrirse ⟨the curtains parted : las cortinas se abrieron⟩ **3 to part with** : deshacerse de — *vt* **1** SEPARATE : separar **2 to part one's hair** : hacerse la raya, peinarse con raya

part² *n* **1** SECTION, SEGMENT : parte *f*, sección *f* **2** PIECE : pieza *f* (de una máquina, etc.) **3** ROLE : papel *m* **4** : raya *f* (del pelo)

partake [pɑr'teɪk, pər-] *vi* **-took** [-'tʊk]; **-taken** [-'teɪkən;]; **-taking 1 to partake of** CONSUME : comer, beber, tomar **2 to partake in** : participar en (una actividad, etc.)

partial ['pɑrʃəl] *adj* **1** BIASED : parcial, tendencioso **2** INCOMPLETE : parcial, incompleto **3 to be partial to** : ser aficionado a

partiality [ˌpɑrʃi'æləti] *n, pl* **-ties** : parcialidad *f*

partially ['pɑrʃəli] *adv* : parcialmente

participant [pər'tisəpənt, pɑr-] *n* : participante *mf*

participate [pər'tisə,peɪt, pɑr-] *vi* **-pated; -pating** : participar

participation [pər,tisə'peɪʃən, pɑr-] *n* : participación *f*

participle ['pɑrtə,sipəl] *n* : participio *m*

particle ['pɑrtɪkəl] *n* : partícula *f*

particular¹ [pər'tɪkjələr] *adj* **1** SPECIFIC : particular, en particular ⟨this partic-

ular person : esta persona en particular⟩ **2** SPECIAL : particular, especial ⟨with particular emphasis : con un énfasis especial⟩ **3** FUSSY : exigente, maniático ⟨to be very particular : ser muy especial⟩ ⟨I'm not particular : me da igual⟩

particular² *n* **1** DETAIL : detalle *m*, sentido *m* **2 in particular** : en particular, en especial

particularly [pər'tɪkjələrli] *adv* **1** ESPECIALLY : particularmente, especialmente **2** SPECIFICALLY : específicamente, en especial

partisan ['pɑrtəzən, -sən] *n* **1** ADHERENT : partidario *m*, -ria *f* **2** GUERRILLA : partisano *m*, -na *f*; guerrillero *m*, -ra *f*

partition¹ [pər'tɪʃən, pɑr-] *vt* : dividir ⟨to partition off (a room) : dividir (una habitación) con un tabique⟩

partition² *n* **1** DISTRIBUTION : partición *f*, división *f*, reparto *m* **2** DIVIDER : tabique *m*, mampara *f*, biombo *m*

partly ['pɑrtli] *adv* : en parte, parcialmente

partner ['pɑrtnər] *n* **1** COMPANION : compañero *m*, -ra *f* **2** : pareja *f* (en un juego, etc.) ⟨dancing partner : pareja de baile⟩ **3** SPOUSE : cónyuge *mf* **4** *or* **business partner** : socio *m*, -cia *f*; asociado *m*, -da *f*

partnership ['pɑrtnər,ʃɪp] *n* **1** ASSOCIATION : asociación *f*, compañerismo *m* **2** : sociedad *f* (de negociantes) ⟨to form a partnership : asociarse⟩

part of speech : categoría *f* gramatical

partridge ['pɑrtrɪʤ] *n, pl* **-tridge** *or* **-tridges** : perdiz *f*

party ['pɑrti] *n, pl* **-ties 1** : partido *m* (político) **2** PARTICIPANT : parte *f*, participante *mf* **3** GROUP : grupo *m* (de personas) **4** GATHERING : fiesta *f* ⟨to throw a party : dar una fiesta⟩

parvenu ['pɑrvə,nu:, -,nju:] *n* : advenedizo *m*, -za *f*

pass¹ ['pæs] *vi* **1** : pasar, cruzarse ⟨a car passed by : pasó un coche⟩ ⟨we passed in the hallway : nos cruzamos en el pasillo⟩ **2** CEASE : pasarse ⟨the pain passed : se pasó el dolor⟩ **3** ELAPSE : pasar, transcurrir **4** PROCEED : pasar ⟨let me pass : déjame pasar⟩ **5** HAPPEN : pasar, ocurrir **6** : pasar, aprobar (en un examen) **7** RULE : fallar ⟨the jury passed on the case : el jurado falló en el caso⟩ **8** *or* **to pass down** : pasar ⟨the throne passed to his son : el trono pasó a su hijo⟩ **9 to let pass** OVERLOOK : pasar por alto **10 to pass as** : pasar por **11 to pass away** *or* **to pass on** DIE : fallecer, morir — *vt* **1** : pasar por ⟨they passed the house : pasaron por la casa⟩ **2** OVERTAKE : pasar, adelantar **3** SPEND : pasar (tiempo) **4** HAND : pasar ⟨pass me the salt : pásame la sal⟩ **5** : aprobar (un examen, una ley)

pass² *n* **1** CROSSING, GAP : paso *m*, desfiladero *m*, puerto *m* ⟨mountain pass : puerto de montaña⟩ **2** PERMIT : pase *m*, permiso *m* **3** : pase *m* (en deportes) **4** SITUATION : situación *f* (difícil) ⟨things have come to a pretty pass! : ¡hasta dónde hemos llegado!⟩
passable ['pæsəbəl] *adj* **1** ADEQUATE : adecuado, pasable **2** : transitable (dícese de un camino, etc.)
passably ['pæsəbli] *adv* : pasablemente
passage ['pæsɪʤ] *n* **1** PASSING : paso *m* ⟨the passage of time : el paso del tiempo⟩ **2** PASSAGEWAY : pasillo *m* (dentro de un edificio), pasaje *m* (entre edificios) **3** VOYAGE : travesía *f* (por el mar), viaje *m* ⟨to grant safe passage : dar un salvoconducto⟩ **4** SECTION : pasaje *m* (en música o literatura)
passageway ['pæsɪʤˌweɪ] *n* : pasillo *m*, pasadizo *m*, corredor *m*
passbook ['pæsˌbʊk] *n* BANKBOOK : libreta *f* de ahorros
passé [pæ'seɪ] *adj* : pasado de moda
passenger ['pæsənʤər] *n* : pasajero *m*, -ra *f*
passerby [ˌpæsər'baɪ, 'pæsər-] *n, pl* **passersby** : transeúnte *mf*
passing ['pæsɪŋ] *n* DEATH : fallecimiento *m*
passion ['pæʃən] *n* : pasión *f*, ardor *m*
passionate ['pæʃənət] *adj* **1** IRASCIBLE : irascible, iracundo **2** ARDENT : apasionado, ardiente, ferviente, fogoso
passionately ['pæʃənətli] *adv* : apasionadamente, fervientemente, con pasión
passive¹ ['pæsɪv] *adj* : pasivo — **passively** *adv*
passive² *n* : voz *f* pasiva (en gramática)
passivity [pæ'sɪvəti] *n* : pasividad *f*
Passover ['pæsˌoːvər] *n* : Pascua *f* (en el judaísmo)
passport ['pæsˌport] *n* : pasaporte *m*
password ['pæsˌwərd] *n* : contraseña *f*
past¹ ['pæst] *adv* : por delante ⟨he drove past : pasamos en coche⟩
past² *adj* **1** AGO : hace ⟨10 years past : hace 10 años⟩ **2** LAST : último ⟨the past few months : los últimos meses⟩ **3** BYGONE : pasado ⟨in past times : en tiempos pasados⟩ **4** : pasado (en gramática)
past³ *n* : pasado *m*
past⁴ *prep* **1** BY : por, por delante de ⟨he ran past the house : pasó por la casa corriendo⟩ **2** BEYOND : más allá de ⟨just past the corner : un poco más allá de la esquina⟩ ⟨we went past the exit : pasamos la salida⟩ **3** AFTER : después de ⟨past noon : después del mediodía⟩ ⟨half past two : las dos y media⟩
pasta ['pɑstə, 'pæs-] *n* : pasta *f*
paste¹ ['peɪst] *vt* **pasted; pasting** : pegar (con engrudo)
paste² *n* **1** : pasta *f* ⟨tomato paste : pasta de tomate⟩ **2** : engrudo *m* (para pegar)
pasteboard ['peɪstˌbord] *n* : cartón *m*, cartulina *f*

pastel [pæ'stɛl] *n* : pastel *m* — **pastel** *adj*
pasteurization [ˌpæstʃərə'zeɪʃən, ˌpæstjə-] *n* : pasteurización *f*
pasteurize ['pæstʃəˌraɪz, 'pæstjə-] *vt* **-ized; -izing** : pasteurizar
pastime ['pæsˌtaɪm] *n* : pasatiempo *m*
pastor ['pæstər] *n* : pastor *m*, -tora *f*
pastoral ['pæstərəl] *adj* : pastoral
past participle *n* : participio *m* pasado
pastry ['peɪstri] *n, pl* **-ries 1** DOUGH : pasta *f*, masa *f* **2 pastries** *npl* : pasteles *mpl*
pasture¹ ['pæstʃər] *v* **-tured; -turing** *vi* GRAZE : pacer, pastar — *vt* : apacentar, pastar
pasture² *n* : pastizal *m*, potrero *m*, pasto *m*
pasty ['peɪsti] *adj* **pastier; -est 1** : pastoso (en consistencia) **2** PALLID : pálido
pat¹ ['pæt] *vt* **patted; patting** : dar palmaditas a, tocar
pat² *adv* : de memoria ⟨to have down pat : saberse de memoria⟩
pat³ *adj* **1** APT : apto, apropiado **2** GLIB : fácil **3** UNYIELDING : firme ⟨to stand pat : mantenerse firme⟩
pat⁴ *n* **1** TAP : golpecito *m*, palmadita *f* ⟨a pat on the back : una palmadita en la espalda⟩ **2** CARESS : caricia *f* **3** : porción *f* ⟨a pat of butter : una porción de mantequilla⟩
patch¹ ['pætʃ] *vt* **1** MEND, REPAIR : remendar, parchar, ponerle un parche a **2 to patch together** IMPROVISE : confeccionar, improvisar **3 to patch up** : arreglar ⟨they patched things up : hicieron las paces⟩
patch² *n* **1** : parche *m*, remiendo *m* (para la ropa) ⟨eye patch : parche para el ojo⟩ **2** PIECE : mancha *f*, trozo *m* ⟨a patch of sky : un trozo de cielo⟩ **3** PLOT : parcela *f*, terreno *m* ⟨cabbage patch : parcela de repollos⟩
patchwork ['pætʃˌwərk] *n* : labor *f* de retazos
patchy ['pætʃi] *adj* **patchier; -est 1** IRREGULAR : irregular, desigual **2** INCOMPLETE : parcial, incompleto
patent¹ ['pætənt] *vt* : patentar
patent² ['pætənt, 'peɪt-] *adj* **1** OBVIOUS : patente, evidente **2** ['pæt-] PATENTED : patentado
patent³ ['pætənt] *n* : patente *f*
patently ['pætəntli] *adv* : patentemente, evidentemente
paternal [pə'tərnəl] *adj* **1** FATHERLY : paternal **2** : paterno ⟨paternal grandfather : abuelo paterno⟩
paternity [pə'tərnəti] *n* : paternidad *f*
path ['pæθ, 'pɑθ] *n* **1** TRACK, TRAIL : camino *m*, sendero *m*, senda *f* **2** COURSE, ROUTE : recorrido *m*, trayecto *m*, trayectoria *f*
pathetic [pə'θɛtɪk] *adj* : patético — **pathetically** [-tɪkli] *adv*
pathological [ˌpæθə'lɑʤɪkəl] *adj* : patológico

pathologist [pə'θaɪlədʒɪst] *n* : patólogo *m*, -ga *f*

pathology [pə'θaɪlədʒi] *n, pl* **-gies** : patología *f*

pathos ['peɪ,θas, 'pæ-, -,θɔs] *n* : patetismo *m*

pathway ['pæθ,weɪ] *n* : camino *m*, sendero *m*, senda *f*, vereda *f*

patience ['peɪʃəns] *n* : paciencia *f*

patient[1] ['peɪʃənt] *adj* : paciente — **patiently** *adv*

patient[2] *n* : paciente *mf*

patio ['pæti,o:] *n, pl* **-tios** : patio *m*

patriarch ['peɪtri,ark] *n* : patriarca *m*

patriarchy ['peɪtri,arki] *n, pl* **-chies** : patriarcado *m*

patrimony ['pætrə,mo:ni] *n, pl* **-nies** : patrimonio *m*

patriot ['peɪtriət] *n* : patriota *mf*

patriotic [,peɪtri'atɪk] *adj* : patriótico — **patriotically** *adv*

patriotism ['peɪtriə,tɪzəm] *n* : patriotismo *m*

patrol[1] [pə'tro:l] *v* **-trolled; -trolling** : patrullar

patrol[2] *n* : patrulla *f*

patrolman [pə'tro:lmən] *n, pl* **-men** [-mən, -,mɛn] : policía *mf*, guardia *mf*

patron ['peɪtrən] *n* **1** SPONSOR : patrocinador *m*, -dora *f* **2** CUSTOMER : cliente *m*, -ta *f* **3** *or* **patron saint** : patrono *m*, -na *f*

patronage ['peɪtrənɪdʒ, 'pæ-] *n* **1** SPONSORSHIP : patrocinio *m* **2** CLIENTELE : clientela *f* **3** : influencia *f* (política)

patronize ['peɪtrə,naɪz, 'pæ-] *vt* **-ized; -izing** **1** SPONSOR : patrocinar **2** : ser cliente de (un negocio) **3** : tratar con condescendencia

patter[1] ['pætər] *vi* **1** TAP : golpetear, tamborilear (dícese de la lluvia) **2 to patter about** : corretear (con pasos ligeros)

patter[2] *n* **1** TAPPING : golpeteo *m*, tamborileo *m* (de la lluvia), correteo *m* (de pies) **2** CHATTER : palabrería *f*, parloteo *m fam*

pattern[1] ['pætərn] *vt* **1** BASE : basar (en un modelo) **2 to pattern after** : hacer imitación de

pattern[2] *n* **1** MODEL : modelo *m*, patrón *m* (de costura) **2** DESIGN : diseño *m*, dibujo *m*, estampado *m* (de tela) **3** NORM, STANDARD : pauta *f*, norma *f*, patrón *m*

patty ['pæti] *n, pl* **-ties** : porción *f* de carne picada (u otro alimento) en forma de ruedita ⟨a hamburger patty : una hamburguesa⟩

paucity ['pɔsəti] *n* : escasez *f*

paunch ['pɔntʃ] *n* : panza *f*, barriga *f*

pauper ['pɔpər] *n* : pobre *mf*, indigente *mf*

pause[1] ['pɔz] *vi* **paused; pausing** : hacer una pausa, pararse (brevemente)

pause[2] *n* : pausa *f*

pave ['peɪv] *vt* **paved; paving** : pavimentar ⟨to pave with stones : empedrar⟩

pavement ['peɪvmənt] *n* : pavimento *m*, empedrado *m*

pavilion [pə'vɪljən] *n* : pabellón *m*

paving ['peɪvɪŋ] → **pavement**

paw[1] ['pɔ] *vt* : tocar, manosear, sobar

paw[2] *n* : pata *f*, garra *f*, zarpa *f*

pawn[1] ['pɔn] *vt* : empeñar, prendar

pawn[2] *n* **1** PLEDGE, SECURITY : prenda *f* **2** PAWNING : empeño *m* **3** : peón *m* (en ajedrez)

pawnbroker ['pɔn,bro:kər] *n* : prestamista *mf*

pawnshop ['pɔn,ʃap] *n* : casa *f* de empeños, monte *m* de piedad

pay[1] ['peɪ] *v* **paid** ['peɪd]; **paying** *vt* **1** : pagar (una cuenta, a un empleado, etc.) **2 to pay attention** : poner atención, prestar atención, hacer caso **3 to pay back** : pagar, devolver ⟨she paid them back : les devolvió el dinero⟩ ⟨I'll pay you back for what you did! : ¡me las pagarás!⟩ **4 to pay off** SETTLE : saldar, cancelar (una deuda, etc.) **5 to pay one's respects** : presentar uno sus respetos **6 to pay a visit** : hacer una visita — *vi* : valer la pena ⟨crime doesn't pay : no hay crimen sin castigo⟩

pay[2] *n* : paga *f*

payable ['peɪəbəl] *adj* DUE : pagadero *m*

paycheck ['peɪ,tʃɛk] *n* : sueldo *m*, cheque *m* del sueldo

payee [peɪ'i:] *n* : beneficiario *m*, -ria *f* (de un cheque, etc.)

payment ['peɪmənt] *n* **1** : pago *m* **2** INSTALLMENT : plazo *m*, cuota *f* **3** REWARD : recompensa *f*

payoff ['peɪ,ɔf] *n* **1** REWARD : recompensa *f* **2** PROFIT : ganancia *f* **3** BRIBE : soborno *m*

payroll ['peɪ,ro:l] *n* : nómina *f*

PC [,pi:'si:] *n, pl* **PCs** *or* **PC's** : PC *mf*, computadora *f* personal

pea ['pi:] *n* : chícharo *m*, guisante *m*, arveja *f*

peace ['pi:s] *n* **1** : paz *f* ⟨peace treaty : tratado de paz⟩ ⟨peace and tranquility : paz y tranquilidad⟩ **2** ORDER : orden *m* (público)

peaceable ['pi:səbəl] *adj* : pacífico — **peaceably** [-bli] *adv*

peaceful ['pi:sfəl] *adj* **1** PEACEABLE : pacífico **2** CALM, QUIET : tranquilo, sosegado — **peacefully** *adv*

peacemaker ['pi:s,meɪkər] *n* : conciliador *m*, -dora *f*; mediador *m*, -dora *f*

peach ['pi:tʃ] *n* : durazno *m*, melocotón *m*

peacock ['pi:,kak] *n* : pavo *m* real

peak[1] ['pi:k] *vi* : alcanzar su nivel máximo

peak[2] *adj* : máximo

peak[3] *n* **1** POINT : punta *f* **2** CREST, SUMMIT : cima *f*, cumbre *f* **3** APEX : cúspide *f*, apogeo *m*, nivel *m* máximo

peaked ['pi:kəd] *adj* SICKLY : pálido

peal[1] ['pi:l] *vi* : repicar

peal[2] *n* : repique *m*, tañido *m* (de campanada) ⟨peals of laughter : carcajadas⟩

peanut ['piː,nʌt] *n* : maní *m*, cacahuate *m Mex*, cacahuete *m Spain*

pear ['pær] *n* : pera *f*

pearl ['pərl] *n* : perla *f*

pearly ['pərli] *adj* **pearlier; -est** : nacarado

peasant ['pɛzənt] *n* : campesino *m*, -na *f*

peat ['piːt] *n* : turba *f*

pebble ['pɛbəl] *n* : guijarro *m*, piedrecita *f*, piedrita *f*

pecan [pɪ'kɑn, -'kæn, 'piː,kæn] *n* : pacana *f*, nuez *f Mex*

peccadillo [,pɛkə'dɪlo] *n, pl* **-loes** *or* **-los** : pecadillo *m*

peccary ['pɛkəri] *n, pl* **-ries** : pécari *m*, pecarí *m*

peck[1] ['pɛk] *vt* : picar, picotear

peck[2] *n* **1** : medida *f* de áridos equivalente a 8.810 litros **2** : picotazo *m* (de un pájaro) ⟨a peck on the cheek : un besito en la mejilla⟩

pectoral ['pɛktərəl] *adj* : pectoral

peculiar [pɪ'kjuːljər] *adj* **1** DISTINCTIVE : propio, peculiar, característico ⟨peculiar to this area : propio de esta zona⟩ **2** STRANGE : extraño, raro — **peculiarly** *adv*

peculiarity [pɪ,kjuːlı'jærəti, -,kjuːli'ær-] *n, pl* **-ties 1** DISTINCTIVENESS : peculiaridad *f* **2** ODDITY, QUIRK : rareza *f*, idiosincrasia *f*, excentricidad *f*

pecuniary [pɪ'kjuːni,ɛri] *adj* : pecuniario

pedagogical [,pɛdə'gɑʤɪkəl, -'goː-] *adj* : pedagógico

pedagogy ['pɛdə,goːʤi, -,gɑ-] *n* : pedagogía *f*

pedal[1] ['pɛdəl] *v* **-aled** *or* **-alled; -aling** *or* **-alling** *vi* : pedalear — *vt* : darle a los pedales de

pedal[2] *n* : pedal *m*

pedant ['pɛdənt] *n* : pedante *mf*

pedantic [pɪ'dæntɪk] *adj* : pedante

pedantry ['pɛdəntri] *n, pl* **-ries** : pedantería *f*

peddle ['pɛdəl] *vt* **-dled; -dling** : vender (en las calles)

peddler ['pɛdlər] *n* : vendedor *m*, -dora *f* ambulante; mercachifle *m*

pedestal ['pɛdəstəl] *n* : pedestal *m*

pedestrian[1] [pə'dɛstriən] *adj* **1** COMMONPLACE : pedestre, ordinario **2** : de peatón, peatonal ⟨pedestrian crossing : paso de peatones⟩

pedestrian[2] *n* : peatón *m*, -tona *f*

pediatric [,piːdi'ætrɪk] *adj* : pediátrico

pediatrician [,piːdiə'trɪʃən] *n* : pediatra *mf*

pediatrics [,piːdi'ætrɪks] *ns & pl* : pediatría *f*

pedigree ['pɛdə,griː] *n* **1** FAMILY TREE : árbol *m* genealógico **2** LINEAGE : pedigrí *m* (de un animal), linaje *m* (de una persona)

peek[1] ['piːk] *vi* **1** PEEP : espiar, mirar furtivamente **2** GLANCE : echar un vistazo

peek[2] *n* **1** : miradita *f* (furtiva) **2** GLANCE : vistazo *m*, ojeada *f*

peel[1] ['piːl] *vt* **1** : pelar (fruta, etc.) **2** *or* **to peel away** : quitar — *vi* : pelarse (dícese de la piel), desconcharse (dícese de la pintura)

peel[2] *n* : cáscara *f*

peep[1] ['piːp] *vi* **1** PEEK : espiar, mirar furtivamente **2** CHEEP : piar **3** **to peep out** SHOW : asomarse

peep[2] *n* **1** CHEEP : pío *m* (de un pajarito) **2** GLANCE : vistazo *m*, ojeada *f*

peer[1] ['pɪr] *vi* : mirar detenidamente, mirar con atención

peer[2] *n* **1** : par *m*, igual *mf* **2** NOBLE : noble *mf*

peerage ['pɪrɪʤ] *n* : nobleza *f*

peerless ['pɪrləs] *adj* : sin par, incomparable

peeve[1] ['piːv] *vt* **peeved; peeving** : fastidiar, irritar, molestar

peeve[2] *n* : queja *f*

peevish ['piːvɪʃ] *adj* : quejoso, fastidioso — **peevishly** *adv*

peevishness ['piːvɪʃnəs] *n* : irritabilidad *f*

peg[1] ['pɛg] *vt* **pegged; pegging 1** PLUG : tapar (con una clavija) **2** FASTEN, FIX : sujetar (con estaquillas) **3** **to peg out** MARK : marcar (con estaquillas)

peg[2] *n* : estaquilla *f* (para clavar), clavija *f* (para tapar)

pejorative [pɪ'ʤɔrətɪv] *adj* : peyorativo — **pejoratively** *adv*

pelican ['pɛlɪkən] *n* : pelícano *m*

pellagra [pə'lægrə, -'leɪ-] *n* : pelagra *f*

pellet ['pɛlət] *n* **1** BALL : bolita *f* ⟨food pellet : bolita de comida⟩ **2** SHOT : perdigón *m*

pell-mell [pɛl'mɛl] *adv* : desordenadamente, atropelladamente

pelt[1] ['pɛlt] *vt* **1** THROW : lanzar, tirar (algo a alguien) **2** **to pelt with stones** : apedrear — *vi* BEAT : golpear con fuerza ⟨the rain was pelting down : llovía a cántaros⟩

pelt[2] *n* : piel *f*, pellejo *m*

pelvic ['pɛlvɪk] *adj* : pélvico

pelvis ['pɛlvɪs] *n, pl* **-vises** *or* **-ves** ['pɛl,viːz] : pelvis *f*

pen[1] ['pɛn] *vt* **penned; penning 1** *or* **pen in** : encerrar (animales) **2** WRITE : escribir

pen[2] *n* **1** CORRAL : corral *m*, redil *m* (para ovejas) **2** : pluma *f* ⟨fountain pen : pluma fuente⟩ ⟨ballpoint pen : bolígrafo⟩

penal ['piːnəl] *adj* : penal

penalize ['piːnəl,aɪz, 'pɛn-] *vt* **-ized; -izing** : penalizar, sancionar, penar

penalty ['pɛnəlti] *n, pl* **-ties 1** PUNISHMENT : pena *f*, castigo *m* **2** DISADVANTAGE : desventaja *f*, castigo *m*, penalty *m* (en deportes) **3** FINE : multa *f*

penance ['pɛnənts] *n* : penitencia *f*

pence → **penny**

penchant ['pɛntʃənt] *n* : inclinación *f*, afición *f*

pencil¹ [ˈpɛntsəl] *vt* **-ciled** *or* **-cilled; -ciling** *or* **-cilling** : escribir con lápiz, dibujar con lápiz
pencil² *n* : lápiz *m*
pendant [ˈpɛndənt] *n* : colgante *m*
pending¹ [ˈpɛndɪŋ] *adj* : pendiente
pending² *prep* **1** DURING : durante **2** AWAITING : en espera de
pendulum [ˈpɛndʒələm, -djʊləm] *n* : péndulo *m*
penetrate [ˈpɛnəˌtreɪt] *vt* **-trated; -trating** : penetrar
penetrating [ˈpɛnəˌtreɪtɪŋ] *adj* : penetrante, cortante
penetration [ˌpɛnəˈtreɪʃən] *n* : penetración *f*
penguin [ˈpɛŋgwɪn, ˈpɛn-] *n* : pingüino *m*
penicillin [ˌpɛnəˈsɪlən] *n* : penicilina *f*
peninsula [pəˈnɪntsələ, -ˈnɪntʃʊlə] *n* : península *f*
penis [ˈpiːnəs] *n*, *pl* **-nes** [-ˌniːz] *or* **-nises** : pene *m*
penitence [ˈpɛnətənts] *n* : arrepentimiento *m*, penitencia *f*
penitent¹ [ˈpɛnətənt] *adj* : arrepentido, penitente
penitent² *n* : penitente *mf*
penitentiary [ˌpɛnəˈtentʃəri] *n*, *pl* **-ries** : penitenciaría *f*, prisión *m*, presidio *m*
penmanship [ˈpɛnmənˌʃɪp] *n* : escritura *f*, caligrafía *f*
pen name *n* : seudónimo *m*
pennant [ˈpɛnənt] *n* : gallardete *m* (de un barco), banderín *m*
penniless [ˈpɛniləs] *adj* : sin un centavo
penny [ˈpɛni] *n*, *pl* **-nies** *or* **pence** [ˈpɛnts] **1** : penique *m* (del Reino Unido) **2** *pl* **-nies** CENT : centavo *m* (de los Estados Unidos)
pension¹ [ˈpɛnʃən] *vt or* **to pension off** : jubilar
pension² *n* : pensión *m*, jubilación *f*
pensive [ˈpɛntsɪv] *adj* : pensativo, meditabundo — **pensively** *adv*
pent [ˈpɛnt] *adj* : encerrado ⟨pent-up feelings : emociones reprimidas⟩
pentagon [ˈpɛntəˌgɑn] *n* : pentágono *m*
pentagonal [pɛnˈtægənəl] *adj* : pentagonal
penthouse [ˈpɛntˌhaʊs] *n* : ático *m*, penthouse *m*
penultimate [pɪˈnʌltəmət] *adj* : penúltimo
penury [ˈpɛnjəri] *n* : penuria *f*, miseria *f*
peon [ˈpiːˌɑn, -ən] *n*, *pl* **-ons** *or* **-ones** [peɪˈoːniːz] : peón *m*
peony [ˈpiːəni] *n*, *pl* **-nies** : peonía *f*
people¹ [ˈpiːpəl] *vt* **-pled; -pling** : poblar
people² *ns & pl* **1** people *npl* : gente *f*, personas *fpl* ⟨people like him : él le cae bien a la gente⟩ ⟨many people : mucha gente, muchas personas⟩ **2** *pl* **peoples** : pueblo *m* ⟨the Cuban people : el pueblo cubano⟩
pep¹ [ˈpɛp] *vt* **pepped; pepping** *or* **to pep up** : animar
pep² *n* : energía *f*, vigor *m*

pepper¹ [ˈpɛpər] *vt* **1** : añadir pimienta a **2** RIDDLE : acribillar (a balazos) **3** SPRINKLE : salpicar ⟨peppered with quotations : salpicado de citas⟩
pepper² *n* **1** : pimienta *f* (condimento) **2** : pimiento *m*, pimentón *m* (fruta) **3** → chili
peppermint [ˈpɛpərˌmɪnt] *n* : menta *f*
peppery [ˈpɛpəri] *adj* : picante
peppy [ˈpɛpi] *adj* **peppier; -est** : lleno de energía, vivaz
peptic [ˈpɛptɪk] *adj* **peptic ulcer** : úlcera *f* estomacal
per [ˈpər] *prep* **1** : por ⟨miles per hour : millas por hora⟩ **2** ACCORDING TO : según ⟨per his specifications : según sus especificaciones⟩
per annum [pərˈænəm] *adv* : al año, por año
percale [ˌpərˈkeɪl, ˈpər-; ˌpərˈkæl] *n* : percal *m*
per capita [pərˈkæpɪtə] *adv & adj* : per cápita
perceive [pərˈsiːv] *vt* **-ceived; -ceiving 1** REALIZE : percatarse de, concientizarse de, darse cuenta de **2** NOTE : percibir, notar
percent¹ [pərˈsɛnt] *adv* : por ciento
percent² *n*, *pl* **-cent** *or* **-cents 1** : por ciento ⟨10 percent of the population : el 10 por ciento de la población⟩ **2** → **percentage**
percentage [pərˈsɛntɪʤ] *n* : porcentaje *m*
perceptible [pərˈsɛptəbəl] *adj* : perceptible — **perceptibly** [-bli] *adv*
perception [pərˈsɛpʃən] *n* **1** : percepción *f* ⟨color perception : la percepción de los colores⟩ **2** INSIGHT : perspicacia *f* **3** IDEA : idea *f*, imagen *f*
perceptive [pərˈsɛptɪv] *adj* : perspicaz
perceptively [pərˈsɛptɪvli] *adv* : con perspicacia
perch¹ [ˈpərʧ] *vi* **1** ROOST : posarse **2** SIT : sentarse (en un sitio elevado) — *vt* PLACE : posar, colocar
perch² *n* **1** ROOST : percha *f* (para los pájaros) **2** *pl* **perch** *or* **perches** : perca *f* (pez)
percolate [ˈpərkəˌleɪt] *vi* **-lated; -lating** : colarse, filtrarse ⟨percolated coffee : café filtrado⟩
percolator [ˈpərkəˌleɪtər] *n* : cafetera *f* de filtro
percussion [pərˈkʌʃən] *n* **1** STRIKING : percusión *f* **2** *or* **percussion instruments** : instrumentos *mpl* de percusión
peremptory [pəˈrɛmptəri] *adj* : perentorio
perennial¹ [pəˈrɛniəl] *adj* **1** : perenne, vivaz ⟨perennial flowers : flores perennes⟩ **2** RECURRENT : perenne, continuo ⟨a perennial problem : un problema eterno⟩
perennial² *n* : planta *f* perenne, planta *f* vivaz
perfect¹ [pərˈfɛkt] *vt* : perfeccionar

perfect² [ˈpərfɪkt] *adj* : perfecto — **perfectly** *adv*
perfection [pərˈfɛkʃən] *n* : perfección *f*
perfectionist [pərˈfɛkʃənɪst] *n* : perfeccionista *mf*
perfidious [pərˈfɪdiəs] *adj* : pérfido
perforate [ˈpərfəˌreɪt] *vt* **-rated; -rating** : perforar
perforation [ˌpərfəˈreɪʃən] *n* : perforación *f*
perform [pərˈfɔrm] *vt* **1** CARRY OUT : realizar, hacer, desempeñar **2** PRESENT : representar, dar (una obra teatral, etc.) — *vi* : actuar (en una obra teatral), cantar (en una ópera, etc.), tocar (en un concierto, etc.), bailar (en un ballet, etc.)
performance [pərˈfɔrmənts] *n* **1** EXECUTION : ejecución *f*, realización *f*, desempeño *m*, rendimiento *m* **2** INTERPRETATION : interpretación *f* ⟨his performance of Hamlet : su interpretación de Hamlet⟩ **3** PRESENTATION : representación *f* (de una obra teatral), función *f*
performer [pərˈfɔrmər] *n* : artista *mf*; actor *m*, -triz *f*; intérprete *mf* (de música)
perfume¹ [pərˈfjuːm, ˈpərˌ-] *vt* **-fumed; -fuming** : perfumar
perfume² [ˈpərˌfjuːm, pərˈ-] *n* : perfume *m*
perfunctory [pərˈfʌŋktəri] *adj* : mecánico, superficial, somero
perhaps [pərˈhæps] *adv* : tal vez, quizá, quizás
peril [ˈpɛrəl] *n* : peligro *m*
perilous [ˈpɛrələs] *adj* : peligroso — **perilously** *adv*
perimeter [pəˈrɪmətər] *n* : perímetro *m*
period [ˈpɪriəd] *n* **1** : punto *m* (en puntuación) **2** : período *m* ⟨a two-hour period : un período de dos horas⟩ **3** STAGE : época *f* (histórica), fase *f*, etapa *f*
periodic [ˌpɪriˈɑdɪk] *or* **periodical** [-dɪkəl] *adj* : periódico — **periodically** [-dɪkli] *adv*
periodical [ˌpɪriˈɑdɪkəl] *n* : publicación *f* periódica, revista *f*
peripheral [pəˈrɪfərəl] *adj* : periférico
periphery [pəˈrɪfəri] *n, pl* **-eries** : periferia *f*
periscope [ˈpɛrəˌskoːp] *n* : periscopio *m*
perish [ˈpɛrɪʃ] *vi* DIE : perecer, morirse
perishable¹ [ˈpɛrɪʃəbəl] *adj* : perecedero
perishable² *n* : producto *m* perecedero
perjure [ˈpərdʒər] *vt* **-jured; -juring** (*used in law*) **to perjure oneself** : perjurar, perjurarse
perjury [ˈpərdʒəri] *n* : perjurio *m*
perk¹ [ˈpərk] *vt* **1** : levantar (las orejas, etc.) **2** *or* **to perk up** FRESHEN : arreglar — *vi* **to perk up** : animarse, reanimarse
perk² *n* : extra *m*
perky [ˈpərki] *adj* **perkier; -est** : animado, alegre, lleno de vida
permanence [ˈpərmənənts] *n* : permanencia *f*

permanent¹ [ˈpərmənənt] *adj* : permanente — **permanently** *adv*
permanent² *n* : permanente *f*
permeability [ˌpərmiəˈbɪləti] *n* : permeabilidad *f*
permeable [ˈpərmiəbəl] *adj* : permeable
permeate [ˈpərmiˌeɪt] *v* **-ated; -ating** *vt* **1** PENETRATE : penetrar, impregnar **2** PERVADE : penetrar, difundirse por — *vi* : penetrar
permissible [pərˈmɪsəbəl] *adj* : permisible, lícito
permission [pərˈmɪʃən] *n* : permiso *m*
permissive [pərˈmɪsɪv] *adj* : permisivo
permit¹ [pərˈmɪt] *vt* **-mitted; -mitting** : permitir, dejar ⟨weather permitting : si el tiempo lo permite⟩
permit² [ˈpərˌmɪt, pərˈ-] *n* : permiso *m*, licencia *f*
pernicious [pərˈnɪʃəs] *adj* : pernicioso
peroxide [pəˈrɑkˌsaɪd] *n* **1** : peróxido *m* **2** → **hydrogen peroxide**
perpendicular¹ [ˌpərpənˈdɪkjələr] *adj* **1** VERTICAL : vertical **2** : perpendicular ⟨perpendicular lines : líneas perpendiculares⟩ — **perpendicularly** *adv*
perpendicular² *n* : perpendicular *f*
perpetrate [ˈpərpəˌtreɪt] *vt* **-trated; -trating** : perpetrar, cometer (un delito)
perpetrator [ˈpərpəˌtreɪtər] *n* : autor *m*, -tora *f* (de un delito)
perpetual [pərˈpɛtʃuəl] *adj* **1** EVERLASTING : perpetuo, eterno **2** CONTINUAL : perpetuo, continuo, constante
perpetually [pərˈpɛtʃuəli, -tʃəli] *adv* : para siempre, eternamente
perpetuate [pərˈpɛtʃuˌeɪt] *vt* **-ated; -ating** : perpetuar
perpetuity [ˌpərpəˈtuːəti, -ˈtjuː-] *n, pl* **-ties** : perpetuidad *f*
perplex [pərˈplɛks] *vt* : dejar perplejo, confundir
perplexed [pərˈplɛkst] *adj* : perplejo
perplexity [pərˈplɛksəti] *n, pl* **-ties** : perplejidad *f*, confusión *f*
persecute [ˈpərsɪˌkjuːt] *vt* **-cuted; -cuting** : perseguir
persecution [ˌpərsɪˈkjuːʃən] *n* : persecución *f*
perseverance [ˌpərsəˈvɪrənts] *n* : perseverancia *f*
persevere [ˌpərsəˈvɪr] *vi* **-vered; -vering** : perseverar
Persian [ˈpərʒən] *n* **1** : persa *mf* **2** : persa *m* (idioma) — **Persian** *adj*
persist [pərˈsɪst] *vi* : persistir
persistence [pərˈsɪstənts] *n* **1** CONTINUATION : persistencia *f* **2** TENACITY : perseverancia *f*, tenacidad *f*
persistent [pərˈsɪstənt] *adj* : persistente — **persistently** *adv*
person [ˈpərsən] *n* **1** HUMAN, INDIVIDUAL : persona *f*, individuo *m*, ser *m* humano **2** : persona *f* (en gramática) **3 in person** : en persona
personable [ˈpərsənəbəl] *adj* : agradable

personage ['pərsənɪdʒ] *n* : personaje *m*
personal ['pərsənəl] *adj* **1** OWN, PRI-
VATE : personal, particular, privado
⟨for personal reasons : por razones per-
sonales⟩ **2** : en persona ⟨to make a personal appearance : presentarse en persona, hacerse acto de presencia⟩ **3**
: íntimo, personal ⟨personal hygiene
: higiene personal⟩ **4** INDISCREET,
PRYING : indiscreto, personal
personal computer *n* : computadora *f*
personal, ordenador *m* personal *Spain*
personal digital assistant *n* : asistente
m personal digital
personality [ˌpərsən'æləti] *n, pl* **-ties 1**
DISPOSITION : personalidad *f*, temperamento *m* **2** CELEBRITY : personalidad *f*, personaje *m*, celebridad *f*
personalize ['pərsənəˌlaɪz] *vt* **-ized;**
-izing : personalizar
personally ['pərsənəli] *adv* **1** : personalmente, en persona ⟨I'll do it personally : lo haré personalmente⟩ **2**
: como persona ⟨personally she's very
amiable : como persona es muy am-
able⟩ **3** : personalmente ⟨personally, I
don't believe it : yo, personalmente, no
me lo creo⟩
personification [pərˌsɑnəfə'keɪʃən] *n*
: personificación *f*
personify [pər'sɑnəˌfaɪ] *vt* **-fied; -fying**
: personificar
personnel [ˌpərsən'ɛl] *n* : personal *m*
perspective [pər'spɛktɪv] *n* : perspectiva *f*
perspicacious [ˌpərspə'keɪʃəs] *adj* : perspicaz
perspiration [ˌpərspə'reɪʃən] *n* : transpiración *f*, sudor *m*
perspire [pər'spaɪr] *vi* **-spired; -spiring**
: transpirar, sudar
persuade [pər'sweɪd] *vt* **-suaded; -suad-**
ing : persuadir, convencer
persuasion [pər'sweɪʒən] *n* : persuasión
f
persuasive [pər'sweɪsɪv, -zɪv] *adj* : persuasivo — **persuasively** *adv*
persuasiveness [pər'sweɪsɪvnəs, -zɪv-] *n*
: persuasión *f*
pert ['pərt] *adj* **1** SAUCY : descarado, impertinente **2** JAUNTY : alegre, animado ⟨a pert little hat : un sombrero co-
queto⟩
pertain [pər'teɪn] *vi* **1** BELONG
: pertenecer (a) **2** RELATE : estar relacionado (con)
pertinence ['pərtənənts] *n* : pertinencia
f
pertinent ['pərtənənt] *adj* : pertinente
perturb [pər'tərb] *vt* : perturbar
perusal [pə'ru:zəl] *n* : lectura *f* cuida-
dosa
peruse [pə'ru:z] *vt* **-rused; -rusing 1**
READ : leer con cuidado **2** SCAN
: recorrer con la vista ⟨he perused the
newspaper : echó un vistazo al peri-
ódico⟩

Peruvian [pə'ru:viən] *n* : peruano *m*, -na
f — **Peruvian** *adj*
pervade [pər'veɪd] *vt* **-vaded; -vading**
: penetrar, difundirse por
pervasive [pər'veɪsɪv, -zɪv] *adj* : penetrante
perverse [pər'vərs] *adj* **1** CORRUPT
: perverso, corrompido **2** STUBBORN
: obstinado, porfiado, terco (sin razón)
— **perversely** *adv*
perversion [pər'vərʒən] *n* : perversión *f*
perversity [pər'vərsəti] *n, pl* **-ties 1** COR-
RUPTION : corrupción *f* **2** STUBBORN-
NESS : obstinación *f*, terquedad *f*
pervert[1] [pər'vərt] *vt* **1** DISTORT : pervertir, distorsionar **2** CORRUPT : pervertir, corromper
pervert[2] ['pərˌvərt] *n* : pervertido *m*, -da
f
pesky ['pɛski] *adj* : molestoso, molesto
peso ['peɪˌso:] *n, pl* **-sos** : peso *m*
pessimism ['pɛsəˌmɪzəm] *n* : pesimismo
m
pessimist ['pɛsəmɪst] *n* : pesimista *mf*
pessimistic [ˌpɛsə'mɪstɪk] *adj* : pesimista
pest ['pɛst] *n* **1** NUISANCE : peste *f*;
latoso *m*, -sa *f fam* ⟨to be a pest : dar
(la) lata⟩ **2** : insecto *m* nocivo, animal
m nocivo ⟨the squirrels were pests : las
ardillas eran una plaga⟩
pester ['pɛstər] *vt* **-tered; -tering** : molestar, fastidiar
pesticide ['pɛstəˌsaɪd] *n* : pesticida *m*
pestilence ['pɛstələnts] *n* : pestilencia *f*,
peste *f*
pestle ['pɛsəl, 'pɛstəl] *n* : mano *f* de
mortero, mazo *m*, maja *f*
pet[1] ['pɛt] *vt* **petted; petting** : acariciar
pet[2] *n* **1** : animal *m* doméstico **2** FA-
VORITE : favorito *m*, -ta *f*
petal ['pɛtəl] *n* : pétalo *m*
petite [pə'ti:t] *adj* : pequeña, menuda,
chiquita
petition[1] [pə'tɪʃən] *vt* : peticionar
petition[2] *n* : petición *f*
petitioner [pə'tɪʃənər] *n* : peticionario
m, -ria *f*
petrify ['pɛtrəˌfaɪ] *vt* **-fied; -fying** : petrificar
petroleum [pə'tro:liəm] *n* : petróleo *m*
petticoat ['pɛtiˌko:t] *n* : enagua *f*, fondo
m Mex
pettiness ['pɛtinəs] *n* **1** INSIGNIFI-
CANCE : insignificancia *f* **2** MEANNESS
: mezquindad *f*
petty ['pɛti] *adj* **-tier; -est 1** MINOR
: menor ⟨petty cash : dinero para gastos menores⟩ **2** INSIGNIFICANT : insignificante, trivial, nimio **3** MEAN
: mezquino
petty officer *n* : suboficial *mf*
petulance ['pɛtʃələnts] *n* : irritabilidad *f*,
mal genio *m*
petulant ['pɛtʃələnt] *adj* : irritable, de
mal genio
petunia [pɪ'tu:njə, -'tju:-] *n* : petunia *f*
pew ['pju:] *n* : banco *m* (de iglesia)

pewter ['pju:t̬ər] *n* : peltre *m*
pH [,pi:'eɪʧ] *n* : pH *m*
phallic ['fælɪk] *adj* : fálico
phallus ['fæləs] *n, pl* **-li** ['fæˌlaɪ] *or* **-luses** : falo *m*
phantasy ['fæntəsi] → **fantasy**
phantom ['fæntəm] *n* : fantasma *m*
pharaoh ['fɛrˌoː, 'feɪˌroː] *n* : faraón *m*
pharmaceutical [,farmə'su:t̬ɪkəl] *adj* : farmacéutico
pharmacist ['farməsɪst] *n* : farmacéutico *m*, -ca *f*
pharmacology [,farmə'kalədʒi] *n* : farmacología *f*
pharmacy ['farməsi] *n, pl* **-cies** : farmacia *f*
pharynx ['færɪŋks] *n, pl* **pharynges** [fə'rɪnˌdʒi:z] : faringe *f*
phase¹ ['feɪz] *vt* **phased; phasing 1** SYNCHRONIZE : sincronizar, poner en fase **2** STAGGER : escalonar **3 to phase in** : introducir progresivamente **4 to phase out** : retirar progresivamente, dejar de producir
phase² *n* **1** : fase *f* (de la luna, etc.) **2** STAGE : fase *f*, etapa *f*
pheasant ['fɛzənt] *n, pl* **-ant** *or* **-ants** : faisán *m*
phenomenal [fɪ'namənəl] *adj* : extraordinario, excepcional
phenomenon [fɪ'naməˌnan, -nən] *n, pl* **-na** [-nə] *or* **-nons 1** : fenómeno *m* **2** *pl* **-nons** PRODIGY : fenómeno *m*, prodigio *m*
philanthropic [,fɪlən'θrapɪk] *adj* : filantrópico
philanthropist [fə'lænt̬θrəpɪst] *n* : filántropo *m*, -pa *f*
philanthropy [fə'lænt̬θrəpi] *n, pl* **-pies** : filantropía *f*
philately [fə'læt̬əli] *n* : filatelia *f*
philodendron [,fɪlə'dɛndrən] *n, pl* **-drons** *or* **-dra** [-drə] : arácea *f*
philosopher [fə'lasəfər] *n* : filósofo *m*, -fa *f*
philosophic [,fɪlə'safɪk] *or* **philosophical** [-fɪkəl] *adj* : filosófico — **philosophically** [-kli] *adv*
philosophize [fə'lasəˌfaɪz] *vi* **-phized; -phizing** : filosofar
philosophy [fə'lasəfi] *n, pl* **-phies** : filosofía *f*
phlebitis [flɪ'baɪt̬əs] *n* : flebitis *f*
phlegm ['flɛm] *n* : flema *f*
phlox ['flaks] *n, pl* **phlox** *or* **phloxes** : polemonio *m*
phobia ['foːbiə] *n* : fobia *f*
phoenix ['fi:nɪks] *n* : fénix *m*
phone¹ ['foːn] *v* → **telephone¹**
phone² *n* → **telephone²**
phoneme ['foːˌni:m] *n* : fonema *m*
phonetic [fə'nɛt̬ɪk] *adj* : fonético
phonetics [fə'nɛt̬ɪks] *n* : fonética *f*
phonics ['fanɪks] *n* : método *m* fonético de aprender a leer
phonograph ['foːnəˌgræf] *n* : fonógrafo *m*, tocadiscos *m*
phony¹ *or* **phoney** ['foːni] *adj* **-nier; -est** : falso

phony² *or* **phoney** *n, pl* **-nies** : farsante *mf*; charlatán *m*, -tana *f*
phosphate ['fasˌfeɪt] *n* : fosfato *m*
phosphorescence [,fasfə'rɛsənts] *n* : fosforescencia *f*
phosphorescent [,fasfə'rɛsənt] *adj* : fosforescente — **phosphorescently** *adv*
phosphorus ['fasfərəs] *n* : fósforo *m*
photo ['foːt̬oː] *n, pl* **-tos** : foto *f*
photocopier ['foːt̬oːˌkapiər] *n* : fotocopiadora *f*
photocopy¹ ['foːt̬oːˌkapi] *vt* **-copied; -copying** : fotocopiar
photocopy² *n, pl* **-copies** : fotocopia *f*
photoelectric [,foːt̬oɪ'lɛktrɪk] *adj* : fotoeléctrico
photogenic [,foːt̬ə'dʒɛnɪk] *adj* : fotogénico
photograph¹ ['foːt̬əˌgræf] *vt* : fotografiar
photograph² *n* : fotografía *f*, foto *f* ⟨to take a photograph of : tomarle una fotografía a, tomar una fotografía de⟩
photographer [fə'tagrəfər] *n* : fotógrafo *m*, -fa *f*
photographic [,foːt̬ə'græfɪk] *adj* : fotográfico — **photographically** [-fɪkli] *adv*
photography [fə'tagrəfi] *n* : fotografía *f*
photosynthesis [,foːt̬o'sɪnt̬θəsɪs] *n* : fotosíntesis *f*
photosynthetic [,foːt̬osɪn'θɛt̬ɪk] *adj* : fotosintético, de fotosíntesis
phrase¹ ['freɪz] *vt* **phrased; phrasing** : expresar
phrase² *n* : frase *f*, locución *f* ⟨to coin a phrase : para decirlo así⟩
phylum ['faɪləm] *n, pl* **-la** [-lə] : phylum *m*
physical¹ ['fɪzɪkəl] *adj* **1** : físico ⟨physical laws : leyes físicas⟩ **2** MATERIAL : material, físico **3** BODILY : físico, corpóreo — **physically** [-kli] *adv*
physical² *n* CHECKUP : chequeo *m*, reconocimiento *m* médico
physician [fə'zɪʃən] *n* : médico *m*, -ca *f*
physicist ['fɪzəsɪst] *n* : físico *m*, -ca *f*
physics ['fɪzɪks] *ns & pl* : física *f*
physiognomy [,fɪzi'agnəmi] *n, pl* **-mies** : fisonomía *f*
physiological ['fɪziə'ladʒɪkəl] *or* **physiologic** [-dʒɪk] *adj* : fisiológico
physiologist [,fɪzi'alədʒɪst] *n* : fisiólogo *m*, -ga *f*
physiology [,fɪzi'alədʒi] *n* : fisiología *f*
physique [fə'zi:k] *n* : físico *m*
pi ['paɪ] *n, pl* **pis** ['paɪz] : pi *f*
pianist [pi'ænɪst, 'pi:ənɪst] *n* : pianista *mf*
piano [pi'ænoː] *n, pl* **-anos** : piano *m*
piazza [pi'æzə, -'atsə] *n, pl* **-zas** *or* **-ze** [-'atˌseɪ] : plaza *f*
picaresque [,pɪkə'rɛsk, ˌpiː-] *adj* : picaresco
picayune [,pɪki'ju:n] *adj* : trivial, nimio, insignificante
piccolo ['pɪkəˌloː] *n, pl* **-los** : flautín *m*
pick¹ ['pɪk] *vt* **1** : picar, labrar (con un pico) ⟨he picked the hard soil : picó la

tierra dura⟩ **2** : quitar, sacar (poco a poco) ⟨to pick meat off the bones : quitar pedazos de carne de los huesos⟩ **3** : recoger, arrancar (frutas, flores, etc.) **4** SELECT : escoger, elegir **5** PROVOKE : provocar ⟨to pick a quarrel : buscar pleito, buscar pelea⟩ **6 to pick a lock** : forzar una cerradura **7 to pick someone's pocket** : robarle algo del bolsillo de alguien ⟨someone picked my pocket! : ¡me robaron la cartera del bolsillo!⟩ — *vi* **1** NIBBLE : picar, picotear **2 to pick and choose** : ser exigente **3 to pick at** : tocar, rascarse (una herida, etc.) **4 to pick on** TEASE : mofarse de, atormentar

pick² *n* **1** CHOICE : selección *f* **2** BEST : lo mejor ⟨the pick of the crop : la crema y nata⟩ **3** → **pickax**

pickax [ˈpɪkˌæks] *n* : pico *m*, zapapico *m*, piqueta *f*

pickerel [ˈpɪkərəl] *n, pl* **-el** *or* **-els** : lucio *m* pequeño

picket¹ [ˈpɪkət] *v* : piquetear

picket² *n* **1** STAKE : estaca *f* **2** STRIKER : huelguista *mf*, integrante *mf* de un piquete

pickle¹ [ˈpɪkəl] *vt* **-led; -ling** : encurtir, escabechar

pickle² *n* **1** BRINE : escabeche *m* **2** GHERKIN : pepinillo *m* (encurtido) **3** JAM, TROUBLE : lío *m*, apuro *m*

pickpocket [ˈpɪkˌpɑkət] *n* : carterista *mf*

pickup [ˈpɪkˌəp] *n* **1** IMPROVEMENT : mejora *f* **2** *or* **pickup truck** : camioneta *f*

pick up *vt* **1** LIFT : levantar **2** TIDY : arreglar, ordenar — *vi* IMPROVE : mejorar

picnic¹ [ˈpɪkˌnɪk] *vi* **-nicked; -nicking** : ir de picnic

picnic² *n* : picnic *m*

pictorial [pɪkˈtoriəl] *adj* : pictórico

picture¹ [ˈpɪktʃər] *vt* **-tured; -turing 1** DEPICT : representar **2** IMAGINE : imaginarse ⟨can you picture it? : ¿te lo puedes imaginar?⟩

picture² *n* **1** : cuadro *m* (pintado o dibujado), ilustración *f*, fotografía *f* **2** DESCRIPTION : descripción *f* **3** IMAGE : imagen *f* ⟨he's the picture of his father : es la viva imagen de su padre⟩ **4** MOVIE : película *f*

picturesque [ˌpɪktʃəˈrɛsk] *adj* : pintoresco

pie [ˈpaɪ] *n* : pastel *m* (con fruta o carne), empanada *f* (con carne)

piebald [ˈpaɪˌbɔld] *adj* : picazo, pío

piece¹ [ˈpiːs] *vt* **pieced; piecing 1** PATCH : parchar, arreglar **2 to piece together** : construir pieza por pieza

piece² *n* **1** FRAGMENT : trozo *m*, pedazo *m* **2** COMPONENT : pieza *f* ⟨a three-piece suit : un traje de tres piezas⟩ **3** UNIT : pieza *f* ⟨a piece of fruit : una (pieza de) fruta⟩ **4** WORK : obra *f*, pieza *f* (de música, etc.) **5** (*in board games*) : ficha *f*, pieza *f*, figura *f* (en ajedrez)

piecemeal¹ [ˈpiːsˌmiːl] *adv* : poco a poco, por partes

piecemeal² *adj* : hecho poco a poco, poco sistemático

pied [ˈpaɪd] *adj* : pío

pier [ˈpɪr] *n* **1** : pila *f* (de un puente) **2** WHARF : muelle *m*, atracadero *m*, embarcadero *m* **3** PILLAR : pilar *m*

pierce [ˈpɪrs] *vt* **pierced; piercing 1** PENETRATE : atravesar, traspasar, penetrar (en) ⟨the bullet pierced his leg : la bala le atravesó la pierna⟩ ⟨to pierce one's heart : traspasarle el corazón a uno⟩ **2** PERFORATE : perforar, agujerear (las orejas, etc.) **3 to pierce the silence** : desgarrar el silencio

piety [ˈpaɪəti] *n, pl* **-eties** : piedad *f*

pig [ˈpɪg] *n* **1** HOG, SWINE : cerdo *m*, -da *f*; puerco *m*, -ca *f* **2** SLOB : persona *f* desaliñada; cerdo *m*, -da *f* **3** GLUTTON : glotón *m*, -tona *f* **4** *or* **pig iron** : lingote *m* de hierro

pigeon [ˈpɪdʒən] *n* : paloma *f*

pigeonhole [ˈpɪdʒənˌhoːl] *n* : casilla *f*

pigeon-toed [ˈpɪdʒənˌtoːd] *adj* : patituerto

piggish [ˈpɪgɪʃ] *adj* **1** GREEDY : glotón **2** DIRTY : cochino, sucio

piggyback [ˈpɪgiˌbæk] *adv & adj* : a cuestas

pigheaded [ˈpɪgˌhɛdəd] *adj* : terco, obstinado

piglet [ˈpɪglət] *n* : cochinillo *m*; lechón *m*, -chona *f*

pigment [ˈpɪgmənt] *n* : pigmento *m*

pigmentation [ˌpɪgmənˈteɪʃən] *n* : pigmentación *f*

pigmy → **pygmy**

pigpen [ˈpɪgˌpɛn] *n* : chiquero *m*, pocilga *f*

pigsty [ˈpɪgˌstaɪ] → **pigpen**

pigtail [ˈpɪgˌteɪl] *n* : coleta *f*, trenza *f*

pike [ˈpaɪk] *n, pl* **pike** *or* **pikes 1** : lucio *m* (pez) **2** LANCE : pica *f* **3** → **turnpike**

pile¹ [ˈpaɪl] *v* **piled; piling** *vt* : amontonar, apilar — *vi* **to pile up** : amontonarse, acumularse

pile² *n* **1** STAKE : pilote *m* **2** HEAP : montón *m*, pila *f* **3** NAP : pelo *m* (de telas)

piles [ˈpaɪlz] *npl* HEMORRHOIDS : hemorroides *fpl*, almorranas *fpl*

pilfer [ˈpɪlfər] *vt* : robar (cosas pequeñas), ratear

pilgrim [ˈpɪlgrəm] *n* : peregrino *m*, -na *f*

pilgrimage [ˈpɪlgrəmɪdʒ] *n* : peregrinación *f*

pill [ˈpɪl] *n* : pastilla *f*, píldora *f*

pillage¹ [ˈpɪlɪdʒ] *vt* **-laged; -laging** : saquear

pillage² *n* : saqueo *m*

pillar [ˈpɪlər] *n* : pilar *m*, columna *f*

pillory [ˈpɪləri] *n, pl* **-ries** : picota *f*

pillow [ˈpɪˌloː] *n* : almohada *f*

pillowcase [ˈpɪˌloːˌkeɪs] *n* : funda *f*

pilot¹ [ˈpaɪlət] *vt* : pilotar, pilotear

pilot² *n* : piloto *mf*

pilot light *n* : piloto *m*

pimento [pəˈmɛnˌtoː] → **pimiento**

pimiento [pə'mɛn̩to:, -'mjɛn-] *n, pl* **-tos** : pimiento *m* morrón

pimp ['pɪmp] *n* : proxeneta *m*

pimple ['pɪmpəl] *n* : grano *m*

pimply ['pɪmpəli] *adj* **-plier; -est** : cubierto de granos

pin¹ ['pɪn] *vt* **pinned; pinning 1** FASTEN : prender, sujetar (con alfileres) **2** HOLD, IMMOBILIZE : inmovilizar, sujetar **3 to pin one's hopes on** : poner sus esperanzas en

pin² *n* **1** : alfiler *m* ⟨safety pin : alfiler de gancho⟩ ⟨a bobby pin : una horquilla⟩ **2** BROOCH : alfiler *m*, broche *m*, prendedor *m* **3** *or* **bowling pin** : bolo *m*

pinafore ['pɪnə̩for] *n* : delantal *m*

pincer ['pɪntsər] *n* **1** CLAW : pinza *f* (de una langosta, etc.) **2 pincers** *npl* : pinzas *fpl*, tenazas *fpl*, tenaza *f*

pinch¹ ['pɪntʃ] *vt* **1** : pellizcar ⟨she pinched my cheek : me pellizcó el cachete⟩ **2** STEAL : robar — *vi* : apretar ⟨my shoes pinch : me aprietan los zapatos⟩

pinch² *n* **1** EMERGENCY : emergencia *f* ⟨in a pinch : en caso necesario⟩ **2** PAIN : dolor *m*, tormento *m* **3** SQUEEZE : pellizco *m* (con los dedos) **4** BIT : pizca *f*, pellizco *m* ⟨a pinch of cinnamon : una pizca de canela⟩

pinch hitter *n* **1** SUBSTITUTE : sustituto *m*, -ta *f* **2** : bateador *m* emergente (en beisbol)

pincushion ['pɪn̩kuʃən] *n* : acerico *m*, alfiletero *m*

pine¹ ['paɪn] *vi* **pined; pining 1 to pine away** : languidecer, consumirse **2 to pine for** : añorar, suspirar por

pine² *n* **1** : pino *m* (árbol) **2** : madera *f* de pino

pineapple ['paɪn̩æpəl] *n* : piña *f*, ananá *m*, ananás *m*

ping–pong ['pɪŋ̩pɑŋ, -̩pɔŋ] *n* : ping-pong *m*

pinion¹ ['pɪnjən] *vt* : sujetar los brazos de, inmovilizar

pinion² *n* : piñón *m*

pink¹ ['pɪŋk] *adj* : rosa, rosado

pink² *n* **1** : clavelito *m* (flor) **2** : rosa *m*, rosado *m* (color) **3 to be in the pink** : estar en plena forma, rebosar de salud

pinkeye ['pɪŋk̩aɪ] *n* : conjuntivitis *f* aguda

pinkish ['pɪŋkɪʃ] *adj* : rosáceo

pinnacle ['pɪnɪkəl] *n* **1** : pináculo *m* (de un edificio) **2** PEAK : cima *f*, cumbre *f* (de una montaña) **3** ACME : pináculo *m*, cúspide *f*, apogeo *m*

pinpoint ['pɪn̩pɔɪnt] *vt* : precisar, localizar con precisión

pint ['paɪnt] *n* : pinta *f*

pinto ['pɪn̩to:] *n, pl* **pintos** : caballo *m* pinto

pinworm ['pɪn̩wərm] *n* : oxiuro *m*

pioneer¹ [̩paɪə'nɪr] *vt* : promover, iniciar, introducir

pioneer² *n* : pionero *m*, -ra *f*

pious ['paɪəs] *adj* **1** DEVOUT : piadoso, devoto **2** SANCTIMONIOUS : beato

piously ['paɪəsli] *adv* **1** DEVOUTLY : piadosamente **2** SANCTIMONIOUSLY : santurronamente

pipe¹ ['paɪp] *v* **piped; piping** *vi* : hablar en voz chillona — *vt* **1** PLAY : tocar (el caramillo o la flauta) **2** : conducir por tuberías ⟨to pipe water : transportar el agua por tubería⟩

pipe² *n* **1** : caramillo *m* (instrumento musical) **2** BAGPIPE : gaita *f* **3** : tubo *m*, caño *m* ⟨gas pipes : tubería de gas⟩ **4** : pipa *f* (para fumar)

pipeline ['paɪp̩laɪn] *n* **1** : conducto *m*, oleoducto *m* (para petróleo), gasoducto *m* (para gas) **2** CONDUIT : vía *f* (de información, etc.)

piper ['paɪpər] *n* : músico *m*, -ca *f* que toca el caramillo o la gaita

piping ['paɪpɪŋ] *n* **1** : música *f* del caramillo o de la gaita **2** TRIM : cordoncillo *m*, ribete *m* con cordón

piquant ['pi:kənt, 'pɪkwənt] *adj* **1** SPICY : picante **2** INTRIGUING : intrigante, estimulante

pique¹ ['pi:k] *vt* **piqued; piquing 1** IRRITATE : picar, irritar **2** AROUSE : despertar (la curiosidad, etc.)

pique² *n* : pique *m*, resentimiento *m*

piracy ['paɪrəsi] *n, pl* **-cies** : piratería *f*

piranha [pə'rɑnə, -'rɑnjə, -'rænjə] *n* : piraña *f*

pirate¹ ['paɪrət] *n* : pirata *mf*

pirate² *vt* **-rated; -rating** : piratear (software, etc.)

pirouette [̩pɪrə'wɛt] *n* : pirueta *f*

pis → **pi**

Pisces ['paɪ̩si:z, 'pɪ-; 'pɪs̩keɪs] *n* : Piscis *mf*

pistachio [pə'stæʃi̩o:, -'stɑ-] *n, pl* **-chios** : pistacho *m*

pistil ['pɪstəl] *n* : pistilo *m*

pistol ['pɪstəl] *n* : pistola *f*

piston ['pɪstən] *n* : pistón *m*, émbolo *m*

pit¹ ['pɪt] *v* **pitted; pitting** *vt* **1** : marcar de hoyos, picar (una superficie) **2** : deshuesar (una fruta) **3 to pit against** : enfrentar a, oponer a — *vi* : quedar marcado

pit² *n* **1** HOLE : fosa *f*, hoyo *m* ⟨a bottomless pit : un pozo sin fondo⟩ **2** MINE : mina *f* **3** : foso *m* ⟨orchestra pit : foso orquestal⟩ **4** POCKMARK : marca *f* (en la cara), cicatriz *f* de viruela **5** STONE : hueso *m*, pepa *f* (de una fruta) **6 pit of the stomach** : boca *f* del estómago

pitch¹ ['pɪtʃ] *vt* **1** SET UP : montar, armar (una tienda) **2** THROW : lanzar, arrojar **3** ADJUST, SET : dar el tono de (un discurso, un instrumento musical) — *vi* **1** *or* **pitch forward** FALL : caerse **2** LURCH : cabecear (dícese de un barco o un avión), dar bandazos

pitch² *n* **1** LURCHING : cabezada *f*, cabeceo *m* (de un barco o un avión) **2** SLOPE : (grado de) inclinación *f*, pendiente *f* **3** : tono *m* (en música) ⟨perfect pitch : oído absoluto⟩ **4** THROW : lanzamiento *m* **5** DEGREE : grado *m*, nivel *m*, punto *m* ⟨the excitement reached a high pitch : la excitación llegó a un punto culminante⟩ **6** *or* **sales pitch** : presentación *f* (de un vendedor) **7** TAR : pez *f*, brea *f*

pitcher [ˈpɪtʃər] *n* **1** JUG : jarra *f*, jarro *m*, cántaro *m*, pichel *m* **2** : lanzador *m*, -dora *f* (en béisbol, etc.)

pitchfork [ˈpɪtʃˌfɔrk] *n* : horquilla *f*, horca *f*

piteous [ˈpɪtiəs] *adj* : lastimoso, lastimero — **piteously** *adv*

pitfall [ˈpɪtˌfɔl] *n* : peligro *m* (poco obvio), dificultad *f*

pith [ˈpɪθ] *n* **1** : médula *f* (de una planta) **2** CORE : meollo *m*, entraña *f*

pithy [ˈpɪθi] *adj* **pithier; -est** : conciso y sustancioso ⟨pithy comments : comentarios sucintos⟩

pitiable [ˈpɪtiəbəl] → **pitiful**

pitiful [ˈpɪtɪfəl] *adj* **1** LAMENTABLE : lastimero, lastimoso, lamentable **2** CONTEMPTIBLE : despreciable, lamentable — **pitifully** [-fli] *adv*

pitiless [ˈpɪtɪləs] *adj* : despiadado — **pitilessly** *adv*

pittance [ˈpɪtənts] *n* : miseria *f*

pituitary [pəˈtuːəˌtɛri, -ˈtjuː-] *adj* : pituitario

pity¹ [ˈpɪti] *vt* **pitied; pitying** : compadecer, compadecerse de

pity² *n, pl* **pities 1** COMPASSION : compasión *f*, piedad *f* **2** SHAME : lástima *f*, pena *f* ⟨what a pity! : ¡qué lástima!⟩

pivot¹ [ˈpɪvət] *vi* **1** : girar sobre un eje **2 to pivot on** : girar sobre, depender de

pivot² *n* : pivote *m*

pivotal [ˈpɪvətəl] *adj* : fundamental, central

pixie *or* **pixy** [ˈpɪksi] *n, pl* **pixies** : elfo *m*, hada *f*

pizza [ˈpiːtsə] *n* : pizza *f*

pizzazz *or* **pizazz** [pəˈzæz] *n* **1** GLAMOR : encanto *m* **2** VITALITY : animación *f*, vitalidad *f*

placard [ˈplækərd, -ˌkɑrd] *n* POSTER : cartel *m*, póster *m*, afiche *m*

placate [ˈpleɪˌkeɪt, ˈplæ-] *vt* **-cated; -cating** : aplacar, apaciguar

place¹ [ˈpleɪs] *vt* **placed; placing 1** PUT, SET : poner, colocar **2** SITUATE : situar, ubicar, emplazar ⟨to be well placed : estar bien situado⟩ ⟨to place in a job : colocar en un trabajo⟩ **3** IDENTIFY, RECALL : identificar, ubicar, recordar ⟨I can't place him : no lo ubico⟩ **4 to place an order** : hacer un pedido

place² *n* **1** SPACE : sitio *m*, lugar *m* ⟨there's no place to sit : no hay sitio para sentarse⟩ **2** LOCATION, SPOT : lugar *m*, sitio *m*, parte *f* ⟨place of work : lugar de trabajo⟩ ⟨our summer place : nuestra casa de verano⟩ ⟨all over the place : por todas partes⟩ **3** RANK : lugar *m*, puesto *m* ⟨he took first place : ganó el primer lugar⟩ **4** POSITION : lugar *m* ⟨everything in its place : todo en

su debido lugar⟩ ⟨to feel out of place : sentirse fuera de lugar⟩ **5** SEAT : asiento *m*, cubierto *m* (a la mesa) **6** JOB : puesto *m* **7** ROLE : papel *m*, lugar *m* ⟨to change places : cambiarse los papeles⟩ **8 to take place** : tener lugar **9 to take the place of** : sustituir a

placebo [pləˈsiːˌboː] *n, pl* **-bos** : placebo *m*

placement [ˈpleɪsmənt] *n* : colocación *f*

placenta [pləˈsɛntə] *n, pl* **-tas** *or* **-tae** [-ti, -ˌtaɪ] : placenta *f*

placid [ˈplæsəd] *adj* : plácido, tranquilo — **placidly** *adv*

plagiarism [ˈpleɪdʒəˌrɪzəm] *n* : plagio *m*

plagiarist [ˈpleɪdʒərɪst] *n* : plagiario *m*, -ria *f*

plagiarize [ˈpleɪdʒəˌraɪz] *vt* **-rized; -rizing** : plagiar

plague¹ [ˈpleɪg] *vt* **plagued; plaguing 1** AFFLICT : plagar, afligir **2** HARASS : acosar, atormentar

plague² *n* **1** : plaga *f* (de insectos, etc.) **2** : peste *f* (en medicina)

plaid¹ [ˈplæd] *adj* : escocés, de cuadros ⟨a plaid skirt : una falda escocesa⟩

plaid² *n* TARTAN : tela *f* escocesa, tartán *m*

plain¹ [ˈpleɪn] *adj* **1** SIMPLE, UNADORNED : liso, sencillo, sin adornos **2** CLEAR : claro ⟨in plain language : en palabras claras⟩ **3** FRANK : franco, puro ⟨the plain truth : la pura verdad⟩ **4** HOMELY : ordinario, poco atractivo **5 in plain sight** : a la vista de todos

plain² *n* : llanura *f*, llano *m*, planicie *f*

plainly [ˈpleɪnli] *adv* **1** CLEARLY : claramente **2** FRANKLY : francamente, con franqueza **3** SIMPLY : sencillamente

plaintiff [ˈpleɪntɪf] *n* : demandante *mf*

plaintive [ˈpleɪntɪv] *adj* MOURNFUL : lastimero, plañidero

plait¹ [ˈpleɪt, ˈplæt] *vt* **1** PLEAT : plisar **2** BRAID : trenzar

plait² *n* **1** PLEAT : pliegue *m* **2** BRAID : trenza *f*

plan¹ [ˈplæn] *v* **planned; planning** *vt* **1** : planear, proyectar, planificar ⟨to plan a trip : planear un viaje⟩ ⟨to plan a city : planificar una ciudad⟩ **2** INTEND : tener planeado, proyectar — *vi* : hacer planes

plan² *n* **1** DIAGRAM : plano *m*, esquema *m* **2** SCHEME : plan *m*, proyecto *m*, programa *m* ⟨to draw up a plan : elaborar un proyecto⟩

plane¹ [ˈpleɪn] *vt* **planed; planing** : cepillar (madera)

plane² *adj* : plano

plane³ *n* **1** : plano *m* (en matemáticas, etc.) **2** LEVEL : nivel *m* **3** : cepillo *m* (de carpintero) **4** → **airplane**

planet [ˈplænət] *n* : planeta *f*

planetarium [ˌplænəˈtɛriəm] *n, pl* **-iums** *or* **-ia** [-iə] : planetario *m*

planetary [ˈplænəˌtɛri] *adj* : planetario

plank [ˈplæŋk] *n* **1** BOARD : tablón *m*, tabla *f* **2** : artículo *m*, punto *m* (de una plataforma política)

plankton ['plæŋktən] n : plancton m
plant[1] ['plænt] vt 1 : plantar, sembrar (semillas) ⟨planted with flowers : plantado de flores⟩ 2 PLACE : plantar, colocar ⟨to plant an idea : inculcar una idea⟩
plant[2] n 1 : planta f ⟨leafy plants : plantas frondosas⟩ 2 FACTORY : planta f, fábrica f ⟨hydroelectric plant : planta hidroeléctrica⟩ 3 MACHINERY : maquinaria f, equipo m
plantain ['plæntən] n 1 : llantén m (mala hierba) 2 : plátano m, plátano m macho Mex (fruta)
plantation [plæn'teɪʃən] n : plantación f, hacienda f ⟨a coffee plantation : un cafetal⟩
planter ['plæntər] n 1 : hacendado m, -da f (de una hacienda) 2 FLOWERPOT : tiesto m, maceta f
plaque ['plæk] n 1 TABLET : placa f 2 : placa f (dental)
plasma ['plæzmə] n : plasma m
plaster[1] ['plæstər] vt 1 : enyesar, revocar (con yeso) 2 COVER : cubrir, llenar ⟨a wall plastered with notices : una pared cubierta de avisos⟩
plaster[2] n 1 : yeso m, revoque m (para paredes, etc.) 2 : escayola f, yeso m (en medicina) 3 **plaster of Paris** ['pæris] : yeso m mate
plaster cast n : vaciado m de yeso
plasterer ['plæstərər] n : revocador m, -dora f
plastic[1] ['plæstɪk] adj 1 : de plástico 2 PLIABLE : plástico, flexible 3 **plastic surgery** : cirugía f plástica
plastic[2] n : plástico m
plasticity [plæ'stɪsəti] n, pl **-ties** : plasticidad f
plate[1] ['pleɪt] vt **plated; plating** : chapar (en metal)
plate[2] n 1 PLAQUE, SHEET : placa f ⟨a steel plate : una placa de acero⟩ 2 UTENSILS : vajilla f (de metal) ⟨silver plate : vajilla de plata⟩ 3 DISH : plato m 4 DENTURES : dentadura f postiza 5 ILLUSTRATION : lámina f (en un libro) 6 **license plate** : matrícula f, placa f de matrícula
plateau [plæ'to:] n, pl **-teaus** or **-teaux** [-'to:z] : meseta f
platform ['plæt,fɔrm] n 1 STAGE : plataforma f, estrado m, tribuna f 2 : andén m (de una estación de ferrocarril) 3 **political platform** : plataforma f política, programa m electoral
plating ['pleɪtɪŋ] n 1 : enchapado m 2 **silver plating** : plateado m
platinum ['plætənəm] n : platino m
platitude ['plætə,tu:d, -,tju:d] n : lugar m común, perogrullada f
platonic [plə'tɑnɪk] adj : platónico
platoon [plə'tu:n] n : sección f (en el ejército)
platter ['plætər] n : fuente f
platypus ['plætɪpəs, -,pʊs] n, pl **platypuses** or **platypi** [-,paɪ, -,pi:] : ornitorrinco m

plausibility [,plɔzə'bɪləti] n, pl **-ties** : credibilidad f, verosimilitud f
plausible ['plɔzəbəl] adj : creíble, convincente, verosímil — **plausibly** [-bli] adv
play[1] ['pleɪ] vi 1 : jugar ⟨to play with a doll : jugar con una muñeca⟩ ⟨to play with an idea : darle vueltas a una idea⟩ 2 FIDDLE, TOY : jugar, juguetear ⟨don't play with your food : no juegues con la comida⟩ 3 : tocar ⟨to play in a band : tocar en un grupo⟩ 4 : actuar (en una obra de teatro) — vt 1 : jugar (un deporte, etc.), jugar a (un juego), jugar contra (un contrincante) 2 : tocar (música o un instrumento) 3 PERFORM : interpretar, hacer el papel de (un carácter), representar (una obra de teatro) ⟨she plays the lead : hace el papel principal⟩ 4 **to play back** : poner (una grabación) 5 **to play down** : minimizar 6 **to play up** : resaltar
play[2] n 1 GAME, RECREATION : juego m ⟨children at play : niños jugando⟩ ⟨a play on words : un juego de palabras⟩ 2 ACTION : juego m ⟨the ball is in play : la pelota está en juego⟩ ⟨to bring into play : poner en juego⟩ 3 DRAMA : obra f de teatro, pieza f (de teatro) 4 MOVEMENT : juego m (de la luz, una brisa, etc.) 5 SLACK : juego m ⟨there's not enough play in the wheel : la rueda no da lo suficiente⟩
playacting ['pleɪ,æktɪŋ] n : actuación f, teatro m
player ['pleɪər] n 1 : jugador m, -dora f (en un juego) 2 ACTOR : actor m, actriz f 3 MUSICIAN : músico m, -ca f
playful ['pleɪfəl] adj 1 FROLICSOME : juguetón 2 JOCULAR : jocoso — **playfully** adv
playfulness ['pleɪfəlnəs] n : lo juguetón, jocosidad f, alegría f
playground ['pleɪ,graʊnd] n : patio m de recreo, jardín m para jugar
playhouse ['pleɪ,haʊs] n 1 THEATER : teatro m 2 : casita f de juguete
playing card n : naipe m, carta f
playmate ['pleɪ,meɪt] n : compañero m, -ra f de juego
play-off ['pleɪ,ɔf] n : desempate m
playpen ['pleɪ,pɛn] n : corral m (para niños)
plaything ['pleɪ,θɪŋ] n : juguete m
playwright ['pleɪ,raɪt] n : dramaturgo m, -ga f
plaza ['plæzə, 'plɑ-] n 1 SQUARE : plaza f 2 **shopping plaza** MALL : centro m comercial
plea ['pli:] n 1 : acto m de declararse ⟨he entered a plea of guilty : se declaró culpable⟩ 2 APPEAL : ruego m, súplica f
plead ['pli:d] v **pleaded** or **pled** ['plɛd]; **pleading** vi 1 : declararse (culpable o inocente) 2 **to plead for** : suplicar, implorar — vt 1 : alegar, pretextar ⟨he pleaded illness : pretextó la enfermedad⟩ 2 **to plead a case** : defender un caso

pleasant ['plɛzənt] *adj* : agradable, grato, bueno — **pleasantly** *adv*

pleasantness ['plɛzəntnəs] *n* : lo agradable, amenidad *f*

pleasantries ['plɛzəntriz] *npl* : cumplidos *mpl*, cortesías *fpl* ⟨to exchange pleasantries : intercambiar cumplidos⟩

please¹ ['pli:z] *v* **pleased; pleasing** *vt* **1** GRATIFY : complacer ⟨please yourself! : ¡cómo quieras!⟩ **2** SATISFY : contentar, satisfacer — *vi* **1** SATISFY : complacer, agradar ⟨anxious to please : deseoso de complacer⟩ **2** LIKE : querer ⟨do as you please : haz lo que quieras, haz lo que te parezca⟩

please² *adv* : por favor

pleased ['pli:zd] *adj* : contento, satisfecho, alegre

pleasing ['pli:zɪŋ] *adj* : agradable — **pleasingly** *adv*

pleasurable ['plɛʒərəbəl] *adj* PLEASANT : agradable

pleasure ['plɛʒər] *n* **1** WISH : deseo *m*, voluntad *f* ⟨at your pleasure : cuando guste⟩ **2** ENJOYMENT : placer *m*, disfrute *m*, goce *m* ⟨with pleasure : con mucho gusto⟩ **3** : placer *m*, gusto *m* ⟨it's a pleasure to be here : me da gusto estar aquí⟩ ⟨the pleasures of reading : los placeres de leer⟩

pleat¹ ['pli:t] *vt* : plisar

pleat² *n* : pliegue *m*

plebeian [plɪ'bian] *adj* : ordinario, plebeyo

pledge¹ ['plɛdʒ] *vt* **pledged; pledging 1** PAWN : empeñar, prendar **2** PROMISE : prometer, jurar

pledge² *n* **1** SECURITY : garantía *f*, prenda *f* **2** PROMISE : promesa *f*

plenteous ['plɛntiəs] *adj* : copioso, abundante

plentiful ['plɛntɪfəl] *adj* : abundante — **plentifully** [-fli] *adv*

plenty ['plɛnti] *n* : abundancia *f* ⟨plenty of time : tiempo de sobra⟩ ⟨plenty of visitors : muchos visitantes⟩

plethora ['plɛθərə] *n* : plétora *f*

pleurisy ['plʊrəsi] *n* : pleuresía *f*

pliable ['plaɪəbəl] *adj* : flexible, maleable

pliant ['plaɪənt] → **pliable**

pliers ['plaɪərz] *npl* : alicates *mpl*, pinzas *fpl*

plight ['plaɪt] *n* : situación *f* difícil, apuro *m*

plod ['plɑd] *vi* **plodded; plodding 1** TRUDGE : caminar pesadamente **2** DRUDGE : trabajar laboriosamente

plot¹ ['plɑt] *v* **plotted; plotting** *vt* **1** DEVISE : tramar **2 to plot out** : trazar, determinar (una posición, etc.) — *vi* CONSPIRE : conspirar

plot² *n* **1** LOT : terreno *m*, parcela *f*, lote *m* **2** STORY : argumento *m* (en el teatro), trama *f* (en un libro, etc.) **3** CONSPIRACY, INTRIGUE : complot *m*, intriga *f*

plotter ['plɑtər] *n* : conspirador *m*, -dora *f*; intrigante *mf*

plow¹ *or* **plough** ['plaʊ] *vt* **1** : arar (la tierra) **2 to plow the seas** : surcar los mares

plow² *or* **plough** *n* **1** : arado *m* **2** → **snowplow**

plowshare ['plaʊˌʃɛr] *n* : reja *f* del arado

ploy ['plɔɪ] *n* : estratagema *f*, maniobra *f*

pluck¹ ['plʌk] *vt* **1** PICK : arrancar **2** : desplumar (un pollo, etc.) — *vi* **to pluck at** : tirar de

pluck² *n* **1** TUG : tirón *m* **2** COURAGE, SPIRIT : valor *m*, ánimo *m*

plucky ['plʌki] *adj* **pluckier; -est** : valiente, animoso

plug¹ ['plʌg] *vt* **plugged; plugging 1** BLOCK : tapar **2** PROMOTE : hacerle publicidad a, promocionar **3 to plug in** : enchufar

plug² *n* **1** STOPPER : tapón *m* **2** : enchufe *m* (eléctrico) **3** ADVERTISEMENT : publicidad *f*, propaganda *f*

plum ['plʌm] *n* **1** : ciruela *f* (fruta) **2** : color *m* ciruela **3** PRIZE : premio *m*, algo muy atractivo

plumage ['plu:mɪdʒ] *n* : plumaje *m*

plumb¹ ['plʌm] *vt* **1** : aplomar ⟨to plumb a wall : aplomar una pared⟩ **2** SOUND : sondear, sondar

plumb² *adv* **1** VERTICALLY : a plomo, verticalmente **2** EXACTLY : justo, exactamente **3** COMPLETELY : completamente, absolutamente ⟨plumb crazy : loco de remate⟩

plumb³ *adj* : a plomo

plumb⁴ *n or* **plumb line** : plomada *f*

plumber ['plʌmər] *n* : plomero *m*, -ra *f*; fontanero *m*, -ra *f*

plumbing ['plʌmɪŋ] *n* **1** : plomería *f*, fontanería *f* (trabajo del plomero) **2** PIPES : cañería *f*, tubería *f*

plume ['plu:m] *n* **1** FEATHER : pluma *f* **2** TUFT : penacho *m* (en un sombrero, etc.)

plumed ['plu:md] *adj* : con plumas ⟨white-plumed birds : aves de plumaje blanco⟩

plummet ['plʌmət] *vi* : caer en picada, desplomarse

plump¹ ['plʌmp] *vi or* **to plump down** : dejarse caer (pesadamente)

plump² *adv* **1** STRAIGHT : a plomo **2** DIRECTLY : directamente, sin rodeos ⟨he ran plump into the door : dio de cara con la puerta⟩

plump³ *adj* : llenito *fam*, regordete *fam*, rechoncho *fam*

plumpness ['plʌmpnəs] *n* : gordura *f*

plunder¹ ['plʌndər] *vi* : saquear, robar

plunder² *n* : botín *m*

plunderer ['plʌndərər] *n* : saqueador *m*, -dora *f*

plunge¹ ['plʌndʒ] *v* **plunged; plunging** *vt* **1** IMMERSE : sumergir **2** THRUST : hundir, clavar — *vi* **1** DIVE : zambullirse (en el agua) **2** : meterse precipitadamente o violentamente ⟨they plunged into war : se enfrascaron en una guerra⟩ ⟨he plunged into depression : cayó en la depresión⟩ **3** DE-SCEND : descender en picada ⟨the road plunges dizzily : la calle desciende vertiginosamente⟩

plunge² *n* **1** DIVE : zambullida *f* **2** DROP : descenso *m* abrupto ⟨the plunge in prices : el desplome de los precios⟩

plural¹ [ˈplʊrəl] *adj* : plural

plural² *n* : plural *m*

plurality [plʊˈrælətɪ] *n, pl* **-ties** : pluralidad *f*

pluralize [ˈplʊrəˌlaɪz] *vt* **-ized; -izing** : pluralizar

plus¹ [ˈplʌs] *adj* **1** POSITIVE : positivo ⟨a plus factor : un factor positivo⟩ **2** (*indicating a quantity in addition*) ⟨a grade of C plus : una calificación entre C y B⟩ ⟨a salary of $30,000 plus : un sueldo de más de $30,000⟩

plus² *n* **1** *or* **plus sign** : más *m*, signo *m* de más **2** ADVANTAGE : ventaja *f*

plus³ *prep* : más (en matemáticas)

plus⁴ *conj* AND : y

plush¹ [ˈplʌʃ] *adj* **1** : afelpado **2** LUXURIOUS : lujoso

plush² *n* : felpa *f*, peluche *m*

plushy [ˈplʌʃi] *adj* **plushier; -est** : lujoso

Pluto [ˈpluːˌtoː] *n* : Plutón *m*

plutocracy [pluːˈtɑkrəsi] *n, pl* **-cies** : plutocracia *f*

plutonium [pluːˈtoːniəm] *n* : plutonio *m*

ply¹ [ˈplaɪ] *v* **plied; plying** *vt* **1** USE, WIELD : manejar ⟨to ply an ax : manejar un hacha⟩ **2** PRACTICE : ejercer ⟨to ply a trade : ejercer un oficio⟩ **3 to ply with questions** : acosar con preguntas

ply² *n, pl* **plies 1** LAYER : chapa *f* (de madera), capa *f* (de papel) **2** STRAND : cabo *m* (de hilo, etc.)

plywood [ˈplaɪˌwʊd] *n* : contrachapado *m*

pneumatic [nʊˈmætɪk, njʊ-] *adj* : neumático

pneumonia [nʊˈmoːnjə, njʊ-] *n* : pulmonía *f*, neumonía *f*

poach [ˈpoːtʃ] *vt* **1** : cocer a fuego lento ⟨to poach an egg : escalfar un huevo⟩ **2 to poach game** : cazar ilegalmente — *vi* : cazar ilegalmente

poacher [ˈpoːtʃər] *n* : cazador *m* furtivo, cazadora *f* furtiva

pock [ˈpɑk] *n* **1** PUSTULE : pústula *f* **2** → **pockmark**

pocket¹ [ˈpɑkət] *vt* **1** : meterse en el bolsillo ⟨he pocketed the pen : se metió la pluma en el bolsillo⟩ **2** STEAL : embolsarse

pocket² *n* **1** : bolsillo *m*, bolsa *f* *Mex* ⟨a coat pocket : el bolsillo de un abrigo⟩ ⟨air pockets : bolsas de aire⟩ **2** CENTER : foco *m*, centro *m* ⟨a pocket of resistance : un foco de resistencia⟩

pocketbook [ˈpɑkətˌbʊk] *n* **1** PURSE : cartera *f*, bolso *m*, bolsa *f* *Mex* **2** MEANS : recursos *mpl*

pocketknife [ˈpɑkətˌnaɪf] *n, pl* **-knives** : navaja *f*

pocket–size [ˈpɑkətˌsaɪz] *adj* : de bolsillo

pockmark [ˈpɑkˌmɑrk] *n* : cicatriz *f* de viruela, viruela *f*

pod [ˈpɑd] *n* : vaina *f* ⟨pea pod : vaina de guisantes⟩

podiatrist [pəˈdaɪətrɪst, po-] *n* : podólogo *m*, -ga *f*

podiatry [pəˈdaɪətri, po-] *n* : podología *f*, podiatría *f*

podium [ˈpoːdiəm] *n, pl* **-diums** *or* **-dia** [-diə] : podio *m*, estrado *m*, tarima *f*

poem [ˈpoːəm] *n* : poema *m*, poesía *f*

poet [ˈpoːət] *n* : poeta *mf*

poetic [poˈɛtɪk] *or* **poetical** [-tɪkəl] *adj* : poético

poetry [ˈpoːətri] *n* : poesía *f*

pogrom [ˈpoːgrəm, pəˈgrɑm, ˈpɑgrəm] *n* : pogrom *m*

poignancy [ˈpɔɪnjəntsi] *n, pl* **-cies** : lo conmovedor

poignant [ˈpɔɪnjənt] *adj* **1** PAINFUL : penoso, doloroso ⟨poignant grief : profundo dolor⟩ **2** TOUCHING : conmovedor, emocionante

poinsettia [pɔɪnˈsɛtiə, -ˈsɛtə] *n* : flor *f* de Nochebuena

point¹ [ˈpɔɪnt] *vt* **1** SHARPEN : afilar (la punta de) **2** INDICATE : señalar, indicar ⟨to point the way : señalar el camino⟩ **3** AIM : apuntar **4 to point out** : señalar, indicar — *vi* **1 to point at** : señalar (con el dedo) **2 to point to** INDICATE : señalar, indicar

point² *n* **1** ITEM : punto *m* ⟨the main points : los puntos principales⟩ **2** QUALITY : cualidad *f* ⟨her good points : sus buenas cualidades⟩ ⟨it's not his strong point : no es su (punto) fuerte⟩ **3** (*indicating a chief idea or meaning*) ⟨it's beside the point : no viene al caso⟩ ⟨to get to the point : ir al grano⟩ ⟨to stick to the point : no salirse del tema⟩ **4** PURPOSE : fin *m*, propósito *m* ⟨there's no point to it : no vale la pena, no sirve para nada⟩ **5** PLACE : punto *m*, lugar *m* ⟨points of interest : puntos interesantes⟩ **6** : punto *m* (en una escala) ⟨boiling point : punto de ebullición⟩ **7** MOMENT : momento *m*, coyuntura *f* ⟨at this point : en este momento⟩ **8** TIP : punta *f* **9** HEADLAND : punta *f*, cabo *m* **10** PERIOD : punto *m* (marca de puntuación) **11** UNIT : punto *m* ⟨he scored 15 points : ganó 15 puntos⟩ ⟨shares fell 10 points : las acciones bajaron 10 enteros⟩ **12 compass points** : puntos *mpl* cardinales **13 decimal point** : punto *m* decimal, coma *f*

point–blank¹ [ˈpɔɪntˈblæŋk] *adv* **1** : a quemarropa ⟨to shoot point-blank : disparar a quemarropa⟩ **2** BLUNTLY, DIRECTLY : a bocajarro, sin rodeos, francamente

point–blank² *adj* **1** : a quemarropa ⟨point-blank shots : disparos a quemarropa⟩ **2** BLUNT, DIRECT : directo, franco

pointed ['pɔɪntəd] *adj* **1** POINTY : puntiagudo **2** PERTINENT : atinado **3** CONSPICUOUS : marcado, manifiesto

pointedly ['pɔɪntədli] *adv* : intencionadamente, directamente

pointer ['pɔɪntər] *n* **1** STICK : puntero *m* (para maestros, etc.) **2** INDICATOR, NEEDLE : indicador *m*, aguja *f* **3** : perro *m* de muestra **4** HINT, TIP : consejo *m*

pointless ['pɔɪntləs] *adj* : inútil, ocioso, vano ⟨it's pointless to continue : no tiene sentido continuar⟩

point of view *n* : perspectiva *f*, punto *m* de vista

pointy ['pɔɪnti] *adj* : puntiagudo

poise¹ ['pɔɪz] *vt* **poised; poising** BALANCE : equilibrar, balancear

poise² *n* : aplomo *m*, compostura *f*

poison¹ ['pɔɪzən] *vt* **1** : envenenar, intoxicar **2** CORRUPT : corromper

poison² *n* : veneno *m*

poison ivy *n* : hiedra *f* venenosa

poisonous ['pɔɪzənəs] *adj* : venenoso, tóxico, ponzoñoso

poke¹ ['po:k] *v* **poked; poking** *vt* **1** JAB : golpear (con la punta de algo), dar ⟨he poked me with his finger : me dio con el dedo⟩ **2** THRUST : introducir, asomar ⟨I poked my head out the window : asomé la cabeza por la ventana⟩ — *vi* **1 to poke around** RUMMAGE : hurgar **2 to poke along** DAWDLE : demorarse, entretenerse

poke² *n* : golpe *m* abrupto (con la punta de algo)

poker ['po:kər] *n* **1** : atizador *m* (para el fuego) **2** : póker *m*, poker *m* (juego de naipes)

polar ['po:lər] *adj* : polar

polar bear *n* : oso *m* blanco

Polaris [po'lærɪs, -'lɑr-] → North Star

polarize ['po:lə,raɪz] *vt* **-ized; -izing** : polarizar

pole ['po:l] *n* **1** : palo *m*, poste *m*, vara *f* ⟨telephone pole : poste de teléfonos⟩ **2** : polo *m* ⟨the South Pole : el Polo Sur⟩ **3** : polo *m* (eléctrico o magnético)

Pole ['po:l] *n* : polaco *m*, -ca *f*

polecat ['po:l,kæt] *n*, *pl* **polecats** *or* **polecat** **1** : turón *m* (de Europa) **2** SKUNK : mofeta *f*, zorrillo *m*

polemical [pə'lɛmɪkəl] *adj* : polémico

polemics [pə'lɛmɪks] *ns & pl* : polémica *f*

polestar ['po:l,stɑr] → North Star

police¹ [pə'li:s] *vt* **-liced; -licing** : mantener el orden en ⟨to police the streets : patrullar las calles⟩

police² *ns & pl* **1** : policía *f* (organización) **2** POLICE OFFICERS : policías *mfpl*

policeman [pə'li:smən] *n*, *pl* **-men** [-mən, -,mɛn] : policía *m*

police officer *n* : policía *mf*, agente *mf* de policía

policewoman [pə'li:s,wʊmən] *n*, *pl* **-women** [-,wɪmən] : policía *f*, mujer *f* policía

policy ['pɑləsi] *n*, *pl* **-cies** **1** : política *f* ⟨foreign policy : política exterior⟩ **2** *or* **insurance policy** : póliza *f* de seguros, seguro *m*

polio¹ ['po:li,o:] *adj* : de polio ⟨polio vaccine : vacuna contra la polio⟩

polio² *n* → **poliomyelitis**

poliomyelitis [,po:li,o:,maɪə'laɪtəs] *n* : poliomielitis *f*, polio *f*

polish¹ ['pɑlɪʃ] *vt* **1** : pulir, lustrar, sacar brillo a ⟨to polish one's nails : pintarse las uñas⟩ **2** REFINE : pulir, perfeccionar

polish² *n* **1** LUSTER : brillo *m*, lustre *m* **2** REFINEMENT : refinamiento *m* **3** : betún *m* (para zapatos), cera *f* (para suelos y muebles), esmalte *m* (para las uñas)

Polish¹ ['po:lɪʃ] *adj* : polaco

Polish² *n* : polaco *m* (idioma)

polite [pə'laɪt] *adj* **-liter; -est** : cortés, correcto, educado

politely [pə'laɪtli] *adv* : cortésmente, correctamente, con buenos modales

politeness [pə'laɪtnəs] *n* : cortesía *f*

politic ['pɑlə,tɪk] *adj* : diplomático, prudente

political [pə'lɪtɪkəl] *adj* : político — **politically** [-tɪkli] *adv*

politician [,pɑlə'tɪʃən] *n* : político *m*, -ca *f*

politics ['pɑlə,tɪks] *ns & pl* : política *f*

polka ['po:lkə, 'po:kə] *n* : polka *f*

polka dot ['po:kə,dɑt] *n* : lunar *m* (en un diseño)

poll¹ ['po:l] *vt* **1** : obtener (votos) ⟨she polled over 1000 votes : obtuvo más de 1000 votos⟩ **2** CANVASS : encuestar, sondear — *vi* : obtener votos

poll² *n* **1** SURVEY : encuesta *f*, sondeo *m* **2 polls** *npl* : urnas *fpl* ⟨to go to the polls : acudir a las urnas, ir a votar⟩

pollen ['pɑlən] *n* : polen *m*

pollinate ['pɑlə,neɪt] *vt* **-nated; -nating** : polinizar

pollination [,pɑlə'neɪʃən] *n* : polinización *f*

pollster ['po:lstər] *n* : encuestador *m*, -dora *f*

pollutant [pə'lu:tənt] *n* : contaminante *m*

pollute [pə'lu:t] *vt* **-luted; -luting** : contaminar

pollution [pə'lu:ʃən] *n* : contaminación *f*

pollywog *or* **polliwog** ['pɑli,wɑg] *n* TADPOLE : renacuajo *m*

polo ['po:,lo:] *n* : polo *m*

poltergeist ['po:ltər,gaɪst] *n* : poltergeist *m*, fantasma *m* travieso

polyester ['pɑli,ɛstər, ,pɑli'-] *n* : poliéster *m*

polygamous [pə'lɪgəməs] *adj* : polígamo

polygamy [pə'lɪgəmi] *n* : poligamia *f*

polygon ['pɑli,gɑn] *n* : polígono *m*

polymer ['pɑləmər] *n* : polímero *m*
Polynesian [,pɑlə'ni:ʒən, -ʃən] *n* : polinesio *m*, -sia *f* — **Polynesian** *adj*
polyunsaturated [,pɑli,ʌn'sætʃə-,reɪṭəd] *adj* : poliinsaturado
pomegranate ['pɑmə,grænət, 'pɑm-,grænət] *n* : granada *f* (fruta)
pommel[1] ['pʌməl] *vt* → **pummel**
pommel[2] ['pʌməl, 'pɑ-] *n* **1** : pomo *m* (de una espada) **2** : perilla *f* (de una silla de montar)
pomp ['pɑmp] *n* **1** SPLENDOR : pompa *f*, esplendor *m* **2** OSTENTATION : boato *m*, ostentación *f*
pom–pom ['pɑm,pɑm] *n* : borla *f*, pompón *m*
pomposity [pɑm'pɑsəṭi] *n, pl* **-ties** : pomposidad *f*
pompous ['pɑmpəs] *adj* : pomposo — **pompously** *adv*
poncho ['pɑn,tʃo:] *n, pl* **-chos** : poncho *m*
pond ['pɑnd] *n* : charca *f* (natural), estanque *m* (artificial)
ponder ['pɑndər] *vt* : reflexionar, considerar — *vi* **to ponder over** : reflexionar sobre, sopesar
ponderous ['pɑndərəs] *adj* : pesado
pontiff ['pɑntɪf] *n* POPE : pontífice *m*
pontificate [pɑn'tɪfə,keɪt] *vi* **-cated; -cating** : pontificar
pontoon [pɑn'tu:n] *n* : pontón *m*
pony ['po:ni] *n, pl* **-nies** : poni *m*, poney *m*, jaca *f*
ponytail ['po:ni,teɪl] *n* : cola *f* de caballo, coleta *f*
poodle ['pu:dəl] *n* : caniche *m*
pool[1] ['pu:l] *vt* : mancomunar, hacer un fondo común de
pool[2] *n* **1** : charca *f* ⟨a swimming pool : una piscina⟩ **2** PUDDLE : charco *m* **3** RESERVE, SUPPLY : fondo *m* común (de recursos), reserva *f* **4** : billar *m* (juego)
poor ['pʊr, 'por] *adj* **1** : pobre ⟨poor people : los pobres⟩ **2** SCANTY : pobre, escaso ⟨poor attendance : baja asistencia⟩ **3** UNFORTUNATE : pobre ⟨poor thing! : ¡pobrecito!⟩ **4** BAD : malo ⟨to be in poor health : estar mal de salud⟩
poorly ['pʊrli, 'por-] *adv* : mal
pop[1] ['pɑp] *v* **popped; popping** *vi* **1** BURST : reventarse, estallar **2** : ir, venir, o aparecer abruptamente ⟨he popped into the house : se metió en la casa⟩ ⟨a menu pops up : aparece un menú⟩ **3** **to pop out** PROTRUDE : salirse, saltarse ⟨my eyes popped out of my head : se me saltaban los ojos⟩ — *vt* **1** BURST : reventar **2** : hacer o meter abruptamente ⟨he popped it into his mouth : se lo metió en la boca⟩
pop[2] *adj* : popular ⟨pop music : música popular⟩
pop[3] *n* **1** : estallido *m* pequeño (de un globo, etc.) **2** SODA : refresco *m*, gaseosa *f*
popcorn ['pɑp,kɔrn] *n* : palomitas *fpl* (de maíz)

pope ['po:p] *n* : papa *m* ⟨Pope John : el Papa Juan⟩
poplar ['pɑplər] *n* : álamo *m*
poplin ['pɑplɪn] *n* : popelín *m*, popelina *f*
poppy ['pɑpi] *n, pl* **-pies** : amapola *f*
populace ['pɑpjələs] *n* **1** MASSES : pueblo *m* **2** POPULATION : población *f*
popular ['pɑpjələr] *adj* **1** : popular ⟨the popular vote : el voto popular⟩ **2** COMMON : generalizado, común ⟨popular beliefs : creencias generalizadas⟩ **3** : popular, de gran popularidad ⟨a popular singer : un cantante popular⟩
popularity [,pɑpjə'lærəṭi] *n* : popularidad *f*
popularize ['pɑpjələ,raɪz] *vt* **-ized; -izing** : popularizar
popularly ['pɑpjələrli] *adv* : popularmente, vulgarmente
populate ['pɑpjə,leɪt] *vt* **-lated; -lating** : poblar
population [,pɑpjə'leɪʃən] *n* : población *f*
populist ['pɑpjəlɪst] *n* : populista *mf* — **populist** *adj*
populous ['pɑpjələs] *adj* : populoso
porcelain ['pɔrsələn] *n* : porcelana *f*
porch ['pɔrtʃ] *n* : porche *m*
porcupine ['pɔrkjə,paɪn] *n* : puerco *m* espín
pore[1] ['por] *vi* **pored; poring 1** GAZE : mirar (con atención) **2 to pore over** : leer detenidamente, estudiar
pore[2] *n* : poro *m*
pork ['pork] *n* : carne *f* de cerdo, carne *f* de puerco
pornographic [,pɔrnə'græfɪk] *adj* : pornográfico
pornography [pɔr'nɑgrəfi] *n* : pornografía *f*
porous ['porəs] *adj* : poroso
porpoise ['pɔrpəs] *n* **1** : marsopa *f* **2** DOLPHIN : delfín *m*
porridge ['pɔrɪdʒ] *n* : sopa *f* espesa de harina, gachas *fpl*
port[1] ['port] *adj* : de babor ⟨on the port side : a babor⟩
port[2] *n* **1** HARBOR : puerto *m* **2** ORIFICE : orificio *m* (de una válvula, etc.) **3** : puerto *m* (de una computadora) **4** PORTHOLE : portilla *f* **5** *or* **port side** : babor *m* (de un barco) **6** : oporto *m* (vino)
portable ['portəbəl] *adj* : portátil
portal ['portəl] *n* : portal *m*
portend [por'tɛnd] *vt* : presagiar, augurar
portent ['por,tɛnt] *n* : presagio *m*, augurio *m*
portentous [por'tɛntəs] *adj* : profético, que presagia
porter ['portər] *n* : maletero *m*, mozo *m* (de estación)
portfolio [port'fo:li,o] *n, pl* **-lios 1** FOLDER : cartera *f* (para llevar papeles), carpeta *f* **2** : cartera *f* (diplomáti-

ca) **3 investment portfolio** : cartera de inversiones

porthole [ˈpɔrtˌhoːl] *n* : portilla *f* (de un barco), ventanilla *f* (de un avión)

portico [ˈpɔrtɪˌko] *n, pl* **-coes** *or* **-cos** : pórtico *m*

portion¹ [ˈpɔrʃən] *vt* DISTRIBUTE : repartir

portion² *n* PART, SHARE : porción *f*, parte *f*

portly [ˈpɔrtli] *adj* **-lier; -est** : corpulento

portrait [ˈpɔrtrət, -ˌtreɪt] *n* : retrato *m*

portray [pɔrˈtreɪ] *vt* **1** DEPICT : representar, retratar **2** DESCRIBE : describir **3** PLAY : interpretar (un personaje)

portrayal [pɔrˈtreɪəl] *n* **1** REPRESENTATION : representación *f* **2** PORTRAIT : retrato *m*

Portuguese [ˌpɔrtʃəˈgiːz, -ˈgiːs] *n* **1** : portugués *m*, -guesa *f* (persona) **2** : portugués *m* (idioma) — **Portuguese** *adj*

pose¹ [ˈpoːz] *v* **posed; posing** *vt* PRESENT : plantear (una pregunta, etc.), representar (una amenaza) — *vi* **1** : posar (para una foto, etc.) **2 to pose as** : hacerse pasar por

pose² *n* **1** : pose *f* ⟨to strike a pose : asumir una pose⟩ **2** PRETENSE : pose *f*, afectación *f*

posh [ˈpɑʃ] *adj* : elegante, de lujo

position¹ [pəˈzɪʃən] *vt* : colocar, situar, ubicar

position² *n* **1** APPROACH, STANCE : posición *f*, postura *f*, planteamiento *m* **2** LOCATION : posición *f*, ubicación *f* **3** STATUS : posición *f* (en una jerarquía) **4** JOB : puesto *m*

positive [ˈpɑzəṭɪv] *adj* **1** DEFINITE : incuestionable, inequívoco ⟨positive evidence : pruebas irrefutables⟩ **2** CONFIDENT : seguro **3** : positivo (en gramática, matemáticas, y física) **4** AFFIRMATIVE : positivo, afirmativo ⟨a positive response : una respuesta positiva⟩

positively [ˈpɑzəṭɪvli] *adv* **1** FAVORABLY : favorablemente **2** OPTIMISTICALLY : positivamente **3** DEFINITELY : definitivamente, en forma concluyente **4** (*used for emphasis*) : realmente, verdaderamente ⟨it's positively awful! : ¡es verdaderamente malo!⟩

possess [pəˈzɛs] *vt* **1** HAVE, OWN : poseer, tener **2** SEIZE : apoderarse de ⟨he was possessed by fear : el miedo se apoderó de él⟩

possession [pəˈzɛʃən] *n* **1** POSSESSING : posesión *f* **2** : posesión *f* (por un demonio, etc.) **3 possessions** *npl* PROPERTY : bienes *mpl*, propiedad *f*

possessive¹ [pəˈzɛsɪv] *adj* **1** : posesivo (en gramática) **2** JEALOUS : posesivo, celoso

possessive² *n or* **possessive case** : posesivo *m*

possessor [pəˈzɛsər] *n* : poseedor *m*, -dora *f*

possibility [ˌpɑsəˈbɪləṭi] *n, pl* **-ties** : posibilidad *f*

possible [ˈpɑsəbəl] *adj* : posible

possibly [ˈpɑsəbli] *adv* **1** CONCEIVABLY : posiblemente ⟨it can't possibly be true! : ¡no puede ser!⟩ **2** PERHAPS : quizás, posiblemente

possum [ˈpɑsəm] → **opossum**

post¹ [ˈpoːst] *vt* **1** MAIL : echar al correo, mandar por correo **2** ANNOUNCE : anunciar ⟨they've posted the grades : han anunciado las notas⟩ **3** AFFIX : fijar, poner (noticias, etc.) **4** STATION : apostar **5 to keep (someone) posted** : tener al corriente (a alguien)

post² *n* **1** POLE : poste *m*, palo *m* **2** STATION : puesto *m* **3** CAMP : puesto *m* (militar) **4** JOB, POSITION : puesto *m*, empleo *m*, cargo *m*

postage [ˈpoːstɪʤ] *n* : franqueo *m*

postal [ˈpoːstəl] *adj* : postal

postcard [ˈpoːstˌkɑrd] *n* : postal *f*, tarjeta *f* postal

poster [ˈpoːstər] *n* : póster *m*, cartel *m*, afiche *m*

posterior¹ [pɑˈstɪriər, po-] *adj* : posterior

posterior² *n* BUTTOCKS : trasero *m*, nalgas *fpl*, asentaderas *fpl*

posterity [pɑˈstɛrəṭi] *n* : posteridad *f*

postgraduate¹ [ˌpoːstˈgræʤuət] *adj* : de postgrado

postgraduate² *n* : postgraduado *m*, -da *f*

posthaste [ˈpoːstˈheɪst] *adv* : a toda prisa

posthumous [ˈpɑstʃəməs] *adj* : póstumo — **posthumously** *adv*

postman [ˈpoːstmən, -ˌmæn] → **mailman**

postmark¹ [ˈpoːstˌmɑrk] *vt* : matasellar

postmark² *n* : matasellos *m*

postmaster [ˈpoːstˌmæstər] *n* : administrador *m*, -dora *f* de correos

postmodern [ˌpoːstˈmɑdərn] *adj* : posmoderno

postmortem [ˌpoːstˈmɔrtəm] *n* : autopsia *f*

postnatal [ˌpoːstˈneɪtəl] *adj* : postnatal ⟨postnatal depression : depresión posparto⟩

post office *n* : correo *m*, oficina *f* de correos

postoperative [ˌpoːstˈɑpərəṭɪv, -ˌreɪ-] *adj* : posoperatorio

postpaid [ˌpoːstˈpeɪd] *adv* : con franqueo pagado

postpone [ˌpoːstˈpoːn] *vt* **-poned; -poning** : postergar, aplazar, posponer

postponement [ˌpoːstˈpoːnmənt] *n* : postergación *f*, aplazamiento *m*

postscript [ˈpoːstˌskrɪpt] *n* : postdata *f*, posdata *f*

postulate [ˈpɑstʃəˌleɪt] *vt* **-lated; -lating** : postular

posture¹ [ˈpɑstʃər] *vi* **-tured; -turing** : posar, asumir una pose

posture² *n* : postura *f*

postwar [ˌpoːstˈwɔr] *adj* : de (la) posguerra

posy ['po:zi] *n, pl* **-sies 1** FLOWER : flor *f* **2** BOUQUET : ramo *m*, ramillete *m*
pot¹ ['pɑt] *vt* **potted; potting** : plantar (en una maceta)
pot² *n* **1** : olla *f* (de cocina) **2 pots and pans** : cacharros *mpl*
potable ['po:ṭəbəl] *adj* : potable
potash ['pɑt,æʃ] *n* : potasa *f*
potassium [pə'tæsiəm] *n* : potasio *m*
potato [pə'teɪṭo] *n, pl* **-toes** : papa *f*, patata *f Spain*
potato chips *npl* : papas *fpl* fritas (de bolsa)
potbellied ['pɑt,bɛlid] *adj* : panzón, barrigón *fam*
potbelly ['pɑt,bɛli] *n* : panza *f*, barriga *f*
potency ['po:tənʦi] *n, pl* **-cies 1** POWER : fuerza *f*, potencia *f* **2** EFFECTIVENESS : eficacia *f*
potent ['po:tənt] *adj* **1** POWERFUL : potente, poderoso **2** EFFECTIVE : eficaz ⟨a potent medicine : una medicina bien fuerte⟩
potential¹ [pə'tɛnʧəl] *adj* : potencial, posible
potential² *n* **1** : potencial *m* ⟨growth potential : potencial de crecimiento⟩ ⟨a child with potential : un niño que promete⟩ **2** : potencial *m* (eléctrico) — **potentially** *adv*
potful ['pɑt,fʊl] *n* : contenido *m* de una olla ⟨a potful of water : una olla de agua⟩
pothole ['pɑt,ho:l] *n* : bache *m*
potion ['po:ʃən] *n* : brebaje *m*, poción *f*
potluck ['pɑt,lʌk] *n* **to take potluck** : tomar lo que haya
potpourri [,po:pʊ'ri:] *n* : popurrí *m*
potshot ['pɑt,ʃɑt] *n* **1** : tiro *m* al azar ⟨to take potshots at : disparar al azar a⟩ **2** CRITICISM : crítica *f* (hecha al azar)
potter ['pɑṭər] *n* : alfarero *m*, -ra *f*
pottery ['pɑṭəri] *n, pl* **-teries** : cerámica *f*
pouch ['paʊʧ] *n* **1** BAG : bolsa *f* pequeña **2** : bolsa *f* (de un animal)
poultice ['po:lṭəs] *n* : emplasto *m*, cataplasma *f*
poultry ['po:ltri] *n* : aves *fpl* de corral
pounce ['paʊnʦ] *vi* **pounced; pouncing** : abalanzarse
pound¹ ['paʊnd] *vt* **1** CRUSH : machacar, machucar, majar **2** BEAT : golpear, machacar ⟨she pounded the lessons into them : les machacaba las lecciones⟩ ⟨he pounded home his point : les hizo entender su razonamiento⟩ — *vi* **1** BEAT : palpitar (dícese del corazón) **2** RESOUND : retumbar, resonar **3** : andar con paso pesado ⟨we pounded through the mud : caminamos pesadamente por el barro⟩
pound² *n* **1** : libra *f* (unidad de peso) **2** : libra *f* (unidad monetaria) **3 dog pound** : perrera *f*
pour ['por] *vt* **1** : echar, verter, servir (bebidas) ⟨pour it into a pot : viértalo

en una olla⟩ **2** : proveer con abundancia ⟨they poured money into it : le invirtieron mucho dinero⟩ **3 to pour out** : dar salida a ⟨he poured out his feelings to her : se desahogó con ella⟩ — *vi* **1** FLOW : manar, fluir, salir ⟨blood was pouring from the wound : la sangre le salía de la herida⟩ **2 it's pouring (outside)** : está lloviendo a cántaros
pout¹ ['paʊt] *vi* : hacer pucheros
pout² *n* : puchero *m*
poverty ['pɑvərṭi] *n* : pobreza *f*, indigencia *f*
powder¹ ['paʊdər] *vt* **1** : empolvar ⟨to powder one's face : empolvarse la cara⟩ **2** PULVERIZE : pulverizar
powder² *n* : polvo *m*, polvos *mpl*
powdery ['paʊdəri] *adj* : polvoriento, como polvo
power¹ ['paʊər] *vt* : impulsar, propulsar
power² *n* **1** AUTHORITY : poder *m*, autoridad *f* ⟨executive powers : poderes ejecutivos⟩ **2** ABILITY : capacidad *f*, poder *m* **3** : potencia *f* (política) ⟨foreign powers : potencias extranjeras⟩ **4** STRENGTH : fuerza *f* **5** : potencia *f* (en física y matemáticas)
powerful ['paʊərfəl] *adj* : poderoso, potente — **powerfully** *adv*
powerhouse ['paʊər,haʊs] *n* : persona *f* dinámica
powerless ['paʊərləs] *adj* : impotente
power plant *n* : central *f* eléctrica
powwow ['paʊ,waʊ] *n* : conferencia *f*
pox ['pɑks] *n, pl* **pox** *or* **poxes 1** CHICKEN POX : varicela *f* **2** SYPHILIS : sífilis *f*
practicable ['præktɪkəbəl] *adj* : practicable, viable, factible
practical ['præktɪkəl] *adj* : práctico
practicality [,præktɪ'kæləṭi] *n, pl* **-ties** : factibilidad *f*, viabilidad *f*
practical joke *n* : broma *f* (pesada)
practically ['præktɪkli] *adv* **1** : de manera práctica **2** ALMOST : casi, prácticamente
practice¹ *or* **practise** ['præktəs] *vt* **-ticed** *or* **-tised; -ticing** *or* **-tising 1** : practicar ⟨he practiced his German on us : practicó el alemán con nosotros⟩ ⟨to practice politeness : practicar la cortesía⟩ **2** : ejercer ⟨to practice medicine : ejercer la medicina⟩
practice² *n* **1** USE : práctica *f* ⟨to put into practice : poner en práctica⟩ **2** CUSTOM : costumbre *f* ⟨it's a common practice here : por aquí se acostumbra hacerlo⟩ **3** TRAINING : práctica *f* **4** : ejercicio *m* (de una profesión)
practitioner [præk'tɪʃənər] *n* **1** : profesional *mf* **2 general practitioner** : médico *m*, -ca *f*
pragmatic [præg'mæṭɪk] *adj* : pragmático — **pragmatically** *adv*
pragmatism ['prægmə,tɪzəm] *n* : pragmatismo
prairie ['prɛri] *n* : pradera *f*, llanura *f*

praise[1] [ˈpreɪz] vt **praised; praising** : elogiar, alabar ⟨to praise God : alabar a Dios⟩

praise[2] n : elogio m, alabanza f

praiseworthy [ˈpreɪzˌwərði] adj : digno de alabanza, loable

prance[1] [ˈprænts] vi **pranced; prancing 1** : hacer cabriolas, cabriolar ⟨a prancing horse : un caballo haciendo cabriolas⟩ **2** SWAGGER : pavonearse

prance[2] n : cabriola f

prank [ˈpræŋk] n : broma f, travesura f

prankster [ˈpræŋkstər] n : bromista mf

prattle[1] [ˈprætəl] vt **-tled; -tling** : parlotear fam, cotorrear fam, balbucear (como un niño)

prattle[2] n : parloteo m fam, cotorreo m fam, cháchara f fam

prawn [ˈprɔn] n : langostino m, camarón m, gamba f

pray [ˈpreɪ] vt ENTREAT : rogar, suplicar — vi : rezar

prayer [ˈprɛr] n **1** : plegaria f, oración f ⟨to say one's prayers : orar, rezar⟩ ⟨the Lord's Prayer : el Padrenuestro⟩ **2** PRAYING : rezo m, oración f ⟨to kneel in prayer : arrodillarse para rezar⟩

praying mantis → mantis

preach [ˈpriːtʃ] vi : predicar — vt ADVOCATE : abogar por ⟨to preach cooperation : promover la cooperación⟩

preacher [ˈpriːtʃər] n **1** : predicador m, -dora f **2** MINISTER : pastor m, -tora f

preamble [ˈpriːˌæmbəl] n : preámbulo m

prearrange [ˌpriːəˈreɪndʒ] vt **-ranged; -ranging** : arreglar de antemano

precarious [prɪˈkæriəs] adj : precario — **precariously** adv

precariousness [prɪˈkæriəsnəs] n : precariedad f

precaution [prɪˈkɔʃən] n : precaución f

precautionary [prɪˈkɔʃəˌnɛri] adj : preventivo, cautelar, precautorio

precede [prɪˈsiːd] v **-ceded; -ceding** : preceder a

precedence [ˈprɛsədənts, prɪˈsiːdənts] n : precedencia f

precedent [ˈprɛsədənt] n : precedente m

precept [ˈpriːˌsɛpt] n : precepto m

precinct [ˈpriːˌsɪŋkt] n **1** DISTRICT : distrito m (policial, electoral, etc.) **2 precincts** npl PREMISES : recinto m, predio m, límites mpl (de una ciudad)

precious [ˈprɛʃəs] adj **1** : precioso ⟨precious gems : piedras preciosas⟩ **2** DEAR : querido **3** AFFECTED : afectado

precipice [ˈprɛsəpəs] n : precipicio m

precipitate [prɪˈsɪpəˌteɪt] v **-tated; -tating** vt **1** HASTEN, PROVOKE : precipitar, provocar **2** HURL : arrojar **3** : precipitar (en química) — vi : precipitarse (en química), condensarse (en meteorología)

precipitation [prɪˌsɪpəˈteɪʃən] n **1** HASTE : precipitación f, prisa f **2** : precipitaciones fpl (en meteorología)

precipitous [prɪˈsɪpətəs] adj **1** HASTY, RASH : precipitado **2** STEEP : escarpado, empinado ⟨a precipitous drop : una caída vertiginosa⟩

précis [preɪˈsiː] n, pl **précis** [-ˈsiːz] : resumen m

precise [prɪˈsaɪs] adj **1** DEFINITE : preciso, explícito **2** EXACT : exacto, preciso ⟨precise calculations : cálculos precisos⟩ — **precisely** adv

preciseness [prɪˈsaɪsnəs] n : precisión f, exactitud f

precision [prɪˈsɪʒən] n : precisión f

preclude [prɪˈkluːd] vt **-cluded; -cluding** : evitar, impedir, excluir (una posibilidad, etc.)

precocious [prɪˈkoːʃəs] adj : precoz — **precociously** adv

precocity [prɪˈkɑsəti] n : precocidad f

preconceive [ˌpriːkənˈsiːv] vt **-ceived; -ceiving** : preconcebir

preconception [ˌpriːkənˈspʃən] n : idea f preconcebida

precondition [ˌpriːkənˈdɪʃən] n : precondición f, condición f previa

precook [ˌpriːˈkʊk] vt : precocinar

precursor [prɪˈkərsər] n : precursor m, -sora f

predator [ˈprɛdətər] n : depredador m, -dora f

predatory [ˈprɛdəˌtori] adj : depredador

predecessor [ˈprɛdəˌsɛsər, ˈpriː-] n : antecesor m, -sora f; predecesor m, -sora f

predestination [priˌdɛstəˈneɪʃən] n : predestinación f

predestine [prɪˈdɛstən] vt **-tined; -tining** : predestinar

predetermine [ˌpriːdɪˈtərmən] vt **-mined; -mining** : predeterminar

predicament [prɪˈdɪkəmənt] n : apuro m, aprieto m

predicate[1] [ˈprɛdəˌkeɪt] vt **-cated; -cating 1** AFFIRM : afirmar, aseverar **2 to be predicated on** : estar basado en

predicate[2] [ˈprɛdɪkət] n : predicado m

predict [prɪˈdɪkt] vt : pronosticar, predecir

predictable [prɪˈdɪktəbəl] adj : previsible — **predictably** [-bli] adv

prediction [prɪˈdɪkʃən] n : pronóstico m, predicción f

predilection [ˌprɛdəlˈɛkʃən, ˌpriː-] n : predilección f

predispose [ˌpriːdɪˈspoːz] vt **-posed; -posing** : predisponer

predisposition [ˌpriːˌdɪspəˈzɪʃən] n : predisposición f

predominance [prɪˈdɑmənənts] n : predominio m

predominant [prɪˈdɑmənənt] adj : predominante — **predominantly** adv

predominate [prɪˈdɑməˌneɪt] vi **-nated; -nating 1** : predominar (en cantidad) **2** PREVAIL : prevalecer

preeminence [priˈɛmənənts] n : preeminencia f

preeminent [priˈɛmənənt] adj : preeminente

preeminently [priˈɛmənəntli] adv : especialmente

preempt [pri'ɛmpt] *vt* **1** APPROPRIATE : apoderarse de, apropiarse de **2** : reemplazar (un programa de televisión, etc.) **3** FORESTALL : adelantarse a (un ataque, etc.)

preen ['pri:n] *vt* : arreglarse (el pelo, las plumas, etc.)

prefabricated [ˌpri:'fæbrəˌkeɪţəd] *adj* : prefabricado

preface ['prɛfəs] *n* : prefacio *m*, prólogo *m*

prefatory ['prɛfəˌtori] *adj* : preliminar

prefer [pri'fər] *vt* **-ferred; -ferring 1** : preferir ⟨I prefer coffee : prefiero café⟩ **2 to prefer charges against** : presentar cargos contra

preferable ['prɛfərəbəl] *adj* : preferible

preferably ['prɛfərəbli] *adv* : preferentemente, de preferencia

preference ['prɛfrənʦ, 'prɛfər-] *n* : preferencia *f*, gusto *m*

preferential [ˌprɛfə'rɛnʧəl] *adj* : preferencial, preferente

prefigure [pri'fɪgjər] *vt* **-ured; -uring** FORESHADOW : prefigurar, anunciar

prefix ['pri:ˌfɪks] *n* : prefijo *m*

pregnancy ['prɛgnənʦi] *n, pl* **-cies** : embarazo *m*, preñez *f*

pregnant ['prɛgnənt] *adj* **1** : embarazada (dícese de una mujer), preñada (dícese de un animal) **2** MEANINGFUL : significativo

preheat [ˌpri:'hi:t] *vt* : precalentar

prehensile [pri'hɛnʦəl, -'hɛnˌsaɪl] *adj* : prensil

prehistoric [ˌpri:hɪs'tɔrɪk] *or* **prehistorical** [-ɪkəl] *adj* : prehistórico

prejudge [ˌpri:'ʤʌʤ] *vt* **-judged; -judging** : prejuzgar

prejudice¹ ['prɛʤədəs] *vt* **-diced; -dicing 1** DAMAGE : perjudicar **2** BIAS : predisponer, influir en

prejudice² *n* **1** DAMAGE : perjuicio *m* (en derecho) **2** BIAS : prejuicio *m*

prelate ['prɛlət] *n* : prelado *m*

preliminary¹ [pri'lɪməˌnɛri] *adj* : preliminar

preliminary² *n, pl* **-naries 1** : preámbulo *m*, preludio *m* **2 preliminaries** *npl* : preliminares *mpl*

prelude ['prɛˌlu:d, 'prɛlˌju:d; 'preɪˌlu:d, 'pri:-] *n* : preludio *m*

premarital [ˌpri:'mærəţəl] *adj* : prematrimonial

premature [ˌpri:mə'tʊr, -'tjʊr, -'ʧʊr] *adj* : prematuro — **prematurely** *adv*

premeditate [pri'mɛdəˌteɪt] *vt* **-tated; -tating** : premeditar

premeditation [priˌmɛdə'teɪʃən] *n* : premeditación *f*

premenstrual [pri'mɛnʦstruəl] *adj* : premenstrual

premier¹ [pri'mɪr, -'mjɪr; 'pri:miər] *adj* : principal

premier² *n* PRIME MINISTER : primer ministro *m*, primera ministra *f*

premiere¹ [prɪ'mjɛr, -'mɪr] *vt* **-miered; -miering** : estrenar

premiere² *n* : estreno *m*

premise ['prɛmɪs] *n* **1** : premisa *f* ⟨the premise of his arguments : la premisa de sus argumentos⟩ **2 premises** *npl* : recinto *m*, local *m*

premium ['pri:miəm] *n* **1** BONUS : prima *f* **2** SURCHARGE : recargo *m* ⟨to sell at a premium : vender (algo) muy caro⟩ **3 insurance premium** : prima *f* (de seguros) **4 to set a premium on** : darle un gran valor (a algo)

premonition [ˌpri:mə'nɪʃən, ˌprɛmə-] *n* : presentimiento *m*, premonición *f*

prenatal [ˌpri:'neɪţəl] *adj* : prenatal

preoccupation [priˌɑkjə'peɪʃən] *n* : preocupación *f*

preoccupied [pri'ɑkjəˌpaɪd] *adj* : abstraído, ensimismado, preocupado

preoccupy [pri'ɑkjəˌpaɪ] *vt* **-pied; -pying** : preocupar

preparation [ˌprɛpə'reɪʃən] *n* **1** PREPARING : preparación *f* **2** MIXTURE : preparado *m* ⟨a preparation for burns : un preparado para quemaduras⟩ **3 preparations** *npl* ARRANGEMENTS : preparativos *mpl*

preparatory [pri'pærəˌtori] *adj* : preparatorio

prepare [pri'pær] *v* **-pared; -paring** *vt* : preparar — *vi* : prepararse

prepay [ˌpri:'peɪ] *vt* **-paid; -paying** : pagar por adelantado

preponderance [pri'pɑndərənʦ] *n* : preponderancia *f*

preponderant [pri'pɑndərənt] *adj* : preponderante — **preponderantly** *adv*

preposition [ˌprɛpə'zɪʃən] *n* : preposición *f*

prepositional [ˌprɛpə'zɪʃənəl] *adj* : preposicional

prepossessing [ˌpri:pə'zɛsɪŋ] *adj* : atractivo, agradable

preposterous [pri'pɑstərəs] *adj* : absurdo, ridículo

prerequisite¹ [pri'rɛkwəzət] *adj* : necesario, esencial

prerequisite² *n* : condición *f* necesario, requisito *m* previo

prerogative [pri'rɑgəţɪv] *n* : prerrogativa *f*

presage ['prɛsɪʤ, pri'seɪʤ] *vt* **-saged; -saging** : presagiar

preschool ['pri:ˌsku:l] *adj* : preescolar ⟨preschool students : estudiantes de preescolar⟩

prescribe [pri'skraɪb] *vt* **-scribed; -scribing 1** ORDAIN : prescribir, ordenar **2** : recetar (medicinas, etc.)

prescription [pri'skrɪpʃən] *n* : receta *f*

presence ['prɛzənʦ] *n* : presencia *f*

present¹ [pri'zɛnt] *vt* **1** INTRODUCE : presentar ⟨to present oneself : presentarse⟩ **2** : presentar (una obra de teatro, etc.) **3** GIVE : entregar (un regalo, etc.), regalar, obsequiar **4** SHOW : presentar, ofrecer ⟨it presents a lovely view : ofrece una vista muy linda⟩

present² ['prɛzənt] *adj* **1** : actual ⟨present conditions : condiciones actuales⟩

2 : presente ⟨all the students were present : todos los estudiantes estaban presentes⟩

present³ ['prɛzənt] *n* **1** GIFT : regalo *m*, obsequio *m* **2** : presente *m* ⟨at present : en este momento⟩ **3** *or* **present tense** : presente *m*

presentable [pri'zɛntəbəl] *adj* : presentable

presentation [ˌpri:ˌzɛn'teɪʃən, ˌprɛzən-] *n* : presentación *f* ⟨presentation ceremony : ceremonia de entrega⟩

presentiment [pri'zɛntəmənt] *n* : presentimiento *m*, premonición *f*

presently ['prɛzəntli] *adv* **1** SOON : pronto, dentro de poco **2** NOW : actualmente, ahora

present participle *n* : participio *m* presente, participio *m* activo

preservation [ˌprɛzər'veɪʃən] *n* : conservación *f*, preservación *f*

preservative [pri'zərvətɪv] *n* : conservante *m*

preserve¹ [pri'zərv] *vt* **-served; -serving** **1** PROTECT : proteger, preservar **2** : conservar (los alimentos, etc.) **3** MAINTAIN : conservar, mantener

preserve² *n* **1** *or* **preserves** *npl* : conserva *f* ⟨peach preserves : duraznos en conserva⟩ **2** : coto *m* ⟨game preserve : coto de caza⟩

preside [pri'zaɪd] *vi* **-sided; -siding 1 to preside over** : presidir ⟨he presided over the meeting : presidió la reunión⟩ **2 to preside over** : supervisar ⟨she presides over the department : dirige el departamento⟩

presidency ['prɛzədəntsi] *n, pl* **-cies** : presidencia *f*

president ['prɛzədənt] *n* : presidente *m*, -ta *f*

presidential [ˌprɛzə'dɛntʃəl] *adj* : presidencial

press¹ ['prɛs] *vt* **1** PUSH : apretar **2** SQUEEZE : apretar, prensar (frutas, flores, etc.) **3** IRON : planchar (ropa) **4** URGE : instar, apremiar ⟨he pressed me to come : insistió en que viniera⟩ — *vi* **1** PUSH : apretar ⟨press hard : aprieta con fuerza⟩ **2** CROWD : apiñarse **3** : abrirse paso ⟨I pressed through the crowd : me abrí paso entre el gentío⟩ **4** URGE : presionar

press² *n* **1** CROWD : multitud *f* **2** : imprenta *f*, prensa *f* ⟨to go to press : entrar en prensa⟩ **3** URGENCY : urgencia *f*, prisa *f* **4** PRINTER, PUBLISHER : imprenta *f*, editorial *f* **5 the press** : la prensa ⟨freedom of the press : libertad de prensa⟩

pressing ['prɛsɪŋ] *adj* URGENT : urgente

pressure¹ ['prɛʃər] *vt* **-sured; -suring** : presionar, apremiar

pressure² *n* **1** : presión *f* ⟨to be under pressure : estar bajo presión⟩ **2** → **blood pressure**

pressurize ['prɛʃəˌraɪz] *vt* **-ized; -izing** : presurizar

prestige [prɛ'sti:ʒ, -'sti:dʒ] *n* : prestigio *m*

prestigious [prɛ'stɪdʒəs] *adj* : prestigioso

presto ['prɛsˌto:] *adv* : de pronto

presumably [pri'zu:məbli] *adv* : es de suponer, supuestamente ⟨presumably, he's guilty : supone que es culpable⟩

presume [pri'zu:m] *vt* **-sumed; -suming** **1** ASSUME, SUPPOSE : suponer, asumir, presumir **2 to presume to** : atreverse a, osar

presumption [pri'zʌmpʃən] *n* **1** AUDACITY : atrevimiento *m*, osadía *f* **2** ASSUMPTION : presunción *f*, suposición *f*

presumptuous [pri'zʌmptʃuəs] *adj* : descarado, atrevido

presuppose [ˌpri:sə'po:z] *vt* **-posed; -posing** : presuponer

pretend [pri'tɛnd] *vt* **1** CLAIM : pretender **2** FEIGN : fingir, simular — *vi* : fingir

pretender [pri'tɛndər] *n* : pretendiente *mf* (al trono, etc.)

pretense *or* **pretence** ['pri:ˌtɛnts, pri'tɛnts] *n* **1** CLAIM : afirmación *f* (falsa), pretensión *f* **2** FEIGNING : fingimiento *m*, simulación *f* ⟨to make a pretense of doing something : fingir hacer algo⟩ ⟨a pretense of order : una apariencia de orden⟩ **3** PRETEXT : pretexto *m* ⟨under false pretenses : con pretextos falsos, de manera fraudulenta⟩

pretension [pri'tɛntʃən] *n* **1** CLAIM : pretensión *f*, afirmación *f* **2** ASPIRATION : aspiración *f*, ambición *f* **3** PRETENTIOUSNESS : pretensiones *fpl*, presunción *f*

pretentious [pri'tɛntʃəs] *adj* : pretencioso

pretentiousness [pri'tɛntʃəsnəs] *n* : presunción *f*, pretensiones *fpl*

pretext ['pri:ˌtɛkst] *n* : pretexto *m*, excusa *f*

prettily ['prɪtəli] *adv* : atractivamente

prettiness ['prɪtinəs] *n* : lindeza *f*

pretty¹ ['prɪti] *adv* : bastante, bien ⟨it's pretty obvious : está bien claro⟩ ⟨it's pretty much the same : es más o menos igual⟩

pretty² *adj* **-tier; -est** : bonito, lindo, guapo ⟨a pretty girl : una muchacha guapa⟩ ⟨what a pretty dress! : ¡qué vestido más lindo!⟩

pretzel ['prɛtsəl] *n* : galleta *f* salada (en forma de nudo)

prevail [pri'veɪl] *vi* **1** TRIUMPH : prevalecer **2** PREDOMINATE : predominar **3 to prevail upon** : persuadir, convencer ⟨I prevailed upon her to sing : la convencí para que cantara⟩

prevailing [pri'veɪlɪŋ] *adj* : imperante, prevaleciente

prevalence ['prɛvələnts] *n* : preponderancia *f*, predominio *m*

prevalent ['prɛvələnt] *adj* **1** COMMON : común y corriente, general **2** WIDESPREAD : extendido

prevaricate [pri'værə,keɪt] *vi* **-cated;
-cating** LIE : mentir
prevarication [pri,værə'keɪʃən] *n* : mentira *f*
prevent [pri'vɛnt] *vt* **1** AVOID : prevenir,
evitar ⟨steps to prevent war : medidas
para evitar la guerra⟩ **2** HINDER : impedir
preventable [pri'vɛntəbəl] *adj* : evitable
preventative [pri'vɛntətɪv] → **preventive**
prevention [pri'vɛntʃən] *n* : prevención
f
preventive [pri'vɛntɪv] *adj* : preventivo
preview ['pri:,vju] *n* : preestreno *m*
previous ['pri:viəs] *adj* : previo, anteri-
or ⟨previous knowledge : conocimien-
tos previos⟩ ⟨the previous day : el día
anterior⟩ ⟨in the previous year : en el
año pasado⟩
previously ['pri:viəsli] *adv* : antes
prewar [,pri:'wɔr] *adj* : de antes de la
guerra
prey ['preɪ] *n*, *pl* **preys** : presa *f*
prey on *vt* **1** : cazar, alimentarse de ⟨it
preys on fish : se alimenta de peces⟩ **2
to prey on one's mind** : hacer presa en
alguien, atormentar a alguien
price[1] ['praɪs] *vt* **priced; pricing** : poner
un precio a
price[2] *n* : precio *m* ⟨peace at any price
: la paz a toda costa⟩
priceless ['praɪsləs] *adj* : inestimable, inapreciable
pricey ['praɪsi] *adj* : caro
prick[1] ['prɪk] *vt* **1** : pinchar **2 to prick
up one's ears** : levantar las orejas —
vi : pinchar
prick[2] *n* **1** STAB : pinchazo *m* ⟨a prick
of conscience : un remordimiento⟩ **2**
→ **pricker**
pricker ['prɪkər] *n* THORN : espina *f*
prickle[1] ['prɪkəl] *vi* **-led; -ling** : sentir un
cosquilleo, tener un hormigueo
prickle[2] *n* **1** : espina *f* (de una planta) **2**
TINGLE : cosquilleo *m*, hormigueo *m*
prickly ['prɪkəli] *adj* **1** THORNY : espinoso **2** : que pica ⟨a prickly sensation : un hormigueo⟩
prickly pear *n* : tuna *f*
pride[1] ['praɪd] *vt* **prided; priding** : estar
orgulloso de ⟨to pride oneself on : preciarse de, enorgullecerse de⟩
pride[2] *n* : orgullo *m*
priest ['pri:st] *n* : sacerdote *m*, cura *m*
priestess ['pri:stɪs] *n* : sacerdotisa *f*
priesthood ['pri:st,hʊd] *n* : sacerdocio *m*
priestly ['pri:stli] *adj* : sacerdotal
prig ['prɪg] *n* : mojigato *m*, -ta *f*; gazmoño *m*, -ña *f*
prim ['prɪm] *adj* **primmer; primmest 1**
PRISSY : remilgado **2** PRUDISH : mojigato, gazmoño
primarily [praɪ'mɛrəli] *adv* : principalmente, fundamentalmente
primary[1] ['praɪ,mɛri, 'praɪməri] *adj* **1**
FIRST : primario **2** PRINCIPAL : principal **3** BASIC : fundamental

primary[2] *n*, *pl* **-ries** : elección *f* primaria
primary color *n* : color *m* primario
primary school → **elementary school**
primate *n* **1** ['praɪ,meɪt, -mət] : primado *m* (obispo) **2** [-,meɪt] : primate *m*
(animal)
prime[1] ['praɪm] *vt* **primed; priming 1**
: cebar ⟨to prime a pump : cebar una
bomba⟩ **2** PREPARE : preparar (una
superficie para pintar) **3** COACH
: preparar (a un testigo, etc.)
prime[2] *adj* **1** CHIEF, MAIN : principal,
primero **2** EXCELLENT : de primera
(categoría), excelente
prime[3] *n* **the prime of one's life** : la flor
de la vida
prime minister *n* : primer ministro *m*,
primera ministra *f*
primer[1] ['prɪmər] *n* **1** READER : cartilla
f **2** MANUAL : manual *m*
primer[2] ['praɪmər] *n* **1** : cebo *m* (para
explosivos) **2** : base *f* (de pintura)
prime time *n* : horas *fpl* de mayor audiencia
primeval [praɪ'mi:vəl] *adj* : primitivo,
primigenio
primitive ['prɪmətɪv] *adj* : primitivo
primly ['prɪmli] *adv* : mojigatamente
primness ['prɪmnəs] *n* : mojigatería *f*,
gazmoñería *f*
primordial [praɪ'mɔrdiəl] *adj* : primordial, fundamental
primp ['prɪmp] *vi* : arreglarse, acicalarse
primrose ['prɪm,ro:z] *n* : primavera *f*,
prímula *f*
prince ['prɪnts] *n* : príncipe *m*
princely ['prɪntsli] *adj* : principesco
princess ['prɪntsəs, 'prɪn,sɛs] *n* : princesa *f*
principal[1] ['prɪntsəpəl] *adj* : principal —
principally *adv*
principal[2] *n* **1** PROTAGONIST : protagonista *mf* **2** : director *m*, -tora *f* (de una
escuela) **3** CAPITAL : principal *m*, capital *m* (en finanzas)
principality [,prɪntsə'pæləti] *n*, *pl* **-ties**
: principado *m*
principle ['prɪntsəpəl] *n* : principio *m*
print[1] ['prɪnt] *vt* : imprimir (libros, etc.)
— *vi* : escribir con letra de molde
print[2] *n* **1** IMPRESSION : marca *f*, huella
f, impresión *f* **2** : texto *m* impreso ⟨to
be out of print : estar agotado⟩ **3** LET-
TERING : letra *f* **4** ENGRAVING : grabado *m* **5** : copia *f* (en fotografía) **6** : estampado *m* (de tela)
printer ['prɪntər] *n* **1** : impresor *m*, -sora
f (persona) **2** : impresora *f* (máquina)
printing ['prɪntɪŋ] *n* **1** : impresión *f*
(acto) ⟨the third printing : la tercera
tirada⟩ **2** : imprenta *f* (profesión) **3**
LETTERING : letras *fpl* de molde
printing press *n* : prensa *f*
print out *vt* : imprimir (de una computadora)
printout ['prɪnt,aʊt] *n* : copia *f* impresa
(de una computadora)
prior ['praɪər] *adj* **1** : previo **2 prior to**
: antes de

priority [praɪˈɔrəti] *n, pl* **-ties** : prioridad *f*

priory [ˈpraɪəri] *n, pl* **-ries** : priorato *m*

prism [ˈprɪzəm] *n* : prisma *m*

prison [ˈprɪzən] *n* : prisión *f*, cárcel *f*

prisoner [ˈprɪzənər] *n* : preso *m*, -sa *f*; recluso *m*, -sa *f* ⟨prisoner of war : prisionero de guerra⟩

prissy [ˈprɪsi] *adj* **-sier; -est** : remilgado, melindroso

pristine [ˈprɪsˌtiːn, prɪsˈ-] *adj* : puro, prístino

privacy [ˈpraɪvəsi] *n, pl* **-cies** : privacidad *f*

private[1] [ˈpraɪvət] *adj* **1** PERSONAL : privado, particular ⟨private property : propiedad privada⟩ **2** INDEPENDENT : privado, independiente ⟨private studies : estudios privados⟩ **3** SECRET : secreto **4** SECLUDED : aislado, privado — **privately** *adv*

private[2] *n* : soldado *m* raso

privateer [ˌpraɪvəˈtɪr] *n* : corsario *m*

privation [praɪˈveɪʃən] *n* : privación *f*

privilege [ˈprɪvlɪdʒ, ˈprɪvə-] *n* : privilegio *m*

privileged [ˈprɪvlɪdʒd, ˈprɪvə-] *adj* : privilegiado

privy[1] [ˈprɪvi] *adj* **to be privy to** : estar enterado de

privy[2] *n, pl* **privies** : excusado *m*, retrete *m* (exterior)

prize[1] [ˈpraɪz] *vt* **prized; prizing** : valorar, apreciar

prize[2] *adj* **1** : premiado ⟨a prize stallion : un semental premiado⟩ **2** OUTSTANDING : de primera, excepcional

prize[3] *n* **1** AWARD : premio *m* ⟨third prize : el tercer premio⟩ **2** : joya *f*, tesoro *m* ⟨he's a real prize : es un tesoro⟩

prizefighter [ˈpraɪzˌfaɪtər] *n* : boxeador *m*, -dora *f* profesional

prizewinning [ˈpraɪzˌwɪnɪŋ] *adj* : premiado

pro[1] [ˈproː] *adv* : a favor

pro[2] *adj* → **professional**[1]

pro[3] *n* **1** : pro *m* ⟨the pros and cons : los pros y los contras⟩ **2** → **professional**[2]

probability [ˌprɑbəˈbɪləti] *n, pl* **-ties** : probabilidad *f*

probable [ˈprɑbəbəl] *adj* : probable — **probably** [-bli] *adv*

probate[1] [ˈproːˌbeɪt] *vt* **-bated; -bating** : autenticar (un testamento)

probate[2] *n* : autenticación *f* (de un testamento)

probation [proˈbeɪʃən] *n* **1** : período *m* de prueba (para un empleado, etc.) **2** : libertad *f* condicional (para un preso)

probationary [proˈbeɪʃəˌneri] *adj* : de prueba

probe[1] [ˈproːb] *vt* **probed; probing 1** : sondar (en medicina y tecnología) **2** INVESTIGATE : investigar, sondear

probe[2] *n* **1** : sonda *f* (en medicina, etc.) ⟨space probe : sonda espacial⟩ **2** INVESTIGATION : investigación *f*, sondeo *m*

probity [ˈproːbəti] *n* : probidad *f*

problem[1] [ˈprɑbləm] *adj* : difícil

problem[2] *n* : problema *m*

problematic [ˌprɑbləˈmætɪk] *or* **problematical** [-tɪkəl] *adj* : problemático

proboscis [prəˈbɑsɪs] *n, pl* **-cises** *also* **-cides** [-səˌdiːz] : probóscide *f*

procedural [prəˈsɜrəl] *adj* : de procedimiento

procedure [prəˈsiːdʒər] *n* : procedimiento *m* ⟨administrative procedures : trámites administrativos⟩

proceed [proˈsiːd] *vi* **1** : proceder ⟨to proceed to do something : proceder a hacer algo⟩ **2** CONTINUE : continuar, proseguir ⟨he proceeded to the next phase : pasó a la segunda fase⟩ **3** ADVANCE : avanzar ⟨as the conference proceeded : mientras seguía avanzando la conferencia⟩ ⟨the road proceeds south : la calle sigue hacia el sur⟩

proceeding [proˈsiːdɪŋ] *n* **1** PROCEDURE : procedimiento *m* **2 proceedings** *npl* EVENTS : acontecimientos *mpl* **3 proceedings** *npl* MINUTES : actas *fpl* (de una reunión, etc.)

proceeds [ˈproːˌsiːdz] *npl* : ganancias *fpl*

process[1] [ˈprɑˌsɛs, ˈproː-] *vt* : procesar, tratar

process[2] *n, pl* **-cesses** [ˈprɑˌsɛsəz, ˈproː-, -səsəz, -səˌsiːz] **1** : proceso *m* ⟨the process of elimination : el proceso de eliminación⟩ **2** METHOD : proceso *m*, método *m* ⟨manufacturing processes : procesos industriales⟩ **3** : acción *f* judicial ⟨due process of law : el debido proceso (de la ley)⟩ **4** SUMMONS : citación *f* **5** PROJECTION : protuberancia *f* (anatómica) **6 in the process of** : en vías de ⟨in the process of repair : en reparaciones⟩

procession [prəˈsɛʃən] *n* : procesión *f*, desfile *m* ⟨a funeral procession : un cortejo fúnebre⟩

processional [prəˈsɛʃənəl] *n* : himno *m* para una procesión

processor [ˈprɑˌsɛsər, ˈproː-, -səsər] *n* **1** : procesador *m* (de una computadora) **2 food processor** : procesador *m* de alimentos

proclaim [proˈkleɪm] *vt* : proclamar

proclamation [ˌprɑkləˈmeɪʃən] *n* : proclamación *f*

proclivity [proˈklɪvəti] *n, pl* **-ties** : proclividad *f*

procrastinate [prəˈkræstəˌneɪt] *vi* **-nated; -nating** : demorar, aplazar las responsabilidades

procrastination [prəˌkræstəˈneɪʃən] *n* : aplazamiento *m*, demora *f*, dilación *f*

procreate [ˈproːkriˌeɪt] *vi* **-ated; -ating** : procrear

procreation [ˌproːkriˈeɪʃən] *n* : procreación *f*

proctor[1] [ˈprɑktər] *vt* : supervisar (un examen)

proctor[2] *n* : supervisor *m*, -sora *f* (de un examen)

procure [prə'kjʊr] vt -cured; -curing 1 OBTAIN : procurar, obtener 2 BRING ABOUT : provocar, lograr, conseguir
procurement [prə'kjʊrmənt] n : obtención f
prod[1] ['prɑd] vt **prodded; prodding** 1 JAB, POKE : pinchar, golpear (con la punta de algo) 2 GOAD : incitar, estimular
prod[2] n 1 JAB, POKE : golpe m (con la punta de algo), pinchazo m 2 STIMULUS : estímulo m 3 **cattle prod** : picana f, aguijón m
prodigal[1] ['prɑdɪgəl] adj SPENDTHRIFT : pródigo, despilfarrador, derrochador
prodigal[2] n : pródigo m, -ga f; derrochador m, -dora f
prodigious [prə'dɪdʒəs] adj 1 MARVELOUS : prodigioso, maravilloso 2 HUGE : enorme, vasto ⟨prodigious sums : muchísimo dinero⟩ — **prodigiously** adv
prodigy ['prɑdədʒi] n, pl -gies : prodigio m ⟨child prodigy : niño prodigio⟩
produce[1] [prə'du:s, -'dju:s] vt -duced; -ducing 1 EXHIBIT : presentar, mostrar 2 YIELD : producir 3 CAUSE : producir, causar 4 CREATE : producir ⟨to produce a poem : escribir un poema⟩ 5 : poner en escena (una obra de teatro), producir (una película)
produce[2] ['prɑ₁du:s, 'pro:-, -₁dju:s] n : productos mpl agrícolas
producer [prə'du:sər, -'dju:-] n : productor m, -tora f
product ['prɑ₁dʌkt] n : producto m
production [prə'dʌkʃən] n : producción f
productive [prə'dʌktɪv] adj : productivo
productivity [₁pro:₁dʌk'tɪvəṭi, ₁prɑ-] n : productividad f
profane[1] [pro'feɪn] vt -faned; -faning : profanar
profane[2] adj 1 SECULAR : profano 2 IRREVERENT : irreverente, impío
profanity [pro'fænəṭi] n, pl -ties 1 IRREVERENCE : irreverencia f, impiedad f 2 : blasfemias fpl, obscenidades fpl ⟨don't use profanity : no digas blasfemias⟩
profess [prə'fɛs] vt 1 DECLARE : declarar, manifestar 2 CLAIM : pretender 3 : profesar (una religión, etc.)
professedly [prə'fɛsədli] adv 1 OPENLY : declaradamente 2 ALLEGEDLY : supuestamente
profession [prə'fɛʃən] n : profesión f
professional[1] [prə'fɛʃənəl] adj : profesional — **professionally** adv
professional[2] n : profesional mf
professionalism [prə'fɛʃənə₁lizəm] n : profesionalismo m
professor [prə'fɛsər] n : profesor m (universitario), profesora f (universitaria); catedrático m, -ca f
proffer ['prɑfər] vt -fered; -fering : ofrecer, dar

proficiency [prə'fɪʃəntsi] n : competencia f, capacidad f
proficient [prə'fɪʃənt] adj : competente, experto — **proficiently** adv
profile ['pro:₁faɪl] n : perfil m ⟨a portrait in profile : un retrato de perfil⟩ ⟨to keep a low profile : no llamar la atención, hacerse pasar desapercibido⟩
profit[1] ['prɑfət] vi : sacar provecho (de), beneficiarse (de)
profit[2] n 1 ADVANTAGE : provecho m, partido m, beneficio m 2 GAIN : beneficio m, utilidad f, ganancia f ⟨to make a profit : sacar beneficios⟩
profitable ['prɑfəṭəbəl] adj : rentable, lucrativo — **profitably** [-bli] adv
profitless ['prɑfətləs] adj : infructuoso, inútil
profligate ['prɑflɪgət, -₁geɪt] adj 1 DISSOLUTE : disoluto, licencioso 2 SPENDTHRIFT : despilfarrador, derrochador, pródigo
profound [prə'faʊnd] adj : profundo
profoundly [prə'faʊndli] adv : profundamente, en profundidad
profundity [prə'fʌndəṭi] n, pl -ties : profundidad f
profuse [prə'fju:s] adj 1 COPIOUS : profuso, copioso 2 LAVISH : pródigo — **profusely** adv
profusion [prə'fju:ʒən] n : abundancia f, profusión f
progenitor [pro'dʒɛnəṭər] n : progenitor m, -tora f
progeny ['prɑdʒəni] n, pl -nies : progenie f
progesterone [pro'dʒɛstə₁ro:n] n : progesterona f
prognosis [prɑg'no:sɪs] n, pl -noses [-₁si:z] : pronóstico m (médico)
program[1] ['pro:₁græm, -grəm] vt -grammed or -gramed; -gramming or -graming : programar
program[2] n : programa m
programmable ['pro:₁græməbəl] adj : programable
programmer ['pro:₁græmər] n : programador m, -dora f
programming ['pro:₁græmɪŋ] n : programación f
progress[1] [prə'grɛs] vi 1 PROCEED : progresar, adelantar 2 IMPROVE : mejorar
progress[2] ['prɑgrəs, -₁grɛs] n 1 ADVANCE : progreso m, adelanto m, avance m ⟨to make progress : hacer progresos⟩ 2 BETTERMENT : mejora f, mejoramiento m
progression [prə'grɛʃən] n 1 ADVANCE : avance m 2 SEQUENCE : desarrollo m (de eventos)
progressive [prə'grɛsɪv] adj 1 : progresista ⟨a progressive society : una sociedad progresista⟩ 2 : progresivo ⟨a progressive disease : una enfermedad progresiva⟩ 3 or **Progressive** : progresista (en política) 4 : progresivo (en gramática)

progressively [prə'grɛsɪvli] *adv* : progresivamente, poco a poco

prohibit [pro'hɪbət] *vt* : prohibir

prohibition [ˌproːə'bɪʃən, ˌproːhə-] *n* : prohibición *f*

prohibitive [pro'hɪbətɪv] *adj* : prohibitivo

project¹ [prə'dʒɛkt] *vt* **1** PLAN : proyectar, planear **2** : proyectar (imágenes, misiles, etc.) — *vi* PROTRUDE : sobresalir, salir

project² ['prɑˌdʒɛkt, -dʒɪkt] *n* : proyecto *m*, trabajo *m* (de un estudiante) ⟨research project : proyecto de investigación⟩

projectile [prə'dʒɛktəl, -ˌtaɪl] *n* : proyectil *m*

projection [prə'dʒɛkʃən] *n* **1** PLAN : plan *m*, proyección *f* **2** : proyección *f* (de imágenes, misiles, etc.) **3** PROTRUSION : saliente *m*

projector [prə'dʒɛktər] *n* : proyector *m*

proletarian¹ [ˌproːlə'tɛriən] *adj* : proletario

proletarian² *n* : proletario *m*, -ria *f*

proletariat [ˌproːlə'tɛriət] *n* : proletariado *m*

proliferate [prə'lɪfəˌreɪt] *vi* **-ated; -ating** : proliferar

proliferation [prəˌlɪfə'reɪʃən] *n* : proliferación *f*

prolific [prə'lɪfɪk] *adj* : prolífico

prologue ['proːˌlɔg] *n* : prólogo *m*

prolong [prə'lɔŋ] *vt* : prolongar

prolongation [ˌproːˌlɔŋ'geɪʃən] *n* : prolongación *f*

prom ['prɑm] *n* : baile *m* formal (de un colegio)

promenade¹ [ˌprɑmə'neɪd, -'nɑd] *vi* **-naded; -nading** : pasear, pasearse, dar un paseo

promenade² *n* : paseo *m*

prominence ['prɑmənənts] *n* **1** PROJECTION : prominencia *f* **2** EMINENCE : eminencia *f*, prestigio *m*

prominent ['prɑmənənt] *adj* **1** OUTSTANDING : prominente, destacado **2** PROJECTING : prominente, saliente

prominently ['prɑmənəntli] *adv* : destacadamente, prominentemente

promiscuity [ˌprɑmɪs'kjuːəʈi] *n, pl* **-ties** : promiscuidad *f*

promiscuous [prə'mɪskjuəs] *adj* : promiscuo — **promiscuously** *adv*

promise¹ ['prɑməs] *v* **-ised; -ising** : prometer

promise² *n* **1** : promesa *f* ⟨he kept his promise : cumplió su promesa⟩ **2 to show promise** : prometer

promising ['prɑməsɪŋ] *adj* : prometedor

promissory ['prɑməˌsori] *adj* : que promete ⟨a promissory note : un pagaré⟩

promontory ['prɑmənˌtori] *n, pl* **-ries** : promontorio *m*

promote [prə'moːt] *vt* **-moted; -moting** **1** : ascender (a un alumno o un empleado) **2** ADVERTISE : promocionar,

hacerle publicidad a **3** FURTHER : promover, fomentar

promoter [prə'moːtər] *n* : promotor *m*, -tora *f*; empresario *m*, -ria *f* (en deportes)

promotion [prə'moːʃən] *n* **1** : ascenso *m* (de un alumno o un empleado) **2** FURTHERING : promoción *f*, fomento *m* **3** ADVERTISING : publicidad *f*, propaganda *f*

promotional [prə'moːʃənəl] *adj* : promocional

prompt¹ ['prɑmpt] *vt* **1** INDUCE : provocar (una cosa), inducir (a una persona) ⟨curiosity prompted me to ask you : la curiosidad me indujo a preguntarle⟩ **2** : apuntar (a un actor, etc.)

prompt² *adj* : pronto, rápido ⟨prompt payment : pago puntual⟩

prompter ['prɑmptər] *n* : apuntador *m*, -dora *f* (en teatro)

promptly ['prɑmptli] *adv* : inmediatamente, rápidamente

promptness ['prɑmptnəs] *n* : prontitud *f*, rapidez *f*

promulgate ['prɑməlˌgeɪt] *vt* **-gated; -gating** : promulgar

prone ['proːn] *adj* **1** LIABLE : propenso, proclive ⟨accident-prone : propenso a los accidentes⟩ **2** : boca abajo, decúbito prono ⟨in a prone position : en decúbito prono⟩

prong ['prɔŋ] *n* : punta *f*, diente *m*

pronoun ['proːˌnaʊn] *n* : pronombre *m*

pronounce [prə'naʊnts] *vt* **-nounced; -nouncing 1** : pronunciar ⟨how do you pronounce your name? : ¿cómo se pronuncia su nombre?⟩ **2** DECLARE : declarar **3 to pronounce sentence** : dictar sentencia, pronunciar un fallo

pronounced [prə'naʊntst] *adj* MARKED : pronunciado, marcado

pronouncement [prə'naʊntsmənt] *n* : declaración *f*

pronunciation [prəˌnʌntsi'eɪʃən] *n* : pronunciación *f*

proof¹ ['pruːf] *adj* : a prueba ⟨proof against tampering : a prueba de manipulación⟩

proof² *n* : prueba *f*

proofread ['pruːfˌriːd] *v* **-read; -reading** *vt* : corregir — *vi* : corregir pruebas

proofreader ['pruːfˌriːdər] *n* : corrector *m*, -tora *f* (de pruebas)

prop¹ ['prɑp] *vt* **propped; propping 1 to prop against** : apoyar contra **2 to prop up** SUPPORT : apoyar, apuntalar, sostener **3 to prop up** SUSTAIN : alentar (a alguien), darle ánimo (a alguien)

prop² *n* **1** SUPPORT : puntal *m*, apoyo *m*, soporte *m* **2** : accesorio *m* (en teatro)

propaganda [ˌprɑpə'gændə, ˌproː-] *n* : propaganda *f*

propagandize [ˌprɑpə'gænˌdaɪz, ˌproː-] *v* **-dized; -dizing** *vt* : someter a propaganda — *vi* : hacer propaganda

propagate ['prɑpə,geɪt] v -gated; -gating vi : propagarse — vt : propagar
propagation [,prɑpə'geɪʃən] n : propagación f
propane ['pro:,peɪn] n : propano m
propel [prə'pɛl] vt -pelled; -pelling : impulsar, propulsar, impeler
propellant or **propellent** [prə'pɛlənt] n : propulsor m
propeller [prə'pɛlər] n : hélice f
propensity [prə'pɛntsəti] n, pl -ties : propensión f, tendencia f, inclinación f
proper ['prɑpər] adj 1 RIGHT, SUITABLE : apropiado, adecuado 2 : propio, mismo ⟨the city proper : la propia ciudad⟩ 3 CORRECT : correcto 4 GENTEEL : fino, refinado, cortés 5 OWN, SPECIAL : propio ⟨proper name : nombre propio⟩ — **properly** adv
property ['prɑpərti] n, pl -ties 1 CHARACTERISTIC : característica f, propiedad f 2 POSSESSIONS : propiedad f 3 BUILDING : inmueble m 4 LAND, LOT : terreno m, lote m, parcela f 5 PROP : accesorio m (en teatro)
prophecy ['prɑfəsi] n, pl -cies : profecía f, vaticinio m
prophesy ['prɑfə,saɪ] v -sied; -sying vt 1 FORETELL : profetizar (como profeta) 2 PREDICT : profetizar, predecir, vaticinar — vi : hacer profecías
prophet ['prɑfət] n : profeta m, profetisa f
prophetic [prə'fɛtɪk] or **prophetical** [-tɪkəl] adj : profético — **prophetically** [-tɪkli] adv
propitiate [pro'pɪʃi,eɪt] vt -ated; -ating : propiciar
propitious [prə'pɪʃəs] adj : propicio
proponent [prə'po:nənt] n : defensor m, -sora f; partidario m, -ria f
proportion¹ [prə'porʃən] vt : proporcionar ⟨well-proportioned : de buenas proporciones⟩
proportion² n 1 RATIO : proporción f 2 SYMMETRY : proporción f, simetría f ⟨out of proportion : desproporcionado⟩ 3 SHARE : parte f 4 **proportions** npl SIZE : dimensiones fpl
proportional [prə'porʃənəl] adj : proporcional — **proportionally** adv
proportionate [prə'porʃənət] adj : proporcional — **proportionately** adv
proposal [prə'po:zəl] n 1 PROPOSITION : propuesta f, proposición f ⟨marriage proposal : propuesta de matrimonio⟩ 2 PLAN : proyecto m, propuesta f
propose [prə'po:z] v -posed; -posing vi : proponer matrimonio — vt 1 INTEND : pensar, proponerse 2 SUGGEST : proponer
proposition [,prɑpə'zɪʃən] n 1 PROPOSAL : proposición f, propuesta f 2 STATEMENT : proposición f
propound [prə'paʊnd] vt : proponer, exponer
proprietary [prə'praɪə,tɛri] adj : propietario, patentado

proprietor [prə'praɪətər] n : propietario m, -ria f
propriety [prə'praɪəti] n, pl -eties 1 DECORUM : decencia f, decoro m 2 **proprieties** npl CONVENTIONS : convenciones fpl, cánones mpl sociales
propulsion [prə'pʌlʃən] n : propulsión f
prosaic [pro'zeɪɪk] adj : prosaico
proscribe [pro'skraɪb] vt -scribed; -scribing : proscribir
prose ['pro:z] n : prosa f
prosecute ['prɑsɪ,kju:t] vt -cuted; -cuting 1 CARRY OUT : llevar a cabo 2 : procesar, enjuiciar ⟨prosecuted for fraud : procesado por fraude⟩
prosecution [,prɑsɪ'kju:ʃən] n 1 : procesamiento m ⟨the prosecution of forgers : el procesamiento de falsificadores⟩ 2 PROSECUTORS : acusación f ⟨witness for the prosecution : testigo de cargo⟩
prosecutor ['prɑsɪ,kju:tər] n : acusador m, -dora f; fiscal mf
prospect¹ ['prɑ,spɛkt] vi : prospectar (el terreno) ⟨to prospect for gold : buscar oro⟩
prospect² n 1 VISTA : vista f, panorama m 2 POSSIBILITY : posibilidad f 3 OUTLOOK : perspectiva f 4 : posible cliente m, -ta f ⟨a salesman looking for prospects : un vendedor buscando nuevos clientes⟩
prospective [prə'spɛktɪv, 'prɑ,spɛk-] adj 1 EXPECTANT : futuro ⟨prospective mother : futura madre⟩ 2 POTENTIAL : potencial, posible ⟨prospective employee : posible empleado⟩
prospector ['prɑ,spɛktər, prɑ'spɛk-] n : prospector m, -tora f; explorador m, -dora f
prospectus [prə'spɛktəs] n : prospecto m
prosper ['prɑspər] vi : prosperar
prosperity [prɑ'spɛrəti] n : prosperidad f
prosperous ['prɑspərəs] adj : próspero
prostate ['prɑ,steɪt] n : próstata f
prosthesis [prɑs'θi:sɪs, 'prɑsθə-] n, pl -theses [-,si:z] : prótesis f
prostitute¹ ['prɑstə,tu:t, -,tju:t] vt -tuted; -tuting 1 : prostituir 2 to prostitute oneself : prostituirse
prostitute² n : prostituto m, -ta f
prostitution [,prɑstə'tu:ʃən, -'tju:-] n : prostitución f
prostrate¹ ['prɑ,streɪt] vt -trated; -trating 1 : postrar 2 to prostrate oneself : postrarse
prostrate² adj : postrado
prostration [prɑ'streɪʃən] n : postración f
protagonist [pro'tægənɪst] n : protagonista mf
protect [prə'tɛkt] vt : proteger
protection [prə'tɛkʃən] n : protección f
protective [prə'tɛktɪv] adj : protector
protector [prə'tɛktər] n 1 : protector m, -tora f (persona) 2 GUARD : protector m (aparato)

protectorate [prə'tɛktərət] *n* : protectorado *m*

protégé ['proːṭə‚ʒeɪ] *n* : protegido *m*, -da *f*

protein ['proː‚tiːn] *n* : proteína *f*

protest[1] [proˈtɛst] *vt* **1** ASSERT : afirmar, declarar **2** : protestar ⟨they protested the decision : protestaron (por) la decisión⟩ — *vi* **to protest against** : protestar contra

protest[2] ['proː‚tɛst] *n* **1** DEMONSTRATION : manifestación *f* (de protesta) ⟨a public protest : una manifestación pública⟩ **2** COMPLAINT : queja *f*, protesta *f*

Protestant ['prɑṭəstənt] *n* : protestante *mf*

Protestantism ['prɑṭəstən‚tɪzəm] *n* : protestantismo *m*

protocol ['proː‚ṭə‚kɔl] *n* : protocolo *m*

proton ['proː‚tɑn] *n* : protón *m*

protoplasm ['proː‚ṭə‚plæzəm] *n* : protoplasma *m*

prototype ['proː‚ṭə‚taɪp] *n* : prototipo *m*

protozoan [‚proː‚ṭə'zoː‚ən] *n* : protozoario *m*, protozoo *m*

protract [proˈtrækt] *vt* : prolongar

protractor [proˈtræktər] *n* : transportador *m* (instrumento)

protrude [proˈtruːd] *vi* **-truded; -truding** : salir, sobresalir

protrusion [proˈtruːʒən] *n* : protuberancia *f*, saliente *m*

protuberance [proˈtuːbərənts, -ˈtjuː-] *n* : protuberancia *f*

proud ['praʊd] *adj* **1** HAUGHTY : altanero, orgulloso, arrogante **2** : orgulloso ⟨she was proud of her work : estaba orgullosa de su trabajo⟩ ⟨too proud to beg : demasiado orgulloso para rogar⟩ **3** GLORIOUS : glorioso — **proudly** *adv*

prove ['pruːv] *v* **proved; proved** *or* **proven** ['pruːvən]; **proving** *vt* **1** TEST : probar **2** DEMONSTRATE : probar, demostrar — *vi* : resultar ⟨it proved effective : resultó efectivo⟩

Provençal [‚proː‚vɑn'sɑl, ‚prɑvən-] *n* **1** : provenzal *mf* **2** : provenzal *m* (idioma) — **Provençal** *adj*

proverb ['prɑ‚vərb] *n* : proverbio *m*, refrán *m*

proverbial [prəˈvərbiəl] *adj* : proverbial

provide [prəˈvaɪd] *v* **-vided; -viding** *vt* **1** STIPULATE : estipular **2 to provide with** : proveer de, proporcionar — *vi* **1** : proveer ⟨the Lord will provide : el Señor proveerá⟩ **2 to provide for** SUPPORT : mantener **3 to provide for** ANTICIPATE : hacer previsiones para, prever

provided [prəˈvaɪdəd] *or* **provided that** *conj* : con tal (de) que, siempre que

providence ['prɑvədənts] *n* **1** PRUDENCE : previsión *f*, prudencia *f* **2** *or* **Providence** : providencia *f* ⟨divine providence : la Divina Providencia⟩ **3 Providence** GOD : Providencia *f*

provident ['prɑvədənt] *adj* **1** PRUDENT : previsor, prudente **2** FRUGAL : frugal, ahorrativo

providential [‚prɑvə'dɛntʃəl] *adj* : providencial

provider [prəˈvaɪdər] *n* **1** PURVEYOR : proveedor *m*, -dora *f* **2** BREADWINNER : sostén *m* (económico)

providing that → **provided**

province ['prɑvɪnts] *n* **1** : provincia *f* (de un país) ⟨to live in the provinces : vivir en las provincias⟩ **2** FIELD, SPHERE : campo *m*, competencia *f* ⟨it's not in my province : no es de mi competencia⟩

provincial [prəˈvɪntʃəl] *adj* **1** : provincial ⟨provincial government : gobierno provincial⟩ **2** : provinciano, pueblerino ⟨a provincial mentality : una mentalidad provinciana⟩

provision[1] [prəˈvɪʒən] *vt* : aprovisionar, abastecer

provision[2] *n* **1** PROVIDING : provisión *f*, suministro *m* **2** STIPULATION : condición *f*, salvedad *f*, estipulación *f* **3 provisions** *npl* : despensa *f*, víveres *mpl*, provisiones *fpl*

provisional [prəˈvɪʒənəl] *adj* : provisional, provisorio — **provisionally** *adv*

proviso [prəˈvaɪ‚zoː] *n, pl* **-sos** *or* **-soes** : condición *f*, salvedad *f*, estipulación *f*

provocation [‚prɑvə'keɪʃən] *n* : provocación *f*

provocative [prəˈvakəṭɪv] *adj* : provocador, provocativo ⟨a provocative article : un artículo que hace pensar⟩

provoke [prəˈvoːk] *vt* **-voked; -voking** : provocar

prow ['praʊ] *n* : proa *f*

prowess ['praʊəs] *n* **1** VALOR : valor *m*, valentía *f* **2** SKILL : habilidad *f*, destreza *f*

prowl ['praʊl] *vi* : merodear, rondar — *vt* : rondar por

prowler ['praʊlər] *n* : merodeador *m*, -dora *f*

proximity [prɑk'sɪməṭi] *n* : proximidad *f*

proxy ['prɑksi] *n, pl* **proxies 1** : poder *m* (de actuar en nombre de alguien) ⟨by proxy : por poder⟩ **2** AGENT : apoderado *m*, -da *f*; representante *mf*

prude ['pruːd] *n* : mojigato *m*, -ta *f*; gazmoño *m*, -ña *f*

prudence ['pruːdənts] *n* **1** SHREWDNESS : prudencia *f*, sagacidad *f* **2** CAUTION : prudencia *f*, cautela *f* **3** THRIFTINESS : frugalidad *f*

prudent ['pruːdənt] *adj* **1** SHREWD : prudente, sagaz **2** CAUTIOUS, FARSIGHTED : prudente, previsor, precavido **3** THRIFTY : frugal, ahorrativo — **prudently** *adv*

prudery ['pruːdəri] *n, pl* **-eries** : mojigatería *f*, gazmoñería *f*

prudish ['pruːdɪʃ] *adj* : mojigato, gazmoño

prune¹ ['pru:n] *vt* **pruned; pruning** : podar (arbustos, etc.), acortar (un texto), recortar (gastos, etc.)
prune² *n* : ciruela *f* pasa
prurient ['prʊriənt] *adj* : lascivo
pry ['praɪ] *v* **pried; prying** *vi* : curiosear, huronear ⟨to pry into other people's business : meterse uno en lo que no le importa⟩ — *vt or* **to pry open** : abrir (con una palanca), apalancar
psalm ['sɑm, 'sɑlm] *n* : salmo *m*
pseudonym ['su:də,nɪm] *n* : seudónimo *m*
psoriasis [sə'raɪəsɪs] *n* : soriasis *f*, psoriasis *f*
psyche ['saɪki] *n* : psique *f*, psiquis *f*
psychedelic¹ [,saɪkə'dɛlɪk] *adj* : psicodélico
psychedelic² *n* : droga *f* psicodélica
psychiatric [,saɪki'ætrɪk] *adj* : psiquiátrico, siquiátrico
psychiatrist [sə'kaɪətrɪst, saɪ-] *n* : psiquiatra *mf*, siquiatra *mf*
psychiatry [sə'kaɪətri, saɪ-] *n* : psiquiatría *f*, siquiatría *f*
psychic¹ ['saɪkɪk] *adj* **1** : psíquico, síquico (en psicología) **2** CLAIRVOYANT : clarividente
psychic² *n* : vidente *mf*, clarividente *mf*
psychoanalysis [,saɪkoə'næləsɪs] *n, pl* **-yses** : psicoanálisis *m*, sicoanálisis *m*
psychoanalyst [,saɪko'ænəlɪst] *n* : psicoanalista *mf*, sicoanalista *mf*
psychoanalytic [,saɪko,ænəl'ɪtɪk] *adj* : psicoanalítico, sicoanalítico
psychoanalyze [,saɪko'ænəl,aɪz] *vt* **-lyzed; -lyzing** : psicoanalizar, sicoanalizar
psychological [,saɪkə'lɑdʒɪkəl] *adj* : psicológico, sicológico — **psychologically** *adv*
psychologist [saɪ'kɑlədʒɪst] *n* : psicólogo *m*, -ga *f*; sicólogo *m*, -ga *f*
psychology [saɪ'kɑlədʒi] *n, pl* **-gies** : psicología *f*, sicología *f*
psychopath ['saɪkə,pæθ] *n* : psicópata *mf*, sicópata *mf*
psychopathic [,saɪkə'pæθɪk] *adj* : psicopático, sicopático
psychosis [saɪ'ko:sɪs] *n, pl* **-choses** [-'ko:,si:z] : psicosis *f*, sicosis *f*
psychosomatic [,saɪkəsə'mætɪk] *adj* : psicosomático, sicosomático
psychotherapist [,saɪko'θɛrəpɪst] *n* : psicoterapeuta *mf*, sicoterapeuta *mf*
psychotherapy [,saɪko'θɛrəpi] *n, pl* **-pies** : psicoterapia *f*, sicoterapia *f*
psychotic¹ [saɪ'kɑtɪk] *adj* : psicótico, sicótico
psychotic² *n* : psicótico *m*, -ca *f*; sicótico *m*, -ca *f*
puberty ['pju:bərti] *n* : pubertad *f*
pubic ['pju:bɪk] *adj* : pubiano, púbico
public¹ ['pʌblɪk] *adj* : público — **publicly** *adv*
public² *n* : público *m*
publication [,pʌblə'keɪʃən] *n* : publicación *f*

publicist ['pʌbləsɪst] *n* : publicista *mf*
publicity [pə'blɪsəti] *n* : publicidad *f*
publicize ['pʌblə,saɪz] *vt* **-cized; -cizing** : publicitar
public school *n* : escuela *f* pública
publish ['pʌblɪʃ] *vt* : publicar
publisher ['pʌblɪʃər] *n* : casa *f* editorial (compañía); editor *m*, -tora *f* (persona)
publishing ['pʌblɪʃɪŋ] *n* : industria *f* editorial
pucker¹ ['pʌkər] *vt* : fruncir, arrugar — *vi* : arrugarse
pucker² *n* : arruga *f*, frunce *m*, fruncido *m*
pudding ['pʊdɪŋ] *n* : budín *m*, pudín *m*
puddle ['pʌdəl] *n* : charco *m*
pudgy ['pʌdʒi] *adj* **pudgier; -est** : regordete *fam*, rechoncho *fam*, gordinflón *fam*
puerile ['pjʊrəl] *adj* : pueril
Puerto Rican¹ [,pwɛrtə'ri:kən, ,portə-] *adj* : puertorriqueño
Puerto Rican² *n* : puertorriqueño *m*, -ña *f*
puff¹ ['pʌf] *vi* **1** BLOW : soplar **2** PANT : resoplar, jadear **3 to puff up** SWELL : hincharse — *vt* **1** BLOW : soplar ⟨to puff smoke : echar humo⟩ **2** INFLATE : inflar, hinchar ⟨to puff out one's cheeks : inflar las mejillas⟩
puff² *n* **1** GUST : soplo *m*, ráfaga *f*, bocanada *f* (de humo) **2** DRAW : chupada *f* (a un cigarrillo) **3** SWELLING : hinchazón *f* **4 cream puff** : pastelito *m* de crema **5 powder puff** : borla *f*
puffy ['pʌfi] *adj* **puffier; -est 1** SWOLLEN : hinchado, inflado **2** SPONGY : esponjoso, suave
pug ['pʌg] *n* **1** : doguillo *m* (perro) **2 or pug nose** : nariz *f* achatada
pugnacious [,pʌg'neɪʃəs] *adj* : pugnaz, agresivo
puke ['pju:k] *vi* **puked; puking** : vomitar, devolver
pull¹ ['pʊl, 'pʌl] *vt* **1** DRAW, TUG : tirar de, jalar **2** EXTRACT : sacar, extraer ⟨to pull teeth : sacar muelas⟩ ⟨to pull a gun on : amenazar a (alguien) con pistola⟩ **3** TEAR : desgarrarse (un músculo, etc.) **4 to pull down** : bajar, echar abajo, derribar (un edificio) **5 to pull in** ATTRACT : atraer (una muchedumbre, etc.) ⟨to pull in votes : conseguir votos⟩ **6 to pull off** REMOVE : sacar, quitar **7 to pull oneself together** : calmarse, tranquilizarse **8 to pull up** RAISE : levantar, subir — *vi* **1** DRAW, TUG : tirar, jalar **2** *(indicating movement in a specific direction)* ⟨they pulled in front of us : se nos metieron delante⟩ ⟨to pull to a stop : pararse⟩ **3 to pull through** RECOVER : recobrarse, reponerse **4 to pull together** COOPERATE : trabajar juntos, cooperar
pull² *n* **1** TUG : tirón *m*, jalón *m* ⟨he gave it a pull : le dio un tirón⟩ **2** ATTRACTION : atracción *f*, fuerza *f* ⟨the pull of gravity : la fuerza de la gravedad⟩ **3**

INFLUENCE : influencia f 4 HANDLE : tirador m (de un cajón, etc.) 5 bell pull : cuerda f
pullet ['pʊlət] n : polla f, gallina f (joven)
pulley ['pʊli] n, pl -leys : polea f
pullover ['pʊl₁oːvər] n : suéter m
pulmonary ['pʊlmə₁nɛri, 'pʌl-] adj : pulmonar
pulp ['pʌlp] n 1 : pulpa f (de una fruta, etc.) 2 MASH : papilla f, pasta f ⟨wood pulp : pasta de papel, pulpa de papel⟩ ⟨to beat to a pulp : hacer papilla (a alguien)⟩ 3 : pulpa f (de los dientes)
pulpit ['pʊl₁pɪt] n : púlpito m
pulsate ['pʌl₁seɪt] vi -sated; -sating 1 BEAT : latir, palpitar 2 VIBRATE : vibrar
pulsation [₁pʌl'seɪʃən] n : pulsación f
pulse ['pʌls] n : pulso m
pulverize ['pʌlvə₁raɪz] vt -ized; -izing : pulverizar
puma ['puːmə, 'pjuː-] n : puma m; león m, leona f (in various countries)
pumice ['pʌməs] n : piedra f pómez
pummel ['pʌməl] vt -meled; -meling : aporrear, apalear
pump¹ ['pʌmp] vt 1 : bombear ⟨to pump water : bombear agua⟩ ⟨to pump (up) a tire : inflar una llanta⟩ 2 : mover (una manivela, un pedal, etc.) de arriba abajo ⟨to pump someone's hand : darle un fuerte apretón de manos (a alguien)⟩ 3 to pump out : sacar, vaciar (con una bomba)
pump² n 1 : bomba f ⟨water pump : bomba de agua⟩ 2 SHOE : zapato m de tacón
pumpernickel ['pʌmpər₁nɪkəl] n : pan m negro de centeno
pumpkin ['pʌmpkɪn, 'pʌŋkən] n : calabaza f, zapallo m Arg, Chile, Peru, Uru
pun¹ ['pʌn] vi punned; punning : hacer juegos de palabras
pun² n : juego m de palabras, albur m Mex
punch¹ ['pʌntʃ] vt 1 HIT : darle un puñetazo (a alguien), golpear ⟨she punched him in the nose : le dio un puñetazo en la nariz⟩ 2 PERFORATE : perforar (papel, etc.), picar (un boleto)
punch² n 1 : perforadora f ⟨paper punch : perforadora de papel⟩ 2 BLOW : golpe m, puñetazo m 3 : ponche m ⟨fruit punch : ponche de frutas⟩
punctilious [pəŋk'tɪliəs] adj : puntilloso
punctual ['pʌŋktʃuəl] adj : puntual
punctuality [₁pʌŋktʃu'æləti] n : puntualidad f
punctually ['pʌŋktʃuəli] adv : puntualmente, a tiempo
punctuate ['pʌŋktʃu₁eɪt] vt -ated; -ating : puntuar
punctuation [₁pʌŋktʃu'eɪʃən] n : puntuación f
puncture¹ ['pʌŋktʃər] vt -tured; -turing : pinchar, punzar, perforar, ponchar Mex
puncture² n : pinchazo m, ponchadura f Mex

pundit ['pʌndɪt] n : experto m, -ta f
pungency ['pʌndʒəntsi] n : acritud f, acrimonia f
pungent ['pʌndʒənt] adj : acre
punish ['pʌnɪʃ] vt : castigar
punishable ['pʌnɪʃəbəl] adj : punible
punishment ['pʌnɪʃmənt] n : castigo m
punitive ['pjuːnət̬ɪv] adj : punitivo
punt¹ ['pʌnt] vt : impulsar (un barco) con una pértiga — vi : despejar (en deportes)
punt² n 1 : batea f (barco) 2 : patada f de despeje (en deportes)
puny ['pjuːni] adj -nier; -est : enclenque, endeble
pup ['pʌp] n : cachorro m, -rra f (de un perro); cría f (de otros animales)
pupa ['pjuːpə] n, pl -pae [-pi, -₁paɪ] or -pas : crisálida f, pupa f
pupil ['pjuːpəl] n 1 : alumno m, -na f (de colegio) 2 : pupila f (del ojo)
puppet ['pʌpət] n : títere m, marioneta f
puppy ['pʌpi] n, pl -pies : cachorro m, -rra f
purchase¹ ['pərtʃəs] vt -chased; -chasing : comprar
purchase² n 1 PURCHASING : compra f, adquisición f 2 : compra f ⟨last-minute purchases : compras de última hora⟩ 3 GRIP : agarre m, asidero m ⟨she got a firm purchase on the wheel : se agarró bien del volante⟩
purchase order n : orden f de compra
pure ['pjʊr] adj purer; purest : puro
puree¹ [pjʊ'reɪ, -'riː] vt -reed; -reeing : hacer un puré con
puree² n : puré m
purely ['pjʊrli] adv 1 WHOLLY : puramente, completamente ⟨purely by chance : por pura casualidad⟩ 2 SIMPLY : sencillamente, meramente
purgative ['pərgət̬ɪv] n : purgante m
purgatory ['pərgə₁tori] n, pl -ries : purgatorio m
purge¹ ['pərdʒ] vt purged; purging : purgar
purge² n : purga f
purification [₁pjʊrəfə'keɪʃən] n : purificación f
purify ['pjʊrə₁faɪ] vt -fied; -fying : purificar
puritan ['pjʊrətən] n : puritano m, -na f — puritan adj
puritanical [₁pjʊriːrə'tænɪkəl] adj : puritano
purity ['pjʊrət̬i] n : pureza f
purl¹ ['pərl] v : tejer al revés, tejer del revés
purl² n : punto m del revés
purloin [pər'lɔɪn, 'pər₁lɔɪn] vt : hurtar, robar
purple ['pərpəl] n : morado m, color m púrpura
purport [pər'port] vt : pretender ⟨to purport to be : pretender ser⟩
purpose ['pərpəs] n 1 INTENTION : propósito m, intención f ⟨on purpose

: a propósito, adrede⟩ 2 FUNCTION : función f 3 RESOLUTION : resolución f, determinación f
purposeful [ˈpərpəsfəl] adj : determinado, decidido, resuelto
purposefully [ˈpərpəsfəli] adv : decididamente, resueltamente
purposely [ˈpərpəsli] adv : intencionadamente, a propósito, adrede
purr¹ [ˈpər] vi : ronronear
purr² n : ronroneo m
purse¹ [ˈpərs] vt **pursed; pursing** : fruncir ⟨to purse one's lips : fruncir la boca⟩
purse² n 1 HANDBAG : cartera f, bolso m, bolsa f Mex ⟨a change purse : un monedero⟩ 2 FUNDS : fondos mpl 3 PRIZE : premio m
pursue [pərˈsuː] vt **-sued; -suing** 1 CHASE : perseguir 2 SEEK : buscar, tratar de encontrar ⟨to pursue pleasure : buscar el placer⟩ 3 FOLLOW : seguir ⟨the road pursues a northerly course : el camino sigue hacia el norte⟩ 4 : dedicarse a ⟨to pursue a hobby : dedicarse a un pasatiempo⟩
pursuer [pərˈsuːər] n : perseguidor m, -dora f
pursuit [pərˈsuːt] n 1 CHASE : persecución f 2 SEARCH : búsqueda f, busca f 3 ACTIVITY : actividad f, pasatiempo m
purveyor [pərˈveɪər] n : proveedor m, -dora f
pus [ˈpʌs] n : pus m
push¹ [ˈpʊʃ] vt 1 SHOVE : empujar 2 PRESS : apretar, pulsar ⟨push that button : aprieta ese botón⟩ 3 PRESSURE, URGE : presionar 4 to push around BULLY : intimidar, mangonear — vi 1 SHOVE : empujar 2 INSIST : insistir, presionar 3 to push off LEAVE : marcharse, irse, largarse fam 4 to push on PROCEED : seguir
push² n 1 SHOVE : empujón m 2 DRIVE : empuje m, energía f, dinamismo m 3 EFFORT : esfuerzo m
push–button [ˈpʊʃˈbʌtən] adj : de botones
pushcart [ˈpʊʃˌkɑrt] n : carretilla f de mano
pushy [ˈpʊʃi] adj **pushier; -est** : mandón, prepotente
pussy [ˈpʊsi] n, pl **pussies** : gatito m, -ta f; minino m, -na f
pussy willow n : sauce m blanco
pustule [ˈpʌsˌtʃuːl] n : pústula f
put [ˈpʊt] v **put; putting** vt 1 PLACE : poner, colocar ⟨put it on the table : ponlo en la mesa⟩ 2 INSERT : meter 3 (indicating causation of a state or feeling) : poner ⟨it put her in a good mood : la puso de buen humor⟩ ⟨to put into effect : poner en práctica⟩ 4 IMPOSE : imponer ⟨they put a tax on it : lo gravaron con un impuesto⟩ 5 SUBJECT : someter, poner ⟨to put to the test : poner a prueba⟩ ⟨to put to death : ejecutar⟩ 6 EXPRESS : expresar, decir ⟨he put it

simply : lo dijo sencillamente⟩ 7 APPLY : aplicar ⟨to put one's mind to something : proponerse hacer algo⟩ 8 SET : poner ⟨I put him to work : lo puse a trabajar⟩ 9 ATTACH : dar ⟨to put a high value on : dar gran valor a⟩ 10 PRESENT : presentar, exponer ⟨to put a question to someone : hacer una pregunta a alguien⟩ — vi 1 to put to sea : hacerse a la mar 2 to put up with : aguantar, soportar
put away vt 1 KEEP : guardar 2 or to put aside : dejar a un lado
put by vt SAVE : ahorrar
put down vt 1 SUPPRESS : aplastar, suprimir 2 ATTRIBUTE : atribuir ⟨she put it down to luck : lo atribuyó a la suerte⟩
put in vi : presentarse ⟨I've put in for the position : me presenté para el puesto⟩ — vt DEVOTE : dedicar (unas horas, etc.)
put off vt DEFER : aplazar, posponer
put on vt 1 ASSUME : afectar, adoptar 2 PRODUCE : presentar (una obra de teatro, etc.) 3 WEAR : ponerse
put out vt INCONVENIENCE : importunar, incomodar
putrefy [ˈpjuːtrəˌfaɪ] v **-fied; -fying** vt : pudrir — vi : pudrirse
putrid [ˈpjuːtrɪd] adj : putrefacto, pútrido
putter [ˈpʌtər] vi or **to putter around** : entretenerse
putty¹ [ˈpʌti] vt **-tied; -tying** : poner masilla m
putty² n, pl **-ties** : masilla f
put up vt 1 LODGE : alojar 2 CONTRIBUTE : contribuir, pagar
puzzle¹ [ˈpʌzəl] vt **-zled; -zling** 1 CONFUSE : confundir, dejar perplejo 2 to puzzle out : dar vueltas a, tratar de resolver
puzzle² n 1 : rompecabezas m ⟨a crossword puzzle : un crucigrama⟩ 2 MYSTERY : misterio m, enigma m
puzzlement [ˈpʌzəlmənt] n : desconcierto m, perplejidad f
pygmy¹ [ˈpɪgmi] adj : enano, pigmeo
pygmy² n, pl **-mies** 1 DWARF : enano m, -na f 2 **Pygmy** : pigmeo m, -mea f
pylon [ˈpaɪˌlɑn, -lən] n 1 : torre f de conducta eléctrica 2 : pilón m (de un puente)
pyramid [ˈpɪrəˌmɪd] n : pirámide f
pyre [ˈpaɪr] n : pira f
pyromania [ˌpaɪroˈmeɪniə] n : piromanía f
pyromaniac [ˌpaɪroˈmeɪniˌæk] n : pirómano m, -na f
pyrotechnics [ˌpaɪrəˈtɛknɪks] npl 1 FIREWORKS : fuegos mpl artificiales 2 DISPLAY, SHOW : espectáculo m, muestra f de virtuosismo ⟨computer pyrotechnics : efectos especiales hechos por computadora⟩
python [ˈpaɪˌθɑn, -θən] n : pitón f, serpiente f pitón

Q

q ['kju:] *n, pl* **q's** *or* **qs** ['kju:z] : deci-moséptima letra del alfabeto inglés

quack¹ ['kwæk] *vi* : graznar

quack² *n* **1** : graznido *m* (de pato) **2** CHARLATAN : curandero *m*, -ra *f*; matasanos *m fam*

quadrangle ['kwɑ‚dræŋgəl] *n* **1** COURTYARD : patio *m* interior **2** → **quadrilateral**

quadrant ['kwɑdrənt] *n* : cuadrante *m*

quadrilateral [‚kwɑdrə'læt̬ərəl] *n* : cuadrilátero *m*

quadruped ['kwɑdrə‚pɛd] *n* : cuadrúpedo *m*

quadruple [kwɑ'dru:pəl, -'drʌ-; 'kwɑdrə-] *v* **-pled; -pling** *vt* : cuadruplicar — *vi* : cuadruplicarse

quadruplet [kwɑ'dru:plət, -'drʌ-; 'kwɑdrə-] *n* : cuatrillizo *m*, -za *f*

quagmire ['kwæg‚maɪr, 'kwɑg-] *n* **1** : lodazal *m*, barrizal *m* **2** PREDICAMENT : atolladero *m*

quail¹ ['kweɪl] *vi* : encogerse, acobardarse

quail² *n, pl* **quail** *or* **quails** : codorniz *f*

quaint ['kweɪnt] *adj* **1** ODD : extraño, curioso **2** PICTURESQUE : pintoresco — **quaintly** *adv*

quaintness ['kweɪntnəs] *n* : rareza *f*, lo curioso

quake¹ ['kweɪk] *vi* **quaked; quaking** : temblar

quake² *n* : temblor *m*, terremoto *m*

qualification [‚kwɑləfə'keɪʃən] *n* **1** LIMITATION, RESERVATION : reserva *f*, limitación *f* ⟨without qualification : sin reservas⟩ **2** REQUIREMENT : requisito *m* **3** **qualifications** *npl* ABILITY : aptitud *f*, capacidad *f*

qualified ['kwɑlə‚faɪd] *adj* : competente, capacitado

qualifier ['kwɑlə‚faɪər] *n* **1** : clasificado *m*, -da *f* (en deportes) **2** : calificativo *m* (en gramática)

qualify ['kwɑlə‚faɪ] *v* **-fied; -fying** *vt* **1** : matizar ⟨to qualify a statement : matizar una declaración⟩ **2** MODIFY : calificar (en gramática) **3** : habilitar ⟨the certificate qualified her to teach : el certificado la habilitó para enseñar⟩ — *vi* **1** : obtener el título, recibirse ⟨to qualify as an engineer : recibirse de ingeniero⟩ **2** : clasificarse (en deportes)

quality ['kwɑlət̬i] *n, pl* **-ties 1** NATURE : carácter *m* **2** ATTRIBUTE : cualidad *f* **3** GRADE : calidad *f* ⟨of good quality : de buena calidad⟩

qualm ['kwɑm, 'kwɑlm, 'kwɔm] *n* **1** MISGIVING : duda *f*, aprensión *f* **2** RESERVATION, SCRUPLE : escrúpulo *m*, reparo *m*

quandary ['kwɑndri] *n, pl* **-ries** : dilema *m*

quantitative ['kwɑntə‚teɪt̬ɪv] *adj* : cuantitativo

quantity ['kwɑntət̬i] *n, pl* **-ties** : cantidad *f*

quantum¹ ['kwɑntəm] *n* : cuanto *m* (en física)

quantum² *adj* : cuántico

quantum theory ['kwɑntəm] *n* : teoría *f* cuántica

quarantine¹ ['kwɔrən‚ti:n] *vt* **-tined; -tining** : poner en cuarentena

quarantine² *n* : cuarentena *f*

quarrel¹ ['kwɔrəl] *vi* **-reled** *or* **-relled; -reling** *or* **-relling** : pelearse, reñir, discutir

quarrel² *n* : pelea *f*, riña *f*, disputa *f*

quarrelsome ['kwɔrəlsəm] *adj* : pendenciero, discutidor

quarry¹ ['kwɔri] *vt* **quarried; quarrying 1** EXTRACT : extraer, sacar ⟨to quarry marble : extraer mármol⟩ **2** EXCAVATE : excavar ⟨to quarry a hill : excavar un cerro⟩

quarry² *n, pl* **quarries 1** PREY : presa *f* **2** *or* **stone quarry** : cantera *f*

quart ['kwɔrt] *n* : cuarto *m* de galón

quarter¹ ['kwɔrt̬ər] *vt* **1** : dividir en cuatro partes **2** LODGE : alojar, acuartelar (tropas)

quarter² *n* **1** : cuarto *m*, cuarta parte *f* ⟨a foot and a quarter : un pie y cuarto⟩ ⟨a quarter after three : las tres y cuarto⟩ **2** : moneda *f* de 25 centavos, cuarto *m* de dólar **3** DISTRICT : barrio *m* ⟨business quarter : barrio comercial⟩ **4** PLACE : parte *f* ⟨from all quarters : de todas partes⟩ ⟨at close quarters : de muy cerca⟩ **5** MERCY : clemencia *f*, cuartel *m* ⟨to give no quarter : no dar cuartel⟩ **6** **quarters** *npl* LODGING : alojamiento *m*, cuartel *m* (militar)

quarterback ['kwɔrt̬ər‚bæk] *n* : mariscal *m* de campo

quarterly¹ ['kwɔrt̬ərli] *adv* : cada tres meses, trimestralmente

quarterly² *adj* : trimestral

quarterly³ *n, pl* **-lies** : publicación *f* trimestral

quartermaster ['kwɔrt̬ər‚mæstər] *n* : intendente *mf*

quartet [kwɔr'tɛt] *n* : cuarteto *m*

quartz ['kwɔrts] *n* : cuarzo *m*

quash ['kwɑʃ, 'kwɔʃ] *vt* **1** ANNUL : anular **2** QUELL : sofocar, aplastar

quaver¹ ['kweɪvər] *vi* **1** SHAKE : temblar ⟨her voice was quavering : le temblaba la voz⟩ **2** TRILL : trinar

quaver² *n* : temblor *m* (de la voz)

quay ['ki:, 'keɪ, 'kweɪ] *n* : muelle *m*

queasiness ['kwi:zinəs] *n* : mareo *m*, náusea *f*

queasy ['kwi:zi] *adj* **-sier; -est** : mareado

queen ['kwi:n] *n* : reina *f*

queenly ['kwi:nli] *adj* **-lier; -est** : de reina, regio

queer ['kwɪr] *adj* : extraño, raro, curioso — **queerly** *adv*

quell ['kwl] *vt* : aplastar, sofocar

quench ['kwɛntʃ] *vt* **1** EXTINGUISH : apagar, sofocar **2** SATISFY : saciar, satisfacer (la sed)

querulous ['kwɛrələs, 'kwɛrjələs, 'kwɪr-] *adj* : quejumbroso, quejoso — **querulously** *adv*

query¹ ['kwɪri, 'kwɛr-] *vt* **-ried; -rying 1** ASK : preguntar, interrogar ⟨we queried the professor : preguntamos al profesor⟩ **2** QUESTION : cuestionar, poner en duda ⟨to query a matter : cuestionar un asunto⟩

query² *n, pl* **-ries 1** QUESTION : pregunta *f* **2** DOUBT : duda *f*

quest¹ ['kwɛst] *v* : buscar

quest² *n* : búsqueda *f*

question¹ ['kwɛstʃən] *vt* **1** ASK : preguntar **2** DOUBT : poner en duda, cuestionar **3** INTERROGATE : interrogar — *vi* INQUIRE : inquirir, preguntar

question² *n* **1** QUERY : pregunta *f* **2** ISSUE : asunto *m*, problema *f*, cuestión *f* **3** POSSIBILITY : posibilidad *f* ⟨it's out of the question : es indiscutible⟩ **4** DOUBT : duda *f* ⟨to call into question : poner en duda⟩

questionable ['kwɛstʃənəbəl] *adj* : dudoso, discutible, cuestionable ⟨questionable results : resultados discutibles⟩ ⟨questionable motives : motivos sospechosos⟩

questioner ['kwɛstʃənər] *n* : interrogador *m*, -dora *f*

question mark *n* : signo *m* de interrogación

questionnaire [ˌkwɛstʃə'nær] *n* : cuestionario *m*

queue¹ ['kju:] *vi* **queued; queuing** *or* **queueing** : hacer cola

queue² *n* **1** PIGTAIL : coleta *f*, trenza *f* **2** LINE : cola *f*, fila *f*

quibble¹ ['kwɪbəl] *vi* **-bled; -bling** : quejarse por nimiedades, andar con sutilezas

quibble² *n* : objeción *f* de poca monta, queja *f* insignificante

quick¹ ['kwɪk] *adv* : rápidamente

quick² *adj* **1** RAPID : rápido **2** ALERT, CLEVER : listo, vivo, agudo **3 a quick temper** : un genio vivo

quick³ *n* **1** FLESH : carne *f* viva **2 to cut someone to the quick** : herir a alguien en lo más vivo

quicken ['kwɪkən] *vt* **1** REVIVE : resucitar **2** AROUSE : estimular, despertar **3** HASTEN : acelerar ⟨she quickened her pace : aceleró el paso⟩

quickly ['kwɪkli] *adv* : rápidamente, rápido, de prisa

quickness ['kwɪknəs] *n* : rapidez *f*

quicksand ['kwɪkˌsænd] *n* : arena *f* movediza

quicksilver ['kwɪkˌsɪlvər] *n* : mercurio *m*, azogue *m*

quick–tempered ['kwɪk'tɛmpərd] *adj* : irascible, de genio vivo

quick–witted ['kwɪk'wɪtəd] *adj* : agudo

quiet¹ ['kwaɪət] *vt* **1** SILENCE : hacer callar, acallar **2** CALM : calmar, tranquilizar — *vi* **to quiet down** : calmarse, tranquilizarse

quiet² *adv* : silenciosamente ⟨a quiet-running engine : un motor silencioso⟩

quiet³ *adj* **1** CALM : tranquilo, calmoso **2** MILD : sosegado, suave ⟨a quiet disposition : un temperamento sosegado⟩ **3** SILENT : silencioso **4** UNOBTRUSIVE : discreto **5** SECLUDED : aislado ⟨a quiet nook : un rincón aislado⟩ — **quietly** *adv*

quiet⁴ *n* **1** CALM : calma *f*, tranquilidad *f* **2** SILENCE : silencio *m*

quietness ['kwaɪətnəs] *n* : suavidad *f*, tranquilidad *f*, quietud *f*

quietude ['kwaɪəˌtu:d, -ˌtju:d] *n* : quietud *f*, reposo *m*

quill ['kwɪl] *n* **1** SPINE : púa *f* (de un puerco espín) **2** : pluma *f* (para escribir)

quilt¹ ['kwɪlt] *vt* : acolchar

quilt² *n* : colcha *f*, edredón *m*

quince ['kwɪnts] *n* : membrillo *m*

quinine ['kwaɪˌnaɪn] *n* : quinina *f*

quintessence [kwɪn'tɛsənts] *n* : quintaesencia *f*

quintet [kwɪn'tɛt] *n* : quinteto *m*

quintuple [kwɪn'tu:pəl, -'tju:-, -'tʌ-; 'kwɪntə-] *adj* : quíntuplo

quintuplet [kwɪn'tʌplət, -'tu:-, -'tju:-; 'kwɪntə-] *n* : quintillizo *m*, -za *f*

quip¹ ['kwɪp] *vi* **quipped; quipping** : bromear

quip² *n* : ocurrencia *f*, salida *f*

quirk ['kwərk] *n* : peculiaridad *f*, rareza *f* ⟨a quirk of fate : un capricho del destino⟩

quirky ['kwərki] *adj* **-kier; -est** : peculiar, raro

quit ['kwɪt] *v* **quit; quitting** *vt* : dejar, abandonar ⟨to quit smoking : dejar de fumar⟩ — *vi* **1** STOP : parar **2** RESIGN : dimitir, renunciar

quite ['kwaɪt] *adv* **1** COMPLETELY : completamente, totalmente **2** RATHER : bastante ⟨quite near : bastante cerca⟩

quits ['kwɪts] *adj* **to call it quits** : quedar en paz

quitter ['kwɪtər] *n* : derrotista *mf*

quiver¹ ['kwɪvər] *vi* : temblar, estremecerse, vibrar

quiver² *n* **1** : carcaj *m*, aljaba *f* (para flechas) **2** TREMBLING : temblor *m*, estremecimiento *m*

quixotic [kwɪk'sɑtɪk] *adj* : quijotesco

quiz¹ ['kwɪz] *vt* **quizzed; quizzing** : interrogar, hacer una prueba a (en el colegio)

quiz² *n, pl* **quizzes** : examen *m* corto, prueba *f*

quizzical ['kwɪzɪkəl] *adj* **1** TEASING : burlón **2** CURIOUS : curioso, interrogativo

quorum ['kworəm] *n* : quórum *m*

quota ['kwo:ʈə] *n* : cuota *f*, cupo *m*
quotable ['kwo:ʈəbəl] *adj* : citable
quotation [kwo'teɪʃən] *n* **1** CITATION : cita *f* **2** ESTIMATE : presupuesto *m*, estimación *f* **3** PRICE : cotización *f*
quotation marks *npl* : comillas *fpl*

quote¹ ['kwo:t] *vt* **quoted; quoting 1** CITE : citar **2** VALUE : cotizar (en finanzas)
quote² *n* **1** → quotation **2 quotes** *npl* → quotation marks
quotient ['kwo:ʃənt] *n* : cociente *m*

R

r ['ɑr] *n*, *pl* **r's** *or* **rs** ['ɑrz] : decimoctava letra del alfabeto inglés
rabbi ['ræ,baɪ] *n* : rabino *m*, -na *f*
rabbit ['ræbət] *n*, *pl* **-bit** *or* **-bits** : conejo *m*, -ja *f*
rabble ['ræbəl] *n* **1** MASSES : populacho *m* **2** RIFFRAFF : chusma *f*, gentuza *f*
rabid ['ræbɪd] *adj* **1** : rabioso, afectado con la rabia **2** FURIOUS : furioso **3** FANATIC : fanático
rabies ['reɪbi:z] *ns & pl* : rabia *f*
raccoon [ræ'ku:n] *n*, *pl* **-coon** *or* **-coons** : mapache *m*
race¹ ['reɪs] *vi* **raced; racing 1** : correr, competir (en una carrera) **2** RUSH : ir a toda prisa, ir corriendo
race² *n* **1** CURRENT : corriente *f* (de agua) **2** : carrera *f* ⟨dog race : carrera de perros⟩ ⟨the presidential race : la carrera presidential⟩ **3** : raza *f* ⟨the black race : la raza negra⟩ ⟨the human race : el género humano⟩
racecourse ['reɪs,kors] *n* : pista *f* (de carreras)
racehorse ['reɪs,hors] *n* : caballo *m* de carreras
racer ['reɪsər] *n* : corredor *m*, -dora *f*
racetrack ['reɪs,træk] *n* : pista *f* (de carreras)
racial ['reɪʃəl] *adj* : racial — **racially** *adv*
racism ['reɪ,sɪzəm] *n* : racismo *m*
racist ['reɪsɪst] *n* : racista *mf*
rack¹ ['ræk] *vt* **1** : atormentar ⟨racked with pain : atormentado por el dolor⟩ **2 to rack one's brains** : devanarse los sesos
rack² *n* **1** SHELF, STAND : estante *m* ⟨a luggage rack : un portaequipajes⟩ ⟨a coatrack : un perchero, una percha⟩ **2** : potro *m* (instrumento de la tortura)
racket ['rækət] *n* **1** : raqueta *f* (en deportes) **2** DIN : estruendo *m*, bulla *f*, jaleo *m fam* **3** SWINDLE : estafa *f*, timo *m fam*
racketeer [,rækə'tɪr] *n* : estafador *m*, -dora *f*
raconteur [,ræ,kɑn'tər] *n* : anecdotista *mf*
racy ['reɪsi] *adj* **racier; -est** : subido de tono, picante
radar ['reɪ,dɑr] *n* : radar *m*
radial ['reɪdiəl] *adj* : radial
radiance ['reɪdiənts] *n* : resplandor *m*
radiant ['reɪdiənt] *adj* : radiante — **radiantly** *adv*
radiate ['reɪdi,eɪt] *v* **-ated; -ating** *vt* : irradiar, emitir ⟨to radiate heat : irradiar el calor⟩ ⟨to radiate happiness : rebosar de alegría⟩ — *vi* **1** : irradiar **2** SPREAD : salir, extenderse ⟨to radiate (out) from the center : salir del centro⟩
radiation [,reɪdi'eɪʃən] *n* : radiación *f*
radiator ['reɪdi,eɪtər] *n* : radiador *m*
radical¹ ['rædɪkəl] *adj* : radical — **radically** [-kli] *adv*
radical² *n* : radical *mf*
radicalism ['rædɪkə,lɪzəm] *n* : radicalismo *m*
radii → **radius**
radio¹ ['reɪdi,o:] *v* : llamar por radio, transmitir por radio
radio² *n*, *pl* **-dios** : radio *m* (aparato), radio *f* (emisora, radiodifusión)
radioactive ['reɪdio'æktɪv] *adj* : radiactivo, radioactivo
radioactivity [,reɪdio,æk'tɪvəti] *n*, *pl* **-ties** : radiactividad *f*, radioactividad *f*
radiologist [,reɪdi'ɑlədʒɪst] *n* : radiólogo *m*, -ga *f*
radiology [,reɪdi'ɑlədʒi] *n* : radiología *f*
radish ['rædɪʃ] *n* : rábano *m*
radium ['reɪdiəm] *n* : radio *m*
radius ['reɪdiəs] *n*, *pl* **radii** [-di,aɪ] : radio *m*
radon ['reɪ,dɑn] *n* : radón *m*
raffle¹ ['ræfəl] *vt* **-fled; -fling** : rifar, sortear
raffle² *n* : rifa *f*, sorteo *m*
raft ['ræft] *n* **1** : balsa *f* ⟨rubber rafts : balsas de goma⟩ **2** LOT, SLEW : montón *m* ⟨a raft of documents : un montón de documentos⟩
rafter ['ræftər] *n* : par *m*, viga *f*
rag ['ræg] *n* **1** CLOTH : trapo *m* **2 rags** *npl* TATTERS : harapos *mpl*, andrajos *mpl*
ragamuffin ['rægə,mʌfən] *n* : pilluelo *m*, -la *f*
rage¹ ['reɪdʒ] *vi* **raged; raging 1** : estar furioso, rabiar ⟨to fly into a rage : enfurecerse⟩ **2** : bramar, hacer estragos ⟨the wind was raging : el viento bramaba⟩ ⟨flu raged through the school : la gripe hizo estragos por el colegio⟩
rage² *n* **1** ANGER : furia *f*, ira *f*, cólera *f* **2** FAD : moda *f*, furor *m*
ragged ['rægəd] *adj* **1** UNEVEN : irregular, desigual **2** TORN : hecho jirones **3** TATTERED : andrajoso, harapiento
ragout [ræ'gu:] *n* : ragú *m*, estofado *m*
ragtime ['ræg,taɪm] *n* : ragtime *m*
ragweed ['ræg,wi:d] *n* : ambrosía *f*
raid¹ ['reɪd] *vt* **1** : invadir, hacer una incursión en ⟨raided by enemy troops

: invadido por tropas enemigas⟩ 2 : asaltar, atracar ⟨the gang raided the warehouse : la pandilla asaltó el almacén⟩ 3 : allanar, hacer una redada en ⟨police raided the house : la policía allanó la vivienda⟩
raid² n 1 : invasión f (militar) 2 : asalto m (por delincuentes) 3 : redada f, allanamiento m (por la policía)
raider ['reɪdər] n 1 ATTACKER : asaltante mf; invasor m, -sora f 2 **corporate raider** : tiburón m
rail¹ ['reɪl] vi 1 **to rail against** REVILE : denostar contra 2 **to rail at** SCOLD : regañar, reprender
rail² n 1 BAR : barra f, barrera f 2 HANDRAIL : pasamanos m, barandilla f 3 TRACK : riel m (para ferrocarriles) 4 RAILROAD : ferrocarril m
railing ['reɪlɪŋ] n 1 : baranda f (de un balcón, etc.) 2 RAILS : verja f
raillery ['reɪləri] n, pl **-leries** : bromas fpl
railroad ['reɪl,roːd] n : ferrocarril m
railway ['reɪl,weɪ] → railroad
raiment ['reɪmənt] n : vestiduras fpl
rain¹ ['reɪn] vi 1 : llover ⟨it's raining : está lloviendo⟩ 2 **to rain down** SHOWER : llover ⟨insults rained down on him : le llovieron los insultos⟩
rain² n : lluvia f
rainbow ['reɪn,boː] n : arco m iris
raincoat ['reɪn,koːt] n : impermeable m
raindrop ['reɪn,drɑp] n : gota f de lluvia
rainfall ['reɪn,fɔl] n : lluvia f, precipitación f
rainstorm ['reɪn,stɔrm] n : temporal m (de lluvia)
rainwater ['reɪn,wɔt̬ər] n : agua f de lluvia
rainy ['reɪni] adj rainier; -est : lluvioso
raise¹ ['reɪz] vt raised; raising 1 LIFT : levantar, subir, alzar ⟨to raise one's spirits : levantarle el ánimo a alguien⟩ 2 ERECT : levantar, erigir 3 COLLECT : recaudar ⟨to raise money : recaudar dinero⟩ 4 REAR : criar ⟨to raise one's children : criar uno a sus niños⟩ 5 GROW : cultivar 6 INCREASE : aumentar, subir 7 PROMOTE : ascender 8 PROVOKE : provocar ⟨it raised a laugh : provocó una risa⟩ 9 BRING UP : sacar (temas, objeciones, etc.)
raise² n : aumento m
raisin ['reɪzən] n : pasa f
raja or **rajah** ['rɑdʒə, -,dʒɑ, -,ʒɑ] n : rajá m
rake¹ ['reɪk] v raked; raking vt 1 : rastrillar ⟨to rake leaves : rastrillar las hojas⟩ 2 SWEEP : barrer ⟨raked with gunfire : barrido con metralla⟩ — vi **to rake through** : revolver, hurgar en
rake² n 1 : rastrillo m 2 LIBERTINE : libertino m, -na f; calavera m
rakish ['reɪkɪʃ] adj 1 JAUNTY : desenvuelto, desenfadado 2 DISSOLUTE : libertino, disoluto
rally¹ ['ræli] v -lied; -lying vi 1 MEET, UNITE : reunirse, congregarse 2 RE-

COVER : recuperarse — vt 1 ASSEMBLE : reunir (tropas, etc.) 2 RECOVER : recobrar (la fuerza, el ánimo, etc.)
rally² n, pl **-lies** : reunión f, mitin m, manifestación f
ram¹ ['ræm] v rammed; ramming vt 1 DRIVE : hincar, clavar ⟨he rammed it into the ground : lo hincó en la tierra⟩ 2 SMASH : estrellar, embestir — vi COLLIDE : chocar (contra), estrellarse
ram² n 1 : carnero m (animal) 2 **battering ram** : ariete m
RAM ['ræm] n : RAM f
ramble¹ ['ræmbəl] vi -bled; -bling 1 WANDER : pasear, deambular 2 **to ramble on** : divagar, perder el hilo 3 SPREAD : trepar (dícese de una planta)
ramble² n : paseo m, excursión f
rambler ['ræmblər] n 1 WALKER : excursionista mf 2 ROSE : rosa f trepadora
rambunctious [ræm'bʌŋkʃəs] adj UNRULY : alborotado
ramification [,ræməfə'keɪʃən] n : ramificación f
ramify ['ræmə,faɪ] vi -fied; -fying : ramificarse
ramp ['ræmp] n : rampa f
rampage¹ ['ræm,peɪdʒ, ræm'peɪdʒ] vi -paged; -paging : andar arrasando todo, correr destrozando
rampage² ['ræm,peɪdʒ] n : alboroto m, frenesí m (de violencia)
rampant ['ræmpənt] adj : desenfrenado
rampart ['ræm,pɑrt] n : terraplén m, muralla f
ramrod ['ræm,rɑd] n : baqueta f
ramshackle ['ræm,ʃækəl] adj : destartalado
ran → run
ranch ['ræntʃ] n 1 : hacienda f, rancho m, finca f ganadera 2 FARM : granja f ⟨fruit ranch : granja de frutas⟩
rancher ['ræntʃər] n : estanciero m, -ra f; ranchero m, -ra f
rancid ['rænsɪd] adj : rancio
rancor ['ræŋkər] n : rencor m
random ['rændəm] adj 1 : fortuito, aleatorio 2 **at ~** : al azar — **randomly** adv
rang → ring
range¹ ['reɪndʒ] v ranged; ranging vt ARRANGE : alinear, ordenar, arreglar — vi 1 ROAM : deambular ⟨to range through the town : deambular por el pueblo⟩ 2 EXTEND : extenderse ⟨the results range widely : los resultados se extienden mucho⟩ 3 VARY : variar ⟨discounts range from 20% to 40% : los descuentos varían entre 20% y 40%⟩
range² n 1 ROW : fila f, hilera f ⟨a mountain range : una cordillera⟩ 2 GRASSLAND : pradera f, pampa f 3 STOVE : cocina f 4 VARIETY : variedad f, gama f 5 SPHERE : ámbito m, esfera f, campo m 6 REACH : registro m (de la voz), alcance m (de un arma de fuego) 7 **shooting range** : campo m de tiro

ranger ['reɪndʒər] *n or* forest ranger
: guardabosque *mf*
rangy ['reɪndʒi] *adj* rangier; -est : alto y
delgado
rank¹ ['ræŋk] *vt* 1 RANGE : alinear, ordenar, poner en fila 2 CLASSIFY : clasificar — *vi* 1 to rank above : ser superior a 2 to rank among : encontrarse
entre, figurar entre
rank² *adj* 1 LUXURIANT : lozano, exuberante (dícese de una planta) 2
SMELLY : fétido, maloliente 3 OUT-
RIGHT : completo, absoluto ⟨a rank injustice : una injusticia manifiesta⟩
rank³ *n* 1 LINE, ROW : fila *f* ⟨to close
ranks : cerrar filas⟩ 2 GRADE, POSI-
TION : grado *m*, rango *m* (militar) ⟨to
pull rank : abusar de su autoridad⟩ 3
CLASS : categoría *f*, clase *f* 4 ranks *npl*
: soldados *mpl* rasos
rank and file *n* 1 RANKS : soldados *mpl*
rasos 2 : bases *fpl* (de un partido, etc.)
rankle ['ræŋkəl] *v* -kled; -kling *vi* : doler — *vt* : irritar, herir
ransack ['ræn,sæk] *vt* : revolver, desvalijar, registrar de arriba abajo
ransom¹ ['ræntsəm] *vt* : rescatar, pagar
un rescate por
ransom² *n* : rescate *m*
rant ['rænt] *vi or* to rant and rave
: despotricar, desvariar
rap¹ ['ræp] *v* rapped; rapping *vt* 1
KNOCK : golpetear, dar un golpe en 2
CRITICIZE : criticar — *vi* 1 CHAT : charlar, cotorrear *fam* 2 KNOCK : dar un
golpe
rap² *n* 1 BLOW, KNOCK : golpe *m*,
golpecito *m* 2 CHAT : charla *f* 3 *or* rap
music : rap *m* 4 to take the rap : pagar el pato *fam*
rapacious [rə'peɪʃəs] *adj* 1 GREEDY
: avaricioso, codicioso 2 PREDATORY
: rapaz, de rapiña 3 RAVENOUS : voraz
rape¹ ['reɪp] *vt* raped; raping : violar
rape² *n* 1 : colza *f* (planta) 2 : violación
f (de una persona)
rapid ['ræpɪd] *adj* : rápido — rapidly *adv*
rapidity [rə'pɪdəti] *n* : rapidez *f*
rapids ['ræpɪdz] *npl* : rápidos *mpl*
rapier ['reɪpiər] *n* : estoque *m*
rapist ['reɪpɪst] *n* : violador *m*, -dora *f*
rapper ['ræpər] *n* : cantante *mf* de rap;
rapero *m*, -ra *f*
rapport [ræ'por] *n* : relación *f* armo-
niosa, entendimiento *m*
rapt ['ræpt] *adj* : absorto, embelesado
rapture ['ræptʃər] *n* : éxtasis *m*
rapturous ['ræptʃərəs] *adj* : extasiado,
embelesado
rare ['rær] *adj* rarer; rarest 1 RAREFIED
: enrarecido 2 FINE : excelente, excepcional ⟨a rare talent : un talento ex-
cepcional⟩ 3 UNCOMMON : raro, poco
común 4 : poco cocido (dícese de la
carne)
rarefy ['rærə,faɪ] *vt* -fied; -fying : rari-
ficar, enrarecer

rarely ['rærli] *adv* SELDOM : pocas veces,
rara vez
raring ['rærən, -ɪŋ] *adj* : lleno de entusiasmo, con muchas ganas
rarity ['rærəti] *n, pl* -ties : rareza *f*
rascal ['ræskəl] *n* : pillo *m*, -lla *f*; pícaro
m, -ra *f*
rash¹ ['ræʃ] *adj* : imprudente, precipitado — rashly *adv*
rash² *n* : sarpullido *m*, erupción *f*
rashness ['ræʃnəs] *n* : precipitación *f*,
impetuosidad *f*
rasp¹ ['ræsp] *vt* 1 SCRAPE : raspar, es-
cofinar 2 to rasp out : decir en voz
áspera
rasp² *n* : escofina *f*
raspberry ['ræz,bɛri] *n, pl* -ries : frambuesa *f*
rat ['ræt] *n* : rata *f*
ratchet ['rætʃət] *n* : trinquete *m*
rate¹ ['reɪt] *vt* rated; rating 1 CONSID-
ER, REGARD : considerar, estimar 2
DESERVE : merecer
rate² *n* 1 PACE, SPEED : velocidad *f*, ritmo *m* ⟨at this rate : a este paso⟩ 2
: índice *m*, tasa *f* ⟨birth rate : índice de
natalidad⟩ ⟨interest rate : tasa de in-
terés⟩ 3 CHARGE, PRICE : precio *m*,
tarifa *f*
rather ['ræðər, 'rʌ-, 'rɑ-] *adv* 1 (*indicating preference*) ⟨she would rather stay
in the house : preferiría quedarse en
casa⟩ ⟨I'd rather not : mejor que no⟩
2 (*indicating preciseness*) ⟨my father, or
rather my stepfather : mi padre, o
mejor dicho mi padrastro⟩ 3 INSTEAD
: sino que, más que, al contrario ⟨I'm
not pleased; rather I'm disappointed
: no estoy satisfecho, sino desilusiona-
do⟩ 4 SOMEWHAT : algo, un tanto
⟨rather strange : un poco extraño⟩ 5
QUITE : bastante ⟨rather difficult : bastante difícil⟩
ratification [,rætəfə'keɪʃən] *n* : ratificación *f*
ratify ['rætə,faɪ] *vt* -fied; -fying : ratificar
rating ['reɪtɪŋ] *n* 1 STANDING : clasificación *f*, posición *f* 2 ratings *npl*
: índice *m* de audiencia
ratio ['reɪʃio] *n, pl* -tios : proporción *f*,
relación *f*
ration¹ ['ræʃən, 'reɪʃən] *vt* : racionar
ration² *n* 1 : ración *f* 2 rations *npl* PRO-
VISIONS : víveres *mpl*
rational ['ræʃənəl] *adj* : racional, razonable, lógico — rationally *adv*
rationale [,ræʃə'næl] *n* 1 EXPLANATION
: explicación *f* 2 BASIS : base *f*, razones
fpl
rationality [,ræʃə'næləti] *n, pl* -ties
: racionalidad *f*
rationalization [,ræʃənələ'zeɪʃən] *n*
: racionalización *f*
rationalize ['ræʃənə,laɪz] *vt* -ized; -izing
: racionalizar
rattle¹ ['rætəl] *v* -tled; -tling *vi* 1 CLAT-
TER : traquetear, hacer ruido 2 to rattle on CHATTER : parlotear *fam* — *vt*

1 : hacer sonar, agitar ⟨the wind rattled the door : el viento sacudió la puerta⟩ **2** DISCONCERT, WORRY : desconcertar, poner nervioso **3 to rattle off** : despachar, recitar, decir de corrido
rattle² *n* **1** CLATTER : traqueteo *m*, ruido *m* **2** *or* **baby's rattle** : sonajero *m* **3** : cascabel *m* (de una culebra)
rattler ['rætələr] → **rattlesnake**
rattlesnake ['rætəl,sneɪk] *n* : serpiente *f* de cascabel
ratty ['ræti] *adj* **rattier; -est** : raído, andrajoso
raucous ['rɔkəs] *adj* **1** HOARSE : ronco **2** BOISTEROUS : escandaloso, bullicioso — **raucously** *adv*
ravage¹ ['rævɪʤ] *vt* **-aged; -aging** : devastar, arrasar, hacer estragos
ravage² *n* : destrozo *m*, destrucción *f* ⟨the ravages of war : los estragos de la guerra⟩
rave ['reɪv] *vi* **raved; raving 1** : delirar, desvariar ⟨to rave like a maniac : desvariar como un loco⟩ **2 to rave about** : hablar con entusiasmo sobre, entusiasmarse por
ravel ['rævəl] *v* **-eled** *or* **-elled; -eling** *or* **-elling** *vt* UNRAVEL : desenredar, desenmarañar — *vi* FRAY : deshilacharse
raven ['reɪvən] *n* : cuervo *m*
ravenous ['rævənəs] *adj* : hambriento, voraz — **ravenously** *adv*
ravine [rə'viːn] *n* : barranco *m*, quebrada *f*
ravish ['rævɪʃ] *vt* **1** PLUNDER : saquear **2** ENCHANT : embelesar, cautivar, encantar
raw ['rɔ] *adj* **rawer; rawest 1** UNCOOKED : crudo **2** UNTREATED : sin tratar, sin refinar, puro ⟨raw data : datos en bruto⟩ ⟨raw materials : materias primas⟩ **3** INEXPERIENCED : novato, inexperto **4** OPEN : abierto, en carne viva ⟨a raw sore : una llaga abierta⟩ **5** : frío y húmedo ⟨a raw day : un día crudo⟩ **6** UNFAIR : injusto ⟨a raw deal : un trato injusto, una injusticia⟩
rawhide ['rɔ,haɪd] *n* : cuero *m* sin curtir
ray ['reɪ] *n* **1** : rayo *m* (de la luz, etc.) ⟨a ray of hope : un resquicio de esperanza⟩ **2** : raya *f* (pez)
rayon ['reɪ,ɑn] *n* : rayón *m*
raze ['reɪz] *vt* **razed; razing** : arrasar, demoler
razor ['reɪzər] *n* **1** *or* **straight razor** : navaja *f* (de afeitar) **2** *or* **safety razor** : maquinilla *f* de afeitar, rastrillo *m* *Mex* **3** SHAVER : afeitadora *f*, rasuradora *f*
reach¹ ['riːʧ] *vt* **1** EXTEND : extender, alargar ⟨to reach out one's hand : extender la mano⟩ **2** : alcanzar ⟨I couldn't reach the apple : no pude alcanzar la manzana⟩ **3** : llegar a, llegar hasta ⟨the shadow reached the wall : la sombra llegó hasta la pared⟩ **4** CONTACT : contactar, ponerse en contacto con — *vi* **1** *or* **to reach out** : extender la mano **2** STRETCH : extenderse **3 to**

reach for : tratar de agarrar
reach² *n* : alcance *m*, extensión *f*
react [ri'ækt] *vi* : reaccionar
reaction [ri'ækʃən] *n* : reacción *f*
reactionary¹ [ri'ækʃə,nɛri] *adj* : reaccionario
reactionary² *n*, *pl* **-ries** : reaccionario *m*, -ria *f*
reactor [ri'æktər] *n* : reactor *m* ⟨nuclear reactor : reactor nuclear⟩
read¹ ['riːd] *v* **read** ['rɛd]; **reading** *vt* **1** : leer ⟨to read a story : leer un cuento⟩ **2** INTERPRET : interpretar ⟨it can be read two ways : se puede interpretar de dos maneras⟩ **3** : decir, poner ⟨the sign read "No smoking" : el letrero decía "No Fumar"⟩ **4** : marcar ⟨the thermometer reads 70° : el termómetro marca 70°⟩ — *vi* **1** : leer ⟨he can read : sabe leer⟩ **2** SAY : decir ⟨the list reads as follows : la lista dice lo siguiente⟩
read² *n* **to be a good read** : ser una lectura amena
readable ['riːdəbəl] *adj* : legible — **readably** [-bli] *adv*
reader ['riːdər] *n* : lector *m*, -tora *f*
readily ['rɛdəli] *adv* **1** WILLINGLY : de buena gana, con gusto **2** EASILY : fácilmente, con facilidad
readiness ['rɛdinəs] *n* **1** WILLINGNESS : buena disposición *f* **2 to be in readiness** : estar preparado
reading ['riːdɪŋ] *n* : lectura *f*
readjust [,riːə'ʤʌst] *vt* : reajustar — *vi* : volverse a adaptar
readjustment [,riːə'ʤʌstmənt] *n* : reajuste *m*
ready¹ ['rɛdi] *vt* **readied; readying** : preparar
ready² *adj* **readier; -est 1** PREPARED : listo, preparado **2** WILLING : dispuesto **3** : a punto de ⟨ready to cry : a punto de llorar⟩ **4** AVAILABLE : disponible ⟨ready cash : efectivo⟩ **5** QUICK : vivo, agudo ⟨a ready wit : un ingenio agudo⟩
ready-made ['rɛdi'meɪd] *adj* : preparado, confeccionado
reaffirm [,riːə'fərm] *vt* : reafirmar
real¹ ['riːl] *adv* VERY : muy ⟨we had a real good time : lo pasamos muy bien⟩
real² *adj* **1** : inmobiliario ⟨real property : bien inmueble, bien raíz⟩ **2** GENUINE : auténtico, genuino **3** ACTUAL, TRUE : real, verdadero ⟨a real friend : un verdadero amigo⟩ **4 for real** SERIOUSLY : de veras, de verdad
real estate *n* : propiedad *f* inmobiliaria, bienes *mpl* raíces
realign [,riːə'laɪn] *vt* : realinear
realignment [,riːə'laɪnmənt] *n* : realineamiento *m*
realism ['riːə,lɪzəm] *n* : realismo *m*
realist ['riːəlɪst] *n* : realista *mf*
realistic [,riːə'lɪstɪk] *adj* : realista
realistically [,riːə'lɪstɪkli] *adv* : de manera realista

reality [ri'æləti] *n*, *pl* **-ties** : realidad *f*
realizable [ˌri:ə'laɪzəbəl] *adj* : realizable, alcanzable
realization [ˌri:ələ'zeɪʃən] *n* : realización *f*
realize ['ri:əˌlaɪz] *vt* **-ized; -izing 1** AC-COMPLISH : realizar, llevar a cabo **2** GAIN : obtener, realizar, sacar ⟨to realize a profit : realizar beneficios⟩ **3** UNDERSTAND : darse cuenta de, saber
really ['rɪli, 'ri:-] *adv* **1** ACTUALLY : de verdad, en realidad **2** TRULY : verdaderamente, realmente **3** FRANKLY : francamente, en serio
realm ['rɛlm] *n* **1** KINGDOM : reino *m* **2** SPHERE : esfera *f*, campo *m*
ream[1] ['ri:m] *vt* : escariar
ream[2] *n* **1** : resma *f* (de papel) **2 reams** *npl* LOADS : montones *mpl*
reap ['ri:p] *v* : cosechar
reaper ['ri:pər] *n* **1** : cosechador *m*, -dora *f* (persona) **2** : cosechadora *f* (máquina)
reappear [ˌri:ə'pɪr] *vi* : reaparecer
reappearance [ˌri:ə'pɪrənts] *n* : reaparición *f*
rear[1] ['rɪr] *vt* **1** LIFT, RAISE : levantar **2** BREED, BRING UP : criar — *vi or* **to rear up** : encabritarse
rear[2] *adj* : trasero, posterior, de atrás
rear[3] *n* **1** BACK : parte *f* de atrás ⟨to bring up the rear : cerrar la marcha⟩ **2 or rear end** : trasero *m*
rear admiral *n* : contraalmirante *mf*
rearrange [ˌri:ə'reɪndʒ] *vt* **-ranged; -ranging** : colocar de otra manera, volver a arreglar, reorganizar
rearview mirror ['rɪrˌvju:-] *n* : retrovisor *m*
reason[1] ['ri:zən] *vt* THINK : pensar — *vi* : razonar ⟨I can't reason with her : no puedo razonar con ella⟩
reason[2] *n* **1** CAUSE, GROUND : razón *f*, motivo *m* ⟨the reason for his trip : el motivo de su viaje⟩ ⟨for this reason : por esta razón, por lo cual⟩ ⟨the reason why : la razón por la cual, el porqué⟩ **2** SENSE : razón *f* ⟨to lose one's reason : perder los sesos⟩ ⟨to listen to reason : avenirse a razones⟩
reasonable ['ri:zənəbəl] *adj* **1** SENSIBLE : razonable **2** INEXPENSIVE : barato, económico
reasonably ['ri:zənəbli] *adv* **1** SENSIBLY : razonablemente **2** FAIRLY : bastante
reasoning ['ri:zənɪŋ] *n* : razonamiento *m*, raciocinio *m*, argumentos *mpl*
reassess [ˌri:ə'sɛs] *vt* : revaluar, reconsiderar
reassurance [ˌri:ə'ʃurənts] *n* : consuelo *m*, palabras *fpl* alentadoras
reassure [ˌri:ə'ʃur] *vt* **-sured; -suring** : tranquilizar
reassuring [ˌri:ə'ʃurɪŋ] *adj* : tranquilizador
reawaken [ˌri:ə'weɪkən] *vt* : volver a despertar, reavivar
rebate ['ri:ˌbeɪt] *n* : reembolso *m*, devolución *f*

rebel[1] [rɪ'bɛl] *vi* **-belled; -belling** : rebelarse, sublevarse
rebel[2] ['rɛbəl] *adj* : rebelde
rebel[3] ['rɛbəl] *n* : rebelde *mf*
rebellion [rɪ'bɛljən] *n* : rebelión *f*
rebellious [rɪ'bɛljəs] *adj* : rebelde
rebelliousness [rɪ'bɛljəsnəs] *n* : rebeldía *f*
rebirth [ˌri:'bərθ] *n* : renacimiento *m*
reboot [ri'bu:t] *vt* : reiniciar (una computadora)
reborn [ri:'bɔrn] *adj* **to be reborn** : renacer
rebound[1] ['ri:ˌbaʊnd, ˌri:'baʊnd] *vi* : rebotar
rebound[2] ['ri:ˌbaʊnd] *n* : rebote *m*
rebuff[1] [rɪ'bʌf] *vt* : desairar, rechazar
rebuff[2] *n* : desaire *m*, rechazo *m*
rebuild [ˌri:'bɪld] *vt* **-built** [-'bɪlt]; **-building** : reconstruir
rebuke[1] [rɪ'bju:k] *vt* **-buked; -buking** : reprender, regañar
rebuke[2] *n* : reprimenda *f*, reproche *m*
rebut [ri'bʌt] *vt* **-butted; -butting** : rebatir, refutar
rebuttal [ri'bʌtəl] *n* : refutación *f*
recalcitrant [ri'kælsətrənt] *adj* : recalcitrante
recall[1] [ri'kɔl] *vt* **1** : llamar, retirar ⟨recalled to active duty : llamado al servicio activo⟩ **2** REMEMBER : recordar, acordarse de **3** REVOKE : revocar
recall[2] [ri'kɔl, 'ri:ˌkɔl] *n* **1** : retirada *f* (de personas o mercancías) **2** MEMORY : memoria *f* ⟨to have total recall : poder recordar todo⟩
recant [ri'kænt] *vt* : retractarse de — *vi* : retractarse, renegar
recapitulate [ˌri:kə'pɪtʃəˌleɪt] *v* **-lated; -lating** : resumir, recapitular
recapture [ˌri:'kæptʃər] *vt* **-tured; -turing 1** REGAIN : volver a tomar, reconquistar **2** RELIVE : revivir (la juventud, etc.)
recast [ri:'kæst] *vt* **-cast; -casting 1** : refundir (metales) **2** REWRITE : refundir, modificar
recede [ri'si:d] *vi* **-ceded; -ceding 1** WITHDRAW : retirarse, retroceder **2** FADE : desvanecerse, alejarse **3** SLANT : inclinarse **4 to have a receding hairline** : tener entradas
receipt [ri'si:t] *n* **1** : recibo *m* **2 receipts** *npl* : ingresos *mpl*, entradas *fpl*
receivable [ri'si:vəbəl] *adj* **accounts receivable** : cuentas por cobrar
receive [ri'si:v] *vt* **-ceived; -ceiving 1** GET : recibir ⟨to receive a letter : recibir una carta⟩ ⟨to receive a blow : recibir un golpe⟩ **2** WELCOME : acoger, recibir ⟨to receive guests : tener invitados⟩ **3** : recibir, captar (señales de radio)
receiver [ri'si:vər] *n* **1** : receptor *m*, -tora *f* (en futbol americano) **2** : receptor *m* (de radio o televisión) **3 telephone receiver** : auricular *m*
recent ['ri:sənt] *adj* : reciente — **recently** *adv*

receptacle [rɪ'sɛptɪkəl] *n* : receptáculo *m*, recipiente *m*

reception [rɪ'sɛpʃən] *n* : recepción *f*

receptionist [rɪ'sɛpʃənɪst] *n* : recepcionista *mf*

receptive [rɪ'sɛptɪv] *adj* : receptivo

receptivity [ˌriː,sɛp'tɪvəʈi] *n* : receptividad *f*

recess¹ ['riː,sɛs, rɪ'sɛs] *vt* **1** : poner en un hueco ⟨recessed lighting : iluminación empotrada⟩ **2** ADJOURN : suspender, levantar

recess² *n* **1** ALCOVE : hueco *m*, nicho *m* **2** BREAK : receso *m*, descanso *m*, recreo *m* (en el colegio)

recession [rɪ'sɛʃən] *n* : recesión *f*, depresión *f* económica

recessive [rɪ'sɛsɪv] *adj* : recesivo

recharge [ˌriː'ʧɑrʤ] *vt* **-charged; -charging** : recargar

rechargeable [ˌriː'ʧɑrʤəbəl] *adj* : recargable

recipe ['rɛsə,piː] *n* : receta *f*

recipient [rɪ'sɪpiənt] *n* : recipiente *mf*

reciprocal [rɪ'sɪprəkəl] *adj* : recíproco

reciprocate [rɪ'sɪprə,keɪt] *vi* **-cated; -cating** : reciprocar

reciprocity [ˌrɛsə'prɑsəʈi] *n, pl* **-ties** : reciprocidad *f*

recital [rɪ'saɪʈəl] *n* **1** PERFORMANCE : recital *m* **2** ENUMERATION : relato *m*, enumeración *f*

recitation [ˌrɛsə'teɪʃən] *n* : recitación *f*

recite [rɪ'saɪt] *vt* **-cited; -citing 1** : recitar (un poema, etc.) **2** RECOUNT : narrar, relatar, enumerar

reckless ['rɛkləs] *adj* : imprudente, temerario — **recklessly** *adv*

recklessness ['rɛkləsnəs] *n* : imprudencia *f*, temeridad *f*

reckon ['rɛkən] *vt* **1** CALCULATE : calcular, contar **2** CONSIDER : considerar

reckoning ['rɛkənɪŋ] *n* **1** CALCULATION : cálculo *m* **2** SETTLEMENT : ajuste *m* de cuentas ⟨day of reckoning : día del juicio final⟩

reclaim [rɪ'kleɪm] *vt* **1** : ganar, sanear ⟨to reclaim marshy land : sanear las tierras pantanosas⟩ **2** RECOVER : recobrar, reciclar ⟨to reclaim old tires : reciclar llantas desechadas⟩ **3** REGAIN : reclamar, recuperar ⟨to reclaim one's rights : reclamar uno sus derechos⟩

recline [rɪ'klaɪn] *vi* **-clined; -clining 1** LEAN : reclinarse **2** REPOSE : recostarse

recluse ['rɛ,kluːs, rɪ'kluːs] *n* : solitario *m*, -ria *f*

recognition [ˌrɛkɪg'nɪʃən] *n* : reconocimiento *m*

recognizable ['rɛkəg,naɪzəbəl] *adj* : reconocible

recognize ['rɛkɪg,naɪz] *vt* **-nized; -nizing** : reconocer

recoil¹ [rɪ'kɔɪl] *vi* : retroceder, dar un culatazo

recoil² ['riː,kɔɪl, rɪ'-] *n* : retroceso *m*, culatazo *m*

recollect [ˌrɛkə'lɛkt] *v* : recordar

recollection [ˌrɛkə'lɛkʃən] *n* : recuerdo *m*

recommend [ˌrɛkə'mɛnd] *vt* **1** : recomendar ⟨she recommended the medicine : recomendó la medicina⟩ **2** ADVISE, COUNSEL : aconsejar, recomendar

recommendation [ˌrɛkəmən'deɪʃən] *n* : recomendación *f*

recompense¹ ['rɛkəm,pɛnʦ] *vt* **-pensed; -pensing** : indemnizar, recompensar

recompense² *n* : indemnización *f*, compensación *f*

reconcile ['rɛkən,saɪl] *v* **-ciled; -ciling** *vt* **1** : reconciliar (personas), conciliar (ideas, etc.) **2 to reconcile oneself to** : resignarse a — *vi* MAKE UP : reconciliarse, hacer las paces

reconciliation [ˌrɛkən,sɪli'eɪʃən] *n* : reconciliación *f* (con personas), conciliación *f* (con ideas, etc.)

recondite ['rɛkən,daɪt, rɪ'kɑn-] *adj* : recóndito, abstruso

recondition [ˌriː kən'dɪʃən] *vt* : reacondicionar

reconnaissance [rɪ'kɑnəzənʦ, -sənʦ] *n* : reconocimiento *m*

reconnoiter *or* **reconnoitre** [ˌriː kə-'nɔɪʈər, ˌrɛkə-] *v* **-tered** *or* **-tred; -tering** *or* **-tring** *vt* : reconocer — *vi* : hacer un reconocimiento

reconsider [ˌriː kən'sɪdər] *vt* : reconsiderar, repensar

reconsideration [ˌriː kən,sɪdə'reɪʃən] *n* : reconsideración *f*

reconstruct [ˌriː kən'strʌkt] *vt* : reconstruir

reconstruction [ˌriː kən'strʌkʃən] *n* : reconstrucción *f*

record¹ [rɪ'kɔrd] *vt* **1** WRITE DOWN : anotar, apuntar **2** REGISTER : registrar, hacer constar **3** INDICATE : marcar (una temperatura, etc.) **4** TAPE : grabar

record² ['rɛkərd] *n* **1** DOCUMENT : registro *m*, documento *m* oficial **2** HISTORY : historial *m* ⟨a good academic record : un buen historial académico⟩ ⟨criminal record : antecedentes penales⟩ **3** : récord *m* ⟨the world record : el récord mundial⟩ **4** : disco *m* (de música, etc.) ⟨to make a record : grabar un disco⟩

recorder [rɪ'kɔrdər] *n* **1** : flauta *f* dulce (instrumento de viento) **2 tape recorder** : grabadora *f*

recording [rɪ'kɔrdɪŋ] *n* : grabación *f*

recount¹ [rɪ'kaʊnt] *vt* **1** NARRATE : narrar, relatar **2** : volver a contar (votos, etc.)

recount² ['riː,kaʊnt, ˌriː'-] *n* : recuento *m*

recoup [rɪ'kuːp] *vt* : recuperar, recobrar

recourse ['riː,kɔrs, rɪ'-] *n* : recurso *m* ⟨to have recourse to : recurrir a⟩

recover [rɪ'kʌvər] *vt* REGAIN : recobrar — *vi* RECUPERATE : recuperarse

recovery [ri'kʌvəri] *n, pl* **-eries** : recuperación *f*

re–create [ˌri:kri'eɪt] *vt* **-ated; -ating** : recrear

recreation [ˌrɛkri'eɪʃən] *n* : recreo *m*, esparcimiento *m*, diversión *f*

recreational [ˌrɛkri'eɪʃənəl] *adj* : recreativo, de recreo

recrimination [riˌkrɪmə'neɪʃən] *n* : recriminación *f*

recruit[1] [ri'kru:t] *vt* : reclutar

recruit[2] *n* : recluta *mf*

recruitment [ri'kru:tmənt] *n* : reclutamiento *m*, alistamiento *m*

rectal ['rɛktəl] *adj* : rectal

rectangle ['rɛkˌtæŋgəl] *n* : rectángulo *m*

rectangular [rɛk'tæŋgjələr] *adj* : rectangular

rectify ['rɛktəˌfaɪ] *vt* **-fied; -fying** : rectificar

rectitude ['rktəˌtu:d, -ˌtju:d] *n* : rectitud *f*

rector ['rɛktər] *n* : rector *m*, -tora *f*

rectory ['rɛktəri] *n, pl* **-ries** : rectoría *f*

rectum ['rɛktəm] *n, pl* **-tums** *or* **-ta** [-tə] : recto *m*

recuperate [ri'ku:pəˌreɪt, -'kju:-] *v* **-ated; -ating** *vt* : recuperar — *vi* : recuperarse, restablecerse

recuperation [riˌku:pə'reɪʃən, -ˌkju:-] *n* : recuperación *f*

recur [ri'kər] *vi* **-curred; -curring** : volver a ocurrir, volver a producirse, repetirse

recurrence [ri'kərənts] *n* : repetición *f*, reaparición *f*

recurrent [ri'kərənt] *adj* : recurrente, que se repite

recyclable [ri'saɪkələbəl] *adj* : reciclable

recycle [ri'saɪkəl] *vt* **-cled; -cling** : reciclar

recycling [ri'saɪkəlɪŋ] *n* : reciclaje *m*

red[1] ['rɛd] *adj* **1** : rojo, colorado ⟨to be red in the face : ponerse colorado⟩ ⟨to have red hair : ser pelirrojo⟩ **2** COMMUNIST : rojo, comunista

red[2] *n* **1** : rojo *m*, colorado *m* **2 Red** COMMUNIST : comunista *mf*

red blood cell *n* : glóbulo *m* rojo

red–blooded ['rɛd'blʌdəd] *adj* : vigoroso

redcap ['rɛdˌkæp] → **porter**

redden ['rɛdən] *vt* : enrojecer — *vi* BLUSH : enrojecerse, ruborizarse

reddish ['rɛdɪʃ] *adj* : rojizo

redecorate [ˌri:'dɛkəˌreɪt] *vt* **-rated; -rating** : renovar, pintar de nuevo

redeem [ri'di:m] *vt* **1** RESCUE, SAVE : rescatar, salvar **2** : desempeñar ⟨she redeemed it from the pawnshop : lo desempeñó de la casa de empeños⟩ **3** : redimir (en religión) **4** : canjear, vender ⟨to redeem coupons : canjear cupones⟩

redeemer [ri'di:mər] *n* : redentor *m*, -tora *f*

redefine [ˌri:dɪ'faɪn] *vt* : redefinir

redemption [ri'dɛmpʃən] *n* : redención *f*

redesign [ˌri:di'zaɪn] *vt* : rediseñar

red–handed ['rɛd'hændəd] *adj* : con las manos en la masa

redhead ['rɛdˌhɛd] *n* : pelirrojo *m*, -ja *f*

red–hot ['rɛd'hɑt] *adj* **1** : al rojo vivo, candente **2** CURRENT : de candente actualidad **3** POPULAR : de gran popularidad

rediscover [ˌri:di'skʌvər] *vt* : redescubrir

redistribute [ˌri:di'strɪˌbju:t] *vt* **-uted; -uting** : redistribuir

red–letter ['rɛd'lɛtər] *adj* **red–letter day** : día *m* memorable

redness ['rɛdnəs] *n* : rojez *f*

redo [ˌri:'du:] *vt* **-did** [-dɪd]; **-done** [-'dʌn]; **-doing** **1** : hacer de nuevo **2** → **redecorate**

redolence ['rɛdələnts] *n* : fragancia *f*

redolent ['rɛdələnt] *adj* **1** FRAGRANT : fragante, oloroso **2** SUGGESTIVE : evocador

redouble [ri'dʌbəl] *vt* **-bled; -bling** : redoblar, intensificar (esfuerzos, etc.)

redoubtable [r'daʊṭəbəl] *adj* : temible

redress [ri'drɛs] *vt* : reparar, remediar, enmendar

red snapper *n* : pargo *m*, huachinango *m Mex*

red tape *n* : papeleo *m*

reduce [ri'du:s, -'dju:s] *v* **-duced; -ducing** *vt* **1** LESSEN : reducir, disminuir, rebajar (precios) **2** DEMOTE : bajar de categoría, degradar **3 to be reduced to** : verse rebajado a, verse forzado a **4 to reduce someone to tears** : hacer llorar a alguien — *vi* SLIM : adelgazar

reduction [ri'dʌkʃən] *n* : reducción *f*, rebaja *f*

redundancy [ri'dʌndəntsi] *n, pl* **-cies 1** : superfluidad *f* **2** REPETITION : redundancia *f*

redundant [ri'dʌndənt] *adj* : superfluo, redundante

redwood ['rɛdˌwʊd] *n* : secoya *f*

reed ['ri:d] *n* **1** : caña *f*, carrizo *m*, junco *m* **2** : lengüeta *f* (para instrumentos de viento)

reef ['ri:f] *n* : arrecife *m*, escollo *m*

reek[1] ['ri:k] *vi* : apestar

reek[2] *n* : hedor *m*

reel[1] ['ri:l] *n* **1 to reel in** : enrollar, sacar (un pez) del agua **2 to reel off** : recitar de un tirón — *vi* **1** SPIN, WHIRL : girar, dar vueltas **2** STAGGER : tambalearse

reel[2] *n* **1** : carrete *m* (de pescar etc.), rollo *m* (de fotos) **2** : baile *m* escocés **3** STAGGER : tambaleo *m*

reelect [ˌri:i'lɛkt] *vt* : reelegir

reenact [ˌri:i'nækt] *vt* : representar de nuevo, reconstruir

reenter [ˌri:'ɛntər] *vt* : volver a entrar

reestablish [ˌri:i'stæblɪʃ] *vt* : restablecer

reevaluate [ˌri:i'væljuˌeɪt] *vt* **-ated; -ating** : revaluar

reevaluation [ˌri:iˌvælju'eɪʃən] *n* : revaluación *f*

reexamine [ˌriːɪgˈzæmən, -g-] *vt* **-ined; -ining** : volver a examinar, reexaminar
refer [rɪˈfər] *v* **-ferred; -ferring** *vt* DIRECT, SEND : remitir, enviar ⟨to refer a patient to a specialist : enviar a un paciente a un especialista⟩ — *vi* **to refer to** MENTION : referirse a, aludir a
referee[1] [ˌrɛfəˈriː] *v* **-eed; -eeing** : arbitrar
referee[2] *n* : árbitro *m*, -tra *f*; réferi *mf*
reference [ˈrɛfrənts, ˈrɛfə-] *n* **1** ALLUSION : referencia *f*, alusión *f* ⟨to make reference to : hacer referencia a⟩ **2** CONSULTATION : consulta *f* ⟨for future reference : para futuras consultas⟩ **3** *or* **reference book** : libro *m* de consulta **4** TESTIMONIAL : informe *m*, referencia *f*, recomendación *f*
referendum [ˌrɛfəˈrɛndəm] *n, pl* **-da** [-də] *or* **-dums** : referéndum *m*
refill[1] [ˌriːˈfɪl] *vt* : rellenar
refill[2] [ˈriːˌfɪl] *n* : recambio *m*
refinance [ˌriːˈfaɪˌnænts] *vt* **-nanced; -nancing** : refinanciar
refine [rɪˈfaɪn] *vt* **-fined; -fining** **1** : refinar (azúcar, petróleo, etc.) **2** PERFECT : perfeccionar, pulir
refined [rɪˈfaɪnd] *adj* **1** : refinado (dícese del azúcar, etc.) **2** CULTURED : culto, educado, refinado
refinement [rɪˈfaɪnmənt] *n* : refinamiento *m*, fineza *f*, finura *f*
refinery [rɪˈfaɪnəri] *n, pl* **-eries** : refinería *f*
reflect [rɪˈflɛkt] *vt* **1** : reflejar ⟨to reflect light : reflejar la luz⟩ ⟨happiness is reflected in her face : la felicidad se refleja en su cara⟩ **2 to reflect that** : pensar que, considerar que — *vi* **1 to reflect on** : reflexionar sobre **2 to reflect badly on** : desacreditar, perjudicar
reflection [rɪˈflɛkʃən] *n* **1** : reflexión *f*, reflejo *m* (de la luz, de imágenes, etc.) **2** THOUGHT : reflexión *f*, meditación *f*
reflective [rɪˈflɛktɪv] *adj* **1** THOUGHTFUL : reflexivo, pensativo **2** : reflectante (en física)
reflector [rɪˈflɛktər] *n* : reflector *m*
reflex [ˈriːˌflɛks] *n* : reflejo *m*
reflexive [rɪˈflɛksɪv] *adj* : reflexivo ⟨a reflexive verb : un verbo reflexivo⟩
reform[1] [rɪˈfɔrm] *vt* : reformar — *vi* : reformarse
reform[2] *n* : reforma *f*
reformation [ˌrɛfərˈmeɪʃən] *n* : reforma *f* ⟨the Reformation : la Reforma⟩
reformatory [rɪˈfɔrməˌtori] *n, pl* **-ries** : reformatorio *m*
reformer [rɪˈfɔrmər] *n* : reformador *m*, -dora *f*
refract [rɪˈfrækt] *vt* : refractar — *vi* : refractarse
refraction [rɪˈfrækʃən] *n* : refracción *f*
refractory [rɪˈfræktəri] *adj* OBSTINATE : refractario, obstinado
refrain[1] [rɪˈfreɪn] *vi* **to refrain from** : abstenerse de

refrain[2] *n* : estribillo *m* (en música)
refresh [rɪˈfrɛʃ] *vt* : refrescar ⟨to refresh one's memory : refrescarle la memoria a uno⟩
refreshing [rɪˈfrɛʃɪŋ] *adj* : refrescante ⟨a refreshing sleep : un sueño reparador⟩
refreshment [rɪˈfrɛʃmənt] *n* **1** : refresco *m* **2 refreshments** *npl* : refrigerio *m*
refrigerate [rɪˈfrɪdʒəˌreɪt] *vt* **-ated; -ating** : refrigerar
refrigeration [rɪˌfrɪdʒəˈreɪʃən] *n* : refrigeración *f*
refrigerator [rɪˈfrɪdʒəˌreɪtər] *n* : refrigerador *m*, -dora *f*, nevera *f*
refuel [riːˈfjuːəl] *v* **-eled** *or* **-elled; -eling** *or* **-elling** *vi* : repostar — *vt* : llenar de combustible
refuge [ˈrɛˌfjuːdʒ] *n* : refugio *m*
refugee [ˌrɛfjʊˈdʒiː] *n* : refugiado *m*, -da *f*
refund[1] [rɪˈfʌnd, ˈriːˌfʌnd] *vt* : reembolsar, devolver
refund[2] [ˈriːˌfʌnd] *n* : reembolso *m*, devolución *f*
refundable [rɪˈfʌndəbəl] *adj* : reembolsable
refurbish [rɪˈfərbɪʃ] *vt* : renovar, restaurar
refusal [rɪˈfjuːzəl] *n* : negativa *f*, rechazo *m*, denegación *f* (de una petición)
refuse[1] [rɪˈfjuːz] *vt* **-fused; -fusing** **1** REJECT : rechazar, rehusar **2** DENY : negar, rehusar, denegar ⟨to refuse permission : negar el permiso⟩ **3 to refuse to** : negarse a
refuse[2] [ˈrɛˌfjuːs, -ˌfjuːz] *n* : basura *f*, desechos *mpl*, desperdicios *mpl*
refutation [ˌrɛfjʊˈteɪʃən] *n* : refutación *f*
refute [rɪˈfjuːt] *vt* **-futed; -futing** **1** DENY : desmentir, negar **2** DISPROVE : refutar, rebatir
regain [riːˈgeɪn] *vt* **1** RECOVER : recuperar, recobrar **2** REACH : alcanzar ⟨to regain the shore : llegar a la tierra⟩
regal [ˈriːgəl] *adj* : real, regio
regale [rɪˈgeɪl] *vt* **-galed; -galing** **1** ENTERTAIN : agasajar, entretener **2** AMUSE, DELIGHT : deleitar, divertir
regalia [rɪˈgeɪljə] *npl* : ropaje *m*, vestiduras *fpl*, adornos *mpl*
regard[1] [rɪˈgɑrd] *vt* **1** OBSERVE : observar, mirar **2** HEED : tener en cuenta, hacer caso de **3** CONSIDER : considerar **4** RESPECT : respetar ⟨highly regarded : muy estimado⟩ **5 as regards** : en cuanto a, en lo que se refiere a
regard[2] *n* **1** CONSIDERATION : consideración *f* **2** ESTEEM : respeto *m*, estima *f* **3** PARTICULAR : aspecto *m*, sentido *m* ⟨in this regard : en este sentido⟩ **4 regards** *npl* : saludos *mpl*, recuerdos *mpl* **5 with regard to** : con relación a, con respecto a
regarding [rɪˈgɑrdɪŋ] *prep* : con respecto a, en cuanto a
regardless [rɪˈgɑrdləs] *adv* : a pesar de todo

regardless of *prep* : a pesar de, sin tener en cuenta ⟨regardless of our mistakes : a pesar de nuestros errores⟩ ⟨regardless of age : sin tener en cuenta la edad⟩
regenerate [ri'ʤɛnəˌreɪt] *v* -ated; -ating *vt* : regenerar — *vi* : regenerarse
regeneration [riˌʤɛnə'reɪʃən] *n* : regeneración *f*
regent ['ri:ʤənt] *n* **1** RULER : regente *mf* **2** : miembro *m* de la junta directiva (de una universidad, etc.)
regime [reɪ'ʒi:m, rɪ-] *n* : régimen *m*
regimen ['rɛʤəmən] *n* : régimen *m*
regiment[1] ['rɛʤəˌmɛnt] *vt* : reglamentar
regiment[2] ['rɛʤəmənt] *n* : regimiento *m*
region ['ri:ʤən] *n* **1** : región *f* **2 in the region of** : alrededor de
regional ['ri:ʤənəl] *adj* : regional — **regionally** *adv*
register[1] ['rɛʤəstər] *vt* **1** RECORD : registrar, inscribir **2** INDICATE : marcar (temperatura, medidas, etc.) **3** REVEAL : manifestar, acusar ⟨to register surprise : acusar sorpresa⟩ **4** : certificar (correo) — *vi* ENROLL : inscribirse, matricularse
register[2] *n* : registro *m*
registrar ['rɛʤəˌstrɑr] *n* : registrador *m*, -dora *f* oficial
registration [ˌrɛʤə'streɪʃən] *n* **1** REGISTERING : inscripción *f*, matriculación *f*, registro *m* **2** *or* **registration number** : matrícula *f*, número *m* de matrícula
registry ['rɛʤəstri] *n, pl* -tries : registro *m*
regress [ri'grɛs] *vi* : retroceder
regression [ri'grɛʃən] *n* : retroceso *m*, regresión *f*
regressive [ri'grɛsɪv] *adj* : regresivo
regret[1] [ri'grɛt] *vt* -gretted; -gretting : arrepentirse de, lamentar ⟨he regrets nothing : no se arrepiente de nada⟩ ⟨I regret to tell you : lamento decirle⟩
regret[2] *n* REMORSE : arrepentimiento *m*, remordimientos *mpl* **2** SADNESS : pesar *m*, dolor *m* **3 regrets** *npl* : excusas *fpl* ⟨to send one's regrets : excusarse⟩
regretful [ri'grɛtfəl] *adj* : arrepentido, pesaroso
regretfully [ri'grɛtfəli] *adv* : con pesar
regrettable [ri'grɛtəbəl] *adj* : lamentable — **regrettably** [-bli] *adv*
regular[1] ['rɛgjələr] *adj* **1** NORMAL : regular, normal, usual **2** STEADY : uniforme, regular ⟨a regular pace : un paso regular⟩ **3** CUSTOMARY, HABITUAL : habitual, de costumbre
regular[2] *n* : cliente *mf* habitual
regularity [ˌrɛgjə'lærəţi] *n, pl* -ties : regularidad *f*
regularly ['rɛgjələrli] *adv* : regularmente, con regularidad
regulate ['rɛgjəˌleɪt] *vt* -lated; -lating : regular
regulation [ˌrɛgjə'leɪʃən] *n* **1** REGULATING : regulación *f* **2** RULE : regla *f*,

reglamento *m*, norma *f* ⟨safety regulations : reglas de seguridad⟩
regulator ['rɛgjəˌleɪţər] *n* **1** : regulador *m* (mecanismo) **2** : persona *f* que regula
regulatory ['rɛgjələˌtori] *adj* : regulador
regurgitate [ri'gərʤəˌteɪt] *v* -tated; -tating : regurgitar, vomitar
rehabilitate [ˌri:hə'bɪləˌteɪt, ˌri:ə-] *vt* -tated; -tating : rehabilitar
rehabilitation [ˌri:həˌbɪlə'teɪʃən, ˌri:ə-] *n* : rehabilitación *f*
rehearsal [ri'hərsəl] *n* : ensayo *m*
rehearse [ri'hərs] *v* -hearsed; -hearsing : ensayar
reheat [ˌri:'hi:t] *vt* : recalentar
reign[1] ['reɪn] *vi* **1** RULE : reinar **2** PREVAIL : reinar, predominar ⟨the reigning champion : el actual campeón⟩
reign[2] *n* : reinado *m*
reimburse [ˌri:əm'bərs] *vt* -bursed; -bursing : reembolsar
reimbursement [ˌri:əm'bərsmənt] *n* : reembolso *m*
rein[1] ['reɪn] *vt* : refrenar (un caballo)
rein[2] *n* **1** : rienda *f* ⟨to give free rein to : dar rienda suelta a⟩ **2** CHECK : control *m* ⟨to keep a tight rein on : llevar un estricto control de⟩
reincarnation [ˌri:ɪnˌkɑr'neɪʃən] *n* : reencarnación *f*
reindeer ['reɪnˌdɪr] *n* : reno *m*
reinforce [ˌri:ən'fors] *vt* -forced; -forcing : reforzar
reinforcement [ˌri:ən'forsmənt] *n* : refuerzo *m*
reinstate [ˌri:ən'steɪt] *vt* -stated; -stating **1** : reintegrar, restituir (una persona) **2** RESTORE : restablecer (un servicio, etc.)
reinstatement [ˌri:ən'steɪtmənt] *n* : reintegración *f*, restitución *f*, restablecimiento *m*
reiterate [ri'ɪţəˌreɪt] *vt* -ated; -ating : reiterar, repetir
reiteration [riˌɪţə'reɪʃən] *n* : reiteración *f*, repetición *f*
reject[1] [ri'ʤɛkt] *vt* : rechazar
reject[2] ['ri:ˌʤɛkt] *n* : desecho *m* (cosa), persona *f* rechazada
rejection [ri'ʤɛkʃən] *n* : rechazo *m*
rejoice [ri'ʤɔɪs] *vi* -joiced; -joicing : alegrarse, regocijarse
rejoin [ˌri:'ʤɔɪn] *vt* **1** : reincorporarse a, reintegrarse a ⟨he rejoined the firm : se reincorporó a la firma⟩ **2** [ri'-] REPLY, RETORT : replicar
rejoinder [ri'ʤɔɪndər] *n* : réplica *f*
rejuvenate [ri'ʤu:vəˌneɪt] *vt* -nated; -nating : rejuvenecer
rejuvenation [riˌʤu:və'neɪʃən] *n* : rejuvenecimiento *m*
rekindle [ˌri:'kɪndəl] *vt* -dled; -dling : reavivar
relapse[1] [ri'læps] *vi* -lapsed; -lapsing : recaer, volver a caer
relapse[2] ['ri:ˌlæps, ri'læps] *n* : recaída *f*

relate [ri'leɪt] v **-lated; -lating** vt **1** TELL : relatar, contar **2** ASSOCIATE : relacionar, asociar ⟨to relate crime to poverty : relacionar la delincuencia a la pobreza⟩ — vi **1** CONNECT : conectar, estar relacionado (con) **2** INTERACT : relacionarse (con), llevarse bien (con) **3 to relate to** UNDERSTAND : identificarse con, simpatizar con

related [ri'leɪt̬əd] adj : emparentado ⟨to be related to : ser pariente de⟩

relation [ri'leɪʃən] n **1** NARRATION : relato m, narración f **2** RELATIVE : pariente mf, familiar mf **3** RELATIONSHIP : relación f ⟨in relation to : en relación con, con relación a⟩ **4 relations** npl : relaciones fpl ⟨public relations : relaciones públicas⟩

relationship [ri'leɪʃən,ʃɪp] n **1** CONNECTION : relación f **2** KINSHIP : parentesco m

relative[1] ['rɛlət̬ɪv] adj : relativo — **relatively** adv

relative[2] n : pariente mf, familiar mf

relativism ['rɛlət̬ɪ,vɪzəm] n : relativismo m

relativity [,rɛlə'tɪvət̬i] n, pl **-ties** : relatividad f

relax [ri'læks] vt : relajar, aflojar — vi : relajarse

relaxation [,ri:,læk'seɪʃən] n **1** RELAXING : relajación f, aflojamiento m **2** DIVERSION : esparcimiento m, distracción f

relaxing [ri'læksɪŋ] adj : relajante

relay[1] ['ri:,leɪ, ri'leɪ] vt **-layed; -laying** : transmitir

relay[2] ['ri:,leɪ] n **1** : relevo m **2** or **relay race** : carrera de relevos

release[1] [ri'li:s] vt **-leased; -leasing 1** FREE : liberar, poner en libertad **2** LOOSEN : soltar, aflojar ⟨to release the brake : soltar el freno⟩ **3** RELINQUISH : renunciar a, ceder **4** ISSUE : publicar (un libro), estrenar (una película), sacar (un disco)

release[2] n **1** LIBERATION : liberación f, puesta f en libertad **2** RELINQUISHMENT : cesión f (de propiedad, etc.) **3** ISSUE : estreno m (de una película), puesta f en venta (de un disco), publicación f (de un libro) **4** ESCAPE : escape m, fuga f (de un gas)

relegate ['rɛlə,geɪt] vt **-gated; -gating** : relegar

relent [ri'lɛnt] vi : ablandarse, ceder

relentless [ri'lɛntləs] adj : implacable, sin tregua

relentlessly [ri'lɛntləsli] adv : implacablemente

relevance ['rɛləvənts] n : pertinencia f, relación f

relevant ['rɛləvənt] adj : pertinente — **relevantly** adv

reliability [ri,laɪə'bɪlət̬i] n, pl **-ties 1** : fiabilidad f, seguridad f (de una cosa) **2** : formalidad f, seriedad f (de una persona)

reliable [ri'laɪəbəl] adj : confiable, fiable, fidedigno, seguro

reliably [ri'laɪəbli] adv : sin fallar ⟨to be reliably informed : saber (algo) de fuentes fidedignas⟩

reliance [ri'laɪənts] n **1** DEPENDENCE : dependencia f **2** CONFIDENCE : confianza f

reliant [ri'laɪənt] adj : dependiente

relic ['rɛlɪk] n **1** : reliquia f **2** VESTIGE : vestigio m

relief [ri'li:f] n **1** : alivio m, desahogo m ⟨relief from pain : alivio del dolor⟩ **2** AID, WELFARE : ayuda f (benéfica), asistencia f social **3** : relieve m (en la escultura) ⟨relief map : mapa en relieve⟩ **4** REPLACEMENT : relevo m

relieve [ri'li:v] vt **-lieved; -lieving 1** ALLEVIATE : aliviar, mitigar ⟨to feel relieved : sentirse aliviado⟩ **2** FREE : liberar, eximir ⟨to relieve someone of responsibility for : eximir a alguien de la responsabilidad de⟩ **3** REPLACE : relevar (a un centinela, etc.) **4** BREAK : romper ⟨to relieve the monotony : romper la monotonía⟩

religion [ri'lɪdʒən] n : religión f

religious [ri'lɪdʒəs] adj : religioso — **religiously** adv

relinquish [ri'lɪŋkwɪʃ, -'lɪn-] vt **1** GIVE UP : renunciar a, abandonar **2** RELEASE : soltar

relish[1] ['rɛlɪʃ] vt : saborear (comida), disfrutar con (una idea, una perspectiva, etc.)

relish[2] n **1** ENJOYMENT : gusto m, deleite m **2** : salsa f (condimento)

relive [,ri:'lɪv] vt **-lived; -living** : revivir

relocate [,ri:'lo:,keɪt, ,ri:lo'keɪt] v **-cated; -cating** vt : reubicar, trasladar — vi : trasladarse

relocation [,ri:lo'keɪʃən] n : reubicación f, traslado m

reluctance [ri'lʌktənts] n : renuencia f, reticencia f, desgana f

reluctant [ri'lʌktənt] adj : renuente, reacio, reticente

reluctantly [ri'lʌktəntli] adv : a regañadientes

rely [ri'laɪ] vi **-lied; -lying 1** DEPEND : depender (de), contar (con) **2** TRUST : confiar (en)

remain [ri'meɪn] vi **1** : quedar ⟨very little remains : queda muy poco⟩ ⟨the remaining 10 minutes : los 10 minutos que quedan⟩ **2** STAY : quedarse, permanecer **3** CONTINUE : continuar, seguir ⟨to remain the same : continuar siendo igual⟩ **4 to remain to** : quedar por ⟨to remain to be done : quedar por hacer⟩ ⟨it remains to be seen : está por ver⟩

remainder [ri'meɪndər] n : resto m, remanente m

remains [ri'meɪnz] npl : restos mpl ⟨mortal remains : restos mortales⟩

remake[1] [ri:'meɪk] vt **-made; -making 1** TRANSFORM : rehacer **2** : hacer una nueva versión de (una película, etc.)

remake² ['ri:ˌmeɪk] n : nueva versión f
remark¹ [ri'mɑrk] vt 1 NOTICE : observar 2 SAY : comentar, observar — vi
to remark on : hacer observaciones sobre
remark² n : comentario m, observación f
remarkable [ri'mɑrkəbəl] adj : extraordinario, notable — **remarkably** [-bli] adv
rematch ['ri:ˌmætʃ] n : revancha f
remedial [ri'mi:diəl] adj : correctivo ⟨remedial classes : clases para alumnos atrasados⟩
remedy¹ ['rɛmədi] vt -died; -dying : remediar
remedy² n, pl -dies : remedio m, medicamento m
remember [ri'mɛmbər] vt 1 RECOLLECT : acordarse de, recordar 2 : no olvidar ⟨remember my words : no olvides mis palabras⟩ ⟨to remember to : acordarse de⟩ 3 : dar saludos, dar recuerdos ⟨remember me to her : dale saludos de mi parte⟩ 4 COMMEMORATE : recordar, conmemorar
remembrance [ri'mɛmbrənts] n 1 RECOLLECTION : recuerdo m ⟨in remembrance of : en conmemoración de⟩ 2 MEMENTO : recuerdo m
remind [ri'maɪnd] vt : recordar ⟨remind me to do it : recuérdame que lo haga⟩ ⟨she reminds me of Clara : me recuerda de Clara⟩
reminder [ri'maɪndər] n : recuerdo m
reminisce [ˌrɛmə'nɪs] vi -nisced; -niscing : rememorar los viejos tiempos
reminiscence [ˌrɛmə'nɪsənts] n : recuerdo m, reminiscencia f
reminiscent [ˌrɛmə'nɪsənt] adj 1 NOSTALGIC : reminiscente, nostálgico 2 SUGGESTIVE : evocador, que recuerda — **reminiscently** adv
remiss [ri'mɪs] adj : negligente, descuidado, remiso
remission [ri'mɪʃən] n : remisión f
remit [ri'mɪt] vt -mitted; -mitting 1 PARDON : perdonar 2 SEND : remitir, enviar (dinero)
remittance [ri'mɪtənts] n : remesa f
remnant ['rɛmnənt] n : restos mpl, vestigio m
remodel [ri'mɑdəl] vt -eled or -elled; -eling or -elling : remodelar, reformar
remonstrate [ri'mɑnˌstreɪt] vi -strated; -strating : protestar ⟨to remonstrate with someone : quejarse a alguien⟩
remorse [ri'mɔrs] n : remordimiento m
remorseful [ri'mɔrsfəl] adj : arrepentido, lleno de remordimiento
remorseless [ri'mɔrsləs] adj 1 PITILESS : despiadado 2 RELENTLESS : implacable
remote [ri'mo:t] adj -moter; -est 1 FAR-OFF : lejano, remoto ⟨remote countries : países remotos⟩ ⟨in the remote past : en el pasado lejano⟩ 2 SECLUDED : recóndito 3 : a distancia, remoto ⟨remote control : control remoto⟩ 4 SLIGHT : remoto 5 ALOOF : distante
remotely [ri'mo:tli] adv 1 SLIGHTLY : remotamente 2 DISTANTLY : en un lugar remoto, muy lejos
remoteness [ri'mo:tnəs] n : lejanía f
removable [ri'mu:vəbəl] adj : removible
removal [ri'mu:vəl] n : separación f, extracción f, supresión f (en algo escrito), eliminación f (de problemas, etc.)
remove [ri'mu:v] vt -moved; -moving 1 : quitar, quitarse ⟨remove the lid : quite la tapa⟩ ⟨to remove one's hat : quitarse el sombrero⟩ 2 EXTRACT : sacar, extraer ⟨to remove the contents of : sacar el contenido de⟩ 3 ELIMINATE : eliminar, disipar
remunerate [ri'mju:nəˌreɪt] vt -ated; -ating : remunerar
remuneration [riˌmju:nə'reɪʃən] n : remuneración f
remunerative [ri'mju:nərətɪv, -ˌreɪ-] adj : remunerativo
renaissance [ˌrɛnə'sɑnts, -'zɑnts, 'rɛnəˌ-] n : renacimiento m ⟨the Renaissance : el Renacimiento⟩
renal ['ri:nəl] adj : renal
rename [ˌri:'neɪm] vt -named; -naming : ponerle un nombre nuevo a
rend ['rɛnd] vt rent ['rɛnt]; rending : desgarrar
render ['rɛndər] vt 1 : derretir ⟨to render lard : derretir la manteca⟩ 2 GIVE : prestar, dar ⟨to render aid : prestar ayuda⟩ 3 MAKE : hacer, volver, dejar ⟨it rendered him helpless : lo dejó incapacitado⟩ 4 TRANSLATE : traducir, verter ⟨to render into English : traducir al inglés⟩
rendezvous ['rɑndɪˌvu:, -deɪ-] ns & pl : encuentro m, cita f
rendition [rɛn'dɪʃən] n : interpretación f
renegade ['rɛnɪˌgeɪd] n : renegado m, -da f
renege [ri'nɪg, -'nɛg] vi -neged; -neging : no cumplir con (una promesa, etc.)
renew [ri'nu:, -'nju:] vt 1 REVIVE : renovar, reavivar ⟨to renew the sentiments of youth : renovar los sentimientos de la juventud⟩ 2 RESUME : reanudar 3 EXTEND : renovar ⟨to renew a subscription : renovar una suscripción⟩
renewable [ri'nu:əbəl, -'nju:-] adj : renovable
renewal [ri'nu:əl, -'nju:-] n : renovación f
renounce [ri'naunts] vt -nounced; -nouncing : renunciar a
renovate ['rɛnəˌveɪt] vt -vated; -vating : restaurar, renovar
renovation [ˌrɛnə'veɪʃən] n : restauración f, renovación f
renown [ri'naun] n : renombre m, fama f, celebridad f
renowned [ri'naund] adj : renombrado, célebre, famoso
rent¹ ['rɛnt] vt : rentar, alquilar

rent[2] *n* **1** : renta *f*, alquiler *m* ⟨for rent : se alquila⟩ **2** RIP : rasgadura *f*
rental[1] [ˈrɛntəl] *adj* RENT : de alquiler
rental[2] *n* : alquiler *m*
renter [ˈrɛntər] *n* : arrendatario *m*, -ria *f*
renunciation [riˌnʌntsiˈeɪʃən] *n* : renuncia *f*
reopen [ˌriːˈoːpən] *vt* : volver a abrir
reorganization [ˌriːˌɔrgənəˈzeɪʃən] *n* : reorganización *f*
reorganize [ˌriːˈɔrgənˌaɪz] *vt* **-nized; -nizing** : reorganizar
repair[1] [riˈpær] *vt* : reparar, arreglar, refaccionar
repair[2] *n* **1** : reparación *f*, arreglo *m* **2** CONDITION : estado *m* ⟨in bad repair : en mal estado⟩
reparation [ˌrɛpəˈreɪʃən] *n* **1** AMENDS : reparación *f* **2 reparations** *npl* COMPENSATION : indemnización *f*
repartee [ˌrɛpərˈtiː, -ˌpɑr-, -ˈteɪ] *n* : intercambio *m* de réplicas ingeniosas
repast [riˈpæst, ˈriːˌpæst] *n* : comida *f*
repatriate [riˈpeɪtriˌeɪt] *vt* **-ated; -ating** : repatriar
repay [riˈpeɪ] *vt* **-paid; -paying** : pagar, devolver, reembolsar
repeal[1] [riˈpiːl] *vt* : abrogar, revocar
repeal[2] *n* : abrogación *f*, revocación *f*
repeat[1] [riˈpiːt] *vt* : repetir
repeat[2] *n* : repetición *f*
repeatedly [riˈpiːtədli] *adv* : repetidamente, repetidas veces
repel [riˈpɛl] *vt* **-pelled; -pelling 1** REPULSE : repeler (un enemigo, etc.) **2** RESIST : resistir **3** REJECT : rechazar, repeler **4** DISGUST : repugnar, darle asco (a alguien)
repellent *or* **repellant** [riˈpɛlənt] *n* : repelente *m*
repent [riˈpɛnt] *vi* : arrepentirse
repentance [riˈpɛntənts] *n* : arrepentimiento *m*
repentant [riˈpɛntənt] *adj* : arrepentido
repercussion [ˌriːpərˈkʌʃən, ˌrɛpər-] *n* : repercusión *f*
repertoire [ˈrɛpərˌtwɑr] *n* : repertorio *m*
repertory [ˈrɛpərˌtori] *n*, *pl* **-ries** : repertorio *m*
repetition [ˌrɛpəˈtɪʃən] *n* : repetición *f*
repetitious [ˌrɛpəˈtɪʃəs] *adj* : repetitivo, reiterativo — **repetitiously** *adv*
repetitive [riˈpɛtətɪv] *adj* : repetitivo, reiterativo
replace [riˈpleɪs] *vt* **-placed; -placing 1** : volver a poner ⟨replace it in the drawer : vuelve a ponerlo en el cajón⟩ **2** SUBSTITUTE : reemplazar, sustituir **3** : reponer ⟨to replace the worn carpet : reponer la alfombra raída⟩
replaceable [riˈpleɪsəbəl] *adj* : reemplazable
replacement [riˈpleɪsmənt] *n* **1** SUBSTITUTION : reemplazo *m*, sustitución *f* **2** SUBSTITUTE : sustituto *m*, -ta *f*; suplente *mf* (persona) **3 replacement part** : repuesto *m*, pieza *f* de recambio
replenish [riˈplɛnɪʃ] *vt* : rellenar, llenar de nuevo

replenishment [riˈplɛnɪʃmənt] *n* : reabastecimiento *m*
replete [riˈpliːt] *adj* : repleto, lleno
replica [ˈrɛplɪkə] *n* : réplica *f*, reproducción *f*
replicate [ˈrɛpləˌkeɪt] *v* **-cated; -cating** *vt* : duplicar, repetir — *vi* : duplicarse
replication [ˌrɛpləˈkeɪʃən] *n* **1** REPRODUCTION : reproducción *f* **2** REPETITION : repetición *f* **3** : replicación *f* (celular)
reply[1] [riˈplaɪ] *vi* **-plied; -plying** : contestar, responder
reply[2] *n*, *pl* **-plies** : respuesta *f*, contestación *f*
report[1] [riˈport] *vt* **1** ANNOUNCE : relatar, anunciar **2** : dar parte de, informar de, reportar ⟨he reported an accident : dio parte de un accidente⟩ ⟨to report a crime : denunciar un delito⟩ **3** : informar acerca de (en un periódico, la televisión, etc.) — *vi* **1** : hacer un informe, informar **2 to report for duty** : presentarse, reportarse
report[2] *n* **1** RUMOR : rumor *m* **2** REPUTATION : reputación *f* ⟨people of evil report : personas de mala fama⟩ **3** ACCOUNT : informe *m*, reportaje *m* (en un periódico, etc.) **4** BANG : estallido *m* (de un arma de fuego)
report card *n* : boletín *m* de calificaciones, boletín *m* de notas
reportedly [riˈportədli] *adv* : según se dice, según se informa
reporter [riˈportər] *n* : periodista *mf*; reportero *m*, -ra *f*
repose[1] [riˈpoːz] *vi* **-posed; -posing** : reposar, descansar
repose[2] *n* **1** : reposo *m*, descanso *m* **2** CALM : calma *f*, tranquilidad *f*
repository [riˈpɑzəˌtori] *n*, *pl* **-ries** : depósito *m*
repossess [ˌriːpəˈzɛs] *vt* : recuperar, recobrar la posesión de
reprehensible [ˌrɛprɪˈhɛntsəbəl] *adj* : reprensible — **reprehensibly** *adv*
represent [ˌrɛprɪˈzɛnt] *vt* **1** SYMBOLIZE : representar ⟨the flag represents our country : la bandera representa a nuestro país⟩ **2** : representar, ser un representante de ⟨an attorney who represents his client : un abogado que representa su cliente⟩ **3** PORTRAY : presentar ⟨he represents himself as a friend : se presenta como amigo⟩
representation [ˌrɛprɪˌzɛnˈteɪʃən, -zən-] *n* : representación *f*
representative[1] [ˌrɛprɪˈzɛntətɪv] *adj* : representativo
representative[2] *n* **1** : representante *mf* **2** : diputado *m*, -da *f* (en la política)
repress [riˈprɛs] *vt* : reprimir
repression [riˈprɛʃən] *n* : represión *f*
repressive [riˈprɛsɪv] *adj* : represivo
reprieve[1] [riˈpriːv] *vt* **-prieved; -prieving** : indultar
reprieve[2] *n* : indulto *m*
reprimand[1] [ˈrɛprəˌmænd] *vt* : reprender

reprimand² *n* : reprimenda *f*
reprint¹ [ri'prɪnt] *vt* : reimprimir
reprint² ['riːˌprɪnt, riˈprɪnt] *n* : reedición *f*
reprisal [riˈpraɪzəl] *n* : represalia *f*
reproach¹ [riˈproːtʃ] *vt* : reprochar
reproach² *n* **1** DISGRACE : deshonra *f* **2** REBUKE : reproche *m*, recriminación *f*
reproachful [riˈproːtʃfəl] *adj* : de reproche
reproduce [ˌriːprəˈduːs, -ˈdjuːs] *v* **-duced; -ducing** *vt* : reproducir — *vi* BREED : reproducirse
reproduction [ˌriːprəˈdʌkʃən] *n* : reproducción *f*
reproductive [ˌriːprəˈdʌktɪv] *adj* : reproductor
reproof [riˈpruːf] *n* : reprobación *f*, reprimenda *f*, reproche *m*
reprove [riˈpruːv] *vt* **-proved; -proving** : reprender, censurar
reptile ['rɛpˌtaɪl] *n* : reptil *m*
republic [riˈpʌblɪk] *n* : república *f*
republican¹ [riˈpʌblɪkən] *adj* : republicano
republican² *n* : republicano *m*, -na *f*
repudiate [riˈpjuːdiˌeɪt] *vt* **-ated; -ating 1** REJECT : rechazar **2** DISOWN : repudiar, renegar de
repudiation [riˌpjuːdiˈeɪʃən] *n* : rechazo *m*, repudio *m*
repugnance [riˈpʌgnənts] *n* : repugnancia *f*
repugnant [riˈpʌgnənt] *adj* : repugnante, asqueroso
repulse¹ [riˈpʌls] *vt* **-pulsed; -pulsing 1** REPEL : repeler **2** REBUFF : desairar, rechazar
repulse² *n* : rechazo *m*
repulsive [riˈpʌlsɪv] *adj* : repulsivo, repugnante, asqueroso — **repulsively** *adv*
reputable ['rɛpjətəbəl] *adj* : acreditado, de buena reputación
reputation [ˌrɛpjəˈteɪʃən] *n* : reputación *f*, fama *f*
repute [riˈpjuːt] *n* : reputación *f*, fama *f*
reputed [riˈpjuːt̬əd] *adj* : reputado, supuesto ⟨she's reputed to be the best : tiene fama de ser la mejor⟩
reputedly [riˈpjuːt̬ədli] *adv* : supuestamente, según se dice
request¹ [riˈkwɛst] *vt* : pedir, solicitar, rogar ⟨to request assistance : solicitar asistencia, pedir ayuda⟩ ⟨I requested him to do it : le pedí que lo hiciera⟩
request² *n* : petición *f*, solicitud *f*, pedido *m*
requiem ['rɛkwiəm, 'reɪ-] *n* : réquiem *m*
require [riˈkwaɪr] *vt* **-quired; -quiring 1** CALL FOR, DEMAND : requerir, exigir ⟨if required : si se requiere⟩ ⟨to require that something be done : exigir que algo se haga⟩ **2** NEED : necesitar, requerir
requirement [riˈkwaɪrmənt] *n* **1** NECESSITY : necesidad *f* **2** DEMAND : requisito *m*, demanda *f*

requisite¹ ['rɛkwəzɪt] *adj* : esencial, necesario
requisite² *n* : requisito *m*, necesidad *f*
requisition¹ [ˌrɛkwəˈzɪʃən] *vt* : requisar
requisition² *n* : requisición *f*, requisa *f*
reread [ˌriːˈriːd] *vt* **-read; -reading** : releer
reroute [ˌriːˈruːt, -ˈraʊt] *vt* **-routed; -routing** : desviar
rerun¹ [riːˈrʌn] *vt* **-ran; -run; -running** : reponer (un programa televisivo)
rerun² ['riːˌrʌn] *n* **1** : reposición *f* (de un programa televisivo) **2** REPEAT : repetición *f*
resale ['riːˌseɪl, ˌriːˈseɪl] *n* : reventa *f* ⟨resale price : precio de venta⟩
rescind [riˈsɪnd] *vt* **1** CANCEL : rescindir, cancelar **2** REPEAL : abrogar, revocar
rescue¹ ['rɛsˌkjuː] *vt* **-cued; -cuing** : rescatar, salvar
rescue² *n* : rescate *m*
rescuer ['rɛskjuər] *n* : salvador *m*, -dora *f*
research¹ [riˈsərtʃ, 'riːˌsərtʃ] *v* : investigar
research² *n* : investigación *f*
researcher [riˈsərtʃər, 'riːˌ-] *n* : investigador *m*, -dora *f*
resemblance [riˈzɛmblənts] *n* : semejanza *f*, parecido *m*
resemble [riˈzɛmbəl] *vt* **-sembled; -sembling** : parecerse a, asemejarse a
resent [riˈzɛnt] *vt* : resentirse de, ofenderse por
resentful [riˈzɛntfəl] *adj* : resentido, rencoroso — **resentfully** *adv*
resentment [riˈzɛntmənt] *n* : resentimiento *m*
reservation [ˌrɛzərˈveɪʃən] *n* **1** : reservación *f*, reserva *f* ⟨to make a reservation : hacer una reservación⟩ **2** DOUBT, MISGIVING : reserva *f*, duda *f* ⟨without reservations : sin reservas⟩ **3** : reserva *f* (de indios americanos)
reserve¹ [riˈzərv] *vt* **-served; -serving** : reservar
reserve² *n* **1** STOCK : reserva *f* ⟨to keep in reserve : guardar en reserva⟩ **2** RESTRAINT : reserva *f*, moderación *f* **3** **reserves** *npl* : reservas *fpl* (militares)
reserved [riˈzərvd] *adj* : reservado
reservoir ['rɛzərˌvwɑr, -ˌvwɔr, -ˌvɔr] *n* : embalse *m*
reset [ˌriːˈsɛt] *vt* **-set; -setting** : reajustar, poner en hora (un reloj), reiniciar (una computadora)
reside [riˈzaɪd] *vi* **-sided; -siding 1** DWELL : residir **2** LIE : radicar, residir ⟨the power resides in the presidency : el poder radica en la presidencia⟩
residence ['rɛzədənts] *n* : residencia *f*
resident¹ ['rɛzədənt] *adj* : residente
resident² *n* : residente *mf*
residential [ˌrɛzəˈdɛntʃəl] *adj* : residencial
residual [riˈzɪdʒuəl] *adj* : residual
residue ['rɛzəˌduː, -ˌdjuː] *n* : residuo *m*, resto *m*

resign [ri'zaɪn] *vt* **1** QUIT : dimitir, renunciar **2 to resign oneself** : aguantarse, resignarse
resignation [ˌrɛzɪg'neɪʃən] *n* : resignación *f*
resignedly [ri'zaɪnədli] *adv* : con resignación
resilience [ri'zɪljənts] *n* **1** : capacidad *f* de recuperación, adaptabilidad *f* **2** ELASTICITY : elasticidad *f*
resiliency [ri'zɪljəntsi] → **resilience**
resilient [ri'zɪljənt] *adj* **1** STRONG : resistente, fuerte **2** ELASTIC : elástico
resin ['rɛzən] *n* : resina *f*
resist [ri'zɪst] *vt* **1** WITHSTAND : resistir ⟨to resist heat : resistir el calor⟩ **2** OPPOSE : oponerse a
resistance [ri'zɪstənts] *n* : resistencia *f*
resistant [ri'zɪstənt] *adj* : resistente
resolute ['rɛzəˌlu:t] *adj* : firme, resuelto, decidido
resolutely ['rɛzəˌlu:tli, ˌrzə'-] *adv* : resueltamente, firmemente
resolution [ˌrɛzə'lu:ʃən] *n* **1** SOLUTION : solución *f* **2** RESOLVE : resolución *f*, determinación *f* **3** DECISION : propósito *m*, decisión *f* ⟨New Year's resolutions : propósitos para el Año Nuevo⟩ **4** MOTION, PROPOSAL : moción *f*, resolución *f* (legislativa)
resolve¹ [ri'zɑlv] *vt* **-solved; -solving 1** SOLVE : resolver, solucionar **2** DECIDE : resolver ⟨she resolved to get more sleep : resolvió dormir más⟩
resolve² *n* : resolución *f*, determinación *f*
resonance ['rɛzənənts] *n* : resonancia *f*
resonant ['rɛzənənt] *adj* : resonante, retumbante
resort¹ [ri'zɔrt] *vi* **to resort to** : recurrir ⟨to resort to force : recurrir a la fuerza⟩
resort² *n* **1** RECOURSE : recurso *m* ⟨as a last resort : como último recurso⟩ **2** HANGOUT : lugar *m* popular, lugar *m* muy frecuentado **3** : lugar *m* de vacaciones ⟨tourist resort : centro turístico⟩
resound [ri'zaʊnd] *vi* : retumbar, resonar
resounding [ri'zaʊndɪŋ] *adj* **1** RESONANT : retumbante, resonante **2** ABSOLUTE, CATEGORICAL : rotundo, tremendo ⟨a resounding success : un éxito rotundo⟩
resource ['ri:ˌsɔrs, ri'sɔrs] *n* **1** RESOURCEFULNESS : ingenio *m*, recursos *mpl* **2 resources** *npl* : recursos *mpl* ⟨natural resources : recursos naturales⟩ **3 resources** *npl* MEANS : recursos *mpl*, medios *mpl*, fondos *mpl*
resourceful [ri'sɔrsfəl, -'zɔrs-] *adj* : ingenioso
resourcefulness [ri'sɔrsfəlnəs, -'zɔrs-] *n* : ingenio *m*, recursos *mpl*, inventiva *f*
respect¹ [ri'spɛkt] *vt* : respetar, estimar
respect² *n* **1** REFERENCE : relación *f*, respeto *m* ⟨with respect to : en lo que respecta a⟩ **2** ESTEEM : respeto *m*, estima *f* **3** DETAIL, PARTICULAR : detalle *m*, sentido *m*, respeto *m* ⟨in some respects : en algunos sentidos⟩ **4 respects** *npl* : respetos *mpl* ⟨to pay one's respects : presentar uno susrespetos⟩
respectability [riˌspɛktə'bɪləti] *n* : respetabilidad *f*
respectable [ri'spɛktəbəl] *adj* **1** PROPER : respetable, decente **2** CONSIDERABLE : considerable, respetable ⟨a respectable amount : una cantidad respetable⟩ — **respectably** [-bli] *adv*
respectful [ri'spɛktfəl] *adj* : respetuoso — **respectfully** *adv*
respectfulness [ri'spɛktfəlnəs] *n* : respetuosidad *f*
respective [ri'spɛktɪv] *adj* : respectivo ⟨their respective homes : sus casas respectivas⟩ — **respectively** *adv*
respiration [ˌrɛspə'reɪʃən] *n* : respiración *f*
respirator ['rɛspəˌreɪtər] *n* : respirador *m*
respiratory ['rɛspərəˌtori, ri'spaɪrə-] *adj* : respiratorio
respite ['rɛspɪt, ri'spaɪt] *n* : respiro *m*, tregua *f*
resplendent [ri'splɛndənt] *adj* : resplandeciente — **resplendently** *adv*
respond [ri'spɑnd] *vi* **1** ANSWER : contestar, responder **2** REACT : responder, reaccionar ⟨to respond to treatment : responder al tratamiento⟩
response [ri'spɑnts] *n* : respuesta *f*
responsibility [riˌspɑntsə'bɪləti] *n, pl* **-ties** : responsabilidad *f*
responsible [ri'spɑntsəbəl] *adj* : responsable — **responsibly** [-bli] *adv*
responsive [ri'spɑntsɪv] *adj* **1** ANSWERING : que responde **2** SENSITIVE : sensible, receptivo
responsiveness [ri'spɑntsɪvnəs] *n* : receptividad *f*, sensibilidad *f*
rest¹ ['rɛst] *vi* **1** REPOSE : reposar, descansar **2** RELAX : quedarse tranquilo **3** STOP : pararse, detenerse **4** DEPEND : basarse (en), descansar (sobre), depender (de) ⟨the decision rests with her : la decisión pesa sobre ella⟩ **5 to rest on** : apoyarse en, descansar sobre ⟨to rest on one's arm : apoyarse en el brazo⟩ — *vt* **1** RELAX : descansar **2** SUPPORT : apoyar **3 to rest one's eyes on** : fijar la mirada en
rest² *n* **1** RELAXATION, REPOSE : reposo *m*, descanso *m* **2** SUPPORT : soporte *m*, apoyo *m* **3** : silencio *m* (en música) **4** REMAINDER : resto *m* **5 to come to rest** : pararse
restart [ri'stɑrt] *vt* **1** : volver a empezar **2** RESUME : reanudar **3** : volver a arrancar (un motor), reiniciar (una computadora) — *vi* **1** : reanudarse **2** : volver a arrancar
restatement [ˌri:'steɪtmənt] *n* : repetición *f*
restaurant ['rɛstəˌrɑnt, -rənt] *n* : restaurante *m*

restful ['rɛstfəl] *adj* **1** RELAXING : relajante **2** PEACEFUL : tranquilo, sosegado

restitution [ˌrɛstə'tu:ʃən, -'tju:-] *n* : restitución *f*

restive ['rɛstɪv] *adj* : inquieto, nervioso

restless ['rɛstləs] *adj* **1** FIDGETY : inquieto, agitado **2** IMPATIENT : impaciente **3** SLEEPLESS : desvelado ⟨a restless night : una noche en blanco⟩

restlessly ['rɛstləsli] *adv* : nerviosamente

restlessness ['rɛstləsnəs] *n* : inquietud *f*, agitación *f*

restoration [ˌrɛstə'reɪʃən] *n* : restauración *f*, restablecimiento *m*

restore [ri'stor] *vt* **-stored; -storing 1** RETURN : volver **2** REESTABLISH : restablecer **3** REPAIR : restaurar

restrain [ri'streɪn] *vt* **1** : refrenar, contener **2 to restrain oneself** : contenerse

restrained [ri'streɪnd] *adj* : comedido, templado, contenido

restraint [ri'streɪnt] *n* **1** RESTRICTION : restricción *f*, limitación *f*, control *m* **2** CONFINEMENT : encierro *m* **3** RESERVE : reserva *f*, control *m* de sí mismo

restrict [ri'strɪkt] *vt* : restringir, limitar, constreñir

restricted [ri'strɪktəd] *adj* **1** LIMITED : limitado, restringido **2** CLASSIFIED : secreto, confidencial

restriction [ri'strɪkʃən] *n* : restricción *f*

restrictive [ri'strɪktɪv] *adj* : restrictivo — **restrictively** *adv*

rest room *n* : servicios *mpl*, baño *m*

restructure [ri'strʌktʃər] *vt* **-tured; -turing** : reestructurar

result¹ [ri'zʌlt] *vi* : resultar ⟨to result in : resultar en, tener por resultado⟩

result² *n* : resultado *m*, consecuencia *f* ⟨as a result of : como consecuencia de⟩

resultant [ri'zʌltənt] *adj* : resultante

resume [ri'zu:m] *v* **-sumed; -suming** *vt* : reanudar — *vi* : reanudarse

résumé *or* **resume** *or* **resumé** ['rɛzə-ˌmeɪ, ˌrɛzə'-] *n* **1** SUMMARY : resumen *m* **2** CURRICULUM VITAE : currículum *m*, currículo *m*

resumption [ri'zʌmpʃən] *n* : reanudación *f*

resurface [ˌri:'sərfəs] *v* **-faced; -facing** *vt* : pavimentar (una carretera) de nuevo — *vi* : volver a salir en la superficie

resurgence [ri'sərdʒənts] *n* : resurgimiento *m*

resurrect [ˌrɛzə'rɛkt] *vt* : resucitar, desempolvar

resurrection [ˌrɛzə'rɛkʃən] *n* : resurrección *f*

resuscitate [ri'sʌsəˌteɪt] *vt* **-tated; -tating** : resucitar, revivir

resuscitation [ri,sʌsə'teɪʃən] *n* : reanimación *f*, resucitación *f*

retail¹ ['ri:ˌteɪl] *vt* : vender al por menor, vender al detalle

retail² *adv* : al por menor, al detalle

retail³ *adj* : detallista, minorista

retail⁴ *n* : venta *f* al detalle, venta *f* al por menor

retailer ['ri:ˌteɪlər] *n* : detallista *mf*, minorista *mf*

retain [ri'teɪn] *vt* : retener, conservar, guardar

retainer [ri'teɪnər] *n* **1** SERVANT : criado *m*, -da *f* **2** ADVANCE : anticipo *m*

retaliate [ri'tæliˌeɪt] *vi* **-ated; -ating** : responder, contraatacar, tomar represalias

retaliation [ri,tæli'eɪʃən] *n* : represalia *f*, retaliación *f*

retard [ri'tard] *vt* : retardar, retrasar

retardation [ˌri:ˌtar'deɪʃən] *n* **1** : retardación *f* **2** *or* **mental retardation** : retraso *m* mental

retarded [ri'tardəd] *adj* : retrasado

retch ['rɛtʃ] *vi* : hacer arcadas

retention [ri'tɛntʃən] *n* : retención *f*

retentive [ri'tɛntɪv] *adj* : retentivo

rethink [ri:'θɪŋk] *vt* **-thought; -thinking** : reconsiderar, repensar

reticence ['rɛtəsənts] *n* : reticencia *f*

reticent ['rɛtəsənt] *adj* : reticente

retina ['rɛtənə] *n*, *pl* **-nas** *or* **-nae** [-əni, -ənˌaɪ] : retina *f*

retinue ['rɛtənˌu:, -ˌju:] *n* : séquito *m*, comitiva *f*, cortejo *m*

retire [ri'taɪr] *vi* **-tired; -tiring 1** RETREAT, WITHDRAW : retirarse, retraerse **2** : retirarse, jubilarse (de su trabajo) **3** : acostarse, irse a dormir

retiree [ri,taɪ'ri:] *n* : jubilado *m*, -da *f*

retirement [ri'taɪrmənt] *n* : jubilación *f*

retiring [ri'taɪrɪŋ] *adj* SHY : retraído

retort¹ [ri'tort] *vt* : replicar

retort² *n* : réplica *f*

retrace [ˌri:'treɪs] *vt* **-traced; -tracing** : volver sobre, desandar ⟨to retrace one's steps : volver uno sobre sus pasos⟩

retract [ri'trækt] *vt* **1** TAKE BACK, WITHDRAW : retirar, retractarse de **2** : retraer (las garras) — *vi* : retractarse

retractable [ri'træktəbəl] *adj* : retractable

retrain [ˌri:'treɪn] *vt* : reciclar, reconvertir

retreat¹ [ri'tri:t] *vi* : retirarse

retreat² *n* **1** WITHDRAWAL : retirada *f*, repliegue *m*, retiro *m* ⟨to beat a retreat : batirse en retirada⟩ **2** REFUGE : retiro *m*, refugio *m*

retrench [ri'trɛntʃ] *vt* : reducir (gastos) — *vi* : economizar

retribution [ˌrɛtrə'bju:ʃən] *n* PUNISHMENT : castigo *m*, pena *f* merecida

retrieval [ri'tri:vəl] *n* : recuperación *f* ⟨beyond retrieval : irrecuperable⟩ ⟨data retrieval : recuperación de datos⟩

retrieve [ri'tri:v] *vt* **-trieved; -trieving 1** : cobrar ⟨to retrieve game : cobrar la caza⟩ **2** RECOVER : recuperar

retriever [ri'tri:vər] *n* : perro *m* cobrador

retroactive [ˌrɛtro'æktɪv] *adj* : retroactivo — **retroactively** *adv*
retrograde ['rɛtrəˌgreɪd] *adj* : retrógrado
retrospect ['rɛtrəˌspɛkt] *n* **in retrospect** : mirando hacia atrás, retrospectivamente
retrospective [ˌrɛtrə'spɛktɪv] *adj* : retrospectivo
return¹ [ri'tərn] *vi* **1** : volver, regresar ⟨to return home : regresar a casa⟩ **2** REAPPEAR : reaparecer, resurgir **3** ANSWER : responder — *vt* **1** REPLACE, RESTORE : devolver, volver (a poner), restituir ⟨to return something to its place : volver a poner algo en su lugar⟩ **2** YIELD : producir, redituar, rendir **3** REPAY : pagar, devolver ⟨to return a compliment : devolver un cumplido⟩
return² *adj* : de vuelta
return³ *n* **1** RETURNING : regreso *m*, vuelta *f*, retorno *m* **2** *or* **tax return** : declaración *f* de impuestos **3** YIELD : rédito *m*, rendimiento *m*, ganancia *f* **4 returns** *npl* DATA, RESULTS : resultados *mpl*, datos *mpl*
reunion [ri'ju:njən] *n* : reunión *f*, reencuentro *m*
reunite [ˌri:ju'naɪt] *v* **-nited; -niting** *vt* : (volver a) reunir — *vi* : (volver a) reunirse
reusable [ri'ju:zəbəl] *adj* : reutilizable
reuse [ri'ju:z] *vt* **-used; -using** : reutilizar, usar de nuevo
revamp [ˌri'væmp] *vt* : renovar
reveal [ri'vi:l] *vt* **1** DIVULGE : revelar, divulgar ⟨to reveal a secret : revelar un secreto⟩ **2** SHOW : manifestar, mostrar, dejar ver
revealing [ri'vi:lɪŋ] *adj* : revelador
reveille ['rɛvəli] *n* : toque *m* de diana
revel¹ ['rɛvəl] *vi* **-eled** *or* **-elled; -eling** *or* **-elling** **1** CAROUSE : ir de juerga **2 to revel in** : deleitarse en
revel² *n* : juerga *f*, parranda *f fam*
revelation [ˌrɛvə'leɪʃən] *n* : revelación *f*
reveler *or* **reveller** ['rɛvələr] *n* : juerguista *mf*
revelry ['rɛvəlri] *n, pl* **-ries** : juerga *f*, parranda *f fam*, jarana *f fam*
revenge¹ [ri'vɛnʤ] *vt* **-venged; -venging** : vengar ⟨to revenge oneself on : vengarse de⟩
revenge² *n* : venganza *f*
revenue ['rɛvəˌnu:, -ˌnju:] *n* : ingresos *mpl*, rentas *fpl*
reverberate [ri'vərbəˌreɪt] *vi* **-ated; -ating** : reverberar
reverberation [riˌvərbə'reɪʃən] *n* : reverberación *f*
revere [ri'vɪr] *vt* **-vered; -vering** : reverenciar, venerar
reverence ['rɛvərənts] *n* : reverencia *f*, veneración *f*
reverend ['rɛvərənd] *adj* : reverendo ⟨the Reverend John Chapin : el reverendo John Chapin⟩

reverent ['rɛvərənt] *adj* : reverente — **reverently** *adv*
reverie ['rɛvəri] *n, pl* **-eries** : ensueño *m*
reversal [ri'vərsəl] *n* **1** INVERSION : inversión *f* (del orden normal) **2** CHANGE : cambio *m* total **3** SETBACK : revés *m*, contratiempo *m*
reverse¹ [ri'vərs] *v* **-versed; -versing** *vt* **1** INVERT : invertir **2** CHANGE : cambiar totalmente **3** ANNUL : anular, revocar — *vi* : dar marcha atrás
reverse² *adj* **1** : inverso ⟨in reverse order : en orden inverso⟩ ⟨the reverse side : el reverso⟩ **2** OPPOSITE : contrario, opuesto
reverse³ *n* **1** OPPOSITE : lo contrario, lo opuesto **2** SETBACK : revés *m*, contratiempo *m* **3** BACK : reverso *m*, dorso *m*, revés *m* **4** *or* **reverse gear** : marcha *f* atrás, reversa *f Col, Mex*
reversible [ri'vərsəbəl] *adj* : reversible
reversion [ri'vərʒən] *n* : reversión *f*, vuelta *f*
revert [ri'vərt] *vi* : revertir
review¹ [ri'vju:] *vt* **1** REEXAMINE : volver a examinar, repasar (una lección) **2** CRITICIZE : reseñar, hacer una crítica de **3** EXAMINE : examinar, analizar ⟨to review one's life : examinar su vida⟩ **4 to review the troops** : pasar revista a las tropas
review² *n* **1** INSPECTION : revista *f* (de tropas) **2** ANALYSIS, OVERVIEW : resumen *m*, análisis *m* ⟨a review of current affairs : un análisis de las actualidades⟩ **3** CRITICISM : reseña *f*, crítica *f* (de un libro, etc.) **4** : repaso *m* (para un examen) **5** REVUE : revista *f* (musical)
reviewer [ri'vju:ər] *n* : crítico *m*, -ca *f*
revile [ri'vaɪl] *vt* **-viled; -viling** : injuriar, denostar
revise [ri'vaɪz] *vt* **-vised; -vising** : revisar, corregir, refundir ⟨to revise a dictionary : corregir un diccionario⟩
revision [ri'vɪʒən] *n* : revisión *f*
revival [ri'vaɪvəl] *n* **1** : renacimiento *m* (de ideas, etc.), restablecimiento *m* (de costumbres, etc.), reactivación *f* (de la economía) **2** : reanimación *f*, resucitación *f* (en medicina) **3** *or* **revival meeting** : asamblea *f* evangelista
revive [ri'vaɪv] *v* **-vived; -viving** *vt* **1** REAWAKEN : reavivar, reanimar, reactivar (la economía), resucitar (a un paciente) **2** REESTABLISH : restablecer — *vi* **1** : renacer, reanimarse, reactivarse **2** COME TO : recobrar el sentido, volver en sí
revoke [ri'vo:k] *vt* **-voked; -voking** : revocar
revolt¹ [ri'vo:lt] *vi* **1** REBEL : rebelarse, sublevarse **2 to revolt at** : sentir repugnancia por — *vt* DISGUST : darle asco (a alguien), repugnar
revolt² *n* REBELLION : rebelión *f*, revuelta *f*, sublevación *f*
revolting [ri'vo:ltɪŋ] *adj* : asqueroso, repugnante

revolution [ˌrɛvəˈluːʃən] *n* : revolución *f*
revolutionary[1] [ˌrɛvəˈluːʃənɛˌri] *adj* : revolucionario
revolutionary[2] *n, pl* **-aries** : revolucionario *m*, -ria *f*
revolutionize [ˌrɛvəˈluːʃənˌaiz] *vt* **-ized; -izing** : cambiar radicalmente, revolucionar
revolve [riˈvɑlv] *v* **-volved; -volving** *vt* ROTATE : hacer girar — *vi* **1** ROTATE : girar ⟨to revolve around : girar alrededor de⟩ **2 to revolve in one's mind** : darle vueltas en la cabeza a alguien
revolver [riˈvɑlvər] *n* : revólver *m*
revue [riˈvjuː] *n* : revista *f* (musical)
revulsion [riˈvʌlʃən] *n* : repugnancia *f*
reward[1] [riˈwɔrd] *vt* : recompensar, premiar
reward[2] *n* : recompensa *f*
rewrite [ˌriːˈrait] *vt* **-wrote; -written; -writing** : escribir de nuevo, volver a escribir
rhapsody [ˈræpsədi] *n, pl* **-dies 1** : elogio *m* excesivo ⟨to go into rhapsodies over : extasiarse por⟩ **2** : rapsodia *f* (en música)
rhetoric [ˈrɛtərik] *n* : retórica *f*
rhetorical [riˈtɔrikəl] *adj* : retórico
rheumatic [rʊˈmætik] *adj* : reumático
rheumatism [ˈruːməˌtizəm, ˈrʊ-] *n* : reumatismo *m*
rhinestone [ˈrainˌstoːn] *n* : diamante *m* de imitación
rhino [ˈraiˌnoː] *n, pl* **rhino** *or* **rhinos** → **rhinoceros**
rhinoceros [raiˈnɑsərəs] *n, pl* **-eroses** *or* **-eros** *or* **-eri** [-ˌrai] : rinoceronte *m*
rhododendron [ˌroːdəˈdɛndrən] *n* : rododendro *m*
rhombus [ˈrɑmbəs] *n, pl* **-buses** *or* **-bi** [-ˌbai, -bi] : rombo *m*
rhubarb [ˈruːˌbɑrb] *n* : ruibarbo *m*
rhyme[1] [ˈraim] *vi* **rhymed; rhyming** : rimar
rhyme[2] *n* **1** : rima *f* **2** VERSE : verso *m* (en rima)
rhythm [ˈriðəm] *n* : ritmo *m*
rhythmic [ˈriðmik] *or* **rhythmical** [-mikəl] *adj* : rítmico — **rhythmically** [-mikli] *adv*
rib[1] [ˈrib] *vt* **ribbed; ribbing 1** : hacer en canalé ⟨a ribbed sweater : un suéter en canalé⟩ **2** TEASE : tomarle el pelo (a alguien)
rib[2] *n* **1** : costilla *f* (de una persona o un animal) **2** : nervio *m* (de una bóveda o una hoja), varilla *f* (de un paraguas), canalé *m* (de una prenda tejida)
ribald [ˈribəld] *adj* : escabroso, procaz
ribbon [ˈribən] *n* **1** : cinta *f* **2 to tear to ribbons** : hacer jirones
rice [ˈrais] *n* : arroz *m*
rich [ˈritʃ] *adj* **1** WEALTHY : rico **2** SUMPTUOUS : suntuoso, lujoso **3** : pesado ⟨rich foods : comida pesada⟩ **4** ABUNDANT : abundante **5** : vivo, intenso ⟨rich colors : colores vivos⟩ **6** FERTILE : fértil, rico

riches [ˈritʃəz] *npl* : riquezas *fpl*
richly [ˈritʃli] *adv* **1** SUMPTUOUSLY : suntuosamente, ricamente **2** ABUNDANTLY : abundantemente **3 richly deserved** : bien merecido
richness [ˈritʃnəs] *n* : riqueza *f*
rickets [ˈrikəts] *n* : raquitismo *m*
rickety [ˈrikəti] *adj* : desvencijado, destartalado
ricksha *or* **rickshaw** [ˈrikˌʃɔ] *n* : cochecillo *m* tirado por un hombre
ricochet[1] [ˈrikəˌʃei] *vi* **-cheted** [-ˌʃeid] *or* **-chetted** [-ˌʃɛtəd]; **-cheting** [-ˌʃeiŋ] *or* **-chetting** [-ˌʃɛtiŋ] : rebotar
ricochet[2] *n* : rebote *m*
rid [ˈrid] *vt* **rid; ridding 1** FREE : librar ⟨to rid the city of thieves : librar la ciudad de ladrones⟩ **2 to rid oneself of** : desembarazarse de
riddance [ˈridənts] *n* : libramiento *m* ⟨good riddance! : ¡adiós y buen viaje!, ¡vete con viento fresco!⟩
riddle[1] [ˈridəl] *vt* **-dled; -dling** : acribillar ⟨riddled with bullets : acribillado a balazos⟩ ⟨riddled with errors : lleno de errores⟩
riddle[2] *n* : acertijo *m*, adivinanza *f*
ride[1] [ˈraid] *v* **rode** [ˈroːd]; **ridden** [ˈridən]; **riding** *vt* **1** : montar, ir, andar ⟨to ride a horse : montar a caballo⟩ ⟨to ride a bicycle : montar en bicicleta, andar en bicicleta⟩ ⟨to ride the bus : ir en autobús⟩ **2** TRAVERSE : recorrer ⟨he rode 5 miles : recorrió 5 millas⟩ **3** TEASE : burlarse de, ridiculizar **4** CARRY : llevar **5** WEATHER : capear ⟨they rode out the storm : capearon el temporal⟩ **6 to ride the waves** : surcar los mares — *vi* **1** : montar a caballo, cabalgar **2** TRAVEL : ir, viajar (en coche, en bicicleta, etc.) **3** RUN : andar, marchar ⟨the car rides well : el coche anda bien⟩ **4 to ride at anchor** : estar fondeado **5 to let things ride** : dejar pasar las cosas
ride[2] *n* **1** : paseo *m*, vuelta *f* (en coche, en bicicleta, a caballo) ⟨to go for a ride : dar una vuelta⟩ ⟨to give someone a ride : llevar en coche a alguien⟩ **2** : aparato *m* (en un parque de diversiones)
rider [ˈraidər] *n* **1** : jinete *mf* ⟨the rider fell off his horse : el jinete se cayó de su caballo⟩ **2** CYCLIST : ciclista *mf* **3** MOTORCYCLIST : motociclista *mf* **4** CLAUSE : cláusula *f* añadida
ridge [ˈridʒ] *n* **1** CHAIN : cadena *f* (de montañas o cerros) **2** : caballete *m* (de un techo), cresta *f* (de una ola o una montaña), cordoncillo *m* (de telas)
ridicule[1] [ˈridəˌkjuːl] *vt* **-culed; -culing** : burlarse de, mofarse de, ridiculizar
ridicule[2] *n* : burlas *fpl*
ridiculous [rəˈdikjələs] *adj* : ridículo, absurdo
ridiculously [rəˈdikjələsli] *adv* : de forma ridícula
rife [ˈraif] *adj* : abundante, común ⟨to be rife with : estar plagado de⟩

riffraff ['rɪf,ræf] *n* : chusma *f*, gentuza *f*
rifle¹ ['raɪfəl] *v* **-fled; -fling** *vt* RANSACK : desvalijar, saquear — *vi* **to rifle through** : revolver
rifle² *n* : rifle *m*, fusil *m*
rift ['rɪft] *n* **1** FISSURE : grieta *f*, fisura *f* **2** BREAK : ruptura *f* (entre personas), división *f* (dentro de un grupo)
rig¹ ['rɪg] *vt* **rigged; rigging 1** : aparejar (un barco) **2** EQUIP : equipar **3** FIX : amañar (una elección, etc.) **4 to rig up** CONSTRUCT : construir, erigir **5 to rig oneself out as** : vestirse de
rig² *n* **1** : aparejo *m* (de un barco) **2 or oil rig** : torre *f* de perforación, plataforma *f* petrolífera
rigging ['rɪgɪŋ, -gən] *n* : jarcia *f*, aparejo *m*
right¹ ['raɪt] *vt* **1** FIX, RESTORE : reparar ⟨to right the economy : reparar la economía⟩ **2** STRAIGHTEN : enderezar
right² *adv* **1** : bien ⟨to live right : vivir bien⟩ **2** PRECISELY : precisamente, justo ⟨right in the middle : justo en medio⟩ **3** DIRECTLY, STRAIGHT : derecho, directamente ⟨he went right home : fue derecho a casa⟩ **4** IMMEDIATELY : inmediatamente ⟨right after lunch : inmediatamente después del almuerzo⟩ **5** COMPLETELY : completamente ⟨he felt right at home : se sintió completamente cómodo⟩ **6** : a la derecha ⟨to look left and right : mirar a la izquierda y a la derecha⟩
right³ *adj* **1** UPRIGHT : bueno, honrado ⟨right conduct : conducta honrada⟩ **2** CORRECT : correcto ⟨the right answer : la respuesta correcta⟩ **3** APPROPRIATE : apropiado, adecuado, debido ⟨the right man for the job : el hombre perfecto para el trabajo⟩ **4** STRAIGHT : recto ⟨a right line : una línea recta⟩ **5** : derecho ⟨the right hand : la mano derecha⟩ **6** SOUND : bien ⟨he's not in his right mind : no está bien de la cabeza⟩
right⁴ *n* **1** GOOD : bien *m* ⟨to do right : hacer el bien⟩ **2** : derecha *f* ⟨on the right : a la derecha⟩ **3 or right hand** : mano *f* derecha **4** ENTITLEMENT : derecho *m* ⟨the right to vote : el derecho a votar⟩ ⟨women's rights : los derechos de la mujer⟩ **5 the Right** : la derecha (en la política)
right angle *n* : ángulo *m* recto
right–angled ['raɪt'æŋgəld] *or* **right–angle** [-gəl] *adj* **1** : en ángulo recto **2 right–angled triangle** : triángulo *m* rectángulo
righteous ['raɪtʃəs] *adj* : recto, honrado — **righteously** *adv*
righteousness ['raɪtʃəsnəs] *n* : rectitud *f*, honradez *f*
rightful ['raɪtfəl] *adj* **1** JUST : justo **2** LAWFUL : legítimo — **rightfully** *adv*
right–hand ['raɪt'hænd] *adj* **1** : situado a la derecha **2** RIGHT-HANDED : para

la mano derecha, con la mano derecha **3 right–hand man** : brazo *m* derecho
right–handed ['raɪt'hændəd] *adj* **1** : diestro ⟨a right-handed pitcher : un lanzador diestro⟩ **2** : para la mano derecha, con la mano derecha **3** CLOCKWISE : en la dirección de las manecillas del reloj
rightly ['raɪtli] *adv* **1** JUSTLY : justamente, con razón **2** PROPERLY : debidamente, apropiadamente **3** CORRECTLY : correctamente
right–of–way ['raɪtə'weɪ, -əv-] *n, pl* **rights–of–way 1** : preferencia (del tráfico) **2** ACCESS : derecho *m* de paso
rightward ['raɪtwərd] *adj* : a la derecha, hacia la derecha
right–wing ['raɪt'wɪŋ] *adj* : derechista
right wing *n* **the right wing** : la derecha
right–winger ['raɪt'wɪŋər] *n* : derechista *mf*
rigid ['rɪdʒɪd] *adj* : rígido — **rigidly** *adv*
rigidity [rɪ'dʒɪdəti] *n, pl* **-ties** : rigidez *f*
rigmarole ['rɪgmə,roːl, 'rɪgə-] *n* **1** NONSENSE : galimatías *m*, disparates *mpl* **2** PROCEDURES : trámites *mpl*
rigor ['rɪgər] *n* : rigor *m*
rigor mortis [,rɪgər'mortəs] *n* : rigidez *f* cadavérica
rigorous ['rɪgərəs] *adj* : riguroso — **rigorously** *adv*
rile ['raɪl] *vt* **riled; riling** : irritar
rill ['rɪl] *n* : riachuelo *m*
rim ['rɪm] *n* **1** EDGE : borde *m* **2** : llanta *f*, rin *m* Col, Mex (de una rueda) **3** FRAME : montura *f* (de anteojos)
rime ['raɪm] *n* : escarcha *f*
rind ['raɪnd] *n* : corteza *f*
ring¹ ['rɪŋ] *v* **rang** ['ræŋ]; **rung** ['rʌŋ]; **ringing** *vi* **1** : sonar ⟨the doorbell rang : el timbre sonó⟩ ⟨to ring for : llamar⟩ **2** RESOUND : resonar **3** SEEM : parecer ⟨to ring true : parecer cierto⟩ — *vt* **1** : tocar, hacer sonar (un timbre, una alarma, etc.) **2** SURROUND : cercar, rodear
ring² *n* **1** : anillo *m*, sortija *f* ⟨wedding ring : anillo de matrimonio⟩ **2** BAND : aro *m*, anillo *m* ⟨piston ring : aro de émbolo⟩ **3** CIRCLE : círculo *m* **4** ARENA : arena *f*, ruedo *m* ⟨a boxing ring : un cuadrilátero, un ring⟩ **5** GANG : banda *f* (de ladrones, etc.) **6** SOUND : timbre *m*, sonido *m* **7** CALL : llamada *f* (por teléfono)
ringer ['rɪŋər] *n* **to be a dead ringer for** : ser un vivo retrato de
ringleader ['rɪŋ,liːdər] *n* : cabecilla *mf*
ringlet ['rɪŋlət] *n* : sortija *f*, rizo *m*
ringworm ['rɪŋ,wərm] *n* : tiña *f*
rink ['rɪŋk] *n* : pista *f* ⟨skating rink : pista de patinaje⟩
rinse¹ ['rɪnts] *vt* **rinsed; rinsing** : enjuagar ⟨to rinse out one's mouth : enjuagarse la boca⟩
rinse² *n* : enjuague *m*
riot¹ ['raɪət] *vi* : amotinarse
riot² *n* : motín *m*, tumulto *m*, alboroto *m*

rioter ['raɪəṭər] *n* : alborotador *m*, -dora *f*

riotous ['raɪəṭəs] *adj* **1** UNRULY, WILD : desenfrenado, alborotado **2** ABUNDANT : abundante

rip¹ ['rɪp] *v* **ripped; ripping** *vt* : rasgar, arrancar, desgarrar — *vi* : rasgarse, desgarrarse

rip² *n* : rasgón *m*, desgarrón *m*

ripe ['raɪp] *adj* **riper; ripest 1** MATURE : maduro ⟨ripe fruit : fruta madura⟩ **2** READY : listo, preparado

ripen ['raɪpən] *v* : madurar

ripeness ['raɪpnəs] *n* : madurez *f*

rip–off ['rɪp͵ɔf] *n* **1** THEFT : robo *m* **2** SWINDLE : estafa *f*, timo *m fam*

rip off *vt* **1** : rasgar, arrancar, desgarrar **2** SWINDLE *fam* : estafar, tifar

ripple¹ ['rɪpəl] *v* **-pled; -pling** *vi* : rizarse, ondear, ondular — *vt* : rizar

ripple² *n* : onda *f*, ondulación *f*

rise¹ ['raɪz] *vi* **rose** ['ro:z]; **risen** ['rɪz-ən]; **rising 1** GET UP : levantarse ⟨to rise to one's feet : ponerse de pie⟩ **2** : elevarse, alzarse ⟨the mountains rose to the west : las montañas se elevaron al oeste⟩ **3** : salir (dícese del sol y de la luna) **4** : subir (dícese de las aguas, del humo, etc.) ⟨the river rose : las aguas subieron de nivel⟩ **5** INCREASE : aumentar, subir **6** ORIGINATE : nacer, proceder **7 to rise in rank** : ascender **8 to rise up** REBEL : sublevarse, rebelarse

rise² *n* **1** ASCENT : ascensión *f*, subida *f* **2** ORIGIN : origen *m* **3** ELEVATION : elevación *f* **4** INCREASE : subida *f*, aumento *m*, alzamiento *m* **5** SLOPE : pendiente *f*, cuesta *f*

riser ['raɪzər] *n* **1** : contrahuella *f* (de una escalera) **2 early riser** : madrugador *m*, -dora *f* **3 late riser** : dormilón *m*, -lona *f*

risk¹ ['rɪsk] *vt* : arriesgar

risk² *n* : riesgo *m*, peligro *m* ⟨at risk : en peligro⟩ ⟨at your own risk : por su cuenta y riesgo⟩

risky ['rɪski] *adj* **riskier; -est** : arriesgado, peligroso, riesgoso

risqué [rɪ'skeɪ] *adj* : escabroso, picante, subido de tono

rite ['raɪt] *n* : rito *m*

ritual¹ ['rɪtʃuəl] *adj* : ritual — **ritually** *adv*

ritual² *n* : ritual *m*

rival¹ ['raɪvəl] *vt* **-valed** *or* **-valled; -valing** *or* **-valling** : rivalizar con, competir con

rival² *adj* : competidor, rival

rival³ *n* : rival *mf*; competidor *m*, -dora *f*

rivalry ['raɪvəlri] *n, pl* **-ries** : rivalidad *f*, competencia *f*

river ['rɪvər] *n* : río *m*

riverbank ['rɪvər͵bæŋk] *n* : ribera *f*, orilla *f*

riverbed ['rɪvər͵bɛd] *n* : cauce *m*, lecho *m*

riverside ['rɪvər͵saɪd] *n* : ribera *f*, orilla *f*

rivet¹ ['rɪvət] *vt* **1** : remachar **2** FIX : fijar (los ojos, etc.) **3** FASCINATE : fascinar, cautivar

rivet² *n* : remache *m*

rivulet ['rɪvjələt] *n* : arroyo *m*, riachuelo *m* ⟨rivulets of sweat : gotas de sudor⟩

roach ['ro:tʃ] → **cockroach**

road ['ro:d] *n* **1** : carretera *f*, calle *f*, camino *m* **2** PATH : camino *m*, sendero *m*, vía *f* ⟨on the road to a solution : en vías de una solución⟩

roadblock ['ro:d͵blɑk] *n* : control *m*

roadrunner ['ro:d͵rʌnər] *n* : correcaminos *m*

roadside ['ro:d͵saɪd] *n* : borde *m* de la carretera

roadway ['ro:d͵weɪ] *n* : carretera *f*, calzada *f*

roam ['ro:m] *vi* : vagar, deambular, errar — *vt* : vagar por

roan¹ ['ro:n] *adj* : ruano

roan² *n* : caballo *m* ruano

roar¹ ['ror] *vi* : rugir, bramar ⟨to roar with laughter : reírse a carcajadas⟩ — *vt* : decir a gritos

roar² *n* **1** : rugido *m*, bramido *m* (de un animal) **2** DIN : clamor *m* (de gente), fragor *m* (del trueno), estruendo *m* (del tráfico, etc.)

roast¹ ['ro:st] *vt* : asar (carne, papas), tostar (café, nueces) — *vi* : asarse

roast² *adj* : asado ⟨roast chicken : pollo asado⟩ **2 roast beef** : rosbif *m*

roast³ *n* : asado *m*

rob ['rɑb] *v* **robbed; robbing** *vt* **1** STEAL : robar **2** DEPRIVE : privar, quitar — *vi* : robar

robber ['rɑbər] *n* : ladrón *m*, -drona *f*

robbery ['rɑbəri] *n, pl* **-beries** : robo *m*

robe¹ ['ro:b] *vt* **robed; robing** : vestirse

robe² *n* **1** : toga *f* (de magistrados, etc.), sotana *f* (de eclesiásticos) ⟨robe of office : traje de ceremonias⟩ **2** BATHROBE : bata *f*

robin ['rɑbən] *n* : petirrojo *m*

robot ['ro:͵bɑt, -bət] *n* : robot *m*

robotic [ro'bɑṭɪk] *adj* : robótico, robotizado

robotics [ro'bɑṭɪks] *ns & pl* : robótica *f*

robust [ro'bʌst, 'ro:͵bʌst] *adj* : robusto, fuerte — **robustly** *adv*

rock¹ ['rɑk] *vt* **1** : acunar (a un niño), mecer (una cuna) **2** SHAKE : sacudir — *vi* SWAY : mecerse, balancearse

rock² *adj* : de rock

rock³ *n* **1** ROCKING : balanceo *m* **2** *or* **rock music** : rock *m*, música *f* rock **3** : roca *f* (substancia) **4** STONE : piedra *f*

rock and roll *n* : rock and roll *m*

rocker ['rɑkər] *n* **1** : balancín *m* **2** *or* **rocking chair** : mecedora *f*, balancín *m* **3 to be off one's rocker** : estar chiflado, estar loco

rocket¹ ['rɑkət] *vi* : dispararse, subir rápidamente

rocket² *n* : cohete *m*

rocking horse *n* : caballito *m* (de balancín)
rock salt *n* : sal *f* gema
rocky ['rɑki] *adj* **rockier; -est 1** : rocoso, pedregoso **2** UNSTEADY : inestable
rod ['rɑd] *n* **1** BAR : barra *f*, varilla *f*, vara *f* (de madera) ⟨a fishing rod : una caña (de pescar)⟩ **2** : medida *f* de longitud equivalente a 5.03 metros (5 yardas)
rode → **ride**[1]
rodent ['ro:dənt] *n* : roedor *m*
rodeo ['ro:diˌo:, ro'deɪˌo:] *n, pl* **-deos** : rodeo *m*
roe ['ro:] *n* : hueva *f*
rogue ['ro:g] *n* SCOUNDREL : pícaro *m*, -ra *f*; pillo *m*, -lla *f*
roguish ['ro:gɪʃ] *adj* : pícaro, travieso
role ['ro:l] *n* : papel *m*, función *f*, rol *m*
roll[1] ['ro:l] *vt* **1** : hacer rodar ⟨to roll the ball : hacer rodar la pelota⟩ ⟨to roll one's eyes : poner los ojos en blanco⟩ **2** : liar (un cigarrillo) **3** *or* **to roll up** : enrollar ⟨to roll (oneself) up into a ball : hacerse una bola⟩ **4** FLATTEN : estirar (masa), laminar (metales), pasar el rodillo por (el césped) **5 to roll up one's sleeves** : arremangarse — *vi* **1** : rodar ⟨the ball kept on rolling : la pelota siguió rodando⟩ **2** SWAY : balancearse ⟨the ship rolled in the waves : el barco se balanceó en las olas⟩ **3** REVERBERATE, SOUND : tronar (dícese del trueno), redoblar (dícese de un tambor) **4 to roll along** PROCEED : ponerse en marcha **5 to roll around** : revolcarse **6 to roll by** : pasar **7 to roll over** : dar una vuelta
roll[2] *n* **1** LIST : lista *f* ⟨to call the roll : pasar lista⟩ ⟨to have on the roll : tener inscrito⟩ **2** *or* **bread roll** : panecillo *m*, bolillo *m* Mex **3** : rollo *m* (de papel, de tela, etc.) ⟨a roll of film : un carrete⟩ ⟨a roll of bills : un fajo⟩ **4** : redoble *m* (de tambores), retumbo *m* (del trueno, etc.) **5** ROLLING, SWAYING : balanceo *m*
roller ['ro:lər] *n* **1** : rodillo *m* **2** CURLER : rulo *m*
roller coaster ['ro:lərˌko:stər] *n* : montaña *f* rusa
roller–skate ['ro:lərˌskeɪt] *vi* **-skated; -skating** : patinar (sobre ruedas)
roller skate *n* : patín *m* (de ruedas)
rollicking ['rɑlɪkɪŋ] *adj* : animado, alegre
rolling pin *n* : rodillo *m*
Roman[1] ['ro:mən] *adj* : romano
Roman[2] *n* : romano *m*, -na *f*
Roman Catholic *n* : católico *m*, -ca *f* — **Roman Catholic** *adj*
Roman Catholicism *n* : catolicismo *m*
romance[1] [ro'mænts, 'ro:ˌmænts] *vi* **-manced; -mancing** FANTASIZE : fantasear
romance[2] *n* **1** : romance *m*, novela *f* de caballerías **2** : novela *f* de amor, novela *f* romántica **3** AFFAIR : romance *m*, amorío *m*

Romanian [rʊ'meɪniən, ro-] *n* **1** : rumano *m*, -na *f* **2** : rumano *m* (idioma) — **Romanian** *adj*
Roman numeral *n* : número *m* romano
romantic [ro'mæntɪk] *adj* : romántico — **romantically** [-tɪkli] *adv*
romp[1] ['rɑmp] *vi* FROLIC : retozar, juguetear
romp[2] *n* : retozo *m*
roof[1] ['ru:f, 'rʊf] *vt* : techar
roof[2] *n, pl* **roofs** ['ru:fs, 'rʊfs; 'ru:vz, 'rʊvz] **1** : techo *m*, tejado *m*, techado *m* **2 roof of the mouth** : paladar *m*
roofing ['ru:fɪŋ, 'rʊfɪŋ] *n* : techumbre *f*
rooftop ['ru:fˌtɑp, 'rʊf-] *n* ROOF : tejado *m*
rook[1] ['rʊk] *vt* CHEAT : defraudar, estafar, timar
rook[2] *n* **1** : grajo *m* (ave) **2** : torre *f* (en ajedrez)
rookie ['rʊki] *n* : novato *m*, -ta *f*
room[1] ['ru:m, 'rʊm] *vi* LODGE : alojarse, hospedarse
room[2] *n* **1** SPACE : espacio *m*, sitio *m*, lugar *m* ⟨to make room for : hacer lugar para⟩ **2** : cuarto *m*, habitación *f* (en una casa), sala *f* (para reuniones, etc.) **3** BEDROOM : dormitorio *m*, habitación *f*, pieza *f* **4** (*indicating possibility or opportunity*) ⟨room for improvement : posibilidad de mejorar⟩ ⟨there's no room for error : no hay lugar para errores⟩
roomer ['ru:mər, 'rʊmər] *n* : inquilino *m*, -na *f*
rooming house *n* : pensión *f*
roommate ['ru:mˌmeɪt, 'rʊm-] *n* : compañero *m*, -ra *f* de cuarto
roomy ['ru:mi, 'rʊmi] *adj* **roomier; -est 1** SPACIOUS : espacioso, amplio **2** LOOSE : suelto, holgado ⟨a roomy blouse : una blusa holgada⟩
roost[1] ['ru:st] *vi* : posarse, dormir (en una percha)
roost[2] *n* : percha *f*
rooster ['ru:stər, 'rʊs-] *n* : gallo *m*
root[1] ['ru:t, 'rʊt] *vi* **1** : arraigar ⟨the plant rooted easily : la planta arraigó con facilidad⟩ ⟨deeply rooted traditions : tradiciones profundamente arraigadas⟩ **2** : hozar (dícese de los cerdos) ⟨to root around in : hurgar en⟩ **3 to root for** : apoyar a, alentar — *vt* **to root out** *or* **to root up** : desarraigar (plantas), extirpar (problemas, etc.)
root[2] *n* **1** : raíz *f* (de una planta) **2** ORIGIN : origen *m*, raíz *f* **3** CORE : centro *m*, núcleo *m* ⟨to get to the root of the matter : ir al centro del asunto⟩
rootless ['ru:tləs, 'rʊt-] *adj* : desarraigado
rope[1] ['ro:p] *vt* **roped; roping 1** TIE : amarrar, atar **2** LASSO : lazar **3 to rope off** : acordonar
rope[2] *n* : soga *f*, cuerda *f*
rosary ['ro:zəri] *n, pl* **-ries** : rosario *m*
rose[1] → **rise**[1]
rose[2] ['ro:z] *adj* : rosa, color de rosa

rose³ *n* **1** : rosal *m* (planta), rosa *f* (flor) **2** : rosa *m* (color)

rosebush [ˈroːzˌbʊʃ] *n* : rosal *m*

rosemary [ˈroːzˌmɛri] *n*, *pl* **-maries** : romero *m*

rosette [roˈzɛt] *n* : escarapela *f* (hecho de cintas), roseta *f* (en arquitectura)

Rosh Hashanah [ˌrɑʃhɑˈʃɑnə, ˌroːʃ-] *n* : el Año Nuevo judío

rosin [ˈrɑzən] *n* : colofonia *f*

roster [ˈrɑstər] *n* : lista *f*

rostrum [ˈrɑstrəm] *n*, *pl* **-trums** *or* **-tra** [-trə] : tribuna *f*, estrado *m*

rosy [ˈroːzi] *adj* **rosier; -est 1** : sonrosado, de color rosa **2** PROMISING : prometedor, halagüeño

rot¹ [ˈrɑt] *v* **rotted; rotting** *vi* : pudrirse, descomponerse — *vt* : pudrir, descomponer

rot² *n* : putrefacción *f*, descomposición *f*, podredumbre *f*

rotary¹ [ˈroːtəri] *adj* : rotativo, rotatorio

rotary² *n*, *pl* **-ries 1** : máquina *f* rotativa **2** TRAFFIC CIRCLE : rotonda *f*, glorieta *f*

rotate [ˈroːˌteɪt] *v* **-tated; -tating** *vi* REVOLVE : girar, rotar — *vt* **1** TURN : hacer girar, darle vueltas a **2** ALTERNATE : alternar

rotation [roˈteɪʃən] *n* : rotación *f*

rote [ˈroːt] *n* **to learn by rote** : aprender de memoria

rotor [ˈroːtər] *n* : rotor *m*

rotten [ˈrɑtən] *adj* **1** PUTRID : podrido, putrefacto **2** CORRUPT : corrompido **3** BAD : malo ⟨a rotten day : un día malísimo⟩

rottenness [ˈrɑtənnəs] *n* : podredumbre *f*

rotund [roˈtʌnd] *adj* **1** ROUNDED : redondeado **2** PLUMP : regordete *fam*, llenito *fam*

rouge [ˈruːʒ, ˈruːdʒ] *n* : colorete *m*

rough¹ [ˈrʌf] *vt* **1** ROUGHEN : poner áspero **2 to rough out** SKETCH : esbozar, bosquejar **3 to rough up** BEAT : darle una paliza (a alguien) **4 to rough it** : vivir sin comodidades

rough² *adj* **1** COARSE : áspero, basto **2** UNEVEN : desigual, escabroso, accidentado (dícese del terreno) **3** : agitado (dícese del mar), tempestuoso (dícese del tiempo), violento (dícese del viento) **4** VIOLENT : violento, brutal ⟨a rough neighborhood : un barrio peligroso⟩ **5** DIFFICULT : duro, difícil **6** CRUDE : rudo, tosco, burdo ⟨a rough cottage : una casita tosca⟩ ⟨a rough draft : un borrador⟩ ⟨a rough sketch : un bosquejo⟩ **7** APPROXIMATE : aproximado ⟨a rough idea : una idea aproximada⟩

rough³ *n* **1 the rough** : el rough (en golf) **2 in the rough** : en borrador

roughage [ˈrʌfɪdʒ] *n* : fibra *f*

roughen [ˈrʌfən] *vt* : poner áspero — *vi* : ponerse áspero

roughly [ˈrʌfli] *adv* **1** : bruscamente ⟨to treat roughly : maltratar⟩ **2** CRUDELY : burdamente **3** APPROXIMATELY : aproximadamente, más o menos

roughneck [ˈrʌfˌnɛk] *n* : matón *m*

roughness [ˈrʌfnəs] *n* : rudeza *f*, aspereza *f*

roulette [ruˈlɛt] *n* : ruleta *f*

round¹ [ˈraʊnd] *vt* **1** : redondear ⟨she rounded the edges : redondeó los bordes⟩ **2** TURN : doblar ⟨to round the corner : dar la vuelta a la esquina⟩ **3 to round off** : redondear (un número) **4 to round off** *or* **to round out** COMPLETE : rematar, terminar **5 to round up** GATHER : reunir

round² *adv* → **around¹**

round³ *adj* **1** : redondo ⟨a round table : una mesa redonda⟩ ⟨in round numbers : en números redondos⟩ ⟨round shoulders : espaldas cargadas⟩ **2 round trip** : viaje *m* de ida y vuelta

round⁴ *n* **1** CIRCLE : círculo *m* **2** SERIES : serie *f*, sucesión *f* ⟨a round of talks : una ronda de negociaciones⟩ ⟨the daily round : la rutina cotidiana⟩ **3** : asalto *m* (en boxeo), recorrido *m* (en golf), vuelta *f* (en varios juegos) **4** : salva *f* (de aplausos) **5 round of drinks** : ronda *f* **6 round of ammunition** : disparo *m*, cartucho *m* **7 rounds** *npl* : recorridos *mpl* (de un cartero), rondas *fpl* (de un vigilante), visitas *fpl* (de un médico) ⟨to make the rounds : hacer visitas⟩

round⁵ *prep* → **around²**

roundabout [ˈraʊndəˌbaʊt] *adj* : indirecto ⟨to speak in a roundabout way : hablar con rodeos⟩

roundly [ˈraʊndli] *adv* **1** THOROUGHLY : completamente **2** BLUNTLY : francamente, rotundamente **3** VIGOROUSLY : con vigor

roundness [ˈraʊndnəs] *n* : redondez *f*

roundup [ˈraʊndˌʌp] *n* **1** : rodeo *m* (de animales), redada *f* (de delincuentes, etc.) **2** SUMMARY : resumen *m*

round up *vt* **1** : rodear (ganado), reunir (personas) **2** SUMMARIZE : hacer un resumen de

roundworm [ˈraʊndˌwərm] *n* : lombriz *f* intestinal

rouse [ˈraʊz] *vt* **roused; rousing 1** AWAKE : despertar **2** EXCITE : excitar ⟨it roused him to fury : lo enfureció⟩

rout¹ [ˈraʊt] *vt* **1** DEFEAT : derrotar, aplastar **2 to rout out** : hacer salir

rout² *n* **1** DISPERSAL : desbandada *f*, dispersión *f* **2** DEFEAT : derrota *f* aplastante

route¹ [ˈruːt, ˈraʊt] *vt* **routed; routing** : dirigir, enviar, encaminar

route² *n* : camino *m*, ruta *f*, recorrido *m*

routine¹ [ruːˈtiːn] *adj* : rutinario — **routinely** *adv*

routine² *n* : rutina *f*

rove [ˈroːv] *v* **roved; roving** *vi* : vagar, errar — *vt* : errar por

rover [ˈroːvər] *n* : vagabundo *m*, -da *f*

row¹ [ˈroː] *vt* **1** : avanzar a remo ⟨to row a boat : remar⟩ **2** : llevar a remo ⟨he rowed me to shore : me llevó hasta la orilla⟩ — *vi* : remar

row² [ˈraʊ] *n* **1** : paseo *m* en barca ⟨to go for a row : salir a remar⟩ **2** LINE, RANK : fila *f*, hilera *f* **3** SERIES : serie *f* ⟨three days in a row : tres días seguidos⟩ **4** RACKET : estruendo *m*, bulla *f* **5** QUARREL : pelea *f*, riña *f*

rowboat [ˈroːˌboːt] *n* : bote *m* de remos

rowdiness [ˈraʊdinəs] *n* : bulla *f*

rowdy¹ [ˈraʊdi] *adj* **-dier; -est** : escandaloso, alborotador

rowdy² *n, pl* **-dies** : alborotador *m*, -dora *f*

rower [ˈroːər] *n* : remero *m*, -ra *f*

royal¹ [ˈrɔɪəl] *adj* : real — **royally** *adv*

royal² *n* : persona de linaje real, miembro de la familia real

royalty [ˈrɔɪəlti] *n, pl* **-ties** **1** : realeza *f* (posición) **2** : miembros *mpl* de la familia real **3 royalties** *npl* : derechos *mpl* de autor

rub¹ [ˈrʌb] *v* **rubbed; rubbing** *vt* **1** : frotar, restregar ⟨to rub one's hands together : frotarse las manos⟩ **2** MASSAGE : friccionar, masajear **3** CHAFE : rozar **4** POLISH : frotar, pulir **5** SCRUB : fregar **6 to rub elbows with** : codearse con **7 to rub someone the wrong way** : sacar de quicio a alguien, caerle mal a alguien — *vi* **to rub against** : rozar

rub² *n* **1** RUBBING : frotamiento *m*, fricción *f* **2** DIFFICULTY : problema *m*

rubber [ˈrʌbər] *n* **1** : goma *f*, caucho *m*, hule *m Mex* **2 rubbers** *npl* OVERSHOES : chanclos *mpl*

rubber band *n* : goma *f* (elástica), gomita *f*

rubber–stamp [ˈrʌbərˈstæmp] *vt* **1** APPROVE : aprobar, autorizar **2** STAMP : sellar

rubber stamp *n* : sello *m* (de goma)

rubbery [ˈrʌbəri] *adj* : gomoso

rubbish [ˈrʌbɪʃ] *n* : basura *f*, desechos *mpl*, desperdicios *mpl*

rubble [ˈrʌbəl] *n* : escombros *mpl*, ripio *m*

ruble [ˈruːbəl] *n* : rublo *m*

ruby [ˈruːbi] *n, pl* **-bies** **1** : rubí *m* (gema) **2** : color *m* de rubí

rudder [ˈrʌdər] *n* : timón *m*

ruddy [ˈrʌdi] *adj* **-dier; -est** : rubicundo (dícese de la cara, etc.), rojizo (dícese del cielo)

rude [ˈruːd] *adj* **ruder; rudest** **1** CRUDE : tosco, rústico **2** IMPOLITE : grosero, descortés, maleducado **3** ABRUPT : brusco ⟨a rude awakening : una sorpresa desagradable⟩

rudely [ˈruːdli] *adv* : groseramente

rudeness [ˈruːdnəs] *n* **1** IMPOLITENESS : grosería *f*, descortesía *f*, falta *f* de educación **2** ROUGHNESS : tosquedad *f* **3** SUDDENNESS : brusquedad *f*

rudiment [ˈruːdəmənt] *n* : rudimento *m*, noción *f* básica ⟨the rudiments of Spanish : los rudimentos del español⟩

rudimentary [ˌruːdəˈmɛntəri] *adj* : rudimentario, básico

rue [ˈruː] *vt* **rued; ruing** : lamentar, arrepentirse de

rueful [ˈruːfəl] *adj* **1** PITIFUL : lastimoso **2** REGRETFUL : arrepentido, pesaroso

ruffian [ˈrʌfiən] *n* : matón *m*

ruffle¹ [ˈrʌfəl] *vt* **-fled; -fling** **1** AGITATE : agitar, rizar (agua) **2** RUMPLE : arrugar (ropa), despeinar (pelo) **3** ERECT : erizar (plumas) **4** VEX : alterar, irritar, perturbar **5** : fruncir volantes en (tela)

ruffle² *n* FLOUNCE : volante *m*

ruffly [ˈrʌfəli] *adj* : con volantes

rug [ˈrʌg] *n* : alfombra *f*, tapete *m*

rugged [ˈrʌgəd] *adj* **1** ROUGH, UNEVEN : accidentado, escabroso ⟨rugged mountains : montañas accidentadas⟩ **2** HARSH : duro, severo **3** ROBUST, STURDY : robusto, fuerte

ruin¹ [ˈruːən] *vt* **1** DESTROY : destruir, arruinar **2** BANKRUPT : arruinar, hacer quebrar

ruin² *n* **1** : ruina *f* ⟨to fall into ruin : caer en ruinas⟩ **2** : ruina *f*, perdición *f* ⟨to be the ruin of : ser la perdición de⟩ **3 ruins** *npl* : ruinas *fpl*, restos *mpl* ⟨the ruins of the ancient temple : las ruinas del templo antiguo⟩

ruinous [ˈruːənəs] *adj* : ruinoso

rule¹ [ˈruːl] *v* **ruled; ruling** *vt* **1** CONTROL, GOVERN : gobernar (un país), controlar (las emociones) **2** DECIDE : decidir, fallar ⟨the judge ruled that . . . : el juez falló que . . . ⟩ **3** DRAW : trazar con una regla — *vi* **1** GOVERN : gobernar, reinar **2** PREVAIL : prevalecer, imperar **3 to rule against** : fallar en contra de

rule² *n* **1** REGULATION : regla *f*, norma *f* **2** CUSTOM, HABIT : regla *f* general ⟨as a rule : por lo general⟩ **3** GOVERNMENT : gobierno *m*, dominio *m* **4** RULER : regla *f* (para medir)

ruler [ˈruːlər] *n* **1** LEADER, SOVEREIGN : gobernante *m*, soberano *m*, -na *f* **2** : regla *f* (para medir)

ruling [ˈruːlɪŋ] *n* : resolución *f*, fallo *m*

rum [ˈrʌm] *n* : ron *m*

Rumanian [rʊˈmeɪniən] → **Romanian**

rumble¹ [ˈrʌmbəl] *vi* **-bled; -bling** : retumbar, hacer ruidos (dícese del estómago)

rumble² *n* : estruendo *m*, ruido *m* sordo, retumbo *m*

ruminant¹ [ˈruːmənənt] *adj* : rumiante

ruminant² *n* : rumiante *m*

ruminate [ˈruːməˌneɪt] *vi* **-nated; -nating** **1** : rumiar (en zoología) **2** REFLECT : reflexionar, rumiar

rummage [ˈrʌmɪdʒ] *v* **-maged; -maging** *vi* : hurgar — *vt* RANSACK : revolver ⟨they rummaged the attic : revolvieron el ático⟩

rummy ['rʌmi] *n* : rummy *m* (juego de naipes)

rumor¹ ['ru:mər] *vt* : rumorear ⟨it is rumored that . . . : se rumorea que . . ., se dice que . . .⟩

rumor² *n* : rumor *m*

rump ['rʌmp] *n* **1** : ancas *fpl*, grupa *f* (de un animal) **2** : cadera *f* ⟨rump steak : filete de cadera⟩

rumple ['rʌmpəl] *vt* **-pled; -pling** : arrugar (ropa, etc.), despeinar (pelo)

rumpus ['rʌmpəs] *n* : lío *m*, jaleo *m fam*

run¹ ['rʌn] *v* **ran** ['ræn]; **run; running** *vi* **1** : correr ⟨she ran to catch the bus : corrió para alcanzar el autobús⟩ ⟨run and fetch the doctor : corre a buscar al médico⟩ **2** : circular, correr ⟨the train runs between Detroit and Chicago : el tren circula entre Detroit y Chicago⟩ ⟨to run on time : ser puntual⟩ **3** FUNCTION : funcionar, ir ⟨the engine runs on gasoline : el motor funciona con gasolina⟩ ⟨to run smoothly : ir bien⟩ **4** FLOW : correr, ir **5** LAST : durar ⟨the movie runs for two hours : la película dura dos horas⟩ ⟨the contract runs for three years : el contrato es válido por tres años⟩ **6** : desteñir, despintar (dícese de los colores) **7** EXTEND : correr, extenderse **8 to run for office** : postularse, presentarse — *vt* **1** : correr ⟨to run 10 miles : correr 10 millas⟩ ⟨to run errands : hacer los mandados⟩ ⟨to run out of town : hacer salir del pueblo⟩ **2** PASS : pasar **3** DRIVE : llevar en coche **4** OPERATE : hacer funcionar (un motor, etc.) **5** : echar ⟨to run water : echar agua⟩ **6** MANAGE : dirigir, llevar (un negocio, etc.) **7** EXTEND : tender (un cable, etc.) **8 to run a risk** : correr un riesgo

run² *n* **1** : carrera *f* ⟨at a run : a la carrera, corriendo⟩ ⟨to go for a run : ir a correr⟩ **2** TRIP : vuelta *f*, paseo *m* (en coche), viaje *m* (en avión) **3** SERIES : serie *f* ⟨a run of disappointments : una serie de desilusiones⟩ ⟨in the long run : a la larga⟩ ⟨in the short run : a corto plazo⟩ **4** DEMAND : gran demanda *f* ⟨a run on the banks : una corrida bancaria⟩ **5** (*used for theatrical productions and films*) ⟨to have a long run : mantenerse mucho tiempo en la cartelera⟩ **6** TYPE : tipo *m* ⟨the average run of students : el tipo más común de estudiante⟩ **7** : carrera *f* (en béisbol) **8** : carrera *f* (en una media) **9 to have the run of** : tener libre acceso de (una casa, etc.) **10 ski run** : pista *f* (de esquí)

runaway¹ ['rʌnə,weɪ] *adj* **1** FUGITIVE : fugitivo **2** UNCONTROLLABLE : incontrolable, fuera de control ⟨runaway inflation : inflación desenfrenada⟩ ⟨a runaway success : un éxito aplastante⟩

runaway² *n* : fugitivo *m*, -va *f*

rundown ['rʌn,daʊn] *n* SUMMARY : resumen *m*

run–down ['rʌn'daʊn] *adj* **1** DILAPIDATED : ruinoso, destartalado **2** SICKLY, TIRED : cansado, débil

rung¹ *pp* → **ring¹**

rung² ['rʌn] *n* : peldaño *m*, escalón *m*

run–in ['rʌn,ɪn] *n* : disputa *f*, altercado *m*

runner ['rʌnər] *n* **1** RACER : corredor *m*, -dora *f* **2** MESSENGER : mensajero *m*, -ra *f* **3** TRACK : riel *m* (de un cajón, etc.) **4** : patín *m* (de un trineo), cuchilla *f* (de un patín) **5** : estolón *m* (planta)

runner–up [,rʌnər'ʌp] *n, pl* **runners–up** : subcampeón *m*, -peona *f*

running ['rʌnɪn] *adj* **1** FLOWING : corriente ⟨running water : agua corriente⟩ **2** CONTINUOUS : continuo ⟨a running battle : una lucha continua⟩ **3** CONSECUTIVE : seguido ⟨six days running : por seis días seguidos⟩

runny ['rʌni] *adj* **-nier; -est 1** WATERY : caldoso **2 to have a runny nose** : moquear

run over *vt* : atropellar — *vi* OVERFLOW : rebosar

runt ['rʌnt] *n* : animal *m* pequeño ⟨the runt of the litter : el más pequeño de la camada⟩

runway ['rʌn,weɪ] *n* : pista *f* de aterrizaje

rupee [ru:'pi:, 'ru:,-] *n* : rupia *f*

rupture¹ ['rʌptʃər] *v* **-tured; -turing** *vt* **1** BREAK, BURST : romper, reventar **2** : causar una hernia en — *vi* : reventarse

rupture² *n* **1** BREAK : ruptura *f* **2** HERNIA : hernia *f*

rural ['rʊrəl] *adj* : rural, campestre

ruse ['ru:s, 'ru:z] *n* : treta *f*, ardid *m*, estratagema *f*

rush¹ ['rʌʃ] *vi* : correr, ir de prisa ⟨to rush around : correr de un lado a otro⟩ ⟨to rush off : irse corriendo⟩ — *vt* **1** HURRY : apresurar, apurar **2** ATTACK : abalanzarse sobre, asaltar

rush² *adj* : urgente

rush³ *n* **1** HASTE : prisa *f*, apuro *m* **2** SURGE : ráfaga *f* (de aire), torrente *m* (de aguas), avalancha *f* (de gente) **3** DEMAND : demanda *f* ⟨a rush on sugar : una gran demanda para el azúcar⟩ **4** : carga *f* (en futbol americano) **5** : junco *m* (planta)

russet ['rʌsət] *n* : color *m* rojizo

Russian ['rʌʃən] *n* **1** : ruso *m*, -sa *f* **2** : ruso *m* (idioma) — **Russian** *adj*

rust¹ ['rʌst] *vi* : oxidarse — *vt* : oxidar

rust² *n* **1** : herrumbre *f*, orín *m*, óxido *m* (en los metales) **2** : roya *f* (en las plantas)

rustic¹ ['rʌstɪk] *adj* : rústico, campestre — **rustically** [-tɪkli] *adv*

rustic² *n* : rústico *m*, -ca *f*; campesino *m*, -na *f*

rustle¹ ['rʌsəl] *v* **-tled; -tling** *vt* **1** : hacer susurrar, hacer crujir ⟨to rustle a newspaper : hacer crujir un periódico⟩ **2** STEAL : robar (ganado) — *vi* : susurrar, crujir

rustle² *n* : murmullo *m*, susurro *m*, crujido *m*

rustler ['rʌsələr] *n* : ladrón *m*, -drona *f* de ganado

rusty ['rʌsti] *adj* **rustier; -est** : oxidado, herrumbroso

rut ['rʌt] *n* **1** GROOVE, TRACK : rodada *f*, surco *m* **2 to be in a rut** : ser esclavo de la rutina

ruthless ['ru:θləs] *adj* : despiadado, cruel — **ruthlessly** *adv*

ruthlessness ['ru:θləsnəs] *n* : crueldad *f*, falta *f* de piedad

Rwandan ['rʊˈandən] *n* : ruandés *m*, -desa *f* — **Rwandan** *adj*

rye ['raɪ] *n* **1** : centeno *m* **2** *or* **rye whiskey** : whisky *m* de centeno

S

s ['ɛs] *n*, *pl* **s's** *or* **ss** ['ɛsəz] : decimonovena letra del alfabeto inglés

Sabbath ['sæbəθ] *n* **1** : sábado *m* (en el judaísmo) **2** : domingo *m* (en el cristianismo)

saber ['seɪbər] *n* : sable *m*

sable ['seɪbəl] *n* **1** BLACK : negro *m* **2** : marta *f* cebellina (animal)

sabotage¹ ['sæbəˌtɑʒ] *vt* **-taged; -taging** : sabotear

sabotage² *n* : sabotaje *m*

sac ['sæk] *n* : saco *m* (anatómico)

saccharin ['sækərən] *n* : sacarina *f*

saccharine ['sækərən, -ˌriːn, -ˌraɪn] *adj* : meloso, empalagoso

sachet [sæˈʃeɪ] *n* : bolsita *f* (perfumada)

sack¹ ['sæk] *vt* **1** FIRE : echar (del trabajo), despedir **2** PLUNDER : saquear

sack² *n* BAG : saco *m*

sacrament ['sækrəmənt] *n* : sacramento *m*

sacramental [ˌsækrəˈmɛntəl] *adj* : sacramental

sacred ['seɪkrəd] *adj* **1** RELIGIOUS : sagrado, sacro ⟨sacred texts : textos sagrados⟩ **2** HOLY : sagrado **3 sacred to** : consagrado a

sacrifice¹ ['sækrəˌfaɪs] *vt* **-ficed; -ficing** **1** : sacrificar **2 to sacrifice oneself** : sacrificarse

sacrifice² *n* : sacrificio *m*

sacrilege ['sækrəlɪdʒ] *n* : sacrilegio *m*

sacrilegious [ˌsækrəˈlɪdʒəs, -ˈliː-] *adj* : sacrílego

sacrosanct ['sækroˌsæŋkt] *adj* : sacrosanto

sad ['sæd] *adj* **sadder; saddest** : triste — **sadly** *adv*

sadden ['sædən] *vt* : entristecer

saddle¹ ['sædəl] *vt* **-dled; -dling** : ensillar

saddle² *n* : silla *f* (de montar)

sadism ['seɪˌdɪzəm, 'sæ-] *n* : sadismo *m*

sadist ['seɪdɪst, 'sæ-] *n* : sádico *m*, -ca *f*

sadistic [səˈdɪstɪk] *adj* : sádico — **sadistically** [-tɪkli] *adv*

sadness ['sædnəs] *n* : tristeza *f*

safari [səˈfɑri, -ˈfær-] *n* : safari *m*

safe¹ ['seɪf] *adj* **safer; safest** **1** UNHARMED : ileso ⟨safe and sound : sano y salvo⟩ **2** SECURE : seguro **3 to be on the safe side** : para mayor seguridad **4 to play it safe** : ir a la segura

safe² *n* : caja *f* fuerte

safeguard¹ ['seɪfˌgɑrd] *vt* : salvaguardar, proteger

safeguard² *n* : salvaguarda *f*, protección *f*

safekeeping ['seɪfˈkiːpɪŋ] *n* : custodia *f*, protección *f* ⟨to put into safekeeping : poner en buen recaudo⟩

safely ['seɪfli] *adv* **1** UNHARMED : sin incidentes, sin novedades ⟨they landed safely : aterrizaron sin novedades⟩ **2** SECURELY : con toda seguridad, sin peligro

safety ['seɪfti] *n*, *pl* **-ties** : seguridad *f*

safety belt *n* : cinturón *m* de seguridad

safety pin *n* : alfiler *m* de gancho, alfiler *m* de seguridad, imperdible *m Spain*

saffron ['sæfrən] *n* : azafrán *m*

sag¹ ['sæg] *vi* **sagged; sagging** **1** DROOP, SINK : combarse, hundirse, inclinarse **2** : colgar, caer ⟨his jowls sagged : le colgaban las mejillas⟩ **3** FLAG : flaquear, decaer ⟨his spirits sagged : se le flaqueó el ánimo⟩

sag² *n* : combadura *f*

saga ['sɑgə, 'sæ-] *n* : saga *f*

sagacious [səˈgeɪʃəs] *adj* : sagaz

sage¹ ['seɪdʒ] *adj* **sager; -est** : sabio — **sagely** *adv*

sage² *n* **1** : sabio *m*, -bia *f* **2** : salvia *f* (planta)

sagebrush ['seɪdʒˌbrʌʃ] *n* : artemisa *f*

Sagittarius [ˌsædʒəˈtɛriəs] *n* : Sagitario *mf*

said → **say**

sail¹ ['seɪl] *vi* **1** : navegar (en un barco) **2** : ir fácilmente ⟨we sailed right in : entramos sin ningún problema⟩ — *vt* **1** : gobernar (un barco) **2 to sail the seas** : cruzar los mares

sail² *n* **1** : vela *f* (de un barco) **2** : viaje *m* en velero ⟨to go for a sail : salir a navegar⟩

sailboat ['seɪlˌboːt] *n* : velero *m*, barco *m* de vela

sailfish ['seɪlˌfɪʃ] *n* : pez *m* vela

sailor ['seɪlər] *n* : marinero *m*

saint ['seɪnt, *before a name* ˌseɪnt *or* sənt] *n* : santo *m*, -ta *f* ⟨Saint Francis : San Francisco⟩ ⟨Saint Rose : Santa Rosa⟩

saintliness ['seɪntlinəs] *n* : santidad *f*

saintly ['seɪntli] *adj* **saintlier; -est** : santo

sake ['seɪk] *n* **1** BENEFIT : bien *m* ⟨for the children's sake : por el bien de los niños⟩ **2** (*indicating an end or a purpose*) ⟨art for art's sake : el arte por el arte⟩ ⟨let's say, for argument's sake, that he's wrong : pongamos que está equivocado⟩ **3 for goodness' sake!** : ¡por (el amor de) Dios!

salable *or* **saleable** ['seɪləbəl] *adj* : vendible

salacious [sə'leɪʃəs] *adj* : salaz — **salaciously** *adv*

salad ['sæləd] *n* : ensalada *f*

salamander ['sælə,mændər] *n* : salamandra *f*

salami [sə'lɑmi] *n* : salami *m*

salary ['sæləri] *n, pl* **-ries** : sueldo *m*

sale ['seɪl] *n* **1** SELLING : venta *f* **2** : liquidación *f*, rebajas *fpl* ⟨on sale : de rebaja⟩ **3 sales** *npl* : ventas *fpl* ⟨to work in sales : trabajar en ventas⟩

salesman ['seɪlzmən] *n, pl* **-men** [-mən, -,men] **1** : vendedor *m*, dependiente *m* (en una tienda) **2 traveling salesman** : viajante *m*, representante *m*

salesperson ['seɪlz,pərsən] *n* : vendedor *m*, -dora *f*; dependiente *m*, -ta *f* (en una tienda)

saleswoman ['seɪlz,wumən] *n, pl* **-women** [-,wimən] **1** : vendedora *f*, dependienta *f* (en una tienda) **2 traveling saleswoman** : viajante *f*, representante *f*

salient ['seɪljənt] *adj* : saliente, sobresaliente

saline ['seɪ,li:n, -,laɪn] *adj* : salino

saliva [sə'laɪvə] *n* : saliva *f*

salivary ['sælə,vɛri] *adj* : salival ⟨salivary gland : glándula salival⟩

salivate ['sælə,veɪt] *vi* **-vated; -vating** : salivar

sallow ['sælo:] *adj* : amarillento, cetrino

sally[1] ['sæli] *vi* **-lied; -lying** SET OUT : salir, hacer una salida

sally[2] *n, pl* **-lies 1** : salida *f* (militar), misión *f* **2** QUIP : salida *f*, ocurrencia *f*

salmon ['sæmən] *ns & pl* **1** : salmón *m* (pez) **2** : color *m* salmón

salon [sə'lɑn, 'sæ,lɑn, sæ'lɔ̃] *n* : salón *m* ⟨beauty salon : salón de belleza⟩

saloon [sə'lu:n] *n* **1** HALL : salón *m* (en un barco) **2** BARROOM : bar *m*

salsa ['sɔlsə, 'sɑl-] *n* : salsa *f* mexicana, salsa *f* picante

salt[1] ['sɔlt] *vt* : salar, echarle sal a

salt[2] *adj* : salado

salt[3] *n* : sal *f*

saltwater ['sɔlt,wɔt̬ər, -,wɑ-] *adj* : de agua salada

salty ['sɔlt̬i] *adj* **saltier; -est** : salado

salubrious [sə'lu:briəs] *adj* : salubre

salutary ['sæljə,tɛri] *adj* : saludable, salubre

salutation [,sæljə'teɪʃən] *n* : saludo *m*, salutación *f*

salute[1] [sə'lu:t] *v* **-luted; -luting** *vt* **1** : saludar (con gestos o ceremonias) **2** ACCLAIM : reconocer, aclamar — *vi* : hacer un saludo

salute[2] *n* **1** : saludo *m* (gesto), salva *f* (de cañonazos) **2** TRIBUTE : reconocimiento *m*, homenaje *m*

Salvadoran [,sælvə'dorən] → **El Salvadoran**

salvage[1] ['sælvɪʤ] *vt* **-vaged; -vaging** : salvar, rescatar

salvage[2] *n* **1** SALVAGING : salvamento *m*, rescate *m* **2** : objetos *mpl* salvados

salvation [sæl'veɪʃən] *n* : salvación *f*

salve[1] ['sæv, 'sav] *vt* **salved; salving** : calmar, apaciguar ⟨to salve one's conscience : aliviarse la conciencia⟩

salve[2] *n* : ungüento *m*

salvo ['sæl,vo:] *n, pl* **-vos** *or* **-voes** : salva *f*

same[1] ['seɪm] *adj* : mismo, igual ⟨the results are the same : los resultados son iguales⟩ ⟨he said the same thing as you : dijo lo mismo que tú⟩

same[2] *pron* : mismo ⟨it's all the same to me : me da lo mismo⟩ ⟨the same to you! : ¡igualmente!⟩

sameness ['seɪmnəs] *n* **1** SIMILARITY : identidad *f*, semejanza *f* **2** MONOTONY : monotonía *f*

sample[1] ['sæmpəl] *vt* **-pled; -pling** : probar

sample[2] *n* : muestra *f*, prueba *f*

sampler ['sæmplər] *n* **1** : dechado *m* (de bordado) **2** COLLECTION : colección *f* **3** ASSORTMENT : surtido *m*

sanatorium [,sænə'toriəm] *n, pl* **-riums** *or* **-ria** [-iə] : sanatorio *m*

sanctify ['sæŋktə,faɪ] *vt* **-fied; -fying** : santificar

sanctimonious [,sæŋktə'mo:niəs] *adj* : beato, santurrón

sanction[1] ['sæŋkʃən] *vt* : sancionar, aprobar

sanction[2] *n* **1** AUTHORIZATION : sanción *f*, autorización *f* **2 sanctions** *npl* : sanciones *fpl* ⟨to impose sanctions on : imponer sanciones a⟩

sanctity ['sæŋktət̬i] *n, pl* **-ties** : santidad *f*

sanctuary ['sæŋktʃu,ɛri] *n, pl* **-aries 1** : presbiterio *m* (en una iglesia) **2** REFUGE : refugio *m*, asilo *m*

sand[1] ['sænd] *vt* : lijar (madera)

sand[2] *n* : arena *f*

sandal ['sændəl] *n* : sandalia *f*

sandbank ['sænd,bæŋk] *n* : banco *m* de arena

sandpaper *n* : papel *m* de lija

sandpiper ['sænd,paɪpər] *n* : andarríos *m*

sandstone ['sænd,sto:n] *n* : arenisca *f*

sandstorm ['sænd,stɔrm] *n* : tormenta *f* de arena

sandwich[1] ['sænd,wɪtʃ] *vt* : intercalar, encajonar, meter (entre dos cosas)

sandwich[2] *n* : sandwich *m*, emparedado *m*, bocadillo *m* Spain

sandy ['sændi] *adj* **sandier; -est** : arenoso

sane ['seɪn] *adj* **saner; sanest 1** : cuerdo **2** SENSIBLE : sensato, razonable

sang → **sing**
sanguine [ˈsæŋgwən] *adj* **1** RUDDY : sanguíneo, rubicundo **2** HOPEFUL : optimista
sanitarium [ˌsænəˈtɛriəm] *n, pl* -**iums** *or* -**ia** [-iə] → **sanatorium**
sanitary [ˈsænətɛri] *adj* **1** : sanitario ⟨sanitary measures : medidas sanitarias⟩ **2** HYGIENIC : higiénico **3 sanitary napkin** : compresa *f*, paño *m* higiénico
sanitation [ˌsænəˈteɪʃən] *n* : sanidad *f*
sanitize [ˈsænəˌtaɪz] *vt* -**tized; -tizing 1** : desinfectar **2** EXPURGATE : expurgar
sanity [ˈsænəti] *n* : cordura *f*, razón *f* ⟨to lose one's sanity : perder el juicio⟩
sank → **sink**
Santa Claus [ˈsæntəˌklɔz] *n* : Papá Noel, San Nicolás
sap¹ [ˈsæp] *vt* **sapped; sapping 1** UNDERMINE : socavar **2** WEAKEN : minar, debilitar
sap² *n* **1** : savia *f* (de una planta) **2** SUCKER : inocentón *m*, -tona *f*
sapling [ˈsæplɪŋ] *n* : árbol *m* joven
sapphire [ˈsæˌfaɪr] *n* : zafiro *m*
sarcasm [ˈsɑrˌkæzəm] *n* : sarcasmo *m*
sarcastic [sɑrˈkæstɪk] *adj* : sarcástico — **sarcastically** [-ˌtɪkli] *adv*
sarcophagus [sɑrˈkɑfəgəs] *n, pl* -**gi** [-ˌgaɪ, -ˌdʒaɪ] : sarcófago *m*
sardine [sɑrˈdiːn] *n* : sardina *f*
sardonic [sɑrˈdɑnɪk] *adj* : sardónico — **sardonically** [-nɪkli] *adv*
sarsaparilla [ˌsæspəˈrɪlə, ˌsɑrs-] *n* : zarzaparrilla *f*
sash [ˈsæʃ] *n* **1** : faja *f* (de un vestido), fajín *m* (de un uniforme) **2** *pl* **sash** : marco *m* (de una ventana)
sassafras [ˈsæsəˌfræs] *n* : sasafrás *m*
sassy [ˈsæsi] *adj* **sassier; -est** → **saucy**
sat → **sit**
Satan [ˈseɪtən] *n* : Satanás *m*, Satán *m*
satanic [səˈtænɪk, seɪ-] *adj* : satánico — **satanically** [-nɪkli] *adv*
satchel [ˈsætʃəl] *n* : cartera *f*, saco *m*
sate [ˈseɪt] *vt* **sated; sating** : saciar
satellite [ˈsætəˌlaɪt] *n* : satélite *m* ⟨spy satellite : satélite espía⟩
satiate [ˈseɪʃiˌeɪt] *vt* -**ated; -ating** : saciar, hartar
satin [ˈsætən] *n* : raso *m*, satín *m*, satén *m*
satire [ˈsæˌtaɪr] *n* : sátira *f*
satiric [səˈtɪrɪk] *or* **satirical** [-ɪkəl] *adj* : satírico
satirize [ˈsætəˌraɪz] *vt* -**rized; -rizing** : satirizar
satisfaction [ˌsætəsˈfækʃən] *n* : satisfacción *f*
satisfactory [ˌsætəsˈfæktəri] *adj* : satisfactorio, bueno — **satisfactorily** [-rəli] *adv*
satisfy [ˈsætəsˌfaɪ] *v* -**fied; -fying** *vt* **1** PLEASE : satisfacer, contentar **2** CONVINCE : convencer **3** FULFILL : satisfacer, cumplir con, llenar **4** SETTLE : pagar, saldar (una cuenta) — *vi* SUFFICE : bastar

saturate [ˈsætʃəˌreɪt] *vt* -**rated; -rating 1** SOAK : empapar **2** FILL : saturar
saturation [ˌsætʃəˈreɪʃən] *n* : saturación *f*
Saturday [ˈsætərˌdeɪ, -di] *n* : sábado *m*
Saturn [ˈsætərn] *n* : Saturno *m*
satyr [ˈseɪtər, ˈsæ-] *n* : sátiro *m*
sauce [ˈsɔs] *n* : salsa *f*
saucepan [ˈsɔsˌpæn] *n* : cacerola *f*, cazo *m*, cazuela *f*
saucer [ˈsɔsər] *n* : platillo *m*
sauciness [ˈsɔsinəs] *n* : descaro *m*, frescura *f*
saucy [ˈsɔsi] *adj* **saucier; -est** IMPUDENT : descarado, fresco *fam* — **saucily** *adv*
Saudi [ˈsaʊdi, ˈsɔ-] → **Saudi Arabian**
Saudi Arabian *n* : saudita *mf*, saudí *mf* — **Saudi Arabian** *adj*
sauna [ˈsɔnə, ˈsaʊnə] *n* : sauna *mf*
saunter [ˈsɔntər, ˈsɑn-] *vi* : pasear, parsearse
sausage [ˈsɔsɪdʒ] *n* : salchicha *f*, embutido *m*
sauté [sɔˈteɪ, so:-] *vt* -**teed** *or* -**téd; -téing** : saltear, sofreír
savage¹ [ˈsævɪdʒ] *adj* : salvaje, feroz — **savagely** *adv*
savage² *n* : salvaje *mf*
savagery [ˈsævɪdʒri, -dʒəri] *n, pl* -**ries 1** FEROCITY : ferocidad *f* **2** WILDNESS : salvajismo *m*
savanna [səˈvænə] *n* : sabana *f*
save¹ [ˈseɪv] *vt* **saved; saving 1** RESCUE : salvar, rescatar **2** PRESERVE : preservar, conservar **3** KEEP : guardar, ahorrar (dinero), almacenar (alimentos) **4** : guardar (en informática)
save² *prep* EXCEPT : salvo, excepto, menos
savior [ˈseɪvjər] *n* **1** : salvador *m*, -dora *f* **2 the Savior** : el Salvador *m*
savor¹ [ˈseɪvər] *vt* : saborear
savor² *n* : sabor *m*
savory [ˈseɪvəri] *adj* : sabroso
saw¹ → **see**
saw² [ˈsɔ] *vt* **sawed; sawed** *or* **sawn** [ˈsɔn]; **sawing** : serrar, cortar (con sierra)
saw³ *n* : sierra *f*
sawdust [ˈsɔˌdʌst] *n* : aserrín *m*, serrín *m*
sawhorse [ˈsɔˌhɔrs] *n* : caballete *m*, burro *m* (en carpintería)
sawmill [ˈsɔˌmɪl] *n* : aserradero *m*
saxophone [ˈsæksəˌfoːn] *n* : saxofón *m*
say¹ [ˈseɪ] *v* **said** [ˈsɛd]; **saying; says** [ˈsɛz] *vt* **1** EXPRESS, UTTER : decir, expresar ⟨to say no : decir que no⟩ ⟨that goes without saying : ni que decir tiene⟩ ⟨no sooner said than done : dicho y hecho⟩ ⟨to say again : repetir⟩ ⟨to say one's prayers : rezar⟩ **2** INDICATE : marcar, poner ⟨my watch says three o'clock : mi reloj marca las tres⟩ ⟨what does the sign say? : ¿qué pone el letrero?⟩ **3** ALLEGE : decir ⟨it's said that she's pretty : se dice que es bonita⟩ — *vi* : decir

say² *n, pl* **says** ['seɪz] : voz *f*, opinión *f* ⟨to have no say : no tener ni voz ni voto⟩ ⟨to have one's say : dar uno su opinión⟩

saying ['seɪɪŋ] *n* : dicho *m*, refrán *m*

scab ['skæb] *n* **1** : costra *f*, postilla *f* (en una herida) **2** STRIKEBREAKER : rompehuelgas *mf*, esquirol *mf*

scabbard ['skæbərd] *n* : vaina *f* (de una espada), funda *f* (de un puñal, etc.)

scabby ['skæbi] *adj* **scabbier; -est** : lleno de costras

scaffold ['skæfəld, -ˌfoːld] *n* **1** *or* **scaffolding** : andamio *m* (para obreros, etc.) **2** : patíbulo *m*, cadalso *m* (para ejecuciones)

scald ['skɔld] *vt* **1** BURN : escaldar **2** HEAT : calentar (hasta el punto de ebullición)

scale¹ ['skeɪl] *v* **scaled; scaling** *vt* **1** : escamar (un pescado) **2** CLIMB : escalar (un muro, etc.) **3 to scale down** : reducir — *vi* WEIGH : pesar ⟨he scaled in at 200 pounds : pesó 200 libras⟩

scale² *n* **1** *or* **scales** : balanza *f*, báscula *f* (para pesar) **2** : escama *f* (de un pez, etc.) **3** EXTENT : escala *f*, proporción *f* ⟨wage scale : escala salarial⟩ **4** : escala *f* (en música, en cartografía, etc.) ⟨to draw to scale : dibujar a escala⟩

scallion ['skæljən] *n* : cebollino *m*, cebolleta *f*

scallop ['skɑləp, 'skæ-] *n* **1** : vieira *f* (molusco) **2** : festón *m* (decoración)

scalp¹ ['skælp] *vt* : arrancar la cabellera a

scalp² *n* : cuero *m* cabelludo

scalpel ['skælpəl] *n* : bisturí *m*, escalpelo *m*

scaly ['skeɪli] *adj* **scalier; -est** : escamoso

scam ['skæm] *n* : estafa *f*, timo *m fam*, chanchullo *m fam*

scamp ['skæmp] *n* : bribón *m*, -bona *f*; granuja *mf*; travieso *m*, -sa *f*

scamper ['skæmpər] *vi* : corretear

scan¹ ['skæn] *vt* **scanned; scanning 1** : escandir (versos) **2** SCRUTINIZE : escudriñar, escrutar ⟨to scan the horizon : escudriñar el horizonte⟩ **3** PERUSE : echarle un vistazo a (un periódico, etc.) **4** EXPLORE : explorar (con radar), hacer un escáner de (en ecografía) **5** : escanear (una imagen)

scan² *n* **1** : ecografía *f*, examen *m* ultrasónico (en medicina) **2** : imagen *f* escaneada (en una computadora)

scandal ['skændəl] *n* **1** DISGRACE, OUTRAGE : escándalo *m* **2** GOSSIP : habladurías *fpl*, chismes *mpl*

scandalize ['skændəlˌaɪz] *vt* **-ized; -izing** : escandalizar

scandalous ['skændələs] *adj* : de escándalo

Scandinavian¹ [ˌskændə'neɪviən] *adj* : escandinavo

Scandinavian² *n* : escandinavo *m*, -va *f*

scanner ['skænər] *n* : escáner *m*, scanner *m*

scant ['skænt] *adj* : escaso

scanty ['skænti] *adj* **scantier; -est** : exiguo, escaso ⟨a scanty meal : una comida insuficiente⟩ — **scantily** [-təli] *adv*

scapegoat ['skeɪpˌgoːt] *n* : chivo *m* expiatorio, cabeza *f* de turco

scapula ['skæpjələ] *n, pl* **-lae** [-ˌliː, -ˌlaɪ] *or* **-las** → **shoulder blade**

scar¹ ['skɑr] *v* **scarred; scarring** *vt* : dejar una cicatriz en — *vi* : cicatrizar

scar² *n* : cicatriz *f*, marca *f*

scarab ['skærəb] *n* : escarabajo *m*

scarce ['skɛrs] *adj* **scarcer; -est** : escaso

scarcely ['skɛrsli] *adv* **1** BARELY : apenas **2** : ni mucho menos, ni nada que se le parezca ⟨he's scarcely an expert : ciertamente no es experto⟩

scarcity ['skɛrsəti] *n, pl* **-ties** : escasez *f*

scare¹ ['skɛr] *vt* **scared; scaring** : asustar, espantar

scare² *n* **1** FRIGHT : susto *m*, sobresalto *m* **2** ALARM : pánico *m*

scarecrow ['skɛrˌkroː] *n* : espantapájaros *m*, espantajo *m*

scarf ['skɑrf] *n, pl* **scarves** ['skɑrvz] *or* **scarfs 1** MUFFLER : bufanda *f* **2** KERCHIEF : pañuelo *m*

scarlet ['skɑrlət] *n* : escarlata *f* — **scarlet** *adj*

scarlet fever *n* : escarlatina *f*

scary ['skɛri] *adj* **scarier; -est** : espantoso, pavoroso

scathing ['skeɪðɪŋ] *adj* : mordaz, cáustico

scatter ['skæt̬ər] *vt* : esparcir, desparramar — *vi* DISPERSE : dispersarse

scavenge ['skævəndʒ] *v* **-venged; -venging** *vt* : rescatar (de la basura), pepenar *CA, Mex* — *vi* : rebuscar, hurgar en la basura ⟨to scavenge for food : andar buscando comida⟩

scavenger ['skævəndʒər] *n* **1** : persona *f* que rebusca en las basuras; pepenador *m*, -dora *f CA, Mex* **2** : carroñero *m*, -ra *f* (animal)

scenario [sə'næriˌoː, -'nɑr-] *n, pl* **-ios 1** PLOT : argumento *m* (en teatro), guión *m* (en cine) **2** SITUATION : situación *f* hipotética ⟨in the worst-case scenario : en el peor de los casos⟩

scene ['siːn] *n* **1** : escena *f* (en una obra de teatro) **2** SCENERY : decorado *m* (en el teatro) **3** VIEW : escena *f* **4** LOCALE : escenario *m* **5** COMMOTION, FUSS : escándalo *m*, escena *f* ⟨to make a scene : armar un escándalo⟩

scenery ['siːnəri] *n, pl* **-eries 1** : decorado *m* (en el teatro) **2** LANDSCAPE : paisaje *m*

scenic ['siːnɪk] *adj* : pintoresco

scent¹ ['sɛnt] *vt* **1** SMELL : oler, olfatear **2** PERFUME : perfumar **3** SENSE : sentir, percibir

scent² *n* **1** ODOR : olor *m*, aroma *m* **2** : olfato *m* ⟨a dog with a keen scent : un perro con un buen olfato⟩ 3 PERFUME : perfume *m*

scented ['sɛntəd] *adj* : perfumado

scepter ['sɛptər] *n* : cetro *m*

sceptic ['skɛptɪk] → **skeptic**

schedule[1] ['skɛˌdʒuːl, -dʒəl, *esp Brit* 'ʃɛdˌjuːl] *vt* -**uled**; -**uling** : planear, programar

schedule[2] *n* 1 PLAN : programa *m*, plan *m* ⟨on schedule : según lo previsto⟩ ⟨behind schedule : atrasado, con retraso⟩ 2 TIMETABLE : horario *m*

scheme[1] ['skiːm] *vi* **schemed; scheming** : intrigar, conspirar

scheme[2] *n* 1 PLAN : plan *m*, proyecto *m* 2 PLOT, TRICK : intriga *f*, ardid *m* 3 FRAMEWORK : esquema *f* ⟨a color scheme : una combinación de colores⟩

schemer ['skiːmər] *n* : intrigante *mf*

schism ['sɪzəm, 'skɪ-] *n* : cisma *m*

schizophrenia [ˌskɪtsəˈfriːniə, ˌskɪzə-, -ˈfrɛ-] *n* : esquizofrenia *f*

schizophrenic [ˌskɪtsəˈfrɛnɪk, ˌskɪzə-] *n* : esquizofrénico *m*, -ca *f* — **schizophrenic** *adj*

scholar ['skɑlər] *n* 1 STUDENT : escolar *mf*; alumno *m*, -na *f* 2 EXPERT : especialista *mf*

scholarly ['skɑlərli] *adj* : erudito

scholarship ['skɑlərˌʃɪp] *n* 1 LEARNING : erudición *f* 2 GRANT : beca *f*

scholastic [skəˈlæstɪk] *adj* : académico

school[1] ['skuːl] *vt* : instruir, enseñar

school[2] *n* 1 : escuela *f*, colegio *m* (institución) 2 : estudiantes *mfpl* y profesores *mpl* (de una escuela) 3 : escuela *f* (en pintura, etc.) ⟨the Flemish school : la escuela flamenca⟩ 4 **school of fish** : banco *m*, cardumen *m*

schoolboy ['skuːlˌbɔɪ] *n* : escolar *m*, colegial *m*

schoolgirl ['skuːlˌgərl] *n* : escolar *f*, colegiala *f*

schoolhouse ['skuːlˌhaʊs] *n* : escuela *f*

schoolmate ['skuːlˌmeɪt] *n* : compañero *m*, -ra *f* de escuela

schoolroom ['skuːlˌruːm, -ˌrʊm] → **classroom**

schoolteacher ['skuːlˌtiːtʃər] *n* : maestro *m*, -tra *f*; profesor *m*, -sora *f*

schoolwork ['skuːlˌwərk] *n* : trabajo *m* escolar

schooner ['skuːnər] *n* : goleta *f*

science ['saɪənts] *n* : ciencia *f*

science fiction *n* : ciencia ficción *f*

scientific [ˌsaɪənˈtɪfɪk] *adj* : científico — **scientifically** [-fɪkli] *adv*

scientist ['saɪəntɪst] *n* : científico *m*, -ca *f*

scintillating ['sɪntəˌleɪtɪŋ] *adj* : chispeante, brillante

scissors ['sɪzərz] *npl* : tijeras *fpl*

sclerosis [skləˈroːsəs] *n, pl* -**roses** : esclerosis *f*

scoff ['skɑf] *vi* **to scoff at** : burlarse de, mofarse de

scold ['skoːld] *vt* : regañar, reprender, reñir

scoop[1] ['skuːp] *vt* 1 : sacar (con pala o cucharón) 2 **to scoop out** HOLLOW : vaciar, ahuecar

scoop[2] *n* : pala *f* (para harina, etc.), cucharón *m* (para helado, etc.)

scoot ['skuːt] *vi* : ir rápidamente ⟨she scooted around the corner : volvió la esquina a toda prisa⟩

scooter ['skuːtər] *n* : patineta *f*, monopatín *m*, patinete *m*

scope ['skoːp] *n* 1 RANGE : alcance *m*, ámbito *m*, extensión *f* 2 OPPORTUNITY : posibilidades *fpl*, libertad *f*

scorch ['skɔrtʃ] *vt* : chamuscar, quemar

score[1] ['skor] *v* **scored; scoring** *vt* 1 RECORD : anotar 2 MARK, SCRATCH : marcar, rayar 3 : marcar, meter (en deportes) 4 GAIN : ganar, apuntarse 5 GRADE : calificar (exámenes, etc.) 6 : instrumentar, orquestar (música) — *vi* 1 : marcar (en deportes) 2 : obtener una puntuación (en un examen)

score[2] *n, pl* **scores** 1 *or pl* **score** TWENTY : veintena *f* 2 LINE, SCRATCH : línea *f*, marca *f* 3 : resultado *m* (en deportes) ⟨what's the score? : ¿cómo va el marcador?⟩ 4 GRADE, POINTS : calificación *f* (en un examen), puntuación *f* (en un concurso) 5 ACCOUNT : cuenta *f* ⟨to settle a score : ajustar una cuenta⟩ ⟨on that score : a ese respecto⟩ 6 : partitura *f* (musical)

scorn[1] ['skɔrn] *vt* : despreciar, menospreciar, desdeñar

scorn[2] *n* : desprecio *m*, menosprecio *m*, desdén *m*

scornful ['skɔrnfəl] *adj* : desdeñoso, despreciativo — **scornfully** *adv*

Scorpio ['skɔrpiˌoː] *n* : Escorpio *mf*, Escorpión *mf*

scorpion ['skɔrpiən] *n* : alacrán *m*, escorpión *m*

Scot ['skɑt] *n* : escocés *m*, -cesa *f*

Scotch[1] ['skɑtʃ] *adj* → **Scottish**[1]

Scotch[2] *npl* **the Scotch** : los escoceses

scot–free ['skɑt'friː] *adj* **to get off scot–free** : salir impune, quedar sin castigo

Scots ['skɑts] *n* : escocés *m* (idioma)

Scottish[1] ['skɑtɪʃ] *adj* : escocés

Scottish[2] *n* → **Scots**

scoundrel ['skaʊndrəl] *n* : sinvergüenza *mf*; bellaco *m*, -ca *f*

scour ['skaʊər] *vt* 1 EXAMINE, SEARCH : registrar (un área), revisar (documentos, etc.) 2 SCRUB : fregar, restregar

scourge[1] ['skɔrdʒ] *vt* **scourged; scourging** : azotar

scourge[2] *n* : azote *m*

scout[1] ['skaʊt] *vi* 1 RECONNOITER : reconocer 2 **to scout around for** : explorar en busca de

scout[2] *n* 1 : explorador *m*, -dora *f* 2 *or* **talent scout** : cazatalentos *mf*

scow ['skaʊ] *n* : barcaza *f*, gabarra *f*

scowl[1] ['skaʊl] *vi* : fruncir el ceño

scowl[2] *n* : ceño *m* fruncido

scram ['skræm] *vi* **scrammed; scramming** : largarse

scramble¹ ['skræmbəl] *v* **-bled; -bling** *vi* **1** : trepar, gatear (con torpeza) ⟨he scrambled over the fence : se trepó a la cerca con dificultad⟩ **2** STRUGGLE : pelearse (por) ⟨they scrambled for seats : se pelearon por los asientos⟩ — *vt* **1** JUMBLE : mezclar **2 to scramble eggs** : hacer huevos revueltos

scramble² *n* : rebatiña *f*, pelea *f*

scrap¹ ['skræp] *v* **scrapped; scrapping** *vt* DISCARD : desechar — *vi* FIGHT : pelearse

scrap² *n* **1** FRAGMENT : pedazo *m*, trozo *m* **2** FIGHT : pelea *f* **3** *or* **scrap metal** : chatarra *f* **4 scraps** *npl* LEFTOVERS : restos *mpl*, sobras *fpl*

scrapbook ['skræp,bʊk] *n* : álbum *m* de recortes

scrape¹ ['skreɪp] *v* **scraped; scraping** *vt* **1** GRAZE, SCRATCH : rozar, rascar ⟨to scrape one's knee : rasparse la rodilla⟩ **2** CLEAN : raspar ⟨to scrape carrots : raspar zanahorias⟩ **3 to scrape off** : raspar (pintura, etc.) **4 to scrape up** *or* **to scrape together** : juntar, reunir poco a poco — *vi* **1** RUB : rozar **2 to scrape by** : arreglárselas, ir tirando

scrape² *n* **1** SCRAPING : raspadura *f* **2** SCRATCH : rasguño *m* **3** PREDICAMENT : apuro *m*, aprieto *m*

scratch¹ ['skrætʃ] *vt* **1** : arañar, rasguñar ⟨to scratch an itch : rascarse⟩ **2** MARK : rayar, marcar **3 to scratch out** : tachar

scratch² *n* **1** : rasguño *m*, arañazo *m* (en la piel), rayón *m* (en un mueble, etc.) **2** : sonido *m* rasposo ⟨I heard a scratch at the door : oí como que raspaban a la puerta⟩

scratchy ['skrætʃi] *adj* **scratchier; -est** : áspero, que pica ⟨a scratchy sweater : un suéter que pica⟩

scrawl¹ ['skrɔl] *v* : garabatear

scrawl² *n* : garabato *m*

scrawny ['skrɔni] *adj* **scrawnier; -est** : flaco, escuálido

scream¹ ['skri:m] *vi* : chillar, gritar

scream² *n* : chillido *m*, grito *m*

screech¹ ['skri:tʃ] *vi* : chillar (dícese de las personas o de los animales), chirriar (dícese de los frenos, etc.)

screech² *n* **1** : chillido *m*, grito *m* (de una persona o un animal) **2** : chirrido *m* (de frenos, etc.)

screen¹ ['skri:n] *vt* **1** SHIELD : proteger **2** CONCEAL : tapar, ocultar **3** EXAMINE : someter a una revisión, hacerle un chequeo (a un paciente) **4** SIEVE : cribar

screen² *n* **1** PARTITION : biombo *m*, pantalla *f* **2** SIEVE : criba *f* **3** : pantalla *f* (de un televisor, una computadora, etc.) **4** MOVIES : cine *m* **5** *or* **window screen** : ventana *f* de tela metálica

screenplay ['skri:n,pleɪ] *n* SCRIPT : guión *m*

screw¹ ['skru:] *vt* : atornillar — *vi* **1 to screw in** : atornillarse **2 to screw up** *fam* : meter la pata

screw² *n* **1** : tornillo *m* (para fijar algo) **2** TWIST : vuelta *f* **3** PROPELLER : hélice *f*

screwdriver ['skru:,draɪvər] *n* : destornillador *m*, desarmador *m* *Mex*

scribble¹ ['skrɪbəl] *v* **-bled; -bling** : garabatear

scribble² *n* : garabato *m*

scribe ['skraɪb] *n* : escriba *m*

scrimmage ['skrɪmɪdʒ] *n* : escaramuza *f*

scrimp ['skrɪmp] *vi* **1 to scrimp on** : escatimar **2 to scrimp and save** : hacer economías

script ['skrɪpt] *n* **1** HANDWRITING : letra *f*, escritura *f* **2** : guión *m* (de una película, etc.)

scriptural ['skrɪptʃərəl] *adj* : bíblico

scripture ['skrɪptʃər] *n* **1** : escritos *mpl* sagrados (de una religión) **2 the Scriptures** *npl* : las Sagradas Escrituras

scriptwriter ['skrɪpt,raɪtər] *n* : guionista *mf*, libretista *mf*

scroll ['skro:l] *n* **1** : rollo *m* (de pergamino, etc.) **2** : voluta *f* (adorno en arquitectura)

scrotum ['skro:təm] *n, pl* **scrota** [-tə] *or* **scrotums** : escroto *m*

scrounge ['skraʊndʒ] *v* **scrounged; scrounging** *vt* **1** BUM : gorrear *fam*, sablear *fam* (dinero) **2 to scrounge around for** : buscar, andar a la busca de — *vi* **to scrounge off someone** : vivir a costa de alguien

scrub¹ ['skrʌb] *vt* **scrubbed; scrubbing** : restregar, fregar

scrub² *n* **1** THICKET, UNDERBRUSH : maleza *f*, matorral *m*, matorrales *mpl* **2** SCRUBBING : fregado *m*, restregadura *f*

scrubby ['skrʌbi] *adj* **-bier; -est** **1** STUNTED : achaparrado **2** : cubierto de maleza

scruff ['skrʌf] *n* **by the scruff of the neck** : por el cogote, por el pescuezo

scrumptious ['skrʌmpʃəs] *adj* : delicioso, muy rico

scruple ['skru:pəl] *n* : escrúpulo *m*

scrupulous ['skru:pjələs] *adj* : escrupuloso — **scrupulously** *adv*

scrutinize ['skru:tən,aɪz] *vt* **-nized; -nizing** : escrutar, escudriñar

scrutiny ['skru:təni] *n, pl* **-nies** : escrutinio *m*, inspección *f*

scuba ['sku:bə] *n* **1** *or* **scuba gear** : equipo *m* de submarinismo **2 scuba diver** : submarinista *mf* **3 scuba diving** : submarinismo *m*

scuff ['skʌf] *vt* : rayar, raspar ⟨to scuff one's feet : arrastrar los pies⟩

scuffle¹ ['skʌfəl] *vi* **-fled; -fling** **1** TUSSLE : pelearse **2** SHUFFLE : caminar arrastrando los pies

scuffle² *n* **1** TUSSLE : refriega *f*, pelea *f* **2** SHUFFLE : arrastre *m* de los pies

scull¹ ['skʌl] *vi* : remar (con espadilla)

scull² *n* OAR : espadilla *f*
sculpt ['skʌlpt] *v* : esculpir
sculptor ['skʌlptər] *n* : escultor *m*, -tora *f*
scuptural ['skʌlptʃərəl] *adj* : escultórico
sculpture¹ ['skʌlptʃər] *vt* **-tured; -turing** : esculpir
sculpture² *n* : escultura *f*
scum ['skʌm] *n* **1** FROTH : espuma *f*, nata *f* **2** : verdín *m* (encima de un líquido)
scurrilous ['skərələs] *adj* : difamatorio, calumnioso, injurioso
scurry ['skəri] *vi* **-ried; -rying** : corretear
scurvy ['skərvi] *n* : escorbuto *m*
scuttle¹ ['skʌṭəl] *v* **-tled; -tling** *vt* : hundir (un barco) — *vi* SCAMPER : corretear
scuttle² *n* : cubo *m* (para carbón)
scythe ['saɪð] *n* : guadaña *f*
sea¹ ['si:] *adj* : del mar
sea² *n* **1** : mar *mf* ⟨the Black Sea : el Mar Negro⟩ ⟨on the high seas : en alta mar⟩ ⟨heavy seas : mar gruesa, mar agitada⟩ **2** MASS : mar *m*, multitud *f* ⟨a sea of faces : un mar de rostros⟩
seabird ['si:ˌbərd] *n* : ave *f* marina
seaboard ['si:ˌbord] *n* : litoral *m*
seacoast ['si:ˌko:st] *n* : costa *f*, litoral *m*
seafarer ['si:ˌfærər] *n* : marinero *m*
seafaring¹ ['si:ˌfærɪŋ] *adj* : marinero
seafaring² *n* : navegación *f*
seafood ['si:ˌfu:d] *n* : mariscos *mpl*
seagull ['si:ˌgʌl] *n* : gaviota *f*
sea horse ['si:ˌhɔrs] *n* : hipocampo *m*, caballito *m* de mar
seal¹ ['si:l] *vt* **1** CLOSE : sellar, cerrar ⟨to seal a letter : cerrar una carta⟩ ⟨to seal an agreement : sellar un acuerdo⟩ **2 to seal up** : tapar, rellenar (una grieta, etc.)
seal² *n* **1** : foca *f* (animal) **2** : sello *m* ⟨seal of approval : sello de aprobación⟩ **3** CLOSURE : cierre *m*, precinto *m*
sea level *n* : nivel *m* del mar
sea lion *n* : león *m* marino
sealskin ['si:lˌskɪn] *n* : piel *f* de foca
seam¹ ['si:m] *vt* **1** STITCH : unir con costuras **2** MARK : marcar
seam² *n* **1** STITCHING : costura *f* **2** LODE, VEIN : veta *f*, filón *m*
seaman ['si:mən] *n*, *pl* **-men** [-mən, -ˌmɛn] **1** SAILOR : marinero *m* **2** : marino *m* (en la armada)
seamless ['si:mləs] *adj* **1** : sin costuras, de una pieza **2** : perfecto ⟨a seamless transition : una transición fluida⟩
seamstress ['si:mpstrəs] *n* : costurera *f*
seamy ['si:mi] *adj* **seamier; -est** : sórdido
séance ['seɪˌɑnts] *n* : sesión *f* de espiritismo
seaplane ['si:ˌpleɪn] *n* : hidroavión *m*
seaport ['si:ˌport] *n* : puerto *m* marítimo
sear ['sɪr] *vt* **1** PARCH, WITHER : secar, resecar **2** SCORCH : chamuscar, quemar

search¹ ['sərtʃ] *vt* : registrar (un edificio, un área), cachear (a una persona), buscar en — *vi* **to search for** : buscar
search² *n* : búsqueda *f*, registro *m* (de un edificio, etc.), cacheo *m* (de una persona)
searchlight ['sərtʃˌlaɪt] *n* : reflector *m*
seashell ['si:ˌʃɛl] *n* : concha *f* (marina)
seashore ['si:ˌʃor] *n* : orilla *f* del mar
seasick ['si:ˌsɪk] *adj* : mareado ⟨to get seasick : marearse⟩
seasickness ['si:ˌsɪknəs] *n* : mareo *m*
seaside → **seacoast**
season¹ ['si:zən] *vt* **1** FLAVOR, SPICE : sazonar, condimentar **2** CURE : curar, secar ⟨seasoned wood : madera seca⟩ ⟨a seasoned veteran : un veterano avezado⟩
season² *n* **1** : estación *f* (del año) **2** : temporada *f* (en deportes, etc.) ⟨baseball season : temporada de beisbol⟩
seasonable ['si:zənəbəl] *adj* **1** : propio de la estación (dícese del tiempo, de las temperaturas, etc.) **2** TIMELY : oportuno
seasonal ['si:zənəl] *adj* : estacional — **seasonally** *adv*
seasoning ['si:zənɪŋ] *n* : condimento *m*, sazón *f*
seat¹ ['si:t] *vt* **1** SIT : sentar ⟨please be seated : siéntense, por favor⟩ **2** HOLD : tener cabida para ⟨the stadium seats 40,000 : el estadio tiene 40,000 asientos⟩
seat² *n* **1** : asiento *m*, plaza *f* (en un vehículo) ⟨take a seat : tome asiento⟩ **2** BOTTOM : fondillos *mpl* (de la ropa), trasero *m* (del cuerpo) **3** : sede *f* (de un gobierno, etc.)
seat belt *n* : cinturón *m* de seguridad
sea urchin *n* : erizo *m* de mar
seawall ['si:ˌwal] *n* : rompeolas *m*, dique *m* marítimo
seawater ['si:ˌwɔtər, -ˌwɑ-] *n* : agua *f* de mar
seaweed ['si:ˌwi:d] *n* : alga *f* marina
seaworthy ['si:ˌwərði] *adj* : en condiciones de navegar
secede [sɪ'si:d] *vi* **-ceded; -ceding** : separarse (de una nación, etc.)
seclude [sɪ'klu:d] *vt* **-cluded; -cluding** : aislar
seclusion [sɪ'klu:ʒən] *n* : aislamiento *m*
second¹ ['sɛkənd] *vt* : secundar, apoyar (una moción)
second² or secondly ['sɛkəndli] *adv* : en segundo lugar
second³ *adj* : segundo
second⁴ *n* **1** : segundo *m*, -da *f* (en una serie) **2** : segundo *m*, ayudante *m* (en deportes) **3** MOMENT : segundo *m*, momento *m*
secondary ['sɛkənˌdri] *adj* : secundario
secondhand ['sɛkəndˈhænd] *adj* : de segunda mano
second lieutenant *n* : alférez *mf*, subteniente *mf*
second–rate ['sɛkəndˈreɪt] *adj* : mediocre, de segunda categoría

secrecy ['si:krəsi] *n, pl* **-cies** : secreto *m*
secret¹ ['si:krət] *adj* : secreto — **secretly** *adv*
secret² *n* : secreto *m*
secretarial [ˌsɛkrə'triəl] *adj* : de secretario, de oficina
secretariat [ˌsɛkrə'triət] *n* : secretaría *f*, secretariado *m*
secretary ['sɛkrəˌtri] *n, pl* **-taries** 1 : secretario *m*, -ria *f* (en una oficina, etc.) 2 : ministro *m*, -tra *f*; secretario *m*, -ria *f* ⟨Secretary of State : Secretario de Estado⟩
secrete [sɪ'kri:t] *vt* **-creted; -creting** 1 : secretar, segregar (en fisiología) 2 HIDE : ocultar
secretion [sɪ'kri:ʃən] *n* : secreción *f*
secretive ['si:krətɪv, sɪ'kri:tɪv] *adj* : reservado, callado, secreto
sect ['sɛkt] *n* : secta *f*
sectarian [sɛk'triən] *adj* : sectario
section ['sɛkʃən] *n* : sección *f*, parte *f* (de un mueble, etc.), sector *m* (de la población), barrio *m* (de una ciudad)
sectional ['sɛkʃənəl] *adj* 1 : en sección, en corte ⟨a sectional diagram : un gráfico en corte⟩ 2 FACTIONAL : de grupo, entre facciones 3 : modular ⟨sectional furniture : muebles modulares⟩
sector ['sɛktər] *n* : sector *m*
secular ['sɛkjələr] *adj* 1 : secular, laico ⟨secular life : la vida secular⟩ 2 : seglar (dícese de los sacerdotes, etc.)
secure¹ [sɪ'kjʊr] *vt* **-cured; -curing** 1 FASTEN : asegurar (una puerta, etc.), sujetar 2 GET : conseguir
secure² *adj* **-curer; -est** : seguro — **securely** *adv*
security [sɪ'kjʊrəti] *n, pl* **-ties** 1 SAFETY : seguridad *f* 2 GUARANTEE : garantía *f* 3 **securities** *npl* : valores *mpl*
sedan [sɪ'dæn] *n* 1 *or* **sedan chair** : silla *f* de manos 2 : sedán *m* (automóvil)
sedate¹ [sɪ'deɪt] *vt* **-dated; -dating** : sedar
sedate² *adj* : sosegado — **sedately** *adv*
sedation [sɪ'deɪʃən] *n* : sedación *f*
sedative¹ ['sɛdətɪv] *adj* : sedante
sedative² *n* : sedante *m*, calmante *m*
sedentary ['sɛdənˌtɛri] *adj* : sedentario
sedge ['sɛdʒ] *n* : juncia *f*
sediment ['sɛdəmənt] *n* : sedimento *m* (geológico), poso *m* (en un líquido)
sedimentary [ˌsɛdə'mɛntəri] *adj* : sedimentario
sedition [sɪ'dɪʃən] *n* : sedición *f*
seditious [sɪ'dɪʃəs] *adj* : sedicioso
seduce [sɪ'du:s, -'dju:s] *vt* **-duced; -ducing** : seducir
seduction [sɪ'dʌkʃən] *n* : seducción *f*
seductive [sɪ'dʌktɪv] *adj* : seductor, seductivo
see¹ ['si:] *v* **saw** ['sɔ]; **seen** ['si:n]; **seeing** *vt* 1 : ver ⟨I saw a dog : vi un perro⟩ ⟨see you later! : ¡hasta luego!⟩ 2 EXPERIENCE : ver, conocer 3 UNDERSTAND : ver, entender 4 ENSURE : asegurarse ⟨see that it's correct : asegúrese

de que sea correcto⟩ 5 ACCOMPANY : acompañar 6 **to see off** : despedir, despedirse de — *vi* 1 : ver ⟨seeing is believing : ver para creer⟩ 2 UNDERSTAND : entender, ver ⟨now I see! : ¡ya entiendo!⟩ 3 CONSIDER : ver ⟨let's see : vamos a ver⟩ 4 **to see to** : ocuparse de
see² *n* : sede *f* ⟨the Holy See : la Santa Sede⟩
seed¹ ['si:d] *vt* 1 SOW : sembrar 2 : despepitar, quitarle las semillas a
seed² *n, pl* **seed** *or* **seeds** 1 : semilla *f*, pepita *f* (de una fruta) 2 SOURCE : germen *m*, semilla *f*
seedless ['si:dləs] *adj* : sin semillas
seedling ['si:dlɪŋ] *n* : plantón *m*
seedpod ['si:dˌpɑd] → **pod**
seedy ['si:di] *adj* **seedier; -est** 1 : lleno de semillas 2 SHABBY : raído (dícese de la ropa) 3 RUN-DOWN : ruinoso (dícese de los edificios, etc.), sórdido
seek ['si:k] *v* **sought** ['sɔt]; **seeking** *vt* 1 : buscar ⟨to seek an answer : buscar una solución⟩ 2 REQUEST : solicitar, pedir 3 **to seek to** : tratar de, intentar de — *vi* SEARCH : buscar
seem ['si:m] *vi* : parecer
seeming ['si:mɪŋ] *adj* : aparente, ostensible
seemingly ['si:mɪŋli] *adv* : aparentemente, según parece
seemly ['si:mli] *adj* **seemlier; -est** : apropiado, decoroso
seep ['si:p] *vi* : filtrarse
seer ['si:ər] *n* : vidente *mf*, clarividente *mf*
seesaw¹ ['si:ˌsɔ] *vi* 1 : jugar en un subibaja 2 VACILLATE : vacilar, oscilar
seesaw² *n* : balancín *m*, subibaja *m*
seethe ['si:ð] *vi* **seethed; seething** 1 : bullir, hervir 2 **to seethe with anger** : rabiar, estar furioso
segment ['sɛgmənt] *n* : segmento *m*
segmented ['sɛgˌmɛntəd, sɛg'mɛn-] *adj* : segmentado
segregate ['sɛgrɪˌgeɪt] *vt* **-gated; -gating** : segregar
segregation [ˌsɛgrɪ'geɪʃən] *n* : segregación *f*
seismic ['saɪzmɪk, 'saɪs-] *adj* : sísmico
seize ['si:z] *v* **seized; seizing** *vt* 1 CAPTURE : capturar, tomar, apoderarse de 2 ARREST : detener 3 CLUTCH, GRAB : agarrar, coger, aprovechar (una oportunidad) 4 **to be seized with** : estar sobrecogido por — *vi* **or to seize up** : agarrotarse
seizure ['si:ʒər] *n* 1 CAPTURE : toma *f*, captura *f* 2 ARREST : detención *f* 3 : ataque *m* ⟨an epileptic seizure : un ataque epiléptico⟩
seldom ['sɛldəm] *adv* : pocas veces, rara vez, casi nunca
select¹ [sə'lɛkt] *vt* : escoger, elegir, seleccionar (a un candidato, etc.)
select² *adj* : selecto
selection [sə'lɛkʃən] *n* : selección *f*, elección *f*

selective [sə'lɛktɪv] *adj* : selectivo
selenium [sə'li:niəm] *n* : selenio *m*
self ['sɛlf] *n, pl* **selves** ['sɛlvz] **1** : ser *m*, persona *f* ⟨the self : el yo⟩ ⟨with his whole self : con todo su ser⟩ ⟨her own self : su propia persona⟩ **2** SIDE : lado (de la personalidad) ⟨his better self : su lado bueno⟩
self–addressed [ˌsɛlfə'drst] *adj* : con la dirección del remitente ⟨include a self-addressed envelope : incluya un sobre con su nombre y dirección⟩
self–appointed [ˌsɛlfə'pɔɪntəd] *adj* : autoproclamado, autonombrado
self–assurance [ˌsɛlfə'ʃʊrənts] *n* : seguridad *f* en sí mismo
self–assured [ˌsɛlfə'ʃʊrd] *adj* : seguro de sí mismo
self–centered [ˌsɛlf'sɛntərd] *adj* : egocéntrico
self–confidence [ˌsɛlf'kɑnfədənts] *n* : confianza *f* en sí mismo
self–confident [ˌsɛlf'kɑnfədənt] *adj* : seguro de sí mismo
self–conscious [ˌsɛlf'kɑntʃəs] *adj* : cohibido, tímido
self–consciously [ˌsɛlf'kɑntʃəsli] *adv* : de manera cohibida
self–consciousness [ˌsɛlf'kɑntʃəsnəs] *n* : vergüenza *f*, timidez *f*
self–contained [ˌsɛlfkən'teɪnd] *adj* **1** INDEPENDENT : independiente **2** RESERVED : reservado
self–control [ˌsɛlfkən'tro:l] *n* : autocontrol *m*, control *m* de sí mismo
self–defense [ˌsɛlfdɪ'fɛnts] *n* : defensa *f* propia, defensa *f* personal ⟨to act in self-defense : actuar en defensa propia⟩ ⟨self-defense class : clase de defensa personal⟩
self–denial [ˌsɛlfdɪ'naɪəl] *n* : abnegación *f*
self–destructive [ˌsɛlfdɪ'strʌktɪv] *adj* : autodestructivo
self–determination [ˌsɛlfdɪˌtərmə'neɪʃən] *n* : autodeterminación *f*
self–discipline [ˌsɛlf'dɪsəplən] *n* : autodisciplina *f*
self–employed [ˌsɛlfɪm'plɔɪd] *adj* : que trabaja por cuenta propia, autónomo
self–esteem [ˌsɛlfɪ'sti:m] *n* : autoestima *f*, amor *m* propio
self–evident [ˌsɛlf'ɛvədənt] *adj* : evidente, manifiesto
self–explanatory [ˌsɛlfɪk'splænəˌtori] *adj* : fácil de entender, evidente
self–expression [ˌsɛlfɪk'sprʃən] *n* : expresión *f* personal
self–government [ˌsɛlf'gʌvərmənt, -vərn-] *n* : autogobierno *m*
self–help [ˌsɛlf'hɛlp] *n* : autoayuda *f*
self–important [ˌsɛlfɪm'pɔrtənt] *adj* **1** VAIN : vanidoso, presumido **2** ARROGANT : arrogante
self–indulgent [ˌsɛlfɪn'dʌldʒənt] *adj* : que se permite excesos
self–inflicted [ˌsɛlfɪn'flɪktəd] *adj* : autoinfligido

self–interest [ˌsɛlf'ɪntrəst, -təˌrst] *n* : interés *m* personal
selfish ['sɛlfɪʃ] *adj* : egoísta
selfishly ['sɛlfɪʃli] *adv* : de manera egoísta
selfishness ['sɛlfɪʃnəs] *n* : egoísmo *m*
selfless ['sɛlfləs] *adj* UNSELFISH : desinteresado
self–made [ˌsɛlf'meɪd] *adj* : próspero gracias a sus propios esfuerzos
self–pity [ˌsɛlf'pɪti] *n, pl* **-ties** : autocompasión *f*
self–portrait [ˌsɛlf'pɔrtrət] *n* : autorretrato *m*
self–propelled [ˌsɛlfpro'pɛld] *adj* : autopropulsado
self–reliance [ˌsɛlfri'laɪənts] *n* : independencia *f*, autosuficiencia *f*
self–respect [ˌsɛlfri'spɛkt] *n* : autoestima *f*, amor *m* propio
self–restraint [ˌsɛlfri'streɪnt] *n* : autocontrol *m*, moderación *f*
self–righteous [ˌsɛlf'raɪtʃəs] *adj* : santurrón, moralista
self–sacrifice [ˌsɛlf'sækrəˌfaɪs] *n* : abnegación *f*
selfsame ['sɛlfˌseɪm] *adj* : mismo
self–service [ˌsɛlf'sərvɪs] *adj* **1** : de autoservicio **2 self-service restaurant** : autoservicio *m*
self–sufficiency [ˌsɛlfsə'fɪʃəntsi] *n* : autosuficiencia *f*
self–sufficient [ˌsɛlfsə'fɪʃənt] *adj* : autosuficiente
self–taught [ˌsɛlf'tɔt] *adj* : autodidacta
sell ['sɛl] *v* **sold** ['so:ld]; **selling** *vt* : vender — *vi* : venderse
seller ['sɛlər] *n* : vendedor *m*, -dora *f*
selves → **self**
semantic [sɪ'mæntɪk] *adj* : semántico
semantics [sɪ'mæntɪks] *ns & pl* : semántica *f*
semaphore ['sɛməˌfor] *n* : semáforo *m*
semblance ['sɛmblənts] *n* : apariencia *f*
semen ['si:mən] *n* : semen *m*
semester [sə'mɛstər] *n* : semestre *m*
semicolon ['sɛmiˌko:lən, 'sɛˌmaɪ-] *n* : punto y coma *m*
semiconductor ['sɛmikənˌdʌktər, 'sɛˌmaɪ-] *n* : semiconductor *m*
semifinal ['sɛmiˌfaɪnəl, 'sɛˌmaɪ-] *n* : semifinal *f*
seminar ['sɛməˌnar] *n* : seminario *m*
seminary ['sɛməˌnɛri] *n, pl* **-naries** : seminario *m*
Semitic [sə'mɪtɪk] *adj* : semita
senate ['sɛnət] *n* : senado *m*
senator ['sɛnətər] *n* : senador *m*, -dora *f*
send ['sɛnd] *vt* **sent** ['sɛnt]; **sending** **1** : mandar, enviar ⟨to send a letter : mandar una carta⟩ ⟨to send word : avisar, mandar decir⟩ **2** PROPEL : mandar, lanzar ⟨he sent it into left field : lo mandó al jardín izquierdo⟩ ⟨to send up dust : alzar polvo⟩ **3 to send into a rage** : poner furioso
sender ['sɛndər] *n* : remitente *mf* (de una carta, etc.)

Senegalese [ˌsɛnəgəˈliːz, -ˈliːs] *n* : sene-galés *m*, -lesa *f* — **Senegalese** *adj*
senile [ˈsiːˌnaɪl] *adj* : senil
senility [sɪˈnɪləti] *n* : senilidad *f*
senior[1] [ˈsiːnjər] *adj* **1** ELDER : mayor ⟨John Doe, Senior : John Doe, padre⟩ **2** : superior (en rango), más antiguo (en años de servicio) ⟨a senior official : un alto oficial⟩
senior[2] *n* **1** : superior *m* (en rango) **2 to be someone's senior** : ser mayor que alguien ⟨she's two years my senior : me lleva dos años⟩
senior citizen *n* : persona *f* de la tercera edad
seniority [ˌsiːˈnjɔrəti] *n* : antigüedad *f* (en años de servicio)
sensation [sɛnˈseɪʃən] *n* : sensación *f*
sensational [sɛnˈseɪʃənəl] *adj* : que causa sensación ⟨sensational stories : historias sensacionalistas⟩
sense[1] [ˈsɛnts] *vt* **sensed; sensing** : sen-tir ⟨he sensed danger : se dio cuenta del peligro⟩
sense[2] *n* **1** MEANING : sentido *m*, sig-nificado *m* **2** : sentido *m* ⟨the sense of smell : el sentido del olfato⟩ **3 to make sense** : tener sentido
senseless [ˈsɛntsləs] *adj* **1** MEANING-LESS : sin sentido, sin razón **2** UN-CONSCIOUS : inconsciente
senselessly [ˈsɛntsləsli] *adv* : sin senti-do
sensibility [ˌsɛntsəˈbɪləti] *n*, *pl* **-ties** : sen-sibilidad *f*
sensible [ˈsɛntsəbəl] *adj* **1** PERCEPTIBLE : sensible, perceptible **2** AWARE : con-sciente **3** REASONABLE : sensato ⟨a sensible man : un hombre sensato⟩ ⟨sensible shoes : zapatos prácticos⟩ — **sensibly** [-bli] *adv*
sensibleness [ˈsɛntsəbəlnəs] *n* : sen-satez *f*, solidez *f*
sensitive [ˈsɛntsətɪv] *adj* **1** : sensible, delicado ⟨sensitive skin : piel sensible⟩ **2** IMPRESSIONABLE : sensible, impre-sionable **3** TOUCHY : susceptible
sensitiveness [ˈsɛntsətɪvnəs] → **sensi-tivity**
sensitivity [ˌsɛntsəˈtɪvəti] *n*, *pl* **-ties** : sen-sibilidad *f*
sensitize [ˈsɛntsəˌtaɪz] *vt* **-tized; -tizing** : sensibilizar
sensor [ˈsɛnˌsor, ˈsɛntsər] *n* : sensor *m*
sensory [ˈsɛntsəri] *adj* : sensorial
sensual [ˈsɛnʧuəl] *adj* : sensual — **sen-sually** *adv*
sensuality [ˌsɛnʧəˈwæləti] *n*, *pl* **-ties** : sensualidad *f*
sensuous [ˈsɛnʧuəs] *adj* : sensual
sent → **send**
sentence[1] [ˈsɛntənts, -ənz] *vt* **-tenced; -tencing** : sentenciar
sentence[2] *n* **1** JUDGMENT : sentencia *f* **2** : oración *f*, frase *f* (en gramática)
sentiment [ˈsɛntəmənt] *n* **1** BELIEF : opinión *f* **2** FEELING : sentimiento *m* **3** → **sentimentality**

sentimental [ˌsɛntəˈmɛntəl] *adj* : senti-mental
sentimentality [ˌsɛntəˌmɛnˈtæləti] *n*, *pl* **-ties** : sentimentalismo *m*, sensiblería *f*
sentinel [ˈsɛntənəl] *n* : centinela *mf*, guardia *mf*
sentry [ˈsɛntri] *n*, *pl* **-tries** : centinela *mf*
sepal [ˈsiːpəl, ˈsɛ-] *n* : sépalo *m*
separable [ˈsɛpərəbəl] *adj* : separable
separate[1] [ˈsɛpəˌreɪt] *v* **-rated; -rating** *vt* **1** DETACH, SEVER : separar **2** DISTIN-GUISH : diferenciar, distinguir — *vi* PART : separarse
separate[2] [ˈsɛprət, ˈsɛpə-] *adj* **1** INDI-VIDUAL : separado, aparte ⟨a separate state : un estado separado⟩ ⟨in a sepa-rate envelope : en un sobre aparte⟩ **2** DISTINCT : distinto
separately [ˈsɛprətli, ˈsɛpə-] *adv* : por separado, separadamente, aparte
separation [ˌsɛpəˈreɪʃən] *n* : separación *f*
sepia [ˈsiːpiə] *n* : color *m* sepia
September [sɛpˈtɛmbər] *n* : septiembre *m*, setiembre *m*
septic [ˈsɛptɪk] *adj* : séptico ⟨septic tank : fosa séptica⟩
sepulchre [ˈsɛpəlkər] *n* : sepulcro *m*
sequel [ˈsiːkwəl] *n* **1** CONSEQUENCE : secuela *f*, consecuencia *f* **2** : contin-uación *f* (de una película, etc.)
sequence [ˈsiːkwənts] *n* **1** SERIES : se-rie *f*, sucesión *f*, secuencia *f* (matemáti-ca o musical) **2** ORDER : orden *m*
sequester [sɪˈkwɛstər] *vt* : aislar
sequin [ˈsiːkwən] *n* : lentejuela *f*
sequoia [sɪˈkwɔɪə] *n* : secoya *f*, secuoya *f*
sera → **serum**
Serb [ˈsərb] *or* **Serbian** [ˈsərbiən] *n* **1** : serbio *m*, -bia *f* **2** : serbio *m* (idioma) — **Serb** *or* **Serbian** *adj*
Serbo–Croatian [ˌsɔrbokroˈeɪʃən] *n* : serbocroata *m* (idioma) — **Serbo–Croatian** *adj*
serenade[1] [ˌsɛrəˈneɪd] *vt* **-naded; -nading** : darle una serenata (a alguien)
serenade[2] *n* : serenata *f*
serene [səˈriːn] *adj* : sereno — **serene-ly** *adv*
serenity [səˈrɛnəti] *n* : serenidad *f*
serf [ˈsərf] *n* : siervo *m*, -va *f*
serge [ˈsɔrʤ] *n* : sarga *f*
sergeant [ˈsɑrʤənt] *n* : sargento *mf*
serial[1] [ˈsɪriəl] *adj* : seriado
serial[2] *n* : serie *f*, serial *m* (de radio o televisión), publicación *f* por entregas
serially [ˈsɪriəli] *adv* : en serie
series [ˈsɪrˌiːz] *n*, *pl* **series** : serie *f*, suce-sión *f*
serious [ˈsɪriəs] *adj* **1** SOBER : serio **2** DEDICATED, EARNEST : serio, dedica-do ⟨to be serious about something : tomar algo en serio⟩ **3** GRAVE : serio, grave ⟨serious problems : problemas graves⟩
seriously [ˈsɪriəsli] *adv* **1** EARNESTLY : seriamente, con seriedad, en serio **2** SEVERELY : gravemente

seriousness ['sɪriəsnəs] *n* : seriedad *f*, gravedad *f*

sermon ['sərmən] *n* : sermón *m*

serpent ['sərpənt] *n* : serpiente *f*

serrated [sə'reɪt̬əd, 'sɛr,eɪt̬əd] *adj* : dentado, serrado

serum ['sɪrəm] *n, pl* **serums** *or* **sera** ['sɪrə] : suero *m*

servant ['sərvənt] *n* : criado *m*, -da *f*; sirviente *m*, -ta *f*

serve ['sərv] *v* **served; serving** *vi* 1 : servir ⟨to serve in the navy : servir en la armada⟩ ⟨to serve on a jury : ser miembro de un jurado⟩ 2 DO, FUNCTION : servir ⟨to serve as : servir de, servir como⟩ 3 : sacar (en deportes) — *vt* 1 : servir ⟨to serve God : servir a Dios⟩ 2 HELP : servir ⟨it serves no purpose : no sirve para nada⟩ 3 : servir (comida o bebida) ⟨dinner is served : la cena está servida⟩ 4 SUPPLY : abastecer 5 CARRY OUT : cumplir, hacer ⟨to serve time : servir una pena⟩ 6 **to serve a summons** : entregar una citación

server ['sərvər] *n* 1 : camarero *m*, -ra *f*; mesero *m*, -ra *f* (en un restaurante) 2 *or* **serving dish** : fuente *f* (para servir comida) 3 : servidor *m* (en informática)

service[1] ['sərvəs] *vt* **-viced; -vicing** 1 MAINTAIN : darle mantenimiento a (una máquina), revisar 2 REPAIR : arreglar, reparar

service[2] *n* 1 HELP, USE : servicio *m* ⟨to do someone a service : hacerle un servicio a alguien⟩ ⟨at your service : a sus órdenes⟩ ⟨to be out of service : no funcionar⟩ 2 CEREMONY : oficio *m* (religioso) 3 DEPARTMENT, SYSTEM : servicio *m* ⟨social services : servicios sociales⟩ ⟨train service : servicio de trenes⟩ 4 SET : juego *m*, servicio *m* ⟨tea service : juego de té⟩ 5 MAINTENANCE : mantenimiento *m*, revisión *f*, servicio *m* 6 : saque *m* (en deportes) 7 **armed services** : fuerzas *fpl* armadas

serviceable ['sərvəsəbəl] *adj* 1 USEFUL : útil 2 DURABLE : duradero

serviceman ['sərvəs,mæn, -mən] *n, pl* **-men** [-mən, -,mɛn] : militar *m*

service station → **gas station**

servicewoman ['sərvəs,wυmən] *n, pl* **-women** [-,wɪmən] : militar *f*

servile ['sərvəl, -,vaɪl] *adj* : servil

serving ['sərvɪŋ] *n* HELPING : porción *f*, ración *f*

servitude ['sərvə,tu:d, -,tju:d] *n* : servidumbre *f*

sesame ['sɛsəmi] *n* : ajonjolí *m*, sésamo *m*

session ['sɛʃən] *n* : sesión *f*

set[1] ['sɛt] *v* **set; setting** *vt* 1 SEAT : sentar 2 *or* **set down** PLACE : poner, colocar 3 ARRANGE : fijar, establecer ⟨to set the date : poner la fecha⟩ ⟨he set the agenda : estableció la agenda⟩ 4 ADJUST : poner (un reloj, etc.) 5 (*indicating the causing of a certain condition*) ⟨to set fire to : prenderle fuego a⟩ ⟨she set it free : lo soltó⟩ 6 MAKE, START : poner, hacer ⟨I set them working : los puse a trabajar⟩ — *vi* 1 SOLIDIFY : fraguar (dícese del cemento, etc.), cuajar (dícese de la gelatina, etc.) 2 : ponerse (dícese del sol o de la luna)

set[2] *adj* 1 ESTABLISHED, FIXED : fijo, establecido 2 RIGID : inflexible ⟨to be set in one's ways : tener costumbres muy arraigadas⟩ 3 READY : listo, preparado

set[3] *n* 1 COLLECTION : juego *m* ⟨a set of dishes : un juego de platos, una vajilla⟩ ⟨a tool set : una caja de herramientas⟩ 2 *or* **stage set** : decorado *m* (en el teatro), plató *m* (en el cine) 3 APPARATUS : aparato *m* ⟨a television set : un televisor⟩ 4 : conjunto *m* (en matemáticas)

setback ['sɛt,bæk] *n* : revés *m*, contratiempo *m*

set in *vi* BEGIN : comenzar, empezar

set off *vt* 1 PROVOKE : provocar 2 EXPLODE : hacer estallar (una bomba, etc.) — *vi or* **to set forth** : salir

set out *vi* 1 : salir (de viaje) — *vt* INTEND : proponerse

settee [sɛ'ti:] *n* : sofá *m*

setter ['sɛt̬ər] *n* : setter *mf* ⟨Irish setter : setter irlandés⟩

setting ['sɛt̬ɪŋ] *n* 1 : posición *f*, ajuste *m* (de un control) 2 : engaste *m*, montura *f* (de una gema) 3 SCENE : escenario *m* (de una novela, etc.) 4 SURROUNDINGS : ambiente *m*, entorno *m*, marco *m*

settle ['sɛt̬əl] *v* **settled; settling** *vi* 1 ALIGHT, LAND : posarse (dícese de las aves), depositarse (dícese del polvo) 2 SINK : asentarse (dícese de los edificios) ⟨he settled into the chair : se arrellanó en la silla⟩ 3 : instalarse (en una casa), establecerse (en una ciudad o región) 4 **to settle down** : calmarse, tranquilizarse ⟨settle down! : ¡tranquilízate!, ¡cálmate!⟩ 5 **to settle down** : sentar cabeza, hacerse sensato ⟨to marry and settle down : casarse y sentar cabeza⟩ — *vt* 1 ARRANGE, DECIDE : fijar, decidir, acordar (planes, etc.) 2 RESOLVE : resolver, solucionar ⟨to settle an argument : resolver una discusión⟩ 3 PAY : pagar ⟨to settle an account : saldar una cuenta⟩ 4 CALM : calmar (los nervios), asentar (el estómago) 5 COLONIZE : colonizar 6 **to settle oneself** : acomodarse, hacerse cómodo

settlement ['sɛt̬əlmənt] *n* 1 PAYMENT : pago *m*, liquidación *f* 2 COLONY : asentamiento *m* 3 RESOLUTION : acuerdo *m*

settler ['sɛt̬ələr] *n* : poblador *m*, -dora *f*; colono *m*, -na *f*

setup ['sɛt̬,ʌp] *n* 1 ASSEMBLY : montaje *m*, ensamblaje *m* 2 ARRANGEMENT : disposición *f* 3 PREPARATION : preparación *f* 4 TRAP, TRICK : encerrona *f*

set up *vt* **1** ASSEMBLE : montar, armar **2** ERECT : levantar, erigir **3** ESTABLISH : establecer, fundar, montar (un negocio) **4** CAUSE : armar ⟨they set up a clamor : armaron un alboroto⟩

seven¹ ['sɛvən] *adj* : siete

seven² *n* : siete *m*

seven hundred¹ *adj* : setecientos

seven hundred² *n* : setecientos *m*

seventeen¹ [ˌsɛvən'tiːn] *adj* : diecisiete

seventeen² *n* : diecisiete *m*

seventeenth¹ [ˌsɛvən'tiːnθ] *adj* : decimoséptimo

seventeenth² *n* **1** : decimoséptimo *m*, -ma *f* (en una serie) **2** : diecisieteavo *m*, diecisieteava parte *f*

seventh¹ ['sɛvənθ] *adj* : séptimo

seventh² *n* **1** : séptimo *m*, -ma *f* (en una serie) **2** : séptimo *m*, séptima parte *f*

seventieth¹ ['sɛvəntiəθ] *adj* : septuagésimo

seventieth² *n* **1** : septuagésimo *m*, -ma *f* (en una serie) **2** : setentavo *m*, setentava parte *f*, septuagésima parte *f*

seventy¹ ['sɛvənti] *adj* : setenta

seventy² *n, pl* **-ties** : setenta *m*

sever ['sɛvər] *vt* **-ered; -ering** : cortar, romper

several¹ ['sɛvrəl, 'sɛvə-] *adj* **1** DISTINCT : distinto **2** SOME : varios ⟨several weeks : varias semanas⟩

several² *pron* : varios, varias

severance ['sɛvrənts, sɛvə-] *n* **1** : ruptura *f* (de relaciones, etc.) **2 severance pay** : indemnización *f* (por despido)

severe [sə'vɪr] *adj* **severer; -est 1** STRICT : severo **2** AUSTERE : sobrio, austero **3** SERIOUS : grave ⟨a severe wound : una herida grave⟩ ⟨severe aches : dolores fuertes⟩ **4** DIFFICULT : duro, difícil — **severely** *adv*

severity [sə'vrəti] *n* **1** HARSHNESS : severidad *f* **2** AUSTERITY : sobriedad *f*, austeridad *f* **3** SERIOUSNESS : gravedad *f* (de una herida, etc.)

sew ['soː] *v* **sewed; sewn** ['soːn] *or* **sewed; sewing** : coser

sewage ['suːɪʤ] *n* : aguas *fpl* negras, aguas *fpl* residuales

sewer¹ ['soːər] *n* : uno que cose

sewer² ['suːər] *n* : alcantarilla *f*, cloaca *f*

sewing ['soːɪŋ] *n* : costura *f*

sex ['sɛks] *n* **1** : sexo *m* ⟨the opposite sex : el sexo opuesto⟩ **2** COPULATION : relaciones *fpl* sexuales

sexism ['sɛkˌsɪzəm] *n* : sexismo *m*

sexist¹ ['sɛksɪst] *adj* : sexista

sexist² *n* : sexista *mf*

sextant ['sɛkstənt] *n* : sextante *m*

sextet [sɛk'stɛt] *n* : sexteto *m*

sexton ['sɛkstən] *n* : sacristán *m*

sexual ['sɛkʃuəl] *adj* : sexual — **sexually** *adv*

sexuality [ˌsɛkʃu'æləti] *n* : sexualidad *f*

sexy ['sɛksi] *adj* **sexier; -est** : sexy

shabbily ['ʃæbəli] *adv* **1** : pobremente ⟨shabbily dressed : pobremente vestido⟩ **2** UNFAIRLY : mal, injustamente

shabbiness ['ʃæbinəs] *n* **1** : lo gastado (de ropa, etc.) **2** : lo mal vestido (de personas) **3** UNFAIRNESS : injusticia *f*

shabby ['ʃæbi] *adj* **shabbier; -est 1** : gastado (dícese de la ropa, etc.) **2** : mal vestido (dícese de las personas) **3** UNFAIR : malo, injusto ⟨shabby treatment : mal trato⟩

shack ['ʃæk] *n* : choza *f*, rancho *m*

shackle¹ ['ʃækəl] *vt* **-led; -ling** : ponerle grilletes (a alguien)

shackle² *n* : grillete *m*

shad ['ʃæd] *n* : sábalo *m*

shade¹ ['ʃeɪd] *v* **shaded; shading** *vt* **1** SHELTER : proteger (del sol o de la luz) **2** *or* **to shade in** : matizar los colores de — *vi* : convertirse gradualmente ⟨his irritation shaded into rage : su irritación iba convirtiéndose en furia⟩

shade² *n* **1** : sombra *f* ⟨to give shade : dar sombra⟩ **2** : tono *m* (de un color) **3** NUANCE : matiz *m* **4** : pantalla *f* (de una lámpara), persiana *f* (de una ventana)

shadow¹ ['ʃædoː] *vt* **1** DARKEN : ensombrecer **2** TRAIL : seguir de cerca, seguirle la pista (a alguien)

shadow² *n* **1** : sombra *f* **2** DARKNESS : oscuridad *f* **3** TRACE : sombra *f*, atisbo *m*, indicio *m* ⟨without a shadow of a doubt : sin sombra de duda, sin lugar a dudas⟩ **4 to cast a shadow over** : ensombrecer

shadowy ['ʃædowi] *adj* **1** INDISTINCT : vago, indistinto **2** DARK : oscuro

shady ['ʃeɪdi] *adj* **shadier; -est 1** : sombreado (dícese de un lugar), que da sombra (dícese de un árbol) **2** DISREPUTABLE : sospechoso (dícese de una persona), turbio (dícese de un negocio, etc.)

shaft ['ʃæft] *n* **1** : asta *f* (de una lanza), astil *m* (de una flecha), mango *m* (de una herramienta) **2** *or* **mine shaft** : pozo *m*

shaggy ['ʃægi] *adj* **shaggier; -est 1** HAIRY : peludo ⟨a shaggy dog : un perro peludo⟩ **2** UNKEMPT : enmarañado, despeinado (dícese del pelo, de las barbas, etc.)

shake¹ ['ʃeɪk] *v* **shook** ['ʃʊk]; **shaken** ['ʃeɪkən]; **shaking** *vt* **1** : sacudir, agitar, hacer temblar ⟨he shook his head : negó con la cabeza⟩ **2** WEAKEN : debilitar, hacer flaquear ⟨it shook her faith : debilitó su confianza⟩ **3** UPSET : afectar, alterar **4 to shake hands with someone** : darle la mano a alguien, estrecharle la mano a alguien — *vi* : temblar, sacudirse

shake² *n* : sacudida *f*, apretón *m* (de manos)

shaker ['ʃeɪkər] *n* **1 salt shaker** : salero *m* **2 pepper shaker** : pimentero *m* **3 cocktail shaker** : coctelera *f*

shake–up ['ʃeɪkˌʌp] *n* : reorganización *f*

shakily ['ʃeɪkəli] *adv* : temblorosamente

shaky [ˈʃeɪki] *adj* **shakier; -est 1** SHAK-
ING : tembloroso **2** UNSTABLE : poco
firme, inestable **3** PRECARIOUS : precario, incierto **4** QUESTIONABLE : dudoso, cuestionable ⟨shaky arguments
: argumentos discutibles⟩
shale [ˈʃeɪl] *n* : esquisto *m*
shall [ˈʃæl] *v aux, past* **should** [ˈʃʊd] *pre-*
sent s & pl **shall 1** (*used to express a*
command) ⟨you shall do as I say : harás
lo que te digo⟩ **2** (*used to express futu-*
rity) ⟨we shall see : ya veremos⟩ ⟨when
shall we expect you? : ¿cuándo te
podemos esperar?⟩ **3** (*used to express*
determination) ⟨you shall have the
money : tendrás el dinero⟩ **4** (*used to*
express a condition) ⟨if he should die
: si muriera⟩ ⟨if they should call, tell
me : si llaman, dímelo⟩ **5** (*used to ex-*
press obligation) ⟨he should have said
it : debería haberlo dicho⟩ **6** (*used to*
express probability) ⟨they should arrive
soon : deben (de) llegar pronto⟩ ⟨why
should he lie? : ¿porqué ha de mentir?⟩
shallow [ˈʃæloʊ] *adj* **1** : poco profundo
(dícese del agua, etc.) **2** SUPERFICIAL
: superficial
shallows [ˈʃæloʊz] *npl* : bajío *m*, bajos
mpl
sham[1] [ˈʃæm] *v* **shammed; shamming**
: fingir
sham[2] *adj* : falso, fingido
sham[3] *n* **1** FAKE, PRETENSE : farsa *f*,
simulación *f*, imitación *f* **2** FAKER : impostor *m*, -tora *f*; farsante *mf*
shamble [ˈʃæmbəl] *vi* **-bled; -bling**
: caminar arrastrando los pies
shambles [ˈʃæmbəlz] *ns & pl* : caos *m*,
desorden *m*, confusión *f*
shame[1] [ˈʃeɪm] *vt* **shamed; shaming 1**
: avergonzar ⟨he was shamed by their
words : sus palabras le dieron vergüen-
za⟩ **2** DISGRACE : deshonrar
shame[2] *n* **1** : vergüenza *f* ⟨to have no
shame : no tener vergüenza⟩ **2** DIS-
GRACE : vergüenza *f*, deshonra *f* **3** PITY
: lástima *f*, pena *f* ⟨what a shame! : ¡qué
pena!⟩
shamefaced [ˈʃeɪmˌfeɪst] *adj* : avergonzado
shameful [ˈʃeɪmfəl] *adj* : vergonzoso —
shamefully *adv*
shameless [ˈʃeɪmləs] *adj* : descarado,
desvergonzado — **shamelessly** *adv*
shampoo[1] [ʃæmˈpuː] *vt* : lavar (el pelo)
shampoo[2] *n, pl* **-poos** : champú *m*
shamrock [ˈʃæmˌrɑk] *n* : trébol *m*
shank [ˈʃæŋk] *n* : parte *f* baja de la pierna
shan't [ˈʃænt] (*contraction of* **shall not**)
→ **shall**
shanty [ˈʃænti] *n, pl* **-ties** : choza *f*, rancho *m*
shape[1] [ˈʃeɪp] *v* **shaped; shaping** *vt* **1**
: dar forma a, modelar (arcilla, etc.),
tallar (madera, piedra), formar (carácter) ⟨to be shaped like : tener forma
de⟩ **2** DETERMINE : decidir, determi-

nar — *vi or* **to shape up** : tomar forma
shape[2] *n* **1** : forma *f*, figura *f* ⟨in the
shape of a circle : en forma de círcu-
lo⟩ **2** CONDITION : estado *m*, condiciones *fpl*, forma *f* (física) ⟨to get in
shape : ponerse en forma⟩
shapeless [ˈʃeɪpləs] *adj* : informe
shapely [ˈʃeɪpli] *adj* **shapelier; -est**
: curvilíneo, bien proporcionado
shard [ˈʃɑrd] *n* : fragmento *m*, casco *m*
(de cerámica, etc.)
share[1] [ˈʃɛr] *v* **shared; sharing** *vt* **1** AP-
PORTION : dividir, repartir **2** : com-
partir ⟨they share a room : comparten
una habitación⟩ — *vi* : compartir
share[2] *n* **1** PORTION : parte *f*, porción *f*
⟨one's fair share : lo que le corresponde
a uno⟩ **2** : acción *f* (en una compañía)
⟨to hold shares : tener acciones⟩
sharecropper [ˈʃɛrˌkrɑpər] *n* : aparcero
m, -ra *f*
shareholder [ˈʃɛrˌhoːldər] *n* : accionista
mf
shark [ˈʃɑrk] *n* : tiburón *m*
sharp[1] [ˈʃɑrp] *adv* : en punto ⟨at two
o'clock sharp : a las dos en punto⟩
sharp[2] *adj* **1** : afilado, filoso ⟨a sharp
knife : un cuchillo afilado⟩ **2** PENE-
TRATING : cortante, fuerte **3** CLEVER
: agudo, listo, perspicaz **4** ACUTE : agudo ⟨sharp eyesight : vista aguda⟩ **5**
HARSH, SEVERE : duro, severo, agudo
⟨a sharp rebuke : una reprimenda mor-
daz⟩ **6** STRONG : fuerte ⟨sharp cheese
: queso fuerte⟩ **7** ABRUPT : brusco, repentino **8** DISTINCT : nítido, definido
⟨a sharp image : una imagen bien
definida⟩ **9** ANGULAR : anguloso
(dícese de la cara) **10** : sostenido (en
música)
sharp[3] *n* : sostenido *m* (en música)
sharpen [ˈʃɑrpən] *vt* : afilar, aguzar ⟨to
sharpen a pencil : sacarle punta a un
lápiz⟩ ⟨to sharpen one's wits : aguzar
el ingenio⟩
sharpener [ˈʃɑrpənər] *n* : afilador *m*
(para cuchillos, etc.), sacapuntas *m*
(para lápices)
sharply [ˈʃɑrpli] *adv* **1** ABRUPTLY : bruscamente **2** DISTINCTLY : claramente,
marcadamente
sharpness [ˈʃɑrpnəs] *n* **1** : lo afilado (de
un cuchillo, etc.) **2** ACUTENESS
: agudeza *f* (de los sentidos o de la
mente) **3** INTENSITY : intensidad *f*,
agudeza *f* (de dolores, etc.) **4** HARSH-
NESS : dureza *f*, severidad *f* **5** ABRUPT-
NESS : brusquedad *f* **6** CLARITY : nitidez *f*
sharpshooter [ˈʃɑrpˌʃuːtər] *n* : tirador
m, -dora *f* de primera
shatter [ˈʃætər] *vt* **1** : hacer añicos ⟨to
shatter the silence : romper el silencio⟩
2 to be shattered by : quedar destrozado por — *vi* : hacerse añicos,
romperse en pedazos

shave¹ [ˈʃeɪv] *v* **shaved; shaved** *or* **shaven** [ˈʃeɪvən]; **shaving** *vt* **1** : afeitar, rasurar ⟨she shaved her legs : se rasuró las piernas⟩ ⟨they shaved (off) his beard : le afeitaron la barba⟩ **2** SLICE : cortar (en pedazos finos) — *vi* : afeitarse, rasurarse

shave² *n* : afeitada *f*, rasurada *f*

shaver [ˈʃeɪvər] *n* : afeitadora *f*, máquina *f* de afeitar, rasuradora *f*

shawl [ˈʃɔl] *n* : chal *m*, mantón *m*, rebozo *m*

she [ˈʃiː] *pron* : ella

sheaf [ˈʃiːf] *n*, *pl* **sheaves** [ˈʃiːvz] : gavilla *f* (de cereales), haz *m* (de flechas), fajo *m* (de papeles)

shear [ˈʃɪr] *vt* **sheared; sheared** *or* **shorn** [ˈʃorn]; **shearing** **1** : esquilar, trasquilar ⟨to shear sheep : trasquilar ovejas⟩ **2** CUT : cortar (el pelo, etc.)

shears [ˈʃɪrz] *npl* : tijeras *fpl* (grandes)

sheath [ˈʃiːθ] *n*, *pl* **sheaths** [ˈʃiːðz, ˈʃiːθs] : funda *f*, vaina *f*

sheathe [ˈʃiːð] *vt* **sheathed; sheathing** : envainar, enfundar

shed¹ [ˈʃd] *vt* **shed; shedding** **1** : derramar (sangre o lágrimas) **2** EMIT : emitir (luz) ⟨to shed light on : aclarar⟩ **3** DISCARD : mudar (la piel, etc.) ⟨to shed one's clothes : quitarse uno la ropa⟩

shed² *n* : cobertizo *m*

she'd [ˈʃiːd] (*contraction of* **she had** *or* **she would**) → **have, would**

sheen [ˈʃiːn] *n* : brillo *m*, lustre *m*

sheep [ˈʃiːp] *ns & pl* : oveja *f*

sheepfold [ˈʃiːpˌfoːld] *n* : redil *m*

sheepish [ˈʃiːpɪʃ] *adj* : avergonzado

sheepskin [ˈʃiːpˌskɪn] *n* : piel *f* de oveja, piel *f* de borrego

sheer¹ [ˈʃɪr] *adv* **1** COMPLETELY : completamente, totalmente **2** VERTICALLY : verticalmente

sheer² *adj* **1** TRANSPARENT : vaporoso, transparente **2** ABSOLUTE, UTTER : puro ⟨by sheer luck : por pura suerte⟩ **3** STEEP : escarpado, vertical

sheet [ˈʃiːt] *n* **1** *or* **bedsheet** [ˈbɛd-ˌʃiːt] : sábana *f* **2** : hoja *f* (de papel) **3** : capa *f* (de hielo, etc.) **4** : lámina *f*, placa *f* (de vidrio, metal, etc.), plancha *f* (de metal, madera, etc.) ⟨baking sheet : placa de horno⟩

sheikh *or* **sheik** [ˈʃiːk, ˈʃeɪk] *n* : jeque *m*

shelf [ˈʃelf] *n*, *pl* **shelves** [ˈʃelvz] **1** : estante *m*, anaquel *m* (en una pared) **2** : banco *m*, arrecife *m* (en geología) ⟨continental shelf : plataforma continental⟩

shell¹ [ˈʃel] *vt* **1** : desvainar (chícharos), pelar (nueces, etc.) **2** BOMBARD : bombardear

shell² *n* **1** SEASHELL : concha *f* **2** : cáscara *f* (de huevos, nueces, etc.), vaina *f* (de chícharos, etc.), caparazón *m* (de crustáceos, tortugas, etc.) **3** : cartucho *m*, casquillo *m* ⟨a .45 caliber shell : un cartucho calibre .45⟩ **4** *or* **racing shell** : bote *m* (para hacer regatas de remos)

she'll [ˈʃiːl, ˈʃɪl] (*contraction of* **she shall** *or* **she will**) → **shall, will**

shellac¹ [ʃəˈlæk] *vt* **-lacked; -lacking** **1** : laquear (madera, etc.) **2** DEFEAT : darle una paliza (a alguien), derrotar

shellac² *n* : laca *f*

shellfish [ˈʃelˌfɪʃ] *n* : marisco *m*

shelter¹ [ˈʃeltər] *vt* **1** PROTECT : proteger, abrigar **2** HARBOR : dar refugio a, albergar

shelter² *n* : refugio *m*, abrigo *m* ⟨to take shelter : refugiarse⟩

shelve [ˈʃelv] *vt* **shelved; shelving** **1** : poner en estantes **2** DEFER : dar carpetazo a

shenanigans [ʃəˈnænɪgənz] *npl* **1** TRICKERY : artimañas *fpl* **2** MISCHIEF : travesuras *fpl*

shepherd¹ [ˈʃepərd] *vt* **1** : cuidar (ovejas, etc.) **2** GUIDE : conducir, guiar

shepherd² *n* : pastor *m*

shepherdess [ˈʃepərdəs] *n* : pastora *f*

sherbet [ˈʃərbət] *or* **sherbert** [-bərt] *n* : sorbete *m*, nieve *f* Cuba, Mex, PRi

sheriff [ˈʃerɪf] *n* : sheriff *mf*

sherry [ˈʃeri] *n*, *pl* **-ries** : jerez *m*

she's [ˈʃiːz] (*contraction of* **she is** *or* **she has**) → **be, have**

shield¹ [ˈʃiːld] *vt* **1** PROTECT : proteger **2** CONCEAL : ocultar ⟨to shield one's eyes : taparse los ojos⟩

shield² *n* **1** : escudo *m* (armadura) **2** PROTECTION : protección *f*, blindaje *m* (de un cable)

shier, shiest → **shy**

shift¹ [ˈʃɪft] *vt* **1** CHANGE : cambiar ⟨to shift gears : cambiar de velocidad⟩ **2** MOVE : mover **3** TRANSFER : transferir ⟨to shift the blame : echarle la culpa (a otro)⟩ — *vi* **1** CHANGE : cambiar **2** MOVE : moverse **3 to shift for oneself** : arreglárselas solo

shift² *n* **1** CHANGE, TRANSFER : cambio *m* ⟨a shift in priorities : un cambio de prioridades⟩ **2** : turno *m* ⟨night shift : turno de noche⟩ **3** DRESS : vestido *m* (suelto) **4** → **gearshift**

shiftless [ˈʃɪftləs] *adj* : perezoso, vago, holgazán

shifty [ˈʃɪfti] *adj* **shiftier; -est** : taimado, artero ⟨a shifty look : una mirada huidiza⟩

shilling [ˈʃɪlɪŋ] *n* : chelín *m*

shimmer [ˈʃɪmər] *vi* GLIMMER : brillar con luz trémula

shin¹ [ˈʃɪn] *vi* **shinned; shinning** : trepar, subir ⟨she shinned up the pole : subió al poste⟩

shin² *n* : espinilla *f*, canilla *f*

shine¹ [ˈʃaɪn] *v* **shone** [ˈʃoːn] *or* **shined; shining** *vi* **1** : brillar, relucir ⟨the stars were shining : las estrellas brillaban⟩ **2** EXCEL : brillar, lucirse — *vt* **1** : alumbrar ⟨he shined the flashlight at it : lo alumbró con la linterna⟩ **2** POLISH : sacarle brillo a, lustrar

shine² *n* : brillo *m*, lustre *m*

shingle¹ [ˈʃɪŋgəl] *vt* **-gled; -gling** : techar

shingle² *n* : tablilla *f* (para techar)
shingles [ˈʃɪŋɡəlz] *npl* : herpes *m*
shinny [ˈʃɪni] *vi* -nied; -nying → shin¹
shiny [ˈʃaɪni] *adj* shinier; -est : brillante
ship¹ [ˈʃɪp] *vt* shipped; shipping 1 LOAD : embarcar (en un barco) 2 SEND : transportar (en barco), enviar ⟨to ship by air : enviar por avión⟩
ship² *n* 1 : barco *m*, buque *m* 2 → spaceship
shipboard [ˈʃɪpˌbord] *n* on ~ : a bordo
shipbuilder [ˈʃɪpˌbɪldər] *n* : constructor *m*, -tora *f* naval
shipment [ˈʃɪpmənt] *n* 1 SHIPPING : transporte *m*, embarque *m* 2 : envío *m*, remesa *f* ⟨a shipment of medicine : un envío de medicina⟩
shipping [ˈʃɪpɪŋ] *n* 1 SHIPS : barcos *mpl*, embarcaciones *fpl* 2 TRANSPORTATION : transporte *m* (de mercancías)
shipshape [ˈʃɪpˌʃeɪp] *adj* : ordenado
shipwreck¹ [ˈʃɪpˌrɛk] *vt* to be shipwrecked : naufragar
shipwreck² *n* : naufragio *m*
shipyard [ˈʃɪpˌjɑrd] *n* : astillero *m*
shirk [ˈʃərk] *vt* : eludir, rehuir ⟨to shirk one's responsibilities : esquivar uno sus responsabilidades⟩
shirt [ˈʃərt] *n* : camisa *f*
shiver¹ [ˈʃɪvər] *vi* 1 : tiritar (de frío) 2 TREMBLE : estremecerse, temblar
shiver² *n* : escalofrío *m*, estremecimiento *m*
shoal [ˈʃoːl] *n* : banco *m*, bajío *m*
shock¹ [ˈʃɑk] *vt* 1 UPSET : conmover, conmocionar 2 STARTLE : asustar, sobresaltar 3 SCANDALIZE : escandalizar 4 : darle una descarga eléctrica a
shock² *n* 1 COLLISION, JOLT : choque *m*, sacudida *f* 2 UPSET : conmoción *f*, golpe *m* emocional 3 : shock *m* (en medicina) 4 *or* electric shock : descarga *f* eléctrica 5 SHEAVES : gavillas *fpl* 6 shock of hair : mata *f* de pelo
shock absorber *n* : amortiguador *m*
shocking [ˈʃɑkɪŋ] *adj* 1 : chocante 2 **shocking pink** : rosa *m* estridente
shoddy [ˈʃɑdi] *adj* shoddier; -est : de mala calidad ⟨a shoddy piece of work : un trabajo chapucero⟩
shoe¹ [ˈʃuː] *vt* shod [ˈʃɑd]; shoeing : herrar (un caballo)
shoe² *n* 1 : zapato *m* ⟨the shoe industry : la industria del calzado⟩ 2 HORSESHOE : herradura *f* 3 **brake shoe** : zapata *f*
shoelace [ˈʃuːˌleɪs] *n* : cordón *m* (de zapatos)
shoemaker [ˈʃuːˌmeɪkər] *n* : zapatero *m*, -ra *f*
shone → shine
shook → shake
shoot¹ [ˈʃuːt] *v* shot [ˈʃɑt]; shooting *vt* 1 : disparar, tirar ⟨to shoot a bullet : tirar una bala⟩ 2 : pegarle un tiro a, darle un balazo a ⟨he shot her : le pegó un tiro⟩ ⟨they shot and killed him : lo mataron a balazos⟩ 3 THROW : lanzar

(una pelota, etc.), echar (una mirada) 4 PHOTOGRAPH : fotografiar 5 FILM : filmar — *vi* 1 : disparar (con un arma de fuego) 2 DART : ir rápidamente ⟨it shot past : pasó como una bala⟩
shoot² *n* : brote *m*, retoño *m*, vástago *m*
shooting star *n* : estrella *f* fugaz
shop¹ [ˈʃɑp] *vi* shopped; shopping : hacer compras ⟨to go shopping : ir de compras⟩
shop² *n* 1 WORKSHOP : taller *m* 2 STORE : tienda *f*
shopkeeper [ˈʃɑpˌkiːpər] *n* : tendero *m*, -ra *f*
shoplift [ˈʃɑpˌlɪft] *vi* : hurtar mercancía (de una tienda) — *vt* : hurtar (de una tienda)
shoplifter [ˈʃɑpˌlɪftər] *n* : ladrón *m*, -drona *f* (que roba en una tienda)
shopper [ˈʃɑpər] *n* : comprador *m*, -dora *f*
shore¹ [ˈʃor] *vt* shored; shoring : apuntalar ⟨they shored up the wall : apuntalaron la pared⟩
shore² *n* 1 : orilla *f* (del mar, etc.) 2 PROP : puntal *m*
shoreline [ˈʃorˌlaɪn] *n* : orilla *f*
shorn → shear
short¹ [ˈʃort] *adv* 1 ABRUPTLY : repentinamente, súbitamente ⟨the car stopped short : el carro se paró en seco⟩ 2 **to fall short** : no alcanzar, quedarse corto
short² *adj* 1 : corto (de medida), bajo (de estatura) 2 BRIEF : corto ⟨short and sweet : corto y bueno⟩ ⟨a short time ago : hace poco⟩ 3 CURT : brusco, cortante, seco 4 : corto (de tiempo, de dinero) ⟨I'm one dollar short : me falta un dólar⟩
short³ *n* 1 **shorts** *npl* : shorts *mpl*, pantalones *mpl* cortos 2 → short circuit
shortage [ˈʃortɪdʒ] *n* : falta *f*, escasez *f*, carencia *f*
shortcake [ˈʃortˌkeɪk] *n* : tarta *f* de fruta
shortchange [ˈʃortˈtʃeɪndʒ] *vt* -changed; -changing : darle mal el cambio (a alguien)
short circuit *n* : cortocircuito *m*, corto *m* (eléctrico)
shortcoming [ˈʃortˌkʌmɪŋ] *n* : defecto *m*
shortcut [ˈʃortˌkʌt] *n* 1 : atajo *m* ⟨to take a shortcut : cortar camino⟩ 2 : alternativa *f* fácil, método *m* rápido
shorten [ˈʃortən] *vt* : acortar — *vi* : acortarse
shorthand [ˈʃortˌhænd] *n* : taquigrafía *f*
short-lived [ˈʃortˈlɪvd, -ˈlaɪvd] *adj* : efímero
shortly [ˈʃortli] *adv* 1 BRIEFLY : brevemente ⟨to put it shortly : para decirlo en pocas palabras⟩ 2 SOON : dentro de poco
shortness [ˈʃortnəs] *n* 1 : lo corto ⟨shortness of stature : estatura baja⟩ 2 BREVITY : brevedad *f* 3 CURTNESS : brusquedad *f* 4 SHORTAGE : falta *f*, escasez *f*, carencia *f*

shortsighted ['ʃɔrt,saɪtəd] → **near-sighted**
shot ['ʃɑt] *n* **1** : disparo *m*, tiro *m* ⟨to fire a shot : disparar⟩ **2** PELLETS : perdigones *mpl* **3** : tiro *m* (en deportes) **4** ATTEMPT : intento *m*, tentativa *f* ⟨to have a shot at : hacer un intento por⟩ **5** RANGE : alcance *m* ⟨a long shot : una posibilidad remota⟩ **6** PHOTOGRAPH : foto *f* **7** INJECTION : inyección *f* **8** : trago *m* (de licor)
shotgun ['ʃɑt,gʌn] *n* : escopeta *f*
should → **shall**
shoulder¹ ['ʃoːldər] *vt* **1** JOSTLE : empujar (con el hombro) **2** : ponerse al hombro (una mochila, etc.) **3** : cargar con (la responsabilidad, etc.)
shoulder² *n* **1** : hombro *m* ⟨to shrug one's shoulders : encogerse los hombros⟩ **2** : arcén *m* (de una carretera)
shoulder blade *n* : omóplato *m*, omoplato *m*, escápula *f*
shouldn't ['ʃʊdənt] (*contraction of* **should not**) → **shall**
shout¹ ['ʃaʊt] *v* : gritar, vocear
shout² *n* : grito *m*
shove¹ ['ʃʌv] *v* **shoved; shoving** : empujar bruscamente
shove² *n* : empujón *m*, empellón *m*
shovel¹ ['ʃʌvəl] *vt* **-veled** *or* **-velled; -veling** *or* **-velling** **1** : mover con (una) pala ⟨they shoveled the dirt out : sacaron la tierra con palas⟩ **2** DIG : cavar (con una pala)
shovel² *n* : pala *f*
show¹ ['ʃoː] *v* **showed; shown** ['ʃoːn] *or* **showed; showing** *vt* **1** DISPLAY : mostrar, enseñar **2** REVEAL : demostrar, manifestar, revelar ⟨he showed himself to be a coward : se reveló como cobarde⟩ **3** TEACH : enseñar **4** PROVE : demostrar, probar **5** CONDUCT, DIRECT : llevar, acompañar ⟨to show someone the way : indicarle el camino a alguien⟩ **6** : proyectar (una película), dar (un programa de televisión) — *vi* **1** : notarse, verse ⟨the stain doesn't show : la mancha no se ve⟩ **2** APPEAR : aparecer, dejarse ver
show² *n* **1** : demostración *f* ⟨a show of force : una demostración de fuerza⟩ **2** EXHIBITION : exposición *f*, exhibición *f* ⟨flower show : exposición de flores⟩ ⟨to be on show : estar expuesto⟩ **3** : espectáculo *m* (teatral), programa *m* (de televisión, etc.) ⟨to go to a show : ir al teatro⟩
showcase ['ʃoː,keɪs] *n* : vitrina *f*
showdown ['ʃoː,daʊn] *n* : confrontación *f* (decisiva)
shower¹ ['ʃaʊər] *vt* **1** SPRAY : regar, mojar **2** HEAP : colmar ⟨they showered him with gifts : lo colmaron de regalos, le llovieron los regalos⟩ — *vi* **1** BATHE : ducharse, darse una ducha **2** RAIN : llover
shower² *n* **1** : chaparrón *m*, chubasco *m* ⟨a chance of showers : una posibil-

idad de chaparrones⟩ **2** : ducha *f* ⟨to take a shower : ducharse⟩ **3** PARTY : fiesta *f* ⟨a bridal shower : una despedida de soltera⟩
show off *vt* : hacer alarde de, ostentar — *vi* : lucirse
show up *vi* APPEAR : aparecer — *vt* EXPOSE : revelar
showy ['ʃoːi] *adj* **showier; -est** : llamativo, ostentoso — **showily** *adv*
shrank → **shrink**
shrapnel ['ʃræpnəl] *ns & pl* : metralla *f*
shred¹ ['ʃred] *vt* **shredded; shredding** : hacer trizas, desmenuzar (con las manos), triturar (con una máquina) ⟨to shred vegetables : cortar verduras en tiras⟩
shred² *n* **1** STRIP : tira *f*, jirón *m* (de tela) **2** BIT : pizca *f* ⟨not a shred of evidence : ni la mínima prueba⟩
shrew ['ʃruː] *n* **1** : musaraña *f* (animal) **2** : mujer *f* regañona, arpía *f*
shrewd ['ʃruːd] *adj* : astuto, inteligente, sagaz — **shrewdly** *adv*
shrewdness ['ʃruːdnəs] *n* : astucia *f*
shriek¹ ['ʃriːk] *vi* : chillar, gritar
shriek² *n* : chillido *m*, alarido *m*, grito *m*
shrill ['ʃrɪl] *adj* : agudo, estridente
shrilly ['ʃrɪli] *adv* : agudamente
shrimp ['ʃrɪmp] *n* : camarón *m*, langostino *m*
shrine ['ʃraɪn] *n* **1** TOMB : sepulcro *m* (de un santo) **2** SANCTUARY : lugar *m* sagrado, santuario *m*
shrink ['ʃrɪŋk] *vi* **shrank** ['ʃræŋk] *or* **shrunk** ['ʃrʌŋk]; **shrunk** *or* **shrunken** ['ʃrʌŋkən]; **shrinking** **1** RECOIL : retroceder ⟨he shrank back : se echó para atrás⟩ **2** : encogerse (dícese de la ropa)
shrinkage ['ʃrɪŋkɪdʒ] *n* : encogimiento *m* (de ropa, etc.), contracción *f*, reducción *f*
shrivel ['ʃrɪvəl] *vi* **-veled** *or* **-velled; -veling** *or* **-velling** : arrugarse, marchitarse
shroud¹ ['ʃraʊd] *vt* : envolver
shroud² *n* **1** : sudario *m*, mortaja *f* **2** VEIL : velo *m* ⟨wrapped in a shroud of mystery : envuelto en un aura de misterio⟩
shrub ['ʃrʌb] *n* : arbusto *m*, mata *f*
shrubbery ['ʃrʌbəri] *n*, *pl* **-beries** : arbustos *mpl*, matas *fpl*
shrug ['ʃrʌg] *vi* **shrugged; shrugging** : encogerse de hombros
shrunk → **shrink**
shuck¹ ['ʃʌk] *vt* : pelar (mazorcas, etc.), abrir (almejas, etc.)
shuck² *n* **1** HUSK : cascarilla *f*, cáscara *f* (de una nuez, etc.), hojas *fpl* (de una mazorca) **2** SHELL : concha *f* (de una almeja, etc.)
shudder¹ ['ʃʌdər] *vi* : estremecerse
shudder² *n* : estremecimiento *m*, escalofrío *m*
shuffle¹ ['ʃʌfəl] *v* **-fled; -fling** *vt* MIX : mezclar, revolver, barajar (naipes) — *vi* : caminar arrastrando los pies

shuffle² *n* **1** : acto *m* de revolver ⟨each player gets a shuffle : a cada jugador le toca barajar⟩ **2** JUMBLE : revoltijo *m* **3** : arrastramiento *m* de los pies

shun [ˈʃʌn] *vi* **shunned; shunning** : evitar, esquivar, eludir

shunt [ˈʃʌnt] *vt* : desviar, cambiar de vía (un tren)

shut [ˈʃʌt] *v* **shut; shutting** *vt* **1** CLOSE : cerrar ⟨shut the lid : tápalo⟩ **2 to shut out** EXCLUDE : excluir, dejar fuera a (personas), no dejar que entre (luz, ruido, etc.) **3 to shut up** CONFINE : encerrar — *vi* : cerrarse ⟨the factory shut down : la fábrica cerró suspuertas⟩

shut–in [ˈʃʌtˌɪn] *n* : inválido *m*, -da *f* (que no puede salir de casa)

shutter [ˈʃʌtər] *n* **1** : contraventana *f*, postigo *m* (de una ventana o puerta) **2** : obturador *m* (de una cámara)

shuttle¹ [ˈʃʌtəl] *v* **-tled; -tling** *vt* : transportar ⟨she shuttled him back and forth : lo llevaba de acá para allá⟩ — *vi* : ir y venir

shuttle² *n* **1** : lanzadera *f* (para tejer) **2** : vehículo *m* que hace recorridos cortos **3** → **space shuttle**

shuttlecock [ˈʃʌtəlˌkɑk] *n* : volante *m*

shut up *vi* : callarse ⟨shut up! : ¡cállate (la boca)!⟩

shy¹ [ˈʃaɪ] *vi* **shied; shying** : retroceder, asustarse

shy² *adj* **shier** *or* **shyer** [ˈʃaɪər]; **shiest** *or* **shyest** [ˈʃaɪəst] **1** TIMID : tímido **2** WARY : cauteloso ⟨he's not shy about asking : no vacila en preguntar⟩ **3** SHORT : corto (de dinero, etc.) ⟨I'm two dollars shy : me faltan dos dólares⟩

shyly [ˈʃaɪli] *adv* : tímidamente

shyness [ˈʃaɪnəs] *n* : timidez *f*

Siamese¹ [ˌsaɪəˈmiːz, -ˈmiːs-] *adj* : siamés ⟨Siamese twins : hermanos siameses⟩

Siamese² *n* **1** : siamés *m*, -mesa *f* **2** : siamés *m* (idioma) **3** *or* **Siamese cat** : gato *m* siamés

sibling [ˈsɪblɪŋ] *n* : hermano *m*, hermana *f*

Sicilian [səˈsɪljən] *n* : siciliano *m*, -na *f* — **Sicilian** *adj*

sick [ˈsɪk] *adj* **1** : enfermo **2** NAUSEOUS : mareado, con náuseas ⟨to get sick : vomitar⟩ **3** : para uso de enfermos ⟨sick day : día de permiso (por enfermedad)⟩

sickbed [ˈsɪkˌbɛd] *n* : lecho *m* de enfermo

sicken [ˈsɪkən] *vt* **1** : poner enfermo **2** REVOLT : darle asco (a alguien) — *vi* : enfermar(se), caer enfermo

sickening [ˈsɪkənɪŋ] *adj* : asqueroso, repugnante, nauseabundo

sickle [ˈsɪkəl] *n* : hoz *f*

sickly [ˈsɪkli] *adj* **sicklier; -est 1** : enfermizo **2** → **sickening**

sickness [ˈsɪknəs] *n* **1** : enfermedad *f* **2** NAUSEA : náuseas *fpl*

side [ˈsaɪd] *n* **1** : lado *m*, costado *m* (de una persona), ijada *f* (de un animal) **2** : lado *m*, cara *f* (de una moneda, etc.) **3** : lado *m*, parte *f* ⟨he's on my side : está de mi parte⟩ ⟨to take sides : tomar partido⟩

sideboard [ˈsaɪdˌbord] *n* : aparador *m*

sideburns [ˈsaɪdˌbərnz] *npl* : patillas *fpl*

sided [ˈsaɪdəd] *adj* : que tiene lados ⟨one-sided : de un lado⟩

side effect *n* : efecto *m* secundario

sideline [ˈsaɪdˌlaɪn] *n* **1** : línea *f* de banda (en deportes) **2** : actividad *f* suplementaria (en negocios) **3 to be on the sidelines** : estar al margen

sidelong [ˈsaɪdˌlɔŋ] *adj* : de reojo, de soslayo

sideshow [ˈsaɪdˌʃoː] *n* : espectáculo *m* secundario, atracción *f* secundaria

sidestep [ˈsaɪdˌstɛp] *v* **-stepped; -stepping** *vi* : dar un paso hacia un lado — *vt* AVOID : esquivar, eludir

sidetrack [ˈsaɪdˌtræk] *vt* : desviar (una conversación, etc.), distraer (a una persona)

sidewalk [ˈsaɪdˌwɔk] *n* : acera *f*, vereda *f*, andén *m* *CA, Col*, banqueta *f Mex*

sideways¹ [ˈsaɪdˌweɪz] *adv* **1** : hacia un lado ⟨it leaned sideways : se inclinaba hacia un lado⟩ **2** : de lado, de costado ⟨lie sideways : acuéstese de costado⟩

sideways² *adj* : hacia un lado ⟨a sideways glance : una mirada de reojo⟩

siding [ˈsaɪdɪŋ] *n* **1** : apartadero *m* (para trenes) **2** : revestimiento *m* exterior (de un edificio)

sidle [ˈsaɪdəl] *vi* **-dled; -dling** : moverse furtivamente

siege [ˈsiːdʒ, ˈsiːʒ] *n* : sitio *m* ⟨to be under siege : estar sitiado⟩

siesta [siˈɛstə] *n* : siesta *f*

sieve [ˈsɪv] *n* : tamiz *m*, cedazo *m*, criba *f* (en mineralogía)

sift [ˈsɪft] *vt* **1** : tamizar, cerner ⟨sift the flour : tamice la harina⟩ **2** *or* **to sift through** : examinar cuidadosamente, pasar por el tamiz

sifter [ˈsɪftər] *n* : tamiz *m*, cedazo *m*

sigh¹ [ˈsaɪ] *vi* : suspirar

sigh² *n* : suspiro *m*

sight¹ [ˈsaɪt] *vt* : ver (a una persona), divisar (la tierra, un barco)

sight² *n* **1** : vista *f* (facultad) ⟨out of sight : fuera de vista⟩ **2** : algo visto ⟨it's a familiar sight : se ve con frecuencia⟩ ⟨she's a sight for sore eyes : da gusto verla⟩ **3** : lugar *m* de interés (para turistas, etc.) **4** : mira *f* (de un rifle, etc.) **5** GLIMPSE : mirada *f* breve ⟨I caught sight of her : la divisé, alcancé a verla⟩

sighting [ˈsaɪtɪŋ] *n* : avistamiento *m*

sightless [ˈsaɪtləs] *adj* : invidente, ciego

sightseer [ˈsaɪtˌsiːər] *n* : turista *mf*

sign¹ [ˈsaɪn] *vt* **1** : firmar ⟨to sign a check : firmar un cheque⟩ **2** *or* **to sign on** HIRE : contratar (a un empleado), fichar (a un jugador) — *vi* **1** : hacer una seña ⟨she signed for him to stop : le hizo una seña para que se parara⟩ **2** : comunicarse por señas

sign² *n* **1** SYMBOL : símbolo *m*, signo *m* ⟨minus sign : signo de menos⟩ **2** GESTURE : seña *f*, señal *f*, gesto *m* **3** : letrero *m*, cartel *m* ⟨neon sign : letrero de neón⟩ **4** TRACE : señal *f*, indicio *m*

signal¹ ['sɪgnəl] *vt* **-naled** *or* **-nalled**; **-naling** *or* **-nalling** **1** : hacerle señas (a alguien) ⟨she signaled me to leave : me hizo señas para que saliera⟩ **2** INDICATE : señalar, indicar — *vi* : hacer señas, comunicar por señas

signal² *adj* NOTABLE : señalado, notable

signal³ *n* : señal *f*

signature ['sɪgnə,t͡ʃʊr] *n* : firma *f*

signet ['sɪgnət] *n* : sello *m*

significance [sɪg'nɪfɪkənts] *n* **1** MEANING : significado *m* **2** IMPORTANCE : importancia *f*

significant [sɪg'nɪfɪkənt] *adj* **1** IMPORTANT : importante **2** MEANINGFUL : significativo — **significantly** *adv*

signify ['sɪgnə,faɪ] *vt* **-fied; -fying** **1** : indicar ⟨he signified his desire for more : haciendo señas indicó que quería más⟩ **2** MEAN : significar

sign language *n* : lenguaje *m* por señas

signpost ['saɪn,po:st] *n* : poste *m* indicador

silence¹ ['saɪlənts] *vt* **-lenced; -lencing** : silenciar, acallar

silence² *n* : silencio *m*

silent ['saɪlənt] *adj* **1** : callado ⟨to remain silent : quedarse callado, guardar silencio⟩ **2** QUIET, STILL : silencioso **3** MUTE : mudo ⟨a silent letter : una letra muda⟩

silently ['saɪləntli] *adv* : silenciosamente, calladamente

silhouette¹ [,sɪlə'wɛt] *vt* **-etted; -etting** : destacar la silueta de ⟨it was silhouetted against the sky : se perfilaba contra el cielo⟩

silhouette² *n* : silueta *f*

silica ['sɪlɪkə] *n* : sílice *f*

silicon ['sɪlɪkən, -,kɑn] *n* : silicio *m*

silk ['sɪlk] *n* : seda *f*

silken ['sɪlkən] *adj* **1** : de seda ⟨a silken veil : un velo de seda⟩ **2** SILKY : sedoso ⟨silken hair : cabellos sedosos⟩

silkworm ['sɪlk,wərm] *n* : gusano *m* de seda

silky ['sɪlki] *adj* **silkier; -est** : sedoso

sill ['sɪl] *n* : alféizar *m* (de una ventana), umbral *m* (de una puerta)

silliness ['sɪlinəs] *n* : tontería *f*, estupidez *f*

silly ['sɪli] *adj* **sillier; -est** : tonto, estúpido, ridículo

silo ['saɪ,lo:] *n*, *pl* **silos** : silo *m*

silt ['sɪlt] *n* : cieno *m*

silver¹ ['sɪlvər] *adj* **1** : de plata ⟨a silver spoon : una cuchara de plata⟩ **2** → **silvery**

silver² *n* **1** : plata *f* **2** COINS : monedas *fpl* **3** → **silverware** **4** : color *m* plata

silverware ['sɪlvər,wær] *n* **1** : artículos *mpl* de plata, platería *f* **2** FLATWARE : cubertería *f*

silvery ['sɪlvəri] *adj* : plateado

similar ['sɪmələr] *adj* : similar, parecido, semejante

similarity [,sɪmə'lærəti] *n*, *pl* **-ties** : semejanza *f*, parecido *m*

similarly ['sɪmələrli] *adv* : de manera similar

simile ['sɪmə,li:] *n* : símil *m*

simmer ['sɪmər] *v* : hervir a fuego lento

simper¹ ['sɪmpər] *vi* : sonreír como un tonto

simper² *n* : sonrisa *f* tonta

simple ['sɪmpəl] *adj* **simpler; -plest** **1** INNOCENT : inocente **2** PLAIN : sencillo, simple **3** EASY : simple, sencillo, fácil **4** STRAIGHTFORWARD : puro, simple ⟨the simple truth : la pura verdad⟩ **5** NAIVE : ingenuo, simple

simpleton ['sɪmpəltən] *n* : bobo *m*, -ba *f*; tonto *m*, -ta *f*

simplicity [sɪm'plɪsəti] *n* : simplicidad *f*, sencillez *f*

simplification [,sɪmpləfə'keɪʃən] *n* : simplificación *f*

simplify ['sɪmplə,faɪ] *vt* **-fied; -fying** : simplificar

simply ['sɪmpli] *adv* **1** PLAINLY : sencillamente **2** SOLELY : simplemente, sólo **3** REALLY : absolutamente

simulate ['sɪmjə,leɪt] *vt* **-lated; -lating** : simular

simulation [,sɪmjə'leɪʃən] *n* : simulación *f*

simultaneous [,saɪməl'teɪniəs] *adj* : simultáneo — **simultaneously** *adv*

sin¹ ['sɪn] *vi* **sinned; sinning** : pecar

sin² *n* : pecado *m*

since¹ ['sɪnts] *adv* **1** : desde entonces ⟨they've been friends ever since : desde entonces han sido amigos⟩ ⟨she's since become mayor : más tarde se hizo alcalde⟩ **2** AGO : hace ⟨he's long since dead : murió hace mucho⟩

since² *conj* **1** : desde que ⟨since he was born : desde que nació⟩ **2** INASMUCH AS : ya que, puesto que, dado que

since³ *prep* : desde

sincere [sɪn'sɪr] *adj* **-cerer; -est** : sincero — **sincerely** *adv*

sincerity [sɪn'serəti] *n* : sinceridad *f*

sinew ['sɪnju:, 'sɪ,nu:] *n* **1** TENDON : tendón *m*, nervio *m* (en la carne) **2** POWER : fuerza *f*

sinewy ['sɪnjui, 'sɪnui] *adj* **1** STRINGY : fibroso **2** STRONG, WIRY : fuerte, nervudo

sinful ['sɪnfəl] *adj* : pecador (dícese de las personas), pecaminoso

sing ['sɪŋ] *v* **sang** ['sæŋ] *or* **sung** ['sʌŋ]; **sung; singing** : cantar

singe ['sɪnd͡ʒ] *vt* **singed; singeing** : chamuscar, quemar

singer ['sɪŋər] *n* : cantante *mf*

single¹ ['sɪŋgəl] *vt* **-gled; -gling** *or* **to single out 1** SELECT : escoger **2** DISTINGUISH : señalar

single² *adj* **1** UNMARRIED : soltero **2** SOLE : solo ⟨a single survivor : un solo sobreviviente⟩ ⟨every single one : cada uno, todos⟩

single³ *n* **1** : soltero *m*, -ra *f* ⟨for married couples and singles : para los matrimonios y los solteros⟩ **2** *or* **single room** : habitación *f* individual **3** DOLLAR : billete *m* de un dólar

single–handed ['sɪŋɡəl'hændəd] *adj* : sin ayuda, solo

singly ['sɪŋɡli] *adv* : individualmente, uno por uno

singular¹ ['sɪŋɡjələr] *adj* **1** : singular (en gramática) **2** OUTSTANDING : singular, sobresaliente **3** STRANGE : singular, extraño

singular² *n* : singular *m*

singularity [ˌsɪŋɡjə'lærəti] *n*, *pl* **-ties** : singularidad *f*

singularly ['sɪŋɡjələrli] *adv* : singularmente

sinister ['sɪnəstər] *adj* : siniestro

sink¹ ['sɪŋk] *v* **sank** ['sæŋk] *or* **sunk** ['sʌŋk]; **sunk; sinking** *vi* **1** : hundirse (dícese de un barco) **2** DROP, FALL : descender, caer ⟨to sink into a chair : dejarse caer en una silla⟩ ⟨her heart sank : se le cayó el alma a los pies⟩ **3** DECREASE : bajar — *vt* **1** : hundir (un barco, etc.) **2** EXCAVATE : excavar (un pozo para minar), perforar (un pozo de agua) **3** PLUNGE, STICK : clavar, hincar **4** INVEST : invertir (fondos)

sink² *n* **1** **kitchen sink** : fregadero *m*, lavaplatos *m* *Chile, Col, Mex* **2** **bathroom sink** : lavabo *m*, lavamanos *m*

sinner ['sɪnər] *n* : pecador *m*, -dora *f*

sinuous ['sɪnjuəs] *adj* : sinuoso — **sinuously** *adv*

sinus ['saɪnəs] *n* : seno *m*

sip¹ ['sɪp] *v* **sipped; sipping** *vt* : sorber — *vi* : beber a sorbos

sip² *n* : sorbo *m*

siphon¹ ['saɪfən] *vt* : sacar con sifón

siphon² *n* : sifón *m*

sir ['sər] *n* **1** (*in titles*) : sir *m* **2** (*as a form of address*) : señor *m* ⟨Dear Sir : Muy señor mío⟩ ⟨yes sir! : ¡sí, señor!⟩

sire¹ ['saɪr] *vt* **sired; siring** : engendrar, ser el padre de

sire² *n* : padre *m*

siren ['saɪrən] *n* : sirena *f*

sirloin ['sər,lɔɪn] *n* : solomillo *m*

sirup → **syrup**

sisal ['saɪsəl, -zəl] *n* : sisal *m*

sissy ['sɪsi] *n*, *pl* **-sies** : mariquita *f fam*

sister ['sɪstər] *n* **1** : hermana *f* **2** **Sister** : hermana *f*, Sor *f* ⟨Sister Mary : Sor María⟩

sisterhood ['sɪstər,hʊd] *n* **1** : condición *f* de ser hermana **2** : sociedad *f* de mujeres

sister–in–law ['sɪstərɪn,lɔ] *n*, *pl* **sisters–in–law** : cuñada *f*

sisterly ['sɪstərli] *adj* : de hermana

sit ['sɪt] *v* **sat** ['sæt]; **sitting** *vi* **1** : sentarse, estar sentado ⟨he sat down : se sentó⟩ **2** ROOST : posarse **3** : sesionar ⟨the legislature is sitting : la legislatu-

ra está en sesión⟩ **4** POSE : posar (para un retrato) **5** LIE, REST : estar (ubicado) ⟨the house sits on a hill : la casa está en una colina⟩ — *vt* SEAT : sentar, colocar ⟨I sat him on the sofa : lo senté en el sofá⟩

sitcom ['sɪt,kɑm] → **situation comedy**

site ['saɪt] *n* **1** PLACE : sitio *m*, lugar *m* **2** LOCATION : emplazamiento *m*, ubicación *f*

sitter ['sɪtər] → **baby–sitter**

sitting room → **living room**

situated ['sɪtʃʊ,eɪtəd] *adj* LOCATED : ubicado, situado

situation [ˌsɪtʃʊ'eɪʃən] *n* **1** LOCATION : situación *f*, ubicación *f*, emplazamiento *m* **2** CIRCUMSTANCES : situación *f* **3** JOB : empleo *m*

situation comedy *n* : comedia *f* de situación

six¹ ['sɪks] *adj* : seis

six² *n* : seis *m*

six–gun ['sɪks,ɡʌn] *n* : revólver *m* (con seis cámaras)

six hundred¹ *adj* : seiscientos

six hundred² *n* : seiscientos *m*

six–shooter ['sɪks,ʃuːtər] → **six–gun**

sixteen¹ [sɪks'tiːn] *adj* : dieciséis

sixteen² *n* : dieciséis *m*

sixteenth¹ [sɪks'tiːnθ] *adj* : decimosexto

sixteenth² *n* **1** : decimosexto *m*, -ta *f* (en una serie) **2** : dieciseisavo *m*, dieciseisava parte *f*

sixth¹ ['sɪksθ, 'sɪkst] *adj* : sexto

sixth² *n* **1** : sexto *m*, -ta *f* (en una serie) **2** : sexto *m*, sexta parte *f*

sixtieth¹ ['sɪkstiəθ] *adj* : sexagésimo

sixtieth² *n* **1** : sexagésimo *m*, -ma *f* (en una serie) **2** : sesentavo *m*, sesentava parte *f*

sixty¹ ['sɪksti] *adj* : sesenta

sixty² *n*, *pl* **-ties** : sesenta *m*

sizable *or* **sizeable** ['saɪzəbəl] *adj* : considerable

size¹ ['saɪz] *vt* **sized; sizing 1** : clasificar según el tamaño **2** **to size up** : evaluar, apreciar

size² *n* **1** DIMENSIONS : tamaño *m*, talla *f* (de ropa), número *m* (de zapatos) **2** MAGNITUDE : magnitud *f*

sizzle ['sɪzəl] *vi* **-zled; -zling** : chisporrotear

skate¹ ['skeɪt] *vi* **skated; skating** : patinar

skate² *n* **1** : patín *m* ⟨roller skate : patín de ruedas⟩ **2** : raya *f* (pez)

skateboard ['skeɪt,bord] *n* : monopatín *m*

skater ['skeɪtər] *n* : patinador *m*, -dora *f*

skein ['skeɪn] *n* : madeja *f*

skeletal ['sklətəl] *adj* **1** : óseo (en anatomía) **2** EMACIATED : esquelético

skeleton ['skɛlətən] *n* **1** : esqueleto *m* (anatómico) **2** FRAMEWORK : armazón *mf*

skeptic ['skɛptɪk] *n* : escéptico *m*, -ca *f*

skeptical ['skɛptɪkəl] *adj* : escéptico

skepticism ['skɛptə,sɪzəm] *n* : escepticismo *m*

sketch[1] ['skɛtʃ] *vt* : bosquejar — *vi* : hacer bosquejos
sketch[2] *n* **1** DRAWING, OUTLINE : esbozo *m*, bosquejo *m* **2** ESSAY : ensayo *m*
sketchy ['skɛtʃi] *adj* **sketchier; -est** : incompleto, poco detallado
skewer[1] ['skju:ər] *vt* : ensartar (carne, etc.)
skewer[2] *n* : brocheta *f*, broqueta *f*
ski[1] ['ski:] *vi* **skied; skiing** : esquiar
ski[2] *n, pl* **skis** : esquí *m*
skid[1] ['skɪd] *vi* **skidded; skidding** : derrapar, patinar
skid[2] *n* : derrape *m*, patinazo *m*
skier ['ski:ər] *n* : esquiador *m*, -dora *f*
skiff ['skɪf] *n* : esquife *m*
skill ['skɪl] *n* **1** DEXTERITY : habilidad *f*, destreza *f* **2** CAPABILITY : capacidad *f*, arte *m*, técnica *f* ⟨organizational skills : la capacidad para organizar⟩
skilled ['skɪld] *adj* : hábil, experto
skillet ['skɪlət] *n* : sartén *mf*
skillful ['skɪlfəl] *adj* : hábil, diestro
skillfully ['skɪlfəli] *adv* : con habilidad, con destreza
skim[1] ['skɪm] *vt* **skimmed; skimming 1** *or* **to skim off** : espumar, descremar (leche) **2** : echarle un vistazo a (un libro, etc.), pasar rozando (una superficie)
skim[2] *adj* : descremado ⟨skim milk : leche descremada⟩
skimp ['skɪmp] *vi* **to skimp on** : escatimar
skimpy ['skɪmpi] *adj* **skimpier; -est** : exiguo, escaso, raquítico
skin[1] ['skɪn] *vt* **skinned; skinning** : despellejar, desollar
skin[2] *n* **1** : piel *f*, cutis *m* (de la cara) ⟨dark skin : piel morena⟩ **2** RIND : piel *f*
skin diving *n* : buceo *m*, submarinismo *m*
skinflint ['skɪn,flɪnt] *n* : tacaño *m*, -ña *f*
skinned ['skɪnd] *adj* : de piel ⟨toughskinned : de piel dura⟩
skinny ['skɪni] *adj* **skinnier; -est** : flaco
skip[1] ['skɪp] *v* **skipped; skipping** *vi* : ir dando brincos — *vt* : saltarse
skip[2] *n* : brinco *m*, salto *m*
skipper ['skɪpər] *n* : capitán *m*, -tana *f*
skirmish[1] ['skərmɪʃ] *vi* : escaramuzar
skirmish[2] *n* : escaramuza *f*, refriega *f*
skirt[1] ['skərt] *vt* **1** BORDER : bordear **2** EVADE : evadir, esquivar
skirt[2] *n* : falda *f*, pollera *f*
skit ['skɪt] *n* : sketch *m* (teatral)
skittish ['skɪtɪʃ] *adj* : asustadizo, nervioso
skulk ['skʌlk] *vi* : merodear
skull ['skʌl] *n* **1** : cráneo *m*, calavera *f* **2 skull and crossbones** : calavera *f* (bandera pirata)
skunk ['skʌŋk] *n* : zorrillo *m*, mofeta *f*
sky ['skaɪ] *n, pl* **skies** : cielo *m*
skylark ['skaɪ,lɑrk] *n* : alondra *f*
skylight ['skaɪ,laɪt] *n* : claraboya *f*, tragaluz *m*

skyline ['skaɪ,laɪn] *n* : horizonte *m*
skyrocket ['skaɪ,rɑkət] *vi* : dispararse
skyscraper ['skaɪ,skreɪpər] *n* : rascacielos *m*
slab ['slæb] *n* : losa *f* (de piedra), tabla *f* (de madera), pedazo *m* grueso (de pan, etc.)
slack[1] ['slæk] *adj* **1** CARELESS : descuidado, negligente **2** LOOSE : flojo **3** SLOW : de poco movimiento
slack[2] *n* **1** : parte *f* floja ⟨to take up the slack : tensar (una cuerda, etc.)⟩ **2**
slacks *npl* : pantalones *mpl*
slacken ['slækən] *vt* : aflojar — *vi* : aflojarse
slacker ['slækər] *n* : vago *m*, -ga *f*; holgazán *m*, -zana *f*
slag ['slæg] *n* : escoria *f*
slain → **slay**
slake ['sleɪk] *vt* **slaked; slaking** : saciar (la sed), satisfacer (la curiosidad)
slam[1] ['slæm] *v* **slammed; slamming** *vt* **1** : cerrar de golpe ⟨he slammed the door : dio un portazo⟩ **2** : tirar o dejar caer de golpe ⟨he slammed down the book : dejó caer el libro de un golpe⟩ — *vi* **1** : cerrarse de golpe **2 to slam into** : chocar contra
slam[2] *n* : golpe *m*, portazo *m* (de una puerta)
slander[1] ['slændər] *vt* : calumniar, difamar
slander[2] *n* : calumnia *f*, difamación *f*
slanderous ['slændərəs] *adj* : difamatorio, calumnioso
slang ['slæŋ] *n* : argot *m*, jerga *f*
slant[1] ['slænt] *vi* : inclinarse, ladearse — *vt* **1** SLOPE : inclinar **2** ANGLE : sesgar, orientar, dirigir ⟨a story slanted towards youth : un artículo dirigido a los jóvenes⟩
slant[2] *n* **1** INCLINE : inclinación *f* **2** PERSPECTIVE : perspectiva *f*, enfoque *m*
slap[1] ['slæp] *vt* **slapped; slapping** : bofetear, cachetear, dar una palmada (en la espalda, etc.)
slap[2] *n* : bofetada *f*, cachetada *f*, palmada *f*
slash[1] ['slæʃ] *vt* **1** GASH : cortar, hacer un tajo en **2** REDUCE : rebajar, rebajar (precios)
slash[2] *n* : tajo *m*, corte *m*
slat ['slæt] *n* : tablilla *f*, listón *m*
slate ['sleɪt] *n* **1** : pizarra *f* ⟨a slate roof : un techo de pizarra⟩ **2** : lista *f* de candidatos (políticos)
slaughter[1] ['slɔtər] *vt* **1** BUTCHER : matar (animales) **2** MASSACRE : masacrar (personas)
slaughter[2] *n* **1** : matanza *f* (de animales) **2** MASSACRE : masacre *f*, carnicería *f*
slaughterhouse ['slɔtər,haʊs] *n* : matadero *m*
Slav ['slɑv, 'slæv] *n* : eslavo *m*, -va *f*
slave[1] ['sleɪv] *vi* **slaved; slaving** : trabajar como un burro
slave[2] *n* : esclavo *m*, -va *f*
slaver ['slævər, 'sleɪ-] *vi* : babear

slavery ['sleɪvəri] n : esclavitud f
Slavic ['slɑvɪk, 'slæ-] adj : eslavo
slavish ['sleɪvɪʃ] adj 1 SERVILE : servil 2 IMITATIVE : poco original
slay ['sleɪ] vt slew ['slu:]; slain ['sleɪn]; slaying : asesinar, matar
slayer ['sleɪər] n : asesino m, -na f
sleazy ['sli:zi] adj sleazier; -est 1 SHODDY : chapucero, de mala calidad 2 DILAPIDATED : ruinoso 3 DISREPUTABLE : de mala fama
sled¹ ['slɛd] v sledded; sledding vi : ir en trineo — vt : transportar en trineo
sled² n : trineo m
sledge ['slɛdʒ] n 1 : trineo m (grande) 2 → sledgehammer
sledgehammer ['slɛdʒˌhæmər] n : almádena f, combo m Chile, Peru
sleek¹ ['sli:k] vt SLICK : alisar
sleek² adj : liso y brillante
sleep¹ ['sli:p] vi slept ['slɛpt]; sleeping : dormir
sleep² n 1 : sueño m 2 to go to sleep : dormirse
sleeper ['sli:pər] n 1 : durmiente mf ⟨to be a light sleeper : tener el sueño ligero⟩ 2 or sleeping car : coche m cama, coche m dormitorio
sleepily ['sli:pəli] adv : de manera somnolienta
sleepiness ['sli:pinəs] n : somnolencia f
sleepless ['sli:pləs] adj : sin dormir, desvelado ⟨to have a sleepless night : pasar la noche en blanco⟩
sleepwalker ['sli:pˌwɔkər] n : sonámbulo m, -la f
sleepy ['sli:pi] adj sleepier; -est 1 DROWSY : somnoliento, soñoliento ⟨to be sleepy : tener sueño⟩ 2 LETHARGIC : aletargado, letárgico
sleet¹ ['sli:t] vi to be sleeting : caer aguanieve
sleet² n : aguanieve f
sleeve ['sli:v] n : manga f (de una camisa, etc.)
sleeveless ['sli:vləs] adj : sin mangas
sleigh¹ ['sleɪ] vi : ir en trineo
sleigh² n : trineo m (tirado por caballos)
sleight of hand [ˌslaɪtəv'hænd] : prestidigitación f, juegos mpl de manos
slender ['slɛndər] adj 1 SLIM : esbelto, delgado 2 SCANTY : exiguo, escaso ⟨a slender hope : una esperanza lejana⟩
sleuth ['slu:θ] n : detective mf; sabueso m, -sa f
slew → slay
slice¹ ['slaɪs] vt sliced; slicing : cortar
slice² n : rebanada f, tajada f, lonja f (de carne, etc.), rodaja f (de una verdura, fruta, etc.), trozo m (de pastel, etc.)
slick¹ ['slɪk] vt : alisar
slick² adj 1 SLIPPERY : resbaladizo, resbaloso 2 CRAFTY : astuto, taimado
slicker ['slɪkər] n : impermeable m
slide¹ ['slaɪd] v slid ['slɪd]; sliding ['slaɪdɪŋ] vi 1 SLIP : resbalar 2 GLIDE : deslizarse 3 DECLINE : bajar ⟨to let

things slide : dejar pasar las cosas⟩ — vt : correr, deslizar
slide² n 1 SLIDING : deslizamiento m 2 SLIP : resbalón m 3 : tobogán m (para niños) 4 TRANSPARENCY : diapositiva f (fotográfica) 5 DECLINE : descenso m
slier, sliest → sly
slight¹ ['slaɪt] vt : desairar, despreciar
slight² adj 1 SLENDER : esbelto, delgado 2 FLIMSY : endeble 3 TRIFLING : leve, insignificante ⟨a slight pain : un leve dolor⟩ 4 SMALL : pequeño, ligero ⟨not in the slightest : en absoluto⟩
slight³ n SNUB : desaire m
slightly ['slaɪtli] adv : ligeramente, un poco
slim¹ ['slɪm] v slimmed; slimming : adelgazar
slim² adj slimmer; slimmest 1 SLENDER : esbelto, delgado 2 SCANTY : exiguo, escaso
slime ['slaɪm] n 1 : baba f (secretada por un animal) 2 MUD, SILT : fango m, cieno m
slimy ['slaɪmi] adj slimier; -est : viscoso
sling¹ ['slɪŋ] vt slung ['slʌŋ]; slinging 1 THROW : lanzar, tirar 2 HANG : colgar
sling² n 1 : honda f (arma) 2 : cabestrillo m ⟨my arm is in a sling : llevo el brazo en cabestrillo⟩
slingshot ['slɪŋˌʃɑt] n : tiragomas m, resortera f Mex
slink ['slɪŋk] vi slunk ['slʌŋk]; slinking : caminar furtivamente
slip¹ ['slɪp] v slipped; slipping vi 1 STEAL : ir sigilosamente ⟨to slip away : escabullirse⟩ ⟨to slip out the door : escaparse por la puerta⟩ 2 SLIDE : resbalarse, deslizarse 3 LAPSE : caer ⟨to slip into error : equivocarse⟩ 4 to let slip : dejar escapar 5 to slip into PUT ON : ponerse — vt 1 PUT : meter, poner 2 PASS : pasar ⟨she slipped me a note : me pasó una nota⟩ 3 to slip one's mind : olvidársele a uno
slip² n 1 PIER : atracadero m 2 MISHAP : percance m, contratiempo m 3 MISTAKE : error m, desliz m ⟨a slip of the tongue : un lapsus⟩ 4 PETTICOAT : enagua f 5 : injerto m, esqueje m (de una planta) 6 slip of paper : papelito m
slipper ['slɪpər] n : zapatilla f, pantufla f
slipperiness ['slɪpərinəs] n 1 : lo resbaloso, lo resbaladizo 2 TRICKINESS : astucia f
slippery ['slɪpəri] adj slipperier; -est 1 : resbaloso, resbaladizo ⟨a slippery road : un camino resbaloso⟩ 2 TRICKY : artero, astuto, taimado 3 ELUSIVE : huidizo, escurridizo
slipshod ['slɪpˌʃɑd] adj : descuidado, chapucero
slip up vi : equivocarse
slit¹ ['slɪt] vt slit; slitting : cortar, abrir por lo largo

slit² *n* **1** OPENING : abertura *f*, rendija *f* **2** CUT : corte *m*, raja *f*, tajo *m*
slither ['slɪðər] *vi* : deslizarse
sliver ['slɪvər] *n* : astilla *f*
slob ['slɑb] *n* : persona *f* desaliñada ⟨what a slob! : ¡qué cerdo!⟩
slobber¹ ['slɑbər] *vi* : babear
slobber² *n* : baba *f*
slogan ['slo:gən] *n* : lema *m*, eslogan *m*
sloop ['slu:p] *n* : balandra *f*
slop¹ ['slɑp] *v* **slopped; slopping** *vt* : derramar — *vi* : derramarse
slop² *n* : bazofia *f*
slope¹ ['slo:p] *vi* **sloped; sloping** : inclinarse ⟨the road slopes upward : el camino sube (en pendiente)⟩
slope² *n* : inclinación *f*, pendiente *f*, declive *m*
sloppy ['slɑpi] *adj* **sloppier; -est** **1** MUDDY, SLUSHY : lodoso, fangoso **2** UNTIDY : descuidado (en el trabajo, etc.), desaliñado (de aspecto)
slot ['slɑt] *n* : ranura *f*
sloth ['slɔθ, 'slo:θ] *n* **1** LAZINESS : pereza *f* **2** : perezoso *m* (animal)
slouch¹ ['slaʊtʃ] *vi* : andar con los hombros caídos, repantigarse (en un sillón)
slouch² *n* **1** SLUMPING : mala postura *f* **2** BUNGLER, IDLER : haragán *m*, -gana *f*; inepto *m*, -ta *f* ⟨to be no slouch : no quedarse atrás⟩
slough¹ ['slʌf] *vt* : mudar de (piel)
slough² ['slu:, 'slaʊ] *n* SWAMP : ciénaga *f*
Slovak ['slo:ˌvɑk, -ˌvæk] *or* **Slovakian** [slo:'vɑkiən, -'væ-] *n* : eslovaco *m*, -ca *f* — **Slovak** *or* **Slovakian** *adj*
Slovene ['slo:ˌvi:n] *or* **Slovenian** [slo:-'vi:niən] *n* : esloveno *m*, -na *f* — **Slovene** *or* **Slovenian** *adj*
slovenly ['slavənli, 'slʌv-] *adj* : descuidado (en el trabajo, etc.), desaliñado (de aspecto)
slow¹ [slo:] *vt* : retrasar, reducir la marcha de — *vi* : ir más despacio
slow² *adv* : despacio, lentamente
slow³ *adj* **1** : lento ⟨a slow process : un proceso lento⟩ **2** : atrasado ⟨my watch is slow : mi reloj está atrasado, mi reloj se atrasa⟩ **3** SLUGGISH : lento, poco activo **4** STUPID : lento, torpe, corto de alcances
slowly [slo:li] *adv* : lentamente, despacio
slowness [slo:nəs] *n* : lentitud *f*, torpeza *f*
sludge ['slʌdʒ] *n* : aguas *fpl* negras, aguas *fpl* residuales
slug¹ ['slʌg] *vt* **slugged; slugging** : pegarle un porrazo (a alguien)
slug² *n* **1** : babosa *f* (molusco) **2** BULLET : bala *f* **3** TOKEN : ficha *f* **4** BLOW : porrazo *m*, puñetazo *m*
sluggish ['slʌgɪʃ] *adj* : aletargado, lento
sluice¹ ['slu:s] *vt* **sluiced; sluicing** : lavar en agua corriente
sluice² *n* : canal *m*
slum ['slʌm] *n* : barriada *f*, barrio *m* bajo

slumber¹ ['slʌmbər] *vi* : dormir
slumber² *n* : sueño *m*
slump¹ ['slʌmp] *vi* **1** DECLINE, DROP : disminuir, bajar **2** SLOUCH : encorvarse, dejarse caer (en una silla, etc.)
slump² *n* : bajón *m*, declive *m* (económico)
slung → **sling**
slunk → **slink**
slur¹ ['slər] *vt* **slurred; slurring** : ligar (notas musicales), tragarse (las palabras)
slur² *n* **1** : ligado *m* (en música), mala pronunciación *f* (de las palabras) **2** ASPERSION : calumnia *f*, difamación *f*
slurp¹ ['slərp] *vi* : beber o comer haciendo ruido — *vt* : sorber ruidosamente
slurp² *n* : sorbo *m* (ruidoso)
slush ['slʌʃ] *n* : nieve *f* medio derretida
slut ['slʌt] *n* PROSTITUTE : ramera *f*, fulana *f*
sly ['slaɪ] *adj* **slier** ['slaɪər]; **sliest** ['slaɪəst] **1** CUNNING : astuto, taimado **2** UNDERHANDED : soplado — **slyly** *adv*
slyness ['slaɪnəs] *n* : astucia *f*
smack¹ ['smæk] *vi* **to smack of** : oler a, saber a — *vt* **1** KISS : besar, plantarle un beso (a alguien) **2** SLAP : pegarle una bofetada (a alguien) **3 to smack one's lips** : relamerse
smack² *adv* : justo, exactamente ⟨smack in the face : en plena cara⟩
smack³ *n* **1** TASTE, TRACE : sabor *m*, indicio *m* **2** : chasquido *m* (de los labios) **3** SLAP : bofetada *f* **4** KISS : beso *m*
small ['smɔl] *adj* **1** : pequeño, chico ⟨a small house : una casa pequeña⟩ ⟨small change : monedas de poco valor⟩ **2** TRIVIAL : pequeño, insignificante
smallness ['smɔlnəs] *n* : pequeñez *f*
smallpox ['smɔlˌpɑks] *n* : viruela *f*
smart¹ ['smɑrt] *vi* **1** STING : escocer, picar, arder **2** HURT : dolerse, resentirse ⟨to smart under a rejection : dolerse ante un rechazo⟩
smart² *adj* **1** BRIGHT : listo, vivo, inteligente **2** STYLISH : elegante — **smartly** *adv*
smart³ *n* **1** PAIN : escozor *m*, dolor *m* **2** **smarts** *npl* : inteligencia *f*
smartness ['smɑrtnəs] *n* **1** INTELLIGENCE : inteligencia *f* **2** ELEGANCE : elegancia *f*
smash¹ ['smæʃ] *vt* **1** BREAK : romper, quebrar, hacer pedazos **2** WRECK : destrozar, arruinar **3** CRASH : estrellar, chocar — *vi* **1** SHATTER : hacerse pedazos, hacerse añicos **2** COLLIDE, CRASH : estrellarse, chocar
smash² *n* **1** BLOW : golpe *m* **2** COLLISION : choque *m* **3** BANG, CRASH : estrépito *m*
smattering ['smæt̬ərɪŋ] *n* **1** : nociones *fpl* ⟨she has a smattering of programming : tiene nociones de programación⟩ **2** : un poco, unos cuantos ⟨a

smattering of spectators : unos cuantos espectadores⟩

smear[1] [ˈsmɪr] vt **1** DAUB : embadurnar, untar (mantequilla, etc.) **2** SMUDGE : emborronar **3** SLANDER : calumniar, difamar

smear[2] n **1** SMUDGE : mancha f **2** SLANDER : calumnia f

smell[1] [ˈsmɛl] v **smelled** or **smelt** [ˈsmɛlt]; **smelling** vt : oler, olfatear ⟨to smell danger : olfatear el peligro⟩ — vi : oler ⟨to smell good : oler bien⟩

smell[2] n **1** : olfato m, sentido m del olfato **2** ODOR : olor m

smelly [ˈsmɛli] adj **smellier; -est** : maloliente

smelt[1] [ˈsmɛlt] vt : fundir

smelt[2] n, pl **smelts** or **smelt** : eperlano m (pez)

smile[1] [ˈsmaɪl] vi **smiled; smiling** : sonreír

smile[2] n : sonrisa f

smirk[1] [ˈsmərk] vi : sonreír con suficiencia

smirk[2] n : sonrisa f satisfecha

smite [ˈsmaɪt] vt **smote** [ˈsmoːt]; **smitten** [ˈsmɪtən] or **smote; smiting 1** STRIKE : golpear **2** AFFLICT : afligir

smith [ˈsmɪθ] n : herrero m, -ra f

smithy [ˈsmɪθi] n, pl **smithies** : herrería f

smock [ˈsmɑk] n : bata f, blusón m

smog [ˈsmɑg, ˈsmɔg] n : smog m

smoke[1] [ˈsmoːk] v **smoked; smoking** vi **1** : echar humo, humear ⟨a smoking chimney : una chimenea que echa humo⟩ **2** : fumar ⟨I don't smoke : no fumo⟩ — vt : ahumar (carne, etc.)

smoke[2] n : humo m

smoke detector [dɪˈtɛktər] n : detector m de humo

smoker [ˈsmoːkər] n : fumador m, -dora f

smokestack [ˈsmoːkˌstæk] n : chimenea f

smoky [ˈsmoːki] adj **smokier; -est 1** SMOKING : humeante **2** : a humo ⟨a smoky flavor : un sabor a humo⟩ **3** : lleno de humo ⟨a smoky room : un cuarto lleno de humo⟩

smolder [ˈsmoːldər] vi **1** : arder sin llama **2** : arder (en el corazón) ⟨his anger smoldered : su rabia ardía⟩

smooth[1] [ˈsmuːð] vt : alisar

smooth[2] adj **1** : liso (dícese de una superficie) ⟨smooth skin : piel lisa⟩ **2** : suave (dícese de un movimiento) ⟨a smooth landing : un aterrizaje suave⟩ **3** : sin grumos ⟨a smooth sauce : una salsa sin grumos⟩ **4** : fluido ⟨smooth writing : escritura fluida⟩

smoothly [ˈsmuːðli] adv **1** GENTLY, SOFTLY : suavemente **2** EASILY : con facilidad, sin problemas

smoothness [ˈsmuːðnəs] n : suavidad f

smother [ˈsmʌðər] vt **1** SUFFOCATE : ahogar, sofocar **2** COVER : cubrir **3** SUPPRESS : contener — vi : asfixiarse

smudge[1] [ˈsmʌʤ] v **smudged; smudging** vt : emborronar — vi : correrse

smudge[2] n : mancha f, borrón m

smug [ˈsmʌg] adj **smugger; smuggest** : suficiente, pagado de sí mismo

smuggle [ˈsmʌgəl] vt **-gled; -gling** : contrabandear, pasar de contrabando

smuggler [ˈsmʌgələr] n : contrabandista mf

smugly [ˈsmʌgli] adv : con suficiencia

smut [ˈsmʌt] n **1** SOOT : tizne m, hollín m **2** FUNGUS : tizón m **3** OBSCENITY : obscenidad f, inmundicia f

smutty [ˈsmʌti] adj **smuttier; -est 1** SOOTY : tiznado **2** OBSCENE : obsceno, indecente

snack [ˈsnæk] n : refrigerio m, bocado m, tentempié m fam ⟨an afternoon snack : una merienda⟩

snag[1] [ˈsnæg] v **snagged; snagging** vt : enganchar — vi : engancharse

snag[2] n : problema m, inconveniente m

snail [ˈsneɪl] n : caracol m

snake [ˈsneɪk] n : culebra f, serpiente f

snakebite [ˈsneɪkˌbaɪt] n : mordedura f de serpiente

snap[1] [ˈsnæp] v **snapped; snapping** vi **1** : intentar morder (dícese de un perro, etc.), picar (dícese de un pez) **2** : hablar con severidad ⟨he snapped at me! : ¡me gritó!⟩ **3** BREAK : romperse, quebrarse (haciendo un chasquido) — vt **1** BREAK : partir (en dos), quebrar **2** : hacer (algo) de un golpe ⟨to snap open : abrir de golpe⟩ **3** RETORT : decir bruscamente **4** CLICK : chasquear ⟨to snap one's fingers : chasquear los dedos⟩

snap[2] n **1** CLICK, CRACK : chasquido m **2** FASTENER : broche m **3** CINCH : cosa f fácil ⟨it's a snap : es facilísimo⟩

snapdragon [ˈsnæpˌdrægən] n : dragón m (flor)

snapper [ˈsnæpər] → **red snapper**

snappy [ˈsnæpi] adj **snappier; -est 1** FAST : rápido ⟨make it snappy! : ¡date prisa!⟩ **2** LIVELY : vivaz **3** CHILLY : frío **4** STYLISH : elegante

snapshot [ˈsnæpˌʃɑt] n : instantánea f

snare[1] [ˈsnær] vt **snared; snaring** : atrapar

snare[2] n : trampa f, red f

snare drum n : tambor m con bordón

snarl[1] [ˈsnɑrl] vi **1** TANGLE : enmarañar, enredar **2** GROWL : gruñir

snarl[2] n **1** TANGLE : enredo m, maraña f **2** GROWL : gruñido m

snatch[1] [ˈsnæʧ] vt : arrebatar

snatch[2] n : fragmento m

sneak[1] [ˈsniːk] vi : ir a hurtadillas — vt : hacer furtivamente ⟨to sneak a look : mirar con disimulo⟩ ⟨he sneaked a smoke : fumó un cigarrillo a escondidas⟩

sneak[2] n : soplón m, -plona f

sneakers [ˈsniːkərz] npl : tenis mpl, zapatillas fpl

sneaky [ˈsniːki] adj **sneakier; -est** : solapado

sneer¹ [ˈsnɪr] *vi* : sonreír con desprecio
sneer² *n* : sonrisa *f* de desprecio
sneeze¹ [ˈsniːz] *vi* **sneezed; sneezing** : estornudar
sneeze² *n* : estornudo *m*
snicker¹ [ˈsnɪkər] *vi* : reírse disimuladamente
snicker² *n* : risita *f*
snide [ˈsnaɪd] *adj* : sarcástico
sniff¹ [ˈsnɪf] *vi* **1** SMELL : oler, husmear (dícese de los animales) **2 to sniff at** : despreciar, desdeñar — *vt* **1** SMELL : oler **2 to sniff out** : olerse, husmear
sniff² *n* **1** SNIFFING : aspiración *f* por la nariz **2** SMELL : olor *m*
sniffle [ˈsnɪfəl] *vi* **-fled; -fling** : respirar con la nariz congestionada
sniffles [ˈsnɪfəlz] *npl* : resfriado *m*
snip¹ [ˈsnɪp] *vt* **snipped; snipping** : cortar (con tijeras)
snip² *n* : tijeretada *f*, recorte *m*
snipe¹ [ˈsnaɪp] *vi* **sniped; sniping** : disparar
snipe² *n, pl* **snipes** *or* **snipe** : agachadiza *f*
sniper [ˈsnaɪpər] *n* : francotirador *m*, -dora *f*
snippet [ˈsnɪpət] *n* : fragmento *m* (de un texto, etc.)
snivel [ˈsnɪvəl] *vi* **-veled** *or* **-velled; -veling** *or* **-velling 1** → **snuffle 2** WHINE : lloriquear
snob [ˈsnɑb] *n* : esnob *mf*, snob *mf*
snobbery [ˈsnɑbəri] *n, pl* **-beries** : esnobismo *m*
snobbish [ˈsnɑbɪʃ] *adj* : esnob, snob
snobbishness [ˈsnɑbɪʃnəs] *n* : esnobismo *m*
snoop¹ [ˈsnuːp] *vi* : husmear, curiosear
snoop² *n* : fisgón *m*, -gona *f*
snooze¹ [ˈsnuːz] *vi* **snoozed; snoozing** : dormitar
snooze² *n* : siestecita *f*, siestita *f*
snore¹ [ˈsnor] *vi* **snored; snoring** : roncar
snore² *n* : ronquido *m*
snort¹ [ˈsnɔrt] *vi* : bufar, resoplar
snort² *n* : bufido *m*, resoplo *m*
snout [ˈsnaʊt] *n* : hocico *m*, morro *m*
snow¹ [ˈsnoː] *vi* **1** : nevar ⟨I'm snowed in : estoy aislado por la nieve⟩ **2 to be snowed under** : estar inundado
snow² *n* : nieve *f*
snowball [ˈsnoːˌbɔl] *n* : bola *f* de nieve
snowdrift [ˈsnoːˌdrɪft] *n* : ventisquero *m*
snowfall [ˈsnoːˌfɔl] *n* : nevada *f*
snowplow [ˈsnoːˌplaʊ] *n* : quitanieves *m*
snowshoe [ˈsnoːˌʃuː] *n* : raqueta *f* (para nieve)
snowstorm [ˈsnoːˌstɔrm] *n* : tormenta *f* de nieve, ventisca *f*
snowy [ˈsnoːi] *adj* **snowier; -est** : nevoso ⟨a snowy road : un camino nevado⟩
snub¹ [ˈsnʌb] *vt* **snubbed; snubbing** : desairar
snub² *n* : desaire *m*
snub–nosed [ˈsnʌbˌnoːzd] *adj* : de nariz respingada

snuff¹ [ˈsnʌf] *vt* **1** : apagar (una vela) **2** : sorber (algo) por la nariz
snuff² *n* : rapé *m*
snuffle [ˈsnʌfəl] *vi* **-fled; -fling** : respirar con la nariz congestionada
snug [ˈsnʌg] *adj* **snugger; snuggest 1** COMFORTABLE : cómodo **2** TIGHT : ajustado, ceñido ⟨snug pants : pantalones ajustados⟩
snuggle [ˈsnʌgəl] *vi* **-gled; -gling** : acurrucarse ⟨to snuggle up to someone : arrimársele a alguien⟩
snugly [ˈsnʌgli] *adv* **1** COMFORTABLY : cómodamente **2** : de manera ajustada ⟨the shirt fits snugly : la camisa queda ajustada⟩
so¹ [ˈsoː] *adv* **1** (*referring to something indicated or suggested*) ⟨do you think so? : ¿tú crees?⟩ ⟨so it would seem : eso parece⟩ ⟨I told her so : se lo dije⟩ ⟨he's ready, or so he says : según dice, está listo⟩ ⟨it so happened that . . . : resultó que . . . ⟩ ⟨do it like so : hazlo así⟩ ⟨so be it : así sea⟩ **2** ALSO : también ⟨so do I : yo también⟩ **3** THUS : así, de esta manera **4** : tan ⟨he'd never been so happy : nunca había estado tan contento⟩ **5** CONSEQUENTLY : por lo tanto
so² *conj* **1** THEREFORE : así que **2 or so that** : para que, así que, de manera que **3 so what?** : ¿y qué?
soak¹ [ˈsoːk] *vi* : estar en remojo — *vt* **1** : poner en remojo **2 to soak up** ABSORB : absorber
soak² *n* : remojo *m*
soap¹ [ˈsoːp] *vt* : enjabonar
soap² *n* : jabón *m*
soapsuds [ˈsoːpˌsʌdz] → **suds**
soapy [ˈsoːpi] *adj* **soapier; -est** : jabonoso ⟨a soapy taste : un gusto a jabón⟩ ⟨a soapy texture : una textura de jabón⟩
soar [ˈsor] *vi* **1** FLY : volar **2** RISE : remontar el vuelo (dícese de las aves) ⟨her hopes soared : su esperanza renació⟩ ⟨prices are soaring : los precios están subiendo vertiginosamente⟩
sob¹ [ˈsɑb] *vi* **sobbed; sobbing** : sollozar
sob² *n* : sollozo *m*
sober [ˈsoːbər] *adj* **1** : sobrio ⟨he's not sober enough to drive : está demasiado borracho para manejar⟩ **2** SERIOUS : serio
soberly [ˈsoːbərli] *adv* **1** : sobriamente **2** SERIOUSLY : seriamente
sobriety [səˈbraɪəti, soː-] *n* **1** : sobriedad *f* ⟨sobriety test : prueba de alcoholemia⟩ **2** SERIOUSNESS : seriedad *f*
so–called [ˈsoːˈkɔld] *adj* : supuesto, presunto ⟨the so-called experts : los expertos, así llamados⟩
soccer [ˈsɑkər] *n* : futbol *m*, fútbol *m*
sociable [ˈsoːʃəbəl] *adj* : sociable
social¹ [ˈsoːʃəl] *adj* : social — **socially** *adv*
social² *n* : reunión *f* social

socialism [ˈsoːʃə,lɪzəm] *n* : socialismo *m*
socialist¹ [ˈsoːʃəlɪst] *adj* : socialista
socialist² *n* : socialista *mf*
socialize [ˈsoːʃə,laɪz] *v* **-ized; -izing** *vt* **1**
NATIONALIZE : nacionalizar **2** : so-
cializar (en psicología) — *vi* : alternar,
circular ⟨to socialize with friends : alternar con amigos⟩
social work *n* : asistencia *f* social
society [səˈsaɪəti] *n, pl* **-eties 1** COM-
PANIONSHIP : compañía *f* **2** : sociedad
f ⟨a democratic society : una sociedad
democrática⟩ ⟨high society : alta so-
ciedad⟩ **3** ASSOCIATION : sociedad *f*,
asociación *f*
socioeconomic [,soːsio,iːkəˈnɑmɪk,
-,ɛkə-] *adj* : socioeconómico
sociology [,soːsiˈɑlədʒi] *n* : sociología *f*
sociological [,soːsiəˈlɑdʒɪkəl] *adj* : sociológico
sociologist [,soːsiˈɑlədʒɪst] *n* : sociólogo
m, -ga *f*
sock¹ [ˈsɑk] *vt* : pegar, golpear, darle un
puñetazo a
sock² *n* **1** *pl* **socks** *or* **sox** [ˈsɑks] : calcetín *m*, media *f* ⟨shoes and socks : za-
patos y calcetines⟩ **2** *pl* **socks** [ˈsɑks]
PUNCH : puñetazo *m*
socket [ˈsɑkət] *n* **1** *or* **electric socket**
: enchufe *m*, toma *f* de corriente **2** : glena *f* (de una articulación) ⟨shoulder
socket : glena del hombro⟩ **3 eye socket** : órbita *f*, cuenca *f*
sod¹ [ˈsɑd] *vt* **sodded; sodding** : cubrir
de césped
sod² *n* TURF : césped *m*, tepe *m*
soda [ˈsoːdə] *n* **1** *or* **soda water** : soda *f*
2 *or* **soda pop** : gaseosa *f*, refresco *m*
3 *or* **ice–cream soda** : refresco *m* con
helado
sodden [ˈsɑdən] *adj* SOGGY : empapado
sodium [ˈsoːdiəm] *n* : sodio *m*
sodium bicarbonate *n* : bicarbonato *m*
de soda
sodium chloride → **salt**
sofa [ˈsoːfə] *n* : sofá *m*
soft [ˈsɔft] *adj* **1** : blando ⟨a soft pillow
: una almohada blanda⟩ **2** SMOOTH
: suave (dícese de las texturas, de los
sonidos, etc.) **3** NONALCOHOLIC : no
alcohólico ⟨a soft drink : un refresco⟩
softball [ˈsɔft,bɔl] *n* : softbol *m*
soften [ˈsɔfən] *vt* : ablandar (algo sólido), suavizar (la piel, un golpe, etc.),
amortiguar (un impacto) — *vi* : ablandarse, suavizarse
softly [ˈsɔftli] *adv* : suavemente ⟨she
spoke softly : habló en voz baja⟩
softness [ˈsɔftnəs] *n* **1** : blandura *f*, lo
blando (de una almohada, de la mantequilla, etc.) **2** SMOOTHNESS : suavidad *f*
software [ˈsɔft,wær] *n* : software *m*
soggy [ˈsɑgi] *adj* **soggier; -est** : empapado
soil¹ [ˈsɔɪl] *vt* : ensuciar — *vi* : ensuciarse

soil² *n* **1** DIRTINESS : suciedad *f* **2** DIRT,
EARTH : suelo *m*, tierra *f* **3** COUNTRY
: patria *f* ⟨her native soil : su tierra na-
tal⟩
sojourn¹ [ˈsoː,dʒərn, soːˈdʒərn] *vi* : pasar
una temporada
sojourn² *n* : estadía *f*, estancia *f*, permanencia *f*
solace [ˈsɑləs] *n* : consuelo *m*
solar [ˈsoːlər] *adj* : solar ⟨the solar system : el sistema solar⟩
sold → **sell**
solder¹ [ˈsɑdər, ˈsɔ-] *vt* : soldar
solder² *n* : soldadura *f*
soldier¹ [ˈsoːldʒər] *vi* : servir como soldado
soldier² *n* : soldado *mf*
sole¹ [ˈsoːl] *adj* : único
sole² *n* **1** : suela *f* (de un zapato) **2**
: lenguado *m* (pez)
solely [ˈsoːli] *adv* : únicamente, sólo
solemn [ˈsɑləm] *adj* : solemne, serio —
solemnly *adv*
solemnity [səˈlɛmnəti] *n, pl* **-ties** : solemnidad *f*
solicit [səˈlɪsət] *vt* : solicitar
solicitous [səˈlɪsətəs] *adj* : solícito
solicitude [səˈlɪsə,tuːd, -,tjuːd] *n* : solicitud *f*
solid¹ [ˈsɑləd] *adj* **1** : macizo ⟨a solid
rubber ball : una bola maciza de cau-
cho⟩ **2** CUBIC : tridimensional **3** COM-
PACT : compacto, denso **4** STURDY
: sólido **5** CONTINUOUS : seguido, continuo ⟨two solid hours : dos horas
seguidas⟩ ⟨a solid line : una línea con-
tinua⟩ **6** UNANIMOUS : unánime **7** DE-
PENDABLE : serio, fiable **8** PURE : macizo, puro ⟨solid gold : oro macizo⟩
solid² *n* : sólido *m*
solidarity [,sɑləˈdærəti] *n* : solidaridad *f*
solidify [səˈlɪdə,faɪ] *v* **-fied; -fying** *vt* : solidificar — *vi* : solidificarse
solidity [səˈlɪdəti] *n, pl* **-ties** : solidez *f*
solidly [ˈsɑlədli] *adv* **1** : sólidamente **2**
UNANIMOUSLY : unánimemente
soliloquy [səˈlɪləkwi] *n, pl* **-quies** : soliloquio *m*
solitaire [ˈsɑlə,tɛr] *n* : solitario *m*
solitary [ˈsɑlə,tɛri] *adj* **1** ALONE : solitario **2** SECLUDED : apartado, retirado
3 SINGLE : solo
solitude [ˈsɑlə,tuːd, -,tjuːd] *n* : soledad *f*
solo¹ [ˈsoː,loː] *vi* : volar en solitario
(dícese de un piloto)
solo² *adv & adj* : en solitario, a solas
solo³ *n, pl* **solos** : solo *m*
soloist [ˈsoːloɪst] *n* : solista *mf*
solstice [ˈsɑlstɪs] *n* : solsticio *m*
soluble [ˈsɑljəbəl] *adj* : soluble
solution [səˈluːʃən] *n* : solución *f*
solve [ˈsɑlv] *vt* **solved; solving** : resolver, solucionar
solvency [ˈsɑlvəntsi] *n* : solvencia *f*
solvent [ˈsɑlvənt] *n* : solvente *m*
Somali [soːˈmɑli, sə-] *n* : somalí *mf* —
Somali *adj*
somber [ˈsɑmbər] *adj* **1** DARK : sombrío, oscuro ⟨somber colors : colores

oscuros⟩ **2** GRAVE : sombrío, serio **3** MELANCHOLY : sombrío, lúgubre

sombrero [səm'brɛr‚oː] *n, pl* **-ros** : sombrero *m* (mexicano)

some¹ ['sʌm] *adj* **1** : un, algún ⟨some lady stopped me : una mujer me detuvo⟩ ⟨some distant galaxy : alguna galaxia lejana⟩ **2** : algo de, un poco de ⟨he drank some water : tomó (un poco de) agua⟩ **3** : unos ⟨do you want some apples? : ¿quieres unas manzanas?⟩ ⟨some years ago : hace varios años⟩

some² *pron* **1** : algunos ⟨some went, others stayed : algunos se fueron, otros se quedaron⟩ **2** : un poco, algo ⟨there's some left : queda un poco⟩ ⟨I have gum; do you want some? : tengo chicle, ¿quieres?⟩

somebody ['sʌmbədi, -‚bɑdi] *pron* : alguien

someday ['sʌm‚deɪ] *adv* : algún día

somehow ['sʌm‚haʊ] *adv* **1** : de alguna manera, de algún modo ⟨I'll do it somehow : lo haré de alguna manera⟩ **2** : por alguna razón ⟨somehow I don't trust her : por alguna razón no me fío de ella⟩

someone ['sʌm‚wʌn] *pron* : alguien

someplace ['sʌm‚pleɪs] → **somewhere**

somersault¹ ['sʌmər‚sɔlt] *vi* : dar volteretas, dar un salto mortal

somersault² *n* : voltereta *f*, salto *m* mortal

something ['sʌmθɪŋ] *pron* : algo ⟨I want something else : quiero otra cosa⟩ ⟨she's writing a novel or something : está escribiendo una novela o no sé qué⟩

sometime ['sʌm‚taɪm] *adv* : algún día, en algún momento ⟨sometime next month : durante el mes que viene⟩

sometimes ['sʌm‚taɪmz] *adv* : a veces, algunas veces, de vez en cuando

somewhat ['sʌm‚hwʌt, -‚hwɑt] *adv* : algo, un tanto

somewhere ['sʌm‚hwɛr] *adv* **1** (*indicating location*) : en algún lugar ⟨it must be somewhere else : estará en otra parte⟩ **2** (*indicating destination*) : a algún lugar

son ['sʌn] *n* : hijo *m*

sonar ['soː‚nɑr] *n* : sonar *m*

sonata [sə'nɑṭə] *n* : sonata *f*

song ['sɔŋ] *n* : canción *f*, canto *m* (de un pájaro)

songbird ['sɔŋ‚bərd] *n* : pájaro *m* cantor

songwriter ['sɔŋ‚raɪṭər] *n* : compositor *m*, -tora *f*

sonic ['sɑnɪk] *adj* **1** : sónico **2 sonic boom** : estampido *m* sónico

son–in–law ['sʌnɪn‚lɔ] *n, pl* **sons–in–law** : yerno *m*, hijo *m* político

sonnet ['sɑnət] *n* : soneto *m*

sonorous ['sɑnərəs, sə'nɔrəs] *adj* : sonoro

soon ['suːn] *adv* **1** : pronto, dentro de poco ⟨he'll arrive soon : llegará pron-

to⟩ **2** QUICKLY : pronto ⟨as soon as possible : lo más pronto posible⟩ ⟨the sooner the better : cuanto antes mejor⟩ **3** : de buena gana ⟨I'd sooner walk : prefiero caminar⟩

soot ['sʊt, 'suːt, 'sʌt] *n* : hollín *m*, tizne *m*

soothe ['suːð] *vt* **soothed; soothing 1** CALM : calmar, tranquilizar **2** RELIEVE : aliviar

soothsayer ['suːθ‚seɪər] *n* : adivino *m*, -na *f*

sooty ['sʊṭi, 'suː-, 'sʌ-] *adj* **sootier; -est** : cubierto de hollín, tiznado

sop¹ ['sɑp] *vt* **sopped; sopping 1** DIP : mojar **2** SOAK : empapar **3 to sop up** : rebañar, absorber

sop² *n* **1** CONCESSION : concesión *f* **2** BRIBE : soborno *m*

sophisticated [sə'fɪstə‚keɪṭəd] *adj* **1** COMPLEX : complejo **2** WORLDLYWISE : sofisticado

sophistication [sə‚fɪstə'keɪʃən] *n* **1** COMPLEXITY : complejidad *f* **2** URBANITY : sofisticación *f*

sophomore ['sɑf‚mor, 'sɑfə‚mor] *n* : estudiante *mf* de segundo año

soporific [‚sɑpə'rɪfɪk, ‚soː-] *adj* : soporífero

soprano [sə'præ‚noː] *n, pl* **-nos** : soprano *mf*

sorcerer ['sɔrsərər] *n* : hechicero *m*, brujo *m*, mago *m*

sorceress ['sɔrsərəs] *n* : hechicera *f*, bruja *f*, maga *f*

sorcery ['sɔrsəri] *n* : hechicería *f*, brujería *f*

sordid ['sɔrdɪd] *adj* : sórdido

sore¹ ['sor] *adj* **sorer; sorest 1** PAINFUL : dolorido, doloroso ⟨I have a sore throat : me duele la garganta⟩ **2** ACUTE, SEVERE : extremo, grande ⟨in sore straits : en grandes apuros⟩ **3** ANGRY : enojado, enfadado

sore² *n* : llaga *f*

sorely ['sorli] *adv* : muchísimo ⟨it was sorely needed : se necesitaba urgentemente⟩ ⟨she was sorely missed : la echaban mucho de menos⟩

soreness ['sornəs] *n* : dolor *m*

sorghum ['sɔrgəm] *n* : sorgo *m*

sorority [sə'rɔrəṭi] *n, pl* **-ties** : hermandad *f* (de estudiantes femeninas)

sorrel ['sɔrəl] *n* **1** : alazán *m* (color o animal) **2** : acedera *f* (hierba)

sorrow ['sɑr‚oː] *n* : pesar *m*, dolor *m*, pena *f*

sorrowful ['sɑrofəl] *adj* : triste, afligido, apenado

sorrowfully ['sɑrofəli] *adv* : con tristeza

sorry ['sɑri] *adj* **sorrier; -est 1** PITIFUL : lastimero, lastimoso **2 to be sorry** : sentir, lamentar ⟨I'm sorry : lo siento⟩ **3 to feel sorry for** : compadecer ⟨I feel sorry for him : me da pena⟩

sort¹ ['sɔrt] *vt* **1** : dividir en grupos **2** CLASSIFY : clasificar **3 to sort out** ORGANIZE : poner en orden **4 to sort out** RESOLVE : resolver

sort[2] *n* **1** KIND : tipo *m*, clase *f* ⟨a sort of writer : una especie de escritor⟩ **2** NATURE : índole *f* **3** out of sorts : de mal humor

sortie ['sɔrṭi, sɔr'ti:] *n* : salida *f*

SOS [ˌɛsˌo:'ɛs] *n* : SOS *m*

so–so ['so:'so:] *adj & adv* : así así, de modo regular

soufflé [su:'fleɪ] *n* : suflé *m*

sought → **seek**

soul ['so:l] *n* **1** SPIRIT : alma *f* **2** ESSENCE : esencia *f* **3** PERSON : persona *f*, alma *f*

soulful ['so:lfəl] *adj* : conmovedor, lleno de emoción

sound[1] ['saʊnd] *vt* **1** : sondar (en navegación) **2** *or* to sound out PROBE : sondear **3** : hacer sonar, tocar (una trompeta, etc.) — *vi* **1** : sonar ⟨the alarm sounded : la alarma sonó⟩ **2** SEEM : parecer

sound[2] *adj* **1** HEALTHY : sano ⟨safe and sound : sano y salvo⟩ ⟨of sound mind and body : en pleno uso de sus facultades⟩ **2** FIRM, SOLID : sólido **3** SENSIBLE : lógico, sensato **4** DEEP : profundo ⟨a sound sleep : un sueño profundo⟩

sound[3] *n* **1** : sonido *m* ⟨the speed of sound : la velocidad del sonido⟩ **2** NOISE : sonido *m*, ruido *m* ⟨I heard a sound : oí un sonido⟩ **3** CHANNEL : brazo *m* de mar, canal *m* (ancho)

soundless ['saʊndləs] *adj* : sordo

soundlessly ['saʊndləsli] *adv* : silenciosamente

soundly ['saʊndli] *adv* **1** SOLIDLY : sólidamente **2** SENSIBLY : lógicamente, sensatamente **3** DEEPLY : profundamente ⟨sleeping soundly : durmiendo profundamente⟩

soundness ['saʊndnəs] *n* **1** SOLIDITY : solidez *f* **2** SENSIBLENESS : sensatez *f*, solidez *f*

soundproof ['saʊndˌpru:f] *adj* : insonorizado

soundtrack ['saʊndˌtræk] *n* : banda *f* sonora

sound wave *n* : onda *f* sonora

soup ['su:p] *n* : sopa *f*

sour[1] ['saʊər] *vi* : agriarse, cortarse (dícese de la leche) — *vt* : agriar, cortar (leche)

sour[2] *adj* **1** ACID : agrio, ácido (dícese de la fruta, etc.), cortado (dícese de la leche) **2** DISAGREEABLE : desagradable, agrio

source ['sors] *n* : fuente *f*, origen *m*, nacimiento *m* (de un río)

sourness ['saʊərnəs] *n* : acidez *f*

south[1] ['saʊθ] *adv* : al sur, hacia el sur ⟨the window looks south : la ventana mira al sur⟩ ⟨she continued south : continuó hacia el sur⟩

south[2] *adj* : sur, del sur ⟨the south entrance : la entrada sur⟩ ⟨South America : Sudamérica, América del Sur⟩

south[3] *n* : sur *m*

South African *n* : sudafricano *m*, -na *f*
— **South African** *adj*

South American[1] *adj* : sudamericano, suramericano

South American[2] *n* : sudamericano *m*, -na *f*; suramericano *m*, -na *f*

southbound ['saʊθˌbaʊnd] *adj* : con rumbo al sur

southeast[1] [saʊ'θi:st] *adj* : sureste, sudeste, del sureste

southeast[2] *n* : sureste *m*, sudeste *m*

southeasterly [saʊ'θi:stərli] *adv & adj* **1** : del sureste (dícese del viento) **2** : hacia el sureste

southeastern [saʊ'θi:stərn] *adj* → **southeast**[1]

southerly ['sʌðərli] *adv & adj* : del sur

southern ['sʌðərn] *adj* : sur, sureño, meridional, austral ⟨a southern city : una ciudad del sur del país, una ciudad meridional⟩ ⟨the southern side : el lado sur⟩

Southerner ['sʌðərnər] *n* : sureño *m*, -ña *f*

South Pole : Polo *m* Sur

southward ['saʊθwərd] *or* **southwards** [-wərdz] *adv & adj* : hacia el sur

southwest[1] [saʊθ'wɛst, *as a nautical term often* saʊ'wɛst] *adj* : suroeste, sudoeste, del suroeste

southwest[2] *n* : suroeste *m*, sudoeste *m*

southwesterly [saʊθ'wɛstərli] *adv & adj* **1** : del suroeste (dícese del viento) **2** : hacia el suroeste

southwestern [saʊθ'wɛstərn] *adj* → **southwest**[1]

souvenir [ˌsu:və'nɪr, 'su:və-] *n* : recuerdo *m*, souvenir *m*

sovereign[1] ['savərən] *adj* : soberano

sovereign[2] *n* **1** : soberano *m*, -na *f* (monarca) **2** : soberano *m* (moneda)

sovereignty ['savərənti] *n*, *pl* **-ties** : soberanía *f*

Soviet ['so:viˌɛt, 'sa-, -viət] *adj* : soviético

sow[1] ['so:] *vt* **sowed**; **sown** ['so:n] *or* **sowed**; **sowing** **1** PLANT : sembrar **2** SCATTER : esparcir

sow[2] ['saʊ] *n* : cerda *f*

sox → **sock**

soy ['sɔɪ] *n* : soya *f*, soja *f*

soybean ['sɔɪˌbi:n] *n* : soya *f*, soja *f*

spa ['spa] *n* : balneario *m*

space[1] ['speɪs] *vt* **spaced**; **spacing** : espaciar

space[2] *n* **1** PERIOD : espacio *m*, lapso *m*, período *m* **2** ROOM : espacio *m*, sitio *m*, lugar *m* ⟨is there space for me? : ¿hay sitio para mí?⟩ **3** : espacio *m* ⟨blank space : espacio en blanco⟩ **4** : espacio *m* (en física) **5** PLACE : plaza *f*, sitio *m* ⟨to reserve space : reservar plazas⟩ ⟨parking space : sitio para estacionarse⟩

spacecraft ['speɪsˌkræft] *n* : nave *f* espacial

spaceflight ['speɪsˌflaɪt] *n* : vuelo *m* espacial

spaceman ['speɪsmən, -ˌmæn] *n, pl* **-men** [-mən, -ˌmɛn] : astronauta *m*, cosmonauta *m*
spaceship ['speɪsˌʃɪp] *n* : nave *f* espacial
space shuttle *n* : transbordador *m* espacial
space suit *n* : traje *m* espacial
spacious ['speɪʃəs] *adj* : espacioso, amplio
spade¹ ['speɪd] *v* **spaded; spading** *vt* : palear — *vi* : usar una pala
spade² *n* **1** SHOVEL : pala *f* **2** : pica *f* (naipe)
spaghetti [spə'gɛti] *n* : espagueti *m*, espaguetis *mpl*, spaghetti *mpl*
spam ['spæm] *n* : spam *m*, correo *m* electrónico no solicitado
span¹ ['spæn] *vt* **spanned; spanning** : abarcar (un período de tiempo), extenderse sobre (un espacio)
span² *n* **1** : lapso *m*, espacio *m* (de tiempo) ⟨life span : duración de la vida⟩ **2** : luz *f* (entre dos soportes)
spangle ['spæŋɡəl] *n* : lentejuela *f*
Spaniard ['spænjərd] *n* : español *m*, -ñola *f*
spaniel ['spænjəl] *n* : spaniel *m*
Spanish¹ ['spænɪʃ] *adj* : español
Spanish² *n* **1** : español *m* (idioma) **2 the Spanish** *npl* : los españoles
spank ['spæŋk] *vt* : darle nalgadas (a alguien)
spar¹ ['spɑr] *vi* **sparred; sparring** : entrenarse (en boxeo)
spar² *n* : palo *m*, verga *f* (de un barco)
spare¹ ['spær] *vt* **spared; sparing 1** : perdonar ⟨to spare someone's life : perdonarle la vida a alguien⟩ **2** SAVE : ahorrar, evitar ⟨I'll spare you the trouble : le evitaré la molestia⟩ **3** : prescindir de ⟨I can't spare her : no puedo prescindir de ella⟩ ⟨can you spare a dollar? : ¿me das un dólar?⟩ **4** STINT : escatimar ⟨they spared no expense : no repararon en gastos⟩ **5 to spare** : de sobra
spare² *adj* **1** : de repuesto, de recambio ⟨spare tire : llanta de repuesto⟩ **2** EXCESS : de más, de sobra ⟨spare time : tiempo libre⟩ **3** LEAN : delgado
spare³ *n or* **spare part** : repuesto *m*, recambio *m*
sparing ['spærɪŋ] *adj* : parco, económico — **sparingly** *adv*
spark¹ ['spɑrk] *vi* : chispear, echar chispas — *vt* PROVOKE : despertar, provocar ⟨to spark interest : despertar interés⟩
spark² *n* **1** : chispa *f* ⟨to throw off sparks : echar chispas⟩ **2** GLIMMER, TRACE : destello *m*, pizca *f*
sparkle¹ ['spɑrkəl] *vi* **-kled; -kling 1** FLASH, SHINE : destellar, centellear, brillar **2** : estar muy animado (dícese de una conversación, etc.)
sparkle² *n* : destello *m*, centelleo *m*
sparkler ['spɑrklər] *n* : luz *f* de bengala
spark plug *n* : bujía *f*

sparrow ['spæroː] *n* : gorrión *m*
sparse ['spɑrs] *adj* **sparser; -est** : escaso — **sparsely** *adv*
spasm ['spæzəm] *n* **1** : espasmo *m* (muscular) **2** BURST, FIT : arrebato *m*
spasmodic [spæz'mɑdɪk] *adj* **1** : espasmódico **2** SPORADIC : irregular, esporádico — **spasmodically** [-dɪkli] *adv*
spastic ['spæstɪk] *adj* : espástico
spat¹ → **spit¹**
spat² ['spæt] *n* : discusión *f*, disputa *f*, pelea *f*
spatial ['speɪʃəl] *adj* : espacial
spatter¹ ['spætər] *v* : salpicar
spatter² *n* : salpicadura *f*
spatula ['spætʃələ] *n* : espátula *f*, paleta *f* (para servir)
spawn¹ ['spɔn] *vi* : desovar, frezar — *vt* GENERATE : generar, producir
spawn² *n* : hueva *f*, freza *f*
spay ['speɪ] *vt* : esterilizar (una perra, etc.)
speak ['spiːk] *v* **spoke** ['spoːk]; **spoken** ['spoːkən]; **speaking** *vi* **1** TALK : hablar ⟨to speak to someone : hablar con alguien⟩ ⟨who's speaking? : ¿de parte de quien?⟩ ⟨so to speak : por así decirlo⟩ **2 to speak out** : hablar claramente **3 to speak out against** : denunciar **4 to speak up** : hablar en voz alta **5 to speak up for** : defender — *vt* **1** SAY : decir ⟨she spoke her mind : habló con franqueza⟩ **2** : hablar (un idioma)
speaker ['spiːkər] *n* **1** : hablante *mf* ⟨a native speaker : un hablante nativo⟩ **2** : orador *m*, -dora *f* ⟨the keynote speaker : el orador principal⟩ **3** LOUDSPEAKER : altavoz *m*, altoparlante *m*
spear¹ ['spɪr] *vt* : atravesar con una lanza
spear² *n* : lanza *f*
spearhead¹ ['spɪrˌhɛd] *vt* : encabezar
spearhead² *n* : punta *f* de lanza
spearmint ['spɪrmɪnt] *n* : menta *f* verde
special ['spɛʃəl] *adj* : especial ⟨nothing special : nada en especial, nada en particular⟩ — **specially** *adv*
specialist ['spɛʃəlɪst] *n* : especialista *mf*
specialization [ˌspɛʃələ'zeɪʃən] *n* : especialización *f*
specialize ['spɛʃəˌlaɪz] *vi* **-ized; -izing** : especializarse
specialty ['spɛʃəlti] *n, pl* **-ties** : especialidad *f*
species ['spiːˌʃiːz, -ˌsiːz] *ns & pl* : especie *f*
specific [spɪ'sɪfɪk] *adj* : específico, determinado — **specifically** [-fɪkli] *adv*
specification [ˌspɛsəfə'keɪʃən] *n* : especificación *f*
specify ['spɛsəˌfaɪ] *vt* **-fied; -fying** : especificar
specimen ['spɛsəmən] *n* **1** SAMPLE : espécimen *m*, muestra *f* **2** EXAMPLE : espécimen *m*, ejemplar *m*
speck ['spɛk] *n* **1** SPOT : manchita *f* **2** BIT, TRACE : mota *f*, pizca *f*, ápice *m*
speckled ['spɛkəld] *adj* : moteado

spectacle ['spɛktɪkəl] *n* **1** : espectáculo *m* **2 spectacles** *npl* GLASSES : lentes *fpl*, gafas *fpl*, anteojos *mpl*, espejuelos *mpl*

spectacular [spɛk'tækjələr] *adj* : espectacular

spectator ['spɛk,teɪtər] *n* : espectador *m*, -dora *f*

specter *or* **spectre** ['spɛktər] *n* : espectro *m*, fantasma *m*

spectrum ['spɛktrəm] *n*, *pl* **spectra** [-trə] *or* **spectrums** **1** : espectro *m* (de colores, etc.) **2** RANGE : gama *f*, abanico *m*

speculate ['spɛkjə,leɪt] *vi* **-lated; -lating 1** : especular (en finanzas) **2** WONDER : preguntarse, hacer conjeturas

speculation [,spɛkjə'leɪʃən] *n* : especulación *f*

speculative ['spɛkjə,leɪtɪv] *adj* : especulativo

speculator ['spɛkjə,leɪtər] *n* : especulador *m*, -dora *f*

speech ['spi:tʃ] *n* **1** : habla *f*, modo *m* de hablar, expresión *f* **2** ADDRESS : discurso *m*

speechless ['spi:tʃləs] *adj* : enmudecido, estupefacto

speed¹ ['spi:d] *v* **sped** ['spɛd] *or* **speeded; speeding** *vi* **1** : ir a toda velocidad, correr a toda prisa ⟨he sped off : se fue a toda velocidad⟩ **2** : conducir a exceso de velocidad ⟨a ticket for speeding : una multa por exceso de velocidad⟩ — *vt* **to speed up** : acelerar

speed² *n* **1** SWIFTNESS : rapidez *f* **2** VELOCITY : velocidad *f*

speedboat ['spi:d,bo:t] *n* : lancha *f* motora

speed bump *n* : badén *m*

speed limit *n* : velocidad *f* máxima, límite *m* de velocidad

speedometer [spɪ'dɑmətər] *n* : velocímetro *m*

speedup ['spi:d,ʌp] *n* : aceleración *f*

speedy ['spi:di] *adj* **speedier; -est** : rápido — **speedily** [-dəli] *adv*

spell¹ ['spɛl] *vt* **1** : escribir, deletrear (verbalmente) ⟨how do you spell it? : ¿cómo se escribe?, ¿cómo se deletrea?⟩ **2** MEAN : significar ⟨that could spell trouble : eso puede significar problemas⟩ **3** RELIEVE : relevar

spell² *n* **1** TURN : turno *m* **2** PERIOD, TIME : período *m* (de tiempo) **3** ENCHANTMENT : encanto *m*, hechizo *m*, maleficio *m*

spellbound ['spɛl,baund] *adj* : embelesado

speller ['spɛlər] *n* : persona *f* que escribe ⟨she's a good speller : tiene buena ortografía⟩

spelling ['spɛlɪŋ] *n* : ortografía *f*

spend ['spɛnd] *vt* **spent** ['spɛnt]; **spending 1** : gastar (dinero, etc.) **2** PASS : pasar (el tiempo) ⟨to spend time on : dedicar tiempo a⟩

spendthrift ['spɛnd,θrɪft] *n* : derrochador *m*, -dora *f*; despilfarrador *m*, -dora *f*

sperm ['spərm] *n*, *pl* **sperm** *or* **sperms** : esperma *mf*

spew ['spju:] *vi* : salir a chorros — *vt* : vomitar, arrojar (lava, etc.)

sphere ['sfɪr] *n* : esfera *f*

spherical ['sfɪrɪkəl, 'sfɛr-] *adj* : esférico

spice¹ ['spaɪs] *vt* **spiced; spicing 1** SEASON : condimentar, sazonar **2** *or* **to spice up** : salpimentar, hacer más interesante

spice² *n* **1** : especia *f* **2** FLAVOR, INTEREST : sabor *m* ⟨the spice of life : la sal de la vida⟩

spick–and–span ['spɪkənd'spæn] *adj* : limpio y ordenado

spicy ['spaɪsi] *adj* **spicier; -est 1** SPICED : condimentado, sazonado **2** HOT : picante **3** RACY : picante

spider ['spaɪdər] *n* : araña *f*

spigot ['spɪɡət, -kət] *n* : llave *f*, grifo *m*, canilla *Arg, Uru*

spike¹ ['spaɪk] *vt* **spiked; spiking 1** FASTEN : clavar (con clavos grandes) **2** PIERCE : atravesar **3** : añadir alcohol a ⟨he spiked her drink with rum : le puso ron a la bebida⟩

spike² *n* **1** : clavo *m* grande **2** CLEAT : clavo *m* **3** : remache *m* (en voleibol) **4** PEAK : pico *m*

spill¹ ['spɪl] *vt* **1** SHED : derramar, verter ⟨to spill blood : derrame sangre⟩ **2** DIVULGE : revelar, divulgar — *vi* : derramarse

spill² *n* **1** SPILLING : derrame *m*, vertido *m* ⟨oil spill : derrame de petróleo⟩ **2** FALL : caída *f*

spin¹ ['spɪn] *v* **spun** ['spʌn]; **spinning** *vi* **1** : hilar **2** TURN : girar **3** REEL : dar vueltas ⟨my head is spinning : la cabeza me está dando vueltas⟩ — *vt* **1** : hilar (hilo, etc.) **2** : tejer ⟨to spin a web : tejer una telaraña⟩ **3** TWIRL : hacer girar

spin² *n* : vuelta *f*, giro *m* ⟨to go for a spin : dar una vuelta (en coche)⟩

spinach ['spɪnɪtʃ] *n* : espinacas *fpl*, espinaca *f*

spinal column ['spaɪnəl] *n* BACKBONE : columna *f* vertebral

spinal cord *n* : médula *f* espinal

spindle ['spɪndəl] *n* **1** : huso *m* (para hilar) **2** : eje *m* (de un mecanismo)

spindly ['spɪndli] *adj* : larguirucho *fam*, largo y débil (dícese de una planta)

spine ['spaɪn] *n* **1** BACKBONE : columna *f* vertebral, espina *f* dorsal **2** QUILL : púa *f* (de un animal) **3** THORN : espina *f* **4** : lomo *m* (de un libro)

spineless ['spaɪnləs] *adj* **1** : sin púas, sin espinas **2** INVERTEBRATE : invertebrado **3** WEAK : débil (de carácter)

spinet ['spɪnət] *n* : espineta *f*

spinster ['spɪntstər] *n* : soltera *f*

spiny ['spaɪni] *adj* **spinier; -est** : con púas (dícese de los animales), espinoso (dícese de las plantas)

spiral¹ ['spaɪrəl] *vi* **-raled** *or* **-ralled;** **-raling** *or* **-ralling** : ir en espiral

spiral² *adj* : espiral, en espiral ⟨a spiral staircase : una escalera de caracol⟩

spiral³ *n* : espiral *f*

spire ['spaɪr] *n* : aguja *f*

spirit¹ ['spɪrət] *vt* **to spirit away** : hacer desaparecer

spirit² *n* **1** : espíritu *m* ⟨body and spirit : cuerpo y espíritu⟩ **2** GHOST : espíritu *m*, fantasma *m* **3** MOOD : espíritu *m*, humor *m* ⟨in the spirit of friendship : en el espíritu de amistad⟩ ⟨to be in good spirits : estar de buen humor⟩ **4** ENTHUSIASM, VIVACITY : espíritu *m*, ánimo *m*, brío *m* **5 spirits** *npl* : licores *mpl*

spirited ['spɪrətəd] *adj* : animado, energético

spiritless ['spɪrətləs] *adj* : desanimado

spiritual¹ ['spɪrɪtʃuəl, -tʃəl] *adj* : espiritual — **spiritually** *adv*

spiritual² *n* : espiritual *m* (canción)

spiritualism ['spɪrɪtʃuə,lɪzəm, -tʃə-] *n* : espiritismo *m*

spirituality [,spɪrɪtʃu'æləti] *n, pl* **-ties** : espiritualidad *f*

spit¹ ['spɪt] *v* **spit** *or* **spat** ['spæt]; **spitting** : escupir

spit² *n* **1** SALIVA : saliva *f* **2** ROTISSERIE : asador *m* **3** POINT : lengua *f* (de tierra)

spite¹ ['spaɪt] *vt* **spited; spiting** : fastidiar, molestar

spite² *n* **1** : despecho *m*, rencor *m* **2 in spite of** : a pesar de (que), pese a (que)

spiteful ['spaɪtfəl] *adj* : malicioso, rencoroso

spitting image *n* **to be the spitting image of** : ser el vivo retrato de

spittle ['spɪtəl] *n* : saliva *f*

splash¹ ['splæʃ] *vt* : salpicar — *vi* **1** : salpicar **2 to splash around** : chapotear

splash² *n* **1** SPLASHING : salpicadura *f* **2** SQUIRT : chorrito *m* **3** SPOT : mancha *f*

splatter ['splætər] → **spatter**

splay ['spleɪ] *vt* : extender (hacia afuera) ⟨to splay one's fingers : abrir los dedos⟩ — *vi* : extenderse (hacia afuera)

spleen ['spli:n] *n* **1** : bazo *m* (órgano) **2** ANGER, SPITE : ira *f*, rencor *m*

splendid ['splɛndəd] *adj* : espléndido — **splendidly** *adv*

splendor ['splɛndər] *n* : esplendor *m*

splice¹ ['splaɪs] *vt* **spliced; splicing** : empalmar, unir

splice² *n* : empalme *m*, unión *f*

splint ['splɪnt] *n* : tablilla *f*

splinter¹ ['splɪntər] *vt* : astillar — *vi* : astillarse

splinter² *n* : astilla *f*

split¹ ['splɪt] *v* **split; splitting** *vt* **1** CLEAVE : partir, hender ⟨to split wood : partir madera⟩ **2** BURST : romper, rajar ⟨to split open : abrir⟩ **3** DIVIDE, SHARE : dividir, repartir — *vi* **1** : par-

tirse (dícese de la madera, etc.) **2** BURST, CRACK : romperse, rajarse **3** *or* **to split up** : dividirse

split² *n* **1** CRACK : rajadura *f* **2** TEAR : rotura *f* **3** DIVISION : división *f*, escisión *f*

splurge¹ ['splərdʒ] *v* **splurged; splurging** *vt* : derrochar — *vi* : derrochar dinero

splurge² *n* : derroche *m*

spoil¹ ['spɔɪl] *vt* **1** PILLAGE : saquear **2** RUIN : estropear, arruinar **3** PAMPER : consentir, mimar — *vi* : estropearse, echarse a perder

spoil² *n* PLUNDER : botín *m*

spoke¹ → **speak**

spoke² ['spo:k] *n* : rayo *m* (de una rueda)

spoken → **speak**

spokesman ['spo:ksmən] *n, pl* **-men** [-mən, -,mɛn] : portavoz *mf*; vocero *m*, -ra *f*

spokeswoman ['spo:ks,wumən] *n, pl* **-women** [-,wɪmən] : portavoz *f*, vocera *f*

sponge¹ ['spʌndʒ] *vt* **sponged; sponging** : limpiar con una esponja

sponge² *n* : esponja *f*

spongy ['spʌndʒi] *adj* **spongier; -est** : esponjoso

sponsor¹ ['spɑntsər] *vt* : patrocinar, auspiciar, apadrinar (a una persona)

sponsor² *n* : patrocinador *m*, -dora *f*; padrino *m*, madrina *f*

sponsorship ['spɑntsər,ʃɪp] *n* : patrocinio *m*, apadrinamiento *m*

spontaneity [,spɑntə'ni:əti, -'neɪ-] *n* : espontaneidad *f*

spontaneous [spɑn'teɪniəs] *adj* : espontáneo — **spontaneously** *adv*

spoof ['spu:f] *n* : burla *f*, parodia *f*

spook¹ ['spu:k] *vt* : asustar

spook² *n* : fantasma *m*, espíritu *m*, espectro *m*

spooky ['spu:ki] *adj* **spookier; -est** : que da miedo, espeluzante

spool ['spu:l] *n* : carrete *m*

spoon¹ ['spu:n] *vt* : comer, servir, o echar con cuchara

spoon² *n* : cuchara *f*

spoonful ['spu:n,ful] *n* : cucharada *f* ⟨by the spoonful : a cucharadas⟩

spoor ['spur, 'spor] *n* : rastro *m*, pista *f*

sporadic [spə'rædɪk] *adj* : esporádico — **sporadically** [-dɪkli] *adv*

spore ['spor] *n* : espora *f*

sport¹ ['sport] *vi* FROLIC : retozar, juguetear — *vt* SHOW OFF : lucir, ostentar

sport² *n* **1** : deporte *m* ⟨outdoor sports : deportes al aire libre⟩ **2** JEST : broma *f* **3 to be a good sport** : tener espíritu deportivo

sporting ['sportɪŋ] *adj* : deportivo ⟨a sporting chance : buenas posibilidades⟩

sportsman ['sportsmən] *n, pl* **-men** [-mən, -,mɛn] : deportista *m*

sportsmanship ['sportsmən,ʃɪp] *n* : espíritu *m* deportivo, deportividad *f* Spain

sportswoman ['sports,wʊmən] *n, pl* **-women** [-,wɪmən] : deportista *f*

sporty ['sporţi] *adj* **sportier; -est** : deportivo

spot¹ ['spɑt] *v* **spotted; spotting** *vt* 1 STAIN : manchar 2 RECOGNIZE, SEE : ver, reconocer ⟨to spot an error : descubrir un error⟩ — *vi* : mancharse

spot² *adj* : hecho al azar ⟨a spot check : un vistazo, un control aleatorio⟩

spot³ *n* 1 STAIN : mancha *f* 2 DOT : punto *m* 3 PIMPLE : grano *m* ⟨to break out in spots : salirle granos a alguien⟩ 4 PREDICAMENT : apuro *m*, aprieto *m*, lío *m* ⟨in a tight spot : en apuros⟩ 5 PLACE : lugar *m*, sitio *m* ⟨to be on the spot : estar en el lugar⟩

spotless ['spɑtləs] *adj* : impecable, inmaculado — **spotlessly** *adv*

spotlight¹ ['spɑt,laɪt] *vt* **-lighted** *or* **-lit** [-,lɪt]; **-lighting** 1 LIGHT : iluminar (con un reflector) 2 HIGHLIGHT : destacar, poner en relieve

spotlight² *n* 1 : reflector *m*, foco *m* 2 **to be in the spotlight** : ser el centro de atención

spotty ['spɑţi] *adj* **spottier; -est** : irregular, desigual

spouse ['spaʊs] *n* : cónyuge *mf*

spout¹ ['spaʊt] *vt* 1 : lanzar chorros de 2 DECLAIM : declamar — *vi* : salir a chorros

spout² *n* 1 : pico *m* (de una jarra, etc.) 2 STREAM : chorro *m*

sprain¹ ['spreɪn] *vt* : sufrir un esguince en

sprain² *n* : esguince *m*, torcedura *f*

sprawl¹ ['sprɔl] *vi* 1 LIE : tumbarse, echarse, despatarrarse 2 EXTEND : extenderse

sprawl² *n* 1 : postura *f* despatarrada 2 SPREAD : extensión *f*, expansión *f*

spray¹ ['spreɪ] *vt* : rociar (una superficie), pulverizar (un líquido)

spray² *n* 1 BOUQUET : ramillete *m* 2 MIST : rocío *m* 3 ATOMIZER : atomizador *m*, pulverizador *m*

spray gun *n* : pistola *f*

spread¹ ['sprɛd] *v* **spread; spreading** *vt* 1 *or* **to spread out** : desplegar, extender 2 SCATTER, STREW : esparcir 3 SMEAR : untar (mantequilla, etc.) 4 DISSEMINATE : difundir, sembrar, propagar — *vi* 1 : difundirse, correr, propagarse 2 EXTEND : extenderse

spread² *n* 1 EXTENSION : extensión *f*, difusión *f* (de noticias, etc.), propagación *f* (de enfermedades, etc.) 2 : colcha *f* (para una cama), mantel *m* (para una mesa) 3 PASTE : pasta *f* ⟨cheese spread : pasta de queso⟩

spreadsheet ['sprɛd,ʃiːt] *n* : hoja *f* de cálculo

spree ['spri] *n* 1 : acción *f* desenfrenada ⟨to go on a shopping spree : comprar como loco⟩ 2 BINGE : parranda *f*, juerga *f* ⟨on a spree : de parranda, de juerga⟩

sprig ['sprɪg] *n* : ramita *f*, ramito *m*

sprightly ['spraɪtli] *adj* **sprightlier; -est** : vivo, animado ⟨with a sprightly step : con paso ligero⟩

spring¹ ['sprɪŋ] *v* **sprang** ['spræŋ] *or* **sprung** ['sprʌŋ]; **sprung; springing** *vi* 1 LEAP : saltar 2 : mover rápidamente ⟨the lid sprang shut : la tapa se cerró de un golpe⟩ ⟨he sprang to his feet : se paró de un salto⟩ 3 **to spring up** : brotar (dícese de las plantas), surgir 4 **to spring from** : surgir de — *vt* 1 RELEASE : soltar (de repente) ⟨to spring the news on someone : sorprender a alguien con las noticias⟩ ⟨to spring a trap : hacer saltar una trampa⟩ 2 ACTIVATE : accionar (un mecanismo) 3 **to spring a leak** : hacer agua

spring² *n* 1 SOURCE : fuente *f*, origen *m* 2 : manantial *m*, fuente *f* ⟨hot spring : fuente termal⟩ 3 : primavera *f* ⟨spring and summer : la primavera y el verano⟩ 4 : resorte *m*, muelle *m* (de metal, etc.) 5 LEAP : salto *m*, brinco *m* 6 RESILIENCE : elasticidad *f*

springboard ['sprɪŋ,bord] *n* : trampolín *m*

springtime ['sprɪŋ,taɪm] *n* : primavera *f*

springy ['sprɪŋi] *adj* **springier; -est** 1 RESILIENT : elástico 2 LIVELY : enérgico

sprinkle¹ ['sprɪŋkəl] *vt* **-kled; -kling** : rociar (con agua), espolvorear (con azúcar, etc.), salpicar

sprinkle² *n* : llovizna *f*

sprinkler ['sprɪŋkələr] *n* : rociador *m*, aspersor *m*

sprint¹ ['sprɪnt] *vi* : echar la carrera, esprintar (en deportes)

sprint² *n* : esprint *m* (en deportes)

sprinter ['sprɪntər] *n* : esprínter *mf*

sprite ['spraɪt] *n* : hada *f*, elfo *m*

sprocket ['sprɑkət] *n* : diente *m* (de una rueda dentada)

sprout¹ ['spraʊt] *vi* : brotar

sprout² *n* : brote *m*, retoño *m*, vástago *m*

spruce¹ ['spruːs] *v* **spruced; sprucing** *vt* : arreglar — *vi* *or* **to spruce up** : arreglarse, acicalarse

spruce² *adj* **sprucer; sprucest** : pulcro, arreglado

spruce³ *n* : picea *f* (árbol)

spry ['spraɪ] *adj* **sprier** *or* **spryer** ['spraɪər]; **spriest** *or* **spryest** ['spraɪəst] : ágil, activo

spun → **spin**

spunk ['spʌŋk] *n* : valor *m*, coraje *m*, agallas *fpl fam*

spunky ['spʌŋki] *adj* **spunkier; -est** : animoso, corajudo

spur¹ ['spər] *vt* **spurred; spurring** *or* **to spur on** : espolear (un caballo), motivar (a una persona), etc.)

spur² *n* **1** : espuela *f*, acicate *m* **2** STIMULUS : acicate *m* **3** : espolón *m* (de aves gallináceas)

spurious ['spjʊriəs] *adj* : espurio

spurn ['spərn] *vt* : desdeñar, rechazar

spurt¹ ['spərt] *vt* SQUIRT : lanzar un chorro de — *vi* SPOUT : salir a chorros

spurt² *n* **1** : actividad *f* repentina ⟨a spurt of energy : una explosión de energía⟩ ⟨to do in spurts : hacer por rachas⟩ **2** JET : chorro *m* (de agua, etc.)

sputter¹ ['spʌtər] *vi* **1** JABBER : farfullar **2** : chisporrotear (dícese de la grasa, etc.), petardear (dícese de un motor)

sputter² *n* **1** JABBER : farfulla *f* **2** : chisporroteo *m* (de grasa, etc.), petardeo *m* (de un motor)

spy¹ ['spaɪ] *v* **spied; spying** *vt* SEE : ver, divisar — *vi* : espiar ⟨to spy on someone : espiar a alguien⟩

spy² *n* : espía *mf*

squab ['skwɑb] *n, pl* **squabs** *or* **squab** : pichón *m*

squabble¹ ['skwɑbəl] *vi* **-bled; -bling** : reñir, pelearse, discutir

squabble² *n* : riña *f*, pelea *f*, discusión *f*

squad ['skwɑd] *n* : pelotón *m* (militar), brigada *f* (de policías), cuadrilla *f* (de obreros, etc.)

squadron ['skwɑdrən] *n* : escuadrón *m* (de militares), escuadrilla *f* (de aviones), escuadra *f* (de naves)

squalid ['skwɑlɪd] *adj* : miserable

squall ['skwɔl] *n* **1** : aguacero *m* tormentoso, chubasco *m* tormentoso **2** **snow squall** : tormenta *f* de nieve

squalor ['skwɑlər] *n* : miseria *f*

squander ['skwɑndər] *vt* : derrochar (dinero, etc.), desaprovechar (una oportunidad, etc.), desperdiciar (talentos, energías, etc.)

square¹ ['skwær] *vt* **squared; squaring** **1** : cuadrar **2** : elevar al cuadrado (en matemáticas) **3** CONFORM : conciliar (con), ajustar (con) **4** SETTLE : saldar (una cuenta) ⟨I squared it with him : lo arreglé con él⟩

square² *adj* **squarer; -est** **1** : cuadrado ⟨a square house : una casa cuadrada⟩ **2** RIGHT-ANGLED : a escuadra, en ángulo recto **3** : cuadrado (en matemáticas) ⟨a square mile : una milla cuadrada⟩ **4** HONEST : justo ⟨a square deal : un buen acuerdo⟩ ⟨fair and square : en buena lid⟩

square³ *n* **1** : escuadra *f* (instrumento) **2** : cuadrado *m*, cuadro *m* ⟨to fold into squares : plegar en cuadrados⟩ **3** : plaza *f* (de una ciudad) **4** : cuadrado *m* (en matemáticas)

squarely ['skwærli] *adv* **1** EXACTLY : exactamente, directamente, justo **2** HONESTLY : honradamente, justamente

square root *n* : raíz *f* cuadrada

squash¹ ['skwɑʃ, 'skwɔʃ] *vt* **1** CRUSH : aplastar **2** SUPPRESS : acallar (protestas), sofocar (una rebelión)

squash² *n* **1** *pl* **squashes** *or* **squash** : calabaza *f* (vegetal) **2** *or* **squash racquets** : squash *m* (deporte)

squat¹ ['skwɑt] *vi* **squatted; squatting** **1** CROUCH : agacharse, ponerse en cuclillas **2** : ocupar un lugar sin derecho

squat² *adj* **squatter; squattest** : bajo y ancho, rechoncho *fam* (dícese de una persona)

squat³ *n* **1** : posición *f* en cuclillas **2** : ocupación *f* ilegal (de un lugar)

squaw ['skwɔ] *n* : india *f* (norteamericana)

squawk¹ ['skwɔk] *vi* : graznar (dícese de las aves), chillar

squawk² *n* : graznido *m* (de un ave), chillido *m*

squeak¹ ['skwi:k] *vi* : chillar (dícese de un animal), chirriar (dícese de un objeto)

squeak² *n* : chillido *m*, chirrido *m*

squeaky ['skwi:ki] *adj* **squeakier; -est** : chirriante ⟨a squeaky voice : una voz chillona⟩

squeal¹ ['skwi:l] *vi* **1** : chillar (dícese de las personas o los animales), chirriar (dícese de los frenos, etc.) **2** PROTEST : quejarse

squeal² *n* **1** : chillido *m* (de una persona o un animal) **2** SCREECH : chirrido *m* (de frenos, etc.)

squeamish ['skwi:mɪʃ] *adj* : impresionable, sensible ⟨he's squeamish about cockroaches : las cucarachas le dan asco⟩

squeeze¹ ['skwi:z] *vt* **squeezed; squeezing** **1** PRESS : apretar, exprimir (naranjas, etc.) **2** EXTRACT : extraer (jugo, etc.)

squeeze² *n* : apretón *m*

squelch ['skwɛltʃ] *vt* : aplastar (una rebelión, etc.)

squid ['skwɪd] *n, pl* **squid** *or* **squids** : calamar *m*

squint¹ ['skwɪnt] *vi* : mirar con los ojos entornados

squint² *adj or* **squint–eyed** ['skwɪnt,aɪd] : bizco

squint³ *n* : ojos *mpl* bizcos, bizquera *f*

squire ['skwaɪr] *n* : hacendado *m*, -da *f*; terrateniente *mf*

squirm ['skwərm] *vi* : retorcerse

squirrel ['skwərəl] *n* : ardilla *f*

squirt¹ ['skwərt] *vt* : lanzar un chorro de — *vi* SPURT : salir a chorros

squirt² *n* : chorrito *m*

stab¹ [stæb] *vt* **stabbed; stabbing** **1** KNIFE : acuchillar, apuñalar **2** STICK : clavar (con una aguja, etc.), golpear (con el dedo, etc.)

stab² *n* **1** : puñalada *f*, cuchillada *f* **2** JAB : pinchazo *m* (con una aguja, etc.), golpe *m* (con un dedo, etc.) **3** **to take a stab at** : intentar

stability [stə'bɪləti] *n, pl* **-ties** : estabilidad *f*

stabilize ['steɪbə,laɪz] *v* **-lized; -lizing** *vt* : estabilizar — *vi* : estabilizarse

stable¹ ['steɪbəl] *vt* **-bled; -bling** : poner (ganado) en un establo, poner (caballos) en una caballeriza

stable² *adj* **-bler; -blest** 1 FIXED, STEADY : fijo, sólido, estable 2 LASTING : estable, perdurable ⟨a stable government : un gobierno estable⟩ 3 : estacionario (en medicina), equilibrado (en psicología)

stable³ *n* : establo *m* (para ganado), caballeriza *f* o cuadra *f* (para caballos)

staccato [stə'kɑtoː] *adj* : staccato

stack¹ ['stæk] *vt* 1 PILE : amontonar, apilar 2 COVER : cubrir, llenar ⟨he stacked the table with books : cubrió la mesa de libros⟩

stack² *n* 1 PILE : montón *m*, pila *f* 2 SMOKESTACK : chimenea *f*

stadium ['steɪdiəm] *n, pl* **-dia** [-diə] *or* **-diums** : estadio *m*

staff¹ ['stæf] *vt* : proveer de personal

staff² *n, pl* **staffs** ['stæfs, stævz] *or* **staves** ['stævz, 'steɪvz] 1 : bastón *m* (de mando), báculo *m* (de obispo) 2 *pl* **staffs** PERSONNEL : personal *m* 3 *or* **stave** : pentagrama *m* (en música)

stag¹ ['stæg] *adv* : solo, sin pareja ⟨to go stag : ir solo⟩

stag² *adj* : sólo para hombres

stag³ *n, pl* **stags** *or* **stag** : ciervo *m*, venado *m*

stage¹ ['steɪdʒ] *vt* **staged; staging** : poner en escena (una obra de teatro)

stage² *n* 1 PLATFORM : estrado *m*, tablado *m*, escenario *m* (de un teatro) 2 PHASE, STEP : fase *f*, etapa *f* ⟨stage of development : fase de desarrollo⟩ ⟨in stages : por etapas⟩ 3 **the stage** : el teatro *m*

stagecoach ['steɪdʒ,koːtʃ] *n* : diligencia *f*

stagger¹ ['stægər] *vi* TOTTER : tambalearse — *vt* 1 ALTERNATE : alternar, escalonar (turnos de trabajo) 2 : hacer tambalear ⟨to be staggered by : quedarse estupefacto por⟩

stagger² *n* : tambaleo *m*

staggering ['stægərɪŋ] *adj* : asombroso

stagnant ['stægnənt] *adj* : estancado

stagnate ['stæg,neɪt] *vi* **-nated; -nating** : estancarse

staid ['steɪd] *adj* : serio, sobrio

stain¹ ['steɪn] *vt* 1 DISCOLOR : manchar 2 DYE : teñir (madera, etc.) 3 SULLY : manchar, empañar

stain² *n* 1 SPOT : mancha *f* 2 DYE : tinte *m*, tintura *f* 3 BLEMISH : mancha *f*, mácula *f*

stainless ['steɪnləs] *adj* : sin mancha ⟨stainless steel : acero inoxidable⟩

stair ['stær] *n* 1 STEP : escalón *m*, peldaño *m* 2 **stairs** *npl* : escalera *f*, escaleras *fpl*

staircase ['stær,keɪs] *n* : escalera *f*, escaleras *fpl*

stairway ['stær,weɪ] *n* : escalera *f*, escaleras *fpl*

stake¹ ['steɪk] *vt* **staked; staking** 1 : estacar, marcar con estacas (una

propiedad) 2 BET : jugarse, apostar 3 **to stake a claim to** : reclamar, reivindicar

stake² *n* 1 POST : estaca *f* 2 BET : apuesta *f* ⟨to be at stake : estar en juego⟩ 3 INTEREST, SHARE : interés *m*, participación *f*

stalactite [stə'læk,taɪt] *n* : estalactita *f*

stalagmite [stə'læg,maɪt] *n* : estalagmita *f*

stale ['steɪl] *adj* **staler; stalest** : viejo ⟨stale bread : pan duro⟩ ⟨stale news : viejas noticias⟩

stalemate ['steɪl,meɪt] *n* : punto *m* muerto, impasse *m*

stalk¹ ['stɔk] *vt* : acechar — *vi* : caminar rígidamente (por orgullo, ira, etc.)

stalk² *n* : tallo *m* (de una planta)

stall¹ ['stɔl] *vt* 1 : parar (un motor) 2 DELAY : entretener (a una persona), demorar — *vi* 1 : pararse (dícese de un motor) 2 DELAY : demorar, andar con rodeos

stall² *n* 1 : compartimiento *m* (de un establo) 2 : puesto *m* (en un mercado, etc.)

stallion ['stæljən] *n* : caballo *m* semental

stalwart ['stɔlwərt] *adj* 1 STRONG : fuerte ⟨a stalwart supporter : un firme partidario⟩ 2 BRAVE : valiente, valeroso

stamen ['steɪmən] *n* : estambre *m*

stamina ['stæmənə] *n* : resistencia *f*

stammer¹ ['stæmər] *vi* : tartamudear, titubear

stammer² *n* : tartamudeo *m*, titubeo *m*

stamp¹ ['stæmp] *vt* 1 : pisotear (con los pies) ⟨to stamp one's feet : patear, dar una patada⟩ 2 IMPRESS, IMPRINT : sellar (una factura, etc.), acuñar (monedas) 3 : franquear, ponerle estampillas a (correo)

stamp² *n* 1 : sello *m* (para documentos, etc.) 2 DIE : cuño *m* (para monedas) 3 *or* **postage stamp** : sello *m*, estampilla *f*, timbre *m* CA, Mex

stampede¹ ['stæm'piːd] *vi* **-peded; -peding** : salir en estampida

stampede² *n* : estampida *f*

stance ['stæns] *n* : postura *f*

stanch ['stɔntʃ, 'stæntʃ] *vt* : detener, estancar (un líquido)

stand¹ ['stænd] *v* **stood** ['stʊd]; **standing** *vi* 1 : estar de pie, estar parado ⟨I was standing on the corner : estaba parada en la esquina⟩ 2 *or* **to stand up** : levantarse, pararse, ponerse de pie 3 (*indicating a specified position or location*) ⟨they stand third in the country : ocupan el tercer lugar en el país⟩ ⟨the machines are standing idle : las máquinas están paradas⟩ 4 (*referring to an opinion*) ⟨how does he stand on the matter? : ¿cuál es su postura respecto al asunto?⟩ 5 BE : estar ⟨the house stands on a hill : la casa está en una colina⟩ 6 CONTINUE : seguir ⟨the order still stands : el mandato sigue vigente⟩ — *vt* **1** PLACE, SET : poner, colocar ⟨he stood them in a row : los colocó en hilera⟩ **2** TOLERATE : aguantar, soportar ⟨he can't stand her : no la puede tragar⟩ **3 to stand firm** : mantenerse firme **4 to stand guard** : hacer la guardia

stand² *n* **1** RESISTANCE : resistencia *f* ⟨to make a stand against : resistir a⟩ **2** BOOTH, STALL : stand *m*, puesto *m*, kiosko *m* (para vender periódicos, etc) **3** BASE : pie *m*, base *f* **4** : grupo *m* (de árboles, etc.) **5** POSITION : posición *f*, postura *f* **6 stands** *npl* GRANDSTAND : tribuna *f*

standard¹ ['stændərd] *adj* **1** ESTABLISHED : estándar, oficial ⟨standard measures : medidas oficiales⟩ ⟨standard English : el inglés estándar⟩ **2** NORMAL : normal, estándar, común **3** CLASSIC : estándar, clásico ⟨a standard work : una obra clásica⟩

standard² *n* **1** BANNER : estandarte *m* **2** CRITERION : criterio *m* **3** RULE : estándar *m*, norma *f*, regla *f* **4** LEVEL : nivel *m* ⟨standard of living : nivel de vida⟩ **5** SUPPORT : poste *m*, soporte *m*

standardization [ˌstændərdəˈzeɪʃən] *n* : estandarización *f*

standardize ['stændərˌdaɪz] *vt* **-ized; -izing** : estandarizar

standard time *n* : hora *f* oficial

stand by *vt* : atenerse a, cumplir con (una promesa, etc.) — *vi* **1** : mantenerse aparte ⟨to stand by and do nothing : mirar sin hacer nada⟩ **2** : estar preparado, estar listo (para un anuncio, un ataque, etc.)

stand for *vt* **1** REPRESENT : significar **2** PERMIT, TOLERATE : permitir, tolerar

standing ['stændɪŋ] *n* **1** POSITION, RANK : posición *f* **2** DURATION : duración *f*

stand out *vi* **1** : destacar(se) ⟨she stands out from the rest : se destaca entre los otros⟩ **2 to stand out against** RESIST : oponerse a

standpoint ['stændˌpɔɪnt] *n* : punto *m* de vista

standstill ['stændˌstɪl] *n* **1** STOP : detención *f*, paro *m* ⟨to come to a standstill : pararse⟩ **2** DEADLOCK : punto *m* muerto, impasse *m*

stand up *vt* : dejar plantado ⟨he stood me up again : otra vez me dejó plantado⟩ — *vi* **1** ENDURE : durar, resistir **2 to stand up for** : defender **3 to stand up to** : hacerle frente (a alguien)

stank → **stink**

stanza ['stænzə] *n* : estrofa *f*

staple¹ ['steɪpəl] *vt* **-pled; -pling** : engrapar, grapar

staple² *adj* : principal, básico ⟨a staple food : un alimento básico⟩

staple³ *n* **1** : producto *m* principal **2** : grapa *f* (para engrapar papeles)

stapler ['steɪplər] *n* : engrapadora *f*, grapadora *f*

star¹ ['star] *v* **starred; starring** *vt* **1** : marcar con una estrella o un aster-

isco **2** FEATURE : estar protagonizado por — *vi* **1** : tener el papel principal ⟨to star in : protagonizar⟩

star² *n* : estrella *f*

starboard ['starbərd] *n* : estribor *m*

starch¹ ['startʃ] *vt* : almidonar

starch² *n* : almidón *m*, fécula *f* (comida)

starchy ['startʃi] *adj* **starchier; -est** : lleno de almidón ⟨a starchy diet : una dieta feculenta⟩

stardom ['stardəm] *n* : estrellato *m*

stare¹ ['stær] *vi* **stared; staring** : mirar fijamente

stare² *n* : mirada *f* fija

starfish ['starˌfɪʃ] *n* : estrella *f* de mar

stark¹ ['stark] *adv* : completamente ⟨stark raving mad : loco de remate⟩ ⟨stark naked : completamente desnudo⟩

stark² *adj* **1** ABSOLUTE : absoluto **2** BARREN, DESOLATE : desolado, desierto **3** BARE : desnudo **4** HARSH : severo, duro

starlight ['starˌlaɪt] *n* : luz *f* de las estrellas

starling ['starlɪŋ] *n* : estornino *m*

starry ['stari] *adj* **starrier; -est** : estrellado

start¹ ['start] *vi* **1** JUMP : levantarse de un salto, sobresaltarse, dar un respingo **2** BEGIN : empezar, comenzar **3** SET OUT : salir (de viaje, etc.) **4** : arrancar (dícese de un motor) — *vt* **1** BEGIN : empezar, comenzar, iniciar **2** CAUSE : provocar, causar **3** ESTABLISH : fundar, montar, establecer ⟨to start a business : montar un negocio⟩ **4** : arrancar, poner en marcha, encender ⟨to start the car : arrancar el motor⟩

start² *n* **1** JUMP : sobresalto *m*, respingo *m* **2** BEGINNING : principio *m*, comienzo *m* ⟨to get an early start : salir temprano⟩

starter ['startər] *n* **1** : participante *mf* (en una carrera, etc.); jugador *m* titular, jugadora *f* titular (en beisbol, etc.) **2** APPETIZER : entremés *m*, aperitivo *m* **3** *or* **starter motor** : motor *m* de arranque

startle ['startəl] *vt* **-tled; -tling** : asustar, sobresaltar

start–up ['startˌʌp] *adj* : de puesta en marcha

starvation [starˈveɪʃən] *n* : inanición *f*, hambre *f*

starve ['starv] *v* **starved; starving** *vi* : morirse de hambre — *vt* : privar de comida

stash ['stæʃ] *vt* : esconder, guardar (en un lugar secreto)

stat ['stæt] → **statistic**

state¹ ['steɪt] *vt* **stated; stating** **1** REPORT : puntualizar, exponer (los hechos, etc.) ⟨state your name : diga su nombre⟩ **2** ESTABLISH, FIX : establecer, fijar

state² *n* **1** CONDITION : estado *m*, condición *f* ⟨a liquid state : un estado líquido⟩ ⟨state of mind : estado de ánimo⟩

⟨in a bad state : en malas condiciones⟩ **2** NATION : estado *m*, nación *f* **3** : estado *m* (dentro de un país) ⟨the States : los Estados Unidos⟩
stateliness ['steɪtlinəs] *n* : majestuosidad *f*
stately ['steɪtli] *adj* **statelier; -est** : majestuoso
statement ['steɪtmənt] *n* **1** DECLARATION : declaración *f*, afirmación *f* **2** *or* **bank statement** : estado *m* de cuenta
stateroom ['steɪt,ruːm, -,rʊm] *n* : camarote *m*
statesman ['steɪtsmən] *n*, *pl* **-men** [-mən, -,mɛn] : estadista *mf*
static¹ ['stætɪk] *adj* : estático
static² *n* : estática *f*, interferencia *f*
station¹ ['steɪʃən] *vt* : apostar, estacionar
station² *n* **1** : estación *f* (de trenes, etc.) **2** RANK, STANDING : condición *f* (social) **3** : canal *m* (de televisión), estación *f* o emisora *f* (de radio) **4** **police station** : comisaría *f* **5** **fire station** : estación *f* de bomberos, cuartel *m* de bomberos
stationary ['steɪʃə,nɛri] *adj* **1** IMMOBILE : estacionario, inmovible **2** UNCHANGING : inmutable, inalterable
stationery ['steɪʃə,nɛri] *n* : papel *m* y sobres *mpl* (para correspondencia)
station wagon *n* : camioneta *f* ranchera, camioneta *f* guayín *Mex*
statistic [stə'tɪstɪk] *n* : estadística *f* ⟨according to statistics : según las estadísticas⟩
statistical [stə'tɪstɪkəl] *adj* : estadístico
statistician [,stætə'stɪʃən] *n* : estadístico *m*, -ca *f*
statue ['stæ,tʃuː] *n* : estatua *f*
statuesque [,stætʃu'ɛsk] *adj* : escultural
statuette [,stætʃu'ɛt] *n* : estatuilla *f*
stature ['stætʃər] *n* **1** HEIGHT : estatura *f*, talla *f* **2** PRESTIGE : talla *f*, prestigio *m*
status ['steɪtəs, 'stæ-] *n* : condición *f*, situación *f*, estatus *m* (social) ⟨marital status : estado civil⟩
statute ['stæ,tʃuːt] *n* : ley *f*, estatuto *m*
staunch ['stɔntʃ] *adj* : acérrimo, incondicional, leal ⟨a staunch supporter : un partidario incondicional⟩ —
staunchly *adv*
stave¹ ['steɪv] *vt* **staved** *or* **stove** ['stoːv]; **staving 1 to stave in** : romper **2 to stave off** : evitar (un ataque), prevenir (un problema)
stave² *n* : duela *f* (de un barril)
staves → **staff**
stay¹ ['steɪ] *vi* **1** REMAIN : quedarse, permanecer ⟨to stay in : quedarse en casa⟩ ⟨he stayed in the city : permaneció en la ciudad⟩ **2** CONTINUE : seguir, quedarse ⟨it stayed cloudy : siguió nublado⟩ ⟨to stay awake : mantenerse despierto⟩ **3** LODGE : hospedarse, alojarse (en un hotel, etc.) — *vt* **1** HALT : detener, suspender (una ejecución, etc.) **2 to stay the course** : aguantar hasta el final

stay² *n* **1** SOJOURN : estadía *f*, estancia *f*, permanencia *f* **2** SUSPENSION : suspensión *f* (de una sentencia) **3** SUPPORT : soporte *m*
stead ['stɛd] *n* **1** : lugar *m* ⟨she went in his stead : fue en su lugar⟩ **2 to stand (someone) in good stead** : ser muy útil a, servir de mucho a
steadfast ['stɛd,fæst] *adj* : firme, resuelto ⟨a steadfast friend : un fiel amigo⟩ ⟨a steadfast refusal : una negativa categórica⟩
steadily ['stɛdəli] *adv* **1** CONSTANTLY : continuamente, sin parar **2** FIRMLY : con firmeza **3** FIXEDLY : fijamente
steady¹ ['stɛdi] *v* **steadied; steadying** *vt* : sujetar ⟨she steadied herself : recobró el equilibrio⟩ — *vi* : estabilizarse
steady² *adj* **steadier; -est 1** FIRM, SURE : seguro, firme ⟨to have a steady hand : tener buen pulso⟩ **2** FIXED, REGULAR : fijo ⟨a steady income : ingresos fijos⟩ **3** CALM : tranquilo, ecuánime ⟨she has steady nerves : es imperturbable⟩ **4** DEPENDABLE : responsable, fiable **5** CONSTANT : constante
steak ['steɪk] *n* : bistec *m*, filete *m*, churrasco *m*, bife *m Arg, Chile, Uru*
steal ['stiːl] *v* **stole** ['stoːl]; **stolen** ['stoːlən]; **stealing** *vt* : robar, hurtar — *vi* **1** : robar, hurtar **2** : ir sigilosamente ⟨to steal away : escabullirse⟩
stealth ['stɛlθ] *n* : sigilo *m*
stealthily ['stɛlθəli] *adv* : furtivamente
stealthy ['stɛlθi] *adj* **stealthier; -est** : furtivo, sigiloso
steam¹ ['stiːm] *vi* : echar vapor ⟨to steam away : moverse echando vapor⟩ — *vt* **1** : cocer al vapor (en cocina) **2 to steam open** : abrir con vapor
steam² *n* **1** : vapor *m* **2 to let off steam** : desahogarse
steamboat ['stiːm,boːt] → **steamship**
steam engine *n* : motor *m* de vapor
steamroller ['stiːm,roːlər] *n* : apisonadora *f*
steamship ['stiːm,ʃɪp] *n* : vapor *m*, barco *m* de vapor
steamy ['stiːmi] *adj* **steamier; -est 1** : lleno de vapor **2** EROTIC : erótico ⟨a steamy romance : un tórrido romance⟩
steed ['stiːd] *n* : corcel *m*
steel¹ ['stiːl] *vt* **to steel oneself** : armarse de valor
steel² *adj* : de acero
steel³ *n* : acero *m*
steely ['stiːli] *adj* **steelier; -est** : como acero ⟨a steely gaze : una mirada fría⟩ ⟨steely determination : determinación férrea⟩
steep¹ ['stiːp] *vt* : remojar, dejar (té, etc.) en infusión
steep² *adj* **1** : empinado, escarpado ⟨a steep cliff : un precipicio escarpado⟩ **2** CONSIDERABLE : considerable, marcado **3** EXCESSIVE : excesivo ⟨steep prices : precios muy altos⟩
steeple ['stiːpəl] *n* : aguja *f*, campanario *m*

steeplechase ['sti:pəl,tʃeɪs] *n* : carrera *f* de obstáculos
steeply ['sti:pli] *adv* : abruptamente
steer¹ ['stɪr] *vt* **1** : conducir (un coche), gobernar (un barco) **2** GUIDE : dirigir, guiar
steer² *n* : buey *m*
steering wheel *n* : volante *m*
stein ['staɪn] *n* : jarra *f* (para cerveza)
stellar ['stɛlər] *adj* : estelar
stem¹ ['stɛm] *v* **stemmed; stemming** *vt* : detener, contener, parar ⟨to stem the tide : detener el curso⟩ — *vi* **to stem from** : provenir de, ser el resultado de
stem² *n* : tallo *m* (de una planta)
stench ['stɛntʃ] *n* : hedor *m*, mal olor *m*
stencil¹ ['stɛntsəl] *vt* **-ciled** *or* **-cilled; -ciling** *or* **-cilling** : marcar utilizando una plantilla
stencil² *n* : plantilla *f* (para marcar)
stenographer [stə'nɑgrəfər] *n* : taquígrafo *m*, -fa *f*
stenographic [,stɛnə'græfɪk] *adj* : taquigráfico
stenography [stə'nɑgrəfi] *n* : taquigrafía *f*
step¹ ['stɛp] *vi* **stepped; stepping 1** : dar un paso ⟨step this way, please : pase por aquí, por favor⟩ ⟨he stepped outside : salió⟩ **2 to step on** : pisar
step² *n* **1** : paso *m* ⟨step by step : paso por paso⟩ **2** STAIR : escalón *m*, peldaño *m* **3** RUNG : escalón *m*, travesaño *m* **4** MEASURE, MOVE : medida *f*, paso *m* ⟨to take steps : tomar medidas⟩ **5** STRIDE : paso *m* ⟨with a quick step : con paso rápido⟩
stepbrother ['stɛp,brʌðər] *n* : hermanastro *m*
stepdaughter ['stɛp,dɔtər] *n* : hijastra *f*
stepfather ['stɛp,fɑðər, -,fa-] *n* : padrastro *m*
stepladder ['stɛp,lædər] *n* : escalera *f* de tijera
stepmother ['stɛp,mʌðər] *n* : madrastra *f*
steppe ['stɛp] *n* : estepa *f*
stepping–stone ['stɛpɪŋ,sto:n] *n* : pasadera *f* (en un río, etc.), trampolín *m* (al éxito)
stepsister ['stɛp,sɪstər] *n* : hermanastra *f*
stepson ['stɛp,sʌn] *n* : hijastro *m*
step up *vt* INCREASE : aumentar
stereo¹ ['stɛri,o:, 'stɪr-] *adj* : estéreo
stereo² *n, pl* **stereos** : estéreo *m*
stereophonic [,stɛrio'fɑnɪk, ,stɪr-] *adj* : estereofónico
stereotype¹ ['stɛrio,taɪp, 'stɪr-] *vt* **-typed; -typing** : estereotipar
stereotype² *n* : estereotipo *m*
sterile ['stɛrəl] *adj* : estéril
sterility [stə'rɪləti] *n* : esterilidad *f*
sterilization [,stɛrələ'zeɪʃən] *n* : esterilización *f*
sterilize ['stɛrə,laɪz] *vt* **-ized; -izing** : esterilizar

sterling ['stərlɪŋ] *adj* **1** : de ley ⟨sterling silver : plata de ley⟩ **2** EXCELLENT : excelente
stern¹ ['stərn] *adj* : severo, adusto — **sternly** *adv*
stern² *n* : popa *f*
sternness ['stərnnəs] *n* : severidad *f*
sternum ['stərnəm] *n, pl* **sternums** *or* **sterna** [-nə] : esternón *m*
stethoscope ['stɛθə,sko:p] *n* : estetoscopio *m*
stevedore ['sti:və,dor] *n* : estibador *m*, -dora *f*
stew¹ ['stu:, 'stju:] *vt* : estofar, guisar — *vi* **1** : cocer (dícese de la carne, etc.) **2** FRET : preocuparse
stew² *n* **1** : estofado *m*, guiso *m* **2 to be in a stew** : estar agitado
steward ['stu:ərd, 'stju:-] *n* **1** MANAGER : administrador *m* **2** : auxiliar *m* de vuelo (en un avión), camarero *m* (en un barco)
stewardess ['stu:ərdəs, 'stju:-] *n* **1** MANAGER : administradora *f* **2** : camarera *f* (en un barco) **3** : auxiliar *f* de vuelo, azafata *f*, aeromoza *f* (en un avión)
stick¹ ['stɪk] *v* **stuck** ['stʌk]; **sticking** *vt* **1** STAB : clavar **2** ATTACH : pegar **3** PUT : poner **4 to stick out** : sacar (la lengua, etc.), extender (la mano) — *vi* **1** ADHERE : pegarse, adherirse **2** JAM : atascarse **3 to stick around** : quedarse **4 to stick out** PROJECT : sobresalir (de una superficie), asomar (por detrás o debajo de algo) **5 to stick to** : no abandonar ⟨stick to your guns : manténgase firme⟩ **6 to stick up** : estar parado (dícese del pelo, etc.), sobresalir (de una superficie) **7 to stick with** : serle fiel a (una persona), seguir con (una cosa) ⟨I'll stick with what I know : prefiero lo conocido⟩
stick² *n* **1** BRANCH, TWIG : ramita *f* **2** : palo *m*, vara *f* ⟨a walking stick : un bastón⟩
sticker ['stɪkər] *n* : etiqueta *f* adhesiva
stickler ['stɪklər] *n* : persona *f* exigente ⟨to be a stickler for : insistir mucho en⟩
sticky ['stɪki] *adj* **stickier; -est 1** ADHESIVE : pegajoso, adhesivo **2** MUGGY : bochornoso **3** DIFFICULT : difícil
stiff ['stɪf] *adj* **1** RIGID : rígido, tieso ⟨a stiff dough : una masa firme⟩ **2** : agarrotado, entumecido ⟨stiff muscles : músculos entumecidos⟩ **3** STILTED : acartonado, poco natural **4** STRONG : fuerte (dícese del viento, etc.) **5** DIFFICULT, SEVERE : severo, difícil, duro
stiffen ['stɪfən] *vt* STRENGTHEN : fortalecer, reforzar (tela, etc.) **2** : hacer más duro (un castigo, etc.) — *vi* **1** HARDEN : endurecerse **2** : entumecerse (dícese de los músculos)
stiffly ['stɪfli] *adv* **1** RIGIDLY : rígidamente **2** COLDLY : con frialdad
stiffness ['stɪfnəs] *n* **1** RIGIDITY : rigidez *f* **2** COLDNESS : frialdad *f* **3** SEVERITY : severidad *f*

stifle ['staɪfəl] vt **-fled; -fling** SMOTHER, SUPPRESS : sofocar, reprimir, contener ⟨to stifle a yawn : reprimir un bostezo⟩

stigma ['stɪgmə] n, pl **stigmata** [stɪg-'mɑtə, 'stɪgmətə] or **stigmas** : estigma m

stigmatize ['stɪgmə,taɪz] vt **-tized; -tizing** : estigmatizar

stile ['staɪl] n : escalones mpl para cruzar un cerco

stiletto [stə'lɛ,to:] n, pl **-tos** or **-toes** : estilete m

still¹ ['stɪl] vt CALM : pacificar, apaciguar — vi : pacificarse, apaciguarse

still² adv **1** QUIETLY : quieto ⟨sit still! : ¡quédate quieto!⟩ **2** : de todos modos, aún, todavía ⟨she still lives there : aún vive allí⟩ ⟨it's still the same : sigue siendo lo mismo⟩ **3** IN ANY CASE : de todos modos, aún así ⟨he still has doubts : aún así le quedan dudas⟩ ⟨I still prefer that you stay : de todos modos prefiero que te quedes⟩

still³ adj **1** MOTIONLESS : quieto, inmóvil **2** SILENT : callado

still⁴ n **1** SILENCE : quietud f, calma f **2** : alambique m (para destilar alcohol)

stillborn ['stɪl,bɔrn] adj : nacido muerto

stillness ['stɪlnəs] n : calma f, silencio m

stilt ['stɪlt] n : zanco m

stilted ['stɪltəd] adj : afectado, poco natural

stimulant ['stɪmjələnt] n : estimulante m — **stimulant** adj

stimulate ['stɪmjə,leɪt] vt **-lated; -lating** : estimular

stimulation [,stɪmjə'leɪʃən] n **1** STIMULATING : estimulación f **2** STIMULUS : estímulo m

stimulus ['stɪmjələs] n, pl **-li** [-,laɪ] **1** : estímulo m **2** INCENTIVE : acicate m

sting¹ ['stɪŋ] v **stung** ['stʌŋ]; **stinging** vt **1** : picar ⟨a bee stung him : le picó una abeja⟩ **2** HURT : hacer escocer (físicamente), herir (emocionalmente) — vi **1** : picar (dícese de las abejas, etc.) **2** SMART : escocer, arder

sting² n : picadura f (herida), escozor m (sensación)

stinger ['stɪŋər] n : aguijón m (de una abeja, etc.)

stinginess ['stɪndʒinəs] n : tacañería f

stingy ['stɪndʒi] adj **stingier; -est 1** MISERLY : tacaño, avaro **2** PALTRY : mezquino, mísero

stink¹ ['stɪŋk] vi **stank** ['stæŋk] or **stunk** ['stʌŋk]; **stunk; stinking** : apestar, oler mal

stink² n : hedor m, mal olor m, peste f

stint¹ ['stɪnt] vt : escatimar ⟨to stint oneself of : privarse de⟩ — vi **to stint on** : escatimar

stint² n : período m

stipend ['staɪ,pɛnd, -pənd] n : estipendio m

stipulate ['stɪpjə,leɪt] vt **-lated; -lating** : estipular

stipulation [,stɪpjə'leɪʃən] n : estipulación f

stir¹ ['stər] v **stirred; stirring** vt **1** AGITATE : mover, agitar **2** MIX : revolver, remover **3** INCITE : incitar, impulsar, motivar **4** or **to stir up** AROUSE : despertar (memorias, etc.), provocar (ira, etc.) — vi : moverse, agitarse

stir² n **1** MOTION : movimiento m **2** COMMOTION : revuelo m

stirrup ['stərəp, 'stɪr-] n : estribo m

stitch¹ ['stɪtʃ] vt : coser, bordar (para decorar) — vi : coser

stitch² n **1** : puntada f **2** TWINGE : punzada f, puntada f

stock¹ ['stɑk] vt : surtir, abastecer, vender — vi **to stock up** : abastecerse

stock² n **1** SUPPLY : reserva f, existencias fpl (en comercio) ⟨to be out of stock : estar agotadas las existencias⟩ **2** SECURITIES : acciones fpl, valores mpl **3** LIVESTOCK : ganado m **4** ANCESTRY : linaje m, estirpe f **5** BROTH : caldo m **6 to take stock** : evaluar

stockade [stɑ'keɪd] n : estacada f

stockbroker ['stɑk,bro:kər] n : corredor m, -dora f de bolsa

stockholder ['stɑk,ho:ldər] n : accionista mf

stocking ['stɑkɪŋ] n : media f ⟨a pair of stockings : unas medias⟩

stock market n : bolsa f

stockpile¹ ['stɑk,paɪl] vt **-piled; -piling** : acumular, almacenar

stockpile² n : reservas fpl

stocky ['stɑki] adj **stockier; -est** : robusto, fornido

stockyard ['stɑk,jɑrd] n : corral m

stodgy ['stɑdʒi] adj **stodgier; -est 1** DULL : aburrido, pesado **2** OLD-FASHIONED : anticuado

stoic¹ ['sto:ɪk] or **stoical** [-ɪkəl] adj : estoico — **stoically** [-ɪkli] adv

stoic² n : estoico m, -ca f

stoicism ['sto:ə,sɪzəm] n : estoicismo m

stoke ['sto:k] vt **stoked; stoking** : atizar (un fuego), echarle carbón a (un horno)

stole¹ → **steal**

stole² ['sto:l] n : estola f

stolen → **steal**

stolid ['stɑlɪd] adj : impasible, imperturbable — **stolidly** adv

stomach¹ ['stʌmɪk] vt : aguantar, soportar

stomach² n **1** : estómago m **2** BELLY : vientre m, barriga f, panza f **3** DESIRE : ganas fpl ⟨he had no stomach for a fight : no quería pelea⟩

stomachache ['stʌmɪk,eɪk] n : dolor m de estómago

stomp ['stɑmp, 'stɔmp] vt : pisotear — vi : pisar fuerte

stone¹ ['sto:n] vt **stoned; stoning** : apedrear, lapidar

stone² n **1** : piedra f **2** PIT : hueso m, pepa f (de una fruta)

Stone Age n : Edad f de Piedra

stony ['stoːni] *adj* **stonier; -est 1** ROCKY : pedregoso **2** UNFEELING : insensible, frío ⟨a stony stare : una mirada glacial⟩
stood → **stand**
stool ['stuːl] *n* **1** SEAT : taburete *m*, banco *m* **2** FOOTSTOOL : escabel *m* **3** FECES : deposición *f* de heces
stoop[1] ['stuːp] *vi* **1** CROUCH : agacharse **2 to stoop to** : rebajarse a
stoop[2] *n* **1** : espaldas *fpl* encorvadas ⟨to have a stoop : ser encorvado⟩ **2** : entrada *f* (de una casa)
stop[1] ['stɑp] *v* **stopped; stopping** *vt* **1** PLUG : tapar **2** PREVENT : impedir, evitar ⟨she stopped me from leaving : me impidió que saliera⟩ **3** HALT : parar, detener **4** CEASE : dejar de ⟨he stopped talking : dejó de hablar⟩ — *vi* **1** HALT : detenerse, parar **2** CEASE : cesar, terminar ⟨the rain won't stop : no deja de llover⟩ **3** STAY : quedarse ⟨she stopped with friends : se quedó en casa de unos amigos⟩ **4 to stop by** : visitar
stop[2] *n* **1** STOPPER : tapón *m* **2** HALT : parada *f*, alto *m* ⟨to come to a stop : pararse, detenerse⟩ ⟨to put a stop to : poner fin a⟩ **3** : parada *f* ⟨bus stop : parada de autobús⟩
stopgap ['stɑp,gæp] *n* : arreglo *m* provisorio
stoplight ['stɑp,laɪt] *n* : semáforo *m*
stoppage ['stɑpɪdʒ] *n* : acto *m* de parar ⟨a work stoppage : un paro⟩
stopper ['stɑpər] *n* : tapón *m*
storage ['storɪdʒ] *n* : almacenamiento *m*, almacenaje *m*
storage battery *n* : acumulador *m*
store[1] ['stor] *vt* **stored; storing** : guardar, almacenar
store[2] *n* **1** RESERVE, SUPPLY : reserva *f* **2** SHOP : tienda *f* ⟨grocery store : tienda de comestibles⟩
storehouse ['stor,haʊs] *n* : almacén *m*, depósito *m*
storekeeper ['stor,kiːpər] *n* : tendero *m*, -ra *f*
storeroom ['stor,ruːm, -,rʊm] *n* : almacén *m*, depósito *m*
stork ['stork] *n* : cigüeña *f*
storm[1] ['storm] *vi* **1** : llover o nevar tormentosamente **2** RAGE : ponerse furioso, vociferar **3 to storm out** : salir echando pestes — *vt* ATTACK : asaltar
storm[2] *n* **1** : tormenta *f*, tempestad *f* **2** UPROAR : alboroto *m*, revuelo *m*, escándalo *m* ⟨a storm of abuse : un torrente de abusos⟩
stormy ['stormi] *adj* **stormier; -est** : tormentoso
story ['stori] *n*, *pl* **stories 1** NARRATIVE : cuento *m*, relato *m* **2** ACCOUNT : historia *f*, relato *m* **3** : piso *m*, planta *f* (de un edificio) ⟨first story : planta baja⟩
stout ['staʊt] *adj* **1** FIRM, RESOLUTE : firme, resuelto **2** STURDY : fuerte, robusto, sólido **3** FAT : corpulento, gordo
stove[1] ['stoːv] *n* : cocina *f* (para cocinar), estufa *f* (para calentar)

stove[2] → **stave**[1]
stow ['stoː] *vt* **1** STORE : poner, meter, guardar **2** LOAD : cargar — *vi* **to stow away** : viajar de polizón
stowaway ['stoːə,weɪ] *n* : polizón *m*
straddle ['strædəl] *vt* **-dled; -dling** : sentarse a horcajadas sobre
straggle ['strægəl] *vi* **-gled; -gling** : rezagarse, quedarse atrás
straggler ['strægələr] *n* : rezagado *m*, -da *f*
straight[1] ['streɪt] *adv* **1** : derecho, directamente ⟨go straight, then turn right : sigue derecho, luego gira a la derecha⟩ **2** HONESTLY : honestamente ⟨to go straight : enmendarse⟩ **3** CLEARLY : con claridad **4** FRANKLY : francamente, con franqueza
straight[2] *adj* **1** : recto (dícese de las líneas, etc.), derecho (dícese de algo vertical), lacio (dícese del pelo) **2** HONEST, JUST : honesto, justo **3** NEAT, ORDERLY : arreglado, ordenado
straighten ['streɪtən] *vt* **1** : enderezar, poner derecho **2 to straighten up** : arreglar, ordenar ⟨he straightened up the house : arregló la casa⟩
straightforward [streɪt'forwərd] *adj* **1** FRANK : franco, sincero **2** CLEAR, PRECISE : puro, simple, claro
straightway ['streɪt'weɪ, -,weɪ] *adv* : inmediatamente
strain[1] ['streɪn] *vt* **1** EXERT : forzar (la vista, la voz) ⟨to strain oneself : hacer un gran esfuerzo⟩ **2** FILTER : colar, filtrar **3** INJURE : lastimarse, hacerse daño en ⟨to strain a muscle : sufrir un esguince⟩
strain[2] *n* **1** LINEAGE : linaje *m*, abolengo *m* **2** STREAK, TRACE : veta *f* **3** VARIETY : tipo *m*, variedad *f* **4** STRESS : tensión *f*, presión *f* **5** SPRAIN : esguince *m*, torcedura *f* (del tobillo, etc.) **6 strains** *npl* TUNE : melodía *f*, acordes *mpl*, compases *fpl*
strainer ['streɪnər] *n* : colador *m*
strait ['streɪt] *n* **1** : estrecho *m* **2 straits** *npl* DISTRESS : aprietos *mpl*, apuros *mpl* ⟨in dire straits : en serios aprietos⟩
straitened ['streɪtənd] *adj* **in straitened circumstances** : en apuros económicos
strand[1] ['strænd] *vt* **1** : varar **2 to be left stranded** : quedar(se) varado, quedar colgado ⟨they left me stranded : me dejaron abandonado⟩
strand[2] *n* **1** : hebra *f* (de hilo, etc.) ⟨a strand of hair : un pelo⟩ **2** BEACH : playa *f*
strange ['streɪndʒ] *adj* **stranger; -est 1** QUEER, UNUSUAL : extraño, raro **2** UNFAMILIAR : desconocido, nuevo
strangely ['streɪndʒli] *adv* ODDLY : de manera extraña ⟨to behave strangely : portarse de una manera rara⟩ ⟨strangely, he didn't call : curiosamente, no llamó⟩

strangeness ['streɪndʒnəs] *n* **1** ODD-NESS : rareza *f* **2** UNFAMILIARITY : lo desconocido

stranger ['streɪndʒər] *n* : desconocido *m*, -da *f*; extraño *m*, -ña *f*

strangle ['stræŋgəl] *vt* **-gled; -gling** : estrangular

strangler ['stræŋglər] *n* : estrangulador *m*, -dora *f*

strap[1] ['stræp] *vt* **strapped; strapping 1** FASTEN : sujetar con una correa **2** FLOG : azotar (con una correa)

strap[2] *n* **1** : correa *f* **2 shoulder strap** : tirante *m*

strapless ['stræpləs] *n* : sin tirantes

strapping ['stræpɪŋ] *adj* : robusto, fornido

stratagem ['strætədʒəm, -ˌdʒɛm] *n* : estratagema *f*, artimaña *f*

strategic [strə'tiːdʒɪk] *adj* : estratégico

strategist ['strætədʒɪst] *n* : estratega *mf*

strategy ['strætədʒi] *n, pl* **-gies** : estrategia *f*

stratified ['strætəˌfaɪd] *adj* : estratificado

stratosphere ['strætəˌsfɪr] *n* : estratosfera *f*

stratospheric [ˌstrætə'sfɪrɪk, -'sfɛr-] *adj* : estratosférico

stratum ['streɪtəm, 'stræ-] *n, pl* **strata** [-tə] : estrato *m*, capa *f*

straw *n* **1** : paja *f* ⟨the last straw : el colmo⟩ **2** *or* **drinking straw** : pajita *f*, popote *m Mex*

strawberry ['strɔˌbɛri] *n, pl* **-ries** : fresa *f*

stray[1] ['streɪ] *vi* **1** WANDER : alejarse, extraviarse ⟨the cattle strayed away : el ganado se descarrió⟩ **2** DIGRESS : desviarse, divagar

stray[2] *adj* : perdido, callejero (dícese de un perro o un gato), descarriado (dícese del ganado)

stray[3] *n* : animal *m* perdido, animal *m* callejero

streak[1] ['striːk] *vt* : hacer rayas en ⟨blue streaked with grey : azul veteado con gris⟩ — *vi* : ir como una flecha

streak[2] *n* **1** : raya *f*, veta *f* (en mármol, queso, etc.), mechón *m* (en el pelo) **2** : rayo *m* (de luz) **3** TRACE : veta *f* **4** : racha *f* ⟨a streak of luck : una racha de suerte⟩

stream[1] ['striːm] *vi* : correr, salir a chorros ⟨tears streamed from his eyes : las lágrimas brotaban de sus ojos⟩ — *vt* : derramar, dejar correr ⟨to stream blood : derramar sangre⟩

stream[2] *n* **1** BROOK : arroyo *m*, riachuelo *m* **2** RIVER : río *m* **3** FLOW : corriente *f*, chorro *m*

streamer ['striːmər] *n* **1** PENNANT : banderín *m* **2** RIBBON : serpentina *f* (de papel), cinta *f* (de tela)

streamlined ['striːmˌlaɪnd] *adj* **1** : aerodinámico (dícese de los automóviles, etc.) **2** EFFICIENT : eficiente, racionalizado

street ['striːt] *n* : calle *f*

streetcar ['striːtˌkɑr] *n* : tranvía *m*

strength ['strɛŋkθ] *n* **1** POWER : fuerza *f* **2** SOLIDITY, TOUGHNESS : solidez *f*, resistencia *f*, dureza *f* **3** INTENSITY : intensidad *f* (de emociones, etc.), lo fuerte (de un sabor, etc.) **4** : punto *m* fuerte ⟨strengths and weaknesses : virtudes y defectos⟩ **5** NUMBER : número *m*, complemento *m* ⟨in full strength : en gran número⟩

strengthen ['strɛŋkθən] *vt* **1** : fortalecer (los músculos, el espíritu, etc.) **2** REINFORCE : reforzar **3** INTENSIFY : intensificar, redoblar (esfuerzos, etc.) — *vi* **1** : fortalecerse, hacerse más fuerte **2** INTENSIFY : intensificarse

strenuous ['strɛnjuəs] *adj* **1** VIGOROUS : vigoroso, enérgico **2** ARDUOUS : duro, riguroso

strenuously ['strɛnjuəsli] *adv* : vigorosamente, duro

stress[1] ['strɛs] *vt* **1** : someter a tensión (física) **2** EMPHASIZE : enfatizar, recalcar **3 to stress out** : estresar

stress[2] *n* **1** : tensión *f* (en un material) **2** EMPHASIS : énfasis *m*, acento *m* (en lingüística) **3** TENSION : tensión *f* (nerviosa), estrés *m*

stressful ['strɛsfəl] *adj* : estresante

stretch[1] ['strɛtʃ] *vt* **1** EXTEND : estirar, extender, desplegar (alas) **2 to stretch the truth** : forzar la verdad, exagerar — *vi* : estirarse

stretch[2] *n* **1** STRETCHING : extensión *f*, estiramiento *m* (de músculos) **2** ELASTICITY : elasticidad *f* **3** EXPANSE : tramo *m*, trecho *m* ⟨the home stretch : la recta final⟩ **4** PERIOD : período *m* (de tiempo)

stretcher ['strɛtʃər] *n* : camilla *f*

strew ['struː] *vt* **strewed; strewed** *or* **strewn** ['struːn]; **strewing 1** SCATTER : esparcir (semillas, etc.), desparramar (papeles, etc.) **2 to strew with** : cubrir de

stricken ['strɪkən] *adj* **stricken with** : aquejado de (una enfermedad), afligido por (tristeza, etc.)

strict ['strɪkt] *adj* : estricto — **strictly** *adv*

strictness ['strɪktnəs] *n* : severidad *f*, lo estricto

stricture ['strɪktʃər] *n* : crítica *f*, censura *f*

stride[1] ['straɪd] *vi* **strode** ['stroːd]; **stridden** ['strɪdən]; **striding** : ir dando trancos, ir dando zancadas

stride[2] *n* : tranco *m*, zancada *f*

strident ['straɪdənt] *adj* : estridente

strife ['straɪf] *n* : conflictos *mpl*, disensión *f*

strike[1] ['straɪk] *v* **struck** ['strʌk]; **striking** *vt* **1** HIT : golpear (a una persona) ⟨to strike a blow : pegar un golpe⟩ **2** DELETE : suprimir, tachar **3** COIN, MINT : acuñar (monedas) **4** : dar (la hora) **5** AFFLICT : sobrevenir ⟨he was stricken with a fever : le sobrevino una fiebre⟩ **6** IMPRESS : impresionar, parecer ⟨her voice struck me : su voz me impresionó⟩ ⟨it struck him as funny : le pareció chistoso⟩ **7** : encender (un fósforo) **8** FIND : descubrir (oro, petróleo) **9** ADOPT : adoptar (una pose, etc.) — *vi* **1** HIT : golpear ⟨to strike against : chocar contra⟩ **2** ATTACK : atacar **3** : declararse en huelga

strike² *n* **1** BLOW : golpe *m* **2** : huelga *f*, paro *m* ⟨to be on strike : estar en huelga⟩ **3** ATTACK : ataque *m*

strikebreaker ['straɪkˌbreɪkər] *n* : rompehuelgas *mf*, esquirol *mf*

strike out *vi* **1** HEAD : salir (para) **2** : ser ponchado (en béisbol) ⟨the batter struck out : poncharon al bateador⟩

striker ['straɪkər] *n* : huelguista *mf*

strike up *vt* START : entablar, empezar

striking ['straɪkɪŋ] *adj* : notable, sorprendente, llamativo ⟨a striking beauty : una belleza imponente⟩ — **strikingly** *adv*

string¹ ['strɪŋ] *vt* **strung** ['strʌŋ]; **stringing** **1** THREAD : ensartar ⟨to string beads : ensartar cuentas⟩ **2** HANG : colgar (con un cordel)

string² *n* **1** : cordel *m*, cuerda *f* **2** SERIES : serie *f*, sarta *f* (de insultos, etc.) **3** strings *npl* : cuerdas *fpl* (en música)

string bean *n* : judía *f*, ejote *m Mex*

stringent ['strɪndʒənt] *adj* : estricto, severo

stringy ['strɪŋi] *adj* **stringier; -est** : fibroso

strip¹ ['strɪp] *v* **stripped; stripping** *vt* : quitar (ropa, pintura, etc.), desnudar, despojar — *vi* UNDRESS : desnudarse

strip² *n* : tira *f* ⟨a strip of land : una faja⟩

stripe¹ ['straɪp] *vt* **striped** ['straɪpt]; **striping** : marcar con rayas o listas

stripe² *n* **1** : raya *f*, lista *f* **2** BAND : franja *f*

striped ['straɪpt, 'straɪpəd] *adj* : a rayas, de rayas, rayado, listado

strive ['straɪv] *vi* **strove** ['stro:v]; **striven** ['strɪvən] *or* **strived; striving** **1 to strive for** : luchar por lograr **2 to strive to** : esforzarse por

strobe ['stro:b] *or* **strobe light** *n* : luz *f* estroboscópica

strode → **stride**

stroke¹ ['stro:k] *vt* **stroked; stroking** : acariciar

stroke² *n* : golpe *m* ⟨a stroke of luck : un golpe de suerte⟩

stroll¹ ['stro:l] *vi* : pasear, pasearse, dar un paseo

stroll² *n* : paseo *m*

stroller ['stro:lər] *n* : cochecito *m* (para niños)

strong ['strɔŋ] *adj* **1** : fuerte **2** HEALTHY : sano **3** ZEALOUS : ferviente

stronghold ['strɔŋˌho:ld] *n* : fortaleza *f*, fuerte *m*, bastión *m* ⟨a cultural stronghold : un baluarte de la cultura⟩

strongly ['strɔŋli] *adv* **1** POWERFULLY : fuerte, con fuerza **2** STURDILY

: fuertemente, sólidamente **3** INTENSELY : intensamente, profundamente **4** WHOLEHEARTEDLY : totalmente

struck → **strike¹**

structural ['strʌktʃərəl] *adj* : estructural

structure¹ ['strʌktʃər] *vt* **-tured; -turing** : estructurar

structure² *n* **1** BUILDING : construcción *f* **2** ARRANGEMENT, FRAMEWORK : estructura *f*

struggle¹ ['strʌgəl] *vi* **-gled; -gling** **1** CONTEND : forcejear (físicamente), luchar, contender **2** : hacer con dificultad ⟨she struggled forward : avanzó con dificultad⟩

struggle² *n* : lucha *f*, pelea *f* (física)

strum ['strʌm] *vt* **strummed; strumming** : rasguear

strung → **string¹**

strut¹ ['strʌt] *vi* **strutted; strutting** : pavonearse

strut² *n* **1** : pavoneo *m* ⟨he walked with a strut : se pavoneaba⟩ **2** : puntal *m* (en construcción, etc.)

strychnine ['strɪkˌnaɪn, -nən, -ˌni:n] *n* : estricnina *f*

stub¹ ['stʌb] *vt* **stubbed; stubbing 1 to stub one's toe** : darse en el dedo (del pie) **2 to stub out** : apagar

stub² *n* : colilla *f* (de un cigarrillo), cabo *m* (de un lápiz, etc.), talón *m* (de un cheque)

stubble ['stʌbəl] *n* **1** : rastrojo *m* (de plantas) **2** BEARD : barba *f*

stubborn ['stʌbərn] *adj* **1** OBSTINATE : terco, obstinado, empecinado **2** PERSISTENT : pertinaz, persistente — **stubbornly** *adv*

stubbornness ['stʌbərnnəs] *n* **1** OBSTINACY : terquedad *f*, obstinación *f* **2** PERSISTENCE : persistencia *f*

stubby ['stʌbi] *adj* **stubbier; -est** : corto y grueso ⟨stubby fingers : dedos regordetes⟩

stucco ['stʌko:] *n, pl* **stuccos** *or* **stuccoes** : estuco *m*

stuck → **stick¹**

stuck–up ['stʌk'ʌp] *adj* : engreído, creído *fam*

stud¹ ['stʌd] *vt* **studded; studding** : tachonar, salpicar

stud² *n* **1** *or* **stud horse** : semental *m* **2** : montante *m* (en construcción) **3** HOBNAIL : tachuela *f*, tachón *m*

student ['stu:dənt, 'stju:-] *n* : estudiante *mf*; alumno *m*, -na *f* (de un colegio)

studied ['stʌdid] *adj* : intencional, premeditado

studio ['stu:diˌo:, 'stju:-] *n, pl* **studios** : estudio *m*

studious ['stu:diəs, 'stju:-] *adj* : estudioso — **studiously** *adv*

study¹ ['stʌdi] *v* **studied; studying 1** : estudiar **2** EXAMINE : examinar, estudiar

study² *n, pl* **studies 1** STUDYING : estudio *m* **2** OFFICE : estudio *m*, gabi-

nete *m* (en una casa) **3** RESEARCH : investigación *f*, estudio *m*
stuff¹ ['stʌf] *vt* : rellenar, llenar, atiborrar ⟨a stuffed toy : un juguete de peluche⟩
stuff² *n* **1** POSSESSIONS : cosas *fpl* **2** ESSENCE : esencia *f* **3** SUBSTANCE : cosa *f*, cosas *fpl* ⟨some sticky stuff : una cosa pegajosa⟩ ⟨she knows her stuff : es experta⟩
stuffing ['stʌfɪŋ] *n* : relleno *m*
stuffy ['stʌfi] *adj* **stuffier; -est 1** CLOSE : viciado, cargado ⟨a stuffy room : una sala mal ventilada⟩ ⟨stuffy weather : tiempo bochornoso⟩ **2** : tapado (dícese de la nariz) **3** STODGY : pesado, aburrido
stumble¹ ['stʌmbəl] *vi* **-bled; -bling 1** TRIP : tropezar, dar un traspié **2** FLOUNDER : quedarse sin saber qué hacer o decir **3 to stumble across** *or* **to stumble upon** : dar con, tropezar con
stumble² *n* : tropezón *m*, traspié *m*
stump¹ ['stʌmp] *vt* : dejar perplejo ⟨to be stumped : no tener respuesta⟩
stump² *n* **1** : muñón *m* (de un brazo o una pierna) **2** *or* **tree stump** : cepa *f*, tocón *m* **3** STUB : cabo *m*
stun ['stʌn] *vt* **stunned; stunning 1** : aturdir (con un golpe) **2** ASTONISH, SHOCK : dejar estupefacto, dejar atónito, aturdir
stung → **sting¹**
stunk → **stink¹**
stunning ['stʌnɪŋ] *adj* **1** ASTONISHING : asombroso, pasmoso, increíble **2** STRIKING : imponente, impresionante (dícese de la belleza)
stunt¹ ['stʌnt] *vt* : atrofiar
stunt² *n* : proeza *f* (acrobática)
stupefy ['stu:pə,faɪ, 'stju:-] *vt* **-fied; -fying 1** : aturdir, atontar (con drogas, etc.) **2** AMAZE : dejar estupefacto, dejar atónito
stupendous [stʊ'pɛndəs, stju-] *adj* **1** MARVELOUS : estupendo, maravilloso **2** TREMENDOUS : tremendo — **stupendously** *adv*
stupid ['stu:pəd, 'stju:-] *adj* **1** IDIOTIC, SILLY : tonto, bobo, estúpido **2** DULL, OBTUSE : lento, torpe, lerdo
stupidity [stʊ'pɪdəti, stju-] *n* : tontería *f*, estupidez *f*
stupidly ['stu:pədli, 'stju:-] *adv* **1** IDIOTICALLY : estúpidamente, tontamente **2** DENSELY : torpemente
stupor ['stu:pər, 'stju:-] *n* : estupor *m*
sturdily ['stərdəli] *adv* : sólidamente
sturdiness ['stərdinəs] *n* : solidez *f* (de muebles, etc.), robustez *f* (de una persona)
sturdy ['stərdi] *adj* **sturdier; -est** : fuerte, robusto, sólido
sturgeon ['stərdʒən] *n* : esturión *m*
stutter¹ ['stʌtər] *vi* : tartamudear
stutter² *n* STAMMER : tartamudeo *m*

sty ['staɪ] *n* **1** *pl* **sties** PIGPEN : chiquero *m*, pocilga *f* **2** *pl* **sties** *or* **styes** : orzuelo *m* (en el ojo)
style¹ ['staɪl] *vt* **styled; styling 1** NAME : llamar **2** : peinar (pelo), diseñar (vestidos, etc.) ⟨carefully styled prose : prosa escrita con gran esmero⟩
style² *n* **1** : estilo *m* ⟨that's just his style : él es así⟩ ⟨to live in style : vivir a lo grande⟩ **2** FASHION : moda *f*
stylish ['staɪlɪʃ] *adj* : de moda, elegante, chic
stylishly ['staɪlɪʃli] *adv* : con estilo
stylishness ['staɪlɪʃnəs] *n* : estilo *m*
stylist ['staɪlɪst] *n* : estilista *mf*
stylize ['staɪ,laɪz, 'staɪə-] *vt* : estilizar
stylus ['staɪləs] *n, pl* **styli** ['staɪ,laɪ] **1** PEN : estilo *m* **2** NEEDLE : aguja *f* (de un tocadiscos)
stymie ['staɪmi] *vt* **-mied; -mieing** : obstaculizar
suave ['swɑv] *adj* : fino, urbano
sub¹ ['sʌb] *vi* **subbed; subbing** → **substitute¹**
sub² *n* **1** → **substitute² 2** → **submarine**
subcommittee ['sʌbkə,mɪti] *n* : subcomité *m*
subconscious¹ [səb'kɑntʃəs] *adj* : subconsciente — **subconsciously** *adv*
subconscious² *n* : subconsciente *m*
subcontract [,sʌb'kɑn,trækt] *vt* : subcontratar
subculture ['sʌb,kʌltʃər] *n* : subcultura *f*
subdivide [,sʌbdə'vaɪd, 'sʌbdə,vaɪd] *vt* **-vided; -viding** : subdividir
subdivision ['sʌbdə,vɪʒən] *n* : subdivisión *f*
subdue [səb'du:, -'dju:] *vt* **-dued; -duing 1** OVERCOME : sojuzgar (a un enemigo), vencer, superar **2** CONTROL : dominar **3** SOFTEN : suavizar, atenuar (luz, etc.), moderar (lenguaje)
subgroup ['sʌb,gru:p] *n* : subgrupo *m*
subhead ['sʌb,hɛd] *or* **subheading** [-,hɛdɪŋ] *n* : subtítulo *m*
subject¹ [səb'dʒɛkt] *vt* **1** CONTROL, DOMINATE : controlar, dominar **2** : someter ⟨they subjected him to pressure : lo sometieron a presiones⟩
subject² ['sʌbdʒɪkt] *adj* **1** : subyugado, sometido ⟨a subject nation : una nación subyugada⟩ **2** PRONE : sujeto, propenso ⟨subject to colds : sujeto a resfriarse⟩ **3 subject to** : sujeto a ⟨subject to congressional approval : sujeto a la aprobación del congreso⟩
subject³ ['sʌbdʒɪkt] *n* **1** : súbdito *m*, -ta *f* (de un gobierno) **2** TOPIC : tema *m* **3** : sujeto *m* (en gramática)
subjection [səb'dʒɛkʃən] *n* : sometimiento *m*
subjective [səb'dʒɛktɪv] *adj* : subjetivo — **subjectively** *adv*
subjectivity [,sʌb,dʒɛk'tɪvəti] *n* : subjetividad *f*
subjugate ['sʌbdʒɪ,geɪt] *vt* **-gated; -gating** : subyugar, someter, sojuzgar

subjunctive [səb'dʒʌŋktɪv] *n* : subjuntivo *m* — **subjunctive** *adj*
sublet ['sʌb,lɛt] *vt* -let; -letting : subarrendar
sublime [sə'blaɪm] *adj* : sublime
sublimely [sə'blaɪmli] *adv* 1 : de manera sublime 2 UTTERLY : absolutamente, completamente
submarine[1] ['sʌbmə,riːn, ,sʌbmə'-] *adj* : submarino
submarine[2] *n* : submarino *m*
submerge [səb'mərdʒ] *v* -merged; -merging *vt* : sumergir — *vi* : sumergirse
submission [səb'mɪʃən] *n* 1 YIELDING : sumisión *f* 2 PRESENTATION : presentación *f*
submissive [səb'mɪsɪv] *adj* : sumiso, dócil
submit [səb'mɪt] *v* -mitted; -mitting *vi* YIELD : rendirse ⟨to submit to : someterse a⟩ — *vt* PRESENT : presentar
subnormal [,sʌb'nɔrməl] *adj* : por debajo de lo normal
subordinate[1] [sə'bɔrdən,eɪt] *vt* -nated; -nating : subordinar
subordinate[2] [sə'bɔrdənət] *adj* : subordinado ⟨a subordinate clause : una oración subordinada⟩
subordinate[3] *n* : subordinado *m*, -da *f*; subalterno *m*, -na *f*
subordination [sə,bɔrdən'eɪʃən] *n* : subordinación *f*
subpoena[1] [sə'piːnə] *vt* -naed; -naing : citar
subpoena[2] *n* : citación *f*, citatorio *m*
subscribe [səb'skraɪb] *vi* -scribed; -scribing 1 : suscribirse (a una revista, etc.) 2 to subscribe to : suscribir (una opinión, etc.), estar de acuerdo con
subscriber [səb'skraɪbər] *n* : suscriptor *m*, -tora *f* (de una revista, etc.); abonado *m*, -da *f* (de un servicio)
subscription [səb'skrɪpʃən] *n* : suscripción *f*
subsequent ['sʌbsɪkwənt, -sə,kwɛnt] *adj* : subsiguiente ⟨subsequent to : posterior a⟩
subsequently ['sʌb,sɪkwɛntli, -kwənt-] *adv* : posteriormente
subservient [səb'sərviənt] *adj* : servil
subside [səb'saɪd] *vi* -sided; -siding 1 SINK : hundirse, descender 2 ABATE : calmarse (dícese de las emociones), amainar (dícese del viento, etc.)
subsidiary[1] [səb'sɪdi,ɛri] *adj* : secundario
subsidiary[2] *n, pl* -ries : filial *f*, subsidiaria *f*
subsidize ['sʌbsə,daɪz] *vt* -dized; -dizing : subvencionar, subsidiar
subsidy ['sʌbsədi] *n, pl* -dies : subvención *f*, subsidio *m*
subsist [səb'sɪst] *vi* : subsistir, mantenerse, vivir
subsistence [səb'sɪstənts] *n* : subsistencia *f*

substance ['sʌbstənts] *n* 1 ESSENCE : sustancia *f*, esencia *f* 2 : sustancia *f* ⟨a toxic substance : una sustancia tóxica⟩ 3 WEALTH : riqueza *f* ⟨a woman of substance : una mujer acaudalada⟩
substandard [,sʌb'stændərd] *adj* : inferior, deficiente
substantial [səb'stæntʃəl] *adj* 1 ABUNDANT : sustancioso ⟨a substantial meal : una comida sustanciosa⟩ 2 CONSIDERABLE : considerable, apreciable 3 SOLID, STURDY : sólido
substantially [səb'stæntʃəli] *adv* : considerablemente
substantiate [səb'stæntʃi,eɪt] *vt* -ated; -ating : confirmar, probar, justificar
substitute[1] ['sʌbstə,tuːt, -,tjuːt] *adj* -tuted; -tuting *vt* : sustituir — *vi* to substitute for : sustituir
substitute[2] *n* 1 : sustituto *m*, -ta *f*; suplente *mf* (persona) 2 : sucedáneo *m* ⟨sugar substitute : sucedáneo de azúcar⟩
substitute teacher *n* : profesor *m*, -sora *f* suplente
substitution [,sʌbstə'tuːʃən, -'tjuː-] *n* : sustitución *f*
subterfuge ['sʌbtər,fjuːdʒ] *n* : subterfugio *m*
subterranean [,sʌbtə'reɪniən] *adj* : subterráneo
subtitle ['sʌb,taɪtəl] *n* : subtítulo *m*
subtle ['sʌtəl] *adj* -tler; -tlest 1 DELICATE, ELUSIVE : sutil, delicado 2 CLEVER : sutil, ingenioso
subtlety ['sʌtəlti] *n, pl* -ties : sutileza *f*
subtly ['sʌtəli] *adv* : sutilmente
subtotal ['sʌb,toːtəl] *n* : subtotal *m*
subtract [səb'trækt] *vt* : restar, sustraer
subtraction [səb'trækʃən] *n* : resta *f*, sustracción *f*
suburb ['sʌ,bərb] *n* : municipio *m* periférico, suburbio *m*
suburban [sə'bərbən] *adj* : de las afueras (de una ciudad), suburbano
subversion [səb'vərʒən] *n* : subversión *f*
subversive [səb'vərsɪv] *adj* : subversivo
subway ['sʌb,weɪ] *n* : metro *m*, subterráneo *m* Arg, Uru
succeed [sək'siːd] *vi* FOLLOW : suceder a — *vi* : tener éxito (dícese de las personas), dar resultado (dícese de los planes, etc.) ⟨she succeeded in finishing : logró terminar⟩
success [sək'sɛs] *n* : éxito *m*
successful [sək'sɛsfəl] *adj* : exitoso, logrado — **successfully** *adv*
succession [sək'sɛʃən] *n* : sucesión *f* ⟨in succession : sucesivamente⟩
successive [sək'sɛsɪv] *adj* : sucesivo, consecutivo — **successively** *adv*
successor [sək'sɛsər] *n* : sucesor *m*, -sora *f*
succinct [sək'sɪŋkt, sə'sɪŋkt] *adj* : sucinto — **succinctly** *adv*
succor[1] ['sʌkər] *vt* : socorrer
succor[2] *n* : socorro *m*

succotash ['sʌkə,tæʃ] *n* : guiso *m* de maíz y frijoles

succulent¹ ['sʌkjələnt] *adj* : suculento, jugoso

succulent² *n* : suculenta *f* (planta)

succumb [sə'kʌm] *vi* : sucumbir

such¹ ['sʌtʃ] *adv* **1** SO : tan ⟨such tall buildings : edificios tan grandes⟩ **2** VERY : muy ⟨he's not in such good shape : anda un poco mal⟩ **3 such that** : de tal manera que

such² *adj* : tal ⟨there's no such thing : no existe tal cosa⟩ ⟨in such cases : en tales casos⟩ ⟨animals such as cows and sheep : animales como vacas y ovejas⟩

such³ *pron* **1** : tal ⟨such was the result : tal fue el resultado⟩ ⟨he's a child, and acts as such : es un niño, y se porta como tal⟩ **2** : algo o alguien semejante ⟨books, papers and such : libros, papeles y cosas por el estilo⟩

suck ['sʌk] *vi* **1** : chupar (por la boca), aspirar (dícese de las máquinas) **2** SUCKLE : mamar — *vt* : sorber (bebidas), chupar (dulces, etc.)

sucker ['sʌkər] *n* **1** : ventosa *f* (de un insecto, etc.) **2** : chupón *m* (de una planta) **3** → **lollipop 4** FOOL : tonto *m*, -ta *f*; idiota *mf*

suckle ['sʌkəl] *v* **-led; -ling** *vt* : amamantar — *vi* : mamar

suckling ['sʌklɪŋ] *n* : lactante *mf*

sucrose ['su:,kro:s, -,kro:z] *n* : sacarosa *f*

suction ['sʌkʃən] *n* : succión *f*

Sudanese [,su:dən'i:z, -'i:s] *n* : sudanés *m*, -nesa *f* — **Sudanese** *adj*

sudden ['sʌdən] *adj* **1** : repentino, súbito ⟨all of a sudden : de pronto, de repente⟩ **2** UNEXPECTED : inesperado, improviso **3** ABRUPT, HASTY : precipitado, brusco

suddenly ['sʌdənli] *adv* **1** : de repente, de pronto **2** ABRUPTLY : bruscamente

suddenness ['sʌdənnəs] *n* **1** : lo repentino **2** ABRUPTNESS : brusquedad *f* **3** HASTINESS : lo precipitado

suds ['sʌdz] *npl* : espuma *f* (de jabón)

sue ['su:] *v* **sued; suing** *vt* : demandar — *vi* **to sue for** : demandar por (daños, etc.)

suede ['sweɪd] *n* : ante *m*, gamuza *f*

suet ['su:ət] *n* : sebo *m*

suffer ['sʌfər] *vi* : sufrir — *vt* **1** : sufrir, padecer (dolores, etc.) **2** PERMIT : permitir, dejar

sufferer ['sʌfərər] *n* : persona que padece (una enfermedad, etc.)

suffering ['sʌfərɪŋ] *n* : sufrimiento *m*

suffice [sə'faɪs] *vi* **-ficed; -ficing** : ser suficiente, bastar

sufficient [sə'fɪʃənt] *adj* : suficiente

sufficiently [sə'fɪʃəntli] *adv* : (lo) suficientemente, bastante

suffix ['sʌ,fɪks] *n* : sufijo *m*

suffocate ['sʌfə,keɪt] *v* **-cated; -cating** *vt* : asfixiar, ahogar — *vi* : asfixiarse, ahogarse

suffocation [,sʌfə'keɪʃən] *n* : asfixia *f*, ahogo *m*

suffrage ['sʌfrɪdʒ] *n* : sufragio *m*, derecho *m* al voto

suffuse [sə'fju:z] *vt* **-fused; -fusing** : impregnar (de olores, etc.), bañar (de luz), teñir (de colores), llenar (de emociones)

sugar¹ ['ʃʊgər] *vt* : azucarar

sugar² *n* : azúcar *mf*

sugarcane ['ʃʊgər,keɪn] *n* : caña *f* de azúcar

sugary ['ʃʊgəri] *adj* **1** : azucarado ⟨sugary desserts : postres azucarados⟩ **2** SACCHARINE : empalagoso

suggest [səg'dʒɛst, sə-] *vt* **1** PROPOSE : sugerir **2** IMPLY : indicar, dar a entender

suggestible [səg'dʒɛstəbəl, sə-] *adj* : influenciable

suggestion [səg'dʒɛstʃən, sə-] *n* **1** PROPOSAL : sugerencia *f* **2** INDICATION : indicio *m* **3** INSINUATION : insinuación *f*

suggestive [səg'dʒɛstɪv, sə-] *adj* : insinuante — **suggestively** *adv*

suicidal [,su:ə'saɪdəl] *adj* : suicida

suicide ['su:ə,saɪd] *n* **1** : suicidio *m* (acto) **2** : suicida *mf* (persona)

suit¹ ['su:t] *vt* **1** ADAPT : adaptar **2** BEFIT : convenir a, ser apropiado a **3** BECOME : favorecer, quedarle bien (a alguien) ⟨the dress suits you : el vestido te queda bien⟩ **4** PLEASE : agradecer, satisfacer, convenirle bien (a alguien) ⟨does Friday suit you? : ¿le conviene el viernes?⟩ ⟨suit yourself! : ¡como quieras!⟩

suit² *n* **1** LAWSUIT : pleito *m*, litigio *m* **2** : traje *m* (ropa) **3** : palo *m* (de naipes)

suitability [,su:tə'bɪləti] *n* : idoneidad *f*, lo apropiado

suitable ['su:təbəl] *adj* : apropiado, idóneo — **suitably** [-bli] *adv*

suitcase ['su:t,keɪs] *n* : maleta *f*, valija *f*, petaca *f Mex*

suite ['swi:t, *for 2 also* 'su:t] *n* **1** : suite *f* (de habitaciones) **2** SET : juego *m* (de muebles)

suitor ['su:tər] *n* : pretendiente *m*

sulfur ['sʌlfər] *n* : azufre *m*

sulfuric acid [,sʌl'fjʊrɪk] *adj* : ácido *m* sulfúrico

sulfurous [,sʌl'fjʊrəs, 'sʌlfərəs, 'sʌlfjə-] *adj* : sulfuroso

sulk¹ ['sʌlk] *vi* : estar de mal humor, enfurruñarse *fam*

sulk² *n* : mal humor *m*

sulky ['sʌlki] *adj* **sulkier; -est** : malhumorado, taimado *Chile*

sullen ['sʌlən] *adj* **1** MOROSE : hosco, taciturno **2** DREARY : sombrío, deprimente

sullenly ['sʌlənli] *adv* **1** MOROSELY : hoscamente **2** GLOOMILY : sombríamente

sully ['sʌli] *vt* **sullied; sullying** : manchar, empañar

sultan ['sʌltən] *n* : sultán *m*
sultry ['sʌltri] *adj* **sultrier; -est 1** : bochornoso ⟨sultry weather : tiempo sofocante, tiempo bochornoso⟩ **2** SENSUAL : sensual, seductor
sum¹ ['sʌm] *vt* **summed; summing 1** : sumar (números) **2** → **sum up**
sum² *n* **1** AMOUNT : suma *f*, cantidad *f* **2** TOTAL : suma *f*, total *f* **3** : suma *f*, adición *f* (en matemáticas)
sumac ['ʃuːˌmæk, 'suː-] *n* : zumaque *m*
summarize ['sʌməˌraɪz] *v* **-rized; -rizing** : resumir, compendiar
summary¹ ['sʌməri] *adj* **1** CONCISE : breve, conciso **2** IMMEDIATE : inmediato ⟨a summary dismissal : un despido inmediato⟩
summary² *n, pl* **-ries** : resumen *m*, compendio *m*
summer ['sʌmər] *n* : verano *m*
summery ['sʌməri] *adj* : veraniego
summit ['sʌmət] *n* **1** : cumbre *f*, cima *f* (de una montaña) **2** *or* **summit conference** : cumbre *f*
summon ['sʌmən] *vt* **1** CALL : convocar (una reunión, etc.), llamar (a una persona) **2** : citar (en derecho) **3** to **summon up** : armarse de (valor, etc.) ⟨to summon up one's strength : reunir fuerzas⟩
summons ['sʌmənz] *n, pl* **summonses 1** SUBPOENA : citación *f*, citatorio *m* Mex **2** CALL : llamada *f*, llamamiento *m*
sumptuous ['sʌmptʃuəs] *adj* : suntuoso
sum up *vt* **1** SUMMARIZE : resumir **2** EVALUATE : evaluar — *vi* : recapitular
sun¹ ['sʌn] *vt* **sunned; sunning 1** : poner al sol **2** to **sun oneself** : asolearse, tomar el sol
sun² *n* **1** : sol *m* **2** SUNSHINE : luz *f* del sol
sunbeam ['sʌnˌbiːm] *n* : rayo *m* de sol
sunblock ['sʌnˌblɑk] *n* : filtro *m* solar
sunburn¹ ['sʌnˌbərn] *vi* **-burned** [-ˌbərnd] *or* **-burnt** [-ˌbərnt]; **-burning** : quemarse por el sol
sunburn² ['sʌnˌbərn] *n* : quemadura *f* de sol
sundae ['sʌndi] *n* : sundae *m*
Sunday ['sʌnˌdeɪ, -di] *n* : domingo *m*
sundial ['sʌnˌdaɪl] *n* : reloj *m* de sol
sundown ['sʌnˌdaʊn] → **sunset**
sundries ['sʌndriz] *npl* : artículos *mpl* diversos
sundry ['sʌndri] *adj* : varios, diversos
sunflower ['sʌnˌflaʊər] *n* : girasol *m*, mirasol *m*
sung → **sing**
sunglasses ['sʌnˌglæsəz] *npl* : gafas *fpl* de sol, lentes *mpl* de sol
sunk → **sink¹**
sunken ['sʌŋkən] *adj* : hundido
sunlight ['sʌnˌlaɪt] *n* : sol *m*, luz *f* del sol
sunny ['sʌni] *adj* **sunnier; -est** : soleado
sunrise ['sʌnˌraɪz] *n* : salida *f* del sol
sunscreen ['sʌnˌskriːn] *n* : filtro *m* solar

sunset ['sʌnˌsɛt] *n* : puesta *f* del sol
sunshine ['sʌnˌʃaɪn] *n* : sol *m*, luz *f* del sol
sunspot ['sʌnˌspɑt] *n* : mancha *f* solar
sunstroke ['sʌnˌstroːk] *n* : insolación *f*
suntan ['sʌnˌtæn] *n* : bronceado *m*
sup ['sʌp] *vi* **supped; supping** : cenar
super ['suːpər] *adj* : súper ⟨super! : ¡fantástico!⟩
superabundance [ˌsuːpərə'bʌndənts] *n* : superabundancia *f*
superb [suˈpərb] *adj* : magnífico, espléndido — **superbly** *adv*
supercilious [ˌsuːpərˈsɪliəs] *adj* : altivo, altanero, desdeñoso
supercomputer ['suːpərkəmˌpjuːtər] *n* : supercomputadora *f*
superficial [ˌsuːpərˈfɪʃəl] *adj* : superficial — **superficially** *adv*
superfluous [suˈpərfluəs] *adj* : superfluo
superhighway ['suːpərˌhaɪˌweɪ, ˌsuː-pər'-] *n* : autopista *f*
superhuman [ˌsuːpərˈhjuːmən] *adj* **1** SUPERNATURAL : sobrenatural **2** HERCULEAN : sobrehumano
superimpose [ˌsuːpərɪmˈpoːz] *vt* **-posed; -posing** : superponer, sobreponer
superintend [ˌsuːpərɪnˈtɛnd] *vt* : supervisar
superintendent [ˌsuːpərɪnˈtɛndənt] *n* : portero *m*, -ra *f* (de un edificio); director *m*, -tora *f* (de una escuela, etc.); superintendente *mf* (de policía)
superior¹ [suˈpɪriər] *adj* **1** BETTER : superior **2** HAUGHTY : altivo, altanero
superior² *n* : superior *m*
superiority [suˌpɪriˈɔrəṭi] *n, pl* **-ties** : superioridad *f*
superlative¹ [suˈpərləṭɪv] *adj* **1** : superlativo (en gramática) **2** SUPREME : supremo **3** EXCELLENT : excelente, excepcional
superlative² *n* : superlativo *m*
supermarket ['suːpərˌmɑrkət] *n* : supermercado *m*
supernatural [ˌsuːpərˈnætʃərəl] *adj* : sobrenatural
supernaturally [ˌsuːpərˈnætʃərəli] *adv* : de manera sobrenatural
superpower ['suːpərˌpaʊər] *n* : superpotencia *f*
supersede [ˌsuːpərˈsiːd] *vt* **-seded; -seding** : suplantar, reemplazar, sustituir
supersonic [ˌsuːpərˈsɑnɪk] *adj* : supersónico
superstar ['suːpərˌstɑr] *n* : superestrella *f*
superstition [ˌsuːpərˈstɪʃən] *n* : superstición *f*
superstitious [ˌsuːpərˈstɪʃəs] *adj* : supersticioso
superstructure ['suːpərˌstrʌktʃər] *n* : superestructura *f*
supervise ['suːpərˌvaɪz] *vt* **-vised; -vising** : supervisar, dirigir
supervision [ˌsuːpərˈvɪʒən] *n* : supervisión *f*, dirección *f*

supervisor [ˈsuːpərˌvaɪzər] *n* : supervisor *m*, -sora *f*
supervisory [ˌsuːpərˈvaɪzəri] *adj* : de supervisor
supine [sʊˈpaɪn] *adj* 1 : en decúbito supino, en decúbito dorsal 2 ABJECT, INDIFFERENT : indiferente, apático
supper [ˈsʌpər] *n* : cena *f*, comida *f*
supplant [səˈplænt] *vt* : suplantar
supple [ˈsʌpəl] *adj* -pler; -plest : flexible
supplement¹ [ˈsʌpləˌmɛnt] *vt* : complementar, completar
supplement² [ˈsʌpləmənt] *n* 1 : complemento *m* ⟨dietary supplement : complemento alimenticio⟩ 2 : suplemento *m* (de un libro o periódico)
supplementary [ˌsʌpləˈmɛntəri] *adj* : suplementario
supplicate [ˈsʌpləˌkeɪt] *v* -cated; -cating *vi* : rezar — *vt* : suplicar
supplier [səˈplaɪər] *n* : proveedor *m*, -dora *f*; abastecedor *m*, -dora *f*
supply¹ [səˈplaɪ] *vt* -plied; -plying : suministrar, proveer de, proporcionar
supply² *n*, *pl* -plies 1 PROVISION : provisión *f*, suministro *m* ⟨supply and demand : la oferta y la demanda⟩ 2 STOCK : reserva *f*, existencias *fpl* (de un negocio) 3 **supplies** *npl* PROVISIONS : provisiones *fpl*, víveres *mpl*, despensa *f*
support¹ [səˈport] *vt* 1 BACK : apoyar, respaldar 2 MAINTAIN : mantener, sostener, sustentar 3 PROP UP : sostener, apoyar, apuntalar, soportar
support² *n* 1 : apoyo *m* (moral), ayuda *f* (económica) 2 PROP : soporte *m*, apoyo *m*
supporter [səˈportər] *n* : partidario *m*, -ria *f*
supportive [səˈportɪv] *adj* : que apoya ⟨his family is very supportive : su familia lo apoya mucho⟩
suppose [səˈpoːz] *vt* -posed; -posing 1 ASSUME : suponer, imaginarse 2 BELIEVE : suponer, creer 3 **to be supposed to** : tener que, deber
supposed [səˈpoːzd, -ˈpoːzəd] *adj* : supuesto — **supposedly** [səˈpoːzədli] *adv*
supposition [ˌsʌpəˈzɪʃən] *n* : suposición *f*
suppository [səˈpɑzəˌtori] *n*, *pl* -ries : supositorio *m*
suppress [səˈprɛs] *vt* 1 SUBDUE : sofocar, suprimir, reprimir (una rebelión, etc.) 2 : suprimir, ocultar (información) 3 REPRESS : reprimir, contener ⟨to suppress a yawn : reprimir un bostezo⟩
suppression [səˈprɛʃən] *n* 1 SUBDUING : represión *f* 2 : supresión *f* (de información) 3 REPRESSION : represión *f*, inhibición *f*
supremacy [sʊˈprɛməsi] *n*, *pl* -cies : supremacía *f*
supreme [sʊˈpriːm] *adj* : supremo

Supreme Being *n* : Ser *m* Supremo
supremely [sʊˈpriːmli] *adv* : totalmente, sumamente
surcharge [ˈsərˌtʃɑrdʒ] *n* : recargo *m*
sure¹ [ˈʃʊr] *adv* 1 ALL RIGHT : por supuesto, claro 2 (*used as an intensifier*) ⟨it sure is hot! : ¡hace tanto calor!⟩ ⟨she sure is pretty! : ¡qué linda es!⟩
sure² *adj* **surer; -est** : seguro ⟨to be sure about something : estar seguro de algo⟩ ⟨a sure sign : una clara señal⟩ ⟨for sure : seguro, con seguridad⟩
surely [ˈʃʊrli] *adv* 1 CERTAINLY : seguramente 2 (*used as an intensifier*) ⟨you surely don't mean that! : ¡no me digas que estás hablando en serio!⟩
sureness [ˈʃʊrnəs] *n* : certeza *f*, seguridad *f*
surety [ˈʃʊrəti] *n*, *pl* -ties : fianza *f*, garantía *f*
surf¹ [ˈsərf] *n* 1 WAVES : oleaje *m* 2 FOAM : espuma *f*
surface¹ [ˈsərfəs] *v* -faced; -facing *vi* : salir a la superficie — *vt* : revestir (una carretera)
surface² *n* 1 : superficie *f* 2 **on the surface** : en apariencia
surfboard [ˈsərfˌbord] *n* : tabla *f* de surf, tabla *f* de surfing
surfeit [ˈsərfət] *n* : exceso *m*
surfer [ˈsərfər] *n* : surfista *mf*
surfing [ˈsərfɪŋ] *n* : surf *m*, surfing *m*
surge¹ [ˈsərdʒ] *vi* **surged; surging** 1 : hincharse (dícese del mar), levantarse (dícese de las olas) 2 SWARM : salir en tropel (dícese de la gente, etc.)
surge² *n* 1 : oleaje *m* (del mar), oleada *f* (de gente) 2 FLUSH : arranque *m*, arrebato *m* (de ira, etc.) 3 INCREASE : aumento *m* (súbito)
surgeon [ˈsərdʒən] *n* : cirujano *m*, -na *f*
surgery [ˈsərdʒəri] *n*, *pl* -geries : cirugía *f*
surgical [ˈsərdʒɪkəl] *adj* : quirúrgico — **surgically** [-kli] *adv*
surly [ˈsərli] *adj* **surlier; -est** : hosco, arisco
surmise¹ [sərˈmaɪz] *vt* -mised; -mising : conjeturar, suponer, concluir
surmise² *n* : conjetura *f*
surmount [sərˈmaʊnt] *vt* 1 OVERCOME : superar, vencer, salvar 2 CLIMB : escalar 3 CAP, TOP : coronar
surname [ˈsərˌneɪm] *n* : apellido *m*
surpass [sərˈpæs] *vt* : superar, exceder, rebasar, sobrepasar
surplus [ˈsərˌplʌs] *n* : excedente *m*, sobrante *m*, superávit *m* (de dinero)
surprise¹ [səˈpraɪz, sər-] *vt* -prised; -prising : sorprender
surprise² *n* : sorpresa *f* ⟨to take by surprise : sorprender⟩
surprising [səˈpraɪzɪŋ, sər-] *adj* : sorprendente — **surprisingly** *adv*
surrender¹ [səˈrɛndər] *vt* 1 : entregar, rendir 2 **to surrender oneself** : entregarse — *vi* : rendirse
surrender² *n* : rendición *m* (de una ciudad, etc.), entrega *f* (de posesiones)

surreptitious [ˌsərəpˈtɪʃəs] *adj* : subrepticio — **surreptitiously** *adv*

surrogate [ˈsərəgət, -ˌgeɪt] *n* : sustituto *m*

surround [səˈraʊnd] *vt* : rodear

surroundings [səˈraʊndɪŋz] *npl* : ambiente *m*, entorno *m*

surveillance [sərˈveɪlənts, -ˈveɪljənts, -ˈveɪənts] *n* : vigilancia *f*

survey[1] [sərˈveɪ] *vt* **-veyed; -veying 1** : medir (un terreno) **2** EXAMINE : inspeccionar, examinar, revisar **3** POLL : hacer una encuesta de, sondear

survey[2] [ˈsərˌveɪ] *n, pl* **-veys 1** INSPECTION : inspección *f*, revisión *f* **2** : medición *f* (de un terreno) **3** POLL : encuesta *f*, sondeo *m*

surveyor [sərˈveɪər] *n* : agrimensor *m*, -sora *f*

survival [sərˈvaɪvəl] *n* : supervivencia *f*, sobrevivencia *f*

survive [sərˈvaɪv] *v* **-vived; -viving** *vi* : sobrevivir — *vt* OUTLIVE : sobrevivir a

survivor [sərˈvaɪvər] *n* : superviviente *mf*, sobreviviente *mf*

susceptibility [səˌsɛptəˈbɪləti] *n, pl* **-ties** : vulnerabilidad *f*, propensión *f* (a enfermedades, etc.)

susceptible [səˈsɛptəbəl] *adj* **1** VULNERABLE : vulnerable, sensible ⟨susceptible to flattery : sensible a halagos⟩ **2** PRONE : propenso ⟨susceptible to colds : propenso a resfriarse⟩

suspect[1] [səˈspɛkt] *vt* **1** DISTRUST : dudar de **2** : sospechar (algo), sospechar de (una persona) **3** IMAGINE, THINK : imaginarse, creer

suspect[2] [ˈsʌsˌpɛkt, səˈspɛkt] *adj* : sospechoso, dudoso, cuestionable

suspect[3] [ˈsʌsˌpɛkt] *n* : sospechoso *m*, -sa *f*

suspend [səˈspɛnd] *vt* : suspender

suspenders [səˈspɛndərz] *npl* : tirantes *mpl*

suspense [səˈspɛnts] *n* : incertidumbre *f*, suspenso *m* (en una película, etc.)

suspenseful [səˈspɛntsfəl] *adj* : de suspenso

suspension [səˈspɛnʧən] *n* : suspensión *f*

suspicion [səˈspɪʃən] *n* **1** : sospecha *f* **2** TRACE : pizca *f*, atisbo *m*

suspicious [səˈspɪʃəs] *adj* **1** QUESTIONABLE : sospechoso, dudoso **2** DISTRUSTFUL : suspicaz, desconfiado

suspiciously [səˈspɪʃəsli] *adv* : de modo sospechoso, con recelo

sustain [səˈsteɪn] *vt* **1** NOURISH : sustentar **2** PROLONG : sostener **3** SUFFER : sufrir **4** SUPPORT, UPHOLD : apoyar, respaldar, sostener

sustainable [səˈsteɪnəbəl] *adj* : sostenible

sustenance [ˈsʌstənənts] *n* **1** NOURISHMENT : sustento *m* **2** SUPPORT : sostén *m*

svelte [ˈsfɛlt] *adj* : esbelto

swab[1] [ˈswɑb] *vt* **swabbed; swabbing 1** CLEAN : lavar, limpiar **2** : aplicar a (con hisopo)

swab[2] *n or* **cotton swab** : hisopo *m* (para aplicar medicinas, etc.)

swaddle [ˈswɑdəl] *vt* **-dled; -dling** [ˈswɑdəlɪŋ] : envolver (en pañales)

swagger[1] [ˈswægər] *vi* : pavonearse

swagger[2] *n* : pavoneo *m*

swallow[1] [ˈswɑlo:] *vt* **1** : tragar (comida, etc.) **2** ENGULF : tragarse, envolver **3** REPRESS : tragarse (insultos, etc.) — *vi* : tragar

swallow[2] *n* **1** : golondrina *f* (pájaro) **2** GULP : trago *m*

swam → **swim**[1]

swamp[1] [ˈswɑmp] *vt* : inundar

swamp[2] *n* : pantano *m*, ciénaga *f*

swampy [ˈswɑmpi] *adj* **swampier; -est** : pantanoso, cenagoso

swan [ˈswɑn] *n* : cisne *f*

swap[1] [ˈswɑp] *vt* **swapped; swapping** : cambiar, intercambiar ⟨to swap places : cambiarse de sitio⟩

swap[2] *n* : cambio *m*, intercambio *m*

swarm[1] [ˈswɔrm] *vi* : enjambrar

swarm[2] *n* : enjambre *m*

swarthy [ˈswɔrði, -θi] *adj* **swarthier; -est** : moreno

swashbuckling [ˈswɑʃˌbʌklɪŋ] *adj* : de aventurero

swat[1] [ˈswɑt] *vt* **swatted; swatting** : aplastar (un insecto), darle una palmada (a alguien)

swat[2] *n* : palmada *f* (con la mano), golpe *m* (con un objeto)

swatch [ˈswɑʧ] *n* : muestra *f*

swath [ˈswɑθ, ˈswoθ] *or* **swathe** [ˈswɑð, ˈswɔð, ˈsweɪð] *n* : franja *f* (de grano segado)

swathe [ˈswɑð, ˈswɔð, ˈsweɪð] *vt* **swathed; swathing** : envolver

swatter [ˈswɑtər] → **flyswatter**

sway[1] [ˈsweɪ] *vi* : balancearse, mecerse — *vt* INFLUENCE : influir en, convencer

sway[2] *n* **1** SWINGING : balanceo *m* **2** INFLUENCE : influjo *m*

swear [ˈswær] *v* **swore** [ˈswor]; **sworn** [ˈsworn]; **swearing** *vi* **1** VOW : jurar **2** CURSE : decir palabrotas — *vt* : jurar

swearword [ˈswærˌwərd] *n* : mala palabra *f*, palabrota *f*

sweat[1] [ˈswɛt] *vi* **sweat** *or* **sweated; sweating 1** PERSPIRE : sudar, transpirar **2** OOZE : rezumar **3** to sweat over : sudar la gota gorda por

sweat[2] *n* : sudor *m*, transpiración *f*

sweater [ˈswɛtər] *n* : suéter *m*

sweatshirt [ˈswɛtˌʃərt] *n* : sudadera *f*

sweaty [ˈswɛti] *adj* **sweatier; -est** : sudoroso, sudado, transpirado

Swede [ˈswiːd] *n* : sueco *m*, -ca *f*

Swedish[1] [ˈswiːdɪʃ] *adj* : sueco

Swedish[2] *n* **1** : sueco *m* (idioma) **2 the Swedish** *npl* : los suecos

sweep[1] [ˈswiːp] *v* **swept** [ˈswɛpt]; **sweeping** *vt* **1** : barrer (el suelo, etc.), limpiar (suciedad, etc.) ⟨he swept the books

aside : apartó los libros de un manotazo⟩ **2** *or* **to sweep through** : extenderse por (dícese del fuego, etc.), azotar (dícese de una tormenta) — *vi* **1** : barrer, limpiar **2** : extenderse (en una curva), describir una curva ⟨the sun swept across the sky : el sol describía una curva en el cielo⟩
sweep² *n* **1** : barrido *m*, barrida *f* (con una escoba) **2** : movimiento *m* circular **3** SCOPE : alcance *m*
sweeper ['swi:pər] *n* : barrendero *m*, -ra *f*
sweeping ['swi:pɪŋ] *adj* **1** WIDE : amplio (dícese de un movimiento) **2** EXTENSIVE : extenso, radical **3** INDISCRIMINATE : indiscriminado, demasiado general **4** OVERWHELMING : arrollador, aplastante
sweepstakes ['swi:p,steɪks] *ns & pl* **1** : carrera *f* (en que el ganador se lleva el premio entero) **2** LOTTERY : lotería *f*
sweet¹ ['swi:t] *adj* **1** : dulce ⟨sweet desserts : postres dulces⟩ **2** FRESH : fresco **3** : sin sal (dícese de la mantequilla, etc.) **4** PLEASANT : dulce, agradable **5** DEAR : querido
sweet² *n* : dulce *m*
sweeten ['swi:tən] *vt* : endulzar
sweetener ['swi:tənər] *n* : endulzante *m*
sweetheart ['swi:t,hɑrt] *n* : novio *m*, -via *f* ⟨thanks, sweetheart : gracias, cariño⟩
sweetly ['swi:tli] *adv* : dulcemente
sweetness ['swi:tnəs] *n* : dulzura *f*
sweet potato *n* : batata *f*, boniato *m*
swell¹ ['swɛl] *vi* **swelled; swelled** *or* **swollen** ['swo:lən, 'swʌl-]; **swelling 1** *or* **to swell up** : hincharse ⟨her ankle swelled : se le hinchó el tobillo⟩ **2** *or* **to swell out** : inflarse, hincharse (dícese de las velas, etc.) **3** INCREASE : aumentar, crecer
swell² *n* **1** : oleaje *m* (del mar) **2** → **swelling**
swelling ['swɛlɪŋ] *n* : hinchazón *f*
swelter ['swɛltər] *vi* : sofocarse de calor
swept → **sweep¹**
swerve¹ ['swərv] *vi* **swerved; swerving** : virar bruscamente
swerve² *n* : viraje *m* brusco
swift¹ ['swɪft] *adj* **1** FAST : rápido, veloz **2** SUDDEN : repentino, súbito — **swiftly** *adv*
swift² *n* : vencejo *m* (pájaro)
swiftness ['swɪftnəs] *n* : rapidez *f*, velocidad *f*
swig¹ ['swɪg] *vi* **swigged; swigging** : tomar a tragos, beber a tragos
swig² *n* : trago *m*
swill¹ ['swɪl] *vt* : chupar, beber a tragos grandes
swill² *n* **1** SLOP : bazofia *f* **2** GARBAGE : basura *f*
swim¹ ['swɪm] *vi* **swam** ['swæm]; **swum** ['swʌm]; **swimming 1** : nadar **2** FLOAT : flotar **3** REEL : dar vueltas ⟨his head was swimming : la cabeza le daba vueltas⟩

swim² *n* : baño *m*, chapuzón *m* ⟨to go for a swim : ir a nadar⟩
swimmer ['swɪmər] *n* : nadador *m*, -dora *f*
swindle¹ ['swɪndəl] *vt* **-dled; -dling** : estafar, timar
swindle² *n* : estafa *f*, timo *m fam*
swindler ['swɪndələr] *n* : estafador *m*, -dora *f*; timador *m*, -dora *f*
swine ['swaɪn] *ns & pl* : cerdo *m*, -da *f*
swing¹ ['swɪŋ] *v* **swung** ['swʌŋ]; **swinging 1** : describir una curva con ⟨he swung the ax at the tree : le dio al arbol con el hacha⟩ **2** : balancear (los brazos, etc.), hacer oscilar **3** SUSPEND : colgar — *vi* **1** SWAY : balancearse (dícese de los brazos, etc.), oscilar (dícese de un objeto), columpiarse, mecerse (en un columpio) **2** SWIVEL : girar (en un pivote) ⟨the door swung shut : la puerta se cerró⟩ **3** CHANGE : virar, cambiar (dícese de las opiniones, etc.)
swing² *n* **1** SWINGING : vaivén *m*, balanceo *m* **2** CHANGE, SHIFT : viraje *m*, movimiento *m* **3** : columpio *m* (para niños) **4 to take a swing at someone** : intentar pegarle a alguien
swipe¹ ['swaɪp] *vt* **swiped; swiping 1** STRIKE : dar, pegar (con un movimiento amplio) **2** WIPE : limpiar **3** STEAL : birlar *fam*, robar
swipe² *n* BLOW : golpe *m*
swirl¹ ['swərl] *vi* : arremolinarse
swirl² *n* **1** EDDY : remolino *m* **2** SPIRAL : espiral *f*
swish¹ ['swɪʃ] *vt* : mover (produciendo un sonido) ⟨she swished her skirt : movía la falda⟩ — *vi* : moverse (produciendo un sonido) ⟨the cars swished by : se oían pasar los coches⟩
swish² *n* : silbido *m* (de un látigo, etc.), susurro *m* (de agua), crujido *m* (de ropa, etc.)
Swiss ['swɪs] *n* : suizo *m*, -za *f* — **Swiss** *adj*
swiss chard *n* : acelga *f*
switch¹ ['swɪtʃ] *vt* **1** LASH, WHIP : azotar **2** CHANGE : cambiar de **3** EXCHANGE : intercambiar **4 to switch on** : encender, prender **5 to switch off** : apagar — *vi* **1** : moverse de un lado al otro **2** CHANGE : cambiar **3** SWAP : intercambiarse
switch² *n* **1** WHIP : vara *f* **2** CHANGE, SHIFT : cambio *m* **3** : interruptor *m*, llave *f* (de la luz, etc.)
switchboard ['swɪtʃ,bord] *n* : conmutador *m*, centralita *f*
swivel¹ ['swɪvəl] *vi* **-veled** *or* **-velled; -veling** *or* **-velling** : girar (sobre un pivote)
swivel² *n* : base *f* giratoria
swollen *pp* → **swell¹**
swoon¹ ['swu:n] *vi* : desvanecerse, desmayarse
swoon² *n* : desvanecimiento *m*, desmayo *m*

665

spoon

swoop¹ ['swu:p] *vi* : abatirse (dícese de las aves), descender en picada (dícese de un avión)

swoop² *n* : descenso *m* en picada

sword ['sɔrd] *n* : espada *f*

swordfish ['sɔrd,fɪʃ] *n* : pez *m* espada

swore, sworn → **swear**

swum *pp* → **swim¹**

swung → **swing¹**

sycamore ['sɪkə,mor] *n* : sicomoro *m*

sycophant ['sɪkəfənt, -,fænt] *n* : adulador *m*, -dora *f*

syllabic [sə'læbɪk] *adj* : silábico

syllable ['sɪləbəl] *n* : sílaba *f*

syllabus ['sɪləbəs] *n, pl* **-bi** [-,baɪ] *or* **-buses** : programa *m* (de estudios)

symbol ['sɪmbəl] *n* : símbolo *m*

symbolic [sɪm'balɪk] *adj* : simbólico — **symbolically** [-kli] *adv*

symbolism ['sɪmbə,lɪzəm] *n* : simbolismo *m*

symbolize ['sɪmbə,laɪz] *vt* **-ized; -izing** : simbolizar

symmetrical [sə'mɛtrɪkəl] *or* **symmetric** [-trɪk] *adj* : simétrico — **symmetrically** [-trɪkli] *adv*

symmetry ['sɪmətri] *n, pl* **-tries** : simetría *f*

sympathetic [,sɪmpə'θɛt̬ɪk] *adj* **1** PLEASING : agradable **2** RECEPTIVE : receptivo, favorable **3** COMPASSIONATE, UNDERSTANDING : comprensivo, compasivo

sympathetically [,sɪmpə'θɛt̬ɪkli] *adv* : con compasión, con comprensión

sympathize ['sɪmpə,θaɪz] *vi* **-thized; -thizing** : compadecer ⟨I sympathize with you : te compadezco⟩

sympathy ['sɪmpəθi] *n, pl* **-thies 1** COMPASSION : compasión *f* **2** UNDERSTANDING : comprensión *f* **3** AGREEMENT : solidaridad *f* ⟨in sympathy with : de acuerdo con⟩ **4** CONDOLENCES : pésame *m*, condolencias *fpl*

symphonic [sɪm'fanɪk] *adj* : sinfónico

symphony ['sɪmpfəni] *n, pl* **-nies** : sinfonía *f*

symposium [sɪm'po:ziəm] *n, pl* **-sia** [-ziə] *or* **-siums** : simposio *m*

symptom ['sɪmptəm] *n* : síntoma *m*

symptomatic [,sɪmptə'mæt̬ɪk] *adj* : sintomático

synagogue ['sɪnə,gag, -,gɔg] *n* : sinagoga *f*

sync ['sɪŋk] *n* : sincronización *f* ⟨in sync : sincronizado⟩

synchronize ['sɪŋkrə,naɪz, 'sɪn-] *v* **-nized; -nizing** *vi* : estar sincronizado — *vt* : sincronizar

syncopate ['sɪŋkə,peɪt, 'sɪn-] *vt* **-pated; -pating** : sincopar

syncopation [,sɪŋkə'peɪʃən, ,sɪn-] *n* : síncopa *f*

syndicate¹ ['sɪndə,keɪt] *vi* **-cated; -cating** : formar una asociación

syndicate² ['sɪndɪkət] *n* : asociación *f*, agrupación *f*

syndrome ['sɪn,dro:m] *n* : síndrome *m*

synonym ['sɪnə,nɪm] *n* : sinónimo *m*

synonymous [sə'nanəməs] *adj* : sinónimo

synopsis [sə'napsɪs] *n, pl* **-opses** [-,si:z] : sinopsis *f*

syntactic [sɪn'tæktɪk] *adj* : sintáctico

syntax ['sɪn,tæks] *n* : sintaxis *f*

synthesis ['sɪnθəsɪs] *n, pl* **-theses** [-,si:z] : síntesis *f*

synthesize ['sɪnθə,saɪz] *vt* **-sized; -sizing** : sintetizar

synthetic¹ [sɪn'θɛt̬ɪk] *adj* : sintético, artificial — **synthetically** [-t̬ɪkli] *adv*

synthetic² *n* : producto *m* sintético

syphilis ['sɪfələs] *n* : sífilis *f*

Syrian ['sɪriən] *n* : sirio *m*, -ria *f* — **Syrian** *adj*

syringe [sə'rɪndʒ, 'sɪrɪndʒ] *n* : jeringa *f*, jeringuilla *f*

syrup ['sərəp, 'sɪrəp] *n* : jarabe *m*, almíbar *m* (de azúcar y agua)

system ['sɪstəm] *n* **1** METHOD : sistema *m*, método *m* **2** APPARATUS : sistema *m*, instalación *f*, aparato *m* ⟨electrical system : instalación eléctrica⟩ ⟨digestive system : aparato digestivo⟩ **3** BODY : organismo *m*, cuerpo *m* ⟨diseases that affect the whole system : enfermedades que afectan el organismo entero⟩ **4** NETWORK : red *f*

systematic [,sɪstə'mæt̬ɪk] *adj* : sistemático — **systematically** [-t̬ɪkli] *adv*

systematize ['sɪstəmə,taɪz] *vt* **-tized; -tizing** : sistematizar

systemic [sɪs'tɛmɪk] *adj* : sistémico

T

t ['ti:] *n, pl* **t's** *or* **ts** ['ti:z] : vigésima letra del alfabeto inglés

tab ['tæb] *n* **1** FLAP, TAG : lengüeta *f* (de un sobre, una caja, etc.), etiqueta *f* (de ropa) **2** → **tabulator 3** BILL, CHECK : cuenta *f* **4 to keep tabs on** : tener bajo vigilancia

tabby ['tæbi] *n, pl* **-bies 1** *or* **tabby cat** : gato *m* atigrado **2** : gata *f*

tabernacle ['tæbər,nækəl] *n* : tabernáculo *m*

table ['teɪbəl] *n* **1** : mesa *f* ⟨a table for two : una mesa para dos⟩ **2** LIST : tabla *f* ⟨multiplication table : tabla de multiplicar⟩ **3 table of contents** : índice *m* de materias

tableau ['tæ'blo:, 'tæ,-] *n, pl* **-leaux** [-'blo:z, -,blo:z] : retablo *m*, cuadro *m* vivo (en teatro)

tablecloth ['teɪbəl,klɔθ] *n* : mantel *m*

tablespoon ['teɪbəl,spu:n] *n* **1** : cuchara *f* (de mesa) **2** → **tablespoonful**

tablespoonful · take on

tablespoonful ['teɪbəl,spu:n,fʊl] *n*
: cucharada *f*
tablet ['tæblət] *n* **1** PLAQUE : placa *f* **2**
PAD : bloc *m* (de papel) **3** PILL : tableta *f*, pastilla *f*, píldora *f* ⟨an aspirin
tablet : una tableta de aspirina⟩
table tennis *n* : tenis *m* de mesa
tableware ['teɪbəl,wær] *n* : vajillas *fpl*,
cubiertos *mpl* (de mesa)
tabloid ['tæ,blɔɪd] *n* : tabloide *m*
taboo¹ [tə'bu:, tæ-] *adj* : tabú
taboo² *n* : tabú *m*
tabular ['tæbjələr] *adj* : tabular
tabulate ['tæbjə,leɪt] *vt* **-lated; -lating**
: tabular
tabulator ['tæbjə,leɪtər] *n* : tabulador *m*
tacit ['tæsɪt] *adj* : tácito, implícito — **tacitly** *adv*
taciturn ['tæsɪ,tərn] *adj* : taciturno
tack¹ ['tæk] *vt* **1** : sujetar con tachuelas
2 to tack on ADD : añadir, agregar
tack² *n* **1** : tachuela *f* **2** COURSE : rumbo *m* ⟨to change tack : cambiar de rumbo⟩
tackle¹ ['tækəl] *vt* **-led; -ling 1** : taclear
(en futbol americano) **2** CONFRONT
: abordar, enfrentar, emprender (un
problema, un trabajo, etc.)
tackle² *n* **1** EQUIPMENT, GEAR : equipo
m, aparejo *m* **2** : aparejo *m* (de un
buque) **3** : tacleada *f* (en futbol americano)
tacky ['tæki] *adj* **tackier; -est 1** STICKY
: pegajoso **2** CHEAP, GAUDY : de mal
gusto, naco *Mex*
tact ['tækt] *n* : tacto *m*, delicadeza *f*, discreción *f*
tactful ['tæktfəl] *adj* : discreto, diplomático, de mucho tacto
tactfully ['tæktfəli] *adv* : discretamente,
con mucho tacto
tactic ['tæktɪk] *n* : táctica *f*
tactical ['tæktɪkəl] *adj* : táctico, estratégico
tactics ['tæktɪks] *ns & pl* : táctica *f*, estrategia *f*
tactile ['tæktəl, -,taɪl] *adj* : táctil
tactless ['tæktləs] *adj* : indiscreto, poco
delicado
tactlessly ['tæktləsli] *adv* : rudamente,
sin tacto
tadpole ['tæd,po:l] *n* : renacuajo *m*
taffeta ['tæfətə] *n* : tafetán *m*, tafeta *f*
Arg, Mex, Uru
taffy ['tæfi] *n, pl* **-fies** : caramelo *m* de
melaza, chicloso *m Mex*
tag¹ ['tæg] *v* **tagged; tagging** *vt* **1** LABEL : etiquetar **2** TAIL : seguir de cerca
3 TOUCH : tocar (en varios juegos)
— *vi* **to tag along** : pegarse, acompañar
tag² *n* **1** LABEL : etiqueta *f* **2** SAYING
: dicho *m*, refrán *m*
tail¹ ['teɪl] *vt* FOLLOW : seguir de cerca,
pegarse
tail² *n* **1** : cola *f*, rabo *m* (de un animal)
2 : cola *f*, parte *f* posterior ⟨a comet's
tail : la cola de un cometa⟩ **3 tails** *npl*
: cruz *f* (de una moneda) ⟨heads or tails
: cara o cruz⟩

tailed ['teɪld] *adj* : que tiene cola
tailgate¹ ['teɪl,geɪt] *vi* **-gated; -gating**
: seguir a un vehículo demasiado de
cerca
tailgate² *n* : puerta *f* trasera (de un vehículo)
taillight ['teɪl,laɪt] *n* : luz *f* trasera (de un
vehículo), calavera *f Mex*
tailor¹ ['teɪlər] *vt* **1** : confeccionar o alterar (ropa) **2** ADAPT : adaptar, ajustar
tailor² *n* : sastre *m*, -tra *f*
tailpipe ['teɪl,paɪp] *n* : tubo *m* de escape
tailspin ['teɪl,spɪn] *n* : barrena *f*
taint¹ ['teɪnt] *vt* : contaminar, corromper
taint² *n* : corrupción *f*, impureza *f*
take¹ ['teɪk] *v* **took** ['tʊk]; **taken** ['teɪkən];
taking *vt* **1** CAPTURE : capturar, apresar **2** GRASP : tomar, agarrar ⟨to take
the bull by the horns : tomar al toro
por los cuernos⟩ **3** CATCH : tomar,
agarrar ⟨taken by surprise : tomado
por sorpresa⟩ **4** CAPTIVATE : encantar,
fascinar **5** INGEST : tomar, ingerir
⟨take two pills : tome dos píldoras⟩ **6**
REMOVE : sacar, extraer ⟨take an orange : saca una naranja⟩ **7** : tomar,
coger (un tren, un autobús, etc.) **8**
NEED, REQUIRE : tomar, requerir
⟨these things take time : estas cosas
toman tiempo⟩ **9** BRING, CARRY : llevar, sacar, cargar ⟨take them with you
: llévalos contigo⟩ ⟨take the trash out
: saca la basura⟩ **10** BEAR, ENDURE
: soportar, aguantar (dolores, etc.) **11**
ACCEPT : aceptar (un cheque, etc.),
seguir (consejos), asumir (la responsabilidad) **12** SUPPOSE : suponer ⟨I take
it that . . . : supongo que . . . ⟩ **13** (*indicating an action or an undertaking*)
⟨to take a walk : dar un paseo⟩ ⟨to take
a class : tomar una clase⟩ **14 to take
place** HAPPEN : tener lugar, suceder,
ocurrir — *vi* : agarrar (dícese de un
tinte), prender (dícese de una vacuna)
take² *n* **1** PROCEEDS : recaudación *f*, ingresos *mpl*, ganancias *fpl* **2** : toma *f* (de
un rodaje o una grabación)
take back *vt* : retirar (palabras, etc.)
take in *vt* **1** : tomarle a, achicar (un vestido, etc.) **2** INCLUDE : incluir, abarcar
3 ATTEND : ir a ⟨to take in a movie : ir
al cine⟩ **4** GRASP, UNDERSTAND : captar, entender **5** DECEIVE : engañar
takeoff ['teɪk,ɔf] *n* **1** PARODY : parodia
f **2** : despegue *m* (de un avión o cohete)
take off *vt* REMOVE : quitar ⟨take off
your hat : quítate el sombrero⟩ — *vi* **1**
: despegar (dícese de un avión o un cohete) **2** LEAVE : irse, partir
take on *vt* **1** TACKLE : abordar, emprender (problemas, etc.) **2** ACCEPT
: aceptar, encargarse de, asumir (una
responsabilidad) **3** CONTRACT : contratar (trabajadores) **4** ASSUME : adoptar, asumir, adquirir ⟨the neighborhood took on a dingy look : el barrio
asumió una apariencia deprimente⟩

takeover [ˈteɪkˌoːvər] *n* : toma *f* (de poder o de control), adquisición *f* (de una empresa por otra)

take over *vt* : tomar el poder de, tomar las riendas de — *vi* : asumir el mando

taker [ˈteɪkər] *n* : persona *f* interesada ⟨available to all takers : disponible a cuantos estén interesados⟩

take up *vt* **1** LIFT : levantar **2** SHORTEN : acortar (una falda, etc.) **3** BEGIN : empezar, dedicarse a (un pasatiempo, etc.) **4** OCCUPY : ocupar, llevar (tiempo, espacio) **5** PURSUE : volver a (una cuestión, un asunto) **6** CONTINUE : seguir con

talc [ˈtælk] *n* : talco *m*

talcum powder [ˈtælkəm] *n* : talco *m*, polvos *mpl* de talco

tale [ˈteɪl] *n* **1** ANECDOTE, STORY : cuento *m*, relato *m*, anécdota *f* **2** FALSEHOOD : cuento *m*, mentira *f*

talent [ˈtælənt] *n* : talento *m*, don *m*

talented [ˈtæləntəd] *adj* : talentoso

talisman [ˈtælɪsmən, -lɪz-] *n*, *pl* **-mans** : talismán *m*

talk¹ [ˈtɔk] *vi* **1** : hablar ⟨he talks for hours : se pasa horas hablando⟩ **2** CHAT : charlar, platicar — *vt* **1** SPEAK : hablar ⟨to talk French : hablar francés⟩ ⟨to talk business : hablar de negocios⟩ **2** PERSUADE : influenciar, convencer ⟨she talked me out of it : me convenció que no lo hiciera⟩ **3 to talk over** DISCUSS : hablar de, discutir

talk² *n* **1** CONVERSATION : charla *f*, plática *f*, conversación *f* **2** GOSSIP, RUMOR : chisme *m*, rumores *mpl*

talkative [ˈtɔkətɪv] *adj* : locuaz, parlanchín, charlatán

talker [ˈtɔkər] *n* : conversador *m*, -dora *f*; hablador *m*, -dora *f*

talk show *n* : programa *m* de entrevistas

tall [ˈtɔl] *adj* : alto ⟨how tall is he? : ¿cuánto mide?⟩

tallness [ˈtɔlnəs] *n* HEIGHT : estatura *f* (de una persona), altura *f* (de un objeto)

tallow [ˈtæloː] *n* : sebo *m*

tally¹ [ˈtæli] *v* **-lied; -lying** *vt* RECKON : contar, hacer una cuenta de — *vi* MATCH : concordar, corresponder, cuadrar

tally² *n*, *pl* **-lies** : cuenta *f* ⟨to keep a tally : llevar la cuenta⟩

talon [ˈtælən] *n* : garra *f* (de un ave de rapiña)

tambourine [ˌtæmbəˈriːn] *n* : pandero *m*, pandereta *f*

tame¹ [ˈteɪm] *vt* **tamed; taming** : domar, amansar, domesticar

tame² *adj* **tamer; -est 1** DOMESTICATED : domesticado, manso **2** DOCILE : manso, dócil **3** DULL : aburrido, soso

tamely [ˈteɪmli] *adv* : mansamente, dócilmente

tamer [ˈteɪmər] *n* : domador *m*, -dora *f*

tamp [ˈtæmp] *vt* : apisonar

tamper [ˈtæmpər] *vi* **to tamper with** : adulterar (una sustancia), forzar (un sello, una cerradura), falsear (documentos), manipular (una máquina)

tampon [ˈtæmˌpɑn] *n* : tampón *m*

tan¹ [ˈtæn] *v* **tanned; tanning** *vt* **1** : curtir (pieles) **2** : broncear — *vi* : broncearse

tan² *n* **1** SUNTAN : bronceado *m* ⟨to get a tan : broncearse⟩ **2** : color *m* canela, color *m* café con leche

tandem¹ [ˈtændəm] *adv or* **in tandem** : en tándem

tandem² *n* : tándem *m* (bicicleta)

tang [ˈtæŋ] *n* : sabor *m* fuerte

tangent [ˈtændʒənt] *n* : tangente *f* ⟨to go off on a tangent : irse por la tangente⟩

tangerine [ˈtændʒəˌriːn, ˌtændʒəˈ-] *n* : mandarina *f*

tangible [ˈtændʒəbəl] *adj* : tangible, palpable — **tangibly** [-bli] *adv*

tangle¹ [ˈtæŋgəl] *v* **-gled; -gling** *vt* : enredar, enmarañar — *vi* : enredarse

tangle² *n* : enredo *m*, maraña *f*

tango¹ [ˈtæŋˌgoː] *vi* : bailar el tango

tango² *n*, *pl* **-gos** : tango *m*

tangy [ˈtæŋi] *adj* **tangier; -est** : que tiene un sabor fuerte

tank [ˈtæŋk] *n* **1** : tanque *m*, depósito *m* ⟨fuel tank : depósito de combustibles⟩

tankard [ˈtæŋkərd] *n* : jarra *f*

tanker [ˈtæŋkər] *n* : buque *m* cisterna, camión *m* cisterna, avión *m* cisterna ⟨an oil tanker : un petrolero⟩

tanner [ˈtænər] *n* : curtidor *m*, -dora *f*

tannery [ˈtænəri] *n*, *pl* **-neries** : curtiduría *f*, tenería *f*

tannin [ˈtænən] *n* : tanino *m*

tantalize [ˈtæntəˌlaɪz] *vt* **-lized; -lizing** : tentar, atormentar (con algo inasequible)

tantalizing [ˈtæntəˌlaɪzɪŋ] *adj* : tentador, seductor

tantamount [ˈtæntəˌmaʊnt] *adj* : equivalente

tantrum [ˈtæntrəm] *n* : rabieta *f*, berrinche *m* ⟨to throw a tantrum : hacer un berrinche⟩

tap¹ [ˈtæp] *vt* **tapped; tapping 1** : ponerle una espita, sacar líquido de (un barril, un tanque, etc.) **2** : intervenir (una línea telefónica) **3** PAT, TOUCH : tocar, golpear ligeramente ⟨he tapped me on the shoulder : me tocó en el hombro⟩

tap² *n* **1** FAUCET : llave *f*, grifo *m* ⟨beer on tap : cerveza de barril⟩ **2** : extracción *f* (de líquido) ⟨a spinal tap : una punción lumbar⟩ **3** PAT, TOUCH : golpecito *m*, toque *m*

tape¹ [ˈteɪp] *vt* **taped; taping 1** : sujetar o arreglar con cinta adhesiva **2** RECORD : grabar

tape² *n* **1** : cinta *f* (adhesiva, magnética, etc.) **2** → **tape measure**

tape measure *n* : cinta *f* métrica

taper¹ [ˈteɪpər] *vi* **1** : estrecharse gradualmente ⟨its tail tapers towards the tip : su cola va estrechándose hacia la punta⟩ 2 *or* **to taper off** : disminuir gradualmente

taper² *n* **1** CANDLE : vela *f* larga y delgada **2** TAPERING : estrechamiento *m* gradual

tapestry ['tæpəstri] *n, pl* **-tries** : tapiz *m*

tapeworm ['teɪpˌwərm] *n* : solitaria *f*, tenia *f*

tapioca [ˌtæpi'oːkə] *n* : tapioca *f*

tar¹ ['tɑr] *vt* **tarred; tarring** : alquitranar

tar² *n* : alquitrán *m*, brea *f*, chapopote *m* Mex

tarantula [tə'ræntʃələ, -'ræntələ] *n* : tarántula *f*

tardiness ['tɑrdinəs] *n* : tardanza *f*, retraso *m*

tardy ['tɑrdi] *adj* **-dier; -est** LATE : tardío, de retraso

target¹ ['tɑrgət] *vt* : fijar como objetivo, dirigir, destinar

target² *n* **1** : blanco *m* ⟨target practice : tiro al blanco⟩ **2** GOAL, OBJECTIVE : meta *f*, objetivo *m*

tariff ['tærɪf] *n* DUTY : tarifa *f*, arancel *m*

tarnish¹ ['tɑrnɪʃ] *vt* **1** DULL : deslustrar **2** SULLY : empañar, manchar (una reputación, etc.) — *vi* : deslustrarse

tarnish² *n* : deslustre *m*

tarpaulin [tɑr'pɔlən, 'tɑrpə-] *n* : lona *f* (impermeable)

tarragon ['tærəˌgɑn, -gən] *n* : estragón *m*

tarry¹ ['tæri] *vi* **-ried; -rying** : demorarse, entretenerse

tarry² ['tɑri] *adj* **1** : parecido al alquitrán **2** : cubierto de alquitrán

tart¹ ['tɑrt] *adj* **1** SOUR : ácido, agrio **2** CAUSTIC : mordaz, acrimonioso — **tartly** *adv*

tart² *n* : tartaleta *f*

tartan ['tɑrtən] *n* : tartán *m*

tartar ['tɑrtər] *n* **1** : tártaro *m* ⟨tartar sauce : salsa tártara⟩ **2** : sarro *m* (dental)

tartness ['tɑrtnəs] *n* **1** SOURNESS : acidez *f* **2** ACRIMONY, SHARPNESS : mordacidad *f*, acrimonia *f*, acritud *f*

task ['tæsk] *n* : tarea *f*, trabajo *m*

taskmaster ['tæskˌmæstər] *n* **to be a hard taskmaster** : ser exigente, ser muy estricto

tassel ['tæsəl] *n* : borla *f*

taste¹ ['teɪst] *v* **tasted; tasting** *vt* : probar (alimentos), degustar, catar (vinos) ⟨taste this soup : prueba esta sopa⟩ — *vi* : saber ⟨this tastes good : esto sabe bueno⟩

taste² *n* **1** SAMPLE : prueba *f*, bocado *m* (de comida), trago *m* (de bebidas) **2** FLAVOR : gusto *m*, sabor *m* **3** : gusto *m* ⟨she has good taste : tiene buen gusto⟩ ⟨in bad taste : de mal gusto⟩

taste bud *n* : papila *f* gustativa

tasteful ['teɪstfəl] *adj* : de buen gusto

tastefully ['teɪstfəli] *adv* : con buen gusto

tasteless ['teɪstləs] *adj* **1** FLAVORLESS : sin sabor, soso, insípido **2** : de mal gusto ⟨a tasteless joke : un chiste de mal gusto⟩

taster ['teɪstər] *n* : degustador *m*, -dora *f*; catador *m*, -dora *f* (de vinos)

tastiness ['teɪstinəs] *n* : lo sabroso

tasty ['teɪsti] *adj* **tastier; -est** : sabroso, gustoso

tatter ['tætər] *n* **1** SHRED : tira *f*, jirón *m* (de tela) **2 tatters** *npl* : andrajos *mpl*, harapos *mpl* ⟨to be in tatters : estar por los suelos⟩

tattered ['tætərd] *adj* : andrajoso, en jirones

tattle ['tætəl] *vi* **-tled; -tling 1** CHATTER : parlotear *fam*, cotorrear *fam* **2 to tattle on someone** : acusar a alguien

tattletale ['tætəlˌteɪl] *n* : soplón *m*, -plona *f fam*

tattoo¹ [tæ'tuː] *vt* : tatuar

tattoo² *n* : tatuaje *m* ⟨to get a tattoo : tatuarse⟩

taught → **teach**

taunt¹ ['tɔnt] *vt* MOCK : mofarse de, burlarse de

taunt² *n* : mofa *f*, burla *f*

Taurus ['tɔrəs] *n* : Tauro *mf*

taut ['tɔt] *adj* : tirante, tenso — **tautly** *adv*

tautness ['tɔtnəs] *n* : tirantez *f*, tensión *f*

tavern ['tævərn] *n* : taberna *f*

tawdry ['tɔdri] *adj* **-drier; -est** : chabacano, vulgar

tawny ['tɔni] *adj* **-nier; -est** : leonado

tax¹ ['tæks] *vt* **1** : gravar, cobrar un impuesto sobre **2** CHARGE : acusar ⟨they taxed him with neglect : fue acusado de incumplimiento⟩ **3 to tax someone's strength** : ponerle a prueba las fuerzas (a alguien)

tax² *n* **1** : impuesto *m*, tributo *m* **2** BURDEN : carga *f*

taxable ['tæksəbəl] *adj* : sujeto a un impuesto

taxation [tæk'seɪʃən] *n* : impuestos *mpl*

tax–exempt ['tæksɪg'zɛmpt, -ɛg-] *adj* : libre de impuestos

taxi¹ ['tæksi] *vi* **taxied; taxiing** *or* **taxying; taxis** *or* **taxies 1** : ir en taxi **2** : rodar sobre la pista de aterrizaje (dícese de un avión)

taxi² *n, pl* **taxis** : taxi *m*, libre *m* Mex

taxicab ['tæksiˌkæb] *n* → **taxi²**

taxidermist ['tæksəˌdərmɪst] *n* : taxidermista *mf*

taxidermy ['tæksəˌdərmi] *n* : taxidermia *f*

taxpayer ['tæksˌpeɪər] *n* : contribuyente *mf*, causante *mf* Mex

TB [ˌtiː'biː] → **tuberculosis**

tea ['tiː] *n* **1** : té *m* (planta y bebida) **2** : merienda *f*, té *m* (comida)

teach ['tiːtʃ] *v* **taught** ['tɔt]; **teaching** *vt* : enseñar, dar clases de ⟨she teaches math : da clases de matemáticas⟩ ⟨she taught me everything I know : me enseñó todo lo que sé⟩ — *vi* : enseñar, dar clases

teacher ['ti:tʃər] *n* : maestro *m*, -tra *f* (de enseñanza primaria); profesor *m*, -sora *f* (de enseñanza secundaria)

teaching ['ti:tʃɪŋ] *n* : enseñanza *f*

teacup ['ti:,kʌp] *n* : taza *f* para té

teak ['ti:k] *n* : teca *f*

teakettle ['ti:,ktəl] *n* : tetera *f*

teal ['ti:l] *n, pl* **teal** *or* **teals** : cerceta *f* (pato)

team¹ ['ti:m] *vi or* **to team up 1** : formar un equipo (en deportes) **2** COLLABORATE : asociarse, juntarse, unirse

team² *adj* : de equipo

team³ *n* **1** : tiro *m* (de caballos), yunta *f* (de bueyes o mulas) **2** : equipo *m* (en deportes, etc.)

teammate ['ti:m,meɪt] *n* : compañero *m*, -ra *f* de equipo

teamster ['ti:mstər] *n* : camionero *m*, -ra *f*

teamwork ['ti:m,wərk] *n* : trabajo *m* en equipo, cooperación *f*

teapot ['ti:,pɑt] *n* : tetera *f*

tear¹ ['tær] *v* **tore** ['tor]; **torn** ['torn]; **tearing** *vt* **1** RIP : desgarrar, romper, rasgar (tela) ⟨to tear to pieces : hacer pedazos⟩ **2** *or* **to tear apart** DIVIDE : dividir **3** REMOVE : arrancar ⟨torn from his family : arrancado de su familia⟩ **4 to tear down** : derribar — *vi* **1** RIP : desgarrarse, romperse **2** RUSH : ir a gran velocidad ⟨she went tearing down the street : se fue como rayo por la calle⟩

tear² *n* : desgarradura *f*, rotura *f*, desgarro *m* (muscular)

tear³ ['tɪr] *n* : lágrima *f*

teardrop ['tɪr,drɑp] *n* → **tear³**

tearful ['tɪrfəl] *adj* : lloroso, triste — **tearfully** *adv*

tease¹ ['ti:z] *vt* **teased; teasing 1** MOCK : burlarse de, mofarse de **2** ANNOY : irritar, fastidiar

tease² *n* **1** TEASING : burla *f*, mofa *f* **2** : bromista *mf*; guasón *m*, -sona *f*

teaspoon ['ti:,spu:n] *n* **1** : cucharita *f* **2** → **teaspoonful**

teaspoonful ['ti:,spu:n,fʊl] *n, pl* **-spoonfuls** [-,fʊlz] *or* **-spoonsful** [-,spu:nz,fʊl] : cucharadita *f*

teat ['ti:t] *n* : tetilla *f*

technical ['tɛknɪkəl] *adj* : técnico — **technically** [-kli] *adv*

technicality [,tɛknə'kæləti] *n, pl* **-ties** : detalle *m* técnico

technician [tɛk'nɪʃən] *n* : técnico *m*, -ca *f*

technique [tɛk'ni:k] *n* : técnica *f*

technological [,tɛknə'lɑdʒɪkəl] *adj* : tecnológico

technology [tɛk'nɑlədʒi] *n, pl* **-gies** : tecnología *f*

teddy bear ['tɛdi] *n* : oso *m* de peluche

tedious ['ti:diəs] *adj* : aburrido, pesado, monótono — **tediously** *adv*

tediousness ['ti:diəsnəs] *n* : lo aburrido, lo pesado

tedium ['ti:diəm] *n* : tedio *m*, pesadez *f*

tee ['ti:] *n* : tee *mf*

teem ['ti:m] *vi* **to teem with** : estar repleto de, estar lleno de

teenage ['ti:n,eɪdʒ] *or* **teenaged** [-eɪdʒd] *adj* : adolescente, de adolescencia

teenager ['ti:n,eɪdʒər] *n* : adolescente *mf*

teens ['ti:nz] *npl* : adolescencia *f*

teepee → **tepee**

teeter¹ ['ti:tər] *vi* : balancearse, tambalearse

teeter² *n* *or* **teeter–totter** ['ti:tər-,tɑtər] → **seesaw**

teeth → **tooth**

teethe ['ti:ð] *vi* **teethed; teething** : formársele a uno los dientes ⟨the baby's teething : le están saliendo los dientes al niño⟩

telecast¹ ['tɛlə,kæst] *vt* **-cast; -casting** : televisar, transmitir por televisión

telecast² *n* : transmisión *f* por televisión

telecommunication ['tɛləkə,mju:nə-'keɪʃən] *n* : telecomunicación *f*

telegram ['tɛlə,græm] *n* : telegrama *m*

telegraph¹ ['tɛlə,græf] *v* : telegrafiar

telegraph² *n* : telégrafo *m*

telepathic [,tɛlə'pæθɪk] *adj* : telepático — **telepathically** [-θɪkli] *adv*

telepathy [tə'lɛpəθi] *n* : telepatía *f*

telephone¹ ['tɛlə,fo:n] *v* **-phoned; -phoning** *vt* : llamar por teléfono a, telefonear — *vi* : telefonear

telephone² *n* : teléfono *m*

telescope¹ ['tɛlə,sko:p] *vi* **-scoped; -scoping** : plegarse (como un telescopio)

telescope² *n* : telescopio *m*

telescopic [,tɛlə'skɑpɪk] *adj* : telescópico

televise ['tɛlə,vaɪz] *vt* **-vised; -vising** : televisar

television ['tɛlə,vɪʒən] *n* : televisión *f*

tell ['tɛl] *v* **told** ['to:ld]; **telling** *vt* **1** COUNT : contar, enumerar ⟨all told : en total⟩ **2** INSTRUCT : decir ⟨he told me how to fix it : me dijo cómo arreglarlo⟩ ⟨they told her to wait : le dijeron que esperara⟩ **3** RELATE : contar, relatar, narrar ⟨to tell a story : contar una historia⟩ **4** DIVULGE, REVEAL : revelar, divulgar ⟨he told me everything about her : me contó todo acerca de ella⟩ **5** DISCERN : discernir, notar ⟨I can't tell the difference : no noto la diferencia⟩ — *vi* **1** SAY : decir ⟨I won't tell : no voy a decírselo a nadie⟩ **2** KNOW : saber ⟨you never can tell : nunca se sabe⟩ **3** SHOW : notarse, hacerse sentir ⟨the strain is beginning to tell : la tensión se empieza a notar⟩

teller ['tɛlər] *n* **1** NARRATOR : narrador *m*, -dora *f* **2** *or* **bank teller** : cajero *m*, -ra *f*

temerity [tə'mɛrəti] *n, pl* **-ties** : temeridad *f*

temp ['tɛmp] *n* : empleado *m*, -da *f* temporal

temper¹ ['tɛmpər] *vt* **1** MODERATE : moderar, temperar **2** ANNEAL : templar (acero, etc.)

temper² *n* **1** DISPOSITION : carácter *m*, genio *m* **2** HARDNESS : temple *m*, dureza *f* (de un metal) **3** COMPOSURE : calma *f*, serenidad *f* ⟨to lose one's temper : perder los estribos⟩ **4** RAGE : furia *f* ⟨to fly into a temper : ponerse furioso⟩

temperament ['tɛmpərmənt, -prə-, -pərə-] *n* : temperamento *m*

temperamental [ˌtɛmpər'mɛntəl, -prə-, -pərə-] *adj* : temperamental

temperance ['tɛmprənts] *n* : templanza *f*, temperancia *f*

temperate ['tɛmpərət] *adj* : templado (dícese del clima, etc.), moderado

temperature ['tɛmpərˌtʃur, -prə-, -pərə-, -tʃər] *n* **1** : temperatura *f* **2** FEVER : calentura *f*, fiebre *f*

tempest ['tɛmpəst] *n* : tempestad *f*

tempestuous [tɛm'pɛstʃuəs] *adj* : tempestuoso

temple ['tɛmpəl] *n* **1** : templo *m* (en religión) **2** : sien *f* (en anatomía)

tempo ['tɛmˌpoː] *n*, *pl* **-pi** [-ˌpiː] *or* **-pos** : ritmo *m*, tempo *m* (en música)

temporal ['tɛmpərəl] *adj* : temporal

temporarily [ˌtɛmpə'rɛrəli] *adv* : temporalmente, provisionalmente

temporary ['tɛmpəˌrɛri] *adj* : temporal, provisional, provisorio

tempt ['tɛmpt] *vt* : tentar

temptation [tɛmp'teɪʃən] *n* : tentación *f*

tempter ['tɛmptər] *n* : tentador *m*

temptress ['tɛmptrəs] *n* : tentadora *f*

ten¹ ['tɛn] *adj* : diez

ten² *n* **1** : diez *m* (número) **2** : decena *f* ⟨tens of thousands : decenas de millares⟩

tenable ['tɛnəbəl] *adj* : sostenible, defendible

tenacious [tə'neɪʃəs] *adj* : tenaz

tenacity [tə'næsəṭi] *n* : tenacidad *f*

tenancy ['tɛnəntsi] *n*, *pl* **-cies** : tenencia *f*, inquilinato *m* (de un inmueble)

tenant ['tɛnənt] *n* : inquilino *m*, -na *f*; arrendatario *m*, -ria *f*

tend ['tɛnd] *vt* : atender, cuidar (de), ocuparse de — *vi* : tender ⟨it tends to benefit the consumer : tiende a beneficiar al consumidor⟩

tendency ['tɛndəntsi] *n*, *pl* **-cies** : tendencia *f*, proclividad *f*, inclinación *f*

tender¹ ['tɛndər] *vt* : entregar, presentar ⟨I tendered my resignation : presenté mi renuncia⟩

tender² *adj* **1** : tierno, blando ⟨tender steak : bistec tierno⟩ **2** AFFECTIONATE, LOVING : tierno, cariñoso, afectuoso **3** DELICATE : tierno, sensible, delicado

tender³ *n* **1** OFFER : propuesta *f*, oferta *f* (en negocios) **2 legal tender** : moneda *f* de curso legal

tenderize ['tɛndəˌraɪz] *vt* **-ized; -izing** : ablandar (carnes)

tenderloin ['tɛndrˌlɔɪn] *n* : lomo *f* (de res o de puerco)

tenderly ['tɛndərli] *adv* : tiernamente, con ternura

tenderness ['tɛndərnəs] *n* : ternura *f*

tendon ['tɛndən] *n* : tendón *m*

tendril ['tɛndrɪl] *n* : zarcillo *m*

tenement ['tɛnəmənt] *n* : casa *f* de vecindad

tenet ['tɛnət] *n* : principio *m*

tennis ['tɛnəs] *n* : tenis *m*

tenor ['tɛnər] *n* **1** PURPORT : tenor *m*, significado *m* **2** : tenor *m* (en música)

tenpins ['tɛnˌpɪnz] *npl* : bolos *mpl*, boliche *m*

tense¹ ['tɛnts] *v* **tensed; tensing** *vt* : tensar — *vi* : tensarse, ponerse tenso

tense² *adj* **tenser; tensest 1** TAUT : tenso, tirante **2** NERVOUS : tenso, nervioso

tense³ *n* : tiempo *m* (de un verbo)

tensely ['tɛntsli] *adv* : tensamente

tenseness ['tɛntsnəs] → **tension**

tension ['tɛntʃən] *n* **1** TAUTNESS : tensión *f*, tirantez *f* **2** STRESS : tensión *f*, nerviosismo *m*, estrés *m*

tent ['tɛnt] *n* : tienda *f* de campaña

tentacle ['tɛntɪkəl] *n* : tentáculo *m*

tentative ['tɛntəṭɪv] *adj* **1** HESITANT : indeciso, vacilante **2** PROVISIONAL : sujeto a cambios, provisional

tentatively ['tɛntəṭɪvli] *adv* : provisionalmente

tenth¹ ['tɛnθ] *adj* : décimo

tenth² *n* **1** : décimo *m*, -ma *f* (en una serie) **2** : décimo *m*, décima parte *f*

tenuous ['tɛnjuəs] *adj* : tenue, débil ⟨tenuous reasons : razones poco convincentes⟩

tenuously ['tɛnjuəsli] *adv* : tenuemente, ligeramente

tenure ['tɛnjər] *n* : tenencia *f* (de un cargo o una propiedad), titularidad *f* (de un puesto académico)

tepee ['tiːˌpiː] *n* : tipi *m*

tepid ['tɛpɪd] *adj* : tibio

tequila [tə'kiːlə] *n* : tequila *m*

term¹ ['tərm] *vt* : calificar de, llamar, nombrar

term² *n* **1** PERIOD : término *m*, plazo *m*, período *m* **2** : término *m* (en matemáticas) **3** WORD : término *m*, vocablo *m* ⟨legal terms : términos legales⟩ **4 terms** *npl* CONDITIONS : términos *mpl*, condiciones *fpl* **5 terms** *npl* RELATIONS : relaciones *fpl* ⟨to be on good terms with : tener buenas relaciones con⟩ **6 in terms of** : con respecto a, en cuanto a

terminal¹ ['tərmənəl] *adj* : terminal

terminal² *n* **1** : terminal *m*, polo *m* (en electricidad) **2** : terminal *f* (de una computadora) **3** STATION : terminal *f*, estación *f* (de transporte público)

terminate ['tərməˌneɪt] *v* **-nated; -nating** *vi* : terminar(se), concluirse — *vt* : terminar, poner fin a

termination [ˌtərmə'neɪʃən] *n* : cese *m*, terminación *f*

terminology [ˌtərmə'nɑlədʒi] *n*, *pl* **-gies** : terminología *f*

terminus ['tərmənəs] *n*, *pl* **-ni** [-ˌnaɪ] *or* **-nuses 1** END : término *m*, fin *m* **2** : terminal *f* (de transporte público)

termite ['tər¸maɪt] *n* : termita *f*
tern ['tərn] *n* : golondrina *f* de mar
terrace¹ ['tɛrəs] *vt* **-raced; -racing** : formar en terrazas, disponer en bancales
terrace² *n* **1** PATIO : terraza *f*, patio *m* **2** : terraplén *m*, terraza *f*, bancal *m* (en agricultura)
terra–cotta [¸tɛrə'kɑtə] *n* : terracota *f*
terrain [tə'reɪn] *n* : terreno *m*
terrapin ['tɛrəpɪn] *n* : galápago *m* norteamericano
terrarium [tə'ræriəm] *n, pl* **-ia** [-iə] *or* **-iums** : terrario *m*
terrestrial [tə'rɛstriəl] *adj* : terrestre
terrible ['tɛrəbəl] *adj* : atroz, horrible, terrible
terribly ['tɛrəbli] *adv* **1** BADLY : muy mal **2** EXTREMELY : terriblemente, extremadamente
terrier ['tɛriər] *n* : terrier *mf*
terrific [tə'rɪfɪk] *adj* **1** FRIGHTFUL : aterrador **2** EXTRAORDINARY : extraordinario, excepcional **3** EXCELLENT : excelente, estupendo
terrify ['tɛrə¸faɪ] *vt* **-fied; -fying** : aterrorizar, aterrar, espantar
terrifying ['tɛrə¸faɪɪŋ] *adj* : espantoso, aterrador
territory ['tɛrə¸tori] *n, pl* **-ries** : territorio *m* — **territorial** [¸tɛrə'toriəl] *adj*
terror ['tɛrər] *n* : terror *m*
terrorism ['tɛrər¸ɪzəm] *n* : terrorismo *m*
terrorist¹ ['tɛrərɪst] *adj* : terrorista
terrorist² *n* : terrorista *mf*
terrorize ['tɛrər¸aɪz] *vt* **-ized; -izing** : aterrorizar
terry ['tɛri] *n, pl* **-ries** *or* **terry cloth** : (tela de) toalla *f*
terse ['tərs] *adj* **terser; tersest** : lacónico, conciso, seco — **tersely** *adv*
tertiary ['tərʃi¸ɛri] *adj* : terciario
test¹ ['tɛst] *vt* : examinar, evaluar — *vi* : hacer pruebas
test² *n* : prueba *f*, examen *m*, test *m* ⟨to put to the test : poner a prueba⟩
testament ['tɛstəmənt] *n* **1** WILL : testamento *m* **2** : Testamento *m* (en la Biblia) ⟨the Old Testament : el Antiguo Testamento⟩
testicle ['tɛstɪkəl] *n* : testículo *m*
testify ['tɛstə¸faɪ] *v* **-fied; -fying** *vi* : testificar, atestar, testimoniar — *vt* : testificar
testimonial [¸tɛstə'moniəl] *n* **1** REFERENCE : recomendación *f* **2** TRIBUTE : homenaje *m*, tributo *m*
testimony ['tɛstə¸moni] *n, pl* **-nies** : testimonio *m*, declaración *f*
test tube *n* : probeta *f*, tubo *m* de ensayo
testy ['tɛsti] *adj* **-tier; -est** : irritable
tetanus ['tɛtənəs] *n* : tétano *m*, tétanos *m*
tête–à–tête [¸tɛtə'tɛt, ¸teɪtə'teɪt] *n* : conversación *f* en privado
tether¹ ['tɛðər] *vt* : atar (con una cuerda), amarrar
tether² *n* : atadura *f*, cadena *f*, correa *f*

text ['tɛkst] *n* **1** : texto *m* **2** TOPIC : tema *m* **3** → **textbook**
textbook ['tɛkst¸bʊk] *n* : libro *m* de texto
textile ['tɛk¸staɪl, 'tɛkstəl] *n* : textil *m*, tela *f* ⟨the textile industry : la industria textil⟩
textual ['tɛkstʃuəl] *adj* : textual
texture ['tɛkstʃər] *n* : textura *f*
Thai ['taɪ] *n* **1** : tailandés *m*, -desa *f* **2** : tailandés *m* (idioma) — **Thai** *adj*
than¹ ['ðæn] *conj* : que, de ⟨it's worth more than that : vale más que eso⟩ ⟨more than you think : más de lo que piensas⟩
than² *prep* : que, de ⟨you're better than he is : eres mejor que él⟩ ⟨more than once : más de una vez⟩
thank ['θæŋk] *vt* : agradecer, darle (las) gracias (a alguien) ⟨thank you! : ¡gracias!⟩ ⟨I thanked her for the present : le di las gracias por el regalo⟩ ⟨I thank you for your help : le agradezco su ayuda⟩
thankful ['θæŋkfəl] *adj* : agradecido
thankfully ['θæŋkfəli] *adv* **1** GRATEFULLY : con agradecimiento **2** FORTUNATELY : afortunadamente, por suerte ⟨thankfully, it's over : se acabó, gracias a Dios⟩
thankfulness ['θæŋkfəlnəs] *n* : agradecimiento *m*, gratitud *f*
thankless ['θæŋkləs] *adj* : ingrato ⟨a thankless task : un trabajo ingrato⟩
thanks ['θæŋks] *npl* **1** : agradecimiento *m* **2 thanks!** : ¡gracias!
Thanksgiving [θæŋks'gɪvɪŋ, 'θæŋks¸-] *n* : el día de Acción de Gracias (fiesta estadounidense)
that¹ ['ðæt] *adv* (*in negative constructions*) : tan ⟨it's not that expensive : no es tan caro⟩ ⟨not that much : no tanto⟩
that² *adj, pl* **those** : ese, esa, aquel, aquella ⟨do you use those children? : ¿ves a aquellos niños?⟩
that³ *conj & pron* : que ⟨he said that he was afraid : dijo que tenía miedo⟩ ⟨the book that he wrote : el libro que escribió⟩
that⁴ *pron, pl* **those** ['ðo:z] **1** : ése, ésa, eso ⟨that's my father : ése es mi padre⟩ ⟨those are the ones he likes : ésos son los que le gustan⟩ ⟨what's that? : ¿qué es eso?⟩ **2** (*referring to more distant objects or time*) : aquél, aquélla, aquello ⟨those are maples and these are elms : aquéllos son arces y éstos son olmos⟩ ⟨that came to an end : aquello se acabó⟩
thatch¹ ['θætʃ] *vt* : cubrir o techar con paja
thatch² *n* : paja *f* (usada para techos)
thaw¹ ['θɔ] *vt* : descongelar — *vi* : derretirse (dícese de la nieve), descongelarse (dícese de los alimentos)
thaw² *n* : deshielo *m*

the[1] [ðə, *before vowel sounds usu* ði:] *adv* **1** (*used to indicate comparison*) ⟨the sooner the better : cuanto más pronto, mejor⟩ ⟨she likes this one the best : éste es el que más le gusta⟩ **2** (*used as a conjunction*) : cuanto ⟨the more I learn, the less I understand : cuanto más aprendo, menos entiendo⟩

the[2] *art* : el, la, los, las ⟨the gloves : los guantes⟩ ⟨the suitcase : la maleta⟩ ⟨forty cookies to the box : cuarenta galletas por caja⟩

theater *or* **theatre** [ˈθiːətər] *n* **1** : teatro *m* (edificio) **2** DRAMA : teatro *m*, drama *m*

theatrical [θiˈætrɪkəl] *adj* : teatral, dramático

thee [ˈðiː] *pron* : te, ti

theft [ˈθɛft] *n* : robo *m*, hurto *m*

their [ˈðɛr] *adj* : su ⟨their friends : sus amigos⟩

theirs [ˈðɛrz] *pron* : (el) suyo, (la) suya, (los) suyos, (las) suyas ⟨they came for theirs : vinieron por el suyo⟩ ⟨theirs is bigger : la suya es más grande, la de ellos es más grande⟩ ⟨a brother of theirs : un hermano suyo, un hermano de ellos⟩

them [ˈðɛm] *pron* **1** (*as a direct object*) : los (*Spain sometimes* les), las ⟨I know them : los conozco⟩ **2** (*as indirect object*) : les, se ⟨I sent them a letter : les mandé una carta⟩ ⟨give it to them : dáselo (a ellos)⟩ **3** (*as object of a preposition*) : ellos, ellas ⟨go with them : ve con ellos⟩ **4** (*for emphasis*) : ellos, ellas ⟨I wasn't expecting them : no los esperaba a ellos⟩

thematic [θiˈmætɪk] *adj* : temático

theme [ˈθiːm] *n* **1** SUBJECT, TOPIC : tema *m* **2** COMPOSITION : composición *f*, trabajo *m* (escrito) **3** : tema *m* (en música)

themselves [ðəmˈsɛlvz, ðɛm-] *pron* **1** (*as a reflexive*) : se, sí ⟨they enjoyed themselves : se divirtieron⟩ ⟨they divided it among themselves : lo repartieron entre sí, se lo repartieron⟩ **2** (*for emphasis*) : ellos mismos, ellas mismas ⟨they built it themselves : ellas mismas lo construyeron⟩

then[1] [ˈðɛn] *adv* **1** : entonces, en ese tiempo ⟨I was sixteen then : tenía entonces dieciséis años⟩ ⟨since then : desde entonces⟩ **2** NEXT : después, luego ⟨we'll go to Toronto, then to Winnipeg : iremos a Toronto, y luego a Winnipeg⟩ **3** BESIDES : además, aparte ⟨then there's the tax : y aparte está el impuesto⟩ **4** : entonces, en ese caso ⟨if you like music, then you should attend : si te gusta la música, entonces deberías asistir⟩

then[2] *adj* : entonces ⟨the then governor of Georgia : el entonces gobernador de Georgia⟩

thence [ˈðɛnts, ˈθɛnts] *adv* : de ahí, de ahí en adelante

theologian [ˌθiːəˈloːdʒən] *n* : teólogo *m*, -ga *f*

theological [ˌθiːəˈlɑdʒɪkəl] *adj* : teológico

theology [θiˈɑlədʒi] *n, pl* **-gies** : teología *f*

theorem [ˈθiːərəm, ˈθɪrəm] *n* : teorema *m*

theoretical [ˌθiːəˈrɛtɪkəl] *adj* : teórico — **theoretically** *adv*

theorist [ˈθiːərɪst] *n* : teórico *m*, -ca *f*

theorize [ˈθiːəˌraɪz] *vi* **-rized; -rizing** : teorizar

theory [ˈθiːəri, ˈθɪri] *n, pl* **-ries** : teoría *f*

therapeutic [ˌθɛrəˈpjuːtɪk] *adj* : terapéutico — **therapeutically** *adv*

therapist [ˈθɛrəpɪst] *n* : terapeuta *mf*

therapy [ˈθɛrəpi] *n, pl* **-pies** : terapia *f*

there[1] [ˈðær] *adv* **1** : ahí, allí, allá ⟨stand over there : párate ahí⟩ ⟨over there : por allí, por allá⟩ ⟨who's there? : ¿quién es?⟩ **2** : ahí, en esto, en eso ⟨there is where we disagree : en eso es donde no estamos de acuerdo⟩

there[2] *pron* **1** (*introducing a sentence or clause*) ⟨there comes a time to decide : llega un momento en que tiene uno que decidir⟩ **2 there is, there are** : hay ⟨there are many children here : aquí hay muchos niños⟩ ⟨there's a good hotel in the center : hay un buen hotel en el centro⟩

thereabouts [ðærəˈbaʊts, ˈðærəˌ-] *or* **thereabout** [-ˈbaʊt, -ˌbaʊt] *adv* *or* **thereabouts** : por ahí, más o menos ⟨at five o'clock or thereabouts : por ahí de las cinco⟩

thereafter [ðærˈæftər] *adv* : después ⟨shortly thereafter : poco después⟩

thereby [ðærˈbaɪ, ˈðærˌbaɪ] *adv* : de tal modo, de ese manera, así

therefore [ˈðærˌfor] *adv* : por lo tanto, por consiguiente

therein [ðærˈɪn] *adv* **1** : allí adentro, ahí adentro ⟨the contents therein : lo que allí se contiene⟩ **2** : allí, en ese aspecto ⟨therein lies the problem : allí está el problema⟩

thereof [ðærˈʌv, -ˈɑv] *adv* : de eso, de esto

thereupon [ˈðærəˌpɑn, -ˌpɔn; ˌðærəˈpɑn, -ˈpɔn] *adv* : acto seguido, inmediatamente (después)

therewith [ðærˈwɪð, -ˈwɪθ] *adv* : con eso, con ello

thermal [ˈθərməl] *adj* **1** : térmico (en física) **2** HOT : termal

thermodynamics [ˌθərmodaɪˈnæmɪks] *ns & pl* : termodinámica *f*

thermometer [θərˈmɑmətər] *n* : termómetro *m*

thermos [ˈθərməs] *n* : termo *m*

thermostat [ˈθərməˌstæt] *n* : termostato *m*

thesaurus [θɪˈsɔrəs] *n, pl* **-sauri** [-ˈsɔrˌaɪ] *or* **-sauruses** [-ˈsɔrəsəz] : diccionario *m* de sinónimos

these → **this**

thesis ['θi:sɪs] *n, pl* **theses** ['θi:ˌsi:z] : tesis *f*

they ['ðeɪ] *pron* : ellos, ellas ⟨they are here : están aquí⟩ ⟨they don't know : ellos no saben⟩

they'd ['ðeɪd] (*contraction of* they had *or* they would) → have, would

they'll ['ðeɪl, 'ðɛl] (*contraction of* they shall *or* they will) → shall, will

they're ['ðɛr] (*contraction of* they are) → be

they've ['ðeɪv] (*contraction of* they have) → have

thiamine ['θaɪəmɪn, -ˌmi:n] *n* : tiamina *f*

thick[1] ['θɪk] *adj* **1** : grueso ⟨a thick plank : una tabla gruesa⟩ **2** : espeso, denso ⟨thick syrup : jarabe espeso⟩ — **thickly** *adv*

thick[2] *n* **1 in the thick of** : en medio de ⟨in the thick of the battle : en lo más reñido de la batalla⟩ **2 through thick and thin** : a las duras y a las maduras

thicken ['θɪkən] *vt* : espesar (un líquido) — *vi* : espesarse

thickener ['θɪkənər] *n* : espesante *m*

thicket ['θɪkət] *n* : matorral *m*, maleza *f*, espesura *f*

thickness ['θɪknəs] *n* : grosor *m*, grueso *m*, espesor *m*

thickset ['θɪk'sɛt] *adj* STOCKY : robusto, fornido

thick–skinned ['θɪk'skɪnd] *adj* : poco sensible, que no se ofende fácilmente

thief ['θi:f] *n, pl* **thieves** ['θi:vz] : ladrón *m*, -drona *f*

thieve ['θi:v] *v* **thieved; thieving** : hurtar, robar

thievery ['θi:vəri] *n* : hurto *m*, robo *m*, latrocinio *m*

thigh ['θaɪ] *n* : muslo *m*

thighbone ['θaɪˌbo:n] *n* : fémur *m*

thimble ['θɪmbəl] *n* : dedal *m*

thin[1] ['θɪn] *v* **thinned; thinning** *vt* : hacer menos denso, diluir, aguar (un líquido), enrarecer (un gas) — *vi* : diluirse, aguarse (dícese de un líquido), enrarecerse (dícese de un gas)

thin[2] *adj* **thinner; -est 1** LEAN, SLIM : delgado, esbelto, flaco **2** SPARSE : ralo, escaso ⟨a thin beard : una barba rala⟩ **3** WATERY : claro, aguado, diluido **4** FINE : delgado, fino ⟨thin slices : rebanadas finas⟩

thing ['θɪŋ] *n* **1** AFFAIR, MATTER : cosa *f*, asunto *m* ⟨don't talk about those things : no hables de esas cosas⟩ ⟨how are things? : ¿cómo van las cosas?⟩ **2** ACT, EVENT : cosa *f*, suceso *m*, evento *m* ⟨the flood was a terrible thing : la inundación fue una cosa terrible⟩ **3** OBJECT : cosa *f*, objeto *m* ⟨don't forget your things : no olvides tus cosas⟩

think ['θɪŋk] *v* **thought** ['θɔt]; **thinking** *vt* **1** : pensar ⟨I thought to return early : pensaba regresar temprano⟩ **2** BELIEVE : pensar, creer, opinar **3** PONDER : pensar, reflexionar **4** CONCEIVE : ocurrirse, concebir ⟨we've thought up a plan : se nos ha ocurrido un plan⟩ —

vi **1** REASON : pensar, razonar **2** CONSIDER : pensar, considerar ⟨think of your family first : primero piensa en tu familia⟩

thinker ['θɪŋkər] *n* : pensador *m*, -dora *f*

thinly ['θɪnli] *adv* **1** LIGHTLY : ligeramente **2** SPARSELY : escasamente ⟨thinly populated : poco populado⟩ **3** BARELY : apenas

thinness ['θɪnnəs] *n* : delgadez *f*

thin–skinned ['θɪn'skɪnd] *adj* : susceptible, muy sensible

third[1] ['θərd] *or* **thirdly** [-li] *adv* : en tercer lugar ⟨she came in third : llegó en tercer lugar⟩

third[2] *adj* : tercero ⟨the third day : el tercer día⟩

third[3] *n* **1** : tercero *m*, -ra *f* (en una serie) **2** : tercero *m*, tercera parte *f*

third world *n* **the Third World** : el Tercer Mundo *m*

thirst[1] ['θərst] *vi* **1** : tener sed **2 to thirst for** DESIRE : tener sed de, estar sediento de

thirst[2] *n* : sed *f*

thirsty ['θərsti] *adj* **thirstier; -est** : sediento, que tiene sed ⟨I'm thirsty : tengo sed⟩

thirteen[1] [ˌθər'ti:n] *adj* : trece

thirteen[2] *n* : trece *m*

thirteenth[1] [ˌθər'ti:nθ] *adj* : décimo tercero

thirteenth[2] *n* **1** : decimotercero *m*, -ra *f* (en una serie) **2** : treceavo *m*, treceava parte *f*

thirtieth[1] ['θərt̬iəθ] *adj* : trigésimo

thirtieth[2] *n* **1** : trigésimo *m*, -ma *f* (en una serie) **2** : treintavo *m*, treintava parte *f*

thirty[1] ['θərt̬i] *adj* : treinta

thirty[2] *n, pl* **thirties** : treinta *m*

this[1] ['ðɪs] *adv* : así, a tal punto ⟨this big : así de grande⟩

this[2] *adj, pl* **these** ['ði:z] : este ⟨these things : estas cosas⟩ ⟨read this book : lee este libro⟩

this[3] *pron, pl* **these** : esto ⟨what's this? : ¿qué es esto?⟩ ⟨this wasn't here yesterday : esto no estaba aquí ayer⟩

thistle ['θɪsəl] *n* : cardo *m*

thong ['θɔŋ] *n* **1** STRAP : correa *f*, tira *f* **2** FLIP-FLOP : chancla *f*, chancleta *f*

thorax ['θor̩æks] *n, pl* **-raxes** *or* **-races** ['θorəˌsi:z] : tórax *m*

thorn ['θorn] *n* : espina *f*

thorny ['θorni] *adj* **thornier; -est** : espinoso

thorough ['θəro:] *adj* **1** CONSCIENTIOUS : concienzudo, meticuloso **2** COMPLETE : absoluto, completo — **thoroughly** *adv*

thoroughbred ['θəroˌbrɛd] *adj* : de pura sangre (dícese de un caballo)

Thoroughbred *n or* **Thoroughbred horse** : pura sangre *mf*

thoroughfare ['θəroˌfær] *n* : vía *f* pública, carretera *f*

thoroughness ['θəronəs] *n* : esmero *m*, meticulosidad *f*

those → **that**

thou [ˈðaʊ] *pron* : tú

though¹ [ˈðoː] *adv* **1** HOWEVER, NEVERTHELESS : sin embargo, no obstante **2 as ~** : como si ⟨as though nothing had happened : como si nada hubiera pasado⟩

though² *conj* : aunque, a pesar de ⟨though it was raining, we went out : salimos a pesar de la lluvia⟩

thought¹ → **think**

thought² [ˈθɔt] *n* **1** THINKING : pensamiento *m*, idea *fpl* ⟨Western thought : el pensamiento occidental⟩ **2** COGITATION : pensamiento *m*, reflexión *f*, raciocinio *m* **3** IDEA : idea *f*, ocurrencia *f* ⟨it was just a thought : fue sólo una idea⟩

thoughtful [ˈθɔtfəl] *adj* **1** PENSIVE : pensativo, meditabundo **2** CONSIDERATE : considerado, atento, cortés — **thoughtfully** *adv*

thoughtfulness [ˈθɔtfəlnəs] *n* : consideración *f*, atención *f*, cortesía *f*

thoughtless [ˈθɔtləs] *adj* **1** CARELESS : descuidado, negligente **2** INCONSIDERATE : desconsiderado — **thoughtlessly** *adv*

thousand¹ [ˈθaʊzənd] *adj* : mil

thousand² *n, pl* **-sands** *or* **-sand** : mil *m*

thousandth¹ [ˈθaʊzəntθ] *adj* : milésimo

thousandth² *n* **1** : milésimo *m*, -ma *f* (en una serie) **2** : milésimo *m*, milésima parte *f*

thrash [ˈθræʃ] *vt* **1** → **thresh 2** BEAT : golpear, azotar, darle una paliza (a alguien) **3** FLAIL : sacudir, agitar bruscamente

thread¹ [ˈθrɛd] *vt* **1** : enhilar, enhebrar (una aguja) **2** STRING : ensartar (cuentas en un hilo) **3 to thread one's way** : abrirse paso

thread² *n* **1** : hilo *m*, hebra *f* ⟨needle and thread : aguja e hilo⟩ ⟨the thread of an argument : el hilo de un debate⟩ **2** : rosca *f*, filete *m* (de un tornillo)

threadbare [ˈθrɛdˈbær] *adj* **1** SHABBY, WORN : raído, gastado **2** TRITE : trillado, tópico, manido

threat [ˈθrɛt] *n* : amenaza *f*

threaten [ˈθrɛtən] *v* : amenazar

threatening [ˈθrɛtənɪŋ] *adj* : amenazador — **threateningly** *adv*

three¹ [ˈθriː] *adj* : tres

three² *n* : tres *m*

3–D [ˈθriːˈdiː] *adj* → **three–dimensional**

three–dimensional [ˈθriːdəˈmɛntʃənəl] *adj* : tridimensional

threefold [ˈθriːˌfoːld] *adj* TRIPLE : triple

three hundred¹ *adj* : trescientos

three hundred² *n* : trescientos *m*

threescore [ˈθriːˈskor] *adj* SIXTY : sesenta

thresh [ˈθrɛʃ] *vt* : trillar (grano)

thresher [ˈθrɛʃər] *n* : trilladora *f*

threshold [ˈθrɛʃˌhoːld, -ˌoːld] *n* : umbral *m*

threw → **throw¹**

thrice [ˈθraɪs] *adv* : tres veces

thrift [ˈθrɪft] *n* : economía *f*, frugalidad *f*

thriftless [ˈθrɪftləs] *adj* : despilfarrador, manirroto

thrifty [ˈθrɪfti] *adj* **thriftier**; **-est** : económico, frugal — **thriftily** [ˈθrɪftəli] *adv*

thrill¹ [ˈθrɪl] *vt* : emocionar — *vi* **to thrill to** : dejarse conmover por, estremecerse con

thrill² *n* : emoción *f*

thriller [ˈθrɪlər] *n* **1** : evento *m* emocionante **2** : obra *f* de suspenso

thrilling [ˈθrɪlɪŋ] *adj* : emocionante, excitante

thrive [ˈθraɪv] *vi* **throve** [ˈθroːv] *or* **thrived**; **thriven** [ˈθrɪvən] **1** FLOURISH : florecer, crecer abundantemente **2** PROSPER : prosperar

throat [ˈθroːt] *n* : garganta *f*

throaty [ˈθroːt̬i] *adj* **throatier**; **-est** : ronco (dícese de la voz)

throb¹ [ˈθrɑb] *vi* **throbbed**; **throbbing** : palpitar, latir (dícese del corazón), vibrar (dícese de un motor, etc.)

throb² *n* : palpitación *f*, latido *m*, vibración *f*

throe [ˈθroː] *n* **1** PAIN, SPASM : espasmo *m*, dolor *m* ⟨the throes of childbirth : los dolores de parto⟩ **2 throes** *npl* : lucha *f* larga y ardua ⟨in the throes of : en el medio de⟩

throne [ˈθroːn] *n* : trono *m*

throng¹ [ˈθrɔŋ] *vt* CROWD : atestar, atiborrar, llenar — *vi* : aglomerarse, amontonarse

throng² *n* : muchedumbre *f*, gentío *m*, multitud *f*

throttle¹ [ˈθrɑt̬əl] *vt* **-tled**; **-tling 1** STRANGLE : estrangular, ahogar **2 to throttle down** : desacelerar (un motor)

throttle² *n* **1** : válvula *f* reguladora **2 at full throttle** : a toda máquina

through¹ [ˈθruː] *adv* **1** : a través, de un lado a otro ⟨let them through : déjenlos pasar⟩ **2** : de principio a fin ⟨she read the book through : leyó el libro de principio a fin⟩ **3** COMPLETELY : completamente ⟨soaked through : completamente empapado⟩

through² *adj* **1** DIRECT : directo ⟨a through train : un tren directo⟩ **2** FINISHED : terminado, acabado ⟨we're through : hemos terminado⟩

through³ *prep* **1** : a través de, por ⟨through the door : por la puerta⟩ ⟨a road through the woods : un camino que atraviesa el bosque⟩ **2** BETWEEN : entre ⟨a path through the trees : un sendero entre los árboles⟩ **3** BECAUSE OF : a causa de, como consecuencia de **4** (*in expressions of time*) ⟨through the night : durante la noche⟩ ⟨to go through an experience : pasar por una experiencia⟩ **5** : a, hasta ⟨from Monday through Friday : de lunes a viernes⟩

throughout¹ [θru:ˈaʊt] *adv* **1** EVERY-
WHERE : por todas partes **2** THROUGH
: desde el principio hasta el fin de (algo)
throughout² *prep* **1** : en todas partes de,
a través de ⟨throughout the United
States : en todo Estados Unidos⟩ **2** : de
principio a fin de, durante ⟨through-
out the winter : durante todo el in-
vierno⟩
throve → **thrive**
throw¹ [θro:] *vt* **threw** [θru:]; **thrown**
[θro:n]; **throwing 1** TOSS : tirar, lanzar, echar, arrojar, aventar *Col, Mex*
⟨to throw a ball : tirar una pelota⟩ **2**
UNSEAT : desmontar (a un jinete) **3**
CAST : proyectar ⟨it threw a long shadow : proyectó una sombra larga⟩ **4 to
throw a party** : dar una fiesta **5 to
throw into confusion** : desconcertar **6
to throw out** DISCARD : botar, tirar (en
la basura)
throw² *n* TOSS : tiro *m*, tirada *f*, lanzamiento *m*, lance *m* (de dados)
thrower [θro:ər] *n* : lanzador *m*, -dora *f*
throw up *v* VOMIT : vomitar, devolver
thrush [θrʌʃ] *n* : tordo *m*, zorzal *m*
thrust¹ [θrʌst] *vt* **thrust; thrusting 1**
SHOVE : empujar bruscamente **2**
PLUNGE, STAB : apuñalar, clavar ⟨he
thrust a dagger into her heart : la
apuñaló en el corazón⟩ **3 to thrust
one's way** : abrirse paso **4 to thrust
upon** : imponer a
thrust² *n* **1** PUSH, SHOVE : empujón *m*,
empellón *m* **2** LUNGE : estocada *f* (en
esgrima) **3** IMPETUS : ímpetu *m*, impulso *m*, propulsión *f* (de un motor)
thud¹ [θʌd] *vi* **thudded; thudding** : producir un ruido sordo
thud² *n* : ruido *m* sordo (que produce
un objeto al caer)
thug [θʌg] *n* : matón *m*
thumb¹ [θʌm] *vt* : hojear (con el pulgar)
thumb² *n* : pulgar *m*, dedo *m* pulgar
thumbnail [θʌmˌneɪl] *n* : uña *f* del pulgar
thumbtack [θʌmˌtæk] *n* : tachuela *f*,
chinche *f*
thump¹ [θʌmp] *vt* POUND : golpear,
aporrear — *vi* : latir con vehemencia
(dícese del corazón)
thump² *n* THUD : ruido *m* sordo
thunder¹ [θʌndər] *vi* **1** : tronar ⟨it
rained and thundered all night : llovió
y tronó durante la noche⟩ **2** BOOM : retumbar, bramar, resonar — *vt* ROAR,
SHOUT : decir a gritos, vociferar
thunder² *n* : truenos *mpl*
thunderbolt [θʌndərˌbo:lt] *n* : rayo *m*
thunderclap [θʌndərˌklæp] *n* : trueno
m
thunderous [θʌndərəs] *adj* : atronador,
ensordecedor, estruendoso
thundershower [θʌndərˌʃaʊər] *n* : lluvia *f* con truenos y relámpagos
thunderstorm [θʌndərˌstɔrm] *n* : tormenta *f* con truenos y relámpagos
thunderstruck [θʌndərˌstrʌk] *adj*
: atónito

Thursday [θərzˌdeɪ, -di] *n* : jueves *m*
thus [ðʌs] *adv* **1** : así, de esta manera **2**
SO : hasta (cierto punto) ⟨the weath-
er's been nice thus far : hasta ahora ha
hecho buen tiempo⟩ **3** HENCE : por
consiguiente, por lo tanto
thwart [θwɔrt] *vt* : frustrar
thy [ðaɪ] *adj* : tu
thyme [taɪm, θaɪm] *n* : tomillo *m*
thyroid [θaɪˌrɔɪd] *n or* **thyroid gland**
: tiroides *mf*, glándula *f* tiroidea
thyself [ðaɪˈself] *pron* : ti, ti mismo
tiara [tiˈærə, -ˈɑr-] *n* : diadema *f*
Tibetan [təˈbɛtən] *n* **1** : tibetano *m*, -na
f **2** : tibetano *m* (idioma) — **Tibetan**
adj
tibia [tɪbiə] *n, pl* **-iae** [-biˌi:] : tibia *f*
tic [tɪk] *n* : tic *m*
tick¹ [tɪk] *vi* **1** : hacer tictac **2** OPER-
ATE, RUN : operar, andar (dícese de un
mecanismo) ⟨what makes him tick?
: ¿qué es lo que lo mueve?⟩ — *vt or* **to
tick off** CHECK : marcar
tick² *n* **1** : tictac *m* (de un reloj) **2** CHECK
: marca *f* **3** : garrapata *f* (insecto)
ticket¹ [tɪkət] *vt* LABEL : etiquetar
ticket² *n* **1** : boleto *m*, entrada *f* (de un
espectáculo), pasaje *m* (de avión, tren,
etc.) **2** SLATE : lista *f* de candidatos
tickle¹ [tɪkəl] *v* **-led; -ling** *vt* **1** AMUSE
: divertir, hacerle gracia (a alguien) **2**
: hacerle cosquillas (a alguien) ⟨don't
tickle me! : ¡no me hagas cosquillas!⟩
— *vi* : picar
tickle² *n* : cosquilleo *m*, cosquillas *fpl*,
picor *m* (en la garganta)
ticklish [tɪkəlɪʃ] *adj* **1** : cosquilloso
(dícese de una persona) **2** DELICATE,
TRICKY : delicado, peliagudo
tidal [taɪdəl] *adj* : de marea, relativo a
la marea
tidal wave *n* : maremoto *m*
tidbit [tɪdˌbɪt] *n* **1** BITE, SNACK : bocado *m*, golosina *f* **2** : dato *m* o noticia *f*
interesante ⟨useful tidbits of information : informaciones útiles⟩
tide¹ [taɪd] *vt* **tided; tiding** *or* **to tide over**
: proveer lo necesario para aguantar
una dificultad ⟨this money will tide you
over until you find work : este dinero
te mantendrá hasta que encuentres em-
pleo⟩
tide² *n* **1** : marea *f* **2** CURRENT : corriente *f* (de eventos, opiniones, etc.)
tidily [taɪdəli] *adv* : ordenadamente
tidiness [taɪdinəs] *n* : aseo *m*, limpieza
f, orden *m*
tidings [taɪdɪŋz] *npl* : nuevas *fpl*
tidy¹ [taɪdi] *vt* **-died; -dying** : asear,
limpiar, poner en orden
tidy² *adj* **-dier; -est 1** CLEAN, NEAT
: limpio, aseado, en orden **2** SUBSTAN-
TIAL : grande, considerable ⟨a tidy sum
: una suma considerable⟩
tie¹ [taɪ] *v* **tied; tying** *or* **tieing** *vt* **1** : atar,
amarrar ⟨to tie a knot : atar un nudo⟩
⟨to tie one's shoelaces : atarse los cor-
dones⟩ **2** BIND, UNITE : ligar, atar **3**
: empatar ⟨they tied the score : em-

pataron el marcador〉 — *vi* : empatar 〈the two teams were tied : los dos equipos empataron〉

tie² *n* **1** : ligadura *f*, cuerda *f*, cordón *m* (para atar algo) **2** BOND, LINK : atadura *f*, ligadura *f*, vínculo *m*, lazo *m* 〈family ties : lazos familiares〉 **3** *or* **railroad tie** : traviesa *f* **4** DRAW : empate *m* (en deportes) **5** NECKTIE : corbata *f*

tier ['tɪr] *n* : hilera *f*, escalón *m*

tiff ['tɪf] *n* : disgusto *m*, disputa *f*

tiger ['taɪgər] *n* : tigre *m*

tight¹ ['taɪt] *adv* TIGHTLY : bien, fuerte 〈shut it tight : ciérralo bien〉

tight² *adj* **1** : bien cerrado, hermético 〈a tight seal : un cierre hermético〉 **2** STRICT : estricto, severo **3** TAUT : tirante, tenso **4** SNUG : apretado, ajustado, ceñido 〈a tight dress : un vestido ceñido〉 **5** DIFFICULT : difícil 〈to be in a tight spot : estar en un aprieto〉 **6** STINGY : apretado, avaro, agarrado *fam* **7** CLOSE : reñido 〈a tight game : un juego reñido〉 **8** SCARCE : escaso 〈money is tight : escasea el dinero〉

tighten ['taɪtən] *vt* : tensar (una cuerda, etc.), apretar (un nudo, un tornillo, etc.), apretarse (el cinturón), reforzar (las reglas)

tightly ['taɪtli] *adv* : bien, fuerte

tightness ['taɪtnəs] *n* : lo apretado, lo tenso, tensión *f*

tightrope ['taɪtˌroːp] *n* : cuerda *f* floja

tights ['taɪts] *npl* : leotardo *m*, malla *f*

tightwad ['taɪtˌwɑd] *n* : avaro *m*, -ra *f*; tacaño *m*, -ña *f*

tigress ['taɪgrəs] *n* : tigresa *f*

tile¹ ['taɪl] *vt* **tiled; tiling** : embaldosar (un piso), revestir de azulejos (una pared), tejar (un techo)

tile² *n* **1** *or* **floor tile** : losa *f*, baldosa *f*, mosaico *m* Mex (de un piso) **2** : azulejo *m* (de una pared) **3** : teja *f* (de un techo)

till¹ ['tɪl] *vt* : cultivar, labrar

till² *n* : caja *f*, caja *f* registradora

till³ *prep & conj* → **until**

tiller ['tɪlər] *n* **1** : cultivador *m*, -dora *f* (de la tierra) **2** : caña *f* del timón (de un barco)

tilt¹ ['tɪlt] *vt* : ladear, inclinar — *vi* : ladearse, inclinarse

tilt² *n* **1** SLANT : inclinación *f* **2** **at full tilt** : a toda velocidad

timber ['tɪmbər] *n* **1** : madera *f* (para construcción) **2** BEAM : viga *f*

timberland ['tɪmbərˌlænd] *n* : bosque *m* maderero

timbre ['tæmbər, 'tɪm-] *n* : timbre *m*

time¹ ['taɪm] *vt* **timed; timing 1** SCHEDULE : fijar la hora de, calcular el momento oportuno para **2** CLOCK : cronometrar, medir el tiempo de (una competencia, etc.)

time² *n* **1** : tiempo *m* 〈the passing of time : el paso del tiempo〉 〈she doesn't have time : no tiene tiempo〉 **2** MOMENT : tiempo *m*, momento *m* 〈this is not the time to bring it up : no es el momento

de sacar el tema〉 **3** : vez *f* 〈she called you three times : te llamó tres veces〉 〈three times greater : tres veces mayor〉 **4** AGE : tiempo *m*, era *f* 〈in your grandparents' time : en el tiempo de tus abuelos〉 **5** TEMPO : tiempo *m*, ritmo *m* (en música) **6** : hora *f* 〈what time is it? : ¿qué hora es?〉 〈it's time for dinner : es hora de comer〉 〈at the usual time : a la hora acostumbrada〉 〈to keep time : ir a la hora〉 〈to lose time : atrasar〉 **7** EXPERIENCE : rato *m*, experiencia *f* 〈we had a nice time together : pasamos juntos un rato agradable〉 〈to have a rough time : pasarlo mal〉 〈have a good time! : ¡que se diviertan!〉 **8 at times** SOMETIMES : a veces **9 for the time being** : por el momento, de momento **10 from time to time** OCCASIONALLY : de vez en cuando **11 in time** PUNCTUALLY : a tiempo **12 in time** EVENTUALLY : con el tiempo **13 time after time** : una y otra vez

timekeeper ['taɪmˌkiːpər] *n* : cronometrador *m*, -dora *f*

timeless ['taɪmləs] *adj* : eterno

timely ['taɪmli] *adj* **-lier; -est** : oportuno

timepiece ['taɪmˌpiːs] *n* : reloj *m*

timer ['taɪmər] *n* : temporizador *m*, cronómetro *m*

times ['taɪmz] *prep* : por 〈3 times 4 is 12 : 3 por 4 son 12〉

timetable ['taɪmˌteɪbəl] *n* : horario *m*

timid ['tɪmɪd] *adj* : tímido — **timidly** *adv*

timidity [tə'mɪdəti] *n* : timidez *f*

timorous ['tɪmərəs] *adj* : timorato, miedoso

timpani ['tɪmpəni] *npl* : timbales *mpl*

tin ['tɪn] *n* **1** : estaño *m*, hojalata *f* (metal) **2** CAN : lata *f*, bote *m*, envase *m*

tincture ['tɪŋktʃər] *n* : tintura *f*

tinder ['tɪndər] *n* : yesca *f*

tine ['taɪn] *n* : diente *m* (de un tenedor, etc.)

tinfoil ['tɪnˌfɔɪl] *n* : papel *m* (de) aluminio

tinge¹ ['tɪndʒ] *vt* **tinged; tingeing** *or* **tinging** TINT : matizar, teñir ligeramente

tinge² *n* **1** TINT : matiz *m*, tinte *m* sutil **2** TOUCH : dejo *m*, sensación *f* ligera

tingle¹ ['tɪŋgəl] *vi* **-gled; -gling** : sentir (un) hormigueo, sentir (un) cosquilleo

tingle² *n* : hormigueo *m*, cosquilleo *m*

tinker ['tɪŋkər] *vi* **to tinker with** : arreglar con pequeños ajustes, toquetear (con intento de arreglar)

tinkle¹ ['tɪŋkəl] *vi* **-kled; -kling** : tintinear

tinkle² *n* : tintineo *m*

tinsel ['tɪntsəl] *n* : oropel *m*

tint¹ ['tɪnt] *vt* : teñir, colorear

tint² *n* : tinte *m*

tiny ['taɪni] *adj* **-nier; -est** : diminuto, minúsculo

tip¹ ['tɪp] *v* **tipped; tipping** *vt* **1** *or* **to tip over** : volcar, voltear, hacer caer **2** TILT : ladear, inclinar 〈to tip one's hat : saludar con el sombrero〉 **3** TAP : tocar, golpear ligeramente **4** : darle una propina (a un mesero, etc.) ⟨I tipped him $5 : le di $5 de propina⟩ **5** : adornar o cubrir la punta de ⟨wings tipped in red : alas que tienen las puntas rojas⟩ **6 to tip off** : dar información a — *vi* TILT : ladearse, inclinarse

tip² *n* **1** END, POINT : punta *f*, extremo *m* ⟨on the tip of one's tongue : en la punta de la lengua⟩ **2** GRATUITY : propina *f* **3** ADVICE, INFORMATION : consejo *m*, información *f* (confidencial)

tip–off [ˈtɪpˌɔf] *n* **1** SIGN : indicación *f*, señal *f* **2** TIP : información *f* (confidencial)

tipple [ˈtɪpəl] *vi* **-pled; -pling** : tomarse unas copas

tipsy [ˈtɪpsi] *adj* **-sier; -est** : achispado

tiptoe¹ [ˈtɪpˌtoː] *vi* **-toed; -toeing** : caminar de puntillas

tiptoe² *adv* : de puntillas

tiptoe³ *n* : punta *f* del pie

tip–top¹ [ˈtɪpˈtɑp, -ˌtɑp] *adj* EXCELLENT : excelente

tip–top² *n* SUMMIT : cumbre *f*, cima *f*

tirade [ˈtaɪˌreɪd] *n* : diatriba *f*

tire¹ [ˈtaɪr] *v* **tired; tiring** *vt* : cansar, agotar, fatigar — *vi* : cansarse

tire² *n* : llanta *f*, neumático *m*, goma *f*

tired [ˈtaɪrd] *adj* : cansado, agotado, fatigado ⟨to get tired : cansarse⟩

tireless [ˈtaɪrləs] *adj* : incansable, infatigable — **tirelessly** *adv*

tiresome [ˈtaɪrsəm] *adj* : fastidioso, pesado, tedioso — **tiresomely** *adv*

tissue [ˈtɪˌʃuː] *n* **1** : pañuelo *m* de papel **2** : tejido *m* ⟨lung tissue : tejido pulmonar⟩

titanic [taɪˈtænɪk, tə-] *adj* GIGANTIC : titánico, gigantesco

titanium [taɪˈteɪniəm, tə-] *n* : titanio *m*

titillate [ˈtɪtəlˌeɪt] *vt* **-lated; -lating** : excitar, estimular placenteramente

title¹ [ˈtaɪtəl] *vt* **-tled; -tling** : titular, intitular

title² *n* : título *m*

titter¹ [ˈtɪtər] *vi* GIGGLE : reírse tontamente

titter² *n* : risita *f*, risa *f* tonta

tizzy [ˈtɪzi] *n, pl* **tizzies** : estado *m* agitado o nervioso ⟨I'm all in a tizzy : estoy todo alterado⟩

TNT [ˌtiːˌɛnˈtiː] *n* : TNT *m*

to¹ [ˈtuː] *adv* **1** : a un estado consciente ⟨to come to : volver en sí⟩ **2 to and fro** : de aquí para allá, de un lado para otro

to² *prep* **1** (*indicating a place*) : a ⟨to go to the doctor : ir al médico⟩ ⟨I'm going to John's : voy a la casa de John⟩ **2** TOWARD : a, hacia ⟨two miles to the south : dos millas hacia el sur⟩ **3** ON : en, sobre ⟨apply salve to the wound : póngale ungüento a la herida⟩ **4** UP TO : hasta, a ⟨to a degree : hasta cierto grado⟩ ⟨from head to toe : de pies a cabeza⟩ **5** (*in expressions of time*) ⟨it's quarter to seven : son las siete menos cuarto⟩ **6** UNTIL : a, hasta ⟨from May to December : de mayo a diciembre⟩ **7** (*indicating belonging or possession*) : de, a ⟨the key to the lock : la llave del candado⟩ **8** (*indicating response*) : a ⟨dancing to the rhythm : bailando al compás⟩ **9** (*indicating comparison or proportion*) : a ⟨it's similar to mine : es parecido al mío⟩ ⟨they won 4 to 2 : ganaron 4 a 2⟩ **10** (*indicating agreement or conformity*) : a, de acuerdo con ⟨made to order : hecho a la orden⟩ ⟨to my knowledge : a mi saber⟩ **11** (*indicating inclusion*) : en cada, por ⟨twenty to the box : veinte por caja⟩ **12** (*used to form the infinitive*) ⟨to understand : entender⟩ ⟨to go away : irse⟩

toad [ˈtoːd] *n* : sapo *m*

toadstool [ˈtoːdˌstuːl] *n* : hongo *m* (no comestible)

toady [ˈtoːdi] *n, pl* **toadies** : adulador *m*, -dora *f*

toast¹ [ˈtoːst] *vt* **1** : tostar (pan) **2** : brindar por ⟨to toast the victors : brindar por los vencedores⟩ **3** WARM : calentar ⟨to toast oneself : calentarse⟩

toast² *n* **1** : pan *m* tostado, tostadas *fpl* **2** : brindis *m* ⟨to propose a toast : proponer un brindis⟩

toaster [ˈtoːstər] *n* : tostador *m*

tobacco [təˈbæːoː] *n, pl* **-cos** : tabaco *m*

toboggan¹ [təˈbɑɡən] *vi* : deslizarse en tobogán

toboggan² *n* : tobogán *m*

today¹ [təˈdeɪ] *adv* **1** : hoy ⟨she arrives today : hoy llega⟩ **2** NOWADAYS : hoy en día

today² *n* : hoy *m* ⟨today is a holiday : hoy es día de fiesta⟩

toddle [ˈtɑdəl] *vi* **-dled; -dling** : hacer pininos, hacer pinitos

toddler [ˈtɑdələr] *n* : niño *m* pequeño, niña *f* pequeña (que comienza a caminar)

to–do [təˈduː] *n, pl* **to–dos** [-ˈduːz] FUSS : lío *m*, alboroto *m*

toe [ˈtoː] *n* : dedo *m* del pie

toenail [ˈtoːˌneɪl] *n* : uña *f* del pie

toffee or **toffy** [ˈtɔfi, ˈtɑ-] *n, pl* **toffees** or **toffies** : caramelo *m* elaborado con azúcar y mantequilla

toga [ˈtoːɡə] *n* : toga *f*

together [təˈɡɛðər] *adv* **1** : juntamente, juntos (el uno con el otro) ⟨Susan and Sarah work together : Susan y Sarah trabajan juntas⟩ **2** ∼ **with** : junto con

togetherness [təˈɡɛðərnəs] *n* : unión *f*, compañerismo *m*

togs [ˈtɑɡz, ˈtɔɡz] *npl* : ropa *f*

toil¹ [ˈtɔɪl] *vi* : trabajar arduamente

toil² *n* : trabajo *m* arduo

toilet [ˈtɔɪlət] *n* **1** : arreglo *m* personal **2** BATHROOM : (cuarto de) baño *m*, servicios *mpl* (públicos), sanitario *m* Col, Mex, Ven **3** : inodoro *m* ⟨to flush the toilet : jalar la cadena⟩

toilet paper *n* : papel *m* higiénico

toiletries [ˈtɔɪlətriz] *npl* : artículos *mpl* de tocador

token ['to:kən] n 1 PROOF, SIGN : prueba f, muestra f, señal m 2 SYMBOL : símbolo m 3 SOUVENIR : recuerdo m 4 : ficha f (para transporte público, etc.)

told → **tell**

tolerable ['talərəbəl] adj : tolerable — **tolerably** [-bli] adv

tolerance ['talərənts] n : tolerancia f

tolerant ['talərənt] adj : tolerante — **tolerantly** adv

tolerate ['talə,reɪt] vt -ated; -ating 1 ACCEPT : tolerar, aceptar 2 BEAR, ENDURE : tolerar, aguantar, soportar

toleration [,talə'reɪʃən] n : tolerancia f

toll[1] ['to:l] vt : tañer, sonar (una campana) — vi : sonar, doblar (dícese de las campanas)

toll[2] n 1 : peaje m (de una carretera, un puente, etc.) 2 CASUALTIES : pérdida f, número m de víctimas 3 TOLLING : tañido m (de campanas)

tollbooth ['to:l,bu:θ] n : caseta f de peaje

tollgate ['to:l,geɪt] n : barrera f de peaje

tomahawk ['tamə,hɔk] n : hacha f de guerra (de los indígenas norteamericanos)

tomato [tə'meɪt̬o, -'ma-] n, pl -toes : tomate m

tomb ['tu:m] n : sepulcro m, tumba f

tomboy ['tam,bɔɪ] n : marimacho mf; niña f que se porta como muchacho

tombstone ['tu:m,sto:n] n : lápida f

tomcat ['tam,kæt] n : gato m (macho)

tome ['to:m] n : tomo m

tomorrow[1] [tə'maro] adv : mañana

tomorrow[2] n : mañana m

tom–tom ['tam,tam] n : tam-tam m

ton ['tən] n : tonelada f

tone[1] ['to:n] vt **toned; toning 1** or **to tone down** : atenuar, suavizar, moderar **2** or **to tone up** STRENGTHEN : tonificar, vigorizar

tone[2] n : tono m ⟨in a friendly tone : en tono amistoso⟩ ⟨a greyish tone : un tono grisáceo⟩

tongs ['taŋz, 'tɔŋz] npl : tenazas fpl

tongue ['tʌŋ] n 1 : lengua f 2 LANGUAGE : lengua f, idioma m

tongue–tied ['tʌŋ,taɪd] adj **to get tongue–tied** : trabársele la lengua a uno

tonic[1] ['tanɪk] adj : tónico

tonic[2] n 1 : tónico m 2 or **tonic water** : tónica f

tonight[1] [tə'naɪt] adv : esta noche

tonight[2] n : esta noche f

tonsil ['tantsəl] n : amígdala f, angina f Mex

tonsillitis [,tantsə'laɪt̬əs] n : amigdalitis f, anginas fpl Mex

too ['tu:] adv 1 ALSO : también 2 EXCESSIVELY : demasiado ⟨it's too hot in here : aquí hace demasiado calor⟩

took → **take**[1]

tool[1] ['tu:l] vt 1 : fabricar, confeccionar (con herramientas) 2 EQUIP : instalar maquinaria en (una fábrica)

tool[2] n : herramienta f

toolbox ['tu:l,baks] n : caja f de herramientas

toot[1] ['tu:t] vt : sonar (un claxon o un pito)

toot[2] n : pitido m, bocinazo m (de un claxon)

tooth ['tu:θ] n, pl **teeth** ['ti:θ] : diente m

toothache ['tu:θ,eɪk] n : dolor m de muelas

toothbrush ['tu:θ,brʌʃ] n : cepillo m de dientes

toothless ['tu:θləs] adj : desdentado

toothpaste ['tu:θ,peɪst] n : pasta f de dientes, crema f dental, dentífrico m

toothpick ['tu:θ,pɪk] n : palillo m (de dientes), mondadientes m

top[1] ['tap] vt **topped; topping 1** COVER : cubrir, coronar **2** SURPASS : sobrepasar, superar **3** CLEAR : pasar por encima de

top[2] adj : superior ⟨the top shelf : la repisa superior⟩ ⟨one of the top lawyers : uno de los mejores abogados⟩

top[3] n 1 : parte f superior, cumbre f, cima f (de un monte, etc.) ⟨to climb to the top : subir a la cumbre⟩ 2 COVER : tapa f, cubierta f 3 : trompo m (juguete) 4 **on top of** : encima de

topaz ['to:,pæz] n : topacio m

topcoat ['tap,ko:t] n : sobretodo m, abrigo m

topic ['tapɪk] n : tema m, tópico m

topical ['tapɪkəl] adj : de interés actual

topmost ['tap,mo:st] adj : más alto

top–notch ['tap'natʃ] adj : de lo mejor, de primera categoría

topographic [,tapə'græfɪk] or **topographical** [-fɪkəl] adj : topográfico

topography [tə'pagrəfi] n, pl -phies : topografía f

topple ['tapəl] v -pled; -pling vi : caerse, venirse abajo — vt : volcar, derrocar (un gobierno, etc.)

topsoil ['tap,sɔɪl] n : capa f superior del suelo

topsy–turvy [,tapsi'tərvi] adv & adj : patas arriba, al revés

torch ['tɔrtʃ] n : antorcha f

tore → **tear**[1]

torment[1] [tɔr'mɛnt, 'tɔr,-] vt : atormentar, torturar, martirizar

torment[2] ['tɔr,mɛnt] n : tormento m, suplicio m, martirio m

tormentor [tɔr'mɛntər] n : atormentador m, -dora f

torn pp → **tear**[1]

tornado [tɔr'neɪdo] n, pl -does or -dos : tornado m

torpedo[1] [tɔr'pi:do] vt : torpedear

torpedo[2] n, pl -does : torpedo m

torpid ['tɔrpɪd] adj 1 SLUGGISH : aletargado 2 APATHETIC : apático

torpor ['tɔrpər] n : letargo m, apatía f

torrent ['tɔrənt] n : torrente m

torrential [tə'rɛntʃəl, ta-] adj : torrencial

torrid ['tɔrɪd] adj : tórrido

torso ['tɔr,so:] n, pl -sos or -si [-,si:] : torso m

tortilla [tɔr'tiːjə] *n* : tortilla *f* (de maíz)
tortoise ['tɔrtəs] *n* : tortuga *f* (terrestre)
tortoiseshell ['tɔrtəs,ʃɛl] *n* : carey *m*, concha *f*
tortuous ['tɔrtʃʊəs] *adj* : tortuoso
torture[1] ['tɔrtʃər] *vt* **-tured; -turing** : torturar, atormentar
torture[2] *n* : tortura *f*, tormento *m* ⟨it was sheer torture! : ¡fue un verdadero suplicio!⟩
torturer ['tɔrtʃərər] *n* : torturador *m*, -dora *f*
toss[1] ['tɔs, 'tɑs] *vt* **1** AGITATE, SHAKE : sacudir, agitar, mezclar (una ensalada) **2** THROW : tirar, echar, lanzar — *vi* : sacudirse, moverse agitadamente ⟨to toss and turn : dar vueltas⟩
toss[2] *n* THROW : lanzamiento *m*, tiro *m*, tirada *f*, lance *m* (de dados, etc.)
toss–up ['tɔs,ʌp] *n* : posibilidad *f* igual ⟨it's a toss-up : quizá sí, quizá no⟩
tot ['tɑt] *n* : pequeño *m*, -ña *f*
total[1] ['toːtəl] *vt* **-taled** *or* **-talled; -taling** *or* **-talling 1** *or* **to total up** ADD : sumar, totalizar **2** AMOUNT TO : ascender a, llegar a
total[2] *adj* : total, completo, absoluto — **totally** *adv*
total[3] *n* : total *m*
totalitarian [toː,tælə'tɛriən] *adj* : totalitario
totalitarianism [toː,tælə'tɛriə,nɪzəm] *n* : totalitarismo *m*
totality [toː'tælətʃi] *n, pl* **-ties** : totalidad *f*
tote ['toːt] *vt* **toted; toting** : cargar, llevar
totem ['toːtəm] *n* : tótem *m*
totter ['tɑtər] *vi* : tambalearse
touch[1] ['tʌtʃ] *vt* **1** FEEL, HANDLE : tocar, tentar **2** AFFECT, MOVE : conmover, afectar, tocar ⟨his gesture touched our hearts : su gesto nos tocó el corazón⟩ — *vi* : tocarse
touch[2] *n* **1** : tacto *m* (sentido) **2** DETAIL : toque *m*, detalle *m* ⟨a touch of color : un toque de color⟩ **3** BIT : pizca *f*, gota *f*, poco *m* **4** ABILITY : habilidad *f* ⟨to lose one's touch : perder la habilidad⟩ **5** CONTACT : contacto *m*, comunicación *f* ⟨to keep in touch : mantenerse en contacto⟩
touchdown ['tʌtʃ,daʊn] *n* : touchdown *m* (en futbol americano)
touching ['tʌtʃɪŋ] *adj* MOVING : conmovedor
touchstone ['tʌtʃ,stoːn] *n* : piedra *f* de toque
touch up *vt* : retocar
touchy ['tʌtʃi] *adj* **touchier; -est 1** : sensible, susceptible (dícese de una persona) **2** : delicado ⟨a touchy subject : un tema delicado⟩
tough[1] ['tʌf] *adj* **1** STRONG : fuerte, resistente (dícese de materiales) **2** LEATHERY : correoso ⟨a tough steak : un bistec duro⟩ **3** HARDY : fuerte, robusto (dícese de una persona) **4** STRICT

: severo, exigente **5** DIFFICULT : difícil **6** STUBBORN : terco, obstinado
tough[2] *n* : matón *m*, persona *f* ruda y brusca
toughen ['tʌfən] *vt* : fortalecer, endurecer — *vi* : endurecerse, hacerse más fuerte
toughness ['tʌfnəs] *n* : dureza *f*
toupee [tuː'peɪ] *n* : peluquín *m*, bisoñé *m*
tour[1] ['tʊr] *vi* : tomar una excursión, viajar — *vt* : recorrer, hacer una gira por
tour[2] *n* **1** : gira *f*, tour *m*, excursión *f* **2** **tour of duty** : período *m* de servicio
tourism ['tʊr,ɪzəm] *n* : turismo *m*
tourist ['tʊrɪst, 'tər-] *n* : turista *mf*
tournament ['tərnəmənt, 'tʊr-] *n* : torneo *m*
tourniquet ['tərnɪkət, 'tʊr-] *n* : torniquete *m*
tousle ['taʊzəl] *vt* **-sled; -sling** : desarreglar, despeinar (el cabello)
tout ['taʊt] *vt* : promocionar, elogiar (con exageración)
tow[1] ['toː] *vt* : remolcar
tow[2] *n* : remolque *m*
toward ['tord, tə'wɔrd] *or* **towards** ['tordz, tə'wɔrdz] *prep* **1** (*indicating direction*) : hacia, rumbo a ⟨heading toward town : dirigiéndose rumbo al pueblo⟩ ⟨efforts towards peace : esfuerzos hacia la paz⟩ **2** (*indicating time*) : alrededor de ⟨toward midnight : alrededor de la medianoche⟩ **3** REGARDING : hacia, con respecto a ⟨his attitude toward life : su actitud hacia la vida⟩ **4** FOR : para, como pago parcial de (una compra o deuda)
towel ['taʊəl] *n* : toalla *f*
tower[1] ['taʊər] *vi* **to tower over** : descollar sobre, elevarse sobre, dominar
tower[2] *n* : torre *f*
towering ['taʊərɪŋ] *adj* : altísimo, imponente
town ['taʊn] *n* : pueblo *m*, ciudad *f* (pequeña)
township ['taʊn,ʃɪp] *n* : municipio *m*
tow truck ['toː,trʌk] *n* : grúa *f*
toxic ['taksɪk] *adj* : tóxico
toxicity [tak'sɪsətʃi] *n, pl* **-ties** : toxicidad *f*
toxin ['taksɪn] *n* : toxina *f*
toy[1] ['tɔɪ] *vi* : juguetear, jugar
toy[2] *adj* : de juguete ⟨a toy rifle : un rifle de juguete⟩
toy[3] *n* : juguete *m*
trace[1] ['treɪs] *vt* **traced; tracing 1** : calcar (un dibujo, etc.) **2** OUTLINE : delinear, trazar (planes, etc.) **3** TRACK : describir (un curso, una historia) **4** FIND : localizar, ubicar
trace[2] *n* **1** SIGN, TRACK : huella *f*, rastro *m*, indicio *m*, vestigio *m* ⟨he disappeared without a trace : desapareció sin dejar rastro⟩ **2** BIT, HINT : pizca *f*, ápice *m*, dejo *m*
trachea ['treɪkiə] *n, pl* **-cheae** [-ki,iː] : tráquea *f*

tracing paper *n* : papel *m* de calcar

track¹ ['træk] *vt* **1** TRAIL : seguir la pista de, rastrear **2** : dejar huellas de ⟨he tracked mud all over : dejó huellas de lodo por todas partes⟩

track² *n* **1** : rastro *m*, huella *f* (de animales), pista *f* (de personas) **2** PATH : pista *f*, sendero *m*, camino *m* **3** *or* **railroad track** : vía *f* (férrea) **4** → **racetrack 5** : oruga *f* (de un tanque, etc.) **6** : pista *f* (deporte) **7 to keep track of** : llevar la cuenta de

track–and–field ['trækənd'fi:ld] *adj* : de pista y campo

tract ['trækt] *n* **1** AREA : terreno *m*, extensión *f*, área *f* **2** : tracto *m* ⟨digestive tract : tracto digestivo⟩ **3** PAMPHLET : panfleto *m*, folleto *m*

traction ['trækʃən] *n* : tracción *f*

tractor ['træktər] *n* **1** : tractor *m* (vehículo agrícola) **2** TRUCK : camión *m* (con remolque)

trade¹ ['treɪd] *v* **traded; trading** *vi* : comerciar, negociar — *vt* EXCHANGE : intercambiar, canjear

trade² *n* **1** OCCUPATION : oficio *m*, profesión *f*, ocupación *f* ⟨a carpenter by trade : carpintero de oficio⟩ **2** COMMERCE : comercio *m*, industria *f* ⟨free trade : libre comercio⟩ ⟨the book trade : la industria del libro⟩ **3** EXCHANGE : intercambio *m*, canje *m*

trade–in ['treɪd,ɪn] *n* : artículo *m* que se canjea por otro

trademark ['treɪd,mɑrk] *n* **1** : marca *f* registrada **2** CHARACTERISTIC : sello *m* característico (de un grupo, una persona, etc.)

trader ['treɪdər] *n* : negociante *mf*, tratante *mf*, comerciante *mf*

tradesman ['treɪdzmən] *n, pl* **-men** [-mən, -ˌmɛn] **1** CRAFTSMAN : artesano *m*, -na *f* **2** SHOPKEEPER : tendero *m*, -ra *f*; comerciante *mf*

trade wind *n* : viento *m* alisio

tradition [trə'dɪʃən] *n* : tradición *f*

traditional [trə'dɪʃənəl] *adj* : tradicional — **traditionally** *adv*

traffic¹ ['træfɪk] *vi* **trafficked; trafficking** : traficar (con)

traffic² *n* **1** COMMERCE : tráfico *m*, comercio *m* ⟨the drug traffic : el narcotráfico⟩ **2** : tráfico *m*, tránsito *m*, circulación *f* (de vehículos, etc.)

traffic circle *n* : rotonda *f*, glorieta *f*

trafficker ['træfɪkər] *n* : traficante *mf*

traffic light *n* : semáforo *m*, luz *f* (de tránsito)

tragedy ['trædʒədi] *n, pl* **-dies** : tragedia *f*

tragic ['trædʒɪk] *adj* : trágico — **tragically** *adv*

trail¹ ['treɪl] *vi* **1** DRAG : arrastrarse **2** LAG : quedarse atrás, retrasarse **3 to trail away** *or* **to trail off** : disminuir, menguar, desvanecerse — *vt* **1** DRAG : arrastrar **2** PURSUE : perseguir, seguir la pista de

trail² *n* **1** TRACK : rastro *m*, huella *f*, pista *f* ⟨a trail of blood : un rastro de sangre⟩ **2** : cola *f*, estela *f* (de un meteoro) **3** PATH : sendero *m*, camino *m*, vereda *f*

trailer ['treɪlər] *n* **1** : remolque *m*, tráiler *m* (de un camión) **2** : caravana *f* (vivienda ambulante)

train¹ ['treɪn] *vt* **1** : adiestrar, entrenar (atletas), capacitar (trabajadores), amaestrar (animales) **2** POINT : apuntar (un arma, etc.) — *vi* : entrenar(se) (físicamente), prepararse (profesionalmente) ⟨she's training at the gym : se está entrenando en el gimnasio⟩

train² *n* **1** : cola *f* (de un vestido) **2** RETINUE : cortejo *m*, séquito *m* **3** SERIES : serie *f* (de eventos) **4** : tren *m* ⟨passenger train : tren de pasajeros⟩

trainee [treɪ'ni:] *n* : aprendiz *m*, -diza *f*

trainer ['treɪnər] *n* : entrenador *m*, -dora *f*

training ['treɪnɪŋ] *n* : adiestramiento *m*, entrenamiento *m* (físico), capacitación *f* (de trabajadores)

traipse ['treɪps] *vi* **traipsed; traipsing** : andar de un lado para otro, vagar

trait ['treɪt] *n* : rasgo *m*, característica *f*

traitor ['treɪtər] *n* : traidor *m*, -dora *f*

traitorous ['treɪtərəs] *adj* : traidor

trajectory [trə'dʒɛktəri] *n, pl* **-ries** : trayectoria *f*

tramp¹ ['træmp] *vi* : caminar (a paso pesado) — *vt* : deambular por, vagar por ⟨to tramp the streets : vagar por las calles⟩

tramp² *n* **1** VAGRANT : vagabundo *m*, -da *f* **2** HIKE : caminata *f*

trample ['træmpəl] *vt* **-pled; -pling** : pisotear, hollar

trampoline [ˌtræmpə'li:n, 'træmpəˌ-] *n* : trampolín *m*, cama *f* elástica

trance ['trænts] *n* : trance *m*

tranquil ['træŋkwəl] *adj* : calmo, tranquilo, sereno — **tranquilly** *adv*

tranquilize ['træŋkwəˌlaɪz] *vt* **-ized; -izing** : tranquilizar

tranquilizer ['træŋkwəˌlaɪzər] *n* : tranquilizante *m*

tranquillity *or* **tranquility** [træŋ'kwɪləti] *n* : sosiego *m*, tranquilidad *f*

transact [træn'zækt] *vt* : negociar, gestionar, hacer (negocios)

transaction [træn'zækʃən] *n* **1** : transacción *f*, negocio *m*, operación *f* **2 transactions** *npl* RECORDS : actas *fpl*

transatlantic [ˌtræntsət'læntɪk, ˌtrænz-] *adj* : transatlántico

transcend [træn'sɛnd] *vt* : trascender, sobrepasar

transcendent [træn'sɛndənt] *adj* : trascendente — **transcendence** [trænt'sɛndənts] *n*

transcendental [ˌtræntˌsɛn'dɛntəl, -sən-] *adj* : trascendental ⟨transcendental meditation : meditación trascendental⟩

transcribe [træn'skraɪb] *vt* **-scribed; -scribing** : transcribir

transcript ['træn₁skrɪpt] *n* : copia *f* oficial

transcription [træn'skrɪpʃən] *n* : transcripción *f*

transfer[1] [træn/s'fər, 'træn/s₁fər] *v* **-ferred; -ferring** *vt* **1** : trasladar (a una persona), transferir (fondos) **2** : transferir, traspasar, ceder (propiedad) **3** PRINT : imprimir (un diseño) — *vi* **1** MOVE : trasladarse, cambiarse **2** CHANGE : transbordar, cambiar (de un transporte a otro) ⟨he transfers at E Street : hace un transborde a la calle E⟩

transfer[2] ['træn/s₁fər] *n* **1** TRANSFER-RING : transferencia *f* (de fondos, de propiedad, etc.), traslado *m* (de una persona) **2** DECAL : calcomanía *f* **3** : boleto *m* (para cambiar de un avión, etc., a otro)

transferable [træn/s'fərəbəl] *adj* : transferible

transference [træn/s'fərən/s] *n* : transferencia *f*

transfigure [træn/s'fɪgjər] *vt* **-ured; -uring** : transfigurar, transformar

transfix [træn/s'fɪks] *vt* **1** PIERCE : traspasar, atravesar **2** IMMOBILIZE : paralizar

transform [træn/s'fɔrm] *vt* : transformar

transformation [₁træn/sfər'meɪʃən] *n* : transformación *f*

transformer [træn/s'fɔrmər] *n* : transformador *m*

transfusion [træn/s'fju:ʒən] *n* : transfusión *f*

transgress [træn/s'grɛs, trænz-] *vt* : transgredir, infringir

transgression [træn/s'grɛʃən, trænz-] *n* : transgresión *f*

transient[1] ['træn/ʃənt, 'trænsiənt] *adj* : pasajero, transitorio — **transiently** *adv*

transient[2] *n* : transeúnte *mf*

transistor [træn'zɪstər, -'sɪs-] *n* : transistor *m*

transit ['træn/sɪt, 'trænzɪt] *n* **1** PASSAGE : pasaje *m*, tránsito *m* ⟨in transit : en tránsito⟩ **2** TRANSPORTATION : transporte *m* (público) **3** : teodolito *m* (instrumento topográfico)

transition [træn'sɪʃən, -'zɪʃ-] *n* : transición *f*

transitional [træn'sɪʃənəl, -'zɪʃ-] *adj* : de transición

transitive ['træn/sətɪv, 'trænzə-] *adj* : transitivo

transitory ['træn/sə₁tori, 'trænzə-] *adj* : transitorio

translate [træn/s'leɪt, trænz-; 'træn/s₁-, 'trænz₁-] *vt* **-lated; -lating** : traducir

translation [træn/s'leɪʃən, trænz-] *n* : traducción *f*

translator [træn/s'leɪtər, trænz-; 'træn/s₁-, 'trænz₁-] *n* : traductor *m*, -tora *f*

translucent [træn/s'lu:sənt, trænz-] *adj* : translúcido

transmission [træn/s'mɪʃən, trænz-] *n* : transmisión *f*

transmit [træn/s'mɪt, trænz-] *vt* **-mitted; -mitting** : transmitir

transmitter [træn/s'mɪtər, trænz-; 'træn/s₁-, 'træns₁-] *n* : transmisor *m*, emisor *m*

transom ['træn/səm] *n* : montante *m* (de una puerta), travesaño *m* (de una ventana)

transparency [træn/s'pærən/si] *n, pl* **-cies** : transparencia *f*

transparent [træn/s'pærənt] *adj* **1** : transparente, traslúcido ⟨a transparent fabric : una tela transparente⟩ **2** OBVIOUS : transparente, obvio, claro — **transparently** *adv*

transpiration [₁træn/spə'reɪʃən] *n* : transpiración *f*

transpire [træn/s'paɪr] *vi* **-spired; -spiring** **1** : transpirar (en biología y botánica) **2** TURN OUT : resultar **3** HAPPEN : suceder, ocurrir, tener lugar

transplant[1] [træn/s'plænt] *vt* : trasplantar

transplant[2] ['træn/s₁plænt] *n* : trasplante *m*

transport[1] [træn/s'port, 'træn/s₁-] *vt* **1** CARRY : transportar, acarrear **2** ENRAPTURE : transportar, extasiar

transport[2] ['træn/s₁port] *n* **1** TRANSPORTATION : transporte *m*, transportación *f* **2** RAPTURE : éxtasis *m* **3** *or* **transport ship** : buque *m* de transporte (de personal militar)

transportation [₁træn/spər'teɪʃən] *n* : transporte *m*, transportación *f*

transpose [træn/s'po:z] *vt* **-posed; -posing** : transponer, trasladar, transportar (una composición musical)

transverse [træn/s'vərs, trænz-] *adj* : transversal, transverso, oblicuo — **transversely** *adv*

trap[1] ['træp] *vt* **trapped; trapping** : atrapar, apresar (en una trampa)

trap[2] *n* : trampa *f* ⟨to set a trap : tender una trampa⟩

trapdoor ['træp'dor] *n* : trampilla *f*, escotillón *m*

trapeze [træ'pi:z] *n* : trapecio *m*

trapezoid ['træpə₁zɔɪd] *n* : trapezoide *m*, trapecio *m*

trapper ['træpər] *n* : trampero *m*, -ra *f*; cazador *m*, -dora *f* (que usa trampas)

trappings ['træpɪŋz] *npl* **1** : arreos *mpl*, jaeces *mpl* (de un caballo) **2** ADORNMENTS : adornos *mpl*, pompa *f*

trash ['træʃ] *n* : basura *f*

trashy ['træʃi] *adj* : de pacotilla

trauma ['trɔmə, 'traʊ-] *n* : trauma *m*

traumatic [trə'mæt̬ɪk, trɔ-, traʊ-] *adj* : traumático

travel[1] ['trævəl] *vi* **-eled** *or* **-elled; -eling** *or* **-elling** **1** JOURNEY : viajar **2** GO, MOVE : desplazarse, moverse, ir ⟨the waves travel at uniform speed : las ondas se desplazan a una velocidad uniforme⟩

travel[2] *n or* **travels** *npl* : viajes *mpl*

traveler *or* **traveller** ['trævələr] *n* : viajero *m*, -ra *f*

traverse [trə'vərs, træ'vərs, 'trævərs] *vt* **-versed; -versing** CROSS : atravesar, extenderse a través de, cruzar

travesty ['trævəsti] *n, pl* **-ties** : parodia *f*

trawl[1] ['trɔl] *vi* : pescar con red de arrastre, rastrear

trawl[2] *n or* **trawl net** : red *f* de arrastre

trawler ['trɔlər] *n* : barco *m* de pesca (utilizado para rastrear)

tray ['treɪ] *n* : bandeja *f*, charola *f Bol, Mex, Peru*

treacherous ['trɛtʃərəs] *adj* **1** TRAITOROUS : traicionero, traidor **2** DANGEROUS : peligroso

treacherously ['trɛtʃərəsli] *adv* : a traición

treachery ['trɛtʃəri] *n, pl* **-eries** : traición *f*

tread[1] ['trɛd] *v* **trod** ['trɑd]; **trodden** ['trɑdən] *or* **trod; treading** *vt* TRAMPLE : pisotear, hollar — *vi* **1** WALK : caminar, andar **2 to tread on** : pisar

tread[2] *n* **1** STEP : paso *m*, andar *m* **2** : banda *f* de rodadura (de un neumático, etc.) **3** : escalón *m* (de una escalera)

treadle ['trɛdəl] *n* : pedal *m* (de una máquina)

treadmill ['trɛd,mɪl] *n* **1** : rueda *f* de andar **2** ROUTINE : rutina *f*

treason ['trizən] *n* : traición *f* (a la patria, etc.)

treasure[1] ['trɛʒər, 'treɪ-] *vt* **-sured; -suring** : apreciar, valorar

treasure[2] *n* : tesoro *m*

treasurer ['trɛʒərər, 'treɪ-] *n* : tesorero *m*, -ra *f*

treasury ['trɛʒəri, 'treɪ-] *n, pl* **-suries** : tesorería *f*, tesoro *m*

treat[1] ['trit] *vt* **1** DEAL WITH : tratar (un asunto) ⟨the article treats of poverty : el artículo trata de la pobreza⟩ **2** HANDLE : tratar (a una persona), manejar (un objeto) ⟨to treat something as a joke : tomar(se) algo a broma⟩ **3** INVITE : invitar, convidar ⟨he treated me to a meal : me invitó a comer⟩ **4** : tratar, atender (en medicina) **5** PROCESS : tratar ⟨to treat sewage : tratar las aguas negras⟩

treat[2] *n* : gusto *m*, placer *m* ⟨it was a treat to see you : fue un placer verte⟩ ⟨it's my treat : yo invito⟩

treatise ['triːtɪs] *n* : tratado *m*, estudio *m*

treatment ['triːtmənt] *n* : trato *m*, tratamiento *m* (médico)

treaty ['triːti] *n, pl* **-ties** : tratado *m*, convenio *m*

treble[1] ['trɛbəl] *vt* **-bled; -bling** : triplicar

treble[2] *adj* **1** → **triple 2** : de tiple, soprano (en música) **3 treble clef** : clave *f* de sol

treble[3] *n* : tiple *m*, parte *f* de soprano

tree ['triː] *n* : árbol *m*

treeless ['triːləs] *adj* : carente de árboles

trek[1] ['trɛk] *vi* **trekked; trekking** : hacer un viaje largo y difícil

trek[2] *n* : viaje *m* largo y difícil

trellis ['trɛlɪs] *n* : enrejado *m*, espaldera *f*, celosía *f*

tremble ['trɛmbəl] *vi* **-bled; -bling** : temblar

tremendous [trɪ'mɛndəs] *adj* : tremendo — **tremendously** *adv*

tremor ['trɛmər] *n* : temblor *m*

tremulous ['trɛmjələs] *adj* : trémulo, tembloroso

trench ['trɛntʃ] *n* **1** DITCH : zanja *f* **2** : trinchera *f* (militar)

trenchant ['trɛntʃənt] *adj* : cortante, mordaz

trend[1] ['trɛnd] *vi* : tender, inclinarse

trend[2] *n* **1** TENDENCY : tendencia *f* **2** FASHION : moda *f*

trendy ['trɛndi] *adj* **trendier; -est** : de moda

trepidation [,trɛpə'deɪʃən] *n* : inquietud *f*, ansiedad *f*

trespass[1] ['trɛspəs, -,pæs] *vi* **1** SIN : pecar, transgredir **2** : entrar ilegalmente (en propiedad ajena)

trespass[2] *n* **1** SIN : pecado *m*, transgresión *f* ⟨forgive us our trespasses : perdónanos nuestras deudas⟩ **2** : entrada *f* ilegal (en propiedad ajena)

tress ['trɛs] *n* : mechón *m*

trestle ['trɛsəl] *n* **1** : caballete *m* (armazón) **2** *or* **trestle bridge** : puente *m* de caballete

triad ['traɪ,æd] *n* : tríada *f*

trial[1] ['traɪəl] *adj* : de prueba ⟨trial period : período de prueba⟩

trial[2] *n* **1** : juicio *m*, proceso *m* ⟨to stand trial : ser sometido a juicio⟩ **2** AFFLICTION : aflicción *f*, tribulación *f* **3** TEST : prueba *f*, ensayo *m*

triangle ['traɪ,æŋgəl] *n* : triángulo *m*

triangular [traɪ'æŋgjələr] *adj* : triangular

tribal ['traɪbəl] *adj* : tribal

tribe ['traɪb] *n* : tribu *f*

tribesman ['traɪbzmən] *n, pl* **-men** [-mən, -,mɛn] : miembro *m* de una tribu

tribulation [,trɪbjə'leɪʃən] *n* : tribulación *f*

tribunal [traɪ'bjuːnəl, trɪ-] *n* : tribunal *m*, corte *f*

tributary ['trɪbjə,tɛri] *n, pl* **-taries** : afluente *m*

tribute ['trɪb,juːt] *n* : tributo *m*

trick[1] ['trɪk] *vt* : engañar, embaucar

trick[2] *n* **1** RUSE : trampa *f*, treta *f*, artimaña *f* **2** PRANK : broma *f* ⟨we played a trick on her : le gastamos una broma⟩ **3** : truco *m* ⟨magic tricks : trucos de magia⟩ ⟨the trick is to wait five minutes : el truco está en esperar cinco minutos⟩ **4** MANNERISM : peculiaridad *f*, manía *f* **5** : baza *f* (en juegos de naipes)

trickery ['trɪkəri] *n* : engaños *mpl*, trampas *fpl*

trickle[1] ['trɪkəl] *vi* **-led; -ling** : gotear, chorrear

trickle² n : goteo m, hilo m
trickster ['trɪkstər] n : estafador m, -dora f; embaucador m, -dora f
tricky ['trɪki] adj **trickier; -est 1** SLY : astuto, taimado **2** DIFFICULT : delicado, peliagudo, difícil
tricycle ['traɪsəkəl, -ˌsɪkəl] n : triciclo m
trident ['traɪdənt] n : tridente m
triennial [traɪ'ɛniəl] adj : trienal
trifle¹ ['traɪfəl] vi **-fled; -fling** : jugar, juguetear
trifle² n : nimiedad f, insignificancia f
trifling ['traɪflɪŋ] adj : trivial, insignificante
trigger¹ ['trɪgər] vt : causar, provocar
trigger² n : gatillo m
trigonometry [ˌtrɪgə'nɑmətri] n : trigonometría f
trill¹ ['trɪl] vi QUAVER : trinar, gorjear — vt : vibrar ⟨to trill the r : vibrar la r⟩
trill² n **1** QUAVER : trino m, gorjeo m **2** : vibración f (en fonética)
trillion ['trɪljən] n : billón m
trilogy ['trɪlədʒi] n, pl **-gies** : trilogía f
trim¹ ['trɪm] vt **trimmed; trimming 1** DECORATE : adornar, decorar **2** CUT : recortar **3** REDUCE : recortar, reducir ⟨to trim the excess : recortar el exceso⟩
trim² adj **trimmer; trimmest 1** SLIM : esbelto **2** NEAT : limpio y arreglado, bien cuidado
trim³ n **1** CONDITION : condición f, estado m ⟨to keep in trim : mantenerse en buena forma⟩ **2** CUT : recorte m **3** TRIMMING : adornos mpl
trimming ['trɪmɪŋ] n : adornos mpl, accesorios mpl
Trinity ['trɪnəti] n : Trinidad f
trinket ['trɪŋkət] n : chuchería f, baratija f
trio ['tri:ˌo:] n, pl **trios** : trío m
trip¹ ['trɪp] v **tripped; tripping** vi **1** : caminar (a paso ligero) **2** STUMBLE : tropezar **3 to trip up** ERR : equivocarse, cometer un error — vt **1** : hacerle una zancadilla (a alguien) ⟨you tripped me on purpose! : ¡me hiciste la zancadilla a propósito!⟩ **2** ACTIVATE : activar (un mecanismo) **3 to trip up** : hacer equivocar (a alguien)
trip² n **1** JOURNEY : viaje m ⟨to take a trip : hacer un viaje⟩ **2** STUMBLE : tropiezo m, traspié m
tripartite [traɪ'pɑrˌtaɪt] adj : tripartito
tripe ['traɪp] n **1** : mondongo m, callos mpl, pancita f Mex **2** TRASH : porquería f
triple¹ ['trɪpəl] vt **-pled; -pling** : triplicar
triple² adj : triple
triple³ n : triple m
triplet ['trɪplət] n **1** : terceto m (en poesía, música, etc.) **2** : trillizo m, -za f (persona)
triplicate ['trɪplɪkət] n : triplicado m
tripod ['traɪˌpɑd] n : trípode m
trite ['traɪt] adj **triter; tritest** : trillado, tópico, manido

triumph¹ ['traɪəmpf] vi : triunfar
triumph² n : triunfo m
triumphal [traɪ'ʌmpfəl] adj : triunfal
triumphant [traɪ'ʌmpfənt] adj : triunfante, triunfal — **triumphantly** adv
trivia ['trɪviə] ns & pl : trivialidades fpl, nimiedades fpl
trivial ['trɪviəl] adj : trivial, intrascendente, insignificante
triviality [ˌtrɪvi'æləti] n, pl **-ties** : trivialidad f
trod, trodden → **tread¹**
troll ['tro:l] n : duende m o gigante m de cuentos folklóricos
trolley ['trɑli] n, pl **-leys** : tranvía m
trombone [trɑm'bo:n] n : trombón m
trombonist [trɑm'bo:nɪst] n : trombón m
troop¹ ['tru:p] vi : desfilar, ir en tropel
troop² n **1** : escuadrón m (de caballería) **2** GROUP : grupo m, banda f (de personas) **3 troops** npl SOLDIERS : tropas fpl, soldados mpl
trooper ['tru:pər] n **1** : soldado m (de caballería) **2** : policía m montado **3** : policía m (estatal)
trophy ['tro:fi] n, pl **-phies** : trofeo m
tropic¹ ['trɑpɪk] or **tropical** [-pɪkəl] adj : tropical
tropic² n **1** : trópico m ⟨tropic of Cancer : trópico de Cáncer⟩ **2 the tropics** : el trópico
trot¹ ['trɑt] vi **trotted; trotting** : trotar
trot² n : trote m
trouble¹ ['trʌbəl] v **-bled; -bling** vt **1** DISTURB, WORRY : molestar, perturbar, inquietar **2** AFFLICT : afligir, afectar — vi : molestarse, hacer un esfuerzo ⟨they didn't trouble to come : no se molestaron en venir⟩
trouble² n **1** PROBLEMS : problemas mpl, dificultades fpl ⟨to be in trouble : estar en un aprieto⟩ ⟨heart trouble : problemas de corazón⟩ **2** EFFORT : molestia f, esfuerzo m ⟨to take the trouble : tomarse la molestia⟩ ⟨it's not worth the trouble : no vale la pena⟩
troublemaker ['trʌbəlˌmeɪkər] n : agitador m, -dora f; alborotador m, -dora f
troublesome ['trʌbəlsəm] adj : problemático, dificultoso — **troublesomely** adv
trough ['trɔf] n, pl **troughs** ['trɔfs, 'trɔvz] **1** : comedero m, bebedero m (de animales) **2** CHANNEL, HOLLOW : depresión f (en el suelo), seno m (de olas)
trounce ['traʊnts] vt **trounced; trouncing 1** THRASH : apalear, darle una paliza (a alguien) **2** DEFEAT : derrotar contundentemente
troupe ['tru:p] n : troupe f
trousers ['traʊzərz] npl : pantalón m, pantalones mpl
trout ['traʊt] n, pl **trout** : trucha f
trowel ['traʊəl] n **1** : llana f, paleta f (de albañil) **2** : desplantador m (de jardinero)
truant ['tru:ənt] n : alumno m, -na f que falta a clase sin permiso

truce ['tru:s] *n* : tregua *f*, armisticio *m*

truck¹ ['trʌk] *vt* : transportar en camión

truck² *n* **1** : camión *m* (vehículo automóvil), carro *m* (manual) **2** DEALINGS : tratos *mpl* ⟨to have no truck with : no tener nada que ver con⟩

trucker ['trʌkər] *n* : camionero *m*, -ra *f*

truculent ['trʌkjələnt] *adj* : agresivo, beligerante

trudge ['trʌdʒ] *vi* **trudged; trudging** : caminar a paso pesado

true¹ ['tru:] *vt* **trued; trueing** : aplomar (algo vertical), nivelar (algo horizontal), centrar (una rueda)

true² *adv* **1** TRUTHFULLY : lealmente, sinceramente **2** ACCURATELY : exactamente, certeramente

true³ *adj* **truer; truest 1** LOYAL : fiel, leal **2** : cierto, verdadero, verídico ⟨it's true : es cierto, es la verdad⟩ ⟨a true story : una historia verídica⟩ **3** GENUINE : auténtico, genuino — **truly** *adv*

true–blue ['tru:'blu:] *adj* LOYAL : leal, fiel

truffle ['trʌfəl] *n* : trufa *f*

truism ['tru:ˌɪzəm] *n* : perogrullada *f*, verdad *f* obvia

trump¹ ['trʌmp] *vt* : matar (en juegos de naipes)

trump² *n* : triunfo *m* (en juegos de naipes)

trumped–up ['trʌmpt'ʌp] *adj* : inventado, fabricado ⟨trumped-up charges : falsas acusaciones⟩

trumpet¹ ['trʌmpət] *vi* **1** : sonar una trompeta **2** : berrear, bramar (dícese de un animal) — *vt* : proclamar a los cuatro vientos

trumpet² *n* : trompeta *f*

trumpeter ['trʌmpətər] *n* : trompetista *mf*

truncate ['trʌŋˌkeɪt, 'trʌn-] *vt* **-cated; -cating** : truncar

trundle ['trʌndəl] *v* **-dled; -dling** *vi* : rodar lentamente — *vt* : hacer rodar, empujar lentamente

trunk ['trʌŋk] *n* **1** : tronco *m* (de un árbol o del cuerpo) **2** : trompa *f* (de un elefante) **3** CHEST : baúl *m* **4** : maletero *m*, cajuela *f Mex* (de un auto) **5 trunks** *npl* : traje *m* de baño (de caballero)

truss¹ ['trʌs] *vt* : atar (con fuerza)

truss² *n* **1** FRAMEWORK : armazón *m* (de una estructura) **2** : braguero *m* (en medicina)

trust¹ ['trʌst] *vi* : confiar, esperar ⟨to trust in God : confiar en Dios⟩ — *vt* **1** ENTRUST : confiar, encomendar **2** : confiar en, tenerle confianza a ⟨I trust you : te tengo confianza⟩

trust² *n* **1** CONFIDENCE : confianza *f* **2** HOPE : esperanza *f*, fe *f* **3** CREDIT : crédito *m* ⟨to sell on trust : fiar⟩ **4** : fideicomiso *m* ⟨to hold in trust : guardar en fideicomiso⟩ **5** : trust *m* (consorcio empresarial) **6** CUSTODY : responsabilidad *f*, custodia *f*

trustee [ˌtrʌs'ti:] *n* : fideicomisario *m*, -ria *f*; fiduciario *m*, -ria *f*

trustful ['trʌstfəl] *adj* : confiado — **trustfully** *adv*

trustworthiness ['trəstˌwərðinəs] *n* : integridad *f*, honradez *f*

trustworthy ['trəstˌwərði] *adj* : digno de confianza, confiable

trusty ['trəsti] *adj* **trustier; -est** : fiel, confiable

truth ['tru:θ] *n, pl* **truths** ['tru:ðz, 'tru:θs] : verdad *f*

truthful ['tru:θfəl] *adj* : sincero, veraz — **truthfully** *adv*

truthfulness ['tru:θfəlnəs] *n* : sinceridad *f*, veracidad *f*

try¹ ['traɪ] *v* **tried; trying** *vt* **1** : enjuiciar, juzgar, procesar ⟨he was tried for murder : fue procesado por homicidio⟩ **2** : probar ⟨did you try the salad? : ¿probaste la ensalada?⟩ **3** TEST : tentar, poner a prueba ⟨to try one's patience : tentarle la paciencia a uno⟩ **4** ATTEMPT : tratar (de), intentar **5** *or* **to try on** : probarse (ropa) — *vi* : tratar, intentar

try² *n, pl* **tries** : intento *m*, tentativa *f*

tryout ['traɪˌaʊt] *n* : prueba *f*

tsar ['zɑr, 'tsɑr, 'sɑr] → **czar**

T–shirt ['ti:ˌʃərt] *n* : camiseta *f*

tub ['tʌb] *n* **1** CASK : cuba *f*, barril *m*, tonel *m* **2** CONTAINER : envase *m* (de plástico, etc.) ⟨a tub of margarine : un envase de margarina⟩ **3** BATHTUB : tina *f* (de baño), bañera *f*

tuba ['tu:bə, 'tju:-] *n* : tuba *f*

tube ['tu:b, 'tju:b] *n* **1** PIPE : tubo *m* **2** : tubo *m* (de dentífrico, etc.) **3** *or* **inner tube** : cámara *f* **4** : tubo *m* (de un aparato electrónico) **5** : trompa *f* (en anatomía)

tubeless ['tu:bləs, 'tju:b-] *adj* : sin cámara (dícese de una llanta)

tuber ['tu:bər, 'tju:-] *n* : tubérculo *m*

tubercular [tʊ'bərkjələr, tjʊ-] → **tuberculous**

tuberculosis [tʊˌbərkjə'lo:sɪs, tjʊ-] *n, pl* **-loses** [-ˌsi:z] : tuberculosis *f*

tuberculous [tʊ'bərkjələs, tjʊ-] *adj* : tuberculoso

tuberous ['tu:bərəs, 'tju:-] *adj* : tuberoso

tubing ['tu:bɪŋ, 'tju:-] *n* : tubería *f*

tubular ['tu:bjələr, 'tju:-] *adj* : tubular

tuck¹ ['tʌk] *vt* **1** PLACE, PUT : meter, colocar ⟨tuck in your shirt : métete la camisa⟩ **2** : guardar, esconder ⟨to tuck away one's money : guardar uno bien su dinero⟩ **3** COVER : arropar (a un niño en la cama)

tuck² *n* : pliegue *m*, alforza *f*

Tuesday ['tu:zˌdeɪ, 'tju:z-, -di] *n* : martes *m*

tuft ['tʌft] *n* : penacho *m* (de plumas), copete *m* (de pelo)

tug¹ ['tʌg] *v* **tugged; tugging** *vi* : tirar, jalar, dar un tirón — *vt* : jalar, arrastrar, remolcar (con un barco)

tug² *n* **1** : tirón *m*, jalón *m* **2** → **tugboat**

tugboat ['tʌgˌbo:t] *n* : remolcador *m*

tug–of–war [ˌtʌgə'wɔr] *n, pl* **tugs–of–war** : tira y afloja *m*
tuition [tu'ɪʃən] *n or* **tuition fees** : tasas *fpl* de matrícula, colegiatura *f Mex*
tulip ['tu:lɪp, 'tju:-] *n* : tulipán *m*
tumble¹ ['tʌmbəl] *v* **-bled; -bling** *vi* **1** : dar volteretas (en acrobacia) **2** FALL : caerse, venirse abajo — *vt* **1** TOPPLE : volcar **2** TOSS : hacer girar
tumble² *n* : voltereta *f*, caída *f*
tumbler ['tʌmblər] *n* **1** ACROBAT : acróbata *mf*, saltimbanqui *mf* **2** GLASS : vaso *m* (de mesa) **3** : clavija *f* (de una cerradura)
tummy ['tʌmi] *n, pl* **-mies** BELLY : panza *f*, vientre *m*
tumor ['tu:mər, 'tju:-] *n* : tumor *m*
tumult ['tu:ˌmʌlt, 'tju:-] *n* : tumulto *m*, alboroto *m*
tumultuous [tʊ'mʌltʃʊəs, tju:-] *adj* : tumultuoso
tuna ['tu:nə, 'tju:-] *n, pl* **-na** *or* **-nas** : atún *m*
tundra ['tʌndrə] *n* : tundra *f*
tune¹ ['tu:n, 'tju:n] *v* **tuned; tuning** *vt* **1** ADJUST : ajustar, hacer más preciso, afinar (un motor) **2** : afinar (un instrumento musical) **3** : sintonizar (un radio o televisor) — *vi* **to tune in** : sintonizar (con una emisora)
tune² *n* **1** MELODY : tonada *f*, canción *f*, melodía *f* **2 in tune** : afinado (dícese de un instrumento o de la voz), sintonizado, en sintonía
tuneful ['tu:nfəl, 'tju:n-] *adj* : armonioso, melódico
tuner ['tu:nər, 'tju:-] *n* : afinador *m*, -dora *f* (de instrumentos); sintonizador *m* (de un radio o un televisor)
tungsten ['tʌŋkstən] *n* : tungsteno *m*
tunic ['tu:nɪk, 'tju:-] *n* : túnica *f*
tuning fork *n* : diapasón *m*
Tunisian [tu:'ni:ʒən, tju:'nɪziən] *n* : tunecino *m*, -na *f* — **Tunisian** *adj*
tunnel¹ ['tʌnəl] *vi* **-neled** *or* **-nelled; -neling** *or* **-nelling** : hacer un túnel
tunnel² *n* : túnel *m*
turban ['tərbən] *n* : turbante *m*
turbid ['tərbɪd] *adj* : turbio
turbine ['tərbən, -ˌbaɪn] *n* : turbina *f*
turboprop ['tərboːˌprɑp] *n* : turbopropulsor *m* (motor), avión *m* turbopropulsado
turbulence ['tərbjələnts] *n* : turbulencia *f*
turbulent ['tərbjələnt] *adj* : turbulento — **turbulently** *adv*
tureen [tə'ri:n, tjʊ-] *n* : sopera *f*
turf ['tərf] *n* SOD : tepe *m*
turgid ['tərdʒɪd] *adj* **1** SWOLLEN : turgente **2** : ampuloso, hinchado ⟨turgid style : estilo ampuloso⟩
Turk ['tərk] *n* : turco *m*, -ca *f*
turkey ['tərki] *n, pl* **-keys** : pavo *m*
Turkish¹ ['tərkɪʃ] *adj* : turco
Turkish² *n* : turco *m* (idioma)
turmoil ['tərˌmɔɪl] *n* : agitación *f*, desorden *m*, confusión *f*

turn¹ ['tərn] *vt* **1** : girar, voltear, volver ⟨to turn one's head : voltear la cabeza⟩ ⟨she turned her chair toward the fire : giró su asiento hacia la hoguera⟩ **2** ROTATE : darle vuelta a, hacer girar ⟨turn the handle : dale vuelta a la manivela⟩ **3** SPRAIN, WRENCH : dislocar, torcer **4** UPSET : revolver (el estómago) **5** TRANSFORM : convertir ⟨to turn water into wine : convertir el agua en vino⟩ **6** SHAPE : tornear (en carpintería) — *vi* **1** ROTATE : girar, dar vueltas **2** : girar, doblar, dar una vuelta ⟨turn left : doble a la izquierda⟩ ⟨to turn around : dar la media vuelta⟩ **3** BECOME : hacerse, volverse, ponerse **4** SOUR : agriarse, cortarse (dícese de la leche) **5 to turn to** : recurrir a ⟨they have no one to turn to : no tienen quien les ayude⟩
turn² *n* **1** : vuelta *f*, giro *m* ⟨a sudden turn : una vuelta repentina⟩ **2** CHANGE : cambio *m* **3** CURVE : curva *f* (en un camino) **4** : turno *m* ⟨they're awaiting their turn : están esperando su turno⟩ ⟨whose turn is it? : ¿a quién le toca?⟩
turnaround ['tərnəˌraʊnd] *n* PROCESSING : procesamiento *m*
turncoat ['tərnˌko:t] *n* : traidor *m*, -dora *f*
turn down *vt* **1** REFUSE : rehusar, rechazar ⟨they turned down our invitation : rehusaron nuestra invitación⟩ **2** LOWER : bajar (el volumen)
turn in *vt* : entregar ⟨to turn in one's work : entregar uno su trabajo⟩ ⟨they turned in the suspect : entregaron al sospechoso⟩ — *vi* : acostarse, irse a la cama
turnip ['tərnəp] *n* : nabo *m*
turn off *vt* : apagar (la luz, la radio, etc.)
turn on *vt* : prender (la luz, etc.), encender (un motor, etc.)
turnout ['tərnˌaʊt] *n* : concurrencia *f*
turn out *vt* **1** EVICT, EXPEL : expulsar, echar, desalojar **2** PRODUCE : producir **3** → **turn off** — *vi* **1** : concurrir, presentarse ⟨many turned out to vote : muchos concurrieron a votar⟩ **2** PROVE, RESULT : resultar
turnover ['tərnˌo:vər] *n* **1** : empanada *f* (salada o dulce) **2** : volumen *m* (de ventas) **3** : rotación *f* (de personal) ⟨a high turnover : un alto nivel de rotación⟩
turn over *vt* **1** TRANSFER : entregar, transferir (un cargo o una responsabilidad) **2** : voltear, darle la vuelta a ⟨turn the cassette over : voltea el cassette⟩
turnpike ['tərnˌpaɪk] *n* : carretera *f* de peaje
turnstile ['tərnˌstaɪl] *n* : torniquete *m* (de acceso)
turntable ['tərnˌteɪbəl] *n* : tornamesa *mf*
turn up *vi* **1** APPEAR : aparecer, presentarse **2** HAPPEN : ocurrir, suceder (inesperadamente) — *vt* : subir (el volumen)
turpentine ['tərpənˌtaɪn] *n* : aguarrás *m*, trementina *f*

turquoise ['tər,kɔɪz, -,kwɔɪz] *n* : turque-sa *f*
turret ['tərət] *n* **1** TOWER : torre *f* pequeña **2** : torreta *f* (de un tanque, un avión, etc.)
turtle ['tərtəl] *n* : tortuga *f* (marina)
turtledove ['tərtəl,dʌv] *n* : tórtola *f*
turtleneck ['tərtəl,nɛk] *n* : cuello *m* de tortuga, cuello *m* alto
tusk ['tʌsk] *n* : colmillo *m*
tussle¹ ['tʌsəl] *vi* -sled; -sling SCUFFLE : pelearse, reñir
tussle² *n* : riña *f*, pelea *f*
tutor¹ ['tuːtər, 'tjuː-] *vt* : darle clases particulares (a alguien)
tutor² *n* : tutor *m*, -tora *f*; maestro *m*, -tra *f* (particular)
tuxedo [,tək'siː,doː] *n, pl* -dos *or* -does : esmoquin *m*, smoking *m*
TV [,tiː'viː, 'tiː,viː] → television
twain ['tweɪn] *n* : dos *m*
twang¹ ['twæŋ] *vt* : pulsar la cuerda de (una guitarra) — *vi* : hablar en tono nasal
twang² *n* **1** : tañido *m* (de una cuerda de guitarra) **2** : tono *m* nasal (de voz)
tweak¹ ['twiːk] *vt* : pellizcar
tweak² *n* : pellizco *m*
tweed ['twiːd] *n* : tweed *m*
tweet¹ ['twiːt] *vi* : piar
tweet² *n* : gorjeo *m*, pío *m*
tweezers ['twiːzərz] *npl* : pinzas *fpl*
twelfth¹ ['twɛlfθ] *adj* : duodécimo
twelfth² *n* **1** : duodécimo *m*, -ma *f* (en una serie) **2** : doceavo *m*, doceava parte *f*
twelve¹ ['twɛlv] *adj* : doce
twelve² *n* : doce *m*
twentieth¹ ['twʌntiəθ, 'twɛn-] *adj* : vigésimo
twentieth² *n* **1** : vigésimo *m*, -ma *f* (en una serie) **2** : veinteavo *m*, veinteava parte *f*
twenty¹ ['twʌnti, 'twɛn-] *adj* : veinte
twenty² *n, pl* -ties : veinte *m*
twice ['twaɪs] *adv* : dos veces ⟨twice a day : dos veces al día⟩ ⟨it costs twice as much : cuesta el doble⟩
twig ['twɪg] *n* : ramita *f*
twilight ['twaɪ,laɪt] *n* : crepúsculo *m*
twill ['twɪl] *n* : sarga *f*, tela *f* cruzada
twin¹ ['twɪn] *adj* : gemelo, mellizo
twin² *n* : gemelo *m*, -la *f*; mellizo *m*, -za *f*
twine¹ ['twaɪn] *v* twined; twining *vt* : entrelazar, entrecruzar — *vi* : enroscarse (alrededor de algo)
twine² *n* : cordel *m*, cuerda *f*, mecate *m* CA, Mex, Ven
twinge¹ ['twɪndʒ] *vi* twinged; twinging *or* twingeing : sentir punzadas
twinge² *n* : punzada *f*, dolor *m* agudo
twinkle¹ ['twɪŋkəl] *vi* -kled; -kling : centellear, titilar (dícese de las estrellas o de la luz) **2** : chispear, brillar (dícese de los ojos)
twinkle² *n* : centelleo *m* (de las estrellas), brillo *m* (de los ojos)
twirl¹ ['twərl] *vt* : girar, darle vueltas a — *vi* : girar, dar vueltas (rápidamente)

twirl² *n* : giro *m*, vuelta *f*
twist¹ ['twɪst] *vt* : torcer, retorcer ⟨he twisted my arm : me torció el brazo⟩ — *vi* : retorcerse, enroscarse, serpentear (dícese de un río, un camino, etc.)
twist² *n* **1** BEND : vuelta *f*, recodo *m* (en el camino, el río, etc.) **2** TURN : giro *m* ⟨give it a twist : hazlo girar⟩ **3** SPIRAL : espiral *f* ⟨a twist of lemon : una rodajita de limón⟩ **4** : giro *m* inesperado (de eventos, etc.)
twisted ['twɪstəd] *adj* : retorcido ⟨a twisted mind : una mente retorcida⟩
twister ['twɪstər] **1** → tornado **2** → waterspout
twitch¹ ['twɪtʃ] *vi* : moverse nerviosamente, contraerse espasmódicamente (dícese de un músculo)
twitch² *n* : espasmo *m*, sacudida *f* ⟨a nervous twitch : un tic nervioso⟩
twitter¹ ['twɪtər] *vi* CHIRP : gorjear, cantar (dícese de los pájaros)
twitter² *n* : gorjeo *m*
two¹ ['tuː] *adj* : dos
two² *n, pl* twos : dos *m*
twofold¹ ['tuː'foːld] *adv* : al doble
twofold² ['tuː,foːld] *adj* : doble
two hundred¹ *adj* : doscientos
two hundred² *n* : doscientos *m*
twosome ['tuːsəm] *n* COUPLE : pareja *f*
tycoon [taɪ'kuːn] *n* : magnate *mf*
tying → tie¹
type¹ ['taɪp] *v* typed; typing *vt* **1** TYPEWRITE : escribir a máquina, pasar (un texto) a máquina **2** CATEGORIZE : categorizar, identificar — *vi* : escribir a máquina
type² *n* **1** KIND : tipo *m*, clase *f*, categoría *f* **2** *or* printing type : tipo *m*
typeface ['taɪp,feɪs] *n* : tipo *m* de imprenta
typewrite ['taɪp,raɪt] *v* -wrote; -written : escribir a máquina
typewriter ['taɪp,raɪtər] *n* : máquina *f* de escribir
typhoid¹ ['taɪ,fɔɪd, taɪ'-] *adj* : relativo al tifus o a la tifoidea
typhoid² *n or* typhoid fever : tifoidea *f*
typhoon [taɪ'fuːn] *n* : tifón *m*
typhus ['taɪfəs] *n* : tifus *m*, tifo *m*
typical ['tɪpɪkəl] *adj* : típico, característico — **typically** *adv*
typify ['tɪpə,faɪ] *vt* -fied; -fying : ser típico o representativo de (un grupo, una clase, etc.)
typist ['taɪpɪst] *n* : mecanógrafo *m*, -fa *f*
typographic [,taɪpə'græfɪk] *or* **typographical** [-fɪkəl] *adj* : tipográfico — **typographically** [-fɪkli] *adv*
typography [taɪ'pɑgrəfi] *n* : tipografía *f*
tyrannical [tə'rænɪkəl, taɪ-] *adj* : tiránico — **tyrannically** [-nɪkli] *adv*
tyrannize ['tɪrə,naɪz] *vt* -nized; -nizing : tiranizar
tyranny ['tɪrəni] *n, pl* -nies : tiranía *f*
tyrant ['taɪrənt] *n* : tirano *m*, -na *f*
tzar ['zɑr, 'tsɑr, 'sɑr] → czar

U

u ['ju:] *n*, *pl* **u's** *or* **us** ['ju:z] : vigésima primera letra del alfabeto inglés

ubiquitous [ju:'bɪkwəṭəs] *adj* : ubicuo, omnipresente

udder ['ʌdər] *n* : ubre *f*

UFO [ˌju:ˌɛf'o:, 'ju:ˌfo:] *n*, *pl* **UFO's** *or* **UFOs** (*u*nidentified *f*lying *o*bject) : ovni *m*, OVNI *m*

Ugandan [ju:'gændən, -'gɑn-; u:'gɑn-] *n* : ugandés *m*, -desa *f* — **Ugandan** *adj*

ugliness ['ʌglinəs] *n* : fealdad *f*

ugly ['ʌgli] *adj* **uglier; -est** **1** UNATTRACTIVE : feo **2** DISAGREEABLE : desagradable, feo ⟨ugly weather : tiempo feo⟩ ⟨to have an ugly temper : tener mal genio⟩

Ukrainian [ju:'kreɪniən, -'kraɪ-] *n* **1** : ucraniano *m*, -na *f* **2** : ucraniano *m* (idioma) — **Ukrainian** *adj*

ukulele [ˌju:kə'leɪli] *n* : ukelele *m*

ulcer ['ʌlsər] *n* : úlcera *f* (interna), llaga *f* (externa)

ulcerate ['ʌlsəˌreɪt] *vi* **-ated; -ating** : ulcerarse

ulceration [ˌʌlsə'reɪʃən] *n* **1** : ulceración *f* **2** ULCER : úlcera *f*, llaga *f*

ulcerous ['ʌlsərəs] *adj* : ulceroso

ulna ['ʌlnə] *n* : cúbito *m*

ulterior [ˌʌl'tɪriər] *adj* : oculto ⟨ulterior motive : motivo oculto, segunda intención⟩

ultimate ['ʌltəmət] *adj* **1** FINAL : último, final **2** SUPREME : supremo, máximo **3** FUNDAMENTAL : fundamental, esencial

ultimately ['ʌltəmətli] *adv* **1** FINALLY : por último, finalmente **2** EVENTUALLY : a la larga, con el tiempo

ultimatum [ˌʌltə'meɪṭəm, -'mɑ-] *n*, *pl* **-tums** *or* **-ta** [-ṭə] : ultimátum *m*

ultrasound ['ʌltrəˌsaʊnd] *n* **1** : ultrasonido *m* **2** : ecografía *f* (técnica o imagen)

ultraviolet [ˌʌltrə'vaɪələt] *adj* : ultravioleta

umbilical cord [ˌʌm'bɪlɪkəl] *n* : cordón *m* umbilical

umbrage ['ʌmbrɪʤ] *n* **to take umbrage at** : ofenderse por

umbrella [ˌʌm'brɛlə] *n* **1** : paraguas *m* **2 beach umbrella** : sombrilla *f*

umpire¹ ['ʌmˌpaɪr] *v* **-pired; -piring** : arbitrar

umpire² *n* : árbitro *m*, -tra *f*

umpteenth [ˌʌmp'ti:nθ] *adj* : enésimo

unable [ˌʌn'eɪbəl] *adj* : incapaz ⟨to be unable to : no poder⟩

unabridged [ˌʌnə'brɪʤd] *adj* : íntegro

unacceptable [ˌʌnɪk'sɛptəbəl] *adj* : inaceptable

unaccompanied [ˌʌnə'kʌmpənid] *adj* : solo, sin acompañamiento (en música)

unaccountable [ˌʌnə'kaʊntəbəl] *adj* : inexplicable, incomprensible — **unaccountably** [-bli] *adv*

unaccustomed [ˌʌnə'kʌstəmd] *adj* **1** UNUSUAL : desacostumbrado, inusual **2** UNUSED : inhabituado ⟨unaccustomed to noise : inhabituado al ruido⟩

unacquainted [ˌʌnə'kweɪnṭəd] *adj* **to be unacquainted with** : desconocer, ignorar

unadorned [ˌʌnə'dɔrnd] *adj* : sin adornos, puro y simple

unadulterated [ˌʌnə'dʌltəˌreɪṭəd] *adj* **1** PURE : puro ⟨unadulterated food : comida pura⟩ **2** ABSOLUTE : completo, absoluto

unaffected [ˌʌnə'fɛktəd] *adj* **1** : no afectado, indiferente **2** NATURAL : sin afectación, natural

unaffectedly [ˌʌnə'fɛktədli] *adv* : de manera natural

unafraid [ˌʌnə'freɪd] *adj* : sin miedo

unaided [ˌʌn'eɪdəd] *adj* : sin ayuda, solo

unambiguous [ˌʌnæm'bɪgjʊəs] *adj* : inequívoco

unanimity [ˌju:nə'nɪməṭi] *n* : unanimidad *f*

unanimous [jʊ'nænəməs] *adj* : unánime — **unanimously** *adv*

unannounced [ˌʌnə'naʊnst] *adj* : sin dar aviso

unanswered [ˌʌn'ænʦərd] *adj* : sin contestar

unappealing [ˌʌnə'pi:lɪŋ] *adj* : desagradable

unappetizing [ˌʌn'æpəˌtaɪzɪŋ] *adj* : poco apetitoso, poco apetecible

unarmed [ˌʌn'ɑrmd] *adj* : sin armas, desarmado

unassisted [ˌʌnə'sɪstəd] *adj* : sin ayuda

unassuming [ˌʌnə'su:mɪŋ] *adj* : modesto, sin pretensiones

unattached [ˌʌnə'tæʧt] *adj* **1** LOOSE : suelto **2** INDEPENDENT : independiente **3** : solo (ni casado ni prometido)

unattractive [ˌʌnə'træktɪv] *adj* : poco atractivo

unauthorized [ˌʌn'ɔθəˌraɪzd] *adj* : sin autorización, no autorizado

unavailable [ˌʌnə'veɪləbəl] *adj* : no disponible

unavoidable [ˌʌnə'vɔɪdəbəl] *adj* : inevitable, ineludible

unaware¹ [ˌʌnə'wær] *adv* → **unawares**

unaware² [ˌʌnə'wær] *adj* : inconsciente

unawares [ˌʌnə'wærz] *adv* **1** : por sorpresa ⟨to catch someone unawares : agarrar a alguien desprevenido⟩ **2** UNINTENTIONALLY : inconscientemente, inadvertidamente

unbalanced [ˌʌn'bælənʦt] *adj* : desequilibrado

unbearable [ˌʌn'bærəbəl] *adj* : insoportable, inaguantable — **unbearably** [-bli] *adv*

unbecoming [ˌʌnbɪ'kʌmɪŋ] *adj* **1** UNSEEMLY : impropio, indecoroso **2** UNFLATTERING : poco favorecedor

unbelievable [ˌʌnbəˈliːvəbəl] *adj* : increíble — **unbelievably** [-bli] *adv*

unbend [ˌʌnˈbɛnd] *vi* -**bent** [-ˈbɛnt]; -**bending** RELAX : relajarse

unbending [ˌʌnˈbɛndɪŋ] *adj* : inflexible

unbiased [ˌʌnˈbaɪəst] *adj* : imparcial, objetivo

unbind [ˌʌnˈbaɪnd] *vt* -**bound** [-ˈbaʊnd]; -**binding** 1 UNFASTEN, UNTIE : desatar, desamarrar 2 RELEASE : liberar

unbolt [ˌʌnˈboːlt] *vt* : abrir el cerrojo de, descorrer el pestillo de

unborn [ˌʌnˈbɔrn] *adj* : aún no nacido, que va a nacer

unbosom [ˌʌnˈbʊzəm, -ˈbuː-] *vt* : revelar, divulgar

unbreakable [ˌʌnˈbreɪkəbəl] *adj* : irrompible

unbridled [ˌʌnˈbraɪdəld] *adj* : desenfrenado

unbroken [ˌʌnˈbroːkən] *adj* 1 INTACT : intacto, sano 2 CONTINUOUS : continuo, ininterrumpido

unbuckle [ˌʌnˈbʌkəl] *vt* -**led**; -**ling** : desabrochar

unburden [ˌʌnˈbərdən] *vt* 1 UNLOAD : descargar 2 **to unburden oneself** : desahogarse

unbutton [ˌʌnˈbʌtən] *vt* : desabrochar, desabotonar

uncalled–for [ˌʌnˈkɔldˌfɔr] *adj* : inapropiado, innecesario

uncanny [ənˈkæni] *adj* -**nier**; -**est** 1 STRANGE : extraño 2 EXTRAORDINARY : raro, extraordinario — **uncannily** [-ˈkænəli] *adv*

unceasing [ˌʌnˈsiːsɪŋ] *adj* : incesante, continuo — **unceasingly** *adv*

unceremonious [ˌʌnˌsɛrəˈmoːniəs] *adj* 1 INFORMAL : sin ceremonia, sin pompa 2 ABRUPT : abrupto, brusco — **unceremoniously** *adv*

uncertain [ˌʌnˈsərtən] *adj* 1 INDEFINITE : indeterminado 2 UNSURE : incierto, dudoso 3 CHANGEABLE : inestable, variable ⟨uncertain weather : tiempo inestable⟩ 4 HESITANT : indeciso 5 VAGUE : poco claro

uncertainly [ˌʌnˈsərtənli] *adv* : dudosamente, con desconfianza

uncertainty [ˌʌnˈsərtənti] *n*, *pl* -**ties** : duda *f*, incertidumbre *f*

unchangeable [ˌʌnˈtʃeɪndʒəbəl] *adj* : inalterable, inmutable

unchanged [ˌʌnˈtʃeɪndʒd] *adj* : sin cambiar

unchanging [ˌʌnˈtʃeɪndʒɪŋ] *adj* : inalterable, inmutable, firme

uncharacteristic [ˌʌnˌkærɪktəˈrɪstɪk] *adj* : inusual, desacostumbrado

uncharged [ˌʌnˈtʃɑrdʒd] *adj* : sin carga (eléctrica)

uncivilized [ˌʌnˈsɪvəˌlaɪzd] *adj* 1 BARBAROUS : incivilizado, bárbaro 2 WILD : salvaje

uncle [ˈʌŋkəl] *n* : tío *m*

unclean [ˌʌnˈkliːn] *adj* 1 IMPURE : impuro 2 DIRTY : sucio

unclear [ˌʌnˈklɪr] *adj* : confuso, borroso, poco claro

Uncle Sam [ˈsæm] *n* : el Tío Sam

unclog [ˌʌnˈklɑg] *vt* -**clogged**; -**clogging** : desatascar, destapar

unclothed [ˌʌnˈkloːðd] *adj* : desnudo

uncomfortable [ˌʌnˈkʌmpfərtəbəl] *adj* 1 : incómodo (dícese de una silla, etc.) 2 UNEASY : inquieto, incómodo

uncommitted [ˌʌnkəˈmɪtəd] *adj* : sin compromisos

uncommon [ˌʌnˈkɑmən] *adj* 1 UNUSUAL : raro, poco común 2 REMARKABLE : excepcional, extraordinario

uncommonly [ˌʌnˈkɑmənli] *adv* : extraordinariamente

uncompromising [ˌʌnˈkɑmprəˌmaɪzɪŋ] *adj* : inflexible, intransigente

unconcerned [ˌʌnkənˈsərnd] *adj* : indiferente — **unconcernedly** [-ˈsərnədli] *adv*

unconditional [ˌʌnkənˈdɪʃənəl] *adj* : incondicional — **unconditionally** *adv*

unconscious[1] [ˌʌnˈkɑntʃəs] *adj* : inconsciente — **unconsciously** *adv*

unconscious[2] *n* : inconsciente *m*

unconsciousness [ˌʌnˈkɑntʃəsnəs] *n* : inconsciencia *f*

unconstitutional [ˌʌnˌkɑntstəˈtuːʃənəl, -ˈtju:-] *adj* : inconstitucional

uncontrollable [ˌʌnkənˈtroːləbəl] *adj* : incontrolable, incontenible — **uncontrollably** [-bli] *adv*

uncontrolled [ˌʌnkənˈtroːld] *adj* : incontrolado

unconventional [ˌʌnkənˈvɛntʃənəl] *adj* : poco convencional

unconvincing [ˌʌnkənˈvɪntsɪŋ] *adj* : poco convincente

uncouth [ˌʌnˈkuːθ] *adj* CRUDE, ROUGH : grosero, rudo

uncover [ˌʌnˈkʌvər] *vt* 1 : destapar (un objeto), dejar al descubierto 2 EXPOSE, REVEAL : descubrir, revelar, exponer

uncultivated [ˌʌnˈkʌltəˌveɪtəd] *adj* : inculto

uncurl [ˌʌnˈkərl] *vt* UNROLL : desenrollar — *vi* : desenrollarse, desrizarse (dícese del pelo)

uncut [ˌʌnˈkʌt] *adj* 1 : sin cortar ⟨uncut grass : hierba sin cortar⟩ 2 : sin tallar, en bruto ⟨an uncut diamond : un diamante en bruto⟩ 3 UNABRIDGED : completo, íntegro

undaunted [ˌʌnˈdɔntəd] *adj* : impávido

undecided [ˌʌndiˈsaɪdəd] *adj* 1 IRRESOLUTE : indeciso, irresoluto 2 UNRESOLVED : pendiente, no resuelto

undefeated [ˌʌndiˈfiːtəd] *adj* : invicto

undeniable [ˌʌndiˈnaɪəbəl] *adj* : innegable — **undeniably** [-bli] *adv*

under[1] [ˈʌndər] *adv* 1 LESS : menos ⟨$10 or under : $10 o menos⟩ 2 UNDERWATER : debajo del agua 3 : bajo los efectos de la anestesia

under[2] *adj* 1 LOWER : (más) bajo, inferior 2 SUBORDINATE : inferior 3 : insuficiente ⟨an under dose of medicine : una dosis insuficiente de medicina⟩

689

under³ *prep* **1** BELOW, BENEATH : debajo de, abajo de ⟨under the table : abajo de la mesa⟩ ⟨we walked under the arch : pasamos por debajo del arco⟩ ⟨under the sun : bajo el sol⟩ **2** : menos de ⟨in under 20 minutes : en menos de 20 minutos⟩ **3** *(indicating rank or authority)* : bajo ⟨under the command of : bajo las órdenes de⟩ **4** SUBJECT TO : bajo ⟨under suspicion : bajo sospecha⟩ ⟨under the circumstances : dadas las circunstancias⟩ **5** ACCORDING TO : según, de acuerdo con, conforme a ⟨under the present laws : según las leyes actuales⟩

underage [ˌʌndərˈeɪʤ] *adj* : menor de edad

underbrush [ˈʌndərˌbrəʃ] *n* : maleza *f*

underclothes [ˈʌndərˌkloːz, -ˌkloːðz] → **underwear**

underclothing [ˈʌndərˌkloːðɪŋ] → **underwear**

undercover [ˌʌndərˈkʌvər] *adj* : secreto, clandestino

undercurrent [ˈʌndərˌkərənt] *n* **1** : corriente *f* submarina **2** UNDERTONE : corriente *f* oculta, trasfondo *m*

undercut [ˌʌndərˈkʌt] *vt* **-cut; -cutting** : vender más barato que

underdeveloped [ˌʌndərdɪˈvɛləpt] *adj* : subdesarrollado, atrasado

underdog [ˈʌndərˌdɔɡ] *n* : persona *f* que tiene menos posibilidades

underdone [ˌʌndərˈdʌn] *adj* RARE : poco cocido

underestimate [ˌʌndərˈɛstəˌmeɪt] *vt* **-mated; -mating** : subestimar, menospreciar

underexposed [ˌʌndərɪkˈspoːzd] *adj* : subexpuesto (en fotografía)

underfoot [ˌʌndərˈfʊt] *adv* **1** : bajo los pies ⟨to trample underfoot : pisotear⟩ **2 to be underfoot** : estorbar ⟨they're always underfoot : están siempre estorbando⟩

undergarment [ˈʌndərˌɡɑrmənt] *n* : prenda *f* íntima

undergo [ˌʌndərˈɡoː] *vt* **-went** [-ˈwɛnt]; **-gone** [-ˈɡɔn]; **-going** : sufrir, experimentar ⟨to undergo an operation : someterse a una intervención quirúrgica⟩

undergraduate [ˌʌndərˈɡræʤuət] *n* : estudiante *m* universitario, estudiante *f* universitaria

underground¹ [ˌʌndərˈɡraʊnd] *adv* **1** : bajo tierra **2** SECRETLY : clandestinamente, en secreto ⟨to go underground : pasar a la clandestinidad⟩

underground² [ˈʌndərˌɡraʊnd] *adj* **1** SUBTERRANEAN : subterráneo **2** SECRET : secreto, clandestino

underground³ [ˈʌndərˌɡraʊnd] *n* : movimiento *m* o grupo *m* clandestino

undergrowth [ˈʌndərˌɡroːθ] *n* : maleza *f*, broza *f*

underhand¹ [ˈʌndərˌhænd] *adv* **1** SECRETLY : de manera clandestina **2** *or*

underhanded : sin levantar el brazo por encima del hombro (en deportes)

underhand² *adj* **1** SLY : solapado **2** : por debajo del hombro (en deportes)

underhanded [ˌʌndərˈhændəd] *adj* **1** SLY : solapado **2** SHADY : turbio, poco limpio

underline [ˈʌndərˌlaɪn] *vt* **-lined; -lining 1** : subrayar **2** EMPHASIZE : subrayar, acentuar, hacer hincapié en

underlying [ˌʌndərˈlaɪɪŋ] *adj* **1** : subyacente ⟨the underlying rock : la roca subyacente⟩ **2** FUNDAMENTAL : fundamental, esencial

undermine [ˌʌndərˈmaɪn] *vt* **-mined; -mining 1** : socavar (una estructura, etc.) **2** SAP, WEAKEN : minar, debilitar

underneath¹ [ˌʌndərˈniːθ] *adv* : debajo, abajo ⟨the part underneath : la parte de abajo⟩

underneath² *prep* : debajo de, abajo de

undernourished [ˌʌndərˈnərɪʃt] *adj* : desnutrido

underpants [ˈʌndərˌpænts] *npl* : calzoncillos *mpl*, calzones *mpl*

underpass [ˈʌndərˌpæs] *n* : paso *m* a desnivel

underprivileged [ˌʌndərˈprɪvlɪʤd] *adj* : desfavorecido

underrate [ˌʌndərˈreɪt] *vt* **-rated; -rating** : subestimar, menospreciar

underscore [ˈʌndərˌskor] *vt* **-scored; -scoring** → **underline**

undersea¹ [ˌʌndərˈsiː] *or* **underseas** [-ˈsiːz] *adv* : bajo la superficie del mar

undersea² *adj* : submarino

undersecretary [ˌʌndərˈsɛkrəˌteri] *n, pl* **-ries** : subsecretario *m*, -ria *f*

undersell [ˌʌndərˈsɛl] *vt* **-sold; -selling** : vender más barato que

undershirt [ˈʌndərˌʃərt] *n* : camiseta *f*

undershorts [ˈʌndərˌʃɔrts] *npl* : calzoncillos *mpl*

underside [ˈʌndərˌsaɪd, ˌʌndərˈsaɪd] *n* : parte *f* de abajo

undersized [ˌʌndərˈsaɪzd] *adj* : más pequeño de lo normal

understand [ˌʌndərˈstænd] *v* **-stood** [-ˈstʊd]; **-standing** *vt* **1** COMPREHEND : comprender, entender ⟨I don't understand it : no lo entiendo⟩ ⟨that's understood : eso se comprende⟩ ⟨to make oneself understood : hacerse entender⟩ **2** BELIEVE : entender ⟨to give someone to understand : dar a alguien a entender⟩ **3** INFER : tener entendido ⟨I understand that she's leaving : tengo entendido que se va⟩ — *vi* : comprender, entender

understandable [ˌʌndərˈstændəbəl] *adj* : comprensible

understanding¹ [ˌʌndərˈstændɪŋ] *adj* : comprensivo, compasivo

understanding² *n* **1** GRASP : comprensión *f*, entendimiento *m* **2** SYMPATHY : comprensión *f* (mutua) **3** INTERPRETATION : interpretación *f* ⟨it's my understanding that . . . : tengo la impresión de que . . ., tengo entendido que ... ⟩ **4** AGREEMENT : acuerdo *m*, arreglo *m*

understate [ˌʌndər'steɪt] *vt* **-stated; -stating** : minimizar, subestimar

understatement [ˌʌndər'steɪtmənt] *n* : atenuación *f* ⟨that's an understatement : decir sólo eso es quedarse corto⟩

understudy ['ʌndərˌstʌdi] *n, pl* **-dies** : sobresaliente *mf*, suplente *mf* (en el teatro)

undertake [ˌʌndər'teɪk] *vt* **-took** [-'tʊk]; **-taken** [-'teɪkən]; **-taking 1** : emprender (una tarea), asumir (una responsabilidad) **2** PROMISE : comprometerse (a hacer algo)

undertaker ['ʌndərˌteɪkər] *n* : director *m*, -tora *f* de funeraria

undertaking ['ʌndərˌteɪkɪŋ, ˌʌndər'-] *n* **1** ENTERPRISE, TASK : empresa *f*, tarea *f* **2** PLEDGE : promesa *f*, garantía *f*

undertone ['ʌndərˌtoːn] *n* **1** : voz *f* baja ⟨to speak in an undertone : hablar en voz baja⟩ **2** HINT, UNDERCURRENT : trasfondo *m*, matiz *m*

undertow ['ʌndərˌtoː] *n* : resaca *f*

undervalue [ˌʌndər'vælˌjuː] *vt* **-ued; -uing** : menospreciar, subestimar

underwater¹ [ˌʌndər'wɔtər, -'wɑ-] *adv* : debajo (del agua)

underwater² *adj* : submarino

under way [ˌʌndər'weɪ] *adv* : en marcha, en camino ⟨to get under way : ponerse en marcha⟩

underwear ['ʌndərˌwær] *n* : ropa *f* interior, ropa *f* íntima

underworld ['ʌndərˌwərld] *n* **1** HELL : infierno *m* **2 the underworld** CRIMINALS : la hampa, los bajos fondos

underwrite ['ʌndərˌraɪt, ˌʌndər'-] *vt* **-wrote** [-ˌroːt, -'roːt]; **-written** [-ˌrɪtən, -'rɪtən]; **-writing 1** INSURE : asegurar **2** FINANCE : financiar **3** BACK, ENDORSE : suscribir, respaldar

underwriter ['ʌndərˌraɪtər, ˌʌndər'-] *n* INSURER : asegurador *m*, -dora *f*

undeserving [ˌʌndi'zərvɪŋ] *adj* : indigno

undesirable¹ [ˌʌndi'zaɪrəbəl] *adj* : indeseable

undesirable² *n* : indeseable *mf*

undeveloped [ˌʌndi'vɛləpt] *adj* : sin desarrollar, sin revelar (dícese de una película)

undies ['ʌndiːz] → **underwear**

undignified [ˌʌn'dɪgnəfaɪd] *adj* : indecoroso

undiluted [ˌʌndaɪ'luːtəd, -də-] *adj* : sin diluir, concentrado

undiscovered [ˌʌndɪ'skʌvərd] *adj* : no descubierto

undisputed [ˌʌndɪ'spjuːtəd] *adj* : indiscutible

undisturbed [ˌʌndɪ'stərbd] *adj* : tranquilo (dícese de una persona), sin tocar (dícese de un objeto)

undivided [ˌʌndɪ'vaɪdəd] *adj* : íntegro, completo

undo [ˌʌn'duː] *vt* **-did** [-'dɪd]; **-done** [-'dʌn]; **-doing 1** UNFASTEN : desabrochar, desatar, abrir **2** ANNUL : anular **3** REVERSE : deshacer, reparar (daños, etc.) **4** RUIN : arruinar, destruir

undoing [ˌʌn'duːɪŋ] *n* : ruina *f*, perdición *f*

undoubted [ˌʌn'daʊtəd] *adj* : cierto, indudable — **undoubtedly** *adv*

undress [ˌʌn'drɛs] *vt* : desvestir, desabrigar, desnudar — *vi* : desvestirse, desnudarse

undrinkable [ˌʌn'drɪŋkəbəl] *adj* : no potable

undue [ˌʌn'duː:, -'djuː] *adj* : excesivo, indebido — **unduly** *adv*

undulate ['ʌnʤəˌleɪt] *vi* **-lated; -lating** : ondular

undulation [ˌʌnʤə'leɪʃən] *n* : ondulación *f*

undying [ˌʌn'daɪɪŋ] *adj* : perpetuo, imperecedero

unearth [ˌʌn'ərθ] *vt* **1** EXHUME : desenterrar, exhumar **2** DISCOVER : descubrir

unearthly [ˌʌn'ərθli] *adj* **-lier; -est** : sobrenatural, de otro mundo

uneasily [ˌʌn'iːzəli] *adv* : inquietamente, con inquietud

uneasiness [ˌʌn'iːzinəs] *n* : inquietud *f*

uneasy [ˌʌn'iːzi] *adj* **-easier; -est 1** AWKWARD : incómodo **2** WORRIED : preocupado, inquieto **3** RESTLESS : inquieto, agitado

uneducated [ˌʌn'ɛʤəˌkeɪtəd] *adj* : inculto, sin educación

unemployed [ˌʌnɪm'plɔɪd] *adj* : desempleado

unemployment [ˌʌnɪm'plɔɪmənt] *n* : desempleo *m*

unending [ˌʌn'ɛndɪŋ] *adj* : sin fin, interminable

unendurable [ˌʌnɪn'dʊrəbəl, -ɛn-, -'djʊr-] *adj* : insoportable, intolerable

unequal [ˌʌn'iːkwəl] *adj* **1** : desigual **2** INADEQUATE : incapaz, incompetente ⟨to be unequal to a task : no estar a la altura de una tarea⟩

unequaled *or* **unequalled** [ˌʌn'iːkwəld] *adj* : sin igual

unequivocal [ˌʌnɪ'kwɪvəkəl] *adj* : inequívoco, claro — **unequivocally** *adv*

unerring [ˌʌn'ɛrɪŋ, -'ər-] *adj* : infalible

unethical [ˌʌn'ɛθɪkəl] *adj* : poco ético

uneven [ˌʌn'iːvən] *adj* **1** ODD : impar (dícese de un número) **2** : desigual, desnivelado (dícese de una superficie) ⟨uneven terrain : terreno accidentado⟩ **3** IRREGULAR : irregular, poco uniforme **4** UNEQUAL : desigual

unevenly [ˌʌn'iːvənli] *adv* : desigualmente, irregularmente

uneventful [ˌʌnɪ'vɛntfəl] *adj* : sin incidentes, tranquilo

unexpected [ˌʌnɪk'spɛktəd] *adj* : imprevisto, inesperado — **unexpectedly** *adv*

unfailing [ˌʌn'feɪlɪŋ] *adj* **1** CONSTANT : constante **2** INEXHAUSTIBLE : inagotable 3 SURE : a toda prueba, indefectible

unfair [ˌʌnˈfær] *adj* : injusto — **unfairly** *adv*

unfairness [ˌʌnˈfærnəs] *n* : injusticia *f*

unfaithful [ˌʌnˈfeɪθfəl] *adj* : desleal, infiel — **unfaithfully** *adv*

unfaithfulness [ˌʌnˈfeɪθfəlnəs] *n* : infidelidad *f*, deslealtad *f*

unfamiliar [ˌʌnfəˈmɪljər] *adj* 1 STRANGE : desconocido, extraño ⟨an unfamiliar place : un lugar nuevo⟩ 2 to be unfamiliar with : no estar familiarizado con, desconocer

unfamiliarity [ˌʌnfəˌmɪliˈærəti] *n* : falta *f* de familiaridad

unfashionable [ˌʌnˈfæʃənəbəl] *adj* : fuera de moda

unfasten [ˌʌnˈfæsən] *vt* : desabrochar, desatar (una cuerda, etc.), abrir (una puerta)

unfavorable [ˌʌnˈfeɪvərəbəl] *adj* : desfavorable, mal — **unfavorably** [-bli] *adv*

unfeeling [ˌʌnˈfiːlɪŋ] *adj* : insensible — **unfeelingly** *adv*

unfinished [ˌʌnˈfɪnɪʃd] *adj* : inacabado, incompleto

unfit [ˌʌnˈfɪt] *adj* 1 UNSUITABLE : inadecuado, impropio 2 UNSUITED : no apto, incapaz 3 : incapacitado (físicamente) ⟨to be unfit : no estar en forma⟩

unflappable [ˌʌnˈflæpəbəl] *adj* : imperturbable

unflattering [ˌʌnˈflæt̬ərɪŋ] *adj* : poco favorecedor

unfold [ˌʌnˈfoːld] *vt* 1 EXPAND : desplegar, desdoblar, extender ⟨to unfold a map : desplegar un mapa⟩ 2 DISCLOSE, REVEAL : revelar, exponer (un plan, etc.) — *vi* 1 DEVELOP : desarrollarse, desenvolverse ⟨the story unfolded : el cuento se desarrollaba⟩ 2 EXPAND : extenderse, desplegarse

unforeseeable [ˌʌnforˈsiːəbəl] *adj* : imprevisible

unforeseen [ˌʌnforˈsiːn] *adj* : imprevisto

unforgettable [ˌʌnfərˈget̬əbəl] *adj* : inolvidable, memorable — **unforgettably** [-bli] *adv*

unforgivable [ˌʌnfərˈgɪvəbəl] *adj* : imperdonable

unfortunate[1] [ˌʌnˈfɔrtʃənət] *adj* 1 UNLUCKY : desgraciado, infortunado, desafortunado ⟨how unfortunate! : ¡qué mala suerte!⟩ 2 INAPPROPRIATE : inoportuno ⟨an unfortunate comment : un comentario poco feliz⟩

unfortunate[2] *n* : desgraciado *m*, -da *f*

unfortunately [ˌʌnˈfɔrtʃənətli] *adv* : desafortunadamente

unfounded [ˌʌnˈfaʊndəd] *adj* : infundado

unfreeze [ˌʌnˈfriːz] *v* -froze [-ˈfroːz]; -frozen [-ˈfroːzən]; -freezing *vt* : descongelar — *vi* : descongelarse

unfriendliness [ˌʌnˈfrɛndlinəs] *n* : hostilidad *f*, antipatía *f*

unfriendly [ˌʌnˈfrɛndli] *adj* -lier; -est : poco amistoso, hostil

unfurl [ˌʌnˈfərl] *vt* : desplegar, desdoblar — *vi* : desplegarse

unfurnished [ˌʌnˈfərnɪʃt] *adj* : desamueblado

ungainly [ˌʌnˈgeɪnli] *adj* : desgarbado

ungodly [ˌʌnˈgɔdli, -ˈgɑd-] *adj* 1 IMPIOUS : impío 2 OUTRAGEOUS : atroz, terrible ⟨at an ungodly hour : a una hora intempestiva⟩

ungrateful [ˌʌnˈgreɪtfəl] *adj* : desagradecido, ingrato — **ungratefully** *adv*

ungratefulness [ˌʌnˈgreɪtfəlnəs] *n* : ingratitud *f*

unhappily [ˌʌnˈhæpəli] *adv* 1 SADLY : tristemente 2 UNFORTUNATELY : desafortunadamente, lamentablemente

unhappiness [ˌʌnˈhæpinəs] *n* : infelicidad *f*, tristeza *f*, desdicha *f*

unhappy [ˌʌnˈhæpi] *adj* -pier; -est 1 UNFORTUNATE : desafortunado, desventurado 2 MISERABLE, SAD : infeliz, triste, desdichado 3 INOPPORTUNE : inoportuno, poco feliz

unharmed [ˌʌnˈhɑrmd] *adj* : salvo, ileso

unhealthy [ˌʌnˈhɛlθi] *adj* -thier; -est 1 UNWHOLESOME : insalubre, malsano, nocivo a la salud ⟨an unhealthy climate : un clima insalubre⟩ 2 SICKLY : de mala salud, enfermizo

unheard-of [ˌʌnˈhərdəv] *adj* : sin precedente, inaudito, insólito

unhinge [ˌʌnˈhɪndʒ] *vt* 1 : desquiciar (una puerta, etc.) 2 DISRUPT, UNSETTLE : trastornar, perturbar

unholy [ˌʌnˈhoːli] *adj* -lier; -est 1 : profano, impío 2 UNGODLY : atroz, terrible

unhook [ˌʌnˈhʊk] *vt* 1 : desenganchar, descolgar (de algo) 2 UNDO : desabrochar

unhurt [ˌʌnˈhərt] *adj* : ileso

unicorn [ˈjuːnəˌkɔrn] *n* : unicornio *m*

unidentified [ˌʌnaɪˈdɛntəˌfaɪd] *adj* : no identificado ⟨unidentified flying object : objeto volador no identificado⟩

unification [ˌjuːnəfəˈkeɪʃən] *n* : unificación *f*

uniform[1] [ˈjuːnəˌfɔrm] *adj* : uniforme, homogéneo, constante

uniform[2] *n* : uniforme *m*

uniformed [ˈjuːnəˌfɔrmd] *adj* : uniformado

uniformity [ˌjuːnəˈfɔrməti] *n, pl* -ties : uniformidad *f*

unify [ˈjuːnəˌfaɪ] *vt* -fied; -fying : unificar, unir

unilateral [ˌjuːnəˈlæt̬ərəl] *adj* : unilateral — **unilaterally** *adv*

unimaginable [ˌʌnɪˈmædʒənəbəl] *adj* : inimaginable, inconcebible

unimportant [ˌʌnɪmˈpɔrtənt] *adj* : intrascendente, insignificante, sin importancia

uninhabited [ˌʌnɪnˈhæbət̬əd] *adj* : deshabitado, desierto, despoblado

uninhibited [ˌʌnɪn'hɪbətəd] *adj* : desenfadado, desinhibido, sin reservas
uninjured [ˌʌn'ɪndʒərd] *adj* : ileso
unintelligent [ˌʌnɪn'tɛlədʒənt] *adj* : poco inteligente
unintelligible [ˌʌnɪn'tɛlədʒəbəl] *adj* : ininteligible, incomprensible
unintentional [ˌʌnɪn'tɛntʃənəl] *adj* : no deliberado, involuntario
unintentionally [ˌʌnɪn'tɛntʃənəli] *adv* : involuntariamente, sin querer
uninterested [ˌʌn'ɪntəˌrɛstəd, -trəstəd] *adj* : indiferente
uninteresting [ˌʌn'ɪntəˌrɛstɪŋ, -trəstɪŋ] *adj* : poco interesante, sin interés
uninterrupted [ˌʌnˌɪntə'rʌptəd] *adj* : ininterrumpido, continuo
union ['ju:njən] *n* **1** : unión *f* **2** *or* **labor union** : sindicato *m*, gremio *m*
unionize ['ju:njəˌnaɪz] *v* **-ized; -izing** *vt* : sindicalizar, sindicar — *vi* : sindicalizarse
unique [jʊ'ni:k] *adj* **1** SOLE : único, solo **2** UNUSUAL : extraordinario
uniquely [jʊ'ni:kli] *adv* **1** EXCLUSIVELY : exclusivamente **2** EXCEPTIONALLY : excepcionalmente
unison ['ju:nəsən, -zən] *n* **1** : unísono *m* (en música) **2** CONCORD : acuerdo *m*, armonía *f*, concordia *f* **3 in ∼** SIMULTANEOUSLY : simultáneamente, al unísono
unit ['ju:nɪt] *n* **1** : unidad *f* **2** : módulo *m* (de un mobiliario)
unitary ['ju:nəˌtɛri] *adj* : unitario
unite [jʊ'naɪt] *v* **united; uniting** *vt* : unir, juntar, combinar — *vi* : unirse, juntarse
unity ['ju:nəti] *n, pl* **-ties** **1** UNION : unidad *f*, unión *f* **2** HARMONY : armonía *f*, acuerdo *m*
universal [ˌju:nə'vərsəl] *adj* **1** GENERAL : general, universal ⟨a universal rule : una regla universal⟩ **2** WORLDWIDE : universal, mundial — **universally** *adv*
universe ['ju:nəˌvərs] *n* : universo *m*
university [ˌju:nə'vərsəti] *n, pl* **-ties** : universidad *f*
unjust [ˌʌn'dʒʌst] *adj* : injusto — **unjustly** *adv*
unjustifiable [ˌʌnˌdʒʌstə'faɪəbəl] *adj* : injustificable
unjustified [ˌʌn'dʒʌstəˌfaɪd] *adj* : injustificado
unkempt [ˌʌn'kɛmpt] *adj* : descuidado, desaliñado, despeinado (dícese del pelo)
unkind [ˌʌn'kaɪnd] *adj* : poco amable, cruel — **unkindly** *adv*
unkindness [ˌʌn'kaɪndnəs] *n* : crueldad *f*, falta *f* de amabilidad
unknowing [ˌʌn'no:ɪŋ] *adj* : inconsciente, ignorante — **unknowingly** *adv*
unknown [ˌʌn'no:n] *adj* : desconocido
unlawful [ˌʌn'lɔfəl] *adj* : ilícito, ilegal — **unlawfully** *adv*
unleash [ˌʌn'li:ʃ] *vt* : soltar, desatar
unless [ən'lɛs] *conj* : a menos que, salvo que, a no ser que

unlike¹ [ˌʌn'laɪk] *adj* **1** DIFFERENT : diferente, distinto **2** UNEQUAL : desigual
unlike² *prep* **1** : diferente de, distinto de ⟨unlike the others : distinto a los demás⟩ **2** : a diferencia de ⟨unlike her sister, she is shy : a diferencia de su hermana, es tímida⟩
unlikelihood [ˌʌn'laɪkliˌhʊd] *n* : improbabilidad *f*
unlikely [ˌʌn'laɪkli] *adj* **-lier; -est 1** IMPROBABLE : improbable, poco probable **2** UNPROMISING : poco prometedor
unlimited [ˌʌn'lɪmətəd] *adj* : ilimitado
unload [ˌʌn'lo:d] *vt* **1** REMOVE : descargar, desembarcar (mercancías o pasajeros) **2** : descargar (un avión, un camión, etc.) **3** DUMP : deshacerse de — *vi* : descargar (dícese de un avión, un camión, etc.)
unlock [ˌʌn'lɑk] *vt* **1** : abrir (con llave) **2** DISCLOSE, REVEAL : revelar
unluckily [ˌʌn'lʌkəli] *adv* : desgraciadamente
unlucky [ˌʌn'lʌki] *adj* **-luckier; -est 1** : de mala suerte, desgraciado, desafortunado ⟨an unlucky year : un año de mala suerte⟩ **2** INAUSPICIOUS : desfavorable, poco propicio **3** REGRETTABLE : lamentable
unmanageable [ˌʌn'mænɪdʒəbəl] *adj* : difícil de controlar, poco manejable, ingobernable
unmarried [ˌʌn'mærid] *adj* : soltero
unmask [ˌʌn'mæsk] *vt* EXPOSE : desenmascarar
unmerciful [ˌʌn'mərsɪfəl] *adj* MERCILESS : despiadado — **unmercifully** *adv*
unmistakable [ˌʌnmɪ'steɪkəbəl] *adj* : evidente, inconfundible, obvio — **unmistakably** [-bli] *adv*
unmoved [ˌʌn'mu:vd] *adj* : impasible ⟨to be unmoved by : permanecer impasible ante⟩
unnatural [ˌʌn'nætʃərəl] *adj* **1** ABNORMAL, UNUSUAL : anormal, poco natural, poco normal **2** AFFECTED : afectado, forzado ⟨an unnatural smile : una sonrisa forzada⟩ **3** PERVERSE : perverso, antinatural
unnecessary [ˌʌn'nɛsəˌsɛri] *adj* : innecesario — **unnecessarily** [-ˌnɛsə'sɛrəli] *adv*
unnerve [ˌʌn'nərv] *vt* **-nerved; -nerving** : turbar, desconcertar, poner nervioso
unnoticed [ˌʌn'no:təst] *adj* : inadvertido ⟨to go unnoticed : pasar inadvertido⟩
unobstructed [ˌʌnəb'strʌktəd] *adj* : libre, despejado
unobtainable [ˌʌnəb'teɪnəbəl] *adj* : inasequible
unobtrusive [ˌʌnəb'stru:sɪv] *adj* : discreto
unoccupied [ˌʌn'ɑkjəˌpaɪd] *adj* **1** IDLE : desempleado, desocupado **2** EMPTY : desocupado, libre, deshabitado
unofficial [ˌʌnə'fɪʃəl] *adj* : extraoficial, oficioso, no oficial

unorganized [ˌʌn'ɔrgəˌnaɪzd] *adj* : desorganizado

unorthodox [ˌʌn'ɔrθəˌdɑks] *adj* : poco ortodoxo, poco convencional

unpack [ˌʌn'pæk] *vt* : desempacar — *vi* : desempacar, deshacer las maletas

unpaid [ˌʌn'peɪd] *adj* : no remunerado, no retribuido ⟨an unpaid bill : una cuenta pendiente⟩

unparalleled [ˌʌn'pærəˌlɛld] *adj* : sin igual

unpatriotic [ˌʌnˌpeɪtri'ɑt̬ɪk] *adj* : antipatriótico

unpleasant [ˌʌn'plɛzənt] *adj* : desagradable — **unpleasantly** *adv*

unplug [ˌʌn'plʌg] *vt* **-plugged; -plugging 1** UNCLOG : destapar, desatascar **2** DISCONNECT : desconectar, desenchufar

unpopular [ˌʌn'pɑpjələr] *adj* : impopular, poco popular

unpopularity [ˌʌnˌpɑpjə'lærət̬i] *n* : impopularidad *f*

unprecedented [ˌʌn'prɛsəˌdɛntəd] *adj* : sin precedentes, inaudito, nuevo

unpredictable [ˌʌnpri'dɪktəbəl] *adj* : impredecible

unprejudiced [ˌʌn'prɛdʒədəst] *adj* : imparcial, objetivo

unprepared [ˌʌnpri'pærd] *adj* : no preparado ⟨an unprepared speech : un discurso improvisado⟩

unpretentious [ˌʌnpri'tɛntʃəs] *adj* : modesto, sin pretensiones

unprincipled [ˌʌn'prɪnɪsəpəld] *adj* : sin principios, carente de escrúpulos

unproductive [ˌʌnprə'dʌktɪv] *adj* : improductivo

unprofitable [ˌʌn'prɑfət̬əbəl] *adj* : no rentable, poco provechoso

unpromising [ˌʌn'prɑməsɪŋ] *adj* : poco prometedor

unprotected [ˌʌnprə'tɛktəd] *adj* : sin protección, desprotegido

unprovoked [ˌʌnprə'vo:kt] *adj* : no provocado

unpublished [ˌʌn'pʌblɪʃt] *adj* : inédito

unpunished [ˌʌn'pʌnɪʃt] *adj* : impune ⟨to go unpunished : escapar sin castigo⟩

unqualified [ˌʌn'kwɑləˌfaɪd] *adj* **1** : no calificado, sin título **2** COMPLETE : completo, absoluto ⟨an unqualified denial : una negación incondicional⟩

unquestionable [ˌʌn'kwɛstʃənəbəl] *adj* : incuestionable, indudable, indiscutible — **unquestionably** [-bli] *adv*

unquestioning [ˌʌn'kwɛstʃənɪŋ] *adj* : incondicional, absoluto, ciego

unravel [ˌʌn'rævəl] *v* **-eled** *or* **-elled; -eling** *or* **-elling** *vt* **1** DISENTANGLE : desenmarañar, desenredar **2** SOLVE : aclarar, desenmarañar, desentrañar — *vi* : deshacerse

unreal [ˌʌn'ri:l] *adj* : irreal

unrealistic [ˌʌnˌri:ə'lɪstɪk] *adj* : poco realista

unreasonable [ˌʌn'ri:zənəbəl] *adj* **1** IRRATIONAL : poco razonable, irrazon-

able, irracional **2** EXCESSIVE : excesivo ⟨unreasonable prices : precios excesivos⟩

unreasonably [ˌʌn'ri:zənəbli] *adv* **1** IRRATIONALLY : irracionalmente, de manera irrazonable **2** EXCESSIVELY : excesivamente

unrefined [ˌʌnri'faɪnd] *adj* **1** : no refinado, sin refinar (dícese del azúcar, de la harina, etc.) **2** : poco refinado, inculto (dícese de una persona)

unrelated [ˌʌnri'leɪt̬əd] *adj* : no relacionado, inconexo

unrelenting [ˌʌnri'lɛntɪŋ] *adj* **1** STERN : severo, inexorable **2** CONSTANT, RELENTLESS : constante, implacable

unreliable [ˌʌnri'laɪəbəl] *adj* : que no es de fiar, de poca confianza, inestable (dícese del tiempo)

unrepentant [ˌʌnri'pɛntənt] *adj* : impenitente

unresolved [ˌʌnri'zɑlvd] *adj* : pendiente, no resuelto

unrest [ˌʌn'rɛst] *n* : inquietud *f*, malestar *m* ⟨political unrest : disturbios políticos⟩

unrestrained [ˌʌnri'streɪnd] *adj* : desenfrenado, incontrolado

unrestricted [ˌʌnri'strɪktəd] *adj* : sin restricción ⟨unrestricted access : libre acceso⟩

unrewarding [ˌʌnri'wɔrdɪŋ] *adj* THANKLESS : ingrato

unripe [ˌʌn'raɪp] *adj* : inmaduro, verde

unrivaled *or* **unrivalled** [ˌʌn'raɪvəld] *adj* : incomparable

unroll [ˌʌn'ro:l] *vt* : desenrollar — *vi* : desenrollarse

unruffled [ˌʌn'rʌfəld] *adj* **1** SERENE : sereno, tranquilo **2** SMOOTH : tranquilo, liso ⟨unruffled waters : aguas tranquilas⟩

unruliness [ˌʌn'ru:linəs] *n* : indisciplina *f*

unruly [ˌʌn'ru:li] *adj* : indisciplinado, díscolo, rebelde

unsafe [ˌʌn'seɪf] *adj* : inseguro

unsaid [ˌʌn'sɛd] *adj* : sin decir ⟨to leave unsaid : quedar por decir⟩

unsanitary [ˌʌn'sænəˌteri] *adj* : antihigiénico

unsatisfactory [ˌʌnˌsæt̬əs'fæktəri] *adj* : insatisfactorio

unsatisfied [ˌʌn'sæt̬əsˌfaɪd] *adj* : insatisfecho

unscathed [ˌʌn'skeɪðd] *adj* UNHARMED : ileso

unscheduled [ˌʌn'skɛˌdʒu:ld] *adj* : no programado, imprevisto

unscientific [ˌʌnˌsaɪən'tɪfɪk] *adj* : poco científico

unscrupulous [ˌʌn'skru:pjələs] *adj* : inescrupuloso, sin escrúpulos — **unscrupulously** *adv*

unseal [ˌʌn'si:l] *vt* : abrir, quitarle el sello a

unseasonable [ˌʌn'si:zənəbəl] *adj* **1** : extemporáneo ⟨unseasonable rain

: lluvia extemporánea⟩ 2 UNTIMELY : extemporáneo, inoportuno

unseemly [ˌʌnˈsiːmli] *adj* **-lier; -est** 1 INDECOROUS : indecoroso 2 INAPPROPRIATE : impropio, inapropiado

unseen [ˌʌnˈsiːn] *adj* 1 UNNOTICED : inadvertido 2 INVISIBLE : oculto, invisible

unselfish [ˌʌnˈsɛlfɪʃ] *adj* : generoso, desinteresado — **unselfishly** *adv*

unselfishness [ˌʌnˈsɛlfɪʃnəs] *n* : generosidad *f*, desinterés *m*

unsettle [ˌʌnˈsɛtəl] *vt* **-tled; -tling** DISTURB : trastornar, alterar, perturbar

unsettled [ˌʌnˈsɛtəld] *adj* 1 CHANGEABLE : inestable, variable ⟨unsettled weather : tiempo inestable⟩ 2 DISTURBED : agitado, inquieto ⟨unsettled waters : aguas agitadas⟩ 3 UNDECIDED : pendiente (dícese de un asunto), indeciso (dícese de una persona) 4 UNPAID : sin saldar, pendiente 5 UNINHABITED : despoblado, no colonizado

unshaped [ˌʌnˈʃeɪpt] *adj* : sin forma, informe

unsightly [ˌʌnˈsaɪtli] *adj* UGLY : feo, de aspecto malo

unskilled [ˌʌnˈskɪld] *adj* : no calificado

unskillful [ˌʌnˈskɪlfəl] *adj* : inexperto, poco hábil

unsnap [ˌʌnˈsnæp] *vt* **-snapped; -snapping** : desabrochar

unsociable *adj* : poco sociable

unsolved [ˌʌnˈsɑlvd] *adj* : no resuelto, sin resolver

unsophisticated [ˌʌnsəˈfɪstəˌkeɪtəd] *adj* 1 NAIVE, UNWORLDLY : ingenuo, de poco mundo 2 SIMPLE : simple, poco sofisticado, rudimentario

unsound [ˌʌnˈsaʊnd] *adj* 1 UNHEALTHY : enfermizo, de mala salud 2 : poco sólido, defectuoso (dícese de una estructura, etc.) 3 INVALID : inválido, erróneo 4 **of unsound mind** : mentalmente incapacitado

unspeakable [ˌʌnˈspiːkəbəl] *adj* 1 INDESCRIBABLE : indecible, inexpresable, incalificable 2 HEINOUS : atroz, nefando, abominable — **unspeakably** [-bli] *adv*

unspecified [ˌʌnˈspɛsəˌfaɪd] *adj* : indeterminado, sin especificar

unspoiled [ˌʌnˈspɔɪld] *adj* 1 : conservado, sin estropear (dícese de un lugar) 2 : que no está mimado (dícese de un niño)

unstable [ˌʌnˈsteɪbəl] *adj* 1 CHANGEABLE : variable, inestable, cambiable ⟨an unstable pulse : un pulso irregular⟩ 2 UNSTEADY : inestable, poco sólido (dícese de una estructura)

unsteadily [ˌʌnˈstɛdəli] *adv* : de modo inestable

unsteadiness [ˌʌnˈstɛdinəs] *n* : inestabilidad *f*, inseguridad *f*

unsteady [ˌʌnˈstɛdi] *adj* 1 UNSTABLE : inestable, variable 2 SHAKY : tembloroso

unstoppable [ˌʌnˈstɑpəbəl] *adj* : irrefrenable, incontenible

unsubstantiated [ˌʌnsəbˈstænʃiˌeɪtəd] *adj* : no corroborado, no demostrado

unsuccessful [ˌʌnsəkˈsɛsfəl] *adj* : fracasado, infructuoso

unsuitable [ˌʌnˈsuːtəbəl] *adj* : inadecuado, impropio, inapropiado ⟨an unsuitable time : una hora inconveniente⟩

unsuited [ˌʌnˈsuːtəd] *adj* : inadecuado, inepto

unsung [ˌʌnˈsʌŋ] *adj* : olvidado

unsure [ˌʌnˈʃʊr] *adj* : incierto, dudoso

unsurpassed [ˌʌnsərˈpæst] *adj* : sin par, sin igual

unsuspecting [ˌʌnsəˈspɛktɪŋ] *adj* : desprevenido, desapercibido, confiado

unsympathetic [ˌʌnˌsɪmpəˈθɛt̬ɪk] *adj* : poco comprensivo, indiferente

untangle [ˌʌnˈteɪŋɡəl] *vt* **-gled; -gling** : desenmarañar, desenredar

unthinkable [ˌʌnˈθɪŋkəbəl] *adj* : inconcebible, impensable

unthinking [ˌʌnˈθɪŋkɪŋ] *adj* : irreflexivo, inconsciente — **unthinkingly** *adv*

untidy [ˌʌnˈtaɪdi] *adj* 1 SLOVENLY : desaliñado 2 DISORDERLY : desordenado, desarreglado

untie [ˌʌnˈtaɪ] *vt* **-tied; -tying** *or* **-tieing** : desatar, deshacer

until[1] [ˌʌnˈtɪl] *prep* : hasta ⟨until now : hasta ahora⟩

until[2] *conj* : hasta que ⟨until they left : hasta que salieron⟩ ⟨don't answer until you're sure : no contestes hasta que (no) estés seguro⟩

untimely [ˌʌnˈtaɪmli] *adj* 1 PREMATURE : prematuro ⟨an untimely death : una muerte prematura⟩ 2 INOPPORTUNE : inoportuno, intempestivo

untold [ˌʌnˈtoːld] *adj* 1 : nunca dicho ⟨the untold secret : el secreto sin contar⟩ 2 INCALCULABLE : incalculable, indecible

untouched [ˌʌnˈtʌtʃt] *adj* 1 INTACT : intacto, sin tocar, sin probar (dícese de la comida) 2 UNAFFECTED : insensible, indiferente

untoward [ˌʌnˈtord, -ˈtoːərd, -təˈword] *adj* 1 : indecoroso, impropio (dícese del comportamiento) 2 ADVERSE, UNFORTUNATE : desafortunado, adverso ⟨untoward effects : efectos perjudiciales⟩ 3 UNSEEMLY : indecoroso

untrained [ˌʌnˈtreɪnd] *adj* : inexperto, no capacitado

untreated [ˌʌnˈtriːt̬əd] *adj* : no tratado (dícese una enfermedad, etc.), sin tratar (dícese de un material)

untroubled [ˌʌnˈtrʌbəld] *adj* : tranquilo ⟨to be untroubled by : no estar afectado por⟩

untrue [ˌʌnˈtruː] *adj* 1 UNFAITHFUL : infiel 2 FALSE : falso

untrustworthy [ˌʌnˈtrʌstˌwərði] *adj* : de poca confianza (dícese de una persona), no fidedigno (dícese de la información)

untruth [ˌʌn'truːθ, 'ʌnˌ-] *n* : mentira *f*, falsedad *f*

untruthful [ˌʌn'truːθfəl] *adj* : mentiroso, falso

unusable [ˌʌn'juːzəbəl] *adj* : inútil, inservible

unused [ˌʌn'juːzd, *in sense 1 usually* -'juːst] *adj* 1 UNACCUSTOMED : inhabituado 2 NEW : nuevo 3 IDLE : no utilizado (dícese de la tierra) 4 REMAINING : restante ⟨the unused portion : la porción restante⟩

unusual [ˌʌn'juːʒʊəl] *adj* : inusual, poco común, raro

unusually [ˌʌn'juːʒʊəli, -'juːʒəli] *adv* : excepcionalmente, extraordinariamente, fuera de lo común

unwanted [ˌʌn'wɑntəd] *adj* : superfluo, de sobre

unwarranted [ˌʌn'wɔrəntəd] *adj* : injustificado

unwary [ˌʌn'wæri] *adj* : incauto

unwavering [ˌʌn'weɪvərɪŋ] *adj* : firme, inquebrantable ⟨an unwavering gaze : una mirada fija⟩

unwelcome [ˌʌn'wɛlkəm] *adj* : importuno, molesto

unwell [ˌʌn'wɛl] *adj* : enfermo, mal

unwholesome [ˌʌn'hoːlsəm] *adj* 1 UNHEALTHY : malsano, insalubre 2 PERNICIOUS : pernicioso 3 LOATHSOME : repugnante, muy desagradable

unwieldy [ˌʌn'wiːldi] *adj* CUMBERSOME : difícil de manejar, torpe y pesado

unwilling [ˌʌn'wɪlɪŋ] *adj* : poco dispuesto ⟨to be unwilling to : no estar dispuesto a⟩

unwillingly [ˌʌn'wɪlɪŋli] *adv* : a regañadientes, de mala gana

unwind [ˌʌn'waɪnd] *v* **-wound** [-'waʊnd]; **-winding** *vt* UNROLL : desenrollar — *vi* 1 : desenrollarse 2 RELAX : relajar

unwise [ˌʌn'waɪz] *adj* : imprudente, desacertado, poco aconsejable

unwisely [ˌʌn'waɪzli] *adv* : imprudentemente

unwitting [ˌʌn'wɪtɪŋ] *adj* 1 UNAWARE : inconsciente 2 INADVERTENT : involuntario, inadvertido ⟨an unwitting mistake : un error inadvertido⟩ — **unwittingly** *adv*

unworthiness [ˌʌn'wərðinəs] *n* : falta *f* de valía

unworthy [ˌʌn'wərði] *adj* 1 UNDESERVING : indigno ⟨to be unworthy of : no ser digno de⟩ 2 UNMERITED : inmerecido

unwrap [ˌʌn'ræp] *vt* **-wrapped; -wrapping** : desenvolver, deshacer

unwritten [ˌʌn'rɪtən] *adj* : no escrito

unyielding [ˌʌn'jiːldɪŋ] *adj* : firme, inflexible, rígido

unzip [ˌʌn'zɪp] *vt* **-zipped; -zipping** : abrir el cierre de

up[1] ['ʌp] *v* **upped** ['ʌpt]; **upping; ups** *vt* INCREASE : aumentar, subir ⟨they upped the prices : aumentaron los precios⟩ — *vi* **to up and** : agarrar y *fam* ⟨she up and left : agarró y se fue⟩

up[2] *adv* 1 ABOVE : arriba, en lo alto ⟨up in the mountains : arriba en las montañas⟩ 2 UPWARDS : hacia arriba ⟨push it up : empújalo hacia arriba⟩ ⟨the sun came up : el sol salió⟩ ⟨prices went up : los precios subieron⟩ 3 (*indicating an upright position or waking state*) ⟨to sit up : ponerse derecho⟩ ⟨they got up late : se levantaron tarde⟩ ⟨I stayed up all night : pasé toda la noche sin dormir⟩ 4 (*indicating volume or intensity*) ⟨to speak up : hablar más fuerte⟩ 5 (*indicating a northerly direction*) ⟨the climate up north : el clima del norte⟩ ⟨I'm going up to Canada : voy para Canadá⟩ 6 (*indicating the appearance or existence of something*) ⟨the book turned up : el libro apareció⟩ 7 (*indicating consideration*) ⟨she brought the matter up : mencionó el asunto⟩ 8 COMPLETELY : completamente ⟨eat it up : cómetelo todo⟩ 9 : en pedazos ⟨he tore it up : lo rompió en pedazos⟩ 10 (*indicating a stopping*) ⟨the car pulled up to the curb : el carro paró al borde de la acera⟩ 11 (*indicating an even score*) ⟨the game was 10 up : empataron a 10⟩

up[3] *adj* 1 (*risen above the horizon*) ⟨the sun is up : ha salido el sol⟩ 2 (*being above a normal or former level*) ⟨prices are up : los precios han aumentado⟩ ⟨the river is up : las aguas están altas⟩ 3 : despierto, levantado ⟨up all night : despierto toda la noche⟩ 4 BUILT : construido ⟨the house is up : la casa está construida⟩ 5 OPEN : abierto ⟨the windows are up : las ventanas están abiertas⟩ 6 (*moving or going upward*) ⟨the up staircase : la escalera para subir⟩ 7 ABREAST : enterado, al día, al corriente ⟨to be up on the news : estar al corriente de las noticias⟩ 8 PREPARED : preparado ⟨we were up for the test : estuvimos preparados para el examen⟩ 9 FINISHED : terminado, acabado ⟨time is up : se ha terminado el tiempo permitido⟩ 10 **to be up** : pasar ⟨what's up? : ¿qué pasa?⟩

up[4] *prep* 1 (*to, toward, or at a higher point of*) ⟨he went up the stairs : subió la escalera⟩ 2 (*to or toward the source of*) ⟨to go up the river : ir río arriba⟩ 3 ALONG : a lo largo, por ⟨up the coast : a lo largo de la costa⟩ ⟨just up the way : un poco más adelante⟩ ⟨up and down the city : por toda la ciudad⟩

upbraid [ˌʌp'breɪd] *vt* : reprender, regañar

upbringing ['ʌpˌbrɪŋɪŋ] *n* : crianza *f*, educación *f*

upcoming [ˌʌp'kʌmɪŋ] *adj* : próximo

update[1] [ˌʌp'deɪt] *vt* **-dated; -dating** : poner al día, poner al corriente, actualizar

update[2] ['ʌpˌdeɪt] *n* : actualización *f*, puesta *f* al día

upend [ˌʌp'end] *vt* 1 : poner vertical 2 OVERTURN : volcar

upgrade¹ [ˈʌpˌgreɪd, ˌʌpˈ-] *vt* **-graded; -grading 1** PROMOTE : ascender **2** IMPROVE : mejorar

upgrade² [ˈʌpˌgreɪd] *n* **1** SLOPE : cuesta *f*, pendiente *f* **2** RISE : aumento *m* de categoría (de un puesto), ascenso *m* (de un empleado) **3** IMPROVEMENT : mejoramiento *m*

upheaval [ˌʌpˈhiːvəl] *n* **1** : levantamiento *m* (en geología) **2** DISTURBANCE, UPSET : trastorno *m*, agitación *f*, conmoción *f*

uphill¹ [ˌʌpˈhɪl] *adv* : cuesta arriba

uphill² [ˈʌpˌhɪl] *adj* **1** ASCENDING : en subida **2** DIFFICULT : difícil, arduo

uphold [ˌʌpˈhoːld] *vt* **-held; -holding 1** SUPPORT : sostener, apoyar, mantener **2** RAISE : levantar **3** CONFIRM : confirmar (una decisión judicial)

upholster [ˌʌpˈhoːlstər] *vt* : tapizar

upholsterer [ˌʌpˈhoːlstərər] *n* : tapicero *m*, -ra *f*

upholstery [ˌʌpˈhoːlstəri] *n*, *pl* **-steries** : tapicería *f*

upkeep [ˈʌpˌkiːp] *n* : mantenimiento *m*

upland [ˈʌplənd, -ˌlænd] *n* : altiplanicie *f*, altiplano *m*

uplift¹ [ˌʌpˈlɪft] *vt* **1** RAISE : elevar, levantar **2** ELEVATE : elevar, animar (el espíritu, la mente, etc.)

uplift² [ˈʌpˌlɪft] *n* : elevación *f*

upon [əˈpɔn, əˈpɑn] *prep* : en, sobre ⟨upon the desk : sobre el escritorio⟩ ⟨upon leaving : al salir⟩ ⟨questions upon questions : pregunta tras pregunta⟩

upper¹ [ˈʌpər] *adj* **1** HIGHER : superior ⟨the upper classes : las clases altas⟩ **2** : alto (en geografía) ⟨the upper Mississippi : el alto Mississippi⟩

upper² *n* : parte *f* superior (del calzado, etc.)

uppercase [ˌʌpərˈkeɪs] *adj* : mayúsculo

upper hand *n* : ventaja *f*, dominio *m*

uppermost [ˈʌpərˌmoːst] *adj* : más alto ⟨it was uppermost in his mind : era lo que más le preocupaba⟩

upright¹ [ˈʌpˌraɪt] *adj* **1** VERTICAL : vertical **2** ERECT : erguido, derecho **3** JUST : recto, honesto, justo

upright² *n* : montante *m*, poste *m*, soporte *m*

uprising [ˈʌpˌraɪzɪŋ] *n* : insurrección *f*, revuelta *f*, alzamiento *m*

uproar [ˈʌpˌror] *n* COMMOTION : alboroto *m*, jaleo *m*, escándalo *m*

uproarious [ˌʌpˈroriəs] *adj* **1** CLAMOROUS : estrepitoso, clamoroso **2** HILARIOUS : muy divertido, hilarante — **uproariously** *adv*

uproot [ˌʌpˈruːt, -ˈrʊt] *vt* : desarraigar

upset¹ [ˌʌpˈsɛt] *vt* **-set; -setting 1** OVERTURN : volcar **2** SPILL : derramar **3** DISTURB : perturbar, disgustar, inquietar, alterar **4** SICKEN : sentar mal a ⟨it upsets my stomach : me sienta mal al estómago⟩ **5** DISRUPT : trastornar, desbaratar (planes, etc.) **6** DEFEAT : derrotar (en deportes)

upset² *adj* **1** DISPLEASED, DISTRESSED : disgustado, alterado **2** to have an upset stomach : estar mal del estómago, estar descompuesto (de estómago)

upset³ [ˈʌpˌsɛt] *n* **1** OVERTURNING : vuelco *m* **2** DISRUPTION : trastorno *m* (de planes, etc.) **3** DEFEAT : derrota *f* (en deportes)

upshot [ˈʌpˌʃɑt] *n* : resultado *m* final

upside-down [ˌʌpˌsaɪdˈdaʊn] *adj* : al revés

upside down [ˌʌpˌsaɪdˈdaʊn] *adv* **1** : al revés **2** : en confusión, en desorden

upstairs¹ [ˌʌpˈstærz] *adv* : arriba, en el piso superior

upstairs² [ˈʌpˌstærz, ˌʌpˈ-] *adj* : de arriba

upstairs³ [ˈʌpˌstærz, ˌʌpˈ-] *ns & pl* : piso *m* de arriba, planta *f* de arriba

upstanding [ˌʌpˈstændɪŋ, ˈʌpˌ-] *adj* HONEST, UPRIGHT : honesto, íntegro, recto

upstart [ˈʌpˌstɑrt] *n* : advenedizo *m*, -za *f*

upswing [ˈʌpˌswɪŋ] *n* : alza *f*, mejora *f* notable ⟨to be on the upswing : estar mejorándose⟩

uptight [ˌʌpˈtaɪt] *adj* : tenso, nervioso

up to *prep* **1** : hasta ⟨up to a year : hasta un año⟩ ⟨in mud up to my ankles : en barro hasta los tobillos⟩ **2** to be up to : estar a la altura de ⟨I'm not up to going : no estoy en condiciones de ir⟩ **3** to be up to : depender de ⟨it's up to the director : depende del director⟩

up-to-date [ˌʌptəˈdeɪt] *adj* **1** CURRENT : corriente, al día ⟨to keep up-to-date : mantenerse al corriente⟩ **2** MODERN : moderno

uptown [ˈʌpˈtaʊn] *adv* : hacia la parte alta de la ciudad, hacia el distrito residencial

upturn [ˈʌpˌtərn] *n* : mejora *f*, auge *m* (económico)

upward¹ [ˈʌpwərd] *or* **upwards** [-wərdz] *adv* **1** : hacia arriba **2** ~ **of** : más de

upward² *adj* : ascendente, hacia arriba

upwind [ˌʌpˈwɪnd] *adv & adj* : contra el viento

uranium [jʊˈreɪniəm] *n* : uranio *m*

Uranus [jʊˈreɪnəs, ˈjʊrənəs] *n* : Urano *m*

urban [ˈərbən] *adj* : urbano

urbane [ˌərˈbeɪn] *adj* : urbano, cortés

urchin [ˈərtʃən] *n* **1** SCAMP : granuja *mf*; pillo *m*, -lla *f* **2** sea urchin : erizo *m* de mar

Urdu [ˈʊrduː, ˈər-] *n* : urdu *m*

urethra [jʊˈriːθrə] *n*, *pl* **-thras** *or* **-thrae** [-ˌriː] : uretra *f*

urge¹ [ˈərdʒ] *vt* **urged; urging 1** PRESS : instar, apremiar, insistir ⟨we urged him to come : insistimos en que viniera⟩ **2** ADVOCATE : recomendar, abogar por **3 to urge on** : animar, alentar

urge² *n* : impulso *m*, ganas *fpl*, compulsión *f*

urgency [ˈərdʒəntsi] *n*, *pl* **-cies** : urgencia *f*

urgent [ˈərʤənt] *adj* **1** PRESSING : urgente, apremiante **2** INSISTENT : insistente **3 to be urgent** : urgir
urgently [ˈərʤəntli] *adv* : urgentemente
urinal [ˈjʊrənəl, *esp Brit* jʊˈraɪnəl] *n* : orinal *m* (recipiente), urinario *m* (lugar)
urinary [ˈjʊrəˌnɛri] *adj* : urinario
urinate [ˈjʊrəˌneɪt] *vi* -**nated; -nating** : orinar
urination [ˌjʊrəˈneɪʃən] *n* : orinación *f*
urine [ˈjʊrən] *n* : orina *f*
urn [ˈərn] *n* **1** VASE : urna *f* **2** : recipiente *m* (para servir café, etc.)
Uruguayan [ˌʊrəˈgwaɪən, ˌjʊr-, -ˈgweɪ-] *n* : uruguayo *m*, -ya *f* — **Uruguayan** *adj*
us [ˈʌs] *pron* **1** (*as direct object*) : nos ⟨they were visiting us : nos visitaban⟩ **2** (*as indirect object*) : nos ⟨he gave us a present : nos dio un regalo⟩ **3** (*as object of preposition*) : nosotros, nosotras ⟨stay with us : quédese con nosotros⟩ ⟨both of us : nosotros dos⟩ **4** (*for emphasis*) : nosotros ⟨it's us! : ¡somos nosotros!⟩
usable [ˈjuːzəbəl] *adj* : utilizable
usage [ˈjuːsɪʤ, -zɪʤ] *n* **1** HABIT : costumbre *f*, hábito *m* **2** USE : uso *m*
use¹ [ˈjuːz] *v* **used** [ˈjuːzd, *in phrase "used to" usually* ˈjuːstu]; **using** *vt* **1** EMPLOY : emplear, usar **2** CONSUME : consumir, tomar (drogas, etc.) **3** UTILIZE : usar, utilizar ⟨to use tact : usar tacto⟩ ⟨he used his friends to get ahead : usó a sus amigos para mejorar su posición⟩ **4** TREAT : tratar ⟨they used the horse cruelly : maltrataron al caballo⟩ **5 to use up** : agotar, consumir, gastar — *vi* (*used in the past with* **to** *to indicate a former fact or state*) : soler, acostumbrar ⟨winters used to be colder : los inviernos solían ser más fríos, los inviernos eran más fríos⟩ ⟨she used to dance : acostumbraba bailar⟩
use² [ˈjuːs] *n* **1** APPLICATION, EMPLOYMENT : uso *m*, empleo *m*, utilización *f* ⟨out of use : en desuso⟩ ⟨ready for use : listo para usar⟩ ⟨to be in use : usarse, estar funcionando⟩ ⟨to make use of : servirse de, aprovechar⟩ **2** USEFULNESS : utilidad *f* ⟨to be of no use : no servir (para nada)⟩ ⟨it's no use! : ¡es inútil!⟩ **3 to have the use of** : poder usar, tener acceso a **4 to have no use for** : no necesitar ⟨she has no use for po-

etry : a ella no le gusta la poesía⟩
used [ˈjuːzd] *adj* **1** SECONDHAND : usado, de segunda mano ⟨used cars : coches usados⟩ **2** ACCUSTOMED : acostumbrado ⟨used to the heat : acostumbrado al calor⟩
useful [ˈjuːsfəl] *adj* : útil, práctico — **usefully** *adv*
usefulness [ˈjuːsfəlnəs] *n* : utilidad *f*
useless [ˈjuːsləs] *adj* : inútil — **uselessly** *adv*
uselessness [ˈjuːsləsnəs] *n* : inutilidad *f*
user [ˈjuːzər] *n* : usuario *m*, -ria *f*
usher¹ [ˈʌʃər] *vt* **1** ESCORT : acompañar, conducir **2 to usher in** : hacer pasar (a alguien) ⟨to usher in a new era : anunciar una nueva época⟩
usher² *n* : acomodador *m*, -dora *f*
usherette [ˌʌʃəˈrɛt] *n* : acomodadora *f*
usual [ˈjuːʒʊəl] *adj* **1** NORMAL : usual, normal **2** CUSTOMARY : acostumbrado, habitual, de costumbre **3** ORDINARY : ordinario, típico
usually [ˈjuːʒʊəli, ˈjuːʒəli] *adv* : usualmente, normalmente
usurp [jʊˈsərp, -ˈzərp] *vt* : usurpar
usurper [jʊˈsərpər, -ˈzər-] *n* : usurpador *m*, -dora *f*
utensil [jʊˈtɛntsəl] *n* **1** : utensilio *m* (de cocina) **2** IMPLEMENT : implemento *m*, útil *m* (de labranza, etc.)
uterine [ˈjuːtəˌraɪn, -rən] *adj* : uterino
uterus [ˈjuːtərəs] *n, pl* **uteri** [-ˌraɪ] : útero *m*, matriz *f*
utilitarian [juːˌtɪləˈtɛriən] *adj* : utilitario
utility [juːˈtɪləti] *n, pl* -**ties** **1** USEFULNESS : utilidad *f* **2 public utility** : empresa *f* de servicio público
utilization [ˌjuːtələˈzeɪʃən] *n* : utilización *f*
utilize [ˈjuːtəlˌaɪz] *vt* -**lized; -lizing** : utilizar, hacer uso de
utmost¹ [ˈʌtˌmoːst] *adj* **1** FARTHEST : extremo, más lejano **2** GREATEST : sumo, mayor ⟨of the utmost importance : de suma importancia⟩
utmost² *n* : lo más posible ⟨to the utmost : al máximo⟩
utopia [jʊˈtoːpiə] *n* : utopía *f*
utopian [jʊˈtoːpiən] *adj* : utópico
utter¹ [ˈʌtər] *vt* : decir, articular, pronunciar (palabras)
utter² *adj* : absoluto — **utterly** *adv*
utterance [ˈʌtərənts] *n* : declaración *f*, articulación *f*

V

v [ˈviː] *n, pl* **v's** *or* **vs** [ˈviːz] : vigésima segunda letra del alfabeto inglés
vacancy [ˈveɪkəntsi] *n, pl* -**cies** **1** EMPTINESS : vacío *m*, vacuidad *f* **2** : vacante *f*, puesto *m* vacante ⟨to fill a vacancy

: ocupar un puesto⟩ **3** : habitación *f* libre (en un hotel) ⟨no vacancies : completo⟩
vacant [ˈveɪkənt] *adj* **1** EMPTY : libre, desocupado (dícese de los edificios,

etc.) **2** : vacante (dícese de los puestos) **3** BLANK : vacío, ausente ⟨a vacant stare : una mirada ausente⟩
vacate [ˈveɪˌkeɪt] vt -**cated; -cating** : desalojar, desocupar
vacation¹ [veɪˈkeɪʃən, və-] vi : pasar las vacaciones, vacacionar Mex
vacation² n : vacaciones fpl ⟨to be on vacation : estar de vacaciones⟩
vacationer [veɪˈkeɪʃənər, və-] n : turista mf, veraneante mf, vacacionista mf CA, Mex
vaccinate [ˈvæksəˌneɪt] vt -**nated; -nating** : vacunar
vaccination [ˌvæksəˈneɪʃən] n : vacunación f
vaccine [vækˈsiːn, ˈvækˌ-] n : vacuna f
vacillate [ˈvæsəˌleɪt] vi -**lated; -lating 1** HESITATE : vacilar **2** SWAY : oscilar
vacillation [ˌvæsəˈleɪʃən] n : indecisión f, vacilación f
vacuous [ˈvækjuəs] adj **1** EMPTY : vacío **2** INANE : vacuo, necio, estúpido
vacuum¹ [ˈvæˌkjuːm, -kjəm] vt : limpiar con aspiradora, pasar la aspiradora por
vacuum² n, pl **vacuums** or **vacua** [ˈvækjuə] : vacío m
vacuum cleaner n : aspiradora f
vagabond¹ [ˈvægəˌbɑnd] adj : vagabundo
vagabond² n : vagabundo m, -da f
vagary [ˈveɪgəri, vəˈgɛri] n, pl -**ries** : capricho m
vagina [vəˈdʒaɪnə] n, pl -**nae** [-ˌniː, -ˌnaɪ] or -**nas** : vagina f
vagrancy [ˈveɪgrəntsi] n, pl -**cies** : vagancia f
vagrant¹ [ˈveɪgrənt] adj : vagabundo
vagrant² n : vagabundo m, -da f
vague [ˈveɪg] adj **vaguer; -est 1** IMPRECISE : vago, impreciso ⟨a vague feeling : una sensación indefinida⟩ ⟨I haven't the vaguest idea : no tengo la más remota idea⟩ **2** UNCLEAR : borroso, poco claro ⟨a vague outline : un perfil indistinto⟩ **3** ABSENTMINDED : distraído
vaguely [ˈveɪgli] adv : vagamente, de manera imprecisa
vagueness [ˈveɪgnəs] n : vaguedad f, imprecisión f
vain [ˈveɪn] adj **1** WORTHLESS : vano **2** FUTILE : vano, inútil ⟨in vain : en vano⟩ **3** CONCEITED : vanidoso, presumido
vainly [ˈveɪnli] adv : en vano, vanamente, inútilmente
valance [ˈvælənts, ˈveɪ-] n **1** FLOUNCE : volante m (de una cama, etc.) **2** : galería f de cortina (sobre una ventana)
vale [ˈveɪl] n : valle m
valedictorian [ˌvælədɪkˈtoriən] n : estudiante mf que pronuncia el discurso de despedida en ceremonia de graduación
valedictory [ˌvæləˈdɪktəri] adj : de despedida
valentine [ˈvælənˌtaɪn] n : tarjeta f que se manda el Día de los Enamorados (el 14 de febrero)

Valentine's Day n : Día m de los Enamorados
valet [ˈvæˌleɪ, væˈleɪ, ˈvælət] n : ayuda m de cámara
valiant [ˈvæljənt] adj : valiente, valeroso
valiantly [ˈvæljəntli] adv : con valor, valientemente
valid [ˈvæləd] adj : válido
validate [ˈvæləˌdeɪt] vt -**dated; -dating** : validar, dar validez a
validity [vəˈlɪdəti, væ-] n : validez f
valise [vəˈliːs] n : maleta f (de mano)
valley [ˈvæli] n, pl -**leys** : valle m
valor [ˈvælər] n : valor m, valentía f
valorous [ˈvælərəs] adj : valeroso, valiente
valuable¹ [ˈvæljuəbəl, ˈvæljəbəl] adj **1** EXPENSIVE : valioso, de valor **2** WORTHWHILE : valioso, apreciable
valuable² n : objeto m de valor
valuation [ˌvæljuˈeɪʃən] n **1** APPRAISAL : valoración f, tasación f **2** VALUE : valuación f
value¹ [ˈvælˌjuː] vt -**ued; -uing 1** APPRAISE : valorar, avaluar, tasar **2** APPRECIATE : valorar, apreciar
value² n **1** : valor m ⟨of little value : de poco valor⟩ ⟨to be a good value : estar bien de precio, tener buen precio⟩ ⟨at face value : en su sentido literal⟩ **2** **values** npl : valores mpl (morales), principios mpl
valueless [ˈvæljuːləs] adj : sin valor
valve [ˈvælv] n : válvula f
vampire [ˈvæmˌpaɪr] n **1** : vampiro m **2** or **vampire bat** : vampiro m
van¹ [ˈvæn] → vanguard
van² n : furgoneta f, camioneta f
vanadium [vəˈneɪdiəm] n : vanadio m
vandal [ˈvændəl] n : vándalo m
vandalism [ˈvændəlˌɪzəm] n : vandalismo m
vandalize [ˈvændəlˌaɪz] vt : destrozar, destruir, estropear
vane [ˈveɪn] n or **weather vane** : veleta f
vanguard [ˈvænˌgɑrd] n : vanguardia f
vanilla [vəˈnɪlə, -ˈnɛ-] n : vainilla f
vanish [ˈvænɪʃ] vi : desaparecer, disiparse, desvanecerse
vanity [ˈvænəti] n, pl -**ties 1** : vanidad f **2** or **vanity table** : tocador m
vanquish [ˈvæŋkwɪʃ, ˈvæn-] vt : vencer, conquistar
vantage point [ˈvæntɪdʒ] n : posición f ventajosa
vapid [ˈvæpəd, ˈveɪ-] adj : insípido, insulso
vapor [ˈveɪpər] n : vapor m
vaporize [ˈveɪpəˌraɪz] v -**rized; -rizing** vt : vaporizar — vi : vaporizarse, evaporarse
vaporizer [ˈveɪpəˌraɪzər] n : vaporizador m
variability [ˌveriəˈbɪləti] n, pl -**ties** : variabilidad f
variable¹ [ˈvɛriəbəl] adj : variable ⟨variable cloudiness : nubosidad variable⟩

variable² *n* : variable *f*, factor *m*
variance ['vɛriənts] *n* **1** DISCREPANCY
: varianza *f*, discrepancia *f* **2** DIS-
AGREEMENT : desacuerdo *m* ⟨at variance with : en desacuerdo con⟩
variant¹ ['vɛriənt] *adj* : variante, divergente
variant² *n* : variante *f*
variation [ˌvɛri'eɪʃən] *n* : variación *f*,
diferencias *fpl*
varicose ['værəˌkoːs] *adj* : varicoso
varicose veins *npl* : varices *fpl*, várices
fpl
varied ['vɛrid] *adj* : variado, dispar,
diferente
variegated ['vɛriəˌgeɪţd] *adj* : abigarrado, multicolor
variety [və'raɪəţi] *n, pl* -**ties** **1** DIVERSI-
TY : diversidad *f*, variedad *f* **2** ASSORT-
MENT : surtido *m* ⟨for a variety of reasons : por diversas razones⟩ **3** SORT
: clase *f* **4** BREED : variedad *f* (de plantas)
various ['vɛriəs] *adj* : varios, diversos
varnish¹ ['varnɪʃ] *vt* : barnizar
varnish² *n* : barniz *f*
varsity ['varsəţi] *n, pl* -**ties** : equipo *m*
universitario
vary ['vɛri] *v* **varied; varying** *vt* : variar,
diversificar — *vi* **1** CHANGE : variar,
cambiar **2** DEVIATE : desviarse
vascular ['væskjələr] *adj* : vascular
vase ['veɪs, 'veɪz, 'vaz] *n* : jarrón *m*, florero *m*
vassal ['væsəl] *n* : vasallo *m*, -lla *f*
vast ['væst] *adj* : inmenso, enorme, vasto
vastly ['væstli] *adv* : enormemente
vastness ['væstnəs] *n* : vastedad *f*, inmensidad *f*
vat ['væt] *n* : cuba *f*, tina *f*
vaudeville ['vɔdvəl, -ˌvɪl; 'vɔdəˌvɪl]
: vodevil *m*
vault¹ ['vɔlt] *vi* LEAP : saltar
vault² *n* **1** JUMP : salto *m* ⟨pole vault
: salto de pértiga, salto con garrocha⟩
2 DOME : bóveda *f* **3** : bodega *f* (para
vino), bóveda *f* de seguridad (de un
banco) **4** CRYPT : cripta *f*
vaulted ['vɔltəd] *adj* : abovedado
vaunted ['vɔntəd] *adj* : cacareado,
alardeado ⟨a much vaunted wine : un
vino muy alardeado⟩
VCR [ˌviːˌsiːˈar] *n* : video *m*, videocasetera *f*
veal ['viːl] *n* : ternera *f*, carne *f* de ternera
veer ['vɪr] *vi* : virar (dícese de un barco),
girar (dícese de un coche), torcer
(dícese de un camino)
vegetable¹ ['vɛʤtəbəl, 'vɛʤəţə-] *adj*
: vegetal
vegetable² *n* **1** : vegetal *m* ⟨the vegetable kingdom : el reino vegetal⟩ **2**
: verdura *f*, hortaliza *f* (para comer)
vegetarian [ˌvɛʤə'tɛriən] *n* : vegetariano *mf*
vegetarianism [ˌvɛʤə'tɛriəˌnizəm] *n*
: vegetarianismo *m*

vegetate ['vɛʤəˌteɪt] *vi* -**tated; -tating**
: vegetar
vegetation [ˌvɛʤə'teɪʃən] *n* : vegetación
f
vegetative ['vɛʤəˌteɪţɪv] *adj* : vegetativo
vehemence ['viːəmənts] *n* : intensidad *f*,
vehemencia *f*
vehement ['viːəmənt] *adj* : intenso, vehemente
vehemently ['viːəməntli] *adv* : vehe-
mentemente, con vehemencia
vehicle ['viːkəl, 'viːˌhɪkəl] *n* **1** *or motor*
vehicle : vehículo *m* **2** MEDIUM : vehículo *m*, medio *m*
vehicular [vi'hɪkjələr, və-] *adj* : vehicular ⟨vehicular homicide : muerte por
atropello⟩
veil¹ ['veɪl] *vt* **1** CONCEAL : velar, disimular **2** : cubrir con un velo ⟨to veil one's
face : cubrirse con un velo⟩
veil² *n* : velo *m* ⟨bridal veil : velo de
novia⟩
vein ['veɪn] *n* **1** : vena *f* (en anatomía,
botánica, etc.) **2** LODE : veta *f*, vena *f*,
filón *m* **3** STYLE : vena *f* ⟨in a humorous vein : en vena humorística⟩
veined ['veɪnd] *adj* : veteado (dícese del
queso, de los minerales, etc.)
velocity [və'lasəţi] *n, pl* -**ties** : velocidad
f
velour [və'lʊr] *or* **velours** [-'lʊrz] *n*
: velour *m*
velvet¹ ['vɛlvət] *adj* **1** : de terciopelo **2**
→ **velvety**
velvet² *n* : terciopelo *m*
velvety ['vɛlvəţi] *adj* : aterciopelado
venal ['viːnəl] *adj* : venal, sobornable
vend ['vɛnd] *vt* : vender
vendetta [vɛn'dɛţə] *n* : vendetta *f*
vendor ['vɛndər] *n* : vendedor *m*, -dora
f; puestero *m*, -ra *f*
veneer¹ [və'nɪr] *vt* : enchapar, chapar
veneer² *n* **1** : enchapado *m*, chapa *f* **2**
APPEARANCE : apariencia *f*, barniz *m*
⟨a veneer of culture : un barniz de cul-
tura⟩
venerable ['vɛnərəbəl] *adj* : venerable
venerate ['vɛnəˌreɪt] *vt* -**ated; -ating**
: venerar
veneration [ˌvɛnə'reɪʃən] *n* : veneración
f
venereal disease [və'nɪriəl] *n* : enfermedad *f* venérea
venetian blind [və'niːʃən] *n* : persiana *f*
veneciana
Venezuelan [ˌvɛnə'zweɪlən, -zʊ'eɪ-] *n*
: venezolano *m*, -na *f* — **Venezuelan**
adj
vengeance ['vɛnʤənts] *n* : venganza *f*
⟨to take vengeance on : vengarse de⟩
vengeful ['vɛnʤfəl] *adj* : vengativo
venial ['viːniəl] *adj* : venial ⟨a venial sin
: un pecado venial⟩
venison ['vɛnəsən, -zən] *n* : venado *m*,
carne *f* de venado
venom ['vɛnəm] *n* **1** : veneno *m* **2** MAL-
ICE : veneno *m*, malevolencia *f*

venomous [ˈvɛnəməs] *adj* : venenoso
vent¹ [ˈvɛnt] *vt* : desahogar, dar salida a ⟨to vent one's feelings : desahogarse⟩
vent² *n* **1** OPENING : abertura *f* (de escape), orificio *m* **2** *or* **air vent** : respiradero *m*, rejilla *f* de ventilación **3** OUTLET : desahogo *m* ⟨to give vent to one's anger : desahogar la ira⟩
ventilate [ˈvɛntəlˌeɪt] *vt* **-lated; -lating** : ventilar
ventilation [ˌvɛntəlˈeɪʃən] *n* : ventilación *f*
ventilator [ˈvɛntəlˌeɪtər] *n* : ventilador *m*
ventricle [ˈvɛntrɪkəl] *n* : ventrículo *m*
ventriloquism [vɛnˈtrɪləˌkwɪzəm] *n* : ventriloquia *f*
ventriloquist [vɛnˈtrɪləˌkwɪst] *n* : ventrílocuo *m*, -cua *f*
venture¹ [ˈvɛnʧər] *v* **-tured; -turing** *vt* **1** RISK : arriesgar **2** OFFER : aventurar ⟨to venture an opinion : aventurar una opinión⟩ — *vi* : arriesgarse, atreverse, aventurarse
venture² *n* **1** UNDERTAKING : empresa *f* **2** GAMBLE, RISK : aventura *f*, riesgo *m*
venturesome [ˈvɛnʧərsəm] *adj* **1** ADVENTUROUS : audaz, atrevido **2** RISKY : arriesgado
venue [ˈvɛnˌju:] *n* **1** PLACE : lugar *m* **2** : jurisdicción *f* (en derecho)
Venus [ˈviːnəs] *n* : Venus *m*
veracity [vəˈræsəti] *n, pl* **-ties** : veracidad *f*
veranda *or* **verandah** [vəˈrændə] *n* : terraza *f*, veranda *f*
verb [ˈvərb] *n* : verbo *m*
verbal [ˈvərbəl] *adj* : verbal
verbalize [ˈvərbəˌlaɪz] *vt* **-ized; -izing** : expresar con palabras, verbalizar
verbally [ˈvərbəli] *adv* : verbalmente, de palabra
verbatim¹ [vərˈbeɪtəm] *adv* : palabra por palabra, textualmente
verbatim² *adj* : literal, textual
verbose [vərˈboːs] *adj* : verboso, prolijo
verdant [ˈvərdənt] *adj* : verde, verdeante
verdict [ˈvərdɪkt] *n* **1** : veredicto *m* (de un jurado) **2** JUDGMENT, OPINION : juicio *m*, opinión *f*
verge¹ [ˈvərʤ] *vi* **verged; verging** : estar al borde, rayar ⟨it verges on madness : raya en la locura⟩
verge² *n* **1** EDGE : borde *m* **2 to be on the verge of** : estar a pique de, estar al borde de, estar a punto de
verification [ˌvɛrəfəˈkeɪʃən] *n* : verificación *f*
verify [ˈvɛrəˌfaɪ] *vt* **-fied; -fying** : verificar, comprobar, confirmar
veritable [ˈvɛrətəbəl] *adj* : verdadero — **veritably** *adv*
vermicelli [ˌvərməˈʧɛli, -ˈsɛli] *n* : fideos *mpl* finos
vermin [ˈvərmən] *ns & pl* : alimañas *fpl*, bichos *mpl*, sabandijas *fpl*
vermouth [vərˈmuːth] *n* : vermut *m*
vernacular¹ [vərˈnækjələr] *adj* : vernáculo

vernacular² *n* : lengua *f* vernácula
versatile [ˈvərsəṭəl] *adj* : versátil
versatility [ˌvərsəˈtɪləṭi] *n* : versatilidad *f*
verse [ˈvərs] *n* **1** LINE, STANZA : verso *m*, estrofa *f* **2** POETRY : poesía *f* **3** : versículo *m* (en la Biblia)
versed [ˈvərst] *adj* : versado ⟨to be well versed in : ser muy versado en⟩
version [ˈvərʒən] *n* : versión *f*
versus [ˈvərsəs] *prep* : versus
vertebra [ˈvərtəbrə] *n, pl* **-brae** [-ˌbreɪ, -ˌbriː] *or* **-bras** : vértebra *f*
vertebrate¹ [ˈvərtəbrət, -ˌbreɪt] *adj* : vertebrado
vertebrate² *n* : vertebrado *m*
vertex [ˈvərˌtɛks] *n, pl* **vertices** [ˈvərtəˌsiːz] **1** : vértice *m* (en matemáticas y anatomía) **2** SUMMIT, TOP : ápice *m*, cumbre *f*, cima *f*
vertical¹ [ˈvərtɪkəl] *adj* : vertical — **vertically** *adv*
vertical² *n* : vertical *f*
vertigo [ˈvərtɪˌgoː] *n, pl* **-goes** *or* **-gos** : vértigo *m*
verve [ˈvərv] *n* : brío *m*
very¹ [ˈvɛri] *adv* **1** EXTREMELY : muy, sumamente ⟨very few : muy pocos⟩ ⟨I am very sorry : lo siento mucho⟩ **2** (*used for emphasis*) ⟨at the very least : por lo menos, como mínimo⟩ ⟨the very same dress : el mismo vestido⟩
very² *adj* **verier; -est 1** EXACT, PRECISE : mismo, exacto ⟨at that very moment : en ese mismo momento⟩ ⟨it's the very thing : es justo lo que hacía falta⟩ **2** BARE, MERE : solo, mero ⟨the very thought of it : sólo pensarlo⟩ **3** EXTREME : extremo, de todo ⟨at the very top : arriba de todo⟩
vesicle [ˈvɛsɪkəl] *n* : vesícula *f*
vespers [ˈvɛspərz] *npl* : vísperas *fpl*
vessel [ˈvɛsəl] *n* **1** CONTAINER : vasija *f*, recipiente *m* **2** BOAT, CRAFT : nave *f*, barco *m*, buque *m* **3** : vaso *m* ⟨blood vessel : vaso sanguíneo⟩
vest¹ [ˈvɛst] *vt* **1** CONFER : conferir ⟨to vest authority in : conferirle la autoridad a⟩ **2** CLOTHE : vestir
vest² *n* **1** : chaleco *m* **2** UNDERSHIRT : camiseta *f*
vestibule [ˈvɛstəˌbjuːl] *n* : vestíbulo *m*
vestige [ˈvɛstɪʤ] *n* : vestigio *m*, rastro *m*
vestment [ˈvɛstmənt] *n* : vestidura *f*
vestry [ˈvɛstri] *n, pl* **-tries** : sacristía *f*
vet [ˈvɛt] *n* **1** → **veterinarian 2** → **veteran²**
veteran¹ [ˈvɛtərən, ˈvɛtrən] *adj* : veterano
veteran² *n* : veterano *m*, -na *f*
Veterans Day *n* : día *m* del Armisticio (celebrado el 11 de noviembre en los Estados Unidos)
veterinarian [ˌvɛtərəˈnɛriən, ˌvɛtəˈnɛr-] *n* : veterinario *m*, -ria *f*
veterinary [ˈvɛtərəˌnɛri] *adj* : veterinario
veto¹ [ˈviːˌtoː] *vt* **1** FORBID : prohibir **2** : vetar ⟨to veto a bill : vetar un proyecto de ley⟩

veto² *n, pl* **-toes** **1** : veto *m* ⟨the power of veto : el derecho de veto⟩ **2** BAN : veto *m*, prohibición *f*

vex [ˈvɛks] *vt* : contrariar, molestar, irritar

vexation [vɛkˈseɪʃən] *n* : contrariedad *f*, irritación *f*

via [ˈvaɪə, ˈviːə] *prep* : por, vía

viability [ˌvaɪəˈbɪləti] *n* : viabilidad *f*

viable [ˈvaɪəbəl] *adj* : viable

viaduct [ˈvaɪəˌdʌkt] *n* : viaducto *m*

vial [ˈvaɪəl] *n* : frasco *m*

vibrant [ˈvaɪbrənt] *adj* **1** LIVELY : vibrante, animado, dinámico **2** BRIGHT : fuerte, vivo (dícese de los colores)

vibrate [ˈvaɪˌbreɪt] *vi* **-brated; -brating 1** OSCILLATE : vibrar, oscilar **2** THRILL : bullir ⟨to vibrate with excitement : bullir de emoción⟩

vibration [vaɪˈbreɪʃən] *n* : vibración *f*

vicar [ˈvɪkər] *n* : vicario *m*, -ria *f*

vicarious [vaɪˈkæriːəs, vɪ-] *adj* : indirecto — **vicariously** *adv*

vice [ˈvaɪs] *n* : vicio *m*

vice admiral *n* : vicealmirante *mf*

vice president *n* : vicepresidente *m*, -ta *f*

viceroy [ˈvaɪsˌrɔɪ] *n* : virrey *m*, -rreina *f*

vice versa [ˌvaɪsɪˈvərsə, ˌvaɪsˈvər-] *adv* : viceversa

vicinity [vəˈsɪnəti] *n, pl* **-ties 1** NEIGHBORHOOD : vecindad *f*, inmediaciones *fpl* **2** NEARNESS : proximidad *f*

vicious [ˈvɪʃəs] *adj* **1** DEPRAVED : depravado, malo **2** SAVAGE : malo, fiero, salvaje ⟨a vicious dog : un perro feroz⟩ **3** MALICIOUS : malicioso

viciously [ˈvɪʃəsli] *adv* : con saña, brutalmente

viciousness [ˈvɪʃəsnəs] *n* : brutalidad *f*, ferocidad *f* (de un animal), malevolencia *f* (de un comentario, etc.)

vicissitudes [vəˈsɪsəˌtuːdz, vaɪ-, -ˌtjuːdz] *npl* : vicisitudes *fpl*

victim [ˈvɪktəm] *n* : víctima *f*

victimize [ˈvɪktəˌmaɪz] *vt* **-mized; -mizing** : tomar como víctima, perseguir, victimizar *Arg, Mex*

victor [ˈvɪktər] *n* : vencedor *m*, -dora *f*

Victorian [vɪkˈtoːriən] *adj* : victoriano

victorious [vɪkˈtoːriəs] *adj* : victorioso — **victoriously** *adv*

victory [ˈvɪktəri] *n, pl* **-ries** : victoria *f*, triunfo *m*

victuals [ˈvɪtəlz] *npl* : víveres *mpl*, provisiones *fpl*

video¹ [ˈvɪdiˌoː] *adj* : de video ⟨video recording : grabación de video⟩

video² *n* **1** : video *m* (medio o grabación) **2** → **videotape²**

video camera *n* : videocámara *f*

videocassette [ˌvɪdiokəˈsɛt] *n* : videocasete *m*, videocassette *m*

videocassette recorder → **VCR**

video game *n* : videojuego *m*, juego *m* de video

videotape¹ [ˈvɪdioˌteɪp] *vt* **-taped; -taping** : grabar en video, videograbar

videotape² *n* : videocinta *f*

vie [ˈvaɪ] *vi* **vied; vying** [ˈvaɪɪŋ] : competir, rivalizar

Vietnamese [viˌɛtnəˈmiːz, -ˈmiːs] *n* **1** : vietnamita *mf* **2** : vietnamita *m* (idioma) — **Vietnamese** *adj*

view¹ [ˈvjuː] *vt* **1** OBSERVE : mirar, ver, observar **2** CONSIDER : considerar, contemplar

view² *n* **1** SIGHT : vista *f* ⟨to come into view : aparecer⟩ **2** ATTITUDE, OPINION : opinión *f*, parecer *m*, actitud *f* ⟨in my view : en mi opinión⟩ **3** SCENE : vista *f*, panorama *f* **4** INTENTION : idea *f*, vista *f* ⟨with a view to : con vistas a, con la idea de⟩ **5 in view of** : dado que, en vista de (que)

viewer [ˈvjuːər] *n or* **television viewer** : telespectador *m*, -dora *f*; televidente *mf*

viewpoint [ˈvjuːˌpɔɪnt] *n* : punto *m* de vista

vigil [ˈvɪdʒəl] *n* **1** : vigilia *f*, vela *f* **2 to keep vigil** : velar

vigilance [ˈvɪdʒələnts] *n* : vigilancia *f*

vigilant [ˈvɪdʒələnt] *adj* : vigilante

vigilante [ˌvɪdʒəˈlænˌtiː] *n* : integrante *mf* de un comité de vigilancia (que actúa como policía)

vigilantly [ˈvɪdʒələntli] *adv* : con vigilancia

vigor [ˈvɪgər] *n* : vigor *m*, energía *f*, fuerza *f*

vigorous [ˈvɪgərəs] *adj* : vigoroso, enérgico — **vigorously** *adv*

Viking [ˈvaɪkɪŋ] *n* : vikingo *m*, -ga *f*

vile [ˈvaɪl] *adj* **viler; vilest 1** WICKED : vil, infame **2** REVOLTING : asqueroso, repugnante **3** TERRIBLE : horrible, atroz ⟨vile weather : tiempo horrible⟩ ⟨to be in a vile mood : estar de un humor de perros⟩

vilify [ˈvɪləˌfaɪ] *vt* **-fied; -fying** : vilipendiar, denigrar, difamar

villa [ˈvɪlə] *n* : casa *f* de campo, quinta *f*

village [ˈvɪlɪdʒ] *n* : pueblo *m* (grande), aldea *f* (pequeña)

villager [ˈvɪlɪdʒər] *n* : vecino *m*, -na *f* (de un pueblo); aldeano *m*, -na *f* (de una aldea)

villain [ˈvɪlən] *n* : villano *m*, -na *f*; malo *m*, -la *f* (en ficción, películas, etc.)

villainess [ˈvɪlənɪs, -nəs] *n* : villana *f*

villainous [ˈvɪlənəs] *adj* : infame, malvado

villainy [ˈvɪləni] *n, pl* **-lainies** : vileza *f*, maldad *f*

vim [ˈvɪm] *n* : brío *m*, vigor *m*, energía *f*

vindicate [ˈvɪndəˌkeɪt] *vt* **-cated; -cating 1** EXONERATE : vindicar, disculpar **2** JUSTIFY : justificar

vindication [ˌvɪndəˈkeɪʃən] *n* : vindicación *f*, justificación *f*

vindictive [vɪnˈdɪktɪv] *adj* : vengativo

vine [ˈvaɪn] *n* **1** GRAPEVINE : vid *f*, parra *f* **2** : planta *f* trepadora, enredadera *f*

vinegar [ˈvɪnɪgər] *n* : vinagre *m*

vinegary [ˈvɪnɪɡəri] *adj* : avinagrado
vineyard [ˈvɪnjərd] *n* : viña *f*, viñedo *m*
vintage¹ [ˈvɪntɪʤ] *adj* **1** : añejo (dícese de un vino) **2** CLASSIC : clásico, de época
vintage² *n* **1** : cosecha *f* ⟨the 1947 vintage : la cosecha de 1947⟩ **2** ERA : época *f*, era *f* ⟨slang of recent vintage : argot de la época reciente⟩
vinyl [ˈvaɪnəl] *n* : vinilo
viola [viːˈoːlə] *n* : viola *f*
violate [ˈvaɪəˌleɪt] *vt* **-lated; -lating 1** BREAK : infringir, violar, quebrantar ⟨to violate the rules : violar las reglas⟩ **2** RAPE : violar **3** DESECRATE : profanar
violation [ˌvaɪəˈleɪʃən] *n* **1** : violación *f*, infracción *f* (de una ley) **2** DESECRATION : profanación *f*
violence [ˈvaɪlənts, ˈvaɪə-] *n* : violencia *f*
violent [ˈvaɪlənt, ˈvaɪə-] *adj* : violento
violently [ˈvaɪləntli, ˈvaɪə-] *adv* : violentamente, con violencia
violet [ˈvaɪlət, ˈvaɪə-] *n* : violeta *f*
violin [ˌvaɪəˈlɪn] *n* : violín *m*
violinist [ˌvaɪəˈlɪnɪst] *n* : violinista *mf*
violoncello [ˌvaɪələnˈtʃeloː, ˌviː-] → **cello**
VIP [ˌviːˌaɪˈpiː] *n, pl* **VIPs** [-ˈpiːz] : VIP *mf*, persona *f* de categoría
viper [ˈvaɪpər] *n* : víbora *f*
viral [ˈvaɪrəl] *adj* : viral, vírico ⟨viral pneumonia : pulmonía viral⟩
virgin¹ [ˈvərdʒən] *adj* **1** CHASTE : virginal ⟨the virgin birth : el alumbramiento virginal⟩ **2** : virgen, intacto ⟨a virgin forest : una selva virgen⟩ ⟨virgin wool : lana virgen⟩
virgin² *n* : virgen *mf*
virginity [vərˈdʒɪnəti] *n* : virginidad *f*
Virgo [ˈvərˌgoː, ˈvɪr-] *n* : Virgo *mf*
virile [ˈvɪrəl, -ˌaɪl] *adj* : viril, varonil
virility [vəˈrɪləti] *n* : virilidad *f*
virtual [ˈvərtʃuəl] *adj* : virtual ⟨a virtual dictator : un virtual dictador⟩ ⟨virtual reality : realidad virtual⟩
virtually [ˈvərtʃuəli, ˈvərtʃəli] *adv* : en realidad, de hecho, casi
virtue [ˈvərˌtʃuː] *n* **1** : virtud *f* **2 by virtue of** : en virtud de, debido a
virtuosity [ˌvərtʃuˈasəti] *n, pl* **-ties** : virtuosismo *m*
virtuoso [ˌvərtʃuˈoːsoː, -zoː] *n, pl* **-sos** *or* **-si** [-ˌsiː, -ˌziː] : virtuoso *m*, -sa *f*
virtuous [ˈvərtʃuəs] *adj* : virtuoso, bueno — **virtuously** *adv*
virulence [ˈvɪrələnts, ˈvɪrjə-] *n* : virulencia *f*
virulent [ˈvɪrələnt, ˈvɪrjə-] *adj* : virulento
virus [ˈvaɪrəs] *n* : virus *m*
visa [ˈviːzə, -sə] *n* : visa *f*
vis-à-vis [ˌviːzəˈviː, -sə-] *prep* : con relación a, con respecto a
viscera [ˈvɪsərə] *npl* : vísceras *fpl*
visceral [ˈvɪsərəl] *adj* : visceral
viscosity [vɪsˈkasəti] *n, pl* **-ties** : viscosidad *f*
viscount [ˈvaɪˌkæʊnt] *n* : vizconde *m*

viscountess [ˈvaɪˌkæʊntɪs] *n* : vizcondesa *f*
viscous [ˈvɪskəs] *adj* : viscoso
vise [ˈvaɪs] *n* : torno *m* de banco, tornillo *m* de banco
visibility [ˌvɪzəˈbɪləti] *n, pl* **-ties** : visibilidad *f*
visible [ˈvɪzəbəl] *adj* **1** : visible ⟨the visible stars : las estrellas visibles⟩ **2** OBVIOUS : evidente, patente
visibly [ˈvɪzəbli] *adv* : visiblemente
vision [ˈvɪʒən] *n* **1** EYESIGHT : vista *f*, visión *f* **2** APPARITION : visión *f*, aparición *f* **3** FORESIGHT : visión *f* (del futuro), previsión *f* **4** IMAGE : imagen *f* ⟨she had visions of a disaster : se imaginaba un desastre⟩
visionary¹ [ˈvɪʒəˌneri] *adj* **1** FARSIGHTED : visionario, con visión de futuro **2** UTOPIAN : utópico, poco realista
visionary² *n, pl* **-ries** : visionario *m*, -ria *f*
visit¹ [ˈvɪzət] *vt* **1** : visitar, ir a ver **2** AFFLICT : azotar, afligir ⟨visited by troubles : afligido con problemas⟩ — *vi* : hacer (una) visita
visit² *n* : visita *f*
visitor [ˈvɪzəʈ̣ər] *n* : visitante *mf* (a una ciudad, etc.), visita *f* (a una casa)
visor [ˈvaɪzər] *n* : visera *f*
vista [ˈvɪstə] *n* : vista *f*
visual [ˈvɪʒuəl] *adj* : visual ⟨the visual arts : las artes visuales⟩ — **visually** *adv*
visualize [ˈvɪʒuəˌlaɪz] *vt* **-ized; -izing** : visualizar, imaginarse, hacerse una idea de — **visualization** [ˌvɪʒəwələˈzeɪʃən] *n*
vital [ˈvaɪʈ̣əl] *adj* **1** : vital ⟨vital organs : órganos vitales⟩ **2** CRUCIAL : esencial, crucial, decisivo ⟨of vital importance : de suma importancia⟩ **3** LIVELY : enérgico, lleno de vida, vital
vitality [vaɪˈtæləti] *n, pl* **-ties** : vitalidad *f*, energía *f*
vitally [ˈvaɪʈ̣əli] *adv* : sumamente
vital statistics *npl* : estadísticas *fpl* demográficas
vitamin [ˈvaɪʈ̣əmən] *n* : vitamina *f* ⟨vitamin deficiency : carencia vitamínica⟩
vitreous [ˈvɪtriəs] *adj* : vítreo
vitriolic [ˌvɪtriˈalɪk] *adj* : mordaz, virulento
vituperation [vaɪˌtuːpəˈreɪʃən, -ˌtjuː-] *n* : vituperio *m*
vivacious [vəˈveɪʃəs, vaɪ-] *adj* : vivaz, animado, lleno de vida
vivaciously [vəˈveɪʃəsli, vaɪ-] *adv* : con vivacidad, animadamente
vivacity [vəˈvæsəti, vaɪ-] *n* : vivacidad *f*
vivid [ˈvɪvəd] *adj* **1** LIVELY : lleno de vitalidad **2** BRILLIANT : vivo, intenso ⟨vivid colors : colores vivos⟩ **3** INTENSE, SHARP : vívido, gráfico ⟨a vivid dream : un sueño vívido⟩
vividly [ˈvɪvədli] *adv* **1** BRIGHTLY : con colores vivos **2** SHARPLY : vívidamente
vividness [ˈvɪvədnəs] *n* **1** BRIGHTNESS : intensidad *f*, viveza *f* **2** SHARPNESS : lo gráfico, nitidez *f*

vivisection [ˌvɪvə'sɛkʃən, 'vɪvəˌ-] *n*
: vivisección *f*
vixen ['vɪksən] *n* : zorra *f*, raposa *f*
vocabulary [vo:'kæbjəˌlɛri] *n, pl* **-laries**
1 : vocabulario *m* 2 LEXICON : léxico
m
vocal ['vo:kəl] *adj* 1 : vocal 2 LOUD,
OUTSPOKEN : ruidoso, muy franco
vocal cords *npl* : cuerdas *fpl* vocales
vocalist ['vo:kəlɪst] *n* : cantante *mf*, vocalista *mf*
vocalize ['vo:kəlˌaɪz] *vt* **-ized; -izing** : vocalizar
vocation [vo'keɪʃən] *n* : vocación *f* ⟨to
have a vocation for : tener vocación
de⟩
vocational [vo'keɪʃənəl] *adj* : profesional ⟨vocational guidance : orientación
profesional⟩
vociferous [vo'sɪfərəs] *adj* : ruidoso, vociferante
vodka ['vɑdkə] *n* : vodka *m*
vogue ['vo:g] *n* : moda *f*, boga *f* ⟨to
be in vogue : estar de moda, estar en
boga⟩
voice[1] ['vɔɪs] *vt* **voiced; voicing** : expresar
voice[2] *n* 1 : voz *f* ⟨in a low voice : en
voz baja⟩ ⟨to lose one's voice
: quedarse sin voz⟩ ⟨the voice of the
people : la voz del pueblo⟩ 2 **to make
one's voice heard** : hacerse oír
voice box → **larynx**
voiced ['vɔɪst] *adj* : sonoro
voice mail *n* : correo *m* de voz
void[1] ['vɔɪd] *vt* : anular, invalidar ⟨to
void a contract : anular un contrato⟩
void[2] *adj* 1 EMPTY : vacío, desprovisto
⟨void of content : desprovisto de con-
tenido⟩ 2 INVALID : inválido, nulo
void[3] *n* : vacío *m*
volatile ['vɑlətəl] *adj* : volátil, inestable
volatility [ˌvɑlə'tɪləti] *n* : volatilidad *f*, inestabilidad *f*
volcanic [vɑl'kænɪk] *adj* : volcánico
volcano [vɑl'keɪˌno:] *n, pl* **-noes** *or* **-nos**
: volcán *m*
vole ['vo:l] *n* : campañol *m*
volition [vo'lɪʃən] *n* : volición *f*, voluntad *f* ⟨of one's own volition : por voluntad propia⟩
volley ['vɑli] *n, pl* **-leys** 1 : descarga *f*
(de tiros) 2 : torrente *m*, lluvia *f* (de insultos, etc.) 3 : salva *f* (de aplausos) 4
: volea *f* (en deportes)
volleyball ['vɑliˌbɔl] *n* : voleibol *m*
volt ['vo:lt] *n* : voltio *m*
voltage ['vo:ltɪdʒ] *n* : voltaje *m*
volubility [ˌvɑljə'bɪləti] *n* : locuacidad *f*
voluble ['vɑljəbəl] *adj* : locuaz
volume ['vɑljəm, -ˌju:m] *n* 1 BOOK : volumen *m*, tomo *m* 2 SPACE : capacidad
f, volumen *m* (en física) 3 AMOUNT

: cantidad *f*, volumen *m* 4 LOUDNESS
: volumen *m*
voluminous [və'lu:mənəs] *adj* : voluminoso
voluntary ['vɑlənˌtɛri] *adj* : voluntario
— **voluntarily** [ˌvɑlən'tɛrəli] *adv*
volunteer[1] [ˌvɑlən'tɪr] *vt* : ofrecer, dar
⟨to volunteer one's assistance : ofrecer
la ayuda⟩ — *vi* : ofrecerse, alistarse
como voluntario
volunteer[2] *n* : voluntario *m*, -ria *f*
voluptuous [və'lʌptʃuəs] *adj* : voluptuoso
vomit[1] ['vɑmət] *v* : vomitar
vomit[2] *n* : vómito *m*
voodoo ['vu:ˌdu:] *n, pl* **voodoos** : vudú
m
voracious [vɔ'reɪʃəs, və-] *adj* : voraz
voraciously [vɔ'reɪʃəsli, və-] *adv* : vorazmente, con voracidad
vortex ['vɔrˌtɛks] *n, pl* **vortices** ['vɔrtə-
ˌsi:z] : vórtice *m*
vote[1] ['vo:t] *vi* **voted; voting** : votar ⟨to
vote Democratic : votar por los
demócratas⟩
vote[2] *n* 1 : voto *m* 2 SUFFRAGE : sufragio *m*, derecho *m* al voto
voter ['vo:tər] *n* : votante *mf*
voting ['vo:tɪŋ] *n* : votación *f*
vouch ['væʊtʃ] *vi* **to vouch for** : garantizar (algo), responder de (algo), responder por (alguien)
voucher ['væʊtʃər] *n* 1 RECEIPT : comprobante *m* 2 : vale *m* ⟨travel voucher : vale de viajar⟩
vow[1] ['væʊ] *vt* : jurar, prometer, hacer
voto de
vow[2] *n* : promesa *f*, voto *m* (en la religión) ⟨a vow of poverty : un voto de
pobreza⟩
vowel ['væʊəl] *n* : vocal *m*
voyage[1] ['vɔɪɪdʒ] *vi* **-aged; -aging** : viajar
voyage[2] *n* : viaje *m*
voyager ['vɔɪɪdʒər] *n* : viajero *m*, -ra *f*
vulcanize ['vʌlkəˌnaɪz] *vt* **-nized; -nizing**
: vulcanizar
vulgar ['vʌlgər] *adj* 1 COMMON, PLE-
BIAN : ordinario, populachero, del vulgo 2 COARSE, CRUDE : grosero, de mal
gusto, majadero *Mex* 3 INDECENT : indecente, colorado (dícese de un chiste,
etc.)
vulgarity [ˌvʌl'gærəti] *n, pl* **-ties**
: grosería *f*, vulgaridad *f*
vulgarly ['vʌlgərli] *adv* : vulgarmente,
groseramente
vulnerability [ˌvʌlnərə'bɪləti] *n, pl* **-ties**
: vulnerabilidad *f*
vulnerable ['vʌlnərəbəl] *adj* : vulnerable
vulture ['vʌltʃər] *n* : buitre *m*, zopilote *m*
CA, Mex
vying → **vie**

W

w ['dʌbəl,ju:] *n, pl* **w's** *or* **ws** [-,ju:z] : vigésima tercera letra del alfabeto inglés

wad¹ ['wɑd] *vt* **wadded; wadding 1** : hacer un taco con, formar en una masa **2** STUFF : rellenar

wad² *n* : taco *m* (de papel), bola *f* (de algodón, etc.), fajo *m* (de billetes)

waddle¹ ['wɑdəl] *vi* **-dled; -dling** : andar como un pato

waddle² *n* : andar *m* de pato

wade ['weɪd] *v* **waded; wading** *vi* **1** : caminar por el agua **2 to wade through** : leer (algo) con dificultad — *vt or* **to wade across** : vadear

wading bird *n* : zancuda *f*, ave *f* zancuda

wafer ['weɪfər] *n* : barquillo *m*, galleta *f* de barquillo

waffle ['wɑfəl] *n* **1** : wafle *m* **2 waffle iron** : waflera *f*

waft ['wɑft, 'wæft] *vt* : llevar por el aire — *vi* : flotar

wag¹ ['wæg] *v* **wagged; wagging** *vt* : menear — *vi* : menearse, moverse

wag² *n* **1** : meneo *m* (de la cola) **2** JOKER, WIT : bromista *mf*

wage¹ ['weɪʤ] *vt* **waged; waging** : hacer, librar ⟨to wage war : hacer la guerra⟩

wage² *n or* **wages** *npl* : sueldo *m*, salario *m* ⟨minimum wage : salario mínimo⟩

wager¹ ['weɪʤər] *v* : apostar

wager² *n* : apuesta *f*

waggish ['wægɪʃ] *adj* : burlón, bromista (dícese de una persona), chistoso (dícese de un comentario)

waggle ['wægəl] *vt* **-gled; -gling** : menear, mover (de un lado a otro)

wagon ['wægən] *n* **1** : carro *m* (tirado por caballos) **2** CART : carrito *m* **3** → **station wagon**

waif ['weɪf] *n* : niño *m* abandonado, animal *m* sin hogar

wail¹ ['weɪl] *vi* : gemir, lamentarse

wail² *n* : gemido *m*, lamento *m*

wainscot ['weɪnskət, -,skɑt, -,skoːt] *or* **wainscoting** [-skəṭɪŋ, -,skɑ-, -,skoː-] *n* : boiserie *f*, revestimiento *m* de paneles de madera

waist ['weɪst] *n* : cintura *f* (del cuerpo humano), talle *m* (de ropa)

waistline ['weɪst,laɪn] → **waist**

wait¹ ['weɪt] *vi* : esperar ⟨to wait for something : esperar algo⟩ ⟨wait and see! : ¡espera y verás!⟩ ⟨I can't wait : me muero de ganas⟩ — *vt* **1** AWAIT : esperar **2** DELAY : retrasar ⟨don't wait lunch : no retrase el almuerzo⟩ **3** SERVE : servir, atender ⟨to wait tables : servir (a la mesa)⟩

wait² *n* **1** : espera *f* **2 to lie in wait** : estar al acecho

waiter ['weɪṭər] *n* : mesero *m*, camarero *m*, mozo *m* *Arg, Chile, Col, Peru*

waiting room *n* : sala *f* de espera

waitress ['weɪtrəs] *n* : mesera *f*, camarera *f*, moza *f* *Arg, Chile, Col, Peru*

waive ['weɪv] *vt* **waived; waiving** : renunciar a ⟨to waive one's rights : renunciar a sus derechos⟩ ⟨to waive the rules : no aplicar las reglas⟩

waiver ['weɪvər] *n* : renuncia *f*

wake¹ ['weɪk] *v* **woke** ['woːk]; **woken** ['woːkən] *or* **waked; waking** *vi or* **to wake up** : despertar(se) ⟨he woke at noon : se despertó al mediodía⟩ ⟨wake up! : ¡despiértate!⟩ — *vt* : despertar

wake² *n* **1** VIGIL : velatorio *m*, velorio *m* (de un difunto) **2** TRAIL : estela *f* (de un barco, un huracán, etc.) **3** AFTERMATH : consecuencias *fpl* ⟨in the wake of : tras, como consecuencia de⟩

wakeful ['weɪkfəl] *adj* **1** SLEEPLESS : desvelado **2** VIGILANT : alerta, vigilante

waken ['weɪkən] → **awake**

walk¹ ['wɔk] *vi* **1** : caminar, andar, pasear ⟨you're walking too fast : estás caminando demasiado rápido⟩ ⟨to walk around the city : pasearse por la ciudad⟩ **2** : ir andando, ir a pie ⟨we had to walk home : tuvimos que ir a casa a pie⟩ **3** : darle base por bolas (a un bateador) — *vt* **1** : recorrer, caminar ⟨she walked two miles : caminó dos millas⟩ **2** ACCOMPANY : acompañar **3** : sacar a pasear (a un perro)

walk² *n* **1** : paseo *m*, caminata *f* ⟨to go for a walk : ir a caminar, dar un paseo⟩ **2** PATH : camino *m* **3** GAIT : andar *m* **4** : marcha *f* (en beisbol) **5 walk of life** : esfera *f*, condición *f*

walker ['wɔkər] *n* **1** : paseante *mf* **2** HIKER : excursionista *mf* **3** : andador *m* (aparato)

walking stick *n* : bastón *m*

walkout ['wɔk,aʊt] *n* STRIKE : huelga *f*

walk out *vi* **1** STRIKE : declararse en huelga **2** LEAVE : salir, irse **3 to walk out on** : abandonar, dejar

walkway ['wɔk,weɪ] *n* **1** SIDEWALK : acera *f* **2** PATH : sendero *m* **3** PASSAGEWAY : pasadizo *m*

wall¹ ['wɔl] *vt* **1 to wall in** : cercar con una pared o un muro, tapiar, amurallar **2 to wall off** : separar con una pared o un muro **3 to wall up** : tapiar, condenar (una ventana, etc.)

wall² *n* **1** : muro *m* (exterior) ⟨the walls of the city : las murallas de la ciudad⟩ **2** : pared *f* (interior) **3** BARRIER : barrera *f* ⟨a wall of mountains : una barrera de montañas⟩ **4** : pared *f* (en anatomía)

wallaby ['wɑləbi] *n, pl* **-bies** : ualabí *m*

walled ['wɔld] *adj* : amurallado

wallet ['wɑlət] *n* : billetera *f*, cartera *f*

wallflower ['wɔl,flaʊər] *n* **1** : alhelí *m* (flor) **2 to be a wallflower** : comer pavo

wallop¹ ['wɑləp] *vt* **1** TROUNCE : darle una paliza (a alguien) **2** SOCK : pegar fuerte

wallop² n : golpe m fuerte, golpazo m
wallow¹ ['wɑˌlo:] vi 1 : revolcarse ⟨to wallow in the mud : revolcarse en el lodo⟩ 2 DELIGHT : deleitarse ⟨to wallow in luxury : nadar en lujos⟩
wallow² n : revolcadero m (para animales)
wallpaper¹ ['wɔlˌpeɪpər] vt : empapelar
wallpaper² n : papel m pintado
walnut ['wɔlˌnʌt] n 1 : nuez f (fruta) 2 : nogal m (árbol y madera)
walrus ['wɔlrəs, 'wɑl-] n, pl **-rus** or **-ruses** : morsa f
waltz¹ ['wɔlts] vi 1 : valsar, bailar el vals 2 BREEZE : pasar con ligereza ⟨to waltz in : entrar tan campante⟩
waltz² n : vals m
wan ['wɑn] adj **wanner; -est** 1 PALLID : pálido 2 DIM : tenue ⟨wan light : luz tenue⟩ 3 LANGUID : lánguido ⟨a wan smile : una sonrisa lánguida⟩ — **wanly** adv
wand ['wɑnd] n : varita f (mágica)
wander ['wɑndər] vi 1 RAMBLE : deambular, vagar, vagabundear 2 STRAY : alejarse, desviarse, divagar ⟨she let her mind wander : dejó vagar la imaginación⟩ — vt : recorrer ⟨to wander the streets : vagar por las calles⟩
wanderer ['wɑndərər] n : vagabundo m, -da f; viajero m, -ra f
wanderlust ['wɑndərˌlʌst] n : pasión f por viajar
wane¹ ['weɪn] vi **waned; waning** 1 : menguar (dícese de la luna) 2 DECLINE : disminuir, decaer, menguar
wane² n **on the wane** : decayendo, en decadencia
wangle ['wæŋgəl] vt **-gled; -gling** FINAGLE : arreglárselas para conseguir
wannabe ['wɑnəˌbi:] n : aspirante mf (a algo); imitador m, -dora f (de alguien)
want¹ ['wɑnt, 'wɔnt] vt 1 LACK : faltar 2 REQUIRE : requerir, necesitar 3 DESIRE : querer, desear
want² n 1 LACK : falta f 2 DESTITUTION : indigencia f, miseria f 3 DESIRE, NEED : deseo m, necesidad f
wanting ['wɑntɪŋ, 'wɔn-] adj 1 ABSENT : ausente 2 DEFICIENT : deficiente ⟨he's wanting in common sense : le falta sentido común⟩
wanton ['wɑntən, 'wɔn-] adj 1 LEWD, LUSTFUL : lascivo, lujurioso, licencioso 2 INHUMANE, MERCILESS : despiadado ⟨wanton cruelty : crueldad despiadada⟩
wapiti ['wɑpəti] n, pl **-ti** or **-tis** : uapití m
war¹ ['wɔr] vi **warred; warring** : combatir, batallar, hacer la guerra
war² n : guerra f ⟨to go to war : entrar en guerra⟩
warble¹ ['wɔrbəl] vi **-bled; -bling** : gorjear, trinar
warble² n : trino m, gorjeo m
warbler ['wɔrblər] n : pájaro m gorjeador, curruca f
ward¹ ['wɔrd] vt **to ward off** : desviar, protegerse contra

ward² n 1 : sala f (de un hospital, etc.) ⟨maternity ward : sala de maternidad⟩ 2 : distrito m electoral o administrativo (de una ciudad) 3 : pupilo m, -la f (de un tutor, etc.)
warden ['wɔrdən] n 1 KEEPER : guarda mf; guardián m, -diana f ⟨game warden : guardabosque⟩ 2 or **prison warden** : alcaide m
wardrobe ['wɔrdˌro:b] n 1 CLOSET : armario m 2 CLOTHES : vestuario m, guardarropa f
ware ['wær] n 1 POTTERY : cerámica f 2 **wares** npl GOODS : mercancía f, mercadería f
warehouse ['wærˌhaʊs] n : depósito m, almacén m, bodega f Chile, Col, Mex
warfare ['wɔrˌfær] n 1 WAR : guerra f 2 STRUGGLE : lucha f ⟨the warfare against drugs : la lucha contra las drogas⟩
warhead ['wɔrˌhɛd] n : ojiva f, cabeza f (de un misil)
warily ['wærəli] adv : cautelosamente, con cautela
wariness ['wærinəs] n : cautela f
warlike ['wærˌlaɪk] adj : belicoso, guerrero
warm¹ ['wɔrm] vt 1 HEAT : calentar, recalentar 2 **to warm one's heart** : reconfortar a uno, alegrar el corazón 3 **to warm up** : calentar (los músculos, un automóvil, etc.) — vi 1 : calentarse 2 **to warm to** : tomarle simpatía (a alguien), entusiasmarse con (algo)
warm² adj 1 LUKEWARM : tibio, templado 2 : caliente, cálido, caluroso ⟨a warm wind : un viento cálido⟩ ⟨a warm day : un día caluroso, un día de calor⟩ ⟨warm hands : manos calientes⟩ 3 : caliente, que abriga ⟨warm clothes : ropa de abrigo⟩ ⟨I feel warm : tengo calor⟩ 4 CARING, CORDIAL : cariñoso, cordial 5 : cálido (dícese de colores) 6 FRESH : fresco, reciente ⟨a warm trail : un rastro reciente⟩ 7 (used for riddles) : caliente
warm–blooded ['wɔrm'blʌdəd] adj : de sangre caliente
warmhearted ['wɔrm'hɑrtəd] adj : cariñoso
warmly ['wɔrmli] adv 1 AFFECTIONATELY : calurosamente, afectuosamente 2 **to dress warmly** : abrigarse
warmonger ['wɔrˌmɑŋgər, -ˌmʌŋ-] n : belicista mf
warmth ['wɔrmpθ] n 1 : calor m 2 AFFECTION : cariño m, afecto m 3 ENTHUSIASM : ardor m, entusiasmo m
warm–up ['wɔrmˌʌp] n : calentamiento m
warn ['wɔrn] vt 1 CAUTION : advertir, alertar 2 INFORM : avisar, informar
warning ['wɔrnɪŋ] n 1 ADVICE : advertencia f, aviso m 2 ALERT : alerta f, alarma f
warp¹ ['wɔrp] vt 1 : alabear, combar 2 PERVERT : pervertir, deformar — vi : pandearse, alabearse, combarse

warp² *n* **1** : urdimbre *f* ⟨the warp and the weft : la urdimbre y la trama⟩ **2** : alabeo *m* (en la madera, etc.)

warrant¹ [ˈwɔrənt] *vt* **1** ASSURE : asegurar, garantizar **2** GUARANTEE : garantizar **3** JUSTIFY, MERIT : justificar, merecer

warrant² *n* **1** AUTHORIZATION : autorización *f*, permiso *m* ⟨an arrest warrant : una orden de detención⟩ **2** JUSTIFICATION : justificación *f*

warranty [ˈwɔrənti, ˌwɔrənˈti:] *n, pl* **-ties** : garantía *f*

warren [ˈwɔrən] *n* : madriguera *f* (de conejos)

warrior [ˈwɔriər] *n* : guerrero *m*, -ra *f*

warship [ˈwɔrˌʃɪp] *n* : buque *m* de guerra

wart [ˈwɔrt] *n* : verruga *f*

wartime [ˈwɔrˌtaɪm] *n* : tiempo *m* de guerra

wary [ˈwæri] *adj* **warier; -est** : cauteloso, receloso ⟨to be wary of : desconfiar de⟩

was → be

wash¹ [ˈwɔʃ, ˈwɑʃ] *vt* **1** CLEAN : lavar(se), limpiar, fregar ⟨to wash the dishes : lavar los platos⟩ ⟨to wash one's hands : lavarse las manos⟩ **2** DRENCH : mojar **3** LAP : bañar ⟨waves were washing the shore : las olas bañaban la orilla⟩ **4** CARRY, DRAG : arrastrar **5 to wash away** : llevarse (un puente, etc.) — *vi* **1** : lavarse (dícese de una persona o la ropa) ⟨the dress washes well : el vestido se lava bien⟩ **2 to wash against** *or* **to wash over** : bañar

wash² *n* **1** : lavado *m* ⟨to give something a wash : lavar algo⟩ **2** LAUNDRY : artículos *mpl* para lavar, ropa *f* sucia **3** : estela *f* (de un barco)

washable [ˈwɔʃəbəl, ˈwɑ-] *adj* : lavable

washboard [ˈwɔʃˌbord, ˈwɑʃ-] *n* : tabla *f* de lavar

washbowl [ˈwɔʃˌboːl, ˈwɑʃ-] *n* : lavabo *m*, lavamanos *m*

washcloth [ˈwɔʃˌklɔθ, ˈwɑʃ-] *n* : toallita *f* (para lavarse)

washed-out [ˈwɔʃtˈaʊt, ˈwɑʃt-] *adj* **1** : desvaído (dícese de colores) **2** EXHAUSTED : agotado, desanimado

washed-up [ˈwɔʃtˈʌp, ˈwɑʃt-] *adj* : acabado (dícese de una persona), fracasado (dícese de un negocio, etc.)

washer [ˈwɔʃər, ˈwɑ-] *n* **1 → washing machine 2** : arandela *f* (de una llave, etc.)

washing [ˈwɔʃɪŋ, ˈwɑ-] *n* WASH : ropa *f* para lavar

washing machine *n* : máquina *f* de lavar, lavadora *f*

washout [ˈwɔʃˌaʊt, ˈwɑʃ-] *n* **1** : erosión *f* (de la tierra) **2** FAILURE : fracaso *m* ⟨she's a washout : es un desastre⟩

washroom [ˈwɔʃˌruːm, ˈwɑʃ-, -ˌrʊm] *n* : servicios *mpl* (públicos), baño *m*, sanitario *m* Col, Mex, Ven

wasn't [ˈwʌzənt] (*contraction of* **was not**) **→ be**

wasp [ˈwɑsp] *n* : avispa *f*

waspish [ˈwɑspɪʃ] *adj* **1** IRRITABLE : irritable, irascible **2** CAUSTIC : cáustico, mordaz

waste¹ [ˈweɪst] *v* **wasted; wasting** *vt* **1** DEVASTATE : arrasar, arruinar, devastar **2** SQUANDER : desperdiciar, despilfarrar, malgastar ⟨to waste time : perder tiempo⟩ — *vi or* **to waste away** : consumirse, chuparse

waste² *adj* **1** BARREN : yermo, baldío **2** DISCARDED : de desecho **3** EXCESS : sobrante

waste³ *n* **1 → wasteland 2** MISUSE : derroche *m*, desperdicio *m*, despilfarro *m* ⟨a waste of time : una pérdida de tiempo⟩ **3** RUBBISH : basura *f*, desechos *mpl*, desperdicios *mpl* **4** EXCREMENT : excremento *m*

wastebasket [ˈweɪstˌbæskət] *n* : cesto *m* (de basura), papelera *f*, zafacón *m* Car

wasteful [ˈweɪstfəl] *adj* : despilfarrador, derrochador, pródigo

wastefulness [ˈweɪstfəlnəs] *n* : derroche *m*, despilfarro *m*

wasteland [ˈweɪstˌlænd, -lənd] *n* : baldío *m*, yermo *m*, desierto *m*

watch¹ [ˈwɑtʃ] *vi* **1 *or* to keep watch** : velar **2** OBSERVE : mirar, ver, observar **3 to watch for** AWAIT : esperar, quedar a la espera de **4 to watch out** : tener cuidado ⟨watch out! : ¡ten cuidado!, ¡ojo!⟩ — *vt* **1** OBSERVE : mirar, observar **2 *or* to watch over** : vigilar, cuidar **3** : tener cuidado de ⟨watch what you do : ten cuidado con lo que haces⟩

watch² *n* **1** : guardia *f* ⟨to be on watch : estar de guardia⟩ **2** SURVEILLANCE : vigilancia *f* **3** LOOKOUT : guardia *mf*, centinela *f*, vigía *mf* **4** TIMEPIECE : reloj *m*

watchdog [ˈwɑtʃˌdɔg] *n* : perro *m* guardián

watcher [ˈwɑtʃər] *n* : observador *m*, -dora *f*

watchful [ˈwɑtʃfəl] *adj* : alerta, vigilante, atento

watchfulness [ˈwɑtʃfəlnəs] *n* : vigilancia *f*

watchman [ˈwɑtʃmən] *n, pl* **-men** [-mən, -ˌmɛn] : vigilante *m*, guarda *m*

watchword [ˈwɑtʃˌwərd] *n* **1** PASSWORD : contraseña *f* **2** SLOGAN : lema *m*, eslogan *m*

water¹ [ˈwɔtər, ˈwɑ-] *vt* **1** : regar (el jardín, etc.) **2 to water down** DILUTE : diluir, aguar — *vi* : lagrimear (dícese de los ojos), hacérsele agua la boca a uno ⟨my mouth is watering : se me hace agua la boca⟩

water² *n* : agua *f*

water buffalo *n* : búfalo *m* de agua

watercolor [ˈwɔtərˌkʌlər, ˈwɑ-] *n* : acuarela *f*

watercourse [ˈwɔtərˌkors, ˈwɑ-] *n* : curso *m* de agua

watercress [ˈwɔtərˌkrɛs, ˈwɑ-] *n* : berro *m*

waterfall ['wɔtər₁fɔl, 'wɑ-] *n* : cascada *f*, salto *m* de agua, catarata *f*

waterfowl ['wɔtər₁faʊl, 'wɑ-] *n* : ave *f* acuática

waterfront ['wɔtər₁frʌnt, 'wɑ-] *n* **1** : tierra *f* que bordea un río, un lago, o un mar **2** WHARF : muelle *m*

water lily *n* : nenúfar *m*

waterlogged ['wɔtər₁lɔgd, 'wɑtər-₁lɑgd] *adj* : lleno de agua, empapado, inundado (dícese del suelo)

watermark ['wɔtər₁mɑrk, 'wɑ-] *n* **1** : marca *f* del nivel de agua **2** : filigrana *f* (en el papel)

watermelon ['wɔtər₁mɛlən, 'wɑ-] *n* : sandía *f*

water moccasin → **moccasin**

waterpower ['wɔtər₁paʊər, 'wɑ-] *n* : energía *f* hidráulica

waterproof¹ ['wɔtər₁pruːf, 'wɑ-] *vt* : hacer impermeable, impermeabilizar

waterproof² *adj* : impermeable, a prueba de agua

watershed ['wɔtər₁ʃɛd, 'wɑ-] *n* **1** : línea *f* divisoria de aguas **2** BASIN : cuenca *f* (de un río)

waterskiing ['wɔtər₁skiːɪŋ, 'wɑ-] *n* : esquí *m* acuático

waterspout ['wɔtər₁spaʊt, 'wɑ-] *n* WHIRLWIND : tromba *f* marina

watertight ['wɔtər₁taɪt, 'wɑ-] *adj* **1** : hermético **2** IRREFUTABLE : irrebatible, irrefutable ⟨a watertight contract : un contrato sin lagunas⟩

waterway ['wɔtər₁weɪ, 'wɑ-] *n* : vía *f* navegable

waterworks ['wɔtər₁wərks, 'wɑ-] *npl* : central *f* de abastecimiento de agua

watery ['wɔtəri, 'wɑ-] *adj* **1** : acuoso, como agua **2** : aguado, diluido ⟨watery soup : sopa aguada⟩ **3** : lloroso ⟨watery eyes : ojos llorosos⟩ **4** WASHEDOUT : desvaído (dícese de colores)

watt ['wɑt] *n* : vatio *m*

wattage ['wɑtɪʤ] *n* : vataje *m*

wattle ['wɑtəl] *n* : carúncula *f* (de un ave, etc.)

wave¹ ['weɪv] *v* **waved; waving** *vi* **1** : saludar con la mano, hacer señas con la mano ⟨she waved at him : lo saludó con la mano⟩ **2** FLUTTER, SHAKE : ondear, agitarse **3** UNDULATE : ondular — *vt* **1** SHAKE : agitar **2** BRANDISH : blandir **3** CURL : ondular, marcar (el pelo) **4** SIGNAL : hacerle señas a (con la mano) ⟨he waved farewell : se despidió con la mano⟩

wave² *n* **1** : ola *f* (de agua) **2** CURL : onda *f* (en el pelo) **3** : onda *f* (en física) **4** SURGE : oleada *f* ⟨a wave of enthusiasm : una oleada de entusiasmo⟩ **5** GESTURE : señal *f* con la mano, saludo *m* con la mano

wavelength ['weɪv₁lɛŋkθ] *n* : longitud *f* de onda

waver ['weɪvər] *vi* **1** VACILLATE : vacilar, fluctuar **2** FLICKER : parpadear, titilar, oscilar **3** FALTER : flaquear, tambalearse

wavy ['weɪvi] *adj* **wavier; -est** : ondulado

wax¹ ['wæks] *vi* **1** : crecer (dícese de la luna) **2** BECOME : volverse, ponerse ⟨to wax indignant : indignarse⟩ — *vt* : encerar

wax² *n* **1** BEESWAX : cera *f* de abejas **2** : cera *f* ⟨floor wax : cera para el piso⟩ **3** *or* **earwax** ['ɪr₁wæks] : cerilla *f*, cerumen *m*

waxen ['wæksən] *adj* : de cera

waxy ['wæksi] *adj* **waxier; -est** : ceroso

way ['weɪ] *n* **1** PATH, ROAD : camino *m*, vía *f* **2** ROUTE : camino *m*, ruta *f* ⟨to go the wrong way : equivocarse de camino⟩ ⟨I'm on my way : estoy de camino⟩ **3** : línea *f* de conducta, camino *m* ⟨he chose the easy way : optó por el camino fácil⟩ **4** MANNER, MEANS : manera *f*, modo *m*, forma *f* ⟨in the same way : del mismo modo, igualmente⟩ ⟨there are no two ways about it : no cabe la menor duda⟩ ⟨no way! : ¡de ninguna manera!⟩ **5** (*indicating a wish*) ⟨have it your way : como tú quieras⟩ ⟨to get one's own way : salirse uno con la suya⟩ **6** STATE : estado *m* ⟨things are in a bad way : las cosas marchan mal⟩ **7** RESPECT : aspecto *m*, sentido *m* **8** CUSTOM : costumbre *f* ⟨to mend one's ways : dejar las malas costumbres⟩ **9** PASSAGE : camino *m* ⟨to get in the way : meterse en el camino⟩ **10** DISTANCE : distancia *f* ⟨to come a long way : hacer grandes progresos⟩ **11** DIRECTION : dirección *f* ⟨come this way : venga por aquí⟩ ⟨which way did he go? : ¿por dónde fue?⟩ **12 by the way** : a propósito, por cierto **13 by way of** VIA : vía, pasando por **14 out of the way** REMOTE : remoto, recóndito **15** → **under way**

wayfarer ['weɪ₁færər] *n* : caminante *mf*

waylay ['weɪ₁leɪ] *vt* **-laid** [-₁leɪd]; **-laying** ACCOST : abordar

wayside ['weɪ₁saɪd] *n* : borde *m* del camino

wayward ['weɪwərd] *adj* **1** UNRULY : díscolo, rebelde **2** UNTOWARD : adverso

we ['wiː] *pron* : nosotros, nosotras

weak ['wiːk] *adj* **1** FEEBLE : débil, endeble **2** : flojo, pobre ⟨a weak excuse : una excusa poco convincente⟩ **3** DILUTED : aguado, diluido ⟨weak tea : té poco cargado⟩ **4** FAINT : tenue (dícese de los colores, las luces, los sonidos, etc.)

weaken ['wiːkən] *vt* : debilitar — *vi* : debilitarse, flaquear

weakling ['wiːklɪŋ] *n* : alfeñique *m fam*; debilucho *m*, -cha *f*

weakly¹ ['wiːkli] *adv* : débilmente

weakly² *adj* **weaklier; -est** : débil, enclenque

weakness ['wiːknəs] *n* **1** FEEBLENESS : debilidad *f* **2** FAULT, FLAW : flaqueza *f*, punto *m* débil

wealth ['wɛlθ] *n* **1** RICHES : riqueza *f* **2** PROFUSION : abundancia *f*, profusión *f*

wealthy ['wɛlθi] *adj* **wealthier; -est** : rico, acaudalado, adinerado

wean ['wi:n] *vt* **1** : destetar (a los niños o las crías) **2 to wean someone away from** : quitarle a alguien la costumbre de

weapon ['wɛpən] *n* : arma *f*

weaponless ['wɛpənləs] *adj* : desarmado

weaponry ['wɛpənri] *n* : armamento *m*

wear[1] ['wær] *v* **wore** ['wor]; **worn** ['worn]; **wearing** *vt* **1** : llevar (ropa, un reloj, etc.), calzar (zapatos) ⟨to wear a happy smile : sonreír alegremente⟩ **2** *or* **to wear away** : desgastar, erosionar (rocas, etc.) **3 to wear out** : gastar ⟨he wore out his shoes : gastó sus zapatos⟩ **4 to wear out** EXHAUST : agotar, fatigar ⟨to wear oneself out : agotarse⟩ — *vi* **1** LAST : durar **2 to wear off** DIMINISH : disminuir **3 to wear out** : gastarse

wear[2] *n* **1** USE : uso *m* ⟨for everyday wear : para todos los días⟩ **2** CLOTHING : ropa *f* ⟨children's wear : ropa de niños⟩ **3** DETERIORATION : desgaste *m* ⟨to be the worse for wear : estar deteriorado⟩

wearable ['wærəbəl] *adj* : que puede ponerse (dícese de una prenda)

wear and tear *n* : desgaste *m*

weariness ['wɪrinəs] *n* : fatiga *f*, cansancio *m*

wearisome ['wɪrisəm] *adj* : aburrido, pesado, cansado

weary[1] ['wɪri] *v* **-ried; -rying** *vt* **1** TIRE : cansar, fatigar **2** BORE : hastiar, aburrir — *vi* : cansarse

weary[2] *adj* **-rier; -est 1** TIRED : cansado **2** FED UP : harto **3** BORED : aburrido

weasel ['wi:zəl] *n* : comadreja *f*

weather[1] ['wɛðər] *vt* **1** WEAR : erosionar, desgastar **2** ENDURE : aguantar, sobrellevar, capear ⟨to weather the storm : capear el temporal⟩

weather[2] *n* : tiempo *m*

weather–beaten ['wɛðər₁bi:tən] *adj* : curtido

weatherman ['wɛðər₁mæn] *n, pl* **-men** [-mən, -₁mɛn] METEOROLOGIST : meteorólogo *m*, -ga *f*

weatherproof ['wɛðər₁pru:f] *adj* : que resiste a la intemperie, impermeable

weather vane → **vane**

weave[1] ['wi:v] *v* **wove** ['wo:v] *or* **weaved; woven** ['wo:vən] *or* **weaved; weaving** *vt* **1** : tejer (tela) **2** INTERLACE : entretejer, entrelazar **3 to weave one's way through** : abrirse camino por — *vi* **1** : tejer **2** WIND : serpentear, zigzaguear

weave[2] *n* : tejido *m*, trama *f*

weaver ['wi:vər] *n* : tejedor *m*, -dora *f*

web[1] ['wɛb] *vt* **webbed; webbing** : cubrir o proveer con una red

web[2] *n* **1** COBWEB, SPIDERWEB : telaraña *f*, tela *f* de araña **2** ENTANGLEMENT, SNARE : red *f*, enredo *m* ⟨a web of intrigue : una red de intriga⟩ **3** : membrana *f* interdigital (de aves) **4** NETWORK : red *f* ⟨a web of highways : una red de carreteras⟩ **5 the Web** : la web

webbed ['wɛbd] *adj* : palmeado ⟨webbed feet : patas palmeadas⟩

Web site *n* : sitio *m* web

wed ['wɛd] *vt* **wedded; wedding 1** MARRY : casarse con **2** UNITE : ligar, unir

we'd ['wi:d] (*contraction of* **we had, we should,** *or* **we would**) → **have, should, would**

wedding ['wɛdɪŋ] *n* : boda *f*, casamiento *m*

wedge[1] ['wɛʤ] *vt* **wedged; wedging 1** : apretar (con una cuña) ⟨to wedge open : mantener abierto con una cuña⟩ **2** CRAM : meter, embutir

wedge[2] *n* **1** : cuña *f* **2** PIECE : porción *f*, trozo *m*

wedlock ['wɛd₁lɑk] → **marriage**

Wednesday ['wɛnz₁deɪ, -di] *n* : miércoles *m*

wee ['wi:] *adj* : pequeño, minúsculo ⟨in the wee hours : a las altas horas⟩

weed[1] ['wi:d] *vt* **1** : desherbar, desyerbar **2 to weed out** : eliminar, quitar

weed[2] *n* : mala hierba *f*

weedy ['wi:di] *adj* **weedier; -est 1** : cubierto de malas hierbas **2** LANKY, SKINNY : flaco, larguirucho *fam*

week ['wi:k] *n* : semana *f*

weekday ['wi:k₁deɪ] *n* : día *m* laborable

weekend ['wi:k₁ɛnd] *n* : fin *m* de semana

weekly[1] ['wi:kli] *adv* : semanalmente

weekly[2] *adj* : semanal

weekly[3] *n, pl* **-lies** : semanario *m*

weep ['wi:p] *v* **wept** ['wɛpt]; **weeping** : llorar

weeping willow *n* : sauce *m* llorón

weepy ['wi:pi] *adj* **weepier; -est** : lloroso, triste

weevil ['wi:vəl] *n* : gorgojo *m*

weft ['wɛft] *n* : trama *f*

weigh ['weɪ] *vt* **1** : pesar **2** CONSIDER : considerar, sopesar **3 to weigh anchor** : levar anclas **4 to weigh down** : sobrecargar (con una carga), abrumar (con preocupaciones, etc.) — *vi* **1** : pesar ⟨it weighs 10 pounds : pesa 10 libras⟩ **2** COUNT : tener importancia, contar **3 to weigh on one's mind** : preocuparle a uno

weight[1] ['weɪt] *vt* **1** : poner peso en, sujetar con un peso **2** BURDEN : cargar, oprimir

weight[2] *n* **1** HEAVINESS : peso *m* ⟨to lose weight : bajar de peso, adelgazar⟩ **2** : peso *m* ⟨weights and measures : pesos y medidas⟩ **3** : pesa *f* ⟨to lift weights : levantar pesas⟩ **4** BURDEN : peso *m*, carga *f* ⟨to take a weight off one's mind : quitarle un peso de encima a uno⟩ **5**

IMPORTANCE : peso *m* **6** INFLUENCE : influencia *f*, autoridad *f* ⟨to throw one's weight around : hacer sentir su influencia⟩

weighty [ˈweɪt̬i] *adj* **weightier; -est 1** HEAVY : pesado **2** IMPORTANT : importante, de peso

weird [ˈwɪrd] *adj* **1** MYSTERIOUS : misterioso **2** STRANGE : extraño, raro — **weirdly** *adv*

welcome¹ [ˈwɛlkəm] *vt* **-comed; -coming** : darle la bienvenida a, recibir

welcome² *adj* : bienvenido ⟨to make someone welcome : acoger bien a alguien⟩ ⟨you're welcome! : ¡de nada!, ¡no hay de qué!⟩

welcome³ *n* : bienvenida *f*, recibimiento *m*, acogida *f*

weld¹ [ˈwɛld] *v* : soldar

weld² *n* : soldadura *f*

welder [ˈwɛldər] *n* : soldador *m*, -dora *f*

welfare [ˈwɛlˌfær] *n* **1** WELL-BEING : bienestar *m* **2** : asistencia *f* social

well¹ [ˈwɛl] *vi or* **to well up** : brotar, manar

well² *adv* **better** [ˈbɛt̬ər]; **best** [ˈbɛst] **1** RIGHTLY : bien, correctamente **2** SATISFACTORILY : bien ⟨to turn out well : resultar bien, salir bien⟩ **3** COMPLETELY : completamente ⟨well-hidden : completamente escondido⟩ **4** INTIMATELY : bien ⟨I knew him well : lo conocía bien⟩ **5** CONSIDERABLY, FAR : muy, bastante ⟨well ahead : muy adelante⟩ ⟨well before the deadline : bastante antes de la fecha⟩ **6 as well** ALSO : también **7** → **as well as**

well³ *adj* **1** SATISFACTORY : bien ⟨all is well : todo está bien⟩ **2** DESIRABLE : conveniente ⟨it would be well if you left : sería conveniente que te fueras⟩ **3** HEALTHY : bien, sano

well⁴ *n* **1** : pozo *m* (de agua, petróleo, gas, etc.), aljibe *m* (de agua) **2** SOURCE : fuente *f* ⟨a well of information : una fuente de información⟩ **3 or stairwell** : caja *f*, hueco *m* (de la escalera)

well⁵ *interj* **1** (*used to introduce a remark*) : bueno **2** (*used to express surprise*) : ¡vaya!

we'll [ˈwi:l, wɪl] (*contraction of* **we shall** *or* **we will**) → **shall, will**

well-balanced [ˈwɛlˈbælənst] *adj* : equilibrado

well-being [ˈwɛlˈbi:ɪŋ] *n* : bienestar *m*

well-bred [ˈwɛlˈbrɛd] *adj* : fino, bien educado

well-defined [ˌwɛldiˈfaɪnd] *adj* : bien definido

well-done [ˈwɛlˈdʌn] *adj* **1** : bien hecho ⟨well-done! : ¡bravo!⟩ **2** : bien cocido

well-known [ˈwɛlˈnoːn] *adj* : famoso, bien conocido

well-meaning [ˈwɛlˈmiːnɪŋ] *adj* : bienintencionado, que tiene buenas intenciones

well-nigh [ˈwɛlˈnaɪ] *adv* : casi ⟨well-nigh impossible : casi imposible⟩

well-off [ˈwɛlˈɔf] → **well-to-do**

well-rounded [ˈwɛlˈraʊndəd] *adj* : completo, equilibrado

well-to-do [ˌwɛltəˈduː] *adj* : próspero, adinerado, rico

Welsh [ˈwɛlʃ] *n* **1** : galés *m*, galesa *f* **2** : galés *m* (idioma) — **Welsh** *adj*

welt [ˈwɛlt] *n* **1** : vira *f* (de un zapato) **2** WHEAL : verdugón *m*

welter [ˈwɛltər] *n* : fárrago *m*, revoltijo *m* ⟨a welter of data : un fárrago de datos⟩

wend [ˈwɛnd] *vi* **to wend one's way** : ponerse en camino, encaminar sus pasos

went → **go¹**

wept → **weep**

were → **be**

we're [ˈwɪr, ˈwər, ˈwiːər] (*contraction of* **we are**) → **be**

werewolf [ˈwɪrˌwʊlf, ˈwɛr-, ˈwər-, -ˌwʌlf] *n, pl* **-wolves** [-ˌwʊlvz, -ˌwʌlvz] : hombre *m* lobo

west¹ [ˈwɛst] *adv* : al oeste

west² *adj* : oeste, del oeste, occidental ⟨west winds : vientos del oeste⟩

west³ *n* **1** : oeste *m* **2 the West** : el Oeste, el Occidente

westerly [ˈwɛstərli] *adv & adj* : del oeste

western [ˈwɛstərn] *adj* **1** : Occidental, del Oeste **2** : occidental, oeste

Westerner [ˈwɛstərnər] *n* : habitante *mf* del oeste

West Indian *n* : antillano *m*, -na *f* — **West Indian** *adj*

westward [ˈwɛstwərd] *adv & adj* : hacia el oeste

wet¹ [ˈwɛt] *vt* **wet** *or* **wetted; wetting** : mojar, humedecer

wet² *adj* **wetter; wettest 1** : mojado, húmedo ⟨wet clothes : ropa mojada⟩ **2** RAINY : lluvioso **3 wet paint** : pintura *f* fresca

wet³ *n* **1** MOISTURE : humedad *f* **2** RAIN : lluvia *f*

we've [ˈwiːv] (*contraction of* **we have**) → **have**

whack¹ [ˈʰwæk] *vt* : golpear (fuertemente), aporrear

whack² *n* **1** : golpe *m* fuerte, porrazo *m* **2** ATTEMPT : intento *m*, tentativa *f*

whale¹ [ˈʰweɪl] *vi* **whaled; whaling** : cazar ballenas

whale² *n, pl* **whales** *or* **whale** : ballena *f*

whaleboat [ˈʰweɪlˌbo:t] *n* : ballenero *m*

whalebone [ˈʰweɪlˌbo:n] *n* : barba *f* de ballena

whaler [ˈʰweɪlər] *n* **1** : ballenero *m*, -ra *f* **2** → **whaleboat**

wharf [ˈʰwɔrf] *n, pl* **wharves** [ˈʰwɔrvz] : muelle *m*, embarcadero *m*

what¹ [ˈʰwɑt, ˈʰwʌt] *adv* **1** HOW : cómo, cuánto ⟨what he suffered! : ¡cómo sufría!⟩ **2 what with** : entre ⟨what with one thing and another : entre una cosa y otra⟩

what² *adj* **1** (*used in questions*) : qué ⟨what more do you want? : ¿qué más quieres?⟩ ⟨what color is it? : ¿de qué color es?⟩ **2** (*used in exclamations*) : qué ⟨what an idea! : ¡qué idea!⟩ **3** ANY, WHATEVER : cualquier ⟨give what help you can : da cualquier contribución que puedas⟩

what³ *pron* **1** (*used in direct questions*) : qué ⟨what happened? : ¿qué pasó?⟩ ⟨what does it cost? : ¿cuánto cuesta?⟩ **2** (*used in indirect statements*) : lo que, que ⟨I don't know what to do : no sé que hacer⟩ ⟨do what I tell you : haz lo que te digo⟩ **3 what for** WHY : porqué **4 what if** : y si ⟨what if he knows? : ¿y si lo sabe?⟩

whatever¹ [hwɑt'ɛvər, ˌhwʌt-] *adj* **1** ANY : cualquier, cualquier . . . que ⟨whatever way you prefer : de cualquier manera que prefiera, como prefiera⟩ **2** (*in negative constructions*) ⟨there's no chance whatever : no hay ninguna posibilidad⟩ ⟨nothing whatever : nada en absoluto⟩

whatever² *pron* **1** ANYTHING : (todo) lo que ⟨I'll do whatever I want : haré lo que quiera⟩ **2** (*no matter what*) ⟨whatever it may be : sea lo que sea⟩ **3** WHAT : qué ⟨whatever do you mean? : ¿qué quieres decir?⟩

whatsoever¹ [ˌhwatso'ɛvər, ˌhwʌt-] *adj* → **whatever¹**

whatsoever² *pron* → **whatever²**

wheal ['hwi:l] *n* : verdugón *m*

wheat ['hwi:t] *n* : trigo *m*

wheaten ['hwi:tən] *adj* : de trigo

wheedle ['hwi:dəl] *vt* -**dled**; -**dling** CAJOLE : engatusar ⟨to wheedle something out of someone : sonsacarle algo a alguien⟩

wheel¹ ['hwi:l] *vt* : empujar (una bicicleta, etc.), mover (algo sobre ruedas) — *vi* **1** ROTATE : girar, rotar **2 to wheel around** TURN : darse la vuelta

wheel² *n* **1** : rueda *f* **2** *or* **steering wheel** : volante *m* (de automóviles, etc.), timón *m* (de barcos o aviones) **3 wheels** *npl* : maquinaria *f*, fuerza *f* impulsora ⟨the wheels of government : la maquinaria del gobierno⟩

wheelbarrow ['hwi:lˌbær‚o:] *n* : carretilla *f*

wheelchair ['hwi:lˌtʃær] *n* : silla *f* de ruedas

wheeze¹ ['hwi:z] *vi* **wheezed**; **wheezing** : resollar, respirar con dificultad

wheeze² *n* : resuello *m*

whelk ['hwɛlk] *n* : buccino *m*

whelp¹ ['hwɛlp] *vi* : parir

whelp² *n* : cachorro *m*, -rra *f*

when¹ ['hwɛn] *adv* : cuándo ⟨when will you return? : ¿cuándo volverás?⟩ ⟨he asked me when I would be home : me preguntó cuándo estaría en casa⟩

when² *conj* **1** (*referring to a particular time*) : cuando, en que ⟨when you are ready : cuando estés listo⟩ ⟨the days when I clean the house : los días en que limpio la casa⟩ **2** IF : cuando, si ⟨how can I go when I have no money?⟩

: ¿cómo voy a ir si no tengo dinero?⟩ **3** ALTHOUGH : cuando ⟨you said it was big when actually it's small : dijiste que era grande cuando en realidad es pequeño⟩

when³ *pron* : cuándo ⟨since when are you the boss? : ¿desde cuándo eres el jefe?⟩

whence ['hwɛnts] *adv* : de donde

whenever¹ [hwɛn'vər] *adv* **1** : cuando sea ⟨tomorrow or whenever : mañana o cuando sea⟩ **2** (*in questions*) : cuándo

whenever² *conj* **1** : siempre que, cada vez que ⟨whenever I go, I'm disappointed : siempre que voy, quedo desilusionado⟩ **2** WHEN : cuando ⟨whenever you like : cuando quieras⟩

where¹ ['hwɛr] *adv* : dónde, adónde ⟨where is he? : ¿dónde está?⟩ ⟨where did they go? : ¿adónde fueron?⟩

where² *conj* : donde, adonde ⟨she knows where the house is : sabe donde está la casa⟩ ⟨she goes where she likes : va adonde quiera⟩

where³ *pron* : donde ⟨Chicago is where I live : Chicago es donde vivo⟩

whereabouts¹ ['hwɛrəˌbauts] *adv* : dónde, por dónde ⟨whereabouts is the house? : ¿dónde está la casa?⟩

whereabouts² *ns & pl* : paradero *m*

whereas [hwɛr'æz] *conj* **1** : considerando que (usado en documentos legales) **2** : mientras que ⟨I like the white one whereas she prefers the black : me gusta el blanco mientras que ella prefiere el negro⟩

whereby [hwɛr'baɪ] *adv* : por lo cual

wherefore ['hwɛrˌfor] *adv* : por qué

wherein [hwɛr'ɪn] *adv* : en el cual, en el que

whereof [hwɛr'ʌv, -'ɑv] *conj* : de lo cual

whereupon ['hwɛrəˌpɑn, -ˌpɔn] *conj* : con lo cual, después de lo cual

wherever¹ [hwɛr'ɛvər] *adv* **1** WHERE : dónde, adónde **2** : en cualquier parte ⟨or wherever : o donde sea⟩

wherever² *conj* : dondequiera que, donde sea ⟨wherever you go : dondequiera que vayas⟩

wherewithal ['hwɛrwɪˌðɔl, -ˌθɔl] *n* : medios *mpl*, recursos *mpl*

whet ['hwɛt] *vt* **whetted**; **whetting** **1** SHARPEN : afilar **2** STIMULATE : estimular ⟨to whet the appetite : estimular el apetito⟩

whether ['hwɛðər] *conj* **1** : si ⟨I don't know whether it is finished : no sé si está acabado⟩ ⟨we doubt whether he'll show up : dudamos que aparezca⟩ **2** (*used in comparisons*) ⟨whether I like it or not : tanto si quiero como si no⟩ ⟨whether he comes or he doesn't : venga o no⟩

whetstone ['hwɛtˌsto:n] *n* : piedra *f* de afilar

whey ['hweɪ] *n* : suero *m* (de la leche)

which¹ ['hwɪtʃ] *adj* : qué, cuál ⟨which tie do you prefer? : ¿cuál corbata prefieres?⟩ ⟨which ones? : ¿cuáles?⟩ ⟨tell me which house is yours : dime qué casa es la tuya⟩

which² *pron* **1** : cuál ⟨which is the right answer? : ¿cuál es la respuesta correcta?⟩ **2** : que, el (la) cual ⟨the cup which broke : la taza que se quebró⟩ ⟨the house, which is made of brick : la casa, la cual es de ladrillo⟩

whichever¹ [*h*wɪtʃˈevər] *adj* : el (la) que, cualquiera que ⟨whichever book you like : cualquier libro que te guste⟩

whichever² *pron* : el (la) que, cualquiera que ⟨take whichever you want : toma el que quieras⟩ ⟨whichever I choose : cualquiera que elija⟩

whiff¹ [ˈ*h*wɪf] *v* PUFF : soplar

whiff² *n* **1** PUFF : soplo *m*, ráfaga *f* **2** SNIFF : olor *m* **3** HINT : dejo *m*, pizca *f*

while¹ [ˈ*h*waɪl] *vt* **whiled; whiling** : pasar ⟨to while away the time : matar el tiempo⟩

while² *n* **1** TIME : rato *m*, tiempo *m* ⟨after a while : después de un rato⟩ ⟨in a while : dentro de poco⟩ **2 to be worth one's while** : valer la pena

while³ *conj* **1** : mientras ⟨whistle while you work : silba mientras trabajas⟩ **2** WHEREAS : mientras que **3** ALTHOUGH : aunque ⟨while it's very good, it's not perfect : aunque es muy bueno, no es perfecto⟩

whim [ˈ*h*wɪm] *n* : capricho *m*, antojo *m*

whimper¹ [ˈ*h*wɪmpər] *vi* : lloriquear, gimotear

whimper² *n* : quejido *m*

whimsical [ˈ*h*wɪmzɪkəl] *adj* **1** CAPRICIOUS : caprichoso, fantasioso **2** ERRATIC : errático — **whimsically** *adv*

whine¹ [ˈ*h*waɪn] *vi* **whined; whining 1** : lloriquear, gimotear, gemir **2** COMPLAIN : quejarse

whine² *n* : quejido *m*, gemido *m*

whinny¹ [ˈ*h*wɪni] *vi* **-nied; -nying** : relinchar

whinny² *n, pl* **-nies** : relincho *m*

whip¹ [ˈ*h*wɪp] *v* **whipped; whipping** *vt* **1** SNATCH : sacar (rápidamente), arrebatar ⟨she whipped the cloth off the table : arrebató el mantel de la mesa⟩ **2** LASH : azotar **3** DEFEAT : vencer, derrotar **4** INCITE : incitar, despertar ⟨to whip up enthusiasm : despertar el entusiasmo⟩ **5** BEAT : batir (huevos, crema, etc.) — *vi* FLAP : agitarse

whip² *n* **1** : látigo *m*, azote *m*, fusta *f* (de jinete) **2** : miembro *m* de un cuerpo legislativo encargado de disciplina

whiplash [ˈ*h*wɪpˌlæʃ] *n or* **whiplash injury** : traumatismo *m* cervical

whippet [ˈ*h*wɪpət] *n* : galgo *m* pequeño, galgo *m* inglés

whir¹ [ˈ*h*wər] *vi* **whirred; whirring** : zumbar

whir² *n* : zumbido *m*

whirl¹ [ˈ*h*wərl] *vi* **1** SPIN : dar vueltas, girar ⟨my head is whirling : la cabeza me

está dando vueltas⟩ **2 to whirl about** : arremolinarse, moverse rápidamente

whirl² *n* **1** SPIN : giro *m*, vuelta *f*, remolino *m* (dícese del polvo, etc.) **2** BUSTLE : bullicio *m*, torbellino *m* (de actividad, etc.) **3 to give it a whirl** : intentar hacer, probar

whirlpool [ˈ*h*wərlˌpuːl] *n* : vorágine *f*, remolino *m*

whirlwind [ˈ*h*wərlˌwɪnd] *n* : remolino *m*, torbellino *m*, tromba *f*

whisk¹ [ˈ*h*wɪsk] *vt* **1** : llevar ⟨she whisked the children off to bed : llevó a los niños a la cama⟩ **2** : batir ⟨to whisk eggs : batir huevos⟩ **3 to whisk away** *or* **to whisk off** : sacudir

whisk² *n* **1** WHISKING : sacudida *f* (movimiento) **2** : batidor *m* (para batir huevos, etc.)

whisk broom *n* : escobilla *f*

whisker [ˈ*h*wɪskər] *n* **1** : pelo *m* (de la barba o el bigote) **2 whiskers** *npl* : bigotes *mpl* (de animales)

whiskey *or* **whisky** [ˈ*h*wɪski] *n, pl* **-keys** *or* **-kies** : whisky *m*

whisper¹ [ˈ*h*wɪspər] *vi* : cuchichear, susurrar — *vt* : decir en voz baja, susurrar

whisper² *n* **1** WHISPERING : susurro *m*, cuchicheo *m* **2** RUMOR : rumor *m* **3** TRACE : dejo *m*, pizca *f*

whistle¹ [ˈ*h*wɪsəl] *v* **-tled; -tling** *vi* : silbar, chiflar, pitar (dícese de un tren, etc.) — *vt* : silbar ⟨to whistle a tune : silbar una melodía⟩

whistle² *n* **1** WHISTLING : chiflido *m*, silbido *m* **2** : silbato *m*, pito *m* (instrumento)

whit [ˈ*h*wɪt] *n* BIT : ápice *m*, pizca *f*

white¹ [ˈ*h*waɪt] *adj* **whiter, -est** : blanco

white² *n* **1** : blanco *m* (color) **2** : clara *f* (de huevos) **3** *or* **white person** : blanco *m*, -ca *f*

white blood cell *n* : glóbulo *m* blanco

whitecaps [ˈ*h*waɪtˌkæps] *npl* : cabrillas *fpl*

white–collar [ˈ*h*waɪtˈkɑlər] *adj* **1** : de oficina **2 white–collar worker** : oficinista *mf*

whitefish [ˈ*h*waɪtˌfɪʃ] *n* : pescado *m* blanco

whiten [ˈ*h*waɪtən] *vt* : blanquear — *vi* : ponerse blanco

whiteness [ˈ*h*waɪtnəs] *n* : blancura *f*

white–tailed deer [ˈ*h*waɪtˈteɪld] *n* : ciervo *f* de Virginia

whitewash¹ [ˈ*h*waɪtˌwɔʃ] *vt* **1** : enjalbegar, blanquear ⟨to whitewash a fence : enjalbegar una valla⟩ **2** CONCEAL : encubrir (un escándalo, etc.)

whitewash² *n* **1** : jalbegue *m*, lechada *f* **2** COVER-UP : encubrimiento *m*

whither [ˈ*h*wɪðər] *adv* : adónde

whiting [ˈ*h*waɪtɪŋ] *n* : merluza *f*, pescadilla *f* (pez)

whitish [ˈ*h*waɪtɪʃ] *adj* : blancuzco

whittle [ˈ*h*wɪtəl] *vt* **-tled; -tling 1** : tallar (madera) **2 to whittle down** : reducir, recortar ⟨to whittle down expenses : reducir los gastos⟩

whiz¹ *or* **whizz** [ˈʰwɪz] *vi* **whizzed; whizzing 1** BUZZ : zumbar **2 to whiz by** : pasar muy rápido, pasar volando

whiz² *or* **whizz** *n, pl* **whizzes 1** BUZZ : zumbido *m* **2 to be a whiz** : ser un prodigio, ser muy hábil

who [ˈhuː] *pron* **1** (*used in direct and indirect questions*) : quién ⟨who is that? : ¿quién es ése?⟩ ⟨who did it? : ¿quién lo hizo?⟩ ⟨we know who they are : sabemos quiénes son⟩ **2** (*used in relative clauses*) : que, quien ⟨the lady who lives there : la señora que vive allí⟩ ⟨for those who wait : para los que esperan, para quienes esperan⟩

whodunit [huːˈdʌnɪt] *n* : novela *f* policíaca

whoever [huːˈɛvər] *pron* **1** : quienquiera que, quien ⟨whoever did it : quienquiera que lo hizo⟩ ⟨give it to whoever you want : dalo a quien quieras⟩ **2** (*used in questions*) : quién ⟨whoever could that be? : ¿quién podría ser?⟩

whole¹ [ˈhoːl] *adj* **1** UNHURT : ileso **2** INTACT : intacto, sano **3** ENTIRE : entero, íntegro ⟨the whole island : toda la isla⟩ ⟨whole milk : leche entera⟩ **4 a whole lot** : muchísimo

whole² *n* **1** : todo *m* **2 as a whole** : en conjunto **3 on the whole** : en general

wholehearted [ˈhoːlˈhɑrtəd] *adj* : sin reservas, incondicional

whole number *n* : entero *m*

wholesale¹ [ˈhoːlˌseɪl] *v* **-saled; -saling** *vt* : vender al por mayor — *vi* : venderse al por mayor

wholesale² *adv* : al por mayor

wholesale³ *adj* **1** : al por mayor ⟨wholesale grocer : tendero al por mayor⟩ **2** TOTAL : total, absoluto ⟨wholesale slaughter : matanza sistemática⟩

wholesale⁴ *n* : mayoreo *m*

wholesaler [ˈhoːlˌseɪlər] *n* : mayorista *mf*

wholesome [ˈhoːlsəm] *adj* **1** : sano ⟨wholesome advice : consejo sano⟩ **2** HEALTHY : sano, saludable

whole wheat *adj* : de trigo integral

wholly [ˈhoːli] *adv* **1** COMPLETELY : completamente **2** SOLELY : exclusivamente, únicamente

whom [ˈhuːm] *pron* **1** (*used in direct questions*) : a quién ⟨whom did you choose? : ¿a quién elegiste?⟩ **2** (*used in indirect questions*) : de quién, con quién, en quién ⟨I don't know whom to consult : no sé con quién consultar⟩ **3** (*used in relative clauses*) : que, a quien ⟨the lawyer whom I recommended to you : el abogado que te recomendé⟩

whomever [huːmˈɛvər] *pron* WHOEVER : quienquiera, quien ⟨marry whomever you please : cásate con quien quieras⟩

whoop¹ [ˈʰwuːp, ˈhwʊp] *vi* : gritar, chillar

whoop² *n* : grito *m*

whooping cough *n* : tos *f* ferina

whopper [ˈʰwɑpər] *n* **1** : cosa *f* enorme **2** LIE : mentira *f* colosal

whopping [ˈʰwɑpɪŋ] *adj* : enorme

whore [ˈhor] *n* : puta *f*, ramera *f*

whorl [ˈʰworl, ˈhwərl] *n* : espiral *f*, espira *f* (de una concha), línea *f* (de una huella digital)

whose¹ [ˈhuːz] *adj* **1** (*used in questions*) : de quién ⟨whose truck is that? : ¿de quién es ese camión?⟩ **2** (*used in relative clauses*) : cuyo ⟨the person whose work is finished : la persona cuyo trabajo está terminado⟩

whose² *pron* : de quién ⟨tell me whose it was : dime de quién era⟩

why¹ [ˈʰwaɪ] *adv* : por qué ⟨why did you do it? : ¿por qué lo hizo?⟩

why² *n, pl* **whys** REASON : porqué *m*, razón *f*

why³ *conj* : por qué ⟨I know why he left : yo sé por qué salió⟩ ⟨there's no reason why it should exist : no hay razón para que exista⟩

why⁴ *interj* (*used to express surprise*) : ¡vaya!, ¡mira!

wick [ˈwɪk] *n* : mecha *f*

wicked [ˈwɪkəd] *adj* **1** EVIL : malo, malvado **2** MISCHIEVOUS : travieso, pícaro ⟨a wicked grin : una sonrisa traviesa⟩ **3** TERRIBLE : terrible, horrible ⟨a wicked storm : una tormenta horrible⟩

wickedly [ˈwɪkədli] *adv* : con maldad

wickedness [ˈwɪkədnəs] *n* : maldad *f*

wicker¹ [ˈwɪkər] *adj* : de mimbre

wicker² *n* **1** : mimbre *m* **2** → **wickerwork**

wickerwork [ˈwɪkərˌwərk] *n* : artículos *mpl* de mimbre

wicket [ˈwɪkət] *n* **1** WINDOW : ventanilla *f* **2** *or* **wicket gate** : postigo *m* **3** : aro *m* (en croquet), palos *mpl* (en críquet)

wide¹ [ˈwaɪd] *adv* **wider; widest 1** WIDELY : por todas partes ⟨to travel far and wide : viajar por todas partes⟩ **2** COMPLETELY : completamente, totalmente ⟨wide open : abierto de par en par⟩ **3 wide apart** : muy separados

wide² *adj* **wider; widest 1** VAST : vasto, extensivo ⟨a wide area : una área extensiva⟩ **2** : ancho ⟨three meters wide : tres metros de ancho⟩ **3** BROAD : ancho, amplio **4** *or* **wide-open** : muy abierto **5 wide of the mark** : desviado, lejos del blanco

wide-awake [ˈwaɪdəˈweɪk] *adj* : (completamente) despierto

wide-eyed [ˈwaɪdˈaɪd] *adj* **1** : con los ojos muy abiertos **2** NAIVE : inocente, ingenuo

widely [ˈwaɪdli] *adv* : extensivamente, por todas partes

widen [ˈwaɪdən] *vt* : ampliar, ensanchar — *vi* : ampliarse, ensancharse

widespread [ˈwaɪdˈsprɛd] *adj* : extendido, extenso, difuso

widow¹ [ˈwɪˌdoː] *vt* : dejar viuda ⟨to be widowed : enviudar⟩

widow² *n* : viuda *f*

widower ['wɪdowər] *n* : viudo *m*

width ['wɪdθ] *n* : ancho *m*, anchura *f*

wield ['wi:ld] *vt* **1** USE : usar, manejar ⟨to wield a broom : usar una escoba⟩ **2** EXERCISE : ejercer ⟨to wield influence : influir⟩

wiener ['wi:nər] → **frankfurter**

wife ['waɪf] *n, pl* **wives** ['waɪvz] : esposa *f*, mujer *f*

wifely ['waɪfli] *adj* : de esposa, conyugal

wig ['wɪg] *n* : peluca *f*

wiggle[1] ['wɪɡəl] *v* **-gled; -gling** *vt* : menear, contonear ⟨to wiggle one's hips : contonearse⟩ — *vi* : menearse

wiggle[2] *n* : meneo *m*, contoneo *m*

wiggly ['wɪɡəli] *adj* **-glier; -est 1** : que se menea **2** WAVY : ondulado

wigwag ['wɪɡ,wæg] *vi* **-wagged; -wagging** : comunicar por señales

wigwam ['wɪɡ,wɑm] *n* : wigwam *m*

wild[1] ['waɪld] *adv* **1** → **wildly 2 to run wild** : descontrolarse

wild[2] *adj* **1** : salvaje, silvestre, cimarrón ⟨wild horses : caballos salvajes⟩ ⟨wild rice : arroz silvestre⟩ **2** DESOLATE : yermo, agreste **3** UNRULY : desenfrenado **4** CRAZY : loco, fantástico ⟨wild ideas : ideas locas⟩ **5** BARBAROUS : salvaje, bárbaro **6** ERRATIC : errático ⟨a wild throw : un tiro errático⟩

wild[3] *n* → **wilderness**

wild card *n* **1** : factor *m* desconocido **2** : comodín *m* (carta o símbolo)

wildcat ['waɪld,kæt] *n* **1** : gato *m* montés **2** BOBCAT : lince *m* rojo

wilderness ['wɪldərnəs] *n* : yermo *m*, desierto *m*

wildfire ['waɪld,faɪr] *n* **1** : fuego *m* descontrolado **2 to spread like wildfire** : propagarse como un reguero de pólvora

wildflower ['waɪld,flauər] *n* : flor *f* silvestre

wildfowl ['waɪld,faul] *n* : ave *f* de caza

wildlife ['waɪld,laɪf] *n* : fauna *f*

wildly ['waɪldli] *adv* **1** FRANTICALLY : frenéticamente, como un loco **2** EXTREMELY : extremadamente ⟨wildly happy : loco de felicidad⟩

wile[1] ['waɪl] *vt* **wiled; wiling** LURE : atraer

wile[2] *n* : ardid *m*, artimaña *f*

will[1] ['wɪl] *v, past* **would** ['wʊd]; *pres sing & pl* **will** *vt* WISH : querer ⟨do what you will : haz lo que quieras⟩ — *v aux* **1** (*expressing willingness*) ⟨no one would take the job : nadie aceptaría el trabajo⟩ ⟨I won't do it : no lo haré⟩ **2** (*expressing habitual action*) ⟨he will get angry over nothing : se pone furioso por cualquier cosa⟩ **3** (*forming the future tense*) ⟨tomorrow we will go shopping : mañana iremos de compras⟩ **4** (*expressing capacity*) ⟨the couch will hold three people : en el sofá cabrán tres personas⟩ **5** (*expressing determination*) ⟨I will go despite them : iré a pesar de

ellos⟩ **6** (*expressing probability*) ⟨that will be the mailman : eso ha de ser el cartero⟩ **7** (*expressing inevitability*) ⟨accidents will happen : los accidentes ocurrirán⟩ **8** (*expressing a command*) ⟨you will do as I say : harás lo que digo⟩

will[2] *vt* **1** ORDAIN : disponer, decretar ⟨if God wills it : si Dios lo dispone, si Dios quiere⟩ **2** : lograr a fuerza de voluntad ⟨they were willing him to succeed : estaban deseando que tuviera éxito⟩ **3** BEQUEATH : legar

will[3] *n* **1** DESIRE : deseo *m*, voluntad *f* **2** VOLITION : voluntad *f* ⟨free will : libre albedrío⟩ **3** WILLPOWER : voluntad *f*, fuerza *f* de voluntad ⟨a will of iron : una voluntad férrea⟩ **4** : testamento *m* ⟨to make a will : hacer testamento⟩

willful *or* **wilful** ['wɪlfəl] *adj* **1** OBSTINATE : obstinado, terco **2** INTENTIONAL : intencionado, deliberado — **willfully** *adv*

willing ['wɪlɪŋ] *adj* **1** INCLINED, READY : listo, dispuesto **2** OBLIGING : servicial, complaciente

willingly ['wɪlɪŋli] *adv* : con gusto

willingness ['wɪlɪŋnəs] *n* : buena voluntad *f*

willow ['wɪ,lo:] *n* : sauce *m*

willowy ['wɪlowi] *adj* : esbelto

willpower ['wɪl,pauər] *n* : voluntad *f*, fuerza *f* de voluntad

wilt ['wɪlt] *vi* **1** : marchitarse (dícese de las flores) **2** LANGUISH : debilitarse, languidecer

wily ['waɪli] *adj* **wilier; -est** : artero, astuto

wimp ['wɪmp] *n* **1** COWARD : gallina *f*, cobarde *mf* **2** WEAKLING : debilucho *m*, -cha *f*, alfeñique *m*

win[1] ['wɪn] *v* **won** ['wʌn]; **winning** *vi* : ganar — *vt* **1** : ganar, conseguir **2 to win over** : ganarse a **3 to win someone's heart** : conquistar a alguien

win[2] *n* : triunfo *m*, victoria *f*

wince[1] ['wɪnts] *vi* **winced; wincing** : estremecerse, hacer una mueca de dolor

wince[2] *n* : mueca *f* de dolor

winch ['wɪntʃ] *n* : torno *m*

wind[1] ['wɪnd] *vt* : dejar sin aliento ⟨to be winded : quedarse sin aliento⟩

wind[2] ['waɪnd] *v* **wound** ['waund]; **winding** *vi* MEANDER : serpentear — *vt* **1** COIL, ROLL : envolver, enrollar **2** TURN : hacer girar ⟨to wind a clock : darle cuerda a un reloj⟩

wind[3] ['wɪnd] *n* **1** : viento *m* ⟨against the wind : contra el viento⟩ **2** BREATH : aliento *m* **3** FLATULENCE : flatulencia *f*, ventosidad *f* **4 to get wind of** : enterarse de

wind[4] ['waɪnd] *n* **1** TURN : vuelta *f* **2** BEND : recodo *m*, curva *f*

windbreak ['wɪnd,breɪk] *n* : barrera *f* contra el viento, abrigadero *m*

windfall ['wɪnd,fɔl] *n* **1** : fruta *f* caída **2** : beneficio *m* imprevisto

wind instrument *n* : instrumento *m* de viento

windlass ['wɪndləs] *n* : cabrestante *m*
windmill ['wɪnd,mɪl] *n* : molino *m* de viento
window ['wɪn,doː] *n* **1** : ventana *f* (de un edificio o una computadora), ventanilla *f* (de un vehículo o avión), vitrina *f* (de una tienda) **2** → **windowpane**
windowpane ['wɪn,doː,peɪn] *n* : vidrio *m*
window-shop ['wɪndoˌʃɑp] *vi* **-shopped; -shopping** : mirar las vitrinas
windpipe ['wɪnd,paɪp] *n* : tráquea *f*
windshield ['wɪnd,ʃiːld] *n* **1** : parabrisas *m* **2 windshield wiper** : limpiaparabrisas *m*
windup ['waɪnd,ʌp] *n* : conclusión *f*
wind up *vt* END : terminar, concluir — *vi* : terminar, acabar
windward¹ ['wɪndwərd] *adj* : de barlovento
windward² *n* : barlovento *m*
windy ['wɪndi] *adj* **windier; -est 1** : ventoso ⟨it's windy : hace viento⟩ **2** VERBOSE : verboso, prolijo
wine¹ ['waɪn] *v* **wined; wining** *vi* : beber vino — *vt* **to wine and dine** : agasajar
wine² *n* : vino *m*
wing¹ ['wɪŋ] *vi* FLY : volar
wing² *n* **1** : ala *f* (de un ave, un avión, o un edificio) **2** FACTION : ala *f* ⟨the right wing of the party : el ala derecha del partido⟩ **3 wings** *npl* : bastidores *mpl* (de un teatro) **4 on the wing** : al vuelo, volando **5 under one's wing** : bajo el cargo de uno
winged ['wɪŋd, 'wɪŋəd] *adj* : alado
wink¹ ['wɪŋk] *vi* **1** : guiñar el ojo **2** BLINK : pestañear, parpadear **3** FLICKER : parpadear, titilar
wink² *n* **1** : guiño *m* (del ojo) **2** NAP : siesta *f* ⟨not to sleep a wink : no pegar el ojo⟩
winner ['wɪnər] *n* : ganador *m*, -dora *f*
winning ['wɪnɪŋ] *adj* **1** VICTORIOUS : ganador **2** CHARMING : encantador
winnings ['wɪnɪŋz] *npl* : ganancias *fpl*
winnow ['wɪ,noː] *vt* : aventar (el grano, etc.)
winsome ['wɪnsəm] *adj* CHARMING : encantador
winter¹ ['wɪntər] *adj* : invernal, de invierno
winter² *n* : invierno *m*
wintergreen ['wɪntər,griːn] *n* : gaulteria *f*
wintertime ['wɪntər,taɪm] *n* : invierno *m*
wintry ['wɪntri] *adj* **wintrier; -est 1** WINTER : invernal, de invierno **2** COLD : frío ⟨she gave us a wintry greeting : nos saludó fríamente⟩
wipe¹ ['waɪp] *vt* **wiped; wiping 1** : limpiar, pasarle un trapo a ⟨to wipe one's feet : limpiarse los pies⟩ **2 to wipe away** : enjugar (lágrimas), borrar (una memoria) **3 to wipe out** ANNIHILATE : aniquilar, destruir
wipe² *n* : pasada *f* (con un trapo, etc.)

wire¹ ['waɪr] *vt* **wired; wiring 1** : instalar el cableado en (una casa, etc.) **2** BIND : atar con alambre **3** TELEGRAPH : telegrafiar, mandarle un telegrama (a alguien)
wire² *n* **1** : alambre *m* ⟨barbed wire : alambre de púas⟩ **2** : cable *m* (eléctrico o telefónico) **3** CABLEGRAM, TELEGRAM : telegrama *m*, cable *m*
wireless ['waɪrləs] *adj* : inalámbrico
wiretapping ['waɪr,tæpɪŋ] *n* : intervención *f* electrónica
wiring ['waɪrɪŋ] *n* : cableado *m*
wiry ['waɪri] *adj* **wirier; -est 1** : hirsuto, tieso (dícese del pelo) **2** : esbelto y musculoso (dícese del cuerpo)
wisdom ['wɪzdəm] *n* **1** KNOWLEDGE : sabiduría *f* **2** JUDGMENT, SENSE : sensatez *f*
wisdom tooth *n* : muela *f* de juicio
wise¹ ['waɪz] *adj* **wiser; wisest 1** LEARNED : sabio **2** SENSIBLE : sabio, sensato, prudente **3** KNOWLEDGEABLE : entendido, enterado ⟨they're wise to his tricks : conocen muy bien sus mañas⟩
wise² *n* : manera *f*, modo *m* ⟨in no wise : de ninguna manera⟩
wisecrack ['waɪz,kræk] *n* : broma *f*, chiste *m*
wisely ['waɪzli] *adv* : sabiamente, sensatamente
wish¹ ['wɪʃ] *vt* **1** WANT : desear, querer **2 to wish (something) for** : desear ⟨they wished me well : me desearon lo mejor⟩ — *vi* **1** : pedir (como deseo) **2** : querer ⟨as you wish : como quieras⟩
wish² *n* **1** : deseo *m* ⟨to grant a wish : conceder un deseo⟩ **2 wishes** *npl* : saludos *mpl*, recuerdos *mpl* ⟨to send best wishes : mandar muchos recuerdos⟩
wishbone ['wɪʃ,boːn] *n* : espoleta *f*
wishful ['wɪʃfəl] *adj* **1** HOPEFUL : deseoso, lleno de esperanza **2 wishful thinking** : ilusiones *fpl*
wishy-washy ['wɪʃi,wɔʃi, -,wɑʃi] *adj* : insípido, soso
wisp ['wɪsp] *n* **1** BUNCH : manojo *m* (de paja) **2** STRAND : mechón *m* (de pelo) **3** : voluta *f* (de humo)
wispy ['wɪspi] *adj* **wispier; -est** : tenue, ralo (dícese del pelo)
wisteria [wɪs'tɪriə] *n* : glicinia *f*
wistful ['wɪstfəl] *adj* : añorante, anhelante, melancólico — **wistfully** *adv*
wistfulness ['wɪstfəlnəs] *n* : añoranza *f*, melancolía *f*
wit ['wɪt] *n* **1** INTELLIGENCE : inteligencia *f* **2** CLEVERNESS : ingenio *m*, gracia *f*, agudeza *f* **3** HUMOR : humorismo *m* **4** JOKER : chistoso *m*, -sa *f* **5 wits** *npl* : razón *f*, buen juicio *m* ⟨scared out of one's wits : muerto de miedo⟩ ⟨to be at one's wits' end : estar desesperado⟩
witch ['wɪtʃ] *n* : bruja *f*
witchcraft ['wɪtʃ,kræft] *n* : brujería *f*, hechicería *f*

witch doctor *n* : hechicero *m*, -ra *f*
witchery [ˈwɪtʃəri] *n*, *pl* **-eries** 1 → **witchcraft** 2 CHARM : encanto *m*
witch-hunt [ˈwɪtʃˌhʌnt] *n* : caza *f* de brujas
with [ˈwɪð, ˈwɪθ] *prep* 1 : con ⟨I'm going with you : voy contigo⟩ ⟨coffee with milk : café con leche⟩ 2 AGAINST : con ⟨to argue with someone : discutir con alguien⟩ 3 (*used in descriptions*) : con, de ⟨the girl with red hair : la muchacha de pelo rojo⟩ 4 (*indicating manner, means, or cause*) : con ⟨to cut with a knife : cortar con un cuchillo⟩ ⟨fix it with tape : arréglalo con cinta⟩ ⟨with luck : consuerte⟩ 5 DESPITE : a pesar de, aún con ⟨with all his work, the business failed : a pesar de su trabajo, el negocio fracasó⟩ 6 REGARDING : con respecto a, con ⟨the trouble with your plan : el problema con su plan⟩ 7 ACCORDING TO : según ⟨it varies with the season : varía según la estación⟩ 8 (*indicating support or understanding*) : con ⟨I'm with you all the way : estoy contigo hasta el fin⟩
withdraw [wɪðˈdrɔ, wɪθ-] *v* **-drew** [-ˈdruː]; **-drawn** [-ˈdrɔn]; **-drawing** *vt* 1 REMOVE : retirar, apartar, sacar (dinero) 2 RETRACT : retractarse de — *vi* : retirarse, recluirse (de la sociedad)
withdrawal [wɪðˈdrɔəl, wɪθ-] *n* 1 : retirada *f*, retiro *m* (de fondos, etc.), retraimiento *m* (social) 2 RETRACTION : retractación *f* 3 **withdrawal symptoms** : síndrome *m* de abstinencia
withdrawn [wɪðˈdrɔn, wɪθ-] *adj* : retraído, reservado, introvertido
wither [ˈwɪðər] *vt* : marchitar, agostar — *vi* 1 WILT : marchitarse 2 WEAKEN : decaer, debilitarse
withhold [wɪθˈhoːld, wɪð-] *vt* **-held** [-ˈhld]; **-holding** : retener (fondos), aplazar (una decisión), negar (permiso, etc.)
within[1] [wɪðˈɪn, wɪθ-] *adv* : dentro
within[2] *prep* 1 : dentro de ⟨within the limits : dentro de los límites⟩ 2 (*in expressions of distance*) : a menos de ⟨within 10 miles of the ocean : a menos de 10 millas del mar⟩ 3 (*in expressions of time*) : dentro de ⟨within an hour : dentro de una hora⟩ ⟨within a month of her birthday : a poco menos de un mes de su cumpleaños⟩
without[1] [wɪðˈaʊt, wɪθ-] *adv* 1 OUTSIDE : fuera 2 **to do without** : pasar sin algo
without[2] *prep* 1 OUTSIDE : fuera de 2 : sin ⟨without fear : sin temor⟩ ⟨he left without his briefcase : se fue sin su portafolios⟩
withstand [wɪθˈstænd, wɪð-] *vt* **-stood** [-ˈstʊd]; **-standing** 1 BEAR : aguantar, soportar 2 RESIST : resistir, resistirse a
witless [ˈwɪtləs] *adj* : estúpido, tonto
witness[1] [ˈwɪtnəs] *vt* 1 SEE : presenciar, ver, ser testigo de 2 : atestiguar (una firma, etc.) — *vi* TESTIFY : atestiguar, testimoniar

witness[2] *n* 1 TESTIMONY : testimonio *m* ⟨to bear witness : atestiguar, testimoniar⟩ 2 : testigo *mf* ⟨witness for the prosecution : testigo de cargo⟩
witticism [ˈwɪtəˌsɪzəm] *n* : agudeza *f*, ocurrencia *f*
witty [ˈwɪti] *adj* **-tier; -est** : ingenioso, ocurrente, gracioso
wives → **wife**
wizard [ˈwɪzərd] *n* 1 SORCERER : mago *m*, brujo *m*, hechicero *m* 2 : genio *m* ⟨a math wizard : un genio en matemáticas⟩
wizened [ˈwɪzənd, ˈwiː-] *adj* : arrugado, marchito
wobble[1] [ˈwɑbəl] *vi* **-bled; -bling** : bambolearse, tambalearse, temblar (dícese de la voz)
wobble[2] *n* : tambaleo *m*, bamboleo *m*
wobbly [ˈwɑbəli] *adj* : bamboleante, tambaleante, inestable
woe [ˈwoː] *n* 1 GRIEF, MISFORTUNE : desgracia *f*, infortunio *m*, aflicción *f* 2 **woes** *npl* TROUBLES : penas *fpl*, males *mpl*
woeful [ˈwoːfəl] *adj* 1 SORROWFUL : afligido, apenado, triste 2 UNFORTUNATE : desgraciado, infortunado 3 DEPLORABLE : lamentable
woke, woken → **wake**[1]
wolf[1] [ˈwʊlf] *vt* *or* **to wolf down** : engullir
wolf[2] *n, pl* **wolves** [ˈwʊlvz] : lobo *m*, -ba *f*
wolfram [ˈwʊlfrəm] → **tungsten**
wolverine [ˌwʊlvəˈriːn] *n* : glotón *m* (animal)
woman [ˈwʊmən] *n, pl* **women** [ˈwɪmən] : mujer *f*
womanhood [ˈwʊmənˌhʊd] *n* 1 : condición *f* de mujer 2 WOMEN : mujeres *fpl*
womanly [ˈwʊmənli] *adj* : femenino
womb [ˈwuːm] *n* : útero *m*, matriz *f*
won → **win**
wonder[1] [ˈwʌndər] *vi* 1 SPECULATE : preguntarse, pensar ⟨to wonder about : preguntarse por⟩ 2 MARVEL : asombrarse, maravillarse — *vt* : preguntarse ⟨I wonder if they're coming : me pregunto si vendrán⟩
wonder[2] *n* 1 MARVEL : maravilla *f*, milagro *m* ⟨to work wonders : hacer maravillas⟩ 2 AMAZEMENT : asombro *m*
wonderful [ˈwʌndərfəl] *adj* : maravilloso, estupendo
wonderfully [ˈwʌndərfəli] *adv* : maravillosamente, de maravilla
wonderland [ˈwʌndərˌlænd, -lənd] *n* : país *m* de las maravillas
wonderment [ˈwʌndərmənt] *n* : asombro *m*
wondrous [ˈwʌndrəs] → **wonderful**
wont[1] [ˈwɔnt, ˈwoːnt, ˈwɑnt] *adj* : acostumbrado, habituado
wont[2] *n* : hábito *m*, costumbre *f*
won't [ˈwoːnt] (*contraction of* **will not**) → **will**[1]
woo [ˈwuː] *vt* 1 COURT : cortejar 2 : buscar el apoyo de (clientes, votantes, etc.)

wood¹ ['wʊd] *adj* : de madera
wood² *n* **1** *or* **woods** *npl* FOREST : bosque *m* **2** : madera *f* (materia) **3** FIREWOOD : leña *f*
woodchuck ['wʊd,tʃʌk] *n* : marmota *f* de América
woodcut ['wʊd,kʌt] *n* **1** : plancha *f* de madera (para imprimir imágenes) **2** : grabado *m* en madera
woodcutter ['wʊd,kʌt̬ər] *n* : leñador *m*, -dora *f*
wooded ['wʊdəd] *adj* : arbolado, boscoso
wooden ['wʊdən] *adj* **1** : de madera ⟨a wooden cross : una cruz de madera⟩ **2** STIFF : rígido, inexpresivo (dícese del estilo, de la cara, etc.)
woodland ['wʊdlənd, -,lænd] *n* : bosque *m*
woodpecker ['wʊd,pɛkər] *n* : pájaro *m* carpintero
woodshed ['wʊd,ʃɛd] *n* : leñera *f*
woodsman ['wʊdzmən] → **woodcutter**
woodwind ['wʊd,wɪnd] *n* : instrumento *m* de viento de madera
woodworking ['wʊd,wərkɪŋ] *n* : carpintería *f*
woody ['wʊdi] *adj* **woodier; -est 1** → **wooded 2** : leñoso ⟨woody plants : plantas leñosas⟩ **3** : leñoso (dícese de la textura), a madera (dícese del aroma, etc.)
woof ['wʊf] → **weft**
wool ['wʊl] *n* : lana *f*
woolen¹ *or* **woollen** ['wʊlən] *adj* : de lana
woolen² *or* **woollen** *n* **1** : lana *f* (tela) **2 woolens** *npl* : prendas *fpl* de lana
woolly ['wʊli] *adj* **-lier; -est 1** : lanudo **2** CONFUSED : confuso, vago
woozy ['wu:zi] *adj* **-zier; -est** : mareado
word¹ ['wərd] *vt* : expresar, formular, redactar
word² *n* **1** : palabra *f*, vocablo *m*, voz *f* ⟨word for word : palabra por palabra⟩ ⟨in one's own words : en sus propias palabras⟩ ⟨words fail me : me quedo sin habla⟩ **2** REMARK : palabra *f* ⟨by word of mouth : de palabra⟩ ⟨to have a word with : hablar (dos palabras) con⟩ **3** COMMAND : orden *f* ⟨to give the word : dar la orden⟩ ⟨just say the word : no tienes que decirlo⟩ **4** MESSAGE, NEWS : noticias *fpl* ⟨is there any word from her? : ¿hay noticias de ella?⟩ ⟨to send word : mandar un recado⟩ **5** PROMISE : palabra *f* ⟨to keep one's word : cumplir uno su palabra⟩ **6 words** *npl* QUARREL : palabra *f*, riña *f* ⟨to have words with : tener unas palabras con, reñir con⟩ **7 words** *npl* TEXT : letra *f* (de una canción, etc.)
wordiness ['wərdinəs] *n* : verbosidad *f*
wording ['wərdɪŋ] *n* : redacción *f*, lenguaje *m* (de un documento)
word processing *n* : procesamiento *m* de textos
word processor *n* : procesador *m* de textos

wordy ['wərdi] *adj* **wordier; -est** : verboso, prolijo
wore → **wear¹**
work¹ ['wərk] *v* **worked** ['wərkt] *or* **wrought** ['rɔt]; **working** *vt* **1** OPERATE : trabajar, operar ⟨to work a machine : operar una máquina⟩ **2** : lograr, conseguir (algo) con esfuerzo ⟨to work one's way up : lograr subir por sus propios esfuerzos⟩ **3** EFFECT : efectuar, llevar a cabo, obrar (milagros) **4** MAKE, SHAPE : elaborar, fabricar, formar ⟨a beautifully wrought vase : un florero bellamente elaborado⟩ **5 to work up** : estimular, excitar ⟨don't get worked up : no te agites⟩ — *vi* **1** LABOR : trabajar ⟨to work full-time : trabajar a tiempo completo⟩ **2** FUNCTION : funcionar, servir
work² *adj* : laboral
work³ *n* **1** LABOR : trabajo *m*, labor *f* **2** EMPLOYMENT : trabajo *m*, empleo *m* **3** TASK : tarea *f*, faena *f* **4** DEED : obra *f*, labor *f* ⟨works of charity : obras de caridad⟩ **5** : obra *f* (de arte o literatura) **6** → **workmanship 7 works** *npl* FACTORY : fábrica *f* **8 works** *npl* MECHANISM : mecanismo *m*
workable ['wərkəbəl] *adj* **1** : explotable (dícese de una mina, etc.) **2** FEASIBLE : factible, realizable
workaday ['wərkə,dei] *adj* : ordinario, banal
workbench ['wərk,bɛntʃ] *n* : mesa *f* de trabajo
workday ['wərk,dei] *n* **1** : jornada *f* laboral **2** WEEKDAY : día *m* hábil, día *m* laborable
worker ['wərkər] *n* : trabajador *m*, -dora *f*; obrero *m*, -ra *f*
working ['wərkɪŋ] *adj* **1** : que trabaja ⟨working mothers : madres que trabajan⟩ ⟨the working class : la clase obrera⟩ **2** : de trabajo ⟨working hours : horas de trabajo⟩ **3** FUNCTIONING : que funciona, operativo **4** SUFFICIENT : suficiente ⟨a working majority : una mayoría suficiente⟩ ⟨working knowledge : conocimientos básicos⟩
workingman ['wərkɪŋ,mæn] *n*, *pl* **-men** [-mən, -,mɛn] : obrero *m*
workman ['wərkmən] *n*, *pl* **-men** [-mən, -,mɛn] **1** → **workingman 2** ARTISAN : artesano *m*
workmanlike ['wərkmən,laik] *adj* : bien hecho, competente
workmanship ['wərkmən,ʃɪp] *n* **1** WORK : ejecución *f*, trabajo *m* **2** CRAFTSMANSHIP : artesanía *f*, destreza *f*
workout ['wərk,aut] *n* : ejercicios *mpl* físicos, entrenamiento *m*
work out *vt* **1** DEVELOP, PLAN : idear, planear, desarrollar **2** RESOLVE : solucionar, resolver ⟨to work out the answer : calcular la solución⟩ — *vi* **1** TURN OUT : resultar **2** SUCCEED : lograr, dar resultado, salir bien **3** EXERCISE : hacer ejercicio

workroom [ˈwərkˌruːm, -ˌrʊm] *n* : taller *m*

workshop [ˈwərkˌʃɑp] *n* : taller *m* ⟨ceramics workshop : taller de cerámica⟩

workstation [ˈwərkˌsteɪʃən] *n* : estación *f* de trabajo (en informática)

world¹ [ˈwərld] *adj* : mundial, del mundo ⟨world championship : campeonato mundial⟩

world² *n* : mundo *m* ⟨around the world : alrededor del mundo⟩ ⟨a world of possibilities : un mundo de posibilidades⟩ ⟨to think the world of someone : tener a alguien en alta estima⟩ ⟨to be worlds apart : no tener nada que ver (uno con otro)⟩

worldly [ˈwərldli] *adj* **1** : mundano ⟨wordly goods : bienes materiales⟩ **2** SOPHISTICATED : sofisticado, de mundo

worldwide¹ [ˈwərldˈwaɪd] *adv* : mundialmente, en todo el mundo

worldwide² *adj* : global, mundial

World Wide Web *n* : World Wide Web *f*

worm¹ [ˈwərm] *vi* CRAWL : arrastrarse, deslizarse (como gusano) — *vt* **1** : desparasitar (un animal) **2 to worm one's way into** : introducirse en ⟨he wormed his way into her confidence : se ganó su confianza⟩ **3 to worm something out of someone** : sonsacarle algo a alguien

worm² *n* **1** : gusano *m*, lombriz *f* **2 worms** *npl* : lombrices *fpl* (parásitos)

wormy [ˈwərmi] *adj* **wormier; -est** : infestado de gusanos

worn *pp* → **wear¹**

worn-out [ˈwornˈaʊt] *adj* **1** USED : gastado, desgastado **2** TIRED : agotado

worried [ˈwərid] *adj* : inquieto, preocupado

worrier [ˈwəriər] *n* : persona *f* que se preocupa mucho

worrisome [ˈwərisəm] *adj* **1** DISTURBING : preocupante, inquietante **2** : que se preocupa mucho (dícese de una persona)

worry¹ [ˈwəri] *v* **-ried; -rying** *vt* : preocupar, inquietar — *vi* : preocuparse, inquietarse, angustiarse

worry² *n, pl* **-ries** : preocupación *f*, inquietud *f*, angustia *f*

worse¹ [ˈwərs] *adv* (*comparative of* **bad** *or of* **ill**) : peor

worse² *adj* (*comparative of* **bad** *or of* **ill**) : peor ⟨from bad to worse : de mal en peor⟩ ⟨to get worse : empeorar⟩ ⟨to feel worse : sentirse peor⟩

worse³ *n* : estado *m* peor ⟨to take a turn for the worse : ponerse peor⟩ ⟨so much the worse : tanto peor⟩

worsen [ˈwərsən] *vt* : empeorar — *vi* : empeorar(se)

worship¹ [ˈwərʃəp] *v* **-shiped** *or* **-shipped; -shiping** *or* **-shipping** *vt* : adorar, venerar ⟨to worship God : adorar a Dios⟩ — *vi* : practicar una religión

worship² *n* : adoración *f*, culto *m*

worshiper *or* **worshipper** [ˈwərʃəpər] *n* : devoto *m*, -ta *f*; adorador *m*, -dora *f*

worst¹ [ˈwərst] *vt* DEFEAT : derrotar

worst² *adv* (*superlative of* **ill** *or of* **bad** *or* **badly**) : peor ⟨the worst dressed of all : el peor vestido de todos⟩

worst³ *adj* (*superlative of* **bad** *or of* **ill**) : peor ⟨the worst movie : la peor película⟩

worst⁴ *n* **the worst** : lo peor, el (la) peor ⟨the worst is over : ya ha pasado lo peor⟩

worsted [ˈwʊstəd, ˈwərstəd] *n* : estambre *m*

worth¹ [ˈwərθ] *n* **1** : valor *m* (monetario) ⟨ten dollars' worth of gas : diez dólares de gasolina⟩ **2** MERIT : valor *m*, mérito *m*, valía *f* ⟨an employee of great worth : un empleado de gran valía⟩

worth² *prep* **to be worth** : valer ⟨her holdings are worth a fortune : sus propiedades valen una fortuna⟩ ⟨it's not worth it : no vale la pena⟩

worthiness [ˈwərðinəs] *n* : mérito *m*

worthless [ˈwərθləs] *adj* **1** : sin valor ⟨worthless trinkets : chucherías sin valor⟩ **2** USELESS : inútil

worthwhile [wərθˈhwaɪl] *adj* : que vale la pena

worthy [ˈwərði] *adj* **-thier; -est 1** : digno ⟨worthy of promotion : digno de un ascenso⟩ **2** COMMENDABLE : meritorio, encomiable

would [ˈwʊd] *past of* **will 1** (*expressing preference*) ⟨I would rather go alone than with her : preferiría ir sola que con ella⟩ **2** (*expressing intent*) ⟨those who would ban certain books : aquellos que prohibirían ciertos libros⟩ **3** (*expressing habitual action*) ⟨he would often take his kids to the park : solía llevar a sus hijos al parque⟩ **4** (*expressing contingency*) ⟨I would go if I had the money : iría yo si tuviera el dinero⟩ **5** (*expressing probability*) ⟨she would have won if she hadn't tripped : habría ganado si no hubiera tropezado⟩ **6** (*expressing a request*) ⟨would you kindly help me with this? : ¿tendría la bondad de ayudarme con esto?⟩

would-be [ˈwʊdˈbiː] *adj* : potencial ⟨a would-be celebrity : un aspirante a celebridad⟩

wouldn't [ˈwʊdənt] (*contraction of* **would not**) → **would**

wound¹ [ˈwuːnd] *vt* : herir

wound² *n* : herida *f*

wound³ [ˈwaʊnd] → **wind²**

wove, woven → **weave¹**

wow [ˈwaʊ] *interj* : ¡guau!, ¡híjole! *Mex*, ¡hala! *Spain*

wrangle¹ [ˈræŋɡəl] *vi* **-gled; -gling** : discutir, reñir ⟨to wrangle over : discutir por⟩

wrangle² *n* : riña *f*, disputa *f*

wrap¹ [ˈræp] *v* **wrapped; wrapping** *vt* **1** COVER : envolver, cubrir ⟨to wrap a package : envolver un paquete⟩

⟨wrapped in mystery : envuelto en misterio⟩ **2** ENCIRCLE : rodear, ceñir ⟨to wrap one's arms around someone : estrechar a alguien⟩ **3 to wrap up** FINISH : darle fin a (algo) — *vi* **1** COIL : envolverse, enroscarse **2 to wrap up** DRESS : abrigarse ⟨wrap up warmly : abrígate bien⟩

wrap² *n* **1** WRAPPER : envoltura *f* **2** : prenda *f* que envuelve (como un chal, una bata, etc.)

wrapper ['ræpər] *n* : envoltura *f*, envoltorio *m*

wrapping ['ræpɪŋ] *n* : envoltura *f*, envoltorio *m*

wrath ['ræθ] *n* : ira *f*, cólera *f*

wrathful ['ræθfəl] *adj* : iracundo

wreak ['ri:k] *vt* : infligir, causar ⟨to wreak havoc : crear caos, causar estragos⟩

wreath ['ri:θ] *n, pl* **wreaths** ['ri:ðz, 'ri:θs] : corona *f* (de flores, etc.)

wreathe ['ri:ð] *vt* **wreathed; wreathing** **1** ADORN : coronar (de flores, etc.) **2** ENVELOP : envolver ⟨wreathed in mist : envuelto en niebla⟩

wreck¹ ['rɛk] *vt* : destruir, arruinar, estrellar (un automóvil), naufragar (un barco)

wreck² *n* **1** WRECKAGE : restos *mpl* (de un buque naufragado, un avión siniestrado, etc.) **2** RUIN : ruina *f*, desastre *m* ⟨this place is a wreck! : ¡este lugar está hecho un desastre!⟩ ⟨to be a nervous wreck : tener los nervios destrozados⟩

wreckage ['rɛkɪʤ] *n* : restos *mpl* (de un buque naufragado, un avión siniestrado, etc.), ruinas *fpl* (de un edificio)

wrecker ['rɛkər] *n* **1** TOW TRUCK : grúa *f* **2** : desguazador *m* (de autos, barcos, etc.), demoledor *m* (de edificios)

wren ['rɛn] *n* : chochín *m*

wrench¹ ['rɛnʧ] *vt* **1** PULL : arrancar (de un tirón) **2** SPRAIN, TWIST : torcerse (un tobillo, un músculo, etc.)

wrench² *n* **1** TUG : tirón *m*, jalón *m* **2** SPRAIN : torcedura *f* **3** *or* **monkey wrench** : llave *f* inglesa

wrest ['rɛst] *vt* : arrancar

wrestle¹ ['rɛsəl] *v* **-tled; -tling** *vi* **1** : luchar, practicar la lucha (en deportes) **2** STRUGGLE : luchar ⟨to wrestle with a dilemma : lidiar con un dilema⟩ — *vt* : luchar contra

wrestle² *n* STRUGGLE : lucha *f*

wrestler ['rɛsələr] *n* : luchador *m*, -dora *f*

wrestling ['rɛsəlɪŋ] *n* : lucha *f*

wretch ['rɛʧ] *n* : infeliz *mf*; desgraciado *m*, -da *f*

wretched ['rɛʧəd] *adj* **1** MISERABLE, UNHAPPY : desdichado, afligido ⟨I feel wretched : me siento muy mal⟩ **2** UNFORTUNATE : miserable, desgraciado, lastimoso ⟨wretched weather : tiempo

espantoso⟩ **3** INFERIOR : inferior, malo

wretchedly ['rɛʧədli] *adv* : miserablemente, lamentablemente

wriggle ['rɪgəl] *vi* **-gled; -gling** : retorcerse, menearse

wring ['rɪŋ] *vt* **wrung** ['rʌŋ]; **wringing** **1** *or* **to wring out** : escurrir, exprimir (el lavado) **2** EXTRACT : arrancar, sacar (por la fuerza) **3** TWIST : torcer, retorcer **4 to wring someone's heart** : partirle el corazón a alguien

wringer ['rɪŋər] *n* : escurridor *m*

wrinkle¹ ['rɪŋkəl] *v* **-kled; -kling** *vt* : arrugar — *vi* : arrugarse

wrinkle² *n* : arruga *f*

wrinkly ['rɪŋkəli] *adj* **wrinklier; -est** : arrugado

wrist ['rɪst] *n* **1** : muñeca *f* (en anatomía) **2** *or* **wristband** ['rɪst-,bænd] CUFF : puño *m*

writ ['rɪt] *n* : orden *f* (judicial)

write ['raɪt] *v* **wrote** ['ro:t]; **written** ['rɪtən]; **writing** : escribir

write down *vt* : apuntar, anotar

write off *vt* CANCEL : cancelar

writer ['raɪtər] *n* : escritor *m*, -tora *f*

writhe ['raɪð] *vi* **writhed; writhing** : retorcerse

writing ['raɪtɪŋ] *n* **1** : escritura *f* **2** HANDWRITING : letra *f* **3 writings** *npl* WORKS : escritos *mpl*, obra *f*

wrong¹ ['rɔŋ] *vt* **wronged; wronging** : ofender, ser injusto con

wrong² *adv* : mal, incorrectamente

wrong³ *adj* **wronger** ['rɔŋər]; **wrongest** ['rɔŋəst] **1** EVIL, SINFUL : malo, injusto, inmoral **2** IMPROPER, UNSUITABLE : inadecuado, inapropiado, malo **3** INCORRECT : incorrecto, erróneo, malo ⟨a wrong answer : una mala respuesta⟩ **4 to be wrong** : equivocarse, estar equivocado

wrong⁴ *n* **1** INJUSTICE : injusticia *f*, mal *m* **2** OFFENSE : ofensa *f*, agravio *m* (en derecho) **3 to be in the wrong** : haber hecho mal, estar equivocado

wrongdoer ['rɔŋ,du:ər] *n* : malhechor *m*, -chora *f*

wrongdoing ['rɔŋ,du:ɪŋ] *n* : fechoría *f*, maldad *f*

wrongful ['rɔŋfəl] *adj* **1** UNJUST : injusto **2** UNLAWFUL : ilegal

wrongly ['rɔŋli] *adv* **1** : injustamente **2** INCORRECTLY : erróneamente, incorrectamente

wrote → **write**

wrought ['rɔt] *adj* **1** SHAPED : formado, forjado ⟨wrought iron : hierro forjado⟩ **2** *or* **wrought up** : agitado, excitado

wrung → **wring**

wry ['raɪ] *adj* **wrier** ['raɪər]; **wriest** ['raɪəst] **1** TWISTED : torcido ⟨a wry neck : un cuello torcido⟩ **2** : irónico, sardónico (dícese del humor)

X

x¹ *n, pl* **x's** *or* **xs** ['ɛksəz] **1** : vigésima cuarta letra del alfabeto inglés **2** : incógnita *f* (en matemáticas)

x² ['ks] *vt* **x–ed** ['ɛkst]; **x–ing** *or* **x'ing** ['ɛksɪŋ] DELETE : tachar

xenon ['zi:ˌnɑn, 'zɛ-] *n* : xenón *m*

xenophobia [ˌzɛnə'fo:biə, ˌzi:-] *n* : xenofobia *f*

Xmas ['krɪsməs] *n* : Navidad *f*

x–ray ['ɛksˌreɪ] *vt* : radiografiar

X ray ['ɛksˌreɪ] *n* **1** : rayo *m* X **2** *or* **X–ray photograph** : radiografía *f*

xylophone ['zaɪləˌfo:n] *n* : xilófono *m*

Y

y ['waɪ] *n, pl* **y's** *or* **ys** ['waɪz] : vigésima quinta letra del alfabeto inglés

yacht¹ ['jɑt] *vi* : navegar (a vela), ir en yate ⟨to go yachting : irse a navegar⟩

yacht² *n* : yate *m*

yak ['jæk] *n* : yac *m*

yam ['jæm] *n* **1** : ñame *m* **2** SWEET POTATO : batata *f*, boniato *m*

yank¹ ['jæŋk] *vt* : tirar de, jalar, darle un tirón a

yank² *n* : tirón *m*

Yankee ['jæŋki] *n* : yanqui *mf*

yap¹ ['jæp] *vi* **yapped; yapping 1** BARK, YELP : ladrar, gañir **2** CHATTER : cotorrear *fam*, parlotear *fam*

yap² *n* : ladrido *m*, gañido *m*

yard ['jɑrd] *n* **1** : yarda *f* (medida) **2** SPAR : verga *f* (de un barco) **3** COURTYARD : patio *m* **4** : jardín *m* (de una casa) **5** : depósito *m* (de mercancías, etc.)

yardage ['jɑrdɪʤ] *n* : medida *f* en yardas

yardarm ['jɑrdˌɑrm] *n* : penol *m*

yardstick ['jɑrdˌstɪk] *n* **1** : vara *f* **2** CRITERION : criterio *m*, norma *f*

yarn ['jɑrn] *n* **1** : hilado *m* **2** TALE : historia *f*, cuento *m* ⟨to spin a yarn : inventar una historia⟩

yawl ['jɔl] *n* : yola *f*

yawn¹ ['jɔn] *vi* **1** : bostezar **2** OPEN : abrirse

yawn² *n* : bostezo *m*

ye ['ji:] *pron* : vosotros, vosotras

yea¹ ['jeɪ] *adv* YES : sí

yea² *n* : voto *m* a favor

year ['jɪr] *n* **1** : año *m* ⟨last year : el año pasado⟩ ⟨he's ten years old : tiene diez años⟩ **2** : curso *m*, año *m* (escolar) **3 years** *npl* AGES : siglos *mpl*, años *mpl* ⟨I haven't seen them in years : hace siglos que no los veo⟩

yearbook ['jɪrˌbʊk] *n* : anuario *m*

yearling ['jɪrlɪŋ, 'jərlən] *n* : animal *m* menor de dos año

yearly¹ ['jɪrli] *adv* : cada año, anualmente

yearly² *adj* : anual

yearn ['jərn] *vi* : anhelar, ansiar

yearning ['jərnɪŋ] *n* : anhelo *m*

yeast ['ji:st] *n* : levadura *f*

yell¹ ['jɛl] *vi* : gritar, chillar — *vt* : gritar

yell² *n* : grito *m*, alarido *m* ⟨to let out a yell : dar un grito⟩

yellow¹ ['jɛlo] *vi* : ponerse amarillo, volverse amarillo

yellow² *adj* **1** : amarillo **2** COWARDLY : cobarde

yellow³ *n* : amarillo *m*

yellow fever *n* : fiebre *f* amarilla

yellowish ['jɛloɪʃ] *adj* : amarillento

yellow jacket *n* : avispa *f* (con rayas amarillas)

yelp¹ ['jɛlp] *vi* : dar un gañido (dícese de un animal), dar un grito (dícese de una persona)

yelp² *n* : gañido *m* (de un animal), grito *m* (de una persona)

yen ['jɛn] *n* **1** DESIRE : deseo *m*, ganas *fpl* **2** : yen *m* (moneda japonesa)

yeoman ['jo:mən] *n, pl* **-men** [-mən, -mɛn] : suboficial *mf* de marina

yes¹ ['jɛs] *adv* : sí ⟨to say yes : decir que sí⟩

yes² *n* : sí *m*

yesterday¹ ['jɛstərˌdeɪ, -di] *adv* : ayer

yesterday² *n* **1** : ayer *m* **2 the day before** : anteayer

yet¹ ['jɛt] *adv* **1** BESIDES, EVEN : aún ⟨yet more problems : más problemas aún⟩ ⟨yet again : otra vez⟩ **2** SO FAR : aún, todavía ⟨not yet : todavía no⟩ ⟨as yet : hasta ahora, todavía⟩ **3** : ya ⟨has he come yet? : ¿ya ha venido?⟩ **4** EVENTUALLY : todavía, algún día **5** NEVERTHELESS : sin embargo

yet² *conj* : pero

yew ['ju:] *n* : tejo *m*

yield¹ ['ji:ld] *vt* **1** SURRENDER : ceder ⟨to yield the right of way : ceder el paso⟩ **2** PRODUCE : producir, dar, rendir (en finanzas) — *vi* **1** GIVE : ceder ⟨to yield under pressure : ceder por la presión⟩ **2** GIVE IN, SURRENDER : ceder, rendirse, entregarse

yield² *n* : rendimiento *m*, rédito *m* (en finanzas)

yin and yang ['jɪnænd'jæŋ, -'jɑŋ] *n* : yin *m* y yang *f*

yodel¹ ['jo:dəl] *vi* **-deled** *or* **-delled; -deling** *or* **-delling** : cantar al estilo tirolés

yodel² *n* : canción *f* al estilo tirolés

yoga ['jo:gə] *n* : yoga *m*

yogurt ['jo:gərt] *n* : yogur *m*, yogurt *m*

yoke¹ ['jo:k] *vt* **yoked; yoking** : uncir (animales)

yoke² *n* **1** : yugo *m* (para uncir animales)

⟨the yoke of oppression : el yugo de la opresión⟩ **2** TEAM : yunta *f* (de bueyes) **3** : canesú *m* (de ropa)
yokel ['jo:kəl] *n* : palurdo *m*, -da *f*
yolk ['jo:k] *n* : yema *f* (de un huevo)
Yom Kippur [ˌjoːmkɪ'pʊr, ˌjam-, -'kɪpər] *n* : el Día *m* del Perdón, Yom Kippur
yon ['jɑn] → **yonder**
yonder[1] ['jɑndər] *adv* : allá ⟨over yonder : allá lejos⟩
yonder[2] *adj* : aquel ⟨yonder hill : aquella colina⟩
yore ['jo:r] *n* **in days of yore** : antaño
you ['ju:] *pron* **1** (*used as subject — familiar*) : tú; vos (*in some Latin American countries*); ustedes *pl*; vosotros, vosotras *pl Spain* **2** (*used as subject — formal*) : usted, ustedes *pl* **3** (*used as indirect object — familiar*) : te, les *pl* (se before *lo, la, los, las*), os *pl Spain* ⟨he told it to you : te lo contó⟩ ⟨I gave them to (all of, both of) you : se los di⟩ **4** (*used as indirect object — formal*) : lo (*Spain sometimes* le), la; los (*Spain sometimes* les), las *pl* **5** (*used as a preposition — familiar*) : ti; vos (*in some Latin American countries*); ustedes *pl*; vosotros, vosotras *pl Spain* **6** (*used after a preposition — formal*) : usted, ustedes *pl* **7** (*used as an impersonal subject*) ⟨you never know : nunca se sabe⟩ ⟨you have to be aware : hay que ser consciente⟩ ⟨you mustn't do that : eso no se hace⟩ **8 with you** (*familiar*) : contigo; con ustedes *pl*; con vosotros, con vosotras *pl Spain* **9 with you** (*formal*) : con usted, con ustedes *pl*
you'd ['ju:d, 'jʊd] (*contraction of* **you had** *or* **you would**) → **have, would**
you'll ['ju:l, 'jʊl] (*contraction of* **you shall** *or* **you will**) → **shall, will**
young[1] ['jʌŋ] *adj* **younger** ['jʌŋgər]; **youngest** [-gəst] **1** : joven, pequeño, menor ⟨young people : los jóvenes⟩ ⟨my younger brother : mi hermano menor⟩ ⟨she is the youngest : es la más pequeña⟩ **2** FRESH, NEW : tierno (dícese de las verduras), joven (dícese del vino) **3** YOUTHFUL : joven, juvenil
young[2] *npl* : jóvenes *mfpl* (de los humanos), crías *fpl* (de los animales)
youngster ['jʌŋkstər] *n* **1** YOUTH : joven *mf* **2** CHILD : chico *m*, -ca *f*; niño *m*, -ña *f*
your ['jʊr, 'jo:r, jər] *adj* **1** (*familiar singular*) : tu ⟨your cat : tu gato⟩ ⟨your

books : tus libros⟩ ⟨wash your hands : lávate las manos⟩ **2** (*familiar plural*) : su, vuestro *Spain* ⟨your car : su coche, el coche de ustedes⟩ **3** (*formal*) : su ⟨your houses : sus casas⟩ **4** (*impersonal*) : el, la, los, las ⟨on your left : a la izquierda⟩
you're ['jʊr, 'jo:r, 'jər, 'ju:ər] (*contraction of* **you are**) → **be**
yours ['jʊrz, 'jo:rz] *pron* **1** (*belonging to one person — familiar*) : (el) tuyo, (la) tuya, (los) tuyos, (las) tuyas ⟨those are mine; yours are there : ésas son mías; las tuyas están allí⟩ ⟨is this one yours? : ¿éste es tuyo?⟩ **2** (*belonging to more than one person — familiar*) : (el) suyo, (la) suya, (los) suyos, (las) suyas; (el) vuestro, (la) vuestra, (los) vuestros, (las) vuestras *Spain* ⟨our house and yours : nuestra casa y la suya⟩ **3** (*formal*) : (el) suyo, (la) suya, (los) suyos, (las) suyas
yourself [jər'sɛlf] *pron, pl* **yourselves** [-'slvz] **1** (*used reflexively — familiar*) : te, se *pl*, os *pl Spain* ⟨wash yourself : lávate⟩ ⟨you dressed yourselves : se vistieron, os vestisteis⟩ **2** (*used reflexively — formal*) : se ⟨did you hurt yourself? : ¿se hizo daño?⟩ ⟨you've gotten yourselves dirty : se ensuciaron⟩ **3** (*used for emphasis*) : tú mismo, tú misma; usted mismo, usted misma; ustedes mismos, ustedes mismas *pl*; vosotros mismos, vosotras mismas *pl Spain* ⟨you did it yourselves? : ¿lo hicieron ustedes mismos?, ¿lo hicieron por sí solos?⟩
youth ['ju:θ] *n, pl* **youths** ['ju:ðz, 'ju:θs] **1** : juventud *f* ⟨in her youth : en su juventud⟩ **2** BOY : joven *m* **3** : jóvenes *mfpl*, juventud *f* ⟨the youth of our city : los jóvenes de nuestra ciudad⟩
youthful ['ju:θfəl] *adj* **1** : de juventud **2** YOUNG : joven **3** JUVENILE : juvenil
youthfulness ['ju:θfəlnəs] *n* : juventud *f*
you've ['ju:v] (*contraction of* **you have**) → **have**
yowl[1] ['jæʊl] *vi* : aullar
yowl[2] *n* : aullido *m*
yo-yo ['jo:ˌjo:] *n, pl* **-yos** : yoyo *m*, yoyó *m*
yucca ['jʌkə] *n* : yuca *f*
Yugoslavian [ˌju:go'slɑviən] *n* : yugoslavo *m*, -va *f* — **Yugoslavian** *adj*
yule ['ju:l] *n* CHRISTMAS : Navidad *f*
yuletide ['ju:lˌtaɪd] *n* : Navidades *fpl*
yuppie ['jʌpi] *n* : yuppy *mf*

Z

z ['zi:] *n, pl* **z's** *or* **zs** : vigésima sexta letra del alfabeto inglés

Zambian ['zæmbiən] *n* : zambiano *m*, -na *f* — **Zambian** *adj*

zany¹ ['zeɪni] *adj* **-nier; -est** : alocado, disparatado

zany² *n, pl* **-nies** : bufón *m*, -fona *f*

zap¹ ['zæp] *vt* **zapped; zapping** **1** ELIMINATE : eliminar **2** : enviar o transportar rápidamente — *vi* : ir rápidamente

zap² *n* **1** ZEST : sabor *m*, sazón *f* **2** BLAST : golpe *m* fuerte

zap³ *interj* : ¡zas!

zeal ['zi:l] *n* : fervor *m*, celo *m*, entusiasmo *m*

zealot ['zɛlət] *n* : fanático *m*, -ca *f*

zealous ['zɛləs] *adj* : celoso — **zealously** *adv*

zebra ['zi:brə] *n* : cebra *f*

zenith ['zi:nəθ] *n* **1** : cenit *m* (en astronomía) **2** PEAK : apogeo *m*, cenit *m* ⟨at the zenith of his career : en el apogeo de su carrera⟩

zephyr ['zɛfər] *n* : céfiro *m*

zeppelin ['zɛplən, -pəlɪn] *n* : zepelín *m*

zero¹ ['zi:ro, 'zɪro] *vi* **to zero in on** : apuntar hacia, centrarse en (un problema, etc.)

zero² *adj* : cero, nulo ⟨zero degrees : cero grados⟩ ⟨zero opportunities : oportunidades nulas⟩

zero³ *n, pl* **-ros** : cero *m* ⟨below zero : bajo cero⟩

zest ['zɛst] *n* **1** GUSTO : entusiasmo *m*, brío *m* **2** FLAVOR : sabor *m*, sazón *f*

zestful ['zɛstfəl] *adj* : brioso

zigzag¹ ['zɪg,zæg] *vi* **-zagged; -zagging** : zigzaguear

zigzag² *adv & adj* : en zigzag

zigzag³ *n* : zigzag *m*

Zimbabwean [zɪm'babwiən, -bweɪ-] *n* : zimbabuense *mf* — **Zimbabwean** *adj*

zinc ['zɪŋk] *n* : cinc *m*, zinc *m*

zing ['zɪŋ] *n* **1** HISS, HUM : zumbido *m*, silbido *m* **2** ENERGY : brío *m*

zinnia ['zɪniə, 'zi:-, -njə] *n* : zinnia *f*

Zionism ['zaɪə,nɪzəm] *n* : sionismo *m*

Zionist ['zaɪənɪst] *n* : sionista *mf*

zip¹ ['zɪp] *v* **zipped; zipping** *vt or* **to zip up** : cerrar el cierre de — *vi* **1** SPEED : pasarse volando ⟨the day zipped by : el día se pasó volando⟩ **2** HISS, HUM : silbar, zumbar

zip² *n* **1** ZING : zumbido *m*, silbido *m* **2** ENERGY : brío *m*

zip code *n* : código *m* postal

zipper ['zɪpər] *n* : cierre *m*, cremallera *f*, zíper *m* CA, Mex

zippy ['zɪpi] *adj* **-pier; -est** : brioso

zircon ['zər,kɑn] *n* : circón *m*, zircón *m*

zirconium [,zər'ko:niəm] *n* : circonio *m*

zither ['zɪðər, -θər] *n* : cítara *f*

zodiac ['zo:di,æk] *n* : zodíaco *m*

zombie ['zɑmbi] *n* : zombi *mf*, zombie *mf*

zone¹ ['zo:n] *vt* **zoned; zoning** **1** : dividir en zonas **2** DESIGNATE : declarar ⟨to zone for business : declarar como zona comercial⟩

zone² *n* : zona *f*

zoo ['zu:] *n, pl* **zoos** : zoológico *m*, zoo *m*

zoological [,zo:ə'lɑʤɪkəl, ,zu:ə-] *adj* : zoológico

zoologist [zo'ɑləʤɪst, zu:-] *n* : zoólogo *m*, -ga *f*

zoology [zo'ɑləʤi, zu:-] *n* : zoología *f*

zoom¹ ['zu:m] *vi* **1** : zumbar, ir volando ⟨to zoom past : pasar volando⟩ **2** CLIMB : elevarse ⟨the plane zoomed up : el avión se elevó⟩

zoom² *n* **1** : zumbido *m* ⟨the zoom of an engine : el zumbido de un motor⟩ **2** : subida *f* vertical (de un avión, etc.) **3** *or* **zoom lens** : zoom *m*

zucchini [zu'ki:ni] *n, pl* **-ni** *or* **-nis** : calabacín *m*, calabacita *f* Mex

Zulu ['zu:lu:] *n* **1** : zulú *mf* **2** : zulú *m* (idioma) — **Zulu** *adj*

zygote ['zaɪ,go:t] *n* : zigoto *m*, cigoto *m*

Common Spanish Abbreviations

SPANISH ABBREVIATION AND EXPANSION		ENGLISH EQUIVALENT	
abr.	abril	**Apr.**	April
A.C., a.C.	antes de Cristo	**BC**	before Christ
a. de J.C.	antes de Jesucristo	**BC**	before Christ
admon., admón.	administración	—	administration
a/f	a favor	—	in favor
ago.	agosto	**Aug.**	August
Apdo.	apartado (de correos)	—	P.O. box
aprox.	aproximadamente	**approx.**	approximately
Aptdo.	apartado (de correos)	—	P.O. box
Arq.	arquitecto	**arch.**	architect
A.T.	Antiguo Testamento	**O.T.**	Old Testament
atte.	atentamente	—	sincerely
atto., atta.	atento, atenta	—	kind, courteous
av., avda.	avenida	**ave.**	avenue
a/v.	a vista	—	on receipt
BID	Banco Interamericano de Desarrollo	**IDB**	Interamerican Development Bank
Bo	banco	—	bank
BM	Banco Mundial	—	World Bank
c/, C/	calle	**st.**	street
C	centígrado, Celsius	**C**	centigrade, Celsius
C.	compañía	**Co.**	company
CA	corriente alterna	**AC**	alternating current
cap.	capítulo	**ch., chap.**	chapter
c/c	cuenta corriente	—	current account, checking account
c.c.	centímetros cúbicos	**cu. cm**	cubic centimeters
CC	corriente continua	**DC**	direct current
c/d	con descuento	—	with discount
Cd.	ciudad	—	city
CE	Comunidad Europea	**EC**	European Community
CEE	Comunidad Económica Europea	**EEC**	European Economic Community
cf.	confróntese	**cf.**	compare
cg.	centígramo	**cg**	centigram
CGT	Confederación General de Trabajadores *or* del Trabajo	—	confederation of workers, workers' union
CI	coeficiente intelectual *or* de inteligencia	**IQ**	intelligence quotient
Cía.	compañía	**Co.**	company
cm.	centímetro	**cm**	centimeter
Cnel.	coronel	**Col.**	colonel
col.	columna	**col.**	column
Col. *Mex*	colonia	—	residential area
Com.	comandante	**Cmdr.**	commander
comp.	compárese	**comp.**	compare
Cor.	coronel	**Col.**	colonel

SPANISH ABBREVIATION AND EXPANSION		ENGLISH EQUIVALENT	
C.P.	código postal	—	zip code
CSF, c.s.f.	coste, seguro y flete	**c.i.f.**	cost, insurance, and freight
cta.	cuenta	**ac., acct.**	account
cte.	corriente	**cur.**	current
c/u	cada uno, cada una	**ea.**	each
CV	caballo de vapor	**hp**	horsepower
D.	Don	—	—
Da., D.ᵃ	Doña	—	—
d.C.	después de Cristo	**AD**	anno Domini (in the year of Our Lord)
dcha.	derecha	—	right
d. de J.C.	después de Jesucristo	**AD**	anno Domini (in the year of Our Lord)
dep.	departamento	**dept.**	department
DF, D.F.	Distrito Federal	—	Federal District
dic.	diciembre	**Dec.**	December
dir.	director, directora	**dir.**	director
dir.	dirección	—	address
Dña.	Doña	—	—
do.	domingo	**Sun.**	Sunday
dpto.	departamento	**dept.**	department
Dr.	doctor	**Dr.**	doctor
Dra.	doctora	**Dr.**	doctor
dto.	descuento	—	discount
E, E.	Este, este	**E**	East, east
Ed.	editorial	—	publishing house
Ed., ed.	edición	**ed.**	edition
edif.	edificio	**bldg.**	building
edo.	estado	**st.**	state
EEUU, EE.UU.	Estados Unidos	**US, U.S.**	United States
ej.	por ejemplo	**e.g.**	for example
E.M.	esclerosis multiple	**MS**	multiple sclerosis
ene.	enero	**Jan.**	January
etc.	etcétera	**etc.**	et cetera
ext.	extensión	**ext.**	extension
F	Fahrenheit	**F**	Fahrenheit
f.a.b.	franco a bordo	**f.o.b.**	free on board
FC	ferrocarril	**RR**	railroad
feb.	febrero	**Feb.**	February
FF AA, FF.AA.	Fuerzas Armadas	—	armed forces
FMI	Fondo Monetario Internacional	**IMF**	International Monetary Fund
g.	gramo	**g., gm, gr.**	gram
G.P.	giro postal	**M.O.**	money order
gr.	gramo	**g., gm, gr.**	gram
Gral.	general	**Gen.**	general
h.	hora	**hr.**	hour
Hnos.	hermanos	**Bros.**	brothers
I + D, I & D, I y D	investigación y desarrollo	**R & D**	research and development
i.e.	esto es, es decir	**i.e.**	that is
incl.	inclusive	**incl.**	inclusive, inclusively
Ing.	ingeniero, ingeniera	**eng.**	engineer

SPANISH ABBREVIATION AND EXPANSION		ENGLISH EQUIVALENT	
IPC	indice de precios al consumo	**CPI**	consumer price index
IVA	impuesto al valor agregado	**VAT**	value-added tax
izq.	izquierda	**l.**	left
juev.	jueves	**Thurs.**	Thursday
jul.	julio	**Jul.**	July
jun.	junio	**Jun.**	June
kg.	kilogramo	**kg**	kilogram
km.	kilómetro	**km**	kilometer
km/h	kilómetros por hora	**kph**	kilometers per hour
kv, kV	kilovatio	**kw, kW**	kilowatt
l.	litro	**l, lit.**	liter
Lic.	licenciado, licenciada	—	—
Ltda.	limitada	**Ltd.**	limited
lun.	lunes	**Mon.**	Monday
m	masculino	**m**	masculine
m	metro	**m**	meter
m	minuto	**m**	minute
mar.	marzo	**Mar.**	March
mart.	martes	**Tues.**	Tuesday
mg.	miligramo	**mg**	milligram
miérc.	miércoles	**Wednes.**	Wednesday
min	minuto	**min.**	minute
mm.	milímetro	**mm**	millimeter
M-N, m/n	moneda nacional	—	national currency
Mons.	monseñor	**Msgr.**	monsignor
Mtra.	maestra	—	teacher
Mtro.	maestro	—	teacher
N, N.	Norte, norte	**N, no.**	North, north
n/o	nuestro	—	our
n.º	número	**no.**	number
N. de (la) R.	nota de (la) redacción	—	editor's note
NE	nordeste	**NE**	northeast
NN.UU.	Naciones Unidas	**UN**	United Nations
NO	noroeste	**NW**	northwest
nov.	noviembre	**Nov.**	November
N.T.	Nuevo Testamento	**N.T.**	New Testament
ntra., ntro.	nuestra, nuestro	—	our
NU	Naciones Unidas	**UN**	United Nations
núm.	número	**num.**	number
O, O.	Oeste, oeste	**W**	West, west
oct.	octubre	**Oct.**	October
OEA, O.E.A.	Organización de Estados Americanos	**OAS**	Organization of American States
OMS	Organización Mundial de la Salud	**WHO**	World Health Organization
ONG	organización no gubernamental	**NGO**	non-governmental organization
ONU	Organización de las Naciones Unidas	**UN**	United Nations
OTAN	Organización del Tratado del Atlántico Norte	**NATO**	North Atlantic Treaty Organization
p.	página	**p.**	page
P, P.	padre	**Fr.**	father

SPANISH ABBREVIATION AND EXPANSION		ENGLISH EQUIVALENT	
pág.	página	**pg.**	page
pat.	patente	**pat.**	patent
PCL	pantalla de cristal líquido	**LCD**	liquid crystal display
P.D.	post data	**P.S.**	postscript
p. ej.	por ejemplo	**e.g.**	for example
PNB	Producto Nacional Bruto	**GNP**	gross national product
p^o	paseo	**Ave.**	avenue
p.p.	porte pagado	**ppd.**	postpaid
PP, p.p.	por poder, por poderes	**p.p.**	by proxy
prom.	promedio	**av., avg.**	average
ptas., pts.	pesetas	—	—
q.e.p.d.	que en paz descanse	**R.I.P.**	may he/she rest in peace
R, R/	remite	—	sender
RAE	Real Academia Española	—	—
ref., ref.^{a}	referencia	**ref.**	reference
rep.	república	**rep.**	republic
r.p.m.	revoluciones por minuto	**rpm.**	revolutions per minute
rte.	remite, remitente	—	sender
s.	siglo	**c., cent.**	century
s/	su, sus	—	his, her, your, their
S, S.	Sur, sur	**S, so.**	South, south
S.	san, santo	**St.**	saint
S.A.	sociedad anónima	**Inc.**	incorporated (company)
sáb.	sábado	**Sat.**	Saturday
s/c	su cuenta	—	your account
SE	sudeste, sureste	**SE**	southeast
seg.	segundo, segundos	**sec.**	second, seconds
sep., sept.	septiembre	**Sept.**	September
s.e.u.o.	salvo error u omisión	—	errors and omissions excepted
Sgto.	sargento	**Sgt.**	sergeant
S.L.	sociedad limitada	**Ltd.**	limited (corporation)
S.M.	Su Majestad	**HM**	His Majesty, Her Majesty
s/n	sin número	—	no (street) number
s.n.m.	sobre el nivel de mar	**a.s.l.**	above sea level
SO	sudoeste/suroeste	**SW**	southwest
S.R.C.	se ruega contestación	**R.S.V.P.**	please reply
ss.	siguientes	—	the following ones
SS, S.S.	Su Santidad	**H.H.**	His Holiness
Sta.	santa	**St.**	Saint
Sto.	santo	**St.**	saint
t, t.	tonelada	**t., tn.**	ton
TAE	tasa anual efectiva	**APR**	annual percentage rate
tb.	también	—	also
tel., Tel.	teléfono	**tel.**	telephone
Tm.	tonelada métrica	**MT**	metric ton
Tn.	tonelada	**t., tn.**	ton
trad.	traducido	**tr., trans., transl.**	translated

SPANISH ABBREVIATION AND EXPANSION		ENGLISH EQUIVALENT	
UE	Unión Europea	**EU**	European Union
Univ.	universidad	**Univ., U.**	university
UPC	unidad procesadora central	**CPU**	central processing unit
Urb.	urbanización	—	residential area
v	versus	**v., vs.**	versus
v	verso	**v., ver., vs.**	verse
v.	véase	**vid.**	see
Vda.	viuda	—	widow
v.g., v.gr.	verbigracia	**e.g.**	for example
vier., viern.	viernes	**Fri.**	Friday
V.M.	Vuestra Majestad	—	Your Majesty
V^{o}B^o, V.^{o}B.^{o}	visto bueno	—	OK, approved
vol, vol.	volumen	**vol.**	volume
vra., vro.	vuestra, vuestro	—	your

Common English Abbreviations

	ENGLISH ABBREVIATION AND EXPANSION	SPANISH EQUIVALENT	
AAA	American Automobile Association	—	—
AD	anno Domini (in the year of Our Lord)	d.C., d. de J.C.	después de Cristo, después de Jesucristo
AK	Alaska	—	Alaska
AL, Ala.	Alabama	—	Alabama
Alas.	Alaska	—	Alaska
a.m., AM	ante meridiem	a.m.	ante meridiem (de la mañana)
Am., Amer.	America, American	—	América, americano
amt.	amount	—	cantidad
anon.	anonymous	—	anónimo
ans.	answer	—	respuesta
Apr.	April	abr.	abril
AR	Arkansas	—	Arkansas
Ariz.	Arizona	—	Arizona
Ark.	Arkansas	—	Arkansas
asst.	assistant	ayte.	ayudante
atty.	attorney	—	abogado, -da
Aug.	August	ago.	agosto
ave.	avenue	av., avda.	avenida
AZ	Arizona	—	Arizona
BA	Bachelor of Arts	Lic.	Licenciado, -da en Filosofía y Letras
BA	Bachelor of Arts (degree)	—	Licenciatura en Filosofía y Letras
BC	before Christ	a.C., A.C., a. de J.C.	antes de Cristo, antes de Jesucristo
BCE	before the Christian Era, before the Common Era	—	antes de la era cristiana, antes de la era común
bet.	between	—	entre
bldg.	building	edif.	edificio
blvd.	boulevard	blvar., br.	bulevar
Br., Brit.	Britain, British	—	Gran Bretaña, británico
Bro(s).	brother(s)	Hno(s).	hermano(s)
BS	Bachelor of Science	Lic.	Licenciado, -da en Ciencias
BS	Bachelor of Science (degree)	—	Licenciatura en Ciencias
c	carat	—	quilate
c	cent	—	centavo
c	centimeter	cm.	centímetro
c	century	s.	siglo
c	cup	—	taza
C	Celsius, centigrade	C	Celsius, centígrado
CA, Cal., Calif.	California	—	California
Can., Canad.	Canada, Canadian	—	Canadá, canadiense
cap.	capital	—	capital
cap.	capital	—	mayúscula
Capt.	captain	—	capitán

ENGLISH ABBREVIATION AND EXPANSION		SPANISH EQUIVALENT	
cent.	century	**s.**	siglo
CEO	chief executive officer	—	presidente, -ta (de una corporación)
ch., chap.	chapter	**cap.**	capítulo
CIA	Central Intelligence Agency	—	—
cm	centimeter	**cm.**	centímetro
Co.	company	**C., Cía.**	compañía
co.	county	—	condado
CO	Colorado	—	Colorado
c/o	care of	**a/c**	a cargo de
COD	cash on delivery, collect on delivery	—	(pago) contra reembolso
col.	column	**col.**	columna
Col., Colo.	Colorado	—	Colorado
Conn.	Connecticut	—	Connecticut
corp.	corporation	—	corporación
CPR	cardiopulmonary resuscitation	**RCP**	reanimación cardiopulmonar, resucitación cardiopulmonar
ct.	cent	—	centavo
CT	Connecticut	—	Connecticut
D.A.	district attorney	—	fiscal (del distrito)
DC	District of Columbia	—	—
DDS	Doctor of Dental Surgery	—	doctor de cirugía dental
DE	Delaware	—	Delaware
Dec.	December	**dic.**	diciembre
Del.	Delaware	—	Delaware
DJ	disc jockey	—	disc-jockey
dept.	department	**dep., dpto.**	departamento
DMD	Doctor of Dental Medicine	—	doctor de medicina dental
doz.	dozen	—	docena
Dr.	doctor	**Dr., Dra.**	doctor, doctora
DST	daylight saving time	—	—
DVM	Doctor of Veterinary Medicine	—	doctor de medicina veterinaria
E	East, east	**E, E.**	Este, este
ea.	each	**c/u**	cada uno, cada una
e.g.	for example (exempli gratia)	**v.g., v.gr.**	verbigracia
EMT	emergency medical technician	—	técnico, -ca en urgencias médicas
Eng.	England, English	—	Inglaterra, inglés
esp.	especially	—	especialmente
EST	eastern standard time	—	—
etc.	et cetera	**etc.**	etcétera
f	false	—	falso
f	female	**f**	femenino
F	Fahrenheit	**F**	Fahrenheit
FBI	Federal Bureau of Investigation	—	—
Feb.	February	**feb.**	febrero
fem.	feminine	—	femenino
FL, Fla.	Florida	—	Florida

ENGLISH ABBREVIATION AND EXPANSION		SPANISH EQUIVALENT	
Fri.	Friday	**vier., viern.**	viernes
ft.	feet, foot	—	pie(s)
g	gram	**g., gr.**	gramo
Ga., GA	Georgia	—	Georgia
gal.	gallon	—	galón
Gen.	general	**Gral.**	general
gm	gram	**g., gr.**	gramo
gov.	governor	—	gobernador, -dora
govt.	government	—	gobierno
gr.	gram	**g., gr.**	gramo
HI	Hawaii	—	Hawai, Hawaii
hr.	hour	**h.**	hora
HS	high school	—	colegio secundario
ht.	height	—	altura
Ia., IA	Iowa	—	Iowa
ID	Idaho	—	Idaho
i.e.	that is (id est)	**i.e.**	id est (esto es, es decir)
IL, Ill.	Illinois	—	Illinois
in.	inch	—	pulgada
IN	Indiana	—	Indiana
Inc.	incorporated	**S.A.**	sociedad anónima
Ind.	Indian, Indiana	—	Indiana
Jan.	January	**ene.**	enero
Jul.	July	**jul.**	julio
Jun.	June	**jun.**	junio
Jr., Jun.	Junior	**Jr.**	Júnior
Kan., Kans.	Kansas	—	Kansas
kg	kilogram	**kg.**	kilogramo
km	kilometer	**km.**	kilómetro
KS	Kansas	—	Kansas
Ky., KY	Kentucky	—	Kentucky
l	liter	**l.**	litro
l.	left	**izq.**	izquierda
L	large	**G**	(talla) grande
La., LA	Louisiana	—	Luisiana, Louisiana
lb.	pound	—	libra
Ltd.	limited	**S.L.**	sociedad limitada
m	male	**m**	masculino
m	meter	**m**	metro
m	mile	—	milla
M	medium	**M**	(talla) mediana
MA	Massachusetts	—	Massachusetts
Maj.	major	—	mayor
Mar.	March	**mar.**	marzo
masc.	masculine	—	masculino
Mass.	Massachusetts	—	Massachusetts
Md., MD	Maryland	—	Maryland
M.D.	Doctor of Medicine	—	doctor de medicina
Me., ME	Maine	—	Maine
Mex.	Mexican, Mexico	**Méx.**	mexicano, México
mg	milligram	**mg.**	miligramo
mi.	mile	—	milla
MI, Mich.	Michigan	—	Michigan
min.	minute	**min**	minuto
Minn.	Minnesota	—	Minnesota
Miss.	Mississippi	—	Mississippi, Misisipí
ml	mililiter	**ml.**	mililitro

ENGLISH ABBREVIATION AND EXPANSION		SPANISH EQUIVALENT	
mm	millimeter	**mm.**	milímetro
MN	Minnesota	—	Minnesota
mo.	month	—	mes
Mo., MO	Missouri	—	Missouri
Mon.	Monday	**lun.**	lunes
Mont.	Montana	—	Montana
mpg	miles per gallon	—	millas por galón
mph	miles per hour	—	millas por hora
MS	Mississippi	—	Mississippi, Misisipí
mt.	mount, mountain	—	monte, montaña
MT	Montana	—	Montana
mtn.	mountain	—	montaña
N	North, north	**N**	Norte, norte
NASA	National Aeronautics and Space Administration	—	—
NC	North Carolina	—	Carolina del Norte, North Carolina
ND, N. Dak.	North Dakota	—	Dakota del Norte, North Dakota
NE	northeast	**NE**	nordeste
NE, Neb., Nebr.	Nebraska	—	Nebraska
Nev.	Nevada	—	Nevada
NH	New Hampshire	—	New Hampshire
NJ	New Jersey	—	Nueva Jersey, New Jersey
NM, N. Mex.	New Mexico	—	Nuevo México, New Mexico
no.	north	**N**	norte
no.	number	**n.º**	número
Nov.	November	**nov.**	noviembre
N.T.	New Testament	**N.T.**	Nuevo Testamento
NV	Nevada	—	Nevada
NW	northwest	**NO**	noroeste
NY	New York	**NY**	Nueva York, New York
O	Ohio	—	Ohio
Oct.	October	**oct.**	octubre
OH	Ohio	—	Ohio
OK, Okla.	Oklahoma	—	Oklahoma
OR, Ore., Oreg.	Oregon	—	Oregon
O.T.	Old Testament	**A.T.**	Antiguo Testamento
oz.	ounce, ounces	—	onza, onzas
p.	page	**p.**	página
Pa., PA	Pennsylvania	—	Pennsylvania, Pensilvania
pat.	patent	**pat.**	patente
PD	police department	—	departamento de policía
PE	physical education	—	educación física
Penn., Penna.	Pennsylvania	—	Pennsylvania, Pensilvania
pg.	page	**pág.**	página
PhD	Doctor of Philosophy	—	doctor, -tora (en filosofía)

ENGLISH ABBREVIATION AND EXPANSION		SPANISH EQUIVALENT	
pkg.	package	—	paquete
p.m., PM	post meridiem	**p.m.**	post meridiem (de la tarde)
P.O.	post office	—	oficina de correos, correo
pp.	pages	**págs.**	páginas
PR	Puerto Rico	**PR**	Puerto Rico
pres.	present	—	presente
pres.	president	—	presidente, -ta
prof.	professor	—	profesor, -sora
P.S.	postscript	**P.D.**	postdata
P.S.	public school	—	escuela pública
pt.	pint	—	pinta
pt.	point	**pto.**	punto
PTA	Parent-Teacher Association	—	—
PTO	Parent-Teacher Organization	—	—
q, qt.	quart	—	cuarto de galón
r.	right	**dcha.**	derecha
rd.	road	**c/, C/**	calle
RDA	recommended daily allowance	—	consumo diario recomendado
recd.	received	—	recibido
Rev.	reverend	**Rdo.**	reverendo
RI	Rhode Island	—	Rhode Island
rpm	revolutions per minute	**r.p.m.**	revoluciones por minuto
RR	railroad	**FC**	ferrocarril
R.S.V.P.	please reply (répondez s'il vous plaît)	**S.R.C.**	se ruega contestación
rt.	right	**dcha.**	derecha
rte.	route	—	ruta
S	small	**P**	(talla) pequeña
S	South, south	**S**	Sur, sur
S.A.	South America	—	Sudamérica, América del Sur
Sat.	Saturday	**sáb.**	sábado
SC	South Carolina	—	Carolina del Sur, South Carolina
SD, S. Dak.	South Dakota	—	Dakota del Sur, South Dakota
SE	southeast	**SE**	sudeste, sureste
Sept.	September	**sep., sept.**	septiembre
so.	south	**S**	sur
sq.	square	—	cuadrado
Sr.	Senior	**Sr.**	Sénior
Sr.	sister	—	sor
st.	state	—	estado
st.	street	**c/, C/**	calle
St.	saint	**S., Sto., Sta.**	santo, santa
Sun.	Sunday	**dom.**	domingo
SW	southwest	**SO**	sudoeste, suroeste
t.	teaspoon	—	cucharadita
T, tb., tbsp.	tablespoon	—	cucharada (grande)
Tenn.	Tennessee	—	Tennessee

ENGLISH ABBREVIATION AND EXPANSION		SPANISH EQUIVALENT	
Tex.	Texas	—	Texas
Thu., Thur., Thurs.	Thursday	**juev.**	jueves
TM	trademark	—	marca (de un producto)
TN	Tennessee	—	Tennessee
tsp.	teaspoon	—	cucharadita
Tue., Tues.	Tuesday	**mart.**	martes
TX	Texas	—	Texas
UN	United Nations	**NU, NN.UU.**	Naciones Unidas
US	United States	**EEUU, EE.UU.**	Estados Unidos
USA	United States of America	**EEUU, EE.UU.**	Estados Unidos de América
usu.	usually	—	usualmente
UT	Utah	—	Utah
v.	versus	**v**	versus
Va., VA	Virginia	—	Virginia
vol.	volume	**vol.**	volumen
VP	vice president	—	vicepresidente, -ta
vs.	versus	**v**	versus
Vt., VT	Vermont	—	Vermont
W	West, west	**O**	Oeste, oeste
WA, Wash.	Washington (estado)	—	Washington
Wed.	Wednesday	**miérc.**	miércoles
WI, Wis., Wisc.	Wisconsin	—	Wisconsin
wt.	weight	—	peso
WV, W. Va.	West Virginia	—	Virginia del Oeste, West Virginia
WY, Wyo.	Wyoming	—	Wyoming
yd.	yard	—	yarda
yr.	year	—	año

Spanish Numbers

Cardinal Numbers

1	uno	28	veintiocho
2	dos	29	veintinueve
3	tres	30	treinta
4	cuatro	31	treinta y uno
5	cinco	40	cuarenta
6	seis	50	cincuenta
7	siete	60	sesenta
8	ocho	70	setenta
9	nueve	80	ochenta
10	diez	90	noventa
11	once	100	cien
12	doce	101	ciento uno
13	trece	200	doscientos
14	catorce	300	trescientos
15	quince	400	cuatrocientos
16	dieciséis	500	quinientos
17	diecisiete	600	seiscientos
18	dieciocho	700	setecientos
19	diecinueve	800	ochocientos
20	veinte	900	novecientos
21	veintiuno	1,000	mil
22	veintidós	1,001	mil uno
23	veintitrés	2,000	dos mil
24	veinticuatro	100,000	cien mil
25	veinticinco	1,000,000	un millón
26	veintiséis	1,000,000,000	mil millones
27	veintisiete	1,000,000,000,000	un billón

Ordinal Numbers

1st	primero, -ra	18th	decimoctavo, -va
2nd	segundo, -da	19th	decimonoveno, -na;
3rd	tercero, -ra		*or* decimonono, -na
4th	cuarto, -ta	20th	vigésimo, -ma
5th	quinto, -ta	21st	vigésimoprimero,
6th	sexto, -ta		vigésimaprimera
7th	séptimo, -ta	22nd	vigésimosegundo,
8th	octavo, -ta		vigésimasegunda
9th	noveno, -na	30th	trigésimo, -ma
10th	décimo, -ma	40th	cuadragésimo, -ma
11th	undécimo, -ca	50th	quincuagésimo, -ma
12th	duodécimo, -ma	60th	sexagésimo, -ma
13th	decimotercero, -ra	70th	septuagésimo, -ma
14th	decimocuarto, -ta	80th	octogésimo, -ma
15th	decimoquinto, -ta	90th	nonagésimo, -ma
16th	decimosexto, -ta	100th	centésimo, -ma
17th	decimoséptimo, -ma	1,000th	milésimo, -ma

English Numbers

Cardinal Numbers

1	one		50	fifty
2	two		60	sixty
3	three		70	seventy
4	four		80	eighty
5	five		90	ninety
6	six		100	one hundred
7	seven		101	one hundred and one
8	eight		200	two hundred
9	nine		300	three hundred
10	ten		400	four hundred
11	eleven		500	five hundred
12	twelve		600	six hundred
13	thirteen		700	seven hundred
14	fourteen		800	eight hundred
15	fifteen		900	nine hundred
16	sixteen		1,000	one thousand
17	seventeen		1,001	one thousand and one
18	eighteen		2,000	two thousand
19	nineteen		10,000	ten thousand
20	twenty		100,000	one hundred thousand
21	twenty-one		1,000,000	one million
30	thirty		1,000,000,000	one billion
40	forty		1,000,000,000,000	one trillion

Ordinal Numbers

1st	first		17th	seventeenth
2nd	second		18th	eighteenth
3rd	third		19th	nineteenth
4th	fourth		20th	twentieth
5th	fifth		21st	twenty-first
6th	sixth		30th	thirtieth
7th	seventh		40th	fortieth
8th	eighth		50th	fiftieth
9th	ninth		60th	sixtieth
10th	tenth		70th	seventieth
11th	eleventh		80th	eightieth
12th	twelfth		90th	ninetieth
13th	thirteenth		100th	hundredth
14th	fourteenth		1,000th	thousandth
15th	fifteenth		1,000,000th	millionth
16th	sixteenth		1,000,000,000th	billionth

Nations of the World

ENGLISH	SPANISH

Africa/África

ENGLISH	SPANISH
Algeria	Argelia
Angola	Angola
Benin	Benin
Botswana	Botswana, Botsuana
Burkina Faso	Burkina Faso
Burundi	Burundi
Cameroon	Camerún
Cape Verde	Cabo Verde
Central African Republic	República Centroafricana
Chad	Chad
Comoro Islands	Islas Comores, Comoras
Congo	Congo
Democratic Republic of Congo	Congo, República Democrática del
Djibouti	Djibouti, Djibuti
Egypt	Egipto
Equatorial Guinea	Guinea Ecuatorial
Eritrea	Eritrea
Ethiopia	Etiopía
Gabon	Gabón
Gambia	Gambia
Ghana	Ghana
Guinea	Guinea
Guinea-Bissau	Guinea-Bissau
Ivory Coast	Costa de Marfil
Kenya	Kenya, Kenia
Lesotho	Lesotho, Lesoto
Liberia	Liberia
Libya	Libia
Madagascar	Madagascar
Malawi	Malawi, Malaui
Mali	Malí
Mauritania	Mauritania
Mauritius	Mauricio
Morocco	Marruecos
Mozambique	Mozambique
Namibia	Namibia
Niger	Níger
Nigeria	Nigeria
Rwanda	Ruanda, Rwanda
São Tomé and Principe	Santo Tomé y Príncipe
Senegal	Senegal
Seychelles	Seychelles
Sierra Leone	Sierra Leona
Somalia	Somalia
South Africa, Republic of	Sudáfrica, República de
Sudan	Sudán
Swaziland	Suazilandia, Swazilandia
Tanzania	Tanzanía, Tanzania
Togo	Togo

ENGLISH	SPANISH
Tunisia	Túnez
Uganda	Uganda
Zambia	Zambia
Zimbabwe	Zimbabwe, Zimbábue

Antarctica/Antártida
No independent countries

Asia/Asia

Afghanistan	Afganistán
Armenia	Armenia
Azerbaijan	Azerbaiyán, Azerbaiján
Bahrain	Bahrein
Bangladesh	Bangladesh
Bhutan	Bhután, Bután
Brunei	Brunei
Cambodia	Camboya
China	China
Cyprus	Chipre
Georgia, Republic of	Georgia
India	India
Indonesia	Indonesia
Iran	Irán
Iraq	Iraq, Irak
Israel	Israel
Japan	Japón
Jordan	Jordania
Kazakhstan	Kazajstán
Korea, North	Corea del Norte
Korea, South	Corea del Sur
Kuwait	Kuwait
Kyrgyzstan	Kirguistán, Kirguizistán
Laos	Laos
Lebanon	Líbano
Malaysia	Malasia
Maldive Islands	Maldivas
Mongolia	Mongolia
Myanmar	Myanmar
Nepal	Nepal
Oman	Omán
Pakistan	Pakistán
Philippines	Filipinas
Qatar	Qatar
Saudi Arabia	Arabia Saudita, Arabia Saudí
Singapore	Singapur
Sri Lanka	Sri Lanka
Syria	Siria
Taiwan	Taiwán
Tajikistan	Tayikistán
Thailand	Tailandia
Turkey	Turquía
Turkmenistan	Turkmenistán

ENGLISH	SPANISH
United Arab Emirates	Emiratos Árabes Unidos
Uzbekistan	Uzbekistán
Vietnam	Vietnam
Yemen	Yemen

Europe/Europa

Albania	Albania
Andorra	Andorra
Austria	Austria
Belarus	Belarús
Belgium	Bélgica
Bosnia and Herzegovina	Bosnia y Hercegovina, Bosnia y Herzegovina
Bulgaria	Bulgaria
Croatia	Croacia
Czech Republic	República Checa
Denmark	Dinamarca
Estonia	Estonia
Finland	Finlandia
France	Francia
Germany	Alemania
Greece	Grecia
Hungary	Hungría
Iceland	Islandia
Ireland	Irlanda
Italy	Italia
Latvia	Letonia
Liechtenstein	Liechtenstein
Lithuania	Lituania
Luxembourg	Luxemburgo
Macedonia	Macedonia
Malta	Malta
Moldavia	Moldavia
Monaco	Mónaco
Netherlands	Países Bajos
Norway	Noruega
Poland	Polonia
Portugal	Portugal
Romania	Rumania, Rumanía
Russian Federation	Rusia, Federación de
San Marino	San Marino
Serbia and Montenegro	Serbia y Montenegro
Slovakia	Eslovaquia
Slovenia	Eslovenia
Spain	España
Sweden	Suecia
Switzerland	Suiza
Ukraine	Ucrania
United Kingdom	Reino Unido
Vatican City	Ciudad del Vaticano

ENGLISH   SPANISH

North America/Norteamérica

Antigua and Barbuda	Antigua y Barbuda
Bahamas	Bahamas
Barbados	Barbados
Belize	Belice
Bermuda	Bermudas
Canada	Canadá
Costa Rica	Costa Rica
Cuba	Cuba
Dominica	Dominica
Dominican Republic	República Dominicana
El Salvador	El Salvador
Grenada	Granada
Guatemala	Guatemala
Haiti	Haití
Honduras	Honduras
Jamaica	Jamaica
Mexico	México, Méjico
Nicaragua	Nicaragua
Panama	Panamá
Saint Kitts-Nevis	Saint Kitts y Nevis
Saint Lucia	Santa Lucía
Saint Vincent and the Grenadines	San Vicente y las Granadinas
Trinidad and Tobago	Trinidad y Tobago
United States of America	Estados Unidos de América

Oceania/Oceanía

Australia	Australia
Fiji	Fiji
Kiribati	Kiribati
Marshall Islands	Islas Marshall
Nauru	Nauru
New Zealand	Nueva Zelanda, Nueva Zelandia
Papua New Guinea	Papua Nueva Guinea
Solomon Islands	Islas Salomón
Tonga	Tonga
Tuvalu	Tuvalu
Vanuatu	Vanuatu
Western Samoa	Samoa del Oeste

South America/Sudamérica

Argentina	Argentina
Bolivia	Bolivia
Brazil	Brasil
Chile	Chile
Colombia	Colombia
Ecuador	Ecuador
Guyana	Guyana
Paraguay	Paraguay
Peru	Perú
Suriname	Surinam
Uruguay	Uruguay
Venezuela	Venezuela

Metric System: Conversions

Length

unit	number of meters	approximate U.S. equivalents	
millimeter	0.001	0.039	inch
centimeter	0.01	0.39	inch
meter	1	39.37	inches
kilometer	1,000	0.62	mile

Longitud

unidad	número de metros	equivalentes aproximados de los EE.UU.	
milímetro	0.001	0.039	pulgada
centímetro	0.01	0.39	pulgada
metro	1	39.37	pulgadas
kilómetro	1,000	0.62	milla

Area

unit	number of square meters	approximate U.S. equivalents	
square centimeter	0.0001	0.155	square inch
square meter	1	10.764	square feet
hectare	10,000	2.47	acres
square kilometer	1,000,000	0.3861	square mile

Superficie

unidad	número de metros cuadrados	equivalentes aproximados de los EE.UU.	
centímetro cuadrado	0.0001	0.155	pulgada cuadrada
metro cuadrado	1	10.764	pies cuadrados
hectárea	10,000	2.47	acres
kilómetro cuadrado	1,000,000	0.3861	milla cuadrada

Volume

unit	number of cubic meters	approximate U.S. equivalents	
cubic centimeter	0.000001	0.061	cubic inch
cubic meter	1	1.307	cubic yards

Volumen

unidad	número de metros cúbicos	equivalentes aproximados de los EE.UU	
centímetro cúbico	0.000001	0.061	pulgada cúbica
metro cúbico	1	1.307	yardas cúbicas

Capacity

unit	number of liters	approximate U.S. equivalents		
		CUBIC	DRY	LIQUID
liter	1	61.02 cubic inches	0.908 quart	1.057 quarts

Capacidad

unidad	número de litros	equivalentes aproximados de los EE.UU.		
		CÚBICO	SECO	LÍQUIDO
litro	1	61.02 pulgadas cúbicas	0.908 cuarto	1.057 cuartos

Mass and Weight

unit	number of grams	approximate U.S. equivalents	
milligram	0.001	0.015	grain
centigram	0.01	0.154	grain
gram	1	0.035	ounce
kilogram	1,000	2.2046	pounds
metric ton	1,000,000	1.102	short tons

Masa y peso

unidad	número de gramos	equivalentes aproximados de los EE.UU.	
miligramo	0.001	0.015	grano
centigramo	0.01	0.154	grano
gramo	1	0.035	onza
kilogramo	1.000	2.2046	libras
tonelada métrica	1,000,000	1.102	toneladas cortas